ITALIAN WINES 2004

Gambero Rosso®

Slow Food Editore

talianwines

2004

ITALIAN WINES 2004
GAMBERO ROSSO®- SLOW FOOD EDITORE

EDITORIAL STAFF FOR THE ORIGINAL EDITION

CHIEF EDITORS
DANIELE CERNILLI AND GIGI PIUMATTI

SENIOR EDITORS
GIANNI FABRIZIO AND MARCO SABELLICO

TECHNICAL SUPERVISION
DARIO CAPPELLONI, NICOLA FRASSON, ELEONORA GUERINI, TIZIANO GAIA,
VITTORIO MANGANELLI, PAOLO ZACCARIA

MEMBERS OF THE FINAL TASTING PANELS
EGIDIO FEDELE DELL'OSTE, FABIO GIAVEDONI, GIACOMO MOJOLI, MARCO OREGGIA,
LEONARDO ROMANELLI, PIERO SARDO, RICCARDO VISCARDI

CONTRIBUTORS
.NINO AJELLO, GILBERTO ARRU, STEFANO ASARO, PAOLO BATTIMELLI, ENRICO BATTISTELLA,
FRANCESCO BEGHI, FRANCESCA BIDASIO DEGLI IMBERTI, ANTONIO BOCO,
SERGIO BONANNO, WALTER BORDO, MICHELE BRESSAN, PASQUALE BUFFA,
DARIO CAPPELLONI, DIONISIO CASTELLO, DANIELE CERNILLI, ROBERTO CHECCHETTO,
VALERIO CHIARINI, ANTONIO CIMINELLI, GIULIO COLOMBA, IAN DOMENICO D'AGATA,
MASSIMO DI CINTIO, GIANNI FABRIZIO, EGIDIO FEDELE DELL'OSTEI, MAURIZIO FAVA,
ROSSANO FERRAZZANO, FAUSTO FERRONI, NICOLA FRASSON, LUCA FURLOTTI, TIZIANO GAIA,
FABIO GIAVEDONI, ELEONORA GUERINI, VITO LACERENZA, MASSIMO LANZA,
GIANCARLO LO SICCO, GIACOMO MOJOLI, GIOVANNI NORESE, MARCO OREGGIA,
FRANCO PALLINI, STEFANO PASTOR, NEREO PEDERZOLLI, PIERPAOLO PENCO,
FRANCESCO PENSOVECCHIO, MASSIMILIANO PERAZZOLI, ANGELO PERETTI,
NICOLA PICCININI, GUIDO PIRAZZOLI, GIGI PIUMATTI, MARIO PLAZIO, PIERPAOLO RASTELLI,
LEONARDO ROMANELLI, FABRIZIO RUSSO, MARCO SABELLICO, DIEGO SORACCO,
HERBERT TASCHLER, MASSIMO TOFFOLO, ANDREA VANNELLI, RICCARDO VISCARDI,
MASSIMO VOLPARI, PAOLO ZACCARIA.

MEMBERS OF REGIONAL TASTING PANELS
ANTONIO ATTORRE, SALVATORE BASTA, PAOLA BERTINOTTI, ALBERTO BETTINI,
ALESSANDRO BULZONI, TEODOSIO BUONGIORNO, REMO CAMURANI, SERGIO CECCARELLI,
ANGELO DAL BON, MARCO DANIELE, PAOLO DE CRISTOFARO, TIZIANA DI MICELI,
ROSANNA FERRARO, PIERO FIORENTINI, RAFFAELE GUZZON, DARIO LAURENZI,
LUCA MANGONI, MIRCO MARCONI, MINO MARTUCCI, MAURIZIO MENICHETTI, ENZO MERZ,
FABIO MONGARETTO, DANNY MURARO, VANNI MURARO, LINDA NANO, ROBERTO NOVARO,
UGO ONGARETTO, RENATO ORLANDO, ROBERTO PALMIERI, LINA PAOLILLO, LIANO PETROZZI,
EMANUELA PIERANGELINI, FULVIO PIERANGELINI, FILIPPO POLIDORI, CRISTIANA POLIMENO,
RENZO PRIORI, SILVANO PROMPICAI, MAURIZIO ROSSI, MARIO SCARFINI, VALENTINO RAMELLI,
HELMUT RIEBSCHLÄGER, RENATO TEDESCO, PAOLO VALDASTRI, GIULIANA VELISCEK,
ALBERTO ZACCONE, VALERIO ZORZI

EDITING
DARIO CAPPELLONI, ELEONORA GUERINI, BIANCA MINARDO, PAOLO ZACCARIA

EDITORIAL CO-ORDINATOR
GIORGIO ACCASCINA

TRANSLATIONS CO-ORDINATED AND EDITED BY
GILES WATSON

TRANSLATORS
MAUREEN ASHLEY, KAREN CHRISTENFELD, HELEN DONALD, DAVID HENDERSON,
STEPHEN JACKSON, ANDREW L MILLER, GILES WATSON, AILSA WOOD

PUBLISHER
GAMBERO ROSSO, INC.
PRESIDENT STEFANO BONILLI
636 BROADWAY - SUITE 1111 - NEW YORK, NY 10012
TEL. 212- 253-5653 FAX 212- 253-8349 - E-MAIL: gamberousa@aol.com

DISTRIBUTION:
USA AND CANADA BY ANTIQUE COLLECTORS' CLUB, MARKET STREET INDUSTRIAL PARK,
WAPPINGER FALLS, NY 12590, USA;
UK AND AUSTRALIA BY GRUB STREET, THE BASEMENT, 10 CHIVALRY ROAD,
LONDON SW11 1HT, UK.

ITALIAN WINES 2004 WAS CLOSED ON 22 SETTEMBRE 2003

PRINTED IN ITALY BY
AMADEUS SPA – STRADA STATALE NETTUNENSE, KM 7,347 – 00040 ARICCIA (RM)

CONTENTS

INTRODUCTION	6
THREE GLASS AWARDS 2004	8
THE STARS	12
GUIDE TO VINTAGES	13
HOW TO USE THE GUIDE	14

THE REGIONS

VALLE D'AOSTA	15
PIEDMONT	21
LIGURIA	165
LOMBARDY	181
TRENTINO	227
ALTO ADIGE	253
VENETO	287
FRIULI VENEZIA GIULIA	353
EMILIA ROMAGNA	431
TUSCANY	463
MARCHE	623
UMBRIA	657
LAZIO	679
ABRUZZO AND MOLISE	695
CAMPANIA	711
BASILICATA	729
PUGLIA	737
CALABRIA	757
SICILY	765
SARDINIA	789

INDEXES

WINES	805
PRODUCERS	852

INTRODUCTION

This is the 17th edition of Gambero Rosso and Slow Food's Italian Wines. Over the years, we have written more than 10,000 pages on the wines of Italy, uncorked more than 100,000 bottles and awarded more than 2,000 Three Glass ratings. We have discovered new wines, promoted vast numbers of wineries and increased awareness of Italy's finest labels in many countries. For years, the Italian edition of the Guide has been flanked by a German one, published by Hallwag, and by an English-language version. Last year, total circulation of the three editions was more than 150,000 copies. The Italian publication was in the upper reaches of the bestseller lists in Italy's leading newspapers. One paper classified it as the 13th-highest selling title in the period from mid November to mid December, when 60 per cent of all Italy's book sales take place. It was a thrilling success, for which we must thank all those who purchased the Guide and made the result possible. But now it is time to tell you how things went this year. As usual, we began work in the month of May, when local tasting panels began to collect sample bottles which would later be evaluated at blind comparative tastings. Wherever possible, we strove to involve protection consortia, chambers of commerce and anyone else who could act as neutral guarantors for the collection of wines and the organization of tasting sessions. Around 70,000 bottles were collected all over Italy for this year's Guide. They had to be procured and properly conserved – no easy matter in this year's heat – and then masked for tasting after they had been sorted into groups of comparable wines. Readers can imagine how much work this involved. We also believe that the supervision of this phase by independent bodies is a very positive factor. These bodies represent all the producers and can check that operations are carried out properly, safeguarding the interests of consumers and monitoring our activities. For this, we are very grateful to our collaborators. We will acknowledge all of them, in the hope that none are inadvertently omitted, and thank the consortia of Marchio Storico del Chianti Classico, Brunello and Rosso di Montalcino, Nobile di Montepulciano, Bolgheri, Vernaccia di San Gimignano, Chianti Rufina, Carmignano, Morellino di Scansano, Montecucco, Monteregio di Massa Marittima, Franciacorta, Oltrepò Pavese, Valtellina, Soave and Valpolicella, the Enoteca Regionale del Roero, the Enoteca Regionale at Dozza, the Enoteca Regionale at Roppolo, the Istituto Agronomico Mediterraneo at Valenzano, the Centro Agroalimentare Umbro at Foligno, the Bolzano Chamber of Commerce, the Caserta Chamber of Commerce, the Trento Chamber of Commerce, the Arezzo Chamber of Commerce, Assivip at Majolati Spontini , the Vineria della Signora in Rosso at Nizza Monferrato, Vinea at Offida and the Anteprima group at Lucca. If we add those who worked at the consortia to the roughly 100 tasters we called in, it is obvious that the Guide requires the contribution of at least 250 individuals every year. In short, a whole lot of people. The 30 or so tasting panels, each comprising at least five judges, worked for about two months, tasting around 25,000 wines. Just under 10,000 wines were rejected outright, and the rest were awarded from zero to two Glasses. In the first phase, we award points out of 100 and select the roughly 1,500 wines that will go forward to the Three Glass taste-offs. At the end of this huge task, the final awards committee meets. Made up of prominent figures on local tasting panels, the committee examines all the wines sent to the final round. Again, all tastings are blind. The judgement here is more drastic, either a yes or a no. Each decision is carefully justified. All the elements of every wine are discussed and analysed, every aspect being awarded a mark. For this Guide, the following panellists joined Daniele Cernilli, Gigi Piumatti, Gianni Fabrizio and Marco Sabellico for at least one of the three final taste-offs over a total of 15 days: Vittorio Manganelli, Dario Cappelloni, Nicola Frasson, Eleonora Guerini, Giacomo Mojoli, Piero Sardo, Egidio Fedele dell'Oste, Marco Oreggia, Leonardo Romanelli, Paolo Zaccaria, Fabio Giavedoni, Riccardo Viscardi and Tiziano Gaia. That makes a total of 17 individuals who are jointly responsible for the assessments that awarded 254 wines from all over Italy our legendary Three Glasses. Above all, they make up a formidable team of some of Italy's finest tasters. Obviously, the evaluation system is collective in nature, with cross checks and controls. Before it is awarded our top prize, a wine will have been tasted at least twice, and often three times. Only the availability of a broad-based, thoroughly reliable team makes this rigorous approach feasible. Our final tastings were held in the months of July and August in three separate locations: at Gambero Rosso's Città del Gusto in Roma; at the Castello di Verduno hotel in Piedmont, and at the Là di Petros restaurant at Colloredo di Monte Albano in Friuli. We used only glasses by Spiegelau, our unwitting sponsor. And here they are, the Italian Wines Three Glass winners, region by region: there were 62 from Tuscany, 60 from Piedmont, 26 from Friuli, 20 from the Veneto, 18 from Alto Adige, 12 from Sicily, nine from Lombardy and Marche, six from Umbria, five each from Campania, Abruzzo and Emilia Romagna, four from Puglia, three each from Sardinia, Trentino and Lazio, two each from Valle d'Aosta and Basilicata, and – sadly – none from Liguria, Calabria or Molise. It's a large number, but without wishing to justify our choices the number of wines tasted was also large, and widespread progress in terms of quality sometimes makes it difficult to draw clear distinctions. Paradoxically, it would be much easier to award prizes to a dozen wines, the very best from Italy's cellars, than to strike one off the longer list. But awarding so few prizes would have two negative repercussions. First, you the consumer would be unable to find any of the wine, and even if you could, the price would be prohibitive because demand would be boosted by the award itself. That's why we have lowered the bar a notch, enabling many more wines to leap to success. As we have said, there are 254 winners this year. Of course, this does not mean that we have been giving awards to indifferent wines. It simply means that we have not drawn the line at "100-pointers", as some American wine writers might put it. We have also given top awards to stupendous territory wines that perhaps belong to minor wine types, or are made from local varieties like Puglia's sussumaniello, Lazio's grechetto or lagrein in Alto Adige. At our tastings, all these performed extraordinarily well. We shall conclude with one or two general remarks. After a 2002 vintage that was very wet almost everywhere, 2003 brought very dry, almost subtropical weather. Production was low in both years, falling well below 48,000,000 hectolitres. From one point of view, this was all to the good, for wine in Italy is suffering from a recession in sales. But it also means that a number of intelligent decisions have to be taken. Producers have to realize that economic conditions do not always leave room for hopelessly optimistic price rises, and that there is increasing demand for less standardized wines, with more personality and closer links to their territories and types. We have attempted to take this into account for our readers' benefit. We discussed how to go beyond the simple grammar of wine and international styles in the way we carried out our tastings and assessments. The release of very favourable vintages, such as '97 and '99, enabled us to award prizes to many classic wines in Piedmont, Tuscany and in other regions. We have striven to penalize over-lavish use of oak, excessive recourse to concentrators, the indiscriminate conversion of entire areas to cabernet and invasive winemaking techniques. There will have to be a change, and we invite producers, winemakers, other professionals and concerned readers to ponder the matter. The way forward for Italian wine is through the promotion of viticulture and the improvement of traditional varieties, not through the standardization imposed by universally adopted oenological techniques. Wine, the finest Italian wine, must speak our language. It is in no one's interest that it should become too expensive for most consumers to afford. These thoughts are dictated more by common sense than by any theory of marketing. But perhaps it is plain common sense that Italy's producers have been lacking of late.

Daniele Cernilli and Gigi Piumatti

THREE GLASS AWARDS 2004

VALLE D'AOSTA

Coteau La Tour '01	Les Crêtes	17
Valle d'Aosta Chardonnay Cuvée Frissonnière Les Crêtes Cuvée Bois 01	Les Crêtes	17

PIEDMONT

Barbaresco '00	Gaja	33
Barbaresco '99	Produttori del Barbaresco	36
Barbaresco Asili '99	Bruno Giacosa	122
Barbaresco Camp Gros '99	Tenuta Cisa Asinari dei Marchesi di Gresy	12
Barbaresco Pajoré '00	Sottimano	124
Barbaresco Rabajà '00	Bruno Rocca	37
Barbaresco Rabajà Ris. '96	Giuseppe Cortese	33
Barbaresco S. Stefanetto '00	Piero Busso	120
Barbaresco Serraboella '00	F.lli Cigliuti	120
Barbaresco Vign. Brich Ronchi '00	Albino Rocca	36
Barbaresco Vign. Starderi '00	La Spinetta	58
Barbera d'Alba Scarrone V. Vecchia '01	Vietti	66
Barbera d'Alba Sup. '01	G. D. Vajra	44
Barbera d'Asti Pomorosso '01	Coppo	55
Barbera d'Asti Sup. '01	La Spinetta	58
Barbera d'Asti Sup. Alfiera '01	Marchesi Alfieri	134
Barbera d'Asti Sup. Montruc '01	Franco M. Martinetti	144
Barbera d'Asti Sup. Nizza La Court '00	Michele Chiarlo	47
Barbera d'Asti Sup. SanSì Sel. '00	Scagliola	48
Barbera d'Asti Sup. Sei V. Insynthesis '01	Cantina Sociale di Vinchio - Vaglio Serra	153
Barolo '99	Bartolo Mascarello	40
Barolo Brunate '99	Poderi Marcarini	95
Barolo Brunate '99	Roberto Voerzio	99
Barolo Bussia '99	Prunotto	27
Barolo Bussia V. Munie '99	Armando Parusso	111
Barolo Case Nere '99	Enzo Boglietti	90
Barolo Cerequio Tenuta Secolo '99	Contratto	55
Barolo Ciabot Mentin Ginestra '99	Domenico Clerico	106
Barolo Cl. '98	Giacomo Borgogno & Figli	38
Barolo Gavarini V. Chiniera '99	Elio Grasso	110
Barolo Lazzarito V. La Delizia '99	Fontanafredda	140
Barolo Le Vigne '99	Luciano Sandrone	42
Barolo nei Cannubi '99	Einaudi	77
Barolo Percristina '98	Domenico Clerico	106
Barolo Rocche dell'Annunziata Ris. '97	Paolo Scavino	65
Barolo S. Giovanni '99	Gianfranco Alessandria	106
Barolo S. Rocco '99	Azelia	63
Barolo S. Stefano di Perno '98	Giuseppe Mascarello e Figlio	105
Barolo Sorì Ginestra '99	Conterno Fantino	108
Barolo V. Big 'd Big '99	Podere Rocche dei Manzoni	112
Barolo V. Bricco Gattera '99	Monfalletto - Cordero di Montezemolo	94
Barolo V. Conca '99	F.lli Revello	96
Barolo V. Merenda '99	Giorgio Scarzello e Figli	42
Barolo V. Rionda Ris. '97	Vigna Rionda - Massolino	142
Barolo Vecchie Vigne '99	Giovanni Corino	92
Barolo Vign. Arborina '99	Elio Altare - Cascina Nuova	89
Barolo Vign. La Villa '99	F.lli Seghesio	114
Gattinara Vign. Castelle '99	Antoniolo	81
Langhe Nebbiolo Sorì S. Lorenzo '99	Gaja	33
Langhe Rosso Alta Bussia '01	Attilio Ghisolfi	109
Langhe Rosso Bric du Luv '01	Ca' Viola	76
Monferrato Rosso Mystère '01	Cascina La Barbatella	126
Nebbiolo d'Alba '01	Hilberg - Pasquero	131
Roero '00	Cascina Val del Prete	130
Roero Audinaggio '01	Cascina Ca' Rossa	50
Roero Bric Valdiana '01	Giovanni Almondo	115
Roero Printi '00	Monchiero Carbone	53
Roero Ròche d'Ampsèj '00	Matteo Correggia	51
Roero Sup. '01	Filippo Gallino	52
Roero Sup. Mombeltramo '00	Malvirà	53

LOMBARDY

Franciacorta Brut Cabochon '99	Monte Rossa	190
Franciacorta Cuvée Annamaria Clementi '96	Ca' del Bosco	196
Franciacorta Extra Brut Comarì del Salem '98	Uberti	198
Franciacorta Gran Cuvée Brut '99	Bellavista	195

Franciacorta Satèn '99	Ferghettina	197
Garda Cabernet Le Zalte '01	Cascina La Pertica	206
Valtellina Sforzato San Domenico '01	Triacca	215
Valtellina Sfursat 5 Stelle '01	Nino Negri	191
Valtellina Sfursat Fruttaio Ca' Rizzieri '00	Aldo Rainoldi	191

TRENTINO

Giulio Ferrari '94	Ferrari	247
Granato '01	Foradori	239
San Leonardo '00	Tenuta San Leonardo	228

ALTO ADIGE

A. A. Bianco Beyond the Clouds '01	Castel Ringberg & Kastelaz Elena Walch	280
A. A. Cabernet Tor di Lupo '00	Cantina Produttori Andriano	254
A. A. Cabernet Sauvignon Lafoa '00	Cantina Produttori Colterenzio	258
A. A. Gewürztraminer Brenntal '02	Cantina Produttori Cortaccia	273
A. A. Gewürztraminer Castel Turmhof '02	Tiefenbrunner	273
A. A. Gewürztraminer Nussbaumerhof '02	Cantina Produttori Termeno	281
A. A. Lagrein Abtei Ris. '00	Cantina Convento Muri-Gries	260
A. A. Lagrein Scuro Barbagòl Ris. '00	Cantina Laimburg	282
A. A. Lagrein Scuro Grieser Prestige Line Ris. '00	Cantina Gries/Cantina di Bolzano	259
A. A. Lagrein Scuro Ris. '00	Josephus Mayr - Erbhof Unterganzner	262
A. A. Lagrein Scuro Taber Ris. '01	C. P. Santa Maddalena/C. di Bolzano	264
A. A. Sauvignon St. Valentin '02	Cantina Produttori San Michele Appiano	258
A. A. Stoan '02	Cantina Produttori Termeno	281
A. A. Terlano Sauvignon '92	Cantina Terlano	279
A. A. Valle Isarco Kerner '02	Manfred Nössing - Hoandlhof	267
A. A. Valle Isarco Kerner Praepositus '02	Abbazia di Novacella	282
A. A. Valle Isarco Sylvaner '02	Kuenhof - Peter Pliger	267
Yngram '00	Hofstätter	281

VENETO

Amarone della Valpolicella '98	Corte Sant'Alda	302
Amarone della Valpolicella Campo dei Gigli '98	Tenuta Sant'Antonio	304
Amarone della Valpolicella Cl. Casa dei Bepi '98	Viviani	314
Amarone della Valpolicella Cl. Caterina Zardini '99	Giuseppe Campagnola	299
Amarone della Valpolicella Cl. Sergio Zenato Ris. '98	Zenato	316
Amarone della Valpolicella Cl. Terre di Cariano '99	Cecilia Beretta	341
Amarone della Valpolicella Cl. Vign. Monte Ca' Bianca '99	Lorenzo Begali	321
Amarone della Valpolicella Roccolo Grassi '99	Roccolo Grassi	303
Amarone della Valpolicella Vign. di Monte Lodoletta '98	Romano Dal Forno	296
Capitel Croce '01	Roberto Anselmi	307
Colli Euganei Rosso Gemola '00	Vignalta	334
Fratta '01	Maculan	290
Il Rosso dell'Abazia '00	Serafini & Vidotto	315
Recioto della Valpolicella Cl. Giovanni Allegrini '00	Allegrini	294
Recioto della Valpolicella Cl. Vigneti di Moron Domini Veneti '01	Cantina Sociale Valpolicella	312
Rosso del Bepi '96	Giuseppe Quintarelli	313
Soave Cl. Calvarino '02	Leonildo Pieropan	331
Soave Cl. Monte Carbonare '02	Suavia	331
Soave Cl. Monte Grande '02	Prà	310
Soave Cl. Sup. Vign. Du Lot '01	Inama	317

FRIULI VENEZIA GIULIA

Breg '99	Gravner	391
COF Bianco Rosazzo Ronco delle Acacie '01	Le Vigne di Zamò	397
COF Bianco Rosazzo Terre Alte '01	Livio Felluga	371
COF Pignolo di Buttrio Vign. Ronc di Juri '00	Girolamo Dorigo	358
COF Refosco P. R. Vign. Montsclapade '00	Girolamo Dorigo	358
COF Refosco P. R. Zuc di Volpe '01	Volpe Pasini	425
COF Sauvignon Blanc '02	Rosa Bosco	394
Collio Bianco '02	Edi Keber	372
Collio Bianco '02	Dario Raccaro	376
Collio Bianco Ronco della Chiesa '01	Borgo del Tiglio	367
Collio Bianco Russiz Disôre '01	Russiz Superiore	361
Collio Pinot Bianco '02	Alessandro Princic	375
Collio Rosso Cjarandon '00	Ronco dei Tassi	377
Collio Sauvignon de La Tour '02	Villa Russiz	363
Collio Sauvignon Segré '02	Castello di Spessa	360
Collio Tocai Friulano '02	Mauro Drius	370
Collio Tocai Friulano '02	Franco Toros	379
Collio Tocai Friulano Ronco delle Cime '02	Venica & Venica	384
Friuli Isonzo Arbis Blanc '02	Borgo San Daniele	367
Friuli Isonzo Merlot '01	Ronco del Gelso	377
Friuli Isonzo Pinot Grigio Gris '01	Lis Neris	421
Friuli Isonzo Sauvignon Piere '01	Vie di Romans	399
Mario Schiopetto Bianco '02	Schiopetto	362
Pignacolusse '00	Jermann Vinnaioli	388
Tiare Blu Gran Cru '00	Livon	419
Vespa Bianco '01	Bastianich	405

EMILIA ROMAGNA

Afederico Merlot '01	Vallona	437
Marzieno '01	Fattoria Zerbina	440
Ronco dei Ciliegi '00	Castelluccio	446
Sangiovese di Romagna Sup. Avi Ris. '00	San Patrignano	439
Sangiovese di Romagna Sup. Terra di Covignano Ris. '01	San Valentino	452

TUSCANY

50 & 50 Avignonesi e Capannelle '99	Capannelle/Avignonesi	497/542
Avvoltore '01	Moris Farms	514
Balifico '00	Castello di Volpaia	569
Bolgheri Montepergoli '01	Enrico Santini	476
Bolgheri Rosso Piastraia '01	Michele Satta	476
Bolgheri Sassicaia '00	Tenuta San Guido	471
Brancaia Il Blu '01	La Brancaia	566
Brunello di Montalcino Poggio alle Mura '98	Castello Banfi	515
Brunello di Montalcino Ris. '97	Casanuova delle Cerbaie	518
Brunello di Montalcino Ris. '97	Fanti - La Palazzetta	524
Brunello di Montalcino Ris. '97	Eredi Fuligni	525
Brunello di Montalcino Ris. '97	Tenuta Il Poggione	528
Brunello di Montalcino Ris. '97	Castello Romitorio	534
Brunello di Montalcino Ris. '97	Uccelliera	537
Brunello di Montalcino Vigna di Pianrosso '98	Ciacci Piccolomini D'Aragona	521
Caberlot '00	Podere Il Carnasciale	514
Camartina '00	Querciabella	504
Castello del Terriccio '00	Castello del Terriccio	482
Cepparello '00	Isole e Olena	467
Chianti Cl. Castello di Ama '00	Castello di Ama	495
Chianti Cl. Castello di Brolio '00	Barone Ricasoli	496
Chianti Cl. Castello di Fonterutoli '00	Castello di Fonterutoli	478
Chianti Cl. Cellole Ris. '00	San Fabiano Calcinaia	482
Chianti Cl. Doccio a Matteo Ris. '00	Caparsa	566
Chianti Cl. Grosso Sanese '01	Podere Il Palazzino	498
Chianti Cl. Poggio Rosso Ris. '00	San Felice	488
Chianti Cl. Rancia Ris. '00	Fattoria di Felsina	485
Chianti Cl. Ris. Ducale Oro '00	Tenimenti Ruffino	564
Chianti Cl. V. il Poggiale Ris. '00	Castellare di Castellina	478
Chianti Rufina Montesodi '01	Marchesi de' Frescobaldi	494
D'Alceo '01	Castello dei Rampolla	556
Fidenzio '00	Podere San Luigi	561
Flaccianello della Pieve '00	Tenuta Fontodi	557
Galatrona '01	Fattoria Petrolo	471
Giséle '01	La Rampa di Fugnano	580
Gratius '00	Il Molino di Grace	557
Il Carbonaione '00	Podere Poggio Scalette	503
Il Pareto '00	Tenute Ambrogio e Giovanni Folonari	493
Il Sasso '01	Piaggia	563
La Massa '01	La Massa	558
Masseto '00	Tenuta dell' Ornellaia	470
Nambrot '01	Tenuta di Ghizzano	561
Nardo '01	Montepeloso	590
Nobile di Montepulciano Asinone '00	Poliziano	547
Nobile di Montepulciano Vign. Antica Chiusina '00	Fattoria del Cerro	544
Oracolo '01	Poggio Amorelli	480
Orcia Guardiavigna '01	Podere Forte	489
Podalirio '01	Querceto di Castellina	481
Podere Le Rocce '00	Le Filigare	468
Poggiassai '01	Fattorie Chigi Saracini	485
Primamateria '01	Poggerino	568
Redigaffi '01	Tua Rita	591
Roccato '00	Rocca delle Macìe	481
Saffredi '01	Le Pupille	509
San Martino '00	Villa Cafaggio	560
Sant'Antimo Pietradonice '00	Casanova di Neri	517
Siepi '01	Castello di Fonterutoli	578
Solaia '00	Marchesi Antinori	492
Stielle '00	Rocca di Castagnoli	500
Stignano '00	San Vincenti	501
Val di Cornia Rosso l'Rennero '01	Gualdo del Re	589
Vignamaggio '00	Villa Vignamaggio	507

MARCHE

Anghelos '01	Tenuta De Angelis	629
Barricadiero '01	Aurora	643
Chaos '01	Fattoria Le Terrazze	642
Kurni '01	Oasi degli Angeli	632
Ludi '01	Ercole Velenosi	626
Pathos '01	Santa Barbara	627
Solo Sangiovese '01	Fattoria Dezi	651
Verdicchio dei Castelli di Jesi Cl. Sup. Massaccio '00	Fazi Battaglia	630
Verdicchio dei Castelli di Jesi Cl. Villa Bucci Ris. '00	Bucci	645

UMBRIA

Campoleone '01	Lamborghini - La Fiorita	671
Cervaro della Sala '01	Castello della Sala	662
Crovello '01	Poggio Bertaio	661
Merlot '01	Castello delle Regine	658
Montefalco Sagrantino '00	Còlpetrone	664
Montefalco Sagrantino 25 Anni '00	Arnaldo Caprai - Val di Maggio	665

LAZIO

Grechetto Latour a Civitella '01	Sergio Mottura	684
Montiano '01	Falesco	688
Vigna del Vassallo '01	Paola Di Mauro	686

ABRUZZO AND MOLISE

Montepulciano d'Abruzzo '97	Edoardo Valentini	701
Montepulciano d'Abruzzo Plateo '98	Agriverde	703
Montepulciano d'Abruzzo Villa Gemma '99	Gianni Masciarelli	706
Trebbiano d'Abruzzo '00	Edoardo Valentini	701
Trebbiano d'Abruzzo Marina Cvetic '01	Gianni Masciarelli	706

CAMPANIA

Falerno del Massico Rosso Vigna Camarato '00	Villa Matilde	714
Montevetrano '01	Montevetrano	721
Naima '01	Viticoltori De Conciliis	720
Pàtrimo '01	Feudi di San Gregorio	723
Serpico '01	Feudi di San Gregorio	723

BASILICATA

Aglianico del Vulture Roinos '01	Eubea	734
Aglianico del Vulture Rotondo '01	Paternoster	731

PUGLIA

Nero '01	Conti Zecca	746
Salice Salentino Rosso Donna Lisa Ris. '99	Leone de Castris	751
Torcicoda '01	Tormaresca	752
Torre Testa '01	Tenute Rubino	739

SICILY

Almanera '01	Fatascià	777
Camelot '01	Firriato	776
Contea di Sclafani Cabernet Sauvignon '01	Tasca d'Almerita	778
Contessa Entellina Milleunanotte '00	Tenuta di Donnafugata	772
Don Antonio '01	Morgante	770
Etna Bianco Sup. Pietramarina '99	Benanti	782
Faro Palari '01	Palari	775
Forti Terre di Sicilia Cabernet Sauvignon '01	Cantina Sociale di Trapani	781
Hugonis '01	Tenute Rapitalà	768
Litra '01	Abbazia Santa Anastasia	768
Sagana '02	Cusumano	779
Syrah '01	Planeta	774

SARDINIA

Alghero Marchese di Villamarina '99	Tenute Sella & Mosca	790
Latinia '01	Cantina Sociale di Santadi	797
Turriga '99	Antonio Argiolas	799

THE YEAR'S BEST WINES

THE SPARKLER		
FRANCIACORTA BRUT CABOCHON '99	MONTE ROSSA	190
THE WHITE		
COLLIO TOCAI FRIULANO '02	TOROS	379
THE RED		
VALTELLINA SFURSAT 5 STELLE '01	NINO NEGRI	191
THE SWEET		
RECIOTO DELLA VALPOLICELLA CL.		
GIOVANNI ALLEGRINI '00	ALLEGRINI	294

WINERY OF THE YEAR

GIANNI MASCIARELLI	706

OENOLOGIST OF THE YEAR

WILLI STÜRZ	

UP-AND-COMING WINERY

IL MOLINO DI GRACE	557

BEST-PRICED WINE

BARBARESCO '99	PRODUTTORI DEL BARBARESCO	36

WINE-GROWER OF THE YEAR

EDOARDO VALENTINI	701

THE STARS

Fully 49 Italian wineries have been awarded Three Glasses at least ten times in the 17 editions of Italian Wines. They represent the very pinnacle of Italian winemaking and you will find among them the prestigious names that have brought Italian wine fame and fortune around the world. At the top of the list is Angelo Gaja, which has been firmly in command for many years. But if we were to add up all the awards made, the Antinori group would come out on top with a total of 37 Three Glass prizes earned by Marchesi Antinori, Castello della Sala, Prunotto, Tormaresca and Guado al Tasso. This year's new entries include Le Vigne di Zamò, which reached a total of 11, including awards made to Abbazia di Rosazzo, whose labels and staff it has inherited. Then there is Ceretto's Bricco Asili – Bricco Rocche, which we should have included last year. Feudi di San Gregorio and Masciarelli have arrived to beef up the south Italian contingent, and finally we have Prunotto, the Piedmont outpost of the Antinori empire. On the home straight, with nine Three Glass awards, there are 12 more wineries that could earn a Star as early as next year. The contenders are Anselmi, Argiolas, Chiarlo, Uberti, Venica, San Leonardo, La Massa, Rocche dei Manzoni, Ronco del Gelso, Cantina di Cortaccia, Frescobaldi and Castello di Brolio.

★ ★ ★

33
GAJA (Piedmont)

★ ★

23
CA' DEL BOSCO (Lombardy)
LA SPINETTA/RIVETTI (Piedmont)

22
ELIO ALTARE (Piedmont)

★

19
ALLEGRINI (Veneto)
CASTELLO DI FONTERUTOLI
(Tuscany)

17
FATTORIA DI FELSINA
(Tuscany)
VINNAIOLI JERMANN
(Friuli Venezia Giulia)

16
DOMENICO CLERICO (Piedmont)

15
MARCHESI ANTINORI
(Tuscany)
POLIZIANO (Tuscany)
PAOLO SCAVINO
(Piedmont)

14
CANTINA PRODUTTORI
SAN MICHELE APPIANO (Alto Adige)
CASTELLO DELLA SALA (Umbria)
GIROLAMO DORIGO
(Friuli Venezia Giulia)
TENIMENTI RUFFINO (Tuscany)
MARIO SCHIOPETTO
(Friuli Venezia Giulia)

EDOARDO VALENTINI (Abruzzo)
VIE DI ROMANS/STELIO GALLO
(Friuli Venezia Giulia)
VILLA RUSSIZ (Friuli Venezia Giulia)

13
BANFI (Tuscany)
BELLAVISTA (Lombardy)
CASTELLO DI AMA (Tuscany)
LIVIO FELLUGA (Friuli Venezia Giulia)
FERRARI (Trentino)
ISOLE E OLENA (Tuscany)
CASCINA LA BARBATELLA (Piedmont)
TENUTA FONTODI (Tuscany)
TENUTA SAN GUIDO (Tuscany)
ROBERTO VOERZIO (Piedmont)

12
PODERI ALDO CONTERNO
(Piedmont)
MATTEO CORREGGIA (Piedmont)
ROMANO DAL FORNO (Veneto)
IOSKO GRAVNER
(Friuli Venezia Giulia)
MIANI (Friuli Venezia Giulia)

11
CANTINA PRODUTTORI COLTERENZIO
(Alto Adige)
GIACOMO CONTERNO (Piedmont)
CONTERNO FANTINO (Piedmont)
FEUDI DI SAN GREGORIO
(Campania)
LE VIGNE DI ZAMÒ - ABBAZIA
DI ROSAZZO (Friuli Venezia Giulia)
MACULAN (Veneto)
PIEROPAN (Veneto)
PLANETA (Sicily)
QUERCIABELLA (Tuscany)
TASCA D'ALMERITA (Sicily)
TENUTA DELL'ORNELLAIA (Tuscany)

10
BRICCO ROCCHE - BRICCO ASILI
(Piedmont)
GIANNI MASCIARELLI (Abruzzo)
PRUNOTTO (Piedmont)

A GUIDE TO VINTAGES, 1971 - 2000

	BARBARESCO	BRUNELLO DI MONTALCINO	BAROLO	CHIANTI CLASSICO	NOBILE DI MONTEPULCIANO	AMARONE
1971	●●●●	●●●	●●●●●	●●●●●	●●●●	●●●●
1974	●●●●	●●	●●●●	●●●	●●●	●●●●
1975	●●	●●●●●	●●	●●●●	●●●●	●●●
1976	●●	●	●●	●●	●●	●●●●
1977	●●	●●●●	●●	●●●●	●●●●	●●●
1978	●●●●●●	●●●●	●●●●●	●●●●●	●●●●●	●●●
1979	●●●●	●●●●	●●●●	●●●●	●●●●	●●●●
1980	●●●●	●●●●	●●●●	●●●●	●●	●●●
1981	●●●	●●●	●●●	●●●	●●●	●●●
1982	●●●●●	●●●●●	●●●●●	●●●●	●●●●	●
1983	●●●●	●●●●	●●●●	●●●●	●●●●	●●●●●
1984	●	●●	●●	●	●	●●
1985	●●●●●	●●●●●	●●●●●	●●●●●	●●●●●	●●●●
1986	●●●	●●●	●●●	●●●●	●●●●	●●●
1987	●●	●●	●●	●●	●●	●●
1988	●●●●●	●●●●●	●●●●●	●●●●●	●●●●●	●●●●●
1989	●●●●●	●●	●●●●●	●	●	●●
1990	●●●●●	●●●●●	●●●●●	●●●●●	●●●●●	●●●●●
1991	●●●	●●●	●●●	●●●	●●●	●●
1992	●●	●●	●●	●	●	●
1993	●●●	●●●●	●●●	●●●●	●●●●●	●●●●
1994	●●	●●●	●●	●●	●●	●●
1995	●●●●	●●●●●	●●●●	●●●●●	●●●●●	●●●●
1996	●●●●●	●●●	●●●●●	●●●	●●●	●●●
1997	●●●●	●●●●	●●●●●	●●●●	●●●●	●●●●
1998	●●●●	●●●●	●●●●	●●●●	●●●	●●●
1999	●●●●●	●●●●●	●●●●●	●●●●●	●●●●●	●●●
2000	●●●●	●●●	●●●●	●●●	●●●	●●●●

HOW TO USE THE GUIDE

KEY
○ WHITE WINES
● RED WINES
◉ ROSÉ WINES

RATINGS

LISTING WITHOUT A GLASS SYMBOL:
A WELL-MADE WINE OF AVERAGE QUALITY
IN ITS CATEGORY

♟
ABOVE AVERAGE TO GOOD IN ITS CATEGORY, EQUIVALENT TO 70-79/100

♟♟
VERY GOOD TO EXCELLENT IN ITS CATEGORY, EQUIVALENT TO 80-89/100

♟♟
VERY GOOD TO EXCELLENT WINE SELECTED FOR FINAL TASTINGS

♟♟♟
EXCELLENT WINE IN ITS CATEGORY, EQUIVALENT TO 90-99/100

(♟, ♟♟, ♟♟♟) WINES RATED IN PREVIOUS EDITIONS OF THE GUIDE ARE
INDICATED BY WHITE GLASSES, PROVIDED THEY ARE STILL DRINKING AT THE
LEVEL FOR WHICH THE ORIGINAL AWARD WAS MADE

STAR ★
INDICATES WINERIES THAT HAVE WON TEN THREE GLASS
AWARDS FOR EACH STAR

PRICE RANGES (1) (2)
1 UP TO $4.20 AND UP TO £2.45
2 FROM $4.21 TO $6.00 AND FROM £2.46 TO £3.50
3 FROM $6.01 TO $9.00 AND FROM £3.51 TO £5.25
4 FROM $9.01 TO $15.60 AND FROM £5.26 TO £9.10
5 FROM $15.61 TO $24.00 AND FROM £9.11 TO £14.00
6 FROM $24.01 TO $36.00 AND FROM £14.01 TO £21.00
7 FROM $36.01 TO $48.00 AND FROM £21.01 TO £28.00
8 MORE THAN $48.01 AND MORE THAN £28.01
(1)Approx. retail prices in USA and UK (2)€ 1,00 = $1.20 = £0.70

ASTERISK *
INDICATES ESPECIALLY GOOD VALUE FOR MONEY

NOTE
PRICES INDICATED REFER TO RETAIL AVERAGES. INDICATIONS OF PRICE NEXT TO
WINES ASSIGNED WHITE GLASSES (AWARDS MADE IN PREVIOUS EDITIONS) TAKE
INTO ACCOUNT APPRECIATION OVER TIME WHERE APPROPRIATE

ABBREVIATIONS
A. A.	Alto Adige
C.	Colli
Cl.	Classico
C.S.	Cantina Sociale (co-operative winery)
Cant.	Cantina (cellar or winery)
Cast.	Castello (castle)
C. B.	Colli Bolognesi
C. P.	Colli Piacentini
COF	Colli Orientali del Friuli
Cons.	Consorzio (consortium)
Coop.Agr.	Cooperativa Agricola (farming co-operative)
DOC	Denominazione di Origine Controllata (category of wines created in 1963)
DOCG	Denominazione di Origine Controllata e Garantita (superior category of wines created in 1963)
Et.	Etichetta (label)
IGT	Indicazione Geografica Tipica (category of wines created in 1992)
M.	Metodo
M.to	Monferrato
OP	Oltrepò Pavese
P.R.	Peduncolo Rosso (red bunchstem)
P.	Prosecco
Rif. Agr.	Riforma Agraria (agrarian reform)
Ris.	Riserva
Sel.	Selezione
Sup.	Superiore
TdF	Terre di Franciacorta
V.	Vigna (vine)
Vign.	Vigneto (vineyard)
V. T.	Vendemmia Tardiva (late harvest)

VALLE D'AOSTA

At last, winemaking in Valle d'Aosta is not just about Costantino Charrère, though he remains the benchmark producer for emerging youngsters. Two of these are coming on nicely. Marco Martin, owner of the Lo Triolet winery and Giorgio Anselmet, who runs the winery of the same name, are both fast-emerging 30-somethings. Martin has made two excellent wines, a Pinot Gris aged in wood and the syrah and fumin Coteau Barrage, which are both interesting and very competitive. Giorgio Anselmet replaced his charismatic father, Renato, at the helm of their winery two years ago, and is making some good whites, such as the Chardonnay, and reds (we particularly liked his monovarietal Syrah). Above all, he makes a great "passito", Declivium, unfortunately released in very small quantities. Costantino Charrère's winery and the Les Crêtes estate place him at the top of the Valle d'Aosta winemaking tree for he won Three Glasses for the fifth time running with one of the best Chardonnays in Italy, the Cuvée Bois. Not satisfied with this success, Charrère came back for more with another Three Glass winner, the Coteau La Tour, made from syrah grapes. Among his other gems are the very good stainless steel-aged Chardonnay, the mouthfilling Fumin, and the tangy, harmonious Petite Arvine. To cap it all, Costantino makes many wines from endangered local varieties like prëmetta and mayolet. The Grosjean brothers deserve to be mentioned for the commendable regularity with which they have produced good results for several years now. Their attention to quality is paying off and production is now up to 60,000 bottles a year. Valle d'Aosta also has a large number of small and very small producers, making less than 10,000 bottles per year, who belong to the Associazione Viticulteurs Encaveurs. Sadly, there simply isn't room to put them all in the Guide, but we recommend tasting their very worthwhile wines. Moving on to the co-operatives, we acknowledge and welcome progress here, too. The Institut Agricole in Aosta stands out for its excellent whites, while the Passito di Moscato released by Crotta di Vegneron is as good as this wine type gets in Valle d'Aosta, or indeed anywhere in Italy. Finally, the Cave du Vin Blanc de Morgex et de La Salle is working well and coming on, thanks to shrewd diversification of the product range.

AOSTA

INSTITUT AGRICOLE RÉGIONAL
RÉGION LA ROCHERE, 1/A
11100 AOSTA
TEL. 0165215811
E-MAIL: s.aguettaz@iaraosta.it

This agricultural college plays a very important educational role in the region, and some of the best growers in Valle d'Aosta have completed their studies here. The winemaking department is in the capable hands of Luciano Rigazio, who is at the head of a fine team. As they did last year, the college winemakers have produced a series of interesting wines of excellent quality, earning better scores for their whites than for the reds. The wines aged in stainless steel and those aged in oak are all very good indeed. The first group includes a classic from this winery, the Pinot Gris. It is pale yellow with greenish highlights and faint, but stylish, aromas of spring flowers and pears. The palate is mouthfilling and warm, with impressive acidity in the finish. The oak-aged whites include an excellent • Chardonnay. A nice straw yellow precedes hints of vanilla, crusty bread and apples on the nose. The palate is enjoyably potent, but nicely balanced. The La Comète, from 100 per cent sauvignon, is also good, with strong varietal aromas of sage and tomato leaves, tempered by toasty nuances from the oak, and a mature, generous palate. The Petite Arvine is minerally, and the acidity enhances the length. The Müller Thurgau is also interesting, showing pear and peach aromas. As we said previously, we were less impressed with the reds.

AYMAVILLES (AO)

COSTANTINO CHARRÈRE
LES MOULINS, 28
11010 AYMAVILLES (AO)
TEL. 0165902135 - 0165902274
E-MAIL: info@lescretesvins.it

Few growers can boast such a strong influence on their region as Costantino Charrère. He divides his time between the winery that bears his own name, and the famed Les Crêtes estate. The Charrère cellar has a history dating back centuries. It was founded in 1750 by Costantino's great-great-grandfather, and the vinification cellars were subsequently transferred to Les Crêtes to improve organization and reduce costs. The production philosophy at Costantino Charrère differs from Les Crêtes in several ways. First of all, only reds are made here, almost all sourced from native local varieties. Second, no more than 30,000 bottles are produced, and the wines coming out now are from 2002, after a rather short period of ageing. One of those we liked best was the Mayolet, made from the local grape variety of the same name. The bright red colour is impressive, with its almost lilac hues, then the nose has rich ripe blackberry fruit, and the palate is enviably fresh-tasting and satisfyingly rounded. Vin Les Fourches, made from grenache, was equally striking, with strong pepper spice and cherry aromas. The palate is remarkably muscular, with a sweet, well-orchestrated and pleasantly stylish entry. The Torrette has liquorice and red peppers on the nose, and a nice long palate. The Prëmetta 2002 suffers from the unfortunate growing year, but Costantino has still managed to make it an enjoyably floral wine.

O	La Comète '01	🍷🍷	5
O	Valle d'Aosta Chardonnay Barrique '01	🍷🍷	5
O	Valle d'Aosta Müller Thurgau '02	🍷🍷	3*
O	Valle d'Aosta Petite Arvine '02	🍷🍷	4*
O	Valle d'Aosta Pinot Gris '02	🍷🍷	4*
●	Rouge du Prieur '01	🍷	5
●	Valle d'Aosta Pinot Noir '02	🍷	3
O	La Comète '00	🍷🍷	5
O	Valle d'Aosta Chardonnay Barrique '00	🍷🍷	5

●	Valle d'Aosta Mayolet '02	🍷🍷	5
●	Valle d'Aosta Torrette '02	🍷🍷	4
●	Vin Les Fourches '02	🍷🍷	5
●	Valle d'Aosta Prëmetta '02	🍷	5
●	Vin de La Sabla '01	🍷🍷	5
●	Vin Les Fourches '01	🍷🍷	5

AYMAVILLES (AO)

LES CRÊTES
LOC. VILLETOS, 50
11010 AYMAVILLES (AO)
TEL. 0165902274
E-MAIL: info@lescretesvins.it

Les Crêtes is without doubt the most famous winery in Valle d'Aosta, as well as a benchmark for smaller local producers, with its 18 hectares of vineyards and 170,000 bottles produced per year. Costantino Charrère works alongside winemaker, Claudio David, and Carlo Bataillon, who is the vineyard manager. The winery also benefits from the external consultancy of winemaker, Massimo Bellocchia. The wines presented this year are really special. In fact, they are astonishing, and two Three Glass prizes were awarded, which is a wonderful achievement by one of the most professional and charismatic figures in Italian winemaking. Let's begin with the superb Chardonnay Cuvée Bois 2001. Strong grapefruit and apples greet the nose, with an unobtrusive hint of wood. The stylish palate has perfect supporting acidity and well-judged strength, then the finish is very long and pleasantly bitterish. The Coteau La Tour 2001, from syrah grapes, is outstanding, with enthralling hints of pepper on the nose and a lovely juicy palate. This must be one of the most extraordinarily stylish reds we tasted this year. The inky Fumin Vigne La Tour 2001 is also good, showing varietal red pepper aromas with wood in the background, and a sweet, juicy entry on the palate. Two other excellent, attractively priced offerings were the standard-label Chardonnay and the Petite Arvine. Unfortunately, we don't have enough space to talk about the other two excellent Les Crêtes wines, the Pinot Noir and Torrette.

CHAMBAVE (AO)

LA CROTTA DI VEGNERON
P.ZZA RONCAS, 2
11023 CHAMBAVE (AO)
TEL. 016646670
E-MAIL: lacrotta@libero.it

La Crotta di Vegneron is the co-operative that is developing most promisingly in Valle d'Aosta now. Much of the credit goes to the 130 suppliers, chair Elio Cornaz and brilliant Piedmontese winemaker, Andrea Costa, who has relocated to the valley. As last year, the star of the range is the Moscato Passito di Chambave, with its amber gold colour. The generous, complex aromas begin with peaches, and develop into hazelnuts, ending with tropical fruit. The palate reveals strength, but also shows plenty of style that prevents the wine from becoming cloying. The long finish won us over, and in fact this is one of the best dried-grape "passito" wines we tasted for the Guide. Also impressive is the pinot grigio-based Malvoisie Flétrì, a sweet wine typical of the Nus area. The aromas are less complex and more floral than the previous wine, but the palate is generously fat and potent. The dry whites included brilliantly crafted moscato-based products that we enjoyed. The Muscat has very vibrant aromas of pears and apricots, in particular, which are reflected on the palate, and the finish is long and lingering, without the bitter note so often found in aromatic wines. The Müller Thurgau is pale straw yellow, with classic aromatic notes on the nose and a sweet, rounded palate refreshed by good acidity. From the red list, we recommend the Quatre Vignobles, a blend of petit rouge, gamay, fumin and pinot noir, and the Fumin. The Nus Rouge and dry Malvoisie are well typed.

O Valle d'Aosta Chardonnay Cuvée Frissonnière Les Crêtes Cuvée Bois '01 ♔♔♔ 7	O Valle d'Aosta Chambave Moscato Passito '01 ♔♔ 6
● Coteau La Tour '01 ♔♔♔ 6	● Valle d'Aosta Chambave Rouge Quatre Vignobles '01 ♔♔ 4*
● Valle d'Aosta Fumin Vigne La Tour '01 ♔♔ 6	O Valle d'Aosta Nus Malvoisie Flétrì '01 ♔♔ 6
O Valle d'Aosta Chardonnay Cuvée Frissonnière Les Crêtes '02 ♔♔ 5	O Valle d'Aosta Chambave Muscat '02 ♔♔ 4*
O Valle d'Aosta Petite Arvine Vigne Champorette '02 ♔♔ 5	● Valle d'Aosta Fumin '01 ♔ 4
● Valle d'Aosta Pinot Noir Vigne La Tour '02 ♔ 5	O Valle d'Aosta Malvoisie '02 ♔ 4
● Valle d'Aosta Torrette Vigne Les Toules '02 ♔ 4	O Valle d'Aosta Müller Thurgau '02 ♔ 4
O Valle d'Aosta Chardonnay Cuvée Frissonnière Les Crêtes Cuvée Bois '00 ♔♔♔ 6	● Valle d'Aosta Nus Rouge '02 ♔ 3
	O Valle d'Aosta Chambave Moscato Passito '00 ♔♔ 6

INTROD (AO)

LO TRIOLET
LOC. JUNOD, 7
11010 INTROD (AO)
TEL. 016595437
E-MAIL: lotriolet@libero.it

Young Marco Martin is taking giant strides forward, and in just a few years, has put together an impressive range of wines. Now, he is practically at the pinnacle of regional wine production. And that's not all. A few months ago, work began on a new winery, a short distance from the enchanting farm holiday centre he runs with his wife. As ever, Marco's parents Renato and Emilia continue to work alongside him among the vines and barrels. Turning to the wines, our favourite this year was the Pinot Gris 2002, aged in small casks, which is sourced from vineyards 700 to 800 metres above sea level. Its pale straw yellow introduces complex aromas of delicious banana and apple fruit that are left undisturbed by the oak notes from barrel ageing. The palate is explosively potent, with lashings of alcohol content, although this is disguised by the well-orchestrated, supporting acidity. The finish is long and mouthfilling. The Coteau Barrage 2002 is made from 85 per cent syrah and 15 per cent fumin grapes. It easily won Two Glasses for its strong, vibrant nose with red fruit, pepper and sweet spices melded together by elegant oak from the barriques. The palate is long and well-rounded, with plenty of juicy fruit. The selection of steel-aged wines is equally impressive, and super value for money, starting with the Pinot Gris and the two reds, the Gamay and the Nus Rouge.

MORGEX (AO)

CAVE DU VIN BLANC DE MORGEX
ET DE LA SALLE
FRAZ. LA RUINE - CHEMIN DES ILES, 19
11017 MORGEX (AO)
TEL. 0165800331
E-MAIL: caveduvinblanc@hotmail.com

This winery does much more than just vinify, age and bottle wines. When you visit the vineyards of the 100 or so member growers, you are astonished by the spectacular natural setting, with Mont Blanc as backdrop to the eye-catching low pergola-trained plots sheltered by dry stone walls, and growing at greater elevations than any others in Europe. Work at the winery is coming on in leaps and bounds. For instance, the decision to bottle the various vineyard selections was the right one and credit must go to winemaker, Gianluca Telloli, and chair, Mauro Jaccod. The most prestigious line includes a Rayon that has everything it takes to appeal to a wide public. Its pale straw yellow ushers in rich aromas of Alpine flowers, pears and apple fruit. The typically strong acidity of the terroir and the native prié blanc grape is tempered by shrewd selection of the riper bunches, a method which will be rigorously adopted from now. The Chaudelune Vin de Glace is a pleasant surprise. It comes from a winter harvest when the grapes were covered with snow and actually frozen. The colour is straw yellow, with golden highlights, and the nose has enjoyable aromas of apples and fresh almonds. The palate is all the more enjoyable for not being excessively sweet. We also liked the Metodo Classico, with its subtly stylish perlage, crusty bread and yeast aromas. The Blanc de Morgex Vini Estremi and the Blanc Fripon, a cuve close sparkling wine, are both interesting.

O	Valle d'Aosta Pinot Gris Élevé en Fût de Chêne '02	♙♙	5
●	Coteau Barrage '02	♙♙	5
O	Valle d'Aosta Pinot Gris Lo Triolet '02	♙♙	4
●	Valle d'Aosta Gamay '02	♙	4*
●	Valle d'Aosta Nus Rouge '02	♙	4*
●	Coteau Barrage '01	♟♟	5
O	Valle d'Aosta Pinot Gris Élevé en Fût de Chêne '01	♟♟	5

O	Chaudelune Vin de Glace '01	♙♙	5
O	Valle d'Aosta Blanc de Morgex et de La Salle Rayon '02	♙♙	4*
O	Valle d'Aosta Blanc de Morgex et de La Salle M. Cl. '00	♙	5
O	Valle d'Aosta Blanc de Morgex et de La Salle '02	♙	4
O	Valle d'Aosta Blanc de Morgex et de La Salle Vini Estremi '02	♙	4
O	Blanc Fripon Extra Dry	♙	3
O	Chaudelune Bianco '99	♟♟	5

QUART (AO)

VILLENEUVE (AO)

F.LLI GROSJEAN
VILLAGGIO OLLIGNAN, 1
11020 QUART (AO)
TEL. 0165775791
E-MAIL: maison.vigneronne@libero.it

ANSELMET
FRAZ. LA CRETE, 194
11018 VILLENEUVE (AO)
TEL. 016595419
E-MAIL: renato.anselmet@tiscalinet.it

This is one of the most consistently good wineries in the whole Valle d'Aosta. Founded over 30 years ago in 1969 by Dauphin Grosjean, the original 3,000 square metres under vine have now expanded to seven hectares, yielding an annual production of over 60,000 bottles. Grosjean has been helped by his five children for some years. Eraldo, Fernando, Marco, Piergiorgio look to Vincent as leader of the team, because he has valuable experience as a winemaker. The estate's land is situated on the border between Saint-Christophe and Quart, two towns close to Aosta. The wine we liked most this year was again the barrique-aged Pinot Noir. The ruby red introduces rich spice and mineral aromas, then appetizing acidity on the palate lends enjoyable elegance. The Fumin 2001 is no less appealing, although this wine perhaps has more room for improvement. The colour is inky dark, and there are strong spicy pepper aromas on the nose. The entry on the palate is enjoyably sweet and mouthfilling, with a long persistent finish. The Gamay 2002 is a nice wine, starting with the red colour streaked with lilac hues. The nose has smoky hints with red fruit and almonds in the background and the nicely long-lasting palate is delicate and interesting with a hint of bitterness. The Blanc de Dauphin is also worth mentioning, made from a mixture of varieties: pinot grigio, müller thurgau and moscato. Lastly the standard label Pinot Noir, Torrette and Petite Arvine are all good.

This is only the second year that Giorgio Anselmet has been running the business, and the results are very encouraging. He is still given valuable help by his father, Renato. The plan is to increase the three and a half hectares of vineyards to five by the end of 2006, on land that is situated on both the left and right banks of the Dora Baltea. Talking of excellent results, the "passito" Declivium. from pinot grigio and gewürztraminer, is truly delicious, and flaunts a beautiful golden yellow with coppery highlights. The explosive nose has aromas of tropical fruit, almonds and roses. The palate is so concentrated that it is almost oily in texture, and the finish is excitingly long. Unfortunately, only a small number of bottles are made. The most impressive whites were the standard-label Chardonnay and the barrique-aged version. The former is more concentrated and has more complex aromas, whereas the oak-conditioned edition holds its own thanks to the freshness and quality of the fruit. Moving on to the reds, we liked the Henry. This 100 per cent Syrah shows deep ruby red with strong, spicy aromas of pepper and vanilla. The palate is powerful and robust, with a nice sweet entry and long-lasting finish. Le Prisonnier is another good wine, made from a complicated blend of cornalin, mayolet, fumin and petit rouge that offers full, complex aromas nicely reflected on the palate. Unfortunately, space restrictions prevent us from saying more about the many wines presented, but they are all well typed and very good, like the Torrette Superiore and the Pinot Noir.

● Valle d'Aosta Fumin '01	♀♀	5
● Valle d'Aosta Pinot Noir Élevé en Barrique '01	♀♀	5
● Valle d'Aosta Gamay '02	♀♀	4*
○ Blanc de Dauphin '02	♀	3
○ Valle d'Aosta Petite Arvine '02	♀	4
● Valle d'Aosta Pinot Noir '02	♀	4
● Valle d'Aosta Torrette '02	♀	4
● Valle d'Aosta Fumin '00	♀♀	5
● Valle d'Aosta Pinot Noir Élevé en Barrique '00	♀♀	4*

● Henry '01	♀♀	5
○ Valle d'Aosta Chardonnay '02	♀♀	5*
○ Valle d'Aosta Chardonnay Élevé en Fût de Chêne '02	♀♀	5
● Valle d'Aosta Torrette Sup. Élevé en Fût de Chêne '02	♀♀	5
○ Declivium	♀♀	6
● Le Prisonnier	♀♀	7
● Valle d'Aosta Pinot Noir '02	♀	4
○ Valle d'Aosta Chardonnay Élevé en Fût de Chêne '01	♀♀	6
● Valle d'Aosta Torrette Sup. Élevé en Fût de Chêne '01	♀♀	5

OTHER WINERIES

Gabriella Minuzzo

Fraz. Sizan, 6
11020 Challand Saint Victor (AO)
tel. 0125967365
e-mail: gabriella.minuzzo@migrazioni.net

Gabriella Minuzzo did well this year. We recommend two wines in particular, the Müller Thurgau, with its complex nose and explosively kaleidoscopic palate, and the excellent Pinot Noir 2001, which shows fruit and vanilla aromas, then a sweet, very juicy palate. The Pinot Noir 2002 is also good.

● Valle d'Aosta Pinot Noir '01	🍷🍷	4
○ Valle d'Aosta Müller Thurgau '02	🍷🍷	4*
● Valle d'Aosta Pinot Noir '02	🍷	4

Caves Cooperatives de Donnas

via Roma, 97
11020 Donnas (AO)
tel. 0125807096 - 0125804481
e-mail: essevi@iol.it

This is another good lower valley co-operative making interesting reds. Best is the Donnas Napoleone selection, a blend of 85 per cent nebbiolo with freisa and neyret. The standard Donnas also scored well for its clear sweet spice and wild berries on the nose, and great complexity on the palate.

● Valle d'Aosta Donnas Napoleone '00	🍷🍷	4
● Valle d'Aosta Donnas '00	🍷	4

Maison Albert Vevey

s.da del Villair, 57
11017 Morgex (AO)
tel. 0165808930
e-mail: mariovevey@tiscalinet.it

It's not easy to make wine at 1,200 metres above sea level, as Albert Vevey knows, but his Blanc de Morgex is good. Green-flecked yellow introduces citrus fruit and Alpine flowers on the nose. The sweetish entry on the mouthfilling palate precedes strong acidity, and a slightly bitterish finish.

○ Valle d'Aosta Blanc de Morgex et de La Salle '02	🍷🍷	4*

Di Barrò

fraz. Veyne, 14
11018 Villeneuve (AO)
tel. 016595260
e-mail: dibarro@mediavallee.it

We tasted three good wines from this cellar, starting with the petit rouge and mayolet Torrette Superiore, with its rich fruit on the nose and full body on the palate. The aromatic barrique-aged Chardonnay is nice. We also liked the Lo Flapì, from part-dried malvoisie grapes.

○ Valle d'Aosta Chardonnay '01	🍷🍷	4*
● Valle d'Aosta Torrette Sup. '01	🍷🍷	5
○ Lo Flapì '02	🍷	7

PIEDMONT

In the 2004 edition of Italian Wines, Piedmont confirms its status as a colossus in domestic winemaking. The number of estates in the region has grown. Many others, deserving of a place in the Guide, had to be excluded because there simply wasn't enough space. There are also more awards. Piedmont has the same haul of Three Glass scores as last year, 60, but many more Two and a Half Glass wines. All this suggests that regional winemaking has found an even more coherent identity than in recent years. This is the age of territory and Piedmont is home to several production macrozones, all with well-defined characteristics. Langhe is becoming increasingly identified with nebbiolo, the variety that goes into both Barolo and Barbaresco, and Roero is steadily gaining respect. Asti Monferrato is witnessing the rise of Barbera d'Asti, which will soon eclipse Barbera d'Alba, showing the importance of the area's leading DOC. The part of Monferrato in the province of Alessandria is doing well, although perhaps held back by its over-concentrated wines, and the north of the region confirms a commitment to quality, with nebbiolo as its leading variety and a large group of dynamic winemakers. Above all, we should remember that wine is a product of nature, the elements, the seasons and the harvest. The bottles sampled this year all came from good, or even exceptional, vintages. The 1999, 2000 and 2001 harvests gave us three great years in a row, a run that was rudely interrupted by a poor harvest in 2002. We won't be able to assess the outcome properly until next year. A glance at the Three Glass wines, and at our extensive summer tasting sessions, reveals the remarkable achievements of Angelo Gaja and brothers Rivetti and Domenico Clerico, the only winemakers to earn double awards. Congratulations to Asti, which won its first Three Glasses for the new subzone of Nizza, and the spectacular performance of the Cantina Sociale di Vinchio e Vaglio. Even without its best selections, another co-operative, Produttori di Barbaresco, astounded the panel with a wine that offers unbeatable value for money. And without wishing to fuel the debate in the Langhe between traditionalists and modernists, we should mention the achievements of some of the great names, including Bartolo Mascarello, Sandrone, Scarzello, Giuseppe Mascarello and Borgogno. In the north, Rosanna Antoniolo celebrates 50 years in the business with Three Glasses that are perfectly timed to crown her illustrious career. Finally, a word on price. Much has been said about indiscriminate hikes blamed on the introduction of the euro and a booming wine market, but let us take a much-needed look at the actual situation. The lists of the estates we visited show very few increases. This only goes to confirm what we have always said. With one or two exceptions, you get more bang for your buck in Piedmont than you do in France, Spain, the United States or Australia.

AGLIANO TERME (AT)

AGLIANO TERME (AT)

DACAPO
S.DA ASTI MARE, 4
14041 AGLIANO TERME (AT)
TEL. 0141964921
E-MAIL: info@dacapo.it

ROBERTO FERRARIS
FRAZ. DOGLIANI, 33
14041 AGLIANO TERME (AT)
TEL. 0141954234
E-MAIL: az.ferraris@virgilio.it

The Dacapo estate was established in 1997. That was when Paolo Dania and Dino Riccomagno decided to merge their experience and know-how in a quality-oriented winery. In the space of just six years, a very short time in which to produce results, the two partners have attained their goal. Today, they produce around 30,000 bottles a year, split between three labels that bear full testament to the territory's vocation. The lion's share naturally belongs to the Barbera d'Asti, available in two interesting versions. The Sanbastiàn selection is from in a rented vineyard in Castagnole Monferrato and embodies the finesse, elegance and fruitiness typical of the Castagnole terroir. Its partner, the Superiore Nizza Vigna Dacapo, comes from one of the estate's own plots in Agliano, the "cradle" of Asti Barbera, which traditionally produces structured, warm, ageable wines. The bright red Sanbastiàn '01, offers complex, clear aromas of berry fruit, sweet spice and black cherry and a marked acidulous vein on the palate that is nicely balanced by the fullness of the body. The Superiore Nizza, again a 2001 but oak-aged for 12 extra months, is more concentrated, as is clear from its colour. It has an intense bouquet of blackberry, plum and coffee, then a palate whose body does not disturb the harmony of a remarkably fragrant, well-rounded structure. The estate also grows at Castagnole the grapes for an excellent Ruché. Its freshness is nicely balanced by a weighty palate, making it one of the most outstanding wines in its category.

We are always delighted when small estates like the one run by Roberto Ferraris take a step up the quality ladder. Last year, we thought this skilled Agliano grower was coming on, and dedicated more space to him in the Guide in the hope of greater things to come. This year, all of his limited range of wines performed brilliantly, and some are truly outstanding. Roberto's seriousness is also evident in the acquisition of three new hectares of vineyards, which gives him a total of nine under vine, and in his desire to maintain his well-tried consulting relationship with eminent oenologist, Giuliano Noè. His 35,000 bottles a year are split across the three Barbera d'Astis that make up his entire production, Agliano has, in fact, become a sort of Barbera d'Asti capital. Berry fruit and subtle spices make the fresh-tasting standard-label Barbera very agreeable, but it is the two selections that best express the mysterious, winning combination of man and nature that lies at the heart of every great wine. The Barbera Nobbio '01 is exquisite. Deep and concentrated to the eye, it has complex aromas of black cherry and autumn leaves with traces of coffee. Its pure fruit palate – no oak here – is soft and fragrant, with a long, harmonious finish. La Cricca, barrique-conditioned for an extra year, is even better. Its intense, well-defined nose offers mineral tones with hints of berry fruit liqueur, while sensuous mouthfeel offers rich, fragrant pulp and superb nose-palate consistency. The finish is leisurely and very well-balanced.

● Barbera d'Asti Sanbastiàn '01	♟♟	4*
● Barbera d'Asti Sup.		
Nizza Vigna Dacapo '01	♟♟	5
● Ruché di Castagnole M.to		
Bric Majoli '02	♟♟	4
● Barbera d'Asti Vigna Dacapo '98	♟♟	4
● Barbera d'Asti Vigna Dacapo '99	♟♟	4
● Barbera d'Asti Sanbastiàn '00	♟♟	4
● Barbera d'Asti Sup.		
Nizza Vigna Dacapo '00	♟♟	5

● Barbera d'Asti Sup. La Cricca '00	♟♟	4
● Barbera d'Asti '01	♟♟	3*
● Barbera d'Asti Sup. Nobbio '01	♟♟	4
● Barbera d'Asti Sup. Nobbio '99	♟♟	4
● Barbera d'Asti La Cricca '99	♟♟	5

AGLIANO TERME (AT)

GARETTO
S.DA ASTI MARE, 30
14041 AGLIANO TERME (AT)
TEL. 0141954068
E-MAIL: tenutagaretto@garetto.it

Alessandro Garetto is one of Asti's golden boys. A combination of verve, determination and indisputable talent has secured him a place in the front rank of local producers and have turned his winery into a major benchmark for Barbera d'Asti, for which Agliano is an important hub. The 15 skilfully managed hectares planted to vine are soon to expand to 20, as some of the estate's plots are not yet in production. The labels Alessandro proposes this year owe much of their success to the excellent position of the plots and the invaluable support of his consulting team, agronomist, Nicola Argamante, and oenologist, Lorenzo Quinterno. With three selections, Barbera d'Asti is the mainstay of the estate's production. Favà '01 has surpassed itself. Its dark, concentrated appearance, ushers in a bouquet of faint, toasty oak mingling with fruit, black cherry and plum. It is dense, full and velvety on the palate, with nice alcohol and a long, balanced finish. The slightly less complex In Pectore from the same vintage is aged partly in barriques and partly in large oak barrels. But what it lacks in complexity it more than makes up for with the remarkable elegance that underpins the whole palate. This year's version is simple and easy-drinking. Alessandro also produces two whites. The Chardonnay Diversamente is fruity and pleasing, with a slightly bitter palate, while the Cortese is straightforward and technically unpretentious, with an attractive, flowery bouquet.

AGLIANO TERME (AT)

AGOSTINO PAVIA E FIGLI
FRAZ. BOLOGNA, 33
14041 AGLIANO TERME (AT)
TEL. 0141954125
E-MAIL: mauro.pavia@crasti.it

The Agostino Pavia estate is a prime example of the philosophy behind many of the small wineries in the Agliano area. It farms a few hectares under vine to meet the needs of the cellar without having to buy in fruit. A limited number of good, terroir-driven labels are released. And attention, not to mention resources, is concentrated on the most representative local variety, barbera. The Pavia family – Agostino works with his sons, Giuseppe and Mauro – have got where they are today through sacrifice and determination. Now, they are now reaping the well-deserved rewards of their labours with a series of excellent-quality wines. They produce three Barbera selections, all Barbera d'Astis. Marescialla comes from a 60-year-old plot and stays in wood for about a year. The '01 version is vibrant red with a purplish edge, and has an intense bouquet of well-defined black cherry and coffee, with faint undertones of spice. The generous, dry palate maintains great balance through to its long finish. The Bricco Blina, aged entirely in stainless steel, is excellent. Soft and elegant, it unveils lovely traces of minerals and autumn leaves. We weren't quite so impressed with the 2001 Moliss, which ages in large barrels and 900-litre casks, but it is still very drinkable and well-balanced. The Monferrato Talin, a newcomer to the ranks this year, is a blend of 85 per cent barbera with cabernet sauvignon, and the result is an austere, intense wine with an elegant bouquet of black berry fruit and liquorice, then a velvety palate. Finally, the Grignolino is light and enjoyable.

● Barbera d'Asti Sup. Favà '01	♀♀	5
● Barbera d'Asti Sup. In Pectore '01	♀♀	4*
● Barbera d'Asti Tra Neuit e Dì '02	♀	3*
○ Cortese dell'Alto M.to Le Due Cioche '02	♀	3
○ Piemonte Chardonnay Diversamente '02	♀	4
● Barbera d'Asti Sup. Favà '97	♀♀	5
● Barbera d'Asti Sup. In Pectore '97	♀♀	4
● Barbera d'Asti Sup. Favà '98	♀♀	5
● Barbera d'Asti Sup. Favà '99	♀♀	5
● Barbera d'Asti Sup. Favà '00	♀♀	5
● Barbera d'Asti Sup. In Pectore '00	♀♀	4

● Monferrato Rosso Talin '00	♀♀	5
● Barbera d'Asti Bricco Blina '01	♀♀	4*
● Barbera d'Asti Sup. La Marescialla '01	♀♀	5
● Barbera d'Asti Moliss '01	♀	4
● Grignolino d'Asti '02	♀	3
● Barbera d'Asti La Marescialla '96	♀♀	5
● Barbera d'Asti La Marescialla '98	♀♀	5
● Barbera d'Asti La Marescialla '99	♀♀	5
● Barbera d'Asti Moliss '99	♀♀	4
● Barbera d'Asti La Marescialla '00	♀♀	5

AGLIÈ (TO)

CIECK
FRAZ. SAN GRATO
S.DA BARDESONO
10011 AGLIÈ (TO)
TEL. 0124330522
E-MAIL: info@cieck.it

The Cieck estate takes its name from the beautiful, elegantly restored "cascina", or farmhouse, in which it is housed. It produces a fine range of wines from varieties native to the Canavese area, with erbaluce obviously leading the way. The estate has Gianfranco Cordero as consultant and several projects under way with the University of Turin, which carries out some of its research here. The wines all have a style that puts the emphasis on precise winemaking and respect for the grape type. The Erbaluces on offer are all excellent but we particularly liked the basic version, which is a delicate, textbook example. Its superbly defined aromas recall spring flowers and chlorophyll, then the palate is subtle and discreet with a long, lingering finish. Vigna Misobolo has greater depth, but opens on a more restrained note. The Erbaluce Calliope, vinified in both stainless steel vats and new barriques, is a well-balanced, very stylish wine whose oak merges well with the varietal notes, which predominate. We were impressed by the San Giorgio, a "metodo classico" Brut. Rigorously well-made in terms of both vinification and bottle fermentation, it is a radically distinctive wine in that it brings out the full character of the erbaluce grape. Cieck Rosso is made from several of the zone's native varieties that grow together in the oldest vineyards. It ages in used barriques and has lovely, complex, deliciously spicy aromas followed by a stylish, well-balanced palate. Caluso Passito Alladium is modern and well made.

AGLIÈ (TO)

SILVA
CASCINE ROGGE, 1/B
10011 AGLIÈ (TO)
TEL. 012433356
E-MAIL: silvastefano@eurexnet.it

In last year's edition of the Guide, we pointed out Giovanni Silva's winery as a rising star in the Canavese firmament. We are happy to say that this year's tastings confirmed the quality achieved by this estate, which is now among the best in the zone. All due recognition for this success must go to the investments Giovanni has made in recent years, including a spotless new cellar with up-to-date equipment, and the support of a first-rate oenologist, Gianfranco Cordero. The extremely delicate Erbaluce Tre Ciochè is a fine version of a difficult vintage, 2002. Pale straw yellow in colour, it offers vivid, varietal aromas then a palate characterized by elegant flowers and a marked acidulous vein that is lent further finesse by lovely minerality. The Erbaluce Ca' Neuva is fermented and matured in oak with a very modern procedure involving large barrels instead of barriques. It is a very harmonious wine whose oaky overtones enhance the bouquet without weighing it down. The restrained, stylish palate is in the same idiom. Tre Ciochè Rosso, a blend of barbera with small proportions of nebbiolo and neretto, is vinified in a rotary fermenter and aged in pre-used barriques. Deep in colour, indeed almost opaque, it offers rich cherry and blackberry aromas with a barely discernible trace of oak. The palate shows more style and consistency than concentration. The lustrous, warm-hued Caluso Passito Poetica has an intriguing bouquet and an intense, chewy, very sweet palate.

● Canavese Rosso Cieck '01	▾▾	4
○ Erbaluce di Caluso		
Vigna Misobolo '02	▾▾	3*
○ Erbaluce di Caluso Calliope '01	▾▾	4
○ Caluso Passito		
Alladium Vigneto Runc '98	▾▾	5
○ Erbaluce di Caluso '02	▾▾	3*
○ Caluso Spumante Brut		
S. Giorgio '99	▾▾	5
○ Erbaluce di Caluso Calliope '00	▿▿	4
● Canavese Rosso Cieck '00	▿▿	4*

● Canavese Rosso Tre Ciochè '01	▾▾	4
○ Erbaluce di Caluso		
Tre Ciochè '02	▾▾	3*
○ Erbaluce di Caluso Ca' Neuva '01	▾▾	4
○ Caluso Passito Poetica '98	▾▾	6
● Canavese Rosso Tre Ciochè '00	▿▿	4

ALBA (CN)

BOROLI
LOC. MADONNA DI COMO, 34
12051 ALBA (CN)
TEL. 0173365477
E-MAIL: info@boroli.it

In our notes last year, we introduced Boroli as a relatively new estate with a big ambition – to make its mark on the oenological map of Italy. This year, we can safely say that all the hard work of Silvano and Elena Boroli has paid off. First of all, renovation of the vineyards is almost complete and the Borolis will soon be able to concentrate on other things. The wines they offered us for tasting were very good indeed. We will start with the Barolos, the estate's premium product. Every member of the cellar team deserves credit, from director of operations, Enzo Alluvione, and son, Daniele, the agronomist, to Achille Boroli, who takes care of the marketing side of the business. The flagship wine is the Barolo Villero, a fine interpretation of this Castiglione Falletto vineyard. Austere on nose and palate, it reveals its elegance at once in its colour. Red fruit and wild berry aromas are laced with soft notes of vanilla from skilfully administered oak, then the palate unveils silky, never assertive tannins. The standard-label Barolo also shows the hand of expert oenologist Beppe Caviola. We awarded very high marks for its complex aromas and immediate drinkability, for it is every bit as good as the Villero. Also superb is the Barbera Bricco dei Fagiani. A fruit-rich, spicy bouquet is followed by pleasing acidity in the mouth that adds length to the finish. Because of the poor vintage, the Borolis have forgone their Moscato Aureum. The 2001 edition was excellent and for 2002, the cellar has released an agreeable, refreshing basic version.

ALBA (CN)

CERETTO
LOC. SAN CASSIANO, 34
12051 ALBA (CN)
TEL. 0173282582
E-MAIL: ceretto@ceretto.com

The various plots belonging to the Ceretto brothers are dotted across some of the most important vineyards in the Langhe, which ensures a high-quality range of wines, each with its own distinct, terroir-driven personality. As usual, we cover Bricco Rocche and Bricco Asili elsewhere in the Guide and concentrate here on the wines produced by La Bernardina (a sparkling wine and a red, Monsordo); Blangé (an Arneis named after the estate); Rossana (Dolcetto Rossana, Barbera Piana and Nebbiolo Lantasco); Arbarei (a good Riesling comes from this vineyard); and Ceretto (Barolo Zonchera, Barbaresco Asij and Barolo Chinato). We open our tasting notes with the lovely Monsordo, from cabernet sauvignon, pinot nero, merlot and nebbiolo. Ruby garnet tinged with orange, it offers wonderful iodine aromas mingling with raspberry and juniper. The palate is succulent, the tannins robust and the long finish is redolent of leather. The Riesling Arbarei has golden highlights and a bouquet that strikes a nice balance between the sweet notes and the minerally varietal vein. The palate is soft and generous. The lively, lingering Barolo Zonchera has citrus, spice and fruit aromas, and the Barolo Chinato is well balanced and complex. Rounding off the long list we have a series of quality wines that includes the captivating Barbera Piana 2001, the classy Barbaresco Asij 2000 and the pleasant Blangé, a white that does very well in the market.

● Barolo Villero '99	♟♟	7
● Barbera d'Alba Sup. Bricco dei Fagiani '00	♟♟	5
● Barolo '99	♟♟	6
○ Moscato d'Asti '02	♟	3
● Barolo Bussia '97	♟♟	8
● Barolo Villero '97	♟♟	8
● Dolcetto d'Alba Madonna di Como '01	♟♟	4
● Barolo Villero '98	♟♟	8

● Langhe Rosso Monsordo La Bernardina '00	♟♟	6
● Barbaresco Asij '00	♟♟	6
● Barbera d'Alba Piana '01	♟♟	5
○ Langhe Arbarei La Bernardina '01	♟♟	5
● Barolo Zonchera '99	♟♟	6
● Barolo Chinato	♟♟	7
● Langhe Nebbiolo Lantasco '01	♟	5
● Dolcetto d'Alba Rossana '02	♟	4
○ Langhe Arneis Blangé '02	♟	4
● Langhe Rosso Monsordo La Bernardina '99	♟♟	6
○ Piemonte Brut M. Cl. La Bernardina '96	♟♟	5

Gianluigi Lano

Fraz. San Rocco Seno d'Elvio
s.da Basso, 38
12051 Alba (CN)
tel. 0173286958

This small family-run winery, which has six hectares planted to vine for an annual production of around 35,000 bottles, has progressed in leaps and bounds. Driving this impressive growth are Gianluigi Lano, his wife Daniela and oenologist Gianfranco Cordero. Top of our list came the clear garnet Barbaresco 2000, which boasts rich, complex aromas of cherry, strawberry and chocolate and a palate that is powerful and very stylish. The Barbera d'Alba Fondo Prà also performed very well. A cornucopia of fruit on the nose ushers in an entry on the palate that is sweet and juicy. The finish gains length from a tangy, acidulous note that braces the progression. The complexity of this wine's bouquet owes much to the expert, shrewdly gauged use of small barrels. The standard-label Barbera offers value for money that is hard to find in other Langhe labels. While less complex in its aromas, it offers a palate that is very fresh-tasting and ready to drink, with notes of clear red fruit and a tangy finish that captivates the senses. Finally, we also sampled the basic Dolcetto 2002, which has an extraordinarily complex bouquet, despite the poor harvest. The Langhe Favorita and Langhe Freisa wines are well managed and hold no surprises.

● Barbaresco '00	TT	6*
● Barbera d'Alba '01	TT	4*
● Barbera d'Alba Fondo Prà '01	TT	5
● Dolcetto d'Alba '02	TT	3*
● Langhe Freisa '02	T	3
○ Langhe Favorita '02	T	3
● Barbaresco '97	YY	6
● Barbera d'Alba Fondo Prà '98	YY	5
● Barbaresco '98	YY	6
● Barbera d'Alba Fondo Prà '99	YY	5
● Barbera d'Alba Fondo Prà '00	YY	5
● Barbaresco '99	YY	6

ALBA (CN)

Pio Cesare

via Cesare Balbo, 6
12051 Alba (CN)
tel. 0173440386
e-mail: piocesare@piocesare.it

The Pio Cesare estate belongs to that hallowed circle of wineries on which are founded the history and the success of Alba's viticulture. Founded in 1881, it is now in the competent hands of Pio Boffa, aided and abetted by oenologist, Paolo Fenocchio, and nephew Cesare Benvenuto, who runs the commercial side of the business. Cellar renovation is proceeding at a brisk pace, but is nevertheless behind schedule, as the old structure must be handled with kid gloves. Boffa has bought several new plots at La Morra, Novello and Serralunga to bring the total number of hectares under vine to 40. We were very impressed by the wines he offered us, and in particular by the Barolo Ornato 1999. Its bouquet releases cocoa powder, wild berries and liquorice, while on the palate it reveals considerable power and energy, buttressed by captivating complexity. The Barbaresco Bricco 1999 is another winner, revelling in a gorgeous red fruit bouquet, with cherry and strawberry to the fore, lifted by chocolate tones. And let's not forget the Barbaresco 2000 and the standard-label Barolo 1999. Made with every bit as much attention to detail and quality as the flagship labels, they both show great class and balance on the palate. The fruity, fragrant Barbera d'Alba Fides is also very good, as is the Langhe Chardonnay PiodiLei 2001, which has banana and pineapple aromas, an underlying hint of vanilla, and a well-rounded palate with a long, long finish. The whites from the 2002 harvest – the Gavi, Roero Arneis and Piemonte Chardonnay L'Altro – are all well managed.

● Barbaresco Bricco '99	TT	8
● Barolo Ornato '99	TT	8
● Barbaresco '00	TT	8
● Barbera d'Alba Fides '00	TT	6
○ Langhe Chardonnay PiodiLei '01	TT	6
● Barolo '99	TT	8
○ Gavi '02	T	4
○ Piemonte Chardonnay L'Altro '02	T	4
○ Roero Arneis '02	T	4
● Barolo Ornato '85	YYY	6
● Barolo Ornato '89	YYY	6
● Barbaresco Bricco '97	YYY	8
● Barbaresco Bricco '98	YY	8
● Barolo Ornato '98	YY	8

ALBA (CN)

PODERI COLLA
LOC. SAN ROCCO SENO D'ELVIO, 82
12051 ALBA (CN)
TEL. 0173290148
E-MAIL: info@podericolla.it

Ten years ago, Tino Colla and his niece, Federica, joined forces to create this new Langhe winery with the staunch support of the very capable Beppe Colla. Today, Poderi Colla is the proud owner of three beautiful properties, Cascine Drago at Alba, Tenuta Roncaglia at Barbaresco and Dardi Le Rose at Monforte. Each enjoys an excellent location and specializes in different categories of wine. Key to the estate's success is the tremendous sense of team spirit that binds the three protagonists, Federica, Beppe and Tino Colla. This year, the wines they offered us were marvellous, in particular the Barolo Bussia Dardi Le Rose 1999 from their Monforte plots. It is a truly superb example of a classic Barolo. The elegance emerges in a bouquet that revels in notes of roses and wild berries, with faint traces of tar. On the palate, the silky, subtle tannins lead into a finish worthy of a genuinely great wine with long, lingering length. The Barbaresco Tenuta Roncaglia is notable for its fruity aromas and for generous flesh that fills the palate. The Nebbiolo has nothing to envy these, revealing a powerful, muscular character that was well in evidence at our tastings. Barbera d'Alba Costa Bruna is more immediate, with just the right amount of fruit and a wealth of complex aromas. The Langhe Sanrocco 2002, a white, is very well managed, in spite of the poor harvest.

ALBA (CN)

★ PRUNOTTO
REG. SAN CASSIANO, 4/G
12051 ALBA (CN)
TEL. 0173280017
E-MAIL: prunotto@prunotto.it

Bought in 1989 by Marchesi Antinori, this historic estate continues to produce excellent results and a quality of wines that keeps the cellar right at the top of the category. Part of the secret of this success has been the decision to invest money in land, the most recent acquisition being in 1997, when a stunning five-hectare vineyard near Barbaresco known as Bric Turot was purchased, and another of similar size in Treiso planted to moscato. Credit for the quality of the wines must also go to the super efforts of all those who maintain the great reputation of this house, notably Albiera Antinori, who is in charge, and Gianluca Torrengo, a young oenologist from Alba. Once again, it is the Barolo Bussia that earned most applause and a Three Glass award. From one of the most prestigious vineyards at Monforte, its elegance is obvious in the intense ruby red colour and aromas of red berries and sweet spices, including vanilla. Austere on the palate without being too severe, it has a modern note in the finish that lends rare finesse. The standard-label Barolo is a little simpler on nose and palate, but also gained high marks for its grace and gentle harmony. Bric Turot comes from the Barbaresco vineyard of that name. It delighted the panel with captivating notes of moreish blackberry and cherry fruit. Prunotto is lucky enough to vinifying grapes from an impressive number of vineyards, turning out very well-made wines such as Barbera d'Alba Pian Romualdo, Nebbiolo d'Alba Occhetti and Dolcetto d'Alba Mosesco.

● Barolo Bussia Dardi Le Rose '99	🍷🍷	7*
● Barbaresco Tenuta Roncaglia '00	🍷🍷	7
● Barbera d'Alba Costa Bruna Tenuta Roncaglia '01	🍷🍷	4
● Nebbiolo d'Alba '01	🍷🍷	4
○ Langhe Bianco Sanrocco '02	🍷	4
● Barolo Bussia Dardi Le Rose '96	🍷🍷	7
● Barbaresco Tenuta Roncaglia '97	🍷🍷	7
● Barbaresco Tenuta Roncaglia '98	🍷🍷	7
● Barolo Bussia Dardi Le Rose '98	🍷🍷	7
● Langhe Bricco del Drago '99	🍷🍷	5

● Barolo Bussia '99	🍷🍷🍷	8
● Barbaresco Bric Turot '00	🍷🍷	8
● Barbera d'Alba Pian Romualdo '01	🍷🍷	6
● Dolcetto d'Alba Mosesco '01	🍷🍷	5
● Nebbiolo d'Alba Occhetti '01	🍷🍷	5
● Barolo '99	🍷🍷	7
● Barbera d'Alba '01	🍷	4
● Barbera d'Asti Fiulòt '02	🍷	4
● Barbera d'Asti Costamiòle '96	🍷🍷🍷	7
● Barolo Bussia '96	🍷🍷🍷	8
● Barbera d'Asti Costamiòle '97	🍷🍷🍷	7
● Barbera d'Asti Costamiòle '99	🍷🍷🍷	7
● Barolo Bussia '98	🍷🍷🍷	8

ALBA (CN)

MAURO SEBASTE
FRAZ. GALLO
VIA GARIBALDI, 222/BIS
12051 ALBA (CN)
TEL. 0173262148
E-MAIL: maurosebaste@maurosebaste.it

It is now 12 years since Mauro Sebaste set out to take his estate to the top rank of Langhe winemaking. His efforts are more than evident in the quality of the wines he presented this year. Thanks in part to the superb soil on which the grapes grow, Mauro's wines made a big impression on our panel. Without doubt, the cream of the crop is the Barolo Prapò, which comes from the vineyard of the same name at Serralunga. Its crisp, persistent aromas of red berry fruit and oak-derived vanilla lead into impressive power and structure on the palate, which render the finish long and leisurely. One notch down we have the Barolo Brunate, another jewel in the Sebaste family crown, whose structure tends more towards elegance than a display of muscle. The bouquet brims with fruit and liquorice, then and the pleasing palate is eminently drinkable. Taking a bit more of a back seat this time, the Barolo Monvigliero is uncomplicated in the glass but is nevertheless a well-managed, premium-quality wine. We very much liked the Langhe Rosso Centobricchi, a blend of 80 per cent barbera with 20 per cent nebbiolo. The bouquet reveals potent aromas of berry fruit and pepper, while the palate has extraordinary power, starting out sweet and moving into a masterly finish. The excellent Nebbiolo Parigi repeats the success it enjoyed last year, in its rather modern, fruit-forward style. The same goes for the Dolcetto d'Alba S. Rosalia, which offers notes of almond, plum and blueberry. Finally, the Roero Arneis is well-made.

ALBA (CN)

SINAGLIO
FRAZ. SAN ROCCO CHERASCA, 9/BIS
12051 ALBA (CN)
TEL. 0173612209
E-MAIL: poderi.sinaglio@tiscalinet.it

The 2002 vintage was not one of the best for the Accomo brothers' estate. Poor weather conditions hampered production and they did not release their Diano d'Alba selections. For that reason, the bottle we liked best was the Barbera Vigna Erta 2001, a wine of impenetrable inky black. The bouquet proffers notes of chocolate, roasted coffee, plum jam and cherry, while the palate is almost too potent, indeed a tad unbalanced, although the finish is long and satisfying. The Nebbiolo d'Alba Giachét 2001 is full of pleasing sensations, starting with its ruby red colour flecked with faint orange highlights. It offers aromas of cherry and strawberry fruit, and sweet vanilla spice, then and lovely mouthfilling flesh on the palate. The deep purple Langhe Rosso Sinaij 2001, a nebbiolo, barbera and freisa blend, has strong notes of balsam, spice, charred oak and super-ripeness. The palate reveals a fairly free hand with the oak, and lively tannins. The Dolcetto 2002 has suffered the effects of the poor vintage, but is skilfully and correctly made. Inky purple in the glass, it has a bouquet of hay, leather and spices, then agreeable fruit on the palate. Last on our list is the Langhe Chardonnay 2002, a straw-yellow wine with green highlights. Its predominant aromas are of pear and apple, with an underlying hint of almond, while the palate shows nice body and good drinkability.

● Langhe Rosso Centobricchi '01	♟♟	5
● Nebbiolo d'Alba Parigi '01	♟♟	4
● Dolcetto d'Alba S. Rosalia '02	♟♟	4*
● Barolo Brunate '99	♟♟	7
● Barolo Prapò '99	♟♟	7
○ Roero Arneis '02	♟	4
● Barolo Monvigliero '99	♟	7
● Nebbiolo d'Alba Parigi '00	♟♟	5
● Barolo Monvigliero '98	♟♟	7
● Barolo Prapò '98	♟♟	7

● Barbera d'Alba Vigna Erta '01	♟♟	4*
● Nebbiolo d'Alba Giachét '01	♟♟	4*
● Langhe Rosso Sinaij '01	♟	4
● Dolcetto di Diano d'Alba '02	♟	3
○ Langhe Chardonnay '02	♟	3
● Langhe Rosso Sinaij '99	♟♟	4
● Barbera d'Alba Vigna Erta '00	♟♟	4
● Barbera d'Alba Vigna Erta '99	♟	4

ALFIANO NATTA (AL)

TENUTA CASTELLO DI RAZZANO
FRAZ. CASARELLO
LOC. RAZZANO, 2
15021 ALFIANO NATTA (AL)
TEL. 0141922124 - 0141922426
E-MAIL: info@castellodirazzano.it

As they strive to make the most of their winery's historic setting, the Olearo family has worked over the last few years to restore its architectural features and replace the equipment in the old cellars. In the meanwhile, they have continued to work in the vineyards. Despite some changes at the top of the range, this year's wines show good consistency and the quality is solid across the board. We awarded the Barbera d'Asti Superiore Vigna del Beneficio Two Glasses for its deep ruby red colour, its aromas of blackberry and blueberry enriched with notes of oak-derived vanilla and balsam, and its well-balanced palate that starts out softly and finishes on a lovely reprise of fruit. We were pleasantly surprised by the Barbera d'Asti Superiore Campasso, which is not just excellent quality for money, but also has personality and character. The bouquet is redolent of ripe plum, blackberry and forest floor, and gentle maturation in 20-hectolitre oak barrels has imbued it with spicy tones. The pinot nero-based Onero missed a Two Glass score by a whisker. But don't be fooled by the high score. It will get even better in the next two or three years. For now, it is ruby, tending to purple, and has rather a closed bouquet, while on the palate there is already evidence of the elegance and grace that it will eventually acquire. The Vigna Caligaris, a very well-structured wine, is a little below par, probably because it is not yet ready and the overall balance is a bit patchy. Both the nose and the palate show traces of oak that have still to mellow out.

ALICE BEL COLLE (AL)

CA' BIANCA
REG. SPAGNA, 58
15010 ALICE BEL COLLE (AL)
TEL. 0144745420
E-MAIL: giv@giv.it

Ca' Bianca, a Gruppo Italiano Vini estate, has an annual production of about 1,000,000 bottles. At around 50 per cent of the total stock, barbera accounts for the lion's share of the vines grown, but all the major Piedmont grape types are represented, including cortese from Novi Ligure and the lampia and michet subvarieties of nebbiolo from La Morra. Manager and oenologist Marco Galeazzo, at the helm since 1987, runs the estate with passion and skill. On its third release, Barbera Chersì is a resounding success. Its red colour is so deep and concentrated that it is almost opaque, and the bouquet is wonderfully intense and generous, with hints of plum, blackberry, walnutskin and vanilla. On the palate, the acidity melds well with the substantial structure. There is considerable depth and length, despite the rather strong oaky tones that have yet to lose their edge. The Gavi won Two Glasses primarily for the character, supreme elegance and style of the palate, where well-balanced acidity makes it very pleasant to drink. Aromas of apples and spring flowers put the finishing touches to the overall harmony. The Barolo is obtained by combining two differently matured versions of the same wine. Some is matured in new barriques while most ages in medium-sized barrels for 24 months. Intense, bright red in appearance, it is redolent of violets and roses tinged with spice, notably cinnamon. The palate has fabulous complexity of flavour and very decent structure. The Barbera d'Asti 2001 shows the typical acidity of the variety, which is nicely offset by the very soft mouthfeel.

● Barbera d'Asti Sup. Campasso '01	ŸŸ	4*
● Barbera d'Asti Sup. Vigna del Beneficio '01	ŸŸ	5
● Barbera d'Asti Sup. Vigna Valentino Caligaris '01	Ÿ	6
● Monferrato Rosso Onero '01	Ÿ	5
● Barbera d'Asti Sup. Vigna del Beneficio '00	ŸŸ	5
● Barbera d'Asti Sup. Vigna Valentino Caligaris '00	ŸŸ	6
● Barbera d'Asti Sup. Campasso '00	Ÿ	4
● Monferrato Rosso Onero '00	Ÿ	5

● Barbera d'Asti Chersì '01	ŸŸ	7
○ Gavi '02	ŸŸ	5
● Barolo '99	ŸŸ	7
● Barbera d'Asti '01	Ÿ	5
● Barbera d'Asti Chersì '99	ŸŸ	6
● Barbera d'Asti Chersì '00	ŸŸ	6
● Barolo '98	ŸŸ	6

ASTI

BARBARESCO (CN)

F.lli Rovero
loc. Valdonata
fraz. San Marzanotto, 218
14100 Asti
tel. 0141592460 - 0141530102
e-mail: grapparovero@inwind.it

Ca' Romè - Romano Marengo
via Rabajà 36
12050 Barbaresco (CN)
tel. 0173635126
e-mail: info@carome.com

Brothers Claudio, Franco and Michele Rovero, ably supported by Michele's young oenologist son, Enrico, run a trio of activities with enormous passion and success. They have an "agriturismo" facility, a distillery and a winery. The 20 hectares of vineyards give them an average annual production of around 90,000 bottles of certified organic wines and each year sees a marked improvement in quality. Once again, our preference was for the Barbera Rouvé, a gorgeous deep purplish ruby colour with berry fruit and pepper aromas and faint overtones of spice and vanilla. Full and rounded on the palate, it strikes a perfect balance between acidity and alcohol. Villa Guani is a deliciously easy drinking, barrique-conditioned Sauvignon with nicely judged oak that never threatens to mask the clear notes of bell pepper, peach and banana. The palate echoes the balance and elegance in a notable structure that leads to a lingering finish. The steel-conditioned Barbera Gustin perfectly embodies the variety in its red fruit and balsam bouquet, tangy acidity and velvety, round tannins. Rocca Schiavino, from 85 per cent cabernet sauvignon and 15 per cent barbera, offers vegetal, plum and cocoa powder, then the palate shows solid structure and long length. The Lajetto is a fruity, tannic Pinot Nero with varietal gamey notes. Villa Drago, a sauvignon vinified in stainless steel vats, is pleasant and well made, and the Grignolino La Casalina flaunts rich fruit and flower aromas but is still held back by strong acidity and over-enthusiastic tannins.

Big changes are afoot at Ca' Romè. Romano Marengo, still the mainstay of the estate, has passed control to his son, Giuseppe, who also acts as oenologist. The two women of the family, daughter Paola and mother Olimpia, who welcomes visitors from Italy and abroad, also have a say in the smooth running of the estate. In addition, work to restructure the cellars is now complete, simplifying internal logistics through the creation of an underground tunnel that links the winemaking area to the spaces where the wine is aged in barriques and large barrels. The bottles on offer this year are superb, and raise the quality bar to new heights, although the estate already has a reputation for high quality products. We particularly liked the Barbaresco Sorì Rio Sordo, which has a nose brimming with fruit and spices, including ginger, pepper, vanilla and violets. The palate unleashes a torrent of sensations that climax in a captivating finish. The Barolo Rapet also performed well. This wine is distinctive for its enticing austerity, which derives from aromas of liquorice, Peruvian bark and chocolate. The Barbaresco Maria di Brun is still very tannic, indicating that it has yet to mature, but this also hints at conspicuous longevity. The rigorous, mouthfilling Barbaresco 2000 and the delicious, very well-structured Barbera d'Alba La Gamberaja 2001 are as good as the selections. The invitingly fruity Langhe Rosso Da Pruvé 2000 and the Barolo Vigna Cerretta 1999 are well-typed examples of their respective categories.

● Barbera d'Asti Sup. Rouvé '00	🍷🍷	5
● Barbera d'Asti Sup. Vigneto Gustin '00	🍷🍷	4
● Monferrato Rosso Rocca Schiavino '00	🍷🍷	4
○ Monferrato Bianco Villa Guani '01	🍷🍷	4
● Monferrato Rosso Lajetto '01	🍷🍷	4
● Grignolino d'Asti Vigneto La Casalina '02	🍷	3
○ Monferrato Bianco Villa Drago '02	🍷	4
● Monferrato Rosso Cabernet '97	🍷🍷	5
● Barbera d'Asti Sup. Rouvé '98	🍷🍷	5
● Monferrato Rosso Cabernet '98	🍷🍷	5
● Barbera d'Asti Sup. Rouvé '99	🍷🍷	5

● Barbaresco Maria di Brun '00	🍷🍷	8
● Barbaresco Sorì Rio Sordo '00	🍷🍷	7
● Barbera d'Alba La Gamberaja '01	🍷🍷	5
● Barolo Rapet '99	🍷🍷	7
● Barbaresco '00	🍷🍷	7
● Langhe Rosso Da Pruvé '00	🍷	5
● Barolo Vigna Cerretta '99	🍷	7
● Barbaresco Maria di Brun '96	🍷🍷	8
● Barbaresco Maria di Brun '97	🍷🍷	8
● Barolo Rapet '97	🍷🍷	7
● Barbaresco Maria di Brun '98	🍷🍷	8
● Barolo Rapet '98	🍷🍷	7

BARBARESCO (CN)

BARBARESCO (CN)

CANTINA DEL PINO
VIA OVELLO, 15
12050 BARBARESCO (CN)
TEL. 0173635147
E-MAIL: cantinadelpino@libero.it

CASCINA LUISIN
VIA RABAJÀ, 23
12050 BARBARESCO (CN)
TEL. 0173635154

The small, neat Cantina del Pino is in the capable hands of Renato Vacca, supported by his father, Adriano. They work six hectares of vineyards, more than half planted to nebbiolo, and produce a total of around 30,000 bottles a year. They presented us with a good range of wines this time, although Renato has other selections maturing in the cellar that he believes are even better. However, let's give them the time they need to mature. The Freisa 2002, produced in a limited quantity of just 1,300 bottles, has a faint prickle that is rather attractive, and distinct, very elegant aromas of strawberry, roses and earth. The palate possesses acidity and extract that make this wine the perfect foil for the famous sausages and salamis of the Langhe. The Dolcetto 2002, which has perhaps felt the effects of the poor vintage more than most, has a delicate, lively colour and rather tart fruit. Its grace and balance on the palate are due to an agile body and skilled winemaking. On another level entirely is the Barbera 2001. From an excellent growing year, it marries power and harmony with generous notes of leather, chocolate and coffee, and hints of red berries and wild herbs. The dark garnet Barbaresco Ovello 2000 (15,000 bottles released) starts out reticent and slightly muddled on the nose but, given time to breathe, offers tobacco, vegetal and citrus peel aromas. The palate shows captivating intensity and warmth, the tannins are robust and rather astringent, and the long finish is full of flavour.

This famous, family-run Barbaresco estate is currently in the hands of father and son team, Luigi and Roberto Minuto. They see eye to eye on managing the estate – Roberto's innovative strategies are complemented by his father's calm experience – and this produces results that are in perfect tune with the estate's brand. They offered us an excellent Barbera Asili 2001, obtained from over 50-year-old vines that grow in a plot less than a hectare in size, in the heart of great Barbaresco nebbiolo country. The Minutos only made 3,000 bottles of this wine, which matured for 18-20 months in barriques, one third of which are new and the rest pre-used. It is a very deep red ruby with an intense, elegant bouquet of fruit jam that melds very nicely with the spicy balsamic tones from the oak. The warm, enfolding palate reveals depth, breadth and balance. The bright garnet ruby Barbaresco Rabajà 1999 was released a year later than its competitors to give it extra ageing time in the bottle. It starts out closed and slightly fuzzy on the nose, then opens to reveal almost salty aromas and a succession of pepper, leather and red berry tones. It performs better on the palate, where the powerful, fruit-led entry is buttressed by tight-knit, fairly astringent tannins. The Nebbiolo 2001, reviewed in error last year, is still very decent. Obtained from a vineyard at San Rocco Seno d'Elvio, it is clear and brilliant in hue, with raspberry fruit aromas and a warm, generous, harmonious palate. The Barbera and the Dolcetto 2002 are well-managed, although both are a little green and acidic.

● Barbaresco Ovello '00	▼▼	6*
● Barbera d'Alba '01	▼▼	4*
● Dolcetto d'Alba '02	▼	3
● Langhe Freisa '02	▼	3
● Barbaresco Ovello '99	▼▼▼	6
● Barbaresco Ovello '97	▼▼	6
● Barbaresco Ovello '98	▼▼	6
● Barbera d'Alba '99	▼▼	4
● Barbera d'Alba '00	▼▼	4

● Barbera d'Alba Asili '01	▼▼	5*
● Langhe Nebbiolo '01	▼▼	6
● Barbaresco Rabajà '99	▼▼	6*
● Barbera d'Alba Maggiur '02	▼	4
● Dolcetto d'Alba Bric Trifüla '02	▼	4
● Barbera d'Alba Asili '00	▼▼▼	5
● Barbera d'Alba Asili Barrique '97	▼▼▼	5
● Barbera d'Alba Asili '99	▼▼▼	5
● Barbaresco Rabajà '98	▼▼	6
● Barbaresco Sorì Paolin '98	▼▼	6
● Barbaresco Sorì Paolin '99	▼▼	6

BARBARESCO (CN)

BARBARESCO (CN)

Cascina Morassino
via Ovello, 32
12050 Barbaresco (CN)
tel. 0173635149

Cisa Asinari dei Marchesi di Gresy
loc. Martinenga - via Rabajà, 43
12050 Barbaresco (CN)
tel. 0173635221 - 0173635222
E-mail: wine@marchesidigresy.com

A round of applause is the very least that Roberto Bianco deserves for this year's range of excellent wines. He is back into the Guide, having ironed the dents out of his pride and rejoined the ranks of major estates. The travails of the last few years briefly derailed this estate, which ahs always aimed for quality, and which was one of the first in Barbaresco to recognize the potential of the nebbiolo-based wine named after the area. The estate hasn't changed. Roberto still manages its four hectares himself for an annual production of no more than 20,000 bottles. He offered us two Barbaresco selections, both products of a favourable vintage, the 2000. The Ovello shines with all its former splendour, thanks to excellent power and complexity. The bouquet is intense and complex, offering a riot of blackberry, blackcurrant, tobacco leaf, sweet spices and earthy tones. It is sumptuous and dry on the palate, then exquisitely balanced and mouthfilling in the lingering finish. This outstanding performance nearly overshadowed the Morassino, another very sound wine that is matured in big barrels and has a legitimate claim to the title of number two estate wine. Austere and tannic, it is distinctive for its refined bouquet and the harmony of its attractively elegant palate. The Barbera d'Alba Vignot also puts on a good show. We cannot remember ever having tasted such an impressive, robust and yet enjoyable version. It has a lovely acidulous vein that is not the least overwhelmed by the oaky tones. Last on the list are the Langhe Nebbiolo and the Dolcetto.

The Cisa Asinari estate has expanded its boundaries. Next year sees the unveiling of two major new wines, a Barbera d'Asti and a single-variety Merlot Monferrato Rosso. These are to be obtained from the new plots purchased at Cassine near Asti, which take the estate's original five hectares of moscato to a total of 13. Moving on to the wines themselves, we must compliment Marco Dotta, vineyard manager and estate oenologist, and Alberto Cisa Asinari. As we have noted at past tastings, the estate's flagship wines are still the Barbarescos. Top of the list is the Camp Gros 1999, a Three Glass monster of finesse and almost matchless class. The nose throws a succession of rich sensations, ranging from violets to pepper to rose and ending on a balsamic note. The same aromas return to lift the warm, velvet-smooth palate. The Martinenga 2000 is also excellent, proffering more subtle, vaguely spicy tones and a full, richly extracted palate that is also very stylish. The Langhe Rosso Virtus, a cabernet sauvignon and barbera blend, is another big hitter. The nose is redolent of red berry fruit and sweet spices, then the palate shows plenty of power and muscle. Unfortunately, we do not have enough space here to pay full tribute to the Gresy range of wines, which are all of high quality. We do feel, however, that we should at least mention in passing the Barbaresco Gaiun 1999, the Moscato d'Asti La Serra, the Langhe Rosso Villa Martis and the Passito L'Altro Moscato.

● Barbaresco Ovello '00	🍷🍷	7
● Barbaresco Morassino '00	🍷🍷	6*
● Barbera d'Alba Vignot '01	🍷🍷	5
● Dolcetto d'Alba '02	🍷	4
● Langhe Nebbiolo '02	🍷	5
● Barbaresco Morassino '99	🍷🍷	6
● Barbaresco Ovello '99	🍷🍷	7

● Barbaresco Camp Gros '99	🍷🍷🍷	8
● Langhe Rosso Virtus '00	🍷🍷	7
● Barbaresco Martinenga '00	🍷🍷	8
○ Piemonte Moscato Passito L'Altro Moscato '01	🍷🍷	5
● Langhe Nebbiolo Martinenga '02	🍷🍷	5
○ Moscato d'Asti La Serra '02	🍷🍷	4
● Barbaresco Gaiun '99	🍷🍷	8
● Langhe Rosso Villa Martis '99	🍷🍷	5
● Dolcetto d'Alba Monte Aribaldo '02	🍷	4
○ Langhe Chardonnay '02	🍷	4
● Barbaresco Gaiun '85	🍷🍷🍷	8
● Barbaresco Gaiun '97	🍷🍷🍷	8
● Barbaresco Camp Gros '98	🍷🍷🍷	8

BARBARESCO (CN)

GIUSEPPE CORTESE
VIA RABAJÀ, 35
12050 BARBARESCO (CN)
TEL. 0173635131
E-MAIL: az.cortesegiuseppe@jumpy.it

Giuseppe Cortese and his young son, Piercarlo, have done a fine job. Now that work to extend their cellars is complete and they are fully operational again, we were able to taste some memorable wines. Some of the credit for these must go to terroir, as the estate has vineyards in Rabajà, one of the most important vineyards in Barbaresco. We start with the Barbaresco Riserva 1996, which debuts this year and will only be produced in particularly favourable years. The Corteses have made 6,000 bottles of this wine, which aged for three years in large barrels and a further three in bottle. Bright red with orange highlights, it boasts fine complex aromas of dried flowers, liquorice, red berries and tobacco. The very muscular but extremely harmonious palate is magnificent, and signs off with a finish that just goes on and on. Not quite up to the same standard but still excellent is the Barbaresco Rabajà 2000. Its nose is a tad heavy on the alcohol, but it has lovely fruity tones, predominantly of cherry and wild strawberry. The flavoursome, generously fleshy palate is backed up by impressive tannins. The Barbera d'Alba Morassina is one of the best in its category, thanks to a lustrous colour and very fruity nose that has just the right hint of vanilla. The palate is well-structured and has that lovely acidity typical of the variety, finishing on an elegant, mineral note. Finally, the Langhe Chardonnay Scapulin is very good. It has a banana and pineapple bouquet and a generous palate rounded off by an intense, citrussy finish.

BARBARESCO (CN)

★ ★ ★ GAJA
VIA TORINO, 36
12050 BARBARESCO (CN)
TEL. 0173635158

We have run out of adjectives to describe the quality of Gaja's wines. There were two more Three Glass awards this year and a range of outstandingly good wines at the final tastings. The flagship wines are the magnificent trio that were the subject of a lively journalistic debate a few years ago as to whether Gaja should release them as non-Barbaresco DOC products. Angelo ages them for a year longer than the Barbaresco, and has now released the 1999 selections on the market. From a great harvest and the great nebbiolo grape, the three wines are a concentration of aromas, elegance and power on the palate. There is little to choose among them, but we preferred the Sorì San Lorenzo, which is already ready to drink but will really come into its own as it matures. Deep ruby red in appearance, it unfolds ripe fruit aromas softened by touches of balsam and toasty oak. The palate is full and the fruit assures a progression of extraordinary length. Not far behind come the Sorì Tildin, lacking only a little of its stablemate's grace, and the Costa Russi, which is still rather tannic and in search of balance. The other Three Glass award goes to the Barbaresco 2000, which stands out at once with its intense ruby red hue. Ripe fruit sensations of blackcurrant and morello cherry mingle with attractive oaky notes on the nose, then the palate is full, very well-structured and enveloping with an impressive tannic weave. The Sperss is up to its usual standards and the sauvignon-based Conteisa and Alteni di Brassica are good, but nothing to get too excited about.

● Barbaresco Rabajà Ris. '96	♟♟♟	8
● Barbaresco Rabajà '00	♟♟	6*
● Barbera d'Alba Morassina '00	♟♟	5
○ Langhe Chardonnay Scapulin '01	♟♟	3
● Barbaresco Rabajà '95	♟♟	6
● Barbaresco Rabajà '96	♟♟	6
● Barbaresco Rabajà '97	♟♟	6
● Barbaresco Rabajà '98	♟♟	6
● Barbaresco Rabajà '99	♟♟	6
● Langhe Nebbiolo '01	♟	5

● Barbaresco '00	♟♟♟	8
● Langhe Nebbiolo		
Sorì S. Lorenzo '99	♟♟♟	8
● Langhe Nebbiolo Sorì Tildin '99	♟♟	8
● Langhe Nebbiolo Sperss '99	♟♟	8
● Langhe Nebbiolo Costa Russi '99	♟♟	8
○ Langhe Alteni di Brassica '00	♟♟	7
● Langhe Nebbiolo Conteisa '99	♟♟	8
● Langhe Darmagi '96	♟♟♟	8
● Langhe Nebbiolo Costa Russi '96	♟♟♟	8
● Langhe Nebbiolo Sperss '96	♟♟♟	8
● Langhe Nebbiolo Sorì Tildin '97	♟♟♟	8
● Langhe Nebbiolo		
Sorì S. Lorenzo '98	♟♟♟	8
● Langhe Nebbiolo Sorì Tildin '98	♟♟♟	8

BARBARESCO (CN)

CARLO GIACOSA
VIA OVELLO, 8
12050 BARBARESCO (CN)
TEL. 0173635116

This small, family-owned estate is run by Carlo Giacosa, wife Carla and daughter, Maria Grazia, with an occasional hand from the other members of the family. Their five hectares planted to vine give them less than 30,000 bottles a year. This year, we were unable to review either the Barbera 2002, whose very limited run was sold out at the time of our visit, or the Barbaresco Montefico 2000, on which we shall reserve judgement until the next edition of the Guide. It has not yet been bottled. The Barbaresco Narin 2000, obtained from the prestigious vineyards of Canova, Cole and Asili, performed well. Its deep, lively garnet colour heralds a complex bouquet of aniseed, dried flowers and raspberry jam, and the rich, powerful palate ends with a big, rather dry, finish. For those who prefer their Nebbiolos youngish but full of character, we recommend the Maria Grazia 2001. It is delicate garnet ruby, with very firm, elegant aromas of dried roses, violets, liquorice and strawberries. The muscular palate has yet to develop fully, but already hints at Barbaresco-style length and strength. A beautiful vineyard at Albesani near Neive has given the Giacosas 5,500 bottles of Barbera Lina 2001. A brilliant purplish ruby wine, it tempts with notes of Peruvian bark, wood resin, cinnamon and lashings of black cherry. The palate is extraordinary for its density and power, signing off with a deliciously long finish. We end with the Dolcetto 2002, which comes from a poor vintage. It has a simple fruity nose and rather a rigorous, tannic palate.

BARBARESCO (CN)

I PAGLIERI
LOC. PAJÉ
VIA RABAJÀ, 8
12050 BARBARESCO (CN)
TEL. 0173635109

The 2004 edition of the Guide catches I Paglieri in a period of transition. The estate, which is at the forefront of the new but serious revival movement in Langhe wines, had only one wine to offer. For years now our publishing deadlines, always tight and frequently hectic, have been at odds with the slower and certainly more natural timetable that Alfredo Roagna and son, Luca, deem vital to the proper evolution of their wines. They did not produce a Langhe Bianco 2002 because of the poor harvest, and the estate's reds, the Barolo La Rocca, La Pira 1999, Barbaresco Pajé 2000 and Barbaresco Crichèt Pajé 1998, have yet to go into bottle or, in some cases, into the maturation barrel. The estate currently has just over 15 hectares to its name, nearly six in the Barolo DOCG zone below the town of Castiglione Falletto and another ten in the Pajé depression near Barbaresco. The Roagnas' lone offering, the Barolo La Rocca e La Pira Riserva 1996, is produced only in the best years. It is obtained not by selecting the fruit when it is harvested, but by combining the best barrels in the cellar. From a potential total of approximately 30,000 bottles, they selected just under 40 hectolitres (5,000 bottles) and aged it in barrels of Slavonian oak for about five years. The result is a wine with a complex bouquet that foregrounds mint and dried flowers, and a palate with austere, juicy tannins.

● Barbaresco Narin '00	🍷🍷	6*
● Barbera d'Alba Lina '01	🍷🍷	4*
● Langhe Nebbiolo Maria Grazia '01	🍷🍷	4*
● Dolcetto d'Alba Cuchet '02	🍷	3
● Barbaresco Montefico '97	🍷🍷	6
● Barbaresco Montefico '98	🍷🍷	6
● Barbaresco Narin '98	🍷🍷	6
● Barbera d'Alba Lina '00	🍷🍷	4
● Barbaresco Montefico '99	🍷🍷	6
● Barbaresco Narin '99	🍷	6

● Barolo La Rocca e La Pira Ris. '96	🍷🍷	8
● Barbaresco Crichèt Pajé '96	🍷🍷	8
● Barolo La Rocca e La Pira '96	🍷🍷	8
● Barbaresco Crichèt Pajé '97	🍷🍷	8
● Barolo La Rocca e La Pira '97	🍷🍷	8
● Opera Prima XIV	🍷🍷	8
○ Langhe Bianco '01	🍷🍷	4
● Barolo La Rocca e La Pira '98	🍷🍷	8
● Barbaresco Pajé '99	🍷🍷	8

BARBARESCO (CN)

MOCCAGATTA
VIA RABAJÀ, 8
12050 BARBARESCO (CN)
TEL. 0173635228 - 0173635152

The Minutos have finished work to extend the vinification area and in the new binning cellar, which provides a haven of cool from the heat of summer. The secret iso an old well, fed by an underground water table, which is now on show behind glass. This year, Sergio and Franco added 2,800 bottles of a new recruit to their ranks, a Nebbiolo made from grapes grown in their younger vineyards. They have released the 2002, whose vegetal tones hint at the unfavourable weather conditions that plagued the vintage. Without doubt, the best wines are the three Barbarescos, whose 30,000 to 35,000 bottles account for almost half of total production. The Basarin 2000, from a vineyard of the same name at Neive, has medium colour, slightly evolved aromas and a pleasant palate that is a little short on zip. The Bric Balin, still oaky at this point in its evolution, is more substantial. Classic tones of roses and violets are layered over sweet, toasty notes of oak and lead into a palate with nice weight, lovely warmth and a reasonably long finish. The Cole, from the vineyards around the cellars, shows its usual superior backbone, robust but not dry tannins, and good body. In fact, it is our pick of the three Barbarescos this year. As for the whites, the 4,500 bottles of the Chardonnay Buschet 2001 matured in new casks, giving the wine a complex, almost oily, mouthfeel and acidity that keeps it perky. The basic version, which in the 2002 vintage produced only 3,500 bottles instead of the usual 8,000 to 10,000, is simpler and easy drinking.

●	Barbaresco Bric Balin '00	♟♟	7
●	Barbaresco Cole '00	♟♟	8
●	Barbaresco Basarin '00	♟♟	7
○	Langhe Chardonnay Buschet '01	♟♟	5
○	Langhe Chardonnay '02	♟	4
●	Langhe Nebbiolo '02	♟	4
●	Barbaresco Bric Balin '90	♟♟♟	8
●	Barbaresco Cole '97	♟♟♟	8
●	Barbaresco Bric Balin '98	♟♟	7
●	Barbaresco Bric Balin '99	♟♟	7
●	Barbaresco Cole '99	♟♟	8
●	Barbara d'Alba Basarin '00	♟♟	6

BARBARESCO (CN)

MONTARIBALDI
FRAZ. TRE STELLE
VIA RIO SORDO, 30/A
12050 BARBARESCO (CN)
TEL. 0173638220
E-MAIL: montaribaldi@tiscali.it

The Taliano family estate is in a truly magnificent position overlooking the entire Barbaresco zone. The big news is the arrival of Giulia, who was born in April and is already charming visitors to the estate with her smile. Work on the cellars proceeds apace and when complete, will enable the Talianos to work more comfortably. A second new arrival is the Barbaresco Palazzina, made from grapes grown in a vineyard that lies below the famous Starderi cru. The Talianos produced 4,500 bottles of the 2002 vintage. A medium ruby introduces subtle aromas that hint faintly at dried flowers, and a fruity, rather predictable palate that could do with a shot of extra energy. The 6,000 bottles of Barbaresco Sörì Montaribaldi is richer in hue. The nose has yet to develop fully, but has undertones of fruit. The palate offers lovely flesh, solid, but not drying, tannins, and a lingering liquorice finish. We liked the Barbera dü Gir 2001, of which 4,500 bottles were produced. It aged in small casks, some of which were new, and boasts a flavoursome, juicy palate with lively acidity that enhances the overall balance. The Nebbiolo Gambarin is a sound, mealtime wine with a lovely fruity nose and a harmonious palate. The Dolcetto Nicolini – only 3,000 bottles were released – is up to its usual standards. The intense, fruit-led nose introduces a powerful, complex palate featuring solid tannins and good balance. The rather rich, chewy Chardonnay Stissa d'le Favole is decent and the Arneis is well made.

●	Barbaresco Sörì Montaribaldi '00	♟♟	7
●	Barbaresco Palazzina '00	♟♟	6
●	Barbera d'Alba dü Gir '01	♟♟	5
●	Dolcetto d'Alba Nicolini '01	♟	4
○	Langhe Chardonnay Stissa d'le Favole '01	♟	5
●	Langhe Nebbiolo Gambarin '01	♟	5
○	Roero Arneis Capural '02	♟	4
●	Barbaresco Sörì Montaribaldi '97	♟♟	6
●	Barbaresco Sörì Montaribaldi '98	♟♟	6
●	Barbera d'Alba dü Gir '00	♟♟	4
●	Barbaresco Sörì Montaribaldi '99	♟	6

BARBARESCO (CN)

PRODUTTORI DEL BARBARESCO
VIA TORINO, 52
12050 BARBARESCO (CN)
TEL. 0173635139
E-MAIL:
produttori@produttoridelbarbaresco.com

The Produttori are a Barbaresco institution. It was set up in 1958 by a determined priest whose aim was to re-establish the former winery created in 1894 by the father of Barbaresco, Domizio Cavazza, and closed by the Fascists in the 1920s. Under the guidance of the first general manager, Celestino Vacca, the 19 original members decided to invest their entire nebbiolo production in the venture, retaining the right to dispose of their other varieties as they pleased. In return, the winery pledged to vinify only nebbiolo grapes. Today's 54 members possess around 20 per cent of the entire DOCG Barbaresco area (90 hectares), almost all in the municipality of Barbaresco. Thanks to the initiative of the more ambitious of the viticulturists, and the work of oenologist, Giovanni Testa, the quality of the range has improved dramatically over the last few years. Only when there is an outstanding great vintage is each of the nine, prestigious crus bottled separately. The harvest of 1998, although good, was not deemed worthy of this honour, which means that we were only able to taste two wines this year. But what wines they are, a Three Glass Barbaresco and a Two Glass Langhe Nebbiolo. The former's 110,000 bottles come from a perfect harvest and matured for 18 months in barrels of Slavonian and Allier oak of varying sizes. The aromas of dried flowers, liquorice and tobacco express all the complexity of Langhe-grown nebbiolo, and the palate promises that legendary Barbaresco velvet smoothness. The other wine is already a Barbaresco in miniature.

BARBARESCO (CN)

ALBINO ROCCA
VIA RABAJÀ, 15
12050 BARBARESCO (CN)
TEL. 0173635145
E-MAIL: roccaalbino@globwine.com

Angelo Rocca, who owns this estate, has 13 hectares from which he obtains the classic Langhe reds plus a little Chardonnay and Cortese. His new Barbaresco, made from grapes grown in the Montersino vineyard between San Rocco and Treiso, has already been bottled in anticipation of its release next year. Of the wines we tasted this time around, we were bowled over by the Barbaresco Brich Ronchi (25,000 bottles), which is so deep and dark in colour that it is almost opaque. The nose is an explosion of toasty oak and rich, generous fruit, especially black berries, with a spicy note of juniper in the background. The alcohol-rich palate starts out full and round, lingering on the finish after revealing solid tannins and exquisite finesse. The Three Glasses were a formality. Predictably, the Loreto is lighter in appearance. It shows a very fruity nose, with an elegant touch of spice, and a powerful, harmonious palate that ends on a nice tannic note. The Dolcetto Vignalunga is scented, juicy, gorgeously fruity, clean and thoroughly enjoyable. It was a very pleasant surprise, given the difficult vintage. The intense ruby Barbera Gepin offers crisp vanilla and morello cherry aromas, the generous, sweet fruit returning on the palate where it is sustained by perfect acidity right through to the full, satisfying finish. As for the whites, the Chardonnay is a rich straw-yellow flecked with gold and has a ripe fruit bouquet, then an attractive tangy palate. The cortese-based Langhe Bianco is as interesting as ever.

● Barbaresco '99	♆♆♆	5*
● Langhe Nebbiolo '01	♆♆	4*
● Barbaresco		
Vigneti in Rio Sordo Ris. '97	♆♆♆	6
● Barbaresco		
Vigneti in Montestefano Ris. '96	♆♆♆	6
● Barbaresco		
Vigneti in Pora Ris. '96	♆♆	6
● Barbaresco		
Vigneti in Montestefano Ris. '97	♆♆	6
● Barbaresco		
Vigneti in Moccagatta Ris. '97	♆♆	6
● Barbaresco		
Vigneti in Ovello Ris. '97	♆♆	6

● Barbaresco		
Vigneto Brich Ronchi '00	♆♆♆	7*
● Barbaresco Vigneto Loreto '00	♆♆	7
● Barbera d'Alba Gepin '01	♆♆	5
● Dolcetto d'Alba Vignalunga '02	♆♆	4*
○ Langhe Chardonnay da Bertü '01	♆	4
○ Langhe Bianco La Rocca '02	♆	5
● Barbaresco		
Vigneto Brich Ronchi '93	♆♆♆	7
● Barbaresco		
Vigneto Brich Ronchi '96	♆♆♆	7
● Barbaresco		
Vigneto Brich Ronchi '97	♆♆♆	7
● Barbaresco Vigneto Loreto '98	♆♆♆	7

BARBARESCO (CN)

BRUNO ROCCA
VIA RABAJÀ, 29
12050 BARBARESCO (CN)
TEL. 0173635112
E-MAIL: info@brunorocca.it

Work to enlarge the cellars is almost complete, giving this winery a very elegant tasting room where visitors can sample the gems that we have come to expect from the accomplished Bruno Rocca. Bruno may not see 50 again but he is still dynamic and always on the go. This year, he celebrates his 25th harvest for he started with the 1978 vintage. The eight hectares under vine give him about 40,000 bottles a year, and the wines he turned out for the panel were exceptional. The Langhe Chardonnay 2001 is so rich and ripe it could almost qualify as a "vendemmia tardiva" (late harvest). Its cornucopia of sweet sensations, notably vanilla, pineapple, melon, butter and roasted hazelnuts, mingle on the nose, lifted by the generous alcohol. Langhe Rosso Rabajolo 2000, a cabernet, nebbiolo and barbera blend, is held back by uncomplicated tanginess, although it was vinified to be more complex. The nose is a little grassy, but the palate is easy drinking. A plot at San Cristoforo near Neive produces the fabulous Barbera 2001. Aromas of cherry jam, vanilla and earth usher in a palate that unveils power, personality and perfectly gauged acidity. A well-deserved Three Glasses went to the Rabajà 2000 for its utterly captivating bouquet of chocolate, spice and raspberry, and a very weighty palate that stuns with its enormous breadth and long, velvety finish. The Coparossa 2000 is also very good, starting out closed and etheric, then releasing notes of red berries, pepper and fruit preserved in alcohol. The fruit-led palate has nice texture and a long, harmonious finish.

● Barbaresco Rabajà '00	♟♟♟	8
● Barbera d'Alba '01	♟♟	6
● Barbaresco Coparossa '00	♟♟	8
● Langhe Rosso Rabajolo '00	♟♟	7
○ Langhe Chardonnay Cadet '01	♟♟	5
● Barbaresco Rabajà '93	♟♟♟	8
● Barbaresco Rabajà '96	♟♟♟	8
● Barbaresco Coparossa '97	♟♟♟	8
● Barbaresco Rabajà '98	♟♟♟	8
● Barbera d'Alba '00	♟♟	6
● Barbaresco Coparossa '99	♟♟	8
● Barbaresco Rabajà '99	♟♟	8

BARBARESCO (CN)

RINO VARALDO
VIA SECONDINE, 2
12050 BARBARESCO (CN)
TEL. 0173635160
E-MAIL: varaldo_rino@hotmail.com

Brothers Rino and Michele Varaldo's cellars are in the centre of Secondine, almost directly under the tower. Their six hectares under vine, half nebbiolo destined for Barbaresco, give an annual production of 45,000 bottles. Two of the wines presented came close to winning a third Glass, the Barolo Vigna di Aldo and the Barbaresco Bricco Libero. The Varaldos made 3,500 bottles of the Barolo, with fruit from Terlo, in 1999. Still closed, it opens out into notes of delightful spiciness, cinchona, flowers and raspberry. The big, powerful palate displays austere tannins and a long, elegant finish. The Bricco Libero 2000, 6,000 bottles of which were obtained from the Gallina and Albesani vineyards at Neive, is etheric and still oak-dominated, but offers small red berry fruit and liquorice aromas. Entry on the palate is full and weighty, then the finish is long with slightly mouth-drying tannins. The much classier Sorì Loreto 2000 has notes of dried herbs and tobacco, followed by liquorice and violets, and a juicy, round palate with slightly green tannins on the finish. Two Glasses also go to the full, succulent, alcohol-rich Barbera Vigna delle Fate 2001 for its lovely mingling of fruit and oak, and to the Langhe Fantasia 4.20, a blend of four varieties (barbera, cabernet, merlot and nebbiolo) barrique-aged for 20 months. Dark, with a grassy, fruity nose, it follows up with a palate that nicely balances the sweetness of the tannins and barbera's acidity. We also liked the fruity, mouthfilling Nebbiolo 2001 and the very harmonious Dolcetto 2002. The Barbera 2002 is less balanced.

● Barbaresco Bricco Libero '00	♟♟	7
● Barolo Vigna di Aldo '99	♟♟	7
● Barbaresco Sorì Loreto '00	♟♟	7
● Barbera d'Alba Vigna delle Fate '01	♟♟	5
● Langhe Rosso Fantasia 4.20 '01	♟♟	5
● Langhe Nebbiolo '01	♟	5
● Dolcetto d'Alba '02	♟	4
● Barbera d'Alba '02		3
● Barbaresco Bricco Libero '97	♟♟♟	7
● Barolo Vigna di Aldo '95	♟♟	7
● Barolo Vigna di Aldo '98	♟♟	7
● Barbaresco Bricco Libero '99	♟♟	7
● Barbaresco Sorì Loreto '99	♟♟	7

BAROLO (CN)

BAROLO (CN)

GIACOMO BORGOGNO & FIGLI
VIA GIOBERTI, 1
12060 BAROLO (CN)
TEL. 017356108
E-MAIL: borgogno-barolo@libero.it

GIACOMO BREZZA & FIGLI
VIA LOMONDO, 4
12060 BAROLO (CN)
TEL. 0173560921 - 017356354
E-MAIL: brezza@brezza.it

This is the first Three Glass award for the historic Borgogno estate. The star is its very traditional Barolo Classico 1998, showing that tradition versus innovation means little in the face of quality. This wine, 45,000 bottles of which were blended from five famous vineyards in the municipality of Barolo, undergoes lengthy maceration and matures only in large barrels. At every stage of our tastings, it stood out for its style and solid, but never excessive, structure. Well-defined aromas of violet and red berry fruit give way to a hint of forest floor, then the already well-integrated palate has sweet tannins and extraordinary length. It's a wine that Cesare and Giorgio Boschis have every reason to be proud of. Close behind comes the Barolo Liste 1998, 4,000 bottles of which were obtained from 25-year-old vines in the famous Liste vineyard at Barolo. Its rich, spicy nose will mature satisfyingly with ageing. Equally good is the standard-label Barolo 1998, made from grapes grown at Barolo, La Morra, Serralunga, Novello and Verduno. The Barbera d'Alba Superiore 2000, matured for 12 months in 100-hectolitre barrels, is also very nice. It has vibrant colour, a flower and fruit nose and marked, but not excessive, freshness. The Dolcetto d'Alba 2002 has nice berry fruit aromas and rather an insubstantial, vegetal palate. The beautiful cellars in the centre of town enable the Boschis to turn out about 150,000 bottles a year with ease, and to store their historic wines, dating back to 1947, in ideal conditions. The older wines can still astound with their purity and freshness.

The Brezzas have purchased the roughly one and a half-hectare plot at Cannubi that they used to rent, bringing their total area under vine to 20 hectares and their annual production to 100,000 units, one third sold at the cellar door or at their restaurant in Barolo. This year, we tasted two 2002 Barberas (accounting for 15,000 units in total), Cannubi and Cannubi Muscatel. The first is simple, fruity and very drinkable, with a clean finish, while the Cannubi Muscatel is more complex, with a trace of morello cherry on the nose and generous fruit on the palate, backed up by good acidity. The large, efficient cellars are equipped with the classic barrels of Slavonian oak are also home to the Nebbiolo 2000, debuting this year and obtained from recently planted vines in the Fossati cru. It offers fresh fruit and lovely balsamic notes, then lively acidity on the palate. Moving on to the Barolos, we enjoyed a terroir-driven Cannubi which offers typical earthy tones and an undertone of dried roses. The elegant palate ends on notes of balsam and pepper. The Bricco Sarmassa is a classic. Its not very dense, garnet colour introduces an intense minty bouquet. The palate has character, sweet fruit and solid but not edgy tannins. This is a wine that will age well. Up last is the vibrant garnet Sarmassa. It offers a violet and spice nose, then sound structure on the palate, where the fruit is sustained by acidity and a mineral vein that comes through on the long finish.

● Barolo Cl. '98	♟♟♟	7
● Barolo '98	♟♟	7
● Barbera d'Alba Sup. '00	♟♟	3*
● Barolo Liste '98	♟♟	8
● Dolcetto d'Alba '02	♟	4
● Barolo Cl. '93	♟♟	8
● Barolo Cl. '96	♟♟	8
● Barolo Liste '96	♟♟	8
● Barolo Cl. '97	♟♟	7
● Barolo Liste '97	♟♟	8

● Barbera d'Alba		
Cannubi Muscatel '00	♟♟	4*
● Barolo Bricco Sarmassa '99	♟♟	8
● Barolo Cannubi '99	♟♟	7
● Barolo Sarmassa '99	♟♟	7
● Barbera d'Alba Cannubi '00	♟	4
● Langhe Nebbiolo '00	♟	5
● Barolo Cannubi '96	♟♟♟	7
● Barolo Bricco Sarmassa '97	♟♟	7
● Barolo Sarmassa '97	♟♟	7
● Barolo Cannubi '97	♟♟	7
● Barolo Sarmassa '98	♟♟	7

BAROLO (CN)

DAMILANO
V.LO SAN SEBASTIANO, 2
12060 BAROLO (CN)
TEL. 017356265 - 017356105
E-MAIL: damilanog@damilanog.com

The large cellars built over 40 years ago have more than enough space and equipment to enable Damilano to develop. However, the dynamic new generation – Mario and Paolo, Giovanni Damilano's sons, and their cousins, Margherita and Guido – are planning to renovate the façade and the interior to launch a project that will promote the new image that they want to create. In an encore of last year's performance, the two Barolo selections (10,000 bottles each) reached the final tastings, and if they continue like this, then things will only get better. The Barolo Liste 1999, from a celebrated Barolo vineyard, spends 24 months in half-new barriques and throws the traditional aromas of plum, morello cherry and wild berries, laced with tar and spice. On the palate, the powerful tannins have yet to be tamed, although the structure has plenty of breadth. The Barolo Cannubi 1999, obtained from 50-year-old vines that grow in one of the most famous crus in the whole of the Langhe, is more original in a certain sense. Sixteen months in barrique and eight more in large barrels have given it a splendid garnet colour and intense, lingering aromas of black cherry and autumn leaves, with an unusual vegetal undertone. Right now, it is readier to drink than the Liste, largely thanks to the balance of tannins and alcohol it has achieved. The Dolcetto d'Alba 2002 has a fairly intense, stylish nose, but the Barbera d'Alba 2001 is better. Actually, it's one of the best wines in its category, with a linger flower and fruit nose and, notably, a full, harmonious palate with a long, clean finish.

BAROLO (CN)

GIACOMO GRIMALDI
VIA LUIGI EINAUDI, 8
12060 BAROLO (CN)
TEL. 017335256

On its second entry in the Guide, the Giacomo Grimaldi estate, run by Giacomo and son Ferruccio, has boosted quality and saw its Barolo Le Coste 1999 reach the finals. Unfortunately, the poor harvest of 2002 forced Giacomo to sacrifice his Dolcetto and Barbera d'Alba Pistìn, but if quality is his prime objective, then he had little choice. The Barolo Le Coste 1999 has come a long way in four short years. Admittedly, the vineyard is one of Barolo's best, but skill is also required in the cellars. The bright garnet colour ushers in a crisp, pervasive, lingering nose. Two years in 60 per cent-new barriques produce the tertiary aromas of spice and leather that are already discernible, but do not overwhelm the fruit. The palate is still tannin-heavy, although the structure and alcohol are more than capable of rising to the challenge. This is a great Barolo with a long life ahead of it. From the 4,000 bottles of Le Coste, we pass to the 5,000 bottles of Nebbiolo d'Alba Valmaggiore 2001, a concentrated, easy-to-drink wine, obtained from low-yielding vines that are almost 40 years old. Its clean aromas of violets and berry fruit introduce a palate that may not have immense structure but does offer soft tannins and good length. The Barbera d'Alba Fornaci 2001 is also decent. It is aged for 18 months in 70 per cent-new barriques, then for a further seven in bottle. This produces a bright, varietal colour and strong oaky tones that are nicely balanced by the richness of the fruit, which returns on the palate and is more than a match for the tangy varietal acidity.

● Barolo Cannubi '99	🍷🍷	7
● Barolo Liste '99	🍷🍷	7
● Barbera d'Alba '01	🍷🍷	5
● Dolcetto d'Alba '02	🍷	4
● Barolo '97	🍷🍷	7
● Barolo Cannubi '97	🍷🍷	7
● Barbera d'Alba '99	🍷🍷	5
● Barbera d'Alba '00	🍷🍷	5
● Barolo Cannubi '98	🍷🍷	7
● Barolo Liste '98	🍷🍷	7

● Barolo Le Coste '99	🍷🍷	8
● Barbera d'Alba Fornaci '01	🍷🍷	6
● Nebbiolo d'Alba Valmaggiore '01	🍷🍷	5
● Nebbiolo d'Alba '00	🍷🍷	4
● Barbera d'Alba Pistìn '01	🍷🍷	4
● Dolcetto d'Alba '01	🍷🍷	3
● Barolo Le Coste '98	🍷🍷	7

BAROLO (CN)

MARCHESI DI BAROLO
VIA ALBA, 12
12060 BAROLO (CN)
TEL. 0173564400
E-MAIL: reception@marchesibarolo.com

Oenologist Roberto Vezza and the owners of this estate have much to be proud of. Two wines reached the finals and the rest included a series of high-quality bottles. Considering that the cellar produces over 1,000,000 bottles a year, this marriage of quality and quantity is quite an achievement. The Barolo Vigneti di Proprietà 1999 is nearly as good as the 1997 and 1998, and its combination of style and generosity, lovely spicy bouquet, skilfully balanced oak and velvety tannins just missed out on Three Glasses. Close behind is Sarmassa 1999, from the historic Barolo cru of the same name. It impresses with complex aromas ranging from red berry fruit to spice, and a harmonious, consistent palate. Just as good is the brilliant garnet Barolo Cannubi 1999, offering oak-derived balsam and nice nose-palate consistency. Perhaps the most traditional of the estate wines is the austere, complex Riserva Grande Annata 1997, which is also good and promises well for the future. Above the estate lies the Paiagallo vineyard, whence the lovely Barbera d'Alba Paiagal 2001 is sourced. Its year in barrique gives it understated oakiness, very clean fruity aromas and a freshness nicely offset by alcohol. The Barbera d'Alba Ruvei 2001 is more vegetal in tone, while the two 2002 Dolcetto d'Albas, the Boschetti and the Madonna di Como, are typical of their vintage with a pleasant wild berry bouquet, but a lightish palate. The Pi Cit 2001 is a successful blend of cabernet and nebbiolo, and the Gavi di Gavi and Roero Arneis are well-made examples of their categories that deservedly earned a Glass.

BAROLO (CN)

BARTOLO MASCARELLO
VIA ROMA, 15
12060 BAROLO (CN)
TEL. 017356125

Legend has it that every family used to have its own store of special bottles known as "scacciaparenti" (relative-chasers). They would be produced on the second or third day of traditional festivals to get rid of difficult relations who, so the story goes, might be reluctant to return home if bottle after bottle of good wine were on offer. This story came to mind at Bartolo when we saw the quality of the 2002 nebbiolo grapes destined for Barolo. Why not make a simpler, fresher, lesser Nebbiolo and call it "scacciaparenti," since it was unlikely to amount to much? We tasted the wine and unfortunately – or perhaps fortunately for the wine – we actually liked it. In fact, we liked it so much we might have continued drinking it if the lunch bell hadn't called us to the table. Maria Teresa, the daughter of the house, regaled us with tales of how difficult it had been to get the grapes into the cellar, and of the patience required to select the bunches worthy of vinification. The harvest yielded just 6,000 bottles of Nebbiolo, and none whatsoever of Barolo. But Mascarello always has a few good Barolos in reserve. The 1999, for example, is perfect, and an effortless Three Glass champion. Deep garnet ruby, it regales the nose with exquisitely refreshing aromas of ripe fruit laced with sweet spices and dried flowers. The already well-balanced palate offers dense yet velvety tannins that make it quite irresistible. Also very harmonious is the Barbera 2001, which bursts with raspberry, balsamic herb and tobacco tones, and then parades all the elegance of its cru on the palate.

● Barolo Sarmassa '99	♟♟	6*
● Barolo		
Vigneti di Proprietà in Barolo '99	♟♟	8
● Barbera d'Alba Paiagal '01	♟♟	4
● Langhe Rosso Pi Cit '01	♟♟	6
● Barolo Riserva Grande Annata '97	♟♟	8
● Barolo Cannubi '99	♟♟	6
● Barbera d'Alba Ruvei '01	♟	4
● Dolcetto d'Alba Boschetti '02	♟	4
● Dolcetto d'Alba Madonna di Como '02	♟	3
○ Gavi di Gavi '02	♟	4
○ Roero Arneis '02	♟	4
● Barolo Estate Vineyard '97	♟♟♟	8
● Barolo		
Vigneti di Proprietà in Barolo '98	♟♟♟	6

● Barolo '99	♟♟♟	8
● Barbera d'Alba		
Vigna S. Lorenzo '01	♟♟	5
● Langhe Nebbiolo '02	♟♟	5
● Barolo '83	♟♟♟	8
● Barolo '84	♟♟♟	8
● Barolo '85	♟♟♟	8
● Barolo '89	♟♟♟	8
● Barolo '98	♟♟♟	8
● Barolo '88	♟♟	8
● Barolo '90	♟♟	8
● Barolo '93	♟♟	8
● Barolo '96	♟♟	8
● Barolo '97	♟♟	8

BAROLO (CN)

E. Pira & Figli - Chiara Boschis

via Vittorio Veneto, 1
12060 Barolo (CN)
tel. 017356247
e-mail: piracb@libero.it

Chiara Boschis is both determined and committed to her chosen career as a producer, and is actively involved in every phase of production. The impressive array of barriques in the spotless, efficient new cellars contains her maturing wines. This year, the new product we announced last time makes its debut in the shape of Via Nuova, a Barolo obtained from the half-hectare plot of 25 to 30-year-old vines behind the cellars that yields 3,000 bottles. Aged in the same way as the Cannubi in new casks, it has a very intense, bright garnet appearance and a nose of red berry fruit, enhanced by oaky tones with undertones of spice and flowers. The palate displays more elegance than power, a strong fruity vein and a tannic finish. This is a fine Barolo, if not quite as complex as the Cannubi, whose 10,000 bottles sport an unusually vibrant, brilliant colour and a cornucopia of fruity aromas with a balsamic, minty vein and just a hint of citrus peel. The palate is flavoursome and juicy, with very firm but not dry, tannins and a very long, rather tangy finish. All in all, a stylish, very balanced wine that will age well. The Barbera 2001, of which barely 2,000 bottles were produced, is aged in pre-used barriques and has a dark, intense colour, then an equally intense nose that reveals distinct notes of cherry and minerally undertones. The palate is full and nicely buttressed by acidity, with a lingering, fruity finish.

● Barolo Cannubi '99	🍷🍷	8
● Barbera d'Alba '01	🍷🍷	5
● Barolo Via Nuova '99	🍷🍷	8
● Barolo Ris. '90	🍸🍸🍸	8
● Barolo '94	🍸🍸🍸	8
● Barolo Cannubi '96	🍸🍸🍸	8
● Barolo Cannubi '97	🍸🍸🍸	8
● Barolo Cannubi '95	🍸🍸	8
● Barbera d'Alba '00	🍸🍸	5

BAROLO (CN)

Giuseppe Rinaldi

via Monforte, 3
12060 Barolo (CN)
tel. 017356156

Beppe Rinaldi has run this estate since he inherited it from his father, Battista, in 1992. It is often hailed as a pioneering force in traditional Barolo-making, employing as it does long macerations on the skins, only large barrels of Slavonian oak and blends of grapes from different vineyards. If this year's consistently high quality is anything to go by, then Beppe should stick firmly to these techniques. Our only complaint is that his production is so limited. The estate has just under seven hectares to its name, giving an annual production of around 10,000 bottles of Brunate-Le Coste and 3,500 of Cannubi S. Lorenzo-Ravera. As in previous years, our preference is for the Barolo Brunate-Le Coste, whose bright, vibrant garnet introduces a black cherry and wild berry nose. The palate has enormous, but never overwhelming, structure and a perfect marriage of alcohol with velvety tannins, which offer lovely walnut sensations that echo throughout the lingering finish. The Barolo Cannubi S. Lorenzo-Ravera 1999 also has a good pedigree, coming from equally prestigious Barolo vineyards. It is less complex than its partner, and readier to drink, or, to be more exact, is less likely to evolve to the same degree. It is actually already mature and harmonious, particularly on the palate. We were privileged to taste the Barbera, the Dolcetto and the unusual Ruché Rosae 2001 and would like to explore them further here, but given the extremely low numbers of bottles released, Beppe prefers not to present them for official tastings, and rightly so.

● Barolo Brunate-Le Coste '99	🍷🍷	7
● Barolo Cannubi S. Lorenzo-Ravera '99	🍷🍷	7
● Barolo Brunate-Le Coste '97	🍸🍸🍸	7
● Barolo Brunate-Le Coste '96	🍸🍸	7
● Barolo Cannubi S. Lorenzo-Ravera '96	🍸🍸	7
● Barolo Cannubi S. Lorenzo-Ravera '97	🍸🍸	7
● Barolo Brunate-Le Coste '98	🍸🍸	7
● Barolo Cannubi S. Lorenzo-Ravera '98	🍸🍸	7

BAROLO (CN)

LUCIANO SANDRONE
VIA PUGNANE, 4
12060 BAROLO (CN)
TEL. 0173560023
E-MAIL: info@sandroneluciano.com

The wines offered this year by Luciano Sandrone won the panel's unconditional approval, despite the fact that the estate's production was penalized in terms of quantity by the poor harvest of 2002. For example, only 13,000 bottles of the Dolcetto were produced, which is less than half the usual total. Starting with the Barolos, Le Vigne (19,000 bottles) is superb. Clear garnet in colour, it boasts a nose of cocoa powder and spice set against a backdrop of sweet oakiness and ripe fruit, then a full, juicy palate ending in a solid finish of gorgeous ripe fruit. We gave it Three Glasses for its splendid performance. The Cannubi Boschis (13,000 bottles) is deeper in hue and proffers aromas of ripe plum, with a suggestion of spice and an alcohol-rich palate that has close-knit, sweet tannins. There is great personality in the lingering finish, into which creeps a hint of the earlier spice. The deep violet, almost black, Barbera is very well made, with an intense, generous, etheric nose of ripe fruit and an astonishingly full-bodied palate with good length. The Pe Mol, a barbera and nebbiolo blend, is similar in hue, and its vibrant aromas include fruit, spice and balsam. The palate is imposingly round, with gorgeous flesh and a delicious finish. The bright garnet Nebbiolo Valmaggiore offers balsamic, earthy aromas with fruity undertones and a firm palate that is still austere. A hint of mint returns on the back palate.

BAROLO (CN)

GIORGIO SCARZELLO E FIGLI
VIA ALBA, 29
12060 BAROLO (CN)
TEL. 017356170
E-MAIL: cantina-scarzello@libero.it

Without taking anything away from Giorgio Scarzello, who has produced some great wines and whose ten-plus years of vineyard experience were crucial for this estate, we think a subtle change took place in 1997. that was when 17-year-old Federico, studying to be an oenologist at the time, joined his father in the cellar. Success followed swiftly, climaxing in this year's brilliant performance that earned a first, well-deserved, Three Glasses for the Barolo Vigna Merenda 1999. Almost a month's fermentation and ageing in 30-hectolitre barrels produced a superb, austere Barolo, in which the succulence of the fruit melds with aromas of pepper, spice and tar, leading into a soft, round, harmonious palate brimming with smooth tannins. A total of 7,000 bottles of this elixir are on offer at a very competitive price for a DOCG wine. The Barolo 1999 (3,500 bottles) underwent shorter fermentation and matured in 900-litre casks previously used for Barbera. Its aromas of redcurrant and jam laced with spice are more closed, but it already shows good nose-palate consistency. The other niche labels (25,000 bottles in all) include 4,000 bottles of Barbera d'Alba Superiore 2000 whose 18-month stay in oak has left traces of wild berries, notably blackberry, liquorice, leather and charred oak, and a palate that impresses with its length. The still alcohol-led Dolcetto d'Alba 2001 is pleasantly rustic with a coherent and simple, but not dull, palate. The Langhe Nebbiolo 2001 is better than last year's version, mingling violet and black cherry tones with a hint of balsam from its French oak.

● Barolo Le Vigne '99	ΨΨΨ	8
● Barolo Cannubi Boschis '99	ΨΨ	8
● Barbera d'Alba '01	ΨΨ	5
● Langhe Rosso Pe Mol '01	ΨΨ	5
● Nebbiolo d'Alba Valmaggiore '01	ΨΨ	6
● Dolcetto d'Alba '02	Ψ	4
● Barolo '83	ΨΨΨ	8
● Barolo '84	ΨΨΨ	8
● Barolo Cannubi Boschis '86	ΨΨΨ	8
● Barolo Cannubi Boschis '87	ΨΨΨ	8
● Barolo Cannubi Boschis '89	ΨΨΨ	8
● Barolo Cannubi Boschis '90	ΨΨΨ	8
● Barolo Cannubi Boschis '98	ΨΨ	8
● Barolo Le Vigne '98	ΨΨ	8

● Barolo Vigna Merenda '99	ΨΨΨ	6*
● Barbera d'Alba Sup. '00	ΨΨ	4*
● Barolo '99	ΨΨ	6
● Dolcetto d'Alba '01	Ψ	4
● Langhe Nebbiolo '01	Ψ	4
● Barolo '95	ΨΨ	6
● Barolo '96	ΨΨ	6
● Barolo '97	ΨΨ	6
● Barolo Vigna Merenda '98	ΨΨ	6
● Barbera d'Alba Sup. '99	ΨΨ	4
● Barolo '98	Ψ	6

BAROLO (CN)

Tenuta La Volta - Cabutto

via San Pietro, 13
12042 Barolo (CN)
tel. 017356168

Bruno and Osvaldo Cabutto's estate looks out over one of the most stunning landscapes in the Langhe. The cellars may be located here, but their 15 hectares planted to vine extend across some of the most prestigious vineyards in the DOCG. Their 3,000 bottles of Riserva del Fondatore, for example, all originate in the Sarmassa cru, even if it doesn't say so on the label. The Barolo Vigna La Volta (25,000 bottles) comes from a lesser known vineyard at approximately 400 metres above sea level that faces southeast. Its 30-day maceration and ageing in barrels of Slavonian oak produce a seductive nose of dried flowers, autumn leaves and mushrooms that leads into a long, generous palate full of smooth tannins. This superb Barolo was a clear contender for the final taste-offs and the Barolo Riserva del Fondatore 1997 is almost as good. The Cabuttos are quick to point out that this "riserva" comes from a selection of grapes in the vineyard and a cellar technique that involves 30 days' maceration, manual pumping over the cap, and maturing in large barrels. This imbues it with stewed plums, tobacco and leather, aromas that only the truly great vintages can sustain without seeming coarse. The Barbera d'Alba Superiore 2001, macerated for 15 days and aged for a year in barriques, impresses with its clean flowery nose and tangy, solidly built palate that indicates good cellarability. Finally, the Dolcetto d'Alba Vigna La Volta 2002 undergoes a five-day maceration and stainless steel ageing, which leave it with pleasing flower and fruit aromas, if rather a lightweight palate.

●	Barolo Vigna La Volta '99	🍷🍷	7
●	Barbera d'Alba Sup. '01	🍷🍷	5
●	Barolo Ris. del Fondatore '97	🍷🍷	8
●	Dolcetto d'Alba Vigna La Volta '02	🍷	3
●	Barolo Ris. del Fondatore '90	🍸🍸	8
●	Barolo Vigna La Volta '97	🍸🍸	7
●	Barolo Ris. del Fondatore '96	🍸🍸	8
●	Barolo Vigna La Volta '98	🍸🍸	7
●	Langhe Vendemmiaio '99	🍸🍸	6

BAROLO (CN)

Terre da Vino

via Bergesia, 6
12060 Barolo (CN)
tel. 0173564611
e-mail: info@terredavino.it

Through its network of 2,500 members, Terre da Vino manages almost 4,000 hectares of vineyards in Monferrato, the Langhe and Roero, and releases over 4,000,000 bottles each year. A tour of the modern cellars reveals just how this huge winery has managed to make quality an integral part of its production philosophy. The labels they offered us this year served to confirm our past enthusiasm. The Barbera d'Alba Croere 2001, made from grapes grown in the municipality of Castagnito and aged in new barriques, has a radiant, deep ruby colour and a typical red berry fruit nose laced with spice and vanilla from the oak. Its magnificent, richly extracted body, marked acidity and velvety tannins firmly buttress the palate and lead into a fabulously lengthy finish. The Barbera d'Asti Superiore La Luna e i Falò 2001 boasts a complex, captivating nose. The Barolo Podere Scarrone and Barolo Paesi Tuoi are both good, but we preferred the first for its pervasive bouquet of toastiness with notes of blackberry, blueberry, tobacco and spice. The Barbaresco 2000 is full and round, while the Nebbiolo La Malora 2001 is not very complex but extremely varietal. The Monferrato Tra Donne Sole, from chardonnay and sauvignon, is straw yellow flecked with gold and stood out for its aromas of banana, ripe apple and citrus fruit. The Moscato Passito La Bella Estate is pleasant, well-rounded and harmonious, and the Asti Spumante Monti Furchi 2002 is well made.

●	Barbera d'Alba Croere '01	🍷🍷	5
●	Barbaresco La Casa in Collina '00	🍷🍷	6
●	Barbera d'Asti Sup. La Luna e i Falò '01	🍷🍷	5
○	Piemonte Moscato Passito La Bella Estate '01	🍷🍷	5
○	Monferrato Bianco Tra Donne Sole '02	🍷🍷	4*
●	Barolo Podere Scarrone '99	🍷🍷	8
●	Langhe Nebbiolo La Malora '01	🍷	5
○	Asti Monti Furchi '02	🍷	4
●	Barolo Paesi Tuoi '99	🍷	7
●	Barbera d'Asti La Luna e i Falò '99	🍸🍸	4
●	Barbera d'Alba Croere '00	🍸🍸	5

BAROLO (CN)

G. D. VAJRA
LOC. VERGNE
VIA DELLE VIOLE, 25
12060 BAROLO (CN)
TEL. 017356257
E-MAIL: gdvajra@tin.it

First, we would like to pay tribute to the excellent quality of the wines Aldo and Milena Vajra presented for this Guide. It is all the more impressive when you consider the number of bottles they now turn out, 120,000 to 150,000 from nearly 40 hectares under vine scattered across several municipalities in the Langhe. La Barbera Superiore 2001 (formerly known as Bricco delle Viole, a label no longer permitted for a Barbera) trounced the competition and took Three Glasses for the second year in a row. Very deep, dark ruby, it unleashes a concentration of fruity, almost super-ripe aromas with touches of dried herbs and sweet spices. The palate is supremely elegant, displaying power, character and class. The Freisa Kyè 2001 is sensational, and quite possibly the best Freisa around. No other really comes close. It has an intense colour and brims with berry fruit aromas, especially strawberry and raspberry, with hints of sweet spice and earthiness. The palate delights with its intensity and fruitiness, its only fault being a lack of complexity in comparison to a Nebbiolo or a Pinot Nero. We also liked the Barolo Bricco delle Viole 1998, which offers cinnamon, vanilla and dried rose, and a fresh, fruity palate of great character and decent balance. There were compliments, too, for the fine Barbera 2000 (30,000 bottles), an elegant, characterful wine with a cinnamon and dried fruit nose. The Dolcetto 2002 is good, and the Langhe Nebbiolo is as good as ever. The Dolcetto d'Alba Coste & Fossati and the riesling-based Langhe Bianco, both 2002, were unavailable for tasting.

BASTIA MONDOVÌ (CN)

BRICCO DEL CUCÙ
FRAZ. BRICCO, 21
12060 BASTIA MONDOVÌ (CN)
TEL. 017460153
E-MAIL: briccocucu@libero.it

It is a pleasure to see how this estate, which until five years ago mainly produced double bottles and demijohns of moderately good red much loved by its Ligurian clients, has developed into one of the leading lights of Dolcetto di Dogliani. There are two reasons for this remarkable about-face. First, there are almost 12 hectares planted mainly to old dolcetto vines, located in the best subzones of Bastia Mondovì and Roccacigliè, and tended with loving care. The second is the unassuming determination of Dario Sciolla who, with the backing of his family, had the courage to take a risk and invest money in modernizing his cellars. Today, stainless steel fermenting vats and oak barrels ranging from 15 to 40 hectolitres in size stand in the place of the old, worn-out barrels. Dario has also purchased a small but efficient bottling line. Rigorous thinning and selections designed to offset the poor harvest of 2002 reduced the estate's normal output to just under half, or 25,000 bottles. The range is underpinned by a fruity, agreeably acidulous Langhe Dolcetto 2002. The Dolcetto di Dogliani 2002 contains most of the best grapes that usually go to make up the Bricco San Bernardo, which probably won't be produced. It is a fresh, harmonious Dolcetto with classic blackberry and cocoa powder aromas. The Bricco San Bernardo 2001, a 5,000-bottle selection obtained from a 50-year-old vineyard and aged for 18 months in large casks, boasts great body, lifted by notes of blackberry jam and juniper berry, that leads into a long, velvety finale.

● Barbera d'Alba Sup. '01	♼♼♼	5
● Langhe Freisa Kyè '01	♼♼	7
● Barolo Bricco delle Viole '98	♼♼	8
● Barbera d'Alba '00	♼♼	4*
● Dolcetto d'Alba '02	♼	4
● Langhe Nebbiolo '02	♼	4
● Barbera d'Alba Sup. '00	♈♈♈	6
● Barolo Bricco delle Viole '95	♈♈	8
● Barolo Bricco delle Viole '96	♈♈	8
● Barbera d'Alba		
Bricco delle Viole '99	♈♈	5
● Dolcetto d'Alba		
Coste & Fossati '01	♈♈	5
○ Langhe Bianco '01	♈♈	5
● Barolo Bricco delle Viole '97	♈♈	8

● Dolcetto di Dogliani Sup.		
Bricco S. Bernardo '01	♼♼	4
● Dolcetto di Dogliani '02	♼♼	3*
● Langhe Dolcetto '02	♼	3*
● Dolcetto di Dogliani Sup.		
Bricco S. Bernardo '99	♈♈	4
● Dolcetto di Dogliani '01	♈♈	3

BERZANO DI TORTONA (AL)   BOSIO (AL)

TERRALBA
FRAZ. INSELMINA
15050 BERZANO DI TORTONA (AL)
TEL. 013180403 - 0131866791

DOMENICO GHIO E FIGLI
VIA CIRCONVALLAZIONE, 2
15060 BOSIO (AL)
TEL. 0143684117 - 0143684320
E-MAIL: ghio@vini.it

Once again, Terralba presented the tasting panel with a fine range of high-quality wines. This year's out and out champion is the 100 per cent-croatina Montegrande, but all the wines we reviewed either reached or scored just below Two Glasses. The Montegrande 2001 was the best wine, and its rich ruby colour alone lets you know that it is a red of extraordinary backbone. It has a diverse and fascinating array of aromas, from distinct notes of red berry fruit and chocolate to grassier undertones of hay. It is powerful on the palate, but shows wonderful balance and a finish reminiscent of chestnut honey. The barbera-based Terralba, another very dark wine, almost made it to the finals, too. Left to breathe for a few minutes, its first minerally impression gives way to fruitier tones. The Monleale, from barbera with an addition of croatina, is particularly notable for its balance on the palate, where the marked acidity is borne up by the soft tannins. The superb Barbera Strà Loja 2001 stands out for its fabulous fruitiness and lovely mouthfeel. The whites were also very decent. The Stato 2001, from timorasso, is one of the best selections of this indigenous variety that we tasted. The white La Vetta did not make Two Glasses, but is nevertheless an interesting and attractively different cortese.

The most creative member of Domenico's numerous family is his nephew Roberto. He is also the estate's front man, responsible for client relations and presenting the range of wines. Roberto is the personification of Bosio wines, which are unconventional, totally unpredictable, reluctant to conform and whose best – and sometimes worst – features are character, individuality and uniqueness. Our pick of the bunch this year is the Dolcetto L'Arciprete. Ruby red with youthful purplish highlights, it has a concentrated nose of mainly plum and blackberry fruit. The fresh palate reveals understated tannins that bring the lovely finish to an elegant close. Obtained from super-ripe, almost raisined, grapes that grow on old vines of very old dolcetto dal raspo rosso, Drac Rosso should not be considered a classic Dolcetto. It is intense ruby, with a nose of Madeira wine, stewed fruit and dried figs, and a palate that manages to be warm and fresh at the same time. The rich straw-yellow Gavi La Cascina has golden highlights in the glass and complex aromas of ripe peach and apricot, exotic fruit, flowers and vanilla. The palate is fresh, tangy and warm, with good structure and length. The golden yellow Drac Bianco, made from super-ripe fruit, is redolent of vanilla, marsala zabaglione and charred oak. On the palate, it is warm and mellow with a strong acid vein, good fullness and length. A Glass each also goes to the basic Gavi for its aromas of pear and acacia blossom, and the graceful, very drinkable Dolcetto.

● Colli Tortonesi Rosso Montegrande '01	🍷🍷	6
● Colli Tortonesi Rosso Terralba '00	🍷🍷	6
○ Colli Tortonesi Bianco Stato '01	🍷🍷	5
● Colli Tortonesi Rosso Monleale '01	🍷🍷	5
● Colli Tortonesi Rosso Strà Loja '01	🍷🍷	5
○ Colli Tortonesi Bianco La Vetta '02	🍷	5
● Colli Tortonesi Rosso Terralba '98	🍷🍷	6
○ Colli Tortonesi Bianco Stato '00	🍷🍷	5
● Colli Tortonesi Rosso Terralba '99	🍷🍷	6

● Dolcetto di Ovada Sup. Drac Rosso '01	🍷🍷	6
● Dolcetto di Ovada Sup. L'Arciprete '01	🍷🍷	4*
○ Gavi La Cascina '02	🍷🍷	4*
○ Gavi Drac Bianco '01	🍷	6
○ Gavi '02	🍷	3
● Dolcetto di Ovada '02	🍷	3
○ Gavi Drac Bianco '00	🍷🍷	5
● Dolcetto di Ovada Sup. Drac Rosso '00	🍷🍷	5
● Dolcetto di Ovada Sup. L'Arciprete '00	🍷	4

BRA (CN)

ASCHERI
VIA PIUMATI, 23
12042 BRA (CN)
TEL. 0172412394
E-MAIL: ascheri@ascherivini.it

The Ascheri family is putting the finishing touches to its impressive new complex in the centre of Bra. Next door to the cellars, they are building a large hotel that will boost the number of beds available in the town that is home to the Slow Food movement. All this is going up next to the now renowned Osteria Muri Vecchi, which is also owned by the Ascheris. Matteo, the winery owner, also has very clear ideas about the production side of things, and this year the estate has attained some of its best results yet. There is a new Barolo in the shape of the Sorano Coste & Bricco selection. It is a concentrated, complex Nebbiolo that will evolve even further when left to age in the bottle. Meanwhile, we can attest to its spicy, earthy bouquet, its generous, warm palate and its balanced finish. Both the Vigna dei Pola and the Sorano also performed well. Vigna dei Pola is an intense ruby, with a fruity nose that reveals undertones of liquorice and roasted coffee, then a round, consistent palate. Sorano is less complex, but its very clean, complex nose of chocolate, redcurrant and sweet spice makes it another easy Two Glass winner. The rest of the range included a fragrant, well-typed Dolcetto Vigna Nirane and another Nebbiolo, the very varietal, tannic Bricco S. Giacomo. The Dolcetto S. Rocco and the Langhe Bianco Montalupa are uncomplicated but well-made.

BRUSNENGO (BI)

BARNI
VIA FORTE, 63
13082 BRUSNENGO (BI)
TEL. 015985977

Filippo Barni has thrown himself wholeheartedly into the business of learning how to combine the ancient, traditional typicity of the Brusnengo territory with the free expression of his own creativity. The restoration of the Mesola vineyard, where maggiorina is still cultivated, has saved a small section of croatina and uva rara vines dating back to 1910 from its state of neglect. With a small addition of nebbiolo, these grapes have given a new lease of life to Mesolone, a historic wine that today offers close-knit aromas of ripe red berry fruit mingling with violet flowers and signing off with a warmer note of Virginia tobacco. The palate displays an elegant, supple tannic element that leads into a characterful finish. The Dosso del Fornetto is a well-balanced Bramaterra, lifted by lingering sweetness and hints of morello cherry and blackberry that have yet to find a point of balance with the oak. The Torrearsa, obtained from vespolina with a substantial dose of cabernet and nebbiolo, has a complex nose of thick, dense plum aromas and traces of medicinal herbs. The Albaciara is a one-off. While the nose is all erbaluce and sauvignon, fresh and dry with notes of chalk and sage, the palate is dominated by big, juicy chardonnay aromas of ripe peach. It signs off with a delicate hint of acidity. The Cantagal, a dried-grape "passito", is in its first vintage and still needs to find a length.

● Barolo Sorano Coste & Bricco '99	▼▼ 8
● Nebbiolo d'Alba Bricco S. Giacomo '01	▼▼ 5
● Dolcetto d'Alba Vigna Nirane '02	▼▼ 4
● Barolo Sorano '99	▼▼ 8
● Barolo Vigna dei Pola '99	▼▼ 7
○ Langhe Bianco Montalupa '01	▼ 6
● Dolcetto d'Alba S. Rocco '02	▼ 4
● Barolo Sorano '96	♈ 7
● Barolo Sorano '97	♈ 7
● Barolo Sorano '98	♈ 7
...ntalupa Rosso '99	♈ 6

● Coste della Sesia Rosso Mesolone '00	▼▼ 5
● Coste della Sesia Rosso Torrearsa '01	▼▼ 5
○ Albaciara Bianco '02	▼▼ 4
● Bramaterra Dosso del Fornetto '99	▼▼ 6
● Mesolone Rosso '98	♈ 5
● Coste della Sesia Rosso Torrearsa '99	♈ 5
● Coste della Sesia Rosso Torrearsa '00	♈ 5
○ Albaciara Bianco '01	♈ 4
● Coste della Sesia Rosso Mesolone '99	♈ 5

CALAMANDRANA (AT)

MICHELE CHIARLO
S.DA NIZZA-CANELLI, 99
14042 CALAMANDRANA (AT)
TEL. 0141769030
E-MAIL: chiarlo@tin.it

Michele Chiarlo has built himself a reputation for quality products. He has been making wine for a long time, in fact ever since he took over the family business in 1956. Chiarlo's estate now has vineyards and cellars in three of Piedmont's most prestigious winemaking areas: Calamandrana in Asti Monferrato, the estate headquarters; Barolo in the heart of the Langhe; and Gavi, Piedmont's most famous white production zone. This year, the Chiarlo family has won the coveted Three Glasses for a wine that has been the main focus of their attention for the last few years, the Barbera La Court from the Nizza subzone. The award pays tribute not only to Michele Chiarlo, but also to everyone else who has put their faith in the potential of this zone. The La Court 2000 selection has enormous character, showing fruit aromas with hints of wild berries and toastiness, then dense texture and fabulous softness on the palate. The bright Barolo Cerequio is, as usual, excellent. It has a fruit and flower bouquet with undertones of charred oak, and a superb palate of extraordinary balance. The Cannubi hints at juniper berries and Peruvian bark, following with tremendous strength on the palate. The Brunate possesses a very intense fruitiness, the Triumviratum 1997 is less approachable, and the Barbaresco Asili is slightly etheric. The Gavi Fornaci flaunts elegant, spicy aromas from cask conditioning, whereas the Gavi Rovereto is simpler. A well-deserved Glass apiece goes to the Countacc!, from nebbiolo, barbera and cabernet, and the Chardonnay Plenilunio.

CALAMANDRANA (AT)

HASTAE
FRAZ. QUARTINO, 6
14042 CALAMANDRANA (AT)
TEL. 0141769146

Where does the name "Hastae" come from? Well, it was the old Roman name for Asti. The six producers who formed this winery chose the name very carefully, as they wanted to their estate to embody the identity of the territory. The six families who own this successful venture have written the history of Asti viticulture and of Barbera: Braida, Coppo, Chiarlo, Prunotto, Vietti and Berta. To achieve their goal of making Barbera d'Asti one of the giants of the Italian wine world, they have put together a team that includes the very best talent on the market, namely agronomist Federico Curtaz, oenologist Riccardo Cotarella, and oenologist Paco Perletto, who directs operations in the cellar. The big event of 2003 was the acquisition of four hectares that were planted to vine over the course of the year. This parcel of land, which they purchased as a consortium, is destined to be the site of experiments to improve their barbera even further. Until then, the Barbera Quorum is obtained from equal quotas of the best fruit brought to the cellars by the six partners. The 2001 vintage has produced a very richly coloured deep ruby wine with purplish highlights. Its intense, concentrated bouquet suggests ripe morello cherry and plum fruit enhanced by traces of sweet vanilla and pepper spice. The palate reveals astounding strength, a wealth of pulp and fruit, and a delicately acidulous, lingering, agreeable finish.

● Barbera d'Asti Sup.		
Nizza La Court '00	♟♟♟	6
● Barolo Cannubi '99	♟♟	8
● Barolo Cerequio '99	♟♟	8
● Barolo Triumviratum Ris. '97	♟♟	8
● Barbaresco Asili '00	♟♟	7
● Barolo Brunate '99	♟♟	8
○ Gavi Fornaci di Tassarolo '01	♟♟	6
○ Piemonte Chardonnay		
Plenilunio '01	♟	5
○ Gavi Rovereto '02	♟	4
● Monferrato Montemareto		
Countacc! '00	♟	6
● Barolo Cerequio '97	♟♟♟	8
● Barolo Cerequio '98	♟♟♟	8

● Barbera d'Asti Quorum '01	♟♟	8
● Barbera d'Asti Quorum '97	♟♟	8
● Barbera d'Asti Quorum '98	♟♟	8
● Barbera d'Asti Quorum '99	♟♟	8
● Barbera d'Asti Quorum '00	♟♟	8

CALAMANDRANA (AT)

CALOSSO (AT)

LA GIRIBALDINA
REG. SAN VITO, 39
14042 CALAMANDRANA (AT)
TEL. 0141718043
E-MAIL: info@giribaldina.com

SCAGLIOLA
FRAZ. SAN SIRO, 42
14052 CALOSSO (AT)
TEL. 0141853183
E-MAIL: scagliola@libero.it

The La Giribaldina estate consists of 15 hectares, and the eight under vine yield an annual production of around 40,000 bottles. Mariagrazia Macchi, husband Francesco Colombo, and their son, Emanuele, have been running it since 1995 and, in this short time, have taken their wines to new heights of quality. some of the credit must go to agronomist, Piero Roseo, and oenologist, Piergiorgio Berta. Their plots are scattered across the municipalities of Calamandrana, where the estate has its headquarters, Vinchio and Vaglio Serra in the Val Sarmassa nature reserve. This year, the Barbera Sarmassa replaces the Rossobaldo and Monte del Mare Barberas, which have gone out of production. The Sarmassa is a lovely garnet ruby and boasts a fruity nose that recalls cherry and redcurrant, with a hint of autumn leaves and spice. These aromas spill over onto the full, concentrated palate, which climaxes in a long, warm finish. We liked the Cala delle Mandrie selection. It still needs to find a more harmonious balance of oak and fruit, but this is nothing that cellaring won't fix. The dense colour and aromas of crushed fruit and earth, with a rather insistent note of charred oak, precede a palate of rich texture. The consistent finish is allows a dryish vein to emerge. The white Ferro di Cavallo, from sauvignon with a small proportion of cortese, expresses clear varietal notes of grapefruit, tomato leaf and sage in a framework of wonderful elegance. The palate is soft and clean, with nice character and a long, tidy finish.

Maggiorino and Mario Scagliola's estate is progressing at a spanking pace. Last year, we praised their fabulous Barbera SanSì Selezione 1999. This year, we repeat the list of superlatives we lavished on this magnificent bottle and we applaud a fine performance from the entire range of wines. The 2002 version of the SanSì Selezione is dense garnet ruby, with the briefest of edges. It releases refined, concentrated notes of small red berry fruit with hints of charred oak, dried leaf and forest floor. The palate is full-bodied but dry, progressing into a lovely, consistent, lingering finish with nuances of liquorice. Three brimming Glasses go to this selection, a tribute to the quality of the estate's winemaking. The SanSì 2001 is also superb with a very, very deep, concentrated in appearance. Left to breathe in the glass, the bouquet opens out into notes of earth and fruit, then the palate reveals a generously satisfying mouthfeel and dry tannins that buttress the structure through to the finish, which echoes the aromas of the bouquet. The keynotes of the pleasant Moscato Volo di Farfalle are its ripe bouquet and dense palate. Rich straw yellow in colour, it hints at peach and sage, followed by a balanced palate with moderate effervescence, generous body and a very satisfying finish. The simple, attractive Barbera Frem shows mineral and violet tones, and fleshy vigour on the palate. The coherent Chardonnay Casot dan Vian suggests fermentation on the nose, then rather a lightweight palate. The Dolcetto Busiord is simple, with black cherry aromas.

● Barbera d'Asti Sup.		
Sarmassa '01	♟♟	5
● Barbera d'Asti Sup.		
Cala delle Mandrie '01	♟♟	5
○ Monferrato Bianco		
Ferro di Cavallo '01	♟♟	4*
● Barbera d'Asti Sup.		
Cala delle Mandrie '00	♟♟	5
○ Monferrato Bianco		
Ferro di Cavallo '00	♟♟	4

● Barbera d'Asti Sup.		
SanSì Sel. '00	♟♟♟	7
● Barbera d'Asti Sup. SanSì '01	♟♟	5
○ Moscato d'Asti		
Volo di Farfalle '02	♟♟	4*
● Barbera d'Asti Frem '02	♟	4
● Langhe Dolcetto Busiord '02	♟	4
○ Piemonte Chardonnay		
Casot dan Vian '02	♟	3
● Barbera d'Asti Sup.		
SanSì Sel. '99	♟♟♟	6
● Barbera d'Asti Sup.		
SanSì Sel. '97	♟♟	5
● Barbera d'Asti Sup.		
SanSì Sel. '98	♟♟	5

CALOSSO (AT)

TENUTA DEI FIORI
FRAZ. RODOTIGLIA
VIA VALCALOSSO, 3
14052 CALOSSO (AT)
TEL. 0141826938
E-MAIL: info@tenutadeifiori.com

Walter Bosticardo is a busy man. In addition to producing wine, he is committed to building up the reputation of the territory. Specifically, he is working to revive and promote Gamba di Pernice, a wine obtained from the grape of the same name. He aims to rescue it from the table wine category where it presently languishes. Walter is also the driving force behind the Associazione Produttori Castello di Calosso, a group of ten winemakers who have vineyards in Calosso, Canelli and Costigliole. What they want to do is release ten Barbera d'Astis under the Castello di Calosso DOC label from vines that are more than 40 years old. They have laid down very specific guidelines for cropping levels and vinification processes. The best of the wines Walter offered us this year was the Barbera Castello di Calosso Rusticardi. It comes from the Rodotiglia vineyard and shows a deep purplish colour introducing aromas of spices and red fruit. These expand across the palate, where barrique-derived oaky tones emerge, merging nicely with the alcohol and extract. The Gamba di Pernice 1999 offers generous, spice-themed aromatics. The palate features vegetal tones and assertive tannins that will smooth out in the cellar. Our retasting of the Gamba di Pernice 1990 confirmed that it has aged well. The Musica and the Rairì 2001 are obtained from super-ripe moscato grapes. The first is more complex and structured, while the Rairì is lighter and more approachable. Both are fine examples their variety, aroma-rich and sweet, but not cloying.

CAMINO (AL)

TENUTA GAIANO
VIA TRINO, 8
15020 CAMINO (AL)
TEL. 0142469440
E-MAIL: tenutagaiano@tiscalinet.it

Tenuta Gaiano is one of the flagship estates of Monferrato and Alessandria, a province that every year produces more and more quality wines, but tends to be overlooked for more famous Piedmont winemaking areas. The estate's Barbera Vigna della Torretta is, as usual, quite magnificent. Almost opaque in colour, it has a bouquet of wild berry fruit, blackberry and blueberry, with undertones of walnutskin and tea leaf. The palate is juicy and mouthfilling, the 14.5 per cent alcohol barely discernible and balanced by solid tannins and moderate acidity. The barrique and steel-aged Barbera del Monferrato Vigna Migliau won Two Glasses for its fabulous overall balance, ruby colour with very deep purple highlights, concentrated nose of stylish blackberry and blueberry tinged with balsam and liquorice, and soft, harmonious, lingering palate. The Birba Rossa, a blend of ruché and freisa with a small proportion of other varieties, is a deep, dark ruby and boasts aromas that range from spring flowers to ripe blackberry to cherry. It has an agreeable, fruity palate and good length in the finish. The Barbera del Monferrato Gallianum shows notes of plum, forest floor and evolved cherries preserved in alcohol. The lingering palate echoes the fruit. Rounding off the list is the Grignolino Gallianum, which is pale ruby with orange highlights. Its bouquet reveals pepper and saffron-led spice, and notes of roses and redcurrants, then the palate shows just the right amount of tannins, nice acidity and a typical, rather bitter finish.

● Barbera d'Asti Rusticardi Castello di Calosso '00	⅋⅋	6
○ Musica Moscato '01	⅋⅋	3*
○ Rairì Moscato '01	⅋	3
● Gamba di Pernice '99	⅋	4
● Barbera d'Asti Rodotiglia Castello di Calosso '99	⅋⅋	6
● Barbera d'Asti Vigneto del Tulipano Nero '00	⅋⅋	4*
● Monferrato Rosso '99	⅋⅋	4*
● Gamba di Pernice '90	⅋	5

● Barbera del M.to Vigna della Torretta '01	⅋⅋	6
● Barbera del M.to Vigna Migliau '01	⅋⅋	5
● Birba Rossa '02	⅋⅋	4
● Barbera del M.to Gallianum '01	⅋	4
● Grignolino del M.to Casalese Gallianum '02	⅋	4
● Barbera del M.to Vigna della Torretta '98	⅋⅋	5
● Barbera del M.to '00	⅋⅋	4
● Barbera del M.to Gallianum '00	⅋⅋	4
● Barbera del M.to Vigna della Torretta '99	⅋⅋	5

CANALE (CN)

CANALE (CN)

CASCINA CA' ROSSA
LOC. CASCINA CA' ROSSA, 56
12043 CANALE (CN)
TEL. 017398348

CASCINA CHICCO
VIA ROMA, 80
12043 CANALE (CN)
TEL. 0173979069
E-MAIL:
cascinachicco@cascinachicco.com

Angelo Ferrio can be considered one of the founding fathers of Roero. In a few short years, his charm and likeable ways have made him a point of reference for both the local territory and for the winemaking world in general, a world that sometimes takes itself a little too seriously. His affable optimism, reminiscent of the calm demeanour of his great friend and colleague, Matteo Correggia, prompts him to make the best of even the most complicated situations, a great advantage if you happen to be a grower. We are used to wines of a certain quality from Ferrio, and this year he did not disappoint. He works his 15 hectares with the help of his father, Alfonso, often in difficult conditions; the famed Audinaggio vineyard, for example, is known for the extremely steep slopes of some of its hillside plots. This year, Angelo has produced a solid range of wines. The Roero Audinaggio 2001 made a triumphant return to its glorious 1996 level and won another Three Glasses. Deep ruby red, it has a complex, forthright nose of sweet spice, mint and wild berries. The enveloping, flavoursome palate is perfectly integrated with the oak, and is supported by a rigorous tannic backbone. The Mompissano is a superb second wine. Fruity and concentrated, it is rounded on the palate and shows very harmonious nose-palate consistency. We loved the Barbera Mulassa del 2001, which successfully strikes a delicate balance between acidity and softness, offering notes of blackberry and liquorice, then a mouthfilling palate with a very lengthy finish. The Arneis Merica is fresh and agreeable.

The Faccenda family estate just outside Canale is making progress. The ultimate aim of the winery's determined, far-sighted project is to become a leading light in Roero winemaking. It's fair to say that the foundations are in place. Winemaking and ageing are carried out in an architectural gem of a building that is well worth a visit. The 20 beautifully tended and superbly located hectares under vine are distributed across three Roero municipalities and in the cellars, young Enrico and Marco keep things running smoothly under the watchful eye of their dynamic father, Federico. It is no surprise, then, that the wines they presented this year were again excellent. The nebbiolo-based products were all very good, but we preferred the Roero Valmaggiore. It is outstanding both on the spice, autumn leaf and coffee nose and in the mouth, where the intense progression is enhanced by soft, enveloping sensations and rounded off by a long, harmonious finish. Also excellent, if a tad light, is the Montespinato, while the warm, potent Nebbiolo Mompissano is up to its usual high standard. The famous Bric Loira selection is the best of the Barolos. Dark and concentrated in colour, it explodes onto the nose with concentrated, clear fruit then reveals a fragrant velvetiness on the palate. The current Barolo is simple and well typed. The panel also liked the dried Arneis "passito", the sweet, mellow Arcàss. Finally, the two whites, the Arneis and the Favorita, are very pleasant.

● Roero Audinaggio '01	♀♀♀	6
● Barbera d'Alba Mulassa '01	♀♀	6
● Roero Mompissano '01	♀♀	6
○ Roero Arneis Merica '02	♀	4
● Roero Vigna Audinaggio '96	♀♀♀	6
● Barbera d'Alba Mulassa '99	♀♀♀	6
● Roero Mompissano '99	♀♀	6
● Roero Vigna Audinaggio '99	♀♀	6
● Roero Vigna Audinaggio '98	♀♀	6
● Barbera d'Alba Mulassa '00	♀♀	6
● Roero Audinaggio '00	♀♀	6

● Roero Valmaggiore '00	♀♀	5
● Barbera d'Alba Bric Loira '01	♀♀	5
○ Arcàss Passito '01	♀♀	6
● Nebbiolo d'Alba Mompissano '01	♀♀	5
● Roero Montespinato '01	♀♀	4*
● Barbera d'Alba Granera Alta '02	♀♀	4*
○ Langhe Favorita '02	♀	3
○ Roero Arneis Anterisio '02	♀	4
● Barbera d'Alba Bric Loira '97	♀♀♀	5
● Barbera d'Alba Bric Loira '98	♀♀♀	5
● Nebbiolo d'Alba Mompissano '99	♀♀♀	5
● Barbera d'Alba Bric Loira '00	♀♀	5
● Roero Valmaggiore '99	♀♀	5

CANALE (CN)

★ MATTEO CORREGGIA
CASE SPARSE GARBINETTO, 124
12043 CANALE (CN)
TEL. 0173978009
E-MAIL: matteo@matteocorreggia.com

Yet again, we find ourselves writing about a magnificent range of wines from the most prestigious estate in Roero. Consistently high quality has become its hallmark, thanks to the efforts of Correggia family, including Ornella, and young technician, Luca Rostagno. But above all, credit must go to the philosophy that Matteo Correggia bequeathed, and the determination with which it is still applied today. The estate has big plans for the future. The great winemaker's legacy is evident in the extraordinary wines we were offered, and an impeccable, distinctive style that pays full tribute to their territory of origin. The Roero Ròche d'Ampsèj, a cult wine in Matteo's lifetime, is now an exquisitely fashioned jewel. Dark and dense, it flaunts a graceful, concentrated bouquet that suggests red berry fruit, coffee and tobacco. The palate has its customary power and balance in every component, and the 2000 vintage is blessed with uncommon length. The other two big 2001 reds are excellent. Barbera Marun is a perfect combination of concentration, power and elegance, while the austere, tannic Nebbiolo La Val dei Preti has a subtle bitterish vein that pervades the palate. There is also an interesting newcomer to the red ranks. It's a Langhe Rosso obtained from half cabernet sauvignon, franc and merlot, and half nebbiolo and barbera. The nose is a riot of fruit, then the enfolding palate reveals rich extract. The Sauvignon performed well, showing intense fruit and a generous palate. The rest of the range is very good.

CANALE (CN)

DELTETTO
C.SO ALBA, 43
12043 CANALE (CN)
TEL. 0173979383
E-MAIL: deltetto@deltetto.com

Tonino Deltetto's wines just keep getting better. His lovely Canale estate is in a state of flux at the moment. There have been a series of significant changes both on the production side, with the release of several new labels onto the market, and in estate organization, where Tonino has been joined by his young son, Carlo. Carlo will be helping to run the 15 hectares under vine that the estate now embraces, and the cellars, which turn out 120,000 bottles a year. Turning to those new labels, we thought that the most delicious on offer was the debut version of the first Deltetto "spumante", a delightful "metodo classico" obtained from a traditional blend of 60 per cent pinot nero and chardonnay. This very impressive sparkler's bouquet is as intense as its palate is soft and velvety. Meanwhile, the estate's historic labels march on apace. The Roero Braja outdid itself in the 2001 vintage. It follows a rigorous, imposing nose with a well-rounded, powerful palate, nicely buttressed by subtle tannins, that leads into a long, balanced finish. The Barolo Bussia is also good and getting better, now displaying rather more style and character. Of the two Barberas, we still prefer the mouthfilling, elegant Bramè selection, but the Rocca delle Marasche is coming along nicely. From a late harvest, it offers lovely fruity sensations of blueberry, blackberry and cherry, then a harmonious palate. The Langhe Nebbiolo is pleasant and all the whites are, as ever, good.

●	Roero Ròche d'Ampsèj '00	♟♟♟	8
●	Barbera d'Alba Marun '01	♟♟	6
●	Nebbiolo d'Alba La Val dei Preti '01	♟♟	6
○	Langhe Bianco Matteo Correggia '02	♟♟	6
●	Langhe Rosso Le Marne Grigie '00	♟♟	6
●	Anthos '02	♟♟	4
○	Roero Arneis '02	♟♟	4*
●	Roero Ròche d'Ampsèj '96	♟♟♟	8
●	Barbera d'Alba Marun '97	♟♟♟	6
●	Roero Ròche d'Ampsèj '97	♟♟♟	8
●	Roero Ròche d'Ampsèj '98	♟♟♟	8
●	Roero Ròche d'Ampsèj '99	♟♟♟	8

●	Roero Braja '01	♟♟	5
○	Deltetto Extra Brut Ris. '00	♟♟	5
●	Barbera d'Alba Bramè '01	♟♟	4
●	Barbera d'Alba Rocca delle Marasche '01	♟♟	6
○	Langhe Bianco Suasì '02	♟♟	4*
○	Roero Arneis S. Michele '02	♟♟	4*
●	Barolo Bussia '99	♟♟	6
●	Langhe Nebbiolo '01	♟	4
○	Langhe Favorita Sarvai '02	♟	4
○	Roero Arneis Daivej '02	♟	4
●	Roero Braja '98	♟♟	5
●	Roero Braja '99	♟♟	5
●	Roero Braja '00	♟♟	5

CANALE (CN)

FUNTANIN
VIA TORINO, 191
12043 CANALE (CN)
TEL. 0173979488

This year, brothers Bruno and Piercarlo Sperone, alias Funtanin, have made radical changes to production at their estate, which is a member of the historic group behind the recent resurgence of Roero winemaking. We have sometimes noticed, as we remarked in last year's edition of the Guide, that the Funtanin reds, particularly the big ones, seemed reluctant to reveal their full potential on first tasting, but after further cellaring, would open up to show their breadth and balance the second time around. From a consumer perspective, we have to say that the brothers have done the right thing in leaving the range's two thoroughbreds, the Roero Bricco Barbisa and the Barbera Ciabot Pierin, to age for an extra year. We'll come back to both of these 2001 vintages next year, along with the Langhe Rosso Menico and the Chardonnay Papé Bianc, neither of which was released this year either. This leaves the 2003 release to market somewhat depleted in numbers and in quality, although the basic reds and the two whites sampled by our panel were very decent. The current Roero on offer is a 2000 vintage. Spicy and earthy in its aromas, it is full and tannic on the palate. The 2001 Barbera is ruby red with purplish highlights. It has a still very fresh, heady nose with strains of violet and blackberry, and an acidulous palate borne up by alcohol and rounded off by a lingering finish. The two Arneis are good, particularly the Pierin di Soc, which has a fruity, bitterish, minerally palate.

CANALE (CN)

FILIPPO GALLINO
FRAZ. VALLE DEL POZZO, 63
12043 CANALE (CN)
TEL. 017398112
E-MAIL: gallino.filippo@libero.it

We have always admired the Gallinos' production philosophy: a limited number of Roero territory-driven labels crafted with the utmost attention to quality. This year's entire range of Roeros, Barbera d'Albas and Arneis is no exception, and the Superiore reds in particular are superb. This is proof that behind every great wine lie the skilled efforts of a tight-knit family team – in this case, Filippo and Maria Gallino with children Gianni and Laura – and first-class vineyards: the Gallinos have 12 hectares occupying excellent positions at Canale. The 2001 harvest gave the family two of the best Roero reds we were privileged to taste for the 2004 Guide. The Roero Superiore and the Barbera Superiore are at their very best, and as always, we found it difficult to choose between them. This time we plumped for the more austere, complex Roero. This Nebbiolo is blessed with a bouquet of rare intensity that offers wonderfully harmonious notes of rain-soaked earth, liquorice and berry fruit. Its rich cornucopia of aromas is the prelude to a palate of fabulous consistency and power that almost overwhelms with its rigorous, tannic entry. The finish is very, very long and balances all the components of the palate extremely well. The Barbera is also very good. It has a generous nose of frank, complex blackberry and plum fruit layered over forest floor. The broad palate is backed up by a bitterish vein and just the right amount of acidity, then the fruit returns in force to permeate the big, embracing finish. The rest of the range, all 2002, is good, well-styled and very drinkable.

●	Barbera d'Alba '01	♟♟	4
○	Roero Arneis Pierin di Soc '02	♟♟	4
●	Roero '00	♟	4
○	Roero Arneis '02	♟	3
●	Barbera d'Alba Ciabot Pierin '98	♟♟	5
●	Roero Sup. Bricco Barbisa '98	♟♟	5
●	Barbera d'Alba Ciabot Pierin '99	♟♟	5
●	Roero Sup. Bricco Barbisa '99	♟♟	5
●	Barbera d'Alba Ciabot Pierin '00	♟♟	5
●	Roero Sup. Bricco Barbisa '00	♟♟	5

●	Roero Sup. '01	♟♟♟	6
●	Barbera d'Alba Sup. '01	♟♟	5
●	Barbera d'Alba '02	♟♟	3*
●	Roero '02	♟♟	4
○	Roero Arneis '02	♟	4
●	Barbera d'Alba Sup. '97	♟♟♟	5
●	Roero Sup. '98	♟♟♟	6
●	Roero Sup. '99	♟♟♟	6
●	Roero Sup. '97	♟♟	6
●	Barbera d'Alba Sup. '99	♟♟	5
●	Barbera d'Alba Sup. '00	♟♟	5
●	Roero Sup. '00	♟♟	6

CANALE (CN)

MALVIRÀ
LOC. CANOVA
VIA CASE SPARSE, 144
12043 CANALE (CN)
TEL. 0173978145
E-MAIL: malvira@malvira.com

Brothers Massimo and Roberto Damonte have surpassed themselves yet again this year. They have released an impressive range of wines that is solid across the board. There are also one or two absolute winners. First things first, however. As announced last year, the Damontes have opened their Relais country hotel, run by the family, comprising nine suites, a restaurant and a "vineria" wine outlet, The setting affords a marvellous panorama over the countryside. It will certainly make an important contribution to the revitalization of tourism in Roero. This work has not, however, distracted the Damontes from their true vocation, winemaking. We congratulate them again on their two great reds, the Roero Mombeltramo and Roero Trinità. There is little to choose between them. The Mombeltramo is powerful, pervasive and balanced, with lovely clean, concentrated fruit, spice and coffee adding gorgeous complexity. The Trinità is more subtle. Its aromas of red berry fruit and liquorice spill over onto the palate and expand into the soft, lingering and very harmonious finish. The whites also deserve a mention, notably the various Arneis, in particular the famous Malvirà, which is very well-made. Despite the poor harvest, masterfully overcome by the Damontes, the three 2002 wines are all very good, as is the flowery, round Saglietto 2001. In fact, there are no disappointments anywhere on the list and the four remaining wines, Barbera, Nebbiolo, Favorita and Langhe Bianco Tre Uve, range from good to very good.

CANALE (CN)

MONCHIERO CARBONE
VIA SANTO STEFANO ROERO, 2
12043 CANALE (CN)
TEL. 017395568
E-MAIL: info@monchierocarbone.com

Shortly after the Guide is published, Francesco Monchiero will celebrate the birth of his first child. In the meantime, he has much else to be proud of, as his family estate establishes ever more firmly its position as a leader in Roero winemaking. Even before Francesco took over, it was his father, Marco, a noted oenologist who also takes an active part in local politics, who put his faith in the potential of the area. Today, their beautiful estate just outside Canale produces wines that are a credit not only to those who make them but also to the territory whose name they bear. Francesco has expanded his vineyards to a dozen or so hectares that yield about 80,000 bottles a year. We'll start our notes with some big news. The Roero Srü, the estate's second wine and an important complement to the flagship Roero Printi, has not been released this year. The Printi confirmed last year's very favourable impressions and won another Three Glasses for the 2000 vintage. Again, it is sumptuous, warm and enfolding. Its considerable power is mitigated by subtle tones of oak and fruity notes that range from redcurrant to blackberry. This is a truly great Nebbiolo that can only improve with cellaring. This year, the very clean, stylishly elegant Barbera MonBirone takes over as number two wine. The other offerings are all good, both the reds from the Barbera Pelisa to the Nebbiolo Regret, and the whites from the Arneis Re Cit to the arneis and chardonnay Langhe Tamardì.

●	Roero Sup. Mombeltramo '00	♟♟♟	6
●	Roero Sup. Trinità '00	♟♟	6
●	Barbera d'Alba S. Michele '00	♟♟	4*
●	Langhe Nebbiolo '00	♟♟	4*
○	Langhe Bianco Tre Uve '01	♟♟	5
○	Roero Arneis Saglietto '01	♟♟	4
○	Roero Arneis Renesio '02	♟♟	4
○	Roero Arneis Trinità '02	♟♟	4
○	Langhe Favorita '02	♟	3
○	Roero Arneis '02	♟	3
●	Roero Sup. '90	♟♟♟	6
●	Roero Sup. '93	♟♟♟	6
●	Roero Sup. '97	♟♟♟	6
●	Roero Sup. Trinità '99	♟♟♟	6
●	Roero Sup. '98	♟♟	6

●	Roero Printi '00	♟♟♟	6
●	Barbera d'Alba MonBirone '01	♟♟	5
○	Langhe Bianco Tamardì '01	♟♟	4
○	Roero Arneis Re Cit '02	♟♟	4
●	Barbera d'Alba Pelisa '01	♟	3*
●	Langhe Nebbiolo Regret '01	♟	4
●	Roero Printi '99	♟♟♟	6
●	Roero Printi '97	♟♟	6
●	Roero Printi '98	♟♟	6
●	Roero Srü '99	♟♟	5
●	Barbera d'Alba MonBirone '00	♟♟	5
●	Roero Srü '00	♟♟	5

CANALE (CN)

PORELLO
C.SO ALBA, 71
12043 CANALE (CN)
TEL. 0173979324
E-MAIL: marcoporello@porellovini.it

Following the progress we noted last year, which saw this estate back in the Guide with a full profile, Marco Porello has been pushing the quality envelope across his entire range of wines. Marco has the estate running just the way he wants it, and this enables him to focus all his energy and attention on the production side of things. The new tasting centre under the castle walls in Guarene is now complete and Marco, with help from his parents and wife, Paola, can now concentrate full-time on his 15 hectares under vine in Canale and Vezza. In the cellars, increasingly careful use of oak plays a large part in the high quality his wines have attained. Standing head and shoulders above the rest are the two big reds. The Roero Torretta 2001 shows its austerity straight away in its garnet ruby and deep, layered bouquet of red berry fruit and sweet spice. The palate is soft, despite its firm backbone, showing good harmony and nose-palate convergence. The Barbera Filatura, another 2001, is a fine example of its type. Fruity and well-defined on the nose, it has a fragrant, dry entry on the palate, where a supple acidulous vein is smoothed by subtle notes of oak. The Nebbiolo is good, its one-year sojourn in big barrels lending fullness and tannins. The simpler wines on offer are all well-managed and pleasant to drink, including this year's Barbera Mommiano, the Arneis Camestrì and the Favorita al Birbét.

CANELLI (AT)

CASCINA BARISÉL
REG. SAN GIOVANNI, 2
14053 CANELLI (AT)
TEL. 0141824849
E-MAIL: barisel@inwind.it

A kilometre or two down the road that leads from Canelli to Asti lies Cascina Barisél, nestling among luxuriant vineyards halfway up the south and southwest-facing hillslopes. The Penna brothers are still living off the legacy of knowledge left by their father, but have very precise ideas and clear objectives of their own. Their wines, for example, are soon to be certified organic. The range is structured around the classic local wine types and includes an excellent straw-yellow Moscato d'Asti 2002 that offers generous aromas of fruit and clear notes of sage and polyflora honey. The nice fleshy palate is invigorated by an elegant, fragrant mousse that stays through to a lingering finish. Making its debut appearance is the Avija, a warm, coppery gold table wine obtained from moscato grapes allowed to raisin both on the vine and on rush mats. It has a bouquet of white-fleshed fruit, notably peach, and citrus, then an enfolding palate with balanced acidity. The finish reveals notes of slightly bitter candied lemon peel that offset the sweetness. The still white Monferrato Bianco Foravia 2002, from 100 per cent favorita, is vinified with particular care and attention to crushing and temperature control to preserve the varietal aromas of white damson and yellow apple. It is pleasing on the palate and has a zesty tang. La Cappelletta was not presented as it has been left to age and realize its full potential, but we tasted the Barbera d'Asti 2001, which has approachable cherry tones and a juicy palate.

● Roero Torretta '01	♙♙	4*	
● Barbera d'Alba Filatura '01	♙♙	4*	
● Nebbiolo d'Alba '01	♙♙	4	
● Barbera d'Alba Mommiano '02	♙	4	
● Birbét '02	♙	3	
○ Langhe Favorita '02	♙	3	
○ Roero Arneis Camestrì '02	♙	3	
● Barbera d'Alba Bric Torretta '00	♟♟	4	
● Roero Bric Torretta '00	♟♟	4	

○ L'Avija '01	♙♙	8	
○ Moscato d'Asti '02	♙♙	4	
● Barbera d'Asti '01	♙	4	
○ Monferrato Bianco Foravia '02	♙	3	
● Barbera d'Asti Sup. La Cappelletta '97	♟♟	5	
● Barbera d'Asti Sup. La Cappelletta '98	♟♟	5	
● Barbera d'Asti Sup. La Cappelletta '99	♟♟	5	
● Barbera d'Asti Sup. La Cappelletta '00	♟♟	5	

CANELLI (AT)

CONTRATTO
VIA G. B. GIULIANI, 56
14053 CANELLI (AT)
TEL. 0141823349
E-MAIL: info@contratto.it

This historic estate was founded a long time ago, as is evident from the elegant Art Nouveau buildings of its impressive headquarters at Canelli. For over 130 years, the charming cellars carved into the tufa have witnessed the miraculous bottle fermentation that is the foundation of its great Metodo Classico Spumante wines. Contratto does not just make sparklers, though. Over the last few years, the estate has been turning its attention more and more to quality reds, which is where we start our tasting notes. The Barolo Secolo 1999, from the Cerequio vineyard, is a seductive deep garnet. The nose releases fresh minty tones that play hide and seek with notes of cocoa powder, liquorice and red fruit jam. We gave it Three effortless Glasses for its superb nose and complex palate. The dark ruby Barbera Panta Rei 2001, made with grapes from plots at Agliano and Nizza Monferrato, possesses a range of clear, pervasive aromas, especially blackberry and cherry, with undertones of balsam and charred oak, then the palate is full and enveloping. The Barbera d'Asti Solus Ad is deep ruby with an austere, supremely refined bouquet. The palate reveals rich extract and the odd rough spot that will mellow out with bottle age. The finish is endless. The Giuseppe Contratto Brut is decent, although its nose is rather dominated by oak. The palate is long and creamy. The Chardonnay La Sabauda 2001 finishes on oak-derived vanilla tones.

CANELLI (AT)

COPPO
VIA ALBA, 66
14053 CANELLI (AT)
TEL. 0141823146
E-MAIL: info@coppo.it

The beautiful 18th-century cellars belonging to the Coppo family estate are very picturesque, their red brick vaults looking down on bottles that are allowed ample time to age. One of these is the Coppo Brut 1997, a very well-made and highly expressive "metodo classico" obtained from pinot nero and redolent of ripe hazelnut and peach. The estate now turns out 400,000 bottles a year, including three Barbera d'Astis. The best of these is undoubtedly the Pomorosso 2001, which has reached the absolute maximum in terms of balance and aromatic complexity. Its deep blood-red colour heralds clear, enveloping notes of ripened tobacco and dried violet, then the palate offers roundness and a noble body of boundless generosity, lifted by harmonious tannins. There was never any doubt about the Three Glass award. Riserva della Famiglia 1999 is not to be missed. Perfectly mature and very aristocratic in structure, it unveils a complex, very classy bouquet. The dry, tasty Camp du Rouss 2001 is less aristocratic but does have richer tones of autumn leaf. The list of whites is dominated by the Monteriolo 2001, which shows chamomile, citrus and tropical fruit then a buttery, invigorating palate. The Piemonte Chardonnay Riserva della Famiglia 1999 is very graceful. Seductive and lingering on nose and palate, it boasts generous notes of pear, ripe pineapple and roasted hazelnut. The Costebianche 2002, with nicely gauged fruitiness, the faintly bitterish Gavi La Rocca 2002, and the Moscato d'Asti Moncalvina 2002, with its varietal nose, are all simpler but convincing.

● Barolo Cerequio Tenuta Secolo '99	♟♟♟	8
● Barbera d'Asti Solus Ad '01	♟♟	6
○ Spumante M. Cl. Brut Ris. Giuseppe Contratto '99	♟♟	6
● Barbera d'Asti Panta Rei '01	♟♟	4
○ Piemonte Chardonnay La Sabauda '01	♟	5
○ Spumante M. Cl. Brut Ris. Giuseppe Contratto '96	♟♟♟	6
○ Asti De Miranda M. Cl. '97	♟♟♟	6
● Barolo Cerequio Tenuta Secolo '97	♟♟♟	8
○ Asti De Miranda M. Cl. '00	♟♟♟	6
● Barbera d'Asti Solus Ad '00	♟♟	6
● Barolo Cerequio Tenuta Secolo '98	♟♟	8

● Barbera d'Asti Pomorosso '01	♟♟♟	7
○ Piemonte Chardonnay Monteriolo '01	♟♟	6
● Barbera d'Asti Riserva della Famiglia '99	♟♟	8
● Barbera d'Asti Camp du Rouss '01	♟♟	4*
○ Coppo Brut Ris. '97	♟♟	6
○ Piemonte Chardonnay Riserva della Famiglia '99	♟♟	8
○ Gavi La Rocca '02	♟	4
○ Moscato d'Asti Moncalvina '02	♟	4
○ Piemonte Chardonnay Costebianche '02	♟	4
● Barbera d'Asti Pomorosso '90	♟♟♟	7
● Barbera d'Asti Pomorosso '99	♟♟♟	7
● Barbera d'Asti Pomorosso '00	♟♟	7
● Barbera d'Asti Riserva della Famiglia '98	♟♟	8

CANELLI (AT)

GANCIA
C.SO LIBERTÀ, 66
14053 CANELLI (AT)
TEL. 01418301

In the beginning, there was Gancia. It was the brilliant Carlo Gancia who invented the first "spumante italiano", a moscato-based product inspired by the winemaking techniques used for France's world-famous Champagne. The year was 1865 and a brand new Italy, in the throes of momentous historical events, was witnessing the birth of a Piedmontese label that was destined to become a legend. One and a half centuries later, the fifth generation of Gancias enters the new millennium in the first rank of international sparkling wine production. But it doesn't stop there. The board of directors, led by Lamberto, Edoardo and Massimiliano Gancia presides over a wine, aperitif and liqueur empire that owns, or has a majority interest in, operations and properties across Italy. Under the technical guidance of Piergiorgio Cane, the Canelli-based winery produces magnificent results, managing to combine huge volume with excellent quality. Outstanding out in the vast range of sparkling wines on offer are the Alta Langa Carlo Gancia, a "metodo classico" with fine perlage and a complex, balanced palate, the aromatic, fruity Asti Modonovo, and the Oltrepò Pavese Brut P.rosé from holdings outside the local territory. Gancia is also looking to include the great Piedmont reds in its line-up. The new Tenuta dei Vallarino property just outside Canelli brings us two excellent Barbera d'Astis and a Monferrato Rosso from nebbiolo, barbera, cabernet and merlot grapes. That Beppe Caviola had a hand in these is a clear indication that this historic house is serious about its new venture.

○	Piemonte Alta Langa Carlo Gancia Cuvée del Fondatore '00	♥♥ 5
●	Barbera d'Asti La Ladra '01	♥♥ 4*
●	Barbera d'Asti Sup. Bricco Asinari '01	♥♥ 6
●	Monferrato Rosso Dialogo '01	♥♥ 6
○	Asti Modonovo	♥♥ 4*
☉	OP Pinot Nero Brut P.rosé	♥ 4

CANELLI (AT)

L'ARMANGIA
FRAZ. SAN GIOVANNI, 14/C
14053 CANELLI (AT)
TEL. 0141824947
E-MAIL: armangia@inwind.it

In the Asti dialect, "armangia" means "return match". The term is familiar in most of the farmsteads in these hills, whose well-tended, prosperous appearance belies their harsh past. Ignazio Giovine's "armangia" came when as a young man he decided to take over his father's estate. It was already dealing in wine, but Ignazio rebuilt it using new, modern techniques. In doing so, he forwent easy profits from a simple products and threw himself into the competitive world of quality wine. Today, he has won his personal return match, played primarily against himself. In the functional, ultra-modern new building where he both lives and works, Ignazio has ample space to handle the grapes from his seven hectares. In good years, he produces around 40,000 bottles. Canelli is a Barbera and Moscato zone, so it is no coincidence that these two wine types are the mainstays of the estate's production. Ignazio makes three Barbera d'Astis. This year's Titon is very good. Its seductive brilliant ruby red introduces an intense fruit-rich bouquet that clearly suggests spice and autumn leaf. The palate is full, enveloping and acidulous, with a long, harmonious finish. The Barbera Vignali, made as part of the Castello di Calosso project, is not quite as open in its aromas, but shows power and concentration on the palate. The Sopra Berruti is a well-typed Barbera from the current vintage. The fresh, flowery Moscato has weathered a poor growing year, but is a bit lean on the palate. The Chardonnay Robi & Robi, made from partly raisined grapes, is good, and the Sauvignon EnneEnne is enjoyable.

●	Barbera d'Asti Vignali Castello di Calosso '00	♥♥ 6
●	Barbera d'Asti Sup. Titon '00	♥♥ 4*
○	Piemonte Chardonnay Robi & Robi '01	♥♥ 3
●	Barbera d'Asti Sopra Berruti '02	♥ 3
○	Moscato d'Asti Il Giai '02	♥ 3
○	Monferrato Bianco EnneEnne '02	♥ 3

CANELLI (AT)

VILLA GIADA
REG. CEIROLE, 4
14053 CANELLI (AT)
TEL. 0141831100
E-MAIL: villagiada@atlink.it

Andrea Faccio and his family run 22 hectares in the municipalities of Canelli, Calosso and Agliano Terme. Villa Giada is also offers "agriturismo" holiday accommodation for those who want to explore the Canelli zone or sample its food and wine. Andrea's range this year is topped by the new Monferrato Rosso (the 2001 is the first release). A blend of nebbiolo and barbera with some cabernet and merlot, it is well made, the dense colour introducing a seductive, layered bouquet of flowers, berry fruit and peach. The palate is dry and full-bodied, ending on a lingering note of vanilla. We have another newcomer in the Primovolo, from equal parts of barbera, merlot and sangiovese, which represents the successful collaboration of three estates. The barbera is from Villa Giada, Montecchia in Veneto provided the merlot and Rocca delle Macìe in Tuscany supplied the sangiovese. The outcome is an interesting wine with persistent vegetal tones and a rich texture. The three Barberas performed well. First, we have the deep garnet Bricco Dani with its very captivating aromas of earth, menthol and crushed flowers. The velvety palate is ever so slightly dry and nicely rounded off by a finish that mirrors the nose. La Quercia shows sweet fruity notes with traces of mineral, then a dense, vigorous palate that powers through to the satisfying finish. The steel-conditioned Ajan hints at cakes and grass, then its palate is invigorating, balanced and reasonably long. A mention also goes to the Bricco Manè, from chardonnay with a little cortese, and the Moscato Ceirole, both of which are enjoyable.

CAREMA (TO)

CANTINA DEI PRODUTTORI
NEBBIOLO DI CAREMA
VIA NAZIONALE, 32
10010 CAREMA (TO)
TEL. 0125811160
E-MAIL: cantinacarema@libero.it

The Carema production zone, bordered on the south by Turin and lying at the foot of the Valle d'Aosta mountains, is distinctive for its high altitude, very poor soil and quite severe weather conditions. The distinctive potential of the site climates and terroir makes it a suitable area for nebbiolo. In fact, the variety has been grown here throughout Carema's long winemaking history, which dates back to the 1500s, and two local subvarieties, picutener and pugnet, produce wines with strong personalities and mountain character. The Cantina's range is well organized and oriented exclusively to the typicity of the DOC zone, which is nicely embodied in the Etichetta Nera, a fine, simple, subtle wine that gently hints at wild roses. Airale and Laurey, historically Carema's two most favourably positioned vineyards, give us the Etichetta Bianca, a fuller wine of greater structure and complexity that boasts a generous, meaty nose and a refined palate. The progression is marked by biting, yet complex, tannins and oscillates between lovely clean sensations of red fruit and a classic echo of crushed flowers. A distinctive minerality pays full tribute to the terroir. The Carema Etichetta Bianca Barricato 1998, produced in very limited numbers, is a Nebbiolo aged in small casks. Skilfully and sensitively made, it is a lovely, balanced wine that is a pleasure to drink.

● Primovolo '00	🍷🍷	6
● Barbera d'Asti Sup. Ajan '01	🍷🍷	4*
● Barbera d'Asti Sup. Bricco Dani '01	🍷🍷	5
● Barbera d'Asti Sup. Vigneto La Quercia '01	🍷🍷	4*
● Monferrato Rosso '01	🍷🍷	5
○ Moscato d'Asti Ceirole '02	🍷	3
○ Monferrato Bianco Bricco Manè '02	🍷	4
● Barbera d'Asti Sup. Bricco Dani '97	🍷🍷	5
● Barbera d'Asti Sup. Bricco Dani '98	🍷🍷	5
● Barbera d'Asti Sup. Bricco Dani '99	🍷🍷	5
● Barbera d'Asti Sup. Bricco Dani '00	🍷🍷	5

● Carema Etichetta Bianca '98	🍷🍷	4*
● Carema Etichetta Bianca Barricato '98	🍷🍷	4
● Carema Etichetta Nera '99	🍷	4
● Carema Etichetta Bianca '95	🍷🍷	4
● Carema Etichetta Bianca Barricato '96	🍷🍷	5
● Carema Etichetta Bianca Barricato '97	🍷🍷	5
● Carema Etichetta Bianca '97	🍷	4
● Carema Etichetta Bianca '96	🍷	4

CASSINASCO (AT)

KARIN E REMO HOHLER
REG. BRICCO BOSETTI, 85
14050 CASSINASCO (AT)
TEL. 0141851209
E-MAIL: remohohler@hotmail.com

Karin and Remo Hohler, from German-speaking Switzerland, took over this small estate in the Cassinasco hills near Canelli in 1990. Their three hectares currently give them an annual production of around 12,000 bottles, a figure that is set to increase. The Hohlers are in the process of planting new vineyards with varieties other than the barbera and moscato that they have grown to date. For this edition of the Guide, we were unable to taste the dry Moscato Cenerentola, as the poor harvest of 2002 obliged Karin and Remo to forgo it. We did, however, taste the two Barberas, the Pian Bosco (about 3,000 bottles) and the Pian Bosco Barrique, which is a cask-aged version of the same wine (about 4,000 bottles). The first has a deep garnet colour and a characterful nose redolent of the woods, particularly in the notes of earth and autumn leaves that accompany the fruit. It is concentrated and dynamic on the palate, which progresses deliciously to a rich, warm finish. The barrique-aged version is even better. It is darker in appearance, with fascinating touches of wild berries and hay in the bouquet. The palate is rounded and a dry vein supports the development right through to the long finish of liquorice-tinged fruit.

CASTAGNOLE DELLE LANZE (AT)

★ ★ LA SPINETTA
FRAZ. ANNUNZIATA, 17
14054 CASTAGNOLE DELLE LANZE (AT)
TEL. 0141877396
E-MAIL: arivetti@libero.it

The impressive array of wines presented by the Rivetti brothers embodies the spirit and the ambition of this leading winemaker. The labels include the great Langhe reds, Barbaresco, Barbera d'Alba and, soon, a Barolo, as well as Asti wine types (Moscato, Monferrato Rosso and Barbera d'Asti), some exquisite whites and an extremely concentrated "passito". There are also reds from the new holding in Tuscany to add to the Piedmont bottles. In short, the Rivettis may continue to surprise us with developments at the winery, but not with the quality of their wines, which is again extraordinary. The Barbarescos are incomparably good. The Starderi selection scored higher than the Gallina and Valeirano thanks to its dense hue and a complex nose that explodes with in-your-face fruitiness, sweet spice, liquorice and chocolate. The majestic palate shows oaky tones, with balsamic aromas emerging gradually in a framework of rare harmony between the sweetness of the tannins and the austerity of the body. This Three Glass champion is flanked by another top scorer, one of the very best Barbera d'Asti Superiores we have ever tasted. A paragon of velvetiness, lifted by the classic acidity of the variety, it is long, warm and exalted on the palate by an elegant note of charred oak. The other big reds, the Barbera Gallina and the Monferrato Pin, are also superb. The whites, too, keep getting better and this year, there is an excellent Sauvignon, released as a Langhe Bianco, and a weighty Chardonnay. The dried-grape Oro is sweet and rich, and the Moscato Bricco Quaglia mouthfilling.

● Barbera d'Asti Pian Bosco '01	♟♟	5
● Barbera d'Asti Pian Bosco Barrique '01	♟♟	5
● Barbera d'Asti Pian Bosco Barrique '98	♟♟	5
● Barbera d'Asti Pian Bosco '99	♟♟	5
● Barbera d'Asti Pian Bosco '00	♟♟	5
● Barbera d'Asti Pian Bosco Barrique '00	♟♟	5

● Barbaresco Vigneto Starderi '00	♟♟♟	8
● Barbera d'Asti Sup. '01	♟♟♟	7
● Barbaresco Vigneto Gallina '00	♟♟	8
● Barbaresco Vigneto Valeirano '00	♟♟	8
● Barbera d'Alba Vigneto Gallina '01	♟♟	7
● Monferrato Rosso Pin '01	♟	7
○ La Spinetta Oro '00	♟♟	6
○ Langhe Bianco '01	♟♟	6
○ Piemonte Chardonnay Lidia '01	♟♟	6
○ Moscato d'Asti Bricco Quaglia '02	♟♟	4
● Barbaresco Vigneto Starderi '98	♟♟♟	8
● Barbaresco Vigneto Valeirano '98	♟♟♟	8
● Barbera d'Asti Sup. '00	♟♟♟	8
● Barbaresco Vigneto Starderi '99	♟♟♟	8

CASTEL BOGLIONE (AT)

CASTEL BOGLIONE (AT)

ARALDICA - IL CASCINONE
V.LE LAUDANO, 2
14040 CASTEL BOGLIONE (AT)
TEL. 014176311
E-MAIL: informazioni@araldicavini.com

CASCINA GARITINA
VIA GIANOLA, 20
14040 CASTEL BOGLIONE (AT)
TEL. 0141762162
E-MAIL: cascinagaritina@cascinagaratina.it

Araldica is a huge enterprise, comprising 290 members who between them have a total of 800 hectares under vine and an enormous annual production of around 4,000,000 bottles. The aim is to make quality wines and to this end, member growers lavish great care and attention on their fruit. The cream of the crop this year is the very impressive pinot nero-based Renero. Ruby with garnet highlights, it possesses the a clear, coherent varietal nose of well-defined strawberry, rhubarb and leather. On the palate, it is well-sustained and attractive, and has a lovely finish that offers notes of pepper, among other aromas. The Sauvignon Camillona is clear straw yellow and hints strongly at citrus fruit, sage and tomato. The palate is livened up by an acidulous vein and reveals a gorgeous array of aromas in the finish. The brilliant Arneis Sorilaria boasts a bouquet of ripe fruit and chamomile, then a full, robust palate that is mature but not soft. The Luce Monaca, a barbera, cabernet and merlot blend, is dense in appearance and offers notes of earth, forest floor and fruit, followed by a fairly substantial palate. The Chardonnay Roleto expresses good varietal typicity framed in medium structure. The Barbera Rive has great texture, but rather a muddled nose. Last but not least, the Nebbiolo Castellero suggests crushed flowers and has a smooth, dry palate.

Gianluca Morino puts his heart into running the family estate, which lies among the beautiful hills of Castel Boglione a stone's throw from Acqui Terme. It embraces 20 hectares, planted predominantly to barbera, as is to be expected given the traditions of the area. And where better to start our notes than with the Barberas. Neuvsent, the Garitina standard bearer, is deep garnet with a short edge, and has a generous, seductive nose of elegant black berry fruit, pepper, green leaf and forest floor. The full, rich palate is surefooted and well-sustained, ending in a lingering finish that reveals lovely undertones of liquorice in the resounding reprise of fruit. The Barbera Bricco Garitta is a very pleasant, well-made example of its category, a jolly, not overly challenging red, which wants for nothing in terms of character and elegance. Deep ruby verging on garnet, it has fresh, clear notes of fruit and liquorice enhanced by complex mineral tones. The palate shows vibrant juicy flesh and an intense finish that mirrors the nose. The Monferrato Rosso Amis, made from barbera, pinot nero and cabernet, is also good. Its concentrated colour precedes a nose that ranges from strawberry to cherry and hints of mint. On the palate, it is full-bodied, well-sustained and rounded off by a lengthy finish that recalls the aromas of the bouquet. Last on the list, there is a nice Brachetto, a convincing Dolcetto, and a very well-managed Barbera del Monferrato Vivace.

● Monferrato Rosso Luce Monaca '01	⚑⚑	5
● Monferrato Rosso Renero '01	⚑⚑	4
○ Monferrato Bianco Camillona '02	⚑⚑	4*
○ Roero Arneis Sorilaria '02	⚑⚑	4
● Langhe Nebbiolo Castellero '00	⚑	5
● Barbera d'Asti Sup. Rive '01	⚑	5
○ Piemonte Chardonnay Roleto '02	⚑	4
● Barbera d'Asti Sup. Rive '99	⚐⚐	4
● Monferrato Rosso Luce Monaca '99	⚐⚐	5
● Barbera d'Asti Sup. Rive '00	⚐⚐	4
● Monferrato Rosso Luce Monaca '00	⚐⚐	5

● Barbera d'Asti Sup. Nizza Neuvsent '01	⚑⚑	5
● Monferrato Rosso Amis '01	⚑⚑	5
● Barbera d'Asti Bricco Garitta '02	⚑⚑	3*
● Brachetto d'Acqui Niades '02	⚑	4
● Barbera del M.to Vivace Morinaccio '02		3
● Dolcetto d'Asti Caranzano '02		3
● Barbera d'Asti Sup. Neuvsent '99	⚐⚐	5
● Monferrato Rosso Amis '99	⚐⚐	4
● Barbera d'Asti Sup. Nizza Neuvsent '00	⚐⚐	5
● Monferrato Rosso Amis '00	⚐⚐	4

CASTELLETTO D'ORBA (AL)   CASTELLINALDO (CN)

LUIGI TACCHINO
VIA MARTIRI DELLA BENEDICTA, 26
15060 CASTELLETTO D'ORBA (AL)
TEL. 0143830115
E-MAIL: luigitacchinovini@libero.it

RAFFAELE GILI
REG. PAUTASSO, 7
12050 CASTELLINALDO (CN)
TEL. 0173639011

The Tacchino estate has geared up for quality. In three years, it has metamorphosed from a 50-year-old commercial outfit, serving mainly the Genoa market, into a more ambitious business that aims to produce good wines from its own vineyards, located in a fabulous position between Castelletto and Lerma. Much of the credit for this goes to Romina, who convinced her father and grandfather, the man with the last word on such matters, to modernize without the traumas that usually accompany such a move. Brother Alessio completes the successful family team. Their lovely, lively ruby red Barbera del Monferrato Albarola 2001 is notable for its sweet blueberry and raspberry fruit aromas. On the palate, it is gratifyingly full and harmonious, with great length in the finish. Eresia 2001 is a Monferrato Rosso with a barbera, cabernet and dolcetto base, and takes its name from grandfather's description of this use of an alien variety, "heresy". Dark ruby, its coffee and cocoa powder nose heralds vegetal, fruity tones. The dry palate has medium structure and is very attractive to drink. The brilliant ruby Dolcetto di Ovada Du Riva 2001 mingles ripe fruit with oaky tones, and has a very dry, warm, tannic palate. The intense straw-yellow Gavi 2002 has generous aromas of apple and pear, flowers and bitter almond. It is fresh and tangy with a slightly bitterish finish. One Glass apiece goes to the agreeable Dolcetto Prabarasco, and the Marsenca 2002 Cortese dell'Alto Monferrato, for its citrus fruit and wild roses, which precede a fresh, bitterish palate.

We were curious to taste the wines of Raffaele Gili, a young Castellina producer who made his Guide debut last year with a range of very interesting labels. We were not disappointed. Raffaele has outdone himself with some truly excellent wines and we are happy to confirm that Roero winemaking has a rising star on its horizon. Watch this space. Nothing, or almost nothing, has changed in the way the estate is run. It still comprises five hectares and its grapes are processed in the lovely cellars on the edge of town. These have been slightly expanded to allow Raffaele and his team to work in greater comfort. We were most impressed with the wines, particularly the very rich ruby red Barbera d'Alba di Castellinaldo, which offers a concentrated, spicy nose with hints of fruit slightly toned down by the oakiness. It is huge and soft on the palate, with a lingering, harmonious finish. The Roero Bric Angelino is also very good. Very dark in appearance, it throws a complex bouquet of autumn leaf and earth, then the round, tannic palate signs off with a long, balanced finish. We were absolutely knocked out by the Langhe Rosso L'Assemblato 2001, a nebbiolo and barbera blend, which makes its first appearance this year. It is as elegant in its aromas as it is powerful on the palate. The Nebbiolo Sansivé also performed well, showing sustained body and an agreeable alcoholic vein. The two whites, the Arneis and the Favorita, are pleasant and well-styled.

● Barbera del M.to Albarola '01	🍷🍷	4*
● Dolcetto di Ovada Du Riva '01	🍷🍷	4*
● Monferrato Rosso Eresia '01	🍷🍷	4*
○ Cortese dell'Alto M.to Marsenca '02	🍷	2
● Dolcetto di Ovada Prabarasco '02	🍷	3
○ Gavi '02	🍷	2
● Monferrato Rosso Eresia '00	🍷🍷	4

● Castellinaldo Barbera d'Alba '01	🍷🍷	5
● Langhe Rosso L'Assemblato '01	🍷🍷	5
● Nebbiolo d'Alba Sansivé '01	🍷🍷	5
● Roero Bric Angelino '01	🍷🍷	5
○ Roero Arneis '02	🍷	3
○ Langhe Favorita '02	🍷	3
● Castellinaldo Barbera d'Alba '99	🍷🍷	5
● Castellinaldo Barbera d'Alba '00	🍷🍷	5
● Nebbiolo d'Alba Sansivé '00	🍷🍷	5
● Roero Bric Angelino '00	🍷🍷	5

CASTELLINALDO (CN)

STEFANINO MORRA
VIA CASTAGNITO, 50
12050 CASTELLINALDO (CN)
TEL. 0173213489

Stefano Morra's estate is back among the ranks of the wineries given a full profile in the Guide. Last year, the rather poor performance of one or two of his labels set him back a bit, but he's back with a vengeance in this edition thanks to a range of high quality products. First, a quick look at the estate. Stefano has ten hectares of vineyards at Castellinaldo, Vezza and Canale. Three just outside the town are new, after an arduous soil preparation and replantation project, and will go into production in a couple of years. Stefano produces around 60,000 bottles a year, with help from his wife, Edda, and her brother-in-law, Gianni. Turning to this year's impressive range, we were privileged to sample one of the best Barbera di Castellinaldos we have ever tasted. Dark and dense in appearance, it proffers a full, complex bouquet of red fruit and spices. The oaky tones that tend to hamper the full expression of this wine type, which undergoes lengthy barrique-ageing, are well under control. On the palate, the wine is round and velvety, echoing the nose in a long, harmonious finish. The two Roeros are excellent. The Superiore releases notes of earth and autumn leaves, and is remarkably beefy on the palate. The elegant Srai, obtained from rigorous vineyard selection, is even more concentrated and balanced. Another Two Glass winner, the Barbera Castlè, is acidulous and succulent. Finally, the two Arneis are sound, notably the San Pietro, which stays for two months in large barrels.

● Castellinaldo Barbera d'Alba '00	ŸŸ	5
● Barbera d'Alba Castlè '01	ŸŸ	4
● Roero Srai '01	ŸŸ	6
● Roero Sup. '01	ŸŸ	4*
○ Roero Arneis Vigneto S. Pietro '01	Ÿ	5
○ Roero Arneis '02	Ÿ	4
● Roero Sup. '00	♀♀	4
● Castellinaldo Barbera d'Alba '99	♀	5

CASTELLINALDO (CN)

FABRIZIO PINSOGLIO
FRAZ. MADONNA DEI CAVALLI, 8
12050 CASTELLINALDO (CN)
TEL. 0173213078

Fabrizio Pinsoglio belongs to the group of young Roero producers who have set out on the difficult but fascinating quest for high quality wines. Fabrizio, born in 1974, was inspired by two mentors who, unfortunately, fate has since snatched from him. The first was his father, Oreste, whose name he has given to his Chardonnay (unavailable this year) and the second was Matteo Correggia, whose enormous talent served in the mid 1990s to direct a then very young Fabrizio along the road to superior winemaking that respects both territory and style. Today, these qualities are firmly embodied in Fabrizio's wines. He has renovated his property, expanded his vineyards to around nine hectares, and increased the number of bottles he produces to over 30,000 a year. The Barbera Bric La Rondolina is the flagship wine in his range. The 2001 is a deep ruby red with clear aromas of berry fruit and spice. The palate mirrors these superbly, showing round and balanced with a dry, lingering finish. The basic version, from 2002, is also good. It is simpler, but well typed and eminently enjoyable. The Roero 2001 is missing from the list of Nebbiolos, as it has been left to age a little longer, but the Nebbiolo d'Alba more than makes up for its absence. It is concentrated and soft with gorgeous overall harmony. As the Oreste was not released this year, the only white left is the Arneis Malinat. Known as one of the best in the DOC, it lives up to its reputation, despite the difficult harvest of 2002, displaying lovely aromas of peachy fruit and wild flowers, then nice texture on the palate.

● Barbera d'Alba Bric La Rondolina '01	ŸŸ	5
● Nebbiolo d'Alba '01	ŸŸ	4*
○ Roero Arneis Vigneto Malinat '02	ŸŸ	3*
● Barbera d'Alba Vigna Giaconi '02	Ÿ	4
● Roero '98	♀♀	4
● Barbera d'Alba Bric La Rondolina '99	♀♀	4
● Roero '99	♀♀	4
● Barbera d'Alba Bric La Rondolina '00	♀♀	5
● Roero '00	♀♀	5

CASTELLINALDO (CN)

VIELMIN
VIA SAN DAMIANO, 16
12050 CASTELLINALDO (CN)
TEL. 0173213298 - 0173611248
E-MAIL: ivan.gili@tin.it

Ivan Gili entered the wine world with clear objectives and the right approach. He has turned the family estate, which used to produce bulk wine, into a modern business that targets the quality market. Ivan is now in the process of reducing his volume with the aim of producing a limited number of quality labels. Last year, Gili had a full Guide profile for the first time for an array of selections that are unavailable this time, either because they have been left to mature longer or because they were not produced after the poor harvest of 2002. We applaud this difficult decision, proof of Ivan's intelligence and honesty, which we are sure will take this young Castellina producer far. Meanwhile, we did sample several very good wines. In the absence of the Roero, the Nebbiolo d'Alba 2001 put on a good show. Clear ruby red, it presents a concentrated fruity bouquet with faint vegetal tones. The palate is reasonably powerful, displaying elegance and a long, harmonious finish. Hot on its heels comes the Barbera from the subzone of Castellinaldo, where regulations dictate 12-month cask conditioning. It is dense in appearance, showing a complex nose of wild red berry fruit, spice and cherry, and a round, fragrant palate. The current Barbera is just as it should be – fresh, light and enjoyable. The two whites are typical examples of their category. The Favorita is aromatic and fruity, the Arneis pleasant and acidulous.

CASTELNUOVO DON BOSCO (AT)

CASCINA GILLI
VIA NEVISSANO, 36
14022 CASTELNUOVO DON BOSCO (AT)
TEL. 0119876984
E-MAIL: info@cascinagilli.it

Gianni Vergnano's range of wines is, as usual, extensive and very good. He has a vineyard holding of around 20 hectares around the beautiful Cascina Gilli, where the winery is based. The philosophy of this estate, a major player in the Castelnuovo area, combines modern, functional equipment with a winemaking approach that faithfully mirrors the territory and its heritage. The Freisa d'Asti and the Malvasia di Castelnuovo Don Bosco are the estate's leading products and we will start our notes with the first. Cascina Gilli produces several selections of Freisa d'Asti but our preference is for the Luna di Maggio, a ruby red wine with fresh, clean aromas of wild rose, red berry fruit and almond. On the palate, it is full, balanced and mirrors the nose. The Freisa Vigna del Forno and the Freisa Vivace are simpler, but agreeable. The other "house" wine is the Malvasia, which is also very good. It has a flowery, fresh and very crisp nose then a palate that combines tannins and effervescence very enjoyably. Vergnano's skilled hand is also evident in the Barbera d'Astis. The Vigna delle More selection is fruity and complex, with exquisite notes of plum and black cherry preceding an acidulous, delicate palate. The Sebrì is more imposing. It's a big, concentrated wine with marked alcohol and a long, very balanced finish. The rest of the range is well typed, including the white Rafé, from chardonnay and cortese, the Monferrato Rosso, a barbera and freisa blend, and the Bonarda.

●	Castellinaldo Barbera d'Alba '01	♟♟	5
●	Nebbiolo d'Alba '01	♟♟	5
●	Barbera d'Alba '02	♟	3
○	Langhe Favorita '02	♟	3
○	Roero Arneis '02	♟	3
●	Castellinaldo Barbera d'Alba '99	♟♟	5
●	Castellinaldo Barbera d'Alba '00	♟♟	5
●	Barbera d'Alba Srëi '01	♟♟	4
●	Roero La Rocca '01	♟♟	5

●	Barbera d'Asti Sebrì '01	♟♟	4
●	Barbera d'Asti		
	Vigna delle More '02	♟♟	3*
●	Malvasia di Castelnuovo		
	Don Bosco '02	♟♟	3*
●	Freisa d'Asti Luna di Maggio '02	♟	3
●	Freisa d'Asti Vigna del Forno '02	♟	3*
●	Freisa d'Asti Vivace '02	♟	3
●	Monferrato Rosso '02	♟	3
●	Piemonte Bonarda '02	♟	3
○	Rafé Vigneto di Costa Bianca '02	♟	3
●	Barbera d'Asti		
	Vigna delle More '01	♟♟	3

CASTIGLIONE FALLETTO (CN)

AZELIA
FRAZ. GARBELLETTO
VIA ALBA-BAROLO, 53
12060 CASTIGLIONE FALLETTO (CN)
TEL. 017362859

After two years of seeing their two big Barolos pipped at the post for a top award, Luigi and Lorella Scavino celebrate a Three Glass win with the Barolo San Rocco 1999, the first time this selection has equalled the past exploits of the better-known Bricco Fiasco. The Scavinos release 8,000 bottles of this elixir from Serralunga's San Rocco vineyard, also known as Costabella. The nose captivates with its quality, generosity and length, then gorgeous notes of liquorice return on a palate that is smooth, sweetly tannic and nicely alcoholic, leading to a long, lingering finish. In comparison, the Barolo Bricco Fiasco 1999 is less inclined to reveal its class. The balance between the fruit and aromas from ageing in 35 per cent new barriques needs a little more time to find its feet, but it will. The Barolo 1999 has little to envy these two. Conditioned in large barrels and pre-used barriques, its bouquet is notable for wild berry tones and traces of spice. The pleasing palate has good harmony and decent length. The Azelia plots at Montelupo yield 10,000 bottles of the Dolcetto d'Alba Bricco dell'Oriolo 2002, whose notes of cherry and raspberry offer quite a fruity nose for the vintage. The palate is agreeable and follows through well. The interesting Langhe Nebbiolo (5,000 bottles), made solely from Serralunga grapes, returns after five years, and at a very reasonable price. The Barbera d'Alba Vigneto Punta 2001's one-year stay in half new barriques has imbued it with vanilla and charred oak, then the palate is fresh and robust with a clean, enjoyable finish.

CASTIGLIONE FALLETTO (CN)

★ BRICCO ROCCHE - BRICCO ASILI
VIA MONFORTE, 63
12060 CASTIGLIONE FALLETTO (CN)
TEL. 0173282582
E-MAIL: ceretto@ceretto.com

Grapes from some of the most prestigious Barolo and Barbaresco vineyards go into the wines of these two estates, owned by the Ceretto brothers. Bricco Rocche produces 45,000 bottles a year from 11 hectares under vine in the municipalities of La Morra (Brunate), Serralunga (Prapò) and Castiglione Falletto (Bricco Rocche). Bricco Asili obtains 25,000 bottles from the Bricco Asili, Faset and Bernardot vineyards, the first two in the municipality of Barbaresco and the third at Treiso. The wines on offer include a very well-made Barbaresco Bricco Asili. It is medium garnet with a lingering bouquet of spice and toastiness, set against the characteristic fruity of the variety. The palate displays nice flesh in a harmonious framework that highlights dry tannins in a finish that reflects the nose. The Bernardot is quite a mature garnet and throws evolved aromas of dried flowers and caramel, layered over faint hints of charred oak. The palate is very rich and supple, nicely buttressed by an alcohol that warms the finish. The Faset is more mature in colour, but the nose and palate are refined and dynamic. The Prapò stands out among the Barolos for its character. Brilliant garnet ruby, it offers intense aromas of fruit and marked oaky tones. The palate delights with rich texture and a long finish. The Bricco Rocche has a sweetish nose and a palate that shows well-gauged tannins. The Brunate is mouthfilling and has shrewdly judged tannins and long length. In short, three Barolos that beautifully embody the characteristics of the vineyards they come from.

● Barolo S. Rocco '99	♟♟♟	8
● Barolo Bricco Fiasco '99	♟♟	8
● Barbera d'Alba Vigneto Punta '01	♟♟	5
● Langhe Nebbiolo '01	♟♟	4*
● Dolcetto d'Alba		
Bricco dell'Oriolo '02	♟♟	4
● Barolo '99	♟♟	7
● Barolo Bricco Fiasco '93	♟♟♟	8
● Barolo Bricco Fiasco '95	♟♟♟	8
● Barolo Bricco Fiasco '96	♟♟♟	8
● Barolo Bricco Fiasco '97	♟♟	8
● Barolo S. Rocco '97	♟♟	8
● Barolo Bricco Fiasco '98	♟♟	8
● Barolo S. Rocco '98	♟♟	8
● Barolo '98	♟♟	7

● Barbaresco Bricco Asili '00	♟♟	8
● Barolo Prapò Bricco Rocche '99	♟♟	8
● Barbaresco Bernardot		
Bricco Asili '00	♟♟	8
● Barbaresco Faset Bricco Asili '00	♟♟	8
● Barolo Bricco Rocche '99	♟♟	8
● Barolo Brunate Bricco Rocche '99	♟♟	8
● Barolo Prapò Bricco Rocche '83	♟♟♟	8
● Barolo Bricco Rocche '89	♟♟♟	8
● Barolo Brunate Bricco Rocche '90	♟♟♟	8
● Barbaresco Bricco Asili '96	♟♟♟	8
● Barbaresco Bricco Asili '97	♟♟♟	8
● Barbaresco Bricco Asili '99	♟♟♟	8

CASTIGLIONE FALLETTO (CN)

BROVIA
FRAZ. GARBELLETTO
VIA ALBA-BAROLO, 54
12060 CASTIGLIONE FALLETTO (CN)
TEL. 017362852
E-MAIL: gibrovia@tin.it

The whole family works on this estate of 20 hectares (15 under vine), which has an annual production of 50,000 to 60,000 bottles. The Barolo Garblèt Sué, from the 1999 harvest, is back this year with 3,000 bottles. It has a classic garnet hue, young fruity aromas with a hint of dried flowers, and a palate that has just the right amount of tannins and acidity to offset the fruit. The superb Rocche dei Brovia stands out for its fine, elegant nose of violet and rose with undertones of spice, and its equally fine, elegant palate leading to a long, delicate finish. The Villero (4,500 units released, as for the Rocche dei Brovia) is unmissable and one of the best versions ever. A vibrant, bright garnet, it has a nose that is still closed, but gradually releases very clear notes of violet with nuances of red fruit. The palate is powerful, very well structured, and impeccable in its crisp fruit aromas. The follow through on the palate is magnificent, and progresses to a lingering finish redolent of liquorice. This is a Barolo for the cellar, and it would be foolish not to wait. Serralunga is the source for the just over 4,000 bottles of Ca' Mia. Its balsamic nose introduces a palate whose potent tannins and alcohol tell you why Barolos from this subzone are so famous. The long finish smacks of chocolate. Dolcetto Ciabot del Re, obtained from the grapes that usually go into the Solatìo, performed well, and the Barbera Brea 2001 is excellent. Its concentrated fruit nose, with cherry to the fore, precedes a very full, fruit-forward palate that is borne up by admirable acidity.

CASTIGLIONE FALLETTO (CN)

CASCINA BONGIOVANNI
VIA ALBA-BAROLO, 4
12060 CASTIGLIONE FALLETTO (CN)
TEL. 0173262184
E-MAIL: cascinabongiovanni@libero.it

Davide Mozzone is young, skilled and enthusiastic. Not content with progress so far, he is considering the addition of an underground cellar and his products, already very good, are bound to get even better. His bid for quality is evident in the decision not to release the Dolcetto di Diano d'Alba 2002, and to delay release of the Barbera d'Alba 2002, but the four wines he did present more than make up for these absences. The top performer is the Barolo Pernanno 1999, from the historic vineyard at Castiglione. It was a very worthy finalist that just missed a third Glass, as it did in 1998. The nose has perfectly gauged oak, revealing notes of cinchona and autumn leaves, but it is the palate that overwhelms with soft tannins, a very well-structured body and a finish of extraordinary length. The other Barolo 1999, sourced from plots at Serralunga, Castiglione Falletto and Monforte, is aged in pre-used barrels. The result is a blend of balance and elegance. The nose has a hint of leather in evidence and is every bit as enjoyable as the palate, which achieves an excellent balance of tannins and alcohol. The Dolcetto d'Alba 2002 is one of the best from the vintage, offering a structured palate that is refined and harmonious, as well as its customary pleasing aromas of wild berry fruit. There were good reviews for the Langhe Rosso Faletto 2001, too, which impressed us above all with its harmonious aromas. From 60 per cent cabernet, with equal parts of merlot and barbera, it ages in 60 per cent-new barriques and offers a structured, reasonably long palate.

●	Barolo Rocche dei Brovia '99	♟♟	8
●	Barolo Villero '99	♟♟	8
●	Barbera d'Alba Brea '01	♟♟	5
●	Dolcetto d'Alba Ciabot del Re '02	♟♟	4*
●	Barolo Ca' Mia '99	♟♟	8
●	Barolo Garblèt Sué '99	♟♟	8
●	Barolo Monprivato '90	♟♟♟	8
●	Barolo Ca' Mia '96	♟♟♟	8
●	Barolo Ca' Mia '97	♟♟	7
●	Barolo Ca' Mia '98	♟♟	8
●	Barolo Rocche dei Brovia '98	♟♟	7
●	Barolo Villero '98	♟♟	7

●	Barolo Pernanno '99	♟♟	7
●	Langhe Rosso Faletto '01	♟♟	6
●	Dolcetto d'Alba '02	♟♟	3*
●	Barolo '99	♟♟	6*
●	Barolo '97	♟♟	6
●	Barolo Pernanno '97	♟♟	7
●	Langhe Rosso Faletto '99	♟♟	6
●	Barolo Pernanno '98	♟♟	7
●	Langhe Rosso Faletto '00	♟♟	6
●	Barbera d'Alba '01	♟♟	5
●	Barolo '98	♟♟	6

CASTIGLIONE FALLETTO (CN)

F.LLI CAVALLOTTO
·LOC. BRICCO BOSCHIS·
VIA ALBA-MONFORTE
12060 CASTIGLIONE FALLETTO (CN)
TEL. 017362814 - 017312060
E-MAIL: info@cavallotto.com

A new generation of Cavallottos has taken over. Oenologists Giuseppe and Alfio, and their sister Laura, know where they want to go and have set their sights high. The foundation they are working from is solid. Their 23 hectares around the winery form an almost perfect amphitheatre, what the French would call a "monopole", ensuring sound grape selections at every harvest. The Cavallottos also own a vineyard in Garbellotto, in an area called Vignolo, which is the birthplace of the very promising Barolo Vignolo Riserva 1998. We'll have to wait until next year to pass final judgement on it, as that's when it will be released onto the market. However, we can give our impressions of the Vignolo Riserva 1997 and the S. Giuseppe Riserva 1997, hastily reviewed last year before their release had been officially sanctioned. If the S. Giuseppe has maintained the austerity and elegance it showed last year, the Vignolo has actually progressed further. It has acquired intensity, richness of bouquet in liquorice, leather and spice aromas, and softness on the palate, where it is enveloping and much more balanced. This performance overshadows the still impressive accomplishment of the fruity, potent Barolo Bricco Boschis 1999, which has balsam and tobacco notes but is a little young on the palate. We liked the Dolcetto Vigna Scot 2002, which is earthy, soft and very full, despite the vintage. The Barbera Vigna del Cuculo 2000 is a refined wine in the classic style.

CASTIGLIONE FALLETTO (CN)

★ PAOLO SCAVINO
FRAZ. GARBELLETTO
VIA ALBA-BAROLO, 59
12060 CASTIGLIONE FALLETTO (CN)
TEL. 017362850
E-MAIL: e.scavino@libero.it

Enrico Scavino and daughter Enrica run one of the loveliest estates in the Langhe and their Barolo Rocche dell'Annunziata has again graced it with Three Glasses. Looking ahead, Enrico is pouring all his energy into his cellars – the new barrique cellars are almost complete – and his vineyards. New plots include Bricco Ambrogio at Roddi, in which he places enormous faith. The Rocche dell'Annunziata 1997 matches the 1996 for quality. Aromas of fruit and clear, clean, tertiary spice notes introduce a superbly typed palate that is very, very long indeed. The balance of extract and alcohol is exemplary. The Bric dël Fiasc 1999 has never been better. The generous, pervasive berry fruit, spice, leather and cocoa powder aromas are backed up by assertive tannins that meld into the sumptuous structure. The Cannubi 1999 is more austere, displaying tertiary aromas of tobacco and spice, followed by a palate that shows just the right amount of tannins. The Carobric 1999, sourced from Cannubi, Rocche and Bric del Fiasc, is a textbook Barolo that combines the best of its various vineyards. At present, it has the most youthful tannins of the three. The basic Barolo 1999 is very good, its flowery aromas lifted by lovely notes of pepper. It may not be massive, but the palate is long. The Barbera 2000 benefits from an extra year's ageing and its harmonious palate lingers over a final note of black cherry. The Corale 2000 flaunts its Piedmont origins (80 per cent nebbiolo and barbera) over its cabernet. The barrique-aged chardonnay and sauvignon Sorriso 2001 has a peach nose and fresh palate.

● Barolo Vignolo Ris. '97	🍷🍷	8
● Barolo Vigna S. Giuseppe Ris. '97	🍷🍷	8
● Barolo Bricco Boschis '99	🍷🍷	7
● Barbera d'Alba		
Vigna del Cuculo '00	🍷	5
● Dolcetto d'Alba Vigna Scot '02	🍷	4
● Barolo Vigna S. Giuseppe Ris. '89	🍷🍷🍷	8
● Barolo Bricco Boschis '96	🍷🍷	7
● Barolo Vignolo Ris. '95	🍷🍷	8
● Barolo Vigna S. Giuseppe Ris. '96	🍷🍷	8
● Barolo Vignolo Ris. '96	🍷🍷	8
● Barolo Bricco Boschis '97	🍷🍷	7

● Barolo Rocche dell'Annunziata		
Ris. '97	🍷🍷🍷	8
● Barolo Bric dël Fiasc '99	🍷🍷	8
● Barbera d'Alba		
Affinata in Carati '00	🍷🍷	6
● Langhe Rosso Corale '00	🍷🍷	7
○ Langhe Bianco Sorriso '01	🍷🍷	6
● Barolo '99	🍷🍷	8
● Barolo Cannubi '99	🍷🍷	8
● Barolo Carobric '99	🍷🍷	8
● Barolo Rocche dell'Annunziata		
Ris. '90	🍷🍷🍷	8
● Barolo Bric dël Fiasc '96	🍷🍷🍷	8
● Barolo Rocche dell'Annunziata		
Ris. '96	🍷🍷🍷	8

CASTIGLIONE FALLETTO (CN)

TERRE DEL BAROLO
VIA ALBA-BAROLO, 5
12060 CASTIGLIONE FALLETTO (CN)
TEL. 0173262053
E-MAIL: tdb@terredelbarolo.com

The production of this major co-operative, which totals over 1,000,000 bottles a year, embraces an enormous range of good-quality, honestly priced labels. They are very representative of the territory and show the strong relationship that exists between this historic estate and the Langhe winemaking tradition. In spite of the poor 2002 harvest, Terre di Barolo turned out several very good wines, starting with the Dolcettos. The Dolcetto d'Alba 2002 is ruby with purplish hints. Its agreeable fruit-led nose of cherry, raspberry and redcurrant introduces a warm, soft palate with decent balance and a stunning finish. The Dolcetto di Diano d'Alba from the same vintage is ruby with purple highlights and reveals aromas of ripe morello fruit with vegetal tones. The Barolo Monvigliero 1999 has vegetal notes and rugged tannins, but the quality of the grapes is good. We suggest you wait until it has matured to its full potential before reaching for the corkscrew. The Verduno Pelaverga 2002 is sound, with a varietal strawberry and spice nose. The Nebbiolo d'Alba 2001 has a lovely rich colour, clean aromatics and a pleasant palate. The Valdisera 2001 stands out among the Barberas for its very deep fruit-rich nose with sweet notes of red berry fruit and cocoa powder. Entry on the palate shows good structure, nicely gauged tannins and controlled acidity. The delightful, tangy Barbera d'Alba Superiore 2001 is simpler and more approachable. Finally, the 1999 Barolo offers aromas of tobacco, spice and liquorice, then a very concentrated palate.

CASTIGLIONE FALLETTO (CN)

VIETTI
P.ZZA VITTORIO VENETO, 5
12060 CASTIGLIONE FALLETTO (CN)
TEL. 017362825
E-MAIL: info@vietti.com

An invisible maze of narrow tunnels and functional, attractive, barrel-filled underground rooms. That sums up the new cellars of this old Castiglione estate, now expertly run by Luca Currado and Mario Cordero. Their wines are all excellent, so we'll let them speak for themselves. The Barbera d'Asti Tre Vigne is well made, its ripe fruit accompanied by notes of spice and an equally fruity, juicy palate. The Barbera d'Alba Scarrone has a balsamic nose with traces of plum and cherry, and a full, lengthy palate. The Vigna Vecchia, another Barbera d'Alba, is similar but richer and still closed. It wins Three Glasses for ageing potential that will carry it through many long year in the cellar. The Crena, a Barbera d'Asti, flaunts warm, evolved red fruit aromas and a big, powerful, rather austere palate. The Barolo Rocche has great class and elegance, faithfully embodying its terroir in notes of dried roses with a hint of leather. The austere, elegant palate has sweet tannins and an incomparable finish. The Villero Riserva 1997 is powerful and wonderfully fleshy, its palate extraordinarily enveloping and its finish long and velvety. The Brunate is very good. Its still oaky bouquet hints at cocoa powder, and the long, varietal, juicy finish reveals a classic earthy note. The Lazzarito is faithful to its origins, with potent extract and a long, lively finish. The decent Barolo Ravera di Novello is readier to drink, while the superb Barbaresco Masseria 2000 shows obvious finesse. The classy Barolo Castiglione, a blend of grapes from the town's various vineyards, is not to be missed.

● Barbera d'Alba Valdisera '01	♟♟	3
● Barolo Monvigliero '99	♟♟	7
● Barbera d'Alba Sup. '01	♟	4
● Nebbiolo d'Alba '01	♟	4
● Dolcetto d'Alba '02	♟	3
● Dolcetto di Diano d'Alba '02	♟	3
● Verduno Pelaverga '02	♟	4
● Barolo '99	♟	6
● Barolo Codana '95	♟♟	6
● Barbera d'Alba Sup. '99	♟♟	5
● Barolo Monvigliero Ris. '96	♟♟	7

● Barbera d'Alba Scarrone		
Vigna Vecchia '01	♟♟♟	7
● Barolo Villero Ris. '97	♟♟	8
● Barolo Rocche di Castiglione '99	♟♟	8
● Barbaresco Masseria '00	♟♟	7
● Barbera d'Asti La Crena '00	♟♟	6
● Barbera d'Alba Scarrone '01	♟♟	6
● Barbera d'Asti Tre Vigne '01	♟♟	4*
● Barolo Brunate '99	♟♟	8
● Barolo Castiglione '99	♟♟	7
● Barolo Lazzarito '99	♟♟	8
● Barolo Ravera '99	♟♟	8
● Barbera d'Alba Scarrone		
Vigna Vecchia '00	♟♟♟	7
● Barbera d'Asti La Crena '99	♟♟♟	6

CASTIGLIONE TINELLA (CN)

CAUDRINA
S.DA BROSIA, 20
12053 CASTIGLIONE TINELLA (CN)
TEL. 0141855126
E-MAIL: romano@caudrina.it

Romano Dogliotti is a leading light in the Moscato d'Asti zone and president of the producers' consortium. He runs a beautiful estate and is soon to complete work on a big new cellar right next to the vineyards that give the Dogliottis (Alessandro, Sergio and Marco work with their father) almost 170,000 bottles of red and white wine a year. Moscato accounts for the lion's share of the range, but they are starting to focus more on other wine types, particularly Barbera d'Asti. We'll review the two house selections, La Solista and Monte Venere, in next year's Guide, but we did taste a very good 2002 Asti. This sparkler brims with refined, very varietal aromas of apples, pears and grass. On the palate, the poor harvest has penalized its fullness, but the wonderful balance and gorgeous citrus vein more than make up for this. Of the two Moscatos, both at the top of their category, we preferred the La Galeisa selection. It has the golden straw-yellow hue of the very best Moscatos and an intensely fruit-forward nose with clear hints of acacia blossom, daisies and honey. The weighty palate is refined, sweet but not too sweet, and signs off with a long, harmonious finish.

CASTIGLIONE TINELLA (CN)

ICARDI
LOC. SAN LAZZARO
VIA BALBI, 30
12053 CASTIGLIONE TINELLA (CN)
TEL. 0141855159
E-MAIL: icardivini@libero.it

Scrupulous work in the vineyards in accordance with low environmental impact management techniques has enabled Claudio Icaro to attain consistently high levels of quality. All his wines have a modern slant, and are characterized by rich fruitiness and measured softness. The Barbera Nuj Suj 2001, barrique-matured for 18 months, is ruby tinged with purple. It has a subtle, complex bouquet that opens on fruity notes of raspberry, cherry and cassis, lifted sweet, complex oakiness. Entry on the palate is full-bodied, and there is plenty of extract. The Nej, from 100 per cent pinot nero, has a generous nose and excellent varietal character. The Barolo Parej stands out for the fullness and intensity of its palate, whose smooth tannins support a pleasant, mouthfilling texture. Making its debut on the market is the Barbaresco Montubert 2000 from plots at Neive that are over 50 years old. The nose is astonishing for its breadth and the elegance of its violet and rose aromas, layered over berry fruit, liquorice and cakes. Claudio took the difficult decision not to release either the red or white Pafoj in the far from thrilling 2002 vintage. The whites were represented by a fragrant Balera. Despite the vintage, the Moscato d'Asti La Rosa Selvatica and the Barbera Tabarin are both good. A final word of praise for the Monferrato Rosso Cascina Bricco del Sole, a blend of nebbiolo, barbera and cabernet sauvignon. The 2001 is extraordinarily expressive, even more so than last year's sumptuous version.

○ Moscato d'Asti La Galeisa '02	♀♀	4*
○ Asti La Selvatica '02	♀♀	4
○ Moscato d'Asti Caudrina '02	♀♀	4
● Barbera d'Asti Sup. Monte Venere '99	♀♀	5
● Barbera d'Asti La Solista '00	♀	4
○ Piemonte Chardonnay Mej '00	♀	4

● Barbera d'Asti Nuj Suj '01	♀♀	6
● Monferrato Rosso Cascina Bricco del Sole '01	♀♀	7
● Barbaresco Montubert '00	♀♀	8
● Langhe Rosso Nej '01	♀♀	6
● Barolo Parej '99	♀♀	8
● Barbera d'Asti Tabarin '02	♀	3
○ Moscato d'Asti La Rosa Selvatica '02	♀	4
○ Piemonte Cortese Balera '02	♀	4
● Langhe Rosso Pafoj '00	♀♀	7
● Barolo Parej '97	♀♀	8
● Monferrato Rosso Cascina Bricco del Sole '00	♀♀	6

CASTIGLIONE TINELLA (CN) CASTIGLIONE TINELLA (CN)

LA MORANDINA
LOC. MORANDINI, 11
12053 CASTIGLIONE TINELLA (CN)
TEL. 0141855261
E-MAIL: lamorandina@tin.it

ELIO PERRONE
S.DA SAN MARTINO, 3/BIS
12053 CASTIGLIONE TINELLA (CN)
TEL. 0141855803
E-MAIL: elioperr@tin.it

Brothers Paolo and Giulio Morando have taken enormous strides in a very short time. Their flagship Moscato d'Asti (70,000 bottles) is flanked by a wide range of other products. These include 25,000 bottles of Barbera d'Asti, 4,000 bottles of stainless steel-matured Chardonnay, 1,000 or so half bottles of Costa del Sole "passito" and a further 1,000 of a new red, whose 2000 version replaces the Costa Nera and flanks the L'Insieme project. The Moscato, sourced from plots scattered across the municipality of Castiglione Tinella, is firmly at the peak of its category, thanks to length and elegance that combines a sumptuous mouthfeel with fresh aromas of peach and sage. The two Barberas come from five hectares in the municipality of Montegrosso d'Asti that still have several pre-phylloxera vines, now about 50 years old. The Varmat, barrique-aged for about 15 months, shows roundness and austere concentration. Its mineral and ripe plum notes are enhanced by touches of charred oak and spice. The Zucchetto is less complex on the nose but offers a satisfying palate of dense, fruity flesh. L'Insieme, a blend of Bricco di Neive nebbiolo and Varmat barbera with a dash of syrah, is aged for 18 months in new barriques. It has so much fruit and balsam that its extraordinary structure appears almost normal. Finally, the Costa del Sole 1997 is obtained from moscato grapes left to raisin on the vine, then fermented and matured in new barriques for three years.

Stefano Perrone is one of the best Moscato d'Asti makers in the business. His estate at Castiglione Tinella lies in the heart of the production area and his ten hectares under vine give him about 80,000 bottles a year. Once again, he presented us with two impressive Moscato selections, both of which took home Two Glasses. The Sourgal is a lovely straw-yellow colour flecked with green, and its nose releases exquisitely balanced notes of apricot and peach. The pervasive palate progresses well to end in a lingering, harmonious finish. The Clarté has a more flowery nose, full of acacia blossom and daisy tones, that is all cleanliness and concentration. The rich palate has attractive prickle and a sweet note that prevents it from cloying. Still on the sweet front, the Bigarò, from mainly brachetto grapes, is well-styled and agreeable. The estate has also distinguished itself in recent years with some very good Barbera d'Astis. The Mongovone turned out another very good performance. It is an original selection presented in elegant one-litre bottles (fewer than 3,000 units are released). The 2001 is fruity with clear aromas of blackberry, black cherry and cassis. The palate is big, round and nicely buttressed by acidity, and the finish is well balanced. The Grivò selection from the same vintage is just a tad simpler. Clear ruby red, it has a clean, fragrant bouquet of roses and cherries, followed by a long, acidic palate that is wonderfully supple.

● L'Insieme '00	🍷🍷	8
● Barbera d'Asti Varmat '01	🍷🍷	6
● Barbera d'Asti Zucchetto '01	🍷🍷	4*
○ Moscato d'Asti '02	🍷🍷	4*
○ Costa del Sole '97	🍷🍷	5
○ Langhe Chardonnay '02	🍷	4
● Barbera d'Asti Varmat '98	🍷🍷	6
● Barbera d'Asti Varmat '99	🍷🍷	6
● Barbera d'Asti Varmat '00	🍷🍷	6
● Costa Nera '00	🍷🍷	7

● Barbera d'Asti Grivò '01	🍷🍷	4*
● Barbera d'Asti Mongovone '01	🍷🍷	6
○ Moscato d'Asti Clarté '02	🍷🍷	3*
○ Moscato d'Asti Sourgal '02	🍷🍷	3*
● Bigarò '02	🍷	3
● Barbera d'Asti Grivò '99	🍷🍷	4
● Barbera d'Asti Grivò '00	🍷🍷	4
● Barbera d'Asti Mongovone '00	🍷🍷	6

CASTIGLIONE TINELLA (CN) CERRINA MONFERRATO (AL)

PAOLO SARACCO
VIA CIRCONVALLAZIONE, 6
12053 CASTIGLIONE TINELLA (CN)
TEL. 0141855113
E-MAIL: info@paolosaracco.com

IULI - CA.VI.MON.
FRAZ. MONTALDO
VIA CENTRALE, 27
15020 CERRINA MONFERRATO (AL)
TEL. 0142461146 - 0142943894
E-MAIL: cavimon@libero.it

When you are asked to name a maestro of Moscato, the name of Paolo Saracco is sure to spring to mind. For years now, he has been one of the leading producers of this Asti wine type. Two factors are responsible for his well-established success: painstaking work in the vineyard (Paolo has almost 30 hectares, most of which enjoy excellent positions); and faultless cellar techniques. This enables him to turn out two wonderful Moscato selections every year. The Moscato d'Autunno is superb. Its limpid straw yellow with green highlights captivates and satisfies the eye. The nose is an understated explosion of peach blossom, acacia blossom, honey and wild herbs, then the fat, full palate mirrors the nose with a strong sweet vein that never for a moment threatens to cloy. The finish is long, harmonious and impressive. The basic Moscato is a little simpler, but very fragrant and sweet. The rest of the range, where whites take the lion's share, include a Langhe Bianco obtained from sauvignon and riesling renano and a Chardonnay. The Langhe Graffagno is varietal and very aromatic, with clear tones of freshly mown grass, tomato leaf and minerals. The palate is round, flavoursome and echoes the nose reassuringly, signing off with a long, harmonious finish. The Chardonnay is good, too, a scrupulously crafted example of its type.

Big news from this beautiful Monferrato estate in the province of Alessandria. Partners Fabrizio Iuli, his sister Cristina, and Claudio Barzaghi have been joined by Gad and Umberta Lerner. Gad Lerner, the well-known Italian TV anchorman, and his wife, that is. Having bought a lovely country house in Odalengo, they decided to "go native" and threw themselves into winemaking with impressive results. The range of wines presented follows the same pattern as previous harvests. It is the product of high quality and skilled work that starts in the vineyard, where the winery makes the most of its old vines and keeps cropping levels to around 50 quintals per hectare. One of the new labels is the Malidea, a Monferrato Rosso obtained from barbera, nebbiolo and cabernet sauvignon at yields of about 40 quintals per hectare. It is deep ruby in appearance, and tempts with aromas of blackberry and plum jam over balsam and vanilla from maturation in barrique. The palate is powerful, but well balanced, and the finish lingers. The Barbera Superiore Barabba got through to the finals, thanks to its wonderful harmony and consistent quality. It has concentrated colour and depth on both nose and palate. The Rossore is a less challenging Barbera, but shows many of its stablemate's distinctive characteristics. Last up was the Barbera Umberta, a wine of superb quality that is also making its first appearance on the estate's list. It differs from the other Barberas in that it is aged in stainless steel, and came very close to earning a second Glass.

○	Piemonte Moscato d'Autunno '02 🍷🍷		4*
○	Langhe Bianco Graffagno '01	🍷🍷	4*
○	Moscato d'Asti '02	🍷🍷	4
○	Langhe Chardonnay Prasuè '02	🍷	4
○	Langhe Bianco Graffagno '98	🍷🍷	4
○	Langhe Chardonnay Bianch del Luv '98	🍷🍷	5
○	Langhe Bianco Graffagno '99	🍷🍷	4
○	Langhe Bianco Graffagno '00	🍷🍷	4
○	Piemonte Moscato d'Autunno '01 🍷🍷		4

●	Barbera del M.to Sup. Barabba '01	🍷🍷	7
●	Monferrato Rosso Malidea '01	🍷🍷	6
●	Barbera del M.to Rossore '02	🍷🍷	5
●	Barbera del M.to Umberta '02	🍷	4
●	Barbera del M.to Barabba '00	🍷🍷	7
●	Rossore '01	🍷🍷	5

COCCONATO (AT)

Cantine Bava

s.da Monferrato, 2
14023 Cocconato (AT)
tel. 0141907083
e-mail: bava@bava.com

Cocconato has been producing wine since 1911 and the Bava family has been in charge for four generations. Today Roberto, Paolo and Giulio, with their father Piero, are at the helm of this historic Piedmont estate. In addition to making and selling quality wine, they also organize promotional events to publicize the territory. The range of wines offered this year includes the chardonnay-based Brut Millesimato Giulio Cocchi, which we particularly liked. It belongs to the interesting new Alta Langa DOC exclusively for "metodo classico" wines. The fairly concentrated straw-yellow colour ushers in a seductive nose redolent of jam and yeasted dough, with creamy nuances. The marked effervescence on the palate never threatens to upset the overall balance of the sensations. The Spumante Rosé Giulio Cocchi is simpler, offering notes of orange blossom and a tangy palate. The Alteserre 2001, a chardonnay-based blend, offers sweet aromas and sound character. The Chardonnay Thou Bianc is more of a lightweight, revealing fruit aromas and a palate of medium structure. The straw-yellow Moscato Bass Tuba is well made, showing a nose of peach, cream and elderflower, then the palate strikes a nice balance between sweetness and prickle. The Stradivario is the pick of the Barberas, but the Libera deserves attention for its sweetness, and the Piano Alto for its richer fullness. Rounding off the range is the Malvasia di Castelnuovo Don Bosco, which has varietal notes of wild roses.

○	Piemonte Alta Langa Brut Giulio Cocchi '00	🍷🍷	6
●	Barbera d'Asti Sup. Nizza Piano Alto '01	🍷🍷	6
○	Monferrato Bianco Alteserre '01	🍷🍷	4*
○	Moscato d'Asti Bass Tuba '02	🍷🍷	4*
⊙	Piemonte Alta Langa Brut Rosé Giulio Cocchi '00	🍷	5
●	Barbera d'Asti Libera '01	🍷	3*
●	Malvasia di Castelnuovo Don Bosco Rosa Canina '02	🍷	4
○	Piemonte Chardonnay Thou Bianc '02		3
●	Barbera d'Asti Sup. Nizza Piano Alto '00	YY	6

COSSOMBRATO (AT)

Carlo Quarello

via Marconi, 3
14020 Cossombrato (AT)
tel. 0141905204

Grignolino is often overlooked as a variety, and rarely accounts for the lion's share of an estate's production. More often than not, it is vinified "with the left hand", as they say in these parts, in a winemaking schedule dominated by the maturation periods required by moscato and barbera. Despite all this, moscato accounts for 90 per cent of Carlo and Bianca Quarello's production. With the help of their son, they meticulously tend their grignolino vines and the results are more than gratifying. Witness the Cré Marcaleone, a round, solidly built Grignolino that year after year demonstrates extraordinarily consistent quality. If it is true that this variety has a genetic predisposition to very marked tannins that emerge in the finished product, then it must also be said that ageing completely transforms their impact on the palate. It is these very tannins, tight knit and very mature, that provide the perfect foil for the generous warmth of grignolino's alcohol and constitute the strong point of Cré Marcaleone. Clear cherry red in appearance, its nose is very well defined and offers clear notes of roses, violets, pepper and mint. The palate has strong personality and the finish is long and eminently satisfying. We shall review the red Crebarné 2000, an 80 per cent barbera and 20 per cent nebbiolo mix, in next year's Guide, as the excellent growing year has produced wine of structure that needs more time in the cellar.

●	Grignolino del M.to Casalese Cré Marcaleone '02	🍷🍷	4*
●	Monferrato Rosso Crebarné '98	YY	5
●	Monferrato Rosso Crebarné '99	YY	5
●	Grignolino del M.to Casalese Cré Marcaleone '01	YY	5

COSTA VESCOVATO (AL)

COSTIGLIOLE D'ASTI (AT)

LUIGI BOVERI
FRAZ. MONTALE CELLI
VIA XX SETTEMBRE, 6
15050 COSTA VESCOVATO (AL)
TEL. 0131838165
E-MAIL: boveriluigimichele@virgilio.it

CARLO BENOTTO
VIA SAN CARLO, 52
14055 COSTIGLIOLE D'ASTI (AT)
TEL. 0141966406

Certain areas of Costa Vescovato in Valle Ossona have clearly visible geological stratifications. A stroll through the vineyards is likely to turn up a fossil or two. This very varied landscape may well be one of the secrets of Luigi Boveri's success for this year, his wines are again of superb quality. There is no secret about Luigi's skill as a red winemaker. It is evident in his Barbera selections, all three of which are very exciting. The Vignalunga, part barrique-aged, is a perfect combination of power and balance. It has toasty, fruit-rich sensations, with morello cherry and raspberry to the fore. In contrast, Poggio delle Amarene is a stainless steel-aged Barbera notable for its generous black cherry fruit bouquet that pays tribute to its name ("amarena" means "black cherry). The palate is gutsy but also very refined and long. Boccanera is notable for its fresh acidity and excellent price-quality ratio. Just because he's a maestro with the reds doesn't mean that Luigi can't make some very good whites. One such is the Filari di Timorasso, which comes from the local variety of the same name and walked away with Two full Glasses. Its initial mineral sensations give way to fruit hints of apple and white peach, with a touch of almond in the finish. The Vigna del Prete also put on a good show. Although not in the Timorasso's class, it is still a tangy Cortese that is very pleasant to drink.

Carlo Benotto dedicates himself heart and soul to his 14 hectares under vine and his cellars. Deservedly, he is rewarded by a fine range of wines whose quality is destined to get even better. Barbera is still his mainstay, but he also has a range of equally native varieties, including nebbiolo and gamba di pernice. The first of these is responsible for the new Monferrato Rosso Nebieul 2000, and is matured in 900-litre casks before going into pre-used barriques. The result is a lively, intensely coloured wine with a plum and wild berry bouquet. The palate reveals soft tannins and good nose-palate consistency. The gamba di pernice grape, named for the reddish colour of its bunchstem, had almost disappeared from the area, but is now enjoying a well-deserved, if slow, revival. Despite youth that comes through in its very tangy palate, the Monferrato Rosso Gamba di Pernice 2001 shows good potential. We were able to confirm this by retasting the 1999 and the 2000, both of which are still good and have a long way to go. Carlo offered us two Barbera d'Asti Superiores. The Balau 2000, which spends a year in big barrels of Allier oak, has a very rich colour and strong oak-derived aromas that do not overwhelm the fruit. The Rupestris 2001 seems readier, from its wild berry and vegetal tones, mingling with vanilla and spice. The palate shows a fine balance of freshness and alcohol. Finally, the Monferrato Dolcetto Plissé 2002 is very decent, despite the poor vintage. Its pleasing, approachable aromas introduce a fairly concentrated structure.

● Colli Tortonesi Barbera Vignalunga '01	🍷	5
● Colli Tortonesi Barbera Poggio delle Amarene '01	🍷🍷	4*
○ Colli Tortonesi Bianco Filari di Timorasso '01	🍷🍷	5
● Colli Tortonesi Barbera Boccanera '02	🍷	3*
○ Colli Tortonesi Cortese Vigna del Prete '02	🍷	3*
● Colli Tortonesi Barbera Vignalunga '98	🍷🍷	5
● Colli Tortonesi Barbera Vignalunga '99	🍷🍷	5
● Colli Tortonesi Barbera Vignalunga '00	🍷🍷	5

● Barbera d'Asti Sup. Balau '00	🍷🍷	4*
● Monferrato Rosso Nebieul '00	🍷🍷	5
● Barbera d'Asti Sup. Rupestris '01	🍷🍷	5
● Monferrato Gamba di Pernice '01	🍷🍷	4
● Monferrato Dolcetto Plissé '02	🍷	3
● Barbera d'Asti Sup. Balau '98	🍷🍷	4
● Barbera d'Asti Sup. Rupestris '99	🍷🍷	5
● Barbera d'Asti Sup. Rupestris '00	🍷🍷	5
● Barbera d'Asti Sup. Balau '99	🍷🍷	4

COSTIGLIOLE D'ASTI (AT)

COSTIGLIOLE D'ASTI (AT)

BERTELLI
VIA SAN CARLO
14055 COSTIGLIOLE D'ASTI (AT)
TEL. 0258314153 - 0141966137

CASCINA CASTLÈT
S.DA CASTELLETTO, 6
14055 COSTIGLIOLE D'ASTI (AT)
TEL. 0141966651
E-MAIL: castlet@tin.it

Big changes have been made to the management of this estate. Aldo Bertelli has stepped in to improve marketing, the only side of the business that was less than effective. Indeed, winelovers have long lamented the fact that they would taste wines of great quality and character, but were then unable to enjoy them when ageing had added complexity. Now, under the watchful eye of Elisabetta Bertelli, the wines will be distributed more judiciously. In the cellar, nothing has changed, and Alberto's magic touch is still evident. For over 15 years now, he has allowed his wines to express themselves, unhampered by set production processes. As well as the indigenous barbera, his seven hectares of vineyards are home to many international varieties brought to Piedmont by the Marchesi Asinari of San Marzano in the 18th century. On the white front, our old friend the Chardonnay Giarone is still very young and not on its best form. The splendid I Fossaretti Bianco, from sauvignon, and the gewürztraminer-based Plissé, which is enjoying a new lease of life, both performed very well. The first possesses a wonderfully rich palate and refreshing notes of grapefruit, while the second has a concentrated bouquet and rather a sweetish palate. Of the reds, our preference went to the marvellous Barbera S. Antonio, with its complex, characterful nose and lingering palate. The Barbera Giarone could do with a few more months in the cellar. The Monferrato Cabernet Fossaretti, redolent of blackcurrants and the San Marsan Rosso, full of white pepper aromas, are worthy companions for the two Barberas.

People who meet Mariuccia Borio are infected by her passionate enthusiasm for the territory, as witnessed by her extensive experiments with uvalina, a late-ripening local grape that has been saved from extinction and is awaiting recovery. We tasted a dried-grape version from 1997 and found it very interesting. Then there are her wines, made with the help of skilled oenologist, Giorgio Gozzelino. Barbera is the estate's chief product and it comes in four versions, although the Passum 2001 is not yet available. The Barbera d'Asti 2002 (60,000 bottles) is approachable and pleasant, with youthful alcohol-rich aromas. The palate mirrors these sensations, but the finish is predictable. The semi-sparkling Barbera del Monferrato Goj 2002 reminded us of a category that has been somewhat overlooked. It is very enjoyable and ready to drink, with lovely tones of violets and roses, as well as perfectly judged prickle. It's an excellent example of its type. The Barbera d'Asti Superiore Litina 2000 is very good. Sourced from low-yielding vines more than 30 years old, it shows a concentrated nose of flowers and wild berries. Eight months of barrel-ageing have added notes of vanilla and the palate is remarkable for its long, sweet finish. The estate is also justly proud of its Moscatos. The charming Piemonte Moscato Passito Avié 2000 was, alas, only released in a quantity of 3,000 half-bottles. Its golden yellow colour and aromas of apricot and yellow plum hint elegantly at sunshine. The Moscato d'Asti 2002 is fresh and pleasing, if less citrussy than others of the vintage.

● Barbera d'Asti S. Antonio Vieilles Vignes '00	♟♟	6
● Barbera d'Asti Giarone '00	♟♟	6
● Monferrato Cabernet Fossaretti '00	♟♟	6
● Monferrato Rosso Mon Mayor '00	♟♟	6
● San Marsan Rosso '00	♟♟	6
○ Monferrato Bianco I Fossaretti '01	♟♟	6
○ Piemonte Chardonnay Giarone '01	♟♟	6
○ Plissé Traminer '01	♟♟	6
○ San Marsan Bianco '01	♟	6
● Barbera d'Asti S. Antonio Vieilles Vignes '98	♟♟	5
● Barbera d'Asti S. Antonio Vieilles Vignes '99	♟♟	6

● Barbera d'Asti Sup. Litina '00	♟♟	5
○ Piemonte Moscato Passito Avié '00	♟♟	6
● Barbera del M.to Goj '02	♟♟	3*
● Barbera d'Asti '02	♟	3
○ Moscato d'Asti '02	♟	4
● Monferrato Rosso Policalpo '97	♟♟	5
● Monferrato Rosso Policalpo '98	♟♟	5
● Monferrato Rosso Policalpo '99	♟♟	6
● Barbera d'Asti Sup. Passum '99	♟♟	5
● Barbera d'Asti Sup. Passum '00	♟♟	5
○ Piemonte Moscato Passito Avié '99	♟♟	5

COSTIGLIOLE D'ASTI (AT)

CASCINA ROERA
FRAZ. BIONZO, 32
14055 COSTIGLIOLE D'ASTI (AT)
TEL. 0141968437

This young estate has produced quality wines ever since it was founded by Piero Nebiolo and Claudio Rosso. This is clear from the wines listed with this review, even if the list is shorter than in previous years for several reasons. First, the harvest of 2002 permitted vinification of only two types of Barbera and second, the estate has taken the laudable decision to delay release of the wines already in bottle so that they have time to find their balance. That's why we were unable to review either the Barbera d'Asti Superiore S. Martino 2001 or the Barbera d'Asti 2002. We'll be back to assess them for in the 2005 Guide. Happily, we were able to taste the estate's best selection, the Barbera d'Asti Superiore Cardin 2001. Only 6,000 bottles were obtained from east-facing limestone plots, but they are fully expressive of their terroir. A lively, very dense ruby colour introduces cherry and fruit aromas, layered over notes of liquorice and oak-derived balsam. On the palate, the body is well balanced and closes cleanly with a nice touch of almond in the finish. As for the whites, the Ciapin Bianco 2002 is a 70-30 blend of chardonnay and arneis matured in stainless steel but left to age unhurriedly on the lees. The bouquet suggests daisies and pears, then the rounded palate is nice and tangy. It's a very well-made wine that is let down only by the shortish finish. The Piemonte Chardonnay Le Aie 2002 is more complex. It is evolved in appearance, and almost coppery in colour, then the nose reveals ripe plum and medlar. The palate is lifted by an almost riesling-like mineral vein.

COSTIGLIOLE D'ASTI (AT)

SCIORIO
VIA ASTI - NIZZA, 87
14055 COSTIGLIOLE D'ASTI (AT)
TEL. 0141966610

In a family business like Mauro and Giuseppe Gozzelino's, rooted solidly in country traditions, change doesn't happen overnight. In 2004, the estate's five hectares will be fully productive and their 20,000 bottles will find ample space in the recently completed cellars. This year, the wonderful Barbera Reginal is missing from the ranks because of a hailstorm. By way of compensation, the range of wines has grown with gratifying results. The Barbera d'Asti Superiore Sciorio 1999 (6,000 bottles) is fermented in cement tanks before going into barriques and large barrels to age for a year. It has intense aromas of rose, wild berries and jam, and a palate with firm acidic backbone. The Barbera d'Asti Superiore Beneficio 1999 comes from almost 40-year-old vines. It is more concentrated in appearance and on the nose, where its the oak comes through distinctly in the vanilla tones. The 1998 version of the Vigna Beneficio Riserva (it was not subsequently released again) is also very good. Only 1,000 magnums were obtained from super-ripe fruit, matured for two years in barriques. It boasts an embracing, concentrated nose of cherry and redcurrant and a palate that still seems young, as its rich texture has yet to balance out. The Monferrato Rosso Antico Vitigno 2000 (almost 1,500 bottles) is based on cabernet sauvignon, which has been grown in the area since the late 1700s. It shows tertiary aromas, clear but sweet tannins and decent structure. The Piemonte Chardonnay Vigna Levi 2001 still foregrounds ripe fruit, banana and peach, but is more balanced and pleasant than the 2000.

● Barbera d'Asti Sup. Cardin '01	♟♟	4*
○ Ciapin Bianco '02	♟♟	3*
○ Piemonte Chardonnay		
Le Aie '02	♟	4
● Barbera d'Asti Sup. Cardin '99	♟♟	5
● Barbera d'Asti Sup. Cardin '00	♟♟	4
● Barbera d'Asti Sup.		
Cardin Ris. '00	♟♟	5
● Barbera d'Asti '01	♟♟	4
● Barbera d'Asti Sup. S. Martino '00	♟	4

● Monferrato Rosso		
Antico Vitigno '00	♟♟	5
● Barbera d'Asti Sup.		
Beneficio Ris. '98	♟♟	5
● Barbera d'Asti Sup. Beneficio '99	♟♟	5
● Barbera d'Asti Sup. Sciorio '99	♟♟	4
○ Piemonte Chardonnay		
Vigna Levi '01	♟	5
● Monferrato Rosso Reginal '97	♟♟	5
● Barbera d'Asti Sup. Beneficio '98	♟♟	5
● Barbera d'Asti Sup. Sciorio '98	♟♟	5
● Barbera d'Asti Sup. Reginal '99	♟♟	5
● Monferrato Rosso		
Antico Vitigno '99	♟♟	5

COSTIGLIOLE D'ASTI (AT)

VALFIERI

S.DA LORETO, 5
14055 COSTIGLIOLE D'ASTI (AT)
TEL. 0141966881
E-MAIL: ncler@tin.it

This year the Clericis – Maria Chiara and brother Angelo – have taken enormous strides and the results speak for themselves. Their Barbera d'Asti 2002 (26,000 bottles) is obtained from a blend of grapes grown on the nine hectares of vineyards managed by the estate at Agliano, Costigliole and Nizza Monferrato, as well as fruit bought in from reliable growers. Despite the recurrent rain that inundated Piedmont just before harvest time, this wine displays all of the usual freshness and fruity richness that make it unbeatable in terms of value for money. The harvest of 2001 was exceptional throughout the region, but it was also very difficult for Valfieri. In early spring, the estate's finest vineyards, at Agliano, were hit by violent hailstorms. As a result, yields plummeted to around 20 quintals per hectare. In autumn, the few remaining bunches ripened to such sweetness that oenologist, Luca Caramellino, had to use every last ounce of his experience to rein in the wine's enormous power. The Barbera Superiore (around 13,000 bottles), which underwent malolactic fermentation and ageing in one third-new barriques, reaches dizzying heights. The 100 per cent merlot Matot and the barbera and nebbiolo-based Cassabò are a little fuller and juicier than usual. The Barbera I Filari Lunghi deserves a separate mention. It 15 degrees of alcohol and cherry jam aromas are very reminiscent of an Amarone.

● Barbera d'Asti Sup. '01	*YY*	4*
● Barbera d'Asti Sup. I Filari Lunghi '01	**YY**	6
● Cassabò Rosso '01	**YY**	5
● Monferrato Rosso Matot '01	**YY**	5
● Barbera d'Asti '02	**YY**	4*
● Barbera d'Asti Sup. I Filari Lunghi '99	YY	5
● Monferrato Rosso Matot '99	YY	5
● Barbera d'Asti I Filari Lunghi '00	YY	5
● Barbera d'Asti Sup. '00	YY	4
● Monferrato Rosso Matot '00	YY	5

DIANO D'ALBA (CN)

CLAUDIO ALARIO

LOC. SERVETTI
VIA SANTA CROCE, 23
12055 DIANO D'ALBA (CN)
TEL. 0173231808
E-MAIL: aziendaalario@tiscali.it

Claudio Alario is noted around Diano for his consistently high quality wines. Already known for his excellent Dolcetto selections, released as Diano d'Alba DOCs, Claudio is making an even bigger name for himself with other Langhe wine types. The first of these is Barolo. We shall have to wait until next year to taste the new label from the Sorano vineyard at Serralunga, but in the meantime we were privileged to sample the best version ever to come out of this estate. The 1999, sourced from the Riva vineyard at Verduno, is a masterpiece of sumptuousness and elegance. Ruby red with a garnet edge, it releases rich notes of coffee, sweet spice and liquorice. The palate expands harmoniously and powerfully, never faltering throughout the softly tannin-rich progression. The finish boasts extraordinary length and balance. The Nebbiolo Cascinotto is simpler, with fine, fruity aromas and pleasing softness and harmony. The Barbera Valletta makes the most of its favourable southeast-facing position and displays fragrant, velvety sensations. Moving on to the area's main wine type, Dolcetto di Diano (sometimes simply known as Diano d'Alba), we are happy to confirm our past impressions. Claudio is one of the most skilled producers of this wine, as is clear from his two 2002 selections. Costa Fiore and Montagrillo emerged unscathed from the poor harvest with clean aromas and complexity on the palate. The first is austere, with strong almond tones and notable tannicity. The second has a blueberry and black berry fruit bouquet, then good nose-palate consistency.

● Barolo Riva '99	*YY*	7
● Barbera d'Alba Valletta '01	**YY**	5
● Nebbiolo d'Alba Cascinotto '01	**YY**	5
● Diano d'Alba Costa Fiore '02	**YY**	4*
● Diano d'Alba Montagrillo '02	**YY**	4*
● Barolo Riva '96	YY	7
● Barolo Riva '97	YY	7
● Barbera d'Alba Valletta '00	YY	5
● Nebbiolo d'Alba Cascinotto '00	YY	5
● Diano d'Alba Costa Fiore '01	YY	4
● Diano d'Alba Montagrillo '01	YY	4
● Barolo Riva '98	YY	7

DIANO D'ALBA (CN)

DOGLIANI (CN)

BRICCO MAIOLICA
FRAZ. RICCA
VIA BOLANGINO, 7
12055 DIANO D'ALBA (CN)
TEL. 0173612049
E-MAIL: accomo@briccomaiolica.it

MARZIANO ED ENRICO ABBONA
VIA TORINO, 242
12063 DOGLIANI (CN)
TEL. 0173721317
E-MAIL: abbona.marziano@tiscalinet.it

Beppe Accomo is charismatic and a man of many talents. As well as managing his own lovely estate, he runs the Bottega del Vino in Diano, an organization that aims to promote the image of the local DOC, with energy and an eye to the future. Outside the world of wine, he helps his father, Angelo, who is a noted livestock breeder. None of this distracts Beppe from his main vocation as a scrupulous, highly talented grower-producer. The range of labels presented this year bears the scars of the poor 2002 growing year, and there are even some "casualties". Missing from the line-up are the Sörì Bricco Maiolica (the Dolcetto cru) and the Nebbiolo Cumot, both of whose absences can be blamed on hail. The estate only presented its basic Dolcetto and has delayed release of the Nebbiolo 2001 until next year. As far as we're concerned, though, Beppe has nothing to worry about since he scored high marks for the wines we did taste. His Barbera Vigna Vigia 2001 is concentrated in appearance and offers a fruity bouquet of cherry, black cherry and mineral nuances. The palate is impressive, enveloping and austere, buttressed by good acidity and substantial overall balance. Given the poor harvest, the Dolcetto is astonishing. Far from being thin or predictable, it displays remarkable fleshy pulp and rigorously defined components on the palate. The Langhe Bianco Rolando, which has an intensely floral, fragrant nose, is also good, and the pinot nero-based Langhe Rosso Lorié is pleasantly spicy and easy to drink.

Marziano Abbona, a true wine entrepreneur, is never still for a minute. In those rare moments when he feels discouraged, it doesn't cross his mind to give up. Instead, his naturally optimistic character prevails and off he goes to buy another plot. His estate, run with the help of his wife and son, is one of the most interesting in the Langhe, not least for its size. It boasts almost 50 hectares planted to vine, 25 of which lie in the municipality of Dogliani. The rest are also to be found in other prestigious zones: 18 hectares in Monforte d'Alba (in the Pressenda, Rinaldi and Bricco del Barone vineyards), six at Novello (Terlo and Ravera), and three rented hectares at Barbaresco (Faset). The only 2002 Dolcetto Marziano produced is the fresh, easy-drinking Vigneto Muntâ, a younger brother of the better-known Papà Celso. The 2001 vintage saw the first bottling of the rich, complex Dolcetto Superiore. It is a Papà Celso selection, matured for more than a year in a 37-quintal barrel made by Garbellotto. The Barbaresco Faset 2000 is excellent, too. In fact, it's quite superb, both powerful on the palate and refined on the nose. The Barbera Rinaldi 2001 (almost 45,000 bottles) is every bit as gutsy, blessed with great fullness and wonderful freshness. The two 1999 Barolos are very respectable and pay tribute to a fine vintage. Flanking these aristocrats, we have the Langhe Due Ricu, a blend of cabernet, nebbiolo and other Italian varieties, and the charming, aromatic Cinerino 2002, a big, palate-enfolding white obtained from a rarely planted Rhône valley grape type.

●	Barbera d'Alba Vigna Vigia '01	▼▼	6
●	Dolcetto di Diano d'Alba '02	▼▼	4
○	Langhe Bianco Rolando '02	▼▼	5
●	Langhe Rosso Lorié '00	▼	6
●	Barbera d'Alba Vigna Vigia '98	♈♈♈	5
●	Diano d'Alba Sörì Bricco Maiolica '00	♈♈	4
●	Barbera d'Alba Vigna Vigia '99	♈♈	5
●	Nebbiolo d'Alba Cumot '99	♈♈	5
●	Barbera d'Alba Vigna Vigia '00	♈♈	5
●	Diano d'Alba Sörì Bricco Maiolica '01	♈♈	4

●	Barbaresco Faset '00	▼▼	6
●	Barbera d'Alba Rinaldi '01	▼▼	4*
●	Dolcetto di Dogliani Sup. '01	▼▼	5
●	Langhe Rosso I Due Ricu '01	▼▼	5
○	Cinerino '02	▼▼	4*
●	Barolo Pressenda '99	▼▼	7
●	Barolo Vigneto Terlo Ravera '99	▼▼	7
●	Nebbiolo d'Alba '01	▼	4
●	Dolcetto di Dogliani Vigneto Muntâ '02	▼	4
●	Dolcetto di Dogliani Papà Celso '00	♈♈♈	4
●	Barolo Pressenda '98	♈♈	7
●	Barbera d'Alba Rinaldi '00	♈♈	4
●	Langhe Rosso I Due Ricu '00	♈♈	5
●	Barolo Vigneto Terlo Ravera '98	♈♈	7
●	Barbaresco Faset '99	♈♈	6

DOGLIANI (CN)

CA' VIOLA
B.TA SAN LUIGI, 11
12063 DOGLIANI (CN)
TEL. 017370547 - 0173742535
E-MAIL: caviola@caviola.com

It's now been two years since Beppe Caviola moved his cellars from Montelupo Albese to Dogliani. Most of his vineyards, however, are at Montelupo and make up a holding of just over seven hectares, split between dolcetto and barbera, with a few rows of nebbiolo and pinot nero. This might sound rather odd for an oenologist whose advice is sought the length and breadth of Italy, from Puglia to Veneto and from Sardinia to Marche, as well as in Piedmont, and known affectionately as "the Dolcetto king". The big news from the estate is the addition of two hectares that Beppe rented at Novello and immediately planted with nebbiolo destined for Barolo. The estate's product list has undergone several changes. First, the Pinot Nero Rangone has gone, to be replaced by L'Insieme, a blend of barbera, nebbiolo and pinot nero, aged for almost 18 months in mainly new barriques. Second, Beppe has created a standard-label Barbera that will serve to take up any slack from Bric du Luv. Finally, the Dolcetto Barturot 2002 was not vinified separately because adverse weather conditions forced Beppe to blend most of his fruit in order to obtain a decent Vilot, which has turned out to be full and fruity. This year, the Bric du Luv 2001 (88 per cent barbera and 12 per cent pinot nero) has a wealth of aromas. Juicy on the palate, and extraordinarily classy, it beats its local rivals hands down. Only L'Insieme 2000 can go the distance with its rich fruit and smooth tannins. Sadly, fewer than 2,000 bottles were released.

DOGLIANI (CN)

QUINTO CHIONETTI & FIGLIO
B.TA SAN LUIGI, 44
12063 DOGLIANI (CN)
TEL. 017371179
E-MAIL:
chionettiquinto@chionettiquinto.com

This estate, an important one for Dolcetto di Dogliani, is entirely focused on the variety. The Chionettis, Quinto, his wife Gianna and daughter-in-law Maria, make nothing but Dolcetto. They are aided in this endeavour by Marco Devalle, in the vineyard and cellar, and his wife Manuela, who works in the office. Quinto was born on the hill of San Luigi and has never so much as considered vineyards outside Dogliani, let alone swapping his variety for an "alien" grape type, such as barbera or nebbiolo. He is a committed single-grape grower and his 14 hectares are devoted entirèly to dolcetto. Quinto's plots generally give him 75,000 bottles divided between the San Luigi and Briccolero vineyard selections. In 2002, however, the poor harvest took its toll, although now it all seems little more than a bad dream. The inevitable result for a producer as conscientious as Quinto was to sacrifice part of his harvest to preserve the quality of the rest. This year only just under 50,000 bottles of the San Luigi will be released. As usual, the estate wines were fermented then aged for a brief spell in stainless steel tanks. The San Luigi 2002 is a classic, deep ruby in appearance with purplish lights. The nose, although not explosive, reveals a swathe of very varietal aromas, including blackberry, raspberry and bitter almond. The palate is reasonably structured for the vintage but fails to open out as it progresses.

● Langhe Rosso Bric du Luv '01	♥♥♥	6
● L'Insieme '00	♥♥	7
● Barbera d'Alba Brichet '02	♥♥	5
● Dolcetto d'Alba Vilot '02	♥♥	4*
● Langhe Rosso Bric du Luv '95	♥♥♥	6
● Dolcetto d'Alba Barturot '96	♥♥♥	5
● Langhe Rosso Bric du Luv '96	♥♥♥	6
● Dolcetto d'Alba Barturot '98	♥♥♥	5
● Langhe Rosso Bric du Luv '98	♥♥♥	6
● Langhe Rosso Bric du Luv '99	♥♥♥	6
● Langhe Dolcetto Barturot '01	♥♥♥	5

● Dolcetto di Dogliani S. Luigi '02	♥♥	4*
● Dolcetto di Dogliani Briccolero '00	♥♥	4
● Dolcetto di Dogliani Briccolero '01	♥♥	4
● Dolcetto di Dogliani S. Luigi '01	♥♥	4

DOGLIANI (CN)

DOGLIANI (CN)

EINAUDI
B.TA GOMBE, 31
12063 DOGLIANI (CN)
TEL. 017370191
E-MAIL: einaudi@poderieinaudi.com

PECCHENINO
B.TA VALDIBERTI, 59
12063 DOGLIANI (CN)
TEL. 017370686
E-MAIL: a.pecchenino@onw.net

The Einaudis are eager to reap the rewards of the new vineyards they have planted at Neviglie and, above all, at Neive, a plot that is likely to yield a new Barbaresco. Meanwhile they continue to turn out excellent wines from their holdings at Dogliani (30 hectares in the Santa Lucia, San Luigi and Gombe vineyards) and Barolo (eight hectares in Cannubi and Via Nuova). Their barrique-conditioned Barolo nei Cannubi repeats last year's extraordinary performance. Its complex balsam and fruit nose calls to mind vanilla, cinnamon, pencil lead and fresh raspberries, then its dense but elegant tannic structure has long, velvety length. The Costa Grimaldi and the basic Barolo, both matured in large barrels, have little to choose between them in terms of nose. They are understandably simpler and do not offer the same amazing thrust on the palate. The other outstanding offering is the Luigi Einaudi, a cabernet sauvignon and nebbiolo blend with a dash of barbera and merlot, aged largely in new barriques. As yet, it is closed and needs to find balance, but its power explodes on the palate in waves of soft, juicy, fruit-led tones. As for the Doglianis, the 2001 Dolcettos put on a good show and we particularly liked the I Filari selection. Mellowed by a stay in oak, it is much less austere than the Tecc. A quick mention goes to the Piemonte Barbera 2001 and the Dolcetto 2002. All in all, it was an authoritative performance from this estate that bears witness to both its potential and the determination of the owners to make further investments.

Brothers Orlando and Attilio Pecchenino, leading lights of the new generation of Dogliani producers, have aimed to produce big-structured wines since they started bottling. In the past, particularly bountiful harvests (1997 and 2000 come to mind) encouraged over-extracted wines, but today's offerings are much more refined. They have lost none of their backbone, however. The estate consists of 25 hectares planted to vine that lie largely on the hillside at San Luigi. It also boasts a new cellar kitted out with everything an oenologist might need down to the micro-oxygenation apparatus used to tone down dolcetto's powerful tannins. We start our notes with the 2002 vintages. Here, as everywhere else, ruthless selection has reduced volume and the most important labels are missing from the line-up. The lone Dolcetto 2002 produced is the San Luigi, a fruity, varietal wine with good body that is still a bit rigid in the finish. The white Vigna Maestro, from chardonnay, sauvignon and arneis, is penalized by slightly intrusive oak that makes it a little heavy, for the time being. Turning to 2001, the Langhe Rosso La Castella has been discontinued and its two component varieties are now vinified separately. The Barbera displays opulent flesh, well supported by acidity, and the Nebbiolo is impressive for the complexity and density of its tannic weave. As we have come to expect, this year's clear winner is the Dolcetto Bricco Botti. Aged for nine months in 25-hectolitre barrels, it combines a wealth of aromas, notably blackberry and cocoa powder, with a round palate.

● Barolo nei Cannubi '99	♟♟♟	8
● Dolcetto di Dogliani I Filari '01	♟♟	5
● Langhe Rosso Luigi Einaudi '01	♟♟	6
● Dolcetto di Dogliani Vigna Tecc '01	♟♟	4*
● Piemonte Barbera '01	♟♟	5
● Barolo '99	♟♟	7
● Barolo Costa Grimaldi '99	♟♟	8
● Langhe Nebbiolo '01	♟	4
○ Langhe Vigna Meira '01	♟	4
● Dolcetto di Dogliani '02	♟	3*
● Langhe Rosso Luigi Einaudi '97	♟♟♟	6
● Langhe Rosso Luigi Einaudi '98	♟♟♟	6
● Langhe Rosso Luigi Einaudi '99	♟♟♟	6
● Barolo nei Cannubi '98	♟♟♟	8

● Dolcetto di Dogliani Sup. Bricco Botti '01	♟♟	6
● Piemonte Barbera Quass '01	♟♟	5
● Langhe Nebbiolo Vigna Botti '01	♟♟	6
● Dolcetto di Dogliani S. Luigi '02	♟♟	4*
○ Langhe Vigna Maestro '02	♟	5
● Dolcetto di Dogliani Sirì d'Jermu '97	♟♟♟	4
● Dolcetto di Dogliani Sirì d'Jermu '98	♟♟♟	4
● Dolcetto di Dogliani Sirì d'Jermu '99	♟♟♟	4
● Dolcetto di Dogliani S. Luigi '00	♟♟♟	4
● Dolcetto di Dogliani Sirì d'Jermu '01	♟♟♟	4

DOGLIANI (CN)

PIRA
B.TA VALDIBERTI, 69
12063 DOGLIANI (CN)
TEL. 017378538
E-MAIL: vini.pira@onw.net

Gianmatteo Pira's well-run estate lies in the municipalities of Monforte and Dogliani, or oenologically speaking, on the border of the Dolcetto d'Alba and Dolcetto di Dogliani production areas. It has 20 hectares to its name, eight of which are planted to vine and give an annual production of about 35,000 bottles of Dolcetto, Barbera, Merlot and Nebbiolo. We open our notes with the estate's three Dolcettos, the best of which is the superb Bricco dei Botti. It has a deep garnet colour and a nose that hints at ripe black berry fruit, camphor and liquorice. The palate is complex and invigorating, with extraordinary texture supported by robust tannins. The Vigna Landes is only marginally less impressive. It has a youthful appearance, aromas of pepper, peach and redcurrant, and a palate that is notable for its freshness and consistency. The Vigna Fornaci (Dolcetto d'Alba) offers green leaf tones mingled with the fruity notes of the grape type. It boasts a well-structured palate with good acidity. We liked the deep coloured Barbera Briccobotti for its morello cherry aromas and its warm, full-bodied, very generous palate. The Barbera Fornaci suggests almond, mint and pepper and has a full, tangy palate that leads to an extremely enjoyable, if not particularly long, finish. The 100 per cent merlot Camerlot has dense, richly extracted aromas of wild berry and black berry fruit, while the Nebbiolo Bricco dell'Asino is surefooted and pleasant.

DOGLIANI (CN)

SAN FEREOLO
LOC. SAN FEREOLO
B.TA VALDIBÀ, 59
12063 DOGLIANI (CN)
TEL. 0173742075
E-MAIL: sanfereolo@sanfereolo.com

The viticultural partnership between estate owner, Nicoletta Bocca, and Francesco Stralla goes from strength to strength. Between them they have ten hectares of vineyards at Dogliani, most of which are planted with old vines. San Fereolo's wines have always been long-lived and solidly austere. Whatever the reason – lengthy fermentation and ageing or simply geography – these characteristics are also the measure of their success. At the bottom of the estate's price and production heap are the 10,000 bottles of Dolcetto Valdibà 2002, which distinguishes itself for its fresh aromas and approachable palate. A step up the quality ladder we have the San Fereolo, matured for one year in Slavonian vats and 900-litre barrels of French oak. The 2001 is labelled Superiore and the 27,000 bottles released make it one of San Fereolo's most important wines. Although still rather closed, the nose has depth and the palate, as usual, needs a few more months in the bottle to smooth out its innate hardness and give full rein to its immense class. One step further up, the Dolcetto 1999 takes us back in time and astonishes with its youth. The Superiore 1593, matured for two full years in vats, then 900-litre barrels, has an extraordinary nose and seductive depth on the palate. Rounding off the list we have a new white obtained from a blend of riesling and gewürztraminer. To date, only 500 bottles have been produced, but this number will certainly increase. Its array of floral and mineral aromas is backed up by big, dry structure. Release of the Brumaio 2001 has been delayed for a year.

●	Dolcetto di Dogliani Vigna Bricco dei Botti '01	▼▼	4*
●	Piemonte Barbera Briccobotti '01	▼▼	6
●	Barbera d'Alba Vigna Fornaci '01	▼▼	5
●	Langhe Rosso Camerlot '01	▼▼	5
●	Dolcetto d'Alba Vigna Fornaci '02	▼▼	4*
●	Dolcetto di Dogliani Vigna Landes '02	▼▼	4*
●	Nebbiolo d'Alba Vigna Bricco dell'Asino '01	▼	5
●	Dolcetto di Dogliani Vigna Bricco dei Botti '99	▽▽	5
●	Piemonte Barbera Briccobotti '99	▽▽	6
●	Dolcetto di Dogliani Vigna Bricco dei Botti '00	▽▽	5

●	Dolcetto di Dogliani Sup. S. Fereolo '01	▼▼	4*
●	Dolcetto di Dogliani Sup. 1593 '99	▼▼	5
●	Dolcetto di Dogliani Valdibà '02	▼▼	4*
○	Langhe Bianco '02	▼▼	4
●	Dolcetto di Dogliani S. Fereolo '97	▽▽▽	4
●	Langhe Rosso Brumaio '97	▽▽▽	5
●	Dolcetto di Dogliani S. Fereolo '99	▽▽▽	4
●	Dolcetto di Dogliani Valdibà '01	▽▽	4

DOGLIANI (CN)

SAN ROMANO
B.TA GIACHELLI, 8
12063 DOGLIANI (CN)
TEL. 017376289
E-MAIL: bchionetti@sanromano.com

Bruno Chionetti runs his small Dogliani estate with aplomb. His eight hectares of vineyards stretch across the hill below Dogliani in the direction of Farigliano. For the moment, San Romano is entirely dedicated to dolcetto, bar the odd row of pinot nero and chardonnay and a hectare of nebbiolo that has yet to go into production. Bruno is proud of his estate's conversion to organic farming, which will be complete in 2005 when he expects to get his certification. Do not confuse respect for nature with technical backwardness, however. Bruno is equally proud of his new cellar, a technological wonder that features computer-controlled fermentation in every vat and allows remote control of every phase of production. The poor harvest of 2002 forced Bruno to divert part of the Vigna del Pilone and part of the Dolianum to make the Dolcetto di Dogliani. The result is a light, rather acidulous red that should be drunk young. The Vigna del Pilone 2002 (the usual 12,000 bottles are reduced to 8,000) is obtained from a rigorous selection. It shows greater body and flesh, as well as aromas of blueberry and bitter almonds, but doesn't sacrifice the freshness responsible for the lean structure of the 2002 Dolcettos. The Dolianum, obtained from a Pilone harvest selection aged for 12 months in new 900-litre casks of Hungarian oak, again emerges as the jewel in the estate's crown. It managed to achieve a difficult balance of freshness and depth on the nose, and of power and style on the palate. The monovarietal Pinot Nero Martin Sec is a model of elegance.

FARA NOVARESE (NO)

DESSILANI
VIA CESARE BATTISTI, 21
28073 FARA NOVARESE (NO)
TEL. 0321829252
E-MAIL: dessilani@onw.net

The beautiful central courtyard of Dessilani at Fara is a picturesque haven of peace and tranquillity. Enzio Lucca is quick to point out the connection between aesthetics and functionality in the various parts of the estate, and loves to hold forth on the relationship of space, free-standing fermentation vessels and real quality. He cannot abide the vulgarity of pre-ordained winemaking protocols and assembly lines. Instead, he advocates "listening to" the wine and "keeping it happy" at each phase of production. The results of this philosophy are clear, with the Caramino again in contention for Three Glasses. The plum and cherry ripeness of the 2000 shows the narrow temperature range experienced during the growing year. It boasts a wonderfully deep bouquet with clear notes of roots and spices. The palate progresses nicely and provides a perfect framework for the well-gauged oak. The Lochera is similar, but rather edgy at present. It has clean, clear aromas of delicate flowers, including violet and wistaria, with a subtle mineral vein that suggests even greater development potential than the Caramino. The Gattinara has a white chocolate and ginger bouquet with a hint of fresh bell pepper, then a refined, lingering palate. The Ghemme possesses feminine aromas of lavender and fern, leading to a less than harmonious palate redolent of dried spices and raspberries. The Sizzano is less complex and alternates chocolate sensations of oak with ripe fruit. The Laio, a dried-grape table wine, overdoes its extreme ripeness and fullness, upsetting the balance of the erbaluce grape.

● Dolcetto di Dogliani Sup.		
Dolianum '01	♟♟	5
● Dolcetto di Dogliani		
Vigna del Pilone '02	♟♟	4*
● Langhe Rosso Martin Sec '01	♟♟	5
● Dolcetto di Dogliani '02	♟	4
● Dolcetto di Dogliani		
Vigna del Pilone '97	♟♟♟	4
● Dolcetto di Dogliani		
Vigna del Pilone '98	♟♟♟	4
● Dolcetto di Dogliani		
Vigna del Pilone '99	♟♟♟	4
● Dolcetto di Dogliani Sup.		
Dolianum '00	♟♟	5

● Fara Caramino '00	♟♟	6
● Fara Lochera '00	♟♟	6
● Gattinara '99	♟♟	6
● Colline Novaresi Nebbiolo '00	♟	5
○ Laio Passito '00	♟	7
○ Colline Novaresi		
Bianco Collefino '02	♟	4
● Ghemme '99	♟	5
● Sizzano '99	♟	6
● Fara Caramino '99	♟♟♟	6
● Fara Caramino '98	♟♟	6
● Ghemme '98	♟♟	6
● Fara Lochera '99	♟♟	6

FARIGLIANO (CN)

ANNA MARIA ABBONA
FRAZ. MONCUCCO, 21
12060 FARIGLIANO (CN)
TEL. 0173797228
E-MAIL: amabbona@amabbona.com

This estate lies right on the edge of Langhe wine country, next to the road that leads to Murazzano. Run by Anna Maria Abbona and her husband, Franco Schellino, it has won quite a name for itself in a short time. The cellars nestle in a deep valley, immersed in peaceful surroundings, and enjoy a stunning view. In the late 1930s, Anna Maria's grandfather planted his dolcetto and barbera rooted cutting here at an elevation of 490 to 550 metres above sea level. Today, these same vines contribute the aromas of the Maioli and Cadò selections. This is dolcetto country, and the estate is given over almost entirely to the variety. The only exception is a small amount of barbera that provides the base for the Langhe Cadò, and a few rows of nebbiolo on which Anna Maria is cutting her teeth before releasing a new label. The 2002 vintage gave us just the two basic Dolcettos, as neither the Maioli nor the Superiore was produced. The Langhe Dolcetto has no particular pretensions and seeks only to stimulate the palate. The Sorì dij But packs a bigger tannic punch and will benefit from more time in bottle. The Cadò 2001, barbera enhanced by a little dolcetto, is big and powerful, with refreshing acidity on the palate. Its stay in barrique is still a little too evident, though. Once again, it is the Superiore, a Maioli selection aged unhurriedly in bottle, that won the panel's vote. Inky black in appearance, it has a cinchona and blackberry jam nose followed by superb roundness on the palate.

FARIGLIANO (CN)

GIOVANNI BATTISTA GILLARDI
CASCINA CORSALETTO, 69
12060 FARIGLIANO (CN)
TEL. 017376306
E-MAIL: gillardi@gillardi.it

Perched on one of the most beautiful hills in Farigliano and surrounded by its vineyards, the Gillardi family's estate looks like a cherry on a fancy cake. Giovanni Battista Gillardi's six and a half hectares are 90 per cent planted to dolcetto, with the remaining ten per cent split among cabernet sauvignon and other French varieties. Giovanni makes it a rule to bring only the best fruit into the cellars to give his son, Giacolino, who vinifies the grapes, a head start. Giacolino's choice of production methods, borne out by frequent tastings, shies away from too much technology. The only technological apparatus in the cellars is the stainless steel fermenting vats and a few rows of small oak casks. The harvest of 2002 reduced the estate's volume by 25 per cent. After an initial vineyard selection at harvest time, a further ten per cent of the crop was rejected at the cellar during a second bout of selection. This means that the output for 2002 will total 30,000 bottles, rather than the usual 40,000. Turning to the Dolcettos, the Vigneto Maestra (15,000 bottles) lacks some of its usual fruitiness and is a bit more rugged. The Cursalet (13,000 bottles) is excellent, despite the fact that its character is wilder and less manageable than we're used to. As we have come to expect, the dolcetto and cabernet-based Yeta is outstanding but the Harys, in particular, is a thoroughbred, nicely honed by its stay in small wood. Only 2,000 bottles of each were released.

● Dolcetto di Dogliani Sup. '01	♟♟	5
● Langhe Rosso Cadò '01	♟♟	5
● Dolcetto di Dogliani Sorì dij But '02	♟♟	4*
● Langhe Dolcetto '02	♟	3
● Langhe Rosso Cadò '98	♟♟	5
● Dolcetto di Dogliani Maioli '00	♟♟	4
● Dolcetto di Dogliani Sup. Maioli '99	♟♟	5
● Langhe Rosso Cadò '99	♟♟	5
● Dolcetto di Dogliani Sup. Maioli '00	♟♟	5
● Langhe Rosso Cadò '00	♟♟	5
● Dolcetto di Dogliani Maioli '01	♟♟	4

● Harys '01	♟♟	7
● Langhe Rosso Yeta '01	♟♟	5
● Dolcetto di Dogliani Cursalet '02	♟♟	4*
● Dolcetto di Dogliani Vigneto Maestra '02	♟	4
● Harys '98	♟♟♟	7
● Harys '99	♟♟♟	7
● Harys '00	♟♟♟	7
● Dolcetto di Dogliani Cursalet '01	♟♟	4
● Langhe Rosso Yeta '00	♟♟	5

FRASSINELLO MONFERRATO (AL) GATTINARA (VC)

CASTELLO DI LIGNANO
VIA CASTELLO DI LIGNANO
15035 FRASSINELLO MONFERRATO (AL)
TEL. 0142925326
E-MAIL: vinidoc@castellodilignano.it

ANTONIOLO
C.SO VALSESIA, 277
13045 GATTINARA (VC)
TEL. 0163833612
E-MAIL: antoniolovini@gattinara.alpcom.it

We tasted a very impressive series of wines at Castello di Lignano. After vinification, the Barbera d'Asti Superiore Vigna Stramba is left to age in medium toast barriques for several months. The result is a fabulous ruby wine verging on purple that unleashes aromas of red berry fruit, plum and raspberry. The well-balanced palate displays nice symmetry of alcohol-derived softness, light tannins and good acidity. The 100 per cent freisa Blasonato is a fine Monferrato Rosso and we gave it Two Glasses. Its deep ruby red colour heralds a nose of pepper and ripe fruit, then the velvety palate balances its various components very well. The Barbera del Monferrato Valisenda shows notes of super-ripeness and jam, slightly veiled by the aromas from its cask ageing. The Grignolino Vigna Tufara came very close to Two Glasses for its clear ruby flecked with orange and a nose of roses, tomato leaf and white pepper. The palate is reasonably harmonious and faintly tannic. We sampled both the 2001 and the 2002 versions of the Monferrato Bianco Grisello, a blend of sauvignon and cortese, and found them to be very different. The 2001 suggests acacia blossom and citrus fruit, whereas the 2002 hints at hazelnut and wisteria. Frassinella, the Castello di Lignano still Freisa, also just missed a Two Glass score. If this wine is anything to go by, we can look forward to great things from this indigenous Piedmont variety.

Alberto Antoniolo is one of the new generation of Piedmont producers who have their own style. A skilled technician, he has a sensitive touch that brings out nebbiolo's traditional characteristics. Factor in his modesty and foresight, rare qualities in today's world, and you have a winemaker capable of producing first-class wines. One such is Osso S. Grato, which has a nose of liquorice and rhubarb, wild roses and violets, with the rusty sensation that tells you it is a Gattinara. It's a thrilling wine, whose austere palate reveals precision, length and vibrant texture. San Francesco, the oldest vineyard on the estate, produces subtle but extremely stylish wines with a delicate nose of redcurrant and ginger, a palate that lingers over sensations of ginger and rhubarb, and a long, mellow mineral note. In vintages like 1999, the basic Gattinara, obtained from a second selection of these two vineyards, is almost on a par with its stablemates. An eminently respectable wine with a ripe fruit nose, it has a dense blackberry palate that hints at rosemary and gunflint. But the surprise of the year is Castelle. It started out as a simple but carefully executed barrique experiment, but the result is a work of art. Shrewdly judged use of 20 per cent new wood imbues it with unusual delicacy. The wealth of aromas and flavours range from golden leaf tobacco to vanilla and cinnamon while remaining true to type. The body is compact, with streamlined and approachable, yet very lively, tannins. This sensational wine captured another Three Glass award for Rosanna Antoniolo's trophy case.

● Monferrato Rosso Blasonato '00	🍷🍷	6
● Barbera d'Asti Sup. Vigna Stramba '01	🍷🍷	5
● Monferrato Rosso Lhennius '01	🍷🍷	5
● Barbera del M.to Sup. Valisenda '01	🍷	5
○ Monferrato Bianco Grisello '01	🍷	4
● Monferrato Freisa La Frassinella '01	🍷	4
● Grignolino del M.to Casalese Vigna Tufara '02	🍷	4
○ Monferrato Bianco Grisello '02	🍷	4

● Gattinara Vigneto Castelle '99	🍷🍷🍷	6
● Gattinara Vigneto Osso S. Grato '99	🍷🍷	7
● Gattinara '99	🍷🍷	7
● Gattinara Vigneto S. Francesco '99	🍷🍷	6
● Coste della Sesia Nebbiolo Juvenia '02	🍷	3
○ Erbaluce di Caluso '02	🍷	4
● Gattinara Vigneto Osso S. Grato '98	🍷🍷	7
● Gattinara '98	🍷🍷	5
● Gattinara Vigneto Castelle '98	🍷🍷	6
● Gattinara Vigneto S. Francesco '98	🍷🍷	6

GATTINARA (VC)

ANZIVINO
C.SO VALSESIA, 162
13045 GATTINARA (VC)
TEL. 0163827172
E-MAIL: anzivino@anzivino.net

There is a regeneration under way at Gattinara, one of Italy's most aristocratic areas, and Anzivino is providing new blood and new challenges. This recently established estate is making a creative contribution, releasing a range of wines that are remarkably consistent in style. Credit for these products goes to the talented technician, Beppe Zatti, an expert with croatina and, above all, vespolina. The Gattinara is made scrupulously in the traditional manner, maturing in barriques. Limpid in the glass, it has confident, almost pungent aromas. The palate is acidulous and opens out to reveal layers of bitter cocoa powder, ripe white cherry and traces of spice. There is decent length and the back palate signs off with a very unusual chalky note. The Bramaterra is well-rounded and tidy, its alcohol foregrounding redcurrant and ripe blackberry followed by a hint of violet and aniseed. A predominantly croatina base gives the Bramaterra a less austere, more powerful, expressive tannic texture than the Gattinara. So much so that we though this was one of the best in its category. Faticato is the result of an interesting experiment based on part-dried nebbiolo grapes. Released very young age as a 2001, it has a rather predictable structure and limited length on its palate, but offers aromas of primary fruit and a wonderful fresh acidity that provides the perfect foil for the wine's richness and the glycerine density. The whole is lifted by a faint hint of medicinal herbs.

GATTINARA (VC)

NERVI
C.SO VERCELLI, 117
13045 GATTINARA (VC)
TEL. 0163833228
E-MAIL: avnervi@libero.it

Nervi is a historic name in Gattinara viticulture. Run by Giorgio Aliata, it is on a permanent mission to improve quality. The heart of the estate is its vineyards and it is here that this quest is most keenly felt. In the cellars, too, even the best traditions are deemed not good enough, and advice is sought from the most experienced winemakers around. All this plus careful experimentation with today's new methods, such as small wood, indicates that Nervi has a rosy future. The Gattinara Molsino, sourced from the beautiful, amphitheatre-shaped vineyard of the same name, strongly embodies the character of the vintage. The 1999 is similar to the 1997, in that it has neither the class of the 1996 nor the elegance of the 1998. It is deep in hue and its delightful, generous aromas of ripe cherry, vanilla and sweet mint hint at maturing in new barriques, although only five per cent of the total weight of fruit saw oak. Typical Gattinara characteristics – strong tannins, powerful minerality and floral notes of roses and wild flowers – echo across the palate to the after-aroma. The structure is slightly unbalanced, however, and a little below the standards we have come to expect from this wine. The basic Gattinara has a fresher, more assured nose that shows the typical sweetness of the vintage. It shows red berry fruit and sweet cocoa powder, then a round, flavoursome palate. The Spanna is a wine of extraordinary quality. Fruit, flowers, minerals and tannins mingle with wonderful complexity, bound together by tight, clean acidity.

● Bramaterra '00	♛♛	5
● Coste della Sesia Faticato '01	♛♛	7
● Gattinara '99	♛♛	6
● Tarlo Rosso '00	♛	4
● Gattinara '98	♕♕	5
● Bramaterra '99	♕♕	5
● Tarlo Rosso '99	♕	4

● Gattinara Vigneto Molsino '99	♛♛	6
● Coste della Sesia Spanna '01	♛	4
● Gattinara '99	♛	5
● Gattinara '97	♕♕	5
● Gattinara Vigneto Molsino '97	♕♕	6
● Gattinara Vigneto Molsino '98	♕♕	6
● Gattinara '98	♕	5

GATTINARA (VC)

GAVI (AL)

GIANCARLO TRAVAGLINI
VIA DELLE VIGNE, 36
13045 GATTINARA (VC)
TEL. 0163833588
E-MAIL: info@travaglinigattinara.it

NICOLA BERGAGLIO
FRAZ. ROVERETO
LOC. PEDAGGERI, 59
15066 GAVI (AL)
TEL. 0143682195

Giancarlo Travaglini has very clear ideas about Gattinara and quality. His decision to focus on a few high-profile labels and large volumes, rather than vinifying single crus in limited numbers, and presumably also at premium prices, has been the subject of much debate. It is, however, an extraordinarily farsighted strategy that benefits the entire DOCG zone enormously every year, particularly in terms of international visibility. The 1998 Riserva is a dazzling garnet colour with an edge that already hints at the classic orange tone. Its minty nose signals the use of special 300-litre casks in addition to large barrels, and the five-year stock rotation adopted in the barrique cellar. Light notes of blackberry and redcurrant heralding a subtle vein of spice come into their own on the palate, where the wine offers clearer, longer tones of cinnamon, white pepper and wood resin. These meld with a vein of acidity and assertive tannins that make their presence felt rather ruggedly. The finish hints at citrus fruit, lifted by delicate floral after-aromas. The Tre Vigne 1999 reveals a more concentrated nose of dark chocolate, coffee and vanilla, with a touch of cedar layered over a generous, if somewhat flat, base of white cherry. The palate is big and expansive, but its classic oak-derived aromas and mineral tones are held back by peppermint and bitter liquorice that tend to overwhelm the sweetness of the fruit.

Gianluigi Bergaglio's well-known estate is one of the cornerstones of Gavi winemaking. Gianluigi, ably assisted by his son Diego, has 15 hectares under vine, four of which went into production in 2003. Total production for 2002 amounted to around 30,000 bottles, which is slightly fewer than usual because of poor weather conditions during the growing year. Nevertheless, Gianluigi managed to muster some interesting wines for us to taste. His Gavi Minaia, the leading vineyard in the DOCG zone, is straw yellow with golden highlights and a fresh nose of citrus and banana, peach and pineapple fruit. It comes into its own on the palate, where it displays an elegance and tidiness that lend both balance and refinement. The finish is slightly bitterish and acidulous. The standard-label Gavi, however, outclassed its thoroughbred stablemate to romp home with Two Glasses. It possesses more complex aromas that range from apple to pear to varietal hints of spring flowers. We particularly liked the palate for its tidiness and intense almondy finish. Finally, this particular wine is exceptionally good value for money, which is an important consideration these days, when all's said and done.

● Gattinara Ris. '98	♀♀	6
● Gattinara Tre Vigne '99	♀♀	6
● Gattinara Ris. '96	♀♀	6
● Gattinara Tre Vigne '97	♀♀	6
● Gattinara Ris. '97	♀♀	6
● Gattinara Tre Vigne '98	♀♀	6
● Gattinara '99	♀♀	5

○ Gavi del Comune di Gavi '02	♀♀	3*
○ Gavi del Comune di Gavi Minaia '02	♀	4
○ Gavi del Comune di Gavi Minaia '01	♀♀	4

GAVI (AL)

GIAN PIERO BROGLIA
TENUTA LA MEIRANA
LOC. LOMELLINA, 14
15066 GAVI (AL)
TEL. 0143642998 - 0143643086
E-MAIL: broglia.azienda@tin.it

Despite the indifferent weather that beset the vintage, Gian Piero Broglia managed to harvest some superb fruit from his vineyards and using his customary magical touch, he transformed it into attractive wines. The headquarters of his estate is the centuries-old "cascina", or farmhouse, called La Meirana, where, we are told, wine has been produced and sold since AD 972. The Gavi La Meirana 2002 is straw yellow with green highlights, introducing a lovely intense bouquet of apples and pears, with traces of very subtle spice. The palate embodies the typical characteristics of the variety, its balanced acidity well buttressed by solid structure. The estate's flagship selection, Gavi Bruno Broglia, is obtained from a blend of steel-matured Gavi and a carefully gauged proportion of the same wine aged in small casks. Its deep straw yellow colour with dazzling, light, golden highlights reveals its personality at once. The nose of very ripe apples and pears ushers in a palate of good length and reasonable structure. Just to show that his cellar can also do reds, Gian Piero presented us with two Monferrato Rossos, both obtained from native varieties. The Bruno Broglia – the 1999 confirmed our favourable impressions from last year – has a predominantly barbera base, with small amounts of international grape types, including cabernet and merlot, giving it impressive harmony on the palate. The dolcetto-based Le Pernici offers aromas of ripe fruit and a palate that is refreshing throughout. We also enjoyed the Gavi Extra Brut for its fine perlage, yeasty aromas and nice weighty palate.

GAVI (AL)

CASTELLARI BERGAGLIO
FRAZ. ROVERETO, 136
15066 GAVI (AL)
TEL. 0143644000
E-MAIL: gavi@castellaribergaglio.it

Castellari Bergaglio has always been a single-variety estate concentrating on cortese. This decision to specialize so narrowly was a courageous one, as it increases the level of risk. It has not, however, prevented Marco Bergaglio and his family from producing a fine range of Gavis, even in a potentially poor growing year. Their brilliant, rich, straw Fornace proffers austere, refined notes of apples and pears, flowers and citrus fruit. It is tangy and round on the palate, with good structure and length. All told, it's a truly splendid effort for a 2002. The jewel in the estate's crown is Pilìn, which is again released as a Gavi DOCG in the 2000 edition. Marco is meticulous about the production techniques he uses for his wines. These include selection of the oldest vines, part-drying the grapes after harvest, barrique fermentation and ageing in the same casks. The result is a soft, creamy-textured wine that is warm and harmonious, with a reasonably long finish rendered slightly bitterish by oak-derived tannins. The Rolona 2002 also won Two Glasses for its concentrated, dazzling straw yellow and fresh nose of green apples and citron. The palate follows through well, showing fresh and zesty with very enjoyable balance. The Gavi Rovereto, sourced from an 80-year-old vineyard, was perhaps presented to the tasting panel a little too soon. Its nose of apple, pineapple and white peach is still closed, and the palate is cool and moderately long.

○ Gavi del Comune di Gavi Bruno Broglia '01	⟡⟡	5
○ Gavi del Comune di Gavi La Meirana '02	⟡⟡	4
● Monferrato Rosso Le Pernici '02	⟡	3
○ Gavi Spumante Extra Brut	⟡	4
● Monferrato Rosso Bruno Broglia '98	♉♉	5
● Monferrato Rosso Bruno Broglia '99	♉♉	5
○ Gavi del Comune di Gavi Bruno Broglia '00	♉♉	5

○ Gavi del Comune di Tassarolo Fornaci '02	⟡⟡	4
○ Gavi del Comune di Gavi Pilìn '00	⟡⟡	5
○ Gavi del Comune di Gavi Rolona '02	⟡⟡	4
○ Gavi del Comune di Gavi Rovereto '02	⟡	5
○ Pilìn '99	♉♉	5
○ Gavi del Comune di Gavi Rolona '01	♉♉	4
○ Gavi Rovereto Vignavecchia '01	♉♉	4

GAVI (AL)

LA GIUSTINIANA
FRAZ. ROVERETO, 5
15066 GAVI (AL)
TEL. 0143682132
E-MAIL: info@lagiustiniana.it

La Giustiniana is one of those historic Gavi wineries housed in noble Genoese 17th-century villas that first vinified cortese for the Ligurian market. The Lombardinis' vast property comprises this estate and Contero di Strevi, both of which are in the capable and reliable hands of Enrico Tomalino. The "IL", which suggests "our Gavi", is a new project that adopts Burgundy-style fermentation with prolonged contact with the fine lees. This produces an intense gold-flecked straw Gavi whose aromas offer spring flowers, acacia blossom, grass and vanilla. The palate is soft, mellow, structured and pleasantly refreshing. The bright, rich straw yellow Gavi Montessora reveals sweet tones of honey, elderflower, minerals and citrus fruit, then an elegantly cool, concentrated palate. The Just Bianco is redolent of peach, apricot, flowers, vanilla and almonds that precede a complex, harmonious palate that lingers attractively. The Gavi Lugarara has a varietal nose of spring flowers and hay, and a refreshing, zesty palate with a tempting mouthfeel. The Monferrato Rosso Just is bright ruby in appearance and boasts notes of red berry fruit, raspberry and spice. The palate is mildly tannic and fresh, with a delicate profile. Turning to the Contero wines, the Moscato d'Asti di Strevi is soft and fresh with good prickle and the sweetness never cloys. The Moscato Passito 2001 offers notes of honey with nuances of peach, dried apricot and vanilla. The palate is velvety and balanced, suggesting chamomile and nuts. The Brachetto d'Acqui Spumante is well typed.

GAVI (AL)

MORGASSI SUPERIORE
CASE SPARSE SERMORIA, 7
15066 GAVI (AL)
TEL. 0143642007
E-MAIL: info@morgassisuperiore.it

The Piacitelli family estate, founded in 1990, grows both the native cortese and timorasso varieties as well as international grapes, in a true spirit of experimentation. The Piacitellis, who release a very varied range of labels and wine types, have invested heavily in their cellars. Their Sarastro is a cabernet sauvignon and barbera blend with a very deep, almost opaque, but quite dazzling red colour. It has concentrated vegetal, toasty and red berry aromas, before the palate shows off the wine's harmony in its freshness, softness and exceptional structure. The rich straw yellow Timorasso opens on mineral and fruity notes of apricot and tropical fruit, then ends on a vaguely spicy tone. The long length on the palate is accompanied by a assured intensity of flavour. The 100 per cent syrah Tamino is very deep ruby red in appearance and offers a warm, generous nose of super-ripe fruit, spice, coffee and caramel sugar. The palate reveals tannins that are already very polished. The Gavi Etichetta Oro is a classic straw yellow, then offers aromas of apples, pears and flowers, decent length on the palate and a typically bitterish aftertaste. We also liked the basic Gavi and a Glass goes to the viognier-based Cherubino, a rich straw yellow wine with notes of tangerine and pineapple layered over gently sweet nuances of oak. The palate is fairly rich and shows medium intensity. The Leporello, a blend of syrah, cabernet sauvignon and barbera, scored well enough to earn One comfortable Glass.

●	Monferrato Rosso Just '00	♥♥	5
○	Gavi del Comune di Gavi IL '01	♥♥	5
○	Just Bianco '01	♥♥	5
○	Moscato Passito di Strevi '01	♥♥	5
○	Gavi del Comune di Gavi Montessora '02	♥♥	4*
○	Moscato d'Asti Contero '02	♥♥	4
●	Brachetto d'Acqui Spumante Contero '02	♥	4
○	Gavi del Comune di Gavi Lugarara '02	♥	4
○	Just Bianco '00	♥♥	5
●	Monferrato Rosso Just '99	♥♥	5

●	Tamino '00	♥♥	8
●	Sarastro '00	♥♥	5
○	Timorasso '01	♥♥	5
○	Cherubino '02	♥	6
○	Gavi del Comune di Gavi '02	♥	4
○	Gavi del Comune di Gavi Etichetta Oro '02	♥	5
●	Leporello '02	♥	4

GAVI (AL)

PRODUTTORI DEL GAVI
VIA CAVALIERI DI VITTORIO VENETO, 45
15066 GAVI (AL)
TEL. 0143642786
E-MAIL: cantina.prodgavi@libero.it

There were three more excellent wines from the Produttori del Gavi cellars, the last under the technical direction of Roberto Sarotto, who was the co-operative's manager and oenologist for three consecutive harvests until June 2003. Credit must also go to the inspired collaboration of the 30 or so members who subscribe to the vineyard selection policy, in the fashion of the great Alto Adige co-operative wineries. As we write, it is not clear who will replace Sarotto, but we sincerely hope that the new management will not change the production policies that have given so much to the estate, to consumers and to the Gavi DOCG zone. The 2002 vintage, severely tested by the extremely wet summer, has produced approximately 150,000 units of three excellent Gavi DOCGs. The Gavi Cascine dell'Aureliana, aged partly in barriques, is rich straw yellow and has a nose of peaches, apricots, chamomile, butter, vanilla and light toastiness. The palate is cool, soft and moderately long, with a slightly bitterish finish. The Gavi Primuva is a bright, intense straw in appearance and offers generous aromas of acacia blossom, chamomile, pear, apple and confectioner's cream. The palate is full, very fresh, soft and unbelievably long. The Gavi La Maddalena, the estate's flagship selection, is an almost voluptuous wine whose best feature is its harmony. The lovely, bright straw yellow heralds notes of ripe fruit, peach and yellow flowers. The freshness of the palate is balanced by the wonderfully mellow, rounded structure. The long finish is simply delicious.

GAVI (AL)

VILLA SPARINA
FRAZ. MONTEROTONDO, 56
15066 GAVI (AL)
TEL. 0143633835
E-MAIL: villasparina@villasparina.it

The earthquake that hit this border area of Piedmont in spring left its mark on Villa Sparina. It was forced to delay the inauguration, originally planned for September, of the new Relais hotel facility that will flank its winemaking business. Fortunately for the devotees of the estate's range of labels, the Moccagatta family's enthusiasm and desire to make high quality products is undiminished. This year's results are quite excellent, with the lovely ruby Monferrato Rosso Rivalta rising above the rest of the range. It is particularly attractive for the vanilla aromas that derive from a stay in barrique, and that open out to meld with fruitier aromas of morello cherry and red berry fruit. The palate has a nice silky sensation and hint at spice and chocolate. Monte Rotondo, a Gavi DOCG, is the best of the whites. Also oak-aged, it offers warm notes of spring flowers and apricot. The palate still has a slight vein of acidity that is accompanied by good aromatic length and a pleasant aftertaste of sweet almonds. We were also very impressed by the Müller Thurgau. It's a gorgeous straw yellow that introduces floral aromas of acacia blossom and wild roses. The Monferrato Rosso Sampò is very dark in appearance and has a rich, youthfully alcoholic nose of lovely wild berry aromas. The palate's tannic weave is suitably restrained. The Dolcetto Maioli has a fresh grassy, floral bouquet. The Gavi di Gavi and the Brut Metodo Classico Villa Sparina are good, but not quite up to the same standard.

○ Gavi Cascine dell'Aureliana '02	ŸŸ	4*
○ Gavi di Gavi La Maddalena '02	ŸŸ	4*
○ Gavi Primuva '02	ŸŸ	3*
○ Gavi Cascine dell'Aureliana '01	♀♀	4

● Monferrato Rosso Rivalta '01	ŸŸ	6
○ Gavi del Comune di Gavi Monte Rotondo '02	ŸŸ	6
● Monferrato Rosso Sampò '00	ŸŸ	4
● Dolcetto d'Acqui Bric Maioli '02	ŸŸ	3*
○ Monferrato Bianco Müller Thurgau '02	ŸŸ	4
○ Gavi del Comune di Gavi '02	Ÿ	4
○ Villa Sparina Brut M. Cl.	Ÿ	5
● Barbera del M.to Rivalta '97	♀♀♀	6
○ Gavi del Comune di Gavi Monte Rotondo '99	♀♀♀	5
● Monferrato Rosso Rivalta '99	♀♀♀	6
● Monferrato Rosso Rivalta '00	♀♀♀	6
○ Gavi del Comune di Gavi Monte Rotondo '01	♀♀	5

GHEMME (NO)

GHEMME (NO)

ANTICHI VIGNETI DI CANTALUPO
VIA MICHELANGELO BUONARROTI, 5
28074 GHEMME (NO)
TEL. 0163840041
E-MAIL: cantalupovigneti@tiscalinet.it

ROVELLOTTI
VIA PRIVATA TAMIOTTI, 3
28074 GHEMME (NO)
TEL. 0163840478
E-MAIL: info@rovellotti.it

Alberto Arlunno, owner of Cantalupo, has a passion for the history of language as well as sound technical expertise that makes him an influential figure in Ghemme winemaking. He is an expert on Ghemme nebbiolo, and now identifies two separate local subvarieties, cò ross and cò bianc, which are important benchmarks for the identity of the DOCG zone. It is no surprise, then, that Alberto's Ghemmes are all 100 per cent nebbiolo. Collis Breclemae 1998 is an austere Ghemme that possesses gamey tones and notes of wild rose. The only thing keeping it out of the final Three Glass tastings is its slightly lightweight structure and well-defined, but not very compelling, fruitiness. The Signore di Bayard 1999, obtained from a selection of grapes aged for 18 months in 50 per cent new barriques, caters for those consumers who like an international style in their wine. We found it very much lacking in balance. The estate's third selection, Collis Carellae, was not produced in 1998. The basic Ghemme is harmonious and coherent, offering a wide range of red berry fruit aromas. Its unassertive tannins make it very easy to drink. The Mimo is an unusual rosé made from 100 per cent nebbiolo. Entry on the palate is sweet and delicate, and ends on a lingering, very refreshing note of geranium. The Villa Horta, from vespolina, and the Primigenia, a red blend, are easy drinking and nicely balanced. The nebbiolo-based Agamium and the white Carolus blend have more flavour and personality.

In the Ricetto di Ghemme, a unique fortified building constructed to shelter local people in mediaeval times, only one window is decorated with a grapevine, the one that belongs to the Rovellotti family. When the Rovellottis recruited the talents of technician Mario Ronco in 1997, the ancient bond that links this family to Ghemme and its viticulture was re-established. Today, the wines made by the skilled hands of Paolo and Antonello Rovellotti bring recognition to an emerging DOCG zone. Release of the Riserva 1999 has been postponed until next year. In the meantime, the basic Ghemme 1999 offers notes of cherry mingled with sweet chocolate tones of oak and intense, enjoyable alcohol. Left to breathe for a while in the glass, the wine reveals itself to be anything but simple, offering delicate floral hints of roses and cyclamen. These sensations echo across the palate, where they combine with an attractive tannic weave, demonstrating the validity of Antonello Rovellotti's traditional vinification procedure, in which a substantial amount of vespolina is added to the nebbiolo. There was another fine performance from the Vespolina 2002, a lovely heady, fragrant wine that will reward anyone who cares to cellar it for a short time with extra complexity and unexpected character. The Valdenrico, a dried-grape erbaluce "passito", is very good indeed. Its aromatic spectrum embraces golden delicious apple, honey and walnutskin and the aristocratic structure is lifted by a faint note of botrytis.

● Ghemme Collis Breclemae '98	� YY	6
● Ghemme '99	YY	5
● Colline Novaresi Agamium '01	Y	4
○ Carolus '02	Y	3
☉ Colline Novaresi Il Mimo '02	Y	3
● Colline Novaresi Primigenia '02	Y	3
● Colline Novaresi Villa Horta '02	Y	3
● Ghemme Signore di Bayard '99	Y	6
● Ghemme Collis Carellae '96	YY	6
● Ghemme Collis Carellae '97	YY	6
● Ghemme Collis Breclemae '97	YY	6
● Ghemme Signore di Bayard '98	YY	6

○ Valdenrico Passito '00	YY	6
● Ghemme '99	YY	5
○ Colline Novaresi Bianco '02	Y	3
● Colline Novaresi Rosso '02	Y	3
● Colline Novaresi Vespolina '02	Y	3
● Ghemme Ris. '97	YY	6
● Ghemme Ris. '98	YY	6
● Ghemme '98	YY	5
○ Valdenrico Passito '99	YY	6

INCISA SCAPACCINO (AT)

ERMANNO E ALESSANDRA BREMA
VIA POZZOMAGNA, 9
14045 INCISA SCAPACCINO (AT)
TEL. 014174019
E-MAIL: vinibrema@inwind.it

INCISA SCAPACCINO (AT)

TENUTA OLIM BAUDA
S.DA PRATA, 22
14045 INCISA SCAPACCINO (AT)
TEL. 014174266
E-MAIL: info@tenutaolimbauda.it

Ermanno Brema and his wife, Alessandra, are at the helm of this estate, which has been making wine since 1887. They farm 13 hectares planted to vine for an annual production of 100,000 bottles. The slopes of Incisa Scapaccino, one of the municipalities in the new subzone of Nizza, are given over mainly to barbera, the traditional Asti variety that is a growing source of satisfaction for producers and consumers alike. Ermanno Brema's most ambitious project for his indigenous grape variety is Bricco della Volpettona. Ruby shading into garnet, it flaunts a very complex nose with clear fruit aromas of black berries, notably plum, and oak-derived undertones of toastiness and cakes. The richness of the texture is obvious on the palate, where it is vibrant and bright through to the dry, lingering finish that echoes the nose. The estate's basic Barbera, Cascina Croce, is limpid in appearance and offers moderately elegant, rather mature aromas. The palate unveils the powerful acidity of the variety in a framework of pleasing tidiness. The Dolcetto Vigna Impagnato has a colour of medium intensity and a nose that is somewhat dominated by oak. The palate is dry and concentrated. Hints of geranium and earth filter through on the nose of the Grignolino Brich Le Roche, then the palate shows medium body. The Barbera Bricconizza has rather an evolved nose, and the Brachetto Carlotta is fresh-tasting.

Tenuta Olim Bauda has 90 hectares scattered across several municipalities. Some 25 hectares are planted to vine and yield an annual production of around 50,000 bottles. Gianni, Dino and Diana Bertolino run their family business with skill and enthusiasm that have earned them good results in just a few short years. The estate has a modern, fully equipped vinification cellar, ageing areas, most of which are in the basement in the oldest wing of the building that houses Olim Bauda, a tasting room and guest accommodation. This year, the Barbera d'Asti Superiore Nizza is missing from the ranks, as the Bertolinos are not yet ready to release their 2001 vintage onto the market. However, the excellent quality of the Barbera d'Asti Superiore 2000 would be enough on its own to justify their profile in the Guide. A rich garnet ruby, it shows a generous bouquet of extraordinary complexity that revels in notes of raspberry, mint and almond, nuanced with faint hints of tar. The palate is slightly dry and shows consistent weight that climaxes in an intense fruit, mint and liquorice finish. The straw yellow Chardonnay is flecked with gold, this 2002 version presenting a fairly coherent nose of apple and spring flowers. The palate is attractively full, simple and fresh with a finish of remarkable length. We liked the current Barbera d'Asti with its intriguing aromas of ripe fruit and the lively acid vein on the tidy palate. Last but not least, the Moscato d'Asti is generous and juicy.

● Barbera d'Asti Sup. Bricco della Volpettona '01	♥♥	6
● Barbera d'Asti Sup. Bricconizza '01	♥	5
● Barbera d'Asti Sup. Cascina Croce '01	♥	3
● Dolcetto d'Asti Vigna Impagnato '02	♥	4
● Grignolino d'Asti Brich Le Roche '02	♥	3
● Piemonte Brachetto Carlotta '02	♥	4
● Barbera d'Asti Sup. Bricco della Volpettona '00	♥♥	6
● Barbera d'Asti Sup. Bricconizza '00	♥♥	5

● Barbera d'Asti Sup. '00	♥♥	5
● Barbera d'Asti '02	♥♥	4*
○ Moscato d'Asti Centive '02	♥♥	4*
○ Piemonte Chardonnay '02	♥	4
● Barbera d'Asti Sup. '98	♥♥	5
● Barbera d'Asti Sup. Nizza '00	♥♥	6
● Barbera d'Asti Sup. '99	♥♥	5

IVREA (TO)

LA MORRA (CN)

FERRANDO
VIA TORINO, 599/A
10015 IVREA (TO)
TEL. 0125641176 - 0125633550
E-MAIL: info@ferrandovini.it

★ ★ ELIO ALTARE - CASCINA NUOVA
FRAZ. ANNUNZIATA, 51
12064 LA MORRA (CN)
TEL. 017350835

The wines presented by Ferrando to the panel this year included a Caluso Passito our tasters very much enjoyed. Obtained from grapes dried in cases for six months, then fermented and matured in barrique, it is brilliant gold with clear notes of chamomile, orange and acacia honey. The palate is deep and concentrated, and the sweetness is very marked. The Erbaluce Etichetta Nera, part vinified in small casks, is good. Its barrique-derived sumptuousness does not detract from its elegance. The stainless steel-aged Erbaluce Etichetta Verde has lovely aromas and a palate with medium structure. Solativo is a "vino da meditazione" sipping wine that rewards investigation. Its sugars come not from partial drying on mats, but from a late harvest in mid December. Contrary to expectations, it reveals barely discernible notes of mould, expressing the erbaluce variety extremely well in the velvet smoothness of the mouthfeel and a stylish, moderately sweet palate. The Canavese Rosso Montodo, sourced from two very old vineyards with a mix of local varieties, missed the Two Glass mark by a whisker. The Caremas weren't quite up to par this year. The basic version has a nose of super-ripe red berry fruit, crushed roses and coffee, then a subtle palate that offsets austerity against softness. The selection offers aromas of very ripe black plum, ground pepper and a fascinating hint of rhubarb. Its palate is more structured and fruity than the standard-label wine but less subtly floral.

Elio Altare, celebrating his 37th harvest and ably assisted by his son in the cellar, has the air of a man who is determined to get a lot more out of life. We can go some way to satisfying him after tasting his stunning Barolo Vigneto Arborina 1999, a paragon of character, harmony and sheer goodness. The bouquet alternates spicy notes with fleshy red berry tones and leads into a sumptuous, dynamic palate. It's already very substantial and will mellow out, becoming more refined over time. Three truly magnificent Glasses. The Barolo 1999 displays its customary texture and maturity in its wonderful structure, which enhances the typical Annunziata aromas. As for the Langhe DOCs, we gave equal marks to the Larigi, whose barbera grapes display soft complexity and delightful breadth, to the Arborina, lifted by first-class nebbiolo fruit and solidly tannic on the palate, and to the astonishing La Villa, which melds the characteristics of barbera and nebbiolo into a velvety cornucopia of sensations. This year, the Dolcetto 2002 was released under the Langhe label. It has nose-palate consistency and flavour, but is penalized by the poor vintage. The same goes for the Barbera d'Alba 2002, with its coherent, compact body. We were happy to retaste L'Insieme 2000, a joint project with other winemakers that is producing increasingly interesting results. Made from a blend of local and other varieties, it is emblematic of the passion, genuine flavours and eloquent class of an affable, combative grower-producer who has put La Morra at the forefront of today's wine scene.

●	Carema Etichetta Nera '98	🍷🍷	6
○	Caluso Passito Vigneto Cariola '98	🍷🍷	7
○	Erbaluce di Caluso Cariola Etichetta Nera '01	🍷🍷	5
○	Erbaluce di Caluso Cariola Etichetta Verde '02	🍷	4
○	Solativo '01	🍷	6
●	Carema Etichetta Bianca '99	🍷	5
●	Canavese Rosso Montodo '01	🍷	3
●	Carema Etichetta Nera '97	🍷🍷	6
●	Carema Etichetta Nera '96	🍷🍷	6
●	Carema Etichetta Nera '95	🍷🍷	6

●	Barolo Vigneto Arborina '99	🍷🍷🍷	8
●	L'Insieme '00	🍷🍷	8
●	Langhe Arborina '01	🍷🍷	8
●	Langhe La Villa '01	🍷🍷	8
●	Langhe Larigi '01	🍷🍷	8
●	Barolo '99	🍷🍷	8
●	Barbera d'Alba '02	🍷	4
●	Langhe Dolcetto '02	🍷	4
●	Langhe Larigi '95	🍷🍷🍷	8
●	Langhe Arborina '96	🍷🍷🍷	8
●	Langhe Arborina '97	🍷🍷🍷	8
●	Langhe Larigi '97	🍷🍷🍷	8
●	Langhe La Villa '99	🍷🍷🍷	8
●	Langhe Larigi '99	🍷🍷🍷	8
●	Barolo Vigneto Arborina '98	🍷🍷🍷	8

LA MORRA (CN)

BATASIOLO
FRAZ. ANNUNZIATA, 87
12064 LA MORRA (CN)
TEL. 017350130 - 017350131
E-MAIL: info@batasiolo.com

Batasiolo is focusing its energies on the cellar's evolving production strategy. It has also renovated the vineyards, to maintain the current level of quality. We were most impressed by the Barolos, despite the absence of Boscareto, one of the flagship wines, which has been left to age for an extra year before release. The Barolo Corda della Briccolina 1999, from plots in Serralunga, has a solid garnet colour and refined, intriguing aromas of black cherry and blackberry. Warm and velvety on the palate, it foregrounds ripe tannins and powers through to a clean, very lengthy finish. The less austere Cerequio 1999 embodies the elegant characteristics of the vineyard it comes from, its nose a lovely mix of spice and mint and its palate balanced and fruity. The basic Barolo also performs very well. The nose is anything but ordinary, flaunting notes of ripe red berry fruit, tobacco and liquorice. The palate is very classy and struts appealingly smooth tannins. The Barolo Bofani 1999 isn't quite up to the same standard, showing a tad one-dimensional and muddled in the nose. The Barbera d'Alba Sovrana 2001 is dense ruby with purple highlights. Its concentrated nose offers evolved notes of fruit, including blackberry and cherry jam, then impressive structure on the palate. The Dolcetto Arsigà 2002 is pleasant, alcohol-rich and very fruity. Of the whites, we preferred the Sunsì, which is more approachable and fragrant than the Chardonnay Serbato. The Moscato d'Asti Bosc d'la Rei has well-gauged sweetness that never cloys, and the citrussy Muscatel Tardì is balanced.

LA MORRA (CN)

ENZO BOGLIETTI
VIA ROMA, 37
12064 LA MORRA (CN)
TEL. 017350330
E-MAIL: enzoboglietti@virgilio.it

The Boglietti brothers' wines have done extremely well this year, winning a series of Glasses that attest the overall quality. We start at the top with the Barolo Case Nere, which won its first Three Glasses. The Bogliettis obtained 3,000 bottles from a beautiful but little known vineyard below La Serra and between Fossati and Cerequio in the municipality of La Morra. The fruit is harvested when almost super-ripe and the wine's alcohol content is about 15 degrees. We were bowled over by the palate, which is bursting with power and personality, yet very soft and full of delicious raspberry jam, herb, dried fig, cinchona and violet aromas. The Brunate 1999 is less approachable but just as complex and mouthfilling, with spicy tones of tobacco and pepper layered over hints of mint and dried rose. The palate is classic, austere, pervasive and crisply defined. The rich fruity Fossati 1999 still suggests charred oak. The Barbera Roscaleto 2001, obtained from a plot in the small village of Boiolo, is another winner. It is soft and elegant with a bouquet of violet, rose, raspberry and liquorice. We retasted the Vigna dei Romani 2000 (reviewed in error last year) and found it more powerful and extreme than the previous version. At last, it has managed to absorb its strong, spicy oak. The Langhe Buio 2001, from nebbiolo with a little barbera, impressed. The Bogliettis have decided not to produce vineyard selections from the 2002 vintage. At the moment, their Dolcetto and Barbera are above average, but the Nebbiolo leaves something to be desired.

● Barolo Corda della Briccolina '99	�♣♣	8
● Barbera d'Alba Sovrana '01	♣♣	5
● Dolcetto d'Alba Arsigà '02	♣♣	5
● Barolo '99	♣♣	6
● Barolo Cerequio '99	♣♣	8
● Barolo Bofani '99	♣	8
○ Piemonte Muscatel Tardì '01	♣	7
○ Langhe Bianco Sunsì '02	♣	5
○ Langhe Chardonnay Serbato '02	♣	4
○ Moscato d'Asti Bosc d'la Rei '02	♣	4
● Barolo Corda della Briccolina '88	♣♣♣	8
● Barolo Corda della Briccolina '89	♣♣♣	8
● Barolo Corda della Briccolina '90	♣♣♣	8
● Barolo Corda della Briccolina '98	♣♣	8

● Barolo Case Nere '99	♣♣♣	8
● Barbera d'Alba		
Vigna dei Romani '00	♣♣	7
● Barolo Brunate '99	♣♣	8
● Barbera d'Alba Roscaleto '01	♣♣	6
● Langhe Rosso Buio '01	♣♣	6
● Barolo Fossati '99	♣♣	8
● Barbera d'Alba '02	♣	4
● Dolcetto d'Alba '02	♣	4
● Langhe Nebbiolo '02	♣	5
● Barbera d'Alba		
Vigna dei Romani '94	♣♣♣	7
● Barolo Fossati '96	♣♣♣	8
● Barolo Brunate '97	♣♣♣	8

LA MORRA (CN)

Gianfranco Bovio

fraz. Annunziata
b.ta Ciotto, 63
12064 La Morra (CN)
tel. 017350667
e-mail: walterporasso@libero.it

Several years ago, Gianfranco Bovio expanded his cellars, adding space and equipment that permit him to manage the fruit from his 22 hectares, half planted to nebbiolo, more easily. Today, this famous estate produces up to 90,000 bottles a year in an unusual array of wines. The able Walter Porasso, who is much more than just a cellarman, is responsible overall, but the estate also has consultancy from Beppe Caviola. The three Barolos offered are all impressive and highlight the consistent quality of this estate. First on the list is the Arborina 1999. It is the only one conditioned in new barriques, yet it is already mature and flavoursome, noble and showing an almost textbook complexity. The Gattera 1999 has a fresher, more penetrating nose, chewier fruit in the mouth and a light spicy vein, ending in a lovely, summarizing finish. The Rocchettevino 1999, aged like the previous wine in medium-large barrels, is sweet and delicately dense, and embodies the best of the territory's characteristics. The estate's next new project, a "riserva" sourced from the Parussi vineyard at Castiglione Falletto, will be released in 2004. The range of reds is rounded off by the deliciously heady Dolcetto d'Alba Dabbene 2002, which offers notes of roses and cherry, and the upfront, ripe plum-led Barbera d'Alba Il Ciotto 2002. We'll end our notes with the two Langhe Chardonnays. La Villa 2002 has varietal fragrances of banana, whereas the golden Alessandro 2001, aged in bottle for a year, is dense with lovely depth and elegance.

●	Barolo Vigna Arborina '99	🍷🍷	7
●	Barolo Vigna Gattera '99	🍷🍷	7
○	Langhe Chardonnay Alessandro '01	🍷🍷	5
●	Barolo Rocchettevino '99	🍷🍷	7
●	Barbera d'Alba Il Ciotto '02	🍷	4
●	Dolcetto d'Alba Dabbene '02	🍷	4
○	Langhe Chardonnay Vigna La Villa '02	🍷	4
●	Barolo Vigna Arborina '90	YYY	8
●	Barolo Rocchettevino '97	YY	8
●	Barolo Vigna Arborina '97	YY	8
●	Barolo Rocchettevino '98	YY	8
●	Barolo Vigna Arborina '98	YY	8
●	Barolo Vigna Gattera '98	YY	8

LA MORRA (CN)

Cascina Ballarin

fraz. Annunziata, 115
12064 La Morra (CN)
tel. 017350365
e-mail: cascina@cascinaballarin.it

As you wind round Annunziata's countless hairpin bends, you will come upon this lovely "cascina", or farmhouse. The estate is creating new spaces for ageing its wines, and also offers seasonal accommodation in an annex next to the cellars. Gianni Viberti is in charge of production, which now totals around 30,000 bottles a year, and his brother Giorgio looks after things on the commercial side. Their Barolo Bussia 1999, of which only 1,400 units were bottled, earned the panel's hearty congratulations for the harmonious fullness that sets it apart from the pack. It shows elegant length on the palate and a complex bouquet redolent of liquorice and red cherry. The Barolo I Tre Ciabot 1999 is less full, and more mature, whereas the Barolo Bricco Rocca 1999 has plenty of character and delightful, generous aromas of raspberry and lavender. The palate shows vigorous, dry structure. The Bricco Rocca vineyard is also the source of the Riserva Tistot 1997, notable for its generous flavours, outstanding nose and refreshing extract on the back palate. Two full Glasses go to the Barbera D'Alba Giuli 2001, as deep in colour as it is rich in black berry fruit and mint on the nose. The rest of the range is not as complex, but all the wines are clean, fragrant and very interesting. The Langhe Bianco 2002, from 80 per cent chardonnay with some favorita and pinot nero, offers lovely notes of tropical fruit and sage that lead into a tangy, aromatic finish. The Dolcetto, Nebbiolo and Langhe Rosso have youthful, floral personalities.

●	Barolo Bussia '99	🍷🍷	8
●	Barbera d'Alba Giuli '01	🍷🍷	5
●	Barolo Bricco Rocca Tistot Ris. '97	🍷🍷	8
●	Barolo Bricco Rocca '99	🍷🍷	8
●	Langhe Rosso Ballarin '01	🍷	5
●	Dolcetto d'Alba Bussia '02	🍷	4
○	Langhe Bianco Ballarin '02	🍷	5
●	Langhe Nebbiolo '02	🍷	5
●	Barolo I Tre Ciabot '99	🍷	7
●	Barolo Bricco Rocca '97	YY	8
●	Barolo Bussia '97	YY	8
●	Barbera d'Alba Giuli '99	YY	5
●	Barbera d'Alba Giuli '00	YY	5

LA MORRA (CN)

LA MORRA (CN)

GIOVANNI CORINO
FRAZ. ANNUNZIATA, 24
12064 LA MORRA (CN)
TEL. 017350219

SILVIO GRASSO
FRAZ. ANNUNZIATA
CASCINA LUCIANI, 112
12064 LA MORRA (CN)
TEL. 017350322

This year, Renato and Giuliano Corino offered us six superb '99 Barolos, each one better than the last. We were overwhelmed, and offer our congratulations for the tasting. The basic version is nice and fruity, very drinkable and ready now, although it will age well. The Roncaglie is a new offering from the house of Corino, its 3,000 bottles sourced from just under half a hectare of three-year-old vines. It is pleasant, wonderfully fruity, long and balanced, with a clean finish. The pale Rocche (3,300 bottles) boasts complex aromas of spice and balsam, with undertones of fruit. Its juicy palate reveals an earthy sensation, with solid yet sweet tannins that are anything but dry, and a very classy finish. Arborina, of which the same number of units were released, is a glorious garnet. The nose is still a little closed, but the palate shows firm tannins and an extremely enjoyable fruit-forward style. Vigna Giachini (10,000 bottles) mingles notes of balsam, rose and violet with fruit. On the palate, its assertive tannins integrate perfectly with the ripe fruit and the initial aromas return on the finish. Last of the magnificent six is the superlative Vecchie Vigne, a lovely, rich garnet wine that has yet to express its full range of aromas. It is positively explosive on the palate, where it parades potent, juicy tannins, rich fruitiness and fabulous balance. The elegant, firmly structured palate of the L'Insieme 2000 brims with aromas. The powerful, fruit-led Barbera Pozzo is good, and the Dolcetto and Barbera are very creditable wines for the vintage.

Federico and Marilena Grasso's ten hectares produce 60-70,000 bottles of the Langhe classics, Dolcetto, Barbera, Nebbiolo and Barolo. We welcome a newcomer this year in the Barolo Giachini 1999, only 3,000 bottles of which were produced from less than a hectare of vineyard. It is vinified with fairly short fermentations, aged in pre-used barriques, and is light garnet in colour. The subtle nose shows cocoa powder and dried roses, then the palate, which is drinking nicely, follows through well to a liquorice finish. All in all, a fine debut. Moving on to the other Barolos, we found the Bricco Luciani offers delicious violets on the nose and tight-knit, firm yet sweet tannins on the very powerful palate, which ends in a long finish. This wine will age very well. We loved the Ciabot Manzoni. Although matured entirely in new barriques, its oaky tones are not excessive. The bright colour ushers in a complex nose of violets and roses, with traces of blackberry fruit, and a palate that stands out for its harmony and balance. Its wonderful thrust carries through to the long, leisurely and very elegant finish. The Pì Vigne is much simpler, with nice aromas but rather a dry palate. The Barbera Fontanile 2001 is a faithful expression of its variety in its freshness, rich, juicy morello fruit and wonderful palate. Release of the Nebbiolo 2001, from Monforte grapes, has been delayed until next year. The Dolcetto 2002 is penalized by the vintage, but has decent fruit and an agreeable palate. Finally, L'Insieme 2000, a nebbiolo, barbera, cabernet sauvignon and merlot blend, is good.

● Barolo Vecchie Vigne '99	♟♟♟	8
● Barolo Rocche '99	♟♟	8
● Barbera d'Alba Pozzo '00	♟♟	6
● L'Insieme '00	♟♟	8
● Barolo '99	♟♟	6
● Barolo Vigna Giachini '99	♟♟	7
● Barolo Vigneto Arborina '99	♟♟	8
● Barolo Vigneto Roncaglie '99	♟♟	7
● Barbera d'Alba '02	♟	4
● Dolcetto d'Alba '02	♟	3
● Barolo Vigna Giachini '89	♟♟♟	8
● Barolo Rocche '90	♟♟♟	8
● Barbera d'Alba Vigna Pozzo '96	♟♟♟	8
● Barbera d'Alba Vigna Pozzo '97	♟♟♟	8
● Barolo Vecchie Vigne '98	♟♟♟	8

● Barolo Bricco Luciani '99	♟♟	8
● Barolo Ciabot Manzoni '99	♟♟	8
● L'Insieme '00	♟♟	8
● Barbera d'Alba Fontanile '01	♟♟	5
● Barolo Giachini '99	♟♟	7
● Dolcetto d'Alba '02	♟	4
● Barolo Pì Vigne '99	♟	7
● Barbera d'Alba '02		4
● Barolo Bricco Luciani '90	♟♟♟	8
● Barolo Bricco Luciani '95	♟♟♟	8
● Barolo Bricco Luciani '96	♟♟♟	8
● Barolo Ciabot Manzoni '97	♟♟	8
● Barolo Bricco Luciani '98	♟♟	8
● Barolo Ciabot Manzoni '98	♟♟	8

LA MORRA (CN)

MARIO MARENGO
VIA XX SETTEMBRE, 36
12064 LA MORRA (CN)
TEL. 017350127 - 017350115

In his tiny cellar at La Morra, skilled, easy-going winemaker Marco Marengo is working hard to create a more complete range of wines. This is a kind of interim phase for Marco, as he is waiting for extension work on his cellars to be completed and he was forced to forgo his classic Dolcetto as a result of the poor harvest. He presented us with just two wines this year, but future vintages will swell the ranks once again, particularly as regards Barolos. Marco's production philosophy is based on diligence in the vineyard, limited racking, and short macerations to preserve aromas as far as possible and enhance the character of the noble raw material he works with. It certainly pays off in the case of the excellent Barolo Brunate 1999. Bright garnet in hue, it releases enveloping aromas of fresh coffee and star-anise contributed by the hallmark elegance of the superb Brunate vineyard. The palate reveals fragrant sensations of effortless class and ends on a leisurely note of bramble. The Nebbiolo d'Alba Valmaggiore 2001 is, as ever, robust and satisfying. Sourced from a vineyard at Vezza near Roero, it has a youthful, citrussy nose and a palate that shows nice breadth and length, with well-judged extract.

LA MORRA (CN)

MAURO MOLINO
FRAZ. ANNUNZIATA, 111
12064 LA MORRA (CN)
TEL. 017350814
E-MAIL: molino.mauro@libero.it

Mauro Molino has produced an extraordinary series of wines this year with his capable son, Matteo, who is helping him to build on his already impressive achievements. The explosive Vigna Conca 1999 and the refined Vigna Gancia 1999 are the stars of the Barolos. The Vigna Conca comes from almost 30-year-old vines and reveals a wealth of redcurrant and black cherry on the nose. It is vivacious, flavoursome and elegant in its long, long finish, and the extract is admirably balanced. The Vigna Gancia comes from younger, southeast-facing plots and offers generous notes of liquorice, leather and mint. It floods the palate with a fabulous spectrum of aromatics and the soft mouthfeel melds with potently pervasive fruit. The austere, very typical Barolo 1999 is rich in mineral and spice tones, and also impressed. The deep ruby Barbera Vigna Gattere 2001 (4,000 bottles) is a lovely wine that proffers dense, delicious aromas of mushrooms, violets and bramble. The palate is warm, lengthy and powerful, with a finish that recalls fresh herbs and spices. Despite the difficult year, the other stainless steel-vinified reds show character. The Langhe Nebbiolo has a rich wild rose bouquet and a fascinating, lively palate. The vibrant Barbera d'Alba tempts with mouthwatering morello cherry, and the purple-red Dolcetto d'Alba releases headily pervasive notes of strawberry. Finally, our congratulations on the characterful and impeccably made L'Insieme 2000, a very successful blend of nebbiolo, barbera, cabernet and merlot that offers rich, pervasive aromas ranging from raspberry to pepper.

● Nebbiolo d'Alba Valmaggiore '01	♟♟	5
● Barolo Brunate '99	♟♟	7
● Barolo Brunate '95	♟♟	8
● Barolo Brunate '96	♟♟	8
● Barolo Bricco Viole '97	♟♟	8
● Barolo Brunate '97	♟♟	8
● Nebbiolo d'Alba Valmaggiore '00	♟♟	5
● Dolcetto d'Alba '01	♟♟	3
● Barolo Bricco Viole '98	♟♟	8

● L'Insieme '00	♟♟	8
● Barbera d'Alba Vigna Gattere '01	♟♟	6
● Barolo Vigna Conca '99	♟♟	8
● Barolo Vigna Gancia '99	♟♟	8
● Barolo '99	♟♟	7
● Barbera d'Alba '02	♟	4
● Dolcetto d'Alba '02	♟	3
● Langhe Nebbiolo '02	♟	4
● Barbera d'Alba Vigna Gattere '96	♟♟♟	5
● Barolo Vigna Conca '96	♟♟♟	8
● Barbera d'Alba Vigna Gattere '97	♟♟♟	6
● Barolo Vigna Conca '97	♟♟♟	8
● Barbera d'Alba Vigna Gattere '00	♟♟♟	6

LA MORRA (CN)

MONFALLETTO
CORDERO DI MONTEZEMOLO
FRAZ. ANNUNZIATA, 67
12064 LA MORRA (CN)
TEL. 017350344
E-MAIL: info@corderodimontezemolo.com

Once again, Gianni and Enrico Cordero presented us with a series of excellent wines. Their annual production hovers around the 100,000 bottle mark, and 55,000 of these are Barolo. We'll start with the Barolos and the bright garnet Monfalletto, whose fruit-led nose introduces an approachable, very enjoyable palate with a hint of flowers in the whistle-clean finish. The Enrico VI has a gorgeous garnet hue and is a little reticent in the nose, which recalls roses and plum fruit. The palate is both full-bodied and robust, with excellent fruit and a trace of liquorice in the lingering finish. The Gattera (5,000 bottles) is the most complex and refined of the range, and earned Three Glasses. It has beautiful garnet tones and offers classy, concentrated notes of fruit and flowers that integrate seamlessly with the oak. The palate is full and rich, with firm but polished tannins, and the long, leisurely finish echoes the fruit with a hint of earth. We liked the Barbera Funtanì for its plum, citrus and raspberry nose, and its rich palate of lovely full fruit. The basic Barbera has a very refined floral nose and a lively, generous, fruit-forward palate. The finish suggests cherry with a hint of minerality. The Nebbiolo comes from a difficult growing year but performed well, offering aromas of spice, herbs and dried flowers. The palate is solid, fairly complex and long. The Dolcetto is decent and simple, with moderate structure. The Chardonnay Elioro is, as usual, very pleasant. Bright in hue, it is full and soft on the palate, then long in the finish. The Arneis is well typed.

LA MORRA (CN)

ANDREA OBERTO
B.TA SIMANE, 11
12064 LA MORRA (CN)
TEL. 017350104

Now that the new cellars are finished, Andrea Oberto and his son, Fabio, can focus all their attention on their vineyards and the superb grapes that go into their premium-quality range of wines. They currently have an annual production of around 70,000 bottles. We start our notes with the Barolos, which are vinified with modern equipment that sprays the cap during fermentation. The cream of the crop is the majestic Vigneto Albarella 1999. Its refined, aristocratic aromas of liquorice, leather and rich fruit progress elegantly to the finish, which is perked up by lively tannins. It is partnered by the complex Vigneto Rocche 1999, which weds notes of blackberry and blackcurrant with a structure that is warm in mid palate and dynamic in the dry, delicious finish. The Barolo 1999 is delicious and true to type, offering tobacco and violet aromas. The Langhe Rosso Fabio 2001, a nebbiolo and barbera blend, is similar, layering mushroom aromas over a richly flavoured, leisurely palate. The Barbera d'Alba Giada 2001 (almost 12,000 bottles) is quite superb. It melds barrique-derived sweetness with generous hints of ripe fruit and traces of balsam, lingering long and deliciously on the palate. The Dolcetto d'Alba Vantrino Albarella 2002 is very good and in fact one of the best of the vintage. Rich, pleasant and supple, it has an upfront, generous palate. The clean, well-made Dolcetto d'Alba 2002, Barbera d'Alba 2002 and Langhe Nebbiolo 2002 all show flowers on the nose and are very pleasant to drink.

●	Barolo Vigna Bricco Gattera '99	♟♟♟	8
●	Barolo Enrico VI '99	♟♟	8
●	Barbera d'Alba Sup. Funtanì '00	♟♟	6
○	Langhe Chardonnay Elioro '00	♟♟	5
●	Barbera d'Alba '01	♟♟	5
●	Langhe Nebbiolo '02	♟♟	5
●	Barolo Monfalletto '99	♟♟	7
●	Dolcetto d'Alba '02	♟	4
○	Langhe Arneis '02	♟	4
●	Barolo Enrico VI '96	♟♟♟	8
●	Barolo Enrico VI '97	♟♟♟	8
●	Barolo Enrico VI '98	♟♟	8
●	Barbera d'Alba Sup. Funtanì '99	♟♟	6

●	Barbera d'Alba Giada '01	♟♟	6
●	Barolo Vigneto Albarella '99	♟♟	8
●	Barolo Vigneto Rocche '99	♟♟	8
●	Langhe Rosso Fabio '01	♟♟	6
●	Dolcetto d'Alba Vigneto Vantrino Albarella '02	♟♟	4
●	Barolo '99	♟♟	7
●	Barbera d'Alba '02	♟	4
●	Dolcetto d'Alba '02	♟	3
●	Langhe Nebbiolo '02	♟	4
●	Barbera d'Alba Giada '96	♟♟♟	6
●	Barolo Vigneto Rocche '96	♟♟♟	8
●	Barbera d'Alba Giada '97	♟♟♟	6
●	Barbera d'Alba Giada '00	♟♟♟	6

LA MORRA (CN)

F.LLI ODDERO
FRAZ. SANTA MARIA, 28
12064 LA MORRA (CN)
TEL. 017350618
E-MAIL: info@odderofratelli.it

The Oddero brothers' estate was founded back in 1878, making it one of the oldest and most important in the area. Their wines are a happy marriage of modernity and respect for tradition. We have two new items to report this year. The first is another Barolo selection, the Brunate, and the second is the debut of a Barbaresco made with grapes from the Gallina vineyard at Neive. We were offered a splendid range of Barolo 1999s to taste and very much liked the intensely garnet Vigna Rionda. Its pervasive bouquet recalls fruit, spice, rosemary and liquorice, with a subtle balsamic hint of resin and mountain pine. The palate reveals a full, warm structure, ripe tannins and a very lengthy finish. The Mondoca di Bussia is more evolved in colour and unveils a rigorous nose of dried roses and tobacco. The palate is firm and dry, with sweet tannins and a clean, leisurely finish. The Barolo Rivera di Castiglione flaunts concentrated, elegant aromas of red berry fruit, tobacco, rain-soaked earth, cocoa powder and liquorice. The warm, firm palate shows close-knit, fairly mature tannins. The Rocche di Castiglione (4,500 bottles) has a deep, austere nose of blackberry and dried violet, and a vibrantly pervasive palate. The basic Barolo is very characterful, and the Barbaresco is potent on the palate and traditional in style. Both are interesting and well made. The Barbera 2001 is quite delightful, offsetting the softness of its fruit with the marked acidity of the variety. Finally, the fresh, pleasant Chardonnay Collaretto 2002 merits One Glass.

● Barolo Vigna Rionda '99	♈♈	8
● Barbaresco '99	♈♈	6
● Barolo '99	♈♈	6*
● Barolo Mondoca di Bussia Soprana '99	♈♈	8
● Barolo Rivera di Castiglione '99	♈♈	7
● Barolo Rocche di Castiglione '99	♈♈	7
● Barbera d'Alba '01	♈	4
○ Langhe Chardonnay Collaretto '02	♈	3
● Barolo Vigna Rionda '89	♈♈♈	8
● Barolo Mondoca di Bussia Soprana '97	♈♈♈	8
● Barolo Vigna Rionda '98	♈♈♈	8

LA MORRA (CN)

PODERI MARCARINI
P.ZZA MARTIRI, 2
12064 LA MORRA (CN)
TEL. 017350222
E-MAIL: marcarini@marcarini.it

This year, Manuel and Luisa Marchetti presented the panel with another range of very interesting products that are very representative of their terroir of origin. Under the watchful eye of oenologist, Armando Cordero, this 19th century cellar produces some excellent Barolo vineyard selections. The Barolo Brunate '99 is a marvel of compactness and depth, revealing a full, flavoursome body, clear notes of ripe blackberry and fine nuances of lavender and mulberry that expand gracefully over elegant tannins. Three brimming Glasses. Hot on its heels was the Barolo La Serra 1999. Drier and more austere, it unleashes a torrent of balsam and morello aromas that buttress a balanced, sustained structure and a finish reminiscent of tobacco. Both these wines embody the enormous character of the variety, clearly reflecting the estate philosophy that puts the accent on the personality of the fruit. Neither are our heroes averse to experimental projects, which they approach with insight and carefully drafted protocols. The Langhe Rosso Donald 2000 was just such an experiment, a blend of 60 per cent barbera, 30 per cent nebbiolo and ten per cent syrah. It is named after young Donald Rossi and its sales will make regular contributions to an organization dedicated to supporting young people. The warm, fruity bouquet offers approachable, alcohol-rich aromas and delicate complexity, then the palate reveals soft, satisfying texture that vaguely hints at pungent spices. We'll end this review with the classic Langhe Nebbiolo Lasarin 2002, a well-typed, coherent wine with an exciting palate.

● Barolo Brunate '99	♈♈♈	7
● Barolo La Serra '99	♈♈	7
● Langhe Rosso Donald '00	♈♈	5
● Langhe Nebbiolo Lasarin '02	♈	4
● Barolo Brunate Ris. '85	♈♈♈	8
● Dolcetto d'Alba Boschi di Berri '96	♈♈♈	5
● Barolo La Serra '95	♈♈	7
● Barolo Brunate '96	♈♈	7
● Barolo La Serra '96	♈♈	7
● Dolcetto d'Alba Boschi di Berri '01	♈♈	4
● Barolo Brunate '98	♈♈	7
● Barolo La Serra '98	♈♈	7

LA MORRA (CN)

LA MORRA (CN)

RENATO RATTI
FRAZ. ANNUNZIATA, 7
12064 LA MORRA (CN)
TEL. 017350185

F.LLI REVELLO
FRAZ. ANNUNZIATA, 103
12064 LA MORRA (CN)
TEL. 017350276
E-MAIL: revello@revellofratelli.com

The new cellars have been under construction for some time but we won't see results until next summer. This is an important second step (the first was expanding the vineyard holding 35 hectares) in a long-term project. Pietro Ratti has a clear plan and first-rate collaborators in Massimo Martinelli, cellarman Federico Oberto and consultant, Beppe Caviola. His Monferrato Villa Pattono 2001 is superb. This blend of barbera, cabernet and merlot comes from the Costigliole d'Asti estate that will soon give us with a Sauvignon Blanc. Villa Pattono is a structured wine, with penetrating, pervasive aromas of black damson, honey and tobacco, depth of flavour and pleasant length. The 1999 Barolo Marcenascos, bearing the former name of the Rocche vineyard, are proof of the excellent growing year and the estate's reliability. Both the simple, elegant basic wine and the prestigious Annunziata selections are outstanding. The Conca vineyard lies just below the abbey and imbues its wine with strong aromas, warmth and a graceful, bitterish finish from the polished, gentle tannins. The Rocche selection is elegant and complex, with a full, harmonious palate and exquisitely long progression on the palate. Barbera d'Alba Torriglione 2001 has sweet fruit tones, generous body and a pleasingly clean finish. Finally, the Nebbiolo d'Alba Ochetti from nearby Roero fails to find consistency in the broad swathe of aromas contributed by the excellent fruit. In total, the cellar releases 200,000 bottles of austere, warm, complex wines to watch with close attention as they mature to their peak.

The Revello brothers know how to bring out the diverse characteristics of their 11 hectares of Annunziata vineyards. They offered us a remarkable assortment of 1999 Barolo selections, led by the Vigna Conca. Deep amaranth red, it releases warm, ripe notes of fig jam. The palate is dense and flavoursome, with a long, tangy finish. The 5,000 bottles released were adjudged worthy of Three Glasses. The Vigna Giachini (also 5,000 units) has an enveloping, spicy bouquet with soft notes of pear and rose. Its luxuriously rich palate brims with cranberry aromas and polished tannins. We have a newcomer in the Vigna Gattera, which takes advantage of its south and southeast-aspected location to acquire elegant nuances of plum and stylish tannins. The palate confirms the solid structure and shows dryish tannins. Aristocratic notes of red jam and tobacco meld in the Rocche dell'Annunziata, a mature, very well-made Barolo with a long finish. Barolos from 1999 are typically austere and rewarding. The Barbera Ciabot du Re 2001 is simply splendid. The rich, penetrating nose is a concentration of blackberry and mulberry fruit, with undertones of incense. The palate is immensely gratifying, showing balance and unusual character. The Nebbiolo 2001 has lovely pepper and morello cherry aromas, and the Barbera and the Dolcetto 2002 have a nice bouquet and a fragrant finish. L'Insieme 2000, from nebbiolo, cabernet sauvignon, barbera and petit verdot, is not to be missed, with its velvety nose, tannic finesse and charming fruit-led profile.

● Monferrato Villa Pattono '01	▼▼	6
● Barolo Rocche Marcenasco '99	▼▼	8
● Barbera d'Alba Torriglione '01	▼▼	5
● Barolo Conca Marcenasco '99	▼▼	8
● Barolo Marcenasco '99	▼▼	7
● Nebbiolo d'Alba Ochetti '01	▼	5
● Barolo Rocche Marcenasco '83	♀♀♀	8
● Barolo Rocche Marcenasco '84	♀♀♀	8
● Barolo Rocche Marcenasco '96	♀♀	8
● Monferrato Villa Pattono '98	♀♀	5
● Barolo Rocche Marcenasco '97	♀♀	8
● Barbera d'Alba Torriglione '00	♀♀	4
● Dolcetto d'Alba Colombè '01	♀♀	4
● Barolo Rocche Marcenasco '98	♀♀	8

● Barolo Vigna Conca '99	▼▼▼	8
● L'Insieme '00	▼▼	8
● Barbera d'Alba Ciabot du Re '01	▼▼	6
● Barolo Vigna Giachini '99	▼▼	7
● Barolo Rocche dell'Annunziata '99	▼▼	8
● Barolo Vigna Gattera '99	▼▼	7
● Langhe Nebbiolo '01	▼	5
● Barbera d'Alba '02	▼	4
● Dolcetto d'Alba '02	▼	4
● Barolo '99	▼	7
● Barolo '93	♀♀♀	8
● Barolo Rocche dell'Annunziata '97	♀♀♀	8
● Barbera d'Alba Ciabot du Re '00	♀♀♀	7
● Barolo Vigna Conca '98	♀♀	8

LA MORRA (CN)

LA MORRA (CN)

ROCCHE COSTAMAGNA
VIA VITTORIO EMANUELE, 8
12064 LA MORRA (CN)
TEL. 0173509225
E-MAIL: barolo@rocchecostamagna.it

MAURO VEGLIO
FRAZ. ANNUNZIATA
CASCINA NUOVA, 50
12064 LA MORRA (CN)
TEL. 0173509212
E-MAIL: mauro.veglio@libero.it

This estate has always been an important part of the history of La Morra, and that history seems almost palpable as you walk through its venerable cellars. But the structure will be modernized soon into a visitor and historical centre, while the actual winemaking will be moved to a new facility at Annunziata. These are the fruits of forward-looking management from Alessando Locatelli, assisted by consultant Beppe Caviola. Together with agronomist Giampiero Romana, Locatelli has already introduced significant vineyard-specific cluster-thinning regimes. In our tastings, we were impressed by the qualities of the Barolo Bricco Francesco '99, from 30 to 40-year-old vineyards. The nose boasts lush, warm aromas, with notes of morello cherry, leather and mint, the wine then developing harmoniously on the palate, with the fruit returning to blend with silky tannins. Just a notch behind is the Barolo Rocche dell'Annunziata '99, from new vineyards. Purplish-red, with rich mineral and mushroom notes, it marries succulent fruit to a crisp acidity. Complexity and eloquence mark the nose of the Langhe Nebbiolo Roccardo '01, lean in structure but full-flavoured and laden with red-fruit preserve. The Barbera d'Alba Annunziata '01 is all balance, especially in the mouth, which bursts with ripe blackberries and sweet tannins, while the Dolcetto d'Alba '02 is subdued yet fruity. Two whites complete the line-up: a heady and appealing Langhe Arneis '02, and the Langhe Chardonnay Flavo '02, which has a stylish, intriguing nose highlighting snappy notes of yellow peach.

Mauro Veglio and his wife Daniela, who is also secretary of the Insieme solidarity project, are single-minded and determined. Change and investment marked their 2003: in particular, their new cellar was completed, so its well-equipped facilities will allow them to get the most from their outstanding vineyards. Their production is now 55,000 bottles from 11 hectares of estate vineyards in La Morra and Monforte. The wines tasted this year were all crowd-pleasers, underlining the great quality achieved by the entire line, which is led by the Barolos and the Barbera Cascina Nuova. We tasted four Barolo selections and liked best the Castelletto, for its dense and impressively structured body. Mauro has sculpted it into a supple and very attractive wine. The nose of the Barolo Arborina ranges through ripe cherry and raspberry fruit to faded rose petal and mineral tones, then the palate demonstrates elegant, balanced complexity. The Barolo Vigneto Rocche fascinates the taster with rich notes of balsam and liquorice. Finally, the Veglio Barolo Vigneto Gattina is absolute textbook nebbiolo. All in all, these are very well-turned out wines, but missing somehow is that edge which the Veglios are capable of. As we said, the Barbera d'Alba Cascina Nuova is outstanding and exuberant in both nose and palate. Despite a less than favourable growing year, both the Barbera and the standard Dolcetto are fine. Let's end with their red l'Insieme, from nebbiolo, barbera and cabernet sauvignon. Loads of character and admirably intense colour and nose make it pure drinking pleasure.

● Barolo Bricco Francesco Rocche dell'Annunziata '99	🍷🍷	7
● Langhe Nebbiolo Roccardo '01	🍷🍷	4
● Barolo Rocche dell'Annunziata '99	🍷🍷	6
● Barbera d'Alba Annunziata '01	🍷	4
● Dolcetto d'Alba '02	🍷	4
○ Langhe Arneis '02	🍷	4
○ Langhe Chardonnay Flavo '02	🍷	4
● Barolo Bricco Francesco Rocche dell'Annunziata '97	🍷🍷	8
● Barolo Rocche dell'Annunziata '97	🍷🍷	7
● Barbera d'Alba Annunziata '00	🍷🍷	5
● Barolo Bricco Francesco Rocche dell'Annunziata '98	🍷🍷	8
● Barolo Rocche dell'Annunziata '98	🍷🍷	7

● Barbera d'Alba Cascina Nuova '01	🍷🍷	6
● Barolo Castelletto '99	🍷🍷	7
● L'Insieme '01	🍷🍷	8
● Barolo Arborina '99	🍷🍷	7
● Barolo Vigneto Gattera '99	🍷🍷	7
● Barolo Vigneto Rocche '99	🍷🍷	8
● Barbera d'Alba '02	🍷	4
● Dolcetto d'Alba '02	🍷	3
● Barbera d'Alba Cascina Nuova '96	🍷🍷🍷	5
● Barolo Vigneto Rocche '96	🍷🍷🍷	8
● Barbera d'Alba Cascina Nuova '99	🍷🍷🍷	6
● Barolo Arborina '97	🍷🍷	7
● Barbera d'Alba Cascina Nuova '00	🍷🍷	6
● Barolo Arborina '98	🍷🍷	7

LA MORRA (CN)

ERALDO VIBERTI
FRAZ. SANTA MARIA
B.TA TETTI DEI TURCHI, 53
12064 LA MORRA (CN)
TEL. 017350308

Eraldo Viberti runs a winery that gets consistently good results and is one of the most dependable contributors to Langhe winemaking. Restructuring of the cellars is now complete, and the wines we sampled were truly delicious. Standing out from the rest is the Barolo '99. It is medium garnet in hue with a full nose that opens with balsam and lightly toasted oak, then plunges into rich fruity morello and strawberry, to end on dried roses and violets, veined with distinct but not intrusive vanilla. The mouth shows tannins in abundance, but they've been well rounded, and the wine has elegance to spare – its strong suit – and impeccable balance throughout. Worthy of note is the Barbera d'Alba Vigna Clara '00, which matured for several months in barrique. A deep red, it flaunts a panoply of aromas, with spice and fruit in rich abundance. Depth, structure, and succulence combine on the palate. A delicate but sappy undergirding lends impressive length. The deep violet Dolcetto d'Alba '02 is redolent of fresh hay and plum jam, with more weight than you would expect from this year, and an agreeably bitterish finish. The Langhe Nebbiolo '01 is exhibits a mellow ruby red, opening to scents of ripe cherry and strawberry, and continues with solid flavours in the mouth.

LA MORRA (CN)

OSVALDO VIBERTI
FRAZ. SANTA MARIA
B.TA SERRA DEI TURCHI, 95
12064 LA MORRA (CN)
TEL. 017350374

Osvaldo Viberti owns a modest winery that is experiencing solid growth thanks to his dedication and talents. He has seven hectares under vine in the La Morra zone, but not all the wine is bottled, so his commercial production is still limited. A lovely ruby red announces his Barolo Serra dei Turchi '99 as a wine of great character, then ripe fruit, liquorice and a spicy sweetness of vanilla plus black pepper open together on the nose. Although the mouth is austere enough, with a generous level of alcohol and tannins, the overall impression is one of finesse and complexity, convincingly seconded by a rich, lengthy finish. Excellent marks, too, for the Barbera d'Alba Mancine '01 which has cherry-red highlights. Full-fruited aromas of morello cherry, strawberry and plum fill out a generous nose. The attack is immediately smooth and succulent, but a zingy, varietal freshness keeps everything lively and bright. The growing year wouldn't have led one to expect such a delicious Dolcetto d'Alba Galletto '02. A ruby red edged with purple ushers in fruity, clean, wondrously lengthy aromas. It's light in the mouth, which is predictable given its youthfulness, but this is a real beauty of a wine with every component nicely in place. The Langhe Nebbiolo is delightful, with a crisp, fruity nose lifted by a touch of spice. Full, rich flavours flow nicely on the palate and a light, bitterish tang signs off a lengthy finish.

● Barbera d'Alba Vigna Clara '00	🍷🍷	5
● Dolcetto d'Alba '02	🍷🍷	4
● Barolo '99	🍷🍷	6
● Langhe Nebbiolo '01	🍷	5
● Barolo '93	🍷🍷🍷	8
● Barolo '97	🍷🍷	8
● Barbera d'Alba Vigna Clara '98	🍷🍷	6
● Gilat Rosso '99	🍷🍷	6
● Barolo '98	🍷🍷	8
● Barbera d'Alba Vigna Clara '99	🍷🍷	6

● Barbera d'Alba Mancine '01	🍷🍷	4*
● Barolo Serra dei Turchi '99	🍷🍷	6
● Dolcetto d'Alba Galletto '02	🍷	3
● Langhe Nebbiolo '02	🍷	4
● Barolo Serra dei Turchi '97	🍷🍷	7
● Barbera d'Alba Mancine '00	🍷🍷	5
● Barolo Serra dei Turchi '98	🍷🍷	7
● Barbera d'Alba Mancine '99	🍷	4

LA MORRA (CN)

GIANNI VOERZIO
S.DA LORETO, 1
12064 LA MORRA (CN)
TEL. 0173509194

Although the fateful Three Glasses did not arrive this year, Gianni and Franca Voerzio's winery remains one of the stars of Langhe winemaking. The sheer elegance of the wines sets their estate apart, and terroir is always to the fore. From the twelve and a half hectares of vineyards in the municipalities of La Morra, Castellinaldo, and Castiglione Tinella, the Voerzios make about 60,000 bottles a year. As ever, the Barolo La Serra (9,200 bottles) leads the pack. Matured in new 500-litre tonneaux, its habitually rich colour precedes a nose marked by finesse and complexity that opens up in raspberry, roasted coffee and cinnamon. The palate expands powerfully, but is held firmly in check by a suite of seductive, caressing tannins. Next in line is the compelling Barbera Ciabot della Luna (9,200 units). A full-bodied wine, it finishes very long, the plentiful blackberry and ripe cherry echoes contributing mightily to its overall savouriness. Fully worth their Two Glasses are the Langhe Serrapiù (5,300 bottles), a classic blend of 60 per cent nebbiolo and 40 per cent barbera matured in new barriques, and the Langhe Nebbiolo (5,200 units), which Gianni finds ages best in 500-litre tonneaux. The Serrapiù comes off as soft and full, despite a touch of hotness from the alcohol, while the second features an intriguing nose and suppleness in the mouth. The wines of the difficult 2002 growing year round out the line, but are hard pressed to repeat the great results of previous years. But the Dolcetto Rochettevino performed well, as did an aromatic Arneis Bricco Cappellina.

LA MORRA (CN)

★ ROBERTO VOERZIO
LOC. CERRETO, 1
12064 LA MORRA (CN)
TEL. 0173509196

The wines of Roberto and Pinuccia Voerzio rank among the finest in the Langhe this year. For about 20 years now, this well-matched winemaking duo have set their sights exclusively on quality, shunning mere quantity in order to coax the best from their fruit. And what vineyards they have, in the best sites at La Morra in some of Barolo's most celebrated crus! In addition, they have been focusing for several years on one particular vineyard, little considered by some and located outside the hamlet of Santa Maria di La Morra. But the Voerzios hit the jackpot, because the Vecchie Viti dei Capalot, blended with fruit from Brunate, has produced one of the finest Barolos in the entire DOCG zone. We will evaluate it for next year's edition. This year, the standout once again is the Barolo Brunate '99, which took our breath away. It's an austere wine, displaying every quality that should mark a classic Barolo: deep ruby colour; a nose still flaunting ripe fruit, but fast acquiring the complexity that will come with ageing; and massive power on the palate, with an almost juicy succulence from rich, rounded tannins. The oaking is perfectly judged. The Cerequio and the La Serra match last year's quality. So does the Barolo Sarmassa, a compendium of Voerzio qualities. The sublimely rich, powerful palate reveals elegant fruit that easily holds its tannins in check. Textbook perfect, too, is the Barbera Vigneto Pozzo, bottled only in magnum.

● Barbera d'Alba Ciabot della Luna '01	🍷🍷	5
● Barolo La Serra '99	🍷🍷	8
● Langhe Nebbiolo Ciabot della Luna '01	🍷🍷	6
● Langhe Rosso Serrapiù '01	🍷🍷	6
● Dolcetto d'Alba Rocchettevino '02	🍷	4
● Langhe Freisa Sotti I Bastioni '02	🍷	4
○ Moscato d'Asti Vignasergente '02	🍷	5
○ Roero Arneis Bricco Cappellina '02	🍷	4
● Barolo La Serra '96	🍷🍷🍷	8
● Barolo La Serra '97	🍷🍷🍷	8
● Barolo La Serra '98	🍷🍷🍷	8
● Barolo La Serra '95	🍷🍷	8

● Barolo Brunate '99	🍷🍷🍷	8
● Barbera d'Alba Vigneto Pozzo dell'Annunziata Ris. '00	🍷🍷	8
● Barolo Cerequio '99	🍷🍷	8
● Barolo La Serra '99	🍷🍷	8
● Barolo Sarmassa '99	🍷🍷	8
● Barolo Cerequio '90	🍷🍷🍷	8
● Barolo Brunate '93	🍷🍷🍷	8
● Barbera d'Alba Vigneto Pozzo dell'Annunziata Ris. '96	🍷🍷🍷	8
● Barolo Brunate '96	🍷🍷🍷	8
● Barolo Cerequio '96	🍷🍷🍷	8
● Barolo Brunate '98	🍷🍷🍷	8
● Barbera d'Alba Vigneto Pozzo dell'Annunziata Ris. '99	🍷🍷🍷	8

LESSONA (BI)

SELLA
VIA IV NOVEMBRE, 110
13853 LESSONA (BI)
TEL. 01599455

LOAZZOLO (AT)

BORGO MARAGLIANO
REG. SAN SEBASTIANO, 2
14050 LOAZZOLO (AT)
TEL. 014487132
E-MAIL: maragliano@inwind.it

It is always a surprise that Lessona has only one producer of note, and that its reputation has not reached a wider circle of wine aficionados. The superb characteristics which Sella infuses into his wines convincingly reflect the unparalleled qualities of the Lessona terroir. They also show the intimate link to the land of this important, historic family. Sella's San Sebastiano allo Zoppo is a nebbiolo of the first rank, whose body and sinew are subtly shaped by a touch of vespolina. The nose opens to supple aromas of vanilla, mulberry, and blueberry, then presents spice and forest floor, finally closing with the classic crushed rose. The palate features an amazingly expressive texture and re-proposes the nose's kaleidoscopic richness. The standard Lessona leads off with an appealingly sharp-edged eloquence, reinforced by its impeccably clean structure. It foregrounds minerals and flowers, the prime characteristics of its terroir. Sella's textbook Bramaterra underlines its white cherry and redcurrant fruit, with coffee notes from its stay in oak, followed by the denomination's typical liquorice root. The palate gives full rein to croatina's lively contributions, plumskin and attractively chewy tannins. Even the least ambitious wine, Orbello, a blend of cabernet and barbera, shows the unmistakable Sella hallmarks: sweet, juicy fruit, nicely supported with oak, underpins perfectly tenored clove and geranium leaf.

The Galliano family farm nine hectares in the heart of the Loazzolo district, at 400 metres above sea level. In addition to chardonnay and pinot noir, they of course grow moscato. In fact, Borgo Maragliano produces one of the most respected examples of the Loazzolo DOC, a dried-grape "passito" of remarkable fullness. Let's begin with that. Brilliant gold leads to a rich, intriguing bouquet bursting with caramel-covered fruit, smokiness and super-ripeness. Perfect balance rules in the mouth, with firm acidity holding the sweetness nicely in check. It tapers out into a harmonious and lengthy finish. The Gallianos produce two sparklers, an 80-20 pinot noir and chardonnay "metodo classico," and a cuve close Chardonnay Brut Giuseppe Galliano. The first is clear in colour, with some slightly forward notes, and is redolent of preserves and yeasted dough. Its progression is consistent and nicely complex. The second is a bit lighter and veined with apple and floral notes. A nice crispness enlivens the palate. The Crevoglio is an undemanding Chardonnay matured in steel to maximize its youthful fruitiness. The Moscato La Caliera releases delicious scents of apricot and grapefruit, which lead into a palate of good complexity and medium weight. Finally, the experimental Calié is an interesting non-wine "wine" offering with only three degrees alcohol. Its raison d'être is to convey as faithfully as possible the fresh aromas of the grape.

● Lessona		
S. Sebastiano allo Zoppo '99	♟♟	6
● Coste della Sesia Rosso		
Orbello '01	♟♟	3*
● Bramaterra '99	♟♟	4*
● Lessona '99	♟♟	5
● Lessona '97	♟♟	5
● Lessona		
S. Sebastiano allo Zoppo '97	♟♟	5
● Lessona '98	♟♟	5
● Lessona		
S. Sebastiano allo Zoppo '98	♟♟	5
● Coste della Sesia Rosso		
Orbello '00	♟	3

○ Loazzolo		
Borgo Maragliano V. T. '00	♟♟	6
○ Giuseppe Galliano Brut M. Cl. '99	♟♟	5
○ Moscato d'Asti La Caliera '02	♟	3
○ Piemonte Chardonnay		
Crevoglio '02	♟	3
○ Giuseppe Galliano		
Chardonnay Brut	♟	3
○ Loazzolo		
Borgo Maragliano V. T. '98	♟♟	6
○ Loazzolo		
Borgo Maragliano V. T. '99	♟♟	6

LOAZZOLO (AT)

FORTETO DELLA LUJA
REG. BRICCO CASA ROSSO, 4
14050 LOAZZOLO (AT)
TEL. 0141831596
E-MAIL: fortetodellaluja@inwind.it

The winery that has long been in the family of Giancarlo Scaglione's mother is in buildings that go back to the seventeenth century. Its distinctive architecture and site make this eight-hectare estate a real jewel of Monferrato. Giancarlo and his equally dedicated children, Gianni and Silvia, are acutely conscious of this heritage and work tirelessly to improve the cellar and its land. The vineyards, planted to moscato, brachetto, barbera and pinot noir, are among the best-sited in the area, with production around 40,000 bottles per year. Their Loazzolo Piasa Rischei moscato enjoys a long-secured reputation as one of Italy's finest sweet wines. The 2000 release displays a luminous gold and a nose of stunning individuality, weaving gorgeous scents of dates, semi-dried grapes and spices with hints of earth and oak. The palate is stunning. An uninterrupted progression expands in intensity and richness, but with disciplined balance. Their Brachetto Passito Forteto Pian dei Sogni also impressed us, showing a light ruby red and boasting a nose ranging from tea to faded rose petal and red fruit jam. The sweetness in the mouth is pure finesse, complemented by barely evident tannins. A deep straw hue announces the Moscato Piasa San Maurizio, whose ripe, generous nose is dominated by candied tangerine. Its satisfying weight is offset by a tangy fizz, and the finish echoes everything that preceded it. The Rosso Le Grive, from barbera and pinot noir, is deep ruby with some garnet and unfolds scents of flowers, citrus and leather. Leanness and confident progression mark the palate.

LU (AL)

CASALONE
VIA MARCONI, 92
15040 LU (AL)
TEL. 0131741280
E-MAIL: info@casalone.com

One cannot help noticing that the winery owned by the Casalone family is in a phase of active growth. In fact, with the assistance of winemaker Giovanni Bailo, the quality has reached impressive levels. The Monferrato Rosso Rus has taken only a few years to become the cellar's standard-bearer and to pull down Two Red Glasses. A dark, almost opaque, red announces this blend of barbera, merlot, and pinot noir, but it is the nose that immediately takes centre stage, unleashing a stupendous breadth of aromas that range from tree moss to forest floor and dried fruits, concluding with blueberry and lively notes of pear. It opens massively onto the palate, but the opulent flavours are sagely tempered and balanced, and it ends with a long, aroma-textured finish. The Barbera d'Asti Rubermillo also offers plenty for the senses, its nose profuse with morello and plum jam. The exemplary structure supports a satisfying vein of spice and bitter almond. Not far behind is the Barbera del Monferrato Bricco Morlantino. It suffers from some initial notes of uncleanness, but a brief airing restores clarity, and an appealing acidic crispness finally captivates. We found the Grignoliono La Capletta excellent as well. Its elegant suppleness commands attention, as does its nose, rich in rose petals and hinting at balsam and resin. Grignolino's typical tannic grip is in evidence, but in moderation. The whites include an impressive aromatic-grape Monemvasia, and there is also a "passito" version. A cask-conditioned Chardonnay, Munsrët, completes the line.

○ Loazzolo Piasa Rischei '00	�♏	7
● Monferrato Rosso Le Grive '01	♏♏	5
● Piemonte Brachetto Forteto Pian dei Sogni '01	♏♏	6
○ Moscato d'Asti Piasa San Maurizio '02	♏♏	4*
○ Loazzolo Piasa Rischei '93	♏♏♏	7
○ Loazzolo Piasa Rischei '94	♏♏♏	7
○ Loazzolo Piasa Rischei '95	♏♏♏	7
○ Loazzolo Piasa Rischei '96	♏♏♏	7
○ Loazzolo Piasa Rischei '97	♏♏♏	7
○ Loazzolo Piasa Rischei '98	♏♏	7
○ Loazzolo Piasa Rischei '99	♏♏	7
● Piemonte Brachetto Forteto Pian dei Sogni '00	♏♏	6

● Monferrato Rosso Rus '01	♏♏	5
● Barbera d'Asti Rubermillo '01	♏♏	4*
○ Monemvasia '02	♏♏	3*
○ Monemvasia Passito '00	♏	5
○ Monferrato Bianco Munsrët '02	♏	4
● Barbera del M.to Bricco Morlantino '01	♏	4
● Piemonte Grignolino La Capletta '02	♏	3
● Barbera d'Asti Rubermillo '99	♏♏	4
● Monferrato Rosso Rus '99	♏♏	5
● Monferrato Rosso Rus '00	♏♏	5

LU (AL)

Tenuta San Sebastiano
cascina San Sebastiano, 41
15040 Lu (AL)
TEL. 0131741353
E-MAIL: dealessi@libero.it

The line of wines offered by Roberto De Alessi reinforces the impression that the Monferrato "terroir" (using the French term for that complex of land, site climate and grower) is expanding the number of its wineries in the Guide and the outstanding performance of estates such as the present one. The Barbera Mepari opens with an almost opaque ruby red, then immediately captivates with rich scents of ripe plum, balsam, and liquorice. The palate is classic Barbera, a light vein of tannin and a delicious acidity dancing together then flowing into a lengthy finish. We tasted the first release of the Monferrato Rosso Do-Sol, a blend of cabernet franc, cabernet sauvignon and pinot noir, and were delighted to discover a wine of rare breed. Colour and nose are the epitome of richness. Deep ruby with flashes of purple is followed by superb aromas of ripe fruit and plum jam, lifted by a whiff of coffee. The complex palate, framed by well-gauged tannins, also impresses. The Barbera del Monferrato has everything in place, and missed Two Glasses by only a hair. A richly faceted nose weaves together violets, blueberries and fruit preserve. It progresses well, the supple roundness laced with a crisp acidity, and finishes long. De Alessi's Grignolino is always dependable, showing impeccable craftsmanship. The variety's characteristics work together in perfect synergy. The late-harvest moscato LV finishes our tasting. Barrique fermented and matured, it is an excellent wine.

MANGO (CN)

Cascina Fonda
loc. Cascina Fonda, 45
12056 Mango (CN)
TEL. 0173677156
E-MAIL: cascinafonda@cascinafonda.com

Marco and Massimo Barbero own this estate, founded in 1963 by their father, Secondino, and recently modernized. They own about 12 hectares of vineyard, plus a hazelnut grove, and concentrate on turning out top-notch Moscatos. Among the wines we tasted, the Vendemmia Tardiva was the real star. A polished offering, it eloquently interprets the varietal qualities of which super-ripe moscato is capable. The medium straw yellow ushers in rich aromas of spring flowers and peach, shaped by tones springing from that super-ripeness. A moderate fizz lifts the palate's satisfyingly fullness, and the lengthy finish presents an enthusiastic encore of nose and palate. Their Moscato Spumante Tardivo holds the bar high, too. Redolent of resin and rose, it is rich in the mouth and long on the end. Sage, peach and apricot emerge from the Moscato d'Asti, matching nicely its deep straw colour, while its zesty acidity exerts admirable control over a generous dollop of sweetness. The Asti Spumante comes across well as lively and pleasant, exhibiting gracefully moscato's aromatic range. Not exactly a heavyweight in the mouth, it is nonetheless a thoroughly enjoyable Asti. The Barbera Bruseisa offers attractively clean aromas of cherry and peach. The mouthfeel may not be huge, but the palate is nicely delineated. We end with the Brachetto, which shows off a brilliant cherry hue and then nuances of rose petals and rhubarb. The mouth is light, complemented by an insistent prickle, and the finish follows through nicely into medium length.

● Barbera del M.to Mepari '01	ⅦⅦ	4*
● Monferrato Rosso Do-Sol '01	ⅦⅦ	7
○ LV '01	Ⅶ	5
● Barbera del M.to '02	Ⅶ	3
● Piemonte Grignolino '02	Ⅶ	3
● Barbera del M.to Mepari '97	ⅨⅨ	4
● Barbera del M.to Mepari '98	ⅨⅨ	4
● Barbera del M.to Mepari '99	ⅨⅨ	4
● Barbera del M.to Mepari '00	ⅨⅨ	4

○ Vendemmia Tardiva '01	ⅦⅦ	5
○ Moscato Spumante Tardivo '01	ⅦⅦ	5
○ Moscato d'Asti '02	ⅦⅦ	4*
● Barbera d'Alba Bruseisa '01	ⅦⅦ	4*
● Piemonte Brachetto '02	Ⅶ	4
○ Asti '02	Ⅶ	4*
○ Piemonte Moscato Passito '00	ⅨⅨ	5

MANGO (CN)

Sergio Degiorgis

via Circonvallazione, 3
12056 Mango (CN)
tel. 014189107
e-mail: degiorgis.sergio@tin.it

Of the eight hectares under vine that belong to Sergio and Patrizia Degiorgis, fully six and a half are planted to moscato, the variety most common in this corner of the Langhe. The fairly high altitude – Mango is at about 500 metres – ensures significant daily temperature fluctuations. This encourages development of crisp, fruity aromas. Sorì del Re is always a remarkably distinctive moscato. The 2000 edition is almost gold and a very rich, ripe, yet well-modulated nose is its hallmark, exuding peaches in syrup and honey. The gorgeous texture impresses instantly, compounding the pleasure with a lively dance of sweetness, crisp acidity and effervescence. Nor does the lingering, rich finish disappoint. The Barbera '01 is not far behind, with deep colour and lovely notes of toasty oak and plum. It progresses beautifully in the mouth, showing energy and self-confidence, then the lingering finish echoes the nose and palate. The 100 per cent freisa Riella is ruby garnet, releasing aromas ranging from fruit to mint and almond. The palate is pleasurably full-bodied, and perfectly mirrors the nose. The somewhat difficult growing year makes its effects felt in the Dolcetto Peso, but the wine's qualities do shine through. Deep in colour, it unfolds notes of fruit and earth. The mouth displays a nice chewiness, with a tad too much tannin, and the finish lasts well.

●	Langhe Rosso Riella '01	▼▼	5
●	Barbera d'Alba '01	▼▼	5
●	Dolcetto d'Alba Bricco Peso '02	▼▼	4
○	Moscato d'Asti Sorì del Re '02	▼▼	4*
●	Langhe Rosso Riella '99	▽▽	5
●	Barbera d'Alba '00	▽▽	5
●	Dolcetto d'Alba Bricco Peso '01	▽▽	4

MOASCA (AT)

La Ghersa

via San Giuseppe, 19
14050 Moasca (AT)
tel. 0141856012
e-mail: info@laghersa.it

Last year's preview of the Barbera Vignassa '00 impressed us. This year's tasting convinced us more than ever of its outstanding quality, achieved by very rigorous fruit selection from the best of La Ghersa's vineyards. Massimo Pastura Barbero is of the firm opinion that a wine should be identified by its terroir, so it's no surprise that the winery's standard-bearer is labelled for the Nizza subzone. Vignassa '00 is dark, with a marvellously complex nose of blackberry, dried leaves and mown hay, offset by those intriguing minerally tones that so often mark the Barberas of this area. In the mouth, there is immediate structural heft, healthy acidity and alcoholic warmth, the last two so evident that they add significant sensory and tactile richness to the remarkably coherent, long finish. One of Massimo's goals is to give distinctiveness and character even to simpler wines. He has certainly succeeded with Barbera Camparò. Fruit, spice and ink unfold in profusion with an attractive salty tang hinted at throughout. In the mouth, it has power and energy to spare, and a fully satisfying finish. We thought the Rosso La Ghersa, from barbera, cabernet and merlot, was a little inferior to previous editions. It has plenty of stuffing and vitality, but some muddled notes mar the composition. The nose of Piagé is a bit one dimensional and rustic, but the wine is enjoyable and drinks well. The cortese, chardonnay, and sauvignon Sivoy is pleasant, showing good fruit and citrus, and impresses on the palate. Delicacy and complexity mark the Moscato Giorgia.

●	Barbera d'Asti Sup. Nizza La Vignassa '00	▼▼	6
●	Barbera d'Asti Sup. Camparò '01	▼▼	4*
○	Monferrato Bianco Sivoy '02	▼	4
○	Moscato d'Asti Giorgia '02	▼	4
●	Monferrato Rosso La Ghersa '00	▼	6
●	Monferrato Rosso Piagé '02	▼	3*
●	Barbera d'Asti Sup. La Vignassa '99	▽▽	6
●	Barbera d'Asti Sup. Camparò '00	▽▽	4
●	Monferrato Rosso La Ghersa '99	▽▽	6

MOMBARUZZO (AT)

MALGRÀ
LOC. BAZZANA
VIA NIZZA, 8
14046 MOMBARUZZO (AT)
TEL. 0141725055 - 0141726377
E-MAIL: wine@malgra.it

We continue to be impressed with Malgrà, after its first appearance in the Guide last year. Four partners run the estate, each with long experience in wine, Nico Conta, Massimiliano Diotto, Ezio Ciarlie and Giorgio Ciarlie. The winery has more than 100 hectares under vine and produces a wide range of outstanding wines. Let's begin with the Mora di Sassi Barbera d'Asti Superiore Nizza (Nizza is at the heart of the 18 municipalities that make up the Nizza subzone of the DOC Barbera d'Asti Superiore.) The '01, crafted by Giuliano Noè, impresses even more than last year's version and sailed into the finals for Three Glasses. A deep ruby garnet introduces lavish scents of berry fruit, mint and black pepper. It progresses in the mouth with great fullness and vigour, flowing seamlessly into a liquorice-veined finish. Not as complex, but still an outstanding performer, is the Barbera Fornace di Cerreto, with garnet-edged ruby and a nose exuding fruit liqueur. Rich mouthfeel is enlivened by the variety's acidulous zip, and it signs off with a harmonious, pleasurable finish. The Gavi Poggio Basco is a delight, its deep straw yellow announcing beguiling aromas of damson, peach and lemon peel. In the mouth, it unfolds a supple complexity that continues through to a wonderfully long finish. Finally, One Glass each went to the ripe, even-handed Barbera Gaiana and to the slightly oak-dominated Chardonnay Innuce.

MOMBERCELLI (AT)

LUIGI SPERTINO
S.DA LEA, 505
14044 MOMBERCELLI (AT)
TEL. 0141959098
E-MAIL: luigi.spertino@libero.it

Luigi Spertino, legendary in the Asti area for his skill at assessing bought-in grapes, decided in 1977 to bottle his own wines. His winery has always been on the map of Grignolino lovers, and he continues to produce this varietal with fruit purchased from the best sites in the municipalities of Castagnole Monferrato, Scurzolengo and San Desiderio, as well as Asti, close to the historic Migliandolo vineyard, which is unfortunately no longer productive. In June 2003, Spertino was fortunate to bring on board his son Mauro, who had been working as winemaker for a famous liqueur firm. The winery's two top red wines are now produced from estate-owned or leased vineyards. The almost 13,000 bottles of Barbera '01 were sourced from vineyards in Mombercelli, Vinchio and Bricco di Nizza, more than half of them over 70 years old, and are great value for money. Matured for 20 months in Slavonian oak tonneaux, it displays equal amounts of power and balance. In contrast, Rosso N°1 '00 is a monovarietal pinot. The 2,500 bottles are produced from just one hectare, and the resulting concentration stands up well to a two and a half year stay in barrique. The typically varietal nose of fruit and gamey notes leads convincingly into a texture of elegant tannins. Mauro's respect for Piedmont's winemaking past prompted him to investigate the old recipes. Thus were born Ottocento Liberty, a traditional vermouth of moscato and wormwood, Ipocrasso, a Barbera flavoured in the mediaeval style, and a grignolino-based Brut that is as delicious as it is singular.

● Barbera d'Asti Sup. Nizza		
Mora di Sassi '01	♟♟	5
● Barbera d'Asti Sup.		
Fornace di Cerreto '01	♟♟	4
○ Gavi del Comune di Gavi		
Poggio Basco '02	♟♟	4
● Barbera d'Asti Sup. Gaiana '01	♟	4
○ Piemonte Chardonnay Innuce '02	♟	5
● Barbera d'Asti Sup. Gaiana '98	♟♟	4
● Barbera d'Asti Sup. Nizza		
Mora di Sassi '00	♟♟	5
● Monferrato Rosso Emmerosso '99	♟♟	4

● Monferrato Rosso N° 1 '00	♟♟	6
● Barbera d'Asti '01	♟♟	4*
● Grignolino Brut		
Andrea Spertino '99	♟♟	5
● Ippocrasso	♟♟	6
○ Ottocento Liberty	♟♟	4*
● Grignolino d'Asti '02	♟	4*
○ Lunà Brut '99	♟	5

MONCHIERO (CN)

Giuseppe Mascarello e Figlio

via Borgonuovo, 108
12060 Monchiero (CN)
tel. 0173792126
e-mail:
mauromascarello@mascarello1881.com

Mauro Mascarello, wife Maria Teresa and their son Giuseppe have a firm grip on the direction of this historic cellar, dedicated to maintaining tradition. Mauro's pride are austere, long-lived wines that even many years later can unleash exciting sensory experiences. From the estate vineyards in Castiglione Falletto and Monforte come great Barolos, from various vineyards, that undergo lengthy fermentations and mature in Slavonian oak barrels. Exceptional, too, is Mascarello's practice of giving his wines an extra year before release so that their qualities will be even more evident. His Barolo Santo Stefano '98 is the best wine we tasted this year: the Three Glasses were a formality. Orange-rimmed garnet in colour, it weaves together medicinal herbs, rose petals, hay and tobacco, then offers a magnificent tannic weave shot through with zesty acidity that tells you this wine will be around for a very long time. It closes with smoky notes of leather and liquorice. The Barolo Monprivato, from one of the most prestigious vineyards in the Langhe, was also excellent. Still stiff and cautious on the nose of mint, hay and dried flowers, it boasts a classic build and stunning sensory complexity. The Barolo Villero glides on tannic silkiness and scented opulence, but the Barolo Bricco was very slightly below par. Among Mascarello's other wines, we especially liked the fruity, easy drinking Dolcetto Santo Stefano di Perno and the Barbera Codana, where the variety's good acidity is wonderfully integrated into the supple, fruity body.

● Barolo S. Stefano di Perno '98	🍷🍷🍷	8
● Barolo Monprivato '98	🍷🍷	8
● Barbera d'Alba Codana '00	🍷🍷	7
● Barolo Villero '98	🍷🍷	8
● Barbera d'Alba Scudetto '00	🍷	5
● Nebbiolo d'Alba S. Rocco '00	🍷	5
● Dolcetto d'Alba S. Stefano di Perno '01	🍷	4
● Barolo Bricco '98	🍷	8
● Barolo Monprivato '85	YYY	8
● Barolo Villero '96	YYY	8
● Barolo Monprivato Cà d' Morissio Ris. '95	YY	8

MONDOVI (CN)

Il Colombo - Barone Riccati

via dei Sent, 2
12084 Mondovi (CN)
tel. 017441607

Carlo Riccati and his wife, Adriana Giusta, assisted by winemaking consultant Beppe Caviola, continue to achieve impressive results. In 2003, they planted a small merlot vineyard, which will eventually go into the Monteregale. The estate currently has four well-sited hectares in outstanding areas, whose fruit produces three first-rate wines. The Dolcetto delle Langhe Monregalesi Il Colombo '02, sourced from very old vineyards, came through that difficult year unscathed. It presents an opaque violet, flecked with lilac, and the nose unleashes rich aromas of blackberry, black pepper and vanilla. Oak is used very judiciously, only tonneaux and never new. It then develops into a real powerhouse, boasting warm, generous flavours, and unfurls a wonderfully long finish that foregrounds hazelnuts and fresh almonds. The Monteregale '01 goes to 6 hectolitre oak tonneaux for one year. Its deep, almost opaque red accompanies lovely scents of hay and drying flowers; the attack is sweet and full, and the finish seductive. Finally, Chiesetta '02 is often considered the simplest wine of the group, but it shows a more than decent complexity. An attractive violet hue and a berry fruit nose precede good roundness and elegant style on the palate. Though the label reads Langhe Dolcetto, it hails from the Langhe Monregalesi DOC zone, and with this kind of quality, it's a real bargain.

● Dolcetto delle Langhe Monregalesi Il Colombo '02	🍷🍷	4*
● Dolcetto delle Langhe Monregalesi Sup. Monteregale '01	🍷🍷	5
● Langhe Dolcetto La Chiesetta '02	🍷🍷	3*
● Dolcetto delle Langhe Monregalesi Il Colombo '97	YYY	4
● Dolcetto delle Langhe Monregalesi Il Colombo '98	YYY	4
● Dolcetto delle Langhe Monregalesi Il Colombo '00	YY	4
● Dolcetto delle Langhe Monregalesi Sup. Monteregale '99	YY	5
● Dolcetto delle Langhe Monregalesi Il Colombo '01	YY	4

MONFORTE D'ALBA (CN)

GIANFRANCO ALESSANDRIA
LOC. MANZONI, 13
12065 MONFORTE D'ALBA (CN)
TEL. 017378576

It is now almost a tradition that Gianfranco Alessandria's Barolo and his Barbera Vittoria engage in a friendly duel for the Three Glass award, and this year the Barolo San Giovanni brings home the prize. This young and already successful grower is admired by both traditionalists and innovators for wines that combine power, elegance, typicity and balance. Precisely these qualities are apparent in the San Giovanni '99, the product of yet another good year. It shows a dark ruby, lightly orange-rimmed colour, and gradually unfolds an aromatic panoply of fruit, spices and balsamic notes that seem to keep expanding in complexity. The palate has superlative structure laden with velvety tannins, continuing impressively into a lengthy finish enriched with toasty oak, coffee and cocoa powder. Also impressive is the Barbera Vittoria '01, a champion that never fails to go the distance. It was still a bit closed when we tasted it, but it shows every sign of revealing, with time, its habitual treasure of cherry, vanilla, and redcurrant, and of delighting the palate with its endless sensory train and lively acidic girding. Gianfranco lavishes care on his standard Barolo, and although it doesn't flaunt the San Giovanni's complexity, it is a worthy stablemate. The always fascinating L'Insieme, a blend of native and international varieties, is good. Alessandria did not bottle a Dolcetto because the '02 did not meet standards. That difficult growing year is represented by the standard Barbera, which is fruity and easy drinking, but a bit lightweight.

MONFORTE D'ALBA (CN)

★ DOMENICO CLERICO
LOC. MANZONI, 67
12065 MONFORTE D'ALBA (CN)
TEL. 017378171
E-MAIL: domenicoclerico@interfree.it

Domenico Clerico and the talented Massimo Conterno served up an outstanding line-up of wines this year, amply demonstrating yet again their mastery of the Langhe area and of their own various crus. The Barolo Percristina '98 and Ciabot Mentin Ginestra '99 went right to the front of the class in this year's Guide. The Percristina enjoys the edge of lengthier bottle age, and unveils the silkiest of tannins after a luxurious charge of berry fruit, spices and chocolate. The wine is ready for uncorking now but will certainly grow in grace through the years. The Ciabot is more massive and still dumb on the nose. After a few minutes, however, it begins to unfold its typical balsamic notes, lacing them with liquorice and rose petal, and mirroring everything deliciously on the palate as it proceeds to a lengthy finish. The Barolo Pajana comes out just a notch below the other two. It displays a mastery of nebbiolo's complex character, while also evidencing shrewd use of barrique. The Arte '01 hits the mark bang on. A blend of 90 per cent nebbiolo with a little of cabernet and barbera, its offers up an impressively rich nose, and luscious tannins frame a stylish, balanced mouthfeel. The Barbera Trevigne is nice, its plentiful fruit and spice lifted by judicious acidity. Although the difficult 2002 year crimps the structure of the Dolcetto Visadì, the wine bravely puts out a terrific, fruited nose. It's a gorgeous quaffer and a classic Dolcetto to drink through the meal. All in all a good year for Clerico, capped by the two remarkable Three Glass awards.

● Barolo S. Giovanni '99	♟♟♟	8
● Barbera d'Alba Vittoria '01	♟♟	7
● L'Insieme '00	♟♟	8
● Barolo '99	♟♟	8
● Barbera d'Alba '02	♟	5
● Barolo '93	♟♟♟	8
● Barbera d'Alba Vittoria '97	♟♟♟	6
● Barbera d'Alba Vittoria '98	♟♟♟	6
● Barolo S. Giovanni '97	♟♟♟	8
● Barolo S. Giovanni '98	♟♟♟	8
● Barbera d'Alba Vittoria '99	♟♟	6

● Barolo Percristina '98	♟♟♟	8
● Barolo Ciabot Mentin Ginestra '99	♟♟♟	8
● Barolo Pajana '99	♟♟	8
● Langhe Rosso Arte '01	♟♟	6
● Barbera d'Alba Trevigne '01	♟♟	5
● Langhe Dolcetto Visadì '02	♟	4
● Barolo Ciabot Mentin Ginestra '85	♟♟♟	8
● Barolo Ciabot Mentin Ginestra '89	♟♟♟	8
● Arte '90	♟♟♟	8
● Barolo Pajana '90	♟♟♟	8
● Barolo Pajana '93	♟♟♟	8
● Barolo Pajana '95	♟♟♟	8
● Barolo Percristina '95	♟♟♟	8
● Barolo Percristina '96	♟♟♟	8
● Barolo Percristina '97	♟♟♟	8

MONFORTE D'ALBA (CN)

★ ALDO CONTERNO
LOC. BUSSIA, 48
12065 MONFORTE D'ALBA (CN)
TEL. 017378150

From 25 hectares of estate vineyards, this magnificent Langhe property produces upwards of 150,000 bottles annually. In our tastings, we were struck by the exceptional character and finesse of the Barolo Gran Bussia Riserva '97. It is a brilliant, orange-rimmed garnet with mature notes of leather, tobacco, liquorice, and tar on a gorgeously expressive nose, redolent of berry fruit and dried rose petals. Firm, ripe tannins enliven a palate that progresses with exemplary style and suppleness into a wondrously long finish. Equally outstanding is the Barolo Colonnello '99. A nice garnet leads into a nose of rare eloquence that takes time to open. The attack is smooth and progresses supply into a ringingly intense finale. The Barolo Cicala is marked by much darker tones, with a nose to match, more austere and reticent than the Colonnello. But the balanced, well proportioned palate more than satisfies, its tannins nicely integrated, and the finish is also pleasing. The Barolo Bussia trots out as a classy champion. The aromas may not be exceptionally full, but its berry fruit, violets and tobacco are charming. An acidic zing provides a good foil to full structure and streamlined tannins. The Langhe Nebbiolo is a classic for the variety. Quartetto, from nebbiolo, barbera, merlot and cabernet, unleashes a wondrous array of rich fruit, offset by grassy notes and sweetish spice that progress into a silky, smooth palate. Floral subtlety and unashamed opulence are the hallmarks of the Langhe Bianco Bussiador.

MONFORTE D'ALBA (CN)

★ GIACOMO CONTERNO
LOC. ORNATI, 2
12065 MONFORTE D'ALBA (CN)
TEL. 017378221

The major changes we discussed last year are now complete. Freisa and dolcetto are gone, to make way for more plantings of nebbiolo and barbera. The Conterno family is now concentrating its attention, with renewed enthusiasm and its customary attention to detail, on the wines which have made their area synonymous with quality, that wines which have written the history of Barolo. The Monfortino Riserva '96 is again up to expectations. Its clear garnet ushers in a stupendous breadth of richly faceted aromas, opening out into dried rose petals, morello cherry, cocoa powder, leather, liquorice, and sweet pipe tobacco. In the mouth, it builds powerfully, with good alcohol and polished tannins keeping pace, to unfurl the length you rightly expect. The Barolo Cascina Francia '99 shows a brooding garnet. The nose seems unresponsive, but then gradually unwinds into fragrances of violets and redcurrants over cherry preserve and liquorice. An alcohol-rich roundness and sweet, dense tannins temper stunning extractive power that pushes through to a lengthy finale. The Barbera d'Alba '01 is dark ruby shot with purple. The attack is rich and warm, progressing with good balance and remarkable brightness from a rich vein of acidity. The nose is still a bit muddled, but promises to develop mown hay and sour cherry.

● Barolo Gran Bussia Ris. '97	𝟀𝟀	8
● Barolo Colonnello '99	𝟀𝟀	8
○ Langhe Bianco Bussiador '00	𝟀𝟀	6
● Langhe Nebbiolo Favot '00	𝟀𝟀	7
● Langhe Rosso Quartetto '00	𝟀𝟀	6
● Barolo Bussia '99	𝟀𝟀	7
● Barolo Cicala '99	𝟀𝟀	8
● Barolo Gran Bussia Ris. '82	𝟀𝟀𝟀	8
● Barolo Gran Bussia Ris. '88	𝟀𝟀𝟀	8
● Barolo Gran Bussia Ris. '89	𝟀𝟀𝟀	8
● Barolo Gran Bussia Ris. '90	𝟀𝟀𝟀	8
● Barolo Vigna del Colonnello '90	𝟀𝟀𝟀	8
● Barolo Gran Bussia Ris. '95	𝟀𝟀𝟀	8
● Barolo Colonnello '97	𝟀𝟀	8
● Barolo Gran Bussia Ris. '96	𝟀𝟀	8

● Barolo Monfortino Ris. '96	𝟀𝟀	8
● Barolo Cascina Francia '99	𝟀𝟀	8
● Barbera d'Alba '01	𝟀𝟀	5
● Barolo Monfortino Ris. '82	𝟀𝟀𝟀	8
● Barolo Cascina Francia '85	𝟀𝟀𝟀	8
● Barolo Monfortino Ris. '85	𝟀𝟀𝟀	8
● Barolo Cascina Francia '87	𝟀𝟀𝟀	8
● Barolo Monfortino Ris. '87	𝟀𝟀𝟀	8
● Barolo Monfortino Ris. '88	𝟀𝟀𝟀	8
● Barolo Cascina Francia '89	𝟀𝟀𝟀	8
● Barolo Cascina Francia '90	𝟀𝟀𝟀	8
● Barolo Monfortino Ris. '90	𝟀𝟀𝟀	8
● Barolo Cascina Francia '97	𝟀𝟀𝟀	8
● Barolo Monfortino Ris. '95	𝟀𝟀	8
● Barolo Cascina Francia '98	𝟀𝟀	8

MONFORTE D'ALBA (CN)

Paolo Conterno
via Ginestra, 34
12065 Monforte d'Alba (CN)
tel. 017378415
E-mail: ginestra@paoloconterno.com

The winery run by Giorgio Conterno, assisted by his parents and his sister Marisa, embraces seven hectares under vine in the prestigious Ginestra vineyard at Monforte. The production of over 50,000 bottles is dedicated to Dolcetto, Barbera and Barolo. The wines reflect qualities that spring from those first-rate plots, partnering complexity and longevity with exemplary balance and finesse. And, of course, they benefit in no little degree from Beppe Caviola's consultancy. The wine that enthused us most this year is the Barolo Ginestra '99, with a run of fully 18,000 bottles. It exhibits a light, orange-rimmed ruby and a captivating bouquet laden with mint, medicinal herbs and berry fruit. Well-gauged acidity complements sinewy power in the mouth, giving this champion generous staying power for years to come. Excellent now, it will bestow greater delights down the road. We cannot express a judgement on the Barolo Ginestra Riserva '98, since by law it can be released only in January 2004. Unofficial tastings predict a great Barolo worthy of a superior vineyard. Dark ruby and an intriguing nose open the Barbera d'Alba '01. The palate beautifully mirrors the bouquet's ripe red berry underpinned by spice and vanilla, and the mouth is refreshed throughout by a good tang of acidity. Impressive, too, is the fruit-centred Dolcetto d'Alba '02, a clean, delicious wine that is ready to uncork.

MONFORTE D'ALBA (CN)

★ Conterno Fantino
via Ginestra, 1
12065 Monforte d'Alba (CN)
tel. 017378204
E-mail: info@conternofantino.it

Giulio Fantino and Claudio Conterno decided to put off for a year the release of their Langhe Rosso Monprà '01, so next year's Guide will be examining it. Their prudent move will allow us to appreciate better the qualities of one of the Langhe's most intriguing blends. The Barolo Ginestra '99 fills in the gap nicely since it had no trouble in earning Three Glasses again. A ruby hue tending to garnet announces a momentarily hesitant nose, which quickly turns gorgeously expressive, foregrounding fruit and floral notes over inviting scents of cherry and roses, tobacco and liquorice. The wine progresses with utter self-confidence, its sweet, silky tannins complementing the firmest of structures and gracing an impressive finish. The Barolo Vigna del Gris holds its own in the contest with the Ginestra. The aromas come tumbling out, rich with mulberry and redcurrant, and generously dusted with notes of cocoa. A lovely combination of balance and finesse delights the palate. The Barolo Parussi is sourced from a vineyard in the lower section of Castiglione Falletto. Slightly lighter in body that the others, it knows how to deliver a perfumed nose of fruit, floral and balsamic fragrances. There's always a bit of barrique protruding from a young Chardonnay Bastia. This year's wine will need some time to integrate toasty oak and vanilla with Bastia's typical ripe peach and apple. The Barbera Vignota and the Dolcetto Bricco Bastia from the unfortunate 2002 harvest are showing lighter than in previous versions, but are drinking beautifully right now.

● Barolo Ginestra '99	♟♟	8
● Barbera d'Alba Ginestra '01	♟♟	5
● Dolcetto d'Alba Ginestra '02	♟	4
● Barolo Ginestra Ris. '93	♟♟	8
● Barolo Ginestra '95	♟♟	8
● Barolo Ginestra '96	♟♟	8
● Barolo Ginestra Ris. '96	♟♟	8
● Barolo Ginestra '97	♟♟	8
● Barolo Ginestra Ris. '97	♟♟	8
● Barolo Ginestra '98	♟♟	8

● Barolo Sorì Ginestra '99	♟♟♟	8
● Barolo Vigna del Gris '99	♟♟	8
○ Langhe Chardonnay Bastia '01	♟♟	5
● Barolo Parussi '99	♟♟	8
● Barbera d'Alba Vignota '02	♟	4
● Dolcetto d'Alba Bricco Bastia '02	♟	4
● Barolo Sorì Ginestra '90	♟♟♟	8
● Barolo Sorì Ginestra '91	♟♟♟	8
● Monprà '94	♟♟♟	8
● Langhe Rosso Monprà '95	♟♟♟	8
● Barolo Vigna del Gris '96	♟♟♟	8
● Langhe Rosso Monprà '97	♟♟♟	8
● Langhe Rosso Monprà '98	♟♟♟	8
● Barolo Vigna del Gris '97	♟♟♟	8
● Barolo Sorì Ginestra '98	♟♟♟	8

MONFORTE D'ALBA (CN)

MONFORTE D'ALBA (CN)

ALESSANDRO E GIAN NATALE FANTINO
VIA G. SILVANO, 18
12065 MONFORTE D'ALBA (CN)
TEL. 017378253

ATTILIO GHISOLFI
LOC. BUSSIA, 27
12065 MONFORTE D'ALBA (CN)
TEL. 017378345

The cellar of the brothers Alessandro and Gian Natale Fantino is emblematic of the grower-producer world throughout the Langhe. A small facility, strictly family-run, it produces just a few, carefully groomed wines in modest numbers (about 40,000 units). Their estate vineyards cover some eight hectares, centred on the outstanding Vigna dei Dardi cru in the hamlet of Bussia. The Fantino line generally stays mainstream, but they unveiled a few new labels this year, all of which are interesting. The first is a Langhe Rosso '01, its youth showing slightly green in the nose and rough on the palate. It's a bit gangly yet in the balance, but it shows sound, full character. The loveliest surprise, however, is the Barolo Riserva Vigna dei Dardi '97. Rarely does a wine present such elegance and a wonderfully lean structure. From the rich depth of the nose unfold scents of leather, tobacco and roast coffee, lifted by delicious blackberry fruit. The polished, voluptuous mouth opens unhesitatingly, echoing the fragrances that condition a long, impeccably balanced finale. The Barolo '99 is excellent on all fronts, and eschews muscularity for finesse and full fruit. The Nepas, a nebbiolo passito, grows ever more intriguing. Unusual notes of dried figs mark both nose and palate, while chewy tannins are well in evidence. Both the complex, nicely rounded Barbera and the zesty, easy drinking Dolcetto are very nice.

Once again, Alta Bussia emerges as one of the Langhe's most outstanding reds, and for the third year in a row earns Three Glasses. It's a 70-30 barbera and nebbiolo blend that weaves a touch of barrique vanilla and notes of roses and cocoa powder into fruity and balsamic aromas. The acidity of the barbera provides a good foil to the nebbiolo's generous tannic charge, while a nice level of alcohol warms the palate. The finish seems endless. Superb, too, is the Barolo Bricco Visette '99, impressing on every level. Dark ruby to the eye, it has a breadth of captivating aromas ranging through red berry fruit, coffee and medicinal herbs. The classic structure of the palate is enfolded by velvet-smooth tannins, finally tapering out into liquorice and leather. A superlative performer, in 13,000 bottles, it comes from a lesser-known vineyard that is now receiving proper treatment from Ghisolfi. We couldn't taste the Langhe Rosso Carlin '01, whose release has been pushed to next year to allow more adequate maturation, nor the Dolcetto, which will no longer be produced, but we were very happy with the Barbera Vigna Lisi '01. The darkest of reds precedes a voluptuous suite of fragrances built on toast and spice then the tannins, acidity, and alcohol dance delightfully on this boldly structured palate. Lastly, we have the second release of Pinay, a fascinating red from pinot noir. Its tannins prove its rootedness in the Langhe, while its game and strawberry notes are classic pinot noir.

●	Barolo Vigna dei Dardi Ris. '97	♟♟	7
●	Nepas Rosso '00	♟♟	6
●	Barbera d'Alba Vigna dei Dardi '01	♟♟	4*
●	Barolo Vigna dei Dardi '99	♟♟	6
●	Dolcetto d'Alba '01	♟	4
●	Langhe Rosso Rosso dei Dardi '01	♟	5
●	Barolo Vigna dei Dardi '93	♟♟	6
●	Barolo Vigna dei Dardi '95	♟♟	6
●	Barolo Vigna dei Dardi '96	♟♟	6
●	Barolo Vigna dei Dardi '97	♟♟	6
●	Barolo Vigna dei Dardi '98	♟♟	6
●	Nepas Rosso '99	♟♟	6

●	Langhe Rosso Alta Bussia '01	♟♟♟	6
●	Barolo Bricco Visette '99	♟♟	7
●	Barbera d'Alba Vigna Lisi '01	♟♟	5
●	Langhe Rosso Pinay '01	♟♟	4
●	Langhe Rosso Alta Bussia '99	♟♟♟	5
●	Langhe Rosso Alta Bussia '00	♟♟♟	5
●	Barolo Bricco Visette '96	♟♟	7
●	Barbera d'Alba Vigna Lisi '98	♟♟	5
●	Barolo Bricco Visette '97	♟♟	7
●	Barbera d'Alba Vigna Lisi '00	♟♟	5
●	Barolo Bricco Visette '98	♟♟	7

MONFORTE D'ALBA (CN)

ELIO GRASSO
LOC. GINESTRA, 40
12065 MONFORTE D'ALBA (CN)
TEL. 017378491
E-MAIL: elio.grasso@isiline.it

The Barolo Vigna Chiniera '99 encores last year's success. Three Glasses were awarded with no quibbling. This champion hardly puts in the shade, though, the other wines produced by this family enterprise, where owner Elio Grasso is capably seconded by his wife Marina and son Gianluca. Their uniquely well-sited estate vineyards allow them to produce consistently fine examples of the classic Langhe wines. Let's consider first the Vigna Chiniera, a Barolo that marries the modern and the traditional. A wine bursting with rich, seductive fragrances of balsam, fruit, and spices that continue seamlessly onto the palate, it boasts a dense complement of sweet tannins underpinning its exemplary structure. In contrast, the Barolo Vigna Casa Maté comes off a bit leaner and tighter. Its Ginestra vineyard terroir has given it massiveness and complex sensory nuances that more cellar time will surely unfold to their fullest. The modernist face of this winery is reflected in the Barolo Runcot. A 30-month stay in new barriques has rendered it pliant and glossy, and vanilla and toasty fragrances interweave nicely with notes of fruit and flowers. Barbera Vigna Martina lived up to our expectations with its more than satisfactory performance this year. Dark, purplish ruby introduces a captivating nose focused on spices and raspberry, then a succulent palate veined with a zesty acidity. No Chardonnay Educato '02 was produced. In its place we have a lovely varietal Chardonnay fermented in steel. The Dolcetto and the Nebbiolo from 2002 both achieve better than satisfactory results.

● Barolo Gavarini Vigna Chiniera '99	𝟁𝟁𝟁	8
● Barolo Runcot '98	𝟁𝟁	8
● Barolo Ginestra Vigna Casa Maté '99	𝟁𝟁	8
● Barbera d'Alba Vigna Martina '00	𝟁𝟁	5
● Dolcetto d'Alba '02	𝟁	4
○ Langhe Chardonnay '02	𝟁	4
● Langhe Nebbiolo Gavarini '02	𝟁	4
● Barolo Gavarini Vigna Chiniera '89	𝟐𝟐𝟐	8
● Barolo Ginestra Vigna Casa Maté '90	𝟐𝟐𝟐	8
● Barolo Ginestra Vigna Casa Maté '93	𝟐𝟐𝟐	8
● Barolo Runcot '96	𝟐𝟐𝟐	8
● Barolo Gavarini Vigna Chiniera '98	𝟐𝟐𝟐	8

MONFORTE D'ALBA (CN)

GIOVANNI MANZONE
VIA CASTELLETTO, 9
12065 MONFORTE D'ALBA (CN)
TEL. 017378114
E-MAIL: manzone.giovanni@tiscalinet.it

Giovanni Manzone's Barolo Gramolere Bricat '99 missed Three Glasses by a fraction. It, and quite a number of other striking wines, speak eloquently of how seriously and determinedly Manzone takes his job. Among other things, he is trying to gain IGT or DOC classification for his white wine from the rossese grape variety. The Bricat, produced in 5,000 bottles, admirably interprets the nebbiolo hallmarks of red berries, rose petals, leather and tobacco. The palate opens out into racy tannins and a confident structure. Equally fine is the Barolo Gramolere '99, with its spicy perfumes and fairly lean palate. The Rosserto is now back, and to great effect. Made from the white grape variant of rossese, it is much more than a curiosity. A brilliant yellow gold in colour, it releases pungent orange peel and citron, then offers good fullness on the palate and well-judged acidity, as well as a pleasingly bitterish finish. We preferred La Serra '00 of the two Barberas. Spicy and slightly smoky notes lend a more than decent complexity to its crisp fruit. The standard-label Barbera '01 offers a good array of varietal characteristics. Some of the Nebbiolo '02 was matured in steel, some in tonneaux. The palate opens with a vigorous attack and echoes nicely the nose's scents of roses and liquorice. The Dolcetto is a well-made wine from a difficult vintage.

● Barolo Gramolere Bricat '99	𝟁𝟁	7
● Barbera d'Alba La Serra '00	𝟁𝟁	5
○ Rosserto Bianco '01	𝟁𝟁	5
● Langhe Nebbiolo il Crutin '02	𝟁𝟁	5
● Barolo Gramolere '99	𝟁𝟁	7
● Barbera d'Alba '01	𝟁	4
● Dolcetto d'Alba '02	𝟁	3
● Barolo Gramolere Ris. '95	𝟐𝟐	8
● Barolo Gramolere Bricat '96	𝟐𝟐	7
● Barolo Gramolere Ris. '96	𝟐𝟐	8
● Barolo Gramolere Bricat '97	𝟐𝟐	7
● Langhe Rosso Tris '98	𝟐𝟐	5
● Barolo Gramolere Ris. '97	𝟐𝟐	8
● Barolo Gramolere Bricat '98	𝟐𝟐	7

MONFORTE D'ALBA (CN)

MONFORTE D'ALBA (CN)

MONTI
FRAZ. CAMIE
LOC. SAN SEBASTIANO, 39
12065 MONFORTE D'ALBA (CN)
TEL. 017378391
E-MAIL: wine@paolomonti.com

ARMANDO PARUSSO
LOC. BUSSIA, 55
12065 MONFORTE D'ALBA (CN)
TEL. 017378257

Pier Paolo Monti, with winemaker Robert Gerbino at his side, has about ten hectares of vineyard in various areas of the municipality of Monforte, giving him an average annual production of 33,000 bottles. He has both native varieties, barbera and nebbiolo, as well the internationals, chardonnay, riesling renano, cabernet sauvignon and merlot. This year he debuts Barolo Monti, sourced from the prestigious Bussia vineyard. And it made a wonderful first appearance: Bussia's imprint is well in evidence in the appealing aromatics bursting with spice and flowers. Dense, glossy tannins accompany a firm attack, and it signs off with a trail of chocolate and cocoa powder. The Barbera d'Alba is the cellar's standard-bearer and put on a good show again this year. A dark ruby verging on purple introduces fragrances built on fruit and spice, with smoky notes throughout. The variety's classic acidity melds well with a gorgeous structure. The Langhe L'Aura '02 has 70 per cent chardonnay, fermented and matured in small oak, and 30 per cent steel-matured riesling renano. A greenish-tinged deep yellow, it offers mineral and citrus on the nose, and a perfect complement of acidity augurs well for cellaring. The Dossi Rossi '01, a 40-40-20 mix of cabernet, merlot and nebbiolo, will need some time to meld the characteristics of the three varieties. Out in front at the moment are the nebbiolo's sturdy tannins, offset with some lovely notes of red berries and vanilla.

The range of wines offered by Marco and Tiziana Parusso stands out as one of the most impressive in the entire Langhe. It is not simply a question of numbers, although these are in fact on the rise, indicating a winery in a strong growth phase. It is rather the overall level of their quality that amazes. Nor can Parusso ever be charged with being in a rut, since every year they present us with new creations that tickle our fancy. We sometimes wonder where exactly this winery, one of the perennial stars of the Piedmont wine scene, is heading. We'll open with the new wines, but with a preliminary remark on important absentees. Pushed back to next year is the renowned Barbera d'Alba Superiore, while the two Langhe Bricco Rovellas, Bianco and Rosso, will appear only in 2005. In the meantime, we enjoyed an interesting Langhe Bianco '02, a monovarietal sauvignon blanc, and a good, varietal Langhe Nebbiolo with judiciously administered tannins. The Barbera d'Asti slot is well represented by Ornati. Dark and intense, it releases crisp aromas of freshly picked berries and spices. The oak is well hidden, giving full rein to luscious flavours that mirror the bouquet, and to a texture lifted by good acidity. Among the many Barolos, the Vigna Munie is outstanding. Austere, massive, with tannins that are pronounced but polished, it explodes with fruit, liquorice, and mint. Just as superb is the Mariondino, which flaunts its usual elegance and depth, and the Vigna Rocche is suppleness and seduction personified. Finally, the Vigna Fiurin and the Piccole Vigne complete the line-up.

●	Barolo Bussia '99	�	8
●	Barbera d'Alba '01	♥♥	6
●	Langhe Rosso Dossi Rossi '01	♥♥	6
○	Langhe Bianco L'Aura '02	♥♥	5
●	Barbera d'Alba '97	♥♥	5
○	Langhe Bianco L'Aura '00	♥♥	5
●	Barbera d'Alba '99	♥♥	5
●	Langhe Rosso Dossi Rossi '99	♥♥	6
○	Langhe Bianco L'Aura '01	♥♥	5

●	Barolo Bussia Vigna Munie '99	♥♥♥	8
●	Barolo Bussia Vigna Rocche '99	♥♥	8
●	Barolo Mariondino '99	♥♥	8
●	Barbera d'Alba Ornati '01	♥♥	5
●	Langhe Nebbiolo '01	♥♥	5
○	Langhe Bianco '02	♥♥	4
●	Barolo Bussia Vigna Fiurin '99	♥♥	8
●	Barolo Piccole Vigne '99	♥♥	7
●	Dolcetto d'Alba Piani Noci '01	♥	4
●	Barolo Bussia Vigna Munie '96	♥♥♥	8
●	Langhe Rosso Bricco Rovella '96	♥♥♥	6
●	Barolo Bussia Vigna Munie '97	♥♥♥	8
●	Barbera d'Alba Sup. '00	♥♥♥	6
●	Barolo Bussia Vigna Munie '98	♥♥	8
●	Barolo Bussia Vigna Rocche '98	♥♥	8

MONFORTE D'ALBA (CN)

FERDINANDO PRINCIPIANO
VIA ALBA, 19
12065 MONFORTE D'ALBA (CN)
TEL. 0173787158

The purchase of two and a half more hectares in the Boscareto vineyard brings to ten the area under vine of the winery run by young Ferdinando Principiano with the help of his father Americo and advice from the talented Beppe Caviola. After several years of restructuring the facilities, full attention can now shift to managing the vineyards and producing outstanding wines. Since Ferdinando decided not to bottle a Dolcetto d'Alba from '02, an unfavourable growing year, production reached only 20,000 bottles, divided among Barbera d'Alba, and the two Barolos, Boscareto and Le Coste. The Barbera La Romualda '01 offers a dark ruby colour and rich aromas ranging through berries, spices, cocoa powder and vanilla, all of which continue on the palate. Harmony reigns among acidity, tannins and an impressive structure, with perceptible, but not excessive, oak. The Barolo Le Coste is from Monforte. A stay in once-used barrels has softened the tannins to real silkiness and captivating notes of fruit, flowers, and balsam make for delicious drinking near term, but this is one for cellaring as well. The Boscareto, from plots in Serralunga, shows that vineyard's hallmark power and complexity. This is an impressively structured Barolo that opens out gradually into plum, tobacco, leather and chocolate, then progresses decisively in the mouth, over a firm foundation of energetic tannins and admirable acidity.

MONFORTE D'ALBA (CN)

PODERE ROCCHE DEI MANZONI
LOC. MANZONI SOPRANI, 3
12065 MONFORTE D'ALBA (CN)
TEL. 017378421
E-MAIL: info@rocchedeimanzoni.it

Construction work at Podere Rocche dei Manzoni seems to be winding up. Still, knowing how Valentino Migliorini operates, we wouldn't be surprised in the least to see him begin some new project to improve his already ambitious facility on the outskirts of Monforte. The most recent initiative, we note, is the "temple," complete with columns and a dome, for the display of the estate's best offerings. In synchrony with these additions is the new mix of wines offered this year for our tasting. Wanting his classic wines to mature further, Valentino held back the three Langhe products, Quatr Nas, Bricco Manzoni and Pinònero, as well as the Brut Zero. However, we did taste two excellent 2000 Barberas, held back last year for similar reasons. We liked the Sorito Mosconi for its supple roundness, while the La Cresta impresses with clean, yet rich fruit and a sinewy vein of crisp acidity. But it's the Barolos that stand out this year at Rocche dei Manzoni. We tasted three crus, and found three thoroughbreds. The Big 'd Big is back big time, amazing us the way it used to in the late 1980s. Here's a wine that puts finesse before power, lengthy and complex, managing to be austere yet sumptuous. Leather and tobacco leaf greet the nose, then the palate is seductive elegance personified. Three resounding Glasses. Its companions were nearly as exciting. The lean, tannic Vigna Cappella di Santo Stefano is especially well done. Of the other wines, the Chardonnay is admirable and the Brut Riserva Elena well made.

● Barolo Boscareto '99		ΨΨ	8
● Barbera d'Alba La Romualda '01		ΨΨ	5
● Barolo Le Coste '99		ΨΨ	8
● Barolo Boscareto '93		ΨΨΨ	8
● Barolo Boscareto '97		ΨΨ	8
● Barbera d'Alba La Romualda '98		ΨΨ	6
● Barbera d'Alba La Romualda '00		ΨΨ	5
● Dolcetto d'Alba S. Anna '01		ΨΨ	4
● Barolo Boscareto '98		ΨΨ	8
● Barolo Le Coste '98		ΨΨ	8

● Barolo Vigna Big 'd Big '99		ΨΨΨ	8
● Barolo			
Vigna Cappella di S. Stefano '99		ΨΨ	8
● Barbera d'Alba Sorito Mosconi '00		ΨΨ	6
● Barbera d'Alba			
Vigna La Cresta '00		ΨΨ	6
○ Langhe Chardonnay L'Angelica '00		ΨΨ	6
● Barolo Vigna d'la Roul '99		ΨΨ	8
○ Valentino Brut Ris. Elena '99		Ψ	5
● Barolo Vigna Big Ris. '89		ΨΨΨ	8
● Barolo Vigna d'la Roul Ris. '90		ΨΨΨ	8
● Barolo			
Vigna Cappella di S. Stefano '96		ΨΨΨ	8
● Langhe Rosso Quatr Nas '96		ΨΨΨ	8
● Langhe Rosso Quatr Nas '99		ΨΨΨ	7

MONFORTE D'ALBA (CN)

FLAVIO RODDOLO
FRAZ. BRICCO APPIANI
LOC. SANT'ANNA, 5
12065 MONFORTE D'ALBA (CN)
TEL. 017378535

Flavio Roddolo is one of those characters out of the spotlight who become, almost inevitably, main actors marked by unique charisma and fascination. Here is a traditional Langhe grower, perhaps one of the few left, who was able to adapt to a changing world both spiritually and mentally, while holding fast to his philosophy of a life linked to the earth and to hard work. It is with humility and deep satisfaction, hallmarks of the unpretentious, that Flavio has won the recognition his wines are now receiving. Visiting his cellar on the sun-kissed Monforte hills can bring you back into touch with the world, and with yourself. Turning to the wines, once again Bricco Appiani stands out as superb. Piedmont's best Cabernet Sauvignon doesn't put a foot wrong. It exploits to the hilt the favourable 2000 harvest to offer an amazing treasure of austerity, warmth, and depth. The nose is varietal, a solid herbaceous vein foregrounded by close-woven fragrances of balsam, spice, and wet earth. The soft attack is nicely matched by a sinewy complement of acids and tannins that leads back to the terroir of which this wine, despite some hints to the contrary, is a true offspring. The Barolo Ravera is equally compelling. Dense garnet ruby introduces rich fruit in the mouth, and an impressive range of plum, bramble and liquorice aromas. The palate is inviting and elegant, reprising the rich bouquet and demonstrating admirable harmony. The remaining wines, Nebbiolo, Barbera, and Dolcetto d'Alba, performed extremely well.

MONFORTE D'ALBA (CN)

RUGGERI CORSINI
LOC. BUSSIA CORSINI, 106
12065 MONFORTE D'ALBA (CN)
TEL. 017378625
E-MAIL: podereruggericorsini@libero.it

Just before you enter Monforte, a dirt road heads down into an out of the way hollow where you find the main facilities of the husband and wife team of Loredana Addari and Nicola Argamante. Some years ago, they purchased an old farm building and then built a new, up-to-date cellar nearby, at the same time acquiring adjacent vineyards on favourably aspected sections of the hill. This has proved effective way of employing their time and resources, so Loredana and Nicola, assisted in the cellar by Lorenzo Addari, can also work as agronomists on the estate's numerous projects. This year, all their wines showed well. The Barbera Armujan is, of course, still their flagship. Dense and dark, it unfolds well-defined scents of blackberry fruit, forest floor and minerals. These continue nicely onto a palate that is at once chewy, tangy and dry. The finish is lengthy, with a light lift of acidity. The 19999 Barolo is showing better and more structured than the 1998. It could still offer more complexity on the nose, but the remainder is distinctly mouthfilling, with copious tannins and good overall balance. The Nebbiolo displays the generous fruit of the variety, then soft, balanced complexity in the mouth. Flying in the face of a difficult 2002, both the Barbera and the Dolcetto are well made and drinking beautifully.

● Bricco Appiani '00	🍷🍷	6
● Barolo Ravera '99	🍷🍷	6
● Barbera d'Alba Sup. '00	🍷🍷	5
● Nebbiolo d'Alba '00	🍷🍷	5
● Dolcetto d'Alba Sup. '01	🍷🍷	4*
● Barolo Ravera '97	🍷🍷🍷	6
● Bricco Appiani '99	🍷🍷🍷	6
● Barolo '96	🍷🍷	6
● Bricco Appiani '97	🍷🍷	6
● Bricco Appiani '98	🍷🍷	6
● Nebbiolo d'Alba '99	🍷🍷	5

● Barbera d'Alba Sup. Armujan '01	🍷🍷	5
● Barolo Corsini '99	🍷🍷	6
● Langhe Nebbiolo '01	🍷	4
● Barbera d'Alba '02	🍷	4
● Dolcetto d'Alba '02	🍷	3
● Barbera d'Alba Sup. Armujan '00	🍷🍷	5
● Barolo Corsini '98	🍷🍷	6

MONFORTE D'ALBA (CN)

F.LLI SEGHESIO
LOC. CASTELLETTO, 19
12065 MONFORTE D'ALBA (CN)
TEL. 017378108

You have to give Aldo and Riccardo Seghesio their due as two of the finest growers in Monforte. Of course, it's true that owning a plot in a vineyard as renowned and well sited as Castelletto can considerably facilitate making outstanding wines. But good terroir can only go so far, and the style and quality of their wines testify even more to the hand of the winemaker, to mastery of technique, and to a refusal to rest on one's laurels. Last year, we went into raptures over the Barbera Vigneto della Chiesa '00. We tasted the following vintage and it echoes those results. Here's a wine with austerity but good alcoholic warmth, given well-gauged acidity and judicious oak. Its complexity on the nose is admirably matched by a stately, full-flavoured progression in the mouth. It's a great performer, and overshadowed only slightly by the plaudits awarded to the Barolo Vigneto La Villa. Frankly, we had not tasted such a stunner since the '91, so the '99 completes a decade of improvements in quality. A dense ruby ushers in complex, multi-faceted aromas luxuriating in notes of spice and earth, layered over forest floor, liquorice and pencil lead. A seductive, warm palate features well-integrated oak tannins, while the nose's complex fruitiness returns to infuse a long, rich finish. The Langhe Bouquet, a nebbiolo, cabernet, and merlot blend, is quite effective. It offers pronounced varietal tones of fresh grass and fruit, then the mouth builds a well-structured and nicely tannic performance of admirable balance. The 2002 Barbera and Dolcetto are well made and lively.

MONLEALE (AL)

RENATO BOVERI
VIA XXV APRILE, 1
15059 MONLEALE (AL)
TEL. 013180560

The results this year are most impressive for the Monleale winery run by 81-year-old Renato Boveri with the help of his sons Fausto and Danilo. All the wines we tasted earned very creditable scores, and if no absolute champion emerged to claim the highest honour, the Monleale came extremely close. The reds were the strongest contenders, starting with that Monleale '99. A powerful, spice-laden nose redolent of plum and cocoa powder follows an intense ruby hue. The palate is a charmer, richly tannic and bursting with long-lingering fruit. The second Barbera, the Sant'Ambrogio, performed well, with its attractive hints of purple, and scents running to spices and plum jam. Two comfortable Glasses went to the Dolcetto Madai!, which spent 24 months in barrique. Further bottle ageing has pushed the wood into the background, and allows room for the wild berries, redcurrant and blackberry in particular, to emerge and shine. The Cereta, too, is dolcetto-based. Mineral and chalky tones keep the nose somewhat in check, but with aeration the wine opens up beautifully, displaying rich floral notes and wild berries. The two cortese-based whites, the Cappelletta and the Munprò, don't rise quite to the level of the reds, but they are nonetheless impressive. The Cappelletta is straightforward and fruity, and the Munprò, a cask-conditioned wine, is more complex.

● Barolo Vigneto La Villa '99	▼▼▼	8
● Barbera d'Alba Vigneto della Chiesa '01	▼	6
● Langhe Rosso Bouquet '01	▼▼	6
● Barbera d'Alba '02	▼	4
● Dolcetto d'Alba Vigneto della Chiesa '02	▼	4
● Barolo Vigneto La Villa '91	▼▼▼	7
● Barbera d'Alba Vigneto della Chiesa '97	▼▼▼	5
● Barbera d'Alba Vigneto della Chiesa '00	▼▼▼	5
● Barbera d'Alba Vigneto della Chiesa '99	▼▼	6
● Barolo Vigneto La Villa '98	▼▼	7

● Colli Tortonesi Barbera Monleale '99	▼▼	5
● Colli Tortonesi Barbera S. Ambrogio '01	▼▼	4
● Colli Tortonesi Rosso Madai! '99	▼▼	5
○ Colli Tortonesi Cortese Munprò '00	▼	5
● Colli Tortonesi Rosso La Cereta '01	▼	4
○ Colli Tortonesi Cortese Cappelletta '02	▼	4
○ Colli Tortonesi Cortese Munprò '97	▼▼	5
● Colli Tortonesi Barbera Monleale '98	▼▼	5

MONLEALE (AL)

VIGNETI MASSA
P.ZZA G. CAPSONI, 10
15059 MONLEALE (AL)
TEL. 013180302

Timorasso is famous, and the media scrutiny of recent years has pushed into international stardom this variety re-introduced by Walter Massa. But Walter's winemaking principles and his love for the land are hardly faddish. His values, passion and dedication are deep rooted. The wines mirror their creator, with no tricks and no compromises, and are eloquent expressions of terroir and season. His Vigna del Gattopardo is new, from a timorasso vineyard dedicated to recently deceased Beppe Zerbino, a journalist and friend. We'll taste its fruits in a few years but for now, we have a great Bigolla '00. A deep-ruby Barbera, with a lean, reticent nose that opens slowly into fruit, spice, and mineral tones, it has great balance, boasting a lush, savoury palate. It is crisp and fruity, but offers good alcoholic warmth and finishes long. The Barbera Cerreta rates high. Dark and opaque, it releases cherries and ripe plum over notes of game and spice. Full, rich, and warm on the palate, it shows exemplary structure and the finish, predictably, is endless. The Monleale also won Two Glasses, showing dark ruby and unfolding a sequence of ripe red berries, roses and spice notes. The mouth is warm and rich with light tannins carrying over into a pleasantly bitterish finish. Grassy and minerally notes open the timorasso-based Costa del Vento, which has a full-bodied warm ripeness supported by crisp acidity, making this a white with a great future. One Glass goes to the cortese-based Casareggio, with pear, apple and spring flower aromas and a crisp, enjoyably vivacious style.

MONTÀ (CN)

GIOVANNI ALMONDO
VIA SAN ROCCO, 26
12046 MONTÀ (CN)
TEL. 0173975256
E-MAIL: almondo@giovannialmondo.com

Domenico Almondo has set quite a pace for his cellar. Last year, this friendly and ever helpful mayor-producer – he occupies Montà's top post – amazed our panel with a glorious vintage of his most impressive red, the Roero Bric Valdiana. Nor was that a fluke, for Domenico brought out several great bottles again this time. There were not many, just his core wines, but all extremely well made, among them that Bric Valdiana icon. The Almondo vineyards have grown to more than ten hectares, but the staff, just family, remains the same: Domenico, his wife Antonella, and his parents Giovanni and Teresina. No one should tinker with a winning team, of course, but Almondo's wines don't so much win – this isn't a competition, after all – as impress with their uncompromising quality. But back to the Bric Valdiana. The '01 is again superb, a ruby garnet hue introducing a rich nose layered with spices and wild berries. Huge and nicely tannic, it shows amazing balance. A champion, then, but one which finds a worthy sparring partner in this year's standard-label Roero. On its Guide debut, and it already surprised us with a great nose and perfection of style. Among the other reds, the very good Barbera has suppleness and balance as its strong cards. As for the whites, the Arneis Bricco delle Ciliegie is a fine example of the variety. The Vigne Sparse is simple but succulent.

● Colli Tortonesi Rosso Bigolla '00	YY	7
○ Colli Tortonesi Bianco Costa del Vento '01	YY	7
● Colli Tortonesi Rosso Cerreta '00	YY	7
● Colli Tortonesi Rosso Monleale '00	YY	6
○ Colli Tortonesi Bianco Casareggio '02	Y	4
● Colli Tortonesi Rosso Bigolla '98	YYY	7
● Colli Tortonesi Rosso Cerreta '99	YY	7
● Colli Tortonesi Rosso Pertichetta '00	YY	6
○ Colli Tortonesi Bianco Costa del Vento '00	YY	7

● Roero Bric Valdiana '01	YYY	6
● Barbera d'Alba Valbianchera '01	YY	5
● Roero '01	YY	5
○ Roero Arneis Bricco delle Ciliegie '02	YY	5
○ Roero Arneis Vigne Sparse '02	Y	4
● Roero Bric Valdiana '00	YYY	6
● Roero Bric Valdiana '97	YY	6
● Roero Sup. Giovanni Almondo '97	YY	7
● Roero Bric Valdiana '98	YY	6
● Barbera d'Alba Valbianchera '99	YY	5
● Roero Bric Valdiana '99	YY	6
● Barbera d'Alba Valbianchera '00	YY	5

MONTÀ (CN)

MICHELE TALIANO
C.SO A. MANZONI, 24
12046 MONTÀ (CN)
TEL. 0173976512 - 0173976100
E-MAIL: taliano@libero.it

MONTEGROSSO D'ASTI (AT)

TENUTA LA MERIDIANA
VIA TANA BASSA, 5
14048 MONTEGROSSO D'ASTI (AT)
TEL. 0141956250 - 0141956172
E-MAIL: tenutalameridiana@tin.it

The small cellar run by Alberto and Ezio Taliano is among the Montà area wineries that have achieved success in recent years, quickly producing top quality results thanks to a well-thought out winemaking philosophy. The valuable assistance of their father, Michele, helps Alberto and Ezio to cover all the area's classic wine genres, plus a delightful Barbaresco sourced from a terrific vineyard in San Rocco Seno d'Elvio. The 2001 is a high achiever, offering intense ruby, then clear notes of berries, hazelnut and liquorice that blend artfully into a gorgeous nose. Supple texture and a seductive fatness make for an irresistible palate, with every moment developing in elegant proportion. But for now, it is Roero that provides the family's best results. The superlative Barbera Laboriosa, by now a benchmark for the variety, invites praise. The vibrant, astonishingly complex 2001 unleashes fragrances of berries and spice then seduces the taster with a synergy of crisp austerity and alcoholic warmth, pushing through to an endless, eloquently harmonious finish. The standard-label, too, is excellent, though of course a bit simpler. Back with the nebbiolos, we have the welcome release of the Roero Ròche dra Bòssora, held back last year for further maturation. The wait was worth it since the 2000 is superb. While modern in style, it bears the clear imprints of variety and terroir, and will improve over time. Finally, the Arneis is a good effort, and both the Langhe Nebbiolo and the Dolcetto are temptingly drinkable wines.

Giampiero Bianco produces about 60,000 bottles each year from about a dozen hectares of vineyards located mostly in Montegrosso, but also in Castelnuovo Calcea, Vinchio and Incisa Scapaccino. The wines tasted this year again revealed the steady improvement in quality of this winery. The Barbera Tra Terra e Cielo is the cellar's star. It shows rich ruby garnet, then unfolds an elegant blend of classic varietal fruit and delicate notes of balsam and spicy oak. Opening to voluptuous structure, it progresses crisp and clean into a lengthy, intensely savoury finale. The other two Barberas, Bricco Sereno and the simpler Le Gagie, also compel attention. The first offers a very intense hue and fragrances ranging from blackberry fruit to black pepper. Varietal notes dominate the palate and fully echo the richness of the bouquet. Le Gagie releases violets, fresh hay and wild berries over nuances of rhubarb, and is well structured and harmonious throughout. We also enjoyed the Rosso Rivaia, a nebbiolo, barbera and cabernet blend with deep colour and gorgeously inviting aromas of fruit and wild berries. A good cut of tannins complements the full body and it ends with a satisfying vibrancy. A well-deserved One Glass goes to the Grignolino Vignamaestra, and also to Puntet, from chardonnay, cortese and favorita. La Meridiana has been carving out a niche for itself these last few years with its determined drive towards quality. Its superb wines are winning it a place among the best wineries in Monferrato.

● Barbera d'Alba Laboriosa '01	♥♥	4*
● Barbaresco Ad Altiora '00	♥♥	6
● Roero Ròche dra Bòssora '00	♥♥	5
○ Roero Arneis Sernì '02	♥♥	4*
● Barbera d'Alba A Bon Rendre '02	♥	4
● Dolcetto d'Alba Ciabot Vigna '02	♥	4
● Langhe Nebbiolo Blagheur '02	♥	4
● Barbaresco Ad Altiora '98	♀♀	6
● Barbera d'Alba Laboriosa '99	♀♀	4
● Roero Ròche dra Bòssora '99	♀♀	4
● Barbera d'Alba Laboriosa '00	♀♀	4

● Barbera d'Asti Sup. Tra Terra e Cielo '00	♥♥	5
● Monferrato Rosso Rivaia '00	♥♥	5
● Barbera d'Asti Le Gagie '00	♥♥	4*
● Barbera d'Asti Sup. Bricco Sereno '00	♥♥	5
● Grignolino d'Asti Vignamaestra '02	♥	3
○ Monferrato Bianco Puntet '02	♥	3
● Barbera d'Asti Sup. Tra Terra e Cielo '98	♀♀	5
● Barbera d'Asti Sup. Bricco Sereno '99	♀♀	5
● Barbera d'Asti Sup. Tra Terra e Cielo '99	♀♀	5
● Monferrato Rosso Rivaia '99	♀♀	5

MONTELUPO ALBESE (CN) MONTEU ROERO (CN)

DESTEFANIS
VIA MORTIZZO, 8
12050 MONTELUPO ALBESE (CN)
TEL. 0173617189
E-MAIL:
marcodestefanis@marcodestefanis.com

ANGELO NEGRO & FIGLI
FRAZ. SANT'ANNA, 1
12040 MONTEU ROERO (CN)
TEL. 017390252
E-MAIL: negro@negroangelo.it

Marco Destefanis' winery is very much a family affair. His parents, Giuseppe and Rosangela, and his wife, Silvia, also work there, ably seconded by the talented Beppe Caviola. We learned this year that they leased two hectares of vines at Torretta, near Montelupo. The 2002 vintage was no less unfavourable in their section of Piedmont, so there will be no release of the Dolcetto Vigna Monia Bassa. But we were far from disappointed by the other wines we tasted. The Barbera d'Alba Superiore '01 was a real pleaser, presenting deep red flecked with light purple, followed by a nice herbaceous, floral bouquet. Entry on the palate is sweet but with good supporting acidity, and the finish is appealing. The Nebbiolo d'Alba '01, displaying brick red tones, opens out with aromas of cut hay, vanilla and berries. A beautiful rounded entry announces hazelnut and toasted almond notes, which continue seamlessly into the finish. The Dolcetto '02 performed very well indeed, especially on the blackberry and plum nose. The palate is slightly acidulous, but very nicely proportioned throughout. The straw-yellow Chardonnay '02 releases hints of banana and spring flowers. The acidity on the palate is nicely restrained and the finale is infused with almond.

At the Negro winery, work proceeds apace to provide this great Roero institution with a more up-to-date facility. Construction is pushing into last phase for the spectacular new premises. The already completed binning cellar merits a visit all on its own. On the wine front, we will soon see the release of the long-awaited Barbaresco sourced from the estate vineyards in Neive. Roero, too, has news: the Roero Prachiosso is to rest another year in bottle, so we will see the '01 next year. In its place, we tasted the standard-label Roero, with three years' maturation to its credit and it thoroughly convincing. In addition to the Barberas, all the nebbiolo wines took top points. This is a clear sign of self-confident expertise with both these varieties on the part of the family staff: Giovanni and Maria with their children Gabriele, Angelo, Manuela and Giuseppe. We note that production is still around 230,000 bottles and that the estate vineyards now total 54 hectares. The Roero Sudisfà is on top form. Fragrances of red berry, spice and liquorice blend beautifully into a voluptuous, expressive nose. Progressing vigorously, it expands into a succulent, well-proportioned mid palate and an appropriately long finish. The two Barbera d'Albas showed well. Bric Bertu in particular is impressive and admirably gauged, in fact a benchmark for the variety. The nicely rounded and richly faceted Gianat stood out among the whites. Impressive, too, is the Bric Millon, from bonarda and croatina.

● Barbera d'Alba Sup. '01	🍷🍷	4
● Nebbiolo d'Alba '01	🍷🍷	4
● Dolcetto d'Alba '02	🍷	3
○ Langhe Chardonnay '02	🍷	3
● Dolcetto d'Alba Vigna Monia Bassa '00	🍷🍷	4
● Nebbiolo d'Alba '00	🍷🍷	4
● Dolcetto d'Alba Vigna Monia Bassa '01	🍷🍷	4

● Roero Sup. Sodisfà '00	🍷🍷	6
● Barbera d'Alba Bric Bertu '01	🍷🍷	5
● Barbera d'Alba Nicolon '01	🍷🍷	4*
○ Roero Arneis Gianat '02	🍷🍷	5
○ Roero Arneis Perdaudin '02	🍷	4
○ Perdaudin Passito '00	🍷	6
● Roero '00	🍷	5
● Langhe Bric Millon '00	🍷	5
● Roero Sup. Sodisfà '98	🍷🍷	6
● Barbera d'Alba Bric Bertu '99	🍷🍷	5
● Barbera d'Alba Bric Bertu '00	🍷🍷	5
● Roero Sup. Sodisfà '99	🍷🍷	6

MONTEU ROERO (CN)

CASCINA PELLERINO
FRAZ. SANT'ANNA
12040 MONTEU ROERO (CN)
TEL. 0173978171
E-MAIL: cascinapellerino@tiscali.it

Cristian Bono, the former "enfant prodige" of Roero winemaking, has reached full professional maturity. We think that, now the quality of his wines has propelled him into the top ranks locally, he will soon be one of the region's big names. His wines convincingly demonstrate talent, and the drive to improve further will power that final leap. Meanwhile the winery, where Cristian's father, Luciano, lends a hand, is becoming a focal point in Roero, with a modern, efficient facility, expanding vineyards – now at nine hectares – and a line that boasts two new wines. Let's take a look first at the new Roero Leoni. Here is a sinewy nebbiolo-based wine of great stature, which three years' ageing has honed to a focused leanness. The palate exudes a seductive opulence and overall, it has the harmony and balance that distinguish great reds are here in abundance. It's a great debut for a wine that will excite comment in years to come. The other new entry, Renè, a table red of nebbiolo, barbera and a bit of cabernet, impresses with a remarkably full body and rich tones of wild berries and cherries, plus a velvety suppleness on the palate. But once again, it is the two classic reds that take the bows. Barbera Gran Madre is all about spice, with a finish built on vigour and concentration. The Roero Vicot parades wild berries caressed by well-judged oak, then an impressive suite of smooth tannins balances tangy flavours. It's a stunning performance from a sumptuous, harmonious wine. All the others – the two standards, Barbera and Roero, plus the Arneis and the Passito – are good.

● Barbera d'Alba Sup.		
Gran Madre '01	♟♟	4
● Roero Vicot '01	♟♟	5
● Roero Leoni '00	♟♟	6
● Renè '01	♟♟	5
○ Poch ma Bon Passito '01	♟	6
● Barbera d'Alba '02	♟	3
● Roero '02	♟	4
○ Roero Arneis Boneur '02	♟	3
● Barbera d'Alba Sup.		
Gran Madre '99	♟♟	5
● Roero Vicot '99	♟♟	5
● Barbera d'Alba Sup.		
Gran Madre '00	♟♟	5
● Roero Vicot '00	♟♟	5

MORSASCO (AL)

LA GUARDIA
REG. LA GUARDIA
15010 MORSASCO (AL)
TEL. 014473076
E-MAIL: guardia@libero.it

The Priarone family is working on the splendid Villa Delfini to make it their winemaking headquarters. Restructuring proceeds apace, with wines already maturing there. The Priarones were the first to realize that wines from upper Monferrato need time to give their best. Almost all their bottles go a year after harvest before release and the results are obvious. The Dolcetto Villa Delfini '00 is magnificent and must be one of the best ever Ovada Dolcettos. A lovely ruby precedes rich aromas of ripe fruit and vanilla. The palate is absolutely impressive, offering a rhythmic duet of tannins and crisp acidity, and sweet fruit pushes the length of an excellent finale. Fruit and spice notes animate the Barbera Vigna di Dante, which has a nice herbaceous lift. Judicious acidity provides elegant balance to its supple texture and full flavours, and it finishes long. Dolcetto and cabernet fruit make up Innominato, which hints at capsicum, spices, red berry fruit and leather. Moderately full bodied, it is pleasantly crisp with a bitterish tang. Continuing the Dolcettos, Il Gamondino shows good plum and cherry fruit complexity. The palate needs some time to pull together, but it impresses with well-judged tannins, acidity and good depth of flavour. Aromas of stewed fruit testify to the fully ripe grapes that produced the Bricco Riccardo. Good tannins help it develop into a savoury, full-bodied delight. Among the whites, the Butàs edges out the Chardonnay Villa Delfini for its personality and distinctiveness, even though the Chardonnay is well made, crisp and enjoyable.

● Barbera del M.to		
Vigna di Dante '00	♟♟	5
● Dolcetto di Ovada Sup.		
Villa Delfini '00	♟♟	5
● Monferrato Rosso Innominato '00	♟♟	5
● Dolcetto di Ovada Sup.		
Il Gamondino '01	♟	4
● Dolcetto di Ovada Sup.		
Vigneto Bricco Riccardo '01	♟	4
○ Piemonte Chardonnay Butàs '01	♟	5
○ Piemonte Chardonnay		
Villa Delfini '01	♟	4
● Barbera del M.to		
Vigna di Dante '99	♟♟	5

MURISENGO (AL)

MURISENGO (AL)

ISABELLA
FRAZ. CORTERANZO
VIA GIANOLI, 64
15020 MURISENGO (AL)
TEL. 0141693000
E-MAIL: calvo@isabellavini.com

LA ZUCCA
FRAZ. SORINA
VIA SORINA, 53/55
15020 MURISENGO (AL)
TEL. 0118193343 - 0141993154
E-MAIL: info@lazucca.com

Gabriele Calvo's winery uncorked another fine group of wines for us this year. All five are superb, with the Barbera d'Astis standing out from the rest. This is somewhat unusual, since we had become used to great performances by the native Monferrato varieties, such as Grignolino Montecastello. Barbera d'Asti Bric Stupui is the more appealing of the two. Dense ruby red shot with purple, it throws a multi-layered nose to match. Over the rich vanilla and ripe wild berries, we catch scents of spicy oak from cask ageing then the palate's alcoholic warmth and nice crisp acidity are both delightful. The finish is long and satisfying. Although the Barbera d'Asti Truccone '01 comes across as a bit less complex, it is still a superb effort, with outstanding fruit from the vineyard it is named after. A fine, purple-flecked ruby introduces emphatic aromas of ripe blackberries and plum. The entrance is velvety and full, followed by a nice encore of fruit and a lengthy finish marked with a lift of acidity. The Barbera del Monferrato, Bricco Montemà, offers pure easy-drinking pleasure. This, uncomplicated wines shows a decently rich nose of blackberry, blueberry and walnut husk, then a tasty, acid-perked palate. The Grignolino Montecastello is not as good as in previous years, but it is nonetheless a fine example of its wine type.

La Zucca is run by the dynamic, fiercely dedicated Ester Accornero. She has effectively promoted the local area not only through her wines, but with her own B&B, which she created by renovating her grandparents' venerable "cascina", or farmhouse. She is just about to open an "agriturismo" facility as well, which will doubtless attract even more visitors and generally stimulate interest in the area's food and wine. Of the wines we tasted, the Grignolino Marmanest '02 earned itself a good Two Glasses. An intense cherry beguiles the eye, and appealing aromatics the nose, with strawberry and rose yielding smoothly to spice and slightly over-ripe fruit. We were greatly impressed by its pliant tannins and superlative balance. The Barbera Martizza showed well, albeit just a notch below previous years. Its deep ruby ushers in a wealth of complex aromas. Blueberries and blackberries are layered over cakes and toasted oak, then the decent body is supported by proportioned acidity. The steel-fermented Barbera 'I Suli, deep red in hue, releases an array of elegant, lingering fragrances and progresses to a zesty sappiness and fruit in the mouth. It's a delicious wine.

● Barbera d'Asti Bric Stupui '00	♟♟	6
● Barbera d'Asti Truccone '01	♟♟	4*
● Monferrato Freisa Bioc '02	♟	4
● Barbera del M.to Bricco Montemà '01	♟	3
● Grignolino del M.to Casalese Montecastello '02	♟	4
● Barbera d'Asti Bric Stupui '98	♟♟	5
● Barbera d'Asti Bric Stupui '99	♟♟	5
● Barbera d'Asti Truccone '00	♟♟	4

● Barbera d'Asti Martizza '01	♟♟	6
● Grignolino del M.to Casalese Marmanest '02	♟♟	4
● Barbera d'Asti 'I Sulì '02	♟	4
● Monferrato Freisa '02	♟	4
● Barbera d'Asti Martizza '99	♟♟	5
● Barbera d'Asti Martizza '00	♟♟	5

NEIVE (CN)

PIERO BUSSO
VIA ALBESANI, 8
12057 NEIVE (CN)
TEL. 017367156
E-MAIL: emanuelabusso@virgilio.it

The modest cellars of friendly Neive-based winemaker, Piero Busso, have hit the jackpot again with a new wine. The Barbaresco Santo Stefanetto '00 is a sensational creation from this little-known Treiso vineyard. Extremely rigorous selection of fruit during growth and at harvest left fruit for only 4,500 bottles. The enrapturing concentration on the nose reveals cocoa powder shot through with sweet spice and citrus, then the mouth fills with rich, succulent fruit charged with dense, stylish tannins. A delight for the senses. Borghese '00 also commands respect. Although slightly closed at the moment, it allows glimpses of raspberry and tobacco, showing nicely complex and distinctive on the palate, with the tannic weave of a great vineyard. The Barbareso Mondino '00, however, is one of those fruity wines that are delightful to enjoy in their youth. Flawlessly made and very distinctive, it has only one drawback – or perhaps charm? – in its uncomplicated, right-now drinkability. A severe attack of downy mildew precluded the production of the Gallina, while an unfavourable year meant no 2002 Dolcetto or Barbera. But '02 did see the production of several thousand bottles of Nebbiolo from a young vineyard at Casasse. A stylish hue introduces luscious aromas of strawberry and forest fruits. It's a wine whose most appealing trait is lively fruitiness. Finally, Two Glasses go to the rich, succulent, well spiced Barbera Majano '01, as well as to the superlative Bianco '01, a chardonnay and sauvignon blanc blend with aromas of tropical fruit and a mouthfilling palate.

NEIVE (CN)

F.LLI CIGLIUTI
VIA SERRABOELLA, 17
12057 NEIVE (CN)
TEL. 0173677185
E-MAIL: cigliutirenato@libero.it

The fewer the wines, the greater the number of Glasses. Oversimplifying a bit, that sums up F.lli Cigliuti's performance in this edition of the Guide. The family decided to hold back the release of several wines, namely the two Barbera d'Albas, Campass and Serraboella, and the Langhe Rosso Bricca Serra. We know that these decisions are difficult, but they are welcome when they enable us to taste wines at a more developed stage, when they yield greater enjoyment. Still, two other wines, both Barbarescos, seem to more than make up for the absence of the others. Serraboella is by now an established champion and again won Three Glasses and there is a new contender in Vigne Erte, which imposed itself by dint of its impressive dimensions and distinctive character. The Serraboella is a nebbiolo of rare intensity. Dark and brooding to the eye, it yields up successive waves of clear fruit, earth, forest floor, pencil lead and sweet spice. It progresses into an explosive show of gutsy tannins, developing into a huge but harmonious wine on every level, with an endless finish. A spectacular performance, with all the stops pulled out, by a talented and well-matched family team. Vigne Erte is, as we said, outstanding. Sourced from a steep vineyard (hence the name) not far from Serraboella, it matures in large barrels. Here we have a distinctly elegant wine, which showcases wonderful nebbiolo austerity and wholly seductive harmony, unfurling finally a lengthy, savoury finish.

●	Barbaresco S. Stefanetto '00	▼▼▼	8
●	Barbaresco Borgese '00	▼▼	7
●	Barbaresco Mondino '00	▼▼	7
●	Barbera d'Alba Majano '01	▼▼	4*
○	Langhe Bianco di Busso '01	▼▼	4*
●	Langhe Nebbiolo '02	▼	5
●	Barbaresco Vigna Borgese '97	▼▼▼	7
●	Barbaresco Bricco Mondino '97	▼▼	7
●	Barbaresco Bricco Mondino '98	▼▼	7
●	Barbaresco Vigna Borgese '98	▼▼	7
●	Barbaresco Bricco Mondino '99	▼▼	7
●	Barbaresco Vigna Borgese '99	▼▼	7

●	Barbaresco Serraboella '00	▼▼▼	7
●	Barbaresco Vigne Erte '00	▼▼	6
●	Barbaresco Serraboella '90	▼▼▼	8
●	Barbaresco Serraboella '96	▼▼▼	8
●	Barbaresco Serraboella '97	▼▼▼	8
●	Barbaresco Serraboella '98	▼▼	8
●	Langhe Rosso Bricco Serra '99	▼▼	7
●	Barbaresco Serraboella '99	▼▼	8
●	Barbera d'Alba Campass '00	▼▼	6
●	Barbera d'Alba Serraboella '00	▼▼	5
●	Langhe Rosso Bricco Serra '00	▼▼	7

NEIVE (CN)

NEIVE (CN)

FONTANABIANCA
VIA BORDINI, 15
12057 NEIVE (CN)
TEL. 017367195
E-MAIL: fontanabianca@libero.it

GASTALDI
VIA ALBESANI, 20
12057 NEIVE (CN)
TEL. 0173677400

Fontanabianca, run by Aldo Pola and Bruno Ferro, is more than just an emerging winery. Over the past few years it has been perfecting its own clearly articulated winemaking philosophy, borne out by tasting results. The most intriguing aspect of tastings at Fontanabianca is how the wines faithfully reflect each individual growing year. The philosophy eschews over-sophisticated techniques that could obscure the elegance and wonderful enjoyability which this area's nebbiolos and barberas so famously express. Take the Barbaresco Sorì Burdin, one of the best 2000 wines. Sporting a lively, deep red just this side of opaque, it's a bit slow to open, but gradually reveals vanilla, tobacco and hazelnut. It's the palate that convinces, though, opening broad, succulent and rich, then adding impressive layers of liquorice and fruit. The wine finishes crisp, dry and seemingly endless. The Barbera Brunet '01 missed Three Glasses by a whisker. From fruit grown on a venerable plot owned by Aldo's father-in-law in the Serracapelli vineyard in Neive, it is dark, purplish ruby, releasing an intricate display of blueberries, cinchona and sweet spices. The firm, decisive entry leads into an opulent, closely-woven texture, signing off with a delightful finale that is all velvet and balance. More on the ready side is the elegant Barbaresco '00, which exhibits strawberry and dried herbs. Finally, both the golden, warmth-laden Arneis '02 and the big, tannic Nebbiolo '01 present very nicely. There will be no 2002 Chardonnay, Dolcetto Bordini or Barbera d'Alba.

Dino Gastaldi may seem a bit unusual for a Langhe grower producer, since he doesn't bottle all the fruit he grows, and the low yields he imposes make those bottles hard to find. Dino plans to remedying this situation over the next few years. For our tastings, he offered the Barbaresco '99 (he didn't make a '98), the Rosso Castlé '98, the Bianco Gastaldi '00 and the Dolcetto Moriolo '02. His estate totals almost 15 hectares: seven and a half of dolcetto, sauvignon blanc and chardonnay at Rodello; five and a half planted mostly to nebbiolo at Neive, in the Albesani, Bricco, and Starderi subzones; and just over one hectare to nebbiolo and merlot in Monforte's Le Coste vineyard; these give him about 20,000 bottles per year. Future production will centre on the following wines: Dolcetto Moriolo, Barbaresco, Barbaresco Albesani, Barolo Le Coste, Rosso Gastaldi, Rosso Castlé and Bianco Gastaldi. Right up there with the best is the Barbaresco '99, exclusively from Albesani fruit, though this does not appear on the label. It has massive power to spare, rounded off only slightly by a lengthy sojourn in barrique. The other offerings consist of the lean, intense, monovarietal Rosso Castlé, the full bodied, minerally Bianco Gastaldi, a blend of 70 per cent sauvignon blanc and 30 per cent chardonnay, and the nicely lean and supple Dolcetto Morolio.

● Barbaresco Sorì Burdin '00	♟♟	8
● Barbera d'Alba Brunet '01	♟♟	5
● Barbaresco '00	♟♟	7
● Langhe Nebbiolo '01	♟	5
○ Langhe Arneis '02	♟	4
● Barbaresco Sorì Burdin '98	♟♟♟	7
● Barbaresco Sorì Burdin '97	♟♟	7
● Barbera d'Alba Brunet '00	♟♟	5
● Barbaresco '99	♟♟	6
● Barbaresco Sorì Burdin '99	♟♟	7

● Barbaresco '99	♟♟	7
○ Langhe Bianco Gastaldi '00	♟♟	6
● Dolcetto d'Alba Moriolo '02	♟♟	4*
● Langhe Rosso Castlé '98	♟♟	7
● Gastaldi Rosso '88	♟♟♟	7
● Gastaldi Rosso '89	♟♟♟	7
● Dolcetto d'Alba Sup. Moriolo '90	♟♟♟	5
● Barbaresco '97	♟♟	7
○ Langhe Bianco Gastaldi '99	♟♟	5
● Langhe Rosso Gastaldi '98	♟♟	7
● Langhe Rosso Castlé '97	♟♟	7

NEIVE (CN)

NEIVE (CN)

BRUNO GIACOSA
VIA XX SETTEMBRE, 52
12057 NEIVE (CN)
TEL. 017367027
E-MAIL: brunogiacosa@brunogiacosa.it

F.LLI GIACOSA
VIA XX SETTEMBRE, 64
12052 NEIVE (CN)
TEL. 017367013
E-MAIL: giacosa@giacosa.it

We still recall the ovation Bruno Giacosa and his wines received after a taste workshop at the 2002 Salone in Turin. It was a tribute to the way Bruno's Barolos and Barbarescos capture the quintessence of nebbiolo, but also to Bruno, the shy yet ever helpful man. In the meantime, Bruno has become grandfather of Francesco Bruno. Leading the range this year is his Barolo Le Rocche del Falletto. Still young in colour, it releases rich balsamic scents over sweet fruit, the warm mouth expanding over dense, well-rounded tannins. Above all, it has exceptional fruit that flows smoothly from attack to the long finish. Earthy notes and dried flowers frame the Falletto's good firm structure and crisp fruit. The finish is plump and seductive. Moving on to the Barberas, the Santo Stefano offers a concentrated, warm, alcohol-rich nose, followed by impressive depth and power, with dense tannins. But the Asili '99 is even better. Stylish faded roses, dried herbs and leather usher in a superbly structured palate, packed with sinewy tannins and an outstandingly elegant succulence that stays through to a savoury finish. It's a superb Barbaresco, as good as the finest wines produced by this exceptional Langhe producer. The Santo Stefano '98 carries Giacosa's red label but hasn't yet developed a nose to match the opulent liveliness of the garnet colour. It yields nice dried flower notes and red fruit, and the mouthfeel is convincingly complex. Both remaining 2001s, the Barbera Falletto and Nebbiolo Valmaggiore, are excellent, and the Arneis is delicious.

Valerio and Renzo Giacosa, with their respective sons, Maurizio and Paolo, continue a family tradition dating back to 1895. In that year, Giuseppe Giacosa, son of tenant farmers in the Bricco area of Neive, left to become an independent grape broker and then wine merchant. Today, this dynamic, forward-looking winery offers superb versions of Langhe classics, along with a brace of Chardonnays for the international market. Tasting their Ca' Lunga reveals what a great performance they have coaxed from the variety. After a lively green-edged straw yellow, it unveils a luxurious aromatic spectrum ranging from rich spice and almond to acacia blossom. It progresses harmoniously in the mouth to an impressively long finish. The Barbaresco Rio Sordo is compelling. Fruit and spice-based aromas follow a nice medium-intense colour, and its juicy palate leads into a satisfying length. Liveliness and richness are the hallmarks of both appearance and nose of the Barolo Vigna Mandorlo, with roasted espresso beans and good ripe fruit preceding a weighty, expansive mouthfeel, though the finish is a tad rough. The deeply coloured Barbera Maria Gioana unfolds nuances of fruit, toasty oak and wild berries. The mouth develops appealing alcohol-warm intensity, and a lengthy finish is nicely laced with notes of cocoa powder. The Arneis boasts a classy nose infused with ripe fruit and sugared almond. On the palate, it shows medium weight and ends well. Finally, the Chardonnay Roera is nicely done.

● Barbaresco Asili '99	♟♟♟	8
● Barbaresco Santo Stefano Ris. '98	♟♟	8
● Barolo Le Rocche del Falletto '99	♟♟	8
● Barbera d'Alba Falletto '01	♟♟	6
● Barbaresco Santo Stefano '99	♟♟	8
● Barolo Falletto '99	♟♟	8
● Nebbiolo d'Alba Valmaggiore '01	♟	5
○ Roero Arneis '02	♟	5
● Barolo Collina Rionda Ris. '82	♟♟♟	8
● Barolo Rocche di Castiglione Falletto '85	♟♟♟	8
● Barolo Falletto '96	♟♟♟	8
● Barbaresco Asili Ris. '96	♟♟♟	8
● Barolo Falletto Ris. '96	♟♟♟	8

● Barbaresco Rio Sordo '00	♟♟	7
● Barbera d'Alba Maria Gioana '00	♟♟	4
○ Langhe Chardonnay Ca' Lunga '01	♟♟	4
● Barolo Vigna Mandorlo '99	♟♟	7
○ Roero Arneis '02	♟	3
○ Langhe Chardonnay Roera '02		3
● Barolo Vigna Mandorlo '97	♟♟	7
● Barbaresco Rio Sordo '98	♟♟	7
● Barolo Vigna Mandorlo '98	♟♟	7
● Barbaresco Rio Sordo '99	♟♟	7
● Barbera d'Alba Maria Gioana '99	♟♟	7

NEIVE (CN)

OTTAVIO LEQUIO - PRINSI
VIA GAIA, 5
12057 NEIVE (CN)
TEL. 017367192
E-MAIL: prinsi@lòibero.it

The impressive performance by their entire line has earned the Lequio family winery at Neive a full profile. It is a real pleasure to recognize the efforts of a modest cellar that exemplifies so clearly the tenacious dedication to sheer quality typical of traditional Langhe small growers. Paterfamilias, Ottavio Lequio, is in his 90s but you'll still find him in the vineyard, helping son Franco and his wife, while young grandson, Daniele, who has finished his winemaking studies in Alba, keeps a close eye on cellar operations and marketing. This multi-generational team intelligently manages 12 hectares of well-sited vineyards, producing about 50,000 bottles per year. Their Barbaresco Prinsi is maturing an extra year, so it's up to the 1999 and 2000 Gallina to do the honours for nebbiolo. The '99 shows deep ruby red and offers delicately nuanced espresso, spices and wild berries. Elegance is the word for the palate, which has impressive linearity that sustains it through to a nice, tannin-framed finish with good length and balance. Matured in large oak and styled for long cellaring, this superb, traditional Barbareso put on an impressive performance. The '00 is following in its steps. The nose already shows nice complexity, and it is clear that both nose and palate will soon develop more depth. The appropriately gutsy, crisp Barbera d'Alba showed well, too. Among the whites, we preferred the Chardonnay to the sauvignon-based Camp'ed Pietrù, for the latter is a bit atypical and too stoney. The remaining two reds, the Dolcetto and the nebbiolo and barbera Calvario, are quite solid.

NEIVE (CN)

UGO LEQUIO
VIA DEL MOLINO, 10
12057 NEIVE (CN)
TEL. 0173677224
E-MAIL: ugolequio@libero.it

Even though he purchases his grapes, Ugo Lequio can always rely on outstanding fruit, thanks to close relationships he has maintained with his suppliers. Add to that his abilities as a meticulous winemaker, and the reasons become clear for the quality he is able to achieve with his 28,000 bottles each year. His winemaking style is very much in the Langhe tradition, and the only wine that sees small oak – 500-litre tonneaux in this case – is his Barbera Gallina. This year's edition shows a ruby still rimmed in youthful purple, with a sound, clean nose of fruit and spice, over a subtle toffee background. It has beautiful, uninterrupted momentum from attack to lengthy finish, and is well structured, full flavoured, and appealing at every moment. The Barbaresco is superlative, exhibiting an intense garnet, mature on the edge, and flaunting a hedonistic mélange of strawberry preserve, dried flowers and liquorice. The palate has richly woven texture and sustained development that concludes in a lengthy echo of the aromatic nose. Complexity and crispness mark the Arneis, which releases nuances of peach and wholemeal. Finally, the Dolcetto displays a violet-flecked ruby with a fairly ripe nose that hints at mown hay. Zesty liveliness in the mouth offsets a modest structure, and it finishes nicely bitterish.

●	Barbaresco Gallina '00	🍷🍷	6*
●	Barbera d'Alba Vigneto Mùc '00	🍷🍷	4
○	Langhe Chardonnay '02	🍷🍷	4
●	Barbaresco Gallina '99	🍷🍷	6*
○	Camp'es Pietrù '01	🍷	5
●	Dolcetto d'Alba San Cristoforo '01	🍷	4
●	Calvario '99	🍷	5
●	Barbaresco Gallina '98	🍷🍷	6*
●	Barbaresco '99	🍷🍷	6

●	Barbaresco Gallina '00	🍷🍷	6*
●	Barbera d'Alba Gallina '01	🍷🍷	4
●	Dolcetto d'Alba '02	🍷	4
○	Langhe Arneis '02	🍷	4
●	Barbaresco Gallina '96	🍷🍷	6
●	Barbaresco Gallina '97	🍷🍷	6
●	Barbera d'Alba Gallina '98	🍷🍷	4
●	Barbaresco Gallina '98	🍷🍷	6
●	Barbera d'Alba Gallina '00	🍷🍷	4

NEIVE (CN)

PAITIN
VIA SERRA BOELLA, 20
12057 NEIVE (CN)
TEL. 017367343 - 0173363123
E-MAIL: info@paitin.it

The Paitin winery celebrated its centenary long ago, for it traces its roots as far back as 1796. In that year, Benedetto Elia bought a beautiful piece of land from Luigi Pellissero. The first Barbaresco was actually bottled in 1893. Secondo Pasquero and his sons, Giovanni and Silvano, are the current incumbents, producing superb wines from their 17 hectares. The estate's thoroughbred is, of course, the Barbaresco Sorì Paitin, with its deep garnet and rich nose proffering red berry fruit, violets, liquorice and cocoa powder. An elegant tannic charge stands out in an impressively massive structure, and the finish, as expected for such a great product, is superbly long. The standard-label Barbaresco is far from standard in quality. Dark purple highlights and rich morello aromas give it a compelling, palpable complexity. We also liked the Barbera d'Alba Campolive '01, with its beguiling carmine tint. Tangy acidity provides a good foil to a palate packed with vanilla-veined fruit. Nebbiolo, barbera, and cabernet combine smoothly in the Langhe Paitin. We liked its fruit and black pepper-laden nose, as well the powerful, succulent palate. Also out of the top drawer is the Nebbiolo d'Alba Ca Veja, while the Arneis Vigna Elisa, the Barbera d'Alba Serra Boella and the Dolcetto d'Alba Sorì Paitin all easily earned One Glass.

● Barbaresco Sorì Paitin Vecchie Vigne '00	🍷🍷	8
● Langhe Paitin '01	🍷🍷	6*
● Barbaresco Sorì Paitin '00	🍷🍷	7
● Barbera d'Alba Campolive '01	🍷🍷	5
● Nebbiolo d'Alba Ca Veja '01	🍷🍷	5
● Barbera d'Alba Serra Boella '02	🍷	4
● Dolcetto d'Alba Sorì Paitin '02	🍷	4
○ Roero Arneis Vigna Elisa '02	🍷	4
● Barbaresco Sorì Paitin '95	🍷🍷🍷	7
● Barbaresco Sorì Paitin '97	🍷🍷🍷	7
● Langhe Paitin '97	🍷🍷🍷	6
● Barbaresco Sorì Paitin Vecchie Vigne '99	🍷🍷🍷	8
● Langhe Paitin '99	🍷🍷	6

NEIVE (CN)

SOTTIMANO
FRAZ. COTTÀ, 21
12057 NEIVE (CN)
TEL. 0173635186
E-MAIL: sottimano@libero.it

It's obvious why the Sottimanos are successful. The family agrees on goals. Anna, Elena, and Claudia do great work in the cellar, while Rino and son, Andrea, scrupulously manage the vineyards, avoiding chemical applications as much as possible and practising severe cluster thinning. Fermentations are designed to maximize fruit aromas and small oak is used sparingly. The Sottimanos are also dispassionate about comparing their wines with other people's and finally, they are totally committed to improving every year. We salute them for releasing a Dolcetto in a difficult vintage, albeit in only one version and in limited production. The Barbera Pairolero is very well crafted, with a nice ruby, gobs of rich ripe fruit, and a full-flavoured, vigorous palate. Over among the Barbarescos, there's great finesse on the nose of the Cottà, whose mouth is built on perfectly gauged sweetness, good structure and tannins to match. Dark, lustrous tones announce the Fausoni, which opens with exuberant cocoa, spices, cinchona and fruit that leads to a juicy, supple mouth and lengthy finish. No less impressive is the Currà, which exhibits lovely ruby garnet and releases clove mixed with ripe fruit. It grows even more intense on the alcohol-boosted palate, although the finish could perhaps be smoother. We've left the best till last. An astounding Pajoré fairly radiates ruby garnet, then flaunts ultra aristocratic fruit and minerally fragrances. Sinewy power and opulent depth mingle confidently in the mouth, and seamlessly continue to create a world-class finale. A spell-binding Three Glasses.

● Barbaresco Pajoré '00	🍷🍷🍷	7
● Barbaresco Cottà '00	🍷🍷	7
● Barbaresco Currà '00	🍷🍷	7
● Barbaresco Fausoni '00	🍷🍷	7
● Barbera d'Alba Pairolero '01	🍷🍷	5
● Dolcetto d'Alba Bric del Salto '02	🍷🍷	3*
● Maté '02	🍷	3
● Barbaresco Fausoni Vigna del Salto '96	🍷🍷🍷	7
● Barbaresco Cottà Vigna Brichet '97	🍷🍷🍷	7
● Barbaresco Cottà '98	🍷🍷🍷	7
● Barbaresco Pajoré '98	🍷🍷🍷	7
● Barbaresco Cottà '99	🍷🍷🍷	7
● Barbaresco Pajoré '99	🍷🍷	7

NEVIGLIE (CN)

F.LLI BERA
CASCINA PALAZZO, 12
12050 NEVIGLIE (CN)
TEL. 0173630194
E-MAIL: info@bera.it

Walter and Attilio Bera's nearly 19 hectares produce 110,000 bottles of impressive wines with no lack of character and verve. The lion's share is represented by three separate Moscatos, the outstanding Su Reimond, the well-made standard label and the Asti. A deep straw introduces the first, its elegant varietal nose centring on nuances of lemon and spring flowers. The mouth reveals an impressive fullness while avoiding heaviness, and a light sparkle lifts its sweetness just the correct degree. Everything returns to infuse a lovely finish. The standard Moscato is a bit lighter, and its fragrances turn more towards citrus and floral, but the palate develops with marked grace and consistency into a tasty, rose-suffused finale. A dense red heralds the barbera-nebbiolo Sassisto. Earth and fruit notes unfold slowly on the nose, then the full-bodied palate appeals with its lively vigour. The hallmark Barbera fruitiness is well out in front in the La Lena, buttressed by a rich vein of chocolate and liquorice. There is vigour and breadth to spare in the mouth. The Chardonnay '02 suggests caramel-covered fruit, then unfolds a closely-woven texture braced by excellent acidity. The Metodo Classico, Dolcetto, standard-label Barbera and Nebbiolo are all well crafted and merit a Glass each.

NIZZA MONFERRATO (AT)

BERSANO & RICCADONNA
P.ZZA DANTE, 21
14049 NIZZA MONFERRATO (AT)
TEL. 0141720211
E-MAIL: wine@bersano.it

One of the key themes in the winemaking credo of Bersano & Riccadonna is value for money: "Each bottle, top of the line or least expensive, must justify the sacrifice the consumer makes to purchase it." To achieve this goal, the group relies on excellent fruit. The 215 hectares of estate vineyards, parcelled into 11 properties, provide a considerable base. The winery also strictly controls cellar practices, focusing technology where it most needed – on the sparklers. Let's begin with the Barbera Generala, a wine as ambitious as it is successful. Dense ruby garnet introduces a velvety, inviting nose that teases out a lovely succession of cocoa, wild berries and cherries. The progression is admirably structured, the pace set by a delicious duet of alcoholic warmth and varietal zestiness. The nose is gracefully reprised in a lengthy finale of perfect consistency. Pomona, a mix of barbera and cabernet, shows very dark, the nose ranging from fruit through to a rich minerality. After massive power on the palate, it signs off with elegant nuances of spice and liquorice. Hints of wood resin and berry fruit fragrances permeate the Barbera Cremosina, leading into a crisp, dry mouthfeel. For the Barbera Nizza, it's chocolate, tobacco, and cherry, and a palate of unapologetic succulence. The Brachetto Castelgaro is a resounding success, the nose delicately hinting at roses and spice, and the palate showing class. Fine, too, are the Moscato and the Metodo Classico.

○	Moscato d'Asti Su Reimond '02	🍷🍷	4
○	Moscato d'Asti '02	🍷🍷	3*
○	Langhe Chardonnay '02	🍷🍷	4
●	Barbera d'Alba Sup. La Lena '01	🍷🍷	4
●	Langhe Sassisto '00	🍷🍷	5
●	Dolcetto d'Alba '02	🍷	3
●	Barbera d'Alba '02	🍷	3
●	Langhe Nebbiolo Alladio '99	🍷	5
○	Bera Brut M. Cl.	🍷	5
●	Barbera d'Alba Sup. '00	🍷🍷	5
●	Langhe Sassisto '99	🍷🍷	4

●	Barbera d'Asti Sup. Generala '01	🍷🍷	7
●	Barbera d'Asti Sup. Nizza '01	🍷🍷	5
●	Monferrato Pomona '01	🍷🍷	7
●	Brachetto d'Acqui Castelgaro '02	🍷🍷	4*
○	Arturo Bersano Talento Brut Ris. M. Cl. '00	🍷	5
●	Barbera d'Asti Cremosina '01	🍷	5
○	Moscato d'Asti '02	🍷	4
●	Barbera d'Asti Sup. Generala '97	🍷🍷🍷	7
●	Barbera d'Asti Sup. Generala '99	🍷🍷	7
●	Monferrato Pomona '99	🍷🍷	7
●	Barbera d'Asti Sup. Generala '00	🍷🍷	7
●	Monferrato Pomona '00	🍷🍷	7
●	Brachetto d'Acqui Castelgaro '01	🍷🍷	4

NIZZA MONFERRATO (AT)

★ CASCINA LA BARBATELLA
S.DA ANNUNZIATA, 55
14049 NIZZA MONFERRATO (AT)
TEL. 0141701434
E-MAIL: sonvico.barbatella@libero.it

Angelo Sonvico's winery has been one of the top-ranked Monferrato producers for years now. Flanked by the expert Giuliano Noè, Angelo believes strongly in Asti's future and in its excellence as a wine area. This year, Monferrato Rosso Mystère, a blend of barbera, cabernet and pinot noir, is splendid. In fact, it's far better than in preceding vintages, and amply merits Three Glasses. Already drinking magnificently, it will improve markedly over time. A deep ruby ushers in a nose of leisurely berry fruit, cocoa powder and fresh herbs. Then, after a confident attack, the well-integrated tannins emerge with impressive power. This has to be the finest version yet, from a growing year that was perfect for all its three components, including the pinot noir. We'll have to wait until next year for the Barbera d'Asti Vigna dell'Angelo '01 from the Nizza subzone, and for the Monferrato Rosso Sonvico '01, but the rest of the offerings are top-notch performers. This is especially true of the Barbera d'Asti Vigna dell'Angelo, whose label differs from the 2000 only in the indication Nizza. Dominated by ripe fruit, the mouth displays invitingly dense pulp and a vein of crisp acidity animates the finish. In addition to his Noè, Sonvico last year released another white, Non è. Although from the same sauvignon and cortese grapes, the two are quite dissimilar. Noè sees less oak than its partner, while Non è exhibits toasty oak and a warm, supple mouthfeel.

NIZZA MONFERRATO (AT)

ANTICA CASA VINICOLA SCARPA
VIA MONTEGRAPPA, 6
14049 NIZZA MONFERRATO (AT)
TEL. 0141721331
E-MAIL: info@scarpavini.it

The updating of the Scarpa operation is proceeding apace. Restructuring and modernization of the historic cellars have been completed, and Maria Piera Zola, Mario Castino and Carlo Castino have now begun the vineyard replanting that will bring real change. The wines we tasted covered the gamut from tradition to modernity. We were very impressed by the Bogliona, the winery's flagship Barbera. Dark ruby announces a nose exuding fruity complexity, redolent of ripe plum, blackberry and cocoa. Its massive structure is veined by pronounced acidity, less intrusively however than in the past, and by glossy, well-defined tannins. No less intriguing is the Rouchet Briccorosa '01, offering a voluptuous suite of herbal and spice fragrances layered over raspberry, redcurrant and liquorice. The same high marks went to the Barbaresco Tettineive '99, a charmer whose mint and faded rose petals usher in an exuberant, richly flavoured palate with nicely rounded tannins. The lively garnet Barolo Tettimorra '99 presents more of a challenge. The nose must be coaxed open, but it eventually presents the taster with a stunning complex of berry fruit, faded violets, coffee beans and intoxicating earthiness. On the opposite side of the stylistic palette is the RossoScarpa '01, a super-tasty mix of dolcetto with a dab of ruché. Gorgeous rose and wild berries are unleashed by the dry fermented Brachetto '01. Other good performers were the Dolcetto and the Freisa from the La Selva di Moirano vineyard, and the Nebbiolo d'Alba Bric du Nota '99.

	Wine	Glasses	Score
●	Monferrato Rosso Mystère '01	♛♛♛	7
●	Barbera d'Asti Sup.		
	Vigna dell'Angelo '01	♛♛	7
○	Monferrato Bianco Non è '01	♛♛	5
○	Monferrato Bianco Noè '02	♛♛	5
●	La Vigna di Sonvico '95	♛♛♛	7
●	La Vigna di Sonvico '96	♛♛♛	7
●	Barbera d'Asti Sup.		
	Vigna dell'Angelo '96	♛♛♛	7
●	Barbera d'Asti Sup.		
	Vigna dell'Angelo '98	♛♛♛	7
●	Monferrato Rosso Sonvico '97	♛♛♛	7
●	Monferrato Rosso Sonvico '98	♛♛♛	7
●	Monferrato Rosso Sonvico '00	♛♛♛	7

	Wine	Glasses	Score
●	Rouchet Briccorosa '01	♛♛	6
●	Barbaresco Tettineive '99	♛♛	8
●	Barbera d'Asti Sup. La Bogliona '00	♛♛	6
●	Dolcetto d'Acqui		
	La Selva di Moirano '01	♛♛	5
●	Monferrato Freisa		
	La Selva di Moirano '01	♛♛	4*
●	Barolo Tettimorra '99	♛♛	8
●	Nebbiolo d'Alba Bric du Nota '99	♛♛	6
●	Brachetto Secco		
	La Selva di Moirano '01	♛	6
●	Monferrato Rosso		
	RossoScarpa '01	♛	4
●	Rouchet Briccorosa '90	♛♛♛	8
●	Barbera d'Asti Sup. La Bogliona '97	♛♛	6

NIZZA MONFERRATO (AT)

FRANCO E MARIO SCRIMAGLIO
VIA ALESSANDRIA, 67
14049 NIZZA MONFERRATO (AT)
TEL. 0141721385 - 0141727052
E-MAIL: piergiorgio@scrimaglio.it

NOVELLO (CN)

ELVIO COGNO
VIA RAVERA, 2
12060 NOVELLO (CN)
TEL. 0173744006
E-MAIL: elviocogno@elviocogno.com

The Scrimaglios have been in Monferrato for centuries and Francesco Scrimaglio launched this estate in the Nizza hills back in the early 20th century. Today, for all the operation's modernity, his successors have faithfully maintained that tight family bond with the land. The Barbera Acsé, to no one's surprise, was a finalist for Three Glasses again this year. It offers a very dense ruby garnet, then fragrances of fruit, black pepper, and mint. The palate is clean, crisp and dry, and the finish nicely mirrors the nose, making it a wine of surpassing elegance and distinction. The dark Barbera Croutin also impressed with lovely creamy nuances, set off by notes of earth. On the palate, it is persistent, full and vigorous, then unfurls a seemingly endless finish laced with liquorice and mint. Sant'Ippolito greets the nose with lively profusion of crisp cherry and blossoms. The palate opens to a strapping structure and a masterful finale. A dark garnet-tinged red announces the barbera-cabernet Monferrato Tantra. The nose captivates with rich forest floor, ushering in a palate as smooth as it is full and a long finish of warmth and generosity. The superbly traditional Barbera Superiore Il Sogno '00 is a joint project of Langhe and Asti producers. The lively Barbera Il Matto is straightforward and enjoyable, sporting a purple-rimmed ruby. If its wet earth and geranium nose is a tad rustic, the flavours are complex and toothsome.

The die has been cast. Long consideration and much critical tasting have convinced Walter Fissore to hold back for a year his Barolo Vigna Elena '99. This will give it more time to mature and to shine in future tastings. Familiar as we are with the qualities of this selection from the Ravera vineyard, we eagerly look forward to its performance after the lengthened cellaring. That aside, Walter, ably assisted by his wife Nadia Cogno, has many reasons for satisfaction. His winery is in the top rank of Langhe producers and the wines tasted this year are superb. Let's begin for once with the more straightforward offerings. We could pretend the Dolcetto '02 came from a very good year but we know that's not the case. Yet the unfavourable vintage has not marred the excellent fruit, or the wine's rich mouthfeel. The same goes for Nas-Cetta, the Langhe's most singular wine. Full fruited and impressively weighty, it has minerally crispness and a wonderful harmony. Up one step, we found the Barbera Bricco dei Merli in great form. A well-defined nose tracks redcurrant and blackberries, the mouth is soft and full, and it ends on a nice note of acidity. Power and balance characterize the Langhe Montegrilli but at the top of the range, there is a remarkable Barolo Ravera. The aromatic breadth of liquorice, roasted coffee beans and sweet spices matches the denseness of its colour. A firm but elegant tannic weave bolsters a suede-smooth palate that concludes with great length and admirable proportion.

● Barbera d'Asti Sup. Nizza Acsé '01 ♍♍	6
● Barbera d'Asti Sup. Bricco S. Ippolito '01 ♍♍	5
● Barbera d'Asti Sup. Croutin '01 ♍♍	5
● Monferrato Rosso Tantra '01 ♍♍	6
● Barbera d'Asti Sup. Il Sogno '00 ♍	4
● Barbera del Monferrato Il Matto '02 ♍	3
● Barbera d'Asti Sup. Acsé '99 ♍♍	6
● Barbera d'Asti Sup. Nizza Acsé '00 ♍♍	6
● Monferrato Rosso Tantra '00 ♍♍	6
● Barbera d'Asti Sup. Croutin '99 ♍♍	5

● Barolo Ravera '99 ♍♍	7
● Barbera d'Alba Bricco dei Merli '01 ♍♍	5
● Langhe Rosso Montegrilli '01 ♍♍	5
● Dolcetto d'Alba Vigna del Mandorlo '02 ♍♍	4*
○ Nas-Cetta '02 ♍♍	4
● Barolo Ravera '95 ♍♍	7
● Barolo Ravera '96 ♍♍	7
● Barolo Ravera '97 ♍♍	7
● Barolo Vigna Elena '97 ♍♍	7
● Langhe Rosso Montegrilli '99 ♍♍	5
● Langhe Rosso Montegrilli '00 ♍♍	5
● Barolo Vigna Elena '98 ♍♍	7

NOVI LIGURE (AL)

IL VIGNALE
LOC. LOMELLINA
VIA GAVI, 130
15067 NOVI LIGURE (AL)
TEL. 014372715
E-MAIL: ilvignale@ilvignale.it

Producing wine began almost as a hobby for Piero and Wilma Cappelletti on their spectacular Vignale estate just opposite historic Villa Lomellina. But their drive and attachment to these hills got the upper hand, and today Il Vignale and its wines enjoy great respect in Gavi. The ingredients of success are a mix of dedication, tradition, forward-looking oenology and the communication talents of the Cappellettis, backed up as always by oenologist Giuseppe Bassi. An intense straw yellow draws immediate attention to the Gavi Vigne Alte '02. Nuances of apple and ripe fruit open to a wondrously rich and well-structured palate of harmony and suppleness. A lengthy, deeply satisfying finish nicely seals the wine's overall elegance. The Vilma Cappelletti '02, some of it oak matured, flaunts a vivacious straw yellow. The nose seemed a bit reticent but still managed an attractive vein of vanilla over pear and apple. Flavours are full, crisp, marked by fruit and softened a touch by the alcohol. The palate signs off fairly long and nicely bitterish. The cabernet-pinot noir Rosso di Malì '01 is a fine example of Il Vignale's innovative side. We retasted previous years and confirmed that cellaring considerably boosts its performance. Perhaps it was youthfulness that unduly lowered previous marks. This year, it easily won Two Glasses for its generous fragrances of fruit and espresso, with distinctive varietal herbaceousness. Modest but effective tannins and well-managed acidity complement its zesty, savoury palate, and the length is good.

NOVI LIGURE (AL)

VIGNE DEL PARETO
S.DA DI GAVI, 105
15067 NOVI LIGURE (AL)
TEL. 010532774 - 01432900
E-MAIL: ilpareto@iol.it

The reliability of Pietro Occhetti's cellar is a given in the presently somewhat unexciting area of Gavi. Now at 50,000 bottles total production, Pareto wins widespread praise from industry figures and consumers alike for each release of its two wines. Fundamental to this success is Occhetti's modesty and dedication. From the beginning, he emphasized quality in the bottle over attention-grabbing but ephemeral marketing campaigns. He also had the great advantage of a vision shared with oenologist Mario Ronco, who has shown himself to be a sensitive interpreter of cortese. We are now looking forward to the imminent debut of the first Pareto reds, and are curious to see if their touch is as skilful with barbera and pinot noir. Gavi Vigne del Pareto '02 sports a sparkling straw yellow. The bouquet is still a bit shy, featuring the varietal range of hedgerow, citrus fruit and bitter almond, but a minerally vein is just beginning to peek out. More impressive results may well be in store. There's plenty of crisp fruit on the full, rich palate, with the deliberately partial malolactic imparting an almost citrussy edge, and it signs off well. A star performer for its category again, the estate's Gavi Ricella Alta '02 selection has a lively straw yellow introducing a strikingly elegant nose of well-balanced floral and fruit aromas. Minerally nuances, almost a Pareto hallmark, are emerging nicely and enrich a palate of notable finesse.

● Monferrato Rosso di Malì '01	♀♀	4	
○ Gavi Vigne Alte '02	♀♀	4*	
○ Gavi Vilma Cappelletti '02	♀	4	
○ Gavi Vilma Cappelletti '01	♀♀	4	

○ Gavi Ricella Alta '02	♀♀	4*	
○ Gavi Vigne del Pareto '02	♀	4	
○ Gavi Ricella Alta '01	♀♀	4	

OTTIGLIO (AL)

CAVE DI MOLETO
REG. MOLETO
15038 OTTIGLIO (AL)
TEL. 0142921468
E-MAIL: moleto@moleto.it

After purchasing this winery in 1999, the Botinellis have striven to produce top-notch wines. But the family has carefully restored a historic settlement dating from Saracen times, in 2001 opening a hotel and restaurant. The estate covers 110 hectares, with 28 under vine, and the property also includes the marl quarries that give the cellar its name. In our tastings, the Monferrato Rosso Pieve di San Michele, a barrique-aged blend of barbera, cabernet, merlot and nebbiolo, aroused great interest. An almost opaque red, it opens to a stunning profusion of super-ripe berry fruit, underpinning beguiling herbal notes and a hint of spice. The palate is solidly built, harmonious and lifted nicely by acidity throughout. Both Barberas are exceptional. The Bricco della Prera, matured in small oak, releases a compelling spectrum of ripe berry and morello cherry, with a touch of toastiness at the end, and its structure is quite thrillingly complex. The steel-vinified Procchio shows purple-edged ruby, then a superb nose and palate. A mix of cabernet and merlot, the Monferrato Rosso Mulej was given an 18-month stay in barrique. It parades lavish herbaceousness and luscious hints of cinnamon and toasty oak. The classically structured palate is no less impressive, with its firm acidic component. Also recommended is the dried-grape Moscato, Oro dei Saraceni.

PIOBESI D'ALBA (CN)

TENUTA CARRETTA
LOC. CARRETTA, 2
12040 PIOBESI D'ALBA (CN)
TEL. 0173619119
E-MAIL: t.carretta@tenutacarretta.it

This estate overlooks the village of Piobesi, in the heart of the Roero. It is full of activity these days as the Miroglio Dracone family, the winery's owners, are investing energy and money in transforming their already impressive operation into a focal point for the entire area. As a winery, Carretta is first rate, and so its wines. But there is also a conference centre, and a Relais hotel with nine suites, and Le Clivie, a top-rated restaurant that moved here from the town. In short, Tenuta Carretta is a complete hospitality centre for visitors and tourists, just the type of facility the Roero needs to add lustre to its image and quality. Now to the wines. We tasted some terrific offerings this year, so plaudits go to the Negro-Monchiero technical team, especially to Gian Domenico Negro, who nurses so many of the winery's initiatives to fruition. The three nebbiolo-based wines are all superb. Barbaresco della Cascina Bordino offers complexity to spare on the nose, then opens powerfully to an impressive structure and a uniquely dynamic follow-through. The flagship territory wine, Roero Bric Paradiso, is equally brilliant, yielding a sensual kaleidoscope of fruit and spice, then a supple palate that nicely echoes the nose. Almost as outstanding is the Barolo Cannubi. A nose of rare eloquence unfolds in subtle fruit and tobacco, and opulent tannins inform a gorgeously structured, glossy palate. Excellent, too, are the Langhe Bric Quercia, from barbera and nebbiolo, the Barbera, and the Nebbiolo, while the Dolcetto and the Arneis are straightforward and well made.

● Monferrato Rosso		
Pieve di San Michele '01	▼▼	5
● Barbera del M.to Procchio '00	▼▼	4*
● Barbera del M.to		
Bricco della Prera '00	▼▼	5
● Monferrato Rosso Mulej '00	▼▼	5
○ Oro dei Saraceni	▼	5

● Barbaresco Cascina Bordino '00	▼▼	7
● Barolo Vigneti in Cannubi '99	▼▼	8
● Roero Sup. Bric Paradiso '01	▼▼	5
● Barbera d'Alba Podium Serre '01	▼▼	5
● Langhe Rosso Bric Quercia '01	▼▼	5
● Nebbiolo d'Alba Vigna Tavoleto '01	▼▼	5
● Dolcetto d'Alba		
Vigna del Pozzo '02	▼	4
○ Roero Arneis Vigna Canorei '02	▼	5
● Barbaresco Cascina Bordino '98	▽▽	8
● Roero Sup. Bric Paradiso '99	▽▽	5
● Roero Sup. Bric Paradiso '00	▽▽	5
● Barolo Vigneti in Cannubi '98	▽▽	8
● Barbaresco Cascina Bordino '99	▽▽	8

PORTACOMARO (AT)

PRIOCCA (CN)

CASTELLO DEL POGGIO
LOC. IL POGGIO, 9
14038 PORTACOMARO (AT)
TEL. 0141202543
E-MAIL: info@poggio.it

CASCINA VAL DEL PRETE
S.DA SANTUARIO, 2
12040 PRIOCCA (CN)
TEL. 0173616534 - 0173616624
E-MAIL: valdelprete@tiscalinet.it

The remains of an ancient settlement, where once stood a Templar fortress, overlook a picturesque vine-filled amphitheatre of over 130 hectares, a magnificent site surrounding the Valle del Tempo. Castello del Poggio does very well with native varieties. The Dolcetto offers a crisp but subtle bouquet built around wild berries, crushed flowers and clove, with a structure that is equally multi-layered. Severe cluster thinning and scrupulous vineyard management have produced a beautiful Grignolino, marked by a lovely hue between ruby and dark cherry. Most of the grapeseeds were discarded after about 36 hours' fermentation, thus eliminating the variety's usual tannic edge. The wine is redolent of typical geraniums and spice, leading into a massively structured, warm, expansive palate. The dark-cloaked Barbera d'Asti Masaréj '01 is superb, exhibiting a well-calibrated mélange of red berries and spices. It then opens to considerable power, tempered by well-integrated tannins and crisp acidity, before finishing quite long. The Barbera Bunéis is sourced from dense-planted vineyards with very low cropping levels of slightly over 40 quintals per hectare. A bit of merlot is added. The aromatics here tend to super-ripe, showing cherry and blackberry preserve, with a definite oak signature. The mouth builds to satisfying intensity with good depth. We finish with the Moscato, which offers a nuanced straw yellow and nicely balanced sweetness.

Mario Roagna is one of the rising stars of Roero winemaking. His career is in a sense emblematic of the entire area's determination to grow and to establish itself as forward looking and quality oriented. Mario's cellar is set in the midst of vines, and standing there you marvel at a vineyard amphitheatre as lovely as it is at times unlucky. For two years in a row, in fact, Mario's vineyards have fallen victim to hail. This forced a drop in production, but also dealt a blow to estate morale, as much hard work came to nothing. But far from giving in to these difficulties, Mario seems to have drawn energy from them, and is determined to better past performances. In fact, his line-up this year is outstanding, starting with the Roero '00, which encored last year's Three Glasses. A vibrantly powerful red introduces an amalgam of fruit, tannin and balance we have rarely seen equalled. The suppleness of the palate speaks of masterly skills with oak, and the spice and fruit make a triumphal return in the finish. We found the Barbera Carolina impressively well rounded, oak gently honing its acidity. It owes its distinctiveness to the cluster thinning that gives Mario such outstanding fruit, the secret of his complex, irresistible wines. Finally, we liked his Arneis Luet for its tangy fruit and glass after glass quaffability.

● Barbera d'Asti Masaréj Gianni Zonin Vineyards '01	🍷🍷	6
● Piemonte Barbera Bunéis Gianni Zonin Vineyards '01	🍷🍷	6
● Grignolino d'Asti '02	🍷	4
○ Moscato d'Asti '02	🍷	4
● Monferrato Dolcetto '02	🍷	4
● Barbera d'Asti Masaréj Gianni Zonin Vineyards '00	🍷🍷	5
● Piemonte Barbera Bunéis Gianni Zonin Vineyards '00	🍷🍷	6

● Roero '00	🍷🍷🍷	6
○ Roero Arneis Luet '02	🍷🍷	4*
● Barbera d'Alba Sup. Carolina '01	🍷🍷	5
● Nebbiolo d'Alba Vigna di Lino '00	🍷🍷🍷	5
● Nebbiolo d'Alba Vigna di Lino '99	🍷🍷	5
● Nebbiolo d'Alba Vigna di Lino '98	🍷🍷	5
● Barbera d'Alba Sup. Carolina '99	🍷🍷	5
● Barbera d'Alba Sup. Carolina '00	🍷🍷	5
● Roero '98	🍷🍷	6
● Roero '99	🍷🍷	6

PRIOCCA (CN)

HILBERG - PASQUERO
VIA BRICCO GATTI, 16
12040 PRIOCCA (CN)
TEL. 0173616197
E-MAIL: hilberg@libero.it

QUARGNENTO (AL)

COLLE MANORA
S.DA BOZZOLE, 4
15044 QUARGNENTO (AL)
TEL. 0131219252
E-MAIL: info@collemanora.it

Michelangelo Pasquero is one of Roero's top producers. You could call his operation a boutique winery, given its diminutive size and the care Pasquero devotes to the smallest detail. For example, the tiny, barrel-girt tasting space is often the venue for lively gatherings and enjoyable winter festivities. "Miclo", whose day job is teaching in Priocca, puts much of himself, his human warmth and his graciousness, into the winery, and that personal style reveals itself in his wines. This Guide has passed more than one favourable judgement on these wines in the past. But this year, the duo of Pasquero-Hilberg (the surname of Miclo's German-born wife Annette) has outdone itself, as we found out when we visited to taste the range. Their Nebbiolo d'Alba has become a benchmark, and the 2001 edition amply confirms this role. The colour is a garnet-veined ruby, then the nose exhibits its usual exuberant medley of floral notes, wild berries and chocolate. The oak is even more restrained than in the past, serving only to underline the seductive, tannin-glossed texture. "Three Glasses" was the inevitable verdict. The Barbera Superiore missed a third Glass by the merest whisker. The dense, velvet nose is laced with cherry, redcurrant, and mint, and followed by a palate that offers superlative texture, good balance and unbelievable opulence. All the other wines are good. The nebbiolo-barbera Langhe Pedrocha is warm and nobly structured, the Barbera d'Alba displays glossy fruit, while the Vareij, a barbera-brachetto mix, is sheer delight to drink.

This winery was purchased in 2000 by Giorgio Schön. Assisted by Donato Lanati and Walter Piccinino, he has put quality first in his current wine production. Giorgio has 75 hectares of estate-owned vineyards, on mostly clayey soils, and new vineyards have been planted recently, some to international varieties. Proof of the trio's skill is the fact that all the wines tasted this year were awarded Two Glasses. We especially liked the Palo Alto, a barrique-matured blend of barbera, cabernet and merlot. It flaunts an almost opaque garnet-flecked ruby, then captivates with extra-ripe berry fruit veined with fresh hay and green pepper. The structure is massive, but kept in check by a nice touch of acidity. A little cabernet is added to barbera for the Barbera Manora. The result shows ruby with purplish highlights, then morello cherry and violets unfold, followed by a lift of spice. The mouth shows good structure and the finish is more than adequate. Mila is a sauvignon and chardonnay blend that is cask-fermented and left on the lees for about eight months. It's a deep straw yellow, and the aromas range from the delicately floral to the richly fruity, with a final note of vanilla. The palate is absolutely elegant, thanks to a tangy complex of flavours that continue long. We found the Mimosa, a monovarietal sauvignon, particularly good.

● Nebbiolo d'Alba '01	🍷🍷🍷	6
● Barbera d'Alba Sup. '01	🍷	6
● Langhe Rosso Pedrocha '01	🍷	5
● Barbera d'Alba '02	🍷	4
● Vareij Rosso '02	🍷	4
● Barbera d'Alba Sup. '97	🍷🍷🍷	6
● Barbera d'Alba Sup. '98	🍷🍷🍷	6
● Nebbiolo d'Alba '99	🍷🍷🍷	6
● Nebbiolo d'Alba '00	🍷🍷🍷	6
● Nebbiolo d'Alba '98	🍷🍷	6
● Barbera d'Alba Sup. '99	🍷🍷	6
● Barbera d'Alba Sup. '00	🍷🍷	6

● Barbera del M.to Manora '00	🍷🍷	4*
● Monferrato Rosso		
Palo Alto '99	🍷🍷	5
○ Mila Bianco '01	🍷🍷	5
○ Monferrato Bianco Mimosa '01	🍷🍷	4

ROCCA GRIMALDA (AL)

CASCINA LA MADDALENA
LOC. PIANI DEL PADRONE, 257
15078 ROCCA GRIMALDA (AL)
TEL. 0143876074
E-MAIL: info@cascina-maddalena.com

Running this winery are three dedicated, experienced women, Ann, Cristina and Marilena, with technical help from oenologist Giovanni Bailo and Domenico's important contribution in the vineyard. Cascina La Maddalena is one of the top producers in the Ovada area, where attention has always focused on the native dolcetto and barbera. The Monferrato Rosso Bricco Maddalena is an outstanding, barrique-matured monovarietal of dense, nearly opaque, ruby. It opens with a beautifully complex spectrum of aromatics, including red berries and blossoms, and hints of spices, then continues into an impressive, harmonious structure which augurs well for further development. The cellar produces two Barberas. The standard label, vinified in steel, earned Two Glasses for its excellent interpretation of the variety. Deep ruby red ushers in lavish berry fruit fragrances and a crisp vein of refreshing acidity. The other Barbera, the Rossa d'Orca, is partly matured in once-used barriques. An intense, purple-tinged ruby in appearance, it releases rich berry fruit on the nose with a nice touch of toasty oak. Perhaps a bit taut in the mouth, it is still quite harmonious. The Dolcetto Bricco del Bagatto '01 catches the eye with its deep ruby, then gorgeous complexity reigns on the nose, where toasty espresso and chocolate notes emerge over a base of rich fruit just this side of over-ripe. The mouth shows moderate tannin and an appealing, full-fleshed texture.

ROCCHETTA TANARO (AT)

BRAIDA
VIA ROMA, 94
14030 ROCCHETTA TANARO (AT)
TEL. 0141644113
E-MAIL: info@braida.it

The Bologna family, it is always our pleasure to note, has devoted itself to carrying on the historic legacy left by Giacomo Bologna, rightly considered the father of Barbera d'Asti as we know it today. The exceptional dedication of the winery staff is mirrored in the high quality displayed across the entire product line. In addition to the owners, Anna, Beppe and Raffaella, also involved in the business are Cristina Bologna and Norbert Reinisch, Beppe's wife and Raffaella's partner, respectively. Our tastings brought some surprises. The venerable Bricco della Bigotta and the Bricco dell'Uccellone were missing. They are deemed to need more maturation time and will be reviewed next year. Their place is well filled by the Ai Suma. It shows deep purple ruby, and scents of ripe cherry over a minerally base emerge on a dense, complex nose. The palate then opens to massive weight and an opulent texture, caressed by delicate acidity. The Montebruna is less complex and a bit husky, but the palate offers good alcoholic warmth. The line-up continues with a very distinctive Moscato, an appealing Brachetto, a barbera and pinot noir Monferrato Rosso and a pair of wines from the Serra dei Fiori estate belonging to the Bologna, Giacosa, and Macaluso families. Of the two, the Langhe Bianco Il Fiore stands out for its lavish, citrussy nose and well-sustained palate.

● Barbera del M.to '01	�♔	4*
● Monferrato Rosso		
Bricco Maddalena '01	♔♔	5
● Barbera del M.to Rossa d'Ocra '01	♔	5
● Dolcetto di Ovada		
Bricco del Bagatto '01	♔	5
● Barbera del M.to Rossa d'Ocra '99	♔♔	5
● Monferrato Rosso		
Bricco Maddalena '99	♔♔	5
● Barbera del M.to Rossa d'Ocra '00	♔♔	5
● Monferrato Rosso		
Bricco Maddalena '00	♔♔	5

● Barbera d'Asti Ai Suma '01	♔♔	8
● Barbera d'Asti Montebruna '01	♔♔	4
○ Langhe Bianco Il Fiore '02	♔♔	4
○ Moscato d'Asti		
Vigna Senza Nome '02	♔♔	4
○ Langhe Bianco Asso di Fiori '01	♔	5
● Monferrato Rosso Il Bacialé '01	♔	4
● Brachetto d'Acqui '02	♔	4
● Barbera d'Asti		
Bricco dell'Uccellone '98	♔♔♔	7
● Barbera d'Asti Ai Suma '00	♔♔	8
● Barbera d'Asti		
Bricco della Bigotta '00	♔♔	7

RODELLO (CN)

F.LLI MOSSIO
FRAZ. CASCINA CARAMELLI
VIA MONTÀ, 12
12050 RODELLO (CN)
TEL. 0173617149
E-MAIL: mossio@mossio.com

Congratulations are always in order for the Mossio family, who own this small model winery set in an area of the Langhe most suited to the production of Dolcetto d'Alba. Cousins Valerio and Remo, who receive important help in areas of the operation from Mauro, Guido and Claudio, have achieved a momentum that allows them to put out great wines even in less than favourable years. The 2002 vintage was certainly one of those in this district, yet the Mossios were able to craft some superb wines, contrary to all expectations. A visit to their winery reveals the keys to their success. The eight hectares of vineyard, all in Rodello, are among the loveliest and most meticulously managed that you could wish to see. The cellars are modest in size, but well organized. The icing on the Mossio cake is that talented Beppe Caviola consults on technical aspects of the winemaking. Mossio's few labels are further reduced this year. There is no standard-label Dolcetto, nor will it reappear, so attention can now be focused on just two wines, both outstanding. Bricco Caramelli came within a whisker of a third Glass. Its almost impenetrable garnet matches the complexity of a nose that shows off ripe plum, blackberry and red berries, nicely layered over a delicately herbaceous, spicy background. The mouth opens velvet, rounded, rich and full, continuing through to a lengthy, harmonious finale. The Piano delli Perdoni shows a bit less concentration, but is well perfumed, elegant and has exemplary balance. As always, the Langhe Rosso, a nebbiolo-barbera mix, is absolutely delicious.

● Dolcetto d'Alba Bricco Caramelli '02	**ΨΨ**	4*
● Langhe Rosso '01	**ΨΨ**	5
● Dolcetto d'Alba Piano delli Perdoni '02	**ΨΨ**	4*
● Dolcetto d'Alba Bricco Caramelli '00	ΨΨΨ	4
● Dolcetto d'Alba Bricco Caramelli '01	ΨΨ	4
● Dolcetto d'Alba Piano delli Perdoni '01	ΨΨ	4

ROSIGNANO MONFERRATO (AL)

VICARA
CASCINA MADONNA DELLE GRAZIE
15030 ROSIGNANO MONFERRATO (AL)
TEL. 0142488054
E-MAIL: vicara@tiscalinetitit

The Visconti-Cassinis-Ravizza partnership moves its wines up the quality ladder each year. The Cantico della Crosia, a Barbera del Monferrato Superiore, sports a dramatically intense, purple-tinged ruby before revealing a nose redolent of vanilla and tobacco over plum and fruit preserve. The palate is built firm but supple. The deep ruby-hued Barbera del Monferrato Volpuva shows classy fruit, invigorating acidity and a good finish. Everything is in exceptional balance. The Grignolino '02 won Two Glasses and is certainly one of the star performers of this native Monferrato grape. Pale ruby in colour, it throws aromas of geranium, roses and spice, progressing into an appealing, lightly tannic palate and a good finale. There were good results, too, for the tightly-knit Monferrato Rubello, with its sparkling ruby hue and fruity nose ripe with cherry and plum preserve, laced with cocoa powder. Velvety fruit flavours on the palate are complemented by moderate tannins. We found the Barbera Vivace among the most appealing of those we tried this year. It nearly earned Two Glasses for its blueberry and redcurrant, with a hint of new-mown hay. The Monferrato l'Uccelletta offers a pale orange-shot ruby and flaunts a remarkable harmonious berry and spice mosaic on the nose. This is followed by understated tannins and well-judged acidity. We conclude with Vicara's Monferrato Bianco Airales. Light gold in colour, with expansive scents of wildflowers, white peach and citrus, it ends satisfyingly long.

● Barbera del M.to Sup. Cantico della Crosia '01	**ΨΨ**	5
● Monferrato Rosso Rubello '01	**ΨΨ**	5
● Barbera del M.to Volpuva '02	**ΨΨ**	3*
● Grignolino del M.to Casalese '02	**ΨΨ**	4
● Monferrato Rosso l'Uccelletta '01	**Ψ**	4
● Barbera del M.to Vivace '02	**Ψ**	3
○ Monferrato Bianco Airales '02	**Ψ**	4
● Barbera del M.to Sup. Cantico della Crosia '99	ΨΨ	5
● Barbera del M.to Sup. '00	ΨΨ	4
● Barbera del M.to Sup. Cantico della Crosia '00	ΨΨ	5
● Monferrato Rosso Rubello '00	ΨΨ	5

SAN GIORGIO CANAVESE (TO)

ORSOLANI
VIA MICHELE CHIESA, 12
10090 SAN GIORGIO CANAVESE (TO)
TEL. 012432386
E-MAIL: orsolani@tiscalinet.it

The winery run by Gigi Orsolani and his father, Francesco, is one of the most reliable in the Canavese area. Although this year's tastings didn't reveal any superstars, the general quality level of the wines is high. La Rustia '02, made of well-ripened erbaluce, succeeds in a difficult growing year. The lengthy nose of apricot and spring flowers is sharply defined and nicely varietal. The attack is clean and the mouth admirably balanced, with a refreshing acidic vein that continues long. We were not quite so enthusiastic about the Vignot Sant'Antonio, again erbaluce, but barrique fermented and matured. The variety is there on the nose, but the oak is much in evidence, bringing peanuts and sweet spice. The mouth, too, still seems out of kilter. We highly recommend the well-crafted Brut Metodo Classico, which offers a fascinating counterpoint of yeastiness and erbaluce's varietal characteristics. The Sulé is produced from erbaluce grapes dried in trays for six months and then cask fermented. It is luminous amber, and unfolds warm, lavish scents of candied apricot, almond paste and apple, proceeding to a palate of exquisite balance. The Carema Le Tabbie, a red vinified at the Cantina Produttori di Carema, shows the great delicacy and elegance of nebbiolo made in this style. It is a wine of compelling grace that exhibits all the variety's best qualities. Acini Sparsi is sourced from very old vineyards, planted to a mixture of native varieties.

SAN MARTINO ALFIERI (AT)

MARCHESI ALFIERI
P.ZZA ALFIERI, 28
14010 SAN MARTINO ALFIERI (AT)
TEL. 0141976015
E-MAIL: alfieri@marchesialfieri.it

The Barbera Alfiera is again this noted winery's top thoroughbred, taking home Three Glasses for the third year in a row. This impressive achievement crowns the superb efforts of sisters Giovanna, Antonella, and Emanuela San Martino di San Germano, ably flanked by oenologist Mario Olivero and outside consultant Giancarlo Scaglione. Alfiera is named for the source vineyard, an outstandingly-sited "sorì", or south-facing parcel, planted in 1937 in the district of San Martino Alfieri. The 2001 displays ruby garnet, then captivating scents of forest floor and black pepper meld with intriguing peach and wood resin aromas to build a complex, confident nose. The palate opens quickly to a dynamic progression that pushes through to an endless, full-fruited finale. The beautifully-crafted La Tota, briefly barrique-matured, immediately won us over with its polished charm. Deep hued, it yields rich scents of cocoa, ginger and earth over a fruit base. Lingering warmth on the palate leads to a finish that explodes in delicious, cherry-dominated fruit. We liked all the remaining wines, beginning with the pinot noir and barbera Rosso dei Marchesi. It proffers inviting mown hay and forest floor aromas, ending with a ringing flourish that caps a firmly tannic texture. The single-grape pinot noir San Germano possesses a solid varietal nose and develops dry, clean and lively in the mouth. We found the Grignolino Sansoero very easy drinking, but still very well-typed.

○ Caluso Passito Sulé '98	🍷🍷	7
○ Erbaluce di Caluso La Rustìa '02	🍷🍷	4*
○ Caluso Spumante Brut M. Cl.	🍷🍷	5
● Carema Le Tabbie '99	🍷🍷	6
● Canavese Rosso Acini Sparsi '01	🍷	5
○ Caluso Bianco		
Vignot S. Antonio '01	🍷	4
○ Caluso Bianco		
Vignot S. Antonio '00	🍷🍷	4
○ Caluso Passito Sulé '97	🍷🍷	7
○ Cuvée Storica Spumante M. Cl.		
Gran Ris. '97	🍷🍷	5
● Carema Le Tabbie '97	🍷🍷	6

● Barbera d'Asti Sup. Alfiera '01	🍷🍷🍷	6
● Barbera d'Asti Sup. La Tota '01	🍷🍷	4*
● Monferrato Rosso dei Marchesi '01	🍷🍷	3*
● Monferrato Rosso		
S. Germano '01	🍷🍷	5
● Piemonte Grignolino Sansoero '02	🍷	4
● Barbera d'Asti Sup. Alfiera '99	🍷🍷🍷	6
● Barbera d'Asti Sup. Alfiera '00	🍷🍷🍷	6
● Barbera d'Asti Sup. Alfiera '98	🍷🍷	6
● Monferrato Rosso		
S. Germano '99	🍷🍷	5

SAN MARZANO OLIVETO (AT)

ALFIERO BOFFA
VIA LEISO, 50
14050 SAN MARZANO OLIVETO (AT)
TEL. 0141856115
E-MAIL: alfieroboffa@tin.it

Alfiero Boffa and his sons, Rossano and Simone, manage a winery operation with 25 hectares of vineyard and an attractive setting for the ageing cellars in the ancient San Marzano fortress. As their Vigne Uniche project demonstrates, the cru concept is a major priority for the Boffa family. It's also worth noting that no Barbera from this cellar is sourced from a vineyard less than 45 years old. Now to the wines. The Velo di Maya is mostly barbera with dollops of other varieties. Garnet-tending ruby is followed by ripe aromas of fruit and rhubarb, a well-structured palate with racy progression, and a satisfying long finale that nicely mirrors the nose. The Barberas are all in the Vigne Uniche category, and the one we most enjoyed was La Riva, from the Nizza subzone. It proffers a delicate palette of spring blossoms, earth and coffee, leading to a self-confident mouth and a luscious finish boasting liquorice and menthol. Leather and earth at first dominate the Collina della Vedova, a tri-variety blend, which then develops good extractive weight. The Vigna delle More seems already a bit developed, with a bracing palate and a decent finish. Unfortunately, the Barbera d'Asti Superiore Vigna Cua Longa and the Vigna Muntrivé do not pass muster.

SAN MARZANO OLIVETO (AT)

TENUTA DELL'ARBIOLA
REG. SALINE, 67
14050 SAN MARZANO OLIVETO (AT)
TEL. 0141856194
E-MAIL: info@arbiola.it

The Terzano family has news a-plenty. The difficult 2002 vintage left its mark on this San Marzano Oliveto winery, so the owners deliberately reduced their line-up. Omitted are the 2002 Monferrato Bianco Arbiola and the Clelie VI, also a Monferrato Bianco. The Monferrato Rosso Arbiola '01, a blend of local varieties, will be released later, and we'll taste this wine, too, further on. Left on their own, as it were, are the two Barbera d'Asti, besides the Moscato. But there's more news. Off the wines for a moment, we can report that the family have acquired a new estate between San Marzano and Calamandrana. It comprises eight full hectares under vine plus farm buildings, where they plan to put in barbera, merlot and cabernet, for some new future products. The last bit of news is the opening of a Relais hotel at the winery. Five spacious rooms await guests, who can purchase wines in the new retail outlet, or taste them in the well-designed tasting room. Finally to the wines. There was an excellent performance from the Barbera Romilda. Its deep ruby red nicely matches an aromatic array featuring rich spice and blackberry, plum and cassis fruit, layered over a touch of mineral and earthy notes. It opens to a full, round mouthfeel that balances velvet softness against lively acidity, and ends long. The Carlotta is a high achiever as well, if a tad less concentrated than the Romilda. The Moscato is lively and light.

● Barbera d'Asti Sup.Nizza Vigna La Riva '00	♟♟	5
● Velo di Maya '00	♟♟	5
● Barbera d'Asti Sup. Collina della Vedova '00	♟	5
● Barbera d'Asti Sup. Vigna delle More '01	♟	5
● Barbera d'Asti Sup. Collina della Vedova '98	♗♗	5
● Velo di Maya '98	♗♗	5
● Barbera d'Asti Sup. Vigna Cua Longa '00	♗♗	4
● Barbera d'Asti Sup. Vigna delle More '00	♗♗	4

● Barbera d'Asti Sup. Nizza Romilda VII '01	♟♟	6
● Barbera d'Asti Carlotta '01	♟♟	4
○ Moscato d'Asti Ferlingot '02	♟	4
● Barbera d'Asti Sup. La Romilda V '99	♗♗	6
● Barbera d'Asti Sup. Nizza Romilda VI '00	♗♗	6
● Monferrato Rosso Arbiola '00	♗♗	5

CA' D'GAL

FRAZ. VALDIVILLA
S.DA VECCHIA DI VALDIVILLA, 1
12058 SANTO STEFANO BELBO (CN)
TEL. 0141847103
E-MAIL: alessandro.boido@virgilio.it

The 2002 growing year forced many producers to wrestle with their conscience. Prolonged rainy spells and even ruinous hail in some cases posed severe threats to the premium offerings of many wineries. Should they go ahead and produce the wines or to skip the year? Sando Boito, owner of this gorgeous cellar-cum-"agriturismo" facility, didn't hesitate. His customary line of wines severely battered, he released the only survivor of nature's vagaries, his Moscato Lumine, to which he added the new Langhe Pian del Gäje '99. Yes, just two wines, but excellent ones, perfectly capable of making up for the others missing in action. Just as important, they are testimony to winemaking conscience and professionalism. Lumine shows a deep, lively straw yellow, flecked with green highlights. The nose releases a rich medley of orange blossom, peach and elderflower, tailing off with nice herbal notes. It offers good, fat body which, in contrast to the leanness of the year, is graceful, well-proportioned and beautifully recapitulates the nose's sensory richness. The finish is gratifyingly long. With little else to present, Sandro brought out some older vintages of the Vigna Vecchia, the other Moscato he produces. The ploy worked, for we were impressed by the staying power of those five to six-year-old wines. The first release of the Langhe is reassuringly good. A blend of 60 per cent freisa, plus barbera and dolcetto, it has nicely proportioned fruit on the nose, progressing consistently with a luscious acid-laced roundness. A wine to watch.

○	Moscato d'Asti Lumine '02	ŶŶ	4*
●	Langhe Rosso Pian del Gäje '99	ŶŶ	4
○	Moscato d'Asti Vigna Vecchia '00	♀♀	4
○	Moscato d'Asti Vigna Vecchia '01	♀♀	4

SANTO STEFANO BELBO (CN)

PIERO GATTI

LOC. MONCUCCO, 28
12058 SANTO STEFANO BELBO (CN)
TEL. 0141840918
E-MAIL: az.agr.gattipiero@hotmail.com

Founded in 1998, the winery run by Rita Gatti and oenologist Sergio Stella produces a little more than 50,000 bottles. The vineyards are on the hillsides at Moncucco, in ideal locations for Moscato. Let's begin our reviews with the Moscato, the cellar's lead wine and among the best we tried this year. The colour is pale straw, and it offers fragrances of markedly elegant, subtly nuanced orange and elder blossom. The effervescence is in perfect balance with the touch of sweetness, and its appealingly austere structure moves seamlessly and consistently into a lengthy finish. The Freisa Violetta shows garnet-tinged ruby, and the nose suggests both raspberry and earth. Its full, tightly-woven texture pleases enormously as the wine glides into a lingering, pleasingly bitterish finish, nicely lifted by scents of cocoa. An 80-20 mix of barbera and freisa goes into Verbeia. After a medium-deep red, the nose is a straightforward presentation of wild berries and fruit, with decent structure in the mouth, good mouthfeel, and a rich finale. The Brachetto '02 ends our review. An intense cherry hue precedes somewhat evolved aromas that privilege crisp pear fragrances. The palate displays satisfactory weight, progressing to a light but pleasurable finish that nicely reprises nose and palate.

●	Langhe Freisa La Violetta '01	ŶŶ	4*
○	Piemonte Moscato '02	ŶŶ	4*
●	Verbeia '01	Ŷ	4
●	Piemonte Brachetto '02	Ŷ	4
●	Verbeia '00	♀♀	4

SANTO STEFANO BELBO (CN)

SERGIO GRIMALDI - CA' DU SINDIC
LOC. SAN GRATO, 15
12058 SANTO STEFANO BELBO (CN)
TEL. 0141840341
E-MAIL: grimaldi.sergio@virgilio.it

Sergio Grimaldi's winery boasts ten hectares under vine sited on the hills of San Grato, where the cellars are located, and at San Maurizio, both in the municipality of Santo Stefano. Sergio and his family are fiercely dedicated to their work, constantly working to raise the quality of the wine by gradually modernizing their equipment. At the same time, they are focusing increased attention on the vines. One of the wines that clearly mirrors those improvements is the Barbera San Grato. The clusters were severely thinned during growth, and the wine spent a brief time in cask. A deep garnet ruby in appearance, it has wide-ranging fragrances, from the classic crushed fruit to subtle tarry notes. The mouth has good weight and progresses impressively to a lingering finale that beautifully reflects the nose. We always like the Moscato Ca' du Sindic Capsula Oro, sourced from venerable vines scattered over the hillside of San Maurizio. This year's edition is a brilliant pale straw, with a finely nuanced rose and peach fruitiness over hints of resin on the ripe, richly-faceted nose. A very delicate fizziness cossets its silky texture, and the lengthy finish is in no hurry to fade away. Down just a notch is the Moscato Capsula Argento, whose fine varietal qualities, and dense but elegant texture make it a lovely wine. Likewise recommended is the floral-scented Brachetto, with luscious flavours and pronounced fizziness.

SANTO STEFANO BELBO (CN)

I VIGNAIOLI DI S. STEFANO
LOC. MARINI, 12
12058 SANTO STEFANO BELBO (CN)
TEL. 0141840419
E-MAIL: ivignaioli@virgilio.it

The winery has about 40 hectares under vine in some of the most exceptional areas at Santo Stefano Belbo. This allows the cellar to produce an impressive 180,000 bottles each year. We tasted three wines, all Moscatos, the area's most important variety. The trio all show top-notch quality, as they have through the years, reflecting a winemaking philosophy that starts with good fruit, then uses the most up-to-date equipment, with no compromises along the way. The management has made considerable efforts recently to raise the Vignaioli di Santo Stefano market profile, introducing for example a very unusual sleek bottle and a label, designed by Giacomo Bersanetti, whose half moon motif evokes the stories of Cesare Pavese. Let's open our review of the wines we tasted with the Moscato d'Asti. A nice medium straw, it tempts with bright aromas of elderflower and peach, which define the notably elegant nose. Its sweetness is well balanced by a soft effervescence, which makes the palate dense and luscious. The Asti is similar in appearance, exuding a breadth of fragrances that ranges through cakes, ripe peach and yeasted dough. It then opens to a crisp, harmonious palate. The Moscato Passito is a lovely shade of amber, showing maturity on the nose and assertive sweetness.

● Barbera d'Asti San Grato '01	♟♟	4*
○ Moscato d'Asti Ca' du Sindic Capsula Oro '02	♟♟	4*
○ Moscato d'Asti Ca' du Sindic Capsula Argento '02	♟	4
● Piemonte Brachetto Ca' du Sindic '02	♟	4
● Barbera d'Asti '00	♟♟	4

○ Piemonte Moscato Passito IL '00	♟♟	5
○ Asti '02	♟♟	4
○ Moscato d'Asti '02	♟♟	4
○ Asti '01	♟♟	4
○ Piemonte Moscato Passito IL '99	♟♟	6

SAREZZANO (AL)

SCURZOLENGO (AT)

MUTTI
LOC. SAN RUFFINO, 49
15050 SAREZZANO (AL)
TEL. 0131884119

CANTINE SANT'AGATA
REG. MEZZENA, 19
14030 SCURZOLENGO (AT)
TEL. 0141203186
E-MAIL: info@santagata.com

The Mutti winery in San Ruffino has won recognition as one of the most reliable producers in this part of Piemonte. Its success is founded on the performance of wines based on the native timorasso grape variety. Andrea Mutti was the first winemaker to adopt his friend Walter Massa's view concerning the variety's future. Today, his versions of this lusty wine with an intriguing personality are among the best anywhere. Castagnoli is one such wine. Its fascinating greenish highlights emerge through a deep straw yellow, and a sure-footed, rich nose reveals mineral notes that yield to tropical fruit and a hint of balsam. The palate is vigorous and full bodied, nicely warmed and softened by a good level of alcohol. The Sauvignon Sull'Aia also reveals Andrea's expert hand with whites, parading seductive floral scents over citrus and banana. Among the reds, we especially liked the San Ruffino, a Barbera that matures in barriques for a longish period. As a result, the wine shows good structure with fine oak-derived spiciness, dense structure and enticing leather and liquorice. Right up with it is the 100 per cent cabernet Rivadestra, also cask-conditioned, which offers well-defined, crisp aromas of red berries and tobacco. There is plenty of complexity to its well-proportioned structure, and all the sensory impressions are admirably gathered together in a long, appealing finish. The barbera Rosso Boscobarona shows less power but is pure drinking pleasure.

A production of over 100,000 bottles, from about a dozen hectares of vineyard, sums up the Monferrato cellar run by the Cavallero brothers. Franco and Claudio offer a number of classics, with Barbera at the top of the list, unsurprisingly enough, given its traditional role in this area. So let's begin with the Barberas. As always, the Cavalé gave a great performance. A deep ruby garnet is followed by a rich aromatic display built solidly on dark berry fruit that lifts up to scents of cakes and toasty oak. The dense structure is impressive, as are its vigorous progression and a finish that mirrors the nose. A step or two down is the Barbera d'Asti Superiore Altea, which has a lighter colour and more perfunctory nose. The weight in the mouth is decent, though, and the wine finishes lively and medium long. Baby is the winery's standard-label Barbera. Fruity all the way through, it is nicely varietal, with a palate that's pleasantly consistent and understated. The Monterovere, a barbera, cabernet, and nebbiolo mix, is superb. Flowers, forest floor and leather come together on the nose, then it progresses with good structure into an exceptionally fine finish that centres on rich liquorice. One Glass went to the Grignolino. Redolent of mint and almond, it is crisp and lean in the mouth. And there was another Glass for the floral, spicy Ruché, which has a luscious, sappy palate.

○	Colli Tortonesi Bianco Castagnoli '01	♟♟	5
●	Colli Tortonesi Rosso Rivadestra '01	♟♟	5
●	Colli Tortonesi Rosso S. Ruffino '01	♟♟	5
●	Colli Tortonesi Rosso Boscobarona '02	♟	3*
○	Colli Tortonesi Bianco Sull'Aia '02	♟	4*
●	Colli Tortonesi Rosso Rivadestra '99	♟♟	5
○	Colli Tortonesi Bianco Castagnoli '00	♟♟	5
●	Colli Tortonesi Rosso S. Ruffino '00	♟♟	5

●	Barbera d'Asti Sup. Cavalé '00	♟♟	5
●	Monferrato Rosso Monterovere '00	♟♟	4
●	Barbera d'Asti Sup. Altea '00	♟	3
●	Barbera d'Asti Baby '01	♟	3
●	Grignolino d'Asti Miravalle '02	♟	3
●	Ruché di Castagnole M.to 'Na Vota '02	♟	4
●	Barbera d'Asti Sup. Cavalé '98	♟♟	5
●	Ruché di Castagnole M.to Pro Nobis '01	♟♟	5
●	Monferrato Rosso Genesi '98	♟♟	6
●	Barbera d'Asti Sup. Cavalé '99	♟♟	5

 SERRALUNGA D'ALBA (CN)

LUIGI BAUDANA
FRAZ. BAUDANA, 43
12050 SERRALUNGA D'ALBA (CN)
TEL. 0173613354
E-MAIL: baudanaluigi@libero.it

The quality of the offerings from this modest winery, which releases about 25,000 bottles from five hectares planted to vine, comes from the passion and dedication which Fiorina and Luigi Baudana pour into their work. This year, they are offering a further Barolo, their Baudana selection. After showing a deep, lively garnet, it opens steadily to enchanting scents of faded roses and liquorice. The palate is chewy, dense and rich, with thrust that pushes into a lengthy finish with good nose-palate consistency. The Cerretta Piani shows a slightly mature, medium ruby garnet, then almost explodes with pronounced aromas of red berry, sweet spice and roast coffee. It continues into a forceful palate, replete with firm, assertive tannins and a gorgeous finale. We found the dark-hued Barbera Donatella scrumptious. The nose beguiles with attractive dark fruit, ink tones and yeasted bread. It's a monster in the mouth, depth and power underpinning broad flavours that overflow into a long, mint-lifted finish. The Dolcetto is uncomplicated but well made. A purple-rimmed garnet ruby is followed by aromas of fruit gums and plenty of alcohol warmth on a crisp and confident palate. Bianco Lorenso is sparkling straw in appearance, then the nose nicely balances fruit and toasty oak, before the palate delivers bracing vitality and good structure.

●	Barolo Cerretta Piani '99	🍷🍷	7
●	Barbera d'Alba Donatella '01	🍷🍷	5
●	Dolcetto d'Alba '02	🍷🍷	4
●	Barolo Baudana '99	🍷🍷	7
○	Langhe Bianco Lorenso '01	🍷	4
●	Barolo Cerretta Piani '96	🍷🍷	7
●	Barolo Cerretta Piani '97	🍷🍷	7
●	Langhe Rosso Lorenso '99	🍷🍷	5
●	Barbera d'Alba Donatella '00	🍷🍷	5
●	Langhe Rosso Lorenso '00	🍷🍷	5
●	Barolo Cerretta Piani '98	🍷🍷	7

CASCINA CUCCO
LOC. CUCCO
VIA MAZZINI, 10
12050 SERRALUNGA D'ALBA (CN)
TEL. 0173613003

The Stroppiana family have been the owners of this lovely cellar for over 30 years. Their 11 hectares under vine are gradually coming into production, allowing them to offer a line built on the classic wines of the area, with Barbera leading the pack. They recently acquired six more hectares at Raddi, planted to barbera, merlot and cabernet. This will enable them to substantially increase production, when most of the new plantings begin to yield fruit in 2005. Meanwhile, 2000 saw the debut of a new red, Mondo, at just 1,400 bottles for the moment. Deep ruby garnet introduces a superb aromatic complex based on fruit, spices and mown hay. The mouth is complex and dense, trailing off nicely into a good finish. A richly-faceted bouquet opens the Barolo Cerrati, revealing a lovely duet of sweet oak tones and classic varietal fruit. Massive and fairly stiff-structured, it offers lengthy pleasure in the finish. The Barolo Cucco is layered with ripe fruit, vanilla, cinnamon and liquorice on the nose, then the structure impresses with its power and breadth. Oak is fairly evident on the finish. The standard-label Barolo evolves a decently nuanced nose, but its strong point is the appealing palate, which has expansive warmth and strong progression. The full-hued Chardonnay had a run of only 2,000 bottles. Buttery notes, spicy herbs and apricots make up an expansive nose, preceding a full structure with good follow-through in the finale.

●	Langhe Rosso Mondo '00	🍷🍷	4
●	Barolo '99	🍷🍷	7
●	Barolo Vigna Cerrati '99	🍷🍷	7
●	Barolo Vigna Cucco '99	🍷🍷	7
○	Langhe Chardonnay '02	🍷	4
●	Barolo Vigna Cucco '97	🍷🍷	7
●	Barolo Vigna Cerrati '98	🍷🍷	7
●	Barolo Vigna Cucco '98	🍷🍷	7

SERRALUNGA D'ALBA (CN)

FONTANAFREDDA
VIA ALBA, 15
12050 SERRALUNGA D'ALBA (CN)
TEL. 0173626111
E-MAIL: fontanafredda@fontanafredda.it

There's important news from this producer, long dedicated to quality. Credit for ongoing achievements goes to the staff headed by Gian Minetti, namely Danilo Drocco on the technical side, vineyard manager, Alberto Grasso, and marketing director, Roberto Bruno. There are redesigned graphics and bottles for the Le Selezioni and Tenimenti Fontanafredda lines. They will be assigned all the top wines, from the Barolos, in Burgundy-style bottles, to the Barberas and the Arneis, in modified Bordeaux-style containers. Finally, the two Serralunga crus of Lazzarito and La Delizia will go into a single wine, bearing the subzone on the label even before new regulations go into effect. But let's taste some wines. Three Glasses go to the Barolo Lazzarito Vigna La Delizia '99, whose nose opens deliberately to youthful but refined fruitiness. It has massive, classic structure and unfurls the longest of elegant finishes. Outstanding, too, is the Barolo Fontanafredda Vigna La Rosa '99, with its textbook spiciness. Anything but lean in the mouth, it has weight, fullness and muscle. The Barolo Paiagallo Vigna La Villa 1999 is from Barolo itself, with 100,000 bottles coming from the three vineyards. It gains in fruit and lush charm what it yields in structure to the wines of Serralunga. Finally, the Barolo Serralunga (120,000 bottles) ably mirrors its terroir and stands shoulder to shoulder with its elder brothers. The Barbaresco Coste Rubin performed nicely, the Barbera Papagena is fine as usual and the Diana d'Alba La Lepre '02 still shows a tad green.

SERRALUNGA D'ALBA (CN)

GABUTTI - FRANCO BOASSO
B.TA GABUTTI, 3/A
12050 SERRALUNGA D'ALBA (CN)
TEL. 0173613165
E-MAIL: gabutti.boasso@libero.it

The Boasso family have been producing wine from their grapes since the early 1970s. Convinced that the only way to outstanding wines is through excellent fruit, Franco Boasso devotes meticulous attention to the six hectares of vineyard. The cellar receives the same attention, from fermentation through maturation, with the family winemaking style guided by tradition. Among the wines tasted, we were especially struck by the Barolo Serralunga. Its colour attracts attention first, the appealing deep, garnet-flecked ruby introducing scents of spice and super-ripe fruit to create a rich, seductive nose. In the mouth, it manages the feat of melding a sensationally rich texture with the smoothest drinkability, then progresses into a lengthy follow-through with a warm touch of alcohol. The Barolo Gabutti '99 is already on the road to maturity, as evidenced by its hue, as well as on the nose. The good power of this area's nebbiolos lends force to the palate. Substantial cellaring will surely tease out its great promise. We found the Dolcetto Mariame, showing garnet-tending ruby, a delicious, elegant mix of cream and lovely ripe fruit. The mouth opens full and soft, and the vigorous progression animates a lengthy sign-off, generously topped with black pepper and red berry. Finally, the current Barbera is nicely straightforward, displaying deep colour and good finesse on the nose, then bracing vigour on the palate.

● Barolo Lazzarito		
Vigna La Delizia '99	♟♟♟	8
● Barolo Fontanafredda		
Vigna La Rosa '99	♟♟	8
● Barbaresco Coste Rubìn '00	♟♟	6*
● Barbera d'Alba Sup. Papagena '01	♟♟	5
● Diano d'Alba Vigna La Lepre '02	♟♟	4*
● Barolo Serralunga d'Alba '99	♟♟	6*
● Barolo Paiagallo Vigna La Villa '99	♟♟	7
● Barolo Vigna La Rosa '98	♟♟♟	8
○ Piemonte Alta Langa		
Talento Brut '96	♟♟	6
● Barolo Vigna La Delizia '98	♟♟	8
● Barolo Vigna La Villa '98	♟♟	7
● Barolo Vigna Lazzarito '98	♟♟	8

● Barolo Serralunga '99	♟♟	7
● Barolo Gabutti '99	♟♟	7
● Barbera d'Alba '02	♟	4
● Dolcetto d'Alba Meriame '02	♟	4
● Barolo Gabutti '96	♟♟	7
● Barolo Gabutti '97	♟♟	7
● Barolo Gabutti '98	♟♟	7

SERRALUNGA D'ALBA (CN)

ETTORE GERMANO
LOC. CERRETTA, 1
12050 SERRALUNGA D'ALBA (CN)
TEL. 0173613528
E-MAIL:
germanoettore@germanoettore.com

Sergio Germano, with help from his father Ettore, is following a winemaking philosophy that continues to bring ever finer results. After last year's Three Glass entry, he offered us another series of very distinctive wines. The Barolo Cerretta all but won the top prize this year, too. A dense colour precedes an equally rich nose, flaunting a raspberry-laden fruitiness well married to nuances of toast and sweet spices. Slightly drying tannins enliven a generously-layered mouth, and the fruit of the nose is nicely mirrored in the long finale. The Barolo Prapò puts on display all the classic nebbiolo fruit, highlighted by lovely scents of balsam, cinchona and coffee. The fine texture of the slightly lean and dry mouth continues into an admirable finish. Pale garnet marks the standard Barolo, along with a nose of peach and coffee that shows good consistency. In the mouth, more than a touch of oak shapes the warm progression. The Barbera Vigna della Madre exudes an appealing blend of mown hay, pastries, forest floor and wild fruit. There's superb extractive weight in the mouth, and the finish shows a good, liquorice-nuanced follow-through. The Balàu, a dolcetto, barbera and merlot blend, lays out lively scents of forest floor, oak toast and tobacco, then opens slowly to a very rich, impressive structure. Oak is fairly obvious on Binel, a mix of riesling and chardonnay, and there is compelling vigour in the mouth. The Chardonnay unfolds delicious notes of smoke and butter over a generous, fruity base, then a smooth, rich palate. The Dolcetto is attractively husky and vigorous.

SERRALUNGA D'ALBA (CN)

LUIGI PIRA
VIA XX SETTEMBRE, 9
12050 SERRALUNGA D'ALBA (CN)
TEL. 0173613106

Assisted by their father Luigi, brothers Giampaolo and Romolo Pira direct a winery that turns out 40,000 bottles a year from the seven hectares they farm. The talented Beppe Caviola oversees the wines, which focus on the area's classics, with four versions of Barolo at the top of the list. After a deep ruby garnet, the Vigna Rionda slowly opens to intense scents of fresh fruit and spices. It progresses into a remarkable, well-proportioned structure and unfurls a very classy finish. The Marenca leans to a slightly more mature hue and evolved nose, the latter layered with the textbook dried fruit and Peruvian bark. The massive structure is bolstered by tannins that a bit more bottle age promises to smooth. A rich aromatic profusion centred on Peruvian bark, faded rose petals and liquorice lends appeal to the Margherita, which is vibrantly deep garnet. We found it a wine of great personality, with good flavour, complexity and alcohol that endows it with warm expansiveness. The standard-label Barolo is nicely vigorous, offering ripe fruit and a harmonious mouth. The Dolcetto d'Alba is ruby shading into garnet, with a fruit-infused nose. The panel liked its energy on the palate, a well as the lengthy finish that rounds off a pleasurably rustic wine. Finally, the Nebbiolo Le Ombre is nicely lean and minerally.

● Barolo Cerretta '99	🍷🍷	8
● Barbera d'Alba		
Vigna della Madre '01	🍷🍷	5
○ Langhe Bianco Binel '01	🍷🍷	4*
● Langhe Rosso Balàu '01	🍷🍷	5
○ Langhe Chardonnay '02	🍷🍷	4
● Barolo Prapò '99	🍷🍷	8
● Dolcetto d'Alba		
Vigneto Lorenzino '02	🍷	4
● Barolo '99	🍷	7
● Barolo Cerretta '98	🍷🍷🍷	7
● Barolo Cerretta '97	🍷🍷	7
● Barbera d'Alba		
Vigna della Madre '00	🍷🍷	5
● Barolo Prapò '98	🍷🍷	7

● Barolo Vigna Rionda '99	🍷🍷	8
● Barolo Vigneto Marenca '99	🍷🍷	8
● Barolo Vigneto Margheria '99	🍷🍷	7
● Langhe Nebbiolo Le Ombre '01	🍷	5
● Dolcetto d'Alba '02	🍷	3
● Barolo '99	🍷	7
● Barolo Vigneto Marenca '97	🍷🍷🍷	8
● Barolo Vigneto Marenca '96	🍷🍷	8
● Barolo Vigneto Margheria '96	🍷🍷	8
● Barolo Vigneto Margheria '97	🍷🍷	8
● Barolo Vigneto Marenca '98	🍷🍷	8
● Barolo Vigneto Margheria '98	🍷🍷	8

SERRALUNGA D'ALBA (CN)

VIGNA RIONDA - MASSOLINO
P.ZZA CAPPELLANO, 8
12050 SERRALUNGA D'ALBA (CN)
TEL. 0173613138
E-MAIL: vignarionda@libero.it

The Massolino family are not new to vineyard selection. The first release of their Barolo Vigna Rionda Riserva goes back to 1982, followed by the Margheria in '85 and the Parafada in '90. Each of these wines displays its own distinctive character; each is clearly rooted in the unique nature and position of its source cru. The Massolinos have shown themselves expert at teasing out every nuance from those vineyards. Three Glasses go to the Vigna Rionda Riserva '97. Cinchona, ginger and liquorice emerge from a nicely evolved nose, the mouth is full structured yet smooth, and it finishes very long. Here is a wine that privileges supple elegance over raw power and the result is absolutely superb. The Parafada releases slightly riper fruit, and the palate shows a tactile velvet. The finish is long, with a subtle vein of oak. The Margheria suggests coffee and fruit preserve, then builds to exceptional structure. The vigorous palate of the standard Barolo is nicely complemented by beguiling wild berries and wood tar. The Barbera Gisep easily seduces with its lavish array of cocoa, cherry fruit and earth tones, and then manages both a terrific structure and delicious drinkability. The nebbiolo and barbera Piria opens to sour cherry, dried leaves and tobacco, while a well-gauged vein of tasty acidity lends vigour to the richly woven palate. Finally, the panel sample a slightly oak-ruled Chardonnay, an upfront Dolcetto, a lean, robust Barbera and a rich, elegant Moscato. In short, we awarded a cabinetful of Glasses that makes this winery one of the most fascinating in all of Barolo.

SIZZANO (NO)

BIANCHI
VIA ROMA, 37
28070 SIZZANO (NO)
TEL. 0321810004 - 0321820823
E-MAIL: e.bianchi@bianchibiowine.it

The Bianchi family have always been reliable producers in Piemonte's northeast. Their line covers the area's major denominations, and their excellent wines are affordably priced, in addition to giving that added value of organic certification. They offer Ghemme and Gattinara crus, Baraggiole and Valferana, respectively, but their standard offerings are just as sound. Their two Gattinaras in particular are quite distinctive, with clean, fruity plum aromas yielding to a crisp, lean palate lifted by the spiciness typical of the area. A stay in barrique gives the Valferana a nice added charge of cocoa, vanilla and wood resin, and it shows a lean, tasty vigour. Both wines turned in Two Glass performances. The two Ghemme versions are very similar. Though solidly varietal, they are a bit more reticent. Their aromatics lean towards the crisp and fruity, with strawberry and raspberry showing, and the Baraggiole's oak is also understated and moderately balsamic. Both were just shy of Two Glasses. The most compelling wine is Primasole, an assemblage of nebbiolo, barbera and merlot matured in once-used barriques and in tonneaux. It proffers lovely scents of chocolate and coffee over stupendous cherry and ripe plum, ending on a nice note of acidity. Another sound wine is the Eloise, a blend of steel-vinified erbaluce with barriqued chardonnay. Peaches and ripe bananas enrich both nose and palate, and the acidity is well-gauged.

● Barolo Vigna Rionda Ris. '97	♥♥♥	8
● Langhe Rosso Piria '00	♥♥	6
● Barbera d'Alba Gisep '00	♥♥	5
● Barolo '99	♥♥	6*
● Barolo Margheria '99	♥♥	7
● Barolo Parafada '99	♥♥	7
○ Langhe Chardonnay '01	♥	4
● Barbera d'Alba '02	♥	4
● Dolcetto d'Alba '02	♥	4
○ Moscato d'Asti di Serralunga '02	♥	4
● Barolo Parafada Ris. '90	♥♥♥	8
● Barolo Vigna Rionda Ris. '90	♥♥♥	8
● Barolo Parafada '96	♥♥♥	8
● Barolo Vigna Rionda Ris. '96	♥♥♥	8

● Primasole Rosso '01	♥♥	4*
● Gattinara '98	♥♥	4*
● Gattinara Vigneto Valferana '98	♥♥	5
○ Eloise Bianco '01	♥	4
● Ghemme '98	♥	4
● Ghemme Colle Baraggiole '98	♥	5
● Sizzano '98	♥	4
○ Passito di Erbaluce		
Autunno degli Artisti '99	♥	6

SPIGNO MONFERRATO (AL)   STREVI (AL)

TRAVERSA - CASCINA BERTOLOTTO
VIA PIETRO PORRO, 70
15018 SPIGNO MONFERRATO (AL)
TEL. 014491223 - 014491551

MARENCO
P.ZZA VITTORIO EMANUELE II, 10
15019 STREVI (AL)
TEL. 0144363133
E-MAIL: marencovini@libero.it

The cellar belonging to the Traversa family has long been prominent in Monferrato, and in the Guide, thanks to an outstanding line of wines. We especially liked the Rosso La Tia, a great example of what a dry Brachetto can offer. Appearing almost purple, its nose offers textbook brachetto characteristics, with rose petal, raspberry and wild strawberry. There is plenty of solid body and alcohol, but at the same time the tannin-smoothed progression is leisurely and supple. The Dolcetto d'Acqui comes in two versions, both top-drawer varietal wines. Notes of ripe fruit preserve come through on the La Muïette, but the rather grainy tannins knock the palate slightly out of balance. Although the Dolcetto La Cresta is slightly less complex, its overall richness edged it ahead of the La Tia. A sound performance by the Barbera del Monferrato I Cheini almost won Two Glasses, but it's still a bit young and gangly. A cortese and favorita blend, Il Barigi, captivates with its acacia blossom, citrus fruit and pineapple. And let's finish with something new, the Sorì di Bertolotto Vin Blanc, a late-harvest moscato dusted off from the family's oenological archives. An amber-flecked gold, it offers minerally notes while unfolding rich acacia honey and ripe apricot.

2002 was trying for the Marenco family, ending with one of the most difficult harvests of recent years. But, as always in farming families, passion and dedication were good supply, and the Marencos found the energy to improve their 65 hectares of magnificent vineyards on the left bank of the Bormida. Their Barbera d'Asti Ciresa '00 presents an intense, deep ruby, followed by a zesty fruitiness centred on raspberry and blackcurrant. Rich, tangy flavours emerge on the palate, and the finale is long and tasty. Close behind is the Bassina, showing purple-flecked ruby, with eloquent, attractively nuanced fruit, and continuing with a crisp, youthful fruitiness of seductive succulence. The Passrì di Scrapona Moscato Passito di Strevi is luscious. Its amber-edged gold-yellow ushers in a voluptuous package of honey, citrus preserve, hazelnut, butter and wood resin. The considerable sweetness is saved from excess by a nice acidity, achieving elegant harmony. The Chardonnay Galet is still quite young, marrying peach and summer flowers to good varietal character. The palate is nicely balanced between a nearly sweet roundness and lively fruit, and it finishes light, with a nice bitterish tang. The standard cork version of the Moscato Scrapona unleashes an elegant nose that enriches the Strevi subzone's classic honey with hints of sage and sweet citrus. Subtle fizziness nicely balances good sweetness on the palate. One Glass each goes to the Pineto, always among the most fragrant Brachettos, and to the "passito" Passrì.

● Dolcetto d'Acqui La Cresta '02	♟♟	4*
● Rosso La Tia '02	♟♟	5
○ Sorì di Bertolotto Vin Blanc '00	♟	5
● Barbera del M.to I Cheini '01	♟	4
● Dolcetto d'Acqui La Muïette '01	♟	4
○ Monferrato Bianco Il Barigi '02	♟	3
● Barbera del M.to I Cheini '99	♟♟	4
● Dolcetto d'Acqui La Muïette '99	♟♟	4
● Rosso La Tia '01	♟♟	5
● Dolcetto d'Acqui La Muïette '00	♟	4

● Barbera d'Asti Ciresa '00	♟♟	5
● Barbera d'Asti Bassina '00	♟♟	4*
○ Piemonte Moscato Passito Passrì di Scrapona '01	♟♟	6
○ Piemonte Chardonnay Galet '02	♟♟	4*
● Passrì Pineto '01	♟	6
● Brachetto d'Acqui Pineto '02	♟	4
○ Moscato d'Asti Scrapona '02	♟	4
● Barbera d'Asti Ciresa '99	♟♟	5
○ Piemonte Moscato Passito Passrì di Scrapona '00	♟♟	6
● Dolcetto d'Acqui Marchesa '01	♟♟	4

STREVI (AL)

TORINO

VIGNE REGALI
VIA VITTORIO VENETO, 22
15019 STREVI (AL)
TEL. 0144363485
E-MAIL: banfi@banfi.com

FRANCO M. MARTINETTI
VIA SAN FRANCESCO DA PAOLA, 18
10123 TORINO
TEL. 0118395937 - 0116273555
E-MAIL: gmartinetti@ciaoweb.it

Last year, we described the recent changes in the top echelons of Vigne Regali, the Strevi operation belonging to the Villa Banfi group. We were eager to taste the wines for the new edition of the Guide, not least to get an idea of the direction the new staff was taking under the president, Attilio Viglierchio, and operations director Alberto Lazzarino. We found the winemaking essentially unchanged, but there was a drastic cut in the number of labels presented. Vigne Regali wants to give its wines more ageing so that they will be in optimum condition at release time. In fact, we tasted only the sparklers and the Gavi Principessa Gavia, but they turned out to be top-notch offerings. Let's begin with the Gavi. The reduced harvest in the difficult 2002 growing year yielded a wine that is inevitably lighter and less rich than previous versions, but exceptional crispness and captivating fruitiness make up for the deficiencies. We liked the Tener Brut best of the sparkling wines. Showing a lovely yeast-charged complexity on the nose, it develops an ultra-savoury, creamy palate of an intriguing suppleness that compels attention. The two remaining wines stand out for their soundness and very good drinkability. The Talento Banfi Brut, an assemblage of chardonnay, pinot noir and pinot bianco, is a delightfully smooth, delicious drinker, and the Alta Langa Cuvée Aurora is clean, straightforward and vigorous.

Here we have a real star on the world food and wine scene, whose dedication, skills, and achievements are a source of real pride for Piemonte. Martinetti is a friend and colleague of top chefs and of the main players in the wine industry, as well as a respected collaborator for the most prestigious international food and wine organizations. His career is studded with major initiatives, professional contributions and difficulties overcome. Take the field of wine. Franco built up a model wine business, with no vineyards and no winery of his own. Or rather, in his own inimitable style, he takes shrewd advantage of the vineyards and facilities of other trusted producers. The result is an extraordinary line of wines, all bearing the clear stamp of his personality. His Barbera Montruc is simply monumental, a Three Glass winner almost before the cork is out. A shimmering, purple-rimmed ruby, it then opens to a stunningly elegant array of fragrances built on violets, blackberry and sweet spices, each nicely defined and exquisitely integrated. The softest of touches from oak ageing lifts the irresistible aromatics. On the palate, the great power is modulated by good acidity and expressed with a finesse that make Montruc a refined and utterly modern interpretation of a long-established tradition. All the other main wines turned in resounding performances. The seductive Barolo shows lean and nicely tannic, and the Monferrato demonstrates its usual elegant complexity. The less demanding standard Barbera is as tasty as they come, and the Gavi Minaia '01 is superlative.

O	Tener Brut N. M.	♟♟	4*
O	Gavi Principessa Gavia '02	♟	4
O	Piemonte Alta Langa Cuvée Aurora '98	♟	4
O	Talento Banfi Brut M. Cl. '99	♟	5
O	Talento Banfi Brut M. Cl. '98	♟♟	5
●	Dolcetto d'Acqui Argusto '99	♟♟	4
●	Barbera d'Asti Vigneto Banin '99	♟♟	5

●	Barbera d'Asti Sup. Montruc '01	♟♟♟	6
O	Colli Tortonesi Bianco Martin '01	♟♟	7
●	Monferrato Rosso Sul Bric '01	♟♟	6
●	Barolo Marasco '99	♟♟	8
O	Gavi Minaia '01	♟♟	6
●	Barbera d'Asti Bric dei Banditi '02	♟	4*
●	Sul Bric '94	♟♟♟	6
●	Sul Bric '95	♟♟♟	6
●	Barbera d'Asti Sup. Montruc '96	♟♟♟	6
●	Barbera d'Asti Sup. Montruc '97	♟♟♟	6
●	Monferrato Rosso Sul Bric '00	♟♟♟	6
O	Minaia '98	♟♟♟	6
O	Colli Tortonesi Martin '00	♟♟	6
●	Barolo Marasco '98	♟♟	8

TORTONA (AL)

LA COLOMBERA
FRAZ. VHÒ
S.DA COMUNALE PER VHO, 7
15057 TORTONA (AL)
TEL. 0131867795
E-MAIL: info@lacolomberavini.it

La Colombera has been active for some 70 years, but lately it has been winning more attention in Piemonte and elsewhere. One of the reasons is that the Tortona area has shown considerable winemaking dynamism in recent years. Pier Carlo Semino, with the entire family by his side, especially his daughter, Elisa, has made great strides in developing the area's native varieties. Let's take for example the barbera-based Elisa, sourced from a 35-year-old vineyard and cask matured. Deep red ushers in ripe fruit aromas of morello cherry, in particular, then smoothness and acidity meld nicely in the mouth to create a wine of restrained power and a long finish. The Dhertona bears witness to the cellar's attention to native grapes, as it is produced with timorasso from a relatively young vineyard. Leading with a deep straw yellow, it yields fruit aromas and hints of spring flowers, above all acacia. Firm structure and a good finish round off this exceptional offering. Also very tasty is the Vegia Rampana, a steel-fermented Barbera. Its fragrant, almost super-ripe, fruit complements an intense ruby red, and the tightly knit structure is the ideal foil for its tangy acidity. We found the Colli Tortonesi Rosso Suciaja attractive. Obtained from vineyards of the dolcetto dal rospo rosso (red-stalked dolcetto, or nibiô in the local dialect). Flaunting a lustrous, deep red, it opens to a rich suite of aromatics ranging from plummy fruit to rich spice. The cortese-based Bricco is crisply fruited and ready to enjoy.

TORTONA (AL)

CLAUDIO MARIOTTO
FRAZ. VHÒ
S.DA PER SAREZZANO, 29
15057 TORTONA (AL)
TEL. 0131868500
E-MAIL: claudio.mariotto@libero.it

The performance of Claudio Mariotto's winery gets better every year. This time, the Derthona and the Poggio del Rosso actually went through to the Three Glass taste-off. The first is from timorasso. It sees no oak, but does undergo substantial lees contact, followed by some months' bottle ageing before release. The superlative qualities of this '01 emerge at once in an exquisite balance of power and appealing mineral notes, laced with tasty fruit. The acidity shows clean and tangy on the palate, which is rounded off by hefty alcohol. The Poggio del Rosso, a red that Claudio dedicated to his father, is making its debut this year. Tobacco, leather and blackberry on the nose provide a fitting introduction to its massive structure, but the dense, supple palate nicely cloaks the power. Full marks, too, for the Barbera Vhò, for many years now the cellar's flagship. A beguiling ruby precedes rich spice and depth on the palate, with the texture played out in soft, mouthfilling tannins that enrich a wonderfully long, delicious finish. Less complex, but ideal for everyday drinking, is the Territorio, which showcases barbera's bright acidity and its classic berry aroma. Those who appreciate a vibrant style will like the Martirella. Coccalina rounds out the line-up, a lovely, easy drinking white to uncork straight away.

● Colli Tortonesi Rosso Suciaja '00	♟♟	5
● Piemonte Barbera Elisa '00	♟♟	5
○ Colli Tortonesi Bianco Derthona '01	♟♟	5
● Colli Tortonesi Rosso Vegia Rampana '01	♟♟	4*
○ Colli Tortonesi Bianco Bricco Bartolomeo '02	♟	3
● Piemonte Barbera Elisa '99	♟♟	5

○ Colli Tortonesi Bianco Derthona '01	♟♟	5
● Colli Tortonesi Rosso Poggio del Rosso '00	♟♟	5
● Colli Tortonesi Rosso Vhò '01	♟♟	5
○ Colli Tortonesi Bianco Coccalina '02	♟	3
● Colli Tortonesi Rosso Martirella '02	♟	3
● Colli Tortonesi Rosso Territorio '02	♟	4*
● Colli Tortonesi Rosso Vhò '99	♟♟	4
● Colli Tortonesi Rosso Vhò '00	♟♟	5

TREISO (CN)

ORLANDO ABRIGO
FRAZ. CAPPELLETTO, 5
12050 TREISO (CN)
TEL. 0173630232
E-MAIL: orlandoabrigo@libero.it

We were quite impressed by this year's wines from the Abrigo family of Treiso. In fact, our tastings during the summer, especially of their reds, led to the award of a full profile in this Guide. The family, father Orlando, his son Gianni, and their respective spouses, operate a handsome cellar surrounded by vineyards near Treiso, in the hamlet of Cappelletto. Five rooms, with swimming pool, for clients and guests are part of the facility. Utilizing fruit from 11 hectares of estate-owned vineyards, the Abrigos produce about 70,000 bottles each year. The range of wines offered is impressive, privileging the classic reds. In the lead is the Barbaresco Vigna Rongallo '00. Its garnet-tinged ruby is followed by a wealth of variegated fragrances, such as dried flowers, almonds, spice and tobacco. A clean backbone of acid and still-rugged tannins are a beautiful foil to the warm, voluptuous palate, and it ends superbly long. The Barbera Montersino passes time in barrique, in contrast to the Vigna Rongallo's large wood, and the palate that emerges is softer and more supple, with nice oak-planed tannins. Its closely-wrought texture is quite appealing, as is its remarkable length. Among the other reds, we found the Barbera d'Alba Vigna Roreto to be a very attractive combination of elegance and strength. The Langhe Livraie, a monovarietal Merlot, is gorgeously smooth. All the other wines performed very well and can be uncorked with confidence.

TREISO (CN)

CA' DEL BAIO
VIA FERRERE, 33
12050 TREISO (CN)
TEL. 0173638219
E-MAIL: cadelbaio@cadelbaio.com

Giulio Grasso, who owns Ca' del Baio, comes from a family involved in growing and winemaking since 1880. He manages 18 hectares, some in the hamlet of Valgrande, near Treiso, and the rest in the fabled Asili vineyard at Barbaresco. His two Barbarescos take their names from these source crus. The Asili shows a lively ruby garnet, then luscious ripe fruit and spice fragrances open evenly on the nose. Texture on the palate may not be excessively complex, but it has exquisite balance, and flows into a superbly fruited finish. A much deeper red announces the Valgrande, with fruit and mown hay infusing a vigorously focused nose that is already slightly evolved. It opens powerfully on the palate to an opulent, full-bodied weave, proceeding steadily into a lean-edged finish. The Barbera Giardin comes in dense ruby garnet and explodes in lovely strawberry and blueberry fruit. The mouth may seem a bit restrained, but the rich, supple mouthfeel impresses, as do its nose-palate consistency and lengthy finish. Pronounced maturity marks the Chardonnay Sermine, with its gold hue and nose of ripe fruit and aromatic herbs. A subtle line of crisp acidity on the palate enlivens a voluptuous texture. The Nebbiolo exudes earthiness and balsamic notes over nice creaminess, then in the mouth, there's good consistency and an attractive leanness.

● Barbaresco Vigna Rongallo '00	¶¶	6
● Barbaresco Vigna Montersino '00	¶¶	6
● Barbera d'Alba Vigna Roreto '01	¶¶	4*
● Langhe Rosso Livraie '99	¶¶	5
● Barbera d'Alba Mervisano '00	¶	4
● Langhe Nebbiolo Settevie '00	¶	4
● Dolcetto d'Alba Vigna dell'Erto '02	¶	3*
○ Langhe Chardonnay Très '02	¶	4*
● Barbaresco Vigna Montersino '99	¶¶	6
● Barbaresco Vigna Rongallo '99	¶	6

● Barbaresco Asili '00	¶¶	6*
● Barbaresco Valgrande '00	¶¶	6*
● Barbera d'Alba Giardin '01	¶¶	5
○ Langhe Chardonnay Sermine '02	¶	4
● Langhe Nebbiolo Bric del Baio '01	¶	5
● Barbaresco Asili '97	¶¶	6
● Barbaresco Asili Barrique '97	¶¶	6
● Barbaresco Asili '99	¶¶	6
● Barbaresco Valgrande '99	¶¶	6
● Barbaresco Valgrande '98	¶	6

TREISO (CN)

ADA NADA
LOC. ROMBONE
VIA AUSARIO, 12
12050 TREISO (CN)
TEL. 0173638127
E-MAIL: info@adanada.it

The Nada family has been making wine since 1919 on this ten-hectare estate, which now includes an "agriturismo" facility. Today, it is managed by Annalisa Nada, husband Elvio, her parents Gian Carlo and Ada, and winery manager, Roberto Rizzi. They produce the traditional Langhe classics, but three Barbarescos are the pick of the crop. Elisa is a new product, sourced from a recently acquired vineyard and named for Annalisa and Elvio's young daughter. The colour reveals significant development. The nose offers well-ripened fruit, and the lean, muscular structure extends into a remarkably rich, lingering finish. The Cichin and the Valeirano are both stand-outs. The first is more rugged, with a nice flinty edge, whereas the second is subtle and graceful, but both display flesh and depth to spare. A garnet hue leads the barbera and nebbiolo Rosso La Bisbetica into a balsam-laced fruitiness. That's followed by a luscious, full palate that drives towards a summarizing finish marked by good length. The rather rustic Vigna 'd Pierin is fairly straightforward, with acceptable definition on the nose and good enough mouthfeel. And another new wine is Desmentià, a cask-conditioned dried-grape Moscato. The hue leans to amber and a super-ripe aromatic mosaic presents dried apricot, tobacco leaf and tamarind. On the palate, it is nicely subtle, and even crisp, making it a perfect partner for mature and blue cheeses.

TREISO (CN)

FIORENZO NADA
LOC. ROMBONE
VIA AUSARIO, 12/C
12050 TREISO (CN)
TEL. 0173638254
E-MAIL: nadafiorenzo@nada.it

The Nada family has owned this attractive cellar since 1921. In the 1960s, the estate was divided among the four sons, with one part going to Fiorenzo. Together with his son Bruno, he still runs his estate with its six hectares under vine in the Rombone and Manzola vineyards. Bruno was the one who, in 1982, persuaded his father to bottle their wine, hitherto sold in bulk. Events proved him right. Wine lovers everywhere vouch for the superlative quality of Nada wines. The Rombone '02 is medium-dense ruby garnet. Tasty fruit on the nose is decisively edged with sweet oak that brings notes of vanilla and pastries. In the mouth, it develops good power, with crispness and nice tannins, and echoes the nose, pushing into good length. The hue on the standard-label Barbaresco is a bit livelier, and lavish strawberry preserve, liquorice and sweet pipe tobacco compose a hedonistic nose. Its dense, opulent mouthfeel makes for wonderful drinkability, with the subtlest of tannins lifting a good finish. The Seifile, an 80-20 barbera and nebbiolo blend, is very well done. A good dark red, it offers up nice scents of wild berries and aromatic herbs. It then unleashes sensory energy that builds to a lengthy finish, with an inviting medley of cocoa and cherry. The Barbera d'Alba '01 is very, very good and already brimming with character, even though sourced from a young vineyard. We missed the Dolcetto, but the unfavourable 2002 growing year precluded quality, so none was released.

● Barbaresco Valeirano '00	♙♙	7
● Barbaresco Cichin '00	♙♙	7
● Barbaresco Elisa '00	♙♙	7
● Langhe Rosso La Bisbetica '00	♙♙	6
○ Desmentià V. T. '00	♙	7
● Barbera d'Alba Vigna 'd Pierin '01	♙	4
● Barbaresco Cichin '98	♙♙	7
● Barbaresco Valeirano '98	♙♙	7
● Barbaresco Valeirano '99	♙♙	7
● Barbaresco Cichin '99	♙♙	7

● Barbaresco Rombone '00	♙♙	8
● Langhe Rosso Seifile '00	♙♙	8
● Barbaresco '00	♙♙	7
● Barbera d'Alba '01	♙♙	5
● Seifile '93	♙♙♙	8
● Langhe Rosso Seifile '95	♙♙♙	8
● Langhe Rosso Seifile '96	♙♙♙	8
● Barbaresco Rombone '97	♙♙♙	8
● Barbaresco Rombone '99	♙♙♙	8
● Barbera d'Alba '00	♙♙	5
● Barbaresco '99	♙♙	7
● Barbaresco Rombone '98	♙♙	8

TREISO (CN)

TREISO (CN)

PELISSERO
VIA FERRERE, 10
12050 TREISO (CN)
TEL. 0173638430
E-MAIL: pelissero@pelissero.com

VIGNAIOLI ELVIO PERTINACE
LOC. PERTINACE, 2
12050 TREISO (CN)
TEL. 0173442238
E-MAIL: c.vignaioli@areacom.it

Giorgio Pelissero's winery has been bottling wine since 1960 and is now in the third generation of family management. It produces about 100,000 bottles yearly, from 20 hectares of vineyard. As always, there are quite a few releases, and they're all top-notch. Let's begin with the well-known Barbaresco Vanto '02. Deep ruby garnet, it boasts a nose dense with chocolate, toasty oak and red berry fruit. The texture is close-knit, and progresses steadily into a superbly long finish. The standard Barbaresco is just as deep in hue, but its rich aromatics turn on vanilla, sweet spices and intense ripe fruit. The palate is all juicy succulence, and oak is prominent on a finely built finish. The barbera and nebbiolo Rosso Long Now lets no light through, and the nose is equally dense, with dark berry fruit finally giving way to nuances of hay and cinnamon. There's rich depth in the mouth, too, and the long, echoing finale shows a strong suite of tannins. The darkest of reds also marks the Barbera Piani, which exudes chocolate, ripe fruit and menthol. Again, a rich, deep mouthfeel, offers a nice fruit follow through, although tannins make themselves felt. The Favorita is always a yummy delight and this year is all exuberant fruit, releasing attractive pear and apricot. The Dolcetto Munfrina may show a bit evolved, but the structure is superb. Elegantly rustic is the description for the Grignolino and the Frisa. The supple and beautifully put together Nebbiolo is almost as youthful and zesty as a nouveau.

This co-operative was founded in 1972 by Mario Belbo, its first president, and 12 other partners. Right from the start, the goal has been top quality. After various re-organizations, the last in 1992, the enterprise today has 80 hectares and an annual output of 200,000 bottles. An impressively deep garnet announces the Barbaresco Castellizzano, an accurate prediction of a complex nose. Elegant dried flowers are layered over lush raspberry and dark liquorice. It then opens to rich, full power on the mouth, and ends as long as you could want. Here's a joyously successful marriage of innovation and tradition. The Nervo is deep hued, with subtle balsamic and fruit notes permeating the nose. Supple tannins contribute to a smooth mouthfeel. The finish may be a tad light, but it does linger surprisingly long. We found the Marcarini crisp, fruity and nicely defined, showing berry fruit and liquorice. The standard Barbaresco is a notch simpler, with resin and coffee ushering in a palate of easy-drinking pleasure. The remaining wines are soundly made, and good fruit shines through. Especially appealing is the lean, tannic and gutsy Langhe Nebbiolo. The Langhe Pertinace, from nebbiolo, barbera and cabernet, may hint at over-ripeness, but again there's great fruit on the palate, and it closes long and well balanced. Only one Dolcetto was produced from the difficult 2002, but it's nicely clean and crisp. The Chardonnay drinks smooth and tasty, with a delicious tart edge.

● Barbaresco Vanotu '00	𝟁𝟁	8
● Langhe Rosso Long Now '01	𝟁𝟁	7
● Barbaresco Annata '00	𝟁𝟁	7
● Barbera d'Alba Piani '02	𝟁𝟁	5
○ Langhe Favorita '02	𝟁𝟁	4
● Dolcetto d'Alba Munfrina '02	𝟁	4
● Langhe Freisa '02	𝟁	4
● Langhe Nebbiolo '02	𝟁	5
● Piemonte Grignolino '02	𝟁	4
● Barbaresco Vanotu '95	𝟁𝟁𝟁	8
● Barbaresco Vanotu '97	𝟁𝟁𝟁	8
● Barbaresco Vanotu '99	𝟁𝟁𝟁	8
● Barbaresco Vanotu '98	𝟁𝟁	8
● Langhe Rosso Long Now '00	𝟁𝟁	6
● Barbera d'Alba Piani '01	𝟁𝟁	4

● Barbaresco Castellizzano '00	𝟁𝟁	6
● Barbaresco Marcarini '00	𝟁𝟁	6
● Barbaresco Nervo '00	𝟁𝟁	6
● Langhe Nebbiolo '01	𝟁𝟁	5
● Barbaresco '00	𝟁	5
● Langhe Pertinace '00	𝟁	5
● Dolcetto d'Alba '02	𝟁	4
○ Langhe Chardonnay '02	𝟁	3
● Barbaresco Vigneto Marcarini '99	𝟁𝟁	6
● Barbaresco Vigneto Nervo '99	𝟁𝟁	6
● Langhe Pertinace '99	𝟁𝟁	5
● Barbaresco Vigneto Castellizzano '99	𝟁	6

VERDUNO (CN)

VERDUNO (CN)

F.LLI ALESSANDRIA
VIA BEATO VALFRÉ, 59
12060 VERDUNO (CN)
TEL. 0172470113
E-MAIL: fratelli.alessandria@tiscalinet.it

BEL COLLE
FRAZ. CASTAGNI, 56
12060 VERDUNO (CN)
TEL. 0172470196
E-MAIL: info@belcolle.it

Frattelli Alessandria is one of the most history-laden cellars in the Langhe. Founded in 1900 by Giovan Battista Alessandria, it is now firmly in the hands of his grandson, Gian, who enjoys the help of his own son, Vittore, and of oenologist Franco Alessandria. Nearly 12 hectares yield them quite a diverse line-up at a production level of 50,000 bottles. Their location in Verduno means, of course, that their flagship is Barolo. It is sourced from two of the best known local vineyards, Monvigliero and San Lorenzo. The former impressed us more, exhibiting absolutely classic colour and nose. The lively garnet is followed by good rose and violet nuances over rich black pepper and liquorice. A healthy dose of alcohol releases a sensational range of flavours on the palate, attractively reinforced by tannins, and the finish is generous. In contrast, the San Lorenzo has a bit less of everything, including aroma and depth on the palate, but good terroir and grapes give it class. The standard-label Barolo isn't designed to reach the levels of the others, but you can't fault its soundness. We found the Langhe Chardonnay Buscät delicious. Straw yellow and lush, appley fragrances introduce an acid-graced, opulent palate. The Langhe Rosso Luna is a very successful blend of barbera, nebbiolo and freisa. Also recommended is the Barbera d'Alba La Priora, which has good fruit and acidity. The Langhe Nebbiolo Prinsiot is well made.

Talented winemaker Paolo Torchio manages this thriving operation. Utilizing fruit from both Langhe and Roero, he produces 150,000 bottles a year of very good quality wines. The wine we liked best was his Barbaresco Roncaglie '00. After a lively ruby, we notice a wide array of fragrances that run through cherry fruit, sweet black pepper and vanilla spice, and floral notes of roses. The texture is pleasantly lean and tannic, and the endless finish pleases enormously. Only a short step behind is the Barolo Monvigliero '99. Orange-flecked ruby introduces an intriguing aromatic medley of wild berry, leather and cinchona, while impeccable balance and sheer drinkability more than offset a slightly drying mouth. Lavish pepper, herbs and strawberry make the Verduno Pelaverga '02 irresistible. A tangy crispness shot with spice completes its seductive appeal. Metaphorically crossing the river Tanaro into Roero, we enjoyed the Monvijé '01, which offers appealing aromas of rose petals and strawberry, an impressively smooth attack and a lengthy finale. Neither the nose nor the palate of the Nebbiolo d'Alba Bricco Reala '02 exhibits such complexity, but it is still soundly crafted, as is the refreshing, well executed Roero Arneis '02.

●	Barbera d'Alba La Priora '01	♟♟	4
○	Langhe Chardonnay Buscät '01	♟♟	4*
●	Langhe Rosso Luna '01	♟♟	5
●	Barolo '99	♟♟	6
●	Barolo Monvigliero '99	♟♟	7
●	Barolo S. Lorenzo '99	♟♟	7
●	Langhe Nebbiolo Prinsiot '01	♟	4
●	Barolo Monvigliero '95	♟♟♟	4
●	Barolo S. Lorenzo '97	♟♟♟	4
●	Barbera d'Alba La Priora '00	♟♟	4
●	Langhe Rosso Luna '00	♟♟	4
●	Barolo S. Lorenzo '98	♟♟	4

●	Barbaresco Roncaglie '00	♟♟	6
●	Roero Monvijé '01	♟♟	4
●	Verduno Pelaverga '02	♟♟	4
●	Barolo Monvigliero '99	♟♟	6
●	Nebbiolo d'Alba Bricco Reala '02	♟	4
○	Roero Arneis '02	♟	4
●	Barolo Monvigliero '96	♟♟	6
●	Barolo Monvigliero '97	♟♟	6
●	Barolo Monvigliero '98	♟♟	6

VERDUNO (CN)

G. B. BURLOTTO
VIA VITTORIO EMANUELE, 28
12060 VERDUNO (CN)
TEL. 0172470122
E-MAIL: burlotto@burlotto.com

With one more hectare now under vine in a barbera vineyard at Roddi, Marina Burlotto's winery has now 12 hectares. They are managed by her husband, Giuseppe, and young son, Fabio. At the same time, they have also upgraded the production area and its equipment. All good news, of course, but the wines tasted for this Guide bring more. We were terrifically impressed by their new Barolo Acclivi, an assemblage of the Verduno area's best vineyards that shows every sign of becoming the winery's star performer. It begins by parading brightly etched aromas of wild berries, cherry and leather. A beautifully disciplined complexity in the mouth is markedly tannic, but well this side of excess. Slightly less complex is the Barolo Vigneto Cannubi '99, but everything is well judged and fits together harmoniously. We ranked the Barbera d'Alba Aves a superlative effort for it floral, flinty nose, but it was the refreshing acidity on the palate that really won us over. High marks also go to the Langhe Bianco, which is sourced from sauvignon grown on the Verduno hills. Varietal tomato leaf and sage are nicely in evidence, and it progresses with a delicious tang, finishing long. The Verduno Pelaverga has its customary well-gauged spice and mineral, lifted by lovely floral notes, and it displays plenty of character and verve in the mouth.

● Barolo Acclivi '99	ΨΨ	7
● Barbera d'Alba Aves '01	ΨΨ	5
○ Langhe Bianco Dives '01	ΨΨ	4*
● Barolo Vigneto Cannubi '99	ΨΨ	7
● Langhe Mores '01	Ψ	5
● Verduno Pelaverga '02	Ψ	4
● Barolo Vigneto Cannubi '96	ΨΨ	7
● Barolo Vigneto Cannubi '97	ΨΨ	7
○ Langhe Bianco Dives '00	ΨΨ	4
● Barolo Vigneto Cannubi '98	ΨΨ	7
● Barolo Vigneto Monvigliero '98	ΨΨ	7

VERDUNO (CN)

CASTELLO DI VERDUNO
VIA UMBERTO I, 9
12060 VERDUNO (CN)
TEL. 0172470284 - 0172470281
E-MAIL:
castellodiverduno@castellodiverduno.com

Castello di Verduno is blessed with a unique history, since it was one of the first wineries to make a Barolo. There's more, for 2003 saw the celebration of the 50th year of Burlotto family ownership of this splendid hotel-cum-fortress. This year saw a fascinating line-up of wines. Let's begin with the superlatively structured Barbaresco Rabajà Riserva '97. The nose offers the expected leather, liquorice and faded flowers, but it is the luscious, succulent palate and endless finish that achieve the rare elegance that make a champion. We thought the Massara '98 an outstanding traditional Barolo. Its fragrances of violets and subtle balsam are graceful yet distinctive, while the massively structured mouth exhibits dense concentration of flavour, then concludes crisp and long. The 100 per cent pelaverga Verduno '02 ranked high as well. It leads with sparking ruby, then flaunts a nose richly spiced with trademark varietal black pepper. The refreshingly crisp, fruity palate makes for remarkably pleasant drinking, qualities sealed by a distinctive, full-fruited finish. Another ringing performance came from the Barbera d'Alba Bricco del Cuculo '01, sourced from one of the finest Barbaresco vineyards. It intrigues the eye with its deep hue, then releases rich cherry and strawberry. The richness continues in succulent fruit on the palate, while tasty varietal acidity lifts the finish. The Langhe Nebbio '01 did well, too, showing that distinctiveness which is the hallmark of excellent grapes. A poor 2002, however, kept the Dolcetto somewhat in the shade.

● Barbaresco Rabajà Ris. '97	ΨΨ	7
● Barbera d'Alba		
Bricco del Cuculo '01	ΨΨ	4*
● Verduno Basadone '02	ΨΨ	4*
● Barolo Massara '98	ΨΨ	7
● Langhe Nebbiolo '01	Ψ	4
● Dolcetto d'Alba Campot '02	Ψ	4
● Barolo Monvigliero '96	ΨΨ	7
● Barolo Massara '97	ΨΨ	7
● Barbaresco Rabajà Ris. '96	ΨΨ	7
● Barolo Massara Ris. '96	ΨΨ	7
● Barbaresco Faset '98	ΨΨ	7
● Barolo Monvigliero '98	ΨΨ	7

VIGNALE MONFERRATO (AL)

VIGNALE MONFERRATO (AL)

GIULIO ACCORNERO E FIGLI
LOC. CA' CIMA
15049 VIGNALE MONFERRATO (AL)
TEL. 0142933317
E-MAIL: info@accornerovini.it

BRICCO MONDALINO
REG. MONDALINO, 5
15049 VIGNALE MONFERRATO (AL)
TEL. 0142933204

Ermanno and Massimo Accornero continue to set the pace for quality winemaking in the province of Alessandria, particularly in Monferrato. They have made courageous decisions. A few years ago, we approved when they drew attention to Monferrato by switching from the Asti DOC designation for their Barbera. Today, we salute their professionalism in keeping back wines not yet ready for release, and in skipping wines in unfavourable years. Now let's celebrate a superb Bricco Battista. The nose still shows very young, but the splendour of its spicy red fruit fragrances makes any reference to age irrelevant. The immediate impressions on the palate are unrestrained power and velvety suppleness, but a tangy savouriness adds even more to the pleasure, as does a lengthy finale. The steel-vinified Giulìn seems to throw its excellent performance in the teeth of the difficult 2002. Showing a vivacious ruby red, it layers rich jasmine over ripe strawberry and cherry fruitiness. Its elegant crispness is a tasty foil to a even, medium structure. Barbera and cabernet give a well-integrated varietal character to the Centenario '02, marrying subtle toasty oak. On the palate, we loved the refreshing tang and good balance. The Grignolino acquits itself well. Classic fruit and spice precede a well-crafted harmony of acidity and tannins. The zesty, full-flavoured Bernardina lays out the typical freisa aromatic array, especially wild berry and cherry. The Brigantino always shows what malvasia fruit can deliver. Lively and intensely aromatic, it is smooth but never cloying.

Last year, we were unable to judge Mauro Gaudio's flagship wines, since he had decided that they needed extra time to age and mature. So after a year's wait, we can now discuss his Barbera Gaudium Magnum '00, the Barbera Zero Legno '00 and the Grignolino Bricco Mondalino '01. It's clear that Mauro was right. Extra cellar time has given them allure and nice focus, expanding eloquent fragrances and generous palates. The best of a very good bunch is the Gaudium Magnum, which opens to clean blackberry and plum, lifted by a hint of spice. The tasty zest of acidity makes for a clean palate, which nicely mirrors the nose, then everything balances well on a long finish. In the same league is the Barbera Zero Legno, with dark ruby announcing equally deep aromatics where tobacco notes entwine with lovely fruit and subtle balsam. The third wine, the Grignolino Bricco Mondalino, displays a more floral, appealingly varietal, nose. It continues crisp and vigorous on an equally typical grignolino palate, and a nicely bitterish tang conditions the long finale. After the three "late developers", we note good performances from two of the standard labels. Both the Grignolino and the Barbera are eminently enjoyable, refreshing and light but by no means lightweight.

● Barbera del M.to Sup.		
Bricco Battista '01	♟♟	6
● Monferrato Rosso Centenario '00	♟♟	6
● Barbera del M.to Giulìn '02	♟♟	4*
● Casorzo Malvasia Brigantino '02	♟	4
● Grignolino del M.to Casalese		
Bricco del Bosco '02	♟	4
● Monferrato Freisa		
La Bernardina '02	♟	3
● Barbera del M.to Sup.		
Bricco Battista '98	♟♟♟	6
● Barbera del M.to Sup.		
Bricco Battista '99	♟♟♟	6
● Barbera del M.to Sup.		
Bricco Battista '00	♟♟	6

● Barbera M.to		
Sel. Gaudium Magnum '00	♟♟	5
● Barbera del M.to Zero Legno '01	♟♟	4
● Barbera del M.to Sup. '01	♟	3
● Grignolino del M.to Casalese		
Bricco Mondalino '01	♟	4
● Grignolino del M.to Casalese '02	♟	3
● Barbera d'Asti		
Sel. Gaudium Magnum '98	♟♟	5
● Barbera d'Asti Il Bergantino '99	♟♟	4
● Barbera d'Asti		
Sel. Gaudium Magnum '99	♟♟	5
● Barbera d'Asti Il Bergantino '00	♟♟	4

Colonna

Fraz. San Lorenzo
Ca' Accatino, 1
15049 Vignale Monferrato (AL)
tel. 0142933239
e-mail: vini.colonna@onw.net

The Colonna winery is utterly dependable for the quality of its wines. Driven by her love of the land, Alessandra has seen to the growth not only of the cellar, but also of local tourism thanks to her Osteria dei Sapori "agriturismo" restaurant. But Alessandra's vision embraces much more than Monferrato. In the last few years, she has been producing a top-notch wine, the Monferrato Rosso Amani, whose proceeds go to help support a solidarity project in Africa. The '00, reviewed in error last year, is a deep red. A nice herbaceousness veins well-ripened berry fruit, and the mouth shows wonderfully long, balanced complexity. The Barbera Alessandra is almost black, while the nose balances ultra-ripe fruit with rich oak toast. That balance continues elegantly in the mouth, and on to an admirably long finish. The intensely lustrous straw yellow of the Armonia is an attention grabber. Super-ripe apples and pears follow on the nose, and the mouth impresses with a lovely, smooth balance. The result is a Chardonnay that may not be huge but does have plenty of character. The Grignolino Sansin shows a light, sparkling ruby, then a gorgeous nose full of spice-laced berry fruit. In the mouth, sweet, dense tannins caress a medium-textured palate. The La Rossa is every inch classic Barbera. This deliciously straightforward pleaser offers fine balance in the mouth as its strong suit.

●	Monferrato Rosso Amani '00	🍷🍷	8
●	Barbera del M.to Alessandra '00	🍷🍷	5
○	Piemonte Chardonnay Armonia '02	🍷🍷	4*
●	Barbera del M.to La Rossa '02	🍷	4
●	Grignolino del M.to Casalese Sansìn '02	🍷	4
●	Barbera del M.to Alessandra '99	YY	6
●	Monferrato Rosso Amani '99	YY	8
●	Barbera del M.to La Rossa '01	YY	4
●	Monferrato Rosso Mondone '99	YY	5

La Scamuzza

Cascina Pomina, 17
15049 Vignale Monferrato (AL)
tel. 0142926214
e-mail: lascamuzza@tiscalinet.it

Laura Zavattaro, an active wine woman, demonstrates again that her winery has arrived in the top ranks of quality producers. It's been quite a journey since far-off 1973, when her husband Massimo Bertone planted their first vineyard and put in barbera, grignolino and freisa, all the Monferrato classics. Their first wine, called Baciamisubito ("kiss me quick"), was for family and friends. Each year saw more progress, with the couple either planting more vines or updating facilities and equipment. Every move was a step towards better quality. Today, the winery enjoys the technical assistance of Mario Ronco. The Barbera del Monferrato Vigneto della Amorosa flaunts a deep ruby hue, then releases rich fragrances of well-ripened red berry fruit over hints of blackberry preserve and spices. The wine then seems to reach out, with a beautifully balanced, silky palate and a vigorous drive creating a resounding finale. Less complex is the Barbera Baciamisubito, with purple-flecked ruby and a well-judged acidity that makes this a delicious, crisp pleasure to drink. The Monferrato Rosso Bricco San Tomaso is a barrique-aged 50-50 blend of barbera and cabernet. A deep, attractive red presages impressive elegance on the nose, which opens to herbal and well-fruited aromas. A massively structured mouth completes a wine of majestic richness.

●	Barbera del M.to Sup. Vigneto della Amorosa '01	🍷🍷	6
●	Monferrato Rosso Bricco San Tomaso '01	🍷🍷	5
●	Barbera del M.to Baciamisubito '02	🍷	4
●	Barbera del M.to Sup. Vigneto della Amorosa '99	YY	5
●	Barbera del M.to Sup. Vigneto della Amorosa '00	YY	5
●	Monferrato Rosso Bricco San Tomaso '00	YY	4

VIGUZZOLO (AL)

CASCINA MONTAGNOLA
S.DA MONTAGNOLA, 1
15058 VIGUZZOLO (AL)
TEL. 0131898558
E-MAIL: info@cascina.montagnola.com

Donatella Giannotti and Bruno Carvi made a difficult decision in 2002, opting to allow their top wines more time to mature instead of releasing them. That decision proved to be the right one, for this year their Barbera Superiore Rodeo went into the final round and earned Two red Glasses. The colour of this well-structured, barrique-aged Barbera already suggests its qualities. On the nose, an initial herbaceousness slowly yields to more forward fragrances of red berry fruit and plum preserve, and to a lovely vein of vanilla. Tannins and months of bottle ageing have sanded away all the rough edges so often encountered in Barberas. The Barbera Amaranto also turned in a fine performance. Made in steel, it exhibits deep ruby and scents of dried hay, and a tasty acidity contributes to complexity in the mouth. Fruit considered substandard unfortunately kept the croatina Pigmento out of the line-up this year. The whites are represented by a new arrival, Riva Rosa, a Cortese that is every bit as impressive as its elder brother, Vergato. Both beguile with fresh-picked fruit and mixed wildflowers. Vergato's palate is the fuller of the two, but stays well this side of heavy. The Chardonnay Risveglio didn't match past performances. A bit more maturation time will most likely bring out more of its qualities.

VINCHIO (AT)

CANTINA SOCIALE DI VINCHIO
VAGLIO SERRA
REG. SAN PANCRAZIO, 1
14040 VINCHIO (AT)
TEL. 0141950903
E-MAIL: info@vinchio.com

Lorenzo Giordano and manager Ernestino Laiolo direct this well-known co-operative, flanked by oenologist, Mauro Cazzola, and with valuable technical help from consultant, Giuliano Noè. This year, we report on two great new Barberas, Bricco Laudana and Sei Vigne Insynthesis. But what really fascinates us is to see one of these Barberas, which we dubbed "the mother of all Barberas", in the top rank of Piedmont wines and easily capturing the sought-after Three Glasses. We are even more pleased, after almost 20 editions of this Guide, that this award goes to a wine from a large Piedmont co-operative winery, something that would have been thought impossible only a few years ago. But this winery has been driving towards ever better quality for over a decade now. Insynthesis, with this 2001 vintage debut, is their most daring project, involving 6,000 bottles of wine made with selected fruit from their most exceptional low-yield vineyards. It exhibits deep garnet, then proffers blackberry and truffle over a subtle resiny balsam, opening to a mouth of sheer elegance. It then powers through to a long, astonishingly rich finish. Only a step below is the Vigne Vecchie, and the Bricco Laudana, of which this is the second release. The ripest red berry fruit infuses the first, whereas the second offers a more floral character. Best of the top Barberas is the Superiore II Sogno. This is the first release of the Bianco Lipiai, a blend of müller thurgau, chardonnay and cortese. Finally, there was One Glass each for the Grignolino, the Barbera Rive Rosse and the Superiore.

● Colli Tortonesi Barbera Sup. Rodeo '00	♟♟	6
● Colli Tortonesi Barbera Amaranto '01	♟♟	4
○ Colli Tortonesi Cortese Riva Rosa '02	♟	3
○ Colli Tortonesi Cortese Vergato '02	♟	4
○ Risveglio Chardonnay '02	♟	6
● Colli Tortonesi Barbera Sup. Rodeo '98	♟♟	6
● Colli Tortonesi Barbera Sup. Rodeo '99	♟♟	6
○ Risveglio Chardonnay '01	♟♟	5

● Barbera d'Asti Sup. Sei Vigne Insynthesis '01	♟♟♟	7
● Barbera d'Asti Sup. Vigne Vecchie '01	♟♟	5
● Barbera d'Asti Sup. Bricco Laudana '01	♟♟	4*
● Barbera d'Asti Sup. II Sogno '00	♟	4
● Barbera d'Asti Sup. '01	♟	4
○ Monferrato Bianco Lipiai '01	♟	3
● Barbera d'Asti Rive Rosse '02	♟	3*
● Grignolino d'Asti '02	♟	3
● Barbera d'Asti Sup. Vigne Vecchie '99	♟♟	5
● Barbera d'Asti Sup. Vigne Vecchie Nizza '00	♟♟	5

OTHER WINERIES

TENUTA LANGASCO
FRAZ. MADONNA DI COMO, 10
12051 ALBA (CN)
TEL. 0173286972

The wines from this cellar are compelling. The Barbera d'Alba leads with deep garnet ruby, then offers complex strawberry, cherry and plum fruit and a lively palate. Sorì Coppa has an elegant nose, a dense, succulent mouthfeel and a lengthy finish. The Dolcetto is delightful.

●	Barbera d'Alba Madonna di Como '01	🍷🍷	4
●	Nebbiolo d'Alba Sorì Coppa '01	🍷🍷	4
●	Dolcetto d'Alba Madonna di Como '02	🍷	3

RONCHI
VIA RABAJÀ, 14
12050 BARBARESCO (CN)
TEL. 0173635156
E-MAIL: az.ronchi@libero.it

This emerging Barbaresco winery enters the Guide for the first time. The Barbaresco from the outstanding 1999 vintage impressed with dense fruit, good progression in the mouth, and remarkable balance. Terlé is also rounded and full. The Chardonnay is crisp, fruity, and ideal for easy drinking.

●	Barbaresco '99	🍷🍷	6
●	Barbera d'Alba Terlé '01	🍷	5
○	Langhe Chardonnay '01	🍷	5

CASCINA ADELAIDE
VIA AIE SOTTANE, 14
12060 BAROLO (CN)
TEL. 0173560503
E-MAIL: wine@cascinaadelaide.com

The Drocco family acquired this Barolo estate some years ago, and modernized the vineyards and facilities. The Cannubi is superb, displaying as much power as any wine from this noted vineyard. Equally excellent are the Langhe Jula, a nebbiolo and barbera mix, and the soft, balanced Barbera Amabilin.

●	Langhe Rosso Jula '01	🍷🍷	6
●	Barolo Cannubi '99	🍷🍷	8
●	Barbera d'Alba Sup. Amabilin '01	🍷	5

LE PIANE
LOC. VIA CERRI, 10
28010 BOCA (NO)
E-MAIL: info@bocapiane.com

This fairly new winery is a rising star. Christoph Künzli, a German in love with the area, runs the cellar with his partners and staff. The Boca is superlative, showing dark, inky red and a nose richly faceted with spice and earthy tones. The seductive palate is fat and fleshy yet harmonious.

●	Boca '99	🍷🍷	5

La Caplana
via Circonvallazione, 4
15060 Bosio (AL)
tel. 0143684182

Quality continues to improve here, and is now at the Two Glass level. The Vigna Vecchia releases fragrances as rich as they are elegant, redolent of blossoms and appley fruit, continuing full-flavoured and harmonious. We found the Dolcetto intriguing, and liked very much the Barbera d'Asti Rubis.

●	Dolcetto di Ovada Barricò '01	🍷🍷	4
○	Gavi del Comune di Gavi Vigna Vecchia '02	🍷🍷	3*
●	Barbera d'Asti Rubis '01	🍷	5

La Smilla
vico Garibaldi, 7
15060 Bosio (AL)
tel. 0143684245
e-mail: info@lasmilla.it

IWe were impressed by the Gavis from La Smilla. The Bergi has hints of citrus against a backdrop of rich floral essences. Its well-structured mouth is beautifully balanced. Two Glasses reward the standard label Gavi's finesse on both nose and palate, with the Comune di Gavi just a whisker below.

○	Gavi del Comune di Bosio I Bergi '01	🍷🍷	4
○	Gavi '02	🍷🍷	3*
○	Gavi del Comune di Gavi '02	🍷	4

Paolo Poggio
via Roma, 67
15050 Brignano Frascata (AL)
tel. 0131784929
e-mail: cantinapoggio@tiscali.it

Paolo Poggi fell just short of last year's performance, even though his wines remain excellent and present no obvious defects. The Derio is the wine that we liked the best, for its good structure and appealing depth on the nose.

●	Colli Tortonesi Barbera Derio '01	🍷🍷	4
●	Colli Tortonesi Barbera Campo La Bà '02	🍷	3
○	Colli Tortonesi Bianco Ronchetto '01	🍷	4

Fabio Fidanza
via Rodotiglia, 55
14052 Calosso (AT)
tel. 0141826921
e-mail: castellodicalosso@tin.it

We tasted two superb selections from this promising new Barbera d'Asti winery. The '01 already shows mature, with a lovely crisp, lightly acid-etched leanness. Castello di Calosso has sumptuous aromas of cassis, blackberry, and cinnamon. The mouth is impressively rugged, but with faultless balance.

●	Barbera d'Asti Sterlino Castello di Calosso '00	🍷🍷	6
●	Barbera d'Asti '01	🍷🍷	4

Mauro Grasso
via Gherzo, 3
14052 Calosso (AT)
tel. 0173291788

Mauro Grasso's Barberas are exceptional. The Sant'Anna presents nice ruby, then sweet spice and red fruit fragrances, with tasty acidity completing a delicious offering. Balsamic notes and generous power give the Romina a more youthful, zesty profile, but the palate is pure velvet.

●	Barbera d'Asti Sant'Anna Castello di Calosso '00	🍷🍷	6
●	Barbera d'Asti Romina '01	🍷🍷	4

Podere Macellio - Renato Bianco
via Roma, 18
10014 Caluso (TO)
tel. 0119833511

After several years, Podere Macellio re-enters the Guide, with two excellent main wines. Calusso Passito has great warmth and depth, with the sweetness in check. The cleanly varietal, well-structured Erbaluce di Calusso shows good balance, while the Spumante Metodo Classico is sound and luscious.

○	Caluso Passito '99	🍷🍷	5
○	Erbaluce di Caluso '02	🍷🍷	3*
○	Caluso Spumante M. Cl. Pas Dosé		4

PIERINO VELLANO
VIA PONTESTURA, 79
15020 CAMINO (AL)
TEL. 0142469127
E-MAIL: info@pierinovellano.it

The Vellano family long wanted to add winemaking to their venerable tradition as wine merchants. Now the Pierino Vellano estate, with some leased vineyards and others of their own being replanted, debuts two excellent Barberas, the cask-matured Gioanòt, and the Pierin, which ages in tonneau.

● Barbera del M.to Gioanòt '00	♈♈	5
● Barbera del M.to Pierin '00	♈♈	5

CORNAREA
VIA VALENTINO, 150
12043 CANALE (CN)
TEL. 017365636 - 0173979091

This historic Roero cellar has long been known for its sound wines. This year's are good. The '02 Arneis is consistent and fruity. But the red side is expanding too, as the superlative Roero Superiore shows. This year's stand-out, though, is an Arneis "passito" that is full, harmonious, endless.

○ Tarasco Passito '99	♈♈	5
● Roero Sup. '00	♈♈	6
○ Roero Arneis '02	♈	4

MALABAILA
P.ZZA CASTELLO, 1
12043 CANALE (CN)
TEL. 0173979044
E-MAIL: castello@malabaila.com

This venerable operation returns to the Guide with many recent improvements, culminating in an impressive line-up. Castelletto reveals the austerity and length of a champion Nebbiolo, and the Barbera is a fragrant seducer. The crisp, minerally Arneis is a delight, as is the Nebbiolo Bric Merli.

● Barbera d'Alba Mezzavilla '00	♈♈	4*
● Roero Sup. Castelletto '00	♈♈	5
● Nebbiolo d'Alba Bric Merli '00	♈	4
○ Roero Arneis Pradvaj '02	♈	4

ENRICO SERAFINO
C.SO ASTI, 5
12043 CANALE (CN)
TEL. 0173967111
E-MAIL: barbero.info@barbero1891.it

Enrico Serafino has for some time been part of the Barbero group, world leader in liqueurs and aperitifs. Their wines, made in magnificent underground cellars, have been gaining in quality. We enjoyed a fruity Barbera, a nicely structured Roero with solid tannins, and a fragrant, tangy Roero Arneis.

● Barbera d'Alba Sup. Parduné '00	♈♈	4*
● Roero Sup. Pasiunà '00	♈♈	4
○ Roero Arneis '02	♈	4

NE. NE.
REG. SERRA MASIO, 30
14053 CANELLI (AT)
TEL. 0141831152

Ne. Ne. is Nervi and Negro, the partners in this Canelli cellar that offers the Asti classics. The undisputed flagship wine is Martleina. The '01 version unleashes rich draughts of almond-edged fruit. The palate is full and dense, showing a good vein of acidity smoothed and balanced by oak.

● Barbera d'Asti Martleina '01	♈♈	5

GIACOMO SCAGLIOLA E FIGLIO
REG. SANTA LIBERA, 20
14053 CANELLI (AT)
TEL. 0141831146
E-MAIL: aziendascagliola@libero.it

This family cellar offers a fine Vigna dei Mandorli '00. It captivates with red fruit and silky spice, then opens on the mouth with power, but with everything well-proportioned. The Monferrato Rosso '00 is glossy with fine-grained tannin. Finally, the Moscato d'Asti is well-crafted and delicious.

● Barbera d'Asti Vigna dei Mandorli '00	♈♈	4*
● Monferrato Rosso La Virasa Vejia '00	♈♈	5
○ Moscato d'Asti Santa Libera '02	♈	3

BEL SIT
VIA PIANI, 30
14054 CASTAGNOLE DELLE LANZE (AT)
TEL. 0141875162

Ezio Rivella gave us two appealing versions of Barbera. La Sichivej is laden with rich blackberry, raspberry, and spice, opening to a smooth, mouthfilling palate, defined by a nice line of acidity. The Monferrato offers elegant minerally and floral notes, and a generous, harmonious palate.

● Barbera d'Asti Sup. Sichivej '01	▼▼	4
● Barbera del M.to '01	▼▼	4

GIANNI DOGLIA
FRAZ. ANNUNZIATA, 56
14054 CASTAGNOLE DELLE LANZE (AT)
TEL. 0141878359
E-MAIL: wine-doglia@libero.it

After a life in the vineyards, Bruno Doglia passed the business to his son, Gianni. For several years, Gianni has been producing Moscato and Barbera, bottling only the best of the four-hectare estate. He delighted us with a fragrant Moscato '02 and a Barbera Superiore '02 with a fleshy mouthfeel.

● Barbera d'Asti Sup. '00	▼▼	5
○ Moscato d'Asti '02	▼▼	3*
● Barbera d'Asti Boscodonne '01	▼	3

CA' DEI MANDORLI
VIA IV NOVEMBRE, 15
14010 CASTEL ROCCHERO (AT)
TEL. 0141760131
E-MAIL: stefanoricagno@cadeimandorli.com

On the border of Asti and Alessandria, Stefano Ricagno runs a 100 hectare plus estate which sources a number of fine local varieties. We found the Brachetto very impressive. It was one of the best tasted, both refreshing and well balanced. The Barbera is also nicely harmonious with plenty of fruit.

● Barbera d'Asti Sup. La Bellalda d'Oro '00	▼▼	5
● Brachetto d'Acqui Le Donne dei Boschi '02	▼▼	4˙

MARSAGLIA
VIA MADAMA MUSSONE, 2
12050 CASTELLINALDO (CN)
TEL. 0173213048
E-MAIL: cantina@cantinamarsaglia.it

The Roero winery of Marina and Emilio Marsaglia is always reliable. We liked the Roero Superiore '00, with its terrific aromatics, mouthfilling palate and long, balanced finale. The nice Castellinaldo Barbera is harmonious and sturdy, offering a rich, intriguing bouquet. The Arneis is well made.

● Castellinaldo Barbera d'Alba '00	▼▼	5
● Roero Sup. Brich d'America '01	▼▼	5
○ Roero Arneis San Servasio '02	▼	4

VILLA FIORITA
VIA CASE SPARSE, 2
14034 CASTELLO DI ANNONE (AT)
TEL. 0141401231 - 0141401852
E-MAIL: villafiorita-wines@villafiorita-wines.com

The Rondolino family is raising quality across the board. This year, we especially liked the lovely, fruit-forward Barbera d'Asti Giorgione, as well as the two Monferrato Rossos. The Nero di Villa opens round and rich, and the Maniero has good depth and alcoholic warmth on the palate.

● Barbera d'Asti Sup. Giorgione '00	▼▼	6
● Monferrato Rosso Nero di Villa '01	▼▼	5
● Monferrato Rosso Maniero '00	▼	5

VALLI UNITE
CASCINA MONTESORO
15050 COSTA VESCOVATO (AL)
TEL. 0131838100

The Valli Unite co-operative is one of the few organic wineries in the area, and all its wines are sound. Two Barberas did well, in particular the Vighet, its character firmed up by a stay in barrique. A clear Two Glass champion.

● Colli Tortonesi Barbera Vighet '01	▼▼	5
● Colli Tortonesi Barbera '01	▼	4

ALFONSO BOERI
FRAZ. BIONZO - VIA BRICCO QUAGLIA, 10
14055 COSTIGLIOLE D'ASTI (AT)
TEL. 0141968171
E-MAIL: boeri@boerivini.it

The Boeri family vineyards and winery are in Costigliole d'Asti, so they really shine with Barbera d'Asti. Their Porlapà is excellent, showing deep red with elegant red fruit on the nose, and a harmonious, nicely bitterish palate. The Martinet rewards with crispness and consistency.

● Barbera d'Asti Sup. Porlapà '00	� past	5
● Barbera d'Asti Sup. Martinet '01	past	4

F.LLI ABRIGO
VIA MOGLIA GERLOTTO, 2
12055 DIANO D'ALBA (CN)
TEL. 017369104

The Abrigo brothers have one of the best wineries in Diano. Dolcetto leads their line-up, with two good labels. The Vigna Pietrin is more dense and generous, but the Sörì dei Berfi pleases mightily. In an area known for good Barberas, the Abrigo's is nicely husky and consistent, with a long finale.

● Barbera d'Alba La Galùpa '01	♟♟	4
● Diano d'Alba Sörì dei Berfi Vigna Pietrìn '02	♟♟	4*
● Diano d'Alba Sörì dei Berfi '02	♟	3

CASAVECCHIA
VIA ROMA, 2
12055 DIANO D'ALBA (CN)
TEL. 017369205

In the Diano area, the Casavecchia brothers stand out for the high quality of their wines. This year, we liked the superb Barolo, with its clean aromatics and generous power. The Nebbiolo is remarkably distinctive. The Dolcetto turned in a good performance, and the Barbera is pleasingly tart.

● Barolo Piantà '99	♟♟	6
● Nebbiolo d'Alba Piadvenza '00	♟♟	4*
● Barbera d'Alba San Quirico '01	♟	4
● Diano d'Alba Sörì Bruni '02	♟	4

CASCINA FLINO
VIA ABELLONI, 7
12055 DIANO D'ALBA (CN)
TEL. 017369231

The wines offered by Paolo Monte suffered a bit from an unfavourable year, but they still did well. We liked the Diano Vigna Vecchia for its clean, focused fragrances and massive power. The nose of the Flin shows a tad too much wood, but the mouth is full-bodied and continues nicely.

● Diano d'Alba Vigna Vecchia '02	♟♟	3*
● Barbera d'Alba Flin '01	♟	4

RICCHINO - TIZIANA MENEGALDO
CASCINA RICCHINO
12055 DIANO D'ALBA (CN)
TEL. 0142488884
E-MAIL: tiziana.menegaldo@tiscalinet.it

This winery, with help from Gian Piero Romana and Beppe Caviola, makes only one wine, superbly. We hope the limited production will grow. The Dolcetto di Diano is lilac-edged purple with ripe fruit preserve on the nose. The palate has zesty fruit and crisp acidity, then almonds infuse the finish.

● Diano d'Alba Rizieri '02	♟♟	4

OSVALDO BARBERIS
B.TA VALDIBÀ, 42
12063 DOGLIANI (CN)
TEL. 017370054
E-MAIL: brekos@jumpy.it

In spite of a poor 2002, this winery offers two nice Dolcettos. We very much liked the Puncin. It shows deep, lively purple, with layered aromas of red berry, cocoa, and bitter almond. The slightly less complex San Lorenzo is nicely fruited and full-bodied, with tasty almond lifting a good finale.

● Dolcetto di Dogliani Puncin '02	♟♟	4*
● Dolcetto di Dogliani San Lorenzo '02	♟	3

FRANCESCO BOSCHIS
FRAZ. SAN MARTINO DI PIANEZZO, 57
12063 DOGLIANI (CN)
TEL. 017370574
E-MAIL: m.boschis@tiscalinet.it

The Boschis family vineyards at Dogliani yield some fascinating wines made from several grape varieties. Both of the Dolcettos are outstanding, but we prefer the rich, concentrated Vigna del Ciliegio. The Barbera d'Alba is compelling, too, showing elegant and consistent, with good acidity.

● Barbera d'Alba Le Masserie '01	♥♥	4*
● Dolcetto di Dogliani Sup.		
Vigna del Ciliegio '01	♥♥	4*
● Dolcetto di Dogliani Pianezzo '02	♥	3

RIBOTE
B.TA VALDIBERTI, 24
12063 DOGLIANI (CN)
TEL. 017370371

The 2002 growing year was not a good one, affecting even Bruno Porro's wines. Notes of cinchona and almond nicely layer his Dolcetto di Dogliani, and its dense palate signs off bitterish. The standard Dolcetto is easy drinking and delicious, but, as expected, it's a bit restrained in body and drive.

● Dolcetto di Dogliani Ribote '02	♥♥	4
● Dolcetto di Dogliani '02	♥	3*

ERALDO REVELLI
LOC. PIANBOSCO, 29
12060 FARIGLIANO (CN)
TEL. 0173797154
E-MAIL: eraldorevelli@tin.it

The Revelli family Dolcettos performed well. The San Matteo pleased us enormously. Voluptuous blackberry, raspberry, and sun-dried tomato introduce a well-structured palate with nice tannins. The Autin Lungh was also good, with a succulent crispness. Otto Filari is a bit simpler, but just as fine.

● Dolcetto di Dogliani		
Autin Lungh '02	♥♥	4
● Dolcetto di Dogliani S. Matteo '02	♥♥	4
● Dolcetto di Dogliani Otto Filari '02	♥	4

LA CHIARA
LOC. VALLEGGE, 24/2
15066 GAVI (AL)
TEL. 0143642293

Roberto Bergaglio introduced Gavi del Comune di Gavi this year and it won Two Glasses. It shows beguiling hedgerow over citrus scents, followed by a balanced mouth and tangy flavours. The long finish shows the variety's bitterish hallmark. The Gavi Vigneto Groppella is good, but it's been better.

○ Gavi del Comune di Gavi		
La Chiara '02	♥♥	3*
○ Gavi del Comune di Gavi		
Vigneto Groppella '01	♥	4

LA SCOLCA
FRAZ. ROVERETO, 170/R
15066 GAVI (AL)
TEL. 0143682176
E-MAIL: info@scolca.it

The Gavi Barrique debuted by the Soldati family immediately earned Two Glasses for its deep straw hue and a bouquet that ranges from vanilla through citrus fruit. The Gavi Etichetta Nera easily held last year's ranking, and the non-vintage Soldati La Scolca Brut put in a solid performance.

○ Gavi Barrique '00	♥♥	6
○ Gavi di Gavi Etichetta Nera '02	♥	6
○ Soldati La Scolca Brut	♥	5

TORRACCIA DEL PIANTAVIGNA
VIA ROMAGNANO, 69/A
28074 GHEMME (NO)
TEL. 0163844711

Alessandro Francoli is making a lot of investments, aiming for top quality. His elegant Jerbion vineyard Gattinara closely reflects its terroir and is one of the best of its type. Tre Confini, his standard Nebbiolo, drinks impressively. The Ghemme is vigorous, but a bit blurred and still awkward.

● Colline Novaresi Nebbiolo		
Tre Confini '02	♥♥	3*
● Gattinara Vigneto Jerbion '98	♥♥	5
● Ghemme '99	♥	5

EUGENIO BOCCHINO
FRAZ. SANTA MARIA - LOC. SERRA, 2
12064 LA MORRA (CN)
TEL. 0173364226
E-MAIL: laperucca@libero.it

Among Eugenio Bocchino's wines this year, we were most impressed by the La Perucca '01. After a deep garnet, it yields cinchona and red berry fruit, then offers a full-fruited, luscious palate. The complex, powerful Barbera d'Alba is fine, as is the Langhe Rosso, despite a heavy hint of oak.

● Barbera d'Alba '01	ΨΨ	4
● Nebbiolo d'Alba La Perucca '01	ΨΨ	6
● Langhe Rosso Suo di Giacomo '01	Ψ	6

F.LLI FERRERO
FRAZ. ANNUNZIATA, 12
12064 LA MORRA (CN)
TEL. 017350691
E-MAIL: renato.ferrero@tiscalinet.it

The Annunziata area of La Morra has long been noted for superb Barolos. The vineyards of the Ferrero family offer even more admirable wines. The Bricco Luciani is ruggedly structured, dense and vigorous, whereas the Manzoni seduces with harmonious elegance. The nebbiolo-based Nebiosè is also good

● Barolo Gattere Bricco Luciani '99	ΨΨ	7
● Barolo Manzoni '99	ΨΨ	7
● Nebiosè '01	Ψ	4

GIANNI GAGLIARDO
B.TA SERRA DEI TURCHI, 88
12064 LA MORRA (CN)
TEL. 017350829
E-MAIL: gagliardo@gagliardo.it

Stefano Gagliardo is in charge of this La Morra cellar, but his father, Barolo legend Gianni, is still on call. The Barolo is the real star, with structure and power galore. The Barbera is also good, but it's more opulent and even-keeled. One Glass each to Langhe Batié and the intriguing Chinato.

● Barbera d'Alba La Matta '00	ΨΨ	5
● Barolo '99	ΨΨ	8
● Langhe Rosso Batié '99	Ψ	6
● Barolo Chinato	Ψ	7

BUSSIA SOPRANA
LOC. BUSSIA, 81
12065 MONFORTE D'ALBA (CN)
TEL. 039305182

Bussia Soprana's 1999 Barolos are superb. The traditional Vigna Colonnello has an array of sweet spice, raspberry, and earth, echoed on a balanced, juicy palate. The Mosconi has a rich nose of with faded rose over liquorice and mint, and a powerful, tannic palate. Bussia is simpler but consistent.

● Barolo Mosconi '99	ΨΨ	7
● Barolo Vigna Colonnello '99	ΨΨ	7
● Barolo Bussia '99	Ψ	7

JOSETTA SAFFIRIO
FRAZ. CASTELLETTO, 32
12065 MONFORTE D'ALBA (CN)
TEL. 017378660
E-MAIL: josettasaffirio@hotmail.com

A Langhe star from the late 1980s is back in the Guide. Sara Vezza, Josetta's young daughter, resurrected the operation in 1999. Only 1,000 bottles of wine exist, a fabulous Barolo di Castelletto di Monforte, but it will soon be joined by a Barbera, a Merlot, and a Rossese fermented off the skins.

● Barolo '99	ΨΨ	8
● Barolo '88	ΨΨΨ	8
● Barolo '89	ΨΨΨ	8

VALERIO ALOI
VIA PIETRO FISSORE, 6
12046 MONTÀ (CN)
TEL. 0173975604

Watch Roero producer Valerio Aloi. His line-up is expanding and his large new facility will allow greater quality. Meanwhile, his two big reds did well. Bricco Valpiana is rich and full-fruited, and the Bricco Morinaldo is luscious and rounded. The Arneis is fruity, crisp, and delicious.

● Barbera d'Alba Bricco Valpiana '01	ΨΨ	4*
● Roero Bricco Morinaldo '01	ΨΨ	4*
○ Roero Arneis Liffrei '02	Ψ	3

CANTINA DEL BRICCHETTO
VIA BRICCHETTO, 4
12057 NEIVE (CN)
TEL. 0173677207

Franco Rocca makes all the area's standards, with Barbaresco his leading label. The Albanesi offers fragrant depth on the nose and a tannic-edged structure of impressive density. We preferred the nicely fruity and tart-crisp Ombranera Barbera to the cask-conditioned Bricco Sterpone.

● Barbaresco Albesani '00	♥♥	6
● Barbera d'Alba Ombranera '01	♥	5

CASTELLO DI NEIVE
VIA CASTELBORGO, 1
12052 NEIVE (CN)
TEL. 017367171
E-MAIL: neive.castello@tin.it

Castello di Neive, part of Barbaresco's history, offers a line-up that is good all round. The Barbaresco Riserva is outstanding. A gorgeous nose leads to a surge of tannins and a mouthfilling progression. Two Glasses, too, for I Cortini, a soft, luscious Pinot Noir. The Barbera d'Alba showed well.

● Langhe Rosso I Cortini '01	♥♥	6
● Barbaresco S. Stefano Ris. '98	♥♥	8
● Barbera d'Alba Mattarello '00	♥	5

DOMENICO FILIPPINO
FRAZ. SERRA CAPELLI, 20
12052 NEIVE (CN)
TEL. 017367507

The Filippino family's wines impressed this year, especially the superb Sorì Capelli '99. Orange-rimmed ruby ushers in rich notes of faded flowers and tobacco, then a generous palate and long finale. A good performance, too, by the complex, caressing Barba Cesco. The Vigna Veja is less intriguing.

● Barbera d'Alba Sup.		
Barba Cesco '00	♥♥	4
● Barbaresco Sorì Capelli '99	♥♥	7
● Barbera d'Alba Vigna Veja '00	♥	4

PUNSET
FRAZ. MORETTA, 5
12057 NEIVE (CN)
TEL. 017367072
E-MAIL: punset@punset.com

Punset farms organically, allowing the estate both to safeguard the environment and to keep quality high. Their Barbaresco Campo Quadro boasts a lean, but richly-faceted nose of blackberry, cassis and spice, then plenty of body and consistency in the mouth. The standard label is also fine.

● Barbaresco Campo Quadro '00	♥♥	7
● Barbaresco '00	♥	6

ROBERTO SAROTTO
FRAZ. RONCO NUOVO, 13
12050 NEVIGLIE (CN)
TEL. 0173630228
E-MAIL: r.sarotto@libero.it

Roberto Sarotto ran Cantina Produttori del Gavi for some time. Now he has his own facility at Neviglie, where he offers the local standards, as well as two Gavis. Elena la Luna has a full, smooth richness, while tannin and good structure inform the Enrico I. The Gavi is fruity, crisp, and delicious.

● Barbera d'Alba Elena la Luna '01	♥♥	4
○ Gavi del Comune di Gavi		
Bric Sassi '02	♥♥	4
● Langhe Rosso Enrico I '99	♥	5

ANTONIO BALDIZZONE
CASCINA LANA
C.SO ACQUI, 187
14049 NIZZA MONFERRATO (AT)
TEL. 0141726734

Antonino Baldizzone's wines are improving apace. We liked best the deep-hued Nizza, with its distinctive red berry fruit, and the palate's sensational depth and opulence. The Vën ëd Michen was impressive as well, with remarkable power, and seemingly endless length in the finish.

● Barbera Sup. Nizza '00	♥♥	5
● Barbera d'Asti Sup.		
Vën ëd Michen '01	♥♥	5

Cascina Giovinale

S.da San Nicolao, 102
14049 Nizza Monferrato (AT)
tel. 0141793005
e-mail: giovinale.ciocca@libero.it

Cascina Giovinale keeps putting out excellent wines and is a main player in the dynamic Nizza area. We liked the Barbera d'Asti del '01, which is clean and fruity, with tasty acidity. Trinum, an interesting cabernet-dolcetto blend, is rounded, with good nose-palate consistency.

●	Barbera d'Asti '01	🍷🍷	4
●	Monferrato Trinum '01	🍷🍷	5

Erede di Armando Chiappone

loc. San Michele, 51
14049 Nizza Monferrato (AT)
tel. 0141721424
e-mail: info@eredechiappone.com

With ten hectares of well-sited vineyards in the Nizza area, quality here is constantly on the rise. Of the wines tasted, the Barbera d'Astis stood out. In the Ru, from Nizza, lovely aromas accentuate a full-bodied velvety mouthfeel. The Brentura impressed us as well.

●	Barbera d'Asti Brentura '01	🍷🍷	4
●	Barbera d'Asti Sup. Nizza Ru '01	🍷🍷	6

La Gironda

S.da Bricco, 12
14049 Nizza Monferrato (AT)
tel. 0141701013

This Asti operation is putting out excellent examples of the DOC area classics. We were very pleased by both the Barbera d'Astis. A fantastic nose and a beefy structure mark the Nizza, but it shows good balance. The elegant La Gena stretches long, and drinks deliciously.

●	Barbera d'Asti Sup. Nizza Le Nicchie '00	🍷🍷	5
●	Barbera d'Asti La Gena '01	🍷🍷	4

Cascina Ulivi

S.da Mazzola, 14
15067 Novi Ligure (AL)
tel. 0143744598 - 01436756430
e-mail: cascinaulivi@libero.it

Stefano Bellotti's philosophy is biodynamics, and his wines are always singular. Fruit and fresh hay waft from his Mounbè, which opens supple and mid bodied. The Filagnotti has a nice Gavi nose over a crisp palate. One Glass goes to Nibiô, and to the generously mineral Montemarino.

●	Piemonte Barbera Mounbè '01	🍷🍷	4*
●	Monferrato Dolcetto Nibiô '01	🍷	4
○	Gavi Filagnotti '02	🍷	3
○	Gavi Montemarino '02	🍷	3

Valditerra

S.da Monterotondo, 75
15067 Novi Ligure (AL)
tel. 0143321451

Laura Valditerra shows total dedication in personally supervising her winery's operations and has lately been turning out good reds. But the Gavi Vigna is the standout, with glorious aromas and a super-savoury palate. The Barbera shows rich and long. The FiorDesAri blend is another winner.

●	Piemonte Barbera '01	🍷🍷	5
○	Gavi Vigna del Lago '02	🍷🍷	5
●	FiorDesAri Rosso '01	🍷	5

Cascina Bondi

loc. Cappellette
15076 Ovada (AL)
tel. 0131299186

Not content with the successful Locanda dell'Olmo at Boscomarengo, the Bondis also make wine at Cascina Banaia on the Cappellette hillslope. The barbera-based Ruvrin is very crisp for such a dense, full wine. The Duién's package of cherry, plum, and flint won it Two Glasses. Le Guie is well made.

●	Dolcetto di Ovada Sup. Duién '01	🍷🍷	4*
●	Monferrato Rosso Ruvrin '01	🍷🍷	5
●	Barbera del M.to Le Guie '02	🍷	4

GAGGINO
VIA S. EVASIO, 29
15076 OVADA (AL)
TEL. 0143822345

Gabriele Gaggino runs this winery with Giovanni Bailo. Its recent performance shows the promise of the Ovada area. The monovarietal barbera Il Ticco has a near-black hue that leads into a nose rich in super-ripe fruit, and the mouth is eloquently proportioned. We also liked Il Capè and Sant'Evasio.

● Monferrato Rosso Il Ticco '01	🍷🍷	5
○ Monferrato Bianco Il Capè '01	🍷🍷	4*
● Dolcetto di Ovada Sup.		
S. Evasio '01	🍷	3

CANTINE VALPANE
VIA CASCINE VALPANE, 10/1
15039 OZZANO MONFERRATO (AL)
TEL. 0142486713
E-MAIL: info@cantinevalpane.com

Two superb wines mark the Guide debut of this winery. Valpane, with time in barrique, exudes mature scents of black pepper and vanilla over rich sour cherry and raspberry. A deeper, younger hue announces the Ljdia, with balsamic notes unfolding over ripe blackberry and raspberry fruit.

● Barbera del M.to Ljdia '00	🍷🍷	5
● Barbera del M.to Valpane '99	🍷🍷	5

FAVARO
VIA CHIUSURE, 1/BIS
10010 PIVERONE (TO)
TEL. 012572606
E-MAIL: favaro.chiusure@hotmail.com

Benito Favaro's recipe is a meticulously groomed hectare of vines and a small, well-equipped cellar. His Passito Sole d'Inverno has superb balance. The poor 2002 vintage penalized the dry Erbaluce. Though sound and lovely, it shows less complex than in past years.

○ Caluso Passito		
Sole d'Inverno '97	🍷🍷	6
○ Erbaluce di Caluso		
Vigna delle Chiusure '02	🍷	4

DANIELE SACCOLETTO
S.S. CASALE-ASTI, 82
15020 SAN GIORGIO MONFERRATO (AL)
TEL. 0142806509
E-MAIL: saccolettovini@virgilio.it

Daniele Saccoletto obstinately practices a rigorous natural and organic viticultural programme, and minimal intervention winemaking. This year, we enjoyed his husky, well-fruited Barbera Aureum '01, as well as the Freisa '01, an appealing, beautifully perfumed quaffer.

● Barbera del M.to Aureum '01	🍷	4
● Monferrato Freisa		
Vigna Fiordaliso '01	🍷	4

GUIDO BERTA
LOC. SALINE, 53
14050 SAN MARZANO OLIVETO (AT)
TEL. 0141856193
E-MAIL: bgpm@inwind.it

From the Barbera d'Asti heartland come two resounding Guido Berta wines. Canto di Luna continues as the cellar's flagship red. The nose nicely focuses rich fruit, then solid acidity gives good progression to a well-developed palate. The Barbera is admirable, showing consistency throughout.

● Barbera d'Asti Sup. '01	🍷🍷	3
● Barbera d'Asti Sup.		
Canto di Luna '01	🍷🍷	4

CARUSSIN
REG. MARIANO, 27
14050 SAN MARZANO OLIVETO (AT)
TEL. 0141831358
E-MAIL: carussin@inwind.it

The Ferro family operate in the centre of the Barbera d'Asti DOC, with Vincenzo Muni consulting. The 13 hectares yield some fine wines. The Nizza area Ferro Carlo is expansive, soundly structured and seductive. La Tranquilla is skilfully crafted. Though younger, it shows maturity and consistency.

● Barbera d'Asti Sup. Nizza		
Ferro Carlo '00	🍷🍷	5
● Barbera d'Asti La Tranquilla '01	🍷🍷	4

FRANCO MONDO
REG. MARIANO, 33
14050 SAN MARZANO OLIVETO (AT)
TEL. 0141834096
E-MAIL: francomondo@inwind.it

Well-performing wines continue to emerge from this modest cellar. Franco Mondo's talent is clear from Barbera Vigna delle Rose. A lively ruby is followed by well-layered red berry and sweet spice, with mouthfilling consistency on the palate. The Balein is delightfully rich-flavoured and weighty.

● Barbera d'Asti Sup.		
Vigna delle Rose '00	♈♈	5
● Barbera del M.to Balein '02	♈	3

GIOVANNI ROSSO
LOC. BAUDANA, 6
12050 SERRALUNGA D'ALBA (CN)
TEL. 0173613142
E-MAIL: wine@giovannirosso.com

Young Davide's appointment as oenologist has brought steady improvements to this winery. We continue to prefer the Cerretta, which is a better structured and fatter Barolo than the admittedly fine Serralunga. The Barbera has still to find its stylistic groove, but it shows good proportion.

● Barbera d'Alba		
Donna Margherita '01	♈♈	5
● Barolo Cerretta '99	♈♈	7
● Barolo Serralunga '99	♈	6

CASTELLO DI TASSAROLO
CASCINA ALBORINA, 1
15060 TASSAROLO (AL)
TEL. 0143342248

Paolo Spinola's new Gavi del Comune di Tassarolo scored well. After a sparkling straw, the aromas are nicely varietal hedgerow, pear, and apricot. The mouth has balance and round, complex flavours. A step behind is Tassarolo S, a crisp, uncomplicated wine redolent of chamomile and Alpine flowers.

○ Gavi del Comune di Tassarolo		
Castello di Tassarolo '02	♈♈	4*
○ Gavi Tassarolo S '02	♈	3

PIOIERO
LOC. PIOIERO, 1
12040 VEZZA D'ALBA (CN)
TEL. 017365492
E-MAIL: info@pioiero.com

We expected and received good results from the ever-reliable Rabino winery in Roero. The wine quality is growing nicely. We found the Roero Superiore superlative, showing well-structured depth. Equally good is the juicy, smooth Barbera. The Arneis and Nebbiolo are both delicious.

● Roero Sup. '01	♈♈	4*
● Barbera d'Alba Sup. '01	♈♈	4
● Nebbiolo d'Alba '01	♈	3
○ Roero Arneis Bric e Val '02	♈	3

MARCO CANATO
CASCINA BALDEA, 18
15049 VIGNALE MONFERRATO (AL)
TEL. 0142933653 - 0142933678
E-MAIL: canatovini@yahoo.it

The Canato family earned their Guide entry. We gave Two Glasses to the Rapet for its remarkable evenness. After a deep ruby, it throws ripe blackberry, aromatic herbs and vanilla. The Grignolino only just missed Two Glasses. Pale garnet, it unveils an array of pepper, roses, wildflowers, and peach.

● Barbera del M.to Rapet '00	♈♈	5
● Grignolino del M.to Casalese		
Celio '02	♈	4

LA CELLA DI SAN MICHELE
VIA CASCINE DI PONENTE, 21
13886 VIVERONE (BI)
TEL. 016198245

Leo Enrieti's cellar is in a romantic monastery on the lake of Viverone. His Erbaluce '02 is scented with crushed flowers and pear-drops. It is well-crafted but perhaps a bit evolved already. The Cella Grande Metodo Classico, with good body and ripeness, is interesting.

○ Erbaluce di Caluso		
San Michele '02	♈	4
○ Caluso Spumante M. Cl.		
Cella Grande	♈	5

LIGURIA

Looking at the overall picture of wine production in Liguria, we find some nice surprises among the reds. Whites, however, are by and large unexciting after an indifferent vintage, some wines dropping down a rung. This is truer of the Levante, the eastern coast, where outstanding performances were rare. But this year's weather was not kind to either coastline. Quality took a hit and production was down a good 30 to 40 per cent. This did not amount to a disaster, of course, but it does raise the question: isn't it about time to adopt a new – in Italy, at any rate – pricing system based on the quality of the vintage and the actual worth of the product? Does it really make sense to keep raising prices? Along-the-line mark-ups deliver a fairly expensive product to the consumer, in many cases restricting purchase to the fairly affluent. It's an oft-posed question, but one still wanting for a satisfactory answer, particularly when restaurants ask you to shell out at least € 15 for a Pigato, a Vermentino or a Cinque Terre. Let's take a closer look now at the various areas. The powerhouse of Liguria winemaking remains the provinces of Imperia and Savona, which can point to Rossese di Dolceacqua, as well as the Ponente coast DOCs of Pigato, Vermentino, Rossese, Ormeasco, and Sciac-trà. Performances were generally sound, but somewhat inconsistent with some laudable exceptions, from La Spezia area producers of Vermentino, Bianco and Rosso in the Colli di Luni DOC, from wineries in the DOCs of Cinque Terre and Cinque Terre Sciacchetrà, and finally from the lacklustre Colline di Levanto DOC. Genoa seems to lack worthy protagonists, despite having two DOCs, Valpolcèvera and Golfo del Tigullio. Let's focus on individual producers who achieved good results. Cascina delle Terre Rosse turned out a string of superb wines. Laura Aschero is back with two distinctive offerings, a Vermentino and a Pigato. Giuncheo remains admirably dedicated to Vermentino and to Rossese di Dolceacqua, a wine type that is also honoured by Mandino Cane and the Terre Bianche winery. We are happy to note exciting performances by Bruna, Lio, Le Rocche del Gatto, Vecchia Cantina, Calleri, Lupi, and by Monticello's sterling Poggio dei Magni, a blend of sangiovese, merlot and other local varieties. That passionate winegrower Emanuele Trevia merits special attention. He richly deserves the spotlight for the success of his La Mattana ("tantrum") red, christened by his daughter, Marta, in tribute to her sometimes headstrong father, and for setting his winery on a course that has brought it well-deserved praise.

ALBENGA (SV)

CALLERI
REG. FRATTI, 2
17031 ALBENGA (SV)
TEL. 018220085

The Calleri brothers are now managing the winery founded by their father in 1968. Their secret is to buy in fruit directly from the vineyards, as if from their own estate's plots. Long-trusted growers in Cisano, Albenga, Pietra Ligure, Cosio and Pornassio work with them selecting the grapes. That quality fruit assures the Calleris of a diverse line-up of distinctive, full-bodied wines, all soundly made, bright and clean. The standard-label Pigato shows flawless quality. Delicate floral and citrus notes open a wonderfully scented nose, yielding to denser layers of musk and sage. They continue in the mouth, enriching a texture that has alcoholic warmth and zesty acidity. The wine's well-crafted balance continues all the way through a powered finale. The other Pigato, Saleasco, is a dependable team mate. Here, we are presented with heady wood resins and fragrant herbs, with a touch of blossoms. The mouth nicely echoes the nose, progressing evenly to a lovely finish with an alluring bitterish tang. We found both Vermentinos appealing. The standard label is undeniably elegant, with an eloquent nose of herbs and wildflowers. Scrumptious, tempting flavours get a delicate lift from alcohol, and it achieves a satisfying fullness. I Muzazzi, on the other hand, flaunts headier aromas of flowers and fruit, notably apples. It progresses clean and smooth, with sound structure, to a good finish. The Olmeasco may not be too complex, but we liked its attractively sunny disposition, which is loaded with cherry fragrances and nicely proportioned.

○	Riviera Ligure di Ponente Pigato '02	▽▽	4*
○	Riviera Ligure di Ponente Pigato Saleasco '02	▽	4
○	Riviera Ligure di Ponente Vermentino '02	▽	4
○	Riviera Ligure di Ponente Vermentino I Muzazzi '02	▽	4
●	Riviera Ligure di Ponente Ormeasco '02		4

ALBENGA (SV)

CASCINA FEIPU DEI MASSARETTI
FRAZ. BASTIA
REG. MASSARETTI, 7
17031 ALBENGA (SV)
TEL. 018220131
E-MAIL: mastroiano@libero.it

Cascina Feipu and Pippo Parodi are names that are always spoken in the same breath, at least by the many admirers the winery has attracted over the years. That loyalty was gained by Parodi's far-sighted efforts to achieve the quality now so widely acclaimed. The venerable adage that "wine is made on the vine" may be true, but, it is also made by the hand of the winemaker. Pippo's has certainly contributed much, especially with his pioneering work to modernize and promote Pigato. For some time now, the reins have been held by his son-in-law, Mirko Mastroianni, and daughter Ivana, so everything is still solidly in the family, and work continues in a well-established direction. Mirko takes care of production, with the assistance of oenologist Mino Moretti, and Ivana looks after sales and marketing. As always, we liked the Pigato. With a lovely clear straw hue, it opens to a note of sweetness, quickly seconded by rich floral fragrances of broom and aniseed. A nicely fruited mouth shows good weight and soft contours. The easy-drinking Rossese is not complex, but it is clean, with a warm touch of alcohol. The Passito II Pippo is new. Produced from mat-dried grapes fermented in small barrels, it sports a cherry hue and an elegant, delicately spicy bouquet, with a medley of rose petals, elegant geranium and wild strawberry. Lovely balance compensates for a somewhat lightweight mouth, and tangy acidity keeps the sweetness at just the right level.

●	Il Pippo Passito '01	▽	4
○	Riviera Ligure di Ponente Pigato '02	▽	4
●	Riviera Ligure di Ponente Rossese '02		4

ALBENGA (SV)

LA VECCHIA CANTINA
FRAZ. SALEA
VIA CORTA, 3
17031 ALBENGA (SV)
TEL. 0182559881

The instincts of a farmer and the strong tug of the earth are obvious in Umberto Calleri. He is justly proud of his work, and of the high quality those efforts have achieved. Additional reasons for quality are the well-sited vineyards Umberto owns, as well as his well-appointed cellar. Winemaking requires a clear idea of what you are doing, and on this score the affable Umberto has no doubts, combining respect for tradition with an even-handed openness to technology. All efforts are focused on coaxing the best from the grape. His range this year included a Vermentino, a Pigato and a Passito, which debuted here with the '98 vintage. The two whites ran almost neck and neck, but we found the Pigato slightly more to our liking. After a lively straw, the nose is not especially rich, but hallmark floral notes do provide an agreeable signature. There's good fruit on top of moderate weight, with an attractive savouriness leading into a finish with warm alcohol and just a touch of the variety's bitterish edge. The Vermentino is a bit loath to open, but stylish scents of peach blossom and broom tease out nicely, then a tasty vein of acidity enlivens the palate and calibrates the structure. The Passito is a delight, flaunting an appealing limpid amber, and seductive hints of citrus fruit, dried apricot, and acacia honey. There's a velvety sweetness, of course, but it's admirably balanced and under control. The rich flavours just keep lingering, with the initial aromas well in evidence.

ALBENGA (SV)

LE ROCCHE DEL GATTO
REG. RUATO, 4
17031 ALBENGA (SV)
TEL. 081221175

The name has changed and two new partners have joined. De Andreis' father Luigi Crosa di Vergagni and daughter Chiara, who heads marketing, are on board and the hectares have risen to six, one of which is leased. Production has risen to about 30,000 bottles. But what really counts is the winemaking philosophy, which remains true to Fausto De Andreis's principles. The vineyards are in various locations, on both flatland and low hills, planted to pigato, vermentino, and rossese (with some Dolceacqua and Campochiesa rossese clones) at 5,000 vines per hectare. Lengthy macerations and frequent pumpovers produce deep coloured wines that are usually fairly aroma-rich. That's a good description of the Pigato, whose elegant, inviting nose has fragrant scrub, broom, and honey. The palate is balanced and expansive, echoing the nose. It progresses solidly to a satisfying finish and took Two well-deserved Glasses. The Crociata, another monovarietal Pigato, is delightful. It leads with gold-flecked straw yellow, but is slow to yield its aromas, centred on apple and almond with spice and mineral nuances. It's well structured, with crisp, tangy flavours that nicely complement the aromatics, and ends on a pleasantly bitterish note. Equally persuasive is the Vermentino, with irresistible floral and fruit aromas that just pour out. The mouth could use more weight, but there's good vigour and a tasty, bitterish conclusion. Finally, the Rosso, a blend of rossese and some minor local varieties, shows nicely floral and fruity, with a suggestion of spice.

○	Colline Savonesi Passito '99	♥♥	6
○	Riviera Ligure di Ponente		
	Pigato '02	♥	4
○	Riviera Ligure di Ponente		
	Vermentino '02	♥	4

○	Riviera Ligure di Ponente		
	Pigato '02	♥♥	4*
○	Riviera Ligure di Ponente		
	Vermentino '02	♥	4
○	Spigau Crociata '02	♥	4
●	Rosso del Gatto '02		4

CAMPOROSSO (IM)

CASTELNUOVO MAGRA (SP)

TENUTA GIUNCHEO
LOC. GIUNCHEO
18033 CAMPOROSSO (IM)
TEL. 0184288639
E-MAIL: info@tenutagiuncheo.it

IL TORCHIO
VIA PROVINCIALE, 202
19030 CASTELNUOVO MAGRA (SP)
TEL. 0187674075

The attractive Tenuta Giuncheo continues the string of superb performances by its wines. Credit goes to constant investment in the operation, as well as to the painstaking efforts of point man Marco Romagnoli, who manages cellar and vines flanked by oenologist Donato Lanati. The vineyards now cover seven hectares, and more will follow, to increase the Vermentino beyond its present three versions. The standard label presents an elegant dance of smoothly fragrant honey, and the charming rusticity of wildflowers and broom. The nicely structured palate tempts with juicy fruit, and a spirited crescendo caps the experience. A stay in barrique of 30 per cent of the fruit for Le Palme lends a touch of gold to its lively yellow. A subtle hint of flowers hovers nicely over rich, appley fruit, and a consistent, harmonious palate lends the whole an alluring elegance. The Eclissi is barrel fermented, remaining in wood for 12 months. Opulent aromas open to a soundly structured mouth that has every component nicely in place. The best of the reds is the Rossese Pian del Vescovo, with its deep ruby and captivating nose lightly scented with balsam. Strawberry and blackberry-laden fruit on a dense, rich palate are in impressive equilibrium with a zesty acidity. Slightly lighter than the '00 release, the syrah-based Sirius has an appropriately varietal nose and offers vigorous, straightforward drinking pleasure.

We've learned that the dynamic Giorgio Tendola has expanded his activities this year by opening an attractive "agriturismo" next to the winery, with six comfortable rooms. In addition, a modern production line has been installed in his olive press-house, so efficiency will improve there. On the wine front, the year was far from favourable, but we found the bottles sound and satisfying. The Colli di Luni Rosso, a 70 per cent sangiovese mix with merlot, filled out with other red varieties, showed very well, just failing to cross the Two Glass threshold. It leads with garnet-tinged ruby, then opens out into a lovely suite of coffee and bitter chocolate underpinned by blackberry and blackcurrant fruit. These are well echoed in a mouth that shows prominent acid, and tannins that are perhaps still a tad rough. Both the progression and the finish are sound. The Vermentino was inviting, a deep yellow straw announcing an intriguing mix of spicy herbs, musk and acacia blossoms. There's marked vigour on the satisfying, velvet palate, but a bit more intensity would be welcome. A varietal almondy touch nicely imprints the finale. One Glass went to the Di Giorgio Bianco, an assemblage of vermentino, trebbiano, albarola and malvasia. It's redolent of spring flowers and piquant Mediterranean scrub, with a clean, refreshing palate that beautifully matches the aromatic array, creating a wine of good balance. Winery production now totals some 30,000 bottles per year.

● Rossese di Dolceacqua Vigneto Pian del Vescovo '01	♟♟	5
○ Riviera Ligure di Ponente Vermentino '02	♟♟	4*
○ Riviera Ligure di Ponente Vermentino Le Palme '02	♟♟	4*
○ Riviera Ligure di Ponente Vermentino Eclissi '01	♟	6
● Sirius '01	♟	7
● Rossese di Dolceacqua Vigneto Pian del Vescovo '00	♟♟	5
● Sirius '00	♟♟	7

● Colli di Luni Rosso '01	♟	5
○ Colli di Luni Vermentino '02	♟	4
○ Di Giorgio Bianco '02	♟	3*
● Di Giorgio Rosso '02		3

CASTELNUOVO MAGRA (SP)   CHIAVARI (GE)

OTTAVIANO LAMBRUSCHI
VIA OLMARELLO, 28
19030 CASTELNUOVO MAGRA (SP)
TEL. 0187674261
E-MAIL: ottavianolambruschi@libero.it

ENOTECA BISSON
C.SO GIANELLI, 28
16043 CHIAVARI (GE)
TEL. 0185314462
E-MAIL: bisson@bissonvini.it

Ottaviano Lambruschi is one of those people you are glad you met. He is honest and industrious, with hands that speak of hard work in the vineyards, testifying to a vocation that one has to be lived totally if satisfactory results are to be achieved. This is particularly true in an area that is not exactly mainstream on Italy's wine scene. Ottaviano has inculcated his deeply held beliefs into his son Fabio, with whom he has established real collaboration in running the winery. They produce 25-30,000 bottles per year with outstanding fruit from about five hectares, almost two of which are leased. Now to the wines. Luscious floral and honey notes give the Sarticola rich length on the nose, and the mouth shows good balance and progression. The renowned Costa Marina vineyard yields a wine of limpid straw yellow that intrigues with its pungent forest floor and Mediterranean brush land. Noticeable acidity in the mouth nicely balances the alcohol. Sangiovese, cabernet and merlot make up the Maniero, with half the blend passing a few months in barriques. The nose is in no hurry to release its plum and morello, and the structure is a bit narrow-shouldered. Still, it's warm and inviting on the palate. The standard Vermentino is honest and straightforward, its deep colour preceding scents of blossoms and country herbs. The Rosso '02 is blended from 60 per cent sangiovese, 10 per cent canaiolo and 10 per cent merlot plus other locals and made in steel. The palate shows a bit immature, but we liked its lively wild berry aromas and its smooth drinkability.

Pietro Lugano, Bisson's amiable manager, can count on ten hectares of estate vineyards, with more coming into production. This will allow him to cut back on bought-in fruit, which at present is less than 20 per cent, for his production, pegged last year at about 60,000 bottles. Add to that the dogged determination that has kept him going through the years, and you have his life's dream becoming a beautiful reality. Located in the province of Genoa, he produces fully ten types of wines, a number that may be the final barrier to his complete success. Reporting on the wines tasted, we found that the Acini Rari performed well indeed, almost winning a second Glass. Its alluring amber prepares you for elegant fragrances of dried fruit, with an odd, barely discernible pungent note. The palate is nicely echoing and satisfying. The other "passito" is just as appealing. We've never seen such a deep-hued version and the luscious medley of walnut, dried apricot, and fig is beguiling. The palate is smooth and long, if just a shade too sweet. The dolcetto-barbera blend Musaico Vigna Intrigoso turned in a solid One Glass performance. Gorgeously crisp cherry preserve is layered over pungent mint and forest floor, all continuing onto a nicely tannin-etched palate with sound, generous structure. The finish is pleasurably bitterish. The cask-aged Il Musaico is quite similar, and also earned One Glass.

●	Colli di Luni Rosso Maniero '02	♟	4
○	Colli di Luni Vermentino Costa Marina '02	♟	4*
○	Colli di Luni Vermentino Sarticola '02	♟	4*
●	Colli di Luni Rosso '02		3
○	Colli di Luni Vermentino '02		4

○	Acini Rari Passito '00	♟	5
○	Caratello Passito '00	♟	5
●	Il Musaico '01	♟	5
●	Golfo del Tigullio Rosso Musaico Vigna Intrigoso '02	♟	4
○	Golfo del Tigullio Vermentino Vigna Intrigoso '02		4

CHIUSANICO (IM)

LA ROCCA DI SAN NICOLAO
FRAZ. GAZZELLI
VIA DANTE, 10
18023 CHIUSANICO (IM)
TEL. 018352850 - 018352304
E-MAIL: info@roccasannicolao.it

The winery's vineyards are set on terraces between 350 and 600 metres above sea level, and receive minimal intervention management, utilizing, for example, cover-cropping in the rows. The Proxi vineyard, which provides the two vineyard designates, is easily recognized by the large rock formation protecting it from cold winds, as well as by the chapel constructed with stone from the ancient Benedictine monastery. The soils are chalky and alkaline, and the vineyards face south to southeast. The planting density ranges from 5,000 vines per hectare for rossese to 6,500 for white varieties. Even if the rankings this year don't match some past vintages, the wines are very appealing and mirror the qualities we found in past years. Leading off with the standard Vermentino, we were impressed with its intriguing combination of rich white-fleshed fruit with delicate scents of wildflowers. The mouth is pleasurably crisp and clean, nicely echoing the nose. The Pigato Vigna Proxi remains in steel about nine months. What the enchanting floral aromas miss in complexity they more than make up for in intensity. Attack and overall balance are sound, though we expected somewhat more body. The Vermentino '02 performs well. The nose presents crisp floral notes and a complement of medicinal herbs, then the mouth is nicely centered on tasty acidity. The Rossese '02 is a top-drawer, youthful quaffer with the expected bitterish tang.

DIANO CASTELLO (IM)

MARIA DONATA BIANCHI
VIA DELLE TORRI, 16
18010 DIANO CASTELLO (IM)
TEL. 0183498233

This estate has been a main player in Liguria for some time now, and it gets better every year. The whites have always been star performers, understandable given this viticultural area. But Emanuele Trevia also presented us with a compelling, well-crafted red, La Mattana. This 50-50 blend of syrah and grenache has been an important item on the winery agenda for some time, and its long development has proved worth the wait. It showcases not only great source fruit and talented winemaking, but Emanuele's personal feelings for his father as well, expressed in a brief dedication on the label. You can certainly cellar it for some time, but it can be enjoyed tonight, too, for its gorgeously crisp nose. Well-judged oak and spice hover over an exuberant fruit-floral package exhibiting lavender, blackberry fruit, and redcurrant. The palate is richly-faceted, brimming with juicy flavours. Structure and balance are simply elegant, as is its dense tannic weave. The Vermentino is superb. Subtle spice gives way to richer scents of apple, wildflowers, and hazelnut, followed by a clean, well-defined palate with fine vigour. The Pigato is equally alluring, flaunting an emphatic medley of citrus, musk, and broom, matched by an explosively fruited mouth of superb weight and length. The cask-aged Eretico Pigato goes on the same pedestal. It offers a rich nose and plenty of savoury flavours on a velvety palate that progresses deliberately to a nicely bitterish finale. The Eretico Vermetino plays a bit below par. The generous, varietal nose fails to find a suitably nuanced mouth.

○ Riviera Ligure di Ponente Pigato Vigna Proxi '02	▼	4
○ Riviera Ligure di Ponente Vermentino '02	▼	4
○ Riviera Ligure di Ponente Vermentino Vigna Proxi '02	▼	5
● Riviera Ligure di Ponente Rossese '02	▼	4

● La Mattana '01	▼▼	6
○ Eretico Pigato '01	▼▼	6
○ Riviera Ligure di Ponente Pigato '02	▼▼	4*
○ Riviera Ligure di Ponente Vermentino '02	▼▼	4*
○ Eretico Vermentino '01	▼	6
○ Riviera Ligure di Ponente Vermentino '01	▽▽	4

DOLCEACQUA (IM)

GIOBATTA MANDINO CANE
VIA ROMA, 21
18035 DOLCEACQUA (IM)
TEL. 0184206120

Giobatta Mandino Cane has always been a consummate professional. He has always focused on the concept of terroir, initially some years ago when introducing his extravirgin olive oil, and later on when producing a Rossese di Dolceacqua. Perfectionist that he is, he honed its character, discarding all the imperfections that were considered "varietal" by winemakers less focused and now eclipsed. His accomplishments have been fully recognized by critics and consumers. A new release this year amply confirms Giobatta's role as pace-setter: L'Intruso is an equal blend of syrah and rossese, released after 18 months in large oak ovals. Good ripe fruit is in gorgeous evidence here, the raspberry, blackberry, and morello cherry clearly etched against a subtle spiciness. The vigorous palate shows impressive depth and fruit, powering though to a well-balanced finale. Of the two Rossese Superiores, the Vigna Arcagna unleashes an elegant aromatic array of captivating richness, ranging through strawberry, blackberry, blackcurrant, and roses, which then infuse a velvety, savoury palate with good alcoholic breadth and balance. The other Superiore, the Vigneto Morghe, also performed well, opening out into rich fruit subtly veined with herbs and spice. A condominium of good tannins, crisp acidity, and satisfactory alcohol admirably complements well-judged structure and goodish density.

●	L'Intruso '01	🍷🍷	5
●	Rossese di Dolceacqua Sup. Vigneto Arcagna '02	🍷🍷	5
●	Rossese di Dolceacqua Sup. Vigneto Morghe '02	🍷	5
●	Rossese di Dolceacqua Sup. Vigneto Morghe '01	🍸🍸	4

DOLCEACQUA (IM)

TERRE BIANCHE
LOC. ARCAGNA
18035 DOLCEACQUA (IM)
TEL. 018431426 - 018431230
E-MAIL: terrebianche@terrebianche.com

After some 20 years, Terre Bianche can be proud of the cellar's accomplishments. Started by Claudio and Paolo Rondelli in the early 1980s, it quickly earned a reputation for its excellent Rossese di Dolceacqua. Vermentino and Pigato followed, and some interesting experiments with both emerged. The reins are now held by Franco Laconi and young Filippo Rondelli, who personally oversee vineyards and cellar, with the talented help of oenologist, Mario Ronco. We were impressed with the overall high performance of the range. Bricco Arcagna, one of the first Rosseses to be cask-aged, did especially well, as always. It boasts a beguiling nose of strawberry fruit, unfolding scents of faded rose and gunflint as well. The rest of the performance is markedly elegant, with an opulent palate nicely matching the aromatics, and it offers a sustained finale. The standard Rossese shows less complexity, but is eminently enjoyable for floral hints over tasty fruit, and for a well-balanced palate of upfront crisp flavours. The Arcana Bianco, a pigato and vermentino mix, turned in a superlative performance. Pungent scents of herbs, walnut husk and pungent scrubland are in glorious evidence, backed by a subtle touch of toasty oak. It opens nicely to a crisp, clean palate that is richly aromatic and nuanced with coffee and white chocolate. Progression to the stellar finish is vigorous. We liked the fragrant, floral Vermentino, whose delicate almondy background seems the perfect foil for its lively, savoury palate. The Pigato offers varietal aromas, succulent mouthfeel and sound balance.

●	Rossese di Dolceacqua Bricco Arcagna '01	🍷🍷	5
○	Arcana Bianco '01	🍷🍷	5
○	Riviera Ligure di Ponente Pigato '02	🍷	4
○	Riviera Ligure di Ponente Vermentino '02	🍷	4
●	Rossese di Dolceacqua '02	🍷	4
●	Rossese di Dolceacqua Bricco Arcagna '00	🍸🍸	4

FINALE LIGURE (SV)

IMPERIA

CASCINA DELLE TERRE ROSSE
VIA MANIE, 3/B
17024 FINALE LIGURE (SV)
TEL. 019698782

COLLE DEI BARDELLINI
LOC. BARDELLINI
VIA FONTANAROSA, 12
18100 IMPERIA
TEL. 0183291370 - 010594513
E-MAIL: info@colledeibardellini.it

Vladimiro Galluzzo's wines this year confirm his winery as one of Liguria's best. Without losing a whit from their reflection of terroir, they continue to show attractively cosmopolitan. For example, the Solitario, a well-gauged assemblage of grenache, barbera, and rossese, is a full-bodied thoroughbred of a wine, with loads of spicy fruit. In many respects, it is the forerunner of modern Ligurian reds. The 2001 meets expectations. A deep ruby precedes the luscious nose, demonstrating a masterful touch of oak married to captivating fruit essences and crisp balsamic spiciness. The palate seems to expand in every direction, creating a mouthfilling, hedonistically smooth repetition of the aromatics. The two Pigatos are consistently good. The basic version has varietal hallmarks of rich peach and summer flowers, which thrust on to infuse a lavish palate that impresses with its crisp, generous flavours. In all, it's a very distinctive wine. A small proportion of the Apogeo Pigato is matured in oak. The nose opens into an exceptional array of scrubland and pine resin fragrances, layered over fruit and flowers and followed by pronounced vigour in the mouth. It shows excellent follow through to a lengthy, bitter-almond finish. The Vermentino turned in a splendid performance. Rich pine resin is successfully married to an intriguing vein of smokiness, with aromas also nicely present on the palate, where balance, power, and concentration admirably meld together. Zesty flavours and light-hearted quaffability are the hallmarks of the 100 per cent lumassina L'Acerbina.

The six and a half hectares at Colle dei Bardellini include four in vineyard on a sunny plateau, not far from the Imperia coast. The wines are consistently good year after year, thanks to the experience and good planning of the smoothly working management team, Pino Sola, Giuliano Noè and Gianni Briatore. Those results are especially visible in the current releases of Vigna U Munte and La Torretta. The first, with 15,000 bottles produced, inclines to the clean-edged spiciness of Mediterranean scrub, broom and musk, then follows with good definition and nicely balanced structure. La Torretta is produced in 10,000 bottles. Here, we find fruit and floral fragrances that are glossy and opulent, then a good sustained progression enlivened by a pronounced citrussy note. It ends well and long. The standard Vermentino is quite well executed, with a nose of alluring delicacy that hints at wildflowers and citrus, over a fruity, pear-like base. The palate shows pliant texture subtly girdered by crisp acidity that brings it into beautiful balance and gives it a savoury thrust. All the varietal characteristics are in evidence in the Pigato, in particular the aromas, which show luscious peach and apricot fruit and floral notes of broom. One might wish a fuller body, but there's no quibbling with that juicy drinkability, capped with a dash of bitter almond.

● Solitario '01	🍷🍷	7
○ Apogeo '02	🍷🍷	5
○ Riviera Ligure di Ponente Pigato '02	🍷🍷	5*
○ Riviera Ligure di Ponente Vermentino '02	🍷🍷	4*
○ L'Acerbina '02	🍷	4
○ Riviera Ligure di Ponente Pigato '99	🍷🍷🍷	4
● Solitario '00	🍷🍷	7
○ Le Banche '01	🍷🍷	5

○ Riviera Ligure di Ponente Pigato '02	🍷	4
○ Riviera Ligure di Ponente Pigato Vigna La Torretta '02	🍷	5
○ Riviera Ligure di Ponente Vermentino '02	🍷	4
○ Riviera Ligure di Ponente Vermentino Vigna U Munte '02	🍷	4

MONTEROSSO AL MARE (SP)   ORTONOVO (SP)

BURANCO
VIA BURANCO, 72
19016 MONTEROSSO AL MARE (SP)
TEL. 0187817677
E-MAIL: info@buranco.org

LA PIETRA DEL FOCOLARE
FRAZ. ISOLA DI ORTONOVO
VIA DOGANA, 209
19034 ORTONOVO (SP)
TEL. 0187662129
E-MAIL: lapietradelfocolare@libero.it

In comparison to Ligurian viticulture as a whole, the estate managed by Kurt and Sonja Wachter looks unusual. The vineyard surround the winery, seeming to form a crown around the modest lemon grove, with olive trees just above. There is something garden-like about it: certainly not what you run into every day here. But the Wachters put hard work into their neat terraces, cultivating vermentino, bosco, albarola, sangiovese, cabernet sauvignon, merlot and syrah. Three very diverse lots go to compose their Cinque Terre. A traditional white-wine fermentation produces one, while a second is cask-fermented and spends about six months on the lees. The third lot remains on the fine lees in steel for 90 days. All three are then assembled, and given a brief rest before bottling. The nose on the '02 is clean and crisp, with a lovely suite of flowers, peach and apricot layered over white chocolate and revealing a light mineral edge. A deliciously crisp palate offers generous echoes of these fragrances, adding a bitter almond fillip to the finish. The Buranco is cabernet and syrah with a dash of merlot and sangiovese, and stays 12 months in new oak. The colour is deep, and the bouquet lingers nicely, exuding intriguing berry fruit, pencil lead and toasty nuances. Balance is satisfactory, but it falls a bit short in body and distinctiveness. Still, the wine serves to indicate some new stylistic directions for the area. The Sciacchetrà appeals with its gold hue and the hedonistic sweetness of its blossoms, dried grapes and acacia honey. The 2001 was produced in 5,300 bottles.

When an unfavourable year dictates a defensive game, it's difficult to produce great wines, especially for wineries with less experience or limited dimensions. The Salvettis' operation, in the Colli di Luni DOC, falls into the latter category, with about six and a half hectares in the areas of Sarticola and Bacchiano. They wisely cut their usual four releases down to two, and it worked. The Vermentino Augusto shows a deep straw yellow, then impresses with a rich melange of pungent herbs and delicate wild flowers over apple and peach fruit. Solid acidity supports an attractive palate that echoes the nose, and a tasty bitter almond note enlivens the finale. We were less pleased with the Santo Paterno. It presents delicate floral essences, and nice apple and pear fruit, but the acidic vein that firms the palate grows bit excessive on the finish, and it could do with tighter structure and more vigorous progression. The Rosso is still at the experimental stage. Sourced from older vineyards of sangiovese, merlot and canaiolo, it spends 14 months in twice-used barriques, then finishes in steel. It's an impressively deep ruby, but with a less than generous nose. Structure and progression are well up to snuff, and it shows a light veil of oak.

● Buranco '01	♀	6
○ Cinque Terre Sciacchetrà '01	♀	8
○ Cinque Terre '02	♀	5
○ Cinque Terre Sciacchetrà '00	♀♀	8

● Colli di Luni Rosso Re Carlo '01	♀	6
○ Colli di Luni Vermentino Augusto '02	♀	5
○ Colli di Luni Vermentino Santo Paterno '02		4
○ Colli di Luni Vermentino Santo Paterno '01	♀♀	4*

PIEVE DI TECO (IM)

PONTEDASSIO (IM)

TOMMASO E ANGELO LUPI
VIA MAZZINI, 9
18026 PIEVE DI TECO (IM)
TEL. 018336161 - 0183291610
E-MAIL: info@vinilupi.it

LAURA ASCHERO
P.ZZA V. EMANUELE, 7
18027 PONTEDASSIO (IM)
TEL. 0183293515

One of the most important hallmarks of this winery is the consistently high quality throughout the line of wines. Behind this policy is owner Tommaso Lupi, well known in the world of Ligurian wine. Ably flanking him are oenologist Donato Lanati, and Tommaso's sons, Massimo in production and Fabio in the vineyards. They look after about nine leased hectares, mostly in Valle Arroscia. This year gave us a top-drawer Vignamare, and it's no longer a blend but 100 per cent pigato. A sparkling straw precedes a stunning array of rich fragrances, exuding beautiful broom and scrub over a base of citrus fruit and apricot, all of which continue flawlessly on a strikingly broad palate. As for the standard whites we tasted, the tip of the hat goes to the Vermentino, in which piney resin nicely backs up floral notes. Alcoholic warmth and good fruit reinforce each other, set off by alluring bitter almond. The Pigato shows pungent spice and subtle fruit, continuing almondy on a well-endowed palate that shows soundly crafted balance and appreciable weight. We were impressed by the sheer aromatic elegance of Le Serre '02, pleasurably echoed on a palate that is dry but textured in velvet. The nose on the Pigato Le Petraie is a bit parsimonious, but the palate shows elegance, and a fine almond tang backgrounds crisp juicy flavours. The only red we tasted was the Ormeasco Le Braje '01. Its deep ruby introduces a slightly evolved bouquet nuanced with morello cherry. The nicely rounded mouth is firmed up by good grip and a light suite of tannins that gives it an inviting crispness.

From 1982 on, this cellar has continuously raised the quality bar, achieving a standard that is as impressive as it is consistent. And results this year amply match last year's good performances. Credit goes to the admirably committed owner, Laura Aschero, one of the few women in Ligurian winemaking. But she is most ably assisted in both cellar and vineyard by her son, Marco Rizzo. Oenologist Gianpaolo Ramò consults. The team also includes daughter-in-law, Carla, with granddaughter Bianca, still at university, signalling her interest as well. Now to the wines. Laura's Vermentino, practically a benchmark for the varietal, did best, if only by a hair. A lustrous deep straw, it unveils fine, velvety fragrances that seem to linger on and on, with floral broom and acacia blossoms offset by rich fruit. Tasty acidic grip graces a full range of succulent flavours and contributes to a good progression and finish. Even the Pigato undergoes the production practice here of a 36 to 48-hour maceration on the skins, followed by the settled must fermenting at 18 degrees Celsius for as long as 30 days. The result is a 2002 with a lush aromatic array featuring scents of Mediterranean scrub, spicy herbs, wildflowers and apricot. The palate is subtly fragrant amidst generous fruit, with sound structure and balance.

○ Vignamare '01	♟♟	5
○ Riviera Ligure di Ponente		
Vermentino Le Serre '02	♟♟	5
● Riviera Ligure di Ponente		
Ormeasco Sup. Le Braje '01	♟	5
○ Riviera Ligure di Ponente		
Pigato '02	♟	4
○ Riviera Ligure di Ponente Pigato		
Le Petraie '02	♟	5
○ Riviera Ligure di Ponente		
Vermentino '02	♟	4
○ Vignamare '00	♟♟	5

○ Riviera Ligure di Ponente		
Pigato '02	♟♟	4*
○ Riviera Ligure di Ponente		
Vermentino '02	♟♟	4*

RANZO (IM)

RANZO (IM)

A MACCIA
FRAZ. BORGO
VIA UMBERTO I, 54
18020 RANZO (IM)
TEL. 0183318003

ALESSANDRI
FRAZ. COSTA PARROCCHIA
18028 RANZO (IM)
TEL. 018253458
E-MAIL: massimoalessandri@libero.it

Loredana Faraldi started this small family-run cellar in the late 1980s. The family owns a parcel of some three hectares in the municipality of Ranzo, north of Imperia, an area hosting some of the denomination's best vineyards. Loredana's vines, at 150-200 metres elevation, are trained to Guyot and spurred cordon (rossese). Rossano Abbona, the young oenologist, plays a major role in the operation. The winery's philosophy is to bring out as much as possible the hallmarks of the pigato variety and to make it ever more distinctive. The '02 Pigato already shows impressive results. It leads with a green-tinged straw yellow, and follows with alluring scents of crisp citrus fruit that unfold over elegant notes of pear. The palate opens to goodish structure and depth, and nicely mirroring the nose. Overall, this is a wine of well-crafted balance. The Rossese is sound and faithful to type, its pale ruby introducing scents of wild red berries that make up a rich, lingering bouquet. The structure could be more complex, but the tang of acidity is enjoyable, and there is judicious proportion throughout, from front palate to satisfying finish. Production of the latest release is around 16,000 bottles.

This year's results confirm, at least in part, our good impressions from last year. The fruit from the 2002 growing year certainly precluded miracles. Nonetheless, the wine that was produced is more than satisfactory. Massimo Alessandri has obstinately set his sights on top quality, ably assisted by talented oenologist, Walter Bonetti. Massimo is gradually increasing his vineyards, but the current total of five hectares, some estate-owned and some leased, gives him a production approaching 25-30,000 bottles, which is just right for an operation of this scale. Since he is in Ranzo, widely recognised as one of the areas most suited to pigato, most of Massimo's vineyards are planted to that grape, and his plots range from 270 to 350 metres above sea level. He has also put in enough syrah and grenache to produce a house red, scheduled for release next year. His present Pigato, the Costa de Vigne, is a bright straw, with a clean, distinct nose showing good citrus fruit and an appealing floral lift. It opens out confidently and vigorously to a very savoury palate, with delicious acid-veined fruit.

○ Riviera Ligure di Ponente Pigato '02	🍷	4
● Riviera Ligure di Ponente Rossese '02	🍷	4

○ Riviera Ligure di Ponente Pigato Costa de Vigne '02	🍷	4

RANZO (IM)

BRUNA
VIA UMBERTO I, 81
18028 RANZO (IM)
TEL. 0183318082
E-MAIL: aziendaagricolabruna@libero.it

RIOMAGGIORE (SP)

WALTER DE BATTÈ
VIA TRARCANTU, 25
19017 RIOMAGGIORE (SP)
TEL. 0187920127

Riccardo Bruna has handed over management of the winery to his daughter, Francesca, but the hand on the tiller is still his. Riccardo is still setting the course and determining the ports of arrival. But this year's releases experienced a few storms, resulting in decreased production and slightly lower quality than normal. However, Riccardo has been hardened by adversity and remains unfazed, even in difficult years. His performance is always well above average. As for this year's line-up, there is no U Bacan, since the quality of the fruit just wasn't there, and the Bruna family's strict principles rule out any cellar tricks. The Pigato Le Russeghine may not have its full complement of qualities, but it's still a champion. Delicately nuanced fruit, peach to the fore, melds with subtle hints of sage. An appreciably crisp acidity lifts the supple palate, and there is sound harmony overall. The Villa Torrachetta is admirably well executed, a standout for both its balance and distinctiveness. The nose flaunts an intriguing complex of fragrances, teasing out summer flowers and wild herbs, then pungent spices, and peach and apricot nuances as well. Next comes a bright, fresh palate with finely crafted progression and a long finish. Finally, the Rossese. Brilliant ruby ushers in richly faceted fruit over delicate raspberry and wild strawberry. The palate is full and dense but crisp edged, with a subtle bitterish vein, conveyed with appreciable vigour and proportion.

Walter is a winemaker who "plans" his wine in the vineyard before making it in the cellar, and he tolerates no compromise unless its purpose is to raise quality still higher. The raw material for his hand-crafted wines comes from 8,000 square metres that he cultivates. The 19 separate plots cling to steep terraces carved into Riomaggiore's rugged slopes. The Cinque Terre we tasted has a production of only 2,500 bottles. About 40 per cent is fermented on the skins, then it goes into used barriques. The remainder undergoes a brief cool fermentation before being racked off into steel. After eight months, the two lots are blended and matured until bottling. During ageing, the must rests on the fine lees, of course, and is racked only as needed. Like its predecessors, the 2002 needs time to be at its best. It shows off its personality right from a deep straw yellow shot with gold, and an ultra distinctive combination of pungent shrub, medicinal herbs and gunflint. Enticing flavours in good consonance with the nose anchor a heady palate, with balance evident at every step. The still-maturing Sciacchetrà '01 has not yet been bottled. We'll be back to review it for the next edition of the Guide.

○ Riviera Ligure di Ponente Pigato Villa Torrachetta '02	🍷🍷	4*
○ Riviera Ligure di Ponente Pigato Le Russeghine '02	🍷	4
● Riviera Ligure di Ponente Rossese '02	🍷	4
○ Riviera Ligure di Ponente Pigato U Bacan '01	🍷🍷	5
○ Riviera Ligure di Ponente Pigato Villa Torrachetta '01	🍷🍷	4

○ Cinque Terre '02	🍷🍷	6
○ Cinque Terre Sciacchetrà '00	🍷🍷	8
○ Cinque Terre '01	🍷🍷	6

SARZANA (SP)

VENDONE (SV)

IL MONTICELLO
VIA GROPPOLO, 7
19038 SARZANA (SP)
TEL. 0187621432
E-MAIL: sub@libero.it

CLAUDIO VIO
FRAZ. CROSA
17032 VENDONE (SV)
TEL. 018276338

Brothers Alessandro and Davide Neri, owners of the winery, currently have available eight and a half hectares under vine, with another plot of about two hectares coming into production for the 2004 harvest. From the wines we tasted this year, the Rosso Poggio dei Magni was the star performer. It's a nicely balanced blend of 70 per cent sangiovese, plus merlot and other local varieties, which sees 11 months in new barriques. The colour falls between ruby and garnet, and hints of dark berry fruit are beautifully integrated with more forceful nuances of spice, chocolate and bitter almond, creating a sumptuous nose of appealing complexity. This wine really takes charge in the mouth, with energetic progression, a raft of tasty tannins and acidity that keeps everything in balance. The Rupestro, nearly 100 per cent sangiovese that sees no oak, is an attractive ruby. A well-defined nose derives decent complexity from a medley of roses, cherries and redcurrant, which return on the attractively balanced palate. The result is a wine that is sure to please. The Vermentino is also appealing. Limpid and clear, it is laden with citrus fruit and herbal spice. The palate is crisp and well defined, resoundingly echoing the aromatics, then adds an enticing drift of lemon. Focused tastings finally convinced the two brothers that from this year on, the Podere Paterno, a cask-aged Vermentino, will be given a few more months of maturation. That's why it was not presented at our tasting.

Verdone is a small town near Albenga, between Valle Arroscia and Val Pennavaira. The remains of a fortress built by the Clavesana family in the hamlet of Castellano testifies to its origins deep in the past. The cellar, managed by Claudio Vio, has some five hectares of vineyard here, in the midst of Mediterranean scrub and soils generally well-suited to pigato. The vineyards are divided into various plots, mostly at 300 metres above sea level, in predominantly sedimentary soils aspected nicely to the south. The poor weather in 2002 reduced production to just around 9,000 total bottles, almost half that of 2001. The Vermentino is a masterful wine. A brilliant straw precedes a gorgeously expressive, fascinating aromatic package that privileges distinctive fragrances of medicinal herbs and pine-tree sap, with additional hints of wildflowers. The mouth is a delicious, carefully balanced amalgam of crisp acid, depth of flavour and sound structure, which continues into a long finish, showing a classic almond edge. Barely a step behind is the Pigato, laced with subtle pine resin, apricot fruit and spicy anise. The warm, heady palate offers a good reflection of the nose. Despite a somewhat lightweight structure, it's soundly balanced. Finally, the Runcu Brujau, a lovely ruby, is a blend of local red varieties. It's a thoroughly pleasurable easy drinker.

● Colli di Luni Rosso Poggio dei Magni '01	🍷🍷	4*
● Colli di Luni Rosso Rupestro '02	🍷	4
○ Colli di Luni Vermentino '02		4

○ Riviera Ligure di Ponente Vermentino '02	🍷🍷	4*
○ Riviera Ligure di Ponente Pigato '02	🍷	4
● Runcu Brujau '02		3

OTHER WINERIES

ANFOSSI
FRAZ. BASTIA - VIA PACCINI, 39
17030 ALBENGA (SV)
TEL. 018220024
E-MAIL: anfossi@aziendaagrariaanfossi.it

This noted Albenga cellar has produced a lovely Pigato among its latest releases. After a straw yellow, its elegant floral display builds on peach and citrus, while a rich, almondy finish concludes the vigorous, well-balanced progression in the mouth. The Rossese '02 is also excellent.

○ Riviera Ligure di Ponente Pigato '02	�	4
● Riviera Ligure di Ponente Rossese '02	�	4

BIOVIO
FRAZ. BASTIA - VIA CROCIATA, 24
17030 ALBENGA (SV)
TEL. 018220776 - 018221856
E-MAIL: giobatta.vio@libero.it

Giobatta Vio's two and a half hectares under vine are beautifully sited in the Albenga hills, and he farms with no chemical applications of any kind. The results are wines such as this fruit-forward Pigato, with nice complexity and plenty of vigour.

○ Riviera Ligure di Ponente Pigato '02	�	4

CASCINA PRAIÉ
LOC. COLLA MICHERI - S.DA CASTELLO
17020 ANDORA (SV)
TEL. 018285745
E-MAIL: m-viglietti@tin.it

Massimo Viglietti and his spouse Anna Maria Corrent, a credentialled agronomist, farm about two and a half hectares. Their winemaking procedures involve a triad of fermentations – off the skins, carbonic maceration, and in cask with lees stirring – giving birth to this intriguing Vermentino.

○ Riviera Ligure di Ponente Vermentino '02	�	4

IL CHIOSO
LOC. BACCANO
19038 ARCOLA (SP)
TEL. 0187986620 - 0187625147

This winery has kept quality high over the years. It repeats last year's performance, winning One Glass for the Vermentino, with 4,000 bottles produced. The light floral and musky notes elegantly caress, then the palate echoes the nose, showing crisp and fruity. The Rosso also struts good quality.

● Colli di Luni Rosso '02	�	3*
○ Colli di Luni Vermentino '02	�	4

'R MESUETO
VIA MASIGNANO, 61
19021 ARCOLA (SP)
TEL. 0187987418
E-MAIL: maurobiassoli@interfree.it

Mauro Biassoli, helped by his spouse Francesca, runs this modest operation with a one-hectare vineyard. His Vermentino, which macerates on the skins for 48 hours, exhibits a deep hue, complexity on the nose, and is nicely supple in the mouth.

○ Colli di Luni Vermentino '02   ♆ 4

GIACOMELLI
VIA PALVOTRISIA, 134
19030 CASTELNUOVO MAGRA (SP)
TEL. 0187674155
E-MAIL: giacomelli71@libero.it

Despite a hardly favourable year, Roberto Petacchi coped very well indeed. His diligence in the vineyard paid off with a Vermentino alive with the hallmark floral aromas, full-flavoured tanginess, and plain overall deliciousness. He produces just over 20,000 bottles.

○ Colli di Luni Vermentino '02   ♆ 4

ENOTECA ANDREA BRUZZONE
VIA BOLZANETO, 94/96
16100 GENOVA
TEL. 0107455157
E-MAIL: andreabruzz@libero.it

The Genoa area does not boast high quality wines, but it does have venerable roots. Andrea Bruzzone sources fruit from various growers in Val Polcèvera, thus keeping in production some of the old native varieties. Crisp, fruity, and ready to drink describes his Treipaexi.

● Val Polcèvera Rosso
Treipaexi '02   ♆ 3*

LA FELCE
VIA BOZZI, 36
19034 ORTONOVO (SP)
TEL. 018766789

Andrea Marcesini's winemaking adventure starts from three hectares of vineyard, nearly all his own. This Rosso, a merlot and cabernet blend, pleases immediately, with heady, youthful aromas of rich fruit and spice. The palate, too, is well crafted, with medium structure and good balance.

● Rosso Golfo dei Poeti '02   ♆ 3*

NICOLA GUGLIERAME
VIA CASTELLO, 10
18020 PORNASSIO (IM)
TEL. 018333037

Ormeasco can be called Superiore after a year's ageing and at a minimum of 12.5 per cent alcohol. This release was matured in oak. It shows a delicate, youthful fruitiness, and the mouth is marked by luscious, crisp flavours, with the variety's hallmark bitter edge.

● Riviera Ligure di Ponente
Ormeasco Sup. '02   ♆ 4

GIAMPAOLO RAMO
VIA S. ANTONIO, 9
18020 PORNASSIO (IM)
TEL. 018333097

Also known as "dolcetto a raspo verde", or "green-stemmed dolcetto", Ormeasco is named after the Piedmont village of Ormea, once the capital of the Marchesato dei Clavesana. Giampaolo Ramò, a talented oenologist and dedicated fan of the variety, makes a Sciac-tra rosé version, as well as a full red.

● Riviera Ligure di Ponente
Ormeasco '02   ♆ 4

INNOCENZO TURCO
VIA BERTONE, 7/A
17040 QUILIANO (SV)
TEL. 019887120 - 0192000026

The Turco family makes a bright-hued version of this venerable, hard-to-find red that shows distinctiveness on the nose, with appealing notes of spice over luscious fruitiness. The body may not be super-heavy, but flavours are warm and generous, and everything ties nicely together.

●	Granaccia di Quiliano Vigneto Cappuccini '01	♟	7

CANTINA CINQUETERRE
LOC. GROPPO - FRAZ. MANAROLA
19010 RIOMAGGIORE (SP)
TEL. 0187920435
E-MAIL: info5t@cantinacinqueterre.com

The Cinqueterre co-operative, founded in 1973 and in its present facilities since 1982, has over 150 members. It produces about 270,000 bottles, including 4,000 of the sweet Sciacchetrà. This release has winning dried-fruit fragrances leading into a honeyed, seductive palate.

○	Cinque Terre Sciacchetrà '01	♟	7

FORLINI CAPPELLINI
LOC. MANAROLA
VIA RICCOBALDI, 45
19010 RIOMAGGIORE (SP)
TEL. 0187920496

Three white grapes, albarola, bosco, and vermentino, go into Cinque Terre, with different proportions in each production area. If the fruit is dried, the result is Sciacchetrà. Both versions are ably crafted by this cellar: the dry wine is sterling and the sweet is delightful.

○	Cinque Terre Sciacchetrà '01	♟	8
○	Cinque Terre '02	♟	5

GIOVANNA MACCARIO
VIA TORRE, 3
18030 SAN BIAGIO DELLA CIMA (IM)
TEL. 0184289947

Giovanna Maccario and Gotz Dringenberg run this winery founded in the mid 18th century, constantly raising its quality level. Their Rossese '02 is soundly varietal. Delicate strawberry and rose nuances, then warm, generous flavours, precede a nice clean, finish that echoes the nose.

●	Rossese di Dolceacqua '02	♟	4

SANTA CATERINA
VIA SANTA CATERINA, 6
19038 SARZANA (SP)
TEL. 0187629429
E-MAIL: akih@libero.it

This cellar's winemaking roots in the area are deep. Ghiaretolo, a monovarietal, cask-aged merlot, leads with deep ruby and fragrances that range from ripe fruit preserve to subtle minerally nuances. Perky tannins and good acidity make for good vigour, which carries through to a lengthy finish.

○	Colli di Luni Bianco '01	♟	4
●	Ghiaretolo '01	♟	4*
○	Colli di Luni Vermentino Poggi Alti '02	♟	4

SANCIO
VIA LAIOLO, 73
17028 SPOTORNO (SV)
TEL. 019747666
E-MAIL: sancioagricola@libero.it

Sancio followed last year's Guide debut Guide with a good performance by their latest releases. The owners, Armando and Riccardo Sancio, take full advantage of six hectares of vineyards, besides offering handsome "agriturismo" facilities.

○	Riviera Ligure di Ponente Pigato '02	♟	4*
○	Riviera Ligure di Ponente Vermentino '02	♟	4*

LOMBARDY

Lombardy continues smoothly along the path to general revitalization of viticulture and winemaking and the region now offers a full range of excellent wines, from long-lived reds to "metodo classico" sparklers that have found here not one, but two, perfect environments. At the end of our tastings, the panel unanimously chose the extraordinary Valtellina Sfursat 5 Stelle '01 as Red of the Year and the Franciacorta Brut Cabochon '99 di Monte Rossa as Sparkler of the Year. In other words, two out of five special awards went to Lombardy. The fact that the number of Three Glass prizes is down two in comparison with the last Guide, falling from 11 to nine, should be taken as merely incidental. The region has great potential, on a par with more celebrated winemaking areas. But one thing needs to be clarified. We should not refer to wines from Lombardy as a whole, since the winemaking terroirs are so different from one another that they ought to be considered autonomous zones, each with its own special characteristics that make for top-quality wines. From the mountain vineyards of the Valtellina to the sunny, glacial hills of Franciacorta, and the gentle slopes of the Oltrepò, all the way to the Lombardy shore of Lake Garda, the region's soils and climates vary greatly, as does the distribution of grape varieties. In fact, the only common element is the potential for making great wines. If we look at the average scores, which are on the rise with respect to previous editions, we can easily infer that the entire region is taking significant steps towards higher quality. Careful promotion of special aspects of the various zones, which offer artistic treasures and reserves of typical products and flavours, as well as excellent restaurants, could combine with state-of-the-art winemaking to transform the mountains, hills and plains of Lombardy into a tourist destination on a par with Tuscany, Piedmont or Sicily. Top prize-winning wines this year came from Valtellina, with three excellent Sfursats, and Franciacorta, where five cuvées earned our highest score. The Garda Bresciano produced another great vintage for Cabernet but the Oltrepò was unable to pick up a Three Glass award, despite numerous nominations. But this is just a temporary situation, related to growing years and individual wineries. And things are changing quickly at the wineries, too. We would put money on it.

ADRO (BS)

ADRO (BS)

CONTADI CASTALDI
LOC. FORNACE BIASCA
VIA COLZANO, 32
25030 ADRO (BS)
TEL. 0307450126
E-MAIL: contadicastaldi@contadicastaldi.it

RONCO CALINO
LOC. QUATTRO CAMINI
FRAZ. TORBIATO - VIA FENICE
25030 ADRO (BS)
TEL. 0307451073

Contadi Castaldi is one of the most technologically advanced estates in Franciacorta. Created from a branch of Bellavista and part of the Terra Moretti group, it has operated autonomously for several years now. Oenologist Mario Falcetti manages the estate and has also worked in research at the prestigious agricultural institute in San Michele all'Adige. Mario has succeeded in the difficult task of running a profitable winery without abandoning his efforts as a researcher and experimenter, in the vineyard as well as the cellar. A visit to the cellar, in the completely restored and renovated former kilns at Adro, is enough to reveal his team's enthusiasm for these activities. The most successful product of their labours is the Franciacorta Satèn '99, which was one of the best tasted this year anywhere. A bright green-flecked straw yellow, it has delicate, well-defined, intense aromas of ripe white peach, apricot and vanilla, then showing rich in fruity pulp on the palate, and a caressingly fresh, supple effervescence and plenty of length. This wine came dangerously close to Three Glasses and we are sure the prize is well within the winery's grasp. The Franciacorta Brut also easily earned Two Glasses. As we waited for the new releases of still reds, we enjoyed the white Terre Bianco '02 and elegant, sweet Pinodisé.

Again this year, Ronco Calino's performance was one of those that don't go unnoticed. Owned by Paolo Radici, a textile industrialist with a passion for wine, the cellar sweeps on and this year all seven wines submitted for our tastings earned outstanding Two Glass scores. Obviously, the big prize still eludes Radici but we feel this estate is one that can aspire to true excellence, with Francesco Polastri as technical director and Professor Leonardo Valenti from the University of Milan overseeing the few dozen hectares under vine. But let's get to the wines. The Franciacorta Brut '98 opens with appealing, unusually spicy aromas lifted by appealing notes of cinnamon and vanilla. The palate is fresh, supple and clean, with continuous progression that signs off with a pleasant toasty note. The Franciacorta Brut is very well crafted, harmonious and pleasant, offering soft aromas of acacia honey and hawthorn. The Satèn has nice ripe, pervasive fruit, and caresses the palate with good, soft density. The Terre di Franciacorta Bianco Sottobosco '01 earned applause for its dense texture, freshness and good fruit. The Pinot Nero, dedicated to pianist Benedetti Michelangeli whose villa owner Radici has now acquired, displays a brilliant ruby red leading into elegant structure, finesse and varietal tones, even though the tannins are still a bit rigid. The two Terre di Franciacortas, Bianco and Rosso, are as good as any.

O	Franciacorta Satèn '99	🍷🍷	6
O	TdF Bianco Curtefranca '02	🍷🍷	4
O	Franciacorta Magno Brut '98	🍷🍷	6
O	Franciacorta Brut	🍷🍷	5
O	Pinodisé	🍷🍷	6
☉	Franciacorta Rosé '99	🍷	6
O	Franciacorta Dosaggio Zero	🍷	5
O	Franciacorta Magno Brut '95	🍷🍷	6
O	Franciacorta Magno Brut '94	🍷🍷	6
O	Franciacorta Satèn Sel. '97	🍷🍷	5*
O	TdF Bianco Manca Pane '00	🍷🍷	5
●	Marco Nero '99	🍷🍷	5

●	Pinot Nero L'Arturo '01	🍷🍷	7
O	TdF Bianco Sottobosco '01	🍷🍷	5
●	TdF Rosso '01	🍷🍷	5
O	TdF Bianco '02	🍷🍷	5
O	Franciacorta Brut '98	🍷🍷	6
O	Franciacorta Brut	🍷🍷	6
O	Franciacorta Satèn	🍷🍷	6
O	TdF Bianco Sottobosco '00	🍷🍷	5
O	Franciacorta Brut '97	🍷🍷	6
●	Pinot Nero L'Arturo '99	🍷🍷	7

BEDIZZOLE (BS)

CANTRINA
FRAZ. CANTRINA
VIA COLOMBERA, 7
25081 BEDIZZOLE (BS)
TEL. 0306871052
E-MAIL: cantrina@libero.it

Cantrina is just a handful of houses near the Chiese river, in hills created by the same glaciers that formed Lake Garda. Dario Dattoli, a restaurateur from Brescia, fell in love with this area about 20 years ago, and began to nurse the idea of a vineyard where international varieties could be planted alongside grapes native to the territory. When Dario passed away prematurely, Cristina Inganni brought the project to life, assisted by Diego Lavo in managing the estate. With the consultancy of Celestino Gaspari's Zymè team, the six hectares of land were replanted and equipment installed. And now here are the first tangible and very convincing results, beginning with the Nepomuceno '00. It's a Garda DOC Merlot with a dense nose of ripe red fruit and small berries preserved in spirits, enhanced by elegant, sweet spice. The big, succulent palate plays off fruity tones against nuances of medicinal herbs. The Corteccio '00 is also good. It's a Pinot Nero with a nose that shows rustic gamey, peppery tones. The palate reveals well-expressed hints of wild berry fruit merging with a clear vegetal note. The Sole di Dario '00 comes from part-dried sauvignon, sémillon and riesling grapes. The amber yellow introduces intriguing dried fruit and apricot aromas that return on the palate, where they meld with the sweetness of honey and candied citron peel. The pleasant white Riné '01 has tropical fruit fragrances and a subtle hint of flowers.

CANEVINO (PV)

CASEO
FRAZ. CASEO, 9
27040 CANEVINO (PV)
TEL. 038599937 - 038599392
E-MAIL: caseo@caseo.it

Ernesto Naro, the owner of Caseo since 1997, has never scrimped on investments to make it successful. The beautiful new vaulted cellar goes into operation shortly, and then oenologist, Marco Goia, will finally have everything he needs to put all his talents to use. For now, the whites are more satisfying, which is not surprising as the vineyards are located at more than 400 metres above sea level. The Sauvignon Blanc I Crocioni '01 is big and round, with a nose of flowers and tropical fruit. The Chardonnay I Ronchi '01 is also very good. The small oak used for ageing is very marked but there is a mature, vigorous wine underneath. The brilliant ruby red Oltrepò Pavese Rosso Canabium '99 has a cherry preserve nose, warmth and good body. The Riserva '98 is slightly inferior for now. Though juicy and fragrant with wild berry fruit, the tannins from the 70 per cent croatina are still harsh. The honeyed Moscato La Dote 2002 is rich and balanced and Malleo '99 is warm and full bodied, but needs further time in bottle to find a balance. The Barbera Donna Clarizia '00, from super-ripe fruit aged 14 months in barriques has marked, intense vanilla, sweet spices and fruit preserves and remarkable structure, well-balanced by the acidity. We had a slight preference for the slightly sparkling "vivace" version of Bonarda Costa delle More '01. The Riesling Le Segrete '00 has typical mineral notes and nice fullness. The "metodo classico" Grande Cuvée '99 is a fresh, unpretentious sparkler.

● Garda Merlot Nepomuceno '00	♟♟	6
○ Sole di Dario '00	♟♟	6
● Garda Pinot Nero Corteccio '99	♟♟	5
○ Riné '01	♟	4
○ Sole di Dario '97	♙♙	4
● Garda Merlot Nepomuceno '99	♙♙	5

○ OP Chardonnay I Ronchi '00	♟♟	5
○ OP Sauvignon Blanc I Crocioni '01	♟♟	4
○ OP La Dote '02	♟♟	4
● OP Rosso Canabium '99	♟♟	5
● OP Barbera Donna Clarizia '00	♟	5
○ OP Riesling Renano Le Segrete '00	♟	4
● OP Bonarda Costa delle More '01	♟	4
● OP Bonarda Vivace Costa delle More '01	♟	4
● OP Rosso Canabium Ris. '98	♟	5
● Malleo '99	♟	5
○ OP Grande Cuvée Caseo Pas Dosé '99	♟	5

CANNETO PAVESE (PV)

F.LLI GIORGI
FRAZ. CAMPONOCE, 39/A
27044 CANNETO PAVESE (PV)
TEL. 0385262151
E-MAIL: fgiorgi@tin.it

Antonio Giorgi runs the estate and his brother, Gianfranco, is in the cellar and together, they turn out reliable wines from their organically farmed vineyards. This year, the highest score goes to the Sangue di Giuda Frizzante '02, one of those emblematic Oltrepò wines from barbera and croatina, with uva rara, vespolina and pinot nero. A ruby red flecked with purple ushers in a fragrant rose and raspberry nose, then a fresh, nicely sweet palate with good length in the finish. The Oltrepò Pavese Rosso Casa Corno '01, from old vineyards of barbera and croatina, ages for 12 months in oak barrels before being racked into barriques. Though good, fruity and full-bodied, we would expect greater complexity from this type of wine. The Extra Brut Metodo Classico Gianfranco Giorgi, from exclusively pinot nero left on the lees for 36 months, has a nice, fine bead, a fairly big bouquet and a nice acid backbone in the mouth, although it finishes a little too quickly. A brand new winery item, Incontro '01, is a cuve close sparkler made with the "Gianfranco Giorgi" method, which is obviously top secret. Pleasant and fragrant, it comes from 100 per cent pinot nero fermented without the skins. There was One full Glass for the Buttafuoco La Manna '02, briefly refermented in a sealed tank, which is sourced from old vines at Casa Ghizzoli near Canneto. It offers broad aromas of wild berries and good structure but we would like to see these grapes vinified in a still version. Finally, there were mentions for the 2002 editions of the Bonarda La Brughera and the semi-sparkling Malvasia.

CANNETO PAVESE (PV)

QUAQUARINI
LOC. MOTEVENEROSO
VIA CASA ZAMBIANCHI, 26
27044 CANNETO PAVESE (PV)
TEL. 038560152

Umberto and Maria Teresa Quaquarini presented a good series of wines. The children of Francesco, and third generation growers at Canneto Pavese, they produce around 700,000 bottles from 55 hectares of vineyards, with 40 hectares on their own estate. The remarkable Buttafuoco Vigna Pregana '99 is from 55 per cent croatina with 30 per cent barbera and 15 per cent ughetta di Canneto aged for 12 months in barrique. Although the tannins from the croatina still have to mellow, the spices and wild berry nose is admirable and there is no lack of pulp in the mouth. It should be left patiently in the cellar for at least another year. The Quaquarini Sangue di Giuda is one of the best in the entire Oltrepò. The 2002 is called, oddly, Acqua Calda, which means "hot water" and is also the name of the vineyard, where there were once volcanic springs. It has intense, persistent, almost caramelly aromas of rose and wild berries and is fresh and sweet without being cloying. The semi-sparkling Bonarda Frizzante '02 earned One full Glass for its fragrant aroma of blackberries and good balance in the mouth. The Oltrepò Pavese Rosso Magister '01, from 40 per cent croatina with 30 per cent pinot nero, shows violets and blackcurrant-led wild berries, then a dry, austere palate with good balance but not much length. The sparkling Pinot Nero, vinified without the skins, is well typed, whereas the Pinot Nero Blau '00 showed some problems with balance and the Riesling Italico '02 seemed a tad forward.

●	OP Sangue di Giuda Frizzante '02	🍷🍷	3*
○	OP Pinot Nero Extra Brut Cl. Gianfranco Giorgi '00	🍷	6
○	OP Pinot Nero Brut Martinotti Incontro '01	🍷	4
●	OP Rosso V. Casa Corno '01	🍷	6
●	OP Buttafuoco Vivace La Manna '02	🍷	3
●	OP Bonarda Vivace La Brughera '02		4
○	OP Malvasia Dolce Frizzante '02		3
○	OP Pinot Nero Brut Cl. Gianfranco Giorgi '96	🍷🍷	4
○	OP Pinot Nero Brut Cl. Mill. Elith '96	🍷🍷	5
●	OP Buttafuoco Casa del Corno '00	🍷🍷	4

●	OP Sangue di Giuda Acqua Calda '02	🍷🍷	3*
●	OP Buttafuoco Vigna Pregana '99	🍷🍷	6
●	OP Rosso Magister '01	🍷	3
●	OP Bonarda Frizzante '02	🍷	3
●	OP Pinot Nero in Bianco Frizzante '02	🍷	3
●	OP Pinot Nero Blau '00		5
●	OP Riesling Italico '02		3

CANNETO PAVESE (PV)

BRUNO VERDI
VIA VERGOMBERRA, 5
27044 CANNETO PAVESE (PV)
TEL. 038588023
E-MAIL: info@verdibruno.it

Paolo Verdi, assisted by oenologist, Enzo Galetti, continues to search for quality. His top wine this year is the Barbera Campo del Marrone '01, aged for 12 months in 500-litre oak casks from Styria, a third of them new. A deep ruby-red flecked with purple, it shows a clean bouquet of violets, cocoa powder, golden tobacco and wild berries with balsamic notes. In the mouth, remarkable body is flanked by well-gauged acidity and outstanding length. The Rosso Riserva Cavariola '00 is just as good. From 65 per cent croatina plus uva rara, ughetta di Canneto and barbera, it sets out its stall with a dark, almost impenetrable ruby red that precedes a broad nose with tertiary aromas of sweet cinnamon and nutmeg spice, liquorice, cedar wood and golden tobacco, lifted by wild berries, especially blueberries. Still young, this wine is already harmonious but will improve even further in bottle as the tannins mellow. The Riesling Renano Vigna Costa '02, one quarter fermented in new oak, is not bad either. It shows vigour and zest, needing only to stay a while longer in bottle to settle down. The Vergomberra Brut '00, left for around 30 months on the lees, has classic aromas of crusty bread and roasted hazelnuts, and good structure. Wines from the 2000 vintage were honest and varietal. They include Pinot Grigio, Bonarda Possessione di Vergombera and Sangue di Giuda Paradiso, which is let down by bitterish tannins.

CAPRIOLO (BS)

LANTIERI DE PARATICO
VIA SIMEONE PARATICO, 50
25031 CAPRIOLO (BS)
TEL. 030736151
E-MAIL: lantierideparatico@numerica.it

Fabio Lantieri de Paratico owns this Capriolo estate. He has 15 hectares of his own vineyards, from which he releases about 125,000 bottles annually. Though Fabio has another job, he still diligently dedicates himself to his cellar and vineyards, making good use of input from oenologist, Cesare Ferrari, and agronomist, Pierluigi Donna. Proof of this winery's growth in quality over the last four or five vintages lies in the most interesting house cuvée, the Franciacorta Arcadia, which offers one of its best editions ever in the '99 vintage. A lovely, deep, bright greenish straw yellow, it has fresh aromas of golden delicious apples that shade into floral notes, and then elegant hints of toasty oak. The palate is exemplary in its fresh-tasting smoothness and in fact resembles a Satèn more than a vintage Brut cuvée. The base Franciacorta Brut has personality and finesse, introduced on the nose with pleasant butterscotch tones that shift into a clean fruitiness. The palate is balanced, consistent and nicely harmonious. The Franciacorta Extra Brut stopped just short of Two Glasses. Nose and palate open on soft notes of apple, pear and ripe peach, but the palate tends to tighten up in the slightly edgy, astringent finish. We felt the Satèn was a tad masked on the nose, though it opens up on the clean, fresh palate, which has good overall harmony. The Terre di Franciacorta Bianco '02 was particularly interesting, and the other wines well made.

○ OP Brut Cl. Vergomberra '00	♀♀	5
● OP Rosso Cavariola Ris. '00	♀♀	5
● OP Barbera Campo del Marrone '01	♀♀	4
○ OP Riesling Renano V. Costa '02	♀♀	4
● OP Bonarda Vivace Possessione di Vergomberra '02	♀	3
○ OP Pinot Grigio '02	♀	3
● OP Sangue di Giuda Dolce Paradiso '02		3
● OP Rosso Cavariola Ris. '96	♀♀	4
● OP Rosso Cavariola Ris. '97	♀♀	4
● OP Rosso Cavariola Ris. '98	♀♀	5
● OP Rosso Cavariola Ris. '99	♀♀	5

○ TdF Bianco '02	♀♀	4*
○ Franciacorta Brut Arcadia '99	♀♀	6
○ Franciacorta Brut	♀♀	4
○ TdF Bianco Colzano '01	♀	4
● TdF Rosso '01	♀	4*
● TdF Rosso Colzano '01	♀	4
○ Franciacorta Extra Brut	♀	5
○ Franciacorta Satèn	♀	5
○ Franciacorta Brut Arcadia '96	♀♀	6
○ Franciacorta Brut Arcadia '97	♀♀	5
○ Franciacorta Brut Arcadia '98	♀♀	5

CAPRIOLO (BS)

RICCI CURBASTRO
VIA ADRO, 37
25031 CAPRIOLO (BS)
TEL. 030736094
E-MAIL: info@riccicurbastro.it

Riccardo Ricci Curbastro again this year presented a wonderful array of wines for our panel. Franciacorta is his main interest, as you can tell on tasting the excellent Extra Brut '99, a cuvée that made a good showing at our finals. The lovely straw yellow flecked with gold accompanies a very fine, continuous perlage, intense aromas of ripe golden delicious apple, yeast and vanilla, then a satisfyingly dry, assertive palate with good length. The soft, fruity Satèn also made a good impression. But all this should not deflect attention from the still wines. Riccardo relies on Alberto Musatti's consultancy for his sparklers but works with New Zealand oenologist, Owen J. Bird, on his still wines. There were three winners here, with the Terre di Franciacorta selections and a sweet wine, all in their best ever editions. The Chardonnay Vigna Bosco Alto '00 is dense, fat and rich in acidity and aromas, melding well with the new oak. The red Santella del Gröm '00 has clear, complex aromas of red fruit with vegetal nuances, tobacco and elegant toasty notes. Solid and balanced in the mouth, it flaunts elegant extract. Finally, the Chardonnay Brolo dei Passoni "passito", from part-dried grapes, is sweet and concentrated, introducing vanilla and apricot on the nose and finishing long and balanced in the mouth. We were less enamoured of the Pinot Nero '00, which is a little evolved and slightly muzzy on the nose. The rest of the range is very well made and attractively priced.

CASTEGGIO (PV)

RICCARDO ALBANI
S.DA SAN BIAGIO, 46
27045 CASTEGGIO (PV)
TEL. 038383622 - 038383345
E-MAIL: Info@vinialbani.it

Riccardo Albani is a man with clear ideas. Going against the trend of most Oltrepò producers, he prefers to focus all his attention and the resources of his estate on just a few labels, sourced from his 16 hectares under vine along the hills of Casteggio. Since this was a year of transition, and several of his major bottles were not yet ready, he only submitted two new wines for tasting. After a few minutes' aeration, the slightly sparkling Bonarda Vivace '02 releases frank, fragrant aromas of roses, raspberries and damp autumn leaves. The soft, delicious palate leads into a finish with good length, supported by a pleasantly tangy touch. The barbera-led Oltrepò Pavese Rosso Costa del Morone '01, sourced from three hectares of old vines, has a wonderfully brilliant ruby red colour, a nose of berry fruit and violets, and good nose-palate consistency. However, there was no way to taste the Albani family flagship wine, Riserva Vigne della Casona, from six and a half hectares of 35 to 40-year-old vines. After having aged part in large wood and part in barrique, the 1999 edition is still maturing in bottle and will be released next year. The '98 we retasted this time still has great structure and depth, although it has one or two problems that may have been caused by a batch of poor-quality corks.

O	Franciacorta Extra Brut '99	♟♟	5
O	Brolo dei Passoni '00	♟♟	5
●	TdF Rosso Santella del Gröm '00	♟♟	4
O	TdF Bianco Vigna Bosco Alto '00	♟♟	4
O	Franciacorta Satèn Brut '98	♟♟	5
●	Pinot Nero Sebino '00	♟	6
O	TdF Bianco Curtefranca '02	♟	3
O	Franciacorta Brut	♟	5
●	TdF Rosso Santella del Gröm '98	♟♟	4*
O	Franciacorta Extra Brut '98	♟♟	5

●	OP Bonarda Vivace '02	♟♟	4
●	OP Rosso Costa del Morone '01	♟	4
●	OP Rosso Vigna della Casona Ris. '96	♟♟	4
●	OP Rosso Vigna della Casona Ris. '97	♟♟	4
●	OP Rosso Vigne della Casona Ris. '98	♟♟	5
●	OP Rosso Costa del Morone '99	♟♟	4

CASTEGGIO (PV)

BELLARIA
FRAZ. MAIRANO
VIA CASTEL DEL LUPO, 28
27045 CASTEGGIO (PV)
TEL. 038383203
E-MAIL: info@vinibellaria.it

From 14 hectares and five more leased, the Massone family makes "only" six types of wine, not many in a zone where some producers have more labels than hectares under vine. Paolo Massone runs the estate with oenologist Giancarlo Scaglione in the cellar and both traditional local varieties and international varieties are vinified. We'll begin with Bricco Sturnèl, which is easy to recognize as a barrique-aged cabernet sauvignon (with 20 per cent barbera) from its grassy aromas with vanillaed notes. An intense ruby introduces pulpy fruit, acidity and a tannic weave that will help it mellow further in the bottle. La Macchia is another IGT red from a vineyard selection. A monovarietal Merlot aged for 18 months in small oak casks, it has a deep ruby-red colour that shades into garnet, a broad bouquet of vanilla, ginger and clove spice and blackberry, with a vegetal note. The palate offers a powerful entry, fine-grained tannins that are still a bit rough, and long length. It's a wine that deserves a little cellar time, even though it is already drinking well. The Chardonnay Costa Soprana '00 cold macerated on the skins for 36 hours before alcoholic fermentation in barrique at a controlled temperature of 18 degrees centigrade. It has a bouquet of honey, banana and vanilla, with good structure, although it lacks a bit of verve. The Barbera Olmetto '00, with 15 per cent croatina and uva rara, is a very different proposition, showing the variety's typical, almost excessive, acidity. The slightly sparkling Bonarda Vivace Bria '02 is good, fresh and simple.

CASTEGGIO (PV)

FRECCIAROSSA
VIA VIGORELLI, 141
27045 CASTEGGIO (PV)
TEL. 0383804465
E-MAIL: info@frecciarossa.com

With 14 of its 35 hectares presently being replanted, the Frecciarossa estate did not submit the historic Villa Odero "riserva" this year since it was still ageing, but the Pinot Nero Giorgio Odero '99 consoled us. It is obtained from grapes harvested by hand in 15-year-old vineyards on clay and chalk soil. After alcoholic fermentation, the wine undergoes malolactic fermentation in French oak barriques, where it ages for 12 months. The ruby red is tinged with garnet and the aromas recall blackcurrants, liquorice and vanilla. The palate is as solid and succulent as it is elegant. The Riesling Renano Gli Orti '02 cold macerated at six degrees Celsius, acquiring a pale straw-yellow hue with greenish flecks, broad peach and apricot aromas, and a fresh, zesty flavour with moderate length. The intense ruby Oltrepò Pavese Rosso Le Praielle '00 has a touch too much volatile acidity that disappears to reveal lovely aromas of wild berry fruit. In the mouth, there is good body, decent depth and still-ripening tannins. One Glass also went to the Bonarda Dardo '02 with its marvellous purple colour. The nose is still a bit closed but the palate is well structured and lively. The Sillery, a Pinot Nero vinified without the skins, has peach and citrus aromas. Finally, the Uva Rara '02, from a native variety rarely vinified on its own, is aromatic, pleasant and easy drinking, if still a bit green.

● Bricco Sturnèl '99	♟♟	5
● La Macchia '99	♟♟	5
● OP Barbera Olmetto '00	♟	4
○ OP Chardonnay Costa Soprana '00	♟	5
● OP Bornarda Vivace La Bria '02	♟	4
● Bricco Sturnèl '97	♟♟	4
● OP Barbera Olmetto '99	♟♟	4

● OP Pinot Nero Giorgio Odero '99	♟♟	5
● OP Rosso Le Praielle '00	♟	4
● OP Bonarda Vivace Dardo '02	♟	3
○ OP Pinot Nero in bianco Sillery '02	♟	4
○ OP Riesling Renano Gli Orti '02	♟	3
● Provincia di Pavia Uva Rara '02		4
● OP Pinot Nero '97	♟♟	4
● OP Rosso Villa Odero Ris. '97	♟♟	4
● OP Pinot Nero '98	♟♟	5
● OP Rosso Villa Odero Ris. '98	♟♟	4

CASTEGGIO (PV)

LE FRACCE
FRAZ. MAIRANO
VIA CASTEL DEL LUPO, 5
27045 CASTEGGIO (PV)
TEL. 038382526
E-MAIL: info@le-fracce.it

Put together a talented, enthusiastic oenologist like Roberto Gerbino, a splendid estate – with a large collection of antique carriages and classic cars – and a foundation, Bussolera Branca, that makes the proper resources available, and you have a rosy picture for this organically farmed estate. Bohemi '99 is an Oltrepò Pavese Rosso from barbera with 25 per cent croatina and 20 per cent pinot nero. The wonderful nose of ripe fruit, roses and violets mingles with a well-mannered hint of oak from 18 months in barrique, and a rich, juicy, velvet-smooth palate. The other 1999 Rosso Oltrepò, Cirgà, is also excellent. It is the same blend as Bohemi but croatina-heavy and never sees wood. There is a broad range of fruit aromas, from wild berries to plum preserve, then a dry, warm palate with tannins from the croatina that are still maturing. The Pinot Grigio Levriere is excellent, especially considering the difficulties of the 2002 harvest. It recalls spring flowers, white peach and citrus, offering freshness and full flavour, with good aromatic persistence. The Garboso '00 is an Oltrepò Pavese Rosso vinified in stainless steel from barbera. Frank, clean and fragrant with wild black berry fruit, it shows warm and soft in the mouth. The Cuvée Bussolera Extra Brut '01, made with the long Charmat method, is mature with good breadth. The Bonarda Rubiosa '02 is nicely fragrant and the Riesling Renano Landò '02 is full flavoured, but a bit lightweight.

CASTEGGIO (PV)

TENUTA PEGAZZERA
LOC. PEGAZZERA
VIA VIGORELLI, 151
27045 CASTEGGIO (PV)
TEL. 0383804646
E-MAIL: tenutapegazzera@libero.it

Tenuta Pegazzera is on the right path. The wines created by oenologist, Corrado Cugnasco, from the 36 hectares of estate vineyards are convincing. First is the Pegazzera Brut Classico '98, from predominatly pinot nero with chardonnay, one of the best sparklers we tasted this year from the Oltrepò Pavese. Flaunting a Champagne style, it has a very fine, persistent perlage and a broad, elegant bouquet with recognizable crusty bread, roasted hazelnuts and golden delicious apples against a background of vanilla, musk and candied fruit. The palate is sound and harmonious, and the flavour lingers. Trames is from botrytized chardonnay and sauvignon grapes fermented in Allier barriques. An impressive wine with a brilliant gold colour, it has dried fruit, vanilla and raisins, then shows sweet but not cloying in the mouth, with good supporting acidity. The Pinot Nero Brut Martinotti '01 and Pinot Nero Petrae '00 are both excellent. The Martinotti, vinified using the long Charmat method, is mature, full, clean and soft, Petrae ages for 12 months in new Allier barriques, and has aromas of cassis, gooseberry and forest floor, with very ripe fruit. The Ligna '00, a warm, full-bodied Cabernet Sauvignon, is very good. The steel-fermented Barbera '01 is well typed, fresh and clean, and the same goes for the full-bodied Bonarda '02. Cardinale, the Oltrepò Pavese Rosso that performed so well last year, revealed a few oxidation problems in the 2001 version. One Glass goes to the Chardonnay La Collegiata and semi-sparkling Pinot Nero in bianco Frizzante, both from 2002.

● OP Rosso Garboso '00	♟♟	4
○ OP Pinot Nero Cuvée Bussolera Extra Brut '01	♟♟	4
○ OP Pinot Grigio Levriere '02	♟♟	4
● OP Rosso Bohemi '99	♟♟	6
● OP Rosso Cirgà '99	♟♟	5*
● OP Bonarda La Rubiosa '02	♟	4
○ OP Riesling Renano Landò '02	♟	4
● OP Rosso Cirgà '97	♟♟	4
● OP Rosso Cirgà '98	♟♟	4

● OP Cabernet Sauvignon Ligna '00	♟♟	4
● OP Pinot Nero Petrae '00	♟♟	4
○ OP Pinot Nero Brut Martinotti '01	♟♟	3*
○ OP Chardonnay La Collegiata '02	♟♟	4
○ OP Pinot Nero Brut Cl. '98	♟♟	5
○ Trames '99	♟♟	7
● OP Barbera '01	♟	3
● OP Rosso Cardinale '01	♟	5
● OP Bonarda Frizzante '02	♟	3
○ OP Pinot Nero in bianco Frizzante '02	♟	3
● OP Cabernet Sauvignon Ligna '98	♟♟	4
● OP Cabernet Sauvignon Ligna '99	♟♟	4
● OP Rosso Cardinale '00	♟♟	5

CASTEGGIO (PV)

RUIZ DE CARDENAS
S.DA DELLA MOLLIE, 35
27045 CASTEGGIO (PV)
TEL. 038382301
E-MAIL: vini@ruizdecardenas.it

Feisty Gianluca Ruiz de Cardenas again earned a full profile for his five hectares under vine in the hills above Casteggio and passion for pinot nero fermented "in rosso" (on the skins) and "metodo classico" sparklers. The fact Gianluca often goes against trends and fashion is shown by his classic "spumante", Galanta, whose name comes from the vineyard, in turn derived from a central European fairy tale. It is not released as a DOC wine for the simple reason that it only contains 30 per cent pinot nero, with 70 per cent partially oak-fermented chardonnay. The '99, disgorged in October 2002 after 34 months on the lees, has broad aromas of yeast, crusty bread and honey. Rich, almost opulent, in the mouth, it has remarkable length. The Blanc de Blancs '99 is not bad, either. Obtained exclusively from chardonnay, it was disgorged recently after 36 months of lees contact, acquiring a lovely fruit-led bouquet and the fine, delicate palate that only a blanc de blancs can offer. Moving on to the reds, all from pinot nero, we liked the typical colour of the Vigna Brumano '00, which aged for 12 months in half-new barriques, and shows a broad nose of wild berries and spices, then backbone and concentration in the mouth. The oak-aged Vigna Miraggi '00 we tasted last year has come on with bottle age, achieving a good balance of tertiary notes and fruit aromas. The steel-aged Baloss '01 is simple and pleasant, albeit a bit lightweight.

CASTELLI CALEPIO (BG)

IL CALEPINO
VIA SURRIPE, 1
24060 CASTELLI CALEPIO (BG)
TEL. 035847178
E-MAIL: info@ilcalepino.it

With 15 hectares under vine at Castelli Calepio, Franco and Marco Plebani's estate specializes in sparklers, but the still wines, especially the reds, are not bad at all. Three "metodo classico" wines are reviewed, led as usual by the Riserva Fra' Ambrogio named after the 16th-century monk, called "Il Calepino", who compiled the first Latin dictionary. The '97 vintage, disgorged in March 2003, stayed for 60 months on the lees after 15 per cent was aged in barriques. A darkish straw yellow precedes a fine, persistent perlage and a broad, mature nose with marked hints of roasted hazelnuts, crusty bread and a hint of lactic acid. With its Champagne style and good length, it is a delight on the palate. The Extra Brut '98 and Brut '99 are simpler. The '98 aged on the lees for 48 months and was disgorged without dosage. It has aromas of yeast and a less fine perlage, whereas the Brut '99 spent 36 months in contact with the lees. Though still a bit bitter, showing yeast and green apple, it will improve in bottle. Moving on to the reds, we thought the Kalos '00, from 100 per cent late-harvest cabernet sauvignon, was not bad at all. It has super-ripe fruit and faintly vegetal notes, then warmth and generosity in the mouth. The Valcalepio Rosso Surie '00 is equally good. A 50-50 Bordeaux blend of cabernet sauvignon and merlot, it is rather evolved, with mostly mature aromas. It may not be complex, but it shows harmony and good textured. One Glass went to the mature, fairly long Valcalepio Bianco '02 whereas the Valcalepio Rosso '01 is a bit edgy and only earned a mention.

● OP Pinot Nero Brumano '00	♥♥	5
○ Galanta Brut Cl. '99	♥♥	5
○ OP Brut Cl. Blanc de Blancs '99	♥♥	4
● OP Pinot Nero Baloss '01	♥	3
● OP Pinot Nero Brumano '96	♥♥	4
● OP Pinot Nero Baloss '97	♥♥	3
● OP Pinot Nero Brumano '98	♥♥	5
● OP Pinot Nero Baloss '99	♥♥	3*
○ OP Brut Cl. Blanc de Blancs '98	♥	4
● OP Pinot Nero Vigna Miraggi '00	♥	5

● Kalos '00	♥♥	6
● Valcalepio Rosso Surie '00	♥♥	4
○ Brut Cl. Ris. Fra Ambrogio '97	♥♥	5
○ Valcalepio Bianco '02	♥	3
○ Extra Brut Cl. Il Calepino '98	♥	5
○ Brut Cl. Il Calepino '99	♥	4
● Valcalepio Rosso '01		3
○ Brut Cl. Ris. Fra Ambrogio '93	♥♥	5
○ Brut Cl. Ris. Fra Ambrogio '95	♥♥	5
○ Extra Brut Cl. Il Calepino '97	♥♥	4

CASTELFAGLIA
FRAZ. CALINO
LOC. BOSCHI, 3
25046 CAZZAGO SAN MARTINO (BS)
TEL. 059812411
E-MAIL: castelfaglia@cavicchioli.it

MONTE ROSSA
FRAZ. BORNATO
VIA LUCA MARENZIO, 14
25040 CAZZAGO SAN MARTINO (BS)
TEL. 030725066 - 0307254614
E-MAIL: info@monterossa.com

The Cavicchioli family from Modena have produced excellent Lambrusco for generations. They acquired this beautiful estate at Cazzago San Martino from the Barboglio family almost 15 years ago. The highly skilled Sandro Cavicchioli makes still wines and sparklers with grapes from the estate's 20 hectares, all in a lovely hilly location at 300 metres above sea level, under the Castello dei Faglia from which the estate takes its name. The range of wines presented is always interesting and although the Brut Monogram '94 caught our eye last year, we will turn our attention to the Satèn as we wait for release of the new vintage of Monogram. The Satèn is a classic of the wine type, showing a fine perlage and creamy mousse, then well-ripened fruit with elegant shades of honey on the nose. It is succulent and almost fat in the mouth and the discreet vanilla tones are never invasive. The soft, dry palate boasts lovely length. The Franciacorta Brut has a leaner body, but is still enjoyable, thanks to the balance and youthful freshness of fruit on the palate and, especially, the nose, where it merges with pleasant notes of yeast and crusty bread. The Extra Brut is in a similar vein but the absence of dosage leaves it with a structure that is less rich, if still fresh and supple. The non-vintage Monogram Brut is good, as are the two Terre di Franciacortas, the Bianco '02 and Rosso '01.

This year, we did more than just award Three Glasses to the splendid prestige cuvée from the Rabotti cellar. We felt Emanuele's extraordinary Franciacorta Brut Cabochon '99 was the best "metodo classico" tasted, emblematic not only of Franciacorta and its great wine country, but also the entire Italian sparkling wine sector. So Emanuele's his father, Paolo, the first chair of the Franciacorta consortium, and mother, Paola Rovetta, who in 1972 converted her beautiful estate to viticulture, will be very happy as well. Three decades have passed since the conversion and Monte Rossa has grown in every respect. There are presently 32 hectares of well-tended vineyards, and a very modern cellar is being completed. Production runs at 200,000 bottles annually, and is now dedicated exclusively to Franciacorta. The Cabochon flaunts a deep golden straw yellow and an extraordinarily fine perlage, ushering in aromas of apples, pears and ripe black berry fruit with complex nuances of oak, toast and spices. In the mouth, it offers spectacular structure and personality, braced by tangy acidity, but also discloses complex notes of flowers, ripe apples and pears, perked up by delicate citrussy notes. The Brut Prima Cuvée also has remarkable elegance and the fruit-forward Satèn is stylish.

O	Franciacorta Brut	♈♈	4	O	Franciacorta Brut Cabochon '99	♈♈♈	8
O	Franciacorta Satèn .	♈♈	5	O	Franciacorta Brut I Cuvée	♈♈	6
●	TdF Rosso '01	♈	4	O	Franciacorta Satèn	♈♈	6
O	TdF Bianco '02	♈	4	O	Franciacorta Extra Brut		
O	Franciacorta Extra Brut	♈	5		Cabochon '93	♈♈♈	6
O	Franciacorta Monogram Brut	♈	4	O	Franciacorta Satèn	♈♈♈	6
O	Franciacorta Monogram Brut '91	♈♈	6	O	Franciacorta Brut Cabochon '97	♈♈♈	6
O	Franciacorta Monogram Brut '94	♈♈	7	O	Franciacorta Brut Cabochon '98	♈♈♈	6
O	Franciacorta Monogram Brut	♈	4	O	Franciacorta Extra Brut '97	♈♈	6

CHIURO (SO)

NINO NEGRI
VIA GHIBELLINI, 3
23030 CHIURO (SO)
TEL. 0342485211
E-MAIL: giv@giv.it

Casimiro Maule is one of Italy's foremost oenologists, yet he has the courage to respect poor vintages and nature's calendar, even if it means passing up the chance of a stellar score at our tastings. Last year, Casimiro's celebrated 5 Stelle did not appear in the Guide, but this time, the Sforzato 5 Stelle '01 not only made it to our finals: the panel were so impressed they awarded it Three Glasses and unanimously acclaimed it Red Wine of the Year. A wine of rare elegance, with an intense garnet colour, it unveils aromas of plums preserved in alcohol and dense notes of blackberries and black cherries. The palate is beefy, continuous and pervasive, with phenomenal body and surprising softness. The excellent Sfursat '00 is distinctive, with supple solidity of structure and spice aromas. Despite more than 40,000 bottles made, it stands out for finesse and roundness. The Vigneto Fracia '01 has class and stops just a step away from excellence, with notes of dried flowers on the nose and an elegant palate of ripe plums. Neither the Sassella Le Tense '00 nor the Inferno Mazer '00 let us down. These are two archetypes of the local viticulture that show how much potential the territory has. The Quadrio '00 has balanced, fruity aromas. From 90 per cent nebbiolo, it has a softness on the palate that comes from its dash of merlot. The forthright, stylish Grumello Sassorosso '00 is round on the palate, with good length. Ca' Brione '02 is stylistically refined. A mix of sauvignon with chardonnay, plus incrocio Manzoni and a little nebbiolo, make this a pleasant, interesting wine.

● Valtellina Sfursat 5 Stelle '01	♆♆♆	7
● Valtellina Sfursat '00	♆♆	8
● Valtellina Sup. Fracia '01	♆♆	8
● Valtellina Sup. Grumello Sassorosso '00	♆♆	6
● Valtellina Sup. Inferno Mazer '00	♆♆	6
● Valtellina Sup. Quadrio '00	♆♆	5
● Valtellina Sup. Sassella Le Tense '00	♆♆	6
○ Ca' Brione '02	♆♆	6
● Valtellina Sfursat 5 Stelle '94	♆♆♆	5
● Valtellina Sfursat 5 Stelle '95	♆♆♆	5
● Valtellina Sfursat 5 Stelle '96	♆♆♆	5
● Valtellina Sfursat 5 Stelle '97	♆♆♆	6
● Valtellina Sfursat 5 Stelle '98	♆♆♆	6
● Valtellina Sfursat 5 Stelle '99	♆♆♆	6

CHIURO (SO)

ALDO RAINOLDI
LOC. CASACCE
VIA STELVIO, 128
23030 CHIURO (SO)
TEL. 0342482225
E-MAIL: rainoldi@rainoldi.com

When Peppino Rainoldi almost won Three Glasses last year, he elegantly commented, "I'll try to do better next year". He kept that promise with a superb Sforzato Ca' Rizzieri '00, which picked up a top award at the final taste-offs. The spicy aromas and crisp sensations of plums preserved in alcohol precede a rich, concentrated palate with hints of chocolate and a long, fruity finale. The Crespino '00 also reached our finals. The concentrated nose with its spicy balsamic notes ushers in a caressing mouthfeel where sweetness is supported by a tannic weave that lends balance and persistence. The Inferno Barrique '99 was a revelation. Outstandingly elegant, it is a thoroughbred Nebbiolo with a nose of dried fruit and coffee. The palate is warm, with soft, glossy tannins. Inferno '00 is less powerful, but has delicate aromas and roundness in the mouth, with good length. The good standard Sforzato '00 has a well-sustained body with leather notes and aromas that recall dried flowers. Although not entirely balanced, the Prugnolo '00 is an easy-drinker. The Sassella Riserva '99 has a great traditional temperament, slowly opening up into deep aromas. The nebbiolo and sauvignon Ghibellino '01 has finally found a style, showing concentrated aromas, complexity in the mouth and balanced acidity.

● Valtellina Sfursat Fruttaio Ca' Rizzieri '00	♆♆♆	7
● Valtellina Sup. Crespino '00	♆♆	5
● Valtellina Sup. Inferno Ris. Barrique '99	♆♆	5
● Valtellina Sfursat '00	♆♆	6
● Valtellina Sup. Inferno '00	♆♆	4
○ Bianco Ghibellino '01	♆♆	4
● Valtellina Sup. Sassella Ris. '99	♆♆	5
● Valtellina Sup. Prugnolo '00	♆	4
● Valtellina Sfursat Fruttaio Ca' Rizzieri '95	♆♆♆	5
● Valtellina Sfursat Fruttaio Ca' Rizzieri '97	♆♆♆	6
● Valtellina Sfursat Fruttaio Ca' Rizzieri '98	♆♆♆	6

COCCAGLIO (BS)

BONOMI - TENUTA CASTELLINO
VIA SAN PIETRO, 46
25030 COCCAGLIO (BS)
TEL. 0307721015
E-MAIL: tenuta.castellino@lombardiacom.it

The Bonomi estate at Coccaglio has grown up over the years around the lovely art deco villa of Castellino, and today includes 13 hectares of vineyards, all well positioned, 300 metres above sea level, in woodland in the natural amphitheatre of Monte Orfano. The Bonomis offered us a series of excellent wines this year. That they were able to do so is due not only to the location of the estate, but also people like cellarmaster Luigi Bersini, consulting agronomist, Pierluigi Donna, and consulting oenologists, Cesare Ferrai and Luca D'Attoma. The Franciacorta Brut '98 is an excellent vintage wine, proof of the stylistic maturity the cellar has now reached. It shows beautiful structure and elegance, with a fatty, but not heavy, palate, good balance and a long fruit and toastiness finale. We also liked the Satèn for its soft, succulent mouthfeel, deep colour and intense notes of yeast and toasted bread. In contrast, the Brut is a fresher, leaner-bodied wine, although just as enjoyable thanks to attractive apricot and citron peel. Two Glasses also went to the Terre Rosso '01 and the fat, glycerine-rich Capineto '00, which flaunts cherry and black berry fruit that fade into delicately vegetal nuances.

CODEVILLA (PV)

MONTELIO
VIA D. MAZZA, 1
27050 CODEVILLA (PV)
TEL. 0383373090

Every year, oenologist Mario Maffi helps Caterina and Giovanna Brazzola to present stylish, reliable wines. The best is always Comprino Mirosa, a monovarietal Merlot dedicated by Caterina and Giovanna to their mother, who passed away in 1999. The 2000, aged for around 16 months in barrique, has a beautiful bouquet of morello cherries, wild berries, autumn leaves and sweet spice, then a warm, soft palate with good balance and length. The Müller Thurgau La Giostra is also excellent, which is unusual in Oltrepò Pavese. From super-ripe grapes, and aged for eight months in Allier tonneaux, it has ripe tropical fruit that integrates well with the oak-derived spice, and a warm, harmonious palate. The other two reds easily passed the Two Glass threshold. The Costarsa '99 is made from 100 per cent pinot nero grapes, part-aged in barriques and part in 25-hectolitre barrels. The typical deep garnet precedes even more typical blackcurrants and morello cherries, plus spice from the oak and faint gamey notes. In the mouth, it is soft and velvety. Equally good is the Oltrepò Pavese Rosso Riserva Solarolo '99, from an increasingly common blend in the Oltrepò DOC of 40 per cent barbera and croatina, plus 20 per cent pinot nero. It is fruity, with notes of ginger, vanilla and liquorice, then warm, harmonious and full bodied in the mouth. The wines from 2002 are decent. The Cortese is zesty and floral; the semi-sparkling Bonarda Frizzante heady and clean, with good body, and the standard Müller Thurgau is simple, with pleasant residual sugar. The Barbera '01 is more tousled than usual.

● TdF Rosso Capineto '00	♀♀	5
● TdF Rosso '01	♀♀	4*
○ Franciacorta Brut '98	♀♀	6
○ Franciacorta Brut	♀♀	5
○ Franciacorta Satèn	♀♀	6
○ TdF Bianco '02	♀	4
○ Franciacorta Brut '95	♀♀	5
○ Franciacorta Brut '96	♀♀	6
○ TdF Bianco Solicano '99	♀♀	4
● TdF Rosso Capineto '99	♀♀	5

● Comprino Mirosa '00	♀♀	6
○ Müller Thurgau La Giostra '01	♀♀	4
● OP Pinot Nero Costarsa '99	♀♀	5
● OP Rosso Solarolo Ris. '99	♀♀	5
○ Müller Thurgau '02	♀	3
● OP Bonarda Frizzante '02	♀	3
○ OP Cortese '02	♀	3
● OP Barbera '01		3
● OP Rosso Ris. Solarolo '97	♀♀	4
● Comprino Mirosa Ris. '98	♀♀	4
● OP Pinot Nero Costarsa '98	♀♀	4
● OP Rosso Ris. Solarolo '98	♀♀	4
● Comprino Mirosa '99	♀♀	6

CORTE FRANCA (BS)

BARONE PIZZINI
FRAZ. TIMOLINE
VIA BRESCIA, 3
25050 CORTE FRANCA (BS)
TEL. 030984136
E-MAIL: inform@baronepizzini.it

Barone Pizzini is one of the most dynamic wineries in Franciacorta. A few years ago, a group of investors took over this prestigious operation, dating from 1870, and entrusted management to the capable, enthusiastic Silvano Brescianini. Over the past few years, the winery has been the focus of a rapid rise in quality, and today is one of the best cellars in Franciacorta. It's a big player, with 40 hectares under vines farmed organically, with a leaning towards biodynamic agriculture. Production is 300,000 bottles annually and the consultants are Alberto Musatti for sparkling wines and Paolo Caciorgna for still products. This year, two wines stood out, a red and a Franciacorta. San Carlo '01 is a classic Bordeaux blend. Intense, dark ruby red, it unfurls concentrated aromas of ripe black berry fruit, tobacco, cocoa and spices, then shows depth on the palate, rich fruit and silk-smooth tannins, signing off with elegant vegetal nuances. The Franciacorta Bagnadore '99 is just as good. It fell a point or two short of Three Glasses, but still offers great appeal with its fresh fruit, caressing effervescence and elegant floral aromas. If a winery should be judged by its standard products, then Barone Pizzini is a certain winner. The Franciacorta Brut is subtle, harmonious and well rounded, features it shares with the very nice Satèn '99. The other wines are also very good.

CORTE FRANCA (BS)

F.LLI BERLUCCHI
LOC. BORGONATO
VIA BROLETTO, 2
25040 CORTE FRANCA (BS)
TEL. 030984451
E-MAIL: info@berlucchifranciacorta.com

The F.lli Berlucchi estate is one of Franciacorta's historic properties. Founded at the end of the 1920s, it has produced Franciacorta DOC wines since 1967. At the helm of the family winery is the energetic and creative Pia Donata Berlucchi, who enthusiastically manages the vineyards and cellar, where Cesare Ferrari consults. The 63 hectares of lovely vineyards in Cortefranca yield the grapes for the cuvées and wines from the Berlucchi cellar, which now boasts an output of about 400,000 bottles a year, mainly Franciacorta. Again this year, we liked the Brut, always a vintage wine at Berlucchi. This time, it was the 1999. A brilliant, green-flecked straw yellow and a creamy mousse precede intriguingly fresh appley aromas, with clear hints of flowers and yeast. The palate tempts with its stylistic precision and perfect cleanliness. Though not very concentrated, it is a paradigm of elegance, freshness and balance. The Pas Dosé is also from the same vintage, and also lean but rigorous in style. It's still a little closed on the nose, but promises well. The trio of sparklers is rounded off by the Franciacorta Rosé '99. The lustrous pale pink hue introduces sweet aromas of wild berries on the nose. The palate is lean, perhaps a little too lean, and deliciously drinkable. The well-made Terre Bianco '02 and Rosso '01 stood out among the still wines, as well as the Dossi delle Querce '00, although past editions have been more interesting.

● San Carlo '01	♟♟	6
○ Franciacorta Bagnadore I '99	♟♟	6
○ Polzina '01	♟♟	5
● TdF Rosso Curtefranca '01	♟♟	4
○ TdF Bianco Curtefranca '02	♟♟	4
○ Franciacorta Satèn '99	♟♟	6
○ Franciacorta Brut	♟♟	5
⊙ Franciacorta Rosé	♟	5
○ Franciacorta Extra Brut Bagnadore V '92	♟♟	5
○ Franciacorta Brut Bagnadore V '93	♟♟	5
● San Carlo '00	♟♟	5
○ TdF Chardonnay Polzina '00	♟♟	5
○ Franciacorta Brut	♟♟	5

○ Franciacorta Brut '99	♟♟	5
○ Franciacorta Pas Dosè '99	♟♟	5
○ TdF Bianco Dossi delle Querce '00	♟	4
● TdF Rosso Curtefranca '01	♟	3
○ TdF Bianco Curtefranca '02	♟	3
⊙ Franciacorta Rosé '99	♟	5
○ Franciacorta Casa delle Colonne '95	♟♟	6
○ Franciacorta Brut '98	♟♟	5
○ Franciacorta Satèn '98	♟♟	5

CORTE FRANCA (BS)

GUIDO BERLUCCHI & C.
FRAZ. BORGONATO
P.ZZA DURANTI, 4
25040 CORTE FRANCA (BS)
TEL. 030984381
E-MAIL: info@berlucchi.it

A new wind is blowing at Berlucchi. This historic Cortefranca estate seems to have embarked on a new path. Emblematic is the excellent performance of the Franciacorta Brut '98 from the Antica Cantina Fratta, a winery owned by the Ziliani family, which specializes, like Berlucchi, in Franciacorta and Terre di Franciacorta DOC whites. Franco Ziliani, who invented Franciacorta by pioneering sparkling winemaking in the early 1960s, has a renewed interest in the zone. This could be a prelude to the hoped-for return to the DOCG zone by Guido Berlucchi & C.. In fact, the winery chose not to release DOCG wines many years ago as the territory was not big enough to supply grapes for their growing international clientele. Whatever happens, this '98 shows an elegant, brilliant straw yellow with invitingly intense aromas of yeast, apricots and citrus peel: It has structure, finesse and character in the mouth, and an elegant, well-sustained progression. The Satèn from the same line has good structure, pleasant complexity and a soft, juicy mouthfeel. We felt the standard Brut was well crafted. On the Berlucchi front, we would point out the elegant, fresh complexity of the Cellarius, and confirm the good opinion we had of the Brut Imperiale '97 when we tasted it last year. The rest of the range is as good as ever.

CORVINO SAN QUIRICO (PV)

TENUTA MAZZOLINO
VIA MAZZOLINO, 26
27050 CORVINO SAN QUIRICO (PV)
TEL. 0383876122
E-MAIL: info@tenuta-mazzolino.com

There is an air of France at Sandra Braggiotti's Tenuta Mazzolino. The two oenologists, Jean-François Coquard and Kyriakos Kynigopoulos, are French (although the latter is obviously of Greek origin), as are most of the varieties planted on the 22 hectares of estate vineyards, supervised by agronomist Roberto Piaggi. As last year, the best wine submitted this time was the Noir, a monovarietal Pinot Nero macerated for three weeks in contact with the skins, and aged for around a year in Allier and Tronçais barriques. A brilliant ruby red introduces aromas of berries, forest floor, leather and spices, then the palate is full and balanced, with remarkable finesse and persistence. The Cabernet Sauvignon Corvino '01 is a bit less concentrated, throwing frank varietal aromas of bell pepper, sun-dried hay and wild berries that mingles with notes of fresh roasted coffee from its 12 months in French oak barriques. The palate reveals good, fruity pulp and ripe tannins, but is not very long. The Chardonnay Blanc '01, fermented in barriques, where it softens out for around a year, has a lovely nose, and the oak is well gauged, but the palate is very forward and seems almost tired. One Glass went to the steel-fermented Bonarda Mazzolino '01, which has frank aromas, but is rather hard in the mouth because of slightly aggressive tannins.

	Wine	Rating	Score
○	Franciacorta Brut Antica Cantina Fratta '98	♟♟	7
○	Cellarius Brut Ris. Speciale	♟♟	5
○	Franciacorta Brut Antica Cantina Fratta	♟♟	6
○	Franciacorta Satèn Antica Cantina Fratta	♟♟	6
○	TdF Bianco Le Arzelle '01	♟	5
○	TdF Bianco '02	♟	5
○	TdF Bianco Antica Cantina Fratta '02	♟	4
○	Cuvée Imperiale Brut	♟	5
○	Cuvée Imperiale Brut Extrême	♟	5
◉	Cuvée Imperiale Max Rosé	♟	5
○	Cuvée Imperiale Brut '97	♟♟	6

	Wine	Rating	Score
●	OP Pinot Nero Noir '01	♟♟	6
●	OP Bonarda Mazzolino '01	♟	4
●	OP Cabernet Sauvignon Corvino '01	♟	4
○	OP Chardonnay Blanc '01	♟	4
●	OP Pinot Nero Noir '89	♟♟	6
●	OP Pinot Nero Noir '90	♟♟	6
●	OP Pinot Nero Noir '95	♟♟	5
●	OP Cabernet Sauvignon Corvino '98	♟♟	4
●	OP Pinot Nero Noir '98	♟♟	5
●	OP Cabernet Sauvignon Corvino '99	♟♟	4
○	OP Chardonnay Blanc '99	♟♟	4
●	OP Pinot Nero Noir '99	♟♟	5
●	OP Pinot Nero Noir '00	♟♟	6
●	OP Cabernet Sauvignon Corvino '00	♟♟	4
○	OP Chardonnay Blanc '00	♟♟	4

DESENZANO DEL GARDA (BS)   ERBUSCO (BS)

PROVENZA
VIA DEI COLLI STORICI
25015 DESENZANO DEL GARDA (BS)
TEL. 0309910006
E-MAIL: provenza@gardanet.it

★ BELLAVISTA
VIA BELLAVISTA, 5
25030 ERBUSCO (BS)
TEL. 0307762000
E-MAIL: info@bellavistasrl.it

The white and red selections to which Fabio Contato puts his name are symbolic of this enthusiastic producer's personality, sometimes meditative, and often bursting with energy. The reflective side is expressed in the velvety red and the energy in the vibrant Lugana, which impressed a year ago in the very seductive 1999 edition. Retasted 12 months later, the Garda Classico '98 has acquired breadth and a more aristocratic mouthfilling quality, which shows how right the cellar was to postpone the release of the '99. We will only be able to assess this wine at some time in the future. For now, we shall restrict ourselves to noting the excellent preview tastings we enjoyed in the cellar, where work continues on the new tasting centre. The Lugana Superiore selection is on its own. In the 2000 version, it offers a nose marked by citrus, peach and vanilla, as well as the varietal vegetal and mineral vein. These are mirrored on the palate, along with delightful layered sensations of fruit and flowers. The other two Luganas have changed labels. The well-balanced Superiore Molin '01, formerly Ca' Molin, offers hints of peach, lime blossom and medicinal herbs, and the '02 Tenuta Maiolo, previously released as Ca' Maiol, has citrus aromas. The cuve close Lugana Spumante is pleasant and soft. The dried-grape Sol Dorè "passito" is sweet and slightly aromatic. The reds include a captivatingly warm, juicy Negresco whose fruit is accompanied by sweet spiciness. The Ca' Maiol is uncompromising and supple.

Vittorio Moretti is an extraordinary character who has been successful in various business sectors. Intuition, passion and the ability to choose the right partners are only some of his gifts, all combined with an outgoing, direct personality. In the world of wine, Vittorio has pulled off a series of masterful coups. As well as Bellavista, he currently owns beautiful estates in Tuscany (Petra at Suvereto and La Badiola in Castiglione della Pescaia) and Lombardy (Contadi Castaldi at Adro): there may be others to follow. And to think his adventure began in the late 1970s, when all he wanted from the vineyard behind his house was a decent wine to give to friends and clients at New Year's parties. Vittorio then met oenologist, Mattia Vezzola, now general manager of Bellavista, the flagship winery of Terre Moretti group. Vittorio and Mattia have expanded the estate to 157 hectares under vine in the best locations in Franciacorta, and it now produces close to 1,000,000 bottles annually. But what about quality? The cuvées from Bellavista, or rather its Gran Cuvées, have now become classics in Italian winemaking: Bellavista is one of the most respected Italian labels in the world. This year, the Gran Cuvée 1999 took the Three Glass prize. This supremely elegant, complex Franciacorta has depth and stunning richness on nose and palate, but it's only the tip of the Bellavista iceberg.

○ Lugana Sup. Sel. Fabio Contato '00	♟♟	6
● Garda Cl. Rosso Negresco '01	♟♟	5
○ Lugana Sup. Molin '01	♟♟	5
● Garda Cl. Rosso Ca' Maiol '02	♟	4
○ Lugana Tenuta Maiolo '02	♟	4
○ Sol Doré '99	♟	7
○ Lugana Brut Sebastian	♟	3
○ Lugana Sup. Sel. Fabio Contato '97	♟♟	5
● Garda Cl. Rosso Sel. Fabio Contato '97	♟♟	6
○ Lugana Sup. Sel. Fabio Contato '98	♟♟	6
○ Lugana Sup. Ca' Molin '99	♟♟	5
○ Lugana Sup. Ca' Molin '00	♟♟	6
● Garda Cl. Rosso Sel. Fabio Contato '98	♟♟	7

○ Franciacorta Gran Cuvée Brut '99	♟♟♟	6
○ TdF Bianco Convento dell'Annunciata '00	♟♟	6
○ Franciacorta Gran Cuvée Pas Operé '98	♟♟	7
○ TdF Bianco Uccellanda '00	♟♟	6
○ TdF Curtefranca Bianco '02	♟♟	4
⊙ Franciacorta Gran Cuvée Brut Rosé '99	♟♟	7
○ Franciacorta Gran Cuvée Satèn	♟♟	7
● Solesine '00	♟	6
● Casotte '01	♟	6
○ Franciacorta Cuvée Brut	♟	5
○ Franciacorta Gran Cuvée Brut '97	♟♟♟	6
○ Franciacorta Gran Cuvée Brut '98	♟♟♟	6

ERBUSCO (BS)

ERBUSCO (BS)

★ ★ CA' DEL BOSCO
VIA CASE SPARSE, 20
25030 ERBUSCO (BS)
TEL. 0307766111
E-MAIL: cadelbosco@cadelbosco.com

CAVALLERI
VIA PROVINCIALE, 96
25030 ERBUSCO (BS)
TEL. 0307760217
E-MAIL: cavalleri@cavalleri.it

Perhaps even Maurizio Zanella never imagined how far the adventure he began in 1968 would bring him. From working the vineyards around his family's country house, to making Ca' del Bosco one of the best-known wine labels in the world is certainly no mean feat. Presently, the most celebrated cellar in Franciacorta and managed by Maurizio as part of the group of wineries owned by the Marzotto family, it embraces 175 hectares under vine and production is set to pass the 1,000,000-bottle a year mark. Quality standards are high, thanks to the top-flight staff led by oenologist, Stefano Cappelli, and a new, large cellar kitted out with state-of-the-art technology: it was designed by Maurizio with some of the best specialists in the world. All this is reflected in a range of wines that runs from excellent to extraordinary, beginning with this year's Three Glass winner, the fabulous 1996 edition of the winery's prestige cuvée, Annamaria Clementi. This is a Franciacorta of wonderful finesse, complexity and elegance that is rich in both structure and fruit, with a soft mouthfeel and effortless length. The Dosage Zéro '99 also made an excellent showing. A wine of exemplary intensity and cleanliness, with aromas of yeast and spices, it is powerful and very fresh on the palate. The Chardonnay '01 missed a top award this year by a whisker. Although balanced and stylish on nose and palate, it has only moderate structure in our opinion, but it is still the best white wine from the whole region. The rest of the Ca' del Bosco range is well up to the high standards we have come to expect.

We'll begin by saying that the Franciacorta Brut Collezione Esclusiva '95, a small release in magnums that enjoyed extended lees contact and was disgorged only recently, is one of the best cuvées we tasted for this edition of the Guide. Sadly, the miserly quantities released prevented us from awarding it Three Glasses. We would like to taste the new vintage for we know that several thousand bottles of this excellent RD (it stands for "récemment dégorgé", or "recently disgorged") are in the lovely cellar at Erbusco, waiting to be released onto the domestic and international markets. In the meantime, we consoled ourselves by drinking the estate's 1999 vintages, an excellent Pas Dosé that combines sound, dense structure with captivating fruity aromas laced with balsamic notes, and the Satèn, subtly soft on the palate and rich in aromas of cakes and raisins on the nose. The approach Giovanni Cavalleri and his daughter, Giulia, have given the winery filters down to the standard-label Franciacorta Brut, one of the best tasted this year. We would also like to point out some good showings on the still wine front. The Terre di Franciacorta Rosso '01 earned Two Glasses, despite youthful rough edges, the Terre Bianco '02 is nice and the classic Rampaneto lived up to its reputation. It's a solidly structured white with rich aromas of golden delicious apples and white peach on the nose, then attractive acidity and good length in the mouth.

○ Franciacorta Cuvée		
Annamaria Clementi '96	♈♈♈	8
● Pinèro '00	♈♈	8
○ TdF Chardonnay '01	♈♈	8
○ Franciacorta Dosage Zéro '99	♈♈	6
● Carmenèro '00	♈♈	8
● Maurizio Zanella '00	♈♈	8
● TdF Rosso Curtefranca '01	♈♈	5
○ TdF Bianco Curtefranca '02	♈♈	4
○ Franciacorta Brut '99	♈♈	6
⊙ Franciacorta Rosé '99	♈♈	7
○ Franciacorta Brut	♈♈	5
○ TdF Chardonnay '99	♈♈♈	6
○ Franciacorta Cuvée		
Annamaria Clementi '95	♈♈♈	8

○ Franciacorta Pas Dosé '99	♈♈	6
○ Franciacorta Satèn '99	♈♈	6
● TdF Rosso '01	♈♈	4
○ TdF Bianco Rampaneto '02	♈♈	4
○ Franciacorta		
Collezione Esclusiva Brut '95	♈♈	6
○ Franciacorta Brut	♈♈	5
● Corniole Merlot '00	♈	6
○ TdF Bianco '02	♈	4
○ Franciacorta Collezione Brut '86	♈♈♈	6
○ Franciacorta Collezione Brut '93	♈♈♈	6
○ Franciacorta Collezione Brut '94	♈♈♈	6
○ Franciacorta		
Collezione Esclusiva Brut '93	♈♈	6
○ Franciacorta Collezione Brut '97	♈♈	6

ERBUSCO (BS)

FERGHETTINA
VIA CASE SPARSE BORGO, 4
25030 ERBUSCO (BS)
TEL. 0307760120
E-MAIL: info@ferghettina.it

Roberto Gatti repeated the successful performance of the 1997 vintage with another excellent Franciacorta Satèn cuvée, the wine closest to his heart. This time, it was the '99. This verdict – it was the best Satèn tasted for this edition of the Guide – confirms his status as one of the top wineries in a Franciacorta already crowded with great producers. In contrast to many business people who invest their passion and capital in winemaking, Roberto could only put the former on the table. He set up his winery 12 years ago with just determination and experience acquired in another local cellar. All this makes him even more likeable, given that today he manages a good 50 hectares of vineyards, almost all of them leased, in the best positions in the territory. Ferghettina now produces more than 200,000 bottles a year, and is experiencing dizzying growth. The entire family collaborates in the effort, particularly Roberto's young daughter Laura, fresh from her degree in oenology at the University of Milan. But on to the wine. The Satèn is a brilliant green-flecked straw yellow, and the very fine perlage is dense and continuous. The nose opens on elegant, complex tones of ripe, but not over-ripe, apples and pears that meld into crystal-clear notes of vanilla, butter and flowers. The controlled, caressing effervescence on the palate is pure Satèn, rich in fruit, freshness and a supple progression that signs off with long, smooth notes of vanilla, chamomile and yeast. In other words, it's marvellous. The rest of the winery's range shows the same exalted levels of quality.

ERBUSCO (BS)

ENRICO GATTI
VIA METELLI, 9
25030 ERBUSCO (BS)
TEL. 0307267999
E-MAIL: info@enricogatti.it

"All things come to those who wait...". The old proverb fits perfectly the well-matched quartet that manages this estate, Lorenzo and Paola Gatti with their respective spouses, Sonia Cherif and Enzo Balzarini. Our heroes have always been committed to the search for absolute quality, and the results are increasingly evident with each passing harvest. Their Satèn '99 was again one of the best tasted this year, and barely missed Three Glasses. It is a powerful, dense Franciacorta, as rich on the nose as it is in the mouth, with ripe fruit, vanilla and yeast over charred notes of toast and tea biscuits. The palate shows dense, structured, well-balanced and persistent. This already excellent cuvée could perhaps be improved by sacrificing some of the structure in favour of freshness and elegance, but far be it from us to give the four advice on how to make wine. In any case, what counts is the quality of this lovely Satèn. To keep it company, there was a rich, convincing Franciacorta Brut that deliciously interprets Erbusco terroir where the Gatti vineyards and cellars are located. Among the other labels, the Terre Rosso '01 came close to Two Glasses for its good concentration, which is slightly masked by a rather too assertive grassy note. The excellent Gatti Rosso '01 is rich in fruit and smooth tannins, and the new oak is well judged. We felt the vanillaed Terre di Franciacorta Bianco '02 was also good, whereas the Gatti Bianco '01 is richer and more complex, showing imposing structure. It's still a little dominated by the new oak, but that will sort itself out in time.

○ Franciacorta Satèn '99	🍷🍷🍷	6
● Merlot Baladello '00	🍷🍷	5
● TdF Rosso '01	🍷🍷	4
○ TdF Bianco '02	🍷🍷	4
○ Franciacorta Extra Brut '96	🍷🍷	6
○ Franciacorta Brut	🍷🍷	5
○ Franciacorta Satèn '97	🍷🍷🍷	5*
○ Franciacorta Satèn '98	🍷🍷	5
○ TdF Bianco Favento '01	🍷🍷	4*
● Merlot Baladello '99	🍷🍷	5

○ Franciacorta Satèn '99	🍷🍷	6
● Gatti Rosso '01	🍷🍷	5
○ TdF Gatti Bianco '01	🍷🍷	5
○ TdF Bianco Curtefranca '02	🍷🍷	4
○ Franciacorta Brut	🍷🍷	5
● TdF Rosso Curtefranca '01	🍷	4
○ Gatti Bianco '96	🍷🍷	4
○ Gatti Bianco '97	🍷🍷	4
● Gatti Rosso '98	🍷🍷	4
○ Franciacorta Satèn '97	🍷🍷	5*
● Gatti Rosso '99	🍷🍷	4*
○ Franciacorta Satèn '98	🍷🍷	5
● Gatti Rosso '00	🍷🍷	5

ERBUSCO (BS)

UBERTI
LOC. SALEM
VIA E. FERMI, 2
25030 ERBUSCO (BS)
TEL. 0307267476
E-MAIL: info@ubertivini.it

Owned by Agostino Uberti and his wife Eleonora, this is one of the most beautiful wineries in Franciacorta. It, and its more than 20 hectares of well-tended vines, are located at Erbusco, the beating heart of this territory and a Lombard "grand cru". While vineyards like Comarì del Salem, which furnishes grapes for the selection of the same name, are excellent, this is not enough to explain the quality of the Uberti cuvées and wines. The real secret of this family-run cellar is that Agostino and Eleonora are perfectly in tune. They share the same ideas of excellence, and together strive for the utmost precision, if not perfection, at every stage of the winemaking process. It goes without saying the Comarì '98 is a masterpiece of freshness, typicity, and expressive depth. It has everything you would expect from an outstandingly good vintage Franciacorta, managing to impress without austerity, delighting nose and palate with vibrant fruit sensations and more complex notes that shade from vanilla to toast and mineral. The Satèn Magnificentia is, as usual, a lovely wine, that shows coherent and fruity, with some aromatic overtones. It may not have the depth of previous versions, but it is still a very fine wine. But then all the Uberti bottles deserve careful attention, from the Bianco dei Frati Priori '01 to the Bianco Maria dei Medici.

ERBUSCO (BS)

GIUSEPPE VEZZOLI
VIA COSTA SOPRA, 22
25030 ERBUSCO (BS)
TEL. 0307267579
E-MAIL: niteovezzoli@libero.it

It takes courage to throw up a secure, satisfying career at 40 and start a new life, especially one on a farm in the country. But that's what Giuseppe Vezzoli did. He left a major career in the engineering industry to return to the family estate at Erbusco and make Franciacorta. It must be something in his blood for the call was irresistible. But going back to the country after a long career in the corporate world also showed a desire to innovate, raise the bar on quality and achieve commercial success. That's how it went and Giuseppe, whose father, Attilio, had never left the vineyard, came back to transform the small family property into one of the emerging wineries at Erbusco, an area already packed with winemaking stars. Giuseppe's cuvées, created with consultancy from Cesare Ferrari, are now among the best we tasted. Once again, we have to say that we are certain major results will not be long in coming for Vezzoli. In the meantime, taste his Franciacorta Brut '99, a wine that reflects an Oltrepò style with its full structure, elegant bottle-ageing aromas and its attractive notes of toasty bread and yeast. Full-flavoured, dense and caressing in its effervescence as only a good Franciacorta can be, it finishes long and intriguing on fruit and balsam notes. The Satèn '99 is just as pleasing with its soft, elegant fullness and expressive depth. The rest of the Vezzoli range, now running at about 85,000 bottles annually, is equally well made. We wish Giuseppe every good fortune.

○ Franciacorta Extra Brut Comarì del Salem '98	▼▼▼	7
● Rosso dei Frati Priori '00	▼▼	6
○ TdF Bianco dei Frati Priori '01	▼▼	5
○ Franciacorta Extra Brut Francesco I	▼▼	5
○ Franciacorta Satén Magnificentia	▼▼	6
○ TdF Bianco Maria Medici '01	▼	5
● TdF Rosso Augustus '01	▼	4
○ Franciacorta Brut Francesco I	▼	5
⊙ Franciacorta Rosé Brut Francesco I	▼	5
○ Franciacorta Brut Comarì del Salem '93	▼▼▼	6
○ Franciacorta Extra Brut Comarì del Salem '95	▼▼▼	6

○ Franciacorta Brut '99	▼▼	6
● Niteo '00	▼▼	6
○ Chardonnay Barbozana '01	▼▼	6
○ Franciacorta Satèn '99	▼▼	6
○ Franciacorta Brut Collezione Oro	▼▼	7
● Attilio Vezzoli '00	▼	8
⊙ Franciacorta Brut Rosé '98	▼	6
○ Franciacorta Brut	▼	6
○ Franciacorta Brut '98	▼▼	6
○ Chardonnay Barbozana '00	▼▼	5
○ Franciacorta Satèn '98	▼▼	6

GRUMELLO DEL MONTE (BG)　MESE (SO)

CARLOZADRA
VIA GANDOSSI, 13
24064 GRUMELLO DEL MONTE (BG)
TEL. 035830244 - 035830804

MAMETE PREVOSTINI
VIA LUCCHINETTI, 65
23020 MESE (SO)
TEL. 034341003
E-MAIL: info@mameteprevostini.com

Carlo Zadra's winery is anomalous at Valcalepio. Carlo is a sparkling wine enthusiast and sources base wines from the hills of his native Trentino, using them to make a range of whistle-clean, value for money "metodo classico" wines. Tradizione '96 is a delightful old-style extra dry wine from chardonnay, pinot nero and pinot meunier grapes left for six years on the lees. The brilliant straw yellow introduces a fine, persistent perlage, aromas of yeast, candied citron, vanilla and sweet spices, and then a soft, rounded palate with good length. The Brut '98 spent three years on its own fermentation yeasts, acquiring a brilliant hue and a broad spectrum of aromas, from crusty bread to citrus, roasted hazelnuts, musk and melted butter. The palate is big, mature, fairly complex and long. The simpler, but very pleasant, Extra Dry Liberty comes from white grapes only (chardonnay and pinot bianco), left for 22 months on the lees. A pale straw yellow ushers in the lively nose and palate, redolent of yeast, crusty bread and almond paste. All three wines were disgorged in September 2002. There was also a red, Don Lodovico '00. A table wine from cabernet sauvignon and pinot nero, it aged for 16 months in oak and shows brilliant ruby red. The nose has the typical grassy sensations of cabernet, mingling with well-gauged oak-derived vanilla and spices. In the mouth, there is good texture, clean fruit and softness. The Nondosato and Moscato Giallo Donna Nunzia were not ready for tasting.

Although Mamete Prevostini did not win Three Glasses this year, he did not miss by much. But then we are dealing with a great little estate that is coming on fast and, above all, bases its production logic on steady quality with an eye on the future. This is all down to the enthusiasm of skilled oenologist, Mamete Prevostini, who attracted plaudits from wine critics for his Sforzato Albareda. About 8,000 bottles of the '01 version were released. The nose introduces itself with intense, varietal aromas, spicy notes and hints of fruit and dried flowers. Rich and concentrated in the mouth, it unveils a soft mouthfeel with exciting sensations of raisins and jam, and an enjoyable, captivating finish. Our tasting of the Corte di Cama '99 was equally exciting. With its breadth and depth, it brings out the potential of nebbiolo grown in Valtellina. Obtained by partially drying some of the grapes, it shows clear-cut raspberry aromas that fuse well with the spicy notes in the finish. There were excellent marks, too, for Sommarovina '01, a Sassella that exalts the territory in a complex bouquet and a palate that is warm and round on entry, with attractive hints of nuts. Though well made and pleasant to drink, the new white blend of 80 per cent chardonnay with sauvignon, müller thurgau and nebbiolo varieties, Opera '01, still needs to take on style and character.

○ Carlozadra Cl. Extra Dry Tradizione '96	🍷🍷	5
○ Carlozadra Cl. Brut '98	🍷🍷	5
○ Carlozadra Extra Dry Liberty	🍷🍷	5
● Don Lodovico '00	🍷	5
○ Carlozadra Cl. Brut Nondosato '92	🍷🍷	5
○ Carlozadra Cl. Brut '93	🍷🍷	5
○ Carlozadra Cl. Brut Nondosato '93	🍷🍷	4
○ Carlozadra Cl. Brut Nondosato '94	🍷🍷	5
○ Carlozadra Cl. Brut '95	🍷🍷	4
○ Carlozadra Cl. Brut '96	🍷🍷	5
○ Carlozadra Extra Dry Liberty '98	🍷🍷	4
○ Carlozadra Cl. Brut Nondosato '95	🍷🍷	5
○ Carlozadra Cl. Brut '97	🍷🍷	5
● Don Lodovico '99	🍷🍷	5

● Valtellina Sforzato Albareda '01	🍷🍷	7
● Valtellina Sup. Corte di Cama '99	🍷🍷	6
● Valtellina Sup. Sassella Sommarovina '00	🍷🍷	5
○ Opera Bianco '01	🍷	5
● Valtellina Sforzato Albareda '00	🍷🍷🍷	7
● Valtellina Sforzato Albareda '99	🍷🍷	6
● Valtellina Sup. Corte di Cama '98	🍷🍷	6
● Valtellina Sup. Sassella Sommarovina '99	🍷🍷	5

MONIGA DEL GARDA (BS)

COSTARIPA
VIA CIALDINI, 12
25080 MONIGA DEL GARDA (BS)
TEL. 0365502010 - 0365503716
E-MAIL: costaripa@tin.it

Moniga del Garda is one of the many jewels of Valtenesi, a green corner of Benaco, or the Lake Garda area, in the province of Brescia. Despite the growing assaults of tourism, the district still adheres to its rural traditions, founded on olives and groppello, the principal local grape variety. And we'll start our review of the wines from Mattia and Imer Vezzola's cellar with a Groppello del Garda Classico, Maim '01. Varietal strawberry aromas greet the nose, returning on the palate, where they are enhanced by hints of ripe red berry fruit and a subtle sweet spiciness. The other Groppello, Castelline '02, is simpler. It's a straightforward, drinkable red that has lovely aromas of wild strawberry and other wild berry fruits, revealing a discreet vegetal note and hint of cloves in the mouth. The Marzemino Le Mazane '02 is very pleasant, combining a nose of fruit veined with chocolate and coffee with a palate of ripe red berry fruit and characteristically exuberant freshness. As last year, the untypical Chiaretto from '01 is rather masked by the oak, but is still interestingly provocative. It can also feature in some quite unexpected food-wine pairings. It is dedicated to the memory of senator Pompeo Molmenti, who is traditionally credited with creating lakeside rosé wines. The Brut Rosè "spumante" is just as unusual, marrying a delicate vegetal note with characteristic hints of berry fruit. The "metodo classico" Brut is clean and floral.

MONIGA DEL GARDA (BS)

MONTE CICOGNA
VIA DELLE VIGNE, 6
25080 MONIGA DEL GARDA (BS)
TEL. 0365503200 - 0365502007
E-MAIL: montecicogna@tin.it

There is a debate on the Lombardy shore of Lake Garda about the potential of part-dried red grapes from the zone, in particular groppello. This is not a matter of fashion, as some winemakers in the zone have been using the technique for decades. Don Lisander, a Garda Classico red from the Monte Cicogna winery, is one of the wines that have, at least in part, espoused this production philosophy. The 1999 version of Cesare Materossi's flagship wine is endowed with marked hints of strawberry jam and elderflower, mingling with subtle geranium petals and sweet spices. The round, full-flavoured palate flaunts fruit and spice, then a restrained liquorice finish. The very interesting white Torrione '02 is a soft Garda Classico from riesling renano. The delicate but elegant aromatic spectrum is lifted by hints of spring flowers that brought it very close to Two Glasses. We were able to taste two different vintages of Del Beana, the Groppello di Moniga, and formed a slight preference for the 2002, which is fresher than the previous vintage and manages to bring out the characteristic body and typical wild strawberry and raspberry sensations of the grape. The same aromatics were present in the 2001, which also shows slightly overdone mineral notes. The power of the fruit in the Garda Classico Rosso Rubinere is a little compromised by the bitter vein. The Lugana '02 is predictable.

● Garda Cl. Groppello Maim '01	♟♟	5
● Marzemino Le Mazane '02	♟♟	4
☉ Garda Cl. Chiaretto Molmenti '01	♟	5
● Garda Cl. Groppello Vign. Le Castelline '02	♟	4
○ Brut Cl. Costaripa	♟	4
☉ Brut Rosè Costaripa	♟	5
● Garda Cl. Groppello Maim '99	♟♟	5
● Garda Cl. Groppello Maim '00	♟♟	5

● Garda Cl. Sup. Don Lisander '99	♟♟	5
● Garda Cl. Rosso Groppello Beana '01	♟	4
● Garda Cl. Rosso Sup. Rubinere '01	♟	4
○ Garda Cl. Bianco Il Torrione '02	♟	4
● Garda Cl. Rosso Groppello Beana '02	♟	4
○ Lugana '02		4
● Garda Cl. Sup. Don Lisander '98	♟♟	5

MONTALTO PAVESE (PV)

DORIA
LOC. CASA TACCONI, 3
27040 MONTALTO PAVESE (PV)
TEL. 0383870143
E-MAIL: az_doria@katamail.com

For the third consecutive year, the Doria family sent Rosso A.D. red, dedicated to the head of the family, Adriano Doria, father of present owner Andrea, to our final taste-offs for the Three Glass award. The wine has a nebbiolo base from an eight-year-old vineyard, and is a selection of old indigenous clones, blended with an Oltrepò Pavese Rosso from a vineyard planted more than 25 years ago. After alcoholic fermentation, it underwent malolactic fermentation in half-new barriques. It was then racked and aged in the same barriques for 14 months. Bottled in July 2001, it aged unhurriedly in bottle before being released for distribution. The colour is a luminous garnet, ushering in a broad spectrum of aromatics that includes black cherry jam, blackberry, coffee, cocoa powder, cloves, vanilla and earthy notes of autumn leaves. Entry on the palate is powerful and austere, then smooth tannins and lively acidity emerge against the warm, elegant depth. It's a fantastic wine. The Querciolo '01 is also very good. From pinot nero barrique-fermented without the skins and barrique-aged, it is old gold and unveils spring flowers, peach, pear, tangerine and vanilla on the nose. The flavour is soft and full, and the palate has good length. The Riesling Renano Roncobianco '01, part-fermented in oak and left on the lees until spring, is dark straw yellow with forthright aromas of tropical fruit against a mineral background. The zesty, fresh-tasting palate is not particularly complex. In contrast, the Roncorosso '00 is less successful than usual. It lacks confidence and balance.

MONTALTO PAVESE (PV)

MARCHESI DI MONTALTO
LOC. COSTA GALLOTTI
27040 MONTALTO PAVESE (PV)
TEL. 0383870358
E-MAIL: fratellimarchesi@libero.it

A grand debut for the Marchesi brothers, who own a 500-hectare estate, 200 planted to vine. Part of the holding is at Montalto Pavese, between 200 and 300 metres above sea level, and part in Pietra de' Giorgi and Cigognola, in the lower range of hills. The Barbera Cascina Bellaria '01 is from a 30-year-old vineyard and won Two Glasses for its brilliant ruby colour, its evolved bouquet of small wild berries, violet, myrtle and spice – from six months in Allier oak – and full, vigorous flavour, backed by good acidity. Wood is handled rather differently in Cà Nuè '01, a monovarietal Pinot Nero macerated on the skins for 20 days. The oak, this time from America, is well defined but doesn't mask the varietal sensations. The jammy mouthfeel makes the palate seem almost chewy. There is no oak in the Monsaltus '02, a chardonnay fermented with cold skin contact, which shows typical aromas of tropical fruit and spring flowers, good structured and very decent length. Marchesi di Montalto releases two IGT Müller Thurgau selections. Biavè '02 is straw yellow flecked with greenish highlights, showing a clean, upfront nose of citrus and vegetal notes, then a simple, enjoyably fresh-tasting palate. In contrast, Canaro '01 spends six months in French barriques, as you can tell from overstated oak-derived aromatics. It's a shame, since the wine is good and would have been lifted by a less heavy-handed use of oak.

● Rosso A.D. '99	♈♈	6
○ OP Pinot Nero in bianco Querciolo '01	♈♈	4
○ OP Riesling Renano Roncobianco '01	♈	4
● OP Rosso Roncorosso '00		5
● Rosso A.D. '97	♈♈	5
○ OP Riesling Renano Roncobianco '00	♈♈	3
● OP Rosso Roncorosso '98	♈♈	4
● Rosso A. D. '98	♈♈	6
○ OP Pinot Nero in bianco Querciolo '00	♈♈	4

● OP Barbera Cascina Bellaria '01	♈♈	4
● OP Pinot Nero Cà Nuè '01	♈♈	4
○ Müller Thurgau Canaro '01	♈	4
○ Müller Thurgau Biavè '02	♈	4
○ OP Chardonnay Monsaltus '02	♈	3

MONTEBELLO DELLA BATTAGLIA (PV)   MONTICELLI BRUSATI (BS)

TENUTA LA COSTAIOLA
VIA COSTAIOLA, 25
27054 MONTEBELLO
DELLA BATTAGLIA (PV)
TEL. 038383169 - 038382069
E-MAIL: lacostaiola@libero.it

LA MONTINA
VIA BAIANA, 17
25040 MONTICELLI BRUSATI (BS)
TEL. 030653278
E-MAIL: info@lamontina.it

The Rossetti brothers opted to appoint Beppe Caviola as consultant, a decision that continues to bear good fruit. Again this year, the range presented was more than positive, and offered products of real excellence. Take, for example, La Vigna Bricca, an Oltrepò Pavese Rosso Riserva '00 from barbera, croatina and pinot nero that aged for 12 months in barrique, it is dark ruby red, unveiling aromas of blackcurrants and blueberries, lifted by sweet spice from the oak. The palate is full-flavoured, dry, soft and long. The Bellarmino '01 is just as good. It's a cold-macerated Riesling Renano, one quarter fermented in Allier and Tronçais barriques. The golden colour has greenish highlights, then the nose offers green apple, pineapple, kiwi fruit, vanilla and gunflint. In the mouth, there is good structure, softness and balance. The other Riesling, Attimo '02, fermented in stainless steel, and shows simpler, floral aromas and a frank, agreeable nature. Aiole '99 is an imposing red. A monovarietal Pinot Nero that aged for a year in oak barriques, it is garnet with orange flecks, throwing a big bouquet of vanilla, coca butter, ginger and wild berry fruit. The warm, dry palate discloses velvety tannins and a well-balanced finale. The Barbera Due Draghi '02 is simple and enjoyable, with blackberry and violet aromas and good support from its vein of acidity. Haris is not a creditable "Charmat lungo"-method sparkler that spent six months on the lees, acquiring a fresh, vegetal bouquet. One Glass went to the green, slightly edgy cuve close Bonarda Giada '02 sparkler.

By now, we are used to superb performances from the Bozza brothers. Their vintage Franciacorta again this year showed admirably at our final tastings, proof of the quality the range has achieved. In the 17th century, La Montina was owned by the family of Paul VI, whose given name was Giovanni Battista Montini. In 1987, the estate was acquired by brothers Vittorio, Giancarlo and Alberto Bozza, who replanted the vineyards and built a cellar that was recently expanded and upgraded. Currently, La Montina farms 35 hectares of vineyards, and can boast an annual production of 300,000 bottles, consisting of a vast range of carefully made Franciacortas and still wines from the local territory. What is striking in the Brut '98 is its freshness on nose and palate, which comes out in nuances of fruit, citrus peel and flowers that combine well with a rich, solid structure that shades into elegant notes of aromatic herbs. Many of the same qualities can also be found in the excellent Extra Brut, which is taut and dry, yet generous with its fruit. The very enjoyable Satèn brings together subtle nuances of vanilla with a body that is lean, but not lightweight. The standard-label Brut is also excellent, confirming the commitment of the skilled winery team, co-ordinated by manager and agronomist Alceo Totò.

● OP Rosso La Vigna Bricca '00	▼▼	4	
○ Bellarmino '01	▼▼	4*	
● Aiole '99	▼▼	5	
● OP Barbera I Due Draghi '02	▼	3	
● OP Bonarda Vivace Giada '02	▼	3	
○ OP Pinot Nero Brut Haris '02	▼	4	
○ OP Riesling Renano Attimo '02	▼	3	
● OP Barbera I Due Draghi '00	♈♈	3*	
● OP Pinot Nero Bellarmino '98	♈♈	4	
● Aiole '98	♈♈	5	
● OP Rosso La Vigna Bricca '99	♈♈	4	

○ Franciacorta Brut '98	▼▼	6	
○ TdF Bianco Vign. Palanca '02	▼▼	3*	
○ Franciacorta Brut	▼▼	5	
○ Franciacorta Extra Brut	▼▼	5	
○ Franciacorta Satèn	▼▼	5	
● TdF Rosso dei Dossi '00	▼	4	
○ Rubinia '01	▼	5	
● TdF Rosso '01	▼	3	
○ Franciacorta Brut '95	♈♈	5	
○ Franciacorta Brut '97	♈♈	5	

MONTICELLI BRUSATI (BS)

Lo Sparviere

via Costa, 2
25040 Monticelli Brusati (BS)
tel. 030652382
e-mail: losparviere@libero.it

Lo Sparviere is the Franciacorta estate of Monique Poncelet and her husband, Ugo Gussalli Beretta, better known as chair of the Beretta company in Gardone Val Trompia and scion of one of Europe's oldest industrial dynasties. The property surrounding the lovely villa and cellar extends for about 150 hectares, 25 of which are planted to vine. Production manager and oenologist, Francesco Polastri, presented us this year with a very convincing array of wines and Franciacortas. The Franciacorta Brut '98 has complexity and intensity. Ripe fruit on the nose mingles with delicate minerally and aromatic notes, then the well-structured palate is rounded, hinting at rather generous dosage. The Franciacorta Extra Brut '97 unfurls elegant tones of tropical fruit, melding with complex hazelnut and mineral nuances. Excellent sparkle, balance and length are all in evidence. The Terre Bianco Il Dossello '01 is charmingly soft, with inviting apple aromas layered with vanilla and toast. The palate has good density and balance, hinting at skilful use of new oak. The red Vino del Cacciatore '01 is pleasant and well-structured, the Terre di Franciacorta Bianco '02 is interesting and the Passito Bianco Esperidio '01 is sweet and well crafted, revealing intriguing honey on the nose.

○	TdF Bianco Il Dossello '01	▼▼	5
○	Franciacorta Extra Brut '97	▼▼	5
○	Franciacorta Brut '98	▼▼	5
○	Passito Esperidio '01	▼	5
●	TdF Rosso Vino del Cacciatore '01	▼	4
○	TdF Bianco '02	▼	4
●	TdF Rosso Il Sergnana '96	▽▽	5
○	Franciacorta Extra Brut	▽▽	5

MONTICELLI BRUSATI (BS)

Villa

via Villa, 12
25040 Monticelli Brusati (BS)
tel. 030652329 - 030652100
e-mail: infor@villa-franciacorta.it

Like many in Franciacorta, Alessandro Bianchi is a businessman with a passion for winemaking who over the years has transformed the family farm into a successful winery. Alessandro's organizational skills have put together a formidable team, led by his son-in-law, Paolo Pizziol, with oenologist, Corrado Cugnasco, agronomist, Ermes Vianelli, and a string of expert collaborators and consultants. Even though the Villa cuvées missed out on Three Glasses, two Franciacortas still came perilously close. More important, the entire range from this winery is excellent and sourced exclusively from the 33 hectares of well-tended vineyards on the estate. The Satèn '99 is charming in its soft, sweet tones on the buttery, vanillaed nose, and the palate, which caresses without being heavy. The panel agreed it was an excellent interpretation of the wine type. The Extra Brut from the same vintage has clean, fruit and flower aromas on the nose, a very fine perlage, and a palate that shows good acid backbone, fruit and persistence. The Brut '99 foregrounds elegant tropical fruit in the intense, well-defined bouquet. Sound body and lovely effervescence on the palate accompany the same notes of pineapple and passion fruit that delight the nose. Best of the still wines is the barrique-aged Merlot Quercus '00, which is enjoyably concentrated and shows soft tannins, then an attractive finale of tobacco-nuanced red and black berry fruit.

○	Franciacorta Extra Brut '99	▼▼	5
○	Franciacorta Satèn '99	▼▼	5
●	Quercus '00	▼▼	6
○	TdF Bianco Marengo '00	▼▼	5
●	TdF Rosso Gradoni '00	▼▼	5
○	Franciacorta Brut '99	▼▼	5
⊙	Franciacorta Rosé Démi Sec '99	▼▼	5
●	TdF Rosso '01	▼	4
○	TdF Bianco '02	▼	4
○	TdF Bianco Pian della Villa '02	▼	4
○	Franciacorta Cuvette Extra Dry '99	▼	6
○	Franciacorta Extra Brut '98	▽▽▽	5*
○	Franciacorta Satèn '98	▽▽	5

MONTÙ BECCARIA (PV)

VERCESI DEL CASTELLAZZO
VIA AURELIANO, 36
27040 MONTÙ BECCARIA (PV)
TEL. 038560067 - 0385262098
E-MAIL: vercesicastellazzo@libero.it

In just the second year since its release, Rosso del Castellazzo is already a contender for the title of best red in Oltrepò. From 75 per cent barbera and 25 per cent cabernet sauvignon, it is matured for 12 months in barrique, and the same again in bottle, before release. A brilliant deep garnet, it has a lovely bouquet of black wild berry fruit and sweet spice, then a big, warm, full-bodied palate with softness and depth. Other showcase wines from the estate include Bonarda Fatila, for many years a benchmark for winemakers who have abandoned the tradition that demands Bonarda should be young and slightly sparkling, preferring to vinify more challenging still, barrique-aged versions. Matured for 26 months in oak barriques, the '99 version is already aromatic, showing wild berry jam and vanilla, then a warm, concentrated palate, although it still needs time in bottle to mellow out the tannins. The Oltrepò Pavese Rosso Pezzalunga '02 is not bad, showing floral, rather than fruity, aromas. A few more months in the cellar will make it better. The Bonarda Luogo della Milla '02, which has 15 per cent barbera, is slow to open, but then reveals wild black berry aromas and sound structure with well-gauged extract. The Barbera Clà '01 is full and satisfying in the mouth, but is also reluctant to open on the nose. The Vespolino, from 100 per cent ughetta, also known as vespolina, has enjoyable spicy aromas, but lacks softness. The fresh and fragrant Gugiarolo '02, a still Pinot Nero fermented off the skins, is a lovely straw yellow with coppery highlights.

MORNICO LOSANA (PV)

CA' DI FRARA
VIA CASA FERRARI, 1
27040 MORNICO LOSANA (PV)
TEL. 0383892299 - 0383892534
E-MAIL: cadifrara@libero.it

Luca and Matteo Bellani, who manage this family winery founded in 1905, have expanded their collection with a new wine, the Io Bianco '01, a blend of chardonnay and malvasia with other white varieties fermented in barrique. The lustrous gold introduces aromas of hedgerow, honey and over-ripe banana laced with mineral notes. The palate is full, rich, mellow and stylish, with a very long finish. Cellar time will help to smooth out the oak. The flagship wine of Ca' di Frara is still the Pinot Grigio Raccolta Tardiva, an Alsace-style wine that has developed an unmistakable style over the years. The 2002 may not be as powerful as in less problematic vintages, but it does have elegance, depth, richness and length, with notes of honeysuckle, pineapple, citron and pear. The Apogeo '02 also gave an excellent performance. From predominantly riesling renano with some riesling italico, it is very fragrant, showing aromas of peaches, apricots, citrus and roses, then a full, soft palate with lovely acidity. The Io Rosso '00, from equal parts of barbera and pinot nero, with 10 per cent other red varieties, has mature aromas of tobacco, cocoa powder and nutmeg, mingled with wild berry fruit and balsamic notes, then richness and depth in the mouth. A step or two behind, but still worth Two Glasses, is the Oltrepò Pavese Rosso Riserva Il Frater '00. Its dense ruby is followed by broad aromas of sweet spices. The acidity and tannins still need time to find a balance with the fruit-rich texture. Finally, we remembered the dry Malvasia Il Raro '02 as being livelier and more fragrant.

● Rosso del Castellazzo '01	🍷🍷	6
● OP Bonarda Fatila '99	🍷🍷	6
● OP Barbera Clà '01	🍷	4
● OP Bonarda Luogo della Milla '02	🍷	4
○ OP Pinot Nero in bianco Gugiarolo '02	🍷	4
● OP Rosso Pezzalunga '02	🍷	4
● Vespolino '02	🍷	4
● Vespolino '00	🍷🍷	3*
● Rosso del Castellazzo '00	🍷🍷	4

○ OP Pinot Grigio V. T. '02	🍷🍷	4
● OP Rosso Il Frater Ris. '00	🍷🍷	5
● Rosso Io '00	🍷🍷	5
○ Bianco Io '01	🍷🍷	5
○ OP Riesling Renano Apogeo '02	🍷🍷	3*
○ OP Malvasia Il Raro '02		4
○ OP Pinot Grigio V. T. '00	🍷🍷	4
○ OP Riesling Renano Apogeo '00	🍷🍷	3*
● OP Rosso Il Frater '98	🍷🍷	5
○ OP Pinot Grigio V. T. '01	🍷🍷	4
○ OP Riesling Renano Apogeo '01	🍷🍷	3*
● OP Rosso Il Frater Ris. '99	🍷🍷	6
● Rosso Io '99	🍷🍷	5

OME (BS)

MAJOLINI
LOC. VALLE
VIA MANZONI, 3
25050 OME (BS)
TEL. 0306527378
E-MAIL: info@majolini.it

In just a few years, Ezio Majolini and his nephew, Simone, have given an incredible stimulus to this winery and brought it much-enhanced prestige. During this period, the Majolini property has acquired 18 hectares under vine, refurbished the cellar with up-to-date technology and excavated new galleries in the solid rock. What is more, Ezio is the new chair of the Franciacorta wine consortium. Add to this the fact that the estate now has input from two excellent consultants, Pierluigi Donna for agronomy and winemaker, Jean Pierre Valade. All this explains the results Majolini wines achieved at our tastings. It's a range that has few rivals in the region. This year, the Franciacorta Electo Brut '98 nearly encored its superb performance with the previous vintage. It has a very fine perlage, complex aromas dominated by yeast and crusty bread, with classic nuances of vanilla. The broad, full palate closes long on honey and hazelnuts. The Satèn Ante Omnia is just as good, showing with excellent structure, flower and fruit aromas, and the soft, elegant mouthfeel of a great "blanc de blancs". The Pas Dosé '98, dedicated to Aligi Sassu (one of the artist's later works, a bronze equestrian statue, is on display at the winery), also shows off elegant aromas and sound structure, but still needs time in the cellar. The Franciacorta Rosé Altera is probably the best tasted this year. Its intense, brilliant rosé precedes a full body. It can even partner white meat, cheese and game.

PARATICO (BS)

BREDASOLE
VIA SAN PIETRO, 44
25030 PARATICO (BS)
TEL. 035910407
E-MAIL: ferrari@bredasole.it

The Ferrari family's Bredasole winery has stood out over the last few vintages for its fast-improving quality. Part of the credit goes to the territory itself, one of the most beautiful, favoured wine locations in the entire DOCG area, but plaudits should also go to Giacomo Ferrari, for taking the right decisions in vineyards and cellar, and to the skilled Corrado Cugnasco, an oenologist who specializes in Franciacortas. The 13 hectares under vine are at the extreme edge of the glacial hills facing Lake Iseo and the Oglio river, and they yield grapes for a complete range of territory-oriented wines. The three Franciacortas tasted this year easily earned Two Glasses each. Our favourite was the Satèn, which is striking in its soft richness and elegant notes of intense ripe fruit and vanilla. Although initially reluctant on the nose, the Brut finally releases captivating aromas of chamomile, wild honey and flowers, then shows rich, complex structure on the palate. Just as convincing, but more minerally, is the Extra Brut, which offers a fresh taste and bright personality. We felt the Terre di Franciacorta Bianco Pio Elemosiniere '01 was also good. It's a blend of chardonnay with small proportions of pinot bianco and pinot nero that offers good, fruity aromas, a lean body and attractive freshness.

O	Franciacorta Electo Brut '98	🍷🍷	6
O	Franciacorta Ante Omnia Satèn '99	🍷🍷	6
●	Deressi '00	🍷🍷	7
O	Ronchello '02	🍷🍷	4
O	Franciacorta Pas Dosé Aligi Sassu '98	🍷🍷	6
O	Franciacorta Brut	🍷🍷	6
⊙	Franciacorta Rosé Altera Brut	🍷🍷	6
●	TdF Rosso Ruc di Gnoc '00	🍷	4
O	Franciacorta Electo Brut '97	🍷🍷🍷	6
O	Franciacorta Electo Brut '95	🍷🍷	6
O	Franciacorta Ante Omnia Satèn '97	🍷🍷	6
O	Franciacorta Ante Omnia Satèn '98	🍷🍷	6

O	Franciacorta Brut	🍷🍷	5*
O	Franciacorta Brut Satèn	🍷🍷	5
O	Franciacorta Extra Brut	🍷🍷	5
O	TdF Bianco Pio Elemosiniere '01	🍷	4
O	TdF Bianco Pio Elemosiniere '00	🍷	4

PASSIRANO (BS)

IL MOSNEL
LOC. CAMIGNONE
VIA BARBOGLIO, 14
25040 PASSIRANO (BS)
TEL. 030653117
E-MAIL: info@ilmosnel.com

A winery that manages to produce a base wine like the Il Mosnel Franciacorta, and furthermore with a production run of 70,000 bottles, deserves all our consideration. Giulio and Lucia Barzanò are fine winemakers. In the course of just a few vintages, they have turned the family estate around, pushing it into the Franciacorta Top Ten, not an easy chart to climb. Here is the standard Brut, which left several much trumpeted prestige cuvées in its wake. It is a brilliant straw yellow with greenish highlights, a very dense, continuous perlage, and an elegant, harmonious bouquet of ripe fruit with a subtle aromatic vein. The fresh palate is perfectly balanced, clearly echoing the peach, apricot and apple on the nose to finish soft and inviting. The Satèn '99 tempts with its restrained style, lovely vanillaed tones and fresh, zesty palate that closes elegantly on tones of vanilla and cakes. The Brut '98 has a more austere personality, as befits a fine vintage. It is acid-rich and already shading into a lovely complexity on the nose and palate. The still wines include the intense, harmonious white Campolarga '02 and the Fontecolo '00, a well-structured, refined red. The excellent white Passito '01 rounds off a nice performance all round. But looking over the records of tastings in the last few years, we noticed the absence of a vintage '97 Franciacorta, which is evidently still ageing. We await it with impatience.

POLPENAZZE DEL GARDA (BS)

CASCINA LA PERTICA
LOC. PICEDO
VIA PICEDO, 24
25080 POLPENAZZE DEL GARDA (BS)
TEL. 0365651471
E-MAIL: asalvetti@cascinalapertica.it

Ruggero Brunori continues to astonish us with the wines he makes on the Cascina La Pertica at Polpenazze del Garda. This year, his 2001 Garda Cabernet Le Zalte took Three comfortable Glasses for the third consecutive year. What is the key to this success? First of all, Ruggero has a passion for winemaking and a trusted team of experts to help him, with Franco Bernabei consulting and Andrea Salvetti as general manager. The result is a model estate whose cellar is equipped with the best in modern technology and 15 hectares of beautiful vineyards, managed biodynamically. Le Zalte has a dark, dense ruby with purple highlights. The nose opens gradually with rich sensations of black and red berry fruit, with blackberry, cherry and blackcurrant to the fore, veering towards toasted oak and tobacco nuanced with vegetal hints. The palate is simply overwhelming. This dense, balanced, harmonious wine has wonderfully smooth tannins, freshness from the small proportion of marzemino, and ends by echoing the fruit it flaunted on the nose. The Garda Chardonnay Le Sincette Brut was another label that particularly impressed us. Lovely ripe white peach, vanilla, toasted bread and yeast on the nose lead to a palate that shows off attractive effervescence, a fresh fruity tone and wonderful length. The Garda Rosso '01 is also good. However, the hailstorm that devastated the vineyards in 2002 prevented release of the other estate labels.

○	Franciacorta Brut	♥♥	5
○	Passito '01	♥♥	6
○	TdF Bianco Campolarga '02	♥♥	4
○	Franciacorta Brut '98	♥♥	7
○	Franciacorta Satèn '99	♥♥	6
●	TdF Rosso Fontecolo '00	♥	5
○	TdF Bianco Sulìf '01	♥	5
○	Franciacorta Extra Brut	♥	5
○	Franciacorta Satèn '96	♀♀	5
○	Franciacorta Satèn '97	♀♀	5
○	Franciacorta Brut '96	♀♀	6
○	Franciacorta Satèn '98	♀♀	6

●	Garda Cabernet Le Zalte '01	♥♥♥	7
○	Garda Chardonnay Le Sincette Brut Ris. '99	♥♥	5
●	Garda Cl. Rosso Le Sincette '00	♥	4
●	Garda Cabernet Le Zalte '99	♀♀♀	5
●	Garda Cabernet Le Zalte '00	♀♀♀	7
●	Garda Cabernet Le Zalte '98	♀♀	5

PROVAGLIO D'ISEO (BS)   ROCCA DE' GIORGI (PV)

BERSI SERLINI
VIA CERRETO, 7
25050 PROVAGLIO D'ISEO (BS)
TEL. 0309823338
E-MAIL: info@bersiserlini.it

ANTEO
LOC. CHIESA
27043 ROCCA DE' GIORGI (PV)
TEL. 038548583 - 038599073
E-MAIL: info@anteovini.it

Over the past three harvests, this historic estate at Provaglio d'Iseo, owned by the Bersi Serlini family, has gone from indifferent performances to turning out a range of truly remarkable wines. All the credit goes to the excellent work done at the estate by Maddalena Bersi Serlini and oenologist, Corrado Cugnasco, who began the challenging task of renovating and modernizing the vineyards and technical equipment. Last year, as we waited for the release of the new vintages still in the cellar, we tried the two '98 vintages, the Brut and Extra Brut, which were very well developed. However, we did not miss them this year because the cellar presented us with another two cuvées that scored well at tasting. At first, the Satèn seemed slightly reduced on the nose, but then it opened up into vanilla and white peach. In the mouth, it is round and fresh, showing a balanced dosage and good overall harmony. The Franciacorta Brut Cuvée n. 4 is also very well made. The textbook aromas of yeast and toasted bread lead into a solid, supple palate that closes with good length. We thought the standard-label Brut was well made and supple, albeit a bit husky on the nose, and the Demi Sec Nuvola was well typed, with intense floral tones. The two Curtefrancas were interesting.

Antonella and Ettore Piero Cribellati's Anteo estate has always been synonymous with quality Oltrepò Pavese sparklers. This year, oenologist Giuseppe Bassi pulled a champion out of his hat, the Extra Brut Nature Ecru '99; from 85 per cent pinot nero, with some chardonnay, left for 30 months on its own yeasts before disgorgement in the spring of 2003. The lustrous straw yellow, creamy mousse and fine, persistent perlage precede frank aromas of melba toast, vanilla and citrus, then a dry, full palate with good length. The non-vintage Brut is also good, revealing more residual sugar than the Extra Brut (nine grams per litre against three), slightly spicy, toasty aromas, and a balanced freshness in the mouth. The Ca' dell'Oca '01 also achieved a Two Glass score. A monovarietal Pinot Nero from old vine, aged for 12 months in barriques from the French Massif Central, it has a typical medium ruby red colour tinged with orange, then aromas of wild berry fruit, cocoa powder and spices. The lovely velvety palate has remarkable length. The Pinot Nero Extra Dry, fermented with brief skin contact, deserved One Glass for its clean, floral bouquet and wild berry notes. The same score went to the fragrant, fruit-led Coste del Roccolo '01 – the vintage is not indicated on the label as it is a table wine – from equal parts of pinot nero and croatina, part-aged in oak barriques. The Bonarda Staffolo '02 is upfront and clean-tasting and the cuve close Pinot Nero Brut is decent, simple and fresh. The Moscato La Volpe and Uva '02 are less successful than on other occasions.

○ Franciacorta Brut Cuvée n. 4	🍷🍷	5
○ Franciacorta Satèn	🍷🍷	6
● TdF Rosso Curtefranca '01	🍷	4
○ TdF Bianco Curtefranca '02	🍷	4
○ Franciacorta Brut	🍷	5
○ Nuvola Démi Sec	🍷	6
○ Franciacorta Extra Brut '98	🍷🍷	6

○ OP Pinot Nero Extra Brut Cl. Anteo Nature Ecru '99	🍷🍷	5
● OP Pinot Nero Ca' dell'Oca '01	🍷🍷	5
○ OP Brut Cl. Anteo	🍷🍷	5
● Coste del Roccolo '01	🍷	4
● OP Bonarda Staffolo '02	🍷	3
○ OP Pinot Nero Brut Martinotti	🍷	4
⊙ OP Pinot Nero Extra Dry Cl. Anteo Rosè	🍷	5
○ OP Moscato La Volpe e L'Uva '02		3

RODENGO SAIANO (BS)

MIRABELLA
VIA CANTARANE, 2
25050 RODENGO SAIANO (BS)
TEL. 030611197
E-MAIL: info@mirabellavini.it

Mirabella, a dynamic winery in Franciacorta created in 1979 by a group of investors with a passion for wine, is back this year with a full profile. We recall these investors included Enrico Job, cinematographer and costume and set designer, as well as husband of celebrated director Lina Wertmüller, to whom a cuvée has been dedicated. Teresio Schiavi, the Mirabella oenologist, presented us this year with a commendable Franciacorta Non Dosato '95. The absence of liqueur de tirage allows excellent raw material to shine in a wine with intense undertones of tropical fruit and yeast on the nose. It is very stylish, elegant and harmonious in the mouth and finishes long on dry notes of apricot. Clear fruity tones are also the distinguishing features of the Selezione Wertmüller, which is enchanting in its elegant softness and the chamomile and white peach in the bouquet. The very decent palate has caressing effervescence and sensations of fruit. A new red wine debuts with the '99 vintage. It's the Nero d'Ombra, a Bordeaux blend with 15 per cent nebbiolo grapes, which ages for a year in stainless steel, a year in barrique and then another 12 months in bottle. It shows good red and black berry fruit, and shades of chocolate and cherry preserve. The palate is dense, soft and structured, hinting at excellent cellaring prospects. The Franciacorta Brut and Terre Rosso Maniero '01 are both good, as are the other labels presented.

ROVESCALA (PV)

AGNES
VIA CAMPO DEL MONTE, 1
27040 ROVESCALA (PV)
TEL. 038575206 - 03385806773
E-MAIL: info@fratelliagnes.it

Rovescala is historic croatina country. Here, the grape is called bonarda, like the wine. In a document from 1192, the "Rovoscalla" wine is called the best in the district and could be used instead of money to pay debts. The Agnes brothers know this variety better than most, and create Bonardas second to none in vitality and typicity. The best this year was dark purple Campo del Monte '02. Aged for a year in oak barrels, it has a wonderfully creamy mousse, clean-tasting aromas of rose, raspberry and strawberry, and is full and ripe in the mouth, with a lively contrast of extract and understated sweetness. The Vignazzo '02 is also good. The grapes ripen earlier than others because of the exposure of the vineyard, and age in large barrels for six months. The wine has big fruity peach and plum aromas, remarkable structure and tannins that are still a bit tough and need to mellow. The still Bonarda Millennium '00 also won Two Glasses. It is obtained from a clone called "pignolo", showing full-bodied, warm and deep, with sensations of autumn leaves and plenty of alcohol. The Possessione del Console '02, another still wine from the same clone, is fragrant, robust and dry with notes of fruit jam. The slightly inferior Poculum '00 is a barrique-aged table wine sourced from the best grapes from the various estate selections aged. The bouquet of berry fruit is enjoyable, and the structure outstanding, but the tannins are too tough. It will improve after a couple of years in bottle. Finally, the pleasant Bonarda Cresta del Ghiffi '01 is made from super-ripe grapes.

●	TdF Rosso Maniero '01	🍷🍷	4
○	Franciacorta Non Dosato '95	🍷🍷	5
●	Nero d'Ombra '99	🍷🍷	6
○	Franciacorta Brut	🍷🍷	4
○	Franciacorta Brut Wertmüller	🍷🍷	4
○	TdF Bianco Palazzina '01	🍷	4
☉	Franciacorta Brut Rosé	🍷	4
○	Franciacorta Satèn	🍷	5
○	Franciacorta Non Dosato '93	🍷🍷	4
○	Franciacorta Non Dosato '94	🍷🍷	5

●	OP Bonarda Millenium '00	🍷🍷	5
●	OP Bonarda Campo del Monte '02	🍷🍷	3*
●	OP Bonarda Possessione del Console '02	🍷🍷	3*
●	OP Bonarda Vignazzo '02	🍷🍷	3*
●	Rosso Poculum '00	🍷	5
●	OP Bonarda Cresta del Ghiffi '01	🍷	4
●	Rosso Poculum '97	🍷🍷	4
●	Rosso Poculum '98	🍷🍷	4
●	OP Bonarda Possessione del Console '00	🍷🍷	3*
●	OP Bonarda Cresta del Ghiffi '99	🍷🍷	4
●	OP Bonarda Possessione del Console '01	🍷🍷	3
●	OP Bonarda Millenium '99	🍷🍷	5
●	Rosso Poculum '99	🍷🍷	5

SAN COLOMBANO AL·LAMBRO (MI) SAN DAMIANO AL COLLE (PV)

PODERI DI SAN PIETRO
VIA MONTI, 37
20078 SAN COLOMBANO AL LAMBRO (MI)
TEL. 0371208054 - 0371208084

BISI
LOC. CASCINA SAN MICHELE
FRAZ. VILLA MARONE, 70
27040 SAN DAMIANO AL COLLE (PV)
TEL. 038575037
E-MAIL: info@aziendagricolabisi.it

When a winery gets a full profile, it means that it is recently established, significant investments have been made, or it has never before produced a champion. All three conditions obtain at Poderi di San Pietro. Founded in 1998, it extends over more than 60 hectares under vine, supervised by the general manager, Daniele Gilberti, with talented oenologist, Roberto Gerbino, in the cellar. The main buildings are under construction in the vast area that once hosted Milan's agricultural consortium. The large climate-controlled barrique cellar and lovely tasting room have yet to be finished but barrel tastings hint at a bright future. But the present is also interesting. The Monastero di Valbissera '98 is a San Colombano, with slightly more croatina than barbera and 15 per cent uva rara, which ages slowly in small oak. Ruby in hue, it opens on aromas of vanilla and wild berries, showing structure and complexity, but the croatina's tannins need to meld with the wine. The 15 per cent merlot in the San Colombano Rosso di Valbissera '01 lend softness to this juicy, fragrant wine with hints of black wild berry fruit. The Solarolo is remarkable. It's an experimental, gold-coloured dried-grape "passito" with hints of over-ripe banana, apple and candied fruit. The tannin-heavy, spicy Bordeaux-blend Trianon '98 also came close to Two Glasses. The list ends with the pleasant cuve close Brut Ca' della Signora '01, the Pinot Nero '98, which lacks a little self-confidence, and a trio of One Glass whites, the still Bianco della Torre '01 and two semi-sparkling wines.

Hard work pays. Claudio and Emilio Bisi's efforts on their family estate, with help from oenologist, Leonardo Valenti, and 30 hectares under vine at San Damiano al Colle, have earned a full review for they have created two wines that made it to our final taste-offs. The Barbera Roncolongo '00 comes from a vineyard with a density of 3,500 plants per hectare both spurred cordon and Guyot-trained. After manual harvesting, the must is left to macerate on the skins for around 20 days before being racked into new Allier barriques for malolactic fermentation and 15 months' ageing. The 2000 edition is just as powerful as, but more refined than, the 1999. With 15 per cent alcohol, it is deep ruby red shading into garnet, and a broad bouquet where the varietal notes of morello cherry, blackcurrants and violets mingle with tertiary aromas of cocoa powder, tobacco, liquorice, carob and vanilla. The palate is powerful, mellow, deep and very long, supported by brisk acidity: velvet on steel. The Primm '00 is just as good. A monovarietal Cabernet Sauvignon from a vineyard planted at 5,600 vines per hectare, it spent 30 days on the skins, acquiring an almost impenetrable garnet colour, then 15 months in new barriques added sweet spice, cocoa powder and vanilla to the varietal sensations of straw, bell pepper and wild berry fruit. The "passito" Villa Marone is fair, although the alcohol is slightly excessive. From 100 per cent aromatic malvasia di Candia, it ferments and ages in oak.

● San Colombano Rosso di Valbissera '01	♛♛	3*
● San Colombano Monastero di Valbissera '98	♛♛	5
○ Solarolo	♛♛	5
○ Bianco della Torre '01	♛	2*
○ Ca' della Signora Brut '01	♛	3
○ Malvasia Letizia '01	♛	1*
○ Serafina '02	♛	2*
● Pinot Nero '98	♛	5
● Trianon '98	♛	5

● OP Barbera Roncolongo '00	♛♛	5
● OP Cabernet Sauvignon Primm '00	♛♛	5
○ Malvasia Villa Marone '00	♛♛	5
● OP Barbera Roncolongo '99	♛♛	5
● OP Cabernet Sauvignon Primm '99	♛	5

SAN PAOLO D'ARGON (BG)   SANTA GIULETTA (PV)

CANTINA SOCIALE BERGAMASCA
VIA BERGAMO, 10
24060 SAN PAOLO D'ARGON (BG)
TEL. 035951098
E-MAIL: csbsanpaolo@libero.it

ISIMBARDA
LOC. CASTELLO
27048 SANTA GIULETTA (PV)
TEL. 0383899256
E-MAIL: info@isimbarda.com

The Cantina Sociale Bergamasca at San Paolo d'Argon works very well. The 150 members farm a total vineyard holding of about 100 hectares under vine. The Valcalepio Bianco '02 is commendable, especially considering the vintage. The spring flowers and tropical fruit precede a palate of medium length, with fresh, pleasant fruit and good structure, supported by marked acidity and suppleness. The Valcalepio Rosso '01, from equal parts of merlot and cabernet sauvignon, has typical notes of herbs and fruit preserves, revealing a soft, balanced mouthfeel. Two '00 "riserva" wines, the Vigna del Conte and Vigna del Castello, are ageing respectively in Allier barriques and tonneaux. We will discuss them next year, but they are very promising, especially the former. The Merlot della Bergamasca '02, sold at an almost unbelievable price for a wine of this quality, has fresh wild berry fruit aromas and a varietal, fairly simple palate, but soft and well behaved. The Cabernet della Bergamasca '01 is simple and rustic on the palate, with the grassy notes typical of the variety and slightly edgy tannins. Finally, the fresh, pleasant Schiava '02 is rosé fermented and flaunts the lovely red of Tropea onions, as well as a fairly broad flower and citrus bouquet.

There is just a part profile for Luigi Meroni's Isimbarda estate this year. In fact, several of the flagship wines were missing, including the Oltrepò Pavese Rosso Monplò, the Riserva Montezavo and the oak-aged white IGT Varmèi. They will be back next year. In the meantime, we consoled ourselves with the Vigna Martina '02, one of the best Riesling Renanos in the entire area. It is sourced from a vineyard planted at a density of 6,000 vines per hectare, situated 350 metres above sea level in the towns of Santa Giuletta and Mornico Losana. Part of the fruit is cold-macerated and around a quarter of the total is aged in oak tonneaux. The wine is straw yellow with greenish flecks. The broad swathe of aromas integrate the typical mineral notes of the variety with sweet spice from the oak. The palate shows good structure, well-supported by acidity and good length. The Bonarda '02, traditionally refermented in a pressure tank in the spring, opens up slowly to reveal a marked alcohol with hints of plums, apples and wild berry fruit. The palate is full, warm, and properly tannic. Another One Glass score goes to the slightly sparkling Pinot Nero, which is fermented off the skins, and shows clean and enjoyably straightforward.

○	Valcalepio Bianco '02	🍷🍷	3*
●	Cabernet della Bergamasca '01	🍷	2
●	Valcalepio Rosso '01	🍷	3
●	Merlot della Bergamasca '02	🍷	2*
☉	Schiava della Bergamasca '02	🍷	2*
○	Moscato Giallo Passito Aureo '00	🍷🍷	5
●	Valcalepio Rosso Riserva Akros Vigna La Tordela '98	🍷🍷	4
●	Valcalepio Rosso Ris. Vigna del Conte '98	🍷🍷	5
●	Valcalepio Rosso Akros Ris. '99	🍷🍷	4

○	OP Riesling Renano Vigna Martina '02	🍷🍷	4
●	OP Bonarda Vivace '02	🍷	3
○	OP Pinot Nero in bianco Vivace '02	🍷	4
●	OP Barbera '98	🍷🍷	3*
●	OP Bonarda Vivace '00	🍷🍷	3*
○	OP Riesling Renano Vigna Martina '00	🍷🍷	4
●	OP Rosso Monplò '98	🍷🍷	4
●	OP Pinot Nero '99	🍷🍷	5
●	OP Rosso Monplò '99	🍷🍷	4
●	OP Rosso Montezavo Ris. '99	🍷🍷	6

SANTA GIULETTA (PV)

PODERE SAN GIORGIO
LOC. CASTELLO, 1
27046 SANTA GIULETTA (PV)
TEL. 0383899168
E-MAIL: info@poderesangiorgio.it

There's a full review for Guido Perdomini's estate, which has made a decisive upturn in quality, thanks in part to the contribution of top oenologist, Donato Lanati. Aged in oak barriques for 10 months, the Barbera Becco Giallo '01 has lovely aromas of violets, jam and spices. It is warm, generous and, compared to the 2000 version, is not held back by varietal acidity. The Re Nero '00 comes from 98 per cent pinot nero with a little pinot tintourier, macerated for about 12 days at controlled temperature, then aged for 18 months in barriques, some new and some used once or twice. A deep garnet red, it has wild berries, morello cherry, fresh flowers and vanilla, as well as nice velvety pulp refreshed by intriguing acidity. The Pinot Grigio '02 is convincingly rich, full, long and varietal, with spring flower aromas. The series of Two Glass wines closes with the Dorè, from super-ripe moscato grapes part-fermented and aged in new Limousin barriques. A light, lustrous gold, it has a bouquet of chamomile, honey and candied fruit. The palate is moderately sweet, well-balanced and attractively long. The part oak-fermented Chardonnay Dama Bianca '02 is fragrant with tropical fruit, but the palate reveals a sweetish vein from excessive residual sugar. Finally, Titanium '00, from cabernet sauvignon, merlot and croatina, is too true to its name. The nose is attractive but the palate is distinctly inflexible.

●	OP Pinot Nero Re Nero '00	🍷🍷	5
○	Moscato Passito Dorè '01	🍷🍷	5
●	OP Barbera Becco Giallo '01	🍷🍷	4
○	OP Pinot Grigio '02	🍷🍷	4
●	Titanium '00	🍷	6
○	OP Chardonnay Dama Bianca '02	🍷	4
●	OP Barbera Becco Giallo '00	YY	4
○	OP Chardonnay Dama Bianca '01	YY	3*

SANTA MARIA DELLA VERSA (PV)

CANTINA SOCIALE LA VERSA
VIA F. CRISPI, 15
27047 SANTA MARIA DELLA VERSA (PV)
TEL. 0385798411

In a short time, Francesco Cervetti has managed to shift the historic Cantina Sociale in Santa Maria La Versa into top gear, thanks to careful selection of the grapes contributed by members and painstaking effort in the cellar. The results can be seen by reading through the list of wines awarded Two Glasses. In first place is the Roccolo line of vineyard selections, created with help from the University of Milan. The Roccolo delle Rose, a "metodo classico" "blanc de blancs" sparkler from chardonnay grapes only, part-fermented in barrique and left on the lees for 36 months. Fragrant golden delicious apples, spring flowers and vanilla on the nose lend great style and personality. The Moscato Passito Lacrimae Vitis '00 is warm, soft, full and reminiscent of wines from Pantelleria. We return to the Oltrepò with a trio of "metodo classico" sparklers that have always been standards from this cellar. Surprisingly, the fragrantly aromatic standard Pinot Nero Brut Classico, seemed a fraction superior to the Carta Oro and the very good Testarossa '00. In contrast to the other two, it spent a year longer on the lees (36 months instead of 24). The "metodo Martinotti lungo" cuve close Monte Calvo '02, a new winery item, is soft and fragrant with tropical fruit. The other wines, starting with the Bonarda Ca' Bella '02, are impeccable, clean and typical.

○	Moscato Passito Lacrimae Vitis '00	🍷🍷	5
○	Spumante Cl. Cuvée Extra Dry Testarossa '00	🍷🍷	6
●	OP Bonarda Frizzante Ca' Bella '02	🍷🍷	4
○	OP Pinot Grigio '02	🍷🍷	4
○	OP Pinot Nero Martinotti Monte Calvo '02	🍷🍷	4
○	OP Pinot Nero Brut Cl.	🍷🍷	4*
○	OP Pinot Nero Brut Cl. Carta Oro	🍷🍷	4
○	Spumante Cl. Brut Roccolo delle Rose	🍷🍷	7
●	OP Buttafuoco Roccolo delle Viole '00	🍷	5
○	Moscato Spumante Martinotti Fior d'Arancio '02	🍷	4
●	OP Bonarda Frizzante '02	🍷	4
○	OP Chardonnay '02	🍷	4
●	OP Barbera Roccolo del Casale '00	YY	3*

SCANZOROSCIATE (BG)

LA BRUGHERATA
FRAZ. ROSCIATE
VIA G. MEDOLAGO, 47
24020 SCANZOROSCIATE (BG)
TEL. 035655202
E-MAIL: info@labrugherata.it

Patrizia Merati's estate covers 10 hectares, of which five are under vine and one is an olive grove. Located at Scanzorosciate, it has shown itself to be one of the most reliable wineries in the Bergamo area. In a problematic vintage like 2002, Patrizia preferred not to produce her Valcalepio Bianco Vescovado Selezione so that all the best grapes would go into the standard Vescovado '02. From equal parts pinot bianco and chardonnay, with 20 per cent pinot grigio, this wine has a lustrous straw-yellow colour with greenish highlights. The nose offers a generous bouquet of hedgerow, peach and apricot, over a light minerally background. The full-flavoured palate has marked acidity and good body. The Valcalepio Rosso Doglio Riserva '99 is also good. Obtained from equal parts of merlot and cabernet sauvignon grapes, and aged for 36 months in large Allier oak barrels, it is almost too evolved, offering generously full, tertiary notes of ripe fruit and brandied morello cherries. The Priore '01 is just as good, a "vino da tavola", or table wine, from cabernet sauvignon barrique-aged for 12 months. Red berry fruit, morello cherry in particular, emerges on the nose and the palate has good structure. One full Glass went to the Valcalepio Rosso Vescovado '01, whose 18 months in large oak barrels has given it softness and a certain aromatic complexity, although grassy tones prevail. The same goes for the spicy, velvety Rosso di Alberico '01. The Moscato di Scanzo Passito Doge '00 shows sage and sweet spices. The structure and complexity are nice, but the balance is not quite perfect.

SIRMIONE (BS)

CA' DEI FRATI
FRAZ. LUGANA
VIA FRATI, 22
25010 SIRMIONE (BS)
TEL. 030919468
E-MAIL: info@cadeifrati.it

The role of the Dal Cero family in experimenting with trebbiano di Lugana ought to be acknowledged. They were the first to dare to use oak for maturing when the idea seemed heretical in the zone. For several years now, they have pursued a philosophy of enhancing longevity in their Lugana whites. Last year, the Brolettino Grande Annata '98 was already impressive for its concentration and power, and this time they have another great interpretation in the 1999 vintage. This is an extreme Lugana that immediately unsettles with its intense gold, shimmering with greenish highlights. The very broad bouquet hints at tea, lime blossom and wistaria, melding citrus sensations with nuts, especially hazelnuts. The palate is sound and vigorous, showing citrus and ripe orange against floral fragrances that return with a clear vegetal note of medicinal herbs. The Lugana Brolettino is as remarkable as ever. The 2001 version has the characteristic minerality of the grape, which melds with a rich bouquet of medicinal herbs and meadows, a fragrance that returns on the palate along with vibrant citrus sensations. The youthfully acidic Lugana '02 is simpler, but very pleasing, and the "spumante" version of Lugana was also enjoyable. The elegant Pratto '01 confirms yet again how successfully trebbiano can be blended with international varieties. The sweet Tre Filer '00 is a version of the same blend from partially dried grapes. The velvety, juicy Ronchedone '00 is the Ca' dei Frati red.

●	Priore '01	𝟐𝟐	5
○	Valcalepio Bianco Vescovado '02	𝟐𝟐	4
●	Valcalepio Rosso Ris. Doglio '99	𝟐𝟐	5
●	Valcalepio Moscato di Scanzo Passito Doge '00	𝟐	8
●	Rosso di Alberico '01	𝟐	5
●	Valcalepio Rosso Vescovado '01	𝟐	4
●	Valcalepio Rosso Ris. Doglio '96	𝟐𝟐	4
●	Valcalepio Rosso Vescovado '98	𝟐𝟐	3*
●	Valcalepio Rosso Ris. Doglio '97	𝟐𝟐	4
●	Rosso di Alberico '99	𝟐𝟐	4
●	Rosso di Alberico '00	𝟐𝟐	4
●	Valcalepio Rosso Ris. Doglio '98	𝟐𝟐	4
●	Moscato di Scanzo Passito Doge '99	𝟐𝟐	6

○	Lugana Il Brolettino Grande Annata '99	𝟐𝟐	6
●	Ronchedone '00	𝟐𝟐	5
○	Lugana Il Brolettino '01	𝟐𝟐	4
○	Pratto '01	𝟐𝟐	5
○	Lugana Brut Cl. Cuvée dei Frati '00	𝟐	4
○	Tre Filer '00	𝟐	5
○	Lugana I Frati '02	𝟐	4
○	Lugana Brolettino Grande Annata '97	𝟐𝟐	5
○	Lugana Il Brolettino '99	𝟐𝟐	4
○	Pratto '99	𝟐𝟐	5
○	Lugana Brolettino Grande Annata '98	𝟐𝟐	6
○	Lugana Il Brolettino '00	𝟐𝟐	4
○	Pratto '00	𝟐𝟐	5

SIRMIONE (BS)

CA' LOJERA
LOC. ROVIZZA
VIA 1886, 19
25019 SIRMIONE (BS)
TEL. 0457551901 - 030919550
E-MAIL: info@calojera.com

In just a few years, Ambra and Franco Tiraboschi's estate has become one of the most interesting in the Garda area. Trebbiano di Lugana is very much at home in the flat, clayey soil of Ca' Lojera, an ancient reclaimed swamp almost on the border of the provinces of Brescia and Verona. It is difficult to choose from the three Luganas, since all of them are fascinating. Lovers of the spirited vegetal notes and subtle minerality of young Garda whites should look to the 2002 vintage. The standard Lugana is one of the best from the zone, its marked suggestions of medicinal herbs mingling with seductive citron and tropical fruit. Freshness and full flavour complement the structure and wonderful length. The 2001 vintage is well represented by the Lugana Superiore, with its explosive floral note. The Lugana Vigna Silva '00 needs time to open and matures for longer than its cellarmates. Its brief stay in oak elegantly amplifies the balsamic vein in the 2002. Nice sensations of hedgerow are accompanied by satisfying citrus, and the palate closes on a subtle note of hazelnut. Ca' Lojera's special skill with whites is obvious in the Garda DOC Chardonnay '02, sourced from very old vineyards on the glacial soil of the province of Mantua. Red grapes also come from these hills, which Virgil knew. The Garda Merlot '02 shines for easy drinkability. The Monte della Guardia '00, a Bordeaux blend, is enjoyable and the rosé is captivating, one of the best we tasted on the shores of Lake Garda.

TEGLIO (SO)

FAY
LOC. SAN GIACOMO
VIA PILA CASELLI, 1
23030 TEGLIO (SO)
TEL. 0342786071
E-MAIL: elefay@tin.it

By now, the Fay family should be considered a team in every sense of the word, especially since the family's original winemaker, Sandro Fay, returned to the estate a short while ago after finishing his term as mayor. His children, Elena and Marco, have certainly wasted no time over the years, managing the commercial, viticultural and winemaking aspects of the estate with dynamism. The results are there for everyone to see and our tastings for this Guide were again more than satisfying. We'll begin with a wonderful example of a territory-focused wine, the Sassella Glicine '00, which shows a complex morello-led bouquet, a warm palate, supported by remarkably concentrated texture, and a long finish of wild berry jam. Around 8,000 bottles are produced of Ca' Morei '00, the legendary Valtellina label with its unmistakable spice and notes of citrus and bitter orange. The palate is soft, with clear hints of cloves and ripe fruit. The Carteria '00 introduces itself with light, pleasing sensations of raisins, then a rounded palate offers sweet touches, supported by a vigorous finish. Last but not least, the very special Sforzato Ronco del Picchio '01 scored well at our final taste-offs. The intense notes of brandied morello cherries mingle attractively with hints of cocoa powder and vanilla. Soft and mouthfilling on the palate, it has sweet notes and a long finish.

O	Lugana Vigna Silva '00	YY	4
O	Lugana Sup. '01	YY	4
O	Garda Chardonnay '02	YY	3*
O	Lugana '02	YY	3*
●	Monte della Guardia Rosso '00	Y	4
●	Garda Merlot '02	Y	4
☉	Monte della Guardia Rosato '02	Y	3
O	Lugana Sup. '99	YY	4
O	Lugana Sup. '00	YY	4

●	Valtellina Sforzato Ronco del Picchio '01	YY	6
●	Valtellina Sup. Sassella Il Glicine '00	YY	5
●	Valtellina Sup. Valgella Ca' Morei '00	YY	5
●	Valtellina Sup. Valgella Carteria '00	YY	5
●	Valtellina Sforzato Ronco del Picchio '99	YY	6
●	Valtellina Sup. Sassella Il Glicine '99	YY	5
●	Valtellina Sup. Valgella Ca' Morei '99	YY	5
●	Valtellina Sup. Valgella Carteria '99	YY	5

TIRANO (SO)

CONTI SERTOLI SALIS
P.ZZA SALIS, 3
23037 TIRANO (SO)
TEL. 0342710404
E-MAIL: info@sertolisalis.com

Over the past few years, Conti Sertoli Salis has shown itself to be one of the Valtellina estates with clear ideas on both quality and business orientation. Credit for this goes to the well-matched team of oenologist, Claudio Introini, and Cesare Sertoli Salis and Gianni Belfiore, both of whom work on marketing and promotion in Italy and abroad. In the absence of a great wine like the Sforzato Canua, to be released next year, we tasted instead a very compelling Corte della Meridiana '00. Made with the ancient "rinforzo" technique, consisting in part-drying some of the fruit and adding it to the wine later, it has a nose of elegant spice with pleasant sensations of red berry fruit, vanilla and quinine. The palate has good texture and a long, velvety finish. Capo di Terra '00, again from nebbiolo grapes harvested when slightly raisined, has an intense, fruity nose, then a round palate mouth with well-supported structure. The Saloncello '02 has appealing aromas of blackberry and raspberry, showing vigorous on the palate, with good consistency. It finishes fresh and fruity. The Sassella '00 is always well typed and in harmony with the territory. It has aromas of nuts and dried flowers, with a silky body and significant length. Broad aromas with notes of raspberry and nutmeg mark the Grumello '00. It is soft and vigorous in the mouth, with sweet sensations, finishing long and persistent. The Torre della Sirena '02 has a clean, fragrant bouquet and a dry palate, with fruity sensations in the finish.

TORRE DE' ROVERI (BG)

LA TORDELA
VIA TORRICELLI, 1
24060 TORRE DE' ROVERI (BG)
TEL. 035580172
E-MAIL: info@latordela.it

This estate, managed for years by Marco Bernardi, has racked up continuing improvements in quality. The stately villa dates from the 16th century and has extensions for "agriturismo" accommodation and raising Avelignese horses. The complex is set in 20 hectares of vineyard along the hills in the depression between Torre de' Roveri and Valle Serradesca. Some 70 per cent of the fruit is harvested mechanically and the best grapes for the various vineyard selections are vinified separately in the recently renovated cellar. The wines presented included a nice Valcalepio Bianco, from the notoriously difficult 2002 growing year. From soft-pressed pinot bianco, pinot grigio and chardonnay, its straw yellow colour is not very bright, and the light, delicate, mainly floral aromas lead into a round palate. The Valcalepio Moscato Passito '00 appears very evolved to the eye and nose. The full, honey-rich body is slightly penalized by an excessively bitter finish. The Valcalepio Rosso '00, tasted last year before its release, has notes of ripe fruit and fresh-cut grass, but the tannins are still a bit aggressive and have not yet mellowed completely ripen in the bottle. We look forward to tasting the Valcalepio Rosso Riserva '00, which is still maturing in tonneaux. It promises to be one of the best wines ever produced in the area around Bergamo.

● Valtellina Sup.		
Corte della Meridiana '00	♟♟	6
● Valtellina Sup. Capo di Terra '00	♟♟	4
● Valtellina Sup. Grumello '00	♟♟	5
● Valtellina Sup. Sassella '00	♟♟	5
● Il Saloncello '02	♟♟	4
○ Torre della Sirena '02	♟	5
● Valtellina Sforzato Canua '97	♟♟♟	6
● Valtellina Sforzato Canua '98	♟♟	6
● Valtellina Sforzato Canua '99	♟♟♟	6
● Valtellina Sforzato Canua '00	♟♟♟	6
● Valtellina Sup. Capo di Terra '99	♟♟	4
● Valtellina Sup.		
Corte della Meridiana '99	♟♟	5

○ Valcalepio Bianco '02	♟♟	3*
○ Valcalepio Moscato Passito '00	♟	6
● Valcalepio Rosso '00	♟♟	3*
● Valcalepio Rosso Ris. '98	♟♟	4
● Cabernet Bergamasca '99	♟	3
○ Valcalepio Moscato Passito '99	♟	6

TORRICELLA VERZATE (PV) VILLA DI TIRANO (SO)

MONSUPELLO
VIA SAN LAZZARO, 5
27050 TORRICELLA VERZATE (PV)
TEL. 0383896043 - 0383896044
E-MAIL: monsupello@monsupello.it

TRIACCA
VIA NAZIONALE, 121
23030 VILLA DI TIRANO (SO)
TEL. 0342701352
E-MAIL: info@triacca.com

Monsupello has shown it is one of the top Oltrepò wineries with a long line of admirable labels. The truth is that this estate almost never gets a wine wrong. The "metodo classico" sparklers, beginning with the creamy, long Cuvée Ca' del Tava '97, are splendidly aromatic and complex. The rich, elegant non-vintage Pinot Nero Brut is also excellent. Another Two full Glasses went to the Oltrepò Pavese Rosso Riserva Mosaico '00, from 60 per cent barbera. Its ruby red shades into garnet, and the broad nose weds fruit jam attractively to the spicy notes from 20 months in barriques, both new and once-used. Warm, rich and deep in the mouth, it flaunts fine-grained tannins. The warm, spicy Cabernet Sauvignon Aplomb '00 is only slightly less concentrated. The following wines were all good: Nature, a "metodo classico" that has twice been awarded Three Glasses; the dried-grape "passito" La Cuenta '98, with its nut and honey tones; the warm, fragrant 2000 Pinot Nero 3309; the forthright, spirited Riesling Renano '02; and Great Ruby '02, a fragrantly aromatic semi-sparkling red. The Chardonnay Senso was not as convincing as usual, but then no one's perfect. One full Glass went to the Barbera Pivena '00 and the very mature Classese '98. All the other wines from the 2002 vintage were attractive, varietal and well typed.

Domenico Triacca has had a lot of satisfaction from investing much of his career and professional enthusiasm in the vineyard. Clonal research into nebbiolo and all-round experimentation into eco-compatibility have given his wines the added value of territory and personality. A wine like Sforzato '01 is proof, winning a well-deserved Three Glass award again this year. From a unique marriage of human skill and the forces of nature, this wine shows austere at first, opening up slowly on the nose with spicy notes and hints of coffee. The palate is elegant, with balanced concentration, a firm tannic weave and a long, expanding finish. The Riserva La Gatta '99 is good, offering refined, clove-laced aromas. An inviting, harmonious entry on the palate leads to a solid, lingering finish. The youthfully alcoholic, uncompromising Casa La Gatta '00 has less structure, but offers a well-rounded palate and an easy drinkability. Two Glasses also went to the Sassella '00, characterized by fresh roast coffee aromas. Its zesty palate has a distinct tannic vein. The Sauvignon Del Frate surprises every time we taste it. The intense golden yellow impresses and the aromatic spectrum is complex, with mineral notes joined on the palate by notes of grapefruit and rue.

● OP Cabernet Sauvignon Aplomb '00	🍷🍷	6
○ OP Brut Cl. Ris. Ca' del Tava '97	🍷🍷	6
○ OP Pinot Nero Brut Cl.	🍷🍷	5
● OP Pinot Nero 3309 '00	🍷🍷	6
○ OP Chardonnay Senso '01	🍷🍷	5
○ OP Riesling Renano '02	🍷🍷	4
● OP Rosso Great Ruby Vivace '02	🍷🍷	4
● OP Rosso Mosaico Ris. '00	🍷🍷	6
○ La Cuenta Passito Giallo '98	🍷🍷	7
○ OP Pinot Nero Cl. Nature	🍷🍷	5
● OP Barbera Ris. Vigna Pivena '00	🍷	6
○ OP Pinot Nero Brut Classese '98	🍷	5
○ OP Pinot Nero Cl. Nature	🍷🍷🍷	4

● Valtellina Sforzato San Domenico '01	🍷🍷🍷	7
● Valtellina Sup. Sassella '00	🍷🍷	5
○ Sauvignon Del Frate '02	🍷🍷	5
● Valtellina Sup. Ris. La Gatta '99	🍷🍷	5
● Valtellina Sup. Casa La Gatta '00	🍷	5
● Valtellina Prestigio Millennium '97	🍷🍷🍷	5
● Valtellina Sforzato '00	🍷🍷🍷	7
● Valtellina Prestigio '99	🍷🍷	6
● Valtellina Prestigio '00	🍷🍷	7
● Valtellina Sup. Ris. Triacca '98	🍷🍷	5

OTHER WINERIES

BATTISTA COLA
VIA SANT'ANNA, 22
25030 ADRO (BS)
TEL. 0307356195
E-MAIL: info@colabattista.it

Battista and Stefano Cola farm their own ten hectares of vineyard on the slopes of Mount Alto di Adro. They showed how good their quality is again this year with the success of the Franciacorta Brut, a fruity, supple wine with lovely fullness.

○	Franciacorta Brut	♈♈	4*
○	Franciacorta Extra Brut	♈	5
○	TdF Bianco '01	♈♈	4

CORNALETO
VIA CORNALETTO, 2
25030 ADRO (BS)
TEL. 0307450507 - 0307450554
E-MAIL: info@cornaleto.it

This historic Franciacorta estate boasts well-aspected vineyards in the municipality of Adro. Owner Vittorio Lancini occasionally sells particularly interesting past vintages like the '92. We enjoyed a more recently produced Satèn '97.

○	Franciacorta Brut Satèn '97	♈♈	6
☉	Franciacorta Rosé Brut '97	♈	6
●	TdF Rosso Baldoc '98	♈♈	6

LEBOVITZ
LOC. GOVERNOLO
V.LE RIMEMBRANZE, 4
46037 BAGNOLO SAN VITO (MN)
TEL. 0376668115

The Lambrusco Mantovano Rosso dei Concari '02 is cold-macerated on the skins. This zesty, fragrant wine has a lovely, creamy, purple mousse, and clear wild berry fruit aromas. However, the Rosso Barriché, also from lambrusco, is less convincing as oak ageing has muddied its aromas.

●	Lambrusco Mantovano		
	Rosso dei Concari '02	♈	2*

ANTICA TESA
LOC. MATTINA
VIA MERANO, 28
25080 BOTTICINO (BS)
TEL. 0302691500

This family-run estate is definitely the best in the Botticino DOC zone. Pierangelo Noventa personally manages his superbly aspected vineyards, on excellent soil. Oenologist Cesare Ferrari consults in the cellar. The barbera, sangiovese, marzemino and schiava Vigna del Gobbio is excellent.

●	Botticino Pià della Tesa '00	♈♈	4
●	Vigna del Gobbio '00	♈♈	5

Cantina Sociale di Broni
via Sansaluto, 81
27043 Broni (PV)
tel. 038551505
E-mail: cantinasocialebroni@tin.it

The historic Broni co-operative is progressing under oenologist, Livio Cagnoni. The Classese '99 has floral fragrances and excellent structure. The Brut Martinotti '02 is simple, sufficiently refined and pleasant. The Oltrepò Pavese Rosso Bronis '98, already tasted last year, confirms its quality.

○ OP Pinot Nero Brut Martinotti '02	♥	3
○ OP Pinot Nero Brut Classese '99	♥	4
● OP Rosso Bronis '98	♀	3

Ca' Tessitori
via Matteotti, 15
27043 Broni (PV)
tel. 038551495

This is the debut of Luigi Giorgi's estate, where Carlo Saviotti consults. The oak-aged Barbera Vignamarona '00 has a clear nose with hints of wild berries and spices. The palate is full and stylish. The Chardonnay '02 has the clean tropical fruit and the Croatina Laetitia is fresh and sparkling.

● OP Barbera Vignamarona '00	♥♥	4
● Croatina Laetitia '02	♥	3
○ OP Chardonnay '02	♥	3

La Marzuola
loc. Marzuola
27045 Calvignano (PV)
tel. 0383871123
E-mail: marzuola@marzuola.it

Red wines by Gabriella Valadè always have excellent raw material. But she has fine-tuning to do during vinification to mellow the rough edges. The Rosso Riserva '99, Pinot Nero '99 and Uva Rara '01, all show clear aromas and juicy fruit, but the tannins protrude.

● Uva Rara '01	♥	3
● OP Pinot Nero '99	♥	4
● OP Rosso Ris. '99	♥	4

Fiamberti
via Chiesa, 17
27044 Canneto Pavese (PV)
tel. 038588019
E-mail: fiambertivini@libero.it

This ancient estate is back in the Guide. The Buttafuoco Vigna Solenga '98 has good structure, with leather and tannins that need bottle age. Monte Acutello '98 is oak-heavy, while Bonarda Vigna Bricco della Sacca '02 is still a little closed.

● OP Bonarda Vivace Vigna Bricco della Sacca '02	♥	4
● OP Buttafuoco Vigna Solenga '98	♥	5
● OP Rosso Ris. Monte Acutello '98	♥	4

La Vigna
Cascina La Vigna
25020 Capriano del Colle (BS)
tel. 0309748061
E-mail: lavignavini@libero.it

Anna Botti and her wine technician husband bring us new wines from Montenetto. The Capriano Riserva '01 is young and evolving. Its intensity and structure took it close to Two Glasses. The Marzemino '01 is simpler and tauter, but still has good prospects for development.

● Capriano del Colle Rosso Monte Bruciato Ris. '01	♥	5
● Marzemino '01		3

F.lli Muratori
via Palazzolo, 168
25031 Capriolo (BS)
tel. 0307461599
E-mail: info@fratellimuratori.com

The Muratori sparklers have shown how good they are. Best this year were the Satèn Cesonato, with its elegant boisé notes, and the Brut Novalia, with elegant tones of sweet cakes and yeast on the nose and a good, harmonious structure.

○ Franciacorta Brut Novalia	♥♥	5
○ Franciacorta Satèn Brut Cesonato	♥♥	6
○ Franciacorta Dosaggio Zero Villa Crespia	♀♀	5

TENUTA LA COSTA
FRAZ. COSTA, 68
27040 CASTANA (PV)
TEL. 0385241527
E-MAIL: tenutalacosta@libero.it

From ten hectares of vineyard, a few kilometres from Broni, Giuseppe Calvi produces an excellent Sangue di Giuda. The typical rose and raspberry 2002 has a wonderful rosé mousse and a palate of good balance and persistence. The rather evolved Buttafuoco Vivace '01 was not quite so successful.

● OP Sangue di Giuda '02	♟♟	3*
● OP Buttafuoco Vivace '02		3

MARCO GIULIO BELLANI
VIA MANZONI, 75
27045 CASTEGGIO (PV)
TEL. 038382122

Laura Bellani, with oenologist, Carlo Saviotti, produces a red Oltrepò Pavese from the Articioc vineyard that is succulent yet still a tad tough in the 2000 version. There are two 1999 "metodo classico" sparklers from a Pinot Nero base: the stylish, structured white and a simpler, enjoyable rosé.

● OP Rosso Articioc '00	♟	4
○ OP Pinot Nero Brut Cl. '99	♟	4
☉ OP Pinot Nero in rosa Brut Cl. '99	♟	4

CANTINA DI CASTEGGIO
VIA TORINO, 96
27045 CASTEGGIO (PV)
TEL. 0383806311
E-MAIL: info@cantinacasteggio.it

Riccardo Cotarella made the fragrant, full-bodied Longobardo '01, a blend of equal parts barbera and croatina with ten per cent cabernet sauvignon and pinot nero. The tangy Sauvignon '02 and the coppery Pinot Grigio '02, are well made and uncomplicated.

● Il Longobardo '01	♟♟	6
○ OP Pinot Grigio Rusan '02	♟	3
○ OP Sauvignon '02	♟	3

CLASTIDIO BALLABIO
VIA SAN BIAGIO, 32
27045 CASTEGGIO (PV)
TEL. 038382566

The semi-sparkling Bonarda from the Vigna delle Cento Pertiche vineyard at this historic Casteggio estate is very reliable. The 2002 version has a nice, clean, forthright nose with aromas of wild berries, roses and violets, then a dry, robust, fruit-led palate.

● OP Bonarda Vivace Le Cento Pertiche '02	♟♟	3*

F.LLI GUERCI
FRAZ. CROTESI, 20
27045 CASTEGGIO (PV)
TEL. 038382725 - 038383907
E-MAIL: guerci_flli@libero.it

The blackberry and forest floor Barbera Vignole '00 is well typed, with marked acidity and good structure. The slightly sparkling Bonarda Vivace '02 is uncertain on the nose but strong in the mouth. The amber Moscato Passito Apricus '01 has big ripe tropical fruit but a muzzy palate.

● OP Barbera Vignole '00	♟	3
○ OP Moscato Passito Apricus '01	♟	5
● OP Bonarda Vivace '02	♟	2

CONTI BETTONI CAZZAGO
VIA MARCONI, 6
25046 CAZZAGO SAN MARTINO (BS)
TEL. 0307750875
E-MAIL: giovanniscand@tiscali.it

Conti Bettoni Cazzago is a historic family that makes a valid range of Franciacortas and still wines from the estate's more than 15 hectares of vineyards. Aside from the Brut Tetellus '97, the Santa Giulia cuvée is particularly interesting this year, with its spirited, captivating style.

○ Franciacorta Brut Tetellus '97	♟♟	5
○ Franciacorta Brut Santa Giulia	♟♟	5

MONTENISA
FRAZ. CALINO
VIA PAOLO VI, 62
25046 CAZZAGO SAN MARTINO (BS)
TEL. 0307750838

At last, the debut of Montenisa, named for the mountain where Dionysius was born. The new Franciacorta estate owned by Marchesi Antinori is managed by Piero's daughters, Albiera, Allegra and Alessia, who acquired the property from the Maggi family. We liked the fruity Satèn and the fresh, soft Brut.

○	Franciacorta Satèn	▼▼	6
○	Franciacorta Brut	▼	5

CA' DEL VÉNT
LOC. CAMPIANI - VIA STELLA, 2
25060 CELLATICA (BS)
TEL. 0302770411
E-MAIL: info@cadelvent.com

The Cellatica Clavis by Massimo Fasoli and Paolo Clerici is as good as ever, but the Franciacorta has also come on, acquiring finesse on the nose and palate, where it shows solid structure and complex minerality.

●	Cellatica Sup. Clavis '99	▼▼	6
○	Franciacorta Brut	▼▼	5
●	Cellatica Sup. Clavis '98	♈♈	6

LE CANTORIE
VIA CASTELLO DI CASAGLIO, 25
25060 CELLATICA (BS)
TEL. 0302523273
E-MAIL: invigna@inwind.it

Mario Gatta and Emiliano Bontempi have built a new winery that vinifies fruit from the 25 hectares under vine at the Gatta estate. The range of wines is well made and runs from Franciacorta to Cellatica DOC. We picked out the two reds, Balench '00 and Curtefranca '01.

●	Balench '00	▼▼	4*
●	TdF Rosso Curtefranca '01	▼▼	3*
○	Franciacorta Satèn '97	♈♈	5
○	TdF Bianco Febo '99	♈	4

PIETRO NERA
VIA IV NOVEMBRE, 43
23030 CHIURO (SO)
TEL. 0342482631
E-MAIL: info@neravini.com

Nera is a historic Valtellina winery that produces a complete range of well made, high quality wines. The Sforzato '99 is very good, the partial drying of the fruit is perfect, and the overall impression is elegant. The Inferno Efesto '00 is fruity and soft on the palate with a lingering finish.

●	Valtellina Sup. Inferno Efesto '00	▼▼	4
●	Valtellina Sforzato '99	▼▼	6
●	Valtellina Sforzato '97	♈♈	6
●	Valtellina Sup. Signorie Ris. '98	♈♈	5

CA' MONTEBELLO
LOC. MONTEBELLO, 10
27040 CIGOGNOLA (PV)
TEL. 038585182
E-MAIL: info@camontebello.it

Ca' Montebello returns to the Guide. The Moscato '02 has a big flower and fruit nose, then an almost opulent palate. Sorbo '00, a blend of barbera, croatina and cabernet sauvignon, offers leather, liquorice and wild black berry fruit, then a dry palate. The Oltrepò Pavese Rosso Custiò '02 is simple.

●	Il Sorbo '00	▼▼	4
○	OP Moscato '02	▼▼	3*
●	OP Rosso Custiò '02	▼	4

MONTERUCCO
VALLE CIMA, 38
27040 CIGOGNOLA (PV)
TEL. 038585151 - 038585411
E-MAIL: monterucco@monterucco.it

The Bonarda Frizzante Vigna Il Modello '02 from the Valenti brothers and oenologist, Carlo Salviotti, shows clean fruit and flower aromas, then a palate with soft, well-defined fruit. The fresh, fruity Barbera '02 is less interesting. The fruit might have done better without bottle fermentation.

●	OP Bonarda Vivace V. Il Modello '02	▼▼	3*
●	OP Barbera Frizzante '02	▼	3

LORENZO FACCOLI & FIGLI
VIA CAVA, 7
25030 COCCAGLIO (BS)
TEL. 0307722761

Lorenzo Faccoli and his sons Gianmario and Claudio cultivate six and a half hectares of vineyards in Coccaglio, producing a well-made range of Franciacortas and still wines. We liked the Dosage Zero '98 for its remarkable structure, complexity and toast and mineral tones. The other labels are good.

O	Franciacorta Dosage Zero '98	♈♈	6
O	Franciacorta Brut	♈	5
O	Franciacorta Extra Brut	♈♈	5*

MONZIO COMPAGNONI
FRAZ. NIGOLINE
C.DA MONTI DELLA CORTE, 2
25040 CORTE FRANCA (BS)
TEL. 0309884157

Marcello Monzio Compagnoni decided to skip the vintage this year. The construction of a new, modern cellar, the decision to release more mature wines and the search for ever better quality were the reasons. We respect this and have kept his place in the Guide, convinced he made the right choice.

●	Rosso di Luna '00	♈♈	5
O	Franciacorta Extra Brut	♈♈	5
O	Franciacorta Satèn	♈♈	6

CANTINE COLLI A LAGO
LOC. SAN MARTINO DELLA BATTAGLIA
CASCINA CAPUZZA
25010 DESENZANO DEL GARDA (BS)
TEL. 0309910279 - 0309910381

Cantina Colli a Lago belongs to Tenute Formentini. From Capuzza, there are two good Luganas. The current base wine is juicy and flavoursome. The Superiore '01 offers flowers and medicinal herbs. The fresh, fruity Campo del Soglio '01 is a nice version of the small San Martino della Battaglia DOC.

O	Lugana Sup. Selva Capuzza '01	♈	4
O	San Martino della Battaglia		
	Campo del Soglio '01	♈	4
O	Lugana Selva Capuzza '02	♈	4

VISCONTI - PODERE SANT'ONORATA
VIA C. BATTISTI, 139
25015 DESENZANO DEL GARDA (BS)
TEL. 0309120681
E-MAIL: vino@luganavisconti.it

There were good results for all three Visconti Luganas, the Sant'Onorata '02 winning by a neck for its pleasant honey and pear fruit, flowers and vegetal notes. The Vigne Sparse was impressive. It's a red with appreciable complexity, and vivid sensations of very ripe fruit.

●	Benaco Bresciano Rosso		
	Vigne Sparse '98	♈♈	4
O	Lugana Sup. S. Onorata '01	♈	4
O	Lugana Collo Lungo Et. Nera '02	♈	3
O	Lugana S. Onorata '02	♈	4

PRINCIPE BANFI - PODERE PIO IX
VIA PER ISEO, 25
25030 ERBUSCO (BS)
TEL. 0307750387 - 0307750385

Owned by Alfredo Principe and Ines Banfi, this Erbusco estate has nine hectares of well-tended vineyards. The wines tasted this year include a noteworthy Franciacorta Brut which is rich in fruit and vanillaed tones, and a soft, well-balanced Satèn.

O	Franciacorta Brut	♈♈	5
O	Franciacorta Satèn	♈	5
O	Franciacorta Extra Brut '98	♈♈	5

SAN CRISTOFORO
FRAZ. VILLA
VIA VILLANUOVA, 2
25030 ERBUSCO (BS)
TEL. 0307760482

Bruno Dotti and Claudia Cavalieri manage their 12 hectares under vine at Erbusco, making a complete range of territory wines and releasing about 70,000 bottles a year. The delicate, complex Franciacorta Brut is as good as usual and the red DossOriane table wine is well made.

O	Franciacorta Brut	♈♈	5
●	DossOriane	♈	4
O	Franciacorta Brut '00	♈♈	5
●	TdF Rosso '00	♈♈	3*

TALLARINI
VIA FONTANILE, 7/9
24060 GANDOSSO (BG)
TEL. 035834003
E-MAIL: info@tallarini.com

As ever, Vincenzo Tallarini's flagship is the powerful, tannic Valcalepio Rosso San Giovannino Riserva '99, with grass, eucalyptus and jam aromas. Valcalepio Bianco '02 shows flowers and tropical fruit, supported by lively acidity. The Valcalepio Rosso '00 is a bit evolved, but has good flesh.

● Valcalepio Rosso Arlecchino '00	♟	4
○ Valcalepio Bianco Arlecchino '02	♟	4
● Valcalepio Rosso		
San Giovannino Ris. '99	♟	5

CABANON
LOC. CABANON, 1
27052 GODIASCO (PV)
TEL. 0383940912
E-MAIL: info@cabanon.it

It was an indifferent year at the organically farmed Cabanon estate. Several of the best wines were missing. The sauvignon-based Cabanon Blanc '02 was good, clean and simple. The Pinot Grigio '02 was equally varietal, showing fresh tropical fruit. Infernot '97 is too evolved and a little below par.

○ Cabanon Blanc '02	♟	4
○ OP Pinot Grigio '02	♟	4
● OP Rosso Infernot '97	♟	6
● OP Barbera Piccolo Principe '98	♟♟	6

CASTELLO DI GRUMELLO
VIA FOSSE, 11
24064 GRUMELLO DEL MONTE (BG)
TEL. 0354420817 - 035830244
E-MAIL: info@castellodigrumelo.it

The Valcalepio Rosso Colle Calvario '00 is a 60-40 mix of cabernet sauvignon and merlot with 12 months in barrique. It has structure and complexity, but a tad too much oak. The soft, fruity standard wine is simpler. The over-citrusy Valcalepio Bianco '02 suffered from a poor vintage.

● Valcalepio Rosso '00	♟	3
● Valcalepio Rosso		
Colle del Calvario '00	♟	5
○ Valcalepio Bianco '02	♟	3

LE CORNE
LOC. CORNE - VIA SAN PANTALEONE
24064 GRUMELLO DEL MONTE (BG)
TEL. 035830215
E-MAIL: italia@lecorne.it

The best wine from Le Corne is the Valcalepio Rosso Messernero Riserva '99, a vigorous red with intense sweet spice and vanilla. The Valcalepio Bianco Gonzaghesco '02 is floral, and the Cabernet Torcularia '01 is succulently soft, with aromas of morello cherries in liqueur and red fruit jam.

● Cabernet della Bergamasca Torcularia '01	♟	3
○ Valcalepio Bianco Gonzaghesco '02	♟	2
● Valcalepio Rosso Messernero Ris. '99	♟	4
● Valcalepio Rosso Messernero Ris. '98	♟♟	4

AVANZI
LOC. S.S. DESENZANO SALÒ
VIA TREVISAGO, 32
25080 MANERBA DEL GARDA (BS)
TEL. 0365551013 - 03042059

The Avanzi family has a major wine and olive oil estate at the busy Manerba crossroads on the western Garda road. The most interesting wine is the Cabernet Vigna Bragagna, which has a sound, forthright palate with cherry notes. The Pinot Nero also has good texture. The Lugana is simple but pleasant.

● Garda Cabernet Sauvignon		
Vigna Bragagna '99	♟♟	5
● Garda Pinot Nero La Valle '00	♟	4
○ Lugana di Sirmione		
Vigna Bragagna '02	♟	3

STEFANO SPEZIA
VIA MATTEOTTI, 90
46010 MARIANA MANTOVANA (MN)
TEL. 0376735012

Stefano Spezia's IGT sparklers are always enjoyable and excellent value. The Ancellotta '02 has a creamy mousse, aromas of forest floor and good continuity. The zesty, easy-drinking Lambrusco is fruitier, showing blackberries and raspberries.

● Ancellotta Frizzante '02	♟	2*
● Lambrusco '02	♟	2*

GIUSEPPE GUGLIELMINI
VIA DEL NERONE, 9
27010 MIRADOLO TERME (PV)
TEL. 038277183

The very dark ruby San Colombano Vigna Battaia '00 with its wild berry aroma, is frank, open and succulent, with fine-grained tannins and good length. The Pinot Nero in bianco '02 shows fragrant flowers and white peach, then good body. The sparkling Riesling Frizzante '02 is a nice aperitif.

●	San Colombano Vigna Battaia '00	♥	2*
○	Pinot Nero in bianco '02	♥	1*
○	Riesling Frizzante '02		1

CANTINE VALTENESI - LUGANA
VIA PERGOLA, 21
25080 MONIGA DEL GARDA (BS)
TEL. 0365502002
E-MAIL: civielle@gardavino.it

The Cantine della Valtenesi e della Lugana co-operatives vinify fruit from around 80 member growers on the Lombardy shore of Lake Garda. All three Luganas are well made. The minerally, tropical fruit and peach Cios Superiore '00 is the most successful. The Bianco Pergola '02 is also very enjoyable.

○	Lugana Sup. Cios '00	♥♥	4
○	Lugana Sup. Pergola '00	♥	4
○	Lugana Pergola '02	♥	3

CA' DEL GÈ
FRAZ. CA' DEL GÈ, 3
27040 MONTALTO PAVESE (PV)
TEL. 0383870179
E-MAIL: info@cadelge.it

There were ups and downs Enzo Padroggi. Problems plagued many of his samples. However, the fresh, soft Barbera '02 is good, with fragrant wild berries. The slightly sparkling Bonarda Vivace '02 is enjoyable, despite roughish tannins. The already mature Riesling Italico '02 is fairly simple.

●	OP Barbera '02	♥	2*
●	OP Bonarda Vivace '02	♥	2*
○	OP Riesling Italico '02	♥	2*

CA' DEL SANTO
LOC. CAMPOLUNGO, 4
27040 MONTALTO PAVESE (PV)
TEL. 0383870545 - 038551026

The Bonarda Vivace Riva Zingari '02 by Laura Bozzi is typical and clean, with violets and wild berry fruit. The generous palate keeps the tannins in check and the price is very affordable. The Pinot Nero Il Nero '01 has varietal aromas of cassis and an approachable palate, but not much length.

●	OP Bonarda Riva Zingari '02	♥♥	3*
●	Pinot Nero Il Nero '01	♥	4
●	Pinot Nero '98	♥♥	3*

TENIMENTI CASTELROTTO - TORTI
FRAZ. CASTELROTTO, 6
27047 MONTECALVO VERSIGGIA (PV)
TEL. 0385951000 - 0385951001
E-MAIL: patrizia@tortino.it

The Bonarda Vivace '02 is fragrant, elegant and almost chewy in the mouth, with exuberant fruit. It's one of the best of its type. The Barbera Selezione Dino Torti '99 is also elegant after barrique ageing. The Pinot Nero Selezione Dino Torti '99 has good structure but excessive wood.

●	OP Bonarda Vivace '02	♥♥	4
●	OP Barbera Sel. Dino Torti '99	♥	6
●	OP Pinot Nero Sel. Dino Torti '99	♥	5

PIETRO TORTI
FRAZ. CASTELROTTO, 9
27047 MONTECALVO VERSIGGIA (PV)
TEL. 038599763 - 038599344
E-MAIL: info@pietrotorti.it

Alessandro Torti's Barbera Campo Rivera '00 is remarkable. Aged for 12 months in Allier oak barriques, it has big aromas of small berry fruit, structure, acidity and finesse. The oak-aged Pinot Nero '00 is also agreeable. The Bonarda '02 has a nice fruity profile, though the tannins could be softer.

●	OP Barbera Campo Rivera '00	♥♥	4
●	OP Pinot Nero '00	♥♥	5
●	OP Bonarda '02	♥	3

RICCHI
VIA FESTONI, 13/D
46040 MONZAMBANO (MN)
TEL. 0376800238
E-MAIL: info@cantinaricchi.it

Aged in oak casks, the Chardonnay Garda Meridiano '02 shows a deep straw yellow, intense banana and honey aromas, and good structure supported by marked acidity. Now the tannins have softened, we can confirm the quality of the full, spicy Garda Merlot Carpino '00.

○	Garda Chardonnay Meridiano '02	♙♙	4
●	Garda Merlot Carpino '00	♙	5

LA GUARDA
FRAZ. CASTREZZONE
VIA ZANARDELLI, 49
25080 MUSCOLINE (BS)
TEL. 0365372948

The Negri family vineyards are in the Muscoline hills, inland from Lake Garda. The Garda Barbera '99 shows fruit lifted by spice and fruit in liqueur, with a nice, subtly bitter finish. The vibrant, spirited Marzemino '99 shows upfront drinkability. The Rosso Superiore '00 has wild berry fruit.

●	Garda Barbera '99	♙♙	4
●	Garda Cl. Rosso Sup. '00	♙	4
●	Garda Marzemino '99	♙	4

LE MARCHESINE
VIA VALLOSA, 31
25050 PASSIRANO (BS)
TEL. 030657005
E-MAIL: info@lemarchesine.com

Only problems of space stop us from giving greater mention to Giovanni and Loris Biatta's winery. The quality of their cuvées is constantly growing and again this year, they have proved themselves fine interpreters of the territory's typicity. French winemaker J. P. Valade consults.

○	Franciacorta Brut '97	♙♙	6
○	Franciacorta Satèn	♙♙	6
○	Franciacorta Brut '95	♙♙	6

LA CASCINA NUOVA
VIA CASCINA NUOVA, 10
25020 PONCARALE (BS)
TEL. 0302540058
E-MAIL: lacascinanuova@virgilio.it

Ambitiously, Franco Poli continues to aim for long-lived wines. But fortune favours the bold. The Capriano Riserva Tenuta Anna '98 is very good. Fragrant notes of blueberry, liquorice and vanilla mingle elegantly, supported by a structure with few equals in the zone.

●	Capriano del Colle Rosso Tenuta Anna Ris. '98	♙♙	4
●	Capriano del Colle Rosso Tenuta Anna Ris. '99	♙	4

CANTINA SOCIALE VAL SAN MARTINO
VIA BERGAMO, 1195
24030 PONTIDA (BG)
TEL. 035795035
E-MAIL: csbpontida@libero.it

The Cantina Sociale Val San Martino co-operative produces a garnet Valcalepio Rosso Riserva '99 with sweet spices, tobacco and hay, then a big, elegant, palate. The nice Valcalepio Bianco '02 shows green apples and the cherry-hued, rosé-fermented Schiava '02 has floral aromas and a decent palate.

●	Valcalepio Rosso Ris. '99	♙♙	4
⊙	Schiava della Bergamasca '02	♙	2*
○	Valcalepio Bianco '02	♙	3

MARANGONA
ANTICA CORTE IALIDY
25010 POZZOLENGO (BS)
TEL. 030919379
E-MAIL: info@marangona.com

You can enjoy Marangona wines in the old farmhouse that belonged to the Gialdi family ("Ialidy" can still be read over the entryway). The range combines satisfaction with easy drinkability. An enjoyable Garda Classico Rosso '01 stands out, alongside the two 2002 Luganas.

●	Garda Cl. Rosso Sup. Antica Corte Ialidy '01	♙	4
○	Lugana Antica Corte Ialidy '02	♙	4
○	Lugana Vecia Musolina '02	♙	3

TENUTA ROVEGLIA
LOC. ROVEGLIA, 1
25010 POZZOLENGO (BS)
TEL. 030918663
E-MAIL: info@tenutaroveglia.it

There are two reds and two whites from the Zweifel-Azzone family. The Cabernets have complexity on the nose, then a palate of ripe red fruit. The Luganas are both agreeable. The 2002 stands out for its peach and apricot nose with vegetal notes and the Superiore integrates fruit with minerality.

● Garda Cabernet Sauvignon '00	♀	4
● Garda Cabernet Sauvignon		
Ca' d'Oro '00	♀	5
○ Lugana Sup. Vigna di Catullo '01	♀	4
○ Lugana '02	♀	3

COMINCIOLI
LOC. PUEGNAGO DEL GARDA
VIA ROMA, 10
25080 PUEGNAGO SUL GARDA (BS)
TEL. 0365651141

Gianfranco Comincioli likes to swim against the tide, and rarely submits wines. He inherited his passion for part-drying groppello grapes from his father, Giovanni Battista, and his bottles age beautifully. An example is Sulèr '00, which has intense super-ripe red berry fruit, pepper and minerality.

● Riviera del Garda Bresciano Sulèr '00	♀♀	7
● Riviera del Garda Bresciano Gropèl '00	♀	5
● Riviera del Garda Bresciano		
Pedemut '00	♀	4

DELAI
VIA MORO, 1
25080 PUEGNAGO SUL GARDA (BS)
TEL. 0365555527

Fronsaga is the best of Sergio Delai's wines (why so many labels?) for its complex, fruit nose, laced with spice and coffee. The palate has ripe red berry fruits. Raspberry and strawberry are the Garda Bresciano Rosso's keynotes. The Groppello, bitterish in the finish, and Sovenigo are both simpler.

● Fronsaga '00	♀♀	5
● Garda Bresciano Groppello '01	♀	4
● Garda Bresciano Rosso '01	♀	4
● Sovenigo '01	♀	4

MONTEACUTO
FRAZ. MONTEACUTO
VIA DOSSO, 4
25080 PUEGNAGO SUL GARDA (BS)
TEL. 0365651291

Though a bit less bright than in previous editions, the Simut '00 is still a very interesting red. From groppello and marzemino, it expands into sensations of morello cherry and jam. More ageing can only improve it, smoothing out the still green tannins. The fresh, vigorous Groppello '01 is good.

● Simut '00	♀	5
● Garda Bresciano Groppello '01	♀	4

PASINI PRODUTTORI
FRAZ. RAFFA - VIA VIDELLE, 2
25080 PUEGNAGO SUL GARDA (BS)
TEL. 0365651419
E-MAIL: info@pasiniproduttori.com

The Vigneto Arzane Groppello '00 displays lavish sweet spices and fruit, then a juicy, agile palate that shows varietal sensations of strawberry and raspberry with cinnamon. The red San Gioan '98 is also good. An earthy, vegetal nose is followed by fruit in liqueur and cocoa powder in the mouth.

● Garda Cl. Groppello		
Vign. Arzane Ris. '00	♀♀	5
● San Gioan I Carati '98	♀	5
○ Brut Cl. Ceppo 326	♀	4

CANTINA SOCIALE
COOPERATIVA DI QUISTELLO
VIA ROMA, 46
46026 QUISTELLO (MN)
TEL. 0376618118

The Cantina Cooperativa di Quistello makes good-value sparklers from organically farmed vineyards. The Gran Rosso del Vicariato '02 has big raspberry aromas and the Lambrusco Mantovano Rossissimo '02 more earthy, gamey tones. The decent Granbianco di Quistello '02 is from chardonnay grapes.

● Gran Rosso del Vicariato '02	♀	1*
● Lambrusco Mantovano		
Rossissimo '02	♀	1*
○ Granbianco di Quistello '02		1

CARLO CONTE GIORGI DI VISTARINO
VILLA FORNACE, 11
27040 ROCCA DE' GIORGI (PV)
TEL. 0385241171
E-MAIL: info@giorgidivistarino.it

There were two very good wines from this winery, founded in 1674, although the Two Glass rating eluded them. The Chardonnay Elaisa '01 has an uncertain bouquet, but the palate recovers with good continuity, The Pinot Nero Pernice '00, barrique-aged like the Chardonnay, has good weight in the mouth.

● OP Pinot Nero Pernice '00	♥	4
○ OP Chardonnay Elaisa '01	♥	4
● OP Pinot Nero Pernice '99	♥♥	5
○ OP Chardonnay Elaisa '99	♥	5

CASTELLO DI LUZZANO
LOC. LUZZANO, 5
27040 ROVESCALA (PV)
TEL. 0523863277
E-MAIL: info@castelloluzzano.it

Eighty hectares under vine on the border of the Oltrepò Pavese and Colli Piacentini make up Castello di Luzzano. Maria Giulia and Giovannella Fugazza, with oenologist, Beppe Caviola, produce a great Oltrepò Pavese Rosso Riserva. The '98 shows vigorous fruit with super-ripe tones and sweet spice.

● OP Rosso Luzzano 270 Ris. '98	♥♥	5
● OP Rosso Luzzano 270 Ris. '97	♥♥	5

ENRICO RICCARDI
VIA CAPRA, 17
20078 SAN COLOMBANO AL LAMBRO (MI)
TEL. 0371897381 - 0371200523
E-MAIL: info@viniriccardi.com

The Passito, fragrant with honey, rose and exotic fruit, has good length. From the local verdea grape, it part-dries on rush mats. The juicy, fairly soft San Colombano Roverone '02 has wild berry fruit. The Bianco del Santo '02 is clean and well made, with aromas of flowers and tropical fruit.

○ Colline del Milanese Passito di Verdea '99	♥♥	4
○ Bianco del Santo '02	♥	2*
● San Colombano Roverone '02	♥	2*

VANZINI
FRAZ. BARBALEONE, 7
27040 SAN DAMIANO AL COLLE (PV)
TEL. 038575019
E-MAIL: info@vanzini-wine.com.it

The Vanzinis' Bonarda Frizzante '02 is fragrant, full and aromatic. The Barbera Vigna Preda '98 is also fairly good. It's still fresh and lively, with nice fruity pulp. The barrique-aged Pinot Nero '01 is clean and well made, and the other wines presented also point to even better things to come.

● OP Bonarda Frizzante '02	♥♥	3*
● OP Barbera Vigna Preda '98	♥♥	5
● OP Pinot Nero '01	♥	5

LE CHIUSURE
FRAZ. PORTESE - VIA BOSCHETTE, 2
25010 SAN FELICE DEL BENACO (BS)
TEL. 0365626243
E-MAIL: info@lechiusure.net

Alessandro Luzzago's winery is now almost the only one left in the municipality. There are two valid products. The better one is Mal Borghetto '00, a warm, mouthfilling wine, with still evolving tannins. The Campei '00 is simpler. Though a tad immature and acidulous, it is well put together.

● Campei '00	♥	4
● Mal Borghetto '00	♥	5
● Garda Cl. Groppello '01		4

BAGNASCO
VIA ROMA, 57
27047 SANTA MARIA DELLA VERSA (PV)
TEL. 0385278019 - 0385798033
E-MAIL: cantinabagnasco@virgilio.it

Paolo Bagnasco's output of 110,000 bottles maintains good quality standards. The Bonarda Frizzante Vigna Matta '02 is forthright and typical, albeit a bit closed. Buttafuoco Frizzante '02 is fruity, simple and pleasing. The '02 Pinot Grigio is also decent, with golden delicious apples to the fore.

● OP Bonarda Vigna Matta '02	♥	4
● OP Buttafuoco Frizzante '02	♥	4
○ OP Pinot Grigio '02	♥	4

LA ROCCHETTA
VIA CERRO, 35
24067 SARNICO (BG)
TEL. 035911937

The Buelli family's winery makes a Valcalepio Rosso, a Valcalepio Bianco and a "metodo classico" Brut. The Rosso has red berry fruit and decent structure. The white is citrusy and clean, if a bit immature. The nice "spumante" is half chardonnay and half pinot bianco, left for 24 months on the lees.

● Valcalepio Rosso '01	♟	3
○ Valcalepio Bianco '02		3
○ La Rocchetta Cl. Brut		4

BONALDI - CASCINA DEL BOSCO
VIA GASPAROTTO, 96
24010 SORISOLE (BG)
TEL. 035571701 - 0354532711
E-MAIL: cascinadelbosco@bonaldi.it

Cantoalto '01, from 80-20 pinot bianco and chardonnay, has vanilla, banana and roast hazelnuts, and good length. There's too much oak, but it should improve with age. The Valcalepio Bianco '02 is fresh, with vegetal tones on the nose. The Valcalepio Rosso '01 is very grassy and less well-mannered.

○ Cantoalto Bianco '01	♟	5
○ Valcalepio Bianco '02	♟	4
● Valcalepio Rosso '01		4

F.LLI BETTINI
LOC. SAN GIACOMO
VIA NAZIONALE, 4/A
23036 TEGLIO (SO)
TEL. 0342786068 - 0342786096

The Sforzato '01 submitted by the Bettinis is well made and as good as ever. Its deep, balsamic aromas lead to a complex, softly persistent palate. The Inferno Prodigio '99 has refined aromas with fruit-forward notes, roundness and good body.

● Valtellina Sup. Sfursat '01	♟♟	7
● Valtellina Sup. Inferno Prodigio '99	♟♟	5

CAVEN CAMUNA
VIA CAVEN, 1
23036 TEGLIO (SO)
TEL. 0342482631

Managed by Pietro Nera, Caven Camuna is on its way to fame in Valtellina. Again this year, we noted a good Nebbiolo Giupa '00 with toasty notes on the nose, a round palate and lovely fine-grained tannins. The complex Inferno Al Carmine '00 has aromas of leather, good structure and a soft palate.

● Valtellina Sup. Giupa '00	♟♟	5
● Valtellina Sup. Inferno Al Carmine '00	♟♟	5
● Valtellina Sup. Giupa '99	♟♟	5

PLOZZA
VIA SAN GIACOMO, 22
23037 TIRANO (SO)
TEL. 0342701297
E-MAIL: info@plozza.ch

The Plozzas are investing in the vineyards as well as the cellar. The results are obvious and the wines impress. We liked the Sforzato '98 for its spicy aromas, dense palate and sweet nuances. The Grumello Riserva '98 is good, showing complexity on the leather-shaded nose and remarkable structure

● Valtellina Sup. Ris. Grumello '98	♟♟	5
● Valtellina Sfurzat Vin da Ca' '97	♟♟	7
● Valtellina Sup. La Scala Ris. '97	♟♟	6

TENUTA IL BOSCO
LOC. IL BOSCO
27049 ZENEVREDO (PV)
TEL. 0385245326
E-MAIL: info@ilbosco.com

The Zonin family's standard-bearers are still ageing in the cellar. The Bonarda Frizzante '02 is clean and fragrant. The Malvasia Frizzante '02 shows spring flowers, and good structure, although it is excessively mature. Only a mention for the nice Phileo, refermented using the long Charmat method.

● OP Bonarda Vivace '02	♟	4
○ OP Malvasia Frizzante '02	♟	4
○ OP Pinot Nero Brut Cl. Phileo		4

TRENTINO

Trentino wine is taking time out for reflection. Quality in general is growing, wineries are enjoying both commercial and critical success, their fame and image are growing steadily but they don't really light any fires. Almost all the wines presented at our tastings this year were technically flawless, confirming the maturity, in terms of style as well as winemaking, acquired by producers in Trentino, whether small growers or large co-operatives. They have a certain "dolomitic" charm, they express a terroir and they evolve well in the bottle. But there's still a gap from here to the top, and only three of our Three Glass prizes were awarded to the region's wineries. It's a pity, because never have there been as many outstanding wines as there were this year at our tastings. The "usual suspects" were present, together with a number of newcomers. Guerrieri Gonzaga, Foradori and Ferrari confirmed their established international status, a statement we make without fear of contradiction. As well as these greats, the agricultural college at San Michele all'Adige is experiencing something of a renaissance, driven by a prestigious tradition. The army of estate wineries marches on, Pojer & Sandri, Cesconi, Maso Furli and Pravis, as do the co-operatives, which are becoming increasingly skilled and expanding both their facilities and quality potential. One example is La Vis, which after the merger with the Cantina Sociale della Valle di Cembra became the third largest producer in Trentino. Again on the subject of co-operatives, Cavit has created a new showcase line and presented wines from the new "SuperDOC", Trentino Superiore. These are the Maso-label wines, a few thousand excellent-quality bottles, sold at very reasonable prices. There is a running debate in Trentino on registered designations of origin, or DOC zones, and smaller winemakers tend to use the IGT Dolomiti typical geographical indication on their labels. For them, it is a mark of distinction that differentiates them from co-operative wineries. The Trento chamber of commerce has undertaken a vast project to promote regional wine with excellent results. Trentino wine is getting better known and more widely appreciated. Success at competitions and comparative tastings has eluded them, but not by much. To take the wine into Italy's front rank, vineyard management has to be reviewed for yields are still too high, the quality of the fruit harvested must be respected, and shortcuts shunned, and the best subzones need to be promoted. In other words, Trentino must make wines with more personality. The basic premises for this last, crucial, advance in quality are in place, and have existed for some time.

AVIO (TN)

AVIO (TN)

CANTINA SOCIALE DI AVIO
VIA DANTE, 14
38063 AVIO (TN)
TEL. 0464684008
E-MAIL: cantinasocialediavio.can@tin.it

TENUTA SAN LEONARDO
LOC. SAN LEONARDO, 3
FRAZ. BORGHETTO ALL'ADIGE
38060 AVIO (TN)
TEL. 0464689004
E-MAIL: info@sanleonardo.it

Avio has always been famous for its vineyards. Documentary proof can be found in the archives of the noble families who took turns to occupy the picturesque castle overlooking the original settlement. This castle has now become the home of the Fondo Ambiente Italiano, the Italian Environmental Fund, where territory and viticulture come together. Wine from the local co-operative, Viticoltori Avio, can be a cultural ambassador for the area, and there is more. Various different grape varieties have been planted along the steep slopes of the castle, including casetta, molinara, enantio and many clones of marzemino from Trentino, Veneto and even Zante, the Greek island that may be the grape's original home. The project supports the territorial marketing launched begun by the co-operative, whose 180 grower members and over 600 hectares under vine are in Campi Sarni and Terra dei Forti. Many people think the terroir is a winner, and results so far are promising. All six wines submitted showed good character and improving quality levels. They are also great value for money. At the top of the cellar's list is Trentino Rosso, a classic Bordeaux blend. Soft and powerful, its vivid hue precedes well-developed tannins, good balance and attractive length. The Pinot Nero behaves well and the Marzemino has great staying power. Best of the whites is the Pinot Bianco. Fragrant notes of country herbs, apple and hazelnut lead into a dense textured and firm, elegant palate.

Wine culture is very much alive here, with roots that go back a thousand years. But the Guerrieri Gonzagas not only conserve: they strive enthusiastically for new goals. Credit for this goes to Marchese Carlo, an indefatigable promoter of good wine and chair of the Casa del Vino della Vallagarina, and to the values of the territory where his family has operated for centuries. Carlo has passed on his commitment to his son, Anselmo, who has been working on the estate for a few harvests now. Anselmo is backed by a top-quality technical staff, including Luigino Tinelli, an admirable estate manager and cellarman, and internationally famous oenologist, Carlo Ferrini, a constant presence for the past couple of years at the Campi Sarni vineyards around the beautiful cellar. The 2000 vintage sees the re-appearance of Villa Gresti, a red from mainly merlot grapes, presented alongside the much-lauded San Leonardo. The cellar releases only three wines, but what wines they are! Villa Gresti '00 has power and class, qualities that will sustain it for many years. Equally impressive is the San Leonardo '00, which confirms its position as one of Trentino's, and indeed Italy's, leading wines. Already splendidly rich in fruit on the nose, it goes on to tempt with perfectly ripe fruit, extraordinary intensity and absolute pleasure on the palate. It, too, will improve over time. That same San Leonardo style is also evident in the Merlot '00, a balanced, soft and very well-structured wine that manages to remain very approachable.

● Trentino Rosso Ris. '00	🍷🍷	5
● Trentino Pinot Nero '00	🍷	4
● Trentino Marzemino '02	🍷	3*
○ Trentino Pinot Bianco '02	🍷	3*
● Trentino Marzemino '00	🍷🍷	3
● Trentino Rosso Ris. '97	🍷🍷	4
● Trentino Rosso Ris. '98	🍷🍷	4
● Trentino Rosso Ris. '99	🍷🍷	4
○ Trentino Vendemmia Tardiva '99	🍷🍷	4
● Enantio '00	🍷	3

● San Leonardo '00	🍷🍷🍷	8
● Villa Gresti '00	🍷🍷	8
● Trentino Merlot '00	🍷🍷	5
● San Leonardo '88	🍷🍷🍷	5
● San Leonardo '90	🍷🍷🍷	5
● San Leonardo '93	🍷🍷🍷	5
● San Leonardo '94	🍷🍷🍷	5
● San Leonardo '95	🍷🍷🍷	5
● San Leonardo '96	🍷🍷🍷	5
● San Leonardo '97	🍷🍷🍷	5
● San Leonardo '99	🍷🍷🍷	8
● Trentino Merlot '99	🍷🍷	4

AVIO (TN)

VALLAROM

FRAZ. VO' SINISTRO
VIA MASI, 21
38063 AVIO (TN)
TEL. 0464684297
E-MAIL: vallarom@libero.it

Barbara and Filippo Scienza have a difficult surname to live up to, but are nonetheless proud to have as their uncle, Professor Attilio Scienza, one of the leading names in oenological research in Italy and internationally, as well as one of the founders of this winery. Now Barbara and Filippo are continuing that task. The wines tasted this year confirm they are working on the right lines, although this has been a year of transition for them. Some wines are still ageing in the cellar (the Cabernet and the red blend sourced from the Campi Sarni vineyard), while others are only now beginning to open up after a few years in bottle. This is the case with the Chardonnay Vigna di Brioni '01. A lovely, deep gold introduces a wine as intense and challenging on the nose as it is impressive in its development on the palate. The Pinot Nero is another serious wine on which meticulous care was lavished. Like the Syrah, it needs cellar time before it fully expresses its elegant, complex personality. The convincing, immediately attractive Vadum Caesaris '02 is a blend of pinot bianco, chardonnay, riesling and sauvignon that reflects the transition we mentioned above. It has class and power, but has yet to find its feet stylistically. Finally, the very pleasant Marzemino '02 shows structure and personality, and will evolve positively in bottle for several years.

○	Chardonnay Vigna Brioni '01	🍷🍷	5
●	Syrah '01	🍷🍷	6
○	Vadum Caesaris '02	🍷🍷	4
●	Pinot Nero '01	🍷	5
●	Marzemino '02	🍷	4
○	Vadum Caesaris '01	YY	3
●	Syrah '00	YY	6
○	Trentino Chardonnay Vigna Brioni '00	YY	5
●	Campi Sarni Rosso '99	YY	4
●	Syrah '99	YY	4
○	Trentino Chardonnay Vigna Brioni '99	YY	4
●	Trentino Pinot Nero '99	YY	4

CALAVINO (TN)

CANTINA TOBLINO

FRAZ. SARCHE
VIA PONTE OLIVETI, 1
38070 CALAVINO (TN)
TEL. 0461564168
E-MAIL: toblino@tin.it

The wines from this co-operative winery are acquiring fullness and typicity. For years, it has worked quietly, implementing the production strategies of its parent company, Cavit, which makes several top selections here opposite the picturesque Castel Toblino, on the lake of the same name. In return, Cantina Toblino rightly insists on safeguarding and promoting Vino Santo Trentino, the highly distinctive local "vino da meditazione" sipping wine. Even the '95 vintage has a refined elegance. Cantina Toblino submitted a large number of labels, some from the first vinification of grapes selected from a 40-hectare estate that was acquired specifically to improve the quality and reputation of the range. Among the whites, there were excellent tasting results for the Traminer Aromatico, which is clean, fragrant and appropriately alcoholic, with good length. We felt the Sauvignon, too, was good. It's another thoroughbred that shows varietal but not too vegetal, with mineral and citrus notes. The other whites are well made and intended for immediate consumption. But the Nosiola is highly evocative of the Valle dei Laghi, and this winery, along with the others in the zone, intends to concentrate on it. The firm-textured Chardonnay has an international style, good backbone and fruity tones on the nose. The Cabernet and Merlot may be less exciting, but like all the other labels, they are offered at very attractive prices.

○	Trentino Nosiola '02	🍷🍷	3*
○	Trentino Traminer Aromatico '02	🍷🍷	3*
○	Trentino Vino Santo '95	🍷🍷	6
●	Trentino Cabernet '01	🍷	3*
●	Trentino Merlot '01	🍷	3*
○	Trentino Chardonnay '02	🍷	3*
○	Trentino Sauvignon '02	🍷	3*
●	Trentino Rebo '01	YY	3*
○	Trentino Vino Santo '94	YY	7
●	Trentino Lagrein Scuro '01	Y	3
○	Trentino Nosiola '01	Y	3
○	Trentino Pinot Grigio '01	Y	3
●	Trentino Pinot Nero '01	Y	3

CALLIANO (TN)

VALLIS AGRI
VIA VALENTINI, 37
38060 CALLIANO (TN)
TEL. 0464834113
E-MAIL: vallisagri@sav.it

SAV, the Società Agricoltori Vallagarina, has started to renew radically its enormous vineyard holdings. Every plot belonging to each of its 750 member-growers has been studied and analysed in compliance with modern agronomic principles, to obtain a complete zoning overview, and select the most suitable grapes to be grown in each vineyard. This co-operative also manages a cheesemaking dairy and numerous other agricultural operations, selling its wine under the Vallis Agri label. Mauro Baldessari, expert oenologist and a man who knows Vallagarina grape growing and winemaking well, looks after the cellar. The most convincing wine submitted to our tasting was the round, soft and very well-developed Cabernet Sauvignon '99. The Aura is delicious and even graceful. It's an unoaked blend of chardonnay and sauvignon that shows big and full, with a layered structure, after a rigorous selection process that began in the vineyard. The very drinkable Pinot Grigio Vigna Reselé '02 has a slight copper tinge, fresh acidity, nice fruit and good length. In contrast, the Marzemino Vigna Fornàs '02, one of Vallagarina's emblematic wines, pays the price of an unexciting vintage. There were mixed results for the Merlot '00, which we tasted more than once, because of a curious note of liquorice with a balsamic aftertaste that detracts from its elegance. It should be better with the next vintage.

CAVEDINE (TN)

GINO PEDROTTI
FRAZ. LAGO DI CAVEDINE
VIA CAVEDINE, 7
38073 CAVEDINE (TN)
TEL. 0461564123
E-MAIL: azagrpedrotti@inwind.it

In addition to attracting tourists to this still little-known corner of Trentino, they have Lake Cavedine lapping at their vineyards and keeping the local climate temperate. "They" are Gino Pedrotti, his wife Rosanna and their children Tullia, Clara and oenologist Giuseppe, who make wine in the traditional style and welcome vacationing gourmets to their simple family "osteria" eatery. Despite their meagre production, the Pedrottis have carved out an important niche in the rich oenological panorama of Trentino. The Vino Santo is responsible for this, as it continues to be a benchmark for other winemakers. It is obtained from nosiola grapes harvested in the vineyards over the lake where the variety has solid roots, and left to part-dry until Easter week. Very sweet and dense, though anything but cloying, it is as well mannered as it is elegant, offering caressing hints of honey. The Pedrottis of course produce other traditional wines, making just a few thousand bottles that represent exceptional value for money. The Schiava is delightfully approachable. Vinified the old-fashioned way, it is very dark wine and shows impressive structure. The Nosiola is just as good. Subtly bitterish and flavoursome, if undemanding, it reveals toast and a touch of the hazelnut that gives it its name ("nosiola" is the local variant of "nocciola", the Italian for "hazelnut"). The green-flecked, fragrant Chardonnay is par for the course, just like the Cabernet, which is concentrated enough to age for a few more years.

○ Trentino Bianco Aura '02	♟♟	4
○ Trentino Pinot Grigio		
Vigna Reselé '02	♟♟	4
● Trentino Cabernet Sauvignon '99	♟♟	4
● Trentino Merlot '00	♟	4
● Trentino Marzemino		
Vigna Fornas '02	♟	4
● Trentino Marzemino		
Vigna Fornas '01	♟♟	4
● Trentino Merlot Borgo Sacco '99	♟♟	5
● Trentino Cabernet Sauvignon '98	♟	5

○ Trentino Vino Santo '91	♟♟	7
○ Chardonnay '02	♟	3
○ Nosiola '02	♟	3
● Schiava Nera '02	♟	3
○ Trentino Vino Santo '89	♟♟	5
○ Trentino Vino Santo '90	♟♟	7
● Merlot '00	♟	3
○ Chardonnay '01	♟	3
○ Nosiola '01	♟	3

CIVEZZANO (TN)

MASO CANTANGHEL
LOC. FORTE
VIA MADONNINA, 33
38045 CIVEZZANO (TN)
TEL. 0461859050
E-MAIL: maso.cantanghel@hotmail.com

Winemaker Piero Zabini has always loved contrasts: soft wines from harsh landscapes; living vines on rock-hard soil; or his soberly elegant cellar, which is in stark contrast to the massive structure that houses it. The Maso Cantanghel headquarters is in fact an Austro-Hungarian fortress with walls more than two metres thick. Built in the First World War, it is now a place where excellent wines are aged and enjoyed. Here, Piero faces a real challenge. He has planted his vines on tableland set between the fort and ancient red marble quarries, on unfertile terrain reclaimed from the mountain. Only quality grapes are grown, further selected at the cellar with the skill and stubbornness of a craft winemaker. The most exciting wine tasted this year was the Cabernet Sauvignon '00, a red with great complexity on nose and palate. Elegant, with sweet tannins, it is already mature and will be even better in a few years' time. Pinot Nero is another of Zabini's challenges. He loves this wine more than most and for all the trouble it gives him, it can also provide him with more gratification than any other, in the right growing year. Its finesse, power, elegance and structure make it one of the few Pinot Neros in Trentino to scale the heights of quality. Next is the Sotsàs '02, named after the marble quarry workers. A mix of sauvignon, chardonnay and incrocio Manzoni, it shows rich, complex and full-flavoured, and will develop well. The Merlot is a little bit simpler and the Tajapreda '02, another quarry-related name, should be enjoyed just as it comes.

FAEDO (TN)

GRAZIANO FONTANA
VIA CASE SPARSE, 9
38010 FAEDO (TN)
TEL. 0461650400

Faedo is a tiny hill town between the flatlands of Campo Rotaliano and the looming cliffs that lead into Valle di Cembra. The village has always been linked to viticulture and is distinguished from other towns by the church, which has two different bell towers, spires pointing heavenward that also mark the different lifestyle of the village's residents. Perhaps Graziano Fontana has chosen the two bell towers of Faedo as his winery's logo for that reason. A genuine winemaker, Graziano has always tried to stand out while at the same time affirming his solid links with local tradition. His wines are simple yet serious. They are driven by the uniqueness of Faedo's territory, and varietal wines, each being made from a single grape. Now on to the 2002 whites, the first to win unanimous approval. The clean, almost minerally Müller Thurgau, the spicy Traminer Aromatico, which is zesty, elegant and free of heaviness, were good, as were the caressing, exquisitely concentrated Chardonnay and a Sauvignon with just the right vegetal note to allow it to stand comparison with wines from Friuli or Alto Adige. Graziano Fontana is an expert "white man", but he can also make reds. He has concentrated all his energies and experience on the Lagrein, and from his hillside plots makes a full, harmonious, fruity version that is silky smooth. Almost as elegant as his Pinot Nero '01, an always satisfying wine. Quality is guaranteed by Faedo, and the skill of growers like Graziano who cultivate grapes as a life choice, not just to make wine.

● Trentino Cabernet Sauvignon Rosso di Pila '00	▼▼	6
● Trentino Pinot Nero Zabini '01	▼▼	6
○ Sotsàs '02	▼▼	5
● Trentino Merlot Tajapreda '02	▼	4
● Trentino Pinot Nero Zabini '00	▽▽	6
○ Trentino Chardonnay Vigna Piccola '01	▽▽	5
● Trentino Cabernet Sauvignon Rosso di Pila '97	▽▽	5
● Trentino Merlot Tajapreda '97	▽▽	3
● Trentino Pinot Nero Zabini '98	▽▽	5
● Trentino Cabernet Sauvignon Rosso di Pila '99	▽▽	6

○ Trentino Traminer di Faedo '01	▼▼	4
○ Trentino Müller Thurgau di Faedo '02	▼▼	4
● Trentino Lagrein di Faedo '01	▼	5
● Trentino Pinot Nero di Faedo '01	▼	4
○ Trentino Chardonnay di Faedo '02	▼	4
○ Trentino Sauvignon di Faedo '02	▼	4
● Trentino Lagrein di Faedo '00	▽▽	4
○ Trentino Müller Thurgau di Faedo '00	▽▽	3*
● Trentino Pinot Nero di Faedo '00	▽▽	4

FAEDO (TN)

ISERA (TN)

POJER & SANDRI
LOC. MOLINI, 4/6
38010 FAEDO (TN)
TEL. 0461650342
E-MAIL: info@pojeresandri.it

DE TARCZAL
FRAZ. MARANO
VIA G. B. MIORI, 4
38060 ISERA (TN)
TEL. 0464409134
E-MAIL: info@detarczal.com

It was a remarkable performance, in every sense of the word, by this cellar. Mario Pojer and Fiorentino Sandri's wines are in a class by themselves, right at the top of Trentino winemaking. They are "dolomitic" both in name – the cellar uses the Dolomiti IGT label to distinguish the products from Trentino DOC wines – and in the nature of the terroir they interpret. All the wines easily won Two Glasses, and three even made it to our final taste-offs, although they missed out on the top prize. That was the case with Besler Biank, a successful blend of pinot bianco, riesling, kerner and incrocio Manzoni. This full, zesty wine is different from the usual fruity products, expressing complex, mineral tones that recall wines from the country tradition. It is sourced from the very steep banks of the river Avisio in Valle di Cembra, where for some years now Mario and Fiorentino have been experimenting with numerous varieties that are on the verge of extinction. Next, the Faye '01 is another wine in a class by itself. Though this Bordeaux blend, with a touch of lagrein, is more convincing on the nose than the palate, it is as elegant as they come. But there's more. Even the Essenzia, a classic late-harvest wine from a complex blend dominated by chardonnay and kerner, shows a splendid balance of sugar and acidity, as well as concentrated sensations of ripe tropical fruit and spices. The Nosiola, Traminer and Sauvignon are all from 2002 and all good, and the same goes for the two Pinot Neros, the Selezione '01 and the '02.

The de Tarczals have been in the wine business for more than three centuries, and always in the same zone. Their home is the slopes at Isera, where Vallagarina opens up to the River Adige and the terrain is perfect for vines. The wines of Ruggero de Tarczal reconcile tradition and innovation, thanks to constant evaluation and ongoing viticultural experimentation that have taken Ruggero as far as Chile, more for a grape-related "cultural exchange" than for commercial reasons. And he does all this without neglecting Isera, Marzemino or his historic winery. The reds were very well received again this year. Three in particular attracted plaudits, in this order, the Cabernet Sauvignon, Merlot and Husar selection of Marzemino. Each has its own characteristics. The Cabernet is pervasive and full bodied, the Merlot is gracefully elegant and the Husar is immediately attractive, in spite of the picture on the label of a sabre-wielding hussar. Though completely in line with tradition, the Marzemino '02 is less convincing. It's still closed on the nose, with floral notes and faintly milky notes, but drinks easily. The other wines, all whites, effortlessly reach the One Glass mark. The best for us was the Pinot Bianco, which is as usual very deep in colour, fragrant and clean on the nose and dry, with decent length on the easy-drinking palate. The Moscato Giallo is different. It's a pleasant, immediate wine that Ruggero, and perhaps the rest of Trentino, should invest in and recover.

○ Besler Biank '01	⟁⟁	5
○ Essenzia Vendemmia Tardiva '01	⟁⟁	5
● Rosso Faye '01	⟁⟁	6
● Pinot Nero Sel. '01	⟁⟁	6
○ Nosiola '02	⟁⟁	4
● Pinot Nero '02	⟁⟁	5
○ Sauvignon '02	⟁⟁	5
○ Trentino Traminer '02	⟁⟁	5
● Rosso Faye '00	⟁⟁⟁	6
○ Essenzia Vendemmia Tardiva '00	⟁⟁	5
○ Bianco Faye '98	⟁⟁	4
○ Cuveé Extra Brut	⟁⟁	5
○ Besler Biank '00	⟁⟁	5
○ Trentino Traminer '01	⟁⟁	4

● Trentino Cabernet Sauvignon '00	⟁⟁	4
● Trentino Merlot '01	⟁⟁	4
● Trentino Marzemino '02	⟁⟁	4
● Trentino Marzemino d'Isera Husar '02	⟁⟁	5
○ Trentino Moscato Giallo '02	⟁	4
○ Trentino Pinot Bianco '02	⟁	4
● Trentino Marzemino d'Isera Husar '00	⟁⟁	3*
● Trentino Cabernet Pianilonghi '99	⟁⟁	4
○ Trentino Chardonnay '99	⟁⟁	3
● Trentino Marzemino d'Isera Husar '99	⟁⟁	4
● Trentino Merlot Campiano '99	⟁⟁	4
○ Trentino Pinot Bianco '99	⟁⟁	3

ISERA (TN)

CANTINA D'ISERA
VIA AL PONTE, 1
38060 ISERA (TN)
TEL. 0464433795
E-MAIL: info@cantinaisera.it

After months of consultation, crop plans and regulations, Trentino has launched an expansion of the DOC, Trentino Superiore. The new specifications were promoted to enhance areas of microproduction, sometimes incorrectly referred to as subzones, and safeguard the uniqueness of indigenous grape varieties, especially Marzemino. One of the first wines in the new category was the Marzemino from this long-established co-operative winery at Isera, the Marzemino capital. The area is so closely tied to the variety that Isera gives an award to the best-kept plot of marzemino each year. For its part, the co-operative has convinced its member-growers to produce less fruit of better quality. The new director, oenologist Fausto Campostrini, means to boost the cellar's wines. We found an early indication in the Sentieri Bordeaux, which shows a gutsy attack and palate. The same goes for the Agiato '02, (the "Accademia degli Agiati", a cultural group, has been active locally for centuries), a copper-tinged Pinot Grigio that is easy on the nose and very convincing in the mouth, showing ripe pear and a dry, pleasantly astringent finish. But Isera is more than just Marzemino. One of Trentino's most interesting Moscato Giallos is made here. It's dry, with a brilliant green-flecked straw-yellow colour, good fragrance and complexity, and with just enough sweetness to make it delicious either with cakes or as an aperitif. Finally, there is a traditional Marzemino, always well typed, and Rebo '02, from a merlot and marzemino cross now classified as an indigenous Trentino variety.

ISERA (TN)

ENRICO SPAGNOLLI
VIA G. B. ROSINA, 4/A
38060 ISERA (TN)
TEL. 0464409054
E-MAIL: enricospagnolli@vinispagnolli.it

If Isera is the capital of Marzemino, then Luigi Spagnolli is its ambassador. The variety arrived in Vallagarina when the Venetian empire extended to the gates of Trento. Today, Marzemino is the symbol of Isera. Every grower in the municipality competes for the title of best-kept vineyard, and the plots are tended like window boxes. Luigi Spagnolli is more of a cellarman than a grower but he lavishes care and dedication on his marzemino grapes even after the harvest, when he part-dries them to enhance the bouquet and consistency of the wine. You note this at once in the Marzemino '01, dedicated to Mozart's Don Giovanni. It has a dark, violet ruby colour, fruity notes, an almost syrupy mouthfeel and remarkable length. The Marzemino '02 is also graceful and refined, showing versatile, intense and varietal. Like the great red winemaker he is, Luigi releases another bottle that is in a class by itself, Pinot Nero. The '01 edition is balanced, and offers a lovely note of ripe black cherry. Among the whites, the Nosiola '02 is a bit insubstantial and more acidulous, whereas the Müller Thurgau offers an intense fragrance, good backbone and a dry, full-flavoured harmony in the mouth. But we should also mention the Moscato Giallo '02, made from a subvariety of moscato. This wine is just as it should be, fragrant, ideal as an aperitif or for sipping on its own.

● Trentino Rosso		
Sentieri Sel. 907 '00	♼♼	4
● Trentino Marzemino Sup.		
Etichetta Verde '02	♼♼	4
○ Trentino Moscato Giallo '02	♼♼	4
○ Trentino Pinot Grigio Agiato '02	♼♼	4
● Trentino Marzemino '02	♼	4
● Trentino Rebo '02	♼	5
● Trentino Marzemino		
Etichetta Verde '98	♿♿	3
● Trentino Rebo '98	♿♿	3
● Trentino Rosso		
Sentieri Sel. 907 '98	♿♿	4
● Trentino Marzemino		
Etichetta Verde '99	♿♿	3

● Trentino Marzemino		
Don Giovanni '01	♼♼	5
● Trentino Pinot Nero '01	♼♼	5
● Trentino Marzemino '02	♼♼	4
○ Trentino Müller Thurgau '02	♼♼	4
○ Trentino Moscato Giallo '02	♼	4
○ Trentino Nosiola '02	♼	4
● Trentino Pinot Nero '00	♿♿	5
● Trentino Pinot Nero '99	♿♿	4

LASINO (TN)

PISONI
LOC. SARCHE
FRAZ. PERGOLESE DI LASINO
VIA SAN SIRO, 7/B
38070 LASINO (TN)
TEL. 0461563216 - 0461564106

A farming and grape-growing family for generations, the Pisonis are mentioned in the annals of the Council of Trent as purveyors of wine to Cardinal Madruzzo. Even then, they were winemakers, vinifying fruit from their plots located around the castles of the nobility in the valley of seven lakes, between Trento and Lake Garda. Today, the Pisonis still make simple, straightforward wines, focusing particular attention on Vino Santo, the exclusive dried-grape "passito dei passiti" made from nosiola grapes pressed at Easter. The Pisoni farming spirit, based on wisdom handed down from one generation to the next, has been brought up to date by the oenological studies of young Marco and Stefano, and is equally evident in the other wines. The good white Sarica blend is obtained from equal parts chardonnay and sauvignon, the latter contributing a lovely vegetal freshness. The rest of the range is all decent, from the Chardonnay to the Nosiola, Pinot Nero and Rebo (a red that carries the name of Rebo Rigotti, the researcher who created this cross of merlot and marzemino in the 1930s), although they suffer from the poor growing year in the Valle dei Laghi.

LASINO (TN)

PRAVIS
LOC. LE BIOLCHE, 1
38076 LASINO (TN)
TEL. 0461564305
E-MAIL: info@pravis.it

Pravis wines are valuable examples of a loving interpretation of the territory. They are uncompromising and unmistakable, precisely because of their intriguing naturalness. These wines are descendants of the Valle dei Laghi winemaking tradition, sourced from many small vineyards scattered among rocks, woods and ponds and caressed by the "ora" wind that blows from Lake Garda. The three partners in Pravis, Giovanni Chistè, Domenico Pedrini and Mario Zambarda, have dedicated a wine to this particular wind, a Nosiola from grapes part-dried on rush mats called "aréle" and also used for drying grapes for the Vino Santo. Fermentation is in small acacia casks. The result is a deep gold, extremely concentrated white with lots of backbone. The Stravino di Stravino '01, also from part-dried grapes, is perhaps the most fascinating white in Trentino, a delightfully opulent wine with good ageing potential. Also good are the Syrae '01, an always satisfying monovarietal Syrah, and the Fratagranda '00, a classic Bordeaux blend that shows solid and complex to the point of austerity, but is also rich in soft fruit. Still with the reds, there is Niergal, an anagram of Lagrein, in its 2001 edition. Fruit-forward and concentrated almost to the limits, it shows well-defined, velvet-smooth structure. The current whites are also very good. Nosiola Le Frate '02 is always a benchmark and the same goes for the Müller Thurgau San Thomà '02 and the hard-to-find Vino Santo '92, an extraordinarily well-typed sweet wine.

●	Trentino Rebo '00	♟	5
○	Sarica Bianco '01	♟	5
○	Trentino Chardonnay '02	♟	4
○	Trentino Nosiola '02	♟	4
○	Trentino Vino Santo '92	♟♟	8
●	Sarica Rosso '98	♟♟	4
●	Sarica Rosso '99	♟♟	5

○	Stravino di Stravino '01	♟♟	7
●	Syrae '01	♟♟	6
○	L'Ora '01	♟♟	6
●	Niergal '01	♟♟	6
○	Müller Thurgau St. Thomà '02	♟♟	4
○	Nosiola Le Frate '02	♟♟	4
●	Trentino Cabernet Fratagranda '00	♟♟	6
●	Trentino Vino Santo '92	♟♟	8
○	Stravino di Stravino '99	♟♟♟	6
●	Niergal '00	♟♟	5
●	Syrae '00	♟♟	6
○	Müller Thurgau St. Thomà '01	♟♟	4
○	Nosiola Le Frate '01	♟♟	4
●	Trentino Cabernet Fratagranda '99	♟♟	6

LAVIS (TN)

LAVIS (TN)

NILO BOLOGNANI
VIA STAZIONE, 19
38015 LAVIS (TN)
TEL. 0461246354
E-MAIL: dibolog@tin.it

CESCONI
FRAZ. PRESSANO
VIA MARCONI, 39
38015 LAVIS (TN)
TEL. 0461240355
E-MAIL: cesconi@cr-surfing.net

The Armilo is an atypical Teroldego in that it is one of the few monovarietals not released as a Rotaliano DOC. Quite the contrary, for the Indicazione Geografica Dolomiti on the label is almost a declaration of independence by Diego Bolognani, a self-taught winemaker who continues a long family tradition. Armilo is named after Diego's parents, Armida and Nilo, and is obtained from grapes harvested in Diego's own vineyards. The Bolognanis are now remodelling the estate, which is becoming less of a winery and more of a full-scale farm, aiming for complete control over the production cycle from grape to glass. The Armilo confirms its status as one of the best wines in Trentino. It came near Three Glasses last year and did so again with the 2001 vintage. Youthfully alcoholic and fragrantly complex, it is also easy-drinking and inviting, showing a dense tannic weave and remarkable balance. It's a great wine, if still a little raw and young. The new release of Gabàn is expected next year so in the meantime, let's get on with the whites. The Müller Thurgau is its usual brilliant straw yellow, then clean on the nose, where it offers sage and hay. The palate is harmonious, dry and inviting. The Sauvignon and Nosiola are both in line with the Bolognani production philosophy, the latter showing more subtle and fruity than in previous years. The Moscato Giallo is as excellent as ever. Fresh, fruity and fragrant, it is soft but not sweet. It's a shame that this wine type has yet to receive the recognition it deserves.

In addition to being friendly, the Cesconis know how to bring out the connection between typical grapes and territory in their wines. This spontaneous gift is made up of respect for country life and the local environment. The Cesconis have only been – very successfully – bottling wine for a few years but they have been involved in growing since 1751. Adelina and Paolo brought their four sons up to value traditional viticulture, lessons later put to use by Alessandro, Franco, Lorenzo and Roberto. The cellar is very new, excavated under the ridges of the hill at Pressano, above Lavis, toward the Cembra valley. The Cesconis grow most of their white grapes here, while red grapes have been planted on a small holding at Drò, towards Lake Garda. All the wines are excellent. Olivar is perhaps the best white we tasted this year in Trentino. Only inclement weather during the growing year kept it from picking up Three Glasses. From a blend of chardonnay, pinot bianco, pinot grigio and sauvignon, it boasts beautiful structure, rich aromas and intense fruit. The Traminer is another top wine, with a rich nose of spice and dried roses, and a palate that is succulent, rather than powerful. Other whites include a deep gold Chardonnay with greenish highlights, then a powerful, close-knit palate, a big, full-flavoured Pinot Grigio and a satisfying Nosiola. The Cabernet and Merlot '01 are both worthwhile, but still very young.

●	Teroldego Armilo '01	♟♟	4*	○	Olivar '02	♟♟	5
○	Trentino Müller Thurgau '02	♟♟	3*	○	Trentino Chardonnay '02	♟♟	4
○	Trentino Nosiola '02	♟♟	3*	○	Trentino Nosiola '02	♟♟	4
○	Trentino Moscato Giallo '02	♟	4	○	Trentino Pinot Grigio '02	♟♟	4
○	Trentino Sauvignon '02	♟	4	○	Trentino Traminer Aromatico '02	♟♟	5
●	Gabàn '00	♟♟	6	●	Trentino Cabernet '01	♟	5
●	Teroldego Armilo '00	♟♟	5	●	Trentino Merlot '01	♟	4
○	Trentino Müller Thurgau '00	♟♟	3	○	Olivar '01	♟♟♟	5
○	Trentino Sauvignon '00	♟♟	3	○	Olivar '00	♟♟	5
				●	Rosso del Pivier '00	♟♟	6
				○	Trentino Chardonnay '00	♟♟	4
				○	Trentino Traminer Aromatico '00	♟♟	4
				○	Trentino Chardonnay '01	♟♟	4
				○	Trentino Pinot Grigio '01	♟♟	4
				○	Trentino Sauvignon '01	♟♟	4

LAVIS (TN)

Vignaiolo Giuseppe Fanti

fraz. Pressano
p.zza della Croce, 3
38015 Lavis (TN)
tel. 0461240809
e-mail: alessandro.fanti@katamail.com

Vines have been grown at Pressano near Lavis since the first farmers the Adige valley fled to these hills from invading armies. For more than a century, the slopes here have been planted entirely to vine. The Fanti family were pioneers of modern viticulture in the zone. A dynasty of growers and skilled winemakers, they are responsible for the successful recovery of Nosiola in the zone. When Giuseppe Fanti released it as a monovarietal in the early 1970s, it was an immediate success and went on to be copied, imitated and promoted. Now his son, oenologist Alessandro, has even more precise ideas. He is re-organizing the winery to handle craft-scale microvinifications of wines that can create genuine excitement. Those intentions are now reality. First, he renovated the vineyards, changed obsolete growing methods and modernized his "caneva", or wine cellar, at the family home in Pressano. There were not many wines, but a lot of compliments. The Portico Rosso, from teroldego with merlot and cabernet, is a fine, full-flavoured red with that now traditional vegetal note. The always admirable and very good Incrocio Manzoni is a powerful yet delicate white that makes up in flavour what it lacks in fragrance. Robur is rich and golden, a monovarietal Chardonnay that should perhaps age for a few years to be at its best. But don't miss Alessandro's Nosiola, a subtly bitter wine with a tangy persistence that is utterly varietal. It's in the style of this small estate, committed to looking after not only the vines but also their habitat, the wine landscape in the hills of Lavis.

●	Portico Rosso '01	🍷🍷	5
○	Incrocio Manzoni '02	🍷🍷	5
○	Trentino Chardonnay Robur '02	🍷🍷	5
○	Trentino Nosiola '02	🍷	4
○	Trentino Chardonnay Robur '99	🍷🍷	4
○	Incrocio Manzoni '00	🍷🍷	4
○	Incrocio Manzoni '01	🍷🍷	5
●	Portico Rosso '97	🍷🍷	4
●	Portico Rosso '98	🍷🍷	4
○	Trentino Chardonnay Robur '98	🍷🍷	3
○	Incrocio Manzoni '99	🍷🍷	3

LAVIS (TN)

La Vis/Valle di Cembra

via del Carmine, 7
38015 Lavis (TN)
tel. 0461246325
e-mail: cantina@la-vis.com

The influence of this co-operative has grown lately with the recent merger with the Cantina Valle di Cembra. It's a synergetic union of two co-operative wineries that have always been close, not just geographically, and it makes Gruppo La Vis the third-largest producer in Trentino, with almost 1,300 member-growers and the same number of hectares under vine. When the Cembra co-operative merged with La Vis, it brought with it wines that were better than we had ever tasted. But both groups have kept their own brands and special qualities. Already having demonstrated that their production philosophies are identical, both will use the same sales and distribution network. La Vis' reputation grows by the year under Fausto Peratoner and his increasingly skilled team of oenologists, (Gianni Gasperi and now also Massimo Tarter at Cembra. The cellars are committed to making good wines. Ritratto Rosso, a good blend of teroldego and lagrein that still has vegetal notes, came close to Three Glasses and all the others are very commendable. The Cabernet Sauvignon, Chardonnay and Pinot Grigio, all from the Ritratti range, are outstanding. We pause here to mention the new arrivals from Valle di Cembra. First is the Müller Thurgau, under three different labels, all perfect in their typicity, with Vigna delle Forche scoring highest. The Pinot Nero, Nosiola and Rupinio, a simple, tasty red from a mix of lagrein and pinot nero, are also good. These exceptional wines are not widely known, but this situation will not last for long. La Vis will spread the word.

●	Ritratto Rosso '00	🍷🍷	6
●	Trentino Cabernet Sauvignon Ritratti '00	🍷🍷	4*
○	Trentino Chardonnay Ritratti '02	🍷🍷	4*
○	Trentino Müller Thurgau Vigna delle Forche V. di Cembra '02	🍷🍷	4
○	Trentino Nosiola V. di Cembra '02	🍷🍷	4
●	Trentino Pinot Nero Coll. Produttori V. di Cembra '00	🍷🍷	5
●	Rupinio V. di Cembra '02	🍷	3*
○	Trentino Pinot Grigio Ritratti '95	🍷🍷🍷	4
○	Ritratto Bianco '99	🍷🍷	5
●	Ritratto Rosso '99	🍷🍷	5

LAVIS (TN)

MASO FURLI
LOC. FURLI
VIA FURLI, 32
38015 LAVIS (TN)
TEL. 0461240667
E-MAIL: masofurli@libero.it

Vineyards cultivated as if they were ornamental gardens, rows planted on small plots of land in the hills above Lavis, and the first crags of the Valle di Cembra, all surround this estate. Given its mountain location, Maso Furli can no longer hope to expand its vineyard holdings, but quality can always be improved. Giorgio and Marco, the Zanoni brothers, understood this when they decided to exploit the unique situation represented by their four hectares of vineyard. They grow three varieties of white grape, with a few rows of reds, and turn out four different labels. Until a few years ago, Zanoni was way off the Trentino winemaking map. Now, all their wines are excellent and among the most representative in Trentino. The Zanonis make their products with tenacity, ability and a spontaneous desire to measure their wines against others, three qualities for which Giorgio and Marco shine. Their whites, the Sauvignon, the Traminer and the Chardonnay, are now models to be imitated for their intense bouquet and clear, concentrated varietal tones. Zanoni wines are obtained with the help of modern technology, but at the same time remain excellent expressions of the territory where they were born. The Zanonis have even patented innovative systems for soft-crushing grapes. Unfortunately, they have not been rewarded as they deserve by recent harvests, and have been able only to confirm the authority of the range, the Traminer in particular.

MEZZOCORONA (TN)

MARCO DONATI
VIA CESARE BATTISTI, 41
38016 MEZZOCORONA (TN)
TEL. 0461604141
E-MAIL: donatimarcovini@libero.it

Faithful to the principle that "wine is born in the vineyard", Marco Donati has intensified work among his rows of vines, mainly located in the celebrated Campo Rotaliano. These are basically teroldego vineyards, and Marco Donati does not joke around with teroldego. He treats it with almost religious devotion, attempting only to curtail its vigorous growth and vinify without altering its amazing characteristics or modifying its temperament. So when the teroldego is at its best, he presents the wine in all its natural glory. In some growing years, the variety performs well; in others, the wine falls short of expectations. We are sad to say this is what happened in 2001. Marco's Teroldego Sangue di Drago is one of the best around, although it is not at the level of the finest vintages. There is class and personality aplenty, but the wine has to deal with the whims of the vintage. We also noted this in the Novai, an unusual blend of teroldego, merlot and cabernet sauvignon. The deep ruby is almost black, and the palate is nice and supple, with a velvety texture, but just a bit too lightweight. The touch of lagrein stands out in the other teroldego and merlot blend, Vino del Maso, an invigoratingly pleasant red. The other wines are all well made, from the fresh, drinkable, traditional-style Teroldego Bagolari, to the other two whites, Terre del Noce, from chardonnay and sauvignon, and the full-flavoured Nosiola, sourced from the hills south of Trento.

● Maso Furli Rosso '00	🍷🍷	5
○ Trentino Chardonnay '01	🍷🍷	5
○ Trentino Sauvignon '02	🍷🍷	5
○ Trentino Traminer Aromatico '02	🍷🍷	5
○ Trentino Chardonnay '99	🍷🍷🍷	3
○ Trentino Chardonnay '00	🍷🍷	4
○ Trentino Traminer Aromatico '00	🍷🍷	4
● Maso Furli Rosso '99	🍷🍷	5
○ Trentino Sauvignon '00	🍷🍷	4
○ Trentino Sauvignon '01	🍷🍷	5
○ Trentino Traminer Aromatico '01	🍷🍷	5
● Maso Furli Rosso '98	🍷🍷	4
○ Trentino Sauvignon '99	🍷🍷	3

● Teroldego Rotaliano Sangue del Drago '01	🍷🍷	6
● Novai '01	🍷🍷	5
● Teroldego Rotaliano Bagolari '02	🍷	4
○ Torre del Noce Bianco '02	🍷	4
○ Trentino Nosiola '02	🍷	4
● Vino del Maso Rosso '02	🍷	4
● Teroldego Rotaliano Sangue del Drago '98	🍷🍷🍷	4
● Novai '00	🍷🍷	5
● Teroldego Rotaliano '00	🍷🍷	3
● Teroldego Rotaliano Sangue del Drago '00	🍷🍷	6
● Vino del Maso Rosso '98	🍷🍷	4
● Mezzedego Rotaliano '99	🍷🍷	3
● Teroldego Rotaliano Sangue del Drago '99	🍷🍷	4
○ Trentino Nosiola '99	🍷🍷	3

MEZZOCORONA (TN)

F.LLI DORIGATI - METIUS
VIA DANTE, 5
38016 MEZZOCORONA (TN)
TEL. 0461605313
E-MAIL: vini@dorigati.it

Teroldego and Trento Classico are two very diverse wines in certain aspects, but they are the two best products from this winery. The Dorigatis' two prized wines are created with painstaking effort. Winemakers for five generations, the family cultivate vines on their own estate and also look after those of other growers on an honour-system contract. The cellar received most accolades for the Methius, a "spumante" of rare elegance. Only a few thousand bottles are produced of this excellent craft wine, now one of the top-ranking Italian designer sparklers. The 1997 vintage yielded an aristocrat of a wine, as always. Intense and complex in its fruity bouquet, with a pervasive mousse, it shows excellent structure and balance. It fell short of our top prize this time, since it is still immature and perhaps less expressive than other vintages. But let's get back to Teroldego. The Riserva Diedri introduces itself with an almost violent purplish colour, then notes of blackberry and raspberry blend well with the oak (the wine is barrique-fermented), and a slightly spicy taste, excellent tannicity, concentration and good length. We felt the standard-label Teroldego was also good, youthfully alcoholic and bright. The Lagrein Kretzer '02, a rosé, is unique of its type in Trentino, has exquisite impact. We also found both the Cabernet and the Rebo '01 very interesting, the latter from a now-traditional local cross of merlot with teroldego. The Pinot Grigio '02 closes the range, offering a flavoursome palate and invitingly husky drinkability.

MEZZOLOMBARDO (TN)

CANTINA ROTALIANA
VIA TRENTO, 65/B
38017 MEZZOLOMBARDO (TN)
TEL. 0461601010
E-MAIL: info@cantinarotaliana.it

The symbol of the Rotaliana cellar is Clesurae, a great, honestly attractive Teroldego that gets richer. But this co-operative does not take any of its wines lightly. There are a dozen or so selections, all well made and all excellent value for money. Cantina Rotaliana has a new facility on the outskirts of Mezzolombardo, even though the historic heart of the co-operative is in the centre of the town. The cellar is committed to quality viticulture, focusing obviously on Teroldego, the bellwether product for the entire local winemaking sector. Clesurae is one of the best Teroldegos around, showing dark ruby, with intense aromas of black and red berry fruits nuanced with delicate vegetal and spicy notes. Powerful in the mouth, it has lashings of glossy tannins and decent length. The other versions of Teroldego also scored well, from the fresh-tasting standard-label to the traditional-style Riserva. The Canevarie selection is also good, showing fruit and dense consistency. But this red wine cellar has a growing reputation in whites, too. The chardonnay-heavy Thamè is very interesting, as are all eight other wines from the Rupe line, including the Pinot Grigio and Müller Thurgau. The intense, elegant notes of ripe fruit, on the nose as well as the palate. They are well gauged and offer upfront frankness. These are wines that show the importance of good decisions in the vineyard by a winery that has convinced members to reduce yields and improve quality.

○ Trento Methius Ris. '97	♈♈	7
● Teroldego Rotaliano Diedri Ris. '00	♈♈	6
● Teroldego Rotaliano '01	♈♈	4
● Trentino Cabernet '01	♈	4
● Trentino Rebo '01	♈	4
⊙ Trentino Lagrein Rosato '02	♈	4
○ Trentino Pinot Grigio '02	♈	4
○ Trento Methius Ris. '92	♈♈♈	5
○ Trento Methius Ris. '95	♈♈♈	5
○ Trento Methius Ris. '94	♈♈	5
● Teroldego Rotaliano '00	♈♈	3*
○ Trentino Pinot Grigio '00	♈♈	3
● Teroldego Rotaliano Diedri Ris. '97	♈♈	5
● Teroldego Rotaliano Diedri Ris. '98	♈♈	5
● Teroldego Rotaliano Diedri Ris. '99	♈♈	5

● Teroldego Rotaliano Ris. '00	♈♈	4
● Teroldego Rotaliano Clesurae '01	♈♈	4
○ Trentino Bianco Thamè '01	♈♈	5
● Teroldego Rotaliano Canevarie '02	♈♈	4
○ Trentino Müller Thurgau La Rupe '02	♈♈	3*
○ Trentino Pinot Grigio La Rupe '02	♈♈	3*
● Teroldego Rotaliano Clesurae '99	♈♈♈	6
● Teroldego Rotaliano Clesurae '00	♈♈	6
● Teroldego Rotaliano '00	♈♈	3*
● Teroldego Rotaliano Canevarie '01	♈♈	4
● Teroldego Rotaliano Ris. '99	♈♈	4

MEZZOLOMBARDO (TN)

NOGAREDO (TN)

FORADORI
VIA DAMIANO CHIESA, 1
38017 MEZZOLOMBARDO (TN)
TEL. 0461601046
E-MAIL: foradori@interline.it

CASTEL NOARNA
FRAZ. NOARNA
VIA CASTELNUOVO, 19
38060 NOGAREDO (TN)
TEL. 0464413295 - 0464435222
E-MAIL: info@castelnoarna.com

This Granato is marvellous. It's a wine that amazes, convinces, satisfies and catches your eye with purple highlights. Dense, viscous and deep-hued, it is a joy on the nose, which invites you to taste. It is difficult to summarize the virtues of a wine this special, which is the best Granato of the past few years. It's worthy of comparison to the 1991, the vintage best loved by Elisabetta Foradori, but it's even fuller and more fascinating. The wine comes from the confidence acquired in the field by a woman who has always aimed for uncompromising excellence, investing in a variety that was little considered for centuries and grown for the abundant harvests it guaranteed, not for the quality of the final result. But all the wines, not just the Granato, from this historic Rotaliano estate have something more that makes them special. Even the traditional Teroldego, called simply Foradori on the label, has the character of a great wine. Purple in colour and spicy on the nose, with a subtly enjoyable hint of earth and tar on nose and palate, the distinguishing feature of Teroldego Rotaliano. Though this wine can be enjoyed young, but it will still give pleasure over time. Since the Ailampa and Karanar, wines released only in favourable vintages, are missing, the white Myrto rounds off the 2002 range. From sauvignon, incrocio Manzoni and pinot bianco, it is as good as it is distinctive, made in the perfect Foradori style that foregrounds elegance and appeal.

The 2002 vintage was very difficult, not just for Marco Zani's estate, but for numerous wineries in Vallagarina. Insistent rain and subsequent humidity penalized top products. The harvest was poor, especially in terms of quantity. The fairly good grapes harvested in the end had high acidity. Consequently, the wines need time to best express themselves. This winery, located in a genuine 11th-century castle overlooking the entire Vallagarina, decided to concentrate on blends, eliminating several labels dedicated to monovarietal wines, and postponing others in need of further ageing until next year. Here is the new item, Salvanél '02, a white named after the mysterious woodland elf mentioned in the transcript of the witch trials that the Inquisition held at this castle. This is a cuvée of all the white varieties produced at the estate, nosiola, riesling, traminer, chardonnay and sauvignon. This approachable, fruit-led wine aspires to drinkability and is on offer at a very reasonable price. Despite the vintage, the Nosiola '02 is also well made. We felt it was the best version Marco has produced in the past few years. Attractively compact, it is perhaps less respectful of the variety's typicity, but certainly has personality. As for the other wines, from the Bianco di Castelnuovo to the red Romeo (the 2001 was not released) and the Mercuria blend, we will have to wait. They are maturing in bottle.

●	Granato '01	🍷🍷🍷	7
○	Myrto '02	🍷🍷	5
●	Teroldego Rotaliano '02	🍷🍷	5
●	Granato '00	🍷🍷🍷	7
●	Granato '91	🍷🍷🍷	5
●	Granato '93	🍷🍷🍷	5
●	Granato '96	🍷🍷🍷	5
●	Teroldego Rotaliano '00	🍷🍷	4
●	Teroldego Rotaliano '01	🍷🍷	4
●	Ailanpa '99	🍷🍷	7
●	Karanar '99	🍷🍷	7
○	Myrto '01	🍷🍷	5

○	Salvanél '02	🍷🍷	3*
○	Trentino Nosiola '02	🍷🍷	4
○	Bianco di Castelnuovo '00	🍷🍷	5
○	Bianco di Castelnuovo '01	🍷🍷	4
●	Mercuria Rosso '00	🍷🍷	5
●	Romeo '99	🍷🍷	5
○	Trentino Chardonnay Campo Grande '99	🍷🍷	4
○	Trentino Nosiola Casot '99	🍷🍷	4

NOMI (TN)

NOMI (TN)

RICCARDO BATTISTOTTI
VIA 3 NOVEMBRE, 21
38060 NOMI (TN)
TEL. 0464834145
E-MAIL: mail@battistotti.com

GRIGOLETTI
VIA GARIBALDI, 12
38060 NOMI (TN)
TEL. 0464834215
E-MAIL: grigolettivini@tin.it

An excellent cellarman, Luciano Battistotti is like good wine: he gets better with age. But nothing else at his family-managed estate seems to change, for you always find friendliness, openness and honest prices. If you look closer, you'll see Luciano's wines are picking up speed on quality. They have acquired character and harmony, and stand out for their sincerity, typicity and cleanliness. This is especially true of the sweet Moscato Rosa, from grapes harvested along the south-facing hill above Nomi, where Luciano garners barely 20 or so hectolitres from a hectare of vineyard. The wine is a rarity. Pleasant on nose and palate, it is rich in spicy aromas, then warm and broad in the mouth, where the sugar is well balanced by vibrant acidity. Balance and elegance are also obvious in the Marzemino, both the standard-label version and the special selection from grapes left to raisin for 45 days in small cases, tucked away in a dry, well-ventilated environment. Luciano Battistotti is particularly proud of the wine from these "uve passe", or part-dried grapes. He has crafted a Marzemino in an early 20th-century style, showing fragrant Parma violets and great structure. Trentino artist Pietro Verdini created the delightful image on the label. Luciano's Chardonnay is also good. Vinified in stainless steel, it shows a nice alcoholic tenor, and a dry, clean palate as well as distinctive notes of ripe fruit and fresh-baked bread.

The Grigolettis are farmers who have vinified their own grapes for several generations. Their vineyards are in the warm hills of Nomi, at Aldeno and Rovereto, on the right bank of the river Adige. This area is well-suited for red varieties like marzemino and others. The soil is alluvial and the temperature range allows high-quality harvests even of merlot, a variety that Aida, Bruno, Carmelo and Marica Grigoletti really shine with. Merlot Antica Vigna is obtained by selecting fruit from a vineyard planted more than 40 years ago, with sturdy vines trained over "pergola trentina" trellises and drastically pruned to yield just a few bunches per plant. The wine is fermented and matured in small oak casks. Concentrated in colour, harmonious and long, it is as successful as the Grigoletti Bordeaux blend, christened Gonzalier, in honour of the guild of Gonzalieri, who carried grapes and must on their backs in a wooden container called a "gonzal". This full-bodied red has a pleasant mouthfeel and elegant balance. But the Grigolettis would never leave out Marzemino, the emblematic wine of Vallagarina. They respect the simple, delicate style of the variety, and their version is frank and quaffable. On the white side of the list, Retiko continues to improve. A blend of chardonnay and sauvignon, it ferments and matures in oak, acquiring a yellow-gold hue, a full palate and nose, and great ageing prospects. Finally, there's an honourable mention for the Chardonnay and the congenial Cabernet.

●	Trentino Marzemino '02	▼▼	4*
●	Trentino Marzemino Verdini '02	▼▼	4
●	Trentino Moscato Rosa '02	▼▼	5
○	Trentino Chardonnay '02	▼	3
●	Trentino Marzemino '00	♈♈	3*
●	Trentino Moscato Rosa '00	♈♈	5
●	Trentino Marzemino Verdini '01	♈♈	4
●	Trentino Moscato Rosa '01	♈♈	5
○	Trentino Chardonnay '01	♈	4

●	Trentino Merlot Antica Vigna di Nomi '01	▼▼	4
●	Gonzalier '99	▼▼	5
○	Retiko '01	▼	5
●	Trentino Cabernet '01	▼	4
○	Trentino Chardonnay L'Opera '02	▼	4
●	Trentino Merlot Antica Vigna di Nomi '00	♈♈	5
●	Gonzalier '97	♈♈	5
●	Trentino Merlot Antica Vigna di Nomi '99	♈♈	4
●	Trentino Marzemino '02	♈	4

ROVERÈ DELLA LUNA (TN)   ROVERETO (TN)

GAIERHOF
VIA IV NOVEMBRE, 51
38030 ROVERÈ DELLA LUNA (TN)
TEL. 0461658514
E-MAIL: informazioni@gaierhof.com

NICOLA BALTER
VIA VALLUNGA II, 24
38068 ROVERETO (TN)
TEL. 0464430101

The Togns were born cellarmen and became growers, a process accompanied by commercial success and a constant focus on good wine. Luigi Togn is the founder of Gaierhof, an estate on the border of Trentino and Alto Adige. It produces typical wines in an international style, most for the export market. The clearly territorial wines are produced at the family estate, Maso Poli, situated above Pressano di Lavis, where as far back as 1526, a statute imposed severe regulations for safeguarding the "... quality of wines from Pressano that should distinguish themselves from those from outside the area". Management of the property is now in the hands of Luigi's daughters, the young – and competent – Romina, Martina and Valentina, with oenologist, Goffredo Pasolli. A dozen or so hectares under vine surround the cellar and production aims for quality. After all, the Togns are used to producing good wines, beginning with the Gaierhof-label range. The Müller Thurgau dei Settecento selection is, as usual, a head above the rest, showing balance, fragrance and tangy acidity. The Traminer and ever-impressive Teroldego Rotaliano selection, which partners the Merlot Riserva, are expressive and appealing. In the Maso Poli line, we liked the elegant Costa Erta. An oak-aged Chardonnay, it is as harmonious as ever on the soft, lingering palate. The Pinot Nero is full flavoured, and shows youthful vigour. Finally, the Sorni Bianco, named after the nearby village of Sorni on the hill of Pressano, is totally convincing.

Authority is not easy to acquire. It takes patience and tireless devotion, like the devotion Nicola Balter and his staff apply daily to the sunniest, flattest area around Rovereto. The position is beautiful, and very suited to viticulture; Nicola makes the best use of it. All his wines have the stamp of originality, which comes from the authority he has acquired over years of devoted winemaking. In other words, Nicola's excellent wines prompt feelings, inspire insights and impart a desire to discover the place where they were created, which most people still do not know. All this has been obvious in his Trento Classico, which acquires complexity and finesse with every passing vintage. A blend of chardonnay and pinot nero from clones selected to provide a base wine for "spumante" base, and planted in good positions. At our blind tastings this year, its scores put it in the thoroughbred category. But this estate's class is also apparent in the Barbanico '00, an lovely blend of 45 per cent lagrein, 35 per cent merlot and cabernet sauvignon, one of the best wines in Trentino. It communicates territory in its compact texture, rich fruit and minerally note in the persistent finish. We also felt the Clarae was interesting. It's an intriguingly full-flavoured, fruit-led white blend with a chardonnay base. We also felt the excellent Sauvignon '02 showed good balance and a vegetal freshness, whereas the Cabernet Sauvignon is youthfully vigorous and still developing, but shows fair promise.

● Teroldego Rotaliano Sup. '01	♟♟	4
○ Trentino Chardonnay Costa Erta '02	♟♟	4
○ Trentino Müller Thurgau Sup. dei Settecento '02	♟♟	4
● Trentino Merlot Ris. '01	♟	4
● Trentino Pinot Nero Maso Poli '01	♟	4
○ Trentino Sorni Bianco Maso Poli '02	♟	4
○ Trentino Traminer '02	♟	4
○ Trentino Chardonnay Costa Erta '00	♟♟	4
○ Trentino Chardonnay Costa Erta '01	♟♟	4
○ Trentino Müller Thurgau dei Settecento '01	♟♟	4
○ Trentino Sorni Bianco Maso Poli '01	♟	4

● Barbanico '00	♟♟	5
○ Trento Brut	♟♟	5
○ Clarae '00	♟♟	5
○ Sauvignon '02	♟♟	4
● Cabernet Sauvignon '01	♟	4
● Barbanico '97	♟♟♟	5
● Barbanico '98	♟♟	5
● Barbanico '99	♟♟	5
● Cabernet Sauvignon '00	♟♟	4
○ Sauvignon '01	♟♟	4
● Cabernet Sauvignon '98	♟♟	4
○ Balter Brut '99	♟♟	5
○ Trento Brut	♟♟	5

ROVERETO (TN)

ROVERETO (TN)

CONTI BOSSI FEDRIGOTTI
VIA UNIONE, 43
38068 ROVERETO (TN)
TEL. 0464439250
E-MAIL: info@fedrigotti.it

LETRARI
VIA MONTE BALDO, 13/15
38068 ROVERETO (TN)
TEL. 0464480200
E-MAIL: info@letrari.it

The Bossi Fedrigottis leave nothing to chance. They have studied, developed and put into practice viticultural growing techniques to create a heritage of knowledge, tradition and innovation that is available to the entire Vallagarina. They have never forgotten the wine that is symbolic of the land, Marzemino. With the new millennium, the estate inaugurated a new phase in its long history of winemaking, which began in 1697. The new course involves the personal contributions of the three siblings, Gianpaolo, well-known writer Isabella and Maria José, who are determined to put their wines back in the big time. The challenge also involved Luca D'Attoma, one of Italy's most successful oenologists. The results are already tangible. The purplish ruby Marzemino is intense in its aromas, warm on the palate, then full and pleasingly bitter in the finish. The Fojaneghe, one of Italy's first Bordeaux blends, has regained its authority and personality. This full, harmonious red has good progression and length in the mouth, thanks to quality-oriented vineyard management and winemaking. The Conte Federico '00 is also convincing. A Bordeaux blend of 50 per cent merlot with equal parts of cabernet sauvignon and franc, it pays the price of youth, for it lacks a little harmony, but also shows great potential. Outstanding among the numerous other wines – they assure us they will cut back the range – are a charming, unusual white version of the Fojaneghe from chardonnay and traminer, the Pinot Grigio '02 and Conte Principe '02, from moscato giallo grapes. All are traditional and attractive.

The stern image of a soldier from long ago, the arquebusier on the Letrari logo, symbolizes the estate's approach to wine: the recovery of tradition integrated with innovation. Leonello Letrari continues his 50 year-long career at the new winery, managed and directed by his children, Paolo Emilio and Lucia, the latter responsible for vinification. The estate has plots scattered across various areas of Vallagarina, from the south, near Avio (the original home of the Letraris, a wine family since 1647), to beyond Rovereto, in Marzemino country. The Letrari range runs from classic sparkling wines to Enantio, Pinot Bianco, Moscato Rosa, Marzemino and Lagrein. It is difficult to discuss the 20 or so excellent wines in our profile. Though all of them merit description, we will restrict ourselves here to the most outstanding. We enjoyed the Ballistarius '00, a Bordeaux blend with a little Lagrein. Dark garnet, it has an intense nose of red berry fruit over deep, complex vegetal hints that mingle with balsam and spice. We would also point out a very traditional, Marzemino that shows youthfully alcoholic and purplish in hue. In the true Letrari style, it flaunts more structure than aroma. We felt the Enantio was good. It comes from lambrusco a foglia frastagliata grapes grown by the Letraris at Terra dei Forti area in Trentino and Veneto, to the south of Avio. The rest of the range is also good.

● Conte Federico '00	♟♟	6
● Fojaneghe Rosso '00	♟♟	4
● Trentino Marzemino '02	♟♟	4
○ Conte Principe '02	♟	5
○ Fojaneghe Bianco '02	♟	4
○ Pinot Grigio '02	♟	4
○ Fojaneghe Bianco '01	♟♟	4
● Trentino Marzemino '01	♟♟	3

● Ballistarius '00	♟♟	6
● Valdadige Terra dei Forti Enantio '01	♟♟	6
○ Fossa Bandita '02	♟♟	4
● Trentino Marzemino '02	♟♟	4
○ Trento Brut Ris. '98	♟♟	5
○ Trentino Pinot Bianco '02	♟	4
● Ballistarius '99	♟♟	7
● Trentino Marzemino Sel. '00	♟♟	4
● Trentino Marzemino '01	♟♟	4
● Ballistarius '97	♟♟	5
○ Trento Brut Letrari Ris. '97	♟♟	5
● Trentino Moscato Rosa '99	♟♟	6

ROVERETO (TN)

ARMANDO SIMONCELLI
VIA NAVICELLO, 7
38068 ROVERETO (TN)
TEL. 0464432373

Armando Simoncelli produces about a dozen different wines that share a cleanness of style and a faithfulness to the local territory. Armando has been busy for 25 years making wine and tending his vineyards to the south of Rovereto, along the river Adige, where once there was a river port. This is alluvial terrain, fertile and well-exposed to sun, so it is ideal for viticulture. Armando's 12 or so hectares under vine are planted mainly to marzemino, which is also the showcase wine of the estate itself. However, the 2002 harvest was less than kind to the tested skills of this authentic viticulturist. Though all his wines are well made using excellent technique and healthy grapes, they were influenced by a growing year that was anything but great. This has led to low extraction of phenolics and less outgoing wines that lack their customary charm. The Marzemino is delicate, as the type dictates, but does not have its usual length on nose or palate. The same one-dimensionality can be noted in the whites, although the Chardonnay '02 is particularly fragrant, and the Trento also failed to live up to expectations. Among the reds, it was the Bordeaux-blend Navesèl that attracted the most positive comments, not just because of its name – that of the river port – but also because the strong cohesion of the cabernet franc and sauvignon with the merlot supports the wine's harmony and structure overall. A very approachable wine, it shows a lovely garnet ruby and is perhaps slightly vegetal on the palate, but the tannins develop well and it offers attractive length.

ROVERETO (TN)

LONGARIVA
FRAZ. BORGO SACCO
VIA R. ZANDONAI, 6
38068 ROVERETO (TN)
TEL. 0464437200 - 0464487322
E-MAIL: info@longariva.it

Marco Manica loves to say that you need to allow a wine plenty of time to understand how it will develop. He and his wife Rosanna have never cut any corners to "have it all and have it now". Each wine is created after patient trials in the vineyard and a lot of cellar experimentation. The 22-hectare estate is a patchwork of small fields in the pleasant hills of Rovereto where Marco, who by now has over 30 years' experience in wine, cultivates various varieties planted with an eye to soil suitability, exposure and elevation. Marco and Rosanna vinify 13 different wines in their cellar, all commendable and all very personal. The couple's technical skill, and above all devotion to their vineyards, shine through in every bottle. By now, they are regular fixtures at our final taste-offs. This time, it was the Chardonnay Praistel, convincing as always although it loses some complexity in the finish. Still, it stood out as especially good. The Sauvignon Cascari, another very varietal and enjoyable white, was equally good. There was a truly excellent series of reds, which are perhaps the wines most favoured by the Manicas, from the Tre Cesure, a Bordeaux blend of refined elegance, to the rich, varietal Cabernet Marognon. The softness of the alcohol in these wines melds with pervasive aromas and velvet-smooth tannins, lending elegance, style and authority. The Pinot Bianco Pergole and coppery Pinot Grigio Graminè are simpler than usual, but still attractively varietal. Finally, the Marzemino is always worthwhile. Like the Manicas, it is pleasant and speaks of territory.

● Trentino Rosso Navesèl '00	♙♙	5
○ Trentino Chardonnay '02	♙	4
● Trentino Lagrein '02	♙	4
● Trentino Marzemino '02	♙	4
● Trentino Merlot '02	♙	4
○ Trento Brut	♙	5
● Trentino Marzemino '00	♙♙	3*
○ Trentino Pinot Bianco '00	♙♙	3*
● Trentino Rosso Navesèl '97	♙♙	4
● Trentino Rosso Navesèl '98	♙♙	4
● Trentino Rosso Navesèl '99	♙♙	4
● Trentino Marzemino '01	♙	4

○ Trentino Chardonnay Praistel '01	♙♙	5
● Trentino Cabernet Sauvignon Marognon Ris. '00	♙♙	5
● Trentino Rosso Tre Cesure Ris. '00	♙♙	5
○ Trentino Sauvignon Cascari '01	♙♙	4
○ Trentino Pinot Bianco Pergole '02	♙♙	5
○ Trentino Pinot Grigio Graminè '99	♙♙	4
● Trentino Marzemino '02	♙	4
○ Trentino Chardonnay Praistel '98	♙♙♙	5
○ Trentino Chardonnay Praistel '00	♙♙	5
○ Trentino Pinot Bianco Pergole '00	♙♙	4
○ Trentino Pinot Bianco Pergole '01	♙♙	4
○ Migoléta '98	♙♙	6
● Trentino Merlot Tovi '98	♙♙	4

SAN MICHELE ALL'ADIGE (TN)

Endrizzi

loc. Masetto, 2
38010 San Michele all'Adige (TN)
tel. 0461650129
e-mail: info@endrizzi.it

The date on the estate trademark is 1885, the year the winery was founded by Francesco Endrici (the local variant of "Endrizzi"). It stands in the vineyards next to the recently created agricultural institute at San Michele. The cellar's successful history has involved the entire Endrici family. Now Paolo, the founder's great-grandson, has relaunched the family estate with the recent construction of a very modern cellar. Helped by his wife Christine, Paolo has transformed the original structure into a small wine museum. Winemaking memorabilia from the late 19th century, and several striking works of modern art, find space among the stone. The cellar is still being restored, and the wines may need time, but the results of this year's tastings are more than positive. The wines submitted include the Masetto Nero '00, an elegant, full-flavoured blend of cabernet sauvignon and merlot with teroldego and lagrein. The nose is delicately spicy, mingling vanilla and chocolate, then the palate shows vigorous tannins, good harmony and a great finish. The Cabernet Sauvignon Maso Kinderleit is good, though marked by a vegetal note. It's a "riserva" carefully selected from new vineyards near the scenic castle of Monreale. Grapes are also sourced from here for Pinot Nero Pian di Castello, a wine that is still on its way. For the time being, it's too young and closed to be fully appreciated. Last but not least, we would mention the dessert wine from super-ripe chardonnay grapes, the Masetto Dulcis, with its citrus aromas and a palate that flaunts a perfect balance of sugars and acidity.

● Masetto Nero '00	▼▼	4
○ Masetto Dulcis '00	▼	5
● Trentino Cabernet Sauvignon Maso Kinderleit Ris. '99	▼	5
● Teroldego Rotaliano Maso Camorz '00	▽▽	5
● Teroldego Rotaliano Maso Camorz '98	▽▽	4
○ Masetto Bianco '99	▽▽	4
● Masetto Nero '99	▽▽	5

SAN MICHELE ALL'ADIGE (TN)

Istituto Agrario Provinciale San Michele all'Adige

via Edmondo Mach, 1
38010 San Michele all'Adige (TN)
tel. 0461615252
e-mail: cantina@ismaa.it

More than just a winery, the Istituto Agrario is a long-established agricultural school where everyone speaks the language of wine. Enrico Paternoster's team bottles products that show how oenological theory and practice can march in step. The school supervises about 60 hectares of vineyards, and is involved in many projects, but their flagship red, Monastero, is the most important and challenging one. In homage to the building where the winery operates, which was once an Augustine monastery, Monastero amazed and convinced us for the second year running. It sets out to be a thoroughbred, backbone given by the almost exclusively cabernet franc grapes, and reveals impeccable vinification technique. It may have been penalized by hurry: another year in bottle would have done wonders for it. The Prepositura performed well again. Five different white grape varieties were harvested late in the autumn to make a "vendemmia tardiva" wine that is extraordinarily powerful on the palate. The sweetness is splendidly balanced by acidity and its golden colour has the vibrant power of a still-young wine. Class and pride also emerge from the white Castel San Michele '02, a blend of chardonnay, pinot bianco and Incrocio Manzoni that shows full and harmonious, with acacia and perfectly ripe golden delicious apples on nose and palate. The other wines submitted for tasting were technically well made, indeed "scholastic". We liked the very pleasing Pinot Bianco '02.

● Trentino Rosso Monastero '01	▼▼	7
○ Prepositura '02	▼▼	5
○ Trentino Bianco Castel San Michele '02	▼▼	4
○ Trentino Pinot Bianco '02	▼▼	4*
○ Trentino Pinot Bianco '00	▽▽	3
○ Trentino Bianco Castel San Michele '00	▽▽	4
● Trentino Rosso Monastero '00	▽▽	5
○ Prepositura '01	▽▽	5
○ Trentino Chardonnay '01	▽▽	4
○ Trentino Pinot Grigio '01	▽▽	4
○ Trentino Bianco Castel San Michele '99	▽▽	3
○ Trentino Pinot Bianco '99	▽▽	3

SAN MICHELE ALL'ADIGE (TN)   TRENTO

ROBERTO ZENI
FRAZ. GRUMO
VIA STRETTA, 2
38010 SAN MICHELE ALL'ADIGE (TN)
TEL. 0461650456
E-MAIL: robezen@tin.it

Andrea and Roberto Zeni began to make wine after finishing their studies at the nearby school in San Michele all'Adige, which stands a few metres from their vineyards. In the beginning, they planned to make mainly white wines, Müller Thurgau and Nosiola in particular. But now, with 30 years' experience, the two brothers have started to broaden their horizons, vinifying reds as well. First is the Teroldego, harvested from one of the best zones in Campo Rotaliano and vinified in a personal style. The Zenis leave it for more than two years in small oak casks, then for several more months in bottle before release. Their patience is rewarded, because the Teroldego Pini is very good. A mouthfilling, harmonious and powerful wine that is cellarable but already satisfying. Among the white wines, the always outstanding Sortì is from pinot bianco, sauvignon and riesling renano, partially fermented in new oak. The Müller Thurgau is fragrant and delicately aromatic. It is sourced from hillside vineyards in Lavis and Faedo, the sunniest spot in the sunny, well-aspected Adige valley. The Sauvignon, harvested in two selections in the middle of August and the end of October, is flavourful and the rare Moscato Rosa '02 is very interesting. Only a few thousand bottles were released, but they are very attractive.

ABATE NERO
FRAZ. GARDOLO
SPONDA TRENTINA, 45
38014 TRENTO
TEL. 0461246566

Trento and "spumante" is a bond sanctioned not only by the DOC reserved for designer sparklers, but also by the widespread desire of local winemakers to make a wine that is reborn in the bottle. A group of enthusiastic friends, each with specific agronomic and oenological skills, in 1975 founded Abate Nero (the name means "black abbot"), a small sparkling wine estate dedicated to the French abbot honoured as the father of Champagne, Dom Pérignon. Today, Eugenio De Castel Terlago still produces a few thousand bottles a year and they get better and better. Abate Nero makes a complete range of "metodo classico" sparklers with the charm and character of all things handcrafted. One such is the Riserva '96, one of the most exciting vintage sparklers we have tasted recently. The excellent structure and progression on a mellow, harmoniously full palate show the winemaker's skilled hand and extraordinary attention to every detail. The balanced Extra Dry is as good as ever, with a subtle, acidulous vein and distinctive softness from the pinot bianco in the cuvée. The vintage '99 confirms the winery's fast-improving quality. This "riserva" has a very fine perlage and excellent richness of flavour, with fruity sensations of ripe apple. The Extra Brut is more immediate, offering easy drinkability and a subtle, typically Trentino-style bouquet. In short, these are stylish wines that stay in character, a fine tribute to the legendary abbot who first made sparkling wine.

● Teroldego Rotaliano Pini '99	♟♟	6
○ Sortì '02	♟♟	5
● Trentino Moscato Rosa '02	♟♟	7
○ Trentino Müller Thurgau Le Croci '02	♟♟	4
○ Trentino Nosiola Maso Nero '02	♟♟	4
○ Trentino Sauvignon Vigneto Ronchi '02	♟♟	4
○ Trentino Pinot Bianco Sortì '01	♟♟	4
○ Trento Brut M. Cl. '95	♟♟	4
● Teroldego Rotaliano Pini '97	♟♟	5
● Trentino Pinot Nero Spiazol '98	♟♟	5
● Trentino Moscato Rosa '01	♟	6
● Teroldego Rotaliano Pini '98	♟	5

○ Trento Brut Ris. '96	♟♟	5
○ Trento Brut Ris. '99	♟♟	5
○ Trento Abate Nero Extra Dry	♟♟	4
○ Trento Extra Brut	♟	5
○ Trento Brut Ris. '88	♟♟	6
○ Trento Brut Ris. '98	♟♟	5

TRENTO

TRENTO

CAVIT
CONSORZIO DI CANTINE SOCIALI
FRAZ. RAVINA - VIA DEL PONTE, 31
38040 TRENTO
TEL. 0461381711
E-MAIL: cavit@cavit.it

CESARINI SFORZA
FRAZ. RAVINA
VIA STELLA, 9
38040 TRENTO
TEL. 0461382200
E-MAIL: sviluppo@cesarinisforza.com

Cavit has a dual operational strategy. It makes big-number wines, mainly for the non-domestic market, and also creates territory-specific wines in the Trentino style that combine globalization with a local orientation. The range perfectly integrates the two aspects. Cavit is the colossus of Trentino co-operatives, an umbrella organization that markets the production of many co-operative wineries and boasts a spectacular turnover of around about € 200,000 a year while still making fine wines in the craft spirit. We are talking about the Progetto Masi products, a dozen or so wine types sourced from around 100 carefully chosen hectares belonging to the best suppliers in more than 30 municipalities. All these wines show character and are as attractive as any from the finest cellars. The most interesting new item is the Müller Thurgau Zeveri '02, made with grapes in part from Valle di Cembra and in part from Vallagarina, from vineyards tended in compliance with the new Trentino Superiore regulations. A particularly fragrant, spicy wine, with a flavoursome tanginess, it is full bodied and destined to improve with a little bottle ageing, as its richness hints. We can confirm the quality of the Chardonnay '02, an imposing wine with good character that is capable of standing shoulder to shoulder with more famous bottles. The Pinot Grigio is good, with faint onionskin highlights introducing a varietal bouquet of pears, and the Pinot Nero, Teroldego and Marzemino are all convincing. Nor should you miss the Firmato, a classy, elegant Trento that sells at an extremely good price.

One of the best-known brands in Trentino "spumante" production, Cesarini Sforza has been active since 1974. The trademark was recently relaunched by new owners, a joint venture between Bologna-based importers, Fratelli Rinaldi, and Cantina La Vis. The technical staff has been renewed, as has the structure of the cellar and even the winery logo. But these innovations have not taken the spotlight off the winery's great traditional label. Proof comes from the classic Trento Talento 1999, a vintage with a powerful personality that puts it among the best in the category. Created from 80 per cent chardonnay and pinot nero, grown in the hills at Trento. The first fermentation is in the usual stainless steel tanks, then the wine goes into small oak casks for six months, to give the nascent sparklers character and charm. Subsequently, it goes into bottle and is left to age for at least 30 months on the lees. The elegant bouquet of stylish yeast and crusty bread precedes a palate of graceful, caressing persuasiveness. A vibrant, harmonious wine, it signs off with a wonderfully mellow finish. The other cuvée is equally convincing. It is made with the "metodo italiano lungo" (long Italian method), perfected and patented by Cesarini Sforza, which involves lees contact of the base wine in large containers for more than six months. The wine has an attractively dry flavour that is fruity, fresh and approachable, making for easy and very satisfying drinkability. The Chardonnay Brut is fragrant and supple.

● Teroldego Rotaliano Bottega Vinai '01	▼▼	4
● Trentino Marzemino dei Ziresi '01	▼▼	4
● Trentino Pinot Nero Bottega Vinai '01	▼▼	4
○ Trentino Chardonnay Bottega Vinai '02	▼▼	4
○ Trentino Müller Thurgau Zeveri '02	▼▼	5
○ Trentino Pinot Grigio Bottega Vinai '02	▼▼	4
○ Trento Brut Firmato	▼▼	4
○ Trento Graal Brut Ris. '93	▽▽▽	4
○ Trentino Vino Santo Aréle '94	▽▽	8
● Trentino Marzemino Maso Romani '00	▽▽	5
○ Trentino Müller Thurgau Bottega de' Vinai '01	▽▽	4
● Teroldego Rotaliano Maso Cervara '97	▽▽	4
● Teroldego Rotaliano Bottega de' Vinai '99	▽▽	3

○ Trento Brut '99	▼▼	4
○ Chardonnay Cuvée Brut	▼	4
○ Cuvée Brut Ris.	▼	4
○ Trento Brut '97	▽▽	4

TRENTO

TRENTO

★ FERRARI
FRAZ. RAVINA
VIA PONTE DI RAVINA, 15
38100 TRENTO
TEL. 0461972311
E-MAIL: info@ferrarispumante.it

LUNELLI
FRAZ. RAVINA
VIA PONTE DI RAVINA, 15
38040 TRENTO
TEL. 0461972311
E-MAIL: info@ferrarispumante.it

The Magnificent Seven from Ferrari. That sums up our final judgement of the sparklers from this Trento winemaker. The results come from constant progress, reinforced by century-long experience of making sparkling wines – Giulio Ferrari started in 1902 – and the 50-year commitment of the Lunelli family, who know just how to promote the fame and prestige of a wine that has been emblematic of Trento for more than a hundred years. The "riserva" dedicated to the "Fondatore" (founder) is one of the best sparklers in Italy, and arguably the world. A satisfying wine of irresistible charm, it is simply spectacular, not just because it is complex and mature (disgorged ten years after the harvest), but also because it is majestic and almost opulent. Well rounded yet vigorously fresh, it discloses citrus and floral notes with hints reminiscent of incense, and a lively, endless perlage. But if the "Giulio" is great, then another two wines are equally good. The Perlé gains depth with each passing year, throwing a lovely nose that is as fresh as the entry on the palate is full. The rosé version, the '99 Perlé Rosé, is unlike any we have ever tasted. Enchanting and butter-rich, it is a wine to drink through the meal. The masterful skill of the Trento-based cellar also comes through in the other labels, from the traditional Brut, produced in millions of units, to the Demi-Sec selection, for those who love to pair sparklers with dessert, and the 100 per cent chardonnay-based Maximum and the pleasant, slightly simpler Rosé. All seven are wines of great class that convince effortlessly.

The entrepreneurial Lunelli brothers are committed to making the most of the vast winemaking legacy acquired over years of "spumante"-related success with the celebrated Ferrari cuvées. Mauro and his brothers have decided to make a clear distinction between sparkler production and still winemaking. Every year, the Lunelli vineyard holding grows (not just in Trentino, but we will discuss this in the near future), as does the quality of the wines released under the family name. The 2000 vintage is the best to date of the Maso Le Viane, a classic blend with a cabernet and merlot base, lent personality by the indigenous varieties grown on the estate near Avio, in the heart of the Campi Sarni, Trentino's top red-grape zone. Maso Le Viane has great intensity and definition, energy as well as balance, and an extremely dynamic progression on nose and palate. The commitment to reds of the Lunellis and their long-serving oenologist, Ruben Larentis, is also clear from Maso Montalto '00, an excellent Pinot Nero. It's Mauro Lunelli's favourite wine, perhaps because the variety is used for "spumante", but more likely because it is the supreme challenge for every winemaker. When we tried the three whites, we liked the Villa San Nicolò '02, a big, gutsy, pleasantly fresh monovarietal Sauvignon. The Villa Gentilotti '02, from chardonnay grapes, is a mature wine that shows complex and mouthfilling. Finally the rich, gratifyingly harmonious Villa Margon '00 is Mauro Lunelli's first still wine, from chardonnay, pinot bianco, sauvignon and incrocio Manzoni.

○	Giulio Ferrari '94	♟♟♟	8
○	Trento Brut Perlé '99	♟♟	6
⊙	Trento Brut Perlé Rosé '99	♟♟	6
⊙	Trento Brut Rosé	♟♟	6
○	Trento Demi Sec	♟♟	5
○	Trento Brut	♟	5
○	Trento Brut Maximum	♟	5
○	Giulio Ferrari '88	♟♟♟	8
○	Giulio Ferrari '89	♟♟♟	8
○	Giulio Ferrari '90	♟♟♟	8
○	Giulio Ferrari '91	♟♟♟	8
○	Giulio Ferrari '92	♟♟♟	8
○	Giulio Ferrari '93	♟♟♟	8
○	Trento Brut Perlé '97	♟♟	5
○	Trento Brut Perlé '98	♟♟	6

●	Trentino Rosso Maso Le Viane '00	♟♟	6
○	Trentino Bianco Villa Margon '00	♟♟	4
●	Trentino Pinot Nero Maso Montalto '00	♟♟	6
○	Trentino Chardonnay Villa Gentilotti '02	♟♟	5
○	Trentino Sauvignon Villa San Nicolò '02	♟♟	4
○	Trentino Chardonnay Villa Margon '01	♟♟	4
○	Trentino Chardonnay Villa Margon '00	♟♟	4
○	Trentino Sauvignon Villa San Nicolò '00	♟♟	5
○	Trentino Sauvignon Villa San Nicolò '01	♟♟	4
○	Trentino Chardonnay Villa Gentilotti '99	♟♟	5
●	Trentino Rosso Maso Le Viane '99	♟♟	6

TRENTO

MASO MARTIS
LOC. MARTIGNANO
VIA DELL'ALBERA, 52
38040 TRENTO
TEL. 0461821057
E-MAIL: masomartis@tin.it

Maso Martis is a city property on the hill of Trento, among the sunny slopes and vineyards of Monte Calisio. This beautiful farm building is surrounded by a dozen hectares of vineyards, excellently managed by owner-growers Antonio and Roberta Stelzer. When they decided to devote themselves to viticulture and winemaking in the 1980s, they thought they would be producing only "spumante". The results were excellent and quick to arrive, convincing them to look beyond bubbles. Their Trento is a small treasure. The Riserva '99, in which pinot nero clear predominates over chardonnay, is one of the best Trentino cuvées. The dense, persistent mousse is very fine, introducing a palate of backbone and structure. Full, caressing and elegant on both palate and nose, it reveals floral aromas with yeast and crusty bread. The Chardonnay selection, L'Incanto '01, shows lovely structure on the palate. A brilliant gold, it ferments in oak, showing complex, deep and elegant, just as you would expect from one of the best Trentino whites. The other estate wines are also convincing. The Cabernet Sauvignon '99 is well defined and full bodied, and the Pinot Nero '01, as always, is one of the best of its type in Trento and further afield. The Trento Brut '00 is also attractively well typed and the Chardonnay '01 (we reviewed the 2000 last year) is pleasant, fruity and cellarable.

VOLANO (TN)

CONCILIO/VIGNETI DELLE MERIDIANE
ZONA INDUSTRIALE, 2
38060 VOLANO (TN)
TEL. 0464411000
E-MAIL: concilio@concilio.it

Concilio and Vigneti delle Meridiane are not the same company, although we are describing both lists in this profile. The two winemaking operations are closely linked both by commercial synergies and many shared beliefs, since they are owned by the same group of investors. Concilio produces ten or so well-made wines sold at very competitive prices on at both the domestic and export markets. Its ultra-modern winery has an overall capacity of more than 12,000,000 litres but respects Trentino traditions and makes wines rich in style and personality. The Bordeaux-blend Mori Vecio, for example, is increasingly convincing. It was probably the first Trentino wine to be barrique-aged in the 1960s. The Sauvignon and Pinot Grigio Maso Guà, both from 2002, are just as good, showing fresh, with backbone and a certain authority of structure. The Teroldego Braide selection is also good. Wines from the Vigneti delle Meridiane, the estate winery situated at Poggio on the hill of Trento, are in line with the quality decisions made by the grower-investors who founded the winery, and shared by member-growers at the historic Cantina Sociale di Trento. These wines are born of painstaking selection of the grapes and great respect for the terroir. The Chardonnay Ravina and Merlot Riserva easily scored Two Glasses and we felt that, on retasting, the Teroldego Cernidor '99 is still as good as ever.

○ Trento Brut Ris. '99	🍷🍷	6
○ Trentino Chardonnay '01	🍷🍷	4
● Trentino Cabernet Sauvignon '00	🍷🍷	5
○ Trentino Chardonnay L'Incanto '01	🍷🍷	4
● Trentino Pinot Nero '01	🍷🍷	5
○ Trento Brut '00	🍷	5
○ Trento Brut Ris. '97	🍷🍷	5
○ Trento Brut Ris. '98	🍷🍷	5

● Vigneti delle Meridiane		
Trentino Merlot Ris. '00	🍷🍷	4
○ Trentino Sauvignon '02	🍷🍷	4
○ Vigneti delle Meridiane		
Trentino Chardonnay Ravina '02	🍷🍷	4
● Teroldego Rotaliano Braide '00	🍷	5
○ Trentino Pinot Grigio Maso Guà '02	🍷	4
○ Vigneti delle Meridiane		
Trentino Chardonnay Ravina '01	🍷🍷	4
● Vigneti delle Meridiane		
Teroldego Cernidor '96	🍷🍷	4
● Trentino Rosso Mori Vecio '97	🍷🍷	4
● Vigneti delle Meridiane		
Teroldego Cernidor '97	🍷🍷	4
● Trentino Rosso Mori Vecio '99	🍷🍷	5

VOLANO (TN)

MASO BASTIE
LOC. BASTIE, 1
38070 VOLANO (TN)
TEL. 0464412747
E-MAIL: masobastie@tin.it

To stroll round this estate is to reconcile oneself with the land. The ordered rows, bordered by low dry-stone walls, the woods brushing against vines and an ultramodern cellar are so perfectly inserted into the rural context they look as if they have been there forever. Patrizia and Giuseppe Torelli are no makeshift winemakers, although their main occupation for years had no connection with wine. They set up their vineyards and cellar with a steady determination, without rushing things. They reserve special attention for sweet wine varieties, and have made space in the cellar for part-drying bunches. But Giuseppe and Patrizia dry more than just sweet wine grapes. They have also been experimenting with drying cabernet and merlot, and have already produced some very interesting results, making wines with personality and character. The Moscato Rosa '01 has an intense, dark colour with ruby flecks that highlight its breeding and add lustre to the intriguing bouquet. Pepper mingles with sensations of cinnamon and nutmeg, also showing a balsamic hint, with notes of pencil lead, then a delicately sweetish flavour that is harmonious and balanced. In contrast, Edys '01 is sweeter. Golden and honey-like, in appearance and aroma, it offsets the freshness of moscato giallo with the allure of the chardonnay and spicy tones of traminer. As for reds, the Torellis only produce the Bordeaux blend, Bastie Alte '99, which is soft and powerful, with balance but perhaps not much complexity. However, we are talking about the first releases.

○ Edys '01	♙♙	5
● Moscato Rosa '01	♙♙	6
● Trentino Bastie Alte Rosso '99	♙	6
● Moscato Rosa '00	♟♟	5
○ Trentino Traminer '01	♟♟	5
○ Edys '99	♟♟	4
● Moscato Rosa '99	♟♟	5

VOLANO (TN)

EUGENIO ROSI
VIA TAVERNELLE, 3/B
38060 VOLANO (TN)
TEL. 0464461375
E-MAIL: tamaramar@virgilio.it

It is not usually possible to stay in the Guide with just one wine, but we had to make this exception. Eugenio Rosi deserves it. Few other winemakers in Trentino are as in love with their work as this innovative Volano viticulturist, a cellarman who turns oenological techniques and procedures on their heads to make different wines as naturally as possible. In the space of a few harvests, Eugenio revolutionized the stagnant Trentino wine scene. Each of his bottles comes from careful experimentation that begins in the vineyard. After drastic pruning, he lets the grapes ripen on the plant almost until the first winter snows, and follows this by part-drying the bunches on special mats, crushing them in late spring, then vinifying them in the cellars of an 18th-century building in Calliano. The cellar is striking in its disarming simplicity. There is little technology and no barriques, only various sizes of wooden casks to respect the special characteristics of each grape. Eugenio merely monitors the development of the wine. That's why he didn't present his youngest wines, only the Marzemino Poiema, a brand-new "creation" waiting to be discovered. The 2001 vintage was vinified with a portion of the grapes part-dried to obtain a different wine, from modern intuition and early 20th-century cellar techniques. This is a gutsy wine with character and expressive depth, a velvet-on-steel Marzemino in the now much-imitated "Rosi style" that is gentle only in name.

● Trentino Marzemino Poiema '01	♙♙	5
● Dòron '00	♟♟	6
● Trentino Rosso Esegesi '99	♟♟	5
● Marzemino dei Ziresi Poiema '00	♟♟	5
● Trentino Rosso Esegesi '98	♟♟	5

OTHER WINERIES

BORGO DEI POSSERI
LOC. POZZO BASSO
38060 ALA (TN)
TEL. 0464671899

One of the new arrivals in Trentino, just now taking its first steps, Borgo dei Posseri has 230 hectares in the Ala hills, only partially under vine. Only one wine has been bottled, but it made a splendid debut. This golden Müller Thurgau is well made and even the label is beautifully designed.

○	Müller Thurgau Quaron '02	♥♥	4

CANTINA DI ALA
VIA BOLZANO, 10
38061 ALA (TN)
TEL. 0464671168
E-MAIL: cantala@tin.it

Cantina di Ala, active for years in lower Vallagarina, aims to promote and develop just two wines, the soft, fragrant Trento Classico, from an exclusively chardonnay base, and a simple, easy-drinking Marzemino selection made in strict accordance with tradition.

○	Trento Brut	♥♥	4
●	Trentino Marzemino		
	Vigne Autari '01	♥	3

ALESSANDRO SECCHI
FRAZ. SERRAVALLE ALL' ADIGE
38060 ALA (TN)
TEL. 0464696647
E-MAIL: info@secchivini.it

The growing year did not allow this dynamic estate to perform at top level, although the wines are still frank, fragrant and very pleasing. We found the lagrein-based Cinabro to be the most convincing of the many labels, but Realgar, Corindone and Berillo d'Oro are also good.

●	Cinabro '01	♥	4
●	Corindone Rosso '01	♥	5
○	Berillo d'Oro '02	♥	4
●	Realgar '02	♥	4

VINICOLA ALDENO
VIA ROMA, 78
38060 ALDENO (TN)
TEL. 0461842511
E-MAIL: viniocola.aldeno@dnet.it

This winery has long been a major, if relatively unnoticed, Merlot maker. The technically perfect wines embody the charm of the alluvial Adige terrain and vineyards set higher up towards Monte Bondone. Aldeno is a Merlot capital and a national competition is held here each year.

●	Trentino Merlot '01	♥♥	4
○	Trentino Moscato Giallo '02	♥	3

ACCADEMIA DEL VINO CADELAGHET
VIA ROMA, 13
38045 CIVEZZANO (TN)
TEL. 0461859045
E-MAIL: info@accademiadelvino.it

This estate's wines are getting more and more convincing. The few thousand bottles are released in no great hurry, when mature and flavoursome. The Cabernet Sauvignon impressed us most, but the Nosiola and Chardonnay are confident and fragrant. The barrique-aged Pinot Nero is nice.

● Trentino Cabernet Sauvignon '00	🍷🍷	5
● Trentino Pinot Nero '99	🍷🍷	5
○ Trentino Chardonnay '01	🍷	4
○ Trentino Nosiola '01	🍷	4

ARCANGELO SANDRI
VIA VANEGGIE, 4
38010 FAEDO (TN)
TEL. 0461650935
E-MAIL: sand_arca@libero.it

Sandri is one of Faedo's most authentic growers, tending high-altitude vineyards cut into the mountain. Daughter Nadia also works on the estate and all the wines are upfront and fragrant. The Lagrein is best, with good fruit and soft texture. The Müller Thurgau, Traminer and Chardonnay are sound.

● Trentino Lagrein '01	🍷🍷	5
○ Trentino Chardonnay '02	🍷	4
○ Trentino Müller Thurgau '02	🍷	4

VILLA CORNIOLE
FRAZ. VERLA
38030 GIOVO (TN)
TEL. 0461684379
E-MAIL: info@villacorniole.com

The cellar here is very new, excavated from the Valle di Cembra rock and surrounded by lovely mountain vineyards. The Pellegrini brothers only vinify grapes from their own vineyards and there are two lines. The wines are well made, well typed and varietal. Below are the best of the ones we tasted.

○ Trentino Müller Thurgau '02	🍷🍷	4
● Teroldego Lagrein '02	🍷	4
○ Trentino Pinot Grigio '02	🍷	4

CASATA MONFORT
VIA CARLO SETTE, 21
38015 LAVIS (TN)
TEL. 0461241484 - 0461246353
E-MAIL: casatamonfort@tin.it

Excellent cellar technique and shrewd grape selection make the Simoni brothers' estate one of the most important and dynamic in Trentino. They produce a broad range of high-quality wines. The aromatic whites are outstanding but the sound Lagrein and appealing Moscato Rosa are just as good.

● Trentino Lagrein '01	🍷🍷	4
○ Trentino Traminer Aromatico '02	🍷🍷	4
⊙ Monfort Rosa '02	🍷	5
○ Trentino Müller Thurgau '02	🍷	4

MOLINO DEI LESSI
LOC. MASI DI SORNI - MASO ROSABEL, 5
38015 LAVIS (TN)
TEL. 0461870275
E-MAIL: enzoce@tin.it

This estate is near an old mill, in a vine-girt gorge between Sorni and Lavis. Oenologist Emma Clauser owns and manages the certified organic property. Output is low but there are two well-made wines. We prefer the invitingly minerally Podere Valtini white, but the Cabernet Sauvignon is elegant.

● Trentino Cabernet Sauvignon '00	🍷🍷	5
○ Riesling Renano Podere Valtini '01	🍷🍷	4

PELZ & PIFFER
LOC. PRESSANO
VIA CLAUDIA AUGUSTA
38015 LAVIS (TN)
TEL. 0461683051

Next year, the new cellar will be ready at this estate on the sunny slopes of Valle di Cembra. Quality is the priority. Among those tasted, the Riesling stood out. The Müller Thurgau is just as good and the Chardonnay is very concentrated.

○ Trentino Riesling '01	🍷🍷	3
○ Chardonnay '02	🍷	3
○ Müller Thurgau '02	🍷	3

CIPRIANO FEDRIZZI
VIA 4 NOVEMBRE, 3
38017 MEZZOLOMBARDO (TN)
TEL. 0461602328

Only limited production hinders this estate winery from competing as a major player in the top-quality Teroldego market. The Due Vigneti selection did not excite us as much as usual but it is still well gauged. Too bad there is not much of it. The standard Teroldego is youthfully alcoholic.

● Teroldego Rotaliano Due Vigneti '01	🍷🍷	6
● Teroldego Rotaliano '02	🍷	3

ZANINI
VIA ROMA, 24
38017 MEZZOLOMBARDO (TN)
TEL. 0461601496
E-MAIL: zaninoscar@jumpy.it

Teroldego is the mainstay of this increasingly reliable estate. The plots are in the Campo Rotaliano and yield grapes that are vinified on-site into vigorous, hearty wines. This year, there was also an elegant selection of Chardonnay and an interesting late-harvest wine, Gocce di Sole.

● Teroldego Rotaliano Le Cervare '01	🍷🍷	4
○ Gocce di Sole '01	🍷	6
○ Trentino Chardonnay I Giardini '01	🍷	4
● Teroldego Rotaliano '02	🍷	3

CANTINA SOCIALE DI NOMI
VIA ROMA, 1
38060 NOMI (TN)
TEL. 0464834195
E-MAIL: cantinanomi@tin.it

Cantina di Nomi is currently re-organizing and has launched an ambitious project for quality wines. But those we tasted were well proportioned and terroir-driven. The Müller Thurgau is good and Marzemino is always flavourful, as are the Pinot Grigio and Moscato Giallo.

○ Trentino Müller Thurgau I Fiori del Trentino '02	🍷🍷	4
● Trentino Marzemino '02	🍷	3
○ Trentino Moscato Giallo Le Comete '02	🍷	4
○ Trentino Pinot Grigio Castel Pietra '02	🍷	4

DALZOCCHIO
LOC. BOSCO DELLA CITTÀ
VIA VALLELUNGA SECONDA, 50
38068 ROVERETO (TN)
TEL. 0464423580 - 0464413664

This estate stands high above Rovereto and its reputation is rising to meet it. There are only two wines, since Elisabetta Dalzocchio has decided to raise quality instead of increasing the number of types. The property is farmed organically and the wines reflect the terroir and estate philosophy.

○ Trentino Chardonnay '01	🍷🍷	5
● Trentino Pinot Nero '01	🍷🍷	6

GIOVANNI POLI
LOC. SANTA MASSENZA
VIA VEZZANO, 37
38070 VEZZANO (TN)
TEL. 0461864119

Giovanni Poli is a master distiller and enthusiastic winemaker. He and his children concentrate on Vino Santo, tending their vineyards and cellar with love. The '96 is delicately sweet and rich in pulp, with good length and elegance.

○ Trentino Vino Santo '96	🍷🍷	6

FRANCESCO POLI
LOC. SANTA MASSENZA, 36
38070 VEZZANO (TN)
TEL. 0461864102
E-MAIL: alessandro.poli@inwind.it

Francesco Poli's small estate is in an equally small village. His specialty is distilling pomace and vinifying nosiola for Vino Santo, a Valle dei Laghi delight. It's a niche production that is worth looking out for.

○ Trentino Vino Santo '96	🍷🍷	6

ALTO ADIGE

We begin with a major announcement. In contrast to events in the rest of Italy, the 2002 harvest in Alto Adige was one of the best in the past few years. We want to state this loud and clear since we would hate to see wines from this vintage, especially the Alto Adige whites, treated as if they were lesser bottles from a poor year. Zones such as the Valle Isarco may actually have had the vintage of the century, or at least come very close. The Kerners, Veltliners, Sylvaners and the few Rieslings are simply out of this world. But things also went very well in other subzones of the region, such as Terlano, in the Oltradige south of Bolzano. Not too much rain, wide day-night temperature variations and perfect ripening produced great aromas and wines with excellent body and acidity levels. All this means long-lived whites, still drinking well four or five years from the harvest. So 2002 was certainly not what you could call an indifferent growing year. We are happy to announce this, since the number of Three Glass awards for Alto Adige this year was slightly lower than last time, only 18 instead of 19. But this is just a temporary setback. Actually, the average level of the wines was the same, if not better. A few high points were missing, but we should point out that all the truly outstanding whites from 2002 will be released next year, and assessed in the 2005 Guide. At any rate, the performance of one special winery should be underscored. The Cantina Produttori at Termeno is the only producer in the region to win two Three Glass awards, and also sent an impressive number of wines to our final taste-offs. That was why we decided to honour winery "Kellermeister" Willi Sturz with the title of Winemaker of the Year. This major prize seeks to reward the work not only of Sturz, obviously, but all Alto Adige's other cellarmasters as well, the top-level technicians who have managed to bring the overall quality of the region's production to levels equalled in few places elsewhere in the entire world. We make this rather bold statement with confidence, in the certainty that is does no more than justice to a region at the forefront of winemaking in Italy and beyond.

ANDRIANO (BZ)

CANTINA PRODUTTORI ANDRIANO
VIA DELLA CHIESA, 2
39010 ANDRIANO (BZ)
TEL. 0471510137
E-MAIL: info@andrianer-kellerei.it

The hospitable Val d'Adige winemaking centre of Andriano is a small village with little more than 700 inhabitants. Its vineyards are found exclusively among the surrounding hills, all on sandy, clayey, alluvial soil. Founded in 1893, La Cantina Produttori Andriano is the oldest co-operative winery in Alto Adige and presently brings together 135 producers with a total surface area of 136 hectares. A good 65 per cent of the wines produced here are reds. Though select products from the Tor di Lupo and Sonnengut lines are now well known, and even famous, we should not forget the wines that are produced with organic growing practices compliant with Bioland guidelines. The Three Glass award went to the excellent Cabernet Tor di Lupo '00, a complex, concentrated wine with ripe tannins, good development and a long, full-flavoured finish. The Terlano Pinot Bianco Sonnengut '02 also made it to our final taste-offs, showing minerally, elegant and concentrated, with notes of damson and tomato leaf, as well as lovely structure. Other very attractive results from the Tor di Lupo line included the elegant, fresh and mineral Terlano Sauvignon Preciosa '02, the Lagrein '01, with ripe fruit on the nose, nice elegance and still slightly green tannins, and the Merlot '01, which is fruity and concentrated but with a lot of wood and drying tannins. The Traminer Aromatico Tor di Lupo '02 is somewhat simple, though full flavoured and well balanced. The Merlot Sonnengut '00 is pleasant, with fresh fruit, tobacco and a certain gamey complexity, but the Chardonnay Tor di Lupo '01 is merely decent, lacking a bit of freshness.

APPIANO/EPPAN (BZ)

JOSEF BRIGL
LOC. SAN MICHELE
VIA MADONNA DEL RIPOSO, 1
39057 APPIANO (BZ)
TEL. 0471662419
E-MAIL: brigl@brigl.com

One of the largest wineries in Alto Adige, Josef Brigl has been a reliable name for some years now and the cellar produces a broad selection of wines, nearly all of which are good quality, and all sold at very reasonable prices. In fact, drinkability and a good value are the winery's hallmarks. We found the Chardonnay 2002 particularly convincing at this year's tastings. It has lovely notes of tropical fruit that shift toward refreshing mint nuances, then ripe white peach shows up again on the big, pervasive palate, accompanied by pleasant balsamic shades. The Lagrein Briglhof '01 is also good, and conveys the typical varietal characteristics of ripe blackberry and black pepper. The palate has no great power, but develops with intensity and continuity. The varietal, well-made Cabernet Briglhof '00 and Gewürztraminer Windegg 2002 are also interesting. The Pinot Nero Kreuzbichler '00, in spite of great recognition in the past, and the Schiava Grigia Kaltenburg and Sauvignon from the 2002 vintage, are all a bit too simple, and less than perfectly balanced. Still, these are utterly respectable results overall, that only lack the true star that would bring this beautiful, historic winery to the top of regional production. The potential is all there.

● A. A. Cabernet Tor di Lupo '00	▼▼▼	5
○ A. A. Terlano Pinot Bianco Cl. Sonnengut '02	▼▼	4
● A. A. Lagrein Scuro Tor di Lupo '01	▼▼	6
● A. A. Merlot Tor di Lupo '01	▼▼	5
○ A. A. Terlano Sauvignon Preciosa Tor di Lupo '02	▼▼	4
● A. A. Merlot Sonnengut '00	▼	4
○ A. A. Chardonnay Tor di Lupo '01	▼	5
○ A. A. Traminer Aromatico Tor di Lupo '02	▼	5
● A. A. Lagrein Scuro Tor di Lupo '00	▼▼▼	5
○ A. A. Traminer Aromatico Sonnengut '01	▼▼	4
○ A. A. Terlano Sauvignon Preciosa Tor di Lupo	▼	4
● A. A. Merlot Siebeneich Tor di Lupo '00	▼▼	4

● A. A. Lagrein Scuro Briglhof '01	▼▼	5
○ A. A. Chardonnay '02	▼▼	3
● A. A. Cabernet Briglhof '00	▼	5
● A. A. Pinot Nero Kreuzbichler '00	▼	5
○ A. A. Gewürztraminer Windegg '02	▼	4
○ A. A. Sauvignon '02	▼	4
● A. A. Schiava Grigia Kaltenburg '02	▼	4
○ A. A. Sauvignon '00	▼▼	4*
● A. A. Lagrein Scuro Briglhof '98	▼▼	5
● A. A. Lagrein Scuro Briglhof '00	▼▼	5
● A. A. Lago di Caldaro Scelto Haselhof Cl. Sup. '01	▼▼	3*
○ A. A. Sauvignon '01	▼▼	4*
● A. A. Cabernet Briglhof '99	▼▼	5

APPIANO/EPPAN (BZ)

APPIANO/EPPAN (BZ)

KÖSSLER - PRAECLARUS
VIA SAN PAOLO, 15
39050 APPIANO/EPPAN (BZ)
TEL. 0471660256 - 0471662182
E-MAIL: ebner@koessler.it

K. MARTINI & SOHN
LOC. CORNAIANO/GIRLAN
VIA LAMM, 28
39050 APPIANO/EPPAN (BZ)
TEL. 0471663156
E-MAIL: info@weinkellerei-martini.it

Founded at the end of the 19th century, in 1878 to be precise, this San Paolo Appiano estate gave us wines as reliable and well-made as ever, thanks to impeccable technique, scrupulous selection of grapes during the harvest and unflagging passion. It should be recalled that part of the range is made up of still wines, almost all released under the Kössler & Ebner label, while others are "metodo classico" sparklers presented with the Praeclarus label, now famous in Italy and beyond. We'll begin with a "spumante", the Praeclarus Noblesse Riserva '94. It's an Extra Brut from 70 per cent chardonnay and pinot bianco, aged on the lees for nine years before disgorgement. A brilliant gold introduces a harmonious bouquet then a powerful palate with hints of roasted hazelnuts, and an elegant closing note of honey and vanilla. The Praeclarus Brut is also very good, showing fullness of flavour and imposing structure. When we moved onto the still wines, we particularly like the Lagrein Merlot Ebner '01 for its lovely notes of spice and ripe blackberry, rich body with assertive tannins but elegant texture, and its beautiful personality. The Cabernet Merlot S. Pauls '01 is also well made, showing concentrated, fruity and linear, with sweet, compact tannins. The Merlot Tschiedererhof '01 and Lagrein '00 may be a bit over-oaked.

A family-run winery founded in 1979 by Karl Martini and his son Gabriel, the Martini estate is located in the midst of beautiful vineyards in the tiny village of Cornaiano, outside Appiano. The rich earth here gives rise to a broad range of wines from this producer, vinified with the proper balance of centuries old tradition and modern technology to preserve bouquet and flavour. Gabriel Martini's pride and joy are his partially barrique-aged wines from the Maturum and Palladium lines, such as the Lagrein Maturum, whose latest release made it to our final tastings last year. The Lagrein Rueslhof '01 has a winning bouquet of ripe fruit, quinine, graphite and coffee. Sweet, very refined and elegant in the mouth, it closes out on a clean, continuous finale. The Sauvignon Palladium '02 introduces itself with an aromatic nose of mint and tomato leaves. The very mineral palate of this well-made wine is fresh and concentrated. The Coldirus Palladium '01, a mix of 60 per cent Lagrein and 40 per cent Cabernet, has a bouquet of blackberry, blueberry, redcurrants and violets on the nose, whereas the palate is a bit simpler, though still refined and elegant. The two schiava-based standard wines were good and well typed. Schiava Palladium '02 and Lago di Caldaro Classico Felton '02 were fresh, fruity and elegant, showing soft with good structure and ready to drink. The Chardonnay Palladium '02 was also well typed but very simple.

O A. A. Spumante Praeclarus Noblesse Ris. '94	♈♈	5
● A. A. Lagrein Merlot Ebner '01	♈♈	6
O A. A. Spumante Praeclarus Brut	♈♈	5
● A. A. Cabernet Kössler & Ebner '00	♈	4
● A. A. Lagrein Scuro '00	♈	5
● A. A. Cabernet-Merlot S. Pauls '01	♈	4
● A. A. Merlot Tschidererhof '01	♈	4
O A. A. Spumante Praeclarus Noblesse Ris. '93	♈♈	5
O A. A. Spumante Praeclarus Brut	♈♈	5
● A. A. Lagrein Merlot Ebner '00	♈♈	6
● A. A. Lagrein Scuro '99	♈♈	5

● A. A. Lagrein Scuro Rueslhof '01	♈♈	4*
● A. A. Lagrein-Cabernet Coldirus Palladium '01	♈♈	4
O A. A. Sauvignon Palladium '02	♈♈	4
● A. A. Lago di Caldaro Cl. Felton '02	♈	3*
● A. A. Schiava Palladium '02	♈	4
O A. A. Chardonnay Palladium '02		4
● A. A. Lagrein Scuro Maturum '99	♈♈	5
● A. A. Lagrein Scuro Maturum '00	♈♈	5
● A. A. Lagrein-Cabernet Coldirus Palladium '00	♈♈	4
O A. A. Chardonnay Palladium '01	♈	4
● A. A. Schiava Palladium '01	♈	3

APPIANO/EPPAN (BZ)

JOSEF NIEDERMAYR
LOC. CORNAIANO/GIRLAN
VIA CASA DI GESÙ, 15
39050 APPIANO/EPPAN (BZ)
TEL. 0471662451
E-MAIL: info@niedermayr.it

Josef Niedermayr is a major player in Alto Adige viticulture. His 16-hectare estate puts out around 350,000 bottles of wines with great personality. Three wines made it to our finals this year and, though none took our highest award, they are proof of the absolute excellence of this historic cellar. We really loved the Lagrein Aus Gries Riserva '01 because of its intense aromas of quinine and ripe blackberry. Full on the palate with sweet, compact tannins, it is very varietal and carries a note of flint. It's a masterful interpretation. The chardonnay and sauvignon-based Aureus 2001 is excellent, though it lacks just a pinch more elegance to be truly great. The Sauvignon Allure '02 has a very varietal nose and unveils a palate of truly remarkable minerality and easy drinkability. But then again, the winery's entire hovers around very high quality levels. The powerful, barrique-aged Euforius '01, from lagrein, cabernet and merlot, has a lovely, long, overwhelming finish. The Gewürztraminer Lage Doss '02 is varietal and fruity, showing concentrated on the palate with a pleasant refreshing acidity. The 50-50 chardonnay and pinot grigio Perelle '01 is powerful and intense. If we really wanted to criticize, we could say we were not entirely convinced by the Pinot Nero Riserva '00, already tasted last year as a cask sample, since we found it currently a bit too marked by the wood. But we are certain Josef will be working hard to make us change our ideas very soon.

APPIANO/EPPAN (BZ)

CANTINA PRODUTTORI CORNAIANO
LOC. CORNAIANO/GIRLAN
VIA SAN MARTINO, 24
39050 APPIANO/EPPAN (BZ)
TEL. 0471662403
E-MAIL: info@girlan.it

Though overall results are positive, there are highs and lows in the range of wines presented this year by the Cantina Produttori Cornaiano. The Cabernet Sauvignon SelectArt Flora Riserva '00 is splendid, introducing itself with intense spicy, balsamic notes and expanding on the concentrated palate with smooth tannins and a very continuous finish, but sadly, we also found the legendary Schiava Gschleier '01 frankly disappointing. But to get back to the many positive notes. The Moscato Rosa Passito Pasithea Rosa '01 is very good, typical and well made, in fact it almost picked up Three Glasses. The Lagrein SelectArt Flora Riserva '00 is concentrated, with dense tannins, and well supported by soft ripe fruit. The Chardonnay SelectArt Flora '01 has great impact on the nose, where pineapple and papaya accompany pleasant nuances of lychees. It is big and balanced on the palate where, again we find tropical fruit, particularly mango, and a wonderfully deep finish. The very interesting Pinot Bianco Plattenriegel '02 is concentrated and introduces nicely complex mineral notes on the palate. The Pinot Nero Trattmannhof SelectArt Flora '01, Sauvignon SelectArt Flora '02, Gewürztraminer SelectArt Flora '02 and Pinot Bianco Passito Pasithea Oro '01 are all simpler wines. Though this is a nice string of glasses, we still have a hunch that this great, historic co-operative winery could do even better and are certain it will as soon as possible.

● A. A. Lagrein Aus Gries Ris. '01	♟♟	6
○ Aureus '01	♟♟	7
○ A. A. Sauvignon Allure '02	♟♟	4
● Euforius '01	♟♟	6
○ A. A. Gewürztraminer Lage Doss '02	♟♟	5
● A. A. Pinot Nero Ris. '00	♟	6
○ Perelle '01	♟	5
○ A. A. Sauvignon Lage Naun '02	♟	4
○ A. A. Terlano Hof zu Pramol '02	♟	4
○ Aureus '95	♟♟♟	6
○ Aureus '98	♟♟♟	6
○ Aureus '99	♟♟♟	6
● A. A. Lagrein Aus Gries Ris. '00	♟♟	5
○ Aureus '00	♟♟	6

● A. A. Moscato Rosa Passito Pasithea Rosa '01	♟♟	6
● A. A. Cabernet Sauvignon SelectArt Flora Ris. '00	♟♟	5
● A. A. Lagrein SelectArt Flora Ris. '00	♟♟	6
○ A. A. Chardonnay Select Art Flora '01	♟♟	5
○ A. A. Pinot Bianco Plattenriegl '02	♟♟	4
○ A. A. Pinot Bianco Passito Pasithea '01	♟	7
● A. A. Pinot Nero Trattmannhof SelectArt Flora '01	♟	5
● A. A. Schiava Gschleier SelectArt Flora '01	♟	5
○ A. A. Gewürztraminer SelectArt Flora '02	♟	5*
○ A. A. Sauvignon SelectArt Flora '02	♟	5

APPIANO/EPPAN (BZ)

APPIANO/EPPAN (BZ)

CANTINA PRODUTTORI SAN PAOLO
LOC. SAN PAOLO
VIA CASTEL GUARDIA, 21
39050 APPIANO/EPPAN (BZ)
TEL. 0471662183
E-MAIL: info@kellereistpauls.com

IGNAZ NIEDRIST
LOC. CORNAIANO/GIRLAN
VIA RONCO, 5
39050 APPIANO/EPPAN (BZ)
TEL. 0471664494

The friendly, likeable Leopold Kager, chair of the Cantina Produttori di San Paolo, should be very satisfied. This lovely Appiano estate presented wines this year with the touch of extra personality that was perhaps missing in earlier vintages. The Terlano Pinot Bianco Plötzner Exclusiv '02 is really very convincing and only just missed Three Glasses. It has intense aromas of damson and white peach, an elegantly complex, concentrated palate with a nice minerally backbone, and a long finish, making it an excellent Pinot Bianco. But then the terrain here is ideal for growing this underrated variety and we are convinced some nice surprises will come from these parts over the next few years. The Sauvignon Gfillhof '02 from the Exclusiv line is truly special. The complex, elegant nose opens up harmoniously on the palate, accompanied by fresh mentholated notes, then the finish is deep and intriguing. The Gewürztraminer Exclusiv St. Justina '02 is good, but a bit simple. On to the reds, where we begin with the fresh, easy-drinking Schiava Sarner Hof Exclusiv '02. Then came the excellent Merlot Huberfeld '01, which shows concentrated and powerful, followed by the Lagrein DiVinus Riserva '00 with its wonderful bouquet. We should point out that all the reds showed a slight excess of wood, particularly the Lagrein. But this is the tiniest of blemishes among such admirable results.

Ignaz Niedrist is one of those producers you always want to award a prize to. He is a professional, and an intelligent winemaker who always looks for balance and elegance, refusing to churn out wines that are overdrawn caricatures of their respective types. It is no accident he has always worked with difficult varieties such as riesling, pinot nero and sauvignon. Indeed, the magnificent Terlano Sauvignon '02 came very close to Three Glasses. It's a great white with aromas that are varietal but not over the top, the notes of white peach and elderflower leading to a round, balanced palate with hints of acidity well integrated into the structure of the wine, and a very elegant finish. The Riesling '02 is also excellent, expressing impeccable balance between benzene aromas and the very fresh, elegant palate with its wonderfully complex mineral notes. All in all, it's a textbook Niedrist wine. The Terlano Pinot Bianco '02 has rare finesse and elegance, showing off the great potential of this variety. The typical Lagrein Berger Gei '01 is full bodied and has remarkable density of extract that marries well with the ripe fruit and lovely notes of leather and tobacco. The Merlot Mühlweg '01 has intense fruit, with slightly over-ripe shades of blackberry and blueberry. It's is concentrated and elegant on the palate with well-integrated oak. Though the Pinot Nero '01 is a bit below expectations, this in no way detracts from the considerable quality. Ignaz Niedrist's great skills and reliability shine throughout the range.

○ A. A. Pinot Bianco Exclusiv Plötzner '02	🍷🍷	4*
● A. A. Lagrein Scuro DiVinus Ris. '00	🍷🍷	6
● A. A. Merlot Exclusiv Huberfeld '01	🍷🍷	4*
○ A. A. Sauvignon Exclusiv Gfillhof '02	🍷🍷	4*
● A. A. Schiava Sarner Hof Exclusiv '02	🍷🍷	4
○ A. A. Gewürztraminer Exclusiv St. Justina '02	🍷	5
● A. A. Merlot DiVinus '97	🍷🍷	5
● A. A: Merlot DiVinus '99	🍷🍷	5
○ A. A. Sauvignon Exclusiv Gfil Hof '01	🍷🍷	4*
○ A. A. Pinot Grigio Exclusiv Egg Leiten '01	🍷🍷	4*

○ A. A. Terlano Sauvignon '02	🍷🍷	5
● A. A. Lagrein Berger Gei '01	🍷🍷	5
○ A. A. Riesling Renano '02	🍷🍷	4*
○ A. A. Terlano Pinot Bianco '02	🍷🍷	4
● A. A. Merlot Mühlweg '01	🍷	5
● A. A. Pinot Nero '01	🍷	6
○ A. A. Terlano Sauvignon '00	🍷🍷🍷	4*
○ A. A. Riesling Renano '99	🍷🍷	4
○ A. A. Riesling Renano '00	🍷🍷	4
● A. A. Lagrein Scuro Berger Gei Ris. '97	🍷🍷	5
● A. A. Lagrein Berger Gei '00	🍷🍷	5
● A. A. Merlot Mühlweg '00	🍷🍷	5
○ A. A. Riesling Renano '01	🍷🍷	4
○ A. A. Terlano Sauvignon '01	🍷🍷	5*

★ Cantina Produttori Colterenzio

loc. Cornaiano/Girlan
strada del Vino, 8
39050 Appiano/Eppan (BZ)
tel. 0471664246
e-mail: info@colterenzio.com

What more is there to say about the innumerable successes of this splendid estate? We could perhaps emphasize the great job that is being done by Wolfgang Raifer, the young oenologist raised on-site. For proof of this, take a quick look below at the impressive number of Glasses earned this year. A shining version of the Cabernet Sauvignon Lafoa '00 won Three Glasses by a landslide. Its truly remarkable concentration and varietal tones show no vegetal excesses, the rich nose of balsamic and fruit aromas introducing compact, sweet tannins in the mouth. It's a masterpiece. The surprise came with its partner, the Cabernet Sauvignon Kastlèt Praedium Riserva '00. This, too, came close to a third Glass for its sheer elegance. The Chardonnay Cornell '01 is a wine that at this point seems to be running on automatic pilot. The broad bouquet reveals broom and acacia honey, then explodes onto the palate with a concentration and elegance that place this well-established wine up there among the great Italian whites. Nothing less than another estate classic, the Gewürztraminer Cornell '02 took advantage of a great harvest to show off a truly majestic interpretation. But the whole range of wines presented by the Cantina Produttori Colterenzio is impressive in both quality and personality. Chair Luis Raifer should be very happy with the results, though we know he will want to do even better, and that is not easy.

●	A. A. Cabernet Sauvignon Lafoa '00	TTT	8
●	A. A. Cabernet Sauvignon Kastelt Ris. '00	TT	5
○	A. A. Chardonnay Cornell '01	TT	5
○	A. A. Gewürztraminer Cornell '02	TT	5
●	A. A. Lagrein Mantsch Ris. '00	TT	5
○	A. A. Pinot Grigio Cornell '01	TT	5
○	A. A. Sauvignon Lafoa '01	TT	6
○	A. A. Pinot Bianco Weisshaus '02	TT	4
●	A. A. Pinot Nero Cornell Schwarzhaus '00	T	6
●	A. A. Cabernet Sauvignon Lafoa '97	YYY	6
○	A. A. Chardonnay Cornell '99	YYY	6
○	A. A. Chardonnay Cornell '00	YYY	6
○	A. A. Chardonnay Altkirch '02	YY	4
●	A. A. Cabernet Sauvignon Lafoa '99	YY	8

★ Cantina Produttori San Michele Appiano

via Circonvallazione, 17/19
39057 Appiano/Eppan (BZ)
tel. 0471664466
e-mail: kellerei@stmichael.it

It is no secret we liked the Lagrein '01 Sanct Valentin, though somewhat less than in the last edition of the Guide. Having said this, the ship piloted by Hans Terzer, the famous cellarmaster from San Michele Appiano, sails on full steam ahead. In fact, a new member has been added to the big Sanct Valentin family, the Pinot Bianco '01 that already shows a lovely personality on its debut. We look forward to the '02 version and are certain we will see some nice wines in the future. There was a warm reception for the Sauvignon Sanct Valentin '02, which easily won our Three Glass award by beguiling the panel with an elegance and balance rarely achieved by a wine that has established itself as one of the great Italian whites. But others also came close, including the Chardonnay '01, the Gewürztraminer '02 and the Cabernet '01, again from the estate's top line. The Pinot Bianco Schulthauser '02 has also returned to top form, introducing intense damson and white peach aromas that lead on to a concentrated palate and stylish, pleasant fresh almond finish. But the average quality of all the wines submitted by this great co-operative winery never ceases to amaze us. Remember, by the way, that overall production runs to almost 2,000,000 units. But apart from these words, take a look at the list of wines below. It shows spectacular quality standards that have been reached, not by accident, but by making the most of the professionalism, far-sightedness and commitment of everyone involved in this splendid winemaking enterprise.

○	A. A. Sauvignon St. Valentin '02	TTT	5
●	A. A. Cabernet St. Valentin '01	TT	6
○	A. A. Chardonnay St. Valentin '01	TT	5
○	A. A. Pinot Grigio St. Valentin '01	TT	5
○	A. A. Gewürztraminer St. Valentin '02	TT	5
○	A. A. Pinot Bianco Schulthauser '02	TT	4*
●	A. A. Pinot Nero Ris. '00	TT	5
●	A. A. Lagrein St. Valentin '01	TT	6
○	A. A. Pinot Bianco St. Valentin '01	TT	5
●	A. A. Pinot Nero St. Valentin '01	TT	6
○	A. A. Bianco Passito Comtess St. Valentin '02	TT	6
○	A. A. Chardonnay Merol '02	TT	4
○	A. A. Pinot Grigio Anger '02	TT	4
○	A. A. Riesling Montiggl '02	TT	4

BOLZANO/BOZEN

ANDREAS BERGER -THURNHOF
VIA CASTEL FLAVON, 7
39100 BOLZANO/BOZEN
TEL. 0471288460
E-MAIL: info@thurnhof.com

Andreas Berger is a great little producer. We say "little" since he only owns three and a half hectares and produces around 12,000 bottles annually. He's "great" because that's what his talent and passion for his wine and land are. So we are sorry the wines the talented Andreas submitted this year were good, but not as great as in the last few vintages. We'll begin with the winery workhorse. The Lagrein '01 has a deep, impenetrable colour and intense spicy aromas with distinct notes of pepper and blueberry. It shows excellent body on the palate and has dense, abundant tannins that are fairly well integrated into the general structure of the wine. It's a lovely Lagrein but not up to the level of the fantastic 1999 edition. The two Cabernet Sauvignons, the 2001 vintage and Riserva 2000, are interesting but slightly below par. The invasive oak in the first wine is not offset by the structure, which does not seem enormous. The Riserva has limited elegance, although it does reveal considerable structure. The Santa Maddalena'02 is as good as usual, with typical sensations of small red berries alongside curious smoky notes. It is fresh and fruity on the palate, and very enjoyable to drink. The Moscato Giallo '02 is also pleasant, with varietal notes of broom and ripe peach. These entirely admirable results only lacked the high point we are certain we will be able to report next year.

BOLZANO/BOZEN

CANTINA GRIES/CANTINA DI BOLZANO
FRAZ. GRIES
P.ZZA GRIES, 2
39100 BOLZANO/BOZEN
TEL. 0471270909 - 0471972944
E-MAIL: info@kellerei-gries.it

The Cantina di Gries, or rather Cantina di Bolzano, repeats its Three Glass performance with an extraordinary version of the Lagrein Scuro Grieser Prestige Line '00. It could well be the best, thanks to its extraordinary ability to read the territory. The intense, varietal wild berry aromas accompany complex notes of oriental spices and tobacco. The soft, full palate then expands with silky tannins, to finish with rare depth and elegance. The Mauritius '00 also reached our final taste-offs. It's a tight-knit blend of Lagrein and Merlot with lots of muscle and dense, ripe tannins. We also continue to enjoy the so-called traditional version of the Lagrein, the Collection Baron Carl Eyrl '01. Fresh, pleasant aromas usher in a not very concentrated mouth that shows good balance and remarkably well-integrated fruit. The pleasant progression leads to an uncommonly clean, elegant finish. The two Merlots, the Siebeneich Prestige Line Riserva '00 and Collection Graf Huyn '01, are also good and well made. As usual, the Moscato Giallo Vinalia '01 is one of the best in the category. Aromas of dates and tropical fruit are accompanied by fresh hints of citron peel before the palate reveals concentration, without sacrificing elegance or typicity. The very well-made Moscato Rosa Rosis '01 is well typed and well interpreted. The other two wines submitted, the Pinot Bianco Collection Dallago '01 and Santa Maddalena Classico Trögler '02, are both very pleasant. In other words, there were better than just positive results for a winery that is a firmly established regional leader.

● A. A. Cabernet Sauvignon Ris. '00	♟♟	5
● A. A. Lagrein Scuro '01	♟♟	5
● A. A. Cabernet Sauvignon '01	♟	5
○ A. A. Moscato Giallo '02	♟	4
● A. A. Santa Maddalena '02	♟	3
● A. A. Lagrein Scuro '99	♟♟♟	4*
● A. A. Lagrein Scuro Ris. '97	♟♟	5
● A. A. Lagrein Scuro '98	♟♟	4
● A. A. Cabernet Sauvignon Ris. '99	♟♟	5
● A. A. Lagrein Scuro '00	♟♟	5
● A. A. Santa Maddalena '01	♟♟	3

● A. A. Lagrein Scuro Grieser Prestige Line Ris. '00	♟♟♟	6
● A. A. Merlot Lagrein Mauritius Ris. '00	♟♟	6
● A. A. Merlot Prestige Line Ris. '00	♟♟	7
● A. A. Lagrein Scuro Grieser Baron Carl Eyrl Ris. '01	♟♟	4*
○ A. A. Moscato Giallo Vinalia '01	♟♟	6
● A. A. Moscato Rosa Rosis '01	♟♟	6
● A. A. Merlot Otto Graf Huyn Ris. '01	♟	5
○ A. A. Pinot Bianco Collection Dellago '01	♟	5
● A. A. Santa Maddalena Cl. Tröglerhof '02	♟	3
○ A. A. Moscato Giallo Vinalia '99	♟♟♟	5
● A. A. Lagrein Scuro Grieser Prestige Line Ris. '99	♟♟♟	6

Cantina Convento Muri-Gries

P.zza Gries, 21
39100 Bolzano/Bozen
tel. 0471282287
e-mail: muri-gries-kg@muri-gries.com

The fact Lagrein has now become one of the most interesting reds on the Italian winemaking scene is remarkable, since it happened in just a few years. Christian Werth, cellarmaster of the Cantina Convento Muri Gries, is no stranger to this development because he is one of its main proponents. His Lagrein Scuro Abtei Riserva is a benchmark for all producers in Alto Adige. This little excursus is our way of introducing the news that this great red has again won Three Glasses for its 2000 version. The bouquet is rich with spice and fruit, as well as notes of tobacco. The attack on the palate is intense and rich, with tannins that are tight-knit but not aggressive, and signs off with almost endless length. It may still be young and in need of more cellar time but it is already great. We were also very impressed with the white Bianco Abtei '01 from chardonnay, pinot bianco and pinot grigio. The complex bouquet of wistaria and candied citron leads to a concentrated, well-balanced palate, with complex balsamic and minty nuances, that drives triumphantly through to the rising finish. But the talented Christian has also made another very nice white, the well-typed, elegant Pinot Grigio '02. And the following wines are all as well made as usual: the standard-label Lagrein, which is fresh, fruity and pleasantly drinkable; the Moscato Rosa Abtei '01, which perhaps only lacks a pinch of elegance; and the easy-drinking Lagrein Rosato '02. In other words, this cellar is more than just Lagrein. It may even win Three Glasses for a white soon.

●	A. A. Lagrein Abtei Ris. '00	🍷🍷🍷	5
○	A. A. Bianco Abtei '01	🍷🍷	4
○	A. A. Pinot Grigio '02	🍷🍷	4
●	A. A. Moscato Rosa '01	🍷	6
●	A. A. Lagrein '02	🍷	4
⊙	A. A. Lagrein Rosato Gries '02	🍷	3*
●	A. A. Lagrein Scuro Abtei Ris. '96	🍸🍸🍸	5
●	A. A. Lagrein Scuro Abtei Ris. '97	🍸🍸🍸	5
●	A. A. Lagrein Scuro Abtei Ris. '98	🍸🍸🍸	5
●	A. A. Lagrein Scuro Abtei Ris. '99	🍸🍸🍸	5
●	A. A. Lagrein Scuro Gries '95	🍸🍸	4
●	A. A. Lagrein Scuro Gries '97	🍸🍸	2
○	A. A. Bianco Abtei '99	🍸🍸	5
○	A. A. Bianco Abtei '00	🍸🍸	4

Franz Gojer Glögglhof

fraz. Santa Maddalena
via Rivellone, 1
39100 Bolzano/Bozen
tel. 0471978775
e-mail: info@gojer.it

The characteristic and quite unmistakable hill of Santa Maddalena rises up over the area north of Bolzano where, in the heart of this tiny subzone, Franz Gojer has been operating a small but very dependable winery since the early 1980s. He turns out around 40,000 bottles a year and the winery flagship is naturally the Santa Maddalena Classico, particularly the Rondell '02 selection that made it our finals this year for its textbook freshness, pleasant drinkability and typicity. This is not one of those wines that cause you to stop and think, prompting learned disquisitions from professionals. Thankfully, it's a wine that you can drink with real pleasure, full stop. The Santa Maddalena Classico '02 is only a shade inferior, and at any rate shows off surprisingly rich fruit and concentration. We found the Lagrein '01 to be in the same elegant, well-typed style, which you could say is a cellar trademark. Clear aromas of wild berries and pencil lead precede sweet, silky tannins on the palate, which has good structure and remarkable elegance. This delicious Lagrein is a very moreish quaffer that managed not to drop any points for typicity or complexity, either. It may have been the vintage, but the Merlot Spitz '01 is a little simple and edgy, a small enough criticism for a winery we can only encourage to continue along its path to quality.

●	A. A. Santa Maddalena Cl. Rondell '02	🍷🍷	4*
●	A. A. Lagrein '01	🍷🍷	4*
●	A. A. Santa Maddalena Cl. '02	🍷🍷	4*
●	A. A. Merlot Spitz '01	🍷	5
●	A. A. Lagrein Scuro Ris. '98	🍸🍸	4
●	A. A. Lagrein Scuro '99	🍸🍸	3
●	A. A. Lagrein Scuro Ris. '99	🍸🍸	4
●	A. A. Lagrein Scuro '00	🍸🍸	4*
●	A. A. Santa Maddalena Cl. Rondell '00	🍸🍸	3*
●	A. A. Merlot Spitz '99	🍸🍸	4
●	A. A. Lagrein Scuro Ris. '00	🍸🍸	5
●	A. A. Merlot Spitz '00	🍸🍸	5
●	A. A. Santa Maddalena Cl. Rondell '01	🍸🍸	4*

BOLZANO/BOZEN

Loacker Schwarzhof

via Santa Justina, 3
39100 Bolzano/Bozen
tel. 0471365125
e-mail: lo@cker.it

The Schwarhof farm has existed since 1334 in the Santa Maddalena production zone. Since 1979, Rainer Loacker and his family have produced special wines here with fascinating, utterly personal characters. Red wines come from Schwarhof and nearby Kohlerhof while grapes for the Loacker-style whites originate in the Kalter Keller vineyard in the Valle Isarco. Since the early days, the Loackers have applied organic farming principles step-by-step in their vineyards and cellars. This hard work has had inconsistent results. Currently, however, the Loackers are remarkably successful at reaping the benefits of their chosen method. The Gewürztraminer Atagis '02 is very convincing in its varietal notes. Minerally and intense, it has a refined, complex and elegantly long palate. It's a great wine. As always well-typed and appealing, the Santa Maddalena Morit '02 is a fruit-forward easy drinker, with sweet tannins and good acidity. The Cabernet Lagrein Kastlet '00 is rich and concentrated, with notes of black pepper, tobacco and blueberries. The Jus Osculi '01, a cuvée of separately fermented Schiava, Lagrein, Cabernet and Pinot Nero, is rather simple, with vegetal notes and dry tannins. The Sylvaner Ysac '02 is fresh and well-typed, with pleasant fruit, while the Pinot Nero Norital '01 is a bit limited, with fruity and smoky notes. At the time of our tastings, we were unconvinced by the Sauvignon Blanc Tasmin '02 and Chardonnay Ateyon '01.

○	A. A. Valle Isarco Gewürztraminer Atagis '02	TTT	5
●	A. A. Cabernet Lagrein Kastlet '00	TT	5
●	A. A. Santa Maddalena Cl. Morit '02	TT	3*
●	A. A. Pinot Nero Norital '01	T	5
●	Cuvée Jus Osculi '01	T	4
○	A. A. Valle Isarco Sylvaner Ysac '02	T	3
○	A. A. Chardonnay Ateyon '00	YY	5
●	Cuvée Jus Osculi '00	YY	4*
●	A. A. Santa Maddalena Cl. Morit '01	YY	4*
○	A. A. Sauvignon Blanc Tasmin '01	YY	4

BOLZANO/BOZEN

R. Malojer Gummerhof

via Weggestein, 36
39100 Bolzano/Bozen
tel. 0471972885
e-mail: info@malojer.it

Organically produced wines are wrongly surrounded by an aura of scepticism that frequently turns into outright mistrust. Taste the wines of Urban and Alfred Malojer and you will be forced to rethink. Six of their wines were submitted for tasting and five achieved Two Glass scores. The Gummerhof winery is located north of Bolzano and produces around 100,000 bottles, split across a dozen or so different wine types, almost all from red grapes typical of the area surrounding Bolzano. There are ten hectares of estate-owned vineyards but grapes are also bought in from trusted small growers. One of the showcase wines is the Cabernet-Lagrein Bautzanum Riserva '01, a powerful, fragrantly harmonious red that integrates the respective characters of the two base varieties very well. The Lagrein Riserva '01 is a bit husky, but has loads of character. The Cabernet Riserva '01 expresses itself in intense black berry fruit aromas leading into great structure on the palate, which signs off with a deep, complex finish. The varietal Merlot Riserva '01 has outstanding personality, featuring freshness and very pleasant drinkability. The Santa Maddalena Classico '02 is simply delicious. It flaunts a youthful exuberance that we find again in the Müller Thurgau from the same vintage. In conclusion, this series of genuine wines may not be perfect, but it is certainly neither boring nor excessive. These are wines that invite you to uncork them and get to know them better.

●	A. A. Cabernet Ris. '01	TT	5
●	A. A. Cabernet-Lagrein Bautzanum Ris. '01	TT	5
●	A. A. Lagrein Scuro Ris. '01	TT	5
●	A. A. Merlot Ris. '01	TT	5
●	A. A. Santa Maddalena Cl. '02	TT	4*
○	A. A. Sauvignon Gur Zu Sand Classic '02	TT	4*
○	A. A. Muller Thurgau '02	T	3
●	A. A. Lagrein Scuro Ris. '97	YY	5
●	A. A. Cabernet-Lagrein Bautzanum Ris. '99	YY	5
●	A. A. Merlot Ris. '99	YY	5
●	A. A. Cabernet Ris. '00	YY	5
●	A. A. Cabernet-Lagrein Bautzanum '00	YY	5
●	A. A. Lagrein Scuro Ris. '00	YY	5
●	A. A. Merlot Ris. '00	YY	5

BOLZANO/BOZEN

JOSEPHUS MAYR
ERBHOF UNTERGANZNER
LOC. CARDANO - VIA CAMPIGLIO, 15
39053 BOLZANO/BOZEN
TEL. 0471365582
E-MAIL: mayr.unterganzner@dnet.it

GEORG MUMELTER
VIA RENCIO, 66
39100 BOLZANO/BOZEN
TEL. 0471973090
E-MAIL: mumelter.g@rolmail.net

The apparent ease with which Josephus Mayr turns out spectacular wines is disconcerting. Whatever the growing year, he gets the best from his vineyards, even though they are not located in Gries, the classic part of the zone. Josephus' vines are situated on the northern slope of the broad, sunny Bolzano valley, next to Santa Maddalena. What could such a talented winemaker do with a vintage as favourable as 2000? Well, here's the answer in one of the greatest versions ever of Lagrein Riserva. The '00 is complex and powerful, but with great character and elegance, the obvious outcome of ripe grapes and great cellar technique used only to bring out the typicity of the variety. Needless to say, it won Three Glasses. The Lamarein '01, from slightly raisined lagrein grapes, missed out for only one reason. It is almost impossible to find in the market. The impenetrable colour precedes deep aromas of ripe blackberries and impressive concentration on the palate, where compact, well-gauged tannins support great fruit. The finish is endless. It's a monster of a wine but not a caricature. The Composition Reif '01, from 80 per cent Cabernet and the rest Lagrein, is a great wine that only needs a few months in bottle to reach its best. The Santa Maddalena Classico '01 is as delicious as ever, and offers enveloping aromas of black berry fruit. The palate is both fresh and concentrated, and the finish has fantastic progression for a so-called simple wine. But our hero is not very interested in simple things, which is why he started producing olive oil a couple of years ago. In Bolzano.

Georg Mumelter is a classic Alto Adige winemaker: taciturn, hardworking and devoted to his land. He produces around 20,000 bottles a year from his three hectares under vine, all very well-typed wines with great character that extremely representative. We'll start with a magnificent Lagrein Riserva '01 that is concentrated and mouthfilling, showing tannins that are compact and smooth. It has great balance and typicity with a long, well-defined finish. As it is a little young, a few months in the bottle will give it better expression. Also just short of Three Glasses is the Cabernet Sauvignon '01, which opens up with deep aromas of blackberry and morello cherry. Though not very concentrated on the palate, it is very well-balanced and elegant with lovely notes of leather and tobacco in the finish. The Santa Maddalena Classico '02 is quite delicious. But this is just confirmation of its textbook drinkability. The Schiava Grigia '02 is fresh and delicious and the Pinot Grigio '02 is also very well-made, with varietal ripe pear and quince on the nose. The powerful palate follows through nicely with lovely refreshing acidity and a fairly elegant finish, showing that this winery can make whites as well. In other words, the date with Three Glasses has been postponed, not cancelled.

●	A. A. Lagrein Scuro Ris. '00	♟♟♟	5
●	Composition Reif '01	♟♟	6
●	Lamarein '01	♟♟	7
●	A. A. Cabernet Sauvignon '00	♟♟	5
●	A. A. Santa Maddalena Cl. '01	♟♟	3*
⊙	A. A. Lagrein Rosato '02	♟	4
●	A. A. Lagrein Scuro Ris. '97	♟♟♟	5
●	A. A. Lagrein Scuro Ris. '98	♟♟♟	5
●	A. A. Lagrein Scuro Ris. '99	♟♟♟	5
●	Lamarein '99	♟♟	6
●	A. A. Santa Maddalena Cl. '00	♟♟	3*
●	Composition Reif '00	♟♟	6
●	Lamarein '00	♟♟	7
●	A. A. Cabernet Sauvignon '99	♟♟	5

●	A. A. Cabernet Sauvignon Griesbauerhof '01	♟♟	5
●	A. A. Lagrein Scuro Ris. '01	♟♟	5
○	A. A. Pinot Grigio Griesbauerhof '02	♟♟	4
●	A. A. Santa Maddalena '02	♟♟	3*
●	A. A. Lagrein Scuro Griesbauerhof '01	♟	4
●	A. A. Schiava Grigia '02	♟	3*
●	A. A. Lagrein Scuro Ris. '99	♟♟♟	5
○	A. A. Pinot Grigio Griesbauerhof '00	♟♟	4
●	Isarcus '00	♟♟	5
●	A. A. Lagrein Scuro Ris. '00	♟♟	5
●	A. A. Santa Maddalena Cl. '01	♟♟	3*

BOLZANO/BOZEN

BOLZANO/BOZEN

JOHANNES PFEIFER PFANNENSTIELHOF
VIA PFANNESTIEL, 9
39100 BOLZANO/BOZEN
TEL. 0471970884
E-MAIL: info@pfannenstielhof.it

HEINRICH PLATTNER - WALDGRIES
SANTA GIUSTINA, 2
39100 BOLZANO/BOZEN
TEL. 0471973245
E-MAIL: info@waldgries.it

Johannes Pfeifer manages this small winery, dating from the mid-16th century and set in the heart of Lagrein country, with unashamed enthusiasm, as well as great competence. He makes 40,000 bottles a year from his four hectares of vineyard. For this round of tastings, Johannes brought out again the Lagrein Riserva '00 we tasted last year as a cask sample. We can only confirm that it is absolutely delicious, and a mere step away from Three Glasses. The complex, varietal aromas of small black berry fruits are lifted by an evident spicy vein. The attack on the palate is sweet and while the structure may not be immense, the balance is impeccable and the elegance irresistible. This splendidly characterful interpretation of the variety has evidently found a secure home at Pfannenstielhof. Only one other wine was submitted for the 2004 edition of the Guide, the fresh, pleasantly fruity and very drinkable Santa Maddalena Classico '02. We are anxiously looking forward to Johannes' offering for next year's tastings, his Lagrein Riserva '01.

The origins of the Plattner family's Waldgries estate can be traced back to the 12th century. It lies in the classic Santa Maddalena zone above Bolzano, covering a sunny hillside amid the vineyards tended with care and devotion by the son of the family, Christian, who also makes his innovative presence felt in the cellar. Plattner-Waldgries has by now become a local benchmark, improving from year to year with wines that are among the best in Alto Adige. Two reached our finals this year. The Lagrein Riserva '01 has balsamic notes and aromas of blueberries and blackberries, leading into a rich, complex palate with sweet, ripe tannins. It is well balanced, with good progression and a long finish. The other star is the soft, flavourful Santa Maddalena Classico '02, which shows intense ripe fruit and excellent drinkability, making it an attractively characteristic representative of this indigenous variety. The other wines presented were also good. The Lagrein Mirell '00 recalls black berry fruits, bramble in particular, with evolved notes, then a full-bodied palate with soft yet assertive tannins and great personality. The concentrated, powerful Cabernet Sauvignon '01 also offers notes of tobacco, blackberry and blueberry. The Terlano Pinot Bianco Riol '02 is concentrated, refined and elegant, foregrounding spring flowers and white peach. However, we found the 2001 vintage Moscato Rosa a bit below average, compared with the past few versions. All things considered, it was a fine performance by Heinrich and Christian Plattner.

● A. A. Lagrein Scuro Ris. '00	♟♟	5
● A. A. Lagrein Scuro '02	♟	4*
● A. A. Santa Maddalena Cl. '02	♟	3
● A. A. Santa Maddalena Cl. '00	♟♟	4
● A. A. Lagrein Scuro '00	♟♟	4*
● A. A. Lagrein Scuro Ris. '99	♟♟	5
● A. A. Lagrein Scuro Ris. '98	♟	5
● A. A. Lagrein Scuro '01	♟	4
● A. A. Pinot Nero '01	♟	4

● A. A. Lagrein Scuro Ris. '01	♟♟	6
● A. A. Santa Maddalena Cl. '02	♟♟	4
● A. A. Lagrein Scuro Mirell '00	♟♟	7
● A. A. Cabernet Sauvignon '01	♟♟	6
○ A. A. Pinot Bianco Riol '02	♟♟	4
● A. A. Moscato Rosa Passito '01	♟	6
● A. A. Lagrein Scuro '02	♟	3
● A. A. Cabernet Sauvignon '99	♟♟♟	6
○ A. A. Bianco Passito Peperum '00	♟♟	6
● A. A. Santa Maddalena Cl. '01	♟♟	4*
● A. A. Lagrein Scuro Ris. Mirell '99	♟♟	7
● A. A. Cabernet Sauvignon '00	♟♟	6
● A. A. Moscato Rosa '00	♟♟	6

BOLZANO/BOZEN

CANTINA PRODUTTORI SANTA MADDALENA/
CANTINA DI BOLZANO
VIA BRENNERO, 15
39100 BOLZANO/BOZEN
TEL. 0471270909 - 0471972944
E-MAIL: info@kellereimagdalena.com

The 2001 growing year was not a great one for wines from Alto Adige, yet the Lagrein Taber Riserva won its fifth Three Glass award with disarming ease. This shows skill at interpreting the variety and the territory (the Taber vineyard is magnificent) while keeping the vintage under perfect control. An impenetrable colour and typical nose of classic blueberry and blackberry notes introduces a concentrated palate, soft tannins and explosive fruit with a spicy finish that is deep and complex. The Cabernet Mumelter Riserva '01 has returned to top form, and flaunts the character of a great wine. It's concentrated, but at the same time deep and balanced with perfectly integrated fruit. As usual, the Sauvignon Mock '02 is among the best in its category. Tomato leaf and tropical fruit emerge in the spectrum of aromatics, the palate is mouthfilling and the finish is clean. The powerful Chardonnay Kleinstein '02 has a vein of tropical fruit. We have never tasted it this good. The fresh, drinkable Lagrein Perl '01 is very pleasant. The two Pinot Neros, Greel '01 and Sandlahner Riserva '01, are both well made. The Gewürztraminer Kleinstein '02 is full flavoured and very elegant. The Santa Maddalena Classico Huck am Bach '02 is good, but we expect more from what is now a classic. Cellarmaster Stefan Filippi should be satisfied with this year's results, which prove that the merger with the Cantina di Gries has been negotiated successfully.

BOLZANO/BOZEN

STEPHAN RAMOSER - FLIEDERHOF
SANTA MADDALENA DI SOTTO, 33
39100 BOLZANO/BOZEN
TEL. 0471979048
E-MAIL: fliederhof@dnet.it

Just another winery until a short while ago, Stefan Ramoser's Fliederhof at Santa Maddalena has this year joined the long profile club in our Guide. Young Stefan thoroughly deserves this position because of the outstanding commitment he lavishes on the old family farm, first mentioned as long ago as 1306. The Fliederhof estate is located in the classic production zone of Santa Maddalena, among the sunny hills and slopes above Bolzano, and has everything it takes to create the great wines for which this territory is famous. In fact, Santa Maddalena and Lagrein are the two main wines at Fliederhof. The Lagrein Riserva '01 introduces itself with notes of sage, saffron, red fruits and chocolate on the nose, going on to show a well-balanced palate with soft, velvety tannins, lovely, fresh structure and long, full-flavoured finale. This particular Lagrein ages in large oak casks that bring out its character and fullness. The standard-label Lagrein '01 is very well-typed, elegantly fruit-led and ready to drink. The Santa Maddalena Classico Fliederhof '02 is also typical and inviting, with red fruit aromas preceding a spicy nose with notes of fresh almonds. The palate is sweet, fresh and elegant, revealing good balance and nice length. The Pfefferer '02 is a real niche product, made from the Alto Adige moscato verde variety. It's a dry wine with a marked floral aroma, excellent bouquet and an elegantly inviting, very fresh structure.

	Wine	Glasses	Price
●	A. A. Lagrein Scuro Taber Ris. '01	♀♀♀	6
●	A. A. Cabernet Mumelterhof Ris. '01	♀♀	6
○	A. A. Sauvignon Mock '02	♀♀	4
●	A. A. Lagrein Scuro Perl '01	♀♀	4
○	A. A. Chardonnay Kleinstein '02	♀♀	4
○	A. A. Gewürztraminer Kleinstein '02	♀♀	5*
●	A. A. Pinot Nero Sandlahner Ris. '00	♀	5
●	A. A. Pinot Nero Greel '01	♀	4
●	A. A. Santa Maddalena Cl. Huck am Bach '02	♀	4
●	A. A. Cabernet Mumelterhof '95	♀♀♀	4
●	A. A. Lagrein Scuro Taberhof Ris. '95	♀♀♀	4
●	A. A. Cabernet Mumelterhof '97	♀♀♀	5
●	A. A. Lagrein Scuro Taberhof '98	♀♀♀	5
●	A. A. Lagrein Scuro Taberhof Ris. '99	♀♀♀	6
●	A. A. Lagrein Scuro Taberhof Ris. '00	♀♀♀	6

	Wine	Glasses	Price
●	A. A. Lagrein Ris. '01	♀♀	5
●	A. A. Santa Maddalena Cl. Fliederhof '02	♀♀	3*
●	A. A. Lagrein '01	♀	3
○	Pfefferer '02	♀	4
●	A. A. Lagrein Ris. '00	♀♀	5
●	A. A. Santa Maddalena Cl. Fliederhof '01	♀	3*

BOLZANO/BOZEN

BOLZANO/BOZEN

GEORG RAMOSER UNTERMOSERHOF
VIA SANTA MADDALENA, 36
39100 BOLZANO/BOZEN
TEL. 0471975481
E-MAIL: untermoserhof@rolmail.net

HEINRICH & THOMAS ROTTENSTEINER
FRAZ. RENCIO
VIA SANTA MADDALENA, 35
39100 BOLZANO/BOZEN
TEL. 0471973549
E-MAIL: info@obermoser.it

Georg Ramoser is a young, enthusiastic producer whose immense labours in the vineyard all aim to drastically reduce yields and safeguard the typicity of his wines. The products of Georg's cellar can be a bit closed and difficult when young, but they have great ageing potential and grow over time. The Lagrein Riserva '01 has genuine character and intensity. Impenetrable in colour, it gives maximum expression to the variety's typical aromas before displaying great concentration in the mouth, even if it falls short of the richness in the 2000 edition. version. The tannins are close-knit and silky, and the palate closes out with a complex, expanding finish. The Merlot Riserva '01 is also good, if perhaps a tad simple. It has lovely notes of ripe blackberry and tobacco, then good structure on the palate, where the tannins are sweet and smooth. The finish is long and the wine is beautifully drinkable. The Cabernet Merlot Riserva '00 is very well balanced, revealing compact fruit and well-integrated oak. The as usual very drinkable Santa Maddalena Classico '02 is almost a paradigm of its variety, a true delight for all those, and there are many, who love this type of wine.

Heinrich Rottensteiner and his son, Thomas, produce around 30,000 bottles from their little more than three hectares of vineyard at Obermoser, in the heart of the Santa Maddalena hills. Their wines come from the vinification of exclusively estate-grown grapes. In other words, these are hand-crafted wines from a family-run winery. The specialties are obviously all the classic wines from the zone, beginning with Lagrein. The Riserva Grafenleiten '01 is a wine with great personality and a stubborn streak to its character. The very prominent tannins are well supported by considerable richness of fruit. The palate still shows some edginess, which is due to the wine's youth, but then it's not in the cellar's style to take the easy way out. The Cabernet-Merlot Putz Riserva '01 is again good, but suffers a little from the leanness imparted by a growing year that was without a doubt inferior to 2000. In spite of this, the '01 has very well-defined wild berry aromas, a decisive flavour and great balance, with a well-integrated touch of oak and very supple finish. The Santa Maddalena Classico '02 is pleasant and light, just as this type of wine should be. The Sauvignon '02 is well typed but nothing more.

● A. A. Lagrein Scuro Ris. '01	🍷🍷	5	● A. A. Cabernet - Merlot	
● A. A. Cabernet - Merlot '00	🍷🍷	5	Putz Ris. '01 🍷🍷	5
● A. A. Merlot Ris. '01	🍷🍷	5	● A. A. Lagrein Scuro	
● A. A. Santa Maddalena Cl '02	🍷	3*	Grafenleiten Ris. '01 🍷🍷	5
● A. A. Lagrein Scuro Ris. '97	🍷🍷🍷	5	● A. A. Santa Maddalena Cl. '02 🍷	3
● A. A. Lagrein Scuro Ris. '98	🍷🍷	5	○ A. A. Sauvignon '02 🍷	4
● A. A. Lagrein Scuro Ris. '99	🍷🍷	5	● A. A. Lagrein Scuro	
● A. A. Merlot '99	🍷🍷	5	Grafenleiten Ris. '97 🍷🍷	5
● A. A. Lagrein Scuro Ris. '00	🍷🍷	5	● A. A. Cabernet - Merlot	
● A. A. Merlot Ris. '00	🍷🍷	5	Putz Ris. '99 🍷🍷	5
			● A. A. Lagrein Scuro	
			Grafenleiten Ris. '00 🍷🍷	5
			● A. A. Cabernet - Merlot	
			Putz Ris. '00 🍷🍷	5

BOLZANO/BOZEN

HANS ROTTENSTEINER
VIA SARENTINO, 1/A
39100 BOLZANO/BOZEN
TEL. 0471282015
E-MAIL: rottensteiner.weine@dnet.it

The winery managed by Toni Rottensteiner with the help of his son, Hannes, sent three wines to our final taste-offs. Though they didn't win the top prize, they still testify to the dependability of this major property just outside Bolzano at the mouth of the beautiful Val Sarentino. The flagship wine is the Gewürztraminer Carcenai '02. The bouquet of citrus, particularly pink grapefruit, and wild roses ushers in a big, rich palate that also manages to display great balance, elegance and excellent depth, closing out on vibrant citron notes. The powerful, concentrated Gewürztraminer Passito Cresta '01 expresses complex tropical fruit and orange peel. One of our favourite wines is still Santa Maddalena Classico Premstallerhof. The '02 edition is a delight and deserved its place in the Three Glass finals. The usual aromas of blueberries and red fruits combine with fresh aromatic herbs. There is freshness on the palate, too, which is magnificently drinkable. The equally well-made Pinot Bianco Carnol '02 introduces elegant wistaria and broom aromas, then medium structure on the palate, where complex mineral notes emerge. The deep finish carries hints of wistaria and medicinal herbs. The Cabernet Select Riserva '00 offers great elegance and power, a lovely tannic weave and a long finish: it's a great Cabernet from a great vintage. The well-made Lagrein Grieser Select Riserva '00 is a tiny bit dilute. The Müller Thurgau '02 is fresh and drinkable, just as it should be, and the Chardonnay '02 has good concentration. A fine collection of Guide stemware.

BOLZANO/BOZEN

ANTON SCHMID - OBERRAUTNER
FRAZ. GRIES
VIA M. PACHER, 3
39100 BOLZANO/BOZEN
TEL. 0471281440
E-MAIL: florianschmid@dnet.it

The Schmid Oberrautner winery at Gries, the famous wine area at Bolzano, has existed since 1482. It has always been family run. Current owner Florian Schmid is the 19th generation to be in charge. Since 2001, we have observed a series of innovations at Schmid Oberrautner. Aside from the new wine shop annexed to the cellar, with wines from all over the world for sale and tasting, we have also noticed steady improvement in the quality of the products from the cellar. As a result, Schmid Oberrautner now has a full Guide profile. First of all, we have to say how much we liked the Lagrein Gries Riserva '00, with its ripe blackberry, polished, tight-knit tannins, and elegant balance on the palate. The progression is well sustained and the finish long. It fully deserved its place at our final taste-offs. The Pinot Nero Mazzon '01 has lovely typical notes of currants and red fruits, showing full-flavoured on the palate, which is powerful, balanced and minerally. The Cabernet Ritsch '01 has distinct toastiness on the nose, with small black fruits, then sweet tannins, medium structure and well-dosed oak emerge on the palate. We found The Lagrein Grieser Riserva Oro '00 a bit simple, but well typed and well made, with notes of coffee, blackberry and blueberries. The Santa Maddalena Steinbauer '02 is very drinkable and fruity, if a bit lean.

○ A. A. Gewürztraminer Cresta '01	♟♟	7
○ A. A. Gewürztraminer Cancenai '02	♟♟	5
● A. A. Santa Maddalena Cl. Premstallerhof '02	♟♟	3*
● A. A. Cabernet Select Ris '00	♟♟	5
○ A. A. Pinot Bianco Carnol '02	♟♟	4
● A. A. Lagrein Scuro Grieser Select Ris. '00	♟	5
○ A. A. Chardonnay '02	♟	4
○ A. A. Müller Thurgau '02	♟	4
○ A. A. Gewürztraminer Cancenai '00	♟♟	4
○ A. A. Gewürztraminer Cresta '00	♟♟	6
● A. A. Cabernet Select Ris '99	♟♟	5
● A. A. Lagrein Scuro Ris. '99	♟♟	4

● A. A. Lagrein Scuro Gries Ris. '00	♟♟	4
● A. A. Cabernet Ritsch '01	♟♟	4
● A. A. Pinot Nero Mazzon '01	♟♟	4
● A. A. Lagrein Scuro Grieser Oro '00	♟	4
● A. A. Lagrein Scuro Grieser '02	♟	3
● A. A. Santa Maddalena Steinbauer '02	♟	3
● A. A. Lagrein Scuro Ris. '95	♟	4
● A. A. Lagrein Scuro Grieser '97	♟	3
● A. A. Lagrein Scuro Gries Ris. '99	♟	4*
● A. A. Lagrein Scuro Saltner '00	♟	4

BRESSANONE/BRIXEN (BZ)

BRESSANONE/BRIXEN (BZ)

KUENHOF - PETER PLIGER
LOC. MARA, 110
39042 BRESSANONE/BRIXEN (BZ)
TEL. 0472850546

MANFRED NÖSSING - HOANDLHOF
FRAZ. KRANEBIH
WEINBERGSTRASSE, 66
39042 BRESSANONE/BRIXEN (BZ)
TEL. 0472832672

The first Sylvaner to win Three Glasses in the history of the Guide could only have come from the great Peter Pliger. We confess our special love for this wine. Every time we have had a chance to taste it, it has amazed us with its balance of aromas, expression on the palate and complexity of the finish. Varietal fruit is layered over hints of benzene reminiscent of a classic Riesling. The rich palate is fresh-tasting and very powerful, braced by an acidity that gives it moreish drinkability. This deep, lustrous wine should be allowed to age for a few years, although it is already drinking superbly. The extraordinary Kaiton '02 recalls the great Alsatian Rieslings, with the added minerality and tanginess that only this terrain, and Peter's artistry, can impart. It has everything from impressive complexity, balance and definition to power, depth and fullness. The only drawback is that winter frost prevented release of more than 1,500 bottles, at prices that are distinctly high. Although apparently a simple wine, the surprising Veltliner '02 embodies the full character of a great vintage. Intense fruity notes on the nose usher in a palate of great concentration and complexity. For the time being, still unsettled mineral notes dominate, but the wine has texture and a deep, caressing finish. Peter believes strongly in this wine so we can look forward to great things. The Gewürztraminer '02 is a perfect Pliger-style, minerally wine. Kuenhof is a benchmark winery, at least for small producers in Valle Isarco and beyond, although Peter himself prefers to avoid the limelight.

Manfred Nössing is a one of a kind, but call him Manni, as it says on his wine labels. He has a swashbuckling, lady-killing air about him. Quick-witted, with a twinkle in his eye, he is not so much a mountaineer as a sort of anti-globalist from Valle Isarco. His wines reflect his character. By bringing out the best of the vintage, Manni has produced dazzling wines that may not yet be perfect but which have a personality of their own. All this is leading up to the announcement that there were Three Glasses this year for the Kerner '02 that Manni calls his "soul wine". An explosion of tropical fruit, including papaya and pink grapefruit, then bell pepper and citron peel precede the minerality that dominates the palate. In the mouth, it is fresh and easy drinking, despite its robust alcohol content. An impressive finish leaves traces of mint and rosemary. The Sylvaner '02 is only just behind. Caressing, complex notes of citrus and tropical fruit are echoed on the zesty, fruit-rich palate, which has razor-sharp definition. This wine of fruit and rock reveals huge elegance, luminosity and freshness, and a finish of fantastic length. The Veltliner '02 throws inebriating aromas of wild flowers, grapefruit and citron, leading to a rich, full palate with complex fruity notes. The finale offers almost briny sensations. Depth, complexity and impressive development combine in the mouth. The powerful Gewürztraminer '02 has character to burn. And a sip of the Müller Thurgau '02 is enough to change your mind about the commonplace that this variety only produces simple wines.

O	A. A. Valle Isarco Sylvaner '02	♆♆♆	4*
O	Kaiton '02	♆♆	4*
O	A. A. Valle Isarco Gewürztraminer '02	♆♆	4*
O	A. A. Valle Isarco Veltliner '02	♆♆	4*
O	Kaiton '99	♆♆♆	4
O	Kaiton '01	♆♆♆	4
O	A. A. Valle Isarco Sylvaner '00	♆♆	4*
O	Kaiton '00	♆♆	4*
O	A. A. Valle Isarco Sylvaner '01	♆♆	4*
O	A. A. Valle Isarco Gewürztraminer '01	♆♆	4*
O	A. A. Valle Isarco Veltliner '01	♆♆	4*

O	A. A. Valle Isarco Kerner '02	♆♆♆	4*
O	A. A. Valle Isarco Sylvaner '02	♆♆	4*
O	A. A. Valle Isarco Gewürztraminer '02	♆♆	4*
O	A. A. Valle Isarco Müller Thurgau '02	♆♆	4*
O	A. A. Valle Isarco Veltliner '02	♆♆	4*
O	A. A. Valle Isarco Sylvaner '99	♆♆	4
O	A. A. Valle Isarco Kerner '00	♆♆	4
O	A. A. Valle Isarco Gewürztraminer '00	♆♆	4
O	A. A. Valle Isarco Gewürztraminer '01	♆♆	4*
O	A. A. Valle Isarco Müller Thurgau '01	♆♆	4
O	A. A. Valle Isarco Sylvaner '01	♆♆	4*

BRESSANONE/BRIXEN (BZ)

CALDARO/KALTERN (BZ)

TASCHLERHOF
VIA MAHR, 107
39042 BRESSANONE/BRIXEN (BZ)
TEL. 0472851091
E-MAIL: wachtler.peter@taschlerhof.com

ERSTE & NEUE
VIA CANTINE, 5/10
39052 CALDARO/KALTERN (BZ)
TEL. 0471963122
E-MAIL: info@erste-neue.it

The 2002 growing year was excellent in Valle Isarco. Witness the entry into the big time of this winery in Mara/Mahr, a village south of Bressanone. Peter Wachtler is one of the young lions who are shaking up winemaking in Aldo Adige. They are enthusiastic, curious and skilful. Inspired by the Peter Pliger, they have found their own interpretations of a territory now revealing itself as one of the most interesting in the region and beyond. Peter Wachtler perfectly matches this description. Born in 1971, he studied oenology at Laimburg and began bottling his own wines in 1999, making around 15,000 bottles annually of Veltliner, Sylvaner and Gewürztraminer from his own two and a half hectares under vine. The plots are at an elevation of about 550 metres in southeast-facing woodland. The wines themselves are varietal and distinctive, with slightly less insistent acidity than those from other producers in the zone, and the typical minerality of Valle Isarco whites. Wachter is about to plant a small vineyard to riesling and only submitted two wines. Both were excellent. The Sylvaner '02 is rather unusual because of its predominant softness and a certain austerity. The big, fat palate has nice ripe fruit and a very special rocky minerality. The Gewürztraminer '02 also stands out from the other Alto Adige Traminers we usually taste. The varietal nose with lovely notes of granny smith apple, apricot and tropical fruit accompanies a palate of austere sweetness and a long, complex finish. They say Peter did a lot of work in the vineyards this year. It shows.

With more than 1,000,000 bottles produced, Prima & Nuova/Erste & Neue is a fixture among the best co-operatives in the region. Their top line of products is released on the market under the Puntay label. One of the best of these is the Chardonnay '01, which introduces itself with interesting balsamic notes and tropical fruit. The palate is concentrated and rich, but with elegant acidity and great depth. The winery flagship, the Cabernet '00, also has great texture. Definition on the nose is very precise, with lovely fruit, then the palate is mouthfilling and concentrated, with ripe, elegant tannins. The finale has admirable continuity and elegance. The Merlot '00 is one of the best of its type, unveiling intense morello cherry. The palate is concentrated, with very prominent tannins that are well supported by fruit, finishing long with complex notes of damp earth and tobacco. The impressively powerful Gewürztraminer '02 has intense aromas of papaya and great concentration on the palate. It may lack a touch of elegance, but it is a wine with enormous impact. The surprising Chardonnay Salt '02 has sound structure, standing out for its lovely balance on the palate and distinctly persistent finish. We expected more from the Pinot Bianco Puntay '02, which we found a bit simple, though still a very well-made, easy-drinking wine. So after our visit, there was a nice line of Glasses for this long-established Caldaro winery.

○ A. A. Valle Isarco Gewürztraminer '02	♀♀	4
○ A. A. Valle Isarco Sylvaner '02	♀♀	4
○ A. A. Valle Isarco Gewürztraminer '00	♀	4
○ A. A. Valle Isarco Sylvaner '00	♀	4
○ A. A. Valle Isarco Gewürztraminer '01	♀	5
○ A. A. Valle Isarco Sylvaner '01	♀	4

● A. A. Chardonnay Puntay '01	♀♀	5
● A. A. Cabernet Puntay '00	♀♀	6
● A. A. Merlot Puntay '00	♀♀	6
○ A. A. Chardonnay Salt '02	♀♀	4*
○ A. A. Gewürztraminer Puntay '02	♀♀	5
● A. A. Cabernet-Merlot Feld '00	♀	5
○ A. A. Pinot Bianco Puntay '02	♀	4
● A. A. Cabernet Puntay '97	♀♀♀	5
○ A. A. Gewürztraminer Puntay '97	♀♀♀	4
○ A. A. Gewürztraminer Puntay '01	♀♀♀	5
○ A. A. Gewürztraminer Puntay '99	♀♀	4
○ A. A. Pinot Bianco Puntay '00	♀♀	4*
○ A. A. Chardonnay Salt '01	♀♀	4*
● A. A. Cabernet Puntay '99	♀♀	5
● A. A. Cabernet-Merlot Feld '99	♀♀	5

CALDARO/KALTERN (BZ)

KETTMEIR
VIA DELLE CANTINE, 4
39052 CALDARO/KALTERN (BZ)
TEL. 0471963135
E-MAIL: kettmeir@kettmeir.com

It was not a very exciting performance from this historic winery at Caldaro, and we say that with sincere regret. In fact, we expected the good vintage to give the cellar the necessary push to shift up from making good, well-typed wines to something a little more earth-shaking. Though this edition of the Guide shows decent scores, they are still well below the potential of one of the greatest wineries in the region. We'll start with the Spumante Brut that won Two Glasses and proved itself to be the winery's best product, along with the Pinot Grigio. The perlage is fine and the aromas delicate, with notes of fresh almonds and wistaria. The pleasant palate has good persistence and an elegant finish. The good, but not exciting, Pinot Grigio '02 spends a short time in barrique. Well-typed on the nose and concentrated in the mouth, it has a sweet, full-flavoured attack and signs off with a long finish. The Chardonnay, Sauvignon and Lago di Caldaro Classico, all from the 2000 vintage, are predictable. The other two reds, the Cabernet Sauvignon Maso Castello '00 and Pinot Nero Maso Reiner '01, are frankly difficult to interpret and we will postpone evaluation for the Guide until next year.

CALDARO/KALTERN (BZ)

TENUTA RITTERHOF
STRADA DEL VINO, 1
39052 CALDARO/KALTERN (BZ)
TEL. 0471963298
E-MAIL: info@ritterhof.it

In 1999, the Ritterhof estate winery passed to the Roner family from the famous Termeno distillery that bears their name. The vineyards, near the winery, extend over the beautiful zones of Termeno and Caldaro. In addition to the more than seven hectares of estate vineyards, another 45 belong to regular suppliers from whom grapes are bought in. The annual output of 200,000 bottles is supervised by oenologist, Bernhard Hannes. Quality is the keystone of the new owners' philosophy and the showcase line, whose labels bear the slogan, Crescendo ("growing"), is proof of this. Four Two Glass wines is a more than creditable result. The Schiava Putzleitn '02 is great. An intense ruby introduces red fruits and cherries. Elegant and refined, it closes with a fresh, clean finish. The powerful Gewürztraminer Klassik '02 has exotic notes of lychees and medicinal herbs. The fruity Merlot Crescendo Riserva '00 discloses blackberry, morello cherry and raspberry, then ripe tannins and a great finish. There are generous notes of yellow peach, damson and broom on the nose of the Pinot Bianco Klassik '02, which is big and caressing, but perhaps a bit short. The Lagrein Riserva Crescendo '00 has great concentration but lacks a bit of freshness and shows a little husky, with dry tannins and a lot of oak. The Cabernet Merlot Crescendo Riserva '00 has faint green notes on the palate, but sweet tannins and a clean finish. Finally, the Perlhof Crescendo '02, a cuvée of Schiava, Lagrein and Merlot, is pleasant, drinkable and youthfully alcoholic, with upfront fruit and sweet tannins.

○ A. A. Spumante Brut	🍷🍷	5
○ A. A. Chardonnay Maso Reiner '02	🍷	4
● A. A. Lago di Caldaro Cl. '02	🍷	3
○ A. A. Pinot Grigio Maso Reiner '02	🍷	4
○ A. A. Sauvignon '02	🍷	4
● A. A. Pinot Nero Maso Reiner '01		4
○ A. A. Pinot Grigio Maso Reiner '00	🍷🍷	4*
○ A. A. Spumante Brut	🍷🍷	5
○ A. A. Pinot Grigio Maso Reiner '01	🍷🍷	4*
● A. A. Cabernet Sauvignon Maso Castello '99	🍷🍷	5

● A. A. Merlot Crescendo Ris. '00	🍷🍷	5
○ A. A. Gewürztraminer '02	🍷🍷	4
○ A. A. Pinot Bianco '02	🍷🍷	3*
● A. A. Schiava Putzleitn '02	🍷🍷	3*
● A. A. Cabernet Merlot Crescendo Ris. '00	🍷	5
● A. A. Lagrein Scuro Crescendo Ris. '00	🍷	5
● A. A. Perlhof Crescendo '02	🍷	4
● A. A. Santa Maddalena Perlhof '01	🍷🍷	4*
○ A. A. Gewürztraminer '01	🍷🍷	4
○ A. A. Pinot Grigio '01	🍷🍷	4

CALDARO/KALTERN (BZ)

Josef Sölva - Niklaserhof
loc. San Nicolo
via Brunner, 31a
39052 Caldaro/Kaltern (BZ)
tel. 0471963432
e-mail: info@niklaserhof.it

"Small producer" does not always mean great quality but the two terms are in perfect agreement at Josef and Johanna Sölva's Niklaserhof, a tiny winery in the Caldaro/Kaltern area. Only 25,000 bottles are produced from the estate's three hectares but all are remarkably good. These wines are not only well made; they also have lots of character. We liked the Pinot Biancos very much, beginning with the standard-label Weingut Niklas '02, which unveils surprising aromas of pink grapefruit and citron peel, then a full structure that shows rather complex mineral notes. Its two stablemates, the Klaser '01 and '02, were also very good, the second in particular unveiling a truly fascinating, slightly minerally, nose that returns on the palate, where concentration and elegance are perfectly balanced. The very rich Sauvignon Weingut Niklas '02 has typical tropical fruit touches, sound structure and lovely elegance. The well-gauged Justisus Kerner '02 has clean citrus notes on the nose. These are echoed on the palate, accompanied by the minerality and complexity of a seriously good wine. The Lagrein Cabernet Klaser '02 took us by surprise with its tones of leather and fresh ground black pepper. Glossy tannins caress the palate, which closes on notes of tobacco and quinine in a well-sustained finish. The fresh, pleasant Bianco Mondevinum '02, from pinot bianco and sauvignon, is always well-executed, and the fruity Lago di Caldaro Scelto Classico '02 drinks deliciously.

CALDARO/KALTERN (BZ)

Peter Sölva & Söhne
via dell'Oro, 33
39052 Caldaro/Kaltern (BZ)
tel. 0471964650
e-mail: info@soelva.com

We'll begin by correcting an error in the last edition of the Guide. We mistakenly cited the Amistar Rosso Edizione '00 after actually tasting the '99. After these apologies, we have to say the overall results from Peter and Stephan Sölva's small winery were better than good, both for the reds as well as the whites. But let's get back to the Amistar Rosso Edizione '00 from lagrein, merlot and cabernet. It has an intense bouquet of cassis, with light fumé notes, a caressing and concentrated palate, potent tannins well-balanced by lovely ripe fruit and a nice touch of oak. The simpler, slightly rustic, Amistar Rosso '01 is still very drinkable. The other three reds, the Lagrein '01, Merlot '01 and Lagrein-Merlot '02 from the Desilvas line are good, though perhaps lacking a pinch more personality and complexity. The whites are very convincing. Amistar Bianco '01, a blend of gewürztraminer, sauvignon and chardonnay aged for around a year in small oak casks, acquiring character and a very compact structure that shows off hints of yellow peach and mint. The long finish is lifted by complex mineral notes. The well-typed, concentrated Gewürztraminer Amistar '02 is overwhelming on the palate, its traces of botrytis and lovely rich flavour endowing it with gutsy personality. The fruity, well-balanced Terlano Desilvas '02 closes out fresh and supple. This small estate winery in Caldaro/Kaltern has every reason to be satisfied with the results of our tastings this year.

● A. A. Lagrein-Cabernet Klaser '00	🍷🍷	5
○ A. A. Pinot Bianco Klaser '01	🍷🍷	4
○ A. A. Pinot Bianco '02	🍷🍷	4*
○ A. A. Pinot Bianco Klaser '02	🍷🍷	4
○ A. A. Sauvignon '02	🍷🍷	4
○ Justinus Kerner '02	🍷🍷	4
○ A. A. Bianco Mondevinum '02	🍷	5
● A. A. Lago di Caldaro Scelto Cl. '02	🍷	3*
○ A. A. Sauvignon '00	🍷🍷	4*
○ A. A. Pinot Bianco Klaser '00	🍷🍷	4
○ A. A. Bianco Mondevinum '01	🍷🍷	5
○ A. A. Sauvignon '01	🍷🍷	4*
○ Justinus Kerner '01	🍷🍷	4

● Amistar Rosso '00	🍷🍷	6
● A. A. Lagrein Scuro Desilvas '01	🍷🍷	5
○ Amistar Bianco '01	🍷🍷	5
○ A. A. Gewürztraminer Amistar '02	🍷🍷	5
● A. A. Lagrein-Merlot Desilvas '02	🍷🍷	5
○ A. A. Terlano Desilvas '02	🍷🍷	5
● A. A. Merlot Desilvas '01	🍷	5
● Amistar Rosso '01	🍷	6
● Amistar Rosso '99	🍷🍷	5
○ Amistar Bianco '99	🍷🍷	4
○ Amistar Bianco '00	🍷🍷	5

CALDARO/KALTERN (BZ)

CASTELBELLO CIARDES/KASTELBELL TSCHARS (BZ)

CANTINA VITICOLTORI DI CALDARO
VIA CANTINE, 12
39052 CALDARO/KALTERN (BZ)
TEL. 0471963149 - 0471963124
E-MAIL: info@kellereikaltern.com

TENUTA UNTERORTL-CASTEL JUVAL
FRAZ. JUVAL, 1/B
39020 CASTELBELLO CIARDES/
KASTELBELL TSCHARS (BZ)
TEL. 0473667580
E-MAIL: familie.aurich@dnet.it

Cantina Produttori di Caldaro only needed a Three Glass wine to round off the kind of excellent performance cellarmaster Helmut Zozin has been putting on for years. Sadly, one of the winery flagships, the Cabernet Sauvignon Campaner, missed our tasting, as the 2001 vintage was not yet in bottle. We consoled ourselves with the excellent Chardonnay Wadleith '02, an intelligent and very affordable wine. The nose opens with delightful tropical fruit then the palate shows concentration and balance, finishing long and supple. The by now classic Moscato Giallo Passito Serenade from 2000 was also just a step away from Three Glasses, showing very concentrated, with lovely notes of sage and apricot. The Pinot Bianco Vial, Pinot Grigio Söll and Sauvignon Premstalerhof are all from the great 2002 vintage, and all among the best in their respective categories. The Pinot Bianco is powerful, elegant and very well-typed, the Pinot Grigio is big, concentrated and well-balanced, and the last of the trio is a Sauvignon of elegance and finesse. The fine Gewürztraminer Campaner '02 has intense floral notes and a rich, fruity palate. The Pinot Nero Riserva '00 was the most convincing red, unveiling a very elegant nose, then opening sweet on the palate, with soft, ripe tannins and then a long, clean finish. The Cabernet Sauvignon-Merlot Riserva Pfarrhof '00, Merlot Lasòn '01 and Lago di Caldaro Pfarrhof '02 are all pleasant and well made. In short, a glance at the number of Glasses earned by Viticoltori di Caldaro makes it clear why this cellar plays a fundamental role in Alto Adige winemaking.

To call Martin and Gisela Aurich passionate producers would be an understatement. This year, they again treated us to some very interesting, distinctive wines from their roughly three hectares at Tenuta Unterortl near Stava. We are in Valle Venosta, 20 kilometres west of Merano, in an area on its way to becoming the new frontline of quality winemaking in Alto Adige. The Riesling Castel Juval '02 fell just short of Three Glasses. A still young varietal wine with complex, aristocratic aromas featuring citron and flint, it has a well-defined palate with a fairly evident acidic component. It is elegant and whistle-clean, yet shows great depth and consistency. This is a bit unusual since we are used to Rieslings from this zone that are heavier and flaunt more concentration. The Pinot Nero '01 is also designed more for elegance than concentration. Classic red fruits accompanied by smoky notes, precede a delicate palate with glossy tannins and a long, clean finish. The Pinot Bianco '02 opens on the nose with intense aromas of fresh almonds and broom, then starts off sweet on the palate, which has a concentrated, mouthfilling progression. In fact, it just needs a bit of depth to make it great.

○ A. A. Passito Serenade '00	♟♟	6
○ A. A. Chardonnay Wadleith '02	♟♟	4*
● A. A. Cabernet Sauvignon - Merlot Pfarrhof Ris. '00	♟♟	6
● A. A. Pinot Nero Ris. '00	♟♟	6
○ A. A. Gewürztraminer Campaner '02	♟♟	5
○ A. A. Pinot Bianco Vial '02	♟♟	4*
○ A. A. Pinot Grigio Söll '02	♟♟	4
○ A. A. Sauvignon Premstalerhof '02	♟♟	4
● A. A. Merlot Lasòn '01	♟	5
● A. A. Lago di Caldaro Pfarrhof '02	♟	4
○ A. A. Gewürztraminer Campaner '99	♟♟♟	4
○ A. A. Sauvignon Premstalerhof '00	♟♟♟	4*
○ A. A. Passito Serenade '99	♟♟♟	6

○ A. A. Valle Venosta Riesling '02	♟♟	5
● A. A. Valle Venosta Pinot Nero '02	♟♟	5
○ A. A. Valle Venosta Pinot Bianco '02	♟	4*
○ A. A. Valle Venosta Riesling '00	♟♟♟	4
○ A. A. Valle Venosta Riesling '98	♟♟	4
○ A. A. Valle Venosta Riesling '99	♟♟	4
● A. A. Valle Venosta Pinot Nero '99	♟♟	5
○ A. A. Valle Venosta Riesling '01	♟♟	4*
○ A. A. Valle Venosta Pinot Bianco '01	♟♟	3*

CERMES/TSCHERMS (BZ)

GRAF PFEIL WEINGUT KRÄNZEL
VIA PALADE, 1
39010 CERMES/TSCHERMS (BZ)
TEL. 0473564549
E-MAIL: weingut@kraenzel-pfeil.com

There were high notes and low notes this year from Graf (count) Pfeil's Weingut Kränzel. This was more than a little surprising since we are accustomed to an array of superb, characterful wines from this pocket-size estate in Cermes/Tscherms, just a few kilometres from Merano. One of the best wines presented was the Chardonnay '02, which combines elegant fruity sensations with fresh notes of mint, then unveils a concentrated, well-balanced palate with a very elegant and distinctive sensory profile. The Passito Dorado '01, from partially dried gewürztraminer and sauvignon grapes, also has lots of character. It tempts the nose with aromas of sage and saffron, then the big, powerful palate reveals confectioner's cream and medicinal herbs, supported by bright acidity, and the finish is a riot of intense tropical fruit. The Schiava Schloss Baslan '02 is attractively fragrant, although we found it less convincing than usual. The Pinot Nero '01 has not yet settled down, but then the variety is a challenge for everyone, even the best winemakers. In other words, we expect this wonderful estate in the Burgraviato district will bounce back quickly to top form.

CHIUSA/KLAUSEN (BZ)

CANTINA PRODUTTORI VALLE ISARCO
VIA COSTE, 50
39043 CHIUSA/KLAUSEN (BZ)
TEL. 0472847553
E-MAIL: info@cantinavalleisarco.it

Founded in 1961, the Cantina Valle Isarco is the youngest co-operative winery in Alto Adige, with 130 members delivering their grapes every autumn to the modern cellar in Chiusa. More than 90 per cent of the grapes are white, and grow on steep slopes between 500 and 900 metres above sea level. Thomas Dorfmann, the dynamic cellarmaster who has taken over from his father, guarantees the constantly improving quality of the wines, which are well-typed, aromatic, fresh and incredibly good value for money in the winery's standard range and offer character, structure and longevity in the showcase Aristos line. Two taste-off finalists stand out, the Pinot Grigio Aristos '02, with damson and pear on the minerally nose and freshness, power, complexity and length on the palate, and the Gewürztraminer Passito Nectaris '01, which has candied citrus peel, dates, honey and aromatic herbs, then a fresh, floral palate with lovely acidity, charming sweetness and remarkable balance. From the 2002 vintage, the Aristos label offers a minerally, concentrated Sylvaner, a caressingly soft Müller Thurgau, and a rich, well-balanced Gewürztraminer that finishes impressively. All are good and well-typed. The Kerner and Veltliner are zesty. From the standard line, the Kerner '02 is surprisingly powerful, fresh and very minerally. Nor should the Dominus '00 be overlooked. Although sourced from a blend of typical Valle Isarco white varieties aged in barrique, it is very modern in style. Finally, the local red, Klausener Laitacher '02, is nice, showing cherries and berry fruit.

○	A. A. Dorado '01	♔♔	6
○	A. A. Chardonnay '02	♔♔	3
●	A. A. Pinot Nero '01	♔	5
●	A. A. Schiava Schloss Baslan '02	♔	4
○	Dorado '97	♔♔	6
○	A. A. Pinot Bianco Et. Nera '98	♔♔	4
○	A. A. Sauvignon '99	♔♔	5
○	A. A. Pinot Bianco Helios '00	♔♔	5
○	A. A. Gewürztraminer Passito '00	♔♔	5
○	A. A. Bianco Passito Dorado '98	♔♔	6
○	A. A. Sauvignon '01	♔♔	4
●	A. A. Cabernet Sauvignon-Merlot Sagittarius '00	♔♔	6
○	A. A. Bianco Helios '01	♔♔	5
○	A. A. Pinot Bianco '01	♔♔	3*

○	A. A. Valle Isarco Gewürztraminer Passito Nectaris '01	♔♔	7
○	A. A. Valle Isarco Pinot Grigio Aristos '02	♔♔	4*
○	A. A. Valle Isarco Gewürztraminer Aristos '02	♔♔	5
○	A. A. Valle Isarco Kerner '02	♔♔	4*
○	A. A. Valle Isarco Müller Thurgau Aristos '02	♔♔	4
○	A. A. Valle Isarco Sylvaner Aristos '02	♔♔	4
○	Dominus '00	♔	5
○	A. A. Valle Isarco Kerner Aristos '02	♔	4
●	A. A. Valle Isarco Klausener Laitacher '02	♔	4
○	A. A. Valle Isarco Veltliner Aristos '02	♔	4
○	A. A. Valle Isarco Müller Thurgau '01	♔♔	3*
○	A. A. Valle Isarco Pinot Grigio '01	♔♔	3*

CORTACCIA/KURTATSCH (BZ)

CORTACCIA/KURTATSCH (BZ)

CANTINA PRODUTTORI CORTACCIA
STRADA DEL VINO, 23
39040 CORTACCIA/KURTATSCH (BZ)
TEL. 0471880115
E-MAIL: info@kellerei-kurtatsch.it

TIEFENBRUNNER
FRAZ. NICLARA
VIA CASTELLO, 4
39040 CORTACCIA/KURTATSCH (BZ)
TEL. 0471880122
E-MAIL: info@tiefenbrunner.com

A great Gewürztraminer, Brenntal '02 from the same zone as the famous Merlot, impressed us from the wines presented this year, and won a richly deserved Three Glass award. The Cortaccia/Kurtatsch zone is excellent for this variety, which needs warmth and a wide day-night temperature variation to reach its peak of ripeness and aromatic concentration. The 2002 version has intense sage and lavender, then a muscular palate that also reveals a nice, refreshing acid backbone. Well typed and extraordinarily well balanced, it closes on elegant tropical fruit and aromatic herbs. The Lagrein Fohrhof '01 has great elegance and flaunts its tannins with finesse and impeccable balance. The very young Cabernet Freienfeld '00 still has to absorb its oak. The complex bouquet offers intense leather and coffee aromas, then the palate shows richness and concentration, with ripe tannins, elegant texture and a very long finish. The Cabernet Kirchhügel '01 has lovely notes of tobacco and quinine, and is very elegant on the easy-drinking palate. The Müller Thurgau Hofstatt and Chardonnay Felsenhof, both from 2002, are very well made. The first has surprising complexity and concentration, whereas the second is powerful, with elegant mineral notes that characterize the long finish. We expected more from the classic Merlot Brenntal '00, which we found a bit thin. The Cabernet-Merlot Soma '00, Pinot Nero Fritzenhof '00, Sauvignon Milla '02 and fresh drinkable Schiava Sonntaler '02 are all as well made as ever. It all adds up to an impressive assortment of Glasses.

We are very pleased to celebrate the first Three Glass award for this historic Alto Adige winery. In fact, Tiefenbrunner's role has been crucial to raising the profile of wines from the province of Bolzano outside their production area and in German-speaking countries. The Gewürztraminer Castel Turmhof is delicious, with intense aromas of broom, lychees and acacia honey. It's concentrated in the mouth, but offers pleasant freshness, developing complexity and depth on its way to a very long finish. The Chardonnay '02, again from the Castel Turmhof line, just missed a third Glass. Elegant tropical fruit aromas are mirrored on the very rich, balanced palate with its stylish flowing finish. The Chardonnay Linticlarus '00 is muscular, but brightened by a well-sustained acidity. The 2002 Feldmarschall is skilfully made from müller thurgau grapes grown in a vineyard at an elevation of nearly 1,000 metres. The floral and citrus peel aromas lead into a supple palate with elegant minerality. Topping off this great all-round performance are the Cuvée Anna '02, from pinot bianco, pinot grigio and chardonnay, the Pinot Nero Linticlarus Riserva '00, a fruity, exquisitely drinkable Schiava Grigia '02, and a great little Pinot Nero with a surprisingly complex finish. The following are all good: the elegant, well-typed Lagrein Linticlarus Riserva '00, the Sauvignon Kirchleiten '02 and the cabernet and merlot Linticlarus Cuvée '00. The merry clink of Glasses rewards the hard work and history of Herbert and Cristof Tiefenbrunner.

○ A. A. Gewürztraminer Brenntal '02	♈♈♈	6
● A. A. Cabernet Freienfeld '00	♈♈	8
● A. A. Lagrein Scuro Fohrhof '01	♈♈	5
● A. A. Cabernet Kirchhügel '01	♈♈	5
○ A. A. Chardonnay Felsenhof '02	♈♈	4
○ A. A. Müller Thurgau Hofstatt '02	♈♈	4
○ A. A. Sauvignon Milla '02	♈♈	4
● A. A. Cabernet-Merlot Soma '00	♈	7
● A. A. Merlot Brenntal '00	♈	7
● A. A. Pinot Nero Fritzenhof '00	♈	6
● A. A. Schiava Grigia Sonntaler '02	♈	4
● A. A. Cabernet Freienfeld '95	♈♈♈	6
● A. A. Cabernet Freienfeld '97	♈♈♈	6
● A. A. Merlot Brenntal '97	♈♈♈	5
● A. A. Lagrein Scuro Fohrhof '00	♈♈♈	5

○ A. A. Gewürztraminer Castel Turmhof '02	♈♈♈	5
○ A. A. Chardonnay Castel Turmhof '02	♈♈	4*
○ A. A. Chardonnay Linticlarus '00	♈♈	5
● A. A. Pinot Nero Linticlarus Ris. '00	♈♈	5
○ A. A. Cuvée Anna Castel Turmhof '02	♈♈	4
● A. A. Grauvernatsch Castel Turmhof '02	♈♈	4*
○ A. A. Sauvignon Kirchleiten '02	♈♈	5
○ Feldmarschall von Fenner '02	♈♈	5
○ A. A. Cuvée Linticlarus '00	♈	5
● A. A. Lagrein Linticlarus Ris. '00	♈	5
○ A. A. Gewürztraminer Castel Turmhof '01	♈♈	5
○ A. A. Chardonnay Castel Turmhof '01	♈♈	4
○ Feldmarschall von Fenner zu Fennberg '01	♈♈	5

CORTINA/KURTINIG (BZ)

PETER ZEMMER - KUPELWIESER
STRADA DEL VINO, 24
39040 CORTINA/KURTINIG (BZ)
TEL. 0471817143
E-MAIL: info@zemmer.com

The Peter Zemmer estate has the same headquarters and ownership as Kupelwieser and together they produce the remarkable quantity of about 700,000 bottles. We were again delighted this year by wines from the Zemmer line, particularly the Chardonnay '02, which showed great character and made it to our finals. The aromas of tropical fruit and damson accompany a concentrated, mouthfilling palate with great balance and a long, supple finish. The very well-typed Pinot Grigio '02 has great power. We noted citrus peel and ripe pear in the rich bouquet, then the palate is concentrated but also very fresh, with elegant, complex mineral notes that accompany a finish in the grand style. It's a lovely Pinot Grigio. Sage and benzene aromas characterize the Riesling '02, which has moderate structure and freshness, intense fruit and a deep, seamless finish. Wines from the Kupelwieser lines are technically well made, but lack that touch more personality that would make them stand out. We felt the Pinot Bianco '02 was the best of the bunch, showing fresh and easy to drink, though perhaps a bit too simple. The Chardonnay '02 was also decent, offering concentration and nice assertive fruit. The Sauvignon Intenditore '02 is well made and attractive. We found the Lagrein Intenditore '01 a bit insubstantial, although it has to be said the growing year was nothing special. The positive note shared by both branches of this winery is good value for money across the range, which is no mean feat nowadays.

EGNA/NEUMARKT (BZ)

CANTINA H. LUN
FRAZ. VILLA
VIA VILLA, 22/24
39044 EGNA/NEUMARKT (BZ)
TEL. 0471813256
E-MAIL: contact@lun.it

H. Lun has been a historic name in Alto Adige viticulture since 1840. Years ago, it was taken over by the Cantina Produttori Cornaiano/Girlan and results have recently been getting very impressive, starting with the Cabernet Sauvignon Albertus '00. The full nose displays ripe blackberry and leather, then the stylish palate offers silky tannins and intense fruit, finishing long and deep, with complex sensations of quinine and damp tobacco. The Bianco Sandbichler '02 is wine of personality, blended from pinot bianco, chardonnay and a smaller percentage of riesling. Peach and damson greet the nose, then the palate is concentrated, fresh and well sustained through to a long, balanced finale. The Sauvignon Albertus '02 is well typed and elegant, enfolding the nose with intense aromas of medicinal herbs and tomato leaves, before the pervasive, full palate shows its elegance. Intense fruit and delightful tobacco mark the Santa Maddalena Föhrner '02, which is also nicely fresh in the mouth. Both the Pinot Nero Sandbichler Riserva '00 and Pinot Grigio '02 are a bit simple and dilute. There's a little too much oak on the Gewürztraminer Albertus '02, which failed to repeat last year's terrific performance. Overall, results are impressive and only one or two details are missing from an otherwise satisfying performance.

Wine		Rating
○ A. A. Chardonnay Zemmer '02	🍷🍷	4*
○ A. A. Pinot Grigio '02	🍷🍷	4*
○ A. A. Riesling '02	🍷🍷	4*
● A. A. Lagrein Scuro Intenditore '01	🍷	5
○ A. A. Chardonnay '02	🍷	4
○ A. A. Pinot Bianco Kupelwieser '02	🍷	4
○ A. A. Sauvignon Intenditore '02	🍷	4
○ A. A. Chardonnay Kupelwieser '00	🍷🍷	4*
○ A. A. Pinot Bianco Kupelwieser '00	🍷🍷	3*
○ A. A. Pinot Grigio '00	🍷🍷	4*
○ A. A. Riesling Kupelwieser '00	🍷🍷	4*
● A. A. Santa Maddalena Kupelwieser '00	🍷🍷	3*
● A. A. Lagrein Scuro Intenditore '00	🍷🍷	5
● Cortinie Rosso '00	🍷🍷	5
○ A. A. Pinot Grigio '01	🍷🍷	4*

Wine		Rating
● A. A. Cabernet Sauvignon Albertus Ris. '00	🍷🍷	5
○ A. A. Bianco Sandbichler '02	🍷🍷	4*
○ A. A. Sauvignon Albertus '02	🍷🍷	4*
● A. A. Pinot Nero Sandbichler Ris. '00	🍷	4
● A. A. Gewürztraminer Albertus '02	🍷	5
● A. A. Santa Maddalena Föhrner '02	🍷	4*
○ A. A. Bianco Sandbichler '00	🍷🍷	4*
● A. A. Pinot Nero Albertus Ris. '00	🍷🍷	5
○ A. A. Bianco Sandbichler '01	🍷🍷	4*
○ A. A. Gewürztraminer Albertus '01	🍷🍷	5
○ A. A. Sauvignon Albertus '01	🍷🍷	5
● A. A. Cabernet Sauvignon Albertus Ris. '99	🍷🍷	6
● A. A. Lagrein Scuro Albertus Ris. '99	🍷🍷	6
○ A. A. Pinot Grigio '02	🍷	4

FIÈ ALLO SCILIAR/VÖLS AM SCHLERN (BZ)

MARLENGO/MARLING (BZ)

MARKUS PRACKWIESER GUMPHOF
NOVALE DI PRESULE, 8
39050 FIÈ ALLO SCILIAR/
VÖLS AM SCHLERN (BZ)
TEL. 0471601190

CANTINA PRODUTTORI BURGGRÄFLER
VIA PALADE, 64
39020 MARLENGO/MARLING (BZ)
TEL. 0473447137
E-MAIL: info@burggraefler.it

On a ridge at the entrance to Valle Isarco, this small estate is now a full-profile Guide reviewee. Although a few hundred metres away geographically, it makes very Eisacktal-style wines, whose minerally complexity is offset by marked acidity. Markus Prackwieser, born in 1972, must love his wines and vineyards on the slopes of the Sciliar. Seen from the valley floor, the estate makes your head spin. Reached by a narrow, twisting road, the vineyards turn out to be perched on insanely steep slopes that would give an acrobat nightmares. It is a very sunny spot, some 400 metres above sea level. The good daytime temperatures help ripen the grapes, then drop noticeably in the evening as breezes rise off the valley. When you talk to Markus, you note his enthusiasm, determination and curiosity. You begin to understand that his amazing results are no coincidence: they come from sheer hard work. The Sauvignon Praesulis '02 proved to be one of the best of its type and almost picked up Three Glasses. The complex nose reveals lovely notes of sage and tomato leaves, then the palate has medium structure, unfolding elegantly into ripe fruit and elderflower sensations. The Pinot Bianco Praesulis '02 was also delicious. The intense mineral notes integrate well into the dominant fruit, and the powerful on the palate never loses its depth and elegance. The Schiava '02 is also good, and the standard-label Pinot Bianco '02 is marvellous, particularly as it is sold at a price that should cause many other producers to blush.

Smooth sailing for the Cantina Produttori del Burgraviato, the district known in German as Burggräfler. Again this year, the cellar presented us with a series of well-made wines at honest prices, something that is becoming ever harder to find. And the excellent Chardonnay '02, which also reached our Three Glass finals, is a bargain. Its wonderful wistaria and tropical fruit lead into a rich, balanced palate with pleasant lychee notes, and a long, crystal-clear finish. The concentrated Pinot Bianco Guggenberg '02 shows off amazingly intense fruit with damson and green apple in the lead. Elegance is the keynote of the delicious Gewürztraminer '02, which shows touches of tropical fruit. The attack on the palate is sweet and concentrated, but also fresh and refined, with a delicious hint of medlar. Among the reds, the Lagrein-Cabernet MerVin '01 has dense, sweet tannins and lovely ripe fruit, accompanied by notes of quinine and graphite. The Merlot MerVin from the same vintage is concentrated and well balanced. Although no monster of complexity, it is pleasant and full bodied. The Pinot Nero MerVin '01 is also convincing, expressing wonderful typicity in notes of blackcurrant and blueberries, nice concentration in the mouth, smooth tannins and a very clean finish. The Moscato Giallo Schickenburg '02 and tasty Meranese Schickenburg '02 are both simpler, but still well typed and pleasant. In other words, one wine in the finals and another five with Two Glasses: not bad for a winery that turns out around 1,500,000 bottles.

O	A. A. Pinot Bianco Praesulis '02	🍷🍷	4*
O	A. A. Sauvignon Praesulis '02	🍷🍷	4*
O	A. A. Pinot Bianco '02	🍷🍷	3*
●	A. A. Schiava '02	🍷	4
O	A. A. Pinot Bianco Praesulis '00	🍷	4
O	A. A. Sauvignon Praesulis '00	🍷	4
O	A. A. Pinot Bianco Praesulis '01	🍷	4
O	A. A. Sauvignon Praesulis '01	🍷	4

O	A. A. Chardonnay '02	🍷🍷	4*
●	A. A. Lagrein-Cabernet MerVin '01	🍷🍷	5
●	A. A. Merlot MerVin '01	🍷🍷	5
●	A. A. Pinot Nero MerVin '01	🍷🍷	5
O	A. A. Gewürztraminer '02	🍷🍷	4
O	A. A. Pinot Bianco Guggenberg '02	🍷🍷	4*
O	A. A. Sauvignon Blanc '02	🍷	4
●	Meranese Schickenburg '02	🍷	3
O	Moscato Giallo Schickenburg '02	🍷	4
O	A. A. Chardonnay Tiefenthaler '00	🍷🍷	4
●	A. A. Lagrein-Cabernet MerVin '00	🍷🍷	5*
●	A. A. Merlot '00	🍷🍷	5
●	A. A. Pinot Nero Tiefenthaler MerVin '00	🍷🍷	5

MELTINA/MÖLTEN (BZ)

VIVALDI - ARUNDA
VIA CENTRO, 53
39010 MELTINA/MÖLTEN (BZ)
TEL. 0471668033
E-MAIL: info@arundavivaldi.it

Joseph Reiterer has been the benchmark for Alto Adige sparkling wine for years now, and is one of the sector's most skilled exponents. He manages this winery in Meltina with his wife Marianna. At around 1,200 metres above sea level, this is definitely the highest sparkling wine cellar in Europe, if not the world. Arunda, or Vivaldi, depending on whether the product is bound for the German or Italian-speaking market, produces several cuvées, always chardonnay-led unless the wine is an actual Blanc del Blancs. The excellent Extra Brut Cuvée Marianna has floral and crusty bread aromas, expands across the palate with tangy crispness before finishing very elegantly. The Vivaldi Brut is balanced and subtle, revealing a nonchalant freshness and harmony as it takes you to a long, fascinating finish. Incidentally, this product of impeccable sparkling winemaking also offers fabulous value for money. The Vivaldi Blanc de Blancs has great finesse, fragrant aromas and a particularly delicate palate. Though still worthwhile, the Vivaldi Extra Brut is more straightforward and lacks a bit of depth and balance.

MERANO/MERAN (BZ)

CANTINA PRODUTTORI DI MERANO
LOC. MAIA BASSA
VIA SAN MARCO, 11
39012 MERANO/MERAN (BZ)
TEL. 0473235544
E-MAIL: info@meranerkellerei.com

This splendid winery, managed by Konrad Innerhofer, will celebrate 50 years of activity in 2004. A half-century of constant growth has brought this major Alto Adige producer to a membership of 205 growers for a total output of more than 1,000,000 bottles. Meraner Kellerei's showcase wine could well be the delicious Goldmuskateller Passito Sissi '01. Firmly established as one of the best sweet wines in the region, it has distinctive tropical fruit fragrances and is concentrated in the mouth, where we find notes of pink grapefruit and chestnut honey, then a long finish that lacks just a touch of freshness. The other winery flagship, the Merlot Freiberg Riserva '02, is slightly too marked by oak but, in spite of this, shows a powerful, compact structure. Although still a bit young, it has a bright future. The two whites, the Pinot Bianco from the Graf Von Meran '02 line and especially the Sauvignon '02 from the same line, are both very good. The first is powerful and concentrated, with intense notes of yellow peach, and the fairly harmonious palate has a long finish. The Sauvignon unveils varietal bell pepper and tomato leaf with great suppleness, and a powerful palate, while maintaining remarkable freshness and elegance. The exquisite Meraner Eines Fürsten Traum '02 has good finesse for its type, and pleasing fresh fruit. The Pinot Nero Zenoberg '00, Gewürztraminer '02 and Cabernet-Merlot '02 from the Graf von Meran line are all simpler. In summary, the few ups and downs look temporary. This major co-operative will certainly be back to amaze us again.

○ A. A. Spumante Extra Brut Cuvée Marianna	�♥	5
○ A. A. Spumante Blanc de Blancs Arunda	♥♥	6
○ A. A. Vivaldi Brut	♥♥	4*
○ A. A. Spumante Extra Brut Vivaldi	♥♥	5
○ A. A. Spumante Extra Brut Cuvée Marianna	♢♢	6

● A. A. Merlot Freiberg Ris. '00	♥♥	6
○ A. A. Moscato Giallo Passito Sissi Graf von Meran '01	♥♥	6
● A. A. Meraner Eines Fürsten Traum '02	♥♥	3*
○ A. A. Pinot Bianco Graf Von Meran '02	♥♥	4
○ A. A. Sauvignon Graf Von Meran '02	♥♥	5
● A. A. Cabernet-Merlot Graf Von Meran '00	♥	6
● A. A. Pinot Nero Zenoberg '00	♥	6
○ A. A. Chardonnay '02	♥	3
○ A. A. Gewürztraminer Graf Von Meran '02	♥	4
● A. A. Lagrein Scuro Segenpichl '00	♢♢	6
○ A. A. Chardonnay Goldegg '01	♢♢	3*

MONTAGNA/MONTAN (BZ)　　NALLES/NALS (BZ)

FRANZ HAAS
VIA VILLA, 6
39040 MONTAGNA/MONTAN (BZ)
TEL. 0471812280 - 0471820510
E-MAIL: info@franz-haas.it

CANTINA PRODUTTORI
NALLES NICLARA MAGRÈ
VIA HEILIGENBERG, 2
39010 NALLES/NALS (BZ)
TEL. 0471678626
E-MAIL: info@kellerei.it

If there were a prize for commitment and hard work, Franz Haas would win hands down. A tenacious experimenter, both in the vineyards (new plantings at more than 12,000 vines per hectare) and cellar (ultra-modern and still under construction), Franz regards viticulture as a vocation. He combines this approach with a production of more than 200,000 bottles a year from grapes grown exclusively in the municipalities of Montagna/Montan and Egna/Neumarkt. Franz's dream is to create a great Pinot Noir. We write the name in French because he wants, more than anything else in the world, to create a great, Burgundy-style wine. We aren't sure whether this is the right choice but in the meantime, his best wine is, at least for us, the fragrant, distinctively varietal Moscato Rosa Schweizer '02, which came, not entirely coincidentally, very close to Three Glasses. The classic damask rose and spice nose precedes a palate of deep ripe fruit supported by a fresh acidity, then a complex, lingering finish. We thought Franz's beloved Pinot Nero Schweizer '01 was good, but not completely convincing. It's a little insubstantial, although well typed and graced with nice finesse. The full-flavoured, mouthfilling Pinot Bianco '02 unfurls elegant mineral notes in the finish. The nose of the Gewürztraminer '02 is complex, with touches of tropical fruit and citrus peel The dry, concentrated palate makes it a pleasure to drink. However, we were puzzled by the Manna '01, a cuvée of Riesling, late-harvest Gewürztraminer, Sauvignon and Chardonnay, but we look forward to tasting future editions.

The Cantina Produttori di Nalles Niclara Magrè harvests and vinifies grapes from its 130 members in three different areas, one around Terlano, the other two in the part of Oltradige south of Cortaccia, and produces more than 700,000 bottles a year. Managed by Gerhard Kofler, the winery has confirmed its status as one of the most interesting in the region. Two wines reached our finals and five won Two Glasses, which is not a bad haul. The aromas of the Cabernet Baron Salvadori Riserva '02 are intense. The sweet entry on the palate sweet unfolds in harmonious elegance amid ripe, fine-grained tannins. Although the excellent Passito Baronesse '01 is very concentrated, nice acidity makes it refreshing and deliciously easy to drink. The Chardonnay '01 and Gewürztraminer '02, both from the Baron Salvadori line, are at the top of their respective categories. The Chardonnay is not as concentrated as the 2000, but still shows great character. Its partner is well-typed and mouthfilling, with a refreshing finish reminiscent of mint. The simply delicious Schiava Galea '02 has rare freshness and elegance. The Terlano Pinot Bianco Sirmian '02 and Pinot Grigio Punggl '02 are excellent value for money. Both show medium structure and bring out the best in their varieties. The Riesling Fidera and Terlano Sauvignon Mantele, both from 2002, are more predictable but still technically impeccable. The inevitable Three Glass award has merely been postponed.

● A. A. Moscato Rosa Schweizer '02	🍷🍷	6
● A. A. Pinot Nero Schweizer '01	🍷🍷	5
○ A. A. Gewürztraminer '02	🍷🍷	5
○ A. A. Pinot Bianco '02	🍷🍷	4
○ Manna '01	🍷	5
● A. A. Moscato Rosa Schweizer '99	🍷🍷🍷	5
● A. A. Moscato Rosa Schweizer '00	🍷🍷🍷	5
● A. A. Pinot Nero Schweizer '95	🍷🍷	5
● A. A. Pinot Nero Schweizer '97	🍷🍷	5
○ A. A. Pinot Bianco '99	🍷🍷	3
○ A. A. Gewürztraminer '00	🍷🍷	4
● A. A. Merlot Schweizer '99	🍷🍷	5
● A. A. Moscato Rosa Schweizer '01	🍷🍷	5
● A. A. Pinot Nero Schweizer '00	🍷🍷	6
○ Manna '00	🍷🍷	5

● A. A. Cabernet Baron Salvadori Ris. '00	🍷🍷	5
○ Baronesse Passito '01	🍷🍷	6
○ A. A. Chardonnay Baron Salvadori '01	🍷🍷	5
○ A. A. Gewürztraminer Baron Salvadori '02	🍷🍷	5
○ A. A. Pinot Grigio Punggl '02	🍷🍷	4*
● A. A. Schiava Galea '02	🍷🍷	4
○ A. A. Terlano Pinot Bianco Sirmian '02	🍷🍷	4*
● A. A. Merlot-Cabernet Sauvignon Anticus Baron Salvadori Ris. '00	🍷	6
○ A. A. Riesling Fidera '02	🍷	4
○ A. A. Terlano Sauvignon Cl. Mantele '02	🍷	4
○ A. A. Chardonnay Baron Salvadori '00	🍷🍷🍷	5
○ A. A. Chardonnay Baron Salvadori '99	🍷🍷	5

NALLES/NALS (BZ)

CASTELLO SCHWANBURG
VIA SCHWANBURG, 16
39010 NALLES/NALS (BZ)
TEL. 0471678622
E-MAIL: info@schwanburg.it

At last, things are looking up. For a few years now, we have been waiting for Castello Schwanburg to rediscover that flair that had made it such a benchmark for the region's producers, and so famous among wine aficionados. That's why we are pleased to report a general improvement in wine quality and greater definition in production. The range is wide here, and all the wines are better than just good, beginning with the Lagrein Riserva '00. This offers a wonderful display of balance, typicity and elegance. The Cabernet Sauvignon Castel Schwanburg '00 is the historic winery flagship. It, too, is very stylish, showing off fine-textured tannins and ripe, juicy fruit. But it was the whites that evinced the clearest reversal of the previous trend. Bianco Pallas '02, a blend of Pinot Bianco, Chardonnay, Riesling and Sauvignon, has aromas of rennet apple refined by elegant mineral notes. The palate is concentrated and well balanced, with a complex, seductive finish. The impeccable Terlano Pinot Bianco Pitzon and Terlano, both from 2002, are lovely expressions of their respective sensory profiles. The Schiava Castel Schwanburg '02 has surprisingly complex characteristics for its type, with captivating cherry notes. All the other wines tasted were good, although we found the Merlot Riserva '00 a little predictable. There only remains to wish winery manager Dieter Rudolf, a major figure in Alto Adige oenology, a quick return to Three Glasses. There is no lack of potential.

NATURNO/NATURNS (BZ)

WEINGUT FALKENSTEIN
FRAZ. VAL VENOSTA
VIA CASTELLO, 15
39025 NATURNO/NATURNS (BZ)
TEL. 0473666054
E-MAIL: falkenstein.naturns@rolmail.com

Reaching Franz Pratzner's tiny winery in the Val Venosta village of Naturno/Naturns is not easy. The very narrow winding road finally arrives at the "falcon's rock", Falkenstein, for fans of this wine craftsman. But Franz's vineyards, four hectares with an overall production of 20,000 bottles a year, are a bit like that, too. The dizzyingly steep slopes, planted at 9-10,000 vines per hectare, are tended with an almost maniacal commitment. Franz was the first producer in Valle Venosta to win Three Glasses with his Riesling '98, in the 2000 Guide, and this unquestionably helped enliven the rather sleepy valley winemaking scene. Well, this year Franz Pratzner was just a step away from winning his third Three Glass prize with the 2002 version of his Riesling. As in all its best versions, it is very powerful on the nose, which explodes with pineapple, sage, juniper and typical petrol notes, then the concentrated palate offers well-expressed minerally sensations. The delicious finish is elegant and endless. The Sauvignon '02 is balanced and fresh, with a supple mouthfeel. It only needs a little more cellar time to settle down. The very distinctive Pinot Bianco '02 presents unusual benzene notes, but still has great character and drinks very enjoyably. To sum up, this is a model winery for growers in Valle Venosta and elsewhere, despite its small size.

● A. A. Cabernet Sauvignon Castel Schwanburg '00	♼♼	7
● A. A. Lagrein Scuro Ris. '00	♼♼	5
○ A. A. Bianco Pallas '02	♼♼	4*
● A. A. Moscato Rosa Castel Schwanburg '02	♼♼	6
● A. A. Schiava Castel Schwanburg '02	♼♼	4
○ A. A. Terlano '02	♼♼	4
○ A. A. Terlano Pinot Bianco Pitzon '02	♼♼	4*
● A. A. Cabernet Sauvignon Ris. '00	♼	5
● A. A. Merlot Ris. '00	♼	5
● A. A. Cabernet Castel Schwanburg '90	♼♼♼	6
● A. A. Cabernet Castel Schwanburg '96	♼♼♼	6
○ A. A. Terlano Pinot Bianco Pitzon '01	♼♼	4*

○ A. A. Valle Venosta Riesling '02	♼♼	6
○ A. A. Valle Venosta Pinot Bianco '02	♼	5
○ Sauvignon '02	♼	5
○ A. A. Valle Venosta Riesling '98	♼♼♼	5
○ A. A. Valle Venosta Riesling '00	♼♼♼	5
○ A. A. Valle Venosta Gewürztraminer '98	♼♼	4
○ A. A. Valle Venosta Gewürztraminer '99	♼♼	4
○ A. A. Valle Venosta Pinot Bianco '99	♼♼	4
○ A. A. Valle Venosta Riesling '99	♼♼	5
○ A. A. Valle Venosta Gewürztraminer V. T. '01	♼♼	5
○ A. A. Valle Venosta Pinot Bianco '01	♼♼	4*
○ A. A. Valle Venosta Riesling '01	♼♼	5

SALORNO/SALURN (BZ)

WEINGUT HADERBURG
LOC. BUCHOLZ
POCHI, 30
39040 SALORNO/SALURN (BZ)
TEL. 0471889097
E-MAIL: haderburg@virgili.it

Back in 1976, Luis and Christine Ochsenreiter were the first growers in Alto Adige to bottle sparkling wine professionally using the "metodo classico". Today, their winery has earned a place among the best "spumante" producers nationwide. The secret of their quality lies in the pair's indisputable skill, as well as the splendid location of their own vineyards. The slightly less than ten-hectare property is at Bucholz, or Pochi, in Salorno/Salurn, one of the best vineyards in Alto Adige. The Pas Dosé '97, from a 90-10 cuvée of Chardonnay and Pinot Nero, stays for five years on the lees and flaunts great class. It is fragrant and fruity, with an extremely clean finish and development. Unfortunately, Haderburg only submitted this one sparkler for tasting, so we were unable to evaluate the cellar's other products. With luck, however, we will be tasting them for the next edition of the Guide. This year, the still wines provided us with some pleasant surprises, in particular the Chardonnay Hausmannhof '02, which displays backbone and unfolds on the palate with admirable harmony. The two Pinot Neros, the Hausmannhof '01 and Riserva '02, were also good, showing well typed and very well made. They may not have enormous complexity, but are nonetheless elegant and easy to drink. The Merlot and Cabernet Sauvignon Erah '00 is less exciting, and a little overpowered by the oak.

TERLANO/TERLAN (BZ)

CANTINA TERLANO
VIA COLLI D'ARGENTO, 7
39018 TERLANO/TERLAN (BZ)
TEL. 0471257135
E-MAIL: office@cantina-terlano.com

Territory and cellar lifespan are the two concepts that could be posted at the entrance to this Terlano winery. The territory is just outside Bolzano in the direction of Merano, where the reddish, mineral-rich porphyritic volcanic soil of Tschoggelberg mountain chain is to be found. The climate is almost Mediterranean. Its uniquely complex wines are unmistakable even at a blind tasting. Cellar lifespan can be gauged by the forthcoming release, in 2009, of a Pinot Bianco 1979. We had the good fortune to taste whites from the 1950s and 1960s that were extraordinarily fresh, lustrous and well defined. The Three Glass award goes to the Terlano Sauvignon '92, with its uniquely complex tertiary notes, perfectly harmonized with tropical fruit. The palate is aristocratic and minerally, with endless depth. The Sauvignon Quarz '01 and Terlano Chardonnay Kreuth '01 are similar, apparently lean-bodied but with incredible length. Though both a little young, they already have great character. "Unique" is a term that crops up often when you're talking about Cantina Terlano, and the Lagrein Porphyr '00 is just that. The young and very talented cellarmaster, Rudi Kofler, has worked his magic, bringing out all its finesse and elegance. The other Lagrein, the Gries Riserva '00, and the Terlano Pinot Bianco Vorberg '00, are both good, as are the other wines submitted for tasting. A final note: not all the wines from this cellar are competitively priced, but take a look at the Terlano and Pinot Bianco '02 from the I Classici line.

●	A. A. Pinot Nero Ris '00	🍷🍷	6
○	A. A. Chardonnay Hausmannhof '02	🍷🍷	4
○	A. A. Spumante Pas Dosé '97	🍷🍷	5
●	A. A. Erah '00	🍷	6
○	A. A. Spumante Hausmannhof '91	🍷🍷	6
○	A. A. Spumante Haderburg Pas Dosé '93	🍷🍷	4
●	A. A. Pinot Nero Hausmannhof Ris. '97	🍷🍷	5
○	A. A. Chardonnay Hausmannhof '99	🍷🍷	3
○	A. A. Chardonnay Hausmannhof '00	🍷🍷	4*
○	A. A. Gewürztraminer Blaspichl '00	🍷🍷	4
○	A. A. Spumante Haderburg Pas Dosé '95	🍷🍷	5
○	A. A. Spumante Hausmannhof Ris. '93	🍷🍷	7
○	A. A. Spumante Pas Dosé '96	🍷🍷	5

○	A. A. Terlano Sauvignon '92	🍷🍷🍷	8
●	A. A. Lagrein Porphyr '00	🍷🍷	6
○	A. A. Terlano Chardonnay Kreuth '01	🍷🍷	5*
○	A. A. Terlano Sauvignon Quarz '01	🍷🍷	6
●	A. A. Lagrein Gries '00	🍷🍷	5
○	A. A. Terlano Nova Domus '00	🍷🍷	6
○	A. A. Terlano Pinot Bianco Vorberg '00	🍷🍷	5*
○	A. A. Gewürztraminer Lunare '01	🍷🍷	6
○	A. A. Terlano Cl. '02	🍷🍷	3*
○	A. A. Terlano Pinot Bianco Cl. '02	🍷🍷	3*
○	A. A. Terlano Sauvignon Winkl '02	🍷🍷	5
●	A. A. Lagrein Gries Ris. '97	🍷🍷🍷	5
○	A. A. Terlano '91	🍷🍷🍷	8
○	A. A. Terlano Sauvignon Quarz '00	🍷🍷	6
○	A. A. Terlano Pinot Bianco Vorberg '99	🍷🍷	4

TERLANO/TERLAN (BZ)

VON BRAUNBACH
LOC. SETTEQUERCE
VIA BOLZANO, 23
39018 TERLANO/TERLAN (BZ)
TEL. 0471910184
E-MAIL: info@braunbach.it

Founded in Bolzano in 1991, the Von Braunbach winery initially intended to produce only sparkling wines. Owner and oenologist, Hans Kleon, and his son Hannes, began releasing still wines as recently as 1997, but today they comprise the bulk of the cellar's output. In fact, Hans and Hannes make a total of 75,000 bottles of still wine, and only 10,000 of traditional "metodo classico" sparklers. Grapes from growers in the zone are sorted into two quality levels: the Von Braunbach line, with one Santa Maddalena and one Chardonnay, both aged in stainless steel, and the more prestigious Calldiv line. The Von Braunbach Brut '99 is excellent, a stylish, elegant "spumante" with notes of damson and citron, showing fresh and very long. It is no accident Hans Kleon has been the best sparkling winemaker in Alto Adige for three years now. In the still wine sector, the Lagrein Calldiv '01 is very well typed and varietal, with notes of ripe blackberry, white pepper and liquorice, then a sweet, soft palate with good structure. The Chardonnay '02 is floral and fresh, with medium structure in the mouth and discreet fruit in the finish. The Cuvée Calldiv, from chardonnay and sauvignon grapes, has good structure and shows fresh and elegant, with a long, full-flavoured finish.

TERMENO (BZ)

CASTEL RINGBERG
& KASTELAZ ELENA WALCH
VIA A. HOFER, 1
39040 TERMENO (BZ)
TEL. 0471860172
E-MAIL: info@walch.it

In the previous edition of the Guide, we called the energetic Elena Walch the "queen of Gewürztraminer". This year, we should perhaps call her the "queen of the reds". Though her winery here in Termeno/Tramin effortlessly won Three Glasses with a white, Beyond the Clouds '01, it was still the reds that amazed us with their character and elegance. The Cabernet Sauvignon Castel Ringberg Riserva '00, an excellent red from the splendid vineyards overlooking Lake Caldaro, has clean, intense balsamic aromas, varietal notes of red fruits, a balanced, elegant flavour and elegant body. It's not a huge wine, but one that puts the accent on finesse. The excellent Lagrein Castel Ringberg Riserva '00, although not from the zone best known for this variety, is powerful and has a refined, aristocratic nose-palate profile. But let's get back to the Bianco and its second Three Glass award in a row. Its distinctive, slightly aromatic nose introduces a palate that lacks the muscle of the 2000 but shines for sheer personality and finesse. The Chardonnay Cardellino '02 is also well made, but we found the Pinot Bianco Kastelaz, Riesling Castel Ringberg and Sauvignon Castel Ringberg, all from the 2002 vintage, slightly under par. We felt the Gewürztraminer Kastelaz '02 was not entirely harmonious and needed fine-tuning. We expected more from this winery workhorse. One final note, prices here appear to be rising constantly, and by too much.

○ A. A. Spumante		
Von Braunbach Brut '99	♈	5
● A. A. Lagrein Scuro Calldiv '01	♈♈	4
○ Cuvée Calldiv '01	♈♈	3*
○ A. A. Chardonnay '02	♈♈	4
● A. A. Lagrein Scuro Calldiv '00	♉♉	4
● A. A. Cabernet Lagrein		
Prestige Calldiv '99	♉♉	5
○ A. A. Spumante		
Von Braunbach Brut	♉♉	5

○ A. A. Bianco Beyond the Clouds '01	♈♈♈	7
● A. A. Cabernet Sauvignon		
Castel Ringberg Ris. '00	♈♈	8
● A. A. Lagrein Castel Ringberg Ris. '00	♈♈	7
○ A. A. Chardonnay Cardellino '02	♈♈	5
○ A. A. Gewürztraminer Kastelaz '02	♈	7
○ A. A. Pinot Bianco Kastelaz '02	♈	5
○ A. A. Riesling Castel Ringberg '02	♈	5
○ A. A. Sauvignon Castel Ringberg '02	♈	5
● A. A. Cabernet Sauvignon		
Castel Ringberg Ris. '97	♉♉♉	5
○ A. A. Gewürztraminer Kastelaz '97	♉♉♉	4
○ A. A. Gewürztraminer Kastelaz '00	♉♉♉	5
○ A. A. Bianco Beyond the Clouds '00	♉♉♉	7
● A. A. Merlot Kastelaz Ris. '00	♉♉	8

TERMENO/TRAMIN (BZ)

HOFSTÄTTER
P.ZZA MUNICIPIO, 7
39040 TERMENO/TRAMIN (BZ)
TEL. 0471860161
E-MAIL: info@hofstatter.com

No introductions are needed for the Hofstätter winery in Termeno. First Paolo, and now Martin, Foradori have earned its reputation with intelligent marketing and the extraordinary quality of the wines. Five reached the finals this year. The Three Glass prize for the Yngram '00, a cuvée of 70 per cent Cabernet Sauvignon base with Petit Verdot and Syrah, surprise some observers. The aromas are very well co-orchestrated. Redcurrants, graphite, spices and liquorice precede a concentrated palate with robust tannins and great length. The Gewürztraminer Kolbenhof '02 is now in a class of its own. Exotic aromas of wild rose, lychees and mango are followed by an intense, full-flavoured palate with well-integrated acidity and an almost interminable finish. We move on to the Pinot Nero Barthenau Vigna S. Urbano, one of the best Italian Pinot Neros. The 2000 version is intense ruby red, then smoke and spice aromas mingle with wild berries. Concentrated in the mouth, it shows ripe, tight-knit tannins, good balance and long length. The amber Joseph '01, a late-harvest Gewürztraminer, reveals intense notes of sage and tropical fruit and a sweet, yet nicely acidic, palate. The Barthenau Vigna S. Michele '02 is a blend of 70 per cent Pinot Bianco, 25 per cent Chardonnay, and five per cent Sauvignon and Riesling. The intense bouquet of white peach, broom and chamomile leads into a stylish palate, with well-integrated wood, nice acidity and a clean finish. The Lagrein Steinraffler '00 and Pinot Bianco '02 are both also good, and the Pinot Nero Riserva '00 and Riesling '02 are well made.

● Yngram '00	♉♉♉	6
● A. A. Pinot Nero S. Urbano '00	♉♉	7
○ A. A. Traminer Aromatico V. T. Joseph '01	♉♉	6
○ A. A. Bianco Vigna S. Michele '02	♉♉	5
○ A. A. Gewürztraminer Kolbenhof '02	♉♉	6
● A. A. Lagrein Scuro Steinraffler '00	♉♉	6
○ A. A. Pinot Bianco '02	♉♉	4
● A. A. Pinot Nero Ris. '00	♉	5
○ A. A. Riesling '02	♉	4
● A. A. Pinot Nero S. Urbano '93	♉♉♉	7
● A. A. Pinot Nero S. Urbano '95	♉♉♉	7
○ A. A. Gewürztraminer Kolbenhof '98	♉♉♉	4
○ A. A. Gewürztraminer Kolbenhof '99	♉♉♉	4
○ A. A. Gewürztraminer Kolbenhof '01	♉♉♉	6

TERMENO/TRAMIN (BZ)

CANTINA PRODUTTORI TERMENO
STRADA DEL VINO, 122
39040 TERMENO/TRAMIN (BZ)
TEL. 0471860126
E-MAIL: info@tramin-wine.it

For the first time in the history of the Guide, eight of the 12 wines presented by this co-operative winery near Termeno/Tramin reached the final taste-offs, and two picked up Three Glasses. The triumph was made even greater by the Winemaker of the Year award for cellarmaster, Willi Stürz, a much-deserved tribute to someone who is as modest as he is talented. This extraordinary result says it all about the winery's reliability and technical expertise. Space is limited so we'll begin our report with what is perhaps the signature wine of Produttori di Termeno, the Gewürztraminer Nussbaumerhof, in the '02 edition, perhaps its greatest ever. As usual, the nose is well typed and well co-ordinated, and the palate is concentrated and powerful, but there is also that extra touch of elegance and complexity to make it a truly great wine. The finish is astonishing, showing depth and aristocratic notes of minerals and aromatic herbs. But the new white, Stoan '02 from chardonnay, gewürztraminer, pinot bianco and sauvignon, is another fantastic wine. We noted tropical fruit and almond on the nose, a caressing, concentrated palate, great balance and a very long finish. We also admired, for different reasons, another two stars in this special performance. The '02 Sauvignon offers great quality at a price that should make many Italian producers bow their heads in shame, and the Pinot Grigio Unterebner '02 for is well typed and harmonious. So when will the talented Willi complete the line-up with a great Pinot Nero?

○ A. A. Gewürztraminer Nussbaumerhof '02	♉♉♉	5
○ A. A. Stoan '02	♉♉♉	5
○ A. A. Gewürztraminer Passito Terminum '01	♉♉	8
● A. A. Lagrein Urbanhof '01	♉♉	6
● A. A. Moscato Rosa Terminum '01	♉♉	6
○ A. A. Gewürztraminer Maratsch '02	♉♉	4*
○ A. A. Pinot Grigio Unterebnerhof '02	♉♉	5
○ A. A. Sauvignon '02	♉♉	4*
● A. A. Loam '00	♉♉	6
○ A. A. Pinot Bianco Tauris '02	♉♉	4*
● A. A. Schiava Freisingerhof '02	♉♉	4
● A. A. Pinot Nero Schiesstandhof '01	♉	6
○ A. A. Gewürztraminer Nussbaumerhof '00	♉♉♉	5
○ A. A. Gewürztraminer Nussbaumerhof '01	♉♉♉	5

VADENA/PFATTEN(BZ)

CANTINA LAIMBURG
LOC. LAIMBURG, 6
39040 VADENA/PFATTEN (BZ)
TEL. 0471969700
E-MAIL: laimburg@provinz.bz.it

Cantina Laimburg made a great comeback with three wines in the finals, including a Three Glass Lagrein. Historically, the winery has been a working laboratory for the adjacent experimental agricultural and forestry centre and Alto Adige owes it much. Every year, the centre turns out competent trained technicians, many in the oenological sector, and lends valid support to the region's viticulture. Many of Alto Adige's winemakers and producers studied here, learning the basics for their subsequent careers. But let's talk about this great Lagrein, the Riserva Barbagòl '00. The complex bouquet shows a sequence of quinine, black berry fruit and graphite. It is concentrated and well balanced on the palate, where close-knit, silk-smooth tannins and well-integrated oak take you joyfully through to a lingering finish. All things considered, perhaps the only problem is its unattractive name. The Pinot Nero Selyèt '01 is also well made, in fact it's one of the best in its category. Elegant and characterful, it offers a supple progression on the palate, signing off with a long, distinctly complex finish. The Sauvignon Oyèll '02 has great style, with none of the slightly wild notes you often find in this wine, and shows good depth, in spite of a structure that is far from enormous. The Riesling '02 is very well made but still young, the full-flavoured Gewürztraminer Eliònd '02 has an interesting mineral vein, and the Cabernet Sauvignon Sass Roà Riserva '00 has great backbone, sweet tannins and a complex, long finish. In short, the cellar presented six magnificent wines.

VARNA/VAHRN (BZ)

ABBAZIA DI NOVACELLA
FRAZ. NOVACELLA
VIA DELL'ABBAZIA, 1
39040 VARNA/VAHRN (BZ)
TEL. 0472836189
E-MAIL: info@kloster-neustift.it

Cantina Abbazia di Novacella is now a legendary benchmark for Valle Isarco winemaking. Labels from here are known throughout Italy and beyond, and are emblematic of Valle Isarco whites. Today, the enthusiastic winemaker, Celestino Lucin, supervises the new, very modern cellar, remodelled a couple of years ago. Grapes for Novacella wines come from 70 hectares of vineyards between 250 and 850 metres above sea level and Urban von Klebersberg, the abbey's dynamic lay administrator, knows how to motivate the member-growers. This year, the results were extraordinary: one Three Glass award and four wines in our taste-offs. Sylvaner, Müller Thurgau, Gewürztraminer, Kerner, Pinot Grigio and Veltliner are all beautifully interpreted in the showcase Praepositus line, and it was the Kerner Praepositus '02 that won the panel's hearts and taste buds. When grown in Valle Isarco, this Austrian variety makes a wine so rich and mouthfillingly delicious that it is impossible to resist. The following are all magnificent: Moscato Rosa '02 is intense, concentrated, balanced and powerful; Gewürztraminer Praepositus '02 is minerally, fresh and tangy, with a long finish; and the Pinot Grigio '02 is fresh, fruit-forward and mineral. Also well typed and very enjoyable are the complex, minerally and long Sylvaner Praepositus '02 and the powerful, well-structured Praepositus Bianco '01. The red Praepositus wines fell below our expectations. The Pinot Nero Riserva '01 is concentrated, but slightly over-oaked, and the Lagrein Riserva '01 is leanish, with rather green tannins.

● A. A. Lagrein Scuro Barbagòl Ris. '00	♟♟♟	6
● A. A. Pinot Nero Selyèt Ris. '01	♟♟	5
○ A. A. Sauvignon Oyèll '02	♟♟	4*
● A. A. Cabernet Sass Roà Ris. '00	♟♟	5
○ A. A. Gewürztraminer Eliònd '02	♟♟	5
○ A. A. Riesling '02	♟♟	4
○ A. A. Gewürztraminer '94	♟♟♟	4
○ A. A. Gewürztraminer '99	♟♟	4
○ A. A. Riesling Renano '99	♟♟	4
○ A. A. Riesling Renano '00	♟♟	4*
● A. A. Lagrein Scuro Ris. '98	♟♟	6
○ A. A. Chardonnay Doa '00	♟♟	5
○ A. A. Sauvignon '01	♟♟	4
● A. A. Cabernet Ris. '99	♟♟	6
● A. A. Lagrein Scuro Ris. '99	♟♟	6

○ A. A. Valle Isarco Kerner Praepositus '02	♟♟♟	5
● A. A. Moscato Rosa '02	♟♟	6
○ A. A. Valle Isarco Gewürztraminer Praepositus '02	♟♟	5
○ A. A. Valle Isarco Pinot Grigio '02	♟♟	4*
○ Praepositus Weiss '01	♟♟	5
○ A. A. Valle Isarco Sylvaner Praepositus '02	♟♟	4
● A. A. Lagrein Praepositus Ris. '01	♟	6
● A. A. Pinot Nero Praepositus Ris. '01	♟	6
○ A. A. Valle Isarco Sauvignon Marklhof '02	♟	4
● A. A. Lagrein Praepositus Ris. '00	♟♟♟	6
○ A. A. Valle Isarco Kerner Praepositus '01	♟♟	5
○ A. A. Valle Isarco Pinot Grigio '01	♟♟	4*

VARNA/VAHRN (BZ)

VARNA/VAHRN (BZ)

KÖFERERHOF
FRAZ. NOVACELLA
VIA PUSTERIA, 3
39040 VARNA/VAHRN (BZ)
TEL. 0472836649
E-MAIL: info@koefererhof.it

PACHERHOF
LOC. NOVACELLA
39040 VARNA/VAHRN (BZ)
TEL. 0472835717
E-MAIL: info@pacherhof.com

This small Novacella estate has five hectares under vine, producing around 27,000 bottles a year. It has followed a course taken by many small producers in Eisacktal. Until 1994, it brought its grapes to the cellar at the Abbazia di Novacella. Then in 1995, 33-year-old Günter Kershbaumer, who studied at the school of oenology in Laimburg, began bottling on his own. The vineyards are located between 630 metres and 660 metres (for the riesling) above sea level, just a few kilometres from Bressanone, in what is becoming the valley's Golden Triangle. This soil is very light and rich in those pebbles that give wines from here a minerality that delights fans of the valley's cellars. Stainless steel is used almost exclusively in the cellar, but there are large oak casks for some of the Pinot Grigio (20 per cent) and Sylvaner (10 per cent). Seven wines were submitted and all earned fine scores for their unique character. We very much liked the Pinot Grigio '02. Smokiness mingles with varietal pear, then the richness of fruit in the mouth is overwhelming. The rather high alcohol content – over 14 degrees – is well balanced by fresh acidity and remarkable minerality. The Sylvaner '02 is a classic. It introduces elegant aromas of tropical fruit, mango and lychees that expand on the palate, where the acid vein is well integrated, then on to a deep finish lifted by complex minerality. All of Günter's wines are a little unapproachable and austere when young, but they are beautifully typed, and interpret the territory to perfection.

It was a great debut for the Pacher estate, located just above the Abbazia di Novacella. Its origins lie somewhere in the 11th century and it has been owned by the Huber family since 1849. Josef Huber and another grower, who owned the nearby Völklhof, were pioneers of viticulture in Valle Isarco. In 1880, the two brought the first white grape varieties, sylvaner and müller thurgau, to the Bressanone area. Today, Andreas Huber farms the six hectares of estate vineyards with his father, Josef. These sandy, gravel-rich calcareous plots, all facing south to southwest, yield lively, aromatic wines, rich in elegance and backbone, that ferment in stainless steel and large wood. The Kerner '02 is a vigorous interpretation of this classic white. The nose is complex, showing notes that run from white peach to apple, and finish off with hints of tropical fruit and citrus peel. The palate is powerful, fresh and well balanced, revealing notes of petrol and ripe fruit, then the finish is long and pervasive. The Sylvaner '02 opens to a broad range of aromas, including sage and petrol. The big, mouthfilling palate takes you through to a firm, full-flavoured finish. It's a surprising wine that needs cellar time to yield its best, so we look forward to next year's tastings.

○ A. A. Valle Isarco Liebelei Passito '01	🍷🍷	6
○ A. A. Valle Isarco Gewürztraminer '02	🍷🍷	5
○ A. A. Valle Isarco Kerner '02	🍷🍷	4*
○ A. A. Valle Isarco Müller Thurgau '02	🍷🍷	4*
○ A. A. Valle Isarco Pinot Grigio '02	🍷🍷	4*
○ A. A. Valle Isarco Riesling '02	🍷🍷	5
○ A. A. Valle Isarco Sylvaner '02	🍷🍷	4*
○ A. A. Valle Isarco Pinot Grigio '99	🍷🍷	4
○ A. A. Valle Isarco Sylvaner '00	🍷🍷	4*
○ A. A. Valle Isarco Gewürztraminer '01	🍷🍷	4
○ A. A. Valle Isarco Kerner '01	🍷🍷	4*
○ A. A. Valle Isarco Müller Thurgau '01	🍷🍷	4
○ A. A. Valle Isarco Pinot Grigio '01	🍷🍷	4
○ A. A. Valle Isarco Riesling '01	🍷🍷	4
○ A. A. Valle Isarco Sylvaner '01	🍷🍷	4*

○ A. A. Kerner '02	🍷🍷	4*
○ A. A. Pinot Grigio '02	🍷🍷	4
○ A. A. Sylvaner '02	🍷🍷	4*

OTHER WINERIES

LORENZ MARTINI
LOC. CORNAIANO/GIRLAN
VIA PRANZOL, 2/D
39050 APPIANO/EPPAN (BZ)
TEL. 0471664136

Lorenz Martini produces only one "spumante" at his small estate. But it's a good one. The Comitissa Brut Riserva '99 is a cuvée of equal parts of Pinot Bianco and Chardonnay. Aged for 40 months on the lees, it has a very fine bead, elegant, complex aromas, mid structure and a harmonious flavour.

○ A. A. Spumante		
Comitissa Brut Ris. '99	🍷🍷	6

STROBLHOF
LOC. SAN MICHELE - VIA PIGANO, 25
39057 APPIANO/EPPAN (BZ)
TEL. 0471662250
E-MAIL: hotel@stroblhof.it

This winery in the village of San Michele Appiano produces little more than 20,000 bottles sourced from about three hectares of vineyards. The Pinot Bianco Strahler '02 and Pinot Nero Pigeno '00 were most convincing at our tastings.

● A. A. Pinot Nero Pigeno '00	🍷🍷	5
○ A. A. Pinot Bianco Strahler '02	🍷🍷	4
● A. A. Pinot Nero Ris. '00	🍷	6
○ A. A. Chardonnay Schwarzhaus '02	🍷	4

EGGER-RAMER
VIA GUNCINA, 5
39100 BOLZANO/BOZEN
TEL. 0471280541 - 3294509871
E-MAIL: egger@suedtirolerwein.de

Toni and Peter Egger specialize in wines from the Bolzano are. Their Lagrein Gries Kristan '01 is very good and sold at reasonable prices. The Lagrein Gries Kristan Riserva '00 is a bit edgy but still well typed.

● A. A. Lagrein Scuro Kristan '01	🍷🍷	4*
● A. A. Lagrein Scuro Gries		
Kristan Ris. '00	🍷	4

HARTMANN LENTSCH
VIA NAZIONALE, 71
39051 BRONZOLO/BRANZOLL (BZ)
TEL. 0471596017
E-MAIL: weingut_lentsch@dnet.it

This estate is a new entry. Hartmann and Klaus Lentsch farm more than 12 hectares, planted to red grapes, at Bronzolo/Branzoll. The Lagrein '00 has typical aromas of wild berries and bitter chocolate but the vigorous palate has a bit too much edge. The Cabernet-Merlot Palestina '00 is simpler.

● A. A. Lagrein '00	🍷🍷	5
● A. A. Cabernet Merlot		
Palestina '00	🍷	5

Castel Sallegg - Graf Kuenburg
v.lo di Sotto, 15
39100 Caldaro/Kaltern (BZ)
TEL. 0471963132 - 0471974140
E-MAIL: castelsallegg@kuenburg.it

There were good results from the historic Castel Sallegg estate. We were particularly struck by the Lagrein Riserva '00, which reveals great character and complexity, then a finish of rare elegance. The Lago di Caldaro Bischofsleiten '02 and Pinot Bianco '02 are both pleasant and well made.

● A. A. Lagrein Ris. '00	🍷🍷	5
● A. A. Lago di Caldaro Scelto Bischofsleiten '02	🍷	4
○ A. A. Pinot Bianco '02	🍷	3

Tenuta Klosterhof
Clavenz, 40
39052 Caldaro/Kaltern (BZ)
TEL. 0471961046
E-MAIL: info@garni-klosterhof.com

Specializing in Goldmuskateller, this small Caldaro winery surprised us this year with an impeccable, concentrated Pinot Bianco Trifall' 02 and an expressive Pinot Nero Panigl Riserva '00. The Moscato Giallo Trifall '02 is always one of the best. Very nice results overall.

● A. A. Pinot Nero '00	🍷🍷	6
○ A. A. Pinot Bianco '02	🍷🍷	4
○ A. A. Moscato Giallo Trifall '02	🍷	4

Brunnenhof
FRAZ. Mazzon
via degli Alpini, 5
39044 Egna/Neumarkt (BZ)
TEL. 0471820687

This estate in the municipality of Egna/Neumarkt makes its guide debut introducing us to an elegant, well-typed Gewürztraminer Mazzon '02. The spectrum of aromatics is textbook stuff. The palate is concentrated, but shows well-supported balance, then the finish is long and supple.

○ A. A. Gewürztraminer Mazzon ' 02	🍷🍷	4

Castello Rametz
FRAZ. Maia Alta - via Labers, 4
39012 Merano/Meran (BZ)
TEL. 0473211011 - 0473290187
E-MAIL: info@rametz.com

This major estate near Merano repeated last year's performance. The Chardonnay '02 is fruity, linear, elegant and pleasant to drink. The Cesuret '00, from chardonnay, is concentrated, powerful and has notes of smoke and tropical fruit. The well-made Riesling '02 is decent.

○ Cèsuret '00	🍷🍷	6
○ A. A. Chardonnay '02	🍷🍷	4*
○ A. A. Riesling '02	🍷	5

Maso Happacherhof
Istituto Tecnico Agrario
via del Monte, 20
39040 Ora/Auer (BZ)
TEL. 0471810538 - 0471810693

Associated with the agricultural technical institute in Ora/Auer, this small, organic estate is well set to join the front ranks of local winemaking. It presented a series of wines that are truly remarkable for clean execution and typicity.

● A. A. Merlot-Cabernet Happacherhof Ris. '00	🍷🍷	5
○ A. A. Chardonnay Passito Aurum Happacherhof '01	🍷🍷	6
● A. A. Lagrein Scuro Happacherhof '01	🍷🍷	5

Steinhauserhof
via Pochi, 37
39040 Salorno/Salurn (BZ)
TEL. 0471889031

Anton Ochsenreiter, owner of this lovely estate at Salorno/Salurn, uncorked a valid Pinot Nero Riserva '00, with varietal aromas and classic notes of strawberry emerging. Though not enormous in the mouth, it still offers great elegance. The Chardonnay Selezione '02 is also interesting.

● A. A. Pinot Nero Ris. '00	🍷🍷	6
○ A. A. Chardonnay Sel. '02	🍷	5
○ A. A. Gewürztraminer Sel. '02	🍷	6
○ A. A. Sauvignon Sel. '02	🍷	5

OSWALD SCHUSTER BEFEHLHOF
VIA VEZZANO, 14
39028 SILANDRO/SCHLANDERS (BZ)
TEL. 0473742197

Oswald Schuster from
Silandro/Schlanders is one of the founders
of modern viticulture in Valle Venosta. As
usual, the Riesling '02 is excellent and
very special, but the Pinot Nero '01 also
has a wonderful touch of elegance, in line
with this micro-winery's subtle style.

● A. A. Pinot Nero '01	♟♟	4
○ A. A. Valle Venosta Riesling '02	♟♟	4*
○ A. A. Müller Thurgau '02	♟	3
○ Fraueler '02	♟	3

TIROLENSIS ARS VINI
39040 VADENA/PFATTEN (BZ)
TEL. 0471969700

Hubert Pohl Köfelgut, Sigmund Kripp
Stachlburg, Franz Pfeil Kränzl, Tenute
Loacker, Georg Mumelter Griesbauerhof,
Josephus Mayr Unterganzner, Andreas
Berger Thurnhof and Laimburg joined
forces to create a blend of Cabernet,
Lagrein and Pinot Nero bottled by
Laimburg oenologist, Urban Piccolruaz.

| ● Tirolensis Ars Vini Rot '00 | ♟♟ | 6 |

ROCKHOF
VIA S. VALENTINO, 9
39040 VILLANDRO/VILLANDERS (BZ)
TEL. 0472847130

Konrad Augschöll's tiny estate has shown
it can make advances in quality, like the
rest of Valle Isarco. The flawlessly crafted
Müller Thurgau and Sylvaner '02 are
excellent, with fragrant varietal aromas.
The Caruess '01 cuvée from
Gewürztraminer, Sylvaner and Pinot Grigio
is surprising.

○ Caruess '01	♟♟	4
○ A. A. Valle Isarco Müller Thurgau '02	♟♟	4
○ A. A. Valle Isarco Sylvaner '02	♟♟	4

VENETO

The larger number of Veneto wineries reviewed in this edition of the Guide perfectly reflects the improved quality of the region's vineyards. More producers are becoming aware that releasing excellent-quality wines onto the market, backed up by a targeted pricing policy, is the only way to bring about progress in the sector. We note this general increase in quality but it is also important to remember that while big wines are still popular right now, Veneto is fast establishing itself as a region with a deep commitment to stylish, balanced wines. In Valpolicella, for example, where richly extracted, solidly built wines are traditional, there are more elegantly drinkable wines about. Balance has been achieved in many different styles, whether the Amarones are modern, like Campagnola's, as traditional as Zenato's, or unmistakably individual, like Quintarelli's. In Veneto, wineries are following different routes to a new identity, seeking less invasive farming methods and authentic, uncompromising wines. This is true of Angiolino Maule at Gambellara and Alessandro Sgaravetti at Monselice, whose wines follow one possible direction. The Breganze and Colli Euganei DOCs are more extensively covered in this year's Guide, demonstrating the areas' huge potential, and the same applies along the river Piave, where the wineries may not have been awarded Three Glasses, but are increasingly oriented towards wines that give full expression to long-established local traditions. The number of wines to receive Three Glasses has also increased and Allegrini's Recioto is the Sweet Wine of the Year. This is not just an acknowledgement of an excellent wine but also pays tribute to a type that embodies the history of Valpolicella. Impressively, over half the wines to win this year's top awards are from this area. There have been significant innovations in large wineries like Cecilia Beretta, Campagnola and the Cantina Sociale Valpolicella, the leading co-operative in Veneto, showing that progress involves the entire winemaking scene. Another new element is the success of the Mezzane valley, which has again confirmed what a great wine area it is. Corte Sant'Alda and Tenuta Sant'Antonio are joined by Roccolo Grassi, a small but expanding winery, admirably managed by Marco Sartori. Soave is paying the price of a difficult year, although the best producers have had good success in expressing the excellent quality of the terroir in their wines, despite the weather. There were Three Glass awards again for Vignalta and Serafini & Vidotto, like Maculan, producers of the stylish, classy wines that Veneto does so well.

ANNONE VENETO (VE)

Bosco del Merlo
via Postumia, 14
30020 Annone Veneto (VE)
tel. 0422768167
e-mail: boscodelmerlo@paladin.it

The positive vibrations from this large winery at Annone Veneto are confirmed this year. Indeed, the products are even more impressive, and for the first time ever in the history of the Guide, a Lison-Pramaggiore DOC wine reached the final tastings for Three Glasses. The rest of the range has also made impressive progress, showing how the determination of the Paladin family, applied to their extensive, well-located vineyards, has succeeded in revolutionizing the quality of their wines in just a few years. The champion is still the Refosco Roggio dei Roveri. This is a very stylish red with a pronounced, attractive floral note on the nose that gradually gives way to understated ripe fruit. Equally impressive is the dry, lingering palate, which has a vein of acidity that bolsters and extends its length. The Tocai Juti is also interesting. Fresh, light flowers and almonds contrast with the well-rounded palate, where a glimpse of iodine and sea-salt from ageing comes through in the aromas. There is another positive edition of Merlot Campo Camino. It shows fragrant, clearly defined grassy and red berry aromas, and an earthiness that lends depth and character. Here, too, the wine is stylish on the palate, its sweet tannins being a common feature throughout the range. The rest of the growing line of products are reliable in quality.

●	Lison-Pramaggiore Refosco P. R. Roggio dei Roveri '00	🍷🍷	6
●	Lison-Pramaggiore Merlot Campo Camino '01	🍷🍷	5
○	Lison-Pramaggiore Cl. Tocai Juti '02	🍷🍷	5
●	360 Ruber Capitae Rosso '00	🍷	6
○	Verduzzo Soandre '01	🍷	5
○	Lison-Pramaggiore Sauvignon Turranio '02	🍷	5
●	Vineargenti Rosso '99	🍷	6
○	Lison-Pramaggiore Cl. Tocai Juti '01	ΥΥ	4
●	Lison-Pramaggiore Refosco P. R. Roggio dei Roveri '99	ΥΥ	5

BAONE (PD)

Giordano Emo Capodilista
via Villa Rita
35030 Baone (PD)
tel. 049637294
e-mail: giordanoemo@libero.it

Giordano Emo Capodilista is a determined producer with strong links to the local Colli Euganei area. He believes it is an excellent terroir that deserves worldwide recognition for its wines, so his decision to take an active role in the protection consortium should be seen in this light. Similarly, he is tireless in his efforts to persuade non quality-oriented colleagues to take the plunge and aim for better wines. This does not prevent Giordano from devoting himself body and soul to his Baone-based winery, with excellent results. For the second year running, the Ireneo, a characterful Cabernet Sauvignon, fell just short of a Third Glass. It is well partnered by a new wine, the astonishing Fior d'Arancio Passito. The Cabernet Sauvignon is dark, with a deep, pronounced nose whose aromas include clear, very ripe cherries, salty, minerally aromas and aromatic herbs, particularly mint and aniseed. The palate is robust and vigorous, and remarkably long. Over time, this liveliness will be transformed into balance and complexity. The Passito is excellent, a very Mediterranean wine with warm, pervasive aromas of dried apricot and candied fruit. It is headily soft on the palate, which offers smooth, even fruitier sensations, and a long, balsamic finish.

●	Colli Euganei Cabernet Sauvignon Ireneo '01	🍷🍷	6
○	Colli Euganei Fiori d'Arancio Passito Donna Daria '01	🍷🍷	6
●	Colli Euganei Cabernet Sauvignon Ireneo '00	ΥΥ	6

BARDOLINO (VR)

GUERRIERI RIZZARDI
VIA VERDI, 4
37011 BARDOLINO (VR)
TEL. 0457210028
E-MAIL: mail@guerrieri-rizzardi.com

Villa Guerrieri Rizzardi is one of the most interesting residences on Veneto's Lake Garda riviera. It stands just outside the eastern gate of the old town of Bardolino, in a huge garden dotted with ancient trees. Maria Cristina Loredan Rizzardi has made one strip of this into a small botanical garden, which is one of the attractions of the new tasting area. Tastings are offered of the products the winery obtains from various holding that extending over some of the finest growing areas in the province of Verona. Maria Rizzardi's son, Giuseppe, supervises winemaking procedures and, drawing on his experience in France, has contributed innovative ideas that are progressively being adopted in the vineyards. The new cellar, now under construction, may provide further possibilities for growth, but the results of the estate's commitment to production are already clear, especially in the two excellent Amarones. The Calcarole throws an intriguing nose of ripe wild cherries with berry fruits and seductive hints of aromatic herbs, followed by a subtle, stylish palate. The standard-label Amarone is also very good, with a well-developed, pervasive nose and firm, velvety palate. The winery's other noteworthy reds include the Valpolicella Poiega, a nicely complex wine named after the spectacular Italian garden, open to visitors, at the Rizzardi villa in Negrar, and the Bardolino Superiore, with its aromatic freshness and floral, grassy notes. The two Soaves are both pleasant, but the simple yet full-bodied Costeggiola is the better of the two.

BARDOLINO (VR)

F.LLI ZENI
VIA COSTABELLA, 9
37011 BARDOLINO (VR)
TEL. 0457210022
E-MAIL: zeni@zeni.it

Gaetano Zeni is being assisted increasingly by his son, Fausto, in the running of the family winery, now almost an institution in Bardolino. First, it is one of the oldest in the area, founded as long ago as 1870, and second because there is a small wine museum on the premises which is popular with tourists. Nearly all the typical Verona DOCs are included in the range of products, but Bardolino is the favourite. The Zeni family have made one of the best ever Superiore versions, here as a DOCG for the first time. It is dense with ripe fruit and combines austerity, fullness and brilliance while retaining an incredibly supple mouthfeel. Another lakeside label, the Lugana Marogne, also yields excellent results, with subtle appley fruit and summer flowers on the nose, and a strong expressive palate. The white Garganega Garda DOC is also tangy and rounded, with an appetizing fragrance of ripe apples. Still in the lake area, the Bianco di Custoza, Bardolino and Lugana from the Vigne Alte line are all very enjoyable. Leading the Valpolicella products are the full, barrique-aged Amarone 2000 and the succulent Valpolicella Superiore Vigne Alte, whose rich fruit and floral notes are lifted by minerally nuances. The standard-label Amarone, Recioto and the Valpolicella Marogne, enhanced with a "ripasso" of unpressed skins after fermentation, are all rather simpler. Finally, the Merlar did well. A modern-style red made from slightly dried cabernet sauvignon grapes, it ages in wood and is intensely fruity.

● Amarone della Valpolicella Cl.		
Calcarole '98	♟♟	8
● Amarone della Valpolicella Cl. '98	♟♟	7
● Bardolino Cl. Sup. Munus '01	♟	5
● Valpolicella Cl. Sup. Poiega '01	♟	4
○ Soave Cl. '02	♟	3
○ Soave Cl. Sup. Costeggiola '02	♟	4
☉ Bardolino Cl. Chiaretto '02		3
● Amarone della Valpolicella Cl. '96	♟♟	7
● Amarone della Valpolicella Cl.		
Calcarole '97	♟♟	7

● Amarone della Valpolicella Cl.		
Barrique '00	♟♟	7
● Merlar Rosso '00	♟♟	6
● Bardolino Cl. Sup. '01	♟♟	4
○ Lugana Marogne '01	♟♟	4
● Valpolicella Cl. Sup.		
Vigne Alte '01	♟♟	3*
● Amarone della Valpolicella Cl. '00	♟	6
● Recioto della Valpolicella Cl.		
Vigne Alte '00	♟	6
● Valpolicella Cl. Sup. Marogne '00	♟	4
● Bardolino Cl. Sup. Vigne Alte '01	♟	3
○ Bianco di Custoza Vigne Alte '02	♟	3
○ Garda Garganega Vigne Alte '02	♟	3*
○ Lugana Vigne Alte '02		3

BASSANO DEL GRAPPA (VI)

VIGNETO DUE SANTI
V.LE ASIAGO, 174
36061 BASSANO DEL GRAPPA (VI)
TEL. 0424502074
E-MAIL: info@duesanti.it

This winery is enthusiastically run by Stefano and Adriano Zonta, who are increasingly successful at producing wines that correspond to their vision as growers. The vineyards lie on hilly ground close to the centre of Bassano, on limestone soil of volcanic and glacial origin. After winning a well-deserved Three Glasses last year, the Zontas have maintained their high standard throughout the production range. The Cabernet Vigneto Due Santi remains a model of style and class. Its characterful, very stylish nose offers tidy aromatic herbs, dried flowers and small berry fruits. The palate is austere yet succulent, and the good texture, tannin density and acidity are beautifully balanced, suggesting excellent ageing potential. The Breganze Rosso has hints of grass, fruit and red peppers on the nose, and a broad, silky, slim and supple palate. The Cabernet is also very good, with a fresh fruity nose, reflected on the dry, dynamic palate with its good finish. Outstanding among the whites are the Sauvignon Due Santi and the Bianco Rivana, which have different characteristics. The Sauvignon has balsamic aromas, with hints of sage and spices, then the powerful, butter-smooth palate progresses well with nice acidity. The Rivana, made from tocai grapes, has a vibrant nose with hints of almonds and spices, and an enthrallingly firm, tangy palate. The Malvasia Campo di Fiori 2002 is ripe, generous and very impressive.

BREGANZE (VI)

★ MACULAN
VIA CASTELLETTO, 3
36042 BREGANZE (VI)
TEL. 0445873733 - 0445873124
E-MAIL: info@maculan.net

Fausto Maculan is a man with a plan. He aims to enhance the character definition of his range of wines, without making radical changes to the production philosophy that has made the name Maculan appreciated around the world. The whites will spend much less time in new wood, facilitating fuller expression, and the reds and sweet wines will focus more on terroir. Our review of the various labels begins with Acininobili, which made its biggest impression in years. The colour is old gold, then the aromas are delightful, with wonderful botrytis in the background complementing the spices and candied citrus fruits. The sweet fruit on the silky, mouthfilling palate is refreshed by a perfect vein of acidity. Wines in the middle range are making progress, especially the Palazzotto and the Dindarello, and we note the innovative Ferrata, a blend of Chardonnay and Sauvignon from the same line. Although affected by the difficult growing year, the aromas are admirably subtle and the handling of the texture is stylish. The nicely spicy, succulent Pinot Nero Altura, and the lean, stylish Merlot Crosara, are both interesting, although the former still has to integrate its oak. The Fratta is again excellently made, and well on the way to becoming a classic among Veneto wines. The 2001 version comes from drastic grape selection. Wood blends subtly with the aromas of blackcurrants, spices and ripe morello cherries, then the edgy, characterful flavour is lifted by a reprise of violets, leather and red peppers that linger through to the austere, compelling finish.

● Breganze Cabernet Vigneto Due Santi '01	♟♟	5
● Breganze Rosso '01	♟♟	4*
○ Breganze Bianco Rivana '02	♟♟	4
○ Breganze Sauvignon Vigneto Due Santi '02	♟♟	4
● Breganze Cabernet '01	♟	4
○ Malvasia Campo di Fiori '02	♟	4
● Breganze Cabernet Vigneto Due Santi '00	♟♟♟	5
● Breganze Cabernet Vigneto Due Santi '98	♟♟	5
● Breganze Cabernet Vigneto Due Santi '99	♟♟	5

● Fratta '01	♟♟♟	8
○ Acininobili '00	♟♟	8
● Breganze Rosso Crosara '01	♟♟	8
● Breganze Cabernet Sauvignon Palazzotto '01	♟♟	5
○ Breganze Torcolato '01	♟♟	7
○ Ferrata '02	♟♟	5
● Breganze Pinot Nero Altura '01	♟.	6
● Brentino '01	♟	4
○ Breganze di Breganze '02	♟	4
○ Dindarello '02	♟	5
○ Pino & Toi '02	♟	3
● Fratta '98	♟♟♟	7
● Fratta '99	♟♟♟	7
● Fratta '00	♟♟♟	7

BREGANZE (VI)

CAVAION VERONESE (VR)

FIRMINO MIOTTI
VIA BROGLIATI CONTRO, 53
36042 BREGANZE (VI)
TEL. 0445873006
E-MAIL: agrifirmino@libero.it

LE FRAGHE
LOC. COLOMBARA, 3
37010 CAVAION VERONESE (VR)
TEL. 0457236832
E-MAIL: info@fraghe.it

The Miottis are a real country family, in the noblest sense of the word. They are capable of producing authentic, original wines in their Breganze hills and they have earned a very favourable review in this Guide. The 25,000-30,000 bottles produced each year come from the estate's five well-aspected hectares, sheltered from the fog off the plains and caressed by breezes that facilitate raisining. The winery building is small and serviceable, and the welcome courteous. Inevitably, we start with Torcolato, Miotti's cult wine, which has been made since the late 19th century. After careful raisining, the grapes are crushed and vinified in the traditional manner, without wood. The result is a fragrant amber-coloured wine with clear hints of candied fruit, pears, gooseberries and honey. On the palate, it is vivid, crystal clear and stylish, despite the rich extract and texture. It also has remarkable ageing potential. There's another good review for the Vespaiolo. Its leanness is often confused with typicity, but despite the mediocre growing year, it has outstanding character. The minerally note on the palate is toned down in the wide spectrum of aromatics, then the tangy finish reveals all the acidity of the grapes. The Pinot Bianco is lean and well-typed, while the Le Colombare, daughter Franca Miotti's brainchild, has fascinating exotic, mineral and citrus hints. Turning to the reds, we found an approachable, stylish Cabernet, which we enjoyed as much as the Valletta, a more powerful, structured wine that also offers smoothness and supple tannins.

You certainly can't say that Matilde Poggi lacks character. It takes guts to write off two wines like the Chardonnay and the Chiaretto, which have enjoyed undisputed success on the market for years. But this atypical winemaker has developed a personal production philosophy in this beautiful, but tricky, area between Lake Garda and the river Adige. She is determined to stick to her guns. The result is that this year, we were only able to taste two wines in bottle, the Garganega and the Bardolino, while Quaiare, the feather in the winery's cap, is still ageing in the cellars of the 15th-century farm complex at the Le Fraghe winery. The Cabernet-based wine will therefore come out later than it used to. The Garganega is made entirely from this native Veronese grape variety, and we can confirm that this is the best version to emerge so far from the Camporengo vineyards. The nose already has a good intense concentration of fruit and the palate is succulent and tangy. The peachy fruit notes are lifted by stylish hints of minerality. The Bardolino is one of the best from the tricky 2002 vintage in this area. It has characteristically enjoyable and intriguing ripe red cherries laced with spirited varietal vegetal tones.

●	Rosso Valletta '00	🍷🍷	6
○	Breganze Torcolato '00	🍷🍷	7
●	Breganze Cabernet '01	🍷🍷	3*
○	Breganze Bianco Le Colombare '02	🍷	3
○	Breganze Vespaiolo '02	🍷	2
○	Breganze Pinot Bianco '02		3

○	Garganega Camporengo '02	🍷🍷	3*
●	Bardolino '02	🍷	3
●	Valdadige Quaiare '96	🍷🍷	5
●	Valdadige Quaiare '97	🍷🍷	5
●	Valdadige Quaiare '98	🍷🍷	5

CINTO EUGANEO (PD)

CA' LUSTRA
LOC. FAEDO
VIA SAN PIETRO, 50
35030 CINTO EUGANEO (PD)
TEL. 042994128
E-MAIL: info@calustra.it

Led by the tireless Franco, indubitably one of the most brilliant winegrowers in the Colli Euganei, the Zanovello family is building an image for their winery that goes beyond the mere wine to acquire an ambitious, far-reaching cultural dimension. A series of interesting projects are under way to restore Villa Alessi, a building whose origins date back to the second century. A wine shop, a B&B, wine courses, academic conferences and other events, including joint projects with universities, are all on the agenda. On the winemaking front, the close-knit cellar team of Ivano Giacomin, Paolo Parpaiola, winemaker, Francesco Polastri, and vineyard manager, Filippo Giannone, offers wines of outstanding density and personality. The Merlot Vigna Sasso Nero is dark ruby red, with a very well-developed variety of aromas that ranges from ripe fruit and aromatic herbs to spices, followed by an attractively long palate with a dense tannic weave. The first Marzemino is a surprise, showing vibrant and rich, with red berry fruits and remarkable character. The excellent Cabernet is almost unbeatable value for money, and the golden Chardonnay Passo Roverello opens with oaky aromas, followed by tropical and citrus fruit, then a firm body and minerally finish. The Pinot Bianco Vigna Pedevenda is supple and fresh-tasting, combining impressive structure with a polished, stylish body. The rest of the wines are also good.

COLOGNOLA AI COLLI (VR)

FASOLI
FRAZ. SAN ZENO
VIA C. BATTISTI, 41
37030 COLOGNOLA AI COLLI (VR)
TEL. 0457650741
E-MAIL: fasoli.gino@mercurio.it

There is a strip of land in the province of Verona which that two important Veneto DOC zones, Soave and Valpolicella, allowing even relatively small estates in the area to release wines under both labels. This is more or less the situation of the Fasoli brothers, Amadio and Natalino, who set space aside for both garganega and corvina on their 14 hectares. While we're on the subject, the Fasolis also grow less traditional varieties – merlot, above all – but their scrupulous vineyard management yields interesting results. The white wines, Soave and Recioto di Soave, take the lead, maintaining a constant high standard of quality thanks to the Fasolis' attentions. The Soave Pieve Vecchia is fermented and aged in 900-litre casks for about a year, and has a rich, vibrant ripe peach nose with hints of oak. The palate is soft and mouthfilling, progressing austerely to a long finish. The winery's flagship Recioto San Zeno is more explosive. It has appealing golden colour and generous, predominantly ripe fruit aromas, with a sunny smooth palate reminiscent of southern dried-grape "passito" wines. The Amarone Alteo is mature, with intriguing aromas and a lively palate. The Merlot Orgno, a big wine with good ageing prospects, just missed out on Two Glasses.

● Colli Euganei Cabernet '01	♈♈	3*
● Colli Euganei Merlot Vigna Sasso Nero Villa Alessi '01	♈♈	4
○ Colli Euganei Chardonnay Vigna Passo Roverello Villa Alessi '02	♈♈	4
● Colli Euganei Marzemino Villa Alessi '02	♈♈	4
○ Colli Euganei Pinot Bianco Vigna Pedevenda Villa Alessi '02	♈♈	4
● Colli Euganei Merlot '01	♈	3
○ Colli Euganei Bianco '02	♈	3
○ Colli Euganei Pinot Bianco '02	♈	3
○ Colli Euganei Sauvignon Vigna Olivetani Villa Alessi '02	♈	4

○ Recioto di Soave S. Zeno '01	♈♈	6
○ Soave Cl. Sup. Pieve Vecchia '01	♈♈	4
● Amarone della Valpolicella Alteo '99	♈♈	7
● Merlot Orgno '01	♈	7
○ Soave Cl. Sup. Pieve Vecchia '99	♈♈	4
○ Liber Bianco '00	♈♈	3
○ Recioto di Soave S. Zeno '99	♈♈	5

CONEGLIANO (TV)

ZARDETTO SPUMANTI
FRAZ. OGLIANO
VIA MARCORÀ, 15/A
31020 CONEGLIANO (TV)
TEL. 0438208909
E-MAIL: info@bubbly.it

This large winery, founded by Pino Zardetto and now managed with aplomb by Fabio, is a benchmark in Conegliano, and has contributed greatly to promoting the local DOC. The premises at Ogliano are currently being renovated, to rationalize the use of space and improve working conditions. Grapes are bought locally, mainly from growers with whom the winery has established a long, loyal working relationship. Zardetto's production is close to 1,000,000 bottles a year, most of it sparkling wines. The star this year was the Prosecco Extra Dry, a sparkling wine with a delicate, fragrant nose that displays the typical aromas of the variety in its hints of golden delicious apples and wild flowers. The palate is also delicate, with a good balance of sugar and acidity, and the sparkle refreshes and perks up the palate. The Zeroventi, named for its 20 grams per litre of residual sugar, is as reliable as ever. The appealingly well-defined appley aromas are reflected on the ripe, mouthfilling palate, where the sweetness is fully integrated into the flavour. The Prosecco Brut is fresh-tasting, with almost biting acidity, whereas the Frizzante is simple but enjoyable. The Chardonnay Extra Brut easily earned One Glass for its fragrance and coherent palate.

DOLCÈ (VR)

ARMANI
VIA CERADELLO, 401
37020 DOLCÈ (VR)
TEL. 0457290033 - 0457290285
E-MAIL: info@albinoarmani.com

Albino Armani loves this area, which has been so inexplicably and embarrassingly relegated to marginal status. He is in the part of Vallagarina that lies on the border of Veneto and Trentino, in the foothills of the Lessini and Baldo mountains. Armani has doggedly pursued his dream of reviving the ancient native casetta grape, which was at last included in the national register of wine grapes a couple of years ago, although it has been grown in the valley for centuries. Its local name is "foja tonda", which comes from the rounded shape of its leaves. While he waits for the new vineyards, planted alongside the beautiful, recently inaugurated cellar, to come onstream, Armani continues to focus on a quality project he and some other local growers are pursuing, in vineyards several decades old. The 2001 Foja Tonda confirms that the project has firm foundations. A red of old-fashioned charm, it has a rich grass and spice nose, and a powerful, generous, typically peppery palate. The other, more modern, red Corvara, from corvina, cabernet sauvignon and merlot, is up to its usual standard, mingling strong hints of fruit with intriguing earthy notes. The range of whites includes Trentino and Valdadige DOCs and wines from the Terra dei Forti subzone. The Sauvignon has hints of melon and mint, while the Chardonnay and Pinot Grigio have peachy fruit and minerality.

O Prosecco Extra Dry	ΥΥ	3
O Chardonnay Extra Brut	Υ	4
O Prosecco di C. Brut Bubbly	Υ	3
O Prosecco di C. Zeroventi Dry	Υ	4
O Prosecco di C. Frizzante Brioso		3
O Prosecco di C. Tranquillo Lungo		3

● Corvara Rosso '00	ΥΥ	5
● Foja Tonda Rosso '01	ΥΥ	4*
O Valdadige Chardonnay Piccola Botte '01	Υ	4
O Trentino Chardonnay Vigneto Capitel '02	Υ	4
O Valdadige Pinot Grigio Vigneto Corvara '02	Υ	4
O Valdadige Terra dei Forti Sauvignon Campo Napoleone '02	Υ	4
● Foja Tonda Rosso '99	ΥΥ	4
● Foja Tonda Rosso '00	ΥΥ	4

FOSSALTA DI PIAVE (VE)

SANTO STEFANO
VIA CADORNA, 92
30020 FOSSALTA DI PIAVE (VE)
TEL. 042167502
E-MAIL: santostefano@ronchiato.it

In recent years, the Piave area has been showing encouraging signs of revival. An increasing number of wineries appear interested in exploiting the remarkable resources the area has to offer. At last, cellars are obtaining premium-quality wines through better vineyard management and lower cropping levels. There is still a long way to go, but thanks to wineries like Santo Stefano, the area is on the right track, and there is hope for the future. Owners Tiziano De Stefani and his son, Alessandro, have been focusing for years on improving the quality of their wines. Finally, they are beginning to reap the fruits of their labours. The most impressive wine, and the one that brought the winery into the Guide for the first time, is Olmera, a blend of tocai and sauvignon. After a few days' maceration on the skins, Olmera is fermented and aged on the yeasts in large wooden barrels for about ten months. The nose is subtle and slightly aromatic, with nice floral and mineral hints. The palate is rounded and tangy, the softness offset by the slight hint of tannin. The Refrontolo Passito Col Vendrame and the Passito Passut, from sauvignon grapes, are both well-made. Last but not least, do not overlook the Brut Cuvée Tombola di Pin 1999, a sparkling wine made with 65 per cent chardonnay and 35 per cent pinot nero grapes.

FUMANE (VR)

★ ALLEGRINI
VIA GIARE, 9/11
37022 FUMANE (VR)
TEL. 0456832011
E-MAIL: info@allegrini.it

When we visited Marilisa and Franco one baking hot morning last summer, we talked sadly of the sudden, tragic death of their brother Walter, and how deeply he would be missed. Walter was the least visible of the three, but as the eldest brother, his role was to catalyse the strong personalities of the other two. In the vineyards, he was a link between the winery founded by his father and today's forward-looking business. The wines we tasted are strongly representative of the current outlook. The Amarone, for example, is less massive than usual, thanks to the remarkable balance of sweetness, acidity and extract. It evidently pursues a new stylistic expression based on power. The opaque colour is impressive, then the closed nose slowly and gradually reveals full, ripe fruit, laced with hints of minerals and spices. Solid on the palate, it has a tannic weave that requires further bottle ageing. The bright, sunny Recioto Giovanni Allegrini 2000, on the other hand, has never been so good. The generous aromas of wild berries are veined with aromatic herbs, fresh flowers and spices in a continually developing whirl of sensation. The sweetness on the palate is so balanced that the wine progresses easily to an incredibly long-lasting finish. The awards of Three Glasses and Sweet Wine of the Year are not only for the wine itself: they are a tribute to a great tradition. All the products are faultless, and a special mention goes to the Palazzo della Torre, a model of concentration and progression on the palate.

O Olmera '02	🍷🍷	6
●, Piave Cabernet Le Ronche '01	🍷	4
● Colli di Conegliano Refrontolo		
Passito Col Vendrame '00	🍷	7
O Brut Cuvée		
Tombola di Pin M. Cl. '99	🍷	5
O Passito Passut '99	🍷	7
O Piave Chardonnay Prà Longo '02		4
O Pinot Grigio Prà Longo '02		5
O Piave Chardonnay Terre Nobili '01	🍷	5

● Recioto della Valpolicella Cl.		
Giovanni Allegrini '00	🍷🍷🍷	8
● Amarone della Valpolicella Cl. '99	🍷🍷	8
● La Grola '00	🍷🍷	6
● Palazzo della Torre '00	🍷🍷	6
● La Poja '99	🍷🍷	8
● Valpolicella Cl. '02	🍷	4
● La Poja '93	🍷🍷🍷	8
● Amarone della Valpolicella Cl. '95	🍷🍷🍷	8
● La Poja '95	🍷🍷🍷	8
● Amarone della Valpolicella Cl. '96	🍷🍷🍷	8
● La Poja '96	🍷🍷🍷	8
● Amarone della Valpolicella Cl. '97	🍷🍷🍷	8
● La Poja '97	🍷🍷🍷	8
● Amarone della Valpolicella Cl. '98	🍷🍷🍷	8

FUMANE (VR)

Le Salette

via Pio Brugnoli, 11/c
37022 Fumane (VR)
tel. 0457701027
e-mail: vinosal@tin.it

The Madonna delle Salette overlooks the picturesque little village of Fumane from on high, and Franco and Monica Scamperle were inspired to name their winery after the sanctuary. The grapes come from the estate's own plots in the various municipal areas of Valpolicella, plus six hectares recently purchased in one of the oldest and most prestigious vineyards of Fumane. The range of wines tasted this year was very good indeed and we are pleased to note that all the wines are perfectly typed. The Valpolicella 2002 is fruity and mature, with a dry finish, and I Progni benefits from excellent texture, smoothed out by intelligent use of wood that never overwhelms its gutsy vein and seductive appearance. The Ca' Carnocchio is slightly inferior, more rounded and jammy, and slightly less reminiscent of the character of Amarone and raisined grapes. Talking of Amarone, the La Marega has an enjoyably attractive and stylish nose, fluctuating between fruit and flowers, while the palate is absolutely typical, thanks to the warmth and length of the flavour. The Amarone Pergole Vece gave a classy performance. The oak is perfectly integrated, the nose is remarkably deep, and the palate is broad and soft, yet dry in the finish. The impression of softness actually derives from the wine's extreme concentration, and a rare balance of alcohol, acidity and tannins. The long juicy finish has Alpine herbs and cocoa powder. Moving on to the Reciotos, the Le Traversagne is approachable and fragrant, while the Pergole Vece is warmer and sweeter, with good texture and a stylish, elegant palate.

●	Amarone della Valpolicella Cl. Pergole Vece '99	YY	8
●	Recioto della Valpolicella Cl. Pergole Vece '00	YY	6
●	Valpolicella Cl. Sup. Ca' Carnocchio '00	YY	5
●	Valpolicella Cl. Sup. I Progni '00	YY	4
●	Amarone della Valpolicella Cl. La Marega '99	YY	6
○	Cesare Passito Bianco '00	Y	5
●	Recioto della Valpolicella Cl. Le Traversagne '00	Y	6
●	Valpolicella Cl. '02	Y	3*
●	Amarone della Valpolicella Cl. Pergole Vece '95	YYY	8

GAMBELLARA (VI)

La Biancara

fraz. Sorio
c.da Biancara, 8
36053 Gambellara (VI)
tel. 0444444244

It's hard to be dispassionate when you're talking about Angiolino Maule. Although we should treat him with the same objectivity we bestow on other growers, his sheer enthusiasm can cloud the view, as it were. The quality of his wines complete the picture of the man. Anything but mainstream, these bottles are almost a liquid transposition of their creator's way of thinking. Tasting Angiolino's Recioto is always a stimulating experience. We think it is Maule's most emblematic wine, and a perfect example of what the raisined garganega grape is can do when it comes into contact with the volcanic terroir of Gambellara. The wine rises above garganega's usual lack of aromas, acquiring the profile of a great sweet wine. This year, the nose has chamomile and citrus fruit, with typically down-to-earth tannin in the soft finish. The Pico 2001 is going through a rather embattled stage in its career and shows more than ever the benefits of bottle ageing, which is smoothing out the hard edges in the nose. The palate is more slender than usual, again because of the unimpressive growing year. The white I Masieri is pleasantly drinkable, whereas Sassaia has a rather evolved colour and a taut, minerally, pleasantly bitterish palate. The impressive Canà Rosso is enviably authentic and floral. Lastly, a wine that is practically unobtainable, a wonderful Merlot of which, alas, only a very few bottles are released. Keep your eyes open!

○	Recioto di Gambellara '00	YY	7
○	Gambellara Cl. Sassaia '02	YY	3*
●	Canà Rosso '01	YY	4
○	Pico '01	YY	4
○	Gambellara Cl. I Masieri '02	Y	4
○	Recioto di Gambellara '97	YY	6
○	Pico '98	YY	4
○	Gambellara Cl. Sassaia '00	YY	3*
○	Recioto di Gambellara '98	YY	6
○	Pico '99	YY	4
○	Gambellara Cl. Sassaia '01	YY	3*
○	Recioto di Gambellara '99	YY	6

GAMBELLARA (VI)

ZONIN
VIA BORGOLECCO, 9
36053 GAMBELLARA (VI)
TEL. 0444640111
E-MAIL: info@zonin.it

This big-league Gambellara producer makes large quantities of simple, enjoyable wines sold at a fair price. But Zonin is also striving to make wines of a different kind, with more depth and concentration. Of course, this applies to the group's parent winery at Gambellara, but it is also true of the many properties it owns in several other regions of Italy. This year, we were pleased to see that the Gambellara Podere il Gangio was more ambitious and showed plenty of character. It's a white with clearly-defined floral aromas and an interesting minerally note throughout. The palate is tangy and well-structured, and the nice finish is fragrant. The two Proseccos performed well. The Brut is lean and dry, whereas the Extra Dry has spring flower aromas, then soft, clean apple on the palate. From the Terre Mediterranee line, we only tasted the Primitivo, which has strikingly exuberant aromas of ripe fruit and printer's ink. The Berengario is well-managed. Although the Recioto di Gambellara Aristòs was awarded Two Glasses, it seemed a little less gutsy than usual. It has fragrant aromas of ripe peaches, croissants and candied citrus fruit on the nose. These are reflected on the warm palate, where there is good sugar and acidity that struggles to keep the wine supple and stylish.

ILLASI (VR)

★ ROMANO DAL FORNO
FRAZ. CELLORE
LOC. LODOLETTA, 1
37030 ILLASI (VR)
TEL. 0457834923
E-MAIL: az.dalforno@tiscalinet.it

We can, without fear of contradiction, describe Romano Dal Forno as a restless man, destined never to be fully satisfied with the results he obtains. Visitors to his extraordinary winery at Cellore will realize how true this is when they see for themselves the marvellous extension work carried out on what was already a beautiful cellar. The same commitment is obvious in the vineyards, especially those recently purchased and replanted at a density of up to 15,000 vines per hectare. Dal Forno is constantly challenging his own assumptions as he pursues his research, and this is reflected in his wines. This year's Valpolicella is a good example. It marks a sea change in the production concept for this type of wine, since it has been made for the first time exclusively from briefly dried grapes. This is a step away from the customary addition of Amarone to Valpolicella made from fresh grapes. As usual, the wine is uncommonly well-textured and the quality of the fruit is astonishing, although the slightly intrusive tannin shows that the change of style needs some fine tuning. Bearing in mind Dal Forno's effort and ambition regarding Valpolicella, the improvements will undoubtedly be quick to appear. Meanwhile, the Amarone put on its usual, now proverbial, show of strength. Even the most experienced tasters will be impressed by the concentration, extract and solid texture. The Three Glasses were a formality, of course.

○ Recioto di Gambellara Podere il Giangio Aristòs '01	♈♈	6
○ Gambellara Cl. Podere il Giangio '01	♈	3
● Primitivo Terre Mediterranee '01	♈	3
● Berengario '98	♈	5
○ Prosecco Brut	♈	3
○ Prosecco Special Cuvée Extra Dry	♈	3
○ Recioto di Gambellara Podere il Giangio Aristòs '98	♈♈	6
○ Recioto di Gambellara Podere il Giangio Aristòs '99	♈♈	6

● Amarone della Valpolicella Vigneto di Monte Lodoletta '98	♈♈♈	8
● Valpolicella Sup. Vigneto di Monte Lodoletta '99	♈♈	8
● Amarone della Valpolicella Vigneto di Monte Lodoletta '91	♈♈♈	8
● Amarone della Valpolicella Vigneto di Monte Lodoletta '93	♈♈♈	8
● Amarone della Valpolicella Vigneto di Monte Lodoletta '95	♈♈♈	8
● Amarone della Valpolicella Vigneto di Monte Lodoletta '96	♈♈♈	8
● Amarone della Valpolicella Vigneto di Monte Lodoletta '97	♈♈♈	8

ILLASI (VR)

SANTI
VIA UNGHERIA, 33
37031 ILLASI (VR)
TEL. 0456520077
E-MAIL: giv@giv.it

Santi is making progress. This traditional Illasi producer put on an outstanding performance this year. Founded back in 1843, Santi has for some time been under the wing of one of Italy's largest wine groups, the Gruppo Italiano Vini, which has subsidiaries in many regions. This large group, whose headquarters are at Calmasino, near Bardolino, has entrusted Santi with the task of interpreting the Verona-area DOCs, using grapes from some of the finest growing areas in the province. This decisive orientation towards improving quality has led to increasingly rigorous selection of grapes and, for some wines, longer ageing in the ancient cellars, which are still in use, at the pretty estate villa in the centre of Illasi. The results can be savoured in this impressive range of wines, led by the Proemio, an Amarone with enviable strength and style. This wine brings together ripe fruit sensations with enchanting grassy notes and fascinating hints of sweet spice. The well-rounded performance of the flagship wine seems to have encouraged the Valpolicella Superiore Le Solance, which is made with the widely used "ripasso" technique, involving the addition of unpressed Amarone skins to the fermented wine; the austere and compact palate is nicely persistent. Once again, the Soave Classico Sanfederici is outstanding, strong hints of ripe fruit providing the essence of its character. The other Soave from the Monteforte vineyards is simpler, but nicely drinkable.

ILLASI (VR)

TRABUCCHI
LOC. MONTE TENDA
37031 ILLASI (VR)
TEL. 0457833233
E-MAIL: azienda.agricola@trabucchi.it

Amongst the vines on Monte Tenda is the Trabucchi family's estate, situated on a natural viewpoint looking out as far as the fortress of Soave. The hot weather of last summer was tempered here by refreshing breezes in the evenings, which cooled the vines. The spacious, futuristic cellar is completely underground so as not to spoil the appearance of one of the most beautiful corners of Valpolicella. There are three floors, each finished in a different colour scheme, for vinification, ageing and storing. This year, we tasted the best Trabucchi wines ever, starting with a great Amarone. Its rich nose is modern and stylish, with an approachable whirl of wild berries and fresh flowers, aromatic herbs and light hints of spice. But this wine comes into its own on the palate. Supple, powerful and soft, it shows a perfect balance of extract and acidity. The early release has, however, deprived it of an even higher score, but it is sure to improve in bottle. The Recioto is also excellent. It shows complex red berry fruit aromas, with hints of dark chocolate and dried flowers, then the sweet, alluring palate is persistent, with lovely tannins in the confident finish. Of the two Valpolicellas, we preferred the Terre di San Colombano, thanks to its harmony. The Terre del Cereolo needs more time to bring calm and balance to its huge texture. However, both deserve Two Glasses.

● Amarone della Valpolicella Proemio '99	♟♟	7
● Valpolicella Cl. Sup. Le Solane '01	♟♟	5
○ Soave Cl. Sanfederici '02	♟♟	5
○ Soave Cl. Monteforte '02	♟	4
● Amarone della Valpolicella Proemio '97	♟♟	6
● Amarone della Valpolicella Proemio '98	♟♟	6

● Amarone della Valpolicella '00	♟♟	7
● Valpolicella Sup. Terre del Cereolo '00	♟♟	6
● Valpolicella Sup. Terre di S. Colombano '00	♟♟	5
● Recioto della Valpolicella '01	♟♟	6
○ Margherita Bianco '02	♟	4
● Amarone della Valpolicella '95	♟♟	8
● Amarone della Valpolicella '96	♟♟	8
● Amarone della Valpolicella '97	♟♟	8
● Amarone della Valpolicella '98	♟♟	8
● Recioto della Valpolicella '00	♟♟	7
● Amarone della Valpolicella '99	♟♟	8

LONGARE (VI)

LONGARE (VI)

COSTOZZA - CONTI DA SCHIO
FRAZ. COSTOZZA
P.ZZA DA SCHIO, 4
36023 LONGARE (VI)
TEL. 0444555099
E-MAIL: giuliodaschio@libero.it

NATALINO MATTIELLO
FRAZ. COSTOZZA
VIA VOLTO, 57
36023 LONGARE (VI)
TEL. 0444555258
E-MAIL: mattiellovini@tin.it

The beautiful gardens at the villa owned by the Conti da Schio, wine producers for over a century, overlook the little square of Costozza near Longare. Their 12 or so hectares under vine are planted using the cordon spur and Guyot training methods, and their locations are the envy of fellow local winegrowers. Claudio De Bortoli, who came here as winemaker in 1995, can take some of the credit for the substantial improvements that have enabled the cellar to make progress in quality. That improvement has earned a full profile in the Guide. Managed by Giulio da Schio, this is one of the most interesting emerging wineries in the Colli Berici area, much of which remains to be undiscovered. The very warm climate of these upland areas translates into sunny wines with ripe fruit aromas and richly extracted palates. The most interesting of these is a Rosso made from cabernet sauvignon grapes and aged in barrique. It is dark and opaque in colour, with charming, approachable red berry fruit aromas that gradually give way to earthy hints of pencil lead. It is generous on the palate, with sweet extract and an attractive acid vein that lengthens and refreshes. The finish is clean and lingering. The Colli Berici Cabernet is only slightly less exciting. A monovarietal Cabernet Franc, it reveals enjoyable fresh floral, grassy hints and an unexpectedly full, harmonious palate. These two excellent reds are joined by a simple, floral Pinot Bianco, with a smooth palate and pleasantly bitterish finish.

Encouraging confirmation from Costozza, Longare, where Andrea Mattiello, who joined his father's winery in 1997, applies himself to his work with passion and scrupulous care. There are three lines from the Colli Berici vineyards: Mattiello, for the native and non-native grape varieties most closely linked to the local area and its traditions; Via Volto, for recently introduced international grape varieties; and lastly, Colle d'Elica, the jewel in the winery crown. And it was Colle d'Elica that again produced the most interesting wine this year, a powerful, rounded Cabernet. It is dark, but not impenetrable, in colour, with clean, pronounced aromas of very approachable, ripe red berry fruits. These gradually give way to floral, minerally and spicy undertones, which are perfectly reflected on the delightfully balanced palate whose tannins are sweet and pleasantly grainy. Although it was not awarded Two Glasses, the Cabernet Sauvignon has improved, showing vibrant, deliciously exuberant aromas of earth and wild berries. It is still slightly assertive on the palate, but should calm down with a little more ageing. The Cabernet 2002 has suffered from the unfortunate growing year, and is no more than well-managed. The whites are not yet showing any results from the attention they have received, except for the good Garganega, with its uncomplicated nose and tangy, harmonious palate.

● Colli Berici Cabernet '01	♟♟	4
● Rosso Costozza '01	♟♟	5
○ Pinot Bianco '02	♟	4

● Colli Berici Cabernet Colle d'Elica '01	♟♟	4*
● Colli Berici Cabernet Sauvignon Via Volto '01	♟	3
○ Colli Berici Garganega '02	♟	2*
● Colli Berici Cabernet '02		2
○ Colli Berici Chardonnay Via Volto '02		2
○ Colli Berici Sauvignon Via Volto '02		3
● Colli Berici Cabernet Colle d'Elica '00	♟♟	4

MARANO DI VALPOLICELLA (VR)

CA' LA BIONDA
FRAZ. VALGATARA
LOC. BIONDA, 4
37020 MARANO DI VALPOLICELLA (VR)
TEL. 0456801198
E-MAIL: casbionda@tin.it

Piero Castellani's winery is situated in a wonderful position on an east-facing slope, and confirms its prominent role in Valpolicella winemaking. Of the estate's 30 hectares, some 20 are planted to vine, including two especially interesting vineyards, Ravazol and Casal Vegri. The latter is entirely given over to the production of Valpolicella, and does not therefore suffer because the best grapes go into Amarone. The leading estate wines are made from raisined grapes, above all the Amarone Ravazzol, which is dark in colour and offers deep, multi-layered aromas ranging from red berries to dried fruit and dried flowers, with a vibrant mineral note in the finish. The palate perfectly reflects these sensations with a decisive, subtly pervasive mouthfeel. The dynamic suppleness on the palate is refreshed by hints of mint and aromatic herbs. The standard-label Amarone is a notch or two lower, with simpler, more approachable expression of fruit on the nose and a dynamic, dry palate that signs off with a clean, long-lasting finish. Despite all the winery's care, the Valpolicella Casal Vegri is still a little ruffled, and the potentially huge palate is still closed. The Recioto is also excellent, with red berries dominating the nose and a generous, opulent palate where the tannins successfully offset the sugary sensations in the finish.

MARANO DI VALPOLICELLA (VR)

GIUSEPPE CAMPAGNOLA
FRAZ. VALGATARA
VIA AGNELLA, 9
37020 MARANO DI VALPOLICELLA (VR)
TEL. 0457703900
E-MAIL: campagnola@campagnola.com

Beppe Campagnola has made huge efforts over the last few years. He has experimented with a range of wines worthy of the great Verona tradition and built a cellar where his team can devote the necessary care, attention and space to production. Finally, the long-awaited results are coming through. Not only in terms of a good review in this Guide, but above all, the cellar can rest assured it has produced a faultless series of wines. The wine that is most emblematic of this new direction is probably the Soave, which is not traditionally a Veronese wine – in fact, it is more of a rival in terms of popularity – but Campagnola makes a very good version, with vibrant, appetizing ripe peach fruit on the nose and a stylish, tangy, persistent palate. Its alter ego, the Valpolicella, has broad fruit enhanced by hints of red peppers and black pepper on the nose, and a dynamic, perfectly balanced and enjoyably well-made palate. Lastly, the Amarone Caterina Zardini, presented at last after its unhurried, lengthy ageing, is generous and enthralling on the nose. Cherry and plum fruit, crushed flowers and spices are just some of the aromas that make up the striking, complex bouquet, then the outstandingly stylish and long-lasting palate manages to communicate the strength, extract, suppleness and class that won this wine a well-deserved Three Glasses.

● Recioto della Valpolicella Cl.		
Vigneto Le Tordare '01	♟♟	6
● Amarone della Valpolicella Cl. '99	♟♟	6
● Amarone della Valpolicella Cl.		
Vigneti di Ravazzol '99	♟♟	7
● Valpolicella Cl. Sup.		
Campo Casal Vegri '00	♟	5
● Valpolicella Cl. Sup.		
Vigneti di Ravazol '01	♟	4
○ Passito Bianco '00	♟♟	6
● Amarone della Valpolicella Cl.		
Vigneti di Ravazol '97	♟♟	6
● Amarone della Valpolicella Cl. '98	♟♟	5
● Amarone della Valpolicella Cl.		
Vigneti di Ravazzol '98	♟♟	6

● Amarone della Valpolicella Cl.		
Caterina Zardini '99	♟♟♟	7
● Amarone della Valpolicella Cl. '00	♟♟	6
● Valpolicella Cl. Sup.		
Vigneti di Purano Le Bine '01	♟♟	4*
○ Soave Cl. Sup. Vigneti		
Monte Foscarino Le Bine '02	♟♟	3*
● Corte Agnella Corvina Veronese '01	♟	4
● Recioto della Valpolicella Cl.		
Casotto del Merlo '01	♟	5
● Amarone della Valpolicella Cl.		
Caterina Zardini '97	♟♟	7
● Amarone della Valpolicella Cl.		
Caterina Zardini '98	♟♟	7
● Amarone della Valpolicella Cl. '99	♟♟	6

MARANO DI VALPOLICELLA (VR)　MARANO DI VALPOLICELLA (VR)

MICHELE CASTELLANI
FRAZ. VALGATARA
VIA GRANDA, 1
37020 MARANO DI VALPOLICELLA (VR)
TEL. 0457701253
E-MAIL: castellani.michele@tin.it

CORTE RUGOLIN
FRAZ. VALGATARA
LOC. RUGOLIN, 1
37020 MARANO DI VALPOLICELLA (VR)
TEL. 0457702153
E-MAIL: rugolin@libero.it

Last year's decision to delay the release of the Amarone Ca' del Pipa was reprised this year for the Amarone Campo Casalin. Sergio Castellani has again demonstrated his desire to allow his wines all they time they need to reach their fullest expression. He is unperturbed by commercial deadlines or strategies. The estate owns about 23 hectares and rents another 25, all of which are scattered over the hills around the winery. The excellent Amarone '99 Ca' del Pipa has made the best of its extra year's ageing. The nose opens out gradually with occasional hints of red and black berry fruit, ripe undertones and hints of musk and autumn leaves. The palate is stylish, subtle yet powerful. Softness, warmth and silkiness progress steadily through to a long, luxurious finish. The Recioto Campo Casalin lives up to its reputation, beginning with concentrated colour and a deep nose redolent of ripe fruit and chocolate. The strong, full-bodied palate reflects the nose well, and the flavour is confident, but never cloying. The Valpolicella Ripasso from the I Castei line has vibrant ripe fruit undertones on the nose, and a nicely rustic, powerful palate with a pleasant reprise of aromatic herbs. The Rosso Sergio 2000 is uncomplicated and a little closed on the nose, but shows fairly good flavour development.

Situated in the foothills at the entrance to the Marano valley, brother and sister Elena and Federico Coati's winery continues to improve year after year. Improvements start in the vineyards, which have been largely replanted with quality-oriented training systems, and the process continues with very competent vinification, to conclude with the important bottle-ageing phase, which is so often crucial to the final result. Since the last harvest, the Coatis have been working with Paolo Grigolli, who in a single year has already managed to add depth and precision to the whole range. The most impressive wine was again the modern-style Amarone Monte Danieli, aged in 900-litre casks and in barriques. The aromas open out naturally into very ripe dried fruit but, unlike previous versions, they are perked up by a lovely hint of aromatic herbs and flowers. The palate has also lost a little of its bold exuberance to become cleaner and more austere. This already excellent Amarone promises to age very well. The Valpolicella Superiore has also great progress, gaining in integrity and harmony. The Valpolicella Classico is good. Fragrant, vibrant fruit on the nose is followed by a lively vein of acid on the palate. The wine may be from a challenging vintage but it perfectly represents the winery's new direction.

● Recioto della Valpolicella Cl.		
Campo Casalin I Castei '01	▼▼	7
● Amarone della Valpolicella Cl.		
Le Vigne Ca' del Pipa '99	▼▼	7
● Rosso Sergio '00	▼	6
● Valpolicella Cl. Sup. Ripasso		
I Castei '00	▼	5
● Recioto della Valpolicella Cl.		
Le Vigne Ca' del Pipa '99	▽▽▽	7
● Amarone della Valpolicella Cl.		
Le Vigne Ca' del Pipa '98	▽▽	8
● Recioto della Valpolicella Cl.		
Le Vigne Ca' del Pipa '00	▽▽	7
● Amarone della Valpolicella Cl.		
Campo Casalin I Castei '99	▽▽	7

● Valpolicella Cl. Sup. di Ripasso '00	▼▼	5
● Amarone della Valpolicella Cl.		
Monte Danieli '99	▼▼	8
○ Aresco Passito '00	▼	6
● Valpolicella Cl. '02	▼	4
● Amarone della Valpolicella Cl.		
Monte Danieli '95	▽▽	5
● Recioto della Valpolicella Cl. '98	▽▽	4
● Amarone della Valpolicella Cl.		
Monte Danieli '97	▽▽	5
● Recioto della Valpolicella Cl. '99	▽▽	4
● Amarone della Valpolicella Cl.		
Monte Danieli '98	▽▽	5

MARANO DI VALPOLICELLA (VR)

F.LLI DEGANI
FRAZ. VALGATARA
VIA TOBELE, 3/A
37020 MARANO DI VALPOLICELLA (VR)
TEL. 0457701850
E-MAIL: aldo.degani@tin.it

The two Degani brothers, Aldo Luca and Zeno, put on an excellent show again, this year presenting a series of high-quality wines with lashings of personality, rare features in a world that is rushing towards standardized flavours. The range of wines made at this little Valgatara winery has features that have died out elsewhere. The wines may seem difficult to interpret but are impossible to forget, like the Amarone '99, a classic wine from the nose on. You will either love it or hate it – we loved it. It is a deep wine, and slow to open out and yield up its fruit, which it hides jealously among folds of iodine and minerally sensations, unveiling it only a little at a time. Austere and unbending on the palate, it flaunts pleasantly rugged tannins that nicely offset the soft sugar. The Recioto La Rosta is a different kettle of fish altogether. Sunny and exuberant, it shows confident red berry fruit and perfectly integrated hints of oak. It is warm, mouthfilling and even fruitier on the palate, with a long clean finish. The fresher Recioto is excellent, like the vibrant Valpolicella Superiore. The Valpolicella Classico is memorable – economically priced and unexpectedly rich and long-lasting. The only slightly less impressive wine was the Amarone La Rosta, which has pronounced, evolved aromas and lacks that dash of vitality we would expect on the palate.

MARANO DI VALPOLICELLA (VR)

GIUSEPPE LONARDI
VIA DELLE POSTE, 2
37020 MARANO DI VALPOLICELLA (VR)
TEL. 0457755154 - 0457755001
E-MAIL: privilegia@lonardivini.it

Giuseppe Lonardi, known to his friends as Bepi, is a good host with a passion for wine and viticulture that has led him to devote more and more of his energies to his vineyards with each passing year. And we, who in addition to compilers of this Guide are above all enthusiastic tasters, can only approve. A remarkable selection of wines was presented this year, starting with the excellent Amarone, from a vintage year that some dismissed too hastily as mediocre. The colour is inky, and the deep, vibrant aromas on the nose are poised between the modern and the traditional. The over-ripe fruit and latent oxidation are traditional while the use of wood and powerful extract are modern. The palate is intriguingly successful at balancing the almost burningly sweet alcohol against the rugged tannins in a long, passionate embrace. The Recioto Le Arele is also very good, with complex aromas of dried flowers and deep undertones of damp earth and wild berries. There is excellent balance on the palate and a very clean finish. The Valpolicella Superiore has also come on in quality, with varietal aromas of bottled fruit and wild cherries that are nicely reflected on the palate, where soft alcohol is well matched by the tannins and vibrant acidity. The other wines are all well made, including the tangy, peppery Valpolicella 2002 and the good red Privilegia, an unusual blend of cabernet franc and raisined corvina grapes.

● Recioto della Valpolicella Cl.		
La Rosta '00	♚♚	6
● Valpolicella Cl. Sup. '00	♚♚	4
● Recioto della Valpolicella Cl. '01	♚♚	5
● Amarone della Valpolicella Cl. '99	♚♚	6
● Valpolicella Cl. Sup. Cicilio '00	♚	4
● Valpolicella Cl. '02	♚	2*
● Amarone della Valpolicella Cl.		
La Rosta '99	♚	6
● Amarone della Valpolicella Cl.		
La Rosta '95	♚♚	5
● Amarone della Valpolicella Cl.		
La Rosta '97	♚♚	5
● Amarone della Valpolicella Cl.		
La Rosta '98	♚♚	5

● Amarone della Valpolicella Cl. '99	♚♚	7
● Recioto della Valpolicella Cl.		
Le Arele '00	♚♚	6
● Valpolicella Cl. Sup. '00	♚♚	5
● Valpolicella Cl. '02	♚	3
● Privilegia Rosso '00	♚	6
● Amarone della Valpolicella Cl. '95	♚♚	7
● Amarone della Valpolicella Cl. '96	♚♚	7
● Amarone della Valpolicella Cl. '97	♚♚	7
● Amarone della Valpolicella Cl. '98	♚♚	7
● Recioto della Valpolicella Cl.		
Le Arele '99	♚♚	6

MARANO DI VALPOLICELLA (VR)

NOVAIA
VIA NOVAIA, 1
37020 MARANO DI VALPOLICELLA (VR)
TEL. 0457755129
E-MAIL: novaia@iper.net

We were right to allow Cesare and Giampaolo Vaona's winery time to bring their newly-planted vineyards onstream. Although they have yet to make it through to the final taste-offs, the wines from this small Marano winery showed they have established themselves and found a personality. They are vibrant, clean and balanced, with the right amount of muscle, in fact practically perfect. In this pleasant corner of Valpolicella, where the winery nestles almost hidden from sight, the Vaona brothers have turned their business inside out in just a few short years, renovating all the vineyards and renovating the beautiful cellar, which is actually built into the rock. Available now after ageing for a suitable length of time, the Valpolicella Classico has concentrated colour, vibrant, youthful fresh fruit aromas and a supple, excellent palate. The Superiore, obviously enough, is deeper and more richly extracted, with balsamic hints alongside the ripe fruit from a stay in barrique. The Recioto has good character and a vibrant vegetal, peppery note on the nose before the predictable fruit sensations. These are reflected perfectly on the palate, were the lovely balance of sweetness and acidity makes this wine beautifully satisfying. The Amarone is even more impressive, with a sumptuously generous aromas ranging from cherries and tobacco to aromatic herbs, to mention just some of the ones we detected. Lively acidity on the palate brightens and expands the mouthfeel.

MEZZANE DI SOTTO (VR)

CORTE SANT'ALDA
LOC. CA' FIUI
VIA CAPOVILLA, 28
37030 MEZZANE DI SOTTO (VR)
TEL. 0458880006
E-MAIL: info@cortesantalda.it

Renovation work on the cellar to re-organize production is complete, and Corte Sant'Alda is now showing off its new look – practical and functional, as well as aesthetically pleasing. There is a superb view from the tower and windows over the Mezzane valley, an area a group of enthusiastic producers are determinedly trying to establish as a fine wine zone. The winery has 17 hectares under vine, two of they manage for a friend to make Soave. Remember that Mezzane is the meeting point of the Soave and Valpolicella DOC zones. Marinella Camerani and Cesar Roman are firmly on the right track. Their very reliable wines have very good quality and plenty of personality. The Amarone Mithas is purplish in colour, with a vibrant bouquet of plums, black cherries, flowers, cedar and hints of balsam. The flavour on the supple, subtle palate is austere and mouthfilling, with polished tannins and a long dry finish. The Amarone '98 is a great wine, brimming with blackberry and cherry fruit, pepper and spice on the warm, vibrant palate. It is even more assertive than its stablemate and easily won Three Glasses. The stylish Valpolicella Mithas is very good, with piquant spice and fruit that opens out gradually. The full, juicy body reveals excellent nose-palate convergence. The rest of the range is uniformly good, with a special mention for the sumptuous Recioto and the delightful Valpolicella Ca' Fiui.

● Recioto della Valpolicella Cl. Le Novaje '00	♥♥	5
● Valpolicella Cl. Sup. I Cantoni '00	♥♥	5
● Valpolicella Cl. '01	♥♥	4
● Amarone della Valpolicella Cl. Le Balze '99	♥♥	8
● Amarone della Valpolicella Cl. '95	♥♥	6
● Recioto della Valpolicella Cl. '99	♥♥	4
● Amarone della Valpolicella Cl. Le Balze '98	♥♥	6

● Amarone della Valpolicella '98	♥♥♥	8
● Valpolicella Sup. Mithas '00	♥♥	6
● Amarone della Valpolicella Mithas '97	♥♥	8
● Valpolicella Sup. Ripasso '00	♥♥	5
● Recioto della Valpolicella '01	♥♥	7
● Valpolicella Ca' Fiui '02	♥♥	4
○ Soave Partenio '02	♥	4
● Amarone della Valpolicella '90	♥♥♥	8
● Amarone della Valpolicella '95	♥♥♥	8
● Amarone della Valpolicella Mithas '95	♥♥♥	8
● Amarone della Valpolicella '97	♥♥	8
● Valpolicella Sup. Mithas '99	♥♥	6

MEZZANE DI SOTTO (VR)

LUIGINO E MARCO PROVOLO
VIA SAN CASSIANO, 2
37030 MEZZANE DI SOTTO (VR)
TEL. 0458880106
E-MAIL: provolomarco@tiscali.it

The Mezzane valley is establishing itself as one of the most interesting areas in Valpolicella. The position, topography and almost Mediterranean climate, with hot days and cool, breezy nights, all play an important role. But none of this would matter very much, had a group of skilled producers not decided to join forces and promote all that potential and their high-profile products. Alongside the more famous, longer-established wineries, we also find Marco and Luigino Provolo's small cellar, which overlooks the western slopes of the Mezzane valley. The products are mainly traditional, including an excellent Valpolicella Superiore '99. The dark but not inky colour is echoed by the deep, vibrant aromas, which range from tempting red berry fruit to dried flowers and Alpine herbs, with perfectly assimilated hints of oak. You can tell the palate comes from a sunny terroir because the soft warm entry and sweet persistent tannins are followed by a long warm finish. The Amarone is only a shade inferior. Alongside the traditional aromas of dried red berries, chocolate and cocoa powder is a modern-style palate, which still lacks accessibility because of the rather over-assertive tannins.

MEZZANE DI SOTTO (VR)

ROCCOLO GRASSI
VIA SAN GIOVANNI DI DIO, 19
37030 MEZZANE DI SOTTO (VR)
TEL. 0458880089
E-MAIL: roccolograssi@libero.it

We never doubted that Marco Sartori would scale the heights of the local wine hierarchy, not just because he wants to excel, but also because he has very high expectations when it comes to quality. Chatting with him, you can see how committed he is to making wines that communicate the wine vocation of this small area. The Mezzane valley is a sunny corridor that soon leaves the plains to move up the sometimes steep, sometimes gentle slopes that become one with the vineyards that cover them. At last, after a few years' finding its feet, the Amarone is now sensational, offering the nose concentrated, deep aromas of ripe, crisp red berry fruit that shyly give way to aromatic herbs, spices and dried flowers. The impressively broad palate is a model of combined strength and style, and leads into a long, lingering finish. The 1999 is outstandingly good, and effortlessly picked up Three Glasses. Marco's other great wine is the Valpolicella 2000, a successful blend of tradition and modernity. This muscular, joyful wine is a paragon of finesse. The Recioto della Valpolicella 2000 is all concentrated fruit and chocolate. What it lacks in elegance it makes up for with enthralling, sumptuous sweetness. The winery is on the border of the Valpolicella and Soave DOCs, so Marco also makes a reliable range of whites, including a deep, punchy Soave and a characterful Recioto di Soave.

● Amarone della Valpolicella '98	🍷🍷	6
● Valpolicella Sup. Campo Torbian '99	🍷🍷	5
● Amarone della Valpolicella San Cassian '95	🍷	7
● Amarone della Valpolicella '97	🍷	6

● Amarone della Valpolicella Roccolo Grassi '99	🍷🍷🍷	8
● Valpolicella Sup. Roccolo Grassi '00	🍷🍷	6
● Recioto della Valpolicella Roccolo Grassi '00	🍷🍷	6
○ Recioto di Soave La Broia '00	🍷🍷	5
○ Soave Sup. La Broia '01	🍷	4
● Amarone della Valpolicella Roccolo Grassi '97	🍷🍷	8
● Amarone della Valpolicella Roccolo Grassi '98	🍷🍷	8
● Valpolicella Sup. Roccolo Grassi '99	🍷🍷	6

MEZZANE DI SOTTO (VR)

TENUTA SANT'ANTONIO
FRAZ. SAN BRICCIO
VIA VALFREDDA
37030 MEZZANE DI SOTTO (VR)
TEL. 0457650383 - 0456150913
E-MAIL: info@tenutasantantonio.it

The Castagnedi brothers again proved that they own one of the most interesting wineries in Valpolicella. They turn out products of increasingly high quality and, no less important, they produce big numbers in line with the ambitions and potential of the area. Working with Paolo Grigolli, they make 300,000 bottles per year from the Monti Garbi holding, most of them Valpolicella and Amarone. All are made to a very high standard. The basic recipe is simple. Scrupulous vineyard management and as little intervention in the cellar lead to wines that express the Mezzane terroir perfectly, and at the same time faithfully mirroring the weather trends of the growing year. This is how the Amarone Campo dei Gigli '98 was crafted. Its wealth of deep, multi-layered aromas include wild berries, lifted by hints of oak, crushed flowers and wild herbs, before closing with distinctive earthy and minerally notes. The terroir is even more clearly expressed on the palate, where the wine is sunny and richly extracted. The tannins and acidity keep the exuberant texture in check, and the finish is stylish and classy. The La Bandina also came close to a top honour. The best features of this Valpolicella are its harmonious aroma and vibrant vein of acidity. The Capitel del Monte is an equally good, and more international, dried-grape cabernet sauvignon "passito". The Castagnedis have skilfully avoided allowing it to slide into sugary sweetness. The rest of the wines are all wonderful, but a special mention goes to the Valpolicella Monti Garbi, which is uniquely even, clean and stylish.

MIANE (TV)

GREGOLETTO
FRAZ. PREMAOR
VIA SAN MARTINO, 81
31050 MIANE (TV)
TEL. 0438970463

The Gregoletto family can trace its roots in the Miane area back to 1792. Here, in the heart of the Conegliano-Valdobbiadene DOC zone, estate manager Luigi has just celebrated his 56th harvest. More than anyone else, Luigi is emblematic of the family's profound attachment to this land. The winery has 15 hectares situated in Miane and San Pietro di Feletto. Annual production averages 250,000 bottles, obtained partly from small batches of grapes bought in from trusted local growers. Although the cellar is actually in the Prosecco DOC, the winery has always kept an open mind and a varied list of wines. It was a leading promoter of the Colli di Conegliano DOC zone and it is no coincidence that the two best wines are the Albio, a white, and the Rosso. The former is a blend of incrocio Manzoni bianco, pinot bianco, chardonnay and small quantities of sauvignon and riesling. The aromas of flowers and aromatic herbs are redolent of peaches, almonds and bananas, and the palate shows plenty of body and length. It's a wine that ages well, as is shown by the delicious 2000. The Rosso is made from merlot, cabernet sauvignon, cabernet franc and a little marzemino. A dense ruby red, it has stylish hints of hay and echoes of autumn leaves, plums and spices. The palate is fresh-tasting, tannic and warm, with a bitter chocolate and coffee finish. The Prosecco Tranquillo is very good, in fact one of the best still versions of this wine. Vineyard management is crucial for Prosecco Tranquillo if the grower wants to make a serious wine. The rest of the Gregoletto products are also very good.

● Amarone della Valpolicella Campo dei Gigli '98	♟♟♟	8
● Cabernet Sauvignon Capitel del Monte '00	♟♟	7
● Valpolicella Sup. La Bandina '99	♟♟	6
● Valpolicella Sup. Monti Garbi '00	♟♟	5
○ Soave Sup. Monte Ceriani '01	♟♟	4
○ Chardonnay Scaia Bianca '01	♟	4
● Amarone della Valpolicella Campo dei Gigli '97	♟♟♟	8
● Cabernet Sauvignon Capitello '97	♟♟♟	6
● Amarone della Valpolicella Campo dei Gigli '95	♟♟	8
● Amarone della Valpolicella Campo dei Gigli '96	♟♟	8

○ Colli di Conegliano Bianco Albio '02	♟♟	4
● Colli di Conegliano Rosso Gregoletto '99	♟♟	6
● Cabernet dei Colli Trevigiani '01	♟	3
● Merlot dei Colli Trevigiani '01	♟	3
○ Chardonnay '02	♟	3
○ Manzoni Bianco '02	♟	3
○ Prosecco di C. Valdobbiadene Tranquillo '02	♟	3
○ Pinot Bianco '02	♟	3
○ Prosecco di C. Valdobbiadene Extra Dry	♟	4
○ Colli di Conegliano Bianco Albio '00	♟♟	3
● Merlot dei Colli Trevigiani '00	♟♟	3

MONSELICE (PD)

BORIN
FRAZ. MONTICELLI
VIA DEI COLLI, 5
35043 MONSELICE (PD)
TEL. 042974384 - 0429700696
E-MAIL: info@viniborin.it

Professor Gianni Borin and his wife, Teresa, have always shown their determination to make constant improvements to their winery, especially as their sons Francesco, an undergraduate student of oenological science, and Giampaolo are starting to become involved in the business. The Borins, spurred on by the new arrivals, are modernizing the cellar and re-organizing the vineyards with the aim of improving grape quality, and thus their wines. This year, the biggest surprise came from the second edition of the Merlot Rocca Chiara. This is a faultless wine with a complex, typically Bordeaux-style nose. The delayed harvest has given it pleasant ripe fruit sensations that contrast with stylish hints of aromatic herbs. On the palate, the tannins are silky and sweet, and the finish is delightfully fresh. The Mons Silicis, a late-harvest Cabernet Sauvignon, does not disappoint and maintains last year's high standard. It opens gradually on the nose, revealing its aromas only gradually. Progression in the mouth is smooth, richly extracted and lingering. The two simpler reds are also attractive. The Merlot Vigna del Foscolo and the Cabernet Vigna Costa made a good impression and both earned themselves One Glass. Similar comments could be made about the entire range of whites, with a special mention for the flavoursome Corte Borin.

MONSELICE (PD)

CASTELLO DI LISPIDA
VIA IV NOVEMBRE, 4
35043 MONSELICE (PD)
TEL. 0429780530
E-MAIL: info@lispida.com

"When we change the way we grow our food, we change our food, we change society, we change our values". This dictum by Masanobu Fukuoka, a Japanese farmer and father of natural farming, sums up Alessandro Sgaravatti's inspiration for his production choices and work. The great challenge is to restore nature's rightful role as a source of nourishment and guide to regenerate the planet. Lispida has ancient origins linked to Augustinian monks who grew vines and olive trees here, and this continued later under the Most Serene Republic of Venice, and then the Conti Corinaldi of Livorno, and now under the Sgaravatti family. The winery is situated in the south-eastern part of the Colli Euganei and the vineyards are on terraced hillsides. No chemical pesticides or fertilizers are used, nor is irrigation. The wines ferment on the skins in open wooden vats, or buried terracotta urns, for long periods, without the addition of selected yeasts or temperature control. They are aged in large barrels and bottled without filtration, following the phases of the moon. The Terraforte '99 is a classic Bordeaux blend. Ruby red with garnet hues, it has aromas of bottled red berries, gamey notes and earthy tones. The full flavour in the mouth has a satisfyingly sustained progression. The Terralba '98 is a Tocai with vibrant fruit and plenty of body. The Amphora 2001 is a new Tocai, fermented and aged in terracotta containers, which macerates on the skins for over six months. The distinct aromas of this particularly subtle and stylish wine include tomato leaves, sage and roses.

● Colli Euganei Cabernet Sauvignon Mons Silicis Ris. '00	🍷🍷	5
● Colli Euganei Merlot Rocca Chiara Ris. '01	🍷🍷	5
○ Colli Euganei Bianco Corte Borin '02	🍷🍷	4*
● Colli Euganei Cabernet Sauvignon Vigna Costa '01	🍷	4
○ Colli Euganei Chardonnay Vigna Bianca '01	🍷	4
● Colli Euganei Merlot Vigna del Foscolo '02	🍷	3
○ Colli Euganei Pinot Bianco Monte Archino '02	🍷	3
○ Colli Euganei Passito Fior d'Arancio '99	🍷	5

○ Amphora '01	🍷🍷	6
○ Terralba '98	🍷🍷	6
● Terraforte '99	🍷🍷	6

MONTEBELLO VICENTINO (VI)

DOMENICO CAVAZZA & F.LLI
C.DA SELVA, 22
36054 MONTEBELLO VICENTINO (VI)
TEL. 0444649166
E-MAIL: vini.cavazza@libero.it

Cavazza has long been admired for the reliability and affordability of its wines, and has invested in resources and ideas to make the very best of its estates in Colli Berici and Gambellara. The Berisi district has again proved interesting for red varieties and the two best wines are those from the Cicogna estate in the heart of this area. The Merlot impressed us with its delicately handled wood and fresh aromas on the nose. The strong, well-rounded palate leads through to a long, minerally finish. The Cabernet is almost as good, showing the hints of red peppers and blackcurrants typical of the variety, and a rather rigid palate due to tannins which still need to settle down, but the liquorice finish is enjoyable. The Syrah needs more attention. Moving on to the Capitel S. Libera label, we found the Merlot again to be the best wine on offer. It's extremely drinkable with deep, juicy fruit. The Cabernet has vegetal notes from the grapes, and is nicely drinkable without being especially complex. Turning to the whites, we thought the clean, uncomplicated Gambellaras were less than forthcoming, but they still have potential to express. While we're on the subject, the newly acquired Vigneto Creari yields 7,000 bottles of a Gambellara that is moving in the right direction. Richer in extract, it has gutsy personality and minerally notes. As we wait for the Recioto, expected to be released next year, we tasted the Vin Santo '99. Dates, apricots and dried fruit on the nose introduce a very sweet palate that is still looking to balance its sugars and acidity.

MONTEBELLO VICENTINO (VI)

LUIGINO DAL MASO
C.DA SELVA, 62
36054 MONTEBELLO VICENTINO (VI)
TEL. 0444649104
E-MAIL: dalmaso@infinito.it

As the new, modern cellar starts to take shape, we note the superlative performance of the wines presented this year by Nicola Dal Maso's winery. We should begin by pointing out that the Gambellara will from now on be called Ca' Fischele to avoid misleading similarities in wine names. The 2002 selection is more promising than usual, thanks especially to a fresh, appetizing colour and pleasant aromas of lemons, golden delicious apples and hay, which are reflected on the palate, with signs off with an almondy note. But the Cabernet Casara Roveri is not as exciting as last year's version. We were more impressed with the generous, harmonious Merlot. The Cabernet Montebelvedere is clean and varietal, with hints of red peppers and smokiness in the nose and a nicely acidic finish. Terra dei Rovi has the makings of a really great wine. It's a Bordeaux blend from vineyards planted in the Colli Berici, where the vines are starting to yield a complexity that can only come with age. The cellar releases 3,500 bottles of this very richly extracted wine, which reveals a closed mineral and spice nose, then greater harmony in the mouth. It is not particularly beefy and remains stylish, despite assertive tannins that have yet to soften. Lastly, there was another excellent performance from the wonderfully clean, fresh Recioto, whose sugar and acidity are superbly balanced. These 6,000 bottles will convince anyone who is still sceptical about whether it is possible to make a great sweet wine in the hills of Gambellara.

	Wine	Rating	Price
●	Colli Berici Cabernet Cicogna '01	🍷🍷	5
●	Colli Berici Merlot Capitel S. Libera '01	🍷🍷	4
●	Colli Berici Merlot Cicogna '01	🍷🍷	5
●	Colli Berici Cabernet Capitel S. Libera '01	🍷	4
○	Dulcis Cicogna '01	🍷	5
●	Syrah Cicogna '01	🍷	6
○	Colli Berici Pinot Bianco Vigneto Campo Corì '02	🍷	4
○	Gambellara Cl. Monte La Bocara '02	🍷	4
○	Gambellara Cl. Vigneto Creari Capitel S. Libera '02	🍷	4
○	Gambellara Vin Santo Capitel S. Libera '99	🍷	8

	Wine	Rating	Price
●	Colli Berici Merlot Casara Roveri '01	🍷🍷	5
○	Recioto di Gambellara Cl. Riva dei Perari '01	🍷🍷	5
●	Terra dei Rovi Rosso '01	🍷🍷	7
●	Colli Berici Cabernet Casara Roveri '01	🍷	5
●	Colli Berici Cabernet Montebelvedere '01	🍷	4
○	Gambellara Cl. Ca' Fischele '02	🍷	3
○	Recioto di Gambellara Cl. Riva dei Perari '00	🍷🍷	5
●	Terra dei Rovi Rosso '00	🍷🍷	5

MONTECCHIA DI CROSARA (VR)

MONTEFORTE D'ALPONE (VR)

CA' RUGATE
VIA PERGOLA, 72
37030 MONTECCHIA DI CROSARA (VR)
TEL. 0456176328
E-MAIL: carugate@carugate.it

ROBERTO ANSELMI
VIA SAN CARLO, 46
37032 MONTEFORTE D'ALPONE (VR)
TEL. 0457611488
E-MAIL: capitelfoscarino@libero.it

The Tessari family moved to Montecchia di Crosara not long ago, but have always been enlightened interpreters of the Monteforte d'Alpone terroir, where the volcanic hills endow the ripe, aromatic Soaves with structure and minerally aromas. Three red wines originate from nearby Valpolicella: the uncomplicated Rio Albo; the Campo Levei, which is smooth and mouthfilling thanks to briefly dried grapes and light oak toastiness; and the Recioto l'Eremita, with its floral, dried fruit nose and subtle, deliciously acidic palate. The white wines of Ca' Rugate have strongly local features thanks to expert vineyard management and the decision to harvest the garganega at various stages of ripeness. The Bucciato, made from very ripe grapes, no longer uses the Soave appellation. This wine has changed a great deal. The whirlwind of aromas we saw in recent years is muted, and the entry on the palate is softened by pleasant residual sugar, leading into a masterful, tropical finish. Ca' Rugate releases 50,000 bottles San Michele, an attractively priced standard wine that unites approachability and serious extract. The Monte Fiorentine performed beautifully with its nice balance of rounded fruit and clear, gutsy mineral echoes, lifted by varietal hints of bitter almonds. The Monte Alto is warm and appealing initially, then veers towards fresher aromas of tangerines and grapefruit. The remarkably full body is wonderfully balanced and the dynamic palate progresses brightly.

Roberto Anselmi's wines gave an excellent account of themselves this year. The 2002 vintage was not as disastrous in Soave as it was elsewhere in Italy. In fact, Soave escaped the hailstorms and enjoyed good weather in the last few weeks when the grapes were ripening. This is not to say that it was an easy year. There was still a real danger of ending up with wines that were too full bodied, and not supple enough on the palate. But none of these problems occurred at Anselmi, and the San Vincenzo was again one of the best garganega-based whites in the area. The vibrant fruity aromas are complemented by delicate mineral and citrus hints that are picked up nicely on the palate, where the wine proves to be highly drinkable and shows good breadth of flavour. The Capitel Foscarino has more structure and depth. It is even less complex on the nose, where varietal aromas mingling with undertones of fermentation. Tangy and rounded on the palate, it signs off with a nicely lingering finish. This wine is bound to be even more impressive a year from now. Not for the first time, Capitel Croce is at the top of the range. Actually this could well be the best ever version. The nose may not yet be fully expressive but there is no mistaking the crystal-clear class on the palate. Rounded and ripe, it progresses slowly and sinuously to a long-lasting finish. The balance of sweetness and acidity is impeccable and this outstanding wine fully deserved its Three Glasses. Completing the range is the I Capitelli "passito", which has a stylish, subtle flavour.

○ Bucciato '01	♈♈	4
○ Soave Cl. Sup. Monte Alto '01	♈♈	4
● Recioto della Valpolicella l'Eremita '01	♈♈	5
○ Recioto di Soave La Perlara '01	♈♈	5
○ Soave Cl. Monte Fiorentine '02	♈♈	4
● Valpolicella Sup. Campo Lavei '01	♈	4
○ Soave Cl. San Michele '02	♈	3*
○ Corte Durlo Passito '99	♈	6
● Valpolicella Rio Albo '02		3
○ Soave Cl. Sup. Monte Alto '96	♈♈♈	3
○ Soave Cl. Sup. Bucciato '99	♈♈♈	4
○ Soave Cl. Sup. Monte Alto '00	♈♈♈	3

○ Capitel Croce '01	♈♈♈	4*
○ I Capitelli '01	♈♈	6
○ Capitel Foscarino '02	♈♈	4*
○ San Vincenzo '02	♈♈	3*
○ Recioto dei Capitelli '87	♈♈♈	7
○ Recioto dei Capitelli '88	♈♈♈	7
○ Recioto di Soave I Capitelli '93	♈♈♈	7
○ Recioto di Soave I Capitelli '96	♈♈♈	7
○ Capitel Croce '99	♈♈♈	4
○ Capitel Croce '00	♈♈♈	4
○ I Capitelli '98	♈♈	7
○ Capitel Foscarino '00	♈♈	4
○ I Capitelli '99	♈♈	7
○ I Capitelli '00	♈♈	7
○ Capitel Foscarino '01	♈♈	4

MONTEFORTE D'ALPONE (VR) MONTEFORTE D'ALPONE (VR)

GINI
VIA MATTEOTTI, 42
37032 MONTEFORTE D'ALPONE (VR)
TEL. 0457611908
E-MAIL: az.agricolagini@tiscalinet.it

LA CAPPUCCINA
FRAZ. COSTALUNGA
VIA SAN BRIZIO, 125
37030 MONTEFORTE D'ALPONE (VR)
TEL. 0456175036 - 0456175840
E-MAIL: lacappuccina@lacappuccina.it

Gini reminds us of a runaway train. The winery charges ahead, apparently oblivious to everything happening round about. Year after year, we note the same high quality, despite some less than ideal vintages, such as 2002. Meanwhile, new white wines are in the pipeline and new vineyards are being planted in Valpolicella. You won't find reviews of the Chardonnay and Sauvignon 2001 because they are not coming out yet, and the Pinot Nero 2000 is still ageing. The Soave has always been a model standard-label wine. The 2002 is wonderfully drinkable and clean, and only very slightly affected by the poor year. Thanks to special efforts during selection, La Froscà is outstanding, especially in its range of aromas. Macerated skins meld with pears, hawthorn and terrifically appealing mineral notes. There is no room for ingratiating softness on the palate, which is lean, rather than fleshy, and has a nicely bitterish finish. Salvarenza has undergone extended ageing. It has obviously benefited, for it follows exuberant tropical fruit, pear, chamomile and flint on the nose with a lively piquant flavour that melts into the varietal almond notes in the vibrant finish. The winery makes 18,000 bottles of this wine from vines up to 80 years old. The modern-style Recioto Col Foscarin manages to combine extract with freshness. The Renobilis version is made exclusively from botrytized grapes, and has an incredibly vast range of aromas, including dried fruit, honey, thyme and noble rot, all of which are reprised on the palate in the exciting progression.

The Tessari brothers' beautiful winery, situated on the eastern border of the Soave Classico zone, has 28 hectares of vineyards, mainly on the flatlands. Don't get the wrong impression, though. Every year, Pietro and Sisto show us how human effort is often more important than the actual location of the vineyard. Replacing pergolas with the more quality-oriented Guyot and cordon spur training systems has enabled them to monitor the fruit regularly, thus obtaining more richly extracted, yet stylish and balanced, wines. The wines from the difficult 2002 vintage are proof of this. In the case of the Soave Fontégo, the results came very close to justifying a third Glass. The wine is a successful blend of garganega and chardonnay, with vibrant, enfolding fruit aromas that foreground peach and golden delicious apples. In the background, there are notes of flowers and minerality that will come out with ageing. The warm, generous palate has a soft entry and stylish, clean progression. The cabernet franc-based Campo Buri put on a classy performance as usual, with a clean polished palate and its strength held firmly in check. The San Brizio, however, still has too much wood, probably a consequence of the poorish year. The Arzìmo Passito has the same problem, although the aromas are rather more impressive. Liquorice, candied citrus fruit and spices join oaky notes, followed by a fleshy, powerful palate that lacks its usual finesse.

○ Soave Cl. Sup. Contrada Salvarenza Vecchie Vigne '01	🍷🍷	5
○ Soave Cl. La Froscà '02	🍷🍷	4
○ Recioto di Soave Renobilis '99	🍷🍷	7
○ Recioto di Soave Col Foscarin '00	🍷🍷	7
○ Soave Cl. '02	🍷	4
○ Soave Cl. Sup. Contrada Salvarenza Vecchie Vigne '96	🍷🍷🍷	5
○ Soave Cl. Sup. Contrada Salvarenza Vecchie Vigne '98	🍷🍷🍷	5
○ Soave Cl. Sup. La Froscà '99	🍷🍷🍷	4
○ Soave Cl. Sup. Contrada Salvarenza Vecchie Vigne '00	🍷🍷🍷	5

○ Soave Sup. Fontégo '02	🍷🍷	4*
○ Arzìmo Passito '00	🍷🍷	5
● Campo Buri '00	🍷🍷	5
○ Soave Sup. San Brizio '01	🍷🍷	4
● Madégo '01	🍷	4
○ Sauvignon '02	🍷	4
○ Soave '02	🍷	3
● Cabernet Franc Campo Buri '95	🍷🍷🍷	5
○ Arzìmo Passito '98	🍷🍷	5
● Cabernet Franc Campo Buri '98	🍷🍷	5
○ Soave Sup. S. Brizio '99	🍷🍷	4
○ Soave Sup. San Brizio '00	🍷🍷	4
○ Soave Sup. Fontégo '01	🍷🍷	4
○ Arzìmo Passito '99	🍷🍷	5
● Campo Buri '99	🍷🍷	5

MONTEFORTE D'ALPONE (VR)   MONTEFORTE D'ALPONE (VR)

LE MANDOLARE
LOC. BROGNOLIGO
VIA FONTANA NUOVA, 1
37030 MONTEFORTE D'ALPONE (VR)
TEL. 0456175083
E-MAIL: info@cantinalemandolare.com

UMBERTO PORTINARI
FRAZ. BROGNOLIGO
VIA SANTO STEFANO, 2
37032 MONTEFORTE D'ALPONE (VR)
TEL. 0456175087
E-MAIL: portinarivini@libero.it

This Brognoligo-based winery is one of this year's new entries. It has been making wine for half a century, and now has 25 hectares under vine. All are located in the Soave Classico DOC, with some excellent plots in subzones such as Castelcerino and Fittà, where good dense Soaves have always been made. The skill of the winery's founder, Giobatta Dal Bosco, is backed up by the business instincts of his daughter, Germana, and her husband, Renzo. They make a perfectly balanced winery team, a balance that is reflected in wines that subtly combine modern and traditional elements. The model is the Soave Il Roccolo 2002, a traditional blend of garganega and trebbiano di Soave. Subtle on the nose, it shows simple, fermentation aromas in the foreground, especially peach and wildflowers. The full-bodied, juicy palate is much fruitier than the nose, with a nice hint of the classic huskiness of the garganega grape. Partial ageing in barrique has toned down its harshness to deliver a harmonious wine. The Recioto Etichetta Nera 2001, entirely aged in wood, has forthright, lively aromas of tropical fruit, candied citrus fruit and sweet spice, followed by good balance of sweetness and acidity on the palate. The Etichetta Bianca version, aged in steel vats, is simpler, with approachable flower and ripe fruit aromas. The Soave Corte Menini 2002 performed well, delivering subtle peach and almond aromas that are nicely reflected on the palate, where the fresh acidity makes the wine dynamic and drinkable.

Umberto Portinari is a resolute man who sticks doggedly to his decisions. While focusing determinedly on his objectives, however, he is always open to dialogue and discussion, for he knows the value of a second opinion. This year, his daughter has joined the business, and his working relationship with winemaker Giampaolo Chiettini continues. Umberto's wines reflect his strong, assertive personality. They ignore current trends and come from scrupulous attention to vineyard management. The two Soaves we tasted this year have rather different characteristics, but scored fairly similar marks at our tastings. They are alike in style, both showing vibrancy and plenty of personality. The Albare is a no-nonsense white with vegetal aromas and hints of flowers and apple fruit. It progresses brightly yet austerely on the palate, and left us with the distinct impression that it will continue to improve with more bottle age. The Ronchetto, a blend of garganega with small quantities of trebbiano di Soave and chardonnay from a vineyard on the volcanic hillside, reveals ripe, warm undertones. The ripe fruit sensations prevail on the juicy palate, which is lovely and drinkable, offering an enjoyably rugged texture.

○ Recioto di Soave Etichetta Nera '01	🍷🍷	5
○ Soave Cl. Il Roccolo '02	🍷🍷	3*
○ Recioto di Soave Etichetta Bianca '01	🍷	5
○ Soave Cl. Corte Menini '02	🍷	3*

○ Soave Vigna Albare Doppia Maturazione Ragionata '02	🍷🍷	4*
○ Soave Cl. Vigna Ronchetto '02	🍷🍷	3
○ Soave Sup. Vigna Albare Doppia Maturazione Ragionata '97	🍷🍷🍷	4
○ Soave Sup. Vigna Albare Doppia Maturazione Ragionata '00	🍷🍷	4
○ Recioto di Soave Oro '00	🍷🍷	5
○ Soave Sup. Santo Stefano '00	🍷🍷	5
○ Soave Cl. Sup. Vigna Ronchetto '01	🍷🍷	3
○ Soave Sup. Vigna Albare Doppia Maturazione Ragionata '01	🍷🍷	4

MONTEFORTE D'ALPONE (VR) MONTEFORTE D'ALPONE (VR)

PRÀ
VIA DELLA FONTANA, 31
37032 MONTEFORTE D'ALPONE (VR)
TEL. 0457612125
E-MAIL: grazianopra@libero.it

TENUTA FALTRACCO
VIA SANTA CROCE, 39
37032 MONTEFORTE D'ALPONE (VR)
TEL. 0457611218
E-MAIL: tenutafaltracco@virgilio.it

The Prà brothers are putting a lot of effort and energy into the construction of their new winery buildings. This will result in the improved organization of grape reception, vinification and ageing spaces. Nevertheless, Graziano and Sergio, with increasing help from Flavio, have in the meantime shown that their winery is solid, and able to keep up a commendable standard of quality. The brothers' Soave Monte Grande 2002, made from garganega grapes with a small percentage of chardonnay, fermented and aged in 20-hectolitre oak barrels, was awarded Three Glasses for the second time. It won the panel over with its broad spectrum of complex aromatics. The minerally hints merge wonderfully with hints of candied citrus fruit, spices and liquorice. The generous impact on the palate is harmonious, the fruit is sweet, the progression excellent progression and the finish a paragon of style. The Soave Colle S. Antonio, made from 100 per cent garganega grapes that are dried slightly before crushing, is also a memorable wine, showing impressively fragrant and delicate on the nose. In the mouth, it is stylish, soft and mouthfilling, gradually opening to lead into a long, powerful finish with plenty of class. The Soave Classico is also coming along well. Despite the difficult growing year, it is one of the very best of its type. Vanilla, apples and nice floral notes alternate on the nose, then the taut palate has great style and an interesting minerally finish.

Elena and Giancarlo Faltracco are two young producers from Monteforte d'Alpone, an area that is invariably exciting and a constant source of oenological surprises. This lovely winery consists of a single plot of almost 15 hectares on the top of Monte Casarsa, in a very sunny position. The cellar is part of a beautiful complex that echoes the traditional architectural style and blends perfectly with the surrounding environment. The range of wines is limited, but all three deserve to be tasted. The Soave Monte Casarsa 2001, aged entirely in stainless steel, is excellent, with vibrant floral aromas on the nose layered over clearly defined apple fruit and veined with hints of minerals and flint. The palate is firm, long-lasting and tangy. The intriguing Basaltico 2000 is a merlot-based red which represents a new direction for the area. It almost won a second Glass. The grapes are left to dry for a month after picking, and the unhurried maturation is in barrique. The colour is dark, introducing juicy ripe red fruit and nice hints of spice and crushed flowers that are beautifully reflected on the palate, which boasts a clean finish. The Recioto 2001 is even more impressive, showing rich aromas of apricots and candied fruit, aromatic herbs and subtle minerally notes. On the palate, the sugar is perfectly integrated into the even, characterful flavour.

○ Soave Cl. Monte Grande '02	♟♟♟	5
○ Soave Cl.Colle S. Antonio '00	♟♟	5
○ Soave Cl. '02	♟♟	4*
○ Soave Cl. Sup. Monte Grande '00	♟♟♟	5
○ Soave Cl. Sup. Monte Grande '99	♟♟	5
○ Soave Cl. Colle S. Antonio '98	♟♟	5
○ Soave Cl. Sup. Monte Grande '01	♟♟	5
○ Soave Cl. Colle S. Antonio '99	♟♟	5

○ Recioto di Soave Santa Croce '01	♟♟	6
○ Soave Cl. Sup. Monte Casarsa '01	♟♟	3*
● Basaltico '00	♟	6

NEGRAR (VR)

NEGRAR (VR)

BERTANI
FRAZ. ARBIZZANO
LOC. NOVARE
37020 NEGRAR (VR)
TEL. 0456011211
E-MAIL: bertani@bertani.net

This classic Negrar-based producer hasn't produced such an impressive range of wines for some years. Two wines got through to the finals and did not miss out on our highest accolade by very much at all. Considerable investment is going into the estate's two cellars, which will result in even better management of the grapes. More modern wines, like the Cabernet Sauvignon Albion, will be vinified and aged at Villa Novare while the traditional Grezzana winery will continue to produce the traditional styles, Amarone above all. In fact, the Bertani Amarone is about as traditional as you can get. Tertiary aromas of herbs, dried flowers and hay dominate the nose, with the fruit appearing subsequently. It is still subtle and stylish, on the palate but the polished tannins that accompany the bottled cherries and raisins are already austere. The Soave Sereole is more modern. Closed and slow to open out, it shows fresh flowers followed by ripe apples and pears, and then hints at oak. The palate is rounded but balanced, with taut, elegant progression. The winery's flagship wine, Secco Bertani, is back at its usual high standard. This Valpantana is more impressive for its thrust on the palate than for finesse of the nose. The Bardolino is equally expressive and the Le Lave, a blend of garganega and chardonnay, is fragrant and mouthfilling. The Due Uve is clean and subtly aromatic, whereas the Valpolicella Monte Riondo is modern in style.

TOMMASO BUSSOLA
LOC. SAN PERETTO
VIA MOLINO TURRI, 30
37024 NEGRAR (VR)
TEL. 0457501740
E-MAIL: t.bussola@tiscalinet.it

This tireless energy of Valpolicella producer, Tommaso Bussola, has led to the purchase of a large property in the Negrar and Grezzana valleys. Bussola wines have never lacked extract, and the grapes from the new vineyards, which are very high up, should further broaden the spectrum of aromatics, lending greater elegance and finesse. In just a few years, Bussola, a cult winemaker for many enthusiasts, will increase the number of bottles he releases. Tommaso is considered a cult because of his style, which involves a strong bond to tradition combined with a readiness to cast his eye over new horizons. The quintessential example of this is his Amarone Vigneto Alto '98. An explosion of dried fruit, crushed flowers and spice sensations is followed by aromas that never stop opening out and continue to develop in the glass. Powerful and warm on the palate, it achieves quite striking balance, thanks to substantial residual sugar. The Valpolicella Superiore 2000 is again very good, showing rich aromas and a volume in the mouth. In contrast, the Recioto TB did not quite manage to repeat its previous performance. The palate is huge, and the considerable residual sugar seems to melt into the dense weave of extract and acidity, but the nose is still a little too hazy. However, cellar time will bring out the best in this wine. Its younger brother, BG, is readier to drink. Its intoxicating aromas of morello cherries and spices are followed by a powerful, full-bodied palate.

○	Soave Cl. Sup. Sereole '02	𝟈𝟈	4*
●	Amarone della Valpolicella Cl. '96	𝟈𝟈	8
●	Valpantena Secco Bertani '01	𝟈𝟈	4
●	Valpolicella Cl. Sup. Monte Riondo '00	𝟈	4
●	Bardolino Cl. Le Nogare '01	𝟈	3
○	Due Uve '02	𝟈	4
○	Le Lave '02	𝟈	4
●	Amarone della Valpolicella Cl. '85	𝟈𝟈𝟈	8
●	Albion Cabernet Sauvignon Villa Novare '97	𝟈𝟈𝟈	7
●	Amarone della Valpolicella Cl. '94	𝟈𝟈	8
●	Albion Cabernet Sauvignon Villa Novare '99	𝟈𝟈	7
●	Amarone della Valpolicella Cl. '95	𝟈𝟈	8

●	Recioto della Valpolicella Cl. TB '00	𝟈𝟈	8
●	Valpolicella Cl. Sup. TB '00	𝟈𝟈	6
●	Amarone della Valpolicella Cl. TB Vigneto Alto '98	𝟈𝟈	8
●	Recioto della Valpolicella Cl. BG '01	𝟈𝟈	7
●	Recioto della Valpolicella Cl. TB '95	𝟈𝟈𝟈	8
●	Recioto della Valpolicella Cl. TB '97	𝟈𝟈𝟈	8
●	Recioto della Valpolicella Cl. TB '98	𝟈𝟈𝟈	8
●	Recioto della Valpolicella Cl. TB '99	𝟈𝟈𝟈	8
●	Amarone della Valpolicella Cl. TB Vigneto Alto '97	𝟈𝟈	8
●	Amarone della Valpolicella Cl. TB '98	𝟈𝟈	8
●	Amarone della Valpolicella Cl. BG '99	𝟈𝟈	7

NEGRAR (VR)

NEGRAR (VR)

CANTINA SOCIALE VALPOLICELLA
VIA CA' SALGARI, 2
37024 NEGRAR (VR)
TEL. 0456014300
E-MAIL: dominiveneti@libero.it

LE RAGOSE
FRAZ. ARBIZZANO
VIA LE RAGOSE, 1
37020 NEGRAR (VR)
TEL. 0457513241
E-MAIL: leragose@libero.it

The commendable efforts, enthusiasm and expertise applied to reconciling the strength of tradition and the advantages of modern technology have taken the Cantina Sociale Valpolicella to our Guide's highest award. It is the first co-operative winery in the Veneto ever to win Three Glasses, making the success a milestone in regional winemaking history. These results do not come from the exploits or techniques of a particular oenologist. They are the culmination of a long process of reviewing work in the vineyards and cellar that began when Daniele Accordini joined the winery. Today, the co-operative carries a range of high-quality products, and the award-winning wine is simply the finest example of this standard of quality. The Recioto Vigneti di Moron is dark in colour, with a deep intense nose that simply bursts with red fruit and wild berries. Enfolded in the fruit are spices, flowers and chocolate that return deliciously on the palate, where the extract is even more evident. The very marked sweetness is controlled well by the dense tannic weave and lifted by refreshing acidity. The palate is rounded off by a long, impressively persistent finish. The Three Glasses go not only to the wine, but also to the work of all the member wineries. The rest of the Domini Veneti line is also memorable, from the austere Amarone Jago to the warm, mouthfilling Soave Ca' de Napa, the deep, powerful Valpolicella La Casetta and the simpler, lighter Vigneti di Torbe. Particular praise goes to the Amarone '99, almost a textbook example of the type.

If you take a walk with Paolo Galli along the slopes and vineyards around the Le Ragose winery, which situated on the eastern border of the Valpolicella Classica DOC, you will enjoy a splendid view over the valleys below. This will give you a better idea of the winery's production philosophy, which is founded on a close relationship with the local area and its best traditions. It soon becomes clear that every vine plant is respected. Nothing is forced, there is no excessive thinning, and local varieties are encouraged, their specific characteristics being nurtured to best advantage. Le Ragose wines reflect this. Never excessive or over-muscled, they have an understated delicacy and style that won the panel over. Valpolicella Superiore Le Sassine '99 has a subtle nose, that is more complex than approachable. Sensations of flowers, fruit and spice introduce a tangy, juicy palate with a long finish. The '98 Amarone has delicate aromas with nice hints of medicinal herbs that return on the taut, well-sustained palate. The Recioto 2000 is also good. It shows very original aromas of olives, aromatic herbs, and tobacco over berry fruit, then the palate is sweet and balanced. The Valpolicella 2002 is enjoyable. Spices, pepper and minerals tempt the nose, then the palate is firm and harmonious.

●	Recioto della Valpolicella Cl. Vigneti di Moron Domini Veneti '01	￥￥￥	6
●	Valpolicella Cl. Sup. La Casetta di Ettore Righetti Domini Veneti '00	￥￥	4*
○	Soave Cl. Vigneti di Ca' de Napa Domini Veneti '02	￥￥	4*
●	Amarone della Valpolicella Cl. Vigneti di Jago Domini Veneti '98	￥￥	7
●	Amarone della Valpolicella Cl. Domini Veneti '99	￥￥	6
○	Costacalda Passito Domini Veneti '00	￥	6
●	Valpolicella Cl. Sup. Vigneti di Torbe Domini Veneti '00	￥	4
●	Recioto della Valpolicella Cl. Domini Veneti '01	￥	5

●	Recioto della Valpolicella Cl. '00	￥￥	6
●	Amarone della Valpolicella Cl. '98	￥￥	8
●	Valpolicella Cl. Sup. Le Sassine '99	￥￥	4
●	Valpolicella Cl. '02	￥	4
●	Amarone della Valpolicella Cl. '86	￥￥￥	8
●	Amarone della Valpolicella Cl. '88	￥￥￥	8
●	Amarone della Valpolicella Cl. '95	￥￥	8
●	Amarone della Valpolicella Cl. '96	￥￥	8
●	Amarone della Valpolicella Cl. '97	￥￥	8
●	Amarone della Valpolicella Cl. Marta Galli '97	￥￥	8

NEGRAR (VR)

Roberto Mazzi
loc. San Peretto
via Crosetta, 8
37024 Negrar (VR)
tel. 0457502072 - 0458266150
e-mail: robertomazzi@iol.it

Stefano and Antonio Mazzi's ambition is to make modern, stylish wines with strong links to the local area and the best of local traditions. To achieve this, they take great care in their vineyards on the well-aspected hills of Calcarole, Castel, Poiega, San Peretto and Villa. Vineyard management is complemented by precision in the cellar, where oenologist Paolo Caciornia is working this year. Extensions and re-organizations are planned for the cellar in the near future. The 1999 growing year was a difficult one in Valpolicella, but the Amarone Punta di Villa is still a very successful wine. The nose is broad and exciting, revealing hints of raisined grapes in the aromatics. Already mature and mouthfilling on the palate, it is very reminiscent of its terroir but maintains a lightness of style and elegant progression. Unlike the Amarone, Valpolicella Vigneto Poiega is a more confident wine. The ripe, warm nose has hints of chocolate and spices, then the palate is full-bodied, juicy and powerful, signing off with a very austere finish. The Valpolicella Superiore is subtler all round, its fairly juicy palate masterfully combining softness with vitality. The Recioto Le Calcarole 2000 was missing when we called but will be released next year.

● Valpolicella Cl. Sup. Vigneto Poiega '00	2 black glasses	4
● Amarone della Valpolicella Cl. Punta di Villa '99	2 black glasses	6
● Valpolicella Cl. Sup. '01	1 black glass	3
● Amarone della Valpolicella Cl. Punta di Villa '97	2 white glasses	7
● Amarone della Valpolicella Cl. Punta di Villa '98	2 white glasses	7
● Recioto della Valpolicella Cl. Le Calcarole '98	2 white glasses	6
● Valpolicella Cl. Sup. Vigneto Poiega '99	2 white glasses	5

NEGRAR (VR)

Giuseppe Quintarelli
via Cere, 1
37024 Negrar (VR)
tel. 0457500016

It is always exciting for us to turn into the San Peretto road and drive up Via del Cerè, looking at the white, renovated dry stone walls here in what is undoubtedly the sanctuary of Valpolicella. We're going to meet Giuseppe Quintarelli, known as Bepi. Holding a fig tree as an old fox might, he was tasting the sweetness of a fruit whose aroma is also present in his wines. In the course of the long, engrossing conversation that followed, our thoughts were stimulated and enriched by occasional tastings of Bepi's wines. We began with the Valpolicella '96, a stylish, elegant product with hints of tobacco, aromatic herbs, leather, black cherries and plums. The soft, mouthfilling palate has with a long finish marked with hints of coffee and smokiness. The newly bottled Valpolicella '97 has a dense hue and a vast bouquet that opens with hints of balsam then shades into sensations of violets, autumn leaves, spices and blackberries. Fresh-tasting and full-bodied, with good extract and alcohol, it seemed to us a fine expression of traditional and modern in true Quintarelli style. Since he did not consider the Amarone '96, to be up to his usual standard, Bepi offered us another Rosso del Bepi. Deep ruby red ushers in a generous nose that ranges from vanilla to damp earth, bottled red fruit, hay and wild berries. Three Glasses were awarded above all for its velvet-smooth, richly stylish palate which combines alcohol, tannin and acidity so successfully that the wine remains light on the palate and extraordinarily drinkable.

● Rosso del Bepi '96	3 black glasses	8
● Valpolicella Cl. Sup. Monte Cà Paletta '96	2 black glasses	8
● Valpolicella Cl. Sup. Monte Cà Paletta '97	2 black glasses	8
● Amarone della Valpolicella Ris. '83	3 white glasses	6
● Amarone della Valpolicella '84	3 white glasses	8
● Amarone della Valpolicella Ris. '85	3 white glasses	8
● Amarone della Valpolicella '86	3 white glasses	6
● Alzero Cabernet Franc '90	3 white glasses	8
● Amarone della Valpolicella Cl. Sup. Monte Cà Paletta '93	3 white glasses	8
● Amarone della Valpolicella Cl. Sup. Ris. '90	2 white glasses	8

NEGRAR (VR)

VILLA SPINOSA
LOC. JAGO
37024 NEGRAR (VR)
TEL. 0457500093
E-MAIL: villaspinosa@valpolicella.it

NEGRAR (VR)

VIVIANI
LOC. MAZZANO
VIA MAZZANO, 8
37020 NEGRAR (VR)
TEL. 0457500286

Villa Spinosa stands in an attractive position on the slopes of the Masua hill, where Enrico Cascella devotes great care and passion to running the family winery. Thanks to the enviable location, the estate's vineyards produce grapes of wonderful quality and character, which are transformed by Enrico into lovely wines in a style midway between traditional and modern. The most obvious example of this is the Valpolicella Antanel 2000. The grapes from a 25- year-old, pergola-trained vineyard are made into wine in the traditional way, with ageing in stainless steel and Slavonian oak barrels. The aromas are clear and fragrant, the fruit in the foreground gradually giving way to more varietal dried flowers and earth. These are reflected weli on the palate where the sweetness of the tannins and fruit-led aromas contrast nicely with the vein of acidity. The Valpolicella Jago 2000 is traditional, with deep rich hints of autumn leaves on the nose, then the entry on the palate is warm and mouthfilling, progressing towards the austere finish that only a vineyard like Jago can provide. The more modern Valpolicella Classico 2002 is aged exclusively in stainless steel. The vibrant, clean, appetizing red berry fruit aromas are complemented by the tangy, peppery palate. The excellent Recioto Francesca Finato Spinosa 2001 has such an explosion of red berry fruit on the nose that the hints of wood from ageing in barriques are deliciously offset by lively varietal aromas. In the mouth, tannins and acidity provide firm support.

Claudio Viviani is one of the great Valpolicella growers. His wines are consistently high in quality, thanks to his hard work and sincere enthusiasm. The winery is at Mazzano, a famous traditional vineyard in the municipality of Negrar, one of the five that make up the Valpolicella Classico DOC zone. Viviani makes 60,000 bottles per year from the nine hectares under vine. The Valpolicella 2002 gives a pretty good idea of the general standard. A deep ruby red precedes appealing grassy aromas with hints of red berry fruit, tobacco and sweet spices, then the palate shows fresh-tasting, medium-bodied and pleasantly peppery. All in all, it's a splendid introduction to a fuller knowledge of the area's wines. The mouthfilling Campo Morar is a concentrated Valpolicella, as well as a great red wine. Blackberries and cherries stand out clearly in the broad, well-typed bouquet, with aromatic undertones and mint, while the very drinkable palate offers cocoa powder and liquorice showing overall finesse. Another wonderful version of Amarone Casa dei Bepi wins Three Glasses, as it did last year. The colour is deep ruby red, and the nose has aromas of violets, chocolate, aromatic herbs, tobacco and autumn leaves. The warm, mouthfilling flavour is full of rich cherry jam, with close-knit tannins and a long finish. The Recioto is as remarkable as ever. The purplish hue introduces heady plum and cherry aromas reminiscent of a tasty red berry tart. Although sumptuous, it is still fresh and supple with a well-orchestrated finish.

● Valpolicella Cl. Sup. Antanel '00	♟♟	3*
● Valpolicella Cl. Sup. Jago '00	♟♟	5
● Recioto della Valpolicella Cl.		
Francesca Finato Spinosa '01	♟♟	6
● Valpolicella Cl. '02	♟	3
● Amarone della Valpolicella Cl. '95	♟♟	6
● Amarone della Valpolicella Cl. '96	♟♟	6
● Amarone della Valpolicella Cl. '97	♟♟	6
● Valpolicella Cl. Sup. Jago '99	♟♟	4

● Amarone della Valpolicella Cl.		
Casa dei Bepi '98	♟♟♟	8
● Recioto della Valpolicella Cl. '00	♟♟	6
● Valpolicella Cl. Sup. Campo Morar '00	♟♟	5
● Valpolicella Cl. '02	♟	3
● Amarone della Valpolicella Cl.		
Casa dei Bepi '95	♟♟♟	8
● Amarone della Valpolicella Cl.		
Tulipano Nero '97	♟♟♟	8
● Amarone della Valpolicella Cl.		
Casa dei Bepi '97	♟♟♟	8
● Amarone della Valpolicella Cl.		
Casa dei Bepi '96	♟♟	8
● Recioto della Valpolicella Cl. '99	♟♟	6
● Valpolicella Cl. Sup. Campo Morar '99	♟♟	5

NERVESA DELLA BATTAGLIA (TV)

PESCHIERA DEL GARDA (VR)

SERAFINI & VIDOTTO
VIA ARDITI, 1
31040 NERVESA DELLA BATTAGLIA (TV)
TEL. 0422773281
E-MAIL:
serafinievidotto@serafinievidotto.com

LA SANSONINA
LOC. LA SANSONINA
37019 PESCHIERA DEL GARDA (VR)
TEL. 0457551905

Francesco Serafini and Antonello Vidotto have almost finished their new cellar and from the next harvest (2003, the year in which we are writing this review), the partners will have more space and better equipment. Two vintages in barrique, one ageing in bottles and another on release needed more comfortable conditions if they were to be cared for properly. Add to this the recently purchased land around the new buildings and you will have some idea of the potential of this little "château" on the banks of the Piave. Turning to more technical matters, Three Glasses went again to a memorable version of the Rosso dell'Abazia, a brilliant example of how elegance and balance are anything but negative features, even in these times of seriously hefty wines. A glimpse at the colour reveals how sophisticated this wine is, a point confirmed by the nose, where aromas of flowers, aromatic herbs and red berry fruits are lifted by faint hints of cedar. The classy palate's beautiful balance hinges on a Bordeaux-like vein of acidity. This sumptuous wine has a long-lasting, crisply vivid finish. The nicely balanced, mouthfilling Phigaia also put on an impressive performance and at this price, it is not to be missed. The particularly well-made Pinot Nero, of which only a few thousand bottles were produced, has an excellent spectrum of aromatics where berry fruits, flowers and rosewood take the lead. The palate is lengthened, and freshened up, by nice acidity.

In the area south of Lake Garda, a series of gentle glacial hills form a delightful natural amphitheatre that has been wine country since time immemorial. Although the traditional variety of this area is trebbiano di Lugana, Carlo Prospero devotes all his energies to vinifying merlot at his winery, and the results are attracting a great deal of attention. Today, the vineyards cover more than 11 hectares, planted at a density of almost 9,000 plants per hectare and trained using the spurred cordon system. The grapes for the single wine produced, Sansonina, are hand-picked and placed in cases, before being crushed and fermented in stainless steel. The wine is then aged unhurriedly in barriques. The packaging is elegant and the wine is stylish, but also very vigorous. The vibrant, clean aromas open out into hints of red berry fruits that gradually give way to flowers and spices. The hints of oak in the background do not disturb the varietal aromas, which are beautifully reflected on the palate. The entry is smooth, mouthfilling and potent, but a vein of acidity softens and expands the mouthfeel through to the long, lingering finale. This is only the third year of production for Sansonina so we are unable to tell as yet how well it will age. But the lovely balance and remarkably rich aromas bode reassuringly well for the ageing prospects.

●	Il Rosso dell'Abazia '00	🍷🍷🍷	7
●	Phigaia After the Red '00	🍷🍷	4*
●	Pinot Nero '00	🍷🍷	7
○	Il Bianco dell'Abazia '01	🍷	4
○	Prosecco Extra Dry	🍷	4
●	Il Rosso dell'Abazia '93	🍷🍷🍷	7
●	Il Rosso dell'Abazia '94	🍷🍷🍷	7
●	Il Rosso dell'Abazia '95	🍷🍷🍷	7
●	Il Rosso dell'Abazia '96	🍷🍷🍷	7
●	Il Rosso dell'Abazia '97	🍷🍷🍷	7
●	Il Rosso dell'Abazia '98	🍷🍷🍷	7
●	Phigaia After the Red '99	🍷🍷	4*
●	Il Rosso dell'Abazia '99	🍷🍷	7
●	Pinot Nero '99	🍷🍷	7

●	Sansonina '00	🍷🍷	7
●	Sansonina '97	🍷🍷	7
●	Sansonina '98	🍷🍷	7

PESCHIERA DEL GARDA (VR)

OTTELLA
FRAZ. S. BENEDETTO DI LUGANA
LOC. OTTELLA, 1
37019 PESCHIERA DEL GARDA (VR)
TEL. 0457551950
E-MAIL: ottella.m@tiscalinet.it

Lake Frassino was left behind by the glaciers in the first ranges of hills around the southern part of Lake Garda. Typical of this area is the treacherous, clayey soil, which shifts like quicksand after rainfall. But this is also a land of miracles, like the legendary birth of octuplets in the 16th century. Their little heads are immortalized in the coat-of-arms of the farm complex named after them, Ottella. But it is no miracle that one of the best Luganas we have ever drunk on the lakeshore was created right here at Ottella, thanks to the commitment of the Montresor family, who have been growing trebbiano grapes here for four generations. Francesco Montresor, who runs the winery with his brother, Michele, and father, Lodovico, has made a 2001 Molceo that expresses the prospects and ambitions opened up by the creation of the Lugana Superiore DOC. Its golden hue introduces an intriguing array of tropical fruit notes on the nose. These mingle with typically minerally hints that return on the palate, laced with dense undertones of citrus fruit, candied citron and sweet spices. The other Lugana, Le Creete, is also very good, and aims rather to bring out the edgy vegetal element typical of local whites, whereas the Lugana 2002 has an uncomplicated, no-nonsense palate. Campo Sireso lives up to its reputation. A blend of corvina, merlot and cabernet grapes, it has strong aromas of ripe fruit and grass. The Rosso Ottella is more simply structured and there was an impressive performance from the Prima Luce Passito, a moscato with well-defined honey aromas.

PESCHIERA DEL GARDA (VR)

ZENATO
FRAZ. S. BENEDETTO DI LUGANA
VIA S. BENEDETTO, 8
37019 PESCHIERA DEL GARDA (VR)
TEL. 0457550300
E-MAIL: info@zenato.it

Three in a row! The Zenato winery picked up its third Three Glass prize with another Amarone, the Riserva '98, which presents an extraordinary blend of elegance and strength of expression. The nose lavishes pervasive sensations of berry fruit, raisins and dried petals, then the seductively supple, meatily full-bodied palate clearly echoes the fruit aromas in a satisfyingly harmonious continuum. This is a gem of a red, reminiscent on closer examination of the fascinatingly velvet-smooth edition ten years before in '88, which brought the first top award to this San Benedetto di Lugana winery. Alongside the good standard-label Amarone 2000, which is less extracted but beautifully made, there are two impressive Valpolicellas, a juicy Superiore 2000 and the muscular Ripassa. Turning to the whites, the top-of-the-range Lugana Sergio Zenato 2001 deserves our applause. In past decades, Sergio Zenato was a pioneer in the production of market-friendly, high-quality Lugana wines, and today the Lugana that bears his name is setting the pace in proving that trebbiano-based whites from lakeside vineyards have serious ageing potential. The nose has hints of candied citron and flint, the long, vividly clear palate opens out gradually, showing both edgy and graceful in its progression. The Vigneto Massoni is also remarkable, and the aromas are so well-typed that the name of the original winery, Santa Cristina, has become emblematic of a certain wine type from the area between Verona and Brescia. The strongly vegetal Lugana San Benedetto is also good. The Rigoletto Passito is enjoyable.

O	Lugana Sup. Molceo '01	▽▽	5
O	Prima Luce Passito '00	▽▽	6
●	Campo Sireso '01	▽▽	5
O	Lugana Le Creete '02	▽▽	4*
O	Lugana '02	▽	4
●	Rosso Ottella '02		4
●	Campo Sireso '98	♈♈	5
●	Campo Sireso '99	♈♈	5
●	Campo Sireso '00	♈♈	5
O	Lugana Sup. Molceo '00	♈♈	5
O	Lugana Le Creete '01	♈♈	4

●	Amarone della Valpolicella Cl.		
	Sergio Zenato Ris. '98	▽▽▽	8
O	Lugana Sergio Zenato '01	▽▽	5
●	Amarone della Valpolicella Cl. '00	▽▽	6
●	Valpolicella Cl. Sup. '00	▽▽	3*
●	Valpolicella Cl. Sup. Ripassa '00	▽▽	4
O	Lugana Vigneto Massoni		
	Santa Cristina '02	▽▽	4
O	Rigoletto Passito '01	▽	6
O	Lugana S. Benedetto '02	▽	3*
●	Amarone della Valpolicella Cl. '97	♈♈♈	6
●	Amarone della Valpolicella Cl.		
	Sergio Zenato Ris. '97	♈♈	8
●	Amarone della Valpolicella Cl. '98	♈♈	6
●	Alberto Rosso '99	♈♈	6

SALGAREDA (TV)

SAN BONIFACIO (VR)

ORNELLA MOLON TRAVERSO
FRAZ. CAMPO DI PIETRA
VIA RISORGIMENTO, 40
31040 SALGAREDA (TV)
TEL. 0422804807
E-MAIL: info@molon.it

INAMA
VIA BIACCHE
37047 SAN BONIFACIO (VR)
TEL. 0456104343
E-MAIL: inama@inamaaziendaagricola.it

Giancarlo Traverso and Ornella Molon work tirelessly here on the banks of the Piave, in a generous land where, paradoxically, life has always been a little too easy for the vines. As a result, the wines from the area never used to achieve really outstanding quality. It took all the skill and ambition of this well-matched couple to take this winery, DOC zone and territory to the level of excellence it enjoys today. Our admiration for the lovely Salgareda winery derives both from the personality of the owners, and their desire to promote an area that deserves much more attention from wine professionals. There was a great performance from Rosso di Villa, obtained mainly from merlot grapes, whose sunny charm brought it close to Three Glasses. Inky dark in colour, it has deep vibrant aromas of blackcurrants and plums with nice hints of dried flowers and sweet spices. It then opens out on the palate very stylishly, the smooth, mouthfilling progression supported by sweet tannins to the long finish. The super sensations from the Merlot demonstrate how suitable this area is for the variety, with its warm, seductive red berry fruit, and the ripe, powerful Chardonnay shows first-class flavour progression. The Traminer is amazingly full and balanced, while the Vite Rossa is a concentrated Bordeaux blend with traditional aromas, enriched by a healthy rustic element that lends character and personality. The rest of the range maintains a very good standard, although the Cabernet needs a little more time to mellow out the edginess of the tannins.

Stefano Inama's wines are better crafted and more elegant each year, without sacrificing their attractively modern, sophistication. Today, Stefano dedicates all his energy to the Alonte estate in the Colli Berici, where he believes he will be able to produce a great red of international calibre in the next few years. Meanwhile, the new vintage Bradisismo is already excellent, a sunny, stylish wine that successfully brings together almost unique strength with moreish drinkability. The range of whites, sourced from 25 hectares in best plots of the excellent Col Foscarino area, has never been so good, starting with the Vin Soave, which is possibly the best standard-label version around. The Vigneti di Foscarino hovers between style and ripe fruit. Its damsons, citrus and ever-present minerally hints fuse with macerated skins in an irresistible cocktail that lingers on the very subtle, elegant palate. Volcanic soil also provides a mineral note in the Vigneto Du Lot, whose perfectly managed wood, and faint hints of pear and ginger enhance fleshier notes of yellow peaches and tropical fruit. The dynamic thrust on the palate is surprisingly well balanced, with nicely crafted sensations and a hint of tannin in the finish. It's a wine that is both firmly rooted in tradition, yet absolutely modern and enjoyable. The two Chardonnays are both good, but the vibrant, ambitious Campo dei Tovi deserves a special mention. Lastly, Vulcaia Fumé is extremely ripe, tropical and floral. Entry on the palate is huge, but we are still waiting for it to find a balance of alcohol, acidity and wood.

●	Rosso di Villa Ris. '00	♉♉	6
●	Piave Cabernet Ornella '00	♉♉	5
●	Piave Merlot Ornella '00	♉♉	5
●	Vite Rossa '00	♉♉	5
○	Piave Chardonnay Ornella '02	♉♉	4*
○	Traminer '02	♉♉	4*
○	Sauvignon Ornella '02	♉♉	4*
○	Bianco di Ornella '00	♉	4
○	Vite Bianca '00	♉	4
●	Piave Raboso Ornella '98	♉	5
●	Vite Rossa '97	♉♉	6
●	Piave Merlot Rosso di Villa '98	♉♉	6
●	Vite Rossa '98	♉♉	6
●	Piave Merlot Ornella '99	♉♉	5
●	Rosso di Villa Ris. '99	♉♉	6

○	Soave Cl. Sup. Vigneto Du Lot '01	♉♉♉	6
○	Soave Cl. Sup. Vigneti di Foscarino '01	♉♉	5
●	Bradisismo Cabernet Sauvignon '00	♉♉	8
○	Chardonnay Campo dei Tovi '01	♉♉	5
○	Sauvignon Vulcaia Fumé '01	♉♉	7
○	Soave Cl. Vin Soave '02	♉♉	4
○	Vulcaia Après Passito '00	♉	8
○	Sauvignon Vulcaia '01	♉	5
○	Chardonnay '02	♉	4
○	Sauvignon Vulcaia Fumé '96	♉♉♉	6
○	Soave Cl. Sup. Vigneto Du Lot '96	♉♉♉	5
○	Soave Cl. Sup. Vigneto Du Lot '99	♉♉♉	5
○	Soave Cl. Sup. Vigneto Du Lot '00	♉♉♉	5

SAN FIOR (TV)

MASOTTINA
LOC. CASTELLO ROGANZUOLO
VIA BRADOLINI, 54
31010 SAN FIOR (TV)
TEL. 0438400775
E-MAIL: info@masottina.it

This winery has a vast range of products but quality is always assured. And every year, we find ourselves remarking on the increasing number of labels worthy of investigation. For some time, the wines from the Vigneto ai Palazzi line, made with grapes from the Piave DOC, have been more impressive. This time round, we liked both the Merlot and the Cabernet. The Merlot is very personal in style. The nose is rather closed initially, but opens out with fresh balsamic notes, and then the supple progression is elegant and enjoyable. The Cabernet has a similar style, again with a rather unapproachable nose that once aerated allows us to glimpse a broad range of aromas, including wild berries and dried grass. The palate is very long, backed up by sweet tannins that avoid astringency. Moving on to the wines from the Colli di Conegliano DOC, the Rosso Montesco has an appealing character, with aromas of ripe fresh fruit and aromatic herbs. We enjoyed the density and extract on the well-balanced palate. A somewhat oily palate aside, the Bianco Rizzardo is well made. The general impression throughout the range of whites is that this important Treviso winery has triumphantly survived the split from Marzio Pol, who was instrumental for progress on the quality front for several years.

SAN GERMANO DEI BERICI (VI)

VILLA DAL FERRO LAZZARINI
VIA CHIESA, 23
36040 SAN GERMANO DEI BERICI (VI)
TEL. 0444868025
E-MAIL: pamivdf@libero.it

We all know that the Colli Berici are not Bordeaux, and that Villa Lazzarini is not in Saint-Emilion, but these two apparently very different places share an underlying philosophy. If nothing else, the magnificent villa would not be at all out of place across the Alps, for it has all the grace of a French "château". Only a few wines are made, usually just one white and one red, and for over a century, the most widely grown varieties in the Berici area have been those typical of Bordeaux, merlot and cabernet above all. The Campo del Lago, obtained from 100 per cent merlot, takes its inspiration from France with an aristocratic style that disdains market trends. Campo del Lago has always been made to last over time, so much so that initially its austerity was often mistaken for leanness. The 2000 version is no exception. Although it is slightly fruitier and more approachable than previous vintages, it is still disinclined to be accessibly drinkable. The red berry fruit on the nose is quite fresh, and laced with hints of tobacco and spices. Don't be misled by the clean definition. The palate is actually complex, and the chewy flesh suggests that this is a wine with good ageing potential. The Pinot Bianco del Rocolo 2001 is an impeccable mix of ripeness and finesse, and the varietal floral and fruity notes are enriched with a nice minerally element. The palate is particularly assertive, and the finish is tangy and refreshing. There are interesting ageing prospects here, too.

● Colli di Conegliano Rosso		
Montesco '00	♈♈	6
● Piave Cabernet Sauvignon		
Vigneto ai Palazzi Ris. '00	♈♈	5
● Piave Merlot		
Vigneto ai Palazzi Ris. '00	♈♈	5
○ Colli di Conegliano Bianco		
Rizzardo '01	♈	5
○ Piave Chardonnay		
Vigneto ai Palazzi Ris. '02	♈	4
○ Piave Pinot Grigio		
Vigneto ai Palazzi '02	♈	4
○ Pinot Brut	♈	4
● Piave Merlot		
Vigneto ai Palazzi Ris. '99	♈♈	5

● Colli Berici Merlot		
Campo del Lago '00	♈♈	5
○ Colli Berici Pinot Bianco		
del Rocolo '01	♈♈	4*
● Colli Berici Merlot		
Campo del Lago '97	♈♈	5
● Colli Berici Merlot		
Campo del Lago '98	♈♈	5
● Colli Berici Merlot Il Massi '00	♈♈	4

SAN MARTINO BUON ALBERGO (VR)

SAN MARTINO BUON ALBERGO (VR)

MARION
LOC. MARCELLISE
VIA BORGO, 1
37036 SAN MARTINO BUON ALBERGO (VR)
TEL. 0458740021
E-MAIL: campedelli@inwind.it

MUSELLA
LOC. MONTE DEL DRAGO
37036 SAN MARTINO BUON ALBERGO (VR)
TEL. 045973385
E-MAIL: musella@musella.it

Named after a former proprietor, this new winery is situated in the so-called "extended" part of Valpolicella, to the east of Verona as far as the border with Soave. Here in the Marcellise valley, the Campedelli family began converting and improving the estate vineyards back in 1994 so that they would be able to release premium-quality wines onto the market, thanks in part to crucial technical help from the Zymè group. Around 20,000 bottles per year are produced from the six hectares of vineyards. The wines are aged and matured for a considerable length of time, but the family intends to extend this even further. The Campedellis plan to install large barrels in the cellar, to be used alongside the existing ones of other sizes, thus ensuring greater balance and improved expression in the wines. The construction of a new, more functional, cellar is planned as the final stage of this restructuring process. Last year, we announced the imminent release of a Teroldego made from lightly raisined grapes, and here it is, in perfect Marion style, combining strength, varietal typicity and finesse with aromas of red berry fruits, liquorice, coffee and autumn leaves. The Valpolicella has a hint of gaminess and bottled red fruit, opening out into varietal aromas of cherries and spices, and is fresh-tasting, tannic and full-bodied. The deep ruby red Cabernet Sauvignon has nice hints of grass, plums and cherries, with generous, lingering flavour lifted by hints of coffee and chocolate.

We will restrict limit our comments on the tastings at Musella to an assessment of wine quality alone, but this would not give a full picture. You really need to savour the atmosphere of this estate, and experience – if only for a half a day – the unspoilt landscape that endows these wines with the Mediterranean character that is so hard to capture elsewhere. This sun-rich, stewed fruit character is clearest in the least traditional wine for the area. Monte del Drago is a well-structured, mouthfilling blend of corvina and cabernet sauvignon, with ripe juicy fruit enhanced with hints of dry flowers. The palate has surprisingly vibrant acidity, which succeeds in the tricky task of livening up such a warm wine. The Amarone is also very good, the modern-style, ripe fruit pushing the oak into the background. The palate is broad and silky, with prominent, sweet tannin. The excellent Valpolicella has bags of personality, as well as aromas of earth, fresh flowers, ripe fruit and spices. It gives a brilliant, long-lasting performance on the palate with smooth, perfectly integrated tannins. The strength and warmth of the Bianco del Drago almost earned it Two Glasses. Tasting the Recioto one year on, we found it more balanced and harmonious, fully confirming last year's Two Glass score.

● Teroldego '99	♟♟	6
● Valpolicella Sup. '99	♟♟	5
● Cabernet Sauvignon '99	♟♟	5
● Cabernet Sauvignon '97	♟♟	6
● Valpolicella Sup. '97	♟♟	6
● Cabernet Sauvignon '98	♟♟	6
○ Passito Bianco '98	♟♟	6
● Valpolicella Sup. '98	♟♟	6

● Valpolicella Sup. '00	♟♟	4*
● Amarone della Valpolicella '99	♟♟	6
● Monte del Drago Rosso '99	♟♟	5
○ Garda Chardonnay Bianco del Drago '01	♟	5
● Amarone della Valpolicella '97	♟♟	5
● Recioto della Valpolicella '00	♟♟	5
● Amarone della Valpolicella '98	♟♟	5

SAN PIETRO DI FELETTO (TV)

Bepin de Eto
via Colle, 32/a
31020 San Pietro di Feletto (TV)
tel. 0438486877
E-mail: bepindeeto@virgilio.it

Bepin de Eto is a traditional winery in the middle of the area around Feletto, which falls into the Prosecco di Conegliano-Valdobbiadene and Colli di Conegliano DOC zones. The estate covers more than 90 hectares, 60 of which are planted to vine. Owner Ettore Ceschin, aided by Marzio Poli, was one of the first to explore this area's potential for red wines, and his Colli di Conegliano Rosso has come close to winning Three Glasses on more than one occasion. The painstaking care that goes into the production of this wine is illustrated by the fact that the '99 was not released this year because the cellar did not consider it ready. The winery's vast range includes a strong selection of whites and sparkling wines, including two new labels this year from the recently purchased Torre Sgarrata estate in Puglia. One is a Primitivo 2002 with rich vibrant aromas and the other, Tindaro 2000, is an enjoyably bright and approachable blend of 80 per cent sangiovese with 20 per cent primitivo. The Veneto wines are as usual well typed, showing characteristic clean, beautifully balanced palates. A special mention goes to the Greccio 2002, a Colli di Conegliano Bianco that is mature and generous on the nose, despite not having aged in wood, and tangy with bags of energy on the palate.

SAN PIETRO IN CARIANO (VR)

Stefano Accordini
fraz. Pedemonte
via Alberto Bolla, 9
37029 San Pietro in Cariano (VR)
tel. 0457701733
E-mail: stefano.accordini@tin.it

Accordini's wines are a harmonious blend of tradition and modernity. His determination to stick to local varieties and avoid superfluous influences from outside is traditional, but there is plenty of innovation in the very clean winemaking and cellar techniques. The modern-style Amarone Il Fornetto selection is released for the third time in a decade. It undergoes long ageing in new wood, and its remarkable strength conveys all the warmth of a great vintage year. Spices, cedarwood, thyme and liquorice appear on the nose, then the palate is lively and mouthfilling. It may be stiffened a little by the prominent tannins but the finish is enormously long. The Amarone Acinatico, on the other hand, is more mature, showing typical aromas of cherries and chocolate on the nose, and an alluring palate with hints of sea salt and black olives in the finish. The Recioto Acinatico is again extremely good. It makes less of an impact than the 2000 version, but it's still very stylish and sophisticated. The fruit is juicy and the nose uncommonly complex, preceding a palate that sidesteps over-extraction, going instead for a more difficult balance of sweetness and drinkability. The other sweet wine is an enthralling garganega-based dried-grape "passito" with plenty of personality and a striking spectrum of aromatics, where tropical fruit, honey and marked minerality come together. The Valpolicella 2002 suffers slightly from a difficult growing year, the beautifully made, flower and fruit Superiore Acinatico, will no doubt improve with bottle ageing, and the Passo Rosso is approachable.

○ Colli di Conegliano Bianco Il Greccio '02	♥♥	4
● Tindaro Torre Sgarrata '00	♥	4
● Cabernet '02	♥	3
○ Incrocio Manzoni 6.0.13 '02	♥	3
● Primitivo Torre Sgarrata '02	♥	4
○ Prosecco di C. Extra Dry	♥	3
○ Prosecco di C. Tranquillo	♥	3
● Colli di Conegliano Rosso Croda Ronca '96	♥♥	6
● Colli di Conegliano Rosso Croda Ronca '97	♥♥	6
● Colli di Conegliano Rosso Croda Ronca '98	♥♥	6

● Recioto della Valpolicella Cl. Acinatico '01	♥♥	7
● Amarone della Valpolicella Cl. Vigneto Il Fornetto '97	♥♥	8
○ Bricco delle Bessole Passito '00	♥♥	7
● Valpolicella Cl. Sup. Acinatico '01	♥♥	5
● Amarone della Valpolicella Cl. Acinatico '99	♥♥	8
● Passo Rosso '01	♥	6
● Valpolicella Cl. '02		3
● Amarone della Valpolicella Cl. Vigneto Il Fornetto '95	♥♥♥	8
● Recioto della Valpolicella Cl. Acinatico '00	♥♥♥	6

SAN PIETRO IN CARIANO (VR)

LORENZO BEGALI
VIA CENGIA, 10
37020 SAN PIETRO IN CARIANO (VR)
TEL. 0457725148
E-MAIL: tiliana@tiscalinet.it

This little Cengia winery is expertly run by the Begali family, and set a very high standard yet again. Helped by Tiliana and Adriana, who tends to remain behind the scenes, Lorenzo and Giordano interpret tradition with an increasingly adroit use of wood in the new extended cellar, aiming for elegance and avoiding structure for its own sake. This philosophy is perfectly embodied by the classy Amarone Ca' Bianca, in which wood serves the exclusive purpose of rounding off the wine's aromatic expression. The deep, variegated nose has generous ripe fruit with no hint of raisining, then the firm, close-knit, tannic weave and vibrant acidity brighten up the huge mouthfeel and make it more dynamic. The clean, impressively long finish convinced us to award Three Glasses. But Begali's outstanding performance does not end there. This year, the Recioto and the Tigiolo both made it through to the final selection. The former has dense, pervasive aromas, and the sweetness on the palate is perfectly integrated into the full but supple flavour. The Tigiolo is a great red. An original blend of corvina, rondinella and slightly dried cabernet grapes, it shows a broad, complex nose and steady progression on the palate, which offers up its rich aromas stylishly yet assertively.

SAN PIETRO IN CARIANO (VR)

BRIGALDARA
FRAZ. SAN FLORIANO
VIA BRIGALDARA, 20
37029 SAN PIETRO IN CARIANO (VR)
TEL. 0457701055
E-MAIL: brigaldara@c-point.it

Stefano Cesari's winery is developing well, both in terms of the quality of his wines and regarding the surface area of his vineyards. This should make Brigaldara an important representative of the Valpolicella zone in the years to come. Stefano has purchased new vineyards located at a very high altitude between the Negrar and Grezzana valleys. Given weather conditions over the past few years, we are sure that the grapes grown here will provide excellent wines. Before extolling the virtues of Stefano's usual thoroughbred Amarone, we would like to devote a couple of lines to an excellent Valpolicella. The wine, a merging of the Superiore with the Valpolicella 2002, was not deliberately conceived to astonish the critics and consumers, but it is incredibly juicy, extremely drinkable and full of fruit that promises well for its ageing prospects. The palate is generous and well-orchestrated, with good definition from the lively acidity and sweet tannins. At this price, it is not to be missed. Once again we were most impressed by the Amarone. Its modern, perfectly ripe fruit mingles perfectly with oak-derived aromas on the nose to achieve the wine's fullest possible expression. The palate is even more impressive, an exemplary combination of extract and agility making it astonishingly drinkable. The only white wine produced, a satisfyingly refreshing Garganega, is also very good. Fans of sweet wines will have to wait until next year though.

● Amarone della Valpolicella Cl. Vigneto Monte Ca' Bianca '99	▼▼▼	8
● Tigiolo '00	▼▼	6
● Recioto della Valpolicella Cl. '01	▼▼	7
● Amarone della Valpolicella Cl. '99	▼▼	7
● Valpolicella Cl. Sup. Vigneto La Cengia '01	▼	5
● Recioto della Valpolicella Cl. '00	♈♈♈	7
● Amarone della Valpolicella Cl. Vigneto Monte Ca' Bianca '97	♈♈♈	8
● Amarone della Valpolicella Cl. '98	♈♈	8
● Amarone della Valpolicella Cl. Vigneto Monte Ca' Bianca '96	♈♈	8
● Amarone della Valpolicella Cl. Vigneto Monte Ca' Bianca '98	♈♈	8

● Amarone della Valpolicella Cl. '99	▼▼	7
● Valpolicella Cl. '01	▼▼	4*
○ Garda Garganega '02	▼	4
● Amarone della Valpolicella Cl. '97	♈♈♈	6
● Amarone della Valpolicella Cl. '98	♈♈♈	6
● Amarone della Valpolicella Cl. '95	♈♈	6
● Amarone della Valpolicella Cl. '96	♈♈	6
● Valpolicella Cl. '99	♈♈	3*
● Recioto della Valpolicella Cl. '00	♈♈	6
● Valpolicella Cl. '00	♈♈	3*

SAN PIETRO IN CARIANO (VR)   SAN PIETRO IN CARIANO (VR)

LUIGI BRUNELLI
VIA CARIANO, 10
37029 SAN PIETRO IN CARIANO (VR)
TEL. 0457701118
E-MAIL: cortecariano@tin.it

MANARA
LOC. SAN FLORIANO
VIA DON CESARE BIASI, 53
37020 SAN PIETRO IN CARIANO (VR)
TEL. 0457701086
E-MAIL: info@manaravini.it

Luigi Brunelli is a skilled, enthusiastic grower, and he can certainly be proud of his new cellar. It links the old farm complex to his more modern vinification buildings, skilfully renovated using traditional materials. The wines performed well overall, although they were not up to last year's standard, partly because the Amarone Campo del Titari and the Recioto will not be ready until next year. This was a wise decision, since the other Amarone selection, Campo Inferi, was not particularly impressive. The palate was tannin-heavy and really needs to age longer. Better results came from the standard-label Amarone, which is traditional in style and very interesting. The nose is already open, and the aromas of herbs, black berry fruit and violets are well defined. The stylish, well-sustained palate has sweet tannins and hints of iodine in the finish make this an especially enjoyable bottle. Also outstanding is the Pariondo, made using the "ripasso" technique of adding Amarone skins after fermentation. It is remarkably well defined, with distinct mineral notes and fresh fruit on the nose, then a juicy, well-sustained palate. The Valpolicella 2002 suffers the effects of a poor year, while the Campo Praesel performs better on the palate than on the nose, which has rather intrusive oak aromas. The Corte Cariano, made from 100 per cent corvina grapes, follows simple aromas with an astonishingly characterful palate, and should age well. The Re Sol "passito" is made from dried garganega grapes and has curious sage, thyme and lemon aromas, as well as a pleasant flavour.

The history of the Manara brothers' winery is similar to that of many wineries of 50 years ago. It was founded by their father, Guido, and started to develop significantly when brothers Giovanni, Lorenzo and Fabio began to work there, and the estate's objectives, needs and aspirations were all revolutionized. We have been aware of Manara's huge potential for a few years now, especially in these latest tastings. The estate's 11 hectares are situated in the hills of the Valpolicello Classico zone, and the wide range of wines respects local traditions. The most impressive bottle on the list was Amarone Postera '99, which shows vibrant vegetal and ripe red fruit aromas. It strongly recalls the Valpolicella tradition in its fairly evolved, fading notes. The strong palate is well sustained by close-knit tannins. The Valpolicella Le Morete 2001 is equally good, and is made using the "ripasso" technique of adding Amarone skins after fermentation. The berry fruit aromas are veiled with vegetal notes and the broad, mouthfilling palate has a warm, vigorous finish. The sweet "passito" wines are a little less impressive. Recioto Della Valpolicella El Rocolo 2000 and Passito Strinà 2001 need to be fresher, and more assertive, with such a high concentration of pulp and sugar.

● Amarone della Valpolicella Cl. '00 ♟♟		6
● Amarone della Valpolicella Cl.		
Campo Inferi '00	♟♟	8
● Valpolicella Cl. Sup.		
Campo Praesel '01	♟♟	3*
● Valpolicella Cl. Sup. Pariondo '01 ♟♟		4
O Passito Re Sol '00	♟	6
● Corte Cariano Rosso '01	♟	4
● Valpolicella Cl. '02	♟	3
● Amarone della Valpolicella Cl.		
Campo del Titari '96	♟♟♟	8
● Amarone della Valpolicella Cl.		
Campo del Titari '97	♟♟♟	8
● Amarone della Valpolicella Cl.		
Campo del Titari '99	♟♟	8

● Valpolicella Cl. Sup. Le Morete '01 ♟♟		4
● Amarone della Valpolicella Cl.		
Postera '99	♟♟	6
● Recioto della Valpolicella Cl.		
El Rocolo '00	♟	6
O Strinà Passito '01	♟	6
● Amarone della Valpolicella Cl.		
Postera '98	♟♟	6

SAN PIETRO IN CARIANO (VR)

ANGELO NICOLIS E FIGLI
VIA VILLA GIRARDI, 29
37029 SAN PIETRO IN CARIANO (VR)
TEL. 0457701261
E-MAIL: info@vininicolis.com

The strong bond that ties the Nicolis brothers to Valpolicella is reflected in the fact that after all the work they have put into building the new cellar, they are now concentrating on extensive purchases of new land to add to their existing 39 hectares under vine. The changes will make this winery increasingly important in the local context. We liked the Recioto 2001 best this year. It has subtle floral hints and dried fruit on the nose, then the palate shows good personality, the enjoyable balance of generous sweetness and well-measured acidity making it juicy, supple and lean. The standard-label Amarone '98 is well made if not terribly lively. The vibrant nose has hints of spice and cocoa powder, then shows a mature palate with a wide range of gradual aromas. The Testal has vegetal hints of flowers and freshly mown grass on the nose, then well-integrated extract endows the broad, mouthfilling palate with balance and elegance. One step below are the standard-label Superiore and the Seccal 2001. The Superiore is enjoyable, showing good personality and generous aromas on the nose, where flowers and aromatic herbs come through. The palate is soft with nice acidity and long length, promising interesting ageing prospects. The Seccal has a less impressive nose but a generous, powerful palate with prominent tannin. The Valpolicella 2002 is very pleasant, with nice fruit and a well-orchestrated, juicy palate. The lively Chardonnay also has good fruit and a good balance of tannin and acidity.

SAN PIETRO IN CARIANO (VR)

SANTA SOFIA
LOC. PEDEMONTE
VIA CA' DEDÉ, 61
37020 SAN PIETRO IN CARIANO (VR)
TEL. 0457701074
E-MAIL: info@santasofia.com

The province of Verona has always made an important contribution to the image of Italian wine. The whole landscape, from the Soave hills down to the gentle slopes of Lake Garda, is dotted with vineyards and the evidence of human intervention, for better or worse. Santa Sofia's complete range includes all, or almost all, the wines of the Verona area, and is still looking for the expressive unity it seemed to have lost in recent years. This time, our tasting revealed a mix of both good and less impressive wines. Once again, we were very impressed with the Amarone, which flaunts a velvety, traditional style and ripe cherries, roses and herbs on the nose. The entry on the palate is fresh and a note of dried grapes lends warmth to the dry finale. The Recioto della Valpolicella is more modern in its use of wood, and in the concentration of the fruit, with rather excessive tannin and sweetness emerging in the finish, which lacks elegance. The Recioto di Soave is warm and sugary, showing candied fruit aromas. If we move on to the dry whites, we find a Soave Montefoscarino that performed well with its refreshing, enthrallingly minerally hints, and the Bianco di Custoza also deserves a mention. The grapes used for the Valpolicella Montegradella are briefly dried, which gives the wine complexity and smoothness, whereas the Arleo is already ready to drink. The other red, Predaia, is made mainly from slightly dried cabernet sauvignon grapes, and has firm, gutsy structure.

● Recioto della Valpolicella Cl. '01	▼▼	6
● Testal '01	▼▼	5
● Amarone della Valpolicella Cl. '98	▼▼	7
● Valpolicella Cl. Sup. '01	▼	4
● Valpolicella Cl. Sup. Seccal '01	▼	4
○ Chardonnay '02	▼	3
● Valpolicella Cl. '02	▼	3
● Amarone della Valpolicella Cl. Ambrosan '93	▼▼▼	8
● Amarone della Valpolicella Cl. Ambrosan '98	▼▼▼	8
● Amarone della Valpolicella Cl. Ambrosan '95	▼▼	8
● Recioto della Valpolicella Cl. '00	▼▼	6

● Amarone della Valpolicella Cl. '98	▼▼	7
● Arleo Rosso '98	▼▼	5
● Predaia Rosso '98	▼▼	5
● Recioto della Valpolicella Cl. '00	▼	6
● Valpolicella Cl. Montegradella '00	▼	5
○ Recioto di Soave Cl. '01	▼	5
● Valpolicella Cl. '01	▼	3
● Bardolino Cl. '02	▼	3
○ Soave Cl. Montefoscarino '02	▼	2
○ Bianco di Custoza Montemagrin '02		2
● Amarone della Valpolicella Cl. Gioé '97	▼▼	5

F.LLI SPERI
FRAZ. PEDEMONTE
VIA FONTANA, 14
37020 SAN PIETRO IN CARIANO (VR)
TEL. 0457701154
E-MAIL: info@speri.com

Owning an estate of more than 60 hectares in the finest area of Valpolicella has its advantages in more difficult years. Let's begin with the Valpolicella 2002, which comes from a difficult growing year but, surprisingly, is much better than other editions. This wine should be drunk young, while the fruit is at its fullest, but it is often given less attention than the more cellarable products. The Valpolicella we tasted perfectly fulfils its role as an approachable, enjoyable wine, thanks to serious selection in the vineyard. La Roverina benefits from the same vineyard management, and is just as drinkable but slightly more concentrated. The Speris have always made well-structured Valpolicellas, without recourse to dried-grape vinification or the "ripasso" technique, and the stylistically impeccable Sant'Urbano has deep fruit and a delightful palate. The Recioto La Roggia is as vigorous on the nose as ever, with Alpine herbs, freshly mown hay and subtle dark chocolate alongside the blackberry jam. The gradual sweetness on the palate blends into soft minerally notes. Lastly, the Amarone '98 is the usual champion of sophistication, evidence of the winery's philosophy that puts elegance before power. The nose is austere, combining velvety mineral hints with clear floral and spicy notes. We were fascinated by the palate, which enhances the rounded fruit with very intense, well-sustained sensations.

F.LLI TEDESCHI
FRAZ. PEDEMONTE
VIA G. VERDI, 4
37020 SAN PIETRO IN CARIANO (VR)
TEL. 0457701487
E-MAIL: tedeschi@tedeschiwines.com

The Tedeschi family name goes back a long way in Valpolicella, to the very roots of fine wine production in this area. It was in the early 17th century that the Tedeschis first bought lands here, and during the 19th century, they purchased two important holdings, Monte Olmi and Monte Fontana, which are still leading Valpolicella vineyards. Antonietta, Sabrina and Riccardo work alongside their father, Renzo, projecting the winery into the future while keeping both feet firmly on the ground, and rooted in tradition. In the wake of last year's excellent results, we noticed a promising improvement in the less prestigious wines, which represent an important slice of today's market. Outstanding among these is the Rosso Capitel San Rocco, a blend of traditional Valpolicella grapes that is naturally enhanced in the early months of the year with a "ripasso" of Recioto and Amarone skins . The aromas are vibrant, showing clear red berry fruit, with lovely hints of crushed flowers. The palate is sweet and juicy, with even more approachable hints of fruit. The finish has assertive but sweet tannins, promising good ageing prospects. There was an excellent performance from the Amarone Monte Olmi. Despite its youth, it is already very expressive with strong, well-orchestrated dried fruit aromas and a lingering, mouthfilling palate. The rest of the products are also interesting, with a special mentions for the delightful Recioto and the deep Rosso della Fabriseria.

● Recioto della Valpolicella Cl.			
La Roggia '00		♈♈	7
● Amarone della Valpolicella Cl.			
Vigneto Monte Sant'Urbano '98		♈♈	7
● Valpolicella Cl. Sup.			
Sant'Urbano '00		♈♈	5*
● Valpolicella Cl. Sup. La Roverina '01		♈	4
● Valpolicella Cl. '02		♈	4
● Amarone della Valpolicella Cl.			
Vigneto Monte Sant'Urbano '93		♈♈♈	8
● Amarone della Valpolicella Cl.			
Vigneto Monte Sant'Urbano '95		♈♈♈	8
● Amarone della Valpolicella Cl.			
Vigneto Monte Sant'Urbano '97		♈♈♈	8

● Amarone della Valpolicella Cl.			
Capitel Monte Olmi '00		♈♈	8
● Capitel S. Rocco			
Rosso di Ripasso '00		♈♈	4*
● Recioto della Valpolicella Cl.			
Capitel Monte Fontana '00		♈♈	8
● Rosso della Fabriseria '01		♈♈	7
● Amarone della Valpolicella Cl. '00		♈	7
● Valpolicella Cl. Sup.			
Capitel dei Nicalò '00		♈	4
● Rosso della Fabriseria '97		♈♈♈	7
● Amarone della Valpolicella Cl.			
Capitel Monte Olmi '99		♈♈♈	7
● Recioto della Valpolicella Cl.			
Capitel Monte Fontana '99		♈♈	5

SAN PIETRO IN CARIANO (VR)

TENUTE GALTAROSSA
VIA ANDREA MONGA, 9
37029 SAN PIETRO IN CARIANO (VR)
TEL. 0456838307
E-MAIL: galta146@yahoo.com

A new great winery has emerged in Valpolicella. This is the former Tenuta Pule, founded by Lorenzo Pullé towards the end of the 18th century. Today's proprietor, Giacomo Galtarossa, has built up a working relationship with the Santi wine producers and together they will go a long way. They are working on what is perhaps the most ambitious project possible in Valpolicella for they are concentrating on making a great Valpolicella Superiore entirely from fresh grapes. The 130-hectare estate is situated in the heart of the Valpolicella Classico zone and 80 hectares are planted to vine. Vineyard manager, Gian Piero Romana, and winemaker, Giuseppe Caviola, have worked together to identify the most suitable vineyards to take part in this project, and the wines tasted this year come from that selection. The results are very impressive and Tenute Galtarossa has earned a Guide profile in the first year it has presented its wines. The most impressive product is the Valpolicella Corte Colombara 2001, a traditional blend of corvina, rondinella and molinara. The grapes are not dried at all and the wine ages in 800-kilogram oak barrels. The colour is not too dark, and there are vibrant red fruit aromas, especially plums and cherries. The palate is full flavoured and mouthfilling, with nice dried flowers and aromatic herbs melding into the fruit. This stylish wine also has nice toasty notes in the finish. The Amarone 2000 is aged in barrels of various sizes, and is deep and chewy. It's much more traditional than the Valpolicella, and shows a generous warm flavour.

SAN PIETRO IN CARIANO (VR)

TOMMASI VITICOLTORI
FRAZ. PEDEMONTE DI VALPOLICELLA
VIA RONCHETTO, 2
37020 SAN PIETRO IN CARIANO (VR)
TEL. 0457701266
E-MAIL: info@tommasiwine.it

Tommasi wines performed very well indeed this year. Add to this a constant commitment to the land and to the extension and specialization of the vineyard holdings, and the overall picture is promising and encouraging. Although rumours from the international market hint that all is not roses, the brothers continue to make the enormous sacrifices necessary for high quality production, with the aim of keeping in check price increases that seemed out of control until last year. The two Amarones are in the lead. Ca' Florian is a magnificent example of an old-fashioned Amarone that lost points for definition but made them up again for its depth and character. The Amarone 2000 is more compact, with straightforward, sweet ripe fruit and a dynamic palate that maintains good control over the extract. The winery's most modern wine, the Crearo della Conca d'Oro, is also very good. This is a blend of cabernet franc with the more traditional corvina and oseleta. The fruit is dried for about a month to produce a wine with generous juicy aromas of fruit and dried flowers, and typical cabernet franc vegetal red pepper. The full-flavoured palate has beautiful suppleness which softens the mouthfeel. The Valpolicella Vigneto Rafael, the Ripasso and the Valpolicella Il Sestante are all a step away from a second Glass, and bottle ageing will give them more harmony and balance. The fragrant, mouthfilling Lugana San Martino is also good, and is now made entirely from the estate's own grapes.

●	Valpolicella Cl. Sup.		
	Corte Colombara '01	♈♈	5
●	Amarone della Valpolicella '00	♈♈	6

●	Amarone della Valpolicella Cl.		
	Ca' Florian '00	♈♈	7
●	Crearo della Conca d'Oro '01	♈♈	5
●	Amarone della Valpolicella Cl. '00	♈♈	7
●	Valpolicella Cl. Sup. I Pianeti		
	Il Sestante '01	♈	4
●	Valpolicella Cl. Sup. Ripasso '01	♈	5
●	Valpolicella Cl. Sup. Vigneto Rafael '01	♈	4
○	Lugana Vigneto San Martino		
	Il Sestante '02	♈	4
●	Crearo della Conca d'Oro '00	♈♈	4
●	Amarone della Valpolicella Cl.		
	Ca' Florian '98	♈♈	6
●	Amarone della Valpolicella Cl.		
	Monte Masua Il Sestante '98	♈♈	6

SAN PIETRO IN CARIANO (VR)   SAN PIETRO IN CARIANO (VR)

MASSIMINO VENTURINI
FRAZ. SAN FLORIANO
VIA SEMONTE, 20
37020 SAN PIETRO IN CARIANO (VR)
TEL. 0457701331 - 0457703320
E-MAIL: azagrventurinimassimino@tin.it

VILLA BELLINI
LOC. CASTELROTTO DI NEGARINE
VIA DEI FRACCAROLI, 6
37020 SAN PIETRO IN CARIANO (VR)
TEL. 0457725630
E-MAIL: archivino@villafiorita.com

Daniele and Mirco Venturini show traditional country passion and determination in tending about ten hectares of vineyards in the Pedemonte area of deepest Valpolicella. The scrupulous care taken over every stage of winemaking, and respect for nature's rhythms, are supported by an ongoing search for the best possible balance of tradition and innovation. The wines obtained particularly flattering results this year and two of them came close to the highest accolade. The Recioto Le Brugnine has lots of personality and expresses a swathe of often contrasting sensations, yet manages to remain admirably balanced. It has a bright garnet colour and ripe, juicy fruit on the nose, with vegetal hints and undertones of violets. The alluring sweetness of the palate is tempered by a vein of freshness that makes it very supple and drinkable. The Amarone '99, a difficult growing year, has lovely deep colour and a concentrated nose with nice mature sensations. However, this wine really comes into its own on the palate, opening out gradually to show well-rounded, full-bodied, stylish and lingering. A notch below is the nicely interpreted Semonte Alto, a full-flavoured, well-structured product that keeps concentration to appropriate levels. The standard-label Valpolicella is again fresh tasting and wonderfully drinkable, and also sells at a practically unbeatable price, which is another point in its favour.

Castelrotto is the last winemaking outpost in southern Valpolicella. The hills around here, almost overlooking Verona, have long been renowned for their high quality grapes. It's not so much that they yield concentration or good colour, as for their vast range of aromas and the balance and personality of the wines they produce. And these are the very qualities you'll find in Villa Bellini wines. Never are they commonplace, nor do they leave you with the impression that you've already tasted them before. Cecilia and Marco's care and enthusiasm translate into depth in their wines, and the sentiments are echoed in the delightful scenery surrounding Villa Bellini itself. The landscape of this corner of Veneto is breathtaking, and the marks of farming can be seen everywhere. The Amarone '99 is an archetype of the country style. The ripe, juicy fruit is neither simple nor accessible on the nose, where it is slightly obscured by hints of iodine, damp earth and iron that give it breadth, charm and huge appeal. The sweetness is well controlled on the palate, and the well-sustained flavour expands gradually. Once the bottle is open, the wine behaves well, showing even lighter and more balanced. The two Valpolicellas impressed. Il Brolo is fresh-tasting, peppery and beautifully tangy on the palate, whereas Il Taso Superiore still needs another year to come into its own. More cellaring will improve the overall harmony and make the aromas a little more interesting.

● Recioto della Valpolicella Cl.		
Le Brugnine '00	♙♙	7
● Amarone della Valpolicella Cl. '99	♙♙	6
● Valpolicella Cl. Sup. Semonte Alto '00	♙♙	4
● Valpolicella Cl. '02	♙	2*
● Recioto della Valpolicella Cl.		
Le Brugnine '97	♙♙♙	6
● Amarone della Valpolicella Cl. '95	♙♙	7
● Amarone della Valpolicella Cl. '96	♙♙	7
● Amarone della Valpolicella Cl. '97	♙♙	7
● Amarone della Valpolicella Cl. '98	♙♙	7
● Recioto della Valpolicella Cl.		
Le Brugnine '98	♙♙	6
● Valpolicella Cl. Sup. Semonte Alto '99	♙♙	4

● Amarone della Valpolicella Cl. '99	♙♙	7
● Valpolicella Cl. Sup. Il Taso '00	♙	4
● Valpolicella Cl. Il Brolo '02	♙	3
● Amarone della Valpolicella Cl. '93	♙♙	7
● Amarone della Valpolicella Cl. '94	♙♙	7
● Amarone della Valpolicella Cl. '95	♙♙	7
● Recioto della Valpolicella Cl. '95	♙♙	6
● Amarone della Valpolicella Cl. '97	♙♙	7
● Amarone della Valpolicella Cl. '98	♙♙	7
● Recioto della Valpolicella Cl. '98	♙♙	6

SAN POLO DI PIAVE (TV)

CASA ROMA

VIA ORMELLE, 19
31020 SAN POLO DI PIAVE (TV)
TEL. 0422855339 - 0422855049
E-MAIL: vinicasaroma@libero.it

Years ago, we compared the Raboso to the barbarian tribes, despised at first but capable of conquering the world. This rash statement no doubt caused some people to smile, but the results speak for themselves today. Casa Roma's wonderful Raboso '99 scored Two Glasses. This is an important achievement for the Peruzzetto cousins who run this 18-hectare winery, making 80,000 bottles per year. It can also be considered a fresh start for this native vine variety. The wine shows absolute typicality in all its features. Vibrant, evolved aromas of morello cherries, plums, hay and herbs meld with perfectly judged tannin and acidity and introduce a subtle, lingering palate. To judge by our tastings of subsequent years, especially the 2002, the wine has considerable potential. The soil here ranges from gravel to clay, which is typical of this DOC zone and endows the wines with a specific identity, as long as yields are limited. More conscientious producers are aware of this. San Dordi is a winner again. The lustrous gold introduces with peach, melon and tomato leaf aromas, then the palate is full bodied and warm, with a pleasant almondy finish. The Cabernet Franc 2002 is a delight. Its purplish ruby red colour heralds typical Veneto aromas of herbs and pepper, with nice hints of raspberries and wild cherries. The flower, spice and mineral Manzoni Bianco 2002 is good, and the Sauvignon, Pinot Grigio and Chardonnay are all admirably forthright. The Verduzzo Passito, tasted for the first time, made a positive impression with honey and carob aromas, rich fruit in syrup and good extract.

○	San Dordi '02	TT	5
●	Piave Raboso '99	TT	5
○	Manzoni Bianco '02	T	3*
●	Piave Cabernet Franc '02	T	3*
○	Piave Chardonnay '02	T	3
○	Piave Pinot Grigio '02	T	3
○	Sauvignon '02	T	3
○	Verduzzo Trevigiano Passito '02	T	5
●	Piave Merlot '02		3
○	San Dordi '01	YY	5
●	Piave Raboso '98	Y	5

SANT'AMBROGIO DI VALPOLICELLA (VR)

MASI

FRAZ. GARGAGNAGO
VIA MONTELEONE, 2
37020 SANT'AMBROGIO DI VALPOLICELLA (VR)
TEL. 0456832511
E-MAIL: masi@masi.it

Amarone is the leading wine in the extensive, diverse range of Masi products. The winery is not only the greatest exponent of Valpolicella's culture and tradition, but also offers variety. The various vineyards on the estate yield wines with distinct sensory characteristics that appeal to all tastes. Depending on the soil and aspect of the vineyard, the wine may be sunny, austere, approachable or reticent, complex and slow to open out. All this is condensed in four Amarones with very individual personalities. Mazzano is deep and multi-layered on the nose, with lovely dried fruit on the palate, all wrapped up in austerity that concedes nothing to sugary softness. Campolongo di Torbe is much sunnier, with approachable aromas of lightly dried red berries on the nose. The residual sugar gives this selection an enchantingly Mediterranean feel. The Costasera is simpler. It is sourced from west-facing vineyards and a minerally note is its most prominent feature. The aromas of the Vaio Armaron Serègo Alighieri are already mature, but the palate doesn't appear to have found its ideal balance just yet. The richly extracted, classy Osar is as excellent as ever. The wine is made from the old Veronese oseleta variety. The rest of the products are very good and the Recioto Amabile degli Angeli missed Two Glasses by a whisker.

●	Amarone della Valpolicella Cl. Mazzano '97	TT	8
●	Amarone della Valpolicella Cl. Campolongo di Torbe '98	TT	8
●	Osar '99	TT	8
●	Grandarella '00	T	6
●	Recioto della Valpolicella Cl. Amabile degli Angeli '00	T	7
○	Possessioni Bianco Serègo Alighieri '02	T	4
●	Amarone della Valpolicella Cl. Vaio Armaron Serègo Alighieri '98	T	8
●	Amarone della Valpolicella Cl. Costasera '99	T	7
●	Toar '99	T	5
●	Campofiorin '99		5

SANT'AMBROGIO DI VALPOLICELLA (VR)

RAIMONDI - VILLA MONTELEONE
FRAZ. GARGANEGA
VIA MONTELEONE, 12
37020 SANT'AMBROGIO DI VALPOLICELLA (VR)
TEL. 0456800533 - 0457704974
E-MAIL: raimondi@mediwork.com

The Raimondi family winery is one of the most representative exponents of local tradition, and their Amarone, in particular, reflects the cellar's focus on wines that are well-made, even if they are not especially modern. At their best, Raimondi wines are as good as any around Verona. These products do not concentrate on the strength and intensity of the fruit, but instead are more gradual, less audacious and unforgettably complex, generous and deep. Much of the credit goes to Lucia Duran, who manages the winery, and winemaker, Federico Giotto, who understands and can express the best of the house style. Amarone Campo San Paolo is the quintessential example of this understanding, with aromas that open out gradually, and a clear but fleeting hint of alcohol giving way to crushed flowers, leather, spices and sweet red berries in a complex and cohesive bouquet. The broad silky palate is warm and mouthfilling, to the point of flabbiness, then moving into a long, lean, delightful finish. The Amarone '99 is only slightly inferior. Equally warm and mouthfilling, it expands without the help of residual sugar. The very interesting Recioto Pal Sun succeeds in blending exuberantly expressive red fruit with a vibrant, stylish hint of flowers, then displays a perfect balance of sugar and acidity on the palate. The two Valpolicellas both perform well. Campo S. Lena is fresh tasting and the vibrant, deep Campo S. Vito will be better still after a few more months' ageing.

SELVAZZANO DENTRO (PD)

LA MONTECCHIA
FRAZ. FERIOLE
VIA MONTECCHIA, 16
35030 SELVAZZANO DENTRO (PD)
TEL. 049637294
E-MAIL: lamontecchia@libero.it

The Colli Euganei are the last strip of hills in the Veneto region and enjoy a warm sunny climate with good temperature variation between night and day. On the one hand, this makes for strong, richly extracted wines, and on the other it helps preserve the integrity of the aromas and their most delicate, stylish subtleties. Businessman Giordano Emo Capodilista has worked here for many years, enthusiastically making mainly red wines from 20 hectares of vineyards. Thanks to input from Andrea Boaretti in the cellar, the wines are some of the finest in the area. Villa Capodilista is an excellent Bordeaux blend of extraordinary finesse. The vibrant aromas include an interesting vegetal hint, and pencil lead alongside plums and berry fruits, then the long, complex palate focuses on elegance and balance. The Fior d'Arancio Passito gave an outstanding performance and has lost some of the excessive concentration it had a few vintages ago. Today, it is subtle and floral on the nose, where a lovely hint of Alpine herbs freshens up the aromas. The sweetness is perfectly integrated on the palate, and the wine is perked up by a fresh vein of acidity. The Godimondo is very good, in fact this tangy, rounded Cabernet Franc came close to winning Two Glasses. The rest of the range is well made and enjoyable, with a special mention for the deep, well-typed Forzaté, made from 100 per cent raboso grapes.

● Amarone della Valpolicella Cl.		
Campo S. Paolo '98	♟♟	8
● Valpolicella Cl. Sup.		
Campo S. Vito '00	♟♟	5
● Amarone della Valpolicella Cl. '99	♟♟	7
● Recioto della Valpolicella Cl.		
Pal Sun '99	♟♟	7
● Valpolicella Cl. Campo S. Lena '02	♟	4
● Amarone della Valpolicella Cl.		
Campo S. Paolo '95	♟♟	8
● Amarone della Valpolicella Cl.		
Campo S. Paolo '97	♟♟	8
● Amarone della Valpolicella Cl. '97	♟♟	6
● Amarone della Valpolicella Cl. '98	♟♟	6

○ Colli Euganei Moscato		
Fior d'Arancio Passito '01	♟♟	7
● Colli Euganei Rosso		
Villa Capodilista '00	♟♟	6
● Colli Euganei Rosso Cà Emo '00	♟	4
● Forzaté Raboso '00	♟	5
● Colli Euganei Merlot '01	♟	4
● Godimondo Cabernet Franc '02	♟	4
○ Colli Euganei Chardonnay '02		4
● Colli Euganei Rosso		
Montecchia '97	♟♟	6
● Colli Euganei Rosso		
Montecchia '98	♟♟	6
● Colli Euganei Rosso		
Villa Capodilista '99	♟♟	6

SOAVE (VR)

CANTINA DEL CASTELLO
CORTE PITTORA, 5
37038 SOAVE (VR)
TEL. 0457680093
E-MAIL: cantinacastello@cantinacastello.it

Following last year's success, Cantina del Castello showed continuity in quality and style in its products of a very high standard. Important work has been done in the vineyards, which will bring results in a few years. Silvana's untimely death has not prevented Arturo Stocchetti from dedicating body and soul to the winery, and his energies seem to have drawn strength from the memory of Silvana's devotion to the cellar. Most of the Pressoni vineyard has been replanted, and the older pergola vines abandoned in favour of quality-oriented training systems. New projects are under way in the cellar, too, and the other Stocchetti warhorse, Carniga, will not be available until next year, allowing it to age to perfection in the cellar. There was another winning performance from the Pressoni. This Soave Classico is a blend of garganega and trebbiano di Soave whose traditional aromas include deep minerally hints and spring flowers. The tangy, well-sustained palate has a long, exciting finish. In contrast, Acini Soave is a very different wine. From late-harvested garganega grapes, it is aged in wooden barrels for a year. Warm ripe fruit aromas precede a soft, mouthfilling palate lifted by hints of oak. The Soave Classico gave a good account of itself with simple hints of apple and pear fruit and an unexpectedly gutsy flavour. As well as his Recioto and Passito, Arturo also makes a traditional Recioto Sur Lie Ardens with a generous, appealing palate.

SOAVE (VR)

CANTINA DI SOAVE
V.LE VITTORIA, 100
37038 SOAVE (VR)
TEL. 0456139811
E-MAIL: cantina@cantinasoave.it

Cantina di Soave has just inaugurated the renovated Via Covergnino property and the more important selections will age in the underground caves of this spectacular building. The 1,200 families that form the backbone of this co-operative are working harder than ever. The traditional standard-bearers, the Rocca Sveva range, will give more space and to Valpolicella and Amarone wines from the neighbouring DOC zone. In this case, most of the grapes come from the extended Valpolicella area, a strip of land stretching from Illasi and Montecchia di Crosara to the Grezzana valley. The warm local climate gives the grapes a Mediterranean feel which translates into sunny, highly-concentrated wines, as shown by the rounded, mature Amarone '97. The ripe fruit tones are veined with aromas of dried flowers and Mediterranean scrubland, reflected well on the broad, mouthfilling palate which is nicely outlined by sweet, silky tannins. The two Valpolicellas are both good, especially the Superiore 2001 with its broad, fascinating range of aromas on the nose and deep, cleanly made palate. The Ripasso has a less impressive nose, but quickly redeems itself on the palate, which is unexpectedly classy with berry fruit and sweetness reminiscent of Pinot Nero. The Soaves are simpler and more evenly made. Villa Rasina is fresh-tasting and Rocca Sveva fruity.

○ Soave Cl. Sup. Acini Soavi '01	🍷🍷	5
○ Soave Cl. Pressoni '02	🍷🍷	4*
○ Acini Dolci Passito '00	🍷🍷	6
○ Recioto di Soave Cl. Corte Pittora '01	🍷	5
○ Recioto di Soave Sur Lie Ardens '01	🍷	5
○ Soave Cl. '02	🍷	4
○ Soave Cl. Sup. Monte Pressoni '01	🍷🍷🍷	4*
○ Soave Cl. Sup. Acini Soavi '00	🍷🍷	5
○ Soave Cl. Sup Monte Carniga '01	🍷🍷	4

● Valpolicella Sup. Rocca Sveva '01	🍷🍷	3*
● Amarone della Valpolicella Rocca Sveva '97	🍷🍷	7
● Valpolicella Sup. Ripasso Rocca Sveva '99	🍷🍷	4
● Garda Cabernet Sauvignon Rocca Sveva '00	🍷	4
○ Soave Cl. Rocca Sveva '02	🍷	3
○ Soave Cl. Villa Rasina '02	🍷	2*
○ Recioto di Soave Rocca Sveva '01		5
● Amarone della Valpolicella Rocca Sveva '95	🍷🍷	7
● Amarone della Valpolicella Rocca Sveva '96	🍷🍷	7

SOAVE (VR)

COFFELE
VIA ROMA, 5
37038 SOAVE (VR)
TEL. 0457680007
E-MAIL: info@coffele.it

We would advise any wine enthusiasts passing through Soave to go and visit the Coffele winery, not only for the high quality of the wines but also for the beautiful setting. The entrance, on the main street of the old town of Soave, leads into a pretty courtyard surrounded by the winery buildings. Here, inside the ancient walls steeped in memories of the past, brother and sister Alberto and Chiara Coffele, helped by their father Giuseppe, are the head and heart of the winery. The estate's 28 hectares of vineyards are situated in the hills of Castelcerino. This year's tastings showed a very promising range of wines, with a high average standard and a few peaks of true excellence. The Soave Ca' Visco was impressive for both its finesse and its wide range of aromas, emphasized by nice minerally notes, then a strong, vigorous palate culminating in a nicely defined finish. The Soave Alzari, aged in wood, has a subtle nose and gave a remarkably stylish performance, showing a soft, nicely balanced palate. The Soave Classico is simpler but still appealing, with fragrant fruity hints. The Recioto Le Sponde and the Passito Le Selle, made exclusively from sauvignon grapes, were very impressive, the former for its liveliness and the latter for its rich aromas, especially the fresh hints of liquorice and fines herbes.

SOAVE (VR)

MONTE TONDO
LOC. MONTE TONDO
VIA S. LORENZO, 89
37038 SOAVE (VR)
TEL. 0457680347
E-MAIL: info@montetondo.it

In many ways, Monte Tondo's history resembles that of many other Soave wineries. The first timid steps were taken in the 1980s, the wine was sold unbottled in demijohns at first, and then came the leap into bottled wines. Today's lovely new winery marks the end of a journey that has made the Magnaboscos into the front rank of Soave winemakers. But if there's one thing that hasn't changed here, it is the modest spirit of people who believe in hard work in the vineyards. The conviction at Monte Tondo is that anything you neglect in the vineyard cannot be remedied in the cellar. Again, the most impressive wine was the oak-aged Casette Foscarin, the well-judged addition of chardonnay grapes lending maturity and sweetness, making the wine pleasantly rounded to drink. In contrast, the garganega grapes give the wine backbone, austerity, deep fruit and mineral hints. The well-structured, floral and extremely cleanly made Mito fell just short of Two Glasses. About 150,000 bottles of Monte Tondo are made each year. This 100 per cent garganega is aged in stainless steel vats and has aromas of pears and jasmine. The fruit is strikingly ripe, but the wine also has remarkable personality, thanks to the down-to-earth tannin from the grape skins and the subtle minerally notes that will expand over the years. The Chardonnay Le Cingelle and Rosso Giunone, made principally from partially dried cabernet franc, are both fresh tasting and approachable. Finally, the Recioto di Soave is enjoyably sweet and slightly masked by oak in the finale.

O Soave Cl. Sup. Alzari '01	♟♟	5
O Soave Cl. Ca' Visco '02	♟♟	4*
O Recioto di Soave Cl. Le Sponde '01	♟♟	6
O Le Selle Passito '00	♟♟	5
O Soave Cl. '02	♟	3*
O Soave Cl. Sup. Ca' Visco '99	♟♟	4
O Soave Cl. Sup. Ca' Visco '00	♟♟	4
O Recioto di Soave Cl. Le Sponde '99	♟♟	5
O Recioto di Soave Cl. Le Sponde '00	♟♟	5
O Soave Cl. Sup. Alzari '00	♟♟	4
O Soave Cl. Sup. Ca' Visco '01	♟♟	4

O Soave Cl. Monte Tondo '02	♟♟	4
O Soave Cl. Casette Foscarin '02	♟♟	4
● Giunone Rosso '01	♟	3
O Recioto di Soave '01	♟	5
O Chardonnay Le Cingelle '02	♟	4
O Soave Mito '02	♟	2*
O Soave Cl. Sup. Vigneti in Casette Foscarin '99	♟♟	5
O Soave Cl. Sup. Vigneti in Casette Foscarin '00	♟♟	5
O Soave Cl. Sup. Vigneti in Casette Foscarin '01	♟♟	5

SOAVE (VR)

★ Leonildo Pieropan
via Camuzzoni, 3
37038 Soave (VR)
tel. 0456190171
e-mail: info@pieropan.it

People who succeed in combining judgement and determination or rather, personality and a precise expression of the relationship between territory and variety, are few and far between in winemaking. Leonildo Pieropan, known as Nino, is one of them. As an area and a DOC, Soave owes a great deal to him. Over the difficult years, his wines were a reliable benchmark for consumers and nowadays, with Soave's renaissance, Nino's products are still absolutely impeccable. It is always astonishing to taste his old vintages. The more than ten-year-old La Rocca and Calvarino are unusually exciting examples of the professionalism and shrewd judgement of this grower, who should be an example to all those aspiring to the profession. The winery's 34 hectares are situated in the heart of the Soave Classico zone and a new vineyard in the Val d'Illasi will yield red wines in a few years' time. The tricky 2002 growing year demonstrated all Nino's skills for he pulled a memorable Soave Classico out of his hat. It is a textbook example of the wine type, floral, fruity and intimately linked to the territory. The Calvarino is simply wonderful. Bright yellow with greenish highlights, it displays subtle herbal notes on the nose, with hints of very healthy ripe peach fruit. The palate is refreshing, juicy, minerally and long lasting, so we gave it Three resounding Glasses. La Rocca has subtle boisé notes as well as honey and rosemary on the nose, with a deep vein of fruit, and a generous, lingering palate.

SOAVE (VR)

Suavia
fraz. Fittà
via Centro, 14
37038 Soave (VR)
tel. 0457675089
e-mail: info@suavia.it

This small winery's products have always stood out for their originality and character. There are various reasons for this, one of which is undoubtedly the work of the Tessari sisters, Arianna, Meri and Valentina. Currently, the trio are at the helm of the family business, managing the considerable resources at their disposal intelligently, reliably and with great determination. The extraordinary vineyards, some over 50 years old, are on hilly land with an ideal growing climate and rich, complex volcanic soil. The Tessaris have deep roots in this area, and seem perfectly in tune with it. You could not say that approachability is the most salient feature of their wines. The Soave Monte Carbonare has a gradually unfolding nose with light, almost rugged green-appley notes and mineral hints to the fore. The wine's power is very apparent on the palate, which has a long, dry finish. The Three Glasses were earned with class and character. The aromatic character of the Soave Le Rive is influenced by barrique fermentation and ageing, and on tasting it shows very potent yet buttery, with an impressively long palate. The Recioto is also interesting, and fresh citrus hints give it a certain elegance.

○ Soave Cl. Calvarino '02	♧♧♧	5
○ Soave Cl. Sup. La Rocca '01	♧♧	6
○ Recioto di Soave Le Colombare '00	♧♧	6
○ Soave Cl. '02	♧♧	4*
○ Soave Cl. Sup. La Rocca '95	♧♧♧	6
○ Soave Cl. Sup. La Rocca '96	♧♧♧	6
○ Soave Cl. Sup. Calvarino '98	♧♧♧	5
○ Soave Cl. Sup. La Rocca '98	♧♧♧	6
○ Soave Cl. Sup. La Rocca '99	♧♧♧	6
○ Soave Cl. Sup. La Rocca '00	♧♧♧	6

○ Soave Cl. Monte Carbonare '02	♧♧♧	4
○ Soave Cl. Sup. Le Rive '01	♧♧	5
○ Recioto di Soave Acinatium '01	♧♧	6
○ Soave Cl. '02	♧	4
○ Soave Cl. Sup. Le Rive '98	♧♧♧	5
○ Soave Cl. Sup. Le Rive '00	♧♧♧	5
○ Soave Cl. Sup. Monte Carbonare '00	♧♧	4
○ Soave Cl. Sup. Le Rive '99	♧♧	5
○ Recioto di Soave Cl. Acinatium '00	♧♧	5
○ Soave Cl. Sup. Monte Carbonare '01	♧♧	4

SOAVE (VR)

SOMMACAMPAGNA (VR)

TAMELLINI
VIA TAMELLINI, 4
37038 SOAVE (VR)
TEL. 0457675328

CAVALCHINA
LOC. CAVALCHINA - FRAZ. CUSTOZA
VIA SOMMACAMPAGNA
37066 SOMMACAMPAGNA (VR)
TEL. 045516002
E-MAIL: cavalchina@cavalchina.com

Gaetano and Piofrancesco Tamellini continue on their reliable way, placing the foundations of their winery solidly on their strong bond with the land. Hard work in the vineyards gives their grapes natural concentration, and this translates into very highly structured wines that need time to develop sufficient balance. The highest expression of this style is to be found in the Recioto, which was erroneously reviewed last year (that was the Recioto '99). The colour is old gold and the heady aromas of ripe peaches, citrus fruit and liquorice are perfectly reflected on the palate, where the considerable sweetness is beautifully integrated. The ripeness of the aromas and noticeable alcohol content make this a highly Mediterranean-style Recioto, unexpectedly aromatic thanks to its well-extracted texture. The Soave 2002 is very good, revealing astounding strength and depth, despite the difficult growing year. The aromas are miles away from the fruit-and-flowers cliché, but show characterful mineral and vegetal nuances. The palate is potent and long lasting. After a soft entry, the dry, masculine progression takes you through to the nice tannin on the finish. The Soave Anguane and Le Bine both still need to find perfect balance and style. Their aromas are still partly closed but they both have dense palates. We are sure that bottle ageing will do great things for both these wines.

Luciano Piona has taken the important decision to postpone the release of some of his wines. He knows that this is the only way to present a mature product with enhanced balance, complexity and style. However, the vast range of wines from the parent winery in Custoza, and the one at Monzambano, Mantua, demonstrate that the improvement in quality no longer concerns only the flagship wines. Even those often wrongly considered to be inferior are involved. The most emblematic wine is probably the Bianco di Custoza, which has approachable floral aromas of tropical fruit, peaches and apples, and an irresistibly appetizing whirlwind of sensations. The acidity on the palate is never intrusive, but highlights the wine's flavour and softness. And all this is available at a bargain price. The excellent Falcone is a Cabernet Sauvignon with mainly fruity aromas, and the considerable body never gets in the way of the palate's suppleness and brisk progression. Also excellent on retasting were the two top-of-the-range whites, the potent, fruit-forward Sauvignon Valbruna 2001 and the Garganega Paroni from the same year, which has more individual sensations. After a year's cellar time, both these wines are still very good indeed. The Bardolino S. Lucia proved to be one of the best around, with its nice full colour and aromas. On the palate, it succeeds in the difficult task of expressing modern, satisfying concentration without sacrificing its proverbial lightness and drinkability.

○ Recioto di Soave		
Vigna Marogne '00	♟♟	5
○ Soave '02	♟♟	4*
○ Soave Cl. Anguane '01	♟	4
○ Soave Cl. Le Bine '01	♟	5
○ Recioto di Soave		
Vigna Marogne '99	♟♟	5
○ Soave Cl. Sup. Anguane '00	♟♟	4

● Bardolino Sup.		
S. Lucia Cavalchina '01	♟♟	4*
● Garda Cabernet Sauvignon		
Vigneto Il Falcone La Prendina '01	♟♟	5
○ Bianco di Custoza '02	♟♟	4*
● Bardolino Cavalchina '02	♟	4
⊙ Bardolino Chiaretto '02	♟	4
● Garda Merlot Casina La Prendina '02	♟	4
⊙ La Rosa Passito '02	♟	4
● Garda Merlot Faial La Prendina '99	♟♟	6
● Garda Merlot La Prendina '00	♟♟	6
○ Garda Garganega Paroni		
La Prendina '01	♟♟	4
○ Garda Sauvignon Valbruna		
La Prendina '01	♟♟	4

SOMMACAMPAGNA (VR)

LE VIGNE DI SAN PIETRO
VIA S. PIETRO, 23
37066 SOMMACAMPAGNA (VR)
TEL. 045510016
E-MAIL: carlo@nerozzi.org

SUSEGANA (TV)

CONTE COLLALTO
VIA 24 MAGGIO, 1
31058 SUSEGANA (TV)
TEL. 0438738241
E-MAIL: collalto@collalto.it

Carlo Nerozzi's wines have never been so impressively good. His decision to stop producing Bardolino has led to a healthy reduction in the number of wines made, enabling the winery to focus its efforts on the remaining types. The ten hectares of vineyards on the little glacial hill of Colle San Pietro are all vertical-trellised and planted at a density well above the local average. Carlo has always been an advocate of concentrated wines with a stylish, even palate, and with the help of Federico Giotto, he has made the best Refolà ever. It shows a captivatingly broad swathe of aromas, ranging from red berry fruit to dried summer flowers and spices, and closes with alluring mineral notes. The palate is even broader, displaying markedly sweet tannins and a vibrant acid backbone. There was further improvement from the supple, classy I Balconi Rossi, a modern Bordeaux blend with a touch of corvina. The Due Cuori is very good again this time. The best features of this moscato giallo "passito" are its floral notes and relaxed flavour, lifted by the depth and strength of the palate. Both versions of the Bianco di Custoza are memorable, which shows how different blends and ageing policies can enable producers to make dissimilar, but equally successful, wines. The standard label is simple and explosively varietal, whereas the Sanpietro is well co-ordinated, the cask conditioning enabling it to bring out the best in the grapes.

The constant aim of this solid winery, firmly rooted in the Marca Trevigiana territory, is to improve and innovate. You can see this at once if you visit the winery, which is continually being enhanced and rendered more efficient with carefully thought-out projects. This year, the most interesting newcomer is an ambitious red wine, Rambaldo VIII, named after an ancestor of the Collalto family. It is a blend of merlot, cabernet, refosco and other native varieties, half of which is aged in large wooden casks and the other half in barrique. The wine still needs to find perfect balance, but there are glimpses of an interesting future in the complexity of the aromas, the good structure and the impressive extract. Wildbacher is one of the winery's most interesting and original products. The typically gamey nose opens with aromas that range from berry fruits to fines herbes and pleasantly clear spicy notes. The palate is impressively long and potent, yet stylish and supple. The Manzoni Rosso 2.15 is a little less complex than the previous two, but still has good personality. The whole range has settled at a good overall level, including the Proseccos, to which the winery devotes increasing attention.

O	Due Cuori Passito '00	♟♟	6
●	Refolà Cabernet Sauvignon '00	♟♟	7
O	Bianco di Custoza Sanpietro '01	♟♟	4
●	I Balconi Rossi '01	♟♟	4
O	Bianco di Custoza '02	♟♟	4
O	Sud '95	♟♟♟	5
●	Refolà Cabernet Sauvignon '96	♟♟	6
●	Refolà Cabernet Sauvignon '97	♟♟	6
●	Refolà Cabernet Sauvignon '98	♟♟	6
O	Bianco di Custoza Sanpietro '00	♟♟	3
●	I Balconi Rossi '00	♟♟	4
●	Refolà Cabernet Sauvignon '99	♟♟	6

●	Rambaldo VIII '00	♟♟	5
●	Incrocio Manzoni 2.15 '02	♟♟	3*
●	Wildbacher '02	♟♟	3*
O	Colli di Conegliano Bianco '02	♟	3
O	Manzoni Bianco '02	♟	3
●	Piave Cabernet '02	♟	3
O	Piave Chardonnay '02	♟	2
●	Piave Merlot '02	♟	3
O	Verdiso '02	♟	2
●	Colli di Conegliano Rosso '99	♟	4
●	Prosecco di C. Brut San Salvatore	♟	4
O	Prosecco di C. Extra Dry	♟	3
●	Piave Cabernet Podere Torrai Ris. '98	♟♟	5

TORREGLIA (PD)

VALDOBBIADENE (TV)

VIGNALTA
FRAZ. LUVIGLIANO
VIA DEI VESCOVI, 5
35038 TORREGLIA (PD)
TEL. 0499933105 - 0429777225
E-MAIL: mrlunghe@tin.it

BRUNO AGOSTINETTO
LOC. SACCOL
VIA PIANDER, 7
31048 VALDOBBIADENE (TV)
TEL. 0423972884 - 335353080
E-MAIL: info@agostinetto.it

Vignalta confirmed its leading position in the Colli Euganei with a phenomenal Gemola 2000. Last year, this wine was extremely young but further bottle ageing has given it complexity and an explosive personality. It must be one of the best versions ever, and fully expresses the warm, mineral, volcanic territory it comes from. Made from mainly merlot grapes, with some cabernet franc, it has a beautiful dense ruby red colour. The nose is spicy and balsamic, with clearly defined cherry fruit subtly surrounded by hints of hay, then shows concentrated, rich and quite long on the palate. Congratulations to the winery's technical staff, winemaker, Francesco Polastri, vineyard manager, Filippo Giannone and cellar manager, Marco Michele Montecchio. The 55 hectares owned by Vignalta include 36 planted to vine. More plots are rented and a small quantity of grapes is bought in, for a total production of about 300,000 bottles a year. Among the other reds, the Rosso Riserva made an excellent impression. Cinnamon, plums and blackberries on the nose precede grassy hints, redcurrant and pencil lead on the freshly tannic, full-bodied palate. The first version of the Merlot Venda is good, offering aromas of cloves, wild cherries and pepper. The whites are led by the Sirio, which is vibrant with roses, pineapple, peaches and spice aromas. This version of a dry moscato has bags of potential and we would like to see all Colli Euganei producers following suit. The Pinot Bianco and the Chardonnay are very good. Lastly, the Fior d'Arancio Passito Alpianae is delicious, with joyously fresh aromas.

Daniele Agostinetto runs the little winery he inherited from his father, Bruno, with determination and passion. Situated in the heart of the Prosecco di Valdobbiadene zone, it is a stone's throw from the Cartizze hill. The wines are all made from grapes grown in the estate's own long-established vineyards, clinging to the steep hillsides surrounding the winery. The range has a highly personal style. Typically enjoyable and approachable like most local products, these wines are also austere and complex and it is these qualities that often provoke contrasting reactions. The winery's most representative product is Mondeserto, made from slowly dried prosecco grapes. Aromas of oxidation on the nose are delicately reminiscent of hazelnuts, contrasting with fresher, fragrant notes of flowers, honey and ripe fruit. The palate is balanced, with very interesting texture, and emphatic echoes of the grapes on the palate and in the afteraroma. Another provocative wine is the Jare, a late-harvested product also made from prosecco grapes aged on the yeasts for nine months. The aromas are fairly complex, and the flavour is unusually alcoholic for a wine from this area. The Brut Nogarole and the Prosecco Extra Dry both exhibit good structure, which promises a decent lifespan in the cellar, and there are hints of almonds on the nose, which is anything but cloying.

● Colli Euganei Rosso Gemola '00	♟♟♟	7
○ Colli Euganei Chardonnay '01	♟♟	5
○ Colli Euganei Moscato Fior d'Arancio Alpianae '01	♟♟	6
● Colli Euganei Rosso Ris. '01	♟♟	5
○ Colli Euganei Pinot Bianco '02	♟♟	4
○ Sirio '02	♟♟	4
● Colli Euganei Merlot Venda '01	♟	4
● Colli Euganei Rosso Gemola '97	♟♟♟	6
● Colli Euganei Rosso Gemola '98	♟♟♟	6
● Colli Euganei Rosso Gemola '99	♟♟♟	6
● Agno Tinto '01	♟♟	5
● Colli Euganei Cabernet Ris. '98	♟♟	7

○ Mondeserto Passito '01	♟♟	7
○ Jare '01	♟	5
○ Nogarole Brut	♟	3
○ Prosecco di V. Extra Dry	♟	3

VALDOBBIADENE (TV)

VALDOBBIADENE (TV)

DESIDERIO BISOL & FIGLI
FRAZ. SANTO STEFANO
VIA FOL, 33
31040 VALDOBBIADENE (TV)
TEL. 0423900138
E-MAIL: bisol@bisol.it

Gianluca Bisol's estate, with 45 hectares under vine, is one of the largest in the zone. This is significant because hereabouts most of the vineyards are owned by farming families and the wineries must buy in their grapes. But the strength of this Santo Stefano winery lies in this vast vineyard holding. The cellar can thus vinify estate-grown grapes, carrying out separate selection and vinification procedures for different grape types from different vineyards. The Prosecco Dry Garnei obtained from scrupulously selected fruit vinified and aged very slowly. In fact, it only becomes available when most ordinary Proseccos have sold out. The sweetness of the ripe peach fruit is overlain with fresh flowers, reflected well on the palate where the creamy mousse contributes to a sophisticated balance of sweetness and acidity. The Duca di Dolle is a different kettle of fish, although it is made with equal care. This Passito di Prosecco is obtained from a solera blend which began ten years ago. It has jammy aromas and a very light hint of acacia honey, then a soft, mouthfilling palate with a charmingly stylish, tangy finish. The performance of the Vigneti del Fol is well up to snuff and as ever this Extra Dry flaunts all the class of this variety. The wide range of Bisol wines is excellent without exception, and includes a second label, Jeio, one for vineyard selections, and a good line-up of "metodo classico" sparklers.

F.LLI BORTOLIN SPUMANTI
FRAZ. SANTO STEFANO
VIA MENEGAZZI, 5
31040 VALDOBBIADENE (TV)
TEL. 0423900135
E-MAIL: info@bortolin.com

The Bortolin winery remains one of the most reliable in the Valdobbiadene area, thanks to careful, restrained vineyard management that aims to obtain the best from every harvest, whether on the estate's own 20 hectares under vine or the others cultivated by trusted local growers. The personal style and character of the wines derive from the skills of Valeriano, who is increasingly reliant on the help of his children Andrea, Diego and Claudia. The Prosecco Brut is one of the best of the type. The clear apple fruit on the nose is matched by an assertive, tangy palate that echoes the typical fragrance of the variety. The Extra Dry version has a broad range of charming aromas, with especially clear citrus fruit and spring flowers that are mirrored well on the palate. The Extra Dry Rù, made in the Rua di Feletto area, also has a very impressive nose, with floral hints and a nice echo of white peaches. The palate is lively and supple, leading to a clean, appley finish. The Cartizze is pale straw yellow, with a fine perlage and nice fruit on the nose. The palate is fresh-tasting, creamy and not too sweet, but not fully satisfying. The Vigneto del Convento Extra Brut and the Dry version are both simple and uncomplicated. The light, well-typed Colli di Conegliano Bianco is made from a blend of incrocio Manzoni bianco, chardonnay and pinot bianco.

O	Prosecco di V. Dry		
	Garnei '02	⅋⅋	5
O	Duca di Dolle Prosecco Passito	⅋⅋	6
O	Prosecco di V. Extra Dry		
	Vigneti del Fol '02	⅋⅋	5
O	Cartizze	⅋⅋	6
O	Prosecco di V. Brut Crede	⅋⅋	4
O	Talento Brut Ris. '98	⅋	5
O	Prosecco di V. Brut Jeio	⅋	4
O	Prosecco di V. Dry Salis	⅋	4
O	Prosecco di V. Tranquillo		
	Molera	⅋	4
O	Prosecco di V. Dry		
	Garnei '01	⅋⅋	5

O	Cartizze	⅋⅋	5
O	Prosecco di V. Brut	⅋⅋	3
O	Prosecco di V. Extra Dry	⅋⅋	3
O	Colli di Conegliano Bianco '02	⅋	4
O	Prosecco di V. Dry	⅋	4
O	Prosecco di V. Extra Dry Rù	⅋	4
O	Spumante Extra Brut		
	Vigneto del Convento	⅋	4

VALDOBBIADENE (TV)

BORTOLOMIOL
VIA GARIBALDI, 142
31049 VALDOBBIADENE (TV)
TEL. 0423974911
E-MAIL: info@bortolomiol.com

Bortolomiol is a big name in the Prosecco area and one of the few wineries to have shaped the history of Veneto sparkling wines. It is still a worldwide leader in the promotion of the wine type. The winery mainly buys its grapes from traditional suppliers, farming families that have sold their grapes to the cellar for generations and today are crucial cogs in the Bortolomiol productive wheel. Sparkling wines, of course, take pride of place in the wide-ranging list. Even in a difficult year like 2002, Bortolomiol managed to make an excellent Banda Rossa. This Prosecco is graceful on the nose, with clearly recognizable apple and pear fruit, and lovely floral hints of jasmine and wistaria. The combination of wine and fizz on the palate is practically perfect, lengthened by a fresh vein of acidity. The Extra Dry gave a good performance, and so does the Tranquillo Canto Fermo where the excellent quality of the grapes is thrown into evidence by the absence of sugar and fizz. The Brut version is not overly impressive on the nose, but has a tangy palate dominated by a strong vein of acidity, while the mature, mouthfilling Dry has greater concentration of sugar. The Cartizze is not on perfect form. It won a Glass, but failed to communicate all the class of this wonderful subzone.

VALDOBBIADENE (TV)

CANEVEL SPUMANTI
LOC. SACCOL
VIA ROCCAT E FERRARI, 17
31049 VALDOBBIADENE (TV)
TEL. 0423975940
E-MAIL: info@canevel.it

With the new, functional winery completed, attention has been focused on the estate's vineyards and, of course, on vinifying the grapes that they yield. Prosecco is not a highly structured or muscular wine, so a lot of care is needed to achieve a good balance of the integrity and richness of the aromas, the acidity and the structure. Roberto De Lucchi, winemaker and guiding light of the winery, has been pursuing this goal by continually fine-tuning all the stages in the winemaking process to allow the wine to express itself with lightness, aromatic finesse and harmony. The Extra Dry versions are particularly successful, especially the Vigneto del Faé, a sparkling wine made with grapes from Refrontolo. The area is well known for producing wines with more structure than finesse, but this one has great style on the palate, where the aromas of golden delicious apples and pears clearly reflect the nose. The low concentration of sugars also makes the wine supple and very versatile with food. The Millesimato is more intriguing, and is made with fruit exclusively from the last harvest. Its slow second fermentation makes it better balanced and more mouthfilling on the palate. The Cartizze is concentrated and varietal, while the Brut is subtler and more elegant, with a nice floral finish. One year on, we tasted the Colli di Conegliano Rosso Vigneto Levina 2000 again. It had developed further, and was as good as we thought it would be.

O	Prosecco di V. Extra Dry Sel. Banda Rossa	🍷🍷	4
O	Prosecco di V. Frizzante Il Ponteggio '02	🍷	4
O	Cartizze	🍷	5
O	Prosecco di V. Brut	🍷	3
O	Prosecco di V. Dry	🍷	3
O	Prosecco di V. Extra Dry	🍷	3*
O	Prosecco di V. Tranquillo Canto Fermo	🍷	3
●	Piave Cabernet Sauvignon Mormorò '01		4
O	Riserva del Governatore Extra Brut '02		4

O	Prosecco di V. Extra Dry Il Millesimato '02	🍷🍷	4
O	Prosecco di V. Extra Dry	🍷🍷	3
O	Prosecco di V. Extra Dry Vigneto del Faé	🍷🍷	3
O	Cartizze	🍷	5
O	Prosecco di V. Brut	🍷	3
O	Prosecco di V. Frizzante Vigneti di S. Biagio	🍷	2
●	Colli di Conegliano Rosso Vigneto Levina '00	🍷🍷	5

VALDOBBIADENE (TV)

COL VETORAZ
FRAZ. SANTO STEFANO
S.DA DELLE TRESIESE, 1
31049 VALDOBBIADENE (TV)
TEL. 0423975291
E-MAIL: colvetoraz@libero.it

Driving along the first few kilometres of the road leading from the centre of Valdobbiadene to Vittorio Veneto, you can admire the most delightful part of the Prosecco hills, with their steep, terraced slopes shaped by the hand of man, and the reassuring presence of the vines. The most attractive spot is the Col Vetoraz winery, its garden almost hanging over the vineyards below. Some of the most stylish and elegant sparkling wines in the whole area are made here, against this lovely backdrop. The care and attention that winemaker, Loris Dall'Acqua, devotes to every stage in production create wines that magically capture the subtlest aromas the grapes can offer. This year, the best sparkling wine was again the Millesimato, with its intoxicating aromas of pears, citrus and jasmine. The palate reflects the nose beautifully, with subtle fizz giving style and length to the mouthfeel. The Brut version is only slightly inferior. Generous and mouthfilling despite the low sugar concentration, its vibrant, flower and blackberry aromas lend a sophisticated tone to the wine. The Extra Dry and Cartizze are reliable as ever. The former has fresh floral aromas and the Cartizze is fruitier, with an interesting balance of acidity, sugar and fizz that makes it soft yet fresh tasting. The Prosecco Tranquillo is light and drinkable, and the Frizzante is tangy and well orchestrated.

VALDOBBIADENE (TV)

LE BELLERIVE - ANGELO RUGGERI
FRAZ. SANTO STEFANO
VIA FOLLO, 26
31040 VALDOBBIADENE (TV)
TEL. 0423900235
E-MAIL: info@lebellerive.it

The church of Santo Stefano in Valdobbiadene overlooks a lovely landscape of vineyards on undulating south-facing hills that soak up every single ray of sunlight and warmth. A little lower down, Remigio and Vittorio Ruggeri's winery nestles in this picturesque framework, drawing inspiration for its excellent products whose best features are consistent, crystal-clear aromas and balance. The range hinges on sparkling wines, of course, which are all made from prosecco grapes. The most striking wine, in our opinion, was the Cartizze, which has approachable, vibrant aromas of spring flowers and tropical fruit. The palate is soft and mouthfilling, and the sugar is perfectly offset by acidity and fizz that lead to a cleanly defined finish. The Extra Dry is equally good. The fragrant nose discloses recognizable varietal aromas of apples and pears, and a subtle floral note that adds style and finesse on the nose. The palate shows good harmony and integrates well with the prickle. The Prosecco Brut is more clearly defined and linear, but what it loses in structure, it gains in vibrant vitality. The Frizzante is well typed but the Dry Funer seemed a little off-form, perhaps because of the difficult growing year. After a good, clean aromatic entry, it fails to develop as it should and remains rather simple.

○ Prosecco di V. Dry Millesimato '02	♀♀	4
○ Cartizze	♀♀	6
○ Prosecco di V. Brut	♀♀	4
○ Prosecco di V. Extra Dry	♀♀	4
○ Prosecco di V. Tranquillo Tresiese '02	♀	4
○ Prosecco di V. Frizzante		4

○ Cartizze	♀♀	5
○ Prosecco di V. Brut	♀♀	3*
○ Prosecco di V. Extra Dry	♀♀	3*
○ Prosecco di V. Frizzante	♀	2
○ Prosecco di V. Dry Funer		3

VALDOBBIADENE (TV)

LE COLTURE
FRAZ. SANTO STEFANO
VIA FOLLO, 5
31040 VALDOBBIADENE (TV)
TEL. 0423900192
E-MAIL: info@lecolture.it

Thanks to their very close links with the land – almost all the grapes processed by the winery are from the estate's own vineyards – brothers Cesare and Renato Ruggeri manage to interpret each vintage with care and sensitivity. The results speak for themselves, and despite the difficulties with the last growing year, which was plagued by frequent rain, the wines have maintained the winery's usual high standard. As usual, the Prosecco Dry Cruner is one of the most interesting wines, not only in this range, but also in the whole zone. The nose is full and pleasantly complex, then the prickle on the palate has a creamy texture, lending the progression balance and harmony as it leads through to a well-defined finale. The Prosecco Extra Dry Pianer also made a good impression, and manages to be approachable but neither commonplace nor predictable. The almost evolved aromas are brought out by fascinating mineral hints, echoed nicely on the austere, long-lasting palate. The Prosecco Brut Fagher has subtle golden delicious apples on the nose and is a little simpler than the wines described above. On the palate, it is dry with a good mouthfeel. The aromas of the Cartizze are not fully open, but the progression is firm and nicely defined. The rest of the range includes the Prosecco Frizzante Mas and the Prosecco Tranquillo Masaré, both of which easily earned One Glass. The Colli Conegliano Rosso is not available yet, because it is stills ageing. We'll be tasting it in time for the next edition of the Guide.

VALDOBBIADENE (TV)

NINO FRANCO
VIA GARIBALDI, 147
31049 VALDOBBIADENE (TV)
TEL. 0423972051
E-MAIL: info@ninofranco.it

Primo Franco is a skilled Valdobbiadene producer and ardent wine enthusiast, and his strong point is an ability to interpret perfectly the growing year. This is of vital importance when dealing with a variety like prosecco, which is certainly not renowned for either strength or concentration. Adaptability enables Primo to obtain the best from every single harvest, even in 2002, a difficult year here, too, although without the disasters experienced in other areas. The unusual condition of the fruit could have yielded heavy, fat wines, but none of this occurred at the Franco winery, where Primo produced an excellent range of wines with typically exuberant, concentrated fruit. This year, the most impressive wine was again the Brut Rive di S. Floriano, with tropical pineapple and grapefruit aromas, and a perfectly balanced palate lightened by acidity and creamy sparkle. The Cartizze is explosive, and the concentration of sugar makes the ripe fruit even more mouthfilling, then on the palate it is soft with a lively vein of acidity. The still Prosecco, Sassi Bianchi, goes well beyond good typing. It's one of the best wines of this vintage, showing tangy and perfectly balanced. The fresh-tasting Brut and the lovely Primo Franco are up to their usual excellent standard.

○	Prosecco di V. Dry Cruner	♈♈	4
○	Prosecco di V. Extra Dry Pianer	♈♈	4
○	Cartizze	♈♈	5
○	Prosecco di V. Tranquillo Masaré '02	♈	3
○	Prosecco di V. Brut Fagher	♈	4
○	Prosecco di V. Frizzante Mas	♈	4
●	Colli di Conegliano Rosso '00	♈	5

○	Prosecco di V. Brut Rive di S. Floriano '02	♈♈	4
○	Prosecco di V. Dry Primo Franco '02	♈♈	4
○	Cartizze	♈♈	5
○	Prosecco di V. Brut	♈♈	3*
○	Prosecco di V. Tranquillo Sassi Bianchi	♈♈	3*
○	Prosecco Brut Rustico	♈	4
○	Prosecco di V. Brut Rive di S. Floriano '01	♈♈	4
○	Prosecco di V. Dry Primo Franco '01	♈♈	4

VALDOBBIADENE (TV)

Ruggeri & C.

via Prà Fontana
31049 Valdobbiadene (TV)
tel. 04239092
e-mail: ruggeri@ruggeri.it

When you think about the physical features and tradition of Valdobbiadene, there are many elements that could seem paradoxical but are drawn together by a single logical thread. Manual work is the only possible solution in this wild landscape with its steep hills, which suggests a growing model of family-run businesses. The network of usually medium or large wineries appears to be at odds the geography of the zone. Talking to Paolo Bisol, though, you realize that the quantity of wine produced is just a detail. The theory and methods behind production reflect a traditional farming mentality that strives to exalt the variety and, to an even greater extent, the territory. The growing number of suppliers around Valdobbiadene should be interpreted in this light. Over 80 per cent of the wine made here comes from this municipality. The Prosecco Extra Dry Giustino B. 2002 is outstanding, with stylish aromas of pears and jasmine that clearly echo the variety and a mature, creamy, mouthfilling palate, still light and smooth to drink, that shows a thrust of acidity despite above average structure. The mouthfilling Cartizze is extraordinarily classy, while the Giall'Oro is intoxicatingly exuberant in the traditional manner. The Dry Santo Stefano is excellent, but the Brut Quartese is a tad less gutsy than usual. A special mention for merit goes to the Prosecco Tranquillo and to the Colli di Conegliano Rosso '99, which tasted one year on, has made positive progress.

○ Prosecco di V. Extra Dry Giustino B. '02	🍷🍷 (grey)	5
○ Cartizze	🍷🍷	5
○ Prosecco di V. Dry S. Stefano	🍷🍷	4
○ Prosecco di V. Extra Dry Giall'Oro	🍷🍷	4*
○ Prosecco di V. Tranquillo La Bastia '02	🍷	4
○ Prosecco di V. Brut Quartese	🍷	4
○ Prosecco di V. Extra Dry Giustino B. '01	ΥΥ	5
● Colli di Conegliano Rosso S. Alberto '99	Υ	5

VALDOBBIADENE (TV)

Santa Eurosia

fraz. San Pietro di Barbozza
via della Cima, 8
31040 Valdobbiadene (TV)
tel. 0423973236
e-mail: info@santaeurasia.it

Scrupulous care in the winery and a tried and tested relationship with the suppliers (only purchased grapes are used here) make this small winery one of the most reliable in the area in terms of quality and value for money. Giuseppe Geronazzo's philosophy is to respect the typical features of the prosecco grape as far as possible, and preserve its local characteristics, with thorough selection of the grapes and by avoiding the excessive use of technology in the cellars. One of the most impressive wines from the 2002 vintage is the Prosecco Extra Dry. Pleasant floral notes and appley fruit on the nose are followed by a juicy, chewy palate rendered even more harmonious by the creamy, well-integrated prickle. The best feature of the excellent Prosecco Dry Millesimato is the firm, well-structured palate, along with a nose that has yet to open fully but is dominated by pleasant floral hints. Among the other wines tasted, the Prosecco Brut showed fresh, fragrant aromas and a nicely defined, well-orchestrated palate. The Prosecco Tranquillo is one of the most interesting in this category, displaying outstandingly varied aromas that range from fresh citrus fruit to nuts and flowers. The Cartizze is subtly expressive.

○ Prosecco di V. Dry Millesimato '02	🍷🍷	4
○ Prosecco di V. Extra Dry	🍷🍷	3*
○ Cartizze	🍷	5
○ Prosecco di V. Brut	🍷	3*
○ Prosecco di V. Tranquillo	🍷	3

VALDOBBIADENE (TV)

VALEGGIO SUL MINCIO (VR)

TANORÉ
FRAZ. SAN PIETRO DI BARBOZZA
VIA MONT DI CARTIZZE, 3
31040 VALDOBBIADENE (TV)
TEL. 0423975770
E-MAIL: tanore@tin.it

CORTE GARDONI
LOC. GARDONI, 5
37067 VALEGGIO SUL MINCIO (VR)
TEL. 0457950382
E-MAIL: cortegardoni@hotmail.com

Brothers Renato and Sergio Follador own this winery set in a splendid hillside position with vineyards in the heart of the Cartizze area at Santo Stefano, San Pietro and Guia. The excellent aspects of the vineyards, the particular type of subsoil and the site climates all help to create perfect conditions for growing the prosecco grape. The most impressive wines tasted were those with most residual sugar, which gives them more expressive aromas. The Prosecco Dry Selezione is pale straw yellow, with mature, vibrant aromas and a lively, supple palate that finds an excellent combination of acidity and sweetness. The beautiful finish is livened up by the stylish, balanced fizz. The Cartizze has a generous, mouthfilling palate with nicely integrated fizz and the long-lasting sweetness that is perfectly gauged. Its aromas are more fruit-based than floral, which promises well for the future. The Prosecco Extra Dry is utterly enjoyable, with appetizing appley aromas on the nose and a supple palate with only slightly aggressive prickle. The Prosecco Tranquillo is much more than just simply enjoyable, showing light floral notes and a well-balanced palate. The aromas are sometimes excessively simple on the taut, vibrant palate of the Prosecco Brut.

The Valeggio area along the river Mincio, with its glacial hills south of Lake Garda on the border between Veneto and Lombardy, has always been considered one of the most interesting for Bardolino production. This was a robust, vigorous wine back in the 1920s. Now that Bardolino Superiore type has been granted DOCG status, Valeggio is still a leader in quality production, thanks in part to the enthusiasm of Gianni Piccoli and his children, who are increasingly involved in the business. The 2001 vintage was the first to flaunt the DOCG neck sticker and Corte Gardoni's Bardolino Superiore points the way to a possible development of this type, blending style and character, and typical fruity fragrance and complex aromas with a sure hand. The vegetal hints and subtle notes of cyclamen, varietal raspberry, blackberry and cherry fruit are present on the nose, and then merge well on the palate. The Bardolino Le Fontane also has red berry fruit and grassy hints, and the mouthfeel is fresh and impressive, showing charmingly edgy, rather than powerful. The Chiaretto, on the other hand, is light-bodied and simpler. The nicely drinkable Becco Rosso is made from corvina grapes, the basis of Bardolino production, and the aromas offer ripe fruit and elegant geraniums. Turning to the whites, the Chardonnay has juicy ripe peach fruit whereas the Bianco di Custoza is more one-dimensional. The performance of the "passito" I Fenili is rather less good than on previous occasions.

O Cartizze	�♔	5
O Prosecco di V. Dry Sel.	♔♔	4
O Prosecco di V. Brut	♔	4
O Prosecco di V. Extra Dry	♔	4
O Prosecco di V. Tranquillo	♔	3*

● Bardolino Sup. '01	♔♔	4
● Bardolino Le Fontane '02	♔♔	3*
● Becco Rosso '01	♔	4
O Garda Chardonnay Vallidium '01	♔	4
☉ Bardolino Chiaretto '02	♔	3
O I Fenili '98		5
O Bianco di Custoza '02		3
O I Fenili '96	♔♔	5
O I Fenili '97	♔♔	5
● Bardolino Sup. '00	♔♔	3

VERONA

VERONA

CANTINA SOCIALE DELLA VALPANTENA
FRAZ. QUINTO
VIA COLONIA ORFANI DI GUERRA, 5/B
37100 VERONA
TEL. 045550032
E-MAIL: info@cantinavalpantena.it

CECILIA BERETTA
LOC. SAN FELICE EXTRA
VIA BELVEDERE, 135
37131 VERONA
TEL. 0458402111
E-MAIL: pasqua@pasqua.it

Luca Degani is the driving force behind this dynamic Verona co-operative, which year after year succeeds in producing a range of wines that just get better and better. One of Luca's wines got through to the final taste-offs for the first time, but that is just the tip of the quality iceberg at the Cantina Sociale della Valpantena. The Valpolicella Valpantena, Falasco and Ritocco are made in remarkably large quantities, sold at very reasonable prices and are surprisingly satisfying to drink. The winery could easily have pushed the most important wine, the Amarone, but the courageous and, we believe, far-sighted decision taken was to make Valpolicella the wine of the future. This is a wine of excellent quality, easily approachable and inexpensive. The best example is the Valpolicella Valpantena, which is rich in red berry fruit, easy-to-like and forthright. The palate is so moreish and satisfying that it will make even the most difficult-to-please drinker happy. The two Valpantenas, Falasco and Ritocco, are equally successful, and both are made using the "ripasso" technique of adding Amarone skins after fermentation. The former is rich with fresh fruit and promises to age well, whereas the Ritocco is even more accessible and enjoyable. The Recioto Tesauro is excellent, with impressive fruit and subtle boisé tones. The palate is richly extracted but highly drinkable. The two Amarones are both good, though we preferred the Valpantena, whose aromas are expressed more forthrightly.

After years in which the Pasqua family were unable to produce wines of a quality that matched their considerable efforts, they have now taken a huge step forward. Part of the credit must surely go to the vineyards, which are coming of age, but let us not forget the hard work of many individuals, the entire technical staff who transform the lovingly tended grapes into great wines. Our favourite was the Amarone Terre di Cariano, which finds a new dimension of aromatic finesse and elegant mouthfeel without sacrificing its soft notes of raisining fruit. The balsamic aromas open out at once into thyme, Alpine herbs and dried roses, giving way to healthy ripe fruit that hints at the generosity of the palate. And the palate is where the wine demonstrates its class. A confident entry develops with suppleness, strength and austerity, requiring no residual sugar to show off its texture, and leading into a long, charming finish. We are sure this wine has a radiant future ahead, and it fully deserves the Three Glasses it was awarded. Only slightly inferior is the Valpolicella Terre di Cariano, which has simpler, more approachable fruit and gradually unveils interesting floral hints. In this case, too, the wine aims for style and length, rather than strength. The rest of the wines are all good, from the Mizzole, a blend of merlot and corvina, to the Brognoligo Soave, and the Karah, a modern-style white made from garganega grapes.

● Recioto della Valpolicella Tesauro '00	♟♟	6
● Amarone della Valpolicella Valpantena '00	♟♟	5
● Valpantena Ripasso Falasco '01	♟♟	4
● Valpantena Ritocco '01	♟♟	4
● Valpantena Sup. '01	♟♟	4
● Recioto della Valpolicella Valpantena '01	♟	5
○ Bianco Garganega Falasco '02	♟	1*
● Corvina Falasco '02	♟	3
● Amarone della Valpolicella Falasco '99	♟	5
● Amarone della Valpolicella Falasco '98	♟♟	5

● Amarone della Valpolicella Cl. Terre di Cariano '99	♟♟♟	7
● Valpolicella Cl. Sup. Terre di Cariano '99	♟♟	4
● Mizzole Rosso '00	♟	4
○ Recioto di Soave Case Vecie '00	♟	6
○ Karah Bianco '02	♟	4
○ Soave Cl. Brognoligo '02	♟	4
● Amarone della Valpolicella Cl. Terre di Cariano '97	♟♟	7
● Amarone della Valpolicella Cl. Terre di Cariano '98	♟♟	7
○ Recioto di Soave Case Vecie '99	♟♟	5

VERONA

VERONA

GIACOMO MONTRESOR
VIA CA' DEI COZZI, 16
37124 VERONA
TEL. 045913399
E-MAIL: montres@tin.it

PASQUA VIGNETI E CANTINE
VIA BELVIGLIERI, 30
37131 VERONA
TEL. 0458402111
E-MAIL: pasqua@pasqua.it

This classic Verona winery has a history over a century long. The technical staff has recently been reinforced and in January Mirco Pozzobon, who has been here for six years, was joined by Vanessa Verdoni. Paolo Montresor's faith in their competence has been promptly rewarded by an improvement in quality throughout the range, which includes two outstanding new wines representing a modern interpretation of tradition, the Amarone and the Valpolicella Castelliere delle Guaite. These two very interesting wines are the standard-bearers of this traditional, well-established winery. Even the packaging shows the care taken in the preparation of the wines. The unusual, removable label offers space for you to note down your tasting impressions. Obviously, the most interesting part is inside the bottle, though. The Amarone has ripe red berry aromas that reveal fresh vegetal hints, then the palate is generous and juicy. The Valpolicella is also excellent. The fruit gives way gradually to floral and spicy aromas on the nose, followed by a fresh-tasting, long palate. The Lugana Gran Guardia is very enjoyable. Its aromas are still uncomplicated, but the ace up its sleeve is the palate. The rest of the range is absolutely reliable, especially the traditional wines from the Verona area.

The Pasqua family is rethinking marketing and production strategies, and demonstrating an attachment to the territory that we feared they had lost. Our impressions during our visit in June have been confirmed by a resizing of the range, sacrificing about 3,000,000 bottles of the lowest quality wine, as well as renewed effort in finishing the new cellar, and an improvement in the quality of the flagship wines. What is even more impressive is that the less prestigious wines are improving as well, and good modern-style wines have been introduced. These are excellent value for money. The leaders are the Valpolicellas, especially the Sagramoso, made from grapes from the extended Valpolicella area. No raisining or "ripasso" is used and the deep fruity note denotes skilful use of wood. Firm and richly extracted on the palate, it is also supple, with pleasantly balanced tannin, alcohol and acidity. The Valpolicella Villa Borghetti is equally interesting, and the notes of over-ripe fruit hint at closer links to tradition. The Morago Appassimento is an excellent Cabernet Sauvignon made from lightly raisined grapes, which give it sweetness and depth. The palate is warm and alluring, with lovely aromatic herbs in the finale. The other wines in the range are all made to a high standard, from the simple Soave Sagramoso to the Kòrae, a 100 per cent corvina in a fragrant, modern idiom.

● Amarone della Valpolicella Cl.		
Castelliere delle Guaite '98	�♙	8
● Valpolicella Cl. Primo Ripasso		
Castelliere delle Guaite '99	♙♙	6
● Recioto della Valpolicella		
Re Teodorico '00	♙	6
● Santomío Rosso '00	♙	6
● Valpolicella Cl. Capitel della Crosara '01	♙	4
○ Bianco di Custoza		
Vigneto Monte Fiera '02	♙	4
○ Lugana Gran Guardia '02	♙	4
○ Sauvignon Sansaia '02	♙	4
○ Soave Cl. Capitel Alto '02	♙	4
● Amarone della Valpolicella Cl.		
Capitel della Crosara '98	♙♙	7

● Valpolicella Sup. Sagramoso '00	♙♙	5
● Valpolicella Cl. Sup. Villa Borghetti '01	♙♙	4
● Morago Appassimento '99	♙♙	6
● Valpolicella Sup.		
Sagramoso Ripasso '00	♙	5
● Kòrae Rosso '01	♙	4
○ Soave Cl.		
Vigneti di Montegrande '02	♙	4
○ Soave Sup. Sagramoso '02	♙	3
● Amarone della Valpolicella Cl.		
Villa Borghetti '99	♙	7
● Amarone della Valpolicella Cl.		
Villa Borghetti '97	♙♙	6
● Amarone della Valpolicella Cl.		
Villa Borghetti '98	♙♙	6

VERONA

TEZZA
LOC. POIANO
VIA MAIOLI, 4
37030 VERONA
TEL. 045550267
E-MAIL: info@tezzawines.it

Tezza is turning out to be one of the most interesting wineries in the extended Valpolicella context, and the brothers are gradually converting the vineyard holding to training systems more suitable for high quality production. Today, their energy is a little dissipated over the large range of wines, but even a quick tasting is enough to show that Flavio, Vanio and Federico are doing their best. The wines express the warm territory in a modern interpretation of tradition, using all that technology can offer and plenty of barrique ageing. The results are very good indeed, starting with the sumptuous Amarone Monte delle Fontane. Deep and generous on the nose, it shows ripe red berry fruit enhanced by well-judged boisé nuances. The potent palate is very stylish, and the mouthfeel is perked up by a vein of acidity. The Recioto Brolo delle Giare is only slightly inferior. The approachable, pervasive nose hints at dried fruit sensations, then the palate is rich and well sustained, with a nice floral element and commendable balance. The two Valpolicellas are good, although they lack the candour and balance of the Amarone and the Recioto. The Cabernet Sauvignon is reliable and varietal in its spectrum of aromatics, although at the moment there is still too much wood.

VIDOR (TV)

ADAMI
FRAZ. COLBERTALDO
VIA ROVEDE, 27
31020 VIDOR (TV)
TEL. 0423982110
E-MAIL: adamispumanti@tin.it

Talking to Franco Adami is a little like taking a journey through the vineyards and history of Valdobbiadene. He always reduces any problem concerning the growing year, harvest or vinification to disarmingly simple terms. There's nature, and there's man – that is Adami's way of thinking – and the latter must produce the best possible expression of whatever the former offers, with no tricks or deception. There are certainly none in the wines made by Franco and his brother Armando. In 2002, the Prosecco area was spared the hailstorms that brought other areas to their knees, and the results were actually very good, although difficult to interpret. The wines are particularly rich in salts, and thus needed to be unusually balanced on the palate to acquire length and freshness, and avoid flabbiness. Skilful work on the base sparkling wines has enabled this Vidor winery to make a memorable range of wines, starting with the house selection. Giardino is more generous and juicy this year than ever before, with a full, exciting range of aromas. The nose has enjoyably well-defined apple, pear and peach fruit, while the palate has perfectly integrated sparkle and a long, nicely defined finish. The other sparkling wines are as excellent as usual, from the long-lasting, fresh-tasting Brut to the lively, creamy Cartizze, and the classy, potent Extra Dry. The Prosecco Tranquillo is especially well managed, like the traditional Sur Lie, which hints at ancient winemaking wisdom in a modern style.

● Recioto della Valpolicella		
Valpantena Brolo delle Giare '00	♈♈	5
● Amarone della Valpolicella		
Monte delle Fontane '99	♈♈	6
● Cabernet Sauvignon		
Terre di Pojan '00	♈	5
● Valpolicella Valpantena Sup.		
Brolo delle Giare '00	♈	5
● Valpolicella Valpantena Sup.		
Monte delle Fontane '00	♈	4
○ Passito Monte delle Fontane '00	♈♈	5
● Amarone della Valpolicella		
Brolo delle Giare '98	♈♈	5

○ Prosecco di V. Dry		
Giardino '02	♈♈	4
○ Cartizze	♈♈	5
○ Prosecco di V.		
Bosco di Gica Brut	♈♈	4
○ Prosecco di V. Extra Dry		
dei Casel	♈♈	4
○ Incrocio Manzoni 6.0.13		
Le Portelle '02	♈	4
○ Prosecco di V. Tranquillo		
Giardino '02	♈	4
○ Prosecco di V. Sur Lie	♈	4
○ Prosecco di V. Dry		
Giardino '01	♈♈	3

VIDOR (TV)

VILLAGA (VI)

SORELLE BRONCA
FRAZ. COLBERTALDO
VIA MARTIRI, 20
31020 VIDOR (TV)
TEL. 0423987201
E-MAIL: info@sorellebronca.com

PIOVENE PORTO GODI
FRAZ. TOARA
VIA VILLA, 14
36020 VILLAGA (VI)
TEL. 0444885142
E-MAIL: tpiovene@protec.it

Piero Balcon is a scrupulous, tireless grower who does not let go until he is sure he has perfect control of the situation. His passion for wine translates into a committed effort to improve his own products. The results get more impressive by the year. Piero's working relationship with Federico Giotto is also bringing innovation to the winery, not so much in terms of new wines as in improved quality. The Colli di Conegliano Rosso 2000 comes from a good growing year, and this shows as soon as you see it in the glass. It is ruby red, with fragrant aromas of wild berries, damp earth and spices, that return deliciously on the palate. The dense tannic weave and vibrant acidity make it long and enjoyably rugged. The Colli Bianco 2002, from now on to be known as Delico, is as good as the previous year. The lively, fresh palate combines good extract with elegant style. Ersiliana and Antonella Bronca have made a new sparkler from a plot renowned for its wine potential, planted to old, and relatively unproductive prosecco clones. The aromas of ripe, deep, fresh fruit precede unusually good structure and length on the palate. The unique nature of this vineyard is reflected in its name, Particella 68. The other sparkling wines all performed well, especially the Brut, which is full and juicy on the palate, where the acidity and bubbles come together in a lovely balance.

Toara is a magical spot in the Colli Berici with evidence of a glorious past. There are also some magnificent vineyards that have been lovingly tended over the years, and enthusiastically replanted in the knowledge that to recreate the prestige of the past, the winery must work to modern criteria. As for the wines themselves, there are two good whites from 2002, which was a difficult year hereabouts, as elsewhere. The Pinot Bianco and the Sauvignon Fostine are both warm and easy drinking. The Pinot Bianco is more floral whereas its stablemate is minerally and varietal. The Tocai Rosso Riveselle has faint aromas of pepper, nutmeg and fresh cherries on the nose, then a palate that is more stylish and assertive than recent versions, although it has lost a little texture. The Rosso Polveriera benefits from the inclusion of the classic Bordeaux varieties, and seems dominated by youthfully lively merlot. The Merlot Fra I Broli is still a little masked by oak, but has aromas of cherry jam, spices and freshly mown grass on the nose, then a chewy, well-rounded palate. The second release of Thovara is the best wine we tasted, with complex, deep sensations in which the fruit blends with subtle mineral and spice hints. The palate is both rugged and stylish, and we are sure it will find perfect balance with a few years' ageing. Lastly, the Cabernet Pozzare is not ready yet, so we will hold fire until next year.

● Colli di Conegliano Rosso Ser Bele '00	▼▼	6
○ Colli di Conegliano Bianco Delico '02	▼▼	4*
○ Prosecco di V. Brut	▼▼	4*
○ Prosecco di V. Extra Dry Particella 68	▼▼	4*
● Piave Cabernet Ardesco '01	▼	4
○ Prosecco di V. Extra Dry	▼	4
● Colli di Conegliano Rosso Ser Bele '97	▼▼	6
● Colli di Conegliano Rosso Ser Bele '98	▼▼	6
● Colli di Conegliano Rosso Ser Bele '99	▼▼	6

● Colli Berici Tocai Rosso Thovara '01	▼▼	6
● Colli Berici Merlot Fra i Broli '01	▼▼	5
○ Colli Berici Pinot Bianco Polveriera '02	▼	3
○ Colli Berici Sauvignon Vigneto Fostine '02	▼	4
● Colli Berici Tocai Rosso Vigneto Riveselle '02	▼	3
● Polveriera Rosso '02	▼	4
● Colli Berici Cabernet Vigneto Pozzare '00	▼▼	5
● Colli Berici Merlot Fra i Broli '00	▼▼	5
● Colli Berici Tocai Rosso Thovara '00	▼▼	6

OTHER WINERIES

Giorgio Poggi

via Poggi, 7
37010 Affi (VR)
tel. 0457236222
e-mail: info@cantinepoggi.com

About 80 hectares of Giorgio Poggi's attractively situated estate are planted to vine. Most of the many wines are made from traditional Garda grapes. The Merlot Naker is good and the Bardolino Superiore Campi Regi is richly extracted, without losing its traditional lightness in the mouth.

●	Bardolino Sup. Campi Regi '01	🍷	4
●	Garda Merlot '01	🍷	3
●	Garda Merlot Naker '99	🍷	4

Lenotti

via S. Cristina, 1
37011 Bardolino (VR)
tel. 0457210484
e-mail: info@lenotti.com

From its large vineyard holding, this Garda winery makes some excellent wines, particularly Bardolino, the emblematic wine of this area. The Superiore Le Olle is one of the best of its type. The richly extracted palate is rendered supple by the nice balance.

●	Bardolino Cl. Sup. Le Olle '01	🍷🍷	4
O	Soave Cl. Capocolle '02	🍷	3
●	Amarone della Valpolicella Cl. '99	🍷	6

Valetti

fraz. Calmasino - via Pragrande, 8
37010 Bardolino (VR)
tel. 0457235075
e-mail: valetti@valetti.it

Moving east from Lake Garda, you come to the Valetti winery at Calmasino. The list focuses on traditional Garda wines, especially Bardolino. The Cabernet Sauvgnon Pardàli came close to Two Glasses while the Bianco di Custoza and Bardolino Superiore are enjoyable and well balanced.

●	Bardolino Cl. Sup. '01	🍷	3
●	Pardàli Cabernet Sauvignon '01	🍷	3*
O	Bianco di Custoza '02	🍷	2*

Villabella

fraz. Calmasino - loc. Ca' Nova, 1
37010 Bardolino (VR)
tel. 0456260655
e-mail: info@vignetivillabella.com

The Delibori and Cristoforetti families manage 350 hectares of vineyards, 200 estate-owned. The best grapes go into Villabella wines, with help from Luca D'Attoma. In the wide-ranging, reliably good range, the stand-outs are the fruit-led, weighty Bardolino and the two very well-made Valpolicellas.

●	Bardolino Cl. Sup. Terre di Cavagion '01	🍷🍷	4*
●	Valpolicella Cl. I Roccoli '01	🍷	4
●	Valpolicella Cl. Sup. Ripasso '99	🍷	4

CANTINA BEATO BARTOLOMEO DA BREGANZE
VIA ROMA, 100
36042 BREGANZE (VI)
TEL. 0445873112

This large Breganze winery plans to make premium-quality wines from a new property. The good Cabernet Sauvignon Kilò impressed us in previous versions and it is joined by the impressively well-orchestrated Merlot Bosco Grande. The enjoyable Torcolato has fresh, light sensations.

● Breganze Cabernet Sauvignon Kilò Ris. '00	♥♥	5
○ Breganze Torcolato '00	♥	6
● Merlot Bosco Grande '01	♥	4

AGOSTINO VICENTINI
FRAZ. SAN ZENO - VIA C. BATTISTI, 62/C
37030 COLOGNOLA AI COLLI (VR)
TEL. 0457650539
E-MAIL: vicentiniagostino@libero.it

Vicentini is an attractive winery on the border of the Soave and Valpolicella DOC zones. The wines of both DOCs are generally good. We recommend the confident, flavoursome, dry Soave, the peppery, well-orchestrated Valpolicella 2002 and the potent Valpolicella Superiore.

○ Soave Vigneto Terrelunghe '02	♥	3
● Valpolicella Vigneto Boccascalucce '02	♥	3
● Valpolicella Sup. Idea Bacco '99	♥	4

CARPENÈ MALVOLTI
VIA ANTONIO CARPENÈ, 1
31015 CONEGLIANO (TV)
TEL. 0438364611
E-MAIL: info@carpene-malvolti.com

This large Conegliano winery has played a crucial role in perfecting Prosecco-making techniques and is still a benchmark estate today. We enjoyed and very much recommend the Cuvée Oro, a stylish, lingering Prosecco Extra Dry.

○ Prosecco di C. Extra Dry Cuvée Oro	♥♥	4*

COLLALBRIGO
LOC. COLLALBRIGO - VIA MARSIGLION, 77
31015 CONEGLIANO (TV)
TEL. 0438455229
E-MAIL: info@collalbrigo.com

With the help of Luca D'Attoma, Tenuta Collalbrigo has begun to improve all its products and the wines are already reacting positively. The Prosecco Brut made an excellent impression, and the strongpoint of the Rosso di Collalbrigo and Merlot is great structure and balance.

● Colli di Conegliano Rosso Collalbrigo '00	♥	4
● Il Merlot '00	♥	4
○ Prosecco di C. Brut	♥	3

G. B. CERLETTI
SCUOLA ENOLOGICA DI CONEGLIANO
VIA ZAMBONI, 20
31015 CONEGLIANO (TV)
TEL. 043861524 - 0438453017

As well as Prosecco di Conegliano, the Scuola Enologica makes an interesting, varied range of local wines. The fruity, vibrantly well-structured Colli di Conegliano Rosso, the sound Manzoni Liquoroso, from unusual varieties, and the impressively well-structured, tangy Incrocio Manzoni are all good.

● Colli di Conegliano Rosso '00	♥	6
● Incrocio Manzoni 2.15 '01	♥	4
☉ Manzoni Liquoroso '02	♥	4
○ Prosecco di C. Extra Dry	♥	3*

VILLA SANDI
LOC. NOGARE - VIA ERIZZO, 112
31035 CROCETTA DEL MONTELLO (TV)
TEL. 0423665033
E-MAIL: info@villasandi.it

There's a new wine on the list, thanks to the working relationship with Riccardo Cotarella. It's Corpore, a merlot-heavy blend with full, enthralling aromas, and gradually expanding flavours on the palate. The Marinali Bianco and Marinali Rosso are reliably good, if not quite so impressive.

● Corpore '01	♥♥	6
● Marinali Rosso '00	♥	5
○ Marinali Bianco '01	♥	5

ANDREOLA ORSOLA
LOC. COL SAN MARTINO
VIA CAL LONGA, 52
31010 FARRA DI SOLIGO (TV)
TEL. 0438989379

This winery's products are less impressive this year, probably because of the difficult growing year. For the time being, we like the varietal Prosecco Extra Dry Dirupo and the Prosecco Tranquillo Romit, which is simple but fresh tasting and satisfyingly drinkable.

O	Prosecco di V. Extra Dry Dirupo	♀	3
O	Prosecco di V. Tranquillo Romit	♀	3

MEROTTO
FRAZ. COL S. MARTINO
VIA TREVISET, 86
31010 FARRA DI SOLIGO (TV)
TEL. 0438898195

Graziano Merotto has worked with his growers for many years, which enables him to obtain good quality grapes to make his very good range of sparkling wines. The three wines we preferred from the wide range are noted below. Average annual production is 500,000 bottles a year.

O	Prosecco di V. Extra Dry Colbelo	♀♀	4
O	Prosecco di V. Dry '02	♀	5
O	Prosecco di V. Brut Barreta	♀	4

SANTA MARGHERITA
VIA ITA MARZOTTO, 8
30025 FOSSALTA DI PORTOGRUARO (VE)
TEL. 0421246111
E-MAIL: santamargherita@stmargherita.com

This large Portogruaro winery can turn out a vast range of well-made wines at interesting prices. The Alto Adige wines are good, especially the Pinot Nero and the vibrant Pinot Bianco. The Merlot is supple and varietal, and the fresh-tasting Pinot Grigio is substantial.

●	A. A. Pinot Nero '01	♀	4
●	Versato Merlot del Veneto '01	♀	4
O	A. A. Pinot Bianco '02	♀	4*
O	Valdadige Pinot Grigio '02	♀	4

I SCRIANI
LOC. FUMANTE - VIA PONTE SCRIVAN, 7
37022 FUMANE (VR)
TEL. 0456839093 - 0456839251
E-MAIL: scriani@libero.it

This Fumane winery continues to prove that small wineries can also make quality wines. All you need are vineyards, commitment and a well-equipped cellar. The range is very good, especially the generous, lively Recioto, The Amarone and Valpolicella are both well structured and enjoyable.

●	Recioto della Valpolicella Cl. Maddalena '00	♀♀	6
●	Valpolicella Cl. Sup. Ripasso '00	♀	4
●	Amarone della Valpolicella Cl. '99	♀	6

LE BERTAROLE
VIA BERTAROLE, 8/A
37022 FUMANE (VR)
TEL. 0456839220
E-MAIL: az.bertarole@tiscalinet.it

We appreciated this winery's remarkably well put-together Valpolicella Superiore, with its supple palate and generous personality. The Amarone has good texture, acidity and a fairly long, harmonious finish. Both are representative of traditional local wines.

●	Valpolicella Cl. Sup. Le Portarine '01	♀♀	4*
●	Amarone della Valpolicella Cl. Vigneto Le Marognole '99	♀	6

VILLA BRUNESCA
VIA SERENISSIMA, 12
31040 GORGO AL MONTICANO (TV)
TEL. 0422800026
E-MAIL: villabrunesca@villabrunesca.it

The estate's 45 hectares are looked after with great passion. The Sauvignon is varietal and the Cabernet Vigna Tilia generous and well structured. The "passito" Bacchico is an interesting blend of traminer, incrocio Manzoni and verduzzo dorato. We also recommend the fresh-tasting, clean Refosco.

O	Bacchico Passito '01	♀	5
●	Piave Cabernet Vigna Tilia '01	♀	4
●	Refosco P. R. '02	♀	3
O	Sauvignon '02	♀	3

Monte Tabor

loc. Monte Tabor - via Sammonte, 45
37031 Illasi (VR)
tel. 0457830511

Monte Tabor is owned by Milan's San Raffaele hospital and farmed using exclusively organic techniques. The Valpolicella Superiore put on an excellent performance, showing subtly enjoyable and weighty. The Amarone deserves One Glass now but holds much promise for future improvement.

● Valpolicella Sup. San Raffaele '99	🍷🍷	5
● Amarone della Valpolicella San Raffaele '99	🍷	8

Lamberti

via Gardesana
37017 Lazise (VR)
tel. 0457580034
e-mail: giv@giv.it

Over 75,000,000 bottles a year come from this large Veronese winery's 170 part owned and part rented hectares. The carefully gauged quality and price of the wines are targeted at the mass market. We recommend the fragrant Bianco di Custoza, the juicy Bardolino and the concentrated Valpolicella.

● Bardolino Cl. Santepietre '02	🍷	4
○ Bianco di Custoza Orchidea Platino '02	🍷	4
● Valpolicella Cl. Santepietre '02	🍷	4

Le Tende

fraz. Colà - loc. Le Tende
37010 Lazise (VR)
tel. 0457590748
e-mail: info@letende.it

This small Lazise winery is committed to making local wines, with the occasional excursion into international territory. The very sound Bianco di Custoza Oro almost won Two Glasses while the Cabernet Sauvignon Cicisbeo and the Bardolino Classico are enjoyable and nicely balanced.

● Bardolino Cl. Sup. '01	🍷	3
● Garda Cabernet Sauvignon Cicisbeo '01	🍷	4
○ Bianco di Custoza Oro '02	🍷	3

La Giaretta

fraz. Valgatara
via del Platano, 6
37020 Marano di Valpolicella (VR)
tel. 0457701791

Francesco Vaona runs this winery, which produces very well-made Valpolicellas and Amarones with plenty of personality. We recommend I Quadretti Valpolicella, which is deep, but shows distinct oak, an enjoyable Valpolicella Superiore and a well-typed, varietal Amarone.

● Valpolicella Cl. Sup. I Quadretti '00	🍷	5
● Amarone della Valpolicella Cl. '99	🍷	6
● Valpolicella Cl. Sup. '99	🍷	4

Amistani Guarda

loc. Pederiva - via Lauretana, 7
31044 Montebelluna (TV)
tel. 0423603722

The winery, taken over by Mionetto in 2001, makes wines from classic red grape Bordeaux varieties, as well as a white "passito". The Cabernet and Merlot, both from the Montello e Colli Asolani DOC, are interesting, as is the flavoursome Ognissanti with its well-balanced sweetness.

● Montello e Colli Asolani Cabernet '00	🍷	4
● Montello e Colli Asolani Merlot '00	🍷	4
○ Ognissanti Passito '01	🍷	6

Cantina di Montecchia

via Alpone, 53
37030 Montecchia di Crosara (VR)
tel. 0457450094
e-mail: cantina@cantinadimontecchia.com

Abele Casagrande achieves increasingly impressive results at Cantina di Montecchia, thanks to ever closer quality-oriented collaboration with member growers. There were good performances again from the Re d'Aurum and the Soave Ca' Vecchie with its fruity nose and firm palate.

○ Monti Lessini Bianco Re d'Aurum '01	🍷	6
○ Soave Cl. Ca' Vecchie I Fossili '02	🍷	2*

BRUNO MARTINELLI
VIA MATTEOTTI, 18
37032 MONTEFORTE D'ALPONE (VR)
TEL. 0456100867

This small, emerging winery in the Monteforte area makes two versions of Soave. The Valentina is aged in oak and its subtle, delicate aromas are echoed on the firm, mouthfilling palate: Two full Glasses. The Classico is simpler and more straightforward, but equally satisfying.

○ Soave Cl. Sup. Valentina '01	♟♟	4
○ Soave Cl. '02	♟	3

CANTINA SOCIALE
DI MONTEFORTE D'ALPONE
VIA XX SETTEMBRE, 24
37032 MONTEFORTE D'ALPONE (VR)
TEL. 0457610110

This co-operative only bottles a few of its wines, with increasingly impressive results. Soave Il Vicario is outstanding. A vibrant wine with a vast range of aromas, it is generous and beautifully balanced on the palate. The Soave Clivus is simpler, and the Durello Metodo Classico enjoyable.

○ Soave Cl. Clivus '02	♟	2*
○ Soave Cl. Il Vicario '02	♟	3*
○ Lessini Durello M. Cl.	♟	4

CASA VINICOLA SARTORI
VIA CASETTE, 2
37024 NEGRAR (VR)
TEL. 0456028011
E-MAIL: sartori@sartorinet.com

Franco Bernabei has joined this large Negrar winery, bringing a blast of innovation. The Valpolicella Montegradella is already benefiting from the new style, with its vibrant fruit and autumn leaf aromas. The rest of the range is good, and we liked the austere, no-nonsense, traditional Amarone.

● Valpolicella Cl. Sup.		
Montegradella '00	♟♟	4*
● Amarone della Valpolicella Cl. '99	♟	6

ITALO CESCON
FRAZ. RONCADELLE - P.ZZA DEI CADUTI, 3
31024 ORMELLE (TV)
TEL. 0422851033
E-MAIL: enoteca.cascon@libero.it

The Cescon family winery makes wines from the generous, but often over-exploited Piave DOC. Careful vineyard management and gentle winemaking produce bottles with plenty of personality, like the vibrant, balanced Raboso. The Chardonnay and Incrocio Manzoni are also well made.

○ Incrocio Manzoni 6.0.13 '02	♟	4
○ Piave Chardonnay La Cesura '02	♟	4
● Piave Raboso La Cesura '98	♟	5

MARTINO ZANETTI
VIA CHISINI, 79
31053 PIEVE DI SOLIGO (TV)
TEL. 0438841608
E-MAIL: casebianche@online.it

Martino Zanetti's winery has been here for years, and continues to make good wines with personality and a strong sense of place. The Camoi is a nicely interpreted, complex, well-orchestrated Bordeaux blend and the Prosecco Vigna del Cuc has interesting structure.

● Camoi Col Sandago '00	♟	5
○ Prosecco di C. Brut		
Vigna del Cuc Case Bianche	♟	4

TENUTA TERACREA
LOC. LISON - VIA ATTIGLIANA, 61
30020 PORTOGRUARO (VE)
TEL. 0421287041 - 0421287900
E-MAIL: tenuta.teracrea@libero.it

At Tenuta Teracrea, Giuseppe, or "Bepi", Bigai maintains a solid link with the past. His wines may set people talking but you can't ignore them. We recommend his flagship wine, the vibrantly salty, tangy Tocai, with its opulent palate. The Malvasia is rugged with plenty of personality.

○ Lison-Pramaggiore		
Tocai Italico '02	♟♟	3*
○ Malvasia del Veneto '02	♟	3

Corte Lenguin
via Ca' dell'Ebreo, 5
37029 San Pietro in Cariano (VR)
tel. 0457701406

Corte Lenguin wines are getting better. Silvio and Lorenzo Vantini run the estate's 13 hectares, making traditional wines, above all a sumptuous Recioto with rich dried fruit and flowers, and a simple, faultlessly made Amarone La Masua. We also recommend the well-typed, standard-label Amarone '99.

- ● Recioto della Valpolicella Cl. '00 🍷🍷 6
- ● Amarone della Valpolicella Cl. '99 🍷 5
- ● Amarone della Valpolicella Cl. La Masua '99 🍷 6

Giuseppe Fornaser
fraz. Bure - via Bure Alto, 1
37029 San Pietro in Cariano (VR)
tel. 0457701651
e-mail: info@montefaustino.com

The Fornaser brothers' small winery has four hectares in the Valpolicella Classico zone, and makes about 25,000 bottles a year. These are very small numbers, considering that the wines are consistently high in quality, especially those made from dried grapes.

- ● Amarone della Valpolicella Cl. Monte Faustino '98 🍷🍷 8
- ● Recioto della Valpolicella Cl. Monte Faustino '99 🍷 6

Marchesi Fumanelli
fraz. San Floriano Valpolicella
loc. Squarano
37020 San Pietro in Cariano (VR)
tel. 0457704875

Armando Pirola runs this splendid 90-hectare winery in the Valpolicella Classico DOC, obtaining excellent results from his working relationship with the Zymè group. The Valpolicella Squarano has deep aromas and an austere palate. The white Terso is rich textured and mouthfilling.

- ● Valpolicella Cl. Sup. Squarano '00 🍷🍷 5
- ○ Terso Bianco '01 🍷 5

Villa Giona
loc. Cengia - via Cengia, 8
37029 San Pietro in Cariano (VR)
tel. 0456855011
e-mail: villagiona@villagiona.it

The first version of this sumptuous red comes from a five-hectare vineyard planted to cabernet sauvignon, merlot and syrah at a density of 9,000 plants per hectare. Intoxicating aromas of wild berries, pepper and pencil lead on the nose precede a balanced palate. You'll hear more about this wine.

- ● Villa Giona '00 🍷🍷 6

Aleardo Ferrari
fraz. Gargagnago - via Giare, 15
37020 Sant'Ambrogio di Valpolicella (VR)
tel. 0457701379

Scrupulous vineyard management is the starting point for the interesting Valpolicella Montepalà, obtained from a vineyard specifically set aside for this wine type, instead of being deprived of its best grapes to make Amarone. The Recioto and Amarone are fragrant and characterful.

- ● Amarone della Valpolicella Cl. '98 🍷🍷 7
- ● Valpolicella Cl. Sup. Montepalà '00 🍷 5
- ● Recioto della Valpolicella Cl. '01 🍷 5

Mosole
via Annone Veneto, 60
30029 Santo Stino di Livenza (VE)
tel. 0421310404
e-mail: mosole@mosole.com

Lucio Mosole has been involved in relaunching the little-known Lison-Pramaggiore DOC for some years. With his 30 hectares of vineyards, and plenty of enthusiasm, he makes a range that focuses on 2002 wines, plus an interesting Cabernet, Hora Sexta, which is aged in oak.

- ● Lison-Pramaggiore Cabernet Hora Sexta '00 🍷 5
- ● Lison-Pramaggiore Merlot '02 🍷 4
- ○ Lison-Pramaggiore Sauvignon '02 🍷 4

RONCOLATO
VIA CARCERA, 21
37038 SOAVE (VR)
TEL. 0457675104
E-MAIL: antonioroncolato@libero.it

Roncolato's wines are released as Soave and Valpolicella DOCs. The Soave Monteleon is excellent, and the cask-conditioned Nicolaio is only slightly inferior. The white Capel del Prete is deep and minerally and the Amarone has plenty of texture, as well as some room for improvement.

○	Soave Cl. Monteleon '02	♟♟	3*
○	Capel del Prete '01	♟	4
○	Soave Cl. Il Nicolaio '01	♟	3
●	Amarone della Valpolicella '98	♟	6

ALBINO PIONA
FRAZ. CUSTOZA - VIA BELLAVISTA, 48
37060 SOMMACAMPAGNA (VR)
TEL. 045516055
E-MAIL: silvio.piona@tin.it

Albino Piona makes a selection of good quality wines at interesting prices from the glacial hills around Lake Garda. The Bianco di Custoza Campo del Sèlese is especially well made, with rich varietal notes in a well-orchestrated flavour. The Bardolino and Passito are both well typed.

○	Bianco di Custoza Sup.		
	Campo del Sèlese '01	♟♟	4
○	La Rabitta Passito Bianco '00	♟	6
●	Bardolino '02	♟	3

IL CARDO
FRAZ. SANTO STEFANO - VIA CAL LONGA, 11
31040 VALDOBBIADENE (TV)
TEL. 0423900295
E-MAIL: vini.ilcardo@libero.it

Silvano and Alberta Follador run this small Valdobbiadene winery with passion, making about 45,000 bottles a year of good wines from vineyards situated in the best subzones of the DOC. Elegant aromas are their main feature, as we realize after tasting the Proseccos and the sound Cartizze.

○	Prosecco di V. Extra Dry	♟♟	3*
○	Cartizze	♟	5
○	Prosecco di V. Brut	♟	3*
○	Prosecco di V. Tranquillo	♟	4

CASA COSTE PIANE
FRAZ. SANTO STEFANO
VIA COSTE PIANE, 2
31040 VALDOBBIADENE (TV)
TEL. 0423900219

Before the cuve close method became popular, sparkling wines underwent bottle fermentation to make moderately sparkling wines with some sediment. Today, Loris Follador is the best exponent of this type. His wines have aromas of fermentation and flowers, and irresistibly dynamic palates.

○	Prosecco di V. Frizzante		
	Sur Lie	♟♟	3*
○	Prosecco di V. Extra Dry		
	San Venanzio	♟	4

SPUMANTI VALDO
VIA FORO BOARIO, 20
31049 VALDOBBIADENE (TV)
TEL. 04239090
E-MAIL: info@valdo.com

This large Valdobbiadene winery makes over 5,000,000 bottles a year, about 20 per cent in the Prestige line, which includes the most interesting products. The Cuvée di Boj is fresh tasting and varietal, while the Cuvée del Fondatore, available a year after the harvest, is rich and mouthfilling.

○	Prosecco di V. Brut		
	Cuvée del Fondatore	♟	4
○	Prosecco di V. Brut		
	Cuvée di Boj	♟	4

CORTE MARZAGO
LOC. LE BUGNE
37067 VALEGGIO SUL MINCIO (VR)
TEL. 0457945104
E-MAIL: info@cortemarzago.com

Lorenzo Fabiano's little winery is one of the most interesting in the Lake Garda area. Lorenzo is committed to the new Bardolino Superiore, and one of its top exponents. Red berry and earthy aromas meld with extract on the light palate. The Bianco di Custoza is pleasantly well typed.

●	Bardolino Sup.		
	Le Bine Vecchie '01	♟♟	3*
○	Bianco di Custoza Sup.		
	Vigna Le Battistine '02	♟	3*

BONOTTO DELLE TEZZE
FRAZ. TEZZE DI PIAVE
VIA DUCA D'AOSTA, 16
31020 VAZZOLA (TV)
TEL. 0438488323

The large Piave plain produces large quantities of wine but also high quality, as long as the vineyards are well treated. Which is what happens at this small but promising winery, as demonstrated by the intriguing Manzoni Bianco, the fresh-tasting Sauvignon and the deep, no-nonsense Raboso.

○	Manzoni Bianco Novalis '01	♥♥	4*
○	Sauvignon Montesanto '01	♥	4
●	Piave Raboso La Potestà '99	♥	6

GIORGIO CECCHETTO
FRAZ. TEZZE DI PIAVE - VIA PIAVE, 67
31020 VAZZOLA (TV)
TEL. 043828598
E-MAIL: info@rabosopiave.com

Giorgio Cecchetto continues to be committed to his favourite variety, raboso, at his modern, well-equipped winery in the vast, generous Piave area. As well as the traditional version, he makes the interesting Gelsaia from dried grapes. The Cabernet and Manzoni Bianco are both good.

●	Piave Raboso Gelsaia '00	♥	6
○	Manzoni Bianco '02	♥	2*
●	Piave Cabernet Sauvignon '02	♥	2*
●	Piave Raboso '99	♥	4

F.LLI BOLLA
P.ZZA CITTADELLA, 3
37122 VERONA
TEL. 0458090911 - 0456836555
E-MAIL: bolla@bolla.it

This large, traditional Verona winery has begun to improve its wines. The results are already clear in the complex Recioto, with its vibrant red berry fruit on the nose and well-judged sweetness. The Amarone Le Origini is austere and vibrant, and the Amarone '99 is simpler but characterful.

●	Recioto della Valpolicella Cl. '01	♥♥	5
●	Amarone della Valpolicella Cl. Le Origini '98	♥	7
●	Amarone della Valpolicella Cl. '99	♥	7

POGGIO TOCCALTA
VIA ARE / ZOVO, 16/B
37027 VERONA
TEL. 0458345559
E-MAIL: glt75@libero.it

This Quinzano winery has been active in the Verona area for over a century, making classic local wines which favour character over perfection. The Valpolicella Superiore is interesting, fruity and weighty, the Amarone is well-typed and the Valpolicella 2002 is enjoyably fresh tasting.

●	Valpolicella Sup. '01	♥♥	5
●	Amarone della Valpolicella '00	♥	7
●	Valpolicella '02	♥	4

DE FAVERI
FRAZ. BOSCO - VIA SARTORI, 21
31020 VIDOR (TV)
TEL. 0423987673
E-MAIL: defaverispumanti@libero.it

Lucio and Mirella Faveri's winery is situated at Bosco, and they are assisted by their children Giorgia and Giordano. Their main product is good quality sparkling wine with beautifully managed refermentation. The Brut is fruity and the Extra Dry and Tranquillo are subtle and even.

○	Prosecco di V. Brut	♥♥	3*
○	Prosecco di V. Extra Dry	♥	3
○	Prosecco di V. Tranquillo	♥	3

CONTE LOREDAN GASPARINI VENEGAZZÙ
FRAZ. VENEGAZZÙ
VIA MARTIGNAGO ALTO, 23
31040 VOLPAGO DEL MONTELLO (TV)
TEL. 0423870024

This traditional Venegazzù winery is pumping up the quality. Lorenzo Palla's enthusiasm is bearing fruit and the wines are more impressive than in previous years. The Venegazzù della Casa almost won Two Glasses, while the Capo di Stato and the Falconera Rosso were very successful.

●	Venegazzù della Casa '00	♥	5
●	Falconera Rosso '01	♥	5
●	Capo di Stato '99	♥	7

FRIULI VENEZIA GIULIA

We shall begin by extending the condolences of winelovers everywhere to the region for the number of sad losses that Friulian winemaking has suffered over the past year. Here, we would like to remember the passing of historic figures such as Douglas S. Attems, founder and first president of the Collio DOC consortium, Tullio Zamò, founder of a winery that has always striven to make the very finest wines, Doro Princic, the shrewd countryman whose fame spread well beyond Friuli as soon as he started to bottle his wine, and Mario Schiopetto, the dean of modern oenology in Friuli, master winemaker and unswerving champion of quality. Yet again, we have had to strike a difficult balance between the space available and the number of cellars that deserve a mention in the Guide. It did not look that way during the 2002 growing year, for the rains were heavy and unremitting, especially at the crucial flowering and veraison stages of the vine growth cycle. It continued to rain until mid August, when there came a break during which it was possible to harvest the white grapes without too much trouble. But then the rain set in again, and its persistence caused problems for the red grape harvest in many cases. Crops were 15 to 45 per cent lower than the average for previous years, and the first results of analysis hinted at wines with marked acidity. Subsequent visits to various cellars quickly changed our minds, however. Tocai, a vine type ideally suited to the region, Malvasia and Ribolla, the white grapes that have been grown for longest in Friuli, were the varieties that yielded the best results in terms of quality. We shall withhold judgement on the reds, since the best of them will be released onto the market from next year. We'll close these notes with a note of warning. The crisis that first hit wine consumption in some of Friuli's traditional markets, such as Germany and the United States, has extended to the most important market, Italy. We can only shake our heads at those producers who have insisted on raising prices again this year, on the pretext that the previous vintage presented low yields. It is true that the increases are modest, but they represent six to ten or 20 per cent, or even more, of the label price. Only a handful of producers have actually lowered prices. However, this is the story told by the official price lists, but of course sometimes the prices actually applied are rather different from those stated.

AQUILEIA (UD)

CA' TULLIO
VIA BELIGNA, 41
33051 AQUILEIA (UD)
TEL. 0431919700
E-MAIL: info@catullio.it

Ca' Tullio is an impressive producer, for many reasons. Founded in 1995, it embraces two vineyards, each just over 30 hectares: Vigneto Sdricca, at Manzano in the heart of the Colli Orientali del Friuli, and Vigneti Beligna, which lies between the splendid Ca' Tullio cellar and the lagoon of Grado, in the Aquileia DOC zone. The young owner, Paolo Calligaris, intends to increase his stock of native vines at Vigneto Sdricca whereas at Beligna, the goal is to promote the plot's historic wines, the easy-drinking Refosco that Ca' Tullio vinifies and matures only in stainless steel, Traminer Aromatico and Riesling. Ca' Tullio's 150,000 bottles a year, just over half with the Aquileia DOC label, are made under the watchful eyes of Francesco Visintin, known as Checco, and Roberta Bassi. This capable and very modest pair use barrels of various sizes for the Sdricca reds and for the Aquileia Duemila blend. All the other wines see only stainless steel. A word about the cellar, where Patrizia Sepulcri looks after visitors. It is an early 20th-century industrial building once used to dry tobacco and grow cuttings. Abandoned in the 1950s, it has now been completely refurbished. Thanks to one or two alterations, it has been adapted for use as a cellar and comfortable "taberna romana", the visitor facilities designed in the style of a scrupulously accurate ancient Roman hostelry. Aquileia Duemila, a blend of 60 per cent refosco with merlot and cabernet sauvignon, is strikingly complex. Enviable structure backs up the fruit and spice.

AQUILEIA (UD)

GIOVANNI DONDA
VIA MANLIO ACIDINIO, 4
33051 AQUILEIA (UD)
TEL. 043191185
E-MAIL: info@vinidonda.it

Gianni Donda has about six hectares under vine, most located on the site of the ancient Circus Maximus of Aquileia. He comes from a family of farmers and viticulturists who moved into the area in 1924. Gianni's vines are Guyot-trained and the wine to be bottled – about 30,000 are released each year – is an increasingly important proportion of the cellar's production. The stainless steel and wood in the cellar are used shrewdly to obtain the best possible results. Donda can call on the consultancy skills of one of Friuli's most scrupulous wine technicians, Giorgi Bertossi, who lends his experience to other wineries in both Aquileia and the Collio. One of the critical factors in the growth of the Aquileia DOC zone we have witnessed in recent years has been collaboration among producers. Tastings, themed meetings and joint promotional activities have created a fertile environment for quality wine production. Donda wines breathe that climate, for all are reliable and convincingly good. The Cabernet Franc forswears varietal herbaceous notes to put the accent on ripe berry fruit and deliciously soft tannins in the mouth. The Sauvignon shows distinct red pepper on nose and palate, where buttery richness and acidity have found an attractive point of equilibrium. Bianco Tàlis, a blend of barrique-fermented and aged sauvignon, pinot grigio and chardonnay, has yet to find its feet.

● Friuli Aquileia Rosso Aquileia Duemila '01	▼▼	4*
● COF Cabernet Sauvignon Sdricca '00	▼	3
● COF Merlot Sdricca '00	▼	4
● Friuli Aquileia Cabernet Franc Vigneti Beligna '02	▼	3
○ Friuli Aquileia Riesling Vigneti Beligna '02	▼	3
○ Friuli Aquileia Traminer Vigneti Beligna '02	▼	3
● COF Refosco P. R. Sdricca '00		4
● Friuli Aquileia Refosco P. R. Vigneti Beligna '02		3

● Friuli Aquileia Cabernet Franc '02	▼▼	3*
○ Friuli Aquileia Sauvignon '02	▼▼	3*
○ Aureo '01	▼	5
● Friuli Aquileia Merlot Ris. '01	▼	4
○ Friuli Aquileia Bianco Tàlis '02	▼	3
○ Friuli Aquileia Pinot Bianco '02	▼	3
○ Friuli Aquileia Pinot Grigio '02	▼	3
● Friuli Aquileia Cabernet Franc '01	▼▼	3

BAGNARIA ARSA (UD)

BAGNARIA ARSA (UD)

MULINO DELLE TOLLE
FRAZ. SEVEGLIANO
VIA MULINO DELLE TOLLE, 15
33050 BAGNARIA ARSA (UD)
TEL. 0432928113
E-MAIL: mulinodelletolle@tin.it

Mulino delle Tolle takes its name from a carved Roman votive head found in a vineyard one day. The estate lies on the remains of two ancient Roman roads, the Via Postumia and the Via Julia Augusta, a relatively short distance from Aquileia. The wine trade, and perhaps production, in the area must have flourished, for entire rows of wine amphorae have been discovered here. Management at Mulino delle Tolle is in the hands of cousins Giorgio and Eliseo Bertossi, the former a wine technician and the latter an agricultural technician. There are 13 hectares under vine and vinification is carried out in a very Spartan cellar. A few kilometres away, on the road to Grado, the Bertossi family runs an "agriturismo" holiday centre, set up in the buildings that were the Italian customs post until the Great War. Where once there was the border between the kingdom of Italy and the Austro-Hungarian empire today stands a hotel – the rooms are named after vine varieties – and a restaurant. Giorgio Bertossi is not just a skilled maker of premium wines, he is also a discriminating taster, ever ready to acknowledge the limits of some of his wines. The Tocai Friulano and Rosso Sabellius, from cabernet franc, merlot and refosco, scored very high marks, but the Malvasia failed to reach the standard for which our many previous tastings had prepared us.

TENUTA BELTRAME
FRAZ. PRIVANO
LOC. ANTONINI, 6/8
33050 BAGNARIA ARSA (UD)
TEL. 0432923670
E-MAIL: tenuta.beltrame@libero.it

Cristian Beltrame and oenologist Giuseppe Golino are an efficient and highly professional team, ever attentive to the market and with a solid grounding in agronomy. Add to that passion and an impressive work ethic, and you will see why the 25 hectares under vine around the lovely noble house on the Aquileia flatlands has been turning out quality wines for years now. This is no nine-day wonder, or lucky break with the weather. Tenuta Beltrame has a clear policy, including delaying release of the reds to improve their balance. This laudable approach has earned all the winery's products at least One Glass in every edition of the Guide, The Cabernet Sauvignon Riserva is a thoroughbred. From the first notes of balsam, bottled fruit and chocolate on the nose, it shows strength. The palate is well-structured with firm but not edgy tannins, and a great finish of bramble tart. The Chardonnay Pribus is equally good, unveiling complex, intense notes of ripe banana, melon, butter, vanilla and tea. The peach-themed finish is irresistible. The Tocai is another fine wine, showing delicate notes of apple and wistaria, then flowers on the palate nuanced with white damson. Sauvignon was the wine that won Tenuta Beltrame its reputation. The house style is an attractive cocktail of elderflower, red pepper and spring flower aromas. Finally, we should note that the warm. fruit-forward Refosco is very much a modern wine.

● Friuli Aquileia Rosso Sabellius '01	♆♆	4
○ Friuli Aquileia Tocai Friulano '02	♆♆	3*
○ Friuli Aquileia Bianco Palmade '02	♆	3
● Friuli Aquileia Cabernet Franc '02	♆	3
○ Friuli Aquileia Malvasia '02	♆	3
○ Friuli Aquileia Sauvignon '02	♆	3
● Friuli Aquileia Refosco P. R. '01		3
○ Friuli Aquileia Chardonnay '02		3

● Friuli Aquileia Cabernet Sauvignon Ris. '00	♆♆	5
● Friuli Aquileia Cabernet Sauvignon '01	♆♆	4
○ Friuli Aquileia Chardonnay Pribus '01	♆♆	4
● Friuli Aquileia Refosco P. R. '01	♆♆	4
○ Friuli Aquileia Sauvignon '02	♆♆	4
○ Friuli Aquileia Tocai Friulano '02	♆♆	4
● Friuli Aquileia Merlot Ris. '00	♆	5
● Tazzelenghe Ris. '00	♆	5
● Friuli Aquileia Cabernet Franc '01	♆	4
● Friuli Aquileia Merlot '01	♆	4
○ Friuli Aquileia Chardonnay '02	♆	4
○ Friuli Aquileia Pinot Grigio '02	♆	4
● Friuli Aquileia Merlot Ris. '99	♆♆	5

BICINICCO (UD)

PRADIO
LOC. FELETTIS
VIA UDINE, 17
33050 BICINICCO (UD)
TEL. 0432990123
E-MAIL: info@pradio.it

The Cielo family's Pradio estate is moving up. Located on the Friulian flatlands, it has 30 hectares under vine yielding about 200,000 bottles a year. Luca Cielo makes no secret of his goal. Despite the rather anonymous large-scale production popular in this area, Luca aims for quality at a reasonable price, a point we would like to underline in this age of over-optimistic pricing policies. With the assistance of agronomic consultant, Beppe Gollino, and wine technician, Beppe Bassi, Luca has renewed the vineyards – increasing planting densities, cutting back on fertilizers, thinning the leaves and bunches – and introduced new cellar techniques, such as maceration on the skins, controlled oxidation of musts, lees contact, and barrique and tonneau fermentation for chardonnay and sauvignon. The results continue to live up to expectations, even in a growing year when quality was bound to be lower than usual. The Pinot Grigio is especially attractive. It may not be a big wine, but the fresh pear aromas linger on the palate nicely. There was a good showing from the Rok, which we erroneously assessed last year. It is a classic Bordeaux blend that is slightly Cabernet Franc-heavy. A creamy texture and notes of warm bramble accompany a well-balanced palate and decent length. The Teraje is very traditional, unveiling crusty bread, banana and yellow plums, the Gaiare is a fruit-forward Tocai with nicely gauged acidity, and the Tuaro has varietal dry leaves and unripe cherry. It's a shame that the vintage did little for its structure or length.

BUTTRIO (UD)

LIVIO E CLAUDIO BUIATTI
VIA LIPPE, 25
33042 BUTTRIO (UD)
TEL. 0432674317
E-MAIL: info@buiattivini.it

We are delighted to see that Claudio Buiatti is back on form, after a short spell in the doldrums. Claudio is fully in line with Friulian tradition in that, with only eight hectares under vine, he releases his wines under as many as 11 different labels. The estate was founded in the early 20th century and the vine stock stands on the hillsides that run from Buttrio to Premariacco. Whites account for almost 70 per cent of the annual 50,000-bottle production, which is sold all over Italy. The cellar is small, but beautifully clean and tidy, qualities that Claudio also transmits to his wines. One of the top Buiatti bottles is the Pinot Grigio, an intensely fruit-rich wine on the nose with a fresh-tasting, elegant palate. The Refosco dal Peduncolo Rosso also has a more exciting palate than nose, showing complexity, body, varietal spice and ripe fruit. The Momon Ros Riserva 2000, a blend of oak-aged merlot and cabernet sauvignon, came very close to winning a second Glass. The Tocai Friulano earned One very full Glass, as did the Pinot Bianco, the Cabernet '01 and the sweet native-grape whites, Picolit and Verduzzo Friulano.

● Friuli Grave Rosso Rok '00	⟐⟐	4*
○ Friuli Grave Pinot Grigio Priara '02	⟐⟐	4*
○ Friuli Grave Chardonnay Teraje '02	⟐	3
● Friuli Grave Refosco P. R. Tuaro '02	⟐	4
○ Friuli Grave Tocai Friulano Gaiare '02	⟐	3
● Friuli Grave Cabernet Sauvignon Crearo '01		4
● Friuli Grave Merlot Roncomoro '02		3
○ Friuli Grave Sauvignon Sobaja '02		4
● Friuli Grave Cabernet Sauvignon Crearo '00	⟐⟐	4

● COF Refosco P. R. '01	⟐⟐	4*
○ COF Pinot Grigio '02	⟐⟐	4*
● COF Rosso Momon Ros Ris. '00	⟐	6
● COF Cabernet '01	⟐	4
○ COF Picolit '01	⟐	6
○ COF Pinot Bianco '02	⟐	4
○ COF Tocai Friulano '02	⟐	4
○ COF Verduzzo Friulano '02	⟐	4
● COF Merlot '01		4
○ COF Sauvignon '02		4

BUTTRIO (UD)

OLIVO BUIATTI
VIA LIPPE, 23
33042 BUTTRIO (UD)
TEL. 0432674316

Olivo Buiatti gave his son a free hand to manage the seven and a half hectares of the family estate. Franco is a hard worker. He is supported by his wife, Simonetta, who helps in the vineyards and also runs a small "frasca", a traditional Friulian country hostelry that sells wine as well as some food. Following long-established countryside traditions, Franco swaps advice and equipment with that great winemaker, Enzo Pontoni of Miani, and his other great friend, Paolo Meroi. The three share the same production philosophy, although Franco shuns Pontoni's more extreme interpretations. The Buiatti winery has a long history, having been founded in 1911. In 1986, it was split between brothers Olivo and Livio. Franco's wine goes into 12,000 bottles each year while the remainder is sold unbottled on the market or at the estate's cellar-door sales outlet. The Tocai Friulano 2001 is every bit as good as it promised to be. The palate is concentrated and well-structured, maintaining its richness and fruit as it progresses over the palate. It has great length, and although not particularly varietal, it is still a remarkable wine. We were impressed by the Poanis Blanc 2002, a malvasia and riesling-heavy blend with proportions of picolit, sauvignon and pinot grigio. The spectrum of aromatics reveals yellow peach, apricot and confectioner's cream, with apple to perk up the finish. Finally, the Cabernet 2001, Merlot 2001 and Merlot 2000 are all good, as is the Tocai Friulano 2002.

●	COF Cabernet '01	🍷🍷	5
○	COF Tocai Friulano '01	🍷🍷	5
○	COF Bianco Poanis Blanc '02	🍷🍷	5
●	COF Merlot '00	🍷	5
●	COF Merlot '01	🍷	5
○	COF Tocai Friulano '02	🍷	4
○	COF Sauvignon '01		5

BUTTRIO (UD)

CONTE D'ATTIMIS-MANIAGO
VIA SOTTOMONTE, 21
33042 BUTTRIO (UD)
TEL. 0432674027
E-MAIL: info@contedattimismaniago.it

It was 1615 when Conte Paolo D'Attimis noted in his memoirs that he had carried out "important work in the district of Buri (Buttrio) ... digging ditches and renewing vine plantations". Many years have passed since then and Alberto, the present owner, who manages the property with thrift and intelligence, has continued the renovation that was begun centuries ago. More than one third of the 110 hectares under vine have been replanted to local biotypes over the past five years, after careful zoning made it possible to optimize the replanting cycle. This year, the historic estate labels have been abandoned in favour of a more elegant, modern look. And the wines? Quality has never been so high and the Malvasia leads a large group of outstanding bottles. The 2002 edition has intense aromas of sweet tobacco, spring flowers, crusty bread and pear, then the palate reveals citrussy notes that last through to the long finish. Vignaricco Rosso, a Bordeaux blend, has intense bramble and plum laced with attractive notes of talcum powder. Ronco Broilo 1999, the new incarnation of Vignaricco Bianco, is a chardonnay and pinot bianco blend with citrus and tropical fruit aromas, nuanced with white chocolate and wild roses. The rounded Cabernet is as good as ever, disclosing deliciously soft tannins. The Sauvignon is also good, its dense, complex aromas redolent of tomato, pineapple and peach. The fat, long palate beautifully mirrors the nose. Finally, elegant hints of banana ice cream and boiled sweets stand out on the Chardonnay.

○	COF Malvasia '02	🍷🍷	4*
●	COF Cabernet '01	🍷🍷	4
○	COF Chardonnay '02	🍷🍷	5
○	COF Sauvignon '02	🍷🍷	4
○	COF Ronco Broilo '99	🍷🍷	5
●	COF Rosso Vignaricco '99	🍷🍷	5
●	COF Tazzelenghe '00	🍷	6
○	COF Picolit '02	🍷	8
○	COF Pinot Grigio '02	🍷	4
●	COF Refosco P. R. '02	🍷	5
○	COF Sauvignon '01	🍷🍷	4
●	COF Cabernet '00	🍷🍷	4
●	Vignaricco Rosso '97	🍷🍷	5

BUTTRIO (UD)

★ GIROLAMO DORIGO
VIA DEL POZZO, 5
33042 BUTTRIO (UD)
TEL. 0432674268
E-MAIL: info@montsclapade.com

Not all that many wineries have a Three Glass wine, and even fewer this year achieved top marks twice, but when the going gets tough, the deepest winemaking roots prevail. And Dorigo's big scores came not from traditional cellar products, like Montsclapade – very good again this year, although with an extra hint of edginess to its austere, terroir-driven profile – or Picolit. The Three Glass winners are native vines, and red ones at that. Some people may have reservations about the fashion for native grapes but it is hardly a problem when the wines are as good as these, whatever the variety they come from. The Dorigo Pignolo is no newcomer to the big league but in recent years, the tannins have been too rigid for the complexity of the immense, extract-rich structure, or the sheer length of the aromatics, to emerge. It has now been established that there are two pignolo clones with very different sensory characteristics, especially those related to phenolics. And it looks as if this year, the Dorigos have finally identified the right selection. But the most gratifying surprise this year was the barriqued Refosco (there's a picture on the label), which has length and weight on the typical chocolate and ripe cherry palate, and an acidity that is less husky than usual. We note the consistently good quality of the Chardonnay and the Sauvignon Ronc di Juri but above all, we would mention the excellent results achieved by the younger, mid-market range that the admirable Alessio has created for less formal winelovers, who may not want to spend a fortune for a top-quality bottle.

BUTTRIO (UD)

DAVINO MEROI
VIA STRETTA DEL PARCO, 1
33042 BUTTRIO (UD)
TEL. 0432674025
E-MAIL: parco.meroi@libero.it

Paolo Meroi has at least one piece of good fortune and two merits. It is his good fortune to combine winemaking with running a restaurant, which gives him a loyal customer base on his own doorstep. His first merit is to have committed to high quality standards; his second is to have achieved them. We have said before that Meroi is one of the most interesting emerging wineries in the area, and recent tastings have confirmed this. Three wines went forward to the national finals this time. The surprising spice, leather, blueberry and barely hinted-at tar of the Ros di Buri is wonderfully echoed on the palate, where the tight-knit tannic weave backs up a fat, warm, mouthfilling structure. The Tocai is as good as ever. Like all Meroi whites, it undergoes severe bunch selection, cold maceration, barrique fermentation and lees stirring. Its elegant milky notes offset ripe fruit, silky extract and a tidy progression through to the classic bitter twist in the finish. Yet again, the Picolit was one of the best we tasted. Its glycerine-rich sweetness is held in check by bright acidity and notes of honey, dried apricot and elderflower. All the other wines repay attention, with special mentions for the minerally Chardonnay and the yellow plum and rue Sauvignon.

● COF Pignolo di Buttrio Vigneto Ronc di Juri '00	ΨΨΨ	8
● COF Refosco P. R. Vigneto Montsclapade '00	ΨΨΨ	6
● COF Montsclapade '00	ΨΨ	7
○ COF Sauvignon Ronc di Juri '01	ΨΨ	6
○ COF Chardonnay Vigneto Ronc di Juri '01	ΨΨ	6
○ COF Picolit Vigneto Montsclapade '01	ΨΨ	8
○ COF Pinot Grigio Vigneto Montsclapade '02	ΨΨ	4*
○ COF Ribolla Gialla Vigneto Ronc di Juri '02	ΨΨ	4*
● COF Cabernet Franc Vigneto Montsclapade '02	Ψ	4

○ COF Picolit '01	ΨΨ	8
● COF Rosso Ros di Buri '01	ΨΨ	6
○ COF Tocai Friulano '02	ΨΨ	6
○ COF Chardonnay '02	ΨΨ	6
○ COF Sauvignon '02	ΨΨ	5
○ COF Bianco Blanc di Buri '02	Ψ	5
● COF Rosso Ros di Buri '99	ΨΨ	6
○ COF Bianco Blanc di Buri '00	ΨΨ	5
○ COF Picolit '00	ΨΨ	8
○ COF Chardonnay '01	ΨΨ	5
● COF Rosso Dominin '99	ΨΨ	7

BUTTRIO (UD)

★ MIANI
VIA PERUZZI, 10
33042 BUTTRIO (UD)
TEL. 0432674327

Almost everything you could say has already been said about Enzo Pontoni and his small winery. He is a legend, and it is hard to find something new to write. If you ask him a few questions, he squints at you as if you had just stepped off a spaceship. "The white? We haven't had any for a few years. The pinot grigio and riesling have been ripped out. I've got 18 hectares in production but I only vinify 15. The rest is new plantings. And then, whichever way you look at it, production is always roughly the same, about 8,000 bottles. The new cellar? Yes, the project will start next year. In the meantime, every storm carries off a bit of the old one. The Refosco? What can I say? I only managed to make the one barrique!…" But when you walk round the vineyards, it's a different story. You just have to look. And when you talk about vintages, and harvest, and grapes, the conversation becomes more precise. In fact, 2002 was not the greatest of vintages. Rain interfered with the harvest, the grapes failed to achieve the right balance, and you needed a specially equipped cellar to handle the subsequent small lots of fruit. That must be why the tastings went as they did. The Merlot was an exception, but it comes from a different vintage. It shows all its characteristic soft fullness, balance and resin and blackcurrant flavours. The whites, however, reveal a struggle for concentration and alcohol that affected the balance of the structure and the fragrance of the aromas. There are slightly untidy notes of greenness and reduction. Difficult wines from difficult times.

BUTTRIO (UD)

PETRUCCO
VIA MORPURGO, 12
33042 BUTTRIO (UD)
TEL. 0432674387 - 04326238340
E-MAIL: petruccovini@libero.it

Paolo Petrucco, an engineer, and his wife, Lina, have been helped for years by oenologist Flavio Cabas as they strive to release onto the market wines that reflect their philosophy. They aim for natural, territory-focused products, and premium quality. To obtain this from the 25 hectares under vine on their 30-hectare estate, they harvest by hand, use soft crushing and cold clarification that shuns fining agents. They are also helped by the location of the vineyards, on a balcony of south-facing hillsides caressed by breezes from the sea. This year, the Petruccos' wines took another step forward. We were impressed by their Pinot Bianco, which enjoyed a favourable vintage. It is fresh and varietal, with classic crusty bread and golden delicious apple aromas. The palate is soft and attractively rich, perked up in the finish by hints of apple. The Tocai throws a sunny nose of citrus and acacia blossom, followed by refreshing acidity in the mouth. We were struck by the delicate, yet intense, flowers of the Sauvignon, which add complexity to a wine with a nose of elderflower, tomato and peach. These aromas are mirrored on a palate that signs off with a long finish of flowers. There are attractive hints of balsam, petit fours and berry fruit salad in the Merlot Vigna del Balbo and the varietal Cabernet is almost as good. Other wines to mention are the less than typical Chardonnay, the tangy Ribolla and the pepper and hay Refosco.

● COF Merlot '00	♟♟	8
○ COF Chardonnay '02	♟♟	7
○ COF Tocai Friulano '02	♟♟	7
○ COF Ribolla Gialla '02	♟	7
○ COF Sauvignon '02	♟	7
○ COF Bianco '96	♟♟♟	7
● COF Rosso '96	♟♟♟	8
○ COF Bianco '97	♟♟♟	7
● COF Rosso '97	♟♟♟	8
○ COF Tocai Friulano '98	♟♟♟	7
○ COF Tocai Friulano '99	♟♟♟	7
○ COF Tocai Friulano '00	♟♟♟	7
● COF Merlot '98	♟♟♟	8
● COF Merlot '99	♟♟♟	8

● COF Merlot V. del Balbo '00	♟♟	4
○ COF Pinot Bianco '02	♟♟	4*
○ COF Sauvignon '02	♟♟	4*
○ COF Tocai Friulano '02	♟♟	4*
● COF Cabernet Franc '01	♟	4
● COF Refosco P. R. '01	♟	4
○ COF Chardonnay '02	♟	4
○ COF Ribolla Gialla '02	♟	4
○ COF Pinot Grigio '02		4
○ COF Chardonnay '01	♟♟	4
● COF Refosco P. R. '00	♟	4

CAPRIVA DEL FRIULI (GO)

CASTELLO DI SPESSA
VIA SPESSA, 1
34070 CAPRIVA DEL FRIULI (GO)
TEL. 0481639914 - 0481808124
E-MAIL: info@castellospessa.com

Castello di Spessa's 30 hectares lie on the hillsides behind the castle itself. Previously owned by various aristocratic families, the castle was acquired in the 19th century by Barone Segre, and in the late 1980s was sold to its current owner, Loretto Pali. He has restored the building, adorning it with objets d'art, cultural events and social gatherings that have given this noble home a new lease of life. The 14th-century cellar lies under the castle's longest wing and was recently connected to an army bunker excavated 15 metres below ground in the 1930s. The constant temperature of 14 degrees Celsius makes the bunker an ideal barrel maturation cellar for the winery's flagship products. Loretto has put together a team that is achieving increasingly impressive results. They are oenologist Domenico Lovat, assisted by Gianni Menotti in the cellar, Marco Simonit in the vineyard and Paolo Della Rovere in charge of distribution. Public relations are the domain of Lucia Luisa. The Sauvignon Segré is stunningly good and won Three Glasses for its terrific peach, red pepper and tomato leaf aromas. The elegant Pinot Bianco is complex and weighty on the palate, the Tocai Friulano has intense apple, pear and herb aromas, the Ribolla Gialla is flavoursome and fresh-tasting, and the warm Merlot Torriani shows good fruit and body, as well as extraordinary nose-palate consistency.

○	Collio Sauvignon Segré '02	♙♙♙	6
●	Collio Merlot Torriani '00	♙♙	6
○	Collio Tocai Friulano '02	♙♙	5
○	Collio Pinot Bianco '02	♙♙	5
○	Collio Ribolla Gialla '02	♙♙	5
○	Collio Pinot Grigio '02	♙♙	5
○	Collio Sauvignon '02	♙♙	5
○	Collio Pinot Bianco '97	♟♟♟	4
○	Collio Pinot Bianco '01	♟♟♟	4
○	Collio Pinot Bianco di Santarosa '00	♟♟	5
○	Collio Sauvignon Segré '01	♟♟	5
●	Collio Rosso Torriani '99	♟♟	5

CAPRIVA DEL FRIULI (GO)

CAPRIVA DEL FRIULI (GO)

PUIATTI
VIA AQUILEIA, 30
34070 CAPRIVA DEL FRIULI (GO)
TEL. 0481809922
E-MAIL: puiatti@puiatti.com

Puiatti is one of the historic names of Friulian winemaking. Established by the charismatic Vittorio Puiatti, the cellar is run today by his children Giovanni and Elisabetta. Until a few years ago, the Puiattis bought most of their fruit from about 60 selected growers. Now, they have about 70 hectares under vine in the Collio and Isonzo DOC zones, most of them estate-owned. The 700,000 bottles released each year are sold all over the world, especially in the United States, where Giovanni is also an importer of premium wines. Over the years, the Puiattis have made a number of production and commercial decisions that go against the trend, maintaining that maceration, lees contact, malolactic fermentation and cask conditioning all jeopardize the aromatic integrity of grape and wine. But at the same time, they have flanked this approach, which seems dated to many, with a far-sighted commitment to communication and marketing, taking full advantage of the explosive creativity of Daniela Zanette. A recently introduced newsletter and an effective interactive website that have made Puiatti a case study in wine communication are only two of the estate's initiatives. On the wine front, it was the Isonzo DOC products that performed better. The 2002 Chardonnay picked up Two Glasses for its minerally nose of flint and citrus, followed by an elegantly "French" palate. The attractively tasty Pinot Grigio also scored high for its well-gauged acidity and the Cabernet Franc proved the best of the reds, with a fresh-tasting, easy-drinking style that foregrounds red berry fruit.

○	Friuli Isonzo Chardonnay '02	♙♙	4
●	Collio Merlot Ruttars '00	♙	5
●	Collio Pinot Nero Ruttars '00	♙	5
●	Friuli Isonzo Cabernet Franc '02	♙	4
○	Friuli Isonzo Pinot Grigio '02	♙	4
●	Collio Cabernet Sauvignon Ruttars '00		6
○	Collio Ribolla Gialla Ruttars '02		5
○	Collio Sauvignon Ruttars '02		5
○	Friuli Isonzo Tocai Friulano '02		4
○	Oltre Vittorio Puiatti Bianco '99	♟♟	7

CAPRIVA DEL FRIULI (GO)

RONCÙS
VIA MAZZINI, 26
34070 CAPRIVA DEL FRIULI (GO)
TEL. 0481809349
E-MAIL: roncus@activeweb.it

Marco Pero, now free of other business commitments, is devoting himself full-time to his vineyard and cellar. These – the vineyard in particular – are Marco's kingdom, and his evident passion transcends mere diligence. He makes changes every year in his search for the "territory wine" that is at the top of his list of priorities. This year, he has lowered yields even further, making further field selections and using only unselected local yeasts. He has made efforts in the vineyard to obtain fruit that is richer in minerals and phenolics, and he has modified some fermentation and maceration procedures to enhance finesse. The white Vecchie Vigne blend is good. It comes from plants more than 40 years old and is malvasia-based, with small proportions of tocai and ribolla. The deep straw hue ushers in complex aromas of tea, dried flowers, yellow peach, melon and candied orange. Broad on the palate, it mingles citrus with pleasant nuances of vanilla. The Tocai is equally praiseworthy. Its elegant ripe apple is accompanied by good, rich structure and length. Val di Miez is from merlot with a little cabernet franc. A fine red with attractive sweet fruit aromas, it has still to find balance on the palate.

CAPRIVA DEL FRIULI (GO)

RUSSIZ SUPERIORE
VIA RUSSIZ, 7
34070 CAPRIVA DEL FRIULI (GO)
TEL. 048199164
E-MAIL: info@marcofelluga.it

This is Marco Felluga's flagship estate. It's not just the quality of the wines yielded by its 60 hectares that make it special, but also the sheer history in the air of a winery whose roots date back to the far-off 13th century. The table you see below, with a Bianco Disôre that soared off with Three Glasses, is the result of that pedigree, and of the work of men and women like oenologist, Raffaella Bruno. Bianco Disôre, a blend of oak-fermented tocai, ribolla, pinot bianco and sauvignon, is as ever a thoroughbred. Its elegant nose discloses cakes, mint and hazelnut over pears and apples. The delicate palate finds a superb balance of flavours that recall in the finish white chocolate, vanilla and especially apricot. The more you taste the Sauvignon 2002, the more it convinces with its full, broad mouthfeel and notes of peach, elderflower and melon. Varietal is the word for the Pinot Bianco. Spring flowers, crusty bread, pear and apple regale nose and palate, where the complex fullness is evident. The Tocai is every bit as good, its sunny tropical fruit and citrus reluctantly giving way to almondy notes in the finish. The Verduzzo has comparable elegance and refinement, combining candied citrus and figs with a hint of palate-refreshing acidity in the finish. Finally, the Rosso degli Orzoni Bordeaux blend is satisfyingly soft and round, with a marked hint of spice.

○ Roncùs Bianco Vecchie Vigne '00	🍷🍷	6
○ Collio Tocai Friulano '02	🍷🍷	5
● Val di Miez '01	🍷	6
○ Friuli Isonzo Sauvignon '02		5
○ Roncùs Bianco Vecchie Vigne '99	🍷🍷	6
○ Collio Tocai Friulano '01	🍷🍷	5
○ Pinot Bianco '01	🍷🍷	5
● Val di Miez '99	🍷🍷	6

○ Collio Bianco Russiz Disôre '01	🍷🍷🍷	6
○ Collio Sauvignon '02	🍷🍷	6
○ Collio Pinot Bianco '02	🍷🍷	6
○ Collio Tocai Friulano '02	🍷🍷	4
○ Verduzzo Friulano '01	🍷🍷	6
○ Collio Pinot Grigio '02	🍷🍷	6
● Collio Rosso Ris. degli Orzoni '99	🍷🍷	8
● Collio Cabernet Franc '01	🍷	6
● Collio Merlot '01	🍷	6
● Collio Rosso Ris. degli Orzoni '94	🍷🍷🍷	7
○ Collio Sauvignon '98	🍷🍷🍷	5
○ Collio Tocai Friulano '99	🍷🍷🍷	5
○ Collio Bianco Russiz Disôre '00	🍷🍷🍷	5

CAPRIVA DEL FRIULI (GO)

★ SCHIOPETTO
VIA PALAZZO ARCIVESCOVILE, 1
34070 CAPRIVA DEL FRIULI (GO)
TEL. 048180332
E-MAIL: azienda@schiopetto.it

Many historic winemakers have passed away this year, but Mario Schiopetto left a particularly significant gap behind him. After years of suffering, an exemplary figure has departed, a self-taught wineman who combined German technology with French finesse to craft uniquely great wines. Mario was always on the cutting edge, and recent decisions at the cellar involving the drastic pruning of labels were implemented at his initiative. His children Maria Angela, Carlo and Giorgio have shown that they want to run the family winery in the great man's spirit. Mario Schiopetto began his career as a winemaker in 1965, when he managed to rent an old winery at Capriva from the archiepiscopal curia of Gorizia. In 1989, he bought the estate, and seven years later acquired the eight-hectare Podere dei Blumeri on the hills at Rosazzo. Today, the estate has a total of 30 or so hectares and an annual production of 200-250,000 units, made by the team of twins Carlo and Giorgio, oenologist, Stefano Menotti, and consultant, Donato Lanati. The Mario Schiopetto Bianco is a fantastically successful wine, blended from chardonnay grown at Blumeri and tocai friulano from the Collio. Some 60 per cent of the wine is vinified in stainless steel while the rest ferments and ages in wood of various sizes. It is a wine that personifies the elegance that has always been the hallmark of the Schiopetto cellar. The Blanc des Rosis, from tocai, pinot grigio, sauvignon, malvasia and ribolla, is superb and the other Schiopetto whites are all excellent.

CAPRIVA DEL FRIULI (GO)

GESTIONI AGRICOLE VIDUSSI
VIA SPESSA, 18
34070 CAPRIVA DEL FRIULI (GO)
TEL. 048180072 - 045913399
E-MAIL: grfirme@tin.it

In 2000, the Vidussi estate was acquired by the Montresor family, which owns the Verona-based winery of the same name. The estate buildings are on the edge of the vineyards that occupy 25 of the property's 50 hectares in Capriva and Pradis near Cormons but the cellar also vinifies grapes from seven hectares at Ipplis, near Premariacco, in the Colli Orientali del Friuli. The vines are beautifully tended and contribute to the spectacular view afforded by the trough of Capriva. The oenologist in charge of winemaking is Luigino De Giuseppe, a young man who has worked in a number of Friulian cellars, as well as in Puglia. His taste for experiment has led him to increase the already high number of labels released by Vidussi. The current total stands at 18. In the 2001 version, Rosso Are di Miute has added one tenth carmenère to its previous mix of merlot and cabernet franc, lifting the wine with a note of spice that comes through on the nose. Bianco Ronchi di Ravéz is a blend of ribolla gialla, malvasia, tocai, chardonnay musqué and picolit, aged in previously used barriques. The soft mouthfeel elicited conflicting reactions from our tasters. But let's move on to the truly superior wines, starting with the Malvasia, which took full advantage of a favourable vintage to acquire rich complexity on the nose, great structure and delicious length. Another serious contender is the Pinot Grigio, which delighted the panel with its nose-palate convergence.

O	Mario Schiopetto Bianco '02	♟♟♟	6
O	Blanc des Rosis '02	♟♟	5
O	Collio Pinot Bianco Amrità '01	♟♟	6
O	Collio Sauvignon Tarsia '01	♟♟	6
O	Collio Pinot Grigio '02	♟♟	5
O	Collio Sauvignon '02	♟♟	5
O	Collio Tocai Friulano '02	♟♟	5
O	Collio Pinot Bianco '02	♟	5
●	Rivarossa '01		5
O	Collio Pinot Bianco Amrità '97	♟♟♟	6
O	COF Sauvignon Podere dei Blumeri '99	♟♟♟	5
O	Collio Pinot Bianco '00	♟♟♟	5
O	Blanc des Rosis '01	♟♟	5
O	Collio Tocai Friulano '01	♟♟	5

O	Collio Malvasia '02	♟♟	4*
O	Collio Pinot Grigio '02	♟♟	4*
O	Collio Bianco Ronchi di Ravéz '01	♟	5
●	Collio Rosso Are di Miute '01	♟	5
O	Collio Chardonnay '02	♟	4
O	Collio Sauvignon '02	♟	4
O	Collio Pinot Bianco '02	♟	4
O	Collio Tocai Friulano Croce Alta '02		4
●	Collio Rosso Are di Miute '00	♟♟	5
O	Collio Tocai Friulano Croce Alta '01	♟♟	4

CAPRIVA DEL FRIULI (GO)

★ Villa Russiz
via Russiz, 6
34070 Capriva del Friuli (GO)
tel. 048180047
e-mail: villarussiz@villarussiz.it

Perhaps the most unusual thing about Villa Russiz is that it is publicly owned. The cellar belongs to the Istituto A. Cerutti, named after the noblewoman who founded an orphanage here after the First World War. Previously, the buildings and land belonged to Elvine von Zahoni, widow of Count Théodore de La Tour en Voivre. Count, or "Graf" in German, de la Tour smuggled the first merlot and cabernet vines from France, which explains why the selections are named after him and his consort, Gräfin Elvine. Today, the institute manages a farm, as well as the cellar, and the income generated finances the activities of nuns working to help young people from underprivileged families. The man behind the cellar's rebirth is Gianni Menotti, whose enthusiasm is matched only by his acknowledged professional skill. All the wines stand out for elegance and longevity, which means that they are at their best from three to eight years after the vintage, for the whites, whereas the reds will happily stay in the cellar for even longer. The Sauvignon de la Tour stays firmly in the top flight for its marriage of rich fruit, softness and fresh acidity, but we also enjoyed the tropical fruit of the Pinot Grigio; the elegance and weight in the mouth of the Pinot Bianco; the supple fullness of the Tocai Friulano; the intriguing chamomile of the Ribolla Gialla; and the freshness and creamy texture of the Chardonnay Gräfin de la Tour.

○ Collio Sauvignon de la Tour '02	🍷🍷🍷	6
○ Collio Chardonnay Gräfin de la Tour '01	🍷🍷	6
○ Collio Pinot Bianco '02	🍷🍷	5
○ Collio Pinot Grigio '02	🍷🍷	5
○ Collio Ribolla Gialla '02	🍷🍷	5
○ Collio Tocai Friulano '02	🍷🍷	5
● Collio Merlot Graf de la Tour '00	🍷🍷	7
○ Collio Malvasia Istriana '02	🍷🍷	5
● Collio Cabernet '01	🍷	5
● Collio Merlot '01	🍷	5
○ Collio Riesling '02	🍷	5
○ Collio Sauvignon '02	🍷	5
○ Collio Chardonnay Gräfin de la Tour '00	🍷🍷🍷 (outline)	6
● Collio Merlot Graf de la Tour '99	🍷🍷🍷 (outline)	7

CARLINO (UD)

Emiro Cav. Bortolusso
via Oltregorgo, 10
33050 Carlino (UD)
tel. 043167596
e-mail: bortolusso@bortolusso.it

The Annia DOC zone, which embraces wine areas between the Latisana and Aquileia DOCs, was created in 1995 thanks to an initiative led by Emiro Bortolusso. Cavalier Bortolusso is no longer with us and now his children, Sergio and Clara, manage the 50 family hectares under vine. The pair have inherited their father's determination and desire to grow, as well as a profound sense of hospitality. For several years, the Bortolussos have been assisted by oenologist, Luigino De Giuseppe, who has contributed to the consolidation and improvement of wine quality. The cellar itself has undergone major restructuring and has been extended with a spectacular new barrel area. The vineyards are close to the sea, so the wines often present significant salinity, which is part of their unique character. The vine stock is 60 per cent red but it is the white varieties that produce the best results. In fact, the 2002 Malvasia scored Two and a Half Glasses. Its elegant nose is a rich bouquet of spring flowers, with attractive lavender, and the complex palate has great balance and even better length. A mark or two lower we find the Tocai Friulano, whose very stylish nose is reflected faithfully on the warm palate, which unveils fruit in the finish. The Pinot Grigio is as good as ever, although the nose is superior to the palate.

○ Friuli Annia Malvasia '02	🍷🍷	4
○ Friuli Annia Tocai Friulano '02	🍷🍷	3*
● Friuli Annia Merlot Privilege '01	🍷	5
○ Friuli Annia Pinot Grigio '02	🍷	3
○ Friuli Annia Pinot Bianco '02		3
○ Friuli Annia Sauvignon '02		3
○ Friuli Annia Verduzzo Friulano '02		4

CERVIGNANO DEL FRIULI (UD)

CA' BOLANI
VIA CA' BOLANI, 2
33052 CERVIGNANO DEL FRIULI (UD)
TEL. 043132670
E-MAIL: info@cabolani.it

Ca' Bolani, purchased by Gianni Zonin in 1970, has a history dating back to the Most Serene Republic of Venice, when it was owned by the noble Bolani family. The alluvial soil is rich in clay veined with gravel. The 550 hectares under vine are organized into three sections, 50 at the winery in Cervignano, 300 at Molin di Ponte, where a small tasting centre has also been opened recently, and 200 at Terzo di Aquileia, the location of the winery's well-appointed hospitality centre. Over half of the vine stock has been converted to new training systems and planting densities, with the declared aim of reducing yields and obtaining top-quality fruit. In recent years, Gianni Zonin, his son, Domenico, or the group oenologist, Franco Giacosa, have treated us to tastings of some stunning wines that have aged slowly in bottle. The success of this policy has prompted the winery to create two distinct lines, adopting the name Gianni Zonin Vineyards for the more prestigious bottles. Nor should we forget the part played by estate manager Lorenzo Costantini, oenologist Roberto Marcolini and agronomist Gabriele Carboni. Conte Bolani, from refosco, merlot and cabernet sauvignon, is a well-structured, complex red with the potential to improve in the cellar. Opimio is from tocai and chardonnay, and reveals breadth in the mouth, whereas the fruit-led Cabernet Franc is a million miles from the asperity that generally characterizes this wine in Friuli.

●	Friuli Aquileia Conte Bolani Rosso Gianni Zonin Vineyards '00	🍷🍷🍷	6
●	Friuli Aquileia Cabernet Franc Gianni Zonin Vineyards '00	🍷🍷	4
○	Friuli Aquileia Opimio Gianni Zonin Vineyards '02	🍷🍷	4
●	Friuli Aquileia Refosco P. R. Gianni Zonin Vineyards '00	🍷	4
●	Friuli Aquileia Cabernet '01	🍷	4
○	Friuli Aquileia Pinot Grigio Gianni Zonin Vineyards '02	🍷	4
○	Friuli Aquileia Traminer Aromatico '02	🍷	4
○	Friuli Aquileia Sauvignon Gianni Zonin Vineyards '01	ΥΥ	4*

CIVIDALE DEL FRIULI (UD)

DAL FARI
LOC. GAGLIANO
VIA DARNAZZACCO, 44/B
33043 CIVIDALE DEL FRIULI (UD)
TEL. 0432731219 - 0432706726
E-MAIL: dalfari@faber_italy.com

Renzo Toffolutti has handed management of the Dal Fari estate to his likeable, enterprising wife, Laura Largajolli. With the assistance of a tip-top team, including consultant Fabio Coser and technician Valentino Giurato, Laura is applying herself to the task with a tenacity that bodes well for the future quality of the wines. In the meantime, the cellar has used for the first time an up-to-the-minute grape dryer, the first in Friuli. The region has typically rainy autumns so the new tool will allow fruit, especially red grapes, to be dried in a controlled manner, lifting the quality of the wines. New plots have been purchased to increase the supply of schioppettino, a historic native Friulian variety, and to start limited production of Picolit. As we wait for the 2002 reds, vinified with the new technology, we can enjoy this year's releases, which are good although there is some room for improvement. We were impressed by the deep purple Cabernet with its intense, varietal notes of sweet spices, hay and ripe bramble. The palate mirrors the nose perfectly and shows great balance, lifted by hints of coffee. Bianco delle Grazie, from chardonnay, sauvignon, tocai and riesling, is convincing with its Tocai-derived almonds and whistle-clean palate.

●	COF Cabernet '01	🍷🍷	4
○	COF Bianco delle Grazie '01	🍷	4
○	COF Chardonnay '02	🍷	3
○	COF Tocai Friulano '02	🍷	4
●	COF Rosso d'Orsone '99	🍷	5
●	COF Merlot '01		4
○	COF Pinot Grigio '02		4
○	COF Bianco delle Grazie '00	ΥΥ	4
○	COF Chardonnay Carato '01	ΥΥ	4

CIVIDALE DEL FRIULI (UD)   CIVIDALE DEL FRIULI (UD)

IL RONCAL
VIA FORNALIS, 148
33043 CIVIDALE DEL FRIULI (UD)
TEL. 0432730138
E-MAIL: info@ilroncal.it

DAVIDE MOSCHIONI
LOC. GAGLIANO
VIA DORIA, 30
33043 CIVIDALE DEL FRIULI (UD)
TEL. 0432730210

Not many decades ago, the Zorzettig family were tenant farmers near Cividale del Friuli. Today, they have scattered all over the area, setting up a number of successful wineries. Several Zorzettig women have married into other important winemaking families, such as Livon and Luisa. Il Roncal was founded in 1987 by Roberto Zorzettig, who started by replanting the vineyards he inherited at Montebello, a hill that dominates Spessa and looks onto the slopes of nearby Rocca Bernarda. Today, Roberto's estate embraces 20 hectares, but the cellar also vinifies fruit bought in from other local producers. The estate buildings are extensive, with space for accommodation, warehousing and the storage of farm tools and equipment. Another wing has been turned over exclusively to vinification. The best of the recent releases is the Pinot Grigio, from young vines planted in 1996 at a density of 5,000 plants per hectare at 180 metres above sea level. There are milky notes but the wine stands our for freshness on nose and palate, rich fruit and long length. Rosso Civon, from schioppettino, refosco and cabernet franc, is not up to the previous vintage's standard, and the same goes for the nonetheless very good Pignolo.

Michele Moschioni has decided to skip a year in his release schedule, so wines from the 2001 vintage will reach the market in 2004. This young producer has 11 hectares under vine, which give him about 35,000 bottles a year. Picolit apart, Michele grows almost exclusively red grapes, with the emphasis on the native pignolo, schioppettino and tazzelenghe varieties. He also has rows of merlot and cabernet sauvignon vines. For years, Michele turned out very concentrated wines, obtained with a vinification technique reminiscent of that used for Amarone. Raisining, however, tended to make the products very similar, masking varietal differences. Having explored that path to the full, Michele revised his vinification process to recover the personalities of the individual grapes. There are two blended wines, Celtico, from merlot and cabernet sauvignon, and Reâl, from half tazzelenghe and equal parts of merlot and cabernet sauvignon. Moschioni's wines benefit from maturation. That is one of the reasons why Michele is one of the not very many producers to release his wines only when they are ready to drink, refusing steadfastly to yield to the siren song of either the market or his loyal direct customers.

○	COF Pinot Grigio '02	🍷🍷	5
●	COF Pignolo '00	🍷	6
●	COF Rosso Civon '00	🍷	5
○	COF Chardonnay '02	🍷	5
○	COF Sauvignon '02	🍷	5
○	COF Tocai Friulano '02		5
○	COF Bianco Ploe di Stelis '01	🍷🍷	4
●	COF Schioppettino '01	🍷🍷	4
●	COF Pignolo '99	🍷	4

●	COF Rosso Celtico '00	🍷🍷	6
●	COF Pignolo '00	🍷🍷	7
●	COF Rosso Reâl '00	🍷🍷	6
●	COF Schioppettino '00	🍷🍷	7

CIVIDALE DEL FRIULI (UD)   CODROIPO (UD)

PAOLO RODARO
FRAZ. SPESSA
VIA CORMONS, 8
33040 CIVIDALE DEL FRIULI (UD)
TEL. 0432716066
E-MAIL: paolorodaro@yahoo.it

VIGNETI PIERO PITTARO
VIA UDINE, 67
33033 CODROIPO (UD)
TEL. 0432904726
E-MAIL: info@vignetipittaro.com

The Rodaros are one of the oldest winemaking families in Friuli. Their activities are documented as long ago as 23 March 1846, in what was then the Lombardo-Venetian Kingdom. They like to describe themselves, with a certain pride, as "country people from Spessa" because they have never lost their links with the territory and rural culture. The Rodaro production strategy is driven by typicity, never yielding an inch to the whimsies of passing fashion. Paolo Rodaro, the man behind the estate, is a master of this approach. He invests substantial effort and resources, which have been further intensified by the recent expansion of the vine stock to a total of 40 hectares. This year, five of Paolo's wines went forward to the final taste-offs and a sixth, the Refosco, missed out by a whisker. The big prize eluded him, but what quality in depth! The first of the top rank is Ronc, a chardonnay and pinot bianco blend with rich sensations of fresh citrus, crusty bread, peach and melon, lifted by a delightful contrast of soft and aromatic hints in the mouth. The traditional Tocai has curious balsam and dried flowers, then an intriguingly intense almond-dominated progression on the palate. The Merlot is concentrated and complex. A minty front palate gives way to fruit tart, vanilla, chocolate and coffee in a lingering finish. Verduzzo Pra Zenâr and Picolit, the two Rodaro sweet wines are likeable. The former has good balance and the Picolit unveils citrus, candied apricot and orange blossom aromas.

After its recent vicissitudes, oenologist Piero Pittaro's winery is back in the Guide. The 85-hectare estate on the lean flatland soil of Codroipo can boast 350 kilometres of vine rows and a headquarters with an interesting wine museum. With the aid of oenologist, Stefano Trinco, and Patrizia Pittaro, the commercial manager, Piero Pittaro presented the panel with a fine range of wines. The best were a vintage Brut and an irresistible Moscato Rosa. Pittaro was one of the first winemakers in Friuli to experiment with the "metodo classico". Over the years, he has fine-tuned techniques and for some time has been making classy sparklers. This year's are especially good. The vintage Brut, from pinot nero, chardonnay and pinot bianco, has tiny, lingering bubbles and broad yeast, nut and fig aromas. The palate is rich with sensations of figs and acacia honey, nicely offset by pear. The other Brut, with a silver label, is uncomplicated and fresh-tasting. Valzer in Rosa is a pastel-labelled Moscato Rosa from super-ripe fruit. Fresh wild roses, apricot and custard-filled wafer on the nose introduce a mouthfilling palate, where restrained sweetness is delightfully contrasted by acidity and raspberry in the long finish. The chardonnay, sauvignon and riesling Bianco shows complex mint, lime blossom and peach. The development on the palate is bright and fresh, echoing the nose satisfyingly. The citrus and tropical fruit Chardonnay Mousqué is intriguing on the nose, but fairly unexciting in the mouth.

● COF Merlot Romain '01		♟♟	7
○ COF Picolit '01		♟♟	7
○ COF Verduzzo Friulano Pra Zenâr '01		♟♟	6
○ Ronc '01		♟♟	4*
○ COF Tocai Friulano '02		♟♟	4*
● COF Refosco P. R. Romain '01		♟♟	6
○ COF Chardonnay '02		♟	4
○ COF Pinot Grigio '02		♟	4
○ COF Ribolla Gialla '02		♟	4
○ COF Sauvignon '02		♟	4
○ COF Sauvignon Bosc Romain '96		♟♟♟	5
○ Ronc '00		♟♟♟	4
● COF Refosco P. R. Romain '00		♟♟	7
○ COF Tocai Friulano '01		♟♟	4

○ Talento Brut Etichetta Oro '94		♟♟	6
● Moscato Rosa Valzer in Rosa '02		♟♟	4*
○ Talento Brut Etichetta Argento		♟	5
○ Friuli Grave Chardonnay Mousqué '02		♟	3
○ Friuli Grave Bianco '02		♟	4
● Friuli Grave Cabernet '00			4

CORMONS (GO)

BORGO DEL TIGLIO
LOC. BRAZZANO
VIA SAN GIORGIO, 71
34070 CORMONS (GO)
TEL. 048162166

Nicola Manferrari's wines continue to attract attention and plaudits. It is obvious that they are the product of a coherent philosophy, original insights, painstaking research and admirable technical skills. This year, we were pleased to welcome back the legendary Ronco della Chiesa, a Tocai that is not released as a DOC wine to sidestep the thorny international problems surrounding the name. In the past, Ronco della Chiesa was one of the trailblazers in promoting the variety, but we should remember the entry on the nose that characterizes Nicola's young white wines: very milky, slightly reduced and not very elegant. You need a broad-rimmed glass and a little patience. Ideally, give the bottle cellar time, but if you have uncorked it young, do let it breathe. The nose will clear and, in this case, acquire power, releasing grapefruit, bananas, peaches and roasted almonds. The palate is harmonious, meaty and well-sustained by acidity and lingering aromas. The other two whites are very good. We liked the Malvasia, and in fact Nicola is in the forefront of winemakers who are promoting this noble local variety. Borgo del Tiglio is equally strong in reds, including the legendary and hard-to-find Rosso della Centa. The dried flower, autumn leaves and plum Rosso Riserva is up there with it, thanks to convincing length.

CORMONS (GO)

BORGO SAN DANIELE
VIA SAN DANIELE, 16
34071 CORMONS (GO)
TEL. 048160552
E-MAIL: info@borgosandaniele.it

Borgo San Daniele is a new estate that has carved a precise niche for itself on the Friulian wine scene, thanks to the sheer personality of the Mauro siblings. Alessandra is the rational thinker in the family and Mauro, active in vineyard and cellar, is its creative spirit. Both share a passion for their work and a sensitivity that they transmit to their wines. Their commitment is obvious in some of the winery's strategic choices. Every year, the Mauros' 45,000 bottles demonstrate a desire to communicate a precise style, one that is driven by constant improvements, although their feet stay firmly planted on the ground of tradition. That is why the pair have decided to use the classic Friulian 20-hectolitre barrel for their whites. Three wines went through to our final tastings, but it was Arbis Blanc 2002, from sauvignon, chardonnay, pinot bianco and tocai, that carried off a third Glass. The sumptuous nose fuses sun-dried hay, pears, apples and caramel before tempting acidity emerges on a palate that builds up to a thrilling finish. The invitingly elegant Pinot Grigio mingles balsam with tropical aromas and has good thrust on the palate. The Tocai is from part super-ripe fruit and reveals some untypical features. In fact, it recalls wines from Alsace or late-harvest Verdicchio in some respects. The acidity on entry is low key, but mineral hints emerge to give the finish the right note of freshness. The pignolo and cabernet Arbis Ros is a likeably refreshing early drinker.

○ Collio Bianco		
Ronco della Chiesa '01	♈♈♈	6
● Collio Rosso Ris. '99	♈♈	6
○ Collio Bianco '00	♈♈	6
○ Collio Malvasia '00	♈♈	6
○ Collio Tocai Friulano		
Ronco della Chiesa '90	♈♈♈	6
○ Collio Chardonnay Sel. '99	♈♈♈	6
○ Collio Chardonnay '00	♈♈♈	5
○ Collio Bianco		
Ronco della Chiesa '00	♈♈	6
○ Collio Studio di Bianco '00	♈♈	6
○ Collio Tocai Friulano '00	♈♈	5
● Collio Rosso Ris. '97	♈♈	5

○ Friuli Isonzo Arbis Blanc '02	♈♈♈	5
○ Friuli Isonzo Pinot Grigio '02	♈♈	5
○ Friuli Isonzo Tocai Friulano '02	♈♈	5
● Friuli Isonzo Arbis Ros '01	♈♈	5
○ Friuli Isonzo Tocai Friulano '97	♈♈♈	5
○ Friuli Isonzo Pinot Grigio '99	♈♈♈	5
● Gortmarin '97	♈♈	5
○ Friuli Isonzo Tocai Friulano '01	♈♈	5
● Arbis Rosso '00	♈	5

CORMONS (GO)

MAURIZIO BUZZINELLI
LOC. PRADIS, 20
34071 CORMONS (GO)
TEL. 048160902
E-MAIL: buzzinelli@libero.it

There may have been too many distractions this year for Maurizio Businelli. This promising young winemaker's cellar is on the hillside at Pradis, one of the finest locations for making superior whites, and Maurizio has recently had to cope with the complete restructuring of his cellar. In fact, work continued as we were writing this profile. In addition, he was looking forward to marrying his long-time partner, Marzia, after the 2003 harvest. So there have been plenty of other things to worry about or prepare for disturbing the serenity necessary for getting the very best out of the fruit. The 2002 vintage yielded Maurizio and his 20 hectares 80,000 bottles of reliably good wine, but without the high scorers that there have been in previous years. Buzzinelli releases his wines under two labels. Ronc dal Luis is for oak-matured wines, whereas the other bottles have no specific label name. Maurizio's Malvasia continues to be a splendid example of how to combine aromas and elegance. The attractively fresh Bianco Ronc dal Luis has a splendid follow-through on the palate, as do the Ribolla Gialla, the Müller Thurgau and the Tocai Friulano.

CORMONS (GO)

PAOLO CACCESE
LOC. PRADIS, 6
34071 CORMONS (GO)
TEL. 048161062
E-MAIL: info@paolocaccese.com

Paolo Caccese's six hectares under vine are all at his lovely cellar in the upper part of Pradis, one of the finest wine locations in the entire Collio. Paolo sets great store by the small dimensions of his estate, which allow it to be run as a family enterprise with only occasional help from outside. And it is quite true that extending a winery's vineyard holding involves radical re-organization, something that many small cellars are unable or unwilling to tackle. In the letter he wrote to the Guide when we were tasting, Paolo bemoaned the heavy rains in July and early August 2002, and the very dry spell after 23 August. This was especially detrimental to the Sauvignon, which failed to develop its normal broad range of aromas. Difficult growing years like 2002 tend to confirm that Paolo Caccese is not wrong to cultivate ten or more different varieties: some of them will yield good-quality grapes. The Tocai Friulano and the Malvasia, two varieties that are so well acclimatized in Friuli that we can regard them as native, again achieved excellent results. The Tocai is tight-knit and fruit-rich, the Malvasia fresh-tasting, complex and flavoursome.

O	Collio Bianco Ronc dal Luis '02	♀	4
O	Collio Malvasia Ronc dal Luis '02	♀	4
O	Collio Müller Thurgau '02	♀	3
O	Collio Pinot Bianco '02	♀	3
O	Collio Ribolla Gialla '02	♀	3
O	Collio Tocai Friulano '02	♀	3
O	Collio Bianco Frututis Ronc dal Luis '01	♀♀	4

O	Collio Malvasia '02	♀♀	4*
O	Collio Tocai Friulano '02	♀♀	4*
O	Collio Müller Thurgau '02	♀	4
O	Collio Pinot Bianco '02	♀	4
O	Collio Pinot Grigio '02	♀	4
●	Collio Cabernet Franc '01		4
O	Collio Sauvignon '02		4
O	Collio Traminer Aromatico '02		4
O	Collio Tocai Friulano '01	♀♀	4*

CORMONS (GO)

CARLO DI PRADIS
LOC. PRADIS, 22/BIS
34071 CORMONS (GO)
TEL. 048162272
E-MAIL: carlodipradis@tin.it

Pradis, between Cormons and Capriva, is especially good wine country and its gentle slopes are outstandingly well-aspected. It is here that we find the cellar of Boris and David Buzzinelli, two brothers who learned the secrets of winemaking from their father, Carlo. The Buzzinellis have about 12 hectares under vine near the winery itself, in the Collio, and on the flatlands below, in the Isonzo DOC zone. The distinction is maintained in the wines, particularly the BorDavi line, the label under which the Isonzo wines are released to make them instantly recognizable. In general, the quality of the range is reliable and uniform, but the hillside products do offer peaks of excellence. Let's take, for example, the Collio Bianco 2001, a blend of steel-fermented tocai friulano, malvasia, pinot bianco and sauvignon aged in five-hectolitre oak casks. Its brilliant straw yellow introduces an elegant nose and sure, lingering progression on the palate, evidence that the vintage imbued the wine with good warmth. The Tocai 2002 lives up to expectations. It's crisp, well-typed and redolent of banana. Among the reds, the Merlot BorDavi 2001 just missed a second Glass for its delicate biscuit and cherry nose and dense, vigorous palate, which impresses with its depth and balance. We preferred the flatlands version of Pinot Grigio 2002 for its greater length and more discreet acidity in the finish.

CORMONS (GO)

COLLE DUGA
LOC. ZEGLA, 10
34071 CORMONS (GO)
TEL. 048161177

Damian Princic's home-cum-winery stands in a vine-clad area with the Italy-Slovenia border running through it. The frontier is marked on the paths through the vineyards by tiny white stones. If you miss them, you can easily find yourself abroad without a passport. In fact, this temptingly permeable border is a magnet for smugglers of goods and people. Evening visitors to Damian's cellar may find themselves challenged by the border police looking for illegal migrants. Damian and his father, Luciano, look after about seven hectares of vineyards near the winery. The cellars themselves are underground and fitted with the necessary stainless steel equipment. There is also a small barrel cellar, which perfectly reflects Damian Princic's serious personality and winemaking style. Last year, Damian came close to Three Glasses with his Merlot 2000 and Tocai Friulano 2001. This time, he was back at the taste-offs with his Pinot Grigio 2002, which combines a stylish nose of apples, pears and tropical fruit with a good follow-through on the full palate. The endless finish is also rich in fruit. Damian's Collio Bianco, from chardonnay, tocai friulano and sauvignon, has impressive breadth of fruit and the Tocai Friulano mingles a fat mouthfeel and alcoholic warmth with outstanding elegance. The Merlot is still young, so its present excellence can only be enhanced by age.

O	Collio Bianco Pradis '01	🍷🍷	4*
O	Collio Tocai Friulano '02	🍷🍷	4*
●	Friuli Isonzo Cabernet BorDavi '01	🍷	4
●	Friuli Isonzo Rosso BorDavi '01	🍷	4
●	Friuli Isonzo Merlot BorDavi '01	🍷	4
O	Collio Pinot Grigio '02	🍷	4
O	Collio Sauvignon '02	🍷	4
O	Friuli Isonzo Pinot Grigio BorDavi '02	🍷	4
●	Collio Merlot '00		5
O	Collio Bianco Pradis '00	🍷🍷	4
●	Collio Merlot '99	🍷🍷	5

O	Collio Pinot Grigio '02	🍷🍷	4*
●	Collio Merlot '01	🍷🍷	4
O	Collio Bianco '02	🍷🍷	4
O	Collio Tocai Friulano '02	🍷🍷	4
O	Collio Chardonnay '02	🍷	4
●	Collio Merlot '00	🍷🍷	4
O	Collio Tocai Friulano '01	🍷🍷	4

CORMONS (GO)

CORMONS (GO)

CANTINA PRODUTTORI DI CORMONS
VIA VINO DELLA PACE, 31
34071 CORMONS (GO)
TEL. 048162471 - 048160579
E-MAIL: info@cormons.com

MAURO DRIUS
VIA FILANDA, 100
34071 CORMONS (GO)
TEL. 048160998
E-MAIL: drius.mauro@adriacom.it

The Cantina Produttori di Cormons is a sizeable winery, in local terms, both for its production and for the professional stimulus it continues to provide for members and winelovers in general. For example, we could mention the independent weather monitoring network, the agricultural techniques that members are expected to use, the systematic analysis of climatic data, organic vineyard management, the focus on product-related health issues and the extremely informative back label on the bottles. The downside is represented by the vast product range. It is far from easy to find your way through the forest of bottles, which on occasion may present contradictory sensory characteristics. There is a new range, Rinascimento, inspired by the health considerations mentioned above. The wines are from organically farmed grapes, crushed and cold macerated in cellar-patented pneumatic presses to extract the antioxidant and heart-protecting qualities of the skins. Partially fermented in large oak casks, the wine ages for several months on the fine lees. We will have to wait to taste these new products but in the meantime, the best of this year's bottles – and not for the first time – was the flagship Vino della Pace. Intended to convey a message of solidarity to the world, it also shows a very convincing, if untypical, palate.

Mauro Drius has 11 hectares under vine in the two Cormons DOC zones (Collio and Friuli Isonzo). In recent years, he has given his estate an increasingly effective orientation. Mauro consistently turns out first-quality wines. They may not be innovative but they are whistle-clean, sophisticated and eloquent witnesses to his undoubted ability to transfer his superb raw material into the bottle. And only a few months after the arrival of a new daughter, the Drius family now receives Three Glasses from the Guide. The star wine is a Tocai, a semi-aromatic variety whose typicity was enhanced by the coolish weather during 2002. Mauro was able to craft both the Collio and Isonzo versions into outstanding wines that embody the characteristics of their terroir. The hillside Tocai has more volume and richness. Its exciting nose hints at apple and almond that are echoed faithfully on the long, harmonious palate. In contrast, the Isonzo version is more vibrant and vertical, its nose showing geraniums and white peach, lifted by a delightful note of botrytis. Mauro's Pinot Bianco, from a very old vineyard, is a wine that never lets you down. Young on the palate, it has plenty of ripe fruit, apple and crusty bread that mingle with appealing elegance. Chamomile and spring flowers grace the nose of the tangy, lingering Malvasia. If it had had a little more finesse, it would have been even better than the reliable Pinot Grigio and Sauvignon.

O	Vino della Pace '00	♟♟	6
O	Collio Collio '02	♟	4
O	Collio Pinot Grigio '02	♟	4
O	Collio Sauvignon '02	♟	4
O	Collio Tocai Friulano Rinascimento '02	♟	4
O	Friuli Isonzo Bianco Pietraverde '02	♟	3
O	Friuli Isonzo Verduzzo Dorè '02	♟	3
O	Malvasia '02	♟	3
O	Pinot Bianco '02	♟	3
O	Friuli Isonzo Sauvignon '02		3

O	Collio Tocai Friulano '02	♟♟♟	4*
O	Friuli Isonzo Tocai Friulano '02	♟♟	4*
●	Friuli Isonzo Merlot '01	♟♟	4
O	Collio Sauvignon '02	♟♟	4
O	Friuli Isonzo Pinot Bianco '02	♟♟	4
O	Friuli Isonzo Pinot Grigio '02	♟♟	4
O	Friuli Isonzo Bianco Vìgnis di Sìris '02	♟	4
O	Friuli Isonzo Malvasia '02	♟	4
O	Friuli Isonzo Pinot Bianco '00	♟♟♟	4
O	Friuli Isonzo Pinot Bianco '01	♟♟	4
●	Friuli Isonzo Merlot '00	♟♟	4

CORMONS (GO)

BRANKO - IGOR ERZETIC
LOC. ZEGLA, 20
34071 CORMONS (GO)
TEL. 0481639826

Branko Erzetic never imagined that his son, Igor, who studied as a wine technician and worked at a number of major Friulian cellars, would one day want to start his own winery. Yet in 1998, Igor started out with a single hectare under vine, first replanting and then adding a further three estate-owned or rented hectares. The few wines Igor has made are simply stellar. Unlike many of his fellow winemakers, Igor concentrated on four white grapes and two red. Except for the Sauvignon, all the wines are part-aged in tonneau. As this is the cellar's principal technique, it is obvious that complicated technology is superfluous. But do visit the winery to experience the Erzetic family's open-armed hospitality. Last year, three out of four wines scored Two and a Half Glasses and this time, four out of five repeated the performance. Obviously, Branko wines are released in very limited numbers and thus far from easy to get hold of. The Tocai Friulano has a superb, fruit-forward palate, remarkable balance and very long length. Red Branko is mainly from merlot. Supple and concentrated, it offers tobacco, liquorice and tar on the nose. The Chardonnay has warm notes of very ripe fruit, then the palate marries complexity and freshness, which are also present in the Pinot Grigio.

CORMONS (GO)

★ LIVIO FELLUGA
FRAZ. BRAZZANO
VIA RISORGIMENTO, 1
34070 CORMONS (GO)
TEL. 048160203
E-MAIL: info@liviofelluga.it

Although he is approaching 90 years of age, Livio Felluga is still emblematic of Friulian winemaking, of which – we should remember – he was one of the founders. His children Maurizio, Elda, Andrea and Filippo have split among them the various areas of estate activity, but Livio continues to map out, with astonishing lucidity, the winery's strategic decisions. Today, the estate extends over 160 hectares, 135 planted to vine, and annual production is around 650,000 bottles that are exported around the globe. Recently, various replantings have been undertaken, as well as improvements to cellar equipment, while the hospitality and tasting rooms at the headquarters have also been refurbished. This year, the Fellugas are celebrating the 20th birthday of Terre Alte, a wine that Maurizio in particular regards as his brainchild. A mix of tocai friulano, sauvignon and pinot bianco, Terre Alte is one of the finest whites produced in Italy. For a few years now, it has undergone brief cask conditioning and the result is an impressively fruit-rich (apricot and yellow peach), creamy textured wine that lingers on the palate. Drinking deliciously now, it will be at its awesome best four to six years after the harvest. Other flagship wines to note are the Shàrjs, a lovely chardonnay and ribolla gialla blend, the Picolit Riserva '99, the Tocai Friulano and the chardonnay and sauvignon Collio Bianco Rosenplatz.

● Red Branko '01	♀♀	5
○ Collio Chardonnay '02	♀♀	5
○ Collio Pinot Grigio '02	♀♀	4
○ Collio Tocai Friulano '02	♀♀	4
○ Collio Sauvignon '02	♀♀	4
○ Collio Pinot Grigio '01	♀♀	4
○ Collio Sauvignon '01	♀♀	4
○ Collio Tocai Friulano '01	♀♀	4
○ Collio Chardonnay '01	♀♀	4

○ COF Bianco Rosazzo Terre Alte '01	♀♀♀	6
○ COF Tocai Friulano '02	♀♀	5
○ Collio Bianco Rosenplatz '02	♀♀	4
○ Shàrjs '02	♀♀	4*
○ COF Rosazzo Picolit Ris. '99	♀♀	8
○ COF Pinot Grigio '02	♀	5
○ COF Sauvignon '02	♀	4
● COF Refosco P. R. '97	♀♀♀	7
○ COF Bianco Rosazzo Terre Alte '97	♀♀♀	6
● COF Refosco P. R. '99	♀♀♀	7
○ COF Bianco Rosazzo Terre Alte '00	♀♀	6
● COF Rosazzo Sossò Ris. '99	♀♀	7

CORMONS (GO)

CORMONS (GO)

EDI KEBER
LOC. ZEGLA, 17
34071 CORMONS (GO)
TEL. 048161184

LA BOATINA
VIA CORONA, 62
34076 CORMONS (GO)
TEL. 048160445 - 0481639914
E-MAIL: info@boatina.com

A few years ago, Edi Keber decided to revamp and extend his cellar and the house under which it stands. This enabled him to set up a by then indispensable new binning cellar, as well as a series of underground tunnels for ageing certain of his wines. The bare marl of the walls is a spectacular visual plus. As we write these notes, work in the house is still under way to provide accommodation for cellar visitors and passing tourists. Over the past several years, Edi has been a welcome rarity on the Friulian wine scene for two main reasons. The first is his pricing policy. Increases are always modest, regardless of the awards that the wine guides have heaped on him. The other reason that sets Edi apart was his decision a few years ago to release no more than four labels a year: Tocai Friulano, Collio Bianco, Collio Rosso and, in exceptional vintages, Merlot. It is one more thing that makes Edi such a sincere, frankly spoken winemaker, as well as a very generous host. As you will note from the table below, the Keber Tocai Friulano is a Three Glass regular every other year. And again, in the even-numbered 2002 vintage, this magnificent white did not quite win top honours. It was the Collio Bianco, a blend of whites from old vines, that brought home the bacon. Crisp, well-defined pear dominates the nose, with a good follow-through on the warm, rich palate, where fresh acidity prolongs the already stunningly impressive length.

Loretto Pali made his fortune manufacturing babies' cots. A few years ago, he decided to invest in wine, a field to which he has devoted an increasing amount of his time and attention. That was when he began taking on top-level consultants, the only ones that could ensure the best results in the shortest time. Domenico Lovat, for many years the cellar's oenologist, has found new stimulus with the arrival of consultant Gianni Menotti. In the vineyard, Loretto expanded the area under vine to 36 hectares, which he planted with assistance from fruitmakers Marco Simonit and Pierpaolo Sirch. Part of the estate complex is an elegant "agriturismo" holiday centre, with attractive accommodation, and a few hundred yards away stands the Ritrovo La Boatina cellar-door sales outlet, also famous for its huge range of cheeses and salamis from all over the world. Pali wants to release his Isonzo DOC wines exclusively under the La Boatina label, keeping the Collio fruit for his other well-known cellar, Castello di Spesso. Rosso Picol Maggiore, from 75 per cent merlot with cabernet sauvignon and a small proportion of cabernet franc, ages half in French oak and half in Slavonian. The result is a starry concentration of warm, ripe red berry fruit, held back a shade by the astringency of the tannins. The lovely Merlot is only a point or two behind.

○ Collio Bianco '02	♟♟♟	4*
○ Collio Tocai Friulano '02	♟	4
○ Collio Tocai Friulano '95	♟♟♟	4
○ Collio Tocai Friulano '97	♟♟♟	4
○ Collio Tocai Friulano '99	♟♟♟	4
○ Collio Tocai Friulano '01	♟♟♟	4
● Collio Merlot '00	♟♟	5
● Collio Rosso '01	♟	5

● Collio Rosso Picol Maggiore '99	♟♟	6
● Collio Merlot '01	♟♟	5
○ Collio Pinot Grigio '02	♟♟	5
○ Collio Sauvignon '02	♟♟	5
○ Collio Tocai Friulano '02	♟♟	5
● Collio Cabernet Sauvignon '01	♟	5
● Collio Cabernet Franc '02	♟	5
○ Collio Chardonnay '02	♟	5
○ Collio Ribolla Gialla '02	♟	5
● Collio Cabernet Sauvignon '00	♟♟	4
○ Collio Sauvignon '01	♟♟	4

CORMONS (GO)

MAGNÀS
VIA CORONA, 47
34071 CORMONS (GO)
TEL. 048160991

Magnàs is a small, family-run winery on the flatlands near Cormons and Gradisca. It takes its name from the owner, Luciano Visintin, nicknamed "Magnàs", who runs it with his son, Andrea, and wife, Sonia. The winery vinifies the grapes from eight hectares of vineyards to produce about 20,000 bottles. There is also a cattle and pig farm, and a delightful holiday centre in the restored farmhouse. In recent years, the estate has focused more on wine, which has led to an across-the-board improvement in the quality of the range. The 2002 wines lack the presence on the palate of previous vintages, but only because the less favourable weather over the year was in general colder. Acidity, freshness and drinkability are the distinguishing characteristics of last year's wines. The gold-flecked, straw-yellow Chardonnay has pineapple and tropical fruit, echoed on a palate supported by fresh acidity. The Pinot Grigio has nicely intense aromas of slightly forward pears. These are mirrored on a moderately broad palate with a bitter twist in the finish. The richly coloured Tocai has a full front palate that thins as it progresses. The vegetal aromas of the Sauvignon are a tad intrusive and the Merlot has still to bring its lively tannins to heel.

○	Friuli Isonzo Chardonnay '02	🍷🍷	4*
●	Friuli Isonzo Merlot '02	🍷	4
○	Friuli Isonzo Pinot Grigio '02	🍷	4
○	Friuli Isonzo Sauvignon '02	🍷	4
○	Friuli Isonzo Tocai Friulano '02	🍷	4
○	Friuli Isonzo Chardonnay '01	🍷🍷 (outline)	4

CORMONS (GO)

GIULIO MANZOCCO
VIA C. BATTISTI, 61
34071 CORMONS (GO)
TEL. 048160590
E-MAIL: vinimanzocco@libero.it

Founded in 1930 when grandfather Amedeo came back from Australia, the Manzocco estate owes first to Giulio, and now to Giulio's son, Dario, the continuity required by an ambitious winery that can call on strong family tradition. Thirty per cent of the seven or so hectares under vine are in the marly Collio and the remainder stand on the gravel of the Isonzo DOC. In the 1960s, the Manzoccos abandoned oak for cement and stainless steel, but now they have gone back to wood for ageing the Verduzzo – which hints at the family's roots in Nimis – and a Merlot selection. But the cellar's highest score was achieved by the Riesling, a variety from the Austrian and German traditions. Elegantly aristocratic banana and grapefruit, with a hint of bottle age, greet the nose, then the palate shows very soft on entry, if a tad dry in the finish. The most successful wines from the Isonzo range are the fresh, subtly spicy Merlot and the intense Sauvignon. In the Collio part of the list, the slightly tousled Pinot Grigio reveals bright acidity, and the Pinot Bianco follows up a milk and cream nose with a faintly pungent palate. The Traminer Aromatico has well-typed spices and rose on the nose that follow through in the mouth. Only excessive residual sugar denied it a higher score at our tasting.

○	Friuli Isonzo Riesling '02	🍷🍷	4*
●	Collio Merlot '01	🍷	4
●	Friuli Isonzo Merlot '01	🍷	4
○	Collio Pinot Bianco '02	🍷	4
○	Collio Pinot Grigio '02	🍷	4
○	Collio Traminer Aromatico '02	🍷	4
○	Friuli Isonzo Sauvignon '02	🍷	4
●	Friuli Isonzo Refosco P. R. '01		4
○	Friuli Isonzo Bianco '02		4
●	Friuli Isonzo Cabernet Franc '02		4

CORMONS (GO)

ROBERTO PICECH - LE VIGNE DEL RIBÉL
LOC. PRADIS, 11
34071 CORMONS (GO)
TEL. 048160347
E-MAIL: picech@libero.it

The porcupine's snout peeking out from a mass of spines on the label of Roberto Picech's wines reflects the nature of the people who live in this borderland: a little prickly at the edges, but with a big heart. That's what Egidio, Roberto's father and the "Ribél" ("rebel") to whom the vineyards are dedicated, was like. But Roberto is approachable, a good mixer and as modern as the wines he obtains from seven hectares at Pradis, in the heart of the Collio at Cormons. This year, major work in the cellar has had an effect on production, which runs at 27,000 bottles. Some of the wines are less than whistle-clean but the fruit they come from is always first class, so standards are nonetheless high. The best of the range this year is the Collio Rosso, a blend of cabernet franc and sauvignon. Don't look for intense aromas, but the wine explodes onto the palate, which has breadth and red berry fruit depth, as well as upfront tannins. The vintage was a good one for Pinot Bianco. The Picech version tempts with crusty bread, white damson and sweet tobacco, finishing on a note of almonds. The Malvasia is redolent of dried flowers, pear and apple, then unveils a note of citrus on the back palate. The Tocai promises miracles in a nose that deliciously offsets fresh almonds against fattier notes of orange ice cream, but the palate lacks breadth although the finish is long. The Bianco Jelka, from ribolla, tocai and malvasia, offers no more than nice ripe fruit, roses and wistaria on the nose. The palate has yet to settle down.

CORMONS (GO)

ALDO POLENCIC
LOC. PLESSIVA, 13
34071 CORMONS (GO)
TEL. 048161027
E-MAIL: info@polencic.com

Aldo Polencic farms his small six-hectare property at Cormons with a determination that is focused on taking the wines to the very top. He is seeking to expand the estate, but refuses to compromise on quality. He is looking for hillside plots with older vines, in order not to muddy the unique profiles of his range. Soon work will be starting on the cellar extension to create new areas for barriques and bottles. This year, Aldo opted to released his Pinot Bianco at once, so we were able to taste two vintages side by side. But let's get back to the wines. They all have outstanding finesse and a well-gauged, very balanced use of small oak barrels. The newer Pinot Bianco, for example, is powerful, with intense yellow peach, petit fours and tropical fruit aromas. In the mouth, a successful contrast of toastiness, butter richness and soft fruit melds into an elegant whole. The 2001 version has greener notes of apple and almond, and a shade less complexity on the palate. The Tocai has marked apple and pear preserve, wistaria and fresh citrus. The warmth and depth of the palate end with hints of vanilla and tropical fruit. The ripe fruit of the Pinot Grigio, and the sweetness supported by robust tannins of the Merlot, are also very attractive.

● Collio Rosso '02	▼▼	4*
○ Collio Malvasia '02	▼▼	4
○ Collio Pinot Bianco '02	▼▼	4
○ Collio Tocai Friulano '02	▼▼	4
○ Collio Bianco Jelka '02	▼	5
○ Collio Bianco Jelka '99	▼▼▼	4
○ Collio Pinot Bianco '01	▼▼	4
● Collio Rosso '01	▼▼	4
● Collio Rosso Ris. '99	▼▼	6

○ Collio Pinot Bianco degli Ulivi '02	▼▼	6
○ Collio Pinot Bianco degli Ulivi '01	▼▼	6
○ Collio Tocai Friulano '02	▼▼	4*
○ Collio Pinot Grigio '02	▼	4
● Collio Merlot degli Ulivi '01	▼	6
○ Collio Tocai Friulano '00	▼▼▼	4
○ Collio Pinot Bianco degli Ulivi '00	▼▼	5

CORMONS (GO)

ISIDORO POLENCIC
LOC. PLESSIVA, 12
34071 CORMONS (GO)
TEL. 048160655

The Isidoro Polencic winery began operations in 1976. It has 25 hectares under vine, almost all in the Collio, with a few plots in the Isonzo DOC. Young but capable Michele Polencic is in charge of the cellar, having served an apprenticeship under his father, expert wineman, Isidoro. About 150,000 bottles a year are released. It should be said straight away that the fresh-tasting, approachable Polencic wines are technically well made and invitingly moreish. We'll start with the Pinot Grigio, a variety that is very much at home here, considering the outstanding results achieved year after year. The 2002 edition is subtly elegant, releasing delightful aromas of pears, apples, flowers and walnutskin. The attack on the palate is intense, the progression bright and refreshing. Bianco, from tocai and pinot bianco grapes, is equally good, unveiling wistaria and acacia blossom flowers over apple and a very fresh-tasting palate. The very varietal Pinot Bianco is clean and tangy. Oblin Ros, an impressively complex Bordeaux blend, foregrounds attractive sour cherry syrup on nose and palate. The mainly chardonnay (with tocai and ribolla) Oblin Blanc just missed out on a second Glass. Melon and orange come through on the nose, but the finish is a little unexciting. The Tocai lacks complexity, the Chardonnay has varietal aromas of banana, and the Sauvignon reveals a charming finish of tomato.

CORMONS (GO)

ALESSANDRO PRINCIC
LOC. PRADIS, 5
34071 CORMONS (GO)
TEL. 048160723
E-MAIL: prcarl@libero.it

Doro Princic is one of the greats of Friulian winemaking who passed away this year. He left behind memories of many long chats together, his legendary ability to assess a wine with one sniff of the glass, his shrewdness and his old countryman's wisdom. Doro's son, Sandro, is a marvellously friendly and hospitable character. He paid tribute to his father's memory with a range in which none of the wines tasted failed to achieve a Two Glass score. In fact, while last year there were two Princic wines in the final round of taste-offs, this year four went forward. Visits to the cellar, if duly booked in advance, are something of a challenge to one's stamina. As Sandro uncorks the bottles, his wife Grazia will bring out plate after plate what she likes to think are mere nibbles. The estate has ten hectares under vine and annual production is more or less 60,000 bottles. For the past couple of years, Sandro has been advised by Luigino De Giuseppe. The new oenologist appears to have added elegance to the weight of the Princic wines. Both Tocais – the Crôs Altis is cask conditioned – are magnificent, the Malvasia is spectacular and the flagship Pinot Bianco is as good as any. Intense golden delicious apple on the nose introduces a tight-knit palate that combines richness and alcohol with refreshing acidity. The Three Glass award is back in the Princic trophy cabinet, a fitting tribute to Doro and a family in Friuli's finest country tradition.

●	Oblin Ros '00	♟♟	5
○	Collio Bianco '02	♟♟	4
○	Collio Pinot Bianco '02	♟♟	4
○	Collio Pinot Grigio '02	♟♟	4
○	Oblin Blanc '01	♟	5
○	Collio Chardonnay '02	♟	4
○	Collio Sauvignon '02	♟	4
○	Collio Tocai Friulano '02	♟	4
○	Collio Pinot Grigio '98	♟♟♟	4
○	Oblin Blanc '00	♟♟	5
●	Oblin Ros '99	♟	5

○	Collio Pinot Bianco '02	♟♟♟	5
○	Collio Malvasia '02	♟♟	5
○	Collio Tocai Friulano '02	♟♟	5
○	Collio Tocai Friulano Crôs Altis '02	♟♟	5
●	Collio Cabernet Franc '01	♟♟	5
○	Collio Pinot Grigio '02	♟♟	5
○	Collio Sauvignon '02	♟♟	5
○	Collio Tocai Friulano '93	♟♟♟	5
○	Collio Pinot Bianco '95	♟♟♟	5
○	Collio Malvasia '01	♟♟	5
○	Collio Pinot Bianco '01	♟♟	4*

CORMONS (GO)

DARIO RACCARO
FRAZ. ROLAT
VIA SAN GIOVANNI, 87
34071 CORMONS (GO)
TEL. 048161425

We have stopped being surprised at the fantastic quality of Dario Raccaro's wines. But it is still astonishing to find that all of them went forward to the finals. True, there were only four, for a total production of 20,000 bottles sourced from four hectares under vine. We believe this is a superb result that rewards a courageous decision taken by Dario several years ago. He slashed the number of labels he was releasing to create three single-variety wines – Tocai Friulano, Malvasia and Merlot – as well as one or two blends, Collio Bianco and, although not in every vintage, Collio Rosso. The limited production comes from a boutique-style cellar and binning cellar. Dario has intelligence and far-sightedness and while he can be argumentative, he is never bitter. In his own way, he is charismatic and in fact is regarded as a fixture in the presidency of the producers' association that manages the local public wine cellar, in tandem with the Cormons local authority. Our tasters were spoiled for choice this year. The Tocai Friulano, fruit-forward on nose and palate, was followed by a tocai, sauvignon and pinot grigio-based Collio Bianco of exceptionally close-knit texture and great length, then a Malvasia that combines elegance, fullness and complexity. There was also a well-structured but not heavy Merlot with admirable concentration and sweet tannins In the end, the Collio Bianco, a magnificent new interpretation of Friulian white wine, came out on top. It's also a bottle with fantastic cellar potential.

CORMONS (GO)

RONCADA
LOC. RONCADA, 5
34071 CORMONS (GO)
TEL. 048161394
E-MAIL: roncada@hotmail.com

Roncada had a difficult time last year but is now back with a full Guide profile. Grapes have been grown on the property since 1914, when the German owners of the day planted the first vines, having acquired the main house and estate from Angelo Levi of Villanova di Farra. Between the wars, the vineyard holding rose to ten hectares. There were several subsequent changes of ownership and in 1956, the estate passed to the Mattioni family from Gorizia. Today, the owner is Silvia Mattioni and the property embraces about 50 hectares, half planted to vine. Cellar management has long been in the reliable hands of Oscar Biasi, a very competent oenologist. A few months ago, crucial cellar improvements began. These will permit high quality standards across the range, which is currently very extensive and includes 16 labels. There were two high-scoring wines, the Pinot Bianco and the Sauvignon. The elegant Pinot Bianco has a well-sustained, tight-knit mouthfeel whereas the Sauvignon offers interesting apple and citrus notes, stylish structure and great length. The Ribolla Gialla, Tocai Friulano and Chardonnay all racked up scores just short of a second Glass. Bianco Chamür is a blend of tocai, malvasia and chardonnay.

○ Collio Bianco '02	♔♔♔	4
○ Collio Tocai Friulano '02	♔♔	5
● Collio Merlot '01	♔♔	6
○ Collio Malvasia '02	♔♔	4
○ Collio Tocai Friulano '00	♔♔♔	4
○ Collio Tocai Friulano '01	♔♔♔	4*
○ Collio Bianco '00	♔♔	4
● Collio Merlot '00	♔♔	4
○ Collio Bianco '01	♔♔	4*
○ Collio Malvasia '01	♔♔	4*

○ Collio Pinot Bianco '02	♔♔	4*
○ Collio Sauvignon '02	♔♔	4*
● Collio Cabernet Sauvignon '01	♔	4
○ Collio Bianco Chamür '02	♔	4
○ Collio Chardonnay '02	♔	4
○ Collio Ribolla Gialla '02	♔	4
○ Collio Tocai Friulano '02	♔	4
● Collio Cabernet Franc '01		4
● Collio Merlot '01		4
● Franconia '01		4

CORMONS (GO)

RONCO DEI TASSI
LOC. MONTE, 38
34071 CORMONS (GO)
TEL. 048160155
E-MAIL: info@roncodeitassi.it

Fabio Coser is an outstanding oenologist and, while shunning the limelight, has helped the many estates he works with in Friuli to improve the quality of their wines. Discreet, thoughtful, and always willing to question his beliefs, he engages his wines in a constant oenological dialogue. For Fabio, wines are not object of worship: they are expressions of their territory and varieties. By putting these ideas into practice, in vineyard and cellar, Fabio obtains bottles that bear his own inimitable hallmark. His 12 hectares under vine in the wooded hills near Cormons have produced two superb wines, a Tocai and the Cjarandon blended red. The Tocai is elegant, well typed and clean, with fresh almonds and williams pear on nose and fragrant palate. The long warm finish foregrounds almonds. The Cjarandon, a classic Bordeaux blend, is surprisingly complex in its cinchona, black cherry, cinnamon, cloves, mint and dried rose aromas. The crisp entry on the palate has warm fruit, then reveals robust tannins that lend it nobility and grace. The Bianco Fosarin, from tocai, malvasia and pinot bianco matured in wood, has very clean rose, peach and tropical fruit, echoed on the palate, which shows freshness and perfectly gauged acidity. The Pinot Grigio has intriguing hints of smokiness and coconut melding attractively with the variety's trademark mineral notes. The Sauvignon still shows the marks of its partial maturing in oak, which are nicely offset by sensations of orange and peach tea.

CORMONS (GO)

RONCO DEL GELSO
VIA ISONZO, 117
34071 CORMONS (GO)
TEL. 048161310
E-MAIL: roncodelgelso@libero.it

For the 2002 vintage, Giorgio Badin has changed the schedule for bottling and release of his wines. His steel-fermented products, Tocai, Sauvignon and Riesling, are still sent to market in spring for the time being, but the others will be given more bottle age and released after the summer. The next stage will be to delay release even further, which is all to the good, as the wines have shown they have ageing potential. This year, the wines provide ample evidence of Giorgio's passion for French-style products. The Merlot wins Three Glasses ten years after its last success, rewarding the cellar's efforts to find a very Bordeaux style of elegance and balance. With so many muscle-bound, over-extracted bottles jostling on wine shop shelves, it goes very much against the trend. Another wine that shows the winemaker's hand is the Riesling 2002, which may be the best version of this variety in Friuli. Rich in tropical fruit, grapefruit, pineapple and aromatic herbs, it shows complexity, freshness and a marvellous vocation for evolution in the cellar. Another "French" wine is the very minerally Chardonnay, which hints at botrytis and whose acidity is nicely marked by a caramel palate of outstanding finesse. The Tocai and Sauvignon are indisputably good. The Tocai, especially, offers very ripe notes interlaced with understated fruit nuances. The Pinot Grigio Sot lis Rivis is a case apart. Ripening on the vine was jeopardized by four separate hailstorms so Badin decided to ripen the fruit to the full, obtaining a wine that has a distinctly Alsatian tenor.

●	Collio Rosso Cjarandon '00	♟♟♟	5
○	Collio Tocai Friulano '02	♟♟	4*
○	Collio Bianco Fosarin '02	♟♟	4
○	Collio Pinot Grigio '02	♟♟	4
○	Collio Sauvignon '02	♟	4
○	Collio Bianco Fosarin '96	♟♟♟	4
○	Collio Sauvignon '98	♟♟♟	4
○	Collio Tocai Friulano '01	♟♟	4
●	Collio Rosso Cjarandon '99	♟	5

●	Friuli Isonzo Merlot '01	♟♟♟	5
○	Friuli Isonzo Chardonnay '02	♟♟	4
○	Friuli Isonzo Riesling '02	♟♟	4
○	Friuli Isonzo Sauvignon '02	♟♟	4
○	Friuli Isonzo Tocai Friulano '02	♟♟	4
●	Friuli Isonzo Cabernet Franc '02	♟	4
○	Friuli Isonzo Pinot Grigio Sot lis Rivis '02	♟	4
○	Friuli Isonzo Tocai Friulano '97	♟♟♟	4
○	Friuli Isonzo Sauvignon '98	♟♟♟	4
○	Friuli Isonzo Pinot Grigio Sot lis Rivis '99	♟♟♟	4
○	Friuli Isonzo Sauvignon '00	♟♟♟	4
○	Friuli Isonzo Tocai Friulano '01	♟♟♟	4

CORMONS (GO)

OSCAR STURM
LOC. ZEGLA, 1
34071 CORMONS (GO)
TEL. 048160720
E-MAIL: sturm@sturm.it

Despite Oscar Sturm's Austrian-sounding surname, he is a member of Italy's Slovene minority. His wife Dunja comes from Slovenia itself and they have three children. Denis, the eldest, studies at the Bocconi University in Milan, as well as taking an enthusiastic part in things in vineyard and cellar. His younger brother Patrick earned a diploma in oenology this year, but for years has been spending periods at wineries outside Friuli. Tajrin, their sister, is at secondary school and lends a hand at the winery when she is not studying. Such a close-knit family could only produce good wines with fine balance. Oscar has 11 hectares under vine, some with plants that are more than 30 years old, and the cellar was extended a few years ago. Today, space is sufficient, but it is getting increasingly restricted as more barrels are brought in. Production potential is 55-70,000 bottles a year. The wine that impressed the panel this year was the Tocai Friulano. A complex, intense, elegant nose ushers in a rich, seamless palate with tangy mineral flavours and very long length. The firm, full Pinot Grigio is again very good, as is the Chardonnay Andritz, which you would think had never seen oak. The sauvignon and pinot grigio Collio Bianco shows exceptional nose-palate consistency.

CORMONS (GO)

SUBIDA DI MONTE
LOC. MONTE, 9
34071 CORMONS (GO)
TEL. 048161011
E-MAIL: subida@libero.it

Young Cristian and Andrea Antonutti were well-taught by their father, Gigi. Now, they are putting that knowledge to good use in the winery with the enthusiasm of youth, making rapid progress in their efforts to raise quality levels. Under the watchful eye of agronomist and friend, Marco Simonit, the family is replanting the vineyards at higher densities (the ten hectares are being planted with gobelet and Guyot-trained vines at 7,000 plants per hectare). In the cellar, the white grapes are given low-temperature skin fermentation to extract their aromas to the full. Cristian and Andrea personally supervise all stages of winemaking to turn out 60,000 excellent bottles each year. Progress is already evident. The Pinot Grigio throws an intriguing nose of melon, wistaria, pear and apple. The rich, deep Tocai Selezione offers broom and citrus, layered over attractive, lingering balsam. These notes are echoed on the palate, which has a very refreshing finish. The Rosso Poncaia is equally good. A tonneau and barrique-aged Bordeaux blend, it convinced us with the complexity of its bottled fruit, cherry and vanilla aromatic spectrum. There is nice balance in the mouth, and the wine should improve further in the cellar. Be sure to check out the very varietal standard Tocai, the subtly fruity Sauvignon, with its tea, lime blossom, apricot and peach aromas, the youthfully alcoholic Cabernet Franc and the Chardonnay, which plays off toastiness and fruit to perfection.

○	Collio Tocai Friulano '02	🍷🍷	4*
○	Chardonnay Andritz '02	🍷🍷	4
○	Collio Bianco '02	🍷🍷	4
○	Collio Pinot Grigio '02	🍷🍷	4
●	Collio Merlot '01	🍷	4
○	Collio Sauvignon '02	🍷	4
○	Chardonnay Andritz '01	🍷🍷	4
○	Collio Pinot Grigio '01	🍷🍷	4
●	Collio Merlot '00	🍷🍷	4

●	Collio Rosso Poncaia '00	🍷🍷	6
○	Collio Pinot Grigio '02	🍷🍷	4*
○	Collio Tocai Friulano Sel. '02	🍷🍷	5
●	Collio Cabernet Franc '01	🍷	4
○	Collio Chardonnay Sel. '01	🍷	5
○	Collio Sauvignon '02	🍷	4
○	Collio Tocai Friulano '02	🍷	4
●	Collio Merlot '01		4
○	Collio Chardonnay Sel. '00	🍷🍷	5
●	Collio Merlot Sel. '99	🍷🍷	6

CORMONS (GO)

FRANCO TOROS
VIA NOVALI, 12
34071 CORMONS (GO)
TEL. 048161327

Franco Toros comes from a long line of farmers. His brother, Renato, is one of the area's best-known and most able pork butchers, which means that visitors to Franco's cellars can sample his wines accompanied with superb cold meats. The cellar was restructured a few years ago and there is an underground passage that serves as an archive of Toros wines. Franco has eight hectares of his own vines, behind the cellar, and a further hectare that he rents on Monte Quarin, the hill that overlooks Cormons. All are south-facing. His vines are planted at high densities to keep yields low, and Franco obtains from them a range of magnificent wines. Three of the six bottles presented this year went forward to the Three Glass taste-offs. A spectacular Tocai Friulano reaped the very best of a vintage that was outstandingly favourable for the variety. The intense, complex aromas disclose elegant pear and delicious peach. These notes are echoed faithfully on the perfectly structured palate, which has fullness, warmth and the longest of finishes. In fact, it is so good that it was crowned White of the Year. Franco's Pinot Bianco also had another great year and marries elegance with generous fruit. And his Pinot Grigio is again one of the best in the region. Its unusually stylish nose introduces a close-knit, seamless progression in the mouth. The Merlot Selezione 2000 flows nicely over the palate but is still young.

○ Collio Tocai Friulano '02	🍷🍷🍷	5
○ Collio Pinot Bianco '02	🍷🍷	5
○ Collio Pinot Grigio '02	🍷🍷	5
● Collio Merlot Sel. '00	🍷🍷	7
○ Collio Sauvignon '02	🍷🍷	5
○ Collio Chardonnay '02	🍷	5
● Collio Merlot Sel. '97	YYY	6
○ Collio Pinot Bianco '00	YYY	4
○ Collio Pinot Bianco '01	YYY	4
● Collio Merlot Sel. '99	YY	7
○ Collio Pinot Grigio '01	YY	4

CORMONS (GO)

VIGNA DEL LAURO
LOC. MONTE, 38
34071 CORMONS (GO)
TEL. 048160155
E-MAIL: info@roncodeitassi.it

The days are long gone when oenologist Fabio Coser and German wine importer Eberhard Spangenberg's Vigna del Lauro was reserved only for the international market. In fact, the cellar's products used to be released in Italy under the Ronco dei Tassi label, which is much better known here. For some time now, Vigna del Lauro has had it own specific identity, which is most obvious in the special timbre of wines from the six-hectare property, mainly located at San Floriano. The Collio Bianco we tasted this year is the best possible proof of this. A blend of pinot bianco with tocai, malvasia and ribolla gialla aged in wood, it opens on complex banana and melon fruit with spring flowers. The same sensations return on the broad, rich palate with its long, milky finish. The Merlot and Chardonnay were close behind. The Merlot has coffee, fruit in alcohol, plain chocolate and curious hints of moss whereas the Chardonnay, aged in wood, unveils stylish, balanced notes of banana and pineapple. The Tocai Friulano is equally good, standing out for its clean nose and good length on the palate. We would also point out the restrained hints of tomato and rue of the Sauvignon, and the Pinot Grigio's williams pear, honey and apple.

○ Collio Bianco '02	🍷🍷	4*
● Collio Merlot '00	🍷🍷	5
○ Friuli Isonzo Chardonnay '02	🍷🍷	4
○ Collio Tocai Friulano '02	🍷🍷	4
○ Collio Pinot Grigio '02	🍷	4
○ Collio Sauvignon '02	🍷	4
○ Collio Sauvignon '99	YYY	4
○ Collio Tocai Friulano '01	YY	4
○ Collio Bianco '01	YY	4
● Collio Merlot '99	YY	5

CORNO DI ROSAZZO (UD) CORNO DI ROSAZZO (UD)

VALENTINO BUTUSSI
VIA PRA' DI CORTE, 1
33040 CORNO DI ROSAZZO (UD)
TEL. 0432759194
E-MAIL: butussi@butussi.it

EUGENIO COLLAVINI
LOC. GRAMOGLIANO
VIA DELLA RIBOLLA GIALLA, 2
33040 CORNO DI ROSAZZO (UD)
TEL. 0432753222
E-MAIL: collavini@collavini.it

Angelo Butussi built his home and cellar fairly recently on the northern outskirts of Corno di Rosazzo. Between the main road and the winery, the family has set up a cellar-door sales outlet that looks like a small church from the outside. Angelo and his wife Pierina are strikingly tall, and so are their children, starting with Filippo who looks after the technical side of things in the cellar. In the vineyards, Angelo is joined by son Tobia, as well as Mattia in his free time from school, and daughter Erica handles marketing and distribution. So the entire Butussi family is involved full-time in the various activities of this estate, which has 12 hectares under vine and releases 75,000 bottles a year. We suspect the Butussis were worried about rain and brought forward the 2002 harvest. There is no other explanation for the marked acidity present in almost all the wines. However, the Tocai Friulano is an exception. Its white peach and almonds return nicely on the full, lingering palate. In the Sauvignon, the acidity actually lifts the aromas, lending the wine elegance and length, but in the other whites, it tends to make the palate a little thin.

For years, Manlio Collavini has been expanding his range of premium-quality wines, but this doesn't mean that his more commercial bottles have been neglected. Quite the reverse, for they are increasingly good value for money. Manlio acknowledges that wine is a product of man's interaction with nature, and when conditions are adverse, as they were in the rainy summer of 2002, he uses a must concentrator. According to Manlio, this merely eliminates excess water in the must. His young oenologist, Walter Bergnach, has gained confidence and experience in using barrels of various sizes, as we were able to confirm. In his wine-related activities, Manlio is increasingly assisted by his sons Giovanni, in the winery, and Luigi at outside events. Nor should we forget the role played by his wife Anna, who has a genuine talent for public relations. The new edition of Merlot dal Pic is as good as ever, its complex nose evoking prune and bramble that introduce a full, expansive, lingering palate. Other good new versions of old favourites are Ribolla Gialla Turian, Pinot Grigio and Tocai Friulano from the Collezione Privata line, Sauvignon Poncanera, Chardonnay Cuccanea, Refosco Pucino and the sweet Verdàc. We would also like to emphasize just how good the standard-label Sauvignon is. Manlio releases 150-200,000 bottles each year, demonstrating that quality, availability and an affordable price can be combined.

○ COF Tocai Friulano '02	♥♥	4*
● COF Cabernet Sauvignon '00	♥	4
○ COF Picolit '01	♥	7
● COF Cabernet Franc '02	♥	4
○ COF Pinot Bianco '02	♥	4
○ COF Sauvignon '02	♥	4
○ COF Verduzzo Friulano '02	♥	3
○ COF Chardonnay '02		4
○ COF Pinot Grigio '02		4
○ COF Ribolla Gialla '02		4
○ COF Picolit '00	♥♥	7

● Collio Merlot dal Pic '00	♥♥	8
○ Verdàc '00	♥♥	6
○ Collio Chardonnay Cuccanea '01	♥♥	6
○ COF Ribolla Gialla Turian '02	♥♥	6
○ Collio Pinot Grigio Collezione Privata '02	♥♥	6
○ Collio Sauvignon Poncanera '02	♥♥	6
○ Collio Tocai Friulano Collezione Privata '02	♥♥	6
● Friuli Isonzo Refosco P. R. Pucino '02	♥♥	5
○ Collio Sauvignon '02	♥	4*
● Collio Cabernet Collezione Privata '00	♥♥	6
● Collio Merlot dal Pic '99	♥♥	8

CORNO DI ROSAZZO (UD)

CORNO DI ROSAZZO (UD)

ADRIANO GIGANTE
VIA ROCCA BERNARDA, 3
33040 CORNO DI ROSAZZO (UD)
TEL. 0432755835
E-MAIL: gigantevini@libero.it

PERUSINI
LOC. GRAMOGLIANO
VIA TORRIONE, 13
33040 CORNO DI ROSAZZO (UD)
TEL. 0432675018 - 0432759151
E-MAIL: info@perusini.com

Adriano Gigante is an easy-going, able winemaker, as well as president of the Consorzio Colli Orientali del Friuli. With wife Giuliana Veliscech and cousin Ariedo Gigante, he runs an estate on the hillslopes at Corno di Rosazzo. The cellar's origins date back to 1957, when miller Ferruccio Gigante realized he was making premium-quality Tocai with the fruit from his small vineyard and decided to take up growing and producing seriously. Today, there are 12 hectares planted to vine, yielding about 60,000 bottles a year. Ferruccio's original vineyard, the "Storico", continues to give the Gigantes great Tocais, but this year the tasting panel was particularly struck by the complexity of the almond and yeast aromas that emerge from a backdrop of tropical fruit. The almondy notes linger on the palate to offset and accompany the complex acidity through to a warm, unhurried finish. The standard-label version is almost as good, its progression on the palate being only a whisker less complex. The Pinot Grigio has distinctive golden delicious apple aromas and an attractive contrast of minerally and fruit notes on the palate. Rue, tomato leaf and rennet permeate nose and palate of the very fresh-tasting Sauvignon. The subtly stylish Picolit is another classy bottle. We would also mention the Chardonnay for its banana aromas and the varietal stewed apple of the Verduzzo. There is hay in the nose of both the Refosco and the Merlot, where it is joined by bramble and plums, whereas the Schioppettino shows concentrated aromas of morello cherry and nutmeg.

Teresa Perusini, known as "Resi", and her husband Giacomo De Pace, are the conscientious owners of a lovely estate that embraces 12 hectares under vine and 48 of woodland and arable farmland. Many years ago, one of the farm buildings on the property was converted into a trattoria called Il Postiglione. Teresa has made good use of the research her grandfather, father and uncle pursued for decades, recovering well-adapted clones of picolit, ribolla gialla and merlot with help from the University of Udine. With assistance from Pierpaolo Sirch in the vineyard, the Perusinis are replanting obsolete or marginal vineyards to obtain better grapes. The cellar has been expanded and a 15-metre high tower erected with experimental materials, to plans drafted by the Faculty of Architecture of the University of Venice. The upper floors house the offices and a panoramic terrace, from which the view can only be described as stunning. The oenologist in charge of the last two vintages has been Roberto Cipresso. The most impressive of the wines presented was certainly the Picolit, a noble wine that is emblematic of Resi's family history and exemplary in its typicity. It elegantly combines flower and fruit aromas, performing equally well in the mouth, where the sweetness is never excessive. Bianco del Postiglione, from equal proportions of riesling renano and pinot bianco, is on the right track but the Bordeaux blend Rosso del Postiglione still has plenty of room for improvement.

O	COF Tocai Friulano Storico '02	🍷🍷	4*
O	COF Picolit '01	🍷🍷	6
O	COF Pinot Grigio '02	🍷🍷	4
O	COF Sauvignon '02	🍷🍷	4
O	COF Tocai Friulano '02	🍷🍷	4
●	COF Merlot '01	🍷	4
●	COF Refosco P. R. '01	🍷	4
●	COF Schioppettino '01	🍷	4
O	COF Verduzzo Friulano '01	🍷	4
O	COF Chardonnay '02	🍷	4
O	COF Tocai Friulano Storico '00	🍷🍷🍷	4
O	COF Picolit '99	🍷🍷	6
O	COF Tocai Friulano Storico '01	🍷🍷	4

O	COF Picolit '02	🍷🍷	7
●	COF Cabernet Franc '01	🍷	4
●	COF Merlot '01	🍷	4
O	COF Bianco del Postiglione '02	🍷	4
O	COF Pinot Bianco '02	🍷	4
O	COF Ribolla Gialla '02	🍷	4
O	COF Sauvignon '02	🍷	4
●	Rosso del Postiglione '01		4
O	COF Pinot Grigio '02		4
●	COF Cabernet Sauvignon '00	🍷🍷	4

CORNO DI ROSAZZO (UD)

LEONARDO SPECOGNA
VIA ROCCA BERNARDA, 4
33040 CORNO DI ROSAZZO (UD)
TEL. 0432755840
E-MAIL: info@specogna.it

Brothers Graziano and Gianni Specogna have been busy in recent months restructuring their winery to rationalize work flow and generally make the cellar much more functional. They are also investing in new winemaking equipment to improve the already very satisfactory quality levels that they have achieved so far. You could say that, in general, the wines lack a little sophistication, and it is this that makes the whites less successful than the reds. This is odd because until a few years ago, the Specogna cellar was known above all for its Tocai: now it finds itself with a reputation for reds. We are very happy to note, however, that the Specogna Tocai Friulano is back on form this year in a very well-typed interpretation. A complex, fresh-tasting, well-structured wine, it is nevertheless also an easy drinker. We hope this is a signal that the cellar's whites are coming back on form. Meanwhile, it was the reds that again earned higher marks at our tastings. Not for the first time, the body, richness and depth of the Merlot Oltre impressed. But even better was the Refosco dal Peduncolo Rosso, which unveiled varietal spice, complex structure and nice harmony. The Pignolo is worth investigation, although it is a little straightforward and lacks concentration.

●	COF Merlot Oltre '00	🍷🍷	6
●	COF Refosco P. R. '01	🍷🍷	5
●	COF Pignolo '01	🍷	6
○	COF Tocai Friulano '02	🍷	4
○	Pinot Grigio '02	🍷	4
○	COF Sauvignon '02	🍷	4
●	COF Merlot '01		4
●	COF Cabernet Franc '02		4
○	COF Verduzzo Friulano '02		4
○	COF Sauvignon '01	🥂🥂	4*
●	COF Merlot Oltre '99	🥂🥂	6

CORNO DI ROSAZZO (UD)

ANDREA VISINTINI
VIA GRAMOGLIANO, 27
33040 CORNO DI ROSAZZO (UD)
TEL. 0432755813
E-MAIL: info@vinivisintini.com

Andrea Visintini, who started this cellar in 1973, has been joined by his children Oliviero and twins Cinzia and Palmira. The handover to the next generation has gone without a hitch, and Andrea can now observe the winery's growth with detached satisfaction. The estate embraces 24 hectares, almost all in the Colli Orientali del Friuli, with small plots in the Collio and Grave del Friuli. The cellar is in a historic listed building and offices have been created from the restored tower of what used to be the castle of Gramogliano. Recently, all the cellar's main containers have been replaced by temperature-controlled stainless steel vats and work will soon be starting on an underground barrique cellar. Annual production is around 100,000 bottles, but there is potential for much more, which explains the extensions that are under way. For years, the Visintinis have implemented a very cautious pricing policy, which makes their wines particularly affordable. The Tocai Friulano dei Colli Orientali is a very fine wine. The nose is redolent of very ripe pears and apples, which are perfectly reflected on the rich, lingering palate. The Bianco, from tocai, pinot bianco, riesling and picolit, is supremely elegant, fresh-tasting and fruit-led. The rest of the range is good, with special mentions for the Riesling and the Traminer Aromatico.

○	COF Tocai Friulano '02	🍷🍷 (grey)	3*
○	COF Bianco '02	🍷🍷	3*
○	COF Riesling '02	🍷🍷	3*
○	COF Traminer Aromatico '02	🍷🍷	3*
○	COF Pinot Bianco '02	🍷	3
○	COF Pinot Grigio '02	🍷	4
○	COF Ribolla Gialla '02	🍷	4
○	COF Sauvignon '02	🍷	3
○	Collio Malvasia '02	🍷	3
○	COF Pinot Bianco '01	🥂🥂	3*
○	COF Bianco '01	🥂🥂	3*

CORNO DI ROSAZZO (UD)

ZOF
FRAZ. SANT'ANDRAT DEL JUDRIO
VIA GIOVANNI XXIII, 32/A
33040 CORNO DI ROSAZZO (UD)
TEL. 0432759673
E-MAIL: info@zof.it

The winery that Daniele Zof runs today was started in 1984 by his father, Alberto. There are nine hectares of estate-owned vineyards located near the cellar, but Daniele also has four hectares that he rents. Last year, he released 60,000 bottles and the rest of the winery's production was sold unbottled. The estate also runs a number of "agriturismo" farm holiday accommodation units. This year, Daniele is celebrating ten years of running the winery with full autonomy and has decided to go it alone, breaking off the consultancy agreement with Donato Lanati, whom he met when he was at university. This year, there is a fine line-up of Glass winners, starting with the Bianco Sonata 2001, from barrique-aged chardonnay and tonneau-aged sauvignon. Both wines in the blend underwent malolactic fermentation and the resulting product has an outstandingly complex, elegant nose, followed by an intriguing palate which, thanks to the alcohol, seems almost soft. We thought the Picolit was very convincing. Its apricot, banana and spice aromas linger impressively. The Tocai Friulano combines freshness with a rich, complex structure dominated by pears and apples. The Ribolla Gialla is a fine example of the variety's freshness on the palate. On the nose, flowers prevail over fruit.

DOLEGNA DEL COLLIO (GO)

CA' RONESCA
LOC. LONZANO 27
34070 DOLEGNA DEL COLLIO (GO)
TEL. 048160034
E-MAIL: caronesca@caronesca.it

Paolo Bianchi, a grower with a thorough arts-based educational background, again surprised us this year with a range of excellent wines, created with the help of expert oenologist, Franco Dalla Rosa. None of the bottles made on his estate in the wild woodlands of the Dolegna hills scored less than One Glass, but two new wines impressed particularly. They were the Pinot Grigio Podere San Giacomo and Chardonnay Il Vino Senza Qualità. As you may have guessed, the Chardonnay's name means "without qualities", a tribute to Robert Musil's novel, "The Man without Qualities", in which the richness and sweetness of love fuse with duty and the daily round in an infinity of sensations. At the same time, the wine's name is also an ironic provocation on the abuse of the term "quality", often utilized in senses that have little to do with the country tradition. But what about the wine itself? It's excellent. Fruit-forward yet delicate, it lingers on the palate with notes of melon. Pinot Grigio Podere San Giacomo came close to Three Glasses for its acacia honey aromas and extremely soft, round mouthfeel, offset by a dry finish. Sauvignon Podere di Ipplis puts aromas first, showing nectarine, melon and elderflower, as well as a refreshing finish, where tomato emerges. The citrussy pinot bianco, malvasia and chardonnay Marnà is back on form. But the fresh-tasting Sermar, from pinot bianco, tocai and ribolla gialla, has a little way to go.

O COF Bianco Sonata '01	🍷🍷	5
O COF Picolit '01	🍷🍷	6
O COF Ribolla Gialla '02	🍷🍷	4*
O COF Tocai Friulano '02	🍷🍷	3*
O COF Chardonnay '02	🍷	4
● COF Merlot '02	🍷	4
O COF Pinot Grigio '02	🍷	4
● COF Refosco P.R. '02	🍷	4
O COF Sauvignon '02	🍷	4
O COF Pinot Grigio '01	🍷🍷	4*

O COF Sauvignon Podere di Ipplis '02	🍷🍷	5
O Collio Pinot Grigio Podere San Giacomo '02	🍷🍷	5
O Collio Bianco Marnà '00	🍷🍷	4*
O Collio Chardonnay Il Vino Senza Qualità '02	🍷🍷	5
O Collio Tocai Friulano '02	🍷🍷	4*
● COF Sariz '99	🍷🍷	5
O COF Picolit '00	🍷	6
O Collio Bianco Sermar '01	🍷	5
O Saramago '01	🍷	5
O Collio Malvasia '02	🍷	4
O Collio Pinot Grigio '02	🍷	4

DOLEGNA DEL COLLIO (GO)

LA RAJADE
LOC. RESTOCINA, 12
34070 DOLEGNA DEL COLLIO (GO)
TEL. 0481639897
E-MAIL: frascadelcollio@libero.it

It's always a pleasure to talk to Romeo and Simone Rossi. Romeo is the man who looks after the vines and cellar. But he is also a hunter who loves to tell stories of what has happened to him in the woods around his vineyards, and how he has shot the odd crop-threatening wild boar that strayed over the border from neighbouring Slovenia. In contrast, Simone is a history buff who enjoys collecting antiquities and organizing costume re-enactments of mediaeval events. The Rossis revamped their cellar a few years ago and now have an attractive tasting area. A few steps from the winery, their mother Lucia runs a delightful, and very successful, "agriturismo" restaurant. The seven hectares under vine are on rather steep hillsides that are difficult to work. The Bianco Caprizi di Marceline ("Marcellina's Caprice", named after the grandmother), is from tocai friulano, chardonnay, verduzzo and ribolla gialla aged for one year in small oak barrels. It has a creamy mouthfeel, firm texture and rich, banana-led fruit. The Cabernet Sauvignon Stratin offers notes of forest floor and tar, keeping its attractive tannins well under control. Still young, it has everything it takes to age very well indeed in the cellar.

○ Collio Bianco		
Caprizi di Marceline '01	♟♟	4*
● Collio Cabernet Sauvignon		
Stratin '01	♟♟	5
● Collio Merlot Ris. '01	♟	5
○ Collio Ribolla Gialla '02	♟	4
○ Collio Sauvignon '02	♟	4
○ Collio Chardonnay '01	♟♟	4
○ Collio Bianco		
Caprizi di Marceline '00	♟	4

DOLEGNA DEL COLLIO (GO)

VENICA & VENICA
LOC. CERÒ
VIA MERNICO, 42
34070 DOLEGNA DEL COLLIO (GO)
TEL. 048161264 - 048160177
E-MAIL: venica@venica.it

The Venicas have carried out major, radical restructuring at their winery, extending the cellar and fitting it out with the latest technology. The offices and dining rooms of their holiday centre have been transferred to the building that was once the family restaurant. This will enable the estate to improve still further the quality of the wines while expanding the hospitality facilities. Brothers Giorgio and Gianni, and Gianni's son Giampaolo, supervise the vineyards with scrupulous care and look after winemaking. When necessary, they are also ready to take part in initiatives promoting their wines, or indeed the entire region. The queen of promotion is, however, Ornella, the former national president of the movement for wine tourism. After leaving that post in the late spring of 2003, she has returned full-time to the family business, taking up the reins of public relations again. We should also mention fruitmakers Pierpaolo Sirch and Marco Simonit, whose contribution has been absolutely crucial to recent Venica successes. This time, the Venicas astounded the panel with an exceptional Tocai Friulano Ronco delle Cime. Concentrated on the nose, it is equally complex on the warm, mellow palate. The standard Tocai Friulano came close to matching the score of the premium version, confirming the extremely favourable vintage for the variety. The Pinot Bianco is as intriguing as ever and the Sauvignon Ronco delle Mele offers a wealth of aromas.

○ Collio Tocai Friulano		
Ronco delle Cime '02	♟♟♟	6
○ Collio Pinot Bianco '02	♟♟	5
○ Collio Sauvignon		
Ronco delle Mele '02	♟♟	6
○ Collio Tocai Friulano '02	♟♟	5
○ Collio Bianco Tre Vignis '01	♟	6
○ Collio Chardonnay		
Ronco Bernizza '02	♟	5
○ Collio Malvasia '02	♟	5
○ Collio Ribolla Gialla '02	♟	5
● Refosco P. R. Bottaz '99	♟	7
○ Collio Tocai Friulano		
Ronco delle Cime '00	♟♟♟	5
○ Collio Sauvignon Ronco delle Mele '01	♟♟♟	5

DUINO AURISINA (TS)

KANTE
FRAZ. SAN PELAGIO
LOC. PREPOTTO, 1/A
34011 DUINO AURISINA (TS)
TEL. 040200255

Edi Kante is more than just a man who practises what we might call extreme viticulture on the rocks and low "doline" hills of the Carso. We are talking about a man of many parts, a lover of painting and horses who is so indissolubly linked to his territory as to have earned the soubriquet "poet of the Carso". It is natural to expect the same character from Edi's wines and when, as may happen, the panel is unable to sense that strong personality, there is a risk that the tasters will be too severe. There is no doubt that, in recent vintages, Kante wines have undergone a change of style. The 2000 wines needed a little cellar time to reveal their true worth, but this year the wines were utterly convincing from our tastings during the summer. First off the blocks is an intriguing, flower and mineral Sauvignon. There is great finesse on the palate, too, and fresh, aromatic notes emerge on the lingering back palate. The Kante Malvasia is back in the ranks of Two Glass winners. Its attractive spices fuse beautifully with the oak and the palate is genuinely stylish. The Chardonnay's strong suit is tropical fruit. The palate has length, if no great breadth, but the gradually increasing momentum on the palate is one of the wine's strong points. The Vitovska shows attractive flowers on the nose, but the palate is a tad short, revealing an almost citrussy vein.

O	Carso Sauvignon '01	🍷🍷	6
O	Carso Chardonnay '01	🍷🍷	6
O	Carso Malvasia '01	🍷🍷	6
O	Carso Vitovska '01	🍷	6
O	Carso Malvasia '98	🍷🍷🍷	6
O	Carso Sauvignon '00	🍷🍷	6

DUINO AURISINA (TS)

ZIDARICH
LOC. PREPOTTO, 23
34011 DUINO AURISINA (TS)
TEL. 040201223
E-MAIL: info@zidarich.it

Prepotto is a tiny village on the Carso plateau, 250 metres above sea level and a few kilometres from the Gulf of Trieste. Its red, iron-rich soil and the Carso limestone give the wines a distinctive personality, thanks in part to site climates that are particularly favourable to viticulture. We need only consider the concentration of excellent wineries that make the Carso, despite its limited dimensions, one of the most dynamic wine areas in the region. Prepotto is the home of Beniamino Zidarich's winery. With help from his sister, Mateja, and the rest of the family, Beniamino has been successfully making premium wines for some years. In the past year, work has begun on an impressive new cellar carved out of the rock, which will provide improved conditions for vinifying the roughly 12,000 bottles released each year. The 2001 wines maintain the winery's consolidated high standards. If we were to make a tiny criticism, we might say that they lack a touch of last year's pulpy fruit. However, they do have greater finesse. The Prulke, from sauvignon, malvasia and vitovska, melds peach and ripe fruit over emerging minerally sensations. Minerality is also a feature of the Vitovska, a sturdy vine variety that resists the "bora" gales. The Zidarich version involves macerating about 50 per cent of the fruit by weight in open vats. Only the faintest hint of oak still masks the delicate aromas of spring flowers. The Terrano has bramble, blueberries and faint vanilla. Weighty on entry, it is thinned by the variety's classic acidity only in the finish. No Malvasia was produced in 2001.

O	Prulke '01	🍷🍷	6
●	Carso Terrano '01	🍷	6
O	Carso Vitovska '01	🍷	6
●	Carso Terrano '00	🍷🍷	5
O	Prulke '00	🍷🍷	5

FAEDIS (UD)

MARCO CECCHINI
LOC. CASALI DE LUCA
VIA COLOMBANI
33040 FAEDIS (UD)
TEL. 0432720563
E-MAIL: info@cecchinimarco.com

In 1998, Marco Cecchini abandoned his studies to make wine. He started with one hectare of vines at Faedis that his grandfather had left him. At first, it was more of a game than a real job, but fortune then took a hand. Marco came into contact with the Terra e Vino group, one of whose leading lights is Alessio Dorigo from the well-known family of growers at Buttrio. Marco quickly realized just how much work it would take to improve quality, and how important it was to have substantial annual production levels. Today, he has four and a half hectares under vine and a further three have been planted. The 2002 vintage yielded 10,000 bottles and 2003 should allow Marco to double that figure. Meanwhile, a small cellar is being built next to the vineyards and will start to be used for the current vintage. As he wants to foreground the territory of Faedis, Marco has concentrated mainly on native grapes, such as tocai, verduzzo, picolit, refosco di Faedis and refosco dal peduncolo rosso. They are complemented by the international varieties, merlot, cabernet franc, cabernet sauvignon and chardonnay. Vineyard management is in the hands of Gibil Crespan and Luca Ronco looks after the cellar. Tovè is a blend of 90 per cent tocai friulano with ten per cent verduzzo, vinified in stainless steel. Its confident progression on the palate is completely seamless. Verlit is a dried-grape Verduzzo with a small proportion of picolit that combines sweetness with a wealth of over-ripe fruit.

FAEDIS (UD)

PAOLINO COMELLI
FRAZ. COLLOREDO DI SOFFUMBERGO
VIA DELLA CHIESA, 8
33040 FAEDIS (UD)
TEL. 0432711226
E-MAIL: comelli@comelli.it

Pierluigi Comelli continues his tireless search for supreme quality on the splendid, 14-hectare Comelli family estate in the hills near Faedis. A notary by trade and a wineman by conviction, "Pigi" has lavished money and time on his winery over recent years. The setting amid fields and woods is delightful, but the site climate is not particularly favourable. Still, high planting densities, a modern cellar and clonal selection have all contributed, under the careful supervision of oenologist Flavio Zuliani, to the winery's ability to release 500 hectolitres of valid wine every year. The quality of the Tocai is a given. Dried flowers, peach, orange and almond caress the nose, echoed by the attack on the palate, which delights with its fresh-tasting, coherent development. The Chardonnay and Merlot missed a second Glass by a whisker. Part of the Chardonnay is barrique-aged. It lacks complexity on the nose, but makes up with soft fruit in the mouth. The Merlot, aged for 14 months in small oak barrels, reveals attractive pepper and fresh plum and fragrant flavours, backed up by robust tannins on the back palate. The Locum Nostrum white, blended mainly from chardonnay and sauvignon, is interesting. The nose foregrounds vanilla, mint, banana and sweet tobacco, but the palate has yet to settle down. The Sauvignon offers nice varietal new-mown grass and rue, while the well-judged Cabernet Sauvignon has lots of youthful alcohol.

○ COF Bianco Tovè '02	🍷🍷	4*
○ COF Verduzzo Friulano Verlit '01	🍷🍷	6
● COF Rosso Careme '00	🍷	4
● COF Refosco P. R. '01	🍷	4

○ COF Tocai Friulano '02	🍷🍷	4*
○ COF Bianco Locum Nostrum '01	🍷	4
● COF Cabernet Sauvignon '01	🍷	4
● COF Merlot '01	🍷	4
○ COF Chardonnay '02	🍷	4
○ COF Sauvignon '02	🍷	4
○ COF Pinot Grigio '02		4
○ COF Bianco Locum Nostrum '99	🍷🍷	4
○ COF Tocai Friulano '01	🍷🍷	4

FARRA D'ISONZO (GO)

FARRA D'ISONZO (GO)

BORGO CONVENTI
S.DA COLOMBARA, 13
34070 FARRA D'ISONZO (GO)
TEL. 0481888004
E-MAIL: info@borgoconventi.it

CASA ZULIANI
VIA GRADISCA, 23
34070 FARRA D'ISONZO (GO)
TEL. 0481888506
E-MAIL: info@icasazuliani.com

Borgo Conventi was founded in 1975 by Gianni Vescovo, who sold it in December 2001 to Luigi Folonari's Tenimenti Ruffino. Folonari's move was prompted by Friuli's undisputed leadership in premium white wines. In fact, for Luigi the new estate was a precious piece to add to the jigsaw puzzle of top-quality reds produced by Tenimenti Ruffino in Tuscany. Currently, Borgo Conventi has 42 hectares under vine in the Collio and Friuli Isonzo DOC zones. The winery headquarters comprise a stupendous home and guest quarters connected to the winemaking cellars by a spectacular barrel storage area. The cellar has the capacity and technology to vinify the grapes harvested in the best possible manner. Indeed, new vineyard purchases will not entail expansion of the existing facilities. Folonari's quality ambitions will of course have to weather the transition period of vineyard and cellar management. We approve of the decision to maintain the typical local production methods, without imposing approaches that belong to other parts of the country. The best wine from the last vintage was the elegant Ribolla Gialla, which shows an apple and flower nose, rich fruit and a characteristic vein of varietal acidity in the mouth. Commitment to native varieties also pays off with the Schioppettino, which has typical black cherry and raspberry notes. We were also intrigued by the Isonzo DOC line released under the I Fiori del Borgo label, which includes an excellent Refosco.

Established in 1923, the Casa Zuliani farm was converted in the 1970s by Bruno Zuliani, who extended the area under vine to the present 17 hectares. Under Claudio Tomadin's management, the cellar earned a reputation for overall reliability, although without any real stars. In 2001, the cellar was extensively renewed, but the crucial factor appears to have been the arrival in that year of Federico Frumento, Bruna Zuliani's grandson. Federico has stimulated Claudio Tomadin's abilities by giving him the assistance of influential vineyard consultants Marco Simonit and Pierpaolo Sirch, as well as the very well-known Gianni Menotti. The first moves involve increasing red grape vine densities and further extending the area under vine, which will rise to 25 hectares. In tribute to the former owners, the Winter family from Vienna, the cellar has released a superb merlot-heavy Bordeaux blend, Winter 2000. Autumn leaves, plum tart and blueberries tempt the nose, then the complex, almost austere palate reveals elegance, body and a long, fruit-led finish. Only about 1,000 bottles of the malvasia, sauvignon and pinot bianco-based Collio Bianco were made, but they intrigued our tasters. Four more wines scored One Glass marks, so Casa Zuliani was able to make a convincing return to the Guide.

● Schioppettino '01		🍷🍷	5
○ Collio Ribolla Gialla '02		🍷🍷	4
○ Collio Pinot Grigio '02		🍷	4
○ Collio Sauvignon '02		🍷	4
○ Collio Tocai Friulano '02		🍷	4
● Friuli Isonzo Refosco P. R. I Fiori del Borgo '02		🍷	4
○ Collio Chardonnay '02			4
● Braida Nuova '91		🍷🍷🍷	7
○ Collio Chardonnay Colle Russian '00		🍷🍷	6
● Braida Nuova '99		🍷	7

● Collio Rosso Winter '00		🍷🍷	6
○ Collio Bianco '02		🍷🍷	4
● Collio Merlot '01		🍷	4
○ Collio Pinot Bianco '02		🍷	4
○ Collio Tocai Friulano '02		🍷	4
○ Friuli Isonzo Sauvignon '02		🍷	3
○ Collio Pinot Grigio '02			4
○ Friuli Isonzo Chardonnay '02			4

FARRA D'ISONZO (GO)

COLMELLO DI GROTTA
LOC. VILLANOVA
VIA GORIZIA, 133
34070 FARRA D'ISONZO (GO)
TEL. 0481888445 - 0481888162
E-MAIL: colmello@xnet.it

Farra d'Isonzo, with its marl and sandstone terrain formed by the raising of the seabed a few million years ago, is the final fraction of the Collio. This is where the alluvial gravel and clay soil of the Isonzo starts. There are several historic wineries at Farra and often, they have plots in both DOC zones. Colmello di Grotta, Francesca Bortolotto Possati's estate, is no exception, its 20 hectares being split evenly between Collio and Isonzo. The difficult 2002 vintage posed problems in the vineyard as many of the plants suffered from the heavy rains. Despite rigorous field selection, and an expert cellarman like Fabio Coser to hand, some of the wines are inevitably a little lacking in structure. The best performers at our tastings were the reds, which are from earlier vintages. We liked the intense, full-bodied Rosso Rondon 2000, an 80-20 mix of merlot and cabernet sauvignon. The Merlot Isonzo 2001 is just as elegant, thanks to ripe, jammy fruit and soft tannins. Best of the whites were the bottles from Collio. The Pinot Grigio, in particular, has complexity and balance on the nose. The varietal acidity is tempered by a fairly full, pear-nuanced palate. Finally, the Tocai did well. It has only moderate body but is clean and even in the mouth.

FARRA D'ISONZO (GO)

★ JERMANN VINNAIOLI
LOC. VILLANOVA
VIA MONTE FORTINO, 21
34070 FARRA D'ISONZO (GO)
TEL. 0481888080
E-MAIL: info@jermannvinnaioli.it

Silvio Jermann still loves to play and experiment with wine. In recent years, he has tried his hand at Pignolo, which he calls Pignacolusse and which this year is the top wine in his range. He has also vinified pinot nero (blau burgunder) and franconia (blau frankisch) to make an instantly successful, thrilling blend called Blau&Blau Mjzzu. Silvio also wanted to try vinification without sulphur dioxide in traditional casks, using long maceration after the manner of Gravner. Così Sia, the premium-priced white he has obtained, is sold exclusively to private customers. Created as a communion wine, one bottle is given to the archdiocese of Gorizia for every 12 bottles sold. At the beginning of the summer, Silvio also inaugurated the Baita, an attractive complex on the outskirts of Capriva with a wine cellar, a restaurant and rooms. In the meantime, work goes on at the new cellar in Ruttars, at the foot of the Capo Martino vineyard. From a purely technical point of view, Pignacolusse 2000 is an improved Jermann interpretation of pignolo and gains Three Glasses. The attack on the nose tells you how good this wine is and it brims with fruit as it expands on the palate. The tannins are kept well under control. The most recent Vintage Tunina was penalized by our tasting, which took place not long after it had gone into bottle. Finally, the Capo Martino 2001 is a symphony of fruit and flowers with great structure on the palate. It is an object lesson in how to use wood.

● Rondon '00	♟♟	5
● Friuli Isonzo Cabernet Sauvignon '01	♟	4
● Friuli Isonzo Merlot '01	♟	4
● Collio Merlot '02	♟	5
○ Collio Pinot Grigio '02	♟	4
○ Collio Sauvignon '02	♟	4
○ Collio Tocai Friulano '02	♟	4

● Pignacolusse '00	♟♟♟	6
○ Capo Martino '01	♟♟	7
○ Vintage Tunina '02	♟♟	7
○ Were Dreams, Now It Is Just Wine! '01	♟♟	7
○ Sauvignon '02	♟♟	5
● Blau&Blau Mjzzu '01	♟♟	7
○ Müller Thurgau '02	♟	5
○ Pinot Bianco '02	♟	5
○ Traminer Aromatico '02	♟	5
○ Pinot Grigio '02		5
● Red Angel '02		5
○ Capo Martino '97	♟♟♟	7
○ Vintage Tunina '99	♟♟♟	7
○ Vintage Tunina '00	♟♟♟	7
○ Vintage Tunina '01	♟♟♟	7

FARRA D'ISONZO (GO)

TENUTA VILLANOVA
LOC. VILLANOVA
VIA CONTESSA BERETTA, 29
34070 FARRA D'ISONZO (GO)
TEL. 0481888013 - 0481888593
E-MAIL: info@tenutavillanova.com

Tenuta Villanova is one of the cornerstones of winemaking in Friuli, and in the Isonzo DOC zone in particular. The history of the estate now stretches back over 500 years. Owned by the Bennati family, it embraces more than 200 hectares in the Collio and Isonzo DOCs. From the point of view of vineyard management, Tenuta Villanova is very modern, but on the commercial front, we note a lack of focus in the 20 or so labels released, ranging from Brut to Moscato Rosa and four kinds of grappa. For the time being, the wines are reassuringly well-typed, albeit without a genuine star. However, the recent arrival of the experienced and vastly competent Mario Zuliani should bring about the necessary changes over the next few harvests. This year, the most convincing wine was the elegant Sauvignon Ronco Cucco 2002, whose understated tropical aromas are picked up nicely on the palate. The Bordeaux blend Fraja (the name means "feast" in Friulian) earned Two Glasses for an admirable concentration that never lapses into looseness, but instead gives the palate length and depth. The Chardonnay Ronco Cucco 2001 still has slightly too evident oak that partially masks the fruit, but this will improve with bottle age. Menj Bianco, a mix of malvasia istriana, pinot bianco and tocai, aims for finesse but lacks the thrust necessary to stand out from the crowd. Still, it is attractive and well made.

GONARS (UD)

DI LENARDO
FRAZ. ONTAGNANO
P.ZZA BATTISTI, 1
33050 GONARS (UD)
TEL. 0432928633
E-MAIL: info@dilenardo.it

As you browse the www.dilenardo.it website, you will see a truth that Massimo di Lenardo is courageous enough to admit. What was the 2002 growing year like? "Rain, rain, rain. No one can remember such a wet July and August". Luckily, September was more clement, but it still wasn't enough to offset high acidity. Full malolactic fermentation was necessary, and there were imbalances in acidity-alcohol ratios, which came through at our tastings. Most of the estate's vineyard holding is in the Grave, the vast alluvial plain between the hills and the coast. In the countryside around Ontagnano in particular, the zone's wines are better-known for their drinkability than for their extract, and this contributed to making this year's products, the whites above all, even leaner and edgier than usual. Di Lenardo wines are made with a weather eye on the United States and the best this time was the Ronco Nolè, a blend of merlot, refosco and cabernet matured in new American barriques. It's a 2001, and comes from a more favourable vintage, but the Pinot Grigio also did well, proving once again that this variety is the workhorse of Friulian winemaking and quite capable of performing admirably in poor years. For the rest of the range, we note that Father's Eyes is a blend of tocai, riesling, sauvignon and chardonnay. Like all Di Lenardo wines, it undergoes controlled oxygenation during fermentation, and is vinified and aged in new wood. The Chardonnay Woody differs from the standard label for its three months' ageing in oak. Toh is the cellar's flagship wine, although this year not the best.

O	Collio Sauvignon Ronco Cucco '02	🍷🍷	5
●	Fraja '99	🍷🍷	7
●	Collio Merlot '00	🍷	4
O	Collio Chardonnay Ronco Cucco '01	🍷	5
O	Collio Tocai Friulano '02	🍷	4
O	Friuli Isonzo Malvasia '02	🍷	4
O	Menj Bianco '02	🍷	4
O	Collio Pinot Grigio '02		4
O	Collio Ribolla Gialla Ronco Cucco '02		5
O	Collio Chardonnay Monte Cucco '97	🍷🍷🍷	4

●	Ronco Nolè Rosso '01	🍷	4
O	Father's Eyes '02	🍷	5
●	Friuli Grave Cabernet '02	🍷	4
O	Friuli Grave Chardonnay '02	🍷	4
O	Friuli Grave Chardonnay Woody '02	🍷	4
●	Friuli Grave Merlot '02	🍷	4
O	Friuli Grave Pinot Bianco '02	🍷	4
O	Friuli Grave Pinot Grigio '02	🍷	4
O	Friuli Grave Sauvignon Blanc '02		4
O	Friuli Grave Tocai Friulano Toh! '02		4
●	Ronco Nolè Rosso '00	🍷🍷	3*
O	Father's Eyes '01	🍷🍷	4

GORIZIA

CONTI ATTEMS
FRAZ. LUCINICO
VIA GIULIO CESARE, 36/A
34070 GORIZIA
TEL. 0481393619
E-MAIL: info@attems.it

After the death of 90-year-old Conte Sigismondo Douglas Attems, the historic winery that bears his family name has come more completely under the control of the Marchesi de' Frescobaldi company. New mother Virginia Attems Fornasir continues to look after public relations while production is under the attentive supervision of Lamberto Frescobaldi. The wisdom of the great Tuscan wine house is clear in the decision to maintain continuity of production by confirming Fabio Coser, the well-known Friulian oenologist, as consultant. In addition, the Frescobaldis have selected from their own staff Gianni Napolitano, a young oenologist, also originally from Friuli. Currently, the estate comprises 32 hectares under vine in the adjoining DOC zones of Collio and Isonzo. A further ten hectares have already been planted and the goal of 50 hectares under vine out of the estate's 75 looks achievable in the short term. The cellars, too, require attention, although they are sufficient for current production needs. The Chardonnay 2002 came out on top, its well-gauged oak adding vanilla and coffee to broad fruit and fusing nicely with notes of yeast and crusty bread. Cicinis, a blend of mainly sauvignon, pinot bianco and tocai friulano, marries freshness and complexity, bringing out the richness of the fruit in the long finish. The Ribolla Gialla is as admirable as ever, impressing with its weight on the palate.

GORIZIA

LA CASTELLADA
FRAZ. OSLAVIA, 1
34170 GORIZIA
TEL. 048133670

Oslavia has always been a very special corner of the Collio. The elevation, aspect, heritage and above all characterful winemakers to be found there have helped to write the oenological history of Friuli. A decade or so ago, this was the most creative, dynamic subzone in the region, or in Italy, if we restrict ourselves to whites. The excesses and insights of Oslavia are still hotly debated even today. The Bensos have always been noted for a style that incorporates all the lessons of the past, without ever going to extremes. They have experimented with large barrels, small wood and maceration techniques. They, too, have travelled to Georgia to try to understand how terracotta is used. For years, the Bensos released only one estate blend and one territory-focused monovarietal. When push came to shove, though, they found a balance that is reflected in their wines. We tasted four offerings this time, all from 2000, and all from the first rank. The Chardonnay unveils aromas of confectioner's cream, top of the milk, banana and yeast, all mirrored nicely on the fresh-tasting palate. The Ribolla Gialla has the classic golden hue of La Castellada wines. It is rounded in the mouth, then a tannin-heavy back palate dries the finish. This time, there is a monovarietal Tocai Friulano, a variety that was out of favour at Oslavia for a period. Oak is still evident on the nose, but the palate offers complexity and richness. The Collio Bianco has milk and cream aromas, and good complexity in the mouth. There are also attractive notes of fresh acidity that bode well for the wine's longevity.

O	Collio Bianco Cicinis '01	🍷🍷	5
O	Collio Chardonnay '02	🍷🍷	4
O	Collio Ribolla Gialla '02	🍷🍷	4
O	Collio Pinot Bianco '02	🍷	4
O	Collio Pinot Grigio '02	🍷	4
O	Collio Sauvignon '02	🍷	4
O	Collio Tocai Friulano '02	🍷	4
O	Collio Ribolla Gialla '01	🍷🍷	5

O	Collio Chardonnay '00	🍷🍷	6
O	Collio Ribolla Gialla '00	🍷🍷	6
O	Collio Tocai Friulano '00	🍷🍷	6
O	Collio Bianco della Castellada '00	🍷🍷	6
O	Collio Chardonnay '94	🍷🍷🍷	6
O	Bianco della Castellada '95	🍷🍷🍷	6
O	Collio Bianco della Castellada '98	🍷🍷🍷	6
O	Collio Bianco della Castellada '99	🍷🍷🍷	6

GORIZIA

GORIZIA

FIEGL
FRAZ. OSLAVIA
LOC. LENZUOLO BIANCO, 1
34170 GORIZIA
TEL. 048131072 - 0481547103
E-MAIL: info@fieglvini.com

★ GRAVNER
FRAZ. OSLAVIA
VIA LENZUOLO BIANCO, 9
34070 GORIZIA
TEL. 048130882
E-MAIL: joskogravner@libero.it

This historic winery has been active for at least 200 years. Today, it is owned by brothers Alessio, Giuseppe and Rinaldo Fiegl, who personally perform almost every stage of winemaking, producing about 100,000 bottles a year from their 18 hectares under vine. The estate stands on the cool hillslopes in the north of the province of Gorizia, on the border with Slovenia. Fiegl releases three lines, the most prestigious being the Collio and the Leopold. On past visits, we pointed out the positive aspects of this rationalization, which assigns the Leopold label to the most complex products, carefully selected and aged for an extra year in bottle. But we also noted that the new list had not achieved a sufficient degree of reliability. Happily, this year our tastings revealed that things have taken a turn for the better, which is encouraging for the future of the cellar. There are still uncertainties in the Leopold range, especially regarding the Chardonnay, but the Merlot and Cuvée Blanc blend of tocai, pinot bianco, sauvignon and ribolla clearly show the potential these wines have. But this year it was the Collio range that truly impressed. The classic apple-led Pinot Bianco with its fullness and nose-palate convergence, the convincingly fresh, richly extracted Ribolla Gialla, and the vigorous, attractively textured Tocai with its elegant nose of pear, honey and yellow plum, all sailed past the Two Glass mark.

Continuous experimentation has been a feature of Josko Gravner's career. It has prompted him to take many courageous, and at times, extreme, decisions in vineyard and cellar. These regard vine training systems, decided with Marco Simonit, as well as the gradual integration of international varieties with ribolla and pignolo. Gravner's use of prolonged maceration is also the result of profound observation and reflection. Open fermentation vessels have been replaced by amphorae from the Caucasus, for which Josko is preparing an underground cellar. According to Gravner, terracotta gives a better result for maceration without sulphur dioxide or temperature control. A few weeks later, the wines are racked into wood vats, where they age for two and a half years before bottling without filtration. Advance tastings confirm that, vintage after vintage, Gravner's wines are exploring ways forward that are as exciting as their maker's personality. These amphorae are no mere exotic curiosities. They are serious cellar tools that produce stunningly rounded wines whose tannins are kept beautifully under control. Breg '99 is from sauvignon, chardonnay, pinot grigio and riesling italico. The golden hue introduces restrained vanilla with no hint of oxidation. After slow aeration, peach, apricot, candied fruit and caramel gently emerge. This "vino da meditazione" sipping wine opens up new horizons in winemaking. The Ribolla is similar in colour and aromas. The palate is slightly less nuanced and there is a touch of candied citrus peel in the finish. The Rosso '98 is less convincing.

○ Collio Pinot Bianco '02	🍷🍷	4*
○ Collio Ribolla Gialla '02	🍷🍷	4*
○ Collio Tocai Friulano '02	🍷🍷	4*
● Collio Merlot '01	🍷	4
○ Collio Pinot Grigio Leopold '01	🍷	5
○ Leopold Cuvée Blanc '01	🍷	4
○ Collio Sauvignon '02	🍷	4
○ Collio Sauvignon Leopold '02	🍷	5
● Collio Merlot Leopold '99	🍷	5
● Cabernet Sauvignon '00	🍷🍷	4*

○ Breg '99	🍷🍷🍷	8
○ Ribolla Gialla '99	🍷🍷	8
● Rosso Gravner '98	🍷	8
○ Collio Chardonnay Ris. '91	🍷🍷🍷	8
○ Collio Breg '98	🍷🍷	8
○ Collio Ribolla Gialla '98	🍷🍷	8

GORIZIA

GORIZIA

DAMIJAN PODVERSIC
VIA BRIGATA PAVIA, 61
34170 GORIZIA
TEL. 048178217
E-MAIL: damijan.go@virgilio.it

PRIMOSIC
FRAZ. OSLAVIA
LOC. MADONNINA DI OSLAVIA, 3
34170 GORIZIA
TEL. 0481535153
E-MAIL: primosic@primosic.com

For some years, the admirable Damijan Podversic has been making wine with enthusiasm and serious commitment. Proof, if proof were needed, can be found in his brave decision to delay bottling his Collio Bianco, Ribolla Gialla and Collio Rosso wines, and with it release of the 2001 vintage. His aim, of course, is to give the wines sufficient time to age in bottle to his satisfaction. In fact, Damijan decided to ferment his white blend on the skins, without temperature control or the use of cultured yeasts or enzymes (he was already vinifying his Ribolla Gialla this way). We'll be reporting on the outcome next year, when we have tasted the wines nearer their release date. For the time being, this year's retastings confirm our previous assessments. Actually, the 1999 and the 2000 seem to have got even better. This is particularly true in the case of the Collio Bianco, a blend of tocai, malvasia and chardonnay (the international variety will be replaced by the more traditional ribolla gialla in the next vintage). It all goes to show how right Damijan was to delay the release of his wines this time round.

In the late 19th century, there are reports of a certain Carlo Primosic who sent wine from the hills in the south of the Austro-Hungarian Empire to the capital, Vienna. When you remember that we are talking about the slopes of Oslavia, whose site climates have made it one of the finest subzones in the Collio, you will understand that we can look forward to good things from this cellar. In previous Guides, we noted the busy efforts of Primosic to rationalize production and improve the range in line with market expectations. After this year's tastings, we can safely say that things are going well. There are three labels, the classics, the more challenging Gmajne wines with an extra year's ageing, and the Riservas, the three flagship bottles. This year, the Riserva Metamorfosis, a Bordeaux blend with a little refosco, scored well for its fruit and dried flowers with pepper and chocolate, and a mature palate. A faint gamey note upset the wine's elegance, denying it a higher score. The Sauvignon Gmajne, a very traditional wine with good weight and bright, pleasant acidity, also impressed, and the ever-reliable, often underrated Pinot Grigio attracted plaudits for its evolved, creamy aromas, soft, consistent mouthfeel and slightly forward note in the finish. The sauvignon, chardonnay and ribolla Klin was a bit disappointing. It has attractive thyme and honey but is also a little dilute. A bitterish finish and over-insistent oak upset the Chardonnay's generous cocktail of quince, hazelnut and banana.

○ Collio Bianco '00	𝟗𝟗	5
● Collio Rosso '00	𝟗𝟗	5
○ Collio Ribolla Gialla '00	𝟗	5

○ Collio Sauvignon Gmajne '01	𝟗𝟗	4*
○ Collio Pinot Grigio Gmajne '01	𝟗𝟗	4*
● Collio Rosso Metamorfosis '99	𝟗𝟗	5
○ Collio Chardonnay Gmajne '01	𝟗	4
○ Collio Bianco Klin '99	𝟗	5
○ Collio Ribolla Gialla Gmajne '01		4
● Collio Rosso Metamorfosis '97	𝟗𝟗	5
○ Collio Chardonnay Gmajne '00	𝟗𝟗	4

GRADISCA D'ISONZO (GO)

MARCO FELLUGA
VIA GORIZIA, 121
34072 GRADISCA D'ISONZO (GO)
TEL. 048199164
E-MAIL: info@marcofelluga.it

It was 1905 when Marco Felluga's grandfather started the family's long love affair with winemaking at Isola d'Istria. Then in 1920, Giovanni followed is father's example, having moved to Grado. Grado is very close to Gradisca so it was not long before the Felluga wine empire began to grow. Today, it includes Castello di Buttrio, Russiz Superiore and a recent acquisition, San Nicolò at Pisignano in Tuscany, as well as the Marco Felluga winery. Marco runs everything with vast experience and commitment, achieving increasingly enviable results. This year, the Marco Felluga estate, with its 130 hectares under vine and 730,000 bottles released every year, came very close to a third Glass for the Tocai, the Carantan Bordeaux blend and the Molamatta white. The Tocai assails the nose with sunny aromas of tropical fruit and yellow peach that give it a Mediterranean personality. After leisurely ageing in barrique, Carantan has plain chocolate, mint and blueberry jam laced with attractive milky notes. The wonderfully poised silky tannins and long, sour cherry finish are also remarkable. Molamatta, from tocai, ribolla and pinot bianco, has a subtle nose of wistaria and citrus, nicely echoed in the mouth, where they come together in an overall impression of great elegance. Marburg, a wine from Castello di Buttrio, is excellent. The pignolo and refosco blend combines balsam and fruit, with sour cherry tart to the fore.

●	Carantan '00	▼▼	6
○	Collio Bianco Molamatta '02	▼▼	6
○	Collio Tocai Friulano '02	▼▼	5
●	Castello di Buttrio Marburg '00	▼▼	6
●	Collio Merlot '01	▼▼	5
○	COF Picolit '00	▼	6
○	Castello di Buttrio Ovestein '01	▼	5
⊙	Moscato Rosa '01	▼	6
●	Refosco '01	▼	5
○	Collio Ribolla Gialla Bellanotte '02	▼	6
○	Collio Chardonnay '02		5
○	Castello di Buttrio Ovestein '00	▽▽	5
●	Castello di Buttrio Marburg '99	▽▽	6
●	Carantan '99	▽	6

GRADISCA D'ISONZO (GO)

SANT'ELENA
VIA GASPARINI, 1
34072 GRADISCA D'ISONZO (GO)
TEL. 048192388
E-MAIL: sant.elena@libero.it

Farming at Sant'Elena on the Gradisca flatlands goes back a long way. Founded in 1893 by the Klodic family, the property was entirely converted to viticulture in the 1960s. Six years ago, the estate was acquired by Dominic Nocerino, the well-known importer of Italian wines into the United States. Nocerino is replanting part of the vine stock with advice from a prestigious expert, Franco Bernabei. The area under vine is now 37 hectares, planted at 5-7,000 vines per hectare, and a new building is under construction. It will bring together the production area and the offices, currently housed in the former farmhouse. There's a lot of investment, but the winery's ideas are clear: not too many labels, all Venezia Giulia IGT (typical geographical indication), to focus on quality. The estate team is also a good one, with Maurizio Drascek in charge of winemaking and Barbara Maniacco looking after the business side. Results were quick in coming. Ròs di Rôl is a monovarietal Merlot with an earthy nose – denoting concentration – that opens slowly in austere authority. The fruit and spice palate is full and chewy, but not excessively so. Tato is an attractively complex Bordeaux blend with depth, harmony and nice notes of morello cherry and geraniums. The slightly "Tuscan-style" Cabernet is good. Impressive, sweet fruit is to the fore, despite one or two youthful rough edges. The Pinot Grigio is more interesting for its slow, complex entry on the palate than for its understated aromas of pear and vanilla.

●	Merlot Ròs di Rôl '00	▼▼	6
●	Cabernet '00	▼▼	4
●	Tato '00	▼▼	6
○	Pinot Grigio '02	▼	4
●	Friuli Isonzo Ròs di Rôl '99	▽▽	5
○	Bianco JN '00	▽▽	5

GRADISCA D'ISONZO (GO)   MANZANO (UD)

FRANCO VISINTIN
VIA ROMA, 37
34072 GRADISCA D'ISONZO (GO)
TEL. 048199974

ROSA BOSCO
LOC. ROSAZZO
VIA ABATE COLONNA, 20
33044 MANZANO (UD)
TEL. 0432751522 - 0432683896

Franco Visintin is not what you would call an "up and coming" winemaker. Although young in spirit, he has been turning out impeccably typed wines for decades and was one of the first growers in the area to bottle on site. Franco's 11 hectares under vine, all in the Isonzo DOC zone, yield almost 50,000 bottles a year and he also has the experience of wine technician Saverio Di Giacomo to call on. The Visintin estate is not well-known outside the region for reasons of commercial strategy. It supplies local restaurateurs and is also the destination of many wine tourists, mainly from Germany and Austria, who appreciate Franco's serious approach and the excellent value for money that his wines represent. For centuries, Gradisca was on the border of the Austro-Hungarian empire with the Venetian republic, and later Italy. In fact, the winery stands where once there was an old customs house with a barrier across the road. The barrier, or "stanga", is the origin of the name of Franco's soft, fruity Bordeaux blend, Stàngja 2000. The Cabernet Franc was harvested when fully ripe and does not have the green, vegetal aromas that for years marked the variety in Friuli. Quite the reverse, for the nose is delicate and the palate shows lovely ripe fruit. Moving on to the whites, we find a convincing sweet spice and rosemary Malvasia. The palate lacks a little breadth and richness on entry but, all in all, it is stylish and eminently drinkable.

For Rosa Bosco, these wines are more than just a wager with fortune, or rather a series of wagers. Rosetta likes a challenge and is not content to do things the easy way. For her, these bottles are a raison d'être, a way of measuring the strength of her convictions. Hence the maniacal grooming of each vine. Hence the endless search to find balance of flavour while respecting varietal characteristics, which in effect means squaring the oenological circle. Hence her painstaking, indeed ground-breaking, barrique management, in a constant struggle against time and logistics. In short, Rosa makes "vins de garage", with the help of a few close friends and a guardian angel called Donato Lanati. And this time, the Bosco molehill has produced a mountain of a wine. It's a superb Sauvignon Blanc, an attractively fresh-tasting wine with juicy peach fruit and a faint hint of deliciously bitter rue that introduce a creamy textured, warm, long and velvet-smooth palate. In contrast with previous editions, the wood here is much better integrated with a rock-solid structure that holds out great promise for an exciting future. Rosetta's other wager also looks a winner. We're talking about the Merlot, which is amazing consistent. This year, it delighted the panel with rich bramble, blueberries and raspberries. The long, seamless palate is lifted by sweet tannins and the follow through is textbook stuff.

● Stàngja Rosso '00	▼▼	4
● Friuli Isonzo Cabernet Franc '01	▼▼	4
● Friuli Isonzo Cabernet Sauvignon '01	▼	3
○ Friuli Isonzo Chardonnay '02	▼	3
○ Friuli Isonzo Malvasia '02	▼	3
○ Friuli Isonzo Pinot Grigio '02	▼	3
● Friuli Isonzo Merlot '01		3

○ COF Sauvignon Blanc '02	▼▼▼	6
● COF Rosso II Boscorosso '01	▼▼	7
● COF Rosso II Boscorosso '98	▼▼	7
○ COF Sauvignon Blanc '99	▼▼	6
● COF Rosso II Boscorosso '99	▼▼	7
○ COF Sauvignon Blanc '00	▼▼	6
● COF Rosso II Boscorosso '00	▼▼	7
○ COF Sauvignon Blanc '01	▼▼	6

MANZANO (UD)

COLUTTA
VIA ORSARIA, 32
33044 MANZANO (UD)
TEL. 0432740315 - 0432751536
E-MAIL: colutta@colutta.it

Giorgio Colutta's cellar came up with a range that surprised our tasters with its overall quality. We certainly did not expect that the wines would be quite so good after such a relatively difficult harvest, and vinification in a cellar in the throes of restructuring. We can only conclude that Antonio Maggio's efforts in the vineyard, where he is assisted by Marco Simonit, and those of oenologist, Clizia Zambiasi, in the cellar, were able to overcome those obstacles. Today, the winery has a cellar with unfaced stone walls and wood beams, a barrique cellar that is separate from the other areas, and a range of equipment that enables the winemaking team to work to the best of its abilities. Colutta vinifies grapes from 20 hectares of vineyard, five planted at a density of 5,600 vines per hectare. Giorgio's aspirations to quality are enthusiastically abetted by the resolute Clizia, a young oenologist from Trento who has settled in Friuli. The best performances this year came from three of the whites, the Chardonnay Selezione Giorgio Colutta, the Tocai Friulano and the Verduzzo Friulano. The elegant Chardonnay, barrique-aged for six months, offers complexity and surefooted progression. The Tocai Friulano nicely marries style with structure. And the Verduzzo Friulano, from fruit part raisined on the vine and part on rush mats, is reminiscent of peaches in syrup, baked apple and dried apricot.

○	COF Chardonnay Sel. Giorgio Colutta '02	▼▼	4
○	COF Tocai Friulano '02	▼▼	4
○	COF Verduzzo Friulano '02	▼▼	5
●	COF Cabernet '01	▼	4
●	COF Merlot Sel. Giorgio Colutta '01	▼	6
○	COF Pinot Grigio '02	▼	4
○	COF Sauvignon '02	▼	4
●	COF Schioppettino '01		5
●	COF Refosco P. R. '02		4
●	COF Rosso Selenard '00	▽▽	5

MANZANO (UD)

MIDOLINI
VIA UDINE, 40
33044 MANZANO (UD)
TEL. 0432754555
E-MAIL: midolini@midolini.com

Lino Midolini is an elderly gentleman who has spent most of his working life among industrial kilns, quarries, waste disposal and construction sites. Now, in his maturity, he has been bewitched by wine. He also decided to transform his domestic balsamic-type vinegar production into a business that has left him with the largest balsamic vinegar factory in the world, mentioned in the Guinness Book of Records. We visited with Lino the new vineyards he replanted a few years ago, admiring his enthusiasm and determination to achieve premium-quality results. Today, vines cover 30 of the estate's 90 hectares and production ranges from 1,200 to 1,500 hectolitres each year. The cellar has a capacity of 3,000 hectolitres so there is plenty of elbow room. Lino is helped at the winery by his daughter, Gloria, who manages personnel, looks after promotional initiatives and takes care of public relations. Supported in the cellar by Ferrante Mian, who has worked there for decades, and with the assistance of oenologist Fabrizio Giacomini and consultant Luca D'Attoma, Gloria has managed to take the cellar back to the superior quality production of the past. Thanks in part to the vintage, the Tocai Friulano is excellent, as are the Soresta'nt Blanc, from part oak-aged tocai friulano and riesling, and the Refosco dal Peduncolo Rosso.

●	COF Refosco P. R. '01	▼▼	4
○	COF Soresta'nt Blanc '01	▼▼	5
○	COF Tocai Friulano '02	▼▼	4*
○	COF Pinot Grigio '02	▼	4
●	COF Refosco P. R. '00	▽▽	4

MANZANO (UD)

RONCHI DI MANZANO

VIA ORSARIA, 42
33044 MANZANO (UD)
TEL. 0432740718 - 0432754098
E-MAIL: info@ronchidimanzano.com

People who have never met Roberta Borghese, owner of Ronchi di Manzano, think she must be a grouch because she studiously avoids public events and other meetings. Nothing could be further from the truth. She's simply very shy and only feels secure in her 20-year experience of wine when she is inside the walls of her own cellar. Roberta has been travelling in recent years, going to the world's finest wine zones, from France to California, always in search of some nugget of wisdom to apply at her own estate. High-density planting – in some cases, up to 9,000 vines per hectare – are no novelty for Roberta, who has been using them for years, and she is disarmingly nonchalant about her expertise with wood, from barriques to 40-hectolitre barrels. The estate was born in the hills ("ronchi") at Manzano, gradually expanding with the acquisition of Ronc di Rosazzo. Now, there are 55 hectares under vine and production runs at over 300,000 bottles a year. Once again, the stars of the estate range are the Merlot Ronc di Subule, a complex, concentrated, full-bodied wine that lingers, the chardonnay, sauvignon, tocai and picolit-based Rosazzo Bianco Ronc di Rosazzo with its intense aromas, the minerally, elegantly seamless Tocai Friulano Superiore, and the Rosazzo Rosso, from merlot, cabernet sauvignon and refosco, which offers black cherry jam and lashings of fruit in the long finish.

●	COF Merlot Ronc di Subule '01	🍷🍷	5
●	COF Rosazzo Rosso Ronc di Rosazzo '01	🍷🍷	4
○	COF Rosazzo Bianco Ronc di Rosazzo '02	🍷🍷	4
○	COF Tocai Friulano Sup. '02	🍷🍷	4
●	COF Cabernet Franc '01	🍷	4
●	COF Cabernet Sauvignon '01	🍷	4
●	COF Merlot '01	🍷	4
●	COF Refosco P. R. '01	🍷	4
○	COF Verduzzo Friulano '01	🍷	4
○	COF Chardonnay '02		4
○	COF Pinot Grigio '02		4
●	COF Merlot Ronc di Subule '99	YYY	5
●	COF Merlot Ronc di Subule '00	YY	5

MANZANO (UD)

RONCO DELLE BETULLE

LOC. ROSAZZO
VIA ABATE COLONNA, 24
33044 MANZANO (UD)
TEL. 0432740547
E-MAIL: info@roncodellebetulle.it

Around here, Rosazzo and its abbey are a secular sanctuary. Oenological pilgrims come to find their cultural roots, refresh their eyes with views over the gentle, vine-clad hills and breathe the olives, must and acacia in the air. They come to visit cellars, meet producers, taste wines and discuss the latest vintage, the market, yields and whether they should be planting reds or whites. If you are a visitor, don't miss Ronco delle Betulle for at least three reasons. The first is the location, the second is Ivana Adami's faultless manners, and the third is her wines. The Franconia is good enough to vie with the best from Austria. Yields are kept to 55 quintals per hectare, maceration lasts 17 days, the wine ages for 12 months in five-hectolitre tonneau and it is bottled without filtration. Pepper and black cherry dominate the confident nose, then good alcohol combines with attractive length in the mouth. The pinot bianco, sauvignon, chardonnay and tocai Narciso Bianco is well made. Yields were only 35 quintals per hectare, and the must fermented and matured for seven months in new barriques. Caramel-covered hazelnuts and apricot usher in a velvety fresh mouthfeel. The Merlot, too, is serious. Yields were below 50 quintals, maceration went on for 15 days and the wine spent 20 months in new and one-year-old barriques, before bottling without filtration. The nose is tousled at first, but then fruit, soft tannins, mouthfilling warmth and great length emerge. The other wines are well-typed, except the Ribolla, one of the estate's flagship wines, which has done better in the past.

○	COF Rosazzo Narciso Bianco '00	🍷🍷	6
●	Franconia '01	🍷🍷	5
●	COF Merlot '99	🍷🍷	5
●	COF Cabernet Sauvignon '01	🍷	5
○	COF Sauvignon '02	🍷	5
○	COF Tocai Friulano '02	🍷	5
○	COF Rosazzo Ribolla Gialla '02		5
●	Narciso Rosso '94	YYY	6
●	COF Rosazzo Narciso Rosso '99	YY	7
○	COF Rosazzo Narciso Bianco '99	YY	6

MANZANO (UD)

MANZANO (UD)

TORRE ROSAZZA
FRAZ. OLEIS
LOC. POGGIOBELLO, 12
33044 MANZANO (UD)
TEL. 0432750180
E-MAIL: bm@borgomagredo.it

★ LE VIGNE DI ZAMÒ
LOC. ROSAZZO
VIA ABATE CORRADO, 4
33044 MANZANO (UD)
TEL. 0432759693
E-MAIL: info@levignedizamo.com

There is important news this year from Torre Rosazza. The estate is owned by the Assicurazioni Generali insurance company and embraces 90 hectares under vine, in two natural amphitheatres 30 kilometres from the coast. A series of initiatives is under way to improve quality. Initial moves include replanting 18 hectares at 5,500 plants per hectare, core boring and mapping of the terrain, and the elimination of the less interesting products. We hope that the friendly estate manager, Piero Totis, and the team co-ordinated by Donato Lanati, will achieve their goals. The reds this year were excellent examples of the push for better quality and actually outperformed the whites, which is rare in Friuli. However, we have to say that the whites were also all worth at least One Glass. The 2000 edition of the historic Altromerlot is delightful. Attractive notes of plum jam and bramble, sweet tobacco and black pepper tempt the nose. These are echoed on the palate, where the lingering, warm finish signs off with cinchona, berry jam and mellow tannins. The Pinot Nero Ronco del Palazzo is as good as ever, showing austere forest fruits and dried roses, then a softly attractive mouthfeel. On its first outing, Bandaròs, a blend of barrique-matured cabernet sauvignon and merlot, impressed us with its balsam and star-anise mingling with hay and plum tart. Softness is not the palate's strong suit, but the vigorous tannins in the unhurried finish demand respect. The other new blend, the white Ronco del Masiero from pinot bianco, pinot grigio and picolit, is also good.

In 1978, Tullio Zamò purchased his first ten hectares of vines on the slopes of Rocca Bernarda, creating a winery – Le Vigne di Zamò – that would quickly earn widespread fame. Tullio passed his enthusiasm for the new venture, and a vocation for hospitality in all forms, to his sons, Pierluigi and Silvano. Sadly, Tullio is no longer with us, for he died at the beginning of the year. The two Zamò brothers suffered a severe blow, but have reacted by concentrating even harder on the winery, which today has 55 hectares under vine, and the other family business in the wood sector. The Zamò vines stand on the finest slopes in the wine country at Rosazzo, Rocca Bernarda and the hills at Buttrio. Their new cellar opened a few years ago, giving them plenty of space and modern technology. Annual production runs at 220-300,000 bottles, depending on the vintage. A few hundred metres from the cellar is the office building, which boasts a superb tasting room and several accommodation units for guests. Oenologist Emilio Del Medico and consultant winemaker Franco Bernabei are responsible for the stunning range of wines presented by Zamò this year, from the Merlot Vigne Cinquant'Anni to the utterly immaculate tocai, chardonnay and pinot bianco Ronco delle Acacie and the Pignolo. Nor should we forget the Tocai Friulano. The version released is impeccable, but we are keen to taste the Cinquant'Anni edition, to be released in 2004.

● COF Pinot Nero		
Ronco del Palazzo '00	♟♟	5
● COF Rosso Bandaròs '01	♟♟	4
● COF Merlot l'Altromerlot '00	♟♟	6
● COF Merlot '01	♟	4
○ COF Picolit '01	♟	6
○ COF Chardonnay '02	♟	4
○ COF Bianco		
Ronco del Masiero '02	♟	4
○ COF Pinot Grigio '02	♟	4
○ COF Ribolla Gialla '02	♟	4
● COF Refosco P. R. '00	♟♟	4
● COF Pinot Nero		
Ronco del Palazzo '99	♟♟	5

○ COF Bianco Rosazzo		
Ronco delle Acacie '01	♟♟♟	5
● COF Merlot V. Cinquant'Anni '00	♟♟	6
● COF Rosazzo Pignolo '99	♟♟	7
● COF Rosso Ronco dei Roseti '00	♟♟	6
○ COF Pinot Bianco Tullio Zamò '01	♟♟	5
● COF Refosco P. R. Re Fosco '01	♟♟	7
○ COF Rosazzo Ribolla Gialla '02	♟♟	4
○ COF Tocai Friulano '02	♟♟	4
○ COF Tocai Friulano		
V. Cinquant'Anni '00	♟♟♟	5
● COF Merlot V. Cinquant'Anni '99	♟♟♟	6

MARIANO DEL FRIULI (GO) MARIANO DEL FRIULI (GO)

EDDI LUISA
FRAZ. CORONA
VIA CORMONS, 19
34070 MARIANO DEL FRIULI (GO)
TEL. 048169680
E-MAIL: azienda@viniluisa.com

MASUT DA RIVE
VIA MANZONI, 82
34070 MARIANO DEL FRIULI (GO)
TEL. 048169200
E-MAIL: info@masutdarive.com

The upper bank of the Isonzo has gravelly soil rich in decalcified limestone with a high aluminium and iron content, known in Italian as "ferrettizato". It is here, at Corona near Manzano, that Tenuta Luisa is located. In charge are Michele, Davide and their father Eddi. In recent years, they have been methodically developing the entire winery. The 55 hectares under vine, all in a single plot, have been replanted. The vines, ready for manual or mechanical harvesting, yield more than 200,000 bottles each year. Major work is going on at the estate headquarters, where a new, bigger cellar is being built along with a hospitality area and a tasting room with a stunning visual impact. "I Ferretti" is the name the Luisas have chosen for their prestige wines, aged in 500-litre tonneaux. It embraces four reds and a white, the Chardonnay 2001, a fresh-tasting, delightfully fluent wine with elegant mineral notes. The excellent Cabernet Sauvignon is austere yet warm and sunny on the nose. A very Mediterranean wine, it has intense progression on the palate, which reveals nice hints of bramble and raspberry. The velvety, very mature Cabernet Franc is also admirable. The dark, concentrated Refosco is one for the cellar. The warm, faintly vanillaed palate of the Merlot has vegetal nuances and just lacks a touch of energy for true greatness. All these wines are released only after an appropriate period in bottle.

The Gallo family has been growing grapes since the early 20th century. The estate has now been passed through the generations to Fabrizio, who runs things with help from his brother, Marco, and his father, Silvano. The younger Gallos have implemented improvements, applying modern vineyard and cellar management techniques. These include new planting patterns, reducing yields in the 17 hectares of estate under vine, and must hyperoxidation. All this has given the 100,000 bottles produced each year elegance and personality. Considering Fabrizio and his family's commitment and serious approach, this is one of the Isonzo cellars from which we can reasonably look forward to truly excellent results in the future. In the meantime, the best wine this year is the Tocai Friulano, in fact it is one of the finest versions from this DOC zone. Long and concentrated on the nose, it gives the impression of being a little closed in the mouth but then progresses surefootedly, broadening slowly to finish in a surprisingly elegant flourish. The Chardonnay Maurùs 2001 still has tannins to be mellowed from its lengthy stay in oak but manages to impress with nice roundness and long, fruit-rich sensations. The Cabernet Sauvignon finds a nice balance of ripe fruit and jam with well-gauged oak. Finally, the full, mature Cabernet Franc has interesting breadth on the palate.

● Friuli Isonzo Cabernet Franc I Ferretti '00	♟♟	5
● Friuli Isonzo Cabernet Sauvignon I Ferretti '00	♟♟	5
○ Friuli Isonzo Chardonnay I Ferretti '01	♟♟	5
● Friuli Isonzo Merlot I Ferretti '00	♟♟	4
● Friuli Isonzo Refosco P. R. I Ferretti '00	♟♟	5
○ Friuli Isonzo Chardonnay '02	♟♟	4
● Rôl '00	♟	5
○ Friuli Isonzo Pinot Bianco '02	♟	4
○ Friuli Isonzo Pinot Grigio '02	♟	4
○ Friuli Isonzo Tocai Friulano '02	♟	4
● Friuli Isonzo Cabernet Franc '02		4

○ Friuli Isonzo Tocai Friulano '02	♟♟	4*
● Friuli Isonzo Cabernet Franc '01	♟♟	4
● Friuli Isonzo Cabernet Sauvignon '01	♟♟	4
○ Friuli Isonzo Chardonnay Maurùs '01	♟♟	5
○ Friuli Isonzo Pinot Bianco '02	♟♟	4
● Friuli Isonzo Merlot '01	♟	4
○ Friuli Isonzo Chardonnay '02	♟	4
○ Friuli Isonzo Pinot Grigio '02	♟	4
○ Friuli Isonzo Sauvignon '02	♟	4
○ Friuli Isonzo Sauvignon '01	♟♟	4

MARIANO DEL FRIULI (GO)   NIMIS (UD)

★ VIE DI ROMANS
VIE DI ROMANS, 1
34070 MARIANO DEL FRIULI (GO)
TEL. 048169600
E-MAIL: viediromans@viediromans.it

DARIO COOS
LOC. RAMANDOLO
VIA PESCIA, 1
33045 NIMIS (UD)
TEL. 0432790320 - 0432797807
E-MAIL: dariocoos@libero.it

For years, the Isonzo plain was a generous reserve of unpretentious wines for local consumption. That tradition still obtains, but for the past 15 years it has been possible to find estates that have made a firm commitment to quality, putting themselves in the front line of white wine production in particular. Gianfranco Gallo was one of the first to put his faith in the potential of the territory and invest not just in production but also in research. His skills and willingness to help younger colleagues have made him a benchmark producer for the DOC zone. His wines reflect a constant striving for improvement that, for example, have prompted him to seek very full ripeness in his grapes. A stunning stainless steel-aged Sauvignon Piere 2001 earned Gianfranco Three Glasses this year. Grapefruit, white peach and damson are reflected on a palate that progresses smoothly, gaining momentum and conviction. The wood-aged Vieris has warmer notes of apricot, peach and melon. Its creamy mouthfeel is still a little stiff but will mellow with bottle age. We loved the Chardonnay Vie di Romans. The depth of the aromas is reminiscent of a Sauternes and the palate is dry, generous, oily and concentrated, summing up the cellar style. Super-ripe notes and alcohol are the keynotes of the stainless steel-aged version, Ciampagnis Vieris. Dessimis is the quintessence of a ripe, concentrated Pinot Grigio, its tropical fruit and structure promising serious ageing potential.

Ten years ago, when Dario Coos was president of the Ramandolo producers' association, he managed to limit the denomination exclusively to those wineries in the municipalities of Nimis and Savorgnano del Torre. The Colli Orientali del Friuli consortium had extended its use to the entire DOC zone. This operation laid the foundations for the Ramandolo producers' subsequent successful application for the first DOCG zone in Friuli-Venezia Giulia. We should remember that verduzzo friulano has many different variations, yielding wines that differ according to the soil and site climate of the vineyards where it is grown. The area around Ramandolo is generally colder than the rest of the zone, which makes the wine more refined. In addition, verduzzo is a white grape that shares some characteristics with red berry varieties, particular regarding its tough skin and the tannin content of the pulp, which is of course transferred to the wine. Sometimes the wine lacks finesse as a result, but today more and more winemakers are able to offer wines like those Dario Coos first released many years ago. His Ramandolo 2000 made a stunning impression on the panel. The sugars have found a perfect balance and the aromas range from tea to herb infusions and very ripe fruit. The dried-grape Romandus '99 and 2000 also earned Two full Glasses. If they have a blemish, it is in their generous sugars and aromas. Finally, the 2000 Picolit convinced the panel more than the preceding vintage.

O Friuli Isonzo Sauvignon Piere '01	♙♙♙	5
O Friuli Isonzo Chardonnay Ciampagnis Vieris '01	♙♙	5
O Friuli Isonzo Chardonnay Vie di Romans '01	♙♙	6
O Friuli Isonzo Pinot Grigio Dessimis '01	♙♙	5
O Friuli Isonzo Sauvignon Vieris '01	♙♙	6
● Friuli Isonzo Maurus '00	♙♙	5
O Friuli Isonzo Bianco Flors di Uis '01	♙	5
O Friuli Isonzo Sauvignon Piere '97	♟♟♟	5
O Friuli Isonzo Pinot Grigio Dessimis '99	♟♟♟	5
O Friuli Isonzo Sauvignon Vieris '00	♟♟♟	5

O COF Ramandolo '00	♙♙	5
O COF Picolit '00	♙♙	7
O COF Ramandolo Passito Romandus '00	♙♙	6
O COF Ramandolo Passito Romandus '99	♙♙	6
O COF Picolit '01	♙	7
O COF Verduzzo Friulano Il Longhino '01	♙	4
O COF Picolit Romandus '99	♟♟	7

NIMIS (UD)

LA RONCAIA
FRAZ. CERGNEU
VIA VERDI, 26
33045 NIMIS (UD)
TEL. 0432790280
E-MAIL: info@laroncaia.com

For some years, this estate has been owned by the Fantinel family. It includes 22 hectares under vine, in the northern part of the Colli Orientali del Friuli at Nimis, Attimis and Ramandolo. The recently built cellar is already having difficulty finding space for all the tonneaux and barriques – there are more than 500 – that the production strategy demands. Marco and Stefano Fantinel are justly proud of the results they have achieved in a relatively short time. The contribution of Hungarian winemaker, Tibor Gal, a man who for ten years was active at the Ornellaia winery, was the crucial factor in the rapid rise of La Roncaia, where technician Massimo Vidoni looks after day-to-day cellar management. As an excellence-oriented producer, Marco Fantinel was one of the staunchest supporters of the DOCG zone for Ramandolo and Picolit, two of his cellar's finest wines. The Ramandolo is dense, sweet and slightly tannic, whereas the Picolit is strikingly reminiscent of sweet wines from Hungary. It comes from the most extensive vineyard of the variety in Friuli, some six and a half hectares at Attimis. Fusco is from native refosco and tazzelenghe with cabernet franc and merlot, and Gheppio is a Bordeaux blend with ten per cent refosco.

NIMIS (UD)

RONCO VIERI
LOC. RAMANDOLO
S.DA INTERPODERALE DELLA MADDALENA
33045 NIMIS (UD)
TEL. 0432904726 - 043286437
E-MAIL: roncovieri@libero.it

Ramandolo is right in the north of the Colli Orientali del Friuli. Its soil and climate are very special. The firm, red clay is rich in iron and trace elements and site climates are strongly influenced by cold northeast winds. There is such a high risk of hail that many vineyards have protection systems in place. It is here that verduzzo friulano vine has given birth to verduzzo giallo, which is known locally as verduzzo di Ramandolo. In 1988, four oenologists got together to purchase Ronco Vieri (the name means "old hilltop"). The quartet were Alvaro Moreale, head oenologist of the Cantina Sociale di Casarsa, his son, Stefano Moreale, Piero Pittaro, producer and former world president of the oenologists' association, and Stefano Trinco, Pittaro's oenologist and current president of the association of Friulian oenologists. The estate has five and a half hectares, three under vine. Vinification is carried out in the new cellar at Tarcento and only three wines, from native grapes, are released. The ever-splendid Ramandolo is sweet but not cloying, with hints of almond paste, apricots and baked apple. The Refosco is fruity and spicy, and the sweet Picolit has a supremely complex range of aromas on the nose.

○ COF Picolit '01	♀♀	8
○ COF Ramandolo '01	♀	6
● COF Refosco '00	♀♀	6
● Il Fusco '00	♀♀	6
○ COF Chardonnay '01	♀♀	5
● COF Rosso Gheppio '00	♀	7
○ COF Ramandolo '00	♀♀	8
● COF Rosso Gheppio '99	♀♀	7

○ COF Ramandolo '00	♀♀	5
○ COF Picolit '01	♀♀	6
● COF Refosco '01	♀	5
○ COF Ramandolo '99	♀♀	4*

PASIAN DI PRATO (UD)

ANTONUTTI
FRAZ. COLLOREDO DI PRATO
VIA D'ANTONI, 21
33030 PASIAN DI PRATO (UD)
TEL. 0432662001
E-MAIL: info@antonuttivini.it

Every year, it is a pleasant surprise to cast an eye over the results of the Antonutti cellar after our tastings. The 40 hectares under vine on the flatlands at Spilimbergo, which provide 30 per cent of the fruit vinified, and the bought-in fruit, yield about 1,000,000 bottles a year, distributed across 20 wine types. These are numbers that don't usually sit with top quality, but this Colloredo-based cellar is the exception that proves the rule. There are great whites and reds again this year, with two outstanding wines in the Pinot Grigio and the Sauvignon. The ripe apricot and yellow peach on the nose of the Pinot Grigio convey a richness that is confirmed on the palate, where there is a warm citrussy finish. The Sauvignon almost assaults the nose with green, piquant bell pepper, nettle and tomato leaf. The melon, peach and pear sweetness in the mouth comes as a surprise, but the nose-palate contrast works beautifully. A notch or two down come the Chardonnays, the standard-label edition offering apricots in syrup and the Riserva Poggio Alto revealing curious green aromas and hints of cake. The Tocai is very varietal, with typical bitter almond nuances. Moving on to the reds, the nose of the Cabernet Sauvignon Riserva '00 is impressive but it is let down by a less than exciting palate.

PAVIA DI UDINE (UD)

F.LLI PIGHIN
FRAZ. RISANO
V.LE GRADO, 1
33050 PAVIA DI UDINE (UD)
TEL. 0432675444
E-MAIL: azpighin@tin.it

For years, the Pighin estate has been prominent on the Friulian winemaking scene, both for its size and for the quality of the range. Things started in 1963, when brothers Luigi, Ercole and Fernando purchased 200 hectares at Risano from a local family. Part of the property was used for orchards and part planted to vine, then in 1967, the new estate headquarters and cellars were built. The following year, the Pighins bought 30 hectares with a cellar and vineyards at Capriva del Friuli, where they carried out major soil stabilization and terracing work. Today, the estate has 150 hectares in the Friuli Grave DOC zone and the 30 already mentioned in the Collio. Every year, the cellar produces about 10,000 hectolitres of Grave wine, and 2,000 from Collio grapes, under the supervision of Paolo Valdesolo. If you visit the fermentation and maturation cellars, with their awesome rows of steel vats and enormous barrel room, you will begin to grasp Pighin's commitment to reliable quality across the entire range. This year, the Pighin's Sauvignons did well, both in the Collio and Grave versions, standing out from most other interpretations of the variety for their distinctive green pepper aromas. The Grave Pinot Grigio, the cellar's workhorse in purely commercial terms, coasted easily to a very full One Glass score.

O	Friuli Grave Pinot Grigio '02	🍷🍷	3*
O	Friuli Grave Sauvignon '02	🍷🍷	3*
●	Friuli Grave Merlot Poggio Alto '99	🍷	4
O	Friuli Grave Chardonnay '02	🍷	3
O	Friuli Grave Chardonnay Poggio Alto '02	🍷	4
O	Friuli Grave Tocai Friulano '02	🍷	3
O	Friuli Grave Sauvignon Blanc Le Selezioni '02		4
●	Friuli Grave Cabernet Sauvignon Ris. '00		4
●	Friuli Grave Merlot '00	🍷🍷	3
O	Friuli Grave Sauvignon Blanc Le Selezioni '01	🍷🍷	4

O	Collio Sauvignon '02	🍷🍷	4
O	Friuli Grave Sauvignon '02	🍷🍷	3
●	Collio Cabernet '01	🍷	4
●	Friuli Grave Cabernet '01	🍷	3
O	Collio Pinot Grigio '02	🍷	4
O	Friuli Grave Chardonnay '02	🍷	4
O	Friuli Grave Pinot Grigio '02	🍷	3
●	Friuli Grave Cabernet Sauvignon '01		3
●	Baredo '98	🍷	5

PAVIA DI UDINE (UD)

SCARBOLO
FRAZ. LAUZACCO
V.LE GRADO, 4
33050 PAVIA DI UDINE (UD)
TEL. 0432675612
E-MAIL: vini@scarbolo.com

Valter Scarbolo is a man of many parts, and may even be over-committed to the wide range of activities he performs. He runs a respected trattoria, which started life as a cellar-door outlet (known as a "frasca" in Friuli). Over time, he developed it into an "agriturismo", and now an increasingly well-patronized restaurant. As well as Scarbolo wines, visitors can also enjoy the cold meats Valter makes as a pork butcher. Since he still – incredibly – has some free time, he also looks after winemaking at the Bastianich estate. Finally, and this is what really interests us, Valter is also a grower who manages about 18 hectares under vine, some estate-owned and some rented, releasing about 150,000 bottles a year. The vines stand on the alluvial flatlands of Friuli in clay and limestone gravel. Some are traditional and some have recently been, or are being, replanted to achieve planting densities of between 5,500 and 6,000 vines per hectare. To satisfy demand, Scarbolo also has to buy in fruit from other local growers. Our hero also has two major winemaking and vineyard consultants, Maurizio Castelli, a Lombard who moved to Tuscany and who has shown he knows how to get the best out of Friulian vineyards, and Emilio Del Medico, a young agronomist who has already earned his spurs in the region. Campo del Viotto is 50 per cent tocai friulano with equal parts of chardonnay and sauvignon. Fermented and aged for ten months in oak, it then stayed in bottle for a year to emerge full-flavoured and fresh as the cellar's flagship wine. The rest of the range is well-made.

PINZANO AL TAGLIAMENTO (PN)

ALESSANDRO VICENTINI ORGNANI
FRAZ. VALERIANO
VIA SOTTOPLOVIA, 2
33090 PINZANO AL TAGLIAMENTO (PN)
TEL. 0432950107
E-MAIL: vicentiniorgnani@libero.it

Despite the challenges of the 2002 vintage in Friuli, Alessandro Vicentini Orgnani produced one of his finest ranges ever this year from his hillside estate. Much of the vine stock has been replanted and Alessandro, who personally supervises all aspects of vineyard and cellar management, with the help of oenologist Fabio Coser, has certainly gained experience. In addition, some of his wines have consolidated past successes, in particular the Ucelut and the Pinot Bianco Braide Cjase. For the third time, the Ucelut came within a whisker of Three Glasses while the Pinot Bianco racked up its sixth successive Two Glass score. We are well aware that it is not easy to obtain results like these in the Grave DOC, which only adds lustre to Alessandro's achievement. Ucelut is a native sweet wine from late-harvested fruit that is then raisined. Amber in hue, it regales the nose with macaroons, caramel-coated figs, cinnamon and candied citrus peel. It stands out from other sweet whites for the contrast on the palate between the initial sweet sensations that echo the nose and the refreshing finish, with a satisfyingly palate-cleaning note of acidity. We thought that this edition of the Pinot Bianco Braide Cjase was one of the best ever. A sunny, Mediterranean bouquet offers tropical fruit and pineapple juice layered over pipe tobacco from the wood. The long spring flower finish is simply delightful. Also good is the fruit-forward Tocai, which has broom, dried flowers and exceptional value for money in its favour.

O	Campo del Viotto Bianco '01	🍷🍷	5
●	Friuli Grave Merlot '01	🍷	4
O	Friuli Grave Sauvignon '02	🍷	3
O	Friuli Grave Tocai Friulano '02	🍷	3
O	Friuli Grave Chardonnay '02		3
O	Friuli Grave Pinot Grigio '02		3
●	Friuli Grave Refosco P. R. Campo del Viotto '99	🍷🍷	5

O	Ucelut Bianco '01	🍷🍷	6
O	Friuli Grave Pinot Bianco Braide Cjase '02	🍷🍷	4*
O	Friuli Grave Tocai Friulano '02	🍷🍷	3*
O	Friuli Grave Sauvignon '02	🍷	3
●	Friuli Grave Cabernet Sauvignon '02		3
●	Friuli Grave Merlot '02		3
O	Friuli Grave Pinot Grigio '02		3
O	Ucelut Bianco '99	🍷🍷	7
O	Ucelut Bianco '00	🍷🍷	7

POVOLETTO (UD)

POVOLETTO (UD)

AQUILA DEL TORRE
FRAZ. SAVORGNANO DEL TORRE
VIA ATTIMIS, 25
33040 POVOLETTO (UD)
TEL. 0432666428 - 0432647942
E-MAIL: info@aquiladeltorre.it

Father and son Claudio and Michele Ciani took over this historic estate in 1996. Having operated under the name of Poderi del Sole since the early 20th century, in the 1970s the winery was releasing a number of widely admired bottles, the best of which was the Picolit. Here are some numbers to give readers an idea of Aquila del Torre. There are 82 hectares in a single property, which includes woodland, various agricultural buildings, the winery itself and 25 hectares under vine. Under the watchful eyes of Marco Simonit and Pierpaolo Sirch, the Cianis have completed a major programme of hydrogeological intervention and vineyard management that is slowing yielding its first results. The main vineyards stand on a spectacular, narrow-terraced double amphitheatre whose higher parts protect the plants from cold north-east winds. Aquila del Torre has taken a strategic decision that goes against the trend in Friuli. After carefully studying the soil and climate of the area, the cellar planted only six varieties, four white and two red. Work on the cellar buildings has also been completed, to the great satisfaction of wine technician Francesco Noro. All this has restricted Aquila del Torre to release only two wines onto the market. Both, a Tocai and a Sauvignon from the Vocalis line of monovarietals, are excellent. The Tocai has further enhanced the features that impressed us during cellar tastings: the nose is intense, complex and elegant, and there is remarkable length on the palate.

TERESA RAIZ
FRAZ. MARSURE DI SOTTO
VIA DELLA ROGGIA, 22
33040 POVOLETTO (UD)
TEL. 0432679556
E-MAIL: info@teresaraiz.it

Great things are afoot at the Teresa Raiz company. The Tosolinis, who owned the business jointly, have split Distillerie Camel, which now belongs to Giovanni, from the wine estate, which is exclusively owned by his brother Paolo. Paolo Tosolini is a wine technician who gained his experience at several leading Friulian wineries, including Mario Schiopetto. Having established that vinification will continue to take place at the Marsure di Sotto site, Paolo also wants to find a winery, in the hills if possible, where he can set up his offices and barrel cellars. Today, Teresa Raiz has 20 hectares of estate-owned vines and buys in first-quality fruit in the area around nearby Savorgnano del Torre, Faedis and Campeglio. The wines obtained from Grave del Friuli fruit are sold under the Corte Le Marsure label while the Teresa Raiz brand is reserved for wines from the Colli Orientali del Friuli. Last year, the Le Marsure Pinot Grigio earned Two Glasses whereas the Colli Orientali del Friuli version only obtained one but this year, the positions are reversed. The Grave wine has an elegant nose of cream but was marked down for an intrusive acidic note in the finish. But the generous fruit of the Teresa Raiz version is more than a match for its acidity. The Decano Rosso Bordeaux blend still lacks balance from nose to palate but we think it will develop nicely. Today, the Rosso is drinking better for this 80-20 mix of merlot and cabernet franc is a shade more evolved.

○ COF Tocai Friulano Vocalis '02	♉♉	5
○ COF Sauvignon Vocalis '02	♉	5
● COF Merlot Vocalis '99	♉♉	5
○ COF Picolit V. T. '99	♉♉	6

● COF Rosso '00	♉♉	5
○ COF Pinot Grigio '02	♉♉	4*
● COF Rosso Decano Rosso '00	♉	6
● COF Cabernet '01	♉	4
● Friuli Grave Merlot '01	♉	3
○ COF Tocai Friulano '02	♉	4
○ Pinot Grigio Corte Le Marsure '02	♉	3
● Querciolo '01		4
○ COF Ribolla Gialla '02		4
○ COF Tocai Friulano '01	♉♉	4
● COF Rosso Decano Rosso '99	♉♉	5

PRATA DI PORDENONE (PN)

VIGNETI LE MONDE
LOC. LE MONDE
VIA GARIBALDI, 2
33080 PRATA DI PORDENONE (PN)
TEL. 0434626096 - 0434622087
E-MAIL: info@vignetilemonde.com

Vigneti Le Monde stands where the Livenza river meets the Meduna. Last year, it won its first Three Glass award in the history of the Guide with a wine from the Grave DOC zone. The 2002 vintage was a challenging one, but it confirmed the quality of Piergiovanni Pistoni Salice's range. As in the past, the panel found a series of remarkable reds and, not for the first time, an excellent Pinot Bianco. It has to be said that although the cellar is not the most modern in Friuli, and the planting densities could do with reconsideration, the soil at Vigneti Le Monde is an ideal habitat for these grapes. Naturally, the almost Venetian ambience, a short distance from the superb Villa Giustinian, and the estate's own 18th-century residence with its lovely hospitality areas, make it easier to work productively. The Pinot Bianco 2002 is youthfully alcoholic, the pear, apple and orange blossom of the nose echoed nicely on the fresh palate. The Cabernet Franc has strikingly intense red berry jam and complex balsam with chocolate, leading into a soft, broad mouthfeel that signs off unhurriedly with cinchona and hay. We also liked the Refosco, a well-structured wine thanks to its tannic weave, warm alcohol and attractive black cherry and bitter chocolate aromas. The structure of the Cabernet Sauvignon Riserva is almost as impressive, but the palate is just a shade less complex.

PRATA DI PORDENONE (PN)

VILLA FRATTINA
FRAZ. GHIRANO
VIA PALAZZETTO, 68
33080 PRATA DI PORDENONE (PN)
TEL. 0434605911
E-MAIL: giuseppe.vavassori@averna.it

Villa Frattina, owned by the Averna group since 1989, extends over 60 hectares of the flatlands around Pordenone. Signora Luisa Averna, who handles promotion with great verve, confirms that the aim is improved quality in vineyard and cellar. Co-ordinating these efforts is consultant winemaker, Donato Lanati, who has the very able Ivan Molaro to call on at the estate. Vineyard management consultant is Professor Attilio Scienza. Obviously, the commitment is to make good wine, whatever the vagaries of the growing year, including the 2002 vintage, which was no great shakes in Friuli. Nevertheless, top-notch staff enabled Villa Frattina to keep the standards of the year's wines well up the scale. Best of all is the blended red Corte dell'Abbà, from cabernet sauvignon, refosco, merlot and cabernet franc, which stayed in barrique for at least 15 months and then aged in bottle for a further four. Well-defined fruit in alcohol, plum jam and bramble mingle with coffee on the nose. The tannins are impressively robust, hinting at a long life in the cellar. The Sauvignon, which is very green on the nose, with evident bell peppers, nearly earned a second Glass. We liked the white blend, Ale di Glesie, from oak-matured chardonnay, pinot grigio, sauvignon and tocai that give the wine hints of petits fours, apples and pears. Finally, the "dark side" of Villa Frattina, and the Pordenone flatlands in general, is evident in a fine selection of red wines.

● Friuli Grave Refosco P. R. Ris. '01	♟♟	5
● Friuli Grave Cabernet Franc '02	♟♟	3*
○ Friuli Grave Pinot Bianco '02	♟♟	3*
○ Friuli Grave Bianco Puja '01	♟	4
● Friuli Grave Cabernet Sauvignon Ris. '01	♟	3
○ Friuli Grave Sauvignon '02	♟	3
● Friuli Grave Rosso Ca' Salice '01		3
○ Friuli Grave Bianco Pra' de Gai '02		3
○ Friuli Grave Chardonnay '02		3
○ Friuli Grave Pinot Grigio '02		4
○ Friuli Grave Pinot Bianco '01	♟♟♟	3
● Friuli Grave Pinot Nero '98	♟♟	4

● Rosso Corte dell'Abbà '00	♟♟	6
● Lison-Pramaggiore Cabernet Franc Faè '00	♟	5
○ Ale di Glesie '01	♟	5
● Refosco P. R. '01	♟	4
● Robbio '01	♟	4
○ Lison-Pramaggiore Chardonnay '02	♟	4
○ Lison-Pramaggiore Sauvignon '02	♟	4
○ Di Gale '02		4
● Lison-Pramaggiore Merlot Faè '00		5
● Lison-Pramaggiore Cabernet Sauvignon '02		4
● Rosso Corte dell'Abbà '99	♟♟	6

PRAVISDOMINI (PN)

PODERE DEL GER
FRAZ. FRATTINA
VIA STRADA DELLA MEDUNA
33076 PRAVISDOMINI (PN)
TEL. 0434644452
E-MAIL: poderedelger@libero.it

The ten hectares recently planted with selected clones of French cabernet franc bring Podere del Ger's total number under vine to 50, and bottles produced to 100,000. This young estate is professionally managed by Gianluigi Spinazzè and his son, Robert, who this year began work on a modern cellar, which will require considerable drainage work as it stands on land with lots of underground water. In the meantime, work in the vineyards goes on under the supervision of flamboyant fruitmaker, Pierpaolo Sirch, and expert oenologist, Romeo Taraborelli. Thanks to these two, the estate has made substantial progress in quality over very few years. When the panel came to visit, it found a series of excellent wines, none of which earned less than One Glass. There were two stars, the El Masut red blend and the original Verduzzo Limine. El Masut is a merlot-heavy mix with cabernet franc, cabernet sauvignon and refosco that undergoes slow maturation in oak. Cherry jam and plum usher in a warm, rich and very complex palate where plain chocolate is underpinned by a robust tannic weave. We called the Verduzzo "original" because it is an oak-aged dry wine with baked apple, mint chocolate and peach tea aromas. The follow through on the palate is impeccable and the warm finish foregrounds peach and macaroons.

PREMARIACCO (UD)

BASTIANICH
VIA CASALI OTTELIO, 7
33040 PREMARIACCO (UD)
TEL. 0432655363
E-MAIL: bastianich@aol.com

Lidia Bastianich and her son Joe, who own a string of successful restaurants in Manhattan and elsewhere in the United States, decided to invest in winemaking in Italy. In 1998, they purchased their first property in Friuli, renting additional vineyards to bring the total to almost 15 hectares. This year, Lidia and Joe rented a cellar, where they will vinify for the next few years until their new headquarters is complete. Joe and Lidia both make frequent visits to the estate, especially at crucial moments of the winemaking year, but quality is guaranteed by a well-matched, first-rank team: Valter Scarbolo is general manager; Emilio Del Medico is vineyard and winemaking consultant; Maurizio Castelli's skills have been on hand from the start; and Andrea Brunisso's experience is available on a day-to-day basis. The Vespa Bianco is as good as ever. From chardonnay and sauvignon half vinified in stainless steel and half in barrique, it contains ten per cent of tonneau-fermented and aged picolit. The resulting wine is intense and elegant, with faint milky notes and a rich, structured palate with good weight and stunning length. Weight and length are also the hallmarks of the Vespa Rosso, obtained from merlot, refosco and cabernet vinified separately in tonneau and barrique. Red berries and forest fruits follow through from nose to the big, full, lingering palate. Tocai Plus is from stainless steel-vinified fruit picked at full ripeness, plus grapes that had almost raisined on the vine and were fermented in oak. It's a wine to wait for, but is already drinking deliciously.

● El Masut '00	♟♟	5
○ Verduzzo Limine '00	♟♟	5
● Lison-Pramaggiore Cabernet Franc '01	♟	3
● Lison-Pramaggiore Merlot '01	♟	3
○ Lison-Pramaggiore Chardonnay '02	♟	3
○ Lison-Pramaggiore Pinot Grigio '02	♟	3
● Lison-Pramaggiore Merlot '00	♟♟	3
○ Verduzzo Limine '99	♟♟	5

○ Vespa Bianco '01	♟♟♟	5
● Vespa Rosso '00	♟♟	5
○ COF Tocai Friulano Plus '01	♟♟	5
○ Vespa Bianco '99	♟♟♟	5
○ Vespa Bianco '00	♟♟♟	5
● Vespa Rosso '98	♟♟	5
○ COF Pinot Grigio Plus '00	♟♟	5
● Calabrone '99	♟♟	7
○ COF Tocai Friulano Plus '00	♟♟	5

PREMARIACCO (UD)

DARIO E LUCIANO ERMACORA
FRAZ. IPPLIS
VIA SOLZAREDO, 9
33040 PREMARIACCO (UD)
TEL. 0432716250
E-MAIL: info@ermacora.it

The 19 hectares under vine at Dario and Luciano Ermacora's Ipplis estate provide the market with 120,000 bottles of premium whites and reds that are textbook examples of varietal typicity. This year, the Ermacoras outdid themselves with a great range of wines, led by their traditional Pinot Bianco and a surprising Sauvignon. In fact, the Pinot Bianco was the subject of a recent vertical tasting that showed how well Dario and Luciano's wines age. Time brings them complexity and their lustre is untarnished. But let's go back to the 2002 Pinot Bianco and the Sauvignon. The Pinot Bianco has varietal crusty bread and apple with hints of fresh citrus and wistaria. The citrus returns in the mouth, then the fresh-tasting finish has an apple theme. We were impressed by the impeccably varietal Sauvignon, which shows fragrant notes of elderflower and ripe bell pepper laced with melon, and a tangy freshness. Only a few marks behind is the Tocai, which opens on fresh, green aromas and concludes with a flowery finish. The nice Pinot Grigio has faint onionskin highlights and full, fruity aromas, the complex Picolit offers rich notes of baked apple, figs, marmalade and peach tea, and a warm, pervasive mouthfeel. There are attractive notes of bramble, cinchona and coffee, as well as robust tannins, in the Merlot. But the Rîul red from refosco, merlot and cabernet sauvignon was let down by an undistinguished back palate.

PREMARIACCO (UD)

LA TUNELLA
FRAZ. IPPLIS
VIA DEL COLLIO, 14
33040 PREMARIACCO (UD)
TEL. 0432716030
E-MAIL: info@latunella.it

Massimo and Marco Zorzettig, with the crucial contribution of their mother, Gabriella, have revamped the philosophy of a winery that once had much higher – perhaps too high – production levels and yields, and bought in substantial quantities of fruit from other growers. Today, the cellar vinifies only grapes from the 69 hectares of estate-owned vines, plus ten rented hectares, and annual production is in excess of 400,000 units. For ten years, Giuseppe Zamparo, better known as Luigino, has been the La Tunella wine technician, making a crucial contribution to the quality levels the cellar has achieved. After this sea change in production, the Zorzettig family courageously decided to modify the cellar's name (it was previously known as Livio Zorzettig, after the deceased father and husband of the present owners) and their customer base. Not satisfied with their large cellar, Massimo and Marco have begun to construct a new headquarters that presages further increases in winery production. The range of wines is very complete and standards are worthy of good mid to upper market products. Our tastings revealed excellent performances from the sweet Picolit and the riesling renano, sauvignon and traminer aromatico-based Noans wines. The traditional whites also did well and if we were looking for faults, we might note that the reds still need some fine tuning.

O COF Pinot Bianco '02	🍷🍷	4*
O COF Sauvignon '02	🍷🍷	4*
● COF Merlot '01	🍷🍷	4
O COF Picolit '01	🍷🍷	7
O COF Pinot Grigio '02	🍷🍷	4
O COF Tocai Friulano '02	🍷🍷	4
● COF Rosso Rîul '00	🍷	5
O COF Verduzzo Friulano '02	🍷	4
O COF Picolit '00	🍷🍷	7
O COF Verduzzo Friulano '01	🍷🍷	4
● COF Rîul Rosso '99	🍷🍷	5
● COF Merlot '00	🍷	4

O COF Picolit '02	🍷🍷	6
O Noans '02	🍷🍷	5
O COF Bianco Campo Marzio '01	🍷🍷	5
O COF Pinot Bianco '02	🍷🍷	4*
O COF Pinot Grigio '02	🍷🍷	4*
O COF Ribolla Gialla '02	🍷🍷	4*
● COF Rosso L'Arcione '00	🍷	5
● COF Cabernet Franc '02	🍷	4
O COF Tocai Friulano '02	🍷	4
● COF Refosco P.R. '02		4
● COF Cabernet Franc '01	🍷🍷	4
O COF Ribolla Gialla '01	🍷🍷	4

PREMARIACCO (UD)

PREMARIACCO (UD)

ROCCA BERNARDA
FRAZ. IPPLIS
VIA ROCCA BERNARDA, 27
33040 PREMARIACCO (UD)
TEL. 0432716914 - 0432716273
E-MAIL: roccabernarda@roccabernarda.com

SCUBLA
FRAZ. IPPLIS
VIA ROCCA BERNARDA, 22
33040 PREMARIACCO (UD)
TEL. 0432716258 - 048192550
E-MAIL: scublavini@libero.it

Things are moving on apace at Rocca Bernarda. In April, Mario Zuliani, the influential estate manager who contributed so much to the rapid improvement in wine quality over the last few years, has resigned, to be substituted by oenologist, Paolo Dolce. Restoration work on the castle has also been completed. This splendid 16th-century residence, which dominates the entire estate, was built by the noble Conti Valvason Maniago family and now houses the estate's offices, cellar-door sales outlet and elegant hospitality facilities. Work in the vineyards continues. New plantings are being made on the sunny south-facing flank of the hill. These pignolo, refosco and merlot vines will be crucial in making further progress on the red wine front. The upshot of all this is that expert oenologist, Marco Monchiero, was able again this year to offer us a fine range of wines, led by the two Rocca Bernarda workhorses, Merlot Centis and Picolit. Both were in the running for Three Glasses. Centis tempted with complex candied citrus, black cherry in spirits, petits fours and attractive balsam aromas that return on the palate. It's a wine that may lack softness, but has elegance in spades. Picolit is a historic wine at Rocca Bernarda. The aromas of noble rot, candied citrus peel, honey, caramel-covered figs and dried roses are accompanied by sweetness that never cloys. We would also like to mention the oily richness of the Pinot Grigio, the typicity of the Tocai and the sunny, baked fruit aromas of the Ribolla Gialla.

Roberto Scubla's estate lies on the slopes of the legendary Rocca Bernarda, where chalky Eocene marl, rich in salts and trace elements, make a particularly favourable winemaking environment. The combination of northerly winds tempered by the effects of the nearby Adriatic produces a temperature range at harvest time that concentrates sugars and flavour precursors, without burning off natural acids. Roberto's winery is an object lesson in this process and some of his wines are Friulian classics. Above all, there is his Pomédes, named after the mountain refuge where the idea germinated during a blizzard. A blend of pinot bianco, tocai and super-ripe riesling wines, fermented for eight months in new wood with lees stirring, and blended for four months in temperature-controlled stainless steel vats, then aged in bottle for a further six months. It's a thoroughbred with a textbook progression that is complete, balanced and eminently long. The Tocai, like all Scubla single-grape whites, is fermented in temperature-controlled stainless steel containers to safeguard freshness and typicity. Its elegant aromas of fresh almonds and medlars, introducing a warm, velvet-smooth palate, are as impressive as Pomédes. The other Scubla classics include a Pinot Bianco with convincing apple aromas, although it is edge to begin with, and Graticcio, a dried-grape Verduzzo from fruit raisined in the "bora" winds. Here, the confectioner's cream, dates and candied orange peel don't quite manage to mellow out the rather too volatile finish. The reds are all good, but we were hoping for more.

●	COF Merlot Centis '01	🍷🍷	6
○	COF Picolit '01	🍷🍷	8
○	COF Pinot Grigio '02	🍷🍷	4*
○	COF Ribolla Gialla '02	🍷🍷	4*
○	COF Tocai Friulano '02	🍷🍷	4*
○	COF Chardonnay '02	🍷	4
○	COF Sauvignon '02	🍷	4
○	COF Picolit '97	🍷🍷🍷	8
○	COF Picolit '98	🍷🍷🍷	8
●	COF Merlot Centis '99	🍷🍷🍷	5
●	COF Merlot Centis '00	🍷🍷	5
○	COF Picolit '00	🍷🍷	8
○	COF Bianco Vineis '01	🍷🍷	5

○	COF Bianco Pomédes '01	🍷🍷	5
○	COF Tocai Friulano '02	🍷🍷	4*
○	COF Verduzzo Friulano Graticcio '00	🍷🍷	6
○	COF Pinot Bianco '02	🍷🍷	4
●	COF Rosso Scuro '00	🍷	5
●	COF Cabernet Sauvignon '01	🍷	5
●	COF Merlot '01	🍷	5
○	COF Sauvignon '02		4
○	COF Bianco Pomédes '98	🍷🍷🍷	5
○	COF Bianco Pomédes '99	🍷🍷🍷	5
○	COF Verduzzo Friulano Graticcio '99	🍷🍷🍷	6
○	COF Bianco Pomédes '00	🍷🍷	5

PREMARIACCO (UD)

VIGNE FANTIN NODA'R
LOC. ORSARIA
VIA CASALI OTTELIO, 4
33040 PREMARIACCO (UD)
TEL. 043428735
E-MAIL: vignefantin@libero.it

Vigne Fantin Noda'r is ten years old. Established in 1993 by Attilio Pignat, it currently has 20 or so hectares on some of the loveliest hillsides in the municipalities of Buttrio and Premariacco. The vineyards are looked after by Stefano Bortolussi and vinification is under the supervision of oenologist, Francesco Spitaleri, who is following in his father's footsteps. The vine stock, planted in 1993-95, is starting to produce top-quality fruit. All the vineyards are Guyot-trained and planted at densities of about 5,000 vines per hectare, with yields kept to little more than one kilogram per vine. Attilio has also decided to renovate and extend the cellar. Moving on to the wines, we find Carato 2000, one of the best whites in Friuli. It is obtained from three quarters riesling and one quarter sauvignon, chardonnay and picolit. Alcoholic and malolactic fermentation are completed in French oak barriques and the blend is released only in the best vintages. Stunningly elegant on the nose, it reveals a complex, rich palate with excellent structure and length. The Tocai Friulano 2002 scored Two good Glasses for its tangy, fresh-tasting palate and seamless consistency. Intense dried pear and apple mingle on the nose of the Verduzzo Friulano with milk of almonds, ushering in a medium-sweet palate. There is good nose-palate consistency.

PREPOTTO (UD)

IOLE GRILLO
FRAZ. ALBANA
VIA ALBANA, 60
33040 PREPOTTO (UD)
TEL. 0432713201 - 0432713322
E-MAIL: info@vinigrillo.it

Recently, Anna Muzzolini, Iole Grillo's daughter, gave the winery a complete overhaul, fitting out a few small holiday flats among other things. The cellar has been extended and rationalized so that there is adequate storage space. The original part of the complex, once a cheese dairy, has been restructured and turned into a barrel cellar. The property, managed by Lino Casella who is also the wine technician, vinifies fruit from eight hectares. Almost all of the vineyards are on the hillsides around the winery, with a small proportion on the narrow stretch of flatland that goes down to the Judrio. This is the river that runs north of Albana and forms the frontier with Slovenia, while to the south it separates the Colli Orientali del Friuli DOC zone from the Collio. Major restructuring going on in the cellar during vinification is nearly always reflected in the wine, and Anna Muzzolini's range is no exception to the rule. The wines were, in fact, a touch below par. We did, however, like the Bianco Santa Justina 2001, from 50 per cent chardonnay and equal parts of ribolla gialla and malvasia. The vines are nearly 40 years old and the musts ferment in 500-litre oak barrels. There is vanilla on the nose, then the palate is complex and well-structured, with lingering fruit. It's a young wine, but should age very well indeed. The rest of the range is well typed, with special mentions for the varietal, full-bodied Cabernet, the fruit-forward, tangy Tocai Friulano and the smooth-drinking Sauvignon, which is lifted by bright acidity.

O	COF Bianco Carato '00	🍷🍷	5
O	COF Verduzzo Friulano '01	🍷🍷	4
O	COF Tocai Friulano '02	🍷🍷	4
●	COF Cabernet '01	🍷	4
●	COF Merlot '01	🍷	4
●	COF Refosco P. R. '01	🍷	4
O	COF Pinot Grigio '02	🍷	4
O	COF Sauvignon '02		4
●	COF Cabernet '00	🍷🍷	4
O	COF Bianco Carato '98	🍷🍷	4

O	COF Bianco Santa Justina '01	🍷🍷	5
●	COF Cabernet '01	🍷	4
●	COF Merlot '02	🍷	4
O	COF Pinot Grigio '02	🍷	4
O	COF Sauvignon '02	🍷	4
O	COF Tocai Friulano '02	🍷	4
●	COF Refosco P. R. '01		4
O	COF Pinot Grigio '01	🍷🍷	4
●	COF Refosco P. R. '00	🍷	4
●	COF Merlot Sel. '99	🍷	4

PREPOTTO (UD)

LA VIARTE
VIA NOVACUZZO, 50
33040 PREPOTTO (UD)
TEL. 0432759458
E-MAIL: laviarte@laviarte.it

Giuseppe Ceschin's estate has passed to his son, Giulio, and continues to be a textbook example of the genuine passion for winemaking to be found in these parts. There are 35 east-facing hectares, 20 under vine that have been wrested from the woodland which, together with the drainage provided by the river Judrio, creates unique site climates. The vineyards are all terraced and the cellar is both large and well equipped. The terraces are planted at 3-3,500 vines per hectare to many different varieties, as is the custom in the area, mixing native vines with international, although it is pedantic to consider certain grapes that have been cultivated in Friuli for more than a century "non-native". The only wine that lived up to its reputation was the intense, floral Tocai. The nose is a little untidy at first, with wet rag on entry, but this – almost a distinguishing feature of La Viarte whites – soon disappears and the palate is soft, zesty and fresh-tasting, with a hint of green in the finish. Moving on to the other wines, we'll be back for the flagship Siùm next year, to keep in step with its release schedule. The other wines are well typed: Sauvignon, Pinot Bianco, Tazzelenghe and Refosco, the best of the bunch. But we were less convinced by the Liende blend, which in the past has been outstanding.

PREPOTTO (UD)

LE DUE TERRE
VIA ROMA, 68/B
33040 PREPOTTO (UD)
TEL. 0432713189

Quite apart from the numbers and points awarded, the fascinating thing about Flavio Basilicata and his wife, Silvana, is their unswerving commitment to concepts and wines that flout traditional canons. They follow their own passions (Pinot Nero), their own insights (Implicito and Sacrisassi Rosso) and their own idea of territory (Sacrisassi Bianco and Merlot). All this is underpinned by a technical rigour that has few equals in the area. The Implicito is a wine to delight connoisseurs. Many others have realized how important picolit is, but to make a single-variety wine and ferment all the sugar is to take this intuition as far as it will go. Opinions are, in fact, mixed but Implicito's impact on Friulian winemaking is undeniable. Our tasters are among those who love it, as one admires any daring enterprise that produces memorable results. The other great product was the Pinot Nero. It's a challenging variety that adapts to the Mediterranean with great difficulty, yet Flavio makes one of Italy's finest. This wine will age without effort to produce the complex tertiary aromas of the other great international reds. Sacrisassi Bianco is straightforward to describe. It has structure, territory from the tocai, a hint of the acidity that tocai lacks from ribolla, and aromas from its elegant sauvignon. And the result is well up to expectations. The refosco and schioppettino Sacrisassi Rosso wasn't firing on all cylinders, its cocoa powder and incense giving way to sweet notes. But the Merlot was very good, confirming that the variety is at home in Friuli.

○	COF Tocai Friulano '02	🍷🍷	5
●	COF Refosco P. R. '00	🍷	5
○	COF Pinot Bianco '02	🍷	5
○	COF Sauvignon '02	🍷	5
●	COF Tazzelenghe '99	🍷	6
●	COF Schioppettino '00		5
○	COF Bianco Liende '01		5
○	COF Pinot Grigio '02		5
○	Siùm '00	🍷🍷	6
○	COF Ribolla Gialla '00	🍷	4

●	COF Pinot Nero '01	🍷🍷	6
○	Implicito '01	🍷🍷	6
○	COF Bianco Sacrisassi '01	🍷🍷	5
●	COF Merlot '01	🍷🍷	6
●	COF Rosso Sacrisassi '01	🍷	6
●	COF Merlot '00	🍷🍷🍷	6
●	COF Rosso Sacrisassi '97	🍷🍷🍷	6
●	COF Rosso Sacrisassi '98	🍷🍷🍷	6
●	COF Merlot '99	🍷🍷	6
●	COF Rosso Sacrisassi '99	🍷🍷	6
○	Implicito '00	🍷🍷	6
●	COF Pinot Nero '00	🍷🍷	6
●	COF Rosso Sacrisassi '00	🍷🍷	6

PREPOTTO (UD)

VALERIO MARINIG

VIA BROLO, 41
33040 PREPOTTO (UD)
TEL. 0432713012
E-MAIL: marinigvalerio@libero.it

The passage from one generation to the next is not always easy. Clashes over production philosophy are almost inevitable. If that is true in all branches of the economy, it is even more evident in winemaking, especially when the shift is from quantity-oriented production to a quality-driven approach. Valerio Marinig is lucky to have had a father, Sergio, who gave him a free hand in the cellar, even though Sergio may have had doubts about the risks associated with the new strategy. However, he was unfailingly supportive, helping with the management of the winery's six hectares and providing a constant supply of experience and good sense. We are impressed at how Valerio, an oenologist, has been able to achieve high quality across the entire range. The small dimensions of the cellar make it difficult to work in, but Valerio obviously knows how to get the best out of what space he has, even managing to find a corner for cask conditioning. Only one of the nine wines tasted just failed to earn One Glass, seven fell into the upper or lower reaches of the One Glass band, and the Tocai Friulano gained a second Glass. For the consumer's information, we should say that Biel Cûr, 1,600 bottles of which were released, is a blend of cabernet sauvignon, schioppettino and refosco.

○	COF Tocai Friulano '02	🍷🍷	3*
●	Biel Cûr Rosso '00	🍷	4
●	COF Merlot '01	🍷	3
○	COF Picolit '01	🍷	6
○	COF Chardonnay '02	🍷	3
○	COF Pinot Bianco '02	🍷	3
○	COF Sauvignon '02	🍷	4
○	COF Verduzzo Friulano '02	🍷	4
●	COF Schioppettino '01		4
○	COF Pinot Bianco '01	ŸŸ	3

PREPOTTO (UD)

PETRUSSA

FRAZ. ALBANA, 49
33040 PREPOTTO (UD)
TEL. 0432713192
E-MAIL: petrussa@petrussa.it

On occasion, results fail to match the winemaker's enthusiasm, but that is not the case with the Petrussas, who have been Guide fixtures for some time. The estate currently has six and a half hectares under vine, with three more rented that are managed directly. Brothers Paolo and Gianni also buy in grapes from a number of small local growers, who provide a viable quantity of fruit to vinify without compromising quality. For many years, the cellar was a triumph of ingenuity over technology but today, it has been completely renovated and can ferment and age in both stainless and oak. The Tocai Friulano took advantage of a good vintage, and Gianni and Paolo's skills, for the fruit is excellent and the vinification impeccable. The wine itself is convincing, well-structured and full-bodied. The panel liked the Bianco Petrussa, a tocai friulano and chardonnay-led blend with a rich, creamy nose of apricots in alcohol, good length and interesting longevity. It should be at its best in a couple of years. Pensiero, from verduzzo friulano, is intense, sweet, beautifully balanced and blessed with a lovely follow through on the palate. The Schioppettino, from Prepotto's leading native grape, is one of the finest versions from the vintage, whereas the merlot, cabernet sauvignon and schioppettino Rosso Petrussa deserves to be cellared for a while. It has marvellous ageing potential.

○	COF Bianco Petrussa '01	🍷🍷	5
●	COF Schioppettino '00	🍷🍷	6
○	COF Tocai Friulano '02	🍷🍷	4*
○	Pensiero '00	🍷🍷	7
●	COF Rosso Petrussa '00	🍷	6
○	COF Pinot Bianco '02	🍷	4
○	COF Sauvignon '02	🍷	4
○	COF Sauvignon S. Elena '01		4
○	Pensiero '99	ŸŸ	7
○	COF Bianco Petrussa '00	ŸŸ	5
●	COF Rosso Petrussa '99	ŸŸ	6

PREPOTTO (UD)

PREPOTTO (UD)

RONCO DEI PINI
VIA RONCHI, 94
33040 PREPOTTO (UD)
TEL. 0432713239
E-MAIL: info@roncodeipini.com

VIGNA PETRUSSA
FRAZ. ALBANA, 47
33040 PREPOTTO (UD)
TEL. 0432713021
E-MAIL: info@vignapetrussa.it

The Novello family, originally from the Veneto, moved to Friuli in 1968, when Vito Novelli purchased a farm from the Rieppi family of Prepotto. The estate included some superbly located hillside vineyards. In 1997, the property was split up and since then, Giuseppe and Claudio Novello have been managing Ronco dei Pini, which has four and a half hectares under vine. The winery also managed a ten-hectare vineyard at Zegla, near Cormons, another excellent wine zone. Ronco dei Pini is a family concern, and the two brothers personally manage the entire production and distribution cycle. In the vineyards, they are assisted by Renato De Noni while Damiano Stramare busies himself in the cellar. Standard-quality production is sold unbottled or under second labels, while the main selections are released as Ronco dei Pini wines. Last year, we complained about a few wobbles in the range, but this time round the overall picture is very positive, beginning with an excellent Verduzzo Friulano Passito 2002. The old gold hue introduces baked apple and honey, then the sweet, elegant palate tempts with a note of caramel and great length. The Pinot Bianco is fresh tasting and stylish, with a lovely follow through on the palate, and the Leucós, from pinot bianco and tocai friulano, flaunts citrus-veined fruit that keeps the oak well in check. A new bottling of the 2001 Cabernet, carried out in July 2003, has been released. It is better than the version we reviewed last year.

Hilde Petrussa Mecchia spent many years in the eastern Veneto. When she left, she returned to her native town, convincing her husband to come with her and start their own estate. Hilde has five scrupulously tended hectares planted to vine and her cellar, too, is spotless, conveying to the visitor an impression of cleanliness that can also be found in the wines. Taking as her starting point the fact that Prepotto is the home of, and finest growing environment for, schioppettino, Hilde persuaded a number of growers to join her in a project to promote the variety. Schioppettino is a red grape that is often vinified to make a sweet wine, and nearly all of the many attempts to produce a serious dry red wine from the variety have met with scant success. Is Hilde tilting at windmills or has she some chance of making her dream come true? Only time will tell. In the meantime, she surprised the panel with a marvellous Tocai Friulano. Its intense nose is followed by a mouthfilling palate and a remarkably fruit-rich finish. Bianco Richenza, which owes its name to a legendary Lombard princess, is a mix of riesling renano, malvasia, verduzzo dorato, tocai friulano and picolit. The grapes are dried in cases and separately fermented. The wine spends 18 months in barrique, acquiring a breadth of aromas that ranges from banana to vanilla and baked apple. In the mouth, it is soft, almost sweet and very long.

○ Verduzzo Friulano Passito '02	♟♟	6
○ COF Pinot Bianco '02	♟♟	4*
○ Leucós Bianco '02	♟♟	5
● Límes Rosso '01	♟	5
○ Collio Chardonnay '02	♟	4
○ COF Tocai Friulano '02	♟	4
○ Collio Pinot Grigio '02	♟	4
● COF Merlot '01		4
○ Collio Sauvignon '02		4
● Límes Rosso '00	♟♟	4*
○ Leucós Bianco '01	♟♟	4*
● COF Cabernet '01	♟	4

○ COF Tocai Friulano '02	♟♟	4*
○ COF Bianco Richenza '01	♟♟	5
● COF Cabernet Franc '01	♟	4
○ COF Picolit '01	♟	6
● COF Refosco P. R. '01	♟	4
○ COF Sauvignon '02	♟	4
○ COF Picolit '00	♟♟	6
○ Richenza '00	♟♟	5

PREPOTTO (UD)

VIGNA TRAVERSO
VIA RONCHI, 73
33040 PREPOTTO (UD)
TEL. 0422804807
E-MAIL: info@molon.it

As soon as they bought their first vineyards in Friuli, Giancarlo Traverso and Ornella Molon set out to achieve dimensions that would make their estate – and substantial investment – productive. Today, they have 45 hectares, 16 planted to wine. Their son, Stefano, supervises the property with enthusiasm. Now, the Friulian vineyards are giving the Traversos considerable satisfaction, thanks to the quality of the wines. Simone Casazza is the oenologist at the Traverso property in the Veneto and also in Friuli, where the experienced Lauro Iacoletig, who has been working on the estate for many years, continues to look after vineyards and cellar. New vines have been planted, and the old vines re-organized and partially replanted, under the direction of Marco Simonit and Pierpaolo Sirch. For the time being, there have been no upheavals in the cellar as the existing equipment enables fruit and wine to be handled with the maximum respect for the natural product. Merlot Sottocastello Rosso is again excellent. It may be a tad over the top but it certainly impresses with its body, fullness, an abundance of fruit and great length. It aged for 14 months in new barrels, half with a capacity of 225 litres and half 112 litres. The Traverso version of Cabernet Franc is impressive for the total absence of the irritating grassy notes that usually characterize this wine in Friuli. Finally, we liked the sugared almond aromas of the Schioppettino and the intense, tangy Tocai Friulano, which is reminiscent of pears.

RONCHI DEI LEGIONARI (GO)

TENUTA DI BLASIG
VIA ROMA, 63
34077 RONCHI DEI LEGIONARI (GO)
TEL. 0481475480
E-MAIL: tenutadiblasig@tiscalinet.it

Tenuta di Blasig is a women's winery. Wine woman Elisabetta Bortolotto Sarcinelli has been running this family cellar since 1990, having taken over from her dynamic mother, Helga. It is destined to pass in the future to her three daughters, Ludovica, Letizia and Antonia, who will carry on the family tradition. They are assisted by oenologist, Erica Orlandino, and the commercial side of things is in the hands of Michele Scamacca. The winery is based in the splendid early 19th-century villa that served as Allied headquarters during the Great War, and was also the base of "Il Vate", writer Gabriele D'Annunzio, when he returned to this area, which he dearly loved. The roughly 60,000 bottles released each year are split into the Classica and Gli Affreschi lines. Fruit to make them comes from the 16 hectares of vineyard, much of it on the border with the Carso district whose nutrient-rich red soil contributes to their quality. Generally, it is the red wines that impress at Tenuta di Blasig, but this year it was the Malvasia that won Two Glasses. A good vintage has given the wine great structure, attractive balsamic herb aromas and a pleasant, fresh-tasting palate. Hot on its heels was the Pinot Grigio Gli Affreschi 2002, which is a little thin on the palate, but has a sea-salt tang and subtle hints of williams pears. We preferred the Cabernet 2002 to the Gli Affreschi Cabernet 2000, albeit not by many marks, but it does have more personality. It is down-to-earth and youthfully alcoholic, whereas its partner is more elegant on nose than palate.

● COF Merlot Sottocastello Rosso '01	♀♀	6
● COF Cabernet Franc '01	♀♀	5
● COF Schioppettino '01	♀♀	5
○ COF Tocai Friulano '02	♀♀	4*
● COF Merlot '01	♀	5
● COF Refosco P. R. '01	♀	5
○ COF Pinot Grigio '02	♀	4
○ COF Ribolla Gialla '02		4
○ COF Sauvignon '02		4
● COF Rosso Sottocastello Ris. '99	♀♀	5
● COF Merlot '00	♀♀	5
● COF Rosso Sottocastello '00	♀♀	6
● COF Cabernet Franc '00	♀♀	4
● COF Schioppettino '00	♀♀	5

○ Friuli Isonzo Malvasia Istriana Gli Affreschi '01	♀♀	4*
● Friuli Isonzo Cabernet Gli Affreschi '00	♀	4
● Rosso Gli Affreschi '00	♀	4
○ Bianco Gli Affreschi '01	♀	4
● Friuli Isonzo Cabernet '02	♀	4
○ Friuli Isonzo Pinot Grigio Gli Affreschi '02	♀	4
● Friuli Isonzo Merlot '02		4
● Friuli Isonzo Merlot Gli Affreschi '00	♀♀	4

RONCHI DEI LEGIONARI (GO)　　SACILE (PN)

DO VILLE
VIA MITRAGLIERI, 2
34077 RONCHI DEI LEGIONARI (GO)
TEL. 0481775561
E-MAIL: info@doville.it

VISTORTA
BRANDINO BRANDOLINI D'ADDA
VIA VISTORTA, 82
33077 SACILE (PN)
TEL. 043471135
E-MAIL: azienda@vistorta.it

The Bonora brothers' winery repeated last year's good showing. Work at the estate is still distributed in the same way, too, for Paolo looks after winemaking and Gianni remains in charge of the vineyards. Their 120,000 bottles each year are split across two lines, the Do Ville for more concentrated wines and Ars Vivendi, for lighter, easier-drinking products. The grapes come from 15 hectares under vine, most on the Friulian flatlands. The name Do Ville was inspired by the discovery nearby of two ancient Roman farms ("villae" in Latin), where wine is believed to have been made many centuries ago. Not for the first time, the Chardonnay Barrique emerged as the most successful wine at our tastings. Confectioner's cream, pears and apples on the nose reveal a complexity and density that is echoed deliciously on the palate. The other wines on the list – and there are fully 15 of them – are hard to describe succinctly. We would point out that releasing so many different wines can easily become a source of confusion for the consumer. However, the potential is certainly there. Focusing on the easy drinkers and a few "riserva" bottles that embody the Do Ville sense of place could give this range a big boost.

The Vistorta estate has always belonged to the Conti Brandolini d'Adda. Founded in 1850, it extends today over about 220 hectares, almost all in Friuli, with just five hectares in the neighbouring Veneto region. The headquarters is in a building in the splendid Vistorta complex, a small rural settlement in the municipality of Sacile that was entirely owned by the noble Venetian family. One "barchessa" wing houses the old barrels, but they are purely decorative in function. The real cellar is at Cordignano, a few kilometres beyond the Veneto border. Brandino graduated in oenology in both the United States and France, the homeland of his consultant winemaker, George Pauli. The oenologist is the affable Alec Ongaro, who has been at Vistorta for almost a decade. There are 35 hectares under vine, and 90 per cent of the 27 hectares planted to red varieties is under merlot. Merlot Vistorta 2000 is a single-grape wine matured in barriques, of which 40 per cent were new, 40 per cent one year old and the remainder two years old. Bottling, without filtration, took place in October 2002. As you taste this wine, you might think you were sampling a young Pomerol, with elegance, balance and outstanding cellarability. We can confirm that impression from tastings of previous vintages. Today, they reveal a complexity that you might never have suspected when they were released.

○ Friuli Isonzo Chardonnay Barrique Do Ville '01	▼▼	4*
● Friuli Isonzo Cabernet Sauvignon Barrique Do Ville '00	▼	4
○ Friuli Isonzo Chardonnay Ars Vivendi '02	▼	4
○ Friuli Isonzo Chardonnay Do Ville '02	▼	3
○ Friuli Isonzo Malvasia Ars Vivendi '02	▼	4
● Friuli Isonzo Merlot Ars Vivendi '02	▼	4
○ Friuli Isonzo Pinot Grigio Ars Vivendi '02	▼	4
○ Friuli Isonzo Pinot Grigio Do Ville '02	▼	3
○ Friuli Isonzo Tocai Friulano Do Ville '02	▼	4
○ Vassilla Bianco	▼	4

● Friuli Grave Merlot Vistorta '00	▼▼	5
● Friuli Grave Merlot Vistorta '95	▼▼	5
● Friuli Grave Merlot Vistorta '97	▼▼	5
● Friuli Grave Merlot Vistorta '98	▼▼	5
● Friuli Grave Merlot Vistorta '99	▼▼	5

SAGRADO (GO)

CASTELVECCHIO
VIA CASTELNUOVO, 2
34078 SAGRADO (GO)
TEL. 048199742
E-MAIL: info@castelvecchio.com

Castelvecchio is the largest estate in the Carso DOC zone. It has 40 hectares under vine, currently being modernized, on the hillside near the old estate residence. The view is simply spectacular, especially at sunset when the chalkstone rocks take on the same colours as the red soil. In recent year, Castelvecchio has devoted much attention to reds, under the watchful eye of manager Gianni Bignucolo. Great wines have been released, thanks in part to the contribution of the Carso plateau's terroir, but 2002 also saw improvements in the whites. A fine example is the fresh-tasting Malvasia, from a variety that has acclimatized marvellously here and which will be an estate workhorse in future. Wisely, the "riserva" wines (Sagrado Rosso '99 and Bianco 2001) were not released. Bignucolo thinks they need more bottle time before they will be ready for the market. The Cabernet Sauvignon 2000 reveals spice and super-ripe fruit. Complex and warm, it is braced by well-gauged acidity that thins the palate only in the finish. Castelvecchio is one of the few wineries in the regions that still produce a top-level Traminer Aromatico. The 2002 edition is dry, well-structured, subtle on the nose and whistle-clean on the palate. All in all, it is a wine that is extremely enjoyable and never cloys. The other reds are also good. The Cabernet Franc is earthy, rather than vegetal, the Refosco dal Peduncolo Rosso is peppery and the alcohol-rich Turmino is a blend of terrano and cabernet franc.

SAN CANZIAN D'ISONZO (GO)

I FEUDI DI ROMANS - LORENZON
LOC. PIERIS
VIA CA' DEL BOSCO, 6
34075 SAN CANZIAN D'ISONZO (GO)
TEL. 048176445
E-MAIL: ifeudi@ifeudi.it

The Lorenzon family has been making and selling farm produce for more than three decades. Their property now has 160 hectares under vine and ten planted to orchards. Recently, owners Enzo and Silvana Lorenzon have been joined in the business by their sons, Davide, who looks after production, and Nicola, in charge of the commercial side. A young but very experienced marketing manager has also come on board in the person of Michela Sfiligoi, an active Friulian wine woman. The new cellar was opened in 1993 and includes an attractive sales outlet for all the estate's products. The cellar turns out a range of fresh, easy-drinking wines, sold in bottle or demijohn, for everyday consumption. The Lorenzons have also reinforced their I Feudi di Romans label for more demanding palates, although value for money is as impressive as ever. Our tastings confirm this. The ten wines presented had a high overall standard and one flagship label that earned Two Glasses. The star is the Pinot Bianco 2002, which has delicacy and length on the nose and nice weight in the mouth. The other wines range from an unabashedly varietal Tocai Sovràn to an attractive fruit-and-alcohol Refosco and the monovarietal, weighty Alfiere Rosso. All are very well-typed, clean on nose and palate, and although they may not be bottles for the cellar, they are certainly drinking deliciously right now.

●	Carso Cabernet Sauvignon '00	🍷🍷	5
○	Carso Traminer Aromatico '02	🍷🍷	4*
●	Carso Cabernet Franc '00	🍷	5
●	Carso Refosco P. R. '00	🍷	5
●	Carso Rosso Turmino '00	🍷	4
○	Carso Malvasia Istriana '02	🍷	4
○	Carso Pinot Grigio '02		4
○	Carso Sauvignon '02		4
●	Carso Cabernet Franc '99	🍷🍷	5
●	Carso Cabernet Sauvignon '99	🍷🍷	5

○	Friuli Isonzo Pinot Bianco '02	🍷🍷	4*
●	Friuli Isonzo Alfiere Rosso '01	🍷	5
●	Friuli Isonzo Cabernet Franc '01	🍷	4
●	Friuli Isonzo Cabernet Sauvignon '01	🍷	4
●	Friuli Isonzo Merlot '01	🍷	4
●	Friuli Isonzo Refosco P. R. '01	🍷	4
○	Friuli Isonzo Pinot Grigio '02		4
○	Friuli Isonzo Sauvignon '02	🍷	4
○	Friuli Isonzo Tocai Friulano Sovràn '02	🍷	4
○	Ribolla Gialla '02	🍷	4

SAN FLORIANO DEL COLLIO (GO)

ASCEVI - LUWA
VIA UCLANZI, 24
34070 SAN FLORIANO DEL COLLIO (GO)
TEL. 0481884140
E-MAIL: p-l@libero.it

For the past three decades, the 30 Ascevi - Luwa hectares in the Collio and Isonzo DOC zones have been managed by Mariano Pintar, recently joined by his children, Luana and Walter. Sauvignon is the cellar's strong suit, to the point that it sometimes "infects" the other labels. Mariano Pintar sets great store by the ripeness of his fruit, yield, low-temperature fermentation, low-temperature skin contact and fermentation times and temperatures to differentiate the two lines. Quite often, however, the differences are not marked, but the Ascevi line is more challenging and Luwa is for easy drinkers. All the whites are steel-fermented and bottle-aged. Yet again, it is the Sauvignons that impress. The Luwa is oily rich and zesty whereas the mint-laced Ronco dei Sassi offers attractive peach and convincing freshness in the mouth, underpinned by firm, close-knit tannins. The Verdana, from sauvignon, chardonnay and ribolla gialla, did well. We have admired it in the past and for some time, it has been putting the accent on sauvignon. The rest of the range is well-made, with a special mention for the Pinot Grappoli. It's a bit of a rough diamond, but it has a great entry on the palate and good body.

SAN FLORIANO DEL COLLIO (GO)

IL CARPINO
LOC. SOVENZA, 14/A
34070 SAN FLORIANO DEL COLLIO (GO)
TEL. 0481884097
E-MAIL: ilcarpino@ilcarpino.com

Il Carpino, in the heart of the Gorizian part of the Collio between Oslavia and San Floriano, is neither large nor old. Its 15-hectare estate was in fact established in 1987. Despite this, it has become a seriously good producer, thanks to the determination of the owners and consultant winemaker, Roberto Cipresso, to ensure the cellar has top-quality fruit. The best grapes are used for the Carpino and Collio selections, which are oak-fermented and aged, and the fruit from the younger grapes goes into the less demanding Vigna Runc line. The Collio line sports a new label this year, an elegant hornbeam ("carpino" in Italian) surmounted by a wavy green line for the whites and a red one for the reds. Best of the wines this year are the sauvignon, chardonnay and ribolla gialla Bianco Carpino, the Chardonnay and the Ribolla. The white blend foregrounds rich notes of white chocolate, sweet tobacco, candied peel and peach tea. The Chardonnay has an impressively confident front palate of banana and dried flower, then a less exciting finish. "Mediterranean" is the word for the Ribolla, which plays off toastiness and orange-dominated fruit to perfection. There are two excellent products in the Vigna Ruc range. The Pinot Grigio reveals penetrating gunflint, yeast and apple aromas and the Merlot has attractive forest fruits on nose and palate.

○ Collio Sauvignon Luwa '02	♀♀	4*
○ Collio Sauvignon Ronco dei Sassi Ascevi '02	♀♀	5
○ Vigna Verdana Ascevi '02	♀♀	5
○ Col Martin Luwa '02	♀	5
○ Collio Pinot Grigio Grappoli Luwa '02	♀	4
○ Collio Sauvignon Ascevi '02	♀	4
○ Friuli Isonzo Tocai Friulano Ascevi '02	♀	3
○ Collio Sauvignon Ascevi '98	♀♀♀	4
○ Collio Pinot Grigio Ascevi '01	♀♀	4

○ Bianco Carpino '01	♀♀	5
○ Collio Chardonnay '01	♀♀	5
○ Collio Ribolla Gialla '01	♀♀	5
● Friuli Isonzo Merlot V. Runc '01	♀♀	4
○ Collio Pinot Grigio V. Runc '02	♀♀	4*
○ Collio Malvasia '01	♀	6
○ Collio Sauvignon '01	♀	5
● Rosso Carpino '01	♀	5
○ Collio Ribolla Gialla V. Runc '02	♀	4
○ Collio Sauvignon V. Runc '02		4
● Rubrum '99	♀♀♀	8
○ Collio Chardonnay '00	♀♀	5
● Rubrum '00	♀♀	8

SAN FLORIANO DEL COLLIO (GO)

SAN FLORIANO DEL COLLIO (GO)

CONTI FORMENTINI
VIA OSLAVIA, 5
34070 SAN FLORIANO DEL COLLIO (GO)
TEL. 0481884131
E-MAIL: m.delpiccolo@giv.it

GRADIS'CIUTTA
LOC. GIASBANA, 10
34070 SAN FLORIANO DEL COLLIO (GO)
TEL. 0481390237
E-MAIL: robigradis@libero.it

The Formentini estate has a history going back almost five centuries. Its significance was underlined a few years ago when it was discovered that a Formentini who married a Hungarian prince took with her to Hungary as part of her dowry some "toccai" vines. The revelation rekindled debate in Friuli over the agreement between the European Union and Hungary concerning the use of the name Tocai. Champions of the right of Friuli to give the name Tocai Friulano to the variety, and the wine it yields, point to this historical precedent. Opponents point out that the word "toccai" simply means "from here" in Slovene. So appeals have been made to the European Court of Justice as the deadline for abandoning the name Tocai Friulano, fixed for 2007, comes inexorably closer. But let's move on from history to the latest news. A few years ago, the Formentini cellar was purchased by the Gruppo Italiano Vini and can now call on the expertise of consultant, Marco Monchiero. Marco Del Piccolo is the estate manager, monitoring the quality of fruit delivered by member growers and its transformation into wine. We particularly liked the Merlot Tajut, with plum tart aromas that are mirrored on the palate, and good weight and body backed up by generous tannins. There have been better versions, though, of the Chardonnay Torre di Tramontana and Collio Bianco Rylint, from chardonnay, pinot grigio and sauvignon, which is named after the 16th-century abbess who encouraged viticulture in the area.

Gradis'ciutta is a new winery, established in 1997 when Robert Princic began to help his father Isidoro. Nevertheless, the family has documents to show that they were making wine at Kozana as long ago as 1780. The 15 hectares under vine are scattered across a number of Collio municipalities and 80 per cent of the harvest is white grapes. All the fruit harvested is brought to the cellar at Giasbana, the nerve centre of the Princic estate. We knew that Robert had everything it takes to make outstanding wines, but we didn't think he would do so quite so quickly. Yet, here he is with a stable of thoroughbreds to add to his collection of Glass-winning products. We'll start with the Pinot Grigio, a subtly elegant wine with aromas of golden delicious apples and a clean, well-rounded mouthfeel. The Ribolla Gialla offers fresh citrus and apple nuanced with wild roses and peach. The panel gave high marks to the Collio Bianco del Tùzz, from late-harvested malvasia, chardonnay and tocai fermented in barrels of various sizes. The rich nose impresses with complex butter, vanilla, tropical fruit, melon and banana, then the entry on the palate is confident and generous with intense fruit. The fresher-tasting pinot grigio, chardonnay, sauvignon and tocai Collio Bianco del Bratinis is also excellent, the Cabernet Franc has lots of youthful fruit and alcohol while the Tocai offers floral aromas.

● Collio Merlot Tajut '01	🍷🍷	6
○ Collio Chardonnay		
Torre di Tramontana '01	🍷	4
○ Collio Bianco Rylint '02	🍷	4
○ Collio Pinot Grigio '02	🍷	5
○ Collio Sauvignon '02	🍷	5
● Pinot Nero Torre di Borea '01		5
○ Collio Chardonnay		
Torre di Tramontana '00	🍷🍷	4*
○ Collio Bianco Rylint '01	🍷🍷	4*

○ Collio Bianco del Tùzz '01	🍷🍷	4
○ Collio Pinot Grigio '02	🍷🍷	4*
○ Collio Ribolla Gialla '02	🍷🍷	4*
○ Collio Bianco del Bratinis '02	🍷🍷	4
○ Collio Chardonnay '02	🍷🍷	4
○ Collio Tocai Friulano '02	🍷🍷	4
● Collio Cabernet Franc '02	🍷🍷	4
● Collio Rosso dei Princic '00	🍷	5
○ Collio Bianco del Bratinis '01	🍷🍷	4
● Collio Cabernet Franc '01	🍷🍷	4

SAN FLORIANO DEL COLLIO (GO)

MARCELLO E MARINO HUMAR
LOC. VALERISCE, 2
34070 SAN FLORIANO DEL COLLIO (GO)
TEL. 0481884094
E-MAIL: humarl@tiscalinet.it

This Collio winery near Gorizia is family run. Brothers Marcello and Marino Humar, and their respective families, look after everything except chemical analyses, performed by an outside laboratory. Since it was founded by Antonio, the brothers' father, the property has grown from the original two mixed hectares of livestock, fruit and vines to a wine estate with 30 hectares under vine. In the 1960s, the Humars began to bottle their own wine and today release 130,000 bottles. The range is broad, and even includes a series of sparkling wines, but the ones that most impressed the panel were the Pinot Bianco and the Picolit. The Pinot Bianco took advantage of a favourable vintage to acquire freshness, subtle notes of golden delicious apples, spring flowers and tangerines, as well as a very long finish. The Picolit gained a second Glass for its intense, attractive orange tart and apricot aromas, as well as gentler nuances of orange blossom. The follow through on the palate is excellent, although the progression is a little unexciting. Another wine that performs better on the nose is the Ribolla Gialla. Acacia blossom, russet apples and almonds are echoed on the palate, which again lacks a little complexity. The Cabernet Franc Rogoves, which we reviewed by mistake last year, shows attractive spice and balsam, the Merlot has pleasing cocoa powder and bramble aromas, the Tocai has roses and citrus and the Chardonnay is agreeably fresh tasting.

SAN FLORIANO DEL COLLIO (GO)

MATIJAZ TERCIC
VIA BUKUJE, 9
34070 SAN FLORIANO DEL COLLIO (GO)
TEL. 0481884193
E-MAIL: tercic@tiscalinet.it

Altitude, and the twin influences of the "bora" gales from the Vipacco valley and breezes from the sea, give San Floriano some of the finest site climates for viticulture in the Gorizia area. To these factors, we could add the clayey marl and sandstone soil of the Collio, which has always offered a superb starting point for local winemakers. San Floriano is also the home of Matijaz Tercic's five-hectare winery, which releases about 22,000 bottles a year and has confirmed its status as one of the most reliable producers on these steep hills. Tercic uses perfectly ripe fruit to make wines that stand out for their breadth and sheer weight on the palate. These are generously rounded wines that are never merely good. The chardonnay-heavy Collio Bianco Planta 2001 has distinct aromas of confectioner's cream, pears and apple from a carefully gauged stay in oak, while the most convincing of the 2002 range is the Pinot Grigio. The aromas range from pear to quince, then the mouthfilling palate is perked up by bright acidity and hints at even better things to come with cellar time. The spicy cinnamon nose of the Merlot 2000 introduces a soft mouthfeel and a satisfying nose-palate consistency.

O Collio Picolit '02	▼▼	6
O Collio Pinot Bianco '02	▼▼	5
● Collio Cabernet Franc Rogoves '00	▼	5
O Collio Chardonnay '02	▼	4
● Collio Merlot '02	▼	4
O Collio Ribolla Gialla '02	▼	4
O Collio Tocai Friulano '02	▼	4
O Friuli Isonzo Traminer Aromatico '02		4
O Collio Pinot Bianco '00	♈♈	4
O Collio Pinot Bianco '01	♈♈	4

O Collio Pinot Grigio '02	▼▼	5
● Collio Merlot '00	▼▼	5
O Collio Bianco Planta '01	▼▼	5
O Collio Chardonnay '02	▼▼	4
O Collio Ribolla Gialla '02	▼	5
O Vino degli Orti '02	▼	5
O Collio Bianco Planta '00	♈♈	4
O Vino degli Orti '01	♈♈	4
● Collio Merlot '99	♈	4

SAN FLORIANO DEL COLLIO (GO)

SAN FLORIANO DEL COLLIO (GO)

FRANCO TERPIN
LOC. VALERISCE, 6/A
34070 SAN FLORIANO DEL COLLIO (GO)
TEL. 0481884215

ZUANI
LOC. GIASBANA, 12
34070 SAN FLORIANO DEL COLLIO (GO)
TEL. 0481391432
E-MAIL: vinizuani@virgilio.it

Franco Terpin's winery is in the San Floriano hills, an unbroken carpet of vines that have influenced both the local landscape and the lives of the people who live there. The Terpin family, in the person of Franco's grandfather, Celestino (known as "Tince"), began to make wine between the First and Second World Wars. Thanks to the hard work of Franco's father, the property now has ten hectares. It was only in 1994 that Franco decided to vinify and bottle on site. Today, the cellar has oenological consultancy from Tuscan Attilio Pagli and vineyard consultancy from Alessandro Zanutta. It has also gained a reputation for the quality of its limited number of wines. They are so good that the 2001 Collio Bianco came very close to Three Glasses for the second time. It's an oak-matured pinot grigio, sauvignon, chardonnay and tocai blend with intense, very complex aromas that range from boiled sweets to melon, vanilla and apricot. The understated front palate gently expands into soft, velvet-smooth flavours that linger delightfully on the finish. The Rosso, from cabernet franc, sauvignon and merlot, is almost as good, The nose shows Peruvian bark, currant jam and black cherries, then the palate presents robust tannins that lend the wine structure and cellarability. The curiously pinkish (from extended skin contact) Pinot Grigio is an interesting wine, with attractive orange and nectarine aromas and toastiness on the palate. Finally, the fruit and vanilla aromas of the Ribolla are distinctly agreeable.

Patrizia Felluga and her son, Antonio, have set out on this new wine adventure with their customary determination. There are seven hectares under vine and output is about 30,000 bottles a year and rising. New plantings and purchases are under way to bring the property to an economically viable size. Last year, the first year of production, promised exceedingly well. The Fellugas were able in a few short months to transform an anonymous vineyard, albeit in an excellent location, and its vinification cellar, into an efficient winery with products that were not just good, but genuinely convincing. Confirmation came this year. The aim, one perhaps imposed by force majeure, is to make territory-driven wines, but the Fellugas' focus on a limited number of products, favouring terroir over variety, is eminently laudable. The mix in the blend may undergo further adjustments, but winemaking is a long, challenging task that demands fine-tuning over time. Careful vineyard management can smooth out some of the rough edges. There are two estate wines, from a slightly unusual blend of tocai, chardonnay, pinot grigio and sauvignon, from various bunch selections, degrees of ripeness and cellar treatment. Vigne, designed for palates that appreciate freshness and fruit, is more approachable and easier to drink. The other version is oak aged, packed with extract and shows decent prospects for the cellar.

○	Collio Bianco '01	🍷🍷	5
●	Collio Rosso '01	🍷🍷	5
○	Collio Ribolla Gialla '01	🍷	5
○	Pinot Grigio Sialis '01	🍷	4
○	Collio Bianco '99	🍷🍷	5
○	Collio Sauvignon '00	🍷🍷	4
○	Collio Bianco '00	🍷🍷	5
●	Collio Rosso '00	🍷	5

○	Collio Bianco Zuani '02	🍷🍷	5
○	Collio Bianco Zuani Vigne '02	🍷🍷	4*
○	Collio Bianco Zuani '01	🍷🍷	5

SAN GIOVANNI AL NATISONE (UD)

ALFIERI CANTARUTTI
VIA RONCHI, 9
33048 SAN GIOVANNI AL NATISONE (UD)
TEL. 0432756317
E-MAIL: alficant@tin.it

It was on the first slopes of the hills at Rosazzo, in a particularly mild location, that Alfieri Cantarutti set up his winery in the late 1970s. Today, it is run by his daughter, Antonella, and her husband, Fabrizio, who manage about 50 hectares under vine. They turn out 110-130,000 bottles a year under 20 or so labels in various ranges. The arrival of the new generation brought with it, naturally enough, a change in the winery's philosophy and the new cellar, now fully functional at last, is the most obvious evidence of this. The product range has also been revamped to combine the demands of the market with Antonella's winemaking outlook. These comments will help us to understand why the Cantarutti cellar has had a stop-and-go history in recent years, and also why the signs of a return to past glories are becoming more tangible. The San Michele line has given rise – and we believe will continue to give rise – to much debate. On the one hand, it is unusual to find such extremes of experimentation in a winery that has always been very traditional, and on the other, the wine itself has a somewhat untidy nose of alcohol and esterified, almost reduced, notes that come together on the palate in a symmetry that is unorthodox, but nonetheless coherent and very individual. Other wines of note are the Pinot Grigio and the Sauvignon. The very attractively priced Canto is under the weather this year and the Tocai, too, fails to convince.

SAN GIOVANNI AL NATISONE (UD)

LIVON
FRAZ. DOLEGNANO
VIA MONTAREZZA, 33
33048 SAN GIOVANNI AL NATISONE (UD)
TEL. 0432757173
E-MAIL: info@livon.it

The Livon group has such vast potential that it can always come up with an outsider when the stable's thoroughbreds are in difficulty. There are three estates in Friuli (but the Livon portfolio extends well beyond the region) that produce three distinct styles. The RoncAlto label includes a superb Collio selection and a limited number of wines for top-of-the-range, terroir-driven bottles that have still to find their feet. The Villa Chiopris line comes from vineyards in the Grave, where they make easy-drinking, attractively priced products (there's a profile in the Other Wineries section). And Livon itself makes three kinds of wine, of which we have chosen the top rank products, bearing the words "Cru" or "Gran Cru" on the label. And there was a Three Glass wine among them this year, somewhat to our surprise, as we had come to view them as eternal bridesmaids at the taste-off wedding. Tiare Blu is a Bordeaux blend with a low proportion of cabernet franc. This has removed the rustic asperity that used to mask the complexity of the fruit sensations, tight-knit structure, pervasive softness of the alcohol and truly convincing concentration. The rest of the range includes the ever-attractive sauvignon, chardonnay, picolit and moscato giallo blend, Braide Alte, and Merlot Tiare Mate. Welcome newcomers are Sauvignon Valbuins and Schioppettino Picotis, perhaps the best interpretation of the variety tasted this year.

○ COF Pinot Grigio		
Ronco San Michele '01	♟♟	5
● COF Merlot		
Ronco San Michele '00	♟	6
○ COF Pinot Grigio '02	♟	4
○ COF Sauvignon '02	♟	4
○ COF Bianco Canto '02		4
○ COF Tocai Friulano '02		4

● Tiare Blu Gran Cru '00	♟♟♟	6
○ Braide Alte Gran Cru '01	♟♟	6
● COF Refosco P. R. Riul Cru '01	♟♟	5
● Collio Cabernet Sauvignon		
RoncAlto '01	♟♟	6
● Collio Merlot Tiare Mate		
Gran Cru '01	♟♟	6
● Schioppettino Picotis Gran Cru '01	♟♟	6
○ Collio Sauvignon Valbuins Cru '02	♟♟	5
○ Collio Pinot Grigio		
Braide Grande Cru '02	♟	5
○ Collio Ribolla Gialla RoncAlto '02	♟	5
○ Braide Alte Gran Cru '96	♟♟♟	6
○ Braide Alte Gran Cru '98	♟♟♟	6
○ Braide Alte Gran Cru '00	♟♟♟	6

Ronco del Gnemiz

via Ronchi, 5
33048 San Giovanni al Natisone (UD)
tel. 0432756238
e-mail: roncodelgnemiz@libero.it

It was 1964 when Enzo Palazzolo acquired this winery, where the Gnemiz family had lived for many years. Today, the tenacious Serena Palazzolo manages the 30 hectares, almost 17 under vine, which have been producing 40,000 interestingly original bottles a year since 1982, the first year of their release. Serena is assisted by oenologist, Roberto Cipresso, and the young but very experienced fruitmakers, Pierpaolo Sirch and Marco Simonit. After last year's wobble, the wines of Ronco del Gnemiz are now back on form, revealing the standards to which we had become accustomed. We'll start with the excellent Rosso del Gnemiz. A Bordeaux blend that stays in barrique for more than two years, it throws a nose of cinchona and cinnamon. After a confident entry, the progression on the palate is laced with liquorice and bramble over robust tannins that provide support without detracting from the elegant style. Bianco Bianco is not a blend. In fact, it's a Malvasia Istriana that we liked for its great balance of toasty oak, fruit salad and intriguing hints of almond and wistaria. The two Sauvignons are equally attractive. The Riserva 2000 is muscular and creamy, whereas the younger version has fresher hints of melon, lime blossom and subtle smokiness. The Pinot Grigio is tangily fresh, with satisfying minerally notes, and the Tocai is elegant.

○	COF Sauvignon Ris. '00	▼▼	6
●	Rosso del Gnemiz '00	▼▼	7
○	Bianco Bianco '01	▼▼	6
○	COF Pinot Grigio '02	▼▼	5
○	COF Sauvignon '02	▼▼	5
○	COF Tocai Friulano '02	▼▼	5
○	COF Chardonnay '00	▼	6
○	COF Bianco '01	▼	4
○	COF Sauvignon Ris. '99	▽▽	6
●	COF Rosso del Gnemiz '99	▽	6

Vignai da Duline

loc. Villanova
via IV Novembre, 136
33048 San Giovanni al Natisone (UD)
tel. 0432758115
e-mail: duline@libero.it

The numbers at Vignai da Duline are modest. The area under vine is less than five hectares, in the hills at Manzano, Corno di Rosazzo and Villanova dello Judrio, and this year's production of wines presented for the Guide tastings, is less than 6,000 bottles. But you just have to chat to the producers and glance around the winery to realize that the cellar is driven by commitment, respect for the countryside, a love of hard work and love of nature. Lorenzo Mucchiutti and Federica Magrini run their property personally and this is translated, thanks in part to their friendship with Alessio Dorigo, into original wines that this year are outstandingly good. Indeed, the red Viburnum went through to the Three Glass taste-offs. A late-harvested blend of mainly merlot with cabernet franc (carmenère), it is an extremely complex wine, both in its bramble and blueberry tart, cherry in alcohol and balsam nose, and for its palate, where a fruit-forward entry opens to reveal cinchona, lingering bramble and a well-structured finish with a firm tannic weave. Two Glasses went to Morus Aurea, a Chardonnay with pistachio, banana and vanilla on nose and palate, and to Morus Nigra, a Refosco that unveils complex hay, bramble tart and petits fours, then a broad palate that echoes the nose and a finish rich in berry fruit sensations. The native-grape Schioppettino is more predictable, with attractive spice but less flesh than we hoped.

●	Viburnum '01	▼▼	4
○	Morus Aurea '01	▼▼	5
●	Morus Nigra '01	▼▼	6
●	Schioppettino '01	▼	4
●	Morus Nigra '00	▽▽	5

SAN LORENZO ISONTINO (GO)

LIS NERIS

VIA GAVINANA, 5
34070 SAN LORENZO ISONTINO (GO)
TEL. 048180105
E-MAIL: lisneris@lisneris.it

Lis Neris has 42 hectares planted to vine and releases almost 450,000 bottles a year. It is also one of the region's most reliable producers. Over the years, Alvaro Pecorari has created his own, well-defined style, based firmly on elegance and attractive drinkability. Joy over another, well-deserved Three Glass award can, however, in no way compensate for the loss of young Francesca, who had begun to assist her father with hospitality at the cellar and also on public occasions in Italy and abroad. The captivating Gris 2001, an oak-conditioned Pinot Grigio, reveals its terroir in a mineral complexity that it combines with sunny Mediterranean fruit. Lis is still the number one wine. A mix of the finest selections of sauvignon, pinot grigio and chardonnay, its soft attack spreads to pervade the mouth with finesse and length. A bit more thrust would have taken Tal Lûc into the top bracket. A dried grape wine from mainly verduzzo, it regales the palate with lavish sensations of figs, chocolate and caramel. The citrus-led Chardonnay Jurosa is always attractive, flowing across the palate with authority. Confini, a blend of traminer aromatico and riesling renano is even more exquisite than usual. An Alsace-style wine, it has substantial residual sugar, nicely offset by its acidic grip. Finally, Lis Neris, a red with generous spice that is mirrored in the mouth, hints at a search for breadth and velvet smoothness.

○	Friuli Isonzo Pinot Grigio Gris '01	🍷🍷🍷	5
○	Lis '01	🍷🍷	6
○	Confini '01	🍷🍷	6
○	Friuli Isonzo Chardonnay Jurosa '01	🍷🍷	5
○	Tal Lûc '01	🍷🍷	8
●	Lis Neris '00	🍷	7
○	Friuli Isonzo Chardonnay '02	🍷	4
○	Friuli Isonzo Pinot Grigio '02	🍷	4
○	Friuli Isonzo Sauvignon Dom Picòl '96	YYY	5
○	Friuli Isonzo Pinot Grigio Gris '98	YYY	5
○	Lis '99	YYY	6
○	Friuli Isonzo Chardonnay Jurosa '00	YYY	5

SAN LORENZO ISONTINO (GO)

PIERPAOLO PECORARI

VIA NICOLO TOMMASEO, 36/C
34070 SAN LORENZO ISONTINO (GO)
TEL. 0481808775
E-MAIL: info@pierpaolopecorari.it

It has been 30 years since Pierpaolo Pecorari took over the family estate and began to grow grapes. In the meantime, he has been joined by his son, Alessandro, who has brought a breeze of enthusiasm and new ideas into the business. With help from expert vineyard manager, Andrea Pittana, the Pecoraris have worked hard on the estate, bringing balance to their 25 hectares and infusing the wines with the minerality and salinity typical of terrain in the upper Isonzo DOC zone. They combine this with a picking schedule that is not overly delayed so that the wines are not too rich or dense, but linear and agile, with good ageing prospects. At the same time, we have noted a growing gap between the reassuringly consistent but lightweight standard-label wines and the heftier selections. In the middle is the Altis range, which means there are now three versions of Pinot Grigio and Sauvignon. In fact, Altis wines still need to find a personality of their own and it fell to the Pinot Grigio Olivers 2001 to take the highest marks. Attractively creamy, velvet-smooth and broad on the palate, it keeps its oak in check, allowing the fresh fruit full rein through to a leisurely finish. The Altis-label Pinot Grigio has an especially inviting nose, and the Merlot Baolar 2000 and Sauvignon Kolàus 2001 are both reliable and complex. The Chardonnay Soris is a more austere, compact wine, with faint tannins and a vein of acidity that hold back an already restrained elegance.

○	Pinot Grigio Olivers '01	🍷🍷	5
●	Merlot Baolar '00	🍷🍷	6
○	Friuli Isonzo Pinot Grigio Altis '01	🍷🍷	5
○	Sauvignon Kolàus '01	🍷🍷	5
○	Chardonnay Soris '01	🍷	5
○	Friuli Isonzo Sauvignon Altis '01	🍷	5
○	Friuli Isonzo Tocai Friulano '02	🍷	4
○	Malvasia '02	🍷	4
○	Friuli Isonzo Chardonnay '02		5
○	Friuli Isonzo Pinot Grigio '02		4
○	Friuli Isonzo Sauvignon '02		4
○	Sauvignon Kolàus '96	YYY	5
●	Refosco P. R. Panta Rei '99	YY	8

SAN MARTINO AL TAGLIAMENTO (PN)

SAN QUIRINO (PN)

TENUTA PINNI
VIA SANT'OSVALDO, 1
33096 SAN MARTINO
AL TAGLIAMENTO (PN)
TEL. 0434899464
E-MAIL: info@tenutapinni.it

RUSSOLO
VIA SAN ROCCO, 58/A
33080 SAN QUIRINO (PN)
TEL. 0434919577
E-MAIL: russolorino@libero.it

Great progress from Tenuta Pinni! This year, it did even better for one wine went forward to the Three Glass taste-offs. Brothers Roberto and Francesco Pinni, who look after winemaking and commercial affairs respectively, are reaping the fruits of the labours they started, with expert oenologist Roberto Fracca, in 1993. The vineyards have been replanted at higher densities and yields are kept low (50-80 quintals per hectare). They have also set up a modern cellar in the "barchessa" wing of the splendid 17th-century villa that is the estate's headquarters. Their 13 hectares under vine produced various wines - the Sauvignon and the Friuli Grave Rosso in particular - that amazed the panel. The Sauvignon comes from very low-yielding vines and offers unusual aromas for the Grave DOC zone. There are peaches, twists of mint and even a hint of noble rot. The very rich palate echoes the nose and signs off with a leisurely finish. The Rosso is a blend of mainly cabernet sauvignon with cabernet franc vinified in barrique. Complex toasty notes of Peruvian bark, milk chocolate, coffee and berry preserve tempt the nose before it explodes onto the palate in a cascade of spices, soft tannins and a bramble-led finish. The Chardonnay is an exciting wine with citrus on the nose and a velvety mouthfeel, while the attractive Pinot Grigio is redolent of golden delicious apples. The Bianco, from chardonnay, sauvignon and pinot grigio, is good but has still to come to terms with the oak. Rounding off the range are two reds, a Refosco with complex herbal aromas and a spicy Cabernet Franc.

Iginio Russolo is the owner of this winery on the Pordenone flatlands. For years, he has been managing vineyard and cellar, and his long experience as an oenologist gives his wines an imprinting that is unique and different from other Grave DOC products. Some time ago, Iginio was joined by his son, Rino, fresh from his own oenological studies. Rino had been helping out with the commercial side of the business, but today he is also active in the cellar. You can be sure that Iginio will be teaching Rino a trick or two, ensuring that the estate's future will be as quality-oriented as its past. For the time being, the Russolos are concentrating on native grapes, replanting two of their 16 hectares to refosco and tocai, while continuing to lavish attention on their workhorses, like Pinot Nero Grifo Nero and Chardonnay I Legni. Year after year, we are astounded at the refined elegance of the Grifo Nero. It is a constant source of amazement how such a difficult variety can give such great results in an area with stony, unfertile soil. This year, it reveals balsam and berry fruit preserve that return on the palate, accompanied by soft, silky tannins. The Chardonnay I Legni is just as good, its delightful nose offering white chocolate, mint, banana and ripe peach. The Müller Thurgau Mussignaz is unusual. Despite the fact that the variety is hardly typical for the Grave, this version is a splendid success. Another Russolo wine to watch is the exciting newcomer, the white Jacot, with its tempting banana and boiled sweet nose.

● Friuli Grave Rosso '00	♓♓	5
○ Friuli Grave Chardonnay '02	♓♓	3*
○ Friuli Grave Sauvignon '02	♓♓	3*
● Friuli Grave Cabernet Franc '01	♓	4
● Friuli Grave Refosco P. R. '01	♓	4
○ Friuli Grave Bianco '02	♓	4
○ Friuli Grave Pinot Grigio '02	♓	3
● Friuli Grave Cabernet Franc '00	♓♓	3

● Pinot Nero Grifo Nero '00	♓♓	5
○ Chardonnay I Legni '01	♓♓	4*
○ Müller Thurgau Mussignaz '02	♓♓	4
● Borgo di Peuma '00	♓	5
● Cabernet I Legni '00	♓	4
● Merlot I Legni '00	♓	4
● Refosco P. R. I Legni '00	♓	4
○ Doi Raps '01	♓	4
○ Malvasia Istriana '02	♓	4
○ Pinot Grigio Ronco Calaj '02	♓	4
○ Bianco Jacot Ronco Calaj '02	♓	4
○ Chardonnay Ronco Calaj '02		4
○ Chardonnay I Legni '00	♓♓	4
● Pinot Nero Grifo Nero '99	♓	5

SPILIMBERGO (PN)

SPILIMBERGO (PN)

FANTINEL
FRAZ. TAURIANO
VIA TESIS, 8
33090 SPILIMBERGO (PN)
TEL. 0427591511
E-MAIL: fantinel@fantinel.com

PLOZNER
FRAZ. BARBEANO
VIA DELLE PRESE, 19
33097 SPILIMBERGO (PN)
TEL. 04272902
E-MAIL: plozner@plozner.it

Mario Fantinel founded this estate in 1969 after a long and successful career in catering. It's a winery of big numbers and a comprehensive range. The 250 hectares under vine are in the Friuli Grave, Collio and Colli Orientali del Friuli DOC zones, which produce fruit for various lines. Vigneti Sant'Helena is the top-flight label, with whites from the Collio and reds from the Grave. It is flanked by Principi, reserved by Fantinel for "vini da meditazione" sipping wines sourced from Collio grapes, Vigneti Santa Caterina, again from Collio fruit, with eye-catching, aesthetically appealing labels, and Borgo Tesis, for wines from the gravelly Grave soil. There is also the Rapsodia range of sparkling wines and Paron Mario which, with Vigneti Fantinel, embodies the cellar's tradition. Finally, Fantinel releases the Collio Bianco Trilogy, a wine that looks to the future. It is, in fact, a project in collaboration with the University of Udine and sets out to highlight the special potential of various vineyard environments. It is not always easy to find your way around this extensive list, and the wines sometimes fail to live up to their makers' expectations. Nevertheless, a number of wines continue to stand out for their precision and personality. Again this year, we liked the Collio Bianco Trilogy from tocai, sauvignon and pinot bianco, the Sant'Helena Refosco and Cabernet Sauvignon, the Borgo Tesis Merlot and, in a year that was less than kind to whites in general, the Pinot Grigio and Sauvignon, again from the Vigneti Sant'Helena range.

It could be the growing success of the wines, or it could be the arrival of Sabina and Marco, owner Valeria Plozner's two children, but there is a distinct air of enthusiasm at Barbeano and it is taking the form of a major investment programme. The replanting of the vineyards at higher densities, restructuring of the cellar, the construction of new vinification and bottling areas, the restyling of bottles and labels, and the search for a trim, modern image are the first steps along this new path. And the wines? Francesco Visentin, the still young but long-serving oenologist, surprised us with a very special Pinot Bianco. The Plozners released 30,000 bottles of this elegant wine that is redolent of acacia blossom and apple, lifted by tropical fruit. The fragrant aromas on the palate are backed up by moderate structure, freshness and excellent thrust, which takes you through to an utterly varietal Pinot Bianco finish. The Tocai is also impressive, its peach and fresh almond aromas introducing a bright palate whose almond echoes the nose, signing off with a citrus finish. Although it was for years the top-scoring Plozner wine, the Sauvignon this time failed to pick up a second Glass. It is very good overall, but lacks concentration in the mouth. We would also point out the typicity of the Pinot Nero, the consistency of the Chardonnay Riserva '98 and the Sauvignon 2001, which are emblematic of the reliability of the Plozner range.

●	Friuli Grave Cabernet Sauvignon		
	Sant'Helena '01	♀	4
●	Friuli Grave Merlot Borgo Tesis '01	♀	4
●	Friuli Grave Refosco P. R.		
	Sant'Helena '01	♀	4
○	Collio Bianco Trilogy '02	♀	5
○	Collio Pinot Grigio Sant'Helena '02	♀	4
○	Collio Sauvignon Sant'Helena '02	♀	4
●	Friuli Grave Merlot Borgo Tesis '00	♀♀	4
○	Collio Bianco Trilogy '01	♀♀	5
●	Barone Rosso Platinum '00	♀	6

○	Friuli Grave Pinot Bianco '02	♀♀	3*
○	Friuli Grave Tocai Friulano '02	♀♀	3*
●	Friuli Grave Pinot Nero '00	♀	3
○	Friuli Grave Chardonnay '02	♀	3
○	Friuli Grave Sauvignon '02	♀	4
●	Friuli Grave Refosco P. R. '01		3
○	Friuli Grave		
	Traminer Aromatico '02		3
○	Friuli Grave Sauvignon '01	♀♀	3
○	Friuli Grave Chardonnay Ris. '98	♀♀	4
●	Friuli Grave Pinot Nero Ris. '99	♀	4

TERZO D'AQUILEIA (UD)

TORREANO (UD)

BROJLI - FRANCO CLEMENTIN
VIA G. GALILEI, 5
33050 TERZO D'AQUILEIA (UD)
TEL. 043132642
E-MAIL: fattoriaclementin@libero.it

JACÙSS
FRAZ. MONTINA
V.LE KENNEDY, 35/A
33040 TORREANO (UD)
TEL. 0432715147
E-MAIL: jacuss@jacuss.com

It was a good, if not great, vintage for Franco Clementin's small winery. The summer rains may have created the problems, as the winery opted for natural techniques to defend the crop. Nor should we forget that this is a certified organic estate. Whatever the case, Franco was able to handle the situation with great skill. Despite the winery's modest dimensions, Clementin has installed a hospitality area. In the large Circolo di Campagna Wigwam room, with its open hearth, adjoining the cellar, visitors can enjoy wines, cold meats and grappas made on site. All this, in addition to Franco's sheer likeability, makes a visit worthwhile. But back to the wines. Best by far was the Verduzzo Friulano del Piccolo Campo, which shows noble rot, lime honey, candied orange peel and dried almonds, followed by firm progression on the palate to a finish that never threatens to cloy. The Traminer has an enthralling bouquet. Intense wild rose, moss and citrus fruits tempt the senses. There is a nice follow through on the palate, although it lacks the power of the nose. The Riesling has the variety's trademark benzene, grapefruit and pear, which return on the palate. The uncomplicated finish offers juicy grapefruit. The two Refoscos are well-typed (we preferred the Campo della Stafula), as is the Pinot Bianco.

Where are brothers Sandro and Andrea Iacuzzi going? They are committed and enthusiastic behind their mask of discretion and shyness, and are almost apologetic when they discuss their "little winery" of ten hectares in the Torreano valley, explaining how hard it is to work there, and the problems they face in the cellar. On the wine front, they presented our tasters with an excellent Refosco and a superb Sauvignon, after last year's magnificent Picolit. The panel was equally impressed to note the quality of the other half a dozen Iacuzzi wines. We knew the brothers were interested in native varieties, but this Refosco is a labour of love. Very warm, powerful, concentrated and rich in aromas of milky coffee, prunes and plain chocolate, it bursts onto the palate yet maintains perfect balance over its substantial tannic weave. The lingering finish signs off with cinchona and plums. The intensely aromatic Sauvignon has rich notes of elderflower and peach before the understated front palate expands to tempt with sensations of fruit salad and peach tea. The two sweet wines are also remarkable. The Picolit offers Mediterranean notes of candied orange peel, caramel-covered figs and petits fours, whereas the baked apple Verduzzo is very varietal. Lindi Uà, a red from cabernet sauvignon, merlot and refosco, is let down by slightly edgy tannins, but we liked the floral theme of the Pinot Bianco, the typicity of the Tocai and the rustic energy of the Tazzelenghe.

O	Verduzzo del Piccolo Campo '02	YY	4
O	Friuli Aquileia Riesling '01	Y	3
●	Refosco Campo della Stafula '01	Y	4
O	Friuli Aquileia Traminer Aromatico '02	Y	3
O	Friuli Aquileia Pinot Bianco '02		3
●	Friuli Aquileia Refosco '02		3
●	Friuli Aquileia Refosco Campo della Stafula '00	YY	4

●	COF Refosco P. R. '00	YY	4*
O	COF Sauvignon '02	YY	4*
O	COF Picolit '00	YY	8
O	COF Verduzzo Friulano '01	YY	4
●	Tazzelenghe '00	Y	4
O	COF Pinot Bianco '02	Y	4
O	COF Tocai Friulano '02	Y	3
●	COF Rosso Lindi Uà '99	Y	4
●	COF Schioppettino '01		4
O	COF Picolit '99	YY	7
●	COF Rosso Lindi Uà '98	Y	4
●	COF Refosco P. R. '99	Y	4

TORREANO (UD)

VALCHIARÒ
LOC. CASALI LAURINI, 3
33040 TORREANO (UD)
TEL. 0432712393
E-MAIL: info@valchiaro.it

Lots of people turn a hobby into a full-time job. Five friends, Emilio, Giampaolo, Lauro, Armando and Galliano, all from the same small town and all with another job, decided a decade or so ago to put together the modest vineyards that gave them wine for domestic consumption. That was how Valchiarò was founded. Over the years, the original ten hectares have grown, as the group bought or rented other plots, and the area under vine is now 15 hectares. The aim of the five friends is to expand to 20 hectares, so as to reach a commercially viable number of bottles, much higher than the total of 50,000 they release now. Overall, the range this year is a very good one. Last year, we incorrectly described the Verduzzo 2000, inadvertently passing it off as the 2001 version. We didn't actually taste the newer wine, which only went into bottle last January. From grapes picked when super-ripe and subsequently dried, the 2001 Verduzzo unveils herbal tea and caramel, which are echoed on the sweet, lingering palate. The Tocai Friulano successfully combines freshness with structure in an elegant whole. The Rosso El Clap ("clap" means "stone", in Friulian) is from merlot, cabernet franc and refosco and reflects the rather cool climate of the Chiarò river valley.

TORREANO (UD)

VOLPE PASINI
FRAZ. TOGLIANO
VIA CIVIDALE, 16
33040 TORREANO (UD)
TEL. 0432715151
E-MAIL: wines@volpepasini.net

It is always a source of amazement that Emilio Rotolo, the strong-willed, autocratic owner of Volpe Pasini, manages to create a smoothly functioning team of individuals who are often as dynamic as he is. We are talking about Riccardo Cotarella, who has shown his skills as a red winemaker in Friuli, but who is also one of the few non-Friulians to produce tip-top whites. We are also talking about Pierpaolo Sirch and Marco Simonit, fruitmakers who work with several of the finest estates in the region and a number of wineries in the south of Italy. The cellar is the responsibility of Alessandro Torresin and the vineyard team is led by Tarcisio Specogna, who has seen 28 vintages at Volpe Pasini. Francesco Rotolo, Emilio's young son, has started his oenology course at the professional school in San Michele all'Adige and is acquiring experience at the winery, when his studies allow it. Emilio is almost always accompanied by Rosa Tomaselli, who looks after public relations. There 34 hectares under vine, which will be supplemented next year by a new property that has just been purchased. The Refosco Zuc di Volpe is one of the finest examples of the variety, rich in fruit, spices and body, and with perfectly gauged tannins. The wood-aged Pinot Grigio Ipso has tropical fruit over milky notes on the nose, then the palate shows astonishing fruit-forward complexity. Focus shows Cotarella's hand in the way the merlot is treated. Red berry fruit and liquorice lead into a palate that offers soft tannins.

O COF Verduzzo Friulano '01	ΨΨ	4*
O COF Tocai Friulano '02	ΨΨ	4*
● COF Rosso El Clap '01	Ψ	4
● COF Refosco P. R. '01	Ψ	4
O COF Sauvignon '02	Ψ	4
O COF Pinot Grigio '02		4
O COF Picolit '00	ΨΨ	7
O COF Verduzzo Friulano '00	ΨΨ	4

● COF Refosco P. R. Zuc di Volpe '01	ΨΨΨ	5
● COF Merlot Focus Zuc di Volpe '01	ΨΨ	6
O COF Pinot Grigio Ipso Zuc di Volpe '01	ΨΨ	5
● COF Cabernet Zuc di Volpe '01	ΨΨ	5
● COF Merlot Togliano '01	ΨΨ	4*
O COF Pinot Bianco Zuc di Volpe '02	ΨΨ	5
O COF Pinot Grigio Zuc di Volpe '02	ΨΨ	4
O COF Ribolla Gialla Zuc di Volpe '02	ΨΨ	4*
O COF Sauvignon Zuc di Volpe '02	ΨΨ	5
O COF Tocai Friulano Zuc di Volpe '02	ΨΨ	4
O COF Chardonnay Zuc di Volpe '01	Ψ	5
O COF Pinot Bianco Zuc di Volpe '99	ΨΨΨ	4
● COF Merlot Focus Zuc di Volpe '99	ΨΨΨ	5
O COF Pinot Bianco Zuc di Volpe '01	ΨΨΨ	4

TRIVIGNANO UDINESE (UD)

FOFFANI
FRAZ. CLAUIANO
P.ZZA GIULIA, 13/14
33050 TRIVIGNANO UDINESE (UD)
TEL. 0432999584
E-MAIL: foffani@foffani.it

After spending much of his working life as a manager in finance, Giovanni Foffani has spent the past ten years personally supervising the production and distribution of wines at his cellar. His wife, Elisabetta Missoni, is a member of the "Donne del Vino" ("wine women") association and looks after hospitality while sons, Guglielmo and Lorenzo, who have recently joined the winery, take care of the technical side and sales, respectively. Of course, it helps to live and work in their magnificent 16th-century villa at Clauiano, now a heritage-listed historic building, where there is documentary proof of winemaking from as early as 1789. Every year, the Foffanis release about 100,000 bottles and this year's range, all of which scored at least One Glass, confirmed the estate's success. Top of the heap is the Merlot, of which 5,000 bottles were made and which ferments for 12 months in large barrels. Its intense purplish hue ushers in complex aromas, including cinchona, pepper, cocoa powder and bramble tart. There is fruit-led softness on the palate, which echoes the nose nicely. The Refosco has a distinctive nose of almost aggressive gamey notes, hay and ripe plum. The Cabernet Sauvignon offers attractive toastiness, backed up by good tannins. Traditionally, the Foffani Sauvignon has been a good wine. This year, the progression on the palate is pleasing, but the nose fails to excite.

VILLA VICENTINA (UD)

VALPANERA
VIA TRIESTE, 5/A
33059 VILLA VICENTINA (UD)
TEL. 0431970395
E-MAIL: valpanera@tin.it

Giampiero Dal Vecchio owns this 52-hectare estate on the flatlands near Aquileia and it is easy to see that he is in love with Refosco. A quick glance through the winery brochure confirms this. The history of the variety is traced from biblical times to Pliny the Elder and Louis Pasteur. There is even a quotation from a novel by Giacomo Casanova. "A good woman … gave us a Refosco that I found exquisite ". They certainly know how to make Refosco here, thanks to enthusiasm, an expert wine technician like Luca Marcolini, yields per plant of less than one and a half kilograms, planting densities of up to 6,500 vines per hectare and late harvesting. The Superiore and Riserva versions are very special. The Superiore stays in barrique for eight months, acquiring bramble jam, cake and sweet spice aromas and a mouthfilling palate. The Riserva has longer maceration and ages for 18 months in barrique. The impenetrable colour is followed by breadth of structure and firm tannins. The delicious finish sets notes of hay against bramble. Another outstanding wine is Rosso Alma, which adds cabernet sauvignon and merlot to the ubiquitous refosco. But the news this year is that Valpanera is also making white wines. The chardonnay, sauvignon and tocai Bianco is a fine wine, with melon, banana and wild rose aromas, then the Chardonnay Carato, which ferments in oak and acacia barrels, offers citrus and tropical fruit on both the nose and the rich, fleshy palate.

● Friuli Aquileia Merlot '01	🍷🍷	4
● Friuli Aquileia Cabernet Sauvignon '00	🍷	4
● Friuli Aquileia Refosco P. R. '01	🍷	4
○ Friuli Aquileia Chardonnay Sup. '02	🍷	3
○ Friuli Aquileia Pinot Grigio Sup. '02	🍷	3
○ Friuli Aquileia Sauvignon Sup. '02	🍷	4
○ Friuli Aquileia Tocai Friulano Sup. '02	🍷	3
○ Friuli Aquileia Sauvignon Sup. '01	🍷🍷	3
● Friuli Aquileia Cabernet Sauvignon '99	🍷	4

● Friuli Aquileia Refosco P. R. Ris. '00	🍷🍷	6
● Friuli Aquileia Refosco P. R. Sup. '01	🍷🍷	5
● Friuli Aquileia Rosso Alma '00	🍷	6
● Friuli Aquileia Refosco P. R. '01	🍷	4
○ Bianco di Valpanera '02	🍷	4
○ Friuli Aquileia Chardonnay Carato '02	🍷	4
● Rosso di Valpanera '01		4
● Friuli Aquileia Refosco P. R. Sup. '00	🍷🍷	3
● Friuli Aquileia Refosco P. R. Ris. '99	🍷🍷	4
● Friuli Aquileia Rosso Alma '99	🍷	4

OTHER WINERIES

FLAVIO PONTONI
VIA PERUZZI, 8
33042 BUTTRIO (UD)
TEL. 0432674352
E-MAIL: flavio@pontoni.it

Flavio Pontoni is an experienced grower-producer from Buttrio. In 2002, he had to bring the harvest of much of his crop forward because of the danger of mould. But he still managed to produce an intense, fragrant Tocai, a full-flavoured, mouthfilling Refosco and an admirable Verduzzo Friulano.

○	COF Tocai Friulano '02	♀	3
○	COF Verduzzo Friulano '02	♀	4
●	Friuli Grave Refosco P.R. '02	♀	3

VALLE
VIA NAZIONALE, 3
33042 BUTTRIO (UD)
TEL. 0432674289
E-MAIL: info@valle.it

Wine expert Gigi Valle and his children, Paolo, Marco and Ilaria, need one more push to get into the big league. Their youthfully alcoholic blended Roldi red and the chocolate and plum Merlot Riserva both attracted the panel's attention.

●	COF Rosso Roldi '01	♀	5
○	COF Sauvignon Sel. Araldica '02	♀	4
●	COF Merlot Gigi Valle Ris. '97	♀	4

VILLA CHIOPRIS
LOC. VISCONE
33048 CHIOPRIS VISCONE (UD)
TEL. 0432757173
E-MAIL: info@livon.it

Villa Chiopris is a Livon-owned winery in the Grave. This is where the group's most competitive wines are made for distribution worldwide. This year, the vintage was not easy, particularly for whites, but the Sauvignon is fragrant and tangy. The Tocai Friulano 2002 is pleasant, if unexciting.

○	Friuli Grave Sauvignon '02	♀♀	3*
○	Friuli Grave Tocai Friulano '02	♀	3*

GIOVANNI CROSATO
VIA CASTELMONTE, 1
33040 CIVIDALE DEL FRIULI (UD)
TEL. 0432701462 - 0432730292
E-MAIL: info@vinicrosato.it

Giovanni Crosato and his wife Lucia Galasso jointly release well-made products from their separate wineries. Both turned out two very good wines. We know how competent this couple are and we look forward to further improvements.

●	Il Rosso Don.Giovanni Lucia Galasso '00	♀	4
○	Chardonnay '02	♀	4
○	Fumé Bianco '02	♀	4
●	Refosco P.R. Lucia Galasso '02	♀	4

TENUTA DI ANGORIS
LOC. ANGORIS, 7
34071 CORMONS (GO)
TEL. 048160923
E-MAIL: info@angoris.it

The long-established Tenuta di Angoris is being re-organized. Experts have taken charge of vineyard and cellar management. The range covers three DOC zones and the best bottles this year were the Collio Tocai and COF Refosco.

●	COF Refosco P. R.		
	Vôs da Vigne '01	♟	4
○	COF Ribolla Gialla Vôs da Vigne '02	♟	4
○	Collio Pinot Grigio Vôs da Vigne '02	♟	4
○	Collio Tocai Friulano Vôs da Vigne '02	♟	4

GRADIMIRO GRADNIK EREDI
LOC. PLESSIVA, 5/BIS
34071 CORMONS (GO)
TEL. 048161395 - 048160737
E-MAIL: gradnik@gradnik.it

Neda Gradnik's wines may not be monsters, but they are reliable. We liked the fresh, fragrant Pinot Bianco, which is as good as ever, the peach aromas of the Tocai, and the fast-improving Collio Rosso 2000. The 12-hectare estate releases 40,000 bottles a year.

●	Collio Rosso '00	♟	5
○	Collio Pinot Bianco '02	♟	4
○	Collio Pinot Grigio '02	♟	4
○	Collio Tocai Friulano '02	♟	4

THOMAS KITZMÜLLER
FRAZ. BRAZZANO - VIA XXIV MAGGIO, 56
34070 CORMONS (GO)
TEL. 048160853
E-MAIL: kitzmuller@tin.it

Last year, Thomas Kitzmüller obtained 11,000 bottles from his three and a half hectares in the Collio and Isonzo DOCs. Small is not always beautiful, but this modest cellar makes lovely wines. The varietal, full-bodied Sauvignon is very good, but so are the Tocai Friulano and Ribolla Gialla.

○	Collio Sauvignon '02	♟♟	3*
○	Collio Ribolla Gialla '02	♟	3
○	Collio Tocai Friulano '02	♟	3

ALFREDO BRACCO
FRAZ. BRAZZANO - VIA XXIV MAGGIO, 28
34070 CORMONS (GO)
TEL. 048160002
E-MAIL: bracchus@libero.it

A new entry for this family winery that grows fruit on six hectares on the Isonzo flatlands, between Brazzano and the river Judrio. Best of the range are a fruit-forward banana and grapefruit Sauvignon with good progression, and a rounded Refosco 2000 with good structure and soft tannins.

○	Isonzo del Friuli Sauvignon '02	♟♟	4
●	Isonzo del Friuli		
	Refosco dal P. R. '00	♟	4

RENATO KEBER
LOC. ZEGLA, 15
34071 CORMONS (GO)
TEL. 048161196 - 0481639844

We are expecting great things from this winery, which has replanted much of its vine stock. For now, there is an excellent Tocai Friulano. This rich, elegant wine is joined by a good blend, Beli Grici, based on pinot bianco, chardonnay and ribolla, which is fresh-tasting and beautifully balanced.

○	Collio Tocai Friulano '01	♟♟	4*
○	Collio Bianco Beli Grici '01	♟	5
○	Collio Pinot Grigio '01		4

SIMON DI BRAZZAN
FRAZ. BRAZZANO
VIA SAN ROCCO, 17
34070 CORMONS (GO)
TEL. 048161182

Young Daniele Drius' cellar is one of Isonzo's most promising newcomers DOC. The Tocai 2002 has a long, refreshing palate, with a very varietal finish of almonds. The Malvasia, also a 2002 vintage, has a milk and flower nose, with freshly ground pepper. We also liked the Merlot and the Sauvignon.

●	Friuli Isonzo Merlot '01	♟	4
○	Friuli Isonzo Malvasia '02	♟	4
○	Friuli Isonzo Sauvignon '02	♟	4
○	Friuli Isonzo Tocai Friulano '02	♟	4

Francesco Vosca
fraz. Brazzano - via Sottomonte, 19
34070 Cormons (GO)
tel. 048162135

The grapes from this small family winery in the superb wine zone of Brazzano go into the small number of reliably good bottles released by Francesco Vosca. The best wines this year are the harmonious Pinot Grigio and the citrus, peach and spring flower Malvasia.

○ Collio Pinot Grigio '02	🍷🍷	4*
● Collio Merlot '01	🍷	4
○ Friuli Isonzo Sauvignon '02	🍷	4
○ Collio Malvasia '02	🍷	4

Alberice
via Bosco Romagno, 4
33040 Corno di Rosazzo (UD)
tel. 0432759460

The Alberice cellar is close to the nature reserve of Bosco Romagno, in the hills at Corno di Rosazzo. It made good progress this year, thanks to an excellent citrus and apple Pinot Grigio and a Chardonnay redolent of bananas and confectioner's cream.

○ COF Chardonnay '02	🍷🍷	4*
○ COF Pinot Grigio '02	🍷🍷	4*
● COF Cabernet Sauvignon '02	🍷	4
○ COF Tocai Friulano '02	🍷	4

Ca di Bon
via Casali Gallo, 1
33040 Corno di Rosazzo (UD)
tel. 0432759316
e-mail: cadibon55@tin.it

There were highs and lows in the wide range of labels presented by Gianni and Ameris Bon. It's a small step in the wrong direction, although we did enjoy the excellent Ribolla Gialla, a good Pinot Grigio and a nice Pinot Bianco, as well as a traditional-style Schioppettino.

○ COF Ribolla Gialla '02	🍷🍷	4*
○ COF Pinot Bianco '02	🍷	4
○ COF Pinot Grigio '02	🍷	4
● COF Schioppettino '02	🍷	4

Le Due Torri
loc. Visinale del Judrio
33040 Corno di Rosazzo (UD)
tel. 0432759150
e-mail: info@le2torri.com

Antonino Volpe's wines varied in quality this time. That's why the cellar has been relegated to the Other Wineries. Fully 15 labels are released for a total of 20,000 bottles. Still, value for money is fantastic in the wines mentioned below.

○ Friuli Grave Tocai Friulano '02	🍷🍷	2*
○ Torri Bianche '02	🍷🍷	3*
○ Friuli Grave Pinot Grigio '02	🍷	2
○ Ribolla Gialla '02	🍷	3

Skerk
loc. Prepotto, 20
34011 Duino Aurisina (TS)
tel. 040200156
e-mail: info@skerk.com

There were good wines again this year from Boris and Sandj Skerk. The spice and spring flower Malvasia would have gained a second Glass with a tad more structure. Not far behind were the Sauvignon and the delicate Vitovska. Less exciting was the red Terrano, which is thinned by exuberant acidity.

○ Carso Malvasia '01	🍷	4
○ Carso Sauvignon '01	🍷	4
● Carso Terrano '01	🍷	5
○ Carso Vitovska '01	🍷	4

Blason
via Roma, 32
34072 Gradisca d'Isonzo (GO)
tel. 048192414
e-mail: v.vecchi@tin.it

Giovanni Blason has brought steady improvement to his family winery, devoting more and more attention to the vineyards. Now, he has 13 hectares in the Isonzo DOC zone. The two best products are the upfront, fruit-led Pinot Grigio and a full-bodied, seamless Cabernet Sauvignon.

● Friuli Isonzo Cabernet Sauvignon Linea Comugna '01	🍷🍷	4
○ Friuli Isonzo Pinot Grigio '02	🍷🍷	3

San Simone
LOC. RONDOVER - VIA PRATA, 30
33080 PORCIA (PN)
TEL. 0434578633
E-MAIL: info@sansimone.it

The Brisotto family has been making wine for four generations on the flatlands of Pordenone. The range is interesting, and at times genuinely exciting. Particularly good are the warm, broad Cabernet Sauvignon Nexus and the varietal Cabernet Franc Sugano.

●	Friuli Grave		
	Cabernet Sauvignon Nexus '01	♀♀	4*
●	Friuli Grave Cabernet Franc		
	Sugano '02	♀	4
○	Friuli Grave Tocai Friulano '02	♀	3

Vigna Angeli
VIA BROLO, 37
33040 PREPOTTO (UD)
TEL. 0432713077
E-MAIL: maurizio.marinig@tin.it

Maurizio and Edi Marinig have 12 hectares. They release 60,000 bottles under the Maurizio Marinig label, and a further 25,000 from hillslopes as Vigna Angeli. Turo, 90 per cent schioppettino and ten pinot nero, is a soft, deep wine. The Cabernet Franc is excellent and the Ribolla Gialla good.

●	COF Rosso Turo '00	♀♀	4*
●	COF Cabernet Franc '02	♀♀	4*
○	COF Ribolla Gialla '02	♀	4
○	COF Tocai Friulano '02	♀	4

Vini Bidoli
VIA FORNACE, 19
33030 RIVE D'ARCANO (UD)
TEL. 0432986118
E-MAIL: bidolivini@bidolivini.com

Another newcomer this year is the estate founded in 1924 by Alessandro Bidoli. His grandchildren Arrigo and Margherita now run the cellar, Arrigo looking after winemaking and Margherita in charge of sales. The two Briccolo reds are especially convincing. The Merlot is milky and the Cabernet fruity.

●	Friuli Grave Cabernet Briccolo '01	♀♀	3*
●	Friuli Grave Merlot Briccolo '01	♀♀	3*
○	Friuli Grave Chardonnay '02	♀	3
○	Friuli Grave Sauvignon '02	♀	3

Muzic
LOC. BIVIO, 4
34070 SAN FLORIANO DEL COLLIO (GO)
TEL. 0481884201
E-MAIL: muzic.az.agr@libero.it

It wasn't a good year for Muzic. Restructuring work in the old cellar, dating from the 16th century, probably upset the routine. The best wine is the Tocai Friulano, whose palate is much more satisfying than the nose might suggest. The rest of the range is decent.

○	Collio Chardonnay '02	♀	4
○	Collio Ribolla Gialla '02	♀	4
○	Collio Sauvignon '02	♀	4
○	Collio Tocai Friulano '02	♀	4

Forchir
FRAZ. PROVESANO - VIA CIASUTIS, 1/B
33095 SAN GIORGIO DELLA RICHINVELDA (PN)
TEL. 042796037
E-MAIL: forchir@forchir.it

We admire the consistency of Forchir wines, almost all worth One Glass, despite big production numbers. We look to oenologist, Gianfranco Bianchini, for a big hitter in the next few years. For now, we like the Traminer and the Bianco Martin Pescatore, a pinot bianco, riesling and traminer mix.

○	Friuli Grave Bianco		
	Martin Pescatore '01	♀	4
●	Friuli Grave Refosco P.R. Refoscone '01	♀	4
○	Friuli Grave Traminer Aromatico '02	♀	3

Alessandra Vidon
FRAZ. DOLEGNANO - VIA DELL'ABBAZIA, 11
33048 SAN GIOVANNI AL NATISONE (UD)
TEL. 0432757470
E-MAIL: lalozeta@tin.it

Alessandra Vidon has taken over and hired valid consultants. Now, she offers some excellent labels. The five-hectare estate releases 20,000 bottles a year, including Pian delle Poiane, a blend of five varieties. But the best wine is a fruity, varietal Sauvignon with body and balance in the mouth.

○	COF Sauvignon '02	♀♀	4*
○	COF Bianco Pian delle Poiane '02	♀	4
○	COF Tocai Friulano '02	♀	4

EMILIA ROMAGNA

Five wines from Emilia Romagna earned Three Glasses in this new edition of Italian Wines. Year after year, the number of bottles that gain our top award increases, a sure sign of the overall improvement in quality of the region's winemaking. We think the result is especially significant because it was achieved largely by the main native variety grown in the territory, sangiovese. Last year, we hailed the first Three Glass award for the Sangiovese di Romagna DOC zone. This year, that result has been consolidated. Two excellent wines from the zone scored top marks, the Sangiovese di Romagna Avi Riserva 2000 from San Patrignano and the Sangiovese di Romagna Terra di Covignano Riserva 2001 from San Valentino. These wineries are in fact located near each other, in the hills just behind Rimini. They were joined by the Ronco dei Ciliegi 2000 from the Castelluccio di Modigliana cellar, a monovarietal sangiovese with great typicity. Another regional Three Glass winner – for the fifth year in succession – was Marzieno 2001 from Fattoria Zerbina. It may be a blend of sangiovese with small proportions of cabernet sauvignon and merlot, but there can be no disputing its typicity as a wine from Romagna. We hope this encouraging trend will continue in future, although next time, our tastings will have to take account of a poor 2002 vintage that has had a varying impact on different parts of the region. We probably won't be finding many truly outstanding wines. In addition to sangiovese, other native varieties, some of them almost unknown elsewhere in Italy, put on good performances this year. Take sauvignon rosso, for example, which is also identified as alicante, and has long been widely planted around Forlì and Faenza. Leone Conti, La Berta and above all Poderi Morini presented us with thoroughly convincing interpretations of this variety. Or consider malbo gentile – there was a good dried-grape version from the Istituto Persolino and an excellent Sette Pievi from the small Vigne dei Boschi winery – or also Longanesi, another local variety. There is an upsurge in the production of Gutturnio, a grape from the Colli Piacentini. Fine wines from Oppizzi, Cardinali, Castelli del Duca, Il Poggiarello, Torre Fornello and other estates bear witness to the commitment of many growers in the area to promoting this vine type. A similar situation prevails around Bologna for Pignoletto, so we can see definite potential for improvement in the wines from this variety. The Colli Bolognesi also produced some excellent interpretations of Bordeaux varieties, especially merlot. The well-deserved Three Glasses earned by Maurizio Vallona's wine on its first outing are flanked by splendid wines from Santarosa, Tenuta Bonzara and Cinti. There were also good selections of Cabernet Sauvignon from Isola and, again, Vallona, Cinti and Santarosa.

BERTINORO (FC)

BERTINORO (FC)

CELLI
VIA CARDUCCI, 5
47032 BERTINORO (FC)
TEL. 0543445183
E-MAIL: celli@celli-vini.com

FATTORIA PARADISO
VIA PALMEGGIANA, 285
47032 BERTINORO (FC)
TEL. 0543445044
E-MAIL:
fattoriaparadiso@fattoriaparadiso.com

The enthusiastic and very friendly owners of the Celli cellar this year turned out a range that confirms the recent improvements we have noted. They have been achieved for both international varieties and for grapes native to Romagna and Bertinoro. We'll start with the Bron & Rusèval Chardonnay 2002, which has a brief stay in barrique and emerges with breadth and fruit-led intensity. The aromas are subtle and the clean palate has length, warmth and harmony, the fruit being lifted by hints of citrus. The varietal, herbaceous Bron & Rusèval red is from sangiovese and cabernet sauvignon. In the mouth, the close-knit, complex structure is backed up by loads of extract and tasty berry fruit, chocolate and liquorice. The muscular finish is only slightly modulated by a hint of bitterness. Powerful alcohol and luscious softness are the distinguishing features of the Albana Passito Solara 2001, which offers intense peach jam and toasted almonds. It's a little predictable in the mouth and over-generous with notes of sweetness. The Sangiovese Riserva Le Grillaie 2000 is traditional, well-typed wine with violet and cherry aromas giving way to balsam, mint and liquorice. Full-bodied and ripe in the mouth, it is pleasant enough, although a tad more freshness would help. Freshness in spades is the keynote of the Sangiovese Le Grillaie 2002, its uncomplicated, attractively fruity partner.

The Pezzi family's tireless determination has made Fattoria Paradiso a benchmark for Romagna's winemakers. The vines enjoy superb locations on the hills around Bertinoro, the cellar has up-to-the-minute equipment and recently the winery decided to hire the consultancy services of leading Tuscan winemaker, Roberto Cipresso. Yet again, Mito 2000 is the cellar's most exciting release. Production runs to 15,000 units of this cabernet sauvignon and merlot blend, which ages unhurriedly in small oak casks. The depth and elegance of the nose embrace soft ripe fruit with spice and vegetal notes, over intriguing toastiness. But the wine comes into its own on the palate. The soft pervasive mouthfeel on entry reveals creamy fruit, silky tannins and the warmth of good alcohol. This swathe of sensations lingers impressively, leaving echoes of a heady sweetness on the taste buds. The Albana Passito Gradisca 2001 again showed just what a classy wine it is. Subtle botrytis, honey and apricot mingle on the palate with good acidity, lending balance to the sweetness and signing off with an elegant persistence. The sweet, alcohol-rich Frutto Proibito, the other Albana Passito, is more traditional in style. Barbarossa 1999 unsheathes impressive structure and rich fruit nicely offset by tight-knit tannins. Drinkability and upfront attractiveness are the keynotes of the well-made Vigna del Molino, Sangiovese 2002. But the Vigna delle Lepri Riserva 2001 from the Castello di Ugarte selection is a little unbending and insistently acidic.

● Sangiovese di Romagna Sup. Le Grillaie Ris. '00	𝅭𝅭	3*
○ Albana di Romagna Passito Solara '01	𝅭𝅭	5
● Bron & Rusèval Sangiovese-Cabernet '01	𝅭𝅭	4
○ Bron & Rusèval Chardonnay '02	𝅭𝅭	4*
○ Albana di Romagna Secco I Croppi '02	𝅭	2
● Sangiovese di Romagna Sup. Le Grillaie '02	𝅭	2
○ Albana di Romagna Passito Solara '00	𝅭𝅭	4
● Bron & Rusèval Sangiovese-Cabernet '00	𝅭𝅭	4
● Sangiovese di Romagna Sup. Le Grillaie Ris. '99	𝅭	3

● Mito '00	𝅭𝅭	7
○ Albana di Romagna Passito Gradisca '01	𝅭𝅭	6
● Sangiovese di Romagna Sup. Vigna del Molino '02	𝅭𝅭	3*
● Barbarossa Il Dosso '99	𝅭𝅭	5
○ Albana di Romagna Passito Frutto Proibito '01	𝅭	6
● Sangiovese di Romagna Sup. Vigna delle Lepri Ris. '01	𝅭	5
○ Jacopo Chardonnay '02	𝅭	4
● Mito '98	𝅭𝅭	5
● Mito '99	𝅭𝅭	5

International Movement
Slow Food®

Exercise your right to the pleasure of food, wine and conviviality
Protect biodiversity
Spread the word about food quality
Educate your taste
Promote clean, sustainable agriculture

Slow Food Presidia
A Foundation promoted by Slow Food funds projects to save and re-launch traditional foods, vegetables and animal species in danger of extinction. To date, Slow Food has developed more than 200 Presidia – 160 in Italy, 50 in the rest of the world – all designed to revitalize local economies and offer prospects for sustainable development.

Slow Food Award
A prize assigned by an international jury to those who protect and promote biodiversity all round the world.

Major Events
The 'Salone del Gusto' in Turin; 'Cheese' in Bra, 'Slow Fish', 'Aux Origines du Goût' in Montpellier, France, and thousands of tastings, meetings and Taste Workshops in Italy and abroad.

University of Pollenzo and Colorno
An international center of training, research and documentation for people in the food and farming worlds.

Slow Food Editore
Publishers of Slow Food's official journal, *Slow: the international herald of taste and culture*, which is mailed to members all over the world, as well as a series of guides, manuals, tourist itineraries and essays on all aspects of food culture and gastronomy.

JOIN !!!

www.slowfood.com

Slow Food – via della Mendicità Istruita, 14 – 12042 Bra (Cuneo) Italy
Tel. +39 0172 419611 – fax +39 0172 414498

SAVOR THE UNIVERSITY WITH TASTE

THE UNIVERSITY OF GASTRONOMIC SCIENCES COMBINES FOOD, TRAVEL, CULTURE AND SCIENCE.

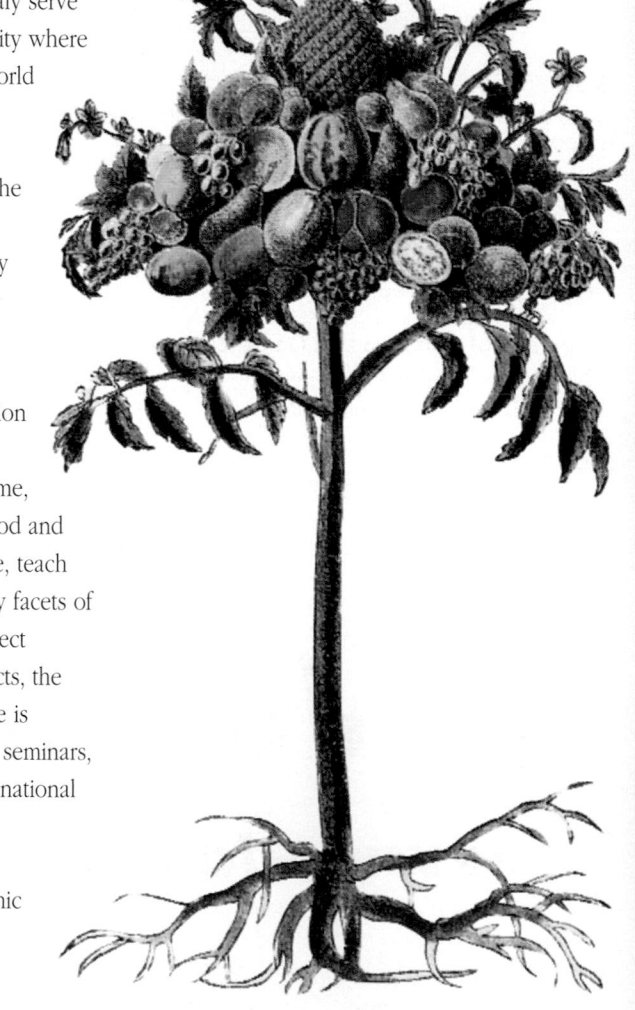

Two historic campuses in Italy serve as the base for the University where 60 students from around the world will participate in an international academic project created by Slow Food. Italy is the starting point for an exploration of the food of many cultures and regions.

A three-year training degree and 2 two-year specialization degrees will create a new professional figure. A gastronome, well versed in the culture of food and communication, able to critique, teach and manage in any of the many facets of food production. Offering a direct contact with flavors and products, the science of gastronomic pleasure is translated into tastings, classes, seminars, specialization courses and international conventions.

The University of Gastronomic Sciences is Food, Culture and Knowledge.

For information, to apply or to contact us: **www.unisg.it**
Address: Piazza Vittorio Emanuele, 9 - 12060 Bra (Cuneo) Pollenzo - Italy
Tel. +39 0172 458 511 - Fax +39 0172 458 500 - E-mail: info@unisg.it

BERTINORO (FC)

GIOVANNA MADONIA
VIA DE' CAPPUCCINI, 130
47032 BERTINORO (FC)
TEL. 0543444361 - 0543445085
E-MAIL: giovanna.madonia@libero.it

Giovanna Madonia started making wine some years ago as a hobby. Since then, she has acquired a skill and professionalism that enable her to release seriously good wines vintage after vintage. This is partly thanks to the contribution of oenologist, Attilio Pagli, and the careful use Giovanna makes of her spare but effective cellar equipment. The panel particularly admired Sterpigno 2000, a single-variety merlot aged slowly in barrique. The nose is a succession of intriguing notes, ripe berry fruit being followed by vanilla, walnut and liquorice. The velvet-soft, creamy palate satisfies from the start, signing off without asperity in a long, elegant finish. Sweet ripeness and spice prevail on the nose of the Sangiovese Riserva Ombroso 2000, to be echoed on the palate, where sweet fleshy fruit is in no hurry to disappear. It's a well-balanced wine with lovely finesse. In contrast, Fermavento 2001 is a powerful, well-structured yet measured Sangiovese which combines vanilla and delicious pulpy flesh with strong berry fruit. The Albana Passito Remoto 2000 was a little under the weather. Its nose brings together curious hints of peach and origanum, then the warm palate reveals lingering alcohol.

BOLOGNA

TERRAGENS FINE WINES
VOLO ROSSO
VIA DEL TIPOGRAFO, 2
40138 BOLOGNA
TEL. 051531803
E-MAIL: info@terragens.com

The Terragens project was launched in 1998 by the Caviro group, makers of the well-known Tavernello box wine. The aim was to create a range of premium-quality wines, committing group members to quality and concentrating exclusively on sangiovese. There then began the long, slow process of mapping the best vineyards in the area between Forlì and Faenza, and subsequently converting them to quality-driven production. Early vinifications, supervised in the cellar by the oenologist and manager, Giordano Zinzani, with consultant Attilio Pagli, yielded very good results. But we should remember that the project has only just begun. There is plenty of room for improvement in the near future. The most interesting product is the IGT Romio, of which 20,000 bottles were released. It is obtained from carefully selected sangiovese grapes and matured in new French oak barriques. The 2001, in particular, shows intense, meaty ripe red berry aromas with jam and spice. The palate has depth, body, austerity and attractive tannins, as well as long length. Large and small wood was used to age the Sangiovese Riserva '99, which has good balance and structure. The even better 2000 edition has a hard, slightly dry finish. The "second-string" Sangiovese Superiore 2001 is a winner. Fully 250,000 bottles were released of this very attractively priced wine. Fresh, clean violets and ripe fruit greet the nose, then the rich palate has balance and softness, braced by vigorous acidity and soft, close-knit tannins.

● Sterpigno Merlot '00	🍷🍷	6
● Sangiovese di Romagna Sup.		
Ombroso Ris. '00	🍷🍷	6
○ Albana di Romagna Passito		
Remoto '00	🍷	5
● Sangiovese di Romagna Sup.		
Fermavento '01	🍷	4
● Sterpigno Merlot '98	🍷🍷	5
● Sangiovese di Romagna Sup.		
Ombroso Ris. '98	🍷🍷	5
○ Albana di Romagna Passito		
Remoto '99	🍷🍷	5
● Sangiovese di Romagna Sup.		
Ombroso Ris. '99	🍷🍷	5

● Romio '00	🍷🍷	4*
● Romio '01	🍷🍷	4*
● Sangiovese di Romagna Sup.		
Romio '01	🍷🍷	2*
● Sangiovese di Romagna Sup.		
Romio Ris. '00	🍷	3
● Sangiovese di Romagna Sup.		
Romio Ris. '99	🍷	3

BOMPORTO (MO)

BORGONOVO VAL TIDONE (PC)

FRANCESCO BELLEI
VIA PER MODENA, 80
41030 BOMPORTO (MO)
TEL. 059818002
E-MAIL: belleifrancesco@libero.it

CASTELLI DEL DUCA
VIA MORETTA, 58
29010 BORGONOVO VAL TIDONE (PC)
TEL. 0522942135
E-MAIL: castelli@medici.it

Giorgio Battilani and Christian Bellei have taken over this winery after the death of Francesco Bellei, who some time ago decided to concentrate on the production of "metodo classico" sparklers. Christian is even more firmly opposed than his father was to the use of pressure tanks for refermentation, and adopted the traditional method to vinify the lambrusco grapes from the vineyards around the cellar at Bomporto. This is no longer a Lambrusco di Sorbara, it's the Extra Cuvée Brut Rosso. Fresh cherries on the nose are followed by a moderately full, fragrant palate, with restrained tannins in the finale. The other sparkling wines are made with chardonnay and pinot nero grapes from hillside vineyards on limestone soil. The site climates are particularly well suited to fruit intended for bottle fermentation and the Cuvée Speciale Brut 1997 is the best of the range. The bubbles are small and the creamy bead lingers. The intense, elegant notes of the rich bouquet tell you the wine is perfectly mature. Finesse and depth in the mouth take you through to a full, and satisfyingly persistent, finish. The Rosé, which aged on the lees for more than three years, is well made and eminently drinkable. The antique rose hue is as subtle as the continuous, lingering perlage, then the nose is complex and evolved, chestnut honey mingling with faint notes of caramel, before an equally complex palate shows depth and personality. Two Glasses also went to the more predictable Extra Cuvée Brut. Flowers on the nose and a fresh palate make this a very moreish sparkler indeed.

After its first releases last year, Castelli del Duca is back with new vintages. The project brings together the skills and resources of the Ermete Medici winery from Reggio Emilia and the Consorzio Terre dei Farnese, which embraces a group of estates in the Colli Piacentini (Cantina Valtidone is a leading light). One of the flagship wines, Gutturnio Riserva Sigillum, was not available for tasting as it needs more bottle age, but the range is a good one nonetheless, and boasts some excellent products. This goes to show just how seriously consultant oenologist, Carlo Corino, is taking his responsibilities in vineyard and cellar. The Malvasia Passito Soleste 2001 is very well crafted, finding a stupendous balance of heady sweetness and acidity that never lets the palate cloy. Intense apricot jam bewitches the nose, returning to linger on the palate, where rich texture and delicious softness tempt the taste buds. Both the light, varietal spice-led Bonarda 2001 and the Gutturnio Classico 2000 are good, the latter showing sumptuous ripe berry fruit aromas and a full, soft palate with nice breadth and close-knit, but fat, tannins. It's an uncomplicatedly delicious wine to drink. The Gutturnio Superiore 2000 is a shade too ripe on the nose and dry in the mouth, while the Sauvignon shows good citrus and decent length on the palate.

⊙	Bellei Extra Cuvée Rosé		
	Brut '96	🍷🍷	7
○	Bellei Cuvée Speciale Brut '97	🍷🍷	6
○	Bellei Extra Cuvée Brut	🍷🍷	4*
●	Extra Cuvée Brut Rosso '01	🍷	5

○	C. P. Malvasia Passito Soleste '01	🍷🍷	5
●	C. P. Gutturnio Cl.		
	Duca Augusto '00	🍷🍷	3*
●	C. P. Bonarda Duca Ottavio '01	🍷🍷	3*
●	C. P. Gutturnio Sup.		
	Duca Alessandro '00	🍷	4
○	C. P. Sauvignon		
	Duchessa Vittoria '02	🍷	3
●	C. P. Gutturnio Sigillum Ris. '99	🍷🍷	5

BRISIGHELLA (RA)

CASALECCHIO DI RENO (BO)

LA BERTA
VIA PIDEURA, 48
48013 BRISIGHELLA (RA)
TEL. 054684998
E-MAIL: be.gio@libero.it

TIZZANO
VIA MARESCALCHI, 13
40033 CASALECCHIO DI RENO (BO)
TEL. 051571208 - 051577665
E-MAIL: visconti@tizzano.191.it

Costantino Giovannini has one of the loveliest wineries in the Faenza hills. Slowly and without fuss, he has tenaciously overcome all kinds of obstacles to make his dream come true, and to be able to release premium wines. He was surprised, at first, when we were optimistic about his prospects, but now he believes in his potential. Costantino always listens carefully to what his brilliant oenologist, Stefano Chioccioli, has to say. The top of the list this year is the Sangiovese Riserva Olmatello 2001, of which 25,000 bottles were released. It has outstanding balance and great concentration. Intense berry fruit is picked up on the full, well-rounded palate, where smooth, close-knit tannins carry you through to a long, soft finish that is slightly dried by the oak. Solano 2002 is a Sangiovese with inviting purplish tinges and massive structure, underpinned by soft yet tight-knit tannins. Sweet, ripe alicante fruit went into the Almante. A riot of local and tropical fruit is let down only by the exuberance of the tannins, which tends to dry out the finish. Ca' di Berta 2001, from cabernet sauvignon and sangiovese, is scheduled for release later on. The barrel sample we tasted was very promising, and we look forward to retasting next time. Infavato, from partially dried malvasia grapes, reveals marked typicity and a palate that is only moderately intense. There is a faintly bitterish twist on the back palate.

Tizzano, owned by Luca Visconti di Modrone, is one of the leading wineries in the Colli Bolognesi. It has 35 hectares under vine, much of it recently replanted or being renovated, in accordance with a well-conceived development programme promoted by manager, Gabriele Forni. The vinification cellar is impressively equipped and the technicians are highly competent. Everything is in place for top-quality production, and we have the impression that Tizzano's potential has not yet come through in the wines. Of course, masterpieces were hard to come by in a difficult vintage like 2002, so we are suspending judgement for the time being. One of the cellar's most representative wines is the Pignoletto Brut, a cuve close sparkler with fresh, fruity aromas and immediate appeal on the palate. Pignoletto Frizzante has a more rustic style, its ripe apple on the nose introducing a full, evolved palate, with a hint of citrus in the finish. The third version of Pignoletto, the Superiore, has not entirely fresh floral notes and a faint suggestion of nail varnish. The dry, subtle palate has a very nice hint of acidity in the finish. The Cabernet Sauvignon 2001 performed very well. The intense, bottled fruit-led nose is followed by body and depth on the palate, and a finish with distinct varietal notes. The Riserva '99 shows ripe fruit and alcohol, which are mirrored unhurriedly on the palate.

●	Sangiovese di Romagna Olmatello Ris. '01	♟♟	5
●	Almante '02	♟♟	5
●	Sangiovese di Romagna Sup. Solano '02	♟♟	4*
○	Infavato Vino da Uve Stramature '01	♟	5
○	Pieve Alta Chardonnay '02	♟	3
●	Sangiovese di Romagna Olmatello Ris. '99	♟♟	5
●	Colli di Faenza Rosso Ca' di Berta '00	♟♟	5
●	Sangiovese di Romagna Olmatello Ris. '00	♟♟	5
●	Sangiovese di Romagna Sup. Solano '01	♟♟	4

●	C. B. Cabernet Sauvignon '01	♟♟	4*
○	C. B. Pignoletto Frizzante '02	♟	3
●	C. B. Cabernet Sauvignon Ris. '99	♟	5
○	C. B. Pignoletto Brut	♟	3
○	C. B. Pignoletto Sup. '02		3
○	C. B. Sauvignon '02		3
●	C. B. Cabernet Sauvignon '00	♟♟	4

CASTEL BOLOGNESE (RA)

CASTEL SAN PIETRO TERME (BO)

STEFANO FERRUCCI
VIA CASOLANA, 3045/2
48014 CASTEL BOLOGNESE (RA)
TEL. 0546651068
E-MAIL: info@stefanoferrucci.it

UMBERTO CESARI
LOC. CASTEL SAN PIETRO
VIA STANZANO, 1120
40050 CASTEL SAN PIETRO TERME (BO)
TEL. 051941896 - 051940234
E-MAIL: info@umbertocesari.it

Domus Caia is the perfect embodiment of the restless enthusiasm and desire to experiment that drive Stefano Ferrucci. The sangiovese fruit is harvested at full ripeness, and placed in wooden boxes to raisin naturally. A few weeks later, it is crushed and slowly macerated. There follows a period of 12 months or more when the wine matures in small oak casks of mixed origin before it ages unhurriedly in bottle before release onto the market. Domus Caia 2000, of which 12,000 units were bottled, has great complexity and outstanding personality. Very intense, fleshy red berry fruit, liquorice and pencil lead usher in an austere, granite-solid palate backed up by alcohol and lingering, close-knit tannins that add silkiness to the finish. The white Stefano Ferrucci comes from malvasia dried on the vine and harvested in mid January, to take advantage of the concentrating effect of cold weather and noble rot. This technique is the usual method for making ice wine, but it is not normally adopted in Romagna, where it nonetheless seems to produce good results. The wine is oily-rich and fat, moderately sweet and very attractive, malvasia's intense varietal aromas leading to a pleasantly dry finish. The sweet, candied peel Albana Passito Domus Aurea is less imposing and the Albana Dolce Lilaria reveals restrained sweetness and full ripe apple. Finally, Sangiovese Centurione has clean fruit aromas and decent structure, particularly if we bear in mind how difficult the vintage was.

Umberto Cesari has a solid, reliable winery that combines big numbers – production runs to almost 2,000,000 bottles a year – with premium-quality vinification. Best of Umberto's wines are two marvellous reds, Liano 2000 and the special Selezione di Sangiovese Tauleto. The cellar bottled almost 50,000 units of Liano, a very successful 70-30 blend of sangiovese and cabernet sauvignon aged in barrique. Layers of ripe fruit and elegant spice insistently tempt the nose, then the stylish, well-balanced palate offers solid structure, a soft, close-knit tannic weave and a lingeringly attractive, irresistibly smooth finish. Tauleto Selezione 1999 (4,000 bottles released) has a firmer, more solid mouthfeel after staying in barrique for 12 months longer than the standard product. A very intense colour is the prelude to dominant aromas of evolved berry fruit jam. A no-nonsense entry on the palate unveils close-knit, austere, yet very smooth tannins and a long, seamless finish. The Sangiovese Riserva 2000 is convincing and well made. In fact, this wine has produced admirably consistent results. Intense fruit, laced with attractive balsam, introduces a full, soft palate with good structure. The performances of both the Sangiovese Ca' Grande and its standard-label partner were significant, for they are solidly well made, despite the poor vintage. The Laurento Chardonnay is dried by the wood, and a tad bitter in the finish, while the Albana Passito Colle del Re 1998 has plenty of body, robust alcohol and moderate sweetness.

● Sangiovese di Romagna Domus Caia Ris. '00	♟♟	6
○ Stefano Ferrucci Vino da Uve Stramature	♟♟	6
○ Albana di Romagna Passito Domus Aurea '01	♟	6
○ Albana di Romagna Dolce Lilaria '02	♟	4
● Sangiovese di Romagna Sup. Centurione '02	♟	4
● Sangiovese di Romagna Auriga '02		3
● Sangiovese di Romagna Domus Caia Ris. '98	♟♟	6
● Sangiovese di Romagna Domus Caia Ris. '99	♟♟	6

● Liano '00	♟♟	5
● Tauleto Sel. Umberto Cesari '99	♟♟	7
● Sangiovese di Romagna Ris. '00	♟♟	4*
○ Laurento Chardonnay '01	♟	4
● Colli d'Imola Cabernet Sauvignon Ca' Grande '02	♟	4
● Sangiovese di Romagna '02	♟	3
● Sangiovese di Romagna Ca' Grande '02	♟	3
○ Albana di Romagna Passito Colle del Re '98	♟	6
○ Albana di Romagna Secco Colle del Re '02		4
○ Malise Pignoletto-Chardonnay '02		4
● Liano '99	♟♟	5
● Tauleto Sangiovese '99	♟♟	5

CASTELL'ARQUATO (PC)

CASTELLO DI SERRAVALLE (BO)

CARDINALI
LOC. MONTEPASCOLO
29014 CASTELL'ARQUATO (PC)
TEL. 0523803502
E-MAIL: info@cardinalidoc.it

VALLONA
FRAZ. FAGNANO
VIA SANT'ANDREA, 203
40050 CASTELLO DI SERRAVALLE (BO)
TEL. 0516703058 - 0516703333

The Cardinali family winery extends over about ten hectares, all planted to vine, on the hills overlooking the mediaeval hamlet of Castell'Arquato. The Guyot-trained vines are planted at 4,000 vines per hectare on calcareous-clay soil. A southeast-facing vineyard provides the grapes for the Gutturnio Riserva Torquato 2000, a successful blend of barbera and bonarda aged in small oak casks. It sailed past the Two Glass cut-off point, asserting itself as one of the finest Gutturnios we tasted this year. Impenetrable and purple-tinged, it shows very ripe red berry fruit laced with subtle spice, mirrored to perfection on the palate, where the balance is outstanding. The steel-vinified Gutturnio Classico Nicchio also foregrounds fruit on the nose, and offers very nice balance on the palate, as well as great nose-palate consistency. Two Glasses was the score awarded to the Cabernet Sauvignon Ronchello '99. Dense in hue, with raspberry and currant aromas accompanied by varietal notes, it unveils a very well-defined palate that flaunts smooth tannins and great length. The Monterosso Solata, from sauvignon, malvasia and ortrugo grapes part vinified in barrique, is interesting. The fruit and mineral aromas introduce good weight in the mouth, where tangy acidity is well in evidence. The Dolce Montepascolo 2001 is obtained from late-harvested, 30-year-old vines of moscato giallo. A slightly rustic nose is followed by a fluent palate that plays off balance and aroma against freshness.

The secret of Maurizio Vallone's success is really no secret at all. You just have to tot up the days he spends out in the vineyards of his 23-hectare estate, cosseting every plant, and then look at his track record as a cellar manager. New plots of merlot vines have come onstream, enabling Maurizio to make his first single-variety wine and the results are outstanding. Merlot Afederico 2001 walked off with Three Glasses for the sheer breadth and austerity of its wonderfully elegant style. Entry on the nose is well defined, showing merlot's varietal pencil lead, spices and herbs rather than fruit sweetness. Soft and densely pulpy in the mouth, it signs off with an severe, ultra-classy finish that lingers forever. The Cabernet Selezione 2001 has explosive ripe fruit, nuanced with pepper and liquorice. The palate has great structure, good balance and a lingering, velvet-smooth finish. This is a wine that has improved steadily over the years, and has not always been adequately appraised by critics. The various versions of Pignoletto are all intriguing. Permartina is the outcome of an experiment with Alsace-style late harvesting. The wine is hardly typical but wins favour for its opulence and tangy palate, not to mention the rich, mineral-nuanced aromas. The standard Pignoletto doesn't seem to have suffered from the poor vintage. In fact, we cannot remember a better version. The Vivace version is fresh tasting and fruity. Passito Altreuve 2000, from pignoletto, albana and sauvignon, has intense apricot and a hint of noble rot, then a dry, subtly sweet palate.

● C. P. Gutturnio Cl. Torquato Ris. '00	🍷🍷	5
● C. P. Cabernet Sauvignon Ronchello '99	🍷🍷	4*
○ Dolce Montepascolo '01	🍷	5
● C. P. Gutturnio Cl. Nicchio '02	🍷	4
○ C. P. Monterosso Val D'Arda Solata '02	🍷	3
● C. P. Gutturnio Cl. Torquato Ris. '99	🍷🍷	5

● Afederico Merlot '01	🍷🍷🍷	5
● Cabernet Sauvignon Sel. '01	🍷🍷	5
○ Altreuve Passito '00	🍷🍷	5
● C. B. Cabernet Sauvignon '01	🍷🍷	4*
○ Permartina '01	🍷🍷	4
○ C. B. Chardonnay '02	🍷🍷	3*
○ C. B. Pignoletto '02	🍷🍷	3*
○ Pignoletto Vivace '02	🍷	3
● C. B. Cabernet Sauvignon Sel. '97	🍷🍷🍷	5
● C. B. Cabernet Sauvignon Sel. '99	🍷🍷🍷	5
● C. B. Cabernet Sauvignon Sel. '00	🍷🍷	5

CASTELVETRO DI MODENA (MO)

CIVITELLA DI ROMAGNA (FC)

CORTE MANZINI
LOC. CÀ DI SOLA
VIA MODENA 131/3
41014 CASTELVETRO DI MODENA (MO)
TEL. 059702658
E-MAIL: cortemanzini@cortemanzini.it

PODERI DAL NESPOLI
LOC. NESPOLI
VILLA ROSSI, 50
47012 CIVITELLA DI ROMAGNA (FC)
TEL. 0543989637
E-MAIL: info@poderidalnespoli.com

In the last Guide, we wagered that the good results obtained by Corte Manzini were no coincidence. We were convinced they derive from the serious approach and winemaking skills that the family devote to their task. We were right. In fact, the new range is even better, despite the challenges of the 2002 vintage. Evidently, Stefano gets better with each passing year. This 30-something agriculture graduate and cellar manager produces, from only ten hectares under vine, an extensive range – from different varieties or selections – of wines that share a common style. All have clean aromas and a very bright, fresh flavour. L'Acino is one of the most exciting Grasparossas in the region. Its intensity and fragrance on the nose are complemented by fullness on the palate, and a perfect balance of soft fruit and tannins. Irresistible pervasiveness in the mouth and intense peach, wild strawberry and blueberry aromas are the hallmarks of the Grasparossa Amabile. Grasparossa Secco has depth and firmness, with a citrus finish, and the Semisecco, a wine that lacks a well-defined identity, is similar, if slightly drier in the finish. Lambrusco di Modena is the estate's least expensive wine, yet it still manages to impress with ripe cherry, nicely balanced tannins and attractive freshness. The fine Rosato is zesty and fruit-forward, the Malvasia dell'Emilia Dolce Incanto has freshness and varietal aromas, and the lively Trebbiano Il Gherlo offers attractive sensations of green apples.

The emphasis on innovation at Poderi dal Nespoli in recent years has been reinforced, especially in the vineyard, where a long-term renovation programme involves the more than 30 hectares under vine. At the same time, there are things afoot in the cellar as new consultant winemaker, the highly successful Alberto Antonini, has taken over. The most convincing proof of these improvements came when we tasted the Nespoli 2001, a Sangiovese from slightly over-ripe fruit. Barrique ageing has round out this wine beautifully, without excess, lending it elegant, intense ripe fruit and liquorice aromas. The soft, creamy texture on the palate releases pervasive notes of chocolate and long length that signs off with delicious nuances of plum jam. There was a good performance from the Borgo dei Guidi, from barrique-conditioned sangiovese, cabernet sauvignon and raboso del Piave. The nose is a tad forward and lacks elegance, but the palate has juicy pulp and concentration, the tannins are firm and mellow, and the back palate is long, although a little more freshness would improve it. The Sangiovese Prugneto 2002 has a close-knit texture and admirable balance. Robust and sinewy, it has attractive acidity and upfront appeal. In contrast, the fruit-forward, fresh-tasting Sangiovese Santodeno 2002 is uncomplicated, approachable and well made.

● Lambrusco Grasparossa di Castelvetro Amabile '02	♟♟	3*
● Lambrusco Grasparossa di Castelvetro L'Acino '02	♟♟	4
○ Malvasia dell'Emilia Dolce Incanto '02	♟	2
○ Il Gherlo Trebbiano di Modena '02	♟	2
◉ Lambrusco di Modena Rosato '02	♟	3
● Lambrusco Grasparossa di Castelvetro Secco '02	♟	3
● Lambrusco Grasparossa di Castelvetro Semisecco '02	♟	3
● Lambrusco di Modena '02	♟	2*

● Il Nespoli '01	♟♟	5
● Borgo dei Guidi '01	♟♟	6
● Sangiovese di Romagna Prugneto '02	♟	4*
● Sangiovese di Romagna Sup. Santodeno '02	♟	3
● Borgo dei Guidi '98	♟♟	6
● Borgo dei Guidi '99	♟♟	6
● Borgo dei Guidi '00	♟♟	6
● Il Nespoli '00	♟♟	5
● Sangiovese di Romagna Vigneto Il Prugneto '01	♟	4

CORIANO (RN)

SAN PATRIGNANO
LOC. SAN PATRIGNANO
VIA SAN PATRIGNANO, 53
47852 CORIANO (RN)
TEL. 0541362362 - 0541756764
E-MAIL: comm3@sanpatrignano.org

San Patrignano has carved a niche for itself on the Romagna wine scene and is definitely here to stay. Its success is the outcome of a well-drafted, carefully thought-out plan driven by state-of-the-art cellar technology, supervised by oenologist, Riccardo Cotarella, and backed up by serious investments in the vineyards. Above all, it can count on the volunteer spirit of all those working in vineyard, cellar and distribution as they attend to their duties. The best wine this year, a Three Glass winner, is a Sangiovese called Avi 2000, which has a superb nose and lashings of personality. The seductively chewy mouthfeel is soft yet well rounded at the same time. Its lingers endlessly on the palate in a welter of red berry fruit, spice, chocolate and cocoa powder. We were also convinced by the sangiovese and cabernet sauvignon Noi 2001 on its first release. The subtle, intense fruit on the nose gives way to the power and sinew of the palate, where the extremely close-knit tannic weave supports a very long, but slightly astringent, finish. The immense potential of cabernet sauvignon, cabernet franc, merlot and petit verdot fails to emerge in the Montepirolo 2000, perhaps because of the difficulties involved in finding a balance of an abundance of fruit, muscular extract and robust oak. The gently complexity of the Sangiovese Aulente is more attractive and the 2002 edition is the best ever. Finally, the intriguing experiment of the 100 per cent sauvignon Vintàn still needs fine-tuning.

●	Sangiovese di Romagna Sup. Avi Ris. '00	🍷🍷🍷	6
●	Colli di Rimini Rosso Noi '01	🍷🍷	5
●	Montepirolo '00	🍷🍷	6
●	Sangiovese di Romagna Sup. Aulente '02	🍷🍷	4*
○	Vintàn '02	🍷	4
●	Montepirolo '99	YYY	6
●	Sangiovese di Romagna Sup. Avi Ris. '99	YYY	6
●	Sangiovese di Romagna Sup. Zarricante Ris. '00	YY	5
●	Sangiovese di Romagna Sup. Avi Ris. '98	YY	6

FAENZA (RA)

LEONE CONTI
LOC. SANTA LUCIA
VIA POZZO, 1
48018 FAENZA (RA)
TEL. 0546642149
E-MAIL: info@leoneconti.it

There were good performances again by the two late-harvest Albanas. It shows that Leone Conti, a cellar committed to this unusual style, has gained experience and familiarity with challenging, non-traditional vinification techniques. Progetto 2 has elegant ripe tropical fruit and botrytis notes, a fatty, almost sweet palate and great balance, with long, minerally length. In contrast, Progetto 1 is dry and alcohol-rich, revealing attractive acidity and decent length. The cellar opted to leave the Albana Passito to mature for a little longer, so we were unable to taste it, but there was a sweet wine, from super-ripe sauvignon fruit, called Tu Chiamale se Vuoi Emozioni Lato B, named after a popular song by the late Lucio Battisti. Full-bodied and distinctly sweet, it has intense candied peel on the back palate. Arcolaio comes from old vines of sauvignon rosso, an unusual variety that is quite commonly planted around Faenza and Forlì. Some commentators think it resembles grenache. The nose combines ripe fruit with a spicy, aromatic and faintly gamey note, then the robustly alcoholic palate takes you through to a long, fruit-led finish. Poderepozzo Le Betulle 2001 is a decently made Sangiovese, but fails to convince with its faintly herbaceous aromas layered over super-ripe fruit. The syrah-based Rossonero is muscular and rich in alcohol. Spice and toastiness on the nose of the Podereviacupa Le Ghiande lead into a fairly substantial body with a faint hint of acidity. Finally, the white Poderepalazzina is fresh, fruity and pleasantly tangy.

●	Arcolaio '01	🍷🍷	5
○	Tu Chiamale se Vuoi Emozioni Lato B '01	🍷🍷	6
○	Albana di Romagna Progetto 1 '02	🍷🍷	3*
○	Albana di Romagna Progetto 2 '02	🍷🍷	4
●	Colli di Faenza Rosso Podereviacupa Le Ghiande '01	🍷	4
●	Rossonero '01	🍷	4
●	Sangiovese di Romagna Sup. Poderepozzo Le Betulle '01	🍷	4
○	Colli di Faenza Bianco Poderepalazzina Le Rive '02	🍷	3
●	Sangiovese di Romagna '02	🍷	3
○	Albana di Romagna Passito Non Ti Scordar di Me '00	YY	6

FAENZA (RA)

FATTORIA ZERBINA
FRAZ. MARZENO
VIA VICCHIO, 11
48010 FAENZA (RA)
TEL. 054640022
E-MAIL: info@zerbina.com

Congratulations to Maria Cristina Geminiani for her Marzieno 2001, a wine that is unfailingly superb. The mainly sangiovese fruit, with a little cabernet sauvignon and merlot, comes from very high-density, bush-trained vines and is matured in new barriques for over a year. Concentrated ripe fruit laced with subtle liquorice lingers on the nose. In the mouth, it is opulent and powerful, with assertive tannins, never putting a foot wrong as it flows seamlessly across the palate. Cleanness, balance, texture and length abound in a perfect performance from this utterly convincing Three Glass winner. The concentrated ripe fruit and velvety mouthfeel of Torre di Ceparano 2001 again make it one of the best Superiore Sauvignons around. Vigna Querce 2001 offers intense ripe cherries then a sustained body with soft, firm tannins. Ceregio is lighter and more approachable, thanks to fresh, fragrant fruit. The albana and chardonnay Tergeno 2001 has a new style, the albana having been harvested late and fermented in wood, while the chardonnay was picked and vinified in the usual manner. It citrus, apples and pears have distinct hints of super-ripeness on nose and palate, with elegant, well-defined minerality and distinct residual sugar in the finish. The good 2000 vintage yielded both versions of Albana Passito. Scacco Matto is getting closer and closer in style to a voluptuous Sauternes, with its stylish notes of botrytis, complex palate and sheer fatty opulence of its fruit. Arrocco is comparable, but more restrained. Although it is a little thin, it has good finesse and persistence.

FAENZA (RA)

PAOLO FRANCESCONI
VIA TULIERO, 154
48018 FAENZA (RA)
TEL. 054643213
E-MAIL: pfrancesconi@racine.ra.it

The story of Paolo Francesconi's estate is similar to that of many other small producers in Romagna. Years ago, Paolo's thoughts were running along the same lines as many of his 30-something contemporaries, tired of watching the family business produce good, but unremunerative, crops and grapes that were handed over to the nearest co-operative. Paolo decided to gradually renew the eight hectares under vine with high-density plantings, applying organic farming techniques, as he always had. He dedicated unremitting care and attention to the new plots that had just come onstream, vinifying the best of the fruit in his small but practical cellar. It's a straightforward story, and like many others, it has led to extremely satisfying results. The panel very much enjoyed the two vintages of Merlot Impavido. Both are deep aubergine in colour, with identical bramble jam aromas that are clearer and more intense in the 2000 edition. The palate is complex and distinctly satisfying. The 2001 is lighter and drinking well now, whereas the 2000 has superb body, with austere, sumptuous extract. The two vintages of Sangiovese Riserva present a similar profile. Both are excellent, revealing austere bottled cherry aromas. Impressive on the palate, they have a good tannic weave that is more prominent in the 2000 version, but softer and more velvety in the following year's wine. Sangiovese Limbecca 2002 has intense fruit on the nose and a full, faintly tannic palate. Finally, Miniato 2001 is more of a lightweight, and its acidity is perhaps excessive.

● Marzieno '01	♟♟♟	6
○ Albana di Romagna Passito Arrocco '00	♟♟	6
○ Albana di Romagna Passito Scacco Matto '00	♟♟	7
● Sangiovese di Romagna Sup. Ceregio Vigna Querce '01	♟♟	4*
● Sangiovese di Romagna Sup. Torre di Ceparano '01	♟♟	4*
○ Tergeno '01	♟♟	4*
● Sangiovese di Romagna Sup. Ceregio '02	♟	3
● Marzieno '98	♟♟♟	6
● Marzieno '99	♟♟♟	6
● Marzieno '00	♟♟♟	6

● Impavido '00	♟♟	5
● Sangiovese di Romagna Vigna delle Iadi Ris. '00	♟♟	4*
● Impavido '01	♟♟	5
● Sangiovese di Romagna Le Iadi Ris. '01	♟♟	4*
● Colli di Faenza Rosso Miniato '01	♟	4
● Colli di Faenza Sangiovese Limbecca '02	♟	3

FAENZA (RA)

ISTITUTO PROFESSIONALE
PER L'AGRICOLTURA E L'AMBIENTE
LOC. PERSOLINO - VIA FIRENZE, 194
48018 FAENZA (RA)
TEL. 054622932
E-MAIL: ipsaa.persolino@mbox.dinamica.it

PODERI MORINI
LOC. ORIOLO DEI FICHI
VIA GESUITA
48018 FAENZA (RA)
TEL. 0546634257
E-MAIL: info@poderimorini.com

The Istituto Persolino is a school that gives its students the chance to train while helping to make excellent wines, experiment with new varieties, and contribute to the rediscovery of historic and native grapes. All this goes on under the watchful eye of oenologist, Sergio Ragazzini, one of the first people in Romagna to promote what today we could view as an early attempt to defend biodiversity. In addition, the school also ensures that experimentation and research are carried out in a context that respects the demands and rules of the market. Malbo gentile is the variety that goes into Amabile Persolino, an excellent red from part-dried grapes. The 2001 vintage was not the most favourable for this wine, for there are untypical dry notes. The ripe black cherry aromas are well-defined and the soft palate is tempting at first, but then reveals dry, tannic astringency on the back palate. The school's fine tradition of dried-grape wines is upheld by the malvasia-based Poesia d'Inverno, a rich, complex product with an intense bouquet. Full and satisfying in the mouth, its vibrant sweetness leads to a finish that matches good alcohol with honey and citrus. The Ultimo Giorno di Scuola (the name means "last day of school") shows elegant noble rot and fullness of flavour, but has a shade too much acidity. Rosso di Nero, from pinot nero grapes, is robust, intense and mouthfilling. The boisterous tannins are reined in by a deliciously soft back palate. Varrone 2001 is reasonably well-rounded and nicely made.

A few years ago, Alessandro Morini decided to take over the 40 hectares under vine owned by his family in the hills around Faenza, at Torre di Oriolo. He set in motion a far-sighted scheme to take his estate upmarket, putting the emphasis on native varieties and building a very modern new cellar. He also opted to hire the services of consultant winemaker, Sergio Ragazzini, an oenologist who know Romagna better than most. Alessandro's laudably responsible approach is bearing its first fruits. He uses the typical Romagna variety, sauvignon rosso, with Spanish alicante to make two wines. One is the intriguing Rubacuori, from fruit dried on rush mats, is in a style reminiscent of vintage port, with intense fruit, understated sweetness and good extract. The other is Traicolli 2001, from grapes harvested late and aged slowly in tonneau. It has acquired wild strawberry and cake aromas, fullness of body, elegance and a velvet smoothness in the long finish. Austrian oak tonneaux are used to mature Augusto, a well-structured, alcohol-rich red from Longanesi grapes that delights with balsam, fruit jam and spice aromas. Alessandro presented three Sangioveses. The one with most breadth and complexity is undoubtedly the Riserva Nonno Rico 2000, which has very good concentration, pulp and persistence. Torre di Oriolo 2001 has generous fruit and balsam notes, as well as a down-soft texture, whereas Beccafico is more rustic and traditional in personality, with a pleasant, balanced flavour.

● Amabile Persolino Rosso Passito '01	♛♛	5
○ Poesia d'Inverno Vino da Uve Stramature '01	♛♛	5
● Rosso di Nero '01	♛♛	4*
○ Albana di Romagna Passito Ultimo Giorno di Scuola '01	♛	5
● Varrone Vigna del Centenario '01	♛	3
○ Albana di Romagna Passito Ultimo Giorno di Scuola '00	豆豆	5
● Amabile Persolino Rosso Passito '00	豆豆	5
○ Poesia d'Inverno Vino da Uve Stramature '00	豆豆	5

● Rubacuori Passito da Uve Stramature '01	♛♛	5
● Augusto '00	♛♛	4*
● Sangiovese di Romagna Sup. Nonno Rico Ris. '00	♛♛	5
○ Albana di Romagna Passito Innamorato '01	♛♛	5
● Traicolli '01	♛♛	5
● Gruccione Merlot '01	♛	4
● Sangiovese di Romagna Sup. Beccafico '01	♛	4
● Sangiovese di Romagna Sup. Torre di Oriolo '01	♛	4
○ Albana di Romagna Secco Sette Note '02	♛	3
○ Colli di Faenza Alba di Luna '02	♛	3

FAENZA (RA)

FORLÌ

TRERÉ
VIA CASALE, 19
48018 FAENZA (RA)
TEL. 054647034
E-MAIL: trere@trere.com

STEFANO BERTI
LOC. RAVALDINO IN MONTE
VIA LA SCAGNA, 18
47100 FORLÌ
TEL. 0543488074
E-MAIL: renbante@tin.it

Last year's progress by Treré was amply confirmed when the panel called this time. The wines have moved on since the last vintage. They are more modern in style, which means they have good concentration, lots of sweetness and fresh aromas. Old wood, and old-style wines, look to be things of the past. Of course, much of the credit for this progress must go to Attilio Pagli, the new consultant oenologist who is keeping an eye on the estate. We were particularly surprised by Sangiovese Renero 2002, an uncomplicated, young wine with intense ripe red berry fruit aromas, close-knit, almost rounded texture and a long, sweet finish. The follow through on the palate is faultless and the extremely attractive flavours are superbly balanced. A more ambitious, and very successful, wine is the Montecorallo 2000, a happy marriage of sangiovese, cabernet sauvignon and merlot grapes. Evident on the nose are fruit preserve and vanilla, then the beefy, full-bodied palate adds chocolate and liquorice, ushering in a long, satisfying finish. Outstanding elegance is the keynote of the more traditional Sangiovese Riserva Amarcord d'un Ross 2000. A muscular wine, it combines great extract with robust tannins, which may be the culprits that introduce a faint bitterish note into a rich, lingering finish. Sangiovese Vigna del Monte has good acidity and reasonable complexity of flavour, but we thought the Vigna dello Sperone was a bit of a lightweight. Both these wines come from a difficult vintage.

Stefano Berti takes his winemaking seriously. After producing a superb product like the Sangiovese Calisto 2001, which is drinking even better now than it was on release, he decided that the poor 2002 vintage did not merit a big-league wine. So he didn't try to make one. Some might raise an eyebrow or two at this, or even begin to doubt Stefano's abilities as a producer. But it is merely the logical consequence of a philosophy that Berti adheres to scrupulously, and which we could sum up like this: wine is a product of the grapes from the vineyard. Stefano's painstaking vineyard management nevertheless enabled him to bring in a decent harvest, although we should not forget that the generally indifferent 2002 vintage was particularly poor in the area around Forlì and Faenza. In the end, he made a Ravaldo, the cellar's second-label Sangiovese. It is reasonably dark and intense, releasing clean, powerful notes of ripe berry fruit and jam, lifted by deliciously fresh flowers. Full and austere on the palate, it combines impressive, close-knit tannins with all the softness of ripe fruit, and its continuity and length on the palate are very good indeed.

● Colli di Faenza Rosso				● Sangiovese di Romagna Sup.		
Montecorallo '00	♀♀	4*		Ravaldo '02	♀♀	4*
● Sangiovese di Romagna				● Sangiovese di Romagna Sup.		
Amarcord d'un Ross Ris. '00	♀♀	4*		Calisto '01	♀♀♀	5
● Colli di Faenza Sangiovese				● Sangiovese di Romagna Sup.		
Renero '02	♀♀	4*		Calisto '00	♀♀	5
● Sangiovese di Romagna						
Vigna del Monte '02	♀	2				
● Sangiovese di Romagna Sup.						
Vigna dello Sperone '02		3				
● Sangiovese di Romagna						
Amarcord d'un Ross Ris. '99	♀♀	4				

FORLÌ

CALONGA

LOC. CASTIGLIONE
VIA CASTEL LEONE, 8
47100 FORLÌ
TEL. 0543753044

The strategy of Maurizio Baravelli and winemaker, Fabrizio Moltard, who has been supervising the cellar since its first vintages, could be summarized as painstakingly careful management of the just over seven hectares of vines, low production levels – totalling about 20,000 bottles – and wines that embody their territory. Above all, the pair have clear ideas and specific objectives. The resulting wines may not be to everyone's liking, but they are characterful, challenging and often need a considerable time in the cellar. That is why release of the two flagship reds was delayed. The Cabernet Sauvignon Castellione and Sangiovese Michelangiolo from 2001 will not be distributed before next year. In the meantime, we tasted the Castellione 2000, which was ageing in the cellars when we called. Just over 3,000 bottles were produced of this wine, from very low yielding vines, and it matured for 12 months in new barriques of French oak. The nose tells you that it comes from great wine country. It is austere, the liquorice faintly nuanced with vegetal notes. The palate is full, the tannins tight-knit and mellow, the structure solid and well sustained. This is a Cabernet Sauvignon with a marvellous future. The younger, steel-vinified Sangiovese Il Bruno is lighter and less demanding. The Albana Passito Kiria 2001 is nicely made, but the Pagadebit bears the scars of the difficult 2002 vintage. Still, it is attractively fresh-tasting, and rewards investigation.

●	Cabernet Sauvignon Castellione '00	🍷🍷	6
○	Albana di Romagna Passito Kiria '01	🍷	4
●	Sangiovese di Romagna Sup. Il Bruno '01	🍷	3
○	Pagadebit di Romagna '02		3
●	Cabernet Sauvignon Castellione '99	YY	6
●	Sangiovese di Romagna Sup. Michelangiolo Ris. '00	YY	6

FORLÌ

DREI DONÀ TENUTA LA PALAZZA

LOC. MASSA DI VECCHIAZZANO
VIA DEL TESORO, 23
47100 FORLÌ
TEL. 0543769371
E-MAIL: dreidona@tin.it

The Drei Donà family produced another good performance with one or two new developments., which concern their younger, more affordable wines. Notturno 2001, of which 35,000 bottles were made, is one of the best young Sangioveses in the region. The new, fresh-tasting, fruit-forward style, with moderate body and well-gauged maturation, makes it an instantly likeable easy drinker. The new white, Varenne (named after a champion Italian racehorse), has fresh aromas and a tangy, tasty palate. Let's move on to the good repeat performances, starting with Graf Noir 1998. From sangiovese, cabernet sauvignon, cabernet franc and Longanesi grapes grown in the same vineyard, it has breadth and intensity on the nose, a no-nonsense palate and an incisive personality. Cabernet Sauvignon Magnificat 1999 offers very complex spice nuanced with vegetal notes, then intensity and depth in a palate that makes no concessions to softness. Tornese 2001, a barrique-fermented and aged Chardonnay, is a full-flavoured, serious white with a hint of resin in the faintly bitter finish. Finally, the Sangiovese Pruno 1999 performed splendidly, only just missing out on a third Glass. The subtle nose is a delightful medley of fruit and spice that soars effortlessly over the contribution of the oak. A fresh, velvety mouthfeel and solid structure contribute to make this a very sophisticated wine, its beautiful balance favouring elegant progression over an exuberance of fruit.

●	Sangiovese di Romagna Sup. Pruno Ris. '99	🍷🍷	5
●	Notturno Sangiovese '01	🍷🍷	3*
●	Graf Noir '98	🍷🍷	6
●	Magnificat Cabernet Sauvignon '99	🍷🍷	6
○	Il Tornese Chardonnay '01	🍷	5
○	Varenne '02	🍷	3
●	Magnificat Cabernet Sauvignon '94	YYY	6
●	Graf Noir '97	YY	6
●	Magnificat Cabernet Sauvignon '98	YY	6
●	Sangiovese di Romagna Sup. Pruno Ris. '98	YY	5

FORLÌ

TENUTA VALLI
LOC. RAVALDINO IN MONTE
VIA DELLE CAMINATE, 38
47100 FORLÌ
TEL. 054524393
E-MAIL: info@tenutavalli.it

Emilio Polgrossi is implementing an extensive, well-thought out scheme to modernize his family winery. He has gradually overhauled his more than 25 hectares under vine, which are now managed organically, and a new cellar means that winemaker Pietro Montanari is able to work in ideal conditions. We can look forward to considerable improvements in quality and, in fact, these are already starting to show. The cellar's most interesting product is the cabernet sauvignon-based Borgo Rosso, which ages for 12 months in French barriques. The very evolved aromas are nuanced with vegetal notes, then the soft, full-bodied palate remarkably long and entirely convincing. The intense, elegantly sweet Albana Passito Mythos 2001 is as well made as ever. Riserva della Beccaccia 2000 was obtained from a selection of the best sangiovese grapes grown at Vigna del Montale, Tenuta Valli's main vineyard. The wine matured slowly in large and small wood to acquire an intense yet subtle nose that alternates spices with fruit preserve. The broad palate has nice balance and structure, without being excessively concentrated. Palazzetto, from sangiovese with a little cabernet, matured in new barriques. Inky black, it has fruit and balsam notes introducing a full body that is a tad heavy on oak-derived aromas. The fresh, fruity Tibano 2002 is an attractively uncomplicated wine, and the more forward, fuller bodied Rosso del Montale is equally good, showing tannins and a bitter twist in the finish.

GAZZOLA (PC)

LURETTA
LOC. CASTELLO DI MOMELIANO
29010 GAZZOLA (PC)
TEL. 0523976500
E-MAIL: luretta.vini@tin.it

First-quality fruit, skilful winemaking and a commitment to characterful wines are the secrets of Lucio Salamini's success. This year's range is no exception to the rule for all the wines impressed, starting with the newcomer, Ala del Drago 2001. It's a Gutturnio Superiore with great depth of colour and intense ripe fruit aromas. The palate is full and nicely balanced, revealing the faintest of balsamic notes. Achab, from pinot nero grapes, has an eloquently varietal nose and a well-defined palate that shows restrained astringency in the finish. The 2001 edition of the Cabernet Sauvignon Corbeau 2001 is as excellent as ever. Deep purplish red, it offers sweet, fruit-led aromas layered over resin and spices, the solid structure and length combine with depth of flavour in a palate that has already found balance, despite the hint of edginess and acidity in the finish. The Vendemmia Tardiva di Malvasia Le Rane 2002 has all the aromatic elegance of the variety, then the well-balanced palate foregrounds peach, pear and candied citrus peel. Malvasia Boccadirosa 2002 also shows good finesse and balance, although it lacks the depth of previous versions, and the Sauvignon I Nani e Le Ballerine is very varietal on the nose, bright and minerally in the mouth. But the most interesting white is the barrique-fermented Chardonnay Selin dl'Armari. Crisp, clean fruit mingles with minerals and vanilla, which the very well-balanced palate echoes beautifully, and the oak has been judged to perfection. All that's missing is the opulence a better vintage would have provided.

O	Albana di Romagna Passito Mythos '01	♙♙	5
●	Borgo Rosso '01	♙♙	4*
●	Sangiovese di Romagna Riserva della Beccaccia Ris. '00	♙♙	4*
●	Sangiovese di Romagna Sup. Il Palazzetto '01	♙	4
●	Sangiovese di Romagna Sup. Rosso del Montale '01	♙	5
●	Sangiovese di Romagna Sup. Il Tibano '02	♙	3
O	Albana di Romagna Secco I Vinchi '02		3
O	Albana di Romagna Passito Mythos '00	♙♙	5

●	C. P. Cabernet Sauvignon Corbeau '01	♙♙	7
●	C. P. Gutturnio Sup. L'Ala del Drago '01	♙♙	5
●	C. P. Pinot Nero Achab '01	♙♙	7
O	C. P. Chardonnay Selin dl'Armari '02	♙♙	5
O	C. P. Malvasia V. T. Le Rane '02	♙♙	7
O	C. P. Malvasia Boccadirosa '02	♙	5
O	C. P. Sauvignon I Nani e Le Ballerine '02	♙	5
●	C. P. Cabernet Sauvignon Corbeau '00	♙♙♙	7
●	C. P. Pinot Nero Achab '00	♙♙	7
O	C. P. Malvasia V. T. Le Rane '01	♙♙	7
●	Come La Pantera e I Lupi nella Sera '01	♙♙	5

IMOLA (BO)

TRE MONTI
LOC. BERGULLO
VIA LOLA, 3
40026 IMOLA (BO)
TEL. 0542657116
E-MAIL: tremonti@tremonti.it

The Navacchia family set out along the road to quality some years ago. Since then, they have never wavered from that path. They are firm believers in science and experimentation, in both vineyard and cellar, and their winemaking style puts softness, balance and fruit on top of the list of priorities. It has to be said that this is a courageous choice in such a heterogeneous area as Romagna, where often muscle and brawn are taken to extremes, not always successfully. The Sangiovese di Romagna Thea 2001 has tempting fresh berry fruit in which bramble and cherry stand out. The palate is elegant, well balanced and soft to the point of sweetness. Well supported by alcohol, it sweeps through to a long, complex and very stylish finish. Boldo 2001 is more herbaceous and edgier, thanks to the cabernet sauvignon that joined the sangiovese in the blend. The French grape also appears to have contributed structure, backed up by a firm tannic weave. The cleanness, style and balance of all the Tre Monti whites comes from a very competent use of oak and skilful fermentation. The Chardonnay Ciardo 2002 tempts with fruit and vanilla, then adds breadth and complexity on a full, well-balanced palate. Salcerella 2002, an ever-reliable mix of albana and chardonnay, is full and generous on nose and palate. Both the Albana Vigna della Rocca and the Trebbiano Vigna del Rio had to cope with the less than exceptional 2002 vintage, but are still two of the best wines of their type in Romagna.

LANGHIRANO (PR)

CARRA
LOC. CASATICO
VIA DELLA NAVE, 10
43013 LANGHIRANO (PR)
TEL. 0521863510 - 0521355260
E-MAIL: info@carradicasatico.com

Bonfiglio Carra is a conscientious young producer who aims to make wines of character and personality. His ten hectares under vine in the hills at Casatico, near Castello di Torrechiara, give him about 100,000 bottles a year. All across the wide range, the wines are clean and unfailingly reliable. We gave Two Glasses this year to the Cinque Torri Brut, a "metodo classico" sparkler from pinot nero and chardonnay grapes with a dense, persistent perlage and a nose of almonds and crusty bread. Fluent and smooth on the palate, it signs off with a subtle, refreshing hint of fruit that echoes the nose. Eden 2000 is a dried-grape "passito" wine from malvasia grapes. The variety's trademark aromas greet the nose, then the palate unveils gentle notes of apricots and honey. The first release of the Merlot has a soft, spicy fruit-led palate that lacks a little depth. When we moved on to the semi-sparkling "frizzante" wines, we found the reds to be suffering after the poor vintage, but the Colli di Parma DOC whites were all good, from the well-defined aromas of the fresh, tangy Sauvignon to the soft, coherent Malvasia Frizzante. Torcularia Bianco, obtained from the first-pressing must of chardonnay, pinot bianco and pinot nero fruit, is nicely balanced on the nose and shows just the right touch of refreshing acidity in the mouth. We finish on a sweet note with the green-flecked straw-yellow Malvasia & Moscato 2002, whose sweet effervescence caresses the palate.

O Albana di Romagna Passito '01	🍷🍷	5
● Colli di Imola Boldo '01	🍷🍷	5
● Sangiovese di Romagna Sup. Thea '01	🍷🍷	5
O Colli di Imola Chardonnay Ciardo '02	🍷🍷	4*
O Colli di Imola Salcerella '02	🍷🍷	5
● Sangiovese di Romagna Ris. '00	🍷	4
O Albana di Romagna Secco Vigna della Rocca '02	🍷	4
● Sangiovese di Romagna Sup. '02	🍷	3
O Trebbiano di Romagna Vigna del Rio '02	🍷	4
● Sangiovese di Romagna Sup. Thea '00	🍷🍷	5

O Cinque Torri Brut	🍷🍷	4
O Eden Passito '00	🍷	5
● Merlot '00	🍷	4
O Colli di Parma Malvasia Frizzante '02	🍷	3
O Colli di Parma Sauvignon Frizzante '02	🍷	3
O Malvasia & Moscato Dolce '02	🍷	3
O Torcularia Bianco '02	🍷	3
O Eden Passito '99	🍷🍷	5

MODENA

CHIARLI 1860
VIA DANIELE MANIN, 15
41100 MODENA
TEL. 0593163311
E-MAIL: info@chiarli.com

It has been more than 135 years since Cleto Chiarli began to fill the first bottles of Lambrusco for diners at his trattoria in the centre of Modena. Now, the family name is a rock-solid beacon in the vast panorama of Lambrusco, thanks in no small measure to the astute management of the winery by the present generation, brothers Anselmo and Mauro Chiarli. Output is distributed across three ranges, the historic leading label, "Cleto Chiarli & Figli", being reserved for premium-quality wines, like Grasparossa Vigneto Enrico Cialdini and Villa Cialdini. Vigneto Enrico Cialdini is obtained from selected fruit from the Enrico Cialdini vineyard, which is named after a hero of the Risorgimento. The nose reveals attractive citrus fruit, which is mirrored on the back palate. Villa Cialdini takes its name from the complex where an efficient modern cellar has recently been installed. Fresh, fragrant aromas usher in a dry palate with good extract. Pruno Nero, from grasparossa fruit slowly macerated at low temperature, is dense and dark, the fruit aromas introducing a full-bodied, richly flavoured palate and nice length. Finally, Nivola is the cellar's most innovative product. This year, it is also the best. From several varieties of lambrusco grape, it impresses with its purplish-black hue and bright, lingering bubbles. The cherry aromas are intense and well-defined, the palate rich and flavourful.

MODIGLIANA (FC)

CASTELLUCCIO
LOC. POGGIOLO
VIA TRAMONTO, 15
47015 MODIGLIANA (FC)
TEL. 0546942486
E-MAIL: info@ronchidicastelluccio.it

Castelluccio is back with another Three Glass winner. Ten years after the triumph of the 1990 Ronco delle Ginestre (still drinking deliciously at a recent tasting), Ronco dei Ciliegi 2000 has joined the top ranks of Italian wine. Over that decade, Castelluccio has undergone many changes. It was recently acquired by Vittorio Fiore, the Tuscan oenologist who first supervised the cellar, and his son Claudio, who is now running the winery with his wife, Veruska. Ronco dei Ciliegi won the panel over because it is far from being an exuberant wine. It is rich, but above all it is very elegant. This great Romagna Sangiovese is, in keeping with tradition, moderately dark in colour. Its delightful ripe fruit, spice, liquorice and mint introduce a delicious palate, where oak has been employed masterfully to round the flavour without distorting it. We found the Ronco delle Ginestre 2000 to be a much more forceful wine, with a muscular power on the palate. A monovarietal Sangiovese, it garlands its bramble jam aromas with distinct toastiness. Massicone 2000 is on its first release. A 50-50 mix of sangiovese and cabernet, it has intense bitter liquorice and pencil lead on the nose. A very close-knit tannic weave backs up dense, sweet fruit, then the finish is slightly dry. The second-label Sangiovese, Le More 2001, is very well made and quite delicious. The two Sauvignons are different in style. Lunaria 2002 is fresh-tasting and distinctly varietal, whereas complexity, mineral notes and character are the keynotes of the oak-fermented Ronco del Re 2000.

● Nivola Lambrusco Scuro '02	𝕐𝕐	2*
● Lambrusco Grasparossa di Castelvetro Vigneto Enrico Cialdini '02	𝕐	3
● Lambrusco Grasparossa di Castelvetro Villa Cialdini '02	𝕐	3
● Lambrusco Grasparossa di Castelvetro Pruno Nero	𝕐	3
● Lambrusco Grasparossa di Castelvetro Gala Amabile		2
● Lambrusco Vecchia Modena Premium '02		3

● Ronco dei Ciliegi '00	𝕐𝕐𝕐	6
● Massicone '00	𝕐𝕐	6
● Ronco delle Ginestre '00	𝕐𝕐	6
○ Ronco del Re '00	𝕐𝕐	6
● Sangiovese di Romagna Sup. Le More '01	𝕐𝕐	4*
○ Lunaria Sauvignon '02	𝕐	4
● Ronco delle Ginestre '90	𝕐𝕐𝕐	6
● Ronco dei Ciliegi '99	𝕐𝕐	6
○ Ronco del Re '99	𝕐𝕐	6
● Ronco delle Ginestre '99	𝕐𝕐	6

MODIGLIANA (FC)

IL PRATELLO
VIA MORANA, 14
47015 MODIGLIANA (FC)
TEL. 0546942038
E-MAIL: pratello@libero.it

To reach Emilio Placci's vineyards and cellar, you have to go up into the mountains at the ancient village of Modigliana. After strolling through woods and fields that have never seen chemical fertilizers, fungicides or intensive farming, you come to Emilio's vineyards. The new plantings are at the cellar and the older vines – red grapes only – nestle in a superbly located valley. Altitudes range from 450 to 600 metres above sea level, harvesting generally takes place late, well into autumn, and the vineyards are managed in strict accordance with the dictates of organic viticulture. The wines themselves reflect both their territory and the unique personality of the man who makes them. They are genuine, sincere and often require patient maturation in the cellar. That is why we were unable to taste the Sangiovese Badia Raustignolo 2000, which Emilio thinks is not yet ready. However, the Calenzone is very good indeed. It's a merlot and cabernet mix that ages in barrique for 24 months and offers intense ripe fruit aromas lifted by spice, vanilla and balsam. The palate has great structure, sweet, tight-knit tannins and a hint of resin in the finish. The Campore, from equal proportions of chardonnay and sauvignon, has a very elegant personality. It ages slowly in barrique, acquiring intense, stylish mineral aromas nuanced with citrus. The tangy, extremely elegant palate takes you through to a mineral-dominated finish. Mantignano 2001 is attractive, uncomplicated and anything but run of the mill.

MODIGLIANA (FC)

VILLA PAPIANO
VIA IBOLA, 26
47015 MODIGLIANA (FC)
TEL. 0546941790 - 0546941790
E-MAIL: info@villapapiano.it

Villa Papiano was founded in 2001 by eight young enthusiasts, and has already earned a place in the front rank of winemaking in Romagna. Four partners are the children of agronomist Remigio Bordini, a well-respected professional with huge experience. The youngest, Francesco, looks after vineyard management and Maria Rosa is in charge of distribution. The Bordini contingent is flanked by Monica Pierleoni and Domenico Angelini Larghetti, formerly in charge of the Carobbio estate, in Chianti Classico, and siblings Ludovica and Uberto Fabbri from Tuscany's Savignola Paolina winery. The group has acquired, and now manages directly, a number of very old vineyards that preserve unique genetic varieties and characteristics. The first vinifications, totalling 30,000 bottles, were supervised in the cellar by oenologist, Lorenzo Landi. There are three very interesting wines, starting with the Sangiovese Le Papesse di Papiano 2001, which has fresh, clean aromas of ripe fruit and a straightforward, but well-defined, flavour. I Probi di Papiano is more evolved but still eminently drinkable. Finally, the Papiano di Papiano 2001 went through to the Three Glass finals on its first outing. It's a mix of 65 per cent merlot with sauvignon rosso and other minor native varieties, and 5,000 bottles were released. The rich, penetrating bouquet has intense berry fruit and jam, then a very elegant, soft palate that shows powerful structure and great length. All in all, the results were excellent and repay the energy and enthusiasm that the winery's partners have devoted to the new enterprise.

● Colli di Faenza Rosso		
Calenzone '00	🍷🍷	6
○ Campore '01	🍷🍷	4
● Colli di Faenza Sangiovese		
Mantignano '01	🍷	4
● Badia Raustignolo '98	🍷🍷	6
● Colli di Faenza Rosso		
Calenzone '99	🍷🍷	6

● Papiano di Papiano '01	🍷🍷	5
● Sangiovese di Romagna		
I Probi di Papiano '01	🍷🍷	4*
● Sangiovese di Romagna		
Le Papesse di Papiano '02	🍷🍷	4*

MONTE SAN PIETRO (BO) MONTE SAN PIETRO (BO)

ISOLA
FRAZ. MONGIORGIO
VIA BERNARDI, 3
40050 MONTE SAN PIETRO (BO)
TEL. 0516768428
E-MAIL: isola1898@interfree.it

SANTAROSA
FRAZ. SAN MARTINO IN CASOLA
VIA SAN MARTINO, 82
40050 MONTE SAN PIETRO (BO)
TEL. 051969203
E-MAIL: santarosavini@katamail.com

The entire Franceschini family helps to run this estate, which also produces high-quality fruit, especially apricots and cherries. Father and son, Marco and Gianluca, are the ones who look after viticulture and winemaking in particular. Marco is busy in the vineyards, where his attentions are scrupulous, while newly qualified agricultural technician, Gianluca, is showing just how knowledgeable and enthusiastic he is about work in the cellar. The most interesting wine is the Cabernet Selezione, which has made steady progress in quality over recent years. The 2001 – 5,000 units were bottled – went through to the final taste-offs, thanks to lovely ripe, chewy berry fruit aromas and impeccable progression on the rich palate, which is austere on entry and velvet-smooth in the long finish. The standard-label 2002 Cabernet throws an intense nose of cherry and raspberry, leading into a broad, deliciously flavoursome palate. The Chardonnay Selezione 2002 is barrique-aged, but the oak is handled with skill and restraint. Fruity on the nose, it has depth, softness and lovely balance on the palate. The steel-vinified Chardonnay 2002 is fresher on the nose and more subdued in the mouth, but gained points for its sheer approachability. Both versions of Pignoletto are well made. The Frizzante sparkler is fresh-tasting, fragrant and full of flavour, whereas the Superiore has intense fruit aromas, with white peach to the fore, nice tanginess and good length in the finale.

The surprisingly good results obtained by Santarosa last year were confirmed this time round. In fact, we can look forward to further improvement. Excellent work in the vineyard, planned by Federico Curtaz and supervised by his very competent agronomist, Chiara Matucci, is backed up by the expertise of winemaker Alberto Antonini. It all adds up to slow, steady progress by Giovanna della Valentina's cellar. The barrique-fermented Chardonnay Giòcoliere 2002 is a first-rate wine. Toastiness alternates with tropical fruit on the nose, then the intense, balanced palate is prodigal with chewy pulp and shows a bitterish twist in the finish. Merlot Giòtondo 2001 has impressively intense, jammy forest fruits lifted by graceful sweet liquorice in the finish. The palate is concentrated, yet the fruit is neither soft nor stewed, and the attractive acidity offsets the softness, making this a very moreish wine. A gentle entry on the palate gives way to austerity, then the finish unveils velvety sweet fruit. The Cabernet Giòrosso 2001 has a similar style to the Giòtondo, but has a crisper, more assertive character. The tannins are closer knit and slightly more astringent, but nonetheless capable of making the long finish very delicious. The Pignoletto Classico is also good. Clean and fruit-forward on the nose, it has substantial body and good balance. Finally, the Pinot Bianco 2002 is not up to the standards of previous vintages, but still shows nice aromas and hefty structure.

●	C. B. Cabernet Sauvignon Sel. '01	🍷🍷	3*
○	C. B. Chardonnay Sel. '02	🍷🍷	3*
●	C. B. Cabernet Sauvignon '02	🍷	3
○	C. B. Chardonnay '02	🍷	3
○	C. B. Pignoletto Frizzante '02	🍷	3
○	C. B. Pignoletto Sup. '02	🍷	3
●	C. B. Cabernet Sauvignon Sel. '00	🍷	3

●	C. B. Cabernet Sauvignon Giòrosso '01	🍷🍷	4*
●	C. B. Merlot Giòtondo '01	🍷🍷	4*
○	C. B. Chardonnay Giòcoliere '02	🍷🍷	4*
○	C. B. Pignoletto Cl. '02	🍷	3
○	C. B. Pinot Bianco '02	🍷	4
●	C. B. Merlot Giòtondo '00	🍷🍷🍷	4
●	C. B. Cabernet Sauvignon Giòrosso '00	🍷🍷	4

MONTE SAN PIETRO (BO)　MONTEVEGLIO (BO)

TENUTA BONZARA
VIA SAN CHIERLO, 37/A
40050 MONTE SAN PIETRO (BO)
TEL. 0516768324 - 051225772
E-MAIL: info@bonzara.it

CORTE D'AIBO
VIA MARZATORE, 15
40050 MONTEVEGLIO (BO)
TEL. 051832583
E-MAIL: cortedaibo@libero.it

For the past two years, release of the Merlot Rocca di Bonacciara and the Cabernet Bonzarone has been delayed, so this year we ought to have found the 2000 versions of both wines waiting for us. But it was not to be. For a number of quite complicated reasons, Francesco Lambertini and long-time estate oenologist, Stefano Chiocciolo, decided not to bottle the two wines, which they believe are not up to the standards of previous vintages. It was a courageous, and expensive, decision, but it also goes to show just how seriously the two take their task. They were, however, able to let us taste the Rocca di Bonacciara 2001, which is already drinking very nicely, unlike the Bonzarone 2001, which we will be tasting next year. The Rocca di Bonacciara sailed through to the final taste-offs, scoring high for the finesse, austerity and cleanness of its aromas. The flavourful palate is irresistibly elegant, with powerful structure, lovely balance and remarkable length. The second-label Merlot, Rosso del Poggio, is as attractive and well made as ever. The fruit-led nose is subtly nuanced with spice, and the light, supremely drinkable palate has lots of flavour. Sauvignon Le Carrate 2002 is very varietal and long on the nose, and the well-made Pignoletto Vigna Antica has nice texture.

Corte d'Aibo is a farmstay estate in a lovely location in the hills near Monteveglio. A co-operative runs the various activities, which include an old farmhouse next to the cellar with four large rooms and a good restaurant. It was set up in 1989 and from the start adhered to the tenets of organic farming. That has been the policy ever since, and organic is still the keyword today. The 17 hectares under vine, of which 12 are currently in production, are managed by Antonio Capelli, while Mario Pirondini looks after the cellar. We were unable to taste the flagship Cabernet Sauvignon Orfeo, which was not made in 1999 because the fruit was felt not to be good enough. The 2000 is still in barrique and will only be ready for us next year. We were, however, very impressed by the Cabernet Le Borre and the Merlot Roncovecchio 2001, both of which cruised to Two Glass scores. The Cabernet has intense, forward aromas with ripe fruit and slightly gamey overtones. It's a tad hard and austere on the palate, but the structure is solid and backed by good alcohol. The finish is clean and lingering. The Merlot has elegant ripe chewy fruit aromas and an impressive entry on the palate. Full-bodied and fleshy, its assertive style leads through to a soft back palate. The very attractive Sauvignon Spugnola 2002 is fruity and fresh-tasting, if not very varietal. A poor vintage means that there is no 2002 edition of the Pignoletto Badessa, the estate's hallmark wine, which undergoes refermentation in bottle.

● C. B. Merlot Rocca di Bonacciara '01	♀♀	5
● C. B. Merlot Rosso del Poggio '02	♀♀	4
○ C. B. Sauvignon Sup. Le Carrate '02	♀♀	3
○ C. B. Pignoletto Cl. Vigna Antica '02	♀	3
○ C. B. Pignoletto Frizzante '02		3
● C. B. Cabernet Sauvignon Bonzarone '97	♀♀♀	5
● C. B. Merlot Rocca di Bonacciara '99	♀♀	5
● C. B. Cabernet Sauvignon Bonzarone '99	♀♀	5

● C. B. Cabernet Sauvignon Le Borre '01	♀♀	4*
● C. B. Merlot Roncovecchio '01	♀♀	4*
○ C. B. Sauvignon Spugnola '02	♀	3

MONTEVEGLIO (BO)

MONTEVEGLIO (BO)

LA MANCINA
FRAZ. MONTEBUDELLO
VIA MOTTA, 8
40050 MONTEVEGLIO (BO)
TEL. 051832691
E-MAIL: info@lamancina.it

There is steady progress at La Mancina, whose 36 hectares under vine make it the most extensive estate in the Colli Bolognesi. Credit for the improvements goes to the ambitious strategy implemented by the young owner, Francesca Zanetti. She has replanted and renewed the vineyards, built a functional new cellar, and put her trust in the skills of Piedmontese oenologist, Giandomenico Negro. It is still early days, but results are already coming through. Three wines in particular impressed the panel. All are reds, which shows once again that Montebudello is ideal country for grapes of that kind. The most interesting wine is the Comandante della Guardia 2000, a barrique-aged Cabernet Sauvignon of which 6,500 bottles were released. A firm entry on the nose reveals fleshy ripe fruit, jam and liquorice, then the full, broad palate offers soft texture braced by attractive acidity. The standard-label 2001 Cabernet is similar in style, but a little less concentrated. The fruit-rich, lingering finish is slightly sweeter, too. The second release of Lanciotto shows that a fresh-tasting Merlot is a winning product. The very pleasant, fruit and alcohol nose leads in to a deliciously drinkable palate. The well-made, varietal Barbera Il Foriere 2001 has clean aromas and a hint of acidity on the palate. Finally, both 2002 versions of Pignoletto are worth investigating. The Frizzante is fresh and fragrant, the intense aromas recalling apple and white peach-led fruit, while the Terre di Montebudello has a full palate and a nice hint of bitterness in the finish.

SAN VITO
FRAZ. OLIVETO
VIA MONTERODANO, 6
40050 MONTEVEGLIO (BO)
TEL. 051964521
E-MAIL: info@agricolasanvito.it

After a few years in the doldrums, when problems on the estate had repercussions on production, Aldo Mazzanti's 14 hectares of well-aspected vineyards at Oliveto have at last yielded a fine range. If we bear in mind that almost all of it come from the testing 2002 vintage, we have to tip our hats to oenologist, Giambattista Zanchetta, who supervises work in the cellar with skilled cellarman, Luciano Manfredini. The best of the wines was the Cabernet Sauvignon Selezione 2001. It has intense ripe fruit and pepper aromas that sign off with subtle hints of smokiness. The palate is round, full and well balanced. There is good alcohol and decent softness, although the finish is a tad dry. The Cabernet Sauvignon 2002 has light, fresh sensations of berry fruit, then the well-balanced structure makes the palate deliciously drinkable. Both versions of Pignoletto are good. The Superiore has a delicate, intense nose of flowers, then the agile, flavoursome palate shows very good length. The Pignoletto Frizzante also has a flower-led nose, lifted by yeasty notes. The tiny bubbles and substantial mouthfeel make the wine very moreish and attractively drinkable The Chardonnay 2002 was fermented and aged in stainless steel. Uncomplicated but full bodied, it gains balance from delicious acidity and is supported by nice aromatic length. The Bianco della Garisenda 2002, a barrique-aged Chardonnay, is more complex and has a more substantial palate.

● C. B. Cabernet Sauvignon Comandante della Guardia '00	♈♈	4*
● C. B. Cabernet Sauvignon '01	♈♈	4*
● C. B. Merlot Lanciotto '02	♈♈	4*
● C. B. Merlot '00	♈	4
● C. B. Barbera Il Foriere '01	♈	4
○ C. B. Pignoletto Frizzante '02	♈	3
○ C. B. Pignoletto Terre di Montebudello '02	♈	4
● C. B. Merlot Lanciotto '01	♈♈	4

● C. B. Cabernet Sauvignon Sel. '01	♈♈	4
● C. B. Cabernet Sauvignon '02	♈♈	3*
○ C. B. Chardonnay '02	♈	3
○ C. B. Chardonnay Bianco della Garisenda '02	♈	3
○ C. B. Pignoletto Frizzante '02	♈	3
○ C. B. Pignoletto Sup. '02	♈	3

PREDAPPIO (FC)

TENUTA PANDOLFA
FRAZ. FIUMANA
VIA PANDOLFA, 35
47010 PREDAPPIO (FC)
TEL. 0543940073
E-MAIL: info@pandolfa.it

There was a great performance from Pezzolo, the estate's flagship bottle vinified with cabernet sauvignon fruit from the Pezzolo vineyard. A year in French barriques, and the same again in bottle, have produced an austere, attractive wine with lashings of personality. The nose is dominated by over-ripe fruit, underpinned by good alcohol and a creamy finish of fresh-baked cakes. A vigorous front palate, with imposing but soft tannins, introduces a finish that is in no hurry to go away. Fosso Le Forche, an unusual blend of sangiovese, montepulciano and nebbiolo aged in barrique for 12 months, has intense bottled morello cherry and elegant spice aromas, over earthy hints of forest floor. It has plenty of personality, robust extract and good acidity, contributed by the nebbiolo, and the finish is long and dry. Sangiovese Canova 2002 is fruit-forward and agile. It's a very successful product, bearing in mind the poorish vintage, and the Chardonnay Cavina is fresh-tasting and undemanding. All in all, it was a good showing from this large, historic estate of nearly 100 carefully managed hectares around the lovely 17th-century villa which Marchese Albicini built, and which today is owned by the Ricci family.

●	Pezzolo Cabernet Sauvignon '00	🍷🍷	6
●	Fosso Le Forche '01	🍷🍷	5
●	Sangiovese di Romagna Canova '02	🍷	3
○	Cavina Chardonnay '02		3
●	Pezzolo Cabernet Sauvignon '99	🍷🍷	6

REGGIO EMILIA

ERMETE MEDICI & FIGLI
LOC. GAIDA
VIA NEWTON, 13/A
42040 REGGIO EMILIA
TEL. 0522942135
E-MAIL: medici@medici.it

Even after a less than favourable vintage like 2002, the Medici family has been able to salvage some very good products. It's an indication that vineyard management at this 60 or so hectare estate is very much quality-oriented, and that experience acquired in the cellar is being put to good use. Proof of this is there for the tasting in the winery's least demanding products. Both the Lambrusco Antica Osteria and the standard-label Reggiano are very well-made wines with fresh, fragrant aromas and attractively clean, sparkling palates. Bearing in mind that these are two of the least expensive wines in this Guide, we can only offer our congratulations. The cellar's two flagship wines, the 2002 Concerto and Assolo, both earned Two Glasses for the first time. They are rather different in style. Assolo is a blend of lambrusco salamino with other varieties, all from the Tenuta I Quercioli vineyard, and 48,000 bottles were released. It's a very fragrant, modern-style Lambrusco with very clean, intense ripe cherry and a broad, full-bodied, flavour-rich palate. Braced by mellow, close-knit tannins, it finds nice balance thanks to good acidity. The 100,000 bottles of Concerto are obtained from the finest lambrusco salamino grapes grown at the Tenuta Rampata vineyard. A more traditional Lambrusco than its partner, it is above all an easy drinker. Intense, fruit-led aromas introduce a full palate with good extract and freshness.

●	Reggiano Assolo '02	🍷🍷	2*
●	Reggiano Lambrusco Secco Concerto '02	🍷🍷	3*
●	Reggiano Lambrusco Secco '02	🍷	1*
●	Lambrusco Antica Osteria	🍷	1*
●	Lambrusco Grasparossa di Castelvetro Dolce Bocciolo '02		2
○	Malvasia dell'Emilia Dolce Nebbie d'Autunno '02		3

RIMINI

SAN VALENTINO
FRAZ. SAN MARTINO IN VENTI
VIA TOMASETTA, 11
47900 RIMINI
TEL. 0541752231
E-MAIL: valerobi@libero.it

Over recent years, quality at the San Valentino estate has been improving steadily. Although the wines are good, they have stopped just short of excellence. In short, the cellar has been unable to take the final step into the very first rank. But with the 2001 vintage, the second supervised by oenologist, Fabrizio Moltard, we are pleased to record that the step has finally been taken. Our congratulations go to Roberto Mascarin, who runs the estate with his sister, Maria Cristina. They have picked up their first Three Glass award for the Sangiovese Terra di Covignano 2001, whose elegant symphony of aromas includes ripe fruit, spices and understated toastiness. In the mouth, the massive structure with its close-knit tannic weave is complemented stupendously by the elegance of the fruit. An austere wine, it makes few concessions to softness or approachability, lingering on the palate with amazing persistence. The Cabernet Sauvignon Luna Nuova 2001 missed out on a third Glass by a whisker. Its long, irresistible nose has fleshy, ripe red berry fruit, then the palate's progression is unstoppable. Elegant on the front palate, it expands over concentrated, well-gauged chewy fruit, then tops this on the back palate with lingering hints of fruit preserve and faint tannins. Scabi may well be the best Sangiovese of 2002, showing depth, intense fruit, chewy pulp and softness in the finish. The same characteristics are evident in the more structured Eclissi di Sole 2001, which is slightly harder and more alcoholic.

RIVERGARO (PC)

LA STOPPA
LOC. ANCARANO
29029 RIVERGARO (PC)
TEL. 0523958159
E-MAIL: info@lastoppa.it

Producing wines that reflect their territorial and varietal origins as naturally as possible is the concept that has always driven the efforts of Elena Pantaleoni and Giulio Armani. Their bottles do not seek extremes of concentration, and could hardly be called approachable, but the depth of sensory experience, which privileges tertiary aromas and ageing-related sensations, needs time in the cellar to emerge. It's a choice that deliberately flies in the face of current market trends, but the numerous La Stoppa fans approve unreservedly. This is more than enough reason for the winery to continue on its path. That said, let's move on to the wines presented for tasting this year. Macchiona 2001, from barbera and bonarda, is garnet-purple with a nose that combines fruit with earthier notes. On the fresh-tasting, assertive palate, the extract is backed up by plenty of body and elegant acidity. The attractive Barbera 2000 comes from an outstanding vintage. It combines great structure with freshness, the natural acidity mingling deliciously with a pleasing tannic weave. The Cabernet Sauvignon Stoppa 2001 is a solid, characterful wine that is still a little stand-offish on the nose, but it has all the richness and depth on the palate of a truly noble wine. The dried-grape, malvasia-based Vigna del Volta is a wine to bank on. Broad, bright aromas of complex peach, citrus peel and apricot jam mingle with malvasia's varietal notes. The well-rounded palate has a touch of freshness in the finish that enhances the length.

● Sangiovese di Romagna Sup. Terra di Covignano Ris. '01	▼▼▼	5
● Colli di Rimini Cabernet Sauvignon Luna Nuova '01	▼▼	5
● Eclissi di Sole '01	▼▼	4*
● Sangiovese di Romagna Sup. Scabi '02	▼▼	3*
○ Fiore Chardonnay '02	▼	4
● Colli di Rimini Cabernet Sauvignon Luna Nuova '00	♈♈	5
● Sangiovese di Romagna Sup. Scabi '01	♈	3

● C. P. Cabernet Sauvignon Stoppa '01	▼▼	5
○ C. P. Malvasia Passito Vigna del Volta '01	▼▼	6
● C. P. Barbera della Stoppa '00	▼▼	4*
● Macchiona '01	▼▼	5
● Stoppa '96	▼▼▼	5
○ C. P. Malvasia Passito Vigna del Volta '97	♈♈♈	5
● C. P. Cabernet Sauvignon Stoppa '00	♈♈	5
○ C. P. Malvasia Passito Vigna del Volta '00	♈♈	5
● C. P. Barbera della Stoppa '99	♈	4

SASSO MARCONI (BO)

FLORIANO CINTI
FRAZ. SAN LORENZO
VIA GAMBERI, 48
40037 SASSO MARCONI (BO)
TEL. 0516751646
E-MAIL: cinti@collibolognesi.com

Each time we call, Floriano Cinti surprises us with a new, and even more attractive, range. Congratulations are due to Floriano and his winemaker, Giovanni Fraulini, who has been assisting the winery for years. Both the Chardonnay and the Pignoletto Classico come from a difficult vintage, but the results are good. The Chardonnay has clean, intense fresh fruit, then a tasty, nicely structured palate lifted by well-judged acidity. The Pignoletto has fresh flowers on the nose, and plenty of body and softness in the mouth, where the flavours linger. The two barrique-aged selections of Merlot and Cabernet Sauvignon are very successful. The Merlot 2001, of which 1,500 bottles were released, has intense ripe fruit, vanilla and liquorice. In the mouth, it has lots of soft, fruity pulp and signs off with an austerely attractive elegance that lingers attractively. The 7,000 bottles of Cabernet 2000 have a nose very similar to the previous wine, albeit less intense. The tannins are close knit and very smooth, the concentration is good, but not excessive, and the wine's gutsy personality powers through to a long finish. The other reds are also impressive. The Cabernet Sauvignon 2001 is pleasant, fruity and faintly grassy, whereas the Merlot 2002 is enjoyable and uncomplicated, with good balance and structure. Varietal aromas on the nose of the Sauvignon Selezione 2002 introduce a longer, more structured palate than the nonetheless well-made and approachable standard-label Sauvignon. And there's a mention for the Pignoletto Frizzante, a subtly textured, tangily fresh crowd pleaser.

TRAVO (PC)

IL POGGIARELLO
LOC. SCRIVELLANO DI STATTO
29020 TRAVO (PC)
TEL. 0523957241 - 0523571610
E-MAIL: info@poggiarellovini.it

Paolo and Stefano Perini turned out another fine range of wines as they continue to fine-tune their winery style. Overall, the quality was good and there were no exceptions to the rule. In fact, there was an admirable high note in the Gutturnio Riserva La Barbona. The dark ruby 2000 editions has berry fruit and spice aromas ushering in a muscular palate where austerity is the keynote. The very solid structure hints at considerable ageing potential. The Gutturnio Perticato Valandrea 2001 is also very good. It may not have the depth of its big brother, but there is good complexity, fresh fruit and decent structure, which all adds up to a deliciously drinkable wine. The Pinot Nero Le Giastre is a well-typed example of the variety, with aromas that follow through well on the attractively sweet palate, where fruit, acidity and extract come together well. The Cabernet Sauvignon Perticato del Novarei has intense fruit and varietal note on the nose. The clean, well-proportioned palate has good structure, although it lacks the depth of the very best vintages. Not for the first time, the top scoring white was the oak-aged Chardonnay La Piana. The green-flecked gold of the 2002 edition introduces a lavish honey and citrus nose, echoed on the palate where a grace note of attractive oaks enhances a structure of excellent depth and volume. The Sauvignon Perticato il Quadri has good varietal aromas and a lightweight body that exposes the limitations of a difficult vintage. Finally, the Malvasia Beatrice Quadri combines impressive aromas with a faint minerally note.

● C. B. Cabernet Sauvignon Sel. '00	♈♈	4*
● C. B. Merlot Sel. '01	♈♈	4*
○ C. B. Chardonnay '02	♈♈	3*
○ C. B. Pignoletto Cl. '02	♈♈	3*
● C. B. Cabernet Sauvignon '01	♈	3
● C. B. Merlot '02	♈	3
○ C. B. Pignoletto Frizzante '02	♈	3
○ C. B. Pinot Bianco '02	♈	3
○ C. B. Sauvignon '02	♈	3
○ C. B. Sauvignon Sel. '02	♈	3
● C. B. Merlot Sel. '00	♈♈	4
● C. B. Cabernet Sauvignon Sel. '99	♈♈	4

● C. P. Gutturnio La Barbona Ris. '00	♈♈	6
● C. P. Cabernet Sauvignon Perticato del Novarei '01	♈♈	6
● C. P. Gutturnio Perticato Valandrea '01	♈♈	5
● C. P. Pinot Nero Perticato Le Giastre '01	♈♈	6
○ C. P. Chardonnay Perticato La Piana '02	♈♈	5
○ C. P. Malvasia Perticato Beatrice Quadri '02	♈	5
○ C. P. Sauvignon Perticato Il Quadri '02	♈	5
● C. P. Cabernet Sauvignon Perticato del Novarei '00	♈♈	5
● C. P. Gutturnio La Barbona Ris. '99	♈♈	6

VIGOLZONE (PC)

VIGOLZONE (PC)

CONTE OTTO BARATTIERI DI SAN PIETRO
LOC. ALBAROLA
29020 VIGOLZONE (PC)
TEL. 0523875111
E-MAIL: ottobarattieri@libero.it

LA TOSA
LOC. LA TOSA
29020 VIGOLZONE (PC)
TEL. 0523870727
E-MAIL: latosa@libero.it

Under the roof of Otto Barattieri's lovely 17th-century villa, set in 40 hectares of vineyards, is a small "vinsantaia" with ten vintages of an almost impossible to find nectar, Albarola Vin Santo. The wine's origins are ancient. The empirical techniques used to make it are a precious heritage, passed down by word of mouth from one generation to the next. Albarola, considered one of Italy's classic "vin santo" wines, has never won Three Glasses, but only because so little of it is produced and certainly not because it does not deserve our top award. Obtained from malvasia di Candia grapes, it is given life by a "mother", a yeast-rich gelatinous substance that encourages fermentation and dates from 1823. For the next nine years, it will remain in small barrels, losing over half of its volume after its very long fermentation. The 1993 vintage produced 390 half-bottles (containing 37.5 centilitres) of a dense, amber wine with a heady nose and a stunning palate. The vast spectrum of aromatics is matched only by the wine's length. The 2001 Gutturnio earned Two Glasses for its lovely, complete nose and polished palate, which combines structure with freshness. The cabernet sauvignon-based Pergolo has a similar range of flavours. The 2001 has a clean nose, but the palate is a little one-dimensional and lacks depth. Best of the semi-sparkling wines from 2002 are the fragrant, fruit and alcohol Gutturnio, which is perked up by spritzy effervescence, and the attractively fresh-tasting Ortugo.

La Tosa is one of the few estates in the region that needs no introduction. We would like to stress once again that Stefano Pizzamiglio stands out for his professionalism and skill, as well as his rare ability to keep questioning what he does and why. He has absolutely no compunction about applying or adapting any of the suggestions or observations that people make. As a result, his decisions are never taken off the cuff, or influenced by fashion. Stefano thinks every move through. All this leads up to our report, which is that some of the wines tasted this year have a different style to past editions. There is less residual sugar, firmer aromas and less approachable palates, but lots more expression. The Sauvignon 2002 is exemplary. Crisp, intense varietal aromas are echoed on the juicy, well-balanced palate and there is plenty of length. Sorriso di Cielo, a monovarietal malvasia di Candia, has intense tropical fruit salad aromas and a balanced palate that is lifted by well-gauged residual sugar. The Frizzante Valnure, a fragrant mix of malvasia, trebbiano and ortrugo, almost claimed a second Glass for its inviting citrussy hints. The fruit-forward, mouthfilling Cabernet Sauvignon Luna Selvatica 2001 had to stand comparison with the marvellous 2000 version, but proved elegant and very drinkable. One very stylish, mouthfilling wine went forward to the Three Glass taste-offs. Gutturnio Vignamorello 2002 is a vineyard selection of barbera and bonarda grapes that marries character with elegance. The meaty, aroma-rich palate is a welter of exciting fruit notes.

○ C. P. Vin Santo Albarola '93	♟♟	7
● C. P. Gutturnio '01	♟♟	4*
● C. P. Cabernet Sauvignon Il Pergolo '01	♟	4
● C. P. Gutturnio Frizzante '02	♟	3
○ C. P. Ortrugo '02	♟	3
○ C. P. Vin Santo Albarola '91	♟♟	7
● Il Faggio '00	♟♟	6
○ C. P. Vin Santo Albarola '92	♟♟	7
● C. P. Cabernet Sauvignon Il Pergolo '00	♟	4

● C. P. Cabernet Sauvignon Luna Selvatica '01	♟♟	5
● C. P. Gutturnio Vignamorello '02	♟♟	4*
○ C. P. Malvasia Sorriso di Cielo '02	♟♟	4*
○ C. P. Sauvignon '02	♟♟	4*
○ C. P. Valnure Frizzante '02	♟	3
● C. P. Cabernet Sauvignon Luna Selvatica '97	♟♟♟	5
● C. P. Cabernet Sauvignon Luna Selvatica '00	♟♟	5
● C. P. Gutturnio Vignamorello '01	♟♟	4
○ C. P. Malvasia Sorriso di Cielo '01	♟♟	4

ZIANO PIACENTINO (PC)

ZIANO PIACENTINO (PC)

GAETANO LUSENTI
FRAZ. VICOBARONE
CASE PICCIONI, 57
29010 ZIANO PIACENTINO (PC)
TEL. 0523868479
E-MAIL: lodovica.lusenti@tin.it

TORRE FORNELLO
LOC. FORNELLO
29010 ZIANO PIACENTINO (PC)
TEL. 0523861001
E-MAIL: vini@torrefornello.it

Our tastings this year confirmed that quality all across the Lusenti range has improved, and that there are some excellent bottles. For years, Lodovica Lusenti has been concentrating on bonarda, releasing a single-variety wine under the name, La Picciona. The edition from 2001, the second year it was made, has a dense, purplish colour and crisp, fragrant aromas whose intense fruit is mirrored on the broad, complex palate. The deep-hued Gutturnio Cresta al Sole 2001 offers rather excessive super-ripe notes that jeopardize the fragrance of the nose, but is vigorous in the mouth, its wealth of juicy fruit nicely enhancing the palate's sweetness and balance. The Cabernet Sauvignon Villante is the wine that most impressed the panel this year. The 2000 edition is an aristocrat, with varietal aromas of black berry fruit, spices and chocolate. The palate has breadth and presence, its oak-derived elegance seamlessly mingling spices, coffee and ripe fruit. Finally, there are two good semi-sparkling wines. The fragrances of Bonarda Amabile bring together flowers and distinct notes of spice, and the Filtrato Dolce di Malvasia 2002 has citrus peel and orange blossom aromas, as well as a generously vibrant, fresh-tasting style.

Torre Fornello has 50 hectares in the heart of Valtidone, a modern cellar and a leading oenologist like Donato Lanati as consultant, so our expectations are high. That's why last year's indifferent performance raised one or two eyebrows. But this year's tastings erased that memory at a stroke. Our congratulations, then, to Enrico Sgorbati, who presented a range of wines befitting a cellar with high ambitions. There's a new release to start with. It's the intense, purple-red oak-aged Bonarda Riserva with rich flower and spice aromas that come back on the solid palate, which has a hint of astringency in the finish. The Gutturnio Riserva Diacono Gerardo is as good as ever. Clean, concentrated aromas nuanced with balsam are the prelude to a firm palate lifted by elegant spice. Sinsäl is also good. Purplish in hue, it has upfront fruit-led aromas as well as a good length on the palate. Ca' Bernesca, from barrique-aged cabernet sauvignon, is excellent. Pervasive and varietal, with well-defined structure, it offers forest fruits and spice, smooth, close-knit tannins and a very long finish. Best of the whites is Pratobianco, a skilful blend of sauvignon, malvasia and chardonnay. Its grassy hints are lifted by subtle aromas and stylish acidity lends attractive drinkability. The Malvasia Donna Luigia has a nicely defined, varietal nose and flows deliciously over the palate. The Frizzante version is also good. Self-assured on the nose, it has a delightful, faintly sweet palate.

● C. P. Cabernet Sauvignon		
Villante '00	🍷🍷	5
● C. P. Bonarda La Picciona '01	🍷🍷	4*
● C. P. Gutturnio Sup. Cresta al Sole '01	🍷🍷	4*
● C. P. Bonarda Amabile '02	🍷	3
○ Filtrato Dolce di Malvasia '02	🍷	3
● C. P. Bonarda La Picciona '00	🍷🍷	4
● C. P. Gutturnio Sup.		
Cresta al Sole '00	🍷🍷	4

● C. P. Cabernet Sauvignon		
Ca' Bernesca '01	🍷🍷	6
● C. P. Bonarda Ris. '00	🍷🍷	5
● C. P. Gutturnio		
Diacono Gerardo 1028 Ris. '01	🍷🍷	5
● C. P. Gutturnio Sup. Sinsäl '02	🍷🍷	4*
○ Pratobianco '02	🍷🍷	4*
● C. P. Bonarda Frizzante '02	🍷	4
○ C. P. Malvasia Donna Luigia '02	🍷	4
○ C. P. Malvasia Secca Frizzante '02	🍷	3
● C. P. Cabernet Sauvignon		
Ca' Bernesca '00	🍷🍷	6
● C. P. Gutturnio		
Diacono Gerardo 1028 Ris. '00	🍷🍷	5

ZOLA PREDOSA (BO)

MARIA LETIZIA GAGGIOLI - VIGNETO BAGAZZANA
VIA RAIBOLINI DETTO IL FRANCIA, 55
40069 ZOLA PREDOSA (BO)
TEL. 051753489 - 0516189198
E-MAIL: nmygag@tin.it

Maria Letizia Gaggioli and her father, Carlo, release a very large number of wines. They're all good products, although some have evidently suffered from the poor 2002 vintage. The new Il Francia Bianco impressed our tasters. This wine, from barrique-fermented sauvignon, pignoletto and chardonnay, has a lovely nose of ripe fruit, herbs and spring flowers, rounded off with a faint toastiness. Breadth and intensity on the palate take you through to a distinctly soft finish, barely marked by a faint note of bitterness. In contrast, Il Francia Rosso 2000 is a monovarietal barrique-aged Cabernet Sauvignon. The nose of full, ripe fruit is veined with subtle spices. Full and flavoursome in the mouth, it has good texture and is very drinkable. The Merlot has red berry fruit on the nose and a palate of balance and firm, attractive structure. The cabernet and merlot Rosso Bagazzana is light and well proportioned. The tasty Pinot Bianco Crilò 2002 has good texture and an attractive nose, whereas the Chardonnay Lavinio has decent body and flavour. Although undeniably concentrated, it is a little short on fragrance and freshness. The white peach and fresh flower Pignoletto Superiore has nice structure and length, but lacks elegance. The Frizzante version has flowers on the nose and a light palate, whereas the pignoletto, chardonnay and pinot bianco Francia Brut is more intense and evolved.

ZOLA PREDOSA (BO)

VIGNETO DELLE TERRE ROSSE
VIA PREDOSA, 83
40068 ZOLA PREDOSA (BO)
TEL. 051755845 - 051759649

The Vallania family have never abandoned their tradition of vinifying both whites and reds exclusively in stainless steel tanks. From the broad range of wines tasted, the panel picked out the Cabernet Sauvignon Cuvée 1999, which matures without hurry. Its clean, elegant, intensely fruity aromas introduce a stylish texture in the mouth, with a close-knit tannic weave. It never threatens to become soft or vanillaed, and in fact is distinctly austere, signing off with a hint of tar. The Merlot Petroso 2000 is extremely elegant on the broad, balanced palate, its full, ripe black berry fruit lingering unhurriedly. The Grannero is attractive. A fragrant red berry and spice Pinot Nero, it is assertive and tasty in the mouth, then the finish is a shade dry. Cherries in alcohol are the hallmark aroma of the Cabernet Sauvignon, which is a little too alcoholic and super-ripe. The close-knit tannins are also a little hard. The Chardonnay Cuvée 2000 is stunningly intense and creamy rich on the nose. The full, fatty palate is backed up by well-judged acidity that has enabled it to evolve yet stay attractively fresh. Admirable finesse and complexity are the distinguishing features of the Riesling Malagò 2002, whose restrained minerality and good ripe fruit expand deliciously over the palate with style and tangy flavour. The Chardonnay 2002 is delicately fruity and deliciously fragrant. Finally, the Vendemmia Tardiva Riesling 2000 is not fully ripe, although the mineral notes are tempting and the finish has a hint of sweetness.

O Il Francia Bianco '02	♟♟	4*
● C. B. Merlot '02	♟♟	4*
● C. B. Cabernet Sauvignon Il Francia Rosso Ris. '00	♟	4
● Bagazzana Rosso '02	♟	4
O C. B. Chardonnay Lavinio '02	♟	3
O C. B. Pignoletto Sup. '02	♟	3
O C. B. Pinot Bianco Crilò '02	♟	3
O C. B. Sauvignon Sup. '02	♟	3
O Il Francia Brut	♟	4
● C. B. Cabernet Sauvignon '02		4
O C. B. Pignoletto Frizzante '02		3
● C. B. Merlot '01	♟♟	4

● C. B. Cabernet Sauvignon Cuvée '99	♟	6
O C. B. Chardonnay Cuvée '00	♟♟	4
● Grannero Pinot Nero '00	♟♟	4
● Petroso Merlot '00	♟♟	4
O C. B. Riesling Malagò '02	♟♟	4
● C. B. Cabernet Sauvignon '00	♟	5
O C. B. Riesling Malagò V. T. '00	♟	5
O C. B. Chardonnay '02	♟	4
O C. B. Sauvignon '02		4
● C. B. Cabernet Sauvignon Cuvée '98	♟♟	6
● C. B. Cabernet Sauvignon '99	♟♟	5

OTHER WINERIES

ERIOLI
VIA MONTEVEGLIO, 64
40053 BAZZANO (BO)
TEL. 051830103

Giorgio Erioli usually gives the panel a very fine Cabernet Sauvignon from his small, beautifully tended vineyard. The 2000 edition has intense bottled morello cherries, a firm palate, good depth and remarkable length.

● C. B. Cabernet Sauvignon		
Terre di Montebudello Ris. '00	🍷🍷	4
● C. B. Cabernet Sauvignon Ris. '99	🍷🍷	4

TENUTA DIAVOLETTO
VIA PAVOLOTTA, 298
47032 BERTINORO (FC)
TEL. 0543445177

This recently founded winery is in the hills of Bertinoro and Polenta. The excellent Leonardo Conti is the winemaker. Mastro Guido 2000 is an elegantly convincing Sangiovese with intense ripe berry fruit and a juicy, velvet-smooth mouthfeel. The Baccanale 2002 is less challenging but still good.

● Sangiovese di Romagna Sup.		
Mastro Guido '00	🍷🍷	4*
● Sangiovese di Romagna Sup.		
Baccanale '02	🍷	3

TENUTA LA VIOLA
VIA COLOMBARONE, 888
47032 BERTINORO (FC)
TEL. 0543445496
E-MAIL: info@tenutalaviola.it

The future looks good for Stefano Gabellini's winery. We enjoyed the two vintages of Colombarone for both are stupendously drinkable. The 2002, in particular, shows intense, ripe berry aromas and good depth. The Riserva 2000 is more complex and evolved.

● Sangiovese di Romagna Sup.		
Il Colombarone '01	🍷🍷	3*
● Sangiovese di Romagna Sup.		
Il Colombarone '02	🍷🍷	3*
● Sangiovese di Romagna Sup. La Badia Ris. '00	🍷	4

CANTINA SOCIALE VALTIDONE
VIA MORETTA, 58
29010 BORGONOVO VAL TIDONE (PC)
TEL. 0523862168
E-MAIL: cantinavaltidone@libero.it

The best of the wines from this major co-operative winery is the Malvasia Passito Luna di Candia 2001, which has tempting candied peel and a sumptuous mouthfeel. The Gutturnio Julius 2000 is full and balanced, whereas the upfront Sauvignon Costa Solara 2002 has a nice nose and reasonable texture.

○ C. P. Malvasia Passito		
Luna di Candia '01	🍷🍷	4*
● C. P. Gutturnio Cl. Julius '00	🍷	3
○ C. P. Sauvignon Costa Solara '02	🍷	3

RONTANA
VIA RONTANA, 50
48013 BRISIGHELLA (RA)
TEL. 030736094
E-MAIL: rontana@libero.it

The Ricci Curbastro family earned their winemaking spurs in Franciacorta and have made a good start in their native Brisighella. Colle Torre Monte 2000, a 40-40-20 blend of cabernet, sangiovese and merlot, has intense, ripe fruit and a full palate. Col Mora is fresh, light and balanced.

● Colli di Faenza Rosso Colle Torre Monte Ris. '00	🍷🍷	5
● Colli di Faenza Sangiovese Col Mora '00	🍷	4

VIGNE DEI BOSCHI
VIA TURA, 7/A
48013 BRISIGHELLA (RA)
TEL. 054651648
E-MAIL: vignedeiboschi@libero.it

Brothers Paolo and Leonardo Babini have ten hectares of high-density vines. Their malbo, merlot and sangiovese went into 1,600 bottles of a lovely wine that came very close to a third Glass. Intense bramble and liquorice introduce a convincing, rock-solid structure and a very long finish.

● Sette Pievi '01	🍷🍷	3*

CANTINE COOPERATIVE RIUNITE
VIA G. BRODOLINI, 24
42040 CAMPEGINE (RE)
TEL. 0522905711
E-MAIL: info@riunite.it

Fruity, fragrant Ottocento Nero is a well-made wine with good body and alcohol. The cellar also offers a well-structured, fresh-tasting Reggiano from the new Cantina del Gallo line and a velvety Cuvée dei Fondatori selection of Grasparossa Amabile Cinghio del Fojonco.

● Lambrusco Grasparossadi Castelvetro Amabile Cinghio del Fojonco	🍷	3
● Lambrusco Ottocento Nero	🍷	3
● Reggiano Lambrusco Inchiostro Cantina del Gallo	🍷	2

FATTORIA CAMERONE
LOC. BIANCANIGO - VIA BIANCANIGO, 1485
48014 CASTEL BOLOGNESE (RA)
TEL. 054650434
E-MAIL: info@fattoriacamerone.it

Good results from Giuseppe Marabini's cellar. Millennium '99, a successful blend of sangiovese and cabernet, is convincingly structured, with austere, lingering aromas. Rosso del Camerone '98 nearly won a second Glass. Oak-aged for two years, it has good body, enhanced by well-gauged acidity.

● Sangiovese di Romagna Sup. Millennium Ris. '99	🍷🍷	4*
● Sangiovese di Romagna Sup. Rosso del Camerone Ris. '98	🍷	4

GIUSEPPE BEGHELLI
VIA CASTELLO, 2257
40050 CASTELLO DI SERRAVALLE (BO)
TEL. 0516704786
E-MAIL: beghelli@collibolognesi.com

Barbera Riserva 2000 is barrique aged and offers a swathe of fruity, faintly spicy, aromas. The varietal palate has enough acidity to make it tempting. The Pignoletto Classico is full, long and very pleasant, while the Sauvignon 2002 has crisp, varietal aromas and pleasing freshness.

● C. B. Barbera Ris. '00	🍷🍷	3*
○ C. B. Pignoletto Cl. '02	🍷	2
○ C. B. Sauvignon '02	🍷	2

VIRGILIO SANDONI
VIA VALLE DEL SAMOGGIA, 780
40050 CASTELLO DI SERRAVALLE (BO)
TEL. 0516703188
E-MAIL: virgiliosandoni@libero.it

Virgilio Sandoni has shown he knows how to make reds. His Cabernet Sauvignon 2001 is intense and clean, with crisp berry fruit and a hint of liquorice. The palate is full, austere and very long. The tasty, fruit-led Barbera Frizzante 2000 is well-made and traditional in style.

● Cabernet Sauvignon '01	🍷🍷	4*
● C. B. Barbera Frizzante '00	🍷	3

TENUTA AMALIA
LOC. DIEGARO DI CESENA - VIA EMILIA PONENTE, 2619
47023 CESENA (FC)
TEL. 0547347037
E-MAIL: cantces@tin.it

Tenuta Amalia has three good Sangioveses. The organic-grape Tito from the San Martino line is forthright on the palate and fresh on the nose. The soft, fruity Riserva Pergami 2000 shows good breadth, and the well-structured Le Case Rosse 2001 offers intense ripe fruit, spice and liquorice.

● Sangiovese di Romagna Tito San Martino '01	▼▼ 3*
● Sangiovese di Romagna Pergami Ris. '00	▼ 4
● Sangiovese di Romagna Sup. Le Case Rosse '01	▼ 4

MONTE DELLE VIGNE
LOC. OZZANO TARO - VIA COSTA, 27
43046 COLLECCHIO (PR)
TEL. 0521809105
E-MAIL: montedellevigne@libero.it

The barbera and merlot Nabucco 2001 is again the finest red in the Colli di Parma DOC zone. The nose is austere, the palate deep and long. The two Frizzante 2002 wines are well made. The Sauvignon is very varietal and fresh tasting, and the Malvasia Frizzante has decent pulp and nice thrust.

● Nabucco '01	▼▼ 5
○ Colli di Parma Malvasia Frizzante '02	▼ 3
○ Colli di Parma Sauvignon Frizzante '02	▼ 3
● Nabucco '00	▼▼ 5

PODERE VECCIANO
VIA CHE GUEVARA, 19
47853 CORIANO (RN)
TEL. 0541658388
E-MAIL: poderevecciano@libero.it

The 2001 vintage brought excellent results at Podere Vecciano, in the hills near Rimini. VignalaVolta is a successful, full-bodied 70-30 blend of barrique-aged sangiovese and cabernet sauvignon. Even more exciting is VignalMonte, a Sangiovese with warm, intense fruit aromas and a velvet mouthfeel.

● Colli di Rimini Rosso VignalaVolta '01	▼▼ 4
● Sangiovese di Romagna Sup. VignalMonte '01	▼▼ 4

TENUTA GODENZA
FRAZ. S. LORENZO IN NOCETO - V.LE DELL'APPENNINO, 654
47100 FORLÌ
TEL. 0543488424
E-MAIL: info@tenutagodenza.it

The complex Alfiere 2001 aged in barrique for 12 months. Elegant ripe fruit and spice usher in an austere, full palate with great length. The Sangiovese Gaudentia shows ripe cherry and a flavoursome palate with smooth, close-knit tannins. The 2000 Riserva Mirus is delicious and nicely balanced.

● Alfiere Cabernet Sauvignon '01	▼▼ 5
● Sangiovese di Romagna Sup. Gaudentia '01	▼▼ 4*
● Sangiovese di Romagna Sup. Mirus Ris. '00	▼ 5

LA MACOLINA
LOC. MONTECATONE
VIA PIEVE SANT'ANDREA, 2
40026 IMOLA (BO)
TEL. 051940234

The 2000 Museum, from sangiovese, cabernet and merlot, is the best version ever. The nose offers berry fruit, liquorice and spices, then the firm palate has balance, finesse and appeal. The Sangiovese Riserva is light and very drinkable. The 1998 Albana Passito is delicious, with nice sweetness.

● Museum '00	▼▼ 5
○ Albana di Romagna Passito La Dolce Vita '98	▼ 5
● Sangiovese di Romagna Ris. '00	▼ 4

TENUTA CA' LUNGA
VIA CA' LUNGA BUORE, 5
40026 IMOLA (BO)
TEL. 0542609257
E-MAIL: paolo@tenutacalunga.it

Paolo Cassetta has revolutionized his family estate, with help from agronomist, Remigio Bordini, and winemaker, Lorenzo Landi. Results are already coming through. Mistero 2002 is a fresh, fruity Sangiovese, and the Riserva 2001 is fuller and more rounded, with a ripe berry fruit and liquorice nose.

● Sangiovese di Romagna Ris. '01	▼▼ 4*
● Sangiovese di Romagna Sup. Mistero '02	▼▼ 4*
○ Colli d'Imola Bianco Euforia '02	3

TENUTA POGGIO POLLINO
VIA MONTE MELDOLA, 2/T
40026 IMOLA (BO)
TEL. 0522942135
E-MAIL: medici@medici.it

Tenuta Poggio Pollino is progressing under oenologist, Carlo Corino. The cabernet and sangiovese Terre di Maestrale 2001 has intense fruit, good body and drinkability. Campo Rosso 2000 is well structured and full bodied, with a long, soft finish. Fresh and well made sums up Vigna di Cambro 2001.

● Sangiovese di Romagna		
Campo Rosso Ris. '00	♟♟	4*
● Colli di Imola Terre di Maestrale '01	♟♟	4*
● Sangiovese di Romagna		
Vigna di Cambro '01	♟	3

ISIDORO LAMORETTI
FRAZ. CASATICO - S.DA DELLA NAVE, 6
43013 LANGHIRANO (PR)
TEL. 0521863590 - 052143013
E-MAIL: lamoretti@tin.it

It was a less than exciting year at Lamoretti. The new edition of the red Vinnalunga was not released, so we'll talk about the semi-sparkling wines. The well-typed Malvasia 2002 has spritzy sparkle and a bitterish finish. The fat, creamy palate of the Moscato 2002 is perked up by nice acidity.

○ Colli di Parma Malvasia		
Frizzante '02	♟	2
○ Moscato '02	♟	2

VILLA DI CORLO
LOC. BAGGIOVARA - S.DA CAVEZZO, 200
41041 MODENA
TEL. 059510736
E-MAIL: info@villadicorlo.com

Villa di Corlo releases two very different wines. One is the traditional, well-made Grasparossa, a fresh, fragrant, medium-bodied wine, and the other is Corleto. Created by oenologist, Luca D'Attoma, it is a well-structured Lambrusco with lots of fruit, good breadth and exciting ageing potential.

● Corleto	♟	3
● Lambrusco Grasparossa		
di Castelvetro	♟	3

CA' SELVATICA
VIA MARZATORE, 16
40050 MONTEVEGLIO (BO)
TEL. 051831837
E-MAIL: caselvatica1@virgilio.it

The 1999 edition of the flagship Barbera Riserva Cabasà is again well-structured, with evolved fruit preserve and spice aromas, then length on the firm palate. The Cabernet Vigna del Falco Nero from the same vintage has good body and definition, as well as an austere personality.

● C. B. Barbera Montebudello		
Sopra i Fichi Cabasà Ris. '99	♟♟	5
● C. B. Cabernet Sauvignon		
Vigna del Falco Nero '99	♟	4

GRADIZZOLO OGNIBENE
VIA INVERNATA, 2
40050 MONTEVEGLIO (BO)
TEL. 051830265 - 051832663
E-MAIL: vinicolaognibene@libero.it

Antonio Ognibene's vines have excellent positions on east-facing hillsides at altitudes of between 200 and 300 metres. This year's good range is led by the Merlot Calastrino. But the Barbera Riserva 2000 is below par, and the standard-label 2001 Barbera is predictable and high on acidity.

● C. B. Merlot Calastrino '01	♟♟	5
● C. B. Barbera Ris. '00	♟	4
● C. B. Barbera '01	♟	3
● C. B. Barbera Ris. '99	♟♟	4*

TENUTA LA TORRETTA
LOC. LA TORRETTA, 62
29010 NIBBIANO VAL TIDONE (PC)
TEL. 0523997008
E-MAIL: tenuta.latorretta@tin.it

Tenuta La Torretta is going places. The best product is the long, full-textured, balsamic Cabernet Sauvignon 2000. The Gutturnio Vigna della Villa 2000 is well made. Still closed on the nose, it has lovely concentration and spice. The Gutturnio Classico 2002 is undemanding and temptingly fruity.

● C. P. Cabernet Sauvignon '00	♟♟	4*
● C. P. Gutturnio		
Vigna della Villa '00	♟	4
● C. P. Gutturnio Cl. '02	♟	3

CANTINE DALL'ASTA
VIA TOSCANA, 47
43100 PARMA
TEL. 0521484086
E-MAIL: cantinedallasta@libero.it

Not for the first time, Mefistofele is one of the region's finest Lambruscos. Intense in hue, with exuberant ripe berry fruit aromas, it has good freshness on the attractively balanced palate. Rich fruit and nice texture are the hallmarks of Le Viole. The Malvasia Torrechiara is nice and fresh.

○	Colli di Parma Malvasia Torrechiara '02	🍷	2
●	Lambrusco dell'Emilia Le Viole '02	🍷	2
●	Lambrusco dell'Emilia Mefistofele '02	🍷	2*

OPPIZZI
LOC. FRAVICA, 191
29010 PIANELLO VAL TIDONE (PC)
TEL. 0523997475

One of the nicest surprises on this year's round of tastings was Oppizzi's Gutturnio Riserva 2000. We sampled it several times, and it was always deliciously soft, with lots of very ripe fruit and a coffee and spice finish. Only 1,400 bottles were released, at a very attractive price.

●	C. P. Gutturnio Ris. '00	🍷🍷	3*

PODERE RIOSTO
VIA DI RIOSTO, 12
40065 PIANORO (BO)
TEL. 051777109 - 051774888
E-MAIL: vendite@podereriosto.it

The Franceschini Galletti family wines are constantly improving. The fresh, fragrant Pignoletto Frizzante is one of the best of its type to be found around Bologna. The still version is even better, showing generous flavours and great length.

○	C. B. Pignoletto Sup. Vigna della Torre '02	🍷🍷	3*
○	C. B. Pignoletto Frizzante Vigna della Torre '02	🍷	3
○	C. B. Sauvignon Vigna del Pino '02	🍷	4

BARACCONE
LOC. CA' DEI MORTI, 1
29028 PONTE DELL'OLIO (PC)
TEL. 0523877147
E-MAIL: cantina.baraccone@libero.it

This small Val Nure winery continues to turn out noteworthy wines. The Gutturnio Riserva Ronco Alto 2000 lived up to expectations by winning Two Glasses for its complex structure and thrust on the palate. As ever, the exuberant Gutturno Frizzante sparkler and the fresh Zagaia are very attractive.

●	C. P. Gutturnio Ronco Alto Ris. '00	🍷🍷	5
●	C. P. Gutturnio Frizzante '02	🍷	3
○	Zagaia Frizzante '02	🍷	3

PERINELLI
LOC. I PERINELLI
29028 PONTE DELL'OLIO (PC)
TEL. 0523571610
E-MAIL: info@perinelli.it

The wines from this 17-hectare estate are interesting. Vigna Vecchia 2001 is a blend of pinot nero, cabernet and barbera with raspberry aromas, great extract and thrust on the palate. The Gutturnio Vivace 2002 is also nice. It has clean aromas and a tangy palate, ending on a fresh, fruity note.

●	Vigna Vecchia '01	🍷🍷	4*
●	C. P. Gutturnio '01	🍷	3
●	C. P. Gutturnio Vivace '02	🍷	3

CASETTO DEI MANDORLI
LOC. PREDAPPIO ALTA - VIA UMBERTO I, 21
47016 PREDAPPIO (FC)
TEL. 0543922361
E-MAIL: casetto@tin.it

The well-made Riggiano 2000 is an unusual blend of sangiovese and terrano. Violet aromas usher in a soft, well-structured palate. The light, slightly acidic, Sangiovese Riserva Vigna del Generale '99 is traditional. Intense fruit, introducing a soft mouthfeel, characterizes the Tre Rocche 2002.

●	Riggiano '00	🍷🍷	4*
●	Sangiovese di Romagna Sup. Tre Rocche '02	🍷	4
●	Sangiovese di Romagna Vigna del Generale Ris. '99	🍷	5

CA' DE' MEDICI
LOC. CADE - VIA DELLA STAZIONE, 32
42040 REGGIO EMILIA
TEL. 0522942141 - 0522941089
E-MAIL: cademedici@cademedici.it

Terra Calda is obtained from a careful selection of the finest hillside lambrusco fruit. The result is one of the best Lambruscos in the region, a full-bodied, aroma-rich, attractively textured wine. The simpler, but still well-made, Piazza San Prospero is refreshingly fruity.

● Terra Calda Rosso Frizzante	♀	3
● Reggiano Lambrusco		
Piazza San Prospero	♀	2*

TENUTA UCCELLINA
VIA GARIBALDI, 51
48026 RUSSI (RA)
TEL. 0544580144

Burson 2000, a Longanesi-based wine, is the cellar's best, with intense aromas and length on the palate. The Albana Passito 2001 has an odd hint of cinchona. Mouthfilling and balanced on the palate, it is a little bitter in the finish. The Sangiovese Riserva 2000 is evolved and alcohol-rich.

● Burson '00	♀♀	3*
● Sangiovese di Romagna Ris. '00	♀	4
○ Albana di Romagna Passito '01	♀	5

CONSORZIO VINI TIPICI DI SAN MARINO
LOC. BORGO MAGGIORE - VIA SERRABOLINO, 89
47890 SAN MARINO
TEL. 0549903124
E-MAIL: mail@consorziovini.sm

About 300 growers on Monte Titano belong to the only winery in the republic of San Marino. Brugneto 2000 is a nice Sangiovese with elegant spice aromas and an austere, lingering palate. The mainly sangiovese Tessano '99 is a little forward, but the Moscato Passito 2001 is intense and attractive.

● San Marino Brugneto '00	♀♀	3*
○ Moscato Passito Oro dei Goti '01	♀	4
● San Marino Tessano Ris. '99	♀	4

CANTINE CAVICCHIOLI & FIGLI
P.ZZA A. GRAMSCI, 9
41030 SAN PROSPERO (MO)
TEL. 059812411
E-MAIL: cantine@cavicchioli.it

The lambrusco salamino-based Robanera is refreshing, full-bodied and tannin-rich, with a nice soft finish. The Grasparossa Amabile from the historic Tre Medaglie line is dry, youthfully alcoholic and delicious, while the light, well-made Sorbara offers intense fruit.

● Lambrusco di Sorbara		
Tre Medaglie	♀	2*
● Lambrusco Grasparossa di		
Castelvetro Amabile Tre Medaglie	♀	2*
● Robanera	♀	3

MORO - RINALDINI
FRAZ. CALERNO - VIA ANDREA RIVASI, 27
42040 SANT'ILARIO D'ENZA (RE)
TEL. 0522679190
E-MAIL: info@rinaldinivini.it

Vigna del Picchio 2000, a late-harvest lambrusco Maestri and ancellotta wine, is full-bodied and distinctly acidic. Moro del Moro '99 is from raisined lambrusco pjcol ross and ancellotta. It has port-like structure and bottled fruit aromas. The Metodo Classico Arita is uncomplicated but well made.

● Vigna del Picchio '00	♀	5
● Moro del Moro '99	♀	6
○ Reggiano Lambrusco Bianco		
Spumante Brut Arita	♀	3

COLONNA - VINI SPALLETTI
VIA SOGLIANO, 100
47039 SAVIGNANO SUL RUBICONE (FC)
TEL. 0541945111 - 0541943446
E-MAIL: spalletticolonna@libero.it

Maolù 2001 is intense, alcohol-rich and moderately sweet, with a delicious candied peel finish. The intense, if a little dry, Villa Rasponi 2000 has vegetal, over-ripe aromas. Finally, the slightly astringent Monaco di Ribano has a spicy, faintly gamey nose.

○ Albana di Romagna Passito		
Maolù '01	♀♀	5
● Il Monaco di Ribano Cabernet '00	♀	5
● Sangiovese di Romagna Sup.		
Villa Rasponi Ris. '00	♀	4

TUSCANY

With 62 Three Glass awards, Tuscany has, for the second time running, won more of our top prizes than any other region of Italy. This is not so strange when you think that it is one of the most important wine regions in the world. What is worth noting, however, is that Tuscany is no longer defined by just one or two serious winemaking areas. Until a few years ago, there was the large and celebrated Chianti zone, Montalcino, Montepulciano and not much else. Now we know that Bolgheri has taken off, Sassicaia having shown them how it's done, but the Val di Cornia zone, not many kilometres to the south, is also providing some very nice surprises. The Maremma di Grosseto has, over the past ten years or so, become the new frontier for first-rate Tuscan wine. Moving inland, we see that new DOC zones like Monteregio, Montecucco and Orcia, are springing up. And even in some areas that no one used to consider suitable for great viticulture, such as the province of Arezzo and the hinterland of Pisa, there are new producers making formidable products. If you add to all this the fact that Carmignano is rapidly modernizing its winegrowing methods, Rufina is doing likewise, and that, even in places like the countryside around Lucca and the inland area near Massa, there are signs of serious quality, it becomes clear that, apart from the odd intractable mountain top and the uncompromising aridity of the Crete Senesi hills, there are DOC zones and wine estates in every corner of this region. So far so good. But there are also problems, and the incorrigible individualism of some producers is responsible for a number of them. Tuscany is home to the Supertuscans, top-of-the-range designer wines that just about every winery produces, and which scorn such niceties as DOC(G) regulations, typicity or terroir. The great Tuscan wines, with the sole exception of Brunello di Montalcino, are, as it were, made to measure. They are the exclusive creations of individual wineries, rather like a haute couture gown. And this involves shunning traditional grape varieties, familiar tastes and local characteristics. The wines, which are often excellent, are almost always breathtakingly expensive. Generally, they are wines without a homeland. It's time for these products to return to their roots. What Tuscan producers need to do in the next few years is to make wines that express a sense of moderation, and give at least some suggestion of actually belonging to the land.

AREZZO

AREZZO

FATTORIA SAN FABIANO - BORGHINI
BALDOVINETTI
LOC. SAN FABIANO
52100 AREZZO
TEL. 057524566
E-MAIL: info@fattoriasanfabiano.it

VILLA CILNIA
FRAZ. BAGNORO
LOC. MONTONCELLO, 27
52040 AREZZO
TEL. 0575365017
E-MAIL: villacilnia@interffre.it

The historic Fattoria San Fabiano winery belongs to the Conti Borghini Baldovinetti De' Bacci and covers 650 hectares, 150 of which are under vine. Part of the estate is in the hills near the ancient walls of Arezzo, and part at the nearby Tenuta di Campriano and the Tenuta Poggio Uliveto at Montepulciano. They have won back a full Guide profile with the release of the '00 version of their standard-bearer, Armaiolo, which was not ready in time for last year's tastings. And indeed a wine of such character makes all the difference to the ranking of an estate. Made from equal parts of sangiovese and cabernet, it shows a nicely concentrated, deep ruby colour and a rich, complex nose featuring black berry fruit mingling well with pleasing vegetal notes and hints of bell pepper and coffee. Only a faintly unripe note in the tannins blemishes the dense, long-lasting palate and prevented the wine from going through to the finals. The Piocaia '01, a blend of sangiovese, cabernet and merlot, is good this time. It combines enjoyable quaffability with hefty structure and impeccably clean execution. Despite a less than felicitous vintage, the '02s are both well focused. The Chianti is fruity and easy to drink, and the white Chiaro, made from chardonnay and trebbiano, is crisp and light with hints of peach and sage. The Nobile di Montepulciano Poggio Uliveto '99, which is fairly traditional in style, shows distinct signs of over-evolution.

Villa Cilnia, which lies on the hillslopes just outside Arezzo, presented a very respectable series of wines, albeit slightly less positive than last year's. The Chianti Colli Aretini '01 offers lovely fruity notes on the nose, then fine-grained tannins and some forward notes in the mouth. While the Riserva '00 is full-bodied, the tannins are somewhat unripe and hard, making for a less than harmonious palate. The other wines did better, from the attractive sangiovese-based Ross'Oro '01, which is soft and warm on the palate with a slightly astringent finish, to the two prestige bottles, Cign'Oro '00 and Vocato '00. Both earned Two Glasses. The former, half sangiovese and a quarter each of cabernet and merlot, has a beautiful deep, intense ruby and a distinctive bouquet with notes of coffee and tamarind, as well as some vegetal hints. In the mouth it is succulent, dense, seductive and fairly well-balanced, but the finish is a bit rigid. The Vocato, mostly sangiovese with a little cabernet, is harmonious and well executed, with delightful fruit and balsamic aromas mirrored on the nicely substantial palate. It's wine that has opted for elegance rather than power.

● Armaiolo '00	🍷🍷	6
● Piocaia '01	🍷🍷	4*
● Chianti '02	🍷	3*
○ Chiaro '02	🍷	3*
● Nobile di Montepulciano Poggio Uliveto '99		5
● Armaiolo '97	🍷🍷	5
● Armaiolo '98	🍷🍷	5
● Armaiolo '99	🍷🍷	6
● Piocaia '00	🍷	4
● Chianti '01	🍷	3

● Cign'Oro '00	🍷🍷	5
● Vocato '00	🍷🍷	5
● Chianti Colli Aretini Ris. '00	🍷	4
● Chianti Colli Aretini '01	🍷	3*
● Ross'Oro '01	🍷	3*
● Cign'Oro '98	🍷🍷	5
● Chianti Colli Aretini '00	🍷🍷	3*
● Chianti Colli Aretini Ris. '99	🍷🍷	4*
● Vocato '99	🍷🍷	4
● Cign'Oro '99	🍷	5

BAGNO A RIPOLI (FI)

LE SORGENTI
LOC. VALLINA
VIA DI DOCCIOLA, 8
50012 BAGNO A RIPOLI (FI)
TEL. 055696004
E-MAIL: info@fattoria-lesorgenti.com

The Ferrari family is sure to be pleased. Their top wine, Scirus '01, made it to our finals, where it was a credit to its makers. In fact, all of the Ferrari wines were excellent, which promises very well indeed. But let's get down to the wines themselves, proof of the dedication lavished by the owners and their oenologist, Paolo Caciorgna. We'll start with that finalist, made from equal parts of merlot and cabernet sauvignon. Opaque to the eye, it is agreeably redolent of wild berries, with blackcurrant to the fore, rounded off by elegant notes of chocolate. The palate is soft, enticing and round, without intrusive harshness. The tannins have been absorbed perfectly into the structure and the finish shows enchanting spicy notes. The Sghiras '02, made from chardonnay with a touch of sauvignon, presents a pleasing bouquet of spring flowers and clear refreshing notes of aromatic herbs. On the palate, fine acidic sinew bolsters the solid body and the finish has very decent length. The Colli Fiorentini '01 is characterized by gamey scents of leather and animal skins, alternating with fruity notes of cherry and plum. The tannins make their presence felt, and so does the acidity, but the contrast is enjoyable. The finish is juicy, warm and lingering. The appealing Calicò Brut '99 displays classic aromas of crusty bread and aromatic herbs, well-calibrated sparkle and notable acidity, nicely balanced by an appropriately soft body. The finish is good and long.

BAGNO A RIPOLI (FI)

PETRETO
VIA ROSANO, 196/A
50012 BAGNO A RIPOLI (FI)
TEL. 0556519021

The Fonseca family have pulled off no mean achievement. It cannot be easy, on the banks of the Arno in the great wine country between Florence and Rufina, to set about making a botrytized white wine. But this is precisely what they did, thanks to their enduring friendship with Nicolò D'Afflitto, still their oenologist and the man who recognized the winemaking potential of this area and its site climates. So where once the classic Chianti grapes flourished, the Fonsecas planted sauvignon and sémillon. The results are nothing short of miraculous. It is interesting to see how each vintage is distinctive in bouquet, flavour and even appearance, because of the great sensitivity of the grapes to the local conditions. The '99 Pourriture Noble displays attractive citrus aromas and a pleasingly seductive palate, nicely underpinned by acidity. The '00 has more noticeable honey and resin on the nose, and is creamy and enticing in the mouth. The '01 reveals fresh notes of peach and apricot, mingling with a flowery fragrance. The attack on the palate is fleshy, powerful and rich, and the length is excellent. The mostly merlot Bocciolè '01 performed well. A lovely vivid ruby introduces a nose remarkable for the strength and complexity of its fruit, with bilberry and blackberry enhanced by notes of cinnamon. After a good attack, the full-bodied palate unfolds to reveal densely packed and enjoyable tannins and a succulent, lingering finish.

● Scirus '01	🍷🍷	6
● Chianti Colli Fiorentini '01	🍷	4
○ Sghiras '02	🍷	4
○ Calicò Brut '99	🍷	5
● Scirus '98	🍷🍷	5
● Scirus '99	🍷🍷	5
● Scirus '00	🍷🍷	6

○ Pourriture Noble '00	🍷🍷	6
● Bocciolè '01	🍷🍷	5
○ Pourriture Noble '01	🍷🍷	6
○ Pourriture Noble '99	🍷🍷	6

BARBERINO VAL D'ELSA (FI) BARBERINO VAL D'ELSA (FI)

CASA EMMA
S. P. DI CASTELLINA IN CHIANTI, 3
50021 BARBERINO VAL D'ELSA (FI)
TEL. 0558072859 - 0558072859
E-MAIL: casaemma@casaemma.com

CASTELLO DELLA PANERETTA
LOC. MONSANTO
S.DA DELLA PANERETTA, 35
50021 BARBERINO VAL D'ELSA (FI)
TEL. 0558059003 - 0558059050
E-MAIL: stefano.paneretta@tin.it

In the absence of Soloìo '01, which was not yet ready for us, Casa Emma at Barberino Val d'Elsa presented only their two Chianti Classicos at our tastings. The Riserva '00 is unquestionably in the style of this winery, which enjoys the advice of the oenologist Nicolò D'Afflitto. It's a meaty, concentrated red and if it seems a little uncertain on the nose at first, a few minutes of breathing time in the glass takes care of the problem. The palate is very confident, engrossing and dense. Perhaps it's a bit one-dimensional, but it does have lots of depth. The Chianti Classico '01 is simpler and a touch dilute, but enjoyable and easy to drink. It's a fragrant red, but lacking in contrasts on nose and palate, and only vaguely suggestive of Chianti. In short, estate style has the upper hand over terroir, and although this makes their wines immediately identifiable, you might have a hard time placing them to a specific Chianti zone. These, however, are only minor quibbles at this level of quality. The estate production as a whole is quite a bit better than just acceptable, and if we were to criticize one thing, it would not be the quality of the wines, but their price, which is not exactly consumer-friendly.

The most important news about this winery is that they have now engaged Nicolò D'Afflitto as their consultant oenologist. Meanwhile, they remain true to their winemaking philosophy, which means they make no concessions to fashion but follow a carefully devised plan, involving the creation of wines with personality that stand out in the company of their peers throughout the country. At this year's tastings, we found the Chianti Classico '01 to be a little under the weather. An intense ruby introduces the less than well-defined nose, where vegetal elements dominate the light fruit. The palate reveals good weight, although balance is tenuous and the acidity, while enjoyable, is a little excessive. On the other hand, Terrine '00, a blend of sangiovese and canaiolo, did very well. The vivid purple hue introduces a lively and intense, if simple, nose, with wild berries coming through well. The palate is dense, showing both sinew and structure, and tightly packed tannins unfold slowly in a firm, mouthfilling palate with an enjoyable, lingering finish. The Vin Santo '98 is a lovely intense gold, opening on the nose with very lively notes of orange that lead to powerful fruity aromas of dried figs and hazelnuts, rounded off by faint hints of resin. After a soft, velvety attack, the palate expands nicely, showing enticingly fleshy body and enough acidity to balance it. Pleasing nuances of dried fruit and nuts appear again on the finish.

●	Chianti Cl. Ris. '00	♟♟	6	● Le Terrine '00	♟♟	6
●	Chianti Cl. '01	♟	4	○ Vin Santo del Chianti Cl. '98	♟♟	4
●	Chianti Cl. Ris. '93	♟♟♟	4	● Chianti Cl. '01	♟	4
●	Soloìo '94	♟♟♟	5	● Chianti Cl. '95	♟♟	4
●	Chianti Cl. Ris. '95	♟♟♟	4	● Chianti Cl. Ris. '95	♟♟	4
●	Chianti Cl. '97	♟♟	4	● Chianti Cl. Torre a Destra Ris. '95	♟♟	4
●	Chianti Cl. Ris. '97	♟♟	4	● Quattrocentenario '95	♟♟	5
●	Soloìo '97	♟♟	5	● Chianti Cl. Torre a Destra Ris. '96	♟♟	4
●	Soloìo '00	♟♟	6	● Quattrocentenario '96	♟♟	5
●	Chianti Cl. Ris. '99	♟♟	8	● Le Terrine '97	♟♟	5
				● Quattrocentenario '97	♟♟	5
				● Chianti Cl. Torre a Destra Ris. '99	♟♟	5
				● Le Terrine '99	♟♟	6
				● Quattrocentenario '99	♟♟	7

BARBERINO VAL D'ELSA (FI)   BARBERINO VAL D'ELSA (FI)

★ ISOLE E OLENA
LOC. ISOLE, 1
50021 BARBERINO VAL D'ELSA (FI)
TEL. 0558072763
E-MAIL: isolena@tin.it

FATTORIA LA RIPA
FRAZ. SAN DONATO IN POGGIO
S. P. PER CASTELLINA IN CHIANTI, 27
50021 BARBERINO VAL D'ELSA (FI)
TEL. 0558072948 - 0558072121
E-MAIL: laripa@laripa.it

Despite the fact that the '00 vintage was not one of the greatest for Paolo De Marchi, the Cepparello, his Supertuscan made from 100 per cent sangiovese, was as good as usual, perhaps even better. This is one of the most elegant, complex sangiovese-based wines, sourced from vines cultivated with an almost maniacal attention to detail. But then, with soil and climate like Paolo's, you don't have many options. The vineyards are high up, over 400 metres above sea level, and if you don't go for excellence, with low yields in particular, the sangiovese grapes may barely manage to ripen. That's the secret of the Cepparello formula: hard work in the vineyards and minimal intervention in the cellar, with enough wood for a wine of this calibre, but not too much. Hence the '00, a wine of exceptional finesse, is almost aristocratic in its elegance. The fine Chianti Classico from '01 promises great things for the other Isole e Olena wines from this vintage. The good Cabernet Sauvignon '00 and the Syrah from the same year, both Collezione De Marchi wines, are not quite up to the level of past versions, but are nevertheless very well executed. It will, however, be quite another story when we taste the '01 vintage, a particularly favourable one for this part of Chianti Classico.

Fattoria La Ripa, which has belonged to the Caramelli family since the early 1940s, is back with its own well-deserved profile after a year's exclusion. The 14 hectares under vine, one tenth of the total estate, are distributed over the municipalities of Castellina in Chianti and Tavernelle Val di Pesa and local grapes account for most of the stock. While you can find some cabernet sauvignon and chardonnay, these are used only for the IGT wines. In fact, elevation and site climates somehow manage to make even the international varieties taste like Chianti natives. The estate presented only two wines at this year's tastings, but they were both spot on. The Chianti Classico '01 attracts attention with its lovely opaque ruby, then after an initial shyness, the nose reveals in rapid succession mineral notes and fruit aromas of ripe cherry, with hints of liquorice. The palate is soft and inviting from the first, showing breadth and generosity with a velvety suppleness straight through the lingering finish. The dense ruby Santa Brigida '00 presents elegant flinty undertones, with a ripe fruit fragrance of blackberry and cherry. The full-bodied palate has grip, chewiness and energy, then the fine progression, with tannins just slightly astringent at mid palate, leads to a delectable rising finish.

● Cepparello '00	♟♟♟	7
● Cabernet Sauvignon '00	♟♟	8
● Syrah '00	♟♟	6
● Chianti Cl. '01	♟♟	4
● Cepparello '86	♟♟♟	6
● Cepparello '88	♟♟♟	6
● Cabernet Sauvignon '90	♟♟♟	6
● Cabernet Sauvignon '95	♟♟♟	6
● Cabernet Sauvignon '96	♟♟♟	6
● Cabernet Sauvignon '97	♟♟♟	6
● Cepparello '97	♟♟♟	5
● Cepparello '98	♟♟♟	6
● Cepparello '99	♟♟♟	6
● Syrah '99	♟♟♟	7

● Santa Brigida '00	♟♟	6
● Chianti Cl. '01	♟♟	5
● Chianti Cl. Ris. '97	♟♟	4
● Chianti Cl. '98	♟♟	3
● Santa Brigida '98	♟♟	6
● Chianti Cl. '99	♟♟	5*
● Santa Brigida '99	♟♟	6

BARBERINO VAL D'ELSA (FI)   BARBERINO VAL D'ELSA (FI)

LE FILIGARE
LOC. LE FILIGARE
VIA SICELLE, 35
50020 BARBERINO VAL D'ELSA (FI)
TEL. 0558072796
E-MAIL: info@filigare.it

MARCHESI TORRIGIANI
LOC. VICO D'ELSA
P.ZZA TORRIGIANI, 15
50021 BARBERINO VAL D'ELSA (FI)
TEL. 0558073001
E-MAIL: az.torri@tin.it

Carlo Burchi's winery has done very well again. The re-organization co-ordinated by oenologist, Luciano Bandini, works so well that one of the wines, the Podere Le Rocce '00, walked off with Three Glasses. The fine Chianti Classico Lorenzo '01 parades fresh, inviting aromas of blackcurrant and cherry, softened by minty nuances. The entry on the palate is tellingly dense, then the well-dosed tannins find perfect balance with the acidity, and a pleasing hint of spice appears on the long finish. The Maria Vittoria Riserva '00 displays an opaque ruby hue. The complex bouquet reveals an assortment of ripe fruit, with hints of clove and cinnamon adding to its elegance. The enjoyable palate is intriguing without being overly powerful, and succulent and well-distributed tannins lead to a pleasing finish. The Pietro '99 did less well than usual. Its intense bouquet is somewhat diminished by slightly coarse vegetal tones and the substantial body is marked by aggressive tannins. Podere Le Rocce '00 offers minty and balsamic notes that shine forth against a fruity backdrop. The palate is velvet-soft and silky, with smooth tannins extending into the depths of a wonderfully elegant texture. A masterful wine!

The general improvement we mentioned last year is continuing apace. The wines are ever more engaging and delicious, which shows that the cellar and consultant oenologist, Luca D'Attoma, are going about things the right way. The estate, right on the border of the Chianti Classico DOCG zone, includes 27 hectares under vine. Sangiovese is the main crop but there is space for other traditional varieties, such as colorino and canaiolo, as well as merlot and cabernet sauvignon. The Torre di Ciardo '01, a blend of sangiovese, colorino, canaiolo and merlot, boasts well-defined aromas of cherry and redcurrant, lifted by light spicy hints of freshly ground pepper. The palate is mouthfilling, and acidity is balanced by prominent, but attractively restrained, tannins. The rising finish is succulent and enjoyably lingering. The Guidaccio '01, from merlot and cabernet sauvignon with a touch of sangiovese, made it to the Three Glass finals. The stylish, complex bouquet offers raspberry and bilberry, with sweet spicy notes of cinnamon and clove, enhanced by a distinct hint of chocolate. After a rounded attack, the palate expands, revealing an almost creamy softness with perfectly blended tannins and a long, deep, satisfying finish.

● Podere Le Rocce '00	????	7
● Chianti Cl. Maria Vittoria Ris. '00	??	6
● Chianti Cl. Lorenzo '01	??	5
● Pietro '99	?	8
● Chianti Cl. '01		5
● Podere Le Rocce '88	???	7
● Chianti Cl. '96	??	4
● Chianti Cl. Ris. '96	??	5
● Podere Le Rocce '97	??	7
● Chianti Cl. '99	??	5
● Pietro '98	??	8
● Chianti Cl. Maria Vittoria Ris. '99	??	6
● Chianti Cl. Lorenzo '00	??	5
● Podere Le Rocce '99	??	7

● Guidaccio '01	??	6
● Torre di Ciardo '01	??	4
● Guidaccio '99	??	5
● Guidaccio '00	??	5
● Torre di Ciardo '00	??	4
● Torre di Ciardo '99	?	4

BARBERINO VAL D'ELSA (FI)

BOLGHERI (LI)

CASTELLO DI MONSANTO
VIA MONSANTO, 8
50021 BARBERINO VAL D'ELSA (FI)
TEL. 0558059000
E-MAIL: monsanto@castellodimonsanto.it

TENUTA GUADO AL TASSO
LOC. BELVEDERE, 140
57020 BOLGHERI (LI)
TEL. 0565749735
E-MAIL: guadoaltasso@antinori.it

There was another very fine showing from Fabrizio Bianchi's winery, where he has assembled an excellent team, including his daughter, Laura, and oenologist Andrea Giovannini. The wines show great character and individuality, which has won them quite a number of admirers. And now for the results of our tastings. The Chardonnay Fabrizio Bianchi '01 presents rather an unusual bouquet, with scents of leather giving way to mineral and dried apricot notes. The palate is solid and fleshy, with slightly conspicuous acidity and a finish of middling length. The Chianti Classico '01 has a lovely ruby hue, but the nose seems over-ripe, with prominent and somewhat simple jammy aromas. The palate is appropriately warm, although the tannins seem a little too aggressive, at least for now. The Riserva '00 is hard to decipher on the nose, but the palate reveals great power and a dense texture, with tightly packed tannins and a mouthfilling sensation. Both the Tinscvil '00 and the Nemo '00 made it to our finals. The former displays eloquent aromas of green bell pepper with ripe fruity nuances of plum and blackberry. In the mouth it is close knit and vibrant, and lively powerful tannins linger through the distinctly rising finish. The fruity bouquet of the Nemo is dominated by raspberry and blackcurrant, nicely underpinned by vanilla. The entry on the palate is soft and inviting, and mellow tannins fuse well with the appealing structure.

At times, it must look as if we don't really like Guado al Tasso, one of the most prestigious red wines in the vast Antinori range. To tell the truth, we have never given it Three Glasses, apart from the award made to the debut vintage, the '90. We find it very good and occasionally, as with the '98 version, we may have been a bit too severe, but we can't help feeling that something is missing for it to be a truly great wine. The '00 is no exception to this rule, which is of course of our own devising and for which we take full responsibility. From cabernet sauvignon with a little merlot and syrah, it is elegant and well executed, offering a soft, engrossing palate. It has the usual spectrum of aromatics, ranging from balsamic tones to leather and tobacco. But it needs just a bit more grip. It has breeding but lacks a little spirit, so to speak. This is more or less the style of the best Antinori wines, which prefer elegance to concentration, but in a Maremma wine we would hope to find something more than a pervasive, agreeable softness. Still, we take our hats off to Guado al Tasso, which has undeniable class. The two lesser wines from this estate are fair, but unexciting. The Bolgheri Rosato Scalabrone '02 has become, perhaps because of an unexceptional vintage, more of a rosé than in the past. Before, it seemed like a slightly pale red. The Bolgheri Vermentino is somewhat acidic and a little too predictable.

● Nemo '00	🍷🍷	7
● Tinscvil '00	🍷🍷	6
● Chianti Cl. Ris. '00	🍷	5
● Chianti Cl. '01	🍷	4
○ Fabrizio Bianchi Chardonnay '01	🍷	5
● Chianti Cl. Il Poggio Ris. '88	🍷🍷🍷	7
● Chianti Cl. Il Poggio Ris. '97	🍷🍷	7
● Chianti Cl. Il Poggio Ris. '98	🍷🍷	7
● Nemo '98	🍷🍷	7
● Tinscvil '98	🍷🍷	5
● Fabrizio Bianchi Sangiovese '99	🍷🍷	7
● Chianti Cl. Il Poggio Ris. '99	🍷🍷	7
● Chianti Cl. Ris. '99	🍷🍷	5
● Nemo '99	🍷🍷	7
● Tinscvil '99	🍷🍷	6

● Bolgheri Rosso Sup.		
Guado al Tasso '00	🍷🍷	8
⊙ Bolgheri Rosato Scalabrone '02	🍷	4
○ Bolgheri Vermentino '02		4
● Bolgheri Rosso Sup.		
Guado al Tasso '90	🍷🍷🍷	8
● Bolgheri Rosso Sup.		
Guado al Tasso '97	🍷🍷	8
● Bolgheri Rosso Sup.		
Guado al Tasso '98	🍷🍷	8
● Bolgheri Rosso Sup.		
Guado al Tasso '99	🍷🍷	8

BOLGHERI (LI)

BOLGHERI (LI)

LE MACCHIOLE
VIA BOLGHERESE, 189/A
57020 BOLGHERI (LI)
TEL. 0565766092
E-MAIL: azagmacchiole@etruscan.li.it

★ TENUTA DELL'ORNELLAIA
VIA BOLGHERESE, 191
57020 BOLGHERI (LI)
TEL. 056571811
E-MAIL: info@ornellaia.it

It saddens us not to be able to award Three Glasses to any of the wines from this small but very important Bolgheri estate. Two years after the death of Eugenio Campolmi, his widow Cinzia and Luca D'Attoma, who has long been their oenologist, are committed to carrying on the work which was so tragically interrupted. It may have been the extreme youth of the wine or, more probably, the fact that the top bottles this time were from '00, a very hot, dry growing year, but none of the wines presented seemed truly first-rate. Two reds, the Bolgheri Rosso Superiore Paleo and the Messorio, a monovarietal merlot, made it to our finals, but they both went overboard with notes of vanilla, and the tannins were slightly aggressive, so they did not get any further. The Scrio '00, a 100 per cent syrah, also lacked balance. The aromas are very balsamic, but the tannins are assertive and the finish is a little bitter. The '01 version of the Bolgheri Superiore Le Macchiole, the simplest wine in the range, is better than last year's. Oaky tones again dominate the Paleo Bianco, a blend of sauvignon, chardonnay and vermentino aged, obviously enough, in barrique.

This famous and prestigious estate, under its new Mondavi-Frescobaldi proprietors, continues to maintain its standards, which have always been high. This year, in particular, we found the entire range admirable, but perhaps there were fewer stars. It could be a matter of policy: the cellar may have preferred overall reliability to the occasional superlative. But the vintage may have played a role, too, since the weather during 2000 had a levelling effect here, as it did elsewhere. Nevertheless, we very much enjoyed the Masseto '00, one of the finest wines in Italy and among the best Merlots anywhere. Admittedly, there is not much of it and the price is out of sight, but with a wine like this, it's hard to complain. The complex bouquet reveals notes of tobacco and leather with balsamic hints, and the palate is astonishing – powerful, yet elegant and very, very long. The Ornellaia '00 is not as successful as it has been in other vintages, in our opinion. The nose shows slightly vegetal tones and the tannins are not backed up by glycerine softness, as was the case in previous editions. It's undoubtedly a great wine, but this is not one of its most successful versions. The other bottles, Le Serre Nuove '01 and Le Volte '01, a blend of cabernet sauvignon, sangiovese and merlot, are both very good.

●	Bolgheri Rosso Sup. Paleo '00	♟♟	8	● Masseto '00	♟♟♟	8
●	Messorio '00	♟	8	● Bolgheri Sup. Ornellaia '00	♟♟	8
●	Scrio '00	♟♟	8	● Bolgheri Rosso Serre Nuove '01	♟♟	7
●	Le Macchiole '01	♟♟	6	● Le Volte '01	♟♟	4
○	Paleo Bianco '01	♟	6	● Masseto '93	♟♟♟	8
●	Bolgheri Rosso Sup. Paleo '95	♟♟♟	8	● Ornellaia '93	♟♟♟	8
●	Bolgheri Rosso Sup. Paleo '96	♟♟♟	8	● Masseto '94	♟♟♟	8
●	Bolgheri Rosso Sup. Paleo '97	♟♟♟	8	● Masseto '95	♟♟♟	8
●	Messorio '97	♟♟♟	8	● Bolgheri Sup. Ornellaia '97	♟♟♟	8
●	Messorio '98	♟♟♟	8	● Masseto '97	♟♟♟	8
●	Messorio '99	♟♟♟	8	● Bolgheri Sup. Ornellaia '98	♟♟♟	8
●	Scrio '97	♟♟	8	● Masseto '98	♟♟♟	8
●	Bolgheri Rosso Sup. Paleo '98	♟♟	8	● Bolgheri Sup. Ornellaia '99	♟♟♟	8
●	Scrio '98	♟♟	8	● Masseto '99	♟♟♟	8
●	Bolgheri Rosso Sup. Paleo '99	♟♟	8			

BOLGHERI (LI)

★ TENUTA SAN GUIDO
LOC. CAPANNE, 27
57020 BOLGHERI (LI)
TEL. 0565762003
E-MAIL: info@sassicaia.com

The panel can't help it. Our tasters are hooked on Sassicaia, and for no other reason than that we are enchanted by Marchese Niccolò Incisa della Rocchetta's wine, to our mind the quintessence of typicity for the Bolgheri zone. Of course, it's made from cabernet sauvignon, which is not a native of Tuscany's coast, as everyone knows. But it seems clear to us that the grape has established roots here and has set up a second home in the Mediterranean, near the celebrated avenue of cypresses and those rather wild Maremma hills that can be glimpsed in the background. It may be that the Sassicaia '00 does not have the extraordinary breeding of the '98 or the '88, but it is still a great Sassicaia. The aromas are just a touch more forward and ripe than usual, however the palate is engrossing, harmonious, extremely elegant and altogether innocent of woody vulgarity. Actually, the way barriques have been used is nothing less than masterful. Since all this takes place under the watchful eye of the oenologist Giacomo Tacchis, we can hardly claim to be surprised. You don't uncork a Sassicaia if you're looking for a display of muscle, so Mr Parker and his school may not be impressed. This a wine that rewards attention and requires time. This year also sees the first release of the second Tenuta San Guido wine. The Guidalberto '01, from merlot, cabernet sauvignon and a little sangiovese, is a perfectly decent wine, but Sassicaia is something else entirely.

●	Bolgheri Sassicaia '00	🍷🍷🍷	8
●	Guidalberto '01	🍷	7
●	Sassicaia '83	🍷🍷🍷	8
●	Sassicaia '84	🍷🍷🍷	8
●	Sassicaia '85	🍷🍷🍷	8
●	Sassicaia '88	🍷🍷🍷	8
●	Sassicaia '90	🍷🍷🍷	8
●	Sassicaia '92	🍷🍷🍷	8
●	Sassicaia '93	🍷🍷🍷	6
●	Bolgheri Sassicaia '95	🍷🍷🍷	8
●	Bolgheri Sassicaia '96	🍷🍷🍷	8
●	Bolgheri Sassicaia '97	🍷🍷🍷	8
●	Bolgheri Sassicaia '98	🍷🍷🍷	8
●	Bolgheri Sassicaia '99	🍷🍷🍷	8

BUCINE (AR)

FATTORIA PETROLO
FRAZ. MERCATALE VALDARNO
LOC. GALATRONA - VIA PETROLO, 30
52020 BUCINE (AR)
TEL. 0559911322
E-MAIL: petrolo@petrolo.it

Before we describe yet another great series of wines from the Sanjust family's estate, there are some innovations to note. The basic wine, Terre di Galatrona, which was made from the youngest vines, has bowed out. The vines are now ready to produce grapes for the two estate selections, Torrione, from sangiovese, and the merlot-based Galatrona. The Sanjusts came to this decision with Carlo Ferrini, the distinguished oenologist and agronomist who has been their adviser for about a year, and its wisdom is incontrovertibly proven by the '01 reds. The Torrione easily captured Two Glasses with one of the best editions from recent years. Its rich, complex nose offers spicy and balsamic notes, rounded out by lovely ripe fruit and is followed by a soft, nicely textured palate. Progression is satisfyingly firm, roughened only on the finish by slightly astringent oak-derived tannins. The again splendid Galatrona picked up another Three Glasses with the superbly elegant '01 version. A concentrated dense ruby, with a youthful brilliance, introduces the enticing bouquet, in which well-defined, pervasive ripe fruit is completed by balsamic, spicy and chocolate notes. All this is carried through onto the very long palate, where the tannins are extraordinarily fine-grained and silky. Even the wine's obvious youthfulness does not in the least detract from its outstanding drinking pleasure. To conclude, the Vin Santo '96 offers nicely blended aromas of almonds, dried figs and candied peel. This warm, lush wine may not be perfectly balanced, but it is attractive and lingering.

●	Galatrona '01	🍷🍷🍷	8
●	Torrione '01	🍷🍷	6
○	Vin Santo del Chianti '96	🍷🍷	6
●	Galatrona '97	🍷🍷🍷	7
●	Galatrona '98	🍷🍷🍷	7
●	Galatrona '99	🍷🍷🍷	7
●	Galatrona '00	🍷🍷🍷	8
●	Galatrona '95	🍷🍷	7
●	Torrione '97	🍷🍷	5
●	Terre di Galatrona '00	🍷🍷	4*
●	Torrione '00	🍷🍷	5
○	Vin Santo del Chianti '95	🍷🍷	5
●	Torrione '99	🍷🍷	5

BUCINE (AR)

CAMPIGLIA MARITTIMA (LI)

FATTORIA VILLA LA SELVA
FRAZ. MONTEBENICHI
LOC. LA SELVA
52021 BUCINE (AR)
TEL. 055998203
E-MAIL: laselva@val.it

JACOPO BANTI
VIA CITERNA, 24
57021 CAMPIGLIA MARITTIMA (LI)
TEL. 0565838802
E-MAIL: info@jacopobanti.it

Glasses have long been a great passion of the owner of this estate, and the ones we award are doubtless a welcome addition to his collection. But this was hardly the only thing that prompted Sergio Carpini to invest significantly in cellar equipment and in planting new, very high-density vines. These efforts, and the advice of that fine oenologist, Stefano Chioccioli, are creating very high hopes for the future. Meanwhile, in the absence of the Felciaia '00, which was not ready in time for our tastings, and of a new wine that for the moment is top secret, we were favourably impressed by the two bottles on offer, each of which won Two Glasses. Selvamaggio '99, a monovarietal cabernet, displays a dense, concentrated ruby hue with youthful highlights, followed by a coffee-dominated nose with slightly reticent fruit and faint grassy notes. The palate has the hardness of youth, but it's warm and opens up nicely on the finish. A little time in the bottle ought to set it to rights. A lovely golden colour introduces one of the best versions yet of the Vin Santo Vigna del Papa, the '97. The rich, elegant bouquet offers singular vegetal notes, then the palate's sweetness is very well balanced by an acidity that makes for a long and enjoyable development.

The gently rolling hills around Campiglia are peculiarly well suited to viticulture and very highly rated by experts in these matters. It is there that you will find a typical Campiglia estate, Jacopo Banti's, which is currently in the charge of Jacopo's son, Lorenzo. Having inherited his father's boundless passion, Lorenzo is thoroughly committed to producing significantly better wines. Investments have been made, especially in the vineyards, and indeed Banti has acquired some new land with excellent locations. The top-quality grapes that the new plots should yield will be an essential first step towards creating a first-rate range of wines. As for this year's tastings, we noticed great discrepancies in the wines. The Val di Cornia Peccato '01 was a particular favourite, and carried off Two Glasses. Its colour is dark and almost opaque. The initially somewhat closed nose is dominated by vegetal tones, then the palate immediately shows velvety and soft, its acidity-tannin balance just right and the fair finish offering sinewy acid grip. The good Aleatico Sciatà '02 displays attractively concentrated fruit and spice on the nose. The palate offers a harmonious sweetness that never cloys and a density that makes it agreeably long. The other wines seemed somewhat unfocused and hard to pin down.

○ Vin Santo del Chianti		
Vigna del Papa '97	♼♼	5
● Selvamaggio '99	♼♼	5
● Selvamaggio '90	♼♼	5
● Felciaia '94	♼♼	5
● Felciaia '95	♼♼	5
● Selvamaggio '95	♼♼	5
● Selvamaggio '96	♼♼	5
● Selvamaggio '97	♼♼	5
● Felciaia '98	♼♼	5
● Felciaia '99	♼♼	5

● Val di Cornia Il Peccato Rosso '01	♼♼	6
● Val di Cornia Aleatico Sciatà '02	♼♼	7
● Val di Cornia Trafui '01		6
○ Val di Cornia Centomini '02		4
○ Val di Cornia Vermentino		
Poggio Angelica '02		4
● Il Peccato Barrique '91	♼♼	3
● Il Peccato Barrique '99	♼♼	5
● Val di Cornia Aleatico '01	♼♼	6
● Val di Cornia		
Il Peccato Barrique '00	♼♼	5

CAPRAIA E LIMITE (FI)

ENRICO PIERAZZUOLI
VIA VALICARDA, 35
50056 CAPRAIA E LIMITE (FI)
TEL. 0571910078
E-MAIL: info@enricopierazzuoli.com

While Enrico Pierazzuoli's ambitious viticultural project has already improved the quality and boosted the personality of his wines, there do seem to have been set-backs along the way. Most probably, these have been due to the vicissitudes of the weather. Perhaps that is why we found this year's range good, and comparable to last year's, but not quite so captivating as it has been on occasion in the past. The Chianti Classico Matroneo '01 presents an intensely fruity bouquet embellished with notes of spice, followed by a weighty palate with prominent but well-behaved tannins and a supple, harmonious structure that finishes long. The Gioveto '00 is again successful, its pleasing aromas of red berry fruit enhanced by toasty and peppery hints. After a soft attack, the palate offers a full-bodied, rich progression with prominent tannins that continue through the remarkably lingering finish. The Carmignano Le Farnete Riserva '99 came close to gaining Two Glasses, as did the Chianti Montalbano Riserva '00. The former is a bit indistinct on the nose and somewhat tannic on the finish, whereas the latter displays an elegant bouquet of black berry fruit and a balanced palate, despite a fair dose of extract. The fruity Chianti Montalbano '01 shows admirable structure. The very decent Carleto '01 boasts floral fragrances mingled with notes of citrus fruit and pear, then the soft, fleshy palate has an enjoyable fruity finish.

CARMIGNANO (PO)

FATTORIA AMBRA
FRAZ. COMEANA
VIA LOMBARDA, 85
59015 CARMIGNANO (PO)
TEL. 055486488
E-MAIL: g.rigoli@agriconsulting.it

The wines from Fattoria Ambra are consistently good. Indeed, this has become one of the most significant estates in the DOCG zone, which is itself rapidly increasing in importance. One of the reasons for this is that producers like Beppe Rigoli pursue excellence without losing sight of local identity. Beppe presented four interesting bottles that should do very well in today's increasingly discriminating market. Once again, the Montalbiolo Riserva – the '00 version this time – was a favourite. An intense ruby introduces fruity aromas that are soon joined by spicy and faintly grassy notes with undertones of oak. After a soft entry, the palate unfolds densely packed, succulent tannins. The finish is long but slightly dusty. Another success is the Santa Cristina in Pilli '01, with its distinct fragrances of red berry fruit and undergrowth, followed by a full-bodied, solid palate that has a fair balance of acidity and extract but a slightly rough, oak-dominated finish. The Elzana Riserva '00 seemed a little under par. The fruit on the nose is fleeting, the palate is dry and only medium-bodied, although the tannins are smooth. The Vigna Montefortini '01 did not repeat its triumphant debut performance of last year. The progression on the palate is warm and soft, but the finish is lean and short. The Barco Reale '02 is enjoyable.

● Gioveto '00	🍷🍷	6
● Chianti Cl. Matroneo '01	🍷🍷	5
● Chianti Montalbano Ris. '00	🍷	5
○ Carleto '01	🍷	5
● Chianti Montalbano '01	🍷	4
● Carmignano Le Farnete Ris. '99	🍷	7
● Carmignano Le Farnete Ris. '97	🍷🍷🍷	5
● Carmignano Le Farnete Ris. '94	🍷🍷	4
● Carmignano Le Farnete Ris. '96	🍷🍷	4
● Chianti Montalbano Ris. '97	🍷🍷	4
● Gioveto '98	🍷🍷	4
● Chianti Cl. Matroneo '00	🍷🍷	4*
● Gioveto '99	🍷🍷	5

● Carmignano Le Vigne Alte di Montalbiolo Ris. '00	🍷🍷	5
● Carmignano Vigna S. Cristina in Pilli '01	🍷🍷	4
● Carmignano Elzana Ris. '00	🍷	5
● Carmignano Vigna di Montefortini '01	🍷	4
● Barco Reale '02	🍷	3
⊙ Vin Ruspo '02		2
● Carmignano Vigna di Montefortini '00	🍷🍷	4*
● Carmignano Elzana Ris. '99	🍷🍷	5
● Carmignano Le Vigne Alte di Montalbiolo Ris. '99	🍷🍷	5*

CARMIGNANO (PO)

TENUTA DI CAPEZZANA
VIA CAPEZZANA, 100
59015 CARMIGNANO (PO)
TEL. 0558706005 - 0558706091
E-MAIL: capezzana@capezzana.it

It would take more than the absence of its top wines, which were still in the process of ageing at the time in question, to keep an estate like Tenuta di Capezzana from impressing at our tastings. The important duty of keeping up the winery's considerable reputation was fulfilled by the remarkable '00 edition of Villa di Trefiano, which sauntered comfortably into our finals and came within an ace of winning Three Glasses. This performance provides further justification for the estate policy of refusing to release wines before they are fully ready, The extra cellar time in bottle is crucial for bringing out the very best in the wine. Villa di Trefiano displays a clean, intense, captivating bouquet that foregrounds ripe fruit, graced with overtones of spice and pepper, as well as toasty notes. The palate is soft, very dense and harmonious, with a solid tannic structure and a lingering, characterful finish. The debut performance of the Trebbiano '01 was excellent. It displays intense fragrances of ripe fruit, citrus and floral tones, then the palate is soft and enchanting, the dense, almost chewy, mouthfeel revealing mineral notes on the finish. The Barco Reale '02 is one of the best of its vintage. A pleasingly fruity nose is echoed on the palate and the satisfying, long finish. The Vin Ruspo '02 is brilliant in hue, fruity in fragrance and easy to drink. Although dense in the mouth, the Vin Santo '97 seemed somewhat inexpressive on the nose.

CARMIGNANO (PO)

PRATESI
LOC. SEANO
VIA RIZZELLI, 10
59011 CARMIGNANO (PO)
TEL. 0558704108
E-MAIL: info@pratesivini.it

There are distinct signs of great things to come in future for Fabrizio Pratesi's estate. Actually, it had already impressed us very favourably last year, when it almost won Three Glasses. This time, the impression is emphatically confirmed and, just as we expected, the Carmignano '01 was amongst the best of its type. Of course, it was a shoo-in for the Three Glass finals. The vibrant, dense colour heralds a complex nose where spicy, toasty tones blend with slightly over-ripe fruity notes of blackberry and raspberry. The palate is full-bodied and juicy on entry, then the powerful structure reveals well-gauged acidity that enlivens the lingering finish. This is a wine with the muscle and sculpted elegance of an athlete's body. The Locorosso '01, which can be considered the second wine of the estate, did not do as well as last year's. Mostly sangiovese-based with a touch of merlot, it presents a dark ruby that suggests a much more concentrated and dense wine. But in fact, its style is based on immediate approachability, with clean aromas of blackberry and blackcurrant, and hints of spice mirrored on the rather one-dimensional palate, which reveals a good balance of acidity and extract.

● Carmignano Villa di Trefiano '00	🍷🍷	6
○ Trebbiano '01	🍷🍷	6
● Barco Reale '02	🍷🍷	4*
☉ Vin Ruspo '02	🍷	3
○ Vin Santo di Carmignano Ris. '97	🍷	6
● Ghiaie della Furba '98	🍷🍷🍷	5
● Carmignano Villa di Capezzana '99	🍷🍷🍷	5
● Ghiaie della Furba '99	🍷🍷	6
● Carmignano Villa di Capezzana '00	🍷🍷	5*
● Ghiaie della Furba '00	🍷🍷	6
● Carmignano Villa di Trefiano '99	🍷🍷	6

● Carmignano '01	🍷🍷	6
● Locorosso Rosso '01	🍷	4
● Carmignano '99	🍷🍷	5
● Carmignano '00	🍷🍷	6

CASTAGNETO CARDUCCI (LI)

CÀ MARCANDA
SANTA TERESA, 272
57022 CASTAGNETO CARDUCCI (LI)
TEL. 0173635158

Ca' Marcanda is Angelo Gaja's new winery in Bolgheri. Naturally, Gaja still has his original estate in Barbaresco, with offshoots in the Barolo zone where he produces Langhe Nebbiolo Sperss and Langhe Nebbiolo Conteisa Cerequio, and the Montalcino winery, Pieve di Santa Restituta. Gaja's intention for Bolgheri is to produce excellent wine in rather larger quantities than he has elsewhere. The vast cellar, in fact, suggests a potential of hundreds of thousands of bottles, and the vineyard holding is similarly extensive. The best wine from the '01 vintage here is called Ca' Marcanda and will, when you read these words, have already been released, since its scheduled debut is 24 October 2003 at the Wine Experience in New York. As our tastings took place earlier, none of it was available. We know that it is a classic Bordeaux blend of cabernet sauvignon and merlot, but that is all we can say. We can, however, tell you that Angelo's second wine, Magari '01, is also a blend of cabernet sauvignon and merlot. It's well executed and reflects the style of Gaja reds in that it is elegant and avoids extremes of assertiveness. The Promis '01, which adds sangiovese and syrah to merlot, is more stylish and even, but also less concentrated and not so long.

CASTAGNETO CARDUCCI (LI)

COLLE MASSARI
LOC. LUNGAGNANO
57022 CASTAGNETO CARDUCCI (LI)
TEL. 0565765069 - 0564990496
E-MAIL: collemassari@tin.it

Pier Mario Meletti Cavallari was the driving force of this estate for over 20 years, when it was called Podere Grattamacco. He has been handing over the reins to Claudio Tipa, who has leased it and is continuing to work with oenologist, Maurizio Castelli. The style of the wines has not changed, for Tipa, a Sicilian entrepreneur but Roman by adoption and connected with the Swiss pharmaceutical group, Serono, seems to have the same sort of passionate dedication that has always inspired Meletti Cavallari. Pier Mario, in fact, still makes much-appreciated contributions to the cellar from time to time. This year's range of wines is slightly less interesting than last year's, primarily because of the less favourable growing year. The Bolgheri Rosso Superiore Grattamacco '00 suffers the consequences of a very hot year that encouraged over-ripeness at the expense of finesse of fragrance. This affected all of Bolgheri and Castagneto Carducci, not just the wines from this estate. Consequently, the aromas are fairly engrossing but also a little forward, with jammy notes of blackberry and faint gamey hints, whereas the palate, despite a long, elegant finish, reveals an uncharacteristic softness.

● Magari '01	♟♟	8
● Promis '01	♟♟	6

● Bolgheri Rosso Sup.		
Grattamacco '00	♟♟	8
● Grattamacco '85	♟♟♟	8
● Bolgheri Rosso Sup.		
Grattamacco '99	♟♟♟	8
● Grattamacco '90	♟♟	8
● Grattamacco '91	♟♟	8
● Grattamacco '92	♟♟	8
● Grattamacco '93	♟♟	8
● Bolgheri Rosso Sup.		
Grattamacco '96	♟♟	8
● Bolgheri Rosso Sup.		
Grattamacco '97	♟♟	8
● Bolgheri Rosso Sup.		
Grattamacco '98	♟♟	8

CASTAGNETO CARDUCCI (LI)

ENRICO SANTINI
LOC. CAMPO ALLA CASA, 74
57020 CASTAGNETO CARDUCCI (LI)
TEL. 0565774375
E-MAIL: enricosantini@interfree.it

We are delighted to welcome Enrico Santini to the ranks of our Three Glass winners. After only three harvests, this very talented winemaker from Bolgheri has hit the bull's eye with a wine that had us sitting up in our seats. This oenological gem, Bolgheri Rosso Superiore Montepergoli '01, offers a very stylish, intense bouquet of red berry fruit, light balsamic notes and already perfectly integrated oak. The palate has excellent body, but what struck us was the finesse of the extract. The tannins are velvety and well incorporated into the wine, providing a pleasing sensation, but also conveying distinct character and grip without excess. In winemaking terms this is something like geometry's squaring of the circle. It is also an indication of a mastery of vinification technique, and of the superlative quality of the grapes that have gone into the wine, in this case merlot and cabernet sauvignon with small amounts of syrah and sangiovese. The other two wines are good as well, although from a less felicitous year. The Bolgheri Rosso Poggio al Moro '02 unites a fairly engaging palate to an admirable structure, especially given its vintage. The Bolgheri Bianco Campo alla Casa '02, from vermentino and sauvignon, is slightly dilute in the mouth, but boasts well-defined, straightforward aromas with distinct notes of apple and pear.

CASTAGNETO CARDUCCI (LI)

MICHELE SATTA
LOC. CASONE UGOLINO, 23
57022 CASTAGNETO CARDUCCI (LI)
TEL. 0565773041
E-MAIL: satta@infol.it

Michele Satta has won his first Three Glass award with a formidable version, the '01, of his Bolgheri Rosso Piastraia. He doesn't even think it his best wine, but it has turned out to be his most typical one and quite a classic. A blend of equal parts of merlot, syrah, cabernet sauvignon and sangiovese, it offers intense fruit and light gamey aromas with distinct notes of leather. The palate is slightly tannic, but there is no end of character and concentration. We preferred it to the Bolgheri Rosso Superiore I Castagni '00, a very pricey blend of merlot, cabernet sauvignon and syrah that Satta considers his top wine. We were not so sure. It wasn't the structure, which is remarkable, but rather the finesse on the nose, which was a little compromised by faintly sulphurous notes at first, and by a suggestion of over-ripeness. The sangiovese-based Cavaliere '00 is as reliable as ever. It's one of the best wines made from this variety in the Bolgheri zone and while it may not be extremely concentrated, it is quite elegant, and the tannins provide grip without aggressiveness. The fair Bolgheri Bianco '02, from trebbiano and vermentino, is the simplest and least exciting wine in the range. Altogether, this was a fine showing, and our only criticism concerns the prices, which have been rocketing up in recent years. We appeal to Michele Satta to have mercy on us poor consumers. We like his wines immensely and don't want to go without simply because we can't afford them.

● Bolgheri Rosso Sup. Montepergoli '01	♟♟♟	7
○ Bolgheri Bianco Campo alla Casa '02	♟	4
● Bolgheri Rosso Poggio al Moro '02	♟	4
● Bolgheri Rosso Sup. Montepergoli '00	♟♟	7

● Bolgheri Rosso Piastraia '01	♟♟♟	7
● Bolgheri Rosso Sup. I Castagni '00	♟♟	8
● Cavaliere '00	♟♟	7
○ Bolgheri Bianco '02	♟	4
● Bolgheri Rosso Piastraia '95	♟♟	7
● Vigna al Cavaliere '95	♟♟	7
● Bolgheri Rosso Piastraia '96	♟♟	7
● Vigna al Cavaliere '96	♟♟	7
● Bolgheri Rosso Piastraia '97	♟♟	7
● Vigna al Cavaliere '97	♟♟	7
● Bolgheri Rosso Piastraia '98	♟♟	7
● Vigna al Cavaliere '98	♟♟	7
● Bolgheri Rosso Piastraia '99	♟♟	7
● Bolgheri Rosso Piastraia '00	♟♟	7
● Cavaliere '99	♟♟	7

CASTELLINA IN CHIANTI (SI)

BUONDONNO
LOC. LA PIAZZA, 37
53011 CASTELLINA IN CHIANTI (SI)
TEL. 0577749754
E-MAIL: buondonno@chianticlassico.com

We were very pleased to be able to write the debut Guide profile for Gabriele Buondonno and Valeria Sodano's estate. It is also a recognition of the unwavering diligence shown by the two agronomists ever since, after coming to Tuscany as tourists, they decided to make wine in compliance with the dictates of organic farming. And at last, their efforts are bearing fruit. We were delighted and astonished by the Chianti Classico Casa Vecchia alla Piazza '01, which made it to our finals. It takes a while to open on the nose, but when it does, it releases complex aromas of leather and tobacco, spicy notes of cinnamon and varied hints of undergrowth. The very pleasing, solid palate reveals crunchy tannins well integrated with the alcohol. The mouthfeel is dense, smooth and altogether satisfying, and to cap it all, there is an excellent rising finish. The Riserva '00 is less successful. A lustrous ruby introduces rather prominent vegetal notes that then give way to elegant autumn leaves. The palate is a bit stiff at first but relaxes to display powerful supporting tannins in an austere, very compact body with a moderately long finish. The very good Campo ai Ciliegi '00, a monovarietal syrah, offers fascinating smoky vegetable aromas that acquire elegance from powerful spicy notes of freshly ground pepper and clove. After a pleasant, not too powerful attack, the palate unfolds smoothly, showing good density. The finish is long and clean.

CASTELLINA IN CHIANTI (SI)

CASTAGNOLI
LOC. CASTAGNOLI
53011 CASTELLINA IN CHIANTI (SI)
TEL. 0577740446
E-MAIL: castagnoli@valdelsa.net

Hans Joachim Dobbelin's organically farmed Castagnoli estate is undoubtedly excellent, although this year's range of wines is less brilliant than last year's. Still, the bottles all have considerable character and fully reflect their terroir. The Riserva '99 is less than totally exciting. The colour is rather pale, and the nose is less than eloquent, releasing only faint hints of cinchona and pencil lead. The good structure in the mouth is founded on the balance of alcohol and tannins, the acidity is marked and the finish is a little short. We were happier with the performance of Le Terrazze del Castello '00. Although not particularly intense in hue, it shows a nose with a range of light, sweet raspberry and strawberry fruit. The palate has good weight and solid, even structure, with attractively expansive tannins, although the finish is in a hurry to sign off. The Vigna Hortulus '00 was a contender at our finals and almost won Three Glasses. This monovarietal Merlot shows a dense, lustrous ruby and reveals a distinctive nose of very elegant vegetal bell pepper and mint, with stylish hints of spice. The soft, silky palate is harmonious and enjoyable, strutting well-absorbed tannins and a lingering finish.

● Chianti Cl.			
Casa Vecchia alla Piazza '01		�果果	5
● Campo ai Ciliegi '00		♈♈	5
● Chianti Cl. Ris. '00		♈	5

● Vigna Hortulus '00		♈♈	6
● Le Terrazze del Castello '00		♈♈	5
● Chianti Cl. Ris. '99		♈	5
● Chianti Cl. Ris. '88		♈♈	5
● Le Terrazze del Castello '98		♈♈	5
● Syrah '98		♈♈	5
● Syrah '99		♈♈	6
● Merlot '99		♈♈	5

CASTELLINA IN CHIANTI (SI)

CASTELLINA IN CHIANTI (SI)

CASTELLARE DI CASTELLINA
LOC. CASTELLARE
53011 CASTELLINA IN CHIANTI (SI)
TEL. 0577742903 - 0577740490
E-MAIL: isodi@tin.it

★ CASTELLO DI FONTERUTOLI
LOC. FONTERUTOLI
VIA OTTONE III, 5
53011 CASTELLINA IN CHIANTI (SI)
TEL. 057773571
E-MAIL: fonterutoli@fonterutoli.it

We want to emphasize how well our tastings went this year at Castellare di Castellina. The winemaking policy adopted by Paolo Panerai in recent years, the undeniable skill of his cellarmaster, Alessandro Cellai, and the magical supervision of Maurizio Castelli have fused into an virtuoso team effort, producing three wines that made it to our finals. One, the Chianti Classico Vigna il Poggiale Riserva '00, hit the Three Glass jackpot, which is the fourth year running for this estate. We are delighted because we consider Castellare di Castellina to be one of the strongholds of traditional Chianti Classico, committed to defending the wine without recourse to exotic styles or grape varieties. The Vigna il Poggiale Riserva '00 is a magnificent wine, combining alcoholic strength with elegant acidity and exceptional length. The Chianti Classico Riserva '00 is also better than ever. The bouquet is less complex, and it has a touch less structure, but it is still an excellent bottle. The sangiovese-based I Sodi di San Niccolò '99, which includes some canaiolo, is still very young, but could develop enormously in the near future. We would recommend it to anyone who is willing to wait a few years. The Chianti Classico '01 is light, fruity and quaffable, and the Coniale '99, a monovarietal Cabernet Sauvignon, is quite enjoyable, but not in the same league as the sangiovese-based reds.

Castello di Fonterutoli did extremely well. Indeed, no other Tuscan producer picked up two Three Glass awards, which is what our heroes did with the two standard-bearers, Siepi '01 and Chianti Classico Castello di Fonterutoli '00. These are two great red wines that, despite their innovative oenological style and the use of non-traditional grape varieties, are true to their Chianti origins. The '01 is one of the best Siepis yet, and a worthy rival for the '95 and the '97. The grapes are sangiovese and merlot, but they grow in the Siepi vineyard, which is considered one of Castellina's first growths. In the first phase of our tastings, we tried it at four different sessions. At first, we found it still overwhelmed by vanilla, which gradually diminished over a few months. In the end, it was showing remarkable complexity on the nose, and structure in the mouth. The Chianti Classico Castello di Fonterutoli '00 is more elegant and nervy, but also more compelling and concentrated than previous versions. Whatever the case, it's a great wine. The fair Chianti Classico '01 is very well executed, soft and pleasing on the palate. The Fonterutoli monovarietal sangiovese, Poggio alla Badiola '02, is simply delicious, despite a not very propitious vintage. Fragrant and straightforward on the nose, it is, when you come to drink it, quite irresistible.

● Chianti Cl. V. il Poggiale Ris. '00	♉♉♉	6
● Chianti Cl. Ris. '00	♉♉	5
● I Sodi di San Niccolò '99	♉♉	8
● Chianti Cl. '01	♉	4
● Coniale '99	♉	7
● Chianti Cl. V. il Poggiale Ris. '97	♉♉♉	6
● I Sodi di San Niccolò '97	♉♉♉	8
● I Sodi di San Niccolò '98	♉♉♉	8
● Chianti Cl. V. il Poggiale Ris. '99	♉♉	6
● I Sodi di San Niccolò '95	♉♉	8
● I Sodi di San Niccolò '96	♉♉	8

● Chianti Cl. Castello di Fonterutoli '00	♉♉♉	8
● Siepi '01	♉♉♉	8
● Chianti Cl. '01	♉♉	6
● Poggio alla Badiola '02	♉♉	4
● Chianti Cl. Castello di Fonterutoli '99	♉♉♉	8
● Siepi '93	♉♉♉	8
● Siepi '94	♉♉♉	8
● Siepi '95	♉♉♉	8
● Siepi '96	♉♉♉	8
● Siepi '97	♉♉♉	8
● Siepi '98	♉♉♉	8
● Siepi '99	♉♉♉	8
● Siepi '00	♉♉♉	8

CASTELLINA IN CHIANTI (SI) CASTELLINA IN CHIANTI (SI)

FAMIGLIA CECCHI
LOC. CASINA DEI PONTI, 56
53011 CASTELLINA IN CHIANTI (SI)
TEL. 05775431
E-MAIL: cecchi@cecchi.net

PODERE COLLELUNGO
LOC. COLLELUNGO
53011 CASTELLINA IN CHIANTI (SI)
TEL. 0577740489
E-MAIL: info@collelungo.com

The average quality of the Cecchi family's wines continues to be good, despite the hefty number of bottles produced. But we feel they could make significant progress if they fine-tuned a few aspects of winemaking: their managerial abilities are beyond doubt. But let's get down to our tastings. The subtle fragrance of the Chianti Classico '01 highlights simple fruity aromas and unusual mineral notes. After a thinnish entry, the palate shows tannins well absorbed into a dense, balanced body. Fruit dominates the nose of the Messer Pietro di Teuzzo '01. The attack on the palate is assertive, with moderate weight mid palate and a pleasant finish. "Well made" and "old fashioned" were our comments on the Chianti Classico Villa Cerna '01. The nose offers not very fashionable aromas of fruit preserved in alcohol, then the palate reveals a solid, powerful body with backbone, structure and well-absorbed tannins. Pleasing notes of rosemary and menthol appear on the finish. We found the Villa Cerna Riserva '00 a little below par. The ripe fruit on the nose lacks clarity and the palate is a little graceless, with its rough and drying tannins. The Spargolo '00, after an initial reticence, offers refreshing balsamic notes together with ripe fruit on the nose. The creaminess of the entry on the palate is soon subdued by excessively astringent tannins, but there is a rising finish. The Vigneto La Gavina '00 shows a simple, not very well-defined nose and a body which, though powerful, is a little dilute at mid palate. The Arcano '02 is, as always, an enjoyable, well-made wine.

There's no denying the consistently high quality of the wine from Podere Collelungo. The superb vineyard sites, with their southern exposure, high elevation and rocky soil, together with painstaking vineyard management and diligence in the cellar, where Alberto Antonini is the consultant oenologist, all help to guarantee impeccable bottles year after year. So we were hardly surprised when both of the wines they presented made it to our finals. We would also point out their loyalty to their territory: there are no Supertuscans on the list here. The excellent performance of the Chianti Classico '01 begins with the remarkable visual impact of its lovely ruby hue, which is both opaque and lustrous. The enticing bouquet brings together admirable balsamic aromas and spicy notes with delightful undertones of wild berries. The palate is vigorous, round and expansive, the tannins unfolding purposefully with no rough edges, and the balance is superlative. The Campo ai Cerchi Riserva '00 presents an attractive brilliant ruby, then a strikingly varied nose, united by the sweetness of the individual aromas, including strawberry, raspberry and inviting spicy notes of vanilla and clove. The palate reveals a soft and delicate, yet weighty and very dense, body, with a creamy texture contributed by the almost imperceptible, perfectly integrated tannins. The finish is a remarkable crescendo of flavour.

●	Spargolo '00	▼▼	7
●	Chianti Cl. Villa Cerna '01	▼▼	5
●	Chianti Cl. Villa Cerna Ris. '00	▼	6
●	Vigneto La Gavina '00	▼	6
●	Chianti Cl. '01	▼	4
●	Chianti Cl. Messer Piero di Teuzzo '01	▼	5
●	Chianti Colli Senesi Arcano '02	▼	4
●	Spargolo '97	♟♟	6
●	Vigneto La Gavina '97	♟♟	5
●	Chianti Cl. Messer Piero di Teuzzo '98	♟♟	4
●	Spargolo '98	♟♟	6
●	Chianti Cl. '99	♟♟	3*
●	Chianti Cl. Villa Cerna '00	♟♟	4
●	Spargolo '99	♟♟	6
●	Vigneto La Gavina '99	♟♟	6

●	Chianti Cl. Campo ai Cerchi Ris. '00	▼▼	8
●	Chianti Cl. '01	▼▼	6
●	Chianti Cl. Ris. '97	♟♟	8
●	Chianti Cl. Roveto '97	♟♟	4
●	Chianti Cl. Roveto '99	♟♟	6
●	Chianti Cl. Ris. '98	♟♟	8
●	Chianti Cl. '99	♟♟	4
●	Chianti Cl. '00	♟♟	5
●	Chianti Cl. Ris. '99	♟♟	8

CASTELLINA IN CHIANTI (SI)   CASTELLINA IN CHIANTI (SI)

POGGIO AMORELLI
LOC. POGGIO AMORELLI
53011 CASTELLINA IN CHIANTI (SI)
TEL. 0571668733
E-MAIL: poggioamorelli@libero.it

FATTORIA NITTARDI
LOC. NITTARDI, 76
53011 CASTELLINA IN CHIANTI (SI)
TEL. 0577740269
E-MAIL: fattorianittardi@chianticlassico.com

It's not every day that a winery graduates to a full profile of its own and wins Three Glasses all in one year, particularly in a zone like Chianti Classico. That distinction has been achieved at Poggio Amorelli by Marco Mazzarini, who is both estate manager and oenologist. All the wines did well. The very good Chianti Classico '01 shows a vivid, rich ruby, followed by distinct balsamic fragrances that enhance the underlying wild berries and flowers, punctuated by notes of spice. The palate is powerful, intense and juicy, and the tannins are well integrated into the structure. The finish is leisurely and attractive. The lively ruby colour of the excellent Chianti Classico Riserva '00 is a perfect introduction to a bouquet of vanilla, raspberry and strawberry, lifted by a hint of cinnamon. The palate is velvety, silky, full and deep, with a good tannic weave aiding the progression to a notable rising finish. But the real masterpiece is the Oracolo '01, made mostly from sangiovese. It owes its status as best estate wine to a lovely ensemble of fragrances, including green bell pepper, stylish notes of spice and excellent lively fruit. The palate offers a firm, dense body, with good concentration and an orderly, velvety progression leading to a relaxed, smooth finish.

A winery located in a spot that, starting in the 12th century, was known as "nectar dei" ("divine nectar") simply has to produce good wine. And the fact that one of its owners was Michelangelo Buonarroti suggests it is a place of rare charm. Whatever the case, these past events may well have contributed to the success of the Femfert family's estate. Their 13 hectares under vine are tended with maniacal care under the meticulous supervision of Carlo Ferrini. Once again, Fattoria Nittardi almost won Three Glasses with the immensely reliable Riserva, which figured well at our finals. The Chianti Classico '01 shows a deep, limpid ruby followed by a broad nose that ranges from notes of vanilla to a red berry fragrance of strawberry and raspberry, underpinned by lovely ripe cherry. The substantial acidity on the palate is nicely integrated into the robust, even structure, leading to an enjoyable lingering finish. The Riserva '00 displays an attractive, decidedly ruby hue with purple nuances. The entry on the nose is dominated by toasty notes of oak, mingled with coffee and liquorice, and softened slightly by a touch of vanilla. Soon, however, a cornucopia of delectable ripe fruit takes over. The palate reveals character and power, the slightly excessive tannins being beautifully absorbed into the soft, smooth, captivatingly supple body. The finish is long and succulent.

● Oracolo '01	▼▼▼	6
● Chianti Cl. Ris. '00	▼▼	5
● Chianti Cl. '01	▼	4

● Chianti Cl. Ris. '00	▼▼	7
● Chianti Cl.		
Casanuova di Nittardi '01	▼▼	5
● Chianti Cl. Ris. '98	▼▼▼	7
● Chianti Cl. Ris. '93	▼▼	4
● Chianti Cl. Ris. '94	▼▼	5
● Chianti Cl. Ris. '95	▼▼	5
● Chianti Cl. Ris. '96	▼▼	5
● Chianti Cl. '97	▼▼	4
● Chianti Cl. Ris. '97	▼▼	5
● Chianti Cl. '98	▼▼	4
● Chianti Cl. Ris. '99	▼▼	7

Enjoy Italy even more.

**$21.95
4 issues**

Gambero Rosso
the insider guide to
top wines
best restaurants
delightful hotels
recipes and routes
ll chosen for you by our experts

Treat yourself to a subscription to Gambero Rosso
Italy's top wine, travel and food magazine

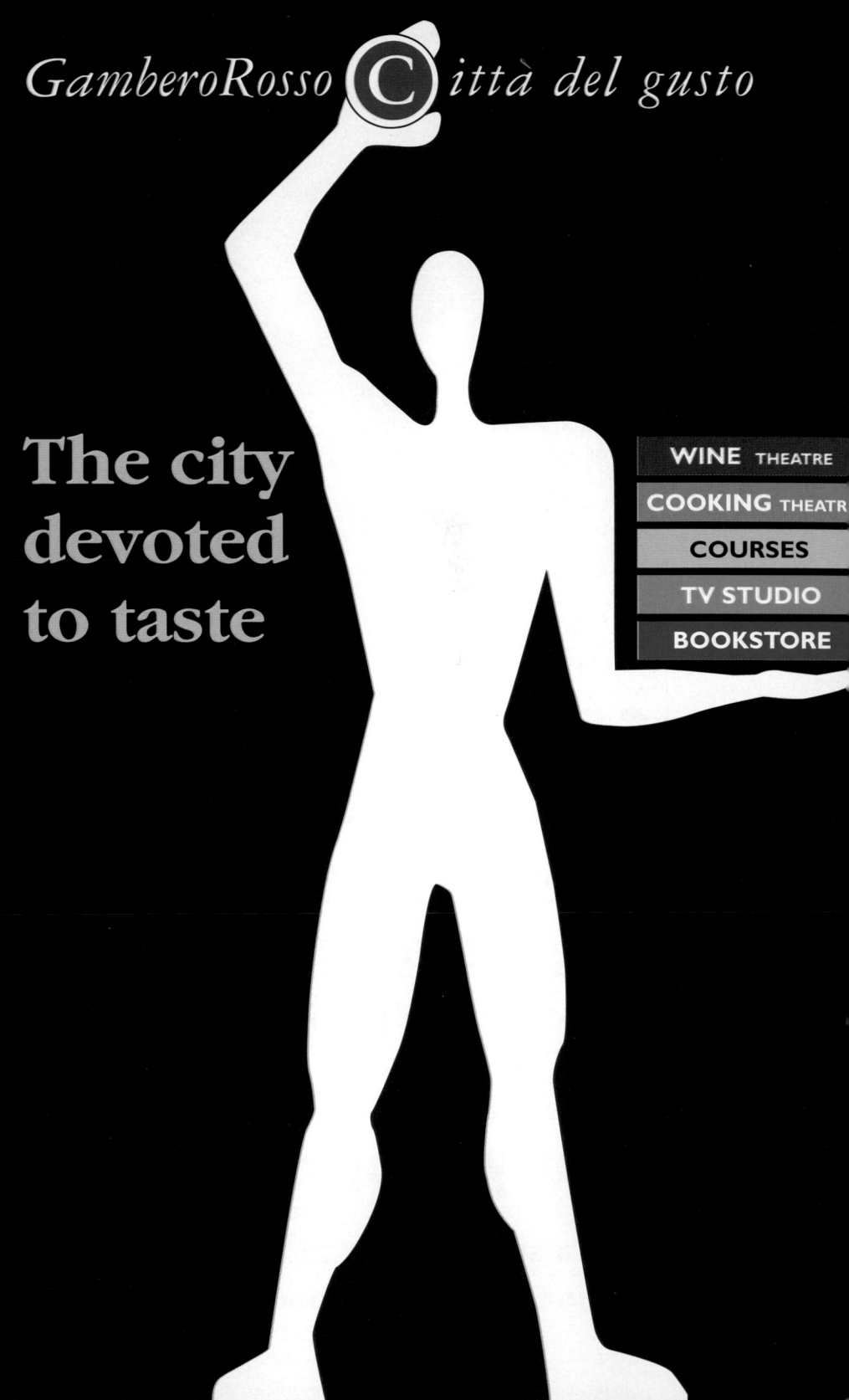

CASTELLINA IN CHIANTI (SI) CASTELLINA IN CHIANTI (SI)

QUERCETO DI CASTELLINA
LOC. QUERCETO, 9
53011 CASTELLINA IN CHIANTI (SI)
TEL. 0577733590
E-MAIL: info@querceto.com

ROCCA DELLE MACÌE
LOC. MACÌE, 45
53011 CASTELLINA IN CHIANTI (SI)
TEL. 05777321
E-MAIL: rocca@roccadellemacie.com

What a splendid showing from the Di Battista family's Querceto di Castellina winery! After last year's debut in the Guide, they have earned Three Glasses this time for their Supertuscan, Podalirio, and their Chianti Classico easily made it to our finals. These things do not happen by chance. At Querceto di Castellina, they are the result of a programme of renovation that has been going on since 1997 under the guidance of oenologist, Gioia Cresti. This year marks the completion of vineyard replanting on their 10 hectares, and the cellar has also been fully renovated. And now for the wines. The Chianti Classico L'Aura '01 shows a vivid purple preceding a pleasingly varied nose of raspberry and blackcurrant, refreshing menthol and stylish spicy notes. The dense palate is powerful from the first and engrossing without lapsing into heaviness. The tannins are nicely integrated in the structure, alcohol and acidity are well balanced, and the finish is long and exciting. The stunning Podalirio '01, from sangiovese and merlot, shows an intense ruby with distinct purple highlights. The generous, complex bouquet releases aromas of concentrated berry fruit, elegant spicy notes of cinnamon and pepper and hints of graceful aromatic herbs. The palate is supple, deep and mouthfilling, the tannins are well gauged and innocent of rough edges, and the full finish lingers attractively.

For the second year in a row, Sergio Zingarelli's winery has taken home Three Glasses for his sangiovese and cabernet sauvignon blend, Roccato. The gear change of some years back has made a real difference, as all the wines prove. The Rubizzo '02 and the Morellino di Scansano '02 are both enjoyable. The well-made and decidedly quaffable Chianti Classico '01 offers vegetal and red berry notes on the nose and densely packed tannins in the mouth. The bouquet of the Riserva '00 is dominated by vegetal notes, with green bell pepper particularly noticeable. The solid palate shows well-judged tannins. The surprising Tenuta Sant'Alfonso Riserva '00 displays scents ranging from ripe fruit to leather. The attack on the palate is powerful, the alcohol has a taming effect on the slightly astringent tannins and the rising finish is tasty. The Fizzano Riserva '00 offers an elegant nose of restrained mixed fruits, followed by a dense, energetic palate with a long finish. The excellent Ser Gioveto '00 made it to our finals. Attractive balsamic notes blend with raspberry to form an engaging bouquet, then the appealing velvety palate reveals good tannic progression to a succulent, forceful finish. Aromas of ripe bell pepper hold sway in the Roccato '00, together with refreshing aromatic herbs. Alcoholic warmth encourages an excellent balance of well-calibrated acidity and tannins, and the intriguing finish is sweet and long.

● Podalirio '01	🍷🍷🍷	5
● Chianti Cl. L'Aura '01	🍷🍷	4
● Podalirio '00	🍷🍷	5
● Podalirio '99	🍷🍷	5
● Chianti Cl. L'Aura '00	🍷	4

● Roccato '00	🍷🍷🍷	7
● Ser Gioveto '00	🍷🍷	7
● Chianti Cl. Tenuta S. Alfonso Ris. '00	🍷🍷	5
● Chianti Cl. Fizzano Ris. '00	🍷	6
● Chianti Cl. Ris. '00	🍷	5
● Chianti Cl. '01	🍷	4
● Rubizzo '02		3
● Morellino di Scansano Campomaccione '02		4
● Roccato '99	🍷🍷🍷	7
● Chianti Cl. Tenuta S. Alfonso '99	🍷🍷	5
● Roccato '98	🍷🍷	7
● Chianti Cl. Ris. '99	🍷	5

CASTELLINA IN CHIANTI (SI)

SAN FABIANO CALCINAIA
LOC. CELLOLE
53011 CASTELLINA IN CHIANTI (SI)
TEL. 0577979232
E-MAIL: info@sanfabianocalcinaia.com

Although San Fabiano Calcinaia has been producing excellent wines regularly for years, it does not always enjoy the success in the market that it deserves. This is due in part to the polite reserve of Guido Serio, the owner of the estate and a real country gentleman. He invests time and money in his vineyards, and in the recently inaugurated and very modern cellar, he listens to the advice of distinguished oenologist, Carlo Ferrini, he devotes himself to his wines, and then he lets them speak for themselves. This year, for the first time, it was not his excellent, but perhaps over-concentrated, sangiovese, cabernet sauvignon and merlot Cerviolo Rosso '01 that won the Three Glasses. Instead, it was the Chianti Classico Cellole Riserva '00, which is more elegant and polished than ever. It comes from a hot growing year, but the vines stand in high, well-ventilated vineyards, so the sangiovese is not at all over-ripe. In fact, it shows a masterful balance of its considerable body and the acidity that contributes greatly to its drinkability. In a nearly tropical vintage like 2000, a result of this kind looks almost miraculous. The basic Chianti Classico '01 is equally excellent, and definitely one of the best of its year. The only fault we can find is with the Cerviolo Bianco '02, which is rather modest this time and a little overwhelmed by oak.

CASTELLINA MARITTIMA (PI)

CASTELLO DEL TERRICCIO
LOC. TERRICCIO
56040 CASTELLINA MARITTIMA (PI)
TEL. 050699709
E-MAIL: castello.terriccio@tin.it

There's a new star wine at Terriccio, shedding its light on a charming, secluded spots in the hinterland of the northern Maremma. Here, human hands and nature have created a garden of olive groves, splendid stables and fine forests, as well as vineyards. Such is the magnitude of this new star that we hardly noticed the absence at our tastings of the old celebrity, Lupicaia, which is enjoying an extra year's ageing time in bottle. The star wine in question, a blend of cabernet sauvignon, petit verdot and syrah which made off with Three Glasses, is Castello del Terriccio '00. Thanks are due to the passionate dedication of Gian Annibale Rossi di Medelana and the capable skills of Carlo Ferrini. The very intriguing bouquet presents crystal-clear, perfectly expressive notes of fresh red berry fruit and superbly judged balsamic and spicy nuances. In the mouth, the keynote is elegance. After a silky entry, it seems to glide into an intense, thrilling mid palate, with tight-knit but soft and absolutely harmonious tannins. It's an overwhelming wine. The Tassinaia '01, obtained from sangiovese, cabernet sauvignon and merlot, is as usual excellent and almost won Three Glasses. Here, too, the nose is fresh and balsamic, and the palate echoes the elegance of its big brother, although it's a bit simpler. Hans Terzer, who has been looking after the estate whites since 2000, has done a good job. We were particularly taken with Con Vento '02, a 100 per cent sauvignon with a typically varietal nose of peaches and figs, then a succulent, well-balanced palate with long length.

● Chianti Cl. Cellole Ris. '00	♈♈♈	6	
● Cerviolo Rosso '01	♈♈	7	
● Chianti Cl. '01	♈♈	4	
○ Cerviolo Bianco '02	♈	5	
● Cerviolo Rosso '96	♈♈♈	6	
● Cerviolo Rosso '97	♈♈♈	6	
● Cerviolo Rosso '99	♈♈♈	6	
● Cerviolo Rosso '98	♈♈♈	6	
● Cerviolo Rosso '00	♈♈♈	7	
● Chianti Cl. Cellole Ris. '96	♈♈	4	
● Chianti Cl. Cellole Ris. '97	♈♈	5	
● Chianti Cl. Cellole Ris. '98	♈♈	5	
○ Cerviolo Bianco '01	♈♈	5	
● Chianti Cl. '00	♈♈	4	
● Chianti Cl. Cellole Ris. '99	♈♈	6	

● Castello del Terriccio '00	♈♈♈	8	
● Tassinaia '01	♈♈	6	
○ Con Vento '02	♈♈	5	
○ Rondinaia '02	♈	5	
● Lupicaia '93	♈♈♈	8	
● Lupicaia '95	♈♈♈	8	
● Lupicaia '96	♈♈♈	8	
● Lupicaia '97	♈♈♈	8	
● Lupicaia '98	♈♈♈	8	
● Lupicaia '99	♈♈♈	8	
● Lupicaia '00	♈♈♈	8	
● Tassinaia '98	♈♈	5	
● Tassinaia '99	♈♈	5	
● Tassinaia '00	♈♈	6	
○ Con Vento '01	♈♈	4	

CASTELNUOVO BERARDENGA (SI) CASTELNUOVO BERARDENGA (SI)

FATTORIA DELL'AIOLA
FRAZ. VAGLIAGLI
53010 CASTELNUOVO
BERARDENGA (SI)
TEL. 0577322615
E-MAIL: info@aiola.net

The Malagodi family's winery continues to alternate years in and out of the Guide, but at this year's tastings, we noticed a distinct improvement, particularly in the basic wines, which augurs well for the immediate future. Winemaking is in the hands of Nicolò D'Afflitto, as it has always been, and the recently completed replanting of the vineyards has produced good results that will continue to be felt. The Chianti Classico '01 releases characteristic fragrances of cherry and violet that are both intense and clear. The palate offers a powerful attack, a significant undergirding of acidity and a dry, very tasty finish. The fine Riserva '00 displays ripe notes of plum and blackberry on the nose and a firm body with densely packed, well-judged tannins and an enchantingly spicy finish. The excellent Cancello Rosso Riserva '99 boasts a more complex range of aromas, including cloves and flowers. The palate is dense, juicy and harmonious, and the finish is succulent. The Logaiolo '00, a blend of cabernet sauvignon and sangiovese, was less exciting. A ripe nose introduces a palate which, although powerful, has yet to find a point of balance for its harder and softer components.

BORGO SCOPETO
LOC. VAGLIAGLI
53010 CASTELNUOVO
BERARDENGA (SI)
TEL. 0577848390 - 0577847166
E-MAIL: caparzo@caparzo.com

This is the first appearance in the Guide for this estate, an offshoot of Tenuta Caparzo at Montalcino, which covers some 500 hectares, of which 37 are under vine. The labours of recent years in both vineyard and cellar under the watchful eye of estate manager Nuccio Turone have borne fruit. We were interested by the Chianti Classico '01. The nose is enhanced by satisfying notes of tar, which accompany engaging hints of tobacco and mixed spices. In the mouth, we found impressive weight and a solid, well-judged body with substantial extract. The unhurried finish is a little bit acidic. The Riserva '00 offers a varied nose with pleasing aromatic herbal notes, particularly thyme, followed by scents of undergrowth, supported by fruity tones of cherry. After a good attack, the palate unveils inviting acidity that makes the wine succulent and pleasing. The Misciano Riserva '00 is less successful. The bouquet is inexpressive, with animal and grassy scents masking the fruit. The wine does better on the soft, even palate which, if not enormous, is savoury and can point to a sweet finale. The bouquet of the Borgonero '00, a blend of sangiovese, cabernet sauvignon and syrah, opens up after an oak-dominated attack and pungent notes of coffee to reveal a suggestion of blackberry jam. The palate is built around the balance of forceful alcohol and tannins, and the finish is enjoyable.

● Chianti Cl. Cancello Rosso Ris. '99	🍷🍷	6
● Chianti Cl. Ris. '00	🍷🍷	5
● Logaiolo '00	🍷	4
● Chianti Cl. '01	🍷	4
● Chianti Cl. Ris. '90	🍷🍷	5
● Chianti Cl. Ris. '94	🍷🍷	4
● Chianti Cl. Ris. '95	🍷🍷	4
● Chianti Cl. Cancello Rosso Ris. '97	🍷🍷	4
● Chianti Cl. Ris. '98	🍷🍷	6
● Logaiolo '98	🍷🍷	4
● Rosso del Senatore '00	🍷	6

● Borgonero '00	🍷🍷	6
● Chianti Cl. '01	🍷🍷	5
● Chianti Cl. Misciano Ris. '00	🍷	6
● Chianti Cl. Ris. '00	🍷	6
● Chianti Cl. Ris. '93	🍷🍷	4
● Chianti Cl. Ris. '98	🍷🍷	4*
● Chianti Cl. Misciano Ris. '98	🍷🍷	5
● Chianti Cl. Misciano Ris. '99	🍷🍷	5

CASTELNUOVO BERARDENGA (SI)

CARPINETA FONTALPINO
FRAZ. MONTEAPERTI
LOC. CARPINETA
53019 CASTELNUOVO BERARDENGA (SI)
TEL. 0577369219
E-MAIL: gioiacresti@interfree.it

The land that yields Do Ut Des is rich, and not just in trace elements and organic matter. History tells us that it was at Montaperti that the Sienese defeated the Florentines in 1260. Do Ut Des, a blend of sangiovese, cabernet sauvignon and merlot, might have been like a lot of other reds, but isn't. In a certain sense, it is a Ghibelline of a wine, almost a heretic. We would expect a prominent, very intense nose, and instead we have to wait a moment before perceiving a delightful red berry fruit liqueur aroma with deep spicy notes. The same sort of thing occurs on the palate. The attack isn't soft and rounded. From the outset, it shows its strong, determined character, with muscular tannins and lively acidity. The well-sustained, full body is crowned by a long, harmonious finish that is elegantly underpinned by oak. This lovely wine came very close indeed to winning Three Glasses, as did last year's release. This is not so much a disappointment as further proof that the cellar is on the right track. The good Chianti Colli Senesi '02 is unquestionably a simpler wine, with a nose that is faintly vegetal, but the palate is well-balanced and substantial. The Carpineta Fontalpino winery, established in 1994 and comprising 11 hectares under vine, belongs to the young, talented oenologist, Gioia Cresti.

CASTELNUOVO BERARDENGA (SI)

CASTELLO DI BOSSI
LOC. BOSSI IN CHIANTI, 28
53019 CASTELNUOVO BERARDENGA (SI)
TEL. 0577359330 - 0577359177
E-MAIL: info@castellodibossi.it

Marco Bacci's Castello di Bossi did extremely well this year. Although it didn't win Three Glasses, three wines went through to the finals, proof that dedication bears fruit. There has been a distinct leap forward after years of investing in vineyard and cellar, first in Chianti, and then in Montalcino and the Maremma, where we shall be seeing results over the next few years. We'll start with the Chianti Classico '01, which offers oaky tones combined with fruit, followed by a good palate in something of a hurry to finish. The very fine Berardo Riserva '00 displays a rather complex nose, where minty and balsamic notes blend with scents of coffee, sweet toasty tones and distinctly juicy aromas of fruit. The full-bodied, engaging palate reveals tannins that have integrated nicely with the alcohol, forming an elegant structure underpinned by acidic sinew that leads to a rising finish. The mostly cabernet sauvignon-based Corbaia '00 came perilously close to earning Three Glasses for an excellent performance. The broad spectrum of aromatics highlights red berry fruit, enhanced by cloves. The captivating palate shows well-calibrated, silky tannins and a very rich, flavourful finish, making this a remarkably drinkable wine. The excellent Girolamo '00, a monovarietal Merlot, has great finesse on the nose, where wild berry notes and vegetal tones hold sway. The palate is even and free of edginess, the tannins are well integrated and the finish lingers.

● Do Ut Des '01	▼▼	6
● Chianti dei Colli Senesi '02	▼	4
● Do Ut Des '97	▼▼	6
● Do Ut Des '98	▼▼	6
● Do Ut Des '99	▼▼	6
● Do Ut Des '00	▼▼	6
● Chianti dei Colli Senesi '01	▼	4

● Chianti Cl. Berardo Ris. '00	▼▼	6
● Corbaia '00	▼▼	7
● Girolamo '00	▼▼	7
● Chianti Cl. '01	▼	5
● Corbaia '99	▼▼▼	8
● Chianti Cl. '99	▼▼	4*
● Corbaia '98	▼▼	8
● Girolamo '98	▼▼	8
● Chianti Cl. '00	▼▼	5*
● Chianti Cl. Berardo Ris. '99	▼▼	6
● Girolamo '99	▼▼	8

CASTELNUOVO BERARDENGA (SI)　CASTELNUOVO BERARDENGA (SI)

FATTORIE CHIGI SARACINI
VIA DELL'ARBIA, 2
53019 CASTELNUOVO BERARDENGA (SI)
TEL. 0577355113
E-MAIL: e.fattoriechigi@mps.it

★ FATTORIA DI FELSINA
VIA DEL CHIANTI, 101
53019 CASTELNUOVO BERARDENGA (SI)
TEL. 0577355117
E-MAIL: felsina@data.it

We had predicted an improvement at Fattorie Chigi Saracini, but not such a big one. Their great diligence, particularly in the vineyards, and the attentive guidance of Carlo Ferrini have made the difference. The improvement process included replanting the vines, reducing the range to two wines and renewing the barrel stock. It then took time for the new vines, covering 60 hectares, to produce grapes of sufficient quality to create a great wine. But let's have a look at our tasting notes. The Chianti Villa Chigi '02 is an uncomplicated but good wine with a pleasingly youthful, grapey fragrance against an admirable background of attractive, well-defined wild berries. In the mouth, it is smooth, supple and remarkably quaffable. Five years after its debut, Poggiassai '00 has won Three Glasses, bowling us over with its boundless elegance. A blend of sangiovese and cabernet sauvignon, it boasts an opaque ruby hue and a stylish, complex bouquet with pleasing notes of chocolate melting into coffee scents and aromas of spice-softened berry fruit. The attack on the palate is creamy and full, then the tidy progression offers perfectly integrated, mellow tannins, followed by an eloquent finish.

When the Fontalloro doesn't make it, they have an ace up their sleeve at Fattoria di Felsina, managed by Giuseppe Mazzocolin. So when the elegant sangiovese-based wine missed out on Three Glasses this year, the Chianti Classico Rancia showed such great style that it slipped in ahead and picked up a top award. The chardonnay-based I Sistri '01 opens on the nose with inviting mineral notes and hints of fresh spice, but cloying vanilla emerges to drown them all out. In the mouth, it is agreeably smooth and moderately long. Pepestrino '02 is pleasant and undemanding. The Chianti Classico '01 is good, particularly on the nose, where elegant minty notes appear with a medley of black berry fruit. The soft and rather less incisive palate reveals considerable acidic backbone and a slightly mouth-puckering finish. The Riserva '00 displays mineral fragrances and good impact on the somewhat dilute palate. The Fontalloro is fine, as we have come to expect. The aromas of the '00 edition are extremely well defined, with sweet wild berries emerging strongly. The palate is velvety and, as usual, remarkably elegant, although lighter bodied than previous versions. The Maestro Raro '98 offers not very clear-cut vegetal aromas and an austere palate with tightly knit, but somewhat astringent, tannins. Rancia '00 displays a complex bouquet of nicely focused red berry fruit and inviting fresh spice, backed up by faint hints of vanilla. After an even, attractively restrained attack, the vibrantly austere palate develops vigorously and enjoyably, revealing fine-grained tannins and a stylish finish.

● Poggiassai '01	♛♛♛	5
● Chianti Villa Chigi '02	♛	3
● Poggiassai '00	♛♛	5*
● Chianti Colli Senesi '00	♛	2*
● Chianti Villa Chigi '01	♛	3*

● Chianti Cl. Rancia Ris. '00	♛♛♛	6
● Fontalloro '00	♛♛	6
● Chianti Cl. Ris. '00	♛	5
● Chianti Cl. '01	♛	4
○ I Sistri '01	♛	4
○ Pepestrino '02	♛	3
● Maestro Raro '98	♛	8
● Chianti Cl. Rancia Ris. '86	♛♛♛	5
● Maestro Raro '91	♛♛♛	5
● Maestro Raro '93	♛♛♛	6
● Fontalloro '97	♛♛♛	6
● Fontalloro '98	♛♛♛	6
● Fontalloro '99	♛♛♛	6
● Chianti Cl. Rancia Ris. '98	♛♛	5
● Chianti Cl. Rancia Ris. '99	♛♛	6

Castello di Monastero

Loc. Monastero d'Ombrone, 19
53019 Castelnuovo Berardenga (SI)
tel. 05775701
e-mail: info@borgomonastero.it

Lionello Marchesi, former owner of several famous Tuscan wineries, is trying his hand at it again. With his passion for the region, he has actually reconstructed a small mediaeval village and set it up to receive overnight visitors, without of course neglecting viticulture. After a year's pause, the winery is back in the Guide, having made a fine showing. The Solo '01, a monovarietal Chardonnay, has an excellent nose with pleasing toasty tones fusing into notes of flint, apple and pear. The appealing palate reveals a robust, but not overblown, body and a succulent, enjoyable finish. The Chianti Classico '01 is a little below par. It has no particular defect on the somewhat fruity nose, but is a bit monotonous, whereas the palate opens out smoothly, displaying dense texture. The Chianti Classico '00 offers distinct aromas of cherry and blackcurrant, as well as riper jammy notes of blackberry. The attack on the palate is excellent, the body solid, balance is exemplary, and the finish savoury and long. The Riserva '99 is striking in its freshness on the nose, thanks to the overlay of balsamic tones on a base of cherry. The palate is fascinating from the first, the pleasingly savoury development unveils well-integrated tannins and the finish is long. The Sangiovese '01 shows a characteristic fragrance of ripe fruit and hints of leather. The dry palate has admirable acidic backbone and powerful, lively tannins. The Infinito '00, gamey and forward on the nose, exhibits a lovely juicy body with crunchy tannins and a lingering flavourful finish.

●	Infinito '00	**YY**	6
○	Solo Chardonnay '01	**YY**	4
●	Chianti Cl. Ris. '99	**YY**	5
●	Chianti Cl. '00	**Y**	4
●	Chianti Cl. '01	**Y**	4
●	Sangiovese '01	**Y**	3
●	Chianti Cl. Ris. '98	YY	4
●	Infinito '99	YY	6

Fattoria di Petroio

Loc. Quercegrossa
via di Mocenni, 7
53019 Castelnuovo Berardenga (SI)
tel. 0577328045 - 0644265210
e-mail: pamela.lenzi@tiscalinet.it

The approachable, intelligent Lenzis – Gian Luigi, a professor of psychiatry at the University of Rome, and Pamela, an elegant American and, incidentally, a great cook – have both become completely wrapped up in their small but excellent wine estate. They take advice from Carlo Ferrini, but they make most decisions themselves, because in the past few years they have gone from being complete neophytes to experts in the arts of viticulture and winemaking. This year, they again presented well-executed wines that are, as they generally tend to be, very enjoyable. But then, here at Castelnuovo Berardenga, or more precisely, at Quercegrossa in the Vagliagli district, the sun shines most of the time, it hardly ever rains and sangiovese ripens beautifully. The Chianti Classico Riserva '00 has come out very well and despite having just been bottled when we were tasting, it went through to our finals, almost winning Three Glasses. It is innocent of the over-ripe notes you can find in many Chianti-zone reds from the '00 vintage, and boasts great concentration, as well as tannins that seem almost hypnotized by the bewitchingly soft extract. The Chianti Classico '01 is very interesting, not least because of its remarkably fair price. But also it's deliciously fruity and quite irresistible.

●	Chianti Cl. Ris. '00	**YY**	6
●	Chianti Cl. '01	**YY**	4*
●	Chianti Cl. Ris. '97	YYY	5
●	Chianti Cl. '93	YY	2
●	Chianti Cl. '95	YY	3
●	Chianti Cl. Ris. '95	YY	4
●	Chianti Cl. '96	YY	3
●	Chianti Cl. Ris. '96	YY	4
●	Chianti Cl. '97	YY	3
●	Chianti Cl. '98	YY	4
●	Chianti Cl. Ris. '98	YY	5
●	Chianti Cl. '99	YY	4*
●	Chianti Cl. Ris. '99	YY	6
●	Chianti Cl. '00	Y	5

CASTELNUOVO BERARDENGA (SI)

POGGIO BONELLI
LOC. POGGIO BONELLI
53019 CASTELNUOVO BERARDENGA (SI)
TEL. 0577355382 - 0577352045
E-MAIL: pogbon@tin.it

The Monte dei Paschi di Siena banking group has invested well. Wines from both its estates, Fattorie Chigi Saracini and Poggio Bonelli, made it to our finals, the latter with both bottles presented. After acquiring Poggio Bonelli, Monte dei Paschi made a careful work plan with the oenological guidance of Carlo Ferrini, starting with replanting and attentive clonal selection in the vineyards, and continuing in the cellar, where all the old barrels were replaced. Improvement was faster than expected. Let's consider the results at our tastings. There was a fine performance from the Chianti Classico '01, with its deep ruby heralding a nose of wild berries enhanced by varied spicy notes. After a soft, moderately dense attack, the palate shows excellent balance of its soft and hard components, then an admirable rising finish. The Tramonto d'Oca '01, a blend of sangiovese and merlot, also did very well, almost winning Three Glasses. A very intense ruby introduces a rich, complex nose opening on toasty notes of coffee that make way for ripe wild berries. The palate reveals an elegant rounded body with fine-grained tannins and a nice balance of alcohol and acidity. The finish is relaxed, still mouthfilling and long.

CASTELNUOVO BERARDENGA (SI)

QUERCIAVALLE
FRAZ. PONTIGNANELLO, 6
LOC. VAGLIAGLI
53019 CASTELNUOVO BERARDENGA (SI)
TEL. 0577356842

This is the Guide debut – and it's a good one – for the estate of cousins Pietro and Paolo Losi, which extends over 50 hectares, 15 under vine. The vine stock is also under the watchful eye of consultant oenologist, Giorgio Baldi. This was one of the historic properties of the Certosa ("charterhouse") at Pontignano and has been in the Losi family since 1954. The current owners began vinification on the estate and marketing their own wines in 1973. They have chosen to concentrate on traditional grape varieties, even in their IGT wines. The Chianti Classico '01 displays an attractive intense ruby followed by aromas of morello cherry and distinct ripe plum. The palate is succulent and dense, showing a smooth tannic texture and a rich, long finish. The Riserva '00 is less well defined. The not very clear-cut nose offers vegetal notes with faint gamey nuances. The palate is smooth, but not very substantial, with drying tannins and a moderately long finish. The not very successful Armonia '00, a monovarietal Sangiovese, shows a nose dominated by a vegetal note, and has a thin, undistinguished body. But the San Brunone '00 is good. Made from sangiovese with a little malvasia nera, it exhibits an impressively engaging nose in which notes of pencil lead add grace to a fragrance of plum jam. The palate is initially round and full, but could do with more length.

● Chianti Cl. '01	🍷🍷	4
● Tramonto d'Oca '01	🍷🍷	6
● Tramonto d'Oca '88	🍷🍷	5
● Tramonto d'Oca '91	🍷🍷	5
● Tramonto d'Oca '99	🍷🍷	6
● Chianti Cl. '00	🍷🍷	4
● Tramonto d'Oca '00	🍷🍷	6
● Chianti Cl. Ris. '99	🍷🍷	5

● San Brunone '00	🍷🍷	6
● Chianti Cl. '01	🍷🍷	4
● Armonia '00	🍷	6
● Chianti Cl. Ris. '00	🍷	5

CASTELNUOVO BERARDENGA (SI) CASTELNUOVO BERARDENGA (SI)

SAN FELICE
LOC. SAN FELICE
53019 CASTELNUOVO BERARDENGA (SI)
TEL. 05773991
E-MAIL: info@agricolasanfelice.it

CASTELLO DI SELVOLE
FRAZ. VAGLIAGLI
LOC. SELVOLE, 1
53019 CASTELNUOVO BERARDENGA (SI)
TEL. 0577322662
E-MAIL: selvole@selvole.com

For the fifth time San Felice, which belongs to the RAS insurance company, has won Three Glasses, this year with the Chianti Classico Riserva Poggio Rosso. It's always good, but really surpassed itself this time. The good Belcaro '02 offers inviting suggestions of pineapple, enhanced by a light floral fragrance and followed by a pleasing impact on the nicely textured palate, which signs off with a moderately long finish. The less successful Ancherona '01 is dominated by green bell pepper on the nose and acidity on the palate. The nose of the Chianti Classico '01 is in thrall to animal and grassy notes, while somewhat prominent acidity rules the palate, at least until the agreeable finish. The Grigio Riserva '00 is reminiscent of an old-fashioned style in its bouquet of alcohol-steeped fruit and flowers. Although the dilute entry on the palate is not very impressive, and the lean body reveals considerable nervy acidity, the finish is savoury and moderately long. The champion Poggio Rosso Riserva '00 boasts a wide range of aromas, from smoky notes to sweet wild berries and fragrant, delicate aromatic herbs. After a meaty entry, the palate is broad, deep and mouthfilling, the tannins melding well with the alcohol. The lingering finish reveals a delightful hint of coffee. Vigorello '99, a blend of sangiovese and cabernet sauvignon, made it to our finals, thanks to its attractive bouquet where ripe fruit steals the show. The palate is muscular and solid, with well-integrated tannins. The wines from the Campogiovanni property at Montalcino also did well.

Guido Busetto and his wife, Nobuko, will not be too cross when they see the results of this year's tastings. Two of the three wines they presented made it to our finals, proof that the work plan they drew up together with oenologist, Stefano Porcinai, is proceeding just as it should. The sangiovese-based Cassero '01, which offers very good value for money, is making its debut, and a fine one it is, too. A vivid ruby ushers in a juicy fragrance of ripe fruit with sweet notes of spice. The supple, smooth palate has weight, structure and mellow tannins. The Chianti Classico '01 is successfully modern in style. Its opaque, lustrous ruby heralds a complex bouquet, with spicy notes of liquorice and coffee against a background of well-integrated ripe red berry fruit. The firm palate reveals densely packed, nicely absorbed tannins and a sweet finish with an excellent lingering fruity tone. The Barullo '00, a monovarietal Sangiovese, shows a lively ruby followed by delicate minty and balsamic nuances over a basso continuo of blackcurrant and raspberry. In the mouth, it is supple, well-balanced and quaffable, before signing off with a smooth, forceful finale.

● Chianti Cl. Poggio Rosso Ris. '00	♟♟♟	6
● Vigorello '99	♟♟	7
● Chianti Cl. Il Grigio Ris. '00	♟	5
○ Ancherona Chardonnay '01	♟	4
● Brunello di Montalcino '98	♟	7
● Brunello di Montalcino V. del Quercione Ris. '97	♟	8
● Chianti Cl. '01	♟	4
○ Belcaro '02	♟	3
● Vigorello '88	♟♟♟	5
● Chianti Cl. Poggio Rosso Ris. '90	♟♟♟	6
● Chianti Cl. Poggio Rosso Ris. '95	♟♟♟	5
● Vigorello '97	♟♟♟	5
● Chianti Cl. Poggio Rosso Ris. '99	♟♟	6

● Barullo '00	♟♟	6
● Chianti Cl. '01	♟♟	3*
● Cassero Rosso '01	♟♟	3*
● Chianti Cl. Ris. '96	♟♟	5
● Barullo '97	♟♟	6
● Chianti Cl. '98	♟♟	4
● Chianti Cl. '99	♟♟	3
● Chianti Cl. '00	♟♟	3*
● Chianti Cl. Ris. '99	♟♟	5
● Barullo '98	♟♟	6

CASTIGLIONE D'ORCIA (SI)

Podere Forte

loc. Petrucci
53023 Castiglione d'Orcia (SI)
tel. 0577887488 - 031636289
e-mail: podereforte@podereforte.it

A Guide debut as striking as that of Podere Forte is probably also the prelude to a new winemaking story. The bleak, uncultivated Val d'Orcia could soon be transformed into an expanse of vines, if this is a fair sample of what the area is capable of. Estate owner, Pasquale Forte, agronomist, Attilio Scienza, and oenologist, Donato Lanati, chose this strip of Tuscany between Montepulciano and Montalcino for an ambitious project. They planted model vineyards on apparently intractable land to produce exemplary wines. The estate covers 110 hectares, of which only two and a half are under vine so far. Output is a mere 6,000 bottles. However, the rooted cuttings which have already been planted will soon bring the vine stock up to 25 hectares. Our panels were astonished by the wines they tasted. The Petrucci '01, named after the historic owners of the estate, is an elegant, harmonious 100 per cent Sangiovese. Ruby red with purplish highlights precede a nose of wild berry fragrances, enhanced by notes of leather and vanilla. The palate is solid and mouthfilling, boasting nicely integrated tannins. The Guardiavigna '01, named after the little watch-house that used to stand guard over the vines (and still does), amply earned its Three Glasses. A blend of sangiovese, cabernet sauvignon, merlot and petit verdot, it shows a bright, lively purplish red. The bouquet is layered and complex, alternating alcohol-steeped cherries, tobacco and liquorice. In the mouth, it reveals character and firm backbone. The entry is soft, mid palate is succulent and chewy, and there's a very long, sweet finish.

● Orcia Guardiavigna '01	🍷🍷🍷	8
● Orcia Petrucci '01	🍷🍷	8

CERTALDO (FI)

Di Fonti

via San Martino, 35
50052 Certaldo (FI)
tel. 0571669437

Di Fonti presented an array of extremely well-executed wines with a consistent, modern style. The standard-bearer is the Fontirosso '00, a blend of sangiovese, cabernet sauvignon and syrah which made it to our finals, where it by no means disgraced itself. A vivid, brilliant ruby red introduces stylish jammy tones of red berry fruit, enhanced by balsamic and peppery notes. The palate reveals powerful fruit and lively tannins supporting a solid structure and leading to a long, enjoyable finish. The equally admirable Il Moro '00, from 100 per cent cabernet sauvignon, throws a nose of black berry fruit and polished notes of spice, followed by an extremely soft palate with smooth tannins and a deep finish. The faint red berry aromas of the Chianti Vigneto Tenebroso '02 are a little dimmed by vegetal tones, but the dry palate is well sustained and agreeable. The Chianti '02 displays animal and earthy aromas that rather compromise the cleanliness of the nose, and a thinnish but harmonious and savoury palate. Lastly, the Fontibianco '02, a monovarietal Chardonnay, boasts a fruit and flower fragrance followed by a structured, but rather one-dimensional, palate. The consultant oenologist at this estate is Giovanni Cappelli.

● Fontirosso '00	🍷🍷	5
● Il Moro '00	🍷🍷	6
● Chianti '02	🍷	3
● Chianti Vigneto Tenebroso '02	🍷	4
○ Fontibianco '02	🍷	4

COLLE DI VAL D'ELSA (SI)

CORTONA (AR)

FATTORIA IL PALAGIO
FRAZ. CASTEL S. GIMIGNANO
LOC. IL PALAGIO
53030 COLLE DI VAL D'ELSA (SI)
TEL. 0577953004
E-MAIL: info@ilpalagio.it

TENIMENTI LUIGI D'ALESSANDRO
FRAZ. CAMUCIA
VIA DI MANZANO, 15
52042 CORTONA (AR)
TEL. 0575618667 - 0575618636
E-MAIL: tenimenti.dalessandro@flashnet.it

Because of the poor growing year, the Vernaccia di San Gimignano Gentilesca selection, one of the best of its kind in recent times, was not presented this year. Nevertheless, Walter Sovran, manager and oenologist of this 115-hectare Zonin-group estate which turns out 600,000 bottles a year, uncorked a range of excellent wines for us. Our favourite, not for the first time, is the Sauvignon '02, which hardly has an equal outside the long-established sauvignon-growing regions of Friuli and Alto Adige. It presents a vivid, brilliant greenish straw and an intense nose reminiscent of tomato leaf and tropical fruit. The tangy, aggressive palate is rich in varietal flavours. The equally fine Chardonnay '02, clean and fruit-led on the nose, has a solid structure in the mouth, enlivened by refreshing acidity, and a leisurely, round finish. These distinctly well-executed wines from international grapes are both great bargains. The Chianti '02 and the Vernaccia di San Gimignano Abbazia Monteoliveto '02 are decently made and pleasant but not very exciting. We are confidently looking forward to the results of a better vintage.

The D'Alessandro brothers' estate embodies the history of Cortona DOC wine. In 1988, with the help of Attilio Scienza, they planted their first experimental vineyard and as a result discovered that their land was peculiarly suited to growing expressively well-typed syrah. In 1990, they started replanting all their vineyards, a process which is still under way. Currently there are 50 hectares under vine, producing some 150,000 bottles a year. The consultant agronomists are Andrea Paoletti and Federico Staderini, and oenological advice is provided by Stefano Chioccioli. Nevertheless, the unpropitious '02 vintage made itself felt here, too, although it must be said that the wines are good. The Bosco '01 is not going to be released until next year, so that this syrah-based wine from a great vintage can benefit from extra ageing time in bottle. The Cortona Syrah '02, made with grapes from the youngest vines, is an intense wine. The fruity aromas are fresh, and we also admired the softness of the tannins and the refreshing acidity on the palate. The enjoyable Vin Santo '99 boasts notes of honey and fig on the nose, and a well-sustained palate just slightly unsettled by acerbic notes on the finish. Lastly, the Fontarca '02, obtained from a blend of chardonnay and viognier, is simple but very attractive.

O Il Palagio Chardonnay '02	🍷🍷 3*	● Cortona Syrah '02	🍷🍷 4*
O Il Palagio Sauvignon '02	🍷🍷 4*	O Cortona Fontarca '02	🍷 5
● Chianti Colli Senesi '02	🍷 3*	O Cortona Vin Santo '99	🍷 6
O Vernaccia di S. Gimignano		● Podere Il Bosco '95	🍷🍷🍷 5
Abbazia di Monteoliveto '02	🍷 3	● Podere Il Bosco '97	🍷🍷🍷 5
O Vernaccia di S. Gimignano		● Podere Il Bosco '96	🍷🍷 5
La Gentilesca '00	🍷🍷 4	● Podere Il Bosco '98	🍷🍷 5
O Il Palagio Chardonnay '01	🍷🍷 3*	● Podere Il Bosco '99	🍷🍷 6
O Il Palagio Sauvignon '01	🍷🍷 3*	O Podere Fontarca '00	🍷🍷 4*
O Vernaccia di S. Gimignano		● Cortona Il Bosco '00	🍷🍷 6
La Gentilesca '01	🍷🍷 4	O Cortona Fontarca '01	🍷🍷 5*

DICOMANO (FI)

EMPOLI (FI)

FRASCOLE
LOC. FRASCOLE, 27/A
50062 DICOMANO (FI)
TEL. 0558386340
E-MAIL: frascole@centroin.it

NOBILE PRIMA
LOC. SANT'ANDREA
VIA SENESE ROMANA, 371
50050 EMPOLI (FI)
TEL. 0571582040
E-MAIL: nobileprima@nobileprima.it

The Lippis have now emerged from the Other Wineries section, earning their first full profile in the Guide for the constancy and enthusiasm of their work in the vineyard. Frascole is a family estate, run personally by Enrico Lippi and his wife with assistance in the cellar from consultant oenologist, Federico Staderini. Located in one of the more obscure parts of Rufina, it has the advantage of well-aspected vineyards, which have been partly replanted in recent years to improve grape quality. We'll start with the Chianti Rufina '01, which has a lovely intense, luminous ruby hue. Excellent ripe fruit aromas of plum mingled with blackcurrant and cherry greet the nose, together with fine notes of spice. The enjoyable palate, well sustained by a good, close-knit tannic weave, is supported by an intriguing acid backbone and a clean lingering finish. The Riserva Il Santo '00 is opaque ruby to the eye. It has an elegant, complex bouquet in which notes of leather and tobacco blend with minty and balsamic nuances, underpinned by wild berries. A rounded entry on the palate leads into a mouthfilling, succulent progression and an attractive rising finish. Lastly, the Vin Santo '94 is a lovely bright amber that introduces sultana and almond aromas. The very sweet palate is faintly cloying but interestingly complex.

This is the debut in the Guide for Nobile Prima, which presented a series of very good wines at our tastings. Indeed, the Schiccato '01, from vines that yield 3,500 kilograms of grapes per hectare, sauntered coolly into our finals. Made from sangiovese only, it spends 15 months maturing in barrique and another four ageing in bottle. The colour is an intense opaque purplish red, and the nose is complex, unveiling black berry fruit, spice and balsamic tones. The palate reveals a powerful structure, tightly knit, smooth tannins and a long, wonderfully sweet finish. The very good, albeit less complex, Vepraio '01 is a blend of colorino and sangiovese aged in barrique for three months. The nose offers notes of subtle oriental spice and tobacco, together with gamey and leather tones underpinned by red berry fruit. The seriously substantial palate has attractively bright tannins and the finish, despite a slight surplus of oak, is enjoyable. The good Chianti Eletto '02 is a little unsettled aromatically, but the weight on the palate is good and it finishes sweet. To conclude, Lacrime di Luna '02, a monovarietal chardonnay, is buttery and faintly fruity on the nose, then full-bodied and long on the palate. Nobile Prima has about eight hectares under vine. Lorenzo Landi consults.

● Chianti Rufina Il Santo Ris. '00		♟♟	5
● Chianti Rufina '01		♟♟	4*
○ Vin Santo del Chianti Rufina '94		♟	5
○ Vin Santo del Chianti Rufina '93		♟♟	5
● Chianti Rufina '00		♟♟	4

● Schiccato '01		♟♟	6
● Vepraio '01		♟♟	6
● Chianti Eletto '02		♟	5
○ Lacrime di Luna '02		♟	5

FAUGLIA (PI)

I Giusti e Zanza
via dei Puntoni, 9
56043 Fauglia (PI)
TEL. 058544354
E-MAIL: info@igiustiezanza.it

As this year's wines proudly testify, the vines Paolo Giusti and Fabio Zanza planted a few years ago have now hit their stride. The path the two owners chose with the help of Stefano Chioccioli has led to constant improvement, further proof that to make a great wine you can't do without first-rate grapes. The vines would seem to be at an ideal age and this time, as never before, the difference between the two estate labels is very clear. Indeed, the Dulcamara '00 easily made it to our finals, only just failing to pick up a third Glass. From a blend of cabernet sauvignon and merlot, it has an intense nose of ripe red berry fruit and a perfectly balanced, elegantly structured palate that lacks only that extra something special. Still, the long finish is mouthfilling and the silky tannins well judged. Belcore '01, from sangiovese and merlot, is as good as ever, an immensely enjoyable, balanced wine with well-behaved tannins. The finish is good and the faint animal nuance on the nose leaves little doubt about the identity of one of its constituent grapes. All in all, this winery is coming on nicely at a steady, natural pace, no small feat in these frenetic, impatient times.

FIRENZE

★ Marchesi Antinori
P.zza degli Antinori, 3
50123 Firenze
TEL. 05523595
E-MAIL: antinori@antinori.it

Antinori's ever-reliable, utterly distinctive wines are produced for various different segments of the market. They range from the ubiquitous, emphatically well-made and affordable Santa Cristina to the refined exclusivity of Solaia, the supreme Antinori red, made from a skilful blend of cabernet sauvignon and a little sangiovese. And the '00 edition carried off Three Glasses, as some ten forebears have before it. The 2000 vintage is one of the most successful versions of this great wine, although not the absolute best. The '95 and the '99 were even better, as was the '97, which was underrated by the international wine press. But Solaia '00 is a superb wine, and a worthy representative of that great tradition. The nose is perhaps a touch forward, but the structure is quite formidable. The Chianti Classico Tenute del Marchese Riserva '00 is very good. In fact, we preferred it to the Tignanello '00, the historic Supertuscan made from sangiovese with a touch of cabernet sauvignon. The Chianti Classico Villa Antinori Riserva '00 is surprisingly good in one of its last appearances as a DOCG. The wine will soon be transformed into an IGT. Lastly, we have nothing but praise for the simple but irreplaceable Santa Cristina, a classic of its category which, in the '01 version, came close to earning Two Glasses.

● Dulcamara '00	▼▼	6
● Belcore '01	▼▼	4
● Dulcamara '97	▽▽	5
● Belcore '98	▽▽	4
● Dulcamara '98	▽▽	6
● Belcore '99	▽▽	4*
● Belcore '00	▽▽	4
● Dulcamara '99	▽▽	6

● Solaia '00	▼▼▼	8
● Chianti Cl.		
Tenute del Marchese Ris. '00	▼▼	6
● Chianti Cl.		
Badia a Passignano Ris. '00	▼▼	6
● Chianti Cl. Villa Antinori Ris. '00	▼▼	4
● Tignanello '00	▼▼	8
● Santa Cristina '01	▼	3
● Solaia '90	▽▽▽	8
● Tignanello '93	▽▽▽	8
● Solaia '95	▽▽▽	8
● Solaia '96	▽▽▽	6
● Solaia '97	▽▽▽	8
● Solaia '98	▽▽▽	8
● Solaia '99	▽▽▽	8

FIRENZE

CASTEL RUGGERO
LOC. BAGNO A RIPOLI - FRAZ. ANTELLA
VIA DI CASTEL RUGGERO, 33
50011 FIRENZE
TEL. 0556499423
E-MAIL: castelruggero@tiscalinet.it

After a long absence, oenologist Nicolò D'Afflitto's Castel Ruggero estate is back in the Guide. The castle in question is fortified and dates from around AD 1000, when it belonged to the Guidis. In the 15th-century, the Alamannis took it over, transforming it into a country residence, and the D'Afflittos became the owners in the early 1900s. The wines presented this year show a clear change of pace. Side by side with the traditional Chiantis, there is now a Supertuscan, a Bordeaux blend which looks extremely promising. The very fine Chianti Classico '01 shows a lovely intense ruby hue, introducing a bouquet that opens on ripe fruit notes of cherry mingled with wild berries, particularly blackcurrant. Stylish hints of cinnamon then enhance the cocktail. After a substantial attack, the palate reveals silky body and a broad, deep development with marvellously integrated tannins, and the finish just goes on and on. Castelruggero '01, from equal parts of merlot and cabernet sauvignon, went straight into our finals, thanks to a splendid bouquet initially dominated by notes of toasty oak, coffee and chocolate, but which then opens to reveal ripe fruit tones laced with hints of cloves. On the rounded, even palate, the tannins meld nicely with alcohol, and the finish is enjoyable and lingering.

FIRENZE

TENUTE AMBROGIO
E GIOVANNI FOLONARI
VIA DE' BARDI, 28
50125 FIRENZE
TEL. 055200281
E-MAIL: folonari@tenutefolonari.com

Ambrogio Folonari and his son Giovanni's group of wineries is making rapid strides. The overall quality of production is definitely on the rise, and there are increasing numbers of outstanding wines. Hence, it comes as no surprise that they have again won Three Glasses for a fine 2000 version of Il Pareto, the Cabernet Sauvignon from their Tenuta di Nozzole estate. It's a classic of its kind, with characteristic Bordeaux-like smoky scents and a firm, powerful body with tight-knit, fine-grained tannins. The excellent Cabreo Il Borgo '00, made from sangiovese and cabernet sauvignon, also attended our finals, thanks to its elegant palate of uncommon grace and balance. The two Chianti Classicos from Nozzole did well, too, and in fact the Riserva La Forra '00 was particularly successful. The Brunello di Montalcino Le Due Sorelle Riserva '97 from Tenuta La Fuga is good, but the Brunello '98 is only fair. The mostly chardonnay-based Le Bruniche '02 is pleasant, but a little unexciting. Bear in mind, however, that it comes from a growing year that was definitely less than wonderful. All in all, these producers deserve to be considered among the serious contenders in premium-quality Tuscan winemaking.

● Castelruggero '01	♟♟	6
● Chianti Cl. '01	♟♟	4
● Chianti Cl. '90	♟♟	4
● Chianti Cl. Ris. '90	♟♟	4
● Chianti Cl. '93	♟♟	3*
● Chianti Cl. Ris. '93	♟♟	4
● Chianti Cl. Ris. '94	♟♟	4
● Chianti Cl. Ris. '95	♟♟	4

● Il Pareto '00	♟♟♟	8
● Cabreo Il Borgo '00	♟♟	6
● Chianti Cl. La Forra Ris. '00	♟♟	5
● Brunello di Montalcino Le Due Sorelle Ris. '97	♟♟	8
● Chianti Cl. Nozzole '01	♟	4
○ Le Bruniche '02	♟	3
● Brunello di Montalcino '98	♟	7
● Chianti Cl. La Forra Ris. '90	♟♟♟	5
● Il Pareto '90	♟♟♟	7
● Il Pareto '93	♟♟♟	7
● Il Pareto '97	♟♟♟	7
● Il Pareto '98	♟♟♟	7
● Cabreomytho '00	♟♟	8
● Il Pareto '99	♟♟	7

FIRENZE

MARCHESI DE' FRESCOBALDI
VIA S. SPIRITO, 11
50125 FIRENZE
TEL. 05527141
E-MAIL: info@frescobaldi.it

The Frescobaldis are back among the Glassware again, this time with one of their classics, Chianti Rufina Montesodi '01. It's a paragon of elegance and power, but we were excited to observe that the quality of all the Frescobaldi wines is seriously good. Consider, for example, the Nipozzano Riserva '00. Millions of bottles leave the cellars each year yet it is a truly excellent wine. Or the Pomino Benefizio, a mostly chardonnay-based white which we recently enjoyed at a vertical tasting that showed how astonishingly well it ages. These results are the product of first-rate organization in vineyard and cellar, co-ordinated by Lamberto Frescobaldi and consultant winemaker, Nicolò D'Afflitto. But let's be more specific about the wines. The Montesodi '01 boasts elegance and finesse on the nose, and a soft, rounded, smooth palate with seamlessly blended tannins and full body. The finish is incredibly long. The Mormoreto '00, a classic Bordeaux blend, has a lovely purple hue, then definite aromas of ripe bell pepper and blackcurrant, laced with light hints of coffee, followed by a powerful, deep, and appropriately long palate with sharp tannins. The Benefizio '01 displays a fragrance of white peach, enhanced by mineral notes, and a succulent, nervy palate with nice breadth and length. The fine Pomino Rosso '00, made from pinot noir, presents flowery notes and hints of spice on the nose, then a lean, elegant, eminently quaffable palate. Pomino Bianco '01 is delicate and enjoyable.

FUCECCHIO (FI)

FATTORIA MONTELLORI
VIA PISTOIESE, 1
50054 FUCECCHIO (FI)
TEL. 0571260641
E-MAIL: montellori@tin.it

Fattoria Montellori has, with remarkable energy, managed to build a solid reputation and become a sort of lone beacon in a little known, and still rather sleepy, wine zone. First, the estate sorted out the vine stock, planting new vineyards in the best sites available and managing them with an eye to excellence of fruit. Then they turned to their cellar, where they introduced modern vinification techniques. And that's how they have produced a range of reliable wines whose quality is steadily improving. We'll start with a newcomer, the Dicatum '01, which is replacing the Castelrapiti. It is a successful monovarietal Sangiovese with grip, balance and great drinkability. The Salamartano '00, however, is struggling to find its feet and does not yet have the complexity of a great wine. The strikingly consistent sauvignon-based Sant'Amato once again offers satisfyingly eloquent, varietal flavour in the '02 version. The sound Montellori Brut boasts a fine bead and a crisp, inviting palate. The Moro '01 shows admirable co-ordination, but is a bit astringent on the finish. Lastly, there are two wines from Le Caselle, the Fattoria Montellori holding near Cerreto Guidi, a juicy, succulent Bramasole '01, made from sangiovese and syrah, and the fresh-tasting, agreeable Chianti '02.

● Chianti Rufina Montesodi '01	♥♥♥	7
● Chianti Rufina Nipozzano Ris. '00	♥♥	4
● Mormoreto '00	♥♥	7
● Pomino Rosso '00	♥♥	5
○ Pomino Il Benefizio '01	♥♥	6
○ Pomino Bianco '02	♥	4
● Pomino Rosso '85	♥♥♥	5
● Chianti Rufina Montesodi '88	♥♥♥	7
● Chianti Rufina Montesodi '90	♥♥♥	7
● Chianti Rufina Montesodi '96	♥♥♥	7
● Chianti Rufina Montesodi '97	♥♥♥	7
● Mormoreto '97	♥♥♥	6
● Chianti Rufina Montesodi '99	♥♥♥	7
● Chianti Rufina Montesodi '00	♥♥	7
● Mormoreto '99	♥♥	7

● Salamartano '00	♥♥	6
● Bramasole '01	♥♥	5
● Dicatum '01	♥♥	6
○ Sant'Amato '02	♥♥	4*
○ Vin Santo dell'Empolese '97	♥♥	5
● V. del Moro '01	♥	4
● Chianti '02	♥	3
● Chianti Fattoria le Caselle '02	♥	3
○ V. del Mandorlo '02	♥	3
○ Montellori Brut '98	♥	5
● Salamartano '96	♥♥	5
● Salamartano '97	♥♥	5
● Salamartano '98	♥♥	6
○ Sant'Amato '00	♥♥	3*
● Salamartano '99	♥♥	6

GAIOLE IN CHIANTI (SI)

AGRICOLTORI DEL CHIANTI GEOGRAFICO
LOC. MULINACCIO
VIA MULINACCIO, 10
53013 GAIOLE IN CHIANTI (SI)
TEL. 0577749489
E-MAIL: info@chiantigeografico.it

Progress continues apace at this co-operative winery, which has shown it knows how to make good standard-label wines and special selections. Credit must go to the entire staff and to the co-operative's manager, Carlo Salvadori, who has imposed a modern approach vineyard and cellar management in order to make best use of resources. The Chianti Classico '01 shows an attractive limpid ruby and a forthright nose that makes up in length for what it lacks in intensity, moving in succession from blackcurrant to raspberry, cherry and plum. The nice palate is clean and not too edgy, and its soft and hard components are well balanced. The bouquet of the more traditional Contessa di Radda selection, another '01, focuses on cherry with some hints of cinnamon. The palate is splendidly concentrated, mouthfilling and generous, and the finish lingers. The Ferraiolo '01 offers a bouquet of refreshing minty tones, together with sweet notes of fruit and spice. The palate, after a juicy attack, becomes a bit dilute at the centre, but then it acquires grip, expanding into a seductive, engrossing finish. The Pulleraia '01, from merlot only, made it to our finals with its excellent nose, where blackcurrant and raspberry jam have the upper hand over stylish spicy notes. The creamy and delightfully dense palate reveals smooth, well-integrated, fine-grained tannins and an excellent finish with no rough edges.

GAIOLE IN CHIANTI (SI)

★ CASTELLO DI AMA
FRAZ. LECCHI IN CHIANTI
LOC. AMA
53013 GAIOLE IN CHIANTI (SI)
TEL. 0577746031
E-MAIL: info@castellodiama.com

We have to say at the outset that we were unable to taste Castello di Ama's two standard-bearers, the Vigna l'Apparita and the Chianti Classico Bellavista, both from '99 and neither of them ready to appear in public. So we decided, with the full agreement of Lorenza Sebasti and Marco Pallanti, who are respectively the estate's co-owner and winemaker, as well as wife and husband, to write about them in next year's Guide. They are seriously good wines that require careful consideration, but they are developing slowly. We managed to console ourselves, however, with a masterly 2000 version of the Chianti Classico Castello di Ama, a red of extraordinary elegance, and even better than the splendid '99 that earned its own Three Glasses last year. At Ama's elevation of 500 metres above sea level, wines acquire an elegance rarely to be found in Chianti Classico, and this '00 is a perfect example of finesse and elegance in a Sangiovese. Since the cellar is not making any Chianti Classico selections from the '00 vintage, grapes from the Bellavista and La Casuccia vineyards have gone into the Castello di Ama. The other wines are fair. The Al Poggio Chardonnay '01 displays a varietal nose, The fragrant Castello di Ama Rosato '02 has been dubbed Ordine del Toson d'Oro ("Order of the Golden Fleece") and confirms that the disastrous weather during the growing year in question was just the thing for producing rosés.

●	Pulleraia '01	🍷🍷	6
●	Ferraiolo. '01	🍷🍷	6
●	Chianti Cl. Montegiachi Ris. '00	🍷	5
●	Chianti Cl. '01	🍷	4
●	Chianti Cl. Contessa di Radda '01	🍷	4
●	I Vigneti del Geografico '97	🍷🍷	5
●	Chianti Cl. '98	🍷🍷	3*
●	Chianti Cl. Montegiachi Ris. '98	🍷🍷	4
●	Pulleraia '99	🍷🍷	5
●	Pulleraia '00	🍷🍷	4*
●	Ferraiolo '00	🍷🍷	5

●	Chianti Cl. Castello di Ama '00	🍷🍷🍷	6
○	Al Poggio Chardonnay '01	🍷🍷	4
☉	Ordine del Toson d'Oro Rosato '02	🍷	3*
●	Chianti Cl. Bellavista '85	🍷🍷🍷	8
●	Chianti Cl. Bellavista '86	🍷🍷🍷	8
●	Chianti Cl. Bertinga '88	🍷🍷🍷	8
●	V. l'Apparita Merlot '88	🍷🍷🍷	8
●	Chianti Cl. Bellavista '90	🍷🍷🍷	8
●	V. l'Apparita Merlot '90	🍷🍷🍷	8
●	V. l'Apparita Merlot '91	🍷🍷🍷	8
●	V. l'Apparita Merlot '92	🍷🍷🍷	8
●	Chianti Cl. La Casuccia '97	🍷🍷🍷	8
●	Chianti Cl. Castello di Ama '99	🍷🍷🍷	5
●	Chianti Cl. Castello di Ama '97	🍷🍷	5
●	Chianti Cl. Castello di Ama '98	🍷🍷	5

GAIOLE IN CHIANTI (SI)

BADIA A COLTIBUONO
LOC. BADIA A COLTIBUONO, 2
53013 GAIOLE IN CHIANTI (SI)
TEL. 057774481
E-MAIL: info@coltibuono.com

Things are humming at the ancient Vallombrosa abbey that belongs to the Stucchi Prinetti family. After investments in vineyard and cellar, they pulled off a master-stroke to the amazement of all and sundry. Historic Coltibuono oenologist, Maurizio Castelli, has returned with the task of forming a working team headed by Emanuela Stucchi Prinetti. Having relinquished her presidency of the Consorzio del Marchio Storico, Emanuela has thrown herself wholeheartedly into this project, assisted, as usual, by her siblings. The Chianti Classico '01 is again well-executed and traditional in style. The attractive clean fragrance hinges on violets and ripe cherries. Well-integrated tannins and good concentration make the palate enjoyable, despite a not very long finish. The Riserva '00 offers a ripe aroma of black cherries preserved in alcohol, followed in quick succession by notes of leather and tobacco. The soft, even and remarkably smooth palate has tight-knit but unobtrusive tannins and an attractive finish, perked up by enjoyable acidity. The Sangioveto '00 shows an intense nose dominated by gamey notes and braced by hints of leather and tobacco, whereas the fruit is hardly perceptible. The structure in the mouth is solid and powerful, and though the tannins still need to settle down, the confident body is dense, and the finish lingers. The Vin Santo '97 exhibits typically evolved aromas, with hazelnut to the fore. The palate is velvety and sweet, but the astringent finish is in a bit of a hurry.

GAIOLE IN CHIANTI (SI)

BARONE RICASOLI
CANTINE DEL CASTELLO DI BROLIO
53013 GAIOLE IN CHIANTI (SI)
TEL. 05777301
E-MAIL: Barone@Ricasoli.it

The triumphal march of Barone Ricasoli is apparently unstoppable. In the barely ten years since Francesco Ricasoli took it in hand, the winery has regained the leading position in Chianti Classico that careless management had caused it to forfeit. Now an image-maker for the whole region wherever wine is drunk, the cellar produces a vast number of bottles without sacrificing the astonishingly high quality of each of the wines. We'll start with the Chianti Classico Castello di Brolio '00, which is clearly the child of its vintage, and hence a little more forward and alcohol-rich than the '99. However, it manages to show an acidic backbone that keeps it from seeming fat on the palate. The Casalferro '01, a blend of sangiovese and cabernet sauvignon, is still extremely young and will probably develop considerably with time. For the moment, notes of vanilla and an over-abundance of alcohol kept it away from Three Glasses. For the first time, the Chianti Classico Rocca Guicciarda Riserva '00 made it to our finals, in its best version yet. The Chianti Classico Brolio '01 is an extraordinary wine of its kind. Remarkably engrossing, and graced with a structure worthy of a much grander red, it's a great little wine. Lastly, the Formulae '01, from almost 100 per cent sangiovese, is soft, enjoyable and a very good buy.

● Sangioveto '00	♟♟	8
○ Vin Santo del Chianti Cl. '97	♟♟	6
● Chianti Cl. Ris. '00	♟	7
● Chianti Cl. '01	♟	5
● Sangioveto '95	♟♟♟	6
● Sangioveto '94	♟♟	6
● Sangioveto '97	♟♟	6
● Chianti Cl. Ris. '98	♟♟	5
● Sangioveto '99	♟♟	8
● Chianti Cl. Ris. '99	♟♟	5

● Chianti Cl. Castello di Brolio '00	♟♟♟	7
● Chianti Cl.		
Rocca Guicciarda Ris. '00	♟♟	5
● Casalferro '01	♟♟	6
● Chianti Cl. Brolio '01	♟♟	4
● Formulae '01	♟♟	3*
● Casalferro '95	♟♟♟	6
● Casalferro '96	♟♟♟	6
● Casalferro '97	♟♟♟	6
● Chianti Cl. Castello di Brolio '97	♟♟♟	6
● Casalferro '98	♟♟♟	6
● Chianti Cl. Castello di Brolio '98	♟♟♟	6
● Casalferro '99	♟♟♟	6
● Chianti Cl. Castello di Brolio '99	♟♟♟	7

GAIOLE IN CHIANTI (SI)

GAIOLE IN CHIANTI (SI)

CAPANNELLE
LOC. CAPANNELLE, 3
53013 GAIOLE IN CHIANTI (SI)
TEL. 0577749691
E-MAIL: info@capannelle.com

IL COLOMBAIO DI CENCIO
LOC. CORNIA
53013 GAIOLE IN CHIANTI (SI)
TEL. 0577747178
E-MAIL: colombaiodicencio@tin.it

Clearly they are going about things the right way at Capannelle. After last year's return to the Guide, James Sherwood's estate is here again with a range of wines that are never predictable, but show great character and strong personality. The watchful eye of Raffaele Rossetti is still on hand, helping to produce, for example, the good Chardonnay '01. Its not very intense golden hue precedes an initial buttery tone, and then the nose unleashes forthright fruity fragrances of peach and banana. In the mouth, the firm body reveals considerable acidity, kept in check by alcohol, but the finish is a tad rushed. The Chianti Classico Capannelle Riserva '99 has a strikingly stylish nose of delightful Alpine herbs and a concentrated, balanced palate that offers lots of acidic sinew and juicy tannins. We were surprised to find the sangiovese and malvasia nera-based '98 Solare at our tastings, since we reviewed the '99 last year. The evolved bouquet shows notes of tobacco and leather dominating tertiary fruit aromas. After a soft, velvety attack, the palate opens out, but the tannins on the finish are a touch inflexible. The 50 & 50 '99, produced in collaboration with Avignonesi from sangiovese and merlot, fully earned its Three Glasses. Irresistible fragrances of wild berries and spice acquire freshness and elegance from balsamic and minty notes. The mouth is particularly fascinating, thanks to its concentration, mouthfilling density and tannins that are soft, fine-grained and seamlessly distributed across the palate. The finish is sweet and satisfying.

Werner Wilhelm should not find it a cause for serious concern that his estate seems to win Three Glasses only in alternate years. This time, both the wines he presented were excellent and his Il Futuro only just missed out on our top award. The consistently high quality and great personality of Werner's wines are tangible signs of his dedication in both vineyard and cellar. With estate manager, Jacopo Morganti, and input from consultant oenologist, Paolo Vagaggini, more Three Glass triumphs look to be on the cards in the near future. The opaque ruby of the very fine Chianti Classico I Massi '01 heralds delicious ripe aromas of red berry fruit, softened by elegant, well-integrated notes of spice. The dense, silky and pleasingly soft palate is balanced and firm, then spicy notes come back on the long, delicious finish. The excellent Il Futuro, which made it to our final taste-offs, is a blend of sangiovese, cabernet sauvignon and merlot. A vividly lustrous, dense ruby introduces enchantingly concentrated fruit notes of blackcurrant jam with cloves. The rich palate is concentrated and substantial, revealing smooth fine-grained tannins and a sweet, if somewhat fleeting, finish.

● 50 & 50 Avignonesi e Capannelle '99	♟♟♟	8
○ Solare '98	♟♟	8
● Chianti Cl. Capannelle Ris. '99	♟♟	7
○ Chardonnay '01	♟	5
● 50 & 50 Avignonesi e Capannelle '97	♟♟♟	8
● Chianti Cl. Capannelle Ris. '98	♟♟	6
● 50 & 50 Avignonesi e Capannelle '98	♟♟	8
● Solare '99	♟♟	8

● Il Futuro '00	♟♟	7
● Chianti Cl. I Massi '01	♟♟	6
● Il Futuro '95	♟♟♟	7
● Il Futuro '97	♟♟♟	7
● Il Futuro '99	♟♟♟	7
● Chianti Cl. '95	♟♟	4
● Il Futuro '98	♟♟	7
● Chianti Cl. I Massi Ris. '98	♟♟	6
● Chianti Cl. I Massi '00	♟♟	6
● Chianti Cl. I Massi Ris. '99	♟♟	6

GAIOLE IN CHIANTI (SI)

GAIOLE IN CHIANTI (SI)

PODERE IL PALAZZINO
FRAZ. MONTI
POD. IL PALAZZINO
53013 GAIOLE IN CHIANTI (SI)
TEL. 0577747008
E-MAIL: palazzino@chianticlassico.com

CASTELLO DI MELETO
LOC. MELETO
53013 GAIOLE IN CHIANTI (SI)
TEL. 0577749217
E-MAIL: market@castellomeleto.it

The Sderci brothers' estate has confirmed its top-rank status. For the second year in a row, Grosso Sanese, one of their Chianti Classico selections, has picked up Three Glasses. Their loyalty to sangiovese and other native grape varieties is still undisputed, but the new, more delicate approach that favours a less edgy and more mouthfilling palate has turned out to be a winner. The oenological fine-tuning, carried out in conjunction consultant oenologist, Luciano Bandini, has produced a clear surge forward. The Chianti Classico La Pieve '01 shows a vivid ruby that introduces a composite bouquet, including very ripe plum and cherry notes alternating with headier tones. The soft, delicate palate flows beautifully, revealing deliciously smooth, perfectly integrated tannins, good acidic backbone and a sweet, lingering finish. The Chianti Classico Argenina '01 has again done well. It kicks off with a ripe nose of cherry jam only just softened by notes of cinnamon. In the mouth, it proves chewy, succulent, mouthfilling and pleasantly drinkable. The Grosso Sanese '01 has a very intense, limpid ruby leading to a fresh, inviting bouquet in which a balsamic note lends elegance to the intense, lingering ripe red berry fragrance. The entry on the palate is creamy, soft and smooth, alcohol and acidity are well balanced, the tannins could hardly be better integrated and there's a tasty rising finish.

This year's results were moderately good. Lots of wines all did pretty well, but nothing stood out. The agreeable, well-made Sangiovese Merlot Pieve di Spaltenna '02 offers captivating aromas and an excellent palate. The keynote of the Chianti Classico '01 is lightness. Berry notes on the nose combine nicely with sweet, spicy hints of vanilla. The wine's outstanding drinkability can be credited to soft tannins, prominent acidity and a lean but adequate body. The Riserva '00 is a bit monotonous on the nose, where a cherry fragrance has it all its own way. The fairly substantial palate reveals slightly assertive tannins but it's easy to drink, if short. The Pieve di Spaltenna Alle Fonti '00, made from sangiovese with a touch of merlot, provides an intense nose of alcohol-steeped cherries together with vegetal hints. The attack on the palate is good and full-bodied, but the centre lacks grip and the moderate finish is a bit acidulous. The Fiore '00, from sangiovese and merlot, presents a ripe-toned bouquet with balsamic and spicy hints. It does better in the mouth, where the entry is soft, the acidic sinew is just right and the expansion on the finish is enjoyable. Rainero '00, a blend of sangiovese, cabernet sauvignon and merlot, is not very clean on the nose, which is masked at first by vegetal tones and notes of incense, but a ripe fruity fragrance then emerges. The medium-bodied, agreeably tidy palate unveils a succulent finish.

● Chianti Cl. Grosso Sanese '01	♉♉♉	8
● Chianti Cl. Argenina '01	♉♉	5
● Chianti Cl. La Pieve '01	♉♉	6
● Chianti Cl. Grosso Sanese '00	♉♉♉	8
● Chianti Cl. Grosso Sanese Ris. '93	♉♉	5
● Chianti Cl. Grosso Sanese Ris. '94	♉♉	5
● Chianti Cl. Grosso Sanese Ris. '97	♉♉	5
● Chianti Cl. '98	♉♉	4
● Chianti Cl. Grosso Sanese Ris. '95	♉♉	5
● Chianti Cl. Grosso Sanese Ris. '96	♉♉	5
● Chianti Cl. Grosso Sanese '98	♉♉	5
● Chianti Cl. Argenina '99	♉♉	4
● Chianti Cl. La Pieve '99	♉♉	4
● Chianti Cl. La Pieve '00	♉♉	6
● Chianti Cl. Argenina '00	♉♉	5

● Fiore '00	♉♉	6
● Alle Fonti Pieve di Spaltenna '00	♉	5
● Chianti Cl. Pieve di Spaltenna '00	♉	4
● Chianti Cl. '01	♉	4
● Rainero '00	♉	7
● Sangiovese Merlot Pieve di Spaltenna '02	♉	3
● Chianti Cl. Ris. '00		5
● Fiore '97	♉♉	5
● Alle Fonti Pieve di Spaltenna '98	♉♉	5
● Chianti Cl. '99	♉♉	4
● Rainero '99	♉♉	5
● Chianti Cl. Ris. '99	♉♉	4

GAIOLE IN CHIANTI (SI)

GAIOLE IN CHIANTI (SI)

S. M. Tenimenti Pile e Lamole
LOC. VISTARENNI
53013 GAIOLE IN CHIANTI (SI)
TEL. 0577738186
E-MAIL: a.ali@stmargherita.com

RIECINE
LOC. RIECINE
53013 GAIOLE IN CHIANTI (SI)
TEL. 0577749098
E-MAIL: riecine@riecine.com

The Chianti Classico Campolungo Riserva is now one of the few red Chiantis that strive to communicate tradition and typicity. It is made exclusively from sangiovese grapes grown at Lamole, a subzone of Greve where there are still very old clones of the variety, some on bush-trained vines. Only large casks are used, not barriques, so there are no vanilla notes to distract the drinker from a decidedly fruity nose and a palate reminiscent of the Chianti of times past, when it had the distinctly rough edges that acidity and tannins can produce. This is not an easy-going wine, and it doesn't make any concessions. It needs a few years' ageing, and then close attention, in order to be understood completely. The '00 does not, we thought, have the complexity of the '99, which was an extraordinary vintage hereabouts, but it does have all the best characteristics of its style. The Campolongo's little brother, Chianti Classico Lamole di Lamole '01, is from a very different vintage and is even better than the Riserva '00, which says a lot about the two years. From the vineyards of Vistarenni, near Gaiole, the other estate in the Marzotto's little Chianti empire, we tasted a good version of the Codirosso, a monovarietal Sangiovese and also from 2000. It is definitely more modern, and more to the taste of those who favour a more international style. The fairish Chianti Classico Villa Vistarenni '01 is a bit dilute and less distinctive. The very fine Vin Santo is complex and sumptuous, but never cloys, thanks to beautifully judged acidity.

Once again, the wines from Sean O'Callaghan's winery afforded the panel great pleasure. There were no Three Glass winners this time, but they showed distinctive personality and an admirable ability to express the characteristics of their terroir. This is due in part to the choice of grape variety, sangiovese, the delight and torment of all Chianti producers. The good Chianti Classico '01 offers a clear-cut, well-focused nose dominated by lively rich fruit, with subtle notes of spice lending elegance. The palate has no rough edges; only mellow smooth tannins and unobtrusive oak. The finish is relaxed and lingering. The unusual attack on the nose of the Riserva '00 includes notes of green bell pepper and boiled sweets, which then make way for ripe fruity tones of raspberry. The palate commands attention, with its very tight-knit but restrained tannins in a meaty, very succulent body. The finish is better balanced, if not terribly long. The mostly sangiovese-based La Gioia '00 came within an ace of Three Glasses. The fine bouquet is a complex succession of mineral notes and aromas of coffee and cinnamon, on a foundation of excellent fruit. We were struck by the easy-drinking nature of the wine, despite its solid, chewy body which reveals very fine-grained tannins. Pervasive on the mouth, it shows an elegant finish without any edginess.

● Chianti Cl. Campolungo Ris. '00	♟♟	7
● Codirosso '00	♟♟	5
● Chianti Cl. Lamole di Lamole '01	♟♟	5
○ Vin Santo Lamole di Lamole '99	♟♟	5
● Chianti Cl. Lamole di Lamole Ris. '00	♟	6
● Chianti Cl. Villa Vistarenni '01	♟	4
● Chianti Cl. Campolungo Ris. '95	♟♟	4
● Chianti Cl. Lamole di Lamole Ris. '95	♟♟	4
● Chianti Cl. Villa Vistarenni '95	♟♟	4
● Codirosso '95	♟♟	5
● Chianti Cl. Campolungo Ris. '97	♟♟	5
● Codirosso '99	♟♟	5
● Chianti Cl. Campolungo Ris. '99	♟♟	5
● Chianti Cl. Villa Vistarenni '00	♟♟	3*
● Lam'oro '00	♟♟	7

● La Gioia '00	♟♟	8
● Chianti Cl. Ris. '00	♟♟	8
● Chianti Cl. '01	♟	5
● Chianti Cl. Ris. '86	♟♟♟	5
● Chianti Cl. Ris. '88	♟♟♟	6
● La Gioia '95	♟♟♟	8
● La Gioia '98	♟♟♟	8
● Chianti Cl. Ris. '99	♟♟♟	8
● Chianti Cl. '97	♟♟	5
● La Gioia '97	♟♟	8
● Chianti Cl. Ris. '98	♟♟	5
● Chianti Cl. '99	♟♟	4
● La Gioia '99	♟♟	8

GAIOLE IN CHIANTI (SI)

GAIOLE IN CHIANTI (SI)

RIETINE
LOC. RIETINE, 27
53013 GAIOLE IN CHIANTI (SI)
TEL. 0577731110 - 0577738482
E-MAIL: fattoria_di_rietine@hotmail.com

ROCCA DI CASTAGNOLI
LOC. CASTAGNOLI
VIA DEL CASTELLO, 3
53013 GAIOLE IN CHIANTI (SI)
TEL. 0577731004
E-MAIL: agricolarocca@libero.it

This year, Galina Lazarides and Mario Gaffuri, who are partners at work and at home, earned a full profile for their fine array of wines. The Rietine estate has 13 hectares under vine out of a total of 29 extending to the hamlet of the same name, actually a cluster of houses around an ancient church. The consultant oenologist here is Andrea Mazzoni. The Chianti Classico '01 presents an attractively intense, vivid ruby, followed by appealing aromas of ripe cherry that mingle with wild berries and nice hints of tobacco. The palate boasts appropriate weight, tightly-knit, well-integrated tannins and an appetizingly succulent finish where faint minerality emerges. The excellent brilliant garnet of the Riserva '99 introduces a striking bouquet of balsamic and minty notes over a fruit base of wild berries. The palate offers a good attack, well-balanced, soft, dense structure with just the right amount of acidity, and a sound, lingering finish. The fine Tiziano '99 is a merlot-based Supertuscan with a delicate nose of faint mint that gives way to aromas of Alpine herbs on a background of very ripe fruit. The enjoyable palate is warm, juicy and mouthfilling, the acidity is well judged and the finish is long.

Formidable is what we could call this year's performance by the wines from Calogero Calì's estate. Thanks to the expert contribution of oenologist, Maurizio Alongi, Rocca di Castagnoli has won its first Three Glasses. Let's see the details. The Molino delle Balze '01 presents eloquent oak tones blended with sweet fruity notes on the nose. The savoury, deep palate drives through to an exciting finish. The simple but clear-cut fragrance of the Chianti Classico '01 is dominated by red berry fruit. In the mouth, the wine proves very drinkable, partly because of just the right amount of lively acidity. The Capraia Riserva '00 offers an attractive nose, with rich fruit emerging from sweet spicy tones. The palate shows a flavourful entry, then reveals well-judged tannins, enticing body and a succulent finish. The Poggio ai Frati Riserva '00 is less successful, despite an enchanting fragrance of coffee and berries. The palate displays moderate density, tight-woven, enjoyable tannins and a rather rushed finish that takes it down a peg. The excellent Buriano '00, from cabernet sauvignon only, boasts an inviting bouquet of wild berries and a creamy but solid body with a lingering finish. The Stielle '00, a blend of sangiovese and cabernet sauvignon, is monumental. The nose flaunts seductive, very elegant notes of wild berries mingling with delicate spicy hints of pepper and cinnamon. The stylish palate shows a smooth body with beautifully integrated tannins and an enjoyable finish. The very good Vin Santo '96 is elegantly redolent of hazelnut, preceding a fleshy, lingering palate.

● Chianti Cl. '01	▼▼	4
● Chianti Cl. Ris. '99	▼▼	5
● Tiziano '99	▼▼	6
● Tiziano '88	♈♈	5
● Tiziano '90	♈♈	5
● Chianti Cl. Ris. '97	♈♈	4
● Chianti Cl. Ris. '98	♈♈	5

● Stielle '00	▼▼▼	8
● Buriano '00	▼▼	8
● Chianti Cl. Capraia Ris. '00	▼▼	6
○ Molino delle Balze '01	▼▼	5
○ Vin Santo del Chianti Cl. '96	▼▼	7
● Chianti Cl. Poggio ai Frati Ris. '00	▼	6
● Chianti Cl. '01	▼	4
● Chianti Cl. Capraia Ris. '98	♈♈	8
● Stielle '98	♈♈	8
● Le Pratole '00	♈♈	8
● Buriano '99	♈♈	8
● Chianti Cl. Capraia Ris. '99	♈♈	8
● Chianti Cl. Poggio ai Frati Ris. '99	♈♈	8
● Stielle '99	♈♈	8

GAIOLE IN CHIANTI (SI)

GAIOLE IN CHIANTI (SI)

SAN GIUSTO A RENTENNANO
FRAZ. MONTI IN CHIANTI
LOC. SAN GIUSTO A RENTENNANO
53013 GAIOLE IN CHIANTI (SI)
TEL. 0577747121
E-MAIL: sangiustorentennano@chiantinet.it

This time, Percarlo, the estate's star bottle, which always causes a stir and often wins Three Glasses, did not appear at our tastings. The reason is simply that it wasn't produced, because the cellar did not consider the vintage worthy. Instead, there was a new Chianti Classico selection called Le Baroncole. This year's was, generally speaking, a somewhat subdued performance. Bouquets wanted cleanness, although structure on the palate was, as usual, good. The Chianti Classico '01 presents a not very inviting nose that reveals some fairly inelegant notes of oak and rich fruity tones of cherry. The palate is appropriately solid but not rounded, nor is the finish very long. The nose of the easy-drinking Chianti Classico Le Baroncole '00 is dominated by a somewhat cloying boiled sweet note. The entry on the palate is firm and powerful, revealing fine-grained, evenly distributed tannins and an enjoyable smooth finish. The '00 La Ricolma, a 100 per cent Merlot, offers inviting aromas of elegantly sweet, ripe wild berries. After a seductive round entry, the palate expands nicely, unveiling well-integrated tannins, nicely judged acidity and a finish that could be just a touch longer. The bouquet of the Vin Santo '96 includes enticing notes of hazelnut and date, but the sweetish palate tends to cloy.

SAN VINCENTI
LOC. SAN VINCENTI
POD. DI STIGNANO, 27
53013 GAIOLE IN CHIANTI (SI)
TEL. 0577734047
E-MAIL: svincent@chiantinet.it

After last year's first-ever Three Glass award, San Vincenti has done it again, this time with their sangiovese-based Supertuscan, Stignano. Little by little, without any fuss, the estate has been getting steadily better, and now it's remarkably good. This is thanks to the owners, Roberto Pucci and Roberta Vannini, and to the peerless expertise of Carlo Ferrini. The remarkably fresh bouquet of the Chianti Classico '01 includes delightful balsamic and herbal tones, matched with fruity notes of sour redcurrant and blueberry. The palate is not imposing, but shows suppleness, flavour and drinkability. The tannins are well behaved and the finish is sweet. The excellent Riserva '00 shows a discreetly elegant nose of blackcurrant and blueberry, over a fruit-rich base of very attractive ripe cherry. The delectable texture of the smooth, powerful palate is in part due to the perfect integration of the tannins into the firm body. The finish is long and sweet. Finally, the mostly sangiovese-based Stignano '00 presents an enchantingly diverse nose in which cherry and strawberry notes are enriched by spicy hints of cinnamon and freshly ground pepper. The entry on the palate is velvety, and as the wine opens out it reveals depth, power and softness, with tannins that meld beautifully into the structure, and a long, rising finish that mirrors the nose perfectly.

● La Ricolma '00	🍷🍷	8
● Chianti Cl. Le Baroncole '00	🍷	6
● Chianti Cl. '01	🍷	5
○ Vin Santo '96	🍷	6
● Percarlo '88	🍷🍷🍷	8
● Percarlo '97	🍷🍷🍷	8
● Percarlo '99	🍷🍷🍷	8
● La Ricolma '97	🍷🍷	8
● La Ricolma '98	🍷🍷	8
● Chianti Cl. Ris. '98	🍷🍷	5
● Percarlo '98	🍷🍷	8
● Chianti Cl. Ris. '99	🍷🍷	6
● La Ricolma '99	🍷🍷	8

● Stignano '00	🍷🍷🍷	7
● Chianti Cl. Ris. '00	🍷🍷	6
● Chianti Cl. '01	🍷🍷	5
● Chianti Cl. Ris. '99	🍷🍷🍷	5*
● Chianti Cl. Ris. '96	🍷🍷	6
● Stignano '96	🍷🍷	5
● Chianti Cl. Ris. '97	🍷🍷	6
● Stignano '97	🍷🍷	7
● Stignano '98	🍷🍷	7
● Chianti Cl. '99	🍷🍷	4
● Chianti Cl. '00	🍷🍷	5
● Stignano '99	🍷🍷	7

GAMBASSI TERME (FI)

SAN VETTORE
LOC. SAN VETTORE, 51
50050 GAMBASSI TERME (FI)
TEL. 0571678005 - 0571678035
E-MAIL: info@sanvettore.it

After some years tagging along in Other Wineries, San Vettore has surged ahead to claim its own profile in the Guide. The 15 hectares under vine of this little estate right at the border of Chianti with the San Gimignano DOC zone are not planted exclusively to the traditional Tuscan varieties. In the most suitable sites, shrewdly chosen by the owner and his expert consultant oenologist, Luciano Bandini, you can find such immigrant grapes as pinot noir, merlot, cabernet sauvignon and syrah for the reds, and whites like traminer, sauvignon blanc and viognier. The organically farmed estate produces about 30,000 bottles a year. Only a few of the wines – and those few only when the grapes seem good enough – spend some time in oak. The Maria Teresa '01, a blend of merlot and cabernet sauvignon, made a fine impression. The nose is focused on dark berry fruit, plum and spice, with faint vegetal hints. The palate, full-bodied, meaty and succulent, shows tight-knit, soft tannins and an appropriately long finish. High marks for both the Maria Margherita '02, a blend of traminer and sauvignon with an intense fruit and flower nose and a mouthfilling palate, and the Traminer '02, which is varietal on the nose and in the mouth. The solid, enjoyable Chianti Riserva '00 almost won Two Glasses, like the Pinot Nero '01, which is faithfully varietal. It should be noted that prices here are by no means excessive.

GAMBASSI TERME (FI)

VILLA PILLO
VIA VOLTERRANA, 24
50050 GAMBASSI TERME (FI)
TEL. 0571680212
E-MAIL: info@villapillo.com

There has been no perceptible decline in the reliability of the wines presented annually by Villa Pillo. The key to this consistent quality is the skilful attention the owners give, particularly during the process of vinification, to preserving intact the varietal qualities that are essential to moulding a wine's personality. In fact, almost all Villa Pillo wines are monovarietal and emblematic of the perfect symbiosis of grape and the excellent site climates in this area. The flagship Syrah '01 is a textbook expression of its grape. The lovely peppery fragrance is carried along by fruity notes, then the attack on the palate is sweet, full-bodied and dense. Progression is nicely balanced and the finish mirrors the bouquet. The equally good Merlot Sant'Adele '01 offers a fruit-led nose shot through with notes of oak and spice, followed by an imposing palate whose balanced tannins lead to a well-defined finish that would benefit from greater complexity. The less successful monovarietal Cabernet Franc, the Vivaldaia '01, is prominently vegetal on the nose, then the palate is fairly balanced and quite agreeable. We preferred the Borgoforte '01, a blend of sangiovese, syrah and cabernet sauvignon with aromas of red berry fruit and spice as well as faint vegetal hints. These are followed by a refreshing, flavourful and pleasingly soft palate.

●	Merlot Maria Teresa '01	♟♟	5
○	Maria Margherita '02	♟♟	4
○	Traminer '02	♟♟	4
●	Chianti Ris. '00	♟	4
●	Pinot Nero '01	♟	5
●	Chianti '02	♟	3
●	Cabernet Sauvignon '00	♟	5
●	Chianti '00	♟	3*
○	Traminer '00	♟	4

●	Merlot Sant'Adele '01	♟♟	6
●	Syrah '01	♟♟	6
●	Borgoforte '01	♟	4
●	Vivaldaia '01	♟	6
●	Syrah '97	♟♟♟	5
●	Syrah '96	♟♟	5
●	Cabernet Sauvignon '97	♟♟	5
●	Merlot '98	♟♟	5
●	Syrah '98	♟♟	5
●	Syrah '99	♟♟	5
●	Merlot Sant'Adele '99	♟♟	5
●	Merlot Sant'Adele '00	♟♟	6
●	Syrah '00	♟♟	6
●	Vivaldaia '99	♟	5
●	Vivaldaia '00	♟	6

GREVE IN CHIANTI (FI)

CARPINETO
LOC. DUDDA, 17/B
50022 GREVE IN CHIANTI (FI)
TEL. 0558549062 - 0558549086
E-MAIL: info@carpineto.com

The '00 vintage was not a very positive one for Carpineto, a winery known for its reliably consistent quality. This says a lot about the vintage, which was somewhat precipitately extolled by the mass media. The Chianti Classico Riserva '99 was decidedly more interesting than the '00, which is nonetheless good, but lacks the personality and grip the older one has in abundance. The aromas are slightly over-ripe, but the palate is unquestionably mouthfilling and very appealing, although not so complex. We can, as usual, find nothing to criticize in its execution. In terms of style and oenological technique, Carpineto is one of the top producers in Chianti. The Farnito Cabernet Sauvignon '00 is a bit below par as well. It seemed a little dilute in the mouth, possibly because of rather prominent alcohol which rather coarsens the fine varietal characteristics of the wine. Ethyl alcohol is tasteless in itself but can, when present in abundance, render the flavour flat and unappealing, unless offset by appropriate acidity and extract. And this is what happened in '00, but not, we hasten to add, only here. The fair Chianti Classico '01 is well made and agreeable, but simpler, as you would expect. We confidently await better days, which are certain to arrive with the seriously good Carpineto '01s.

GREVE IN CHIANTI (FI)

PODERE POGGIO SCALETTE
LOC. RUFFOLI
VIA BARBIANO, 7
50022 GREVE IN CHIANTI (FI)
TEL. 0558546108
E-MAIL: poggio.scalette@tiscali.it

There was another triumph for the Fiore family estate, run by Vittorio and his son, Juri. The Carbonaione '00, from 100 per cent sangiovese, made a splendid showing at our finals and won Three Glasses for the third time. Last year, we mentioned that we would like to do a vertical tasting of all its vintages, and now we have. We were most interested to see how very well it ages. With the passage of time, Carbonaione manages to rein in the odd tannic rough edge that has occasionally kept us from giving it our unqualified praise. This would happen particularly in what were considered exceptional vintages: the bigger structure probably requires more time to achieve balance. But let's get down to the '00. A bright, very dense, vivid ruby introduces a lovely bouquet that includes blackcurrant and blueberry, subtle elegant spicy notes of vanilla and cloves, and a light floral fragrance, with inviting balsamic tones. After a warm attack, the palate shows well-balanced body with beautifully tidy, fine-grained, mouthfilling tannins, and the finish is confident, deep and enchantingly fruity. The second family jewel, the cabernet sauvignon and merlot blend called Piantonaia which we so admired last year, was not presented at our tastings this time. Our suspicion is that, since the cellar makes only 1,200 bottles, a rave review could have caused some distribution problems.

● Chianti Cl. Ris. '00	♟♟	5
● Farnito Cabernet Sauvignon '00	♟	6
● Chianti Cl. '01	♟	5
● Dogajolo '01	♟	4
● Rosso di Montepulciano '02	♟	3*
● Farnito Cabernet Sauvignon '93	♟♟	5
● Chianti Cl. Ris. '94	♟♟	4
● Farnito Cabernet Sauvignon '95	♟♟	5
● Chianti Cl. Ris. '97	♟♟	4
● Chianti Cl. '98	♟♟	3
● Chianti Cl. Ris. '98	♟♟	5
○ Farnito Chardonnay '99	♟♟	4
● Chianti Cl. Ris. '99	♟♟	5
● Chianti Cl. '00	♟♟	4
● Farnito Cabernet Sauvignon '99	♟♟	6

● Il Carbonaione '00	♟♟♟	8
● Il Carbonaione '96	♟♟♟	8
● Il Carbonaione '98	♟♟♟	8
● Il Carbonaione '92	♟♟	8
● Il Carbonaione '93	♟♟	8
● Il Carbonaione '94	♟♟	8
● Il Carbonaione '95	♟♟	8
● Il Carbonaione '97	♟♟	8
● Piantonaia '00	♟♟	8
● Il Carbonaione '99	♟♟	8

GREVE IN CHIANTI (FI)

GREVE IN CHIANTI (FI)

CASTELLO DI QUERCETO
LOC. QUERCETO - FRAZ. LUCOLENA
VIA DUDDA, 61
50020 GREVE IN CHIANTI (FI)
TEL. 05585921
E-MAIL: querceto@castellodiquerceto.it

★ QUERCIABELLA
VIA BARBIANO, 17
50022 GREVE IN CHIANTI (FI)
TEL. 055853834
E-MAIL: info@querciabella.com

The wines from Alessandro François' estate are always very good indeed, although perhaps if he didn't make so many of them they would be even better. The complex nose of the Chianti Classico '01 has vegetal tones and ripe fruit. The palate reveals grip and crunchy tannins, nicely integrated into a body with an admirable balance of acidity and alcohol. The not very exciting Riserva '99 offers dominant vegetal aromas that usher in a very dilute palate with mouth-drying tannins. The more successful Chianti Classico Il Picchio Riserva '99 displays a complex nose including cinnamon, blackberry jam and faint hints of leather. The attack on the palate is well judged, if not particularly powerful, and the orderly progression reveals close-knit, well-integrated tannins that brace the progression to a rising, lingering finish. The sangiovese-based La Corte '00 has an excessively grassy fragrance, but is more appealing in the mouth, where a compact body slowly opens out, leaving a few rough edges for the finish. In contrast, the very good Cignale '00, a blend of cabernet sauvignon and merlot, boasts a harmonious bouquet with a clear-cut fruit base lifted by telling notes of spice. The tidy mellow tannins blend nicely with the alcohol, and the finish is succulent. After an enticing fruit-forward nose, the Sole di Alessandro '00 is a bit lightweight on the palate, which is enjoyable but hasn't got much grip. The fairish Querciolaia '00, from sangiovese and cabernet sauvignon, is not altogether clean on the nose, but proves to be full-bodied and supported by compact, crunchy tannins.

Sadly, we begin this profile with some very sorrowful news: Giuseppe Castiglioni, known to his friends as Pepito, the man who willed this extraordinary Chianti winery into existence, has left us. We were amongst those who had the good fortune to know him, and we will never forget his enthusiasm and vast generosity. He will be greatly missed. Some years ago, Pepito handed over control of Querciabella to his son, Sebastiano, who continues to work with a first-class team, as the results demonstrate. The vineyards are managed in accordance with the tenets of biodynamics, to the obvious advantage of the wines. The Camartina '00, made from sangiovese and cabernet sauvignon, is an absolute gem. It has its customary intense fruit aromas mingling with mineral and smoky notes. The palate struck us as extremely elegant, as it always does, but with a touch more body than usual. The Palafreno '00, a blend of sangiovese and merlot, is softer and more engrossing on the palate, then the nose is a bit more forward, offering notes of tobacco and raspberry. This is a new Querciabella offering, but it already looks set to become one of the lions of the Tuscan wine world. The mostly chardonnay-based Batàr '01 is a classic barrique-aged white with notes of vanilla and tropical fruit on the nose and a very succulent palate. It's good, but not as complex as it has been. Lastly, the Chianti Classico '01, partly made with the grapes that used to go into the Riserva, which will no longer be produced, is a particularly felicitous version of a typical, very elegant red wine.

● Cignale '00	♙♙	8
● La Corte '00	♙♙	7
● Chianti Cl. '01	♙♙	4
● Il Sole di Alessandro '00	♙	7
● Querciolaia '00	♙	6
● Chianti Cl. Il Picchio Ris. '99	♙	6
● Chianti Cl. Ris. '99	♙	6
● Chianti Cl. Ris. '95	♙♙	4
● Cignale '97	♙♙	6
● La Corte '97	♙♙	5
● Querciolaia '97	♙♙	5
● Chianti Cl. Il Picchio Ris. '98	♙♙	6
● La Corte '98	♙♙	7
● Cignale '98	♙♙	8

● Camartina '00	♙♙♙	8
● Palafreno '00	♙♙	6
○ Batàr '01	♙♙	7
● Chianti Cl. '01	♙♙	5
● Camartina '88	♙♙♙	8
● Camartina '90	♙♙♙	8
● Camartina '94	♙♙♙	8
● Camartina '95	♙♙♙	8
○ Batàr '97	♙♙♙	7
○ Batàr '98	♙♙♙	7
● Camartina '97	♙♙♙	8
● Camartina '99	♙♙♙	8
○ Batàr '99	♙♙	7
○ Batàr '00	♙♙	7

GREVE IN CHIANTI (FI)

SAVIGNOLA PAOLINA
VIA PETRIOLO, 58
50022 GREVE IN CHIANTI (FI)
TEL. 0558546036
E-MAIL: savignola@bcc.tin.it

The Fabbri family's estate at Greve in
Chianti piloted its Supertuscan all the way
to the final taste-offs. Our only complaint is
the great discrepancy in quality between
their standard wines and the special
selection, but we rather suspect this
problem will be overcome shortly as a
result of the general re-organization the
Fabbris have undertaken with oenologist,
Lorenzo Landi, of their four hectares under
vine, planted primarily to sangiovese. And
now to the wines themselves. We were not
thrilled by the Chianti Classico '01, which
shows pale ruby, preceding a slightly
unclean nose and scratchy, mouth-drying
tannins. The Riserva '00, which did better,
displays an intense, lustrous colour, a
moderately intense nose with notes of
animal skin and leather and, eventually,
ripe fruit, then a full-bodied mouthfilling
palate. The tannins are prominent to the
point of aggressiveness and underpinned
by a fair amount of alcohol. The finish is
medium long. Granaio '01, a monovarietal
sangiovese, shows a lovely vivid purple,
then a variety of aromas, starting with
plum and cherry, which give way to
elegant notes of spice. The palate's
substantial, dense attack develops
confidently to reveal well-integrated
tannins which are, however, a bit
astringent on the finish.

GREVE IN CHIANTI (FI)

TORRACCIA DI PRESURA
LOC. STRADA IN CHIANTI
VIA DELLA MONTAGNOLA, 130
50027 GREVE IN CHIANTI (FI)
TEL. 0558588656 - 055490563
E-MAIL: torracciadipresura@torracciadipresura.it

Paolo Osti's wines continue to improve
slowly but surely. His 23 hectares under
vine are planted for the most part to native
varieties. The Chianti Classico '01 offers
graceful notes of tobacco and toasty
tones, all nicely co-ordinated on the nose.
After a not very impressive, faintly dilute
attack, the palate opens out, revealing
appropriate solidity, and then delightful
succulent fruit on the finish. The nose of
the Chianti Classico Il Tarocco selection,
another '01, opens to green bell pepper
over a ripe fruit-rich background of cherry,
and then makes way for notes of leather.
The strikingly dense texture in the mouth
shows signs of fatigue towards the finish.
The Tarocco Riserva '00 boasts an
appealing bouquet of crushed fresh fruit,
particularly cherry and blackcurrant,
blending with spicy notes of incense and
camphor. In the mouth, it seems less
confident. The tannins are rough and a
little too assertive, and although it's
agreeable, it's not very long. The fine
Lucciolaio '00, a blend of sangiovese and
cabernet sauvignon, made it to our finals.
It presents an intriguing aroma of cooked
green bell pepper melding with clear-cut,
clean notes of fruit. The palate is firm and
substantial, and the densely woven, well-
paced tannins are nicely supported by
significant alcohol but are just a bit
astringent on the otherwise good finish.

● Granaio '01	♟♟	6
● Chianti Cl. Ris. '00	♟	5
● Chianti Cl. '01	♟	4
● Chianti Cl. Ris. '85	♟♟	5
● Chianti Cl. Ris. '90	♟♟	5
● Chianti Cl. Ris. '95	♟♟	4
● Granaio '00	♟♟	6
● Chianti Cl. Ris. '99	♟♟	5
● Chianti Cl. '00	♟	4

● Lucciolaio '00	♟♟	6
● Chianti Cl. '01	♟♟	4
● Chianti Cl. Il Tarocco Ris. '00	♟	4
● Chianti Cl. Il Tarocco '01	♟	4
● Chianti Cl. Il Tarocco '96	♟♟	3
● Chianti Cl. Il Tarocco Ris. '98	♟♟	4
● Chianti Cl. '00	♟♟	4
● Chianti Cl. Il Tarocco '00	♟♟	4

GREVE IN CHIANTI (FI)

GREVE IN CHIANTI (FI)

CASTELLO UZZANO
VIA DI UZZANO, 23
50022 GREVE IN CHIANTI (FI)
TEL. 0558544851
E-MAIL: uzzano@val.it

CASTELLO DI VERRAZZANO
LOC. VERRAZZANO
50022 GREVE IN CHIANTI (FI)
TEL. 055854243
E-MAIL: info@verrazzano.com

The Sorelli brothers' estate has made a fine debut in the Guide. Engaging consultant oenologist, Giovanni Cappelli, seems to have been just the right move to prod their production out of its moderately good rut onto a decidedly more interesting track. The Castello Uzzano estate near Greve comprises 30 hectares, almost all of which are under vine. There was a great performance from the Chianti Classico '01. The lovely opaque ruby of the Chianti Classico '01 heralds an eloquent and remarkably fruity nose of cherry and redcurrant notes with undertones of chocolate and coffee. The nicely rounded palate reveals well-paced, fine-grained tannins and a perfect balance of alcohol and acidity, leading to a notably elegant finish. The excellent Il Grevone '00, made mostly from sangiovese, has a complex nose of oak notes, reinforced by distinct, attractive hints of chocolate and ripe plum. In the mouth, it is full-bodied, strikingly vigorous, and very relaxed in its progression, with well-integrated tannins and a satisfying but slightly rushed finish. The less successful Riserva '00 has a ripe fruit nose dominated by alcohol-steeped berries and rather astringent tannins on the palate.

The wines from Castello di Verrazzano are always reliably consistent, well executed and a faithful expression of their terroir. The property is located in one of the northernmost corners of the vast Chianti Classico zone, and the wines themselves come, in great part, from vineyards with north-facing aspects. As a result, the reds are more subtle and elegant – more "northern", we might say – than most Chianti wines, and should be judged bearing this in mind. The product we liked best this time was the Bottiglia Particolare '00, from sangiovese and a little cabernet sauvignon. The child of what was, in Greve, a quite propitious vintage, it displays its customary finesse, including an orderly, aristocratic palate. The very good Sassello '00, a monovarietal sangiovese and the estate's flagship, proclaims its varietal and geographical origins unmistakably, and does so to great effect. It is not, and could never be, a full-bodied, powerful wine, but its varietal, stylish aromas and the elegance of the structure make it very representative of this subzone. The more straightforward Chianti Classico '01 is fragrant, easy drinking and charming.

● Il Grevone '00	🍷🍷	6
● Chianti Cl. '01	🍷🍷	4
● Chianti Cl. Ris. '00	🍷	5
● Vin Santo del Chianti '96		5

● Bottiglia Particolare '00	🍷🍷	7
● Sassello '00	🍷🍷	8
● Chianti Cl. '01	🍷	5
● Chianti Cl. Ris. '90	🍷🍷🍷	5
● Sassello '97	🍷🍷🍷	6
● Sassello '93	🍷🍷	6
● Sassello '95	🍷🍷	6
● Chianti Cl. Ris. '96	🍷🍷	5
● Bottiglia Particolare '97	🍷🍷	6
● Chianti Cl. '97	🍷🍷	4
● Chianti Cl. Ris. '97	🍷🍷	5
● Bottiglia Particolare '98	🍷🍷	6
● Chianti Cl. '99	🍷🍷	4
● Chianti Cl. Ris. '99	🍷🍷	5
● Sassello '99	🍷🍷	6

GREVE IN CHIANTI (FI)

CASTELLO DI VICCHIOMAGGIO
LOC. LE BOLLE
VIA VICCHIOMAGGIO, 4
50022 GREVE IN CHIANTI (FI)
TEL. 055854079
E-MAIL: vicchiomaggio@vicchiomaggio.it

John Matta's range of bottles shows considerable personality and confirms that this estate has what it takes to produce first-class good wine. The nose of the Chianti Classico San Jacopo '01 opens on an aromatic herbal note that gives way to prominent mineral tones, followed by an appealing cherry fragrance. The attack on the palate is well balanced, but the succulent finish appears too soon. The Riserva Petri '00 is not overly clean on the nose, where pronounced vegetal tones are interlaced with ripe red berry fruit. The wine does better in the mouth. The body is solid and although the tannins stand out assertively, they are not excessive. The Riserva La Prima '00 made it to our finals. A bouquet of spicy pepper and cloves mingling with ripe wild berries, introduces a captivating palate with perfectly absorbed tannins and a long, savoury finish. The not very successful Ripa delle Mandorle '01, from sangiovese and cabernet sauvignon, is poorly defined on the nose and its oak-derived tannins are decidedly mouth-drying. On its debut, the cabernet, merlot and sangiovese Semifonte di Semifonte '01 was already a candidate for Three Glasses. Rich fruit on the nose reveals appealing notes of fresh pepper and roasting coffee beans. The palate has crunchy tannins and a generous body that's just a bit niggardly on the finish. The Ripa delle More '00, from sangiovese with a touch of cabernet sauvignon, also did very well. Vanilla is the keynote on the nose, which means the oak needs more time to integrate, then the palate offers concentration, deep flavour and an engaging finish.

GREVE IN CHIANTI (FI)

VILLA VIGNAMAGGIO
VIA DI PETRIOLO, 5
50022 GREVE IN CHIANTI (FI)
TEL. 055854661 - 0558546653
E-MAIL: info@vignamaggio.com

This year, we were particularly taken by the special selections Vignamaggio presented, but the various Chianti Classicos seemed less interesting. It may be a question of the vintages, but whatever the case, the two Supertuscans were superb. And most probably, we'll be seeing great sangiovese-based bottles soon as well. But to get down to the wines. The nose of the Chianti Classico '01 releases faint notes of redcurrants, slightly masked by cherries. The attack on the enjoyably succulent palate is confident, and the finish is attractive. The not very distinguished Terre di Prenzano '01 offers raspberry fragrances and a very fluent palate that makes for easy drinking. The Castello di Monna Lisa Riserva '00 is initially held back by grassy tones on the nose, but alcohol-steeped cherries eventually emerge. The palate is solid, and densely packed tannins accompany the savoury finish. Obsession '00, a blend of merlot, syrah and cabernet sauvignon, made it to our finals with its concentrated bouquet of blackberry jam, shading into spicy notes. Admirable acid bite and structure are immediately apparent on the deep palate, which also finishes enjoyably. Vignamaggio '00, a monovarietal Cabernet Franc, walked off with Three Glasses. The sumptuous bouquet unveils a measured balance of coffee, balsamic notes and fruit. The palate unfolds slowly to disclose a surprisingly delicate acid backbone, well-blended tannins and an unusually satisfying, persistent finish. The excellent Vin Santo '98 is intensely jammy on the nose, and opulent and long-lasting on the palate.

● Semifonte di Semifonte '01	♉♉	6
● Chianti Cl. La Prima Ris. '00	♉♉	5
● Ripa delle More '00	♉♉	6
● Chianti Cl. Petri Ris. '00	♉	5
● Chianti Cl. San Jacopo '01	♉	4
● Ripa delle Mandorle '01	♉	4
● Ripa delle More '94	♉♉♉	5
● Ripa delle More '97	♉♉♉	6
● Ripa delle More '96	♉♉	5
● Chianti Cl. La Prima Ris. '98	♉♉	5
● Chianti Cl. Petri Ris. '98	♉♉	4
● Ripa delle More '98	♉♉	6
● Ripa delle More '99	♉♉	6
● Chianti Cl. La Prima Ris. '99	♉♉	5

● Vignamaggio '00	♉♉♉	7
● Obsession '00	♉♉	7
○ Vin Santo del Chianti Classico '98	♉♉	6
● Chianti Cl. Monna Lisa Ris. '00	♉	6
● Chianti Cl. '01	♉	5
● Chianti Cl. Terre di Prenzano '01	♉	4
● Chianti Cl. Monna Lisa Ris. '95	♉♉♉	4
● Chianti Cl. Monna Lisa Ris. '99	♉♉♉	6
● Chianti Cl. Monna Lisa Ris. '97	♉♉	5
● Chianti Cl. Monna Lisa Ris. '98	♉♉	5
● Obsession '98	♉♉	6
● Vignamaggio '98	♉♉	5
● Obsession '99	♉♉	7
● Vignamaggio '99	♉♉	6
● Chianti Cl. '00	♉♉	4

GREVE IN CHIANTI (FI)

VITICCIO
VIA SAN CRESCI, 12/A
50022 GREVE IN CHIANTI (FI)
TEL. 055854210
E-MAIL: info@fattoriaviticcio.com

Alessandro Landini's estate has again done very well, and if there was no absolute champion, the plan he has mapped out with oenologist, Gabriella Tani, is sure to improve the already fine quality of the wines. After initial dumbness, the nose of the Chianti Classico '01 opens to attractive aromas, with well-defined wild berries to the fore. The substantial, mouthfilling palate reveals tight-knit, well-integrated tannins and a long succulent finish. The Riserva '00 shows a nicely varied nose dominated by refreshing cherries. The palate is powerful and muscular, the compact tannins blend into the forceful, but still slightly taut, body and the finish is delicious. The Riserva Beatrice '00, as the back label indicates, contains a generous proportion of cabernet sauvignon, a fact confirmed by the balsam and blackberry notes on the nose. The powerful broad palate flaunts perfect balance of alcohol and acidity. The tannins are just a touch intrusive, but the finish is positive. The sangiovese-based Prunaio '00 is a little stiff at first, but after a while aromas of ripe wild berries, with light stylish vanilla, emerge to delight. The soft, silky palate boasts well-paced, unobtrusive tannins and a very enjoyable finish. The Monile '00, which is mostly cabernet sauvignon, presents somewhat excessive vegetal tones that overshadow the fruit on the nose. In the mouth, it is full-bodied and soft, if not particularly complex, and the finish is clean.

GROSSETO

TENUTA BELGUARDO
LOC. MONTEBOTTIGLI - VIII ZONA
58100 GROSSETO
TEL. 057773571
E-MAIL: fonteruoli@fonteruoli.it

The 35 hectares under vine at Tenuta Belguardo, which was acquired by the Mazzei family in 1997, will have increased to 75 by 2005. Meanwhile, results are already excellent. The presence on the labels of their current range of three wines of the polyhedron Leonardo da Vinci drew for "De Divina Proportione" is perhaps emblematic of the ambitious aims of this new project, in which the Mazzeis are assisted, as usual, by oenologist, Carlo Ferrini. The Tenuta Belguardo '01, a blend of cabernet sauvignon, merlot and sangiovese and the "grand vin" of the estate, shows great breeding. A brilliant, very concentrated ruby introduces a remarkably effective nose of red berry fruit and rich spicy tones. We were struck by the massive tannic structure on the palate, combined with great finesse and a long sweet finish. The equally aristocratic Serrata di Belguardo '01 displays a dark purplish red and a red berry fragrance, with intense balsamic and spicy notes. It has so much personality, and such a full body, that it seems to continue forever in the mouth. The Poggio Bronzone '01 is one of the best Morellinos we've tasted. A lovely opaque ruby, it offers clean scents of cherries preserved in alcohol, wild berries and vanilla. The palate is soft and lifted by fine-grained tannins. The finish lingers.

● Chianti Cl. Beatrice Ris. '00	♟♟	6
● Chianti Cl. Ris. '00	♟♟	6
● Prunaio '00	♟♟	7
● Chianti Cl. '01	♟♟	5
● Monile '00	♟	7
● Prunaio '99	♟♟♟	7
● Prunaio '96	♟♟	5
● Monile '97	♟♟	5
● Prunaio '97	♟♟	5
● Monile '98	♟♟	5
● Chianti Cl. Ris. '99	♟♟	6
● Chianti Cl. '00	♟♟	5
● Chianti Cl. Beatrice Ris. '99	♟♟	6
● Monile '99	♟♟	7

● Serrata di Belguardo '01	♟♟	5
● Tenuta Belguardo '01	♟♟	8
● Morellino di Scansano		
Poggio Bronzone '01	♟♟	6
● Tenuta Belguardo '00	♟♟	6

GROSSETO

GROSSETO

LE PUPILLE
LOC. ISTIA D'OMBRONE
PIAGGE DEL MAIANO, 92/A
58040 GROSSETO
TEL. 0564409517 - 0564409518
E-MAIL: lepupille@tin.it

POGGIO ARGENTIERA
LOC. BANDITELLA DI ALBERESE
S.S. 1 AURELIA KM 170,700
58010 GROSSETO
TEL. 0564405099
E-MAIL: info@poggioargentiera.com

Elisabetta Geppetti and Stefano Rizzi's winery gets stronger every year. The 420-hectare estate includes 60 hectares dedicated to viticulture, ensuring a copious harvest and considerable visibility on the market. Christian Le Sommer's skill in the cellar guarantees a generally high level of production, with the possibility of some really excellent bottles. And this time it's the Saffredi '01, their standard-bearer since its debut in 1987, which has again made off with Three Glasses. A blend of cabernet sauvignon, merlot and alicante, it's not one of your big, muscular wines, but a very stylish, balanced red. The colour is an intense ruby with violet highlights, and notes of violet and wild berries appear on the nose, softened by hints of vanilla. The palate is harmonious and very well-balanced, despite the outstanding concentration and structure. The Poggio Valente '01, from sangiovese and alicante, came very close to winning Three Glasses as well. Elegant aromas of black cherry and tobacco introduce a soft, substantial palate with a long fruit-forward finish. The excellent Solalto '01, a late-harvested blend of traminer, sauvignon and semillon, is a sweet treat. The fresh nose offers a very distinct fragrance of orange marmalade. The palate is dense to the point of viscosity, the sweetness is nicely balanced by acidity and the finish is pleasingly redolent of citrus fruit. The Morellino '02, the cellar's standard red, is well made and agreeable, whereas the Poggio Argentato '02 is faintly fruity on the nose, then crisp, but perhaps a bit acerbic, in the mouth.

This estate near the coast looks onto the Maremma nature park. It embraces 24 hectares under vine and has been selling its wine only since 1998. Nevertheless, when people know what they're about, they can make astonishingly rapid progress. That's why Poggio Argentiera is already one of the most important pieces in the richly varied and exciting mosaic of Maremma wine. Giampaolo Paglia, an agronomist and the dynamic owner of this estate, has engaged the help of oenologist, Fabrizio Moltard. Their new wine missed carrying off Three Glasses by a hair's breadth. Finisterre '01, from a blend of equal parts of alicante and syrah, is, to put it as simply as possible, very good indeed. In the glass, it is vivid ruby red. The intensely fruit-led nose is enlivened by spicy notes of pepper, then wonderfully soft tannins create a mouthfilling sensation, and the finish is long and sweet. The CapaTosta '01 is again one of the most exciting Morellinos we know, and very much a creature of its terroir. Obtained from a selection of their best grapes, it has a nose of jammy red berry fruit with notes of vanilla. The palate is warm, succulent, richly tannic and delightfully fruity on the finish. Lastly, the BellaMarsilia '02 is a distinctly well-executed wine that offers cherry fragrances with some vegetal notes, and a not very weighty palate that contrives to be delightfully easy drinking.

● Saffredi '01	♟♟♟	8
● Morellino di Scansano		
Poggio Valente '01	♟♟	6
○ Solalto '01	♟♟	4
● Morellino di Scansano '02	♟	4
○ Poggio Argentato '02		4
● Saffredi '97	♟♟♟	8
● Morellino di Scansano		
Poggio Valente '98	♟♟♟	6
● Morellino di Scansano Poggio Valente '99	♟♟♟	6
● Saffredi '00	♟♟♟	8
● Saffredi '99	♟♟	8
○ Solalto '00	♟♟	4*
● Morellino di Scansano '01	♟♟	3*
○ Poggio Argentato '01	♟♟	3*

● Finisterre '01	♟♟	7
● Morellino di Scansano		
CapaTosta '01	♟♟	6
● Morellino di Scansano		
BellaMarsilia '02	♟	4
● Morellino di Scansano CapaTosta '00	♟♟♟	6*
● Morellino di Scansano		
CapaTosta '98	♟♟	6
● Morellino di Scansano CapaTosta '99	♟♟	6
● Morellino di Scansano BellaMarsilia '01	♟♟	4
● Morellino di Scansano		
BellaMarsilia '98	♟	4
● Morellino di Scansano		
BellaMarsilia '99	♟	4
● Morellino di Scansano BellaMarsilia '00	♟	4

IMPRUNETA (FI)

FATTORIA DI BAGNOLO
LOC. BAGNOLO
VIA IMPRUNETANA PER TAVARNUZZE, 48
50023 IMPRUNETA (FI)
TEL. 0552313403
E-MAIL: fbagnolo@tin.it

There is a well-earned profile for Marco Bartolini Baldelli's estate at Impruneta, a zone that is proving very suitable for top-quality viticulture, after years of being celebrated primarily for its extravirgin olive oil. Fattoria di Bagnolo has ten hectares under vine, planted mostly to sangiovese, but allowing space for international varieties such as cabernet sauvignon, and for other local grapes, like colorino. The arrival of Lorenzo Landini as consultant oenologist made progress possible, and the wines are now softer and smoother. The Chianti Colli Fiorentini '01 presents a lovely intense ruby followed by striking aromas of vanilla and wild berries, together with appealing fresh cherry. After a soft, delicate entry, the palate acquires vigour, thanks to close-knit tannins and well-judged acidity. The finish is pleasing and persistent. The colour of the Riserva '00 is opaque purple. The fine array of scents includes fresh raspberry and cherry, with attractive notes of tobacco and leather. The attack in the mouth is firm, and the palate then shows good structure, with tightly packed, succulent tannins and a captivating savoury finish. The Capro Rosso '01, a blend of sangiovese, cabernet sauvignon and colorino, boasts a nose that ranges from ripe blackberry and cherry fruit to subtle spicy notes of pepper and cinnamon. The palate is immediately rich and engrossing, revealing tannins that are perfectly integrated into the impressive body, and a lively, forceful finish.

IMPRUNETA (FI)

LA QUERCE
VIA IMPRUNETANA, 41
50023 IMPRUNETA (FI)
TEL. 0552011380
E-MAIL: laquerce@inwind.it

Massimo Marchi's La Querce is one of the Impruneta estates that has been featured for longest in the Guide. The efforts of Massimo Ferretti, who is in charge of the vineyards, and the advice of consultant oenologist, Alberto Antonini, have helped bring about a solid, enduring improvement in quality. The eight hectares under vine are planted to sangiovese and to the complementary colorino grape. The lively purple-hued Chianti Sorrettole '02 exhibits very enticing scents of wild berries with a generous hint of pepper and clove spice. The palate is enjoyably savoury and smooth, with good acidic bite, densely woven, well-paced tannins and an appetizing finish. Massimo did not present their Colli Fiorentini La Torretta '02 at our tastings because, starting with this vintage, it will have more ageing time in bottle. But meanwhile there's the very good La Querce '01, a blend of sangiovese and colorino with a surprisingly intense opaque ruby and an impressive bouquet of minty and balsamic tones that alternate with pleasing notes of green bell pepper. These eventually make room for hints of chocolate and stewed fruit, before the massive entry on the palate. The progression is rich and enticing, with tannins seamlessly melding into the powerful body, and the finish is admirably long.

● Chianti Colli Fiorentini Ris. '00	▼▼	4
● Capro Rosso '01	▼▼	5
● Chianti Colli Fiorentini '01	▼	3
● Capro Rosso '99	▽▽	4
● Capro Rosso '00	▽▽	5

● La Querce '01	▼▼	5
● Chianti Sorrettole '02	▼▼	3*
● Chianti Colli Fiorentini		
La Torretta '00	▽▽	3*
● La Querce '00	▽▽	5
● Chianti Colli Fiorentini		
La Torretta '01	▽▽	4

IMPRUNETA (FI)

LUCCA

LANCIOLA
VIA IMPRUNETANA, 210
50023 IMPRUNETA (FI)
TEL. 055208324
E-MAIL: info@lanciola.net

TENUTA DI VALGIANO
FRAZ. VALGIANO
VIA DI VALGIANO, 7
55010 LUCCA
TEL. 0583402271
E-MAIL: info@valgiano.it

We are never pleased to see a winery with great potential that doesn't quite live up to expectations. We're not talking, in this case, about a serious stumble, but we feel that Lanciola, which was one of the first in the Colli Fiorentini to produce really good wine, can and should do even better. We'll start with the Terricci '00, the estate Supertuscan, from cabernet sauvignon and sangiovese. An opaque ruby introduces ripe fruit scents of plum and blackberry, with grassy overtones. The palate, after a good impact, is warm, juicy and enjoyable, unveiling densely packed, yet polished, tannins and a succulent long finish. The chardonnay-based Ricciobianco '02, which is replacing the Terricci Chardonnay, displays a nice, untypical nose that ranges from spring flowers to hazelnuts, with distinct, very elegant mineral tones. After a good entry, the mouthfillingly fleshy palate shows pervasive flavours perked up by lively acidity and supported by lingering succulence. The Chianti Colli Fiorentini '01 is a lovely bright ruby that ushers in a striking variety of attractive fruit fragrances, with cherry and redcurrant to the fore. The palate is flavoursome, warm and enjoyable, showing tidy tannins. The Chianti Classico Le Masse di Greve '01 is less successful than usual. The nose offers very inviting aromas of ripe fruit and spice, but in the mouth it is still a little unco-ordinated, probably because of its youth. Finally, the Vin Santo '98 is redolent of hazelnut and dried fruit, exhibiting good structure on the palate, but it could have had more volume.

All of Valgiano's wines were presented at our tastings this time, and the cellar missed a Three Glass award by the narrowest of margins. It's a pity, but we are sure they won't bat an eyelid. Instead, they will carry on making ever better wines. The vivacious Moreno Petrini, his other half, Laura Di Collobiano, and estate oenologist, Saverio Petrillo, would seem to have very clear ideas. They want wines with elegance and structure, but which also show good acid bite and plenty of confidence. The nose of their selection, the sangiovese-based Tenuta Valgiano '00, is just a little uncertain, which gets in the way of the blackberry and elegant balsamic notes. The wine does much better on the palate, which is full-bodied and succulent, revealing soft, well-integrated tannins. Although this red unfolds delightfully, it could perhaps do with a touch more flesh. We also thought very highly of the Scasso dei Cesari '00, a monovarietal Sangiovese with a limited production. It's not an easy wine to get into, partly because the nose is not altogether open yet, and partly because the very concentrated palate shows lively varietal acidity. The third estate red, a blend of sangiovese, merlot and syrah, is the Palistorti '01, which is a little over-ripe on the nose but proves pleasing and even on the straightforward, harmonious palate. We were less pleased by the white, Giallo dei Muri. The '02 version seemed unexciting. The fresh nose of apples, pears and almonds is not mirrored on the palate, which is a little bitter on the finish.

● Terricci '00	♟♟	5
● Chianti Colli Fiorentini '01	♟	3
● Chianti Cl. Le Masse di Greve '01	♟	5
○ Ricciobianco '02	♟	6
○ Vin Santo Colli Fiorentini '98	♟	5
● Terricci '96	♟♟	4
● Chianti Cl. Le Masse di Greve Ris. '97	♟♟	4
● Terricci '97	♟♟	4
● Chianti Cl. Le Masse di Greve Ris. '98	♟♟	4
● Chianti Cl. Le Masse di Greve '99	♟♟	3*
● Chianti Cl. Le Masse di Greve '00	♟♟	5
● Chianti Cl. Le Masse di Greve Ris. '99	♟♟	4
● Terricci '99	♟♟	5

● Colline Lucchesi Tenuta di Valgiano '00	♟♟	8
● Scasso dei Cesari '00	♟♟	8
● Colline Lucchesi Rosso dei Palistorti '01	♟	5
○ Colline Lucchesi Bianco Giallo dei Muri '02		4
● Scasso dei Cesari '95	♟♟	4
● Scasso dei Cesari '96	♟♟	4
○ Colline Lucchesi Bianco Giallo dei Muri '97	♟♟	3
● Scasso dei Cesari '97	♟♟	5
● Colline Lucchesi Rosso Scasso dei Cesari '98	♟♟	6
○ Scasso del Bugiardo '99	♟♟	5
● Colline Lucchesi Tenuta di Valgiano '99	♟♟	8
● Colline Lucchesi Rosso dei Palistorti '00	♟♟	5

MAGLIANO IN TOSCANA (GR)   MAGLIANO IN TOSCANA (GR)

FATTORIA DI MAGLIANO
LOC. STERPETI, 10
58051 MAGLIANO IN TOSCANA (GR)
TEL. 0564593040
E-MAIL: info@fattoriadimagliano.it

COSTANZA MALFATTI
LOC. S. ANDREA - POD. 353
58051 MAGLIANO IN TOSCANA (GR)
TEL. 0564592535

Fattoria di Magliano made a great first entrance in the Guide. This fine property, in the heart of Morellino DOC country, covers 85 hectares, of which 37 are given over to high-density vineyards currently producing 72,000 bottles annually. Agostino Lenci, the owner, is assisted among the vines by Valerio Barbieri and in the cellar by Graziana Grassini, a pupil of the great Giacomo Tachis. The wines stood out at our tastings because of their intense sense of place. Morellino di Scansano Heba '02 displays well-defined aromas of cherry jam and a solid, warm, rounded palate with a pleasing follow through on the finish. The Heba '01, on the other hand, offers balsamic and gamey scents, and then strikingly robust structure in which the oak is perhaps just a touch too prominent. The Poggio Bestiale '01, named after its vineyard, was a most delightful surprise. Indeed, it went straight into our finals and very nearly carried off Three Glasses. This blend of merlot, cabernet sauvignon and cabernet franc is profoundly expressive of its territory. Elegant spicy aromas embellished with stylish hints of tar introduce a soft, enticingly full-bodied palate with powerful but extremely smooth tannins. Lastly, the Pagliatura '02, a monovarietal Vermentino, is fresh and fragrant. It may not be very complex in the mouth but it is distinctly enjoyable.

Costanza Malfatti's estate has performed extremely well ever since 1998, the first year her wine was released onto the market. All along, she has concentrated on just one DOC zone and one territory. Over the years, the wine has become increasingly elegant and complex, and this year it came within an ace of Three Glasses. Wine from the Maremma tends to be full-bodied and rich in alcohol. If the winemaker is competent, and lucky, it can lighten its often very ripe fruit with crisp acidity and attractive tannins. When this happens, you can sense the perfect balance of richness and local flavour of a specific terroir. That was the case when we tasted the Morellino '01, which the panel thought was an exciting wine and one of the best of its kind. A blend of sangiovese, alicante and cabernet sauvignon, it's intense, with a lustrous ruby and a nose of freshly roasted coffee with light gamey nuances, underpinned by pronounced ripe fruit. The soft, dense palate reveals solid structure and mellow tannins matched by just enough acidity to make it refreshing and enjoyable all the way through the long finish. The estate extends over eight hectares under vine and produces some 20,000 bottles a year, calling on oenologist, Paolo Caciornia, for advice in the cellar.

●	Poggio Bestiale '01	▼▼	5	● Morellino di Scansano '01	▼▼	6
●	Morellino di Scansano Heba '02	▼▼	4*	● Morellino di Scansano '99	♀♀	3*
●	Morellino di Scansano Heba '01	▼	3	● Morellino di Scansano '00	♀♀	5
○	Pagliatura '02	▼	4			

MAGLIANO IN TOSCANA (GR)

MANTELLASSI
LOC. BANDITACCIA, 26
58051 MAGLIANO IN TOSCANA (GR)
TEL. 0564592037
E-MAIL: info@fatt-mantellassi.it

It was back in the early 1970s that the Mantellassis invested their hopes in wine. They were the first to bottle Morellino, and their contribution to creating a DOC in Scansano, which finally came about in 1978, was decisive. The estate is now particularly important, covering 215 hectares, of which 50 are under vine and produce about 500,000 bottles annually. Mantellassi's wines, made with the assistance of oenologist, Marco Stefanini, are usually pleasing, well executed and very true to type, although until this year none had stood out. But Morellino San Giuseppe '02, named after one of the estate farms, is remarkable and almost won Three Glasses. Made mostly from sangiovese, with a little cabernet sauvignon and malvasia nera aged for six months in barrique, it shows a handsome ruby red followed by a wonderfully clean bouquet with quince jam to the fore. The exceptionally drinkable palate is fragrant and rich, the mouthfeel is tempting and the tannins vibrant and exceptional quaffability. We were not quite so thrilled by the Querciolaia '00, a monovarietal alicante aged in barrique for a year and produced here since '77. The nose, at least at our tastings, was not particularly well developed and the structure in the mouth was a bit lightweight, although pleasantly soft.

MASSA

CIMA
FRAZ. ROMAGNANO
VIA DEL FAGIANO, 1
54100 MASSA
TEL. 0585831617
E-MAIL: info@aziendagricolacima.it

The entire family lends a hand at Aurelio Cima's beautiful estate, all committed to the quest for excellence. The location, which enjoys fresh Mediterranean breezes and the stark, protecting profile of the Apuan Alps, is very favourable to viticulture. The family's winemaking style, reflected in all their bottles, is characterized by opulence of fruit, perfectly ripe grapes and great concentration. Unfortunately, the use of barriques makes the wines verge on the repetitive. There is no question about the quality of the Cima wines, but more careful use of oak, or a further year's ageing in bottle before release, would make all the difference. For now, the wines tend to be much of a muchness, despite the different grape varieties. This year, Romalbo, a blend of sangiovese and massaretta, again made it to our finals. The '01 shows a vivid colour then the nose offers intense, slightly over-ripe fruit, with a distinct hint of rosemary. The palate is powerful and the long finish is redolent of vanilla. It just lacks a little elegance. The merlot-based Montervo '01 performed very well. It's still young and reluctant to open out altogether, but it's also intense, close knit and meaty. The good Anchigi '01, a monovarietal Sangiovese, is sweet and even. We were less impressed by the Massaretta '01 and the Vermentino Nero '01, which are bitterish on the finish. Our favourite from the whites was the Candia Alto '02, with its enticing honey and spice nose followed by a full-bodied, succulent palate. The crisp Candia '02 is leaner, but still inviting.

●	Morellino di Scansano San Giuseppe '02	⟡⟡	4
●	Querciolaia '00	⟡	5
●	Morellino di Scansano Ris. '96	⟡⟡	3
●	Querciolaia '96	⟡⟡	4
●	Morellino di Scansano Le Sentinelle '97	⟡⟡	4
●	Morellino di Scansano Le Sentinelle Ris. '98	⟡⟡	4
●	Morellino di Scansano San Giuseppe '99	⟡	3
●	Morellino di Scansano San Giuseppe '01	⟡	4
●	Morellino di Scansano Le Sentinelle Ris. '99	⟡	6
●	Versoio '99	⟡	6

●	Romalbo '01	⟡⟡	6
●	Anchigi '01	⟡⟡	5
●	Montervo '01	⟡⟡	6
○	Candia dei Colli Apuani Vign. Candia Alto '02	⟡⟡	5
●	Massaretta '01	⟡	6
●	Vermentino Nero '01	⟡	5
○	Candia dei Colli Apuani '02	⟡	4
●	Massaretta '99	⟡⟡	6
●	Montervo '99	⟡⟡	6
●	Romalbo '99	⟡⟡	6
●	Montervo '00	⟡⟡	6
●	Romalbo '00	⟡⟡	6
●	Massaretta '00	⟡⟡	5

MASSA MARITTIMA (GR)

MORIS FARMS
LOC. CURANUOVA
FATTORIA POGGETTI
58020 MASSA MARITTIMA (GR)
TEL. 0566919135
E-MAIL: morisfarms@morisfarms.it

Moris Farms, one of the stars of Maremma, has carved a nice for itself in the highly competitive Tuscan wine world with a range of consistently fine, characterful wines. The cellar receives grapes from two different estates, at Poggio La Mozza near Grosseto, where 30 of the 56 hectares are under vine, and at Poggetti near Massa Marittima, which extends over 420 hectares, 40 of which are planted to vine. Adolfo Parenti, who has been in charge since the late 1970s, created Avvoltore with the help of vineyard manager, Andrea Paoletti, and winemaker, Attilio Pagli. That was in 1988 and Avvoltore has since become a classic of this area. A blend of cabernet sauvignon, sangiovese and syrah that takes its name from the Poggio dell'Avvoltore vineyard at the Massa Marittima estate, Avvoltore has again earned Three Glasses. The dark ruby introduces clear-cut scents of ripe wild berries and spicy notes of pepper. The palate is almost velvety in its softness, the full body unveiling close-knit tannins and a finish that goes on and on. The very fine Morellino Riserva '00 has a clean fragrance of ripe fruit and a captivating tannic weave in the mouth. The pleasing, but simpler, Morellino '02 is refreshing and harmonious. Lastly, the Monteregio '01, which has a slightly muffled nose, performs better on the palate, where it proves substantial and lingering.

MERCATALE VALDARNO (AR)

PODERE IL CARNASCIALE
POD. CARNASCIALE
52020 MERCATALE VALDARNO (AR)
TEL. 0559911142

In the early 1970s, a German family named Rogosky bought this little estate, and some years later, Wolf Rogosky, who died a few years ago, and his consultants, agronomist, Remigio Bordini, and oenologist, Vittorio Fiore, decided to plant an unusual grape at extremely high density. It was a clone from a variety first identified in the Colli Euganei, apparently a genetic mutation of cabernet with some of the characteristics of merlot. And it is from this grape, the only variety planted at Podere Il Carnasciale and now universally identified with the wine, that the cellar makes Caberlot. It has become something of a cult wine, partly because it is excellent, but also because it is available only in a very limited number of magnums. The low production was why we never given it Three Glasses. But this year, in acknowledgement of its remarkably consistent quality, we decided to ignore the question of limited availability and address the quality. The estate, now run by Bettina Rogosky, has begun to extend its vineyards, which will result in a doubling of the current vineyard holding and eventually lead to an increase in production (now just 1,800 magnums). Meanwhile, fruit from the younger vines will go into a second wine, also released in small numbers but in the more affordable format of 75-centilitre bottles. As usual, the '00 Caberlot is superb. A red of character, this is not one of your easy-drinkers. The nose is a broad, complex concentration of oriental spices, cocoa and black berry fruit. Despite its youth, the palate is remarkable for its grip, concentration and length.

● Avvoltore '01	▼▼▼	6
● Morellino di Scansano Ris. '00	▼▼	5
● Monteregio di Massa Marittima Rosso '01	▼	4
● Morellino di Scansano '02	▼	4
● Avvoltore '99	▼▼▼	6
● Avvoltore '00	▼▼▼	6
● Avvoltore '94	▼▼	6
● Morellino di Scansano Ris. '94	▼▼	4
● Avvoltore '95	▼▼	6
● Avvoltore '97	▼▼	5
● Morellino di Scansano Ris. '97	▼▼	4
● Avvoltore '98	▼▼	5
● Morellino di Scansano Ris. '98	▼▼	4
● Morellino di Scansano '01	▼▼	3*
● Morellino di Scansano Ris. '99	▼▼	5

● Caberlot '00	▼▼▼	8
● Caberlot '96	▼▼	6
● Caberlot '97	▼▼	6
● Caberlot '98	▼▼	6
● Caberlot '99	▼▼	8

MONTAIONE (FI)

LA PIEVE
LOC. LA PIEVE
VIA S. STEFANO
50050 MONTAIONE (FI)
TEL. 0571697764 - 0571697934
E-MAIL: simonetognetti@virgilio.it

It often happens that a brilliant debut in the Guide is followed by a less successful second year and the winery does not even appear in Other Wineries. However, thanks to the boundless energy of Simone Tognetti, now a full-time grower, this was not the case at La Pieve. Our tasters were very impressed for the fine debut last year has turned out to be a further stimulus for the planned re-organization of the cellar and vineyards. New vines have been planted with the best rootstocks in sites and at elevations that are perfect for the production of first-class grapes. The wines we tasted were well executed and characterful. The style is similar to last year's, but they are a touch more individual, as exemplified by the Chianti Fortebraccio '01. The fruity nose is laced with oak tones and hints of spice and coffee. The palate is dense in texture, and the progression is supple, succulent and nicely balanced, leading to a fruit-rich, appealingly long, finish. The Rosso del Pievano '01, a blend of sangiovese and cabernet sauvignon, is still a bit closed on the nose, but then releases notes of pencil lead and oak to lift the fruit. The full-bodied, tangy palate reveals well-paced tannins and a successful finish, which is little taut, because of the wine's youth. The two vintages of standard Chianti are unpretentious, enjoyable and a very good buy.

MONTALCINO (SI)

★ CASTELLO BANFI
LOC. SANT'ANGELO SCALO
CASTELLO DI POGGIO ALLE MURA
53024 MONTALCINO (SI)
TEL. 0577840111
E-MAIL: banfi@banfi.it

The Banfi mega-winery is one of Italy's best producers. Admirably managed by Enrico Viglierchio, it continues its quest for ever better wines. The square in front of headquarters is piled high with wood to make barriques for barrel maturation of the wines. The oak is sourced in France but Banfi age it on site at the winery so as to have more control over quality. All this care is reflected in the wines, which are technically impeccable. All the bottles presented won at least One Glass, which is very good going for a start. Two went through to the final taste-offs and five received Two Glasses. One small disappointment was the Brunello Poggio all'Oro Riserva '97, which was unforthcoming at our tastings, probably as a result of the excessive extract that thins the finish. Still, it should improve with more time in bottle. The good news is that the spectacular Brunello Poggio alle Mura '98 won Three glorious Glasses. The fruit on the nose is nicely matched by spice and the tight-knit, mouthfilling palate flaunts an elegant progression and a fine finish. The very good Excelsus, a classic Bordeaux blend of cabernet sauvignon and merlot, shows a well-judged bouquet and makes a great impact on the palate.

● Chianti Fortebraccio '01	♟♟	3*
● Rosso del Pievano '01	♟♟	4
● Chianti '01	♟	3*
● Chianti '02	♟	3*
● Chianti '00	♟♟	2*
● Chianti Fortebraccio '00	♟♟	3*
● Rosso del Pievano '00	♟♟	4

● Brunello di Montalcino Poggio alle Mura '98	♟♟♟	8
● Sant'Antimo Excelsus '00	♟♟	8
● Merlot Mandrielle '00	♟♟	5
● Sant'Antimo Colvecchio '00	♟♟	6
● Sant'Antimo Cum Laude '00	♟♟	6
● Centine '01	♟♟	4*
● Sant'Antimo Summus '00	♟	8
● Sant'Antimo Tavernelle '00	♟	5
● Col di Sasso '01	♟	3
● Rosso di Montalcino '01	♟	6
○ Sant'Antimo Fontanelle Chardonnay '02	♟	6
○ Sant'Antimo Serena Sauvignon Blanc '02	♟	6
● Brunello di Montalcino Poggio all'Oro Ris. '97	♟	8
● Brunello di Montalcino '98	♟	8
● Brunello di Montalcino Poggio all'Oro Ris. '95	♟♟♟	8

MONTALCINO (SI)

MONTALCINO (SI)

FATTORIA DEI BARBI
LOC. PODERNOVI, 170
53024 MONTALCINO (SI)
TEL. 0577841111
E-MAIL: info@fattoriadeibarbi.it

CASTELLO DI CAMIGLIANO
LOC. CAMIGLIANO
VIA D'INGRESSO, 2
53024 MONTALCINO (SI)
TEL. 0577816061 - 0577844068
E-MAIL: camigliano@virgilio.it

This historic estate is one of the best-known Montalcino wineries worldwide. The reason is the brilliant insight of its founder, who produced a good Brunello at an affordable price, putting the wine within the reach of a much larger wine-drinking public. This estate policy is still in force almost a century later, which goes to show that great ideas can stand the test of time. Stefano Cinelli Colombini manages Fattoria dei Barbi with brio, adhering to DOCG and DOC regulations, but with an open mind that contemplates technological improvements with equanimity. Getting down to the wine, we gave Two Glasses to both the Morellino di Scansano Vivaio dei Barbi '00 and the Brunello Riserva '97. The Brunello exhibits a ruby hue shading to garnet at the rim, and an enchanting nose with notes of tobacco and jam. The palate shows good development, thanks in part to elegant, well-balanced tannins without any rough edges, and a lingering finish. The Rosso di Montalcino '01 is extremely fruity in fragrance, revealing attractive acidity and nice drinkability. Brunello Vigna del Fiore '98, a vineyard selection, is still too young. Oak on the nose restricts the spectrum of aromatics and, on the palate, makes the tannins a bit hard. Ageing should do a lot for it. The Brunello '98 is simple but well co-ordinated, with a supple, attractive structure. All the other wines are enjoyable.

We knew that Castello di Camigliano was getting better, but not this much better! They made a splendid showing with both their Brunellos and the newer DOC, Sant'Antimo. Our compliments to the Ghezzi family, who were right to believe in the potential of this western part of Montalcino. And we also applaud Lorenzo Landi, the remarkably skilled oenologist who succeeded in transforming this potential into such individual wines. Two of them, in fact, made it to our finals, the Camigliano '01 and the '98 Brunello. Curiously, this standard Brunello scored higher than the estate's Gualto selection, which nevertheless easily earned Two Glasses. The difference was in the bouquet. The '98 Brunello's is richer, its well-defined, clean fruit enhanced by balsamic and honeyed notes. The palate is also interesting. The richness of the fruit never gets in the way of drinkability, thanks to well-judged tannins and the acidity that underpins all that extract, and the finish is warm and generous. The Gualto '98 also has a rich palate, but it is still a bit edgy, though that should improve with bottle age. The cabernet-based Camigliano '01 is splendid. Opaque with bluish highlights, it offers a full nose of blackcurrant and blueberry with elegant notes of oak, then the well-balanced palate reveals admirable densely knit and juicy tannins.

● Morellino di Scansano		
Vivaio dei Barbi '00	▼▼	4*
● Brunello di Montalcino Ris. '97	▼▼	8
● Brusco dei Barbi '00	▼	3
● Rosso di Montalcino '01	▼	4
● Brunello di Montalcino '98	▼	6
● Brunello di Montalcino V. del Fiore '98	▼	8
● Birbone Toscano '99	▼	6
● Brunello di Montalcino		
Vigna del Fiore Ris. '90	♈♈	6
● Brunello di Montalcino '93	♈♈	5
● Brunello di Montalcino		
Vigna del Fiore Ris. '93	♈♈	8
● Brunello di Montalcino		
Vigna del Fiore Ris. '95	♈♈	8

● Sant'Antimo Cabernet Sauvignon		
Camigliano '01	▼▼	4
● Brunello di Montalcino '98	▼▼	6
● Brunello di Montalcino Gualto '98	▼▼	8
● Rosso di Montalcino '01	▼	4
● Brunello di Montalcino Ris. '90	♈♈	6
● Brunello di Montalcino Ris. '95	♈♈	7
● Sant'Antimo Cabernet Sauvignon		
Camigliano '00	♈♈	5
● Brunello di Montalcino '97	♈♈	7

MONTALCINO (SI)

TENUTA CAPARZO
LOC. CAPARZO
S.P. DEL BRUNELLO KM 1,700
53024 MONTALCINO (SI)
TEL. 0577848390 - 0577847166
E-MAIL: caparzo@caparzo.com

Tenuta Caparzo is a solidly established Montalcino winery. Some changes in ownership recently have in no way damaged its image, thanks to the ability of the manager, Sante Turone. The well-aspected plots are principally in the northern part of Montalcino and include two of the best Brunello vineyards, Montosoli, which provides the Brunello La Casa, and upper Castelgiocondo in the western part of Montalcino. This year's best bottle was the Brunello La Casa '98, which is very faithful to its vineyard, showing an elegant soft palate with fine-grained tannins and a harmonious, lingering finish. The fine nose, which has overcome its past shyness, displays balsamic and spicy nuances, foregrounding fruit tones of bilberry. The Brunello '98 offers a classic varietal nose of sour cherry and very ripe red berries, with enchanting notes of oak. These lead into a medium-bodied but very well-balanced and wonderfully sweet palate. It's a child of its vintage and hence not the most muscular of Brunellos. We expected more from the Brunello Riserva '97. After a good impact on the nose, with somewhat prominent oak, it shows a slightly simple palate, particularly for its year. The two Rosso di Montalcinos get One Glass apiece, although we preferred La Caduta '01 with its floral aromas and refreshing acidity. The Rosso Caparzo '02 is fruity and eminently drinkable.

MONTALCINO (SI)

CASANOVA DI NERI
POD. FIESOLE
53028 MONTALCINO (SI)
TEL. 0577834455
E-MAIL: giacner@tin.it

Improvement at Casanova di Neri over the past decade has been constant, and behind it all is Giacomo Neri. With considerable panache, he has turned his estate into one of the most reliable in Montalcino. A careful blend of technological innovation in the cellar, replanting in the vineyards and respect for the terroir has produced wines of great individuality and admirable definition. This year, we finally managed to taste the marvellous Pietradonice '00, obtained exclusively from cabernet sauvignon grown on the estate vineyards near the unsurfaced road that winds from Castelnuovo dell'Abate to Sant'Angelo in Colle. These vines reflect the past experience of the estate and the extraordinary ability of their consultant oenologist, Carlo Ferrini. And now to the excellent wines themselves. Two, both splendid reds, made it into our finals and the entire range was very good indeed. The sumptuous Brunello Cerretalto '97 offers a varietally spicy nose and an opulent but never cloying palate, thanks to admirably balanced tannins. The finish is broad, captivating and very long. Pietradonice, its first time out, has hit the jackpot. Notes of cedar and pencil lead add elegance to the aromas of blueberry fruit on the nose, a prelude to a wonderfully dense, exceptionally harmonious palate. Our favourite from the '98 Brunellos was the austere, very traditional standard-label version. The Tenuta Nuova seemed a little over-oaked. The Rosso di Montalcino '01 is very pleasant.

● Brunello di Montalcino La Casa '98 ŢŢ		8
● Rosso di Montalcino '01 Ţ		5
● Rosso di Montalcino La Caduta '01 Ţ		5
● Rosso Caparzo Sangiovese '02 Ţ		4
● Brunello di Montalcino Ris. '97 Ţ		7
● Brunello di Montalcino '98 Ţ		7
● Brunello di Montalcino La Casa '93 ŢŢŢ		7
● Brunello di Montalcino La Casa '95 ŢŢ		7
● Brunello di Montalcino La Casa '97 ŢŢ		7
● Sant'Antimo Ca' del Pazzo '98 ŢŢ		6

● Sant'Antimo Pietradonice '00 ŢŢŢ		8
● Brunello di Montalcino		
Cerretalto '97 ŢŢ		8
● Brunello di Montalcino '98 ŢŢ		7
● Rosso di Montalcino '01 ŢŢ		5
● Brunello di Montalcino		
Tenuta Nuova '98 Ţ		7
● Brunello di Montalcino		
Cerretalto Ris. '88 ŢŢŢ		8
● Brunello di Montalcino		
Cerretalto '95 ŢŢŢ		8
● Brunello di Montalcino		
Tenuta Nuova '97 ŢŢŢ		7
● Brunello di Montalcino Tenuta Nuova '95 ŢŢ		7
● Brunello di Montalcino Cerretalto '96 ŢŢ		8

MONTALCINO (SI)

CASANUOVA DELLE CERBAIE
LOC. CASANOVA DELLE CERBAIE, 335
53024 MONTALCINO (SI)
TEL. 0577849284
E-MAIL: casanuovacerbaie@jumpy.it

After its fine showing last time with the Brunello '97, Casanuova delle Cerbaie has gained a full profile and Three Glasses. Credit must go to the Morandinis, who fell in love with the area and Brunello, then bought this estate three years ago. A lot is going on. They will soon be planting 12 more hectares to vine, mostly sangiovese, but including some international varieties in the less well-aspected sites. The current vineyards are on opposite sides of Montalcino. The ones close to the winery are in the north and a further seven hectares are near Castello della Velona, facing Monte Amiata, to the south. This is a shrewd arrangement, as it minimizes the effects of unfavourable vintages like '02. The winery is also investing in the new cellar near Badia, not far from the road to Buonconvento where the new vineyards are to be planted. This year's range is excellent. The new wine, the sangiovese and merlot Cerbaione '01, is very good indeed and almost earned another Three Glasses. A dark, very intense colour introduces a complex nose of red and black berry fruit laced with hints of oak. The palate also does well, with rich tannins that avoid bitterness, but are still a bit young. The texture is very dense and the generous finish echoes the nose. The marvellous Brunello Riserva '97 offers a sour cherry fragrance enhanced by pleasing notes of candied peel. The palate is massive, elegant and lingering, with lots of depth on the finish. Both the Rosso di Montalcino '01 and the Brunello '98 are very well executed, the latter being let down by sulphurous notes on the nose.

MONTALCINO (SI)

CASISANO COLOMBAIO
LOC. CASISANO, 52
53024 MONTALCINO (SI)
TEL. 0577835540
E-MAIL: tatiana@brunello.org

Casisano Colombaio has earned its own profile with palpable improvement throughout its range. The winery is on the road to Sant'Angelo in Colle, and near it are the seven hectares planted to sangiovese for Brunello. The buildings were recently renewed and are an admirable compromise of practicality and aesthetics. In recent years, improvement has been steady, thanks to the program laid out by oenologist, Paolo Vagaggini, who has reduced the yield per vine to make the wines more distinctive. The excellent Brunello Riserva '97 is one of the best of its vintage. The lovely deep, intense ruby red in the glass already suggests a complex, well-co-ordinated wine. The fruit on the nose mingles enticingly with oak-derived toastiness and spices. The mouthfeel is concentrated and graced with excellent tannins that lead to a seductive finish. The '98 Brunellos pay the price of a cold year and the high elevation of the vineyards. They each got One Glass, but we preferred the Brunello Vigna del Colombaio for its clean, intense bouquet of blackberry, cinchona and vanilla introducing a soft attack on the palate. Sadly, this is followed by an unexciting progression, with slightly intrusive oak. The standard Brunello is redolent of chocolate and fruit, then rather aggressive tannins cut into the finish in the mouth. The Rosso di Montalcino '01 is less successful.

● Brunello di Montalcino Ris. '97	▼▼▼	7
● Cerbaione '01	▼▼	6
● Rosso di Montalcino '01	▼	5
● Brunello di Montalcino '98	▼	6
● Brunello di Montalcino '97	▼▼	7

● Brunello di Montalcino Ris. '97	▼▼	7
● Brunello di Montalcino '98	▼	6
● Brunello di Montalcino V. del Colombaio '98	▼	8
● Rosso di Montalcino '01		4
● Brunello di Montalcino Ris. '95	▼▼	7
● Brunello di Montalcino V. del Colombaio '96	▼▼	8
● Brunello di Montalcino V. del Colombaio '97	▼▼	8

MONTALCINO (SI)

MONTALCINO (SI)

CASTELGIOCONDO
LOC. CASTELGIOCONDO
53024 MONTALCINO (SI)
TEL. 057784131
E-MAIL: info@frescobaldi.it

CASTIGLION DEL BOSCO
LOC. CASTIGLION DEL BOSCO
53024 MONTALCINO (SI)
TEL. 0577808348 - 0577807078
E-MAIL: info@castigliondelbosco.it

As if to show that the cellar wanted to prove us wrong in what we wrote last year, Castelgiocondo presented a great Brunello '98 that nudged the Lamaione down into second place. This entertaining rivalry is an example of how important the growing year is, even for two varieties as different as sangiovese and merlot. Tenuta di Castelgiocondo, a Frescobaldi family property, covers 800 hectares. There are 250 hectares under vine, and 150 of these are dedicated to Brunello. These are seriously big numbers, particularly at Castelgiocondo, which has been known for over a century as an exceptional place to grow the sangiovese grape. The Brunello '98 is amongst the finest of its vintage. The bouquet is broad, unveiling classic varietal blackberry and sour cherry. The palate is rich, but never boring, thanks to the excellent balance of tannins and acidity, which also accounts for its elegance. Altogether this is an admirable performance, especially given the vast quantities produced. The merlot-based Lamaione '00 comes from an indifferent vintage. The very hot, dry summer has given it lots of weight, but not very much in terms of elegance. The nose offers mineral tones, together with very warm, almost jammy notes of black berry fruit. Assertive tannins tend to cramp the palate's style but it shows very good concentration. The rather disappointing Brunello Ripa al Convento '97 is dominated by oak that overwhelms the fruit on the nose, and the palate shows some tannin-related stiffness. We were unable to taste the Rosso di Montalcino '01.

Every year, this fine Montalcino estate with its 50 hectares under vine gives us plenty to write about regarding the excellence of its wines. This time, there is important business news as well. Massimo Ferragamo, from the well-known Italian fashion house that bears his name, is the new owner, and with that change come others. The consultant oenologist is now Nicolò D'Afflitto, who knows Montalcino like the back of his hand. We'll be seeing the results of these innovations in the years to come. Meanwhile, Castiglion del Bosco has consolidated the gains of recent years. The best wine this time was the Rosso di Montalcino '01, which won Two Glasses, as did the 2000 edition. A brilliant ruby introduces an array of aromas including vanilla and very warm fruit. It's an easy-drinking wine that refreshes and pleases at first sip. The Brunellos have gone down a notch this time, getting only One Glass each. The '98 offers good structure but slightly over-assertive tannins. However, the very clean bouquet that speaks well for the attentions lavished on the wine in the maturation cellar. The Brunello Riserva '97 is a disappointment after the lovely '96. The aromas suggest rhubarb and oak, and the palate is soft and even.

● Brunello di Montalcino '98	♟♟	7
● Lamaione '00	♟♟	8
● Brunello di Montalcino Ripa al Convento '97	♟	8
● Brunello di Montalcino Ris. '88	♟♟♟	6
● Brunello di Montalcino Ris. '90	♟♟♟	6
● Brunello di Montalcino '93	♟♟	5
● Brunello di Montalcino '95	♟♟	5
● Lamaione '98	♟♟	8
● Brunello di Montalcino '97	♟♟	7
● Lamaione '99	♟♟	8

● Rosso di Montalcino '01	♟♟	5
● Brunello di Montalcino Ris. '97	♟	7
● Brunello di Montalcino '98	♟	6
● Brunello di Montalcino Ris. '95	♟♟	7
● Brunello di Montalcino '96	♟♟	6
● Brunello di Montalcino '97	♟♟	6
● Rosso di Montalcino '00	♟♟	5

MONTALCINO (SI)

MONTALCINO (SI)

CENTOLANI
LOC. FRIGGIALI
S.DA MAREMMANA
53024 MONTALCINO (SI)
TEL. 0577849314 - 0577849454
E-MAIL: agricolacentolani@libero.it

CERBAIONA
LOC. CERBAIONA
53024 MONTALCINO (SI)
TEL. 0577848660

Centolani's 40 hectares planted to sangiovese for Brunello are split across properties at Friggiali and Pietranera. The two estates are very different in their soil characteristics, as well as in site climate. The grapes are kept separate, and the Centolani labels indicate the provenance of the fruit for Brunello as well as Rosso di Montalcino. The Pietranera area is on the southeastern edge of Montalcino, just below the recently restored Castello della Velona. It has basaltic volcanic soil, which is quite unusual for Montalcino. Friggiali, on the other hand, is in the west and the clay and marl soil is not so loose-packed as at Pietranera. The cellar, which is at Friggiali, has been extended, and there is now a charming courtyard with a portico. Inside are casks of the traditional large dimensions, but the number of barriques keeps growing. As for the wines, our tastings were encouraging. The potential of this estate and its terroirs has not yet been fully realized, but the vintage may have played its part in that. Of the two Brunellos, we preferred the Friggiali '98 for its complex earthy tones and notes of bramble, followed by a balanced palate, although the tannins need more time to soften. The Brunello Pietranera '98, with its slightly over-ripe fruity tone, is a notch below. The successful Brunello Riserva '97 shows great elegance and structure, as well as a rich fruit-led bouquet. Our favourite '01 Rosso di Montalcino is the attractively fruity Pietranera. The nose of the Friggiali seemed over-evolved.

We're pleased to find Cerbaiona still in the front ranks. With the excellent assistance of Nora, and the amusing company of their numerous cats, the "commander", as the owner, Diego Molinari, is known in Montalcino, is again producing wine. His excellent Brunello '98 has the polish of the great years, after a brief less graceful period in the mid 1990s, caused in part by some not very glorious vintages. As usual, these good results are not a matter of chance. All the casks have recently been replaced, and replanting has begun in part of the vineyard, so as not to reduce the already limited production. After experimenting with barriques, Molinari has decided not to use them, for a very simple reason. He doesn't like the nose they give to a wine. In amongst the mid-sized barrels, we noticed some larger casks. These are used for the second wine, Cerbaiona, which was not presented for tasting. The '98 Brunello is an austere wine that reflects its vintage, as well as its terroir, the central slopes of the eastern part of Montalcino. The nose offers aromas of plum and sour cherry with a very moderate note of oak. The impact on the palate is uncompromising, then the solid tannins concede nothing to fashions for feather-bed softness, and the lovely finish echoes the nose.

● Brunello di Montalcino Ris. '97	𝟕𝟕	7
● Brunello di Montalcino Tenuta Friggiali '98	𝟕𝟕	8
● Rosso di Montalcino Pietranera '01	𝟕	6
● Rosso di Montalcino Tenuta Friggiali '01	𝟕	6
● Brunello di Montalcino Pietranera '98	𝟕	8
● Brunello di Montalcino Pietranera '97	𝟤𝟤	7
● Brunello di Montalcino Tenuta Friggiali '97	𝟤𝟤	7

● Brunello di Montalcino '98	𝟕𝟕	8
● Brunello di Montalcino '88	𝟕𝟕𝟕	8
● Brunello di Montalcino '90	𝟕𝟕𝟕	8
● Brunello di Montalcino '97	𝟕𝟕𝟕	8
● Brunello di Montalcino '93	𝟤𝟤	8

MONTALCINO (SI)

CIACCI PICCOLOMINI D'ARAGONA
FRAZ. CASTELNUOVO DELL'ABATE
B.GO DI MEZZO, 62
53020 MONTALCINO (SI)
TEL. 0577835616
E-MAIL: info@ciacci-piccolomini.com

This now historic winery was one of the first to demonstrate the potential of the Castelnuovo dell'Abate side of Montalcino. The estate includes excellent plots near the abbey of Sant'Antimo, and also along the unsurfaced road to Sant'Angelo in Colle. It is here that Ciacci Piccolomini D'Aragona is building a new cellar that will replace the lovely facilities underneath the noble family home in the village. The new underground structure will be temperature controlled throughout and is to be used also for extending the bottle-ageing period of the cellar's Brunellos, in accordance with the new regulations. At this year's tastings, the wines did very well, making some significant additions to the estate Glassware. The splendid Brunello '98 displays a ruby hue shading to garnet at the rim of the glass. The confident nose, effectively supported by alcohol, offers jammy notes of blackberry and cherry. The authoritative palate reveals tight-knit, mouthfilling tannins and a finish with an exemplary follow through. This first-rate Brunello comes from a vintage that is too often dismissed as mediocre. The very good Brunello Riserva '97 releases notes of black berry fruit on the nose, enhanced by delightful toasty and floral tones. In the mouth, there are smooth tannins and a lingering full finish. There was One Glass each for the Rosso di Montalcino '01, with its fresh, slightly unripe fragrance, and the Ateo '00, a blend of sangiovese and cabernet with a solid palate which, however, is a little tannin-heavy. The Fabius '00 is over-ripe and under par.

MONTALCINO (SI)

TENUTA COL D'ORCIA
LOC. SANT'ANGELO SCALO
53020 MONTALCINO (SI)
TEL. 057780891
E-MAIL: coldorcia.direzione@tin.it

Tenuta Col d'Orcia is one of the largest estates in Montalcino. It has 140 hectares under vine, 110 of which are dedicated to DOCG or DOC wines. This year, somewhat ironically, the best bottles presented were made from grapes that are not permitted by the regulations. The Nearco '00 gave a great debut performance, and very nearly picked up Three Glasses. A cleverly judged blend of merlot, cabernet sauvignon and syrah, it ages for 18 months in barrique before bottling. Some 25,000 bottles were produced, so it should be possible to find one. Even the nose is characteristic of its terroir. Heady and overwhelming, it shows fruit notes of blackcurrant and blueberry that precede a muscular palate with a splendid progression and a most intriguing finish. The tannins are close knit but not astringent. The Olmaia '99 is not quite so good, but still very good indeed. A monovarietal Cabernet Sauvignon, it is held back on the palate by an overdose of tannins that make it a little inflexible. More bottle age should help the wine to come round. As for the classic Montalcino wines, the news is not equally cheering. The Brunello '98 is well executed, but fades on the finish, whereas the Rosso di Montalcino '01 offers an austere, captivating palate. The not very harmonious Rosso di Montalcino Banditella '01 has a muzzy nose.

● Brunello di Montalcino Vigna di Pianrosso '98	🍷🍷🍷	7
● Brunello di Montalcino Ris. '97	🍷🍷	8
● Sant'Antimo Ateo '00	🍷	6
● Rosso di Montalcino Vigna della Fonte '01	🍷	5
● Sant'Antimo Fabius '00		6
● Brunello di Montalcino Vigna di Pianrosso '88	🍷🍷🍷	8
● Brunello di Montalcino Vigna di Pianrosso '90	🍷🍷🍷	8
● Brunello di Montalcino Vigna di Pianrosso '97	🍷🍷	8

● Nearco '00	🍷🍷	7
● Olmaia '99	🍷🍷	7
● Rosso di Montalcino '01	🍷	4
● Brunello di Montalcino '98	🍷	6
● Rosso di Montalcino Banditella '01		5
● Brunello di Montalcino Poggio al Vento Ris. '85	🍷🍷🍷	8
● Brunello di Montalcino Poggio al Vento Ris. '88	🍷🍷🍷	8
● Brunello di Montalcino Poggio al Vento Ris. '90	🍷🍷🍷	8
● Olmaia '94	🍷🍷🍷	7
● Brunello di Montalcino Poggio al Vento Ris. '95	🍷🍷🍷	8

MONTALCINO (SI)

MONTALCINO (SI)

TENUTA DI COLLOSORBO
FRAZ. CASTELNUOVO DELL'ABATE
LOC. VILLA A SESTA, 25
53020 MONTALCINO (SI)
TEL. 0577835534
E-MAIL: info@collosorbo.com

ANDREA COSTANTI
COLLE AL MATRICHESE
53024 MONTALCINO (SI)
TEL. 0577848195
E-MAIL: costanti@inwind.it

After a few years' absence, Collosorbo is back in the Guide with an excellent range of wines. Located in one of the best areas of Montalcino, along the magnificent unsurfaced road to the village of Sesta, it has some 12 hectares of vines growing fruit for Brunello, although they are not all currently producing. Recently a further eight hectares were planted to various grapes to make Sant'Antimo DOC wines, so now we find merlot and syrah in addition to the traditional sangiovese. There have also been some changes in the cellar. Casks have been replaced, and the cellar staff have started to use small barrels, as was already clear from our tastings. So side by side, there are barrels with capacities ranging from 160 to 540 litres. We found a distinct improvement in the wines we tasted, particularly the younger ones. Hence the performance of the Sorbus '01, a blend of sangiovese and a little cabernet sauvignon, should come as no surprise. The colour is dark, the nose complex and rich, and the fruit tones meld nicely into balsamic notes and hints of pencil lead. The palate reveals great power and softness, fine-grained tannins and engrossing depth. The very good Brunello Riserva '97 has an inviting colour and a rich bouquet of red berry fruit. The well-structured palate progresses admirably, showing nicely integrated tannins and fair acidity. The successful Rosso di Montalcino '01 offers aromas of sour cherry and coffee, followed by a lively palate, thanks to crunchy tannins. A notch down is the Brunello '98, a well-executed, but not particularly complex, wine.

This historic Montalcino winery has again shown that it can be relied on. With more than five hectares dedicated to sangiovese for Brunello, Andrea Costanti's estate makes wine that is expressive of its terroir. The vineyards, at 420 metres above sea level, lie along the road that climbs from Torrenieri towards Montalcino. There are rosebushes at the head of each row, which not only add to the beauty of the vineyard, but also act as a sort of warning system about the health of the vines. The fairly loose soil is one of the reasons for the great finesse of bouquet of the wines, which show no notes of over-ripe grapes. In fact, these wines are never overblown: elegance is their hallmark. This year's best bottle was the Brunello Riserva '97, a perfect example of the aforesaid qualities. The nose presents classic morello cherry notes interlaced with stylish balsamic tones. The palate reveals sweet alcohol and good structure, but the still youthful tannins get in the way of the progression. The other wines earned One Glass each. Our favourite was the Brunello '98, which nearly got Two Glasses. The very floral nose also has an interesting note of peach, and the easy-drinking palate is nicely balanced, which is what we'd expect from this terroir in a cool year. The better of the two Rosso di Montalcinos is Calbello '01, with its rich nose of cinchona and sour cherry preceding well-integrated tannins. The Ardingo '00, a cabernet and merlot blend, is well executed, but a bit too simple to aspire to more than One Glass. The good Vermiglio '00 is warm and engrossing on the palate.

● Rosso Sorbus '01	♟♟	6
● Rosso di Montalcino '01	♟♟	5
● Brunello di Montalcino Ris. '97	♟♟	8
● Brunello di Montalcino '98	♟	8
● Rosso di Montalcino		
Vigna del Cassero Ris. '90	♟♟	6
● Rosso di Montalcino '99	♟♟	4
● Brunello di Montalcino '91	♟	5

● Brunello di Montalcino Ris. '97	♟♟	8
● Rosso di Montalcino Calbello '01	♟	5
● Ardingo '00	♟	7
● Vermiglio '00	♟	6
● Rosso di Montalcino '01	♟	6
● Brunello di Montalcino '98	♟	7
● Brunello di Montalcino '88	♟♟♟	8
● Brunello di Montalcino '93	♟♟	8
● Brunello di Montalcino Ris. '95	♟♟	8
● Brunello di Montalcino '97	♟♟	7
● Ardingo '99	♟♟	7

MONTALCINO (SI)

TENUTA DI SESTA
FRAZ. CASTELNUOVO DELL'ABATE
LOC. SESTA
53020 MONTALCINO (SI)
TEL. 0577835612 - 0577596014
E-MAIL: tenutadisesta@libero.it

Ask Montalcino growers where they would most like to buy more vineyards, and chances are they'll say, "Sesta". This area, between Sant'Angelo in Colle and Castelnuovo dell'Abate, has unique characteristics. Despite its position to the south of Montalcino, ventilation is ideal and a subsoil layer of clay keeps the vines from suffering many of the ill effects of hot, dry seasons. For some years, Giovanni Ciacci's winery had to invest in cellar restructuring to be able to make full use of the potential of this land. In the past, we have often been unconvinced by the aromas of wines at our tastings, but new casks in the cellar have done a lot to overcome these problems. This year, the wines have definitely improved. Some five to ten per cent of all the wine is now barrique aged. The very interesting Brunello Riserva '97 nearly made it into our finals. A fairly intense ruby introduces a classic nose of alcohol-steeped morello cherries with notes of tobacco. The successful palate shows character and an elegant progression accompanied by fine-grained tannins. The Rosso di Montalcino '01 offers aromas of rhubarb and hay. The richness of the palate is not quite sufficient to match the exuberant tannins, which make the wine a bit too taut. The Brunello '98 also got just One Glass. The nose releases faintly vegetal notes and the palate is rather lightweight.

MONTALCINO (SI)

CASATO PRIME DONNE
DONATELLA CINELLI COLOMBINI
LOC. CASATO
53024 MONTALCINO (SI)
TEL. 0577849421 - 0577662108
E-MAIL: vino@cinellicolombini.it

A few years ago, Donatella Cinelli Colombini left her family winery to follow her own ideas of how Brunello should be made. The experience she took with her enabled her to forge ahead and, very soon thereafter, she began presenting distinctive wines with an innovative style. Of course, success only comes with time, but Donatella's ideas have already proved to be sound. The Rosso di Montalcino '01 and the Leone Rosso '01 both did better than last year's versions, and the debutant Orcia Cenerentola '01, a blend of sangiovese and foglia tonda, earned Two Glasses. The upward trend of the more recent wines indicates progress in vinification. For the Brunellos, we shall have to wait the prescribed length of time, but all the indications are promising. The Rosso, a dark ruby red in the glass, flaunts the estate style on the nose with quite distinct notes of oak that meld nicely blended with the fruit. The palate reveals good extract and moderate richness. Although balance was not perfect when we tasted, we felt it would improve by the end of the summer. The Leone Rosso '01, a step down, shows a fragrant nose with quite prominent cherry. The palate is simple, flavourful and fresh. We preferred the standard '98 Brunello to the Prime Donne '98, a blend assembled by a team of well-known female tasters. The Brunello has an attractive personality, with notes of chocolate and red berry fruit on the nose and a dense, characteristically varietal, palate. Prime Donne, however, is not very eloquent on the nose and has yet to absorb its tannins fully.

● Brunello di Montalcino Ris. '97	♈♈	8
● Rosso di Montalcino '01	♈	5
● Brunello di Montalcino '98	♈	8
● Brunello di Montalcino Ris. '95	♉♉	8
● Brunello di Montalcino '97	♉♉	8
● Rosso di Montalcino '99	♈	4

● Orcia Cenerentola '01	♈♈	6
● Rosso di Montalcino '01	♈♈	5
● Brunello di Montalcino '98	♈♈	7
● Brunello di Montalcino Prime Donne '98	♈	7
● Leone Rosso '01	♈	4
● Brunello di Montalcino Prime Donne '95	♉♉	7
● Brunello di Montalcino Prime Donne '96	♉♉	7
● Brunello di Montalcino Prime Donne '97	♉♉	7

MONTALCINO (SI)

MONTALCINO (SI)

DONNA OLGA
LOC. FRIGGIALI
S.DA MAREMMANA
53024 MONTALCINO (SI)
TEL. 0577849454

FANTI - LA PALAZZETTA
FRAZ. CASTELNUOVO DELL'ABATE
VIA BORGO DI SOTTO, 40
53020 MONTALCINO (SI)
TEL. 0577835631

After its fine debut last year with the '97 Brunello, Tenuta Donna Olga has earned a full profile thanks to the excellent Brunello '98, among the best from its vintage and a worthy representative of the southwestern section of Montalcino. The Donna Olga estate covers 11 hectares, of which just four are dedicated to sangiovese for Brunello. The rest is woodland and olive groves. The estate, as the name suggests, belongs to a woman, which is not unique in Montalcino. Olga Peluso herself is well known in the wine world as the owner of another local estate. Here, however, her idea is to use the experience she has gained over the years to produce exclusively Brunello. Part of her profits go to charity. The team Olga has selected hardly requires an introduction. Consultant, Riccardo Cotarella, is the technical supervisor, assisted by the very able Marco Simonit and Pierpaolo Sirch, responsible for managing the vineyards located near the road that goes towards Grosseto from Montalcino. The vines are planted at a high density – about 7,000 plants per hectare – and fermentation takes place in small barrels. The result is very interesting, indeed. The wine's nose is richly fruity, with notes of sour cherry and black berry fruit jam blended with spicy and smoky nuances. The palate is sweet and rich, and the perfectly integrated tannins give the finish breadth and depth. This is an excellent Brunello, and a fine example of technology enhancing terroir.

One of the trickiest things we have to do when writing the Guide is decide on the review format for a producer. In Montalcino, the difficulty is compounded by the high general level of the wines. Attentive readers will have noted the fine showing this small Castelnuovo dell'Abate winery made last year, so this time, given the excellence of Flavio Fanti's wines and the improvement of the estate over time, a full profile seemed in order. The roughly five hectares of vineyards are located near the celebrated abbey of Sant'Antimo and are planted at a density of 5,000 vines per hectare. Flavio is very strict about grape selection at harvest time. In his cellar, there are various kinds of barrels. The oak is Slavonian or French, and the sizes vary from barriques to 200-litre casks. Recently, the estate started up a very attractive country inn near the cellar. As for the wines, the Brunello Riserva '97 is fantastic and strolled off with Three Glasses, having won us over particularly with its interpretation of terroir. The varietal fruit tones of cherry and blackberry on the nose show extraordinary intensity and are accompanied by spicy notes of oak. The palate is meaty and elegant, with smooth, succulent tannins and an incredibly long finish. The '98 Brunello shows the same style, but less complexity, probably because of its vintage. The intense, concentrated ruby ushers in a broad, fruit-forward nose nicely underpinned by oak. Here, too, the tannins are well matched by glycerine and alcohol. The likeable Rosso di Montalcino '01 is fragrant and fruity, with well-gauged acidity.

● Brunello di Montalcino Donna Olga '98	🍷🍷	8
● Brunello di Montalcino Donna Olga '97	🍷🍷	7
● Rosso di Montalcino '00	🍷	7

● Brunello di Montalcino Ris. '97	🍷🍷🍷	8
● Brunello di Montalcino '98	🍷🍷	7
● Rosso di Montalcino '01	🍷	5
● Brunello di Montalcino '95	🍷🍷	7
● Brunello di Montalcino '97	🍷🍷	7

MONTALCINO (SI)

FANTI - SAN FILIPPO
FRAZ. CASTELNUOVO DELL'ABATE
POD. PALAZZO
53020 MONTALCINO (SI)
TEL. 0577835795
E-MAIL: balfanti@tin.it

Filippo Fanti, the dynamic president of the Consorzio di Tutela dei Vini di Montalcino, manages to do two things at once, piling up successes at his estate as well. A great promoter of the Castelnuovo dell'Abate area, which generally produces austere, powerful wines that need lots of ageing time, Filippo has long sought to produce more immediately drinkable wines that still reflect the territory. And he has succeeded, thanks in part to the expert assistance of oenologist, Stefano Chioccioli, who consulted here for a number of years. The improvement project is still under way. It involves steadily increasing the number of small barrels in the cellar, which is also scheduled to expand, and a sizeable extension of the area under vine, which will include grapes other than sangiovese. All the new vines will be planted at high density. The Brunello from the controversial '98 vintage made it to our finals, missing Three Glasses by not very much. It shows the maturity of the estate style and is reminiscent of its recent predecessors. The tropical fruit nose is very distinctive and very fresh, then the sweet, soft palate reveals well-knit tannins and a finish enhanced by peppery notes. It's a very modern, easy-to-like wine. The other two bottles Filippo presented got One Glass each. The Rosso di Montalcino '01 is redolent of cherries steeped in alcohol and shows balance in the mouth, whereas the Rosso Sant'Antimo '01 is grassy on the nose and drinks nicely.

MONTALCINO (SI)

EREDI FULIGNI
VIA S. SALONI, 32
53024 MONTALCINO (SI)
TEL. 0577848039 - 0577848127

We are very pleased indeed to be awarding Three Glasses to Eredi Fuligni, which has for years produced austere, elegant wines as stylish as their creator, Roberto Guerrini. As well as a wine producer, Guerrini is a university professor and a great music lover. A man of many interests, clear-headed and quite untroubled by the wine fashions of the moment, he has always sought an estate style that would privilege terroir to the utmost. The vineyards are in the eastern part of Montalcino, near the road to Buonconvento, on the middle slopes that have fairly loose, not very clayey soil. His wines are consistently well executed, and the '97 Brunello Riserva, helped by a fine growing year, left no room for doubt at our tastings. A fascinating note of plum blends with graceful balsamic tones on the nose. The palate, after a soft attack, immediately reveals a dense, but not excessive texture, in which acidity and very fine-grained tannins are nicely underpinned by glycerine. The finish, which admirably mirrors the bouquet, is very long. The S.J. '01, made from sangiovese and merlot, also made it to our finals with its rich nose of cedar and red berry fruit and a faint vegetal nuance, followed by a most enjoyable palate. There were two very full Glasses for the Brunello '98, a model of elegance and richness. A step down, the Rosso di Montalcino Ginestreto '01 offers persuasively well-defined aromas, but the palate is not particularly complex.

● Brunello di Montalcino '98	♟♟	7
● Rosso di Montalcino '01	♟	4
● Sant'Antimo Rosso '01	♟	4
● Brunello di Montalcino Ris. '95	♟♟♟	7
● Brunello di Montalcino '97	♟♟♟	7

● Brunello di Montalcino Ris. '97	♟♟♟	8
● S. J. '01	♟♟	4
● Brunello di Montalcino Vigneti dei Cottimelli '98	♟♟	7
● Rosso di Montalcino Ginestreto '01	♟	4
● Brunello di Montalcino Vigneti dei Cottimelli Ris. '95	♟♟	7
● Brunello di Montalcino Vigneti dei Cottimelli '96	♟♟	7
● Brunello di Montalcino Vigneti dei Cottimelli '97	♟♟	7

MONTALCINO (SI)

GREPPONE MAZZI
TENIMENTI RUFFINO
LOC. GREPPONE
53024 MONTALCINO (SI)
TEL. 05583605
E-MAIL: info@ruffino.it

Greppone Mazzi, which belongs to the Ruffini group, has always produced wines that are very true to type, but generally lack the personality and sometimes even the complexity that would make them stand out from the multitude of other Brunellos. Yet all the prerequisites for a great wine were there, as we can now see from the '98 Brunello, which is unquestionably the best wine the cellar has ever presented. A brilliant, very concentrated ruby is the prelude to a complex nose with heady and pervasive notes of cherry jam, as well as varietal blackberry nuances. The palate is equally satisfying. This isn't an extremely powerful wine, but it is a notably well-paced one, in which the glycerine is both support and contrast to the rich acidity and tannins, giving the wine balance and throughout the very enjoyable progression. The intense finish beautifully mirrors the bouquet. Another reason this Brunello made it to our finals is its great elegance, which is characteristic of the local territory. The Greppone Mazzi estate includes more than ten hectares under vine currently producing, some of which were recently replanted. It's at a fairly high altitude on the eastern side of Montalcino, where the soil is rather loose. This, together with specific choices made at the winery, has created wines that aim to fascinate rather than overwhelm.

MONTALCINO (SI)

TENUTA IL GREPPO
VILLA GREPPO, 183
53024 MONTALCINO (SI)
TEL. 0577848087
E-MAIL: biondisanti@biondisanti.it

As has been the case for some time, we are including all the wine sold by Biondi Santi in this profile, that is bottles from the Villa Poggio Salvi at Montalcino, as well as those from Il Greppo, and, in the Scansano DOC zone, the production from Castello di Montepò. The Villa Poggio Salvi wines, which have been getting better from year to year, again did well. One Glass went to the Rosso di Montalcino Poggio Salvi '01, which shows a not very deep ruby. The nose is sound, although the fruit is somewhat crowded out by oak-derived smoky notes that will probably fade with some cellar time in the bottle. The good acid bite keeps the wine fresh-tasting, and fruity tones reappear on the finish. We gave Two full Glasses to the Brunello '98. Classic aromas of leather and ripe red berry fruit are interlaced with notes of vanilla, and the palate is pleasing and balanced. The wines from the historic Tenuta Il Greppo made a good showing. The Rosso di Montalcino '00 offers a full bouquet of tobacco and cherry, followed by a rich palate. The Brunello Riserva '97, which at € 400 can hardly be described as affordable, did not make it to our finals because of its rather slack texture, although the balance and elegance contribute to a lovely finish. The nose is agreeable, too, with its mineral and jammy notes melding with a classic tone of leather. As for the wines not made at Montalcino, we should mention that we retasted the good Schidione '98, a blend of sangiovese, cabernet sauvignon and merlot, and also the slender Montepaone '98, a monovarietal Cabernet Sauvignon.

● Brunello di Montalcino '98	▼▼	8
● Brunello di Montalcino Ris. '90	♀♀	7
● Brunello di Montalcino '95	♀♀	7
● Brunello di Montalcino '97	♀♀	8
● Brunello di Montalcino '93	♀	7

● Brunello di Montalcino Ris. '97	▼▼	8
● Brunello di Montalcino		
Poggio Salvi '98	▼▼	7
● Rosso di Montalcino '00	▼	6
● Rosso di Montalcino		
Poggio Salvi '01	▼	4
● Brunello di Montalcino '95	♀♀	6
● Brunello di Montalcino '97	♀♀	8
● Schidione '98	♀♀	8
● Sassoalloro '00	♀♀	5
● Montepaone '98	♀	6

MONTALCINO (SI)

IL PALAZZONE
LOC. DUE PORTE, 245
53024 MONTALCINO (SI)
TEL. 0577835764
E-MAIL: palazzone@virgilio.it

Il Palazzone, with its vineyards high in the Montalcino hills that give such characterful wines, continues to advance. The new American owner, Dick Parsons, has had a profound effect on the estate style in his attempt to produce more full-bodied wines. And he seems to have been successful. After the excellent performance last year of the Rosso di Montalcino '00, his Brunellos are now also showing great breeding. Furthermore, we understand that the estate is to be expanded. The '98 Brunello displays a handsome concentrated ruby that introduces aromas of particularly fresh red berry fruit. The attack on the palate is soft, the tannins are fine-grained and mellow, and the finish is long, thanks in part to the acidity typical of this area, and mirrors the nose. An easy Two Glasses. The Brunello Riserva '97, which does not disgrace its vintage, is a different sort of wine. The advantage of this part of Montalcino is that, in hot years, you can get perfect grapes with no hint of the over-ripeness which prevails elsewhere. So here we have a full, elegant bouquet with fresh notes of cherry and redcurrant. The graceful, lingering palate shows succulent, well-integrated tannins, and a rousing, fruit-forward finish.

MONTALCINO (SI)

IL POGGIOLO
LOC. POGGIOLO, 259
53024 MONTALCINO (SI)
TEL. 0577848412 - 3483411848
E-MAIL: info@ilpoggiolomontalcino.com

Rudy Cosimi, who was a champion motorcyclist and is now racing cars, also manages Il Poggiolo. As usual, the cellar presented quite a number of bottles. Rudy's aim for this estate halfway up the hills of Montalcino is to demonstrate the variety of the territory's characteristics by producing various different Brunellos. Unfortunately, it also has to be said that Il Poggiolo does not release very much wine, so it can be very hard to find what you're looking for. Having said that, we must admit that the bottles that do emerge are good and remarkably consistent. Some of the selections, in the first few years after their release on the market, can be a bit intrusively spicy, but time takes care of that. We were unable to taste the Rosso di Montalcino '01, which was not yet in bottle at the time of our tastings. As for the Brunellos, the Poggiolo Riserva '97 is splendid. The intense blackberry aromas enhanced by mineral notes are typical of this estate. The opulent palate is underpinned by perfectly calibrated acidity and tannins that provide elegance, leading to a very intense finish. The good Brunello Beato Riserva '97 offers hints of anise and coffee and, in the mouth, very smooth tannins. The Brunello Terra Rossa Riserva '97 also collected Two Glasses. It has those mineral notes on the nose, but here they support lovely sour cherry tones, and the palate flaunts perfect balance. The '98 Brunellos are good, but not exciting, which is in keeping with their vintage. Our favourite of the three is the Terra Rossa, which is the richest and most complex.

● Brunello di Montalcino Ris. '97	🍷🍷	8
● Brunello di Montalcino '98	🍷🍷	8
● Brunello di Montalcino Ris. '95	🍷🍷	7
● Rosso di Montalcino '00	🍷🍷	5
● Brunello di Montalcino '97	🍷🍷	8

● Brunello di Montalcino Poggiolo Ris. '97	🍷🍷	8
● Brunello di Montalcino Beato Ris. '97	🍷🍷	8
● Brunello di Montalcino Terra Rossa Ris. '97	🍷🍷	8
● Brunello di Montalcino Beato '98	🍷	7
● Brunello di Montalcino Poggiolo '98	🍷	7
● Brunello di Montalcino Terra Rossa '98	🍷	7
● Brunello di Montalcino Terra Rossa '97	🍷🍷	7
● Brunello di Montalcino Beato '97	🍷🍷	7

MONTALCINO (SI)

MONTALCINO (SI)

TENUTA IL POGGIONE
FRAZ. SANT'ANGELO IN COLLE
P.ZZA CASTELLO, 14
53020 MONTALCINO (SI)
TEL. 0577844029
E-MAIL: ilpoggioine@tin.it

PODERE LA FORTUNA
LOC. LA FORTUNA, 83
53024 MONTALCINO (SI)
TEL. 0577848308
E-MAIL: azaglafortuna@inwind.it

Something's been stirring in the last few years at the historic Tenuta Il Poggione estate. Fabrizio Bindocci has taken an innovative turn, but without distorting the estate style, always deeply rooted in the history of Brunello and the Montalcino territory. The number of small barrels in the cellar has been growing year by year. At present, they are used only for San Leonardo, the Tenuta Il Poggione IGT, but with the new Brunello regulations reducing the minimum barrel maturation time to two years, there could be some changes ahead for the first wine, too. Meanwhile, we can revel in the stupendous Brunello Riserva '97, the best Brunello ever to leave the cellar. Classic in style, it offers a bouquet that ranges from tobacco to peach, apricot and the varietal alcohol-steeped morello cherry. The substantial body helps to restrain the heavyweight acidity and tannins that do credit to the vintage. This is a wine with a great future, and more ageing time in bottle will add balance to all that richness on the palate. The other wines are all good, as usual, and very fairly priced. The San Leopoldo '00, made from cabernet and sangiovese, got Two Glasses for its very spicy nose of black pepper, admirable length and sheer individuality. The very successful Il Poggione '00, which displays exuberant freshness on the nose and a simple, satisfying palate, almost won Two Glasses as well. The other DOCG wines earned One Glass each. Our clear favourite was the '98 Brunello, which is, as usual, reliable and very traditional in style.

For some time now, the wines from Gioberto Zannoni's estate have been making a positive impression, and this year they moved up a gear. Two of the bottles presented at our tastings made it to the finals, a very good showing and a boost for the northeastern area of Montalcino. From the roughly nine hectares under sangiovese vines for Brunello, Podere La Fortuna produced the excellent '97 Riserva, which matured slowly in tonneau. It's quite an eye-catcher with its extremely concentrated ruby hue. The nose is a blend of cherry and blackberry fruit with stylish balsam and spice tones. The power of the palate, which reveals a very precise sense of place, is balanced by acidity and tannins that contribute to a lovely progression. The Sant'Antimo '01 on its first time out is already a splendid wine. It's a blend of equal parts of sangiovese and cabernet sauvignon, the latter from the new estate vineyards in the Torrenieri area. An intense purplish red introduces a nose of candied citron peel, blueberry and red berry fruit. The great elegance and length on the palate can be attributed to fine-grained tannins and to rich glycerine on the finish, which is a mirror image of the bouquet. The delicious '98 Brunello won Two Glasses. The vintage was indifferent, but this wine shows only its good side, thanks to the beautifully judged concentration and elegance of the palate, which make it a delight to drink. The nose offers well-defined cherries. Down a step, the Rosso di Montalcino '01 seemed a little unexciting.

●	Brunello di Montalcino Ris. '97	♟♟♟	8
●	San Leopoldo '00	♟♟	5
●	Brunello di Montalcino '98	♟	6
●	Il Poggione '00	♟	3
●	Rosso di Montalcino '01	♟	4
○	Moscadello di Montalcino '02	♟	4
●	Brunello di Montalcino '90	♟♟	6
●	Brunello di Montalcino '95	♟	6

●	Sant'Antimo La Fortuna '01	♟♟	6
●	Brunello di Montalcino Ris. '97	♟♟	7
●	Brunello di Montalcino '98	♟♟	6
●	Rosso di Montalcino '01	♟	4
●	Brunello di Montalcino Ris. '93	♟♟	7
●	Brunello di Montalcino Ris. '95	♟♟	7
●	Brunello di Montalcino '97	♟♟	7

MONTALCINO (SI)

LA GERLA
LOC. CANALICCHIO
POD. COLOMBAIO
53024 MONTALCINO (SI)
TEL. 0577848599
E-MAIL: lagerla@tin.it

The Rossis, who are well known in advertising, are Guide regulars because their consistently well-executed wines are always worth a profile. La Gerla is located on a hillside north of Montalcino where the soil is marly and there's not much clay. Rather cool years like '98 can be a challenge. The two Brunellos from that vintage which were presented at our tastings differ in style. The Poggio agli Angeli, the estate's vineyard selection, declares its barrel ageing with notes of oak that soften the intense morello cherry on the nose. The balance on the palate is good, but the not very long finish keeps the wine from moving up to Two Glasses. The very traditional nose of the Brunello '98 opens with brief sulphurous notes, then releases captivating varietal aromas of tobacco, sour cherry and other red berry fruit. The attack on the palate is interesting, but the tannins are not enhanced by the understated acidity, which is typical of the terroir. Apart from their divergent styles, which can be traced to different ways of using oak, the two wines are characteristic of both their area and their growing year. The other wines, from warmer vintages, are better. The Brunello Riserva '97, a Two Glass winner, offers a nose of some finesse, where fruity notes of peach and apricot rub shoulders with light floral tones, and then an attractively meaty palate. The good Birba '00, a monovarietal Sangiovese, shows deep colour, a fruit-led nose of blueberry and redcurrant, and a rich and finish that lingers on the palate.

MONTALCINO (SI)

LA PODERINA
FRAZ. CASTELNUOVO DELL'ABATE
LOC. PODERINA
53020 MONTALCINO (SI)
TEL. 0577835737
E-MAIL: poderina@tin.it

This was not a bad year for SAI Agricola's Montalcino estate. The Brunello did well enough to make it to our finals and has now established its own distinctive style. The dark red with ruby highlights ushers in a rich nose on which notes of oak are well integrated into the blackberry and sour cherry fruit. The palate is equally imposing. A very soft attack precedes lovely progression in which acidity and tannins are perfectly balanced by glycerine and alcohol, producing a wonderfully long finish. This is a modern Brunello that nevertheless manages not to distort the characteristics of the terroir. The Moscadello di Montalcino Vendemmia Tardiva '01 is a wine of great breeding. Indeed, it shows what can be done in these parts with a sweet, late-harvested wine. The enticing aromas of candied peel, peach and spring flowers are remarkably clean and long-lasting. The length on the palate is excellent too, although the sweetness tends to dwarf the acidity. The Rosso di Montalcino exhibits a vibrant colour with deep purplish highlights, an intense cherry nose and impressive balance on the palate, which reveals soft, tight-knit tannins. The Brunello Poggio Banale '98 did well, too, although it has yet to come out.

● Birba '00	♟♟	5	○ Moscadello V. T. '01	♟♟	6
● Brunello di Montalcino Ris. '97	♟♟	8	● Brunello di Montalcino '98	♟♟	7
● Rosso di Montalcino '01	♟	4	● Brunello di Montalcino Poggio Banale '98	♟♟	8
● Brunello di Montalcino '98	♟	7	○ Rosso di Montalcino '01	♟	5
● Brunello di Montalcino Poggio agli Angeli '98	♟	8	● Brunello di Montalcino Ris. '88	♟♟♟	7
● Brunello di Montalcino Ris. '95	♟♟	7	● Brunello di Montalcino Poggio Banale '97	♟♟♟	8
● Brunello di Montalcino Vigna gli Angeli '97	♟♟	8	● Brunello di Montalcino Ris. '90	♟♟	7
			○ Moscadello V. T. '99	♟♟	5
			○ Moscadello V. T. '00	♟♟	6

MONTALCINO (SI)

MONTALCINO (SI)

La Togata - Tenuta Carlina
loc. Tavernelle
pod. Poderuccio
53024 Montalcino (SI)
tel. 0668803000
E-mail: brunello@latogata.com

Le Chiuse
loc. Pullera, 228
53024 Montalcino (SI)
tel. 0577848595
E-mail: info@lechiuse.com

When we reviewed La Togata's '90 Brunello there were some raised eyebrows: a bottle from a minuscule winery that bought grapes! In a few years, the winery has grown considerably and now possesses 22 hectares under vine, all of which are producing. The new holdings are planted at high density – about 6,000 vines per hectare – in various parts of Montalcino. The latest addition is in Montosoli, one of the most celebrated Montalcino vineyards. The new cellar has also been expanded and soon will have a new wing, allowing a more rational arrangement of barrels and bottles. On the wine front, our tastings confirmed the consistent excellence of this estate. Indeed, the Brunello Riserva '97 very nearly repeated the triumph of the standard version from the same vintage and all the other wines got Two Glasses. But back to the finalist. The '97 Brunello Riserva has a lovely nose of intense fruit, with perfectly calibrated oak and a hint of cinnamon. The admirably powerful, elegant palate reveals a confident progression to a great finish, which is both broad and deep. The '98 Brunello shows a different style. Aromas of flowers and fresh fruit lead to a good palate with slightly prominent tannins that are not too spiky. The Rosso di Montalcino '01 is hesitant at first, then opens on the nose to reveal fresh cherry. In the mouth, it's enjoyable and well paced. The interesting sangiovese-based Azzurreta '01 is very harmonious and elegant.

Le Chiuse, one of Montalcino's female-owned estates, has for some time been showing the consistency of quality essential if you want to turn a good estate into a great one. The winery is on the northern slopes of Montalcino, facing the celebrated Montosoli vineyard, which is where, on her more than five hectares of sangiovese for Brunello, Simonetta Valiani produces her wines. And this year, they are remarkably good, including a superb '98 Brunello that went through to our finals. Despite the vintage, which was inferior to '97, this Brunello shows enviable complexity. We noted some stylistic changes. Maturation was clearly managed differently, so that spicy and toasty notes of oak play more of a role than in the past. This very intense-hued wine has prominent aromas of red berry fruit and blackberries, together with a well-defined intense note of spice. Length in the mouth is good, and the smooth tannins meld beautifully with the alcohol to provide a dense, rich texture. Two Glasses went to the Brunello Riserva '97, which opens rather slowly on the nose, but is admirably clean. The palate shows the excellent quality of the fruit, but also slightly aggressive tannins which have a rather drying effect on the finish. The Rosso di Montalcino '01 got One Glass for its tobacco aromas and an intriguing acidity that makes it deliciously drinkable.

● Brunello di Montalcino Ris. '97	♥♥	8
● Azzurreta '01	♥♥	6
● Rosso di Montalcino '01	♥♥	6
● Brunello di Montalcino '98	♥♥	7
● Brunello di Montalcino '97	♥♥♥	7
● Brunello di Montalcino '90	♥♥	7
● Brunello di Montalcino Ris. '95	♥♥	7
● Brunello di Montalcino '96	♥♥	7

● Brunello di Montalcino '98	♥♥	8
● Brunello di Montalcino Ris. '97	♥♥	8
● Rosso di Montalcino '01	♥	5
● Brunello di Montalcino '97	♥♥	7
● Brunello di Montalcino '96	♥	6
● Rosso di Montalcino '99	♥	4

Lisini

Loc. Sant'Angelo in Colle
53020 Montalcino (SI)
tel. 0577844040
e-mail: azienda@lisini.com

After its brief absence, this Montalcino estate, long one of the favourites of Brunello devotees, has regained its full profile. The over ten hectares under vine are situated in the splendid wine country of Sesta. In recent years, we noted a slight decline in quality, but that period seems to be over. This time, we found some fascinating stylistic changes. The Rosso di Montalcino '00 is a lesson in the importance of bottle ageing. Released a bit later than its peers, it shows the good qualities of its vintage without any of the defects. Well-defined, prominent aromas of ripe fruit and sour cherry jam on the nose blend with spicy notes of oak. The palate shows some changes, too, in its smoothness, lovely stylish tannins and very satisfying finish. The estate flagship, Brunello di Montalcino Ugolaia '97, gave a fine performance. This edition has recaptured the aromatic harmony and the intensity of the earliest vintages. It boasts a lovely personality, showing quite austere on the nose, with fresh fruity notes of sour cherry and blueberry beautifully enhanced by balsamic tones. The good palate unveils an even progression and tight-knit but not rigid tannins, then tangy acidity supports a rich, enjoyable finish. The '98 Brunello, with its over-evolved aromas, is less successful.

● Rosso di Montalcino '00	**ΨΨ**	5
● Brunello di Montalcino Ugolaia '97	**ΨΨ**	8
● Brunello di Montalcino '98		7
● Brunello di Montalcino Ugolaia '91	ΨΨΨ	8
● Brunello di Montalcino Ugolaia '90	ΨΨ	8
● Brunello di Montalcino Ugolaia '94	ΨΨ	8

Luce

Loc. Castelgiocondo
53024 Montalcino (SI)
tel. 0577848492

The 2000 vintage was not an easy one on the Grosseto side of Montalcino. High summer temperatures and drought in the warmest months caused grapes to dry on the vine, and despite very careful bunch selection at harvest time, the wines from this vintage have quite prominent jammy aromas. Luce is the most talked about joint venture in Montalcino (it belongs to the Frescobaldis and the Californian Mondavis) but it was no exception. The wines this time showed the effects of the growing year quite distinctly. The Luce '00, a blend of sangiovese and merlot, has a lovely dark ruby hue that extends to the rim of the glass. The nose shows varietal aromas of morello cherry and oak-derived spice, but betrays its vintage with warm notes of plum and blackberry. The attack on the rich palate is dense and smooth, but the progression reveals slightly aggressive if not bitter tannins. The finish is good, although the spice comes back a little intrusively. The Lucente '01 did less well. Its very elegant clean, fruit-led nose releases aromas of ripe sour cherry and the palate is very nicely balanced, but not particularly complex.

● Luce '00	**ΨΨ**	8
● Lucente '01	**Ψ**	5
● Luce '94	ΨΨΨ	8
● Luce '93	ΨΨ	8
● Luce '95	ΨΨ	8
● Luce '96	ΨΨ	8
● Luce '97	ΨΨ	8
● Lucente '97	ΨΨ	5
● Luce '98	ΨΨ	8
● Lucente '99	ΨΨ	5
● Luce '99	ΨΨ	8
● Lucente '00	ΨΨ	5

MONTALCINO (SI)

MASTROJANNI
FRAZ. CASTELNUOVO DELL'ABATE
POD. LORETO SAN PIO
53024 MONTALCINO (SI)
TEL. 0577835681

After many years at the helm of the family estate, Antonio Mastrojanni has decided to take a break from winemaking. He's a man we admire, partly because he's so likeable and also because of his excellent wines. We wish him the best of luck in his new endeavours. Meanwhile, the winery, headed by oenologist, Andrea Machetti, who can call on the advice of the consultant, Maurizio Castelli, continues to present good wines, even if there was no absolute champion this time. The estate possesses some 24 hectares under vine in the easternmost part of Castelnuovo dell'Abate, and 17 are dedicated to DOCG wines, while the others are planted mostly to cabernet sauvignon. The restructuring of the cellar is finished and the new casks, including barriques and 500-litre barrels, are all in place. These changes have benefited the San Pio, a blend of sangiovese and cabernet sauvignon whose '99 version is a thoroughbred. The very intense ruby with purplish highlights heralds a remarkably rich nose that releases notes of leather and very concentrated black and red berry fruit. The full-bodied palate offers smooth tannins to support the tightly woven texture. The Rosso di Montalcino '01 easily picked up Two Glasses. This is a very terroir-driven Rosso, with heady notes of jam and fruit steeped in spirits, and then good structure on the palate. It needs some more bottle age to mellow the tannins. The good '98 Brunello shows a distinctly mineral note on the nose, and excellent balance in the mouth. There was no '98 Brunello Schiena d'Asino, as the cellar did not consider the vintage up to snuff.

● Rosso di Montalcino '01	▼▼	4
● San Pio '99	▼▼	6
● Brunello di Montalcino '98	▼	8
● Brunello di Montalcino Ris. '88	YYY	7
● Brunello di Montalcino '90	YYY	7
● Brunello di Montalcino Schiena d'Asino '90	YYY	7
● Brunello di Montalcino Schiena d'Asino '93	YYY	7
● Brunello di Montalcino '97	YYY	7

MONTALCINO (SI)

TENUTE SILVIO NARDI
LOC. CASALE DEL BOSCO
53024 MONTALCINO (SI)
TEL. 0577808269
E-MAIL: info@tenutenardi.com

There are some people who make a profound difference to the history of their wineries, and Emilia Nardi is one of them. When she took the reins of the family estate, the wines were mediocre and house policy was based mostly on keeping prices down. In ten years, she revolutionized Tenute Silvio Nardi, both technically and commercially, taking a number of risky decisions that have turned out very well. Her Brunello Manachiara project is a prime example. It was greeted with scepticism by many in the profession, but has produced one of the most reliable wines of Montalcino. Yet a great estate, and Emilia has more than 50 hectares for Brunello, needs more than one top-class wine. Luckily, the Rosso di Montalcino '01 is quite delicious and one of the top three from its vintage. A fragrant nose of black and red berry fruit with mineral notes is followed by a soft, mouthfilling palate with a very enjoyable finish. The Brunello Manachiara '98 also came close to winning Three Glasses. The aromas are similar to those of the Rosso, but enriched by spicy and balsamic notes. The sumptuous palate has great extract, well-integrated tannins and an exceptionally lingering finish that echoes the nose. The '98 Brunello easily scored Two Glasses. The more forward nose releases floral tones and hints of peach, then the palate is elegant, concentrated and very harmonious.

● Rosso di Montalcino '01	▼▼	4
● Brunello di Montalcino Manachiara Cru '98	▼▼	8
● Brunello di Montalcino '98	▼▼	6
● Brunello di Montalcino Manachiara Cru '97	YYY	7
● Brunello di Montalcino Manachiara '95	YY	8

MONTALCINO (SI)

SIRO PACENTI
LOC. PELAGRILLI, 1
53024 MONTALCINO (SI)
TEL. 0577848662
E-MAIL: pacentisiro@libero.it

Giancarlo Pacenti, who has for some years been working with various universities, both in Italy and abroad, is constantly engaged in research for the improvement of his wines. The new fermentation vats, which should help with tannin extraction and offer better temperature control, are a recent example. And the wines do get better from year to year, in finesse and intensity. The winery now owns plots throughout the Montalcino zone, which means that a proper balance can be struck in the wines. The cellar, which is temperature-controlled throughout, has now been invaded by barriques. The only large casks to be found are used for blending wines. All these developments have led to the creation of Brunellos with a specific, very recognizable style, and they in turn have led to the success of this winery. The '98 Brunello shows the effects of a cool vintage, which produced less rich, but nicely ripened, grapes. The eloquent nose offers varietal notes of sour cherry with hints of leather. The palate has good balance and decent sweetness. The very fine Rosso di Montalcino '01, which is one of the best of its vintage, is full bodied and extremely refreshing. It is a textbook second wine, in the Bordeaux sense, that still expresses its own style.

MONTALCINO (SI)

POGGIO ANTICO
LOC. POGGIO ANTICO
53024 MONTALCINO (SI)
TEL. 0577848044

After a few years' absence from our tastings, Poggio Antico, which won several Three Glass awards in the 1980s, has its Guide profile back again. At the helm of the estate is Paola Gloder, who is Milanese by birth and, despite her youth, one of the great ladies of Brunello. For advice in the cellar she turns to consummate oenologist, Carlo Ferrini. The recently expanded vineyards now include more than 17 hectares dedicated to Brunello, and the very promising replanting programme currently under way will increase the number of vines per hectare to well over 5,000. There have also been changes in the cellar, where casks are getting smaller and barriques are being used even for the Brunello. The estate is near the road to Grosseto, just beyond Passo del Lume Spento. The three Brunellos Paola presented this year are a clear expression of their territory, showing an austere elegance that disdains ostentatious muscularity. The two '98s did equally well, although we prefer the Altero for its more striking nose, which features prominent notes of red berry fruit. In the mouth, they both properly reflect their vintage, revealing lively tannins that don't get in the way of drinkability. The '97 Riserva is a short neck behind the front runners. Mineral tones on the nose accompany toasty oak, and soft tannins contribute to the lovely balance on the palate.

● Rosso di Montalcino '01	♟♟	6
● Brunello di Montalcino '98	♟♟	8
● Brunello di Montalcino '95	♟♟♟	8
● Brunello di Montalcino '96	♟♟♟	8
● Brunello di Montalcino '97	♟♟♟	8
● Brunello di Montalcino '93	♟♟	8

● Brunello di Montalcino '98	♟♟	7
● Brunello di Montalcino Altero '98	♟♟	7
● Brunello di Montalcino Ris. '97	♟	8
● Brunello di Montalcino '85	♟♟♟	7
● Brunello di Montalcino Ris. '85	♟♟♟	8
● Brunello di Montalcino '88	♟♟♟	7
● Brunello di Montalcino Ris. '88	♟♟	8
● Altero '90	♟♟	5
● Brunello di Montalcino '90	♟♟	7
● Rosso di Montalcino '93	♟	3

MONTALCINO (SI)

MONTALCINO (SI)

CASTELLO ROMITORIO
LOC. ROMITORIO, 279
53024 MONTALCINO (SI)
TEL. 0577897220 - 0577847212
E-MAIL: inf@castelloromitorio.it

PODERE SALICUTTI
POD. SALICUTTI, 174
53024 MONTALCINO (SI)
TEL. 0577847003
E-MAIL: leanza@poderesalicutti.it

There are three good reasons for visiting this estate. The castle, which is in the process of being restored, is lovely. Placed between it and the winery are some sculptures by the owner, Sandro Chia, a noted representative of the Transavanguardia movement. And of course, the wines are very good. Eight of the roughly 20 hectares under vine are planted to Montalcino DOCG varieties, the rest hosting international varieties, such as cabernet sauvignon and chardonnay. Before getting down to the wines, we should mention that the labels, designed by Chia himself, are eagerly contended each year by the art-loving fans of this winery. The demand for the Brunello Riserva '97 will probably not be diminished by its Three Glasses. This is the best wine yet to come out of Castello Romitorio and, although modern in style, it preserves the distinctive Montalcino characteristics. Its fascinatingly fleshy mouthfeel is nicely backed up by the acidity typical of vineyards at high elevations. The nose also testifies to a more even-handed use of oak than usual, which enhances the very intense fruit tones of blackberry without distorting them. The '98 Brunello is also fine, although the tannins leave a slightly dusty sensation. Bit the palate is agreeable and flows nicely to an appropriately concentrated finish. The nose offers intense fruit notes and hints of leather. The Rosso di Montalcino '01 earned One Glass for its floral nose and nicely executed, if not particularly incisive, palate.

Francesco Leanza's wines always arouse interest because they are consistently excellent and have great individuality. Podere Salicutti has almost completed restructuring the cellar, where order and attention to detail reign supreme. Care of the vineyards also borders on the obsessive, as necessary condition for an estate that is organically farmed. Turning to the wines themselves, we can give a very good report on the Rosso di Montalcino '01. It has returned to its past glory, earning Two red Glasses and establishing itself as one of the best of its vintage. This enormously impressive wine shows lovely ruby and offers fruit-led aromas mingling with notes of oak. The attack and progression on the palate are good, and the emphatic tannins are well supported by the wine's structure and succulence. The '98 Brunello, which also won Two Glasses, is at its best on the full-bodied palate, which is boosted by already well-integrated tannins. The nose is a bit sulphurous at first, but with a little breathing time, it opens to reveal fruit aromas. The Dopoteatro '98 earned no more than One Glass because of slightly edgy tannins.

●	Brunello di Montalcino Ris. '97	♟♟♟	8	● Rosso di Montalcino '01	♟♟	5
●	Brunello di Montalcino '98	♟♟	8	● Brunello di Montalcino '98	♟♟	7
●	Rosso di Montalcino '01	♟	6	● Dopoteatro '01	♟	6
●	Brunello di Montalcino '93	♟♟	7	● Brunello di Montalcino '97	♟♟♟	8
●	Brunello di Montalcino '95	♟♟	7	● Brunello di Montalcino '95	♟♟	8
●	Romito del Romitorio '98	♟♟	6	● Dopoteatro '98	♟♟	5
●	Brunello di Montalcino '96	♟♟	7	● Brunello di Montalcino '96	♟♟	8
●	Sant'Antimo Rosso			● Dopoteatro '99	♟♟	5
	Romito del Romitorio '99	♟♟	6			

MONTALCINO (SI)

SALVIONI - LA CERBAIOLA
P.ZZA CAVOUR, 19
53024 MONTALCINO (SI)
TEL. 0577848499

We were very pleased indeed to find a Brunello from this estate in our finals again. In the second half of the 1980s, La Cerbaiola presented a series of splendid Brunellos with a very distinctive style. After 1990, there was a slight dip in quality, caused mostly by a string of less than memorable vintages which particularly affected those who are relaxed about barrel replacement or do not possess extensive vineyard holdings. In fact, La Cerbaiola currently has only one plot, although there are plans afoot to expand the hectares under vine, and so expand production. Giulio Salvioni is assisted in vineyard and cellar by his son, Davide. The '98 Brunello reflects both the estate style and the vintage. On the palate, it is a palpable demonstration that a good wine does not necessarily mean massive structure and extreme concentration. Instead, you can achieve great results by striving for balance, of which this wine is a shining example. The tannins are smooth, extremely fine-grained and well integrated with the fruit and acidity. The finish is elegant and lingering, and the wine is very drinkable indeed. The nose is built along the same lines: well defined, clean and delightfully redolent of sour cherries.

MONTALCINO (SI)

SOLARIA - CENCIONI
POD. CAPANNA, 102
53024 MONTALCINO (SI)
TEL. 0577849426
E-MAIL: solaria.cencioni@infinito.it

Patrizia Cencioni has produced an excellent '98 Brunello, which is not bad going, given the less than helpful growing year. The location of the vineyards in the eastern section of Montalcino, and their mid-slope position, tend to foster richness on the nose but you would suppose, rather less in the mouth. But this admirable Brunello is the result of fanatical care in the vineyard, with rigorous bunch selection and very low yields per vine. At last, this year sees the availability of the new cellar. It's a quite lovely, entirely temperature-controlled, underground structure that will increase the efficiency of cellar work and provide plenty of space under the cross vaults for ageing the new estate wines. The aforementioned '98 Brunello presents a strikingly rich nose of berry fruit, ranging from the classic morello cherry to hints of ripe blackberry, with undertones of spice. The super progression on the palate reveals smooth tannins well integrated into the rich structure of the wine. The cabernet-based Solarianne '00, which has a multicoloured label, shows some of the effects of a hot year. Aromas of blackcurrant jam and candied peel mingle with over-ripe notes that attenuate the elegance of the wine. The opulence on the palate is not entirely offset by vibrant acidity and seems a bit flabby. The good Rosso di Montalcino '01 is refreshingly tangy and distinctly easy drinking.

● Brunello di Montalcino '98	♀♀	8
● Brunello di Montalcino '87	♀♀♀	8
● Brunello di Montalcino '88	♀♀♀	8
● Brunello di Montalcino '89	♀♀♀	8
● Brunello di Montalcino '90	♀♀♀	8
● Brunello di Montalcino '97	♀♀♀	8
● Brunello di Montalcino '93	♀♀	8
● Brunello di Montalcino '95	♀♀	8

● Brunello di Montalcino '98	♀♀	8
● Solarianne '00	♀	8
● Rosso di Montalcino '01	♀	5
● Brunello di Montalcino '97	♀♀♀	7
● Brunello di Montalcino '95	♀♀	7
● Brunello di Montalcino '96	♀♀	7
● Solarianne '98	♀♀	8
● Solarianne '99	♀♀	8

MONTALCINO (SI)

TALENTI
FRAZ. SANT'ANGELO IN COLLE
LOC. PIAN DI CONTE
53020 MONTALCINO (SI)
TEL. 0577844064 - 0577844156
E-MAIL: az.talenti@tin.it

Riccardo Talenti took the family estate in hand a few years ago and began a general modernization of vineyards and cellar, where he acquired a number of smaller casks while replacing the older ones. This revolution has not upset the estate style, but it has improved the wines. Much of the credit goes to consultant oenologist, Carlo Ferrini, for his ability to interpret Talenti's wishes. The winery owns some nine hectares dedicated to Brunello in one vineyard, near Sant'Angelo in Colle, which is enviably aspected and has quite loose-packed soil. This year's tastings were very positive for the entire range of Talenti wines, a good sign if ever there was one. Three wines earned Two Glasses. The best, as both wine type and vintage might suggest, was the Brunello Riserva '97, which neatly embodies the virtues of the new order which began that very year. After a little breathing time, the nose releases very well-defined flower and fruit notes, then the attractive, distinctive palate unveils tight-knit, well-integrated tannins. The fine '98 Brunello is admirably fresh on the nose and offers nicely calibrated acidity and tannins on the palate. The Talenti '01, a blend of sangiovese with a little colorino, canaiolo and syrah, shows a rich nose of ink, cedar and black berry fruit, with clear hints of oak, followed by a well-balanced palate. The Rosso di Montalcino '01 didn't get more than One Glass as it is very shy on the nose.

MONTALCINO (SI)

TENIMENTI ANGELINI
LOC. VAL DI CAVA
53024 MONTALCINO (SI)
TEL. 057780411
E-MAIL: tenimenti.mcalzolari@angelini.it

From this year, we are grouping all the Tenimenti Angelini properties in a single profile, for the Val di Suga winery in Montalcino, Tre Rose in Montepulciano and San Leonino in Chianti. The technical staff, headed by Mario Calzolari with the assistance of Fabrizio Ciufoli, cope marvellously. At Montalcino, they are replanting the vineyards at higher vine densities. The Montalcino wines, however, were not up to their customary level. The two selections, which have often received our highest award in the past, seem to have suffered the effects of the poorish '98 vintage. The Brunello Vigna del Lago '98 earned a single Glass. After slight initial hesitation, the nose opens to show fruit and oak-derived aromas. The attack on the palate is good, but the progression is hampered by edgy tannins. The Brunello Spuntali '98 did no better, for it too shows assertive, rather astringent tannins. In contrast, the news from Montepulciano is excellent. The Nobile Simposio '00 made it to our finals and the Nobile La Villa, also from '00, won Two Glasses. The Simposio offers an intense nose of fruit and flowers that meld with the oak, and although the palate is still a bit aggressive, the texture is firm and substantial, and the finish very long. The Nobile La Villa is less impressive with its slightly vegetal aromas and jammy notes. It shows elegance and smooth tannins on the palate, however. From the Chianti estate at San Leonino, we tasted the Salivolpe '07, a monovarietal Syrah that got all the way to our finals when the panel tasted its opulent, summarizing palate.

● Brunello di Montalcino '98	♛♛	7
● Talenti Rosso '01	♛♛	5
● Brunello di Montalcino Ris. '97	♛♛	7
● Rosso di Montalcino '01	♛	4
● Brunello di Montalcino '88	♛♛♛	5
● Brunello di Montalcino Ris. '88	♛♛	6
● Brunello di Montalcino '89	♛♛	5
● Brunello di Montalcino '90	♛♛	5
● Brunello di Montalcino Ris. '90	♛♛	6
● Talenti Rosso '00	♛♛	5
● Brunello di Montalcino '97	♛♛	7

● Nobile di Montepulciano		
Simposio '00	♛♛	6
● Salivolpe '97	♛♛	7
● Nobile di Montepulciano		
La Villa '00	♛♛	6
● Motu Proprio '00	♛	7
● Rosso di Montalcino '01	♛	4
● Brunello di Montalcino		
Vigna del Lago '98	♛	8
● Brunello di Montalcino		
Vigna Spuntali '98	♛	8
● Brunello di Montalcino '98		6
● Brunello di Montalcino Vigna Spuntali '93	♛♛♛	8
● Brunello di Montalcino		
Vigna Spuntali '95	♛♛♛	8

MONTALCINO (SI)

MONTALCINO (SI)

MONTALCINO (SI)

UCCELLIERA
FRAZ. CASTELNUOVO DELL'ABATE
POD. UCCELLIERA, 45
53020 MONTALCINO (SI)
TEL. 0577835729
E-MAIL: amco@uccelliera-montalcino.it

TENUTA VAL DI CAVA
LOC. VAL DI CAVA
53024 MONTALCINO (SI)
TEL. 0577848261

We were extremely pleased to give Three Glasses to Andrea Cortonesi, who has quietly but determinedly helped Uccelliera to grow. A passionate and painstaking grower, he tends his vines so that the wines they produce will express to the full the potential of sangiovese from Montalcino. Andrea's care, with some help from the great '97 vintage, has been rewarded. His Brunello Riserva '97 is a benchmark for the style Andrea has in mind: moderation with no excess of any kind, elegance and a genuine sense of place. An intense ruby is the prelude to a nose that offers varietal morello enhanced by floral notes and hints of peach and apricot. The fine progression on the palate is supported by excellent balance, which can probably be traced to the perfect ripeness of the grapes and the low yields per vine. The tannins are not absolutely smooth, but this is still quite a young wine, and thorough ageing in bottle should mellow the palate and lend it greater harmony. The finish is rich and mouthfilling. The excellent '98 Brunello made it to our finals. After a little breathing time, the nose releases intense fruit, then the palate is stylish and lingering. The good Rosso di Montalcino '01 has floral aromas, and the sangiovese-based Rapace '00 shows some faint hints of over-ripeness.

For years, the able and very likeable Vincenzo Abbruzzese has been a worthy representative of the most northerly part of Montalcino. From his almost 20 hectares under vine, which are planted exclusively to sangiovese, Vincenzo makes his wines with dedication and scrupulous care. The new cellar, which is temperature-controlled and very practical, is delivering the goods, so we look forward to great things from Val di Cava, its owner's past experience and the new ideas. We can see the beginnings in the youngest wines, but for the new-styled Brunello we shall have to wait, DOCG regulations being what they are. The Rosso di Montalcino '01, is a distinct improvement over past editions, particularly in the richness of the aromas. Chocolate and eucalyptus usher in a full-flavoured palate with succulent tannins and a distinctive finish, supported by delightful acidity. The Brunellos Vincenzo presented failed to get more than One Glass each, which is less than expected, particularly for the Riserva Madonna del Piano '97. The palate is rich and the tannins need mellowing, but they are clearly fine-grained, and the nose, which is rather dumb, also wants time. The harmonious '98 Brunello offers a mineral and fruit nose, and an easy-drinking approachability.

● Brunello di Montalcino Ris. '97	♟♟♟	8
● Brunello di Montalcino '98	♟♟	7
● Rosso di Montalcino '01	♟♟	6
● Rapace '00	♟	7
● Brunello di Montalcino '93	♟♟	5
● Rapace '98	♟♟	6
● Brunello di Montalcino '97	♟♟	7
● Rapace '99	♟♟	6

● Rosso di Montalcino '01	♟♟	4
● Brunello di Montalcino '98	♟	8
● Brunello di Montalcino Madonna del Piano Ris. '97	♟	8
● Brunello di Montalcino '88	♟♟	8
● Brunello di Montalcino Madonna del Piano Ris. '88	♟♟	8
● Brunello di Montalcino '89	♟♟	8
● Brunello di Montalcino Madonna del Piano Ris. '90	♟♟	8
● Brunello di Montalcino '93	♟♟	8
● Brunello di Montalcino Madonna del Piano Ris. '95	♟♟	8
● Brunello di Montalcino Madonna del Piano Ris. '96	♟♟	8

MONTALCINO (SI)

VILLA LE PRATA
LOC. LE PRATA, 261
53024 MONTALCINO (SI)
TEL. 0577848325
E-MAIL: alcoyle@tin.it

During the rush in the 1980s and 1990s to snap up wineries in Montalcino, one group, members of the legal profession, did particularly well, oenologically speaking. A lawyer bought Villa Le Prata, but the person who turned the estate around is his daughter, Benedetta Losapio, who is assisted by oenologist, Gioia Cresti. The four hectares of land are near the winery and at Castello della Velona, which means that the cellar has several options for dealing with any given vintage. One hectare is planted to merlot, which is part of the blend that went into the '01 Le Prata, a very convincing wine on both nose and palate. This year marks the release of the best wine Villa Le Prata has ever made, and one of the best of its vintage. The '98 Brunello is simply splendid, and if it didn't win Three Glasses it wasn't by much. The intense ruby with purplish highlights already gives you some idea of the riches in store, and the abundant, wide-ranging nose in fact delivers varietal ripe sour cherry and blackberry followed by distinct oak-derived balsamic and spicy tones that never mask the underlying fruit. The excellent palate reveals great richness and an astonishing progression nicely underpinned by fine-grained, but never intrusive, tannins. It's a great Brunello, but unfortunately there isn't much of it. The Rosso di Montalcino '01 is less balanced than usual. Although the entry on the palate is good, the aggressive tannins hinder the progression and cut short the finish. Earthy notes on the nose kept it from getting more than One Glass.

MONTALCINO (SI)

VISCONTI
LOC. CASTELNUOVO DELL'ABATE
53020 MONTALCINO (SI)
TEL. 0577835631

Montalcino keeps growing, in viticultural terms, and wines from new estates are constantly appearing on the market. The Visconti winery can be considered the revelation of the year. Its size is about average for Montalcino, for there are five hectares under vine currently producing, three dedicated to Brunello and two to Rosso. There can be no complaint about the site, which is virtually at the abbey of Sant'Antimo. That means Castelnuovo dell'Abate, which become one of the top areas in Montalcino. The vineyards are still young, and planted at a density of 5,500 vines per hectare, which looks about right for ripening sangiovese in these parts. The cellar has casks of various sizes, but none are large. They range from the now ubiquitous barrique to 700-litre barrels. We were very favourably impressed by the '98 Brunello. A deep ruby red introduces a rich, intense nose of blackberry and red berry fruit. The excellent palate has smooth, tight-knit tannins and a broad, satisfying finish. The Rosso di Montalcino '01 picked up Two effortless Glasses. The nose mingles cherry jam and blackberry, and the enjoyable palate is remarkably fresh and admirably long. Altogether, it was a fine performance by Carla Visconti, who is assisted in the cellar by Maurizio Castelli, an oenologist who needs no introduction.

● Brunello di Montalcino '98	￥￥	6
● Le Prata '01	￥￥	5
● Rosso di Montalcino Tirso '01	￥	5
● Brunello di Montalcino '93	￥￥	7
● Le Prata '99	￥￥	5
● Rosso di Montalcino Tirso '99	￥￥	4
● Brunello di Montalcino '97	￥￥	7
● Le Prata '00	￥￥	5
● Rosso di Montalcino Tirso '00	￥￥	4

● Brunello di Montalcino '98	￥￥	7
● Rosso di Montalcino '01	￥￥	4

MONTE SAN SAVINO (AR)

GIACOMO MARENGO
FRAZ. CAPRAIA
LOC. PALAZZUOLO
52048 MONTE SAN SAVINO (AR)
TEL. 0575847083 - 0575847048
E-MAIL: marengoe@tin.it

The brief Other Wineries review must have been a squeeze for this lovely, and large, estate. It covers 2,600 hectares, of which 81 are under vine, some in the province of Arezzo and some in Siena, on the hillsides in Val d'Ambra and Val di Chiana where Etruscan antiquities have been found. But neither historical nor geographical merits are responsible for the newly earned profile. The reason is this year's admirable range of wines. The Stroncoli '99, made mostly from cabernet with a little sangiovese, is the best recent version. Dark and concentrated in the glass, it presents a nose of clear-cut, ripe fruit nicely lifted by hints of coffee, spice and well-judged oak. The palate is soft, warm and meaty, and the tannins are noticeable, but fine-grained. House policy here favours traditional vinification, with large casks for sangiovese and barriques for international varieties, and a good representative is the impeccably styled Chianti Riserva La Commenda '99. It has a nose of red berry fruit, liquorice and earth, with a hint of forwardness. The palate is dense, vibrant and long, with assertive tannins and acidity. The other "riserva", Castello di Rapale '99, is full-bodied, but over-evolved notes come through. The interesting Cuvée Sant'Anna '01, a blend of chardonnay with some sauvignon, offers notes of peach, apricot and tropical fruit with mineral hints, but at our tastings these were crushed by oak-derived vanilla and butter. However, the structure and acidity of the wine suggest that it should develop nicely. The other two Chiantis are well executed and well typed.

MONTE SAN SAVINO (AR)

SAN LUCIANO
LOC. SAN LUCIANO, 90
52048 MONTE SAN SAVINO (AR)
TEL. 0575848518
E-MAIL: info@sanlucianovini.it

Commitment, dedication to the land and spontaneous enthusiasm are some of the qualities that have helped the Ziantoni family turn San Luciano into one of the best wineries around Arezzo. And they continue to offer a range of good wines at reasonable prices, no bad thing as things stand at the moment. As usual, the top of the range is the D'Ovidio, this time the 2000 edition, a blend of sangiovese, montepulciano, cabernet and merlot. Although not quite so good as the '99, it is appealing, distinctive and well made. The notes of fruit jam, tobacco and coffee on the nose carry through onto the palate, where the tannins have a few rough edges and the finish is slightly bitter. This wine needs time before it can show itself to greatest effect, and in fact the '99, which we retasted, is in splendid form. There are two other reds. The Boschi Salviati '01, mostly sangiovese with a little montepulciano and cabernet, exhibits some faint earthy notes that get in the way of the fruit on the nose, but it comes into its own on the succulent, full-bodied palate. The Colle Carpito '01, made from sangiovese with a touch of montepulciano, almost won Two Glasses with its sweetly fruity bouquet and easy-drinking nature. Neither of the whites, the Resico, a blend of chardonnay, trebbiano and vermentino, or the Luna di Monte, from trebbiano, chardonnay and grechetto, were helped by the unfortunate 2002 vintage. They are well executed and straightforward, but not outstanding.

O	Cuvèe Sant'Anna '01	𝟏𝟏	6
●	Chianti La Commenda Ris. '99	𝟏𝟏	5
●	Stroncoli '99	𝟏𝟏	6
●	Chianti Castello di Rapale '00	𝟏	4*
●	Chianti Le Tornaie '01	𝟏	3*
●	Chianti Castello di Rapale Ris. '99	𝟏	4
●	Stroncoli '97	𝟏𝟏	5
●	Chianti La Commenda Ris. '97	𝟏𝟏	5
●	Chianti Castello di Rapale Ris. '98	𝟏	4
●	Stroncoli '98	𝟏	6

●	D'Ovidio '00	𝟏𝟏	7
●	Boschi Salviati '01	𝟏𝟏	5*
●	Colle Carpito '01	𝟏	4*
O	Resico '02	𝟏	4
O	Valdichiana Luna di Monte '02	𝟏	4*
●	D'Ovidio '98	𝟏𝟏	5
●	Boschi Salviati '99	𝟏𝟏	4*
●	D'Ovidio '99	𝟏𝟏	5*
●	Boschi Salviati '00	𝟏𝟏	4*
O	Resico '01	𝟏𝟏	3*
●	Colle Carpito '00	𝟏	3

Fattoria del Buonamico

Loc. Cercatoia
via Provinciale di Montecarlo, 43
55015 Montecarlo (LU)
tel. 058322038
e-mail: buonamico@buonamico.com

Change is in the air at Fattoria del Buonamico, and has been for the last few years. It's farewell to wines that are no more than well executed and nicely balanced. Now, there are bottles that express the territory and reflect the passion of the winemaker, who has invested heavily in renewing both vineyards and cellar. The results have not been long in coming, especially when you consider how much time it takes vines to start producing promising grapes. The '99 Cercatoja Rosso, a blend of sangiovese, cabernet sauvignon, cabernet franc and syrah, made it to our finals. An emphatic vegetal note upstages notes of jammy black berry fruit and inviting hints of spice on the nose. The elegant, supple palate is very enjoyable, and lingers nicely. There is a nice balance of silky tannins and the unassertive but crucially important acidity. Fortino Syrah '99 seems a bit below par and less convincing than last year's version. The nose is not perfectly clean and, at least when we were tasting, the palate lacked balance. The two Montecarlos, the Bianco and the Rosso, seem to be suffering the effects of the undistinguished 2002 vintage. The white offers fresh aromas of apple and pear, and a pleasing palate that is a bit dilute on the finish, and the red throws berry fruit and intriguing gamey notes, but its palate is a bit predictable and slightly bitter on the finish. The '00 Vasario, a blend of pinot blanc, sauvignon and sémillon, again shows excessive oak-derived notes of honey and vanilla.

● Cercatoja Rosso '99	TT	6
○ Vasario '00	T	5
○ Montecarlo Bianco '02	T	4
● Montecarlo Rosso '02	T	4
● Il Fortino Syrah '99	T	7
● Il Fortino Syrah '95	YY	7
● Cercatoja Rosso '96	YY	6
● Il Fortino Syrah '96	YY	7
● Cercatoja Rosso '97	YY	6
● Il Fortino Syrah '98	YY	7
● Montecarlo Rosso '01	YY	4*
● Cercatoja Rosso '98	YY	6

Gino Fuso Carmignani

Loc. Cercatoia Alta
via della Tinaia, 7
55015 Montecarlo (LU)
tel. 058322381

Much has been written about Gino "Fuso" Carmignani. His eccentricity, his effervescent conversation, the bizarre names he chooses for his wines, his great stories, practical jokes and endless other quirks are legendary. Not to mention jazz, and the passion he brings to his work, which above all means getting his hands dirty, and the conviction that the path he has chosen must be followed to the end, without deviation of any kind. Sometimes, the results are immediate and exactly as planned, and at other times he seems to alternate good and less successful years. This time his wines were middling. Nothing disastrous, of course, but when someone has got you used to splendid bottles, it's hard to accept even the smallest slip. And the '01 For Duke is not a complete success. While it is probably true that you don't imagine a blend of sangiovese and syrah to be unexciting, after last year's bright and delightfully dissonant version, our hopes were sky-high. The fruit on the nose is a bit forward, and the palate seems tight and not particularly inclined to open up. A little cellar time should help, though. The '01 Merlo-t della Topa Nera is more successful. The nose is very intense and concentrated, as is the colour. The palate is hard, rough, characterful and intriguing. You couldn't accuse it of being an easy wine, but it certainly is exciting.

● Il Merlo-t della Topa Nera '01	TT	7
● For Duke '01	T	7
● For Duke '95	YY	4
● For Duke '97	YY	5
● Montecarlo Rosso Sassonero '97	YY	2
● For Duke '98	YY	5
○ Montecarlo Bianco Stati d'Animo '99	YY	4
● Il Merlo-t della Topa Nera '98	YY	7
● For Duke '99	YY	5
● For Duke '00	YY	7
○ Montecarlo Bianco Stati d'Animo '01	YY	5*

MONTECARLO (LU)

MONTECARLO (LU)

FATTORIA DI MONTECHIARI
VIA MONTECHIARI, 27
55015 MONTECARLO (LU)
TEL. 058322189

FATTORIA DEL TESO
VIA POLTRONIERA
55015 MONTECARLO (LU)
TEL. 0583286288
E-MAIL: info@fattoriadelteso.com

Over the years, Moreno Panettoni and Catherine Pirmez have managed to transform a very nice Montecarlo estate into a corner of paradise. The vines are extraordinarily beautiful, trained very low and, most important, very densely planted, with extremely low yields. Dedicated attention is lavished on every phase of production, from vineyard management to the scrupulous care in the cellar, where the pair's first concern is to preserve the potential of the grapes. And this year two of their wines were finalists. The Cabernet '00, a blend of cabernet sauvignon, cabernet franc and a little merlot, was particularly successful. The fresh nose releases notes of black berry fruit lifted by vegetal hints. The palate, which tends towards elegance and charm rather than muscularity, is velvety, racy and lingering. The sangiovese-based Rosso '00, if not quite as good, is excellent, but perhaps needs more cellar time to integrate the oak. The nose has well-defined blackberry and characteristic gamey notes, then the austere, succulent palate reveals tight-knit but well-blended tannins. The new wine, the Merlot '00, is also good. The vines were planted six years ago and are now producing. The result is a smooth, very dense and compact wine. The Nero '01, a monovarietal Pinot Noir, is immensely moreish and enjoyable. The inviting nose offers notes of red berry fruit, and the lovely, even palate, which is innocent of rough edges, has a fragrant, slightly peppery finish. The pleasing '01 Chardonnay offers a seductive nose of acacia blossom, apples and pears, followed by a succulent palate.

Fattoria del Teso keeps getting better. Restructuring has started to produce the hoped-for results, as have the contributions of Federico Curtaz in the vineyard and Francesco Bartoletti in the cellar. Our favourite from the wines we tasted was the Anfidiamante '00, a blend of sangiovese, syrah, merlot and canaiolo. Intense in colour, it offers aromas of blackberry and blueberry enhanced by notes of spice and roasting coffee beans. The palate is soft but vibrant, thanks to the perfectly judged acidity, and the oak is beautifully integrated. The '02 wines bear the marks of a difficult growing year. They are approachable, pleasing and characteristic wines, and although there may be the occasional rough edge, these are never overdone. The '02 Montecarlo Rosso has well-defined aromas of red berry fruit and spice, then a fragrant, lingering palate. The Montecarlo Bianco '02 also has a clear-cut, clean nose, in this case with inviting notes of honey and spring flowers. In the mouth, it is surprisingly succulent, lively, lean and well balanced. The other white, the Stella del Teso '02, is also very agreeable, showing an intriguing nose of yeast, almonds and tropical fruit. On the inviting palate, the softness of the wood provides a pleasing counterpoint to the lively acidity. Finally, the Vin Santo '97 is unctuous and very long.

● Montechiari Cabernet '00	♆♆	7
● Montechiari Rosso '00	♆♆	6
● Montechiari Merlot '00	♆♆	7
○ Montechiari Chardonnay '01	♆	6
● Montechiari Nero '01	♆	6
● Montechiari Cabernet '97	♆♆♆	8
● Montechiari Pinot Nero '97	♆♆	6
● Montechiari Cabernet '98	♆♆	8
○ Montechiari Chardonnay '00	♆♆	6
● Montechiari Nero '98	♆♆	6
○ Montechiari Chardonnay '99	♆♆	6
● Montechiari Cabernet '99	♆♆	8
● Montechiari Nero '00	♆♆	6
● Montechiari Rosso '99	♆♆	6

● Anfidiamante '00	♆♆	6
○ Montecarlo Bianco '02	♆	4
● Montecarlo Rosso '02	♆	4
○ Stella del Teso '02	♆	4
○ Vin Santo '97	♆	5
○ Vin Santo '90	♆♆	5
● Montecarlo Rosso '01	♆♆	3*
○ Stella del Teso '01	♆♆	4
○ Vin Santo '94	♆♆	5
● Anfidiamante '99	♆♆	6

MONTEMURLO (PO)

TENUTA DI BAGNOLO
DEI MARCHESI PANCRAZI
FRAZ. BAGNOLO - VIA MONTALESE, 156
50045 MONTEMURLO (PO)
TEL. 0574652439
E-MAIL: giuseppe@pancrazi.it

Wines from Tenuta di Bagnolo never fail to intrigue, and this year we found for the first time a high level of quality throughout the entire range. We also witnessed the first appearance of a new version of the Pinot Nero, the special Vigna Baragazza '01 selection. A fairly intense ruby introduces an initially toasty and gamey nose that then opens onto notes of black berry fruit with hints of autumn leaves. The soft but substantial palate reveals forceful, tight-knit tannins building to an enjoyably lingering finish. It's at once a concentrated, distinctive and easily drinkable wine. The successful Villa di Bagnolo '01 offers a somewhat discordant nose with notes of caramel and earth against a background of red berry fruit. The pleasantly textured palate shows smooth tannins and a dry finish, underlined by a bitterish tone. Wines from the San Donato estate include the '01 Casaglia, a monovarietal Colorino, which has moved up a step. It shows better definition on the nose and a well-sculpted personality. The sumptuous palate offers enormous structure, lots of fruit, a dense, soft tannic weave and an admirably long finish. The '02 San Donato earned One Glass for its enticingly fresh aromas of red berry fruit, mingling with almost aromatic nuances and grassy notes. The palate shows a pleasing balance of acidity and tannins, and a short, dry finish.

MONTEPULCIANO (SI)

AVIGNONESI
FRAZ. VALIANO DI MONTEPULCIANO
VIA COLONICA, 1 - FATTORIA LE CAPEZZINE
53045 MONTEPULCIANO (SI)
TEL. 0578724304
E-MAIL: avignonesi@avignonesi.it

The Falvo family winery is a Montepulciano benchmark. It consists of four separate estates, Le Capezzine, I Poggetti, La Lombarda and La Selva, the last of which extends over 220 hectares, about 115 of which are dedicated to viticulture, and is located in the Cortona DOC zone. This year the 50 & 50, created 1988 with the innovative idea of blending Capanelle's Chianti sangiovese with merlot from this Montepulciano winery, has returned to its glory days. The '99 easily swept up Three Glasses. In the glass, it is a deep, intense, almost opaque red. The nose offers well-defined of wild berries and vanilla, then after a soft attack, the palate opens out, flaunting marvellous roundness, tight-knit, powerful tannins and an impressively long finish underpinned by oak-derived sweetness. The '91 Occhio di Pernice, an Avignonesi classic that is much more than a straightforward Vin Santo, also made it to our finals. The bouquet discloses striking hints of balsam and saffron. The palate is extremely concentrated, viscous and infinitely long. The very good Cortona Desiderio '00 throws a fruit-forward nose with some hints of over-ripeness and a concentrated, solid palate. The good '00 Nobile is graceful and clean on the nose, then substantial in the mouth. The fine Rosso di Montepulciano '02 is warm and supple and finally, the '02 Bianco and Rosso Avignonesi are the bottom-of-the-line wines. Don't worry, they're both very well executed and enjoyable.

● Casaglia '01	🍷🍷	5
● Pinot Nero Vigna Baragazza '01	🍷🍷	5
● Pinot Nero Villa di Bagnolo '01	🍷🍷	6
● San Donato '02	🍷	3
● Pinot Nero Villa di Bagnolo '92	🍷🍷	5
● Pinot Nero Villa di Bagnolo '93	🍷🍷	5
● Pinot Nero Villa di Bagnolo '94	🍷🍷	5
● Pinot Nero Villa di Bagnolo '95	🍷🍷	5
● Pinot Nero Villa di Bagnolo '97	🍷🍷	5
● Pinot Nero Villa di Bagnolo '98	🍷🍷	5
● Casaglia '99	🍷🍷	4
● Casaglia '00	🍷🍷	4*
● Pinot Nero Villa di Bagnolo '00	🍷🍷	6

● 50 & 50 Avignonesi e Capannelle '99	🍷🍷🍷	8
○ Vin Santo Occhio di Pernice '91	🍷🍷	8
● Cortona Desiderio '00	🍷🍷	6
● Rosso di Montepulciano '02	🍷🍷	3
● Nobile di Montepulciano '00	🍷	4
○ Bianco Avignonesi '02	🍷	2
● Rosso Avignonesi '02	🍷	3
○ Vin Santo '89	🍷🍷🍷	8
● 50 & 50 Avignonesi e Capannelle '97	🍷🍷🍷	8
○ Vin Santo Occhio di Pernice '89	🍷🍷🍷	8
○ Vin Santo Occhio di Pernice '90	🍷🍷🍷	8
○ Vin Santo '92	🍷🍷	8
● 50 & 50 Avignonesi e Capannelle '98	🍷🍷	8
● Nobile di Montepulciano '99	🍷🍷	4

MONTEPULCIANO (SI)

BINDELLA
FRAZ. ACQUAVIVA
VIA DELLE TRE BERTE, 10/A
53040 MONTEPULCIANO (SI)
TEL. 0578767777
E-MAIL: info@bindella.it

Rudi Bindella, Swiss by birth and Tuscan by adoption, established this winery in 1984. The property covers 64 hectares, of which 30 are planted to vine and generally yield well-made wines. This year was no exception. The new selection, I Quadri '00, is sourced from the best estate grapes and made a very promising debut. A lovely, almost opaque dark ruby introduces an intensely spicy nose with pleasing chocolate nuances. There is no lack of body on the well-sustained, rounded palate. The nice Nobile '00 is a blend of prugnolo gentile, canaiolo, colorino and mammolo that offers distinct vegetal hints laced with the ripe fruit on the nose. The palate show admirable grip, but rather prominent alcoholic warmth. The Vallocaia '00, made from prugnolo and cabernet sauvignon, has a rather closed, almost reduced, nose with distinct gamey tones and notes of leather. The palate is attractively textured and fruity on the finish. Finally, the Vin Santo Dolce Sinfonia '98 made a good showing. A blend of trebbiano and malvasia, it flaunts a classic nose with a clear aromas of raisined fruit and a palate with a fine balance of residual sugar and lively acidity that delivers a very long finish.

MONTEPULCIANO (SI)

BOSCARELLI
FRAZ. CERVOGNANO
VIA DI MONTENERO, 28
53040 MONTEPULCIANO (SI)
TEL. 0578767277 - 0578767608
E-MAIL: info@poderiboscarelli.com

Boscarelli, which belongs to the De Ferraris, is a historic Montepulciano winery dating back to 1962. Right from the first, the family decided to rediscover the flavours and fragrance of traditional Vino Nobile. The estate now has 13 hectares under vine and the consultant oenologist is Maurizio Castelli. They are definitely traditionalists at Boscarelli, but they have their ups and downs. This year's range exhibits some of each. The mostly prugnolo gentile-based Vigna del Nocio '00, the estate's selection, has a vivid dark ruby hue. The clean nose embraces notes of liquorice on a fruit background, and the well-calibrated palate is enjoyably succulent. The fairly well-defined nose offers prominent ripe fruit and distinct vegetal notes. The palate is pleasing, the tannins provide grip and the finish is fruity. The Boscarelli '01, from prugnolo gentile with a small proportion of cabernet sauvignon, is redolent of grass and oak on the nose. The tannins in the mouth are rather aggressive, and the long finish presents some bitter notes. The De Ferrari '01 is a deliberately less complex wine. The nose is predominantly vegetal, with undertones of red berry fruit. The entry on the palate is soft and heady, and the length is admirable.

● Nobile di Montepulciano		
I Quadri '00	♟♟	5
● Nobile di Montepulciano '00	♟	4
● Vallocaia '00	♟	6
○ Vin Santo Dolce Sinfonia '98	♟	6
● Vallocaia '94	♟♟	6
● Vallocaia '95	♟♟	6
● Nobile di Montepulciano '97	♟♟	4
○ Vin Santo Dolce Sinfonia '96	♟♟	6
● Vallocaia '98	♟♟	6
● Nobile di Montepulciano '99	♟♟	4
● Rosso di Montepulciano		
Fosso Lupaio '01	♟	4
○ Vin Santo Dolce Sinfonia '97	♟	6

● Nobile di Montepulciano		
V. del Nocio '00	♟♟	7
● Nobile di Montepulciano '00	♟	5
● Boscarelli '01	♟	8
● De Ferrari '01	♟	4
● Nobile di Montepulciano		
V. del Nocio Ris. '91	♟♟♟	7
● Boscarelli '95	♟♟	8
● Boscarelli '97	♟♟	8
● Nobile di Montepulciano V. del Nocio '97	♟♟	5
● Nobile di Montepulciano '98	♟♟	5
● Nobile di Montepulciano		
V. del Nocio '99	♟♟	7
● Boscarelli '99	♟♟	8
● Nobile di Montepulciano '99	♟♟	5

MONTEPULCIANO (SI)

FATTORIA DEL CERRO
FRAZ. ACQUAVIVA
VIA GRAZIANELLA, 5
53040 MONTEPULCIANO (SI)
TEL. 0578767722 - 0577767700
E-MAIL: fattoriadelcerro@tin.it

Fattoria del Cerro has again produced a Three Glass winner in Antica Chiusina '00. Like its predecessors, it makes an enormous impact. The colour is dense and tinged with purple. The equally dense nose releases prominent notes of wild berries, laced with balsamic tones. The meaty palate offers lingering cherry and vanilla. The excellent Manero '01 also came close to getting our top award. This monovarietal Sangiovese shows lots of ripe fruit on the nose, with a seasoning of pepper. The palate is full bodied, expansive and intense on the finish. The Fattoria del Cerro sweet wines did extremely well. The '98 Sangallo Vin Santo is redolent of honey and figs, and the sweetness in the mouth, which never cloys, is in no hurry to disappear. The Corte d'Oro '01, made from late-harvested sauvignon blanc and moscato, is a delightful newcomer to the range. A fresh bouquet of citrus fruit leads to a tight-knit, well-balanced palate with an intense finish that echoes the nose. The characterful merlot-based Poggio Golo '01 is a bit vegetal in fragrance and shows considerable acid bite. Both the '00 Nobile, with its aromas of undergrowth, and the dry, tannic Nobile Riserva '99, are good wines. The uncomplicated but well-executed Bravìolo '02, from 100 per cent trebbiano, displays a floral nose. Finally, the quite delightful chardonnay-based Poggio a Tramontana '02 is pleasingly succulent in the mouth. Fattoria del Cerro's consultant oenologist is Lorenzo Landi.

MONTEPULCIANO (SI)

DEI
VIA DI MARTIENA, 35
53045 MONTEPULCIANO (SI)
TEL. 0578716878
E-MAIL: info@cantinedei.com

This estate at Villa Martiena has, since 1974, belonged to the Dei family, which immediately set about its new venture with enthusiastic dedication. In 1991, Maria Caterina Dei abandoned her acting career so as to be able to work full-time on the property, which now includes 36 hectares under vine. With the help of consultant oenologist, Niccolò D'Afflitto, her efforts produce a range of admirable wines. They are good and, in fact, getting better. Again this year, one of them very nearly carried off Three Glasses. We refer to the Nobile Bossona Riserva '99, a blend of prugnolo gentile, canaiolo and mammolo that was aged in 300-litre casks of Slavonian oak. It is a fine example of a very well-interpreted traditional Nobile di Montepulciano. The nose may not be overwhelmingly intense, but it is remarkably balanced and elegant, with its aromas of jammy fruit and violets enhanced by notes of spice and tobacco. On the dry, close-knit palate, it reveals robust, nicely integrated tannins. The '00 Nobile is good, although not so complex. The ripe fruity tones on the nose are a touch simple, but admirably clean. After a good attack, the palate, is mouthfilling, Sadly, the oak on the finish is responsible for some not entirely harmonious sweetish notes.

● Nobile di Montepulciano Vign. Antica Chiusina '00	▲▲▲	7
● Manero '01	▲	7
○ Corte d'Oro V. T. '01	▲▲	6
○ Vin Santo di Montepulciano Sangallo '98	▲▲	5
● Nobile di Montepulciano '00	▲	4
● Poggio Golo '01	▲	7
○ Bravìolo '02	▲	2
○ Poggio a Tramontana '02	▲	4
● Nobile di Montepulciano Ris. '99	▲	5
● Nobile di Montepulciano Vign. Antica Chiusina '98	▼▼▼	7
● Nobile di Montepulciano Vign. Antica Chiusina '99	▼▼▼	7
● Manero '99	▼▼	7

● Nobile di Montepulciano Bossona Ris. '99	▲▲	6
● Nobile di Montepulciano '00	▲	5
● Nobile di Montepulciano Ris. '93	▼▼	4
● Nobile di Montepulciano Ris. '97	▼▼	5
● Sancta Catharina '00	▼▼	6
● Nobile di Montepulciano '99	▼▼	5*
● Nobile di Montepulciano Ris. '98	▼▼	5

MONTEPULCIANO (SI)

FASSATI
FRAZ. GRACCIANO
VIA DI GRACCIANELLO, 3/A
53040 MONTEPULCIANO (SI)
TEL. 0578708708 - 06844311
E-MAIL: info@fazibattaglia.it

In 1969 the Sparaco family, owners of Fazi Battaglia, took over the venerable Fassati winery. Winemaking at the estate, which now has 70 hectares under vine, is managed by oenologist, Roberto De Frassini, with advice from consultant Franco Bernabei. The wines did very well at this year's tastings and one of them, the Nobile Gersemi '00 vineyard selection, made it to our finals. Obtained from careful selection at harvest of the best prugnolo gentile grapes, together with a little merlot and cabernet sauvignon, it is a wine of considerable personality. Well-defined aromas of red berry fruit with hints of spice on the nose lead to a rich, pleasingly dense palate where soft tannins take you through to a summarizing finish. The Salarco Riserva '99 is good, although we had hoped for something better. The nose is fairly complex, with notes of cherry and hints of liquorice and violet, but not entirely open. The palate is full-bodied and engrossing, and the finish is dry. The fine Pasiteo '00 is distinctly redolent of sweet fruit. The palate boasts a soft attack, a well-sustained progression and nicely integrated tannins. The Chianti Gaggiole Riserva '00 is simpler but agreeable. The fruity tones on the nose are faint, and the palate is clean but à bit thin. Finally, the Rosso di Montepulciano Selciaia '02 was not a great success, with its very weak aromas and acidulous flavour.

MONTEPULCIANO (SI)

FATTORIA LA BRACCESCA
FRAZ. GRACCIANO
S. S. 326, 15
53040 MONTEPULCIANO (SI)
TEL. 0578724252
E-MAIL: labraccesca@antinori.it

This Antinori estate extends over some 240 hectares under vine in the Montepulciano and Cortona zones, and the vineyards in the latter have shown themselves to be particularly well suited to the cultivation of syrah. On the whole, La Braccesca's wines seem to have hit their stride. The Cortona Bramasole '00 easily sauntered into our finals and nearly left with Three Glasses. Made from syrah with just a touch of merlot, it was barrique-aged for 14 months and then given an additional year in bottle before being released. The colour is a very vivid, brilliantly opaque ruby. The nose shows distinct pepper, with a background note of red berry fruit and some vanilla. The palate is dense, soft, well-sustained and quite free of roughness of any sort, its power enhanced by silky tannins. The '00 Nobile is good, if not exceptional, and traditional in style. It was aged for 12 months, mostly in large casks with a small part maturing in barrique. Vegetal notes take precedence over the mild fruit and herbal hints on the nose. Things are better on the palate, which reveals excellent balance, considerable structure, well-calibrated tannins and a long finish with some mildly bitter notes. The '02 Sabazio offers a pleasantly fruity nose and a simple but even, enjoyable palate.

● Nobile di Montepulciano Gersemi '00 🏆🏆		6
● Chianti Le Gaggiole Ris. '00 🏆		4
● Nobile di Montepulciano Pasiteo '00 🏆		5
● Nobile di Montepulciano		
Salarco Ris. '99 🏆		6
● Rosso di Montepulciano Selciaia '02		3
● Nobile di Montepulciano Pasiteo '97 🏆🏆		5
● Nobile di Montepulciano		
Salarco Ris. '97 🏆🏆		6
● Chianti Le Gaggiole Ris. '98 🏆🏆		3*
● Nobile di Montepulciano Pasiteo '98 🏆🏆		5
● Nobile di Montepulciano		
Salarco Ris. '98 🏆🏆		6
● Nobile di Montepulciano Pasiteo '99 🏆🏆		5
● Chianti Le Gaggiole Ris. '99 🏆		4

● Cortona Bramasole '00 🏆🏆		6
● Nobile di Montepulciano '00 🏆		5
● Rosso di Montepulciano		
Sabazio '02 🏆		4
● Nobile di Montepulciano Ris. '99 🏆		5
● Nobile di Montepulciano '98 🏆🏆		5
● Rosso di Montepulciano		
Sabazio '00 🏆		3
● Rosso di Montepulciano		
Sabazio '01 🏆		3
● Nobile di Montepulciano '99 🏆		5

MONTEPULCIANO (SI)

LA CALONICA
FRAZ. VALIANO
VIA DELLA STELLA, 27
53040 MONTEPULCIANO (SI)
TEL. 0578724119
E-MAIL: lacalonica@libero.it

The vineyards at La Calonica, which has been in the Cattani family since 1972, cover about 38 hectares in the Montepulciano and Cortona zones. In recent years, La Calonica has been doing well, and this year was no exception. The Nobile Riserva '99 is a blend of sangiovese with a little merlot and canaiolo aged mostly in Slavonian oak casks with a small proportion of barrique-aged wine. Its appealingly intense, concentrated ruby ushers in notes of violets and light hints of spice that precede a generous, well-balanced palate. The Nobile '00, from sangiovese and canaiolo, spends two years in large casks. Good red berry fruit rubs shoulders with prominent vegetal tones on the nose. The palate is dry and well-ordered, although the finish slips away rather quickly. The Girifalco '01, an assemblage of sangiovese, merlot and cabernet sauvignon aged for 15 months in barrique, has a pleasingly fruity nose with some intrusive grassiness. The palate is juicy but a bit acidulous and the finish is long. The '02 La Calonica, an intentionally simple red made from a blend of merlot and sangiovese, was a pleasant surprise. The nose offers straightforward, fresh fruit and the palate, if not massively structured, is mouthfilling. The Rosso di Montepulciano '02, which has unripe notes on both nose and palate, is not up to the standard of the other wines. We retasted the '00 Signorelli '00, reviewed last year, and found it quite intriguing.

MONTEPULCIANO (SI)

LA CIARLIANA
FRAZ. GRACCIANO
VIA CIARLIANA, 31
53040 MONTEPULCIANO (SI)
TEL. 0578758423
E-MAIL: info@laciarliana.it

La Ciarliana, which Luigi Frangiosa acquired in 1995, didn't start selling its wines until 1998. There are eight hectares planted to vine under the watchful consulting eye of oenologist, Paolo Vagaggini. Despite its youth, this winery has already hit its stride, and the wines give ample evidence of the care taken in the cellar. The vines, however, will need more time to produce truly excellent grapes. The Santo Pellegrino '01, a monovarietal Cabernet Sauvignon, shows a lustrous dark ruby colour, and a complex nose of distinct black berry fruit and pepper. The solid palate boasts a soft attack, then a mouthfilling, substantial progression to an enjoyable, if slightly bitter, finish. The well-made Riserva '99 offers a clean nose that releases notes of red berry fruit and vanilla. The palate may not be overwhelmingly structured, but it's well typed and lingers. The '00 Nobile also maintains estate standards, offering ripe fruity notes of plum on the nose and, in the mouth, smooth tannins, good balance and roundness. In fact, all it lacks is a spark of individuality to help it stand out from the crowd. Lastly, the '01 Rosso is a simpler but agreeably approachable wine. The fruit on the nose is fresh and sound, and the entry, development and finish on the palate are well paced and evenly distributed.

● Nobile di Montepulciano Ris. '99	ŸŸ	6
● Nobile di Montepulciano '00	Ÿ	5
● Girifalco '01	Ÿ	6
● La Calonica '02	Ÿ	4
● Rosso di Montepulciano '02		4
● Signorelli '98	ŸŸ	7
● Nobile di Montepulciano '98	ŸŸ	5
● Signorelli '99	ŸŸ	7
● Girifalco '00	ŸŸ	6
● Signorelli '00	ŸŸ	7
● Nobile di Montepulciano '99	ŸŸ	5

● Santo Pellegrino '01	ŸŸ	6
● Nobile di Montepulciano '00	Ÿ	5
● Rosso di Montepulciano '01	Ÿ	4
● Nobile di Montepulciano Ris. '99	Ÿ	6
● Nobile di Montepulciano Ris. '98	ŸŸ	6
● Nobile di Montepulciano '99	ŸŸ	5

MONTEPULCIANO (SI)

LODOLA NUOVA - TENIMENTI RUFFINO
FRAZ. VALIANO
VIA LODOLA, 1
53045 MONTEPULCIANO (SI)
TEL. 0578734032
E-MAIL: info@ruffino.it

Ruffino's Lodola Nuova presented only one wine this year, but it is an extraordinary red. This Nobile di Montepulciano '00 - not a "riserva" or even a selection - comfortably made it to our final taste-offs and almost collected Three Glasses. This is no small achievement, and if you consider its modest price, you will understand why we're so excited, and why we have set aside a profile for this winery in Valiano, between Cortona and Arezzo. It's not easy to find a wine that so pleasingly combines a fragrant bouquet, easy-drinking approachability, very respectable structure and a finish that you would hardly expect in this price range. One can only applaud Ruffino's winemaking philosophy and the work of the man at the helm, Luigi Folonari. Particular credit must go to Folonari, who has whipped the estate into shape, taking a few risky decisions to drive it into Tuscany's top ranks. We also had a preview taste of the '00 Riserva, which will be released in May 2004. It is even better than the standard version, as you might have predicted. We'll be reviewing it next year, when we hope to find intact the splendid wine our tasting from the barrel seemed to promise.

MONTEPULCIANO (SI)

★ POLIZIANO
LOC. MONTEPULCIANO STAZIONE
VIA FONTAGO, 1
53040 MONTEPULCIANO (SI)
TEL. 0578738171
E-MAIL: az.agr.poliziano@iol.it

Federico Carletti, with friend and former fellow student, Carlo Ferrini, continues to work with his initial enthusiasm. Yet again, he has won Three Glasses for the incredibly good Asinone '00. Made from prugnolo gentile with just a little canaiolo and mammolo, this vineyard selection is a generally very successful attempt to make a great wine from the refractory sangiovese grape, of which prugnolo gentile is a local variant. The nose reveals intense spicy tones against a background of black berry fruit. The harmonious, full-bodied and deep palate reveals silky tannins and a long, sweet finish. Then comes the '00 Le Stanze, which did not miss Three Glasses by much. This now classic Bordeaux-blend Tuscan wine offers balsamic and spicy aromas and a dense, overwhelming palate. The excellent Nobile '00 is astonishingly easy to drink, and the fine '02 Rosso is one of the few Montepulciano wines from its vintage to make a good showing. This is the debut in the Guide for the wines from Poliziano's Maremma estate, which promises to follow in the footsteps of its illustrious parent. The winery, which is located at Magliano in Toscana, is called Lohsa and has 19 hectares under vine. The excellent Morellino '02 boasts a peppery nose and a soft, enjoyable palate. The Mandrione dell'Osa '01, a blend of cabernet sauvignon, alicante and petit verdot, is already a fascinating wine. The nose releases notes of roasted coffee and red berry fruit jam, then the palate has first-rate texture, smooth tannins and noticeable oak. A few months in the bottle should suffice to get it all in balance.

● Nobile di Montepulciano '00	♈♈	4*
● Nobile di Montepulciano '99	♈♈	4
● Nobile di Montepulciano Ris. '99	♈♈	5

● Nobile di Montepulciano Asinone '00	♈♈♈	7
● Nobile di Montepulciano '00	♈♈	5
● Le Stanze '01	♈♈	7
● Mandrione dell'Osa '01	♈♈	6
● Morellino di Scansano Lohsa '02	♈	4
● Rosso di Montepulciano '02	♈	4
● Le Stanze '97	♈♈♈	7
● Nobile di Montepulciano Asinone '97	♈♈♈	6
● Le Stanze '98	♈♈♈	7
● Nobile di Montepulciano Asinone '98	♈♈♈	6
● Le Stanze '00	♈♈♈	7
● Nobile di Montepulciano Asinone '99	♈♈♈	6
● Le Stanze '99	♈♈	7
● Rosso di Montepulciano '01	♈♈	3*
● Nobile di Montepulciano '99	♈♈	4

MONTEPULCIANO (SI)

MONTEPULCIANO (SI)

REDI
VIA DI COLLAZZI, 5
53045 MONTEPULCIANO (SI)
TEL. 0578716092 - 0578716093
E-MAIL: info@cantinadelredi.com

SALCHETO
LOC. SANT'ALBINO
VIA DI VILLA BIANCA, 15
53045 MONTEPULCIANO (SI)
TEL. 0578799031
E-MAIL: posta@salcheto.it

As usual, Redi presented a wide range of wines from Cantina del Redi, Vecchia Cantina and Terre di Rubinoro. This very important Montepulciano winery produces almost 30 per cent of all the Vino Nobile on the market and has recently invested heavily in renovating the vinification cellars and constructing new, modern ageing rooms. Although they have managed to reconcile quantity with quality, there is still work to be done, perhaps particularly as regards attention to grape condition. The wines we tasted this year were, however, fairly good. Outstanding among them was Orbaio '01, with its lovely nose of ripe fruit enhanced by spicy tones, and an unfussy palate with mellow tannins. The sound Briareo '00 is a bit vegetal on the nose, but reveals lively tannins on the substantial palate. The '00 Nobile from Cantina del Redi is clean and nicely calibrated, which earned it good marks. Both the Nobile Vecchia Cantina '00 and the Nobile Terre di Rubinoro '00, were encouragingly well balanced and affordable. The Rosso di Montepulciano Redi '02, on the other hand, is weak in fragrance but fairly dense in the mouth. The Rosso Vecchia Cantina '02 lacks a little harmony on the nose then shows simple and straightforward on the palate. The '02 Argo did better, displaying an agreeably fruity nose and a succulent palate.

First of all, we wish a hearty farewell and all the best to Fabrizio Piccin and Cecilia Naldoni, who are leaving this historic estate after years of dedicated work. Good luck to Michele Manelli, who will be staying at the helm on his own. The wines this year maintained their customary high standard, and the Nobile Salco '00 very nearly got Three Glasses, which is not bad at all for a wine in its second year of production. Made exclusively from carefully selected prugnolo gentile grapes and aged in barrique, it shows an intense, luminous ruby hue, followed by an elegantly varied and deep bouquet of vanilla tones and ripe red berry fruit notes. In the mouth, it offers full body, densely packed tannins, a generous mid palate and a long, silky finish. The other wines did well, although there was some unevenness. The '02 Rosso was really rather good, considering its vintage. The fruit on the nose is just faintly over-ripe, and the wine is fluent and enjoyable, if not very complex. The fine Chianti Colli Senesi '02 has aromas of sound, clean red berry fruit and a basically admirable palate, although the tannins are a little rough and there is a slightly bitter hint on the finish. We had hoped for something more from the Nobile '00. The red berry fruit fragrance is nicely calibrated, but the palate doesn't show the structure and sinew typical of a Nobile, although it is as soft and long as you could wish. Salcheto started up in 1984 and has a total of 26 hectares of land, of which 16 are under vine. Paolo Vagaggini consults.

●	Nobile di Montepulciano Briareo '00	🍷🍷	6
●	Orbaio '01	🍷🍷	5
●	Nobile di Montepulciano '00	🍷	5
●	Nobile di Montepulciano Terre di Rubinoro '00	🍷	4
●	Nobile di Montepulciano Vecchia Cantina '00	🍷	3
●	Argo '02	🍷	4
●	Rosso di Montepulciano '02	🍷	3
●	Rosso di Montepulciano Vecchia Cantina '02	🍷	3
●	Orbaio '00	🍷🍷	5
●	Nobile di Montepulciano '99	🍷🍷	5
●	Nobile di Montepulciano Terre di Rubinoro '99	🍷🍷	4*

●	Nobile di Montepulciano Salco '00	🍷🍷	6
●	Nobile di Montepulciano '00	🍷	5
●	Chianti dei Colli Senesi '02	🍷	4
●	Rosso di Montepulciano '02	🍷	4
●	Nobile di Montepulciano '97	🍷🍷🍷	5
●	Nobile di Montepulciano Ris. '97	🍷🍷	5
●	Nobile di Montepulciano '98	🍷🍷	5
●	Nobile di Montepulciano Salco '99	🍷🍷	6
●	Nobile di Montepulciano '99	🍷🍷	5
●	Chianti dei Colli Senesi '01	🍷	4
●	Rosso di Montepulciano '01	🍷	4

MONTEPULCIANO (SI)

LE TRE BERTE
LOC. TRE BERTE - FRAZ. ACQUAVIVA
S. S. 326 EST, 85
53045 MONTEPULCIANO (SI)
TEL. 057867143
E-MAIL: info@letreberte.it

It's always a pleasure to find a new winery that manages to stand out in the competitive hurly-burly of Montepulciano. And the Montefoschi family's Le Tre Berte has done just that, making an excellent debut in the Guide. The Montefoschis are gradually replanting their 18 hectares under vine. Cellar technique is basically traditional, involving the use of large casks, but barriques are not unknown here. The family feel they want them for certain wines. Current production is about 40,000 bottles a year, and Lorenzo Landi keeps a watchful consulting eye on the entire process. The Nobile Poggio Tocco '00 made quite an impression at our tastings, slipping into the finals and almost walking off with Three Glasses. The lustrous colour goes all the way to the edge of the glass, then the nose unfolds balsamic and spicy notes on a blanket of red berry fruit. The well-calibrated palate has a soft entry, rich progression and tightly knit but well-behaved tannins. The Rosso di Montepulciano Poggio Tocco '02 is clearly a less complex wine, but still very agreeable. The notes of red berry fruit on the nose are light but distinct, and the palate is well executed and smooth, if perhaps a bit predictable. Lastly, the Chianti Colli Senesi Poggio Tocco '01 is redolent of red berry fruit, with some vegetal tones. After a soft attack, the palate loses a little steam in the centre, but picks up again on the enjoyable long finish. The Montefoschi's pricing policy is praiseworthy across the range.

MONTEPULCIANO (SI)

TENUTA VALDIPIATTA
VIA DELLA CIARLIANA, 25/A
53040 MONTEPULCIANO (SI)
TEL. 0578757930
E-MAIL: info@valdipiatta.it

Giulio Caporali's Tenuta Valdipiatta has about 25 hectares under vine. He has made considerable investments both in the vineyards and in the cellar and Paolo Vagaggini is the consultant oenologist. All of this suggests that Giulio has done everything possible to ensure the production of genuinely good wines. Yet there are many vineyard and winemaking variables to contend with, some of them beyond all control, and this year Giulio's wines are good but not excellent. Trincerone '01, made from canaiolo and merlot, was our favourite. It presents a lightly balsamic nose that opens to hints of red berry fruit and pepper, and a round, mouthfilling palate with smooth, perfectly judged tannins. The very well-executed Nobile '00 offers clean scents of ripe fruit on the nose, and an immediately sweet palate supported by solid extract and rounded off by a warm finale. The sangiovese-based Vigna d'Alfiero '00 is decidedly under par. This famously tricky grape is often thoroughly intractable and, in fact, the nose is dominated by animal and toasty notes, then aggressive tannins take over in the mouth. The Rosso '02 is rather anonymous, but frank. Somewhat over-ripe scents introduce a slightly rough palate, particularly on the finish. Tre Fonti '00, a blend of sangiovese, canaiolo and cabernet sauvignon, is decent. The nose is a bit oak-driven, and the palate soft, but a note of bitterness intrudes on the finish.

● Nobile di Montepulciano Poggio Tocco '00	♈♈	4*
● Chianti Colli Senesi Poggio Tocco '01	♈	3
● Rosso di Montepulciano Poggio Tocco '02	♈	3

● Trincerone '01	♈♈	6
● Nobile di Montepulciano '00	♈	5
● Nobile di Montepulciano V. d'Alfiero '00	♈	6
● Tre Fonti '00	♈	6
● Rosso di Montepulciano '02	♈	4
● Nobile di Montepulciano V. d'Alfiero '99	♈♈♈	6
● Nobile di Montepulciano '97	♈♈	5
● Nobile di Montepulciano Ris. '97	♈♈	5
● Nobile di Montepulciano '98	♈♈	5
● Trincerone '99	♈♈	6
● Trincerone '00	♈♈	6
● Nobile di Montepulciano Ris. '98	♈♈	5
● Nobile di Montepulciano '99	♈♈	5
● Rosso di Montepulciano '01	♈	4
● Tre Fonti '99	♈	6

MONTEPULCIANO (SI)

MONTEROTONDO MARITTIMO (GR)

VILLA SANT'ANNA
FRAZ. ABBADIA
53040 MONTEPULCIANO (SI)
TEL. 0578708017 - 03355283775
E-MAIL: simona@villasantanna.it

SERRAIOLA
FRAZ. FRASSINE
LOC. SERRAIOLA
58025 MONTEROTONDO MARITTIMO (GR)
TEL. 0566910026
E-MAIL: info@serraiola.it

One could say that Villa Sant'Anna is a matriarchal estate. Simona Ruggeri Fabroni has passed on her great love of wine to her daughters, Margherita and Anna, on whose shoulders rest this winery's hopes for the future. They have 12 hectares under vine and Carlo Ferrini is consultant oenologist. In terms of Glasses, the results are very much the same as last year's, although we actually found this year's wines more convincing. The team is working well here, and it is just a question of time – not very much, we hope – before great bottles start to appear. For the present, their Nobile '00 is a splendid wine. Its brilliant ruby has lustrous garnet highlights, and the well-defined nose recalls ripe fruit, violets and elegant spices. The palate is edgy at first, then soft and round as it opens out, revealing a dry and slightly piquant flavour. The very good '96 Vin Santo is distinctly traditional, made in a style that seems almost forgotten by the producers of sweet wine these days. The richly varied bouquet includes notes of citrus, dried fruit and, particularly, almonds and walnuts. The palate is creamy and not too sweet, but enjoyably semi-dry. The Rosso '02 is also good. It shows a clean and uncomplicated, but very intense, nose then a full-bodied palate with well-integrated tannins and acidity lending delightful drinkability. Nor is the Chianti Colli Senesi '02 disappointing. It shows clean, light notes of spices and tannins that are lively, perhaps even a little too lively.

Fiorella Lenzi's Serraiola, thanks to the valuable assistance of Fabrizio Moltard both in the vineyards and in the cellar, got through the difficult '02 vintage with some panache, racking up a collection of Glasses comparable to last year's. This is an encouraging sign of continuity. The top wine is still the Campo Montecristo '01, made mostly from merlot with some syrah and sangiovese. The quite complex nose includes prominent red berry fruit laced with hints of vanilla and pepper. In the mouth, it is soft, broad and long. The Lentisco '01 is named after the mastic tree, a characteristic denizen of the Mediterranean scrubland. The wine, however, shows a rather poorly defined nose that finally allows ripe red berry fruit to emerge. The palate is more convincing, thanks to its good structure. Moving on to the whites, we found the Violina '02 offers intense, if not entirely clean aromas of peaches and apricots. There is intensity on the palate as well, which is almost fat and perhaps a little too rich in alcohol. The two '02 Serraiola wines, the red and the white, are both pleasant.

● Nobile di Montepulciano '00	𝑌𝑌	5
○ Vin Santo '96	𝑌𝑌	7
● Chianti Colli Senesi '01	𝑌	4
● Rosso di Montepulciano '02	𝑌	4
● Nobile di Montepulciano '96	𝑌𝑌	5
● Rosso di Montepulciano '00	𝑌𝑌	4
● Nobile di Montepulciano '98	𝑌𝑌	5
○ Vin Santo '95	𝑌𝑌	7
● Nobile di Montepulciano '99	𝑌𝑌	5
● Chianti Colli Senesi '00	𝑌	4
● Rosso di Montepulciano '01	𝑌	4

● Campo Montecristo '01	𝑌𝑌	6
● Monteregio di Massa Marittima Lentisco '01	𝑌	4
○ Monteregio di Massa Marittima Serraiola '02	𝑌	4
● Monteregio di Massa Marittima Serraiola '02	𝑌	4
○ Monteregio di Massa Marittima Violina '02	𝑌	4
○ Vermentino '02	𝑌	4
○ Monteregio di Massa Marittima Violina '00	𝑌𝑌	4*
● Campo Montecristo '99	𝑌𝑌	5
● Campo Montecristo '00	𝑌𝑌	6
○ Monteregio di Massa Marittima Violina '01	𝑌𝑌	4*

MONTESPERTOLI (FI)

TENUTA CASTIGLIONI
FRAZ. MONTAGNANA VAL DI PESA
VIA MONTEGUFONI, 35
50020 MONTESPERTOLI (FI)
TEL. 0571671387
E-MAIL: info@frescobaldi.it

What was a pleasant surprise last year is, this time, a superb confirmation. This lovely estate, which belongs to Marchesi Frescobaldi and is situated in the Florentine hills that are so viticulture-friendly, only just missed getting Three Glasses for the Giramonte '01. It was confirmation that the wine deserves its status as yet another of the many Frescobaldi oenological pearls. This blend of sangiovese and merlot is a wine of great breeding that is remarkable for its fruity opulence and an aristocratic, vibrant tannic and acidic structure that is typical of the sangiovese grape. Giramonte is a modern red, in that it can already be drunk with pleasure, but it would probably benefit considerably from a lengthy stay in the cellar. It presents a nose of red berry fruit and spices, followed by a remarkably soft, round palate that shows masses of fruit, tannins that have still to be completely tamed, and a finish of less than exceptional length. The distinctly varietal Cabernet Sauvignon '01 earned Two Glasses. Its intense colour precedes a nose where lashings of ripe fruit is enhanced by oak-derived spicy notes and vegetal nuances. In the mouth, it is soft, appropriately sweet, well balanced and nicely supported by perfectly judged tannins, signing off with a lingering finale. The good Chianti '02 offers fresh, inviting notes of fresh fruit on the nose and fair structure on the palate, which makes it balanced and enjoyable.

● Giramonte '01	🍷🍷	8
● Cabernet Sauvignon '01	🍷🍷	5
● Chianti '02	🍷	3*
● Giramonte '00	🍷🍷🍷	8
● Chianti '01	🍷🍷	3*
● Giramonte '99	🍷🍷	6
● Cabernet Sauvignon '00	🍷	4

MONTESPERTOLI (FI)

LE CALVANE
FRAZ. MONTAGNANA
VIA CASTIGLIONI, 1/5
50020 MONTESPERTOLI (FI)
TEL. 0571671073
E-MAIL: lecalvane@interfree.it

All the signs from Le Calvane seem to indicate quite clearly not only that the cellar can be counted on for consistently high quality, but also that it is aiming even higher. The wines presented at our annual tastings are proof of this, and included another new label, Matriarca '00, a monovarietal merlot that aroused considerable interest. After initial shyness on the nose, it releases aromas of plums, tobacco, spices and some vegetal nuances. The appealing palate is substantial, broad, soft and well-balanced, but the finish is a bit astringent and not really long enough. The other estate jewel is Borro del Boscone '00, which is as reliable as ever, although it was still a little closed at the time of our tastings. Obtained from cabernet sauvignon only, it shows an intense red, followed by concentrated aromas of berry fruit lifted by herbal and subtle spicy notes. The full-bodied, harmonious palate reveals densely packed tannins and a slightly bitter aftertaste. The Chianti Il Trecione Riserva '00 seemed a bit under par. Its nose is muffled at first, but then opens to attractive fruity tones on a distinctly oaky background. In the mouth, it displays well-articulated, balanced structure that leads to a nice, succulent finish. The Chianti Quercione '01 is quite simple and frank, flaunting a tangy note of acidity.

● Borro del Boscone '00	🍷🍷	6
● Matriarca '00	🍷🍷	6
● Chianti Colli Fiorentini Il Trecione Ris. '00	🍷	5
● Chianti Colli Fiorentini Quercione '01	🍷	3
● Borro del Boscone '97	🍷🍷🍷	5
● Borro del Boscone '95	🍷🍷	5
● Borro del Boscone '96	🍷🍷	5
● Borro del Boscone '98	🍷🍷	6
● Borro del Boscone '99	🍷🍷	6
● Chianti Colli Fiorentini Quercione '00	🍷	3
● Chianti Colli Fiorentini Il Trecione Ris. '99	🍷	4

MONTESPERTOLI (FI)

Poggio a Poppiano

fraz. Poppiano
via di Poppiano, 19
50025 Montespertoli (FI)
tel. 055213084
e-mail: fezileri@tin.it

After a year's pause, Clemente Zileri Dal Verme's winery is back in the Guide, and a flourish. The wines they presented at our tastings are excellent, well executed and stylistically interesting. The Calamita '01, a blend of sangiovese and merlot aged for eight months in barriques, shows intense fruit on the nose, enriched by toasty notes and light hints of vanilla. The impressive structure on the palate is supported by tight-knit tannins that are perhaps a little too marked, and the finish is rich and persistent. The Calamita '00, which is slightly less intriguing, still almost won Two Glasses. The nose of fragrant ripe fruit and balsam is a little marred by vegetal notes. In the mouth, it shows plenty of temperament, and even perhaps too much bite. The tannins are crunchy and the aftertaste has a hint of bitterness. Flocco '00, which made the best impression at our tastings, is a blend of cabernet sauvignon, cabernet franc, sangiovese and merlot aged in barrique for 14 months. The complex nose offers layered aromas ranging from red berry fruit, to pepper and notes of coffee. Entry on the palate is soft, the progression is seamless and broad, and the finish is deep, sweet and very pleasurable. Poggio a Poppiano has 86 hectares, 25 of which are under vine.

● Flocco '00	🍷🍷	5
● Calamita '01	🍷🍷	4
● Calamita '00	🍷	4
● Flocco '97	♀♀	5
● Flocco '98	♀♀	5
● Calamita '99	♀♀	4
○ Vin Santo '89	♀♀	5
● Flocco '99	♀♀	5

MONTESPERTOLI (FI)

Castello di Poppiano

fraz. Poppiano
via di Fezzana, 45
50025 Montespertoli (FI)
tel. 05582315
e-mail: poppiano@mclink.it

The improvements that have been taking place for the last few years at Castello di Poppiano under the expert guidance of oenologist, Giorgio Marone, continue apace. In fact this year, the wines were cleaner and more intriguing than in the past, on both nose and palate. The Tricorno '99, a blend of sangiovese, cabernet sauvignon and merlot, shows a vivid colour and an intense nose that releases elegant spicy and balsamic notes over a faintly vegetal, toasty background. The palate is soft, mouthfilling and well built, with round tannins and a broad and lingering finish. Toscoforte '01 comes from sangiovese with ten per cent syrah, and offers scents of red berry fruit alternating with vegetal notes and hints of green peppercorns. The substantial palate drives along with a balanced, vigorous progression to a refreshingly succulent finish. The successful Syrah '01 shows finesse on the varietal peppery nose, which it melds with fruity tones. The warm, inviting palate displays balanced, harmonious structure and an echo of spice on the finish. The fair Chianti Colli Fiorentini Il Cortile '01 is initially poorly defined on the nose, but notes of red berry fruit soon emerge. The palate is its strong point, however. A soft, juicy attack reveals smooth, unobtrusive tannins that fuse into a good structure. The less exciting Chianti Riserva '99 has a jammy fragrance of blackberries and blueberries, then an enchantingly soft impact on the palate, which is let down by a slightly perfunctory finish.

● Syrah '01	🍷🍷	4
● Toscoforte '01	🍷🍷	4
● Tricorno '99	🍷🍷	6
● Chianti Colli Fiorentini Il Cortile '01	🍷	3
● Chianti Colli Fiorentini Ris. '99	🍷	4
● Syrah '00	♀♀	4
● Tricorno '98	♀♀	6
● Toscoforte '98	♀	4
● Syrah '99	♀	4
● Chianti Colli Fiorentini Il Cortile '00	♀	3
● Toscoforte '00	♀	4
● Chianti Colli Fiorentini Ris. '98	♀	4

MONTEVARCHI (AR)

LA RENDOLA
LOC. RENDOLA, 85
52025 MONTEVARCHI (AR)
TEL. 0559707594
E-MAIL: info@renideo.com

This young, interesting winery belongs to the Renideo group, which owns other estates in Puglia and Armenia. It earned an entry with a performance that may not have any outright champions but does show considerable improvement and a consistently high level of quality. The winery is situated in the hills of Montevarchi, and has some 19 hectares under vine. The Rendola wine best known to connoisseurs is unquestionably the Merlot, which, in the '01 version, was our favourite. The colour is a brilliant, concentrated ruby, and the nose successfully melds ripe plum aromas with notes of chocolate and balsam. They all follow through onto the dense palate, which is tarnished only by some over-evolved hints and by astringent tannins on the finish. Captivatingly easy to like, the Incanto '01 is a blend of merlot and sangiovese that offers sweet aromas of raspberries and strawberries. These are mirrored on the medium-bodied palate, which makes an appealing entry but is not very deep. The well-executed, sangiovese-based La Pineta '01 is balanced and quite approachable. The better or the two whites, in our opinion, was the Chardonnay '01. Although the oak is noticeable, it's a fresh, savoury wine with pleasing notes of citrus fruits and summer flowers, and an interesting mineral nuance.

MURLO (SI)

FATTORIA CASABIANCA
FRAZ. CASCIANO
LOC. MONTE PESCINI
53100 MURLO (SI)
TEL. 0577811033 - 0577811026
E-MAIL: infovini@fattoriacasabianca.it

The Fattoria Casabianca covers 650 hectares, of which 140 are under vine. Some of these have been recently replanted at a high density. Indoors, the well-equipped modern cellar will soon have a new barrel room for the barriques. Oenologist Alberto Antonini and the agronomist, Federico Curtaz, keep a watchful eye on developments. The Casabianca wines did very well at our tastings, especially the Tenuta Casabianca '00. A blend of sangiovese, cabernet sauvignon and merlot, it is aged first in 40-hectolitre barrels, and then for another 12 months in barrique. The colour is concentrated, and the nose offers jammy notes of red berry fruit laced with hints of ink and pepper. The palate is soft from the start, progressing with nice roundness to a rich finish. The good, though less ambitious, Campo Lungo '02 is made from a blend of sangiovese, canaiolo and ciliegiolo that spends no time in wood. The nose has of red berry fruit with faint vegetal hints, then the dry palate contributes husky tannins and a long finish. The Chianti.Colli Senesi '02 aged for some months in barriques used for the second time. It has fresh notes of red berry fruit on the nose, then the quite tangy attack in the mouth is well balanced by a long dry finish. We were intrigued by our retasting of the Poggio Cenni '00, which we reviewed last year.

○	Chardonnay '01	♟♟	5
●	L'Incanto '01	♟♟	5
●	Merlot Rendola '01	♟♟	6
●	La Pineta '01	♟	4
○	Aliera '02		4
●	Merlot Rendola '00	♟♟	6
●	L'Incanto '00	♟	4

●	Tenuta Casabianca '00	♟♟	6
●	Campo Lungo '02	♟	3
●	Chianti Colli Senesi '02	♟	3
●	Tenuta Casabianca '98	♟♟	6
●	Chianti Colli Senesi Poggio Cenni Ris. '99	♟♟	5
●	Tenuta Casabianca '99	♟♟	6
●	Chianti Colli Senesi Poggio Cenni '00	♟	3
●	Campo Lungo '01	♟	2*

ORBETELLO (GR)

LA PARRINA
LOC. PARRINA
58010 ORBETELLO (GR)
TEL. 0564862636
E-MAIL: parrina@dada.it

PALAIA (PI)

SAN GERVASIO
LOC. SAN GERVASIO
56036 PALAIA (PI)
TEL. 0587483360 - 0587629233
E-MAIL: sangervasio@sangervasio.com

La Parrina's name apparently comes from the Spanish "parra", meaning a vine-clad pergola. Meanwhile, the winery continues to make progress. It is the only winery in Maremma's Parrina DOC zone, established in 1971, and covers 450 hectares of land, some 65 of which are under vine. La Parrina belongs to Marchesa Franca Spinola and has always concentrated on such traditional grapes as sangiovese, trebbiano and ansonica, despite the fact that the 1993 change in the DOC rules allowed the inclusion of cabernet sauvignon, merlot, chardonnay and sauvignon, further increasing the potential of this pocket-sized denomination. The contributions of Giuseppe Caviola in the cellar and Federico Curtaz among the vines are clearly perceptible, and we were very favourably impressed by the wines at our tastings. Radaia, a monovarietal Merlot, is again intriguing in the '01 version. The aromas range from intense fruit to intriguing spicy notes. The attack on the palate is soft, and the progression well-rounded, but the tannins are a bit mouth-puckering on the finish. The Parrina Riserva '00 displays intense scents of red berry fruit and a balanced, savoury palate. A step down is the Muraccio '01, which shows vegetal nuances on the nose and a structured palate with a slightly bitter finish. The bottom-of-the-range bottles are the Parrina Rosso '02, a simple, but well-made wine, and the Parrina Bianco '02, which shows some over-evolved hints on the nose, but is agreeably succulent in the mouth. Ansonica Costa dell'Argentario '02 offers a clean, uncomplicated nose and a crisp, graceful palate.

The future, it would seem, has finally arrived. If the investments in the cellar and vineyards were palpable on our previous visits to San Gervasio in recent years, the wines were inevitably lagging behind. It is no great secret that vines needs time before they can produce great grapes, and that great grapes are a prerequisite for great wine. Well, the necessary time has finally passed, and at this year's tastings, a glance at the wine in our glasses was enough to tell that Luca Tommasini's dedication had at last made a real difference. The excellent I Renai '00, a monovarietal Merlot, came very close to carrying off Three Glasses. The stunningly clean, incisive nose releases fresh, intense and very well-defined notes of fruit. The palate got our vote for its remarkable elegance and complexity, the tight-knit yet silky tannins in no way jarring with the graceful structure. A whisker less exciting, but still splendid, sangiovese-based A Sirio '00 has not yet come together perfectly on the nose, but still shows pleasing spicy notes. The austere palate has elegant tannins and characteristic varietal acidity. It's a pity that the oak is so intrusive. The good, though much simpler, Sangervasio '02 is a new offering made mostly from sangiovese with some cabernet sauvignon and merlot. All their other wines are admirably well made.

● Radaia '01	♟♟	7
● Parrina Rosso Ris. '00	♟	5
● Parrina Rosso Muraccio '01	♟	4
○ Ansonica Costa dell'Argentario '02	♟	3
● Parrina Rosso '02	♟	3
○ Parrina Bianco '02	♟	2
● Parrina Rosso Ris. '98	♟♟	4
● Radaia '00	♟♟	7
● Parrina Rosso Muraccio '00	♟♟	4*
○ Ansonica Costa dell'Argentario '01	♟♟	3*
● Parrina Rosso Ris. '99	♟♟	5
● Parrina Rosso Muraccio '99	♟	4
○ Parrina Bianco '01	♟	2*
● Parrina Rosso '01	♟	3*

● I Renai '00	♟♟	7
● A Sirio '00	♟♟	6
● Sangervasio Rosso '02	♟	4
○ Bianco Pisano S. Torpè Casina de' Venti '2002	♟	4
○ Bianco Pisano S. Torpè Recinaio Vin Santo '98		6
● A Sirio '96	♟♟	4
● A Sirio '97	♟♟	5
● A Sirio '98	♟♟	5
● I Renai '98	♟♟	6
● I Renai '99	♟♟	7

PANZANO (FI)

PANZANO (FI)

CAROBBIO
VIA SAN MARTINO IN CECIONE, 26
50020 PANZANO (FI)
TEL. 0558560133
E-MAIL: info@carobbiowine.com

FATTORIA CASALOSTE
VIA MONTAGLIARI, 32
50020 PANZANO (FI)
TEL. 055852725
E-MAIL: casaloste@casaloste.it

It was another good year for this historic winery at Panzano, which also saw a changing of the guard. Remigio Bordini is now in charge of the entire operation, and Lorenzo Landi oversees the cellar. There was no absolute champion among the wines, but the results were nevertheless excellent. The fine Chianti Classico '01 offers strikingly subtle spices, sweet rich fruit and balanced minty tones on the nose. The rich palate has well-paced tannins and a lovely texture that leads to a long, complex finish. The Riserva '00 was a little disappointing. The nose is not very eloquent, showing only faint hints of fruit. Balance is better in the mouth, which reveals a full body, powerful tannins that are just a bit astringent and a moderately long finish. The cabernet sauvignon-based Pietraforte '00 reached our finals thanks in part to an intriguing nose of aromatic tones that blend beautifully with black berry fruit and teasing faint balsamic nuances. The palate is smooth and enjoyable from the start, then unveils a dense, characterful body, but the finish is not very long. The '99 version is also well built. The nose shows lovely, well-defined fruit, and the well-balanced palate is substantial. Leone di Carobbio '99, made from sangiovese only, offers aromas of raspberries and redcurrants enhanced by notes of cloves. In the mouth, a soft attack leads into a mellow progression, evenly distributed tannins and a long, savoury finish.

We admire Giovanni Battista D'Orsi and his wife Emilia, who own this small Panzano estate. Giovanni is a man who is not afraid of a fight, and so passionately devoted to his work that he has probably not yet forgiven us for being consigned to Other Wineries last year. Naturally, we're pleased that his wines were well worth a full profile this time. Their excellence confirms the potential of the estate, where it is still Giovanni himself who tends the vines. In the cellar, Battista D'Orsi takes advice from Gabriella Tani, who has been his friend and collaborator from the beginning. The Chianti Classico '01 offers extremely intense aromas of berry fruit and undergrowth. The palate is immediately pervasive, showing good weight, well-distributed tannins and a rising finish. The less successful Riserva '00 shows the same depth and intensity of colour as the standard version. Its aromas are somewhat one-dimensional and not very eloquent, focusing principally on notes of ripe fruit. The Don Vincenzo Riserva '99 is an incredibly dense ruby and performs rather better. After initial reticence, the nose offers scents of fur and leather that then make room for concentrated ripe fruit notes of blackberries and plums. The palate is full-bodied. It's not enormous, but does have good balance, and it's braced by good tannic texture. The lovely finish lingers.

● Pietraforte del Carobbio '00	♟♟	6
● Pietraforte del Carobbio '99	♟♟	6
● Chianti Cl. '01	♟♟	4
● Leone di Carobbio '99	♟♟	6
● Chianti Cl. Ris. '00	♟	5
● Chianti Cl. Ris. '99	♟♟♟	5*
● Leone di Carobbio '93	♟♟	5
● Leone di Carobbio '94	♟♟	5
● Pietraforte del Carobbio '95	♟♟	5
● Chianti Cl. Ris. '97	♟♟	5
● Pietraforte del Carobbio '97	♟♟	6
● Leone di Carobbio '97	♟♟	6
● Chianti Cl. Ris. '98	♟♟	5
● Chianti Cl. '99	♟♟	4
● Chianti Cl. '00	♟♟	4*

● Chianti Cl. '01	♟♟	5
● Chianti Cl. Don Vincenzo Ris. '99	♟♟	8
● Chianti Cl. Ris. '00	♟	6
● Chianti Cl. Ris. '94	♟♟	4
● Chianti Cl. '95	♟♟	3
● Chianti Cl. Don Vincenzo Ris. '95	♟♟	5
● Chianti Cl. Ris. '95	♟♟	4
● Chianti Cl. Don Vincenzo Ris. '96	♟♟	5
● Chianti Cl. '98	♟♟	3
● Chianti Cl. Don Vincenzo Ris. '97	♟♟	8
● Chianti Cl. Ris. '99	♟♟	7

PANZANO (FI)

CASTELLO DEI RAMPOLLA
VIA CASE SPARSE, 22
50020 PANZANO (FI)
TEL. 055852001
E-MAIL: castellodeirampolla.cast@tin.it

This is an unusual year for the Rampolla siblings' estate. They collected their usual Three Glasses for the top wine, D'Alceo, but the rest of their range, except the Vendemmia Tardiva, is not up to its usual stratospheric standard. The Chianti Classico '01 failed to light any fires. It's pale, though lively, in colour, and the nose struggles to open, releasing only delicate fruit notes of raspberries and redcurrants. The palate is sound but austere, with firm, crunchy tannins that are slow to unfold, and a moderately long finish. In contrast, the D'Alceo '01, from cabernet sauvignon with a little petit verdot, is quite splendid. An incredibly concentrated colour is the prelude to a wonderfully broad bouquet. The medley of red berry fruit is lifted by distinctive spicy notes of pepper and liquorice that alternate with scents of fresh aromatic herbs and balsamic tones. In the mouth, it shows grip and character. The attack is vigorous and the body full and dense. Progression in the mouth is good, revealing admirably smooth tannins, and an elegant aromatic note in the finish. Sammarco '00, a 90-10 blend of cabernet sauvignon and sangiovese, is a little disappointing. Attractive notes of green peppers are most noticeable on the nose, the palate boasts good structure, and although it isn't perfectly balanced, it does have a pleasing finish. It may just need some cellar time. The Trebianco Vendemmia Tardiva '99, a late-harvested white, presents a beautiful golden colour and sweet scents of fruit. The concentrated, rich, velvety palate takes you through to an enjoyable finish.

PANZANO (FI)

CENNATOIO INTERVINEAS
VIA DI SAN LEOLINO, 35
50020 PANZANO (FI)
TEL. 055852134 - 0558963230
E-MAIL: info@cennatoio.it

Leandro Alessi's winery is assisted by winemaker, Gabriella Tani. It made a fine showing this year with a range of excellent wines, two of which made it into our finals. The Riserva '00 offers clear-cut, pleasing fresh fruit scents of cherries and plums which are joined after a while by spicy notes, with cinnamon and pepper alternately taking the lead. After a forceful attack, the palate shows soft, calibrated tannins integrating into a rich, powerful structure. The finish is long and even. The Arcibaldo '00, made from sangiovese and cabernet sauvignon, has a seductive nose of sweet scents of coffee and chocolate, interspersed with ripe red berry fruit tones and stylish, subtle vanilla. The palate is inviting and round from the first, and offers an admirably expansive, deep progression with smooth, well-absorbed tannins and an elegant, lingering finish. The Etrusco '00, a fine example of a monovarietal Sangiovese, shows a bouquet based on ripe fruity notes of plums and cherries that are subsequently joined by inviting spicy notes. In the mouth, it is immediately creamy and soft, the tannins are tidy, and the finish is engagingly succulent. The Mammolo '00, from 100 per cent merlot, came awfully close to a third Glass. The complex nose reveals delectable notes of freshly ground pepper, aromatic herbs and spices on an intriguingly varied fruit base. The palate is soft but not flabby, revealing tight-knit, fine-grained tannins well distributed across the solid, powerful structure. A graceful note of pepper comes back on the finish.

● D'Alceo '01	▼▼▼	8
○ Trebianco V. T. '99	▼▼	4
● Sammarco '00	▼	8
● Chianti Cl. '01	▼	5
● Sammarco '85	▼▼▼	8
● Sammarco '86	▼▼▼	8
● Sammarco '94	▼▼▼	8
● La Vigna di Alceo '96	▼▼▼	8
● La Vigna di Alceo '97	▼▼▼	8
● La Vigna di Alceo '98	▼▼▼	8
● La Vigna di Alceo '99	▼▼▼	8
● D'Alceo '00	▼▼▼	8
● Sammarco '98	▼▼	8
● Sammarco '99	▼▼	8

● Arcibaldo '00	▼▼	8
● Mammolo '00	▼▼	8
● Chianti Cl. Ris. '00	▼▼	5
● Etrusco '00	▼▼	7
● Etrusco '94	▼▼▼	5
● Chianti Cl. Ris. '95	▼▼	4
● Rosso Fiorentino '95	▼▼	5
● Etrusco '97	▼▼	5
● Chianti Cl. Ris. '97	▼▼	4
● Rosso Fiorentino '97	▼▼	5
● Etrusco '98	▼▼	5
● Arcibaldo '99	▼▼	7
● Etrusco '99	▼▼	7

PANZANO (FI)

★ TENUTA FONTODI
VIA SAN LEOLINO, 89
50020 PANZANO (FI)
TEL. 055852005
E-MAIL: fontodi@fontodi.com

Tenuta Fontodi di Panzano has triumphantly rejoined the ranks of the Three Glass winners, where it was once a habitual presence and will, we hope, continue to be. This year, the occasional aromatic imperfections of its best wines are a thing of the past, and the sangiovese-based Flaccianello '00 is as good as its very best versions. A nose of elegant fruit with an unusual note of varietal violets precedes a vibrant palate underpinned by good acid bite, setting up the long finish of a real thoroughbred. We liked it even more than the Chianti Classico Vigna del Sorbo Riserva, also a '00. This wine has a touch of cabernet sauvignon which, for us, jeopardizes the essence of the nose and makes it softer in the mouth, but also less expressive of its terroir. In contrast, the typical gamey aromas of the syrah grape are powerfully and intensely present on the nose of Syrah Case Via '00, one of the most characteristic representatives of this variety in Italy. The very fine Chianti Classico '01 gives us a clear foretaste of how good this vintage was. As we are beginning to realize, the 2001 growing year was quite extraordinary in these parts. In conclusion, we can only offer our compliments to Giovanni Manetti and his long-time consultant, Franco Bernabei, who continue to show where winemaking passion and skill can take you.

PANZANO (FI)

IL MOLINO DI GRACE
LOC. SAN LEOLINO, 31
50022 PANZANO (FI)
TEL. 0558561010
E-MAIL: info@ilmolinodigrace.it

It's not every day that an estate presents its wines at our tastings for the first time, gains a full Guide profile, and walks off with Three Glasses. But that's what happened here. The winery belongs to Frank Grace, a London-based American who has entrusted it to his manager, Gerard Hirmer. Help in the cellar is on hand from distinguished winemaker, Franco Bernabei. The range consists of four wines, and we'll start with the Chianti Classico '00. It offers pleasing aromas of plums and blackberries, laced with harmonious vegetal and flinty tones. The powerful palate unfolds easily, despite rather abundant alcohol. The Riserva '99 is less convincing. The nose is over-evolved and seems almost tired, although occasional intriguing spicy notes emerge, with ripe rich fruit. The palate is simple and straightforward, the tannins well integrated, and the finish is not particularly long. In contrast, the Margone Riserva '99 is very well executed. After a time, attractive hints of pencil lead on the nose blend with ripe cherry fruit. The savoury, not extraordinarily powerful, but very well-balanced palate unveils a pleasant hint of acidity, well-judged tannins, decent concentration and good length. Finally, we come to the Gratius '00, a monovarietal Sangiovese and Three Glass winner. The stunningly impressive bouquet reels off elegant notes of coffee and cocoa powder, together with initially subdued fruit that expands to redress the balance. The deliciously well-rounded palate proffers an admirable tannic weave that accompanies and enhances the very long finish.

● Flaccianello della Pieve '00	♟♟♟	7
● Chianti Cl. V. del Sorbo Ris. '00	♟♟	7
● Syrah Case Via '00	♟♟	7
● Chianti Cl. '01	♟♟	5
● Chianti Cl. V. del Sorbo Ris. '90	♟♟♟	7
● Flaccianello della Pieve '90	♟♟♟	7
● Flaccianello della Pieve '91	♟♟♟	7
● Chianti Cl. V. del Sorbo Ris. '94	♟♟♟	7
● Syrah Case Via '95	♟♟♟	7
● Flaccianello della Pieve '97	♟♟♟	7
● Syrah Case Via '98	♟♟♟	7
● Syrah Case Via '99	♟♟	7

● Gratius '00	♟♟♟	6
● Chianti Cl. Ris. Il Margone '99	♟♟	5
● Chianti Cl. '00	♟	4
● Chianti Cl. Ris. '99	♟	5

PANZANO (FI)

La Marcellina
VIA CASE SPARSE, 74
50020 PANZANO (FI)
TEL. 055852126
E-MAIL: marcellina@ftbcc.it

The Castellacci family's estate has earned its second profile in the Guide and again shows great, but as yet unfulfilled promise. Such problems as there are can be found on the nose of the wines, which are more convincing in the mouth. The Chianti Classico Sassocupo '01 shows a very intense, opaque colour. At first, the sweet ripe fruity notes the nose releases are quite indefinable, but after a time, you can pick out clearly identifiable blackberries and plums. The not very powerful palate is supple and savoury, the acidity is prominent, and there's a tidy, rising finish. The Comignole '01 selection is less interesting because of its distinctly animal scents of leather and fur, as well as a lack of balance in the mouth. The Sassocupo Riserva '00 is not altogether clean on the nose, which shows some slight hints of over-ripeness, together with fresh vegetal notes and juicy plum. In the mouth, it does better, showing firmness, weight, smooth tannins that are only slightly drying, and a satisfactory, if not very long, finish. The Camporosso '00 is a little disappointing, particularly on the nose, which is initially masked by rather crude animal and vegetal scents. The situation is rosier on the palate, where it shows an intriguing attack and powerful, well-paced tannins, which also detract a little from the finish by drying it out.

PANZANO (FI)

La Massa
VIA CASE SPARSE, 9
50020 PANZANO (FI)
TEL. 055852722
E-MAIL: fattoria.lamassa@tin.it

Every now and then (who knows why?), we seem to delight in rechristening Giampaolo Motta, the owner of La Massa, Giancarlo. And, like the true Neapolitan he is, he never misses the chance to pull our legs about the oversight. But let's get on to more serious matters. The Giorgio Primo is being released a year late, and won't be on the shelves until the spring. We heartily approve of this decision, which shows that the cellar continues to focus on elegance. Meanwhile, fans of this lovely Panzano estate needn't worry because, almost as if by magic, there has now emerged in its place, under the watchful eye of the great consultant oenologist, Carlo Ferrini, a new wine. The IGT La Massa '01 went straight to the top of the charts and earned Three Glasses. It takes the place of the standard Chianti, and is made from 70 per cent sangiovese with equal amounts of cabernet sauvignon and merlot. A luminous ruby introduces intense fruit fragrances of raspberries and strawberries, enhanced by light balsamic hints. The dense, creamy palate reveals tannins that fuse nicely with the alcohol, and take you through to a long, enjoyable finish.

● Chianti Cl. Sassocupo '01	♟♟	4
● Camporosso '00	♟	6
● Chianti Cl. Sassocupo Ris. '00	♟	6
● Chianti Cl. Comignole '01	♟	5
● Camporosso '97	♟♟	5
● Chianti Cl. Comignole '00	♟♟	5
● Chianti Cl. La Marcellina '00	♟♟	5
● Camporosso '99	♟♟	5

● La Massa '01	♟♟♟	5
● Chianti Cl. Giorgio Primo '93	♟♟♟	7
● Chianti Cl. Giorgio Primo '94	♟♟♟	7
● Chianti Cl. Giorgio Primo '95	♟♟♟	7
● Chianti Cl. Giorgio Primo '96	♟♟♟	7
● Chianti Cl. Giorgio Primo '97	♟♟♟	7
● Chianti Cl. Giorgio Primo '98	♟♟♟	7
● Chianti Cl. Giorgio Primo '99	♟♟♟	7
● Chianti Cl. Giorgio Primo '00	♟♟♟	7

PANZANO (FI)

LE CINCIOLE
VIA CASE SPARSE, 83
50020 PANZANO (FI)
TEL. 055852636
E-MAIL: cinciole@chianticlassico.com

Luca Orsini and Valeria Viganò have won back their full profile with an excellent performance. We have never been so impressed by their wines before, and indeed their Chianti Classico '01 made it into our finals. After a period of intensive restructuring, when the oldest vines were replaced by new stock, the cellar was redesigned more rationally, and Stefano Chioccioli took over as consultant oenologist, the wines have at last taken a giant step forward. They have lost the excessive roughness they once had and much greater balance is now emerging. Some of the new plots are planted to cabernet sauvignon and merlot, which will be the basis for a completely new wine. But we'll start our round-up with the Chianti Classico '01. The nose is initially dominated by pleasant notes of green bell peppers that open to embrace sweet ripe fruity tones. The palate shows distinctive character, presenting an even, round attack, strong progression and even tannins, with no rough edges, that merge in a deep, very satisfying finish. The Petresco Riserva '00 is ruby with vivid purplish highlights, and offers a lovely nose of berry fruit blending with riper tones, as well as some spice and mineral hints. The palate is smooth, if not particularly substantial, but has good balance and succulence that are nicely supported by moderate acidity. The finish is very attractive indeed.

PANZANO (FI)

PANZANELLO
VIA CASE SPARSE, 86
50020 PANZANO (FI)
TEL. 055852470
E-MAIL: info@panzanello.it

Andrea and Iole Sommaruga, who moved to Panzano from Rome some years ago, continue to work dedicatedly, assisted by their consultant, Gioia Cresti, one of the best oenologists in Tuscany. At Panzanello, which is about 500 metres above sea level, over Le Cinciole and not far from La Massa, working with sangiovese is no easy matter. The tiniest false move or momentary distraction in the vineyards can quickly lead to disaster. If the grapes don't manage to ripen properly, the wines will become harsh and sharp, and vegetal on the nose. Hence hard work is a requirement, rather than an option, if you want to make good wines. It can also happen that the wines need more time to express all their qualities. This lengthy prologue serves to explain why the release of the '01 Manuzio '01 has been postponed. It is a 100 per cent sangiovese from a vintage that was sensational in these parts, and the structure and complexity make further ageing in bottle essential. Things aren't too bad, however, since we can console ourselves with an excellent Chianti Classico Riserva '00, which is richer and more powerful than previous versions. Moreover, the standard-label Chianti Classico '01 offers us some indication of what the flagship wines will be like when they are released in the second half of 2004. We'd like to call attention to this winery's extremely fair pricing policy, a particularly commendable feature in times like these.

● Chianti Cl. '01	▼▼	4
● Chianti Cl. Petresco Ris. '00	▼▼	6
● Chianti Cl. '93	♼♼	3
● Chianti Cl. '94	♼♼	3
● Chianti Cl. '95	♼♼	3
● Chianti Cl. Valle del Pozzo Ris. '95	♼♼	4
● Chianti Cl. Valle del Pozzo Ris. '96	♼♼	4
● Chianti Cl. Petresco Ris. '97	♼♼	4
● Chianti Cl. Petresco Ris. '98	♼♼	5

● Chianti Cl. Panzanello Ris. '00	▼▼	5
● Chianti Cl. Panzanello '01	▼▼	4
● Chianti Cl. Panzanello '98	♼♼	3
● Chianti Cl. Panzanello Ris. '98	♼♼	4
● Il Manuzio '99	♼♼	5
● Il Manuzio '00	♼♼	6
● Chianti Cl. Panzanello '00	♼♼	4
● Chianti Cl. Panzanello Ris. '99	♼♼	5

PANZANO (FI)

VECCHIE TERRE DI MONTEFILI
VIA SAN CRESCI, 45
50022 PANZANO (FI)
TEL. 055853739
E-MAIL: info@vecchieterredimontefili.com

Roccaldo Acuti's Vecchie Terre di Montefili seems to have embarked on a second youth. Last year, we happily recorded the return to prominence of his Bruno di Rocca, a Supertuscan made from sangiovese and cabernet, and this year the monovarietal Sangiovese IGT Anfiteatro provided a delightful surprise. It all goes to show that Panzano has fantastic natural resources that can be reflected in the wines, provided they are managed with care. Now to our tastings. The Chianti Classico '01 shows a lovely, vivid ruby. The traditional-style nose offers ripe fruit with hints of leather and fur. The palate is somewhat dilute, but nonetheless pleasant, and though the acidity is not quite integrated and the tannins are a little spiky, the finish is clean and enjoyable. The very good Anfitreatro '00 offers an impressive swathe of aromas including violets, redcurrants and brandied fruit. The supple, mouthfilling palate shows grip, and the tannins are very feisty, leading to a finish that is sweet and lingers. The Bruno di Rocca '00 very nearly won Three Glasses again. The complex nose displays quite advanced tertiary aromas, including tobacco and fur that mask the notes of cherry and blackcurrant fruit. The velvety, seductively round palate offers a tidy progression with powerful tannins that tend to dry the mouth on the finish. Some more time in the bottle can only do it good.

PANZANO (FI)

VILLA CAFAGGIO
VIA SAN MARTINO IN CECIONE, 7
50020 PANZANO (FI)
TEL. 055852949 - 0558549094
E-MAIL: basilica.cafaggio@tiscalinet.it

The team consisting of owner, Stefano Farkas, and Stefano Chioccioli, the consultant oenologist, continues to function to perfection. They renewed their annual subscription to Three Glasses, awarded, as usual, to the mainly sangiovese-based Supertuscan, San Martino. But let's get down to details. The Chianti Classico '01 shows a lovely, very intense ruby and fresh, rich fruit aromas of plums and cherries. In the mouth, it is supple and savoury, offering a sweet, lingering finish. The Riserva '00 also did well. The nose offers fresh, well-defined fruit, with redcurrants to the fore, then elegant hints of spices. The vibrant palate is well proportioned, even and attractively juicy, leading to a long, enjoyable finish. The sangiovese San Martino '00 shows a lovely, very vivid purple, introducing a concentrated, intense bouquet of ripe, rich fruity notes of plums, and toasty aromas, especially coffee. The firm, concentrated, palate is admirably supported by tidy, tight-knit tannins, then the finish is savoury, long and delightful. Cortaccio '00, a monovarietal Cabernet Sauvignon, is initially reluctant to declare itself, but soon opens up to reveal good vegetal notes of green bell peppers and jammy hints of blackberries. The palate is taut, dense and pervasive, and the boisterous tannins are held in check by alcohol. It finishes invitingly.

● Anfiteatro '00	🍷🍷	8
● Bruno di Rocca '00	🍷🍷	8
● Chianti Cl. '01	🍷	5
● Chianti Cl. Ris. '85	🍷🍷🍷	6
● Chianti Cl. Anfiteatro Ris. '88	🍷🍷🍷	6
● Anfiteatro '94	🍷🍷🍷	8
● Anfiteatro '95	🍷🍷	8
● Bruno di Rocca '95	🍷🍷	8
● Anfiteatro '96	🍷🍷	8
● Bruno di Rocca '96	🍷🍷	8
● Anfiteatro '97	🍷🍷	8
● Bruno di Rocca '97	🍷🍷	8
● Anfiteatro '98	🍷🍷	8
● Bruno di Rocca '98	🍷🍷	8
● Bruno di Rocca '99	🍷🍷	8

● San Martino '00	🍷🍷🍷	8
● Cortaccio '00	🍷🍷	8
● Chianti Cl. Ris. '00	🍷🍷	6
● Chianti Cl. '01	🍷	4
● Cortaccio '93	🍷🍷🍷	6
● Cortaccio '97	🍷🍷🍷	6
● San Martino '97	🍷🍷🍷	5
● San Martino '98	🍷🍷🍷	6
● San Martino '99	🍷🍷🍷	7
● San Martino '96	🍷🍷	5
● San Martino '93	🍷🍷	5
● San Martino '94	🍷🍷	5
● San Martino '95	🍷🍷	5
● Cortaccio '98	🍷🍷	6
● Cortaccio '99	🍷🍷	7

PECCIOLI (PI)

TENUTA DI GHIZZANO
FRAZ. GHIZZANO
VIA DELLA CHIESA, 13
56030 PECCIOLI (PI)
TEL. 0587630096
E-MAIL: info@tenutadighizzano.com

It sometimes happens that a wine is a distinct expression of its terroir, or its grape. On other occasions, it may be particularly closely linked to its producer. When you taste a wine like that while talking to the person who conceived and made it, you feel that the invisible cord binding wine and winemaker has magically become perceptible. This is the case with Nambrot. Made from merlot, cabernet sauvignon and a small percentage of local grapes, the '01 version is the most successful yet, earning Three Glasses for the second year running. It doesn't flaunt muscles or overwhelming concentration. Instead, it's a wine of extraordinary elegance, offering a heady spectrum of aromatics that features delightful ripe fruit embellished with hints of freshly roasted coffee, and then a smooth, mouthfilling palate where tannins and acidity are in perfect balance. This enthralling wine offers its riches with beguiling shyness to anyone who is willing to pay attention. Ginevra Venerosi Pesciolini, with advice from oenologist Carlo Ferrini, seems to have achieved her goal. She has created an elegant, harmonious jewel of a wine. Meanwhile, the Veneroso '01 was not presented at our tastings this year. We heartily approve of the decision to let the wine age for another year in bottle, giving it the time it needs to absorb the contribution of the oak. We await it impatiently, confident that it will be another splendid success.

PIOMBINO (LI)

PODERE SAN LUIGI
VIA DELL'ARSENALE, 16
57025 PIOMBINO (LI)
TEL. 0565220578 - 056530380

It might come as a surprise to see the panel awarding Three Glasses to Podere San Luigi since this estate has been bottling its wines for only a few years. Yet the perseverance and passionate dedication shown by Annamaria Toni and Elio Tolomei fully deserve the distinction. They have both always believed in the great potential of this area, and of the possibility, backed by their experience in the vineyards, of producing a characterful red wine here. Armed with expert advice from Alberto Antonini on matters oenological, and with input from Federico Curtaz on the viticultural side, they have been working very hard, especially in the vineyards, to produce this magnificent champion, Fidenzio '00. A classic Bordeaux blend of cabernet sauvignon, cabernet franc and merlot, it struck our tasters as one of the most interesting new wines in this area. The intense, luminous colour is firm right to the rim, introducing a deep, complex bouquet of perfectly ripe fruit that reflects the vineyard's superb location. The entry on the palate is enormous, the sweetness and power revealing an elegant tight-knit tannic weave then a very long, velvety, harmonious and spicy finish. "Superlative" is the only word for this wine.

● Nambrot '01	𝟁𝟁𝟁	8
● Nambrot '00	𝟁𝟁𝟁	8
● Veneroso '85	𝟁𝟁	5
● Veneroso '86	𝟁𝟁	5
● Veneroso '88	𝟁𝟁	5
● Veneroso '90	𝟁𝟁	7
● Nambrot '97	𝟁𝟁	8
● Nambrot '98	𝟁𝟁	8
● Veneroso '98	𝟁𝟁	7
● Nambrot '99	𝟁𝟁	8
● Veneroso '99	𝟁𝟁	7
● Veneroso '00	𝟁𝟁	7

● Fidenzio '00	𝟁𝟁𝟁	7
● Fidenzio '98	𝟁𝟁	5
● Fidenzio '99	𝟁𝟁	6
○ La Goccia '00	𝟁	2*

PITIGLIANO (GR)

TENUTA ROCCACCIA
LOC. ROCCACCIA
VIA POGGIO CAVALLUCCIO
58017 PITIGLIANO (GR)
TEL. 0564617020
E-MAIL: roccaccia@tiscalinet.it

Tenuta Roccaccia's 90 hectares, of which 30 are under vine, show the great potential of the Sovana DOC zone. The estate is run by the owners, the Goracci siblings, with assistance from consultant oenologist, Alberto Antonini. The cellar presented an assortment of good wines at our tastings, and the Fontenova '01, a blend of sangiovese and ciliegiolo in equal parts, did particularly well. The dark, nearly opaque, colour introduces balsamic notes and scents of black berry fruit on the nose, then a fleshy, elegant palate with soft, smooth tannins. The Poggio Cavalluccio '01, obtained from 100 per cent ciliegiolo, is just as good. Its broad nose reveals balsamic notes and hints of cinnamon. There's plenty of substance in the mouth, but the long finish shows a faint touch of bitterness. The sangiovese, alicante and ciliegiolo Sovana '02 offers a ripe fruit nose and then delicious drinkability, backed up by somewhat assertive but well-calibrated tannins. The Aleatico Riserva '99 has character and drinks beautifully. It's a well-executed "passito" wine from part-dried grapes that is more successful on the nose, which has well-defined plum jam, than in the mouth, where it is dense but bitterish on the finish. The Chardonnay '01 was the best of the whites, thanks to an intense fruit nose, and a fresh, enjoyable palate with great balance. The Bianco di Pitigliano '02 is a simple wine, with grassy notes on both nose and palate.

POGGIBONSI (SI)

GRANDUCATO
VIA BORGACCIO, 19
53036 POGGIBONSI (SI)
TEL. 0577936057
E-MAIL: granducato@capsi.it

After last year's debut in the Other Wineries section, Granducato has earned a profile of its own. The name is the label on wines released by the Consorzio Agrario di Siena, a major co-operative established over a century ago, which has more than 3,700 members and Luciano Bandini as consultant oenologist. All the wines presented at our tastings were remarkably good. We'll start with the Chianti Colli Senesi '02, which offers a nose of inviting spicy notes against an eloquent fruit backdrop. The palate is taut and vibrant, with depth of flavour, well-distributed, unobtrusive tannins and a lovely relaxed finish. The good Morellino di Scansano Gretaio '01 shows an intense colour and slightly over-ripe aromas of stewed plums and blackberry jam. The soft, concentrated palate shows nicely balanced and integrated tannins that take you through to an enjoyable, if not particularly long, finish. The Chianti Classico Riserva '00 has an attractively vivid ruby hue. Initially closed on the nose, it soon releases uncomplicated, but very clean, fruit. The sound, no-nonsense palate is well-executed and full-bodied, with attractive, tight-knit tannins and a leisurely finish. The straightforward, traditional-style Vernaccia di San Gimignano '02 offers classic aromas of apples and spring flowers before the fairly austere palate reveals considerable acid bite and a medium-length finish.

● Fontenova '01	🍷🍷	5
○ Chardonnay '01	🍷🍷	3*
● Poggio Cavalluccio '01	🍷🍷	6
● Sovana Rosso Aleatico Ris. '99	🍷	6
○ Bianco di Pitigliano '02	🍷	2*
● Sovana Rosso La Roccaccia '02	🍷	3*
● Fontenova '98	🍷🍷	4
● Sovana Rosso La Roccaccia '99	🍷🍷	3
● Sovana Rosso La Roccaccia '00	🍷🍷	3*
● Fontenova '99	🍷🍷	6
● Poggio Cavalluccio '00	🍷🍷	6
● Fontenova '00	🍷🍷	5
● Sovana Rosso La Roccaccia '01	🍷🍷	3

● Chianti Cl. Ris. '00	🍷🍷	4*
● Chianti Colli Senesi '02	🍷🍷	3*
● Morellino di Scansano Gretaio '01	🍷	3
○ Vernaccia di S. Gimignano '02	🍷	3
● Morellino di Scansano Gretaio '00	🍷	3
● Seragio '00	🍷	4
○ Vernaccia di S. Gimignano '01	🍷	3

POGGIBONSI (SI)

POGGIO A CAIANO (PO)

MELINI
LOC. GAGGIANO
53036 POGGIBONSI (SI)
TEL. 0577998511
E-MAIL: giv@giv.it

PIAGGIA
VIA CEGOLI, 47
59016 POGGIO A CAIANO (PO)
TEL. 0558705401
E-MAIL: aziendapiaggia@virgilio.it

We were very much looking forward to tasting the Chianti Classico La Selvanella Riserva '00, but it turned out to be "the wine that never was". It hadn't gone into bottle when we arrived to taste, so we were forced to postpone the pleasure until next year. This is a pity because La Selvanella is one of the standard-bearers of the authentic Chianti tradition. The cellar uses only sangiovese grapes and large barrels, and the vineyards, tended like gardens, cover just under 50 hectares on the crest of a little hill near Lucarelli, in the municipality of Radda but only two kilometres from Panzano. We have resigned ourselves to wait and will be back next year. The way the '98 and '99 editions are developing suggests that we may have underestimated this wine, so we look forward to making amends with the '00, a vintage that was particularly favourable to high-lying vineyards like La Selvanella. On this year's visit, we consoled ourselves with the '01 Bonorli, which is as good as it usually is, and as the growing year allows it to be. This hefty, muscular Merlot is somewhat in the Australian style, but it's not bad at all. The Vernaccia di San Gimignano Le Grillaie '02, suffering the effects of a poor year, is not quite its normal vivacious self.

Mauro Vannucci, a textile manufacturer with a passion for the land and for making wine, and his daughter, Silvia, own Piaggia, a winery that has earned them their fourth consecutive Three Glass award. After a hat trick of excellent Carmignano Riservas, the '97, '98 and '99, it was the turn of the Il Sasso '01 to step up to the podium. It's a great red wine made from 70 per cent sangiovese, 20 per cent cabernet, and merlot that immediately tells you it's serious with a dark, inky ruby that is tinged with purple at the rim. At first, it shows slightly reduced on the nose because of its great concentration, but then it opens gradually and elegantly onto intense, very ripe notes of berry fruit with delicate spicy nuances and a graceful vegetal hint. The palate is simply overwhelming. Extreme concentration and elegance combine in an explosion of fruit and perfectly amalgamated, chewy tannins and extraordinary length. Wonderfully stylish notes of chocolate and tobacco accompany the finish. The Riserva '00 is up there with it. A bouquet of blackberries, and cherry and blueberry jam with subtle balsamic notes and hints of vanilla introduces the muscular – again – palate. The sheer power overwhelms you with gobs of fruit and aromatic herbs, adding just the merest suggestion of bitterness on the finish. Two bottles, and two great wines, testify to the Vannuccis' diligent dedication, as well as to the expertise of their consultants, oenologist Alberto Antonini and the agronomist, Federico Curtaz. Congratulations!

●	Bonorli '01	7	
○	Vernaccia di S. Gimignano		
	Le Grillaie '02	5	
●	Chianti Cl. La Selvanella Ris. '86	6	
●	Chianti Cl. La Selvanella Ris. '90	5	
●	Chianti Cl. La Selvanella Ris. '93	6	
●	Chianti Cl. La Selvanella Ris. '95	6	
●	Chianti Cl. La Selvanella Ris. '96	6	
●	Chianti Cl. La Selvanella Ris. '97	6	
●	Chianti Cl. La Selvanella Ris. '98	6	
●	Bonorli '99	5	
●	Chianti Cl. La Selvanella Ris. '99	6	
●	Bonorli '00	5	

●	Il Sasso '01	5	
●	Carmignano Ris. '00	6	
●	Carmignano Ris. '97	5	
●	Carmignano Ris. '98	6	
●	Carmignano Ris. '99	6	
●	Carmignano Ris. '94	4	
●	Carmignano Ris. '95	4	
●	Carmignano Ris. '96	4	
●	Il Sasso '99	5	
●	Il Sasso '00	5*	

PONTASSIEVE (FI)

★ Tenimenti Ruffino
via Aretina, 42/44
50065 Pontassieve (FI)
TEL. 05583605
E-MAIL: info@ruffino.it

We've gone back in time, at least as far as the Riserva Ducale Oro is concerned. After more than a decade, it has won Three Glasses again, upstaging the other estate gem, Romitorio di Santedame. This is a particularly striking success, given the vast number of bottles of the Riserva released. It would seem that the Folinaris, busy though they are expanding their property, still devote considerable attention to what could be considered the family jewels. But let's get on to the wines. The chardonnay-based Solatia '01 is dominated by oak. On the nose, toasty and honeyed tones are evident, the mouth is dense, savoury, very fleshy and moderately long. The Chianti Classico Santedame '01 displays eloquent fruit with cherries to the fore. The palate unfurls compelling progression and the very tidy tannins provide support without harshness. The less interesting Modus '01, made from sangiovese, cabernet and merlot, is creamy and excessively concentrated, but hasn't got much personality. The Romitorio di Santedame '01, a blend of colorino, sangiovese and merlot, made it into our final taste-offs. The nose, which reveals notes of liquorice, vegetal tones and over-ripe fruit, is somewhat restrained. The dense, very concentrated palate shows somewhat rigid tannins that have trouble expanding. The Riserva Ducale Oro '00 shows a thrillingly powerful fruit nose, on which wild berry notes blend perfectly with nuances of cinnamon and cloves. The dense, creamy mouthfeel of the excellent palate boasts fine-grained, well-gauged tannins and a pervasive rising finish.

PONTASSIEVE (FI)

Fattoria Selvapiana
loc. Selvapiana, 43
50065 Pontassieve (FI)
TEL. 0558369848
E-MAIL: selvapiana@tin.it

We have spoken about important signs of innovation here at the Giuntini family estate, and now at last we can report that tangible results are coming through. A Selvapiana wine was invited to our finals, which is of course a good thing. But more important, the entire range shows solid improvement, thanks to the recently completed vineyard replanting programme. But let's take a look at the finalist, La Fornace '00, a blend of cabernet, merlot and a small amount of sangiovese. The lively ruby introduces a fruit-forward nose of well-defined blackcurrants and raspberries, lifted by an enjoyable touch of vanilla. The soft, mouthfilling palate offers beautifully integrated, well-paced tannins and a sweet, persistent finish. The intense ruby-hued Riserva Bucerchiale '00 presents varietal fruit aromas of cherries and plums, enlivened by spicy notes of cinnamon, in particular. The full-bodied palate is nicely underpinned by perceptible, but tasty, tannins, leading to a rising, succulent finish. The Chianti Rufina '01 offers a fresh, attractive nose of blueberries and cherries laced with faint mint and balsam. Pleasantly bright and intriguing in the mouth, it drinks easily and tastily. The Vin Santo '97 has a lovely amber colour and a strikingly complex nose in which tropical fruit mingles with notes of tamarind and hazelnut. The excellent palate is rich, dense and velvety, and the finish is sweet and engaging.

● Chianti Cl. Ris. Ducale Oro '00	♛♛♛	5
● Romitorio di Santedame '01	♛♛	7
● Chianti Cl. Santedame '01	♛	5
● Modus '01	♛	7
○ Solatia '01	♛	5
● Chianti Cl. Ris. Ducale Oro '90	♛♛♛	5
● Romitorio di Santedame '98	♛♛♛	6
● Romitorio di Santedame '99	♛♛♛	7
● Romitorio di Santedame '00	♛♛♛	7
● Chianti Cl. Ris. Ducale Oro '99	♛♛	5

● La Fornace '00	♛♛	5
● Chianti Rufina		
Bucerchiale Ris. '00	♛♛	5
○ Vin Santo della Rufina '97	♛♛	5
● Chianti Rufina '01	♛	4
● Chianti Rufina		
Bucerchiale Ris. '95	♛♛	5
● Chianti Rufina Fornace Ris. '98	♛♛	5
● Chianti Rufina		
Bucerchiale Ris. '99	♛♛	5
● La Fornace '99	♛♛	5

RADDA IN CHIANTI (SI)

RADDA IN CHIANTI (SI)

CASTELLO D' ALBOLA
LOC. PIAN D'ALBOLA, 31
53017 RADDA IN CHIANTI (SI)
TEL. 0577738019
E-MAIL: info@albola.it

BORGO SALCETINO
LOC. LUCARELLI
53017 RADDA IN CHIANTI (SI)
TEL. 0577733541 - 0432757173
E-MAIL: info@livon.it

This year saw a fairly subdued performance from the Zonin family's Castello d'Albola estate. The flagship wine, Acciaiolo, was absent from our tastings, and the range was, on the whole, disappointing, especially after last year's signs of improvement. This is, we have no doubt, only a momentary lapse. The reasonably convincing Le Fagge Chardonnay '01 is pale gold, and offers sweet scents of tropical fruit and honey. It's initially inviting in the mouth, and full-bodied at mid palate, but runs out of steam on the rushed finish. The simple, savoury Chianti Classico '01 has a pale ruby hue and a fresh floral bouquet of violets with brandied cherries, while the palate is lightweight but tasty, with plenty of acid bite favouring easy drinking. The good Chianti Classico Le Ellere '01 is distinctly redolent of wild berry fruit, particularly wild strawberries, which are nuanced with spicy tones. In the mouth, it has good co-ordination, decent density, and tannins that are spiky, but pleasant and well integrated. The finish is medium long. The Riserva '00 offers a fresh, youthfully alcoholic nose of aromatic herbs and forest floor with faint hints of berries. Acidity is in the foreground on the edgy palate, where the tannins are evident but not intrusive. The finish is good but short. The fair Vin Santo '94 offers a nose of autumn leaves and a not very smooth, but clean and full-bodied palate.

This estate, owned by the Livon family, has confirmed the progress shown last year, demonstrating that the Livons understand the potential of this area. After an initial phase dedicated to a high-density replanting of the vineyard holdings, and to the re-organization of the cellar, results have come quickly. The Chianti Classico '01 made an excellent impression, indeed it swept into our final round of tastings. The vivid purple hue immediately reveals its modern style. The nose offers a swathe of aromas ranging from minty notes to red-fleshed fruit, particularly plums. The powerful, invitingly warm palate has balanced acidity, integrated tannins and a definitely rising finish. The Lucarello Riserva '00 is less of a success. The nose is dominated at first by murky odours of fur and leather, as well as vegetal notes, whereas in the mouth it shows considerable power. It's an austere wine, with a slightly flabby body and prominent tannins that dry the mouth on the finish. The Rossole '01, a blend of sangiovese and merlot, did well without really shining. Notes of coffee and chocolate on the nose intermingle with ripe cherry fruit. The palate is dense and fairly concentrated, revealing broad progression, well-distributed tannins and a harmonious finish with a pleasantly lingering note of pepper.

● Chianti Cl. Ris. '00	🍷🍷	5
● Chianti Cl. '01	🍷	4
● Chianti Cl. Le Ellere '01	🍷	5
○ Le Fagge Chardonnay '01	🍷	5
○ Vin Santo '94	🍷	5
● Acciaiolo '95	🍷🍷🍷	6
● Chianti Cl. Ris. '97	🍷🍷	5
● Acciaiolo '98	🍷🍷	6
○ Le Fagge Chardonnay '99	🍷🍷	4
○ Le Fagge Chardonnay '00	🍷🍷	5
● Chianti Cl. Le Ellere '00	🍷🍷	4*
● Le Marangole '00	🍷🍷	6
● Acciaiolo '99	🍷🍷	7
● Chianti Cl. Ris. '99	🍷🍷	5

● Chianti Cl. '01	🍷🍷	4
● Rossole '01	🍷🍷	5
● Chianti Cl. Lucarello Ris. '00	🍷	5
● Chianti Cl. Lucarello Ris. '96	🍷🍷	5
● Chianti Cl. '97	🍷🍷	4
● Chianti Cl. Lucarello Ris. '97	🍷🍷	5
● Chianti Cl. '98	🍷🍷	4
● Rossole '98	🍷🍷	5
● Rossole '99	🍷🍷	5
● Rossole '00	🍷🍷	5
● Chianti Cl. Lucarello Ris. '99	🍷🍷	5
● Chianti Cl. '00	🍷🍷	4

RADDA IN CHIANTI (SI)

CAPARSA
LOC. CAPARSINO, 48
53017 RADDA IN CHIANTI (SI)
TEL. 0577738174 - 0577738639
E-MAIL: caparsa@ecoitaly.net

This year's tastings show quite clearly that the management has been making the right decisions in vineyard and cellar at Caparsa. In last year's profile, we expressed the hope that the Cianferoni family's estate would produce more consistent results, thereby consolidating its position. No sooner said than done. In their second year in the Guide, the Cianferonis have won Three Glasses, which also acknowledges the distance they have come since 1965, when the estate was acquired by Reginaldo Cianferoni, a great respecter of tradition who has stamped his personality on the winemaking philosophy. The 12 hectares under vine are planted to all the classic Chianti grapes, including malvasia and trebbiano from which, vintage permitting, they produce their Vin Santo sometimes with a proportion of canaiolo, a red variety. The Chianti Classico Caparsino '00 presents a lovely ruby hue. The nose offers a wide array of well-defined, clean aromas with strawberries and raspberries to the fore, enriched by hints of cloves. In the mouth, it is silky and soft, with well-paced tannins and a long, warm, engrossing finish. The Riserva Doccio a Matteo '00, the cellar's Three Glass winner, boasts an astonishingly broad and complex nose on which spicy notes of black pepper mingle with sweet scents of vanilla and ripe cherries. The excellent palate is soft and smooth on entry, the progression is seamless and even, and a delightful note of red berry fruit accompanies the long finish.

RADDA IN CHIANTI (SI)

LA BRANCAIA
LOC. POPPI, 42
53017 RADDA IN CHIANTI (SI)
TEL. 0577742007
E-MAIL: brancaia@brancaia.it

After all the innovations noted in last year's profile, we have no news to report except that work continues to be carried out with the customary care and attention. The results of our tastings are, curiously enough, exactly the same as last year's. For the sixth time, La Brancaia took home Three Glasses, emphasizing the consistency of quality that informs all the wines produced. The champion, Brancaia Il Blu, is a blend of merlot and sangiovese. Impenetrably dense to the eye, it shows a lively ruby, then subtly graceful and elegant aromas of blackcurrants and blueberries blend beautifully with pleasing oak-derived toastiness on the nose. After a subtle entry, the palate reveals softness and balance, and a tannic structure in harmonious counterpoint with the well-judged alcohol. The superb finish has just the right degree of succulence. The Chianti Classico '01 offers stylish fruit aromas underpinned by notes of mint. In the mouth, it is substantial and velvet-smooth, and the discreet tannins open out to a lingering finish. The Brancaia Tre '01 presents gamey aromas of animal skins alternating with notes of leather, with ripe plums leading the way. The good palate offers even progression, a smooth tannic weave, and a not very expansive finish.

● Chianti Cl.		
Doccio a Matteo Ris. '00	♚♚♚	6
● Chianti Cl. Caparsino '00	♚♚	5
● Chianti Cl.		
Doccio a Matteo Ris. '99	♚♚	7
○ Vin Santo '95	♚	7
● Chianti Cl. Caparsino '99	♚	6

● Brancaia Il Blu '01	♚♚♚	7
● Chianti Cl. Brancaia '01	♚♚	6
● Brancaia Tre '01	♚♚	5
● Brancaia '94	♚♚♚	6
● Brancaia '97	♚♚♚	6
● Brancaia '98	♚♚♚	6
● Brancaia '99	♚♚♚	6
● Brancaia Il Blu '00	♚♚♚	7
● Brancaia '95	♚♚	6
● Brancaia '96	♚♚	6
● Chianti Cl. Brancaia '00	♚♚	5*
● Chianti Cl. '99	♚♚	5
● Brancaia Tre '00	♚♚	5*

RADDA IN CHIANTI (SI)

RADDA IN CHIANTI (SI)

LIVERNANO
LOC. LIVERNANO
53017 RADDA IN CHIANTI (SI)
TEL. 0577738353
E-MAIL: info@livernano.it

MONTEVERTINE
LOC. MONTEVERTINE
53017 RADDA IN CHIANTI (SI)
TEL. 0577738009
E-MAIL: info@montevertine.it

Many wineries would be very happy with the results of this year's Livernano tastings: all the wines got Two Glasses. But it is also the case that Marco Montanari has accustomed us to even better things, which we suspect will return in the near future. The lovely golden Anima '01, made from chardonnay, sauvignon and traminer, is at first a little difficult to decipher on the nose. Then delicate notes of pine resin blend with floral fragrances redolent of jasmine, as well as fruit aromas. The palate is somewhat austere, decently meaty, deep and smooth, with a finish of admirable finesse. The Puro Sangue '01, from 100 per cent sangiovese, shows a vibrant ruby. On the nose, the fruit is initially masked by elegant vegetal nuances, supported by hints of tobacco and leather. The smooth, juicy palate reveals well-integrated tannins, admirable balance of alcohol and acidity, and a not very long but nonetheless pleasing finish. In conclusion, the intensely ruby-hued Livernano '01, a blend of merlot, cabernet and sangiovese, offers a lively bouquet of intriguing pepper, elegant, sound vegetal tones, and good, crisply defined fruit. In the mouth, it is sinewy, firm and free of rough edges, thanks to the excellent extract. The finish is enjoyably juicy.

We are, of course, pleased to be able to report the good impression made again at our tastings by the wines from this historic estate, which is managed with great enthusiasm by Martino Manetti. It is their standard-bearer that interested us particularly, because it so authentically expresses its terroir through the sangiovese grape, without compromise or the addition of other varieties. There's news to report. The cellar has begun production of a Vin Santo that we will be able to taste in a few years. For the whites, this year was the turn of the '99 version of the M. It shows a bright straw yellow, then a nose of Peruvian bark, pine resin and stewed fruit. In the mouth, it is a tad slender, but the acidity is powerful and the finish is savoury and succulent. The Montevertine '00 is rather pale, but the nose offers a surprisingly subtle bouquet of minerals alternating with notes of leather, tobacco, and sweet fruit. The palate is light and soft, with very fine-grained tannins and a finish of no great depth. The Pergole Torte '00 again shows the sound traditional style of this estate, founded on a dedication to monovarietal sangiovese wines. Evolved aromas on the nose are joined by ripe fruit notes of cherries, deliciously laced with hints of pencil lead. The palate is austere and taut, flowing nicely but showing substance and alcohol, with good extract. The succulent finish is absolutely convincing.

○ Anima '01		♀♀	7
● Livernano '01		♀♀	7
● Puro Sangue '01		♀♀	7
● Livernano '97		♀♀♀	8
● Livernano '98		♀♀♀	8
● Livernano '99		♀♀♀	8
● Nardina '95		♀♀	5
● Puro Sangue '95		♀♀	6
● Livernano '96		♀♀	6
● Puro Sangue '97		♀♀	6
○ Anima '98		♀♀	5
● Puro Sangue '98		♀♀	6
● Puro Sangue '99		♀♀	7
● Livernano '00		♀♀	8
● Puro Sangue '00		♀♀	7

● Le Pergole Torte '00		♀♀	8
● Montevertine '00		♀	6
○ M '99		♀	5
● Le Pergole Torte '83		♀♀♀	8
● Montevertine Ris. '85		♀♀♀	5
● Le Pergole Torte '86		♀♀♀	8
● Le Pergole Torte '88		♀♀♀	8
● Le Pergole Torte '90		♀♀♀	8
● Le Pergole Torte '92		♀♀♀	8
● Montevertine Ris. '97		♀♀	5
● Montevertine Ris. '98		♀♀	6
● Le Pergole Torte '99		♀♀	8

RADDA IN CHIANTI (SI)

POGGERINO
LOC. POGGERINO
53017 RADDA IN CHIANTI (SI)
TEL. 0577738958
E-MAIL: info@poggerino.com

Two of Piero Lanza Ginori's wines made it into our finals, and one of the two, Primamateria '01, won Three Glasses, sure indications that Piero is on the right track. Signs of progress are to be found in the aromas of these wines, which are much cleaner and better defined, while the palates are livelier and better put together than in the past. The Chianti Classico '01 did well. It shows a lively ruby and a vanload of complex aromas, in which ripe woodland berries are joined by intriguing spice, with cinnamon, cloves and pepper holding centre stage. The attractive, tasty palate has weight and substance, thanks to fine-grained, evenly distributed tannins, then the finish is long and complex. The Bugialla Riserva '00 has a good ruby colour with purple highlights. Its nose is shy at first, but then opens to reveal aromas of fruits and flowers that make room for spicy hints of cinnamon. The palate is impressive. After a subdued attack, it expands emphatically, revealing excellent balance and a forceful rising finish. The lustrous purplish Primamateria '01, from sangiovese and merlot, offers a handsome nose founded on wild berry fruit and lifted by subtle yet distinct spicy notes of cloves. The deep, eloquent palate is initially austere and compact, but unfolds into a long, pleasing finish.

RADDA IN CHIANTI (SI)

FATTORIA DI TERRABIANCA
LOC. SAN FEDELE A PATERNO
53017 RADDA IN CHIANTI (SI)
TEL. 0577738544
E-MAIL: info@terrabianca.com

This year, there is more good news from Roberto Guldener's winery. His Campaccio '00 came very close indeed to winning Three Glasses. In fact, all his wines did well, if not quite so brilliantly as last year, since the vintages in question took their toll. What has not changed is this winemaker's commitment to excellence, both in the vineyards and in the cellar. The Croce Riserva '00 has a lovely ruby colour, but is not very seductive on the nose, which is fruity and jammy but a bit simple. After a measured attack, the pleasing palate offers reasonable concentration, well-behaved tannins, and a clear acid bite on the finish. The Piano del Cipresso '00 has invitingly fresh scents of menthol, balsam and plums. It is soft and well-balanced in the mouth, though it fades away a bit quickly. Obtained from cabernet sauvignon and merlot, Ceppaie '00 is somewhat disappointing, mostly because the nose is not altogether clean, the sweetish notes clouding the raspberry tones. The palate is enjoyable, but a bit unsettled and short. The 2000 Campaccio, mostly sangiovese, is excellent. The aromas offer a lovely mixture of oak and chocolate notes mingling with a delightful assortment of ripe woodland berries. The palate expands impressively, delivering velvety sensations that reveal the presence of supple, well-integrated tannins, and then closes on a pleasant, lightly acidulous note.

Primamateria '01	🍷🍷🍷	6
Chianti Cl. '01	🍷🍷	4
Chianti Cl. Bugialla Ris. '00	🍷🍷	6
Chianti Cl. Ris. '90	🍷🍷🍷	5
Chianti Cl. Bugialla Ris. '94	🍷🍷	5
Chianti Cl. Bugialla Ris. '95	🍷🍷	5
Chianti Cl. Bugialla Ris. '96	🍷🍷	5
Chianti Cl. Bugialla Ris. '97	🍷🍷	5
Primamateria '98	🍷🍷	5
Primamateria '99	🍷🍷	5
Primamateria '00	🍷🍷	6
Chianti Cl. Bugialla Ris. '99	🍷🍷	6

Campaccio '00	🍷🍷	5
Piano del Cipresso '00	🍷🍷	5
Ceppate '00	🍷	7
Chianti Cl. Vigna della Croce Ris. '00	🍷	5
Campaccio '95	🍷🍷	5
Chianti Cl. Vigna della Croce Ris. '95	🍷🍷	4
Piano del Cipresso '97	🍷🍷	5
Ceppate '98	🍷🍷	6
Ceppate '99	🍷🍷	7
Campaccio '99	🍷🍷	5
Chianti Cl. Vigna della Croce Ris. '99	🍷🍷	5
Piano del Cipresso '99	🍷🍷	5

RADDA IN CHIANTI (SI)

VIGNAVECCHIA
SDRUCCIOLO DI PIAZZA, 7
53017 RADDA IN CHIANTI (SI)
TEL. 0577738090 - 0577738326
E-MAIL: vignavecchia@vignavecchia.com

Without much fuss, but with astonishing regularity, the Beccari family's estate produces positive results that earn it a place in the Guide. There are about 20 hectares under vine, with south and southwest-facing aspects, very near Radda in Chianti where the winery is located. Federico Staderini is consultant oenologist, and vine management is in the hands of Franco Beccari, the owner. Franco is the grandson of Odoardo Beccari, the gentleman pictured on the labels, who established the winery in 1876 after touring the world as a zoologist and botanist. Now let's turn to the wines. The Riserva '00 is not very exciting, and barely earned its One Glass. The aromas are pleasant, but the acidity-dominated palate is lightweight. The Raddese '00 is much better. A monovarietal sangiovese, it shows an opaque ruby, then a nose of ripe, succulent, plum and cherry fruit, enhanced by spicy hints of cinnamon and cloves. The palate reveals good texture and well-judged, solid structure, with acidity and tannins in perfect balance. The slightly astringent finish is nonetheless inviting and successful. The Canvalle '99 is also very good. Made from cabernet sauvignon, it boasts a graceful, delicate fragrance that foregrounds wild berries, with elegant hints of vanilla and pepper. In the mouth, it immediately shows its strength, which is modulated and enhanced by a soft roundness and a captivating long finish.

RADDA IN CHIANTI (SI)

CASTELLO DI VOLPAIA
LOC. VOLPAIA
P.ZZA DELLA CISTERNA, 1
53017 RADDA IN CHIANTI (SI)
TEL. 0577738066
E-MAIL: info@volpaia.com

At last, this historic Chianti winery has a Three Glass winner. The success crowns the work mapped out last year by Giovannella Stianti and her husband Carlo Mascheroni, which involved, among other things, the arrival as consultant oenologist of Riccardo Cotarella. Across the range improvement also produced a high note in the Balifico '00. The very fine Chianti Classico '01 displays an impressive nose with a variety of berries well supported by elegant spicy notes. The impact on the palate is remarkable, thanks to the density and well-calibrated acidity that makes it enjoyably moreish. The 2000 Riserva is also excellent. After some initial hesitation, the nose unveils appetizing hints of green peppers together with ripe fruit, then the intriguingly seductive palate flaunts nicely integrated tannins and a good long finish. The Coltassala Riserva made it to the finals, thanks to a complex nose of blackberry jam and elegant spices. The palate is smooth from the start, showing well-incorporated tannins, balanced acidity and a convincing finish. The Balifico '00, a blend of sangiovese and cabernet sauvignon, was a magnificent Three Glass winner. The wide range of aromas is dominated at first by coffee and liquorice, but then makes way for delightful wild berries. The graceful, elegant palate opens out evenly, revealing character and balance, then a long and extremely satisfying finish. The decent Vin Santo '95 is a little closed on the nose and creamy, if a bit short, in the mouth.

●	Raddese '00	𝟮𝟮	6
●	Canvalle '99	𝟮𝟮	6
●	Chianti Cl. Ris. '00	𝟮	5
●	Canvalle '93	𝟮𝟮	5
●	Canvalle '96	𝟮𝟮	5
●	Chianti Cl. Ris. '96	𝟮𝟮	4
●	Chianti Cl. Ris. '97	𝟮𝟮	4
●	Chianti Cl. Ris. '99	𝟮𝟮	5
●	Raddese '99	𝟮𝟮	6

●	Balifico '00	𝟯𝟯𝟯	7
●	Chianti Cl. Coltassala Ris. '00	𝟮𝟮	7
●	Chianti Cl. Ris. '00	𝟮𝟮	6
●	Chianti Cl. '01	𝟮𝟮	5
○	Vin Santo del Chianti Cl. '95	𝟮	6
○	Val d'Arbia '02		4
●	Chianti Cl. Ris. '95	𝟮𝟮	5
●	Coltassala '95	𝟮𝟮	6
●	Chianti Cl. '97	𝟮𝟮	4
●	Chianti Cl. Ris. '97	𝟮𝟮	5
●	Coltassala '97	𝟮𝟮	6
●	Chianti Cl. '99	𝟮𝟮	4*
○	Vin Santo del Chianti Cl. '93	𝟮𝟮	6
●	Chianti Cl. Coltassala Ris. '99	𝟮𝟮	6
●	Chianti Cl. Ris. '99	𝟮𝟮	5

RAPOLANO TERME (SI)

RUFINA (FI)

CASTELLO DI MODANELLA
LOC. VILLAGGIO DI MODANELLA
53040 RAPOLANO TERME (SI)
TEL. 0577704604
E-MAIL: info@modanella.com

FATTORIA DI BASCIANO
V.LE DUCA DELLA VITTORIA, 159
50068 RUFINA (FI)
TEL. 0558397034
E-MAIL: masirenzo@virgilio.it

The 22 hectares under vine at Castello di Modanella are divided into separate vineyards for each wine type. The Vignacce vineyard is planted to the cabernet sauvignon that goes into Le Voliere; the Centro vineyard furnishes the organically grown sangiovese that becomes the Campo d'Aia; merlot grapes from Osteria go into Poggio Montino; and the Scuola vineyard is where the canaiolo grapes for Poggio L'Aiole are cultivated. With the help of the oenologist Fabrizio Ciufoli, the cellar produces some 28,000 bottles a year, and the ones we tasted made a good impression. The Cabernet Sauvignon Le Voliere '00, aged in barriques for 18 months, turned out to be the best of the lot, a clear indication that this variety is particularly well suited to the local soil. The nose releases clean notes of blackberries and blackcurrants, then the mouthfilling palate offers good progression, underpinned by tight-packed, and mellow tannins. Campo d'Aia '00 is also good. Made entirely of sangiovese, and aged for a year in barriques, it shows a fruity nose, then lots of alcohol and somewhat rough tannins in the mouth. The acceptable Poggio Montino '00, from 100 per cent merlot, is somewhat vegetal on the nose and tidy on the mouth, although the finish is astringent. The less successful Poggio l'Aiolo '01 is a monovarietal canaiolo that sees no wood. The nose is too vegetal and the palate is unbalanced.

It seems almost superfluous to submit the Masi family's wines to our tasting panels. Year after year, the same excellent quality levels are maintained with impressive regularity. They cannot be said to be a model of typicity, but they show an able hand has been at work with the grapes. We'll start with the Chianti Rufina '01, which shows an intense ruby and very concentrated, distinct fruit aromas. In the mouth, it is round, nicely tannic and long. The Riserva '00 displays a dark, dense colour, followed by a nose of wild berries and toasted coffee beans, as well as light grassy hints. The palate shows a seductive entry, well supported by oak, then offers an excellent mid palate and a delightfully savoury succulence on the finish. The Corto '01, obtained mostly from sangiovese, has sweet aromas of fresh cream and redcurrant and raspberry jam, enhanced by spicy notes, with cinnamon to the fore. The attack on the palate is gentle and concentrated, with perfectly judged acidity, and the long finish is quite delightful. I Pini '01, a blend of sangiovese and cabernet sauvignon, reveals a complex fruit nose of plums and blackcurrants, with the occasional sweet note of spice. The palate is aggressive but very dense, boasting tannins that fuse nicely with the alcohol, and a lingering finish. Made from the same grape varieties as I Pini, Erta e China '01 has an enticing bouquet in which wild berries interweave with spices. The palate is impressive, mouthfilling and satisfyingly long.

●	Le Voliere Cabernet Sauvignon '00	♟♟	6	● Chianti Rufina Ris. '00	♟♟	5
●	Campo d'Aia '00	♟	5	● Chianti Rufina '01	♟♟	3*
●	Poggio Montino '00	♟	5	● Erta e China '01	♟♟	3*
●	Poggio l'Aiole '01		5	● I Pini '01	♟♟	5
●	Campo d'Aia '97	♟♟	5	● Il Corto '01	♟♟	5
●	Le Voliere Cabernet Sauvignon '97	♟♟	5	● Chianti Rufina Ris. '98	♟♟	3*
●	Poggio Montino '97	♟♟	4	● Erta e China '99	♟♟	3*
●	Le Voliere Cabernet Sauvignon '98	♟♟	5	● Il Corto '99	♟♟	4
●				● Chianti Rufina '00	♟♟	3*
●	Le Voliere Cabernet Sauvignon '99	♟♟	5*	● Erta e China '00	♟♟	3*
●	Campo d'Aia '99	♟	5	● I Pini '00	♟♟	4
●	Poggio Montino '99	♟	5	● Il Corto '00	♟♟	5
●				● Chianti Rufina Ris. '99	♟♟	5

SAN CASCIANO IN VAL DI PESA (FI)

CASTELVECCHIO
VIA CERTALDESE, 30
50020 SAN CASCIANO IN VAL DI PESA (FI)
TEL. 0558248032 - 0558248921
E-MAIL: info@castelvecchio.it

FATTORIA CORZANO E PATERNO
FRAZ. SAN PRANCAZIO IN VAL DI PESA
VIA PATERNO, 8
50020 SAN CASCIANO IN VAL DI PESA (FI)
TEL. 0558249114 - 0558248179
E-MAIL: corzpaterno@ftbcc.it

The Rocchi family's winery is constantly busy. The replanting program is still in full swing, and the barrel room now boasts barriques and tonneaux. The next step, we hear, will be to construct a more functional cellar. In the meantime, they have acquired a new consultant oenologist, Luigi D'Attoma, who has already demonstrated that he knows how to put a wine together. What was lacking in the wines of Castelvecchio was the roundness and fullness that they have now acquired. This is particularly noticeable in Brecciolino '01, obtained from cabernet sauvignon, sangiovese, and colorino. It shows a deep intense colour that introduces captivating aromas of ripe fruits, mingled with balsam and well-defined spicy notes. The rich, well-rounded palate shows smooth, succulent tannins and a lingering finish. The very agreeable Riserva '01 has clear, intense aromas with cherries to the fore, but tobacco and leather play supporting roles. The tannins are perhaps a bit prominent, but evenly distributed, and there's a long, rising finish. The admirable Colli Fiorentini '01 offers floral aromas, good fruit and hints of spice on the nose. There's considerable acid bite, but it's balanced, and the finish is long. Bringing up the rear is the simple but well-made Santa Caterina '01, which has scents of red flowers and an intriguing taste of delightful freshness.

The Corzano e Paterno estate lies on 145 hectares of land, 15 of which are under vine, and produces about 65,000 bottles a year. It has long since taught us to expect wines of high quality that are true to type and very characterful and the cellar did quite well again this year, the Passito di Corzano '96 making a great impression. Actually, it very nearly earned Three Glasses. This "passito", made from the classic combination of part-dried trebbiano and malvasia grapes, stayed on the lees for five years in 100-litre oak barrels. The consequent deep, immediate aromas of walnuts blend with a note sweet biscuits, ushering in a palate that is sumptuous, velvet-smooth and sweet. The Corzano '00, a blend of sangiovese, cabernet sauvignon, and merlot aged for 14 months in barrique, also did very well. The nose exhibits intriguing gamy and leather-like aromas, together with light hints of tobacco against a backdrop of red berry fruit. In the mouth, it shows massive structure and an intense, fruit-led finish with some tannic edginess. The Chianti Terre di Corzano '01 was also successful. It is simpler, but nonetheless very well executed. The red berry fruit aromas are slightly masked by distinct vegetal tones, but the palate is pleasingly dry, with harmonious tannins and an enjoyable finish. The winery is managed by its owner, Aljosha Goldschmidt, who is also the agronomist and oenologist.

● Carmignano Ris. '00	▼▼	5
● Chianti dei Colli Fiorentini Ris. '01	▼▼	5
● Il Brecciolino '01	▼▼	6
● Carmignano '00	▼	4
● Barco Reale '01	▼	3
● Chianti dei Colli Fiorentini '01	▼	3
● Chianti Santa Caterina '01	▼	3
⊙ Vin Ruspo '02	▼	3
● Chianti dei Colli Fiorentini Ris. '00	▼▼	5
● Il Brecciolino '00	▼▼	6

○ Passito di Corzano '96	▼▼	7
● Il Corzano '00	▼▼	7
● Chianti Terre di Corzano '01	▼	4
● Il Corzano '97	▼▼▼	5
● Chianti Terre di Corzano '97	▼▼	3
● Chianti I Tre Borri '98	▼▼	6
● Il Corzano '98	▼▼	6
● Chianti I Tre Borri '99	▼▼	6
● Il Corzano '99	▼▼	6
● Chianti Terre di Corzano '00	▼▼	5
○ Aglaia '01	▼▼	5
○ Passito di Corzano '95	▼▼	6

CASTELLI DEL GREVEPESA
FRAZ. MERCATALE IN VAL DI PESA
VIA GREVIGIANA, 34
50020 SAN CASCIANO IN VAL DI PESA (FI)
TEL. 055821911
E-MAIL: info@castellidelgrevepesa.it

TENUTA IL CORNO
FRAZ. SAN PANCRAZIO
VIA MALAFRASCA, 64
50020 SAN CASCIANO IN VAL DI PESA (FI)
TEL. 055824851
E-MAIL: ilcorno@iol.it

The Castelli del Grevepesa co-operative is getting better every year under the attentive guidance of its manager, Luigi D'Agnolo, and oenologist, Gabriella Tani. The wines are interesting, well executed and never anonymous. The Clemente VII Riserva '00 shows attractive character. The dense, luminous colour is a prelude to a nose initially dominated by delightful notes of aromatic herbs and bell peppers, which are then joined by hints of roasted coffee beans and stewed prunes. After a good attack, the palate reveals densely packed tannins throughout the solid progression, slightly dominated by acidity, to the rich but not very concentrated finish. The lovely bright Syrah '01 offers inviting scents of pepper alternating with fruit notes of blackcurrants. The palate is pleasant if a little dilute, and the acidity fails to integrate. The Coltifredi '00, from sangiovese only, earned a place in our finals thanks to its elegant bouquet, in which strawberries and raspberries merge with a warm note of liquorice. The palate is solid, dense and meaty from entry, and the tannins are succulent, but the finish is in a bit of a hurry. The Gualdo al Luco '00, made from sangiovese and cabernet sauvignon, is not completely successful on the nose, where vegetal notes overshadow the delicate fruit undertones. The palate is even and tasty, but hasn't got much grip, though the moderately long finish is enjoyable.

We ought to be happy with the wines we tasted this year from Tenuta Il Corno, owned by the Frova family, but we are so confident that they are going to get very much better that we were frustrated and impatient for greater delights. This is particularly true of the Colorino '00. An opaque colour introduces a confident nose of great depth, in which blackberry and cherry jam mix with notes of liquorice and tobacco. In the mouth, there is density and concentration, the extremely tight-knit tannins melding nicely into the fine structure. The long finish is slightly marred by bitterish notes. The Corno Rosso '00, a blend of sangiovese, cabernet and colorino, is more relaxed, showing fresh fruit aromas of plums, together with aromatic herbs. The well-balanced palate offers nicely judged acidity, and a light but compact body, leading to a finish that is long and sweet. The chardonnay-based Corno Bianco '01 displays elegant notes of lemons and aromatic herbs on the nose. The flavour is mouthfilling, and the fresh but succulent finish is well sustained. The very successful Chianti San Camillo '01 almost won Two Glasses. Powerfully fruit-forward and seductive, it also suggests violets and a little spice on the nose. The palate is enjoyable from the start, with its well-paced, attractive tannins, showing good length and drinkability. The Vin Santo '95 has ill-defined aromas and a somewhat awkward palate, and did not impress.

● Chianti Cl. Clemente VII Ris. '00	♟♟	5
● Coltifredi '00	♟♟	6
● Gualdo al Luco '00	♟	6
● Syrah '01	♟	5
● Gualdo al Luco '95	♟♟	5
● Gualdo al Luco '96	♟♟	5
● Coltifredi '97	♟♟	6
● Gualdo al Luco '97	♟♟	5
● Chianti Cl. Castelgreve Ris. '98	♟♟	5*
● Gualdo al Luco '98	♟♟	6
● Syrah '00	♟♟	5
● Coltifredi '99	♟♟	6

● Colorino '00	♟♟	6
● Corno Rosso '00	♟♟	6
● Chianti Colli Fiorentini		
San Camillo '01	♟	4
○ Corno Bianco '01	♟	6
○ Vin Santo '95		4
● Colorino '96	♟♟	4
● Colorino '97	♟♟	6
● Corno Rosso '99	♟♟	4
○ Corno Bianco '00	♟♟	5
● Colorino '99	♟♟	6

SAN CASCIANO IN VAL DI PESA (FI)	SAN CASCIANO IN VAL DI PESA (FI)

IL MANDORLO
VIA CERTALDESE, 2/B
50020 SAN CASCIANO IN VAL DI PESA (FI)
TEL. 0558228211
E-MAIL: info@il-mandorlo.it

ISPOLI
FRAZ. MERCATALE VAL DI PESA
VIA SANTA LUCIA, 2
50020 SAN CASCIANO IN VAL DI PESA (FI)
TEL. 055821613
E-MAIL: ispoli@tin.it

Looking at the scores from our tastings, you might think time had stood still. Il Mandorlo's wines were a mirror image of last year's. That's a good sign, since last year's range did very well, and an indication of the reliability and continuity achieved by Conticelli brothers' estate. They concentrate on three labels, two versions of Chianti Classico and a Supertuscan made from sangiovese and cabernet. The boldly ruby-hued Chianti Classico '01 at first displays a definite vegetal note that then makes way for fruit notes of plums and blackberries. The palate is dense, and although the acidity is slightly overdone, the progression is nicely underpinned by crunchy tannins and smoothing alcohol that lead to a tasty finish. The very good Rotone Riserva '00 is an opaque ruby, offering aromas of blackberries, very ripe, almost jammy, redcurrants and blueberries. After a good attack, the medium-bodied palate reveals slightly drying tannins, but shows warm, juicy and very enjoyable through to the convincing finish. The Terrato '00, a blend of sangiovese and cabernet sauvignon, is very dense in colour, and rich if not entirely tidy on the nose, where fruit alternates with toasty notes of oak and a range of spices. The palate is more engaging, thanks to a solid, complex structure, taut, austere body, lovely tannic texture and successful finish.

This Mercatale estate, which belongs to the Matheis, a husband and wife winemaking team, did very well this year, three of the wines going through to our final taste-offs. The Chianti Classico '01 offers delicate, clean notes of raspberries and strawberries interlaced with graceful hints of vanilla on the nose. The palate is soft and creamy, and the tannins meld perfectly into the firm, smooth body. The finish is pleasurable and long-lasting. The Riserva '00 is even better. It shows good depth of colour and nose, with rich, complex aromas ranging from stylish notes of mint to clean, clear-cut notes of woodland berries. The full-bodied, round palate reveals very smooth, well-paced tannins, an optimum balance of alcohol and acidity, and a long gustatory crescendo on the finish. Ispolaia '00, obtained from cabernet and sangiovese, is again splendid. A lively ruby leads into a nose of redcurrants and raspberries, with a teasing touch of vanilla at the end. The palate then pleases with its firm, meaty body, densely packed, well-integrated tannins and a lovely hint of spice on the finish. Lastly, the Podere Ispoli '01, a blend of sangiovese and merlot from newly planted vines, has an inviting nose of extremely elegant mint, balsamic tones and ripe red berries. The palate offers good stuffing, a dense, mouthfilling, juicy body and just a little too much acidity.

● Chianti Cl. Ris. Il Rotone '00	♟♟	5
● Terrato '00	♟♟	6
● Chianti Cl. '01	♟♟	4
● Terrato '98	♟♟	5
● Chianti Cl. '99	♟♟	4
● Chianti Cl. '00	♟♟	4
● Chianti Cl. Ris. Il Rotone '99	♟♟	5
● Terrato '99	♟♟	5

● Chianti Cl. Ris. '00	♟♟	6
● Ispolaia Rosso '00	♟♟	6
● Chianti Cl. '01	♟♟	5
● Podere Ispoli Rosso '01	♟	4
● Ispolaia Rosso '96	♟♟	4
● Chianti Cl. '97	♟♟	3
● Chianti Cl. Ris. '97	♟♟	4
● Chianti Cl. '98	♟♟	3
● Ispolaia Rosso '98	♟♟	4
● Chianti Cl. '99	♟♟	4
● Chianti Cl. '00	♟♟	4*
● Ispolaia Rosso '99	♟♟	5

SAN CASCIANO IN VAL DI PESA (FI)

SAN CASCIANO IN VAL DI PESA (FI)

LA SALA
LOC. PONTEROTTO
VIA SORRIPA, 34
50020 SAN CASCIANO IN VAL DI PESA (FI)
TEL. 055828111
E-MAIL: info@lasala.it

FATTORIA LE CORTI
LOC. LE CORTI
VIA SAN PIERO DI SOTTO, 1
50020 SAN CASCIANO IN VAL DI PESA (FI)
TEL. 055829301
E-MAIL: info@principecorsini.com

Every time we come back to the wines from this lovely estate in Chianti, we wonder why this vast area in central Tuscany is not officially divided into smaller zones. What in the world do the soft, seductive reds from La Sala have in common with the muscular wines from Castelnuovo Berardenga or Monti in Chianti? Laura Baronti, who has long been the owner and inspiration of this cellar, is committed to producing wines that reflect the characteristics of the San Casciano terroir, which typically yields tidy, attractively distinctive wines without massive muscle power. That's a perfect description of the '00 Il Campo all'Albero '00, thanks at least in part to a year that further encouraged its typical softness. This extremely agreeable red may be a bit less complex than earlier versions, but it is very enjoyable, and also reasonably priced, something that disturbs us not at all. The simpler, more approachable Chianti Classico '01 may have less punch than the '00 we liked so much last year, but is still very pleasant and well balanced. We didn't taste the Chianti Classico Riserva '00 for a very good reason. It wasn't sent to us, not having yet gone into bottle. We'll be trying it next year.

Only one wine from this estate in San Casciano Val di Pesa was presented at our tastings. Part of the problem was the 2000 growing year, which was not at all favourable to vineyard selections. As a result, the Chianti Classico '01 was the sole representative from the Chianti vineyards. It has a classical nose of ripe fruit and little hints of spice, then the palate shows a solid but vibrant body with substantial, well-balanced tannins. The real innovation, however, is a wine produced in Maremma at Tenuta Marsiliana, which has belonged to the Corsini family since the 18th century, but has only recently been reconverted to farming. It has about 150 hectares that are cultivable, only 18 of which are under vine, although more planting is planned. The idea is to add some other varieties, like cabernet sauvignon, merlot and sangiovese, to create a blend expressive of the terroir. That is the story behind the new winemaking adventure of Duccio Corsini, aided by invaluable consultant oenologist, Carlo Ferrini. On its first outing, La Marsiliana '00 went straight to our finals with a superb performance. Attractive sweet aromas of elegant but quite distinct wild berries and chocolate lead to a meaty, dense palate with subtly fine-grained, well-paced tannins and a convincing, notably elegant, finish.

● Campo all'Albero '00	⚑⚑	6
● Chianti Cl. '01	⚑⚑	5
● Chianti Cl. Ris. '00	⚑	6
● Campo all'Albero '94	⚑⚑	4
● Campo all'Albero '95	⚑⚑	4
● Campo all'Albero '96	⚑⚑	5
● Chianti Cl. Ris. '96	⚑⚑	4
● Campo all'Albero '97	⚑⚑	5
● Chianti Cl. Ris. '97	⚑⚑	4
● Campo all'Albero '98	⚑⚑	5
● Chianti Cl. Ris. '98	⚑⚑	4
● Chianti Cl. '00	⚑⚑	4*
● Campo all'Albero '99	⚑⚑	6
● Chianti Cl. Ris. '99	⚑⚑	5

● Marsiliana '00	⚑⚑	6
● Chianti Cl. '01	⚑⚑	4
● Chianti Cl. Don Tommaso '99	⚑⚑⚑	5
● Chianti Cl. Don Tommaso '00	⚑⚑	5
● Chianti Cl. Don Tommaso '97	⚑⚑	5
● Chianti Cl. Don Tommaso '96	⚑⚑	5
● Chianti Cl. Cortevecchia Ris. '99	⚑⚑	4
● Chianti Cl. Cortevecchia Ris. '97	⚑⚑	4
● Chianti Cl. '00	⚑	4
● Chianti Cl. '99	⚑	4
● Chianti Cl. '98	⚑	4

SAN CASCIANO IN VAL DI PESA (FI)

SAN CASCIANO IN VAL DI PESA (FI)

MACHIAVELLI
LOC. SANT'ANDREA IN PERCUSSINA
50020 SAN CASCIANO IN VAL DI PESA (FI)
TEL. 055828471
E-MAIL: giv@giv.it

FATTORIA POGGIOPIANO
VIA DI PISIGNANO, 28/30
50020 SAN CASCIANO IN VAL DI PESA (FI)
TEL. 0558229629
E-MAIL: poggiopiano@ftbcc.it

The cellars of this large estate, owned by Gruppo Italiano Vini, are just where Niccolò Machiavelli lived when he was exiled from Florence. From the vineyards, which flank the mediaeval town of Sant'Andrea in Percussina, you can see the dome Brunelleschi erected for Florence cathedral and, in the distance, Fiesole on its hill. For years, the Antica Fattoria Machiavelli has been managed by Nunzio Capurso, one of the key figures on the Chianti wine scene. The most important wine, Chianti Classico Vigna di Fontalle, was not ready in time for our tastings this year, so this is something of a provisional profile. We were not altogether convinced by the '00 version of Il Principe, made from pinot nero, which is masked by oak-derived tones and over-ripeness on the nose. The palate is full-bodied and elegant, but it doesn't quite make up for first impressions. The decent, but also somewhat atypical, Ser Niccolò Solatio del Tani '00 is a Cabernet Sauvignon that behaves like a Sangiovese, so cannot be called entirely varietal. The '02 Il Piano, a white obtained from red-skinned grapes, is not much more than agreeable, although it has plenty of body and quite intense aromas.

It did not receive a top award, but otherwise Poggiopiano gave another excellent performance. The Rosso di Sera was again in our finals, and in fact nearly won Three Glasses, but what is most important is the incredible consistency of Fattoria Poggiopiano. Established in 1993, it belongs to the Bartoli family, which succeeded in reaching a very high level of quality in a very few years. Another important point is that the wines, made entirely from local grapes, albeit often from recent clones, are definitely cellarable, as was demonstrated by a recent vertical tasting of the flagship wine. The Chianti Classico '01 also did well. A lovely vivid ruby introduces a nose that demands your attention. Wild berries precede nuances of oak, to be followed by attractive hints of spice. The succulent palate reveals skilfully extracted tannins with no rough edges, powerful progression and an altogether admirable finish. Rosso di Sera '01, a blend of sangiovese and colorino, has a lively and enticing purple that leads on to a nose where spicy notes of cloves and cinnamon stand out against a backdrop of redcurrants and raspberries. In the mouth, the body is taut, intriguing and delightfully smooth, showing excellent balance as it develops. The flavour lingers, growing in depth and elegance.

● Il Principe '00	▼	8
● Ser Niccolò Solatio del Tani '00	▼	7
○ Bianco di Toscana Il Piano '02	▼	5
● Chianti Cl. V. di Fontalle Ris. '95	▼▼▼	5
● Il Principe '95	▼▼▼	4
● Chianti Cl. V. di Fontalle Ris. '97	▼▼▼	5
● Il Principe '96	▼▼	5
● Il Principe '97	▼▼	5
● Il Principe '98	▼▼	5
● Chianti Cl. V. di Fontalle Ris. '99	▼▼	5
● Il Principe '99	▼▼	6

● Rosso di Sera '01	▼▼	8
● Chianti Cl. '01	▼▼	5
● Rosso di Sera '95	▼▼▼	5
● Rosso di Sera '97	▼▼▼	5
● Rosso di Sera '98	▼▼▼	6
● Rosso di Sera '99	▼▼▼	6
● Rosso di Sera '96	▼▼	5
● Chianti Cl. '99	▼▼	4*
● Rosso di Sera '00	▼▼	8
● Chianti Cl. '00	▼▼	4

SAN GIMIGNANO (SI)

BARONCINI
LOC. CASALE, 43
53037 SAN GIMIGNANO (SI)
TEL. 0577940600

The signs of change at the Baroncini estate, already evident last year, have been confirmed by the wines submitted to this year's tastings. Bruna and Stefano Baroncini both have a deep understanding of their land and are passionately committed to it. Casato '01, made from sangiovese and a little merlot, did extremely well again, showing a dense brilliant colour and aromas of blackberries and pepper. The medium-bodied palate is fruit-forward, extremely well balanced and enjoyable. The intense colour of the very fine Cortegiano '01 goes all the way to the rim, then the nose is reminiscent of black berry fruit with balsamic notes. The palate, solid and confident from the first, displays a lively tannic structure well supported by appealing fruit, followed by a slightly dilute and vegetal finish. The well-executed, sound Vernaccia Dometaia Riserva '01 is one of the best versions of recent years. The nose is intriguing and the flavour is fresh and harmonious, with a characterful soft, sweet finish. The '01 La Faina, with its somewhat unfocused aromas and not very inviting palate, and the '02 La Vernaccia Poggio ai Cannicci Sovestro '02, which is vegetal in fragrance and uncomplicated on the smooth-flowing palate, both seemed somewhat under par. The two Chiantis are extremely well typed.

SAN GIMIGNANO (SI)

CA' DEL VISPO
LOC. LE VIGNE
VIA FUGNANO, 31
53037 SAN GIMIGNANO (SI)
TEL. 0577943053

We still feel the loss of Roberto Vispi, founder, with the Dal Din brothers, of Ca' del Vispo, one of the most interesting wineries in San Gimignano. Its stature was confirmed at our tastings, where the wines evinced a reassuring consistency of quality, thanks in part to the new management team that has taken up the reins of this estate. Once again Cruter, this time the '01, is their most successful wine. Made entirely from merlot, it shows an intense, almost opaque colour and slightly over-ripe, fruit-rich aromas. The dense, mouthfilling palate unveils abundant fruit, underpinned by a firm tannic structure, and then a long, elegant finish. The Poggio Solivo '01 is almost as good. Its ruby hue with garnet highlights precedes a nose of morello cherries and flowers. The soft, structured palate is supported by a lively vein of acidity that gives the finish its delightful freshness. The fine Rovai '01 shows red berry fruit with vegetal hints on the nose, followed by a soft, medium-bodied and beautifully balanced palate. The Basolo '01, with its initially shy nose and dense, round, faintly vegetal palate, is fair, as is the Colle Leone '01, redolent of red and black berry fruit on nose and palate, and slightly bitter on the finish. The white wines were disappointing, probably because of the difficult vintage.

O	Vernaccia di S. Gimignano		
	Dometaia Ris. '00	🍷🍷	4
●	Chianti Messere '01	🍷🍷	5
●	Cortegiano Sovestro '01	🍷🍷	5
●	S. Gimignano Rosso Il Casato '01	🍷🍷	5
O	Vernaccia di S. Gimignano		
	Poggio ai Cannici Sovestro '02	🍷	4
O	La Faina '01		4
●	Chianti Colli Senesi Sup.		
	Vigna S. Domenico Sovestro '02		4
●	Morellino di Scansano Terranera		
	Aia della Macina Ris. '96	🍷🍷	4
O	La Faina '99	🍷🍷	4
●	Cortegiano Sovestro '00	🍷	5

●	Cruter '01	🍷🍷	4
●	Poggio Solivo '01	🍷🍷	5
●	Rovai '01	🍷🍷	4
●	Basolo '01	🍷	4
●	Colle Leone '01	🍷	4
O	Vernaccia di S. Gimignano '02		3
O	Vernaccia di S. Gimignano		
	Vigna in Fiore '02		4
●	Basolo '99	🍷🍷	4
●	Cruter '99	🍷🍷	4
●	Cruter '00	🍷🍷	4*
●	Rovai '00	🍷🍷	4

SAN GIMIGNANO (SI)

SAN GIMIGNANO (SI)

CASA ALLE VACCHE
FRAZ. PANCOLE
LOC. LUCIGNANO, 73/A
53037 SAN GIMIGNANO (SI)
TEL. 0577955103
E-MAIL: casaallevacche@cybermarket.it

VINCENZO CESANI
FRAZ. PANCOLE
VIA PIAZZETTA, 82/D
53037 SAN GIMIGNANO (SI)
TEL. 0577955084
E-MAIL: cesanivini@novamedia.it

The enthusiastic, dedicated Ciappi brothers seek as ever to express the Lucignano terroir through their wines. And their 16 hectares under vine, coaxed along by expert winemaker Luigino Casagrande, regularly yield a range of fine bottles with distinctive personalities. The most successful this time was the San Gimignano Rosso Acantho '00, which has a dense ruby colour, aromas of black berry fruit, nicely fused with oak-derived tones, and well-balanced progression on the palate, thanks to tight-knit tannins and well-gauged acidity. The finish is fair, although slightly vegetal. The somewhat simpler - perhaps because of the poor growing year - but nonetheless well-made sangiovese and merlot Aglieno '02 is intense in colour and on the nose offers fruit overlaid with sweet touches of vanilla. The palate has good texture and plentiful fruit, but the development is a bit limited, and the finish is rushed. Casa alle Vacche managed to turn out some interesting whites despite the unpropitious '02 vintage. Both I Macchioni and Crocus are more than just acceptable. The former presents vegetal and citrus notes on the nose, and a crisp, well-balanced palate with a shortish finish. The intense straw Crocus proffers aromas of almonds mingled with toasty tones, and is soft and medium-bodied in the mouth. The cellar's standard Vernaccia is very fresh and easy to drink, while the Chianti Colli Senesi '02 is pleasant and beautifully made.

The estate that belongs to the Cesanis is one of the finest in San Gimignano, thanks to the couple's clear ideas about what they want to accomplish, and their proud determination to respect Tuscan tradition using only local grapes. The excellence of the wines is now established fact. So much so that their standard-bearer, the monovarietal sangiovese Luenzo, very nearly walked away with Three Glasses. Its very concentrated, almost opaque, ruby precedes a complex, dense bouquet of stylish spice and ripe fruit. The rich, full-bodied palate shows admirable finesse and a lingering finish dominated by tannins that, though very fine-grained, are not yet fully amalgamated into the structure. The Vernaccia di San Gimignano Sanice '02 is especially good. Its intense straw yellow is enhanced by greenish highlights, preceded by lovely ripe fruity tones on the nose that meld with mineral and vanilla nuances. The full-bodied, well-structured palate is harmonious, signing off with the varietal almondy finish. Altogether, it's a delightful, well-made wine, despite the poor vintage. The Vernaccia di San Gimignano '02 is less communicative, but still convincing, for its aromas of unripe apples and lemon verbena, introducing a crisp, well-balanced palate with a lingering almondy flavour. The Chianti Colli Senesi '01 came close to getting Two Glasses for its fragrant fruit and reasonable density on the palate.

● S. Gimignano Rosso Acantho '00 🍷🍷		6
● Aglieno '02 🍷		4
● Chianti Colli Senesi '02 🍷		3
○ Vernaccia di S. Gimignano '02 🍷		3
○ Vernaccia di S. Gimignano Crocus '02 🍷		4
○ Vernaccia di S. Gimignano I Macchioni '02 🍷		4
● Aglieno '00 🍷🍷		3
● Aglieno '01 🍷🍷		4*
● S. Gimignano Rosso Acantho '99 🍷🍷		5

● Luenzo '01 🍷🍷		6
○ Vernaccia di S. Gimignano Sanice '02 🍷🍷		4
● Chianti Colli Senesi '01 🍷		4
○ Vernaccia di S. Gimignano '02 🍷		3
● Luenzo '97 🍷🍷🍷		5
● Luenzo '99 🍷🍷🍷		5
● Luenzo '95 🍷🍷		4
● Luenzo '96 🍷🍷		4
● Luenzo '98 🍷🍷		5
● Luenzo '00 🍷🍷		6

SAN GIMIGNANO (SI)

SAN GIMIGNANO (SI)

GUICCIARDINI STROZZI
FATTORIA CUSONA
LOC. CUSONA, 5
53037 SAN GIMIGNANO (SI)
TEL. 0577950028
E-MAIL: info@guicciardinistrozzi.it

This historic winery has been working overtime in recent years to produce wines that are not only excellent but consistently so. And the success they have achieved can be attributed to the brilliant efforts in vineyard and cellar of their expert oenologist, Ivaldo Volpini, but also to their renewed entrepreneurial enthusiasm, which has led to the acquisition of new vineyards in Maremma. Our tastings confirmed this positive trend. And an intriguing edition of the Guicciardini Strozzi Merlot, the Selvascura '01, made it into our finals. This is a wine that has all the characteristics of the grape from which it is made, showing a deep violet red and an intensely rich, fruit-led nose with some vegetal hints. The palate is mouthfilling and round on entry, then loses some strength at mid palate, but regains balance on the lingering fruity finish. The very distinctive Millanni '01, from sangiovese with a little cabernet sauvignon and merlot, has an intense, complex nose of black berry fruit blended with spice and balsam notes. The vigorous, solid palate achieves a nice balance of alcohol and acidity, thanks to soft tannins, finishing dry and long. The sangiovese-based Sodole '01 repeats the fine performance of earlier versions. The varietal nose of red berry fruit and spices unveils enchanting finesse. The palate is immediately soft, showing good acid and tannic sinew. The estate whites still show less confidence. The '02 Perlato selection is simple and lemony on the finish, and the Vernaccia '01 is dominated by oak. The Morellino di Scansano '02 is fruity but very vegetal.

IL LEBBIO
LOC. SAN BENEDETTO, 11/C
53037 SAN GIMIGNANO (SI)
TEL. 0577944725 - 0577944461
E-MAIL: illebbio@libero.it

The Niccolini brothers' desire to produce first-class wine is clearly demonstrated by their choice of Luciano Bandini as consultant oenologist. And things have definitely been getting better, although the whites still lag behind the reds. At our tastings, the Polito '00, a blend of sangiovese, colorino and cabernet sauvignon, made a particularly good showing. The well-defined nose offers red berry fruit and subtle, nicely integrated oak-derived notes. The palate is substantial and sweet enough, then elegant and harmonious in its development, and long and fruity on the finish. The Cicogio '02, from ciliegiolo, colorino, and sangiovese, is similar in style and also won Two Glasses. The full-bodied palate avoids excessive extraction, showing proper balance, followed by sound fruit on the finish. The '02 I Grottoni, a blend of cabernet sauvignon and sangiovese with a little merlot, is less convincing. On the nose, the notes of red berry fruit and vegetal tones are somewhat muffled, before the palate reveals acid and tannic rough edges that need some smoothing. The most successful of the whites is the Malvasia '02, which flaunts scents of tropical fruits and a well-balanced palate finishing on a citrus note. Both the Vernaccias are merely correct.

●	Selvascura '01	🍷🍷	5
●	Millanni '01	🍷🍷	7
●	Sodole '01	🍷🍷	6
●	Morellino di Scansano Titolato Strozzi '02		3
○	Vernaccia di S. Gimignano Ris. '01		4
○	Vernaccia di S. Gimignano Perlato '02		4
●	Millanni '99	🍷🍷🍷	7
●	Millanni '95	🍷🍷	6
●	Millanni '96	🍷🍷	6
●	Millanni '97	🍷🍷	6
●	Millanni '98	🍷🍷	6
●	Selvascura '99	🍷🍷	5
●	Millanni '00	🍷🍷	7
●	Selvascura '00	🍷🍷	5
●	Sodole '00	🍷🍷	6

●	Polito '00	🍷🍷	6
●	Cicogio '02	🍷🍷	4
●	I Grottoni '02	🍷	4
○	Malvasia '02	🍷	3
○	Vernaccia di S. Gimignano '02		3
○	Vernaccia di S. Gimignano Tropie '02		4
●	I Grottoni '97	🍷🍷	2
●	Cicogio '98	🍷🍷	3
●	I Grottoni '99	🍷🍷	3
●	Polito '98	🍷🍷	4
●	I Grottoni '01	🍷🍷	4
●	Polito '99	🍷🍷	6

SAN GIMIGNANO (SI)

SAN GIMIGNANO (SI)

IL PALAGIONE
VIA PER CASTEL SAN GIMIGNANO, 36
53030 SAN GIMIGNANO (SI)
TEL. 0577953134 - 029550069
E-MAIL: palagione@tin.it

IL PARADISO
LOC. STRADA, 21/A
53037 SAN GIMIGNANO (SI)
TEL. 0577941500
E-MAIL: 0577941500@iol.it

This recently established winery in the outer hills of San Gimignano has become one of the most interesting newcomers in the zone. Monica Rota and Giorgio Comotti, co-owners of the lovely estate, give their all to achieve their objective of making wines that stand out for elegance and faithfulness to the terroir. The results show they are well on their way. Antair '01, from sangiovese plus cabernet and merlot, again reached our finals. Its dense, dark ruby leads to a generous nose of blackcurrants and plums with toasty notes and hints of vanilla. The palate is full-bodied from the first, revealing splendid extract, rich fruit and spices, a vigorous expansive development and a long finish reminiscent of coffee and fruit. The whites are sound and reliable, despite the not very inspiring vintage. Enif '02, a blend of 60 per cent trebbiano with malvasia, offers a spectrum of aromatics ranging from flowers to citrus fruits. The moderately structured palate is soft and well-balanced, preceding a good, faintly bitter finish. The decently executed Vernaccia Hydra '02 offers aromas of almonds and flowers, then a tangy, slightly savoury palate which is a bit lightweight and shortish. The Chianti Colli Senesi Caelum '01 is lively and shows decent structure.

Vasco Ceti and his wife Grazia's Il Paradiso has been a benchmark winery in San Gimignano since the early 1970s. Vasco is a traditionalist, but also a tireless experimenter and whatever time he has over from his medical practice is dedicated to his beloved estate. This now covers 27 hectares and produces an array of wines of enviable quality. Like some other producers in this Vernaccia-making zone, Vasco has found most success with his reds. And this year, again, his most interesting bottle is a red, which just missed Three Glasses. Il Paradiso, which is advised by the able Paolo Caciorgna and by the Matura group, is clearly destined to rack up many future successes. The Saxa Calida '01, from half merlot and half cabernet sauvignon, shows a dark, impenetrable ruby, then intense aromas of blackberries and ripe plums, enlivened by notes of citron peel, tobacco and delicate nuances of printer's ink and new-mown hay. The palate boasts considerable weight and power, caressingly smooth tannins and rich fruit. In short, a superb wine, which failed to get our highest award only because of a slight imbalance on the finish. However, it should grow in elegance over the years. The Sangiovese Paterno II '00 is excellent, as usual, whereas the whites were held back by an uninspiring vintage.

● Antair '01	🍷🍷	6
● Chianti Colli Senesi Caelum '01	🍷	4
○ Enif '02	🍷	3*
○ Vernaccia di S. Gimignano Hydra '02	🍷	4
● Antair '00	🍷🍷	6
○ Enif '01	🍷	3
○ Vernaccia di S. Gimignano Hydra '01	🍷	3

● Saxa Calida '01	🍷🍷	7
● Paterno II '00	🍷🍷	6
● Bottaccio '01	🍷	5
● Chianti Colli Senesi '02	🍷	3
○ Vernaccia di S. Gimignano '02	🍷	3
○ Vernaccia di S. Gimignano Biscondola '02	🍷	4
● Saxa Calida '99	🍷🍷🍷	5
● Saxa Calida '00	🍷🍷🍷	6
● Paterno II '97	🍷🍷	5
● Saxa Calida '98	🍷🍷	5
● Paterno II '98	🍷🍷	5
● Paterno II '99	🍷🍷	6

SAN GIMIGNANO (SI)

SAN GIMIGNANO (SI)

LA LASTRA
FRAZ. SANTA LUCIA
VIA R. DE GRADA, 9
53037 SAN GIMIGNANO (SI)
TEL. 0577941781
E-MAIL: staff@lalastra.it

LA RAMPA DI FUGNANO
LOC. FUGNANO, 55
53037 SAN GIMIGNANO (SI)
TEL. 0577941655
E-MAIL: info@rampadifugnano.it

La Lastra again presented a very good line-up of bottles and has every hope, with the expert assistance of Enrico Paternostro, of producing really excellent wines in the near future. The Vernaccia di San Gimignano Riserva '01 nearly made it to our finals. Its rich straw yellow precedes a nose lifted by the judicious use of new oak, which melds with fruit and mineral tones. The juicy, velvet-smooth palate is underpinned by well-balanced acidity that helps produce an agreeably long finish. The top wine, the mostly sangiovese-based Rovaio '00, again easily earned Two Glasses, showing improvement in the definition of its aromas, which are reminiscent of ripe, sound red berry fruit. The palate is substantial, but the tannins are little too evident, especially on the finish which, though good, is a little too dry. Well-made and true to its vintage, the Vernaccia di San Gimignano '02 offers a clear-cut nose of fruit and aromatic herbs. The palate is soft, warm and well-balanced, and the pleasing finish has the characteristic Vernaccia almondy tone. The good Chianti Colli Senesi '02 is enticingly redolent of red berry fruit and spice. The fairly characterful palate is fresh, fruity and well balanced, making it just the sort of wine to drink with dinner every day.

La Rampa di Fugnano, the lovely estate that belongs to Gisela Traxler and Herbert Ehrenbold, who are Swiss by birth and Tuscan by adoption, has upheld the wine reputation of the "city of towers". An extraordinary '01 version of the merlot-based Gisèle coolly walked off with Three Glasses, repeating the success of the '97 edition. That vintage was a surprise, but all subsequent versions of the wine have been superb, if not quite so splendid. But it was inevitable that Gisèle should rejoin the front rank, as it has done. Everything at the winery, advised by consultant oenologist Paolo Caciorgna and the Matura group, is done with a view to achieving the highest possible quality. The ten hectares of very carefully tended vines produce excellent grapes, which serve to make not only the flagship red, but also the other wines in their very fine range. Gisèle, however, is an extraordinary wine. Its deep, dark ruby hue with a purplish rim ushers in a very intense, elegant nose of blackberries, blueberries and blackcurrants shading into nuances of tobacco, chocolate, and spices. The palate has harmonious structure, masses of rich fruit, perfect balance and tannins of extraordinary finesse, then the long, enticing finish echoes the fruit and spice of the bouquet. The very elegant white '01 Vi Ogni è holds its own even in this distinguished company. Made from viognier, which may help to explain the name, it is both succulent and intense. The other wines are excellent, too.

● Rovaio '00		��	5
○ Vernaccia di S. Gimignano Ris. '01		��	4
● Chianti Colli Senesi '02		�	3
○ Vernaccia di S. Gimignano '02		�	3
● Rovaio '97		♟♟	5
● Rovaio '98		♟♟	5
○ Vernaccia di S. Gimignano Ris. '00		♟♟	4
● Rovaio '99		♟♟	5

● Gisèle '01		���	6
○ Vi Ogni è '01		��	4
○ Vernaccia di S. Gimignano Alata '02		��	3
● Bombereto '01		�	5
● Chianti dei Colli Senesi Via dei Franchi '02		♟	4
● Gisèle '97		♟♟♟	5
● Gisèle '98		♟♟	6
● Gisèle '99		♟♟	6
● Gisèle '00		♟♟	7

SAN GIMIGNANO (SI)

SAN GIMIGNANO (SI)

TENUTA LE CALCINAIE
LOC. SANTA LUCIA
VIA GRAMSCI, 14
53037 SAN GIMIGNANO (SI)
TEL. 0577943007
E-MAIL: aziendalecalcinaie@libero.it

MONTENIDOLI
LOC. MONTENIDOLI
53037 SAN GIMIGNANO (SI)
TEL. 0577941565
E-MAIL: montenidoli@valdelsa.net

Simone Santini's wines have brought Tenuta Le Cancinaie back into its accustomed place in the Guide. This remarkably determined young winegrower is so keen on maintaining high standards that he presents his wines only when he feels they are worthy of the honour. His San Gimignano Rosso Teodoro '99, a blend of sangiovese with small amounts of cabernet sauvignon and merlot, passed muster, fortunately for us. A deep ruby colour with garnet highlights introduces – after a little breathing time – aromas of black berry fruit mingling with earthy notes and hints of leather. The solid palate has tight-knit, assertive tannins that give a certain austerity to the moderately long, dry finish. The interesting Vernaccia di San Gimignano Vigna ai Sassi '01 includes in its blend a small percentage of chardonnay fermented and aged in barrique. It shows a lively straw, then a forthright nose with heady notes of alcohol, as well as mineral tones. The softness and warmth of the palate suggest a certain fleshiness and the fluent finish lacks a hint of acidic vibrancy, showing a persistent sweetness. The pleasing and very easy-drinking Vernaccia di San Gimignano '02 has a dainty nose of fruits and flowers. In the mouth, it offers good body, balance, and a pleasing acidic bite. The fruit-rich, vigorous Chianti Colli Senesi '01 is worth a Glass.

"Truth is the daughter of Time". We begin our entry on Montenidoli with this apophthegm, which has been on our minds ever since a recent visit to Elisabetta Fagiuoli, a woman who is emblematic of San Gimignano wine and the philosophy of her own winery. According to Elisabetta, wines should be released – and drunk – when they express that magical, hotly debated union of grape and terroir. This year, we tasted the Vernaccia di San Gimignano Carato '98, which is still very much alive, as you can see from its golden straw colour and fresh, intensely complex nose of ripe fruit and lovely mineral tones, laced with well-gauged vanilla. The soft, engrossing palate is compact and continuous, still supported by clear, balanced acidity through to a long finish. The Vernaccia di San Gimignano Tradizionale 2002 also put on a good show. First, it presents floral aromas of peaches and apricots, then moving on to mineral tones. On the palate, it is soft and well-balanced, finishing in a lively fashion with an attractive twist of almonds. Still young and just a little below par, the Vernaccia di San Gimignano Fiore '02 shows soft and alcohol-rich at first, but is agreeably drinkable. Passing to the reds, we found that the excellent and very youthful Sono Montenidoli '99 displays a vibrantly confident, succulent palate with a long, elegant finish. The Chianti Colli Senesi '00 drinks rather differently. Attractively distinctive, as usual, it has good balance, but also slightly mouth-puckering tannins. The Canaiuolo '02 offers delicate aromas and refreshing drinkability.

● Teodoro '99	♥♥	5
● Chianti Colli Senesi '01	♥	4
○ Vernaccia di S. Gimignano V. ai Sassi '01	♥	4
○ Vernaccia di S. Gimignano '02	♥	3
○ Vernaccia di S. Gimignano V. ai Sassi '00	♀♀	4
● Teodoro '98	♀♀	4
● Chianti Colli Senesi '00	♀	3
● Teodoro '96	♀	4

○ Vernaccia di S. Gimignano Tradizionale '02	♥♥	3*
○ Vernaccia di S. Gimignano Carato '98	♥♥	5
● Sono Montenidoli '99	♥♥	5
● Chianti Colli Senesi '00	♥	4
⊙ Canaiuolo '02	♥	3
○ Vernaccia di S. Gimignano Fiore '02	♥	4
○ Vernaccia di S. Gimignano Carato '00	♀♀	5
● Sono Montenidoli '98	♀	5
● Chianti Colli Senesi '99	♀	4

SAN GIMIGNANO (SI)

SAN GIMIGNANO (SI)

MORMORAIA
LOC. SANT'ANDREA, 15
53037 SAN GIMIGNANO (SI)
TEL. 0577940096
E-MAIL: info@mormoraia.it

PALAGETTO
VIA MONTEOLIVETO, 46
53037 SAN GIMIGNANO (SI)
TEL. 0577943090
E-MAIL: palagetto@iol.it

Another important red has been added to the Mormoraia list. It's Mitylus '00, a wine that shows Giuseppe Passoni isn't content to rest on his laurels, but nurtures further ambitions that we hope he achieves. The wine, a blend of sangiovese, merlot and syrah, is a very intense ruby, with an enticing nose of blackberries nuanced with spice and pepper. The palate is soft, structured and well paced, and the finish is pleasant if not very long. This is a very promising start. Neita '00, made from sangiovese with some cabernet sauvignon and merlot, is less exciting. The nose offers well-defined notes of red berry fruit, and the development in the mouth is even and well co-ordinated. It's a pity that it shows over-evolved on the finish. The whites are a little uneven. Vernaccia di San Gimignano '02 earns its One Glass honestly. It shows light straw, then attractive fruit and spring flower aromas, before the soft, pleasantly balanced palate delivers its trademark almondy aftertaste. The Vernaccia di San Gimignano Riserva '01 did much better. The nose has considerable finesse and the palate is warm, round and convincing, but it lacks sufficient acidity to give it vivacity and keep it from seeming a bit one-dimensional. The Ostrea Grigia '01, made from vernaccia and chardonnay, is a tad lightweight, at least compared to previous editions. The aromas are not very intense, and the palate, although satisfying, could do with its customary vigour.

This year, the Palagetto winery offered a somewhat reduced line-up. Neither the standard-bearer Sottobosco, nor the Vernaccia Riserva, was present at our roll call. This was because of a decision to extend their ageing time so they will be at their best on release. The white IGT l'Niccolò '02, a blend of equal parts of chardonnay and vermentino fermented and aged in barrique, was particularly successful. It shows an almost golden straw yellow and a nose of tropical fruits, as well as still slightly prominent oak-derived tones. The palate is soft, dense and almost fleshy, displaying remarkable harmony and long length. The Vernaccia Santa Chiara '02 also did well, with its intense, sweet aromas of bananas, summer flowers and vanilla. The dense, soft palate shows nicely gauged acidity and the finish is long, but somewhat oak-heavy. The standard Vernaccia '02 is less impressive. The colour is a bit pale, and the nose reveals faint vegetal and fruit notes, but the palate offers enjoyably lively acidity and balance. The easy-drinking Chianti Colli Senesi '01 is initially dumb on the nose but is fruit-rich and well-balanced in the mouth. We were less pleased by the Chianti Colli Senesi Riserva '00, which was harsh and austere in the mouth.

● Mitylus '00		▼▼	6
○ Vernaccia di S. Gimignano Ris. '01	▼▼		5
● Neitea '00		▼	5
○ Ostrea Grigia '01		▼	4
○ Vernaccia di S. Gimignano '02		▼	4
● Neitea '95		♉♉	4
● Neitea '96		♉♉	4
● Neitea '97		♉♉	4
● Neitea '98		♉♉	5
○ Ostrea Grigia '00		♉♉	4
● Neitea '99		♉♉	5

○ l'Niccolò '02		▼▼	4
○ Vernaccia di S. Gimignano			
Vigna Santa Chiara '02		▼▼	3*
● Chianti Colli Senesi '01		▼	3*
○ Vernaccia di S. Gimignano '02		▼	3
● Chianti Colli Senesi Ris. '00			4
● Sottobosco '00		♉♉	5
○ Vernaccia di S. Gimignano Ris. '00	♉♉		4
○ l'Niccolò '01		♉♉	5
○ Vernaccia di S. Gimignano			
Vigna Santa Chiara '01		♉	4

SAN GIMIGNANO (SI)

GIOVANNI PANIZZI
FRAZ. SANTA MARGHERITA
LOC. RACCIANO, 34
53037 SAN GIMIGNANO (SI)
TEL. 0577941576
E-MAIL: panizzi@panizzi.it

Giovanni Panizzi has earned his place in Tuscany's wine history. He is one of a generation of entrepreneurs from Lombardy who in the 1970s and 1980s, colonized many parts of Tuscany, partly for the fun of it and partly out of genuine passion, establishing first-rank wineries. Today, Giovanni has firm roots in the "city of towers" and 30 hectares under vine in the Santa Margherita area, where he produces 200,000 bottles of wine annually, almost all of it Vernaccia. This year, Giovanni's Riserva '01, long a benchmark for the whole DOCG zone, didn't seem as great as its predecessors. It has its customary lovely structure, and on the nose, shows good fruit and a well-gauged use of wood, but it was neither as concentrated nor as long as we have come to expect. The Vernaccia '02 had a poor growing year to contend with but is nonetheless admirable for its subtle fruit aromas and fresh, enjoyable palate. The Rosso Folgore '02, made from 75 percent sangiovese with cabernet sauvignon and merlot, easily earned Two Glasses. Concentrated and soft, it parades its ripe, very fine-grained tannins. The Rosso Ceraso '02 and the Chianti Colli Senesi Vertunno '01, both reds, are generously fruit-driven and enjoyable.

SAN GIMIGNANO (SI)

TERUZZI & PUTHOD
LOC. CASALE, 19
53037 SAN GIMIGNANO (SI)
TEL. 0577940143
E-MAIL: info@teruzzieputhod.it

Enrico Teruzzi and his wife Carmen came to San Gimignano from their native Milan back in 1974 to take charge of their recently acquired estate. In those days, the world of Tuscan, and indeed Italian, wine had yet to undergo the conceptual and technical changes that were to lead to Italy's viticultural renaissance. Enrico was one of the leaders of that movement, and if Vernaccia now enjoys a certain prestige on the international market, it is probably thanks to him, his tireless experiments and his savvy salesmanship. Today, the estate extends over 2,180 hectares, about 100 of them are under vine, and production runs at 1,300,000 bottles a year, sold throughout the world with increasing success. The Teruzzi & Puthod range is based on classics like Vernaccia di San Gimignano, exemplary for its cleanness, and the Vigna a Rondolino selection, which has a sinewy palate and lovely fruit. Enrico's most important wine, however, is the vernaccia-based Terre di Tufi, and we particularly liked the '01 version. It's a big, powerful wine that is well able to handle its lengthy stay in new wood. Complex and long, it ought to develop beautifully over the years. We also like the Carmen Puthod '01 very much. It's a white Sangiovese vinified without the skins that has complex aromas reminiscent of white chocolate and peaches, and a dense palate supported by tangy acidity. The fruity red Peperino '01 is good, too.

● S. Gimignano Rosso Folgòre '00	🍷🍷	6
○ Vernaccia di S. Gimignano Ris. '01	🍷🍷	5
● Chianti Colli Senesi Vertunno '01	🍷	4
● Ceraso '02	🍷	3
○ Vernaccia di S. Gimignano '02	🍷	4
○ Vernaccia di S. Gimignano Ris. '98	🍷🍷🍷	6
○ Vernaccia di S. Gimignano Ris. '97	🍷🍷	5
○ Vernaccia di S. Gimignano Ris. '99	🍷🍷	6
○ Vernaccia di S. Gimignano Ris. '00	🍷🍷	6

○ Terre di Tufi '01	🍷🍷	5
○ Carmen Puthod '01	🍷🍷	4
● Peperino '01	🍷	4
○ Vernaccia di S. Gimignano '02	🍷	4
○ Vernaccia di S. Gimignano Vigna a Rondolino '02	🍷	4
○ Carmen Puthod '97	🍷🍷	4
○ Terre di Tufi '97	🍷🍷	5
○ Carmen Puthod '98	🍷🍷	4
○ Terre di Tufi '98	🍷🍷	4
○ Terre di Tufi '99	🍷🍷	5
○ Carmen Puthod '00	🍷🍷	4
○ Terre di Tufi '00	🍷🍷	5

SAN GIMIGNANO (SI)

F.LLI VAGNONI
LOC. PANCOLE, 82
53037 SAN GIMIGNANO (SI)
TEL. 0577955077

The Vagnoni brothers, Luigi and Giovanni, are originally from the Marche, as are many other winemakers in San Gimignano, and they belong to the small group of leading producers in this charming zone. The 120,000 bottles they produce from their 20 hectares of beautiful vines at Pancole are, as usual, technically flawless, and include some outstanding wines. Their '01 Riserva I Mocali is again one of the best Vernaccias of its year, and did well at our finals. A brilliant straw yellow introduces the intense fruit-rich nose that makes way for hints of vanilla and toasted oak. The dense, structured palate offers lovely fresh, juicy fruit, excellent balance and nuances of liquorice and new oak as it signs off. It is one of the best examples of Vernaccia from cool areas like Pancole, where the wines tend to be intensely fragrant and elegant. The Vernaccia '02, from a challenging vintage, is still well made, pleasant, fruity and round. Two of the other wines earned One Glass each, the red I Sodi Lunghi '00, made from sangiovese with a little colorino and merlot, and the San Gimignano Rosso San Biagio '00, a successful 50-50 blend of sangiovese and merlot.

SARTEANO (SI)

TENUTA DI TRINORO
VIA RIBATTOLA, 2
53047 SARTEANO (SI)
TEL. 0578267110

Long an enthusiastic connoisseur of great wines, Andrea Franchetti gained experience in Bordeaux and the United States and then decided to produce wine himself at his estate in Sarteano. It lies in Val d'Orcia, in the province of Siena, between Monte Amiata and Monte Cetona near the Umbrian and Lazio borders. In 1992, Andrea planted 16 hectares of vines at an elevation of between 500 and 700 metres. The vineyards are planted to cabernet franc, cabernet sauvignon, merlot, petit verdot and also cesanese d'Affile, at the extremely high density of nearly 10,000 vines per hectare. Thanks to the high altitude and continental climate, the growing season here is a long one, and harvesting finishes well into November. Rigorous bunch thinning is followed after harvest by fermentation in open vats, before the wines are aged unhurriedly in new barriques. Andrea's bottles have enjoyed great success as "vins de garage", rather like Château Valandraud and Dominio de Pingus. The very low yields (15 hectolitres per hectare) and organic vineyard management mean that the wines acquire a unique personality. Very little is produced, and the bottles are hard to find in Italy. The flagship wine, the massively structured Tenuta di Trinoro, is made from 48 per cent cabernet franc, 22 per cent merlot, 18 per cent cabernet sauvignon and petit verdot. Le Cupole '02 is almost as interesting. It's also worth trying the Cincinnato, a fragrant cesanese-based red, and the Passopisciaro, made from nerello mascalese that grows in a 1,000 metre high, 100-year-old vineyard on the north side of Mount Etna.

○	Vernaccia di S. Gimignano Mocali Ris. '01	♥♥	5
●	I Sodi Lunghi '00	♥	5
●	San Gimignano Rosso San Biagio '00	♥	5
○	Vernaccia di S. Gimignano '02	♥	3
●	Chianti Colli Senesi '01		3
○	Vin Brusco del Solatio '02		3
○	Vernaccia di S. Gimignano Mocali '97	♥♥	4
○	Vernaccia di S. Gimignano Mocali '98	♥♥	4
○	Vernaccia di S. Gimignano Mocali '99	♥♥	4
○	Vernaccia di S. Gimignano Mocali Ris. '00	♥♥	4

●	Cincinnato '01	♥♥	8
●	Passopisciaro '01	♥♥	6
●	Le Cupole di Trinoro '02	♥♥	8
●	Tenuta di Trinoro '01	♥♥	8
●	Le Cupole di Trinoro '01	♥	8

SCANSANO (GR)

PODERE AIA DELLA MACINA
LOC. FOSSO LOMBARDO, 87
58054 SCANSANO (GR)
TEL. 0577940600
E-MAIL: baroncini@iol.it

SCANSANO (GR)

ERIK BANTI
LOC. FOSSO DEI MOLINI
58054 SCANSANO (GR)
TEL. 0564508006
E-MAIL: info@erikbanti.com

In Ambrogio Lorenzetti's 14th-century "Buon Governo" fresco in Siena's Palazzo Comunale, you can see a red house set in vineyards in the landscape that slopes down from the city to Maremma. The house, on the Roggettone hill, was, and still is, called Aia della Macina. The estate now belongs to Bruna Baroncini and Franco Azara, the continued excellence of whose delightful wines is monitored by consultant oenologist, Riccardo Cotarella. The range they presented this year is good, well-executed and expressive of the local terroir. Poggio Roggettone '02, a blend of sangiovese, ciliegiolo and alicante, is a striking example. Its intense ruby introduces a well-defined, ripe fruit fragrance of black cherries, and a broad palate with densely packed, nicely integrated tannins. The lingering finish is rich in intense fruit. Terranera Riserva '00 shows more acidic bite, but is very enjoyable. The ruby red shades to garnet at the rim, and there are subtle ripe jam aromas on the nose. There's good structure on the palate, where the tannins are chewy and mellow, and the lively acidity contributes refreshing tanginess. The finish is long, dry and enjoyable. The excellent Labruna '02, made from vermentino and ansonica, is crisp, spirited and intensely fruity. The extremely interesting Morellino Anteo '02 from Riccardo Azara's Rocca dei Venti offers succulent, crunchy fruit and good structure. It's made from grapes grown on a neighbouring estate and is distributed by Aia della Macina.

Erik Banti, one of the historic Morellino producers, released its first bottle in 1981 and now occupies an important position locally, thanks to 50 hectares under vine that yield almost 350,000 bottles a year. The estate oenologist is Nicola Scottini. The wines he presented at this year's tastings were good and, most important, eminently representative of their terroir. The most successful is the Morellino '02, a blend of sangiovese, grenache, canaiolo and malvasia nera. It is an honest, straightforward wine, like the land from which it comes, and the nose offers clean, pleasing notes of red berry fruit. The structured, dry, refreshing palate is underpinned by attractive acidity and tight-knit, succulent tannins. The good Carato '01 releases scents of ripe fruit with gamy notes. The palate is compact and lingering, though the acidity is prominent. The Ciabatta Riserva '00 is evanescent on the nose, and there are some forward notes. On the palate, the tannins are tasty, and the finish is long and enjoyable, if a little bitter. The Poggio Maestrino '00, a blend of sangiovese, merlot, syrah and cabernet sauvignon, is concentrated and redolent of red berry fruit and spices. In the mouth, the tannins demand a little too much attention, and could do with some mellowing. The finish is very enjoyable, despite overbearing oak.

● Morellino di Scansano Poggio Roggettone '02	ŶŶ	4*
● Morellino di Scansano Terranera Ris. '00	ŶŶ	5
○ Labruna '02	ŶŶ	4*
● Morellino di Scansano Anteo - Rocca dei Venti '02	ŶŶ	4
○ Labruna '00	ŶŶ	3*
● Morellino di Scansano '00	ŶŶ	3
○ Labruna '01	ŶŶ	4*
● Morellino di Scansano Poggio Roggettone '99	ŶŶ	3*
● Morellino di Scansano '01	ŶŶ	3*
● Morellino di Scansano Anteo - Rocca dei Venti '01	ŶŶ	4
● Morellino di Scansano Terranera Ris. '98	Ŷ	4

● Morellino di Scansano '02	ŶŶ	4
● Morellino di Scansano Ciabatta Ris. '00	Ŷ	5
● Poggio Maestrino '00	Ŷ	6
● Morellino di Scansano Carato '01	Ŷ	4
● Aquilaia '90	ŶŶ	4
● Ciabatta '90	ŶŶ	4
● Aquilaia '94	ŶŶ	4
● Morellino di Scansano '94	ŶŶ	3
● Aquilaia '95	ŶŶ	4
● Aquilaia '96	ŶŶ	4

SCANSANO (GR)

Cantina Cooperativa
del Morellino di Scansano
loc. Saragiolo
58054 Scansano (GR)
tel. 0564507288 - 0564507979
e-mail: coopmorel@libero.it

This co-operative came into being in 1972 as a way of dealing with the crisis in the mining industry. Ever since, it has been run with passion and dedication by the uncomplicated but expert growers of the Maremma. It is now one of the most modern wine co-operatives around, known for the consistently fine quality of its technically impeccable wines, which clearly reflect the land they come from. The advice of the consultant oenologist, Paolo Caciorgna, and the care taken in the vineyards by member growers, are producing notable results. At our tastings, the wines performed well and, amazingly enough, they don't cost a king's ransom. The Morellino Vignabenefizio '02, a monovarietal sangiovese, was the most outstanding of the range. Clear notes of sour cherries on the nose are sweetened by delicate vanilla tones. The palate is full-bodied and pleasingly tannic, and cherries reappear on the finish. The fine Morellino Vin del Fattore '02 offers well-defined aromas of wild berries and a dry, round palate with a long, slightly acidulous, finish. The Roggiano '02 is a Morellino with ripe fruity aromas and a generous, if rather simple, palate. The Roggiano Riserva '00 is strikingly true to type. The fruit on the nose is a little hesitant to emerge, and tannins have the upper hand on the palate. Finally, the '02 Rasenno, a blend of trebbiano, malvasia and chardonnay, is fresh and intensely fragrant, with plenty of flavour and a lingering finish.

SINALUNGA (SI)

Farnetella
s.da Siena-Bettolle, km 37
53048 Sinalunga (SI)
tel. 0577355117
e-mail: felsina@dada.it

People often make mistakes about numbers and dates. We certainly did last year when we ended Farnetella's profile with the promise that we would describe our tasting of the '99 Poggio Granoni in this year's Guide. The vintage we actually had in mind was the '97. Now that that's all clear, we can report that Farnetella continues to produce excellent wines. We'll start with their only white, the Sauvignon '01. It shows pale gold, and proffers a pleasant medley of aromas ranging from spring flowers to graceful fruity notes, with apricots and peaches taking the lead. The immediately inviting palate unveils distinct acid sinew in a medium body, and a tasty, succulent finish. The Lucilla '01, a blend of sangiovese and cabernet, presents a concentrated, not fully expressed nose with marked notes of fur and leather. Things improve on the palate, where the body is strikingly taut and vigorous, the tannins open out steadily and the finish is splendid. The Poggio Granoni '97, made from sangiovese with small amounts of cabernet, merlot and syrah, came awfully close to winning Three Glasses. A garnet hue introduces a mellow nose on which notes of leather, tobacco and very fine spices contribute to the elegance of the ripe fruity tones. In the mouth, it is velvety, soft and drinkable, with tidy, restrained tannins and a solid body that leads into a succulent finish. Lastly, the Nero di Nubi '99, from pinot nero only, is unexciting. The aromas could be cleaner, and the tannins intrude.

●	Morellino di Scansano Vignabenefizio '02	🍷🍷	4*
●	Morellino di Scansano Roggiano Ris. '00	🍷	5
○	Bianco di Pitigliano Rasenno '02	🍷	3
●	Morellino di Scansano Roggiano '02	🍷	3
●	Morellino di Scansano Vin del Fattore '02	🍷	4
●	Morellino di Scansano Vignabenefizio '96	🍷🍷	2
●	Morellino di Scansano Sicomoro '00	🍷🍷	5
●	Morellino di Scansano Roggiano '00	🍷	3
●	Morellino di Scansano Vignabenefizio '00	🍷	3
●	Morellino di Scansano Roggiano '01	🍷	4
●	Morellino di Scansano San Rabano Ris. '98	🍷	5

●	Poggio Granoni '97	🍷🍷	8
●	Lucilla '01	🍷🍷	4
○	Sauvignon '01	🍷	4
●	Nero di Nubi '99		5
●	Poggio Granoni '93	🍷🍷🍷	6
●	Poggio Granoni '95	🍷🍷🍷	8
●	Chianti Colli Senesi '96	🍷🍷	3
●	Chianti Colli Senesi '98	🍷🍷	3
●	Lucilla '00	🍷🍷	4
○	Sauvignon '00	🍷🍷	4
●	Chianti Colli Senesi '01	🍷🍷	3*

SORANO (GR)

SORANO (GR)

SASSOTONDO
LOC. PIAN DI CONATI, 52
58010 SORANO (GR)
TEL. 0564614218
E-MAIL: sassotondo@ftbcc.it

PODERE SOPRA LA RIPA
FRAZ. SOVANA
LOC. PODERE SOPRA RIPA
58010 SORANO (GR)
TEL. 0564616885
E-MAIL: fr.ventura@sopralarupa.com

Carla Benini and Edoardo Ventimiglia's Sassotondo went all out for organic farming and the ciliegiolo grape. The decision paid off. The attention now being focused on the variety, which has become the symbol of the Sovana DOC zone, is largely thanks to Sassotondo, which can call on the invaluable assistance of agronomist, Remigio Bordini, in the vineyards and oenologist, Attilio Pagli, in the cellar. The estate now extends over 72 hectares, of which about 11 are under vine, and the wines did well at this year's tastings, even though they had begun to get us used to even better things. The San Lorenzo '01, from 100 per cent ciliegiolo aged in barriques for 18 months, presents delicate aromas of ripe cherries, enhanced by refreshing balsamic notes. The palate is elegant, thanks in part to tight-knit but not astringent tannins, and to the nicely balanced acidity that makes it tangy and enjoyable. Franze '01, a blend of sangiovese with some ciliegiolo and merlot, offers scents of ripe fruit with faint vegetal nuances. The palate is full-bodied, and the finish long, but the tannins are still a little edgy. The mostly ciliegiolo-based Sassotondo Rosso '02 is a bit high-strung, but boasts a pleasantly fruit-rich nose and good length, although the acidity is quite noticeable. Sassotondo Numero Sei '01, a blend of greco di Tufo, sauvignon and chardonnay, is a tad indistinct on the nose, but the full-bodied, lingering palate is more interesting.

The Ventura brothers' Podere Sopra la Ripa, where Alberto Antonini is cellar manager, missed Three Glasses by not very much at all. This year, the Ea '01, a name that harks back to Etruscan mythology, is quite superb. Obtained from sangiovese and ciliegiolo, separately fermented and aged in barrique for 18 months, and given a further six months in bottle after blending, is strikingly complex and expressive of its terroir. It shows an opaque, luminous ruby hue in the glass, and a nose of fresh fruit, enhanced by distinct balsamic notes. The attack on the palate is soft, and the progression reveals enormous body and ripe, almost velvety, tannins. The finish is long and succulent. The other red was not quite so successful, mostly because of slightly unripe, sour notes that can probably be traced to both the difficult 2002 vintage, which was felt much more here than in other parts of Maremma, and also to the new vineyards, planted in 1999 and only just starting to come onstream. That's why the '02 Ripa seemed less interesting. It's a blend of sangiovese, ciliegiolo and alicante, and the nose releases faint hints of ripe fruit, mingled with prominent vegetal notes. The straightforward, fairly soft palate shows densely packed tannins.

●	San Lorenzo '01	♈♈	6
●	Sovana Rosso Sup. Franze '01	♈	5
●	Sassotondo Rosso '02	♈	4
○	Numero Sei '01		7
●	San Lorenzo '97	♈♈	4
●	San Lorenzo '98	♈♈	5
●	Sassotondo Rosso '98	♈♈	3
●	Sovana Rosso Sup. Franze '98	♈♈	4
●	Sassotondo Rosso '99	♈♈	3
●	San Lorenzo '99	♈♈	5
●	Sovana Rosso Sup. Franze '99	♈♈	4
●	San Lorenzo '00	♈♈	6
●	Sovana Rosso Sup. Franze '00	♈♈	5
●	Sassotondo Rosso '01	♈♈	4*

●	Ea '01	♈♈	6
●	Ripa '02	♈	5
●	Ripa '00	♈♈	3*
●	Ea '99	♈♈	4
●	Ea '00	♈♈	7
●	Ripa '01	♈♈	5

SUVERETO (LI)

SUVERETO (LI)

LORELLA AMBROSINI
LOC. TABARO, 96
57028 SUVERETO (LI)
TEL. 0565829301
E-MAIL: loreambrowine@katamail.com

BULICHELLA
LOC. BULICHELLA, 131
57028 SUVERETO (LI)
TEL. 0565829892
E-MAIL: bulichella@etruscan.li.it

Lorella Ambrosini and Roberto Fanetti seem to have hit their stride. This year's entire range confirmed the better overall quality, clearly demonstrating that last year's improvements were no fluke. The secret of this progress is that the owners understood that to keep abreast of the times, they had to re-assess everything that was being done, both in the vineyards and in the cellar. They sought the assistance of expert oenologist, Lorenzo Landi, who has made an important contribution to the creation of better focused wines. Once again, Riflesso Antico, this time the '01, a 100 per cent montepulciano d'Abruzzo, made it to our finals. It shows a markedly vivid, opaque colour, and a dense nose with layers of ripe black berry fruit, balsamic notes and hints of toasty oak. In the mouth, it has breadth and power, as well as generous fruit and extract. The finish is somewhat compressed, with tannins that are not yet perfectly integrated into the structure of the wine. The Subertum '01 easily won Two Glasses, displaying a beautiful, concentrated colour and intense scents of woodland berries, mineral notes and faint vegetal hints on the nose. The substantial palate bursts with fruit, unveiling a youthful tannic structure that ought to age very well indeed. The less convincing Tabarò '02 seemed simple, dilute and somewhat vegetal on the back palate.

Bulichella, a strictly organically farmed estate, has installed itself in a leading position in the interesting Suvereto zone. Actually, it almost won Three Glasses with a new wine, the Col di Pietre Rosse '00. A blend of cabernet sauvignon and merlot, this red aged for some 20 months in barrique, where it also underwent malolactic fermentation. An intense, lively ruby red is the prelude to a complex, assertive nose that releases rich fruity notes of blackcurrants and blueberries, mingling perfectly with coffee and oak-derived aromas. The flavour is full-bodied, soft and mouthfilling, with smooth, close-knit tannins, opening out to a very long and intriguingly elegant finish. The very fine Tuscanio Rosso '01, obtained from sangiovese and merlot, offers good ripe fruit on the nose after a faint initial note of reduction. The fairly dense, dynamic palate shows good balance and moderate persistence. The Tuscanio Bianco '02, a monovarietal Vermentino, nearly got Two Glasses for its fresh, complex fragrance of fruit, flowers and aromatic herbs, leading to an enchanting, enjoyably fresh-tasting palate. We found neither the Val di Cornia Rosso Rubino '02 nor the Val di Cornia Aleatico '01 particularly interesting.

● Riflesso Antico '01	🍷🍷	6
● Val di Cornia Subertum '01	🍷🍷	6
● Val di Cornia Rosso Tabarò '02	🍷	3
● Val di Cornia Subertum '00	🍷🍷	6
● Val di Cornia Rosso Tabarò '01	🍷🍷	3
○ Armonia '01	🍷	4

● Val di Cornia		
Col di Pietre Rosse '00	🍷🍷	6
● Val di Cornia Rosso		
Tuscanio '01	🍷🍷	6
○ Val di Cornia Bianco		
Tuscanio '02	🍷	4
● Val di Cornia Aleatico '01		5
● Val di Cornia Rosso Rubino '02		4
● Val di Cornia Rosso		
Tuscanio '99	🍷🍷	5
● Val di Cornia Rosso		
Tuscanio '00	🍷🍷	6

SUVERETO (LI)

GUALDO DEL RE
LOC. NOTRI, 77
57028 SUVERETO (LI)
TEL. 0565829888 - 0565829361
E-MAIL: gualdo@infol.it

After a fine performance last year, Nico Rossi has carried off a triumphal Three Glass prize this time. The efforts expended in recent years by this first-rate grower, who, under the watchful eye of his mother, Barbara Tamburini, has striven to find a style that reflects the characteristics of the land, have met with well-deserved recognition. The Val di Cornia Rosso l'Rennero '01, from merlot only, was an easy Three Glass winner. This great wine flaunts an elegant bouquet of fruit, shot through with oak-derived spice and toastiness. The vibrantly rich, broad palate unfolds mouthfilling tannins that make the wine seamlessly expansive, contributing to a long finish. The Federico Primo '01, a Cabernet Sauvignon, also gave a stunning performance. Dark-hued, it shows a dense nose with aromas of black berry fruit, spices, balsamic notes and toastiness. The palate is substantial, confident, perfectly balanced and compelling, then the long finish offers a pleasing reprise of the bouquet. The Gualdo del Re Riserva '00 is less engaging. Wood gets the better of fruit on nose and palate, and is prominent even on the drying finish. Both interesting and respectable whites, the Valentina '02 and the Eliseo '02, flaunt bright acidity.

SUVERETO (LI)

INCONTRI
LOC. FOSSONI, 38
57028 SUVERETO (LI)
TEL. 0565829401
E-MAIL: blocloko@hotmail.com

Incontri has not taken any time out for reflection. The wines presented at our tastings continue to be consistently pleasurable. There are a number of reasons for this, including a pinch of ambition on the part of the owners, the exceptional mesoclimate of the zone and the intelligently executed replanting of the vineyards, thanks in part to the invaluable aid of consultant, Alberto Antonini. The estate flagship, Lagobruno '01, easily collected Two Glasses. Concentrated, intense aromas of ripe fruit nuanced with toasty notes and balsam usher in a full-bodied palate with supple, lively tannins, expansive progression and a tasty, lingering finish. The equally convincing Vermentino Ildebrandino '02 is a pleasing white that offers typically varietal fruit and flower notes, lifted by hints of Mediterranean undergrowth. The palate is crisp, warm, harmonious and fairly long. The Lorenzo degli Incontri '02 is fleeting in fragrance but confident, distinctive, enjoyable and fluent in the mouth. The Val di Cornia Vignanuova '02 is predictable and not particularly distinguished.

● Val di Cornia Rosso l'Rennero '01	�♀♀	8
● Federico Primo '01	♀♀	6
● Val di Cornia Gualdo del Re '00	♀	6
○ Val di Cornia Bianco Eliseo '02	♀	3
○ Val di Cornia Valentina '02	♀	4
● Federico Primo '93	♀♀	5
● Federico Primo '96	♀♀	5
○ Lumen '00	♀♀	4
● Federico Primo '00	♀♀	6
● Val di Cornia Rosso l'Rennero '00	♀♀	8
● Federico Primo '99	♀♀	6

● Lagobruno '01	♀♀	5
○ Val di Cornia Vermentino Ildebrandino '02	♀♀	4
● Val di Cornia Lorenzo degli Incontri '02	♀	4
○ Val di Cornia Bianco Vignanuova '02		3
● Lagobruno '99	♀♀	5
● Lagobruno '00	♀♀	5
● Val di Cornia Rosso Rubizzo '00	♀	3
● Val di Cornia Lorenzo degli Incontri '01	♀	4

SUVERETO (LI)

MONTEPELOSO
LOC. MONTEPELOSO, 82
57028 SUVERETO (LI)
TEL. 0565828180
E-MAIL: montepeloso@virgilio.it

Nardo, a winery of undeniable breeding, has again swept up Three Glasses. This places Fabio Chiarellotto's Montepeloso among the top estates in the area, and also adds lustre to the wines of Val di Cornia, a constantly developing zone with all the ingredients for producing great wine. The Nardo '01, made from sangiovese with a little cabernet sauvignon, is an exemplary expression of its terroir. Its great character and elegance are immediately evident on the nose, which offers a broad range of aromas. Ripe fruit, spices and balsamic and oak-derived notes are all present. The palate reveals a vigorous, powerful structure, a densely packed but extremely smooth tannic texture, and an expansive, mouthfilling progression leading to a lingering fruity finish. The excellent Gabbro '01, a Cabernet Sauvignon, very nearly earned Three Glasses of its own. The remarkably dense red ushers in a ripe fruit-forward fragrance, laced with hints of spice and stylish balsamic notes. The palate has a sumptuous, velvet-smooth attack, then shows broad progression, notably tight-knit tannins and a finish of amazing length. The Eneo '01 is also very good. It's a fruity wine with a chewy palate, a long finish and really delightful overall balance.

SUVERETO (LI)

RUSSO
LOC. PODERE LA METOCCHINA
VIA FORNI, 71
57028 SUVERETO (LI)
TEL. 0565845105
E-MAIL: azrusso@katamail.com

We are sure that failure to repeat last year's Three Glasses will not cause the Russo brothers any loss of sleep. The estate has already demonstrated such firm foundations that the future looks very rosy indeed, and the investments the Russos have made in recent years shouldn't hurt either. The cellar, which draws on the expert advice of Alberto Antonini, has all it takes to become one of the top wineries in Val di Cornia. The Barbicone '01, a blend of sangiovese with ten per cent colorino, in any case sailed effortlessly into the final taste-offs. It presents a lovely dense colour, and a nose of ripe fruit and oak that meld in exciting synergy. The abundance of fruit and structure in the mouth translates into a meaty, elegant and lingering palate. The fine Sassobucato '01 shows a deep nose that releases distinct notes of ripe fruit. The palate shows its extraordinary stuffing on entry and follows up with a full, satisfying body. The attractive, easy-drinking Ceppitaio '02 is very well balanced, although rather dominated by vegetal tones on both nose and palate.

● Nardo '01	♟♟♟	8
● Gabbro '01	♟♟	8
● Eneo '01	♟♟	5
● Nardo '00	♟♟♟	8
● Nardo '97	♟♟	8
● Gabbro '98	♟♟	8
● Nardo '98	♟♟	8
● Gabbro '99	♟♟	6
● Nardo '99	♟♟	8
● Gabbro '00	♟♟	8

● Val di Cornia Rosso		
Barbicone '01	♟♟	5
● Sassobucato '01	♟♟	6
● Val di Cornia Rosso		
Ceppitaio '02	♟	4
● Val di Cornia Rosso		
Barbicone '00	♟♟♟	5*
● Sassobucato '00	♟♟	6
● Val di Cornia Rosso		
Ceppitaio '01	♟♟	3*

SUVERETO (LI)

TAVARNELLE VAL DI PESA (FI)

TUA RITA
LOC. NOTRI, 81
57025 SUVERETO (LI)
TEL. 0565829237
E-MAIL: info@tuarita.it

PODERE LA CAPPELLA
FRAZ. SAN DONATO IN POGGIO
S.DA CERBAIA, 10
50020 TAVARNELLE VAL DI PESA (FI)
TEL. 0558072727
E-MAIL: poderelacappella@libero.it

There is no doubt that the brightest star in the oenological firmament of Suvereto is, at the moment, Tua Rita. Apart from the consistently excellent quality of the wines, the cellar was a pioneer in developing Val di Cornia, which has become one of the most prestigious growing zones in Tuscany. If someone were to voice any doubts about what we say, and that person had only seen the winery at its inception, we would invite him to return to it today and see in person what the owners have managed to do in the course of ten years. Not only the densely planted vineyards that have covered the hillside like an unstoppable tide, but also the recently built, state-of-the-art cellar, would make our case more emphatically than mere words. Meanwhile, the wines just keep getting better. Indeed the Redigaffi '01, the fifth of the series to win Three Glasses (in a row) and clearly among the top five Merlots in Italy, is a wine of superlative quality and instantly recognizable style. The impenetrable colour serves as an introduction to an intense, richly varied nose where blackberries, blackcurrants and spices blend in a harmonious bouquet. In the mouth, the tannins are tight-knit but extremely elegant, and the fruit is succulent, sound and impeccably good quality. The progression is balanced and expansive, and the finish never ends. The very good Giusto di Notri '01, a cabernet-merlot blend is concentrated and bewitchingly silky.

Bruno Rossigni's estate has won back its own profile with a convincing performance, which is something of a surprise since the flagship merlot-based Cantico will not be presented until next year. The wines we did taste show greater aromatic definition and a distinctive style, obvious prerequisites for a significant step forward. Structure on the palate, which has never been wanting here, is once again the cellar's strong suit. But let's look at the tasting notes. The Chianti Classico Querciolo Riserva '00 shows a vivid, luminous ruby. The nose is initially complex and slightly closed, with fur and leather notes calling the shots, but then makes way for delicate aromas of tobacco that finally yield to a rich, fruity fragrance of ripe cherries. The palate is reluctant to open, but after a while the tightly packed, assertive tannins relax and lend support to the solid, powerful body. The rising succulent finish leaves a lovely fruity aftertaste. The very fine Corbezzolo '00, made mostly from sangiovese, sauntered into our finals thanks to its complex bouquet of rich fruit, alternating with notes of tobacco and leather. After a powerful but soft and smooth attack, the palate reveals still not completely absorbed tannins and perfectly balanced alcohol and acidity. The finish is moderately long.

●	Redigaffi '01	🍷🍷🍷	8
●	Giusto di Notri '01	🍷🍷	8
●	Perlato del Bosco Rosso '01	🍷	6
●	Giusto di Notri '94	🍷🍷🍷	5
●	Giusto di Notri '95	🍷🍷🍷	5
●	Redigaffi '96	🍷🍷🍷	8
●	Redigaffi '98	🍷🍷🍷	8
●	Redigaffi '99	🍷🍷🍷	8
●	Redigaffi '00	🍷🍷🍷	8
●	Giusto di Notri '99	🍷🍷	6
●	Giusto di Notri '00	🍷🍷	8
●	Perlato del Bosco Rosso '00	🍷🍷	5

●	Corbezzolo '00	🍷🍷	7
●	Chianti Cl. Querciolo Ris. '00	🍷🍷	6
●	Corbezzolo '96	🍷🍷	5
●	Corbezzolo '97	🍷🍷	5
●	Chianti Cl. Querciolo '98	🍷🍷	4
●	Corbezzolo '98	🍷🍷	5
●	Cantico '98	🍷🍷	5
●	Chianti Cl. Querciolo '99	🍷🍷	4
●	Corbezzolo '99	🍷🍷	7

TAVARNELLE VAL DI PESA (FI)

TERRANUOVA BRACCIOLINI (AR)

POGGIO AL SOLE
LOC. BADIA A PASSIGNANO
S.DA RIGNANA, 2
50028 TAVARNELLE VAL DI PESA (FI)
TEL. 0558071850
E-MAIL: poggioalsole@bcc.it

TENUTA SETTE PONTI
LOC. ORENO
52020 TERRANUOVA BRACCIOLINI (AR)
TEL. 055977443
E-MAIL:
tenutasetteponti@tenutasetteponti.it

The '00 vintage was, in our opinion, not a very good one for the Chianti Classico Casasilia, one of the landmark wines in Chianti over the last five years. Although it is again an excellent, elegantly varietal red, it lacks the grip and the concentration of extract that made it a champion from '97 to '99. It's more run-of-the-mill, softer, less complex, with intense aromas and a mouthfilling flavour, but a little heavy-handed with the alcohol, which limits the light and shade on nose and palate. Nothing serious, and certainly nothing to be surprised at, given the vintage. Nor could it change our minds about this excellent winery and its enthusiastic, dedicated owner, Giovanni Davaz. This year, the Syrah '01, one of the best of its category, was more interesting. It displays typical gamy scents and berry notes, and very respectable structure in the mouth. The Seraselva '00, a blend of cabernet sauvignon and merlot, also made a subdued appearance this time, but it has never been, in our opinion, this estate's top wine. The '00 version reprises the slight over-ripeness brought on by an extremely hot growing year, which forced an early harvest. The fine Chianti Classico '01 is much better than the '00 we tasted last year. This goes to confirm our impression that 2000 was not a particularly good year in the major parts of Chianti Classico.

The Sette Ponti estate, which once belonged to two Savoia D'Aosta princesses, Margherita and Maria Cristina, was purchased by the father of the present owner, Antonio Moretti. Who knows whether they imagined they would one day produce wines on a level with the most celebrated labels of Tuscany, not to say Italy? Yet this is just what has happened, thanks to the natural vocation of the territory, the determination of the owners, and the technical mastery of a first-rate staff under the guidance of the distinguished Carlo Ferrini. The splendid Oreno '01 came close to repeating last year's Three Glass triumph. A blend of cabernet sauvignon, merlot and sangiovese, it shows a dense, very concentrated colour with the purplish highlights of youth. The rich, powerful nose displays clearly defined notes of black berry fruit and coffee, and also nicely balanced toasty notes from its excellent, already well-integrated wood. The palate has a subtle balance of volume, concentration and elegance, as well as generous, fine-grained tannins, and a slightly rigid but attractively long finish. The Crognolo '01, obtained almost exclusively from sangiovese, nearly made it into our finals. Prominent spicy notes of cinnamon, white pepper and vanilla from the not yet fully absorbed oak appear against a lovely background of the ripe red berry fruit you expect from a good sangiovese. The dense, succulent palate reveals rather hard tannins at mid palate and on the finish.

●	Syrah '01	🍷🍷	7
●	Chianti Cl. Casasilia '00	🍷🍷	7
●	Seraselva '00	🍷🍷	7
●	Chianti Cl. '01	🍷🍷	5
●	Chianti Cl. Casasilia '97	🍷🍷🍷	7
●	Chianti Cl. Casasilia '98	🍷🍷🍷	7
●	Syrah '99	🍷🍷🍷	7
●	Chianti Cl. Casasilia '99	🍷🍷🍷	7
●	Chianti Cl. Casasilia Ris. '95	🍷🍷	7
●	Seraselva '95	🍷🍷	7
●	Seraselva '96	🍷🍷	7
●	Syrah '97	🍷🍷	7
●	Syrah '98	🍷🍷	7
●	Seraselva '99	🍷🍷	7
●	Syrah '00	🍷🍷	7

●	Oreno '01	🍷🍷	6
●	Crognolo '01	🍷🍷	5
●	Oreno '00	🍷🍷🍷	6
●	Crognolo '98	🍷🍷	4
●	Oreno '99	🍷🍷	6
●	Crognolo '99	🍷🍷	4
●	Crognolo '00	🍷🍷	5

VAGLIA (FI)

VINCI (FI)

ORTAGLIA
LOC. PRATOLINO
VIA SAN JACOPO, 331
50036 VAGLIA (FI)
TEL. 055409136
E-MAIL: ortaglia@iol.it

CANTINE LEONARDO DA VINCI
VIA PROVINCIALE MERCATALE, 291
50059 VINCI (FI)
TEL. 0571902444
E-MAIL: info@cantineleonardo.it

Dieter Lange, a German lawyer, has earned a profile for his Ortaglia estate, in part because it is completely atypical. In 1586, when Francesco I De' Medici wanted to give his mistress, Bianca Cappello, a love token in the form of a summer retreat where they could meet, he chose this isolated spot, where he constructed a cosily intimate house. In 1990, the present owner built an up-to-date winery around this enchanting residence. With the assistance of consultant oenologist, Maurizio Castelli, and after a careful study of the site climates and the soil, Dieter decided to plant just chardonnay, sauvignon and moscato. Only later, in 1999, did cabernet sauvignon, malbec and merlot make their appearance in the vineyards of Villa Ortaglia, and they now cover five of the 11 hectares under vine. This year marks the debut of Francesco I, a blend of the three red varieties. Alternating aromas of ripe fruit and mint pave the way for a soft, engrossingly opulent palate whose well-knit tannins are perfectly blended with the alcohol. The finish is very appealing. The Moscato Villa Ortaglia '01 is a real surprise. Delightful, intense aromas of oranges accompany scents of tropical fruits and roses. The palate is dense and extremely full-bodied, and the finish very long indeed. The mostly chardonnay-based N° 1 is very agreeable. Well-defined mineral notes share the stage with very delicate fruit. Finally, the Chardonnay '98 has ripe aromas and medium body.

Cantine Leonardo da Vinci is an excellent example of what the traditional co-operative winery of years ago can become by dint of constant improvement. They aim for high quality here, whatever they do, and the cellar continues to amaze us with its standard Chianti. Millions of bottles are released, all of which are convincing and agreeable. In the '02 version, fruit aromas stand out, enhanced by lovely peppery notes, and the supple body is underpinned by acidic backbone. The sangiovese-based San Zio '01, which is less successful than usual, is not particularly well-defined on the nose, but the palate is powerful and solidly structured. The well-executed Sant'Ippolito '01, a blend of syrah and merlot, opens on the nose with creamy notes which then make way for woodland berry tones. The palate shows good concentration, tight-packed tannins and a long, enjoyable finish. The Merlot degli Artisti '01 offers a variety of elegant and delicate aromas with wild berries to the fore, supported by notes of liquorice and pepper. The substantial palate has silky tannins and a pleasing, if not lingering, finish. The successful Vin Santo Tegrino d'Anchiano '98 shows a nose of dried figs alternating with notes of toasted hazel nuts and sweet hints of honey. The immediately appealing palate is velvety, fleshy and very full-bodied, then the lingering finish is supported by well-dosed acidity. Lastly, the Ser Piero '02, a Chardonnay, again offers excellent value for money. Redolent of bananas and tropical fruit, it is crisp and inviting in the mouth.

●	Francesco I '01	♟♟	4
○	Moscato Villa Ortaglia '01	♟♟	6
○	N° 1 '01	♟	4
○	Chardonnay '98	♟	5
○	Bianca Capello '01	♟♟	4

●	Merlot degli Artisti '01	♟♟	6
●	Sant'Ippolito '01	♟♟	5
○	Vin Santo Tegrino d'Anchiano '98	♟♟	4
●	San Zio '01	♟	4
●	Chianti Leonardo '02	♟	3
○	Ser Piero '02	♟	3
●	San Zio '97	♟♟	4
●	Sant'Ippolito '97	♟♟	5
●	San Zio '98	♟♟	4
●	Sant'Ippolito '98	♟♟	5
●	San Zio '99	♟♟	4
●	Sant'Ippolito '99	♟♟	5
●	Merlot degli Artisti '00	♟♟	6
●	San Zio '00	♟♟	4*

OTHER WINERIES

POGGIO SACCONE
VIA CANALI, 51
58031 ARCIDOSSO (GR)
TEL. 0564967401
E-MAIL: poggiosaccone@tiscali.it

Yet again, Poggio Saccone turned out to be one of the best Montecuccos around. The nose has clean notes of berry fruit jam and liquorice. The palate is almost austere, with plenty of punch backed up by crunchy yet discreet tannins. The finish is long and echoes the nose.

● Montecucco Sangiovese '01		🍷🍷	5
● Montecucco Sangiovese '00		🍷🍷	4

MALENCHINI
LOC. GRASSINA - VIA LILLIANO, 82
50015 BAGNO A RIPOLI (FI)
TEL. 055642602
E-MAIL: dimalen@tin.it

The Lilliano estate has changed its name but is still focusing on quality. Both products are geniunely good. The Colli Fiorentini '01 offers attractive spice-laced berry aromas and a soft, mouthfilling palate. There is jam on the nose of the Bruzzico '00, and silky tannins on the palate.

● Bruzzico '00		🍷🍷	5
● Chianti dei Colli Fiorentini '01		🍷🍷	4
● Bruzzico '99		🍷🍷	5
● Chianti dei Colli Fiorentini '00		🍷	4

I BALZINI
LOC. PASTINE, 19
50021 BARBERINO VAL D'ELSA (FI)
TEL. 0556580484 - 0558075503
E-MAIL: segreteria@disantoassociati.com

The I Balzini wines have made encouraging progress. The Black Label '99 earned Two Glasses for a crisply defined nose and a sweet, consistent palate with nicely rounded tannins. But the Balzini Rosso '99 was less convincing because of the somewhat forward nose and finish.

● I Balzini Black Label '99		🍷🍷	7
● I Balzini Rosso '99		🍷	6
● I Balzini Rosso '97		🍷🍷	6

FATTORIA SANT'APPIANO
VIA SANT'APPIANO, 11
50021 BARBERINO VAL D'ELSA (FI)
TEL. 0558075541
E-MAIL: pierfrancesco17@supereva.it

The flagship Monteloro '01 put on a fine performance. Dark ruby, with a slightly hesitant nose, it has a full, sustained mouthfeel, with well-extracted tannins and an intriguing, moderately long finish. The Chianti is decent. A fresh, pleasantly acidulous wine, it sells at a very honest price.

● Monteloro '01		🍷🍷	4*
● Chianti '02		🍷	3
● Monteloro '00		🍷🍷	4*

Spadaio e Piecorto
via San Silvestro, 1
50021 Barberino Val d'Elsa (FI)
tel. 0558072915 - 0558072238

The Stefanelli estate confirmed last year's good impression, despite the absence of the Alleroso Supertuscan. The Chianti Classico '01 is intense, offering fruit and spice on the nose, and shows character in the mouth. The compact palate and firm, fine-grained tannins, usher in a tasty finish.

● Chianti Cl. '01	♟♟	5

Caccia al Piano 1868
loc. Castagneto Carducci
via Bolgherese, 279
57022 Bolgheri (LI)
tel. 0565763366

The LeVia GraVia '01 is merlot-based with a little cabernet sauvignon. It's also a very fine red that nearly won a third Glass. Bolgheri Rosso Ruit Hora '02 suffered from a less than ideal vintage, but is well-made and clean on the nose.

● Bolgheri Levia Gravia '01	♟♟	8
● Bolgheri Ruit Hora '02	♟	6
● Bolgheri Levia Gravia '00	♟♟	8

Giovanni Chiappini
loc. Le Preselle - pod. Felciaino, 189/b
57020 Bolgheri (LI)
tel. 0565749665
e-mail: chiappini.giovanni@tiscali.it

It's the second year for Chiappini's Guado dei Gemoli, and his second very upbeat assessment. The '01 may even be superior to the '00. However, the Felciaino '02 is a tad weaker than the '01. A well-made, attractive wine, it is just a bit dilute on the palate.

● Bolgheri Guado de' Gemoli '01	♟♟	7
● Felciaino '02	♟	4
● Bolgheri Guado de' Gemoli '00	♟♟	6

Le Volpaiole
via Fonte Carboli, 13
57021 Campiglia Marittima (LI)
tel. 0565843194

There was a great showing from the Volpaiole estate red. Vibrant dark ruby in hue, the black berry fruit on the nose melds perfectly with the wood's spice and vanilla. On the palate, it mouthfilling and well-structured, with attractive finesse in the finish.

● Val di Cornia Rosso '01	♟♟	5
● Val di Cornia Rosso '97	♟♟	4

Cecilia
loc. La Pila - la Casina, 8
57034 Campo nell'Elba (LI)
tel. 024989864 - 0565977322
e-mail: vini.cecilia@virgilio.it

Cecilia comes back to the Guide with a surprisingly good Aleatico. The fresh nose unveils roses and raspberries, then the palate derives balance from acidity that bolsters its sugars. The Ansonica dell'Elba and Elba Rosso, both from '02, are delightfully well made.

● Elba Aleatico '01	♟♟	6
○ Elba Ansonica '02	♟	4
● Elba Rosso '02	♟	4

Fattoria Castellina
via Palandri, 27
50056 Capraia e Limite (FI)
tel. 057157631 - 057157066
e-mail: fmontomoli@tiscali.it

There was a great debut from Fattoria Castellina, whose three labels are models of reliability. The 100 per cent Merlot Daino Bianco '01 is firm and elegant. Corum '01, a blend of sangiovese, syrah and cabernet sauvignon, and the Chianti Montalbano '02, are ready to uncork and nicely structured.

● Daino Bianco '01	♟♟	7
● Corum '01	♟	5
● Chianti Montalbano '02	♟	3*

ARTIMINO
V.LE PAPA GIOVANNI XXIII, 1
59015 CARMIGNANO (PO)
TEL. 0558751423 - 0558751424
E-MAIL: fattoria@artimino.com

An up-and-down showing from Artimino. The Vigna dell'Iris '01 is well made, firm and structured, though the finish is mouth drying. The Carmignano '00 is decent on the palate but fuzzy on the nose. Villa Medicea Riserva '99 is green on the nose, then lean and dry in the mouth.

● Vigna dell'Iris '01	♈♈	6
● Carmignano Villa Artimino '00	♈	4
● Carmignano Villa Medicea Ris. '99		5

CASTELVECCHIO
LOC. SEANO
VIA DELLE MANNELLE, 19
59011 CARMIGNANO (PO)
TEL. 0558705451

Fattoria Castelvecchio turned out a nice Carmignano Riserva '00. Spices and grassy notes over fruit on the nose are followed by a sweet, well-sustained palate with subdued tannins. The Carmignano '00 has a refreshing, well-structured palate and the Vin Ruspo '02 is again attractive.

● Carmignano Ris. '00	♈♈	5
● Carmignano '00	♈	4
● Barco Reale '01	♈	3
⊙ Vin Ruspo '02	♈	3

CERALTI
FRAZ. DONORATICO - VIA DEI CERALTI, 77
57024 CASTAGNETO CARDUCCI (LI)
TEL. 0565763989
E-MAIL: info@ceralti.com

In the midst of so many prestigious cellars and awesomely expensive wines, Cantina Ceralti deserves praise for its Bolgheri wines at affordable prices. The Rosso Alfeo '01 is clean and correct, albeit not immense, and the well-typed Vermentino is undemanding but easy-drinking.

● Bolgheri Rosso Alfeo '01	♈	5
○ Bolgheri Vermentino Ceralti '02	♈	4

PODERE GUADO AL MELO
VIA PER LAMENTANO
57022 CASTAGNETO CARDUCCI (LI)
TEL. 0586679038
E-MAIL: info@guadoalmelo.it

The already impressive panorama of Castagneto Carducci has been enhanced by the arrival of this promising estate, under Michele Scienza. Only one wine was presented but it was a delicious, drinkable one, especially if we bear in mind the indifferent vintage. We await developments with impatience.

● Bolgheri Rosso '02	♈	4

MACCHIALANZI
LOC. MONTENERO D'ORCIA
58040 CASTEL DEL PIANO (GR)
TEL. 0564954140
E-MAIL: dainnocenti@interfree.it

The only Macchialanzi wine presented did well at our tastings. The Scoglio Riserva '00 is predominantly sangiovese with pinot nero, and has delicious fruit notes over nice vanilla. Entry in the mouth is unremarkable but it picks up pace mid palate, with good balance and a tight tannic weave.

● Lo Scoglio Ris. '00	♈♈	5

MONTESALARIO
LOC. MONTENERO D'ORCIA
58040 CASTEL DEL PIANO (GR)
TEL. 0564954173
E-MAIL: montesalario@interfree.it

The nose of the Montecucco '01 is muzzy, with gamey notes over berry fruit. The palate is quite attractive, although the wine seemed edgy and the tannins rough. The Riserva '00 is a better bottle. The clean nose reveals gamey notes and tobacco, then the tasty palate signs off with a slow finish.

● Montecucco Sangiovese Ris. '00	♈♈	5
● Montecucco Sangiovese '01	♈	4
● Montecucco Sangiovese '00	♈♈	5

ORCIAVERDE
LOC. MONTENERO D'ORCIA - PODERE 369
58040 CASTEL DEL PIANO (GR)
TEL. 0564954112
E-MAIL: orciaverde@jvirgilio.it

There was a fine Guide debut for
Orciaverde, and cellarman Paolo
Vagaggini. The Sangiovese '01 has berry
fruit and cinnamon on the nose, good
texture and tangy appeal. Hints of balsam
and forward notes emerge from the
Riserva '99, which has good texture in the
mouth, but intrusive tannins.

●	Montecucco Sangiovese '01	🍷🍷	4
●	Montecucco Sangiovese Ris. '99	🍷	5

TENUTA DI BIBBIANO
VIA BIBBIANO, 76
53011 CASTELLINA IN CHIANTI (SI)
TEL. 0577743065
E-MAIL: drmaya@virgilio.it

A first Guide entry for the Marrocchesi
family, whose 20 plus hectares under vine
are at Castellina in Chianti. The
Montornello '01 selection has generous
fruit aromas graced by notes of spice.
There is good body in the full palate,
where even, close-knit tannins usher in a
tasty finish.

●	Chianti Cl. Montornello '01	🍷🍷	6
●	Chianti Cl. Vigna del Capannino Ris. '99	🍷	7

LA CASTELLINA
VIA FERRUCCIO, 26
53011 CASTELLINA IN CHIANTI (SI)
TEL. 0577740454
E-MAIL: castellina@italyexpo.com

The monovarietal Sangiovese Reale '99 is
very nice. Crisp notes of ripe cherries
mingle with spice on the nose, then the
compact body and even, close-knit
tannins herald a long finish. Both Riserva
wines present slightly drying tannins.

●	Reale '99	🍷🍷	6
●	Chianti Cl. Ris. '99	🍷	5
●	Chianti Cl. Squarcialupi Ris. '99	🍷	5

CASTELLO LA LECCIA
LOC. LA LECCIA
53011 CASTELLINA IN CHIANTI (SI)
TEL. 0577743148 - 0577743076
E-MAIL: laleccia@chianticlassico.com

The Chianti Classico '01 did well. Minty
aromas introduce a gutsy, mouthfilling
palate with plenty of substance. We were
less impressed by the Bruciagna '00
selection, which has a pleasant palate but
somewhat cloying aromas.

●	Chianti Cl. '01	🍷🍷	4
●	Chianti Cl. Bruciagna '00	🍷	5

GAGLIOLE
LOC. GAGLIOLE, 42
53011 CASTELLINA IN CHIANTI (SI)
TEL. 0577740369 - 0577741791
E-MAIL: aziendagagliole@tin.it

The Gagliole '01, a sangiovese-led blend,
did very well again this year. Its lustrous
ruby hue precedes a complex, clean nose
redolent of redcurrant and blueberry. Entry
on the palate is neat, the mouthfeel is
rigorous and enfolding, then the finish is
tangily delicious.

●	Gagliole Rosso '01	🍷🍷	6

CASALE DELLO SPARVIERO
LOC. CASALE, 93
53011 CASTELLINA IN CHIANTI (SI)
TEL. 0577743062
E-MAIL: campoperi@libero.it

We tasted only one wine here, but it was a
good one. There are 90 hectares under
vine, and Attilio Pagli consults. The
Riserva '99 deservedly made the finals.
Strawberry and forest fruit aromas
precede elegance and structure on the
quite powerful palate. The good finish has
a note of spice.

●	Chianti Cl. Ris. '99	🍷🍷	5

Tramonti

Loc. Tramonti
53011 Castellina in Chianti (SI)
tel. 0577740512
e-mail dumhapoint@acadia.net

Martin Kolk and Kyle Wolfe's Castellina in Chianti winery never misses a beat. The Chianti Classico '01 performed admirably. An excellent entry on the nose mingles attractive pepper with rich fruit, where cherry and strawberry stand out. In the mouth, it is full-flavoured, delicious and long.

● Chianti Cl. '01	▼▼	5
● Chianti Cl. '00	▽▽	5

Villa Trasqua

Loc. Trasqua
53011 Castellina in Chianti (SI)
tel. 0577743075
e-mail: info@villatrasqua.it

Overall quality is as high as ever at Villa Trasqua, but the Trasgaia '99 failed to thrill as it usually does. Mint and balsam aromas alternate with spice on the nose, and the soft, creamy palate reveals a lip-smacking finish. The fragrant, beautifully textured Chianti Classico '01 is easy-drinking.

● Trasgaia '99	▼▼	5
● Chianti Cl. '01	▼	4
● Trasgaia '98	▽▽	5

Canonica a Cerreto

Loc. Canonica a Cerreto
53019 Castelnuovo Berardenga (SI)
tel. 0577363261
e-mail: info@canonicacerreto.it

A good showing from the Lorenzi estate. The sangiovese and merlot Sandiavolo '00 went through to the final tastings. Its fine fruit aromas are lifted by elegant spice and the full palate shows discreet extract. The Chianti Classico '01 has a ripe fruit nose, but the palate is dried by the oak.

● Sandiavolo '00	▼▼	5
● Chianti Cl. '01	▼▼	4*
● Chianti Cl. '00	▽▽	4*

Fattoria di Dievole

Fraz. Vagliagli
53010 Castelnuovo Berardenga (SI)
tel. 0577322613 - 0577322712
e-mail: dievole@dievole.it

More ups and downs at Fattoria di Dievole, noted for its label design. The Riserva Novecento '00 has aromas of ripe black berry fruit and spices. The standard Chianti is well made and enjoyable, if tannin-heavy, and the Plenum '99 has grassy aromas and an austere body, although it finishes quickly.

● Chianti Cl. Novecento Ris. '00	▼▼	6
● Chianti Cl. '01	▼	4
● Plenum '99	▼	7

Podere Le Boncie

Loc. San Felice - s.da delle Boncie, 5
53019 Castelnuovo Berardenga (SI)
tel. 0577359383
e-mail: leboncie@libero.it

It's easier than you think to make a good wine. But making a characterful wine with a sense of place and varietal identity is an art. Great artists have paint-stained hands, great winemakers have dirt under their fingernails and Giovanna Morganti makes wines with personality.

● Chianti Cl. Le Trame '00	▼▼	4
● Chianti Cl. Le Trame '99	▽▽	4

Pacina

Loc. Pacina
53019 Castelnuovo Berardenga (SI)
tel. 0577355044
e-mail: pacinina@libero.it

Giovanna Tezzi's winery made a mark this year with the Malena, which is always irresistible. A 50-50 blend of sangiovese and syrah, it reveals a sprinkling of pepper in its nose of ripe fruit. There's plenty of structure on the palate, although the finish is a tad edgy.

● Malena '01	▼▼	4
● Malena '00	▽▽	5

BORGO CASIGNANO
VIA CASIGNANO, 212
52020 CAVRIGLIA (AR)
TEL. 055 967090
E-MAIL: fatbel@tin.it

A small winery in the hill country near Cavriglia, Borgo Casignano uses organic methods to produce two wines. The Solatio '01 is remarkably clean and delicious, with good depth on the palate. The Chianti '00 is decent, too, with spice and berry aromas, moderate body and marked acidity.

● Chianti '00	♀	4
● Solatio '01	♀	5
● Solatio '00	♀♀	5

FATTORIA DI PETRIOLO
VIA DI PETRIOLO, 7
50050 CERRETO GUIDI (FI)
TEL. 0571509491 - 057180251
E-MAIL: info@villapetriolo.com

For a few years now, Villa Petriolo has been making excellent wines. Golpaja '01 shows jam on the nose but its strong suit is a palate of lively but well-balanced acidity and sweet, well-rounded tannins. The Chianti can offer decent texture and fruit, good balance and a very attractive price.

● Golpaja '01	♀♀	5
● Chianti Villa Petriolo '02	♀	3
● Golpaja '99	♀♀	4
● Golpaja '00	♀♀	4

FATTORIA DI FIANO
LOC. FIANO
VIA DI FIRENZE, 11
50050 CERTALDO (FI)
TEL. 0571669048

Ugo Bing's wines are beginning to develop their own personality. Fianesco '01 is the best version of this wine he has made. The dense, firm palate is rich in fruit and soft, sweet tannins. The Chianti is equally pleasant. showing medium structure, a gentle entry and nicely balanced progression.

● Fianesco '01	♀♀	6
● Chianti Colli Fiorentini '01	♀	4*
● Fianesco '99	♀♀	4
● Fianesco '00	♀♀	5

COLLE SANTA MUSTIOLA
VIA DELLE TORRI, 86/A
53043 CHIUSI (SI)
TEL. 057820525

Fabio Cenni presented only one wine, Poggio ai Chiari '01, a sangiovese blend with some colorino. The nose is a little muzzy at first, but then opens into ripe fruit laced with gamey nuances. Tannins are prominent on the palate, but there is no edginess. Nice fruit comes back in the finish.

● Poggio ai Chiari '01	♀♀	7
● Poggio ai Chiari '94	♀♀	3
● Poggio ai Chiari '99	♀♀	5
● Poggio ai Chiari '00	♀♀	5

FICOMONTANINO
LOC. FICOMONTANINO
53043 CHIUSI (SI)
TEL. 057821180 - 065561283
E-MAIL: alessandrogiannelli@tiscalinet.it

Ficomontanino impressed this year. Lucumone '01 is a monovarietal Cabernet Sauvignon with balsam on the nose and a soft, tight-knit mouthfeel. The well-structured, enfolding Tutulus '00 also performed well. The Tutulus '01 is nice, with grassy note on the nose and a hint of edginess on the palate.

● Chianti Colli Senesi Tutulus '00	♀♀	4
● Lucumone '01	♀♀	5
● Chianti Colli Senesi Tutulus '01	♀	4

LE CAPANNACCE
LOC. CAPANNACCE
FRAZ. PARI
58040 CIVITELLA PAGANICO (GR)
TEL. 0564908848

Alberto Porta's Poggio Crocino is very good this year. This elegant, deep ruby blend of sangiovese, syrah and grenache foregrounds black berry fruit and balsam on the nose, then the full-bodied palate leads into a long finish. Le Capannacce '00 and the Montecucco Rosso '00 are not so impressive.

● Poggio Crocino '00	♀♀	6
● Capannacce '00	♀	4
● Montecucco '00	♀	4

A. Vegni - Capezzine
Loc. Centoia
52040 Cortona (AR)
tel. 0575613026 - 0575613106
e-mail: vegni@tin.it

The agricultural college founded a century ago with Angelo Vegni's bequest has, over the years, earned praise for its well-made, attractively priced bottles. The two wines presented are up to snuff, especially the Chardonnay '02, whose peach and vegetal nose is echoed satisfyingly on the palate.

● Cortona Sangiovese '00	🍷	5
○ Cortona Chardonnay '02	🍷	3*

Fattoria Fabbri
loc. S. Marco in Villa, 2
52044 Cortona (AR)
tel. 0575630502
e-mail: info@fattoriafabbri.com

The panel was impressed when it tasted the Vin Santo '89, the only wine that this long-established Cortona winery presented. It is a distinctive sweet wine in the traditional mould but never cloys, thanks to great balance and a wide range of aromas. The length of the finish is incredible.

○ Vin Santo '89	🍷🍷	6

Fattoria Uccelliera
via Prov. Lorenzana Cucigliana, 1
56043 Fauglia (PI)
tel. 050662747
e-mail: info@uccelliera.com

Castellaccio Rosso performed well again in the'00 edition. Its rich, complex nose reveals black berry fruit, vegetal notes and faint spice. The even, attractive palate has perhaps a little too much oak. Rich and juicy sums up the Castellaccio Bianco '01.

● Castellaccio Rosso '00	🍷🍷	6
○ Castellaccio Bianco '01	🍷	5

Bibi Graetz
via di Vincigliata, 19
50014 Fiesole (FI)
tel. 055597289
e-mail: bibi.graetz@virgilio.it

Bibi Graetz started making wine for fun but very soon created a bottle with character. Testamatta '01 is further proof of her skills, with its intense fruit aromas and elegant, muscular structure.

● Testamatta '01	🍷🍷	8
● Testamatta '00	🍸🍸	8

Camposilio
loc. Vaglia - via Basciano, 805
50036 Firenze
tel. 055696456
e-mail: info@camposilio.it

Alessandro Rustioni is back in the Guide. His Camposilio '00, a blend of sangiovese, cabernet sauvignon and merlot, leads with mint and balsam on the nose. The palate is full and deliciously substantial, though the tannins are a shade too prominent.

● Camposilio '00	🍷🍷	6
● I Venti di Camposilio '01	🍷	4
● Camposilio '98	🍸🍸	6

Il Grillesino
b.go degli Albizi, 14
50122 Firenze
tel. 055243101 - 055245012
e-mail: compagniadelvino@lbonet.it

The Compagnia del Vino always obtains excellent wines from the Il Grillesino vineyards at Grancia near Grosseto. Ceccante '00, a sangiovese and cabernet sauvignon blend, is concentrated, full-bodied and mouthfilling. The Morellino Riserva '01 has nice mineral notes and the Morellino '02 is good.

● Ceccante '00	🍷🍷	7
● Morellino di Scansano Ris. '01	🍷🍷	5
● Morellino di Scansano '02	🍷	3
● Ceccante '99	🍸🍸	6

Fattoria Santa Vittoria
LOC. POZZO - VIA PIANA, 43
52045 FOIANO DELLA CHIANA (AR)
TEL. 057566807 - 0575966026
E-MAIL: marnicc@iol.it

The Fattoria Santa Vittoria wines nearly earned a second Glass. Scannagallo '01 has good structure but lacks definition on the nose and the tannins are hard. On retasting, the Poggio al Tempio '01 was deliciously drinkable, but the sweet, balanced Vin Santo '94 is unsettled on the nose.

●	Scannagallo '01	▼	4
○	Vin Santo '94	▼	5
○	Val di Chiana Grechetto '02		3

Castello di Cacchiano
FRAZ. MONTI IN CHIANTI
LOC. CACCHIANO
53010 GAIOLE IN CHIANTI (SI)
TEL. 0577747018

There was no Chianti Classico from Giovanni Ricasoli-Firidolfi's estate this time. The Rosso '01 has an attractive nose, firmness on the palate and is very drinkable. As ever, the Vin Santo is good. Its slightly citrussy aromas usher in a velvet-rich, enfolding mouthfeel and outstanding length.

○	Vin Santo '97	▼▼	8
●	Castello di Cacchiano Rosso '01	▼	4
○	Castello di Cacchiano Bianco '02		3

Montiverdi
LOC. MONTIVERDI
53013 GAIOLE IN CHIANTI (SI)
TEL. 0577749305 - 028378808

Only the two Riservas stand out in the wide range of Montiverdi labels. Villa Maisano Riserva '99 is notably clean on the nose and has a solid, muscular palate with a tasty finish. The Riserva '99 is less successful. The aromas are muzzy and the very full mouthfeel is dilute mid palate.

●	Chianti Cl. Villa Maisano Ris. '99	▼▼	5
●	Chianti Cl. Ris. '99	▼	5

Rocca di Montegrossi
LOC. MONTI IN CHIANTI
53010 GAIOLE IN CHIANTI (SI)
TEL. 0577747977

The 2001 vintage was difficult for Rocca di Montegrossi. There were no selections and all the fruit went into the standard-label Chianti base, a moreish, fruit-forward wine. The amber '97 Vin Santo is as good as ever, showing hazelnut, date and dry fig aromas. The palate is smooth, creamy and long.

○	Vin Santo del Chianti Cl. '95	▼▼	7
●	Chianti Cl. '01	▼	5
●	Chianti Cl. Vigneto S. Marcellino Ris. '99	▼▼▼	5

I Sodi
LOC. MONTI IN CHIANTI
53010 GAIOLE IN CHIANTI (SI)
TEL. 0577332543

An interesting Chianti Classico '01 earned an Other Wineries profile for I Sodi, the Casini family estate at Gaiole. The ten hectares under vine are planted to traditional varieties. The nose is intense and foregrounds cherries, then the palate is reasonably full-bodied. The Riserva '00 is good.

●	Chianti Cl. '01	▼▼	4
●	Chianti Cl. Ris. '99	▼	5

Castello di Tornano
LOC. TORNANO
53013 GAIOLE IN CHIANTI (SI)
TEL. 0577746067
E-MAIL: castellotornano@libero.it

There was only one wine from the Selvolini family's 15 hectares at Gaiole in Chianti. It was an intriguing one, though, for the intense, ruby Chianti Classico has clean fruit aromas, with a hint of spice. It reveals good body, close-knit tannins and tangy acidity before the tasty finish.

●	Chianti Cl. '01	▼▼	4

IL TAGLIATO
VIA BARBIANO, 21
50022 GREVE IN CHIANTI (FI)
TEL. 0558547118

There was a Guide debut this year for Il Tagliato, which makes only one wine, a characterful blend of sangiovese and merlot. Balzi d'Istrice '01 is vibrant ruby with fresh, juicy aromas. The palate has grip, texture and an even tannin weave. It flags a bit mid palate, but the finish is delicious.

● Balze d'Istrice '01	♙♙	8

LA MADONNINA - TRIACCA
LOC. STRADA IN CHIANTI
VIA PALAIA, 39
50027 GREVE IN CHIANTI (FI)
TEL. 055858003

It was only a middling year for the Triacca family estate. Bello Stento '01 has youthful fruit and alcohol aromas and a slender body. The Riserva La Palaia '00 is fuller and more elegant, whereas Il Mandorlo '00 reveals rather too obvious vegetal aromas.

● Chianti Cl. V. La Palaia '00	♙	5
● Il Mandorlo '00	♙	5
● Chianti Cl. Bello Stento '01	♙	4

TENUTA LA NOVELLA
LOC. SAN POLO IN CHIANTI
VIA MUSIGNANA, 11
50022 GREVE IN CHIANTI (FI)
TEL. 0558337749

The cellar work supervised by Gabriella Tani, and David Picci's watchful eye in the vineyard, have enabled Tenuta La Novella to make progress. Their eight hectares have yielded two lovely Chiantis, a standard '01 and a Riserva '00. The first is drinking now, the second has good structure.

● Chianti Cl. '01	♙♙	6
● Chianti Cl. Ris. '00	♙♙	8
● Chianti Cl. Ris. '99	♙♙	6

MONTECALVI
VIA CITILLE, 85
50022 GREVE IN CHIANTI (FI)
TEL. 0558544665
E-MAIL: bollij@tin.it

It was a poor year at Montecalvi. Although the style is there, lack of fruit on the palate has made the wine less interesting than usual. Pale ruby precedes a nose of violet flowers with hints of cherry. The attack is subdued, and progression thinnish. The finish is clean, but not very long.

● Montecalvi '00	♙♙	6

RISECCOLI
VIA CONVERTOIE, 9
50022 GREVE IN CHIANTI (FI)
TEL. 055853598
E-MAIL: info@riseccoli.com

The Saeculum '01 was not ready for the panel so Riseccoli presented two decent versions of their Chianti Classico. The Riserva '00 is a shade dilute and very alcohol-forward, but the standard-label '01 has more character, and even seemed a little young.

● Chianti Cl. Ris. '00	♙	6
● Chianti Cl. '01	♙	4
● Saeculum '00	♙♙	8
● Chianti Cl. Ris. '99	♙♙	5

FATTORIA SANTO STEFANO
LOC. GRETI - VIA DI COLLEGALLE, 3
50022 GREVE IN CHIANTI (FI)
TEL. 0558572298
E-MAIL: info@fattoriasantostefano.net

The Bendinelli family debut in the Guide was crowned by Chianti Classico Drugo '01, which sailed through to our final tastings. The vibrant ruby introduces intense berry fruit and spice on the nose. There's juicy pulp on the palate, which has close-knit, fine-grained tannins and impressive length.

● Cl. Classico Drugo '01	♙♙	5

VILLA CALCINAIA
FRAZ. GRETI - VIA CITILLE, 84
50022 GREVE IN CHIANTI (FI)
TEL. 055854008
E-MAIL: villacalcinaia@villacalcinaia.it

The Capponi family has had another good year. This time, the '01 Chianti Classico took centre stage, thanks to intense forest fruit aromas layered over spice, and a firm, well-balanced body. The Riserva '00 was dried out by the wood and the Casarsa '00 lacks softness and texture.

● Chianti Cl. '01	♟♟	4
● Casarsa '00	♟	7
● Chianti Cl. Ris. '00	♟	6

VILLA CASALE
LOC. GRETI
50022 GREVE IN CHIANTI (FI)
TEL. 0558544859

At Greti, a stone's throw from Greve in Chianti, Heinz Echler makes premium wines with lots of personality. Insolito '00 has intense aromas of bramble and plum, good body and close-knit, but very mellow, tannins. The nice, undemanding Chianti Classico '01 offers an elegant nose and nimble body.

● Chianti Cl. L'Insolito '00	♟♟	7
● Chianti Cl. '01	♟	4

SANTA LUCIA
FRAZ. FONTEBLANDA
VIA AURELIA NORD, 66
58010 GROSSETO
TEL. 0564885474

This year, Luciano Scotti's wines are good. Betto '01, from sangiovese, merlot and cabernet sauvignon, is an exciting red. Elegant on the nose, it shows soft and well-structured in the mouth. The Losco '02 has hints of strawberry. On the palate, there is good body but little length.

● Betto '01	♟♟	4
● Capalbio Rosso Losco '02	♟	3
● Morellino di Scansano Rosso		
Tore del Moro '00	♟♟	4*

FATTORIA COLLAZZI
LOC. TAVARNUZZE - VIA COLLERAMOLE, 101
50029 IMPRUNETA (FI)
TEL. 0552022528 - 0552374902
E-MAIL: collazzi@leonet.it

The Marchi estate has finished replanting and today has 20 hectares under vine. The Collazzi is always good. A very successful blend of cabernet sauvignon, cabernet franc and merlot, its captivatingly intense nose ushers in a soft, gently enfolding mouthfeel.

● Collazzi '01	♟♟	7
● Collazzi '99	♟♟	5
● Collazzi '00	♟♟	7

FATTORIA MONTANINE
LOC. CHIESANUOVA - VIA VOLTERRANA, 45
50029 IMPRUNETA (FI)
TEL. 0552373055
E-MAIL: lemontanine@libero.it

Fattoria Montanine put on a brilliant first show for the Guide. Prominent were the '00 and '01 vintages of Casanova Rosso, from sangiovese with merlot, syrah and malvasia nera. They are similar in style, but we preferred the '00 for its rock solid nose and hefty yet balanced palate.

● Casanova Rosso '00	♟♟	4
● Casanova Rosso '01	♟	4
● Chianti Ris. '01	♟	4
● Chianti '02	♟	3

VIGLIANO
FRAZ. SAN MARTINO ALLA PALMA
VIA CARCHERI, 309
50010 LASTRA A SIGNA (FI)
TEL. 0558727006 - 055284647

The Marchionni winery is going from strength to strength. The white was absent this time, but the estate Supertuscan, Vigna dell'Erta '01, is an easy drinker with tempting aromas and plenty of structure. The Rosso '01 is a winner, thanks to upfront aromas, appeal and good length.

● Vigna dell'Erta '01	♟♟	5
● Rosso Vigliano '01	♟	3
● Vigna dell'Erta '98	♟♟	5
● Vigna dell'Erta '99	♟♟	5

TENUTA VITERETA
VIA CASA NUOVA, 108
52020 LATERINA (AR)
TEL. 057589058
E-MAIL: vitareta@inwind.it

The most exciting newcomer in the province of Arezzo made a fine debut. Cabernet Villa Bernetti '01 nearly made it to the final taste-offs, showing great depth and elegance in a aromatic profile of crisp fruit, spice and balsamic notes, partly from oak. The rest of the range is well done.

● Villa Bernetti '01	▼▼	5
● Capitoni '01	▼	4
● Grondino Rosso '01	▼	3*
○ Grondino Bianco '02	▼	3*

TENUTA IL BORRO
FRAZ. SAN GIUSTINO VALDARNO
52020 LORO CIUFFENNA (AR)
TEL. 055977053
E-MAIL: vino@ilborro.it

Tenuta Il Borro, where Niccolò D'Afflitto consults, releases only one wine, which went right through to the finals. It's a merlot and cabernet-based blend with syrah and petit verdot that offers a complex nose and a firm palate, where the tannins are still a tad stiff. Time will sort this out.

● Il Borro '01	▼▼	8
● Il Borro '00	▼▼	8
● Il Borro '99	▼▼	8

FATTORIA DI ROMIGNANO
VIA SETTEPONTI LEVANTE, 30
52024 LORO CIUFFENNA (AR)
TEL. 055977635 - 3292161691
E-MAIL: romignano@tiscali.it

This organic estate in the hills between the river Arno and Pratomagno did well. Sabòt '01 really hit the spot. The nose foregrounds sweet fruit, vanilla and spice, echoed on the palate, which adds tonic acidity and good progression. The Chianti Terra Antica '00 is attractive.

● Sabòt '01	▼▼	6
● Chianti Terra Antica '00	▼	3*

FATTORIA COLLE VERDE
FRAZ. MATRAIA - LOC. CASTELLO
55010 LUCCA
TEL. 0583402310
E-MAIL: info@colleverde.it

Francesca Pardini and Piero Tartagni's cellar has stormed back into the Guide. Nero della Spinosa '00, a monovarietal Syrah, went through to the taste-offs. Dense and gamey on the nose, it unleashes muscle in a palate whose tannins have yet to mellow. Brania delle Ghiandaie '00 is also very good.

● Nero della Spinosa '00	▼▼	6
● Colline Lucchesi Rosso		
Brania delle Ghiandaie '00	▼▼	5
○ Colline Lucchesi Bianco		
Terre di Matraja '02		3

VALLE DEL SOLE
LOC. MONTE S. QUIRICO
VIA DELLE QUERCE, 325
55060 LUCCA
TEL. 0583395093

There was a good showing from this Lucca estate. Libente '01, from sangiovese and some merlot, is nice. Its berry fruit and dried flower nose introduces a well-balanced, upfront palate. We were less impressed by the Ebrius '01, with its lack of focus on the nose and poor continuity on the palate.

● Libente '01	▼▼	4
● Ebrius '01	▼	5

COL DI BACCHE
S.DA DI CUPI
58051 MAGLIANO IN TOSCANA (GR)
TEL. 0577738526

Alberto Carnasciali's ten-hectare Col di Bacche estate, supervised by Lorenzi Landi, made a fine Guide debut. The soft, delicious Morellino '02 has typical notes of ripe fruit. Cupinero '01, a blend of sangiovese and merlot, shows spice on the nose, then a balanced, juicy, long palate.

● Cupinero '01	▼▼	5
● Morellino di Scansano '02	▼	4

LA STELLATA
VIA FORNACINA, 18
58014 MANCIANO (GR)
TEL. 0564620190
E-MAIL: lastellata@tiscalinet.it

After a year's absence, Manlio Giorni and Clara Divizia's small La Stellata winery is back in the Guide. Their Lunaia Rosso '01, from mainly sangiovese, has elegant berry fruit aromas, followed by a warm, soft entry in the mouth. The finish is attractive, if a little thin.

● Lunaia Rosso '01	𝟁𝟁	4
● Lunaia Rosso '97	𝟁𝟁	3
● Lunaia Rosso '98	𝟁𝟁	4

ALTESINO
LOC. ALTESINO, 54
53028 MONTALCINO (SI)
TEL. 0577806208
E-MAIL: altesino@iol.it

There was a rather disappointing showing from this major producer. All the wines were unfocused on the nose at first. But we liked the Brunello Montosoli '98, whose personality and concentration show how good the local soil is. It's a pity the nose is forward, with hay and tobacco masking the fruit.

● Alte d'Altesi '00	𝟁	6
● Rosso di Montalcino '01	𝟁	5
● Brunello di Montalcino Ris. '97	𝟁	8
● Brunello di Montalcino Montosoli '98	𝟁	8

ARGIANO
FRAZ. SANT'ANGELO IN COLLE
LOC. ARGIANO, 74
53020 MONTALCINO (SI)
TEL. 0577844037

This year, Argiano has released a new wine. Suolo '00 is a terroir-driven, monovarietal Sangiovese from the oldest estate vines, aged in small wood. The nose soon reveals warm tobacco and berry fruit, but the tannins are intrusive. The long Brunello '98 has crisp aromas and a tasty palate.

● Brunello di Montalcino '98	𝟁𝟁	8
● Suolo '00	𝟁	8
● Rosso di Montalcino '01		5
● Solengo '01		8

ROBERTO BELLINI
LOC. PODERE BRIZIO, 11
53024 MONTALCINO (SI)
TEL. 0577846004
E-MAIL: poderebrizio@inwind.it

Bellini's return to Montalcino is marked by the release of the Brunello '98, a nice if less than complex wine. The fruit is well-defined, with morello cherry coming through, and the palate has good balance, thanks to a nice tannic weave. The Pupà Pepu '01 earned Two effortless Glasses.

● Pupà Pepu '01	𝟁𝟁	8
● Podere Brizio '01	𝟁	7
● Brunello di Montalcino '98	𝟁	8
● Podere Brizio '00	𝟁𝟁	5

BRUNELLI - LE CHIUSE DI SOTTO
LOC. LE CHIUSE DI SOTTO, 320
53024 MONTALCINO (SI)
TEL. 0577849342

Gianni Brunelli continues the good work he started last year with a fine Rosso di Montalcino '01. The deep ruby is accompanied by a pleasantly fruit-forward, harmonious personality. The less impressive Brunello '98 is mouth-drying in the finish. This cellar is one to watch.

● Rosso di Montalcino '01	𝟁𝟁	6
● Brunello di Montalcino '98	𝟁	8

CANALICCHIO DI SOPRA
FRAZ. CASACCIA
LOC. CANALICCHIO DI SOPRA, 343
53024 MONTALCINO (SI)
TEL. 0577848316 - 0577846221

Canalicchio di Sopra makes attractively priced, well-made, traditional wines. Since '97, it has also made a terroir-driven Brunello Riserva with a fruit nose lifted by faint smokiness. The palate melds structure and juicy tannins. The fine Brunello '98 is less richly extracted, but very drinkable.

● Brunello di Montalcino Ris. '97	𝟁𝟁	8
● Rosso di Montalcino '01	𝟁	5
● Brunello di Montalcino '98	𝟁	7

CERBAIA
LOC. CERBAIA
53024 MONTALCINO (SI)
TEL. 0577848301 - 066793628

Fabio Pellegrini's cellar put on a fine performance, including its best-ever Brunello. Vigna Cerbaia Riserva '97 is good. Cherry and red berry fruit greet the nose, backed by hints of tobacco and autumn leaves. And the palate is impeccable, with a progression worthy of the finest Brunellos.

● Brunello di Montalcino Ris. '97	♥♥	7
● Brunello di Montalcino '98	♥	7
● Rosso di Montalcino Ris. '01		4

COLLELCETO
POD. LA PISANA
53024 MONTALCINO (SI)
TEL. 0577816022
E-MAIL: info@collelceto.it

Yet another newcomer. The fine Brunello '98 has a very modern style. The nose is exotically redolent of cedar, as well as intense, well-defined morello cherry and cherry. The superbly extracted palate is rich in juicy tannins. Overall, it is well-made, if lacking a little elegance.

● Brunello di Montalcino '98	♥♥	7
● Rosso di Montalcino '01		4

CORTE PAVONE
LOC. CASANOVA
53024 MONTALCINO (SI)
TEL. 0471365125 - 0577848110
E-MAIL: lo@cker.it

The Tuscan branch of the Alto Adige-based Loacker company continues to grow. The wines are rigorously made and richly flavoursome. The Brunello Riserva '97 is nice. Slowly, hints of redcurrant and ripe cherry emerge, then the palate unveils acidity that complements the seriously good extract.

● Brunello di Montalcino Ris. '97	♥♥	8
● Brunello di Montalcino '98	♥	7
● Rosso di Montalcino '01		5

FATTOI
LOC. SANTA RESTITUTA
POD. CAPANNA, 101
53024 MONTALCINO (SI)
TEL. 0577848613

Fattoi lies west of Montalcino. It did well with both the Brunello '98 and the Riserva '97. The fruit-led nose of the Brunello is still slightly closed, but it has good stuffing and mellow tannins that meld with the rich palate. The Riserva is distant on the nose and the tannins are still young.

● Brunello di Montalcino Ris. '97	♥♥	8
● Rosso di Montalcino '01	♥	4
● Brunello di Montalcino '98	♥	6

FOSSACOLLE
LOC. TAVERNELLE, 7
53024 MONTALCINO (SI)
TEL. 0577816013

Located near Tavernelle, Fossacolle releases only Brunello di Montalcino, but it's good. The '98 is hardly muscular, yet the aromas are intriguing, flowers and yellow peach fusing nicely with spice from the wood. The tannins are still intrusive but cellar time should settle them down.

● Brunello di Montalcino '98	♥♥	7

IL MARRONETO
FRAZ. MADONNA DELLE GRAZIE
LOC. IL MARRONETO, 307
53024 MONTALCINO (SI)
TEL. 0577849382

Il Marroneto makes characterful wines. The Brunello di Montalcino '98 reflects a cellar philosophy that favours austere elegance. A vibrant ruby ushers in a nose of apricot and melon over tobacco. Attractive intensity of flavour also helps to make this classic wine a very enjoyable one.

● Brunello di Montalcino '98	♥♥	8
● Brunello di Montalcino '97	♀♀	8

IL PARADISO DI FRASSINA
LOC. FRASSINA, 41
53024 MONTALCINO (SI)
TEL. 0577839031
E-MAIL: alparadiso@tiscalinet.it

Carlo Cignozzi has made a fine winemaking debut after years as a consultant. He gave us two wines in two editions. We liked the newer sangiovese-based Gea for its morello cherry and bramble nose, and balance in the mouth. Do '00 is promising, revealing balanced green notes and concentration.

● Sant'Antimo Do '00	♈♈	6
● Sant'Antimo Do '01	♈	6
● Sant'Antimo Gea '01	♈	6
● Sant'Antimo Gea '00		6

LA FORNACE
POD. FORNACE
53024 MONTALCINO (SI)
TEL. 0577848465
E-MAIL: lafornace@tin.it

What a good performance! The most obvious sign of change in the wines comes from the Brunello Riserva '97, which has a complex nose of bramble and morello cherry with coffee. The aromas mirrored on the palate, where excellent balance favours an unhurried finish. The other wines are well made.

● Brunello di Montalcino Ris. '97	♈♈	8
● Rosso di Montalcino '01	♈	4
● Brunello di Montalcino '98	♈	6

LA RASINA
LOC. RASINA, 132
53024 MONTALCINO (SI)
TEL. 0577848536
E-MAIL: larasina@larasina.it

This small estate on the eastern slopes of Montalcino makes good wines that have been improving for several years. The Brunello '98 is very persuasive, its dark ruby and nose of torrefaction and bramble preceding a robust palate, with delicate tannins. The Rosso di Montalcino '01 is good.

● Brunello di Montalcino '98	♈♈	7
● Rosso di Montalcino '01	♈	4

PODERE LA VIGNA
LOC. TORRENIERI
53028 MONTALCINO (SI)
TEL. 0577834252
E-MAIL: podere.lavigna@virgilio.it

Alvaro Rubegni's estate lies beyond the village of Torrenieri, a part of Montalcino still to be discovered by winelovers. All the wines presented are good, but the Brunello '98 stands out, its modern, tropical aromas and juicy pulp lending balance and drinkability. The other wines are attractive.

● Brunello di Montalcino '98	♈♈	7
● Maritato '01	♈	5
● Rosso di Montalcino '01	♈	5

LE GODE DI RIPACCIOLI
LOC. LE GODE, 343
53024 MONTALCINO (SI)
TEL. 0577848547 - 0577847089
E-MAIL: azienda.legode@libero.it

"Terroir" is this estate's motto. The vines in Montalcino's Montosoli vineyard yielded two wines this year. The Brunello '98 has a complex nose of fruit and toastiness, and good body. The fruit-led Rosso di Montalcino '01 came close to a second Glass for its fresh acidity and sheer attractiveness.

● Brunello di Montalcino '98	♈♈	6
● Rosso di Montalcino '01	♈	4
● Brunello di Montalcino '96	♈♈	6
● Brunello di Montalcino '97	♈♈	7

LE MACIOCHE
S. P. 55 DI SANT'ANTIMO KM 4,85
53024 MONTALCINO (SI)
TEL. 0577849168 - 0632600127

There was a fine display from Le Macioche and the Brunello Riserva '97 reached the finals. Its intense nose has wild cherries, vanilla and bramble, beautifully reflected on the long, harmonious palate, thanks to juicy, close-knit tannins. The fruity Brunello '98 is also great. Watch this cellar.

● Brunello di Montalcino Ris. '97	♈♈	7
● Brunello di Montalcino '98	♈	7
● Rosso di Montalcino '01		4

MOCALI
LOC. MOCALI
53024 MONTALCINO (SI)
TEL. 0577849485
E-MAIL: azmocali@tiscali.it

Tiziano Ciacci's wines have personality, although some lack definition on the nose. The Brunello Vigna delle Raunate '98 is good. Its brilliant ruby introduces a nose of intense fruit and a palate whose elegant harmony lends it complexity and delicious drinkability. The Brunello '98 is also good.

● Brunello di Montalcino Vigna delle Raunate '98	♈♈	7
● Rosso di Montalcino '01	♈	5
● Brunello di Montalcino Ris. '97	♈	8
● Brunello di Montalcino '98	♈	7

CANTINA DI MONTALCINO
LOC. VAL DI CAVA
53024 MONTALCINO (SI)
TEL. 0577848704
E-MAIL: info@cantinadimontalcino.it

The Villa di Corsano '01 did very well. It reveals intense aromas of coffee, chocolate and ripe fruit, as well as a soft, well-rounded mouthfeel and excellent length. The Brunello '98 has nice cherry and plum on the nose, then good body and structure on the palate.

● Villa di Corsano '01	♈♈	6
● Brunello di Montalcino '98	♈♈	6
● Rosso di Montalcino '01	♈	4
● Villa di Corsano '00	♈♈	6

OLIVETO
FRAZ. CASTELNUOVO DELL'ABATE
LOC. OLIVETO
53020 MONTALCINO (SI)
TEL. 0577807170 - 0577835542

Oliveto is at Castelnuovo dell'Abate, south of Montalcino, where it has long produced fine Rosso di Montalcino. The '01 edition is nice, if ruffled by unripe notes on the nose. Still, the body is tidy. Leccio '01 earned Two Glasses. Its depth of aromas and flavour are enhanced by youthful tannins.

● Il Leccio '01	♈♈	5
● Rosso di Montalcino Il Roccolo '01	♈	5
● Brunello di Montalcino '98		7
● Rosso di Montalcino Il Roccolo '99	♈♈	5

PALAZZO
VIA COMUNALI, 144
53024 MONTALCINO (SI)
TEL. 0577848479
E-MAIL: az.palazzo@tin.it

Palazzo did very well, presenting the panel with well-made, well-typed wines. The Brunello '98 earned Two Glasses for its broad nose of fruit and balsam, lifted by understated hints of oakiness. The palate is firm and chewy, the delicately delicious tannins melding perfectly into the texture.

● Brunello di Montalcino '98	♈♈	7
● Alcineo '00	♈	6
● Rosso di Montalcino '01	♈	4
● Brunello di Montalcino Ris. '97	♈	7

PIAN DELLE VIGNE
LOC. PIAN DELLE VIGNE
53024 MONTALCINO (SI)
TEL. 0577816066
E-MAIL: piandellevigne@antinori.it

The Antinoris' Montalcino estate presented a good Brunello '98, if not yet one of the very best. It is well made, and the clean nose shows bramble and oak, but it lacks real complexity in the mouth. We are confident progress will continue, for the Antinoris are lavishing resources on this winery.

● Brunello di Montalcino '98	♈	7

PIAN DELL'ORINO
LOC. PIAN DELL'ORINO, 189
53024 MONTALCINO (SI)
TEL. 0577849301
E-MAIL: info@piandellorino.it

This reliable cellar makes good wine near the legendary Greppo estate. And the Brunello '98? It's lovely. Elegant and well-balanced, it has a nose of warm fruit and toastiness. The Rosso di Montalcino '01 is pleasant. There's bramble on the nose and young tannins do not mask the enfolding finish.

● Brunello di Montalcino '98	♈♈	8
● Rosso di Montalcino '01	♈	6
● Piandorino '99	♈	6

PIANCORNELLO
LOC. PIANCORNELLO
53014 MONTALCINO (SI)
TEL. 0577844105

Piancornello is a cellar that releases fine wines at honest prices. The Brunello '98, from a coolish year, is delicious, a broad nose of fruit fusing nicely with the oak. But progression on the palate is hampered by edgy tannins that hold back the finish. The Rosso '01 is very drinkable.

● Brunello di Montalcino '98	🍷🍷	7
● Rosso di Montalcino '01	🍷	5

AGOSTINA PIERI
FRAZ. S. ANGELO SCALO
LOC. PIANCORNELLO
53024 MONTALCINO (SI)
TEL. 0577844163

The wines from this cellar are always good. The Rosso '01 has floral aromas and a hint of grass. There is good body, but the tannins are intrusive. The Brunello '98, with its chocolate, berry fruit and elegant geraniums aromas, is a better bet. Perfectly ripe grapes ensure balance in the mouth.

● Brunello di Montalcino '98	🍷🍷	7
● Rosso di Montalcino '01	🍷	5
● Rosso di Montalcino '95	🍷🍷🍷	5

POGGIO DI SOTTO
FRAZ. CASTELNUOVO DELL'ABATE
LOC. POGGIO DI SOTTO
53020 MONTALCINO (SI)
TEL. 0577835502

We preferred the Rosso di Montalcino '00 to the more prestigious Brunello, whose '98 edition did not seem up to snuff. Piero Palmucci releases his Rosso di Montalcino a year later than most, but it's well worth the wait. The structure is impressive and the finish echoes the nose to perfection.

● Rosso di Montalcino '00	🍷🍷	7
● Brunello di Montalcino '98	🍷	8
● Brunello di Montalcino '96	🍷🍷	8
● Brunello di Montalcino '97	🍷🍷	8

POGGIO SAN POLO
LOC. PODERE SAN POLO, 161
53024 MONTALCINO (SI)
TEL. 0577835522
E-MAIL: info@poggiosanpolo.com

The new vineyards on the eastern edge of Montalcino are lovely, and the Brunello '98 is good, too. Refreshing on the nose, it has flavour, elegance and appeal. The Rosso di Montalcino '01 is simpler but still attractive, thanks to its cherry fragrance and drinkability.

● Brunello di Montalcino '98	🍷🍷	7
● Rosso di Montalcino '01	🍷	5
● Mezzopane '01		6
● Mezzopane '00	🍷🍷	6

SESTI - CASTELLO DI ARGIANO
FRAZ. SANT'ANGELO IN COLLE
53020 MONTALCINO (SI)
TEL. 0577844113
E-MAIL: giuseppesesti@libero.it

This estate at Argiano scored well in tastings. The flowers on the nose of the Brunello '98 are lifted by classic notes of leather and tobacco. It has flavour, substance and tidy elegance. The Brunello Riserva '97 is less convincing. The mineral nose reveals geraniums and the palate lacks balance.

● Brunello di Montalcino '98	🍷🍷	8
● Sant'Antimo Terra di Siena '00	🍷	6
● Brunello di Montalcino Ris. '97	🍷	8

LA VELONA
LOC. CASTELNUOVO DELL'ABATE
53024 MONTALCINO (SI)
TEL. 0577835525

A Guide debut for this new winery, which for now releases only one wine, a Rosso di Montalcino. The nose is clear and fresh, offering a typical note of ripe cherry. The palate is nice and juicy, flaunting a perfect balance of acidity and tannins: an easy-drinking wine with a long finish.

● Rosso di Montalcino '01	🍷🍷	4

VITANZA
POD. RENAIONE, 291
53024 MONTALCINO (SI)
TEL. 0577846031 - 03479731898
E-MAIL: tenutavitanza@hotmail.com

Rosalba Vitanza's winery is expanding and her seven hectares yield some interesting modern wines. The Brunello '98 reached the finals for its rich, concentrated, fruit-led nose and a mouthfilling palate with a tight weave. The Brunello Riserva '97 has a warm nose, but rather boisterous tannins.

● Brunello di Montalcino '98	🍷🍷	8
● Brunello di Montalcino Ris. '97	🍷	8
● Quadrimendo '01		6
● Rosso di Montalcino '01		6

FATTORIA LA TORRE
VIA PROVINCIALE DI MONTECARLO, 7
55015 MONTECARLO (LU)
TEL. 058322981
E-MAIL: info@fattorialatorre.it

The first release of the Esse Syrah, an '01, was a successful one. The colour is vibrant and the nose intense, with good fruit and delightful spice. There is nice weight on the full, well-rounded palate, where the tannins have mellowed. The finish is dominated by oak-derived sweetness and vanilla.

● Esse '01	🍷🍷	8

WANDANNA
VIA DEL MOLINETTO
55015 MONTECARLO (LU)
TEL. 0583228989 - 0583228226
E-MAIL: vigneto-wandanna@libero.it

We were sorry to see Wandanna lose its full profile. The estate's two flagship wines were absent, and the rest of the range was less convincing than in recent years. The best wines are the three fresh, drinkable whites. The Montecarlo Rosso '02 is disappointing, so we look forward to our next visit.

○ Labirinto '01	🍷	5
○ Montecarlo Bianco '02	🍷	4
● Montecarlo Rosso '02		4

FATTORIA SORBAIANO
LOC. SORBAIANO
56040 MONTECATINI VAL DI CECINA (PI)
TEL. 058830243
E-MAIL: fattoriasorbaiano@libero.it

We were expecting more from Sorbaiano, but it still needs to find a length. Pian del Conte '01, a monovarietal Sangiovese, is poorly focused on nose and palate, and the finish is dry and slightly untogether. Montescudaio Bianco '02 is well-defined on the palate, but wobbles on the nose.

● Pian del Conte '01	🍷	5
○ Montescudaio Bianco '02	🍷	3

CANNETO
VIA DEI CANNETI, 14
53045 MONTEPULCIANO (SI)
TEL. 0578758277
E-MAIL: canneto@dccmp.com

Canneto is back in the Guide after a year's therapy with Carlo Ferrini. The wines are better made and very enjoyable. The Riserva '99 has a fruity nose and a balanced, intense palate. The nice dry Nobile '00 shows firm tannins. The Rosso '01 drinks well and the Vendemmia Tardiva '99 is good.

● Nobile di Montepulciano Ris. '99	🍷🍷	5
● Nobile di Montepulciano '00	🍷	4
● Rosso di Montepulciano '01	🍷	3
○ Vendemmia Tardiva '99	🍷	5

CONTUCCI
VIA DEL TEATRO, 1
53045 MONTEPULCIANO (SI)
TEL. 0578757006
E-MAIL: info@contucci.it

The wines from this historic Montepulciano estate were all decent. The Riserva '99 shows ripe fruit on the nose, with the odd forward note. The palate is broad, but the tannins intrude. Despite some green notes, the nose of the Rosso '02 is attractive. The palate is tasty, but needs to mellow.

● Rosso di Montepulciano '02	🍷	4
● Nobile di Montepulciano Ris. '99	🍷	7
● Nobile di Montepulciano '98	🍷🍷	5
● Nobile di Montepulciano '99	🍷🍷	5

CORTE ALLA FLORA
VIA DI CERVOGNANO, 23
53040 MONTEPULCIANO (SI)
TEL. 0578766003
E-MAIL: corteflora@tin.it

The panel had an enjoyable visit to Corte alla Flora. The Nobile '00 stands out for a complex nose of currants and pepper, followed by a soft, well-knit mouthfeel. The Riserva '99 is tousled on the nose, but firm in the mouth. Finally, the Rosso '01 is nice, with gamey notes and a fruity finish.

● Nobile di Montepulciano '00	♥♥	5
● Rosso di Montepulciano '01	♥	4
● Nobile di Montepulciano Ris. '99	♥	6

FATTORIA DI GRACCIANO
FRAZ. GRACCIANO
VIA UMBRIA, 63
53040 MONTEPULCIANO (SI)
TEL. 0578707097

There was a fine debut from Ambrogio and Giovanni Folonari's Montepulciano estate. The intense ruby Calvano '00 offers whistle-clean cherry that melds into the understated toastiness. Its firm structure is backed up by soft tannins that guarantee a sweet, if not overly long, finish.

● Nobile di Montepulciano		
Calvano '00	♥	5
○ Vin Santo '89	♥♥	5
● Nobile di Montepulciano Ris. '90	♥♥	5

IL FAGGETO
FRAZ. S. ALBINO
VIA FONTELELLERA, 21
53040 MONTEPULCIANO (SI)
TEL. 0577940600 - 3482654560

The Montepulciano branch of the Baroncini winery did well. Vigna Pietra del Diavolo '00 has a full nose of berry fruit laced with vanilla. The structure is good, the tannins tight-knit, and the finish signs off with conviction. Lupaio '02 is simpler, and fuzzy on the nose, but drinks delightfully.

● Nobile di Montepulciano		
Pietra del Diavolo '00	♥♥	5
● Rosso di Montepulciano Lupaio '02	♥	3
● Nobile di Montepulciano		
Pietra del Diavolo '99	♥♥	4

NOTTOLA
LOC. NOTTOLA - S.S. 326, 15
53045 MONTEPULCIANO (SI)
TEL. 0578707060 - 0577684711
E-MAIL: nottola@bccmp.com

The Giomarelli family's wines have personality. The Nobile '00 shows clean fruit on the nose, with hints of super-ripeness. There's good weight on the palate, but the finish tails off too quickly. Rosso '02 is an easy drinker. The ripe fruit aromas are well-defined, but the palate is dull.

● Nobile di Montepulciano '00	♥	5
● Rosso di Montepulciano '02	♥	4
● Nobile di Montepulciano		
Vigna del Fattore '99	♥♥	5

FATTORIA DI PATERNO
FRAZ. SANT'ALBINO
VIA FONTELELLERA, 11
53045 MONTEPULCIANO (SI)
TEL. 0578799194 - 068081881

The Nobile Riserva '99 reveals green notes, but the structured palate confirms it as a coherent wine. The Nobile '00 is delicious, though clean fruit on the nose lets too many hints of oak-derived toastiness come through. But the attack on the palate is nice, and there is great breadth mid palate.

● Nobile di Montepulciano '00	♥	4
● Nobile di Montepulciano Ris. '99	♥	5

POGGIO ALLA SALA
VIA DELLE CHIANE, 3
53045 MONTEPULCIANO (SI)
TEL. 0578767224
E-MAIL: info@poggioallasala.it

Simone Gattavecchi's cellar made an fine Guide debut. The Nobile '00 has a nose of berry fruit with toasty notes from the oak. The robust palate boasts close-knit, ripe tannins. The Nobile Riserva '99 is still fresh on the nose, but the palate is a little dull. The Rosso '02 fades in the finish.

● Nobile di Montepulciano '00	♥♥	5
● Rosso di Montepulciano '02	♥	4
● Nobile di Montepulciano Ris. '99	♥	6

Terra Antica
via Sanguineto, 3
53045 Montepulciano (SI)
tel. 0578766056
e-mail: terraantica@libero.it

Terra Antica's Nobile '00 has a nice nose of ripe fruit and spices. The palate has good depth and balance, with sweet tannins. But the Riserva '99 is less convincing. The nose is clean, but there are intrusive vegetal notes. The sangiovese fruit seems untamed, and the acidity is a bit boisterous.

- ● Nobile di Montepulciano '00 🍷🍷 5
- ● Nobile di Montepulciano Ris. '99 🍷 5
- ● Terra Antica '99 ♡♡ 8

Suveraia
loc. Campetroso
58025 Monterotondo Marittimo (GR)
tel. 050564428

Suveraia's wines are a happy compromise of tradition and modernity. Bacucco '01 has structure and power in spades. The 100 per cent sangiovese Rosso di Campetroso '02 shows unfocused varietal notes and slightly unruly tannins. Monteregio Bianco '02 is elusive on the nose, but balanced overall.

- ● Monteregio di Massa Marittima Bacucco '01 🍷🍷 6
- ○ Monteregio di Massa Marittima Bianco '02 🍷 2
- ● Monteregio di Massa Marittima Rosso di Campetroso '02 🍷 3

Tenuta Cortina e Mandorli
via Mandorli, 95
50025 Montespertoli (FI)
tel. 0571674162
e-mail: cortina.mandorli@tiscali.it

This was our first visit to this winery. Poggioaicozzi '01 is a blend of sangiovese and merlot with a firm palate and sweet, satisfying finish. The Gioiello '00 Merlot is soft and broad, with gentle tannins and intensity in the finish. Chianti Montespertoli Poggignano '01 has a nice tannic weave.

- ● Il Gioiello '01 🍷🍷 6
- ● Poggioaicozzi '01 🍷🍷 5
- ● Chianti Montespertoli Poggignano '01 🍷 3
- ○ Vin Santo Le Solaie '98 🍷 5

Tenuta Maiano
via Bignola, 39
50025 Montespertoli (FI)
tel. 0571608644
e-mail: gfranconigi@libero.it

Tenuta Maiano is another promising newcomer. The Moranna '01 is a sangiovese with a small proportion of merlot that varies from year to year. It offers a very full mouthfeel and a fruit-led finish. Both Chiantis are fruity, fresh-tasting, pleasant to drink and easy on the pocket.

- ● Moranna '01 🍷🍷 6
- ● Chianti '01 🍷 3*
- ○ Campo ai Sassi '02 🍷 3
- ● Chianti '02 🍷 3*

Poggio Capponi
fraz. Pulica - via Montelupo, 184
50025 Montespertoli (FI)
tel. 0571671914
e-mail: info@poggiocapponi.it

Poggio Capponi has excellent potential. The Chianti '02 is very good. Attractive fruit introduces a soft palate with rounded tannins and decent progression. The Chardonnay '02 is juicy, with an intense nose and rich palate. Tinorso '00 and Chianti Montespertoli Petriccio '01 are also worth a look.

- ○ Chardonnay '02 🍷🍷 4*
- ● Chianti '02 🍷🍷 3*
- ● Tinorso '00 🍷 4
- ● Chianti Montespertoli Petriccio '01 🍷 4

Fattoria Castello Sonnino
via Volterrana Nord, 10
50025 Montespertoli (FI)
tel. 0571657481 - 0571609198
e-mail: sonnino@mbr.it

The signs of vitality we noted last year have faded. Best of the bottles was the Sanleone '01, which has lots of juicy fruit on the mouthfilling palate. Cantinino '01 is fuzzy on the nose and suffers from over-emphatic acidity in the mouth. The Chianti Montespertoli are well-made, but no more.

- ● Sanleone '01 🍷🍷 7
- ● Cantinino '01 🍷 5
- ● Chianti Montespertoli Castello di Sonnino '01 🍷 4
- ● Chianti Castello di Montespertoli '02 3

Mannucci Droandi
Fraz. Caposelvi, 61
52020 Montevarchi (AR)
Tel. 0559707276
E-mail: mannuccidroandi@tin.it

Roberto Mannucci Droandi's estate is in two parts, one in the Colli Aretini and the other in the Chianti Classico DOC zone at Starda di Gaiole. The winery is improving all the time. A full-bodied, well-balanced Campolucci '00 stood out, but the Chianti Classico Riserva Ceppeto '00 wasn't far behind.

● Campolucci '00	♥♥	5
● Chianti Cl. Ceppeto Ris. '00	♥♥	5
● Chianti '00	♥	4

Varramista
Loc. Varramista - via Ricavo, 31
56020 Montopoli in Val d'Arno (PI)
Tel. 057144711
E-mail: info@varramista.it

This year, Varramista put on a less than brilliant performance that left the panel puzzled. Varramista '01 has a great nose but lacks the gutsy feel of the previous edition. The palate is a tad meagre, and even one-dimensional. But Frasca '01 is a very good wine.

● Frasca '01	♥♥	4
● Varramista '01	♥	7
● Varramista '00	♥♥♥	7

La Selva
Loc. S. Donato
via Podere La Selva, 138
58015 Orbetello (GR)
Tel. 0564885669

La Selva has 13 hectares and Attiglio Pagli consults. For its Guide debut, it presented some good organic wines. The best is the cabernet sauvignon and merlot Prima Causa '01, with spicy notes and silk-smooth tannins. Colli dell'Uccellina '01 is good and the two Morellinos are easy drinkers.

● Prima Causa '01	♥♥	5
● Colli dell'Uccellina '01	♥	4
● Morellino di Scansano '01	♥	3
● Morellino di Scansano '02	♥	3

Vignole
Loc. La Massa
via Case Sparse, 14
50022 Panzano (FI)
Tel. 0574592025 - 055852197

The Nistri family confirmed previous good impressions. Congius '00 was the best wine, showing chocolate and forest fruit aromas, good body and texture, and a long finish. The easy-drinking Chianti Classico '00 impressed, as did the Riserva '99, which has nice structure but mouth-drying tannins.

● Congius '00	♥♥	6
● Chianti Cl. '00	♥	4
● Chianti Cl. Ris. '99	♥	5

Agri Peccioli
P.zza del Popolo, 10
56037 Peccioli (PI)
Tel. 0587672675
E-mail: agripeccioli@tin.it

Agri Peccioli is another promising cellar that has entered the Guide for one wine in particular, the San Verano '00. This red from sangiovese, merlot and syrah has an alluring nose of berry fruit and sun-dried grass, then a juicy, upfront palate. The IGT white, La Castellaccia '02, is also good.

● San Verano '00	♥♥	5
○ La Castellaccia '02	♥	2*
● Chianti '02		2

Pasqualetti Viticoltori
via Risorgimento, 50
56037 Peccioli (PI)
Tel. 0587635321
E-mail: viticoltori@pasqualetti-viticoltori.com

This Peccioli-based cellar made a fine debut with its Scarlet '99, a sangiovese blend with small proportions of colorino and cabernet sauvignon. The nose unveils berry fruit, spice and gamey hints before the intense, even-textured palate shows its length.

● Scarlet '99	♥♥	5
● Chianti san Crispino '00		4

TENUTA DI POGGIO COSMIANO
VIA POGGIO COSMIANO, 25
56037 PECCIOLI (PI)
TEL. 0587635113

There was a good showing this year from Poggio Cosmiano, which made the finals with Mirasco '01, a blend of sangiovese, cabernet sauvignon and merlot. The nose opens slowly into attractive berry fruit and the easy-drinking palate has lots of juicy pulp. The other IGT, Poggio Cosmiano '01, is good.

● Mirasco '01	♟♟	4
● Poggio Cosmiano '01	♟♟	5

TRAVIGNOLI
VIA TRAVIGNOLI, 78
50060 PELAGO (FI)
TEL. 0558361098
E-MAIL: travignol@tin.it

Travignoli is back in the Guide as the Busi family came up with a very respectable range this year. The convincing Riserva '00 has a nice complex nose and powerful structure. Tegolaia '99, a mix of sangiovese and cabernet sauvignon, flows across the palate, showing good density and length.

● Chianti Rufina Ris. '00	♟♟	4
● Tegolaia '99	♟♟	5
● Chianti Rufina '01	♟	4
● Chianti Rufina Ris. '97	♟♟	3

FATTORIA DI PRESCIANO
LOC. PIEVE A PRESCIANO
VIA GIOVANNI XXIII, 2
52020 PERGINE VALDARNO (AR)
TEL. 0575897160

There's a new name and set-up at the mid-market Le Ginestre winery. Best of the wines tasted was Vin Santo Vinum Passum '98, with dried and candied fruit aromas and good balance on the palate. The attractive, fruit-forward Alfiere Nero '02 is an easy drinker from sangiovese, merlot and canaiolo.

○ Colli Etruria Centrale		
Vinum Passum '98	♟♟	5
● Alfiere Nero '02	♟	3*
○ Chardonnay Brut Cometti	♟	3*
○ Priscus '00		5

SEDIME
POD. SEDIME, 63
53026 PIENZA (SI)
TEL. 0578748436
E-MAIL: capitoni.marco@libero.it

Marco Capitoni and cellarman, Fabrizio Ciufoli, are on the right road. The '02 edition of Capitoni '02 is a very good wine. An 85-15 sangiovese-merlot blend, it has a clean nose with the odd grassy nuance. On the palate, it is soft, well-structured and intense, with a twist of acidity in the finish.

● Orcia Rosso Capitoni '02	♟♟	5
● Orcia Rosso Capitoni '01	♟	5

DANIELE ROCCHI
LOC. FIORENTINA
L.GO ZAMBELLI, 11
57025 PIOMBINO (LI)
TEL. 056535226

There was an impeccable performance from the Rivellino '01, a sangiovese and cabernet sauvignon blend that very nearly earned a third Glass. It has only moderate breadth in the mouth, but drinks beautifully and lingers on the palate. Val di Cornia Vermentino '02 has a nice, fresh-tasting palate.

● Val di Cornia Rivellino '01	♟♟	6
○ Val di Cornia Vermentino '02	♟	4

SAN GIUSTO
LOC. SALIVOLI, 16
57025 PIOMBINO (LI)
TEL. 056541198

We are confident that creases in Piero Bonti's range will soon be ironed out. Rosso degli Appiani '00 has super-ripe notes on the nose and lacks balance in the mouth, with mouth-drying tannins in the finish. The San Giusto '01 is similar in style, but has better balance and progression.

● San Giusto '01	♟♟	4
● Rosso degli Appiani '00	♟	6
● Rosso degli Appiani '99	♟♟	6

SANT'AGNESE
LOC. CAMPO ALLE FAVE, 1
57025 PIOMBINO (LI)
TEL. 0565277069
E-MAIL: gigliapa@hotmail.it

What a fine Guide debut for the Giglis, who went on to the final taste-offs with the merlot and cabernet sauvignon Spirto '01. Its elegantly deep aromas are complemented by a broad palate with lots of volume. Another good wine is the Libatio Lunae '01, from sangiovese with some cabernet sauvignon.

● Spirto '01	🍷🍷	6
● Libatio Lunae '01	🍷🍷	5

LE FONTI
LOC. SAN GIORGIO
53036 POGGIBONSI (SI)
TEL. 0577935690
E-MAIL: fattoria.lefonti@tin.it

The Imbertis' winery did less well than expected. The 100 per cent sangiovese Vito Arturo '00 impressed with intense spice aromas and concentration. The Chianti Classico '01 has yet to absorb its oak. The Riserva '00 is better balanced, with intensity on the nose, but a slightly dilute mid palate.

● Vito Arturo '00	🍷🍷	6
● Chianti Cl. Ris. '00	🍷	6
● Chianti Cl. '01	🍷	4

CASTELLO DEL TREBBIO
VIA S. BRIGIDA, 9
50060 PONTASSIEVE (FI)
TEL. 0558304900
E-MAIL: trebbio@tin.it

"Untypical but characterful" sums up the range from Castello del Trebbio, owned by the Baj-Macario family. Lastricato Riserva '98 has attractive balsamic notes on the nose, a silky mouthfeel and tight-knit tannins. The Pazzesco '99 is opulent and lingers impressively.

● Chianti Rufina Lastricato Ris. '98	🍷🍷	5
● Pazzesco '99	🍷🍷	6
● Pazzesco '97	🍷🍷	4

FATTORIA LAVACCHIO
VIA DI MONTEFIESOLE, 55
50065 PONTASSIEVE (FI)
TEL. 0558317472 - 0558396168
E-MAIL: info@fattorialavacchio.com

Fattoria Lavacchio has made a quantum leap in the quality of its reds. Above all, the Chianti Rufina '01 is a winner, thanks to delicate, stylish aromas, soft structure and plenty of muscle. The Cortigiano '00 offers ripe fruit aromas, solid body and well-gauged tannins.

● Cortigiano '00	🍷🍷	5
● Chianti Rufina '01	🍷🍷	4
● Chianti Rufina Ris. '00	🍷	5
○ Oro del Cedro V. T. '02	🍷	5

CASTELLANI
P. O. BOX 20 - FRAZ. SANTA LUCIA
56025 PONTEDERA (PI)
TEL. 0578292900

The Castellani family winery has joined the Guide. Their offices are near Pisa, but the vineyards are at Radda in Chianti. This year, the Castellanis began distributing their range in Italy. The Riserva '99 has ripe aromas, a well-knit body and good power. The weighty, syrah-based Rosso is spicy.

● Chianti Cl. Vigneti di Campomaggio Ris. '99	🍷🍷	5
● Rosso di Campomaggio '99	🍷🍷	6
● Chianti Cl. Vigneti di Campomaggio '01	🍷	4

FATTORIA SANTA LUCIA
VIA SAN GERVASIO, 4
56025 PONTEDERA (PI)
TEL. 058752481
E-MAIL: fattoriasantalucia@virgilio.it

What a fine Ciliegiolo, barrique-aged for 12 months! Vibrantly intense in the glass, it offers cherry and plum aromas laced with nice oak. The intense fruit palate is mouthfilling, with fine tannins. The Chianti has good weight, softness and balance, then the finish is long, fragrant and fruity.

● Ciliegiolo La Tesa '02	🍷🍷	4
● Chianti Santa Lucia '02	🍷	3*

Azienda Agricola Il Colle
VIA TORRE, 17
55016 PORCARI (LU)
TEL. 0583298062
E-MAIL: sales@vinimontrasio.com

Il Colle's range is a very respectable one. This Lucca estate did well with its monovarietal Merlot Fruttuoso '01. The nose is very varietal, with bell peppers in evidence. The palate is coherent and very drinkable. The IGT Selvatelle '02 and Colline Lucchesi '02 red are also very nice.

● Colline Lucchesi Fruttuoso '01	🍷🍷	5
● Colline Lucchesi Rosso '02	🍷	3
● Selvatelle '02	🍷	4

Colle Bereto
LOC. COLLE BERETO
53017 RADDA IN CHIANTI (SI)
TEL. 0577738083
E-MAIL: colle.bereto@collebereto.it

For the Pinzauti cellar, quality is a given. The best wine is still Il Tocco, whose '01 edition leads with fruit on the nose, a good attack in the mouth and slightly mouth-drying tannins. Both Chiantis are well-structured and the Cenno '01 has moderate aromatic breadth, but the palate is too rigid.

● Il Tocco '01	🍷🍷	6
● Chianti Cl. Ris '00	🍷	5
● Chianti Cl. '01	🍷	4
● Il Cenno '01	🍷	5

Fattoria di Montemaggio
LOC. MONTEMAGGIO
53017 RADDA IN CHIANTI (SI)
TEL. 0577738323
E-MAIL: fattoria_montemaggio@libero.it

We could repeat last year's comments on this winery, but would need to reverse the order. The Chianti Classico '01 did well, its broad nose, fruit and nimble body impressively backed up by firm, even tannins. But the Riserva '00 was a disappointment.

● Chianti Cl. '01	🍷🍷	4
● Chianti Cl. Ris. '00		6

Castello di Monterinaldi
LOC. LUCARELLI
53017 RADDA IN CHIANTI (SI)
TEL. 0577733533
E-MAIL: info@monterinaldi.it

Castello di Monterinaldi presented only one wine for tasting, the cabernet sauvignon Pesanella '00. Its dense ruby hue ushers in marked vegetal notes alternating with bramble and plum fruit. The meaty palate has power and prominent tannins, then the juicy finish lingers as it should.

● Pesanella '00	🍷🍷	5

Podere Capaccia
LOC. CAPACCIA
53017 RADDA IN CHIANTI (SI)
TEL. 0577738385
E-MAIL: capaccia@chianticlassico.com

There were ups and downs again at Podere Capaccia. The vineyards are 500 metres above sea level, which sometimes puts sangiovese to the test, with results that are less than optimal. But the Querciagrande '99 offers intense, varietal aromas that are perhaps a little less complex than we hoped.

● Querciagrande '99	🍷	6
● Querciagrande '88	🍷🍷🍷	6

Podere Terreno alla Via della Volpaia
VIA DELLA VOLPAIA
53017 RADDA IN CHIANTI (SI)
TEL. 0577738312
E-MAIL: podereterreno@chiantinet.it

Marie Sylvie Haniez has brought her cellar back to the Guide thanks to her Chianti Classico Riservas. The '99 is a shade forward on the nose, but soft in the mouth, though the '00 is better. Its invitingly fresh aromas introduce a vigorous body with good texture, spiky tannins and long length.

● Chianti Cl. Ris. '00	🍷🍷	6
● Chianti Cl. Ris. '99	🍷	6

VAL DELLE CORTI
LOC. CASE SPARSE VAL DELLE CORTI, 144
53017 RADDA IN CHIANTI (SI)
TEL. 0577738215
E-MAIL: gbianchi@chiantinet.it

The Radda-based Bianchi family's three hectares at Val delle Corti yield very good wines. We liked their Riserva '00 for its whistle-clean nose, which lifts the ripe fruit, and for the body and sheer character of the palate. Bright, even tannins take you through to a convincing finish.

● Chianti Cl. Ris. '00	♥♥	5

LA REGOLA
VIA A. GRAMSCI, 1
56046 RIPARBELLA (PI)
TEL. 0586698145 - 058881363
E-MAIL: info@laregola.com

La Regola wasn't quite up to snuff this year. The flagship Montescudaio La Regola '01 was good, but not as nice as previous editions. Berry fruit, incense and hay on the nose introduce a muscular, meaty palate that is sweet at first, albeit dryish in the finish. The rest of the range is decent.

● Montescudaio Rosso La Regola '01	♥♥	6
○ Montescudaio Bianco Lauro '02	♥	4
● Montescudaio Rosso Ligustro '02	♥	4

I CAMPETTI
LOC. CAMPETTI - FRAZ. RIBOLLA
VIA DELLA COLLACCHIA, 2
58027 ROCCASTRADA (GR)
TEL. 0564579663

I Campetti has won plaudits in the past for its whites. This year, there were some interesting reds. Vico '01 is mouthfilling and spicy, whereas the Baccio '00 has good concentration. The white Accesa '02 has an attractive, if perhaps overly marked, twist of bitter almonds in the finish.

● Monteregio di Massa Marittima Rosso Baccio '00	♥♥	5
● Vico '01	♥♥	6
○ Malvasia L'Accesa '02	♥	3

COLOGNOLE
LOC. COLOGNOLE - VIA DEL PALAGIO, 15
50068 RUFINA (FI)
TEL. 0558319870
E-MAIL: info@colognole.it

The Coda Nunziante family again turned out a convincing range of wines. We'll start with the Chianti Rufina '01, which reveals crisp notes of cherry and a weighty body, with bright acidity and satisfying length of flavour. The Riserva del Don '00 is less successful.

● Chianti Rufina '01	♥♥	3
● Chianti Rufina Ris. del Don '00	♥	5
● Chianti Rufina '99	♥♥	3*

CASTELLO IL PALAGIO
FRAZ. MERCATALE VAL DI PESA
VIA CAMPOLI, 130
50020 SAN CASCIANO IN VAL DI PESA (FI)
TEL. 055821630

Castello Il Palagio is a newcomer to the Guide, with 25 hectares under vine. The best wine was the Riserva '99 with crisp fruit and a firm body. The tannins are tight, but never intrusive. The standard Chianti and the Rosso '02 are good. The Vin Santo '97 has dried fruit aromas and smooth texture.

● Chianti Cl. Ris. Castello Il Palagio '99	♥♥	5
● Chianti Cl. Castello Il Palagio '01	♥	4
● Rosso del Palagio '02	♥	3
○ Vin Santo del Chianti Cl. '97	♥	7

LA LOGGIA
LOC. MONTEFIRIDOLFI - VIA COLLINA, 40
50020 SAN CASCIANO IN VAL DI PESA (FI)
TEL. 0558244288
E-MAIL: info@fattorialaloggia.com

The Chianti from this Monteridolfi estate, in the municipality of San Casciano Val di Pesa, is a pleasant surprise. Its attractive forest fruits and sweet spice aromas took it through to the finals. The front palate is soft and enfolding, the body firm, and the tannins have melded into the acidity.

● Chianti Cl. Terra dei Cavalieri '01	♥♥	4

Villa Sant'Andrea

loc. Montefiridolfi
via di Fabbrica, 63
50020 San Casciano in Val di Pesa (FI)
tel. 0558244254

The Villa Sant'Andrea wines put on a good show, especially the Chianti Classico '01. We liked the elegant aromas of fruit and attractive spice. The fruit notes of the Vin Santo '99 are equally irresistible. Dates and almonds usher in a firm, velvet-smooth palate.

● Chianti Cl. '01	🍷🍷	4
○ Vin Santo Chianti Cl. '99	🍷🍷	5
● Chianti Cl. Ris. '99	🍷	5

Castello di Montauto

loc. Montauto
53037 San Gimignano (SI)
tel. 0577941130 - 05775431
e-mail: info@castellodimontauto.it

The Chardonnay Sagrato '02 put in a good showing, but the Cecchi family devote a lot of attention to Vernaccia, which they release in two versions. The Vernaccia di San Gimignano '02 is upfront and well made, and the Vernaccia di San Gimignano Castello di Montauto '02 is oak-fermented and aged.

○ Chardonnay Sagrato '02	🍷🍷	5
○ Vernaccia di S. Gimignano Castello di Montauto '02	🍷	3
○ Vernaccia di S. Gimignano '02		2

Pietrafitta

loc. Cortennano
53037 San Gimignano (SI)
tel. 0577943200
e-mail: info@pietrafitta.com

After recent exploits, this year's showing from the historic Pietrafitta winery was disappointing. The Vernaccia Borghetto '02 is dumb on the nose and lacks balance. The Vernaccia Riserva La Costa '01 is soft, but has little grip or length. The Vernaccia '02 is well typed and undemanding.

○ Vernaccia di S. Gimignano V. La Costa Ris. '01	🍷	4
○ Vernaccia di S. Gimignano V. Borghetto '02	🍷	4
○ Vernaccia di S. Gimignano '02		3

San Lorenzo

loc. Casaglia, 30
53037 San Gimignano (SI)
tel. 05779510123
e-mail: sanlorenzo@cybermarket.it

Life sometimes surprises you. Jelleme Horward is a distinguished-looking American gentleman who has settled in delightful San Gimignano, and certainly knows a thing or two about viticulture and winemaking. Just try his wines. You'll see they are all inspired by a single idea: pleasure.

○ Malvasia Toscana '02	🍷	4
● Rolenzo '00	🍷	5
● Sangiovese '01	🍷	4
○ Vernaccia di S. Gimignano '02	🍷	4

San Quirico

loc. Pancole, 39
53037 San Gimignano (SI)
tel. 0577955007
e-mail: az.agr.sanquirico@libero.it

San Quirico releases traditional wines at competitive prices. The Vernaccia di San Gimignano '02, with flowers on the nose and the trademark almond aftertaste, or the exuberantly tannic Chianti Colli Senesi '01, are good examples. The San Gimignano Rosso Il Botticello '00 is nice, but over-oaked.

● S. Gimignano Rosso Il Botticello '00	🍷	4
● Chianti Colli Senesi '01	🍷	3*
○ Vernaccia di S. Gimignano '02	🍷	3*

Fattorie Santo Pietro

loc. Pancole
53037 San Gimignano (SI)
tel. 0577955110
e-mail: info@santopietro.it

Fattoria Santo Pietro at Pancole has joined the Guide. The Spinaio Merlot '00 is fairly convincing for its good extractive weight and faint bitterish hints in the finish. The Vernaccia di San Gimignano '02 shows vanilla mingling with ripe fruit on the nose, then a soft, well-structured palate.

● Lo Spinaio Merlot '00	🍷	5
○ Vernaccia di S. Gimignano '02	🍷	4

SIGNANO
P.ZZA SAN AGOSTINO, 17
53037 SAN GIMIGNANO (SI)
TEL. 0577940164 - 0577942587

Signano made a fine job of the San Gimignano Rosso '00. The soft, mellow tannins are beautifully integrated into the substantial palate, and the finish has very decent length. There are two Chianti Colli Senesi wines. We preferred the Poggiarelli '01 for its superior texture and personality.

●	S. Gimignano Rosso '00	♟♟	5
●	Chianti Colli Senesi '01	♟	3
●	Chianti Colli Senesi Poggiarelli '01	♟	4

PIETRO BECONCINI
FRAZ. LA SCALA - VIA MONTORZO, 13
56028 SAN MINIATO (PI)
TEL. 0571366684
E-MAIL: beconcinipietro@virgilio.it

We have switched preferences this year. The Maurleo '02 is the better of the two wines for its upfront vegetal nose and exuberant bramble fruit. The palate is even, attractive and slightly bitterish in the finish. Reciso '01 is less appealing as both nose and palate show too much oak.

●	Maurleo '02	♟♟	4
●	Reciso '01	♟	5

SANTE MARIE
LOC. SANTE MARIE
53027 SAN QUIRICO D'ORCIA (SI)
TEL. 0577898192

A fine Guide debut by this small Orcia DOC outfit. Curzio '01 is a monovarietal Sangiovese, aged in tonneaux for six months, with a clean, intensely spicy nose. Entry in the mouth is soft, then the progression reveals robust, but never intrusive tannins. The long finish is lifted by notes of cherry.

●	Orcia Rosso Curzio '01	♟♟	4

PODERE SAN MICHELE
VIA CADUTA, 3/A
57027 SAN VINCENZO (LI)
TEL. 0565704808
E-MAIL: info@poderesanmichele.it

Giorgio and Tiziana Socci's mainly sangiovese-based Allodio '01 again showed just how serious and individual it is. Concentrated in the glass and on the nose, it impresses with the integrity of its fruit and the firmness of the body, where wood still prevails.

●	Allodio Rosso '01	♟♟	6
●	Allodio Rosso '99	♟♟	5
●	Allodio Rosso '00	♟♟	5

SAN MICHELE A TORRI
VIA SAN MICHELE, 36
50014 SCANDICCI (FI)
TEL. 055769111
E-MAIL: sanmichele@dada.it

This Scandicci winery, which also owns several hectares in Chianti Classico, put on a very good show. The muscular, upfront Murtas '01 impresses, even though it tends to finish a little unsatisfactorily because of the hardish tannins. The two Chiantis were less convincing, particularly on the nose.

●	Murtas '01	♟♟	6
●	Chianti Cl. La Gabbiola Ris. '00	♟	5
●	Chianti Cl. La Gabbiola '01	♟	4

LA CARLETTA
LOC. PRESELLE - POD. CARLETTA, 80
58050 SCANSANO (GR)
TEL. 0564585045
E-MAIL: sante.massini@tiscalinet.it

Good news from this Morellino DOC estate: the sangiovese, alicante, cabernet sauvignon and merlot Tempio '01 is very good, unveiling delicious notes of tobacco and liquorice on the nose. The palate is broad and tannin-rich, with a hint of edginess. Our retasting of Fonte Tinta '01 was a pleasure.

●	Il Tempio '01	♟♟	6
●	Morellino di Scansano		
	Fonte Tinta '01	♟	5*

PROVVEDITORE
LOC. SALAIOLO
58054 SCANSANO (GR)
TEL. 0564599237
E-MAIL: provveditore@tin.it

Alessandro Bargagli is helped in the cellar by Marco Stefanini at this 30-hectare estate. The best of the wines was the Campo La Chiesa, a sangiovese, alicante and cabernet sauvignon mix with a peppery nose and weighty, characterful palate. The Sassato '02 and Primo Ris. '00 are both attractive.

● Campo La Chiesa '00	♀♀	6
● Morellino di Scansano		
Primo Ris. '00	♀	6
● Morellino di Scansano Sassato '02	♀	4

BOTRONA
LOC. BOTRONA - S. P. DEL PUNTONE
58020 SCARLINO (GR)
TEL. 0566866129

This is the first release for these two excellent reds. Bramante '01 is a monovarietal Merlot with intense fruit and full body, but the youthful tannins tend to dry out the finish. Vedetta '01 is 100 per cent cabernet sauvignon and unveils red berry fruit over vanilla. The finish delectably sweet.

● Bramante '01	♀♀	5
● Vedetta '01	♀♀	5

LA PIEROTTA
LOC. LA PIEROTTA
58020 SCARLINO (GR)
TEL. 056637218
E-MAIL: lapierotta@scarlino.net

The best wine in the range is the 100 per cent syrah Solare '01, with crisp notes of black pepper and liquorice, then softness and muscle on the palate. Scarilius '01 has ripe fruit and tobacco aromas but is a little short. The 100 per cent vermentino Monteregio Bianco '02 is fresh and citrussy.

● Solare '01	♀♀	5
● Monteregio di Massa Marittima		
Scarilius '01	♀	4
○ Monteregio di Massa Marittima '02	♀	3

SAN GIORGIO A LAPI
S.DA DI COLLE PINZUTO, 30
53100 SIENA
TEL. 0577356836
E-MAIL: info@sangiorgioalapi.it

The Simoni family is back in the Guide. Bandecca Riserva '00 has a crisp nose and good texture, with a sweet finish. Eremo '01 nearly earned a second Glass for balsam aromas and flavourful tannins. The Chianti Classico '01 is not bad, and the agreeable Colli Senesi '01 is a little predictable.

● Chianti Cl. Bandecca Ris. '00	♀♀	6
● Chianti Cl. '01	♀	5
● Chianti Colli Senesi '01	♀	4
● Eremo '01	♀	6

TENUTA DI TRECCIANO
LOC. TRECCIANO
53018 SOVICILLE (SI)
TEL. 0577314357
E-MAIL: trecciano@libero.it

Tenuta di Trecciano's Cabernet Sauvignon '01 is good, with an intense fruit nose and elegant palate. Terra Rossa Riserva '01 has a clean nose that vegetal notes disturb. The palate is straightforward, but well balanced. The '02 Terra di Siena's fruit-rich nose and well-typed palate are also nice.

● Cabernet Sauvignon '01	♀♀	4
● Chianti dei Colli Senesi		
Terra Rossa Ris. '01	♀	4
● Chianti dei Colli Senesi		
Terra di Siena '02	♀	2

PETRA
LOC. S. LORENZO ALTO, 131
57021 SUVERETO (LI)
TEL. 0565845308
E-MAIL: info.petra@libero.it

The Petra estate, owned by the Franciacorta-based Bellavista winery, is still finding its feet. Both wines presented are well made, but failed to light any fires. Their structure is unexciting, although they show good balance. In the mouth, vegetal notes tend to dominate.

● Petra Rosso '00	♀	6
● Petra Rosso '01	♀	6
● Petra Rosso '97	♀♀	5
● Petra Rosso '98	♀♀	6

PETRICCI E DEL PIANTA
LOC. S. LORENZO, 20
57028 SUVERETO (LI)
TEL. 0565845140
E-MAIL: info@petriccidelpianta.it

The most outstanding of the wines presented was the Cerosecco '01. A moderately complex nose foregrounds forest fruits and green notes. It is juicy and reasonably chewy, with a vegetal finish. The Val di Cornia Bianco Casetta '02 is shy on the nose, but the palate is even and attractive.

● Cerosecco '01	🍷🍷	5
○ Val di Cornia di Casetta Bianco '02	🍷	3
● Val di Cornia Aleatico Stillo '01	🍷🍷	7

RUBBIA AL COLLE
LOC. POGGETTO
57028 SUVERETO (LI)
TEL. 0565827026
E-MAIL: info@fratellimuratori.com

The 80 hectares under vine at Tenuta Rubbia al Colle lie in the municipalities of Suvereto and Campiglia Marittima. Two very creditable wines were presented. The frank, drinkable Rumpotino '01 comes from sangiovese, canaiolo and ciliegiolo, and the mainly merlot Olpaio '00 is firm and attractive.

● Olpaio '00	🍷🍷	6
● Rumpotino '01	🍷🍷	5

FATTORIA MONTECCHIO
FRAZ. SAN DONATO IN POGGIO
VIA MONTECCHIO, 4
50020 TAVARNELLE VAL DI PESA (FI)
TEL. 0558072907 - 0558072235

The fine Pietracupa '99, from sangiovese and cabernet sauvignon, went through to the finals. An intense ruby wine, it has a delectable nose of coffee over currant and blueberry fruit. The front palate is potent, the body firm, and the close-knit tannic weave is even. But the finish is bitterish.

● Pietracupa '99	🍷🍷	5
● Chianti Cl. Ris. '99		5

FATTORIA POGGIO ROMITA
LOC. ROMITA
VIA DEL CERRO, 10
50028 TAVARNELLE VAL DI PESA (FI)
TEL. 0558077253

The Sistinis always put quality first. Sassaia '01 has intense aromas of evident balsam and a pleasing hint of toastiness. The palate is full-bodied and firm, the muscular tannins are fine-grained and the finish convinces. Both the Chianti Classico '01 and the Riserva '00 are delicious.

● La Sassaia '01	🍷🍷	6
● Chianti Cl. Frimaio Ris. '00	🍷	6
● Chianti Cl. Frimaio '01	🍷	4

COOPERATIVA AGRICOLA VALDARNESE
LOC. PATERNA, 96
52028 TERRANUOVA BRACCIOLINI (AR)
TEL. 055977052

The organic wines from CAV, managed by Marco Noferi, are reliable. Chianti Paterna '01 is a fruity, no-nonsense wine. The 100 per cent sangiovese Vignanova '00 has breadth and complexity, progressing well on the palate. The soft mouthfeel is backed up by oak tannins that dry out the finish a little.

● Vignanova '00	🍷🍷	4*
● Chianti dei Colli Aretini Paterna '01	🍷	3*
● Vignanova '99	🍷🍷	4*

BADIA DI MORRONA
VIA DI BADIA, 8
56030 TERRICCIOLA (PI)
TEL. 0587658505 - 0587656013
E-MAIL: info@badiadimorrona.it

This year, Badia di Morrona wines are well made. Vigna Alta '00, from 100 per cent sangiovese, is full-bodied, but the oak is still too prominent. N'Antia '00 is very easy-drinking, black berry fruit on the nose mingling with toasty oak. The Suvera '02 is a rich white from a difficult vintage.

● N'Antia '00	🍷	6
● Vigna Alta '00	🍷	6
○ La Suvera '02	🍷	5

Casanova della Spinetta
LOC. CASANOVA
56030 TERRICCIOLA (PI)
TEL. 0141877396

There was a fine debut from the Rivetti family's new Tuscan estate. Their Sezzana '01 throws crisp berry fruit and bramble, lifted by delicious spicy notes. The palate is full, uncomplicated and very drinkable, the finish long and expansive.

● Sezzana '01	🍷🍷	5

Podere La Chiesa
VIA DI CASANOVA, 13
56030 TERRICCIOLA (PI)
TEL. 0587653286
E-MAIL: mamajero@libero.it

Podere La Chiesa has a distinctive style and knows how to interpret the territory. Sabiniano di Casanova '01, a blend of sangiovese, cabernet sauvignon and merlot, went through to our finals and came close to a third Glass. It is elegant and long, with a tight-knit but sweet, smooth tannic weave.

● Sabiniano di Casanova '01	🍷🍷	5
● Sabiniano di Casanova '00	🍷🍷	5

Pieve de' Pitti
VIA PIEVE DE' PITTI, 7
56030 TERRICCIOLA (PI)
TEL. 0587635724
E-MAIL: wine@pievedepitti.it

This 30-hectare estate is planted mainly to sangiovese. A fine example is the Moro di Pava '01, a monovarietal Sangiovese with a characteristically gamey nose and a straightforward but enjoyable palate that dries out in the finish. A wine that will benefit from cellar time.

● Moro di Pava '01	🍷🍷	5

Trequanda
LOC. PIAN DELLE FONTI, 100
53020 TREQUANDA (SI)
TEL. 0577662001
E-MAIL: azienda.trequanda@virgilio.it

Yet another fine debut from an Orcia DOC estate. Invidia '01 is a sangiovese-heavy blend with some cabernet sauvignon. The nose is a cocktail of berry fruit lifted by notes of tobacco. In the mouth, the wine shows personality, power and attractive drinkability.

● Orcia Rosso Invidia '01	🍷🍷	5

Tenuta Bacco e Petroio
LOC. SOVIGLIANA
VIA VILLA ALESSANDRI, 18
50053 VINCI (FI)
TEL. 0571509583

Tenuta Bacco e Petroio's calling card is a wide range of good wines. The 100 per cent sangiovese Petroio Primo '00 has full flavour, soft mouthfeel, well-extracted tannins and carefully gauged acidity. The white Orpello '02 stands out for its floral aromas and fresh-tasting, balanced palate.

● Petroio Primo '00	🍷🍷	5
○ Orpello '02	🍷🍷	5
● Sangiovese '01	🍷	5
● Chianti '02	🍷	4

Streda in Belvedere
VIA DI STREDA, 32
50059 VINCI (FI)
TEL. 0571729195
E-MAIL: streda@streda.net

There was a good Guide debut by this estate in the Vinci hills. The Syrah '01 has black berry fruit and peppery notes on the nose. The palate is soft and fruit-rich, with well-knit tannins and a sweet finish. The Chianti '02 has intense notes of fruit, good concentration and drinks very well.

● Syrah '01	🍷🍷	6
● Chianti '02	🍷🍷	4
● Casanova '01	🍷	5

MARCHE

Nine Three Glass winners in Marche confirm that winemaking quality in the region is going in the right direction. Improvements are most evident in the red wine sector, both in DOC zones with a long tradition of quality and in areas that until recently produced wines exclusively for the mass market or for blending. If we remember, for example, that in the mid 1980s, Piceno, now one of the most exciting DOC zones in the region, had only a handful of producers who actually bottled. Most of what today are considered the leading cellars only began to make seriously good wines six to eight years ago. In short, Marche winemaking is in its infancy, and has plenty of scope for improvement. The first objective – wines that are free of defects, rich, full-bodied and concentrated – has generally been achieved without difficulty. This has come about through the application of new vineyard management techniques, including low yields and selection at harvest, and thanks to the great potential of an extraordinary vine type, montepulciano. But the attempt to endow Marche wines with personality and elegance, the qualities that differentiate a good product from an excellent one, has proved more challenging. Extract and concentration are not absolute values. If they are pursued too diligently, they can produce unbalanced wines that are muscular but uninteresting, giants with feet of clay, as it were, that have little or no ageing potential. The next challenge for all Marche winemakers is to turn out wines of finesse, typicity and elegance, like the ones that triumphed at the taste-offs this year. They include Anghelos by De Angelis, Ludi from Velenosi and Barricadiero from Aurora, three stunning Piceno wines blended from montepulciano and Bordeaux varieties. Then there's Chaos from Le Terrazze and Santa Barbara's Pathos, from the area around Monte Conero. And Kurni from Oasi degli Angeli, a very individual single-grape montepulciano, or the breathtakingly elegant Sangiovese Solo from Dezi. On the white front, we like two wines that are superficially very different, but actually have something in common. We were impressed by the superb progression of Bucci's Verdicchio Riserva, and by its sophisticated balance and tangy flavour. Massaccio from Fazi Battaglia stood out for its generous, ripe fruit and outstanding depth on the palate. The characteristic they share is also the reason they are so different. Both are successful, individual interpretations of different territories, and wonderful marriages of soil type and grape variety with the style of the winemaker that created them.

ANCONA

ANCONA

LANARI
FRAZ. VARANO
VIA POZZO, 142
60029 ANCONA
TEL. 0712861343
E-MAIL: cantinalanari@libero.it

The Lanari estate is in the heart of the Monte Conero park. Despite creeping urbanization, the area still offers a superb natural setting that alternates Mediterranean scrubland with olive groves and fields of lavender. Luca Lanari, the young owner, is serious and enthusiastic about his work, and about the search for quality. More than capable of endowing his wines with a distinct personality, Luca appears to be able to do this even when the vintage has not been great, for he presented us with a meaty, powerful Conero that is elegant yet still drinks deliciously. Luca's Rosso Conero 2002 is an inky dark but still fluid purple and its cherry, bramble and plum are lifted by youthful alcohol. Entry on the palate is muscular, then the astringency of the tannins is mellowed by concentration and upfront alcohol. Distinct notes of fruit are evident on the back palate. Fibbio 2001, a selection of barrique-aged montepulciano, is dark, dense and purplish. Morello cherry and blueberry explode onto the nose, mingling with nutmeg, liquorice and tobacco. Surprisingly soft in the mouth, the elegant concentration never compromises its easy-drinking attractiveness.

MAURIZIO MARCHETTI
FRAZ. PINOCCHIO
VIA DI PONTELUNGO, 166
60131 ANCONA
TEL. 071897386 - 071897385
E-MAIL: info@marchettiwines.it

Maurizio Marchetti's estate has been active for more than a century and its 13 hectares under vine are located in the best part of the Rosso Conero zone. A fruitful relationship with Tuscan oenologist Lorenzo Landi has led to some excellent results and Villa Bonomi 2001 is by far the best Rosso Conero we tasted for this edition of the Guide. An intense, austere nose offers firm notes of ripe plum, liquorice, bitter cocoa and cloves. This complexity and finesse are mirrored on the full, concentrated palate, where the beautifully extracted tannins of the normally boisterous montepulciano grape are in a silky, tight-knit mood. The standard Rosso Conero is intense, purple red. The jammy notes on the nose usher in a finish reminiscent of bottled black cherries and overall, the palate has firm texture and warm alcohol. Only 20 per cent of Marchetti's area under vine is dedicated to white grapes, which may reflect a lower degree of commitment to white wines. The Verdicchio 2002 is very well typed, and is actually more interesting than the Tenuta del Cavaliere selection. The panel found the latter less than perfectly balanced, with an intense citrus nose and distinct residual sugar on the palate.

● Rosso Conero Fibbio '01	🍷🍷	6
● Rosso Conero '02	🍷🍷	4*
● Rosso Conero Fibbio '99	🍷🍷🍷	6
● Rosso Conero Fibbio '97	🍷🍷	6
● Rosso Conero Fibbio '98	🍷🍷	6
● Rosso Conero Fibbio '00	🍷🍷	6

● Rosso Conero		
Villa Bonomi Ris. '00	🍷🍷	5
● Rosso Conero '01	🍷	4
○ Verdicchio dei Castelli di Jesi Cl. '02	🍷	2
○ Verdicchio dei Castelli di Jesi Cl.		
Sup. Tenuta del Cavaliere '02	🍷	4
● Rosso Conero		
Villa Bonomi Ris. '97	🍷🍷	5
● Rosso Conero		
Villa Bonomi Ris. '98	🍷🍷	5
● Rosso Conero '00	🍷🍷	4

ANCONA

ALESSANDRO MORODER
VIA MONTACUTO, 112
60062 ANCONA
TEL. 071898232
E-MAIL: info@moroder-vini.it

The Moroder winery is at Montacuto, a small village in the heart of the Conero park. There has 46 hillside hectares, of which 26 are planted to specialized vines. The estate has belonged to the Moroder family since the early 19th century but it is only in the past 15 years that it has been performing at top level, largely thanks to the efforts of Alessandro and his wife, Serenella. Their recently built cellar is tangible proof of their commitment and our tastings confirmed how well the cellar interprets territory-focused wine types. Rosa di Montacuto 2002, a rosé from montepulciano, sangiovese and alicante nero, is cyclamen-hued and flower-fragranced. The floral aromas follow through onto the palate, where they are braced by good acidity and rounded off by cherry and redcurrant. The Rosso Conero 2001 is purple, with a slightly tousled, closed nose. On the palate, the attractive texture offsets freshness against concentration to produce a dry, tangy wine. The flagship Dorico 2000, a Rosso Conero from a selection of montepulciano, is deep ruby and overlays bramble and blueberry with understated oak on the nose. The palate puts the accent on elegance, rather than power and soft tannins take you through to a generously complex back palate. The dried-grape Oro 2001 is amber, revealing white chocolate and dried fig aromas before the refreshing palate signs off with spice and candied citrus peel.

ANCONA

ALBERTO SERENELLI
VIA BARTOLINI, 2
60129 ANCONA
TEL. 07135505
E-MAIL: albertoserenelli@tiscalinet.it

This year, Alberto Serenelli presented the panel with an extremely valid range. Of course, he has already shown that he knows how to make a good wine, particularly a red one. His small estate – the seven hectares yield almost 25,000 bottles a year – enable Alberto to take a craft approach to his work, which is of course ideal when you want to produce premium-quality wines. The excellent 2000 version of Boranico is ample confirmation. A 50-50 blend of montepulciano and merlot, it shows inky purplish red and a very intense nose of morello cherries and faint spice. The palate is a riot of chewy fruit, with good balance between the close-knit tannins and the power of the alcohol. The finish is fairly long and slightly astringent. The montepulciano-based Afro 2000 is an ambitious, expensive wine, of which 2,500 bottles were released. The good depth on the palate is backed by vigorous alcohol and nice long cherry and coffee aromas. Sergio Paolucci, the winery's consultant oenologist, has a reputation as a white winemaker and the trebbiano and malvasia Biancospino 2002 is confirmation of his skills. This is the best version ever. The flowers on the nose reveal hints of the minerals that come through on the palate, which has good, tangy thrust. We were slightly disappointed by the Marro 2001, which is a little closed on the nose, although the palate is admirably textured.

● Rosso Conero Dorico '00		♟♟	5
○ Oro '01		♟	5
● Rosso Conero '01		♟	4
⊙ Rosa di Montacuto '02			3
● Rosso Conero Dorico '90		♟♟♟	5
● Rosso Conero Dorico '93		♟♟♟	5
● Rosso Conero Dorico '97		♟♟	5
● Rosso Conero Dorico '98		♟♟	5
● Rosso Conero '00		♟♟	4

● Boranico '00		♟♟	5
● Afro '00		♟♟	8
○ Biancospino '02		♟♟	4*
● Rosso Conero Marro '01		♟	4
● Rosso Conero Marro '00		♟♟	4
● Rosso Conero Varano '99		♟♟	7

APPIGNANO (MC)

FATTORIA DI FORANO
C.DA FORANO, 40
62010 APPIGNANO (MC)
TEL. 073357102
E-MAIL: villaforano@libero.it

Although there are plenty of other excellent wines in the province, Macerata is known almost exclusively for its Verdicchio di Matelica. Consumers and wine professionals tend to neglect other areas of Macerata, where in fact the wineries are enjoying a fantastic revival. It has to be said, however, that interest and investment in modern techniques have only recently become a feature of local wineries' plans. Fattoria di Forano is one of Giovanni Lucangeli's agricultural holdings. Having realized what good wine country the area is, he decided to invest resources and staff to make top-notch wines. He set up a new cellar and hired oenologist, Giancarlo Soverchia, and since the turn around, Lucangeli's wines have always scored well at our tastings. The wine types on show are the classics of the DOCs, Colli Maceratesi Bianco and Rosso Piceno. Bianco Villa Forano, from mainly maceratino fruit mixed with 20 per cent trebbiano and malvasia, is grey-flecked straw yellow. The mineral aromas mingle with hazelnut and elderflower. Ripe pear and almond are prominent on the palate, braced by refreshing, compact structure. Rosso Piceno 2000 is a classic, dark purple montepulciano and sangiovese blend with aromas ranging from morello cherry to plum, vanilla and tobacco. The smooth tannins never threaten the balanced concentration and the finish has good fruit and spice.

ASCOLI PICENO

ERCOLE VELENOSI
LOC. BRECCIAROLO
VIA DEI BIANCOSPINI, 11
63100 ASCOLI PICENO
TEL. 0736341218
E-MAIL: info@velenosivini.com

Ludi 2001, a blend of 60 per cent montepulciano with cabernet sauvignon and merlot, of which 7,000 bottles were released, was again one of the best wines in the region. The penetrating, pervasive nose offers luscious ripe cherry and bramble-led fruit, layered over liquorice and pencil lead. The austere, elegant palate has an impressive entry and lovely progression, with very close-knit yet well-rounded tannins underlining the wine's assertive palate. Roggio del Filare 2000 offers an intense, complex nose of concentrated fruit and jam, nuanced with alcohol. It is fleshy on the palate, where mellow tannins emerge. It just lacks a little depth because of astringency in the finish. Brecciarolo 2000, the most widely distributed of the cellar's Rosso Piceno wines, is uncomplicated but extremely drinkable. A total of 150,000 bottles were released. Villa Angela Chardonnay 2002 has fruit-led, fragrant aromas laced with crusty bread. The palate is fairly intense but thinnish, with moderate structure and a bitterish finish. Rêve 2001, a selection of barrique-fermented chardonnay, has oak on both the nose and the well-structured, opulent palate, which lacks a little focus because it is dry and bitterish. The fresh-tasting, linear Falerio Vigna Solaria 2002 has spirited acidity. All in all, the range is a creditable one, confirming the progress made by a cellar that can now call on celebrated consultant oenologist, Attilio Pagli.

○ Colli Maceratesi Bianco		
Villa Forano '02	♥♥	3*
● Rosso Piceno Villa Forano '00	♥	3
● Rosso Piceno Bulciano '98	♥♥	4
○ Colli Maceratesi Bianco		
Monteferro '01	♥♥	4
● Rosso Piceno Bulciano '99	♥♥	4

● Ludi '01	♥♥♥	6
● Rosso Piceno Sup.		
Roggio del Filare '00	♥♥	5
○ Velenosi Brut M. Cl.	♥♥	5
○ Falerio dei Colli Ascolani		
Vigna Solaria '02	♥	3
○ Villa Angela Chardonnay '02	♥	3
○ Rêve		
Chardonnay di Villa Angela '01	♥	5
● Rosso Piceno Sup. Il Brecciarolo '00	♥	3
○ Linagre		
Sauvignon di Villa Angela '02		3
● Ludi '00	♥♥♥	6
● Rosso Piceno Sup.		
Roggio del Filare '99	♥♥	5

BARBARA (AN)

SANTA BARBARA
B.GO MAZZINI, 35
60010 BARBARA (AN)
TEL. 0719674249
E-MAIL: info@vinisantabarbara.it

After a number of attempts, Stefano Antonucci has finally done it. Last year, he came painfully close to a third Glass, but this time Pathos, a mix of syrah, merlot and cabernet sauvignon, was simply fantastic. Its class and power were obvious right from the first tastings. Elegant notes of balsam mingle with red berry fruit, pepper and cocoa powder to tempt the nose, then the palate brings together all its assertive components expanding into glorious breadth and depth. It's not easy to find fault, although we note, regretfully, that the low production of only 4,200 bottles means that Pathos '01 will quickly become a collector's item. Only a couple of marks lower is the Verdicchio 2001 that Stefano named after himself. Intense fruit on the nose ushers in a characterful palate that is already balanced and offers good progression. The Rosso Stefano Antonucci is attractively soft, with delicate spice, but lacks the depth that a flagship wine really ought to have. Maschio da Monte 2001, from montepulciano, is held back by over-ripe fruit that unsettles the nose and palate with notes of super-ripeness. Partly because of the cool weather, Le Vaglie 2002 is not quite as soft as usual, showing acid that lends spirit and character to its well-defined varietal aromas. The rest of the range is as reliable as ever. The two Nidastore 2002 wines are refreshing, while the Pignocco 2002 has attractive aromas and firm texture.

BARCHI (PU)

VALENTINO FIORINI
VIA GIARDINO CAMPIOLI, 5
61030 BARCHI (PU)
TEL. 072197151
E-MAIL: carla@fioriniwines.it

The superb landscape of the Pesaro hinterland owes much of its charm to the gentle hills, and the rest to its beautifully tended farmland. At Barchi, a village in the heart of this area, Valentino Fiorini's winery has been active for some time. Today, it is run by his daughter, Carla, an oenologist, who personally supervises all stages of production, accepting advice now and again from her friend, also an oenologist, Roberto Potentini. This year, the Bartis 2000 was still ageing so the best of the reds was the Luigi Fiorini '98. A monovarietal sangiovese, it is austere and evolved, with evident tertiary notes. The tannins are still a little rough, and the acidity is evident, but progression shows depth and finesse. Tenuta Campioli has flowers on the nose. In the mouth, refreshing fruit and acidity take you through to a subtle almond-nuanced finish. Vigna Sant'Ilario was less exciting than usual, not so much for any defects of structure as for an understandable reluctance to show its trademark tangy freshness. A few months in bottle will improve this consequence of the poorish 2002 vintage. Finally, the best wine is Monsavium '97. From biancame, also known as bianchello, raisined in special drying rooms in the estate villa, it stayed in small wood for five years, then in bottle for a further 12 months, and now offers elegant evolved notes of dried apricots, restrained sweetness and remarkable length.

● Pathos '01	▼▼▼	7
○ Verdicchio dei Castelli di Jesi Cl. Stefano Antonucci Ris. '01	▼▼	4
○ Verdicchio dei Castelli di Jesi Cl. Le Vaglie '02	▼▼	4*
● Rosso Piceno Il Maschio da Monte '01	▼	5
● Stefano Antonucci Rosso '01	▼	5
● Pignocco Rosso '02	▼	3
○ Verdicchio dei Castelli di Jesi Cl. Nidastore '02	▼	3
○ Verdicchio dei Castelli di Jesi Cl. Nidastore Vigne Alte '02	▼	3
○ Verdicchio dei Castelli di Jesi Cl. Pignocco '02	▼	3
● Pathos '00	▼▼	7

○ Monsavium Passito '97	▼▼	5
○ Bianchello del Metauro Tenuta Campioli '02	▼	3
● Colli Pesaresi Sangiovese Luigi Fiorini '98	▼	5
○ Bianchello del Metauro Vigna Sant'Ilario '02		2
● Bartis '98	▼▼	4
○ Monsavium Passito '96	▼▼	5
● Bartis '99	▼▼	4

BELVEDERE OSTRENSE (AN) CAMERANO (AN)

LUCIANO LANDI
VIA GAVIGLIANO, 16
60030 BELVEDERE OSTRENSE (AN)
TEL. 073162353
E-MAIL: aziendalandi@aziendalandi.it

SPINSANTI
VIA GALLETTO, 29
60021 CAMERANO (AN)
TEL. 071731797 - 07195537
E-MAIL: agaggiotti@tiscali.it

This year, Luciano Landi and oenologist Sergio Paolucci have released their Goliardo 2001, a wine which benefits from much research, hard work and an appropriate ageing period. The result is truly outstanding, showing an impenetrable ruby that comes from a blend of montepulciano, merlot and cabernet sauvignon. The intense, extremely elegant nose offers layered hints of balsam, ripe cherries, attractive spice and coffee. The wine's harmony is obvious from entry on the palate, where it progresses powerfully yet softly to a long finish that echoes the nose wonderfully. Luciano's other delightful creation is a dessert wine from dried lacrima grapes. Impressively intense varietal rose petal and violets meld superbly with hints of vanilla. The palate is dense and sweet, and has a long, flowery finish. Lacrima is the Landi family's specialty grape. The Gavigliano 2002 is the best version we tasted this year. A full, lingering nose introduces an assertive entry on the palate, where restrained tannins are joined by intense aromas. The standard Lacrima is more predictable, but the excellent ripeness of the fruit is still perceptible in the wine's nice structure. There was an interesting performance by the Torre del Re 2001, a 50-50 mix of lacrima and montepulciano with a firm nose and a suggestion of over-extraction on the palate. The ripe Verdicchio Classico 2002 is well typed.

Catia Spinsanti and husband Andrea began their winemaking adventure when they decided to take over the vineyards from which Catia's father obtained wine for the family and for sale unbottled. Both Catia and Andrea treat winemaking as a passion, as well as a source of income, and it shows. Part of the credit goes to consultant oenologist, Umberto Trombelli, a man who knows the territory well and who has taken over from the competent Giorgio Baldi. Sassòne 2001 is one of the best reds in the region. It's a monovarietal montepulciano with a dense, rich hue that tells you all about its concentration and power. The characterful nose evokes well-defined cherry, coffee and cloves, then the close-knit, silk-smooth tannins are nicely sustained by vigorous alcohol in the long finish. Rosso Conero Camars 2002, made with montepulciano fruit from old vines, is steel fermented. It has suffered as a result of the poor vintage and lacks meaty extract. Instead, it puts the accent on elegance, crisply defined fruit and the depth that comes from bracing acidity. The other Rosso Conero, Adino 2002, is also vinified without oak. In style, it is comparable to the Camars, if less complex, fresher and lighter in concentration. There is no denying its drinkability, though.

● Goliardo '01	♟♟	6
● Lacrima di Morro d'Alba		
Passito '01	♟♟	5
● Lacrima di Morro d'Alba		
Gavigliano '02	♟♟	4*
● Torre di Re '01	♟	4
● Lacrima di Morro d'Alba '02	♟	4
○ Verdicchio dei Castelli di Jesi Cl. '02		3

● Sassòne '01	♟♟	5
● Rosso Conero Camars '02	♟♟	4
● Rosso Conero Adino '02	♟	4
● Sassòne '00	♟♟	5
● Rosso Conero Adino '01	♟♟	4
● Rosso Conero Camars '01	♟♟	4

CAMERANO (AN)

CASTEL DI LAMA (AP)

SILVANO STROLOGO
VIA OSIMANA, 89
60021 CAMERANO (AN)
TEL. 071732359 - 071731104
E-MAIL: s.strologo@libero.it

TENUTA DE ANGELIS
VIA SAN FRANCESCO, 10
63030 CASTEL DI LAMA (AP)
TEL. 073687429
E-MAIL: info@tenutadeangelis.it

This small winery was started by a farming family belonging to the Istituzione Santa Casa di Loreto. In the 1960s, they decided to strike out on their own, planting their vineyards mainly to montepulciano. Later, the Strologos' estate passed from Sante to his son, Silvano, who set about modernizing operations with the help of agronomist and oenologist, Giancarlo Soverchia. Recently, a new cellar has been built and currently work is under way on a new binning cellar and barrique ageing area. Yields are low and selection severe on the eight-hectare property. The super-ripe fruit is harvested by hand and then soft-crushed and slowly fermented at controlled temperatures to produce two premium-quality reds, Julius and Traiano. Like its predecessors, the 2002 edition of Julius 2002 is impressive value for money. The dense amaranth-flecked purple releases aromas of black cherries in alcohol, then the palate melds concentration with power in a close-knit tannic weave that braces a slightly muzzy, over-evolved flavour. The vermilion Traiano 2001 has ruby highlights. The nose foregrounds over-ripe prunes, cherries in alcohol, tobacco and leather. The palate is imposing, echoing the stewed aromas in a meaty texture and signing off with a finish that is perhaps rather too opulent.

Some 75 per cent of the De Angelis family's 57 hectares under vine is planted to sangiovese, montepulciano, merlot and cabernet sauvignon, which explains why the cellar makes such successful red wines. For the flagship Anghelos, oenologist Roberto Potentini carefully selects the fruit from particularly well-positioned vineyards to give us, every year since it was first produced in 1997, one of the best wines in Piceno. The Anghelos 2001 embodies all the sophisticated elegance of the '99 edition, which won Three Glasses on release, and the serious power of the 2000. The nose has intense red berry fruit and sweet spice, with faint hints of green pepper from the cabernet sauvignon. The elegant freshness of the sangiovese gives the wine structure and depth on the palate, and the tight-knit tannins of the montepulciano lend shape and substance to the body. The Three Glasses at the final taste-offs were fully deserved. Oro 2001 is very good. Very ripe on the nose, it has cherries and subtle hint of vanilla followed by a mouthfilling richness on the palate. However, it lacks the extra complexity that would have taken it to the very top level. Some time in bottle should improve things. The Rosso Piceno Superiore 2001 has an eloquent nose, assertive tannins and long, attractive persistence on the palate. The three standard-label wines from 2002 are satisfying easy drinkers.

● Rosso Conero Traiano '01	♟♟	5
● Rosso Conero Julius '02	♟♟	4*
● Rosso Conero Traiano '00	♟♟♟	5
● Rosso Conero Julius '00	♟♟	3
● Rosso Conero Traiano '99	♟♟	5
● Rosso Conero Julius '01	♟♟	3

● Anghelos '01	♟♟♟	5
● Rosso Piceno Sup. '01	♟♟	3*
● Rosso Piceno Sup. Oro '01	♟♟	5
○ Falerio dei Colli Ascolani '02	♟	1*
○ Prato Grande Chardonnay '02	♟	2
● Rosso Piceno '02	♟	2
● Anghelos '99	♟♟♟	5
● Anghelos '98	♟♟	5
● Anghelos '00	♟♟	5
● Rosso Piceno Sup. Oro '00	♟♟	4

CASTELPLANIO (AN)

Fazi Battaglia

via Roma, 117
60031 Castelplanio (AN)
tel. 0731813444 - 06844311
e-mail: info@fazibattaglia.it

Fazi Battaglia came to the public's attention when it created the famous amphora-shaped bottle which for years was synonymous with Verdicchio all over the world. Verdicchio Massaccio 2000 is a wine to which the estate has dedicated much energy, and in fact it won Three Glasses on its first release. From slightly over-ripe fruit, it proffers an intriguing nose that precisely, intensely conjures up acacia blossom, honey and orange peel, bound together by a hint of botrytis. The imposing, elegant palate has vigorous alcohol yet expands easily and harmoniously in its progression. Our congratulations go to the Sparaco family and the estate staff, led by Dino Porfiri, Franco Bernabei and Mirco Pompili. They really earned those Three Glasses. Le Moie 2002 also did well. Its pear, apple and sweet almond lead into the pervasive balance of a full-bodied, tangily flavoursome palate. The Passo del Lupo 2000 is very good. Austere and dynamic, it hints at exciting evolution that is beginning to emerge in the notes of liquorice. San Sisto 2000 is soft and smoky on both nose and palate, also revealing admirable substance. The standard Rosso Conero 2002 is a nice product, with fresh morello cherry and a full, tannin-rich finish. The fresh, but rather acidic, Titulus 2002 scored no more than a mention. We'll close with the voluptuous Arkezia 2000, from verdicchio grapes dried on the vine. The intense candy floss and dried apricot nose ushers in a deliciously sweet palate.

○ Verdicchio dei Castelli di Jesi Cl. Sup. Massaccio '00	🍷🍷🍷	5
○ Arkezia Muffo di S. Sisto '00	🍷🍷	6
● Rosso Conero Passo del Lupo Ris. '00	🍷🍷	6
○ Verdicchio dei Castelli di Jesi Cl. San Sisto Ris. '00	🍷🍷	5
○ Verdicchio dei Castelli di Jesi Cl. Sup. Le Moie '02	🍷🍷	4*
● Rosso Conero '02	🍷	4
○ Verdicchio dei Castelli di Jesi Cl. Titulus '02		3
● Rosso Conero Passo del Lupo Ris. '98	🥂🥂	6

CASTELRAIMONDO (MC)

Collestefano

loc. Colle Stefano, 3
62022 Castelraimondo (MC)
tel. 0737640439
e-mail: info@collestefano.com

After he had finished his oenology studies and acquired some cellar experience in Germany and Alsace, Fabio Marchionni decided to take over his family's four hectares of exclusively verdicchio vines in 1998. He was aiming for quality and to get it, he opted for organic viticulture, which meant back-breaking effort in the vineyard and maniacal attention to detail in the cellar. After four years of dedication and sacrifice, the cool weather conditions of the 2002 vintage gave him the chance to make an excellent wine, thanks especially to his vineyards' elevation very high up the hillsides at 500 or 600 metres above sea level, where the temperature range between day and night is considerable. Only the finest fruit was selected and then vinified traditionally in stainless steel. There was no malolactic fermentation, a procedure that Fabio has steadfastly refused to apply to his wines. Collestefano 2002 has intense spring flowers, green apple and hawthorn that still allow an elegantly assertive hint of minerality to come through. The stylish, aristocratic palate has incisive progression and marked acidity that imbues the wine with plenty of personality. This is a genuine, terroir-driven product, whose 25,000 bottles are on sale at a very attractive price. The 2002 is stunning, while the 2001 is very good, and drinking deliciously at present.

○ Verdicchio di Matelica Collestefano '02	🍷🍷	4*
○ Verdicchio di Matelica Collestefano '01	🍷🍷	4*

CASTIGNANO (AP)

CANTINE DI CASTIGNANO
C.DA SAN VENANZO, 31
63032 CASTIGNANO (AP)
TEL. 0736822216 - 0736822220
E-MAIL: mail@cantinedicastignano.com

One of the great merits of the Cantine di Castignano, a co-operative winery, is that it produces reasonable quantities of good wine at competitive prices. In fact, they are increasingly good value for money. The co-operative chair, Dante Remia, and manager, Pio Iommi, with winemaking consultancy from Pierluigi Lorenzetti, supervise members' vineyard holdings totalling 520 hectares, most of it planted to red varieties. Templaria 2001, a 70-30 blend of merlot and sangiovese, has an intriguing spicy nose, with tempting notes of cinnamon. The palate is soft, with good volume on entry and excellent drinkability, the initial aromas returning on the finish. A soft mouthfeel is also the distinctive feature of the Gramelot 2001, from passerina, verdicchio, malvasia and trebbiano. The spring flowers and apple nose introduces a glycerine-rich palate that is let down by insufficient acidity. The Falerio dei Colli Ascolani 2002 is fresher-tasting and more elegant, suggesting chamomile then revealing good length and balance on the palate. Overall, this was a good showing that does full justice to a co-operative determined to offer the best quality possible.

CIVITANOVA MARCHE (MC)

BOCCADIGABBIA
LOC. FONTESPINA
C.DA CASTELLETTA, 56
62012 CIVITANOVA MARCHE (MC)
TEL. 073370728
E-MAIL: info@boccadigabbia.com

The Boccadigabbia winery is one of the properties that once belonged to the Bonaparte family and Napoleon III. The French varieties that go into its current production were in fact planted at that time. Recently, the property has expanded with the acquisition of Cantina Villamagna at Macerata. Currently, the cellar can call on about 25 hectares, about 60 per cent planted to red grapes. Yet again, this year's tastings gave us an impressive overview of the range, as always very quality-oriented. The deep ruby Rosso Piceno 2001 is distinctly good. It combines a fruit-forward, spicy nose with a fresh palate, where the creamy, pervasive tannic weave leads to an unhurried finish. The merlot-based Pix is a wine with personality. The alcohol on the nose soon gives way to spices and autumn leaves, then the power of the palate is offset nicely by the softly elegant texture that is the wine's hallmark. Akronte, a monovarietal cabernet sauvignon, has always been a lovely, stylish wine. The 2000 edition shows breadth and complexity on the nose, although the meaty palate is overwhelmed by still edgy tannins that tend to dry out the finish. The pinot nero-based Girone 2000 is also excellent. An attractive ruby ushers in a nose that mingles fruit with herbaceous notes. There is lots of fruit on the juicy palate, which has very good length. Both whites are well made. The aromas – intriguing in the Mont'Anello 2001, approachable in the Castelletta 2002 – are discreet and introduce a substantial, well-balanced palate.

●	Templaria '01	♥♥	4*
○	Gramelot '01	♥	4
○	Falerio dei Colli Ascolani '02	♥	2*
○	Gramelot '00	♀♀	4
●	Templaria '00	♀♀	4

●	Akronte '00	♥♥	8
●	Pix Merlot '00	♥♥	7
●	Rosso Piceno '01	♥♥	4*
●	Girone '00	♥♥	7
○	Mont'Anello Bianco '01	♥	4
○	La Castelletta Pinot Grigio '02	♥	4
●	Akronte '94	♀♀♀	8
●	Akronte '93	♀♀♀	8
●	Akronte '95	♀♀♀	8
●	Akronte '97	♀♀♀	8
●	Akronte '98	♀♀♀	8
●	Saltapicchio Sangiovese '99	♀♀	7

CUPRA MARITTIMA (AP)

OASI DEGLI ANGELI
C.DA SANT'EGIDIO, 50
63012 CUPRA MARITTIMA (AP)
TEL. 0735778569
E-MAIL: info@kurni.it

Kurni is a unique wine, born of the labours and intelligence of Marco Casolanetti and Eleonora Rossi. Vinification procedure is rather complicated, as is appropriate for grapes of outstanding quality and concentration. A small proportion of the fruit is part-dried in boxes. Maceration is protracted, and takes place in a low-temperature environment. After the lees have settled naturally, the wine is simply racked off, with no clarification or filtration. It ages in new barriques, selected by grain and seasoning to offer the best possible micro-oxygenation, for nine months, and then is matured further in more new wood for the same length of time. It will spend a few more months in bottle before release. Kurni has been conceived to give its best over the medium to long term, so it may not always convince if tasted soon after it leaves the cellar. Care should be taken to let the wine breathe, perhaps carefully pouring it a few times from one decanter into a second. If you are patient, the wine will open and reveal all its gloriously assertive aromas. It will unfurl intense black berry fruit, which returns even more insistently on the back palate. Bramble and blueberry are well to the fore, lifted by elegant printer's ink and currants. In the mouth, the rich fruit is even more evident and velvet-smooth, close-knit tannins underpin a structure that is a paragon of balance.

CUPRAMONTANA (AN)

COLONNARA
VITICOLTORI IN CUPRAMONTANA
VIA MANDRIOLE, 6
60034 CUPRAMONTANA (AN)
TEL. 0731780273
E-MAIL: info@colonnara.it

Colonnara is a well-managed co-operative winery with a management team of expert professionals. Corrado Cugnasco, Cesare Ferrari and Pierluigi Gagliardini closely supervise the work of the roughly 200 members, who grow grapes on a total of just under 300 hectares. There were plenty of good results this year, and the top of the range turned out to be Tùfico 2001. From super-ripe verdicchio grapes, it reveals elegant apple, hazelnut and chamomile subtly nuanced with honey. The palate has good weight and mirrors the nose beautifully. Vigna San Marco 2002 has less complexity and elegance, but offers instead textbook typicity and nice depth on the palate. The Brut Millesimato '97, a single-variety Verdicchio vinified using the "metodo classico", is again one of the best sparklers in the region. Elegant on the nose, it has just the right note of acidity and palate-caressing prickle in the mouth. Tornamagno '98 is a blend of montepulciano, sangiovese grosso and sangiovese montanino. The soft mouthfeel has very ripe fruit, well-rounded tannins and a finish that focuses on coffee and cherries in alcohol. Lyricus 2002 is a Rosso Piceno that puts the accent on fragrant aromas and attractive drinkability. Sanctorum 2000 is a new product. Obtained from part-dried verdicchio, it offers upfront sultanas on the nose, then the palate shows restrained sweetness and a long, rich finish.

● Kurni '01	♈♈♈	8
● Kurni '97	♈♈♈	8
● Kurni '98	♈♈♈	8
● Kurni '00	♈♈♈	8
● Kurni '99	♈♈	8

○ Verdicchio dei Castelli di Jesi Cl. Sup. Tùfico V. T. '01	♈♈	4
○ Verdicchio dei Castelli di Jesi Cl. Sup. Vigna San Marco '02	♈♈	4*
○ Colonnara Spumante Brut M. Cl. Millesimato '97	♈♈	5
● Tornamagno '98	♈♈	5
○ Verdicchio dei Castelli di Jesi Cl. Romitello delle Mandriole Ris. '00	♈	4
○ Verdicchio dei Castelli di Jesi Passito Sanctorum '00	♈	5
● Rosso Piceno Lyricus '02	♈	3
○ Verdicchio dei Castelli di Jesi Cl. Sup. Tùfico V. T. '00	♈♈	4

CUPRAMONTANA (AN)

FABRIANO (AN)

VALLEROSA BONCI
VIA TORRE, 13
60034 CUPRAMONTANA (AN)
TEL. 0731789129
E-MAIL: info@vallerosa-bonci.com

ENZO MECELLA
VIA DANTE, 112
60044 FABRIANO (AN)
TEL. 073221680
E-MAIL: enzomecella@enzomecella.com

The Bonci family started making and selling wine at least three generations ago. Today, they have 50 hectares, of which 35 are planted to vine at an average altitude of 450 metres. They are located in the best wine country in Cupramontana, the districts of San Michele, Colonnara, Torre, Carpaneto, Alvareto and Pietrone. Bonci Verdicchios are special in that they faithfully reflect the conditions of the vintage. They are territory-driven wines that you could never accuse of being made to a formula. Classico Viatorre still has unripe notes. Its simplicity in the mouth is a merit that should not be underestimated in a vintage like 2002, because it makes the wine attractively easy to drink. The San Michele is good. Although it, too, suffered from the poor vintage, its lovely aromas range from lime blossom to chamomile, and the palate has a fragrance that persists, despite the appreciable concentration. It may not be the most massive of wines, but it is a very elegant one. Le Case 2001 has attractive citrus and ripe fruit that lead in to an impeccably tidy palate. Good balance and nose-palate consistency take you through to the long finish, where almond and hazelnut emerge. The amber Passito Rojano 2001's generous dried fruit introduces an approachable palate with good concentration but lacking complexity, and a finish that verges on the sugary. The verdicchio-based "spumante" sparkler unveils fresh aromas that mingle with hints of crusty bread. The attractive fragrance persists on the palate, backing up the nice almond paste flavour and a faintly minerally finish.

Enzo Mecella is back in the ranks to the region's best winemakers after his products attracted very favourable comments at our various tastings. The cellar carefully selects fruit from 15 hectares of rented vineyards, and uses barriques with great skill. It was, in fact, the first cellar in Marche to see the potential of small wood and to take advantage of it. Enzo avoids the muscular, super-concentrated style others have adopted, preferring elegance and finesse, as befits a character who likes to go his own way and ignore the passing fashions to which the world of wine is often prey. Verdicchio di Matelica Casa Fosca 2001 is a bright straw yellow in the glass, then the spectrum of aromatics fuses minerals with fruit sensations that return on the palate. Tangy flavour and well-gauged concentration make this wine an easy drinker, and the intense finish lingers appreciably. Braccano is an 80-20 mix of ciliegiolo and merlot. Dark ruby, it proffers intense spice and balsam that lift the bouquet. Fresh herbs and elegant body emerge on the palate, where well-defined tannins add length to the finish. Longobardo 2000, is from cabernet with a little merlot. The ruby-flecked purple introduces a nose free of grassy notes, but rich in oak-derived aromas that provide a backdrop for rhubarb, leather and tobacco. The good, fleshy palate has smooth extract and an elegant, temptingly attractive texture, signing off with a fine, long finish.

O Verdicchio dei Castelli di Jesi Cl. Sup. S. Michele '02	♔♔	4*
O Bonci Brut M. Cl. '97	♔♔	4*
O Verdicchio dei Castelli di Jesi Cl. Sup. Le Case '01	♔	5
O Verdicchio dei Castelli di Jesi Passito Rojano '01	♔	5
O Verdicchio dei Castelli di Jesi Cl. Viatorre '02	♔	3
O Verdicchio dei Castelli di Jesi Cl. Sup. S. Michele '00	♔♔♔	4*
● Rosso Piceno Casa Nostra '00	♔♔	6
O Verdicchio dei Castelli di Jesi Passito Rojano '00	♔♔	5

● Braccano '00	♔♔	4*
● Longobardo Rosso '00	♔♔	4*
O Verdicchio di Matelica Casa Fosca Sotto le Querce '01	♔♔	4*
● Longobardo Rosso '99	♔♔	4

FANO (PU)

CLAUDIO MORELLI
V.LE ROMAGNA, 47/B
61032 FANO (PU)
TEL. 0721823352
E-MAIL: clamoro@libero.it

GROTTAMMARE (AP)

VINICOLA DEL TESINO
VIA SAN LEONARDO, 35
63013 GROTTAMMARE (AP)
TEL. 0735735869
E-MAIL: carminucci@carminucci.com

Each year, Claudio Morelli presents the finest examples of a wine – Bianchello del Metauro – that he interprets with great rigour, differentiating the products from his various vineyards. Claudio has a total of 20 hectares in locations with diverse soil types, aspects and site climates. There are three versions from 2002, of which the best is certainly the uncomplicated and inexpensive San Cesareo. The broad bouquet progresses nicely with ripe fruit and dried flowers, as well as faint mineral notes in the finish. The palate is refreshing, full and broad, showing good balance and ending on a bitterish twist. The La Vigna delle Terrazze selection is a fairly intense straw yellow and has light, refreshing pear and apple aromas. The palate is a little light on extract, and the acidity in the finish is excessive. The tangy, reasonably elegant Borgo Torre made a better impression with its good length on the palate. There were good performances from the reds, where the hand of consultant winemaker, Riccardo Cotarella is more evident. Magliano 2000, a blend of 50 per cent sangiovese, 30 per cent cabernet sauvignon and 20 per cent merlot that ages in barrique, greets the nose with intense, very ripe blueberry, bramble and wild strawberry. The palate is muscular, but well-balanced, and the slightly edgy tannins are close knit, expanding into attractive balsamic notes on the finish. Ripe fruit and liquorice are the keynotes of the Sangiovese 2001, an attractive wine that is a tad too tannic and dry on the back palate.

Piero and Giovanni Carminucci's winery has always put very little of its wine into bottle, selling most of its output unbottled. But thanks to shrewd advice from oenologist, Pierluigi Lorenzetti, quality has steadily improved over the years. The Chardonnay Naumachos, which usually has intense, vanilla-mellowed banana and pineapple tropical fruit, is even more delightful this year, offering elegant summer flowers and citrus peel. In the mouth, the thrust of the alcohol and weight of glycerine are simply sumptuous, a nice vein of acidity adding welcome freshness. The velvet-soft, rich mouthfeel lingers deliciously on the back palate. Rosso Piceno Grotte sul Mare 2002 has pleasing fruit on the nose and a fluid mouthfeel that retains plenty of personality. In contrast, the Rosso Piceno Superiore Naumachos 2000 is less assertive. Its robust structure is marred by the excessive ripeness of the fruit and signs of over-evolution. Both Falerios are nice, but we preferred the Naumachos 2002, which has more depth. Fresh and intense, it combines fruit on the palate with a tangy finish that never wavers. Grotte sul Mare 2002 earned One Glass for its pleasant drinkability and subtle almondy finish.

●	Magliano '00	🍷🍷	4
○	Bianchello del Metauro S. Cesareo '02	🍷🍷	2*
●	Colli Pesaresi Sangiovese Sant'Andrea in Villis '01	🍷	4
○	Bianchello del Metauro Borgo Torre '02	🍷	3
○	Bianchello del Metauro La Vigna delle Terrazze '02	🍷	3
●	Suffragium '00	🍷🍷	4
●	Magliano '99	🍷🍷	4

○	Chardonnay Naumachos '01	🍷🍷	4*
●	Rosso Piceno Grotte sul Mare '02	🍷🍷	3*
●	Rosso Piceno Sup. Naumachos '00	🍷	4
○	Falerio dei Colli Ascolani Grotte sul Mare '02	🍷	2
○	Falerio dei Colli Ascolani Naumachos '02	🍷	3
○	Litora Naumachos '99	🍷🍷	5
●	Rosso Piceno Sup. Naumachos '99	🍷	4

JESI (AN)

MONTECAPPONE
VIA COLLE OLIVO, 2
60035 JESI (AN)
TEL. 0731205761
E-MAIL: gianmiri@hotmail.it

Montecappone is a lovely property that has recently been improved, although in the past it was no more than an ordinary, if perfectly respectable farm. Gianluca Mirizzi saw that the 45 hillside hectares could yield wines of great quality, so he left his native Rome and moved to Jesi. He has still has a lot of work to do restructuring the estate, which has been in operation since 1968, but he is getting there. One of the reasons for progress is that he has taken on consultant oenologist, Lorenzo Landi. Moving on to the wines, we found Gianluca's verdicchio-based Tabano Bianco 2002 to be remarkable. The delicate, harmonious nose melds vegetal notes with ripe apple and subtle vanilla, before the opulent front palate ushers in a soft progression through to the generous swathes of fruit in the finish. Tabano Rosso 2001 has distinct bramble, cherry, vanilla and coffee. The weight on the palate is carried forward by nice acidity, good alcohol and lashings of extract. The 2002 version of Montesecco is a monovarietal sangiovese. It lacks the complexity of previous editions but drinks quite deliciously. Verdicchio Montesecco 2002 offers very varietal acacia blossom and a refreshingly tangy palate.

LORETO (AN)

GIOACCHINO GAROFOLI
LOC. VILLA MUSONE
VIA ARNO, 9
60025 LORETO (AN)
TEL. 0717820162 - 0717820163
E-MAIL: mail@garofolivini.it

More than 2,000,000 bottles released each year do not in any way compromise the quality of Garofoli wines. Even what we might consider standard-label products are cleaner and better typed than the flagbearers of many other wineries. Finally, Garofoli has kept prices to reasonable levels, despite the many awards the cellar has won, which can only mean that it is a serious winemaker. Macrina 2002 is unchallenging on the nose, but the palate is a welter of fruit. The 2001 edition of Podium is reticent on the nose. The palate is more convincing, showing full, soft notes of apricot and hazelnut in a perfect balance of freshness and power. The barrique-aged Serra Fiorese 2000 earned good marks. Restrained toastiness never threatens the citrus, elderflower and acacia blossom aromas. In the mouth, it is opulent, harmonious and fresh. The two Rosso Picenos, Ambro and Farnio, are easy drinkers and impeccably clean on both the youthful fruit and alcohol nose and the nicely poised palate. Rosso Conero Piancarda 2000 is purple, with subtle spice and morello cherry introducing softness and pleasing length in the mouth. The exquisite Rosso Conero Grosso Agontano 2000 is dense ruby, mingling fruit and faint gamey hints on the nose. The juicy palate amalgamates the extract into an admirably concentrated structure. The balance is perfect and the length admirable. We'll conclude with a sparkler. The verdicchio-based '96 Brut melds yeast into floral aromas on the nose. The palate is creamy, with even texture and attractive freshness.

○ Esino Bianco Tabano '02	🍷🍷	4
● Esino Rosso Tabano '01	🍷🍷	5
● Rosso Piceno Montesecco '02	🍷	4
○ Verdicchio dei Castelli di Jesi Cl.		
Montesecco '02	🍷	4
● Rosso Piceno Montesecco '01	🍷🍷	4

● Rosso Conero Grosso Agontano Ris. '00	🍷🍷	5
● Rosso Conero Piancarda '00	🍷🍷	4
○ Verdicchio dei Castelli di Jesi Cl.		
Serra Fiorese Ris. '00	🍷🍷	5
○ Verdicchio dei Castelli di Jesi Cl.		
Sup. Podium '01	🍷🍷	4*
● Rosso Piceno Colle Ambro '00	🍷	3
○ Verdicchio dei Castelli di Jesi Cl.		
Sup. Macrina '02	🍷	3*
○ Brut Riserva M. Cl. '96	🍷	4
● Rosso Piceno Farnio '02		3
○ Verdicchio dei Castelli di Jesi Cl.		
Sup. Podium '99	🍷🍷🍷	4
○ Verdicchio dei Castelli di Jesi Cl.		
Serra Fiorese Ris. '99	🍷🍷🍷	4*

MAIOLATI SPONTINI (AN)

MONTESCHIAVO
FRAZ. MONTESCHIAVO
VIA VIVAIO
60030 MAIOLATI SPONTINI (AN)
TEL. 0731700385 - 0731700297
E-MAIL: info@monteschiavo.it

The Pieralisi family are well known as manufacturers of farm machinery. In 1995, they bought the estate and equipment of a co-operative winery and, over the last few years, they have devoted considerable effort to improving the quality of its range. We tasted two wines at Monteschiavo that are among the finest territory-driven products in the area, Pallio di S. Floriano 2002 and Adeodato 2001. The former is a very typical Verdicchio. Fermented and aged in steel only, it has intense, distinct, sweet almond, acacia blossom and apple aromas. The palate is tangy, with good thrust and breadth, as well as attractive lingering acidity in the finish. The Rosso Conero Adeodato is very elegant. The structure hinges on close-knit tannins, but never threatens to become edgy. The finish echoes the palate deliciously with ripe cherries, cocoa powder and subtle minty notes. Esio 2001, from montepulciano and cabernet, trades a little elegance for character and sheer, gutsy personality. Conti Cortesi 2000 is even on the palate after offering attractive spice and fruit on the nose. Nativo 2002, an unfiltered Verdicchio, looks like a good bet for the cellar. Lacrima 2002, with impressively intense roses and violets on the nose, is ready for drinking straight away.

●	Rosso Conero Adeodato '01	YY	6
○	Verdicchio dei Castelli di Jesi Cl. Sup. Pallio di S. Floriano '02	YY	3*
●	Esio '01	YY	5
●	Rosso Conero Conti Cortesi '00	Y	4
○	Verdicchio Castelli di Jesi Cl. Passito Arché '00	Y	4
○	Verdicchio dei Castelli di Jesi Cl. Le Giuncare Ris. '01	Y	4
●	Lacrima di Morro d'Alba '02	Y	4
○	Verdicchio dei Castelli di Jesi Cl. Sup. Nativo '02	Y	3
●	Rosso Conero Adeodato '00	YYY	6
●	Esio '00	YY	5

MATELICA (MC)

BELISARIO CANTINA SOCIALE
DI MATELICA E CERRETO D'ESI
VIA MERLONI, 12
62024 MATELICA (MC)
TEL. 0737787247
E-MAIL: belisario@belisario.it

Cantina Sociale Belisario is a point of reference for a large number of growers who bring fruit from the Matelica area. It is also a safe haven for the many small producers who make useful income growing grapes in vineyards that are often tiny. However, all have to work to the vineyard management standards set by Mario Ghergo, a serious professional. Belisario is such a well-established co-operative that it manages 80 hectares under vine directly, as well as supervising the members' 150. In the cellar, oenologist and manager, Roberto Pontini, a Verdicchio di Matelica expert, regularly obtains superb results from his specialist wine type. This year, the Vigneti Belisario 2002 was the most exciting bottle in the range. Obtained from a single, organically managed, vineyard, it has an impressively elegant nose with well-defined spring flowers, ripe apple and sweet almond, then harmony and length characterize the palate. Cerro, however, was not up to our expectations. Uneven ripening, brought on by the summer rain in 2002, has upset its usual structure and composure, although the flowery personality is the same as ever. In contrast, the softness and rather evolved aromatics of the Cambrugiano reveal how warm the summer of 2000 was. As usual, Terre di Valbona, Ferrante and Colferraio are utterly typical and eminently drinkable. The San Leopardo 2000, from sangiovese, merlot, montepulciano and cabernet, performed well. Complex aromas introduce an intense palate with hints of liquorice and pepper in the finish.

○	Verdicchio di Matelica Vigneti Belisario '02	YY	4*
●	San Leopardo '00	YY	4
○	Verdicchio di Matelica Cambrugiano Ris. '00	Y	4
○	Esino Bianco Ferrante '02	Y	1*
●	Esino Rosso Colferraio '02	Y	1*
○	Verdicchio di Matelica Terre di Valbona '02	Y	2*
○	Verdicchio di Matelica Vigneti del Cerro '02	Y	3
○	Verdicchio di Matelica Cambrugiano Ris. '99	YY	4

MATELICA (MC)

BISCI
VIA FOGLIANO, 120
62024 MATELICA (MC)
TEL. 0737787490
E-MAIL: bisciwines@libero.it

Verdicchio is an extraordinary variety that demands special care during production, especially when it is made in the Matelica valley. But the winemaker's reward is a wine of character, with bracing acidity and generous alcohol, and capable of ageing unhurriedly, something that cannot be said of many whites. These are the qualities we find in Bisci's Verdicchio Riserva 1998. The lustrous straw yellow introduces hints of minerals and balsam on the nose. In the mouth, concentration and succulent flesh are backed up by nice acidity, and the finish is enchantingly fragrant. The straw-yellow Verdicchio 2001 has ripe fruit aromas introducing a coherent, juicy mouthfeel with attractive tropical fruit on the back palate. Villa Castiglioni 2001, a blend of sangiovese and cabernet sauvignon, is dark purple. Initially closed on the nose, it soon opens into plum, aniseed and balsam, then the soft, fleshy palate reveals plenty of length. Rosso Fogliano 2001 is an unusual mix of montepulciano, barbera, cabernet franc and merlot. Deep vermilion precedes ripe red berry fruit and leather, then the caressingly even palate shows excellent balance of extract and concentrated fruit, signing off with spicy notes. The Bisci estate, located in the provinces of Macerata and Ancona, covers 105 hectares, of which about 20 are under vine (14 are planted to verdicchio and six to sangiovese or cabernet).

●	Rosso Fogliano '01	▼▼	3*
●	Villa Castiglioni '01	▼▼	5
○	Verdicchio di Matelica Ris. '98	▼▼	4
○	Verdicchio di Matelica '01	▼	4
○	Verdicchio di Matelica Vigneto Fogliano '00	YY	4

MATELICA (MC)

LA MONACESCA
C.DA MONACESCA
62024 MATELICA (MC)
TEL. 0733812602
E-MAIL: info@monacesca.it

In 1966, Casimiro Cifola bought the first lot of his present property, planting all of it to verdicchio. Later, he set up a vinification cellar in the municipality of Potenza Picena. It was 1973 when he bottled his first Verdicchio di Matelica della Monacesca, a wine of which he releases 140,000 units a year now. In 1994, he decided to plant a vineyard at Contrada Valle to red varieties, sangiovese and merlot. His aim was to restore lustre to Rosso Matelica, a wine that in the early 1900s more than held it own at international competitions. Monacesca wines are utterly reliable, thanks to the winery's organization and the contribution of oenologists, Roberto Potentini and Fabrizio Ciufoli. Verdicchio di Matelica Mirum 2001 is an object lesson in elegance. The aromas range from ripe fruit to aniseed and candied ginger, and are echoed on the richly extracted palate, minerals prevailing on the finish. Camerte, from sangiovese grosso and merlot, has exuberant liquorice on the nose, mellowed subsequently by fruit and spice. The tannic weave on the palate is evident, but not over-assertive, and the fruit is rich and pulpy, unveiling impressive balance in the long finish. Verdicchio La Monacesca 2002 has delicious notes of spring flowers and ripe pears, laced with elegant mineral on the back palate. The full palate is braced by attractive acidity, and the lingering finish is soft and fruit forward.

○	Verdicchio di Matelica Mirum Ris. '01	▼▼	5
○	Verdicchio di Matelica La Monacesca '02	▼▼	4*
●	Camerte '01	▼▼	7
○	Mirus '91	YYY	5
○	Mirum '94	YYY	5
○	Verdicchio di Matelica La Monacesca '94	YYY	5
●	Camerte '99	YYY	7
●	Camerte '00	YY	7
○	Verdicchio di Matelica Mirum '00	YY	5
○	Verdicchio di Matelica La Monacesca '01	YY	4

MONDAVIO (PU)

FATTORIA LAILA
VIA S. FILIPPO SUL CESANO, 27
61040 MONDAVIO (PU)
TEL. 0721979353
E-MAIL: fattorialaila@tin.it

It might comes as a surprise that a Pesaro cellar should produce DOC wines from other provinces. The reason is the Fattoria Laila has 31 hectares under vine in the hills of Corinaldo, in the Verdicchio dei Castelli di Jesi zone. It was here that in 1990 Andrea Croscenzi decided to turn his hand to viticulture, starting with limited production that he sold unbottled. With help from oenologist, Lorenzo Landi, the cellar became more specialized and quality-oriented over the years, earning Fattoria Laila a profile in the Guide. The Verdicchio 2002 has acacia and lime blossom, then a fragrant, chewy palate that mirrors the nose endlessly in a highly attractive finish. Verdicchio Lailum 2002 is less convincing. It is not so much a lesser wine as the victim of a poor vintage, and has still to find a point of balance. The nose is closed and vegetal, and although the palate has decent concentration, it is acidic and untidy. Rosso Piceno 2002's dark vermilion ushers in an upfront, fruit and alcohol, easy-drinking palate that may not be concentrated, but is very well balanced. But the montepulciano-based Lailum 2001 is remarkable. An intense purple tells you this is a serious wine and then the complex nose, laced with understated vanilla, weaves berry fruit with leather and tobacco. Sumptuous and deep in the mouth, it has a juicy mouthfeel, braced by assertive yet mellow tannins that prolong the back palate into hints of morello cherry, cinnamon and liquorice.

MONTECAROTTO (AN)

FATTORIA SAN LORENZO
VIA SAN LORENZO, 6
60036 MONTECAROTTO (AN)
TEL. 073189656
E-MAIL: az-crognaletti@libero.it

Natalino Crognaletti makes bright, characterful wines that are instantly recognizable as his handiwork. He began producing them in 1995, when his father handed the family cellar over to him. From a shy start, the business – and Natalino's enthusiasm – grew apace. He has earned his inclusion in the Guide for the impassioned originality and professional skill with which he makes his wines. Verdicchio di Gino 2002 is typicity in a bottle. Fresh aromas and a fragrant palate are bolstered by subtle tanginess through to an upfront finish. In contrast, Vigna delle Oche Riserva 2000 foregrounds balance. Fruit prevails on the nose, and the power of the palate is tempered by bright freshness, rounded off with excellent length. And Vigna delle Oche Superiore 2001 is the epitome of elegance. Complex aromas accompany a stylish palate lent originality by lees contact. The structure is firm, and the long finish signs off with juicy fruit. Rosso Piceno di Gino 2001 is all youthful fruit and alcohol. Simplicity is the leading virtue of this gently fruit-led wine. Quadratura del Cerchio 2000 goes beyond mere originality. Natalino made it after receiving a challenge from other winemaking friends, and the nose combines the herbaceous notes of carmenère with montepulciano's ripe cherry and barbera's spices. The palate is tangy and the finish good. Finally, Vigneto del Solleone 2000 is solidity. It has a concentrated ruby hue and the nose mingles oak-derived aromas with ripe morello cherry and cocoa powder. The vigorous palate is compact and well-structured, with a juicy spice-rich finish.

●	Lailum '01	🍷🍷	5
●	Rosso Piceno '02	🍷	4
○	Verdicchio dei Castelli di Jesi '02	🍷	3
○	Verdicchio dei Castelli di Jesi Lailum '02	🍷	4
●	Lailum '00	🍷🍷	5
●	Rosso Piceno '01	🍷🍷	4

●	Vigneto del Solleone '00	🍷🍷	6
○	Verdicchio dei Castelli di Jesi Cl. Sup. Vigna delle Oche '01	🍷🍷	4*
●	La Quadratura del Cerchio '00	🍷	6
○	Verdicchio dei Castelli di Jesi Cl. Vigna delle Oche Ris. '00	🍷	5
●	Rosso Piceno di Gino '01	🍷	3
○	Verdicchio dei Castelli di Jesi Cl. di Gino '02		2

MONTECAROTTO (AN)

MONTECAROTTO (AN)

LAURENTINA
VIA SAN PIETRO 19/A
60036 MONTECAROTTO (AN)
TEL. 073189435
E-MAIL: laurentina@katamail.com

TERRE CORTESI MONCARO
VIA PIANDOLE, 7/A
60036 MONTECAROTTO (AN)
TEL. 073189245
E-MAIL: terrecortesi@moncaro.com

Founded in 1997 and equipped with a modern, highly functional cellar from the start, Laurentina has managed to combine quality with admirable faithfulness to the most traditional manifestations of the territory. About 50,000 bottles are turned out each year, all muscular and well typed, especially the Verdicchios. Management of the 13 hectares under vine, nine of which are estate owned, is in the hands of consultant oenologist and agronomist, Giancarlo Soverchia. Vigneto di Tobia 2002 is a textbook traditional-style Verdicchio. Subtle, fleeting hints of lime blossom and spring flowers tempt the nose, then the palate shows tanginess and power, with extract that bolsters and prolongs the sensations of the finish. The Loretello 2001 selection is more complex. Acacia blossom and vanilla introduce a palate with distinct ripe fruit and golden delicious apples, well integrated into the rich concentration. Rosso Piceno Talliano 2001 is vibrant ruby and the nose opens on oak-derived notes that give way to red berry fruit and morello cherry. The close-knit palate is underpinned by smooth tannins and the finish returns to the succulence of ripe cherries.

Sometimes, you can find good quality and high volume production living happily together. Proof is here, at the Terre Cortesi Moncaro co-operative, which produces about 6,000,000 bottles a year yet wins more than its share of awards. This points to solid organization – oenologists Giuliano D'Ignazi and Gianni Mazzoli have abundant experience and the consultant is Riccardo Cotarella – and efficient management. The operation has more than 1,500 hectares under vine and three vinification cellars in various DOC zones. One of the most interesting products is Barocco 2000, a 50-50 blend of montepulciano and cabernet sauvignon. Intense aromas of ripe fruit and spice, an incisive personality of integrity and freshness, and meaty, juicy flesh take you through to a very elegant finish. Fresh fruit jam and spice dominate the nose of the Rosso Conero Vigneti del Parco 2000, which reveals a generously soft mouthfeel and tight-knit, assertive tannins. The Cimerio is built along similar lines, but longer and more velvety in the finish, and Roccaviva has substantial tannins, which it keeps well under control. Passito Tordiruta 2000 has pervasive aromas of apricot jam, lifted by nice notes of noble rot. Opulently full in the mouth, it is distinctly sweet but not cloying, as there is good acidity to provide a counterpoint. There was a good performance from the white Verde Ca' Ruptae 2002, which offers fresh fruit aromas and a full, deliciously tangy palate. Also good is the Vigna Novali 2000, a fruit-led, subtly flowery wine with complexity, elegance and distinct minerality in the mouth.

●	Rosso Piceno Talliano '01	▼▼	5
○	Verdicchio dei Castelli di Jesi Cl. Loretello '01	▼	4
○	Verdicchio dei Castelli di Jesi Cl. Vigneto di Tobia '02	▼	3
●	Rosso Piceno Talliano '00	♉♉	5
●	Esino Rosso Laurano '01	♉♉	4

●	Barocco '00	▼▼	4*
○	Verdicchio dei Castelli di Jesi Passito Tordiruta '00	▼▼	5
○	Verdicchio dei Castelli di Jesi Cl. Sup. Verde Ca' Ruptae '02	▼▼	3*
●	Rosso Conero Cimerio Ris. '00	▼▼	4
●	Rosso Conero Vigneti del Parco Ris. '00	▼▼	5
●	Rosso Piceno Roccaviva '00	▼▼	3*
○	Verdicchio dei Castelli di Jesi Cl. Vigna Novali Ris. '00	▼▼	4
○	Verdicchio dei Castelli di Jesi Cl. Le Vele '02	▼▼	3*
●	Geos '01	▼	3
○	Falerio dei Colli Ascolani Terre Cortesi '02	▼	2

MONTEGRANARO (AP)

RIO MAGGIO
C.DA VALLONE, 41
63014 MONTEGRANARO (AP)
TEL. 0734889587
E-MAIL: info@riomaggio.it

Simone and Tiziana Santucci run their estate competently and enthusiastically, aided by advice from first-rank oenologist, Giancarlo Soverchia. The quality of their range never wavers. Every year, we note good results in the local DOC wines and in the Artias line, which is reserved for French grape varieties. The Chardonnay 2002 has elegant, intense, ripe tropical fruit, echoed on the lingering finish. The structure is generous and very well balanced. The 2002 Sauvignon failed to repeat its predecessor's exploit, undoubtedly because of the less favourable vintage. There is a well-defined varietal note on the nose, accompanied by fresh fruit and citrus. The palate at once shows slightly over-exuberant acidity, that remains on the long finish. The Pinot Nero 2001 aged for a year in French barriques, emerging with a garnet hue and firm, intense dried fruit and spices. The palate is evolved but completely free of oxidative notes. Balance and exceptional elegance are the keynotes, then the temptingly soft finish lingers deliciously. GrAnarijS 2001 has reasonable breadth on the nose, where ripe and bottled fruit mingle with spices and wood resin. The dense mouthfeel and close-knit tannic weave are dried a little by the oak, which holds back the finish. The well-made Falerio Telusiano 2002 has meadow grass aromas, then a fairly intense palate and good acidity.

MONTEPRANDONE (AP)

IL CONTE
VIA COLLE NAVICCHIO, 28
63030 MONTEPRANDONE (AP)
TEL. 073562593
E-MAIL: ilcontevini@tiscalinet.it

The De Angelis family has 21 hectares under vine in the hills behind San Benedetto del Tronto, all enviably well located for wine production. Marino and Emmanuel respectively look after vineyard and cellar management, with advice on modern vinification techniques from consultant oenologist, Pierluigi Lorenzetti. Our recent tastings confirmed last year's excellent performance, which won the cellar a Guide profile right from the start. The Marinus 2001 put on a good show. There are over-ripe notes on the nose, tempered by coffee and faint vanilla, then the palate reveals all its gutsy extract and excellent length. Navicchio 2001 is a white from mainly chardonnay, with proportions of malvasia and verdicchio. An opulent wine with lavish tropical fruit, it reveals a subtle hint of vanilla on the back palate that betrays its stay in barrique. The oak-derived aromas are nicely integrated, but the wine, sadly, fails to do justice to its terroir and personality. Zipolo 2000, from 60 per cent montepulciano and the remainder sangiovese and merlot, is less convincing than the '99 edition. The fruit is excessively ripe, over-ripe notes of jam and rose-water dominate the nose and palate, and the very soft mouthfeel is accompanied by serious alcohol. Donello 2002, an elegant, deep Sangiovese, is attractive. Aurato is a 2002 Falerio that is anything but run of the mill.

● Artias Pinot Nero '01	🍷🍷	5
○ Artias Chardonnay '02	🍷🍷	4*
● Rosso Piceno GrAnarijS '01	🍷	5
○ Artias Sauvignon '02	🍷	4
○ Falerio dei Colli Ascolani Telusiano '02	🍷	3
○ Falerio dei Colli Ascolani '02		2
● Rosso Piceno GrAnarijS '99	🍷🍷	5
● Artias Pinot Nero '00	🍷🍷	5
○ Artias Sauvignon '01	🍷🍷	4
● Rosso Piceno GrAnarijS '00	🍷	5

● Rosso Piceno Marinus '01	🍷🍷	4*
● Zipolo '00	🍷	5
○ Navicchio '01	🍷	5
● Donello Sangiovese '02	🍷	4
○ Falerio dei Colli Ascolani Aurato '02	🍷	3
○ Navicchio '00	🍷🍷	4
● Zipolo '99	🍷🍷	5
● Rosso Piceno Marinus '00	🍷	4

MORRO D'ALBA (AN)

MAROTTI CAMPI
LOC. SANT'AMICO, 14
60030 MORRO D'ALBA (AN)
TEL. 0731618027
E-MAIL: wine.marotticampi@tin.it

For more than a century, the Marotti Campi family has owned 52 beautifully aspected hillside hectares at Morro d'Alba, where high-density plots stand side by side with older plantings. Cropping levels are kept low by severe winter pruning and thinning at veraison, when the berries begin to colour on the vine. After the harvest, the fruit is vinified at once in the new temperature-controlled cellar, built to provide technological support in bringing out the typicity of the fruit and the characteristics of the vintage. Salmariano 2001 is vibrant in hue, and its vanillaed nose has ripe fruit aromas. Soft succulence is the keynote in the mouth. Ripe fruit and cakes return, and the palate signs off with a touch of hazelnut. Luzano 2002 is the antithesis of the Salmariano. Flowers and faint grassy hints prevail on the nose, then the fragrant, uncomplicated palate is instantly approachable, and shows moderate length. The Lacrima Rùbico 2002 has a classic nose of roses and violets. Assertive extract in the mouth masks the fruit, which emerges only on the back palate. Orgiolo 2001 is dark purple, the nose mingling vanilla with dried flowers. There is nice concentration on the palate, where vanilla returns with a vein of acidity that lends drinkability. Xyris is a part-fermented must from lacrima grapes, with good aromas and low alcohol. Onyr 2001 is a copper-flecked straw-yellow dried-grape "passito" with faint hints of nuts, a subtle texture and a bitterish finish.

MORROVALLE (MC)

CAPINERA
C.DA CROCETTE, 16
62010 MORROVALLE (MC)
TEL. 0733222444
E-MAIL: info@capinera.com

This winery is in the municipality of Morrovalle and, since it was established in 1982, has been run by the Capinera family. They have 40 hectares in total, seven planted to mainly red grape vines. The limestone and clay soil is at an average elevation above sea level of about 200 metres. In recent years, the Capineras have implemented a serious plan to replace older vines with practical modern plantings. Low cropping levels, of no more than 60 quintals, and scrupulous bunch selection, complete the cellar's strategy to improve quality year after year. The Murrano 2002 is uncomplicated, but far from ordinary. Fresh flowers come together with an instantly attractive, approachable palate. The Chardonnay 2002 is a deep straw, with herbaceous and tropical fruit aromas. The front palate is tangy and refreshing, echoing the nose, and juicy fruit accompanies the nicely poised finish. The limpid ruby Rosso Piceno Duca Guarnerio 2001 melds delicious fruit and flowers on the nose. Attractive fruit returns in the mouth, where elegance and freshness take precedence over muscle. Cardinal Minio 2001 is a monovarietal Merlot. Amaranth red in the glass, it flaunts ripe fruit aromas shading into tobacco and leather. The very refreshing palate also has nice concentration, braced by smooth, close-knit tannins, and the finish plays off intense fruit against light balsam and spice.

O Verdicchio dei Castelli di Jesi Cl.		
Salmariano Ris. '01	♟♟	4
● Lacrima di Morro d'Alba		
Orgiolo '01	♟	4
● Lacrima di Morro d'Alba Rùbico '02	♟	3
O Verdicchio dei Castelli di Jesi Cl.		
Luzano '02	♟	3
O Verdicchio dei Castelli di Jesi		
Passito Onyr '01		4
● Xyris Filtrato di Lacrima		3
● Lacrima di Morro d'Alba		
Orgiolo '00	♟♟	4

● Cardinal Minio '01	♟♟	4
O La Capinera Chardonnay '02	♟♟	3*
● Rosso Piceno		
Duca Guarnerio '01	♟	4
O Colli Maceratesi Bianco		
Murrano '02	♟	2
O La Capinera Chardonnay '00	♟♟	3

NUMANA (AN)

NUMANA (AN)

CONTE LEOPARDI DITTAJUTI
VIA MARINA II, 26
60026 NUMANA (AN)
TEL. 0717390116
E-MAIL: leopar@tin.it

FATTORIA LE TERRAZZE
VIA MUSONE, 4
60026 NUMANA (AN)
TEL. 0717390352
E-MAIL: a.terni@fastnet.it

This estate now has a total of 35 hectares, much of it in the hillside Coppo vineyard in the Conero park. It is an excellent location, and only two kilometres from the sea. Over recent years, investment has upgraded the cellar equipment, and production is now running at more than 80,000 bottles a year. Bianco del Coppo 2002, a sauvignon-based wine, is a deep straw yellow with a very varietal nose. The palate has a few rough edges, as the acidity has not yet been fully integrated, and the aromas are reminiscent of citrus and rue. Fructus 2002 is a model of an easy-drinking Rosso Conero that puts the accent on fragrant aromas and a soft mouthfeel. This version had to deal with a difficult vintage and its alcohol-rich sensations are unexciting, the texture thin and short. Rosso Conero Vigneti del Coppo 2001 is a lovely, limpid, purple-flecked ruby with direct, fruit and alcohol aromas and a decently fresh palate that shows good concentration and softness. Pigmento '99 is a single-variety montepulciano. The dark ruby ushers in a full, attractive nose that mingles fruit with light hints of vanilla. The palate has oak-derived aromas, soft tannins and succulent fruit that expands over spice in the finish. Casirano 2001, from nearly equal parts of montepulciano, cabernet and syrah, is dark purple, with a fruit-forward nose lifted by faint grassy and spicy notes. The soft, direct texture combines with juicy pulp and ripe fruit, signing off with tobacco and leather.

The bad weather that hit the Monte Conero area just before the 2001 harvest destroyed much of the late-ripening montepulciano crop. As a result, Sassi Neri was not made. However, the small quantity of fruit that did survive was of excellent quality. Antonio and Giorgina Terni, oenologist Attilio Pagli and agronomist, Leonardo Valenti, decided to use some of the grapes for their Chaos 2001 and the rest to make Visions of J, a super-selection of very high-quality fruit from exceptionally good conditions. In fact previously, we have only been able to enjoy one edition, the 1997. Visions of J will be released in a year's time, but for the moment we can enjoy the superlative Chaos 2001, which earned Three Glasses in its own right. A blend of syrah, merlot and montepulciano, it tempts the nose with balsam, adding successive notes of clearly distinguishable white pepper, bitter chocolate and bramble that come together in a whole of rare finesse. The concentration and power of the palate are lifted by a depth of flavour that only wines of great elegance can flaunt, and enhanced by the sheer length of the seemingly endless finish. Rosso Conero 2002 was not ready for us when we arrived for the Guide tastings. The steel-vinified Le Cave 2002, a Chardonnay, has very ripe fruit aromas that return on a very full and enjoyable palate.

● Casirano Rosso '01	♟♟	4*
● Rosso Conero Pigmento '99	♟♟	6
● Rosso Conero Vigneti del Coppo '01	♟	4
○ Bianco del Coppo Sauvignon '02		3
● Rosso Conero Fructus '02		3
● Casirano Rosso '00	♟♟	4
● Rosso Conero Pigmento '98	♟♟	6
○ Calcare Sauvignon '01	♟	4

● Chaos '01	♟♟♟	7
○ Le Cave Chardonnay '02	♟♟	4*
● Chaos '97	♟♟♟	7
● Rosso Conero Visions of J '97	♟♟♟	8
● Rosso Conero Sassi Neri '98	♟♟♟	6
● Rosso Conero Sassi Neri '99	♟♟♟	6
● Chaos '99	♟♟	7
● Chaos '00	♟♟	7
● Rosso Conero Sassi Neri '97	♟♟	6
● Rosso Conero Sassi Neri '00	♟♟	6

OFFIDA (AP)

AURORA
LOC. S. MARIA IN CARRO
C.DA CIAFONE, 98
63035 OFFIDA (AP)
TEL. 0736810007
E-MAIL: enrico@viniaurora.it

Aurora was established in the early 1980s as a free community with a strong vocation for recovering a direct relationship with the land. Resources were entirely self-managed and the speculations of the market were kept, as far as possible, at arm's length. Then as now, a firm political bond holds together all those who take part in the enterprise, finding practical expression in solidarity and co-operation-oriented initiatives. Production criteria are strictly organic, and very close to the tenets of biodynamic viticulture. The completeness and integrity of the project are evident in all the products of the Aurora range. Barricadiero 2001, of which 7,000 bottles were released, was convincing at all our tastings. From 75 per cent montepulciano, with cabernet and merlot, it combines power and concentration with poise and attractive elegance. The aromas are wide-ranging and distinctive, the juicy, ripe fruit being lifted by subtle spice, liquorice and currants. It lingers on the palate without missing a beat, showing all the fullness, finesse and austerity of a great Three Glass winner. Rosso Piceno Superiore 2001 has well-defined, intensely fruity aromas, then the palate's unbending framework of acidity and extract is nicely offset by soft fruit. The purplish Rosso Piceno 2002 has fragrant ripe fruit and spices, then a nice, firm texture in the mouth. It is refreshing, attractive and eminently drinkable. The firm-bodied, alcohol-rich Fiobbo 2002, from pecorino grapes, offers intense fruit on nose and palate.

OFFIDA (AP)

CIÙ CIÙ
LOC. SANTA MARIA IN CARRO
C.DA CIAFONE, 106
63035 OFFIDA (AP)
TEL. 0736810001
E-MAIL: info@ciuciu.com

The curious name of the Bartolomei winery is actually the nickname (it's pronounced "choo choo") that a former head of the family had in the local area. Today, Walter and Massimiliano manage an estate of 70 hectares planted to vine and a modern cellar. Their unswerving goal is to improve quality, to which end they have hired the services of oenologist, Pierluigi Lorenzetti, who keeps an eye on many Piceno cellars. Orum 2001 is a Rosso Piceno Superiore that was created as a traditional-style wine. The admirably complex aromas are followed by extract-rich structure and sure-footed progression. The spicy, deep Saggio 2002 is a monovarietal Sangiovese that is a shade too stiff in the finish. Cellar time should help the palate to smooth out its rough edges. Oppidum is from montepulciano grapes harvested when super-ripe, and could well become the cellar's flagship bottle in future years. The 2000 has impressive structure, but its finish, like the Saggio's, is held back by rather inflexible tannins. Gotico 2001 is very ripe on nose and palate, but lacks a little finesse and freshness. Moving on to the whites, we find a pleasantly fruity, chardonnay-based Gaudeo 2002, as well as a more complex, characterful Le Merlettaie, from native pecorino grapes. Its brief stay in large ovals has tempered the grape's substantial acidity and enhanced its fruitiness.

● Barricadiero '01	♟♟♟	4*
● Rosso Piceno Sup. '01	♟♟	3*
○ Offida Pecorino Fiobbo '02	♟	4
● Rosso Piceno '02	♟	3
● Barricadiero '00	♟♟	4
● Rosso Piceno Sup. '00	♟	3

● Oppidum '00	♟♟	5
● Rosso Piceno Sup. Orum '01	♟♟	3*
● Saggio Sangiovese '02	♟♟	5
● Rosso Piceno Sup. Gotico '01	♟	4
○ Falerio dei Colli Ascolani '02	♟	2
○ Gaudeo '02	♟	3
○ Offida Pecorino Le Merlettaie '02	♟	3
● Rosso Piceno Bacchus '02	♟	3
● Saggio Sangiovese '01	♟♟	5

OFFIDA (AP)

SAN GIOVANNI
C.DA CIAFONE, 41
63035 OFFIDA (AP)
TEL. 0736889032
E-MAIL: sangiovanni@vinisangiovanni.it

Gianni Di Lorenzo has his feet firmly on the ground, as befits a true country gentleman. A law graduate, he has never actually practised that noble profession. Instead, the love of the land that he inherited from his father, Silvano, drew him to the 32 hectares under vine that he manages in one of the finest locations in Piceno. It is to Gianni's credit that he has never tried to overdo things. Progress has been by small, careful steps. His very competent oenologist, Primo Narcisi, shares this view. Both are now enjoying the results, starting with the historic – for this territory – invitation of a Falerio dei Colli Ascolani to the final taste-offs. Actually, Marta 2001 is an untypical Falerio and the words "vendemmia tardiva" ("late harvest") on the label are a tad misleading. From slightly over-ripe fruit, Marta 2001 has finesse on the nose and balanced, expansive elegance in the mouth. Softness is braced by alcohol, not residual sugar, and the well-gauged acidity banishes any trace of cloying sweetness. But the star is Zeii 2000. Obtained mainly from montepulciano with some merlot and cabernet sauvignon, it has power, structure and a tight-knit, ripe tannic weave. The aromas range from aromatic herbs to distinct hints of ripe cherries, as well as liquorice and bitter chocolate. Both Leo Guelfus wines are very good. The Falerio 2002 is very fresh and drinkable and the firm Rosso Piceno 2001 is well balanced. Zagros 2002 is a single-variety trebbiano with intriguing vegetal nuances and serious alcohol. The Ophites wines are well typed and attractively priced.

OSIMO (AN)

UMANI RONCHI
S. S. 16, KM. 310+400, 74
60027 OSIMO (AN)
TEL. 0717108019
E-MAIL: wine@umanironchi.it

Umani Ronchi vinifies fruit from 230 hectares and releases 4,500,000 bottles every year. But big numbers are no threat to quality, thanks in large part to the patient labours of winemaker Cristina Cantarini and consultant Beppe Caviola. We'll start with the 2002 Verdicchios. Casal di Serra is fragrant on the nose and fresh on the palate, whereas Villa Bianchi is racy and temptingly soft. Le Busche 2001, from equal parts of verdicchio and chardonnay, offers lime blossom and a succulent palate. Sultano 2001, from super-ripe fruit, shows stewed fruit aromas and an inelegantly soft mouthfeel. Plenio 2000 tempts the nose with vanilla and the palate with its juicy citrus. Montepulciano Jorio 2001 shows good depth that reveals layered bramble and cherry aromas. The tannins are lively but not over-assertive. San Lorenzo is a well-made Conero that lacks a little complexity. The Pelago 2000 has an exciting nose that perfectly melds fruit and spices, then the broad, deep palate offers nice concentration and smooth tannins that back up the long finish. The Cùmaro 2000 is very good. The subtle, elegant nose introduces good structure in the mouth. The tannins are smooth and the pulp juicy before morello cherry and spice return on the clean finish. The Serrano 2002 is delicious. The alcohol-led nose, with its light fruit, ushers in an aroma-rich structure that makes this a very easy drinker. Finally, Maximo 2000 is from sauvignon grapes attacked by noble rot. The nuts and dried flowers on the nose are followed by an unctuously rich palate with a wealth of residual sugar.

● Zeii '00	♟♟	5
○ Falerio dei Colli Ascolani Marta V. T. '01	♟♟	4*
● Rosso Piceno Sup. Leo Guelfus '01	♟♟	4
○ Falerio dei Colli Ascolani Leo Guelfus '02	♟♟	3*
○ Zagros '02	♟♟	4
○ Falerio dei Colli Ascolani Ophites '02	♟	2*
● Rosso Piceno Ophites '02	♟	3
● Rosso Piceno Sup. Leo Guelfus '00	♟♟	4
● Rosso Piceno Sup. Rosso del Nonno '00	♟♟	5

● Pelago '00	♟♟	7
● Rosso Conero Cùmaro '00	♟♟	5
● Montepulciano d'Abruzzo Jorio '01	♟♟	4*
○ Verdicchio dei Castelli di Jesi Cl. Sup. Casal di Serra '02	♟♟	4*
○ Maximo '00	♟	5
● Rosso Conero S. Lorenzo '00	♟	4
○ Verdicchio dei Castelli di Jesi Cl. Plenio Ris. '00	♟	4
○ Le Busche '01	♟	5
○ Verdicchio dei Castelli di Jesi Cl. Sup. Sultano '01	♟	5
● Rosso Conero Serrano '02	♟	3*
○ Verdicchio dei Castelli di Jesi Cl. Sup. Villa Bianchi '02	♟	3

OSTRA VETERE (AN)

PEDASO (AP)

BUCCI
FRAZ. PONGELLI
VIA CONA, 30
60010 OSTRA VETERE (AN)
TEL. 071964179 - 026570558
E-MAIL: bucciwines@villabucci.com

CASTELLO FAGETO
VIA VALDASO, 52
63016 PEDASO (AP)
TEL. 0734931784
E-MAIL: castellofageto@tiscalinet.it

Ampelio Bucci has remained utterly unmoved by the turmoil and passing trends that in recent years have affected Verdicchio, continuing instead to release his ever-reliable wines made in his own inimitable style. This is a tribute to the widely acknowledged quality of his wines, and in particular of the policies implemented by his very traditional winemaker, Giorgio Grai. Cooling tanks have no place in the cellar, where large barrels of Slavonian oak, more than 40 years old, are the containers of choice for maturation. Villa Bucci Riserva 2000, of which 20,000 bottles were released, is yet again one of the finest whites in the region, the distinctively elegant, perfectly evolved style delighting with its finesse. The superbly balanced aromas, which follow through impeccably on the palate, reveal intense yet subtle flowers, dried hay and crusty bread. The beautifully gauged structure is deliberately understated and tempts not with the volume of its fruit but with the unusual elegance of the mineral notes that linger on the palate long after the wine has been swallowed. Tenuta Pongelli 2001, a 50-50 mix of montepulciano and sangiovese, shows intense red berry fruit, morello cherry and blueberry in particular. The palate is full, alcohol-rich, elegant and wonderfully judged in its concentration, the long finish revealing distinct softness and fruit. The Verdicchio 2002 has elegant fresh and dried flowers that linger on the finish. The structure is attractive and the flavours are nicely balanced.

The energetic Claudio di Ruscio's winery confirmed the flattering profiles it has earned in previous Guides. Founded in 1988, it has 22 hectares planted to vine and releases about 60,000 bottles a year. Most of the production – 70 per cent – goes abroad, but the cellar has also been consolidating its position in the regional market. The reason for this is a careful promotion of local denominations, which the estate interprets in a modern idiom with the help of consultant oenologists, Maurilio Chioccia and Pierluigi Lorenzetti. Rusus 2001 is the wine the panel liked best. Its bright ruby introduces an exciting nose whose balsamic notes mingle well with spice and a hint of black cherry. There's weighty alcohol on the front palate before firm tannins take you through to a long finish. The Falerio and the Rosso Piceno, both from the 2002 vintage, were aged without wood. The reductive environment of the stainless steel tanks ensures that the crisp fruit on nose and palate is very well defined. Spring flowers and ripe apple are evident in the Falerio, whereas attractive, juicy cherry combines beautifully with the soft mouthfeel of the Rosso Piceno. We gave One Glass to the Serrone, a Bordeaux blend from which Claudio is hoping for great things. It has lots of structure and force, but the nose is masked by the over-ripeness of the fruit, which detracts from the overall finesse. The Tristo di Elisena 2002 has tantalizing honey on the nose and a mouthfilling palate, but lacks a little acidity.

O	Verdicchio dei Castelli di Jesi Cl. Villa Bucci Ris. '00	♛♛♛ 6
●	Rosso Piceno Tenuta Pongelli '01	♛♛ 4*
O	Verdicchio dei Castelli di Jesi Cl. '02	♛ 4
O	Verdicchio dei Castelli di Jesi Cl. Villa Bucci Ris. '98	♛♛♛ 6
O	Verdicchio dei Castelli di Jesi Cl. Villa Bucci Ris. '99	♛♛♛ 6
O	Verdicchio dei Castelli di Jesi Cl. Villa Bucci Ris. '97	♛♛ 6
●	Rosso Piceno Tenuta Pongelli '00	♛♛ 4

●	Rosso Piceno Rusus '01	♛♛ 4
●	Serrone '00	♛ 5
O	Falerio dei Colli Ascolani '02	♛ 3
●	Rosso Piceno '02	♛ 4
O	Tristo di Elisena '02	♛ 4
●	Rosso Piceno Rusus '00	♛♛ 4
O	Tristo di Elisena '01	♛♛ 4

PESARO

FATTORIA MANCINI
S.DA DEI COLLI, 35
61100 PESARO
TEL. 072151828
E-MAIL: info@fattoriamancini.com

PIAGGE (PU)

GUERRIERI
VIA SAN FILIPPO, 24
61030 PIAGGE (PU)
TEL. 0721890152
E-MAIL: info@aziendaguerrieri.it

This interesting Colli Pesaresi estate is finding a distinctive personality of its own. Some of the wines have been dropped from the range to give more space to native varieties and Luigi Mancini's passion, pinot nero. The good results he has achieved show that the move was a good one, and hints at even better things to come. Impero Bianco 2001, from pinot nero grapes fermented without the skins, has attractive ripe fruit, still slightly masked by oak, and dries the mouth with a bitterish finish. Roncaglia 2002, from the native albanella grape, has a broad, clean nose of intense fresh flowers, pears and apples. In the mouth, it is well balanced and quite delicious. Fleshy, ripe red berry fruit, with elegant balsam and liquorice, are the keynotes on the nose of the Sangiovese 2001. Its muscular yet soft structure is nicely balanced, the mellow, close-knit tannins just drying the lingering finish. The Pinot Nero Impero 2001, from old vines in the Focara subzone, is elegant and restrained on the nose, where subtle red berry fruit and spice prevail. The temptingly soft entry on the palate expands with lovely poise, offsetting sweet fruit against liquorice. Blu 2000 performed very well. It's an unusual blend of pinot nero and local varieties with an intense nose of full, well-defined wild berries. The palate is powerful, unveiling a soft tannic weave and great personality. The finish is long, balanced and irresistible.

There were more good results from Luca Guerrieri's cellar. The 28 hectares under vine, owned by the family for more than a century, yield wines with good texture. The wines are also well made, thanks to the efforts of Michele Tarini in the cellar under the supervision of experienced oenologist, Roberto Potentini. The best of the range is the Sangiovese Riserva Galileo 2000. From a really excellent vintage, it offers intense aromas of red berry jam and cherries in alcohol. Entry on the palate is restrained, beautifully poised and very elegant. The structure is good, but not excessive, and the lingering persistence leaves intense ripe cherry and strawberry aromas on the back palate. Bianchello del Metauro Celso 2002, skilfully aged in barrique, flaunts a rich, intense range of aromas, where crisply defined ripe tropical fruit predominates. Slightly dry in the mouth, it has distinct acidity that holds back the lovely ripe fruit finish just a fraction. The standard-label Bianchello is more predictable and lighter, its fresh aromas lacking a little definition before the palate reveals decent intensity and good tangy flavour. Finally, we would also like to mention that the Guerrieri estate makes excellent extravirgin olive oil. In fact, it's one of the best producers in Italy.

● Blu '00		¶¶	6
● Colli Pesaresi Focara			
Pinot Nero Impero '01		¶¶	6
● Colli Pesaresi Sangiovese '01		¶¶	4
○ Colli Pesaresi Roncaglia '02		¶¶	3*
○ Impero Bianco '01		¶	6
● Blu '98		¶¶	6
● Impero Pinot Nero Sel. F M '98		¶¶	6
● Colli Pesaresi Sangiovese '00		¶¶	4
○ Impero Bianco '00		¶¶	6
● Blu '99		¶	6

● Colli Pesaresi Sangiovese			
Galileo Ris. '00		¶¶	5
○ Bianchello del Metauro '02		¶	3
○ Bianchello del Metauro Celso '02	¶		4
● Colli Pesaresi Sangiovese '02			3

POGGIO SAN MARCELLO (AN)   POTENZA PICENA (MC)

SARTARELLI
VIA COSTE DEL MOLINO, 24
60030 POGGIO SAN MARCELLO (AN)
TEL. 073189732
E-MAIL: info@sartarelli.it

SANTA CASSELLA
C.DA SANTA CASSELLA, 7
62018 POTENZA PICENA (MC)
TEL. 0733671507
E-MAIL: santacassella@tiscalinet.it

At Sartarelli, more than 60 hectares under vine make it possible for more than 320,000 bottles a year to be released. Over time, they have gained a reputation for quality among Verdicchio lovers. The estate began operations in the mid 1960s, when all the fruit was vinified by outside cellars. In 1972, Sartarelli took the decision to vinify in house, and as a result the cellar gradually took on its current orientation, which aims to produce well-typed, territory-driven Verdicchios from the subzones of Coste del Molino, Balciana and Tralivio. The cellar's base Verdicchio 2002 is a textbook example of typicity. The fairly intense, fragrant aromas usher in a palate where refreshing acidity and good concentration combine deliciously, with a faint trace of sweetness in the finish. Tralivio 2002 is green-flecked straw yellow and offers a broad range of complex hazelnut, golden delicious apple and acacia blossom aromas. Vigorous and soft in the mouth, its outstanding concentration and refreshing drinkability are rounded off by a long finish that focuses on fruit and roasted almonds. Balciana 2001 is a deep yellow, with green and gold highlights. The assertive aromas reveal noble rot layered over golden delicious apples, tangerines, thyme and moss. The brightness of the palate is tempered by a velvety, fleshy softness that extends the finish. Ripe fruit returns on the back palate, with subtle citrus and a faint bitterish twist.

The historic Santa Cassella cellar has been making wine since the 18th century, but it is only in the past few decades that the Sgarbi and Gigotti families have really concentrated on their 25 hectares, helped by consultants Umberto Santoni, who looks after the vineyards, and Pierluigi Lorenzetti, in charge of the cellar. We were surprised how good the Colli Maceratesi Bianco 2002 is. Its subtle, intense flower and citrus introduce a palate with good body and a fine balance of sugar and acidity. The attractively long finish is redolent of spring flowers. However, the most exciting wine is the Conte Leopoldo 2001, a blend of 85 per cent cabernet sauvignon with 15 per cent montepulciano. The French grape's trademark vegetal notes are layered over persistent bramble and cloves. The expansive entry on the palate has well-gauged structure, the mellow tannins underpinning a long finish. Both whites, Guardia Vecchia and Donna Eleonora 2002, are very attractive. Guardia Vecchia, from steel-fermented chardonnay, has delicious banana and melon, a tangy, tidy palate and lovely nose-palate consistency. Donna Eleonora is a blend of chardonnay and sauvignon aged in wood. The sweet vanilla never masks the swathe of tropical fruit, which returns on the palate over softer sensations. Finally, the 70-30 malvasia and chardonnay Donna Angela 2002 is only decent, as the over-generous residual sugar makes it a little cloying. Neither is the Giardin Vecchio 2002 more than moderately good. It's an aromatic "vino da meditazione" sipping wine with a very sweet palate.

○ Verdicchio dei Castelli di Jesi Cl. Sup. Contrada Balciana '01	▼▼	6
○ Verdicchio dei Castelli di Jesi Cl. Sup. Tralivio '02	▼▼	4*
○ Verdicchio dei Castelli di Jesi Cl. '02	▼	3
○ Verdicchio dei Castelli di Jesi Cl. Sup. Contrada Balciana '94	♀♀♀	6
○ Verdicchio dei Castelli di Jesi Cl. Sup. Contrada Balciana '95	♀♀♀	6
○ Verdicchio dei Castelli di Jesi Cl. Sup. Contrada Balciana '97	♀♀♀	6
○ Verdicchio dei Castelli di Jesi Cl. Sup. Contrada Balciana '98	♀♀♀	6

● Conte Leopoldo '01	▼▼	4
○ Colli Maceratesi Bianco '02	▼▼	2*
○ Donna Eleonora '02	▼▼	4
○ Guardia Vecchia '02	▼▼	3*
○ Donna Angela '02	▼	4
○ Giardin Vecchio '02	▼	4
● Rosso Piceno '02		3
● Conte Leopoldo '00	♀♀	4
○ Donna Eleonora '01	♀♀	4
● Rosso Piceno '01	♀♀	3

RIPATRANSONE (AP)

LA CANTINA DEI COLLI RIPANI
VIA TOSCIANO, 28
63038 RIPATRANSONE (AP)
TEL. 07359505
E-MAIL: info@colliripani.com

RIPATRANSONE (AP)

LE CANIETTE
C.DA CANALI, 23
63038 RIPATRANSONE (AP)
TEL. 07359200
E-MAIL: info@lecaniette.it

Careful management by member growers of the more than 1,100 hectares under vine ensures this large co-operative winery releases a fine range of wines. The most interesting one is the barrique-aged Rosso Piceno Leo Ripanus 2000. The flower and spice aromas are closed at first, and not very elegant. Entry on the palate is restrained, but then it expands in the mouth with good structure, well-gauged balance and great length. The Castellano 2000 has a more traditional style. The nose is forward, with spicy notes to the fore and vegetal sensations. There is nice breadth in the mouth, so it is a pity that the fruit is not as bright and fresh as it might be. Falerio Brezzolino 2002 is vibrantly fruity on the nose, then shows decent structure and balance in the mouth, where the finish unfolds attractively. The Ninfa Ripana 2002 has fresh flowers and elegant mineral aromas. Full-bodied and alcohol-rich in the mouth, it has good progression but lacks a little vivacity and acidic grip. The barrique-aged Chardonnay Leukon 2002 has intense tropical fruit aromas that give way to vanilla. The fat, soft palate has rich, ripe fruit and distinctly attractive length that is slightly masked by a faint bitterish note. Anima Mundi 2001 is a dried-grape wine from passerina with nice butter and apricot jam aromas that linger on the palate in the long finish. Uncompromisingly sweet, it never cloys as it is braced by attractive acidity and robust alcohol.

We should point out straight away that Nero di Vite was not available. It is the cellar's flagship product, and a wine that has frequently proved to be one of the region's very finest. The 2001 vintage yielded a wine so powerful that it will require longer barrique ageing than usual so we'll be reviewing it for next year's Guide. Still, the Vagnoni family presented us with some very well-made products, starting with the Morellone, a wine of superior character. The assertive, intense ripe berry fruit aromas are lifted by sweet spice and liquorice. Dense and velvety on the palate, thanks to smooth, close-knit tannins, it progresses surefootedly to a long finish. The 4,000 bottles of Rosso Bello Memoria Storica N° 1 from the 1998 vintage are in fact a successful experiment by the cellar. After a few months in stainless steel vats, it went into bottle, where it remained for more than four years. The panel found that it was perfect on tasting. The dense fruit was still bright and whole, and there were no hints of oxidation or decline. A wine of marked personality and considerable elegance, it opens new, exciting horizons for the grapes and vineyards of Piceno. Sibilla Appenninica is from dried passerina grapes. Heady apricot jam and caramel-covered fruit tempt the nose against a backdrop of almonds and hazelnuts. The admirable development of the fruit is enhanced by the oily, dense palate, which is sweet but not over-sugary.

● Rosso Piceno Sup. Leo Ripanus '00	♟♟	4*
● Rosso Piceno Sup. Castellano '00	♟	3
○ Passito Anima Mundi '01	♟	5
○ Falerio dei Colli Ascolani Brezzolino '02	♟	3
○ Leukon Chardonnay '02	♟	4
○ Offida Passerina Ninfa Ripana '02	♟	2*
● Rosso Piceno Transone '02		2
● Rosso Piceno Sup. Castellano '99	♟♟	3

● Rosso Piceno Morellone '01	♟♟	5
● Rosso Piceno Rosso Bello Memoria Storica N° 1 '98	♟♟	5
○ Vino Passito Sibilla Appenninica '99	♟♟	5
○ Falerio dei Colli Ascolani Lucrezia '02		3
● Rosso Piceno Morellone '98	♟♟	5
● Rosso Piceno Nero di Vite '98	♟♟	5
● Rosso Piceno Morellone '99	♟♟	5
● Rosso Piceno Morellone '00	♟♟	5
● Rosso Piceno Nero di Vite '00	♟♟	5
● Rosso Piceno Rosso Bello '01	♟	4

RIPATRANSONE (AP)

SAN SAVINO - PODERI CAPECCI
LOC. SAN SAVINO
C.DA SANTA MARIA IN CARRO, 13
63038 RIPATRANSONE (AP)
TEL. 073590107
E-MAIL: cantina.sansavino@libero.it

The Capecci family winery is competently managed by Simone, with the help of agronomist and winemaker, Federico Giotto. The pair produce a range of distinctly well-made wines that have just one weakness, which is most evident in the two flagship wines, Fedus and Ver Sacrum: the fruit is a tad too concentrated. They would be much more elegant and enjoyable if they had more freshness. The Sangiovese Fedus 2001 shows a broad, well-sustained structure, its aromas first hinting at forest floor, then mushrooms and violets, before shifting to berry fruit in alcohol. After a firm entry, the palate tends to dry out on the alcohol-rich finish. Ver Sacrum 2001 is from montepulciano and unfurls over-ripe, jammy notes of bramble, blueberry and plum. The progression on the palate is well-sustained, leading to a slightly heavy, very alcoholic finish that unhurriedly echoes the wild berry aromas of the nose. Rosso Piceno 2002 Collemura is fruit-led on the nose and slightly dry in the mouth, but still very drinkable. The Superiore Picus 2001 is rather more complex. The ripe, juicy fruit on the nose is rounded off by bitter liquorice, then the beefy structure underpins austere flavours that reveal a hint of tannic astringency on the back palate. The white Ciprea 2002, from pecorino, has intense apricot and ripe peach on nose and palate, which has good breadth, nice freshness and rich, tangy flavours.

SAN MARCELLO (AN)

MAURIZIO MARCONI
VIA MELANO, 23
60030 SAN MARCELLO (AN)
TEL. 0731267223
E-MAIL: info@vinoearte.it

Maurizio Marconi's property lies in the municipality of San Marcello, in the hills in the heart of Verdicchio Classico country, and has 11 hectares under vine. Vinification is carried out in the estate-owned cellar, which was restructured in 1996. Modern technology is used in tandem with traditional techniques which, in the case of Verdicchio, include fermentation and ageing in large wood. The standard range comprises three very approachable wines. Verdicchio Borgo is well typed and very drinkable, Lacrima Casato has exemplary balance and a classic nose of dried roses, and Rubino, a mix of montepulciano, sangiovese and lacrima, has generous aromas and a soft, juicy mouthfeel. The Falcone Reale line features labels designed by artist Alvaro Tonti and offers more elegance. Verdicchio Corona Reale 2002 has typical aromas of lime and chamomile, a soft, consistent nose, an appealing palate and a hint of almond in the finish. Lacrima Il Falconiere 2002 has well-defined rose and dried flower aromas, then a fragrant palate with perfect balance that makes the wine deliciously approachable. Finally, we sampled the two Sapore di Generazioni wines. The Verdicchio 2002 foregrounds grassy notes on the nose. These return on the fresh-tasting palate, whose meaty structure backs up the finish very nicely. Lacrima 2002 has textbook rose, bramble and raspberry aromas. After a fresh entry, the palate shows good structure and a laudably intense finish.

● Fedus Sangiovese '01	♀♀	6
● Rosso Piceno Sup. Picus '01	♀♀	5
● Ver Sacrum '01	♀♀	6
○ Offida Pecorino Ciprea '02	♀♀	4
● Rosso Piceno Collemura '02	♀	3
● Sangiovese Moggio '98	♀♀♀	6
● Mito '98	♀♀	6
● Fedus Sangiovese '00	♀♀	6
● Rosso Piceno Sup. Picus '00	♀♀	5
● Ver Sacrum '00	♀♀	6
○ Offida Pecorino Ciprea '01	♀♀	4

● Lacrima di Morro d'Alba			
Falconiere '02	♀♀	4*
● Lacrima di Morro d'Alba			
Sapore di Generazioni '02	♀♀	5
○ Verdicchio dei Castelli di Jesi Cl.			
Sup. Sapore di Generazioni '02	♀♀	5
● Rubino '02	♀	3
○ Verdicchio dei Castelli di Jesi Cl.			
Sup. Corona Reale '02	♀	4
● Lacrima di Morro d'Alba			
Casato '02		3
○ Verdicchio dei Castelli di Jesi Cl.			
Borgo '02		3
● Lacrima di Morro d'Alba			
Sapore di Generazioni '01	♀♀	5

SAN SEVERINO MARCHE (MC) SERRA DE' CONTI (AN)

ANTICO TERRENO OTTAVI
FRAZ. CÀGNORE, 6
62027 SAN SEVERINO MARCHE (MC)
TEL. 0733637804
E-MAIL: info@vinocagnore.it

CASALFARNETO
VIA FARNETO, 16
60030 SERRA DE' CONTI (AN)
TEL. 0731889001
E-MAIL: info@casalfarneto.it

The history of the Ottavi family dates back to 1500, when the hillside estate at Càgnore was described in a notary's document. The area is well known as wine country, since the soil and site climates are very suitable for viticulture. Montepulciano, sangiovese grosso and the native vernaccia nera provide wines that combine texture with freshness and longevity. In 1985, the property was acquired by Cesare Maria Ottavi, who embarked on an investment programme to relaunch the winery. In 1997, oenologist Giancarlo Soverchia came on board as consultant. Currently, the estate has eight hectares planted to red varieties, and releases about 10,000 bottles. Càgnore 2001, a blend of sangiovese, montepulciano and vernaccia, is purple, with aromas that lean towards the vegetal rather than fruit. The beautifully soft front palate is lifted by mellow tannins, offering great drinkability and a long finish. Pianetta 2000, from vernaccia nera, has the variety's trademark dark vermilion and spicy aromas. There is a hint of rustic vigour on the front palate from tannins that have still to settle down. Collemorra 2000 is a monovarietal Sangiovese that marries liquorice and wild berry aromas. The palate has sufficient structure to keeps the boisterous tannins in check and sensations of red berry fruit mingle with flowery notes in the attractive finish. Ribballa 2000, from 100 per cent montepulciano, foregrounds ripe cherry on the nose and massive tannins on the palate. The astringency never masks the juicy fruit, which a very favourable vintage has endowed with great concentration and flesh.

Casalfarneto was set up in 1995. Massimo Arcangeli and Danilo Solustri share a great love and respect for their territory. They manage the vineyards using low-impact techniques that involve limited use of agrochemicals and natural soil amelioration. This sense of tradition is accompanied by modern agronomic and winemaking methods, supervised by the crucially important consultant, Roberto Potentini. After careful selection, the ripest grapes go into the Grancasale. The 2002 comes from a rather rainy year that produced more markedly vegetal aromas. These combine attractively with elegant lime blossom and fresh almond. In the mouth, the green notes modulate into delicious mossy nuances and the good acidity perfectly offsets the palate's deep, soft texture. It's a wine that is drinking well now, but will certainly improve in the cellar. The Fontevecchia 2002 is less expressive, but has lots of personality. Chamomile and broom on the nose follow through well on the palate. The structure may be less close-knit and soft, but the wine gains in drinkability and sheer freshness. Five hectares planted to montepulciano, sangiovese, cabernet and merlot give the cellar a fragrant red, Fiorile, which we will be assessing with the new vintage of Cimaio, a barrique-aged verdicchio selection, in the next edition of the Guide.

● Collemorra di Càgnore '00	♟♟	5
● Ribballa di Càgnore '00	♟♟	5
● Pianetta di Càgnore '00	♟	5
● Càgnore '01	♟	4

○ Verdicchio dei Castelli di Jesi Cl. Sup. Grancasale '02	♟♟	4*
○ Verdicchio dei Castelli di Jesi Cl. Sup. Fontevecchia '02	♟	3
○ Verdicchio dei Castelli di Jesi Cl. Sup. Grancasale '00	♟♟	4
○ Verdicchio dei Castelli di Jesi Cl. Sup. Cimaio '00	♟♟	4
○ Verdicchio dei Castelli di Jesi Cl. Sup. Grancasale '01	♟♟	4

SERVIGLIANO (AP)

FATTORIA DEZI
C.DA FONTE MAGGIO, 14
63029 SERVIGLIANO (AP)
TEL. 0734710090
E-MAIL: mauridez@tin.it

The magnificent results that the Dezi family continues to reap confirm that the project they launched a few years ago – converting vineyards, focusing on the cultivation of top-quality fruit, appropriate cellar equipment and well-gauged maturation – was based on solid ground. The overall quality of the wines we tasted provides further evidence that our favourable assessment of the winery is well founded. Sangiovese Solo 2001 is one of the finest versions of the variety in Marche and beyond. The fully ripe fruit reveals plum jam on the nose, with delicate spice, black liquorice and currants. The meaty flesh in the mouth is accompanied by smooth, very tight-knit tannins and assertive, but nicely balanced, alcohol. The harmony is simply perfect. To round things off, nice acidity makes this a deliciously moreish wine. Regina del Bosco 2000 is 100 per cent montepulciano and interprets the style of the Solo with the personality and authority of that variety. The nose has intense ripe fruit, lifted by light, elegant balsamic hints of eucalyptus and liquorice. The no-nonsense palate beautifully contrasts acidity and extract with softness. Dezio 2001 is the cellar's second label. A blend of montepulciano with a small proportion of sangiovese, it reveals intense morello cherry and bottled cherry aromas. The palate may have assertive, indeed slightly rough, tannins, but the admirable progression leads into a well-balanced finish.

SPINETOLI (AP)

SALADINI PILASTRI
VIA SALADINI, 5
63030 SPINETOLI (AP)
TEL. 0736899534
E-MAIL: saladpil@tin.it

We are fans of the estate managed by Conte Saladini Pilastri, with the aid of commercial manager, Pietro Piccioni. We commend their decision to make good wines with admirable consistency while keeping prices to very reasonable levels. Vigna Monteprandone 2001 met with our full approval. Dense and compact from glass to back palate, it also has elegance and controlled power that come out in the fruit notes over spice and light toastiness. Estate manager, Domenico D'Angelo, and consultant winemaker, Alberto Antonini, also presented us with other excellent wines. Nearest in quality to Monteprandone was Pregio del Conte 2001, from montepulciano and aglianico. The nose has earthy notes with liquorice, black berry fruit and coffee. The vigorous tannins lend substance to the palate, but tend to dry out the finish. A welter of red berry fruit and spice is the keynote of the Vigna Montetinello 2001, which has a full front palate and long finish. In comparison with the preceding wines, the Vigna Piediprato 2001 has marked oak-derived notes, but maintains its consistency and intense fruitiness. The Rosso Piceno 2002 has reliable fruit aromas. Finally, the Vigna Palazzi 2002 is slightly over-evolved on the nose, whereas the standard Falerio is predictable, but has harmonious floral aromas.

● Solo Sangiovese '01	♟♟♟	6
● Regina del Bosco '00	♟	5
● Dezio Vigneto Beccaccia '01	♟♟	4*
● Solo Sangiovese '00	♟♟♟	6
● Rosso Piceno		
Regina del Bosco '98	♟♟	6
● Solo Sangiovese '99	♟♟	6
● Dezio Vigneto Beccaccia '00	♟♟	4
○ Le Solagne V. T. '01	♟♟	5

● Rosso Piceno Sup.		
Vigna Monteprandone '01	♟♟	4*
● Pregio del Conte '01	♟♟	3*
● Rosso Piceno Sup.		
Vigna Montetinello '01	♟♟	3*
● Rosso Piceno Vigna Piediprato '01	♟	3
○ Falerio dei Colli Ascolani '02	♟	2*
● Rosso Piceno '02	♟	3
○ Falerio dei Colli Ascolani		
Vigna Palazzi '02		2
● Rosso Piceno Sup.		
Vigna Monteprandone '00	♟♟♟	4
● Pregio del Conte '00	♟♟	4
● Rosso Piceno Sup.		
Vigna Montetinello '00	♟♟	3

STAFFOLO (AN)

CORONCINO
C.DA CORONCINO, 7
60039 STAFFOLO (AN)
TEL. 0731779494
E-MAIL: coroncino@libero.it

Lucio Canestrari has a very personal approach to Verdicchio. His style is distinctive, and very much appreciated by lovers of the wine. Boisterous fruit on the front palate gives way to subtly elegant spice backed up by a texture that is always fresh and lively. The wines are obtained from selections from three vineyards in the municipalities of Cupramontana (Spescia vineyard), Staffolo (Coroncino vineyard) and San Paolo di Jesi (Cerrete vineyard). The total vineyard holding is more than seven hectares. Bacco 2002 is an attractive standard wine with complex aromas and satisfying structure in which the fruit is evident. Coroncino 2001 is upfront on nose and palate. You might think it was a little straightforward at first, but then vibrant fruit expands on the nose, to be echoed on the intense palate with good freshness and length. Gaiospino 2001 has quite remarkable concentration. The aromas have impressive breadth, revealing chlorophyll, apple and lime blossom. The soft palate reveals a nice balance of generous alcohol and fresh acidity. Mouthfilling and sumptuous, it closes on delicate but persistent almondy notes. The Stracacio 2000 is a blend of verdicchio and incrocio Bruni (verdicchio x riesling). Two years' ageing in barrique and tonneau, then 12 months in bottle, have lent this wine exceptional complexity on the nose, where cakes, vanilla and almond paste emerge. The palate is fatty, partly because of the warm alcohol and partly from the residual sugar that bolsters the flavour on the long finish.

○	Verdicchio dei Castelli di Jesi Cl. Sup. Gaiospino '01	🍷🍷	5
○	Verdicchio dei Castelli di Jesi Cl. Sup. Stracacio '00	🍷🍷	6
○	Verdicchio dei Castelli di Jesi Cl. Sup. Il Coroncino '01	🍷🍷	4*
○	Verdicchio dei Castelli di Jesi Cl. Bacco '02	🍷	3
○	Verdicchio dei Castelli di Jesi Cl. Sup. Gaiospino '97	YYY	5
○	Verdicchio dei Castelli di Jesi Cl. Sup. Gaiospino '99	YY	5
○	Verdicchio dei Castelli di Jesi Cl. Sup. Gaiospino '00	YY	5

STAFFOLO (AN)

F.LLI ZACCAGNINI & C.
VIA SALMAGINA, 9/10
60039 STAFFOLO (AN)
TEL. 0731779892
E-MAIL: info@zaccagnini.it

The cellar managed by Rosella Zaccagnini with consultant oenologist, Alberto Musatti, presented us with a fine, and fairly extensive, range from the 25 hectares under vine. Cesolano 1997, from part-dried verdicchio grapes, is very well made. Intense butter and vanilla aromas, moderate sugar and good acidity lead to a rich, pervasive finish. Vigna Vescovi 2000 is a good blend of 70 per cent cabernet sauvignon, 20 per cent pinot nero and ten per cent montepulciano with a clean, elegant nose. Complex texture and good depth are immediately obvious on the very ripe, evolved palate, which is faintly alcoholic in the finish. The Rosso Conero 1999 has a spice and balsam nose, then a lightweight, ripe palate. The 20,000 bottles of Brut Riserva are tangily fresh tasting and very well made. The cuvée is blended from equal proportions of verdicchio and international varieties (pinot nero, pinot bianco and chardonnay). The various Verdicchios performed decently overall. Maestro di Staffolo 2000 has sweet aromas that lack a little definition. The structure and breadth in the mouth are attractive, and there is good balance, as well as a faintly bitterish finish. Pier delle Vigne 2000 is rather predictable. The Salmàgina is the fullest of the 2002 Verdicchios, with nice breadth on the attractively minerally palate, but not quite enough acidity. Casa Lisà 2002 is less than perfectly clean on the nose, but fresh and tasty on the palate, whereas the standard-label Verdicchio has intense pineapple and tropical fruit, a soft mouthfeel and assertive alcohol nicely offset by fresh acidity.

●	Vigna Vescovi '00	🍷🍷	4
○	Cesolano '97	🍷🍷	5
○	Verdicchio dei Castelli di Jesi Cl. Maestro di Staffolo Ris. '00	🍷	5
○	Verdicchio dei Castelli di Jesi Cl. Sup. Pier delle Vigne '00	🍷	4
○	Verdicchio dei Castelli di Jesi Cl. Casa Lisà '02	🍷	2
○	Verdicchio dei Castelli di Jesi Cl. Sup. '02	🍷	3
○	Verdicchio dei Castelli di Jesi Cl. Sup. Salmàgina '02	🍷	4
●	Rosso Conero '99	🍷	3
○	Zaccagnini Brut Ris.	🍷	4

OTHER WINERIES

DEL CARMINE
VIA DEL CARMINE, 51
60020 ANCONA
TEL. 071889403
E-MAIL: carmine@commetodi.com

Don't be fooled by the Ancona address, which is just an office. All vinification is carried out at the cellar in Matelica. There's an excellent verdicchio-based Aja Lunga 2002. Elegant aniseed and flowers on nose and palate are backed up by good progression and finesse.

O Verdicchio di Matelica		
Aja Lunga '02	♥♥	4*
O Verdicchio di Matelica Petrara '02		3

LUCANGELI AYMERICH DI LACONI
LOC. TAVIGNANO
62011 CINGOLI (MC)
TEL. 0733617303
E-MAIL: tavignano@libero.it

As we wait for the prestige Rosso selection that oenologist, Giancarlo Soverchia has decided to leave in the ageing cellar, we enjoyed the flowery Verdicchio dei Castelli di Jesi Tavignano. It's very drinkable, but just a little rustic on the nose.

O Verdicchio dei Castelli di Jesi Cl.		
Sup. Tavignano '02	♥	3

SAPUTI
C.DA FIASTRA, 2
62020 COLMURANO (MC)
TEL. 0733508137
E-MAIL: saputi@mercurio.it

Saputi has always turned out well-made, traditional wines. The rustic extract of the Montenereto 2001 comes as no surprise, but the spicy Castru Vecchiu is rounder. Noi Due, from super-ripe fruit, offers strawberry aromas and a very soft mouthfeel.

● Rosso Piceno Castru Vecchiu '00	♥	4
● Rosso Piceno Montenereto '01	♥	3
O Noi Due '02	♥	3

CONTRADA CASTELLETTA
C.DA CASTELLETTA, 16
63023 FERMO (AP)
TEL. 0734621023

This promising new winery is supervised by oenologist, Alberto Antonini. It has a winner in the first release of Vespro 2001. A dense, purplish montepulciano and syrah blend with intense cherry, pepper and cocoa powder aromas, it reveals structure and persistence in the mouth.

● Vespro '01	♥♥	5

Mario & Giorgio Brunori
V.LE DELLA VITTORIA, 103
60035 JESI (AN)
TEL. 0731207213
E-MAIL: brunorivini@libero.it

Despite being released just a few months after the harvest, Brunori wines have good finesse and ageing prospects. The fresh-tasting, tangy, varietal San Nicolò 2002 is a case in point. The more complex Le Gemme 2002 has intriguing minerality that is not masked by the generous fruit.

○ Verdicchio dei Castelli di Jesi Cl. Le Gemme '02	▼ 3
○ Verdicchio dei Castelli di Jesi Cl. Sup. San Nicolò '02	▼ 4

Benito Mancini
FRAZ. MOIE - VIA SANTA LUCIA, 7
60030 MAIOLATI SPONTINI (AN)
TEL. 0731702975
E-MAIL: mancini@manciniwines.it

The very elegant, dynamic Verdicchio Villa Talliano 2001 is very good. Intense minerality on nose and palate is accompanied by good pulp, attractive acidic grip and nice balance. The tasty, fruity Ghibellino 2002 is fresher and more subtle on the palate.

○ Verdicchio dei Castelli di Jesi Cl. Sup. Villa Talliano '01	▼▼ 4*
○ Verdicchio dei Castelli di Jesi Cl. Ghibellino '02	▼ 3

Poggio Montali
VIA FONTE ESTATE, 6
60030 MONTE ROBERTO (AN)
TEL. 0731702825
E-MAIL: poggiomontali@libero.it

Monte Roberto uses local varieties with good success. Poggio al Cerro 2001 is a spicy, robust Rosso Conero that is just beginning to develop tertiary aromas. Fontelleccio 2001 has elegant vanilla and ripe flowers, with a good follow through on the mouthfilling palate.

● Rosso Conero Poggio al Cerro '01	▼▼ 6
○ Verdicchio dei Castelli di Jesi Cl. Sup. Fontelleccio '01	▼ 5

Azzoni Avogadro Carradori
C.SO CARRADORI, 13
62010 MONTEFANO (MC)
TEL. 0733850002
E-MAIL: fdeglia@tin.it

This Montefano-based winery has made excellent progress. Passatempo 2001, the cellar's best product by far, is a lovely combination of balsamic aromas and a tidy palate. Cantalupo 2002 is let down by persistent vegetal notes, and the Grechetto 2002 shows a nice vein of acidity.

● Passatempo '01	▼▼ 4*
● Cantalupo Rosso '02	▼ 3
○ Grechetto '02	▼ 3

Mario Lucchetti
VIA SANTA MARIA DEL FIORE, 17
60030 MORRO D'ALBA (AN)
TEL. 073163314
E-MAIL: info@lucchettiwines.com

The Lucchetti specialty is still their fresh, fruity Lacrima, the trademark wine of the hillsides above Senigallia, but it was the Verdicchio that performed best. A very varietal nose of ripe apple and almonds introduces a full-flavoured palate with delicious acidity.

○ Verdicchio dei Castelli di Jesi '02	▼▼ 2*
● Lacrima di Morro d'Alba Guardengo '02	4

Stefano Mancinelli
VIA ROMA, 62
60030 MORRO D'ALBA (AN)
TEL. 073163021
E-MAIL: manvin@tin.it

Stefano is a Lacrima specialist and, in some respects, the putative father of the DOC zone. His best wines are Re Sole '99, a sweet, juicy and very fragrant product, and Lacrima Sensazioni di Frutto 2002, whose flowery aromas are enhanced thanks to carbonic maceration during vinification.

● Lacrima di Morro d'Alba Sensazioni di Frutto '02	▼ 4
● Re Sole '99	▼ 5

Vicari

via Sanguinetti, 31/A
60030 Morro d'Alba (AN)
TEL. 073163164
E-MAIL: info@vicarivini.it

The Vicari family specialize in vinifying lacrima grapes, as is demonstrated by an excellent del Pozzo Buono selection. The varietal flowers are accompanied by measured tannins and good length. The fragrant, fresh Verdicchio 2002 has a tangy, almondy finish.

● Lacrima di Morro d'Alba		
del Pozzo Buono '02	�	4
○ Verdicchio dei Castelli di Jesi Cl.		
del Pozzo Buono '02	♀	2

Malacari

via Enrico Malacari, 6
60020 Offagna (AN)
TEL. 0717207606
E-MAIL: malacari@tin.it

We were surprised to find the normally excellent Malacari cellar punching below its weight. The Rosso Conero Grigiano 2001 selection is as good as ever, with a spicy nose and ripe palate. But the standard-label Rosso Conero base is less exciting. The nose is too rustic, as is the palate.

● Rosso Conero Grigiano '01	♀	5
● Rosso Conero '01		4
● Rosso Conero '00	♀♀	3
● Rosso Conero Grigiano '00	♀♀	5

Villa Pigna

c.da Ciafone, 63
63035 Offida (AP)
TEL. 073687525
E-MAIL: villapigna@villapigna.com

The Rozzi family earned praise for the Cabernasco 2000, a single-variety cabernet sauvignon with moderately complex aromas and a dry palate. There were complimentary remarks, too, for the Rosso Piceno 2002, a straightforward but fruity wine that flows nicely over the palate.

● Cabernasco '00	♀	5
● Rosso Piceno '02	♀	2
● Rozzano '00	♀♀	5

Cocci Grifoni

loc. San Savino - c.da Messieri, 12
63038 Ripatransone (AP)
TEL. 073590143
E-MAIL: info@tenutacoccigrifoni.it

Podere Colle Vecchio 2002, a monovarietal pecorino, is the best Cocci Grifoni wine. Good acidity and subtle flowery aromas give it plenty of personality. Best of the reds was the slightly husky Rosso Piceno 2002, a now traditional product of this Ripatransone cellar.

○ Offida Pecorino Podere		
Colle Vecchio '02	♀	3
● Rosso Piceno '02	♀	2

La Fontursia

c.da Fontursia
63038 Ripatransone (AP)
TEL. 07359496 - 073591231
E-MAIL: lafontursia@tin.it

The Veccia family uses only native varieties to make local wine types. The best in the range were the substantial Fontursio 2000, which offers very close-knit tannins and alcohol-driven progression, and the bright, zesty Pecorino Crivellino 2002, with its fresh peanuts on the back palate.

● Rosso Piceno Fontursio '00	♀♀	4*
○ Offida Pecorino Crivellino '02	♀	4

Cavallaro

via Tassanare, 4
60030 Rosora (AN)
TEL. 0731814158

The Crocetta Riserva 2001 is good. Oenologist Umberto Trombelli's hard work is beginning to yield the results the Cavallaro family hoped for. Weighty and full bodied, it is equally intense on the nose, where layered apple, acacia blossom and almonds emerge. Moro 2002 is a ripe, fruit-led red.

○ Verdicchio dei Castelli di Jesi Cl.		
Crocetta Ris. '01	♀♀	5
● Rosso Piceno Il Moro '02	♀	4

AMATO CECI
VIA BATTINEBBIA, 4
60038 SAN PAOLO DI JESI (AN)
TEL. 0731779197 - 0731779052
E-MAIL: info@vignamato.com

The cellar managed by Maurizio Ceci presented the panel with a very good Rosolaccio 2001. It is subtle and persistent on the nose, where delightful nutmeg tails off into berry fruit and ushers in a broad, weighty palate. Vignamato 2002 needs more time. It has body, but was untogether when we tasted.

●	Esino Rosso Rosolaccio '01	🍷🍷	4
○	Verdicchio dei Castelli di Jesi Cl.		
	Sup. Vignamato '02	🍷	3

ENRICO CECI
VIA SANTA MARIA D'ARCO, 7
60038 SAN PAOLO DI JESI (AN)
TEL. 0731119033
E-MAIL: cecienrico@virgilio.it

A decent Rosso Piceno Santa Maria d'Arco 2001 has been added to the range at Enrico Ceci's winery. Dense, meaty extract is held back by the excessive ripeness of the fruit. But the vegetal Verdicchio 2002 is very good, with its fresh-tasting palate and lime blossom aromas.

●	Rosso Piceno		
	Santa Maria d'Arco '01	🍷	4
○	Verdicchio dei Castelli di Jesi Cl.		
	Sup. Santa Maria d'Arco '02	🍷	4

PIERSANTI
BORGO SANTA MARIA, 60
60038 SAN PAOLO DI JESI (AN)
TEL. 0731779020
E-MAIL: piersanti@tin.it

Carlo, Giuliano and Ottavio Piersanti treated us to a richly extracted, vigorously alcoholic Rosso Conero Rubjo 1999. The very nice Ori di Verdicchio 2001 selection has a soft mouthfeel and aromas veined by oak toastiness.

●	Rosso Conero Rubjo '99	🍷🍷	4*
○	Verdicchio dei Castelli di Jesi Cl.		
	Sup. Ori di Verdicchio '01	🍷	4

FONTE DELLA LUNA
MEDORO CIMARELLI
VIA SAN FRANCESCO, 1/A
60039 STAFFOLO (AN)
TEL. 0731779307

Grizio 2001 is one of the best Rosso Picenos from around Ancona. Its very ripe fruit tempts with intense varietal aromas that oak ageing never masks The palate is meaty and well-gauged. Frà Moriale 2002 is a tangy Verdicchio with good depth. Apple mingles with almondy notes in the leisurely finish.

●	Rosso Piceno Grizio '01	🍷🍷	4*
○	Verdicchio dei Castelli di Jesi Cl.		
	Sup. Frà Moriale '02	🍷	4

ESTER HAUSER
C.DA CORONCINO, 1/A
60039 STAFFOLO (AN)
TEL. 0731770203

A few thousand bottles of Cupo were released. From montepulciano with a little cabernet sauvignon, it never fails to impress with its concentration and power, and the 2000 vintage is no exception. In fact, it is even more intense than usual, and showing attractive cherry and cocoa powder aromas.

●	Il Cupo '00	🍷🍷	6

LA RIPE
LOC. RIPALTA - VIA PIANA, 20
61029 URBINO (PU)
TEL. 0721893019
E-MAIL: info@laripe.com

The Lucarelli family's reds put on quite a good show. The more substantial of the two Sangioveses is Goccione 2001, redolent of cinchona and liquorice. La Ripe 2001, however, has a little too much acidity and tannin edginess.

●	Colli Pesaresi Sangiovese		
	Goccione '01	🍷	5
●	Colli Pesaresi Sangiovese		
	La Ripe '01	🍷	4

UMBRIA

Umbria's wine scene is still small, if we look at it in terms of quantities produced. But when we turn our attention to a series of quality indicators, things change considerably. First of all it is astounding that such a small region can boast two DOCG zones, Sagrantino di Montefalco and Torgiano Rosso Riserva. Moving on to Guide criteria, we find that this year fully six wines have earned Three Glasses, which is twice the number won by Trentino, Lazio or Sardinia. It is also ahead of Puglia, Abruzzo and Emilia Romagna, all more important regions, at least on paper. There are still two truly outstanding areas. The first, Orvieto and the adjacent Colli Amerini in the province of Terni, is important for its potential while the second, Montefalco, is home to sagrantino, a variety with a long tradition and is now the jewel in the region's crown. Two of our top prizewinners come from the former area. The first is the classic Cervaro della Sala from Castello della Sala, a white from chardonnay with a little grechetto that has won Three Glasses 13 times in the Guide's 17 years of existence. As such, it is one of the wines that has claimed the greatest number of top awards ever. Alongside it is a newcomer, a Merlot from the small Castello delle Regine in the Colli Amerini. From Montefalco, there are two Sagrantinos, the 25 Anni selection from Marco and Arnaldo Caprai, which wins Three Glasses for the eighth consecutive year, and Sagrantino di Colpetrone from Saiagricola, another wine well worth tracking down. But it is another area, Colli del Trasimeno, that provided the real surprise. Despite its less exalted status, Colli del Trasimeno also produced two Three Glass wines – for the very first time ever. It is a real triumph for this ancient, traditional winemaking area. The two award winners are Campoleone from Lamborghini and Poggio Bertaio's Crovello, both "Super Umbrians" of extraordinary class. Lungarotti, the most representative estate in the region, has not yet returned to the heights, although its signs of recovery are much stronger than before. While it is still indisputably a focal point, to some extent it continues to pay for the inertia in winemaking that it suffered until a couple of years ago. However, the quality of the wines is growing by leaps and bounds all across the extensive range. The time can not be far off when one or more of them will again win Three Glass status for this famous estate.

AMELIA (TR)

CASTELLO DELLE REGINE
FRAZ. LE REGINE
VIA DI CASTELLUCCIO
05022 AMELIA (TR)
TEL. 0744702005
E-MAIL: castellodelleregine@virgilio.it

Castello delle Regina, situated in San Liberato, straddling the townships of Narni and Amelia, has already staked its place as one of Umbria's most impressive estates, despite having just two commercial vintages behind it. It has 51 hectares of its own vines and a further 28 hectares on lease, majoring on varieties such as sangiovese, merlot and cabernet sauvignon, grapes that have been present in Terni province for over 80 years. Winemaking assistance comes from talented oenologist, Franco Bernabei. This year, Castello delle Regine has taken Three Glasses for its Umbria Merlot '01. The colour is a good dark purple, and the nose is full, complex and highly refined. Notes of wild blackberry and ripe cherry mingle with pronounced sensations of sweet spices and well-amalgamated wood. Full and long on the palate, it satisfies a tightly woven, mouthfilling tannic presence. Princeps '01, produced mainly from cabernet sauvignon, with some sangiovese and merlot, came a close second. Its powerful, vegetal character on both nose and palate were well worth Two Glasses. A further Two Glasses go to the estate's newest wine, Bianco delle Regine '02, from sauvignon, chardonnay, riesling and pinot grigio. It has a fresh, fruity nose, with distinct scents of medlar and ripe damson, and good concentration on the palate. The two sangiovese wines, Podernovo and the Castello delle Regine selection, are in the One Glass band. Both offer excellent concentration and drinkability.

AMELIA (TR)

CANTINA DEI COLLI AMERINI
LOC. FORNOLE DI AMELIA
ZONA INDUSTRIALE
05020 AMELIA (TR)
TEL. 0744989721
E-MAIL: colliamerini@virgilio.it

The landscape around the fine village of Amelia is blanketed with gentle, neatly cultivated hills, with rows of vines standing out proudly. Winemaking traditions go back a long way here, yet they have not always been given the importance they deserve. This situation led to the founding of the Colli Amerini co-operative in 1975. It now has 350 members with a combined ownership of 700 hectares, and Riccardo Cotarella has been their advisor for over a decade. As a result, the name of Umbria's best-known oenologist has become linked with the wine that can be claimed to have relaunched the entire area, and which still represents the winery's pride and joy: Carbio, a blend of merlot, sangiovese, montepulciano and ciliegiolo. The '00 has aromas that range from lightly vegetal to firmer, more penetrating notes of redcurrant and cherry. The palate is solidly concentrated, with coffee-like flavours and a good level of tannin, but it is still a little oaky on the finish. While we wait for time to run its course, we can enjoy the simpler, more immediate Colli Amerini Rosso Terre Arnolfe '02, made from the same varieties. The nose is fresh, with aromas of not completely ripe cherry, then the attractive, rather subtle palate veers more towards berry fruits, mainly raspberry, and the finish has a pleasing touch of bitterness. However, Torraccio '01, a 100 per cent sangiovese, is below par, with preponderant oak on the nose and a palate that has still to come together.

●	Merlot '01	🍷🍷🍷	7
●	Princeps '01	🍷🍷	6
○	Bianco delle Regine '02	🍷🍷	4
●	Podernovo '01	🍷	4
●	Sangiovese '01	🍷	5
●	Merlot '00	🍷🍷	7
●	Podernovo '00	🍷🍷	4
●	Princeps '00	🍷🍷	6

●	C. Amerini Rosso Sup. Carbio '00	🍷🍷	5
●	Umbria Sangiovese Torraccio '01	🍷	5
●	C. Amerini Rosso Terre Arnolfe '02	🍷	3*
●	C. Amerini Rosso Sup. Carbio '98	🍷🍷	4
●	Umbria Sangiovese Torraccio '99	🍷🍷	5
●	Umbria Aleatico Bartolomeo '00	🍷	4

BASCHI (TR)

Vaglie

via Amelia, 48
05023 Baschi (TR)
tel. 0744957425
e-mail: a.lumini@tiscali.it

Baschi is one of the few townships lying in all three DOCs in the Orvieto area. The estate has seen a considerable leap in the quality - and the quantity - of its wines over the past few years. Not surprisingly, owners Alessandro Bonino and his wife Elisabetta, are now thinking big. They have already started work on a new cellar, to replace the narrow spaces they currently have to work in. We'll see how that goes. This year we found their best wine to be Umbria Rosso Momenti '02, a sangiovese and merlot blend. Although the nose is still a little closed, the spectrum on the palate is much as we are used to. There's great concentration on initial impact, with roundness of fruit and some oak toast from the barriques used. Umbria Rosso Vaglie '02, from montepulciano, sangiovese, canaiolo and ciliegiolo, is not dissimilar in style. The colour is deep ruby, the nose has coffee and hints of blackberry, and the palate is powerful and well-structured with tightly knit tannins and a silky finish. It also shows good balance, as does the Umbria Rosso Masseo '01. It may be less concentrated, but it is elegant, revealing aromas of fruit, cinchona and pencil lead. The fabulous overall balance and the cleanness of the ripe, crisp, apricot-like fruit on Orvieto Classico Superiore Matricale '02 nudged it towards Two Glasses. It also has fair depth on the palate, highlighted by hints of sweet pastries on the clean, even finish. Vendemmia Tardiva l'Alba '01, on the other hand, is distinguished by its sage-led, herby character.

●	Momenti '02	▼▼	3*
○	L'Alba '01	▼	4
●	Masseo '01	▼	4
○	Orvieto Cl. Sup. Matricale '02	▼	4
●	Umbria Rosso Vaglie '02	▼	2*
●	Momenti '00	▽▽	3*
●	Masseo '99	▽▽	4
●	Momenti '01	▽▽	3*
●	Umbria Rosso Vaglie '01	▽▽	2*

BEVAGNA (PG)

Adanti

voc. Arquata
06031 Bevagna (PG)
tel. 0742360295
e-mail: info@cantineadanti.com

The Adanti estate, housed in a splendid 16th-century monastery, was founded in the 1960s. Without doubt, it is one of the focal points of the sagrantino-producing countryside. Adanti has around 30 hectares of vine, 22 of them in production, and a wide range of grapes, from grechetto and sagrantino through to the international merlot, cabernet and chardonnay varieties. The last few years have seen a complete overhaul of practices here. There have been new plantings in the vineyards and an expansion of the cellar, with new vinification equipment, a new barrel cellar and the passing of winemaking control to the skilled Graziana Grassini. Even cellarman, Alvaro Palini, who has worked here for ever, is handing over to his son, Daniele, although he will remain at the winery to show how, at Adanti, renewal runs alongside continuity. The wines are clearly benefiting from all this. The Sagrantino di Montefalco Passito '99 is very good, showing aromas of blackberry, liqueur cherries and chocolate, and a concentrated, fleshy, very clean palate. It has powerful but ripe tannins without any clumsiness, and finishes long. Umbria Rosso Arquata '00, from mainly cabernet and merlot, is comparable. The nose is perhaps a little closed but the palate displays breadth and elegance. Slim yet not faint, it continually reprises its morello cherry and blackberry jam in a ripe, soft tannic weave. The powerful yet soft Sagrantino di Montefalco '99, with its pervasive finish, and the concentrated Rosso di Montefalco Riserva '00, which has slightly rough-edged tannins, scored just shy of a second Glass.

●	Rosso d'Arquata '00	▼▼	5
●	Montefalco Sagrantino Passito '99	▼▼	7
●	Montefalco Rosso Arquata Ris. '00	▼	5
●	Montefalco Sagrantino Arquata '99	▼	6
●	Rosso d'Arquata '97	▽▽	5
●	Montefalco Sagrantino Arquata '98	▽▽	5
●	Rosso d'Arquata '98	▽▽	5

CASTEL VISCARDO (TR)

CANTINA MONRUBIO
LOC. LE PRESE, 22
FRAZ. MONTERUBIAGLIO
05010 CASTEL VISCARDO (TR)
TEL. 0763626064
E-MAIL: cantina.monrubio@tiscalinet.it

Monterubiaglio, lying just a few kilometres from Orvieto, is a small area with close links to wine and the land. It is also a leading player on the zone's economic and social stage. So it is not surprising to find one of the longest-lived co-operatives of the region here. It was founded in 1957 and wines were first vinified in 1966, although it took until the 1980s, when Riccardo Cotarella took over responsibility for production, for it to make its mark quality-wise. Nowadays, there are 250 members, all well co-ordinated by Tommaso Picciolini, the co-op's president. From the wide range of wines submitted, we felt that the best, as before, was Umbria Rosso Palaia, this time the '01 edition. It is a classic Bordeaux blend and ages for a year in barrique. Red berry fruits on the nose harmonize perfectly with firmer notes of coffee and sweet pipe tobacco. The palate is a touch less ripe, and has dense but still green tannins. There is certainly no lack of power and structure in the mouth. Another promising wine, which came close to Two Glasses, is the 100 per cent cabernet Nociano '01. It shows good concentration, and well-rounded, succulent fruit, but still has to assimilate the oakiness which remains overt on both nose and palate. The final red is Monrubio '02. A little less complex than the others, it has similarly evident notes of oak. The two Orvieto Classicos are well typed. Secco Macchia del Pozzo '02, with its hints of sage, is easy drinking, whereas the Superiore Soana '02 is more floral and citrus-like.

CASTIGLIONE DEL LAGO (PG)

DUCA DELLA CORGNA
VIA ROMA, 236
06061 CASTIGLIONE DEL LAGO (PG)
TEL. 0759652493
E-MAIL: ducacorgna@libero.it

Cantina del Trasimeno, overseen by notary Paolo Biavati, has 270 grape-supplying members with vineyards mainly on the Tuscan side of this lakeside area, close to the regional border. Duca della Corgna is the name of the winery's top line, which derives from a recent quality-directed project involving notable investment and major vineyard improvements (so far a dozen members have taken part). Oenologist Lorenzo Landi consults. Results have not been slow in coming. Despite skipping a vintage with their two leading Colli del Trasimeno wines, Rosso Corniolo and Gamay Divina Villa Etichetta Nera, the range on offer is very satisfying. Colli del Trasimeno Gamay Divina Villa Etichetta Bianca '02 nearly made it to the Three Glass finals. Aged without wood, it shows evenness and clean fruit as its most notable characteristics. The lack of disparity between nose and palate, both yielding small black berry fruit, mostly blueberry, and the pleasure given by the fresh, mid structured, but beautifully balanced, palate are also major plus points. The impressive Colli del Trasimeno Baccio del Bianco '02 shows a nose full of ripe tropical fruit, refined and freshened by a waft of sage, then a rich palate, recalling damson and white peach, takes the wine through to a long finish. It is also extraordinarily good value for money. The series is brought to a close by Colli del Trasimeno Baccio del Rosso '02, which is sound but not as good as last year's, and Colli del Trasimeno Grechetto Nuricante '02, which has a touch of sweetness and hints of resin.

● Palaia '01	♙♙	4*
● Nociano '01	♙	3
● Monrubio '02	♙	2*
○ Orvieto Cl. Secco		
Macchia del Pozzo '02	♙	1*
○ Orvieto Cl. Sup. Soana '02	♙	3*
● Palaia '98	♟♟	5
● Palaia '99	♟♟	5
● Palaia '00	♟♟	4

○ C. del Trasimeno		
Baccio del Bianco '02	♙♙	2*
● C. del Trasimeno Gamay		
Divina Villa Et. Bianca '02	♙♙	4*
● C. del Trasimeno		
Baccio del Rosso '02	♙	3*
○ C. del Trasimeno Grechetto		
Nuricante '02	♙	3*
● C. del Trasimeno Rosso		
Corniolo '01	♟♟	4
● C. del Trasimeno		
Baccio del Rosso '01	♟♟	2*
● C. del Trasimeno Gamay		
Divina Villa Et. Bianca '01	♟♟	4

CASTIGLIONE DEL LAGO (PG) CASTIGLIONE DEL LAGO (PG)

FANINI
LOC. PETRIGNANO DEL LAGO
VOC. I CUCCHI
06060 CASTIGLIONE DEL LAGO (PG)
TEL. 0755173122
E-MAIL: mfdp@unipg.it

POGGIO BERTAIO
FRAZ. CASAMAGGIORE
VIA FRATTAVECCHIA, 29
06061 CASTIGLIONE DEL LAGO (PG)
TEL. 075956921
E-MAIL: poggiobertaio@tiscalinet.it

Known by the name Morolli until the end of the 1980s, the Fanini estate lies at Petrignano sul Trasimeno, the final reaches of a zone that slopes down steeply towards the Tuscan border. Just over ten kilometres away, Montepulciano is visible in the distance. The estate set out on its current course in 1991 when Francesca Fanini took control. Working together with her husband, Marco Fornaciari da Passano, lecturer in applied botany at Perugia University's Faculty of Agriculture, Francesca has continued to invest heavily in developing her estate, which is of considerable interest both in terms of site climates and grape material. There have been new, high density plantings in line with current quality dictates, selection of the estate's best clones, soil and climate analyses and, last but not least, oenological consultancy from young, skilled Fabrizio Ciufoli. Best of the wines submitted this year, we felt, was the Merlot '01 which, as in previous vintages, earned Two Glasses. Ruby red tinged with purple, it has aromas of small, ripe berry fruits and a youthful splash of violet. The fruit and spice palate is full, revealing good structure and length. The ripe plum Sangiovese Vigna la Pieve '00, which has good power but an unimpressive finish, is decent, as is Chardonnay Robbiano '02 which is rather over-evolved on the nose.

This Castiglione del Lago estate had been producing wine for private consumption and for friends and acquaintances for years. Then Ugo and Fabrizio Ciufoli, sons of founder Fabio and respectively the estate agronomist and oenologist, finally decided to embark upon a new venture: bottling to sell commercially. They were after their "ideal wine", and they haven't done at all badly, to judge by the bottles submitted to us for tasting this year. At its second release, Crovello '01, from equal parts of merlot and cabernet sauvignon, aged 12 months in barrique, is quite simply awesome, and walked away with Three Glasses. Purple-ruby in hue, it opens on a full, powerful, pervasively elegant nose rich in ripe, red berry fruits, where wild cherry and plum stand out in particular. It is further enhanced by notes of black pepper and clove, and well-judged hints of oak. The palate is most enjoyable, too. Rich, fleshy and long, it offers vigorous tannins and a beautiful velvet-like finish. Further confirmation of Poggio Bertaio's proficiency came from Cimbolo '01, a 100 per cent sangiovese. Another high scorer, it shows dark ruby, then the nose is elegant and refined, with overt ripe fruit and gentle sweet oakiness. The palate is warm with good body and well-judged, elegant tannins.

● Merlot '01	♟♟	5
● Sangiovese Vigna La Pieve '00	♟	5
○ Chardonnay Robbiano '02	♟	5
○ Chardonnay Robbiano '00	♟♟	4
● Merlot '00	♟♟	5
○ Chardonnay Robbiano '01	♟♟	5
● Sangiovese Vigna La Pieve '99	♟♟	5

● Crovello '01	♟♟♟	8
● Cimbolo '01	♟♟	6
● Cimbolo '98	♟♟	5
● Cimbolo '99	♟♟	5
● Cimbolo '00	♟♟	6
● Crovello '00	♟♟	7

CORCIANO (PG)

IL TOPPELLO
FRAZ. MANTIGNANA
VIA TOPPELLO
06075 CORCIANO (PG)
TEL. 0755841456
E-MAIL: iltoppello@tin.it

This is the Guide debut of the new, promising Cantina Il Toppello. Set up in 2000 and situated at Mantignana, in the Trasimeno zone, it extends over 130 hectares. The seven under vine yield an annual production of around 45,000 bottles. Winemaking is co-ordinated by the skilled Fabrizio Ciufoli. We found the wines submitted for tasting to be excellent. In fact, they were so good that we gave the estate a full entry. So let's take a look at the range. At its first release, Selciaio, a 100 per cent sangiovese given 12 months in barrique, went straight into the Two Glass category. The colour is dark ruby red and the nose complex and powerful, with clear notes of autumn leaves, enhanced by elegant, sweet spicy scents led by liquorice and black pepper. The palate is refined yet powerful, full and very fleshy, strongly evoking plum and ripe cherry. There is also good length and excellent tannic vigour. Just a short way behind comes Rocceto '01, from sangiovese with a small percentage of merlot, and aged 12 months in barrique. A dark purple introduces the clean, full nose, whose delicate nuances of red berry fruits are a little in thrall to slightly excessive oak toast. The palate has good structure, complexity and fruit, with firm, sweet oaky notes and tannins of excellent vigour and character.

FICULLE (TR)

★ CASTELLO DELLA SALA
LOC. SALA
05016 FICULLE (TR)
TEL. 076386051
E-MAIL: castellodellasala@antinori.it

Thirteen Three Glasses wines in 13 years is certainly not a result that can pass unnoticed. This time, another absolutely splendid edition of Cervaro della Sala keeps the wine in the front rank. Here in Ficulle, at Castello della Sala, the Antinori family makes what is without doubt one of their very best wines. And we are talking about one of Italy's most internationally famous estates. Castello della Sala has been in Antinori ownership since 1940. There are 160 hectares of vineyard and output is 1,500,000 bottles a year. But let's move on to the wines themselves. Cervaro della Sala '01 is quite simply dazzling. It just oozes class, right from its luminous, warm, deep straw-yellow hue. The nose is decisive, powerful and quite unique. Very few Italian whites can marry class, finesse and power so well. There is not a hint of heaviness, despite overt vanilla and raisined sensations from its stay in barrique and the full, fresh, lithe palate is just as superb. The 100 per cent Chardonnay '02 falls not far short. A delight to drink, it offers complex, clean florality and well-judged oak. As excellent as ever is Muffato della Sala '00, from sauvignon blanc, grechetto, traminer and riesling, has elegant, ripe notes of tropical fruit and exemplary sweetness on the palate. Equally outstanding is the oak-fermented, full-bodied Conte della Vipara '01, from sauvignon with a little chardonnay, which proffers clean, pervasive fruit. However, just One Glass goes to the '00 Pinot Nero, which is a little over-evolved and bitter on the finish.

●	Selciaio '01	♟♟	7
●	Rocceto '01	♟	7
●	Rocceto '00	♟♟	7

○	Cervaro della Sala '01	♟♟♟	6
○	Muffato della Sala '00	♟♟	6
○	Conte della Vipera '01	♟♟	5
○	Chardonnay della Sala '02	♟♟	4
●	Pinot Nero Vigneto Consola '00	♟	6
○	Cervaro della Sala '90	♟♟♟	6
○	Cervaro della Sala '92	♟♟♟	6
○	Cervaro della Sala '93	♟♟♟	6
○	Cervaro della Sala '94	♟♟♟	6
○	Cervaro della Sala '95	♟♟♟	6
○	Cervaro della Sala '96	♟♟♟	6
○	Cervaro della Sala '97	♟♟♟	6
○	Cervaro della Sala '98	♟♟♟	6
○	Cervaro della Sala '99	♟♟♟	6
○	Cervaro della Sala '00	♟♟♟	6

FOLIGNO (PG)

FOLIGNO (PG)

SAN LORENZO
VIA SAN LORENZO VECCHIO, 30
06034 FOLIGNO (PG)
TEL. 074222553
E-MAIL: sanlorenzovecchio@libero.it

TERRE DE' TRINCI
VIA FIAMENGA, 57
06034 FOLIGNO (PG)
TEL. 0742320165
E-MAIL: cantina@terredetrinci.com

San Lorenzo, in the hills between Spello and Foligno at the foot of Monte Subasio, is well worth a visit. The breathtaking landscape – rising to 600 metres – is full of olive trees and vines seemingly suspended between earth and sky. The heart of the estate, a 14th-century Franciscan monastery, was bought by Aldo De Luca in 1969. He intended to make the property the hub of a new farming enterprise and the estate now has 400 hectares, with 40 of vineyard. It is in the hands and heart of Aldo's daughter, Flaminia, who grew up here and is in love with the land that surrounds her. Oenological consultancy from Maurilio Chioccia has brought a considerable boost to quality in the last two years, as the wines clearly show. Let's start with Sangiovese Chiostro '01, which hopped straight to Two Glasses. Its nose is decidedly fruity and perhaps still a little too youthful, but it's super-clean, even and anything but banal. The harmonious, elegant palate, which prefers subtlety to extreme depth and concentration, mirrors it to perfection, especially in the echoing notes of blackberry and raspberry. The rather marked acidity could stem from the wine's youth, but is perfectly acceptable. San Lorenzo '01, from sagrantino, cabernet sauvignon and merlot, has aromas of berry fruit jam and cinnamon. The palate starts sweet and soft, the tannins are overt but not aggressive, and the finish is reasonably long. Cleos '02, an immediate, lightish, attractively fruity Ciliegiolo, is good, as is Sagrantino di Montefalco '02, although its balance isn't perfect.

The Terre de' Trinci co-operative has now earned a full Guide entry for two years running. Located near Foligno, its farming tradition goes back to ancient times. It has always been considered the hub of wine production in Montefalco. Terre de' Trinci currently sources from 300 hectares of vineyard belonging to its 350 members, and output can reach around 500,000 bottles a year. Co-ordinated by the tireless Lodovico Mattoni and, for winemaking, by the able Maurilio Chioccia, its traditionally styled Montefalco wines performed very well this year. The Terre de' Trinci Montefalco Sangrantino is the winery's flagship wine, and remains its best. The 2000 has a good, bright, dark ruby colour. The nose shows power and character, with clean, pervasive notes of plum and ripe cherry lifted by spicy scents, especially clove and black pepper. The palate is soft and mouthfilling with good concentration and texture, marked tannins and a firm finish. Also good are the Montefalco Rosso '01, with fresh raspberry and mulberry blossom aromas and a slim, softly structured palate, and the Sagrantino Passito '00, which is super-ripe on the nose and concentrated on the palate, with well-judged sweetness. Cajo '01, from sagrantino, merlot and cabernet, is a little under par. Previous vintages have been tighter and cleaner on the nose. The winery's only white, Luna '02, is well typed and fresh.

● Sangiovese Chiostro '01	♟♟	4*
● Montefalco Sagrantino '00	♟	8
● Rosso San Lorenzo '01	♟	4
● Cleos '02	♟	5
● De Luca Rosso '00	♀	3
● Cleos '01	♀	5
● Montefalco Sagrantino '99	♀	5

● Montefalco Sagrantino '00	♟♟	6
● Montefalco Sagrantino Passito '00	♟	6
● Montefalco Rosso '01	♟	4
● Umbria Rosso Cajo '01	♟	4
○ Umbria Bianco Luna '02	♟	4
● Umbria Rosso Cajo '00	♀♀	4
● Montefalco Rosso Ris. '99	♀♀	4
● Montefalco Sagrantino '99	♀♀	6
● Montefalco Sagrantino '97	♀	5
● Umbria Rosso Cajo '99	♀	4

GUALDO CATTANEO (PG)

GUALDO CATTANEO (PG)

CÒLPETRONE
FRAZ. MARCELLANO
VIA DELLA COLLINA, 4
06035 GUALDO CATTANEO (PG)
TEL. 0578767722 - 0578767700
E-MAIL: colpetrone@tin.it

PODERE PERTICAIA
VIA E. CATTANEO, 39
06035 GUALDO CATTANEO (PG)
E-MAIL: guidoguardigli@libero.it

In just a few years, Colpetrone has become a key Montefalco estate, thanks mainly to a terrific Sagrantino that again this year easily won Three Glasses. For the fifth time. The estate, which joined the Saiagricola group in 1995, has 47 of hectares under vine, 33 of which are in production, and produces 58,000 bottles a year. Expert guidance comes from oenologist Lorenzo Landi, who doesn't miss a beat. This year's excellent Montefalco Sagrantino, the '00, has a good, deep purple-red colour. The nose is broad and complex, with harmonious notes of slightly raisined red berry fruits, sensations of cherry and blackberry, and sweet spicy tones of cinnamon and clove well integrated into the fruit. The palate is mouthfilling yet refined, powerful yet harmonious, with warmth and a dense tannic layer that coalesces beautifully into the whole. Montefalco Rosso '01 is also first-rate and again manages to marry complexity on nose and palate with softness and drinkability. The colour is deep purple. The fresh, fruity nose has distinct aromas of blackberry and blackcurrant, then the lively palate reveals good flesh, with soft, restrained tannins. No less impressive is Montefalco Sagrantino Passito, which has found few to rival it over the past few years. The '00 shows dark ruby, then the nose brims with ripe blackberry, pencil lead and cocoa powder. It is also elegant and spicy, with overt notes of cinnamon. The palate shows great refinement, its well-judged sweetness preceding elegant berry fruit jam on the finish.

Having left the Saiagricola group in 2000, Guido Guardigli decided that it was too early to put on the bedroom slippers. Like the courageous, challenge-stimulated person that he is, bought himself a nice property at Casale di Montefalco and returned to the firing line. Set among vineyards and olive grove at 320 to 350 metres, his estate has 20 hectares of gravelly soil, with water from a nearby natural spring. Vineyard accounts for 14 hectares, half destined for sagrantino and the rest split among sangiovese, merlot and cabernet franc. All these varieties may go into Rosso di Montefalco, a wine that Guardigli rates highly. The vinification and bottling area will soon be amplified. In the meantime, the historic cellar at the 18th-century residence in Gualdo Cattaneo has been taken over for bottle maturation. The wines tasted this year included the '00 Sagrantino, which has impressive structure, weight and concentration. It's an imposing, mouthfilling wine, with warm sensations of vanilla and chocolate on a fruity, blackberry-like base, and a long finish. The less powerful, less complex but highly drinkable Rosso di Montefalco '01 is very attractive and is characterized by restrained blueberry-like fruitiness.

● Montefalco Sagrantino '00	♟♟♟	6
● Montefalco Sagrantino Passito '00	♟♟	6
● Montefalco Rosso '01	♟♟	4
● Montefalco Sagrantino '96	♟♟♟	4
● Montefalco Sagrantino '97	♟♟♟	5
● Montefalco Sagrantino '98	♟♟♟	5
● Montefalco Sagrantino '99	♟♟♟	6
● Montefalco Sagrantino '95	♟♟	4
● Montefalco Rosso '97	♟♟	3
● Montefalco Sagrantino Passito '97	♟♟	6
● Montefalco Rosso '98	♟♟	3
● Montefalco Sagrantino Passito '98	♟♟	6
● Montefalco Rosso '99	♟♟	4
● Montefalco Sagrantino Passito '99	♟♟	6
● Montefalco Rosso '00	♟♟	4*

● Montefalco Sagrantino '00	♟♟	6
● Montefalco Rosso '01	♟	4

MONTEFALCO (PG)

ANTONELLI - SAN MARCO
LOC. SAN MARCO, 59
06036 MONTEFALCO (PG)
TEL. 0742379158
E-MAIL: info@antonellisanmarco.it

An unbroken plot of 170 hectares immersed in the Montefalco countryside is the heart of the Antonelli San Marco estate, for some time now a well-established presence in the Guide. The estate was founded way back in 1881, when Francesco Antonelli bought it from the bishopric of Spoleto. Now, it comprises 30 hectares planted to vine and a newly refurbished cellar, including areas for barrique and bottle-ageing. All is managed by expert oenologist Manlio Erba. The estate put in a good performance this year and the '00 vintage of its flagship wine, Montefalco Sagrantino, made it to the Three Glasses finals. The colour is a good, dark ruby. The nose is rich, powerful, complex and nicely evolved, with elegant ripe red fruits and a subtle sweet oakiness. The elegant, warm, well-calibrated palate is equally good, offering clear tones of cherry and ripe plum, then excellent tannins on the finish. The two Montefalco Rosso wines are also good, both gaining One Glass. The '00 Riserva has a refined, balanced nose with delicate scents of slightly raisined fruit and well-gauged oak. The palate is elegant, clearly recalling ripe morello cherry and clove, and there is a characterful tannic finish. The standard-label '01 focuses more on youth. Its dark ruby introduces a nose of ripe blackberry and black pepper, then the soft, easy drinking palate shows lively fruitiness and balanced tannins.

MONTEFALCO (PG)

ARNALDO CAPRAI - VAL DI MAGGIO
LOC. TORRE
06036 MONTEFALCO (PG)
TEL. 0742378802 - 0742378523
E-MAIL: info@arnaldocaprai.it

What more can we say about an estate that has picked up Three effortless Glasses seven years running? No surprise, then, that the Montefalco Sagrantino 25 Anni was a winner again this year. Surely Marco Caprai must be more than satisfied with his achievements. Above all, this young go-getter has raised the profile of the entire Montefalco zone, which was practically unknown a few years ago. If it is now the promised land for many Italian producers, Marco deserves the credit. The '00 25 Anni displays great character right from the first sight of its deep, dark purple hue. The nose is full, powerful and pervasive, with elegant notes of ripe blackberry and cherry, a finely-balanced dose of oak adding finesse. The refined, all-enveloping palate is generous and powerful, showing ripe red berry fruit, elegant spicy notes and great length. Although still young and tannic, it is already impressive. There has never been a better Collepiano than this year's '00, which won Two red Glasses to crown a fine performance. The estate's newest wine, the merlot and cabernet sauvignon-based red, Outsider '00, is excellent. Rich blackberry and blueberry interweave with elegant sweet spiciness on the nose, and the soft, long palate flaunts elegant tannins. Grecante '02 is another Two Glass winner and without doubt the best Grechetto in the region. There is ripe medlar and white peach on the nose, then the palate is both fleshy and zesty. Both Montefalco Rosso '01 and Poggio Belvedere '01 are good and make attractive drinking.

● Montefalco Sagrantino '00	♆♆	6
● Montefalco Rosso Ris. '00	♆	5
● Montefalco Rosso '01	♆	4
● Montefalco Sagrantino '94	♆♆	6
● Montefalco Sagrantino Passito '95	♆♆	4
● Montefalco Sagrantino '95	♆♆	6
● Montefalco Sagrantino '96	♆♆	6
● Montefalco Sagrantino '97	♆♆	6
● Montefalco Sagrantino Passito '97	♆♆	6
● Montefalco Sagrantino '98	♆♆	6
● Montefalco Sagrantino '99	♆♆	6

● Montefalco Sagrantino 25 Anni '00	♆♆♆	8
● Montefalco Sagrantino Collepiano '00	♆♆	6
● Rosso Outsider '00	♆♆	7
○ Colli Martani Grechetto Grecante '02	♆♆	4
● Montefalco Rosso '01	♆	5
● Poggio Belvedere '01	♆	4
● Montefalco Sagrantino 25 Anni '93	♆♆♆	8
● Montefalco Sagrantino 25 Anni '94	♆♆♆	8
● Montefalco Sagrantino 25 Anni '95	♆♆♆	8
● Montefalco Sagrantino 25 Anni '96	♆♆♆	8
● Montefalco Sagrantino 25 Anni '97	♆♆♆	8
● Montefalco Sagrantino 25 Anni '98	♆♆♆	8
● Montefalco Sagrantino 25 Anni '99	♆♆♆	8
● Montefalco Sagrantino Collepiano '99	♆♆	6
● Montefalco Sagrantino Collepiano '98	♆♆	6

MONTEFALCO (PG)

ROCCA DI FABBRI
LOC. FABBRI
06036 MONTEFALCO (PG)
TEL. 0742399379
E-MAIL: faroaldo@roccadifabbri.com

Rocca di Fabbri was founded in 1984. Its owners realized immediately that the grape varieties recommended by the laws of the day were definitely not those best suited to Montefalco's terrain. So, with valuable assistance from Giacomo Tachis, they embarked on a large-scale replanting project, which will be complete in a couple of years, also implementing ambitious winemaking plans. The estate, which has almost 60 hectares of vineyard, is currently in the capable hands of sisters Roberta and Simona Vitali, with winemaking consultancy from Giorgio Marone. This year, we particularly liked the Sagrantino di Montefalco '00, which easily earned Two Glasses. The super-ripe fruit on the nose, clearly evoking blackberry and plum, follows through well on the clean palate, where fair complexity and structure is well supported by a good swathe of acidity and nice length. Rosso di Montefalco '01 also has lots of personality. Strongly spicy aromas of coffee, black pepper and liquorice precede a palate of medium density and a clean, full finish. It is sweetness and alcohol reminiscent of liqueur fruits, however, that mark out the '99 Sagrantino di Montefalco Passito, enhanced by an aromatic spectrum with violet highlights. We finish with Faroaldo '00 from equal parts of sagrantino and cabernet sauvignon. It is a good wine but the excess of oak-derived flavours, especially vanilla, leaves a question mark hanging over it.

MONTEFALCO (PG)

SCACCIADIAVOLI
LOC. CANTINONE, 31
06036 MONTEFALCO (PG)
TEL. 0742371210 - 0742378272
E-MAIL: scacciadiavoli@tin.it

Cantinone (it means "big cellar") is a place name that reverberates with the wine traditions of this strip of the Montefalco zone. It was here that Principe Ugo Boncompagni built his cellar at the end of the 19th century. He did so using methods that were not just advanced for the times, but remain so even today. The building is on four floors, allowing the grapes, and then the must, to move "a caduta", under gravity, from one part to the next, just as the modern precepts of biodynamics demand. The Pambuffetti family, owners of the building since 1952, took care not to upset this arrangement when they began restoration work on the entire complex a couple of years ago. Indeed, the whole project is sensitive to the historical layout. Significant investment, along with diligent renewal of the vineyards and the involvement of both Guido Guardigli, technical director, and Stefano Chioccioli, consultant oenologist, are projecting the estate towards ever higher goals. As for this year's wines, the Sagrantino di Montefalco '00 put on a good showing. The nose may still be a little quiet but the overall style impressed. There is enough concentration, it has good flesh, the tannins are dense and fairly ripe, the aromatic length is promising, and it is nicely peppery. The Montefalco Rosso '01 is not bad either, with liquorice and vanilla layered over the fruit on the nose, and a warm, rounded palate with good balance.

● Montefalco Sagrantino '00	🍷🍷	7
● Faroaldo '00	🍷	6
● Montefalco Rosso '01	🍷	4
● Montefalco Sagrantino Passito '99	🍷	6
● Faroaldo '97	🍷🍷	5
● Montefalco Sagrantino Passito '97	🍷🍷	5
● Faroaldo '98	🍷🍷	6
● Colli Martani Sangiovese Satiro '99	🍷🍷	3*
● Faroaldo '99	🍷🍷	5
● Colli Martani Sangiovese Satiro '00	🍷	4
● Montefalco Rosso '00	🍷	5
● Montefalco Sagrantino '99	🍷	6

● Montefalco Sagrantino '00	🍷🍷	6
● Montefalco Rosso '01	🍷	4
● Montefalco Sagrantino '98	🍷🍷	5
● Montefalco Rosso '00	🍷🍷	4
● Montefalco Sagrantino Passito '99	🍷🍷	7
● Montefalco Sagrantino '99	🍷	6

MONTEGABBIONE (TR) | ORVIETO (TR)

TENUTA CORINI
VOC. CASINO, 53
05010 MONTEGABBIONE (TR)
TEL. 0763837535
E-MAIL: tenutacorini@yahoo.it

BARBERANI - VALLESANTA
LOC. CERRETO
VIA MICHELANGELI, 8
05018 ORVIETO (TR)
TEL. 0763341820
E-MAIL: barberani@barberani.it

Tenuta Corini is the real excitement of this year's Umbrian tastings. The Montegabbione family, from the village of the same name, spent 30 years in Switzerland before returning to their homeland and creating this winemaking estate. Their aim is to bring this corner of Umbria, and its as yet undiscovered winemaking potential, to people's notice. They also took on the skilled Riccardo Cotarella to advise on cellar operations. It was the red wines that struck us particularly. Two were submitted, both from '01. Frabusco, at its first release but already the estate flagship, is from sangiovese, montepulciano and merlot, and spends several months in barrique. It was a delightful surprise, from its deep ruby red colour onwards and sailed into the Three Glass finals. The intense, balsam-like nose has elegant aromas of red berry fruits with pervasive sweet spices thanks to careful use of oak. It is powerful and full of extract on the palate, with flavours of wild berries and a good weight of tannin. The highly distinctive Pinot Nero Camerti, which takes its name from the ancient people who first settled Umbria, is one of the best in the region. Its elegance and varietal purity gained it Two Glasses. A light ruby red introduces a harmonious nose of wild berries, pipe tobacco and a nice touch of oak, while the palate is soft and characterful with good tannic vigour and excellent structure. Our compliments. And welcome to the Guide!

Barberani has one of the oldest winemaking traditions in the Orvieto area. But this doesn't mean that it has remained fixed in time. The cellar, built in 1985, has been progressively re-equipped with the most modern systems, and there has been steady replanting in the vineyards, with particular attention being paid more recently to red varieties. These burst of innovation haven't led to the past being forgotten, though. Just as much care has been taken over rediscovering the wines of tradition, such as the sweet version that made Orvieto famous worldwide. So let's start with that. Orvieto Classico Superiore Calcaia '00 comes from grapes attacked by botrytis, the famous noble rot, and has a highly complex nose of apricot, incense and spices. It completely fills the mouth and, though sweet, does not cloy, thanks to good acidity. Villa Monticelli Rosso '00, from sangiovese, cabernet and merlot, is modern in style. Its blackberry, blueberry and ripe cherry fruit nuances are beautifully integrated with the toasty, coffee-like hints from the use of small oak barrels. There is plenty of warmth on the palate, although there's also a hint of greenness that slightly disturbs the balance. Lago di Corbara Foresco '00 comes from the same varieties but is considerably less complex. At a retaste this year, we found it to be developing well in bottle. The nose has a touch of raisined blackberry and plum. The palate has roundness and medium structure, and develops evenly and well.

● Frabusco '01	🍷🍷	6
● Pinot Nero Camerti '01	🍷🍷	6

● Lago di Corbara Rosso Villa Monticelli '00	🍷🍷	5
○ Orvieto Cl. Sup. Calcaia '00	🍷🍷	6
○ Moscato Passito Villa Monticelli '97	🍷🍷	6
● Lago di Corbara Foresco '98	🍷🍷	5
● Lago di Corbara Foresco '99	🍷🍷	5
○ Moscato Passito Villa Monticelli '99	🍷🍷	6
● Lago di Corbara Foresco '00	🍷🍷	4

ORVIETO (TR)

ORVIETO (TR)

BIGI
LOC. PONTE GIULIO
05018 ORVIETO (TR)
TEL. 0763316224
E-MAIL: giv@giv.it

CARDETO
FRAZ. SFERRACAVALLO
LOC. CARDETO
05018 ORVIETO (TR)
TEL. 0763341286 - 0763343189
E-MAIL: cardecom@tin.it

The Orvieto zone is certainly one of the parts of Umbria most steeped in wine history but it's also an area of great change and modernization. In the last few years, new DOCs have appeared to cover red wine production, and even the most traditional denomination, Orvieto itself, has recently undergone an update to its production parameters. Bigi, a winery founded as far back as 1880 and now owned by Gruppo Italiano Vini, has followed a more or less similar course, allying modern winemaking techniques to respect for the heritage of an area so well suited to wine production. The result is wines that combine quality, quantity and good prices. The new arrival this year is Sartiano '01, which hit Two Glasses on its first outing. The nose has already gained great complexity, with aromas that range from fruit to incense and smoky scents. Despite its youth, the palate has good depth and richness, showing nice harmony and balance. Overall, it is a well-made red with a very long finish, that holds its head high against its almost exclusively white stablemates. One of these is a good Grechetto '02, with nuances of peach and herbs. It's not complex but most attractive, as is the ever-present Orvieto Classico Vigneto Torricella. The '02 is less complex than last year's, but still admirable for its slender structure, refreshing zip and distinct notes of white damson.

Cardeto has again lived up to expectations. A series of really good wines was submitted for this year's Guide, all produced on the 1,000 hectares of vineyard owned by the co-operative's 350 members. Established in 1949, Cardeto now produces a large range, totalling around 5,000,000 bottles a year, under the expert guidance of Maurilio Chioccia, the winery's renowned oenologist, and Eugenio Ranchino on the viticultural side. Let us start with Cardeto's leading wine, Nero della Greca, from sangiovese with a little merlot. No vintage has ever merited our praises like the '01, which easily achieved Two red Glasses. The nose is deep and complex, with elegant ripe fruit and an added dimension from distinct vegetal scents followed by balsam. The palate is full and long, with a good shot of tannin and a pleasing finish. The latest release, '02, of Orvieto L'Armida is again of very good quality, with fresh pineapple and melon on the nose and a well-judged level of sweetness. The clean, elegant Colbadia '02 is also one of the top Orvietos, and has aromas of white peach and sharp damson, then good concentration on the palate. The Febeo '02, with a nose of fresh sage and a fresh, attractive palate, is another likeable wine, while the simpler, fruity red Rupestro '02 has aromas of sharp cherries and drinks very easily.

● Sartiano '01	♟♟	4*
○ Grechetto '02	♟	3
○ Orvieto Cl. Vigneto Torricella '02	♟	4
● Umbria Sangiovese '97	♟♟	2*
○ Orvieto Cl. Vigneto Torricella '00	♟♟	3*
○ Orvieto Cl. Vigneto Torricella '01	♟♟	3*
● Umbria Sangiovese '99	♟	2*

● Nero della Greca '01	♟♟	5
○ Orvieto Cl. Sup. Colbadia '02	♟♟	4*
○ Orvieto Cl. Sup. L'Armida '02	♟♟	5
○ Orvieto Cl. Sup. Febeo '02	♟	4
● Rupestro '02	♟	3
● Arciato '98	♟♟	3*
● Nero della Greca '98	♟♟	4
○ Orvieto Cl. Sup. L'Armida '00	♟♟	4
● Arciato '99	♟♟	3*
● Nero della Greca '99	♟♟	4
● Arciato '01	♟♟	5
● Nero della Greca '00	♟♟	5
○ Orvieto Cl. Sup. Colbadia '01	♟♟	4*

ORVIETO (TR)

ORVIETO (TR)

DECUGNANO DEI BARBI
LOC. FOSSATELLO DI CORBARA, 50
05019 ORVIETO (TR)
TEL. 0763308255
E-MAIL: info@decugnanodeibarbi.com

LA CARRAIA
LOC. TORDIMONTE, 56
05018 ORVIETO (TR)
TEL. 0763304013
E-MAIL: info@lacarraia.it

The wines of Decugnano dei Barbi, Orvieto's leading estate, rank alongside the best in the region. The winery, founded in 1973 and owned by Claudio Barbi, continues to show great dynamism and forward thinking, so there are numerous developments to be seen on the estate. First comes an elegant new facility for visitors. The design was inspired by an ancient church, and it has a spacious tasting room, a kitchen and guestrooms. Then there is plenty of action in the wine area, overseen by skilled oenologist Corrado Cugnasco, with experiments in progress, new vines in production and new wines in prospect. The first of these to emerge is Pinot Nero '01 which, after prolonged bottle ageing, is finally on the market. It is a good light ruby red and the varietal nose is complex, offering wild berries, tobacco and leather. The palate is rich and even, with overt ripe red berry fruit and, on the finish, hints of sweet spices. Lago di Corbara "IL", from sangiovese with cabernet sauvignon, merlot and syrah, always makes a great impression and the '00 is no exception. It's elegant and harmonious on the nose, then soft and long on the palate. The estate's long tradition of "vini da meditazione", serious, reflective dessert wines, is honoured by Pourriture Noble and this year we found the '01 really impressive. Full of pineapple and mango, it has just the right amount of sweetness. Orvieto Classico "IL" '02 is also first-rate, with its melon and white peach tones. The Brut Classico Millesimato '00, Orvieto '02 and Lago di Corbara '01 are all well worth One Glass.

Odoardo Gialletti and Riccardo Cotarella have formed a solid partnership. What's more, it's a highly successful, at this estate set in the heart of Orvieto Classico. They have 128 hectares of vineyard and produce a more than respectable 650,000 bottles or so a year. Quality at all levels is always high and consistent. This year, there wasn't that extra something that would have given really significant scores, but the wines submitted had both character and complexity, as the panel discovered. Tizzonero '01, from montepulciano, sangiovese and cabernet sauvignon, and aged six months in barrique, is a case in point. It made a very good impression at the tasting finals. The nose is fruity and vegetal, with field berries and ripe blackberry. The palate is elegant and beautifully textured, although perhaps slightly too firm in acid and tannin. Sangiovese '02 is highly enjoyable. Its aromas of blackberry and blueberry and a fresh palate make for excellent drinking. Orvieto Classico Poggio Calvelli '02 is as well-typed as ever, although the difficult vintage means that it only just gained One Glass. The only low point this year is the much-lauded Fobiano. The '01 is well below par with, quite honestly, too much oak on the nose and an over-firm, slightly thin and excessively oaky palate.

● Lago di Corbara "IL" '00	♥♥	6
● Lago di Corbara Pinot Nero '01	♥♥	7
○ Orvieto Cl. Sup. Pourriture Noble '01	♥♥	6
○ Orvieto Cl. Sup. "IL" '02	♥♥	5
○ Decugnano dei Barbi Brut M. Cl. '00	♥	5
● Lago di Corbara '01	♥	4
○ Orvieto Cl. Sup. Decugnano dei Barbi '02	♥	4
● "IL" Rosso '98	♥♥♥	5
● "IL" Rosso '94	♥♥	5
● "IL" Rosso '95	♥♥	5
● "IL" Rosso '96	♥♥	5
● "IL" Rosso '97	♥♥	5
○ Orvieto Cl. Sup. "IL" '00	♥♥	4
○ Orvieto Cl. Sup. "IL" '01	♥♥	5
● "IL" Rosso '99	♥♥	6

● Tizzonero '01	♥♥	4
● Umbria Sangiovese '02	♥♥	3*
● Fobiano '01	♥	5
○ Orvieto Cl. Poggio Calvelli '02	♥	3
● Fobiano '98	♥♥♥	5
● Fobiano '99	♥♥♥	6
● Fobiano '95	♥♥	4
● Fobiano '96	♥♥	4
● Fobiano '97	♥♥	4
● Fobiano '00	♥♥	5
● Tizzonero '00	♥♥	3*
● Umbria Sangiovese '01	♥♥	3*

ORVIETO (TR)

TENUTA LE VELETTE
LOC. LE VELETTE, 23
05019 ORVIETO (TR)
TEL. 076329090
E-MAIL: tenuta.le.velette@libero.it

ORVIETO (TR)

PALAZZONE
LOC. ROCCA RIPESENA, 68
05010 ORVIETO (TR)
TEL. 0763344921
E-MAIL: palazzone@palazzone.com

Corrado and Cecilia Bottai's Le Velette estate is among those that best express the potential of Umbria's terrain. It lies in the township of Orvieto and has 104 hectares under vine, including an important area given over to experimental varieties. The white grapes typical of the area – grechetto, verdello, drupeggio and malvasia – are grown, as well as the international chardonnay and sauvignon blanc. For the reds, there are sangiovese and canaiolo, and so-called "improver" varieties, such as cabernet sauvignon and merlot. At the helm of cellar operations we find Gabriella Tani who has been here since 1989. This year, the estate again produced a highly promising range. Le Velette's two vineyard selections, Calanco and Gaudio, remain its best wines. Both gained Two Glasses. Calanco, from sangiovese with some cabernet sauvignon, is a thoroughbred that won Three Glasses for the '95 vintage. This year's version, the '00, is a good dark ruby-purple. The complex aromas of ripe cherry and blackberry mingling with subtle hints of black pepper are broad and powerful. The palate is balanced and very long, revealing vegetal tones and well delineated tannins. Gaudio, 100 per cent Merlot and also from the '00 vintage, is no less impressive. It has clean vegetal aromas of mown hay and complex notes of super-ripe red berry fruit leading to a full, harmonious palate with excellent extract, racy acidity and vigorous tannins. Traluce '02, from sauvignon, and Orvieto Secco '02 are, as usual, attractive and good drinking.

Renovation has begun on the ancient property that gave its name to the entire estate of Palazzone. The building, which hails from the end of the 13th century, will become a "locanda", or guestroom complex, including a restaurant, a tasting room and a meetings room. The task of restoration, so close to the heart of estate owner Giovanni Dubini, continues. There are 46 hectares, 24 of them planted to vine, with the accent on white varieties because this is what local traditions demand and because Giovanni is not the sort to follow market trends blindly. This year, he gave us a great Orvieto Classico Superiore Terre Vineate '02 with captivating aromas of banana and hazelnut, a refreshing palate recalling bergamot and white damson, and an attractive almondy finish. The white L'Ultima Spiaggia '02, from the unusual viognier, is also very good. Attractive and refreshing, it has good body and notes of oak, fruit and sage. The Sangiovese '01 also picked up a comfortable Two Glasses for its aromas and elegant flavours of roast coffee, pepper and ripe blackberry, and a ripe, smooth tannic weave on the warm, powerful palate. A notch down came Muffa Nobile '02, from 100 per cent sauvignon, with its unmistakable candied fruit, the perfumed Grechetto '02 and Orvieto Classico Superiore Campo del Guardiano '02, the last of these possibly a little over-evolved. We finish with two reds, Rubbio '02, a Sangiovese with that puts firmness first, and Umbria Rosso Armaleo '01, which is considerably less impressive than the previous vintage.

●	Calanco '00	🍷🍷	5
●	Gaudio '00	🍷🍷	5
○	Orvieto Cl. Secco '02	🍷	3
○	Traluce '02	🍷	4
●	Calanco '95	🍷🍷🍷	5
●	Calanco '91	🍷🍷	5
●	Calanco '96	🍷🍷	5
●	Calanco '97	🍷🍷	5
●	Gaudio '97	🍷🍷	5
●	Calanco '98	🍷🍷	5
●	Gaudio '98	🍷🍷	5
●	Calanco '99	🍷🍷	5
●	Gaudio '99	🍷🍷	5

●	Sangiovese '01	🍷🍷	6
○	L'Ultima Spiaggia '02	🍷🍷	4
○	Orvieto Cl. Sup. Terre Vineate '02	🍷🍷	3*
●	Armaleo '01	🍷	6
○	Grechetto '02	🍷	3
○	Muffa Nobile '02	🍷	5
○	Orvieto Cl. Sup. Campo del Guardiano '02	🍷	4
●	Rubbio '02	🍷	3
●	Armaleo '95	🍷🍷🍷	6
●	Armaleo '97	🍷🍷🍷	6
●	Armaleo '98	🍷🍷🍷	6
●	Armaleo '00	🍷🍷🍷	6
○	Muffa Nobile '98	🍷🍷	4
●	Rubbio '00	🍷🍷	3*
●	Rubbio '01	🍷🍷	3*

PANICALE (PG)

LAMBORGHINI - LA FIORITA
LOC. SODERI, 1
06064 PANICALE (PG)
TEL. 0758350029
E-MAIL: info@lamborghinionline.it

Patrizia Lamborghini's La Fiorita estate kept its now customary appointment with our Three Glass award. For some years now, she has been astounding us with the excellence of her wines. These hail from the Panicale hills, a short hop from Lake Trasimeno, and the estate, which was founded in 1968, now has 32 hectares of cordon spur-trained vineyard, with merlot, sangiovese and ciliegiolo the dominant varieties. Consultant oenologist Riccardo Cotarella overseeing cellar operations. Umbria Rosso Campoleone '01 is absolutely fascinating. From a 50-50 blend of merlot and sangiovese, and given a good 12 months of barrique ageing, it is a good, dark purple-red colour. The nose is full of sweet oakiness and complex notes of ripe red berry fruits, leading to spicy, pervasive aromas of black pepper, vanilla and cocoa powder. It is full and powerful on the palate, which is austere with noble tannins, flavours of ripe blackberry, blackcurrant and sweet spices, and great character and depth. It should be stressed that there are a good 40,000 bottles of this Three Glass wine and the price is more than fair. Lamborghini's second wine, Trescone '01, from 50 per cent sangiovese with ciliegiolo and merlot, is also well made and earned a One Glass score. Fresh and vegetal on the nose, it shows delicate oakiness and distinct notes of ripe plum. The palate has medium structure with young tannins and is nicely soft.

PENNA IN TEVERINA (TR)

RIO GRANDE
LOC. MONTECCHIE
05028 PENNA IN TEVERINA (TR)
TEL. 0744993102
E-MAIL: info@aziendaagricolariogrande.com

The wines of this attractive estate, in the hands of Francesco Pastore since 1988 and lying right on the regional border with Lazio, continue to be excellent. The estate now has around 54 hectares in total, of which 12 were planted in the early 1990s, with precedence given to international varieties, such as chardonnay and cabernet sauvignon. There is also a modern cellar, built under the main villa. Casa Pastore Rosso '01, a 50-50 blend of sangiovese and cabernet sauvignon aged a year in small oak casks, was again, we felt, the estate's best wine. It is a good ruby red tinged with purple. The broad nose has vegetal notes of bell pepper with elegant nuances of pencil lead. There is strong initial impact on the medium-bodied palate, which is possibly still a little green but has tannins of good texture and a long, clean finish. I Ricordi '00, a 100 per cent cabernet of pronounced varietal character on both nose and palate, is on the same wavelength. Although still young, it already has good overall balance, especially on the palate, where its attack is soft, its texture good and its finish tight. Although not quite as good as last year's, the '02 Poggio Muralto, from sangiovese with a little merlot, is quite agreeable. It puts the emphasis on fruity aromas, most markedly ripe cherry, and its slim, attractive palate.

● Campoleone '01	♛♛♛	6
● Trescone '01	♛	4
● Campoleone '99	♛♛♛	6
● Campoleone '00	♛♛♛	6
● Campoleone '97	♛♛	5
● Campoleone '98	♛♛	5
● Trescone '97	♛	3
● Trescone '98	♛	3
● Trescone '00	♛	3

● I Ricordi '00	♛♛	4
● Casa Pastore Rosso '01	♛♛	5
● Poggio Muralto '02	♛	4
● Casa Pastore Rosso '98	♛♛	4
● Casa Pastore Rosso '99	♛♛	5
● Poggio Muralto '00	♛♛	3*
● I Ricordi '98	♛♛	4
● Casa Pastore Rosso '00	♛♛	5
● Poggio Muralto '01	♛♛	4

PERUGIA

CARINI
FRAZ. CANNETO - COLLE UMBERTO
S.DA DEL TEGOLARO
06070 PERUGIA
TEL. 0755829103
E-MAIL: agrariacarini@libero.it

Brothers Carlo and Marco Carini's estate, a 140-hectare complex with numerous farmhouses, a "borgo", or internal village, and two small lakes, started operations in 2000 when the two inherited it from their father, Armando. The vines, covering roughly ten hectares of marly soil, lie between the slopes of Monte Tezio and the Lake Trasimeno flatlands, at altitudes of 270 to 400 metres. These promising conditions are complemented by the new, modern vinification cellar – a marvel of technology and style – and the attractive barrique cellar. The skilled hands of consultant oenologist Maurilio Chioccia and young agronomist Michele Baiocco, have given the estate's two wines that shot of class that has been so admired in the two vintages so far released. The red, from '01, a sort of long-aged version of last year's Tegolaro, is called Selezione Dedicata Armando, as it is dedicated to the founder of the estate. Produced in very limited numbers – no more than 1,600 bottles – from merlot with small amounts of sangiovese and cabernet sauvignon, it shows a good ruby. The nose homes in on the ripeness of the fruit, which heralds a base of firm, rich extract on the palate. The finish is also fair, although the tannins are a little dusty. The white, Umbria Bianco Poggio Canneto '02, from chardonnay, pinot bianco and grechetto, is decidedly impressive, with its attractive nuances of ripe fruit and pink grapefruit. When the vintage is taken into account, its uncommonly good structure becomes even more impressive and signals impeccable standards, especially in the vineyard.

CASTELLO DI ANTIGNIANO - BROGAL VINI
LOC. BASTIA UMBRA
VIA DEGLI OLMI, 9
06083 PERUGIA
TEL. 0758001501 - 0758000525
E-MAIL: amministrazione@vignabaldo.com

The Antigniano brand is assigned to the most important of the Brogal wines, those destined mainly for wine shops and restaurants. The estate, which has its main offices and bottling centre at Bastia, has vineyards and cellars both in Torgiano, where there are 52 hectares of vineyard, and Montefalco (30 hectares) and, uniquely, produces both Umbria's DOCGs. It also receives highly beneficial input from Riccardo Cotarella, which is, of course, not so unique. But let's get on to the wines. Torgiano Rosso Riserva Santa Caterina '99 is a very fine wine, with resonant notes of ripe blackberry and white pepper on both nose and palate. The palate also has good depth and concentration, although the fairly assertive tannins still need to soften down. The full, well-developed Torgiano Cabernet Sauvignon '99 and the fresh Antigniano Rosso '02 with its lightly minty finish are, in contrast, both ready to drink. Both are also fruit-driven with medium-structured palates. Another successful wine is the Grechetto. Its nose may still need to open out but the palate is clean and attractive, offering long notes of fruit, grass, sage and rosemary. On the Antigniano Montefalco front, a retaste of the '99 Sagrantino found the complexity and good structure we noted last year still intact.

●	Tegolaro Sel. Dedicata Armando '01	🍷🍷	6
○	Poggio Canneto '02	🍷🍷	4
●	Tegolaro '01	🍷🍷	6
○	Poggio Canneto '01	🍷	5

●	Torgiano Rosso Ris. Santa Caterina '99	🍷🍷	6
○	Grechetto dell'Umbria '02	🍷	3
●	Antigniano Rosso '02	🍷	3
●	Torgiano Cabernet Sauvignon '99	🍷	5
●	Torgiano Rosso Ris. Santa Caterina '97	🍷🍷	4
●	Torgiano Cabernet Sauvignon '98	🍷🍷	4
●	Montefalco Sagrantino '99	🍷🍷	6
●	Torgiano Cabernet Sauvignon '97	🍷	4
●	Montefalco Sagrantino '98	🍷	5

PERUGIA

GORETTI
LOC. PILA
S.DA DEL PINO, 4
06070 PERUGIA
TEL. 075607316
E-MAIL: goretti@vinigoretti.com

The estate of brothers Stefano and Gianluca Goretti has always been a Guide regular and is known as one of the most dynamic in Umbria. Its 13th-century tower has been restored to create an innovative, multi-purpose area with a wine shop, tasting room, kitchens and guestrooms. New vineyards have been planted and the modernization of its vinification plant is now almost completed. The most obvious development this year is the first release of the wines from the holding at Montefalco, especially because this new line, Le Mura Saracene, is highly impressive. The Sagrantino '98 is excellent with a good dark ruby colour and intense blackberry, blueberry and pepper on the nose. The palate is powerful, concentrated and ripe, with already-smooth tannins and a pervasive finish, enhanced by a light thread of balsam. Rosso di Montefalco '00 is clearly less complex, yet its primary, youthful aromas and its notes of cherry gently fading into delicate florality give it a personality of its own. Turning to the long-standing holding at Pila, in the Colli Perugini DOC, Fontanella Rosso '02, from sangiovese, merlot and montepulciano, deservedly won Two Glasses. There are aromas of wild rose and plum, well sustained by a long, well-balanced palate. The Colli Perugini Chardonnay '02, which is strongly varietal yet not predictable, is straw coloured, and has fully ripe fruit to fill the nose, offering a counterpoint to its lively, invigorating palate. Finally, there is the Vin Santo, which is well made and well styled in line with the traditions of the area.

SPELLO (PG)

SPORTOLETTI
LOC. CAPITAN LORETO
VIA LOMBARDIA, 1
06038 SPELLO (PG)
TEL. 0742651461
E-MAIL: office@sportoletti.com

This estate has been involved in agriculture since time immemorial, and for some years now its wines have been among the best in Umbria. Family-run, it is located at Spello and has 20 hectares planted to mainly international varieties, such as cabernet sauvignon, merlot and chardonnay, plus some sangiovese and the indigenous grechetto. It only began bottling in 1979. Riccardo Cotarella has consulted over the last few years – the years when Sportoletti has seen greatest success – but the estate's standing really comes from its leading wine, Villa Fidelia, made from merlot with small amounts of cabernets sauvignon and franc. This year, the '01 gained Two Glasses. The colour is a good purple-red and the nose elegant and finely-tuned, with firm vegetal tones and harmonious notes of ripe blackberry and blueberry, oriental spices and cinnamon. The palate is full, showimg slightly racy acidity and nicely hewn tannins but is a touch drying on the finish. The '01 release of Assisi Rosso, from sangiovese and merlot, is again successful. There is character, and delightful freshness, on the nose, then a clean, soft, vegetal palate of great drinkability. Grechetto di Assisi '02, with distinct scents of sharp damson and an attractively fresh palate, also gained One Glass.

● Fontanella Rosso '02	🍷🍷	2*
● Montefalco Sagrantino Le Mure Saracene '98	🍷🍷	6
● Montefalco Rosso Le Mure Saracene '00	🍷	4
○ Colli Perugini Chardonnay '02	🍷	3*
○ Umbria Vin Santo	🍷	4
● Colli Perugini Rosso L'Arringatore '95	🍷🍷	3*
● Colli Perugini Rosso L'Arringatore '98	🍷🍷	4
● Fontanella Rosso '01	🍷🍷	1*

● Villa Fidelia Rosso '01	🍷🍷	7
○ Assisi Grechetto '02	🍷	3
● Assisi Rosso '02	🍷	4
● Villa Fidelia Rosso '98	🍷🍷🍷	6
● Villa Fidelia Rosso '97	🍷🍷	4
● Villa Fidelia Rosso '99	🍷🍷	6
● Assisi Rosso '00	🍷🍷	4*
● Villa Fidelia Rosso '00	🍷🍷	7
● Assisi Rosso '01	🍷🍷	4

SPOLETO (PG)

SPOLETODUCALE
LOC. PETROGNANO, 54
06049 SPOLETO (PG)
TEL. 074356224
E-MAIL: spoletoducale@libero.it

After achieving fine reviews in the Other Wineries section for the past few years, this Colli Spoletini co-operative is now deservedly promoted to a full entry. Situated just a stone's throw from Castel Ritaldi, which explains why it produces Sagrantino, Spoletoducale started operations in 1969. It now has a reliable base of 600 members, led by new president Roberto Angelini Rota, and recently launched a quality line called Casale Triocco. For the present, it involves just 11 members who have agreed to drastic modifications in their vineyards. The aim is to improve grape quality and, to judge by our tastings, they are well on the way to achieving it. Sagrantino di Montefalco '00 is highly distinctive, and both the Rosso di Montefalco '01 and the Colli Martani Grechetto Arcato '02 are very good. But let's take one wine at a time. The Sagrantino is dark ruby red. The aromas are not yet fully expressed but the palate is powerful, concentrated, notably but not excessively alcoholic, and has flavours of blackberry and mulberry that fill the mouth as the wine slowly proceeds to its very long finish. The Rosso is quite different in style, as indeed it should be. All upfront fruit, cleanliness and ripeness on the nose, it has great drinkability on the palate. Finally comes the Grechetto, another traditional wine that may well have its quality zenith in Colli Martani. This example has medium structure, delicately floral aromas and a refreshing finish.

STRONCONE (TR)

LA PALAZZOLA
LOC. VASCIGLIANO
05039 STRONCONE (TR)
TEL. 0744607735 - 0744272357

La Palazzola, situated at Stroncone close to Terni, is indisputably one of the few very high quality estates in southern Umbria. It is owned by the eclectic Stefano Grilli, who in just a few years has completely transformed it into a well-organized winemaking centre, with separate vinification, barrique ageing and binning cellars. The wines showed well again this year: perhaps not as well as in some years, but well enough to convince us that even greater elegance and vigour are achievable. The estate's best wine is still Rubino, from cabernet sauvignon with a little merlot. The '01 is purple-ruby in colour. The nose is full of cassis and ripe blackberry, with underlying sensations of eastern spices, most notably black pepper. The palate has excellent character, fullness and length, the acid backbone is nicely held in place and the well-judged tannins are very elegant. The Sangiovese '01 is well-typed. It shows light ruby, introducing a fresh, fruity nose and then a soft, easy drinking palate. The Riesling Brut is as mouthfilling as ever, the '98 adding weight to the belief that Grilli is one of the best fizzmakers in central-southern Italy. It is deep straw, with a fine, creamy mousse. The complex nose reveals elegant reductive notes, then the palate is fresh with good acidic structure. We finish with Vendemmia Tardiva '00. A light amber-yellow ushers in tropical fruit and iodine-like saltiness on the nose, then super-ripeness with a good level of sweetness on the palate.

● Montefalco Sagrantino Casale Triocco '00	♀♀	5
● Montefalco Rosso Casale Triocco '01	♀♀	4*
○ Colli Martani Grechetto Arcato Casale Triocco '02	♀	2*
● Montefalco Rosso '00	♀♀	3*
● Arcato Sangiovese '00	♀	3

● Rubino '01	♀♀	5
○ La Palazzola V. T. '00	♀	5
○ Riesling Brut M. Cl. '98	♀	4
● Sangiovese '01	♀	3
● Merlot '97	♀♀♀	5
● Rubino '95	♀♀	4
● Rubino '96	♀♀	5
● Rubino '97	♀♀	5
○ La Palazzola V. T. '98	♀♀	5
● Merlot '98	♀♀	5
● Rubino '98	♀♀	5
● Merlot '99	♀♀	5
○ La Palazzola V. T. '99	♀♀	5
● Rubino '99	♀♀	5
● Rubino '00	♀♀	5

TODI (PG)

TORGIANO (PG)

TODINI
FRAZ. COLLEVALENZA
06059 TODI (PG)
TEL. 075887122 - 075887222
E-MAIL: agricola@agricolatodini.com

LUNGAROTTI
VIA MARIO ANGELONI, 16
06089 TORGIANO (PG)
TEL. 075988661
E-MAIL: lungarotti@lungarotti.it

We have been following Agricola Todini carefully for some time now. To judge by the quality of the wines tasted, we were wise to do so. The estate extends over 300 hectares of green hillside just six kilometres from Todi. Some 25 hectares are dedicated to vineyards, cultivated in line with modern precepts. At the heart of the holding is the Relais, a fabulous period building with guestrooms and a restaurant serving Umbrian specialities, matched with the estate's wines. Credit for the quality of the range goes to agronomist Roberto Corsetti, who works with the ever-reliable Maurilio Chioccia, supervisor of cellar operations. Nero della Cervara Selezione '01, from equal parts of cabernet sauvignon and merlot, aged 12 months in barrique, is excellent. Full and rich on both nose and palate, it is still a little oak dominated. Colli Martani Sangiovese Rubro '01 is equally admirable. Its nose is still a little closed, although good fruitiness, recalling ripe plum, is beginning to emerge. Fairly pronounced acidity, assuring good ageing potential, marks out the palate, which also has encouragingly good extract. Overall, it's a promising wine, perhaps a little rustic but honest, resorting neither to cliché nor artifice. Similar things could be said about its white partner, Colli Martani Grechetto di Todi '02, the most native of native varieties. Distinct aromas of white damson and lime blossom set the scene for a fresh, lively palate that has more to offer than structure. All in all, it's an enticingly enjoyable wine and a delight to drink.

There is no doubt that Lungarotti is the estate that has shaped Umbria's recent wine history. For good or ill, every aspect of the region's wine scene is tied in some way to the figure of the patriarchal Giorgio Lungarotti. His daughters, Chiara and Teresa, are now running the estate and after some years of ups and downs, they seems at last to be bringing the range back to the splendid standards that once marked it out. Naturally, this is no mere coincidence. Behind the quality revival are significant investments in vineyards and cellar. Above all, there is a new winemaking team, led by Vincenzo Pepe, the estate's oenologist, with Lorenzo Landi and Denis Dubourdieu as super-consultants. Results have followed quickly, the first signs already being apparent in the wines tasted for this year's Guide. The best is Giubilante '01, a red from montepulciano, sangiovese, canaiolo and cabernet. It is a good dark purple, with a complex nose of blackberry and blueberry, its oak well assimilated into the fruit. The palate is warm and powerful, yet very elegant, with firm, decisive extract on the finish. The excellent Cabernet Sauvignon '00 is strongly varietal and very clean on both nose and palate. A taste of Rosso Rubesco Riserva Vigna Monticchio '97, with its super-ripe red berry fruit nose and full, powerful palate, shows clearly why this wine was once rated so highly. Rubesco '00 is well-typed and good drinking, as is the rather retro-styled San Giorgio '97. The Chardonnay Aurente '01 scores just One Glass, as it is a little over-evolved and rather oak-dominated.

● Colli Martani Sangiovese Rubro '01	♟♟	6
● Nero della Cervara Sel. '01	♟♟	8
○ Colli Martani Grechetto di Todi '02	♟	4
● Colli Martani Sangiovese Rubro '99	♟	3
● Colli Martani Sangiovese Rubro '00	♟	5

● Giubilante '01	♟♟	5
● Cabernet Sauvignon '00	♟♟	4
● Torgiano Rosso V. Monticchio Ris. '97	♟♟	6
● Torgiano Rosso Rubesco '00	♟	4
○ Chardonnay Aurente '01	♟	5
● San Giorgio '97	♟	6
● Torgiano Rosso V. Monticchio Ris. '78	♟♟♟	6
● Torgiano Rosso V. Monticchio Ris. '88	♟♟	5
● Torgiano Rosso V. Monticchio Ris. '90	♟♟	5
● San Giorgio '93	♟♟	6
● Cabernet Sauvignon '98	♟♟	4
○ Chardonnay Aurente '00	♟♟	5
● Giubilante '00	♟♟	5
● San Giorgio '95	♟♟	6
● Cabernet Sauvignon '99	♟♟	4

OTHER WINERIES

TENUTA DI SALVIANO
LOC. CIVITELLA DEL LAGO
VOC. SALVIANO, 44
05020 BASCHI (TR)
TEL. 0744950459

This estate, owned by the Principi Corsini, makes very nice wines. The best is the red Lago di Corbara Solideo '00, which has a fruity, complex nose and a lively palate of fair concentration. The '02 Orvieto Classico Superiore, with its fresh, pervasive sage and tropical fruit, is as good as ever.

● Lago di Corbara Solideo '00	♟	4
○ Orvieto Cl. Sup. '02	♟	4

FATTORIA MILZIADE ANTANO
LOC. COLLE ALLODOLE
06031 BEVAGNA (PG)
TEL. 0742360371

Milziade Antano is considered one of Montefalco's traditionalists. Sadly, his wines have been a tad tired recently. The best is the raisiny, warm Sagrantino di Montefalco Passito '00. The ripe blackberry Rosso di Montefalco Riserva '01 and the slightly dilute Sagrantino di Montefalco '00 are nice.

● Montefalco Sagrantino '00	♟	5
● Montefalco Sagrantino Passito '00	♟	5
● Montefalco Rosso Ris. '01	♟	5

DI FILIPPO
VIA CONVERSINO, 160/A
06033 CANNARA (PG)
TEL. 0742731242
E-MAIL: difilippo@bcsnet.it

Two good, well-styled reds mark out Roberto and Italo Di Filippo's estate this year: Terre di San Nicola '99, with a nose giving cooked plum and oaky notes, and Poggio Madrigale '98, well-made but slightly over-evolved on both nose and palate.

● Poggio Madrigale '98	♟	4
● Terre di S. Nicola Rosso '99	♟	3
● Terre di S. Nicola Rosso '97	♟♟	3*
● Poggio Madrigale '97	♟♟	4

PIEVE DEL VESCOVO
VIA G. LEOPARDI, 82
06073 CORCIANO (PG)
TEL. 0756978874
E-MAIL: lucciaio@pievedelvescovo.com

After rethinking many aspects of production, Pieve del Vescovo returns to our Guide with new gloss. Its pleasing '00 Lucciaio offers complex fruit and vegetal hints on the nose, and a soft palate of medium concentration with good tannic weight. Riccardo Cotarella has long been the consultant here.

● C. del Trasimeno Rosso Lucciaio '00	♟	5
● C. del Trasimeno Rosso Lucciaio '97	♟♟	4
● C. del Trasimeno Rosso Lucciaio '98	♟♟	4
● C. del Trasimeno Rosso Lucciaio '99	♟♟	5

LE CRETE
VOC. MARTINOZZI, 89
05024 GIOVE (TR)
TEL. 0744992443
E-MAIL: az.agr.lecrete@virgilio.it

After a good first showing last year, Le Crete has confirmed its standing. Particularly good is the red Petranera '02. The good purple-ruby introduces a complex nose ripe red berry fruits and sweet oakiness. The palate is clean and well structured, with good concentration and tannic weight.

● Petranera '02	♀	5
● Petranera '01	♀♀	5

PUCCIARELLA
LOC. VILLA DI MAGIONE
06063 MAGIONE (PG)
TEL. 0758409147
E-MAIL: azienda.pucciarella@virgilio.it

Owned by the Cariplo bank, Pucciarella is a new entry to the Guide. All the wines are well made and earned One Glass scores. The fresh, tropical fruit Chardonnay Arsiccio '01 is nice. Empireo '01 is equally good, if a tad forward. Vin Santo Eletto has distinctive notes of dried figs and walnutskin.

○ Chardonnay Arsiccio '01	♀	4
● Empireo '01	♀	4
○ Vin Santo Eletto	♀	4

TERRE DEL CARPINE
VIA FORMANUOVA, 87
06063 MAGIONE (PG)
TEL. 075840298
E-MAIL: cit@trasinet.com

This is a wait-and-see year for the Terre del Carpine co-operative. Still, we enjoyed an excellent, clean '01 Merlot with sweet fruit and vegetal scents coming through well on the nose. The '01 Colli del Trasimeno Rosso Barca is well typed, but a touch too dilute on the palate to merit Two Glasses.

● C. del Trasimeno Rosso Barca '01	♀	2*
● Merlot '01	♀	3
● C. del Trasimeno Rosso Barca '00	♀♀	2*

UMBRIA VITICOLTORI ASSOCIATI
LOC. CERRO
06055 MARSCIANO (PG)
TEL. 0758748989
E-MAIL: info@viniumbri.it

The 3,300 members of this co-operative produce two good wines. The Chardonnay Raffaellesco '01, has appley fruit, florality and sweet oakiness on the nose, then a palate of good body and depth. Sagrantino di Montefalco Raffaellesco '99 shows super-ripe fruit on the nose and well-judged tannicity.

○ Chardonnay Raffaellesco '01	♀	3*
● Montefalco Sagrantino Raffaellesco '99	♀	6
○ Chardonnay Vigne Umbre '98	♀♀	2*

FATTORIA LE POGGETTE
LOC. LE POGGETTE
05026 MONTECASTRILLI (TR)
TEL. 0744940338

Fattoria Le Poggette has 18 hectares of vine on the hills straddling Montecastrilli and San Gemini. Umbria Rosso Torre Maggiore was absent this year. However, Colli Amerini Rosso Superiore '01 has fair concentration and good aromatic depth, and the nice, ripe plum-like Canaiolo '01 also showed well.

● C. Amerini Rosso Sup. '01	♀	3
● Canaiolo '01	♀	4
● C. Amerini Rosso Sup. '00	♀♀	3
● Torre Maggiore '99	♀♀	5

TENUTA ALZATURA
LOC. FRATTA - ALZATURA, 108
06036 MONTEFALCO (PG)
TEL. 0742399435
E-MAIL: info@tenuta-alzatura.it

After its good debut last year, we had high hopes of Tenuta Alzatura. But its sole wine, Sagrantino di Montefalco Uno di Due, has yet to take off. The '99 is well typed, but not much more. The nose is over-ripe and the palate lacks concentration. Let's wait for the new vineyards to start producing.

● Montefalco Sagrantino Uno di Due '99	♀	7
● Montefalco Sagrantino Uno di Uno '98	♀♀	7

RUGGERI
VIA MONTEPENNINO, 5
06036 MONTEFALCO (PG)
TEL. 0742379294

Ruggeri, a small Montefalco estate, makes its return to the Guide this year. Its flagship Sagrantino di Montefalco Passito '00 has raisined red berry fruits and a warm, complex palate. The '01 Rosso di Montefalco is very nice, with good fruit on the nose and a good weight of tannin on the palate.

●	Montefalco Sagrantino Passito '00	♟	6
●	Montefalco Rosso '01	♟	4

FREDDANO
FRAZ. FOSSATELLO, 34
05018 ORVIETO (TR)
TEL. 0763308248
E-MAIL: giuliofreddano@tiscalinet.it

Giulio Freddano's estate, based near Orvieto, has slipped back into the Other Wineries section. His wines are good, but not quite good enough. Lago di Corbara Fontauro leads the range, but this year's '01 has excessive oak and insufficient concentration. Grechetto Vertunno '02 is well typed.

●	Lago di Corbara Fontauro '01	♟	4
○	Grechetto Vertunno '02	♟	3
●	Lago di Corbara Fontauro '99	♟♟	4
●	Lago di Corbara Fontauro '00	♟♟	4

TORDIMARO
LOC. TORDIMONTE, 37
05019 ORVIETO (TR)
TEL. 0763304227
E-MAIL: tordimaro@tiscalinet.it

Another good showing for Tordimano. Rosso Orvietano Il Tordimaro '00 is just a notch below Two Glasses and has pervasive ripe blackberry aromas. Torrello '01 is also good, with vegetal aromas of wild berries and good fleshiness. The well-made '01 Passito is full of tropical fruit.

●	Rosso Orvietano Il Tordimaro '00	♟	5
○	Passito '01	♟	5
●	Umbria Torrello '01	♟	4

CHIORRI
LOC. SANT' ENEA - VIA TODI, 100
06070 PERUGIA
TEL. 075607141
E-MAIL: info@chiorri.it

Marta and Monica Mariotti run this estate at Sant'Enea, near Perugia, with their father Tito. The best wines are two vintages of Colli Perugini Rosso. The '01, tasted last year, has a clean, ripe blackberry nose, and the '02, a touch thin on the palate, has vegetal hints and fresh red berry fruit.

●	Colli Perugini Rosso '02	♟	3
●	Colli Perugini Rosso '00	♟♟	2*
●	Colli Perugini Rosso '01	♟♟	3*

CANTINE PERUSIA
LOC. PONTE PATTOLI
S.DA PATTOLI - RESINA, 1/A-16
06100 PERUGIA
TEL. 075694175

Maurilio Chioccia consults for this co-operative on the outskirts of Perugia. Vencaia Terre di Braccio '02, a white from trebbiano, malvasia and grechetto, has a clean nose and excellent concentration on the palate. Terre di Braccio '02, with raisined red berry fruitiness, is good, too.

○	Vencaia Bianco Terre di Braccio '02	♟♟	3*
●	Valmora Rosso Terre di Braccio '02	♟	4

I GIRASOLI DI SANT'ANDREA
LOC. MOLINO VITELLI
06010 UMBERTIDE (PG)
TEL. 0759410798 - 0759410837
E-MAIL: igirasolidisandrea@tiscalinet.it

I Girasoli di Sant'Andrea did well this year with two more than respectable wines. The mainly sangiovese Il Doge '01 is the estate's best wine, with a spicy nose and a well-textured palate. Ca' Andrea '02 is more fruit-driven, with cherry flavours, good freshness and concentration in the mouth.

●	Il Doge '01	♟	6
●	Ca' Andrea '02	♟	4
●	Il Doge '00	♟	6

LAZIO

For many years, winemaking in Lazio cruised along, safe in the knowledge that the large and not particularly quality-conscious market of Rome would ensure that, whatever happened, everything would get sold in the end. Now, however, there are stirrings. A lot has to do with better technical standards, both in grape growing and winemaking. Nevertheless, with the exception of one large winery, Fontana Candida, all the initiative is coming from a handful of small and medium-sized producers, rather than taking the form of a general, bottom-up trend. The heroic pioneers of fine winemaking in Lazio are Paola and Armando Di Mauro, Giulio and Fabrizio Santarelli, Antonio Santarelli, Piero Costantini, Francesco Trimani, Riccardo and Renzo Cotarella, Sergio Mottura, Enrico Massimo Zandotti and Christine Vaselli. There's not a single co-operative winery because in Lazio, these turn out wines that are at best well made but scale no great heights. Neither have any large, national wine companies – except Gruppo Italiano Vini – shown interest in producing wine in the region. Yet there are few places in Italy as well suited to wine production as certain parts of Lazio. And we don't mean just the Castelli Romani, where urban sprawl has, with or without legal sanction, already turned fields that were once covered with vines and olives into building land. No, we are thinking of Tuscia Laziale, between Montalto di Castro and Tarquinia, where the soils and the lie of the land are strikingly similar to those in the nearby and currently very fashionable Maremma of Grosseto. We are thinking of the hills around Lake Bolsena, where the Falesco estate produces Montiano, a Merlot that rivals the best of the wines produced from the same grape in Tuscany and Friuli. We are thinking of the Ciociaria hills, of Piglio and its cesanese grape which, if worked judiciously, could give reds of similar body and concentration to the best Montepulciano d'Abruzzo, for example. And we are also aware that in the adjacent regions of Tuscany and Campania, small areas attract much more attention. A DOC like Cori, for example, which is based on a single variety, nerobuono, and is set in a wonderful landscape, would probably be on everyone's lips if situated elsewhere. We shall console ourselves by citing this year's three Three Glass awards, the highest number ever awarded to the region: Grechetto Latour a Civitella '01 from Mottura; Montiano '01 from Falesco; and Vigna del Vassallo '01 from Paola Di Mauro. And to Paola Di Mauro we also proffer our best wishes for being as sharp and sprightly at 80 as she was when she was 50. Could her wines have something to do with this?

ANAGNI (FR)

ANAGNI (FR)

CASALE DELLA IORIA
LOC. LA GLORIA
S.DA PROVINCIALE ANAGNI - PALIANO KM 4.200
03012 ANAGNI (FR)
TEL. 077556031
E-MAIL: perinelli@tiscalinet.it

COLACICCHI
LOC. ROMAGNANO
03012 ANAGNI (FR)
TEL. 064469661
E-MAIL: info@colacicchi.it

Cellar modernization continues at Paolo Perinelli's estate, for now the only property in the Piglio area that is focusing determinedly on innovation. Support comes from the skilled Roberto Mazzer, a young oenologist who has put his weight behind the Ciociaria cause. There is no Torre del Piano '02, at least there wasn't at the time of our tastings. It had not yet been cleared for release by Mazzer and, naturally, Perinelli went along with him. We'll come back to it next year. For now, we'll concentrate on Cesanese Casale della Ioria. As in many other parts of Italy, the 2002 vintage was not without its problems and difficulties. However, very good work was done in the cellars to get the best out of what could be salvaged, and the wine is actually rather good. There is some lack of complexity, and the texture is a little loose, but the fruit is good and delicate spiciness emerges. It is a wine best enjoyed for the next couple of years when, after the requisite bottle ageing, it should be at its peak. The year's real success is Passerina del Frusinate '02, a wine that is always regarded with diffidence locally. Yet Perinelli and Mazzer have learned how to shape it and give it verve, zestiness and freshness that meld into a wine of great harmony. And the price couldn't be fairer.

What a Schiaffo ("slap in the face") this is! There was an incredible showing from what should be a minor wine for Colacicchi. Instead, the 2002 vintage of Schiaffo, a classic Bordeaux blend with a little cesanese di Affile, is a jewel of a wine and more powerfully eloquent than ever before. It's a clear sign that the Trimani family, who own this long-standing estate originally farmed by the Colacicchi family, have been working hard on the wine. Romagnano Rosso '00, from the same grape blend, is on similar lines, with good concentration and no little weight. Naturally, the fine '00 vintage has played its part but, in any event, this is a wine that we have always followed with great interest. The '98 Torre Ercolana, the estate classic and practically the forebear of the rest of the range, also showed very well. It, too, comes from a cabernet, merlot and cesanese blend, but the proportions are not revealed. Although the '98 vintage was not one of the best, the wine has good, restrained body and very nice length, more than holding its own against the two outsiders. So far, so delicious. Next comes Romagnano Bianco '02, which is from five grapes, with malvasia del Lazio predominating. Given the vintage, it is naturally rather low key. There is some complexity, and the structure is not immense, but it is sufficient to give the wine decent presence.

● Cesanese del Piglio Casale della Ioria '02	♥	4
○ Passerina del Frusinate '02	♥	3
● Cesanese del Piglio Torre del Piano '00	♥♥	5
● Cesanese del Piglio Torre del Piano '01	♥♥	5
● Cesanese del Piglio Casale della Ioria '01	♥♥	4

● Romagnano Rosso '00	♥♥	5
● Schiaffo '02	♥♥	4
● Torre Ercolana '98	♥♥	6
○ Romagnano Bianco '02	♥	4
● Torre Ercolana '90	♥♥	5
● Torre Ercolana '91	♥♥	5
● Torre Ercolana '93	♥♥	5
○ Romagnano Bianco '94	♥♥	4
○ Romagnano Bianco '97	♥♥	4
● Torre Ercolana '97	♥♥	6
● Romagnano Rosso '99	♥♥	5

APRILIA (LT)

CASALE DEL GIGLIO
LOC. LE FERRIERE
S.DA CISTERNA-NETTUNO, KM 13
04010 APRILIA (LT)
TEL. 0692902530
E-MAIL: casaledelgiglio@tin.it

Antonio Santarelli is a skilled, respected producer but he's not yet had recognition in proportion to the results he's achieved. The range of wines released, under expert guidance from Paolo Tiefenthaler, is extensive and again this year several are outstanding, notably the '00 Cabernet Sauvignon. The style tends to Californian, with clearly balsamic aromas and a full, broad palate, rich in ripe wild cherries and rhubarb on the long finish. Madreselva '99 scored similarly. This is a splendid, barrique-aged blend from equal parts of merlot, cabernet sauvignon and petit verdot. It is penetrating and complex on the nose, with dried roses and small wild berry fruits, and has a full, attractively vegetal and nicely tannic palate. The best of the whites is Antinoo '00, from chardonnay enhanced by a good dose of viognier. The grapes were carefully selected and vinified with a skilled hand. The result is a structured, but not over-oaky, wine with good pineapple-like aromas and elegance on the palate. Sauvignon '02, full of yellow damson fruitiness, delicate flowers and attractive harmony, is also very good, while the '02 versions of Satrico, Chardonnay and the rosé Albiola offer their usual reliability and appeal. Best of the monovarietal reds are Petit Verdot, which has surprisingly good complexity and personality, and the full-bodied Merlot. Two notes to finish off. Aphrodisium '01, a late-harvest white, with fresh aromas of sage and lily of the valley, enters the lists this year but Mater Matuta is absent, as it was not ready in time for our tastings. It will be back next year.

ATINA (FR)

GIOVANNI PALOMBO
LOC. PONTE MELFA
C.SO MUNANZIO PLANCO
03042 ATINA (FR)
TEL. 0776610200
E-MAIL: vinipalombo@hotmail.com

This year, Duca Cantelmi leaves the stage to its less aristocratic companions. We will doubtless be meeting up with the "duke" again in the near future but for now, the main thing to report is the fine performance of Colle della Torre '01, a 90-10 mix of merlot and cabernet that almost reached the Three Glass finals. This "Pomerol from Ciociaria" has the sort of complex silkiness that lends fascination and a tight, dense weave. It is clear that Giovanni and Stephan Palombo, with their skilled oenologist, Roberto Mazzer, have made notable strides forward. However, we think that their real strong suit is still their range of top-notch everyday wines, the ones that are accessible to a wide range of consumers. Take, for example, Bianco delle Chiaie '02, a successful blend of malvasia del Lazio and vermentino. It holds together well and has a beautifully fragrant nose, then liveliness, presence and an overall complexity in the mouth that you very rarely come across. There's also the Rosso delle Chiaie '02, from a judicious blend of merlot and cabernet. It is tight-knit and very elegant, with notes of spices and jam that are in no hurry to fade away. And all this comes at a very keen price. We finish with the very well-styled Cabernet di Atina '02. It shows good concentration, and there is fair breadth spanning the various nuances of its aromas. The palate is fresh, even and satisfying.

● Cabernet Sauvignon '00	⟨⟨	5
○ Antinoo '00	⟨⟨	4
● Merlot '01	⟨⟨	3*
● Petit Verdot '01	⟨⟨	4
○ Sauvignon '02	⟨⟨	3*
● Madreselva '99	⟨⟨	5
○ Aphrodisium '01	⟨	7
○ Satrico '02	⟨	2
● Shiraz '01	⟨	4
⊙ Albiola '02	⟨	3
○ Chardonnay '02	⟨	3
● Mater Matuta '99	⟨⟨	6
● Madreselva '98	⟨⟨	4
○ Antinoo '99	⟨⟨	4
● Cabernet Sauvignon '99	⟨⟨	5*

● Colle della Torre '01	⟨⟨	6
○ Bianco delle Chiaie '02	⟨⟨	3
● Rosso delle Chiaie '02	⟨⟨	4*
● Atina Cabernet '02	⟨	5
● Cabernet Duca Cantelmi '97	⟨⟨	5
● Colle della Torre '97	⟨⟨	4
● Cabernet Duca Cantelmi '98	⟨⟨	5
● Colle della Torre '98	⟨⟨	4
● Cabernet Duca Cantelmi '99	⟨⟨	6
● Colle della Torre '00	⟨⟨	6
● Atina Cabernet '01	⟨⟨	5

CASTIGLIONE IN TEVERINA (VT)

PAOLO D'AMICO
FRAZ. VAIANO
LOC. PALOMBARO
01024 CASTIGLIONE IN TEVERINA (VT)
TEL. 0761948868 - 0668134079

CASTIGLIONE IN TEVERINA (VT)

TRAPPOLINI
VIA DEL RIVELLINO, 65
01024 CASTIGLIONE IN TEVERINA (VT)
TEL. 0761948381
E-MAIL: trappolini@tin.it

Possibly it is the sight of the nearby ravines that has instilled patience and calm in the D'Amico husband and wife team. Their estate is clearly aiming high, but it keeps a very low profile on the region's crowded wine scene. They leave the honour and the duty of embodying their estate philosophy to two tried and tested experts, Carlo Corino and Fabrizio Moltard. That philosophy is indeed perfectly represented by their two first-class wines, both exclusively from chardonnay. Falesia is the more powerful of the pair. The '01 is a deep, bright straw yellow tinged with gold. The nose, minerally and with warm aromas of honey and tomato leaf, has a complexity that is more often associated with France than Lazio. The palate is fat and fruity, but never cloys, with hints of tropical fruit, showing very long, with an admirably even texture. The second wine, Calanchi di Vaiano (the name means "ravines of Vaiano") '01, sees no wood, which enhances the impact of its varietal primary aromas. The end of 2003 or early 2004 sees the first release of a series of rather serious reds. We will have more to say about them very shortly.

It seems incredible, but in a growing year like 2002, which was challenging to say the least, Paolo and Roberto Trappolini managed to bring improvements to their wines, even the standard-label products. If you don't believe us, try the '02 Est Est Est di Montefiascone, which is surprisingly aromatic and also has a rather good streak of citrus. It is nicely savoury and even offers the luxury of a warm, vaguely tropical finish. An added plus is its excellent value for money. Another fine demonstration of something new going on in the cellar comes from Brecceto '02, a 50-50 blend of chardonnay and the indigenous grechetto, given a brief stay in wood. It is a thoroughly enjoyable, tasty, fruit-forward wine whose notes of vanilla are perfectly integrated into the whole. Here, too, the price is absolutely fair. However, Paterno '01, from 100 per cent sangiovese, was not quite as good as we had hoped. The wine is from a vintage that inspired mixed opinions, but which was hardly kind to grape growers. The complexity that so excited us last time round has been muddied this time. Similar considerations apply to Cenereto '02, from equal parts of sangiovese and montepulciano. It is reasonably complex but not very long, and is still unknit and uneven. It can only improve with time. The icing on the cake is Idea '02. Maybe it's just a bit of fun, or it could be the desire to get to grips with a neglected variety like aleatico, but whatever the case, we like the wine just as it is, sweet as a ratafia, dense and energizing.

O	Falesia '01	♥♥ 5	●	Paterno '01	♥♥	4
O	Calanchi di Vaiano '01	♥ 4	O	Brecceto '02	♥♥	3
O	Falesia '98	♟♟ 5	●	Idea '02	♥♥	4
O	Falesia '99	♟♟ 5	●	Cenereto '02	♥	2
O	Calanchi di Vaiano '00	♟♟ 4	O	Est Est Est di Montefiascone '02	♥	2
O	Falesia '00	♟♟ 5	●	Paterno '96	♟♟	3
			●	Idea '98	♟♟	4
			●	Paterno '98	♟♟	3
			●	Idea '99	♟♟	4
			●	Paterno '99	♟♟	3*
			●	Paterno '00	♟♟	4
			O	Brecceto '01	♟♟	3*
			●	Idea '01	♟♟	4

CASTIGLIONE IN TEVERINA (VT)   CERVETERI (RM)

CRISTINE VASELLI
P.ZZA DEL POGGETTO, 12
01024 CASTIGLIONE IN TEVERINA (VT)
TEL. 0761947008 - 0668307065
E-MAIL: info@christinevaselli.it

CANTINA CERVETERI
VIA AURELIA, KM 42,700
00052 CERVETERI (RM)
TEL. 069905677 - 069905697
E-MAIL: cantina@virgilio.it

Nothing has been allowed to get in the way of Christine Vaselli's progress with Le Poggere. In any case, apprehensions vanished when it was first entrusted to the tender loving care of high-calibre technician, Riccardo Cotarella. There are no longer any signs of the initial hiccups with the wine, so Christine has decided to involve herself in two new projects, a new pinot nero-based red to appear with the 2003 vintage, which will no doubt be up to the standards of its big brother, and the creation of a new estate in the Marche where, with Riccardo and Renzo Cotarella's daughters, she will be working on the creation of a great Rosso Conero. It is obvious that this elegant young lady has no fear of putting herself to the test. Let's get back to Le Poggere which, we remind you, comes from a felicitous blend of cabernet sauvignon and merlot. The '01 growing year, which was not especially brilliant, has not dented its solid polyphenolic structure at all. The wine has a strikingly dense, tight weave, enhanced by several months in oak barrels. The nose is in perfect harmony, and reveals similar complexity. In short, here we have a great, international-style red, not dissimilar to certain Australian wines in its fullness of body, richness and depth from start to finish.

A step forwards has been taken at the Cerveteri co-operative. True, we were a bit critical of it in last year's Guide, but now we're happy to record the improvements, however modest they may be. Besides, we can't ignore the importance of the winery and the influence it exerts over a good part of northern Lazio. Neither the reds nor the whites from the Fontana Morella line of wines were submitted for tasting this year, as it was felt that the results obtained from the difficult 2002 vintage weren't up to our standards. But the Vigna Grande line was submitted, and stimulated great interest. Vigna Grande Bianco '02, from the tried and trusted blend of malvasia, trebbiano and chardonnay, is very good indeed, displaying impressive, persistent fragrance. The price is just right, too. The same applies to the beautifully made Vigna Grande Rosso '00, from merlot, montepulciano and sangiovese. The '02 Malvasia Villanova slipped a little in the rankings compared with last year, a sure sign that malvasia in Lazio was a particular victim of the poor weather. Menade '01, from the same varieties as the red Vigna Grande but in different proportions, is well styled, but lacks a bit of flesh and is rather uneven in texture. Tertium '00, from montepulciano and sangiovese, performed better and is a dense, deep wine of some character which, we feel, could well improve further with ageing.

● Le Poggere '01	🍷🍷	5
● Santa Giulia '91	🍷🍷	2
● Santa Giulia '92	🍷🍷	3
○ Orvieto Cl. Torre Sant'Andrea '93	🍷🍷	2
○ Orvieto Cl. Torre Sant'Andrea '94	🍷🍷	1
○ Orvieto Cl. Torre Sant'Andrea '95	🍷🍷	2
● Orvietano Rosso Torre Sant'Andrea '99	🍷🍷	5
● Le Poggere '00	🍷🍷	6

● Cerveteri Rosso Vigna Grande '00	🍷🍷	4
○ Cerveteri Bianco Vigna Grande '02	🍷🍷	4*
● Tertium '00	🍷	4
● Menade '01		2
○ Malvasia del Lazio Villanova '02		2
● Cerveteri Rosso Vigna Grande '97	🍷🍷	3
● Tertium '97	🍷🍷	3
● Cerveteri Rosso Vigna Grande '98	🍷🍷	3*
● Tertium '99	🍷🍷	4
○ Cerveteri Bianco Vigna Grande '01	🍷🍷	2*
● Cerveteri Rosso Vigna Grande '99	🍷🍷	3*

CIVITELLA D'AGLIANO (VT)   CORI (LT)

SERGIO MOTTURA
LOC. POGGIO DELLA COSTA, 1
01020 CIVITELLA D'AGLIANO (VT)
TEL. 0761914533
E-MAIL: vini@motturasergio.it

COLLE SAN LORENZO
VIA GRAMSCI, 52
04010 CORI (LT)
TEL. 069678001
E-MAIL: collesanlorenzo@libero.it

We don't know if Monsieur Latour has ever been to Civitella. It doesn't really matter. The important element in this estate's story is that the Beaune "négociant", Louis Latour, supplied Sergio Mottura with a number of barriques some years ago for Mottura to experiment with. As a beginning, it was not unlike so many others. But the tenacity and clear-thinking of this Piedmontese, and the support of his adviser, the highly skilled Marco Monchiero from Canale, may have been what set Latour a Civitella apart and led to its emergence. Now, the '01 edition has become Lazio's new Three Glass wine. It is made exclusively from grechetto and it is still aged in those small barrels from Beaune. It stirred up a lot of excitement at the tastings for its warm, silky softness, shot through with complex, almost tropical fruit nuances, and sustained length, which stays sweetly warm on the finish. Despite all this, we haven't forgotten that other fine wines also emerge from the Mottura cellar. Consider Muffo '01, for instance, made Sauternes-style from super-ripe grapes, or the sound Poggio della Costa '02, a strongly varietal Grechetto with fragrant notes of almond and sweet cicely. The value for money '02 Orvieto is fresh and fragrant on the palate and also showed well. Although overshadowed by the whites, Civitella's reds are more than decent, especially Magone, from pinot nero and other local varieties. The '01 is less incisive than in previous versions, but it is still a good wine. Civitella Rosso '02 and Vigna Tragugnano '02 deserve a mention.

There's no Colle Amato this year and it's a pity. The Ferretti brothers decided that it was better to hold fire, after the uninspiring growing year. And you can't make a mistake with an estate's leading wine. Syrah-lovers can get their fix in another way, though, in the new Shiraz '01. Its colour is a good purplish-red and there is excellent characteristic spiciness on the nose, which is also full of red and black berry fruitiness. All it lacks is a bit of concentration and length. Neither is intensity the strong point of the '01 Merlot, which reveals a somewhat restrained array of polyphenols and a rather lightly textured palate. Make no mistake, though, this is still a wine well above average. It's just that we are used to greater things from this estate. Costa Vecchia is a more than just decent wine that we would never fail to mention, and the '02 stands up well. From a multi-variety blend, it has a nicely dense structure, refined aromas and ripe, but well-behaved tannins. The '02 Chardonnay is also characterful. Careful vinification has given a wine of balanced structure, with good body but no heaviness, and good fruit that melds into the vanilla notes typical of ageing in small oak barrels.

○	Grechetto Latour a Civitella '01	🍷🍷🍷	4
○	Muffo '01	🍷🍷	5
○	Grechetto Poggio alla Costa '02	🍷	4
●	Magone '01	🍷	5
○	Orvieto Secco '02	🍷	3
●	Civitella Rosso '02		4
○	Orvieto Cl. Vigna Tragugnano '02		3
○	Muffo '97	🍷🍷	3
○	Grechetto Latour a Civitella '98	🍷🍷	4
○	Muffo '98	🍷🍷	3
○	Grechetto Latour a Civitella '99	🍷🍷	4
○	Grechetto Latour a Civitella '00	🍷🍷	5
●	Magone '00	🍷🍷	5
○	Muffo '00	🍷🍷	5

●	Merlot '01	🍷	4
●	Shiraz '01	🍷	4
○	Chardonnay del Lazio '02	🍷	4
●	Costa Vecchia '02	🍷	4
●	Colle Amato '97	🍷🍷	3
●	Colle Amato Pietrapinta '97	🍷🍷	5
●	Colle Amato '98	🍷🍷	3
●	Colle Amato Pietrapinta '98	🍷🍷	5*
●	Colle Amato '99	🍷🍷	5
○	Chardonnay del Lazio '00	🍷🍷	3
●	Colle Amato '00	🍷🍷	5
○	Chardonnay del Lazio '01	🍷🍷	3*

FRASCATI (RM)

CASALE MARCHESE
VIA DI VERMICINO, 68
00044 FRASCATI (RM)
TEL. 069408932
E-MAIL: info@casalemarchese.it

As announced last year, Casale Marchese has started to revive its range. Two people are mainly responsible for this, Paolo Peira, the young, talented oenologist who is re-organizing the estate set-up, and Alessandro Carletti, whom the family has asked to take on even greater management responsibility. We are still at a provisional stage, but the new regime is already making itself felt. Meanwhile, let's have a look at the wines. Vigna del Cavaliere is a well-tested Bordeaux blend that includes a few indigenous grapes, and is vinified in stainless steel before being given a year in barrique and a further year in bottle. With the '00, it remains at the top of the charts. There are distinct aromas of wild rose and wild berry fruits, then the palate has considerable complexity, with good body and tannicity, a tight structure and vanilla on the tasty finish. The '02 Rosso comes mainly from montepulciano, with some merlot and cabernet. The style is fresh, herbaceous and attractively fruity, and the palate is rounded, with the merest touch of mint on the finish. The classic Frascati Superiore had to cope with the difficult '02 vintage but, thanks to a content of 60 per cent early-picked malvasia puntinata, it has vibrancy of character, good aromatic freshness and intensity on the nose. Future developments include cellar refurbishments and the emergence of two new wines already mapped out. We wish Paolo and Alessandro every success.

FRASCATI (RM)

CANTINE SAN MARCO
LOC. VERMICINO
VIA DI MOLA CAVONA, 26/28
00044 FRASCATI (RM)
TEL. 069409403 - 069422689
E-MAIL: info@sanmarcofrascati.it

Everything starts from the link with the land and its vineyards. After almost 30 years dedicated mainly to Frascati, Umberto Notarnicola and Bruno Violo, the San Marco oenologist, have decided to part the waves with a boldly eclectic range of wines. The grapes, which come from 280 directly-supervised growers plus 12 hectares of co-operative-owned vineyard and 45 hectares on lease, are selected and vinified separately by variety and site. This takes effort, but balances out batches of varying ripeness and means the cellar tackle monovarietals in the modern style. The Solo line contains only single varietals, all produced exclusively in stainless steel to enhance their natural fruit characteristics. Soloshiraz '02 is full of personality, with an intense, balanced nose giving wild red berry fruits and incisive spiciness. Also good is Solomalvasia '02, which has aromas of broom and a round, ripe, almondy palate. The two Meraco wines were also designed to provoke. Meraco Frascati Superiore '01 is the only wine in the range that is barrique fermented. It has fresh notes of thyme and tropical fruit, with just perceptible oak and a pleasant finish. Meraco '98 is a blend of cesanese, sangiovese and cabernet, matured at length in barriques of varying ages. There is breadth and complexity on the nose, with leather, cherry and saffron, then a full palate with ripe tannins. Shiraz-Cabernet Sauvignon '02 has a stimulating spiciness and nice structure. The classic Frascati Superiore Selezione is also moving on for the '02 has impressive style, aroma and length.

● Vigna del Cavaliere '00	♟♟	5
○ Frascati Sup. '02	♟	4
● Rosso di Casale Marchese '02	♟	4
● Vigna del Cavaliere '96	♟♟	4
● Rosso di Casale Marchese '97	♟♟	3
● Vigna del Cavaliere '97	♟♟	4
● Vigna del Cavaliere '99	♟♟	5

○ Frascati Sup. Sel. '02	♟♟	3*
● Soloshiraz '02	♟♟	4
● Meraco Rosso '98	♟♟	4
○ Frascati Sup. Bianco Meraco '01	♟	4
○ Solomalvasia '02	♟	4
● Shiraz-Cabernet Sauvignon '02	♟	4

GROTTAFERRATA (RM)

CASTEL DE PAOLIS
VIA VAL DE PAOLIS
00046 GROTTAFERRATA (RM)
TEL. 069413648
E-MAIL: info@casteldepaolis.it

Yet again, there are interesting developments at Giulio and Fabrizio Santarelli's estate. First, extensive works are under way on a new cellar to be ready in summer 2004. Then there has been the decision to turn Campo Vecchio Bianco '02 into an IGT Lazio, allowing the inclusion of several indigenous varieties present in the estate's vineyards. The result is a fruity, floral wine full of fragrance and flavour, and with an elegant finish. Vigna Adriana, a white of great structure and finesse, which brings out the best elements in both the 65 per cent malvasia puntinata and, particularly, the 35 per cent viognier in the mix, had already made the same move. The '02 has full, penetrating aromas of tropical fruit and an intense, invigorating palate with a good thrust of acidity that refreshes through to the long finish, despite evident alcohol. The concentrated Quattro Mori '01, from 60 per cent syrah and, in reducing proportions, merlot, cabernet sauvignon and petit verdot, is anything but simplistic. It put up a first-rate performance to equal that of the Vigna Adriana. The blood red colour leads to clean sensations of coffee and ripe plum, which grow as tobacco emerges on the nose and a silky tannic weave appears on the palate. Campo Vecchio Rosso '01 shows well, too, with distinct, dense spiciness and notes of wild berry fruit, plus a refined tannicity. We finish with two more than decent wines. The '02 Frascati Superiore shows its habitual power and harmony, and Cannellino '02 has unusual aromas of sage and lavender.

MARINO (RM)

PAOLA DI MAURO
LOC. FRATTOCCHIE
VIA COLLE PICCHIONE, 46
00040 MARINO (RM)
TEL. 0693546329
E-MAIL: info@collepicchioni.it

This year, Paola Di Mauro marked her 80th spring. She remains bright, wise and affectionately outgoing. The first person in Lazio to go uncompromisingly for quality, Paola is determined to see her wines and estate are fully appreciated. Her son, Armando, is in charge of the vineyards and the cellar, working in synergy with Riccardo Cotarella, as much a family friend as a consultant. Paola's grandson, Valerio, is now also part of the team. Vigna del Vassallo '01, a fine Bordeaux blend vinified in stainless steel and aged in a mix of large old barrels and barriques, is simply fabulous. There are intense, elegant aromas of red berry fruits, violets and sweet spices to precede a palate that is balanced and structured with ripe tannins that develop well to a long, soft finish. Also excellent is Marino Selezione Oro '02, from white grapes grown on the estate. The bright gold ushers in well-defined aromas of spring flowers and crisp apples that are as stimulating as the full, long flavour, which leads to a dry, typically almondy finish. Le Vignole is steadily evolving as a wine and the '01 is particularly good, evincing a more accomplished use of sauvignon in the blend. This adds personality and finesse to a most attractive wine of good balance, fruit and body. The perfumed, flavoursome Marino Etichetta Verde '02 is surprisingly good, avoiding any trace of banality with its exemplary elegance and typing. The '02 Rosso is as sound as ever and has good intensity and pleasing fruit. The new, welcoming cellar will be ready in 2004, and there may well be some new wines, too.

O Vigna Adriana '02		5
● Quattro Mori '01		6
● Campo Vecchio Rosso '01		4
O Campo Vecchio Bianco '02		3*
O Frascati Cannellino '02		5
O Frascati Sup. '02		4
O Frascati Sup. '99		4
O Frascati Sup. V. Adriana '00		5
● Quattro Mori '99		5
● Quattro Mori '00		6
● Campo Vecchio Rosso '00		4
O Frascati Sup. '01		4
O Frascati Sup. Campo Vecchio '01		4*
O Vigna Adriana '01		5

● Vigna del Vassallo '01		6
O Le Vignole '01		4
O Marino Colle Picchioni Oro '02		4*
O Marino Etichetta Verde '02		3*
● Colle Picchioni Rosso '02		4
● Vigna del Vassallo '85		5
● Vigna del Vassallo '88		5
● Vigna del Vassallo '00		6
● Vigna del Vassallo '98		5
O Marino Colle Picchioni Oro '99		4
● Vigna del Vassallo '99		5*
● Colle Picchioni Rosso '00		4*
O Marino Colle Picchioni Oro '00		4*
● Colle Picchioni Rosso '99		4
O Marino Colle Picchioni Oro '01		4

MONTE PORZIO CATONE (RM)

FONTANA CANDIDA
VIA FONTANA CANDIDA, 11
00040 MONTE PORZIO CATONE (RM)
TEL. 069401881
E-MAIL: giv@giv.it

The figures speak for themselves. The 200 growers are followed every step of the way and their 97 hectares of vineyard in the heart of the Frascati DOC yield around 8,000,000 bottles a year. It all adds up to a winery of impressive dimensions that exports all over the world. Under the expert guidance of Francesco Bardi, Fontana Candida combines typicity effortlessly with quality and a forward-looking outlook. The wines themselves are the proof, especially the terrific sangiovese and merlot Kron '01, a tight-knit, impeccably styled red with intense aromas of tobacco and ripe red berry fruits. Thanks to its stay in oak, it shows ripe tannins and a full, fragrant finish. The other red, Merlot del Lazio '02, has firm aromatics, admirable vigour and good fruit impact. The '02 Malvasia Terre dei Grifi retains the qualities of previous vintages. There is solid structure and personality, with all the characteristics of the variety, from golden delicious apples to fresh almond. When we moved on to the various Frascatis, we were surprised by the accomplished Santa Teresa '02. Despite being squeezed into a simpler, less rich style by the vintage, it is still inviting and delicately fruity. The other two '02 Frascatis, Terre dei Grifi, which is clean and even on the palate, and the flawlessly well-typed, ever-reliable Superiore, are up to their usual standards. The group is completed by the Frascati Cannellino, which is as pleasantly straightforward and lightly sweet as it should be.

MONTE PORZIO CATONE (RM)

POGGIO LE VOLPI
VIA FONTANA CANDIDA, 3/C
00040 MONTE PORZIO CATONE (RM)
TEL. 069419491

Poggio Le Volpi made a great Guide debut with its flavoursome, characterful wines. The leading player behind its changes, after nearly a century of family-run activity, is Felice Mergè. With a group of young partners, Felice runs the estate's almost 13 hectares of vineyards to both organic and biodynamic tenets. Recently, there has been much investment, both in the vineyards, to ensure top-quality grapes, and in the cellar, where there is now good equipment and enough space to work well. Assisting with the wines is oenologist, Maurilio Chioccia. There is just one red, Baccarossa '01, but it is a very good one. From equal parts of montepulciano and merlot, it ages a year in barrique and eight months in bottle. There are lively aromas of rose and liquorice, then refined tannins on the rich, full, long palate. Frascati Superiore '02 is bright gold and has a fresh, mineral nose with clean scents of apple and fresh almond. The palate also reflects this well, and offers a soft finish. The other dry white, Donnaluce '02, comes solely from chardonnay, partially vinified and aged in small barrels. It has varietal sensations of tropical fruit and just perceptible butteriness before opening out to give a progression of vibrantly zesty tones. Finally comes Cannellino '02 from semi-dried, extra-ripe malvasia puntinata, together with ten per cent botrytized chardonnay. It is an impressive wine with honey, camomile and dried fruits. Another red is on its way. It may be from cesanese, a troublesome grape but one that has great character. We'll see.

● Kron '01	♟♟	6
○ Malvasia del Lazio Terre dei Grifi '02	♟♟	3*
○ Frascati Sup. '02	♟	4*
○ Frascati Sup. Santa Teresa '02	♟	4
○ Frascati Sup. Terre dei Grifi '02	♟	3*
● Merlot del Lazio '02	♟	4
○ Frascati Cannellino		3
○ Frascati Sup. Santa Teresa '97	♟♟	2
○ Frascati Sup. Santa Teresa '98	♟♟	2
○ Malvasia del Lazio Terre dei Grifi '99	♟♟	3
○ Frascati Sup. Santa Teresa '01	♟♟	4*
○ Malvasia del Lazio Terre dei Grifi '01	♟♟	3*
○ Frascati Sup. Terre dei Grifi '00	♟	2
○ Frascati Sup. '01	♟	2*
○ Frascati Sup. Terre dei Grifi '01	♟	2*

● Bacca Rossa '01	♟♟	5
○ Donnaluce '02	♟♟	4
○ Frascati Sup. '02	♟♟	2*
○ Frascati Cannellino '02	♟	4

MONTE PORZIO CATONE (RM) MONTEFIASCONE (VT)

VILLA SIMONE
VIA FRASCATI COLONNA, 29
00040 MONTE PORZIO CATONE (RM)
TEL. 069449717
E-MAIL: info@pierocostantini.it

FALESCO
LOC. ARTIGIANA LE GUARDIE
01027 MONTEFIASCONE (VT)
TEL. 0761825669 - 0761825803
E-MAIL: falesco@leonet.it

Piero Costantini was one of the pioneers of the Castelli Romani wine renaissance, and he still plays an important role here. Piero continues to travel, to listen and take note of methods used in the best wineries around the world and then to adapt them, in collaboration with his oenologist, Alberto Corti. Again this year, the top of the range is his newest wine, Ferro e Seta, a 50-50 blend of cesanese and sangiovese, which was a marvellous surprise at its first release and now, at its second, is equally splendid. The '01 vintage yielded 130,000 bottles that offer a deep ruby colour, then rich, penetrating aromas of black berry fruits and fresh spices. The broad, intense palate reveals elegant tannins and a long, flavoursome finish. It seems that the friendly suggestions from expert winemaker, Carlo Ferrini, are having some effect. Torraccia '01, from the same blend, is also very good, with plentiful fruit on the nose, as well as on the savoury, lively palate, which is full of extract. And the '02 Frascatis? The best is still Vigna dei Preti, from four hectares of high-altitude vineyard. Its very attractive character of fragrant spring flowers and apples, and refined acidity, derives mainly from the malvasia and bombino in the blend. Next come the delicate, well-fruited Vigneto Filonardi selection and the Superiore, where freshness, drinkability and typicity come through strongly. Frascati Cannellino '00, from selected late-harvest grapes, also showed well with candied fruits and honey, and impressive softness and style.

Montiano '01 makes it number eight for it's the eighth vintage of the wine to get Three Glasses. The is the only Lazio wine ever to win so many awards and a sure sign that the evergreen Riccardo Cotarella, a one-man band at this admirable estate, is still playing very sweet music. The wine is simply fantastic. The nose is intense, with spiciness and wild black berry fruit jam, then there is superb consistency, length and elegance on the palate. A second wine also reached the finals this year, Marciliano '00, based on cabernet franc and cabernet sauvignon, nearly winning a second Three Glass prize. Falesco could so easily have scored a double triumph, but the whole range is in great form. Take for example the '02 Merlot. It's certainly not a powerful wine but it has great balance to make it thoroughly enjoyable and a suitable partner for a wide range of dishes. Even that minor miracle, Vitiano '02, performed excellently. It's a great everyday wine, so tight-knit and concentrated that it gives real satisfaction from the very first sip. The whites are also full of panache, especially Poggio dei Gelsi '02, a classic Montefiascone wine that can be relied on to give great pleasure. The same comments apply to the more modest but deliciously fragrant and vibrant standard-label Est Est Est di Montefiascone '02. As for the estate's newest wine, the aleatico-based Pomele '02, which offers blackberry and blackcurrant fruit, then the sweetness on its palate, we reckon it would be an ideal accompaniment for relaxed conversation.

●	Ferro e Seta '01	🍷🍷	6
○	Frascati Sup. Cannellino Sel. '00	🍷🍷	5
●	Torraccia '01	🍷🍷	4
○	Frascati Sup. V. dei Preti '02	🍷	4
○	Frascati Sup. Vign. Filonardi '02	🍷	4
○	Frascati Sup. Villa Simone '02		3
○	Frascati Sup. Vign. Filonardi '97	🍷🍷	3
○	Frascati Sup. Cannellino '98	🍷🍷	4
○	Frascati Sup. Vign. Filonardi '99	🍷🍷	3
○	Frascati Sup. Vign. Filonardi '00	🍷🍷	3
●	Ferro e Seta '00	🍷🍷	6
○	Frascati Sup. V. dei Preti '01	🍷🍷	4*
○	Frascati Sup. Cannellino Sel. '99	🍷🍷	5

●	Montiano '01	🍷🍷🍷	6
●	Marciliano '00	🍷🍷	6
○	Est Est Est di Montefiascone Poggio dei Gelsi '02	🍷🍷	3*
●	Vitiano '02	🍷🍷	3*
○	Est Est Est di Montefiascone '02	🍷	2
●	Merlot dell'Umbria '02	🍷	4
●	Pomele '02	🍷	5
●	Montiano '94	🍷🍷🍷	5
●	Montiano '95	🍷🍷🍷	5
●	Montiano '96	🍷🍷🍷	5
●	Montiano '97	🍷🍷🍷	5
●	Montiano '98	🍷🍷🍷	5
●	Montiano '99	🍷🍷🍷	6
●	Montiano '00	🍷🍷🍷	6

ROMA

ROMA

CONTE ZANDOTTI
VIA VIGNE COLLE MATTIA, 8
00132 ROMA
TEL. 0620609000 - 066160335
E-MAIL: info@cantinecontezandotti.it

VINI PALLAVICINI
FRAZ. COLONNA
VIA CASILINA, KM 25,500
00030 ROMA
TEL. 069438816 - 064814344
E-MAIL: saitacolonna@vinipallavicini.com

The rise of this winery continues apace. Its name is linked to Conte Enrico Zandotti but the cellar is now run full time by his son, Leone Massimo, who has various carefully thought-out plans for new wines – a dried-grape "passito" is on the cards – and for improving those already on the list. Responsibility for this work lies with oenologist, Marco Ciarla, who also looks after the estate's 35 hectares of vineyard. He has one very fine wine, Malvasia Rumon, already under his belt and the '02 flaunts excellent harmony and great character. The aromas are penetratingly intense, ranging from apple to fresh walnuts. The palate is full-bodied, pleasingly incisive and deep, with a full flavour and plenty of length. The '02 Frascati Superiore is in its usual style, with clear-cut, elegant typicity, the structure balanced by zippy fruit and a fine array of aromas. New on the red front is Merlot '02, which is vinified in stainless steel and, when we tasted, gave red berry fruit and spices. A retaste of La Petrosa '99, made in large barrels from sangiovese grosso, cabernet sauvignon and a small amount of the rare ottonese variety, confirmed its class. Its impressively complex, fully expressed character combines distinct notes of blackberry and leather, followed by a broad, elegant palate with a full, attractive finish. The list finishes with Frascati Cannellino '02, from super-ripe grapes, which has clean aromas of williams pears and spring flowers, signing off with an attractive finish.

Principessa Maria Camilla Pallavicini runs this winery, founded in 1939. Today, it has 70 hectares of vineyard in the municipalities of Rome, Colonna and Cerveteri, turning out about 1,000,000 bottles a year. The growth has also been structural for there's a modern cellar, and help from skilled agronomists, as well as the young Friulian oenologist, Carlo Roveda, is at hand. The range of wines is good and includes three reds. The excellent Soleggio '01, a Cabernet Sauvignon, is the most distinguished of these. It spends a year in small oak and six months in bottle, acquiring a distinct purple hue, a decisive, austere nose of ripe fruit, and a well-structured, well-knit palate with a spicy finish. La Cavata '01, from cabernet franc, cabernet sauvignon, sangiovese and montepulciano, has good style, offering aromas of blackberry, pepper and ground coffee beans, then full body, softened by oak. The oak-free Torre Pasolina '01, from cabernet and petit verdot, is less full but has a lively, fruit-driven character. On the white front, we have the clean Frascati Selezione Verde '02, with apples on the nose and a zesty palate. The attractively youthful, incisively acidic La Giara '02 is made solely from malvasia puntinata, and Il Pagello '02, from falanghina, greco and grechetto, has a citrus and jasmine nose, then a fresh, elegant palate. We finish on a high note with Stillato '01, from malvasia grapes dried on the vine. This has pervasive scents of yellow peaches and honey, and is creamily full on the palate, which is lightly scored by a varietal almondy finish.

O	Malvasia del Lazio Rumon '02	¶¶	3*
O	Frascati Sup. '02	¶¶	3*
O	Frascati Cannellino '02	¶	5
●	Merlot '02	¶	4
O	Frascati Sup. '98	¶¶	2
●	La Petrosa '98	¶¶	4
●	La Petrosa '99	¶¶	4
O	Malvasia del Lazio Rumon '98	¶¶	3
O	Frascati Sup. '99	¶¶	2
O	Malvasia del Lazio Rumon '01	¶¶	3*
O	Frascati Sup. '01	¶¶	2*

●	Cabernet Sauvignon Soleggio '01	¶¶	4
O	Malvasia Puntinata Stillato '01	¶¶	4
●	La Cavata '01	¶¶	3*
●	Torre Pasolina '01	¶	3
O	Pagello '02	¶	4
O	Frascati Sup. Sel. Verde '02	¶	3
O	Malvasia Puntinata La Giara '02	¶	2
●	Cabernet Sauvignon Soleggio '00	¶¶	4

TERRACINA (LT)

CANTINA SANT'ANDREA
LOC. BORGO VODICE
VIA RENIBBIO, 1720
04019 TERRACINA (LT)
TEL. 0773755028
E-MAIL: info@cantinasantandrea.it

Gabriele Pandolfo was born in Tunisia, and weaned on the French-Sicilian school of winemaking. Now with his competent son, Andrea, he has established a fine estate in the part of southwest Lazio known as the Agro Pontino. The jewel of the estate is without doubt the range based on the emblematic traditional local grape, moscato. Oppidum '02 is entirely from moscato di Terracina, given a long maceration and vinified to dryness. The golden colour leads to a clean, penetrating, varietal nose, rich in the floral and fruity notes that return elegantly on the balanced, flavoursome palate. Il Templum '02 is a sweeter version, from late-harvested grapes, which is delicately perfumed and has a rounded palate with a clean, attractively fragrant finish. There had to be a "passito" and it's Capitolium '00, made from low-yielding grapes dried in shallow cases. The colour is bright orange, then the nose has alluring scents of dried figs and chestnut honey. The palate is harmoniously full, nicely structured and long. Best of the reds is Preludio '01, a mix of merlot and sangiovese that gives clear cherry tones, attractive herbaceousness and a good tannic weave. Last on our list is Circeo Bianco Riflessi '02, a fresh, pleasantly aromatic wine.

VELLETRI (RM)

COLLE DI MAGGIO
VIA PASSO DEI CORESI, 25
00049 VELLETRI (RM)
TEL. 0696453072
E-MAIL: colledimaggio@colledimaggio.it

Velletri is the focus of the Lazio wine scene, both for the area's viticultural heritage and for today's clutch of wine-producing and wine-teaching establishments. Colle di Maggio is more significant for quality than size. Its wines, from both indigenous and non-native varieties, form a happy marriage of elegance and longevity. For example, there is Villa Tulino '01, a Burgundy-style Chardonnay, with an all-enveloping nose of white peach and coconut, fusing with softly pervasive oak toast and vibrant acidity on the palate. Its red partner, Villa Tulino '99, from barrique-fermented shiraz, petit verdot, merlot and cabernet sauvignon, is also very good. The intense nose gives morello cherry and spices. The palate is warm, complex and enlivened by balsam on the finish. The Bordeaux blend once called Le Anfore has swapped a consonant and become Le Ancore. The '00 is a little weighed down by its jamminess but still satisfies, showing leather and cinnamon. The '01 Porticato, another white blend, is interesting, its fruit-forward fragrance revealing a pronounced citrus tang and hints of spring flowers. The convincing performance of the two classics, red and white Velitrae '01, is evidence of the skills of oenologist Paolo Peira, who is overseeing the estate's growth and consolidation. The white has youthful immediacy and a distinct, fresh, flavoursome character, whereas the red is clean and well structured, with attractive red berry fruit on the finish. There are new wines in the pipeline and more attention is to be focused on indigenous varieties.

○ Moscato di Terracina Passito Capitolium '00	♈♈	4
○ Moscato di Terracina Secco Oppidum '02	♈♈	4*
● Circeo Rosso Preludio alla Notte '01	♈	3
○ Circeo Bianco Riflessi '02	♈	2
○ Moscato di Terracina Amabile Templum '02	♈	3

○ Villa Tulino Bianco '01	♈♈	6
● Villa Tulino Rosso '99	♈♈	6
● Le Ancore '00	♈	5
○ Porticato Bianco '01	♈	4
○ Velitrae Bianco '01	♈	4
● Velitrae Rosso '01	♈	4
● Le Anfore '98	♈♈	4
○ Porticato Bianco '99	♈♈	4
○ Villa Tulino Bianco '00	♈♈	6
● Villa Tulino Rosso '97	♈♈	6
● Le Anfore '99	♈♈	5

OTHER WINERIES

ANTONELLO COLETTI CONTI
VIA VITTORIO EMANUELE, 116
03012 ANAGNI (FR)
TEL. 0775728610
E-MAIL: coletticonti@libero.it

Antonello Coletti Conti is getting there. The dream of his own cellar is coming together piece by piece. We are pleased to se the Cesanese del Piglio Hernicus coming on. The '02 was again made at the Cantina Sociale del Piglio, with help from manager Domenico Tagliente, but it's got good stuffing.

● Cesanese del Piglio Haernicus '02	♀	4

MAZZIOTTI
LOC. MELONA-BONVINO
VIA CASSIA, KM 110
01023 BOLSENA (VT)
TEL. 0644291377

The arrival of Valeria, Flaminia Mazziotti's daughter, coincided with cellar re-organization. The red Volgente '01, from merlot, sangiovese and montepulciano, is complex and structured. Est Est Est di Montefiascone '02 is aromatic. The white Canuleio '02 was not ready, so comment is deferred.

● Volgente Rosso '01	♀	4
○ Est Est Est di Montefiascone '02	♀	3

CASALE DEI CENTO CORVI
VIA DELLA TOMBA
00052 CERVETERI (RM)
TEL. 069943486
E-MAIL: cgiorgia@inwind.it

Kottabos and Zilath, each in red and white versions, are promising, well-made wines from rich blends. Chardonnay, trebbiano and malvasia go into the whites and merlot, montepulciano, syrah and sangiovese in the reds. The Cerbero selection was not ready for our tasting. We'll review it next year.

● Zilath Rosso '01	♀♀	4
● Kottabos Rosso '01	♀	4
○ Zilath Bianco '02		4

MARCO CARPINETI
S. P. CORI-VELLETRI KM 14,300
04010 CORI (LT)
TEL. 069679860
E-MAIL: info@marcocarpineti.it

Making wine to organic precepts is not easy, but Marco Carpineti has taken up the cudgels. His Cori Bianco '01 has a tight, complex weave and anything but an easy-drinking, fresh white. Its deep gold, though, may be a disadvantage, suggesting a non-existent heaviness. Applause for Marco's courage.

○ Cori Bianco '01	♀	3
● Cori Rosso '01		4

L'OLIVELLA
VIA DI COLLE PISANO, 1
00044 FRASCATI (RM)
TEL. 069424527 - 069425656
E-MAIL: info@racemo.it

Life at this small Frascati cellar goes on calmly. Frascati Superiore '02 is as sound as ever, despite the poor vintage. Its alter ego Racemo '99 is also good, showing fair power and character. Best of all, though, is Concento '01, from cesanese and shiraz, giving good weight and fair complexity.

● Concento '01	♟	3
● Racemo Rosso '99	♟	4
○ Frascati Sup. Racemo '02		4

TENUTA DI PIETRA PORZIA
VIA PIETRA PORZIA, 60
00044 FRASCATI (RM)
TEL. 069464392
E-MAIL: pietraporzia@libero.it

A 50-hectare farm lying in an amphitheatre of hills, meticulously tended vines and a modern, technological cellar: this is what produced Pietra Porzia's Frascati Superiore. The Etichetta Nera, containing some malvasia del Lazio and aged in small casks, is admirable.

○ Frascati Sup. Regillo		
Etichetta Nera '02	♟	4

CASALE VALLECHIESA
VIA PIETRA PORZIA, 19/23
00044 FRASCATI (RM)
TEL. 069417270 - 0695460086
E-MAIL: info@casalevallechiesa.it

Bruno Gasperini's estate enters the Guide for the first time, partly thanks to Marco Ciarla's skilled adaptation of what has been a more openly commercial range. The '02 Frascati Superiore was more impressive than previous vintages on both nose and palate, meriting One Glass.

○ Frascati Sup. Vallechiesa '02	♟	3

TENUTA CUSMANO
VIA ANAGNINA, 20
00046 GROTTAFERRATA (RM)
TEL. 069410333
E-MAIL: info@tenutacusmano.it

The Cusmano family has been active since 1981 in Valle Marciana, a natural amphitheatre between Grottaferrata and Marino that is ideal for viticulture. Our current favourite is Frascati Superiore S. Nilo Millenium '02, a monovarietal malvasia del Lazio that has fair complexity and a decent array of aromas. An estate to watch.

○ Frascati Sup. S. Nilo Millenium '02	♟	3

GOTTO D'ORO
VIA DEL DIVINO AMORE, 115
00040 MARINO (RM)
TEL. 0693022211
E-MAIL: info@gottodoro.it

Wines from this large co-operative are always reliable. Output is 8,000,000 bottles a year, all well priced, and the style is easy drinking yet attractive and well made. Frascati Superiore '02 is fresh and balanced, Marino Superiore '02 has attractive citrus and Merlot '02 is upfront and varietal.

○ Frascati Sup. '02	♟	2
○ Marino Sup. '02	♟	2*
● Merlot del Lazio '02	♟	3

CANTINA CERQUETTA
VIA DI FONTANA CANDIDA, 20
00040 MONTE PORZIO CATONE (RM)
TEL. 069424147
E-MAIL: cerquetta@cantinacerquetta.it

Another new winery. No, it's not that we weren't aware of its existence, merely that the wines have improved. Take the Frascati Superiore '02, a fine example of careful winemaking with aromas that respect typical Frascati style, and a notable but not too heavy, structure. A Frascati in fine form.

○ Frascati Sup. '02	♟	3

AZ. AGR. CASALE MATTIA
VIA MONTE MELLONE, 19
00040 MONTECOMPATRI (RM)
TEL. 069426249 - 069486930
E-MAIL: info@casalemattia.it

Casale Mattia has again come up with a large range. We drew the Malvasia Bianca and Frascati Superiore '02 out of the pack, each with a good array of aromas in line with modern production criteria. But we'd like to see the estate's high aims leading to wines of greater attack.

○ Frascati Sup. Sel. Oro '02	♀	4
○ Malvasia Bianca '02	♀	3

TENUTA LE QUINTE
VIA DELLE MARMORELLE, 71
00040 MONTECOMPATRI (RM)
TEL. 069438756

Checco Papi has passed on, but his son Elio follows in his winemaking footsteps. Sadly, the poor '02 vintage made itself felt here, too. The famous Montecompatri Virtù Romane '02 has good structure, but not enough fruit to go with it. The red Rasa di Marmorata '01 is more impressive all round.

○ Montecompatri Colonna Virtù Romane '02	♀	3
● Rasa di Marmorata '01	♀	3

CANTINE CIOLLI
VIA DEL CORSO
00035 OLEVANO ROMANO (RM)
TEL. 069564547
E-MAIL: vitivinicola-ciolli@libero.it

This zone is overshadowed by the nearby Piglio DOC, but the Ciolli winery is bringing it out of the gloom. Cesanese di Olevano Cirsium 2001 put up a great showing. Malolactic fermentation and barrique ageing have given new elegance. There are just 2,000 bottles so don't miss out.

● Cesanese di Olevano Cirsium '01	♀♀	5
● Cesanese di Olevano Silene '01		4

CANTINA SOCIALE CESANESE DEL PIGLIO
VIA PRENESTINA, KM 42
03010 PIGLIO (FR)
TEL. 0775502355 - 0775502356
E-MAIL: cantinasocialecesanese@tin.it

We might be incurable romantics, but every time we encounter this wine we stop and reflect. Production problems, uneven grapes from suppliers, insufficient winemaking resources – yet the wine still comes out well. The price seems just right, too. Domenico Tagliente still directs the show.

● Cesanese del Piglio Etichetta Rossa '02	♀	2*

TERRE DEL CESANESE
VIA MAGGIORE, 105
03010 PIGLIO (FR)
TEL. 0775501125

The project seemed too ambitious, doomed not to last. But no, despite endless difficulties this team of affiliated producers presses ahead. Cesanese del Piglio '01 is keeping its promises and is very elegant and consistent, with incisive complexity. The price is a little above average.

● Cesanese del Piglio '01	♀♀	5

MARISA POUCHAIN TAFFURI
VIA DELLA GIUSTINIANA, 1012
04027 PONZA (LT)
TEL. 0630310113

We'll indulge ourselves by mentioning this tiny estate, set up more as a gamble than for commercial reasons. Vino di Bianca '02, from chardonnay, biancolella, sauvignon and malvasia is fresh, medium bodied, aromatic and easy to drink. It's ideal with fish but sadly, there are only 7,000 bottles.

○ Vino di Bianca '02	♀	4

MIGLIARESE
VIA CROCELLE
03047 SAN GIORGIO A LIRI (FR)
TEL. 0771772211 - 3200284565
E-MAIL: migliaresegiuseppe@libero.it

Migliarese is a modern estate inspired by the past. "Kelle Terre" are the first two words of the oldest text in Italian. Kelle Terre Olivella '01, from olivella, is good, as are the white Ausente '02, from native grapes, and Kelle Terre Efelidi '01, a sweet "passito" wine from moscato di Terracina.

● Olivella '01	♈ 4
○ Ausente '02	♈ 4
○ Efelidi '01	4

PURI CHARLOTTE
VIA CASSIA, KM 119,7
01023 SAN LORENZO NUOVO (VT)
TEL. 0763727160
E-MAIL: charlotte.puri@tin.it

Charlotte Puri is a young, clear-thinking, go-getter, as her red Montemore '02 shows. From sangiovese, montepulciano and merlot, and aged for seven months in barrique, it is already characterful and should improve with age. The white Calenne '02, based mainly on procanico, also promises well.

| ● Montemoro '02 | ♈ 6 |
| ○ Calenne '02 | 5 |

GIOVANNI TERENZI
LOC. LA FORMA - VIA PRENESTINA, 140
03010 SERRONE (FR)
TEL. 0775594286
E-MAIL: terenzigiovanni@libero.it

Giovanni Terenzi makes muscular wines, noted for consistency. Three are based on cesanese, Velobra, Colle Forma and the powerful Vajoscuro, all '01. They aim to be half way between traditional vinification and a modern outlook. There is just one problem, the distinctly ambitious prices.

● Cesanese del Piglio	
Colle Forma '01	♈ 6
● Cesanese del Piglio Vajoscuro '01	♈ 7
● Cesanese del Piglio Velobra '01	3

SANT'ISIDORO
LOC. PORTACCIA
01016 TARQUINIA (VT)
TEL. 0766864154 - 0766869716
E-MAIL: s.isidoro@tin.it

Amazing planning and effort went into Soremidio '01, which cruised into the finals on its first release. It is entirely from montepulciano yielding at 4,000 kilograms per hectare and aged in Allier and Nevers oak barriques. The other red, Corithus '01, and the white Forca di Palma '02 are nice.

● Soremidio '01	♈♈ 5
● Corithus '01	4
○ Forca di Palma '02	3

FEDERICI
VIA S. APOLLARIA VECCHIA, 30
00039 ZAGAROLO (RM)
TEL. 0695461022
E-MAIL: vinifederici@tiscalinet.it

The Federici estate was founded in 1960. It has modern equipment and a solid winemaker in Marco Ciarla, who turns out wines for today's consumers. Rosso Le Ripe '01, from montepulciano, merlot and cabernet, showed well. The white Zagarolo '02 and Le Ripe '02 suffered from the poor vintage.

● Le Ripe Rosso '01	♈ 4
○ Le Ripe Bianco '02	4
○ Zagarolo Sup. '02	3

GIANCARLO LORETI
C.SO G. GARIBALDI, 8
00039 ZAGAROLO (RM)
TEL. 069575956 - 069549104
E-MAIL: info@aziendaagricolaloreti.com

Four generations of grape growers have, until now, been producing absolutely traditional wines. But Cesare has decided to change, adjusting the traditional blend to give more structure and complexity of flavour. The result is a dense, warm, complex Zagarolo Superiore '02. The start of a new era?

| ○ Zagarolo Sup. '02 | ♈ 2* |

ABRUZZO AND MOLISE

Five Three Glasses awards and two national prizes: Winery of the Year for Masciarelli and Grower of the Year to Edoardo Valentini, in recognition of his over 50 years as a vine grower. For Abruzzo, the 2004 Guide will be one to remember. Obviously, it is these two superstars who have grabbed the headlines but their triumphs should also be taken as recognition of the great vocation of Abruzzo's wine country, and also act as a stimulus to other producers. It is no coincidence that numerous front-ranking estates, and several more just behind them, are getting down to things, with ever more impressive results. In their enthusiasm, and desire to emulate Masciarelli and Valentini, they have to show the courage that these two displayed in decision-making, their rigorous approach and the strong individuality they have given their wines. If Abruzzo is to have a chance of becoming the new frontier of Italian wine, its producers will have to develop their own oenological profiles before their wines can. In other words, to hit the heights it is not enough simply to take on the latest hotshot oenologist or come out with massive, super-concentrated wines. We support those growers who work hard, without taking short cuts. Thank goodness there is no shortage of them in Abruzzo. Most are from the long-standing estates, some emerging when a younger generation, more open to new ideas, takes over management. But there are also newcomers. There is no point in naming names; just turn the pages and see how the various wineries have done, noting how their wines have been evolving over the years. Abruzzo will be on firmer ground when it learns how to nurture more effectively its most famous varieties, montepulciano and trebbiano, and others that are coming back strongly, such as pecorino and passerina. It will also have to raise the profile of its subzones. Colline Teramane which, from the 2003 vintage, is Montepulciano d'Abruzzo DOCG (on sale from 2005) is the first of these, but already delimited subzones in the region's other three provinces are on their way. There is also movement, albeit slower than in Abruzzo, in the small region of Molise and people with ideas who are willing to make considerable investment in wine estates are arriving in the market place. Here, too, the revival is being led by varieties such as montepulciano and aglianico, trebbiano and falanghina, in good wine country such as the hilly area stretching between Campomarino and Larino. There are also interesting wineries we have had to exclude from the Guide for reasons of space. We'll list them here: in Molise, Masserie Flocco; and in Abruzzo, Santoleri, La Quercia, Fattoria Licia, Podere Castorani, D'Onofrio, Pepe and Valle Martello, and the Roxan, Madonna dei Miracoli, Citra and Miglianico co-operatives.

ATESSA (CH)

ATRI (TE)

TERRA D'ALIGI - SPINELLI
FRAZ. PIAZZANO
VIA PIANA LA FARA, 90
66041 ATESSA (CH)
TEL. 0872897916
E-MAIL: info@terradaligi.it

VILLA MEDORO
FRAZ. FONTANELLE
64030 ATRI (TE)
TEL. 0858708142
E-MAIL: villamed@tiscali.it

Adriano and Carlo Spinelli's estate in the hills overlooking the river Sangro was founded in 1973 but in its current form dates from 1995, when the cellar equipment was brought up to standard and a new line of wines, Terra d'Aligi, created. Both the number of wines in the range and their quality grows year by year, and the label has become better known, gaining its own identity as a separate branch of the estate. This now has around 40 hectares of vine. Last year, young oenologist Riccardo Brighigna was taken on as consultant to aim for even higher quality. And there it is in Tolos '01, a new wine in an enticing, modern style, which scored impressively at our tastings. It is an intense ruby red of notable viscosity, a density that is also discernible on the nose, which has good red berry fruitiness gently integrating into the oak. The tannin is only just apparent initially on the palate, which then develops with fullness, but also freshness and sinuosity, to its liquorice-like finish. Tatone '00 is in similar style, but is less muscular and has more incisive tannins. There is good nose-palate harmony, and even, balanced development right through to the back of the mouth. The three wines in the less expensive range are the uncomplicated but well-made Montepulciano d'Abruzzo '01, the finely profiled Trebbiano d'Abruzzo '02 and the excellently typed Cerasuolo '02, which again has the qualities already found in previous vintages.

First appearing in the Guide last year in the Other Wineries section, Villa Medora is forging ahead with the determination that marks out its young proprietor, Federica Morricone, and has now earned a full entry. The estate has ancient roots, but an overhaul is under way, starting in the more than 30 hectares of vineyard. Production reaches almost 200,000 bottles, split across three versions of Montepulciano d'Abruzzo, one Trebbiano d'Abruzzo and a Cerasuolo, all good value for money. Last year's promise was confirmed by this year's tastings and a new wine, Adrano '98, a 100 per cent montepulciano from the Colline Teramane subzone, made a strong impression. It is an even-hued garnet and the nose has very ripe red berry fruits with a light spiciness. The tannins are still marked, and it develops well on the palate, giving softness and good fruit-oak integration. There is more emphasis on freshness on Rosso del Duca '01, which has a ripe red and black cherry nose enlivened by balsam. The palate is full and round with close-knit tannins, good overall acid-alcohol balance, and wild berry fruits and liquorice on the finish. The third red, the standard-label '00 Montepulciano d'Abruzzo, is happily uncomplicated, without losing its varietal character or drinkability. The same attractiveness is found on the perfumed '02 Cerasuolo, with its fresh, fruity palate, and the '02 Trebbiano d'Abruzzo.

● Montepulciano d'Abruzzo Tolos '00	♟♟	5
● Montepulciano d'Abruzzo Tatone '00	♟♟	4
● Montepulciano d'Abruzzo '01	♟	3
☉ Montepulciano d'Abruzzo Cerasuolo '02	♟	3
○ Trebbiano d'Abruzzo '02	♟	3
● Montepulciano d'Abruzzo Tatone '98	♟♟	4
● Montepulciano d'Abruzzo '00	♟	3

● Montepulciano d'Abruzzo Colline Teramane Adrano '98	♟♟	5
● Montepulciano d'Abruzzo Rosso del Duca '00	♟♟	4
● Montepulciano d'Abruzzo '00	♟	3
☉ Montepulciano d'Abruzzo Cerasuolo '02	♟	3
○ Trebbiano d'Abruzzo '02	♟	3
● Montepulciano d'Abruzzo Rosso del Duca '98	♟♟	4

BOLOGNANO (PE)

CICCIO ZACCAGNINI
C.DA POZZO
65020 BOLOGNANO (PE)
TEL. 0858880195
E-MAIL: zaccagniniwines@tin.it

CAMPOMARINO (CB)

BORGO DI COLLOREDO
FRAZ. NUOVA CLITERNIA
C.DA ZEZZA, 8
86042 CAMPOMARINO (CB)
TEL. 087557453
E-MAIL: info@borgodicolloredo.com

Marcello Zaccagnini and skilled oenologist, Concezio Marulli, have once more come up with a large number of impressive wines. The estate, founded in 1978 by the late Ciccio Zaccagnini, has around 20 hectares of vine with a further 50 leased. Various selection and experimentation programmes are under way. And it is a selection of the best grapes that gives the estate's standard bearers, the two San Clemente wines, both barrique-aged. The San Clemente Montepulciano d'Abruzzo '01 stood out this year, almost winning Three Glasses. It is an impenetrably deep ruby, tinged with purple. Its aromas range across small wild berry fruits and liquorice, with hints of vanilla and chocolate. The palate perfectly echoes these sensations, its tannins are bedding down, it is mouthfilling and long, and it shows the potential to gain further complexity with bottle age. The same is true of the San Clemente Chardonnay '02, even though its nose is already open, yielding varietal aromas of tropical fruit lent elegance by excellent use of oak. The other wines are as characterful as usual. Capisco '99 is lively, silky and long, with enticing aromas of red fruits and spices. The two Tralcetto versions of Montepulciano d'Abruzzo are well typed, with the '00 Selezione offering a better delineated nose and a confident, balanced follow through on the palate. The Cerasuolo Myosotis '02, one of the region's best, deserves a mention, as do the two dried-grape "passito" wines. The red in particular, from montepulciano and cannonau, has never before had such a good balance of sweetness and acidity.

Brothers Enrico and Pasquale Di Giulio, respectively oenologist and agronomist, produce a series of good-value wines reflecting the quality-directed efforts they initiated some years ago. This family-run estate has 50 hectares of vines situated on the hills around Campomarino, over half in the process of being budded over with other indigenous Mediterranean varieties. It is now emerging that the area is well suited to whites, as well as the structured reds for which it is known. An example is the '02 Falanghina. This is the third vintage of the wine. It has fragrant mint and fresh flowers on the nose, and a crisp, long palate. Gironia Bianco '02, based on trebbiano, bombino bianco and malvasia, is more complex. Straw coloured, it is reluctant to open on the nose but then yields white peach and citrus fruit, sensations that are also found on the well-structured palate. There is also ageing potential. The three reds are first rate. While the '00 Aglianico has retained the warmth and style of the previous vintage, the essence of the '01 Montepulciano is its drinkability. Ruby red, it is lively with black and red cherry, and hints of liquorice on both nose and palate. But it is Gironia '00, from montepulciano and aglianico, that takes the honours here. In its best incarnation ever, it is a garnet-tinged ruby red with a nose of ripe red fruit, cherry and plum in particular, as well as tobacco and sweet spices. The palate is initially soft, with gentle tannins, opening confidently and with richness.

● Montepulciano d'Abruzzo Abbazia S. Clemente '01	♙♙	6
● Montepulciano d'Abruzzo Tralcetto Sel. '00	♙♙	4*
● Passito Rosso '01	♙♙	4
○ Chardonnay Abbazia S. Clemente '02	♙♙	5
⊙ Montepulciano d'Abruzzo Cerasuolo Myosotis '02	♙♙	4
● Capsico Rosso '99	♙♙	5
● Montepulciano d'Abruzzo Tralcetto '01	♙	3
○ Bianco di Ciccio '02	♙	3
○ Ibisco Bianco '02	♙	4
⊙ Montepulciano d'Abruzzo Cerasuolo '02	♙	3
○ Passito Bianco '02	♙	4
● Montepulciano d'Abruzzo Abbazia S. Clemente '00	♙♙	5

● Biferno Rosso Gironia '00	♙♙	4
● Molise Montepulciano '01	♙♙	3*
○ Biferno Bianco Gironia '02	♙♙	3*
○ Molise Falanghina '02	♙♙	3*
⊙ Biferno Rosato Gironia '02	♙	3
○ Molise Trebbiano '02	♙	2*
● Aglianico '00	♙♙	4

CAMPOMARINO (CB)

COLONNELLA (TE)

DI MAJO NORANTE
FRAZ. NUOVA CLITERNIA
C.DA RAMITELLI, 4
86042 CAMPOMARINO (CB)
TEL. 087557208
E-MAIL: dimajo@tin.it

LEPORE
C.DA CIVITA
64010 COLONNELLA (TE)
TEL. 086170860
E-MAIL: vini@lepore.it

Even though the fateful Three Glasses did not arrive this year, Alessio Di Majo's winery is still the focal point for Molise wine production. The wide range, produced with guidance from consultant Riccardo Cotarella, is not just well priced but continues to get better. Take Aglianico Contado, for instance. The '00 is deep-hued and has a broad spread of aromas, from tomato leaf to new mown grass, small red berry fruits and spices. The palate is balanced and substantial with ripe tannins and an oaky note. Don Luigi '01, from mainly montepulciano, seems to have suffered from the very hot vintage, as it is fairly inexpressive. This comes through both on the nose, which gives ripe cherry and vanilla but appears reluctant to open up, and on the palate, which has elegance and good structure but tannins that have still to soften. The montepulciano and aglianico-based Ramitello '00 has already bedded down well. It is a concentrated red colour and its most attractive fruity, balsamic, coffee-like nose is well supported by an imposing palate. The other three reds, the Sangiovese, the Prugnolo and the inexpensive Molì, are simple without being simplistic. A grand Biblos '01 emerges on the white front. It has full, fresh floral aromas with grapefruit and almond, and a well-rounded, long palate. Both the Greco and the Falanghina are clean and well made but the thoroughly enjoyable Apianae, a dessert wine from moscato, merits deeper attention for its delicate, refined sensations of peach blossom, its balanced acidity and its roundness on the palate.

Gaspare Lepore, assisted by Giampiero Cichetti for sales and Umberto Svizzeri for winemaking, is seeing the fruits of his labours, initiated a little over a decade ago. Works spreads over his 40 hectares or so on the vine-clad Colonnella hills and in his cellar, where additional equipment is to be installed. There was no Colline Teramane Riserva to be tasted as the '99 was not produced, because of the vagaries of the vintage. The other two Montepulciano d'Abruzzos held their place. The Re '01 is a wine very much in line with the estate's style, showing plum, tobacco and liquorice on a mature, incisive nose and also on the substantial palate, whose tannins are steadily integrating into the fruit. The standard version, from the hot '02 vintage, suffers from over-concentration, giving almost excessive colour and nose, but without the same impact on the palate. For the whites, a well-typed Trebbiano '02 is partnered by three wines from passerina. Lepore has been advocating the repropagation of this indigenous variety for years. The simplest, Passera delle Vigne '02, seems to have paid the price of sustaining the other two. The best remains Sol, now '00, which after oak-free vinification and long ageing is a perfect ensemble of lively, stalky aromas of elderflower, aniseed and balsamic herbs that convince after due appreciation. The barrique-aged Passerina Do, on the other hand, has never really enthused us and the '01 is no exception. The fresh yet structured Cerasuolo '02 is, as usual, admirable.

● Molise Aglianico Contado '00	♟♟	4
○ Apianae '00	♟♟	4
● Biferno Rosso Ramitello '00	♟♟	4
○ Biblos '01	♟♟	4
● Molise Don Luigi '01	♟♟	6
● Prugnolo '00	♟♟	4*
○ Molì Bianco '02	♟	2*
● Molì Rosso '02	♟	2*
○ Molise Falanghina '02	♟	4
○ Molise Greco '02	♟	3
● Sangiovese '02	♟	3
● Molise Don Luigi '99	♟♟♟	5
● Molise Aglianico Contado '99	♟♟♟	4*

○ Controguerra Passerina Sol '00	♟♟	4
● Montepulciano d'Abruzzo Colline Teramane Re '01	♟♟	5
● Montepulciano d'Abruzzo '02	♟♟	4
○ Controguerra Passerina Do '01	♟	4
○ Controguerra Passerina Passera delle Vigne '02	♟	4
◉ Montepulciano d'Abruzzo Cerasuolo '02	♟	3
○ Trebbiano d'Abruzzo '02	♟	3
● Montepulciano d'Abruzzo Colline Teramane Re '00	♟♟	5
● Montepulciano d'Abruzzo Luigi Lepore Ris. '98	♟♟	5

CONTROGUERRA (TE)

Dino Illuminati
c.da San Biagio, 18
64010 Controguerra (TE)
tel. 0861808008
e-mail: info@illuminativini.it

Dino Illuminati and his family have that measured, aristocratic approach to their work that befits those from estates that have seen much of the zone's history go by. Moreover, they have a vineyard holding of over 90 hectares, which allows for the production of a good number of wines, and the estate remains one of the most reliable in the region. Top honours eluded them this year but two wines went into the finals, and their proclivity for reds looks likely to bring some even sharper offerings next time round. For now, though, Claudio Cappellacci and Giorgio Marone's labours have resulted in a '00 Lumen from montepulciano and cabernet sauvignon that is not as immediate as in lesser years but just as admirable. There is even, ripe fruit shot through with oak, and a refined palate that draws you in with its solid structure and long finish. Despite coming from the poorer '99 vintage, Zanna still has the austere, traditional style that brings full, untrammelled enjoyment of the variety's characteristics. Of course, it is without that generous openness that we have become used to, but in compensation there is more elegance and zest on the palate. The other Montepulciano d'Abruzzo, the fresh, well-structured Riparosso '02, with over 700,000 bottles produced, remains good value and has pervasive fruit, well supported by light spiciness. The most complex of the whites, Daniele, has found its feet with the '01, showing intriguing acacia flower and citrus aromas, then good length. Ciafrè '02, a blend of local white varieties, and Costalupo '02 are both enjoyable.

CONTROGUERRA (TE)

Camillo Montori
piane Tronto
64010 Controguerra (TE)
tel. 0861809943 - 0861809900
e-mail: montorivini@katamail.com

In the past few years, we have tended to reserve judgement on Camillo Montori, prompted mainly by our esteem for a producer who was in the front line in the battles to gain DOC status for Controguerra and DOCG for Montepulciano Colline Teramane. It was also a time of transition for him, with the arrival of daughters Beatrice in administration and Laura, an oenologist, in the cellar full-time. Last year, success returned in a big way, and now Leneo Moro '00, from montepulciano and cabernet, came within an inch of Three Glasses. An intense ruby introduces the nose of small red berry fruits, gunflint and tobacco. The palate is vigorous, and brings together depth, freshness, a tight weave of tannin, well-defined density and a liquorice aftertaste. The traditional approach that underlies Fonte Cupa '00 is revealed in the sensations of morello cherry and leather that permeate into lively structure and good length on the palate. The inexpensive Montepulciano d'Abruzzo '01 is attractively supple and the second vintage of the Sauvignon, the '02, has a varietal nose centred on warm, elegant, herby and tropical fruits tones, then a firm acid backbone. Trebbiano Fonte Cupa '02 is simpler and more direct, with a lively colour and a fresh nose of golden delicious apples and sweet herbs. The '01 Leneo d'Oro, from barrique-fermented chardonnay, is one of the best editions of this wine. It has perfectly judged oaking that softens and broadens the fruit without damaging the palate's necessary freshness.

● Controguerra Rosso Lumen '00	♟♟	8
● Montepulciano d'Abruzzo Zanna '99	♟	5
○ Controguerra Bianco Daniele '01	♟♟	4*
● Montepulciano d'Abruzzo Riparosso '02	♟♟	3*
○ Controguerra Bianco Ciafrè '02	♟	4 -
○ Controguerra Bianco Costalupo '02	♟	2*
◉ Montepulciano d'Abruzzo Cerasuolo Campirosa '02	♟	3
○ Brut M. Cl. '98	♟	4
● Controguerra Passito Nicò '99	♟	7
● Controguerra Rosso Lumen '97	♟♟♟	6
● Controguerra Rosso Lumen '98	♟♟	6
● Montepulciano d'Abruzzo Zanna '98	♟♟	5
● Controguerra Rosso Lumen '99	♟♟	8

○ Controguerra Leneo Moro '00	♟♟	7
● Montepulciano d'Abruzzo Colline Teramane Fonte Cupa '00	♟♟	5
○ Sauvignon '02	♟♟	4*
○ Trebbiano d'Abruzzo Fonte Cupa '02	♟♟	4*
○ Controguerra Leneo d'Oro '01	♟	5
● Montepulciano d'Abruzzo '01	♟	3
◉ Montepulciano d'Abruzzo Cerasuolo Fonte Cupa '02	♟	4
○ Trebbiano d'Abruzzo '02	♟	3
● Montepulciano d'Abruzzo Colline Teramane Fonte Cupa '98	♟♟	4*
● Controguerra Leneo Moro '98	♟♟	6

FRANCAVILLA AL MARE (CH)   GIULIANOVA (TE)

FRANCO PASETTI
C.DA PRETARO
VIA SAN PAOLO, 21
66023 FRANCAVILLA AL MARE (CH)
TEL. 08561875 - 0856920041
E-MAIL: info@pasettivini.it

FARAONE
LOC. COLLERANESCO
VIA NAZIONALE PER TERAMO, 290
64020 GIULIANOVA (TE)
TEL. 0858071804
E-MAIL: faraone.vini@tin.it

Mimmo Pasetti feels strongly about living up to the name of his family estate. So after the division of the family properties, it was not unreasonable for him to choose a noted, able oenologist like Romeo Taraborrelli to work with. Together, they have adjusted several aspects of wine production, including increasing ageing times, which prevented us from tasting the Montepulciano d'Abruzzo Tenuta di Testarossa. We did manage to try Tenuta di Testarossa Bianco '02, from chardonnay, pecorino and trebbiano, but only just, because it had been bottled only a few weeks earlier. We found it even more fleshy and structured than the already impressive versions of previous years. The colour is deep straw, the nose gives apple, banana, citrus fruit and notes of incense, and then the palate is broad and quite deep, with good freshness of flavour and an almondy finish. Another white, Zarachè '02, stood out among some promising newcomers, nearly gaining Two Glasses. It is from local grapes – the label says trebbiano and cococciola – and is modern in style, offering enticing softness, freshness of fruit and a satisfying palate. The second Montepulciano d'Abruzzo, Fattoria Pasetti '01, seemed a touch under par, with too much oak for its fruit. Cerasuolo '02 showed well and is one of the best tasted this year. An intense, bright cherry colour ushers in good flesh on the nose and a zesty palate. Finally, Pecorino '02 has an orange blossom nose but needs better acid-alcohol balance.

In his own quiet way, Giovanni Faraone brings something more to his wines each year, following additional investment to complete his underground cellar and acquire land for new vineyard plantings. This will bring his total to around ten hectares, yielding 50,000 bottles split among five wine types, as well as the "metodo classico" sparkling wines for which he is currently devising new formulas. He has always had a passion for sparklers and despite being surrounded by general indifference in Abruzzo, has remained a sort of fizz pioneer. For his two reds, and trebbiano and passerina-based whites, Giovanni seems to have his strategies well in place. The white Santa Maria dell'Arco selection was not available for tasting but the less expensive Le Vigne '02, vinified in stainless steel is, again, one of the most original and most talked about wines in the region. Light straw in colour, it shows elderflower, balsamic herbs and tropical fruits on the nose. The acidity on the palate would be almost intrusive, were it not for the good supporting alcoholic structure and a long, almondy finish. It should develop well, realizing its potential after three to four years. The Montepulciano d'Abruzzo '01 from the same line has a purple ruby colour, a nose whose fruit is augmented by light spiciness, then good extractive weight, non-invasive tannins and a pepper and cinnamon-like finish on the palate. The red Santa Maria dell'Arco '00 showed less rigour in winemaking. The nose is more vegetal than fruit-based, although the palate is supple and has average depth.

O Tenuta di Testarossa Bianco '02 🍷🍷		5
● Montepulciano d'Abruzzo		
Fattoria Pasetti '01	🍷	4
⊙ Montepulciano d'Abruzzo		
Cerasuolo Tenuta Pasetti '02	🍷	3
O Pecorino Fattoria Pasetti '02	🍷	4
O Zarachè '02	🍷	4
● Montepulciano d'Abruzzo		
Tenuta di Testarossa '98	🍷🍷	4
O Tenuta di Testarossa Bianco '01 🍷🍷		5
● Montepulciano d'Abruzzo		
Tenuta di Testarossa '99	🍷🍷	5

● Montepulciano d'Abruzzo		
Le Vigne '01	🍷🍷	3*
O Trebbiano d'Abruzzo Le Vigne '02 🍷🍷		3*
● Montepulciano d'Abruzzo		
S. Maria dell'Arco '00	🍷	4
⊙ Montepulciano d'Abruzzo		
Cerasuolo Le Vigne '02	🍷	3
● Montepulciano d'Abruzzo		
S. Maria dell'Arco '98	🍷🍷	4
● Montepulciano d'Abruzzo		
Le Vigne '00	🍷🍷	3*
● Montepulciano d'Abruzzo		
S. Maria dell'Arco '99	🍷🍷	4
O Trebbiano d'Abruzzo Le Vigne '01	🍷	3

LORETO APRUTINO (PE)

NOCCIANO (PE)

★ EDOARDO VALENTINI
VIA DEL BAIO, 2
65014 LORETO APRUTINO (PE)
TEL. 0858291138

NESTORE BOSCO
C.DA CASALI, 7
65010 NOCCIANO (PE)
TEL. 085847345 - 085847139
E-MAIL: info@nestorebosco.com

Writing Edoardo and Francesco Valentini's entry is harder every year. Especially now that Edoardo has been awarded the new Grower of the Year award, we risk waxing rhetorical about their unique vision of wine production – just 40,000 bottles from 60 hectares – and the rigour of their approach. Another danger is attempting to describe the wines at the moment of tasting instead of conveying their ageing capacity. Let's see what we can do. Montepulciano d'Abruzzo '97 has a deep, bright, garnet ruby colour and an unmistakable timbre to the nose which emerges gradually. It's elegant, rich, fleshy and earthy, with ripe red and black cherry, and roasted coffee beans. The palate is incredibly well knit and has freshness and alcoholic weight beautifully enmeshed. It, too, opens slowly, revealing practically infinite depth. The high score of well over 90/100 reached by Trebbiano d'Abruzzo '00 might make you think that it's the best of recent years. But time can bring surprises for the '96, from a "year ruined by bad weather", is now astounding. So let's just play it as it lies. An intense, bright hue precedes a nose at first reticent, then giving musk, freshly mown grass, mineral notes and balsam in distinct succession. The palate shows character, depth and good minerally piquancy, with citrus and ripe peach fruit emerging ever more clearly, and a very long, liquorice-like finish. The Cerasuolo, again one of the best, has a rose petal colour, aromas of Mediterranean scrubland and the structure of a red. Who knows, maybe one day we'll send it, too, into the Three Glass finals.

The Bosco family live in the Nocciano hills, where they make wine sourced from over 50 hectares of vineyard, part owned, part leased, in one of the most attractive underground cellars of the region Their long-standing winery now regains its status with a full entry, having had a difficult few years, including typographical errors which we are pleased to correct. Last year, the two leading wines, Pan and Don Bosco, both Montepulciano d'Abruzzo '98, took Two Glasses each, as indicated below. It was decided to skip the '99 vintage for this pair as it was unsuitable for ageing. So the new releases of Pan, aged in barriques, and Don Bosco, matured in large casks are from '00, by which time new consultant oenologist Riccardo Brighigna was already in place. Pan showed greater character at the time of tasting. Its nose was still rather oaky but there was good expressiveness and balance on the palate, with its red berry fruit and liquorice continuing right through to the finish. Don Bosco will probably get there, but despite good structure, it was held in by excessive tannin and a lack of harmony. Linfa '02, a young wine from a blend of international grapes, is characterized by easy drinkability. Chardonnay Pan '01 showed well. You can hardly not admire the gentle touch with the oaking, although it lacks the thrust that would have helped it to withstand this underpinning over time.

○	Trebbiano d'Abruzzo '00	⟨⟩	6
●	Montepulciano d'Abruzzo '97	⟨⟩	7
⊙	Montepulciano d'Abruzzo Cerasuolo '01	⟨⟩	6
●	Montepulciano d'Abruzzo '88	⟨⟩	6
○	Trebbiano d'Abruzzo '88	⟨⟩	5
●	Montepulciano d'Abruzzo '90	⟨⟩	6
●	Montepulciano d'Abruzzo '92	⟨⟩	6
○	Trebbiano d'Abruzzo '92	⟨⟩	5
●	Montepulciano d'Abruzzo '95	⟨⟩	6
○	Trebbiano d'Abruzzo '99	⟨⟩	8
○	Trebbiano d'Abruzzo '98	⟨⟩	5
⊙	Montepulciano d'Abruzzo Cerasuolo '00	⟨⟩	7

●	Montepulciano d'Abruzzo Pan '00	⟨⟩	5
●	Montepulciano d'Abruzzo Don Bosco '00	⟨⟩	4
○	Chardonnay Pan '01	⟨⟩	4
●	Linfa '02	⟨⟩	4
●	Montepulciano d'Abruzzo Pan '98	⟨⟩	5
●	Montepulciano d'Abruzzo Don Bosco '98	⟨⟩	4

NOTARESCO (TE)

BRUNO NICODEMI
C.DA VENIGLIO
64024 NOTARESCO (TE)
TEL. 085895493
E-MAIL: fattorie.nicodemi@libero.it

OFENA (AQ)

LUIGI CATALDI MADONNA
LOC. PIANO, 1
67025 OFENA (AQ)
TEL. 0854911680
E-MAIL: azagrluigicataldimadonna@tin.it

Last year, we were already gearing ourselves up for the release of the '00 Montepulciano d'Abruzzo Riserva, since the '99 was not produced. We were not disappointed. It scored well, indicating the sort of results being achieved at Alessandro and Elena Nicodemi's winery by the team lead by Paolo Caciorgna. They have put in huge amounts of effort over the past two years. The 30 hectares of directly owned vineyard have completely changed face and the wines seem to have gained focus, reflecting their origins more strongly. It is as if there were a driving force to this long-standing estate, moving things ever forward. Of course, all this augurs well for the future. For now, though, the flagship '00 Riserva is purple red and has pervasive, fleshy red berry fruits on the nose. The palate is perfectly balanced, the tannins are tight and the relationship between acid and alcohol allows the fruit to remain long, evolving into roasted coffee beans on the finish. The standard '01 Montepulciano d'Abruzzo, aged in large casks, is structured and elegant with typical black cherry melding into lively spicy and vegetal sensations. Of the two Trebbiano d'Abruzzos, the '02 Selezione is naturally a notch or two superior in intensity of aroma and richness of flavour. However the standard '02 is a textbook example of cleanliness and drinking pleasure. The same applies to the '02 Cerasuolo, which is ruby coloured, with a fruity nose and a fragrant palate.

For the first time, Luigi Cataldi Madonna's leading wine, Tonì, came within striking distance of Three Glasses, the '00 showing a personality and sense of completeness that were not quite there in the past. This doesn't surprise us, we had been expecting great things from this winery. Why else would they change their winemaking regime, as they have recently, handing over its management to Tuscan oenologist, Lorenzo Landi? The estate lies at 380 metres, on the western slopes of the Grand Sasso and has 25 hectares of vineyard with a highly site-specific terroir. But let's return to the wines, all impressive and each with its own origin and style. The elegant, purple-ruby Tonì has fruity, leathery and vaguely minerally aromas, elements that also come through on the robust, mouthfilling palate. Malandrino '01, a cru from the Cona vineyard, is really good, showing rich, with soft tannins, and substantial, but not heavy. It is let down only by a rather closed nose. The standard-label Montepulciano d'Abruzzo '01 displays some youthful cut-and-thrust, with lightly spicy fruit and inviting flavour development on the palate. The two Cerasuolos have similar characteristics, both as ever among the region's best for their combination of finesse and structure. The Piè delle Vigne selection would have done even better had the colour not been so deep. Finally comes the '02 Trebbiano d'Abruzzo, more complete and longer than ever before, with fruit on the nose and zestiness on the palate.

● Montepulciano d'Abruzzo Colline Teramane Ris. '00	♙♙	5
● Montepulciano d'Abruzzo '01	♙♙	4
○ Trebbiano d'Abruzzo Sel. '02	♙♙	4
⊙ Montepulciano d'Abruzzo Cerasuolo '02	♙	3
○ Trebbiano d'Abruzzo '02	♙	3
● Montepulciano d'Abruzzo Colline Teramane Bacco '98	♟♟	5
● Montepulciano d'Abruzzo '00	♟♟	4
○ Trebbiano d'Abruzzo Sel. '01	♟	4

● Montepulciano d'Abruzzo Tonì '00	♙♙	6
● Montepulciano d'Abruzzo '01	♙♙	3*
● Montepulciano d'Abruzzo Malandrino '01	♙♙	5
⊙ Montepulciano d'Abruzzo Cerasuolo '02	♙♙	3*
⊙ Montepulciano d'Abruzzo Cerasuolo Pié delle Vigne '02	♙♙	4
○ Trebbiano d'Abruzzo '02	♙♙	3*
● Montepulciano d'Abruzzo Tonì '98	♟♟	5
● Montepulciano d'Abruzzo '00	♟♟	3*
● Occhiorosso '00	♟♟	5
⊙ Montepulciano d'Abruzzo Cerasuolo Pié delle Vigne '01	♟♟	4
● Montepulciano d'Abruzzo Tonì '99	♟♟	6

ORTONA (CH)

AGRIVERDE
LOC. CALDARI
VIA MONTE MAIELLA, 118
66020 ORTONA (CH)
TEL. 0859032101 - 0859039054
E-MAIL: info@agriverde.it

Agriverde's Plateo is the surprise of this year's tastings. Its success is the pay-off for the considerable investment made in the construction of a futuristic, bioarchitecture-inspired cellar and converting the estate's 30 or so hectares, to which should be added another 20 on lease. In truth, even Plateo's first two releases inspired more than a little interest but with the '98, it has hit its strike. Credit is due to the whole team, including proprietor Giannicola De Carlo and his right hand man, Paride Marino, who wisely took on the bright, local oenologist, Riccardo Brighigna, a consultant capable of rapidly bringing about major change. Plateo is a highly concentrated, modern-styled Montepulciano d'Abruzzo, aged in new barriques. Its colour is still purple and the aromas range from liqueur fruits to sweet spices. Full and solid in the mouth, it shows soft tannins and plentiful length, leaving sensations of liquorice and coffee. Rather than Solarea '99, which reflects a problematic vintage, Plateo's partner is the rich, refreshingly youthful '01 Montepulciano d'Abruzzo from the Riseis line. The '02 Cerasuolo is well structured and pleasingly fruity, as usual. The most immediate and honest of the whites is the organically produced Trebbiano d'Abruzzo Natum '02, which nudged Two Glasses (the red Natum is organic, too). There are two Chardonnays, one partly, the other totally oak fermented, but Tresor '02 had the more inviting fruit and acid backbone.

ORTONA (CH)

FARNESE
LOC. CASTELLO CALDORA
VIA DEI BASTIONI
66026 ORTONA (CH)
TEL. 0859067388
E-MAIL: farnesevini@tin.it

Farnese Vini is one of the most successful Abruzzo brand names. The wines are made from local and international varieties, and are mostly sold on export markets. The company grew out of an idea of Camillo De Iuliis, Valentino Sciotti and oenologist Filippo Baccalaro, who is flanked by Marco Flacco, and is based on close relationships with growers and wineries in the area, as well as with a number of consultant winemakers, some from abroad. This has given Farnese Vini a fairly broad range of wines, all offering good value, and an output totalling around 10,000,000 bottles. Most of the wines are released six to eight months after the harvest so their styles aim more for pleasure than complexity. Both versions of Montepulciano d'Abruzzo are examples of this, as is Sangiovese Farneto Valley '02, whose straightforwardly well-typed palate makes it the best of the bunch. In comparison, Sangiovese Don Camillo '02 has a softer, yet more structured, profile with intriguing hints of spice underlying its ripe fruit. Opis '98 and Montepulciano d'Abruzzo Riserva both disappoint, as they lack grip on the palate and, quite apart from its inscrutable label, the montepulciano and primitivo Edizione 5 Autoctoni is dominated by oak. All the whites are nicely even but two stand out, Trebbiano d'Abruzzo Farneto Valley '02, which is well structured, with intense, pervasive apple and ripe citrus fruit on both nose and the crisp palate, and the lower priced Chardonnay Farneto '02, where fermentation in oak has added structure, integrating and softening the primary fruit characteristics.

● Montepulciano d'Abruzzo Plateo '98	ΨΨΨ	6
● Montepulciano d'Abruzzo Riseis '01	ΨΨ	4
○ Chardonnay Vallée du Vin '01	Ψ	4
○ Chardonnay Tresor '02	Ψ	2*
◉ Montepulciano d'Abruzzo Cerasuolo Riseis '02	Ψ	3
● Montepulciano d'Abruzzo Natum '02	Ψ	3
○ Trebbiano d'Abruzzo Natum '02	Ψ	2*
○ Trebbiano d'Abruzzo Riseis '02	Ψ	3
● Montepulciano d'Abruzzo Solàrea '99	Ψ	4
● Montepulciano d'Abruzzo Plateo '95	ΨΨ	5
● Montepulciano d'Abruzzo Plateo '97	ΨΨ	6

● Edizione 5 Autoctoni '01	Ψ	5
○ Chardonnay Farneto '02	Ψ	2*
○ Chardonnay Opis '02	Ψ	5
● Montepulciano d'Abruzzo Casale Vecchio '02	Ψ	4
● Montepulciano d'Abruzzo Farneto Valley '02	Ψ	3
● Sangiovese Don Camillo '02	Ψ	4
● Sangiovese Farneto Valley '02	Ψ	3
○ Trebbiano d'Abruzzo Farneto Valley '02	Ψ	3
● Montepulciano d'Abruzzo Opis Ris. '98	Ψ	5

ORTONA (CH)

Sarchese Dora

c.da Caldari Stazione, 65
66026 Ortona (CH)
tel. 0859031249

Esmeralda and Nicola D'Auria own 17 hectares and produce 110,000 bottles with consultancy from the skilled Leonardo Seghetti. Montepulciano d'Abruzzo Rosso di Macchia '00, of which great things are expected, was not ready in time for our tastings, so it was left to the impressive Montepulciano d'Abruzzo Pietrosa, a Two Glass season ticket holder, to wave the estate's banner. Its lively ruby colour is tinged with purple, the nose mingles intense fruit and spicy notes, and there is good, well-knit substance on the palate. All this makes it an archetypal Montepulciano, albeit a little old-style. Just one step down comes Cerasuolo '02, recalling wild cherries on both appearance and nose, then offering a fairly rich, but not yet fully developed, palate. Chardonnay Pietrosa '02 is well typed and even, but the Trebbiano d'Abruzzo '02 from the same line has just that much more finesse on the nose, fragrance on the palate, and balance. Bianco della Rocca, from chardonnay, has a strong band of fans and so merits a word apart. Its intense, bright hue is followed by aromas of cooked apple and dried flowers. The palate is soft, showing a little weak in the centre but strong on the finish, and held in place by good alcohol. Finally, we are strong advocates of the work that this small estate is doing on montepulciano passito, so we must mention Suavis, even though there are only a few thousand bottles made. It offers warm aromas of dried flowers, black cherry jam and coffee, then lively softness and length, but without any cloying.

● Montepulciano d'Abruzzo Pietrosa '01	🍷🍷	3*
● Passito Suavis '00	🍷	6
○ Bianco della Rocca '02	🍷	3
○ Chardonnay Pietrosa '02	🍷	2*
⊙ Montepulciano d'Abruzzo Cerasuolo '02	🍷	3*
○ Trebbiano d'Abruzzo Pietrosa '02	🍷	2*
● Montepulciano d'Abruzzo Rosso di Macchia '98	YY	5
● Montepulciano d'Abruzzo Pietrosa '00	YY	3*
● Montepulciano d'Abruzzo Rosso di Macchia '99	YY	5

PESCARA

Contesa di Rocco Pasetti

loc. Collecorvino
c.da Caparrone, 9
65100 Pescara
tel. 0854549622
e-mail: info@contesa.it

It's too soon to say whether noted Abruzzo oenologist Rocco Pasetti and his wife Patrizia have won their bet, but in the last two years, they have shown plenty of dedication to bringing firm reliability to their wines. The estate rose from the division of the family's properties. The new cellar is not yet built so all currently hangs on the 25 hectares of vineyard, planted mainly with montepulciano, pecorino and trebbiano. The wines already show great promise, especially the two Montepulciano d'Abruzzos, from different but very good vintages (the estate skipped the disappointing '99). The '00 Contesa has deep colour and an intense, fruity, pervasive nose with ripe black and red cherry and light balsamic notes. The palate is full, with soft tannins, and develops well, leading to traces of chocolate and roast coffee beans on the finish. Vigna Corvino '01 is only a touch less complex. Its freshness and balance on both nose and palate, its undertones of red berry fruits and liquorice, and its typicity of variety and provenance, make it one of the best of the less expensive wines. Similar aromas and typicity are found on Cerasuolo '02 while over among the whites, the original styling of Pecorino '02 stands out. It's a lively, well-balanced wine with subtle yet persistent tones of golden delicious apples and ripe citrus fruits. Finally comes the first release of Contesa Bianco, the '02, from trebbiano, pecorino and chardonnay partly vinified in barriques and tonneaux. It has nice roundness and elegance to its fruit, and a good acid backbone that promises ageing potential.

● Montepulciano d'Abruzzo Contesa '00	🍷🍷 (grey)	5
● Montepulciano d'Abruzzo Vigna Corvino '01	🍷🍷	3*
○ Contesa Bianco '02	🍷🍷	4*
⊙ Montepulciano d'Abruzzo Cerasuolo '02	🍷🍷	3*
○ Pecorino Contesa '02	🍷🍷	4
○ Trebbiano d'Abruzzo '02	🍷	3
● Montepulciano d'Abruzzo Vigna Corvino '00	YY	3*
● Montepulciano d'Abruzzo Contesa '98	YY	5

ROSCIANO (PE)

MARRAMIERO
C.DA SANT'ANDREA, 1
65020 ROSCIANO (PE)
TEL. 0858505766
E-MAIL: azmarram@tin.it

We have become used to good quality from Enrico Marramiero's estate. The 30 hectares or so of vines are farmed by a team under manager, Antonio Chiavaroli, and oenologist, Romeo Taraborrelli, and its new, well-equipped cellar turns out around 300,000 bottles each year. The best of the whites is Chardonnay Punta di Colle '00. Barrique ageing gives a bright gold colour and plenty of impact on the ripe peach-like nose, with its delicate notes of butter and vaguely mineral scents. The palate has good extract and balance, showing caramel and liquorice on the finish. The other oaked white, the trebbiano-based Altare '02, is in a lower key, lacking the attack it has had in previous years. Anima '02 is slimmer and graceful, offering apple and ripe citrus scents. The third Trebbiano d'Abruzzo, Dama '02, brings clearly fragrant aroma and an attractively zesty palate. Inferi '99 leads the three Montepulciano d'Abruzzos with an unmistakable round, comforting style that shoots out ripe aromas of black cherry, blackberry, tobacco and vanilla in succession. The oak is well integrated and there is good density on the palate, which has a faintly vegetal finish. The quieter Incanto '00 is next in line, then comes the good value Dama '01, whose youthful vigour assures great drinkability. We finish with Marramiero Brut, without doubt one of the region's best "metodo classico" sparklers. Deep yellow, it has a fairly fine mousse, ripe peachy fruit and is lively yet soft.

ROSETO DEGLI ABRUZZI (TE)

ORLANDI CONTUCCI PONNO
LOC. PIANA DEGLI ULIVI, 1
64026 ROSETO DEGLI ABRUZZI (TE)
TEL. 0858944049
E-MAIL: orlandi.contucci@libero.it

Marina Orlandi Contucci was not short of things to sort out last year, including the completion of a new cellar and organizing new plantings on her 27 hectares of vines, of which over half are montepulciano. There is a new Montepulciano d'Abruzzo Colline Teramane Riserva, from '98, a well-structured wine that aged in small oak barrels. Its red berry fruit is delicate on the nose, then fuller and more incisive on the palate. Liburnio '00, from montepulciano blended with international varieties, is an elegant-looking purple. The nose has small red berry fruits interlaced with notes of cocoa powder and tar that become more intriguing as the expand and deepen on the palate. One step down come Cabernet Sauvignon '00 and the standard Montepulciano d'Abruzzo '01. The former has a nicely full, varietal nose that doesn't carry through to the palate. The Montepulciano d'Abruzzo is held back by its youth as the tannins have yet to settle down and its fruit is still inexpressive, but it should improve in bottle. The same goes for Sauvignon Ghiaiolo '02, the most complex of the whites and one which should bring increasing pleasure over time. In contrast, Chardonnay Roccesco '02 is even and has good, delicate varietal typing, but seems to have suffered the most from what was a difficult year for early-ripening whites in this zone. Trebbiano d'Abruzzo '02, though, is truly impressive. Bright straw precedes floral and fruit notes on both nose and the palate, which is soft yet lively, with an attractive almondy aftertaste.

○ Chardonnay Punta di Colle '00	♟♟	5
● Montepulciano d'Abruzzo Inferi '99	♟♟	6
● Montepulciano d'Abruzzo Incanto '00	♟	5
● Montepulciano d'Abruzzo Dama '01	♟	4
◉ Montepulciano d'Abruzzo Cerasuolo Dama '02	♟	3
○ Trebbiano d'Abruzzo Altare '02	♟	5
○ Trebbiano d'Abruzzo Anima '02	♟	4
○ Trebbiano d'Abruzzo Dama '02	♟	3
○ Marramiero Brut Cl.	♟	6
● Montepulciano d'Abruzzo Inferi '96	♟♟	5
● Montepulciano d'Abruzzo Inferi '97	♟♟	5
● Montepulciano d'Abruzzo Inferi '98	♟♟	5
○ Chardonnay Punta di Colle '99	♟♟	5

● Liburnio '00	♟♟	7
○ Trebbiano d'Abruzzo Colle della Corte '02	♟♟	4*
● Montepulciano d'Abruzzo delle Colline Teramane Ris. '98	♟♟	6
● Cabernet Sauvignon Colle Funaro '00	♟	5
● Montepulciano d'Abruzzo La Regia Specula '01	♟	4
○ Chardonnay Roccesco '02	♟	4
◉ Montepulciano d'Abruzzo Cerasuolo Vermiglio '02	♟	3
○ Sauvignon Ghiaiolo '02	♟	4
● Cabernet Sauvignon Colle Funaro '98	♟♟	5
● Liburnio '98	♟♟	7
● Liburnio '99	♟♟	7
● Cabernet Sauvignon Colle Funaro '99	♟♟	5

SAN MARTINO SULLA MARRUCINA (CH)

★ GIANNI MASCIARELLI
VIA GAMBERALE, 1
66010 SAN MARTINO SULLA MARRU-
CINA (CH)
TEL. 087185241
E-MAIL: info@masciarelli.it

The Winery of the Year award has gone to Gianni Masciarelli and Marina Cvetic. They deserve it for what they have achieved in 20 years of winemaking, and for what they are still doing as investments and vineyard purchases continue. They now have over 100 hectares, radiating out from their enclave in San Martino to cover all four of Abruzzo's provinces. Marina's brilliant but well-reasoned ideas and Gianni's ingenious, impulsive intuition take them to ever greater heights. In fact, a good five wines reached the Three Glass finals this year. Villa Gemma '99 is a small marvel of class and power, especially when the vintage is taken into account. There is wonderful richness of fruit, which melds beautifully with aristocratic oak, giving spicy scents which come through on the palate, too, right to its final liquorice note. Last year, we said that the Trebbiano d'Abruzzo Marina Cvetic '00 had "reached a high point" and that it managed "to combine great extract, a nose of finesse, fruit warmth and mineral freshness, power and depth of flavour". For the '01, we can add elegance, more length and revelatory varietal purity. What about the other two Marina Cvetic reds? Montepulciano d'Abruzzo '00 is velvety on its black and red cherry nose and has soft tannins on a long, evenly developing, balanced palate. The '98 Cabernet Sauvignon is possibly the best release ever, with perfectly extracted, warm blackcurrant and blueberry fruit caressed by tarry notes. The other wines all performed well. Cerasuolo Villa Gemma '02 is the best of them.

SANT'OMERO (TE)

VALORI
VIA TORQUATO AL SALINELLO, 8
64027 SANT'OMERO (TE)
TEL. 086188461

The affably outgoing Luigi Valori was involved in floriculture until, one day several years back, partly as a gamble, partly out of sudden enthusiasm, he turned his attentions to a small wine estate in his area. From the beginning, he has had precise objectives and clear ideas, which he has followed with unremitting energy. He has fixed up the ten hectares or so of vineyards, part in S. Omero and part in Controguerra, and with guidance from Attilio Pagli, he has renovated the cellar from top to bottom. Good things emerged from the very first year, most notably the two Montepulciano d'Abruzzos, and now there's a Trebbiano d'Abruzzo, Preludio '02. This is one of the best we tasted this year. It may not be perfectly true stylistically but it is intriguing on the nose, with soft peach and apricot scents, and shows full and mouthfilling, with a firm centre palate and good overall balance. The two reds, though different, have a common thread in their high, almost excessive concentration, which distances them from full typicity and probably means they will need longer development in bottle. The more ambitious of the pair, Vigna S. Angelo '01, reveals its density even as it runs down the glass. Its aromas range from black cherry to blackberry, and on to coffee. Similar sensations emerge from the palate, which is soft, fleshy and quite massive, which means it is not so nuanced. The standard Montepulciano d'Abruzzo '02 has a similar purple colour, but reveals small red berry fruits interwoven with a green, almost herbaceous spiciness.

O	Trebbiano d'Abruzzo Marina Cvetic '01	♟♟♟	6
●	Montepulciano d'Abruzzo Villa Gemma '99	♟♟♟	8
●	Montepulciano d'Abruzzo Marina Cvetic S. Martino Rosso '00	♟♟	5
O	Chardonnay Marina Cvetic '01	♟♟	6
●	Cabernet Sauvignon Marina Cvetic '98	♟♟	8
●	Montepulciano d'Abruzzo '01	♟♟	3*
☉	Montepulciano d'Abruzzo Cerasuolo '02	♟♟	4
O	Villa Gemma Bianco '02	♟♟	4
O	Trebbiano d'Abruzzo '02	♟	2*
●	Montepulciano d'Abruzzo Villa Gemma '95	♟♟♟	6
O	Trebbiano d'Abruzzo Marina Cvetic '98	♟♟♟	4
●	Montepulciano d'Abruzzo Villa Gemma '97	♟♟♟	6
●	Montepulciano d'Abruzzo Villa Gemma '98	♟♟♟	7
O	Trebbiano d'Abruzzo Marina Cvetic '00	♟♟	6

●	Montepulciano d'Abruzzo '02	♟♟	4
●	Montepulciano d'Abruzzo V. S. Angelo '01	♟♟	5
O	Trebbiano d'Abruzzo Preludio '02	♟♟	3*
●	Montepulciano d'Abruzzo '00	♟♟	3*
●	Montepulciano d'Abruzzo '01	♟♟	4
●	Montepulciano d'Abruzzo Vigna S. Angelo '00	♟	4

SPOLTORE (PE)

FATTORIA LA VALENTINA
VIA COLLE CESI, 10
65010 SPOLTORE (PE)
TEL. 0854478158
E-MAIL: info@fattorialavalentina.it

Sabatino Di Properzio has raised the stakes, coming up with another wine, Bellovedere, to join Spelt as a contender for Three Glass. He owns 15 hectares, and buys in from another 20, from a tried and trusted group of nearby growers. The consultant is Luca D'Attoma, the much talked-about winemaker from Tuscany who shapes wines of rare class and beautifully tuned concentration. Bellovedere '00 (Bellovedere is the old name for Spoltore) is the most recent of the estate's four variants of Montepulciano d'Abruzzo and it makes a great impact. Ruby garnet in colour, it displays pronounced aromas of black cherry and blackcurrant, and balsam from the oak. The palate tells a similar tale, and has an admirable alcohol-rich structure, giving richness and power. Spelt is quite different. Here the difficult '99 vintage, which was salvaged at the last minute, has given finesse and a more restrained fleshiness. It is soft and elegant on the palate with good fruit and there is refreshing spiciness throughout. With the '00 Binomio, the result of a meeting of minds between Sabatino Di Properzio and Stefano Inama, we are back with a more extreme style, in which the typical characteristics of montepulciano are not immediately obvious. It has a deep purple colour, introducing a nose of red berry fruits and musk, then a warm palate with slightly raw tannins that temporarily loses balance mid way and signs off with a sweet, chocolate finish. Finally, we admired the lively fruits and spices on the least expensive of the four Montepulciano d'Abruzzos.

TOCCO DA CASAURIA (PE)

FILOMUSI GUELFI
VIA F. FILOMUSI GUELFI, 11
65028 TOCCO DA CASAURIA (PE)
TEL. 085986908

Lorenzo Filomusi Guelfi is unmoved by fashions. He has our admiration for the humility and dignity he applies to his decision-making each year. He and his wines have absolutely nothing to do with standardization, or adherence to dictates in any form, except those Lorenzo believes in deeply. This is possibly why it is so easy to recognise in his wines that ten-hectare or so slice of land, Tenuta del Ceppete, one of the best-aspected and ventilated slopes at Tocco da Casauria. The wines also reveal the distinctive characteristics of montepulciano, which is planted on most of Lorenzo's vineyards. The white chardonnay and sauvignon, plus tiny amounts of malvasia and trebbiano, end up in the attractive Scuderie del Cielo '02, which has captivating aromas and a fine, even palate. Montepulciano d'Abruzzo Vigna Fonte Dei '98 is bright garnet, showing clear tones of morello cherry and liquorice on the nose with a slightly spicy undertone. The palate follows suit and has soft tannins, good but not excessive alcoholic vigour, and an earthy, leathery, liquorice-like finish. The '01 Montepulciano d'Abruzzo is more in a traditional style, linking balsam with more fruity sensations and giving a palate that successfully plays off more austere tannins against a gentle roundness. The '02 Cerasuolo, one of the year's best, has wild cherry on the nose and fresh Mediterranean spices on its nicely full palate, which finishes with a long, delicate almondy streak.

● Montepulciano d'Abruzzo Bellovedere '00 ♈♈		7
● Montepulciano d'Abruzzo Spelt '99 ♈♈		5
● Montepulciano d'Abruzzo Binomio '00	♈♈	6
● Montepulciano d'Abruzzo '01	♈♈	3*
☉ Montepulciano d'Abruzzo Cerasuolo '02	♈	3
○ Trebbiano d'Abruzzo '02	♈	3
● Montepulciano d'Abruzzo Binomio '98	♈♈	5
● Montepulciano d'Abruzzo Bellovedere '00	♈♈	7
● Montepulciano d'Abruzzo Spelt '98 ♈♈		5
● Montepulciano d'Abruzzo '00	♈♈	3*
● Montepulciano d'Abruzzo Binomio '99 ♈♈		6

● Montepulciano d'Abruzzo '01	♈♈	4
☉ Montepulciano d'Abruzzo Cerasuolo '02	♈♈	3*
● Montepulciano d'Abruzzo V. Fonte Dei '98	♈♈	6
○ Scuderie del Cielo Bianco '02	♈	3
● Montepulciano d'Abruzzo V. Fonte Dei '97	♈♈	4
● Montepulciano d'Abruzzo '00	♈♈	4
● Montepulciano d'Abruzzo '98	♈	3
● Montepulciano d'Abruzzo '99	♈	3

TOLLO (CH)

CANTINA TOLLO
VIA GARIBALDI, 68
66010 TOLLO (CH)
TEL. 087196251
E-MAIL: produzione@cantinatollo.it

If we could dedicate Cantina Tollo's entry to someone, it would be lawyer Tommaso Perantuono, who in 2003 was re-elected after 42 years in charge to chair this, the region's largest co-operative, by its 1,300 members. Recent years have seen ongoing investments for Cantina Tollo, their timing determined by a team under general manager, Giancarlo Di Ruscio, his righthand man on the sales side, Maurizio Primavera, and vice president, Tonino Verna. On the wine front, the new bottles from the Vigneto 2000 project immediately got off to a good start. Take the Montepulciano d'Abruzzo Aldiano '01, for instance, which impressed on its second release. Aged in variously sized barrels, it is purplish garnet and the nose is rounded, with ripe fruit, leather and tobacco. The palate is well structured, but not too incisive. Cagiolo '99 is aged in barrique and has a solid purple hue introducing aromas of plum and wild cherry that, as expected, open out only slowly. The palate is imposing and nicely broad, with soft tannins and good length. The winery's two classics, the '99 Colle Secco and Colle Secco Rubino, are different in mould, the former's characteristic huskiness contrasting with the greater elegance of the Rubino. The '02 Valle d'Oro affirms its role as leader among the Cerasuolos. Over the years, this wine has taken numerous awards for its consistent ability to combine the rich fruit of montepulciano with the fresh elegance that is crucial to a rosé.

VACRI (CH)

FATTORIA BUCCICATINO
VIA STERPARA, 33
66010 VACRI (CH)
TEL. 0871720273
E-MAIL: buccicatino@libero.it

Each year, Umberto Buccicatino puts another small piece into place in the realization of his ambitious plans. Land purchase and new plantings will bring him 16 hectares in total, all situated close by the cellars. These have themselves been adorned with new wood of various sizes for the ageing of the four reds that make up a large part of the 100,000-plus bottles produced each year. This, and consultancy from oenologist Romeo Taraborrelli, lie behind the Montepulciano d'Abruzzo '01, the least demanding but possibly the most successful wine in the range. Its colour and its typical nose of red and black cherries with additional light spiciness are best described as "honest". Even the certain rusticity in its tannins, which lead to sustained development in the mouth, is not unpleasing. There is fair balance, and wafts of chocolate and coffee mark the finish. At the time of tasting, the oak seemed rather marked on both the Stilla Rubra '00 selection and the less expensive Don Giovanni '01. On the Stilla Rubra, it tended to mask the good underlying fruit, whereas on the lighter bodied Don Giovanni, it gave vanilla on both nose and palate. The idea, though, is to benefit both by giving them a certain amount of bottle age. The fourth red is Cabernet Sauvignon '00. This has a clearly recognizable profile, with black cherry and blackcurrant alongside more vegetal notes, all well integrated with sweet spiciness from the oak. The palate is elegant and quite long, with notable alcohol. The fragrant, harmonious Trebbiano d'Abruzzo '02 is highly attractive.

●	Montepulciano d'Abruzzo Aldiano '01	ΨΨ	4
☉	Montepulciano d'Abruzzo Cerasuolo Valle d'Oro '02	ΨΨ	2*
●	Montepulciano d'Abruzzo Colle Secco Rubino '99	ΨΨ	3*
●	Montepulciano d'Abruzzo Cagiòlo '99	ΨΨ	6
○	Trebbiano d'Abruzzo Aldiano '02	Ψ	3
○	Trebbiano d'Abruzzo Colle Secco '02	Ψ	2*
●	Montepulciano d'Abruzzo Colle Secco '99	Ψ	3*
●	Montepulciano d'Abruzzo Colle Secco Rubino '98	ΨΨ	4*
●	Montepulciano d'Abruzzo Aldiano '00	ΨΨ	5
●	Montepulciano d'Abruzzo Cagiòlo '97	ΨΨ	5
●	Montepulciano d'Abruzzo Cagiòlo '98	ΨΨ	5

●	Montepulciano d'Abruzzo '01	ΨΨ	3
●	Cabernet Sauvignon '00	Ψ	6
●	Montepulciano d'Abruzzo Stilla Rubra '00	Ψ	6
●	Montepulciano d'Abruzzo Don Giovanni '01	Ψ	5
○	Trebbiano d'Abruzzo '02	Ψ	3
●	Cabernet Sauvignon '98	Ψ	7
●	Montepulciano d'Abruzzo Don Giovanni '00	Ψ	6
●	Montepulciano d'Abruzzo Stilla Rubra '99	Ψ	6

OTHER WINERIES

SAN LORENZO
C.DA PLAVIGNANO, 2
64075 CASTILENTI (TE)
TEL. 0861999325 - 0861998542
E-MAIL: info@sanlorenzovini.com

The 150 hectares of vine are owned by the Galasso and Barbone families. Advised by oenologist, Riccardo Brighigna, it moves steadily on. Again the best wine is the elegant, barrique-fermented Chardonnay Alhena, the '01. The new Montepulciano d'Abruzzo Escol '00, dense and mouthfilling, is also good.

○	Chardonnay Alhena '01	🍷🍷	5
●	Montepulciano d'Abruzzo Escol '00	🍷	5
○	Chardonnay Chioma di Berenice '02	🍷	4
○	Chardonnay Alhena '00	🍷🍷	5

ANTONIO E ELIO MONTI
C.DA PIGNOTTO, 62
64010 CONTROGUERRA (TE)
TEL. 086189042
E-MAIL: emilmon@tin.it

The Monti family estate, which has had Riccardo Cotarella as consultant for a couple of years now, continues to produce well. There are two good Montepulciano d'Abruzzos. The less expensive version is enjoyable. Pignotto '01 has a ripe, spicy nose and good substance on the palate.

●	Montepulciano d'Abruzzo Pignotto '01	🍷	7
●	Montepulciano d'Abruzzo Pignotto '00	🍷🍷	5
●	Montepulciano d'Abruzzo '01	🍷🍷	5

CHIUSA GRANDE
C.DA CASALI
65010 NOCCIANO (PE)
TEL. 085847460 - 0858470818
E-MAIL: fdeusan@libero.it

Franco D'Eusanio, proprietor of this new, 30-hectare, organically farmed estate, submitted his standard wines while awaiting the release of the Perla Nera selection. Rocco Secco '01 is made in classic Montepulciano d'Abruzzo mould, full of ripe fruitiness and good structure.

●	Montepulciano d'Abruzzo Rocco Secco '01	🍷🍷	3
○	Trebbiano d'Abruzzo Matté '02	🍷	3
●	Montepulciano d'Abruzzo Rocco Secco '00	🍷	3
●	Montepulciano d'Abruzzo Perla Nera '98	🍷	4

IL FEUDUCCIO DI SANTA MARIA D'ORNI
VIA FEUDUCCIO, 1/A
66036 ORSOGNA (CH)
TEL. 0871891646
E-MAIL: ilfeuduccio@libero.it

Il Feuduccio is businessman Gaetano Lamaletto's estate. There are 30 hectares of vineyard and an attractive cellar. Rocco Cipollone takes care of sales, Franco Bernabei the winemaking. After last year's cheering results, the new releases are also interesting, especially the Margae selection.

●	Montepulciano d'Abruzzo Margae '98	🍷🍷	8
●	Montepulciano d'Abruzzo Margae '99	🍷🍷	8
●	Montepulciano d'Abruzzo '00	🍷	5
●	Montepulciano d'Abruzzo Ursonia '99	🍷	6

CHIARIERI
VIA SANT'ANGELO, 10
65019 PIANELLA (PE)
TEL. 085971365 - 085973313
E-MAIL: chiarieri@tin.it

Giovanni and Ciriaco Chiarieri's estate has now taken on Marco Masciulli as consultant, a promising move. Meantime, the two attractive, traditionally styled versions of Montepulciano d'Abruzzo remain on form. Vinum Hannibal '99 is more complex. The less expensive Granaro '02 has youthful appeal.

● Montepulciano d'Abruzzo Hannibal '99	♟♟	5
● Montepulciano d'Abruzzo Granaro '02	♟	4
● Montepulciano d'Abruzzo Hannibal '98	♟♟	4
● Montepulciano d'Abruzzo Granaro '01	♟	2*

VALLE REALE
LOC. SAN CALISTO
65026 POPOLI (PE)
TEL. 0459808025 - 0458876118
E-MAIL: info@vallereale.it

The Pizzolo family from Veneto continue to invest in the Pescara area. Although the new cellar is not yet built, the quality of the two Montepulciano d'Abruzzos continues to grow. There is good definition on both '01s. S. Calisto is full and firm; the standard wine is structured but more immediate.

● Montepulciano d'Abruzzo San Calisto '01	♟♟	5
● Montepulciano d'Abruzzo '01	♟	4
● Montepulciano d'Abruzzo San Calisto '00	♟♟	5
● Montepulciano d'Abruzzo '00	♟	4

CANTINA SOCIALE FRENTANA
VIA PERAZZA, 32
66020 ROCCA SAN GIOVANNI (CH)
TEL. 087260152
E-MAIL: info@cantinafrentana.it

The new course taken by Cantina Frentana and its 440 members seems to be going more than just smoothly. More interesting wines are joining the two Montepulciano d'Abruzzos. The '00 selection, Rubesto, should improve with bottle age, and the inexpensive standard '01 we tasted last year is excellent.

● Montepulciano d'Abruzzo Rubesto '00	♟	3
● Montepulciano d'Abruzzo Rubesto '98	♟♟	3*
● Montepulciano d'Abruzzo Frentano '00	♟	2*
● Montepulciano d'Abruzzo Frentano '01	♟♟	2*

F.LLI BARBA
VIA PATINI, 7
64026 ROSETO DEGLI ABRUZZI (TE)
TEL. 0858990104
E-MAIL: barba@webzone.it

The Barba estate has 60 hectares and a well-equipped cellar at Scerne di Pineto. Major improvements are now under way, led by members of Roberto Cipresso's team, to ensure that the two Montepulciano d'Abruzzos and two trebbiano-based whites are enticingly modern, as well as good and inexpensive.

● Trebbiano d'Abruzzo Colle Morino '00	♟	2*
● Montepulciano d'Abruzzo Linea Oro '01	♟	3
● Trebbiano d'Abruzzo Vigna Franca '01	♟	4
● Montepulciano d'Abruzzo Colle Morino '02	♟	2*

BARONE CORNACCHIA
C.DA TORRI
64010 TORANO NUOVO (TE)
TEL. 0861887412
E-MAIL: barone.cornacchia@tin.it

Vigna Le Coste and Poggio Varano, the two top wines of Barone Piero Cornacchia's attractive 40-hectare estate, were not available for tasting this year but the standard Montepulciano d'Abruzzo '01 stood up well. It is one of the top value for money Abruzzo wines of the year.

● Montepulciano d'Abruzzo '01	♟♟	3*
● Controguerra Rosso Ris. Villa Torri '00	♟	5
○ Trebbiano d'Abruzzo '02	♟	2*
● Montepulciano d'Abruzzo V. Le Coste '00	♟♟	4

TORRE ZAMBRA
V.LE REGINA MARGHERITA, 18
66010 VILLAMAGNA (CH)
TEL. 0871300121 - 3356223114

The poor '99 vintage affected Brume Rosse, a wine that usually picks up Two Glasses. The number of Riccardo De Cerchio's wines worthy of mention is growing, in particular two fresh, well-structured Trebbiano d'Abruzzos. Romeo Taraborrelli is consultant.

○ Trebbiano d'Abruzzo Diogene '01	♟	4
○ Trebbiano d'Abruzzo Colle Maggio '02	♟	3
● Montepulciano d'Abruzzo Brume Rosse '99	♟	5
● Montepulciano d'Abruzzo Brume Rosse '98	♟♟	5

CAMPANIA

Campania continues, rightly, to mount an impassioned defence of its indigenous varieties and the typicity of its wines. Apart from very occasional, and extremely felicitous, exceptions, such as Patrimo from Feudi di San Gregorio and the legendary Montevetrano from Silvia Imparato, the Campanian wine scene is almost completely dominated by products obtained from its traditional grape types. These are greco, fiano, falanghina, biancolella, forastera, coda di volpe and ginestrella for the whites, and aglianico, piedirosso and a few examples of primitivo and sciascinoso for the reds. But that's not all. Non-DOC "Superwines" are enjoying no great success in Campania. There are examples of IGT Aglianico, for instance, and some are high-profile ones, such as De Conciliis' Naima or Feudi di San Gregorio's Serpico. But it is the DOC wines that reign supreme. Into this scenario comes the recent promotion of Greco di Tufo and Fiano di Avellino to DOCG. From the 2003 vintage, they will join Taurasi, bringing the number of DOCGs in the province of Avellino to three. This is second only to Siena, and equal to the number in the provinces of Florence and Verona. Such a situation would have seemed impossible only five or six years ago, and it is an eloquent testimonial to how things are moving in the region. Sadly, this year's whites had to cope with the particularly difficult 2002 vintage which, with the exception of the northeast, was problematical throughout the country. In Campania, it hit particularly hard, with rain right through the harvest period. This diluted the aromas of fiano and created considerable problems for greco, which has compact bunches and so always risks developing rot when there is high humidity. On the other hand, the '99, '00 and '01 vintages were all very good for the reds, and a number of wines are showing excellently. Overall, we are seeing substantial consistency in overall quality levels but we also notice a disconcerting tendency for prices to increase. We would hope that Campania's producers are not going to fall into the same trap that has created so many problems for their colleagues in Piedmont and Tuscany. They need to keep a clear view of what the facts of the market place actually are when pricing their wines.

ATRIPALDA (AV)

CARINARO (CE)

MASTROBERARDINO
VIA MANFREDI, 75/81
83042 ATRIPALDA (AV)
TEL. 0825614111
E-MAIL: mastro@mastro.it

CANTINE CAPUTO
VIA CONSORTILE
81032 CARINARO (CE)
TEL. 0815033955
E-MAIL: cantine@caputo.it

Mastroberardino is a prestigious winery and a landmark on the regional wine scene. As usual, the range of wines submitted was as extensive as it was impressive. Despite the problematic '02 vintage, which affected practically all Italy, the estate's whites included an ever-dependable Fiano di Avellino, which managed to achieve great personality and particularly good varietal character. We preferred the basic version to the Radici, which is still very young, and the More Maiorum, which needs more time in bottle and will be reviewed next year. Pompeiano Avalon '02, from coda di volpe, was impressive. Remaining with the whites, the two '02 Greco di Tufo wines, the basic version and the Nova Serra, were not at all bad. But the strongest white is still Taurasi Radici, the traditional standard bearer. The current release, '99, is very sound, both as regards the vintage and the winemaking. The nose is complex and though the palate is still a touch aggressive with slightly drying tannins, the wine reached the finals and missed Three Glasses by a whisker. We found the more innovative wines to be less impressive, especially Naturalis Historia '99, from aglianico with a little piedirosso, which flirts with a rather more international style. We didn't feel this was completely in tune with a winery that has always made respect for tradition its keynote.

Cantine Caputo gave us one of the greatest surprises of this year's regional tastings. Without fuss or beating of drums, Mario and Nicola Caputo submitted a range of highly respectable wines with some genuine high points. The most impressive was Sannio Aglianico Clanius '02, which ended up as the top Campanian red from this unfortunate vintage, performing as if it had come from a far more felicitous year. The tannins are not too aggressive, and it shows good structure and varietal aromas. It is, perhaps, very slightly over-ripe, but overall it's a very well-made wine. Terre del Volturno Aglianico Zicorà '01 is refined and balanced, showing good use of wood, and has all the characteristics of the '00, only better. Fiano di Avellino '02 is also very good and one of the best examples of the vintage, with a typically almond-like and mineral nose introducing an elegant, finely tuned and nicely deep palate. The other wines also showed well, notably a delicious, light Vesuvio Lacryma Christi Rosso '02. Then came a pleasing Greco di Tufo '02, one of the highest scoring examples of Asprinio di Aversa, '02 again, and a sound Terre del Volturno Casavecchia '01. The last of these proves the worth of the indigenous Casavecchia, prince of wines when the Bourbons ruled Naples but only recently restored to its ancient glories.

●	Taurasi Radici '99	♟♟	7
○	Avalon Bianco '02	♟♟	5
○	Fiano di Avellino '02	♟♟	5
○	Fiano di Avellino Radici '02	♟	5
○	Greco di Tufo '02	♟	5
○	Greco di Tufo Novaserra '02	♟	5
●	Naturalis Historia '99	♟	7
●	Taurasi Radici '90	♟♟♟	8
○	Fiano di Avellino More Maiorum '96	♟♟	6
●	Taurasi Radici '96	♟♟	7
●	Taurasi Radici '98	♟♟	7

●	Sannio Agliatico Clanius '02	♟♟	5
●	Terre del Volturno Aglianico Zicorrà '01	♟♟	6
○	Fiano di Avellino '02	♟♟	5
○	Asprinio d'Aversa Fescine '02	♟	4
○	Greco di Tufo '02	♟	4
●	Terre del Volturno Casavecchia Rosso '01	♟	6
●	Vesuvio Lacryma Christi Rosso '02	♟	4
●	Sannio Aglianico '00	♟♟	4*
●	Terre del Volturno Aglianico Zicorrà '00	♟♟	6
●	Sannio Aglianico Clanius '01	♟♟	5

CASTEL CAMPAGNANO (CE)   CASTELLABATE (SA)

CASTELLO DUCALE
VIA CHIESA, 35
81010 CASTEL CAMPAGNANO (CE)
TEL. 0824972460
E-MAIL: info@castelloducale.com

LUIGI MAFFINI
FRAZ. SAN MARCO
LOC. CENITO
84071 CASTELLABATE (SA)
TEL. 0974966345
E-MAIL: maffini@costacilento.it

Castello Ducale was founded in 1997 and so has been in existence for only seven years, yet Antonio Donato's estate is already at home among Campania's top wineries. It is a very small property, with a production of just 50,000 bottles or thereabouts from 12 hectares of vine. These lie partly in the Sannio area around Benevento, and partly in the province of Caserta. Everything is driven by the policy of maximizing what the area's indigenous varieties and the special characteristics of the land have to offer, creating a single focus in both vineyards and cellar. And results are coming. The '01 Aglianico Contessa Ferrara, IGT Terre del Volturno, achieved a Two Glasses score thanks to its good concentration and strong character, although there is still a slight youthful stalkiness. The sound Casavecchia Sammichele '02 comes, naturally, from casavecchia. This was famous in the past as it was chosen by the Bourbons as the main grape for wine production at court in the days of the Kingdom of the Two Sicilies. Finally, Pallagrello Bianco del Vantaglio, also '02 and also from an indigenous variety, has reasonable complexity on the nose and fair concentration on the palate.

Is there no stopping Luigi Maffini and his Cenito? The '01 is possibly the best we have ever seen. From aglianico and piedirosso, it's not just a fine red, but shows a class and elegance that were previously missing. The oak is well integrated, the nose complex, rather than just simply fruity, and there are light smoky notes. The palate is full, as you would expect from a wine with such a Mediterranean background, and it shows excellent concentration. The only slightly jarring note in what is otherwise a symphony of sensations came from the merest touch of bitterness on the finish. It's a great wine, though, and likely to improve further over the next few months. The white Kratos '02, from fiano, is also first rate, nicely full and fleshy, even though it's a tad less impressive than last year's. The base wine of the range, Kleos '02, from piedirosso, sangiovese and aglianico, is less complex but well made. It has suffered a touch from the vintage, but maintains a fair degree of finesse, as well as goodish body, again bearing the vintage in mind. All this begins to explain why the estate is right up there in the forefront of winemaking, not just in Cilento but in the entire region. And the artifice of this development, not to mention its soul, is Luigi Maffini, agronomist, oenologist and, above all, a wine man of rare competence and passion.

● Aglianico Contessa Ferrara '01	♟♟	5
● Casavecchia Sammichele '02	♟	4
○ Pallagrello Bianco del Vantaglio '02	♟	4
● Aglianico Contessa Ferrara '00	♀	5
○ Pallagrello Bianco del Vantaglio '01	♀	4

● Cenito '01	♟♟	7
○ Kràtos '02	♟♟	4
● Kléos '02	♟	4
● Cenito '97	♟♟	7
● Cenito '98	♟♟	7
● Kléos '99	♟♟	4
● Cenito '99	♟♟	7
● Kléos '00	♟♟	4*
● Cenito '00	♟♟	7
○ Kràtos '01	♟♟	4*

CELLOLE (CE)

VILLA MATILDE
S.S. DOMITIANA, 18 - KM. 4,700
81030 CELLOLE (CE)
TEL. 0823932088
E-MAIL: info@fattoriavillamatilde.com

FOGLIANISE (BN)

CANTINA DEL TABURNO
VIA SALA
82030 FOGLIANISE (BN)
TEL. 0824871338
E-MAIL: info@cantinadeltaburno.it

In relatively few years, Villa Matilde has become one of the most important, and most solid, estates in the entire south of Italy. All this is down to Salvatore (known as Tani) and Maria Ida Avallone, brother and sister but, more important, real achievers of great ability. The whole enterprise is guided by Riccardo Cotarella, who consults. He may well be ubiquitous, but for the numerous estates he follows (some say there are over 80), he brings reassurance and gives an authoritative seal of quality. Once again, Villa Matilde's wines are outstanding. Falerno del Massico Vigna Camarato '00 joined its predecessors in earning Three Glass honours. We'd venture to suggest that it's the best edition ever. It could rival any red in the Mediterranean for power and complexity, Rhône and Priorato included. Vigna Camarato comes from aglianico grown on the volcanic soils of Mount Massico near the coast. Here, the variety becomes softer and fuller, picking up an almost balsamic tone, with aromas of Mediterranean scrubland and pine resin. Aglianico Rocca dei Leoni '01, which we first evaluated last year, and the astoundingly concentrated Cecubo '01, from piedirosso, primitivo and abbuoto, both showed very well. The '02 whites are, though, less impressive, with Falerno del Massico Vigna Caracci under par and both the standard-label Falerno and Falanghina Rocca dei Leoni displaying honest good typing but little more. Falerno Rosso '01 is sound. We would have expected it to perform better.

It could be the vintage, or perhaps it's the adoption of a winemaking style directed less towards concentration, but this year Cantina del Taburno's best reds were not as attractive as they usually are. They are still big, rich, powerful wines, but they seem to lack the roundness that gave them the edge in other vintages. That said, we should also make it clear that we are nevertheless in the presence of a vast, highly impressive range. In addition, the winery is one of those most responsible for what is a full-blown renaissance of winemaking in the province of Benevento, and this is one of the clearest trends emerging anywhere in the region. But let's get on to this year's wines. Bue Apis '01, from aglianico, is still dominated by smokiness and is still a touch oaky, although it has admirable evenness and balance on the palate. Delius '01, another Aglianico, is similar in style. There's less character but just as much elegance. Given the troublesome vintage, the performance of the '02 Greco was remarkable. Apart from those coming from the classic zones for the variety, it was the best Greco we tasted this year. The other '02 whites, Coda di Volpe Amineo, Taburno Falanghina Folius and the basic Taburno Falanghina, are attractive and well made, but inexorably betray their lesser vintage. Aglianico del Taburno Fidelis '00 is pleasant.

● Falerno del Massico Rosso Vigna Camarato '00	♟♟♟	6
● Cecubo '01	♟♟	5
● Aglianico Rocca dei Leoni '01	♟	5
● Falerno del Massico Rosso '01	♟	4
○ Falanghina Rocca dei Leoni '02	♟	3
○ Falerno del Massico Bianco '02	♟	3
○ Falerno del Massico Bianco Vigna Caracci '02	♟	4
● Falerno del Massico Rosso Vigna Camarato '97	♟♟♟	6
● Falerno del Massico Rosso Vigna Camarato '98	♟♟♟	6
○ Falerno del Massico Bianco Vigna Caracci '01	♟♟	4*

● Bue Apis '01	♟♟	8
● Delius '01	♟♟	6
○ Greco del Taburno '02	♟♟	3*
● Aglianico del Taburno Fidelis '00	♟	3
○ Taburno Coda di Volpe Amineo '02	♟	3
○ Taburno Falanghina '02	♟	3
○ Taburno Falanghina Folius '02	♟	5
● Bue Apis '99	♟♟♟	7
● Bue Apis '00	♟♟♟	7
● Delius '99	♟♟	6
● Delius '00	♟♟	6

FORIO (NA)

D'AMBRA VINI D'ISCHIA
FRAZ. PANZA
VIA MARIO D'AMBRA, 16
80075 FORIO (NA)
TEL. 081907246 - 081907210
E-MAIL: info@dambravini.com

The D'Ambra family has always been the leading grape grower on Ischia. It is difficult work, for the land where vineyards are to be planted has to be clawed from the flanks of Mount Epomeo, a volcano that every so often lets you know that it's not completely dormant. The soils are tufa-based with a characteristic greenish colour and small plots of vines, looking more like vegetable gardens than real vineyards, are scattered all over the place. Everything is on steep, terraced slopes, which are incredibly beautiful to look at, but dreadfully difficult to work. However, this year, too, Andrea D'Ambra has carried out his small miracle and presented us with a very impressive range of wines, starting with Kyme Bianco '01. This is obtained with grape varieties from the Greek Aegean archipelagos and the Chalkis peninsula. Andrea planted them on Ischia, taking his lead from the island's ancient colonists who came from those parts of Greece. The wine is even more impressive than last year's, good as that was. There is less rusticity, the nose is fruity and minerally, and its body is quite something, making it a great Mediterranean white. The whites from '02, though, have paid the price of a so-so vintage (here it rained less than elsewhere). Ischia Biancolella Frassitelli is not all that powerful, but very drinkable. Ischia Biancolella and the slightly raisined Ischia Forastera are well made and sound. Ischia Rosso Dedicato a Mario D'Ambra '00 is more evolved than we would have liked and Ischia Per' e Palummo '02 is uncomplicatedly attractive, but could have been better.

FURORE (SA)

CANTINE GRAN FUROR
DIVINA COSTIERA
VIA G. B. LAMA, 14
84010 FURORE (SA)
TEL. 089830348
E-MAIL: info@granfuror.it

The couple, and working partners, Andrea Ferraioli and Marisa Cuomo, produce their 50,000 or so bottles from around ten hectares of vines, some owned, some leased, and from bought-in grapes. This might not seem very much but in an area like the Sorrento Peninsula, these numbers are quite significant. This is a "bonsai" zone, not for the size of the vines but by reason of their extension. Everything is hard, tiring work. The sites, though spectacular, are on vertiginous slopes and the vines are terraced. Wines here come from pride, passion and a real sense of belonging, more than from any financial considerations. That's why we are particularly pleased that the winery's best red, the '00 Costa d'Amalfi Furore Riserva, demonstrated such class that it reached our finals. It is powerful, with smokiness on the nose and possibly a touch of rusticity on the palate but, of its type, is quite outstanding. The straight Costa d'Amalfi Furore '02, though naturally less of a heavyweight, is also first rate. Fragrant, even and very drinkable, it is also very well priced. The whites showed less well than usual, which is hardly surprising given the '02 vintage, with Fior d'Uva a touch evolved. Yet paradoxically Furore Bianco is fresher and more successful, revealing good winemaking skills.

○ Kyme Bianco '01	♈♈	6
○ Ischia Biancolella Tenuta Frassitelli '02	♈♈	5
● Ischia Rosso Dedicato a Mario d'Ambra '00	♈	6
○ Ischia Biancolella '02	♈	3
○ Ischia Forastera '02	♈	3
● Ischia Per''e Palummo '02	♈	3
○ Ischia Biancolella Tenuta Frassitelli '00	♈♈	5*
○ Ischia Biancolella Tenuta Frassitelli '01	♈♈	5*
○ Kyme Bianco '00	♈♈	6
● Ischia Rosso Dedicato a Mario d'Ambra '99	♈♈	6

● Costa d'Amalfi Furore Rosso Ris. '00	♈♈	7
● Costa d'Amalfi Furore Rosso '02	♈♈	4*
○ Costa d'Amalfi Furore Bianco '02	♈	4
○ Costa d'Amalfi Furore Bianco Fiord'Uva '02	♈	7
● Costa d'Amalfi Furore Rosso Ris. '97	♈♈	7
○ Costa d'Amalfi Furore Bianco Fiord'uva '00	♈♈	7*
● Costa d'Amalfi Furore Rosso Ris. '98	♈♈	7
● Costa d'Amalfi Furore Rosso Ris. '99	♈♈	7
○ Costa d'Amalfi Furore Bianco Fiord'Uva '01	♈♈	7

GALLUCCIO (CE)

GUARDIA SANFRAMONDI (BN)

TELARO
LOC. SORRENTO
VIA CINQUE PIETRE, 2
81045 GALLUCCIO (CE)
TEL. 0823925841
E-MAIL: info@vinitelaro.it

CORTE NORMANNA
C.DA SAPENZIE, 20
82034 GUARDIA SANFRAMONDI (BN)
TEL. 0824817004 - 0824817008
E-MAIL: info@cortenormanna.it

The Telaro brothers might well be considered the kings of the Galluccio DOC, an area in Caserta province that has recently come to light for its great vocation for wines from traditional, highly local varieties. The brothers' experiments with late-harvested falanghina, for example, are bringing notable results, as their '02 Falanghina di Roccamonfina shows. It's surprisingly good, managing to combine perfume and fruit with mineral scents that make the nose much more complex and interesting than you would have imagined. On the palate too, the depth and flesh that the over-ripe grapes give make it a most drinkable wine, whilst retaining considerable density. The most interesting of the reds were, we felt, the deep, full-bodied Galluccio Ara Mundi Riserva '00 and the Galluccio Aglianico Montecaruso '01, the best release of this wine ever. The rest of the range is also good. The '02 whites, Falanghina, Greco and Fiano, have immediate charm, good varietal characteristics and plenty of fruit. However, the Galluccio Calivierno Riserva '00, although still very decent, is a tad evolved and without the attack that really impressed us with the '98. Overall, though, things are on the up here, especially as regards the impeccable winemaking displayed in the various wines.

Balsamic, with typically Aglianico fruit and smokiness on the nose; powerful, fleshy but also a touch austere and tannic on the palate; very long. This, more or less, was the tasting note. Then came the wait to see which famous label from which noted estate it was. When the wine was uncovered, the whole tasting panel was absolutely astounded: Sannio Aglianico '01, Corte Normanna. This is a small estate in Guardia Sanframondi in the heart of the Sannio area at Benevento, owned by brothers Alfredo and Gaetano Falluto. Winemaking is followed by Roberto Mazzer, one of the new names in Italian oenology, who operates mainly in Lazio and Campania. The wine was sent up to the finals and even there, it more than held its own, coming within a hair of Three Glasses. Not bad for a first release! The estate's other two reds are good, too. Solopaca Guiscardo '01 is pleasant, nicely balanced and not too full in body. Sannio Aglianico Tre Pietre '99 is also attractive, but perhaps, for our tastes, a little past its best. The whites, though, were less convincing, so much so that we awarded no glasses and mention only the Falanghina Palombaia '02. You have to do better to score serious points in this sector.

● Galluccio Ara Mundi Ris. '00	🍷🍷	5
● Galluccio Aglianico Montecaruso '01	🍷🍷	4
○ Falanghina di Roccamonfina V.T. '02	🍷🍷	4
● Galluccio Calivierno Ris. '00	🍷	5
○ Fiano di Roccamonfina le Cinque Pietre '02	🍷	4
○ Galluccio Falanghina Ripa Bianca '02	🍷	3
○ Greco di Roccamonfina le Cinque Pietre '02	🍷	4
● Galluccio Aglianico Montecaruso '99	🍷🍷	4*
● Galluccio Calivierno Ris. '98	🍷🍷	5

● Sannio Aglianico '01	🍷🍷	4*
● Solopaca Rosso Guiscardo '01	🍷	4
● Sannio Aglianico Tre Pietre '99	🍷	4
○ Sannio Falanghina La Palombaia '02		3
● Sannio Aglianico Tre Pietre '98	🍷	4

LAPIO (AV)

COLLI DI LAPIO - CLELIA ROMANO
FRAZ. ARIANIELLO
83030 LAPIO (AV)
TEL. 0825982191 - 0825982184

It might be only a tiny winery with just four hectares of vine and a production of 30,000 bottles. You could also say it was hardly representative of Fiano di Avellino. Yet for us, Clelia Romano is the queen of Fiano. She manages to produce a uniquely individual, instantly recognizable version of the wine, even in lesser years, like 2002. This year, we also caught up with the '01 which we didn't manage to taste for the 2003 Guide. If that was a lapse on one side, on the other we now find ourselves with a white of great class. The gently aromatic nose would seem to confirm the hypothesis that the fiano variety is related to the huge moscato family. More significantly, though, it has a mouthfilling softness that remains from first to last, through, almost, to the aftertaste. The '02 is a little more minerally on its flinty, grapefruit-like nose, and the palate is slimmer but also more aristocratic with particularly racy, though not very typical, acidity. The range comes to a close with Aglianico Donna Chiara '01, a sound, well-made red that risks being outclassed and ending up playing second fiddle to the two Fianos.

MONTEFREDANE (AV)

PIETRACUPA
C.DA VADIAPERTI, 17
83030 MONTEFREDANE (AV)
TEL. 0825607418

Sabino Loffredo is a skilled, committed grape grower. His wines, though, are almost always characterized by a sort of initial sullenness that can put off tasters who go no further than the initial impact, without thinking about how the wine might develop. The whites in particular need a bit of time. Loffredo's oenological and viticultural researches are directed towards improving his wines' ageing potential, and this inevitably implies some initial acidic edginess. If we were now to retaste the '01 Greco di Tufo "G", we'd find a wine of complexity and minerality, a sort of Campanian Riesling, with acidity that is still lively but softer and more elegant. All this is even more relevant this year with wines coming from a much more difficult vintage. In fact, the "G" was not even produced. But we do have a Fiano di Avellino of great typicity, which falls from grace a little for a lack of length, but which promises to develop well, for a decent period of time and with fair class. Greco di Tufo '02 is good, too, though it lacks the complexity and length of the previous vintage. The reds are fair. Taurasi '99 is very elegant, showing almost Burgundian in style, with no excess oak on the nose, and Irpinia Aglianico Quirico '01 is acceptable, with a tannic stalkiness that is not completely supported by the wine's body.

O Fiano di Avellino '01	♟♟	5
O Fiano di Avellino '02	♟♟	5
● Irpinia Aglianico Donna Chiara '01	♟	5
O Fiano di Avellino '00	♟♟	4*

O Fiano di Avellino '02	♟♟	4
● Taurasi '99	♟♟	6
● Quirico '01	♟	5
O Greco di Tufo '02	♟	4
O Greco di Tufo "G" '01	♟♟	4*
O Fiano di Avellino '01	♟	4
O Taurasi '98	♟	6

MONTEFUSCO (AV)

COLLI IRPINI
LOC. SERRA
VIA SERRA DI MONTEFUSCO
83030 MONTEFUSCO (AV)
TEL. 0825963972
E-MAIL: info@colliirpini.com

Colli Irpini is a large winery with a production capacity of 1,000,000 bottles a year. The wines come partly from vines in the Irpinia zone, partly from the Sannio part of Benevento, and practically all the styles permitted from both zones are made. This is the winery's first appearance in the Guide, and it won its spurs with a very broad range. We will report on only part of the list, both for reasons of space and because despite some highly promising, well-made wines, there were others that did not completely convince us. That said, we have nothing but praise for the muscle and power of Sannio Aglianico '01, a red of good typicity, that is slightly rustic possibly but full of character. It has a well-knit, balsamic nose with red berry fruits and hints of spiciness; and is full-flavoured, rich and long, with a touch of astringency. A further plus point is its excellent value for money. The two versions of Falanghina del Sannio, both '02, are good, the simpler, lighter, straight version as well as the more concentrated selection, Simposium. Greco di Tufo '02 is pleasing and both releases of Fiano di Avellino '02 are well typed, with the selection Sirios coming out on top for its greater concentration, especially on the palate. One final note. This is one of the very few wineries that is entirely run by women. Ownership is in the hands of agronomist, Rosa Pesa, and her partners Federica Costanza and Sabina Gubitosa.

MONTEFUSCO (AV)

TERREDORA
VIA SERRA
83030 MONTEFUSCO (AV)
TEL. 0825968215
E-MAIL: info@terredora.com

This is one of the most important wineries in southern Italy. It has over 150 hectares of vine but, more important, it also has the dedication and professionalism of Walter Mastroberardino and his children Lucio, Paolo and Daniela behind it. The watchwords are reliability and good pricing, elements that make for happy customers all round the world. And even in a growing year best forgotten, like '02, results were pretty good. The two styles of Greco di Tufo were among the best versions of this wine tasted this year. Both are technically impeccable, with good typicity, plenty of fruit and a welcome acidity that should ensure they hold well over time. Falanghina del Beneventano has surprisingly good complexity and elegance. Its companion, Falanghina dell'Irpinia, is a touch less aromatic, with a hint more neutrality and dilution. Among the reds, Aglianico Il Principio performed quite well, but we would have hoped for something better from the Taurasi, which was quite evolved and had some edginess to its tannins that the richness of extract was incapable of absorbing. Our overall judgement, though, can only be very positive, especially when you consider the excellent value for money offered by the range.

● Sannio Aglianico '01	♟♟	3*
○ Fiano di Avellino '02	♟	5
○ Fiano di Avellino Sirios '02	♟	5
○ Greco di Tufo '02	♟	5
○ Sannio Falanghina '02	♟	4
○ Sannio Falanghina Simposium '02	♟	5

○ Falanghina del Beneventano '02	♟♟	4
○ Greco di Tufo Loggia della Serra '02	♟♟	4
○ Greco di Tufo Terra degli Angeli '02	♟♟	4
● Irpinia Aglianico Il Principio '01	♟	4
○ Fiano di Avellino Terre di Dora '02	♟	4
○ Irpinia Falanghina '02	♟	4
● Taurasi Fatica Contadina '99	♟	6
○ Fiano di Avellino Terre di Dora '00	♟♟	4*
● Taurasi Fatica Contadina '97	♟♟	6
○ Fiano di Avellino Terre di Dora '01	♟♟	4*

MONTEMARANO (AV)

SALVATORE MOLETTIERI
C.DA MUSANNI, 19
83040 MONTEMARANO (AV)
TEL. 082763722 - 082763424
E-MAIL: info@salvatoremolettieri.it

The estate is very small, with just seven hectares and 20,000 bottles produced. Yet Salvatore and Giacomo Molettieri's wines are becoming great talking points, and not just in Italy. The two partners pour their heart and soul into the, lavishing great craftsmanship on their creations and giving them both personality and an ability to communicate the characteristics of their environment. The terrain is not easy for the vines grow at 600 metres, which gives the wines a distinct tenor. They seem more northern, more extreme, and appear to have more in common with wines from the other end of the peninsula. They are also difficult to find, and prices are not always within everyone's reach, a small black mark that we have to mention. But let's describe the range. The two Taurasi wines, the standard-label '99 and the '98 Riserva, are both distinguished. Paradoxically, we continue to prefer the younger version, perhaps because it is more immediate and easier drinking, whereas the Riserva is very austere, and even a shade aggressive. The other two reds, Cinque Querce and Ischia Piana, both '01s also based on aglianico, are sound. Despite its name, Ischia Piana is sourced from grapes grown locally, not on the island of Ischia. These are two uncomplicated wines, with attractiveness and elegance as their strong suits. The overall impression, though, is of a search for identity and wines that express their provenance without conceding anything to immediate pleasure. These are wines you have to wait for and understand, and which require serious attention to be fully appreciated.

PRATOLA SERRA (AV)

LA CASA DELL'ORCO
FRAZ. S. MICHELE
VIA LIMATURO, 52
83039 PRATOLA SERRA (AV)
TEL. 0825967038 - 082537247
E-MAIL: lacasadellorco@libero.it

Lawyer Pellegrino Musto, of the rather menacingly named La Casa del Orco ("the ogre's den") estate, should be very pleased with the performance of this year's wines. We reckon his '02 whites are some of the best in Campania. It was not an easy year to handle, yet Musto's cellars produced wines that deserve careful consideration and clearly show an unexpected perfection of styling. His '02 is, we feel, the year's best Fiano di Avellino. It has a clearly defined, clean, lightly perfumed nose of extreme typicity. The palate is full, soft and well concentrated, so much so that you find yourself asking how the estate managed to turn out such a good wine from such a poor vintage. Similar comments apply to the Greco di Tufo, also '02, with the additional point that the year was even more challenging for the greco grape. The variety is prone to rot when it rains a great deal, as the bunches are tight-packed and the water trapped inside can't evaporate. Despite this, Musto's Greco has a good, citrus-like nose, with some minerality, and a structure well supported by a nice acid backbone. The other two wines submitted, the well-typed, attractive Coda di Volpe dell'Irpinia '02 and the Taurasi '99, are also good. However, we would have hoped for a bit more from the latter given the favourable vintage.

● Taurasi		
Vigna Cinque Querce Ris. '98	♆♆	8
● Taurasi Vigna Cinque Querce '99	♆♆	7
● Aglianico Cinque Querce '01	♆	5
● Irpinia Ischia Piana '01	♆	5
● Taurasi Vigna Cinque Querce '94	♆♆	7
● Taurasi Vigna Cinque Querce '96	♆♆	7
● Taurasi Vigna Cinque Querce '97	♆♆	7
● Taurasi		
Vigna Cinque Querce Ris. '97	♆♆	8
● Taurasi Vigna Cinque Querce '98	♆♆	7

○ Fiano di Avellino '02	♆♆	4*
○ Greco di Tufo '02	♆♆	4*
○ Irpinia Bianco Coda di Volpe '02	♆	3
● Taurasi '99	♆	6

PRIGNANO CILENTO (SA)   QUARTO (NA)

VITICOLTORI DE CONCILIIS
LOC. QUERCE, 1
84060 PRIGNANO CILENTO (SA)
TEL. 0974831090
E-MAIL: info@viticoltorideconciliis.it

CANTINE GROTTA DEL SOLE
VIA SPINELLI, 2
80010 QUARTO (NA)
TEL. 0818762566 - 0818761320
E-MAIL: grottadelsole@grottadelsole.it

After waiting many years, we are finally able to award Bruno De Conciliis' most archetypal wine, the 100 per cent-aglianico Naima, top honours. The '01 seems to have captured, as if by magic, all the sun of the Cilento zone, along with all the power and strength its ancient soils have to yield. It's a wine of majestic structure, as rich and full as a great Mediterranean red should be. Tight-knit as the best examples of Côte Rotie or Priorato, it also reveals the balsam, the sharp red berry fruits and the light smokiness that only aglianico from this particular part of Campania can impart. All credit, then, to Bruno De Conciliis for having given us a wine of this calibre. We sincerely hope that he will be able to repeat the achievement many times more. Acting as pageboys to this sovereign of Campanian wines come a well-styled version of Fiano Donnaluna and a pleasant, most drinkable Aglianico Donnalunga, both '02. They are not outstanding, but given that few people can always drink stellar bottles, it is good to know that we also have wines like these that you can drink regularly without having to take out a second mortgage.

Grotta del Sole's presence in the Guide this year is somewhat provisory, as its best wines were bottled just prior to our tastings and their assessment has had to be deferred to next year. But the most important news comes on the technical front. Gennaro Martusciello, the winery's joint owner and its guiding spirit, has decided to bring in Attilio Pagli to advise on the winemaking side and Federico Curtaz for viticulture. This is sure to bring stylistic developments in the wines that will emerge in the fullness of time. As far as this year's wines are concerned, we decided to look at only three, those we felt were expressing their characteristics clearly, definitively and unequivocally at the time. And the most attractive, most typical and most enjoyable of the trio was the slightly sparkling red, Gragnano, which has its roots firmly buried in true Neapolitan tradition. Falanghina Coste di Cuma, which ages one year, partly in barriques and partly in stainless steel, is quite evolved on the nose, but has fair concentration on the palate. Campi Flegrei Piedirosso Montegauro Riserva '99 has a complex nose but a rather austere and one-dimensional palate. It is one of the estate's top wines but we'd have preferred a younger example.

● Naima '01	♟♟♟	6
● Donnaluna Aglianico '02	♟	4
○ Donnaluna Fiano '02	♟	4
● Naima '98	♟♟	6
● Naima '99	♟♟	6
● Donnaluna Aglianico '00	♟♟	4*
● Zero - D'Orta-De Conciliis '99	♟♟	6
● Merlanico - De Conciliis - Barone Pizzini '00	♟♟	6
● Zero - D'Orta-De Conciliis '00	♟♟	6
● Donnaluna Aglianico '01	♟	4

○ Campi Flegrei Falanghina Coste di Cuma '01	♟	4
● Penisola Sorrentina Gragnano '02	♟	3
● Campi Flegrei Piedirosso Montegauro Ris. '99	♟	5
● Quarto di Sole '98	♟♟	5
○ Quarto di Luna '00	♟♟	4*
○ Quarto di Luna '99	♟	5

SALZA IRPINA (AV)

DI MEO
C.DA COCCOVONI, 1
83050 SALZA IRPINA (AV)
TEL. 0825981419
E-MAIL: info@dimeo.it

The good things that Roberto Di Meo brought to last year's Guide were with us again this year. We still think that he does much better with his reds than his whites, which are certainly very individual but also a touch rustic. On the red side, his two top wines, the "Supercampanian" Don Generoso from aglianico with a little piedirosso, and Taurasi Riserva, did very well indeed at our tastings, as they always do. The '01 Don Generoso in particular is an excellently made, full-bodied wine in a modern style that is also elegant. The '98 Taurasi, a "riserva" of course, stands up well in its category and earned a slot among the top ten wines from this DOCG. But precisely because of all these high-calibre reds, we would have hoped that the winery could offer a more carefully made Greco or Fiano. The basics are all there. You feel, for instance, that the difficult '02 vintage was handled very well in viticultural terms. But then there is that slight lack of conviction on the nose, that excessive fermentative hint, that touch of roughness on the palate which makes you realize that, despite their undeniable qualities, they could have been so much better.

SAN CIPRIANO PICENTINO (SA)

MONTEVETRANO
LOC. NIDO
VIA MONTEVETRANO, 3
84099 SAN CIPRIANO PICENTINO (SA)
TEL. 089882285
E-MAIL: montevetrano@tin.it

With the '01, Montevetrano hit the top spot for the eighth time in nine years of appearances in the Guide. Only the '94 didn't make it. We didn't even judge the '91 and '92. Only a few bottles were made and they circulated exclusively among a small group of fans. This means that, for us, taken over the past 15 years, this prized red from a mix of cabernet sauvignon, merlot and aglianico, is one of the six or seven best wines in Italy. It was the first wine from outside Umbria to benefit from the consultancy of Riccardo Cotarella but, more important, it is indisputably the oenological offspring of "the princess of Italian wine", Silvia Imparato. Her story is already well known. She is beautiful, elegant and cultured. For many years, she was a photographer but is now best known for her achievements with wine. The '01 Montevetrano is a real dream. It's a marvellous wine, a masterpiece, the best, we believe, she has ever produced. It is elegant, complex and extraordinarily eloquent. In fact, it is quite incredible to think that it comes from an area where fine wine – or wine full stop – had never been made before her arrival: San Cipirello is just outside Salerno, not La Morra or Pauillac. But miracles do occur, and passion can make them occur. Silvia is a woman with strong passions, even when she's growing grapes.

Wine	Glasses	Score
● Don Generoso '01	♈♈	8
● Taurasi Ris. '98	♈♈	6
○ Fiano di Avellino Colle dei Cerri '02	♈	5
○ Greco di Tufo '02	♈	4
○ Sannio Falanghina '02		3
● Don Generoso '00	♈♈	8
● Taurasi Ris. '97	♈♈	6

Wine	Glasses	Score
● Montevetrano '01	♈♈♈	8
● Montevetrano '93	♈♈♈	8
● Montevetrano '95	♈♈♈	8
● Montevetrano '96	♈♈♈	8
● Montevetrano '97	♈♈♈	8
● Montevetrano '98	♈♈♈	8
● Montevetrano '99	♈♈♈	8
● Montevetrano '00	♈♈♈	8
● Montevetrano '94	♈♈	8

SANT'AGATA DE' GOTI (BN)

MUSTILLI
VIA CAUDINA, 10
82019 SANT'AGATA DE' GOTI (BN)
TEL. 0823717433
E-MAIL: info@mustilli.com

The name Mustilli conjures up a family that has given dignity to grape growing and winemaking in Sant'Agata dei Goti, an area in the province of Benevento, for over 40 years. And if today the zone is literally exploding with high quality wine, and a renaissance of viticulture in general, it is all down to people like Mustilli, who were able to show what wine production in this lesser-known part of Campania could become before others had even thought about it. Currently, the estate is benefiting increasingly from the input of the two daughters of Leonardo Mustilli, its bard and inspiration. Anna Chiara looks after winemaking and viticulture, whereas Paola runs the commercial side. Consultancy comes from the highly experienced, much respected Tuscan oenologist, Mauro Orsoni. Let's come to this year's wines. The Falanghina and Piedirosso, the estate's bankers, are fairly good. Both come from '02, so were unlikely to be outstanding. However, they retain good typing and have some attractive aspects on both nose and palate. Although Cesco di Nece '99, from 100 per cent aglianico, is in our opinion a little too old, it also has character. Had it been released a year earlier, it would probably have retained more primary notes and more immediacy on the nose. Overall, however, the range does justice to the fame of this renowned, traditional estate.

○ S. Agata dei Goti Falanghina '02	▼	4
● S. Agata dei Goti Piedirosso '02	▼	4
● Sant'Agata dei Goti Aglianico Cesco di Nece '99	▼	5
● Gheppio '00	▽▽	4*
● S. Agata dei Goti Rosso Conte Artus '00	▽	4

SERINO (AV)

VILLA RAIANO
VIA PESCATORE, 19
83028 SERINO (AV)
TEL. 0825592826 - 0825595781
E-MAIL: info@villaraiano.it

It was just seven years ago that Villa Raiano exploded onto the Campanian wine scene. In this short space of time, it has managed to carve out place in the sun for itself among Avellino's wineries. Owner Sabino Basso and his son Simone, the estate director, already have some distinguished results under their belts, thanks in part to input from consultant Luigi Moro, one of Italian oenology's gurus. And remember that in agriculture, and viticulture in particular, things tend to move very slowly. This year, it is again the Taurasi, this time from the excellent '99 vintage, that stands proudly at the top of the range. It is a red of great character, even though it still has one or two youthful rough edges. These will no doubt be smoothed out with a few years in bottle. Both versions of Fiano di Avellino '02 are sound, despite the growing year being what it was. Our preference just went to the Ripa Alta for its more complex, more decisive nose and its slightly more solid structure. The simpler Falanghina is decent, with a rather attractive gentle perfume. We finish with Irpinia Aglianico '01, an IGT red that echoes some of the characteristics of the Taurasi, if with less depth. All in all, we have a good quality range here, even though it wasn't helped by the very difficult '02 vintage, which was especially hard on whites.

● Taurasi '99	▼▼	7
● Irpinia Aglianico '01	▼	5
○ Falanghina Beneventano '02	▼	4
○ Fiano di Avellino '02	▼	4
○ Fiano di Avellino Ripa Alta '02	▼	5
○ Greco di Tufo '01	▽▽	4
● Taurasi '98	▽▽	6

SESSA AURUNCA (CE)

GALARDI
FRAZ. SAN CARLO
S.P. SESSA-MIGNANO
81030 SESSA AURUNCA (CE)
TEL. 0823925003
E-MAIL: galardi@napoli.com

This is a phenomenal story, and no mistake. In a very short space of time, Terre di Lavoro and its meagre production of just 10,000 bottles has become one of the most famous "vins de garage à l'italienne", almost a sort of Italian version of Bordeaux's Le Pin or Valandraud. It is also one of the Italian wines most highly rated by American critic Robert Parker Jr, and one of the proudest feathers in the cap of super-consultant Riccardo Cotarella. But above all, Terre di Lavoro is the result of the dedication and love for their land of the three cousins, Maria Luisa Murena, Francesco and Dora Catello, and Dora's husband, Arturo Celentano, who own this pocket-sized winery. None of the world's finest wines could exist without impassioned producers behind them and Terre di Lavoro is no exception. The name comes from a part of the province of Caserta and the wine itself is made from aglianico with a little piedirosso. It has great personality, even if its overtly smoky nose and its austere, complex character with some unexpected stalkiness might not appeal to everyone. But it is certainly unique. It's a wine that doesn't fit into categories or bow to fashion, and one that derives from its environment, not a particular style of winemaking. It's an extreme wine, if you like, but at the end of the day, what great wine isn't?

SORBO SERPICO (AV)

★ FEUDI DI SAN GREGORIO
LOC. CERZA GROSSA
83042 SORBO SERPICO (AV)
TEL. 08259866
E-MAIL: feudi@feudi.it

Yet again, numerous Feudi wines gained very high scores, marching on like a great, south Italian oenological army. Serpico '01, from aglianico, and the stellar Patrimo '01, from merlot, are well up to expectations and show extremely high quality. Both are powerful, concentrated reds, but they also have the acidity to give them excellent ageing potential. Piano di Montevergine is one of the best examples of Taurasi around. However, the real surprise came from two reds produced in Basilicata and Puglia respectively, Aglianico del Vulture Efesto '01 and Primitivo di Manduria Ognisole '01. Both have good typicity, but what really stands out is the proficiency of the winemaking. Taurasi Selve dei Luoti '99 also showed very well. In contrast, the whites, which are the backbone of the estate's output, seemed a little below par. The vintage certainly didn't help, but even so we'd have expected a somewhat better performance. The '02 Campanaro is simpler and lighter than in the past. It has gained in drinkability but lost in complexity. The Greco, Fiano and Falanghina all seem to have come out of the same mould: fermentative aromas, fair acidity, not all that much body. They are understated, well typed and technically well made, but with less character than the previous few releases. We hope that this is just the result of a vintage that is best forgotten as quickly as possible. But the estate's consolation will be the star it now gains for having won ten Three Glass awards.

● Terra di Lavoro '01	♀♀	7
● Terra di Lavoro '99	♀♀♀	7
● Terra di Lavoro '94	♀♀	7
● Terra di Lavoro '95	♀♀	7
● Terra di Lavoro '97	♀♀	7
● Terra di Lavoro '98	♀♀	7
● Terra di Lavoro '00	♀♀	7
● Terra di Lavoro '96	♀	7

● Pàtrimo '01	♀♀♀	8
● Serpico '01	♀♀♀	8
● Aglianico del Vulture Efesto '01	♀♀	6
● Primitivo di Manduria Ognisole '01	♀♀	6
○ Campanaro '02	♀♀	6
● Taurasi Piano di Montevergine Ris. '99	♀♀	6
● Taurasi Selve di Luoti '99	♀♀	6
○ Fiano di Avellino '02	♀	5
○ Greco di Tufo '02	♀	5
○ Sannio Falanghina '02	♀	4
● Taurasi Piano di Montevergine '96	♀♀♀	6
● Pàtrimo '99	♀♀♀	8
● Serpico '99	♀♀♀	8
● Pàtrimo '00	♀♀♀	8
● Serpico '00	♀♀♀	8

TAURASI (AV)

TORRECUSO (BN)

ANTONIO CAGGIANO
C.DA SALA
83030 TAURASI (AV)
TEL. 082774723
E-MAIL: info@cantinecaggiano.it

FONTANAVECCHIA
VIA FONTANAVECCHIA
82030 TORRECUSO (BN)
TEL. 0824876275

The year 2004 is the tenth vintage on the estate owned by Antonio Caggiano and his son Giuseppe. They have been ten years of great work and much success, for the Caggiano wines are always among the first choices of those aficionados who go for more traditional styles. Taurasi Vigna Macchia dei Goti is for many the quintessence of typicity, even though it is aged in small barrels. The 20,000 bottles released are quickly snapped up by winelovers everywhere. The '00 again showed very well, even though we felt it did not have the aristocratic complexity of the '99. It is elegant, and has noticeable tannin and very impressive complexity on the nose. Salae Domini, also 100 per cent aglianico, is more modern, possibly winking at a more international style. It is also more approachable, if a little simpler. Fiano di Avellino Bechàr can always be relied on and even the '02 has a mineral nose and surprisingly good structure. Fiagre, from fiano and greco, and Greco di Tufo Devon, both '02, are as well styled as ever but Taurì '01, another monovarietal aglianico, performed less brilliantly than usual. It appears a little coarser than it has been in past editions.

Libero Rollo, Torrecuso's proprietor, has eight and a half hectares of vines, some owned directly, some leased. In addition, he bolsters his limited output with small quantities of locally grown grapes that are bought in. One way or another, he turns out 100,000 bottles, still a small number but not insignificant. Everything is from local grape varieties. The main axis of production comes from various versions of Aglianico del Taburno. The one we liked the best was the '01 Grave Morae, a rich, powerful, rather well-balanced red that we felt could stand up to a good few years' in the cellar. It is the first time we've tasted the wine, so we prefer to be cautious, but we feel it might be one of the great hopes of Campanian winemaking. We shall see in good time. Aglianico Vigna Cataratte Riserva is nice, as usual, and a bit edgy, as it often is. The current vintage, '99, is more imposing, but also more closed and stalky than the previous one. Almost preferable, we'd say, is the very pleasing straight version, Aglianico del Taburno '01, which apart from its intrinsic qualities on nose and palate also stands out as good value for money. Finally comes the fresh, pleasant Aglianico del Taburno Rosato '02, which was a pleasure to drink, especially during the torrid summer of 2003.

● Taurasi Macchia dei Goti '00	♟♟	7
● Salae Domini '01	♟♟	6
○ Fiano di Avellino Bechar '02	♟♟	5
● Taurì '01	♟	4
○ Fiagre '02	♟	4
○ Greco di Tufo Devon '02	♟	5
● Taurasi Vigna Macchia dei Goti '99	♟♟♟	7
● Taurasi Vigna Macchia dei Goti '98	♟♟	7
○ Fiano di Avellino Béchar '00	♟♟	5
● Taurì '99	♟♟	4
○ Fiano di Avellino Béchar '01	♟♟	5
● Taurì '00	♟	4

● Aglianico del Taburno Grave Morae '01	♟♟	6
● Aglianico del Taburno '01	♟	4
⊙ Aglianico del Taburno Rosato '02	♟	3
● Aglianico del Taburno Vigna Cataratte Ris. '99	♟	6
● Aglianico del Taburno Vigna Cataratte Ris. '95	♟♟	6
● Aglianico del Taburno Vigna Cataratte '96	♟♟	6
● Orazio '00	♟♟	6
● Orazio '01	♟♟	6
● Aglianico del Taburno Vigna Cataratte Ris. '97	♟	6
● Aglianico del Taburno Vigna Cataratte Ris. '98	♟	6

TORRECUSO (BN)

FATTORIA LA RIVOLTA
C.DA RIVOLTA
82030 TORRECUSO (BN)
TEL. 0824872921
E-MAIL: pcotron@tin.it

That wine, in moderate quantities, can be beneficial to health is nothing new. Many know about the illuminating scientific paper entitled "The French Paradox" and the miraculous properties of resveratrol on the heart and circulatory system. There has been widespread comment on the research, both written and spoken. So it shouldn't come as a surprise that a professional pharmacist becomes involved in wine production. In this case, his name is Paolo Cotroneo and he turned to grape growing and winemaking in the Taburno zone some years ago. Aglianico, the leading grape of this vast hilly area in the northeast of the region, is one of the varieties richest in polyphenols, including resveratrol. In fact, making quality wine with aglianico may be as good for the health as it is for the taste buds. And never have Cotroneo's wines turned out so well. His Aglianico del Taburno Terre di Rivolta Riserva '00 is a great glass of wine that shows rich, with just a hint of stalkiness, and with good complexity on the nose. If wine really does you good, then it should be in every well-stocked cellar of good bottles. The standard-label Aglianico del Taburno, from '00, is pleasing and recalls its elder brother, but aims less high and is, of course, less complex and less concentrated. On the other hand, the '02 version of Falanghina is not one of the best, being a tad over-evolved on the nose and showing only average weight in the mouth.

TUFO (AV)

BENITO FERRARA
FRAZ. S. PAOLO
S. PAOLO, 14/A
83010 TUFO (AV)
TEL. 0825998194
E-MAIL: info@benitoferrara.it

The Greco wines of Gabriella Ferrara, even in the minor key that the '02 vintage sang, showed their usual power and that slightly raisined style that has always marked them out. The Vigna Cicogna is obviously the more impressive of the pair, and isn't as different from previous releases as the vintage might lead you to expect. It is an imposing, fleshy wine, with plenty of alcohol and intense, pervasive aromas. Without doubt, it is an outstanding example of its type. The straight Greco di Tufo showed slightly less confidently, and is a touch shorter and less concentrated than usual. But then the rainy '02 vintage has to have some influence somewhere. What's for sure is that if Gabriella Ferrara and her consultant, Paolo Caciorgna, managed to obtain wines like this in such a vintage, just imagine what sort of fireworks might emerge from the '03, which is already looking very promising for greco grown in its classic zones. Concluding the range comes Aglianico dell'Irpinia, another '02. It is a little lighter than the '01 but not all that much, and has clear aromas of black cherry and tobacco. It is also fully flavoured and still slightly tannic but, all things considered, a balanced and enjoyable wine.

● Aglianico del Taburno Terre di Rivolta Ris. '00	♟♟	6
● Aglianico del Taburno '00	♟	4
○ Taburno Falanghina '02		3
● Aglianico del Taburno Terre di Rivolta Ris. '99	♟	6

○ Greco di Tufo Vigna Cicogna '02	♟♟	5
○ Greco di Tufo '02	♟	5
● Irpinia Aglianico '02	♟	4
○ Greco di Tufo Vigna Cicogna '99	♟♟	4
○ Greco di Tufo Vigna Cicogna '00	♟♟	5
○ Greco di Tufo '01	♟♟	5
○ Greco di Tufo Vigna Cicogna '01	♟♟	5

OTHER WINERIES

MARIANNA
VIA FILANDE, 6
83100 AVELLINO
TEL. 0825627252 - 0825627224
E-MAIL: info@vinimarianna.it

Ciriaco Coscia's winery returns to the Guide with a slightly improved range. Taurasi Riserva '98 in particular showed as a well-made wine with good typicity. From the whites, we liked the fresh, appealing Coda di Volpe best.

○	Irpinia Coda di Volpe '02	♀	4
●	Taurasi Ris. '98	♀	6

FATTORIA CIABRELLI
VIA ITALIA, 3
82030 CASTELVENERE (BN)
TEL. 0824940565
E-MAIL: fattoria@ciabrelli.it

There were two well-made wines from Ciabrelli, a rather impressive version of its habitual Beneventano Aglianico, which is notable for its complex, almost balsamic nose, and an intense Beneventano Barbera. This has good typicity, given that barbera is almost as widespread here as in Piedmont.

●	Beneventano Aglianico '01	♀♀	4
●	Beneventano Barbera '01	♀	4
●	Beneventano Aglianico '00	♀	4

ANTICA MASSERIA VENDITTI
VIA SANNITICA, 122
82030 CASTELVENERE (BN)
TEL. 0824940306
E-MAIL: masseria@venditti.it

There were few wines this year: many were retastes of those first assessed a year earlier. The only truly interesting one was the full, concentrated Sannio Bianco '02, which shows pervasive aromas and a slightly evolved character. Solopaca Rosso Bosco Caldaia '01 is evolving well of the retastes.

○	Sannio Bianco '02	♀	4
●	Sannio Barbera Barbetta Vàndari '01	♀	4
●	Sannio Rosso '01	♀	4
●	Solopaca Rosso Bosco Caldaia '01	♀	5

CANTINA DEL BARONE
VIA NOCELLETO, 19
83020 CESINALI (AV)
TEL. 0825666751
E-MAIL: info@cantinadelbarone.it

A minute winery with only 20,000 bottles from just three hectares of vine. The wines are really well made, though. Taurasi '99 is an excellent example of a typical, traditional red. The rest offer good winemaking, at the least. This is likely to be one of the stars of Campania in the near future.

●	Taurasi '99	♀♀	6
●	Irpinia Aglianico Nocelleto '01	♀	4
○	Fiano di Avellino '02	♀	4

FATTORIA TORRE GAIA
VIA BOSCO CUPO, 11
82030 DUGENTA (BN)
TEL. 0824978172
E-MAIL: info@torre-gaia.com

Falanghina Opera di Torre Gaia '02 is lovely. It has good typicity, with attractive fruit, and is well supported by acidity. Greco Koinè, again '02, is pleasant, but we would have liked a bit more character from the '01 Aglianico Re Sole ("Sun King"), especially given its imposing name.

● Beneventano Aglianico Re Sole '01	▼	4
○ Sannio Falanghina Opera '02	▼	3
○ Sannio Greco Koinè '02	▼	4

URCIUOLO
VIA CONTRADA RAPONE, 1
83020 FORINO (AV)
TEL. 0825761649
E-MAIL: antonurc@tin.it

A first entry in the Guide for this winery run by two men, Ciro and Antonello Urciuolo, who have not yet turned 30. Their Fiano is good for both its price and its typicity. Taurasi '99 has great character. It is tightly knit and concentrated, with dense tannicity well supported by rich fruit.

● Taurasi '99	▼▼	6
○ Fiano di Avellino '02	▼	3

PIETRATORCIA
FRAZ. CUOTTO
VIA PROVINCIALE PANZA, 267
80075 FORIO (NA)
TEL. 081908206 - 081907232

We much prefer Pietratorcia's reds to its whites, which seem a little over-evolved. Scherìa Rosso '01, from aglianico and syrah with small amounts of piedirosso and guarnaccia, is decent. Also good is Ischia Rosso Vigne di Janno Piro from the typical blend of mainly guarnaccia and per'e palummo.

● Scheria Rosso '00	▼	6
● Ischia Rosso		
Vigne di Janno Piro '01	▼	5
● Scheria Rosso '99	▽	6

DE LUCIA
C.DA STARZE
82034 GUARDIA SANFRAMONDI (BN)
TEL. 0824864259
E-MAIL: info@carlodelucia.com

Just one wine from Carlo De Lucia this year. But it's a white of considerable interest, Sannio Falanghina Vigna delle Ginestre Vendemmia Tardina '02. In spite of the depressing vintage, it has notable body and intense, fairly pervasive aromas.

○ Sannio Falanghina		
Vigna delle Ginestre V.T. '02	▼	4

LA GUARDIENSE
LOC. SANTA LUCIA, 104
82034 GUARDIA SANFRAMONDI (BN)
TEL. 0824864352
E-MAIL: janare@inwind.it

This leading co-operative has over 1,000 members and handles grapes from 2,500 hectares of vine covering the Guardiolo and Sannio DOCs. The most characterful is the even, well-made Guardiolo Rosso '02. The whites are fair, with a slight preference going to the Fiano for its fuller body.

○ Guardiolo Falanghina Senete '02	▼	4
● Guardiolo Rosso '02	▼	4
○ Sannio Fiano Colle di Tilio '02	▼	4

D'ANTICHE TERRE - VEGA
C.DA LO PIANO - S. S. 7 BIS
83030 MANOCALZATI (AV)
TEL. 0825675689 - 0825675358
E-MAIL: info@danticheterre.it

Wines here are always well styled and well made, but may lack a bit of character and personality. In any event, Fiano di Avellino '02 is good and Coriliano '02, from aglianico, piedirosso and sciascinoso, not bad. The typical, concentrated Taurasi '99 has more to offer.

○ Fiano di Avellino '02	▼	4
● Irpinia Rosso Coriliano '02	▼	3*
● Taurasi '99	▼	5

MONTE PUGLIANO
VIA SAN VITO, 21/A
84090 MONTECORVINO PUGLIANO (SA)
TEL. 0828350176
E-MAIL: info@montepugliano.com

With an output of more than 800,000 bottles, Monte Pugliano is one of the largest wineries in the province of Salerno. Most of its wines are IGT Colli di Salerno but some come from other parts of the region. This year, we liked two very well typed '02 wines from Benevento, Falanghina and Aglianico.

● Beneventano Aglianico '02	▼	4
○ Falanghina del Beneventano '02	▼	4
● Aglianico Castellaccio Ris. '01	♀	5

OCONE
LOC. LA MADONNELLA
VIA DEL MONTE, 56
82030 PONTE (BN)
TEL. 0824874040

The time can not be far off when Domenico Ocone reclaims a full entry. We have already noted some significant improvements. Aglianico La Madonnella is a well-made, very well-priced red. Falanghina Vigna del Monaco and Coda di Volpe are well-typed, attractive whites.

○ Taburno Coda di Volpe '02	▼	3
○ Taburno Falanghina Vigna del Monaco '02	▼	4
● Aglianico del Taburno La Madonnella '99	▼	4*

ETTORE SAMMARCO
VIA CIVITA, 9
84010 RAVELLO (SA)
TEL. 089872774
E-MAIL: info@ettoresammarco.it

Two excellent whites from the Sorrento Peninsula. Grotta Piana '02, from ginestrella, falanghina (called "bianca zita" locally) and biancolella ("bianca tenera"), is barrique-aged. Selva delle Monache, from biancolella and falanghina, sees no wood.

○ Costa d'Amalfi Ravello Bianco Grotta Piana '02	▼	5
○ Costa d'Amalfi Ravello Bianco Selva delle Monache '02	▼	4

FATTORIA PRATTICO
S.S. 430 - KM 17,100
81040 ROCCA D'EVANDRO (CE)
TEL. 0823925313
E-MAIL: info@fattoriaprattico.it

One of the rising estates from Roccamonfina, in the province of Caserta. It makes around 100,000 bottles from the zone's typical varieties. Best this year is the well-made, attractive Aglianico Vigna ai Cerri '01. Falanghina Vigna del Prete '02 is fair. Value for money is excellent across the board.

● Aglianico Vigna ai Cerri '01	▼	3
○ Falanghina Vigna del Prete '02	▼	3*

DE FALCO
VIA FIGLIOLA
80040 SAN SEBASTIANO AL VESUVIO (NA)
TEL. 0817713755
E-MAIL: defalcovini@tin.it

If you happen to like Gragnano, the slightly sparkling red produced on the foothills of Monti Lattari, on the Sorrento peninsula, don't miss this one from Gabriele De Falco's winery. It's really good. Also nice are Vesuvio Lacryma Christi, Greco di Tufo and Fiano di Avellino, all '02.

● Pen. Sorr. Gragnano '02	▼▼	4*
○ Fiano di Avellino '02	▼	4
○ Greco di Tufo '02	▼	4
● Vesuvio Lacryma Christi Rosso '02	▼	4

MASSERIA FELICIA
LOC. SAN TERENZANO
VIA PROV. APPIA CARANO
81030 SESSA AURUNCA (CE)
TEL. 0817362201

This small Massico estate in the province of Caserta makes its tiny quantities of wine from just over three hectares of vine. The best is the elegant, tidy Falerno del Massico Rosso Etichetta Bronzo '01. The second wine, Ariapetrina '02, from aglianico and piedirosso, is light and easy drinking.

● Falerno del Massico Rosso Etichetta Bronzo '01	▼▼	6
● Ariapetrina '02	▼	5

BASILICATA

These days, what emerges from Basilicata is no longer either a surprise or a novelty for quality wine aficionados. The region arouses ever greater interest and attracts in consequence considerable investment. Much of the incoming money is concentrated in the Vulture zone, where aglianico dominates and where a series of factors, including volcanic soils, altitudes and marked day-to-night temperature fluctuations make it an area of high viticultural potential. Aglianico, the "hellenicus" of ancient times, is one of Italy's most noble indigenous varieties. It is cited in the works of Horace and in ancient times was reported as giving a wine of superb flavour, widely regarded as practically a miracle cure. The grape was extolled by Hannibal's doctors and veterinary surgeons, who called for its wine after the battle of Cannae to help heal the wounds of both soldiers and horses. With such a historical legacy, these stunning lands were surely destined sooner or later to come up with wines that could take their place alongside the world's best. Today, we have a whole series of excellent wines from which to choose, and which are quite distinct from each other, despite their common provenance and grape variety.

Apart from the two Aglianico del Vultures that were awarded Three Glasses, several others reached the Three Glass finals, most of them only just missing the top prize. This speaks volumes for average quality in Vulture, which has now established itself as a leading premium wine district. But let's have a look at the two wines that clinched Three Glasses. Roinos, from Eubea-Sasso, is fabulous. It is the first release of this Aglianico but it should come as no surprise that it did so well so soon, since the estate has always produced exceedingly classy wines, including Aglianico Covo dei Briganti, a firm fixture in the tasting finals. In that sense, Roinos is in effect the affirmation of a top-quality estate. The other Three Glass wine is one of the region's classics, Rotondo from Paternoster. It is the supreme incarnation of a modern Aglianico, a powerful yet wonderfully elegant example of velvet on steel. We are convinced that this style is the future of Vulture, rather than bottles produced by the continuing drive towards ever greater ripeness in the grapes and ever richer extract in the wines. That particular route often ends up in the loss of the aglianico grape's innate elegance.

BARILE (PZ)

BARILE (PZ)

CONSORZIO VITICOLTORI
ASSOCIATI DEL VULTURE
S. S. 93
85022 BARILE (PZ)
TEL. 0972770386
E-MAIL: coviv@tiscalinet.it

ELENA FUCCI
C.DA SOLAGNA DEL TITOLO
85022 BARILE (PZ)
TEL. 0972770736

This co-operative is based in Barile, a delightful small town nestling in a breathtaking landscape of hills, vines, castles and farmhouses. Under the guidance of that superior oenologist, Sergio Paternoster, the winery has become the hub for Vulture's many viticultural undertakings that are not yet set up to vinify and mature their wines themselves. The co-operative handles the grapes of members who are situated across all 15 municipalities in the Aglianico del Vulture DOC zone, most of them on the slopes of the volcano, the heartland of the zone. And the wines? They simply keep getting better. Vetusto '00, which spends eight months in new barriques, is the standard-bearer, and Carpe Diem '01, after 12 months in second-year barriques and 12 in large old wood, is not just remarkable quality, but also represents unbeatable value for money. Both came within a hair of Three Glasses. Vetusto is the more concentrated, especially on the palate, where there are attractive, balanced notes of new oak. Carpe Diem is almost as long and complex, but has more zip. The baseline Aglianico is excellent, too, with crisp fruit and balanced alcohol. It would go as well with a sandwich as with serious meat dishes. To finish, a curiosity: Malvasia della Basilicata Topazio '02 is an aromatic dry white made from an indigenous subvariety of malvasia. So, in short we have great reds, wines from indigenous grapes others have tended to forget and fantastic prices. Well done everybody!

The estate is in the name of the 22-year old Fucci daughter, a student of agriculture at the University of Pisa, specializing in oenology, but the real driving force is Elena's father, Nicola. Actually, he is more a force of nature. The family has been growing grapes for three generations but until recently, the only wine bottled was a typical "farmer's wine". Nicola's grandfather, Generoso Fucci, was a tenant farmer of the former owner of Villa Rotondo, where he lived. Nicola's father was born there, too, and became very attached to the villa and its surrounding lands. So when the villa and its 24 hectares went on sale in 1970, Fucci, with the Paternoster family, bought it and then divided it between them. Fucci originally took 15 hectares but he lost eight under a compulsory purchase order for the construction of a highway (Italy's politicians are so far-sighted, don't you think?). He now has three hectares under vine, the rest being olive grove. They lie in one of the parts of Vulture best suited to viticulture, in effect an Aglianico "grand cru". The parcel is called Solagna del Titolo and, with valuable assistance from Sergio Paternoster whom we are bound to hear more of, Nicola has pulled out of the bag one of southern Italy's best reds, Aglianico del Vulture Titolo. It is bright ruby tinged with purple. The nose has fragrance and great finesse, with spices, peppermint and black cherries ushering in a palate that is aristocratic, very fresh and elegant. The spectrum of aromatics includes attractive notes of balsam and small wild black berry fruits.

● Aglianico del Vulture Vetusto '00	🍷🍷	6
● Aglianico del Vulture Carpe Diem '01	🍷🍷	4
● Aglianico del Vulture '02	🍷🍷	3*
○ Malvasia della Basilicata Topazio '02	🍷	2*
● Aglianico del Vulture Carpe Diem '93	🍷🍷	3
● Aglianico del Vulture Carpe Diem '95	🍷🍷	3
● Aglianico del Vulture '96	🍷🍷	2
● Aglianico del Vulture Vetusto '97	🍷🍷	4
● Aglianico del Vulture Carpe Diem '99	🍷🍷	4*
● Aglianico del Vulture Vetusto '98	🍷🍷	6
● Aglianico del Vulture Carpe Diem '00	🍷🍷	6
● Aglianico del Vulture Vetusto '99	🍷🍷	6
● Aglianico del Vulture '01	🍷🍷	4

● Aglianico del Vulture Titolo '01	🍷🍷	6
● Aglianico del Vulture Titolo '00	🍷🍷	5

BARILE (PZ)

TENUTA LE QUERCE
C.DA LE QUERCE
85022 BARILE (PZ)
TEL. 0971470709 - 0972725102
E-MAIL: tenutalequerce@tin.it

This leading estate was founded in 1996, when it was bought by the Pietrafesa family, who already had a share in the long-established, 18-hectare Cantine Sasso winery. The intention was to market both the Sasso and the Tenuta Le Querce ranges. Sasso wines are well made and aimed at the middle market, but Tenuta Le Querce is a gem of an estate where no half measures are taken. There are two spectacular underground cellars, two agronomists, Claudio Santini and Professor Leonardo Valenti from Milan University, two oenologists, Valenti – in a dual role here – and Daniel Kern. The numerous developments include as the switch from "alberello" bushes to cordon spur training and various research projects into clones, indigenous varieties and microvinifications – and very good wines. This time, there were no half measures among the wines, either. All are deeply coloured and so concentrated that they have almost lost aglianico's typical elegance. The '01 vintage of Vigna della Corona, the estate's top wine and a previous Three Glass finalist, is a great wine of impressive power and fascination, but the richness of extract and the almost resinous oakiness lessen its drinkability rather than make it memorable. Rosso di Costanza '01, the best release ever, is a similar monster of a wine. Viola '01, the fresh, fragrant standard wine, is very sound, and there is great character from Tamurro Nero '01, a new wine from a rediscovered indigenous variety that is being further developed. Tenuta Le Querce has everything it needs to become a leader in Basilicata, and in the rest of Italy.

BARILE (PZ)

PATERNOSTER
VIA NAZIONALE, 23
85022 BARILE (PZ)
TEL. 0972770224
E-MAIL: paternoster.vini@tiscalinet.it

No one who loves wine can remain impassive before the sight of the Scoscio, the vast hill in the Cantine area of Barile, its tufa perforated by hundreds of grottoes laid out as cellars. It was here that local families used to keep their wines; believing that this special location played a fundamental role in the maturation of their best Aglianicos. And if that isn't sufficient proof Barile's wine leanings, there are the three generations of the Paternosters, one of Italy's great wine families. Vito Paternoster runs this, the oldest Vulture estate, with a sure hand and produces the best range of Aglianico anywhere. It's an embarrassment of riches when you have to choose between Rotondo and Don Anselmo. Both are extraordinary, both are refined but powerful at the same time, both are well but not over-extracted and yet have great structure, and both are fresh-tasting and elegant. Rotondo '01 is the softer, more immediate wine, with wonderful tannins and finesse. It picked up Three Glasses. Don Anselmo '99 is more austere and a little closed, needing another year or so in bottle to express its full potential. Synthesi '01 is most attractive and also capable of improving significantly with some months' bottle age. The estate's other wines are often overlooked, but they are very good, especially Barigliott '02, a lightly sparkling Aglianico that is ideal at partnering cold meats. It has particularly good structure this year. Bianco di Corte, a monovarietal Fiano, and Clivus '02, a very nice sweet Moscato, are also worth investigating.

● Aglianico del Vulture Rosso di Costanza '01	♟♟	6
● Aglianico del Vulture Vigna della Corona '01	♟♟	8
● Aglianico del Vulture Sasso '00	♟	3
● Aglianico del Vulture Il Viola '01	♟	4
● Aglianico del Vulture Minorco Sasso '01	♟	5
● Tamurro Nero '01	♟	6
● Aglianico del Vulture Rosso di Costanza '98	♟♟	6
● Aglianico del Vulture Federico II '99	♟♟	5
● Aglianico del Vulture Rosso di Costanza '99	♟♟	6
● Aglianico del Vulture Vigna della Corona '00	♟♟	8
● Aglianico del Vulture Rosso di Costanza '00	♟♟	6

● Aglianico del Vulture Rotondo '01	♟♟♟	6
● Aglianico del Vulture Don Anselmo '99	♟♟	6
● Aglianico del Vulture Synthesi '01	♟♟	4
○ Bianco di Corte '02	♟♟	4
○ Moscato della Basilicata Clivus '02	♟♟	3*
● Barigliott '02	♟	3
● Aglianico del Vulture Rotondo '98	♟♟♟	5*
● Aglianico del Vulture Rotondo '00	♟♟♟	6
● Aglianico del Vulture Don Anselmo Ris. '93	♟♟	5
● Aglianico del Vulture Don Anselmo Ris. '94	♟♟	5
● Aglianico del Vulture Don Anselmo Ris. '95	♟♟	5
● Aglianico del Vulture Rotondo '97	♟♟	4
● Aglianico del Vulture Don Anselmo Ris. '97	♟♟	5
● Aglianico del Vulture Don Anselmo '98	♟♟	6
● Aglianico del Vulture Synthesi '00	♟♟	4*

BARILE (PZ)

RIONERO IN VULTURE (PZ)

TENUTA DEL PORTALE
C.DA LE QUERCE
85022 BARILE (PZ)
TEL. 0972724691

BASILISCO
VIA UMBERTO I, 129
85028 RIONERO IN VULTURE (PZ)
TEL. 0972720032
E-MAIL: basilisco@interfrre.it

Barile's wine vocation is summed up in the city's coat of arms, in which a baby Jesus grasps a bunch of grapes in his fist. The town is also home to Tenuta del Portale, the estate owned by Filena Ruppi, the wife of Donato d'Angelo, another important name in Aglianico del Vulture production. Ruppi comes from Locorotondo but moved to Basilicata when she married D'Angelo. She has always stood out as someone who becomes passionately involved in whatever she does, and a person of great energy. She has always been part of the wine world too. Her father worked for a large winery in northern Italy, and her own serious approach led to her sign up for a university course in viticulture and winemaking. Filena is not coy about her love for traditionally styled wines. She does not appreciate wines she calls "jammy" so her estate's range follows her preferences, as well as the tracks laid down by her husband. The products are well made, not too intensely coloured or over-extracted, and they are always a joy to drink. The one we best liked this year was Aglianico del Vulture Le Vigne a Capanno '00, which aged for 15 months in barrique. It is a bright ruby colour and there is ripe plum on the nose. The palate could do with a bit more structure but has enough acidity to give it good definition. The standard Aglianico del Vulture '00 is also very pleasing, and shows attractively crisp, fresh and fruity.

Michele Cutolo, a practising gastroenterologist, is very different from many of the other folk from outside the world of wine who have recently bought vineyard plots and holdings all over the peninsula. For a start, he is very attached to his land. He believes in its traditions and wants to do what he can to help the area grow. In addition, he has dedicated himself totally to producing an Aglianico he can be proud of. His decision last year to delay releasing the wine so that it could age longer is a clear sign of his serious-minded approach. The estate is set in a fabulous landscape on the slopes of Vulture, with vineyards planted at between 300 and 450 metres, and has a 15th-century cellar where he vinifies, ages and matures his wines, first made in 1992. The estate name comes from the Byzantine coin, dating from AD 380, that is shown on the labels, which portrays Emperor Theodosius II. Basilisco '00 is a violet-tinged ruby. The nose gives extra-ripe fruit and bottled plums and cherries, then the palate is rich and fleshy, with black berry fruits. The tannins are excellently textured but a little too assertive. In short, it's a great wine but it needs time. This year a new oenologist, the highly professional Luciano Landi, was taken on.

● Aglianico del Vulture '00	♀	4
● Aglianico del Vulture		
Le Vigne a Capanno '00	♀	5
● Aglianico del Vulture '98	♀♀	4
● Aglianico del Vulture		
Le Vigne a Capanno '99	♀♀	5
● Aglianico del Vulture Ris. '98	♀	4
● Aglianico del Vulture '99	♀	3

● Aglianico del Vulture Basilisco '00	♀♀	6
● Aglianico del Vulture Basilisco '98	♀♀	5
● Aglianico del Vulture Basilisco '99	♀♀	5

RIONERO IN VULTURE (PZ) RIONERO IN VULTURE (PZ)

CANTINE DEL NOTAIO
VIA ROMA, 159
85028 RIONERO IN VULTURE (PZ)
TEL. 0972717111 - 0972721371
E-MAIL: gerardo.giura@tin.it

D'ANGELO
VIA PROVINCIALE, 8
85028 RIONERO IN VULTURE (PZ)
TEL. 0972721517
E-MAIL: dangelowine@tiscalinet.it

Who knows how many times Gerardo Giuratrabocchetti, owner of this estate, has been asked whether he's the notary ("notaio") in the cellar's name. He's not, though. The notary is his father for Gerardo graduated in agrarian sciences and is an agronomist. Despite the beautiful cellars where the wines mature, carved out of the tufa rock in the 17th century, the estate was founded only in 1998. But in the brief period since then, Gerardo has managed to create a viable brand image that is immediately recognized and admired all over Italy. This is an exceptional achievement, and is partly owed to his far-sightedness in taking on as consultant, Luigi Moio, who teaches at Naples and Foggia universities and who has been behind a number of the best wines emerging from southern Italy in recent years. The estate's top wine, and consistently one of the best Aglianicos around, is La Firma. This year it missed Three Glasses by a hair. The nose is a delight, with balsam, tobacco and violets. The palate is silky soft, with the very ripe tannins that are the wine's trademark. Partnering it is Repertorio. This still has a little too much oak toast but we don't doubt that careful bottle ageing will render it more than attractive. Finally, we shouldn't forget Autentica, from 70 per cent late-harvest moscato and malvasia, Basilicata's best sweet wine and one of the best in Italy. It is unusually refined and with just a touch more acidity, would have been truly memorable.

D'Angelo, another great name in Basilicata winemaking, is a long-standing estate that continues to resist the lure of fashion. The cellar shuns the stylistic revolutions of the last few years and prefers to maintain balanced tannins and austerity of fruit and colour in its wines. This choice runs counter to the trend but deserves our respect, for the wines are very good. We were very impressed by a new wine, Aglianico del Vulture Donato D'Angelo '00, created in celebration of the owner's 50th birthday. It comes from a single plot and is produced only in good vintages, the latest version being the '01. Aged for 12 months in new barriques and a further 12 months in large old barrels, it is a softer wine than the others in the range. Its garnet-tinged ruby red introduces aromas of wild cherry and tobacco, then a palate of plentiful fruit richness and notable length. Canneto, a legend among Aglianico lovers, is as good as ever, showing evolved and distinctly aristocratic in character. Vigna Caselle Riserva '98 comes from less volcanic soils with more limestone and clay. It has black cherry and leather on the nose, and the palate is warm and full. Serra delle Querce, an 80-20 mix of aglianico and merlot, left us a bit perplexed last year, but this year the '99 made a very good impression. It comes from 12 hectares that grow a unique clone of aglianico, known as the D'Angelo clone, which is being followed by Professor Costacurta from Milan. Finally, Vigna dei Pini '02, from 60 per cent chardonnay, 20 per cent pinot bianco and incrocio Manzoni also showed well.

● Aglianico del Vulture La Firma '01 ♟♟		6
● Aglianico del Vulture		
Il Repertorio '01	♟♟	5
○ L'Autentica '01	♟♟	6
● Aglianico del Vulture La Firma '00 ♟♟♟		6
● Aglianico del Vulture La Firma '99 ♟♟		6
● Aglianico del Vulture		
Il Repertorio '99	♟♟	5
● Aglianico del Vulture		
Il Repertorio '00	♟♟	5
○ L'Autentica '00	♟♟	6

● Aglianico del Vulture Donato D'Angelo '00 ♟♟		5
● Canneto '00	♟♟	5
● Serra delle Querce '99	♟♟	5
● Aglianico del Vulture '00	♟	4
○ Vigna dei Pini '02	♟	3
● Aglianico del Vulture V.Caselle Ris. '98 ♟		4
● Canneto '93	♟♟	5
● Canneto '94	♟♟	5
● Aglianico del Vulture V. Caselle Ris. '95	♟♟	5
● Canneto '95	♟♟	5
● Canneto '97	♟♟	5
● Canneto '98	♟♟	5
● Aglianico del Vulture V. Caselle Ris. '97 ♟♟		4
● Serra delle Querce '98	♟♟	6
● Canneto '99	♟♟	5

RIONERO IN VULTURE (PZ) RIONERO IN VULTURE (PZ)

DI PALMA
VIA BRINDISI - C.DA SCAVONI
85028 RIONERO IN VULTURE (PZ)
TEL. 0972722891 - 0972722515
E-MAIL: info@cantinedipalma.com

EUBEA
VIA ROMA, 209
85028 RIONERO IN VULTURE (PZ)
TEL. 0972723574

Di Palma is an estate that is aiming high. Its owner, Antonio Di Palma, who is also vice president of the Aglianico del Vulture producers' consortium, is highly committed and is investing considerable amounts. You should see all those barriques! The vineyards lie in the three Vulture municipalities of Rionero, Ripacandida and Venosa, on soil that is highly suited to viticulture, and seven of its ten hectares are cultivated organically. There is the additional benefit of Sergio Paternoster's unique skills: he is the oenologist who has shaped many of the great Aglianicos of recent times. Aglianico Il Nibbio Grigio '00, which sports a black label, spends eight to 12 months in new barriques and is absolutely excellent. This wine of great elegance and concentration has a nose that offers mint, bottled cherries and sage, then the palate shows good consistency of flavour and reveals an appealingly savoury, almost salty tang on the finish. The tannins are refined and mouthfilling, and there is considerable length. We were less impressed, though, by the already quite evolved Nibbio Grigio '99, whose label is red. It is sourced exclusively from Venosa and aged in second-year barriques. Solo '02, from aglianico which sees no oak, is a well-styled easy drinker, but just too simplistic. This year, the estate has started to produce two sparkling wines, Moro, from aglianico, and a Moscato, which we hope to see at next year's tastings.

This is a winery whose wines have a traditional soul but look to the future. There are continual innovations in vineyards and cellars, but these are never revolutionary. For example, barriques are used, but most judiciously. The best example of this marriage of tradition and innovation comes from the new wine Roinos '01, an Aglianico that picked up Three Glasses with ease. The name of the wine was originally going to be Cristina, after the owners' daughter, but in the end it was put together from the first syllable of Roberto, their three-year-old grandson, and "oinos", the Ancient Greek word for wine. It was a good choice, as one of young Roberto's favourite play areas is a strip of vineyard with over 60-year-old vines, the ones that give birth to the wine. This Aglianico has amazing power and almost terrifying extract but, unlike so many undrinkable sledgehammers of wines, Roinos has spectacular vivacity. It's a splendid piece of winemaking. Aglianico Etichetta Nera and the oak-free Aglianico Eubea were not submitted this year, so we're still with the '00s, which remain good. Neither have we moved on from the '00 vintage for the winery's other great wine, Aglianico del Vulture Covo dei Brigante. An unsuitable vintage also meant that the usually excellent sweet wine Seduzione was not produced. We'll be talking about all these next year. Roinos is more than enough to be going on with.

● Aglianico del Vulture Nibbio Grigio '00	♟♟	5
● Aglianico del Vulture Nibbio Grigio '99	♟	4
● Solo '02		3
● Aglianico del Vulture Nibbio Grigio '97	♟♟	5
● Aglianico del Vulture Nibbio Grigio '98	♟♟	4

● Aglianico del Vulture Roinos '01	♟♟♟	8
● Aglianico del Vulture Il Covo dei Briganti '99	♟♟	6
● Aglianico del Vulture Il Covo dei Briganti '00	♟♟	6
○ Seduzione '01	♟	5
● Aglianico del Vulture Il Covo dei Briganti '98	♟	4

VENOSA (PZ)

VENOSA (PZ)

TERRE DEGLI SVEVI
LOC. PIAN DI CAMERA
85029 VENOSA (PZ)
TEL. 0972374175 - 0577998511
E-MAIL: terredeglisvevi@giv.it

CANTINA DI VENOSA
LOC. VIGNALI
VIA APPIA
85029 VENOSA (PZ)
TEL. 097236702
E-MAIL: info@cantinadivenosa.it

This estate, owned by Gruppo Italiano Vini, was set up in 1998 and owns 95 hectares in the municipalities of Maschito and Venosa. It produces just one wine, Aglianico del Vulture Re Manfredi, named after the son of Emperor Frederick II of Swabia, who knew this area well, and even the label shows the coat of arms of the imperial house of Swabia with its eagle. Re Manfredi has already found its niche in the market, both in Italy and abroad, gaining critical acclaim and commercial success from its very first release. It has the not insignificant advantage of being both very well made and produced in quite some quantity. The 140,000 unit annual production is considerable for a wine of such quality. These points should be emphasized wherever possible, especially in a national and international wine scene where there are endless wines produced in such small quantities that they are almost impossible to find. Last year, at its first appearance on these pages, Re Manfredi '99 grabbed Three Glasses. This year, the '00 comes within a whisker of similar honours. It is a great red in the modern idiom, with a very typical, varietal array of aromas and great cleanliness of style. The colour is ruby red tinged with garnet, then the nose first gives small wild black berry fruits, interwoven with a strong note of tobacco, and afterwards releases delicate nuances of leather and rosemary. The palate is warm, mouthfilling, pleasantly dry, beautifully textured and very long.

Horace's ode "Nunc est bibendum" is inscribed on a scroll here – the Latin poet was born at Venosa – and we have to say that when it comes to wines as good as this, "now" is always the "time to drink". The Venosa co-operative is Basilicata's largest. When it was founded in 1957, it had just 20 members. Today, there are more than 500, providing it with over 900 hectares of vineyard to draw from. The holdings include plots in the more prestigious parts of the municipalities of Venosa, Ripacandida, Ginestra and Maschito. Not all of the cellar's production is bottled, but the wine that is stands out for quality and fair pricing. This year, Luigi Cantatore has taken over as winemaker from Oronzo Calò. The best wine is Aglianico del Vulture Carato Venusio '99, which comes from a particularly fierce selection of fully ripe grapes. A garnet-tinged ruby red, it has aromas of cherry and tobacco with rather odd hints of cola, but there is great elegance and refined tannicity on the palate. It will improve considerably with further bottle age. Strange as it may seem, the other great wine from the winery is a dry Moscato and despite, regrettably, having been given the English name Dry Muscat, it is quite simply one of the best of its type in Italy. The '02 seemed a mite less appealing than the previous version but only because of a touch too much bitterness on the palate. This, however, does nothing to diminish it as one of the most welcome of tasting surprises. Finally, the least complex of the Aglianicos, Terre di Orazio '00, is as well typed and well made as ever.

● Aglianico del Vulture Re Manfredi '00	🍷🍷	5
● Aglianico del Vulture Re Manfredi '99	🍷🍷🍷	5*
● Aglianico del Vulture Re Manfredi '98	🍷🍷	5

○ Dry Muscat Terre di Orazio '02	🍷🍷	3*
● Aglianico del Vulture Carato Venusio '99	🍷🍷	5
● Aglianico del Vulture Terre di Orazio '00	🍷	4
● Aglianico del Vulture '94	🍷🍷	3
● Aglianico del Vulture Carato Venusio '97	🍷🍷	4
● Aglianico del Vulture Terre di Orazio '98	🍷🍷	3
● Aglianico del Vulture Vignali '98	🍷🍷	2
● Basilicata Rosso Vignali '00	🍷🍷	2*
● Aglianico del Vulture Terre di Orazio '99	🍷🍷	3*

OTHER WINERIES

BASILIUM
C.DA PIPOLI
85011 ACERENZA (PZ)
TEL. 0971741449
E-MAIL: info@basilium.it

Gratifying results for this co-operative founded in 1976, whose Aglianicos you can go for without a moment's hesitation. The deep, complex Aglianico del Vulture Valle del Trono is typical and well made. Aglianico del Vulture Le Gastaldie Sicone '01 is lighter and fresher, but with good structure.

● Aglianico del Vulture		
Valle del Trono '00	♟♟	7
● Aglianico del Vulture		
Le Gastaldie Sicone '01	♟	5

ALLEGRETTI
P.ZZA CARACCIOLO, 4
85022 BARILE (PZ)
TEL. 0972770549
E-MAIL: info@aglianicodelvulture.it

This very young estate, founded in 2001, is a new entry in the Guide. Its Aglianico style is one of restrained innovation. Aglianico del Vulture Il Barile Vecchio '00 is spot on: really creamy, very fruity and with refined tannins.

● Aglianico del Vulture		
Il Barile Vecchio '00	♟♟	5

ARMANDO MARTINO
VIA LUIGI LAVISTA, 2/A
85028 RIONERO IN VULTURE (PZ)
TEL. 0972721422
E-MAIL: martinovini@tiscalinet.it

This long-standing estate's wines didn't quite come up to expectations. Both Aglianico del Vulture Oraziano '98, aged 12 months in barrique, and the oak-free Rosso Carolin '02 are good, but the rest of the range didn't seem particularly clean, which surprised us.

● Rosso Carolin '02	♟	3
● Aglianico del Vulture Oraziano '98	♟	5
● Aglianico del Vulture		
Bel Poggio '99	♟♟	3*

F.LLI NAPOLITANO
VIA MATTEOTTI, 40
85028 RIONERO IN VULTURE (PZ)
TEL. 0972721040
E-MAIL: info@vininapolitano.it

A welcome return to the Guide for this long-standing estate, which makes sound Aglianico. We liked Elea '00, which ages six months in large, old barrels, and Casale Santa Maria '00, with four months in barrique as well as six in large wood. Both are most attractive, richly fruited and fragrant.

● Aglianico del Vulture		
Casale Santa Maria '00	♟	4
● Aglianico del Vulture Elea '00	♟	4
● Aglianico del Vulture Elea '98	♟♟	5

PUGLIA

The most telling figures to emerge from our tastings in Puglia are as follows. For the 2003 Guide, we tasted just under 300 samples. This year, on our arrival at Valenzano's Istituto Agronomico Mediterraneo, where the tastings were held, we found 720 bottles, give or take one or two, waiting for us. That is 44 per cent up on the previous year. What does this mean? Simply that Puglia is going through an exciting period of development. Every year, dozens of grape growers decide to bottle their own wine, bolstered by markets, both in Italy and abroad, that are ever more receptive to the region's products, which remain market leaders in value for money. Then there is the growing number of large companies, from other regions or even countries, that are creating wineries and setting up new estates here, or just coming down to Italy's "heel" at harvest time to select grapes and vinify them locally, adding brands and labels to their existing range. Thanks in part to these "cultural exchanges", and the involvement of big-name wineries, the region's current dynamism has impinged on the average quality of wines across the board, which has risen exponentially. Umbrian, Tuscan, Piedmontese and even Californian and Australian oenologists have found that the areas around Salento, Taranto and others have huge tracts where they can put their experience to good use, passing it on consciously or unconsciously to their Puglian counterparts. It's a stimulating state of affairs, although there is a risk that typicity might be sacrificed. Local grapes and wine types might yield to reds of international style. But in Puglia, territory and tradition are so powerful that no-one can escape them. Puglia's indigenous varieties have extraordinary character, and here on their native land they express it to the full, giving us exactly the sort of wines the market wants. Powerful, spicy, full of fruit… is that not exactly the profile of Primitivo? A structured, warm, complex wine that ages well? Just like the best Negroamaros. Something fleshy and attractive? What about uva di Troia wines? Then there are the rosés, which are acquiring cult status here. This year's Three Glass winners represent the entire spectrum: from Conti Zecca's Nero '01 symbolizing the "new" Puglia in its union of negroamaro and cabernet; to Leone de Castris' Salice Salentino Donna Lisa Riserva '99, a great traditional wine interpreted with one eye on the new; to Torcicoda '01, made by Antinori-Tormaresca, an excellent Primitivo in an international style; and finally to Torretesta '01, from susumaniello, a grape as indigenous as they get. Rubino has crafted it into a delicious "glocal" red.

ALEZIO (LE)

ROSA DEL GOLFO
VIA GARIBALDI, 56
73011 ALEZIO (LE)
TEL. 0331993198
E-MAIL: calo@rosadelgolfo.com

Damiano Calò has one overriding aim. He doesn't just want to produce excellent wines, he wants to make the best rosé in Italy. The idea comes from his father, Mino, whose passion for rosé led him to name his estate, Rosa del Golfo, after the wine type. The flagship wine of the same name has been one of Italy's best rosés for decades, if not the best. Once young Damiano had picked up the paternal reins, he too went for quality. Assisted by oenologist Angelo Solci, he began to give us a succession of beautifully made, elegant wines, led by Rosa del Golfo. It is the epitome of a Puglian rosé. From negroamaro with a touch of malvasia nera, the deep pink colour ushers in intense aromas of ripe, red and white berry fruits, with wafts of Mediterranean scrubland and flowers. The fruit-rich, fresh palate is firm with good grip and length. And it goes with practically everything. But Damiano wanted an even more complex, deeper experience from the wine so the Vigna Mazzì selection emerged, from an old vineyard where much research and experimentation had gone on. The new wine is more concentrated, without losing freshness or drinkability, and its aromas are more complex, with an added dimension from the new oak that makes its subtle mark on the palate, too. The structure is slightly more complex, and you can detect a very light, controlled astringency within its fruit. It is a fine wine, and marks the beginning of a new era for rosé wines and for this estate. And don't forget that there are many other good wines here, too.

ANDRIA (BA)

CONTE SPAGNOLETTI ZEULI
C.DA S. DOMENICO
SS. 98 KM. 21
70031 ANDRIA (BA)
TEL. 0883569511
E-MAIL: c.szo@tiscali.it

Puglia can boast many long-standing estates that don't rest on their laurels and always maintain high quality standards. One such is Spagnoletti Zeuli. Founded in the 17th century, this leading estate owns 120 hectares and is skilfully run by Onofrio and Emanuela Spagnolotti Zeuli, admirably assisted by oenologist Leonardo Pinto. They produce 400,000 excellently made bottles a year, all good value. Wine and olive oil have been produced here since time immemorial and the current aim is to bottle the entire wine production directly. It was difficult to choose among the estate's reds this year. Each seemed as good as the others. But in the end it was Vigna Grande '02 that won us over. A dry, austere Castel del Monte, made from 100 per cent uva di Troia, it shows great finesse. Terranera Riserva '01 is also first-rate, and was also a prizewinner at the Vinitaly wine fair. It comes from the unusual but successful blend of 40 per cent nero di Troia, 40 per cent montepulciano and cabernet, and ages for 12 months in barrique. The oak-derived balsam, tamarind and tobacco on the palate is currently excessive, but we have no doubt that with more bottle age, the wine will be excellent. Pezza La Ruca '01 takes its name from its 15-hectare parcel. An oak-free 50-50 blend of nero di Troia and montepulciano, it too is splendidly fresh and a joy to drink. La Piana '02, a white from the classic mix of pampanuto and bombino bianco, is also very fresh and attractive, making it an ideal wine to drink as an aperitif or with starters.

○	Bolina '02	♀♀	3*
☉	Rosa del Golfo '02	♀♀	3*
☉	Vigna Mazzì '02	♀♀	4*
●	Quarantale '98	♀♀	5
●	Portulano '01	♀	4
●	Primitivo '01	♀	4
☉	Rosa del Golfo '98	♀♀	3
☉	Rosa del Golfo '99	♀♀	4
●	Quarantale '97	♀♀	5

●	Castel del Monte Pezza La Ruca '01	♀♀	4*
●	Castel del Monte Terranera Ris. '01	♀♀	5
●	Castel del Monte Vigna Grande '02	♀♀	4
○	Castel del Monte Bianco La Piana '02	♀	3
●	Castel del Monte Pezza La Ruca '00	♀♀	4
●	Castel del Monte Ris. del Conte '00	♀♀	6

ANDRIA (BA)

RIVERA
FRAZ. C.DA RIVERA
S. S. 98, KM 19.800
70031 ANDRIA (BA)
TEL. 0883569501 - 0883569510
E-MAIL: info@rivera.it

A great estate, like Rivera, is can be recognized, among other things, by its readiness to launch changes and improvements. Rivera already produces one of Puglia's best – and best-value – reds in Il Falcone, from 70 per cent nero di Troia with montepulciano. But determination to remain at the top led to the arrival a year ago of Puer Apuliae, made exclusively from nero di Troia. The first release, reviewed in last year's Guide, impressed mightily but this year's version took Puer Apuliae into the top ranks of Italy's red. The '01 missed Three Glasses by a whisker. It is an elegant wine, with great refinement on the palate. Anything but the usual hyper-concentrated, jammy monster, it is tight, firm, aristocratic and wonderfully textured. Our reasons for congratulating the estate certainly don't finish here. The rest of the range is, as ever, very sound. Il Falcone itself, the '00, failed to enthral as it is a little dilute on the palate this year, but the house pink, Rosé '02, is absolutely terrific. Unlike the rosés from the Salento, which are based on negroamaro, this is 100 per cent bombino nera and shows fresh, fruity and very enjoyable. Cappellaccio Riserva '00, a traditional Puglian Aglianico, and Triusco '01, an interesting blend of primitivo from Manduria and primitivo from Gioia del Colle, are both well made. Unlike many other Puglian estates, Rivera does well with whites. You won't go wrong with any of Chardonnay Lama di Corvo, Preludio No. 1, Fedora or Locorotondo, all '02.

BRINDISI

TENUTE RUBINO
VIA MEDAGLIE D'ORO, 15/A
72100 BRINDISI
TEL. 0831571955 - 0831502912
E-MAIL: info@tenuterubino.it

It is difficult to talk about "surprises" from Tenute Rubino when it is known as one of the leading estates in Puglia. Not only has it picked up another Three Glasses after last year, this time with an extraordinary '01 Torre Testa, a 100 per cent susumaniello at its first release, but another wine also went through to the finals. In fact, the entire range scored Two Glasses or better, and there's no finer guarantee than that. The Rubini family has an excellent winemaker in Luca Petrelli, and Riccardo Cotarella consults, but above all, the cellar can call on 160 hectares of vineyard where new cordon spur-trained plantings at a density of 6,000 vines per hectare sit alongside "alberello" (bush-trained) vines that are over 75 years old. These give the susumaniello grapes that go into Torre Testa, although this indigenous variety once risked extinction. The wine has a nose of great richness and complexity, ripe fruit melding into coffee and chocolate. The full, fleshy palate is just as delicious, offering nicely weighty texture as well as freshness and attractive elegance. Jaddico '02, from 70 per cent negroamaro with 15 per cent each montepulciano and malvasia nera, almost equals it. There are wild berry fruits on the nose, then the palate is dense and full of fleshiness, with fresh fruit and a long, liquorice-like finale. Visellio '02, from Primitivo, is still a little closed, but rich and beautifully concentrated. It is admirable, as is the rest of the range, the fresh, balanced Punta Aquila '02 and the excellent value red and white versions of Marmorelle.

● Castel del Monte Nero di Troia Puer Apuliae '01	🍷🍷	7
● Castel del Monte Rosso Il Falcone Ris. '00	🍷🍷	4
○ Castel del Monte Chardonnay Preludio N° 1 '02	🍷🍷	3*
⊙ Castel del Monte Rosè '02	🍷🍷	2*
● Castel del Monte Aglianico Cappellaccio Ris. '00	🍷	4
● Triusco '01	🍷	4*
○ Castel del Monte Bianco Fedora '02	🍷	2*
○ Castel del Monte Chardonnay Lama di Corvo '02	🍷	5
○ Castel del Monte Sauvignon Terre al Monte '02	🍷	3
● Castel del Monte Rosso Il Falcone Ris. '99	🍷🍷	4*

● Torre Testa '01	🍷🍷🍷	6
● Brindisi Rosso Jaddico '02	🍷🍷	5*
○ Marmorelle '02	🍷🍷	3*
● Primitivo Punta Aquila '02	🍷🍷	4
● Primitivo Visellio '02	🍷🍷	5
● Marmorelle '02	🍷🍷	3*
● Primitivo Visellio '01	🍷🍷🍷	5*
● Brindisi Rosso Gallico '00	🍷🍷	5*
● Primitivo Visellio '00	🍷🍷	4*
● Brindisi Rosso Jaddico '01	🍷🍷	5

CELLINO SAN MARCO (BR)

Tenute Albano Carrisi
C.DA BOSCO
72020 CELLINO SAN MARCO (BR)
TEL. 0831619211
E-MAIL: tenute@albanocarrisi.com

Since Albano Carrisi turned to quality production, his wines have been reliably consistent, and this year is no exception. The estate is increasing in size, too. There are now 65 hectares in production and the winemaking specialists, oenologist Giuseppe Rizzo, agronomist Gianfranco Pagano and consultant Leonardo Pinto, are a very sound team. The surprise, though, is that the jewel in the Carrisi crown this year is not Platone, which made notably less impact than in the past two vintages, but Taras '02. It impressed the tasting panel so much that it went straight through to the Three Glass finals. It is from 100 per cent primitivo, with eight months barrique ageing, and has a dark ruby colour. A deep, full nose ranges from plum to morello cherry, coffee and chocolate, then a medium bodied, moderately intense palate shows an elegant tannic weave. It is not particularly concentrated, but has good balance and fruit. The disappointing Platone '00, from a 50-50 blend of negroamaro and primitivo, has a mix of plum jam and herbaceous notes on both nose and palate. It may be that the heat in 2000 played havoc with a wine that has always flaunted extract and richness of fruit. From the rest of the range, we liked the fresh, attractive Basiliano '01, a traditionally vinified monovarietal negroamaro, which has cherry and tamarind notes, and Don Carmelo Bianco '02, a tasty 100 percent chardonnay, which has good structure, considering the vintage.

CELLINO SAN MARCO (BR)

Cantina Due Palme
VIA SAN MARCO, 130
72020 CELLINO SAN MARCO (BR)
TEL. 0831617909
E-MAIL: info@cantineduepalme.it

For the second year running, the Due Palme co-operative is up there with the region's best wineries. This means it has found the secret of combining high quality with big numbers: 300 members cultivate 800 hectares and release 2,000,000 bottles a year. For the time being, there is no really stupendous wine that might win Three Glasses, but there are three that earned Two Glasses. Not many wineries in the region can say as much. Canonico '02, exclusively from negroamaro, is first rate. It has a vanilla, pepper and raspberry jam nose and big, slightly alcoholic palate, with good richness of fruit and pleasing finish, although there is a touch too much sweetness. Brindisi Rosso '01, from 80 per cent negroamaro and 20 per cent malvasia nera, scored similarly well. Oak and vanilla integrate with super-ripe fruit on the nose, while the palate has good weight and depth, tightly grained, soft tannins and a sweet finish revealing a certain amount of residual sugar. Salice Salentino Selvarossa Riserva '00 is on the same lines. The nose has alluring aromas of cherry jam, while there are very ripe red berry fruits and sweet, oaky nuances on the palate. We have just one criticism. We would be very happy to taste more wines of this quality in Puglia, especially at such competitive prices, but the cellar relies a little too much on sweetness to make the wines attractive and they tend to seem rather samey.

● Taras '02	♟♟	7
● Platone '00	♟♟	8
● Il Basiliano '01	♟	3
○ Don Carmelo '02	♟	5
● Platone '98	♟♟♟	8
● Don Carmelo '97	♟♟	3*
● Platone '99	♟♟	8

● Salice Salentino		
Selvarossa Ris. '00	♟♟	5
● Brindisi Rosso '01	♟♟	3*
● Canonico '02	♟♟	4*
● Primitivo '01	♟♟	3*
● Tenuta Albrizzi '01	♟♟	4*
● Squinzano Rosso '01	♟♟	3*
● Salice Salentino		
Selvarossa Ris. '98	♟♟	4

CELLINO SAN MARCO (BR)   CERIGNOLA (FG)

MASSERIA LI VELI
S.S. CELLINO-CAMPI KM 1
72020 CELLINO SAN MARCO (BR)
TEL. 0831617906
E-MAIL: info@liveli.it

TORRE QUARTO
C.DA QUARTO, 5/O
71042 CERIGNOLA (FG)
TEL. 0885418453 - 0885418456
E-MAIL: torrequartocantine@isnet.it

Winemaking in Puglia benefits from collaborative efforts. That would seem to be the conclusion from recent experiences at Masseria Li Veli, a joint venture between Angelo Maci and the leading Tuscan estate, Avignonesi. The estate, with its 45 hectares of vineyard, performed excellently. There were three Two Glass scores, all with wines made exclusively from negroamaro, the differences being predominantly the length of barrique and bottle-ageing. The most distinctive wine submitted, the Salice Salentino Riserva Morgana Alta '00, matures for 24 months. Although the garnet-ruby colour, and liqueur cherries on the nose, might suggest premature development, the palate is soft and elegant, medium bodied, lively and attractive to drink. Passamante '01 is aged for 12 months. It has fresh, fruity aromas with hints of cocoa powder, while there is sage and rosemary herbiness, and rather strange hints of iodine, on the palate, which has soft tannins and good overall balance, despite a slight excess of alcohol. The other Salice Salentino, Pezzo Morgana '01, also has 12 months in barrique but longer in bottle. It shows good complexity on the nose with clear tones of red berry fruits. The palate is fruity, attractive and elegant, but just a touch dilute.

This Cerignola-based estate, once owned by the dukes of La Rochefoucauld, is back among Puglia's elite. There is much replanting going on, as the high-yielding "tendone" overhead training system is replaced with cordon spur and Guyot regimens, and a series of experiments in the cellar involving the use of barriques and the larger tonneaux. The wines submitted this year showed that these changes have paid off handsomely, even though the grapes came from the difficult 2002 vintage. The most exciting product is the estate's flagship wine, Bottaccia, from 100 per cent uva di Troia, which reached the Three Glass finals. It is a bright ruby colour. The nose is particularly complex, with fresh, fruity aromas of blackcurrant, blackberry and cherry, followed by touches of balsam and chocolate, then the palate is elegant, balanced and long, with good fruit. In fact, it's a pleasure to drink and quite remarkable, especially for the price. Another first-rate bottle is Tarabuso '02, made solely from primitivo. The colour is dark ruby tinged with purple, the nose gives liqueur cherries, and the palate is nicely full and well structured, with attractive, slightly sweet fruitiness and fair length. It may not be as elegant as the Bottaccia, but it does have good solidity and is very enjoyable. All the other wines are more than satisfactory, and all earned One Glass. Among them, the fresh, fragrant Puglia Bianco '02 stands out as one of the region's best whites this year.

●	Salice Salentino		
	Morgana Alta Ris. '00	▼▼	6
●	Passamante '01	▼▼	4*
●	Salice Salentino		
	Pezzo Morgana '01	▼▼	5
●	Salice Salentino		
	Pezzo Morgana '00	♈♈	5

●	Bottaccia '02	▼▼	3*
●	Tarabuso '02	▼▼	3*
●	Quarto Ducale '01	▼	4
●	Don Marcello '02	▼	3
○	Puglia Bianco '02	▼	4
●	Bottaccia '01	♈♈	4
●	Tarabuso '01	♈♈	4

COPERTINO (LE)

MASSERIA MONACI
LOC. TENUTA MONACI
73043 COPERTINO (LE)
TEL. 0832947512
E-MAIL: vini@masseriamonaci.com

Year by year, this estate consolidates its reputation as one of the most exciting in southern Italy. It also continues to breathe new life into Copertino, a DOC which is beginning to spread its wings. Last year, the estate distinguished itself with Le Braci, one of the best southern reds to appear at our tastings. It immediately won Three Glasses for successfully combining the warm soul of Italy's southern reds with the elegance of some of the best wines from the north. Le Braci was not produced this year, but the estate's sure hand was again apparent when Sine Die emerged from the cellar. This stunning Aglianico del Vulture may have missed out on Three Glasses by a hair's breadth, but it is still one of the best reds of the year. It has the clear stamp of classy oenologist, Severino Garofano. The grapes give fully ripe but not cooked flavours, there is great richness of extract and the silky texture caresses the palate. Full flavoured and concentrated, it is also elegant and a very fine wine indeed. Le Briciole, an aromatic dessert wine with attractive notes of hazelnut and acacia honey, and Santa Brigida '02, from chardonnay and sauvignon, with citrus and elderflower on the nose and an uncomplicated, supple palate, are both most successful.

CORATO (BA)

TORREVENTO
LOC. CASTEL DEL MONTE
S. S. 170, KM 28
70033 CORATO (BA)
TEL. 0808980923 - 0808980929
E-MAIL: info@torrevento.it

Torrevento, a large Castel del Monte winery, began operations only recently, in 1989, but distinguished itself at once for its good-quality, competitively priced range. The wine comes from 150 hectares, of which 120 are owned directly. Any cellar that makes around 1,200,000 bottles of good, affordable wine is well worth a second glance. Winelovers should take note, and the estate should be held up as an example. The wines were again very impressive this year, possibly more so than ever before. We were very pleasantly surprised by the '02 Rosato, one of the best rosés the estate has ever produced. From bombino nero and montepulciano, its attractively youthful aromas of small red berry fruit and unusual complexity on the palate are quite striking. Castel del Monte Rosso '00, from 80 per cent uva di Troia and aglianico, came a very close second. It is bright ruby, the fragrances evoke leather and small black berry fruits, and the price is excellent. Vigna Pedale '00, made solely from uva di Troia, is also successful but, as in other vintages, it seems a touch rustic and some way from the elegance that this indigenous variety can give. A retaste of Kebir '00 gave very positive results. The nose has good complexity and the wine is strikingly long. Finally, Castel del Monte Bianco '02, from 70 per cent bombino bianco and pampanuto, is very fresh, easy to drink and most attractive. It's ideal as a cheerful, light-hearted aperitif, or may be drunk with not too weighty fish dishes.

● Aglianico del Vulture		
Sine Die '99	🍷🍷	6
○ Le Briciole Passito	🍷	5
○ Santa Brigida '02	🍷	3
● Le Braci '00	🍷🍷🍷	7*
● Copertino Rosso Eloquenzia '00	🍷	3*

⊙ Castel del Monte Rosato '02	🍷🍷	3*
○ Castel del Monte Bianco '02	🍷	3*
● Castel del Monte Rosso '00	🍷	3*
● Castel del Monte Rosso		
Vigna Pedale Ris. '00	🍷	4
○ Moscato di Trani		
Dulcis in Fundo '02	🍷	4
● Castel del Monte Rosso		
Vigna Pedale Ris. '98	🍷🍷	3
○ Moscato di Trani		
Dulcis in Fundo '00	🍷🍷	4*
● Kebir '00	🍷🍷	6
● Castel del Monte Rosso		
Vigna Pedale Ris. '99	🍷🍷	4

FASANO (BR)

BORGO CANALE
LOC. SELVA DI FASANO
V.LE CANALE DI PIRRO, 23
72015 FASANO (BR)
TEL. 0804331351 - 0805046156
E-MAIL: info@borgocanale.it

This estate does not own any vineyards but manages to achieve notable consistency of quality. The secret lies in its long term contracts with reliable grape growers, plus 50 hectares or so on lease, and the work of its top-notch cellar staff. Since 2002, Borgo Canale has also had the services of the prestigious oenologist Donato Lanati, thereby ensuring good quality across its annual production of 800,000 or so well-priced bottles. This year, we were particularly pleased by the whites. Divo, from verdeca, chardonnay and vermentino, is outstanding and one of the best Puglian whites of the '02 vintage. The nose is refined, with citrus and jasmine flowers, and the palate is fresh and elegant. The vintage means that it doesn't have great body, but it does have attractive white peach and citrus flavours and is pleasingly long. Locorotondo Talnè '02, based mainly on verdeca and bianco d'Alessano, with ten per cent fiano, is also very good and one of the best in the DOC. Its bright straw introduces aromas of pineapple, pears, apples and hazelnuts. The medium-bodied palate is fresh and attractively zesty. Also showing well is Rosa di Selva '02, a heady rosé with almost as much backbone and substance as a young red wine. All the reds are good, all easily achieving One Glass, which underlines the reliability of this estate across its entire range.

GRAVINA IN PUGLIA (BA)

CANTINA COOPERATIVA BOTROMAGNO
VIA ARCHIMEDE, 22
70024 GRAVINA IN PUGLIA (BA)
TEL. 0803265865
E-MAIL: info@botromagno.it

Gravina's co-operative, founded only in 1991, works from a grape pool of 200 hectares, of which it owns 45 directly. The cellar also benefits from the great experience of Severino Garofano, the oenologist who works alongside Matteo De Rosa, and who, over the years, has been responsible for many of the region's most famous wines. This year, we particularly liked both vintages of Pier delle Vigne submitted. From a successful blend of 60 per cent aglianico and montepulciano, the wine takes its name from the counsellor to Frederick II of Swabia and seems to be getting better by the year. We felt that the two vintages tasted this year were the best ever. The '99 is lighter and livelier, whereas the '98 is more structured, with greater body and has more evident, albeit not excessive, hints of raisining. Both have pleasing aromas of ripe red berry fruit, with a delicate spicing of tobacco. Botromagno is practically the sole producer of Gravina, the typical white of the area, made from 60 per cent greco and 40 per cent malvasia. The '02 showed well with vegetal aromas of asparagus and sage, and a clean, supple palate. The '99 vintage of Gravisano, an excellent dried-grape Malvasia produced only in good vintages, was first reviewed in the 2003 Guide and is still very sound. However, despite the rarity in Puglia of a rosé made from montepulciano, we found the '02 Silvium '02 less interesting. Its rather gamey aromas were neither very attractive nor very convincing.

○	Divo '02	♟♟	4*
○	Locorotondo Talné '02	♟♟	3*
●	Primitivo Mo e Mo '01	♟	4
●	Prospero '01	♟	6
○	Puglia Chardonnay Sannà '01	♟	5
●	Primitivo Maestro '02	♟	4
◉	Rosa di Selva '02	♟	3
●	Primitivo Maestro '97	♟♟	3
○	Puglia Chardonnay Sannà '00	♟♟	6

●	Pier delle Vigne '98	♟♟	4
●	Pier delle Vigne '99	♟♟	4
○	Gravina '02	♟	3
●	Primitivo '02	♟	4
◉	Murgia Rosato Silvium '02		3
●	Pier delle Vigne '94	♟♟	2
●	Gravisano '97	♟♟	6
○	Pier delle Vigne '97	♟♟	4*
○	Gravisano '99	♟♟	4*
○	Gravina '01	♟	3

GUAGNANO (LE)

ANTICA MASSERIA DEL SIGILLO
VIA PROVINCIALE, 37
73010 GUAGNANO (LE)
TEL. 0832706331
E-MAIL: sigillo2001@libero.it

This well-run estate, overseen by oenologist Oronzo Alò, was set up just five years ago at Guagnano in the heart of the Salento. Already, it is one of the most promising of Puglia's newcomers. Its mix of old, bush-trained, mainly primitivo vines and newer plantings allow it to make wines that combine tradition and modernity with gratifying success. Indeed, for the second year running, its Terre del Guiscardo reached the Three Glass taste-offs. This year's '01 is from 60 per cent primitivo, with equal amounts of merlot and cabernet sauvignon. Half the wine is aged in stainless steel, and half in barrique. The result is a bright ruby wine whose nose gives vegetal notes of freshly mown hay, followed by sensations of balsam and sweet oakiness. The palate is full, soft, attractive and long, faithfully mirroring the nose. Sigillo Primo Chardonnay is as good as ever. The '02 may be a touch less full than usual, because of the difficult vintage, but it has elegant, floral aromas and is attractively fruity on the palate. The '02 Sigillo Primo Primitivo, a monovarietal, showed fairly well, too. It is already rather forward, as the garnet tinges to its ruby colour reveal, but there are liqueur fruits on the nose and the attractive, nicely traditional palate is clean with medium depth.

●	Terre del Guiscardo '01	▼▼	4*
○	Sigillo Primo Chardonnay '02	▼▼	3*
●	Primitivo Sigillo Primo '02	▼	3
●	Terre del Guiscardo '00	▼▼	4
●	Primitivo Sigillo Primo '01	▼▼	3*
○	Sigillo Primo Chardonnay '01	▼▼	3*

GUAGNANO (LE)

CANTELE
S.P. SALICE SALENTINO - SAN DONACI KM 35,6
73010 GUAGNANO (LE)
TEL. 0832705010
E-MAIL: cantele@cantele.it

Augusto and Domenico Cantele continue as before, demonstrating notable consistency of quality, at least in their estate's leading wines. Quantities are equally notable. Augusto and Domenico co-ordinate a long-standing group of trusted growers who supply grapes from a total of 250 hectares. They have also recent acquired an additional 20 hectares that they own outright and their total output is almost 3,000,000 bottles a year. It was the indigenous reds, more than the Chardonnays, which have possibly suffered from the difficult 2002 vintage, that kept the estate's head held high this year. Amativo '01, from 60 per cent primitivo and negroamaro, was particularly appreciated by the tasting panel and in fact made it to the Three Glass finals, the third successive vintage to do so. The purple-tinged ruby ushers in a refined, complex nose with aromas of fresh fruit and walnut, layered over spices and chocolate from nice oaking. The palate is elegant, lively and long, with ripe fruit and liquorice. The emphasis overall is on elegance rather than power, and the palate has great personality. Teresa Manara Rosso '99, from 85 per cent negroamaro and aglianico, showed very well, too. It is more typically Salento in style, with raisiny fruit and hints of alcohol on the nose. The palate is full and warm, with plum and cherry flavours. Varius '01 comes from negroamaro, cabernet sauvignon and montepulciano, and is more youthful and immediate, with plenty of fresh fruit and light wafts of balsam. Both Teresa Manara Chardonnay '02 and Salice Salentino Riserva '99 are well typed.

●	Amativo '01	▼▼	5*
●	Teresa Manara '99	▼▼	4
●	Varius '01	▼	4
○	Chardonnay Teresa Manara '02	▼	4
●	Salice Salentino Rosso Ris. '99	▼	3
●	Salice Salentino Rosso Ris. '96	▼▼	4
●	Salice Salentino Rosso Ris. '97	▼▼	4
●	Amativo '99	▼▼	6
●	Amativo '00	▼▼	4*
○	Chardonnay Teresa Manara '01	▼▼	4

GUAGNANO (LE)

COSIMO TAURINO
S.S. 605
73010 GUAGNANO (LE)
TEL. 0832706490
E-MAIL: info@taurinovini.it

Founded by Cosimo Taurino, who abandoned his pharmacy in 1970 to dedicate himself to his family's vineyards, this winery rapidly became one of the most important in the region. It has even gained significant market share abroad. Severino Garofano, an oenologist with a profound knowledge of southern Italian winemaking, has been on board right from the very beginning. Today, Cosimo's heirs, son Francesco and daughter Rosanna, are running the estate, with Garofano still consulting. Taurino's flagship is Patriglione, a negroamaro-based red, with a touch of malvasia nera, that comes from the vineyard of the same name. It is produced only in good years and it was the '97 we tasted this time. Its good garnet-ruby introduces complex aromas of liqueur cherries and red berry fruit jam, which lead to quite evolved oak tones. The high alcohol makes the palate powerful, warm and soft, but there are rather astringent tannins and slightly unbalanced acidity. This prevented the panel awarding it its umpteenth Three Glass prize. We found the sweet Le Ricordanze '01, from sémillon and riesling, had great promise. It shows dried rose and marzipan aromas and delicately sweet, floral palate. The '99 Notarpanaro, from negroamaro with 15 per cent malvasia nera, has its usual good structure, concentrated ripe fruit and nice balance. However, when compared with last year's version, the '02 I Sierri, from chardonnay and malvasia bianca, seemed subdued. Salice Salentino '00 and the rosé Scaloti '02 are worthy of mention, but no more.

LEPORANO (TA)

VIGNE & VINI
VIA AMENDOLA, 36
74020 LEPORANO (TA)
TEL. 0995332254
E-MAIL: vigne&vini@italiainrete.net

The Vigne & Vini wines showed excellently this year, and there are continuing gains in both quality and quantity at the winery. In fact, the enterprise is a benchmark for all the many Puglian "maisons de négoce", those wineries that have few or no vines of their own and buy in grapes or lease vineyards. The figures at Vigne & Vini are: 500,000 bottles, 20 hectares of estate-owned vineyard, 135 hectares leased and four wines that won Two Glasses. Tatu '02, from 90 per cent primitivo with a little aglianico, is surprisingly good. The nose is highly complex, with notes of tobacco, coffee, cocoa powder and oriental spices. The palate is soft and elegant, but with good piquancy and a fine acid backbone. Schiaccianoci '02, from negroamaro with 20 per cent malvasia nera vinified and aged in stainless steel, scored similarly highly. It is full and fruity, with a slim vegetal streak, but has good balance and a long, pleasingly liquorice-like finish. It is a fine example of how you can retain freshness and attractiveness on a traditionally styled wine, without overdoing extract. Another Two Glasses went to Primitivo di Manduria Papale '01, whose uncomplicated nose is followed by an elegant, lively palate, full of fruit and laced with ripe tannins. There might not be any great depth, but there is certainly balance and good length. Zinfandel '02 is similar in style and quality, but has a more alluring red berry fruit and chocolate nose.

○ Le Ricordanze Passito '01	♙♙	6
● Patriglione '97	♙♙	8
● Notarpanaro '99	♙♙	5
○ I Sierri '02	♙	4
● Salice Salentino Rosso '00		5
☉ Scaloti '02		4
● Patriglione '85	♛♛♛	5
● Patriglione '88	♛♛♛	8
● Patriglione '94	♛♛♛	6
● Notarpanaro '97	♛♛	5

● Primitivo di Manduria Papale '01	♙♙	4
● Primitivo Zinfandel '02	♙♙	4*
● Primitivo Tatu '02	♙♙	4*
● Schiaccianoci '02	♙♙	4*
● Primitivo di Manduria		
Dolce Naturale Chicca '00	♛♛	5
● Primitivo di Manduria Papale '00	♛♛	4

LEVERANO (LE)

CONTI ZECCA
VIA CESAREA
73045 LEVERANO (LE)
TEL. 0832925613 - 0832910394
E-MAIL: info@contizecca.it

Few wines gain Three Glasses year after year. Yet, Conti Zecca's Nero has hit the bull's eye for the fourth year in succession, this time with the '01. Adjectives such as "classic" and phrases like "it has found itself stylistically" are now fully justified. Congratulations to Alcibiade Zecca and to the excellent team that forged this success, most prominently Fernando Romano, oenologist and estate director, and Giorgio Marone, consultant oenologist. Until about ten years ago, the estate was known for its carefully honed range of good value wines. Then there was a cellar update and the long, laborious task of studying and maximizing the potential of each vineyard in the total of 320 hectares. This culminated in the creation of a prestige line, led off by the majestic Nero. Obtained from 70 per cent negroamaro and 30 per cent cabernet sauvignon, and aged in new barriques, it is a good, deep, dark ruby, tending to purple at the rim. The nose is intense, with sweet red and black ripe berry fruit, and all the perfumes of the Mediterranean south. The palate is tightly knit, showing abundant body and fruit, complex toasty notes, nuances of tobacco and chocolate, and amazing softness and length. The best of the rest include a warm, spicy Primitivo '01; a deep Leverano Riserva Terra '00 with good definition; and an excellent, tight-knit Salice Salentino Riserva '00 from the Cantalupi vineyard, with superbly judged oak. The remaining wines from the large range are all good quality and very fairly priced.

LIZZANO (TA)

MILLE UNA
L.GO CHIESA, 11
74020 LIZZANO (TA)
TEL. 0999552638 - 3355997054
E-MAIL: milleuna2002@supereva.it

This new estate was set up in 2001, since when it has proved a delightful surprise. There are has 12 hectares in direct ownership and a further 18 leased, and management is split among the four founding partners: Dario Cavallo looks after sales; Michele Schifone is the general manager and is also involved in winemaking; Bruno De Conciliis is the agronomist; and Saverio Petrilli the oenologist. The quartet submitted a first-rate series of reds, led by Capitolo Laureto '01, one of the four or five negroamaro-based wines we liked best this year. Despite 15 months in barrique, it is lively and attractive, without excessive weight, and has pleasant notes of plum, coffee and wild black berries. Ori di Taranto '01, from primitivo aged for 12 months in a mixture of stainless steel and barrique, was not only good but is also the best value wine in the group. Bacmione '01, from 100 per cent primitivo aged for nine months in barrique and three in stainless steel, and its big brother, Primitivo Sharazad '01, with 15 months in barrique, are also noteworthy. The only disappointment in all this good news, we regret to say, is the ambitious pricing of most of the range. Like the estate itself, the wines have no track record or tradition behind them to reassure drinkers. But then, this isn't a problem that is unique to Mille Una.

● Nero '01	🍷🍷🍷	6
● Leverano Rosso Terra Ris. '00	🍷🍷	6
● Salice Salentino Cantalupi Ris. '00	🍷🍷	4*
● Primitivo '01	🍷🍷	4*
● Salice Salentino Rosso		
Cantalupi '01	🍷🍷	3*
● Donna Marzia Rosso '01	🍷	3*
● Leverano Rosso V. del Saraceno '01	🍷	3*
● Zinfandel '01	🍷	3*
☉ Donna Marzia Rosato '02	🍷	2*
○ Leverano Bianco V. del Saraceno '02	🍷	3*
☉ Leverano Rosato V. del Saraceno '02	🍷	3*
● Nero '98	🍷🍷🍷	5
● Nero '99	🍷🍷🍷	5*
● Nero '00	🍷🍷🍷	6

● Bacmione '01	🍷🍷	5
● Capitolo Laureto '01	🍷🍷	8
● Ori di Taranto '01	🍷🍷	4*
● Shahrazad '01	🍷🍷	8
● Majara '01	🍷	4
● Rubis '01	🍷	4
● Shahryar '01	🍷	8
● Tretarante '01	🍷	8

LOCOROTONDO (BA)

VINI CLASSICI CARDONE
VIA MARTIRI DELLA LIBERTÀ, 28
70010 LOCOROTONDO (BA)
TEL. 0804311624 - 0804312561
E-MAIL: info@cardonevini.com

Cardone has repeated last year's excellent showing, consolidating its place in the Guide. The estate may be fairly small, with an annual production of less than 100,000 bottles, but oenologist Sandro Rosato's excellent input ensures the wines are good. Primitivo '01, made exclusively from the grape and aged a year in barrique, almost made the finals with its excellent fruit-oak balance. The colour is an intense ruby, then the nose brims with Mediterranean scrubland, fresh cherry, liquorice and chocolate. The palate is lively and vigorous, yet long and elegant, with herbiness and coffee on the finish. It's a fine example of a modern, yet very varietal primitivo. There was also an excellent performance by Carmerum '00, a sweet, primitivo-based wine that attains a nice balance of acidity, tannin and residual sugar. Archita '01, from primitivo, negroamaro and aglianico, also easily won Two Glasses, with sweet spices and cocoa powder on the nose, then a soft palate of plum and ripe cherry flavours. Nausica '02 is excellent. Its intense, refined nose and fresh, attractive palate with red berry fruits make it one of the best rosés of the vintage. Just one notch down come two wines in a young, fresh style. Primaio '02 is very pleasing but not quite as good as the '01, and Locorotondo '02, which accounts for half the estate's entire production, is attractively fresh and zesty this year, making it one of the best in the DOC.

LOCOROTONDO (BA)

CANTINA SOC.COOPERATIVA
DEL LOCOROTONDO
VIA MADONNA DELLA CATENA, 99
70010 LOCOROTONDO (BA)
TEL. 0804311644 - 0804311298
E-MAIL: info@locorotondodoc.com

The Locorotondo co-operative was founded back in 1932. It currently has around 1,000 members and produces 2,500,000 bottles, all good quality and very fairly priced. Cummerse Rosso did very well again this year, the '99 gaining Two well deserved Glasses. It comes from an unusual mix of aglianico, cabernet sauvignon and uva di Troia, aged 24 months in barrique and stainless steel. The real surprise, though, came from the '00 Primitivo di Manduria Terre di Don Peppe, which showed much better than the previous release. Improvements are also evident in Casale San Giorgio Rosato. The attractive pink colour, the delightful aromas of cherry and wild fennel, and the rounded, attractively off-dry palate of the '02 gained it Two Glasses. Roccia Rosso '02 is a well made red. From 60 per cent negroamaro and 20 per cent each of malvasia nera and montepulciano, it aged for three to four months in barrique and stainless steel. Among the whites, all the estate evergreens are as good as ever. The Locorotondo Vigneti in Tallinjano '02, though, is possibly a touch less fresh and enjoyable than usual. It comes from the classic blend of 65 per cent verdeca and bianco d'Alessano, with a little fiano. The fruit is grown on "alberello" (bush-trained) vines averaging 40 years old, located in the small area of Tallinajo, and the mix reflects verdeca's freshness and bianco d'Alessano's structure and its apple and white peach aromas. Congratulations to the entire team, especially manager Donato Pinto, Benedetto Lo Russo, the oenologist, and agronomist Giuseppe Rotolo.

● Carmerum '00	ŶŶ	4
● Archita '01	ŶŶ	5
● Primitivo '01	ŶŶ	4
⊙ Nausica '02	ŶŶ	4
○ Locorotondo '02	Ŷ	3
● Primitivo Primaio '02	Ŷ	4
● Primitivo '00	ŶŶ	4
● Salento Rosso '00	ŶŶ	5
● Primitivo Primaio '01	ŶŶ	3*

● Primitivo di Manduria Terre di Don Peppe '00	ŶŶ	6
⊙ Casale San Giorgio Rosato '02	ŶŶ	3*
● Cummerse Rosso '99	ŶŶ	4*
○ Locorotondo Riserva del Presidente '01	Ŷ	5
○ Locorotondo '02	Ŷ	3
○ Locorotondo Vign. In Tallinajo '02	Ŷ	4
○ Moscato Olimpia '02	Ŷ	4
● Roccia Rosso '02	Ŷ	4
● Cummerse Rosso '98	ŶŶ	4*

MANDURIA (TA)

MANDURIA (TA)

ACCADEMIA DEI RACEMI
VIA SANTO STASI PRIMO - Z. I.
74024 MANDURIA (TA)
TEL. 0999711660
E-MAIL:
accademia@accademiadeiracemi.it

FELLINE
VIA SANTO STASI PRIMO Z. I.
74024 MANDURIA (TA)
TEL. 0999711660
E-MAIL:
accademia@accademiadeiracemi.it

Gregory Perrucci's Accademia dei Racemi groups the production of several small estates, providing assistance in the vineyards and during winemaking. It also handles sales, using the Accademia brand name. The team is top notch, with Salvatore Mero looking after viticulture, Elisabetta Gorla sales and Roberto Cipresso the winemaking. The concepts underlying its activities are the salvaging of old bush-trained vines that have been abandoned or risk being uprooted, and the protection of typical Puglian vines and wine styles, adapted in line with modern oenological know-how. The team is doing an excellent job, to judge by the wines submitted for tasting. Primitivo di Manduria Zinfandel '02 from the 26-hectare Sinfarosa property, owned by Perrucci, is a varietally true, spicy, highly concentrated wine of great elegance that is one of the best in the DOC. It scored just a couple of points shy of Three Glasses. The rest of the range includes Salice Salentino Te Deum '02, from Casale Bevagna, which stands out for its dark ruby colour and nose of super-ripe red and black berry fruit, interlaced with notes of balsam and Mediterranean scrubland. It also has solidity and elegance, qualities it shares with Ottavianello Dedalo '02 from the Torre Guaceto estate, just outside Brindisi. Anarkos '02 is a highly successful blend of primitivo, negroamaro and malvasia nera from the Accademia's various estates. It's excellent, and very well priced.

Primitivo was recreated right here, on this estate which has done so much to improve the image of Puglian viticulture and its wines. The Ferrucci brothers, who are both passionate and knowledgeable about their land and its wines, spent years on study trips to the USA and France before starting to work with Roberto Cipresso, at that time a rising star on the Italian wine scene. Their similar enthusiasms and attitudes to winemaking gave rise to their first Primitivo di Manduria, the '97, which caused a sensation. For many, it was literally too good to be true and so branded as "untraditional" or, worse, "assisted" by other varieties. This was not the case. It was simply that never before had such a clean Primitivo, with such intensity of flavour, been released. It was simply impossible to reconcile with existing "traditional" wines. Since then, the estate has remained firmly at the top of the Puglian tree and this year's wines again set the pace. Vigna del Feudo '02, a promising blend of ottavianello (the cinsault of France's Rhône valley), malvasia nera and primitivo, is excellent, despite still being a touch closed. A concentrated nose of wild berry fruit and oriental spices, introduces a fruit-rich palate. Also highly impressive is the '02 Primitivo di Manduria. This improves greatly in the glass, releasing delicate aromas of liqueur cherries. We were a touch disappointed by the '02 Alberello, though. This 50-50 blend of primitivo and negroamaro seemed a little too evolved for its age.

● Primitivo di Manduria Zinfandel Sinfarosa '02	▼▼	5*
● Anarkos '02	▼▼	4*
● Ottavianello Dedalo Torre Guaceto '02	▼▼	5
● Primitivo di Manduria Giravolta Tenuta Pozzopalo '02	▼▼	5
● Salice Salentino Rosso Te Deum Laudamus Casale Bevagna '02	▼▼	5
● Primitivo Portile Masseria Pepe '02	▼	4
● Sinfarosa Primitivo '02	▼	4
● Primitivo di Manduria Dunico Millennium Masseria Pepe '00	♀♀	6
● Primitivo di Manduria Zinfandel Sinfarosa '01	♀♀	5

● Vigna del Feudo '02	▼▼	5*
● Primitivo di Manduria '02	▼▼	4
● Alberello '02	▼	3
● Vigna del Feudo '97	♀♀♀	4
● Vigna del Feudo '00	♀♀	5*
● Primitivo di Manduria '00	♀♀	4*
● Primitivo di Manduria '01	♀♀	4*

MANDURIA (TA)

PERVINI
VIA SANTO STASI PRIMO - Z. I.
74024 MANDURIA (TA)
TEL. 0999711660
E-MAIL:
accademia@accademiadeiracemi.it

The Perrucci family are leading players in the regeneration of Puglian winemaking, both with their Accademia dei Racemi and with their own estate, founded in 1993, which is more or less the top of the tree. The work of retrieving and raising the profile of old "alberello" or bush-trained, vines goes on, and their vineyard holding continues to grow. Currently they own 32 hectares outright and have another 50 or so under their direct control. This year, it was I Monili '02, from primitivo with ten per cent montepulciano, that was the estate's Two Glasses banner-waver. The nose, although still a little quiet, has attractive fruit led by red berries, and floral notes of violets, but it is the structure and length of the full, powerful, palate that really convince. The '02 Primitivo di Manduria Archidamo is again highly successful. A good plum and cherry nose leads to a palate that may not be particularly full but is clean and lively, with attractive ripe fruit flavours. A step below lies Bizantino Rosso '02, from a 30 per cent barrique-aged 60-40 blend of negroamaro and primitivo. This has a bright ruby colour, aromas of ripe plum, wild red berry fruit and tobacco, and a most attractive, deep, soft palate with good concentration and flavours of plum jam and sweet spices. Also worthy of note is the well-made, but slightly predictable, Primitivo di Manduria Primo Amore '01, a sweet wine with raisiny fruit and good acid-tannin balance.

MARTINA FRANCA (TA)

VINICOLA MIALI
VIA MADONNINA, 1
74015 MARTINA FRANCA (TA)
TEL. 0804303222
E-MAIL: carlomiali@cantinemiali.com

Miali, founded in 1886, is a family-run estate now aiming for quality to be able to do battle on international markets. The whole family is involved in running the estate, with Michele Antonio the oenologist, Francesco the general manager and Carlo Miali in charge of sales. They produce over 580,000 bottles from around 40 hectares of leased vineyards, plus an excellent, oak-free Aglianico del Vulture that is lively and easy drinking. In fact, the reds dominated this year's tastings for it seems there is still some work to be done on the whites. The biggest impression was made by Primitivo Mater '01 which, after a year in barrique, has iodine and Mediterranean scrubland on the nose, and mouthfilling tannins on the fruit-forward palate. The uncomplicated, attractively lively Bardiglio '01, from 60 per cent negroamaro and malvasia nera, and the slightly sweet Primitivo di Manduria, with its raisiny fruit, are both well styled. The main problem with the whites is that they lack stuffing, and show signs of oxidation. The cheaper line, Sevillane, was also fairly unexciting. However, we had a chance to retaste the '00 Castel del Monte Rosso and found it to be developing excellently. Overall, the Miali family deserve credit for this year's results, as well as for their very fair pricing policy.

● Primitivo I Monili '02	♟♟	3*
● Primitivo di Manduria Archidamo '02	♟♟	4*
● Primitivo di Manduria Primo Amore '01	♟	4
● Bizantino '02	♟	3*
● Primitivo di Manduria Archidamo '98	♟♟	3
● Primitivo di Manduria Archidamo '00	♟♟	4*
● Primitivo di Manduria Archidamo '01	♟♟	4

● Primitivo Mater '01	♟♟	5
● Bardiglio Rosso '01	♟	4
● Primitivo di Manduria '01	♟	2*
● Aglianico del Vulture '99	♟	2*
● Castel del Monte Rosso '00	♟	2
● Primitivo di Manduria '00	♟	4

MONTERONI DI LECCE (LE)   SALICE SALENTINO (LE)

CASA VINICOLA APOLLONIO
VIA SAN PIETRO IN LAMA, 7
73047 MONTERONI DI LECCE (LE)
TEL. 0832327182
E-MAIL: info@apolloniovini.it

CASTELLO MONACI
C.DA MONACI
73015 SALICE SALENTINO (LE)
TEL. 0831665700
E-MAIL: giv@giv.it

This estate, focused mainly on Copertino, is a new entry in the Guide. It owns 50 hectares of vineyard, all with traditional "alberello" (bush) training, and produces 1,000,000 bottles a year. The '00 Copertino was one of the greatest, and most cheering, surprises of our Puglian tastings. It is based on 70 per cent negroamaro with equal parts of montepulciano, sangiovese, and malvasia nera di Lecce, and is well-typed, traditionally styled, yet modern. Attractiveness is a major virtue. The colour is dark ruby, introducing a fresh, fruity nose laced with chocolate, coffee and aniseed. The palate is full, firm and nicely fleshy, with assertive but not aggressive tannins, and excellent balance and length. In short, it is a wine that slips comfortably into the Two Glasses category. The two other Copertino wines submitted, Divoto Riserva '97 and '93 (that's right, '93), are both very good, if not quite as delicious as the straight '00. The riservas come mainly from negroamaro, with 30 per cent montepulciano. The '97 has aromas of pepper and cherry, but the alcohol tends to intrude. The palate is round, evolved and sound, with sweet spiciness which gives an unusual, almost chilli-like finish. The '93, another pleasant surprise, has iodine, Mediterranean scrubland and strawberry jam on the nose. Evolved but not over the hill, it has a mouthfilling, full-bodied palate, with attractive notes of raisined fruit, and tannins that are fully softened and smoothed out. The rest of the range showed well, too, confirming that the whole operation is well run.

After its debut in the Guide last year with a short entry, this fine estate, owned by the Gruppo Italiano Vini (GIV) group, now gains a full entry, thanks above all to Artas '01. This delight came within a whisker of Three Glasses, and must be one of this year's best Puglian reds. The fruit, 85 per cent primitivo with the remainder negroamaro, is all grown on very low yielding (4,000 to 5,000 kilograms per hectare) "alberello" (bush-trained) vines about 50 years old, scattered over a variety of terrains. The geological diversity found in very small distances here is summed up in the local saying, "the land changes palm by palm". At Casello Monaci, they believe that primitivo gives its best results from the plots known as "crostini", where the soil is fairly poor but rich in iron salts, and thus reddish coloured. Artas is emblematic of the fine results obtained by Francesco Bardi, GIV's big-league oenologist, and Leonardo Sergio, his self-proclaimed disciple. The colour is dark ruby, brightly tinged with purple, then the nose gives liqueur cherries, leather and black pepper. The palate has beautiful texture and silky tannins. The most impressive of the other wines produced by the estate this year is Primitivo '02. The '02 Salice Salentino Rosso is also good, fully meriting its One Glass.

● Copertino '00	♈♈	4*	● Artas '01	♈♈	5*
● Copertino Divoto Ris. '93	♈♈	8	● Primitivo '02	♈	3*
● Copertino Divoto '97	♈♈	5	● Salice Salentino '02	♈	3
● Salice Salentino '00	♈	4	● Primitivo '01	♀	3
● Valle Cupa '00	♈	4	● Salice Salentino '01	♀	3
● Elfo '02	♈	3			

SALICE SALENTINO (LE)

LEONE DE CASTRIS
VIA SENATORE DE CASTRIS, 26
73015 SALICE SALENTINO (LE)
TEL. 0832731112 - 0832731113
E-MAIL: info@leonedecastris.com

We can say without fear of contradiction that the performance of Leone de Castris this year was unmatched anywhere in Puglia and was one of the best in all Italy. It is hard to know where to begin with the praise. Every wine is as good as the next, from the least expensive and least complicated through to the biggies. However, "noblesse oblige", as they say. We must start with Donna Lisa Riserva '99, 100 per cent negroamaro and a wine of extraordinary quality that scooped Three Glasses. Last year's '98 seemed too green and vegetal, but this time there are no reservations. This is a great wine of rare elegance. Balsamic and spicy, it has length and loads of fruit. Next come the first-class Primitivo di Manduria Santera '01 and Primitivo del Salento La Rena '01. We would like, though, to spend a little time on the wines that are rarely mentioned, but which deserve greater attention, such as Messapia. From 100 per cent verdeca, the '02 has appealing citrus aromas and is as attractive a white as you can find. Then there are the winery's two rosés, both of which are great. This may be no surprise in the case of Five Roses Anniversario '02, but it is a great pleasure to point out that this year the standard Five Roses '02 is just as good, and a great match for salami or white meats. Finally comes the sound, hugely attractive Aleatico Negrino '01, an ideal way to finish a good evening, along with a chocolate-based dessert. Our congratulations to Piernicola Leone de Castris and his winemaking team.

SAN DONACI (BR)

FRANCESCO CANDIDO
VIA A. DIAZ, 46
72025 SAN DONACI (BR)
TEL. 0831635674 - 0831635675
E-MAIL: candido.wines@tin.it

This major winery produces around 2,000,000 bottles a year of very good, very fairly priced wines from roughly 250 hectares, of which it owns 160 directly. Here, too, the oenologist in control is Severino Garofano, something of an institution in these parts. The winery has always stood out for its way with negroamaro, a variety that finds some of its most successful and most typical expressions at this cellar. There could be no better example than the '99 Cappello di Prete, a monovarietal negroamaro aged for six months in barrique which, as usual textbook stuff, apart from a few rustic hints on the palate, which is, in any case fairly common in traditionally vinified Negroamaro. The '97 Duca d'Aragona, from 80 per cent negroamaro with the rest montepulciano, and aged for 12 months in barrique followed by another 12 in bottle, is as sound as ever, although we were less convinced by it than in the past because it seemed quite evolved. Immensum '01, from negroamaro with 20 per cent cabernet sauvignon, is well made but strongly tannic. Vigna Vinera '02 and Portafalsa '02 are the most interesting of the whites. The former comes from 60 per cent chardonnay and 40 per cent sauvignon that stay in barrique for five months. The Portafalsa is a monovarietal Chardonnay and sees no oak. It is a little straightforward, but its uncomplicated freshness makes it very pleasant drinking.

● Salice Salentino Rosso		
Donna Lisa Ris. '99	♟♟♟	6
● Primitivo di Manduria Santera '01	♟♟	3*
● Primitivo La Rena '01	♟♟	3*
○ Salice Salentino Bianco		
Donna Lisa '01	♟♟	5
☉ Five Roses '02	♟♟	3*
☉ Five Roses Anniversario '02	♟♟	4
○ Messapia '02	♟♟	3*
● Illemos '99	♟♟	5
● Aleatico Negrino '01	♟	4
● Negroamaro E lo Veni '01	♟	3
○ Moscato Pierale '02	♟	4
● Salice Salentino Rosso		
Donna Lisa Ris. '95	♟♟♟	5

● Immensum '01	♟♟	4
● Duca d'Aragona '97	♟♟	5
● Cappello di Prete '99	♟♟	3*
● Salice Salentino Ris. '00	♟	3
○ Salice Salentino Bianco		
Portafalsa '02	♟	3
☉ Salice Salentino Rosato		
Le Pozzelle '02	♟	2
○ Vigna Vinera '02	♟	3
● Duca d'Aragona '96	♟♟	5
● Immensum '00	♟♟	4
● Cappello di Prete '98	♟♟	3*
○ Paule Calle '99	♟♟	4

SAN PIETRO VERNOTICO (BR)   SAN SEVERO (FG)

TORMARESCA
VIA MATERNITÀ ED INFANZIA, 21
72027 SAN PIETRO VERNOTICO (BR)
TEL. 0805486943
E-MAIL: tormaresca@tormaresca.it

D'ALFONSO DEL SORDO
C.DA SANT'ANTONINO
71016 SAN SEVERO (FG)
TEL. 0882221444 - 0882335588
E-MAIL: info@dalfonsodelsordo.it

What else is there to be said about the Antinori family and their prince of oenologists, Renzo Cotarella, here admirably supported by Davide Sarcinella? They arrived in Puglia just a short time ago, founding Tormaresca in 1989, and immediately began turning out reds and whites of formidable quality. In fact, the estate is already a leader on the Puglian wine scene. It produces around 1,000,000 bottles a year from 610 hectares under vine, of which 350 are owned directly. There is a new wine this year, Torcicoda '01, from 100 per cent primitivo, and it immediately claimed Three Glasses. Its dark ruby ushers in aromas of morello cherry, tobacco and leather, then mouthfilling tannins and fabulous fruit regale the palate. It is also excellent value. The '01 Bocca di Lupo, from 90 per cent aglianico and cabernet, is again very good, with violet and lavender florality and blackcurrant and cherry fruitiness on the nose, richness and depth on the palate, and good nose-palate convergence. The '01 Masseria Maime is a shade less impressive than last year's, although it is still one of the best wines from negroamaro in circulation. The nose is floral with light oakiness and the palate has good fruit and texture, but here the oak is still too distinct. We still have to wait for the new vintage of Pietrabianca, one of the best white wines in southern Italy. In the meantime, we found the '02 Chardonnay quite spectacular in its marriage of attractiveness, substance and highly praiseworthy pricing. Well done everyone.

D'Alfonso del Sordo's quality improvements continue. The massive work being carried out on the 90 hectares of vineyard and in the cellar, all co-ordinated by Professor Luigi Moio since 2001 and monitored by oenologist Rocco Marino, are taking this estate to the top rank of regional winemaking. The stemware below speaks volumes for the quality of the range. Cava del Re '02, from cabernet sauvignon only, came within an inch of Three Glasses. The nose is fresh and youthfully lively, with distinct black wild berry fruit. The palate is fresh and full, with clearly defined flavours, yet also richly fleshy and very long. Guado San Leo '02, 100 per cent uva di Troia, is also good, showing that wine can be great in Puglia, whether it comes from indigenous or international varieties. The colour is purplish ruby, the nose is fruity with violet florality and the still youthful, well-extracted palate unveils flavours of vanilla and aniseed. There are fewer than 5,000 bottles a year of each of these, but the estate's other Two Glass wines, Catapanus '02 and San Severo Rosato Posta Arignano '02, are produced in abundance. The former, made solely from bombino bianco, is rich, full-flavoured and notably long. Its partner has become one of the most serious candidates for the title of "best rosé in Puglia". It has intense, elegant aromas, with clear notes of wild strawberries and almond blossom. The palate is clean, fresh, well structured and full of fruit. It is also one of the region's best value for money wines. The rest of the range is more than just good.

●	Torcicoda '01	🍷🍷🍷	5*
●	Castel del Monte Rosso Bocca di Lupo '01	🍷🍷	5
●	Masseria Maime '01	🍷🍷	5
○	Tormaresca Chardonnay '02	🍷🍷	3*
●	Masseria Maime '00	🍷🍷🍷	5*
●	Castel del Monte Rosso Bocca di Lupo '99	🍷🍷	5*
●	Castel del Monte Rosso Bocca di Lupo '00	🍷🍷	5
○	Castel del Monte Chardonnay Pietrabianca '01	🍷🍷	5
●	Tormaresca Rosso '01	🍷🍷	3*

●	Cava del Re Cabernet Sauvignon '02	🍷🍷	6
○	Bombino Bianco Catapanus '02	🍷🍷	2*
●	Guado San Leo '02	🍷🍷	6
⊙	San Severo Rosato Posta Arignano '02	🍷🍷	2*
●	Doganera Merlot '02	🍷	6
○	San Severo Bianco Candelaro '02	🍷	4
●	San Severo Rosso Posta Arignano '02	🍷	2
●	Cava del Re Cabernet Sauvignon '01	🍷🍷	6
●	Guado San Leo '01	🍷🍷	6

OTHER WINERIES

Sergio Botrugno
LOC. CASALE - VIA ARCIONE, 1
72011 BRINDISI
TEL. 0831413618
E-MAIL: sergiobotrugno@virgilio.it

Sergio Botrugno runs this estate with oenologist Cosimo Spina. Some wines are unexciting, but we note a desire to improve. Brindisi Rosso, from negroamaro and malvasia nera, is good and Ottavianello promising. Botrus, a malvasia nera "passito", and the dry malvasia bianca Pinea follow.

● Brindisi Rosso Arcione '01	♟♟	4*
● Botrus '01	♟	4
● Ottavianello '02	♟	4
○ Pinea '02		2

Alessia Imperatori
VIA GIGANTE, 2
72020 CELLINO SAN MARCO (BR)
TEL. 0831617689

This ambitious estate is a partnership between Imperatori and Marco Maci. Now in the Guide, it turns out impressive-looking bottles that do not always convince. Alessia Imperatori Rosso '01, from 70-30 negramaro and malvasia nera, is good. Salice Salentino Rosso '99 and Primitivo '01 are both nice.

● Alessia Imperatori Rosso '01	♟♟	4
● Primitivo '01	♟	5
● Salice Salentino '99	♟	4

Paradiso
VIA MANFREDONIA, 39
71042 CERIGNOLA (FG)
TEL. 0885428720
E-MAIL: info@cantineparadiso.it

Angelo Paradiso and his oenologist, Luigi Cantatore, can be proud of their Guide debut. A very well-made range of wines is led by the Primitivo and the merlot-based Solace Daunia '01 which, after an additional year in bottle, outplays the '02. Belmantello, 100 per cent uva di Troia, is also good.

● Primitivo '01	♟♟	3*
● Solace '01	♟♟	3*
● Belmantello '02	♟	3

Santa Lucia
S.DA SAN VITTORE, 1
70033 CORATO (BA)
TEL. 0818721168 - 0817642888
E-MAIL: info@vinisantalucia.com

This is an estate to follow. Giuseppe and Roberto Perrone Capano are guiding it towards major success. Castel del Monte Riserva Le More, from 100 per cent uva di Troia, is aristocratic and full of small, sweet berry fruits. Also good is Fiano Gazza Ladra, with its attractive vanilla and damson.

● Castel del Monte Le More Ris. '00	♟♟	5
○ Gazza Ladra '02	♟	4

LOMAZZI & SARLI
C.DA PARTEMIO - S.S. BINDISI - TARANTO
72022 LATIANO (BR)
TEL. 0831725898 - 337282775
E-MAIL: vinilomazzi@quipo.it

Lomazzi & Sarli submitted the best sweet Puglian wine for tasting this year. A highly concentrated Aleatico, it proffers coffee and cocoa powder aromas. The Malvasia Bianca is also good, but the other wines are less impressive. Still, Franco Bernabei is at the helm so improvements must come.

● Aleatico Dimastrodonato '00	🍷🍷	4*
● Salice Salentino '00	🍷	3
○ Malvasia Partemio '02	🍷	3

AGRICOLE VALLONE
VIA XXV LUGLIO, 5
73100 LECCE
TEL. 0832308041

Vallone, one of the great names in Puglia, only has a short profile because some of its classic labels, such as Graticciaia were still ageing when we tasted. Valesio Sauvignon was a delightful surprise and this year's top Puglian Sauvignon.

⊙ Brindisi Rosato V. Flaminio '02	🍷	3
○ Sauvignon Corte Valesio '02	🍷	3*
● Graticciaia '97	🍷🍷	7

CANTINA SOC. COOPERATIVA LEVERANO
VIA MARCHE, 1
73045 LEVERANO (LE)
TEL. 0832925053 - 0832921985
E-MAIL: info@cantinavecchiatorre.it

This co-operative turns out 1,000,000 value for money bottles each year. This time, it performed well and scored high. Salice Salentino Rosso is one of the best produced this year. Leverano Rosso, Primitivo Vecchia Torre and Arneide, a blend of negramaro, primitivo and montepulciano, are also good.

● Salice Salentino Rosso Vecchia Torre '00	🍷🍷	2*
● Arneide '00	🍷	5
● Primitivo Vecchia Torre '00	🍷	3
● Leverano Rosso '01	🍷	2*

I PASTINI - CARPARELLI
SEDE PRODUTTIVA C/O AZ. VITIVINICOLA
TORREVENTO - CORATO
70033 LOCOROTONDO (BA)
TEL. 0808980923 - 0808980929

Nicola and Pasquale Carparelli produce around well-made 200,000 bottles. Primitivo del Tarantino, the prettily-named Aleatico Elogio della Lentezza ("eulogy of slowness") and the Locorotondo are all sound. The last is a tad oxidative on the nose but makes up for it with a fresh, enjoyable palate.

● Aleatico Elogio della Lentezza '01	🍷	4
● Primitivo del Tarantino '01	🍷	4
○ Locorotondo '02	🍷	3

COOP. SVEVO - LUCERA
V.LE ORAZIO
71036 LUCERA (FG)
TEL. 0881547809

Traditional but well-made wines that you can rely on. Absolutely. This year, the montepulciano and sangiovese Barbarossa is better than the Saraceno, from the same blend but aged in large barrels. Praise goes to Cioccarello, one of the year's best rosés, and Sumarill, from 100 per cent uva di Troia.

● Barbarossa '01	🍷🍷	3*
● U' Summarill '00	🍷	5
● Saraceno '01	🍷	2
⊙ Cioccarello '02	🍷	2*

MORELLA
VIA SAN PIETRO IN BEVAGNA, 65
74024 MANDURIA (TA)
TEL. 0999713967
E-MAIL: azag_terrerosse@libero.it

Morella's range was formerly marketed by Calatrasi Puglia. The oenologist is still Lisa Kilbee, and the wines remain good. The Primitivo and the full, silky Malbek, from 70 per cent primitivo and malbec, are worthy of note, but neither Primitivo Old Vines' English name nor the wine itself impressed.

● Malbek Terre Rosse '01	🍷🍷	4
● Primitivo Terre Rosse '01	🍷🍷	4

CONS. PROD. VINI E MOSTI ROSSI
VIA F. MASSIMO, 19
74024 MANDURIA (TA)
TEL. 0999735332
E-MAIL: consvini@libero.it

This admirable co-operative has good wines, Primitivo Elegia in particular. Again it flaunts a clean, typically varietal nose and a mouthfilling, silky palate. The winery's other Primitivo, Memoria, is also very sound, but just a little shorter and less concentrated than the star.

● Primitivo di Manduria Elegia '01	🍷🍷	5
● Primitivo di Manduria Memoria '01	🍷	3

LE FABRICHE
LOC. C.DA LE FABBRICHE
S.P. MARUGGIO - TORRICELLA
74020 MARUGGIO (TA)
TEL. 0999738284 - 3356616380

There are no new wines this year from Le Fabriche, run by Alessia Perrucci and Barone Pizzini from Franciacorta. Oenologist Beppe Caviola advised them to leave the bottles to age longer before release. They are likely to be very impressive, so we await their appearance with optimism.

● Primitivo '01	🍷🍷	5
● Puglia Rosso '01	🍷	4

MOCAVERO
VIA RUBICHI, 2
73047 MONTERONI DI LECCE (LE)
TEL. 0832327194

A new entry, Mocavero is run by brothers, Francesco and Marco Mocavero, with Benedetto Lo Russo as oenologist. Santufili, from primitivo grown on over 70-year-old bush-trained vines, and Tela di Ragno, from aglianico are cabernet sauvignon, are both spot on. Just below comes Salice Salentino Puteus.

● Tela di Ragno '00	🍷🍷	5
● Santufili '98	🍷🍷	4
● Salice Salentino Puteus '98	🍷	3

BARSENTO
FRAZ. C.DA SAN GIACOMO
STR. PROVINCIALE MARTINA FRANCA
70015 NOCI (BA)
TEL. 0804979657

This is an estate to watch. It opted for indigenous varieties long before they became fashionable, and the wines respect tradition. Malicchia Mapicchia is one of the best examples of sweet Primitivo, and the malvasia nera Magilda is a pleasant, harmonious rosé. Malvasia Bianca Alberano is also good.

○ Alberano '02	🍷	5
⊙ Magilda Rosato '02	🍷	4
● Malicchia Mapicchia '02	🍷	4

LA CORTE
VIA TREPUZZI
73051 NOVOLI (LE)
TEL. 0559707594
E-MAIL: info@renideo.com

Much care goes into production at La Corte. Bottles and labels have attractive designs and the interesting wines are fruit-forward and concentrated, but manage to avoid excess. The best are Ré, a selected blend of negramaro and primitivo from the best sites, and Zinfandel.

● Ré '01	🍷🍷	5
● Zinfandel '01	🍷	5

CANT. COOP. DELLA RIFORMA FONDIARIA
VIA MADONNA DELLE GRAZIE, 8/A
70037 RUVO DI PUGLIA (BA)
TEL. 0803601611
E-MAIL: info@cantinacrifo.it

Good wines, good prices and a group of wines from rarely seen native grapes, such as moscatello selvatico. Augustale '00, a fine single-variety uva di Troia almost scored Two Glasses. Also good is Castel del Monte Rosso Riserva, but the moscatello dessert wine Augustale Oro needs more acidity.

● Augustale '00	🍷	4
● Castel del Monte Rosso Ris. '99	🍷	3
○ Augustale Oro '00		4

CANTINA COOPERATIVA SANDONACI
VIA MESAGNE, 62
72025 SAN DONACI (BR)
TEL. 0831681085

This 1,000-member co-operative, founded in 1933, joins the Guide with a good range. Croce del Moro, a barrique-aged Primitivo, is nice, as is the negramaro-based Anticaia Riserva. Well done oenologist, Leonardo Pinto, and president, Rocco Vincenti: the cellar has been bottling for only four years.

● Croce del Moro '02	♟♟	4
● Salice Salentino Anticaia Ris. '99	♟♟	4
● Salice Salentino Anticaia '00	♟	3

VINAGRI
VIA TUTURANO, 21
72025 SAN DONACI (BR)
TEL. 0831635073
E-MAIL: info@vinagripuglia.it

This estate, owned by Paolo Leo, with Benedetto Lo Russo as oenologist, makes its debut in the Guide. The wines are very well made, especially Limitone dei Greci, from primitivo and malvasia nera, and Orfeo, 100 per cent negroamaro, both nearly earning a second Glass.

● Limitone dei Greci '00	♟	3
● Orfeo '01	♟	4

SANTA BARBARA
VIA MATERNITÀ E INFANZIA, 23
72027 SAN PIETRO VERNOTICO (BR)
TEL. 0831652749

Oenologist Pietro Giorgiani has again come up with a good series of reds. The best of the bunch are Sumanero, a susumaniello, negramaro and malvasia nera mix that came close to Two Glasses, Brindisi Rosso and Aleatico. The whites are less impressive, hinting at oxidation and lacking freshness.

● Aleatico '00	♟	4
● Brindisi Rosso '00	♟	2*
● Sumanero '00	♟	2

VINICOLA MEDITERRANEA
VIA MATERNITÀ INFANZIA, 22
72027 SAN PIETRO VERNOTICO (BR)
TEL. 0831676323 - 0831659329
E-MAIL: medvini@libero.it

The skilled hand of oenologist Cosimo Spina is evident in the ever-better wines here. Crucially, the entire range is very reliable. Primitivo Dolce Naturale is as good as ever, and the Negramaro and Primitivo Scalee are just as delicious. One step down come Squinzano and Brindisi Rosso.

● Negroamaro '00	♟♟	3*
● Primitivo Dolce Naturale '00	♟♟	4*
● Brindisi Rosso '00	♟	3
● Primitivo Scalee '00	♟	2*

CASTEL DI SALVE
FRAZ. DEPRESSA - P.ZZA CASTELLO, 8
73030 TRICASE (LE)
TEL. 0833771041 - 0833771012
E-MAIL: casteldisalve@tiscalinet.it

It's a "wait and see" year for this newish estate, which has impressed us in the past. Priante, a 50-50 blend of negramaro and montepulciano, and Lama del Tenente, from primitivo and montepulciano with ten per cent malvasia nera, are both good, although Lama del Tenente might have been better.

● Lama del Tenente '00	♟	5
● Priante '01	♟	4
● Priante '00	♟♟	4
● Lama del Tenente '99	♟♟	5

MICHELE CALÒ & FIGLI
VIA MASSERIA VECCHIA, 1
73058 TUGLIE (LE)
TEL. 0833596242
E-MAIL: michelecalo@staff.it

Recently, this long-established estate has disappointed. Mjère Rosso, from negroamaro and malvasia nera, is sound, and the rosé is well-typed, but the cellar can do better. Too many wines were oxidized, or lacked freshness. It's a pity, because grape quality is good. We hope for better next year.

⊙ Alezio Rosato Mjere '02	♟	4
● Mjére '01		4
⊙ Alezio Rosato Mjère '01	♟♟	3*
● Mjére '00	♟	4

CALABRIA

We have no need to revise our comments in last year's Guide. Our tastings again show that, even in Calabria, things are moving in the right direction. This time, there was no Three Glass star, it is true, no virtuoso solo performance, but in general Calabria's quality levels, particularly at the medium-high end of the market, are definitely moving upwards. This is confirmed by the number of wines – five – that reached the tasting finals. Yet we cannot avoid pointing out, however regretfully, the gap between these and the rest of the region's wines. Apart from the five or six high-flying names, nothing really new is emerging. Calabria is a narrow region, with sea on both sides, so it has unsurpassed site climates and soils that offer supreme potential for high quality in all wine types. It seems, though, that many producers here are torn between firmly rooted traditions and their impulse to innovate. They just can't find the right balance, and often remain hesitantly stuck in the middle of the stream. An extra ounce of daring could be all that is needed to see them safely across. There is also little point in stressing that the region's most widespread grape variety, gaglioppo, is difficult to handle when some cellars obtain consistently good wines from it. But we are delighted to say that new plantings have opted largely for native varieties. The versatile magliocco is now found outside its traditional areas, but nerello, gaglioffo, calabrese, mantonico, pecorello and greco, too, have all become more widely planted. Finally, it appears that inflation has not had much of an effect on Calabrian wines, which remain very competitively priced. Librandi is, as usual, an outstanding performer with two wines with Two red Glasses. These are Gravello, which with just a little more oomph might have snatched that third Glass, and Efeso, a new, absolutely fascinating monovarietal white from mantonico. Vigna Garrone, from the Odoardi brothers, a powerful, elegant wine of notable concentration and finesse, did not manage to repeat its Three Glass triumph of last year, although it did come very close indeed. Fattoria San Francesco's Ronco dei Quattro Venti, a fine rendition of Cirò, performed very well, but at the final taste-off it was the estate's Brisi, a fabulous dried-grape "passito" wine, that really stood out. Terraccia, the new offering from Demitrio Stancati's winery, is also first class. It stormed through to the final taste-offs, even though it was only at its first release.

CASIGNANA (RC)

CIRÒ (KR)

STELITANO
C.DA PALAZZI, 1
89030 CASIGNANA (RC)
TEL. 0964913023
E-MAIL: stelitano@interfree.it

FATTORIA SAN FRANCESCO
LOC. QUATTROMANI
S. P. EX S. S. 106
88813 CIRÒ (KR)
TEL. 096232228
E-MAIL: info@fattoriasanfrancesco.it

The Stelitano family had been producing for others for three generations when, a decade ago, they decided to bottle under their own name. It was young Francesco and Angela who led this change. Francesco takes care of the commercial side and Angela, an oenologist, oversees winemaking. The pair were in perfect agreement that viticulture would be exclusively organic. Neither was there any debate about what to produce: the first wine was to be a Greco di Bianco. For two youngsters to set out on their winemaking careers producing just one dried-grape "passito" wine might seem an odd choice, but not round here, where the style is part of a centuries' old tradition. It is no coincidence that one of the very first DOCs approved for Calabria covers this area. And quite apart from ensuring that an ancient family tradition remained alive, the Stelitano siblings' choice is also helping to save a wine from the risk of extinction. Greco di Bianco production has fallen drastically in the last few years and much of what is still produced is made solely for home consumption. The Stelitano Greco has a great deal to offer. The colour is a bright, golden yellow, introducing a nose that gives apricots, dates, prunes and honey. The palate is fleshy and sweet, with good acidity to balance the softness, and a very long finish. More recently, another "passito", Locride, made exclusively from mantonico has joined the Greco. It is less complex but just as attractive.

"Innovation in tradition" could be Fattoria San Francesco's motto. The words sum up a production philosophy that yields constantly high quality wines of enviable stylistic consistency. Francesco Siciliani is a law graduate, as the diploma hanging on the wall proudly attests, which may give him an edge in running this family estate, one of the longest-standing Cirò producers. With high-calibre consultant oenologist, Fabrizio Ciufoli, at his side, Francesco began working mainly with indigenous varieties, starting obviously enough with gaglioppo. The two wines that reached the finals this year show just how far he's come. They were only a step away from Three Glasses. The '00 Brisi, a "vino da meditazione" sipping wine from 100 per cent greco, repeated the excellent showing of the '99 by sailing into the finals. The focus is on softness, but there is no sense of cloying. It has good concentration, aromas of honey and cooked apples and pears, a rich, rounded palate and candied orange peel on the finish. The second high-scoring wine is the '01 vintage of the estate's classic, Ronco dei Quattroventi, a Cirò Classico aged in barrique for over a year. It has good concentration, there is fully ripe red berry fruit and a hint of spice on the nose, then the palate is notably full and fleshy. Also of great interest is Donna Madda '01, with its good dark ruby colour, soft fruitiness on the nose, fair structure and more fruit on the finish. Something more from the standard wines would have been the final touch.

○	Greco di Bianco '01	🍷🍷	6
○	Locride '01	🍷	6

○	Brisi '00	🍷🍷	7
●	Cirò Rosso Cl. Ronco dei Quattro Venti '01	🍷🍷	6
●	Cirò Rosso Cl. Donna Madda '01	🍷🍷	5
●	Cirò Rosso Cl. '01		5
●	Martà '01		3
☉	Cirò Rosato Cl. Ronco dei Quattroventi '02		5
○	Pernicolò '02		4
●	Cirò Rosso Cl. Ronco dei Quattro Venti '00	🍷🍷	6
○	Brisi '99	🍷🍷	7

CIRÒ MARINA (KR)

LIBRANDI
LOC. SAN GENNARO
S. S. 106
88811 CIRÒ MARINA (KR)
TEL. 096231518
E-MAIL: librandi@librandi.it

The work on native Calabrian varieties by Attilio Scienza and Donato Lanati, a project that is close to the hearts of the Librandi brothers, honours a winery that which has pressed forward without being lured off course by fashion. And when you taste a wine like Efeso '01, you have to acknowledge the wisdom of the choice for this monovarietal Mantonico swept confidently into the Three Glasses finals. It is a deep straw colour ushers in an intense nose of apricot jam and figs. There's spiciness, too, revealing the use of oak, but with a skilled touch that ensures it is not too invasive. The palate is full and fleshy, its structure and alcohol well balanced by freshness. Two red Glasses also went to Gravello '00, a wine that in recent years has been performing excellently. Somehow, though, it has never yet achieved that final touch that would bring it a third Glass. Magno Megonio '01 is also first rate. It comes solely from magliocco, a variety found only in Calabria, where it arrived over 2,000 years ago from Greece. The wine is well balanced, with elegant aromas of small red berry fruits laced with floral nuances, and plenty of fruit on the palate which has good texture and dense, refined tannins. Le Passule, a dried-grape "passito" from greco, showed very well, as did the good value Critone. It's an easy-drinking, but not simplistic, wine that has a fresh, clean nose of peaches, apricots, golden delicious apples and spring flowers, supported by good acidity and structure. In short, Librandi's range is a beacon of reliability in a region that this year did not shine.

CIRÒ MARINA (KR)

MALENA
LOC. PIRAINETTO
88811 CIRÒ MARINA (KR)
TEL. 096231758
E-MAIL: info@malena.it

Malena is now at its second appearance in our Guide and even if the intervening year did not bring exciting leaps forward, there are continuing, steady quality improvements and the overall level remains sound. Recently, Cataldo Malena has been joined by his younger brother, Antonio, in running the winery. Both are in their 20s. It has been a transitional year for them, with now completed work under way on a new cellar to give them less cramped working areas and more modern equipment. The brothers' bond with their lands runs deep, and they have been planting new vines, which should start to bear fruit with the '03 vintage. For now, interest centres on Similoro '02, from chardonnay, a wine of fair structure and good balance that is fruity on the nose, fresh and attractive to drink. Also attractive is the latest release of Cirò Rosato, the '02, with clean aromas of cherry and strawberry plus a waft of florality. It is clean on the palate, too, which has a good balance of acidity and softness. Bacco '02, the estate's other rosé, is also good, showing nicely styled, fresh, attractive and gently fruity. Nevertheless, it was reasonable to expect a little more from the reds, given the good performance of Pian della Corte in last year's Guide.

●	Gravello '00	🍷🍷	6
○	Efeso '01	🍷🍷	8
○	Le Passule '01	🍷🍷	5
●	Magno Megonio '01	🍷🍷	7
○	Critone '02	🍷🍷	4
●	Melissa Asylia '02	🍷🍷	4*
⊙	Terre Lontane '02	🍷🍷	4
●	Cirò Rosso Cl. Sup. Duca Sanfelice Ris. '00	🍷	4
○	Cirò Bianco '02	🍷	3
⊙	Cirò Rosato '02	🍷	3
●	Cirò Rosso Cl. '02	🍷	3
●	Gravello '98	🍷🍷🍷	5
●	Magno Megonio '99	🍷🍷	7
●	Magno Megonio '00	🍷🍷	7
●	Gravello '99	🍷🍷	6

●	Cirò Rosso Cl. Sup. '01	🍷	2*
⊙	Bacco Rosato '02	🍷	3*
○	Cirò Bianco '02	🍷	2*
⊙	Cirò Rosato '02	🍷	2*
○	Similoro Bianco '02	🍷	3*
●	Cirò Rosso Cl. Sup. Ris. Pian della Corte '98	🍷🍷	4*
●	Cirò Rosso Cl. Sup. '00	🍷	2*

COSENZA

CROTONE

DEMETRIO SERRACAVALLO
VIA PIAVE, 51
87100 COSENZA
TEL. 098421144

ROBERTO CERAUDO
LOC. MARINA DI STRONGOLI
C.DA DATTILO
88815 CROTONE
TEL. 0962865613
E-MAIL: info@dattilo.it

Demetrio Stancanti is as easy-to-like as they come. He began to look after his family's estate almost by chance but quickly became gripped by a love for vines and wine. It wasn't long before he decided to leave the medical profession and throw himself body and soul into winemaking. In a few short years, Demetrio has completely replanted the vineyards, using more modern training systems and selected clones, as well as adding international varieties like cabernet and chardonnay, to the local grapes. Once he'd dealt with the vineyards, he turned straight to the cellar, refurbishing it from top to bottom. Now, he is concentrating his energies on one white variety, the indigenous pecorello, which he believes will give his whites more depth and concentration. All this work has not got in the way of giving the wines a new look. There are new names and new labels (we hope that the presentation is now definitive). More important, Demetrio's labours have not prevented him from bringing improvements to the whole range. Take Terraccia '00, which went through to the finals. From magliocco dolce with ten per cent cabernet sauvignon, it is a thick, dark, ruby colour. The nose is intense but still a bit closed, revealing ripe black berry fruits, blackberry in particular, and a clear streak of herbiness. The flavours hold well on the palate, which has freshness and body in good balance, plenty of flesh and a long aftertaste. The excellent value Sette Chiese '02, from the same blend but with 40 per cent cabernet, also performed well and is only a little less concentrated than Terraccia.

If you are ever on the eastern, or Ionian, side of Calabria, make a visit to Roberto Ceraudo's estate, set in a marvellous corner of what was once Magna Graecia. The farm nestles among hills carpeted with vineyards and olive groves that slope down gently to the sea, and at its centre is the ancient farmhouse and cellars. Much is new here. Until last year, the estate was called Dattilo, the number of wines has gone from three to five and, vitally, work has finally finished on the new barrel cellar. It is completely underground and the estate wines can now mature at controlled temperature. On the quality front, there has been some improvement overall, although there is still much to be done. The '02 Imyr, a 100 per cent Chardonnay aged in small French oak barrels, is again impressive. The nose is fruit-led and the rich palate shows good freshness, as well as flesh and length. Petraro '00 is very decent, with good concentration and pervasive aromas. There's also a touch of edginess that should soon soften down. Grayasusi '02, a well-made, attractive rosé with small red berry fruit on the nose, then freshness, structure and fruit on the palate, also gained One Glass. Dattilo, wholly from gaglioppo, and Petelia, based on chardonnay and greco, are the two new wines, but they probably need to be run in a bit more as they didn't totally convince.

●	Terraccia '00	♟♟	4	○ Imyr '02	♟♟	5
●	Sette Chiese '02	♟♟	3*	● Petraro '00	♟	6
○	Besidie '02		2	☉ Grayasusi '02	♟	4
●	Valle del Crati '01	♟♟	3*	● Dattilo '00		5
●	Valle del Crati Ris. '99	♟♟	4	○ Petelia '02		4
				○ Imyr '01	♟♟	4
				● Petraro '99	♟	4

LAMEZIA TERME (CZ)

CANTINE LENTO
VIA DEL PROGRESSO, 1
88046 LAMEZIA TERME (CZ)
TEL. 096828028
E-MAIL: info@cantinelento.it

With the 40 of the new holding now in production, this long-standing estate now has a total area under vine of 70 hectares at its disposal. They like to keep everything in the family here so, as well as family head, Salvatore, in the cellars, his wife, Giovanna, and two daughters, Danila and Manuela, are also fully involved in running the estate. Even oenologist Antonio Zaffina is part of the family, as he's Salvatore's brother-in-law. The family have always been supporters of indigenous varieties, principally greco. Now they are looking for their forthcoming wines to magliocco, whose characteristics are earning it an ever greater following throughout the region. Once again, our tastings revealed consistent reliability. The latest vintage of Lamezia Greco has particularly good balance. The nose is fruit-based, preceding a palate with freshness, flesh, fruit and good aromatic length. Federico II '00 showed very well, despite being a touch less complex than the previous vintage, as did Contessa Emburga Capsula Nera ("black capsule") '02, which differs from the Capsula Oro ("gold capsule") version in that it undergoes a short time in barrique. Obtained from sauvignon, it shows soft and balanced. Lamezia Rosso Riserva '98 is well typed, with refined tannins and good harmony. Finally comes the attractive, fresh, structured Lamezia Rosato, with enticing notes of blackcurrant and cherry on the nose. Consistency of quality now seems firmly established, so perhaps it's time quality to take a serious stride forward.

LAMEZIA TERME (CZ)

STATTI
TENUTA LENTI
88046 LAMEZIA TERME (CZ)
TEL. 0968456138 - 0968453655
E-MAIL: statti@statti.com

It was another year of fairly good results for young Alberto and Antonio Statti. Their modern cellar has now been completed and contains a very well-equipped analysis laboratory that will give them far greater scope for experimentation. The planting programme, aimed at bringing the area under vine from 35 newly replanted hectares to 100 in just three years, is still under way. The native varieties, magliocco, greco, mantonico and gaglioppo, have been chosen to cover roughly 80 per cent of the new vineyards and international varieties will occupy the rest. Overseeing all this work with consultant, Fabrizio Zardini, is now a young cellar oenologist, Luca Cerutti, and two agronomists. There were good things and less good things on the tasting front, but with all the structural changes that have been going on, some slip-ups are more than excusable, and in any event easily recoverable. The '01 Nosside, an unfortified dried-grape "passito" from mantonico and greco di Bianco, again deservedly took Two Glasses. The nose has sweet aromas of candied fruits, honey and spices, then the palate is warm, soft and sweet. Good acidity brings fine overall harmony and the aromas return on the long aftertaste. Arvino '01 is soft and cherry-like, but needs a little more flesh. In short, everything is in place for quality to soar. We shall await the next few vintages with anticipation.

● Federico II '00		▼▼	5
○ Contessa Emburga Capsula Nera '02		▼▼	4
○ Lamezia Greco '02		▼▼	4
○ Bianco Lieò '02		▼	3
○ Lamezia Bianco Tenuta Romeo '02		▼	4
☉ Lamezia Rosato Tenuta Romeo '02		▼	4
● Lamezia Rosso Ris. '98		▼	5
○ Contessa Emburga Capsula Oro '02			4
○ Villa Caracciolo '02			3
● Federico II '99		▼▼	6
● Lamezia Rosso Ris. '97		▼▼	6

○ Nosside '01		▼▼	5
● Cauro '00		▼	5
● Arvino '01		▼	3
● Lamezia Rosso '01			3
○ Lamezia Bianco '02			3
○ Lamezia Greco '02			4
○ Nosside '00		▼▼	5
● Arvino '00		▼	3

LUZZI (CS)

NOCERA TERINESE (CZ)

LUIGI VIVACQUA
C.DA SAN VITO
87040 LUZZI (CS)
TEL. 0984543404 - 098428825
E-MAIL: luigi@vivacqua.it

ODOARDI
C.DA CAMPODORATO
88047 NOCERA TERINESE (CZ)
TEL. 098429961 - 096891159
E-MAIL: odoardi@tin.it

Following the death of lawyer Luigi Vivacqua, his wife Filomena Bosco and nephew Filippo Bosa are now looking after the estate. Luca D'Attoma, from Tuscany, remains as oenological consultant. For now output is static at around 100,000 bottles, but this should start to increase next year, when ten hectares which were planted recently come onstream. Native varieties, such as magliocco and mantonico, were chosen for the new plantings, together with some cabernet and merlot. Both new and old vineyards are sited in a lovely area with good aspect, on hills that slope down gently to the river Crati. Work in the cellar has finally been completed, so now the entire winemaking process can take place at controlled temperatures. There were no real peaks among the wines submitted this year, but quality was even and sound throughout. From the whites, the chardonnay-based Donna Aurelia '02 gave a good showing, with an elegant, well fruited nose and a palate of attractively fresh drinkability. San Vito di Luzzi Rosso '02 is also good. Fruity on the nose, it is full on the palate and distinguished by freshness of fruit and soft extract. It fully merits One Glass, as do the San Vito di Luzzi Bianco and Rosato. Marinò '00, from gaglioppo and merlot, has good structure and fair fleshiness, and is most attractive overall.

Giovan Battista and Gregorio Odoardi did not manage to repeat last year's success, when Vigna Garrone claimed Three Glasses, but their wines are still of the highest quality and stand out in a region that, for various reasons, is having trouble taking off. The Odoardi brothers, who have skilled Tuscan oenologist, Stefano Chioccioli, as consultant, believe strongly in the potential of their land, to the extent of doubling the area under vine and replanting the entire existing vineyard holding at a density of over 10,000 plants per hectare. Recently, they finished planting a new plot of 40 hectares exclusively to native grapes such as magliocco, greco nero, aglianico and nerello. This year's Vigna Garrone, the '00, lost one of last year's Glasses but still managed to show fleshy, harmonious and powerful The palate is marvellously rich in fruit and has dense, noble tannins. Vigna Mortilla '00, a powerful, rich wine of great finesse and notable concentration, is also excellent. Two Glasses go to Valeo '01 too, a "vino da meditazione" sipping wine from a local subvariety of moscato called "di Valeo '01", which was once planted in small batches between rows to give farmers additional sustenance during the day. The wine has fresh, floral aromas, lavender in particular, and a pleasantly aromatic, sweet but not cloying palate. The picture is completed by Savuto '01, a most appealing wine that is excellent value for money, and Pian della Corte '02, an attractively perfumed, floral white.

●	Marinò Rosso '00	🍷	4
○	Chardonnay Donna Aurelia '02	🍷	4
○	San Vito di Luzzi Bianco '02	🍷	3
☉	San Vito di Luzzi Rosato '02	🍷	3
●	San Vito di Luzzi Rosso '02	🍷	3
●	San Vito di Luzzi Rosso '00	🍷🍷	3*
●	Marinò Rosso '99	🍷🍷	4

●	Scavigna Vigna Garrone '00	🍷🍷	8
●	Savuto Sup. Vigna Mortilla '00	🍷🍷	5
●	Savuto '01	🍷🍷	5
○	Valeo '01	🍷🍷	7
○	Scavigna Pian della Corte '02	🍷	5
●	Scavigna Vigna Garrone '99	🍷🍷🍷	8
●	Savuto '00	🍷🍷	5
●	Savuto Sup. Vigna Mortilla '99	🍷🍷	6

OTHER WINERIES

CAPARRA & SICILIANI
BIVIO S. S. 106
88811 CIRÒ MARINA (KR)
TEL. 0962371435
E-MAIL: caparra&siciliani@cirol.it

After last year's pause, we were expecting something more from this long-standing estate, although the uninspiring vintage will certainly have had its effect. From the large range we recommend the two that we felt had most style, Curiale and Cirò Rosso.

● Cirò Rosso Cl. '01	♈	3
○ Cirò Bianco Curiale '02	♈	4
● Lamezia Rosso Mastro Giurato '01		5
☉ Cirò Rosato Le Formelle '02		4

CANTINA ENOTRIA
LOC. SAN GENNARO - S. S. JONICA 106
88811 CIRÒ MARINA (KR)
TEL. 0962371181
E-MAIL: cantinaenotria@infinito.it

Cantina Enotria is a consortium of producers, drawing from over 150 hectares of vineyard and with a vinification and storage cellar of modern conception. The classic DOC Cirò line is well typed, the Bianco in particular. This has a clean, appley nose, and is fresh and attractive to drink.

○ Cirò Bianco '02	♈	3*
☉ Cirò Rosato '02	♈	3*
● Cirò Rosso Cl. Sup.		
Piana delle Fate Ris. '99		6

IPPOLITO 1845
VIA TIRONE, 118
88811 CIRÒ MARINA (KR)
TEL. 096231106
E-MAIL: ippolito1845@ippolito1845.it

The Ippolito winery was founded in 1845 as a small family concern and now has over 100 hectares of vines. The wines in the I Pitagorici line are well typed and, given all the work under way in vineyards and cellar, are bound to improve in the future. The Cirò Rosato is one of the year's best.

● Cirò Rosso Cl. Sup. I Pitagorici '00	♈	3
○ Cirò Bianco I Pitagorici '02	♈	3
☉ Cirò Rosè I Pitagorici '02	♈	3
● Cirò Rosso Cl. Ripe del Falco Ris. '88		5

VINICOLA ZITO
VIA SCALARETTO
88811 CIRÒ MARINA (KR)
TEL. 096231853
E-MAIL: info@zito.it

This is a long-standing winery, dedicated solely to the classic Cirò wines, all sourced from estate-owned vineyards. The traditionally vinified Cirò Classico Superiore is good, with spices, chocolate and cherry aromas, refined tannins and fair drinkability. The fresh, fruity Bianco is also nice.

● Cirò Rosso Cl. Sup. '01	♈	3
○ Cirò Bianco '02	♈	2
☉ Cirò Rosato '02	♈	2
● Cirò Rosso Cl. Ris. '97	♈	3

TENUTA TERRE NOBILI
C.DA CARIGLIALTO
87046 MONTALTO UFFUGO (CS)
TEL. 0984934005
E-MAIL: lidia.matera@libero.it

Two new wines for agronomist, Lidia Matera, who works with oenologist, Claudio Fuoco. Both won One Glass. Alarico is a nice red with enticing, ripe red berry fruit aromas, and the intriguing Granato is a "passito" from nerello and magliocco. The latest release of Cariglio is concentrated and soft.

●	Alarico '01	♀	3*
●	Granato Vino Passito '01	♀	5
●	Cariglio '02	♀	3
○	Santa Chiara '02		3
●	Cariglio '01	♀♀	3*

VINTRIPODI CALABRIA
VIA VECCHIA COMUNALE, 28
89051 REGGIO CALABRIA
TEL. 096548438
E-MAIL: info@vintripodi.it

The Tripodi brothers run this long-standing family winery with great commitment. The range of wines is extensive. This year, we particularly liked the Greco di Bianco, a "vino da meditazione" sipping wine with delicate aromas of quince and apricot, and a sweet palate that does not cloy.

○	Greco di Bianco '01	♀	6
●	Magna Grecia Rosso '01	♀	3
○	Mantonico di Bianco '01	♀	6
●	Cerasuolo di Scilla '02	♀	3
☉	Zephyro Rosato '02	♀	2*

LUIGI VIOLA & FIGLI
VIA ROMA, 18
87010 SARACENA (CS)
TEL. 098134071

Moscato di Saracena has been known since mediaeval times but had practically disappeared recently until Luigi Viola took it up again, with major success. His love for Moscato prevented him bottling the '02, as it was below expectations. We are holding his Guide place and look forward to next year.

○	Moscato di Saracena '01	♀♀	4*
○	Moscato di Saracena '00	♀♀	4

VAL DI NETO
FRAZ. CORAZZO - VIA NAZIONALE
88831 SCANDALE (KR)
TEL. 096254079
E-MAIL: valdineto@libero.it

Good results for a young, dynamic estate that has made considerable vineyard investment. All the wines submitted were modern in style. The best was Lumia, a fresh Melissa Bianco with attractive aromas of apples and pears. Also pleasing were the decently typed Melissa Rosso and Amistà.

●	Melissa Rosso '01	♀	3*
●	Rosso Archè '01	♀	4
○	Melissa Lumia '02	♀	2*
☉	Rosato Amistà '02	♀	3
●	Rosso Maradea '01		4

SICILY

The improvements in wine quality in Sicily, a region that for long remained dormant while techniques and image were being revolutionized elsewhere in the country, has now become something of a phenomenon. This year, 12 wines were awarded Three Glasses, three more than last time. But to get a proper idea of the amazing speed of change here, you have to realize that as recently as 1999, there were just five wines in the top spot. The Guide has increased in size, and we have dedicated more pages to Sicily, but there are still large numbers of wineries that deserve a profile but have had to be excluded for reasons of space, or squeezed into the Other Wineries section. The number of samples that arrived for tasting until a couple of years ago was between 250 and 300. This year there were 700. All this should help explain the atmosphere reigning among Sicily's producers. Old vineyards are being restored, new ones are being planted in areas where the terrain is suitable for viticulture, capital and know-how are flooding in, and many wine undertakings from elsewhere have set up new estates among Sicily's sun-drenched vines. The results of this feverish activity is there before us. Just turn the pages that follow and you'll see what is happening in greater detail, area by area and estate by estate. But first let's have a look at who are this year's leading players. Tasca d'Almerita returns to Three Glass honours with an absolute stunner of a Cabernet Sauvignon. It is years since it has been so classy and it epitomizes the fabulous vitality that drives this leading estate. Planeta, Firriato, Morgante and Sant'Anastasia are fixtures in our roll of honour. It would be more of a shock if they weren't among the Three Glasses winners. The Cantina Sociale di Trapani came up with an irresistible Cabernet, and Donnafugata has an equally alluring Nero d'Avola, the fabulous Milleunanotte '00. Faro Palari, a wine that is as unusual as it is fascinating, picks up its umpteenth award. Cusumano returns to the spotlight with the excellent Sagana, a thoroughbred of a nero d'Avola, and Rapitalà made the grade with Hugonis '01, another nero d'Avola but blended with merlot. Then come the newcomers. After years of fine quality wine production Benanti has now come through with Pietramarina, a white of extraordinary class. It is obtained from carricante grown on the cool, sun-drenched slopes of Etna, a hotspot for winemaking developments. Then Fatascià, an offshoot of Sant'Anastasia, gained the first prize of its young career with another nero d'Avola, Almanera. And all that without Feudo Principi di Butera, which did not bring out any new vintages of the top wines, and that artist of craft-made, reflective dessert wines, Marco De Bartoli, did not submit anything new either.

ACATE (RG)

CANTINA VALLE DELL'ACATE
C.DA BIDINI, SNC
97011 ACATE (RG)
TEL. 0932874166
E-MAIL: info@valledellacate.com

Tané is the name of the wine from this estate that nearly claimed Three Glasses. But it is also Sicilian dialect for Gaetana, and Gaetana Jacono is the dynamic ex-pharmacist from Vittoria who has dedicated body and soul to this, her family estate. It lies at Bidini, with lands stretching between Acate and Vittoria, where the vine has been cultivated since the beginning of the 19th century. New nero d'Avola plantings, modernization of the old cellar and general renovations have turned Valle d'Acate and its 100 hectares of vines into one of eastern Sicily's leading estates. As for the wines, Tané is made exclusively from nero d'Avola. The '00 was almost certain to reach the finals, judging by what we saw of it last year when we tasted a cask sample. Red berry fruits and spices fill the nose, and the palate is warm, full and round. The '01 Cerasuolo di Vittoria, from nero d'Avola and frappato, also showed as well as the previous release, with a ripe fruity nose and finely balanced tannins. The '01 Bidis, a chardonnay and inzolia blend, is as good as ever. Pervasive aromas of vanilla and ripe banana precede a soft yet complex palate. Moro '01, made solely from nero d'Avola, performed well and Frappato '02, with attractive blueberry and raspberry fruit, is very promising. All the other wines are well made and well styled.

ALCAMO (TP)

CEUSO
VIA ENEA, 18
91011 ALCAMO (TP)
TEL. 0924507860 - 092422836
E-MAIL: info@ceuso.it

It is difficult not to feel immediate empathy with the Melia brothers and their remarkable winemaking enterprise. Their boundless passion, their love for the countryside and the vine, and their diligence during winemaking to ensure high quality wines all win you over. their wines are not only excellent. They also have a distinct touch of originality, something that sets them apart and lends the personality that only wines that are practically hand crafted can offer. That is why for years we have been affectionately calling them "garagistes", like the pocket-sized fine wine producers in France. The Melia team's success, and the plaudits raining down, have not changed their long-term plans. Their vineyard holding, currently 25 hectares, continues to grow and work continues apace on the new estate headquarters, a traditional "baglio", or enclosed farmstead, dating from 1860 and set up even then for winemaking. Work should soon be finished, allowing the brothers to focus on their main activities, although the wines have continued to gain quality in the meantime. New labels are on their way, too. The '01 vintage of Fastaia, a nero d'Avola, cabernet franc and merlot mix, is exceptional and went straight into the Three Glass finals. Deep and elegant, it has great personality and is extremely seductive. Ceuso Custera '00, the estate's first wine, is practically as good and was beaten by Fastaia only by a hair. The 100 per cent nero d'Avola Scurati '02, the first of the new labels to emerge, is excellent too.

●	Tanè '00	♟♟	6
○	Bidis '01	♟♟	4*
●	Cerasuolo di Vittoria '01	♟♟	4*
●	Il Moro '01	♟♟	4*
●	Frappato '02	♟	4
○	Inzolia '02	♟	3
○	Bidis '99	♟♟	2*
○	Bidis '00	♟♟	4
●	Cerasuolo di Vittoria '00	♟♟	3*
●	Il Moro '00	♟♟	4*

●	Fastaia '01	♟♟	5
●	Ceuso Custera '00	♟♟	6
●	Scurati '02	♟♟	4
●	Ceuso '96	♟♟	5
●	Ceuso Custera '97	♟♟	5
●	Ceuso Custera '98	♟♟	5
●	Ceuso Custera '99	♟♟	6
●	Fastaia '00	♟♟	5

BUTERA (CL)

FEUDO PRINCIPI DI BUTERA
C.DA DELIELLA
93011 BUTERA (CL)
TEL. 0934347726
E-MAIL: info@feudobutera.it

A few years ago, the Gambellara-based Zonin family achieved their goal of setting up a major estate in Sicily. It has very quickly risen to the heights. There are 180 hectares of beautiful vineyard and a modern cellar at the estate, Feudo Principi di Buttera, which has already become one of Sicily's benchmarks. This is perhaps not so surprising given, that the general manager of Zonin's holdings is Franco Giacosa, an oenologist with considerable experience in Sicily. The range of wines submitted for this year's tastings was quite excellent, even though new vintages of some of the top wines, such as San Rocco and Merlot Calat, were absent. This was a wise decision as it gives these substantially structured wines the time they need to come round in bottle. Deliella '01, from 100 per cent nero d'Avola, finished just short of Three Glasses but stands out for the intensity of its fruit on nose and palate, its full body and its long, tobacco and oak-toast finish. Retasting San Rocco and Calat '01 confirmed their class. What impressed us, however, was the improvement across the whole range, from the Cabernet to the Merlot and on to the excellent '02 Insolia. All these wines showed striking cleanliness and intense varietal purity, providing further proof, if any were needed, of the skills of oenologist Gaetano Maccarrone and agronomist Calogero Rampanti, both working under Giacosa's supervision.

CAMPOREALE (PA)

FATTORIE AZZOLINO
C.DA AZZOLINO
90043 CAMPOREALE (PA)
TEL. 092436123
E-MAIL: fattorieazzolino@tiscalinet.it

The celebrated north-south marriage that is the joint venture between this Sicilian winery and the Cantina Sociale di Nomi, from Trentino, is proving very successful. The dynamic, businesslike Franco Sacco, managing director of the estate, is busier than ever. The vineyard holding, now at 24 hectares, is increasing and the cellars at Camporeale, where the winemaking is carried out, are increasingly active, with new wines in the pipeline. However for now, technical motives and reasons of space mean that the wines are transferred to Trentino for bottling and storage. And Trentino also currently houses Fattorie Azzolino's barrique cellar. In the hiatus before everything can be carried out in Sicily, winemakers from the Cantina Sociale di Nomi, under its director, Fernando Bolner, take care of the oenological side. Next year, a winemaker from Sicily will join them. Relations are harmonious and there is great satisfaction on both sides, especially as the wines to date have had notable success. The deep gold Chardonnay '02 is a lovely, elegant wine, possibly even more elegant than the '01. Its pronounced personality, power, roundness and length on both nose and palate took it with sure stride into the Three Glass finals. The '01 vintages of both Di 'More, from nero d'Avola and cabernet sauvignon, and the Nero d'Avola are considerably better than previous releases, with better defined, cleaner aromas. The delicate Tranùi '02, the estate's newest wine, is very promising.

● Deliella '01	🍷🍷	8
● Cabernet Sauvignon '01	🍷🍷	4*
○ Insolia '02	🍷🍷	4*
● Merlot '01	🍷	4
● Nero d'Avola '01	🍷	4
○ Chardonnay '02	🍷	4
● Cabernet Sauvignon '00	🍷🍷🍷	7
● Deliella '00	🍷🍷🍷	6
● San Rocco '01	🍷🍷	7
● Calat '01	🍷🍷	7

○ Chardonnay '02	🍷🍷	5
● Di 'More '01	🍷🍷	5
● Nero D'Avola '01	🍷🍷	4
○ Tranùi '02	🍷	3
○ Chardonnay '01	🍷🍷	5
● Di 'More '00	🍷	5
● Nero D'Avola '00	🍷	3

CAMPOREALE (PA)

TENUTE RAPITALÀ
C.DA RAPITALÀ
90143 CAMPOREALE (PA)
TEL. 092437233
E-MAIL: giv@giv.it

There's Rapitalà wine on the Three Glass podium again. This crowns the efforts at Hugues and Gigi de la Gatinais' winery where, since the arrival of Gruppo Italiano Vino, the wines have returned to the national and international spotlight. The 105 hectares of beautifully cared-for vineyard, with its geometrically perfect rows, carpet the gentle hills in the areas of Camporeale and Alcamo at 300 to 600 metres, creating an unforgettable landscape. But let's get to the wines, which are in the hands of a team of skilled winemakers, most notably Piedmontese oenologist, Marco Monchiero. Hugonis '01, from cabernet sauvignon and nero d'Avola, is the wine that gained Three Glasses. An exciting red, it offers ripe red berry fruit and spices on the nose, and a full, fleshy, powerful palate. The '01 Solinero, made solely from syrah, is an excellent wine with attractive aromas of wild cherry, pencil lead and black pepper, and tight, balanced tannins. Nuhar '01 is attractively intriguing, with softness and silky tannins. Casalj '02, from catarratto and chardonnay, evokes green tomatoes and sage on the nose, and has a long, gentle palate, and Conte Hugues Bernard '01 is well styled and attractive. Cielo d'Alcamo is a new, late-harvest wine made from sauvignon and catarratto grapes picked in November. The first release, '01, has intense scents of fruit in syrup and a long, sweet finish.

CASTELBUONO (PA)

ABBAZIA SANTA ANASTASIA
C.DA SANTA ANASTASIA
90013 CASTELBUONO (PA)
TEL. 0921671959 - 0916932060
E-MAIL: info@abbaziasantanastasia.it

We have now reached the fifth top award for Litra, that great red from cabernet sauvignon produced by Francesco Lena here at Castelbuono in the province of Palermo. The estate was only set up in 1990, yet in these few years it has been able to power itself into the front line of the crowded Sicilian quality wine scene. This is without doubt all down to Lena, who immediately took some sound managerial decisions, entrusting the overseeing of winemaking first to Giacomo Tachis, and then to Riccardo Cotarella. Some 60 of the estate's 400 hectares are now under vine and this year the range of wines has grown, both in number and in quality. For the past few vintages, Francesco has been working with his daughter Stefania, whose love of winemaking knows no bounds. Just take a look at how we have written up the Fatascia winery, which she owns, if you want proof. But let's get back to Litra. The '01 is one of its most eloquent incarnations ever. It has a deep dark ruby hue. The most elegant nose evokes ripe, plum laced with vegetal nuances and cedar wood, and the palate is full of succulent fruit, with perfectly honed, ripe tannins and a long, harmonious finish of cherry jam, tobacco and spices. The close-knit, fresh Inzolia '02 and Passomaggio '01, from nero d'Avola and merlot, are both very fine. And although Chardonnay Gemelli '02 is a touch under par, Bianco di Passomaggio, a successful blend of chardonnay, sauvignon and inzolia, makes a convincing first appearance.

● Hugonis '01	🍷🍷🍷	7
● Solinero '01	🍷🍷	8
● Nuhar '01	🍷🍷	6
○ Cielo d'Alcamo '01	🍷	7
○ Conte Hugues Bernard '01	🍷	4
○ Casalj '02	🍷	5
● Solinero '00	🍷🍷🍷	6
● Hugonis '00	🍷🍷	6
○ Alcamo Rapitalà Gran Cru '00	🍷	5
○ Conte Hugues Bernard '00	🍷	4

● Litra '01	🍷🍷🍷	8
● Passomaggio '01	🍷🍷	4*
○ Inzolia '02	🍷🍷	3*
● Nero d'Avola '01	🍷	3
○ Bianco di Passomaggio '02	🍷	3
○ Gemelli '02	🍷	5
☉ Nerello Mascalese '02	🍷	3
● Litra '96	🍷🍷🍷	7
● Litra '97	🍷🍷🍷	7
● Litra '99	🍷🍷🍷	7
● Litra '00	🍷🍷🍷	7

CASTELDACCIA (PA)

CASTIGLIONE DI SICILIA (CT)

DUCA DI SALAPARUTA - VINI CORVO
VIA NAZIONALE, S. S. 113
90014 CASTELDACCIA (PA)
TEL. 091945201
E-MAIL: vinicorvo@vinicorvo.it

COTTANERA
C.DA IANNAZZO
S.P. 89
95030 CASTIGLIONE DI SICILIA (CT)
TEL. 0942963601
E-MAIL: staff@cottanera.it

Duca di Salaparuta was founded in 1824, when Giuseppe Alliata, Principe di Villafranca and Duca di Salaparuta, decided to make wine from the grapes on his holding at Casteldaccia, in the small area of Corvo. It was a white, from inzolia, and had huge success. Even today, it may well be the wine that best symbolizes Sicily. A little over 40 years ago, the by then well-known winery was sold by the family to the regional authority's investment company, which ensured it continuing success. Then in 2001, ILLVA Saronno, which already owned Florio, took over. Two years on, we can take a look at the results of this changeover, and they are strongly positive. The company has been split into two: Vini Corvo, which produces the better known wines, and Duca di Salaparuta, for the higher quality output. A first-class winemaking team has been put in place, overseen by Giacomo Tachis as oenological consultant. The cellar's progress is best demonstrated by the superb Duca Enrico '01, the famous Nero d'Avola. A modern, enticing, elegant but concentrated red, it missed Three Glasses by a hair. Equally good were the Megara '01, from frappato and syrah, a fruit-led wine with tight structure and good spiciness, and the full, fruity Triskelè '00, which has tempting aromas of the Mediterranean, thanks to a mix of 80 per cent nero d'Avola, cabernet and merlot. The whites include Bianca di Valguarnera, from inzolia, which is as good as ever. Colomba Platina and Kados are enjoyable, as is Corvo Bianco, the best known wine of a company that turns out some 14,000,000 bottles a year.

The estate of brothers Guglielmo and Vincenzo Cambria lies 700 metres high in one of the most beautifully evocative settings imaginable. It is surrounded by outcrops of lava and hazelnut and chestnuts woods cut through by the Alcantara river. Although missing Three Glasses by a whisker, Cottanera has built on the good things we saw last year and submitted a range of wines of extraordinary quality. But then viticultural consultancy from Professor Leonardo Valenti, of the Agriculture Faculty at Milan University, and the assiduous, committed work of oenologist Giulio Vecchio and agronomist Luciana Biondo, could hardly fail to bring results. We particularly liked Ardenza '01, which is rich and concentrated on the nose but powerful and very long on the palate. It is, as usual, from 100 per cent mondeuse, and shows caressingly soft, rounded and elegant. Sole di Sesta is entirely from Syrah and the '01 revealed solid quality with attractive jammy notes, elegant tannins and attractive sensations of dark chocolate. Also very good was Grammonte '01, from merlot, which has toasty nuances and a wide array of balsamic and tobacco-like aromas. The new wine, Nume '01, from cabernet sauvignon, has excellent definition on the palate and a long finish. The spicy, harmonious Fatagione '01 confirmed expectations while red and white versions of Barbazzale, both '02, were as good as usual.

●	Duca Enrico '00	🍷🍷	6
●	Triskelè '00	🍷🍷	6
○	Bianca di Valguarnera '01	🍷🍷	6
●	Megara '01	🍷🍷	4
●	Terre d'Agala '00	🍷	4
●	Corvo Rosso '01	🍷	4*
○	Corvo Bianco '02	🍷	3*
○	Corvo Colomba Platino '02	🍷	4
○	Corvo Glicine '02	🍷	3*
○	Kados '02	🍷	4
○	Brut Ris.	🍷	4
●	Duca Enrico '92	🍷🍷🍷	8
○	Bianca di Valguarnera '00	🍷🍷	6
●	Duca Enrico '99	🍷🍷	8

●	L'Ardenza '01	🍷🍷	6
●	Sole di Sesta '01	🍷🍷	6
●	Fatagione '01	🍷🍷	5
●	Grammonte '01	🍷🍷	6
●	Nume '01	🍷🍷	5
○	Barbazzale Bianco '02	🍷	3
●	Barbazzale Rosso '02	🍷	3
●	Sole di Sesta '00	🍷🍷🍷	7
●	Grammonte '99	🍷🍷	5
●	L'Ardenza '99	🍷🍷	5
●	Sole di Sesta '99	🍷🍷	5
●	Grammonte '00	🍷🍷	7
●	L'Ardenza '00	🍷🍷	7
●	Fatagione '99	🍷	4

COMISO (RG)

AVIDE
C.DA MASTRELLA
97013 COMISO (RG)
TEL. 0932967456
E-MAIL: avide@avide.it

Avide, from Comiso, has achieved its best result ever: one wine in the finals and a range that reflects the characteristics of one of Sicily's most attractive areas. The estate's roots go deep. It was founded a century ago when Giuseppina De Stefano, a wealthy landowner, joined lawyer Giuseppe Demostene, whose family had been practising law for generations. Time went by and many things changed, Today, it is Giuseppe Demostene's grandson, Giovanni Calcaterra, also a lawyer, who runs the estate. Calcaterra looks after marketing strategy, entrusting winemaking to the highly capable Giovanni Rizzo, and has a major plan under way to move the winery to Villa Demostene, his ancestors' country residence set among vines and carob trees. Cerasuolo di Vittoria Barocco '00 is an excellent wine that almost earned Three Glasses. It is obtained from nero d'Avola and frappato, and has ripe fruit and liquorice on the nose. Good body and notable structure on the long palate is supported by an imposing raft of tannins. Another Cerasuolo, Etichetta Nera '01, has clear varietal notes on the nose, and is full and harmonious. Sigillo '01, from nero d'Avola and cabernet sauvignon, has redcurrant and blueberry on the nose. It also has good definition on the palate, as does the nero d'Avola 3 Carati '01, which offers intense aromas and a clean finish. The white damson-like Vigne D'Oro '01, made solely from inzolia, is a worthy stablemate and Lacrimae Bacci, a dessert wine, is pleasantly sweet but not frivolous. The Herea line is good.

GROTTE (AG)

MORGANTE
C.DA RACALMARE
92020 GROTTE (AG)
TEL. 0922945579
E-MAIL: morgante_vini@virgilio.it

Congratulations to the Morgante family, who can be rightly proud of the four Three Glass awards in a row they have racked up in the last four editions of the Guide. This year it is the '01 vintage of Don Antonio that breached the top barrier, a great result and a just reward for a fine wine. However, it should be remembered that in these parts, so dear to authors Leonardo Sciascia and Luigi Pirandello, nothing occurs by chance. In the case of Antonio Morgante and his son Carmelo, success is the result of a policy set in place in 1994, and fine-tuned with the arrival of top-flight oenologist Riccardo Cotarella, whose arrival has brought quite extraordinary results. The estate, with around 200 hectares of vineyard, lies in hilly country 25 kilometres from the coast, in an area with typically Mediterranean climate. The superb vineyards where the nero d'Avola for Don Antonio is grown are at Racalmare and have clayey-limestone soils. This year's '01 is full of small wild berry fruit and oriental spices on the nose. The palate has a solid structure, but is soft and opens in the mouth to give intense flavour. The simpler version, Nero d'Avola '01, is a fine example of the variety. It comes from vineyards with different cropping levels but the result is still surprisingly good. It's rich, with good fruit and clear tones of liquorice, and a full palate of great charm.

● Cerasuolo di Vittoria Barocco '00	🍷🍷	6
● Cerasuolo di Vittoria		
Etichetta Nera '01	🍷🍷	3*
● Sigillo Rosso '01	🍷🍷	6
○ Vigne d'Oro '01	🍷🍷	6
● 3 Carati '01	🍷🍷	6
○ Lacrimæ Bacchi '02	🍷🍷	6
○ Herea Bianco '02	🍷	3
● Herea Rosso '02	🍷	3
● Cerasuolo di Vittoria Barocco '98	🍷🍷	6
● Sigillo Rosso '00	🍷🍷	6
○ Vigne d'Oro '00	🍷🍷	5
● 3 Carati '00	🍷🍷	3
● Cerasuolo di Vittoria Barocco '99	🍷🍷	6

● Don Antonio '01	🍷🍷🍷	5
● Nero d'Avola '01	🍷🍷	3*
● Don Antonio '98	🍷🍷🍷	5
● Don Antonio '99	🍷🍷🍷	5
● Don Antonio '00	🍷🍷🍷	6
● Nero d'Avola '99	🍷🍷	3*
● Nero d'Avola '00	🍷🍷	4*
● Nero d'Avola '98	🍷	3

MARSALA (TP)

MARSALA (TP)

BAGLIO HOPPS
C.DA BIESINA, KM. 12,2
VIA SALEMI
91025 MARSALA (TP)
TEL. 0923967020
E-MAIL: info@bagliohopps.com

MARCO DE BARTOLI
C.DA FORNARA, 292
91025 MARSALA (TP)
TEL. 0923962093 - 0923918344
E-MAIL: marcodebartoli@tin.it

Fabio and Giacomo Hopps are direct descendants of the transplanted Englishman, James Hopps, who was one of the pioneers of Marsala. Yet until several years ago, they had nothing to do with wine: Giacomo was a lawyer and Fabio worked in a bank. Then came the moment when the oenology gene in the family chromosomes emerged, and the pair decided to take up grape growing. To be more precise, they focused on wine, tourism and the hotel business, too, achieving success in all three fields. But their hearts and minds were on the family's traditional wine. Their 18th-century "baglio", or traditional enclosed farmstead, in the Marsala countryside was restored to new life, with an up-to-date cellar, and the vineyards were renewed with the help of an able consultant oenologist, the expansive Antonino Galfano. Commitment and tenacity have produced some very fine wines for us to report on each year. Incantri '01, from the much-loved merlot grape, is quite simply delicious. The good deep ruby colour leads on to a complex, imposing array of aromas foregrounding blackcurrant, cocoa powder and ripe black cherry. The palate is most attractive, showing good balance and great depth, characteristics that assured its inclusion in the final tastings. The estate's other two major reds, the elegant Syrah '00 and the '01 Nero d'Avola, whose delicate balsamic note gives it distinctive character, are practically as good. All the other wines impressed and are well styled.

Marco De Bartoli is extraordinary. Even 20 years ago, his enthusiasm, his courageous and often unconventional decisions, and his desire to take on the best in the world, set people talking. Sicilian winemaking, and especially Marsala, owes him a great deal. He has always campaigned strongly for the renewal that has now brought Sicily to prominence on the international stage. But he has a brusque, outspoken character, which in a place like Sicily is bound to cause problems. Never mind. De Bartoli ploughs his own furrow regardless, and lets his wines speak for him. In the last few decades, Marco's dessert wines have been among the best you can find. Try, for example, his Marsala Superiore Riserva 1986, a blend of old wines, the youngest of which comes from '86. Its depth and complexity are simply amazing. Yet, its strengths were less apparent when it was first released. Only now is it shining more and more clearly with each tasting. As we wait for new releases, we can try the more youthful, and absolutely captivating, Marsala Vigna La Miccia or the Vecchio Samperi Ventennale, a solera method wine that exudes elegance in a thousand different ways. But De Bartoli is not just Marsala. With son Renato, he makes a range of wines that stood out this year for excellent overall quality. For a start, there is the Passito di Pantelleria '99 from the vines at Bukkuram. It is dense, sweet and strongly Mediterranean in character. The Rosso di Marco '00, from merlot, has intense fruit, enlivened by intriguing, spicy nuances. All the other wines are worth investigating.

●	Incantari '01	♙♙	6
●	Syrah '00	♙♙	5
●	Nero d'Avola '01	♙♙	5
○	Sulana '02	♙♙	4
●	Diana '01	♙	5
○	Bianca delle Gazzere '02	♙	4
○	James Hopps Marsala Sup.	♙	6
○	Grillo '01	♟♟	5
●	Diana '00	♟	4

○	Passito di Pantelleria Bukkuram '99	♙♙	7
○	Grappoli del Grillo '02	♙♙	4
○	Marsala Sup. Vigna La Miccia	♙♙	5
○	Pietranera '02	♙♙	5
○	Sole e Vento '02	♙	4
○	Vecchio Samperi Ris. 30 Anni Solera	♟♟	6
○	Marsala Sup. '86	♟♟	7
○	Marsala Sup. Ris. 20 Anni	♟♟	6
○	Passito di Pantelleria '00	♟♟	7
○	Vecchio Samperi Ventennale	♟♟	6

MARSALA (TP)

MARSALA (TP)

TENUTA DI DONNAFUGATA
VIA SEBASTIANO LIPARI, 18
91025 MARSALA (TP)
TEL. 0923724200
E-MAIL: info@donnafugata.it

CANTINE FLORIO
VIA VINCENZO FLORIO, 1
91025 MARSALA (TP)
TEL. 0923781111
E-MAIL: marsala@cantineflorio.com

Milleunanotte ("Arabian nights") is a fabulous wine and it would have been much appreciated in the famous story. Sheherazade could have offered it to Sultan Shariar, despite the Koranic ban, and saved herself a long night telling tales. At the first sip, the Caliph would have fallen in love with her for sure. Digressions apart, this year the '00 vintage of this finest of wines, from nero d'Avola with some perricone and cabernet sauvignon, came out as one of the best in Sicily. It swept away with Three Glasses, uniting power, concentration and fruit richness on the one hand, with spectacular finesse, superb balance and outstandingly incisive freshness on the other. A rich array of balsamic and spicy nuances, with oak kept well in check, leads to a remarkably long finish. This wine is the most obvious sign that Carlo Ferrini is now consulting, but it's not the only one. Tancredi, from nero d'Avola and cabernet, has never been as good as this '01 release, which performed proudly at our finals. The '02 release of the chardonnay and ansonica Chiarandà del Merlo confirms that it is one of the best whites in Sicily. Two brimming Glasses also go to Passito Ben Ryé '02 and Angheli, a successful mix of merlot and nero d'Avola. The rest of the range is good, although we expected a bit more from the nero d'Avola-based Sedara and Lighea, from ansonica plus aromatic varieties. But what counts is that Giacomo Rallo and his daughter José's Donnafugata has returned to the island's elite. And looks set to stay there.

This winery, under the wing of the ILLVA Saronno group since 1998, acquired the new title of CVDS – it stands for Case Vinicole di Sicilia – in January 2003. The new business includes Duca di Salaparuta, incorporated into Florio to optimize the two company structures. However, the name Florio remains synonymous with Marsala. The winery dates from 1833, when Vincenzo Florio, a smart businessman with many interests, built a structure of over 100,000 square metres for producing the Marsala wine that had been discovered and made internationally famous by the English Woodhouse and Ingham families at the turn of the 19th century. Nowadays, Florio Marsala still ages in these same, 200-year-old overground cellars. Some 5,000,000 litres of wine rest in large, Slavonian oak casks and in traditional small wooden "caratelli" under the high tufa vaults. We particularly appreciated the great elegance of Vergine Baglio Florio '90, with its clean, intense bouquet, full of hints of spice, honey and nuts, and its warm, long palate. Just as impressive in their respective styles are the silky, caressing Vecchioflorio Superiore Riserva Ambra Semisecco '96 and Vecchioflorio Superiore Ambra Secco, an exceedingly clean, attractive Marsala in the classic mould. There is also space in the wide range for two sweet fortified dessert wines, based on zibibbo, from Pantelleria. Grecale is attractively fruity and excellent value for money and the more refined Morsi di Luce undergoes long ageing in barrique.

● Contessa Entellina Milleunanotte '00	♉♉♉	7
● Contessa Entellina Tancredi '01	♉♉	5
● Angheli '01	♉♉	5
○ Contessa Entellina Chiarandà del Merlo '02	♉♉	6
○ Passito di Pantelleria Ben Ryé '02	♉♉	7
● Sedàra '01	♉	3
○ Anthìlia '02	♉	3
○ Contessa Entellina Chardonnay La Fuga '02	♉	4
○ Contessa Entellina Vigna di Gabri '02	♉	4
○ Lighea '02	♉	3
○ Contessa Entellina Chiarandà del Merlo '99	♉♉♉	5

○ Morsi di Luce '00	♉♉	6
○ Marsala Vergine Baglio Florio '90	♉♉	6
○ Marsala Sup. Ris. Ambra Semisecco Vecchioflorio '96	♉♉	4
○ Marsala Sup. Secco Ambra Vecchioflorio	♉♉	4
○ Marsala Sup. Vecchioflorio '00	♉	3
○ Grecale Vino Liquoroso '02	♉	4*
○ Marsala Vergine Baglio Florio '85	♉♉	5
○ Marsala Vergine Baglio Florio '86	♉♉	5
○ Marsala Vergine Baglio Florio Oro '88	♉♉	6
○ Marsala Vergine Baglio Florio '87	♉	5
○ Marsala Vergine Baglio Florio '89	♉	6

MARSALA (TP)

CARLO PELLEGRINO
VIA DEL FANTE, 39
91025 MARSALA (TP)
TEL. 0923719911
E-MAIL: info@carlopellegrino.it

Pietro Alagna, Michele Sala and Massimo Bellina, respectively president, managing director and export director, should be very happy. The great, historic winery they lead continues to make swift strides forward, claiming new records year after year. Turnover has leapt to over € 18,000,000 and production is currently running at over 7,000,000 bottles. But that's not all. Estate-owned land has increased to 400 hectares and by the end of 2003 the wines produced in the first of the new cellars will be on the market, with another two ready to start operations in 2005. All this is to satisfy the growing demand from an enormous, loyal customer base throughout the world. They are looked after by an efficient sales network with over 120 years of business experience, in many cases passed down from one generation to the next. Wine quality is perfectly tuned to large volumes and to the market. Gorgo Tondo Bianco '02, a successful blend of grillo and chardonnay, has freshness and good structure, and is invitingly attractive. The newly released Grillo '02 scored similarly, with fruit, flowers and herbs on the clean, even nose and a palate of personality, showing depth, good structure and length. Among the reds, the '01 Gorgo Tondo Rosso, an enticing blend of nero d'Avola and cabernet sauvignon, is as seriously aristocratic as ever. The other wines, Marsalas included, are well made and most attractive. All are offered at keen prices.

MARSALA (TP)

CANTINE RALLO
VIA VINCENZO FLORIO, 2
91025 MARSALA (TP)
TEL. 0923721633 - 092372163

Francesco and Andrea Vesco forge ahead with their plans for estate modernization, launched two years ago with the purchase of a historic establishment and a cellar in the centre of Marsala. Current output is 2,000,000 bottles, produced from 50 hectares of vines owned outright and a quota of grapes bought in. In 2003, thoughts turned to company image and the packaging was completely revamped. Now the Cantina Rallo look, as well as the set-up, is in line with objectives and policies. The middle band of the range consists of wines made predominantly from indigenous varieties, with good typicity and similarly good prices, although the traditional line of Marsala and "passito" wines is equally important. First in line for price and drinkability comes the crisp, floral Alcamo Carta d'Oro '02, from catarratto and grillo, and the fresh, characterful Grillo Gruali '01. Both earned Two Glasses. Marsala Vergine Soleras Riserva 12 Anni, with dried fruit and almonds on the nose, complex structure and lively acidity, is a much more imposing wine, as is the sweet, very clean Moscato Passito Moscato Passito di Pantelleria, which has soft fruitiness. Even the Moscato di Pantelleria, which is not a dried-grape wine, is well made and does not cloy. The single-variety Nero d'Avola '01 and Vesco Rosso '01, a blend of indigenous and international grapes, hang together well despite rustic touches. The successful Chardonnay '02 is fresh, supple, minty and a touch green.

● Delia Nivolelli Cabernet Sauvignon '00	🍷🍷	4*
● Nero d'Avola Cabernet '00	🍷🍷	4
○ Gorgo Tondo Bianco '02	🍷🍷	3*
● Gorgo Tondo Rosso '01	🍷🍷	4
○ Grillo '02	🍷🍷	3
○ Passito di Pantelleria Nes '01	🍷🍷	6
○ Marsala Sup. Oro	🍷🍷	4
○ Marsala Sup. Ris. Dom Pellegrino	🍷🍷	4
○ Marsala Vergine Soleras	🍷🍷	4
● Etna Rosso Ulysse '01	🍷	4
○ Cent'Are Bianco '02	🍷	3
○ Chardonnay '02	🍷	4

○ Gruali '01	🍷🍷	3
○ Alcamo Carta d'Oro '02	🍷🍷	2
○ Marsala Vergine Soleras Ris. 12 anni	🍷🍷	5
○ Passito di Pantelleria	🍷🍷	5
● Nero d'Avola '01	🍷	3
● Vesco Rosso '01	🍷	4
○ Chardonnay '02	🍷	4
○ Moscato di Pantelleria	🍷	3
○ Vesco Bianco '02		4
○ Passito di Pantelleria Mare d'Ambra	🍷🍷	4
● Merlot '99	🍷🍷	4
○ Marsala Vergine Soleras Ris. 12 anni	🍷🍷	5
● Vesco Rosso '99	🍷	4
● Vesco Rosso '00	🍷	4

MAZARA DEL VALLO (TP) MENFI (AG)

AJELLO
C.DA GIUDEO
91025 MAZARA DEL VALLO (TP)
TEL. 091309107
E-MAIL: azajello@tin.it

★ PLANETA
C.DA DISPENSA INT. 1
92013 MENFI (AG)
TEL. 091327965
E-MAIL: planeta@planeta.it

The wines of Salvatore Ajello, a hardworking agricultural entrepreneur, put up an excellent performance this year. His estate now has 70 hectares under vine, a figure that continues to grow year by year. The new cellar is ready, as is a modern guest wing and a tasting room flooded with light in the family's 19th-century, "baglio" (traditional enclosed farmstead). Good things are also emerging from the collaboration with headstrong, brilliant consultant oenologist, Vincenzo Bambina. Its fruits include two new wines, a Nero d'Avola and a Grillo, both monovarietals. The excellent '01 Furat, a fascinating blend of nero d'Avola, cabernet sauvignon, merlot and syrah, is simply majestic. Its colour is intense; its nose pronounced and elegant, with spices, blueberries and cherries. The palate has soft, silky tannins that make it a delight to drink. Of course, it reached the finals but missed the coveted Three Glasses, though only just. Bizir '02, from chardonnay, grillo and inzolia, is interesting. Its good golden colour leads to an intense, persistent nose of tropical fruit, thyme and sage, and a well-structured palate that is balanced, warm and mouthfilling. It will improve further with a few more months bottle age. Shams '02, the winery's latest product, is a promising "passito" from moscato, catarratto, grillo and inzolia. It is sweet, gentle and deep, with delicious ripe fruitiness and a winning balance of acidity and softness.

In less than ten years, the Planeta family has risen to stardom on the world's wine stage. This substantial producer has expanded from its original vineyard in Menfi and the first estate buildings at Sambuca di Sicilia to embrace four holdings – Sambuca, Menfi, Noto and Vittoria: all in the region's most significant wine areas – and 350 hectares of vine. The entire Planeta family has been involved, from Diego, who brought his considerable wine experience to bear, and Francesca, who ably combines a number of roles, including that of mother, to Alessio and Santi. All have lavished skill and enthusiasm on the project. Carlo Corino, oenologist, and Fabrizio Moltard, the agronomist, then added the decisive touches. Highest acclaim this year goes to a triumphant Syrah '01, a perfect expression of this renowned international variety, and one that displays all its strengths. It has an impenetrably dark ruby hue. It explodes on the nose with fully ripe red and black berry fruit mingling with elegant notes of newly mown hay and, more dominantly, spices, from cinnamon to nutmeg, finishing on a deep waft of white pepper. Powerful, muscular and full-bodied on the palate, it maintains beautiful balance, suppleness and length. Another serious contender for top honours was the harmonious, concentrated Cabernet Burdese '01, with its perfectly judged new oak. The Merlot is rich, with ripe tannins, the Chardonnay, as usual, simply excellent. What about the rest of the range? Amazing. And sold at affordable prices, too.

● Furat '01	🍷🍷	5		● Syrah '01	🍷🍷🍷	5*
○ Bizir '02	🍷🍷	5		● Burdese '01	🍷🍷	5*
○ Shams '02	🍷🍷	5		○ Chardonnay '02	🍷🍷	5*
● Furat '99	🍷🍷	5		● Santa Cecilia '01	🍷🍷	5*
● Furat '00	🍷🍷	5		○ Alastro '02	🍷🍷	4*
○ Bizir '01	🍷	5		● Cerasuolo di Vittoria '02	🍷🍷	4*
				○ La Segreta Bianco '02	🍷🍷	3*
				● La Segreta Rosso '02	🍷🍷	3*
				● Merlot '01	🍷🍷	5*
				○ Chardonnay '00	🍷🍷🍷	5
				○ Cometa '00	🍷🍷🍷	5
				● Merlot '99	🍷🍷🍷	5
				● Burdese '00	🍷🍷🍷	5
				○ Cometa '01	🍷🍷🍷	5

MENFI (AG)

SETTESOLI
S.S. 115
92013 MENFI (AG)
TEL. 092577111 - 092577102
E-MAIL: info@mandrarossa.it

The business drive of this European-level economic colossus, and its 2,300 members, never ceases to amaze us. Year by year, the tastings reveal surefooted, confident quality improvements, and a miraculous ability to combine large volumes with characterful, well-made wines. Expert oenologist, Carlo Corino, a consultant of international renown, has created a string of attractive, good-quality, great-value wines. These have earned enviable market success, just as far-sighted president, Diego Planeta, forecast when he launched his major development plan some years ago. So it is not just coincidence that Bendicò Mandrarossa '01, an enticing blend of nero d'Avola, merlot and syrah, was up with Italy's best this year in the Three Glasses finals. A dark ruby, with a gentle, inviting nose of cassis and spice, it has a balanced, harmonious palate that hangs together brilliantly and brims with personality: just what you would expect from a wine of such standing and importance. Nor is it coincidental that we found impeccable winemaking and great drinking pleasure in everything we tasted from this admirable co-operative. We need do no more than cite as examples the expressive, yet delicate, Furetta Mandrarossa '02 from chardonnay and grecanico, and the structured Cabernet Sauvignon Mandrarossa '02. And the prices are as good as the wines themselves.

MESSINA

PALARI
LOC. SANTO STEFANO BRIGA
C.DA BARNA
98135 MESSINA
TEL. 090630194 - 090694281
E-MAIL: vinipalari@tin.it

Last year we said, somewhat tongue in cheek, that winemaking architect Salvatore Geraci from Messina only makes great Faro in even numbered years. Just to prove us wrong, he has made a truly great '01. OK, we were wrong. We'll forgive Salvatore, known as "Turi", because of his friendliness, affable ways and dedication to the cause of fine wine. Seriously, though, Palari '01 is a wine of such extraordinary elegance and depth that Three Glasses were a mere formality. In a region where super-wines tend to be powerful and muscular, a red like Palari risks passing unnoticed. Its quest for balance, lively elegance and finesse make its varietal nuances more typical, we'd say, of a Burgundy, and not some New World cult wine. But a cult wine is precisely what Palari actually is. It is obtained from nerello cappuccio and nerello mascalese, with small amounts of local varieties such as nocera and acitana, and is aged around a year and a half in small new oak casks, the successful result of the sensory researches that Salvatore and his consultant oenologist, Donato Lanati, have been carrying out for years. The estate also produces a reliable second wine, Rosso del Soprano, from the same grapes.

● Bendicò Mandrarossa '01	♟♟	5
○ Chardonnay Mandrarossa '01	♟♟	4
● Cabernet Sauvignon Mandrarossa '02	♟♟	4
○ Fiano Mandrarossa '02	♟♟	4*
○ Furetta Mandrarossa '02	♟♟	5
○ Grecanico Mandrarossa '02	♟♟	4*
● Merlot Mandrarossa '02	♟♟	4
● Syrah Mandrarossa '02	♟♟	4
○ Vendemmia Tardiva Mandrarossa '02	♟♟	5
○ Feudo dei Fiori Mandrarossa '02	♟	4
● Nero d'Avola Mandrarossa '02	♟	4
● Bendicò Mandrarossa '00	♟♟	5
○ Furetta Mandrarossa '01	♟♟	5
○ Vendemmia Tardiva Mandrarossa '01	♟♟	4

● Faro Palari '01	♟♟♟	7
● Rosso del Soprano '01	♟	5
● Faro Palari '96	♟♟♟	7
● Faro Palari '98	♟♟♟	7
● Faro Palari '00	♟♟♟	7
● Faro Palari '97	♟♟	7
● Faro Palari '99	♟♟	7

MILO (CT)

BARONE DI VILLAGRANDE
VIA DEL BOSCO
95025 MILO (CT)
TEL. 0957082175 - 0957494339
E-MAIL: info@villagrande.it

The attractive building where Carlo Asmundo and Maria Nicolosi house their estate is made of lava, and is very old. Inside, there are venerable ageing cellars, and old casks and new barriques are bathed in an endless interplay of light and shade that lends a sense of magic and fascination to the place. Outside, the vines stretch over the volcanic (naturally) soil of Milo at 650 metres above sea level. We found Sciara '00, from merlot, nerello mascalese and other varieties grown in the Villagrande vineyards, was the most interesting of the range. A complex wine, it has cherries and blackberry on the nose with notes of liquorice, and a spicy finish on the palate. Fiore di Villagrande '02, an Etna Bianco Superiore, is quite special, with delightful notes of green apple and vanilla, and a full, long palate. From Capo Gramignazzi on the island of Salina comes the Malvasia delle Lipari Passito, made from malvasia and corinto. The '02 is successful again. It is more intense on the nose than the previous release, strongly evoking ripe summer fruits, most notably apricot and peach, and some herbs. The palate is elegant, full and attractively honeyed. The estate's other wines are also very good.

PACECO (TP)

FIRRIATO
VIA TRAPANI, 4
91027 PACECO (TP)
TEL. 0923882755
E-MAIL: info@firriato.it

There are several developments at Firriato this year, all good. The first is that a stupendous version of Camelot, the '01, swept in to pick up Three Glasses with ease. A blend of cabernet sauvignon and merlot, it is always one of the best of its category, but this year its fabulous fruit and great class really stood out. Soft, harmonious and balanced, it is irresistibly seductive and quite bowls you over. The other developments regard the estate set-up. Salvatore De Gaetano has become the estate's sole owner and his wife Vinzia has decided to take the estate onto a broader stage. She is the face of Firriato around the world, and is getting seriously good results. There are changes on the technical side, too. The famous international team of consultants, led by Kym Milne, which has given the winery so much lustre, remains in place, but the role of house oenologist, held by the highly skilled, reserved Peppe Pellegrino, has been boosted. The increasing attention Firriato is devoting to indigenous varieties, and the terrain on which they grow, sees him taking on more of a leading role. Moving back to the wines, Harmonium, from 100 per cent nero d'Avola, is right up behind Camelot. Both it and Santagostino Rosso Baglio Soria, a nero d'Avola and syrah blend, reached the finals. The fine Ribeca '01, a new wine from nero d'Avola and perricone, was much admired. The perricone variety is on the verge of dying out. To find it at 40 per cent in a wine, and see the depth and breadth it bestows, marks a milestone for indigenous vines. Everything else is simply excellent.

●	Sciara di Villagrande Rosso '00	▼▼	5
○	Etna Bianco Sup. Fiore di Villagrande '02	▼▼	4*
○	Malvasia delle Lipari Passito '02	▼▼	5
●	Etna Rosso '01	▼	3
○	Etna Bianco '02	▼	3
●	Sciara di Villagrande Rosso '98	♈♈	4
○	Etna Bianco Sup. '01	♈♈	3*
●	Etna Bianco Sup. Fiore di Villagrande '01	♈♈	3*

●	Camelot '01	▼▼▼	7
●	Harmonium '01	▼▼	6
●	Ribeca '01	▼▼	6
●	Santagostino Rosso Baglio Soria '01	▼▼	5
●	Altavilla della Corte Rosso '01	▼▼	4*
●	Chiaramonte Rosso '01	▼▼	4*
●	Feudi Bordonaro Rosso '01	▼▼	3*
○	Altavilla della Corte Bianco '02	▼▼	3*
○	Chiaramonte Bianco '02	▼▼	3*
○	Feudi Bordonaro Bianco '02	▼▼	3*
○	Santagostino Bianco Baglio Soria '02	▼▼	5
●	Camelot '98	♈♈♈	5
●	Harmonium '00	♈♈♈	5
●	Camelot '00	♈♈	6

PALERMO

FATASCIÀ
VIA G. GALILEI, 95
90145 PALERMO
TEL. 0916932060
E-MAIL: info@led-srl.it

The estate's vineyards are at Castelbuono and form a part of the Lena family's huge holding. Meanwhile, Gianfranco Lena and Giuseppe Natoli, who run the administrative side, are based at Palermo, with Santi Buzzotta, the dynamic sales director and Daniele Virdone, marketing. The technical side is left to – who else? – Riccardo Cotarella, who is ably supported by Stefania Lena. Last year, we felt it was right to bring this young estate into our Guide and, just one year on, the boys have stormed off with Three Glasses for a fantastic version of Almanera, the '01. This is made exclusively from nero d'Avola from vines yielding just 6,500 tons per hectare. It ages five months in French oak casks, then nine months in bottle, and can be found on wine shop shelves for just € 7. Well done! Another wine that may not have matched Almanera's complete triumph but came very close is Rosso del Presidente '01, from cabernet franc and nero d'Avola. Rich, intense and full of personality, it is delicately herbaceous and has great depth on the palate. L'Insolente '01, from merlot and cabernet sauvignon, came over as firm, pleasantly tannic and full bodied. L'Enigma '02, from a good grillo-based blend, is fresh, tangily flavoured and great to drink. Ylenia '01, from grapes left to dry on the vine, is excellent, showing attractively delicate notes of raisining.

PALERMO

SPADAFORA
VIA AUSONIA, 90
90144 PALERMO
TEL. 091514952 - 0916703322
E-MAIL: info@spadafora.com

Two Spadafora wines made the finals but, as last year, the crowning achievement of Three Glasses eluded the cellar by a hair's breadth. But it is possibly just as important to note that in general, the wines, especially the reds, get better, and ever more impressive, from one year to the next. In 1988, Francesco Spadafora, who inherited the estate from his father, started to introduce modern cultivation methods and updated vinification techniques for his grapes. These come from 100 hectares or so of vineyard on a property covering approximately 180 hectares in the sun-drenched area of Virzì in the muncipality of Monreale, 60 kilometres from Palermo. Schietto Syrah '01 and Sole dei Padri '01 are both made from 100 per cent syrah. The yields differ only minimally, although the former ages longer. Both have outstanding personality and both show attractive wild berry fruit, spices and white pepper on the nose. There are differences between them, but they are subtle ones. On the palate, they are mouthfilling, harmonious and notably long. There is plenty to impress in the rest of the estate's range, starting with the cabernet sauvignon-based Schietto Rosso '01, which is full of walnutskin and liquorice on the nose and has great impact on the palate. Then there is Don Pietro Rosso '01, from cabernet sauvignon, merlot and nero d'Avola. It has a wide range of aromas and a well balanced palate. Rosso Virzì '02, from nero d'Avola and syrah, has a complex nose recalling black cherries. Monreale Alhambra '02, a catarratto and inzolia blend, is good.

● Almanera '01	♟♟♟	3*
● Rosso del Presidente '01	♟♟	5
● L'Insolente '01	♟♟	7
○ Ylenia '01	♟♟	6
○ L'Enigma '02	♟♟	5
● L'Insolente '00	♟♟	5
● Almanera '00	♟♟	3*
○ Ylenia '00	♟	6

● Schietto Syrah '01	♟	6
● Sole dei Padri '01	♟	8
● Don Pietro Rosso '01	♟♟	4
● Schietto Rosso '01	♟♟	6
● V. Virzì Rosso '02	♟♟	4
○ Don Pietro Bianco '02	♟	4
○ Monreale Alhambra '02	♟	3
● Schietto Rosso '98	♟♟	3
● Schietto Rosso '99	♟♟	5
● Schietto Rosso '00	♟♟	5
● Don Pietro Rosso '00	♟♟	4
● Schietto Syrah '00	♟♟	5
● Sole dei Padri '00	♟♟	8
● V. Virzì Rosso '01	♟♟	3*

PALERMO

★ TASCA D'ALMERITA
LOC. SCLAFANI BAGNI
C.DA REGALEALI
90029 PALERMO
TEL. 0921544011 - 0916459711
E-MAIL: info@tascadalmerita.it

What can we say about Tasca d'Almerita?
It is one of the most important estates in
Sicily, with a history going back to 1830,
when the Tasca family acquired the
Regaleali property. Since then, they have
been successfully producing excellent
wine, but the great leap in quality came in
the 1960s, when Regaleali Bianco, Rosso
and Rosato gained amazing success.
Then there was a further leap forward in
the mid 1980s when the modern cellars at
Vallelunga Pratameno in the heart of Sicily
where the setting where Giuseppe Tasca
developed the Chardonnay and Cabernet
Sauvignon that would become
international classics. Today, his son Lucio
is at the helm, and he has gathered
around him a technical team of the
highest standing, led by oenologist Luigi
Guzzo, who for the past two vintages has
had Carlo Ferrini as consultant. The cellar
renovations have been completed, too.
The upshot of all this is a top-quality range
of wines, led by the Cabernet Sauvignon
'01. It's a red of rare power and finesse,
with impeccable varietal character. It
reflects perfectly a terrain that, though
bathed by strong sun, lies at 450 to 750
metres, and so is among the island's
coolest terroirs. Pervasive, complex
spiciness marks the estate's return to the
very top of the Italian ladder, an event also
underlined by the performances of wines
such as Cygnus '01, a deep, finely tannic
nero d'Avola, Camastra, a nero d'Avola-
based blend, and the classic Rosso del
Conte, from nero d'Avola and perricone
grown on old bush-trained vines. But
everything here is of the highest quality.

PANTELLERIA (TP)

SALVATORE MURANA
C.DA KHAMMA, 276
91017 PANTELLERIA (TP)
TEL. 0923915231

Salvatore Murana is a remarkable
Pantelleria grape grower, with a perfect
mix of enthusiasm, the patience of Job
and a craftsman's diligence. These
strengths bear fruit in the vineyard,
especially on Pantelleria's difficult soils,
which are battered by salt-bearing winds,
as well as in the cellar. Murana's sweet
wines from zibibbo grapes have made
history. Despite their tiny production, they
have enjoyed worldwide success, and
have brought many to discover the
fabulous aromas engendered by this lump
of volcanic rock in the Mediterranean. If
you ever visit Pantelleria, it is not difficult
to find Salvatore. He'll either be on his
knees looking after his bush-trained vines,
which are planted in small dips dug out of
the soil and sheltered by low walls to
protect the plants from the salt and winds.
Or he'll be on call at the local fire station.
His wines bear the name of the locality
where the grapes grow, so we have
Martingana, Khamma and Mueggen, three
similar but subtly different expressions of
his lands. This year, Martingana didn't
quite make Three Glasses. Still, it is an
elegant, concentrated wine, full of apricot
and dried figs aromas, and intensely
sweet, with deep, elegant flavours of fruit
and caramel. Mueggen '01 is a light
amber colour. The nose is fresh and
perfumed, the palate dense but not
cloying, strongly echoing the fruit and
zibibbo-like grapiness of the nose. The
intensely aromatic Gadì, again from
zibibbo but vinified dry, is very good, as
are È Serre '02, a delightful white from
catarratto, and the red Talìa '01, from nero
d'Avola and cabernet.

● Contea di Sclafani		
Cabernet Sauvignon '01	♟♟♟	6
● Contea di Sclafani Rosso del Conte '01	♟♟	6
● Cygnus '01	♟♟	5
○ Almerita Brut '00	♟♟	6
● Camastra '01	♟♟	5
○ Contea di Sclafani Nozze d'Oro '01	♟♟	4*
○ Leone d'Almerita '02	♟	4
○ Regaleali Bianco '02	♟	3*
☉ Regaleali Rosato '02	♟	4*
● Cabernet Sauvignon '99	♟♟♟	7
● Contea di Sclafani		
Cabernet Sauvignon '00	♟♟	6
○ Chardonnay '01	♟♟	6
● Regaleali Rosso '01	♟	4

○ Moscato Passito di Pantelleria		
Martingana '99	♟♟	8
○ Moscato di Pantelleria		
Mueggen '01	♟♟	7
○ Moscato di Pantelleria Turbé '01	♟♟	5
○ È Serre '02	♟♟	4
○ Gadì '02	♟♟	4
● Talia '01	♟♟	4
○ Moscato Passito di Pantelleria		
Martingana '97	♟♟♟	8
○ Moscato Passito di Pantelleria		
Martingana '98	♟♟♟	8
○ Moscato Passito di Pantelleria		
Khamma '00	♟♟	7

PARTINICO (PA)

PIAZZA ARMERINA (EN)

CUSUMANO
C.DA SAN CARLO S.S. 113
90047 PARTINICO (PA)
TEL. 0918903456 - 0918900589
E-MAIL: cusumano@cusumano.it

MAURIGI
C.DA BUDONETTO
94015 PIAZZA ARMERINA (EN)
TEL. 093585240 - 091321788
E-MAIL: info@maurigi.it

Three Glasses once more adorn the Cusumano sideboard for Sagana '02, a splendid example of clean, varietal, complex nero d'Avola. Despite its excellence, the price is moderate, in line with a firm estate policy that demands relationships with consumers to be based on mutual respect. And so the hard work of the two dynamic brothers, Diego and Alberto, has once more been rewarded. These two divide up their work with a natural ease. Alberto, assisted by top Piedmontese consultant, Mario Ronco, looks after the technical side. This is more demanding than in the past as 177 hectares in the Ficuzza woodland, near Palermo, have been added to the 140 hectares already owned. Only 14 hectares of the new holding are vineyard, but the rest will be planted within two years. The more communicative, determined Diego looks after PR and sales. He takes care of export markets, and so is forever travelling. The exciting results and turnover achieved repay all this commitment. Jalé '02 comes from the new holding at Ficuzza, and is made entirely from chardonnay grown at 700 metres. The golden colour ushers in a broad array of aromas with notable persistence and intensity. The palate is classy. Its warm, round, Mediterranean style perfectly balances acidity and softness. Justly, it went through to the Three Glass finals. As did the estate's other great wine, the delightful Noà '02, a terrific blend of nero d'Avola, merlot and cabernet sauvignon. All the other wines are lovely.

What strikes you about Francesco Maurigi is his urge to put himself to the test, his need for a challenge, and his lack of concern about swimming against the tide or the heritage of history. Who else would plant vines in an area that had never seen them before, and then choose international varieties while everyone else was slaving over the clones of nero d'Avola and catarratto that are so much in vogue? But variety is the spice of life, and Maurigi happily continues to plough his own furrow. He's also carrying out rigorous experiments in the vineyard and the cellar, aiming for even more impressive results. So let's look forward to more surprises and other wines with the elegance and finesse that mark out the estate. Even here it is flying in the face of the trend for the super-big, massively concentrated wines, all muscle and brawn, that other producers go for. This year, it is Terre di Maria '01, a most successful blend of cabernet sauvignon, merlot, syrah and pinot noir, that towers above the rest. Complex, soft, gloriously elegant, beautifully balanced and quite fascinating, it came very close to that Three Glass threshold. Maurigi can, however, rest assured that its wonderful drinkability was greatly appreciated by both the regional and national tasting panels. More evidence that this is Maurigi's year for reds was Saia Grande '02, from syrah, merlot and pinot noir. It is more elegant than before and very good indeed. Also excellent is Terre di Sofia '02, a monovarietal Chardonnay. Coste all'Ombra '02 is not yet ready.

● Sagana '02	🍷🍷🍷	5
○ Jalé '02	🍷🍷	5
● Noà '02	🍷🍷	5
○ Angimbé '02	🍷🍷	4*
● Benuara '02	🍷🍷	4*
○ Alcamo Nadaria '02	🍷	3*
○ Nadarìa Inzolia '02	🍷	3
● Nadarìa Merlot '02	🍷	3
● Nadarìa Nero d'Avola '02	🍷	3*
○ Nadarìa Syrah '02	🍷	3
● Noà '00	🍷🍷🍷	5
● Sagana '00	🍷🍷	5
● Noà '01	🍷🍷	5
● Sagana '01	🍷🍷	5
○ Cubia '02	🍷🍷	5

● Terre di Maria '01	🍷🍷	6
● Saia Grande '02	🍷🍷	5
○ Terre di Sofia '02	🍷🍷	5
○ Coste all'Ombra '02	🍷	5
○ Terre di Sofia '01	🍷🍷	5
● Terre di Maria '00	🍷🍷	6
○ Coste all'Ombra '01	🍷🍷	5
● Saia Grande '01	🍷🍷	5

SAN CIPIRELLO (PA)

CALATRASI - ACCADEMIA DEL SOLE
C.DA PIANO PIRAINO
90040 SAN CIPIRELLO (PA)
TEL. 0918576767 - 0919578080
E-MAIL: info@calatrasi.it

This important estate is in great form. Split across three production facilities, in Puglia, Tunisia and Sicily, it has its operations centre in Sicily, where most of the wine comes from, and the winery's soul is at home. Everything is masterminded and co-ordinated by the sole director and leading partner, Maurizio Micciché, a rheumatologist with a calling as a grape grower. All the wines, across all the lines, have exemplary clarity of style and cleanliness. The careful vinification techniques employed also ensure that the characteristics of each variety are undisturbed and well in evidence. Vioca di Plaia '02, from catarratto and viognier, is impeccable, with delicate aromas of fruit and flowers, refined notes of thyme and sage, good structure and excellent drinkability. Also first rate is the elegant Terre di Ginestra 651 '01, one of the cellar's leading wines. It's a sort of cru, a blend of nero d'Avola and syrah grown at high altitude. Terre di Ginestra Nero d'Avola '02 is a similarly good wine and a fine interpretation of Sicily's most important red grape. It has good concentration and nice varietal characteristics, with red berry fruits and humus, and vigorous, well modulated tannins. D'Istinto Syrah '02 also has good drinkability. The other wines in the D'Istinto line are fault-free.

SCIACCA (AG)

AZIENDE VINICOLE MICELI
C.DA PIANA SCUNCHIPANI, 190
92019 SCIACCA (AG)
TEL. 092580188
E-MAIL: segreteria@midmiceli.it

Since 1995, Gianni Tartaglia, Antonio Massaro and Giuseppe Lo Re have been running this winery, which operates from two centres, Sciacca and the island of Pantelleria. From its 50 or so hectares of estate-owned vineyard, and additional bought-in grapes, it produces around 1,000,000 bottles a year in various styles. There are easy drinking reds and whites, selections, crus, dry and semi-sparkling aromatic wines, "passito" wines from Pantelleria and fortified wines. The jewel in the crown is the richly textured, sumptuously aromatic Moscato di Pantelleria Entelechia. We found the more accessible Passito Nun, blended over three vintages, to be in splendid form, too. The '02 vintage of the complex, individual, dry Moscato Yrnm is again a minor masterpiece. Intensely perfumed, it reveals notes of Mediterranean balsam and a long, elegant, gently bitterish finish. The pleasant, if unusual, slightly sparkling Zibibbo Garighe is a mass of florality. The most serious of the reds, Majo San Lorenzo '01, from merlot and cabernet, stands out for the cleanliness of its aromas and its softness on the palate. It evokes a long stay in barrique with intense notes of hazelnut and coffee cream. The racy, spicy Syrah '01 is similar in style. Then there is the Le Lune line with Salgalaluna '02, a fruity, attractively soft Grillo, and Primoquarto '02, from nero d'Avola and sangiovese, a pleasantly supple, youthful, easy-drinking wine with a cherry and plum nose. Among the whites, Viognier Initio '01 and Chardonnay Dedicato '01 are interesting and developing well.

●	Terre di Ginestra 651 '01	♍♍	6
●	D'Istinto Syrah '02	♍♍	4
●	Terre di Ginestra Nero d'Avola '02	♍♍	5
○	Vioca di Plaia '02	♍♍	3*
○	D'Istinto Bianco '02	♍	3
○	D'Istinto Catarratto-Chardonnay '02	♍	4
○	D'Istinto Chardonnay '02	♍	4
○	D'Istinto Ljetas Bianco '02	♍	3
●	D'Istinto Nero d'Avola '02	♍	4
●	D'Istinto Sangiovese-Merlot '02	♍	4
●	Terre di Ginestra 651 '00	♛♛	7
●	Terre di Ginestra Nero d'Avola '01	♛♛	4

○	Moscato di Pantelleria Entelechia	♍♍	7
●	Majo San Lorenzo '01	♍♍	6
○	Syrah '01	♍♍	5
○	Pantelleria Secco Yrnm '02	♍♍	4
○	Passito di Pantelleria Nun	♍♍	5
○	Garighe Zibibbo '02	♍	4
●	Nero d'Avola '02	♍	4
○	Passito di Pantelleria Tanit	♍	5
○	Dedicato '01		6
○	Initio '01		5
○	Salgalaluna '02		4
●	Primoquarto Rosso '02		4

TRAPANI

Fondo Antico

fraz. Rilievo
via Fiorame, 56
91020 Trapani
tel. 0923864339
e-mail: info@fondoantico.com

One thing that strikes you as soon as you get to this winery near Trapani, on the ancient farm owned by the Polizzotti-Scuderi family, is the luxuriant plantation of palm trees that surrounds the estate. The vines are just as well cared for and grow on excellently aspected terrain. Inside, the cellar contains modern, technologically advanced equipment. Wine has not been made here for long: it was 1995 when the vineyards were replanted. Some of the old vineyards were saved, the ones that were still productive, growing grillo and nero d'Avola on "alberello" bush-trained vines. Other indigenous and international varieties were given space and wine production was entrusted to one of the best, the brilliant young Sicilian oenologist, Vincenzo Bambina. Il Canto '01 is a nero d'Avola and cabernet sauvignon blend that sailed into the finals, very nearly winning a third Glass. It stands out for finesse and personality, while the months it spent in French oak have helped it become rounder and more incisive on the palate. Nero d'Avola '02 is also first rate, with red berry fruit and spices on the nose, and a powerful, fleshy palate. The '02 Grillo Parlante (the punning name means "Jiminy Cricket"), made exclusively from selected grillo grapes, entices with silky tropical fruit on the nose and good length on its well-structured palate. The '02 vintage of Il Coro, from chardonnay and grillo, is also good, showing summer fruit and finishing full and round.

●	Il Canto di Fondo Antico '01	YY (grey)	5
○	Grillo Parlante '02	**YY**	4*
●	Nero d'Avola '02	**YY**	4*
○	Il Coro '02	**Y**	4
○	Il Coro '01	YY	5
●	Il Canto di Fondo Antico '00	Y	5

TRAPANI

Cantina Sociale di Trapani

loc. Fontanelle
c.da Ospedaletto
91100 Trapani
tel. 0923539349
e-mail: info@cantinasocialetrapani.com

A constantly growing co-operative that has developed considerably in the last few years, employing winemaking skills and very careful selection of grapes from different sites to make a range of precisely planned quality wines: that, in short, is the Cantina Sociale di Trapani. Its tireless president, Roberto Adragna, his children, Francesca and Goffredo, and the brilliant young local oenologist, Nicola Centonze, who gives the essential technical backup, continue to offer attractive, well-made wines, especially under the Forti Terre di Sicilia label. And the Three Glass prize that eluded him by so little last year has finally arrived. The wine is a fantastic Cabernet Sauvignon '01. It has a good, intense red colour, a nose of blackcurrant, blackberry and dark chocolate; and a full, powerful palate that has impact and exceptionally silky tannins. Nero d'Avola '01 showed excellently, too, with aromas of morello cherry, blackcurrant and blueberry, and an initially soft palate that is pleasingly long. Il Rosso '02, from nero d'Avola and cabernet sauvignon, is exciting, with concentration on the nose, warmth on the palate and good length. Rocche Rosse '02, from merlot and cabernet sauvignon, is equally good and pleasantly herbaceous, with a full palate and moderate tannins. The whites, the '02 Chardonnay and Il Bianco '02, based on inzolia and chardonnay, are as good as ever. Both are dry, well made and reflect the characteristics of the grapes from which they are made.

●	Forti Terre di Sicilia Cabernet Sauvignon '01	YYY (grey)	5
●	Forti Terre di Sicilia Nero d'Avola '01	**YY**	4
○	Forti Terre di Sicilia Chardonnay '02	**YY**	4
○	Forti Terre di Sicilia Il Bianco '02	**Y**	3
●	Forti Terre di Sicilia Il Rosso '02	**Y**	3
●	Forti Terre di Sicilia Rocche Rosse '02	**Y**	4
●	Forti Terre di Sicilia Cabernet Sauvignon '99	YYY	5
	Forti Terre di Sicilia Cabernet Sauvignon '98	YY	3
●	Forti Terre di Sicilia Il Rosso '99	YY	2
○	Forti Terre di Sicilia Chardonnay '00	YY	3*
●	Forti Terre di Sicilia Cabernet Sauvignon '00	YY	5
○	Forti Terre di Sicilia Chardonnay '01	YY	4*

VIAGRANDE (CT)

BENANTI
VIA G. GARIBALDI, 475
95029 VIAGRANDE (CT)
TEL. 0957893438 - 0957893533
E-MAIL: benanti@vinicolabenanti.it

In little over ten years, Giuseppe Benanti has created a winery that has few equals in southern Italy for the way it is organized and the quality of its output. The brilliant, creative and very businesslike Giuseppe has applied the methods and techniques that gave him success in the pharmaceuticals sector to his real love, wine. Nothing more, nothing less, except his choice of the exceptional, and partly forgotten, lands of Etna as the setting for his dream. These are lands with unique climatic conditions and a wealth of indigenous varieties. From the original nucleus around the cellars in Viagrande, Giuseppe has restored or, in fact, saved, dozens of hectares (he now has 90) of "alberello", or bush-trained, vines which had been abandoned in favour of easier sites in the plains. The Benanti vines stand at between 450 and 1,000 metres, a unique situation for vine growth in Sicily. One wine, in our opinion, is perfectly epitomizes the uniqueness and extraordinary nature of this terrain, Etna Bianco Superiore Pietramarina '99, from 100 per cent carricante. It is a remarkable wine. Rich, with mineral and almondy aromas of great complexity, it is endowed with a powerful structure and an acid backbone that will allow it to evolve elegantly for well over five years. It therefore fully merits our Three Glasses. But the really impressive thing about the Benanti wines is that this now very large range offers tremendous quality all down the line, including wines from the vineyards in Pachino, in Sicily's south-eastern corner, and those from zibibbo grown on Pantelleria.

VITTORIA (RG)

COS
VILLA FONTANE
S.P. ACATE - CHIARAMONTE, KM 14,500
97019 VITTORIA (RG)
TEL. 0932876145
E-MAIL: info@cosvittoria.it

Every year, Giusto Occhipinti and "Titta" Cilia prove to their many admirers by the excellence of their wines that the serious, demanding undertaking they embarked upon so many years ago was backed up by astute foresight. They were also among the very first to adopt Steiner's biodynamic theories. This means no chemical fertilization of the vines and no cultured yeasts in fermentation. Their motto is, "wine is not made, it is only helped along, with respect and love". So they go through their vineyards many times, picking only ripe grapes, and bunches are laid in unusually small, six-kilogram cases that are carefully washed every time they are used. But these are just some examples of their attention to detail. It is exacting work, driven by great passion, profound study and respect for the land, to bring out the very best it is able to give. This year Contrade – Labirinto '99, an estate cru from selected nero d'Avola grapes, was particularly admired. It is warm, Mediterranean, full of fascination, and has a deep ruby colour as well as a varietal nose with refined notes of humus, spices and ripe red berry fruit. Cerasuolo di Vittoria Vastunaca '02 is very fine, too. The interplay of nero d'Avola and frappato gives excellent balance on both nose and palate, generating great elegance. The complex, intriguing, powerfully structured Scyri '01, from 100 per cent nero d'Avola, is good enough to convince the most demanding of palates. All the other wines are impeccably well made.

O Etna Bianco Sup. Pietramarina '99	♇♇♇	5
● Etna Rosso		
Serra della Contessa '00	♇♇	6
● Etna Rosso Rovittello '99	♇♇	5
O Edelmio '00	♇♇	5
● Etna Rosso Rosso di Verzella '00	♇♇	4*
● Nerello Cappuccio '00	♇♇	6
● Nero d'Avola '00	♇♇	6
O Passito di Pantelleria Mueggen '00	♇♇	6
O Minnella '02	♇♇	6
● Lamoremio '99	♇♇	6
● Nerello Mascalese '00	♇	6
O Etna Bianco Bianco di Caselle '02	♇	4

● Scyri '00	♇♇	6
● Cerasuolo di Vittoria		
V. di Vastunaca '02	♇♇	4
● Contrade - Labirinto '99	♇♇	8
● Cerasuolo di Vittoria '01	♇	5
● Pojo di Lupo '01	♇	5
O Ramì '02	♇	4
● Scyri '98	♈♈	5
● Contrade - Dedalo '98	♈♈	8
● Contrade - Labirinto '98	♈♈	8
● Scyri '99	♈♈	6

OTHER WINERIES

MARTORANA
VIA SALERNO, 7
92100 AGRIGENTO
TEL. 0922410352
E-MAIL: vinimartorana@sicilia.it

The Martorana family has 13 hectares of nero d'Avola on the road from Agrigento to Porto Empedocle. Nero d'Avola Ragabo '02 is a fine, concentrated wine with excellent structure, and harmony, with dense tannins. The soft, balanced Nero d'Avola '02 is varietal and attractive.

● Nero d'Avola Ragabo '02		4
● Nero d'Avola '02		3

FEUDO MONTONI
C.DA MONTONI VECCHI
92022 CAMMARATA (AG)
TEL. 091513106
E-MAIL: feudomontoni@virgilio.it

The Nero d'Avola Selezione Speciale cru is the fruit of Fabio Sieci's dedication. This second release, the '01, is a wine of great class and harmony. It will make its many fans very happy indeed. The powerful palate is well delineated and its tannins have unusual elegance and softness.

● Nero d'Avola Sel. Speciale '01	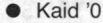	6
● Nero d'Avola '01		4

VINICOLA FALCONE
VIA DELLE ROSE, 117
91021 CAMPOBELLO DI MAZARA (TP)
TEL. 092447361
E-MAIL: info@vinicolafalcone.it

Behind the ambitious Altius project lies a sound team, including the dynamic Giovanni Falcone, one of wine's go-getters. The mix of nero d'Avola and cabernet sauvignon works perfectly. The ripe cherry, blackcurrant and blackberry nose is broad, and the palate mouthfilling, warm and Mediterranean.

● Altius '01		6

ALESSANDRO DI CAMPOREALE
C.DA MANDRANOVA
90043 CAMPOREALE (PA)
TEL. 092437238 - 092437038
E-MAIL: info@alessandrodicamporeale.it

The Alessandro brothers have delivered again. Their syrah-based Kaid '01 is more attractive than ever, and went through to the Three Glass finals. A lovely ruby leads to a refined, complex array of aromas, led by ripe red berry fruits. The palate is fleshy, Mediterranean and lifted by silky tannins.

● Kaid '01		5

SALLIER DE LA TOUR
VIA ATRIO PRINCIPE, 18
90043 CAMPOREALE (PA)
TEL. 092436797
E-MAIL: info@sallierdelatour.it

Filiberto Sallier de La Tour, Principe di Camporeale, has created three magnificent wines, all released for the first time. Sallier de La Tour '00, from nero d'Avola, syrah, cabernet sauvignon and merlot, is deep, with lovely fruit and elegance. Its two companions are equally fine.

● Sallier de La Tour '00	🍷🍷	5
● Cabernet '01	🍷🍷	4
● Syrah '01	🍷🍷	4

FEUDI DI ZANGARA
VIA P.PE DI VILLAFRANCA, 50
91022 CASTELVETRANO (TP)
TEL. 0916888068
E-MAIL: info@feudidizangara.it

This 31-hectare, organically certified estate marks its first appearance in the Guide with Two Glasses for the high-profile Camedrio, from merlot. It looks sumptuously opaque. There are black berry fruit jam and elegant spice on the nose, then the soft, silky palate finishes long.

● Camedrio '01	🍷🍷	3*

GULFI
C.DA ROCCAZZO
VIA MARIA SANTISSIMA DEL ROSARIO, 90
97012 CHIARAMONTE GULFI (RG)
TEL. 0932921654

Vito Catania, aided by skilled oenologist Salvo Foti, turns out a striking set of highly successful nero d'Avola crus. All are distinct, all have a complex, elegant nose, and all are deliciously powerful and fleshy, with exemplary balance and harmony. The white Valcanzjria '02 is also excellent.

● Nero Ibleo '01	🍷🍷	4
● Nerobaroni '01	🍷🍷	7
● Nerobufaleffj '01	🍷🍷	6
○ Valcanzjria '02	🍷🍷	4*

FEUDI DI SAN GIULIANO
C.DA MAZZAPORRO DUCHESSA
90030 CONTESSA ENTELLINA (PA)
TEL. 0923952148
E-MAIL: info@feudidisangiuliano.it

The Spanò family's 50 hectares of vines lie in the Alto Belice hills at 250 metres. The arm, soft Cabernet Timpaia is full of fruit and spices, and again wins Two Glasses. The white Vento di Majo, a blend of chardonnay, inzolia and catarratto, is fresh, supple and pleasant.

● Contessa Entellina Timpaia '02	🍷🍷	5
○ Cjat Omé '02	🍷	4
○ Contessa Entellina Vento di Majo '02	🍷	3
○ Nikasio '02	🍷	3

FRANCESCA E GIAMBATTISTA CURTO
C.DA SULLA - VIA G. GALILEI, 4
97014 ISPICA (RG)
TEL. 0932950161
E-MAIL: az.curto@tin.it

The family has long experience in agriculture and winemaking. Francesca Curto looks after the vines and handles PR. There are two well-made wines from old bush-trained nero d'Avola vineyards at Ispica and Pachino. Both have nice small red berry fruit, spices and hints of raisining.

● Curto Fontanelle Rosso '00	🍷🍷	5
● Curto Rosso '01	🍷🍷	3*

BARONE LA LUMIA
C.DA POZZILLO
92027 LICATA (AG)
TEL. 0922770057
E-MAIL: info@vogliedisicilia.it

Production is about 400,000 bottles, from 40 hectares of vines at Licata. This year's wines have good intensity and typicity. Best from the top line are Don Totò, 100 per cent nero d'Avola, and Halikàs, from inzolia, with warm aromas of orange marmalade and cedarwood, and a long, flavoursome palate.

● Don Totò '01	🍷🍷	6
○ Halykàs '01	🍷🍷	3
● Signorio Rosso '01	🍷	5
○ Sogno di Dama '01	🍷	4

TENUTA SCILIO
LOC. ARRIGO
S.P. LINGUAGLOSSA-ZAFFERANA, KM 2
95014 LINGUAGLOSSA (CT)
TEL. 095932822 - 095647789

The vineyards, all estate-owned, lie in the heart of the Valle Galfina. Tenuta Scilio - Etna Rosso, from nerello mascalese and nerello mantellato, is a bright ruby red, with black berries, chocolate and leather, and an edgy but elegant weave. Balance marks out the whole range.

● Etna Rosso - Tenuta Scilio '01	🍷🍷	3*
● Sikélios Rosso '00	🍷	4
● Etna Rosso Orpheus '99	🍷	4
☉ Etna Rosato - Tenuta Scilio '02		2

CURATOLO
C.DA MISILLA, 204
91025 MARSALA (TP)
TEL. 0923964415
E-MAIL: curatolovini@tiscali.it

Winemaking goes back generations here and the wines come from family-owned vineyards. The admirable Nero d'Avola '01 has a complex nose and a pleasant array of flavours. The two whites, Sarmaro '02 and Tumoli '02, are promising, with good structure and elegant tropical fruit aromas.

● Nero d'Avola '01	🍷🍷	4
○ Sarmaro Bianco '02	🍷	3
○ Tumoli Grillo '02	🍷	4

TERRE DI SANTA MARIA
VIA SANITÀ, 16
91025 MARSALA (TP)
TEL. 0923715115
E-MAIL: info@terredisantamaria.it

Great results from the Giacalone brothers' estate, where Stefania Lena consults. Paliotto, from merlot and cabernet sauvignon grown on the Kelbi plateau near Mazara del Vallo, is intense, solid and concentrated. Moranera, 100 per cent nero d'Avola which sees no wood, is rich and full of character.

● Il Paliotto '01	🍷🍷	5
● Moranera '01	🍷🍷	4

CANTINE FORACI
C.DA SERRONI
91026 MAZARA DEL VALLO (TP)
TEL. 0923934286
E-MAIL: info@foraci.it

Cantine Foraci makes a triumphant entry into the Guide with a range of well made, balanced wines. O'feo Nero d'Avola '00 was greatly admired by the tasting panel. It manages to combine good structure, varietal aromas and softness. Alcamo Conte Ruggero '02 is attractive. Everything else showed well.

● O'feo Nero d'Avola '00	🍷🍷	4
● Galhasi Nero d'Avola '01	🍷	3
○ Alcamo Conte Ruggero '02	🍷	3
○ Galhasi Inzolia Chardonnay '02	🍷	3

AGARENO
VIA FAVIGNANA II, 12
92013 MENFI (AG)
TEL. 0925570409
E-MAIL: info@agareno.it

A fairly new, very modern co-op whose members' grapes come from some of the best areas in western Sicily. The powerful, decisively flavoured '01 Moscafratta, from nero d'Avola, cabernet and merlot, is as good as ever. Gurra '01, 100 per cent nero d'Avola, and Galici '02 are both good.

● Moscafratta '01	🍷🍷	5
○ Galici '02	🍷	3
● Gurra '01	🍷	4

CANTINE COLOSI
VIA MILITARE RITIRO, 23
98152 MESSINA
TEL. 09053852
E-MAIL: info@cantinecolosi.com

Great improvements here. Malvasia Passita '01, from vineyards on Salina, has a good golden colour, aromas of summer fruit, elegance and length. Passito di Pantelleria '01 is similarly good, with ripe apricot and dried figs. Malvasia Naturale '01 impresses with its sober elegance.

○ Malvasia delle Lipari Passita '01	🍷🍷	6
○ Passito di Pantelleria '01	🍷🍷	5
○ Malvasia delle Lipari Naturale '01	🍷	6
○ Moscato di Pantelleria Passito '01	🍷	4

GRASSO
VIA ALBERO, 5
98057 MILAZZO (ME)
TEL. 0909281082
E-MAIL: casavinicolagrasso@tiscalinet.it

The determination of Paola and Alessio Grasso is beginning to bear fruit for their wines are gaining recognition. Their Caporosso '00, from nero d'Avola and sangiovese, is simply delicious, with its deep hue and round, full palate. Almost as good is the unusual Faro '00, from a hard to find DOC.

●	Caporosso '00	▼▼	3*
●	Faro - Di Stefano e Grasso '00	▼▼	7
●	Mamertino Rosso '00	▼▼	4
○	Baldovino Bianco '02	▼▼	2*

POLLARA
C.DA MALVELLO - S. P. 4 BIS KM 2
90046 MONREALE (PA)
TEL. 0918462922 - 0918463512
E-MAIL: pollara@neomedia.it

The estate of siblings Pippo, Vincenzo and Lea Pollara is in the hills of Corleone, in the central Sicily's Monreale DOC. Giada Bianco, from damaskino, and Rosso Narciso, mainly from nero d'Avola, are well made. Also good are the international varietals, including a Merlot and a Pinot Bianco.

●	Merlot Principe di Corleone '00	▼	5
○	Giada Principe di Corleone '02	▼	4
●	Narciso Principe di Corleone Rosso '02	▼	3
○	Pinot Bianco Principe di Corleone '02	▼	3

TAMBURELLO
C.DA PIETRAGNELLA - VIA P.PE PATERNÒ, 42
90144 MONREALE (PA)
TEL. 0918465272
E-MAIL: dagala@libero.it

Mirella Tamburello has recently seen through a refurbishment of this winery, now more attractive than ever. Pietragavina Perricone '02, from admirably restored perricone vines, is first rate. The ripe cherry Nero d'Avola '01 is nicely concentrated. The rest are well styled and prices are good.

●	Monreale Pietragavina Perricone '02	▼▼	4*
●	Dagala Rosso '01	▼	3
●	Monreale Pietragavina Nero d'Avola '01	▼	4
○	Dagala Bianco '02	▼	2

MARCHESI PLATAMONE
LOC. NUBIA - VIA GARIBALDI, 204
91027 PACECO (TP)
TEL. 0923868031 - 0923868135
E-MAIL: fattorieplatamone@libero.it

Rita and Enrico Platamone's estate, on the glorious salt flats of Nubia, makes its first entrance in the Guide with a range of well-styled, well-made wines. Particularly good is Tor di Nubia '02, from grillo, a pleasant, individual wine with attractive tropical fruits and good drinkability.

○	Donna Rita '02	▼	4
○	Grillo Tor di Nubia '02	▼	3
●	Tor di Nubia Nero D'Avola '02	▼	3
●	Venus '02	▼	4

AGRICOLA BONSULTON
C.DA CIMILLIA
91017 PANTELLERIA (TP)
TEL. 091513405
E-MAIL: bonsulton@tin.it

Roberto Casano is one of the stalwarts of grape growing on Pantelleria. From his 15 hectares of well-kept vineyard at Bonsulton comes a Passito that in years like '00 is an excellent example of this sweet wine. Alongside is a good fresh, dry white from zibibbo, with good structure and fragrance.

○	Passito di Pantelleria '00	▼▼	6
○	Moscato di Pantelleria '02	▼	5
○	Pantelleria Bianco Secco '02	▼	4

CASE DI PIETRA
C.DA NIKÀ
91017 PANTELLERIA (TP)
TEL. 0642012644
E-MAIL: casedipietra@tiscalinet.it

The enthusiastic Guido Tariciotti hit bull's eye this year with Nikà '01, an excellent version of his traditional Passito di Pantelleria. Honey, dried figs and dates lead to a powerful, concentrated, yet soft, palate. It's all too drinkable. The dry wine from zibibbo, Nikà '02, is as nice as ever.

○	Passito di Pantelleria Nikà '01	▼▼	5
○	Nikà '02	▼	4

SOLIDEA
C.DA KADDIUGGIA
91017 PANTELLERIA (TP)
TEL. 0923913016
E-MAIL: solideavini@libero.it

Every year, Giacomo and Solidea D'Ancona release wines that are excellently made and stylistically in line with the island's traditions. Passito Solidea '02 fascinates with its broad varietal nose and delicious aromas of apricot, dates and honey. Ilios '02, entirely from zibibbo, is also lovely.

O	Ilios '02	🍷🍷	4
O	Moscato di Pantelleria Solidea '02	🍷🍷	5
O	Passito di Pantelleria Solidea '02	🍷🍷	6

CANTINA SOCIALE LA TORRE
C.DA BOVO MONTAGNA
92020 RACALMUTO (AG)
TEL. 0922942194
E-MAIL: cantina.latorre@tin.it

This well-organized co-operative again put on a welcome good showing. Villa Noce Nero d'Avola '01 clearly comes from very good grapes and has ripe blackberry and spices on the nose. Bovo '01 is well structured and nicely drinkable. Girgenti '00 is a successful mix of nero d'Avola and sangiovese.

●	Bovo '01	🍷🍷	3*
●	Villa Noce Nero d'Avola '01	🍷🍷	3*
●	Girgenti '00	🍷	3

TERRE DI SALEMI
C.DA FIUMELUNGO
S.S. 188 - VIA MACELLO, 5
91018 SALEMI (TP)
TEL. 092464373

.This estate lies in the vine-clad hills of Salemi, between Alcamo and Marsala. The premium Villa Ragut - Barone di Mandralia line offers a nicely complex and richly nuanced Merlot. Viognier '02, from the same range, is evolving well. Alcamo Borgoluna, from inzolia and chardonnay, is pleasant.

●	Merlot '02	🍷🍷	4
●	Nero d'Avola '01	🍷	4
O	Viogner '02	🍷	4
O	Alcamo Borgoluna '02	🍷	4

GASPARE DI PRIMA
VIA G. GUASTO, 27
92017 SAMBUCA DI SICILIA (AG)
TEL. 0925941201 - 0925941279
E-MAIL: info@diprimavini.it

This estate put up its usual good showing. The '01 Villamaura Syrah is as nice, with an attractively spicy nose and a concentrated, harmonious palate. Pepita Rosso '01, a blend of merlot, nero d'Avola and syrah, is from vines at Pepita Roccarossa. It's well structured, with gentle, balanced tannins.

●	Villamaura Syrah '01	🍷🍷	7
●	Pepita Rosso '01	🍷🍷	5
O	Pepita Bianco '02	🍷	4

FEOTTO DELLO JATO
C.DA FEOTTO
90048 SAN GIUSEPPE JATO (PA)
TEL. 0918572650
E-MAIL: info@feottodellojato.it

This year's wines confirm how good the reds are at this recently set up winery. The '02 Rosso di Turi, a great selection of merlot, is even more elegant than before and went through to the finals. The pleasing monovarietal Syrah '01 is incisive. The whites still need some final touches.

●	Rosso di Turi '02	🍷🍷	5
●	Syrah '01	🍷🍷	5

GIROLAMO & C. TOLA
C.DA GIANBASCIO E. BOSCO FALCONERIA
90048 SAN GIUSEPPE JATO (PA)
TEL. 0918781591
E-MAIL: info@vinitola.it

The vineyards at 420 metres include both local and international varieties. The wines are even better than last year's. The mouthfilling Nero d'Avola e Syrah '01 and Nero d'Avola e Merlot '01 are excellent, both showing spicy aromas. The ripe cherry and blackberry Nero d'Avola '02 is also good.

●	Nero D'Avola e Merlot '01	🍷🍷	4
●	Nero D'avola e Syrah '01	🍷🍷	4
●	Rosso '01	🍷	3
●	Nero D'avola '02	🍷	3

CO.DI.VIN. - TENUTA DI MARIA
C.DA SALINELLA
91029 SANTA NINFA (TP)
TEL. 092467635
E-MAIL: tenutadimaria@sifree.it

A first entry for siblings Paolo, Rosario and Valentina Di Maria. The Marchese di Montefusco Bianco, an unoaked catarratto and grecanico mix, is fresh and fruity. The 100 per cent nero d'Avola Rosso is intense and well structured. Next year, the winery's name will change to "Tenute Di Maria".

●	Marchese di Montefusco Rosso '02	🍷🍷	4
○	Marchese di Montefusco Bianco '02	🍷	3

BARONE SCAMMACCA DEL MURGO
VIA ZAFFERANA, 13
95010 SANTA VENERINA (CT)
TEL. 095950520
E-MAIL: murgo@murgo.it

The wines from this small estate, owned by ambassador Scammacca, get better every year, and perfectly reflect the very special terrain of Etna. Tenuta San Michele '00, a monovarietal Cabernet Sauvignon, has delicate aromas of blueberry and liquorice, and a full, round palate. But everything is good.

●	Tenuta San Michele '00	🍷🍷	5
●	Etna Rosso '01	🍷🍷	3*

PUPILLO
C.DA TARGIA
96100 SIRACUSA
TEL. 0931494029
E-MAIL: solacium@tin.it

Lying near the ruins of Eurialo castle, this estate keeps alive the family's ancient winemaking traditions. Quality improves each year. We felt that the best was Moscato di Siracusa Vigna di Mela '02, with citrus and chamomile scents and a full, intense palate, but the range is consistently good.

○	Moscato di Siracusa Pollio '02	🍷🍷	6
○	Moscato di Siracusa Solacium '02	🍷🍷	6
○	Moscato di Siracusa Vigna di Mela '02	🍷🍷	7
○	Cyane '02	🍷	4

ADRAGNA
VIA REGINA ELENA, 4
91100 TRAPANI
TEL. 092326401
E-MAIL: classica@classica.it

Roberto Adragna's family estate extends over the slopes of Mount Erice, which is where he grows the cabernet and merlot for Roccagiglio '01. It has a broad nose of ripe fruit, concentration and complexity. Also good is the round, mouthfilling Chardonnay '02, which has elegant tropical fruit.

●	Roccagiglio '01	🍷🍷	6
○	Chardonnay '02	🍷🍷	5
●	Nero d'Avola '02	🍷	4

CENTONZE
C.DA FONTANELLE OSPEDALETTO
VIA ERICE FORESTE, 19
91100 TRAPANI
TEL. 0923557513

Giovanni Centonze and his children, Nicola and Carla, are all oenologists. They made a great Guide debut. Luce e Colori '02, from sangiovese and nero d'Avola, is delicious and powerful, yet smooth on the palate. Also nice is the varietal, deep Nero d'Avola '01, and indeed the rest of the range.

●	Luce e Colori Rosso '02	🍷🍷	3*
●	Nero d'Avola '01	🍷🍷	4
●	Luce e Colori Bianco '02	🍷	3

TERRE DI SHEMIR
LOC. GUARRATO
91100 TRAPANI
TEL. 0923865323
E-MAIL: info@casesparse.it

Eclectic Swiss globetrotter, journalist and producer of great olive oils, Wolfango Jezek is now confirmed as an honorary Sicilian winemaker. Selvaggio Rosso, from nero d'Avola, syrah and petit verdot, is seductive, with nice structure and notable elegance. Ispirazione '01, from inzolia, is good.

●	Selvaggio Rosso '01	🍷🍷	6
○	Ispirazione '01	🍷	5

SARDINIA

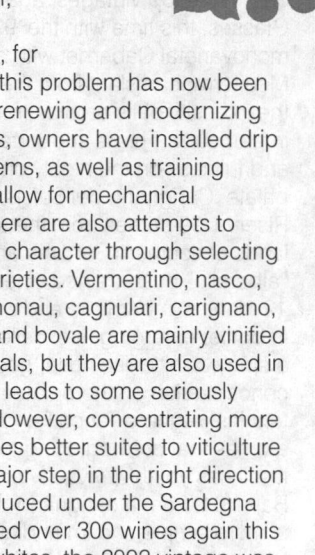

Vitality on the Sardinian wine front is on the increase, as is the quality of the wines. If in the past, outcomes depended on the weather, especially the sparse rainfall, for many estates this problem has now been overcome. In renewing and modernizing their vineyards, owners have installed drip irrigation systems, as well as training systems that allow for mechanical harvesting. There are also attempts to enhance wine character through selecting indigenous varieties. Vermentino, nasco, nuragus, cannonau, cagnulari, carignano, monica, girò and bovale are mainly vinified as monovarietals, but they are also used in blends, which leads to some seriously good wines. However, concentrating more on the subzones better suited to viticulture would be a major step in the right direction for wines produced under the Sardegna DOC. We tasted over 300 wines again this year. For the whites, the 2002 vintage was mediocre at best. The reds were more interesting, though, partly because most were not from this vintage. There are also several new, small estates, coyly beginning to release some promising, characterful wines on the market. Worthy of note, not to mention stemware, are Mura and Depperu with their Vermentino di Sardegna offerings; Naitana, Columbu and Porcu with Malvasia di Bosa and Malvasia della Planargia; Perda Rubia and Arcadu with Cannonau; and Su Baroni with the red of the same name. The established greats who performed well include Sella & Mosca, who won a further Three Glasses, as did Argiolas, with its habitually starry Turriga, and the Cantina Sociale di Santadi co-operative with Latinia. As before, right at the top of the list of wines that went into the finals come the extraordinary Canayli and Piras from the Cantina Sociale di Gallura, without doubt the winery that offers the best value for money on the island. Mancini, with the excellent red Saccaia, and Soletta, with Cannonau di Sardegna Firmadu, are both making very good wines, and improvements continue to come from Pala, Deiana and Pedra Majore, each now producing a diversified, good-quality range. Cherchi has taken a leap forward with Vermentino Tuvaoes and the Cagnulari and Luzzana reds. Gabbas, too, has put everything into cannonau-based reds, most notably Arbeskia, which nearly picked up Three Glasses. The reds from the Cantina Sociale di Dorgali, Cannonau Le Ghiaie from Meloni, Cannonau from Loi and Monica Duca di Mandas from Trexenta are all top notch. Most noteworthy of the new wines are the red Yanna from the Villa di Quartu estate and the Cannonau di Capo Ferrato wines from Castiadas. In the dessert wine sector, we have Angialis from Argiolas, Dolce Valle from Soletta and Vernaccia di Oristano Antico Gregori from Contini, these too almost at Three Glasses level.

ALGHERO (SS)

ALGHERO (SS)

CANTINA SOCIALE
SANTA MARIA LA PALMA
LOC. SANTA MARIA LA PALMA
07041 ALGHERO (SS)
TEL. 079999008 - 079999044
E-MAIL: vini@santamarialapalma.it

After nearly half a century of existence, this co-operative has managed to group together over 300 members who farm around 630 hectares of vineyard in total, much of it destined for DOC wine. Attention is mainly concentrated on Vermentino and Cannonau, although in recent years we have had pleasant surprises from innovative varieties such as chardonnay and sauvignon, as well as the indigenous cagnulari. The latest arrival is barrique-fermented Vermentino di Sardegna Palmador '01, from grapes yielding lower than DOC regulation limits. A little dark in colour, its nose is broad and complex with oak still evident, then there is good impact on the palate, even though the acidity is attenuated by its softness. The other whites are good, too, especially Alghero Chardonnay '01. It's not as good as last year's edition but is attractive on the nose and immediate on the palate. The simple, well-typed, traditional Vermentino di Sardegna wines, I Papiri '02 and Aragosta '02, both earned One Glass. The reds came out slightly better overall. Whereas Cannonau di Sardegna '00 does not have great intensity on the nose, it is clean and fairly long on the palate. The classic Cannonau di Sardegna Le Bombarde '02 is one of the winery's most enticing reds, especially when value for money is taken into account. It's a little closed on the nose, but the uncomplicated palate has attractive vegetal notes.

TENUTE SELLA & MOSCA
LOC. I PIANI
07041 ALGHERO (SS)
TEL. 079997700
E-MAIL: sella-mosca@alghero.it

For some years now, Sella & Mosca has been working over the 600-odd hectares of vineyard, confirming that the winery is modern, dynamic and forward-looking, but without losing sight of tradition and the past. Marchese di Villamarina, produced only in the top vintages, again won Three Glasses, this time with the '99. It is a monovarietal Cabernet with a Mediterranean slant from the breadth and the intensity of its aromas, morello cherry in particular. This is supported by warmth and fullness on the highly characterful palate. Carignano del Sulcis Terremare Riserva '99 comes from the sun-baked lands of southern Sardinia and from "alberello" bush-trained vines. It is given 12 months in barrique and a further year in bottle, emerging in excellent form, with a spicy, vanilla-like nose, good fruit concentration on the palate and soft tannins. Alghero Tanca Farrà '00 is rich in aromas that are beginning to develop, yet it still has youthful vivacity on the palate. Raim '01, from a carignano-based blend, is more simple and immediate. Moving on to the whites, we found both the full, pervasive Le Arenarie '02, a good Sauvignon with a Sardinian twist, and Vermentino di Gallura Monteoro '02, rich on the nose and soft on the palate. Both, though, could do with a little more bottle age. One step down, but still attractive, comes Alghero Terre Bianche Torbato '02 which has aromas of apple and tropical fruits. Vermentino di Sardegna La Cala '02 is good but not as attractive as the previous vintage.

○ Vermentino di Sardegna Palmador '01	♟♟	5
● Cannonau di Sardegna '00	♟	3
● Alghero Cagnulari '01	♟	4
○ Alghero Chardonnay '01	♟	4
● Cannonau di Sardegna Le Bombarde '02	♟	4
○ Vermentino di Sardegna Aragosta '02	♟	3
○ Vermentino di Sardegna I Papiri '02	♟	3
○ Alghero Chardonnay '00	♟♟	4
● Alghero Cagnulari '00	♀	4
● Cannonau di Sardegna Le Bombarde '01	♀	3

● Alghero Marchese di Villamarina '99	♟♟♟	6
○ Alghero Le Arenarie '02	♟♟	3
○ Vermentino di Gallura Sup. Monteoro '02	♟♟	4
● Alghero Tanca Farrà '00	♟	4
● Raim '01	♟	3
○ Alghero Torbato Terre Bianche '02	♟	3
○ Vermentino di Sardegna La Cala '02	♟	3*
● Alghero Marchese di Villamarina '92	♟♟♟	7
● Alghero Marchese di Villamarina '93	♟♟♟	7
● Alghero Marchese di Villamarina '95	♟♟♟	7
● Alghero Marchese di Villamarina '97	♟♟♟	6
● Alghero Tanca Farrà '99	♟♟	4

ARZACHENA (SS)

CAPICHERA
S.S. ARZACHENA - S. ANTONIO KM. 6
07021 ARZACHENA (SS)
TEL. 078980800 - 078980612
E-MAIL: capichera@tiscalinet.it

We are getting used to change with the Ragnedda brothers. Last year, all their whites were bottled as table wines but this year's Vigna 'Ngena '02 has returned to DOCG. It's not worth going into the pros and cons because the important thing is that this estate's wines are a major focus on the fine wine market. The '02 vintage of Capichera Vendemmia Tardiva was not produced and red Assajè was set for release in late autumn, and so was not available in time for our tastings. From those we could taste, we found the traditional Capichera '02 to be as impressive as ever in the breadth of its fruit-rich nose. The palate is full, soft and concentrated, and there is good length of flavour. Vermentino di Gallura Vigna 'Ngena '02 is fresh and more immediate, with captivating perfume and great drinkability both now and for the future. But although Vermentino is naturally the estate's battle-horse, for some years now the reds, too, have been claiming considerable attention. After casting regionwide in its selection process, the cellar opted to put the emphasis on carignano, a variety with great potential, and one much loved by those who go for blends or need to integrate other varieties. From its first arrival, the carignano-based Mantenghìa has aimed fairly high in the market place, both in terms of quality and price, which is in line with estate traditions. The '01 is an ensemble of spices and ripe fruits with some jam. The palate has body and fullness, as well as soft yet noticeable tannins, and it has the potential to develop and improve with time.

●	Mante'nghja '01	🍷🍷	8
○	Capichera '02	🍷🍷	7
○	Vermentino di Gallura Vigna 'Ngena '02	🍷🍷	6
○	Capichera V.T. '00	🍷🍷🍷	7
○	Capichera V.T. '01	🍷🍷	8
●	Mante'nghja '00	🍷🍷	8
○	Capichera '01	🍷🍷	7
○	Capichera Vigna 'Ngena '01	🍷🍷	6
●	Assajè Rosso '01	🍷	6

CABRAS (OR)

ATTILIO CONTINI
VIA GENOVA, 48/50
09072 CABRAS (OR)
TEL. 0783290806
E-MAIL: vinicontini@tiscalinet.it

The Contini estate is the undisputed leader in the province of Oristano and its attentions focus more and more on diversification of the range, away from Vernaccia di Oristano. This year, though, we tasted two great vintages of the estate's battle-horse, '93 and '86. The '93 is all simplicity and freshness, whereas the '86 fully reflects the wine's typical characteristics. The amber hue ushers in considerable breadth on the nose, with toasted hazelnuts predominating. The palate is soft, rounded out by the alcohol and glycerine, and long, signing off with a slightly bitterish finish. We were also greatly impressed by Antico Gregori, a Vernaccia from a blend of the best vintages of the past 50 years. It has a full, complex bouquet with almonds, chocolate and candied peel. As it opens in the mouth, it reveals its alcoholic power, which is kept in check by good acidity. This keeps the palate fresh and assures the wine's long ageing potential. Karmis '02, from vernaccia, is fresh, rounded and well fruited. From the reds, we tasted an excellent Cannonau di Sardegna Riserva '00. The aromas are nicely evolved, with attractive notes of oak, then the palate is full, showing well-gauged extract. The '99 Il Barile is not quite as good as the previous release. The nose is vegetal and balsamic, then the palate is full and soft with a bitterish finish. The '99 vintage of the traditional red Nieddera is uncomplicated, well made and very enjoyable.

●	Cannonau di Sardegna Ris. '00	🍷🍷	4
○	Vernaccia di Oristano Ris. '86	🍷🍷	6
●	Barrile '99	🍷🍷	7
○	Vernaccia di Oristano Antico Gregori	🍷🍷	7
○	Karmis '02	🍷	4
○	Vernaccia di Oristano '93	🍷	4
●	Nieddera Rosso '99	🍷	4
○	Vernaccia di Oristano '88	🍷🍷	3
○	Vernaccia di Oristano Ris. '90	🍷🍷	3
○	Vernaccia di Oristano Ris. '83	🍷🍷	4
●	Barrile '98	🍷🍷	4

CARDEDU (NU)

CASTIADAS (CA)

ALBERTO LOI
s.s. 125 CARDEDU
08040 CARDEDU (NU)
TEL. 070240866 - 078275807
E-MAIL: albertoloi@libero.it

CANTINA SOCIALE DI CASTIADAS
LOC. OLIA SPECIOSA
09040 CASTIADAS (CA)
TEL. 0709949004

The Loi siblings have 50 years of history behind them, all based on Cannonau. There's still plenty going on at the estate, though, for the Lois have rethought their vineyards and set up a new, more rational planting scheme. Now, they are updating their cellars. The estate extends over 50 hectares or so of hillside on the slopes of the Gennargentu mountains, and reach quite close to the sea. The winery is easily visible from the nearby road, which is known as the Orientale Sarda. There is a well-equipped tasting room with views over the vineyards to the sea. More than ten of the cellar's wines are based on cannonau, some with proportions of indigenous or innovative varieties. Tuvara '99, an IGT aged around two years in barrel, mainly barriques, then given another ten months in bottle, was most impressive. The nose is rich and complex, with spiciness and a sweet oakiness that dominates the jam and blackberry fruit. The palate is full, warm, rounded and lightly tannic, finishing long. Cannonau di Sardegna Jerzu Sa Mola '01 showed well, with its aromas of prune and its warm palate, while the other Cannonau di Sardegna, Jerzu Riserva Cardedo '00, is fresher and more immediate on both nose and palate. The "riserva", Alberto Loi '99, is a very decent red, although we were hoping for something more from it. There are aromas of ripe fruit and spiciness, and the extract and acidity on the palate have kept it youthful, giving ample further ageing potential. Astangia '01 is simpler but well styled, with aromas of blackberry.

This co-operative languished for many years, despite the significant potential of its wines. Probably a lack of ambition and good oenological decision-making were to blame. However, now that there is a new administration under chair, Michele Internicola, who has instated a more competent, dynamic technical set-up, the winery is regaining its right place in the regional scene. The production zone, Sarrabus, is in the southeast, one of the hottest and driest spots on the island. The subsoils retain humidity, however. The co-operative's 72 members jointly own around 350 hectares of vineyard, producing mostly cannonau from "alberello" bush-trained and low cane-trained vines. Sangiovese and carignano are grown in the area, and for some years now there have been experiments with varieties such as merlot and cabernet, to excellent effect. The best of the range, according to our tastings, is Parolto '00, a red IGT from 70 per cent cannonau with equal parts of cabernet and carignano. The nose is rich, with an intense streak of balsam and vegetal hints. The palate, too, is lively and balanced, despite powerful structure buoyed up by high alcohol. Cannonau di Sardegna Capo Ferrato '01 is also impressive for its aromas of Mediterranean scrubland and, again, balsamic notes. The palate is concentrated, full and soft, with an attractive finish. We also awarded Two Glasses to the '00 Riserva. There are strong floral notes of eucalyptus on the nose and it has a fleshy, harmonious palate. The winery is the sole producer of Cannonau di Sardegna under the subzone denomination Capo Ferrato.

● Tuvara '99	🍷🍷	6
● Cannonau di Sardegna Jerzu		
Cardedo Ris. '00	🍷	4
● Astangia '01	🍷	5
● Cannonau di Sardegna Jerzu		
Sa Mola '01	🍷	3
● Cannonau di Sardegna Jerzu		
Alberto Loi Ris. '99	🍷	5
● Tuvara '98	🍷🍷	6
● Astangia '99	🍷🍷	4
● Cannonau di Sardegna		
Sa Mola Rubia '00	🍷	3
○ Leila '01	🍷	4
● Cannonau di Sardegna		
Alberto Loi Ris. '98	🍷	4
● Cannonau di Sardegna Cardedo Ris. '99	🍷	4

● Cannonau di Sardegna		
Capo Ferrato Ris. '00	🍷🍷	4*
● Parolto '00	🍷🍷	4*
● Cannonau di Sardegna		
Capo Ferrato '01	🍷🍷	3*

CODRONGIANOS (SS)

DOLIANOVA (CA)

TENUTE SOLETTA
LOC. SIGNOR'ANNA
07040 CODRONGIANOS (SS)
TEL. 079435067
E-MAIL: tenutesoletta@libero.it

CANTINE DI DOLIANOVA
LOC. SANT'ESU
S.S. 387, KM. 17,150
09041 DOLIANOVA (CA)
TEL. 070744101 - 07074410226
E-MAIL: cantinedolianova@tiscalinet.it

Development continues apace at the Soletta siblings' newish estate, just a few kilometres from Sassari. They produce a fairly limited, but ever improving, range of wines from a few dozen hectares of vineyard that is almost like a sample collection, so large is the number of varieties cultivated. The real excitement of the range comes from the moscato-based Dolce Valle '00, aged two years and given a further few months in bottle. It not only fully merits Two Glasses but is one of the best sweet wines on the island. The aromas of flowers, dried fruit, honey and Mediterranean scrubland, are deep and broad. The palate is full, warm, full of character, doesn't cloy and has a long, clean finish. Cannonau di Sardegna Firmadu '00 is also first-rate, confirming that the '00 vintage was really excellent at Soletta. The nose has an array of vegetal and herby aromas that return on the well-structured palate, the tannic impact is moderate and the finish clean. Cannonau di Sardegna Riserva '98 is simpler, but has similar style on the nose. It does, however, show more acidity and astringency on the palate, and the tannins are still green. On the white front, One Glass goes to Vermentino di Sardegna '02. Aged in barrique for several months, it integrates fruit and vanilla on the nose, then the palate has good structure and appealing zestiness.

This winery just outside Cagliari always provides a broad, well-diversified range and every year there is something new, whether it be wines or presentation. The names they choose, though, Terresicci, Montesicci, Prendas and Perlas, for example, might possibly be confusing for non-Sardinian Italians. There are also separate lines for restaurants, wine shops and wholesalers. Whites predominate, although we also found excellent potential for reds from our tastings. The white Montesicci '02 is again impressive for the richness of its aromas and its depth on the palate. Best of the reds was Cannonau di Sardegna Blasio Riserva '00, with its concentrated blackberry nose and its full, soft palate. Terresicci '01, from barbera sarda with a little syrah and montepulciano, showed less well but is nevertheless lightly spicy, balanced and well styled. Monica di Sardegna Arenada '01 and Cannonau di Sardegna Anzenas '01 are both well made and well typed. The pink Sibiola is as attractive as ever, with fresh aromas that sneak up on you. It is without doubt one of the best on the island. The traditional whites are dominated by Vermentino di Sardegna. Naeli '02 has uncomplicated, youthful drinkability, whereas Prendas '02 is fuller and better structured. The Prendas also has some affinities, over and above the name, with Nuragus di Cagliari Perlas '02, which offers an intense nose and a fresh, zesty palate.

● Cannonau di Sardegna		
Firmadu '00	🍷🍷	3*
○ Dolce Valle Moscato Passito '00	🍷🍷	4
○ Vermentino di Sardegna '02	🍷	4
● Cannonau di Sardegna Ris. '98	🍷	4
● Cannonau di Sardegna Ris. '97	🍷	4

● Cannonau di Sardegna		
Blasio Ris. '00	🍷🍷	4
○ Montesicci '02	🍷🍷	4
● Cannonau di Sardegna		
Anzenas '01	🍷	3
● Monica di Sardegna Arenada '01	🍷	3*
● Terresicci '01	🍷	6
○ Nuragus di Cagliari Perlas '02	🍷	2*
⊙ Sibiola Rosato '02	🍷	3*
○ Vermentino di Sardegna Naeli '02	🍷	4
○ Vermentino di Sardegna		
Prendas '02	🍷	3
○ Montesicci '01	🍷🍷	4
● Falconaro '00	🍷🍷	5
○ Moscato di Cagliari '99	🍷🍷	4

DORGALI (NU)

CANTINA SOCIALE DORGALI
VIA PIEMONTE, 11
08022 DORGALI (NU)
TEL. 078496143
E-MAIL: info@c.s.dorgali.com

After the efforts made over some years now to improve wine quality, this co-operative has regained a full entry. It remains an important benchmark, not just for the quantities it produces, but for the image of the cannonau grape in general. Cannonau-based wines predominate, despite the influx of more innovative varieties, and there are also robust proportions of cannonau in many of the local IGT wines. It was, in fact, in the IGT category that we found the winery's two most impressive products, both of which gained Two Glasses. Fuìli '00 has a very rich nose brimming with fruit and vanilla. There is initial softness and roundness on the palate, with light tannins, and a bitterish tang on the finish that helps maintain the length. Norìolo '00 has lively, vegetal aromas that also come through on the palate. Its freshness, softness, fine balance and harmony make it good to drink right through a meal, even with strongly flavoured foods. Another IGT is the well-styled, still youthful Filieri Rosso '02, which has red berry fruitiness. We awarded it One Glass, as we did Cannonau di Sardegna Vigna di Isalle '01. This has a clean, ripe fruits nose, fullness on the palate, good tannins and a bitterish finish.

JERZU (NU)

ANTICHI PODERI JERZU
VIA UMBERTO I, 1
08044 JERZU (NU)
TEL. 078270028
E-MAIL: antichipoderi@tiscalinet.it

The changes that have recently taken place at this co-operative have borne fruit. From a set-up where sugar was the only criterion, there has been steady movement towards selection, particularly in the vineyard. It is also true that the best wines often come from the toughest soils. Because at Ogliastra, the coastal strip apart, soils are impervious and many vineyards have been abandoned as growers find them too difficult to work. Those that remain are "alberello", or bush-trained, and give yields of 3,000 to 4,000 kilograms per hectare. The grapes ripen well, retaining good acidity and this is the base from which the winery is working. It has also dropped its "co-op" tag, taking the name Antichi Poderi Jerzu to make it appear more estate-like. Not all the wines are real crus but there is definitely far more attention being paid to grape selection. A good example is Cannonau di Sardegna Josto Miglior Riserva '99. It has a broad array of aromas, centred on vanilla and blackberry, the palate is fairly round and full, and there is good nose-palate harmony. The other Cannonau, Chuerra '99, is on the same lines, but has more upfront alcohol. Radames, a cannonau-based IGT with some carignano and cabernet, offers more, since the other two grapes, which are not typical of the area, often impart greater elegance and finesse to cannonau. The '99 vintage has stepped up a gear. The rich nose gives jam, with spice and ripe plum, then in the mouth it tends to roundness, and is warm and long, leaving the palate clean and dry. Also good is the still young, fresh Cannonau di Sardegna '00.

● Fuìli '00	♟♟	5
● Norìolo '00	♟♟	5
● Cannonau di Sardegna		
V. di Isalle '01	♟	3
● Filieri Rosso '02	♟	4
● Fuìli '98	♟♟	5
● Fuìli '99	♟♟	5
● Cannonau di Sardegna		
V. di Isalle '99	♀	3
● Cannonau di Sardegna		
V. di Isalle '00	♀	3

● Radames '99	♟♟	5
● Cannonau di Sardegna '00	♟	4
● Cannonau di Sardegna		
Ris. Chuerra '99	♟	5
● Cannonau di Sardegna		
Riserva Josto Miglior '99	♟	5
● Cannonau di Sardegna		
Ris. Chuerra '97	♟♟	4
● Cannonau di Sardegna		
Riserva Josto Miglior '98	♟♟	4
● Cannonau di Sardegna		
Marghìa '98	♀	4
● Radames '98	♀	4
● Cannonau di Sardegna		
Ris. Chuerra '98	♀	4

MONTI (SS)

MONTI (SS)

PEDRA MAJORE
VIA ROMA, 106
07020 MONTI (SS)
TEL. 078943185
E-MAIL: pedramajore@tiscalinet.it

CANTINA SOCIALE DEL VERMENTINO
VIA SAN PAOLO, 1
07020 MONTI (SS)
TEL. 078944012 - 078944631
E-MAIL: cantina@vermentinomonti.it

The Pedra Majore estate, owned by the Isoni family, was set up quite recently. All it took was for Giovanni Battista, a noted politician with a great love of wine, to show his determination to make his mark in this none too easy sector, for the brothers and sisters joined him. They went straight for quality, hiring as consultant a professional who has no need of introduction, Donato Lanati. Rightly convinced that it's the vines that make the wine, Lanati was free to pick his vineyards not just from position and the composition of the soil, but also by their site climate. The over-riding aim is to maximize what the local traditional varieties have to offer. The early years could be considered experimental. So far Vermentino di Sardegna Superiore Hysonj '02 is the most satisfying of the wines, partly thanks to the finesse of its aromas, but more for its structure and the harmonious softness of the palate. The enticing Vermentino di Gallura I Graniti '02, the estate's war-horse, is a touch simpler. Vermentino di Sardegna Le Conche '02 is clean and well typed, with lively aromas. Red Murighessa '02, from a well-judged blend of cannonau, carignano, syrah and other local grapes, has particular potential. It ages briefly in pre-used small oak casks, and has several months in bottle before release. Its main appeal is its youthful drive, with blackberry-like fruit and zestiness on the palate. Mirju, from "extra ripe" moscato grapes, as the label declares, is most impressive. The nose is broad and intense, with ripe fruit and honey, then the palate is soft, warm and long.

In quantity terms, this winery, between Gallura and Logudoro, is one of the most important in northern Sardinia. Its members' lands are mostly granite-based and fertile, making them particularly suitable for Vermentino, which is produced in various styles. Vermentino di Gallura Funtanaliras is always first class and the '02 has lively aromas recalling tropical fruits, and a soft, warm palate with a slightly bitterish finish. Vermentino di Gallura Aghiloia '02, while not exceptional, comes closest in style to the traditions of the zone. Its nose is a little almondy and there is considerable alcoholic power on a palate that still maintains balance with the acidity. Its less ambitious stablemate, S'Eleme '02, is simpler and more immediate, with attractive, delicate aromas. The range of reds increased some years ago. The one most characteristic of the area is Abbaìa, from a blend of cannonau, malaga, pascale and monica. The '02 is balanced and harmonious with medium structure, and has still-youthful aromas of red berry fruits. The characterful Galana '99, in theory the winery's main product, comes from a broad blend of cabernet sauvignon, sangiovese, carignano, cagnulari and other red grapes. It has fruit and spice amalgamated with sweet oakiness on the nose, and is soft and fairly well balanced on the palate, lacking only a little length. Cannonau di Sardegna Tamara '00 is attractive in its heady, slightly herbaceous nose and its fresh, harmonious, even palate that shows good body.

O Vermentino di Gallura Sup. Hysonj '02	♟♟	5
O Mirju Passito	♟♟	5
● Murighessa '02	♟	4
O Vermentino di Gallura I Graniti '02	♟	4
O Vermentino di Sardegna Le Conche '02	♟	3
O Vermentino di Gallura I Graniti '00	♟♟	3*
O Vermentino di Gallura Hysonj '01	♟♟	4*
O Vermentino di Gallura I Graniti '01	♟♟	3*

O Vermentino di Gallura Funtanaliras '02	♟♟	5
● Cannonau di Sardegna Tamara '00	♟	5
● Abbaìa '02	♟	2*
O Vermentino di Gallura S'Eleme '02	♟	2
O Vermentino di Gallura Sup. Aghiloia '02	♟	3
● Galana '99	♟	6
● Abbaìa '01	♟	2*
● Galana '98	♟	6
● Cannonau di Sardegna Tamara '99	♟	4

NUORO

GIUSEPPE GABBAS
VIA TRIESTE, 65
08100 NUORO
TEL. 078431351 - 078433745

OLBIA (SS)

PIERO MANCINI
LOC. CALA SACCAIA
07026 OLBIA (SS)
TEL. 078950717
E-MAIL: poero.mancini@tiscalinet.it

"Chi fa per se fa per tre" is an old Italian proverb meaning roughly "If you want something done well do it yourself". And it's true. Giuseppe Gabbas could shout it from the rooftops, now that he is vinifying his own wines in his own new cellar, due to be fully operational by the end of 2003. Around the cellar lie 15 hectares or so of vineyard, mainly cannonau, which on these deep, granite-based soils produces its most classic characteristics. The natural aridity here is exacerbated by the altitude and where things become extreme irrigation is used. The new consultant is Lorenzo Landi from Tuscany, a red wine specialist. The range showed very well indeed and Arbeskia '00 came very close to Three Glasses. Sourced from cannonau with small amounts of sangiovese, cabernet and merlot, it is released after a year in barrique and a further year in bottle. The breadth and complexity on the nose is impressive, with jam, oak toast and tobacco, then the palate shows warm and mouthfilling, with great body, hardly perceptible tannins and a long, clean finish. Cannonau di Sardegna Lillovè '02, though still young, showed better than the previous vintage. The fruity nose with its vegetal hints is attractive, and the palate is soft and full, but still lively with well-judged tannins. Red Avra '01, from grapes left to dry on the vine in the traditional manner, is most pleasing. It has aromas of raisined grapes and cooked plums. The structure is solid and well supported by acidity and residual sugars.

The character of this estate is gradually becoming better defined. There is increasing attention to provenance, not because of fashion but in acknowledgement of the fact that soil and climate determine individuality. This was one of the objectives of Piero Mancini, the winery's founder, and his plans and aims are now being put into effect by his children, led by Alessandro. The vineyards, which lie in various parts of the Gallura zone, such as Cucaione, Montelittu and Balaiana, already stand out clearly. Although much of the output is white, Vermentino in particular, there is growing interest in the reds. The '01 Saccaia, for example, from cannonau, cabernet sauvignon and merlot, has again scored well, and gains Two Glasses. The broad, pervasive nose discloses morello cherry and ripe plum, then it is full and fleshy on the palate, with soft tannins and a clean, long finish. Cannonau di Sardegna '01 is also good, but slimmer and with an evolved nose, yet possibly still too young given its marked tannins. Vermentino di Gallura Saraìna '02 stands out among the whites, with a well-fruited nose and mineral notes on both nose and palate. Cucaione '02 is simpler with delicate aromas of almond trees and a fresh, clean palate. The straight Vermentino di Sardegna '02 and the rosé Colli del Limbara Montepino '02 are both attractive and well styled, and merit One Glass each.

● Arbeskia '00	▼▼	5
● Avra '01	▼▼	4
● Cannonau di Sardegna Lillové '02	▼▼	4
● Dule '00	▽▽	4
● Arbeskia '99	▽▽	5
● Dule '01	▽▽	4
● Avra '00	▽	4
● Cannonau di Sardegna Lillovè '01	▽	4

● Saccaia '01	▼▼	3*
● Cannonau di Sardegna '01	▼	4
⊙ Montepino Colli del Limbara '02	▼	4
○ Vermentino di Gallura Cucaione '02	▼	4
○ Vermentino di Gallura Saraina '02	▼	5
○ Vermentino di Sardegna '02	▼	2*
● Saccaia '00	▽▽	3*
● Cannonau di Sardegna '00	▽	3
○ Vermentino di Gallura Cucaione '01	▽	3
○ Vermentino di Gallura Saraina '01	▽	4

SANTADI (CA)

CANTINA SOCIALE DI SANTADI
VIA SU PRANU, 12
09010 SANTADI (CA)
TEL. 0781950127 - 0781953007
E-MAIL: pgserafini@cantinadisantadi.it

We are happy to confirm that there is no single wine that symbolizes this estate, since every year there is more than one Three Glass candidate. This year, it is Latinia '01 that wins the honours. The winery's only dessert wine, made solely from nasco grapes left to dry on the vine and aged briefly in four year old barriques, Nasco is not an aromatic variety but still offers great intensity and richness on the nose. There are dried fruits and fruit in syrup with touches of vanilla, then the palate is sweet but not cloying, thanks to notable acidity which, together with the alcohol and glycerine, gives finesse and elegance. Terre Brune '99, a wine of great structure and harmony of flavour, made it to the final taste-offs. It shows ripe fruit and dried flowers on the nose, while softness marks out the palate. Araja '01, a harmonious, balanced red, based on carignano with a little sangiovese, is excellent, as is the fresh, fruity Nuragus di Cagliari Petraia '02 and the softer, more fleshy Vermentino di Sardegna Cala Silente '02, which has a long, clean finish. All deserved their Two Glasses. Carignano Rocca Rubia Riserva '00 is still young, with a morello cherry nose and a tannic palate, but should improve well with age. Grotta Rossa '01, full and structured with a slightly bitterish finish, is along the same lines. The '02 Monica di Sardegna Antigua is as attractive as ever, with delicate, youthful, ripe fruit aromas followed by fair structure and soft tannins that leave the mouth clean. Villa Solais '02 merits One Glass for its attractive flavours and enticing aromas.

SANT'ANTIOCO (CA)

SARDUS PATER
VIA RINASCITA, 46
09017 SANT'ANTIOCO (CA)
TEL. 0781800274 - 078183937
E-MAIL: cantine@cantinesarduspater.com

This potential of this winery, which for too long had to work vast quantities of fruit that ended up in other regions of Italy, is at last beginning to emerge. The current administration has decided to turn the page and is engaged in giving the area's wines the image they deserve, bringing in younger staff, in both sales and winemaking. Recent tastings have revealed the extent of the improvements. Carignano del Sulcis Issolus '01 is the most impressive of the reds. It is intense and pervasive on its wild berry fruit nose. The palate is very soft and balanced. Sulky '99, from carignano with some cabernet and syrah, is also very good. Its nose is fairly intense but the wine really comes to life on the full, even palate, which has marked tannin and acidity, important signs that it will develop and improve with age. Monica di Sardegna Insula '01 has good style and is well made with red berry fruit aromas and a pleasingly soft, lively palate. We have left Naam '01 to last. Its name in Phoenician means good, or attractive, and it is from 100 per cent moscato. There are intense aromas of very ripe fruit, then plentiful alcohol, glycerine and residual sugars lead to a powerful palate which is nonetheless refined, elegant and long.

	Wine	Rating	Score
○	Latinia '01	🍷🍷🍷	5
●	Carignano del Sulcis Sup. Terre Brune '99	🍷	7
●	Araja '01	🍷🍷	4
○	Nuragus di Cagliari Pedraia '02	🍷🍷	3*
○	Vermentino di Sardegna Cala Silente '02	🍷🍷	4*
●	Carignano del Sulcis Rocca Rubia Ris. '00	🍷	5
●	Carignano del Sulcis Grotta Rossa '01	🍷	3
●	Monica di Sardegna Antigua '02	🍷	3*
○	Vermentino di Sardegna Villa Solais '02	🍷	3*
●	Terre Brune '94	🍷🍷🍷	6
○	Latinia '99	🍷🍷🍷	4*
●	Carignano del Sulcis Sup. Terre Brune '98	🍷🍷🍷	6

	Wine	Rating	Score
●	Carignano del Sulcis Issolus '01	🍷🍷	3*
○	Naam '01	🍷🍷	5
●	Sulky '99	🍷🍷	6
●	Monica di Sardegna Insula '01	🍷	3
●	Carignano del Sulcis Ris. '98	🍷🍷	4
●	Sulky '98	🍷🍷	5
●	Carignano del Sulcis Issolus '00	🍷	3

SELARGIUS (CA)

MELONI VINI
VIA GALLUS, 79
09047 SELARGIUS (CA)
TEL. 070852822
E-MAIL: info@meloni-vini.com

Meloni Vini has over a century of history behind it and you can be sure that there has been no shortage of wine passing through this cellar. We make this point because for years output has been very high as the winery's direction has been towards gaining large market share, both in Italy and abroad. Currently there are about ten different lines, from wines in tetrapak to those for restaurants. There is even an organic range. From the many wines that we tasted Cannonau di Sardegna Le Ghiaie again stood out. The '99 is better than the '98 on the nose. It is fuller, giving oak, tobacco and liquorice, and there is also good structure and balance on the palate. Girò di Cagliari Donna Jolanda '97 stands up well, too. It is a little closed on its ripe plum and blackberry nose, and shows better on the attractively soft palate. Malvasia di Cagliari '96 comes from the same line. Despite its age, it has retained liveliness in its secondary aromas while, on the palate, the acidity attenuates its sweetness without reducing its length. From the organic range, we particularly liked Monica di Sardegna Il Germoglio '01. Its aromas are fresh and a little vegetal. The palate is dry, zesty and fairly balanced. Vermentino di Sardegna Le Sabbie '02, also organic, has aromas of fresh flowers and a fruity palate that give enjoyable drinkability.

SENNORI (SS)

TENUTE DETTORI
LOC. BADDE NIGOLOSU
S.P. 29, KM 10
07046 SENNORI (SS)
TEL. 079514711
E-MAIL: info@tenutedettori.it

Young Alessandro Dettori puts great dedication and passion into making his wines. They are unusual in that they have little to do with "modern" wine, as it is understood by most consumers and producers. Alessandro gets grapes of great concentration from his more than 100-year-old "alberello" bush-trained vines, and he vinifies them absolutely traditionally. That's not all. His declared aim is to let the land and tradition speak, and to produce wine as his family has always done, using methods that he proudly describes as "archaic". The result of all this is a completely unique range of wines that are not easy to understand. On the one hand, they are highly concentrated, with great structure and alcohol, having been neither clarified nor filtered. On the other, Alessandro's non-interventionist attitude, and his desire to let nature run its course, means that some of them show marked tendencies towards oxidation and a series of imbalances that an educated palate cannot help noticing. That said, it has to be recognized that some of his wines, Cannonau Dettori in particular, can at times be truly inspiring. They take us back in time to a world where, for good or ill, it was nature, not man, that was at the centre of the universe. This year, we picked out Dettori Rosso '01, made solely from Cannonau. It has 16.5 per cent alcohol and over seven grams per litre residual sugar. An "extreme", complex wine, it is almost sweet, yet distinctly tannic, alcoholic and long. As its creator says, it is an excellent companion for moments of contemplation.

● Girò di Cagliari Donna Jolanda '97	🍷🍷	4
● Cannonau di Sardegna Le Ghiaie '99	🍷🍷	4*
● Monica di Sardegna Il Germoglio '01	🍷	3
○ Vermentino di Sardegna Le Sabbie '02	🍷	4
○ Malvasia di Cagliari Donna Jolanda '96	🍷	4
○ Nasco di Cagliari Donna Jolanda '94	🍷🍷	4
○ Moscato di Cagliari Donna Jolanda '95	🍷🍷	4
○ Moscato di Cagliari Donna Jolanda '98	🍷🍷	4

● Dettori Rosso '01	🍷🍷	8
● Dettori Rosso '00	🍷	8
● Tenores '00	🍷	8
● Tuderi '00	🍷	6
○ Dettori Bianco '01	🍷	5

SENORBI (CA)

CANTINA SOCIALE DELLA TREXENTA
V.LE PIEMONTE, 28
09040 SENORBI (CA)
TEL. 0709808863 - 0709809378
E-MAIL: trexentavini@tiscalinet.it

Work to raise quality, from the vineyards onwards, continues incessantly at this co-operative. The indigenous grapes that have already proved their worth when vinified as monovarietals remain the focus of attention, although there are some equally good wines being made using varieties from the mainland. Alter Nos is the best of the latest additions to the range. It is from cannonau and cabernet, aged over 18 months in barrique and given a further five or six months in bottle. The '00 has a broad, complex nose with aromas of raspberry jam, which soften its incisive vegetal and oaky notes. The palate is soft, full and nicely harmonious, sustained by good structure, and has a long, clean finish. That the winery uses barriques well is confirmed by Tanca Su Conti '98, which shows a spicy nose of black and morello cherry, then a full, mouthfilling, fruit-led palate with a slightly bitter finish. The other reds also showed well, both the zesty, well balanced Cannonau di Sardegna Baione '00 and Monica di Sardegan Duca di Mandas '02 with its still youthful, lively, vegetal aromas and its pleasant, harmonious palate. Among the whites, Sant'Efeis '01, from vermentino, chardonnay, sauvignon and nuragus, created with Alter Nos in honour of Cagliari's patron saint, is focused on elegance and softness. Vermentino di Sardegna Tanca Sa Contissa '02 is zippier and more traditional in style.

SERDIANA (CA)

ANTONIO ARGIOLAS
VIA ROMA, 56/58
09040 SERDIANA (CA)
TEL. 070740606 - 070743264
E-MAIL: argiolaspa@tin.it

No Sardinian estate has matched Argiolas. This tight-knit family has produced wines of quality for three generations and every year, we discover anew how much dedication goes into their wines. The jewel in the crown is Turriga, and the '99 thoroughly deserved its Three Glasses. It has a broad, complex nose with sweet oakiness, wild berry fruits and morello cherry. The palate is soft, tending to roundness, with well-judged tannins and a long, clean finish. The estate's other main red, the gutsy Korem '01, is also excellent, with good structure and finesse on the nose giving elegance and personality. We tasted the freshly bottled '02 vintages of Monica di Sardegna Perdera and Cannonau di Sardegna Costera because the '01s were already sold out. Both were clean, well made and charming. The Perdera is soft and balanced, and the Costera still young and a bit tannic. The huge care taken in the vineyards also means that excellent whites can be produced. Cerdeña '01 is certainly not an easy wine but it is fascinating, with great richness and depth on the nose, where the oak integrates well with vermentino's varietal aromas, then a fleshy, dense palate. The '02 Argiolas is good, but previous vintages have been better. From the more traditional whites, we went for Nuragus S'Elegas '02, for its nose in particular. The Vermentino Costamolino '02 is fresh and lively and the rosé Serralori '02 is good, too. The icing on the cake is the sweet Angialis '02, a concentrate of honey and dried fruits in a harmonious, elegant whole, which again came within a whisker of Three Glasses.

● Alter Nos '00	♟♟	6
● Tanca Su Conti '98	♟♟	5
● Cannonau di Sardegna Baione '00	♟	4
○ Sant'Efeis '01	♟	6
● Monica di Sardegna Duca di Mandas '02	♟	3*
○ Vermentino di Sardegna Tanca Sa Contissa '02		3
● Tanca Su Conti '96	♟♟	4
● Monica di Sardegna Duca di Mandas '00	♟♟	2*
● Monica di Sardegna Duca di Mandas '01	♟♟	2*
○ Moscato di Cagliari Simieri '01	♟♟	4

● Turriga '99	♟♟♟	8
○ Angialis '00	♟♟	7
○ Cerdeña '01	♟♟	8
● Korem '01	♟♟	6
● Cannonau di Sardegna Costera '02	♟♟	4*
● Monica di Sardegna Perdera '02	♟♟	4*
○ Nuragus di Cagliari S'Elegas '02	♟♟	3*
○ Vermentino di Sardegna Costamolino '02	♟♟	4*
○ Argiolas '02	♟	4
☉ Serralori Rosato '02	♟	3*
● Turriga '93	♟♟♟	7
● Turriga '94	♟♟♟	7
● Turriga '95	♟♟♟	7
● Turriga '97	♟♟♟	7
● Turriga '98	♟♟♟	8

SERDIANA (CA)

F.LLI PALA
VIA VERDI, 7
09040 SERDIANA (CA)
TEL. 070740284
E-MAIL: cantinapala@tiscalinet.it

This is a small winery with 50 years of history behind it and vineyards that run across the low hills of Parteolla and Trexenta, lands highly suited to viticulture. This makes for high potential but it's not, we feel, completely realized yet. Brothers Enrico and Mario Pala, admirably supported by manager Angius, have for some years been using a small cellar in the village for bottling. They have been aiming at quality, not quantity, and at building a good image for the traditional wines of this area, while keeping a watchful eye on market developments and requirements. Hence their two leading wines are IGTs, S'Arai and Entemari. We'll report on the '01 S'Arai next year as the estate wanted to give it longer in bottle before release. We support this decision as far too many estates rush to put wines on the market that are still too young and sharp. Entemari '02 is more ready, although still developing. The vegetal nose has good intensity but the palate is better, with alcohol and glycerine that give softness and power. Vermentino di Sardegna Crabilis '02 has a broad array of aromas, but again there is more satisfaction from the palate, which has balance and attractive freshness. Nuragus di Cagliari Salnico '02 is clean, with vegetal aromas and immediacy on the palate. The traditionally styled reds showed well. Cannonau di Sardegna Triente '02 is still young and heady, and the tannins make the palate a little edgy, and the Monica di Sardegna Elima '02 is simpler and more approachable.

SETTIMO SAN PIETRO (CA)

FERRUCCIO DEIANA
VIA GIALETO, 7
09040 SETTIMO SAN PIETRO (CA)
TEL. 070767960 - 070749117
E-MAIL: deiana.ferruccio@tiscalinet.it

The estate is at its second year of bottling but has a long, interesting history behind it. For many years, Ferruccio Deiana selected wines for wholesale markets in Italy and abroad. Now, his attractive winery, set in the vineyards of Parteolla, makes products of almost all types, apart from sparkling and slightly sparkling wines. The best results come from the whites, especially Pluminus '02, an IGT based on vermentino and chardonnay. An elegant nose with oak well integrated into the grape-derived aromas leads to an even more interesting palate of fullness and length that leaves the mouth clean and fresh. Vermentino di Sardegna Arvali '02 also won Two Glasses for its fruity appeal, which recalls the fine whites from Gallura, followed by a full, almondy palate. The other Vermentino di Sardegna, Donnikala '02, showed well, too. The nose is floral, clean and elegant, with some tropical fruits. These sensations are echoed on the palate, which leaves the mouth fresh and clean. The reds are promising, but still young. Cannonau di Sardegna Sileno '01 has good intensity on the nose, with blackberry and morello cherry, then grows in structure and harmony on the palate. Monica di Sardegna Karel '02 is very lively on both nose and palate, where acidity predominates. The sweet Oirad '02, from moscato, malvasia and nasco, has aromas of quince and cooked fruit, which are also perceptible on the palate, and long length. A retaste of the red '00 Ajana confirmed it as one of the most interesting wines on the island. We eagerly await the new vintage.

○ Entemari '02	♟♟	6
● Cannonau di Sardegna Triente '02	♟	4
● Monica di Sardegna Elima '02	♟	4
○ Nuragus di Cagliari Salnico '02	♟	4
○ Vermentino di Sardegna Crabilis '02	♟	4
● S'Arai '98	♟♟	5
○ Entemari '00	♟♟	4
○ Vermentino di Sardegna Crabilis '00	♟♟	3*
● S'Arai '99	♟♟	5
● S'Arai '00	♟♟	5
○ Vermentino di Sardegna Crabilis '01	♟♟	3*

● Monica di Sardegna Karel '02	♟♟	4
○ Pluminus '02	♟♟	7
○ Vermentino di Sardegna Arvali '02	♟♟	4*
● Cannonau di Sardegna Sileno '01	♟	4
○ Oirad '02	♟	6
○ Vermentino di Sardegna Donnikalia '02	♟	4
● Ajana '00	♟♟	7
● Cannonau di Sardegna Sileno '00	♟	4
● Monica di Sardegna Karel '01	♟	4

TEMPIO PAUSANIA (SS)

USINI (SS)

CANTINA SOCIALE GALLURA
VIA VAL DI COSSU, 9
07029 TEMPIO PAUSANIA (SS)
TEL. 079631241
E-MAIL: info@cantinagallura.it

GIOVANNI CHERCHI
LOC. SA PALA E SA CHESSA
VIA OSSI, 22
07049 USINI (SS)
TEL. 079380273
E-MAIL: vinicolacherchi@tiscalinet.it

For many years, we have been praising Dino Addis, the manager here. Not that we have anything against other oenologists, but working in a co-operative with so many members is not easy. Yet Addis has managed to mould members and staff into a team, turning out excellent wines at prices that are more than fair. The '02 was only a so-so vintage but on-going, stringent grape selection has brought some worthy results. Top of the bunch is Vermentino di Sardegna Superiore Canayli '02. It is extraordinarily balanced on the palate, despite powerful structure, and there are broad, intense aromas of tropical fruit with some almond. Piras '02, considered Canayli's "younger brother", also stood out. It is full and pervasive with floral aromas and an attractive palate giving almondy notes that hold right through to the finish. Balajana '02, a well-made wine in traditional style, scored similarly, with almond blossom on the nose and a fleshy, structured palate. Gemellae '02 and Mavriana '02, are also good. Both are Vermentino di Gallura wines and both are fresh and easy drinking. Campos '02 is one of the region's best rosés, with a seductive colour and a clean, fresh, cherry-like nose. Dolmen '99 stands out among the reds. There are red berry fruits and vegetal nuances on the nose, then the nebbiolo character emerges on the rich, concentrated palate, with its well-balanced tannins. The '02 Karana showed well, although it is not as good as last year's. We finish with the delicious, fresh, elegant Moscato di Tempio Pausania '02, which has well-judged sweetness and finishes long.

Giovanni Cherchi is now, apparently at least, just supervising activities at his winery, where his sons have taken over. However, like most older farmers, he is not used to standing and watching. Instead, he moves constantly between the vineyard and the new cellar, which is not yet completed, keeping his hand in and giving advice. Meanwhile, the wines are improving by leaps and bounds. The flagship remains Vermentino di Sardegna Tuvaoes. The '02 is particularly rich in fresh, clean aromas reminiscent of fine sauvignon, and it has considerable depth on a palate that is full, harmonious and long. Even the lesser version, Pigalva, although slimmer in structure, has attractive floral aromas and a pleasing freshness in the mouth. Luzzana has become a giant among the reds, the '01 even vying for Three Glasses. From a well-judged blend of cagnulari and cannonau, aged briefly in barrique, it derives strong vegetal and floral notes of geranium, a firm structure and good acid-tannin balance. Cagnulari's worth as a monovarietal is shown by the '02. Even though the vintage was not outstanding, the wine is still pleasing on the nose and soft on the palate. Cannonau di Sardegna '02 is also characterful, with a lively, perfumed nose and a fresh, zesty palate. We reckon these latest reds will fill out with more bottle age, but sadly commercial constraints mean that most consumers will drink them too young, and therefore never get full pleasure from them. That means the producer is denied full pleasure, as well.

○	Balajana '02	🍷🍷	4
○	Moscato di Tempio Pausania '02	🍷🍷	4
○	Vermentino di Gallura Piras '02	🍷🍷	3*
○	Vermentino di Gallura Sup. Canayli '02	🍷🍷	3*
●	Dolmen '99	🍷🍷	5
⊙	Campos Rosato del Limbara '02	🍷	2*
●	Nebbiolo dei Colli del Limbara Karana '02	🍷	2*
○	Vermentino di Gallura Gemellae '02	🍷	3*
○	Vermentino di Gallura Mavriana '02	🍷	2*
○	Vermentino di Gallura Sup. Canayli '01	🍷🍷	3*
○	Balajana '01	🍷🍷	4
○	Moscato di Tempio Pausania '01	🍷🍷	3
○	Vermentino di Gallura Piras '01	🍷🍷	4*

●	Luzzana '01	🍷🍷	6
○	Vermentino di Sardegna Tuvaoes '02	🍷🍷	5
●	Cagnulari '02	🍷	5
●	Cannonau di Sardegna '02	🍷	5
○	Vermentino di Sardegna Pigalva '02	🍷	4
○	Vermentino di Sardegna Boghes '00	🍷🍷	5
○	Vermentino di Sardegna Pigalva '01	🍷🍷	3*
○	Vermentino di Sardegna Tuvaoes '01	🍷🍷	4
●	Luzzana '00	🍷	5
●	Cagnulari '01	🍷	4

OTHER WINERIES

COLUMBU

VIA MARCONI, 1
08013 BOSA (NU)
TEL. 0785373380 - 0785359190
E-MAIL: rafaelcolumbu@tiscali.it

The Columbu range has been extended by the addition of a younger wine, Planaria Alvarega '02, which is fresh, fruity and easy drinking. Malvasia di Bosa '96 is rich and incisive on the nose, with a long finish evoking toasted hazelnuts and bitter almonds.

○ Planargia Alvarega '02	▼	5
○ Malvasia di Bosa '96	▼	6
○ Malvasia di Bosa '94	∇	5

GIGI PICCIAU

FRAZ. PIRRI - VIA ITALIA, 196
09134 CAGLIARI
TEL. 070560224
E-MAIL: picciau@tin.it

Gigi Picciau remains a producer of traditionally inclined wines that reflect their origins. His range includes a number of dessert wines, produced only in suitable vintages. From the most recent vintage, the '02, we tasted an attractive, fresh-tasting Vermentino di Sardegna.

○ Vermentino di Sardegna '02	▼	3
● Cannonau di Sardegna '99	∇	3

MURA

LOC. AZZANIDO, 1
07020 LOIRI PORTO SAN PAOLO (SS)
TEL. 078941070 - 078923929
E-MAIL: vinimura@tiscalinet.it

Enthusiasm is building up and quality improving at this small estate. Vermentino di Gallura Sienda '02 is traditional, with intense aromas and softness on the palate. Red Baja '01 has surprising intensity and harmony, plus marked aromas of blackberry and morello cherry, then a full palate.

● Baja '01	▼▼	6
● Vermentino di Gallura Sienda '02	▼	4
● Nebidu '01	∇	4
○ Vermentino di Gallura Sienda '01	∇	5

ANDREA DEPPERU

VIA GORIZIA 1
07025 LURAS (SS)
TEL. 079647314

The small Depperu estate is becoming a major focal point for Vermentino di Gallura production. The '02 is memorable, mainly for its breadth and its clean, fresh aromas on the nose. The palate is full and has great structure.

○ Vermentino di Gallura Sup. Saruinas '02	▼▼	4
○ Vermentino di Gallura Sup. Saruinas '00	∇∇	3*
○ Vermentino di Gallura Sup. Saruinas '01	∇	4

GIANVITTORIO NAITANA
VIA ROMA, 2
08010 MAGOMADAS (NU)
TEL. 078535333 - 03490801807

Naitana moves forward a step at a time in his never-ending search for ever greater quality in his Malvasia. He extracts from the grape a nectar of captivating aromas of flowers and ripe peaches, followed by a soft, warm and long palate.

○	Planargia Murapiscados '02	♟♟	5
○	Planargia Murapiscados '99	♟♟	4
○	Planargia Murapiscados '00	♟♟	5
○	Planargia Murapiscados '01	♟♟	5

SU BARONI
VIA ROMA, 48
09010 MASAINAS (CA)
TEL. 0781964844
E-MAIL: giancarlo.vacca@tiscali.it

A young estate of promise, especially for carignano-based reds. The flagship wine, Su Baroni '01, is quite extraordinary. Broad and intense on its fruity, vegetal nose; it shows good impact on the palate, which is warm and harmonious. The white Candiani '02, from vermentino, is good and very fresh.

●	Su Baroni '01	♟♟	5
○	Candiani '02	♟	4
●	Su Baroni '00	♟♟	5
○	Candiani '01	♟	3

F.LLI PORCU
LOC. SU E GIAGU
08019 MODOLO (NU)
TEL. 078535420

The Porcu siblings always manage to produce good Malvasia di Bosa, even in '98, which was not a great vintage for them. The aromas are almondy, with medium intensity, and there is good length of flavour.

○	Malvasia di Bosa '98	♟	5
○	Malvasia di Bosa '97	♟♟	3*

CANTINA SOCIALE IL NURAGHE
S.S. 131, KM 62
09095 MOGORO (OR)
TEL. 0783990285
E-MAIL: nuraghe@essenet.it

This co-operative has a great new offering in Sardegna Semidano Puisteris, one of the best '02 whites on the island. The nose is rich, herby and well fruited, and there is great structure and personality. Best of the reds is the attractive, but still youthful, Cannonau di Sardegna Vignaruja '02.

○	Sardegna Semidano Sup. Puisteris '02	♟♟	5
●	Cannonau di Sardegna Vignaruja '02	♟	4
●	Cannonau di Sardegna Vignaruja '01	♟	3

PERDARUBIA
VIA ASPRONI, 29
08100 NUORO
TEL. 0782615367
E-MAIL: info.perdarubia@tin.it

This small estate from the eastern coast, which has been producing Cannonau for over 50 years, returns to the Guide. The '00, though still young, has pervasive aromas of fruit and black cherry jam. It is tannic and warm on the palate, with good acidity, and should age well for some years.

●	Cannonau di Sardegna '00	♟	4

PISANU
VIA EMANUELA LOI, 10/A
09024 NURAMINIS (CA)
TEL. 0709143240
E-MAIL: pisanuvini@libero.it

This is the first Guide entry for this small estate in Cagliari's Campidano plain. There are two promising reds. Bizante '01, from cannonau and carignano, has aromas of ripe blackberry and is soft on the palate. Brunk'è '99, is solely from cannonau. It's vegetal on the nose and fresher in the mouth.

●	Bizante '01	♟	4
●	Cannonau di Sardegna Brunk'è Ris. '99		4

GOSTOLAI
VIA NINO BIXIO, 87
08025 OLIENA (NU)
TEL. 0784288417
E-MAIL: gostolai.arcadu@tiscalinet.it

A small estate with a fair range of cannonau-based wines. The sweet version, Su Gucciu '02, is very good, showing rich on the nose and soft in the mouth. Nepente di Oliena '02 is still young but nice on the nose, then full and ripely tannic on the palate. Puer Sed Formosus '01 is also pleasant.

● Su Gucciu '02	🍷🍷	4
● Puer sed Formosus '01	🍷	3
● Cannonau di Sardegna Nepente di Oliena '02	🍷	4

CANTINA COOPERATIVA DI OLIENA
VIA NUORO, 112
08025 OLIENA (NU)
TEL. 0784287509

This is one of the island's smallest co-operatives. It produces almost exclusively Cannonau di Sardegna with the Riserva, Corrasi, as the flagship. The '00 is very warm and full, with evolved notes of ripe fruit. Cannonau '02 is soft and similarly structured, but here the nose is still youthful.

● Cannonau di Sardegna Corrasi Nepente di Oliena Ris. '00	🍷	5
● Cannonau di Sardegna Nepente di Oliena '02	🍷	4

CANTINA DI QUARTU
VIA MARCONI, 489
09045 QUARTU SANT'ELENA (CA)
TEL. 070826033

This almost 80-year-old winery gains its first Guide profile. The zone is famous for dessert wines, but it also gives nice reds, like Monica di Sardegna Tuerra '01. The fresh, youthful nose has medium intensity and there is good nose-palate consistency. The Malvasia di Cagliari Nuscara '01 is good.

○ Malvasia di Cagliari Nuscara '01	🍷	4
● Monica di Sardegna Tuerra '01	🍷	3*

VILLA DI QUARTU
VIA GARIBALDI, 96
09045 QUARTU SANT'ELENA (CA)
TEL. 070820947 - 070826997
E-MAIL: villadiquartu@tiscali.it

This estate deserves more space for the range and quality of its wines. The new Yanna '00, from carignano and bovale, is excellent, with aromas of blackberry and plum, and a full, structured palate. Also good are the two Cepola wines, the '02 white and the '01 red. Check out the dessert wines, too.

● Yanna '00	🍷🍷	6
● Cepola Rosso '01	🍷	4
○ Cepola Bianco '02	🍷	4
○ Nasco di Cagliari Gutta'e Axina '00	🍷🍷	4

JOSTO PUDDU
VIA SAN LUSSORIO, 1
09070 SAN VERO MILIS (OR)
TEL. 078353329
E-MAIL: puddu.vini@tiscalinet.it

Terras '01, from nieddera, sangiovese and carignano, with a year's barrique ageing, is a fine newcomer from a winery better known for Vernaccia di Oristano. There are aromas of jam, oaky notes and good body. Vernaccia di Oristano '80, almondy on the nose and soft on the palate, is also excellent.

● Terras Rosso '01	🍷🍷	6
○ Vernaccia di Oristano '80	🍷🍷	6
● Monica di Sardegna Torremora '98	🍷	3
● Cannonau di Sardegna Antares '00	🍷	4

CANTINA SOCIALE DEL MANDROLISAI
C.SO IV NOVEMBRE
08038 SORGONO (NU)
TEL. 078460113
E-MAIL: cant.mandrolisai@tiscalinet.it

This co-operative lies in the heart of Sardinia and has considerable potential yet to be realized. The wine that exemplifies it is Mandrolisai Rosso Superiore, which shows nuances of sweet oak and cherry. The palate is full, a little astringent and has a lightly bitter undertone.

● Mandrolisai Rosso Sup. '99	🍷	4

IINDEX OF WINES

3 Carati, Avide	770
360 Ruber Capitae Rosso, Bosco del Merlo	288
50 & 50 Avignonesi e Capannelle, Avignonesi	542
50 & 50 Avignonesi e Capannelle, Capannelle	497
A. A. Bianco Abtei, Cant. Convento Muri-Gries	260
A. A. Bianco Beyond the Clouds, Castel Ringberg & Kastelaz Elena Walch	280
A. A. Bianco Helios, Graf Pfeil Weingut Kränzel	272
A. A. Bianco Mondevinum, Josef Sölva - Niklaserhof	270
A. A. Bianco Pallas, Castello Schwanburg	278
A. A. Bianco Passito Comtess St. Valentin, Cant. Prod. San Michele Appiano	258
A. A. Bianco Passito Dorado, Graf Pfeil Weingut Kränzel	272
A. A. Bianco Passito Peperum, Heinrich Plattner - Waldgries	263
A. A. Bianco Sandbichler, Cant. H. Lun	274
A. A. Bianco Vigna S. Michele, Hofstätter	281
A. A. Cabernet Baron Salvadori Ris., Cant. Prod. Nalles Niclara Magrè	277
A. A. Cabernet Briglhof, Josef Brigl	254
A. A. Cabernet Castel Schwanburg, Castello Schwanburg	278
A. A. Cabernet Freienfeld, Cant. Prod. Cortaccia	273
A. A. Cabernet Kirchhügel, Cant. Prod. Cortaccia	273
A. A. Cabernet Kössler & Ebner, Kössler - Praeclarus	255
A. A. Cabernet Lagrein Kastlet, Loacker Schwarzhof	261
A. A. Cabernet Lagrein Prestige Calldiv, Von Braunbach	280
A. A. Cabernet - Merlot, Georg Ramoser Untermoserhof	265
A. A. Cabernet Merlot Crescendo Ris., Tenuta Ritterhof	269
A. A. Cabernet Merlot Palestina, Hartmann Lentsch	284
A. A. Cabernet Mumelterhof, Cant. Prod. Santa Maddalena/Cant. di Bolzano	264
A. A. Cabernet Mumelterhof Ris., Cant. Prod. Santa Maddalena/Cant. di Bolzano	264
A. A. Cabernet Puntay, Erste & Neue	268
A. A. Cabernet Ris., Cant. Laimburg	282
A. A. Cabernet Ris., R. Malojer Gummerhof	261
A. A. Cabernet Ritsch, Anton Schmid - Oberrautner	266
A. A. Cabernet Sass Roà Ris., Cant. Laimburg	282
A. A. Cabernet Sauvignon, Andreas Berger -Thurnhof	259
A. A. Cabernet Sauvignon, Josephus Mayr - Erbhof Unterganzner	262
A. A. Cabernet Sauvignon, Heinrich Plattner - Waldgries	263
A. A. Cabernet Sauvignon Albertus Ris., Cant. H. Lun	274
A. A. Cabernet Sauvignon Castel Ringberg Ris., Castel Ringberg & Kastelaz Elena Walch	280
A. A. Cabernet Sauvignon Castel Schwanburg, Castello Schwanburg	278
A. A. Cabernet Sauvignon Griesbauerhof, Georg Mumelter	262
A. A. Cabernet Sauvignon Kastelt Ris., Cant. Prod. Colterenzio	258
A. A. Cabernet Sauvignon Lafoa, Cant. Prod. Colterenzio	258
A. A. Cabernet Sauvignon Maso Castello, Kettmeir	269
A. A. Cabernet Sauvignon Ris., Andreas Berger -Thurnhof	259
A. A. Cabernet Sauvignon Ris., Castello Schwanburg	278
A. A. Cabernet Sauvignon SelectArt Flora Ris., Cant. Prod. Cornaiano	256
A. A. Cabernet Sauvignon-Merlot Pfarrhof Ris., Cant. Viticoltori di Caldaro	271
A. A. Cabernet Sauvignon-Merlot Sagittarius, Graf Pfeil Weingut Kränzel	272
A. A. Cabernet Select Ris, Hans Rottensteiner	266
A. A. Cabernet St. Valentin, Cant. Prod. San Michele Appiano	258
A. A. Cabernet Tor di Lupo, Cant. Prod. Andriano	254
A. A. Cabernet-Lagrein Bautzanum, R. Malojer Gummerhof	261
A. A. Cabernet-Lagrein Bautzanum Ris., R. Malojer Gummerhof	261
A. A. Cabernet-Merlot Feld, Erste & Neue	268
A. A. Cabernet-Merlot Graf Von Meran, Cant. Prod. di Merano	276
A. A. Cabernet-Merlot Putz Ris., Heinrich & Thomas Rottensteiner	265
A. A. Cabernet-Merlot S. Pauls, Kössler - Praeclarus	255
A. A. Cabernet-Merlot Soma, Cant. Prod. Cortaccia	273
A. A. Chardonnay, Josef Brigl	254
A. A. Chardonnay, Graf Pfeil Weingut Kränzel	272
A. A. Chardonnay, Cant. Prod. Burggräfler	275
A. A. Chardonnay, Cant. Prod. di Merano	276
A. A. Chardonnay, Castello Rametz	285
A. A. Chardonnay, Hans Rottensteiner	266
A. A. Chardonnay, Von Braunbach	280
A. A. Chardonnay, Peter Zemmer - Kupelwieser	274
A. A. Chardonnay Altkirch, Cant. Prod. Colterenzio	258
A. A. Chardonnay Ateyon, Loacker Schwarzhof	261
A. A. Chardonnay Baron Salvadori, Cant. Prod. Nalles Niclara Magrè	277
A. A. Chardonnay Cardellino, Castel Ringberg & Kastelaz Elena Walch	280
A. A. Chardonnay Castel Turmhof, Tiefenbrunner	273
A. A. Chardonnay Cornell, Cant. Prod. Colterenzio	258
A. A. Chardonnay Doa, Cant. Laimburg	282
A. A. Chardonnay Felsenhof, Cant. Prod. Cortaccia	273
A. A. Chardonnay Goldegg, Cant. Prod. di Merano	276
A. A. Chardonnay Hausmannhof, Weingut Haderburg	279
A. A. Chardonnay Kleinstein, Cant. Prod. Santa Maddalena/Cant. di Bolzano	264
A. A. Chardonnay Kupelwieser, Peter Zemmer - Kupelwieser	274
A. A. Chardonnay Linticlarus, Tiefenbrunner	273
A. A. Chardonnay Maso Reiner, Kettmeir	269
A. A. Chardonnay Merol, Cant. Prod. San Michele Appiano	258
A. A. Chardonnay Palladium, K. Martini & Sohn	255
A. A. Chardonnay Passito Aurum Happacherhof, Maso Happacherhof - Istituto Tecnico Agrario	285
A. A. Chardonnay Puntay, Erste & Neue	268
A. A. Chardonnay Salt, Erste & Neue	268
A. A. Chardonnay Schwarzhaus, Stroblhof	284
A. A. Chardonnay Sel., Steinhauserhof	285
A. A. Chardonnay Select Art Flora, Cant. Prod. Cornaiano	256
A. A. Chardonnay St. Valentin, Cant. Prod. San Michele Appiano	258
A. A. Chardonnay Tiefenthaler, Cant. Prod. Burggräfler	275
A. A. Chardonnay Tor di Lupo, Cant. Prod. Andriano	254
A. A. Chardonnay Wadleith, Cant. Viticoltori di Caldaro	271
A. A. Chardonnay Zemmer, Peter Zemmer - Kupelwieser	274
A. A. Cuvèe Anna Castel Turmhof, Tiefenbrunner	273
A. A. Cuvée Linticlarus, Tiefenbrunner	273
A. A. Dorado, Graf Pfeil Weingut Kränzel	272
A. A. Erah, Weingut Haderburg	279
A. A. Gewürztramier Puntay, Erste & Neue	268
A. A. Gewürztramier Kleinstein, Cant. Prod. Santa Maddalena/Cant. di Bolzano	264
A. A. Gewürztraminer Amistar, Peter Sölva & Söhne	270
A. A. Gewürztraminer, Franz Haas	277
A. A. Gewürztraminer, Cant. Laimburg	282
A. A. Gewürztraminer, Cant. Prod. Burggräfler	275
A. A. Gewürztraminer, Cant. Prod. Colterenzio	258
A. A. Gewürztraminer, Tenuta Ritterhof	269
A. A. Gewürztraminer Albertus, Cant. H. Lun	274
A. A. Gewürztraminer Baron Salvadori, Cant. Prod. Nalles Niclara Magrè	277
A. A. Gewürztraminer Blaspichl, Weingut Haderburg	279
A. A. Gewürztraminer Brenntal, Cant. Prod. Cortaccia	273
A. A. Gewürztraminer Campaner, Cant. Viticoltori di Caldaro	271
A. A. Gewürztraminer Cancenai, Hans Rottensteiner	266
A. A. Gewürztraminer Castel Turmhof, Tiefenbrunner	273
A. A. Gewürztraminer Cornell, Cant. Prod. Colterenzio	258
A. A. Gewürztraminer Cresta, Hans Rottensteiner	266
A. A. Gewürztraminer Elyònd, Cant. Laimburg	282
A. A. Gewürztraminer Exclusiv St. Justina, Cant. Prod. San Paolo	257
A. A. Gewürztraminer Graf Von Meran, Cant. Prod. di Merano	276
A. A. Gewürztraminer Kastelaz, Castel Ringberg & Kastelaz Elena Walch	280
A. A. Gewürztraminer Kolbenhof, Hofstätter	281
A. A. Gewürztraminer Lage Doss, Josef Niedermayr	256
A. A. Gewürztraminer Lunare, Cant. Terlano	279
A. A. Gewürztraminer Maratsch, Cant. Prod. Termeno	281
A. A. Gewürztraminer Mazzon, Brunnenhof	285
A. A. Gewürztraminer Nussbaumerhof, Cant. Prod. Termeno	281
A. A. Gewürztraminer Passito, Graf Pfeil Weingut Kränzel	272
A. A. Gewürztraminer Passito Terminum, Cant. Prod. Termeno	281
A. A. Gewürztraminer Puntay, Erste & Neue	268
A. A. Gewürztraminer Sel., Steinhauserhof	285
A. A. Gewürztraminer SelectArt Flora, Cant. Prod. Cornaiano	256
A. A. Gewürztraminer St. Valentin, Cant. Prod. San Michele Appiano	258
A. A. Gewürztraminer Windegg, Josef Brigl	254
A. A. Grauvernatsch Castel Turmhof, Tiefenbrunner	273
A. A. Kerner, Pacherhof	283
A. A. Lago di Caldaro Cl., Kettmeir	269
A. A. Lago di Caldaro Cl. Felton, K. Martini & Sohn	255
A. A. Lago di Caldaro Pfarrhof, Cant. Viticoltori di Caldaro	271
A. A. Lago di Caldaro Scelto, Erste & Neue	268
A. A. Lago di Caldaro Scelto Bischofsleiten, Castel Sallegg - Graf Kuenburg	285
A. A. Lago di Caldaro Scelto Cl., Josef Sölva - Niklaserhof	270
A. A. Lago di Caldaro Scelto Haselhof Cl. Sup., Josef Brigl	254
A. A. Lagrein, Cant. Convento Muri-Gries	260
A. A. Lagrein, Franz Gojer Glögglhof	260
A. A. Lagrein, Hartmann Lentsch	284
A. A. Lagrein, Stephan Ramoser - Fliederhof	264
A. A. Lagrein Abtei Ris., Cant. Convento Muri-Gries	260
A. A. Lagrein Aus Gries Ris., Josef Niedermayr	256
A. A. Lagrein Berger Gei, Ignaz Niedrist	257
A. A. Lagrein Castel Ringberg Ris., Castel Ringberg & Kastelaz Elena Walch	280
A. A. Lagrein Gries, Cant. Terlano	279
A. A. Lagrein Gries Ris., Cant. Terlano	279
A. A. Lagrein Linticlarus Ris., Tiefenbrunner	273
A. A. Lagrein Mantsch Ris., Cant. Prod. Colterenzio	258
A. A. Lagrein Merlot Ebner, Kössler - Praeclarus	255
A. A. Lagrein Porphyr, Cant. Terlano	279
A. A. Lagrein Praepositus Ris., Abbazia di Novacella	282
A. A. Lagrein Ris., Castel Sallegg - Graf Kuenburg	285

A. A. Lagrein Ris., Stephan Ramoser - Fliederhof 264
A. A. Lagrein Rosato,
   Josephus Mayr - Erbhof Unterganzner 262
A. A. Lagrein Rosato Gries, Cant. Convento Muri-Gries 260
A. A. Lagrein Scuro, Andreas Berger -Thurnhof 259
A. A. Lagrein Scuro, Franz Gojer Glögglhof 260
A. A. Lagrein Scuro, Kössler - Praeclarus 255
A. A. Lagrein Scuro, Johannes Pfeifer Pfannenstielhof 263
A. A. Lagrein Scuro, Heinrich Plattner - Waldgries 263
A. A. Lagrein Scuro Abtei Ris., Cant. Convento Muri-Gries 260
A. A. Lagrein Scuro Albertus Ris., Cant. H. Lun 274
A. A. Lagrein Scuro Barbagòl Ris., Cant. Laimburg 282
A. A. Lagrein Scuro Berger Gei Ris., Ignaz Niedrist 257
A. A. Lagrein Scuro Briglhof, Josef Brigl 254
A. A. Lagrein Scuro Calldiv, Von Braunbach 280
A. A. Lagrein Scuro Crescendo Ris., Tenuta Ritterhof 269
A. A. Lagrein Scuro Desilvas, Peter Sölva & Söhne 270
A. A. Lagrein Scuro DiVinus Ris., Cant. Prod. San Paolo 257
A. A. Lagrein Scuro Fohrhof, Cant. Prod. Cortaccia 273
A. A. Lagrein Scuro Grafenleiten Ris.,
   Heinrich & Thomas Rottensteiner 265
A. A. Lagrein Scuro Gries, Cant. Convento Muri-Gries 260
A. A. Lagrein Scuro Gries Kristan Ris., Egger-Ramer 284
A. A. Lagrein Scuro Gries Ris., Anton Schmid - Oberrautner 266
A. A. Lagrein Scuro Griesbauerhof, Georg Mumelter 262
A. A. Lagrein Scuro Grieser, Anton Schmid - Oberrautner 266
A. A. Lagrein Scuro Grieser Baron Carl Eyrl Ris.,
   Cant. Gries/Cant. di Bolzano 259
A. A. Lagrein Scuro Grieser Oro,
   Anton Schmid - Oberrautner 266
A. A. Lagrein Scuro Grieser Prestige Line Ris.,
   Cant. Gries/Cant. di Bolzano 259
A. A. Lagrein Scuro Grieser Select Ris., Hans Rottensteiner 266
A. A. Lagrein Scuro Happacherhof,
   Maso Happacherhof - Istituto Tecnico Agrario 285
A. A. Lagrein Scuro Intenditore,
   Peter Zemmer - Kupelwieser 274
A. A. Lagrein Scuro Kristan, Egger-Ramer 284
A. A. Làgrein Scuro Maturum, K. Martini & Sohn 255
A. A. Lagrein Scuro Mirell, Heinrich Plattner - Waldgries 263
A. A. Lagrein Scuro Perl,
   Cant. Prod. Santa Maddalena/Cant. di Bolzano 264
A. A. Lagrein Scuro Ris., Andreas Berger -Thurnhof 259
A. A. Lagrein Scuro Ris., Franz Gojer Glögglhof 260
A. A. Lagrein Scuro Ris., Cant. Laimburg 282
A. A. Lagrein Scuro Ris., R. Malojer Gummerhof 261
A. A. Lagrein Scuro Ris.,
   Josephus Mayr - Erbhof Unterganzner 262
A. A. Lagrein Scuro Ris., Georg Mumelter 262
A. A. Lagrein Scuro Ris.,
   Johannes Pfeifer Pfannenstielhof 263
A. A. Lagrein Scuro Ris., Heinrich Plattner - Waldgries 263
A. A. Lagrein Scuro Ris., Georg Ramoser Untermoserhof 265
A. A. Lagrein Scuro Ris., Hans Rottensteiner 266
A. A. Lagrein Scuro Ris., Anton Schmid - Oberrautner 266
A. A. Lagrein Scuro Ris., Castello Schwanburg 278
A. A. Lagrein Scuro Ris. Mirell, Heinrich Plattner - Waldgries 263
A. A. Lagrein Scuro Rueslhof, K. Martini & Sohn 255
A. A. Lagrein Scuro Saltner, Anton Schmid - Oberrautner 266
A. A. Lagrein Scuro Segenpichl, Cant. Prod. di Merano 276
A. A. Lagrein Scuro Steinraffler, Hofstätter 281
A. A. Lagrein Scuro Taber Ris.,
   Cant. Prod. Santa Maddalena/Cant. di Bolzano 264
A. A. Lagrein Scuro Taberhof,
   Cant. Prod. Santa Maddalena/Cant. di Bolzano 264
A. A. Lagrein Scuro Taberhof Ris.,
   Cant. Prod. Santa Maddalena/Cant. di Bolzano 264
A. A. Lagrein Scuro Tor di Lupo, Cant. Prod. Andriano 254
A. A. Lagrein SelectArt Flora Ris., Cant. Prod. Cornaiano 256
A. A. Lagrein St. Valentin, Cant. Prod. San Michele Appiano 258
A. A. Lagrein Urbanhof, Cant. Prod. Termeno 281
A. A. Lagrein-Cabernet Coldirus Palladium,
   K. Martini & Sohn 255
A. A. Lagrein-Cabernet Klaser, Josef Sölva - Niklaserhof 270
A. A. Lagrein-Cabernet MerVin, Cant. Prod. Burggräfler 275
A. A. Lagrein-Merlot Desilvas, Peter Sölva & Söhne 270
A. A. Loam, Cant. Prod. Termeno 281
A. A. Meraner Eines Fürsten Traum, Cant. Prod. di Merano 276
A. A. Meranese Schickenburg, Cant. Prod. Burggräfler 275
A. A. Merlot, R. Malojer Gummerhof 261
A. A. Merlot, Cant. Prod. Burggräfler 275
A. A. Merlot, Georg Ramoser Untermoserhof 265
A. A. Merlot Brenntal, Cant. Prod. Cortaccia 273
A. A. Merlot Crescendo Ris., Tenuta Ritterhof 269
A. A. Merlot Desilvas, Peter Sölva & Söhne 270
A. A. Merlot DiVinus, Cant. Prod. San Paolo 257
A. A. Merlot Exclusiv Huberfeld, Cant. Prod. San Paolo 257
A. A. Merlot Freiberg Ris., Cant. Prod. di Merano 276
A. A. Merlot Kastelaz Ris.,
   Castel Ringberg & Kastelaz Elena Walch 280
A. A. Merlot Lagrein Mauritius Ris.,
   Cant. Gries/Cant. di Bolzano 259
A. A. Merlot Lasòn, Cant. Viticoltori di Caldaro 271
A. A. Merlot MerVin, Cant. Prod. Burggräfler 275
A. A. Merlot Mühlweg, Ignaz Niedrist 257
A. A. Merlot Otto Graf Huyn Ris., Cant. Gries/Cant. di Bolzano 259
A. A. Merlot Prestige Line Ris., Cant. Gries/Cant. di Bolzano 259
A. A. Merlot Puntay, Erste & Neue 268
A. A. Merlot Ris., R. Malojer Gummerhof 261
A. A. Merlot Ris., Georg Ramoser Untermoserhof 265
A. A. Merlot Ris., Castello Schwanburg 278
A. A. Merlot Schweitzer, Franz Haas 277
A. A. Merlot Siebeneich Tor di Lupo, Cant. Prod. Andriano 254
A. A. Merlot Sonnengut, Cant. Prod. Andriano 254
A. A. Merlot Spitz, Franz Gojer Glögglhof 260
A. A. Merlot Tor di Lupo, Cant. Prod. Andriano 254

A. A. Merlot Tschidererhof, Kössler - Praeclarus 255
A. A. Merlot-Cabernet Happacherhof Ris.,
   Maso Happacherhof - Istituto Tecnico Agrario 285
A. A. Merlot-Cabernet Sauvignon Anticus Baron
   Salvadori Ris., Cant. Prod. Nalles Niclara Magrè 277
A. A. Moscato Giallo, Andreas Berger -Thurnhof 259
A. A. Moscato Giallo Passito Sissi Graf von Meran,
   Cant. Prod. di Merano 276
A. A. Moscato Giallo Schickenburg, Cant. Prod. Burggräfler 275
A. A. Moscato Giallo Trifall, Tenuta Klosterhof 285
A. A. Moscato Giallo Vinalia, Cant. Gries/Cant. di Bolzano 259
A. A. Moscato Rosa, Abbazia di Novacella 282
A. A. Moscato Rosa, Cant. Convento Muri-Gries 260
A. A. Moscato Rosa, Heinrich Plattner - Waldgries 263
A. A. Moscato Rosa Castel Schwanburg,
   Castello Schwanburg 278
A. A. Moscato Rosa Passito, Heinrich Plattner - Waldgries 263
A. A. Moscato Rosa Passito Pasithea Rosa,
   Cant. Prod. Cornaiano 256
A. A. Moscato Rosa Rosis, Cant. Gries/Cant. di Bolzano 259
A. A. Moscato Rosa Schweizer, Franz Haas 277
A. A. Moscato Rosa Terminum, Cant. Prod. Termeno 281
A. A. Müller Thurgau, Oswald Schuster Befelhlof 286
A. A. Muller Thurgau, R. Malojer Gummerhof 261
A. A. Müller Thurgau, Hans Rottensteiner 266
A. A. Müller Thurgau Hofstatt, Cant. Prod. Cortaccia 273
A. A. Passito Serenade, Cant. Viticoltori di Caldaro 271
A. A. Perlhof Crescendo, Tenuta Ritterhof 269
A. A. Pinot Bianco, Castel Sallegg - Graf Kuenburg 285
A. A. Pinot Bianco, Graf Pfeil Weingut Kränzel 272
A. A. Pinot Bianco, Markus Prackwieser Gumphof 275
A. A. Pinot Bianco, Franz Haas 277
A. A. Pinot Bianco, Hofstätter 281
A. A. Pinot Bianco, Tenuta Klosterhof 285
A. A. Pinot Bianco, Tenuta Ritterhof 269
A. A. Pinot Bianco, Santa Margherita 347
A. A. Pinot Bianco, Josef Sölva - Niklaserhof 270
A. A. Pinot Bianco Carnol, Hans Rottensteiner 266
A. A. Pinot Bianco Collection Dellago,
   Cant. Gries/Cant. di Bolzano 259
A. A. Pinot Bianco Et. Nera, Graf Pfeil Weingut Kränzel 272
A. A Pinot Bianco Exclusiv Plötzner, Cant. Prod. San Paolo 257
A. A. Pinot Bianco Graf Von Meran, Cant. Prod. di Merano 276
A. A. Pinot Bianco Guggenberg, Cant. Prod. Burggräfler 275
A. A. Pinot Bianco Helios, Graf Pfeil Weingut Kränzel 272
A. A. Pinot Bianco Kastelaz,
   Castel Ringberg & Kastelaz Elena Walch 280
A. A. Pinot Bianco Klaser, Josef Sölva - Niklaserhof 270
A. A. Pinot Bianco Kupelwieser, Peter Zemmer - Kupelwieser 274
A. A. Pinot Bianco Passito Pasithea, Cant. Prod. Cornaiano 256
A. A. Pinot Bianco Plattenriegl, Cant. Prod. Cornaiano 256
A. A. Pinot Bianco Praesulis, Markus Prackwieser Gumphof 275
A. A. Pinot Bianco Puntay, Erste & Neue 268
A. A. Pinot Bianco Riol, Heinrich Plattner - Waldgries 263
A. A. Pinot Bianco Schulthauser,
   Cant. Prod. San Michele Appiano 258
A. A. Pinot Bianco St. Valentin,
   Cant. Prod. San Michele Appiano 258
A. A. Pinot Bianco Strahler, Stroblhof 284
A. A. Pinot Bianco Tauris, Cant. Prod. Termeno 281
A. A. Pinot Bianco Vial, Cant. Viticoltori di Caldaro 271
A. A. Pinot Bianco Weisshaus, Cant. Prod. Colterenzio 258
A. A. Pinot Grigio, Cant. Convento Muri-Gries 260
A. A. Pinot Grigio, Cant. H. Lun 274
A. A. Pinot Grigio, Pacherhof 283
A. A. Pinot Grigio, Tenuta Ritterhof 269
A. A. Pinot Grigio, Peter Zemmer - Kupelwieser 274
A. A. Pinot Grigio Anger,
   Cant. Prod. San Michele Appiano 258
A. A. Pinot Grigio Cornell, Cant. Prod. Colterenzio 258
A. A. Pinot Grigio Exclusiv Egg Leiten,
   Cant. Prod. San Paolo 257
A. A. Pinot Grigio Griesbauerhof, Georg Mumelter 262
A. A. Pinot Grigio Maso Reiner, Kettmeir 269
A. A. Pinot Grigio Punggl, Cant. Prod. Nalles Niclara Magrè 277
A. A. Pinot Grigio Söll, Cant. Viticoltori di Caldaro 271
A. A. Pinot Grigio St. Valentin,
   Cant. Prod. San Michele Appiano 258
A. A. Pinot Grigio Unterebnerhof, Cant. Prod. Termeno 281
A. A. Pinot Nero, Oswald Schuster Befelhlof 286
A. A. Pinot Nero, Graf Pfeil Weingut Kränzel 272
A. A. Pinot Nero, Tenuta Klosterhof 285
A. A. Pinot Nero, Ignaz Niedrist 257
A. A. Pinot Nero, Johannes Pfeifer Pfannenstielhof 263
A. A. Pinot Nero, Santa Margherita 347
A. A. Pinot Nero Albertus Ris., Cant. H. Lun 274
A. A. Pinot Nero Cornell Schwarzhaus,
   Cant. Prod. Colterenzio 258
A. A. Pinot Nero Fritzenhof, Cant. Prod. Cortaccia 273
A. A. Pinot Nero Greel, Cant. Prod. Santa Maddalena/
   Cant. di Bolzano 264
A. A. Pinot Nero Hausmannhof Ris., Weingut Haderburg 279
A. A. Pinot Nero Kreuzbichler, Josef Brigl 254
A. A. Pinot Nero Linticlarus Ris., Tiefenbrunner 273
A. A. Pinot Nero Maso Reiner, Kettmeir 269
A. A. Pinot Nero Mazzon, Anton Schmid - Oberrautner 266
A. A. Pinot Nero MerVin, Cant. Prod. Burggräfler 275
A. A. Pinot Nero Norital, Loacker Schwarzhof 261
A. A. Pinot Nero Pigeno, Stroblhof 284
A. A. Pinot Nero Praepositus Ris., Abbazia di Novacella 282
A. A. Pinot Nero Ris, Weingut Haderburg 279
A. A. Pinot Nero Ris., Hofstätter 281
A. A. Pinot Nero Ris., Josef Niedermayr 256
A. A. Pinot Nero Ris., Cant. Prod. San Michele Appiano 258
A. A. Pinot Nero Ris., Steinhauserhof 285
A. A. Pinot Nero Ris., Stroblhof 284

A. A. Pinot Nero Ris., Cant. Viticoltori di Caldaro 271
A. A. Pinot Nero S. Urbano, Hofstätter 281
A. A. Pinot Nero Sandbichler Ris., Cant. H. Lun 274
A. A. Pinot Nero Sandlahner Ris.,
Cant. Prod. Santa Maddalena/Cant. di Bolzano 264
A. A. Pinot Nero Schiesstandhof, Cant. Prod. Termeno 281
A. A. Pinot Nero Schweizer, Franz Haas 277
A. A. Pinot Nero Selyèt Ris., Cant. Laimburg 282
A. A. Pinot Nero St. Valentin,
Cant. Prod. San Michele Appiano 258
A. A. Pinot Nero Tiefenthaler MerVin, Cant. Prod. Burggräfler 275
A. A. Pinot Nero Trattmannhof SelectArt Flora,
Cant. Prod. Cornaiano 256
A. A. Pinot Nero Zenoberg, Cant. Prod. di Merano 276
A. A. Resling Castel Ringberg,
Castel Ringberg & Kastelaz Elena Walch 280
A. A. Riesling, Hofstätter 281
A. A. Riesling, Cant. Laimburg 282
A. A. Riesling, Castello Rametz 285
A. A. Riesling, Peter Zemmer - Kupelwieser 274
A. A. Riesling Fidera, Cant. Prod. Nalles Niclara Magrè 277
A. A. Riesling Kupelwieser, Peter Zemmer - Kupelwieser 274
A. A. Riesling Montiggl,
Cant. Prod. San Michele Appiano 258
A. A. Riesling Renano, Cant. Laimburg 282
A. A. Riesling Renano, Ignaz Niedrist 257
A. A. Santa Maddalena, Andreas Berger -Thurnhof 259
A. A. Santa Maddalena, Georg Mumelter 262
A. A. Santa Maddalena Cl., Franz Gojer Glögglhof 260
A. A. Santa Maddalena Cl., R. Malojer Gummerhof 261
A. A. Santa Maddalena Cl.,
Josephus Mayr - Erbhof Unterganzner 262
A. A. Santa Maddalena Cl., Georg Mumelter 262
A. A. Santa Maddalena Cl., Johannes Pfeifer Pfannenstielhof 263
A. A. Santa Maddalena Cl., Heinrich Plattner - Waldgries 263
A. A. Santa Maddalena Cl, Georg Ramoser Untermoserhof 265
A. A. Santa Maddalena Cl., Heinrich & Thomas Rottensteiner 265
A. A. Santa Maddalena Cl. Fliederhof,
Stephan Ramoser - Fliederhof 264
A. A. Santa Maddalena Cl. Huck am Bach,
Cant. Prod. Santa Maddalena/Cant. di Bolzano 264
A. A. Santa Maddalena Cl. Morit, Loacker Schwarzhof 261
A. A. Santa Maddalena Cl. Premstallerhof,
Hans Rottensteiner 266
A. A. Santa Maddalena Cl. Rondell,
Franz Gojer Glögglhof 260
A. A. Santa Maddalena Cl. Tröglerhof,
Cant. Gries/Cant. di Bolzano 259
A. A. Santa Maddalena Föhrner, Cant. H. Lun 274
A. A. Santa Maddalena Kupelwieser,
Peter Zemmer - Kupelwieser 274
A. A. Santa Maddalena Perlhof, Tenuta Ritterhof 269
A. A. Santa Maddalena Steinbauer,
Anton Schmid - Oberrautner 266
A. A. Sauvignon, Josef Brigl 254
A. A. Sauvignon, Graf Pfeil Weingut Kränzel 272
A. A. Sauvignon, Kettmeir 269
A. A. Sauvignon, Cant. Laimburg 282
A. A. Sauvignon, Cant. Prod. Termeno 281
A. A. Sauvignon, Heinrich & Thomas Rottensteiner 265
A. A. Sauvignon, Josef Sölva - Niklaserhof 270
A. A. Sauvignon Albertus, Cant. H. Lun 274
A. A. Sauvignon Allure, Josef Niedermayr 256
A. A. Sauvignon blanc, Cant. Prod. Burggräfler 275
A. A. Sauvignon Blanc Tasmin, Loacker Schwarzhof 261
A. A. Sauvignon Castel Ringberg,
Castel Ringberg & Kastelaz Elena Walch 280
A. A. Sauvignon Exclusiv Gfil Hof, Cant. Prod. San Paolo 257
A. A. Sauvignon Exclusiv Gfillhof, Cant. Prod. San Paolo 257
A. A. Sauvignon Graf Von Meran, Cant. Prod. di Merano 276
A. A. Sauvignon Gur Zu Sand Classic, R. Malojer Gummerhof 261
A. A. Sauvignon Gur zur Sand Classic,
R. Malojer Gummerhof 261
A. A. Sauvignon Intenditore, Peter Zemmer - Kupelwieser 274
A. A. Sauvignon Kirchleiten, Tiefenbrunner 273
A. A. Sauvignon Lafoa, Cant. Prod. Colterenzio 258
A. A. Sauvignon Lage Naun, Josef Niedermayr 256
A. A. Sauvignon Milla, Cant. Prod. Cortaccia 273
A. A. Sauvignon Mock,
Cant. Prod. Santa Maddalena/Cant. di Bolzano 264
A. A. Sauvignon Oyèll, Cant. Laimburg 282
A. A. Sauvignon Palladium, K. Martini & Sohn 255
A. A. Sauvignon Praesulis, Markus Prackwieser Gumphof 275
A. A. Sauvignon Premstalerhof, Cant. Viticoltori di Caldaro 271
A. A. Sauvignon Sel., Steinhauserhof 285
A. A. Sauvignon SelectArt Flora, Cant. Prod. Cornaiano 256
A. A. Sauvignon St. Valentin,
Cant. Prod. San Michele Appiano 258
A. A. Schiava, Markus Prackwieser Gumphof 275
A. A. Schiava Castel Schwanburg, Castello Schwanburg 278
A. A. Schiava Freisingerhof, Cant. Prod. Termeno 281
A. A. Schiava Galea, Cant. Prod. Nalles Niclara Magrè 277
A. A. Schiava Grigia, Georg Mumelter 262
A. A. Schiava Grigia Kaltenburg, Josef Brigl 254
A. A. Schiava Grigia Sonntaler, Cant. Prod. Cortaccia 273
A. A. Schiava Gschleier SelectArt Flora,
Cant. Prod. Cornaiano 256
A. A. Schiava Palladium, K. Martini & Sohn 255
A. A. Schiava Putzleitn, Tenuta Ritterhof 269
A. A. Schiava Sarner Hof Exclusiv, Cant. Prod. San Paolo 257
A. A. Schiava Schloss Baslan, Graf Pfeil Weingut Kränzel 272
A. A. Spumante Blanc de Blancs Arunda, Vivaldi - Arunda 276
A. A. Spumante Brut, Kettmeir 269
A. A. Spumante Brut, Vivaldi - Arunda 276
A. A. Spumante Comitissa Brut Ris., Lorenz Martini 284
A. A. Spumante Extra Brut Cuvée Marianna,
Vivaldi - Arunda 276
A. A. Spumante Extra Brut Vivaldi, Vivaldi - Arunda 276
A. A. Spumante Haderburg Pas Dosé,
Weingut Haderburg 279
A. A. Spumante Hausmannhof, Weingut Haderburg 279
A. A. Spumante Hausmannhof Ris., Weingut Haderburg 279
A. A. Spumante Pas Dosé, Weingut Haderburg 279
A. A. Spumante Pas Dosé, Weingut Haderburg 279
A. A. Spumante Praeclarus Brut, Kössler - Praeclarus 255
A. A. Spumante Praeclarus Noblesse Ris.,
Kössler - Praeclarus 255
A. A. Spumante Von Braunbach Brut, Von Braunbach 280
A. A. Stoan, Cant. Prod. Termeno 281
A. A. Sylvaner, Pacherhof 283
A. A. Terlano, Castello Schwanburg 278
A. A. Terlano, Cant. Terlano 279
A. A. Terlano Chardonnay Kreuth, Cant. Terlano 279
A. A. Terlano Cl., Cant. Terlano 279
A. A. Terlano Desilvas, Peter Sölva & Söhne 270
A. A. Terlano Hof zu Pramol, Josef Niedermayr 256
A. A. Terlano Nova Domus, Cant. Terlano 279
A. A. Terlano Pinot Bianco, Ignaz Niedrist 257
A. A. Terlano Pinot Bianco Cl., Cant. Terlano 279
A. A. Terlano Pinot Bianco Cl. Sonnengut,
Cant. Prod. Andriano 254
A. A. Terlano Pinot Bianco Pitzon, Castello Schwanburg 278
A. A. Terlano Pinot Bianco Sirmian,
Cant. Prod. Nalles Niclara Magrè 277
A. A. Terlano Pinot Bianco Vorberg, Cant. Terlano 279
A. A. Terlano Sauvignon, Ignaz Niedrist 257
A. A. Terlano Sauvignon, Cant. Terlano 279
A. A. Terlano Sauvignon Cl. Mantele,
Cant. Prod. Nalles Niclara Magrè 277
A. A. Terlano Sauvignon Preciosa Tor di Lupo,
Cant. Prod. Andriano 254
A. A. Terlano Sauvignon Quarz, Cant. Terlano 279
A. A. Terlano Sauvignon Winkl, Cant. Terlano 279
A. A. Traminer Aromatico Sonnengut,
Cant. Prod. Andriano 254
A. A. Traminer Aromatico Tor di Lupo,
Cant. Prod. Andriano 254
A. A. Traminer Aromatico V. T. Joseph, Hofstätter 281
A. A. Traminer Aromatico Windegg, Josef Brigl 254
A. A. Valle Isarco Gewürztraminer, Köfererhof 283
A. A. Valle Isarco Gewürztraminer, Kuenhof - Peter Pliger 267
A. A. Valle Isarco Gewürztraminer,
Manfred Nössing - Hoandlhof 267
A. A. Valle Isarco Gewürztraminer, Taschlerhof 268
A. A. Valle Isarco Gewürztraminer Aristos,
Cant. Prod. Valle Isarco 272
A. A. Valle Isarco Gewürztraminer Atagis,
Loacker Schwarzhof 261
A. A. Valle Isarco Gewürztraminer Passito Nectaris,
Cant. Prod. Valle Isarco 272
A. A. Valle Isarco Gewürztraminer Praepositus,
Abbazia di Novacella 282
A. A. Valle Isarco Kerner, Köfererhof 283
A. A. Valle Isarco Kerner, Manfred Nössing - Hoandlhof 267
A. A. Valle Isarco Kerner, Cant. Prod. Valle Isarco 272
A. A. Valle Isarco Kerner Aristos, Cant. Prod. Valle Isarco 272
A. A. Valle Isarco Kerner Praepositus, Abbazia di Novacella 282
A. A. Valle Isarco Klausener Laitacher,
Cant. Prod. Valle Isarco 272
A. A. Valle Isarco Liebelei Passito, Köfererhof 283
A. A. Valle Isarco Müller Thurgau, Köfererhof 283
A. A. Valle Isarco Müller Thurgau,
Manfred Nössing - Hoandlhof 267
A. A. Valle Isarco Müller Thurgau, Cant. Prod. Valle Isarco 272
A. A. Valle Isarco Müller Thurgau, Rockhof 286
A. A. Valle Isarco Müller Thurgau Aristos,
Cant. Prod. Valle Isarco 272
A. A. Valle Isarco Pinot Grigio, Abbazia di Novacella 282
A. A. Valle Isarco Pinot Grigio, Köfererhof 283
A. A. Valle Isarco Pinot Grigio, Cant. Prod. Valle Isarco 272
A. A. Valle Isarco Pinot Grigio Aristos, Cant. Prod. Valle Isarco 272
A. A. Valle Isarco Riesling, Köfererhof 283
A. A. Valle Isarco Sauvignon Marklhof, Abbazia di Novacella 282
A. A. Valle Isarco Sylvaner, Köfererhof 283
A. A. Valle Isarco Sylvaner, Kuenhof - Peter Pliger 267
A. A. Valle Isarco Sylvaner, Manfred Nössing - Hoandlhof 267
A. A. Valle Isarco Sylvaner, Rockhof 286
A. A. Valle Isarco Sylvaner, Taschlerhof 268
A. A. Valle Isarco Sylvaner Aristos, Cant. Prod. Valle Isarco 272
A. A. Valle Isarco Sylvaner Praepositus,
Abbazia di Novacella 282
A. A. Valle Isarco Sylvaner Ysac, Loacker Schwarzhof 261
A. A. Valle Isarco Veltliner, Kuenhof - Peter Pliger 267
A. A. Valle Isarco Veltliner, Manfred Nössing - Hoandlhof 267
A. A. Valle Isarco Veltliner Aristos, Cant. Prod. Valle Isarco 272
A. A. Valle Venosta Gewürztramlner, Weingut Falkenstein 278
A. A. Valle Venosta Gewürztramlner V. T., Weingut Falkenstein 278
A. A. Valle Venosta Pinot Bianco, Weingut Falkenstein 278
A. A. Valle Venosta Pinot Bianco,
Tenuta Unterortl-Castel Juval 271
A. A. Valle Venosta Pinot Nero, Tenuta Unterortl-Castel Juval 271
A. A. Valle Venosta Riesling, Oswald Schuster Befehlhof 286
A. A. Valle Venosta Riesling, Weingut Falkenstein 278
A. A. Valle Venosta Riesling,
Tenuta Unterortl-Castel Juval 271
A Sirio, San Gervasio 554
Abbaia, Cant. Soc. del Vermentino 795
Acciaiolo, Castello d' Albola 565
Acini Dolci Passito, Cant. del Castello 329
Acini Rari Passito, Enoteca Bisson 169
Acininobili, Maculan 290
Afederico Merlot, Vallona 437

Afro, Alberto Serenelli	625
Aglaia, Fattoria Corzano e Paterno	571
Aglianico, Borgo di Colloredo	697
Aglianico Castellaccio Ris., Monte Pugliano	727
Aglianico Cinque Querce, Salvatore Molettieri	719
Aglianico Contessa Ferrara, Castello Ducale	713
Aglianico del Taburno, Fattoria La Rivolta	725
Aglianico del Taburno, Fontanavecchia	724
Aglianico del Taburno Fidelis, Cant. del Taburno	714
Aglianico del Taburno Grave Morae, Fontanavecchia	724
Aglianico del Taburno La Madonnella, Ocone	728
Aglianico del Taburno Rosato, Fontanavecchia	724
Aglianico del Taburno Terra di Rivolta Ris., Fattoria La Rivolta	725
Aglianico del Taburno Vigna Cataratte, Fontanavecchia	724
Aglianico del Taburno Vigna Cataratte Ris., Fontanavecchia	724
Aglianico del Vulture, Cons. Viticoltori Ass. del Vulture	730
Aglianico del Vulture, D'Angelo	733
Aglianico del Vulture, Vinicola Miali	749
Aglianico del Vulture, Tenuta del Portale	732
Aglianico del Vulture, Cant. di Venosa	735
Aglianico del Vulture Basilisco, Basilisco	732
Aglianico del Vulture Bel Poggio, Armando Martino	736
Aglianico del Vulture Carato Venusio, Cant. di Venosa	735
Aglianico del Vulture Carpe Diem, Cons. Vitic. Ass. del Vulture	730
Aglianico del Vulture Casale Santa Maria, F.lli Napolitano	736
Aglianico del Vulture Don Anselmo, Paternoster	731
Aglianico del Vulture Don Anselmo Ris., Paternoster	731
Aglianico del Vulture Donato D'Angelo, D'Angelo	733
Aglianico del Vulture Efesto, Feudi di San Gregorio	723
Aglianico del Vulture Elea, F.lli Napolitano	736
Aglianico del Vulture Federico II, Tenuta Le Querce	731
Aglianico del Vulture Il Barile Vecchio, Allegretti	736
Aglianico del Vulture Il Covo dei Briganti, Eubea	734
Aglianico del Vulture Il Repertorio, Cantine del Notaio	733
Aglianico del Vulture Il Viola, Tenuta Le Querce	731
Aglianico del Vulture La Firma, Cantine del Notaio	733
Aglianico del Vulture Le Gastaldie Sicone, Basilium	736
Aglianico del Vulture Le Vigne a Capanno, Tenuta del Portale	732
Aglianico del Vulture Minorco Sasso, Tenuta Le Querce	731
Aglianico del Vulture Nibbio Grigio, Di Palma	734
Aglianico del Vulture Oraziano, Armando Martino	736
Aglianico del Vulture Re Manfredi, Terre degli Svevi	735
Aglianico del Vulture Ris., Tenuta del Portale	732
Aglianico del Vulture Roinos, Eubea	734
Aglianico del Vulture Rosso di Costanza, Tenuta Le Querce	731
Aglianico del Vulture Rotondo, Paternoster	731
Aglianico del Vulture Sasso, Tenuta Le Querce	731
Aglianico del Vulture Sine Die, Masseria Monaci	742
Aglianico del Vulture Synthesi, Paternoster	731
Aglianico del Vulture Terre di Orazio, Cant. di Venosa	735
Aglianico del Vulture Titolo, Elena Fucci	730
Aglianico del Vulture Valle del Trono, Basilium	736
Aglianico del Vulture Vetusto, Cons. Vitic. Ass. del Vulture	730
Aglianico del Vulture Vigna Caselle Ris., D'Angelo	733
Aglianico del Vulture Vigna della Corona, Tenuta Le Querce	731
Aglianico del Vulture Vignali, Cant. di Venosa	735
Aglianico Rocca dei Leoni, Villa Matilde	714
Aglianico Vigna ai Cerri, Fattoria Prattico	728
Aglieno, Casa alle Vacche	577
Agno Tinto, Vignalta	334
Ailanpa, Foradori	239
Aiole, Tenuta La Costaiola	202
Ajana, Ferruccio Deiana	800
Akronte, Boccadigabbia	631
Al Poggio Chardonnay, Castello di Ama	495
Alarico, Tenuta Terre Nobili	765
Alastro, Planeta	774
Albaciara Bianco, Barni	46
Albana di Romagna Dolce Lilaria, Stefano Ferrucci	436
Albana di Romagna Passito, Tre Monti	445
Albana di Romagna Passito, Tenuta Uccellina	462
Albana di Romagna Passito Arrocco, Fattoria Zerbina	440
Albana di Romagna Passito Colle del Re, Umberto Cesari	436
Albana di Romagna Passito Domus Aurea, Stefano Ferrucci	436
Albana di Romagna Passito Frutto Proibito, Fattoria Paradiso	432
Albana di Romagna Passito Gradisca, Fattoria Paradiso	432
Albana di Romagna Passito Innamorato, Poderi Morini	441
Albana di Romagna Passito Kiria, Calonga	443
Albana di Romagna Passito La Dolce Vita, La Macolina	459
Albana di Romagna Passito Maolù, Colonna - Vini Spalletti	462
Albana di Romagna Passito Mythos, Tenuta Valli	444
Albana di Romagna Passito Non Ti Scordar di Me, Leone Conti	439
Albana di Romagna Passito Remoto, Giovanna Madonia	433
Albana di Romagna Passito Scacco Matto, Fattoria Zerbina	440
Albana di Romagna Passito Solara, Celli	432
Albana di Romagna Passito Ultimo Giorno di Scuola, Ist. Prof. per l'Agricoltura e l'Ambiente	441
Albana di Romagna Progetto 1, Leone Conti	439
Albana di Romagna Progetto 2, Leone Conti	439
Albana di Romagna Secco Colle del Re, Umberto Cesari	436
Albana di Romagna Secco I Croppi, Celli	432
Albana di Romagna Secco I Vinchi, Tenuta Valli	444
Albana di Romagna Secco Sette Note, Poderi Morini	441
Albana di Romagna Secco V. della Rocca, Tre Monti	445
Alberano, Barsento	755
Alberello, Felline	748
Alberto Rosso, Zenato	316
Albiola, Casale del Giglio	681
Albion Cabernet Sauvignon Villa Novare, Bertani	311
Alcamo Borgoluna, Terre di Salemi	787
Alcamo Carta d'Oro, Cantine Rallo	773
Alcamo Conte Ruggero, Cantine Foraci	785
Alcamo Nadaria, Cusumano	779
Alcamo Rapitalà Gran Cru, Tenute Rapitalà	768
Alcineo, Palazzo	608
Ale di Glesie, Villa Frattina	404
Aleatico, Santa Barbara	756
Aleatico Dimastrodonato, Lomazzi & Sarli	754
Aleatico Elogio della Lentezza, I Pastini - Carparelli	754
Aleatico Negrino, Leone de Castris	751
Alessia Imperatori Rosso, Alessia Imperatori	753
Alezio Rosato Mjere, Michele Calò & Figli	756
Alezio Rosato Mjère, Michele Calò & Figli	756
Alfiere Cabernet Sauvignon, Tenuta Godenza	459
Alfiere Nero, Fattoria di Presciano	614
Alghero Le Arenarie, Tenute Sella & Mosca	790
Alghero Marchese di Villamarina, Tenute Sella & Mosca	790
Alghero Tanca Farrà, Tenute Sella & Mosca	790
Alghero Torbato Terre Bianche, Tenute Sella & Mosca	790
Aliera, La Rendola	553
Alle Fonti Pieve di Spaltenna, Castello di Meleto	498
Allodio Rosso, Podere San Michele	619
Almanera, Fatascià	777
Almante, La Berta	435
Almerita Brut, Tasca d'Almerita	778
Altavilla della Corte Bianco, Firriato	776
Altavilla della Corte Rosso, Firriato	776
Alte d'Altesi, Altesino	605
Alter Nos, Cant. Soc. della Trexenta	799
Altero, Poggio Antico	533
Altius, Vinicola Falcone	783
Altreuve Passito, Vallona	437
Alzero Cabernet Franc, Giuseppe Quintarelli	313
Amabile Persolino Rosso Passito, Ist. Prof. per l'Agricoltura e l'Ambiente	441
Amarone della Valpolicella, Corte Sant'Alda	302
Amarone della Valpolicella, Musella	319
Amarone della Valpolicella, Poggio Toccalta	352
Amarone della Valpolicella, Luigino e Marco Provolo	303
Amarone della Valpolicella, Giuseppe Quintarelli	313
Amarone della Valpolicella, Roncolato	351
Amarone della Valpolicella, Tenute Galtarossa	325
Amarone della Valpolicella, Trabucchi	297
Amarone della Valpolicella Alteo, Fasoli	292
Amarone della Valpolicella Brolo delle Giare, Tezza	343
Amarone della Valpolicella Campo dei Gigli, Tenuta Sant'Antonio	304
Amarone della Valpolicella Cl., Allegrini	294
Amarone della Valpolicella Cl., Lorenzo Begali	321
Amarone della Valpolicella Cl., Bertani	311
Amarone della Valpolicella Cl., F.lli Bolla	352
Amarone della Valpolicella Cl., Brigaldara	321
Amarone della Valpolicella Cl., Luigi Brunelli	322
Amarone della Valpolicella Cl., Ca' La Bionda	299
Amarone della Valpolicella Cl., Giuseppe Campagnola	299
Amarone della Valpolicella Cl., Corte Lenguin	350
Amarone della Valpolicella Cl., F.lli Degani	301
Amarone della Valpolicella Cl., Aleardo Ferrari	350
Amarone della Valpolicella Cl., Guerrieri Rizzardi	289
Amarone della Valpolicella Cl., I Scriani	347
Amarone della Valpolicella Cl., La Giaretta	348
Amarone della Valpolicella Cl., Le Ragose	312
Amarone della Valpolicella Cl., Lenotti	345
Amarone della Valpolicella Cl., Giuseppe Lonardi	301
Amarone della Valpolicella Cl., Angelo Nicolis e Figli	323
Amarone della Valpolicella Cl., Novaia	302
Amarone della Valpolicella Cl., Raimondi - Villa Monteleone	328
Amarone della Valpolicella Cl., Santa Sofia	323
Amarone della Valpolicella Cl., Casa Vinicola Sartori	349
Amarone della Valpolicella Cl., F.lli Tedeschi	324
Amarone della Valpolicella Cl., Tommasi Viticoltori	325
Amarone della Valpolicella Cl., Massimino Venturini	326
Amarone della Valpolicella Cl., Villa Bellini	326
Amarone della Valpolicella Cl., Villa Spinosa	314
Amarone della Valpolicella Cl., Zenato	316
Amarone della Valpolicella Cl., F.lli Zeni	289
Amarone della Valpolicella Cl. Acinatico, Stefano Accordini	320
Amarone della Valpolicella Cl. Ambrosan, Angelo Nicolis e Figli	323
Amarone della Valpolicella Cl. Barrique, F.lli Zeni	289
Amarone della Valpolicella Cl. BG, Tommaso Bussola	311
Amarone della Valpolicella Cl. Ca' Florian, Tommasi Viticoltori	325
Amarone della Valpolicella Cl. Calcarole, Guerrieri Rizzardi	289
Amarone della Valpolicella Cl. Campo Casalin I Castei, Michele Castellani	300
Amarone della Valpolicella Cl. Campo del Titari, Luigi Brunelli	322
Amarone della Valpolicella Cl. Campo Inferi, Luigi Brunelli	322
Amarone della Valpolicella Cl. Campo S. Paolo, Raimondi - Villa Monteleone	328
Amarone della Valpolicella Cl. Campolongo di Torbe, Masi	327
Amarone della Valpolicella Cl. Capitel della Crosara, Giacomo Montresor	342
Amarone della Valpolicella Cl. Capitel Monte Olmi, F.lli Tedeschi	324
Amarone della Valpolicella Cl. Casa dei Bepi, Viviani	314
Amarone della Valpolicella Cl. Castelliere delle Guaite, Giacomo Montresor	342
Amarone della Valpolicella Cl. Caterina Zardini, Giuseppe Campagnola	299
Amarone della Valpolicella Cl. Costasera, Masi	327
Amarone della Valpolicella Cl. Domini Veneti, Cant. Soc. Valpolicella	312
Amarone della Valpolicella Cl. Gioé, Santa Sofia	323
Amarone della Valpolicella Cl. La Marega, Le Salette	295
Amarone della Valpolicella Cl. La Masua, Corte Lenguin	350
Amarone della Valpolicella Cl. La Rosta, F.lli Degani	301
Amarone della Valpolicella Cl. Le Balze, Novaia	302
Amarone della Valpolicella Cl. Le Origini, F.lli Bolla	352
Amarone della Valpolicella Cl. Le Vigne Ca' del Pipa, Michele Castellani	300
Amarone della Valpolicella Cl. Marta Galli, Le Ragose	312
Amarone della Valpolicella Cl. Mazzano, Masi	327
Amarone della Valpolicella Cl. Monte Danieli, Corte Rugolin	300

Amarone della Valpolicella Cl. Monte Faustino, Giuseppe Fornaser	350
Amarone della Valpolicella Cl. Monte Masua Il Sestante, Tommasi Viticoltori	325
Amarone della Valpolicella Cl. Pergole Vece, Le Salette	295
Amarone della Valpolicella Cl. Postera, Manara	322
Amarone della Valpolicella Cl. Punta di Villa, Roberto Mazzi	313
Amarone della Valpolicella Cl. Sergio Zenato Ris., Zenato	316
Amarone della Valpolicella Cl. Sup. Monte Cà Paletta, Giuseppe Quintarelli	313
Amarone della Valpolicella Cl. Sup. Ris., Giuseppe Quintarelli	313
Amarone della Valpolicella Cl. TB, Tommaso Bussola	311
Amarone della Valpolicella Cl. TB Vign. Alto, Tommaso Bussola	311
Amarone della Valpolicella Cl. Terre di Cariano, Cecilia Beretta	341
Amarone della Valpolicella Cl. Tulipano Nero, Viviani	314
Amarone della Valpolicella Cl. Vaio Armaron Serègo Alighieri, Masi	327
Amarone della Valpolicella Cl. Vign. di Jago Domini Veneti, Cant. Soc. Valpolicella	312
Amarone della Valpolicella Cl. Vign. di Ravazvol, Ca' La Bionda	299
Amarone della Valpolicella Cl. Vign. di Ravazzol, Ca' La Bionda	299
Amarone della Valpolicella Cl. Vign. Il Fornetto, Stefano Accordini	320
Amarone della Valpolicella Cl. Vign. Le Marognole, Le Bertarole	347
Amarone della Valpolicella Cl. Vign. Monte Ca' Bianca, Lorenzo Begali	321
Amarone della Valpolicella Cl. Vign. Monte Sant'Urbano, F.lli Speri	324
Amarone della Valpolicella Cl. Villa Borghetti, Pasqua Vigneti e Cantine	342
Amarone della Valpolicella Falasco, Cant. Soc. della Valpantena	341
Amarone della Valpolicella Mithas, Corte Sant'Alda	302
Amarone della Valpolicella Monte delle Fontane, Tezza	343
Amarone della Valpolicella Proemio, Santi	297
Amarone della Valpolicella Ris., Giuseppe Quintarelli	313
Amarone della Valpolicella Rocca Sveva, Cant. di Soave	329
Amarone della Valpolicella Roccolo Grassi, Roccolo Grassi	303
Amarone della Valpolicella San Cassian, Luigino e Marco Provolo	303
Amarone della Valpolicella San Raffaele, Monte Tabor	348
Amarone della Valpolicella Valpantena, Cant. Soc. della Valpantena	341
Amarone della Valpolicella Vign. di Monte Lodoletta, Romano Dal Forno	296
Amativo, Cantele	744
Amistar Bianco, Peter Sölva & Söhne	270
Amistar Rosso, Peter Sölva & Söhne	270
Amphora, Castello di Lispida	305
Anarkos, Accademia dei Racemi	748
Ancellotta Frizzante, Stefano Spezia	221
Ancherona Chardonnay, San Felice	488
Anchigi, Cima	513
Anfidiamante, Fattoria del Teso	541
Anfiteatro, Vecchie Terre di Montefili	560
Angheli, Tenuta di Donnafugata	772
Anghelos, Tenuta De Angelis	629
Angialis, Antonio Argiolas	799
Angimbé, Cusumano	779
Anima, Livernano	567
Ansonica Costa dell'Argentario, La Parrina	554
Antair, Il Palagione	579
Anthilia, Tenuta di Donnafugata	772
Anthos, Matteo Correggia	51
Antigniano Rosso, Castello di Antigniano - Brogal Vini	672
Antinoo, Casale del Giglio	681
Aphrodisium, Casale del Giglio	681
Apianae, Di Majo Norante	698
Apogeo, Cascina delle Terre Rosse	172
Aquilaia, Erik Banti	585
Araja, Cant. Soc. di Santadi	797
Arbeskia, Giuseppe Gabbas	796
Arbis Rosso, Borgo San Daniele	367
Arcana Bianco, Terre Bianche	171
Arcàss Passito, Cascina Chicco	50
Arcato Sangiovese, Spoletoducale	674
Archita, Vini Classici Cardone	747
Arciato, Cardeto	668
Arcibaldo, Cennatoio Intervineas	556
Arcolaio, Leone Conti	439
Ardingo, Andrea Costanti	522
Aresco Passito, Corte Rugolin	300
Argiolas, Antonio Argiolas	799
Argo, Redi	548
Ariapetrina, Masseria Felicia	728
Arkezia Muffo di S. Sisto, Fazi Battaglia	630
Arleo Rosso, Santa Sofia	323
Armaleo, Palazzone	670
Armonia, Lorella Ambrosini	588
Armonia, Querciavalle	487
Arneide, Cant. Soc. Coop. Leverano	754
Artas, Castello Monaci	750
Arte, Domenico Clerico	106
Artias Chardonnay, Rio Maggio	640
Artias Pinot Nero, Rio Maggio	640
Artias Sauvignon, Rio Maggio	640
Arturo Bersano Talento Brut Ris. M. Cl., Bersano & Riccadonna	125
Arvino, Statti	761
Arzimo Passito, La Cappuccina	308
Asprinio d'Aversa Fescine, Cantine Caputo	712
Assajè Rosso, Capichera	791
Assisi Grechetto, Sportoletti	673
Assisi Rosso, Sportoletti	673
Astangia, Alberto Loi	792
Asti, I Vignaioli di S. Stefano	137
Asti De Miranda M. Cl., Contratto	55
Asti La Selvatica, Caudrina	67
Asti Modonovo, Gancia	56
Asti Monti Furchi, Terre da Vino	43
Asti Spumante, Cascina Fonda	102
Atina Cabernet, Giovanni Palombo	681
Attilio Vezzoli, Giuseppe Vezzoli	198
Augustale, Cant. Coop. della Riforma Fondiaria	755
Augustale Oro, Cant. Coop. della Riforma Fondiaria	755
Augusto, Poderi Morini	441
Aureo, Giovanni Donda	354
Aureus, Josef Niedermayr	256
Ausente, Migliarese	694
Avalon Bianco, Mastroberardino	712
Avra, Giuseppe Gabbas	796
Avvoltore, Moris Farms	514
Azzurreta, La Togata - Tenuta Carlina	530
Bacca Rossa, Poggio Le Volpi	687
Bacchico Passito, Villa Brunesca	347
Bacco Rosato, Malena	759
Bacmione, Mille Una	746
Badia Raustignolo, Il Pratello	447
Bagazzana Rosso, Maria Letizia Gaggioli - Vigneto Bagazzana	466
Baja, Mura	802
Balajana, Cant. Soc. Gallura	801
Baldovino Bianco, Grasso	786
Balench, Le Cantorie	219
Balifico, Castello di Volpaia	569
Ballistarius, Letrari	242
Balter Brut, Nicola Balter	241
Balze d'Istrice, Il Tagliato	602
Barbanico, Nicola Balter	241
Barbaresco, Ca' Rome' - Romano Marengo	30
Barbaresco, Fontanabianca	121
Barbaresco, Gaja	33
Barbaresco, Gastaldi	121
Barbaresco, Gianluigi Lano	26
Barbaresco, Ottavio Lequio - Prinsi	123
Barbaresco, Fiorenzo Nada	147
Barbaresco, F.lli Oddero	95
Barbaresco, Vignaioli Elvio Pertinace	148
Barbaresco, Pio Cesare	26
Barbaresco, Produttori del Barbaresco	36
Barbaresco, Punset	161
Barbaresco, Ronchi	154
Barbaresco Ad Altiora, Michele Taliano	116
Barbaresco Albesani, Cant. del Bricchetto	161
Barbaresco Annata, Pelissero	148
Barbaresco Asij, Ceretto	25
Barbaresco Asili, Ca' del Baio	146
Barbaresco Asili, Michele Chiarlo	47
Barbaresco Asili, Bruno Giacosa	122
Barbaresco Asili Barrique, Ca' del Baio	146
Barbaresco Asili Ris., Bruno Giacosa	122
Barbaresco Basarin, Moccagatta	35
Barbaresco Bernardot Bricco Asili, Bricco Rocche - Bricco Asili	63
Barbaresco Borgese, Piero Busso	120
Barbaresco Bric Balin, Moccagatta	35
Barbaresco Bric Turot, Prunotto	27
Barbaresco Bricco, Pio Cesare	26
Barbaresco Bricco Asili, Bricco Rocche - Bricco Asili	63
Barbaresco Bricco Libero, Rino Varaldo	37
Barbaresco Bricco Mondino, Piero Busso	120
Barbaresco Camp Gros, Tenuta Cisa Asinari dei Marchesi di Gresy	32
Barbaresco Campo Quadro, Punset	161
Barbaresco Cascina Bordino, Tenuta Carretta	129
Barbaresco Castellizzano, Vignaioli Elvio Pertinace	148
Barbaresco Cichin, Ada Nada	147
Barbaresco Cole, Moccagatta	35
Barbaresco Coparossa, Bruno Rocca	37
Barbaresco Coste Rubin, Fontanafredda	140
Barbaresco Cottà, Sottimano	124
Barbaresco Cottà V. Brichet, Sottimano	124
Barbaresco Crichèt Pajé, I Paglieri	34
Barbaresco Currà, Sottimano	124
Barbaresco Elisa, Ada Nada	147
Barbaresco Faset, Marziano ed Enrico Abbona	75
Barbaresco Faset, Castello di Verduno	150
Barbaresco Faset Bricco Asili, Bricco Rocche - Bricco Asili	63
Barbaresco Fausoni, Sottimano	124
Barbaresco Fausoni V. del Salto, Sottimano	124
Barbaresco Gaiun, Tenuta Cisa Asinari dei Marchesi di Gresy	32
Barbaresco Gallina, Ugo Lequio	123
Barbaresco Gallina, Ottavio Lequio - Prinsi	123
Barbaresco La Casa in Collina, Terre da Vino	43
Barbaresco Marcarini, Vignaioli Elvio Pertinace	148
Barbaresco Maria di Brun, Ca' Rome' - Romano Marengo	30
Barbaresco Martinenga, Tenuta Cisa Asinari dei Marchesi di Gresy	32
Barbaresco Masseria, Vietti	66
Barbaresco Mondino, Piero Busso	120
Barbaresco Montefico, Carlo Giacosa	34
Barbaresco Montubert, Icardi	67
Barbaresco Morassino, Cascina Morassino	32
Barbaresco Narin, Carlo Giacosa	34
Barbaresco Nervo, Vignaioli Elvio Pertinace	148
Barbaresco Ovello, Cant. del Pino	31
Barbaresco Ovello, Cascina Morassino	32
Barbaresco Pajé, I Paglieri	34
Barbaresco Pajoré, Sottimano	124
Barbaresco Palazzina, Montaribaldi	35
Barbaresco Rabajà, Giuseppe Cortese	33
Barbaresco Rabajà, Cascina Luisin	31

Barbaresco Rabajà, Bruno Rocca	37
Barbaresco Rabajà Ris., Castello di Verduno	150
Barbaresco Rio Sordo, F.lli Giacosa	122
Barbaresco Ris. Giuseppe Cortese, Giuseppe Cortese	33
Barbaresco Rombone, Fiorenzo Nada	147
Barbaresco Roncaglie, Bel Colle	149
Barbaresco S. Stefanetto, Piero Busso	120
Barbaresco S. Stefano Ris., Castello di Neive	161
Barbaresco Santo Stefano, Bruno Giacosa	122
Barbaresco Santo Stefano Ris., Bruno Giacosa	122
Barbaresco Serraboella, F.lli Cigliuti	120
Barbaresco Sorì Burdin, Fontanabianca	121
Barbaresco Sorì Capelli, Domenico Filippino	161
Barbaresco Sori Loreto, Rino Varaldo	37
Barbaresco Sörì Montaribaldi, Montaribaldi	35
Barbaresco Sorì Paitin, Paitin	124
Barbaresco Sorì Paitin Vecchie Vigne, Paitin	124
Barbaresco Sorì Paolin, Cascina Luisin	31
Barbaresco Sorì Rio Sordo, Ca' Rome' - Romano Marengo	30
Barbaresco Tenuta Roncaglia, Poderi Colla	27
Barbaresco Tettineive, Antica Casa Vinicola Scarpa	126
Barbaresco V. Borgese, Piero Busso	120
Barbaresco V. Erte, F.lli Cigliuti	120
Barbaresco V. Montersino, Orlando Abrigo	146
Barbaresco V. Rongallo, Orlando Abrigo	146
Barbaresco Valeirano, Ada Nada	147
Barbaresco Valgrande, Ca' del Baio	146
Barbaresco Vanotu, Pelissero	148
Barbaresco Vign. Brich Ronchi, Albino Rocca	36
Barbaresco Vign. Castellizzano, Vignaioli Elvio Pertinace	148
Barbaresco Vign. Gallina, La Spinetta	58
Barbaresco Vign. in Moccagatta Ris., Produttori del Barbaresco	36
Barbaresco Vign. in Montestefano Ris., Produttori del Barbaresco	36
Barbaresco Vign. in Ovello Ris., Produttori del Barbaresco	36
Barbaresco Vign. in Pora Ris., Produttori del Barbaresco	36
Barbaresco Vign. in Rio Sordo Ris., Produttori del Barbaresco	36
Barbaresco Vign. Loreto, Albino Rocca	36
Barbaresco Vign. Marcarini, Vignaioli Elvio Pertinace	148
Barbaresco Vign. Nervo, Vignaioli Elvio Pertinace	148
Barbaresco Vign. Starderi, La Spinetta	58
Barbaresco Vign. Valeirano, La Spinetta	58
Barbarossa, Coop. Svevo - Lucera	754
Barbarossa Il Dosso, Fattoria Paradiso	432
Barbazzale Bianco, Cottanera	769
Barbazzale Rosso, Cottanera	769
Barbera d'Alba, Gianfranco Alessandria	106
Barbera d'Alba, Elio Altare - Cascina Nuova	89
Barbera d'Alba, F.lli Bera	125
Barbera d'Alba, Eugenio Bocchino	160
Barbera d'Alba, Enzo Boglietti	90
Barbera d'Alba, Cant. del Pino	31
Barbera d'Alba, Cascina Bongiovanni	64
Barbera d'Alba, Giacomo Conterno	107
Barbera d'Alba, Giovanni Corino	92
Barbera d'Alba, Damilano	39
Barbera d'Alba, Sergio Degiorgis	103
Barbera d'Alba, Funtanin	52
Barbera d'Alba, Gabutti - Franco Boasso	140
Barbera d'Alba, Filippo Gallino	52
Barbera d'Alba, Silvio Grasso	92
Barbera d'Alba, Hilberg - Pasquero	131
Barbera d'Alba, Gianluigi Lano	26
Barbera d'Alba, Giovanni Manzone	110
Barbera d'Alba, Mauro Molino	93
Barbera d'Alba, Monfalletto - Cordero di Montezemolo	94
Barbera d'Alba, Monti	111
Barbera d'Alba, Fiorenzo Nada	147
Barbera d'Alba, Andrea Oberto	94
Barbera d'Alba, F.lli Oddero	95
Barbera d'Alba, Cascina Pellerino	118
Barbera d'Alba, E. Pira & Figli - Chiara Boschis	41
Barbera d'Alba, Prunotto	27
Barbera d'Alba, F.lli Revello	96
Barbera d'Alba, Bruno Rocca	37
Barbera d'Alba, Ruggeri Corsini	113
Barbera d'Alba, Luciano Sandrone	42
Barbera d'Alba, F.lli Seghesio	114
Barbera d'Alba, G. D. Vajra	44
Barbera d'Alba, Rino Varaldo	37
Barbera d'Alba, Mauro Veglio	97
Barbera d'Alba, Vielmin	62
Barbera d'Alba, Vigna Rionda - Massolino	142
Barbera d'Alba A Bon Rendre, Michele Taliano	116
Barbera d'Alba Affinata in Carati, Paolo Scavino	65
Barbera d'Alba Annunziata, Rocche Costamagna	97
Barbera d'Alba Asili, Cascina Luisin	31
Barbera d'Alba Asili Barrique, Cascina Luisin	31
Barbera d'Alba Aves, G. B. Burlotto	150
Barbera d'Alba Basarin, Moccagatta	35
Barbera d'Alba Bramè, Deltetto	51
Barbera d'Alba Brea, Brovia	64
Barbera d'Alba Bric Bertu, Angelo Negro & Figli	117
Barbera d'Alba Bric La Rondolina, Fabrizio Pinsoglio	61
Barbera d'Alba Bric Luina, Cascina Chicco	50
Barbera d'Alba Bric Torretta, Porello	54
Barbera d'Alba Bricco dei Merli, Elvio Cogno	127
Barbera d'Alba Bricco del Cuculo, Castello di Verduno	150
Barbera d'Alba Bricco delle Viole, G. D. Vajra	44
Barbera d'Alba Bricco Valpiana, Valerio Aloi	160
Barbera d'Alba Brichet, Ca' Viola	76
Barbera d'Alba Brunet, Fontanabianca	121
Barbera d'Alba Campass, F.lli Cigliuti	120
Barbera d'Alba Campolive, Paitin	124
Barbera d'Alba Cannubi, Giacomo Brezza & Figli	38
Barbera d'Alba Cannubi Muscatel, Giacomo Brezza & Figli	38
Barbera d'Alba Cascina Nuova, Mauro Veglio	97
Barbera d'Alba Castellinaldo, Raffaele Gili	60
Barbera d'Alba Castlè, Stefanino Morra	61
Barbera d'Alba Ciabot della Luna, Gianni Voerzio	99
Barbera d'Alba Ciabot du Re, F.lli Revello	96
Barbera d'Alba Ciabot Pierin, Funtanin	52
Barbera d'Alba Codana, Giuseppe Mascarello e Figlio	105
Barbera d'Alba Costa Bruna Tenuta Roncaglia, Poderi Colla	27
Barbera d'Alba Croere, Terre da Vino	43
Barbera d'Alba Donatella, Luigi Baudana	139
Barbera d'Alba Donna Margherita, Giovanni Rosso	164
Barbera d'Alba dù Gir, Montaribaldi	35
Barbera d'Alba Elena la Luna, Roberto Sarotto	161
Barbera d'Alba Falletto, Bruno Giacosa	122
Barbera d'Alba Fides, Pio Cesare	26
Barbera d'Alba Filatura, Porello	54
Barbera d'Alba Flin, Cascina Flino	158
Barbera d'Alba Fondo Prà, Gianluigi Lano	26
Barbera d'Alba Fontanile, Silvio Grasso	92
Barbera d'Alba Fornaci, Giacomo Grimaldi	39
Barbera d'Alba Gallina, Ugo Lequio	123
Barbera d'Alba Gepin, Albino Rocca	36
Barbera d'Alba Giada, Andrea Oberto	94
Barbera d'Alba Giardin, Ca' del Baio	146
Barbera d'Alba Ginestra, Paolo Conterno	108
Barbera d'Alba Gisep, Vigna Rionda - Massolino	142
Barbera d'Alba Giuli, Cascina Ballarin	91
Barbera d'Alba Granera Alta, Cascina Chicco	50
Barbera d'Alba Il Ciotto, Gianfranco Bovio	91
Barbera d'Alba La Galùpa, F.lli Abrigo	158
Barbera d'Alba La Gameraja, Ca' Rome' - Romano Marengo	30
Barbera d'Alba La Matta, Gianni Gagliardo	160
Barbera d'Alba La Priora, F.lli Alessandria	149
Barbera d'Alba La Romualda, Ferdinando Principiano	112
Barbera d'Alba La Serra, Giovanni Manzone	110
Barbera d'Alba Laboriosa, Michele Taliano	116
Barbera d'Alba Le Masserie, Francesco Boschis	159
Barbera d'Alba Lina, Carlo Giacosa	34
Barbera d'Alba Madonna di Como, Tenuta Langasco	154
Barbera d'Alba Maggiur, Cascina Luisin	31
Barbera d'Alba Majain, Piero Busso	120
Barbera d'Alba Mancine, Osvaldo Viberti	98
Barbera d'Alba Maria Gioana, F.lli Giacosa	122
Barbera d'Alba Marun, Matteo Correggia	51
Barbera d'Alba Mattarello, Castello di Neive	161
Barbera d'Alba Mervisano, Orlando Abrigo	146
Barbera d'Alba Mezzavilla, Malabaila	156
Barbera d'Alba Mommiano, Porello	54
Barbera d'Alba MonBirone, Monchiero Carbone	53
Barbera d'Alba Morassina, Giuseppe Cortese	33
Barbera d'Alba Mulassa, Cascina Ca' Rossa	50
Barbera d'Alba Nicolon, Angelo Negro & Figli	117
Barbera d'Alba Ombranera, Cant. del Bricchetto	161
Barbera d'Alba Ornati, Armando Parusso	111
Barbera d'Alba Paiagal, Marchesi di Barolo	40
Barbera d'Alba Pairolero, Sottimano	124
Barbera d'Alba Pelisa, Monchiero Carbone	53
Barbera d'Alba Pian Romualdo, Prunotto	27
Barbera d'Alba Piana, Ceretto	25
Barbera d'Alba Piani, Pelissero	148
Barbera d'Alba Pistìn, Giacomo Grimaldi	39
Barbera d'Alba Podium Serre, Tenuta Carretta	129
Barbera d'Alba Pozzo, Giovanni Corino	92
Barbera d'Alba Rinaldi, Marziano ed Enrico Abbona	75
Barbera d'Alba Rocca delle Marasche, Deltetto	51
Barbera d'Alba Roscaleto, Enzo Boglietti	90
Barbera d'Alba Ruvei, Marchesi di Barolo	40
Barbera d'Alba S. Michele, Malvirà	53
Barbera d'Alba San Quirico, Casavecchia	158
Barbera d'Alba Scarrone, Vietti	66
Barbera d'Alba Scarrone V. Vecchia, Vietti	66
Barbera d'Alba Scudetto, Giuseppe Mascarello e Figlio	105
Barbera d'Alba Serra Boella, Paitin	124
Barbera d'Alba Serraboella, F.lli Cigliuti	120
Barbera d'Alba Sorito Mosconi, Podere Rocche dei Manzoni	112
Barbera d'Alba Sovrana, Batasiolo	90
Barbera d'Alba Srëi, Vielmin	62
Barbera d'Alba Sup., F.lli Bera	125
Barbera d'Alba Sup., Giacomo Borgogno & Figli	38
Barbera d'Alba Sup., Destefanis	117
Barbera d'Alba Sup., Filippo Gallino	52
Barbera d'Alba Sup., Hilberg - Pasquero	131
Barbera d'Alba Sup., Armando Parusso	111
Barbera d'Alba Sup., Flavio Roddolo	113
Barbera d'Alba Sup., Giorgio Scarzello e Figli	42
Barbera d'Alba Sup., Tenuta La Volta - Cabutto	43
Barbera d'Alba Sup., Terre del Barolo	66
Barbera d'Alba Sup., G. D. Vajra	44
Barbera d'Alba Sup. Amabilin, Cascina Adelaide	154
Barbera d'Alba Sup. Armujan, Ruggeri Corsini	113
Barbera d'Alba Sup. Barba Cesco, Domenico Filippino	161
Barbera d'Alba Sup. Bricco dei Fagiani, Boroli	25
Barbera d'Alba Sup. Carolina, Cascina Val del Prete	130
Barbera d'Alba Sup. Funtanì, Monfalletto - Cordero di Montezemolo	94
Barbera d'Alba Sup. Gran Madre, Cascina Pellerino	118
Barbera d'Alba Sup. La Lena, F.lli Bera	125
Barbera d'Alba Sup. Papagena, Fontanafredda	140
Barbera d'Alba Sup. Parduné, Enrico Serafino	156
Barbera d'Alba Terlé, Ronchi	154
Barbera d'Alba Torriglione, Renato Ratti	96
Barbera d'Alba Trevigne, Domenico Clerico	106
Barbera d'Alba V. Bruseisa, Cascina Fonda	102
Barbera d'Alba V. Clara, Eraldo Viberti	98
Barbera d'Alba V. dei Dardi, Alessandro e Gian Natale Fantino	109
Barbera d'Alba V. del Cuculo, F.lli Cavallotto	65
Barbera d'Alba V. della Madre, Ettore Germano	141

Barbera d'Alba V. delle Fate, Rino Varaldo 37
Barbera d'Alba V. Erta, Sinaglio 28
Barbera d'Alba V. Fornaci, Pira 78
Barbera d'Alba V. Gattere, Mauro Molino 93
Barbera d'Alba V. Giaconi, Fabrizio Pinsoglio 61
Barbera d'Alba V. La Cresta, Podere Rocche dei Manzoni 112
Barbera d'Alba V. Lisi, Attilio Ghisolfi 109
Barbera d'Alba V. Martina, Elio Grasso 110
Barbera d'Alba V. Pozzo, Giovanni Corino 92
Barbera d'Alba V. Roreto, Orlando Abrigo 146
Barbera d'Alba V. S. Lorenzo, Bartolo Mascarello 40
Barbera d'Alba V. Veja, Domenico Filippino 161
Barbera d'Alba V. Vigia, Bricco Maiolica 75
Barbera d'Alba Valbianchera, Giovanni Almondo 115
Barbera d'Alba Valdisera, Terre del Barolo 66
Barbera d'Alba Valletta, Claudio Alario 74
Barbera d'Alba Vign. della Chiesa, F.lli Seghesio 114
Barbera d'Alba Vign. Gallina, La Spinetta 58
Barbera d'Alba Vign. Mùc, Ottavio Lequio - Prinsi 123
Barbera d'Alba Vign. Pozzo dell'Annunziata Ris., Roberto Voerzio 99
Barbera d'Alba Vign. Punta, Azelia 63
Barbera d'Alba Vigna Clara, Eraldo Viberti 98
Barbera d'Alba Vigna 'd Pierin, Ada Nada 147
Barbera d'Alba Vigna dei Romani, Enzo Boglietti 90
Barbera d'Alba Vignot, Cascina Morassino 32
Barbera d'Alba Vignota, Conterno Fantino 108
Barbera d'Alba Vittoria, Gianfranco Alessandria 106
Barbera d'Asti, Cascina Barisél 54
Barbera d'Asti, Ca' Bianca 29
Barbera d'Asti, Cascina Castlèt 72
Barbera d'Asti, Cascina Roera 73
Barbera d'Asti, Roberto Ferraris 22
Barbera d'Asti, Fabio Fidanza 155
Barbera d'Asti, Cascina Giovinale 162
Barbera d'Asti, Sergio Grimaldi - Ca' du Sindic 137
Barbera d'Asti, Tenuta Olim Bauda 88
Barbera d'Asti, Luigi Spertino 104
Barbera d'Asti, Valfieri 74
Barbera d'Asti Ai Suma, Braida 132
Barbera d'Asti Baby, Cantine Sant'Agata 138
Barbera d'Asti Bassina, Marenco 143
Barbera d'Asti Boscodonna, Gianni Doglia 157
Barbera d'Asti Bric dei Banditi, Franco M. Martinetti 144
Barbera d'Asti Bric Stupui, Isabella 119
Barbera d'Asti Bricco Blina, Agostino Pavia e Figli 23
Barbera d'Asti Bricco dell'Uccellone, Braida 132
Barbera d'Asti Bricco della Bigotta, Braida 132
Barbera d'Asti Bricco Garitta, Cascina Garitina 59
Barbera d'Asti Camp du Rouss, Coppo 55
Barbera d'Asti Carlotta, Tenuta dell'Arbiola 135
Barbera d'Asti Chersì, Ca' Bianca 29
Barbera d'Asti Ciresa, Marenco 143
Barbera d'Asti Costamiòle, Prunotto 27
Barbera d'Asti Cremosina, Bersano & Riccadonna 125
Barbera d'Asti Fiulòt, Prunotto 27
Barbera d'Asti Frem, Scagliola 48
Barbera d'Asti Giarone, Bertelli 72
Barbera d'Asti Grivò, Elio Perrone 68
Barbera d'Asti I Filari Lunghi, Valfieri 74
Barbera d'Asti 'I Sulì, La Zucca 119
Barbera d'Asti Il Bergantino, Bricco Mondalino 151
Barbera d'Asti La Crena, Vietti 66
Barbera d'Asti La Cricca, Roberto Ferraris 22
Barbera d'Asti La Gena, La Gironda 162
Barbera d'Asti La Ladra, Gancia 56
Barbera d'Asti La Luna e i Falò, Terre da Vino 43
Barbera d'Asti La Marescialla, Agostino Pavia e Figli 23
Barbera d'Asti La Solista, Caudrina 67
Barbera d'Asti La Tranquilla, Carussin 163
Barbera d'Asti Le Gagie, Tenuta La Meridiana 116
Barbera d'Asti Libera, Cantine Bava 70
Barbera d'Asti Martizza, La Zucca 119
Barbera d'Asti Martleina, Ne. Ne. 156
Barbera d'Asti Masaréj Gianni Zonin Vineyards,
   Castello del Poggio 130
Barbera d'Asti Moliss, Agostino Pavia e Figli 23
Barbera d'Asti Mongovone, Elio Perrone 68
Barbera d'Asti Montebruna, Braida 132
Barbera d'Asti Nuj Suj, Icardi 67
Barbera d'Asti Panta Rei, Contratto 55
Barbera d'Asti Pian Bosco, Karin e Remo Hohler 58
Barbera d'Asti Pian Bosco Barrique, Karin e Remo Hohler 58
Barbera d'Asti Pomorosso, Coppo 55
Barbera d'Asti Quorum, Hastae 47
Barbera d'Asti Riserva della Famiglia, Coppo 55
Barbera d'Asti Rive Rosse, Cant. Soc. di Vinchio - Vaglio Serra 153
Barbera d'Asti Rodotiglia Castello di Calosso, Tenuta dei Fiori 49
Barbera d'Asti Romina, Mauro Grasso 155
Barbera d'Asti Rubermillo, Casalone 101
Barbera d'Asti Rubis, La Caplana 155
Barbera d'Asti Rusticardi Castello di Calosso, Tenuta dei Fiori 49
Barbera d'Asti S. Antonio Vieilles Vignes, Bertelli 72
Barbera d'Asti San Grato,
   Sergio Grimaldi - Ca' du Sindic 137
Barbera d'Asti Sanbastiàn, Dacapo 22
Barbera d'Asti Sant'Anna Castello di Calosso,
   Mauro Grasso 155
Barbera d'Asti Sebrì, Cascina Gilli 62
Barbera d'Asti Sel. Gaudium Magnum, Bricco Mondalino 151
Barbera d'Asti Solus Ad, Contratto 55
Barbera d'Asti Sopra Berruti, L'Armangia 56
Barbera d'Asti Sterlino Castello di Calosso, Fabio Fidanza 155
Barbera d'Asti Sup., Guido Berta 163
Barbera d'Asti Sup., Gianni Doglia 157
Barbera d'Asti Sup., Tenuta Olim Bauda 88
Barbera d'Asti Sup., La Spinetta 58

Barbera d'Asti Sup., Valfieri 74
Barbera d'Asti Sup., Cant. Soc. di Vinchio - Vaglio Serra 153
Barbera d'Asti Sup. Acsé, Franco e Mario Scrimaglio 127
Barbera d'Asti Sup. Ajan, Villa Giada 57
Barbera d'Asti Sup. Alfiera, Marchesi Alfieri 134
Barbera d'Asti Sup. Altea, Cantine Sant'Agata 138
Barbera d'Asti Sup. Balau, Carlo Benotto 71
Barbera d'Asti Sup. Beneficio, Sciorio 73
Barbera d'Asti Sup. Beneficio Ris., Sciorio 73
Barbera d'Asti Sup. Bricco Asinari, Gancia 56
Barbera d'Asti Sup. Bricco Dani, Villa Giada 57
Barbera d'Asti Sup. Bricco della Volpettona,
   Ermanno e Alessandra Brema 88
Barbera d'Asti Sup. Bricco Laudana,
   Cant. Soc. di Vinchio - Vaglio Serra 153
Barbera d'Asti Sup. Bricco S. Ippolito, Franco e Mario Scrimaglio 127
Barbera d'Asti Sup. Bricco Sereno, Tenuta La Meridiana 116
Barbera d'Asti Sup. Bricconizza, Ermanno e Alessandra Brema 88
Barbera d'Asti Sup. Cala delle Mandrie, La Giribaldina 48
Barbera d'Asti Sup. Camparò, La Ghersa 103
Barbera d'Asti Sup. Campasso, Tenuta Castello di Razzano 29
Barbera d'Asti Sup. Canto di Luna, Guido Berta 163
Barbera d'Asti Sup. Cardin, Cascina Roera 73
Barbera d'Asti Sup. Cardin Ris., Cascina Roera 73
Barbera d'Asti Sup. Cascina Croce,
   Ermanno e Alessandra Brema 88
Barbera d'Asti Sup. Cavalé, Cantine Sant'Agata 138
Barbera d'Asti Sup. Collina della Vedova, Alfiero Boffa 135
Barbera d'Asti Sup. Croutin, Franco e Mario Scrimaglio 127
Barbera d'Asti Sup. Favà, Garetto 23
Barbera d'Asti Sup. Fornace di Cerreto, Malgrà 104
Barbera d'Asti Sup. Gaiana, Malgrà 104
Barbera d'Asti Sup. Generala, Bersano & Riccadonna 125
Barbera d'Asti Sup. Giorgione, Villa Fiorita 157
Barbera d'Asti Sup. I Filari Lunghi, Valfieri 74
Barbera d'Asti Sup. Il Sogno, Franco e Mario Scrimaglio 127
Barbera d'Asti Sup. Il Sogno, Cant. Soc. di Vinchio - Vaglio Serra 153
Barbera d'Asti Sup. In Pectore, Garetto 23
Barbera d'Asti Sup. La Bellalda d'Oro, Casa' dei Mandorli 157
Barbera d'Asti Sup. La Bogliona, Antica Vinicola Scarpa 126
Barbera d'Asti Sup. La Cappelletta, Cascina Barisél 54
Barbera d'Asti Sup. La Cricca, Roberto Ferraris 22
Barbera d'Asti Sup. La Luna e i Falò, Terre da Vino 43
Barbera d'Asti Sup. La Marescialla, Agostino Pavia e Figli 23
Barbera d'Asti Sup. La Romilda V, Tenuta dell'Arbiola 135
Barbera d'Asti Sup. La Tota, Marchesi Alfieri 134
Barbera d'Asti Sup. La Vignassa, La Ghersa 103
Barbera d'Asti Sup. Litina, Cascina Castlèt 72
Barbera d'Asti Sup. Martinet, Alfonso Boeri 158
Barbera d'Asti Sup. Monte Venere, Caudrina 67
Barbera d'Asti Sup. Montruc, Franco M. Martinetti 144
Barbera d'Asti Sup. Neuvsent, Cascina Garitina 59
Barbera d'Asti Sup. Nizza, Bersano & Riccadonna 125
Barbera d'Asti Sup. Nizza, Tenuta Olim Bauda 88
Barbera d'Asti Sup. Nizza Acsé, Franco e Mario Scrimaglio 127
Barbera d'Asti Sup. Nizza Ferrero Carlo, Carussin 163
Barbera d'Asti Sup. Nizza La Court, Michele Chiarlo 47
Barbera d'Asti Sup. Nizza La Vignassa, La Ghersa 103
Barbera d'Asti Sup. Nizza Le Nicchie, La Gironda 162
Barbera d'Asti Sup. Nizza Mora di Sassi, Malgrà 104
Barbera d'Asti Sup. Nizza Neuvsent, Cascina Garitina 59
Barbera d'Asti Sup. Nizza Piano Alto, Cantine Bava 70
Barbera d'Asti Sup. Nizza Romilda VI, Tenuta dell'Arbiola 135
Barbera d'Asti Sup. Nizza Romilda VII, Tenuta dell'Arbiola 135
Barbera d'Asti Sup. Nizza V. Dacapo, Dacapo 22
Barbera d'Asti Sup. Nizza V. La Riva, Alfiero Boffa 135
Barbera d'Asti Sup. Nobbio, Roberto Ferraris 22
Barbera d'Asti Sup. Passum, Cascina Castlèt 72
Barbera d'Asti Sup. Porlapà, Alfonso Boeri 158
Barbera d'Asti Sup. Reginal, Sciorio 73
Barbera d'Asti Sup. Rive, Araldica - Il Cascinone 59
Barbera d'Asti Sup. Rouvé, F.lli Rovero 30
Barbera d'Asti Sup. Rupestris, Carlo Benotto 71
Barbera d'Asti Sup. S. Martino, Cascina Roera 73
Barbera d'Asti Sup. SanSì, Scagliola 48
Barbera d'Asti Sup. SanSì Sel., Scagliola 48
Barbera d'Asti Sup. Sarmassa, La Giribaldina 48
Barbera d'Asti Sup. Sciorio, Sciorio 73
Barbera d'Asti Sup. Sei V. Insynthesis,
   Cant. Soc. di Vinchio - Vaglio Serra 153
Barbera d'Asti Sup. Sichivej, Bel Sit 157
Barbera d'Asti Sup. Titon, L'Armangia 56
Barbera d'Asti Sup. Tra Terra e Cielo, Tenuta La Meridiana 116
Barbera d'Asti Sup. V. Cua Longa, Alfiero Boffa 135
Barbera d'Asti Sup. V. del Beneficio, Tenuta Castello di Razzano 29
Barbera d'Asti Sup. V. dell'Angelo, Cascina La Barbatella 126
Barbera d'Asti Sup. V. delle More, Alfiero Boffa 135
Barbera d'Asti Sup. V. delle Rose, Franco Mondo 164
Barbera d'Asti Sup. V. Stramba, Castello di Lignano 81
Barbera d'Asti Sup. V. Valentino Caligaris,
   Tenuta Castello di Razzano 29
Barbera d'Asti Sup. Vën ëd Michen,
   Antonio Baldizzone - Cascina Lana 161
Barbera d'Asti Sup. Vign. Gustin, F.lli Rovero 30
Barbera d'Asti Sup. Vign. La Quercia, Villa Giada 57
Barbera d'Asti Sup. Vigne Vecchie,
   Cant. Soc. di Vinchio - Vaglio Serra 153
Barbera d'Asti Sup. Vigne Vecchie Nizza,
   Cant. Soc. di Vinchio - Vaglio Serra 153
Barbera d'Asti Tabarin, Icardi 67
Barbera d'Asti Tra Neuit e Dì, Garetto 23
Barbera d'Asti Tre Vigne, Vietti 66
Barbera d'Asti Truccone, Isabella 119
Barbera d'Asti V. Dacapo, Dacapo 22
Barbera d'Asti V. dei Mandorli,
   Giacomo Scagliola e Figlio 156

Barbera d'Asti V. delle More, Cascina Gilli — 62
Barbera d'Asti Varmat, La Morandina — 68
Barbera d'Asti Vign. Banin, Vigne Regali — 144
Barbera d'Asti Vign. del Tulipano Nero, Tenuta dei Fiori — 49
Barbera d'Asti Vignali Castello di Calosso, L'Armangia — 56
Barbera d'Asti Zucchetto, La Morandina — 68
Barbera del M.to, Cascina La Maddalena — 132
Barbera del M.to, Tenuta Gaiano — 49
Barbera del M.to, Tenuta San Sebastiano — 102
Barbera del M.to Albarola, Luigi Tacchino — 60
Barbera del M.to Alessandra, Colonna — 152
Barbera del M.to Aureum, Daniele Saccoletto — 163
Barbera del M.to Baciamisubito, La Scamuzza — 152
Barbera del M.to Balein, Franco Mondo — 164
Barbera del M.to Barabba, Iuli - Ca.Vi.Mon. — 69
Barbera del M.to Bricco della Prera, Cave di Moleto — 129
Barbera del M.to Bricco Montemà, Isabella — 119
Barbera del M.to Bricco Morlantino, Casalone — 101
Barbera del M.to Gallianum, Tenuta Gaiano — 49
Barbera del M.to Gioanòt, Pierino Vellano — 156
Barbera del M.to Giulin, Giulio Accornero e Figli — 151
Barbera del M.to Goj, Cascina Castlèt — 72
Barbera del M.to I Cheini, Traversa - Cascina Bertolotto — 143
Barbera del M.to La Rossa, Colonna — 152
Barbera del M.to Le Guie, Cascina Bondi — 162
Barbera del M.to Ljdia, Cantine Valpane — 163
Barbera del M.to Manora, Colle Manora — 131
Barbera del M.to Mepari, Tenuta San Sebastiano — 102
Barbera del M.to Pierin, Pierino Vellano — 156
Barbera del M.to Procchio, Cave di Moleto — 129
Barbera del M.to Rapet, Marco Canato — 164
Barbera del M.to Rivalta, Villa Sparina — 86
Barbera del M.to Rossa d'Ocra, Cascina La Maddalena — 132
Barbera del M.to Rossore, Iuli - Ca.Vi.Mon. — 69
Barbera del M.to Sup., Bricco Mondalino — 151
Barbera del M.to Sup., Vicara — 133
Barbera del M.to Sup. Barabba, Iuli - Ca.Vi.Mon. — 69
Barbera del M.to Sup. Bricco Battista, Giulio Accornero e Figli — 151
Barbera del M.to Sup. Cantico della Crosia, Vicara — 133
Barbera del M.to Sup. Valisenda, Castello di Lignano — 81
Barbera del M.to Sup. Vign. della Amorosa, La Scamuzza — 152
Barbera del M.to Umberta, Iuli - Ca.Vi.Mon. — 69
Barbera del M.to V. della Torretta, Tenuta Gaiano — 49
Barbera del M.to V. di Dante, La Guardia — 118
Barbera del M.to V. Migliau, Tenuta Gaiano — 49
Barbera del M.to Valpane, Cantine Valpane — 163
Barbera del M.to Vivace, Vicara — 133
Barbera del M.to Vivace Il Morinaccio, Cascina Garitina — 59
Barbera del M.to Volpuva, Vicara — 133
Barbera del M.to Zero Legno, Bricco Mondalino — 151
Barbera del Monferrato, Bel Sit — 157
Barbera del Monferrato Il Matto, Franco e Mario Scrimaglio — 127
Barbera M.to Sel. Gaudium Magnum, Bricco Mondalino — 151
Barbera Sup. Nizza, Antonio Baldizzone - Cascina Lana — 161
Barco Reale, Fattoria Ambra — 473
Barco Reale, Tenuta di Capezzana — 474
Barco Reale, Castelvecchio — 596
Bardiglio Rosso, Vinicola Miali — 749
Bardolino, Le Fraghe — 291
Bardolino, Albino Piona — 351
Bardolino Cavalchina, Cavalchina — 332
Bardolino Chiaretto, Cavalchina — 332
Bardolino Chiaretto, Corte Gardoni — 340
Bardolino Cl., Santa Sofia — 323
Bardolino Cl. Chiaretto, Guerrieri Rizzardi — 289
Bardolino Cl. Le Nogare, Bertani — 311
Bardolino Cl. Santepietre, Lamberti — 348
Bardolino Cl. Sup., Le Tende — 348
Bardolino Cl. Sup., Valetti — 345
Bardolino Cl. Sup., F.lli Zeni — 289
Bardolino Cl. Sup. Le Olle, Lenotti — 345
Bardolino Cl. Sup. Munus, Guerrieri Rizzardi — 289
Bardolino Cl. Sup. Terre di Cavagion, Villabella — 345
Bardolino Cl. Sup. V. Alte, F.lli Zeni — 289
Bardolino Le Fontane, Corte Gardoni — 340
Bardolino Sup., Corte Gardoni — 340
Bardolino Sup. Campi Regi, Giorgio Poggi — 345
Bardolino Sup. Le Bine Vecchie, Corte Marzago — 351
Bardolino Sup. S. Lucia Cavalchina, Cavalchina — 332
Baredo, F.lli Pighin — 401
Barigliott, Paternoster — 731
Barocco, Terre Cortesi Moncaro — 639
Barolo, F.lli Alessandria — 149
Barolo, Gianfranco Alessandria — 106
Barolo, Elio Altare - Cascina Nuova — 89
Barolo, Azelia — 63
Barolo, Batasiolo — 90
Barolo, Giacomo Borgogno & Figli — 38
Barolo, Boroli — 25
Barolo, Ca' Bianca — 29
Barolo, Cascina Bongiovanni — 64
Barolo, Giovanni Corino — 92
Barolo, Cascina Cucco — 139
Barolo, Damilano — 39
Barolo, Einaudi — 77
Barolo, Gianni Gagliardo — 160
Barolo, Ettore Germano — 141
Barolo, Bartolo Mascarello — 40
Barolo, Mauro Molino — 93
Barolo, Andrea Oberto — 94
Barolo, F.lli Oddero — 95
Barolo, Pio Cesare — 26
Barolo, Luigi Pira — 141
Barolo, E. Pira & Figli - Chiara Boschis — 41
Barolo, Prunotto — 27
Barolo, F.lli Revello — 96

Barolo, Flavio Roddolo — 113
Barolo, Josetta Saffirio — 160
Barolo, Luciano Sandrone — 42
Barolo, Giorgio Scarzello e Figli — 42
Barolo, Paolo Scavino — 65
Barolo, Terre del Barolo — 66
Barolo, Eraldo Viberti — 98
Barolo, Vigna Rionda - Massolino — 142
Barolo Acclivi, G. B. Burlotto — 150
Barolo Arborina, Mauro Veglio — 97
Barolo Baudana, Luigi Baudana — 139
Barolo Bofani, Batasiolo — 90
Barolo Boscareto, Ferdinando Principiano — 112
Barolo Bric dël Fiasc, Paolo Scavino — 65
Barolo Bricco, Giuseppe Mascarello e Figlio — 105
Barolo Bricco Boschis, F.lli Cavallotto — 65
Barolo Bricco delle Viole, G. D. Vajra — 44
Barolo Bricco Fiasco, Azelia — 63
Barolo Bricco Francesco Rocche dell'Annunziata, Rocche Costamagna — 97
Barolo Bricco Luciani, Silvio Grasso — 92
Barolo Bricco Rocca, Cascina Ballarin — 91
Barolo Bricco Rocca Tistot Ris., Cascina Ballarin — 91
Barolo Bricco Rocche, Bricco Rocche - Bricco Asili — 63
Barolo Bricco Sarmassa, Giacomo Brezza & Figli — 38
Barolo Bricco Viole, Mario Marengo — 93
Barolo Bricco Visette, Attilio Ghisolfi — 109
Barolo Brunate, Enzo Boglietti — 90
Barolo Brunate, Michele Chiarlo — 47
Barolo Brunate, Mario Marengo — 93
Barolo Brunate, Poderi Marcarini — 95
Barolo Brunate, Mauro Sebaste — 28
Barolo Brunate, Vietti — 66
Barolo Brunate, Roberto Voerzio — 99
Barolo Brunate Bricco Rocche, Bricco Rocche - Bricco Asili — 63
Barolo Brunate Ris., Poderi Marcarini — 95
Barolo Brunate-Le Coste, Giuseppe Rinaldi — 41
Barolo Bussia, Boroli — 25
Barolo Bussia, Bussia Soprana — 160
Barolo Bussia, Cascina Ballarin — 91
Barolo Bussia, Aldo Conterno — 107
Barolo Bussia, Deltetto — 51
Barolo Bussia, Monti — 111
Barolo Bussia, Prunotto — 27
Barolo Bussia Dardi Le Rose, Poderi Colla — 27
Barolo Bussia V. Fiurin, Armando Parusso — 111
Barolo Bussia V. Munie, Armando Parusso — 111
Barolo Bussia V. Rocche, Armando Parusso — 111
Barolo Ca' Mia, Brovia — 64
Barolo Cannubi, Giacomo Brezza & Figli — 38
Barolo Cannubi, Cascina Adelaide — 154
Barolo Cannubi, Michele Chiarlo — 47
Barolo Cannubi, Damilano — 39
Barolo Cannubi, Marchesi di Barolo — 40
Barolo Cannubi, E. Pira & Figli - Chiara Boschis — 41
Barolo Cannubi, Paolo Scavino — 65
Barolo Cannubi Boschis, Luciano Sandrone — 42
Barolo Cannubi S. Lorenzo-Ravera, Giuseppe Rinaldi — 41
Barolo Carobric, Paolo Scavino — 65
Barolo Cascina Francia, Giacomo Conterno — 107
Barolo Case Nere, Enzo Boglietti — 90
Barolo Castelletto, Mauro Veglio — 97
Barolo Castiglione, Vietti — 66
Barolo Cerequio, Batasiolo — 90
Barolo Cerequio, Michele Chiarlo — 47
Barolo Cerequio, Roberto Voerzio — 99
Barolo Cerequio Tenuta Secolo, Contratto — 55
Barolo Cerretta, Ettore Germano — 141
Barolo Cerretta, Giovanni Rosso — 164
Barolo Cerretta Piani, Luigi Baudana — 139
Barolo Chinato, Ceretto — 25
Barolo Chinato, Gianni Gagliardo — 160
Barolo Ciabot Manzoni, Silvio Grasso — 92
Barolo Ciabot Mentin Ginestra, Domenico Clerico — 106
Barolo Cicala, Aldo Conterno — 107
Barolo Cl., Giacomo Borgogno & Figli — 38
Barolo Codana, Terre del Barolo — 66
Barolo Collina Rionda Ris., Bruno Giacosa — 122
Barolo Colonnello, Aldo Conterno — 107
Barolo Conca Marcenasco, Renato Ratti — 96
Barolo Corda della Briccolina, Batasiolo — 90
Barolo Corsini, Ruggeri Corsini — 113
Barolo Costa Grimaldi, Einaudi — 77
Barolo Enrico VI, Monfalletto - Cordero di Montezemolo — 94
Barolo Estate Vineyard, Marchesi di Barolo — 40
Barolo Falletto, Bruno Giacosa — 122
Barolo Falletto Ris., Bruno Giacosa — 122
Barolo Fontanafredda V. La Rosa, Fontanafredda — 140
Barolo Fossati, Enzo Boglietti — 90
Barolo Gabutti, Gabutti - Franco Boasso — 140
Barolo Garblèt Suè, Brovia — 64
Barolo Gattere Bricco Luciani, F.lli Ferrero — 160
Barolo Gavarini V. Chiniera, Elio Grasso — 110
Barolo Giachini, Silvio Grasso — 92
Barolo Ginestra, Paolo Conterno — 108
Barolo Ginestra Ris., Paolo Conterno — 108
Barolo Ginestra V. Casa Maté, Elio Grasso — 110
Barolo Gramolere, Giovanni Manzone — 110
Barolo Gramolere Bricat, Giovanni Manzone — 110
Barolo Gramolere Ris., Giovanni Manzone — 110
Barolo Gran Bussia Ris., Aldo Conterno — 107
Barolo I Tre Ciabot, Cascina Ballarin — 91
Barolo La Rocca e La Pira, I Paglieri — 34
Barolo La Rocca e La Pira Ris., I Paglieri — 34
Barolo La Serra, Poderi Marcarini — 95
Barolo La Serra, Gianni Voerzio — 99

Barolo La Serra, Roberto Voerzio	99
Barolo Lazzarito, Vietti	66
Barolo Lazzarito V. La Delizia, Fontanafredda	140
Barolo Le Coste, Giacomo Grimaldi	39
Barolo Le Coste, Ferdinando Principiano	112
Barolo Le Rocche del Falletto, Bruno Giacosa	122
Barolo Le Vigne, Luciano Sandrone	42
Barolo Liste, Giacomo Borgogno & Figli	38
Barolo Liste, Damilano	39
Barolo Manzoni, F.lli Ferrero	160
Barolo Marasco, Franco M. Martinetti	144
Barolo Marcenasco, Renato Ratti	96
Barolo Margheria, Vigna Rionda - Massolino	142
Barolo Mariondino, Armando Parusso	111
Barolo Massara, Castello di Verduno	150
Barolo Massara Ris., Castello di Verduno	150
Barolo Mondoca di Bussia Soprana, F.lli Oddero	95
Barolo Monfalletto, Monfalletto - Cordero di Montezemolo	94
Barolo Monfortino Ris., Giacomo Conterno	107
Barolo Monprivato, Brovia	64
Barolo Monprivato, Giuseppe Mascarello e Figlio	105
Barolo Monprivato Cà d' Morissio Ris., Giuseppe Mascarello e Figlio	105
Barolo Monvigliero, F.lli Alessandria	149
Barolo Monvigliero, Bel Colle	149
Barolo Monvigliero, Castello di Verduno	150
Barolo Monvigliero, Mauro Sebaste	28
Barolo Monvigliero, Terre del Barolo	66
Barolo Monvigliero Ris., Terre del Barolo	66
Barolo Mosconi, Bussia Soprana	160
Barolo nei Cannubi, Einaudi	77
Barolo Ornato, Pio Cesare	26
Barolo Paesi Tuoi, Terre da Vino	43
Barolo Paiagallo V. La Villa, Fontanafredda	140
Barolo Pajana, Domenico Clerico	106
Barolo Parafada, Vigna Rionda - Massolino	142
Barolo Parafada Ris., Vigna Rionda - Massolino	142
Barolo Parej, Icardi	67
Barolo Parussi, Conterno Fantino	108
Barolo Percristina, Domenico Clerico	106
Barolo Pernanno, Cascina Bongiovanni	64
Barolo Pì Vigne, Silvio Grasso	92
Barolo Piantà, Casavecchia	158
Barolo Piccole Vigne, Armando Parusso	111
Barolo Podere Scarrone, Terre da Vino	43
Barolo Prapò, Ettore Germano	141
Barolo Prapò, Mauro Sebaste	28
Barolo Prapò Bricco Rocche, Bricco Rocche - Bricco Asili	63
Barolo Pressenda, Marziano ed Enrico Abbona	75
Barolo Rapet, Ca' Rome' - Romano Marengo	30
Barolo Ravera, Elvio Cogno	127
Barolo Ravera, Flavio Roddolo	113
Barolo Ravera, Vietti	66
Barolo Ris., E. Pira & Figli - Chiara Boschis	41
Barolo Ris. del Fondatore, Tenuta La Volta - Cabutto	43
Barolo Riserva Grande Annata, Marchesi di Barolo	40
Barolo Riva, Claudio Alario	74
Barolo Rivera di Castiglione, F.lli Oddero	95
Barolo Rocche, Giovanni Corino	92
Barolo Rocche dei Brovia, Brovia	64
Barolo Rocche dell'Annunziata, F.lli Revello	96
Barolo Rocche dell'Annunziata, Monte Costamagna	97
Barolo Rocche dell'Annunziata Ris., Paolo Scavino	65
Barolo Rocche di Castiglione, F.lli Oddero	95
Barolo Rocche di Castiglione, Vietti	66
Barolo Rocche di Castiglione Falletto, Bruno Giacosa	122
Barolo Rocche Marcenasco, Renato Ratti	96
Barolo Rocchettevino, Gianfranco Bovio	91
Barolo Runcot, Elio Grasso	110
Barolo S. Giovanni, Gianfranco Alessandria	106
Barolo S. Lorenzo, F.lli Alessandria	149
Barolo S. Rocco, Azelia	63
Barolo S. Stefano di Perno, Giuseppe Mascarello e Figlio	105
Barolo Sarmassa, Giacomo Brezza & Figli	38
Barolo Sarmassa, Marchesi di Barolo	40
Barolo Sarmassa, Roberto Voerzio	99
Barolo Serra dei Turchi, Osvaldo Viberti	98
Barolo Serralunga, Gabutti - Franco Boasso	140
Barolo Serralunga, Giovanni Rosso	164
Barolo Serralunga d'Alba, Fontanafredda	140
Barolo Sorano, Ascheri	46
Barolo Sorano Coste e Bricco, Ascheri	46
Barolo Sorì Ginestra, Conterno Fantino	108
Barolo Tettimorra, Antica Casa Vinicola Scarpa	126
Barolo Triumviratum Ris., Michele Chiarlo	47
Barolo V. Albarella, Andrea Oberto	94
Barolo V. Arborina, Gianfranco Bovio	91
Barolo V. Arborina, Mauro Veglio	97
Barolo V. Big 'd Big, Podere Rocche dei Manzoni	112
Barolo V. Big Ris., Podere Rocche dei Manzoni	112
Barolo V. Bricco Gattera, Monfalletto - Cordero di Montezemolo	94
Barolo V. Cappella di S. Stefano, Podere Rocche dei Manzoni	112
Barolo V. Cerrati, Cascina Cucco	139
Barolo V. Cerretta, Ca' Rome' - Romano Marengo	30
Barolo V. Conca, Mauro Molino	93
Barolo V. Conca, F.lli Revello	96
Barolo V. Cucco, Cascina Cucco	139
Barolo V. d'la Roul, Podere Rocche dei Manzoni	112
Barolo V. d'la Roul Ris., Podere Rocche dei Manzoni	112
Barolo V. dei Dardi, Alessandro e Gian Natale Fantino	109
Barolo V. dei Dardi Ris., Alessandro e Gian Natale Fantino	109
Barolo V. dei Pola, Ascheri	46
Barolo V. del Gris, Conterno Fantino	108
Barolo V. di Aldo, Rino Varaldo	37
Barolo V. Elena, Elvio Cogno	127
Barolo V. Gancia, Mauro Molino	93
Barolo V. Gattera, Gianfranco Bovio	91
Barolo V. Gattera, F.lli Revello	96
Barolo V. Gattera, Mauro Veglio	97
Barolo V. Giachini, Giovanni Corino	92
Barolo V. Giachini, F.lli Revello	96
Barolo V. La Delizia, Fontanafredda	140
Barolo V. La Rosa, Fontanafredda	140
Barolo V. La Villa, Fontanafredda	140
Barolo V. La Volta, Tenuta La Volta - Cabutto	43
Barolo V. Lazzarito, Fontanafredda	140
Barolo V. Mandorlo, F.lli Giacosa	122
Barolo V. Merenda, Giorgio Scarzello e Figli	42
Barolo V. Nuova, E. Pira & Figli - Chiara Boschis	41
Barolo V. Rionda, F.lli Oddero	95
Barolo V. Rionda, Luigi Pira	141
Barolo V. Rionda Ris., Vigna Rionda - Massolino	142
Barolo V. Rocche, Andrea Oberto	94
Barolo V. Rocche, Mauro Veglio	97
Barolo Vecchie Vigne, Giovanni Corino	92
Barolo Vign. Arborina, Elio Altare - Cascina Nuova	89
Barolo Vign. Arborina, Giovanni Corino	92
Barolo Vign. Cannubi, G. B. Burlotto	150
Barolo Vign. di Proprietà in Barolo, Marchesi di Barolo	40
Barolo Vign. in Cannubi, Tenuta Carretta	129
Barolo Vign. La Villa, F.lli Seghesio	114
Barolo Vign. Marenca, Luigi Pira	141
Barolo Vign. Margheria, Luigi Pira	141
Barolo Vign. Monvigliero, G. B. Burlotto	150
Barolo Vign. Roncaglie, Giovanni Corino	92
Barolo Vign. Terlo Ravera, Marziano ed Enrico Abbona	75
Barolo Vigna Colonnello, Bussia Soprana	160
Barolo Vigna del Colonnello, Aldo Conterno	107
Barolo Vigna S. Giuseppe Ris., F.lli Cavallotto	65
Barolo Vignolo Ris., F.lli Cavallotto	65
Barolo Villero, Boroli	25
Barolo Villero, Brovia	64
Barolo Villero, Giuseppe Mascarello e Figlio	105
Barolo Villero Ris., Vietti	66
Barolo Zonchera, Ceretto	25
Barone Rosso Platinum, Fantinel	423
Baronesse Passito, Cant. Prod. Nalles Niclara Magrè	277
Barricadiero, Aurora	643
Barrile, Attilio Contini	791
Bartis, Valentino Fiorini	627
Barullo, Castello di Selvole	488
Basaltico, Tenuta Faltracco	310
Basilicata Rosso Vignali, Cant. di Venosa	735
Basolo, Ca' del Vispo	576
Batàr, Querciabella	504
Becco Rosso, Corte Gardoni	340
Belcaro, San Felice	488
Belcore, I Giusti e Zanza	492
Bellarmino, Tenuta La Costaiola	202
Bellei Cuvée Speciale Brut, Francesco Bellei	434
Bellei Extra Cuvée Brut, Francesco Bellei	434
Bellei Extra Cuvée Rosé Brut mill., Francesco Bellei	434
Belmantello, Paradiso	753
Benaco Bresciano Rosso Vigne Sparse, Visconti Podere Sant'Onorata	220
Bendicò Mandrarossa, Settesoli	775
Beneventano Aglianico, Fattoria Ciabrelli	726
Beneventano Aglianico, Monte Pugliano	727
Beneventano Aglianico Re Sole, Fattoria Torre Gaia	727
Beneventano Barbera, Fattoria Ciabrelli	726
Benuara, Cusumano	779
Bera Brut M. Cl., F.lli Bera	125
Berengario, Zonin	296
Berillo d'Oro, Alessandro Secchi	250
Besidie, Demetrio Serracavallo	760
Besler Biank, Pojer & Sandri	232
Betto, Santa Lucia	603
Bianca Capello, Ortaglia	593
Bianca delle Gazzere, Baglio Hopps	771
Bianca di Salaparuta, Duca di Salaparuta - Vini Corvo	769
Bianchello del Metauro, Guerrieri	646
Bianchello del Metauro Borgo Torre, Claudio Morelli	634
Bianchello del Metauro Celso, Guerrieri	646
Bianchello del Metauro La Vigna delle Terrazze, Claudio Morelli	634
Bianchello del Metauro S. Cesareo, Claudio Morelli	634
Bianchello del Metauro Tenuta Campioli, Valentino Fiorini	627
Bianchello del Metauro Vigna Sant'Ilario, Valentino Fiorini	627
Bianco Avignonesi, Avignonesi	542
Bianco Bianco, Ronco del Gnemiz	420
Bianco Carpino, Il Carpino	415
Bianco del Coppo Sauvignon, Conte Leopardi Dittajuti	642
Bianco del Santo, Enrico Riccardi	225
Bianco della Castellada, La Castellada	390
Bianco della Rocca, Sarchese Dora	704
Bianco della Torre, Poderi di San Pietro	209
Bianco delle Chiaie, Giovanni Palombo	681
Bianco delle Regine, Castello delle Regine	658
Bianco di Castelnuovo, Castel Noarna	239
Bianco di Ciccio, Ciccio Zaccagnini	697
Bianco di Corte, Paternoster	731
Bianco di Custoza, Cavalchina	332
Bianco di Custoza, Corte Gardoni	340
Bianco di Custoza, Valetti	345
Bianco di Custoza, Le Vigne di San Pietro	333
Bianco di Custoza Montemagrin, Santa Sofia	323
Bianco di Custoza Orchidea Platino, Lamberti	348
Bianco di Custoza Oro, Le Tende	348
Bianco di Custoza Sanpietro, Le Vigne di San Pietro	333
Bianco di Custoza Sup. Campo del Sèlese, Albino Piona	351
Bianco di Custoza Sup. V. Le Battistine, Corte Marzago	351
Bianco di Custoza V. Alte, F.lli Zeni	289
Bianco di Custoza Vign. Monte Fiera, Giacomo Montresor	342

Bianco di Ornella, Ornella Molon Traverso	317
Bianco di Passomaggio, Abbazia Santa Anastasia	768
Bianco di Pitigliano, Tenuta Roccaccia	562
Bianco di Pitigliano Rasenno, Cant. Coop. del Morellino di Scansano	586
Bianco di Toscana Il Piano, Machiavelli	575
Bianco di Valpanera, Valpanera	426
Bianco Faye, Pojer & Sandri	232
Bianco Garganega Falasco, Cant. Soc. della Valpantena	341
Bianco Ghibellino, Aldo Rainoldi	191
Bianco Gli Affreschi, Tenuta di Blasig	412
Bianco Io, Ca' di Frara	204
Bianco Jacot Ronco Calaj, Russolo	422
Bianco JN, Sant'Elena	393
Bianco Lieò, Cantine Lento	761
Bianco Pisano S. Torpè Casina de' Venti, San Gervasio	554
Bianco Pisano S. Torpè Recinaio Vin Santo, San Gervasio	554
Biancospino, Alberto Serenelli	625
Biblos, Di Majo Norante	698
Bidis, Cant. Valle dell'Acate	766
Biel Cûr Rosso, Valerio Marinig	410
Biferno Bianco Gironia, Borgo di Colloredo	697
Biferno Rosato Gironia, Borgo di Colloredo	697
Biferno Rosso Gironia, Borgo di Colloredo	697
Biferno Rosso Ramitello, Di Majo Norante	698
Bigarò, Elio Perrone	68
Birba, La Gerla	529
Birba Rossa, Tenuta Gaiano	49
Birbét, Porello	54
Birbone Toscano, Fattoria dei Barbi	516
Bizante, Pisanu	803
Bizantino, Pervini	749
Bizir, Ajello	774
Blanc de Dauphin, F.lli Grosjean	19
Blanc des Rosis, Schiopetto	362
Blanc Frigon Extra Dry, Cave du Vin Blanc de Morgex et de La Salle	18
Blau&Blau Mjzzu, Jermann Vinnaioli	388
Blu, Fattoria Mancini	646
Bocciolè, Petreto	465
Bolgheri Bianco, Michele Satta	476
Bolgheri Bianco Campo alla Casa, Enrico Santini	476
Bolgheri Guado de' Gemoli, Giovanni Chiappini	595
Bolgheri Levia Gravia, Caccia al Piano 1868	595
Bolgheri Rosato Scalabrone, Tenuta Guado al Tasso	469
Bolgheri Rosso, Podere Guado al Melo	596
Bolgheri Rosso Alfeo, Ceralti	596
Bolgheri Rosso Piastraia, Michele Satta	476
Bolgheri Rosso Poggio al Moro, Enrico Santini	476
Bolgheri Rosso Serre Nuove, Tenuta dell' Ornellaia	470
Bolgheri Rosso Sup. Grattamacco, Colle Massari	475
Bolgheri Rosso Sup. Guado al Tasso, Tenuta Guado al Tasso	469
Bolgheri Rosso Sup. I Castagni, Michele Satta	476
Bolgheri Rosso Sup. Montepergoli, Enrico Santini	476
Bolgheri Rosso Sup. Paleo, Le Macchiole	470
Bolgheri Ruit Hora, Caccia al Piano 1868	595
Bolgheri Sassicaia, Tenuta San Guido	471
Bolgheri Sup. Ornellaia, Tenuta dell' Ornellaia	470
Bolgheri Vermentino, Tenuta Guado al Tasso	469
Bolgheri Vermentino Ceralti, Ceralti	596
Bolina, Rosa del Golfo	738
Bombereto, La Rampa di Fugnano	580
Bombino Bianco Catapanus, D'Alfonso del Sordo	752
Bonci Brut M. Cl., Vallerosa Bonci	633
Bonorli, Melini	563
Boranico, Alberto Serenelli	625
Borgo dei Guidi, Poderi dal Nespoli	438
Borgo di Peuma, Russolo	422
Borgo Rosso, Tenuta Valli	444
Borgoforte, Villa Pillo	502
Borgonero, Borgo Scopeto	483
Borro del Boscone, Le Calvane	551
Boscarelli, Boscarelli	543
Boschi Salviati, San Luciano	539
Botrus, Sergio Botrugno	753
Bottaccia, Torre Quarto	741
Bottaccio, Il Paradiso	579
Botticino Pià della Tesa, Antica Tesa	216
Bottiglia Particolare, Castello di Verrazzano	506
Bovo, Cant. Soc. La Torre	787
Braccano, Enzo Mecella	633
Brachetto d'Acqui, Braida	132
Brachetto d'Acqui Castelgaro, Bersano & Riccadonna	125
Brachetto d'Acqui Le Donne dei Boschi, Ca' dei Mandorli	157
Brachetto d'Acqui Niades, Cascina Garitina	59
Brachetto d'Acqui Pineto, Marenco	143
Brachetto d'Acqui Spumante Contero, La Giustiniana	85
Brachetto Secco La Selva di Moirano, Antica Casa Vinicola Scarpa	126
Bradisismo Cabernet Sauvignon, Inama	317
Braida Nuova, Borgo Conventi	387
Braide Alte Grand Cru, Livon	419
Bramante, Botrona	620
Bramasole, Fattoria Montellori	494
Bramaterra, Anzivino	82
Bramaterra, Sella	100
Bramaterra Dosso del Fornetto, Barni	46
Brancaia, La Brancaia	566
Brancaia Il Blu, La Brancaia	566
Brancaia Tre, La Brancaia	566
Braviolo, Fattoria del Cerro	544
Brecceto, Trappolini	682
Breg, Gravner	391
Breganze Bianco Le Colombare, Firmino Miotti	291
Breganze Bianco Rivana, Vigneto Due Santi	290
Breganze Cabernet, Firmino Miotti	291
Breganze Cabernet, Vigneto Due Santi	290
Breganze Cabernet Sauvignon Kilò Ris., Cant. Beato Bartolomeo Da Breganze	346
Breganze Cabernet Sauvignon Palazzotto, Maculan	290
Breganze Cabernet Vign. Due Santi, Vigneto Due Santi	290
Breganze di Breganze, Maculan	290
Breganze Pinot Bianco, Firmino Miotti	291
Breganze Pinot Nero Altura, Maculan	290
Breganze Rosso, Vigneto Due Santi	290
Breganze Rosso Crosara, Maculan	290
Breganze Sauvignon Vign. Due Santi, Vigneto Due Santi	290
Breganze Torcolato, Cant. Beato Bartolomeo Da Breganze	346
Breganze Torcolato, Maculan	290
Breganze Torcolato, Firmino Miotti	291
Breganze Vespaiolo, Firmino Miotti	291
Brentino, Maculan	290
Bricco Appiani, Flavio Roddolo	113
Bricco delle Bessole Passito, Stefano Accordini	320
Bricco Sturnèl, Bellaria	187
Bricoli, Vigliano	603
Brindisi Rosato V. Flaminio, Agricole Vallone	754
Brindisi Rosso, Cant. Due Palme	740
Brindisi Rosso, Santa Barbara	756
Brindisi Rosso, Vinicola Mediterranea	756
Brindisi Rosso Arcione, Sergio Botrugno	753
Brindisi Rosso Gallico, Tenute Rubino	739
Brindisi Rosso Jaddico, Tenute Rubino	739
Brindisi Rosso V. Flaminio, Agricole Vallone	754
Brisi, Fattoria San Francesco	758
Brolo dei Passoni, Ricci Curbastro	186
Bron & Rusèval Chardonnay, Celli	432
Bron & Rusèval Sangiovese-Cabernet, Celli	432
Brunello di Montalcino, Argiano	605
Brunello di Montalcino, Castello Banfi	515
Brunello di Montalcino, Fattoria dei Barbi	516
Brunello di Montalcino, Roberto Bellini	605
Brunello di Montalcino, Brunelli - Le Chiuse di Sotto	605
Brunello di Montalcino, Castello di Camigliano	516
Brunello di Montalcino, Canalicchio di Sopra	605
Brunello di Montalcino, Tenuta Caparzo	517
Brunello di Montalcino, Casanova di Neri	517
Brunello di Montalcino, Casanuova delle Cerbaie	518
Brunello di Montalcino, Casisano Colombaio	518
Brunello di Montalcino, Castelgiocondo	519
Brunello di Montalcino, Castiglion del Bosco	519
Brunello di Montalcino, Cerbaia	606
Brunello di Montalcino, Cerbaiona	520
Brunello di Montalcino, Tenuta Col d'Orcia	521
Brunello di Montalcino, Collelceto	606
Brunello di Montalcino, Tenuta di Collosorbo	522
Brunello di Montalcino, Corte Pavone	606
Brunello di Montalcino, Andrea Costanti	522
Brunello di Montalcino, Tenuta Di Sesta	523
Brunello di Montalcino, Casato Prime Donne Donatella Cinelli Colombini	523
Brunello di Montalcino, Fanti - La Palazzetta	524
Brunello di Montalcino, Fanti - San Filippo	525
Brunello di Montalcino, Fattoi	606
Brunello di Montalcino, Tenute Ambrogio e Giovanni Folonari	493
Brunello di Montalcino, Fossacolle	606
Brunello di Montalcino, Greppone Mazzi - Tenimenti Ruffino	526
Brunello di Montalcino, Tenuta Il Greppo	526
Brunello di Montalcino, Il Marroneto	606
Brunello di Montalcino, Il Palazzone	527
Brunello di Montalcino, Tenuta Il Poggione	528
Brunello di Montalcino, La Fornace	607
Brunello di Montalcino, Podere La Fortuna	528
Brunello di Montalcino, La Gerla	529
Brunello di Montalcino, La Poderina	529
Brunello di Montalcino, La Rasina	607
Brunello di Montalcino, La Togata - Tenuta Carlina	530
Brunello di Montalcino, Le Chiuse	530
Brunello di Montalcino, Le Gode di Ripaccioli	607
Brunello di Montalcino, Le Macioche	607
Brunello di Montalcino, Lisini	531
Brunello di Montalcino, Mastrojanni	532
Brunello di Montalcino, Mocali	608
Brunello di Montalcino, Cantina di Montalcino	608
Brunello di Montalcino, Tenute Silvio Nardi	532
Brunello di Montalcino, Oliveto	608
Brunello di Montalcino, Siro Pacenti	533
Brunello di Montalcino, Palazzo	608
Brunello di Montalcino, Pian dell'Orino	608
Brunello di Montalcino, Pian delle Vigne	608
Brunello di Montalcino, Piancornello	609
Brunello di Montalcino, Agostina Pieri	609
Brunello di Montalcino, Poggio Antico	533
Brunello di Montalcino, Poggio di Sotto	609
Brunello di Montalcino, Poggio San Polo	609
Brunello di Montalcino, Castello Romitorio	534
Brunello di Montalcino, Podere Salicutti	534
Brunello di Montalcino, Salvioni - La Cerbaiola	535
Brunello di Montalcino, San Felice	488
Brunello di Montalcino, Solaria - Cencioni	535
Brunello di Montalcino, Talenti	536
Brunello di Montalcino, Tenimenti Angelini	536
Brunello di Montalcino, Uccelliera	537
Brunello di Montalcino, Tenuta Val di Cava	537
Brunello di Montalcino, Villa Le Prata	538
Brunello di Montalcino, Visconti	538
Brunello di Montalcino, Vitanza	610
Brunello di Montalcino Altero, Poggio Antico	533
Brunello di Montalcino Beato, Il Poggiolo	527
Brunello di Montalcino Beato Ris., Il Poggiolo	527
Brunello di Montalcino Cerretalto, Casanova di Neri	517
Brunello di Montalcino Cerretalto Ris., Casanova di Neri	517
Brunello di Montalcino Donna Olga, Donna Olga	524

Brunello di Montalcino Gualto, Castello di Camigliano 516
Brunello di Montalcino La Casa, Tenuta Caparzo 517
Brunello di Montalcino Le Due Sorelle Ris.,
    Tenute Ambrogio e Giovanni Folonari 493
Brunello di Montalcino Madonna del Piano Ris.,
    Tenuta Val di Cava 537
Brunello di Montalcino Manachiara, Tenute Silvio Nardi 532
Brunello di Montalcino Manachiara Cru, Tenute Silvio Nardi 532
Brunello di Montalcino Montosoli, Altesino 605
Brunello di Montalcino Pietranera, Centolani 520
Brunello di Montalcino Poggio agli Angeli, La Gerla 529
Brunello di Montalcino Poggio al Vento Ris., Tenuta Col d'Orcia 521
Brunello di Montalcino Poggio all'Oro Ris., Castello Banfi 515
Brunello di Montalcino Poggio alle Mura, Castello Banfi 515
Brunello di Montalcino Poggio Banale, La Poderina 529
Brunello di Montalcino Poggio Salvi, Tenuta Il Greppo 526
Brunello di Montalcino Poggiolo, Il Poggiolo 527
Brunello di Montalcino Poggiolo Ris., Il Poggiolo 527
Brunello di Montalcino Prime Donne,
    Casato Prime Donne Donatella Cinelli Colombini 523
Brunello di Montalcino Ripa al Convento, Castelgiocondo 519
Brunello di Montalcino Ris., Altesino 605
Brunello di Montalcino Ris., Fattoria dei Barbi 516
Brunello di Montalcino Ris., Castello di Camigliano 516
Brunello di Montalcino Ris., Canalicchio di Sopra 605
Brunello di Montalcino Ris., Tenuta Caparzo 517
Brunello di Montalcino Ris., Casanuova delle Cerbaie 518
Brunello di Montalcino Ris., Casisano Colombaio 518
Brunello di Montalcino Ris., Castelgiocondo 519
Brunello di Montalcino Ris., Castiglion del Bosco 519
Brunello di Montalcino Ris., Centolani 520
Brunello di Montalcino Ris., Cerbaia 606
Brunello di Montalcino Ris., Ciacci Piccolomini D'Aragona 521
Brunello di Montalcino Ris., Tenuta di Collosorbo 522
Brunello di Montalcino Ris., Corte Pavone 606
Brunello di Montalcino Ris., Andrea Costanti 522
Brunello di Montalcino Ris., Tenuta Di Sesta 523
Brunello di Montalcino Ris., Fanti - La Palazzetta 524
Brunello di Montalcino Ris., Fanti - San Filippo 525
Brunello di Montalcino Ris., Fattoi 606
Brunello di Montalcino Ris., Eredi Fuligni 525
Brunello di Montalcino Ris., Greppone Mazzi - Tenimenti Ruffino 526
Brunello di Montalcino Ris., Tenuta Il Greppo 526
Brunello di Montalcino Ris., Il Palazzone 527
Brunello di Montalcino Ris., Tenuta Il Poggione 528
Brunello di Montalcino Ris., La Fornace 607
Brunello di Montalcino Ris., Podere La Fortuna 528
Brunello di Montalcino Ris., La Gerla 529
Brunello di Montalcino Ris., La Poderina 529
Brunello di Montalcino Ris., La Togata - Tenuta Carlina 530
Brunello di Montalcino Ris., Le Chiuse 530
Brunello di Montalcino Ris., Le Macioche 607
Brunello di Montalcino Ris., Mastrojanni 532
Brunello di Montalcino Ris., Mocali 608
Brunello di Montalcino Ris., Palazzo 608
Brunello di Montalcino Ris., Poggio Antico 533
Brunello di Montalcino Ris., Castello Romitorio 534
Brunello di Montalcino Ris., Talenti 536
Brunello di Montalcino Ris., Uccelliera 537
Brunello di Montalcino Ris., Vitanza 610
Brunello di Montalcino Schiena d'Asino, Mastrojanni 532
Brunello di Montalcino Tenuta Friggiali, Centolani 520
Brunello di Montalcino Tenuta Nuova, Casanova di Neri 517
Brunello di Montalcino Terra Rossa, Il Poggiolo 527
Brunello di Montalcino Terra Rossa Ris., Il Poggiolo 527
Brunello di Montalcino Ugolaia, Lisini 531
Brunello di Montalcino V. del Colombaio, Casisano Colombaio 518
Brunello di Montalcino V. del Fiore, Fattoria dei Barbi 516
Brunello di Montalcino V. del Quercione Ris., San Felice 488
Brunello di Montalcino Vigna del Fiore Ris., Fattoria dei Barbi 516
Brunello di Montalcino Vigna del Lago, Tenimenti Angelini 536
Brunello di Montalcino Vigna delle Raunate, Mocali 608
Brunello di Montalcino Vigna di Pianrosso,
    Ciacci Piccolomini D'Aragona 521
Brunello di Montalcino Vigna gli Angeli, La Gerla 529
Brunello di Montalcino Vigna Spuntali, Tenimenti Angelini 536
Brunello di Montalcino Vigneti dei Cottimelli, Eredi Fuligni 525
Brunello di Montalcino Vigneti dei Cottimelli Ris., Eredi Fuligni 525
Bruno di Rocca, Vecchie Terre di Montefili 560
Brusco dei Barbi, Fattoria dei Barbi 516
Brut Cl. Ceppo 326, Pasini Produttori 224
Brut Cl. Costaripa, Costaripa 200
Brut Cl. Il Calepino, Il Calepino 189
Brut Cl. Ris. Fra Ambrogio, Il Calepino 189
Brut Cuvée Tombola di Pin M. Cl., Santo Stefano 294
Brut M. Cl., Dino Illuminati 699
Brut Ris., Duca di Salaparuta - Vini Corvo 769
Brut Riserva M. Cl., Gioacchino Garofoli 635
Brut Rosè Costaripa, Costaripa 200
Bruzzico, Malenchini 594
Bucciato, Ca' Rugate 307
Bue Apis, Cant. del Taburno 714
Buranco, Buranco 173
Burdese, Planeta 774
Buriano, Rocca di Castagnoli 500
Burson, Tenuta Uccellina 462
C. Amerini Rosso Sup., Fattoria Le Poggette 677
C. Amerini Rosso Sup. Carbio, Cant. dei Colli Amerini 658
C. Amerini Rosso Terre Arnolfe, Cant. dei Colli Amerini 658
C. B. Barbera, Gradizzolo 460
C. B. Barbera Frizzante, Virgilio Sandoni 458
C. B. Barbera Il Foriere, La Mancina 450
C. B. Barbera Montebudello Sopra i Fichi Cabasà Ris.,
    Ca' Selvatica 460
C. B. Barbera Ris., Giuseppe Beghelli 458
C. B. Barbera Ris., Gradizzolo 460

C. B. Cabernet Sauvignon, Floriano Cinti 453
C. B. Cabernet Sauvignon,
    Maria Letizia Gaggioli - Vigneto Bagazzana 466
C. B. Cabernet Sauvignon, Isola 448
C. B. Cabernet Sauvignon, La Mancina 450
C. B. Cabernet Sauvignon, San Vito 450
C. B. Cabernet Sauvignon, Tizzano 435
C. B. Cabernet Sauvignon, Vallona 437
C. B. Cabernet Sauvignon, Vigneto delle Terre Rosse 466
C. B. Cabernet Sauvignon Bonzarone, Tenuta Bonzara 449
C. B. Cabernet Sauvignon Comandante della Guardia,
    La Mancina 450
C. B. Cabernet Sauvignon Cuvée, Vigneto delle Terre Rosse 466
C. B. Cabernet Sauvignon Giòrosso, Santarosa 448
C. B. Cabernet Sauvignon Il Francia Rosso Ris.,
    Maria Letizia Gaggioli - Vigneto Bagazzana 466
C. B. Cabernet Sauvignon Le Borre, Corte d'Aibo 449
C. B. Cabernet Sauvignon Ris., Erioli 457
C. B. Cabernet Sauvignon Ris., Tizzano 435
C. B. Cabernet Sauvignon Sel., Floriano Cinti 453
C. B. Cabernet Sauvignon Sel., Isola 448
C. B. Cabernet Sauvignon Sel., San Vito 450
C. B. Cabernet Sauvignon Sel., Vallona 437
C. B. Cabernet Sauvignon Terre di Montebudello Ris., Erioli 457
C. B. Cabernet Sauvignon V. del Falco Nero, Ca' Selvatica 460
C. B. Chardonnay, Floriano Cinti 453
C. B. Chardonnay, Isola 448
C. B. Chardonnay, San Vito 450
C. B. Chardonnay, Vallona 437
C. B. Chardonnay, Vigneto delle Terre Rosse 466
C. B. Chardonnay Bianco della Garisenda, San Vito 450
C. B. Chardonnay Cuvée, Vigneto delle Terre Rosse 466
C. B. Chardonnay Giòcoliere, Santarosa 448
C. B. Chardonnay Lavinio,
    Maria Letizia Gaggioli - Vigneto Bagazzana 466
C. B. Chardonnay Sel., Isola 448
C. B. Merlot, Floriano Cinti 453
C. B. Merlot, Maria Letizia Gaggioli - Vigneto Bagazzana 466
C. B. Merlot, La Mancina 450
C. B. Merlot Calastrino, Gradizzolo 460
C. B. Merlot Giòtondo, Santarosa 448
C. B. Merlot Lanciotto, La Mancina 450
C. B. Merlot Rocca di Bonacciara, Tenuta Bonzara 449
C. B. Merlot Roncovecchio, Corte d'Aibo 449
C. B. Merlot Rosso del Poggio, Tenuta Bonzara 449
C. B. Merlot Sel., Floriano Cinti 453
C. B. Pignoletto, Vallona 437
C. B. Pignoletto Brut, Tizzano 435
C. B. Pignoletto Cl., Giuseppe Beghelli 458
C. B. Pignoletto Cl., Floriano Cinti 453
C. B. Pignoletto Cl., Santarosa 448
C. B. Pignoletto Cl. V. Antica, Tenuta Bonzara 449
C. B. Pignoletto Frizzante, Floriano Cinti 453
C. B. Pignoletto Frizzante, Maria Letizia Gaggioli - Vigneto Bagazzana 466
C. B. Pignoletto Frizzante, Isola 448
C. B. Pignoletto Frizzante, La Mancina 450
C. B. Pignoletto Frizzante, San Vito 450
C. B. Pignoletto Frizzante, Tenuta Bonzara 449
C. B. Pignoletto Frizzante, Tizzano 435
C. B. Pignoletto Frizzante V. della Torre, Podere Riosto 461
C. B. Pignoletto Sup., Maria Letizia Gaggioli - Vigneto Bagazzana 466
C. B. Pignoletto Sup., Isola 448
C. B. Pignoletto Sup., San Vito 450
C. B. Pignoletto Sup., Tizzano 435
C. B. Pignoletto Sup. V. della Torre, Podere Riosto 461
C. B. Pignoletto Terre di Montebudello, La Mancina 450
C. B. Pinot Bianco, Floriano Cinti 453
C. B. Pinot Bianco, Santarosa 448
C. B. Pinot Bianco Crilò, Maria Letizia Gaggioli - Vigneto Bagazzana 466
C. B. Riesling Malagò, Vigneto delle Terre Rosse 466
C. B. Riesling Malagò V. T., Vigneto delle Terre Rosse 466
C. B. Sauvignon, Giuseppe Beghelli 458
C. B. Sauvignon, Floriano Cinti 453
C. B. Sauvignon, Tizzano 435
C. B. Sauvignon, Vigneto delle Terre Rosse 466
C. B. Sauvignon Sel., Floriano Cinti 453
C. B. Sauvignon Spugnula, Corte d'Aibo 449
C. B. Sauvignon Sup., Maria Letizia Gaggioli - Vigneto Bagazzana 466
C. B. Sauvignon Sup. Le Carrate, Tenuta Bonzara 449
C. B. Sauvignon V. del Pino, Podere Riosto 461
C. del Trasimeno Baccio del Bianco, Duca della Corgna 660
C. del Trasimeno Baccio del Rosso, Duca della Corgna 660
C. del Trasimeno Gamay Divina Villa Et. Bianca, Duca della Corgna 660
C. del Trasimeno Grechetto Nuricante, Duca della Corgna 660
C. del Trasimeno Rosso Barca, Terre del Carpine 677
C. del Trasimeno Rosso Corniolo, Duca della Corgna 660
C. del Trasimeno Rosso Lucciaio, Pieve del Vescovo 676
C. di Rimini Rosso VignalaVolta, Podere Vecciano 459
C. P. Barbera della Stoppa, La Stoppa 452
C. P. Bonarda Amabile, Gaetano Lusenti 455
C. P. Bonarda Duca Ottavio, Castelli del Duca 434
C. P. Bonarda Frizzante, Torre Fornello 455
C. P. Bonarda La Picciona, Gaetano Lusenti 455
C. P. Bonarda Ris., Torre Fornello 455
C. P. Cabernet Sauvignon, Tenuta La Torretta 460
C. P. Cabernet Sauvignon Ca' Bernesca, Torre Fornello 455
C. P. Cabernet Sauvignon Corbeau, Luretta 444
C. P. Cabernet Sauvignon Il Pergolo,
    Conte Otto Barattieri di San Pietro 454
C. P. Cabernet Sauvignon Luna Selvatica, La Tosa 454
C. P. Cabernet Sauvignon Perticato del Novarei, Il Poggiarello 453
C. P. Cabernet Sauvignon Ronchello, Cardinali 437
C. P. Cabernet Sauvignon Stoppa, La Stoppa 452
C. P. Cabernet Sauvignon Villante, Gaetano Lusenti 455
C. P. Chardonnay Perticato La Piana, Il Poggiarello 453
C. P. Chardonnay Selin dl'Armari, Luretta 444

C. P. Gutturnio, Conte Otto Barattieri di San Pietro 454
C. P. Gutturnio, Perinelli 461
C. P. Gutturnio Cl., Tenuta La Torretta 460
C. P. Gutturnio Cl. Duca Augusto, Castelli del Duca 434
C. P. Gutturnio Cl. Julius, Cant. Soc. Valtidone 457
C. P. Gutturnio Cl. Nicchio, Cardinali 437
C. P. Gutturnio Cl. Torquato Ris., Cardinali 437
C. P. Gutturnio Diacono Gerardo 1028 Ris., Torre Fornello 455
C. P. Gutturnio Frizzante, Baraccone 461
C. P. Gutturnio Frizzante, Conte Otto Barattieri di San Pietro 454
C. P. Gutturnio La Barbona Ris., Il Poggiarello 453
C. P. Gutturnio Perticato Valandrea, Il Poggiarello 453
C. P. Gutturnio Ris., Oppizzi 461
C. P. Gutturnio Ronco Alto Ris., Baraccone 461
C. P. Gutturnio Sigillum Ris., Castelli del Duca 434
C. P. Gutturnio Sup. Cresta al Sole, Gaetano Lusenti 455
C. P. Gutturnio Sup. Duca Alessandro, Castelli del Duca 434
C. P. Gutturnio Sup. L'Ala del Drago, Luretta 444
C. P. Gutturnio Sup. Sinsàl, Torre Fornello 455
C. P. Gutturnio V. della Villa, Tenuta La Torretta 460
C. P. Gutturnio Vignamorello, La Tosa 454
C. P. Gutturnio Vivace, Perinelli 461
C. P. Malvasia Boccadirosa, Luretta 444
C. P. Malvasia Donna Luigia, Torre Fornello 455
C. P. Malvasia Passito Luna di Candia, Cant. Soc. Valtidone 457
C. P. Malvasia Passito Soleste, Castelli del Duca 434
C. P. Malvasia Passito V. del Volta, La Stoppa 452
C. P. Malvasia Passito Vigna del Volta, La Stoppa 452
C. P. Malvasia Perticato Beatrice Quadri, Il Poggiarello 453
C. P. Malvasia Secca Frizzante, Torre Fornello 455
C. P. Malvasia Sorriso di Cielo, La Tosa 454
C. P. Malvasia V. T. Le Rane, Luretta 444
C. P. Monterosso Val D'Arda Solata, Cardinali 437
C. P. Ortrugo, Conte Otto Barattieri di San Pietro 454
C. P. Pinot Nero Achab, Luretta 444
C. P. Pinot Nero Perticato Le Giastre, Il Poggiarello 453
C. P. Sauvignon, La Tosa 454
C. P. Sauvignon Costa Solara, Cant. Soc. Valtidone 457
C. P. Sauvignon Duchessa Vittoria, Castelli del Duca 434
C. P. Sauvignon I Nani e Le Ballerine, Luretta 444
C. P. Sauvignon Perticato Il Quadri, Il Poggiarello 453
C. P. Valnure Frizzante, La Tosa 454
C. P. Vin Santo Albarola, Conte Otto Barattieri di San Pietro 454
Ca' Andrea, I Girasoli di Sant'Andrea 678
Ca' Brione, Nino Negri 191
Ca' della Signora Brut, Poderi di San Pietro 209
Cabanon Blanc, Cabanon 221
Caberlot, Podere Il Carnasciale 514
Cabernasco, Villa Pigna 655
Cabernet, Bepin de Eto 320
Cabernet, Sallier de La Tour 784
Cabernet, Sant'Elena 393
Cabernet Bergamasca, La Tordela 214
Cabernet dei Colli Trevigiani, Gregoletto 304
Cabernet della Bergamasca, Cant. Soc. Bergamasca 210
Cabernet della Bergamasca Torcularia, Le Corne 221
Cabernet Duca Cantelmi, Giovanni Palombo 681
Cabernet Franc Campo Buri, La Cappuccina 308
Cabernet I Legni, Russolo 422
Cabernet Sauvignon, Nicola Balter 241
Cabernet Sauvignon, Fattoria Buccicatino 708
Cabernet Sauvignon, Casale del Giglio 681
Cabernet Sauvignon, Tenuta Castiglioni 551
Cabernet Sauvignon, Feudo Principi di Butera 767
Cabernet Sauvignon, Fiegl 391
Cabernet Sauvignon, Isole e Olena 467
Cabernet Sauvignon, Lungarotti 675
Cabernet Sauvignon, Marion 319
Cabernet Sauvignon, San Vettore 502
Cabernet Sauvignon, Virgilio Sandoni 458
Cabernet Sauvignon, Tasca d'Almerita 778
Cabernet Sauvignon, Tenuta di Trecciano 620
Cabernet Sauvignon, Villa Pillo 502
Cabernet Sauvignon Capitel del Monte, Tenuta Sant'Antonio 304
Cabernet Sauvignon Capitello, Tenuta Sant'Antonio 304
Cabernet Sauvignon Castellione, Calonga 443
Cabernet Sauvignon Colle Funaro, Orlandi Contucci Ponno 705
Cabernet Sauvignon Mandrarossa, Settesoli 775
Cabernet Sauvignon Marina Cvetic, Gianni Masciarelli 706
Cabernet Sauvignon Sel., Vallona 437
Cabernet Sauvignon Soleggio, Vini Pallavicini 689
Cabernet Sauvignon Terre di Pojan, Tezza 343
Cabreo Il Borgo, Tenute Ambrogio e Giovanni Folonari 493
Cabreomytho, Tenute Ambrogio e Giovanni Folonari 493
Càgnore, Antico Terreno Ottavi 650
Cagnulari, Giovanni Cherchi 801
Calabrone, Bastianich 405
Calamita, Poggio a Poppiano 552
Calanchi di Vaiano, Paolo d'Amico 682
Calanco, Tenuta Le Velette 670
Calat, Feudo Principi di Butera 767
Calcare Sauvignon, Conte Leopardi Dittajuti 642
Calenne, Puri Charlotte 694
Calicò Brut, Le Sorgenti 465
Caluso Bianco Vignot S. Antonio, Orsolani 134
Caluso Passito, Podere Macellio - Renato Bianco 155
Caluso Passito Alladium Vign. Runc, Cieck 24
Caluso Passito Poetica, Giovanni Silva 24
Caluso Passito Sole d'Inverno, Favaro 163
Caluso Passito Sulé, Orsolani 134
Caluso Passito Vign. Cariola, Ferrando 89
Caluso Spumante Brut M. Cl., Orsolani 134
Caluso Spumante M. Cl. Cella Grande, La Cella di San Michele 164
Caluso Spumante M. Cl. Pas Dosé,
Podere Macellio - Renato Bianco 155
Calvario, Ottavio Lequio - Prinsi 123

Camartina, Querciabella 504
Camastra, Tasca d'Almerita 778
Camedrio, Feudi di Zangara 784
Camelot, Firriato 776
Camerte, La Monacesca 637
Camoi Col Sandago, Martino Zanetti 349
Camp'ed Pietrù, Ottavio Lequio - Prinsi 123
Campaccio, Fattoria di Terrabianca 568
Campanaro, Feudi di San Gregorio 723
Campei, Le Chiusure 225
Campi Flegrei Falanghina Coste di Cuma,
Cantine Grotta del Sole 720
Campi Flegrei Piedirosso Montegauro Ris.,
Cantine Grotta del Sole 720
Campi Sarni Rosso, Vallarom 229
Campo ai Ciliegi, Buondonno 477
Campo ai Sassi, Tenuta Maiano 612
Campo all'Albero, La Sala 574
Campo Buri, La Cappuccina 308
Campo d'Aia, Castello di Modanella 570
Campo del Viotto Bianco, Scarbolo 402
Campo La Chiesa, Provveditore 620
Campo Lungo, Fattoria Casabianca 553
Campo Montecristo, Serraiola 550
Campo Sireso, Ottella 316
Campo Vecchio Bianco, Castel De Paolis 686
Campo Vecchio Rosso, Castel De Paolis 686
Campofiorin, Masi 327
Campoleone, Lamborghini - La Fiorita 671
Campolucci, Mannucci Droandi 613
Campore, Il Pratello 447
Camporosso, La Marcellina 558
Campos Rosato del Limbara, Cant. Soc. Gallura 801
Camposilio, Camposilio 600
Canà Rosso, La Biancara 295
Canaiolo, Fattoria Le Poggette 677
Canaiuolo, Montenidoli 581
Canavese Rosso Acini Sparsi, Orsolani 134
Canavese Rosso Cieck, Cieck 24
Canavese Rosso Montodo, Ferrando 89
Canavese Rosso Tre Ciochè, Giovanni Silva 24
Candia dei Colli Apuani, Cima 513
Candia dei Colli Apuani Vign. Candia Alto, Cima 513
Candiani, Vitivincola Su Baroni 803
Canneto, D'Angelo 733
Cannonau di Sardegna, Giovanni Cherchi 801
Cannonau di Sardegna, Antichi Poderi Jerzu 794
Cannonau di Sardegna, Piero Mancini 796
Cannonau di Sardegna, Perdarubia 803
Cannonau di Sardegna, Gigi Picciau 802
Cannonau di Sardegna Alberto Loi Ris., Alberto Loi 792
Cannonau di Sardegna Antares, Josto Puddu 804
Cannonau di Sardegna Anzenas, Cantine di Dolianova 793
Cannonau di Sardegna Baione, Cant. Soc. della Trexenta 799
Cannonau di Sardegna Blasio Ris., Cantine di Dolianova 793
Cannonau di Sardegna Brunk'è Ris., Pisanu 803
Cannonau di Sardegna Cardedo Ris., Alberto Loi 792
Cannonau di Sardegna Corrasi Nepente di Oliena Ris.,
Cant. Coop. di Oliena 804
Cannonau di Sardegna Costera, Antonio Argiolas 799
Cannonau di Sardegna Firmadu, Tenute Soletta 793
Cannonau di Sardegna Jerzu Alberto Loi Ris., Alberto Loi 792
Cannonau di Sardegna Jerzu Cardedo Ris., Alberto Loi 792
Cannonau di Sardegna Jerzu Sa Mola, Alberto Loi 792
Cannonau di Sardegna Le Ghiaie, Meloni Vini 798
Cannonau di Sardegna Lillové, Giuseppe Gabbas 796
Cannonau di Sardegna Lillovè, Giuseppe Gabbas 796
Cannonau di Sardegna Marghia, Antichi Poderi Jerzu 794
Cannonau di Sardegna Nepente di Oliena, Gostolai 804
Cannonau di Sardegna Nepente di Oliena, Cant. Coop. di Oliena 804
Cannonau di Sardegna Ris., Attilio Contini 791
Cannonau di Sardegna Ris., Tenute Soletta 793
Cannonau di Sardegna Ris. Chuerra, Antichi Poderi Jerzu 794
Cannonau di Sardegna Riserva Josto Miglior, Antichi Poderi Jerzu 794
Cannonau di Sardegna Sa Mola Rubia, Alberto Loi 792
Cannonau di Sardegna Sileno, Ferruccio Deiana 800
Cannonau di Sardegna Tamara, Cant. Soc. del Vermentino 795
Cannonau di Sardegna Triente, F.lli Pala 800
Cannonau di Sardegna V. di Isalle, Cant. Soc. Dorgali 794
Cannonau di Sardegna Vignaruja, Cant. Soc. Il Nuraghe 803
Canonico, Cant. Due Palme 740
Cantalupo, Azzoni Avogadro Carradori 654
Cantico, Podere La Cappella 591
Cantinino, Fattoria Castello Sonnino 612
Cantoalto Bianco, Bonaldi - Cascina del Bosco 226
Canvalle, Vignavecchia 569
Capalbio Rosso Losco, Santa Lucia 603
Capel del Prete, Roncolato 351
Capichera, Capichera 791
Capichera V.T., Capichera 791
Capichera Vigna 'Ngena, Capichera 791
Capitel Croce, Roberto Anselmi 307
Capitel Foscarino, Roberto Anselmi 307
Capitel S. Rocco Rosso di Ripasso, F.lli Tedeschi 324
Capitolo Laureto, Mille Una 746
Capitoni, Tenuta Vitereta 604
Capo di Stato, Conte Loredan Gasparini Venegazzù 344
Capo Martino, Jermann Vinnaioli 388
Caporosso, Grasso 786
Cappello di Prete, Francesco Candido 751
Capriano del Colle Rosso Monte Bruciato Ris., La Vigna 217
Capriano del Colle Rosso Tenuta Anna Ris., La Cascina Nuova 223
Capro Rosso, Fattoria di Bagnolo 510
Capsico Rosso, Ciccio Zaccagnini 697
Carantan, Marco Felluga 393
Caratello Passito, Enoteca Bisson 169

Cardinal Minio, Capinera	641
Carema Et.Bianca, Ferrando	89
Carema Et. Bianca, Cant. dei Produttori Nebbiolo di Carema	57
Carema Et. Bianca Barricato, Cantina dei Produttori Nebbiolo di Carema	57
Carema Et. Nera, Ferrando	89
Carema Et. Nera, Cant. dei Produttori Nebbiolo di Carema	57
Carema Le Tabbie, Orsolani	134
Cariglio, Tenuta Terre Nobili	765
Carignano del Sulcis Grotta Rossa, Cant. Soc. di Santadi	797
Carignano del Sulcis Issolus, Sardus Pater	797
Carignano del Sulcis Ris., Sardus Pater	797
Carignano del Sulcis Rocca Rubia Ris., Cant. Soc. di Santadi	797
Carignano del Sulcis Sup. Terre Brune, Cant. Soc. di Santadi	797
Carleto, Enrico Pierazzuoli	473
Carlozadra Cl. Brut, Carlozadra	199
Carlozadra Cl. Brut Nondosato, Carlozadra	199
Carlozadra Cl. Extra Dry Tradizione, Carlozadra	199
Carlozadra Extra Dry Liberty, Carlozadra	199
Carmen Puthod, Teruzzi & Puthod	583
Carmenèro, Ca' del Bosco	196
Carmerum, Vini Classici Cardone	747
Carmignano, Castelvecchio	596
Carmignano, Pratesi	474
Carmignano Elzana Ris., Fattoria Ambra	473
Carmignano Le Farnete Ris., Enrico Pierazzuoli	473
Carmignano Le Vigne Alte di Montalbiolo Ris., Fattoria Ambra	473
Carmignano Ris., Castelvecchio	596
Carmignano Ris., Piaggia	563
Carmignano Vigna di Montefortini, Fattoria Ambra	473
Carmignano Vigna S. Cristina in Pilli, Fattoria Ambra	473
Carmignano Villa Artimino, Artimino	596
Carmignano Villa di Capezzana, Tenuta di Capezzana	474
Carmignano Villa di Trefiano, Tenuta di Capezzana	474
Carmignano Villa Medicea Ris., Artimino	596
Carolus, Antichi Vigneti di Cantalupo	87
Carso Cabernet Franc, Castelvecchio	414
Carso Cabernet Sauvignon, Castelvecchio	414
Carso Chardonnay, Kante	385
Carso Malvasia, Kante	385
Carso Malvasia, Skerk	429
Carso Malvasia Istriana, Castelvecchio	414
Carso Pinot Grigio, Castelvecchio	414
Carso Refosco P. R., Castelvecchio	414
Carso Rosso Turmino, Castelvecchio	414
Carso Sauvignon, Castelvecchio	414
Carso Sauvignon, Kante	385
Carso Sauvignon, Skerk	429
Carso Terrano, Skerk	429
Carso Terrano, Zidarich	385
Carso Traminer Aromatico, Castelvecchio	414
Carso Vitovska, Kante	385
Carso Vitovska, Skerk	429
Carso Vitovska, Zidarich	385
Cartizze, Adami	343
Cartizze, Desiderio Bisol & Figli	335
Cartizze, F.lli Bortolin Spumanti	335
Cartizze, Bortolomiol	336
Cartizze, Canevel Spumanti	336
Cartizze, Il Cardo	351
Cartizze, Col Vetoraz	337
Cartizze, Le Bellerive - Angelo Ruggeri	337
Cartizze, Le Colture	338
Cartizze, Nino Franco	338
Cartizze, Ruggeri & C.	339
Cartizze, Santa Eurosia	339
Cartizze, Tanorè	340
Caruess, Rockhof	286
Casa Pastore Rosso, Rio Grande	671
Casaglia, Tenuta di Bagnolo dei Marchesi Pancrazi	542
Casale San Giorgio Rosato, Cant. Soc.Coop. del Locorotondo	747
Casalferro, Barone Ricasoli	496
Casalj, Tenute Rapitalà	768
Casanova, Streda in Belvedere	622
Casanova Rosso, Fattoria Montanine	603
Casarsa, Villa Calcinaia	603
Casavecchia Sammichele, Castello Ducale	713
Casirano Rosso, Conte Leopardi Dittajuti	642
Casorzo Malvasia Brigantino, Giulio Accornero e Figli	151
Casotte, Bellavista	195
Cassabò Rosso, Valfieri	74
Cassero Rosso, Castello di Selvole	488
Castel del Monte Aglianico Cappellaccio Ris., Rivera	379
Castel del Monte Bianco, Torrevento	742
Castel del Monte Bianco Fedora, Rivera	379
Castel del Monte Bianco La Piana, Conte Spagnoletti Zeuli	738
Castel del Monte Chardonnay Lama di Corvo, Rivera	379
Castel del Monte Chardonnay Pietrabianca, Tormaresca	752
Castel del Monte Chardonnay Preludio N° 1, Rivera	379
Castel del Monte Le More Ris., Santa Lucia	753
Castel del Monte Nero di Troia Puer Apuliae, Rivera	379
Castel del Monte Pezza La Ruca, Conte Spagnoletti Zeuli	738
Castel del Monte Ris. del Conte, Conte Spagnoletti Zeuli	738
Castel del Monte Rosato, Torrevento	742
Castel del Monte Rosè, Rivera	379
Castel del Monte Rosso, Vinicola Miali	749
Castel del Monte Rosso, Torrevento	742
Castel del Monte Rosso Bocca di Lupo, Tormaresca	752
Castel del Monte Rosso Il Falcone Ris., Rivera	379
Castel del Monte Rosso Ris., Cant. Coop. della Riforma Fondiaria	755
Castel del Monte Rosso Vigna Pedale Ris., Torrevento	742
Castel del Monte Sauvignon Terre al Monte, Rivera	379
Castel del Monte Terranera Ris., Conte Spagnoletti Zeuli	738
Castel del Monte Vigna Grande, Conte Spagnoletti Zeuli	738
Castellaccio Bianco, Fattoria Uccelliera	600
Castellaccio Rosso, Fattoria Uccelliera	600
Castellinaldo Barbera d'Alba, Marsaglia	157
Castellinaldo Barbera d'Alba, Stefanino Morra	61
Castellinaldo Barbera d'Alba, Vielmin	62
Castello del Terriccio, Castello del Terriccio	482
Castello di Buttrio Marburg, Marco Felluga	393
Castello di Buttrio Ovestein, Marco Felluga	393
Castello di Cacchiano Bianco, Castello di Cacchiano	601
Castello di Cacchiano Rosso, Castello di Cacchiano	601
Castelruggero, Castel Ruggero	493
Cauro, Statti	761
Cava del Re Cabernet Sauvignon, D'Alfonso del Sordo	752
Cavaliere, Michele Satta	476
Cavina Chardonnay, Tenuta Pandolfa	451
Ceccante, Il Grillesino	600
Cecubo, Villa Matilde	714
Cellarius Brut Ris. Speciale, Guido Berlucchi & C.	194
Cellatica Sup. Clavis, Ca' del Vént	219
Cenereto, Trappolini	682
Cenito, Luigi Maffini	713
Cent'Are Bianco, Carlo Pellegrino	773
Centine, Castello Banfi	515
Cepola Bianco, Villa di Quartu	804
Cepola Rosso, Villa di Quartu	804
Cepparello, Isole e Olena	467
Ceppate, Fattoria di Terrabianca	568
Ceraso, Giovanni Panizzi	583
Cerasuolo di Scilla, Vintripodi Calabria	764
Cerasuolo di Vittoria, COS	782
Cerasuolo di Vittoria, Planeta	774
Cerasuolo di Vittoria, Cant. Valle dell'Acate	766
Cerasuolo di Vittoria Barocco, Avide	770
Cerasuolo di Vittoria Etichetta Nera, Avide	770
Cerasuolo di Vittoria V. di Vastunaca, COS	782
Cerbaione, Casanuova delle Cerbaie	518
Cercatoja Rosso, Fattoria del Buonamico	540
Cerdeña, Antonio Argiolas	799
Cerosecco, Petricci e Del Pianta	621
Cervaro della Sala, Castello della Sala	662
Cerveteri Bianco Vigna Grande, Cant. Cerveteri	683
Cerveteri Rosso Vigna Grande, Cant. Cerveteri	683
Cerviolo Bianco, San Fabiano Calcinaia	482
Cerviolo Rosso, San Fabiano Calcinaia	482
Cesanese del Piglio, Terre del Cesanese	693
Cesanese del Piglio Casale della Ioria, Casale della Ioria	680
Cesanese del Piglio Colle Forma, Giovanni Terenzi	694
Cesanese del Piglio Etichetta Rossa, Cant. Soc. Cesanese del Piglio	693
Cesanese del Piglio Haernicus, Antonello Coletti Conti	691
Cesanese del Piglio Torre del Piano, Casale della Ioria	680
Cesanese del Piglio Vajoscuro, Giovanni Terenzi	694
Cesanese del Piglio Velobra, Giovanni Terenzi	694
Cesanese di Olevano Cirsium, Cantine Ciolli	693
Cesanese di Olevano Silene, Cantine Ciolli	693
Cesare Passito Bianco, Le Salette	295
Cesolano, F.lli Zaccagnini & C.	652
Cèsuret, Castello Rametz	285
Ceuso, Ceuso	766
Ceuso Custera, Ceuso	766
Chaos, Fattoria Le Terrazze	642
Chardonnay, Adragna	788
Chardonnay, Fattorie Azzolino	767
Chardonnay, Capannelle	497
Chardonnay, Casale del Giglio	681
Chardonnay, Giovanni Crosato	427
Chardonnay, Feudo Principi di Butera	767
Chardonnay, Gregoletto	304
Chardonnay, Inama	317
Chardonnay, La Rendola	553
Chardonnay, Angelo Nicolis e Figli	323
Chardonnay, Ortaglia	593
Chardonnay, Carlo Pellegrino	773
Chardonnay, Pelz & Piffer	251
Chardonnay, Planeta	774
Chardonnay, Poggio Capponi	612
Chardonnay, Cantine Rallo	773
Chardonnay, Tenuta Roccaccia	562
Chardonnay, Tasca d'Almerita	778
Chardonnay Abbazia S. Clemente, Ciccio Zaccagnini	697
Chardonnay Alhena, San Lorenzo	709
Chardonnay Andritz, Oscar Sturm	378
Chardonnay Arsiccio, Pucciarella	677
Chardonnay Aurente, Lungarotti	675
Chardonnay Barbozana, Giuseppe Vezzoli	198
Chardonnay Brut Cometti, Fattoria di Presciano	614
Chardonnay Campo dei Tovi, Inama	317
Chardonnay Chioma di Berenice, San Lorenzo	709
Chardonnay Cuvée Brut, Cesarini Sforza	246
Chardonnay del Lazio, Colle San Lorenzo	684
Chardonnay della Sala, Castello della Sala	662
Chardonnay Donna Aurelia, Luigi Vivacqua	762
Chardonnay Extra Brut, Zardetto Spumanti	293
Chardonnay Farneto, Farnese	703
Chardonnay I Legni, Russolo	422
Chardonnay Le Cingelle, Monte Tondo	330
Chardonnay Mandrarossa, Settesoli	775
Chardonnay Marina Cvetic, Gianni Masciarelli	706
Chardonnay Naumachos, Vinicola del Tesino	634
Chardonnay Opis, Farnese	703
Chardonnay Pan, Nestore Bosco	701
Chardonnay Pietrosa, Sarchese Dora	704
Chardonnay Punta di Colle, Marramiero	705
Chardonnay Raffaellesco, Umbria Viticoltori Associati	677
Chardonnay Robbiano, Fanini	661
Chardonnay Roccesco, Orlandi Contucci Ponno	705
Chardonnay Ronco Calaj, Russolo	422
Chardonnay Scaia Bianca, Tenuta Sant'Antonio	304
Chardonnay Soris, Pierpaolo Pecorari	421

Chardonnay Tresor, Agriverde	703
Chardonnay Vallée du Vin, Agriverde	703
Chardonnay Vigna Brioni, Vallarom	229
Chardonnay Vigne Umbre, Umbria Viticoltori Associati	677
Chaudelune Bianco,	
Cave du Vin Blanc de Morgex et de La Salle	18
Chaudelune Vin de Glace,	
Cave du Vin Blanc de Morgex et de La Salle	18
Cherubino, Morgassi Superiore	85
Chianti, Agri Peccioli	613
Chianti, Tenuta Bacco e Petroio	622
Chianti, Borgo Casignano	599
Chianti, Tenuta Castiglioni	551
Chianti, Di Fonti	489
Chianti, La Pieve	515
Chianti, Tenuta Maiano	612
Chianti, Mannucci Droandi	613
Chianti, Fattoria Montanine	603
Chianti, Fattoria Montellori	494
Chianti, Poggio Capponi	612
Chianti, San Vettore	502
Chianti, Fattoria Sant'Appiano	594
Chianti, Streda in Belvedere	622
Chianti Castello di Montespertoli, Fattoria Castello Sonnino	612
Chianti Castello di Rapale, Giacomo Marengo	539
Chianti Castello di Rapale Ris., Giacomo Marengo	539
Chianti Cl., Agricoltori del Chianti Geografico	495
Chianti Cl., Fattoria dell' Aiola	483
Chianti Cl., Castello d' Albola	565
Chianti Cl., Badia a Coltibuono	496
Chianti Cl., Borgo Salcetino	565
Chianti Cl., Borgo Scopeto	483
Chianti Cl., Canonica a Cerreto	598
Chianti Cl., Carobbio	555
Chianti Cl., Carpineto	503
Chianti Cl., Casa Emma	466
Chianti Cl., Fattoria Casaloste	555
Chianti Cl., Castel Ruggero	493
Chianti Cl., Castellare di Castellina	478
Chianti Cl., Castello dei Rampolla	556
Chianti Cl., Castello della Paneretta	466
Chianti Cl., Castello di Bossi	484
Chianti Cl., Castello di Fonterutoli	478
Chianti Cl., Famiglia Cecchi	479
Chianti Cl., Colle Bereto	616
Chianti Cl., Podere Collelungo	479
Chianti Cl., Fattoria di Felsina	485
Chianti Cl., Tenuta Fontodi	557
Chianti Cl., I Sodi	601
Chianti Cl., Il Colombaio di Cencio	497
Chianti Cl., Il Mandorlo	573
Chianti Cl., Il Molino di Grace	557
Chianti Cl., Podere Il Palazzino	498
Chianti Cl., Isole e Olena	467
Chianti Cl., Ispoli	573
Chianti Cl., La Brancaia	566
Chianti Cl., Castello La Leccia	597
Chianti Cl., Tenuta La Novella	602
Chianti Cl., Fattoria La Ripa	467
Chianti Cl., La Sala	574
Chianti Cl., Le Cinciole	559
Chianti Cl., Fattoria Le Corti	574
Chianti Cl., Le Filigare	468
Chianti Cl., Le Fonti	615
Chianti Cl., Castello di Meleto	498
Chianti Cl., Castello di Monastero	486
Chianti Cl., Castello di Monsanto	469
Chianti Cl., Fattoria di Montemaggio	616
Chianti Cl., Fattoria Nittardi	480
Chianti Cl., Fattoria di Petroio	486
Chianti Cl., Podere Capaccia	616
Chianti Cl., Poggerino	568
Chianti Cl., Poggio al Sole	592
Chianti Cl., Poggio Amorelli	480
Chianti Cl., Poggio Bonelli	487
Chianti Cl., Fattoria Poggiopiano	575
Chianti Cl., Castello di Querceto	503
Chianti Cl., Querciabella	504
Chianti Cl., Querciavalle	487
Chianti Cl., Riecine	499
Chianti Cl., Rietine	500
Chianti Cl., Riseccoli	602
Chianti Cl., Rocca delle Macìe	481
Chianti Cl., Rocca di Castagnoli	500
Chianti Cl., Rocca di Montegrossi	601
Chianti Cl., San Fabiano Calcinaia	482
Chianti Cl., San Felice	488
Chianti Cl., San Giorgio a Lapi	620
Chianti Cl., San Giusto a Rentennano	501
Chianti Cl., San Vincenti	501
Chianti Cl., Savignola Paolina	505
Chianti Cl., Castello di Selvole	488
Chianti Cl., Spadaio e Piecorto	595
Chianti Cl., Castello di Tornano	601
Chianti Cl., Torraccia di Presura	505
Chianti Cl., Tramonti	598
Chianti Cl., Castello Uzzano	506
Chianti Cl., Vecchie Terre di Montefili	560
Chianti Cl., Castello di Verrazzano	506
Chianti Cl., Villa Vignamaggio	507
Chianti Cl., Vignole	613
Chianti Cl., Villa Cafaggio	560
Chianti Cl., Villa Calcinaia	603
Chianti Cl., Villa Casale	603
Chianti Cl., Villa Sant'Andrea	618
Chianti Cl., Villa Trasqua	598
Chianti Cl., Viticcio	508
Chianti Cl., Castello di Volpaia	569
Chianti Cl. Anfiteatro Ris., Vecchie Terre di Montefili	560
Chianti Cl. Argenina, Podere Il Palazzino	498
Chianti Cl. Badia a Passignano Ris., Marchesi Antinori	492
Chianti Cl. Bandecca Ris., San Giorgio a Lapi	620
Chianti Cl. Beatrice Ris., Viticcio	508
Chianti Cl. Bellavista, Castello di Ama	495
Chianti Cl. Bello Stento, La Madonnina - Triacca	602
Chianti Cl. Berardo Ris., Castello di Bossi	484
Chianti Cl. Bertinga, Castello di Ama	495
Chianti Cl. Brancaia, La Brancaia	566
Chianti Cl. Brolio, Barone Ricasoli	496
Chianti Cl. Bruciagna, Castello La Leccia	597
Chianti Cl. Bugialla Ris., Poggerino	568
Chianti Cl. Campo ai Cerchi Ris., Podere Collelungo	479
Chianti Cl. Campolungo Ris., S. M. Tenimenti Pile e Lamole	499
Chianti Cl. Cancello Rosso Ris., Fattoria dell' Aiola	483
Chianti Cl. Capannelle Ris., Capannelle	497
Chianti Cl. Caparsino, Caparsa	566
Chianti Cl. Capraia Ris., Rocca di Castagnoli	500
Chianti Cl. Casa Vecchia alla Piazza, Buondonno	477
Chianti Cl. Casanuova di Nittardi, Fattoria Nittardi	480
Chianti Cl. Casasilia, Poggio al Sole	592
Chianti Cl. Casasilia Ris., Poggio al Sole	592
Chianti Cl. Castelgreve Ris., Castelli del Grevepesa	572
Chianti Cl. Castello di Ama, Castello di Ama	495
Chianti Cl. Castello di Brolio, Barone Ricasoli	496
Chianti Cl. Castello di Fonterutoli, Castello di Fonterutoli	478
Chianti Cl. Castello Il Palagio, Castello Il Palagio	617
Chianti Cl. Cellole Ris., San Fabiano Calcinaia	482
Chianti Cl. Ceppeto Ris., Mannucci Droandi	613
Chianti Cl. Clemente VII Ris., Castelli del Grevepesa	572
Chianti Cl. Coltassala Ris., Castello di Volpaia	569
Chianti Cl. Comignole, La Marcellina	558
Chianti Cl. Contessa di Radda, Agricoltori del Chianti Geografico	495
Chianti Cl. Doccio a Matteo Ris., Caparsa	566
Chianti Cl. Don Vincenzo Ris., Fattoria Casaloste	555
Chianti Cl. Fizzano Ris., Rocca delle Macìe	481
Chianti Cl. Frimaio, Fattoria Poggio Romita	621
Chianti Cl. Frimaio Ris., Fattoria Poggio Romita	621
Chianti Cl. Giorgio Primo, La Massa	558
Chianti Cl. Grosso Sanese, Podere Il Palazzino	498
Chianti Cl. Grosso Sanese Ris., Podere Il Palazzino	498
Chianti Cl. I Massi, Il Colombaio di Cencio	497
Chianti Cl. I Massi Ris., Il Colombaio di Cencio	497
Chianti Cl. Il Grigio Ris., San Felice	488
Chianti Cl. Il Picchio Ris., Castello di Querceto	503
Chianti Cl. Il Poggio Ris., Castello di Monsanto	469
Chianti Cl. Il Tarocco, Torraccia di Presura	505
Chianti Cl. Il Tarocco Ris., Torraccia di Presura	505
Chianti Cl. L'Aura, Querceto di Castellina	481
Chianti Cl. L'Insolito, Villa Casale	603
Chianti Cl. La Casuccia, Castello di Ama	495
Chianti Cl. La Forra Ris., Tenute Ambrogio e Giovanni Folonari	493
Chianti Cl. La Gabbiola, San Michele a Torri	619
Chianti Cl. La Gabbiola Ris., San Michele a Torri	619
Chianti Cl. La Marcellina, La Marcellina	558
Chianti Cl. La Pieve, Podere Il Palazzino	498
Chianti Cl. La Pieve, La Pieve	515
Chianti Cl. La Prima Ris., Castello di Vicchiomaggio	507
Chianti Cl. La Selvanella Ris., Melini	563
Chianti Cl. Lamole di Lamole, S. M. Tenimenti Pile e Lamole	499
Chianti Cl. Lamole di Lamole Ris., S. M. Tenimenti Pile e Lamole	499
Chianti Cl. Le Baroncole, San Giusto a Rentennano	501
Chianti Cl. Le Ellere, Castello d' Albola	565
Chianti Cl. Le Masse di Greve, Lanciola	511
Chianti Cl. Le Masse di Greve, Lanciola	511
Chianti Cl. Le Masse di Greve Ris., Lanciola	511
Chianti Cl. Le Trame, Podere Le Boncie	598
Chianti Cl. Lorenzo, Le Filigare	468
Chianti Cl. Lucarello Ris., Borgo Salcetino	565
Chianti Cl. Maria Vittoria Ris., Le Filigare	468
Chianti Cl. Matroneo, Enrico Pierazzuoli	473
Chianti Cl. Messer Piero di Teuzzo, Famiglia Cecchi	479
Chianti Cl. Misciano Ris., Borgo Scopeto	483
Chianti Cl. Monna Lisa Ris., Villa Vignamaggio	507
Chianti Cl. Montegiachi Ris., Agricoltori del Chianti Geografico	495
Chianti Cl. Montornello, Tenuta di Bibbiano	597
Chianti Cl. Nozzole, Tenute Ambrogio e Giovanni Folonari	493
Chianti Cl. Panzanello, Panzanello	559
Chianti Cl. Panzanello Ris., Panzanello	559
Chianti Cl. Petresco Ris., Le Cinciole	559
Chianti Cl. Petri Ris., Castello di Vicchiomaggio	507
Chianti Cl. Pieve di Spaltenna, Castello di Meleto	498
Chianti Cl. Poggio ai Frati Ris., Rocca di Castagnoli	500
Chianti Cl. Poggio Rosso Ris., San Felice	488
Chianti Cl. Querciolo, Podere La Cappella	591
Chianti Cl. Querciolo Ris., Podere La Cappella	591
Chianti Cl. Rancia Ris., Fattoria di Felsina	485
Chianti Cl. Ris., Fattoria dell' Aiola	483
Chianti Cl. Ris., Castello d' Albola	565
Chianti Cl. Ris., Badia a Coltibuono	496
Chianti Cl. Ris., Borgo Scopeto	483
Chianti Cl. Ris., Buondonno	477
Chianti Cl. Ris., Carobbio	555
Chianti Cl. Ris., Carpineto	503
Chianti Cl. Ris., Casa Emma	466
Chianti Cl. Ris., Fattoria Casaloste	555
Chianti Cl. Ris., Castagnoli	477
Chianti Cl. Ris., Castel Ruggero	493
Chianti Cl. Ris., Castellare di Castellina	478
Chianti Cl. Ris., Castello della Paneretta	466
Chianti Cl. Ris., Cennatoio Intervineas	556
Chianti Cl. Ris, Colle Bereto	616
Chianti Cl. Ris., Podere Collelungo	479

Chianti Cl. Ris., Fattoria di Felsina	485
Chianti Cl. Ris., Granducato	562
Chianti Cl. Ris., I Sodi	601
Chianti Cl. Ris., Il Molino di Grace	557
Chianti Cl. Ris., Ispoli	573
Chianti Cl. Ris., La Castellina	597
Chianti Cl. Ris., Tenuta La Novella	602
Chianti Cl. Ris., Fattoria La Ripa	467
Chianti Cl. Ris., La Sala	574
Chianti Cl. Ris., Le Filigare	468
Chianti Cl. Ris., Le Fonti	615
Chianti Cl. Ris., Castello di Meleto	498
Chianti Cl. Ris., Castello di Monastero	486
Chianti Cl. Ris., Castello di Monsanto	469
Chianti Cl. Ris., Fattoria Montecchio	621
Chianti Cl. Ris., Fattoria di Montemaggio	616
Chianti Cl. Ris., Montiverdi	601
Chianti Cl. Ris., Fattoria Nittardi	480
Chianti Cl. Ris., Fattoria di Petroio	486
Chianti Cl. Ris., Podere Terreno alla Via della Volpaia	616
Chianti Cl. Ris., Poggerino	568
Chianti Cl. Ris., Poggio Amorelli	480
Chianti Cl. Ris., Poggio Bonelli	487
Chianti Cl. Ris., Castello di Querceto	503
Chianti Cl. Ris., Querciavalle	487
Chianti Cl. Ris., Riecine	499
Chianti Cl. Ris., Rietine	500
Chianti Cl. Ris., Riseccoli	602
Chianti Cl. Ris., Rocca delle Macìe	481
Chianti Cl. Ris., San Giusto a Rentennano	501
Chianti Cl. Ris., San Vincenti	501
Chianti Cl. Ris., Savignola Paolina	505
Chianti Cl. Ris., Castello di Selvole	488
Chianti Cl. Ris., Casale dello Sparviero	597
Chianti Cl. Ris., Castello Uzzano	506
Chianti Cl. Ris., Val delle Corti	617
Chianti Cl. Ris., Vecchie Terre di Montefili	560
Chianti Cl. Ris., Castello di Verrazzano	506
Chianti Cl. Ris., Vignavecchia	569
Chianti Cl. Ris., Vignole	613
Chianti Cl. Ris., Villa Cafaggio	560
Chianti Cl. Ris., Villa Calcinaia	603
Chianti Cl. Ris., Villa Sant'Andrea	618
Chianti Cl. Ris., Viticcio	508
Chianti Cl. Ris., Castello di Volpaia	569
Chianti Cl. Ris. Castello Il Palagio, Castello Il Palagio	617
Chianti Cl. Ris. Ducale Oro, Tenimenti Ruffino	564
Chianti Cl. Ris. Il Margone, Il Molino di Grace	557
Chianti Cl. Ris. Il Rotone, Il Mandorlo	573
Chianti Cl. Rocca Guicciarda Ris., Barone Ricasoli	496
Chianti Cl. Roveto, Podere Collelungo	479
Chianti Cl. San Jacopo, Castello di Vicchiomaggio	507
Chianti Cl. Santedame, Tenimenti Ruffino	564
Chianti Cl. Sassocupo, La Marcellina	558
Chianti Cl. Sassocupo Ris., La Marcellina	558
Chianti Cl. Squarcialupi Ris., La Castellina	597
Chianti Cl. Tenuta S. Alfonso, Rocca delle Macìe	481
Chianti Cl. Tenuta S. Alfonso Ris., Rocca delle Macìe	481
Chianti Cl. Tenute del Marchese Ris., Marchesi Antinori	492
Chianti Cl. Terra dei Cavalieri, La Loggia	617
Chianti Cl. Terre di Prenzano, Villa Vignamaggio	507
Chianti Cl. Torre a Destra Ris., Castello della Paneretta	466
Chianti Cl. V. del Sorbo Ris., Tenuta Fontodi	557
Chianti Cl. V. di Fontalle Ris., Machiavelli	575
Chianti Cl. V. il Poggiale Ris., Castellare di Castellina	478
Chianti Cl. V. La Palaia, La Madonnina - Triacca	602
Chianti Cl. Valle del Pozzo Ris., Le Cinciole	559
Chianti Cl. Vigna del Capannino Ris., Tenuta di Bibbiano	597
Chianti Cl. Vigna della Croce Ris., Fattoria di Terrabianca	568
Chianti Cl. Vigneti di Campomaggio, Castellani	615
Chianti Cl. Vigneti di Campomaggio Ris., Castellani	615
Chianti Cl. Vigneto S. Marcellino Ris., Rocca di Montegrossi	601
Chianti Cl. Villa Antinori Ris., Marchesi Antinori	492
Chianti Cl. Villa Cerna, Famiglia Cecchi	479
Chianti Cl. Villa Cerna Ris., Famiglia Cecchi	479
Chianti Cl. Villa Maisano Ris., Montiverdi	601
Chianti Cl. Villa Vistarenni, S. M. Tenimenti Pile e Lamole	499
Chianti Colli Aretini, Villa Cilnia	464
Chianti Colli Aretini Ris., Villa Cilnia	464
Chianti Colli Fiorentini, Fattoria di Bagnolo	510
Chianti Colli Fiorentini, Fattoria di Fiano	599
Chianti Colli Fiorentini, Lanciola	511
Chianti Colli Fiorentini, Le Sorgenti	465
Chianti Colli Fiorentini Il Cortile, Castello di Poppiano	552
Chianti Colli Fiorentini Il Trecione Ris., Le Calvane	551
Chianti Colli Fiorentini La Torretta, La Querce	510
Chianti Colli Fiorentini Quercione, Le Calvane	551
Chianti Colli Fiorentini Ris., Fattoria di Bagnolo	510
Chianti Colli Fiorentini Ris., Castello di Poppiano	552
Chianti Colli Fiorentini San Camillo, Tenuta Il Corno	572
Chianti Colli Senesi, Casa alle Vacche	577
Chianti Colli Senesi, Fattoria Casabianca	553
Chianti Colli Senesi, Vincenzo Cesani	577
Chianti Colli Senesi, Fattorie Chigi Saracini	485
Chianti Colli Senesi, Farnetella	586
Chianti Colli Senesi, Granducato	562
Chianti Colli Senesi, Fattoria Il Palagio	490
Chianti Colli Senesi, Il Paradiso	579
Chianti Colli Senesi, La Lastra	580
Chianti Colli Senesi, Tenuta Le Calcinaie	581
Chianti Colli Senesi, Montenidoli	581
Chianti Colli Senesi, Palagetto	582
Chianti Colli Senesi, San Giorgio a Lapi	620
Chianti Colli Senesi, San Quirico	618
Chianti Colli Senesi, Signano	619
Chianti Colli Senesi, F.lli Vagnoni	584
Chianti Colli Senesi, Villa Sant'Anna	550
Chianti Colli Senesi Arcano, Famiglia Cecchi	479
Chianti Colli Senesi Caelum, Il Palagione	579
Chianti Colli Senesi Poggiarelli, Signano	619
Chianti Colli Senesi Poggio Cenni, Fattoria Casabianca	553
Chianti Colli Senesi Poggio Cenni Ris., Fattoria Casabianca	553
Chianti Colli Senesi Poggio Tocco, Le Tre Berte	549
Chianti Colli Senesi Ris., Palagetto	582
Chianti Colli Senesi Sup. Vigna S. Domenico Sovestro, Baroncini	576
Chianti Colli Senesi Tutulus, Ficomontanino	599
Chianti Colli Senesi Vertunno, Giovanni Panizzi	583
Chianti dei Colli Aretini Paterna, Coop. Agricola Valdarnese	621
Chianti dei Colli Fiorentini, Castelvecchio	571
Chianti dei Colli Fiorentini, Malenchini	594
Chianti dei Colli Fiorentini Ris., Castelvecchio	571
Chianti dei Colli Senesi, Carpineta Fontalpino	484
Chianti dei Colli Senesi, Salcheto	548
Chianti dei Colli Senesi Terra di Siena, Tenuta di Trecciano	620
Chianti dei Colli Senesi Terra Rossa Ris., Tenuta di Trecciano	620
Chianti dei Colli Senesi Via dei Franchi, La Rampa di Fugnano	580
Chianti Eletto, Nobile Prima	491
Chianti Fattoria le Caselle, Fattoria Montellori	494
Chianti Fortebraccio, La Pieve	515
Chianti I Tre Borri, Fattoria Corzano e Paterno	571
Chianti La Commenda Ris., Giacomo Marengo	539
Chianti Le Gaggiole Ris., Fassati	545
Chianti Le Tornaie, Giacomo Marengo	539
Chianti Leonardo, Cantine Leonardo da Vinci	593
Chianti Messere, Baroncini	576
Chianti Montalbano, Fattoria Castellina	595
Chianti Montalbano, Enrico Pierazzuoli	473
Chianti Montalbano Ris., Enrico Pierazzuoli	473
Chianti Montespertoli Castello di Sonnino, Fattoria Castello Sonnino	612
Chianti Montespertoli Petriccio, Poggio Capponi	612
Chianti Montespertoli Poggignano, Tenuta Cortina e Mandorli	612
Chianti Ris., Fattoria Montanine	603
Chianti Ris., San Vettore	502
Chianti Rufina, Fattoria di Basciano	570
Chianti Rufina, Colognole	617
Chianti Rufina, Frascole	491
Chianti Rufina, Fattoria Lavacchio	615
Chianti Rufina, Fattoria Selvapiana	564
Chianti Rufina, Travignoli	614
Chianti Rufina Bucerchiale Ris., Fattoria Selvapiana	564
Chianti Rufina Fornace Ris., Fattoria Selvapiana	564
Chianti Rufina Il Santo Ris., Frascole	491
Chianti Rufina Lastricato Ris., Castello del Trebbio	615
Chianti Rufina Montesodi, Marchesi de' Frescobaldi	494
Chianti Rufina Nipozzano Ris., Marchesi de' Frescobaldi	494
Chianti Rufina Ris., Fattoria di Basciano	570
Chianti Rufina Ris., Fattoria Lavacchio	615
Chianti Rufina Ris., Travignoli	614
Chianti Rufina Ris. del Don, Colognole	617
Chianti san Crispino, Pasqualetti Viticoltori	613
Chianti Santa Caterina, Castelvecchio	571
Chianti Santa Lucia, Fattoria Santa Lucia	615
Chianti Sorrettole, La Querce	510
Chianti Terra Antica, Fattoria di Romignano	604
Chianti Terre di Corzano, Fattoria Corzano e Paterno	571
Chianti Vigneto Tenebroso, Di Fonti	489
Chianti Villa Chigi, Fattorie Chigi Saracini	485
Chianti Villa Petriolo, Fattoria di Petriolo	599
Chiaramonte Bianco, Firriato	776
Chiaramonte Rosso, Firriato	776
Ciabatta, Erik Banti	585
Ciapin Bianco, Cascina Roera	73
Cicogio, Il Lebbio	578
Cielo d'Alcamo, Tenute Rapitalà	768
Cign'Oro, Villa Cilnia	464
Cignale, Castello di Querceto	503
Ciliegiolo La Tesa, Fattoria Santa Lucia	615
Cimbolo, Poggio Bertaio	661
Cinabro, Alessandro Secchi	250
Cincinnato, Tenuta di Trinoro	584
Cinerino, Marziano ed Enrico Abbona	75
Cinque Terre, Buranco	173
Cinque Terre, Walter De Battè	176
Cinque Terre, Forlini Cappellini	180
Cinque Terre Sciacchetrà, Buranco	173
Cinque Terre Sciacchetrà, Walter De Battè	176
Cinque Terre Sciacchetrà, Forlini Cappellini	180
Cinque Torri Brut, Carra	445
Cioccarello, Coop. Svevo - Lucera	754
Circeo Bianco Riflessi, Cant. Sant'Andrea	690
Circeo Rosso Preludio alla Notte, Cant. Sant'Andrea	690
Cirò Bianco, Cant. Enotria	763
Cirò Bianco, Librandi	759
Cirò Bianco, Malena	759
Cirò Bianco, Vinicola Zito	763
Cirò Bianco Curiale, Caparra & Siciliani	763
Cirò Bianco I Pitagorici, Ippolito 1845	763
Cirò Rosato, Cant. Enotria	763
Cirò Rosato, Librandi	759
Cirò Rosato, Malena	759
Cirò Rosato, Vinicola Zito	763
Cirò Rosato Cl. Ronco dei Quattroventi, Fattoria San Francesco	758
Cirò Rosato Le Formelle, Caparra & Siciliani	758
Cirò Rosè I Pitagorici, Ippolito 1845	763
Cirò Rosso Cl., Caparra & Siciliani	763
Cirò Rosso Cl., Librandi	759
Cirò Rosso Cl., Fattoria San Francesco	758
Cirò Rosso Cl. Donna Madda, Fattoria San Francesco	758
Cirò Rosso Cl. Ripe del Falco Ris., Ippolito 1845	763
Cirò Rosso Cl. Ris., Vinicola Zito	763
Cirò Rosso Cl. Ronco dei Quattro Venti, Fattoria San Francesco	758

Cirò Rosso Cl. Sup., Malena	759
Cirò Rosso Cl. Sup., Vinicola Zito	763
Cirò Rosso Cl. Sup. Duca Sanfelice Ris., Librandi	759
Cirò Rosso Cl. Sup. I Pitagorici, Ippolito 1845	763
Cirò Rosso Cl. Sup. Piana delle Fate Ris., Cant. Enotria	763
Cirò Rosso Cl. Sup. Ris. Pian della Corte, Malena	759
Civitella Rosso, Sergio Mottura	684
Cl. Classico Drugo, Fattoria Santo Stefano	602
Clarae, Nicola Balter	241
Cleos, San Lorenzo	663
Codirosso, S. M. Tenimenti Pile e Lamole	499
COF Bianco, Miani	359
COF Bianco, Ronco del Gnemiz	420
COF Bianco, Andrea Visintini	382
COF Bianco Blanc di Buri, Davino Meroi	358
COF Bianco Campo Marzio, La Tunella	406
COF Bianco Canto, Alfieri Cantarutti	419
COF Bianco Carato, Vigne Fantin Noda'r	408
COF Bianco del Postiglione, Perusini	381
COF Bianco delle Grazie, Dal Fari	364
COF Bianco Liende, La Viarte	409
COF Bianco Locum Nostrum, Paolino Comelli	386
COF Bianco Petrussa, Petrussa	410
COF Bianco Pian delle Poiane, Alessandra Vidon	430
COF Bianco Ploe di Stelis, Il Roncal	365
COF Bianco Poanis Blanc, Olivo Buiatti	357
COF Bianco Pomédes, Scubla	407
COF Bianco Richenza, Vigna Petrussa	411
COF Bianco Ronco del Masiero, Torre Rosazza	397
COF Bianco Rosazzo Ronco delle Acacie, Le Vigne di Zamò	397
COF Bianco Rosazzo Terre Alte, Livio Felluga	371
COF Bianco RosazzoTerre Alte, Livio Felluga	371
COF Bianco Sacrisassi, Le Due Terre	409
COF Bianco Santa Justina, Iole Grillo	408
COF Bianco Sonata, Zof	383
COF Bianco Tovè, Marco Cecchini	386
COF Bianco Vineis, Rocca Bernarda	407
COF Cabernet, Livio e Claudio Buiatti	356
COF Cabernet, Olivo Buiatti	357
COF Cabernet, Colutta	395
COF Cabernet, Conte D'Attimis-Maniago	357
COF Cabernet, Dal Fari	364
COF Cabernet, Iole Grillo	408
COF Cabernet, Teresa Raiz	403
COF Cabernet, Ronco dei Pini	411
COF Cabernet, Vigne Fantin Noda'r	408
COF Cabernet Franc, Valentino Butussi	380
COF Cabernet Franc, La Tunella	406
COF Cabernet Franc, Perusini	381
COF Cabernet Franc, Petrucco	359
COF Cabernet Franc, Ronchi di Manzano	396
COF Cabernet Franc, Leonardo Specogna	382
COF Cabernet Franc, Vigna Angeli	430
COF Cabernet Franc, Vigna Petrussa	411
COF Cabernet Franc, Vigna Traverso	412
COF Cabernet Franc Vign. Montsclapade, Girolamo Dorigo	358
COF Cabernet Sauvignon, Alberice	429
COF Cabernet Sauvignon, Valentino Butussi	380
COF Cabernet Sauvignon, Paolino Comelli	386
COF Cabernet Sauvignon, Perusini	381
COF Cabernet Sauvignon, Ronchi di Manzano	396
COF Cabernet Sauvignon, Ronco delle Betulle	396
COF Cabernet Sauvignon, Scubla	407
COF Cabernet Sauvignon Sdricca, Ca' Tullio	354
COF Cabernet Zuc di Volpe, Volpe Pasini	425
COF Chardonnay, Alberice	429
COF Chardonnay, Valentino Butussi	380
COF Chardonnay, Paolino Comelli	386
COF Chardonnay, Conte D'Attimis-Maniago	357
COF Chardonnay, Dal Fari	364
COF Chardonnay, Adriano Gigante	381
COF Chardonnay, Valerio Marinig	410
COF Chardonnay, Davino Meroi	358
COF Chardonnay, Miani	359
COF Chardonnay, Petrucco	359
COF Chardonnay, Rocca Bernarda	407
COF Chardonnay, Paolo Rodaro	366
COF Chardonnay, La Roncaia	400
COF Chardonnay, Il Roncal	365
COF Chardonnay, Ronchi di Manzano	396
COF Chardonnay, Ronco del Gnemiz	420
COF Chardonnay, Torre Rosazza	397
COF Chardonnay, Zof	383
COF Chardonnay Carato, Dal Fari	364
COF Chardonnay Sel. Giorgio Colutta, Colutta	395
COF Chardonnay Vign. Ronc di Juri, Girolamo Dorigo	358
COF Chardonnay Zuc di Volpe, Volpe Pasini	425
COF Malvasia, Conte D'Attimis-Maniago	357
COF Merlot, Livio e Claudio Buiatti	356
COF Merlot, Olivo Buiatti	357
COF Merlot, Paolino Comelli	386
COF Merlot, Dal Fari	364
COF Merlot, Dario e Luciano Ermacora	406
COF Merlot, Adriano Gigante	381
COF Merlot, Iole Grillo	408
COF Merlot, Le Due Terre	409
COF Merlot, Valerio Marinig	410
COF Merlot, Miani	359
COF Merlot, Perusini	381
COF Merlot, Petrussa	410
COF Merlot, Ronchi di Manzano	396
COF Merlot, Ronco dei Pini	411
COF Merlot, Ronco delle Betulle	396
COF Merlot, Scubla	407
COF Merlot, Leonardo Specogna	382
COF Merlot, Torre Rosazza	397
COF Merlot, Vigna Traverso	412
COF Merlot, Vigne Fantin Noda'r	408
COF Merlot, Zof	383
COF Merlot Centis, Rocca Bernarda	407
COF Merlot Focus Zuc di Volpe, Volpe Pasini	425
COF Merlot Gigi Valle Ris., Valle	427
COF Merlot l'Altromerlot, Torre Rosazza	397
COF Merlot Oltre, Leonardo Specogna	382
COF Merlot Romain, Paolo Rodaro	366
COF Merlot Ronc di Subule, Ronchi di Manzano	396
COF Merlot Ronco San Michele, Alfieri Cantarutti	419
COF Merlot Sdricca, Ca' Tullio	354
COF Merlot Sel., Iole Grillo	408
COF Merlot Sel. Giorgio Colutta, Colutta	395
COF Merlot Sottocastello Rosso, Vigna Traverso	412
COF Merlot Togliano, Volpe Pasini	425
COF Merlot V. Cinquant'Anni, Le Vigne di Zamò	397
COF Merlot V. del Balbo, Petrucco	359
COF Merlot Vocalis, Aquila del Torre	403
COF Montsclapade, Girolamo Dorigo	358
COF Picolit, Livio e Claudio Buiatti	356
COF Picolit, Valentino Butussi	380
COF Picolit, Ca' Ronesca	383
COF Picolit, Conte D'Attimis-Maniago	357
COF Picolit, Dario Coos	399
COF Picolit, Dario e Luciano Ermacora	406
COF Picolit, Marco Felluga	393
COF Picolit, Adriano Gigante	381
COF Picolit, Jacùss	424
COF Picolit, La Tunella	406
COF Picolit, Valerio Marinig	410
COF Picolit, Davino Meroi	358
COF Picolit, Perusini	381
COF Picolit, Rocca Bernarda	407
COF Picolit, Paolo Rodaro	366
COF Picolit, La Roncaia	400
COF Picolit, Ronco Vieri	400
COF Picolit, Torre Rosazza	397
COF Picolit, Valchiarò	425
COF Picolit, Vigna Petrussa	411
COF Picolit, Zof	383
COF Picolit Romandus, Dario Coos	399
COF Picolit V. T., Aquila del Torre	403
COF Picolit Vign. Montsclapade, Girolamo Dorigo	358
COF Pignolo, Davide Moschioni	365
COF Pignolo, Il Roncal	365
COF Pignolo, Leonardo Specogna	382
COF Pignolo di Buttrio Vign. Ronc di Juri, Girolamo Dorigo	358
COF Pinot Bianco, Livio e Claudio Buiatti	356
COF Pinot Bianco, Valentino Butussi	380
COF Pinot Bianco, Ca di Bon	429
COF Pinot Bianco, Dario e Luciano Ermacora	406
COF Pinot Bianco, Jacùss	424
COF Pinot Bianco, La Tunella	406
COF Pinot Bianco, La Viarte	409
COF Pinot Bianco, Valerio Marinig	410
COF Pinot Bianco, Perusini	381
COF Pinot Bianco, Petrucco	359
COF Pinot Bianco, Petrussa	410
COF Pinot Bianco, Ronco dei Pini	411
COF Pinot Bianco, Scubla	407
COF Pinot Bianco, Andrea Visintini	382
COF Pinot Bianco Tullio Zamò, Le Vigne di Zamò	397
COF Pinot Bianco Zuc di Volpe, Volpe Pasini	425
COF Pinot Grigio, Alberice	429
COF Pinot Grigio, Livio e Claudio Buiatti	356
COF Pinot Grigio, Valentino Butussi	380
COF Pinot Grigio, Ca di Bon	429
COF Pinot Grigio, Alfieri Cantarutti	419
COF Pinot Grigio, Colutta	395
COF Pinot Grigio, Paolino Comelli	386
COF Pinot Grigio, Conte D'Attimis-Maniago	357
COF Pinot Grigio, Dal Fari	364
COF Pinot Grigio, Dario e Luciano Ermacora	406
COF Pinot Grigio, Livio Felluga	371
COF Pinot Grigio, Adriano Gigante	381
COF Pinot Grigio, Iole Grillo	408
COF Pinot Grigio, La Tunella	406
COF Pinot Grigio, La Viarte	409
COF Pinot Grigio, Midolini	395
COF Pinot Grigio, Perusini	381
COF Pinot Grigio, Petrucco	359
COF Pinot Grigio, Teresa Raiz	403
COF Pinot Grigio, Rocca Bernarda	407
COF Pinot Grigio, Paolo Rodaro	366
COF Pinot Grigio, Il Roncal	365
COF Pinot Grigio, Ronchi di Manzano	396
COF Pinot Grigio, Ronco del Gnemiz	420
COF Pinot Grigio, Torre Rosazza	397
COF Pinot Grigio, Valchiarò	425
COF Pinot Grigio, Vigna Traverso	412
COF Pinot Grigio, Vigne Fantin Noda'r	408
COF Pinot Grigio, Andrea Visintini	382
COF Pinot Grigio, Zof	383
COF Pinot Grigio Ipso Zuc di Volpe, Volpe Pasini	425
COF Pinot Grigio Plus, Bastianich	405
COF Pinot Grigio Ronco San Michele, Alfieri Cantarutti	419
COF Pinot Grigio Vign. Montsclapade, Girolamo Dorigo	358
COF Pinot Grigio Vign. Sdricca, Ca' Tullio	354
COF Pinot Grigio Zuc di Volpe, Volpe Pasini	425
COF Pinot Nero, Le Due Terre	409
COF Pinot Nero Ronco del Palazzo, Torre Rosazza	397
COF Ramandolo, Dario Coos	399
COF Ramandolo, La Roncaia	400
COF Ramandolo, Ronco Vieri	400
COF Ramandolo Passito Romandus, Dario Coos	399

COF Refosco, La Roncaia	400	
COF Refosco, Ronco Vieri	400	
COF Refosco P. R., Livio e Claudio Buiatti	356	
COF Refosco P. R., Marco Cecchini	386	
COF Refosco P. R., Colutta	395	
COF Refosco P. R., Conte D'Attimis-Maniago	357	
COF Refosco P. R., Livio Felluga	371	
COF Refosco P. R., Adriano Gigante	381	
COF Refosco P. R., Iole Grillo	408	
COF Refosco P. R., Jacùss	424	
COF Refosco P.R., La Tunella	406	
COF Refosco P. R., Midolini	395	
COF Refosco P. R., Petrucco	359	
COF Refosco P. R., Ronchi di Manzano	396	
COF Refosco P. R., Leonardo Specogna	382	
COF Refosco P. R., Torre Rosazza	397	
COF Refosco P. R., Valchiarò	425	
COF Refosco P. R., Vigna Petrussa	411	
COF Refosco P. R., Vigna Traverso	412	
COF Refosco P. R., Vigne Fantin Noda'r	408	
COF Refosco P.R., Zof	383	
COF Refosco P. R. Re Fosco, Le Vigne di Zamò	397	
COF Refosco P. R. Riul, Livon	419	
COF Refosco P. R. Romain, Paolo Rodaro	366	
COF Refosco P. R. Sdricca, Ca' Tullio	354	
COF Refosco P. R. Vign. Montsclapade, Girolamo Dorigo	358	
COF Refosco P. R. Vôs da Vigne, Tenuta di Angoris	428	
COF Refosco P. R. Zuc di Volpe, Volpe Pasini	425	
COF Ribolla Gialla, Valentino Butussi	380	
COF Ribolla Gialla, Ca di Bon	429	
COF Ribolla Gialla, La Tunella	406	
COF Ribolla Gialla, La Viarte	409	
COF Ribolla Gialla, Miani	359	
COF Ribolla Gialla, Perusini	381	
COF Ribolla Gialla, Petrucco	359	
COF Ribolla Gialla, Teresa Raiz	403	
COF Ribolla Gialla, Rocca Bernarda	407	
COF Ribolla Gialla, Paolo Rodaro	366	
COF Ribolla Gialla, Torre Rosazza	397	
COF Ribolla Gialla, Vigna Angeli	430	
COF Ribolla Gialla, Vigna Traverso	412	
COF Ribolla Gialla, Andrea Visintini	382	
COF Ribolla Gialla, Zof	383	
COF Ribolla Gialla Turian, Eugenio Collavini	380	
COF Ribolla Gialla Vign. Ronc di Juri, Girolamo Dorigo	358	
COF Ribolla Gialla Vôs da Vigne, Tenuta di Angoris	428	
COF Ribolla Gialla Zuc di Volpe, Volpe Pasini	425	
COF Riesling, Andrea Visintini	382	
COF Ronco Broilo, Conte D'Attimis-Maniago	357	
COF Rosazzo Bianco Ronc di Rosazzo, Ronchi di Manzano	396	
COF Rosazzo Narciso Bianco, Ronco delle Betulle	396	
COF Rosazzo Narciso Rosso, Ronco delle Betulle	396	
COF Rosazzo Picolit Ris., Livio Felluga	371	
COF Rosazzo Pignolo, Le Vigne di Zamò	397	
COF Rosazzo Ribolla Gialla, Ronco delle Betulle	396	
COF Rosazzo Ribolla Gialla, Le Vigne di Zamò	397	
COF Rosazzo Rosso Ronc di Rosazzo, Ronchi di Manzano	396	
COF Rosazzo Sossò Ris., Livio Felluga	371	
COF Ross El Clap, Valchiarò	425	
COF Rosso, Miani	359	
COF Rosso, Teresa Raiz	403	
COF Rosso Bandaròs, Torre Rosazza	397	
COF Rosso Careme, Marco Cecchini	386	
COF Rosso Celtico, Davide Moschioni	365	
COF Rosso Civon, Il Roncal	365	
COF Rosso d'Orsone, Dal Fari	364	
COF Rosso Decano Rosso, Teresa Raiz	403	
COF Rosso del Gnemiz, Ronco del Gnemiz	420	
COF Rosso Dominin, Davino Meroi	358	
COF Rosso Gheppio, La Roncaia	400	
COF Rosso Il Boscorosso, Rosa Bosco	394	
COF Rosso L'Arcione, La Tunella	406	
COF Rosso Lindi Uà, Jacùss	424	
COF Rosso Momon Ros Ris., Livio e Claudio Buiatti	356	
COF Rosso Petrussa, Petrussa	410	
COF Rosso Reâl, Davide Moschioni	365	
COF Rosso Rîul, Dario e Luciano Ermacora	406	
COF Rosso Roldi, Valle	427	
COF Rosso Ronco dei Roseti, Le Vigne di Zamò	397	
COF Rosso Ros di Buri, Davino Meroi	358	
COF Rosso Sacrisassi, Le Due Terre	409	
COF Rosso Scuro, Scubla	407	
COF Rosso Selenard, Colutta	395	
COF Rosso Sottocastello, Vigna Traverso	412	
COF Rosso Sottocastello Ris., Vigna Traverso	412	
COF Rosso Turo, Vigna Angeli	430	
COF Rosso Vignaricco, Conte D'Attimis-Maniago	357	
COF Sariz, Ca' Ronesca	383	
COF Sauvignon, Livio e Claudio Buiatti	356	
COF Sauvignon, Olivo Buiatti	357	
COF Sauvignon, Valentino Butussi	380	
COF Sauvignon, Alfieri Cantarutti	419	
COF Sauvignon, Colutta	395	
COF Sauvignon, Paolino Comelli	386	
COF Sauvignon, Conte D'Attimis-Maniago	357	
COF Sauvignon, Dario e Luciano Ermacora	406	
COF Sauvignon, Livio Felluga	371	
COF Sauvignon, Adriano Gigante	381	
COF Sauvignon, Iole Grillo	408	
COF Sauvignon, Jacùss	424	
COF Sauvignon, La Viarte	409	
COF Sauvignon, Valerio Marinig	410	
COF Sauvignon, Davino Meroi	358	
COF Sauvignon, Miani	359	
COF Sauvignon, Perusini	381	
COF Sauvignon, Petrucco	359	

COF Sauvignon, Petrussa	410	
COF Sauvignon, Rocca Bernarda	407	
COF Sauvignon, Paolo Rodaro	366	
COF Sauvignon, Il Roncal	365	
COF Sauvignon, Ronco del Gnemiz	420	
COF Sauvignon, Ronco delle Betulle	396	
COF Sauvignon, Scubla	407	
COF Sauvignon, Leonardo Specogna	382	
COF Sauvignon, Valchiarò	425	
COF Sauvignon, Alessandra Vidon	430	
COF Sauvignon, Vigna Petrussa	411	
COF Sauvignon, Vigna Traverso	412	
COF Sauvignon, Vigne Fantin Noda'r	408	
COF Sauvignon, Andrea Visintini	382	
COF Sauvignon, Zof	383	
COF Sauvignon Blanc, Rosa Bosco	394	
COF Sauvignon Bosc Romain, Paolo Rodaro	366	
COF Sauvignon Podere dei Blumeri, Schiopetto	362	
COF Sauvignon Podere di Ipplis, Ca' Ronesca	383	
COF Sauvignon Ris., Ronco del Gnemiz	420	
COF Sauvignon Ronc di Juri, Girolamo Dorigo	358	
COF Sauvignon Sel. Araldica, Valle	427	
COF Sauvignon Vocalis, Aquila del Torre	403	
COF Sauvignon Zuc di Volpe, Volpe Pasini	425	
COF Schioppettino, Ca di Bon	429	
COF Schioppettino, Colutta	395	
COF Schioppettino, Adriano Gigante	381	
COF Schioppettino, Jacùss	424	
COF Schioppettino, La Viarte	409	
COF Schioppettino, Valerio Marinig	410	
COF Schioppettino, Davide Moschioni	365	
COF Schioppettino, Petrussa	410	
COF Schioppettino, Il Roncal	365	
COF Schioppettino, Vigna Traverso	412	
COF Soresta'nt Blanc, Midolini	395	
COF Tazzelenghe, Conte D'Attimis-Maniago	357	
COF Tazzelenghe, La Viarte	409	
COF Tocai Friulano, Alberice	429	
COF Tocai Friulano, Livio e Claudio Buiatti	356	
COF Tocai Friulano, Olivo Buiatti	357	
COF Tocai Friulano, Valentino Butussi	380	
COF Tocai Friulano, Alfieri Cantarutti	419	
COF Tocai Friulano, Colutta	395	
COF Tocai Friulano, Paolino Comelli	386	
COF Tocai Friulano, Dal Fari	364	
COF Tocai Friulano, Dario e Luciano Ermacora	406	
COF Tocai Friulano, Livio Felluga	371	
COF Tocai Friulano, Adriano Gigante	381	
COF Tocai Friulano, Iole Grillo	408	
COF Tocai Friulano, Jacùss	424	
COF Tocai Friulano, La Tunella	406	
COF Tocai Friulano, La Viarte	409	
COF Tocai Friulano, Valerio Marinig	410	
COF Tocai Friulano, Davino Meroi	358	
COF Tocai Friulano, Miani	359	
COF Tocai Friulano, Midolini	395	
COF Tocai Friulano, Petrucco	359	
COF Tocai Friulano, Petrussa	410	
COF Tocai Friulano, Flavio Pontoni	427	
COF Tocai Friulano, Teresa Raiz	403	
COF Tocai Friulano, Rocca Bernarda	407	
COF Tocai Friulano, Paolo Rodaro	366	
COF Tocai Friulano, Il Roncal	365	
COF Tocai Friulano, Ronco dei Pini	411	
COF Tocai Friulano, Ronco del Gnemiz	420	
COF Tocai Friulano, Ronco delle Betulle	396	
COF Tocai Friulano, Scubla	407	
COF Tocai Friulano, Leonardo Specogna	382	
COF Tocai Friulano, Valchiarò	425	
COF Tocai Friulano, Alessandra Vidon	430	
COF Tocai Friulano, Vigna Angeli	430	
COF Tocai Friulano, Vigna Petrussa	411	
COF Tocai Friulano, Vigna Traverso	412	
COF Tocai Friulano, Le Vigne di Zamò	397	
COF Tocai Friulano, Vigne Fantin Noda'r	408	
COF Tocai Friulano, Andrea Visintini	382	
COF Tocai Friulano, Zof	383	
COF Tocai Friulano Plus, Bastianich	405	
COF Tocai Friulano Storico, Adriano Gigante	381	
COF Tocai Friulano Sup., Ronchi di Manzano	396	
COF Tocai Friulano V. Cinquant'Anni, Le Vigne di Zamò	397	
COF Tocai Friulano Vocalis, Aquila del Torre	403	
COF Tocai Friulano Zuc di Volpe, Volpe Pasini	425	
COF Traminer Aromatico, Andrea Visintini	382	
COF Verduzzo Friulano, Livio e Claudio Buiatti	356	
COF Verduzzo Friulano, Valentino Butussi	380	
COF Verduzzo Friulano, Colutta	395	
COF Verduzzo Friulano, Dario e Luciano Ermacora	406	
COF Verduzzo Friulano, Adriano Gigante	381	
COF Verduzzo Friulano, Jacùss	424	
COF Verduzzo Friulano, Valerio Marinig	410	
COF Verduzzo Friulano, Flavio Pontoni	427	
COF Verduzzo Friulano, Ronchi di Manzano	396	
COF Verduzzo Friulano, Leonardo Specogna	382	
COF Verduzzo Friulano, Valchiarò	425	
COF Verduzzo Friulano, Vigne Fantin Noda'r	408	
COF Verduzzo Friulano Graticcio, Scubla	407	
COF Verduzzo Friulano Il Longhino, Dario Coos	399	
COF Verduzzo Friulano Pra Zenâr, Paolo Rodaro	366	
COF Verduzzo Friulano Verlit, Marco Cecchini	386	
Col di Sasso, Castello Banfi	515	
Col Martin Luwa, Ascevi - Luwa	415	
Collazzi, Fattoria Collazzi	603	
Colle Amato, Colle San Lorenzo	684	
Colle Amato Pietrapinta, Colle San Lorenzo	684	
Colle Carpito, San Luciano	539	

Colle della Torre, Giovanni Palombo 681
Colle Leone, Ca' del Vispo 576
Colle Picchioni Rosso, Paola Di Mauro 686
Collemorra di Càgnore, Antico Terreno Ottavi 650
Colli Berici Cabernet, Costozza - Conti da Schio 298
Colli Berici Cabernet, Natalino Mattiello 298
Colli Berici Cabernet Capitel S. Libera,
    Domenico Cavazza & F.lli 306
Colli Berici Cabernet Casara Roveri, Luigino Dal Maso 306
Colli Berici Cabernet Cicogna, Domenico Cavazza & F.lli 306
Colli Berici Cabernet Colle d'Elica, Natalino Mattiello 298
Colli Berici Cabernet Montebelvedere, Luigino Dal Maso 306
Colli Berici Cabernet Sauvignon Via Volto, Natalino Mattiello 298
Colli Berici Cabernet Vigneto Pozzare, Piovene Porto Godi 344
Colli Berici Chardonnay Via Volto, Natalino Mattiello 298
Colli Berici Garganega, Natalino Mattiello 298
Colli Berici Merlot Campo del Lago, Villa dal Ferro Lazzarini 318
Colli Berici Merlot Capitel S. Libera, Domenico Cavazza & F.lli 306
Colli Berici Merlot Casara Roveri, Luigino Dal Maso 306
Colli Berici Merlot Cicogna, Domenico Cavazza & F.lli 306
Colli Berici Merlot Fra i Broli, Piovene Porto Godi 344
Colli Berici Merlot Il Massi, Villa dal Ferro Lazzarini 318
Colli Berici Pinot Bianco Campo Corì,
    Domenico Cavazza & F.lli 306
Colli Berici Pinot Bianco del Rocolo, Villa dal Ferro Lazzarini 318
Colli Berici Pinot Bianco Polveriera, Piovene Porto Godi 344
Colli Berici Sauvignon Via Volto, Natalino Mattiello 298
Colli Berici Sauvignon Vigneto Fostine, Piovene Porto Godi 344
Colli Berici Tocai Rosso Thovara, Piovene Porto Godi 344
Colli Berici Tocai Rosso Vigneto Riveselle, Piovene Porto Godi 344
Colli d'Imola Bianco Euforia, Tenuta Ca' Lunga 459
Colli d'Imola Cabernet Sauvignon Ca' Grande, Umberto Cesari 436
Colli dell'Uccellina, La Selva 613
Colli di Conegliano Bianco, F.lli Bortolin Spumanti 335
Colli di Conegliano Bianco, Conte Collalto 333
Colli di Conegliano Bianco Albio, Gregoletto 304
Colli di Conegliano Bianco Delico, Sorelle Bronca 344
Colli di Conegliano Bianco Il Greccio, Bepin de Eto 320
Colli di Conegliano Bianco Rizzardo, Masottina 318
Colli di Conegliano Reafrontolo Passito Col Vendrame,
    Santo Stefano 294
Colli di Conegliano Rosso, Collalbrigo 346
Colli di Conegliano Rosso, Conte Collalto 333
Colli di Conegliano Rosso, Le Colture 338
Colli di Conegliano Rosso, G. B. Cerletti Scuola Enol. di Conegliano 346
Colli di Conegliano Rosso Croda Ronca, Bepin de Eto 320
Colli di Conegliano Rosso Gregoletto, Gregoletto 304
Colli di Conegliano Rosso Montesco, Masottina 318
Colli di Conegliano Rosso S. Alberto, Ruggeri & C. 339
Colli di Conegliano Rosso Ser Bele, Sorelle Bronca 344
Colli di Conegliano Rosso Vign. Levina, Canevel Spumanti 336
Colli di Faenza Alba di Luna, Poderi Morini 441
Colli di Faenza Bianco Poderepalazzina Le Rive,
    Leone Conti 439
Colli di Faenza Rosso Ca' di Berta, La Berta 435
Colli di Faenza Rosso Calenzone, Il Pratello 447
Colli di Faenza Rosso Colle Torre Monte Ris., Rontana 458
Colli di Faenza Rosso Miniato, Paolo Francesconi 440
Colli di Faenza Rosso Montecorallo, Treré 442
Colli di Faenza Rosso Podereviacupa Le Ghiande, Leone Conti 439
Colli di Faenza Sangiovese Col Mora, Rontana 458
Colli di Faenza Sangiovese Limbecca, Paolo Francesconi 440
Colli di Faenza Sangiovese Mantignano, Il Pratello 447
Colli di Faenza Sangiovese Renero, Treré 442
Colli di Imola Boldo, Tre Monti 445
Colli di Imola Chardonnay Ciardo, Tre Monti 445
Colli di Imola Salcerella, Tre Monti 445
Colli di Imola Terre di Maestrale, Tenuta Poggio Pollino 460
Colli di Luni Bianco, Santa Caterina 180
Colli di Luni Rosso, Il Chioso 178
Colli di Luni Rosso, Il Torchio 168
Colli di Luni Rosso, Ottaviano Lambruschi 169
Colli di Luni Rosso Maniero, Ottaviano Lambruschi 169
Colli di Luni Rosso Poggio dei Magni, Il Monticello 177
Colli di Luni Rosso Re Carlo, La Pietra del Focolare 173
Colli di Luni Rosso Rupestro, Il Monticello 177
Colli di Luni Vermentino, Giacomelli 179
Colli di Luni Vermentino, Il Chioso 178
Colli di Luni Vermentino, Il Torchio 168
Colli di Luni Vermentino, Ottaviano Lambruschi 169
Colli di Luni Vermentino, Il Monticello 177
Colli di Luni Vermentino, 'R Mesueto 179
Colli di Luni Vermentino Augusto, La Pietra del Focolare 173
Colli di Luni Vermentino Costa Marina, Ottaviano Lambruschi 169
Colli di Luni Vermentino Poggi Alti, Santa Caterina 180
Colli di Luni Vermentino Santo Paterno, La Pietra del Focolare 173
Colli di Luni Vermentino Sarticola, Ottaviano Lambruschi 169
Colli di Parma Malvasia Frizzante, Carra 445
Colli di Parma Malvasia Frizzante, Isidoro Lamoretti 460
Colli di Parma Malvasia Frizzante, Monte delle Vigne 459
Colli di Parma Malvasia Torrechiara, Cantine Dall'Asta 461
Colli di Parma Sauvignon Frizzante, Carra 445
Colli di Parma Sauvignon Frizzante, Monte delle Vigne 459
Colli di Rimini Cabernet Sauvignon Luna Nuova, San Valentino 452
Colli di Rimini Rosso Noi, San Patrignano 439
Colli Etruria Centrale Vinum Passum, Fattoria di Presciano 614
Colli Euganei Bianco, Ca' Lustra 292
Colli Euganei Bianco Corte Borin, Borin 305
Colli Euganei Cabernet, Ca' Lustra 292
Colli Euganei Cabernet Ris., Vignalta 334
Colli Euganei Cabernet Sauvignon Ireneo,
    Giordano Emo Capodilista 288
Colli Euganei Cabernet Sauvignon Mons Silicis Ris., Borin 305
Colli Euganei Cabernet Sauvignon V. Costa, Borin 305
Colli Euganei Chardonnay, La Montecchia 328
Colli Euganei Chardonnay, Vignalta 334

Colli Euganei Chardonnay Passo Roverello Villa Alessi,
    Ca' Lustra 292
Colli Euganei Chardonnay V. Bianca, Borin 305
Colli Euganei Fiori d'Arancio Passito Donna Daria,
    Giordano Emo Capodilista 288
Colli Euganei Marzemino Villa Alessi, Ca' Lustra 292
Colli Euganei Merlot, Ca' Lustra 292
Colli Euganei Merlot, La Montecchia 328
Colli Euganei Merlot Rocca Chiara Ris., Borin 305
Colli Euganei Merlot V. del Foscolo, Borin 305
Colli Euganei Merlot V. Sasso Nero Villa Alessi, Ca' Lustra 292
Colli Euganei Merlot Venda, Vignalta 334
Colli Euganei Moscato Fior d'Arancio Alpianae, Vignalta 334
Colli Euganei Moscato Fior d'Arancio Passito, La Montecchia 328
Colli Euganei Passito Fior d'Arancio, Borin 305
Colli Euganei Pinot Bianco, Ca' Lustra 292
Colli Euganei Pinot Bianco, Vignalta 334
Colli Euganei Pinot Bianco Monte Archino, Borin 305
Colli Euganei Pinot Bianco V. Pedevenda Villa Alessi, Ca' Lustra 292
Colli Euganei Rosso Cà Emo, La Montecchia 328
Colli Euganei Rosso Gemola, Vignalta 334
Colli Euganei Rosso Montecchia, La Montecchia 328
Colli Euganei Rosso Ris., Vignalta 334
Colli Euganei Rosso Villa Capodilista, La Montecchia 328
Colli Euganei Sauvignon V. Olivetani Villa Alessi, Ca' Lustra 292
Colli Maceratesi Bianco, Santa Cassella 647
Colli Maceratesi Bianco Monteferro, Fattoria di Forano 626
Colli Maceratesi Bianco Murrano, Capinera 641
Colli Maceratesi Bianco Villa Forano, Fattoria di Forano 626
Colli Martani Grechetto Arcato Casale Triocco, Spoletoducale 674
Colli Martani Grechetto di Todi, Todini 675
Colli Martani Grechetto Grecante, Arnaldo Caprai - Val di Maggio 665
Colli Martani Sangiovese Rubro, Todini 675
Colli Martani Sangiovese Satiro, Rocca di Fabbri 666
Colli Perugini Chardonnay, Goretti 673
Colli Perugini Rosso, Chiorri 678
Colli Perugini Rosso L'Arringatore, Goretti 673
Colli Pesaresi Focara Pinot Nero Impero, Fattoria Mancini 646
Colli Pesaresi Roncaglia, Fattoria Mancini 646
Colli Pesaresi Sangiovese, Fattoria Mancini 646
Colli Pesaresi Sangiovese, Guerrieri 646
Colli Pesaresi Sangiovese Galileo Ris., Guerrieri 646
Colli Pesaresi Sangiovese Goccione, La Ripe 656
Colli Pesaresi Sangiovese La Ripe, La Ripe 656
Colli Pesaresi Sangiovese Luigi Fiorini, Valentino Fiorini 627
Colli Pesaresi Sangiovese Sant'Andrea in Villis, Claudio Morelli 634
Colli Tortonesi Barbera, Valli Unite 157
Colli Tortonesi Barbera Amaranto, Cascina Montagnola 153
Colli Tortonesi Barbera Boccanera, Luigi Boveri 71
Colli Tortonesi Barbera Campo La Bà, Paolo Poggio 155
Colli Tortonesi Barbera Derio, Paolo Poggio 155
Colli Tortonesi Barbera Monleale, Renato Boveri 114
Colli Tortonesi Barbera Poggio delle Amarene, Luigi Boveri 71
Colli Tortonesi Barbera S. Ambrogio, Renato Boveri 114
Colli Tortonesi Barbera Sup. Rodeo, Cascina Montagnola 153
Colli Tortonesi Barbera Vighet, Valli Unite 157
Colli Tortonesi Barbera Vignalunga, Luigi Boveri 71
Colli Tortonesi Bianco Bricco Bartolomeo, La Colombera 145
Colli Tortonesi Bianco Casareggio, Vigneti Massa 115
Colli Tortonesi Bianco Castagnoli, Mutti 138
Colli Tortonesi Bianco Coccalina, Claudio Mariotto 145
Colli Tortonesi Bianco Costa del Vento, Vigneti Massa 115
Colli Tortonesi Bianco Derthona, La Colombera 145
Colli Tortonesi Bianco Derthona, Claudio Mariotto 145
Colli Tortonesi Bianco Filari di Timorasso, Luigi Boveri 71
Colli Tortonesi Bianco La Vetta, Terralba 45
Colli Tortonesi Bianco Martin, Franco M. Martinetti 144
Colli Tortonesi Bianco Ronchetto, Paolo Poggio 155
Colli Tortonesi Bianco Stato, Terralba 45
Colli Tortonesi Bianco Sull'Aia, Mutti 138
Colli Tortonesi Cortese Cappelletta, Renato Boveri 114
Colli Tortonesi Cortese Munprò, Renato Boveri 114
Colli Tortonesi Cortese Riva Rosa, Cascina Montagnola 153
Colli Tortonesi Cortese Vergato, Cascina Montagnola 153
Colli Tortonesi Cortese Vigna del Prete, Luigi Boveri 71
Colli Tortonesi Rosso Bigolla, Vigneti Massa 115
Colli Tortonesi Rosso Boscobarona, Mutti 138
Colli Tortonesi Rosso Cerreta, Vigneti Massa 115
Colli Tortonesi Rosso Croatina Pertichetta, Vigneti Massa 115
Colli Tortonesi Rosso La Cereta, Renato Boveri 114
Colli Tortonesi Rosso Madai!, Renato Boveri 114
Colli Tortonesi Rosso Martirella, Claudio Mariotto 145
Colli Tortonesi Rosso Monleale, Terralba 45
Colli Tortonesi Rosso Monleale, Vigneti Massa 115
Colli Tortonesi Rosso Montegrande, Terralba 45
Colli Tortonesi Rosso Poggio del Rosso, Claudio Mariotto 145
Colli Tortonesi Rosso Rivadestra, Mutti 138
Colli Tortonesi Rosso S. Ruffino, Mutti 138
Colli Tortonesi Rosso Strà Loja, Terralba 45
Colli Tortonesi Rosso Suciaja, La Colombera 145
Colli Tortonesi Rosso Terralba, Terralba 45
Colli Tortonesi Rosso Territorio, Claudio Mariotto 145
Colli Tortonesi Rosso Vegia Rampana, La Colombera 145
Colli Tortonesi Rosso Vhò, Claudio Mariotto 145
Colline del Milanese Passito di Verdea, Enrico Riccardi 225
Colline Lucchesi Bianco Giallo dei Muri, Tenuta di Valgiano 511
Colline Lucchesi Bianco Terre di Matraja,
    Fattoria Colle Verde 604
Colline Lucchesi Fruttuoso, Azienda Agricola Il Colle 616
Colline Lucchesi Rosso, Azienda Agricola Il Colle 616
Colline Lucchesi Rosso Brania delle Ghiandaie,
    Fattoria Colle Verde 604
Colline Lucchesi Rosso dei Palistorti, Tenuta di Valgiano 511
Colline Lucchesi Rosso Scasso dei Cesari, Tenuta di Valgiano 511
Colline Lucchesi Rosso Terre di Matraja, Fattoria Colle Verde 604
Colline Lucchesi Tenuta di Valgiano, Tenuta di Valgiano 511

Colline Novaresi Agamium, Antichi Vigneti di Cantalupo	87
Colline Novaresi Bianco, Rovellotti	87
Colline Novaresi Bianco Collefino, Dessilani	79
Colline Novaresi Il Mimo, Antichi Vigneti di Cantalupo	87
Colline Novaresi Nebbiolo, Dessilani	79
Colline Novaresi Nebbiolo Tre Confini, Torraccia del Piantavigna	159
Colline Novaresi Primigenia, Antichi Vigneti di Cantalupo	87
Colline Novaresi Rosso, Rovellotti	87
Colline Novaresi Vespolina, Rovellotti	87
Colline Novaresi Villa Horta, Antichi Vigneti di Cantalupo	87
Colline Savonesi Passito, La Vecchia Cantina	167
Collio Bianco, Borgo del Tiglio	367
Collio Bianco, Casa Zuliani	387
Collio Bianco, Colle Duga	369
Collio Bianco, Edi Keber	372
Collio Bianco, Damijan Podversic	392
Collio Bianco, Isidoro Polencic	375
Collio Bianco, Dario Raccaro	376
Collio Bianco, Oscar Sturm	378
Collio Bianco, Franco Terpin	418
Collio Bianco, Vigna del Lauro	379
Collio Bianco Beli Grici, Renato Keber	428
Collio Bianco Caprizi di Marceline, La Rajade	384
Collio Bianco Chamûr, Roncada	376
Collio Bianco Cicinis, Conti Attems	390
Collio Bianco del Bratinis, Gradis'ciutta	416
Collio Bianco del Tùzz, Gradis'ciutta	416
Collio Bianco della Castellada, La Castellada	390
Collio Bianco Fosarin, Ronco dei Tassi	377
Collio Bianco Frututis Ronc dal Luis, Maurizio Buzzinelli	368
Collio Bianco Jelka, Roberto Picech - Le Vigne del Ribél	374
Collio Bianco Klin, Primosic	392
Collio Bianco Marnà, Ca' Ronesca	383
Collio Bianco Molamatta, Marco Felluga	393
Collio Bianco Planta, Matijaz Tercic	417
Collio Bianco Pradis, Carlo di Pradis	369
Collio Bianco Ronc dal Luis, Maurizio Buzzinelli	368
Collio Bianco Ronchi di Ravéz, Gestioni Agricole Vidussi	362
Collio Bianco Ronco della Chiesa, Borgo del Tiglio	367
Collio Bianco Rosenplatz, Livio Felluga	371
Collio Bianco Russiz Disôre, Russiz Superiore	361
Collio Bianco Rylint, Conti Formentini	416
Collio Bianco Sermar, Ca' Ronesca	383
Collio Bianco Tre Vignis, Venica & Venica	384
Collio Bianco Trilogy, Fantinel	423
Collio Bianco Zuani, Zuani	418
Collio Bianco Zuani Vigne, Zuani	418
Collio Cabernet, F.lli Pighin	401
Collio Cabernet, Villa Russiz	363
Collio Cabernet Collezione Privata, Eugenio Collavini	380
Collio Cabernet Franc, Paolo Caccese	368
Collio Cabernet Franc, Gradis'ciutta	416
Collio Cabernet Franc, La Boatina	372
Collio Cabernet Franc, Alessandro Princic	375
Collio Cabernet Franc, Roncada	376
Collio Cabernet Franc, Russiz Superiore	361
Collio Cabernet Franc, Subida di Monte	378
Collio Cabernet Franc Rogoves, Marcello e Marino Humar	417
Collio Cabernet Sauvignon, La Boatina	372
Collio Cabernet Sauvignon, Roncada	376
Collio Cabernet Sauvignon RoncAlto, Livon	419
Collio Cabernet Sauvignon Ruttars, Puiatti	360
Collio Cabernet Sauvignon Stratin, La Rajade	384
Collio Chardonnay, Conti Attems	390
Collio Chardonnay, Borgo Conventi	387
Collio Chardonnay, Borgo del Tiglio	367
Collio Chardonnay, Il Carpino	415
Collio Chardonnay, La Castellada	390
Collio Chardonnay, Colle Duga	369
Collio Chardonnay, Branko - Igor Erzetic	371
Collio Chardonnay, Marco Felluga	393
Collio Chardonnay, Gradis'ciutta	416
Collio Chardonnay, Marcello e Marino Humar	417
Collio Chardonnay, La Boatina	372
Collio Chardonnay, La Rajade	384
Collio Chardonnay, Muzic	430
Collio Chardonnay, Isidoro Polencic	375
Collio Chardonnay, Roncada	376
Collio Chardonnay, Ronco dei Pini	411
Collio Chardonnay, Matijaz Tercic	417
Collio Chardonnay, Franco Toros	379
Collio Chardonnay, Gestioni Agricole Vidussi	362
Collio Chardonnay Colle Russian, Borgo Conventi	387
Collio Chardonnay Cuccanea, Eugenio Collavini	380
Collio Chardonnay Gmajne, Primosic	392
Collio Chardonnay Gräfin de la Tour, Villa Russiz	363
Collio Chardonnay Il Vino Senza Qualità, Ca' Ronesca	383
Collio Chardonnay Monte Cucco, Tenuta Villanova	389
Collio Chardonnay Ris., Gravner	391
Collio Chardonnay Ronco Bernizza, Venica & Venica	384
Collio Chardonnay Ronco Cucco, Tenuta Villanova	389
Collio Chardonnay Sel., Borgo del Tiglio	367
Collio Chardonnay Sel., Subida di Monte	378
Collio Chardonnay Torre di Tramontana, Conti Formentini	416
Collio Collio, Cant. Prod. di Cormons	370
Collio Malvasia, Borgo del Tiglio	367
Collio Malvasia, Ca' Ronesca	383
Collio Malvasia, Paolo Caccese	368
Collio Malvasia, Il Carpino	415
Collio Malvasia, Roberto Picech - Le Vigne del Ribél	374
Collio Malvasia, Alessandro Princic	375
Collio Malvasia, Dario Raccaro	376
Collio Malvasia, Venica & Venica	384
Collio Malvasia, Gestioni Agricole Vidussi	362
Collio Malvasia, Andrea Visintini	382
Collio Malvasia, Francesco Vosca	429
Collio Malvasia Istriana, Villa Russiz	363
Collio Malvasia Ronc dal Luis, Maurizio Buzzinelli	368
Collio Merlot, Carlo di Pradis	369
Collio Merlot, Casa Zuliani	387
Collio Merlot, Colle Duga	369
Collio Merlot, Colmello di Grotta	388
Collio Merlot, Marco Felluga	393
Collio Merlot, Fiegl	391
Collio Merlot, Marcello e Marino Humar	417
Collio Merlot, Edi Keber	372
Collio Merlot, La Boatina	372
Collio Merlot, Giulio Manzocco	373
Collio Merlot, Dario Raccaro	376
Collio Merlot, Roncada	376
Collio Merlot, Russiz Superiore	361
Collio Merlot, Oscar Sturm	378
Collio Merlot, Subida di Monte	378
Collio Merlot, Matijaz Tercic	417
Collio Merlot, Vigna del Lauro	379
Collio Merlot, Villa Russiz	363
Collio Merlot, Tenuta Villanova	389
Collio Merlot, Francesco Vosca	429
Collio Merlot dal Pic, Eugenio Collavini	380
Collio Merlot Graf de la Tour, Villa Russiz	363
Collio Merlot Leopold, Fiegl	391
Collio Merlot Ris., La Rajade	384
Collio Merlot Ruttars, Puiatti	360
Collio Merlot Sel., Subida di Monte	378
Collio Merlot Sel., Franco Toros	379
Collio Merlot Tajut, Conti Formentini	416
Collio Merlot Tiare Mate Grand Cru, Livon	419
Collio Merlot Torriani, Castello di Spessa	360
Collio Müller Thurgau, Maurizio Buzzinelli	368
Collio Müller Thurgau, Paolo Caccese	368
Collio Picolit, Marcello e Marino Humar	417
Collio Pinot Bianco, Conti Attems	390
Collio Pinot Bianco, Maurizio Buzzinelli	368
Collio Pinot Bianco, Paolo Caccese	368
Collio Pinot Bianco, Casa Zuliani	387
Collio Pinot Bianco, Castello di Spessa	360
Collio Pinot Bianco, Fiegl	391
Collio Pinot Bianco, Gradimiro Gradnik Eredi	428
Collio Pinot Bianco, Marcello e Marino Humar	417
Collio Pinot Bianco, Giulio Manzocco	373
Collio Pinot Bianco, Roberto Picech - Le Vigne del Ribél	374
Collio Pinot Bianco, Isidoro Polencic	375
Collio Pinot Bianco, Alessandro Princic	375
Collio Pinot Bianco, Roncada	376
Collio Pinot Bianco, Russiz Superiore	361
Collio Pinot Bianco, Schiopetto	362
Collio Pinot Bianco, Franco Toros	379
Collio Pinot Bianco, Venica & Venica	384
Collio Pinot Bianco, Gestioni Agricole Vidussi	362
Collio Pinot Bianco, Villa Russiz	363
Collio Pinot Bianco Amrità, Schiopetto	362
Collio Pinot Bianco degli Ulivi, Aldo Polencic	374
Collio Pinot Bianco di Santarosa, Castello di Spessa	360
Collio Pinot Grigio, Conti Attems	390
Collio Pinot Grigio, Borgo Conventi	387
Collio Pinot Grigio, Ca' Ronesca	383
Collio Pinot Grigio, Paolo Caccese	368
Collio Pinot Grigio, Carlo di Pradis	369
Collio Pinot Grigio, Casa Zuliani	387
Collio Pinot Grigio, Castello di Spessa	360
Collio Pinot Grigio, Colle Duga	369
Collio Pinot Grigio, Colmello di Grotta	388
Collio Pinot Grigio, Conti Formentini	416
Collio Pinot Grigio, Cant. Prod. di Cormons	370
Collio Pinot Grigio, Branko - Igor Erzetic	371
Collio Pinot Grigio, Gradis'ciutta	416
Collio Pinot Grigio, Gradimiro Gradnik Eredi	428
Collio Pinot Grigio, Renato Keber	428
Collio Pinot Grigio, La Boatina	372
Collio Pinot Grigio, Giulio Manzocco	373
Collio Pinot Grigio, F.lli Pighin	401
Collio Pinot Grigio, Aldo Polencic	374
Collio Pinot Grigio, Isidoro Polencic	375
Collio Pinot Grigio, Alessandro Princic	375
Collio Pinot Grigio, Ronco dei Pini	411
Collio Pinot Grigio, Ronco dei Tassi	377
Collio Pinot Grigio, Russiz Superiore	361
Collio Pinot Grigio, Schiopetto	362
Collio Pinot Grigio, Oscar Sturm	378
Collio Pinot Grigio, Subida di Monte	378
Collio Pinot Grigio, Matijaz Tercic	417
Collio Pinot Grigio, Franco Toros	379
Collio Pinot Grigio, Gestioni Agricole Vidussi	362
Collio Pinot Grigio, Vigna del Lauro	379
Collio Pinot Grigio, Villa Russiz	363
Collio Pinot Grigio, Tenuta Villanova	389
Collio Pinot Grigio, Francesco Vosca	429
Collio Pinot Grigio Ascevi, Ascevi - Luwa	415
Collio Pinot Grigio Braide Grande Grand Cru, Livon	419
Collio Pinot Grigio Collezione Privata, Eugenio Collavini	380
Collio Pinot Grigio Gmajne, Primosic	392
Collio Pinot Grigio Grappoli Luwa, Ascevi - Luwa	415
Collio Pinot Grigio Leopold, Fiegl	391
Collio Pinot Grigio Podere San Giacomo, Ca' Ronesca	383
Collio Pinot Grigio Sant'Helena, Fantinel	423
Collio Pinot Grigio V. Runc, Il Carpino	415
Collio Pinot Grigio Vôs da Vigne, Tenuta di Angoris	428
Collio Pinot Nero Ruttars, Puiatti	360
Collio Ribolla Gialla, Conti Attems	390
Collio Ribolla Gialla, Borgo Conventi	387
Collio Ribolla Gialla, Maurizio Buzzinelli	368
Collio Ribolla Gialla, Il Carpino	415

Collio Ribolla Gialla, La Castellada	390
Collio Ribolla Gialla, Castello di Spessa	360
Collio Ribolla Gialla, Fiegl	391
Collio Ribolla Gialla, Gradis'ciutta	416
Collio Ribolla Gialla, Marcello e Marino Humar	417
Collio Ribolla Gialla, Thomas Kitzmüller	428
Collio Ribolla Gialla, La Boatina	372
Collio Ribolla Gialla, La Rajade	384
Collio Ribolla Gialla, Muzic	430
Collio Ribolla Gialla, Damijan Podversic	392
Collio Ribolla Gialla, Roncada	376
Collio Ribolla Gialla, Matijaz Tercic	417
Collio Ribolla Gialla, Franco Terpin	418
Collio Ribolla Gialla, Venica & Venica	384
Collio Ribolla Gialla, Villa Russiz	363
Collio Ribolla Gialla Bellanotte, Marco Felluga	393
Collio Ribolla Gialla Gmajne, Primosic	392
Collio Ribolla Gialla RoncAlto, Livon	419
Collio Ribolla Gialla Ronco Cucco, Tenuta Villanova	389
Collio Ribolla Gialla Ruttars, Puiatti	360
Collio Ribolla Gialla V. Runc, Il Carpino	415
Collio Riesling, Villa Russiz	363
Collio Rosso, Gradimiro Gradnik Eredi	428
Collio Rosso, Edi Keber	372
Collio Rosso, Roberto Picech - Le Vigne del Ribél	374
Collio Rosso, Damijan Podversic	392
Collio Rosso, Franco Terpin	418
Collio Rosso Are di Miute, Gestioni Agricole Vidussi	362
Collio Rosso Cjarandon, Ronco dei Tassi	377
Collio Rosso dei Princic, Gradis'ciutta	416
Collio Rosso Metamorfosis, Primosic	392
Collio Rosso Picol Maggiore, La Boatina	372
Collio Rosso Poncaia, Subida di Monte	378
Collio Rosso Ris., Borgo del Tiglio	367
Collio Rosso Ris., Roberto Picech - Le Vigne del Ribél	374
Collio Rosso Ris. degli Orzoni, Russiz Superiore	361
Collio Rosso Torriani, Castello di Spessa	360
Collio Rosso Winter, Casa Zuliani	387
Collio Sauvignon, Conti Attems	390
Collio Sauvignon, Borgo Conventi	387
Collio Sauvignon, Paolo Caccese	368
Collio Sauvignon, Carlo di Pradis	369
Collio Sauvignon, Il Carpino	415
Collio Sauvignon, Castello di Spessa	360
Collio Sauvignon, Eugenio Collavini	380
Collio Sauvignon, Colmello di Grotta	388
Collio Sauvignon, Conti Formentini	416
Collio Sauvignon, Cant. Prod. di Cormons	370
Collio Sauvignon, Mauro Drius	370
Collio Sauvignon, Branko - Igor Erzetic	371
Collio Sauvignon, Fiegl	391
Collio Sauvignon, Thomas Kitzmüller	428
Collio Sauvignon, La Boatina	372
Collio Sauvignon, La Rajade	384
Collio Sauvignon, Muzic	430
Collio Sauvignon, F.lli Pighin	401
Collio Sauvignon, Aldo Polencic	374
Collio Sauvignon, Isidoro Polencic	375
Collio Sauvignon, Alessandro Princic	375
Collio Sauvignon, Roncada	376
Collio Sauvignon, Ronco dei Pini	411
Collio Sauvignon, Ronco dei Tassi	377
Collio Sauvignon, Russiz Superiore	361
Collio Sauvignon, Schiopetto	362
Collio Sauvignon, Oscar Sturm	378
Collio Sauvignon, Subida di Monte	378
Collio Sauvignon, Franco Terpin	418
Collio Sauvignon, Franco Toros	379
Collio Sauvignon, Gestioni Agricole Vidussi	362
Collio Sauvignon, Vigna del Lauro	379
Collio Sauvignon, Villa Russiz	363
Collio Sauvignon Ascevi, Ascevi - Luwa	415
Collio Sauvignon de la Tour, Villa Russiz	363
Collio Sauvignon Gmajne, Primosic	392
Collio Sauvignon Leopold, Fiegl	391
Collio Sauvignon Poncanera, Eugenio Collavini	380
Collio Sauvignon Ronco Cucco, Tenuta Villanova	389
Collio Sauvignon Ronco dei Sassi Ascevi, Ascevi - Luwa	415
Collio Sauvignon Ronco delle Mele, Venica & Venica	384
Collio Sauvignon Ruttars, Puiatti	360
Collio Sauvignon Sant'Helena, Fantinel	423
Collio Sauvignon Segré, Castello di Spessa	360
Collio Sauvignon Tarsia, Schiopetto	362
Collio Sauvignon V. Runc, Il Carpino	415
Collio Sauvignon Valbuins Cru, Livon	419
Collio Studio di Bianco, Borgo del Tiglio	367
Collio Tocai Friulano, Conti Attems	390
Collio Tocai Friulano, Borgo Conventi	387
Collio Tocai Friulano, Borgo del Tiglio	367
Collio Tocai Friulano, Maurizio Buzzinelli	368
Collio Tocai Friulano, Ca' Ronesca	383
Collio Tocai Friulano, Paolo Caccese	368
Collio Tocai Friulano, Carlo di Pradis	369
Collio Tocai Friulano, Casa Zuliani	387
Collio Tocai Friulano, La Castellada	390
Collio Tocai Friulano, Castello di Spessa	360
Collio Tocai Friulano, Colle Duga	369
Collio Tocai Friulano, Colmello di Grotta	388
Collio Tocai Friulano, Mauro Drius	370
Collio Tocai Friulano, Branko - Igor Erzetic	371
Collio Tocai Friulano, Marco Felluga	393
Collio Tocai Friulano, Fiegl	391
Collio Tocai Friulano, Gradis'ciutta	416
Collio Tocai Friulano, Gradimiro Gradnik Eredi	428
Collio Tocai Friulano, Marcello e Marino Humar	417
Collio Tocai Friulano, Edi Keber	372
Collio Tocai Friulano, Renato Keber	428
Collio Tocai Friulano, Thomas Kitzmüller	428
Collio Tocai Friulano, La Boatina	372
Collio Tocai Friulano, Muzic	430
Collio Tocai Friulano, Roberto Picech - Le Vigne del Ribél	374
Collio Tocai Friulano, Aldo Polencic	374
Collio Tocai Friulano, Isidoro Polencic	375
Collio Tocai Friulano, Alessandro Princic	375
Collio Tocai Friulano, Dario Raccaro	376
Collio Tocai Friulano, Roncada	376
Collio Tocai Friulano, Ronco dei Tassi	377
Collio Tocai Friulano, Roncùs	361
Collio Tocai Friulano, Russiz Superiore	361
Collio Tocai Friulano, Schiopetto	362
Collio Tocai Friulano, Oscar Sturm	378
Collio Tocai Friulano, Subida di Monte	378
Collio Tocai Friulano, Franco Toros	379
Collio Tocai Friulano, Venica & Venica	384
Collio Tocai Friulano, Vigna del Lauro	379
Collio Tocai Friulano, Villa Russiz	363
Collio Tocai Friulano, Tenuta Villanova	389
Collio Tocai Friulano Collezione Privata, Eugenio Collavini	380
Collio Tocai Friulano Croce Alta, Gestioni Agricole Vidussi	362
Collio Tocai Friulano Crôs Altis, Alessandro Princic	375
Collio Tocai Friulano Rinascimento, Cant. Prod. di Cormons	370
Collio Tocai Friulano Ronco della Chiesa, Borgo del Tiglio	367
Collio Tocai Friulano Ronco delle Cime, Venica & Venica	384
Collio Tocai Friulano Sel., Subida di Monte	378
Collio Tocai Friulano Vôs da Vigne, Tenuta di Angoris	428
Collio Traminer Aromatico, Paolo Caccese	368
Collio Traminer Aromatico, Giulio Manzocco	373
Colonnara Spumante Brut M. Cl. Millesimato, Colonnara Viticoltori in Cupramontana	632
Colorino, Tenuta Il Corno	572
Coltassala, Castello di Volpaia	569
Coltifredi, Castelli del Grevepesa	572
Come La Pantera e I Lupi nella Sera, Luretta	444
Cometa, Planeta	774
Composition Reif, Josephus Mayr - Erbhof Unterganzner	262
Comprino Mirosa, Montelio	192
Comprino Mirosa Ris., Montelio	192
Con Vento, Castello del Terriccio	482
Concento, L'Olivella	692
Confini, Lis Neris	421
Congius, Vignole	613
Coniale, Castellare di Castellina	478
Conte della Vipera, Castello della Sala	662
Conte Federico, Conti Bossi Fedrigotti	242
Conte Hugues Bernard, Tenute Rapitalà	768
Conte Leopoldo, Santa Cassella	647
Conte Principe, Conti Bossi Fedrigotti	242
Contea di Sclafani Cabernet Sauvignon, Tasca d'Almerita	778
Contea di Sclafani Nozze d'Oro, Tasca d'Almerita	778
Contea di Sclafani Rosso del Conte, Tasca d'Almerita	778
Contesa Bianco, Contesa di Rocco Pasetti	704
Contessa Emburga Capsula Nera, Cantine Lento	761
Contessa Emburga Capsula Oro, Cantine Lento	761
Contessa Entellina Chardonnay La Fuga, Tenuta di Donnafugata	772
Contessa Entellina Chiarandà del Merlo, Tenuta di Donnafugata	772
Contessa Entellina Milleunanotte, Tenuta di Donnafugata	772
Contessa Entellina Tancredi, Tenuta di Donnafugata	772
Contessa Entellina Vigna di Gabri, Tenuta di Donnafugata	772
Contrade - Dedalo, COS	782
Contrade - Labirinto, COS	782
Controguerra Bianco Ciafré, Dino Illuminati	699
Controguerra Bianco Costalupo, Dino Illuminati	699
Controguerra Bianco Daniele, Dino Illuminati	699
Controguerra Leneo d'Oro, Camillo Montori	699
Controguerra Leneo Moro, Camillo Montori	699
Controguerra Passerina Do, Lepore	698
Controguerra Passerina Passera delle Vigne, Lepore	698
Controguerra Passerina Sol, Lepore	698
Controguerra Passito Nicò, Dino Illuminati	699
Controguerra Rosso Lumen, Dino Illuminati	699
Controguerra Rosso Ris. Villa Torri, Barone Cornacchia	710
Copertino, Casa Vinicola Apollonio	750
Copertino Divoto, Casa Vinicola Apollonio	750
Copertino Divoto Ris., Casa Vinicola Apollonio	750
Copertino Rosso Eloquenzia, Masseria Monaci	742
Coppo Brut Ris., Coppo	55
Corbaia, Castello di Bossi	484
Corbezzolo, Podere La Cappella	591
Cori Bianco, Marco Carpineti	691
Cori Rosso, Marco Carpineti	691
Corindone Rosso, Alessandro Secchi	250
Corithus, Sant'Isidoro	694
Corleto, Villa di Corlo	460
Corniole Merlot, Cavalleri	196
Corno Bianco, Tenuta Il Corno	572
Corno Rosso, Tenuta Il Corno	572
Corpore, Villa Sandi	346
Cortaccio, Villa Cafaggio	560
Corte Agnella Corvina Veronese, Giuseppe Campagnola	299
Corte Cariano Rosso, Luigi Brunelli	322
Corte d'Oro V. T., Fattoria del Cerro	544
Corte Durlo Passito, Ca' Rugate	307
Corte Valesio Sauvignon, Agricole Vallone	754
Cortegiano Sovestro, Baroncini	576
Cortese dell'Alto M.to Le Due Cioche, Garetto	23
Cortese dell'Alto M.to Marsenca, Luigi Tacchino	60
Cortigiano, Fattoria Lavacchio	615
Cortinie Rosso, Peter Zemmer - Kupelwieser	274
Cortona Bramasole, Fattoria La Braccesca	545
Cortona Chardonnay, Vegni - Capezzine	600
Cortona Desiderio, Avignonesi	542

Cortona Fontarca, Tenimenti Luigi D'Alessandro	490
Cortona Il Bosco, Tenimenti Luigi D'Alessandro	490
Cortona Sangiovese, Vegni - Capezzine	600
Cortona Syrah, Tenimenti Luigi D'Alessandro	490
Cortona Vin Santo, Tenimenti Luigi D'Alessandro	490
Corum, Fattoria Castellina	595
Corvara Rosso, Armani	293
Corvina Falasco, Cant. Soc. della Valpantena	341
Corvo Bianco, Duca di Salaparuta - Vini Corvo	769
Corvo Colomba Platino, Duca di Salaparuta - Vini Corvo	769
Corvo Glicine, Duca di Salaparuta - Vini Corvo	769
Corvo Rosso, Duca di Salaparuta - Vini Corvo	769
Costa d'Amalfi Furore Bianco, Cantine Gran Furor Divina Costiera	715
Costa d'Amalfi Furore Bianco Fiord'Uva, Cantine Gran Furor Divina Costiera	715
Costa d'Amalfi Furore Rosso, Cantine Gran Furor Divina Costiera	715
Costa d'Amalfi Furore Rosso Ris., Cantine Gran Furor Divina Costiera	715
Costa d'Amalfi Ravello Bianco Grotta Piana, Ettore Sammarco	728
Costa d'Amalfi Ravello Bianco Selva delle Monache, Ettore Sammarco	728
Costa del Sole, La Morandina	68
Costa Nera, La Morandina	68
Costa Vecchia, Colle San Lorenzo	684
Costacalda Passito Domini Veneti, Cant. Soc. Valpolicella	312
Coste all'Ombra, Maurigi	779
Coste del Roccolo, Anteo	207
Coste della Sesia Faticato, Anzivino	82
Coste della Sesia Nebbiolo Juvenia, Antoniolo	81
Coste della Sesia Rosso Mesolone, Barni	46
Coste della Sesia Rosso Orbello, Sella	100
Coste della Sesia Rosso Torrearsa, Barni	46
Coste della Sesia Spanna, Nervi	82
Coteau Barrage, Lo Triolet	18
Coteau La Tour, Les Crêtes	17
Crearo della Conca d'Oro, Tommasi Viticoltori	325
Critone, Librandi	759
Croatina Laetitia, Ca' Tessitori	217
Croce del Moro, Cant. Coop. Sandonaci	756
Crognolo, Tenuta Sette Ponti	592
Crovello, Poggio Bertaio	661
Cruter, Ca' del Vispo	576
Cubia, Cusumano	779
Cummerse Rosso, Cant. Soc.Coop. del Locorotondo	747
Cupinero, Col di Bacche	604
Curto Fontanelle Rosso, Francesca e Giambattista Curto	784
Curto Rosso, Francesca e Giambattista Curto	784
Cuvée Brut Ris., Cesarini Sforza	246
Cuvée Calldiv, Von Braunbach	280
Cuvée Extra Brut, Pojer & Sandri	232
Cuvée Imperiale Brut, Guido Berlucchi & C.	194
Cuvée Imperiale Brut Extrême, Guido Berlucchi & C.	194
Cuvée Imperiale Max Rosé, Guido Berlucchi & C.	194
Cuvée Jus Osculi, Loacker Schwarzhof	261
Cuvée Sant'Anna, Giacomo Marengo	539
Cuvée Storica Spumante M. Cl. Gran Ris., Orsolani	134
Cyane, Pupillo	788
Cygnus, Tasca d'Almerita	778
D'Alceo, Castello dei Rampolla	556
D'Istinto Bianco, Calatrasi - Accademia del Sole	780
D'Istinto Catarratto-Chardonnay, Calatrasi - Accademia del Sole	780
D'Istinto Chardonnay, Calatrasi - Accademia del Sole	780
D'Istinto Ljetas Bianco, Calatrasi - Accademia del Sole	780
D'Istinto Nero d'Avola, Calatrasi - Accademia del Sole	780
D'Istinto Sangiovese-Merlot, Calatrasi - Accademia del Sole	780
D'Istinto Syrah, Calatrasi - Accademia del Sole	780
d'Ovidio, San Luciano	539
Dagala Bianco, Tamburello	786
Dagala Rosso, Tamburello	786
Daino Bianco, Fattoria Castellina	595
Dattilo, Roberto Ceraudo	760
De Ferrari, Boscarelli	543
De Luca Rosso, San Lorenzo	663
Declivium, Anselmet	19
Decugnano dei Barbi Brut M. Cl., Decugnano dei Barbi	669
Dedicato, Aziende Vinicole Miceli	780
Delia Nivolelli Cabernet Sauvignon, Carlo Pellegrino	773
Deliella, Feudo Principi di Butera	767
Delius, Cant. del Taburno	714
Deltetto Extra Brut Ris., Deltetto	51
Deressi, Majolini	205
Desmentìa V. T., Ada Nada	147
Dettori Bianco, Tenute Dettori	798
Dettori Rosso, Tenute Dettori	798
Dezio Vign. Beccaccia, Fattoria Dezi	651
Di Gale, Villa Frattina	404
Di Giorgio Bianco, Il Torchio	168
Di Giorgio Rosso, Il Torchio	168
Di 'More, Fattorie Azzolino	767
Diana, Baglio Hopps	771
Diano d'Alba Costa Fiore, Claudio Alario	74
Diano d'Alba Montagrillo, Claudio Alario	74
Diano d'Alba Rizieri, Ricchino - Tiziana Menegaldo	158
Diano d'Alba Sörì Bricco Maiolica, Bricco Maiolica	75
Diano d'Alba Sörì Bruni, Casavecchia	158
Diano d'Alba Sörì dei Berfi, F.lli Abrigo	158
Diano d'Alba Sörì dei Berfi V. Pietrìn, F.lli Abrigo	158
Diano d'Alba V. La Lepre, Fontanafredda	140
Diano d'Alba V. Vecchia, Cascina Flino	158
Dicatum, Fattoria Montellori	494
Dindarello, Maculan	290
Divo, Borgo Canale	743
Do Ut Des, Carpineta Fontalpino	484
Dogajolo, Carpineto	503
Doganera Merlot, D'Alfonso del Sordo	752
Doi Raps, Russolo	422
Dolce Montepascolo, Cardinali	437
Dolce Valle Moscato Passito, Tenute Soletta	793
Dolcetto d'Acqui Argusto, Vigne Regali	144
Dolcetto d'Acqui Bric Maioli, Villa Sparina	86
Dolcetto d'Acqui La Cresta, Traversa - Cascina Bertolotto	143
Dolcetto d'Acqui La Muïètte, Traversa - Cascina Bertolotto	143
Dolcetto d'Acqui La Selva di Moirano, Antica Casa Vinicola Scarpa	126
Dolcetto d'Acqui Marchesa, Marenco	143
Dolcetto d'Alba, Luigi Baudana	139
Dolcetto d'Alba, F.lli Bera	125
Dolcetto d'Alba, Enzo Boglietti	90
Dolcetto d'Alba, Giacomo Borgogno & Figli	38
Dolcetto d'Alba, Cant. del Pino	31
Dolcetto d'Alba, Cascina Bongiovanni	64
Dolcetto d'Alba, Giovanni Corino	92
Dolcetto d'Alba, Damilano	39
Dolcetto d'Alba, Destefanis	117
Dolcetto d'Alba, Alessandro e Gian Natale Fantino	109
Dolcetto d'Alba, Elio Grasso	110
Dolcetto d'Alba, Silvio Grasso	92
Dolcetto d'Alba, Giacomo Grimaldi	39
Dolcetto d'Alba, Gianluigi Lano	26
Dolcetto d'Alba, Ugo Lequio	123
Dolcetto d'Alba, Giovanni Manzone	110
Dolcetto d'Alba, Mario Marengo	93
Dolcetto d'Alba, Mauro Molino	93
Dolcetto d'Alba, Monfalletto - Cordero di Montezemolo	94
Dolcetto d'Alba, Cascina Morassino	32
Dolcetto d'Alba, Andrea Oberto	94
Dolcetto d'Alba, Vignaioli Elvio Pertinace	148
Dolcetto d'Alba, Luigi Pira	141
Dolcetto d'Alba, F.lli Revello	96
Dolcetto d'Alba, Rocche Costamagna	97
Dolcetto d'Alba, Ruggeri Corsini	113
Dolcetto d'Alba, Luciano Sandrone	42
Dolcetto d'Alba, Giorgio Scarzello e Figli	42
Dolcetto d'Alba, Terre del Barolo	66
Dolcetto d'Alba, G. D. Vajra	44
Dolcetto d'Alba, Rino Varaldo	37
Dolcetto d'Alba, Mauro Veglio	97
Dolcetto d'Alba, Eraldo Viberti	98
Dolcetto d'Alba, Vigna Rionda - Massolino	142
Dolcetto d'Alba Arsigà, Batasiolo	90
Dolcetto d'Alba Barturot, Ca' Viola	76
Dolcetto d'Alba Boschetti, Marchesi di Barolo	40
Dolcetto d'Alba Boschi di Berri, Poderi Marcarini	95
Dolcetto d'Alba Bric del Salto, Sottimano	124
Dolcetto d'Alba Bric Trifùla, Cascina Luisin	31
Dolcetto d'Alba Bricco Bastia, Conterno Fantino	108
Dolcetto d'Alba Bricco Caramelli, F.lli Mossio	133
Dolcetto d'Alba Bricco dell'Oriolo, Azelia	63
Dolcetto d'Alba Bricco Peso, Sergio Degiorgis	103
Dolcetto d'Alba Bussia, Cascina Ballarin	91
Dolcetto d'Alba Campot, Castello di Verduno	150
Dolcetto d'Alba Ciabot del Re, Brovia	64
Dolcetto d'Alba Ciabot Vigna, Michele Taliano	116
Dolcetto d'Alba Colombè, Renato Ratti	96
Dolcetto d'Alba Coste & Fossati, G. D. Vajra	44
Dolcetto d'Alba Cuchet, Carlo Giacosa	34
Dolcetto d'Alba Dabbene, Gianfranco Bovio	91
Dolcetto d'Alba Galletto, Osvaldo Viberti	98
Dolcetto d'Alba Ginestra, Paolo Conterno	108
Dolcetto d'Alba Madonna di Como, Boroli	25
Dolcetto d'Alba Madonna di Como, Tenuta Langasco	154
Dolcetto d'Alba Madonna di Como, Marchesi di Barolo	40
Dolcetto d'Alba Meriame, Gabutti - Franco Boasso	140
Dolcetto d'Alba Monte Aribaldo, Tenuta Cisa Asinari dei Marchesi di Gresy	32
Dolcetto d'Alba Moriolo, Gastaldi	121
Dolcetto d'Alba Mosesco, Prunotto	27
Dolcetto d'Alba Munfrina, Pelissero	148
Dolcetto d'Alba Nicolini, Montaribaldi	35
Dolcetto d'Alba Piani Noci, Armando Parusso	111
Dolcetto d'Alba Piano delli Perdoni, F.lli Mossio	133
Dolcetto d'Alba Rocchettevino, Gianni Voerzio	99
Dolcetto d'Alba Rossana, Ceretto	25
Dolcetto d'Alba S. Anna, Ferdinando Principiano	112
Dolcetto d'Alba S. Rocco, Ascheri	46
Dolcetto d'Alba S. Rosalia, Mauro Sebaste	28
Dolcetto d'Alba S. Stefano di Perno, Giuseppe Mascarello e Figlio	105
Dolcetto d'Alba San Cristoforo, Ottavio Lequio - Prinsi	123
Dolcetto d'Alba Sorì Paitin, Paitin	124
Dolcetto d'Alba Sup., Flavio Roddolo	113
Dolcetto d'Alba Sup. Moriolo, Gastaldi	121
Dolcetto d'Alba V. del Mandorlo, Elvio Cogno	127
Dolcetto d'Alba V. del Pozzo, Tenuta Carretta	129
Dolcetto d'Alba V. dell'Erto, Orlando Abrigo	146
Dolcetto d'Alba V. Fornaci, Pira	78
Dolcetto d'Alba V. La Volta, Tenuta La Volta - Cabutto	43
Dolcetto d'Alba V. Nirane, Ascheri	46
Dolcetto d'Alba V. Vantrino Albarella, Andrea Oberto	94
Dolcetto d'Alba Vign. della Chiesa, F.lli Seghesio	114
Dolcetto d'Alba Vign. Lorenzino, Ettore Germano	141
Dolcetto d'Alba Vigna Monia Bassa, Destefanis	117
Dolcetto d'Alba Vignalunga, Albino Rocca	36
Dolcetto d'Alba Vilot, Ca' Viola	76
Dolcetto d'Asti Caranzana, Cascina Garitina	59
Dolcetto d'Asti V. Impagnato, Ermanno e Alessandra Brema	88
Dolcetto delle Langhe Monregalesi Il Colombo, Il Colombo - Barone Riccati	105
Dolcetto delle Langhe Monregalesi Sup. Monteregale, Il Colombo - Barone Riccati	105
Dolcetto di Diano d'Alba, Bricco Maiolica	75

Dolcetto di Diano d'Alba, Terre del Barolo	66
Dolcetto di Dogliani, Bricco del Cucù	44
Dolcetto di Dogliani, Einaudi	77
Dolcetto di Dogliani, Ribote	159
Dolcetto di Dogliani, San Romano	79
Dolcetto di Dogliani Autin Lungh, Eraldo Revelli	159
Dolcetto di Dogliani Briccolero, Quinto Chionetti & Figlio	76
Dolcetto di Dogliani Cursalet, Giovanni Battista Gillardi	80
Dolcetto di Dogliani I Filari, Einaudi	77
Dolcetto di Dogliani Maioli, Anna Maria Abbona	80
Dolcetto di Dogliani Otto Filari, Eraldo Revelli	159
Dolcetto di Dogliani Papà Celso, Marziano ed Enrico Abbona	75
Dolcetto di Dogliani Pianezzo, Francesco Boschis	159
Dolcetto di Dogliani Puncin, Osvaldo Barberis	158
Dolcetto di Dogliani Ribote, Ribote	159
Dolcetto di Dogliani S. Fereolo, San Fereolo	78
Dolcetto di Dogliani S. Luigi, Quinto Chionetti & Figlio	76
Dolcetto di Dogliani S. Luigi, Pecchenino	77
Dolcetto di Dogliani S. Matteo, Eraldo Revelli	159
Dolcetto di Dogliani San Lorenzo, Osvaldo Barberis	158
Dolcetto di Dogliani Sirì d'Jermu, Pecchenino	77
Dolcetto di Dogliani Sorì dij But, Anna Maria Abbona	80
Dolcetto di Dogliani Sup., Anna Maria Abbona	80
Dolcetto di Dogliani Sup., Marziano ed Enrico Abbona	75
Dolcetto di Dogliani Sup. 1593, San Fereolo	78
Dolcetto di Dogliani Sup. Bricco Botti, Pecchenino	77
Dolcetto di Dogliani Sup. Bricco S. Bernardo, Bricco del Cucù	44
Dolcetto di Dogliani Sup. Dolianum, San Romano	79
Dolcetto di Dogliani Sup. Maioli, Anna Maria Abbona	80
Dolcetto di Dogliani Sup. S. Fereolo, San Fereolo	78
Dolcetto di Dogliani Sup. V. del Ciliegio, Francesco Boschis	159
Dolcetto di Dogliani V. Bricco dei Botti, Pira	78
Dolcetto di Dogliani V. del Pilone, San Romano	79
Dolcetto di Dogliani V. Landes, Pira	78
Dolcetto di Dogliani V. Tecc, Einaudi	77
Dolcetto di Dogliani Valdibà, San Fereolo	78
Dolcetto di Dogliani Vign. Maestra, Giovanni Battista Gillardi	80
Dolcetto di Dogliani Vign. Muntâ, Marziano ed Enrico Abbona	75
Dolcetto di Ovada, Domenico Ghio e Figli	45
Dolcetto di Ovada Barricò, La Caplana	155
Dolcetto di Ovada Bricco del Bagatto, Cascina La Maddalena	132
Dolcetto di Ovada Du Riva, Luigi Tacchino	60
Dolcetto di Ovada Prabarasco, Luigi Tacchino	60
Dolcetto di Ovada Sup. Drac Rosso, Domenico Ghio e Figli	45
Dolcetto di Ovada Sup. Duién, Cascina Bondi	162
Dolcetto di Ovada Sup. Il Gamondino, La Guardia	118
Dolcetto di Ovada Sup. L'Arciprete, Domenico Ghio e Figli	45
Dolcetto di Ovada Sup. S. Evasio, Gaggino	163
Dolcetto di Ovada Sup. Vign. Bricco Riccardo, La Guardia	118
Dolcetto di Ovada Sup. Villa Delfini, La Guardia	118
Dolcetto Diano d'Alba, Sinaglio	28
Dolmen, Cant. Soc. Gallura	801
Dominus, Cant. Prod. Valle Isarco	272
Don Antonio, Morgante	770
Don Carmelo Bianco, Tenute Albano Carrisi	740
Don Carmelo Rosso, Tenute Albano Carrisi	740
Don Generoso, Di Meo	721
Don Lodovico, Carlozadra	199
Don Marcello, Torre Quarto	741
Don Pietro Bianco, Spadafora	777
Don Pietro Rosso, Spadafora	777
Don Totò, Barone La Lumia	784
Donello Sangiovese, Il Conte	640
Donna Angela, Santa Cassella	647
Donna Eleonora, Santa Cassella	647
Donna Marzia Rosato, Conti Zecca	746
Donna Marzia Rosso, Conti Zecca	746
Donna Rita, Marchesi Platamone	786
Donnaluce, Poggio Le Volpi	687
Donnaluna Aglianico, Viticoltori De Conciliis	720
Donnaluna Fiano, Viticoltori De Conciliis	720
Dopoteatro, Podere Salicutti	534
Dorado, Graf Pfeil Weingut Kränzel	272
Dòron, Eugenio Rosi	249
DossOriane, San Cristoforo	220
Dry Muscat Terre di Orazio, Cant. di Venosa	735
Duca d'Aragona, Francesco Candido	751
Duca di Dolle Prosecco Passito, Desiderio Bisol & Figli	335
Duca Enrico, Duca di Salaparuta - Vini Corvo	769
Due Cuori Passito, Le Vigne di San Pietro	333
Due Uve, Bertani	311
Dulcamara, I Giusti e Zanza	492
Dulcis Cicogna, Domenico Cavazza & F.lli	306
Dule, Giuseppe Gabbas	796
È Serre, Salvatore Murana	778
Ea, Podere Sopra la Ripa	587
Ebrius, Valle del Sole	604
Eclissi di Sole, San Valentino	452
Edelmio, Benanti	782
Eden Passito, Carra	445
Edizione 5 Autoctoni, Farnese	703
Edys, Maso Bastie	249
Efelidi, Migliarese	694
Efeso, Librandi	759
El Masut, Podere del Ger	405
Elba Aleatico, Cecilia	595
Elba Ansonica, Cecilia	595
Elba Rosso, Cecilia	595
Elfo Salento Rosso, Casa Vinicola Apollonio	750
Eloise Bianco, Bianchi	142
Empireo, Pucciarella	677
Enantio, Cant. Soc. di Avio	228
Eneo, Montepeloso	590
Enif, Il Palagione	579
Entemari, F.lli Pala	800
Erbaluce di Caluso, Antoniolo	81
Erbaluce di Caluso, Cieck	24
Erbaluce di Caluso, Podere Macellio - Renato Bianco	155
Erbaluce di Caluso 13 Mesi, Favaro	163
Erbaluce di Caluso Ca' Neuva, Giovanni Silva	24
Erbaluce di Caluso Calliope, Cieck	24
Erbaluce di Caluso Cariola Et. Nera, Ferrando	89
Erbaluce di Caluso Cariola Et. Verde, Ferrando	89
Erbaluce di Caluso La Rustìa, Orsolani	134
Erbaluce di Caluso San MIchele, La Cella di San Michele	164
Erbaluce di Caluso Spumante Brut S. Giorgio, Cieck	24
Erbaluce di Caluso Tre Ciochè, Giovanni Silva	24
Erbaluce di Caluso V. Misobolo, Cieck	24
Eremo, San Giorgio a Lapi	620
Eretico Pigato, Maria Donata Bianchi	170
Eretico Vermentino, Maria Donata Bianchi	170
Erta e China, Fattoria di Basciano	570
Esino Bianco Ferrante, Belisario Cant. Soc. di Matelica e Cerreto d'Esi	636
Esino Bianco Tabano, Montecappone	635
Esino Rosso Colferraio, Belisario Cant. Soc. di Matelica e Cerreto d'Esi	636
Esino Rosso Laurano, Laurentina	639
Esino Rosso Rosolaccio, Amato Ceci	656
Esino Rosso Tabano, Montecappone	635
Esio, Monteschiavo	636
Esse, Fattoria La Torre	610
Essenzia Vendemmia Tardiva, Pojer & Sandri	232
Est Est Est di Montefiascone, Falesco	688
Est Est Est di Montefiascone, Mazziotti	691
Est Est Est di Montefiascone, Trappolini	682
Est Est Est di Montefiascone Poggio dei Gelsi, Falesco	688
Etna Bianco, Barone di Villagrande	776
Etna Bianco Bianco di Caselle, Benanti	782
Etna Bianco Sup., Barone di Villagrande	776
Etna Bianco Sup. Fiore di Villagrande, Barone di Villagrande	776
Etna Bianco Sup. Pietramarina, Benanti	782
Etna Rosato - Tenuta Scilio, Tenuta Scilio	785
Etna Rosso, Barone Scammacca del Murgo	788
Etna Rosso, Barone di Villagrande	776
Etna Rosso Orpheus, Tenuta Scilio	785
Etna Rosso Rosso di Verzella, Benanti	782
Etna Rosso Rovittello, Benanti	782
Etna Rosso Serra della Contessa, Benanti	782
Etna Rosso - Tenuta Scilio, Tenuta Scilio	785
Etna Rosso Ulysse, Carlo Pellegrino	773
Etrusco, Cennatoio Intervineas	556
Euforius, Josef Niedermayr	256
Extra Brut Cl. Il Calepino, Il Calepino	189
Extra Cuvée Brut Rosso, Francesco Bellei	434
Fabrizio Bianchi Chardonnay, Castello di Monsanto	469
Fabrizio Bianchi Sangiovese, Castello di Monsanto	469
Falanghina Beneventano, Villa Raiano	722
Falanghina del Beneventano, Monte Pugliano	727
Falanghina del Beneventano, Terredora	718
Falanghina di Roccamonfina V.T., Telaro	716
Falanghina Rocca dei Leoni, Villa Matilde	714
Falanghina Vigna del Prete, Fattoria Prattico	728
Falconaro, Cantine di Dolianova	793
Falconera Rosso, Conte Loredan Gasparini Venegazzù	344
Falerio dei Colli Ascolani, Castello Fageto	645
Falerio dei Colli Ascolani, Cantine di Castignano	631
Falerio dei Colli Ascolani, Ciù Ciù	643
Falerio dei Colli Ascolani, Tenuta De Angelis	629
Falerio dei Colli Ascolani, Rio Maggio	640
Falerio dei Colli Ascolani, Saladini Pilastri	651
Falerio dei Colli Ascolani Aurato, Il Conte	640
Falerio dei Colli Ascolani Brezzolino, La Cantina dei Colli Ripani	648
Falerio dei Colli Ascolani Grotte sul Mare, Vinicola del Tesino	634
Falerio dei Colli Ascolani Leo Guelfus, San Giovanni	644
Falerio dei Colli Ascolani Lucrezia, Le Caniette	648
Falerio dei Colli Ascolani Marta V. T., San Giovanni	644
Falerio dei Colli Ascolani Naumachos, Vinicola del Tesino	634
Falerio dei Colli Ascolani Ophites, San Giovanni	644
Falerio dei Colli Ascolani Telusiano, Rio Maggio	640
Falerio dei Colli Ascolani Terre Cortesi, Terre Cortesi Moncaro	639
Falerio dei Colli Ascolani V. Palazzi, Saladini Pilastri	651
Falerio dei Colli Ascolani V. Solaria, Ercole Velenosi	626
Falerno del Massico Bianco, Villa Matilde	714
Falerno del Massico Bianco Vigna Caracci, Villa Matilde	714
Falerno del Massico Rosso, Villa Matilde	714
Falerno del Massico Rosso Etichetta Bronzo, Masseria Felicia	728
Falerno del Massico Rosso Vigna Camarato, Villa Matilde	714
Falesia, Paolo d'Amico	682
Fara Caramino, Dessilani	79
Fara Lochera, Dessilani	79
Farnito Cabernet Sauvignon, Carpineto	503
Farnito Chardonnay, Carpineto	503
Faro - Di Stefano e Grasso, Grasso	786
Faro Palari, Palari	775
Faroaldo, Rocca di Fabbri	666
Fastaia, Ceuso	766
Fatagione, Cottanera	769
Father's Eyes, Di Lenardo	389
Federico II, Cantine Lento	761
Federico Primo, Gualdo del Re	589
Fedus Sangiovese, San Savino - Poderi Capecci	649
Felciaino, Giovanni Chiappini	595
Feldmarschall von Fenner, Tiefenbrunner	273
Feldmarschall von Fenner zu Fennberg, Tiefenbrunner	273
Ferraiolo, Agricoltori del Chianti Geografico	495
Ferrata, Maculan	290
Ferro e Seta, Villa Simone	688
Feudi Bordonaro Bianco, Firriato	776
Feudi Bordonaro Rosso, Firriato	776
Feudo dei Fiori Mandrarossa, Settesoli	775
Fiagre, Antonio Caggiano	724

Fianesco, Fattoria di Fiano	599	Franciacorta Collezione Brut, Cavalleri	196
Fiano di Avellino, Cant. del Barone	726	Franciacorta Collezione Esclusiva Brut, Cavalleri	196
Fiano di Avellino, Cantine Caputo	712	Franciacorta Cuvée Annamaria Clementi, Ca' del Bosco	196
Fiano di Avellino, Colli di Lapio - Clelia Romano	717	Franciacorta Cuvée Brut, Bellavista	195
Fiano di Avellino, Colli Irpini	718	Franciacorta Cuvette Extra Dry, Villa	203
Fiano di Avellino, D'Antiche Terre - Vega	727	Franciacorta Dosage Zéro, Ca' del Bosco	196
Fiano di Avellino, De Falco	728	Franciacorta Dosage Zero, Lorenzo Faccoli & Figli	220
Fiano di Avellino, Feudi di San Gregorio	723	Franciacorta Dosaggio Zero, Contadi Castaldi	182
Fiano di Avellino, La Casa dell'Orco	719	Franciacorta Dosaggio Zero Villa Crespia,	
Fiano di Avellino, Mastroberardino	712	Villa Crespia - F.lli Muratori	217
Fiano di Avellino, Pietracupa	717	Franciacorta Electo Brut, Majolini	205
Fiano di Avellino, Urciuolo	727	Franciacorta Extra Brut, Bersi Serlini	207
Fiano di Avellino, Villa Raiano	722	Franciacorta Extra Brut, Bredasole	205
Fiano di Avellino Bechar, Antonio Caggiano	724	Franciacorta Extra Brut, CastelFaglia	190
Fiano di Avellino Béchar, Antonio Caggiano	724	Franciacorta Extra Brut, Battista Cola	216
Fiano di Avellino Colle dei Cerri, Di Meo	721	Franciacorta Extra Brut, Lorenzo Faccoli & Figli	220
Fiano di Avellino More Maiorum, Mastroberardino	712	Franciacorta Extra Brut, Ferghettina	197
Fiano di Avellino Radici, Mastroberardino	712	Franciacorta Extra Brut, Il Mosnel	206
Fiano di Avellino Ripa Alta, Villa Raiano	722	Franciacorta Extra Brut, La Montina	202
Fiano di Avellino Sirios, Colli Irpini	718	Franciacorta Extra Brut, Lantieri de Paratico	185
Fiano di Avellino Terre di Dora, Terredora	718	Franciacorta Extra Brut, Lo Sparviere	203
Fiano di Roccamonfina le Cinque Pietre, Telaro	716	Franciacorta Extra Brut, Monte Rossa	190
Fiano Mandrarossa, Settesoli	775	Franciacorta Extra Brut, Monzio Compagnoni	220
Fidenzio, Podere San Luigi	561	Franciacorta Extra Brut, Principe Banfi Podere Pio IX	220
Filieri Rosso, Cant. Soc. Dorgali	794	Franciacorta Extra Brut, Ricci Curbastro	186
Filtrato Dolce di Malvasia, Gaetano Lusenti	455	Franciacorta Extra Brut, Villa	203
Finisterre, Poggio Argentiera	509	Franciacorta Extra Brut Bagnadore V, Barone Pizzini	193
FiorDesAri Rosso, Valditerra	162	Franciacorta Extra Brut Cabochon, Monte Rossa	190
Fiore, Castello di Meleto	498	Franciacorta Extra Brut Comarì del Salem, Uberti	198
Fiore Chardonnay, San Valentino	452	Franciacorta Extra Brut Francesco I, Uberti	198
Five Roses, Leone de Castris	751	Franciacorta Gran Cuvée Brut, Bellavista	195
Five Roses Anniversario, Leone de Castris	751	Franciacorta Gran Cuvée Brut Rosé, Bellavista	195
Flaccianello della Pieve, Tenuta Fontodi	557	Franciacorta Gran Cuvée Pas Operé, Bellavista	195
Flocco, Poggio a Poppiano	552	Franciacorta Gran Cuvée Satèn, Bellavista	195
Fobiano, La Carraia	669	Franciacorta Magno Brut, Contadi Castaldi	182
Foja Tonda Rosso, Armani	293	Franciacorta Monogram Brut, CastelFaglia	190
Fojaneghe Bianco, Conti Bossi Fedrigotti	242	Franciacorta Non Dosato, Mirabella	208
Fojaneghe Rosso, Conti Bossi Fedrigotti	242	Franciacorta Pas Dosè, F.lli Berlucchi	193
Fontalloro, Fattoria di Felsina	485	Franciacorta Pas Dosé, Cavalleri	196
Fontanella Rosso, Goretti	673	Franciacorta Pas Dosé, Mirabella	208
Fontenova, Tenuta Roccaccia	562	Franciacorta Pas Dosé Aligi Sassu, Majolini	205
Fontibianco, Di Fonti	489	Franciacorta Rosé, Barone Pizzini	193
Fontirosso, Di Fonti	489	Franciacorta Rosé, F.lli Berlucchi	193
For Duke, Gino Fuso Carmignani	540	Franciacorta Rosé, Ca' del Bosco	196
Forca di Palma, Sant'Isidoro	694	Franciacorta Rosé, Contadi Castaldi	182
Formulae, Barone Ricasoli	496	Franciacorta Rosé Altera Brut, Majolini	205
Forti Terre di Sicilia Cabernet Sauvignon, Cant. Soc. di Trapani	781	Franciacorta Rosé Brut, Cornaleto	216
Forti Terre di Sicilia Chardonnay, Cant. Soc. di Trapani	781	Franciacorta Rosé Brut Francesco I, Uberti	198
Forti Terre di Sicilia Il Bianco, Cant. Soc. di Trapani	781	Franciacorta Rosé Démi Sec, Villa	203
Forti Terre di Sicilia Il Rosso, Cant. Soc. di Trapani	781	Franciacorta Satèn, Barone Pizzini	193
Forti Terre di Sicilia Nero d'Avola, Cant. Soc. di Trapani	781	Franciacorta Satèn, F.lli Berlucchi	193
Forti Terre di Sicilia Rocche Rosse, Cant. Soc. di Trapani	781	Franciacorta Satèn, Bersi Serlini	207
Forzaté Raboso, La Montecchia	328	Franciacorta Satèn, Bonomi - Tenuta Castellino	192
Fossa Bandita, Letrari	242	Franciacorta Satèn, CastelFaglia	190
Fosso le Forche, Tenuta Pandolfa	451	Franciacorta Satèn, Cavalleri	196
Frabusco, Tenuta Corini	667	Franciacorta Satèn, Contadi Castaldi	182
Fraja, Tenuta Villanova	389	Franciacorta Satèn, Ferghettina	197
Francesco I, Ortaglia	593	Franciacorta Satèn, Enrico Gatti	197
Franciacorta Ante Omnia Satèn, Majolini	205	Franciacorta Satèn, Il Mosnel	206
Franciacorta Bagnadore I, Barone Pizzini	193	Franciacorta Satèn, La Montina	202
Franciacorta Brut, Barone Pizzini	193	Franciacorta Satèn, Lantieri de Paratico	185
Franciacorta Brut, F.lli Berlucchi	193	Franciacorta Satèn, Le Cantorie	219
Franciacorta Brut, Bersi Serlini	207	Franciacorta Satèn, Le Marchesine	223
Franciacorta Brut, Bonomi - Tenuta Castellino	192	Franciacorta Satèn, Mirabella	208
Franciacorta Brut, Bredasole	205	Franciacorta Satèn, Monte Rossa	190
Franciacorta Brut, Ca' del Bosco	196	Franciacorta Satèn, Montenisa	219
Franciacorta Brut, Ca' del Vént	219	Franciacorta Satèn, Monzio Compagnoni	220
Franciacorta Brut, CastelFaglia	190	Franciacorta Satèn, Principe Banfi Podere Pio IX	220
Franciacorta Brut, Cavalleri	196	Franciacorta Satèn, Ronco Calino	182
Franciacorta Brut, Battista Cola	216	Franciacorta Satèn, Giuseppe Vezzoli	198
Franciacorta Brut, Contadi Castaldi	182	Franciacorta Satèn, Villa	203
Franciacorta Brut, Lorenzo Faccoli & Figli	220	Franciacorta Satèn Antica Cant. Fratta, Guido Berlucchi & C.	194
Franciacorta Brut, Ferghettina	197	Franciacorta Satèn Brut, Ricci Curbastro	186
Franciacorta Brut, Enrico Gatti	197	Franciacorta Satèn Brut Cesonato, Villa Crespia - F.lli Muratori	217
Franciacorta Brut, Il Mosnel	206	Franciacorta Satén Magnificentia, Uberti	198
Franciacorta Brut, La Montina	202	Franciacorta Satèn Sel., Contadi Castaldi	182
Franciacorta Brut, Lantieri de Paratico	185	Franconia, Roncada	376
Franciacorta Brut, Le Marchesine	223	Franconia, Ronco delle Betulle	396
Franciacorta Brut, Lo Sparviere	203	Frappato, Cant. Valle dell'Acate	766
Franciacorta Brut, Majolini	205	Frasca, Varramista	613
Franciacorta Brut, Mirabella	208	Frascati Cannellino, Castel De Paolis	686
Franciacorta Brut, Montenisa	219	Frascati Cannellino, Conte Zandotti	689
Franciacorta Brut, Principe Banfi Podere Pio IX	220	Frascati Cannellino, Fontana Candida	687
Franciacorta Brut, Ricci Curbastro	186	Frascati Cannellino, Poggio Le Volpi	687
Franciacorta Brut, Ronco Calino	182	Frascati Sup., Cant. Cerquetta	692
Franciacorta Brut, San Cristoforo	220	Frascati Sup., Casale Marchese	685
Franciacorta Brut, Giuseppe Vezzoli	198	Frascati Sup., Castel De Paolis	686
Franciacorta Brut, Villa	203	Frascati Sup., Conte Zandotti	689
Franciacorta Brut Antica Cant. Fratta, Guido Berlucchi & C.	194	Frascati Sup., Fontana Candida	687
Franciacorta Brut Arcadia, Lantieri de Paratico	185	Frascati Sup., Gotto d'Oro	692
Franciacorta Brut Bagnadore V, Barone Pizzini	193	Frascati Sup., Poggio Le Volpi	687
Franciacorta Brut Cabochon, Monte Rossa	190	Frascati Sup. Bianco Meraco, Cantine San Marco	685
Franciacorta Brut Collezione Oro, Giuseppe Vezzoli	198	Frascati Sup. Campo Vecchio, Castel De Paolis	686
Franciacorta Brut Comarì del Salem, Uberti	198	Frascati Sup. Cannellino, Villa Simone	688
Franciacorta Brut Cuvée n. 4, Bersi Serlini	207	Frascati Sup. Cannellino Sel., Villa Simone	688
Franciacorta Brut Francesco I, Uberti	198	Frascati Sup. Racemo, L'Olivella	692
Franciacorta Brut I Cuvée, Monte Rossa	190	Frascati Sup. Regillo Etichetta Nera, Tenuta di Pietra Porzia	692
Franciacorta Brut Novalia, Villa Crespia - F.lli Muratori	217	Frascati Sup. S. Nilo Millenium, Tenuta Cusmano	692
Franciacorta Brut Rosé, Mirabella	208	Frascati Sup. Santa Teresa, Fontana Candida	687
Franciacorta Brut Rosé, Giuseppe Vezzoli	198	Frascati Sel., Cantine San Marco	685
Franciacorta Brut Santa Giulia, Conti Bettoni Cazzago	218	Frascati Sup. Sel. Oro, Az. Agr. Casale Mattia	693
Franciacorta Brut Satèn, Bredasole	205	Frascati Sup. Sel. Verde, Vini Pallavicini	689
Franciacorta Brut Satèn, Cornaleto	216	Frascati Sup. Terre dei Grifi, Fontana Candida	687
Franciacorta Brut Tetellus, Conti Bettoni Cazzago	218	Frascati Sup. V. Adriana, Castel De Paolis	686
Franciacorta Brut Wertmüller, Mirabella	208	Frascati Sup. V. dei Preti, Villa Simone	688
Franciacorta Casa delle Colonne, F.lli Berlucchi	193	Frascati Sup. Vallechiesa, Casale Vallechiesa	692

Frascati Sup. Vign. Filonardi, Villa Simone	688
Frascati Sup. Villa Simone, Villa Simone	688
Fratta, Maculan	290
Fraueler, Oswald Schuster Befehlhof	286
Freisa d'Asti Luna di Maggio, Cascina Gilli	62
Freisa d'Asti V. del Forno, Cascina Gilli	62
Freisa d'Asti Vivace, Cascina Gilli	62
Friuli Annia Malvasia, Emiro Cav. Bortolusso	363
Friuli Annia Merlot Privilege, Emiro Cav. Bortolusso	363
Friuli Annia Pinot Bianco, Emiro Cav. Bortolusso	363
Friuli Annia Pinot Grigio, Emiro Cav. Bortolusso	363
Friuli Annia Sauvignon, Emiro Cav. Bortolusso	363
Friuli Annia Tocai Friulano, Emiro Cav. Bortolusso	363
Friuli Annia Verduzzo Friulano, Emiro Cav. Bortolusso	363
Friuli Aquileia Bianco Palmade, Mulino delle Tolle	355
Friuli Aquileia Bianco Tàlis, Giovanni Donda	354
Friuli Aquileia Cabernet, Ca' Bolani	364
Friuli Aquileia Cabernet Franc, Tenuta Beltrame	355
Friuli Aquileia Cabernet Franc, Giovanni Donda	354
Friuli Aquileia Cabernet Franc, Mulino delle Tolle	355
Friuli Aquileia Cabernet Franc Gianni Zonin Vineyards, Ca' Bolani	364
Friuli Aquileia Cabernet Franc Vign. Beligna, Ca' Tullio	354
Friuli Aquileia Cabernet Sauvignon, Tenuta Beltrame	355
Friuli Aquileia Cabernet Sauvignon, Foffani	426
Friuli Aquileia Cabernet Sauvignon Ris., Tenuta Beltrame	355
Friuli Aquileia Chardonnay, Tenuta Beltrame	355
Friuli Aquileia Chardonnay, Mulino delle Tolle	355
Friuli Aquileia Chardonnay Carato, Valpanera	426
Friuli Aquileia Chardonnay Pribus, Tenuta Beltrame	355
Friuli Aquileia Chardonnay Sup., Foffani	426
Friuli Aquileia Conte Bolani Rosso Gianni Zonin Vineyards, Ca' Bolani	364
Friuli Aquileia Malvasia, Mulino delle Tolle	355
Friuli Aquileia Merlot, Tenuta Beltrame	355
Friuli Aquileia Merlot, Foffani	426
Friuli Aquileia Merlot Ris., Tenuta Beltrame	355
Friuli Aquileia Merlot Ris., Giovanni Donda	354
Friuli Aquileia Opimio Gianni Zonin Vineyards, Ca' Bolani	364
Friuli Aquileia Pinot Bianco, Brojli - Franco Clementin	424
Friuli Aquileia Pinot Bianco, Giovanni Donda	354
Friuli Aquileia Pinot Grigio, Tenuta Beltrame	355
Friuli Aquileia Pinot Grigio, Giovanni Donda	354
Friuli Aquileia Pinot Grigio Gianni Zonin Vineyards, Ca' Bolani	364
Friuli Aquileia Pinot Grigio Sup., Foffani	426
Friuli Aquileia Refosco, Brojli - Franco Clementin	424
Friuli Aquileia Refosco Campo della Stafula, Brojli - Franco Clementin	424
Friuli Aquileia Refosco P. R., Tenuta Beltrame	355
Friuli Aquileia Refosco P. R., Foffani	426
Friuli Aquileia Refosco P. R., Mulino delle Tolle	355
Friuli Aquileia Refosco P. R., Valpanera	426
Friuli Aquileia Refosco P. R. Gianni Zonin Vineyards, Ca' Bolani	364
Friuli Aquileia Refosco P. R. Ris., Valpanera	426
Friuli Aquileia Refosco P. R. Sup., Valpanera	426
Friuli Aquileia Refosco P. R. Vign. Beligna, Ca' Tullio	354
Friuli Aquileia Riesling, Brojli - Franco Clementin	424
Friuli Aquileia Riesling Vign. Beligna, Ca' Tullio	354
Friuli Aquileia Rosso Alma, Valpanera	426
Friuli Aquileia Rosso Aquileia Duemila, Ca' Tullio	354
Friuli Aquileia Rosso Sabellius, Mulino delle Tolle	355
Friuli Aquileia Sauvignon, Tenuta Beltrame	355
Friuli Aquileia Sauvignon, Giovanni Donda	354
Friuli Aquileia Sauvignon, Mulino delle Tolle	355
Friuli Aquileia Sauvignon Gianni Zonin Vineyards, Ca' Bolani	364
Friuli Aquileia Sauvignon Sup., Foffani	426
Friuli Aquileia Tocai Friulano, Tenuta Beltrame	355
Friuli Aquileia Tocai Friulano, Mulino delle Tolle	355
Friuli Aquileia Tocai Friulano Sup., Foffani	426
Friuli Aquileia Traminer Aromatico, Brojli - Franco Clementin	424
Friuli Aquileia Traminer Aromatico, Ca' Bolani	364
Friuli Aquileia Traminer Vign. Beligna, Ca' Tullio	354
Friuli Grave Bianco, Tenuta Pinni	422
Friuli Grave Bianco, Pittaro	366
Friuli Grave Bianco Martin Pescatore, Forchir	430
Friuli Grave Bianco Pra' de Gai, Vigneti Le Monde	404
Friuli Grave Bianco Puja, Vigneti Le Monde	404
Friuli Grave Cabernet, Di Lenardo	389
Friuli Grave Cabernet, F.lli Pighin	401
Friuli Grave Cabernet, Pittaro	366
Friuli Grave Cabernet Briccolo, Vini Bidoli	430
Friuli Grave Cabernet Franc, Vigneti Le Monde	404
Friuli Grave Cabernet Franc, Tenuta Pinni	422
Friuli Grave Cabernet Franc Sugano, San Simone	430
Friuli Grave Cabernet Sauvignon, F.lli Pighin	401
Friuli Grave Cabernet Sauvignon, Alessandro Vicentini Orgnani	402
Friuli Grave Cabernet Sauvignon Crearo, Pradio	356
Friuli Grave Cabernet Sauvignon Nexus, San Simone	430
Friuli Grave Cabernet Sauvignon Ris., Antonutti	401
Friuli Grave Cabernet Sauvignon Ris., Vigneti Le Monde	404
Friuli Grave Cabernet Sauvignon Sant'Helena, Fantinel	423
Friuli Grave Chardonnay, Antonutti	401
Friuli Grave Chardonnay, Vini Bidoli	430
Friuli Grave Chardonnay, Di Lenardo	389
Friuli Grave Chardonnay, Vigneti Le Monde	404
Friuli Grave Chardonnay, F.lli Pighin	401
Friuli Grave Chardonnay, Tenuta Pinni	422
Friuli Grave Chardonnay, Plozner	423
Friuli Grave Chardonnay, Scarbolo	402
Friuli Grave Chardonnay Mousqué, Pittaro	366
Friuli Grave Chardonnay Poggio Alto, Antonutti	401
Friuli Grave Chardonnay Ris., Plozner	423
Friuli Grave Chardonnay Teraje, Pradio	356
Friuli Grave Chardonnay Woody, Di Lenardo	389
Friuli Grave Merlot, Antonutti	401
Friuli Grave Merlot, Di Lenardo	389
Friuli Grave Merlot, Teresa Raiz	403
Friuli Grave Merlot, Scarbolo	402
Friuli Grave Merlot, Alessandro Vicentini Orgnani	402
Friuli Grave Merlot Borgo Tesis, Fantinel	423
Friuli Grave Merlot Briccolo, Vini Bidoli	430
Friuli Grave Merlot Poggio Alto, Antonutti	401
Friuli Grave Merlot Roncomoro, Pradio	356
Friuli Grave Merlot Vistorta, Vistorta - Brandino Brandolini d'Adda	413
Friuli Grave Pinot Bianco, Di Lenardo	389
Friuli Grave Pinot Bianco, Vigneti Le Monde	404
Friuli Grave Pinot Bianco, Plozner	423
Friuli Grave Pinot Bianco Braide Cjase, Alessandro Vicentini Orgnani	402
Friuli Grave Pinot Grigio, Antonutti	401
Friuli Grave Pinot Grigio, Di Lenardo	389
Friuli Grave Pinot Grigio, Le Due Torri	429
Friuli Grave Pinot Grigio, Vigneti Le Monde	404
Friuli Grave Pinot Grigio, F.lli Pighin	401
Friuli Grave Pinot Grigio, Tenuta Pinni	422
Friuli Grave Pinot Grigio, Scarbolo	402
Friuli Grave Pinot Grigio, Alessandro Vicentini Orgnani	402
Friuli Grave Pinot Grigio Priara, Pradio	356
Friuli Grave Pinot Nero, Vigneti Le Monde	404
Friuli Grave Pinot Nero, Plozner	423
Friuli Grave Pinot Nero Ris., Plozner	423
Friuli Grave Refosco P. R., Tenuta Pinni	422
Friuli Grave Refosco P. R., Plozner	423
Friuli Grave Refosco P.R., Flavio Pontoni	427
Friuli Grave Refosco P. R. Campo del Viotto, Scarbolo	402
Friuli Grave Refosco P.R. Refoscone, Forchir	430
Friuli Grave Refosco P. R. Ris., Vigneti Le Monde	404
Friuli Grave Refosco P. R. Sant'Helena, Fantinel	423
Friuli Grave Refosco P. R. Tuaro, Pradio	356
Friuli Grave Rosso, Tenuta Pinni	422
Friuli Grave Rosso Ca' Salice, Vigneti Le Monde	404
Friuli Grave Rosso Rok, Pradio	356
Friuli Grave Sauvignon, Antonutti	401
Friuli Grave Sauvignon, Vini Bidoli	430
Friuli Grave Sauvignon, Vigneti Le Monde	404
Friuli Grave Sauvignon, F.lli Pighin	401
Friuli Grave Sauvignon, Tenuta Pinni	422
Friuli Grave Sauvignon, Plozner	423
Friuli Grave Sauvignon, Scarbolo	402
Friuli Grave Sauvignon, Alessandro Vicentini Orgnani	402
Friuli Grave Sauvignon, Villa Chiopris	427
Friuli Grave Sauvignon Blanc, Di Lenardo	389
Friuli Grave Sauvignon Blanc Le Selezioni, Antonutti	401
Friuli Grave Sauvignon Sobaja, Pradio	356
Friuli Grave Tocai Friulano, Antonutti	401
Friuli Grave Tocai Friulano, Le Due Torri	429
Friuli Grave Tocai Friulano, Plozner	423
Friuli Grave Tocai Friulano, San Simone	430
Friuli Grave Tocai Friulano, Scarbolo	402
Friuli Grave Tocai Friulano, Alessandro Vicentini Orgnani	402
Friuli Grave Tocai Friulano, Villa Chiopris	427
Friuli Grave Tocai Friulano Gaiare, Pradio	356
Friuli Grave Tocai Friulano Toh!, Di Lenardo	389
Friuli Grave Traminer Aromatico, Forchir	430
Friuli Grave Traminer Aromatico, Plozner	423
Friuli Isonzo Alfiere Rosso, I Feudi di Romans - Lorenzon	414
Friuli Isonzo Arbis Blanc, Borgo San Daniele	367
Friuli Isonzo Arbis Ros, Borgo San Daniele	367
Friuli Isonzo Bianco, Giulio Manzocco	373
Friuli Isonzo Bianco Flors di Uis, Vie di Romans	399
Friuli Isonzo Bianco Pietraverde, Cant. Prod. di Cormons	370
Friuli Isonzo Bianco Vignis di Siris, Mauro Drius	370
Friuli Isonzo Cabernet, Tenuta di Blasig	412
Friuli Isonzo Cabernet BorDavi, Carlo di Pradis	369
Friuli Isonzo Cabernet Franc, I Feudi di Romans - Lorenzon	414
Friuli Isonzo Cabernet Franc, Eddi Luisa	398
Friuli Isonzo Cabernet Franc, Giulio Manzocco	373
Friuli Isonzo Cabernet Franc, Masut da Rive	398
Friuli Isonzo Cabernet Franc, Puiatti	360
Friuli Isonzo Cabernet Franc, Ronco del Gelso	377
Friuli Isonzo Cabernet Franc, Franco Visintin	394
Friuli Isonzo Cabernet Franc I Ferretti, Eddi Luisa	398
Friuli Isonzo Cabernet Gli Affreschi, Tenuta di Blasig	412
Friuli Isonzo Cabernet Sauvignon, Colmello di Grotta	388
Friuli Isonzo Cabernet Sauvignon, I Feudi di Romans - Lorenzon	414
Friuli Isonzo Cabernet Sauvignon, Masut da Rive	398
Friuli Isonzo Cabernet Sauvignon, Franco Visintin	394
Friuli Isonzo Cabernet Sauvignon Barrique Do Ville, Do Ville	413
Friuli Isonzo Cabernet Sauvignon I Ferretti, Eddi Luisa	398
Friuli Isonzo Cabernet Sauvignon Linea Comugna, Blason	429
Friuli Isonzo Chardonnay, Casa Zuliani	387
Friuli Isonzo Chardonnay, Lis Neris	421
Friuli Isonzo Chardonnay, Eddi Luisa	398
Friuli Isonzo Chardonnay, Magnàs	373
Friuli Isonzo Chardonnay, Masut da Rive	398
Friuli Isonzo Chardonnay, Pierpaolo Pecorari	421
Friuli Isonzo Chardonnay, Puiatti	360
Friuli Isonzo Chardonnay, Ronco del Gelso	377
Friuli Isonzo Chardonnay, Vigna del Lauro	379
Friuli Isonzo Chardonnay, Franco Visintin	394
Friuli Isonzo Chardonnay Ars Vivendi, Do Ville	413
Friuli Isonzo Chardonnay Barrique Do Ville, Do Ville	413
Friuli Isonzo Chardonnay Ciampagnis Vieris, Vie di Romans	399
Friuli Isonzo Chardonnay Do Ville, Do Ville	413
Friuli Isonzo Chardonnay I Ferretti, Eddi Luisa	398
Friuli Isonzo Chardonnay Jurosa, Lis Neris	421
Friuli Isonzo Chardonnay Maurùs, Masut da Rive	398
Friuli Isonzo Chardonnay Vie di Romans, Vie di Romans	399
Friuli Isonzo Malvasia, Mauro Drius	370
Friuli Isonzo Malvasia, Simon di Brazzan	428
Friuli Isonzo Malvasia, Tenuta Villanova	389
Friuli Isonzo Malvasia, Franco Visintin	394
Friuli Isonzo Malvasia Ars Vivendi, Do Ville	413
Friuli Isonzo Malvasia Istriana Gli Affreschi, Tenuta di Blasig	412

Friuli Isonzo Maurus, Vie di Romans 399
Friuli Isonzo Merlot, Tenuta di Blasig 412
Friuli Isonzo Merlot, Colmello di Grotta 388
Friuli Isonzo Merlot, Mauro Drius 370
Friuli Isonzo Merlot, I Feudi di Romans - Lorenzon 414
Friuli Isonzo Merlot, Magnàs 373
Friuli Isonzo Merlot, Giulio Manzocco 373
Friuli Isonzo Merlot, Masut da Rive 398
Friuli Isonzo Merlot, Ronco del Gelso 377
Friuli Isonzo Merlot, Simon di Brazzan 428
Friuli Isonzo Merlot, Franco Visintin 394
Friuli Isonzo Merlot Ars Vivendi, Do Ville 413
Friuli Isonzo Merlot BorDavi, Carlo di Pradis 369
Friuli Isonzo Merlot Gli Affreschi, Tenuta di Blasig 412
Friuli Isonzo Merlot I Ferretti, Eddi Luisa 398
Friuli Isonzo Merlot V. Runc, Il Carpino 415
Friuli Isonzo Pinot Bianco, Mauro Drius 370
Friuli Isonzo Pinot Bianco, I Feudi di Romans - Lorenzon 414
Friuli Isonzo Pinot Bianco, Eddi Luisa 398
Friuli Isonzo Pinot Bianco, Masut da Rive 398
Friuli Isonzo Pinot Grigio, Tenuta di Blasig 412
Friuli Isonzo Pinot Grigio, Blason 429
Friuli Isonzo Pinot Grigio, Borgo San Daniele 367
Friuli Isonzo Pinot Grigio, Mauro Drius 370
Friuli Isonzo Pinot Grigio, I Feudi di Romans - Lorenzon 414
Friuli Isonzo Pinot Grigio, Lis Neris 421
Friuli Isonzo Pinot Grigio, Eddi Luisa 398
Friuli Isonzo Pinot Grigio, Magnàs 373
Friuli Isonzo Pinot Grigio, Masut da Rive 398
Friuli Isonzo Pinot Grigio, Pierpaolo Pecorari 421
Friuli Isonzo Pinot Grigio, Puiatti 360
Friuli Isonzo Pinot Grigio, Franco Visintin 394
Friuli Isonzo Pinot Grigio Altis, Pierpaolo Pecorari 421
Friuli Isonzo Pinot Grigio Ars Vivendi, Do Ville 413
Friuli Isonzo Pinot Grigio BorDavi, Carlo di Pradis 369
Friuli Isonzo Pinot Grigio Dessimis, Vie di Romans 399
Friuli Isonzo Pinot Grigio Do Ville, Do Ville 413
Friuli Isonzo Pinot Grigio Gris, Lis Neris 421
Friuli Isonzo Pinot Grigio Sot lis Rivis, Ronco del Gelso 377
Friuli Isonzo Refosco P. R., I Feudi di Romans - Lorenzon 414
Friuli Isonzo Refosco P. R., Giulio Manzocco 373
Friuli Isonzo Refosco P. R. I Ferretti, Eddi Luisa 398
Friuli Isonzo Refosco P. R. I Fiori del Borgo, Borgo Conventi 387
Friuli Isonzo Refosco P. R. Pucino, Eugenio Collavini 380
Friuli Isonzo Riesling, Giulio Manzocco 373
Friuli Isonzo Riesling, Ronco del Gelso 377
Friuli Isonzo Ròs di Ról, Sant'Elena 393
Friuli Isonzo Rosso BorDavi, Carlo di Pradis 369
Friuli Isonzo Sauvignon, Casa Zuliani 387
Friuli Isonzo Sauvignon, Cant. Prod. di Cormons 370
Friuli Isonzo Sauvignon, I Feudi di Romans - Lorenzon 414
Friuli Isonzo Sauvignon, Magnàs 373
Friuli Isonzo Sauvignon, Giulio Manzocco 373
Friuli Isonzo Sauvignon, Masut da Rive 398
Friuli Isonzo Sauvignon, Pierpaolo Pecorari 421
Friuli Isonzo Sauvignon, Ronco del Gelso 377
Friuli Isonzo Sauvignon, Roncùs 361
Friuli Isonzo Sauvignon, Simon di Brazzan 428
Friuli Isonzo Sauvignon, Francesco Vosca 429
Friuli Isonzo Sauvignon Altis, Pierpaolo Pecorari 421
Friuli Isonzo Sauvignon Dom Picòl, Lis Neris 421
Friuli Isonzo Sauvignon Piere, Vie di Romans 399
Friuli Isonzo Sauvignon Vieris, Vie di Romans 399
Friuli Isonzo Tocai Friulano, Borgo San Daniele 367
Friuli Isonzo Tocai Friulano, Mauro Drius 370
Friuli Isonzo Tocai Friulano, Eddi Luisa 398
Friuli Isonzo Tocai Friulano, Magnàs 373
Friuli Isonzo Tocai Friulano, Masut da Rive 398
Friuli Isonzo Tocai Friulano, Pierpaolo Pecorari 421
Friuli Isonzo Tocai Friulano, Puiatti 360
Friuli Isonzo Tocai Friulano, Ronco del Gelso 377
Friuli Isonzo Tocai Friulano, Simon di Brazzan 428
Friuli Isonzo Tocai Friulano Ascevi, Ascevi - Luwa 415
Friuli Isonzo Tocai Friulano Do Ville, Do Ville 413
Friuli Isonzo Tocai Friulano Sovràn, I Feudi di Romans - Lorenzon 414
Friuli Isonzo Traminer Aromatico, Marcello e Marino Humar 417
Friuli Isonzo Verduzzo Dorè, Cant. Prod. di Cormons 370
Fronsaga, Delai 224
Fuili, Cant. Soc. Dorgali 794
Fumé Bianco, Giovanni Crosato 427
Furat, Ajello 774
Furetta Mandrarossa, Settesoli 775
Gabàn, Nilo Bolognani 235
Gabbro, Montepeloso 590
Gadì, Salvatore Murana 778
Gagliole Rosso, Gagliole 597
Galana, Cant. Soc. del Vermentino 795
Galanda Brut Cl., Ruiz de Cardenas 189
Galatrona, Fattoria Petrolo 471
Galhasi Inzolia Chardonnay, Cantine Foraci 785
Galhasi Nero d'Avola, Cantine Foraci 785
Galici, Agareno 785
Galluccio Aglianico Montecaruso, Telaro 716
Galluccio Ara Mundi Ris., Telaro 716
Galluccio Calivierno Ris., Telaro 716
Galluccio Falanghina Ripa Bianca, Telaro 716
Gamba di Pernice, Tenuta dei Fiori 49
Gambellara Cl. Ca' Fischele, Luigino Dal Maso 306
Gambellara Cl. I Masieri, La Biancara 295
Gambellara Cl. Monte La Bocara, Domenico Cavazza & F.lli 306
Gambellara Cl. Podere il Giangio, Zonin 296
Gambellara Cl. Sassaia, La Biancara 295
Gambellara Cl. Vign. Creari Capitel S. Libera,
    Domenico Cavazza & F.lli 306
Gambellara Vin Santo Capitel S. Libera,
    Domenico Cavazza & F.lli 306

Garda Barbera, La Guarda 223
Garda Bresciano Groppello, Delai 224
Garda Bresciano Groppello, Monteacuto 224
Garda Bresciano Rosso, Delai 224
Garda Cabernet Le Zalte, Cascina La Pertica 206
Garda Cabernet Sauvignon, Tenuta Roveglia 224
Garda Cabernet Sauvignon Ca' d'Oro, Tenuta Roveglia 224
Garda Cabernet Sauvignon Cicisbeo, Le Tende 348
Garda Cabernet Sauvignon Rocca Sveva, Cant. di Soave 329
Garda Cabernet Sauvignon Vign. Il Falcone La Prendina, Cavalchina 332
Garda Cabernet Sauvignon Vigna Bragagna, Avanzi 221
Garda Chardonnay, Ca' Lojera 213
Garda Chardonnay Bianco del Drago, Musella 319
Garda Chardonnay Le Sincette Brut Ris.,
    Cascina La Pertica 206
Garda Chardonnay Meridiano, Ricchi 223
Garda Chardonnay Vallidium, Corte Gardoni 340
Garda Cl. Bianco Il Torrione, Monte Cicogna 200
Garda Cl. Bianco Pergola, Cantine Valtenesi - Lugana 222
Garda Cl. Chiaretto Molmenti, Costaripa 200
Garda Cl. Groppello, Le Chiusure 225
Garda Cl. Groppello Maim, Costaripa 200
Garda Cl. Groppello Vign. Arzane Ris., Pasini Produttori 224
Garda Cl. Groppello Vign. Le Castelline, Costaripa 200
Garda Cl. Rosso Ca' Maiol, Provenza 195
Garda Cl. Rosso Groppello Beana, Monte Cicogna 200
Garda Cl. Rosso Le Sincette, Cascina La Pertica 206
Garda Cl. Rosso Negresco, Provenza 195
Garda Cl. Rosso Sel. Fabio Contato, Provenza 195
Garda Cl. Rosso Sup., La Guarda 223
Garda Cl. Rosso Sup. Antica Corte Ialidy, Marangona 223
Garda Cl. Rosso Sup. Rubinere, Monte Cicogna 200
Garda Cl. Sup. Don Lisander, Monte Cicogna 200
Garda Garganega, Brigaldara 321
Garda Garganega Paroni La Prendina, Cavalchina 332
Garda Garganega Vigne Alte, F.lli Zeni 289
Garda Marzemino, La Guarda 223
Garda Merlot, Ca' Lojera 213
Garda Merlot, Giorgio Poggi 345
Garda Merlot Carpino, Ricchi 223
Garda Merlot Casina La Prendina, Cavalchina 332
Garda Merlot Faial La Prendina, Cavalchina 332
Garda Merlot La Prendina, Cavalchina 332
Garda Merlot Naker, Giorgio Poggi 345
Garda Merlot Nepomuceno, Cantrina 183
Garda Pinot Nero Corteccio, Cantrina 183
Garda Pinot Nero La Valle, Avanzi 221
Garda Sauvignon Valbruna La Prendina, Cavalchina 332
Garganega Camporengo, Le Fraghe 291
Garighe Zibibbo, Aziende Vinicole Miceli 780
Gastaldi Rosso, Gastaldi 121
Gatti Bianco, Enrico Gatti 197
Gatti Rosso, Enrico Gatti 197
Gattinara, Antoniolo 81
Gattinara, Anzivino 82
Gattinara, Bianchi 142
Gattinara, Dessilani 79
Gattinara, Nervi 82
Gattinara, Giancarlo Travaglini 83
Gattinara Ris., Giancarlo Travaglini 83
Gattinara Tre Vigne, Giancarlo Travaglini 83
Gattinara Vign. Castelle, Antoniolo 81
Gattinara Vign. Jerbion, Torraccia del Piantavigna 159
Gattinara Vign. Molsino, Nervi 82
Gattinara Vign. Valferana, Bianchi 142
Gattinara Vigneto Osso S. Grato, Antoniolo 81
Gattinara Vigneto S. Francesco, Antoniolo 81
Gaudeo, Ciù Ciù 643
Gaudio, Tenuta Le Velette 670
Gavi, Ca' Bianca 29
Gavi, Domenico Ghio e Figli 45
Gavi, La Smilla 155
Gavi, Pio Cesare 26
Gavi, Luigi Tacchino 60
Gavi Barrique, La Scolca 159
Gavi Cascine dell'Aureliana, Produttori del Gavi 86
Gavi del Comune di Bosio I Bergi, La Smilla 155
Gavi del Comune di Gavi, Nicola Bergaglio 83
Gavi del Comune di Gavi, La Smilla 155
Gavi del Comune di Gavi, Morgassi Superiore 85
Gavi del Comune di Gavi, Villa Sparina 86
Gavi del Comune di Gavi Bric Sassi, Roberto Sarotto 161
Gavi del Comune di Gavi Bruno Broglia,
    Gian Piero Broglia - Tenuta La Meirana 84
Gavi del Comune di Gavi Et. Oro, Morgassi Superiore 85
Gavi del Comune di Gavi IL, La Giustiniana 85
Gavi del Comune di Gavi La Chiara, La Chiara 159
Gavi del Comune di Gavi La Meirana,
    Gian Piero Broglia - Tenuta La Meirana 84
Gavi del Comune di Gavi Lugarara, La Giustiniana 85
Gavi del Comune di Gavi Minaia, Nicola Bergaglio 83
Gavi del Comune di Gavi Monte Rotondo, Villa Sparina 86
Gavi del Comune di Gavi Montessora, La Giustiniana 85
Gavi del Comune di Gavi Pilìn, Castellari Bergaglio 84
Gavi del Comune di Gavi Poggio Basco, Malgrà 104
Gavi del Comune di Gavi Rolona, Castellari Bergaglio 84
Gavi del Comune di Gavi Rovereto, Castellari Bergaglio 84
Gavi del Comune di Gavi V. Vecchia, La Caplana 155
Gavi del Comune di Gavi Vign. Groppella, La Chiara 159
Gavi del Comune di Tassarolo Castello di Tassarolo,
    Castello di Tassarolo 164
Gavi del Comune di Tassarolo Fornaci, Castellari Bergaglio 84
Gavi di Gavi, Marchesi di Barolo 40
Gavi di Gavi Et. Nera, La Scolca 159
Gavi di Gavi La Maddalena, Produttori del Gavi 86
Gavi Drac Bianco, Domenico Ghio e Figli 45

Gavi Filagnotti, Cascina Ulivi	162
Gavi Fornaci di Tassarolo, Michele Chiarlo	47
Gavi La Cascina, Domenico Ghio e Figli	45
Gavi La Rocca, Coppo	55
Gavi Minaia, Franco M. Martinetti	144
Gavi Montemarino, Cascina Ulivi	162
Gavi Primuva, Produttori del Gavi	86
Gavi Principessa Gavia, Vigne Regali	144
Gavi Ricella Alta, Vigne del Pareto	128
Gavi Rovereto, Michele Chiarlo	47
Gavi Rovereto Vignavecchia, Castellari Bergaglio	84
Gavi Spumante Extra Brut, Gian Piero Broglia - Tenuta La Meirana	84
Gavi Tassarolo S, Castello di Tassarolo	164
Gavi V. del Lago, Valditerra	162
Gavi Vigne Alte, Il Vignale	128
Gavi Vigne del Pareto, Vigne del Pareto	128
Gavi Vilma Cappelletti, Il Vignale	128
Gazza Ladra, Santa Lucia	753
Gemelli, Abbazia Santa Anastasia	768
Geos, Terre Cortesi Moncaro	639
Ghemme, Antichi Vigneti di Cantalupo	87
Ghemme, Bianchi	142
Ghemme, Dessilani	79
Ghemme, Rovellotti	87
Ghemme, Torraccia del Piantavigna	159
Ghemme Colle Baraggiole, Bianchi	142
Ghemme Collis Breclemae, Antichi Vigneti di Cantalupo	87
Ghemme Collis Carellae, Antichi Vigneti di Cantalupo	87
Ghemme Ris., Rovellotti	87
Ghemme Signore di Bayard, Antichi Vigneti di Cantalupo	87
Gheppio, Mustilli	722
Ghiaie della Furba, Tenuta di Capezzana	474
Ghiaretolo, Santa Caterina	180
Giada Principe di Corleone, Pollara	786
Giardin Vecchio, Santa Cassella	647
Gilat Rosso, Eraldo Viberti	98
Gioveto, Enrico Pierazzuoli	473
Giramonte, Tenuta Castiglioni	551
Girgenti, Cant. Soc. La Torre	787
Girifalco, La Calonica	546
Girò di Cagliari Donna Jolanda, Meloni Vini	798
Girolamo, Castello di Bossi	484
Girone, Boccadigabbia	631
Gisèle, La Rampa di Fugnano	580
Giubilante, Lungarotti	675
Giulio Ferrari, Ferrari	247
Giunone Rosso, Monte Tondo	330
Giuseppe Galliano Brut M. Cl., Borgo Maragliano	100
Giuseppe Galliano Chardonnay Brut, Borgo Maragliano	100
Giusto di Notri, Tua Rita	591
Gocce di Sole, Zanini	252
Godimondo Cabernet Franc, La Montecchia	328
Golfo del Tigullio Rosso Musaico Vigna Intrigoso, Enoteca Bisson	169
Golfo del Tigullio Vermentino Vigna Intrigoso, Enoteca Bisson	169
Goliardo, Luciano Landi	628
Golpaja, Fattoria di Petriolo	599
Gonzialer, Grigoletti	240
Gorgo Tondo Bianco, Carlo Pellegrino	773
Gorgo Tondo Rosso, Carlo Pellegrino	773
Gortmarin, Borgo San Daniele	367
Graf Noir, Drei Donà Tenuta La Palazza	443
Gramelot, Cantine di Castignano	631
Grammonte, Cottanera	769
Gran Rosso del Vicariato, Cant. Soc. Coop. di Quistello	224
Granaccia di Quiliano Vigneto Cappuccini, Innocenzo Turco	180
Granaio, Savignola Paolina	505
Granato, Foradori	239
Granato Vino Passito, Tenuta Terre Nobili	765
Granbianco di Quistello, Cant. Soc. Coop. di Quistello	224
Grandarella, Masi	327
Grannero Pinot Nero, Vigneto delle Terre Rosse	466
Grappoli del Grillo, Marco De Bartoli	771
Graticciaia, Agricole Vallone	754
Gratius, Il Molino di Grace	557
Grattamacco, Colle Massari	475
Gravello, Librandi	759
Gravina, Cant. Coop. Botromagno	743
Gravisano, Cant. Coop. Botromagno	743
Grayasusi, Roberto Ceraudo	760
Grecale Vino Liquoroso, Cantine Florio	772
Grecanico Mandrarossa, Settesoli	775
Grechetto, Azzoni Avogadro Carradori	654
Grechetto, Bigi	668
Grechetto, Palazzone	670
Grechetto dell'Umbria, Castello di Antignano - Brogal Vini	672
Grechetto Latour a Civitella, Sergio Mottura	684
Grechetto Poggio della Costa, Sergio Mottura	684
Grechetto Vertunno, Freddano	678
Greco del Taburno, Cant. del Taburno	714
Greco di Bianco, Stelitano	758
Greco di Bianco, Vintripodi Calabria	764
Greco di Roccamonfina le Cinque Pietre, Telaro	716
Greco di Tufo, Cantine Caputo	712
Greco di Tufo, Colli Irpini	718
Greco di Tufo, De Falco	728
Greco di Tufo, Di Meo	721
Greco di Tufo, Benito Ferrara	725
Greco di Tufo, Feudi di San Gregorio	723
Greco di Tufo, La Casa dell'Orco	719
Greco di Tufo, Mastroberardino	712
Greco di Tufo, Pietracupa	717
Greco di Tufo, Villa Raiano	722
Greco di Tufo Devon, Antonio Caggiano	724
Greco di Tufo Loggia della Serra, Terredora	718
Greco di Tufo Novaserra, Mastroberardino	712
Greco di Tufo Terra degli Angeli, Terredora	718
Greco di Tufo Vigna Cicogna, Benito Ferrara	725
Grignolino Brut Andrea Spertino, Luigi Spertino	104
Grignolino d'Asti, Castello del Poggio	130
Grignolino d'Asti, Agostino Pavia e Figli	23
Grignolino d'Asti, Luigi Spertino	104
Grignolino d'Asti, Cant. Soc. di Vinchio - Vaglio Serra	153
Grignolino d'Asti Brich Le Roche, Ermanno e Alessandra Brema	88
Grignolino d'Asti Miravalle, Cantine Sant'Agata	138
Grignolino d'Asti Vign. La Casalina, F.lli Rovero	30
Grignolino d'Asti Vignamaestra, Tenuta La Meridiana	116
Grignolino del M.to Casalese, Bricco Mondalino	151
Grignolino del M.to Casalese, Vicara	133
Grignolino del M.to Casalese Bricco del Bosco, Giulio Accornero e Figli	151
Grignolino del M.to Casalese Bricco Mondalino, Bricco Mondalino	151
Grignolino del M.to Casalese Celio, Marco Canato	164
Grignolino del M.to Casalese Cré Marcaleone, Carlo Quarello	70
Grignolino del M.to Casalese Gallianum, Tenuta Gaiano	49
Grignolino del M.to Casalese Marmanest, La Zucca	119
Grignolino del M.to Casalese Montecastello, Isabella	119
Grignolino del M.to Casalese Sansìn, Colonna	152
Grignolino del M.to Casalese V.Tufara, Castello di Lignano	81
Grillo, Baglio Hopps	771
Grillo, Carlo Pellegrino	773
Grillo Parlante, Fondo Antico	781
Grillo Tor di Nubia, Marchesi Platamone	786
Grondino Bianco, Tenuta Vitereta	604
Grondino Rosso, Tenuta Vitereta	604
Gruali, Cantine Rallo	773
Gruccione Merlot, Poderi Morini	441
Guado San Leo, D'Alfonso del Sordo	752
Gualdo al Luco, Castelli del Grevepesa	572
Guardia Vecchia, Santa Cassella	647
Guardiolo Falanghina Senete, La Guardiense	727
Guardiolo Rosso, La Guardiense	727
Guidaccio, Marchesi Torrigiani	468
Guidalberto, Tenuta San Guido	471
Gurra, Agareno	785
Halykàs, Barone La Lumia	784
Harmonium, Firriato	776
Harys, Giovanni Battista Gillardi	80
Henry, Anselmet	19
Herea Bianco, Avide	770
Herea Rosso, Avide	770
Hugonis, Tenute Rapitalà	768
I Balconi Rossi, Le Vigne di San Pietro	333
I Balzini Black Label, I Balzini	594
I Balzini Rosso, I Balzini	594
I Capitelli, Roberto Anselmi	307
I Fenili, Corte Gardoni	340
I Grottoni, Il Lebbio	578
I Monili, Pervini	749
I'Niccolò, Palagetto	582
I Pini, Fattoria di Basciano	570
I Renai, San Gervasio	554
I Ricordi, Rio Grande	671
I Sierri, Cosimo Taurino	745
I Sistri, Fattoria di Felsina	485
I Sodì di San Niccolò, Castellare di Castellina	478
I Sodi Lunghi, F.lli Vagnoni	584
I Venti di Camposilio, Camposilio	600
I Vigneti del Geografico, Agricoltori del Chianti Geografico	495
Ibisco Bianco, Ciccio Zaccagnini	697
Idea, Trappolini	682
Il Basiliano, Tenute Albano Carrisi	740
Il Bianco dell'Abazia, Serafini & Vidotto	315
Il Borro, Tenuta Il Borro	604
Il Brecciolino, Castelvecchio	571
Il Canto di Fondo Antico, Fondo Antico	781
Il Carbonaione, Podere Poggio Scalette	503
Il Cenno, Colle Bereto	616
Il Coro, Fondo Antico	781
Il Corto, Fattoria di Basciano	570
Il Corzano, Fattoria Corzano e Paterno	571
Il Cupo, Ester Hauser	656
Il Doge, I Girasoli di Sant'Andrea	678
Il Faggio, Conte Otto Barattieri di San Pietro	454
Il Fortino Syrah, Fattoria del Buonamico	540
Il Francia Bianco, Maria Letizia Gaggioli - Vigneto Bagazzana	466
Il Francia Brut, Maria Letizia Gaggioli - Vigneto Bagazzana	466
Il Fusco, La Roncaia	400
Il Futuro, Il Colombaio di Cencio	497
Il Gherlo Trebbiano di Modena, Corte Manzini	438
Il Gioiello, Tenuta Cortina e Mandorli	612
Il Grevone, Castello Uzzano	506
Il Leccio, Oliveto	608
Il Longobardo, Cant. di Casteggio	218
Il Mandorlo, La Madonnina - Triacca	602
Il Manuzio, Panzanello	559
Il Merlo-t della Topa Nera, Gino Fuso Carmignani	540
Il Merlot, Collalbrigo	346
Il Monaco di Ribano Cabernet, Colonna - Vini Spalletti	462
Il Moro, Di Fonti	489
Il Moro, Cant. Valle dell'Acate	766
Il Musaico, Enoteca Bisson	169
Il Nespoli, Poderi dal Nespoli	438
Il Palagio Chardonnay, Fattoria Il Palagio	490
Il Palagio Sauvignon, Fattoria Il Palagio	490
Il Paliotto, Terre di Santa Maria	785
Il Pareto, Tenute Ambrogio e Giovanni Folonari	493
Il Peccato Barrique, Jacopo Banti	472
Il Pippo Passito, Cascina Feipu dei Massaretti	166
Il Poggione, Tenuta Il Poggione	528
Il Principe, Machiavelli	575
Il Rosso dell'Abazia, Serafini & Vidotto	315

Il Rosso Don.Giovanni Lucia Galasso, Giovanni Crosato	427
Il Saloncello, Conti Sertoli Salis	214
Il Sasso, Piaggia	563
Il Sole di Alessandro, Castello di Querceto	503
Il Sorbo, Ca' Montebello	219
Il Tempio, La Carletta	619
Il Tocco, Colle Bereto	616
Il Tornese Chardonnay, Drei Donà Tenuta La Palazza	443
Ilios, Solidea	787
Illemos, Leone de Castris	751
Immensum, Francesco Candido	751
Impavido, Paolo Francesconi	440
Impero Bianco, Fattoria Mancini	646
Impero Pinot Nero Sel. F M, Fattoria Mancini	646
Implicito, Le Due Terre	409
Imyr, Roberto Ceraudo	760
Incantari, Baglio Hopps	771
Incrocio Manzoni, Vignaiolo Giuseppe Fanti	236
Incrocio Manzoni 2.15, Conte Collalto	333
Incrocio Manzoni 2.15, G. B. Cerletti Scuola Enol. di Conegliano	346
Incrocio Manzoni 6.0.13, Bepin de Eto	320
Incrocio Manzoni 6.0.13, Italo Cescon	349
Incrocio Manzoni 6.0.13 Le Portelle, Adami	343
Infavato Vino da Uve Stramature, La Berta	435
Infinito, Castello di Monastero	486
Initio, Aziende Vinicole Miceli	780
Insolia, Feudo Principi di Butera	767
Inzolia, Abbazia Santa Anastasia	768
Inzolia, Cant. Valle dell'Acate	766
Ippocrasso, Luigi Spertino	104
Irpinia Aglianico, Benito Ferrara	725
Irpinia Aglianico, Villa Raiano	722
Irpinia Aglianico Donna Chiara, Colli di Lapio - Clelia Romano	717
Irpinia Aglianico Il Principio, Terredora	718
Irpinia Aglianico Nocelleto, Cant. del Barone	726
Irpinia Bianco Coda di Volpe, La Casa dell'Orco	719
Irpinia Coda di Volpe, Marianna	726
Irpinia Falanghina, Terredora	718
Irpinia Ischia Piana, Salvatore Molettieri	719
Irpinia Rosso Coriliano, D'Antiche Terre - Vega	727
Isarcus, Georg Mumelter	262
Ischia Biancolella, D'Ambra Vini d'Ischia	715
Ischia Biancolella Tenuta Frassitelli, D'Ambra Vini d'Ischia	715
Ischia Forastera, D'Ambra Vini d'Ischia	715
Ischia Per''e Palummo, D'Ambra Vini d'Ischia	715
Ischia Rosso Dedicato a Mario d'Ambra, D'Ambra Vini d'Ischia	715
Ischia Rosso Vigne di Janno Piro, Pietratorcia	727
Isonzo del Friuli Refosco dal P. R., Alfredo Bracco	428
Isonzo del Friuli Sauvignon, Alfredo Bracco	428
Ispolaia Rosso, Ispoli	573
Jacopo Chardonnay, Fattoria Paradiso	432
Jalé, Cusumano	779
James Hopps Marsala Sup., Baglio Hopps	771
Jare, Bruno Agostinetto	334
Just Bianco, La Giustiniana	85
Justinus Kerner, Josef Sölva - Niklaserhof	270
Kados, Duca di Salaparuta - Vini Corvo	769
Kaid, Alessandro di Camporeale	783
Kaiton, Kuenhof - Peter Pliger	267
Kalos, Il Calepino	189
Karah Bianco, Cecilia Beretta	341
Karanar, Foradori	239
Karmis, Attilio Contini	791
Kebir, Torrevento	742
Kléos, Luigi Maffini	713
Kòrae Rosso, Pasqua Vigneti e Cantine	342
Korem, Antonio Argiolas	799
Kottabos Rosso, Casale dei Cento Corvi	691
Kràtos, Luigi Maffini	713
Kron, Fontana Candida	687
Kurni, Oasi degli Angeli	632
Kyme Bianco, D'Ambra Vini d'Ischia	715
L'Acerbina, Cascina delle Terre Rosse	172
L'Alba, Vaglie	659
L'Ardenza, Cottanera	769
L'Autentica, Cantine del Notaio	733
L'Avija, Cascina Barisél	54
L'Enigma, Fatascià	777
L'Incanto, La Rendola	553
L'Insieme, Gianfranco Alessandria	106
L'Insieme, Elio Altare - Cascina Nuova	89
L'Insieme, Ca' Viola	76
L'Insieme, Giovanni Corino	92
L'Insieme, Mauro Molino	93
L'Insieme, La Morandina	68
L'Insieme, F.lli Revello	96
L'Insieme, Mauro Veglio	97
L'Insolente, Fatascià	777
L'Intruso, Giobatta Mandino Cane	171
L'Ora, Pravis	234
L'Ultima Spiaggia, Palazzone	670
La Calonica, La Calonica	546
La Capinera Chardonnay, Capinera	641
La Castellaccia, Agri Peccioli	613
La Castelletta Pinot Grigio, Boccadigabbia	631
La Cavata, Vini Pallavicini	689
La Comète, Institut Agricole Régional	16
La Corte, Castello di Querceto	503
La Cuenta Passito Giallo, Monsupello	215
La Faina, Baroncini	576
La Fornace, Fattoria Selvapiana	564
La Gioia, Riecine	499
La Goccia, Podere San Luigi	561
La Grola, Allegrini	294
La Macchia, Bellaria	187
La Massa, La Massa	558
La Mattana, Maria Donata Bianchi	170
La Palazzola V. T., La Palazzola	674
La Petrosa, Conte Zandotti	689
La Pineta, La Rendola	553
La Poja, Allegrini	294
La Quadratura del Cerchio, Fattoria San Lorenzo	638
La Querce, La Querce	510
La Rabitta Passito Bianco, Albino Piona	351
La Ricolma, San Giusto a Rentennano	501
La Rocchetta Cl. Brut, La Rocchetta	226
La Rosa Passito, Cavalchina	332
La Sassaia, Fattoria Poggio Romita	621
La Segreta Bianco, Planeta	774
La Segreta Rosso, Planeta	774
La Spinetta Oro, La Spinetta	58
La Suvera, Badia di Morrona	621
La Vigna di Alceo, Castello dei Rampolla	556
La Vigna di Sonvico, Cascina La Barbatella	126
Labirinto, Wandanna	610
Labruna, Podere Aia della Macina	585
Lacrima di Morro d'Alba, Luciano Landi	628
Lacrima di Morro d'Alba, Monteschiavo	636
Lacrima di Morro d'Alba Casato, Maurizio Marconi	649
Lacrima di Morro d'Alba del Pozzo Buono, Vicari	655
Lacrima di Morro d'Alba Gavigliano, Luciano Landi	628
Lacrima di Morro d'Alba Guardengo, Mario Lucchetti	654
Lacrima di Morro d'Alba Il Falconiere, Maurizio Marconi	649
Lacrima di Morro d'Alba Orgiolo, Marotti Campi	641
Lacrima di Morro d'Alba Passito, Luciano Landi	628
Lacrima di Morro d'Alba Rùbico, Marotti Campi	641
Lacrima di Morro d'Alba Sapore di Generazioni, Maurizio Marconi	649
Lacrima di Morro d'Alba Sensazioni di Frutto, Stefano Mancinelli	654
Lacrimæ Bacchi, Avide	770
Lacrime di Luna, Nobile Prima	491
Lago di Corbara, Decugnano dei Barbi	669
Lago di Corbara Fontauro, Freddano	678
Lago di Corbara Foresco, Barberani - Vallesanta	667
Lago di Corbara Pinot Nero, Decugnano dei Barbi	669
Lago di Corbara Rosso Villa Monticelli, Barberani - Vallesanta	667
Lago di Corbara Solideo, Tenuta di Salviano	676
Lagobruno, Incontri	589
Lailum, Fattoria Laila	638
Laio Passito, Dessilani	79
Lam'oro, S. M. Tenimenti Pile e Lamole	499
Lama del Tenente, Castel di Salve	756
Lamaione, Castelgiocondo	519
Lamarein, Josephus Mayr - Erbhof Unterganzner	262
Lambrusco, Stefano Spezia	221
Lambrusco Antica Osteria, Ermete Medici & Figli	451
Lambrusco dell'Emilia Le Viole, Cantine Dall'Asta	461
Lambrusco dell'Emilia Mefistofele, Cantine Dall'Asta	461
Lambrusco di Modena, Corte Manzini	438
Lambrusco di Modena Rosato, Corte Manzini	438
Lambrusco di Sorbara Tre Medaglie, Cantine Cavicchioli & Figli	462
Lambrusco Grasparossa di Castelvetro, Villa di Corlo	460
Lambrusco Grasparossa di Castelvetro Amabile, Corte Manzini	438
Lambrusco Grasparossa di Castelvetro Amabile Tre Medaglie, Cantine Cavicchioli & Figli	462
Lambrusco Grasparossa di Castelvetro Cinghio del Fojonco, Cantine Cooperative Riunite	458
Lambrusco Grasparossa di Castelvetro Dolce Bocciolo, Ermete Medici & Figli	451
Lambrusco Grasparossa di Castelvetro Gala Amabile, Chiarli 1860	446
Lambrusco Grasparossa di Castelvetro L'Acino, Corte Manzini	438
Lambrusco Grasparossa di Castelvetro Pruno Nero, Chiarli 1860	446
Lambrusco Grasparossa di Castelvetro Secco, Corte Manzini	438
Lambrusco Grasparossa di Castelvetro Semisecco, Corte Manzini	438
Lambrusco Grasparossa di Castelvetro Vign. Enrico Cialdini, Chiarli 1860	446
Lambrusco Grasparossa di Castelvetro Villa Cialdini, Chiarli 1860	446
Lambrusco Mantovano Rossissimo, Cant. Soc. Coop. di Quistello	224
Lambrusco Mantovano Rosso dei Concari, Lebovitz	216
Lambrusco Ottocento Nero, Cantine Cooperative Riunite	458
Lambrusco Vecchia Modena Premium, Chiarli 1860	446
Lamezia Bianco, Statti	761
Lamezia Bianco Tenuta Romeo, Cantine Lento	761
Lamezia Greco, Cantine Lento	761
Lamezia Greco, Statti	761
Lamezia Rosato Tenuta Romeo, Cantine Lento	761
Lamezia Rosso, Statti	761
Lamezia Rosso Mastro Giurato, Caparra & Siciliani	763
Lamezia Rosso Ris., Cantine Lento	761
Lamoremio, Benanti	782
Langhe Alteni di Brassica, Gaja	33
Langhe Arbarei La Bernardina, Ceretto	25
Langhe Arborina, Elio Altare - Cascina Nuova	89
Langhe Arneis, Fontanabianca	121
Langhe Arneis, Ugo Lequio	123
Langhe Arneis, Monfalletto - Cordero di Montezemolo	94
Langhe Arneis, Rocche Costamagna	97
Langhe Arneis Blangé, Ceretto	25
Langhe Bianco, I Paglieri	34
Langhe Bianco, Armando Parusso	111
Langhe Bianco, San Fereolo	78
Langhe Bianco, La Spinetta	58
Langhe Bianco, G. D. Vajra	44
Langhe Bianco Asso di Fiori, Braida	132
Langhe Bianco Ballarin, Cascina Ballarin	91
Langhe Bianco Binel, Ettore Germano	141
Langhe Bianco Bussiador, Aldo Conterno	107
Langhe Bianco di Busso, Piero Busso	120
Langhe Bianco Dives, G. B. Burlotto	150
Langhe Bianco Gastaldi, Gastaldi	121
Langhe Bianco Graffagno, Paolo Saracco	69
Langhe Bianco Il Fiore, Braida	132

Langhe Bianco L'Aura, Monti	111	Langhe Nebbiolo Ciabot della Luna, Gianni Voerzio	99
Langhe Bianco La Rocca, Albino Rocca	36	Langhe Nebbiolo Conteisa, Gaja	33
Langhe Bianco Lorenso, Luigi Baudana	139	Langhe Nebbiolo Costa Russi, Gaja	33
Langhe Bianco Matteo Correggia, Matteo Correggia	51	Langhe Nebbiolo Favot, Aldo Conterno	107
Langhe Bianco Montalupa, Ascheri	46	Langhe Nebbiolo Gambarin, Montaribaldi	35
Langhe Bianco Rolando, Bricco Maiolica	75	Langhe Nebbiolo Gavarini, Elio Grasso	110
Langhe Bianco Sanrocco, Poderi Colla	27	Langhe Nebbiolo il Crutin, Giovanni Manzone	110
Langhe Bianco Sorriso, Paolo Scavino	65	Langhe Nebbiolo La Malora, Terre da Vino	43
Langhe Bianco Suasì, Deltetto	51	Langhe Nebbiolo Lantasco, Ceretto	25
Langhe Bianco Sunsì, Batasiolo	90	Langhe Nebbiolo Lasarin, Poderi Marcarini	95
Langhe Bianco Tamardì, Monchiero Carbone	53	Langhe Nebbiolo Maria Grazia, Carlo Giacosa	34
Langhe Bianco Tre Uve, Malvirà	53	Langhe Nebbiolo Martinenga,	
Langhe Bric Millon, Angelo Negro & Figli	117	Tenuta Cisa Asinari dei Marchesi di Gresy	32
Langhe Bricco del Drago, Poderi Colla	27	Langhe Nebbiolo Prinsiot, F.lli Alessandria	149
Langhe Chardonnay, F.lli Bera	125	Langhe Nebbiolo Regret, Monchiero Carbone	53
Langhe Chardonnay, Tenuta Cisa Asinari dei Marchesi di Gresy	32	Langhe Nebbiolo Roccardo, Rocche Costamagna	97
Langhe Chardonnay, Cascina Cucco	139	Langhe Nebbiolo Settevie, Orlando Abrigo	146
Langhe Chardonnay, Destefanis	117	Langhe Nebbiolo Sorì S. Lorenzo, Gaja	33
Langhe Chardonnay, Ettore Germano	141	Langhe Nebbiolo Sorì Tildìn, Gaja	33
Langhe Chardonnay, Elio Grasso	110	Langhe Nebbiolo Sperss, Gaja	33
Langhe Chardonnay, Moccagatta	35	Langhe Nebbiolo V. Botti, Pecchenino	77
Langhe Chardonnay, La Morandina	68	Langhe Paitin, Paitin	124
Langhe Chardonnay, Vignaioli Elvio Pertinace	148	Langhe Pertinace, Vignaioli Elvio Pertinace	148
Langhe Chardonnay, Ronchi	154	Langhe Rosso, F.lli Mossio	133
Langhe Chardonnay, Sinaglio	28	Langhe Rosso Alta Bussia, Attilio Ghisolfi	109
Langhe Chardonnay, Vigna Rionda - Massolino	142	Langhe Rosso Arte, Domenico Clerico	106
Langhe Chardonnay Alessandro, Gianfranco Bovio	91	Langhe Rosso Balàu, Ettore Germano	141
Langhe Chardonnay Bastia, Conterno Fantino	108	Langhe Rosso Ballarin, Cascina Ballarin	91
Langhe Chardonnay Bianch del Luv, Paolo Saracco	69	Langhe Rosso Batié, Gianni Gagliardo	160
Langhe Chardonnay Buscät, F.lli Alessandria	149	Langhe Rosso Bouquet, F.lli Seghesio	114
Langhe Chardonnay Buschet, Moccagatta	35	Langhe Rosso Bric du Luv, Ca' Viola	76
Langhe Chardonnay Ca' Lunga, F.lli Giacosa	122	Langhe Rosso Bric Quercia, Tenuta Carretta	129
Langhe Chardonnay Cadet, Bruno Rocca	37	Langhe Rosso Bricco Rovella, Armando Parusso	111
Langhe Chardonnay Collaretto, F.lli Oddero	95	Langhe Rosso Bricco Serra, F.lli Cigliuti	120
Langhe Chardonnay da Bertu, Albino Rocca	36	Langhe Rosso Brumaio, San Fereolo	78
Langhe Chardonnay Elioro, Monfalletto - Cordero di Montezemolo	94	Langhe Rosso Buio, Enzo Boglietti	90
Langhe Chardonnay Flavo, Rocche Costamagna	97	Langhe Rosso Cadò, Anna Maria Abbona	80
Langhe Chardonnay L'Angelica, Podere Rocche dei Manzoni	112	Langhe Rosso Camerlot, Pira	78
Langhe Chardonnay PiodiLei, Pio Cesare	26	Langhe Rosso Castlé, Gastaldi	121
Langhe Chardonnay Prasuè, Paolo Saracco	69	Langhe Rosso Centobricchi, Mauro Sebaste	28
Langhe Chardonnay Roera, F.lli Giacosa	122	Langhe Rosso Corale, Paolo Scavino	65
Langhe Chardonnay Scapulin, Giuseppe Cortese	33	Langhe Rosso Da Pruvé, Ca' Rome' - Romano Marengo	30
Langhe Chardonnay Serbato, Batasiolo	90	Langhe Rosso Donald, Poderi Marcarini	95
Langhe Chardonnay Sermine, Ca' del Baio	146	Langhe Rosso Dossi Rossi, Monti	111
Langhe Chardonnay Stissa d'le Favole, Montaribaldi	35	Langhe Rosso Enrico I, Roberto Sarotto	161
Langhe Chardonnay Très, Orlando Abrigo	146	Langhe Rosso Fabio, Andrea Oberto	94
Langhe Chardonnay V. La Villa, Gianfranco Bovio	91	Langhe Rosso Faletto, Cascina Bongiovanni	64
Langhe Darmagi, Gaja	33	Langhe Rosso Fantasia 4.20, Rino Varaldo	37
Langhe Dolcetto, Anna Maria Abbona	80	Langhe Rosso Gastaldi, Gastaldi	121
Langhe Dolcetto, Elio Altare - Cascina Nuova	89	Langhe Rosso I Cortini, Castello di Neive	161
Langhe Dolcetto, Bricco del Cucù	44	Langhe Rosso I Due Ricu, Marziano ed Enrico Abbona	75
Langhe Dolcetto Barturot, Ca' Viola	76	Langhe Rosso Jula, Cascina Adelaide	154
Langhe Dolcetto Busiord, Scagliola	48	Langhe Rosso L'Assemblato, Raffaele Gili	60
Langhe Dolcetto La Chiesetta, Il Colombo - Barone Riccati	105	Langhe Rosso La Bisbetica, Ada Nada	147
Langhe Dolcetto Visadì, Domenico Clerico	106	Langhe Rosso Le Marne Grigie, Matteo Correggia	51
Langhe Favorita, Cascina Chicco	50	Langhe Rosso Livraie, Orlando Abrigo	146
Langhe Favorita, Raffaele Gili	60	Langhe Rosso Long Now, Pelissero	148
Langhe Favorita, Gianluigi Lano	26	Langhe Rosso Lorenso, Luigi Baudana	139
Langhe Favorita, Malvirà	53	Langhe Rosso Lorié, Bricco Maiolica	75
Langhe Favorita, Pelissero	148	Langhe Rosso Luigi Einaudi, Einaudi	77
Langhe Favorita, Porello	54	Langhe Rosso Luna, F.lli Alessandria	149
Langhe Favorita, Vielmin	62	Langhe Rosso Martin Sec, San Romano	79
Langhe Favorita Sarvai, Deltetto	51	Langhe Rosso Mondo, Cascina Cucco	139
Langhe Freisa, Cant. del Pino	31	Langhe Rosso Monprà, Conterno Fantino	108
Langhe Freisa, Gianluigi Lano	26	Langhe Rosso Monsordo La Bernardina, Ceretto	25
Langhe Freisa, Pelissero	148	Langhe Rosso Montegrilli, Elvio Cogno	127
Langhe Freisa Kyè, G. D. Vajra	44	Langhe Rosso Nej, Icardi	67
Langhe Freisa La Violetta, Piero Gatti	136	Langhe Rosso Pafoj, Icardi	67
Langhe Freisa Sotti I Bastioni, Gianni Voerzio	99	Langhe Rosso Pe Mol, Luciano Sandrone	42
Langhe La Villa, Elio Altare - Cascina Nuova	89	Langhe Rosso Pedrocha, Hilberg - Pasquero	131
Langhe Larigi, Elio Altare - Cascina Nuova	89	Langhe Rosso Pi Cit, Marchesi di Barolo	40
Langhe Mores, G. B. Burlotto	150	Langhe Rosso Pian del Gäje, Ca' d'Gal	136
Langhe Nebbiolo, Azelia	63	Langhe Rosso Pinay, Attilio Ghisolfi	109
Langhe Nebbiolo, Enzo Boglietti	90	Langhe Rosso Piria, Vigna Rionda - Massolino	142
Langhe Nebbiolo, Giacomo Brezza & Figli	38	Langhe Rosso Quartetto, Aldo Conterno	107
Langhe Nebbiolo, Piero Busso	120	Langhe Rosso Quatr Nas, Podere Rocche dei Manzoni	112
Langhe Nebbiolo, Cascina Ballarin	91	Langhe Rosso Rabajolo, Bruno Rocca	37
Langhe Nebbiolo, Castello di Verduno	150	Langhe Rosso Riella, Sergio Degiorgis	103
Langhe Nebbiolo, Giuseppe Cortese	33	Langhe Rosso Rosso dei Dardi,	
Langhe Nebbiolo, Deltetto	51	Alessandro e Gian Natale Fantino	109
Langhe Nebbiolo, Einaudi	77	Langhe Rosso Seifile, Fiorenzo Nada	147
Langhe Nebbiolo, Fontanabianca	121	Langhe Rosso Serrapiù, Gianni Voerzio	99
Langhe Nebbiolo, Cascina Luisin	31	Langhe Rosso Sinaij, Sinaglio	28
Langhe Nebbiolo, Malvirà	53	Langhe Rosso Suo di Giacomo, Eugenio Bocchino	160
Langhe Nebbiolo, Bartolo Mascarello	40	Langhe Rosso Tris, Giovanni Manzone	110
Langhe Nebbiolo, Moccagatta	35	Langhe Rosso Villa Martis, Tenuta Cisa Asinari dei Marchesi di Gresy	32
Langhe Nebbiolo, Mauro Molino	93	Langhe Rosso Virtus, Tenuta Cisa Asinari dei Marchesi di Gresy	32
Langhe Nebbiolo, Monfalletto - Cordero di Montezemolo	94	Langhe Rosso Yeta, Giovanni Battista Gillardi	80
Langhe Nebbiolo, Cascina Morassino	32	Langhe Sassisto, F.lli Bera	125
Langhe Nebbiolo, Andrea Oberto	94	Langhe V. Maestro, Pecchenino	77
Langhe Nebbiolo, Armando Parusso	111	Langhe V. Meira, Einaudi	77
Langhe Nebbiolo, Pelissero	148	Langhe Vendemmiaio, Tenuta La Volta - Cabutto	43
Langhe Nebbiolo, Vignaioli Elvio Pertinace	148	Latinia, Cant. Soc. di Santadi	797
Langhe Nebbiolo, Produttori del Barbaresco	36	Laurento Chardonnay, Umberto Cesari	436
Langhe Nebbiolo, F.lli Revello	96	Le Ancore, Colle di Maggio	690
Langhe Nebbiolo, Ruggeri Corsini	113	Le Anfore, Colle di Maggio	690
Langhe Nebbiolo, Giorgio Scarzello e Figli	42	Le Banche, Cascina delle Terre Rosse	172
Langhe Nebbiolo, G. D. Vajra	44	Le Braci, Masseria Monaci	742
Langhe Nebbiolo, Rino Varaldo	37	Le Briciole Passito, Masseria Monaci	742
Langhe Nebbiolo, Eraldo Viberti	98	Le Brusche, Tenute Ambrogio e Giovanni Folonari	493
Langhe Nebbiolo, Osvaldo Viberti	98	Le Busche, Umani Ronchi	644
Langhe Nebbiolo Alladio, F.lli Bera	125	Le Cave Chardonnay, Fattoria Le Terrazze	642
Langhe Nebbiolo Blagheur, Michele Taliano	116	Le Cupole di Trinoro, Tenuta di Trinoro	584
Langhe Nebbiolo Bric del Baio, Ca' del Baio	146	Le Fagge Chardonnay, Castello d' Albola	565
Langhe Nebbiolo Castellero, Araldica - Il Cascinone	59	Le Lave, Bertani	311
		Le Macchiole, Le Macchiole	470

Le Marangole, Castello d' Albola 565
Le Passule, Librandi 759
Le Pergole Torte, Montevertine 567
Le Poggere, Cristine Vaselli 683
Le Prata, Villa Le Prata 538
Le Pratole, Rocca di Castagnoli 500
Le Prisonnier, Anselmet 19
Le Ricordanze Passito, Cosimo Taurino 745
Le Ripe Bianco, Federici 694
Le Ripe Rosso, Federici 694
Le Selle Passito, Coffele 330
Le Solagne V. T., Fattoria Dezi 651
Le Stanze, Poliziano 547
Le Terrazze del Castello, Castagnoli 477
Le Terrine, Castello della Paneretta 466
Le Vignole, Paola Di Mauro 686
Le Voliere Cabernet Sauvignon, Castello di Modanella 570
Le Volte, Tenuta dell' Ornellaia 470
Leila, Alberto Loi 792
Leone d'Almerita, Tasca d'Almerita 778
Leone di Carobbio, Carobbio 555
Leone Rosso, Casato Prime Donne Donatella Cinelli Colombini 523
Leopold Cuvée Blanc, Fiegl 391
Leporello, Morgassi Superiore 85
Lessini Durello M. Cl., Cant. Soc. di Monteforte d'Alpone 349
Lessona, Sella 100
Lessona S. Sebastiano allo Zoppo, Sella 100
Leucós Bianco, Ronco dei Pini 411
Leukon Chardonnay, La Cant. dei Colli Ripani 648
Leverano Bianco V. del Saraceno, Conti Zecca 746
Leverano Rosato V. del Saraceno, Conti Zecca 746
Leverano Rosso, Cant. Soc. Coop. Leverano 754
Leverano Rosso Terra Ris., Conti Zecca 746
Leverano Rosso V. del Saraceno, Conti Zecca 746
Liano, Umberto Cesari 436
Libatio Lunae, Sant'Agnese 615
Libente, Valle del Sole 604
Liber Bianco, Fasoli 292
Liburnio, Orlandi Contucci Ponno 705
Lighea, Tenuta di Donnafugata 772
Límes Rosso, Ronco dei Pini 411
Limitone dei Greci, Vinagri 756
Linagre Sauvignon di Villa Angela, Ercole Velenosi 626
Linfa, Nestore Bosco 701
Lis, Lis Neris 421
Lis Neris, Lis Neris 421
Lison-Pramaggiore Cabernet Franc, Podere del Ger 405
Lison-Pramaggiore Cabernet Franc Faè, Villa Frattina 404
Lison-Pramaggiore Cabernet Hora Sexta, Mosole 350
Lison-Pramaggiore Cabernet Sauvignon, Villa Frattina 404
Lison-Pramaggiore Chardonnay, Podere del Ger 405
Lison-Pramaggiore Chardonnay, Villa Frattina 404
Lison-Pramaggiore Cl. Tocai Jutì, Bosco del Merlo 288
Lison-Pramaggiore Merlot, Mosole 350
Lison-Pramaggiore Merlot, Podere del Ger 405
Lison-Pramaggiore Merlot Campo Camino, Bosco del Merlo 288
Lison-Pramaggiore Merlot Faè, Villa Frattina 404
Lison-Pramaggiore Pinot Grigio, Podere del Ger 405
Lison-Pramaggiore Refosco P. R. Roggio dei Roveri, Bosco del Merlo 288
Lison-Pramaggiore Sauvignon, Mosole 350
Lison-Pramaggiore Sauvignon, Villa Frattina 404
Lison-Pramaggiore Sauvignon Turranio, Bosco del Merlo 288
Lison-Pramaggiore Tocai Italico, Tenuta Teracrea 349
Litora Naumachos, Vinicola del Tesino 634
Litra, Abbazia Santa Anastasia 768
Livernano, Livernano 567
Lo Flapì, Di Barrò 20
Loazzolo Borgo Maragliano V. T., Borgo Maragliano 100
Loazzolo Piasa Rischei, Forteto della Luja 101
Locorosso Rosso, Pratesi 474
Locorotondo, Vini Classici Cardone 747
Locorotondo, I Pastini - Carparelli 754
Locorotondo, Cant. Soc.Coop. del Locorotondo 747
Locorotondo Riserva del Presidente,
    Cant. Soc.Coop. del Locorotondo 747
Locorotondo Talné, Borgo Canale 743
Locorotondo Vign. In Tallinajo, Cant. Soc.Coop. del Locorotondo 747
Locride, Stelitano 758
Logaiolo, Fattoria dell' Aiola 483
Longobardo Rosso, Enzo Mecella 633
Lucciolaio, Torraccia di Presura 505
Luce, Luce 531
Luce e Colori Bianco, Centonze 788
Luce e Colori Rosso, Centonze 788
Lucente, Luce 531
Lucilla, Farnetella 586
Lucumone, Ficomontanino 599
Ludi, Ercole Velenosi 626
Ludus, Marco Carpineti 691
Luenzo, Vincenzo Cesani 577
Lugana, Ca' Lojera 213
Lugana, Monte Cicogna 200
Lugana, Ottella 316
Lugana, Tenuta Roveglia 224
Lugana Antica Corte Ialidy, Marangona 223
Lugana Brolettino Grande Annata, Ca' dei Frati 212
Lugana Brut Cl. Cuvée dei Frati, Ca' dei Frati 212
Lugana Brut Sebastian, Provenza 195
Lugana Collo Lungo Et. Nera, Visconti Podere Sant'Onorata 220
Lugana di Sirmione Vigna Bragagna, Avanzi 221
Lugana Gran Guardia, Giacomo Montresor 342
Lugana I Frati, Ca' dei Frati 212
Lugana Il Brolettino, Ca' dei Frati 212
Lugana Il Brolettino Grande Annata, Ca' dei Frati 212
Lugana Le Creete, Ottella 316
Lugana Marogne, F.lli Zeni 289

Lugana Pergola, Cantine Valtenesi - Lugana 222
Lugana S. Benedetto, Zenato 316
Lugana S. Onorata, Visconti Podere Sant'Onorata 220
Lugana Selva Capuzza, Cantine Colli a Lago 220
Lugana Sergio Zenato, Zenato 316
Lugana Sup., Ca' Lojera 213
Lugana Sup. Ca' Molin, Provenza 195
Lugana Sup. Cios, Cantine Valtenesi - Lugana 222
Lugana Sup. Molceo, Ottella 316
Lugana Sup. Molin, Provenza 195
Lugana Sup. Pergola, Cantine Valtenesi - Lugana 222
Lugana Sup. S. Onorata, Visconti Podere Sant'Onorata 220
Lugana Sup. Sel. Fabio Contato, Provenza 195
Lugana Sup. Selva Capuzza, Cantine Colli a Lago 220
Lugana Sup. Vigna di Catullo, Tenuta Roveglia 224
Lugana Tenuta Maiolo, Provenza 195
Lugana V. Alte, F.lli Zeni 289
Lugana Vecia Musolina, Marangona 223
Lugana Vign. Massoni Santa Cristina, Zenato 316
Lugana Vign. San Martino Il Sestante, Tommasi Viticoltori 325
Lugana Vigna Silva, Ca' Lojera 213
Lumen, Gualdo del Re 589
Lunà Brut, Luigi Spertino 104
Lunaia Rosso, La Stellata 605
Lunaria Sauvignon, Castelluccio 446
Lupicaia, Castello del Terriccio 482
Luzzana, Giovanni Cherchi 801
LV, Tenuta San Sebastiano 102
M, Montevertine 567
M.to Bianco Airales, Vicara 133
M.to Bianco EnneEnne, L'Armangia 56
M.to Bianco Foravia, Cascina Barisél 54
M.to Bianco I Fossaretti, Bertelli 72
M.to Bianco Il Barigi, Traversa - Cascina Bertolotto 143
M.to Bianco Il Capè, Gaggino 163
M.to Bianco Mimosa, Colle Manora 131
M.to Bianco Villa Drago, F.lli Rovero 30
M.to Bianco Villa Guani, F.lli Rovero 30
M.to Cabernet Fossaretti, Bertelli 72
M.to Dolcetto, Castello del Poggio 130
M.to Dolcetto Nibiô, Cascina Ulivi 162
M.to Dolcetto Plissé, Carlo Benotto 71
M.to Freisa La Selva di Moirano, Antica Casa Vinicola Scarpa 126
M.to Freisa V. Fiordaliso, Daniele Saccoletto 163
M.to Gamba di Pernice, Carlo Benotto 71
M.to Montemareto Countacc!, Michele Chiarlo 47
M.to Pieve di San Michele, Cave di Moleto 129
M.to Pomona, Bersano & Riccadonna 125
M.to Rosso Antico Vitigno, Sciorio 73
M.to Rosso Bricco Maddalena, Cascina La Maddalena 132
M.to Rosso Bricco San Tomaso, La Scamuzza 152
M.to Rosso Bruno Broglia, Gian Piero Broglia - Tenuta La Meirana 84
M.to Rosso Cabernet, F.lli Rovero 30
M.to Rosso Cascina Bricco del Sole, Icardi 67
M.to Rosso Crebarné, Carlo Quarello 70
M.to Rosso dei Marchesi, Marchesi Alfieri 134
M.to Rosso Do-Sol, Tenuta San Sebastiano 102
M.to Rosso Eresia, Luigi Tacchino 60
M.to Rosso Genesi, Cantine Sant'Agata 138
M.to Rosso Il Bacialé, Braida 132
M.to Rosso Il Ticco, Gaggino 163
M.to Rosso l'Uccelletta, Vicara 133
M.to Rosso Lajetto, F.lli Rovero 30
M.to Rosso Le Grive, Forteto della Luja 101
M.to Rosso Malidea, Iuli - Ca.Vi.Mon. 69
M.to Rosso Matot, Valfieri 74
M.to Rosso Mon Mayor, Bertelli 72
M.to Rosso Monterovere, Cantine Sant'Agata 138
M.to Rosso Mulej, Cave di Moleto 129
M.to Rosso N° 1, Luigi Spertino 104
M.to Rosso Nebieul, Carlo Benotto 71
M.to Rosso Palo Alto, Colle Manora 131
M.to Rosso Policalpo, Cascina Castlèt 72
M.to Rosso Rocca Schiavino, F.lli Rovero 30
M.to Rosso Rosso Scarpa, Antica Casa Vinicola Scarpa 126
M.to Rosso Rubello, Vicara 133
M.to Rosso Ruvrin, Cascina Bondi 162
M.to Rosso S. Germano, Marchesi Alfieri 134
M.to Rosso Sul Bric, Franco M. Martinetti 144
M.to Rosso Talin, Agostino Pavia e Figli 23
M.to Trinum, Cascina Giovinale 162
Macchiona, La Stoppa 452
Madégo, La Cappuccina 308
Madreselva, Casale del Giglio 681
Maestro Raro, Fattoria di Felsina 485
Magari, Cà Marcanda 475
Magilda Rosato, Barsento 755
Magliano, Claudio Morelli 634
Magna Grecia Rosso, Vintripodi Calabria 764
Magnificat Cabernet Sauvignon, Drei Donà Tenuta La Palazza 443
Magno Megonio, Librandi 759
Magone, Sergio Mottura 684
Majara, Mille Una 746
Majo San Lorenzo, Aziende Vinicole Miceli 780
Mal Borghetto, Le Chiusure 225
Malbek Terre Rosse, Morella 754
Malena, Pacina 598
Malicchia Mapicchia, Barsento 755
Malise Pignoletto - Chardonnay, Umberto Cesari 436
Malvasia, Cant. Prod. di Cormons 370
Malvasia, Il Lebbio 578
Malvasia, Pierpaolo Pecorari 421
Malvasia Bianca, Az. Agr. Casale Mattia 693
Malvasia Campo di Fiori, Vigneto Due Santi 290
Malvasia del Lazio Rumon, Conte Zandotti 689
Malvasia del Lazio Terre dei Grifi, Fontana Candida 687

Malvasia del Lazio Villanova, Cant. Cerveteri	683
Malvasia del Veneto, Tenuta Teracrea	349
Malvasia dell'Emilia Dolce Incanto, Corte Manzini	438
Malvasia dell'Emilia Dolce Nebbie d'Autunno, Ermete Medici & Figli	451
Malvasia della Basilicata Topazio, Cons. Vitic. Ass. del Vulture	730
Malvasia delle Lipari Naturale, Cantine Colosi	785
Malvasia delle Lipari Passita, Cantine Colosi	785
Malvasia delle Lipari Passito, Barone di Villagrande	776
Malvasia di Bosa, Columbu	802
Malvasia di Bosa, F.lli Porcu	803
Malvasia di Cagliari Donna Jolanda, Meloni Vini	798
Malvasia di Cagliari Nuscara, Cant. di Quartu	804
Malvasia di Castelnuovo Don Bosco, Cascina Gilli	62
Malvasia di Castelnuovo Don Bosco Rosa Canina, Cantine Bava	70
Malvasia Istriana, Russolo	422
Malvasia L'Accesa, I Campetti	617
Malvasia Letizia, Poderi di San Pietro	209
Malvasia & Moscato Dolce, Carra	445
Malvasia Partemio, Lomazzi & Sarli	754
Malvasia Puntinata La Giara, Vini Pallavicini	689
Malvasia Puntinata Stillato, Vini Pallavicini	689
Malvasia Toscana, San Lorenzo	618
Malvasia Villa Marone, Bisi	209
Mamertino Rosso, Grasso	786
Mammolo, Cennatoio Intervineas	556
Mandrione dell'Osa, Poliziano	547
Mandrolisai Rosso Sup., Cant. Soc. del Mandrolisai	804
Manero, Fattoria del Cerro	544
Manna, Franz Haas	277
Mante'nghja, Capichera	791
Mantonico di Bianco, Vintripodi Calabria	764
Manzoni Bianco, Casa Roma	327
Manzoni Bianco, Giorgio Cecchetto	352
Manzoni Bianco, Conte Collalto	333
Manzoni Bianco, Gregoletto	304
Manzoni Bianco Novalis, Bonotto delle Tezze	352
Manzoni Liquoroso, G. B. Cerletti Scuola Enol. di Coneglianо	346
Marchese di Montefusco Bianco, Co.di.vin. - Tenuta Di Maria	788
Marchese di Montefusco Rosso, Co.di.vin. - Tenuta Di Maria	788
Marciliano, Falesco	688
Marco Nero, Contadi Castaldi	182
Margherita Bianco, Trabucchi	297
Maria Margherita, San Vettore	502
Marinali Bianco, Villa Sandi	346
Marinali Rosso, Villa Sandi	346
Marino Colle Picchioni Oro, Paola Di Mauro	686
Marino Etichetta Verde, Paola Di Mauro	686
Marinò Rosso, Luigi Vivacqua	762
Marino Sup., Gotto d'Oro	692
Mario Schiopetto Bianco, Schiopetto	362
Marmorelle Bianco, Tenute Rubino	739
Marmorelle Rosso, Tenute Rubino	739
Marramiero Brut Cl., Marramiero	705
Marsala Sup. Oro, Carlo Pellegrino	773
Marsala Sup. Oro Vigna La Miccia, Marco De Bartoli	771
Marsala Sup. Ris. 1986, Marco De Bartoli	771
Marsala Sup. Ris. 20 Anni, Marco De Bartoli	771
Marsala Sup. Ris. Ambra Semisecco Vecchioflorio, Cantine Florio	772
Marsala Sup. Ris. Dom Pellegrino, Carlo Pellegrino	773
Marsala Sup. Secco Ambra Vecchioflorio, Cantine Florio	772
Marsala Sup. Vecchioflorio, Cantine Florio	772
Marsala Vergine Baglio Florio, Cantine Florio	772
Marsala Vergine Baglio Florio Oro, Cantine Florio	772
Marsala Vergine Soleras, Carlo Pellegrino	773
Marsala Vergine Soleras Ris. 12 anni, Cantine Rallo	773
Marsiliana, Fattoria Le Corti	574
Martà, Fattoria San Francesco	758
Marzemino, La Vigna	217
Marzemino, Vallarom	229
Marzemino dei Ziresi Poiema, Eugenio Rosi	249
Marzieno, Fattoria Zerbina	440
Masetto Bianco, Endrizzi	244
Masetto Dulcis, Endrizzi	244
Masetto Nero, Endrizzi	244
Maso Furli Rosso, Maso Furli	237
Massaretta, Cima	513
Masseo, Vaglie	659
Masseria Maime, Tormaresca	752
Masseto, Tenuta dell' Ornellaia	470
Massicone, Castelluccio	446
Maté, Sottimano	124
Mater Matuta, Casale del Giglio	681
Matriarca, Le Calvane	551
Maurizio Zanella, Ca' del Bosco	196
Maurleo, Pietro Beconcini	619
Maximo, Umani Ronchi	644
Megara, Duca di Salaparuta - Vini Corvo	769
Melissa Asylia, Librandi	759
Melissa Lumia, Val di Neto	764
Melissa Rosso, Val di Neto	764
Menade, Cant. Cerveteri	683
Menj Bianco, Tenuta Villanova	389
Meraco Rosso, Cantine San Marco	685
Mercuria Rosso, Castel Noarna	239
Merlanico - De Conciliis - Barone Pizzini, Viticoltori De Conciliis	720
Merlar Rosso, F.lli Zeni	289
Merlot, Carra	445
Merlot, Casale del Giglio	681
Merlot, Castagnoli	477
Merlot, Castello delle Regine	658
Merlot, Colle San Lorenzo	684
Merlot, Conte Zandotti	689
Merlot, Fanini	661
Merlot, Feudo Principi di Butera	767
Merlot, La Palazzola	674
Merlot, Planeta	774
Merlot, Cantine Rallo	773
Merlot, Terre del Carpine	677
Merlot, Terre di Salemi	787
Merlot, Villa Pillo	502
Merlot Baladello, Ferghettina	197
Merlot Baolar, Pierpaolo Pecorari	421
Merlot Bosco Grande, Cant. Beato Bartolomeo Da Breganze	346
Merlot degli Artisti, Cantine Leonardo da Vinci	593
Merlot dei Colli Trevigiani, Gregoletto	304
Merlot del Lazio, Fontana Candida	687
Merlot del Lazio, Gotto d'Oro	692
Merlot dell'Umbria, Falesco	688
Merlot della Bergamasca, Cant. Soc. Bergamasca	210
Merlot I Legni, Russolo	422
Merlot Mandrarossa, Settesoli	775
Merlot Mandrielle, Castello Banfi	515
Merlot Maria Teresa, San Vettore	502
Merlot Orgno, Fasoli	292
Merlot Principe di Corleone, Pollara	786
Merlot Rendola, La Rendola	553
Merlot Ròs di Ròl, Sant'Elena	393
Merlot Sant'Adele, Villa Pillo	502
Mesolone Rosso, Barni	46
Messapia, Leone de Castris	751
Messorio, Le Macchiole	470
Mezzopane, Poggio San Polo	609
Migoléta, Longariva	243
Mila Bianco, Colle Manora	131
Millanni, Guicciardini Strozzi - Fattoria Cusona	578
Minaia, Franco M. Martinetti	144
Minnella, Benanti	782
Mirasco, Tenuta di Poggio Cosmiano	614
Mirju Passito, Pedra Majore	795
Mirum, La Monacesca	637
Mirus, La Monacesca	637
Mito, Fattoria Paradiso	432
Mito, San Savino - Poderi Capecci	649
Mitylus, Mormoraia	582
Mizzole Rosso, Cecilia Beretta	341
Mo.to Bianco Bricco Manè, Villa Giada	57
Mo.to Rosso, Villa Giada	57
Modus, Tenimenti Ruffino	564
Molì Bianco, Di Majo Norante	698
Molì Rosso, Di Majo Norante	698
Molino delle Balze, Rocca di Castagnoli	500
Molise Aglianico Contado, Di Majo Norante	698
Molise Don Luigi, Di Majo Norante	698
Molise Falanghina, Borgo di Colloredo	697
Molise Falanghina, Di Majo Norante	698
Molise Greco, Di Majo Norante	698
Molise Montepulciano, Borgo di Colloredo	697
Molise Trebbiano, Borgo di Colloredo	697
Momenti, Vaglie	659
Mondeserto Passito, Bruno Agostinetto	334
Monemvasia, Casalone	101
Monemvasia Passito, Casalone	101
Monferrato Bianco Alteserre, Cantine Bava	70
Monferrato Bianco Camillona, Araldica - Il Cascinone	59
Monferrato Bianco Ferro di Cavallo, La Giribaldina	48
Monferrato Bianco Grisello, Castello di Lignano	81
Monferrato Bianco Lipiai, Cant. Soc. di Vinchio - Vaglio Serra	153
Monferrato Bianco Müller Thurgau, Villa Sparina	86
Monferrato Bianco Munsrèt, Casalone	101
Monferrato Bianco Noè, Cascina La Barbatella	126
Monferrato Bianco Non è, Cascina La Barbatella	126
Monferrato Bianco Puntet, Tenuta La Meridiana	116
Monferrato Bianco Sivoy, La Ghersa	103
Monferrato Bianco Tra Donne Sole, Terre da Vino	43
Monferrato Freisa, La Zucca	119
Monferrato Freisa Bioc, Isabella	119
Monferrato Freisa La Bernardina, Giulio Accornero e Figli	151
Monferrato Freisa La Frassinella, Castello di Lignano	81
Monferrato Rosso, Cascina Gilli	62
Monferrato Rosso, Tenuta dei Fiori	49
Monferrato Rosso Amani, Colonna	152
Monferrato Rosso Amis, Cascina Garitina	59
Monferrato Rosso Arbiola, Tenuta dell'Arbiola	135
Monferrato Rosso Blasonato, Castello di Lignano	81
Monferrato Rosso Centenario, Giulio Accornero e Figli	151
Monferrato Rosso di Malì, Il Vignale	128
Monferrato Rosso Dialogo, Gancia	56
Monferrato Rosso Emmerosso, Malgrà	104
Monferrato Rosso Innominato, La Guardia	118
Monferrato Rosso Just, La Giustiniana	85
Monferrato Rosso La Ghersa, La Ghersa	103
Monferrato Rosso La Virasa Vejia, Giacomo Scagliola e Figlio	156
Monferrato Rosso Le Pernici, Gian Piero Broglia - Tenuta La Meirana	84
Monferrato Rosso Lhennius, Castello di Lignano	81
Monferrato Rosso Luce Monaca, Araldica - Il Cascinone	59
Monferrato Rosso Maniero, Villa Fiorita	157
Monferrato Rosso Mondone, Colonna	152
Monferrato Rosso Mystère, Cascina La Barbatella	126
Monferrato Rosso Nero di Villa, Villa Fiorita	157
Monferrato Rosso Onero, Tenuta Castello di Razzano	29
Monferrato Rosso Piagé, La Ghersa	103
Monferrato Rosso Pin, La Spinetta	58
Monferrato Rosso Reginal, Sciorio	73
Monferrato Rosso Renero, Araldica - Il Cascinone	59
Monferrato Rosso Rivaia, Tenuta La Meridiana	116
Monferrato Rosso Rivalta, Villa Sparina	86
Monferrato Rosso Rus, Casalone	101
Monferrato Rosso Sampò, Villa Sparina	86
Monferrato Rosso Sonvico, Cascina La Barbatella	126
Monferrato Rosso Tantra, Franco e Mario Scrimaglio	127
Monferrato Villa Pattono, Renato Ratti	96

Monfort Rosa, Casata Monfort 251
Monica di Sardegna Antigua, Cant. Soc. di Santadi 797
Monica di Sardegna Arenada, Cantine di Dolianova 793
Monica di Sardegna Duca di Mandas, Cant. Soc. della Trexenta 799
Monica di Sardegna Elima, F.lli Pala 800
Monica di Sardegna Il Germoglio, Meloni Vini 798
Monica di Sardegna Insula, Sardus Pater 797
Monica di Sardegna Karel, Ferruccio Deiana 800
Monica di Sardegna Perdera, Antonio Argiolas 799
Monica di Sardegna Torremora, Josto Puddu 804
Monica di Sardegna Tuerra, Cant. di Quartu 804
Monile, Viticcio 508
Monprà, Conterno Fantino 108
Monreale Alhambra, Spadafora 777
Monreale Pietragavina Nero d'Avola, Tamburello 786
Monreale Pietragavina Perricone, Tamburello 786
Monsavium Passito, Valentino Fiorini 627
Mont'Anello Bianco, Boccadigabbia 631
Montalupa Rosso, Ascheri 46
Monte del Drago Rosso, Musella 319
Monte della Guardia Rosato, Ca' Lojera 213
Monte della Guardia Rosso, Ca' Lojera 213
Montecalvi, Montecalvi 602
Montecarlo Bianco, Fattoria del Buonamico 540
Montecarlo Bianco, Fattoria del Teso 541
Montecarlo Bianco, Wandanna 610
Montecarlo Bianco Stati d'Animo, Gino Fuso Carmignani 540
Montecarlo Rosso, Fattoria del Buonamico 540
Montecarlo Rosso, Fattoria del Teso 541
Montecarlo Rosso, Wandanna 610
Montecarlo Rosso Sassonero, Gino Fuso Carmignani 540
Montechiari Cabernet, Fattoria di Montechiari 541
Montechiari Chardonnay, Fattoria di Montechiari 541
Montechiari Merlot, Fattoria di Montechiari 541
Montechiari Nero, Fattoria di Montechiari 541
Montechiari Pinot Nero, Fattoria di Montechiari 541
Montechiari Rosso, Fattoria di Montechiari 541
Montecompatri Colonna Sup. Virtù Romane, Tenuta Le Quinte 693
Montecucco Sangiovese, Orciaverde 597
Montecucco Sangiovese, Poggio Saccone 594
Montecucco Sangiovese Ris., Orciaverde 597
Montefalco Rosso, Antonelli - San Marco 665
Montefalco Rosso, Arnaldo Caprai - Val di Maggio 665
Montefalco Rosso, Còlpetrone 664
Montefalco Rosso, Podere Perticaia 664
Montefalco Rosso, Rocca di Fabbri 666
Montefalco Rosso, Ruggeri 678
Montefalco Rosso, Scacciadiavoli 666
Montefalco Rosso, Spoletoducale 674
Montefalco Rosso, Terre de' Trinci 663
Montefalco Rosso Casale Triocco, Spoletoducale 674
Montefalco Rosso Le Mure Saracene, Goretti 673
Montefalco Rosso Ris., Fattoria Milziade Antano 676
Montefalco Rosso Ris., Antonelli - San Marco 665
Montefalco Rosso Ris., Terre de' Trinci 663
Montefalco Sagrantino, Fattoria Milziade Antano 676
Montefalco Sagrantino, Antonelli - San Marco 665
Montefalco Sagrantino, Castello di Antigniano - Brogal Vini 672
Montefalco Sagrantino, Còlpetrone 664
Montefalco Sagrantino, Podere Perticaia 664
Montefalco Sagrantino, Rocca di Fabbri 666
Montefalco Sagrantino, San Lorenzo 663
Montefalco Sagrantino, Scacciadiavoli 666
Montefalco Sagrantino, Terre de' Trinci 663
Montefalco Sagrantino 25 Anni, Arnaldo Caprai - Val di Maggio 665
Montefalco Sagrantino Casale Triocco, Spoletoducale 674
Montefalco Sagrantino Collepiano, Arnaldo Caprai - Val di Maggio 665
Montefalco Sagrantino Le Mure Saracene, Goretti 673
Montefalco Sagrantino Passito, Fattoria Milziade Antano 676
Montefalco Sagrantino Passito, Antonelli - San Marco 665
Montefalco Sagrantino Passito, Còlpetrone 664
Montefalco Sagrantino Passito, Rocca di Fabbri 666
Montefalco Sagrantino Passito, Ruggeri 678
Montefalco Sagrantino Passito, Scacciadiavoli 666
Montefalco Sagrantino Passito, Terre de' Trinci 663
Montefalco Sagrantino Raffaellesco, Umbria Vitic. Associati 677
Montefalco Sagrantino Uno di Due, Tenuta Alzatura 677
Montefalco Sagrantino Uno di Uno, Tenuta Alzatura 677
Montello e Colli Asolani Cabernet, Amistani Guarda 348
Montello e Colli Asolani Merlot, Amistani Guarda 348
Montellori Brut, Fattoria Montellori 494
Monteloro, Fattoria Sant'Appiano 594
Montemoro, Puri Charlotte 694
Montepaone, Tenuta Il Greppo 526
Montepino Colli del Limbara, Piero Mancini 796
Montepirolo, San Patrignano 439
Montepulciano d'Abruzzo, Barone Cornacchia 710
Montepulciano d'Abruzzo, Fattoria Buccicatino 708
Montepulciano d'Abruzzo, Luigi Cataldi Madonna 702
Montepulciano d'Abruzzo, Filomusi Guelfi 707
Montepulciano d'Abruzzo, Il Feuduccio di Santa Maria d'Orni 709
Montepulciano d'Abruzzo, Fattoria La Valentina 707
Montepulciano d'Abruzzo, Lepore 698
Montepulciano d'Abruzzo, Gianni Masciarelli 706
Montepulciano d'Abruzzo, Antonio e Elio Monti 709
Montepulciano d'Abruzzo, Camillo Montori 699
Montepulciano d'Abruzzo, Bruno Nicodemi 702
Montepulciano d'Abruzzo, Terra d'Aligi - Spinelli 696
Montepulciano d'Abruzzo, Edoardo Valentini 701
Montepulciano d'Abruzzo, Valle Reale 710
Montepulciano d'Abruzzo, Valori 706
Montepulciano d'Abruzzo, Villa Medoro 696
Montepulciano d'Abruzzo Abbazia S. Clemente, Ciccio Zaccagnini 697
Montepulciano d'Abruzzo Aldiano, Cantina Tollo 708
Montepulciano d'Abruzzo Bellovedere, Fattoria La Valentina 707
Montepulciano d'Abruzzo Binomio, Fattoria La Valentina 707

Montepulciano d'Abruzzo Brume Rosse, Torre Zambra 710
Montepulciano d'Abruzzo Cagiòlo, Cantina Tollo 708
Montepulciano d'Abruzzo Casale Vecchio, Farnese 703
Montepulciano d'Abruzzo Cerasuolo, Luigi Cataldi Madonna 702
Montepulciano d'Abruzzo Cerasuolo, Contesa di Rocco Pasetti 704
Montepulciano d'Abruzzo Cerasuolo, Filomusi Guelfi 707
Montepulciano d'Abruzzo Cerasuolo, Fattoria La Valentina 707
Montepulciano d'Abruzzo Cerasuolo, Lepore 698
Montepulciano d'Abruzzo Cerasuolo, Gianni Masciarelli 706
Montepulciano d'Abruzzo Cerasuolo, Bruno Nicodemi 702
Montepulciano d'Abruzzo Cerasuolo, Sarchese Dora 704
Montepulciano d'Abruzzo Cerasuolo, Terra d'Aligi - Spinelli 696
Montepulciano d'Abruzzo Cerasuolo, Edoardo Valentini 701
Montepulciano d'Abruzzo Cerasuolo, Villa Medoro 696
Montepulciano d'Abruzzo Cerasuolo, Ciccio Zaccagnini 697
Montepulciano d'Abruzzo Cerasuolo Campirosa, Dino Illuminati 699
Montepulciano d'Abruzzo Cerasuolo Dama, Marramiero 705
Montepulciano d'Abruzzo Cerasuolo Fonte Cupa, Camillo Montori 699
Montepulciano d'Abruzzo Cerasuolo Le Vigne, Faraone 700
Montepulciano d'Abruzzo Cerasuolo Myosotis, Ciccio Zaccagnini 697
Montepulciano d'Abruzzo Cerasuolo Pié delle Vigne,
    Luigi Cataldi Madonna 702
Montepulciano d'Abruzzo Cerasuolo Riseis, Agriverde 703
Montepulciano d'Abruzzo Cerasuolo Tenuta Pasetti, Franco Pasetti 700
Montepulciano d'Abruzzo Cerasuolo Valle d'Oro, Cantina Tollo 708
Montepulciano d'Abruzzo Cerasuolo Vermiglio,
    Orlandi Contucci Ponno 705
Montepulciano d'Abruzzo Colle Morino, F.lli Barba 710
Montepulciano d'Abruzzo Colle Secco, Cantina Tollo 708
Montepulciano d'Abruzzo Colle Secco Rubino, Cantina Tollo 708
Montepulciano d'Abruzzo Colline Teramane Adrano, Villa Medoro 696
Montepulciano d'Abruzzo Colline Teramane Bacco, Bruno Nicodemi 702
Montepulciano d'Abruzzo Colline Teramane Fonte Cupa,
    Camillo Montori 699
Montepulciano d'Abruzzo Colline Teramane Re, Lepore 698
Montepulciano d'Abruzzo Colline Teramane Ris., Bruno Nicodemi 702
Montepulciano d'Abruzzo Contesa, Contesa di Rocco Pasetti 704
Montepulciano d'Abruzzo Dama, Marramiero 705
Montepulciano d'Abruzzo delle Colline Teramane Ris.,
    Orlandi Contucci Ponno 705
Montepulciano d'Abruzzo Don Bosco, Nestore Bosco 701
Montepulciano d'Abruzzo Don Giovanni, Fattoria
Buccicatino 708
Montepulciano d'Abruzzo Escol, San Lorenzo 709
Montepulciano d'Abruzzo Farneto Valley, Farnese 703
Montepulciano d'Abruzzo Fattoria Pasetti, Franco Pasetti 700
Montepulciano d'Abruzzo Frentano, Cant. Soc. Frentana 710
Montepulciano d'Abruzzo Granaro, Chiarieri 710
Montepulciano d'Abruzzo Hannibal, Chiarieri 710
Montepulciano d'Abruzzo Incanto, Marramiero 705
Montepulciano d'Abruzzo Inferi, Marramiero 705
Montepulciano d'Abruzzo Jorio, Umani Ronchi 644
Montepulciano d'Abruzzo La Regia Specula, Orlandi Contucci Ponno 705
Montepulciano d'Abruzzo Le Vigne, Faraone 700
Montepulciano d'Abruzzo Linea Oro, F.lli Barba 710
Montepulciano d'Abruzzo Luigi Lepore Ris., Lepore 698
Montepulciano d'Abruzzo Malandrino, Luigi Cataldi Madonna 702
Montepulciano d'Abruzzo Margae,
    Il Feuduccio di Santa Maria d'Orni 709
Montepulciano d'Abruzzo Marina Cvetic S. Martino
    Rosso, Gianni Masciarelli 706
Montepulciano d'Abruzzo Natum, Agriverde 703
Montepulciano d'Abruzzo Opis Ris., Farnese 703
Montepulciano d'Abruzzo Pan, Nestore Bosco 701
Montepulciano d'Abruzzo Perla Nera, Chiusa Grande 709
Montepulciano d'Abruzzo Pietrosa, Sarchese Dora 704
Montepulciano d'Abruzzo Pignotto, Antonio e Elio Monti 709
Montepulciano d'Abruzzo Plateo, Agriverde 703
Montepulciano d'Abruzzo Riparosso, Dino Illuminati 699
Montepulciano d'Abruzzo Riseis, Agriverde 703
Montepulciano d'Abruzzo Rocco Secco, Chiusa Grande 709
Montepulciano d'Abruzzo Rosso del Duca, Villa Medoro 696
Montepulciano d'Abruzzo Rosso di Macchia, Sarchese Dora 704
Montepulciano d'Abruzzo Rubesto, Cant. Soc. Frentana 710
Montepulciano d'Abruzzo S. Maria dell'Arco, Faraone 700
Montepulciano d'Abruzzo San Calisto, Valle Reale 710
Montepulciano d'Abruzzo Solàrea, Agriverde 703
Montepulciano d'Abruzzo Spelt, Fattoria La Valentina 707
Montepulciano d'Abruzzo Stilla Rubra, Fattoria Buccicatino 708
Montepulciano d'Abruzzo Tatone, Terra d'Aligi - Spinelli 696
Montepulciano d'Abruzzo Tenuta di Testarossa, Franco Pasetti 700
Montepulciano d'Abruzzo Tolos, Terra d'Aligi - Spinelli 696
Montepulciano d'Abruzzo Tonì, Luigi Cataldi Madonna 702
Montepulciano d'Abruzzo Tralcetto, Ciccio Zaccagnini 697
Montepulciano d'Abruzzo Tralcetto Sel., Ciccio Zaccagnini 697
Montepulciano d'Abruzzo Ursonia,
    Il Feuduccio di Santa Maria d'Orni 709
Montepulciano d'Abruzzo V. Fonte Dei, Filomusi Guelfi 707
Montepulciano d'Abruzzo V. Le Coste, Barone Cornacchia 710
Montepulciano d'Abruzzo Vigna Corvino,
    Contesa di Rocco Pasetti 704
Montepulciano d'Abruzzo Vigna S. Angelo, Valori 706
Montepulciano d'Abruzzo Villa Gemma, Gianni Masciarelli 706
Montepulciano d'Abruzzo Zanna, Dino Illuminati 699
Monteregio di Massa Marittima, La Pierotta 620
Monteregio di Massa Marittima Bacucco, Suveraia 612
Monteregio di Massa Marittima Bianco, Suveraia 612
Monteregio di Massa Marittima Lentisco, Serraiola 550
Monteregio di Massa Marittima Rosso, Moris Farms 514
Monteregio di Massa Marittima Rosso Baccio, I Campeti 617
Monteregio di Massa Marittima Rosso di Campetroso, Suveraia 612
Monteregio di Massa Marittima Scarilius, La Pierotta 620
Monteregio di Massa Marittima Serraiola, Serraiola 550
Monteregio di Massa Marittima Violina, Serraiola 550
Montervo, Cima 513
Montescudaio Bianco, Fattoria Sorbaiano 610

Montescudaio Bianco Lauro, La Regola	617
Montescudaio Rosso La Regola, La Regola	617
Montescudaio Rosso Ligustro, La Regola	617
Montesicci, Cantine di Dolianova	793
Montevertine, Montevertine	567
Montevertine Ris., Montevertine	567
Montevetrano, Montevetrano	721
Monti Lessini Bianco Re d'Aurum, Cant. di Montecchia	348
Montiano, Falesco	688
Morago Appassimento, Pasqua Vigneti e Cantine	342
Moranera, Terre di Santa Maria	785
Moranna, Tenuta Maiano	612
Morellino di Scansano, Podere Aia della Macina	585
Morellino di Scansano, Erik Banti	585
Morellino di Scansano, Col di Bacche	604
Morellino di Scansano, Il Grillesino	600
Morellino di Scansano, La Selva	613
Morellino di Scansano, Le Pupille	509
Morellino di Scansano, Costanza Malfatti	512
Morellino di Scansano, Moris Farms	514
Morellino di Scansano Anteo - Rocca dei Venti, Podere Aia della Macina	585
Morellino di Scansano BellaMarsilia, Poggio Argentiera	509
Morellino di Scansano Campomaccione, Rocca delle Macìe	481
Morellino di Scansano CapaTosta, Poggio Argentiera	509
Morellino di Scansano Carato, Erik Banti	585
Morellino di Scansano Ciabatta Ris., Erik Banti	585
Morellino di Scansano Fonte Tinta, La Carletta	619
Morellino di Scansano Gretaio, Granducato	562
Morellino di Scansano Heba, Fattoria di Magliano	512
Morellino di Scansano Le Sentinelle, Mantellassi	513
Morellino di Scansano Le Sentinelle Ris., Mantellassi	513
Morellino di Scansano Lohsa, Poliziano	547
Morellino di Scansano Poggio Bronzone, Tenuta Belguardo	508
Morellino di Scansano Poggio Roggettone, Podere Aia della Macina	585
Morellino di Scansano Poggio Roncone, Podere Aia della Macina	585
Morellino di Scansano Poggio Valente, Le Pupille	509
Morellino di Scansano Primo Ris., Provveditore	620
Morellino di Scansano Ris., Il Grillesino	600
Morellino di Scansano Ris., Mantellassi	513
Morellino di Scansano Ris., Moris Farms	514
Morellino di Scansano Roggiano, Cant. Coop. del Morellino di Scansano	586
Morellino di Scansano Roggiano Ris., Cant. Coop. del Morellino di Scansano	586
Morellino di Scansano Rosso Tore del Moro, Santa Lucia	603
Morellino di Scansano San Giuseppe, Mantellassi	513
Morellino di Scansano San Rabano Ris., Cant. Coop. del Morellino di Scansano	586
Morellino di Scansano Sassato, Provveditore	620
Morellino di Scansano Sicomoro, Cant. Coop. del Morellino di Scansano	586
Morellino di Scansano Terranera Aia della Macina Ris., Baroncini	576
Morellino di Scansano Terranera Ris., Podere Aia della Macina	585
Morellino di Scansano Titolato Strozzi, Guicciardini Strozzi - Fattoria Cusona	578
Morellino di Scansano Vignabenefizio, Cant. Coop. del Morellino di Scansano	586
Morellino di Scansano Vin del Fattore, Cant. Coop. del Morellino di Scansano	586
Morellino di Scansano Vivaio dei Barbi, Fattoria dei Barbi	516
Mormoreto, Marchesi de' Frescobaldi	494
Moro del Moro, Moro - Rinaldini	462
Moro di Pava, Pieve de' Pitti	622
Morsi di Luce, Cantine Florio	772
Morus Aurea, Vignai da Duline	420
Morus Nigra, Vignai da Duline	420
Moscadello di Montalcino, Tenuta Il Poggione	528
Moscadello V. T., La Poderina	529
Moscafratta, Agareno	785
Moscato, Isidoro Lamoretti	460
Moscato d'Asti, Cascina Barisél	54
Moscato d'Asti, F.lli Bera	125
Moscato d'Asti, Bersano & Riccadonna	125
Moscato d'Asti, Boroli	25
Moscato d'Asti, Cascina Castlèt	72
Moscato d'Asti, Castello del Poggio	130
Moscato d'Asti, Gianni Doglia	157
Moscato d'Asti, Cascina Fonda	102
Moscato d'Asti, I Vignaioli di S. Stefano	137
Moscato d'Asti, La Morandina	68
Moscato d'Asti, Paolo Saracco	69
Moscato d'Asti Bass Tuba, Cantine Bava	70
Moscato d'Asti Bosc d'la Rei, Batasiolo	90
Moscato d'Asti Bricco Quaglia, La Spinetta	58
Moscato d'Asti Ca' du Sindic Capsula Argento, Sergio Grimaldi - Ca' du Sindic	137
Moscato d'Asti Ca' du Sindic Capsula Oro, Sergio Grimaldi - Ca' du Sindic	137
Moscato d'Asti Caudrina, Caudrina	67
Moscato d'Asti Ceirole, Villa Giada	57
Moscato d'Asti Centive, Tenuta Olim Bauda	88
Moscato d'Asti Clarté, Elio Perrone	68
Moscato d'Asti Contero, La Giustiniana	85
Moscato d'Asti di Serralunga, Vigna Rionda - Massolino	142
Moscato d'Asti Ferlingot, Tenuta dell'Arbiola	135
Moscato d'Asti Giorgia, La Ghersa	103
Moscato d'Asti Il Giai, L'Armangia	56
Moscato d'Asti La Caliera, Borgo Maragliano	100
Moscato d'Asti La Galeisa, Caudrina	67
Moscato d'Asti La Rosa Selvatica, Icardi	67
Moscato d'Asti La Serra, Tenuta Cisa Asinari dei Marchesi di Gresy	32
Moscato d'Asti Lumine, Ca' d'Gal	136
Moscato d'Asti Moncalvina, Coppo	55
Moscato d'Asti Piasa San Maurizio, Forteto della Luja	101
Moscato d'Asti Santa Libera, Giacomo Scagliola e Figlio	156
Moscato d'Asti Scrapona, Marenco	143
Moscato d'Asti Sorì del Re, Sergio Degiorgis	103
Moscato d'Asti Sourgal, Elio Perrone	68
Moscato d'Asti Su Reimond, F.lli Bera	125
Moscato d'Asti V. Senza Nome, Braida	132
Moscato d'Asti V. Vecchia, Ca' d'Gal	136
Moscato d'Asti Vignasergente, Gianni Voerzio	99
Moscato d'Asti Volo di Farfalle, Scagliola	48
Moscato della Basilicata Clivus, Paternoster	731
Moscato di Cagliari, Cantine di Dolianova	793
Moscato di Cagliari Donna Jolanda, Meloni Vini	798
Moscato di Cagliari Simieri, Cant. Soc. della Trexenta	799
Moscato di Pantelleria, Agricola Bonsulton	786
Moscato di Pantelleria, Cantine Rallo	773
Moscato di Pantelleria Entelechia, Aziende Vinicole Miceli	780
Moscato di Pantelleria Mueggen, Salvatore Murana	778
Moscato di Pantelleria Passito, Cantine Colosi	785
Moscato di Pantelleria Solidea, Solidea	787
Moscato di Pantelleria Turbé, Salvatore Murana	778
Moscato di Saracena, Luigi Viola & Figli	764
Moscato di Scanzo Passito Doge, La Brugherata	212
Moscato di Siracusa Pollio, Pupillo	788
Moscato di Siracusa Solacium, Pupillo	788
Moscato di Siracusa Vigna di Mela, Pupillo	788
Moscato di Tempio Pausania, Cant. Soc. Gallura	801
Moscato di Terracina Amabile Templum, Cantina Sant'Andrea	690
Moscato di Terracina Passito Capitolium, Cantina Sant'Andrea	690
Moscato di Terracina Secco Oppidum, Cantina Sant'Andrea	690
Moscato di Trani Dulcis in Fundo, Torrevento	742
Moscato Giallo Passito Aureo, Cant. Soc. Bergamasca	210
Moscato Olimpia, Cant. Soc.Coop. del Locorotondo	747
Moscato Passito di Pantelleria Khamma, Salvatore Murana	778
Moscato Passito di Pantelleria Martingana, Salvatore Murana	778
Moscato Passito di Strevi, La Giustiniana	85
Moscato Passito Dorè, Podere San Giorgio	211
Moscato Passito Lacrimae Vitis, Cant. Soc. La Versa	211
Moscato Passito Oro dei Goti, Cons. Vini Tipici di San Marino	462
Moscato Passito Villa Monticelli, Barberani - Vallesanta	667
Moscato Pierale, Leone de Castris	751
Moscato Rosa, Marco Felluga	393
Moscato Rosa, Maso Bastie	249
Moscato Rosa Valzer in Rosa, Pittaro	366
Moscato Spumante Martinotti Fior d'Arancio, Cant. Soc. La Versa	211
Moscato Spumante Tardivo, Cascina Fonda	102
Moscato Villa Ortaglia, Ortaglia	593
Motu Proprio, Tenimenti Angelini	536
Muffa Nobile, Palazzone	670
Muffato della Sala, Castello della Sala	662
Muffo, Sergio Mottura	684
Müller Thurgau, Montelio	192
Müller Thurgau, Pelz & Piffer	251
Müller Thurgau, Jermann Vinnaioli	388
Müller Thurgau Biavè, Marchesi di Montalto	201
Müller Thurgau Canaro, Marchesi di Montalto	201
Müller Thurgau La Giostra, Montelio	192
Müller Thurgau Mussignaz, Russolo	422
Müller Thurgau Quaron, Borgo dei Posseri	250
Müller Thurgau St. Thomà, Pravis	234
Murgia Rosato Silvium, Cant. Coop. Botromagno	743
Murighessa, Pedra Majore	795
Murtas, San Michele a Torri	619
Museum, La Macolina	459
Musica Moscato, Tenuta dei Fiori	49
Myrto, Foradori	239
N° 1, Ortaglia	593
N'Antia, Badia di Morrona	621
Naam, Sardus Pater	797
Nabucco, Monte delle Vigne	459
Nadaria Inzolia, Cusumano	779
Nadaria Merlot, Cusumano	779
Nadaria Nero d'Avola, Cusumano	779
Nadaria Syrah, Cusumano	779
Naima, Viticoltori De Conciliis	720
Nambrot, Tenuta di Ghizzano	561
Narciso Principe di Corleone Rosso, Pollara	786
Narciso Rosso, Ronco delle Betulle	396
Nardina, Livernano	567
Nardo, Montepeloso	590
Nas-Cetta, Elvio Cogno	127
Nasco di Cagliari Donna Jolanda, Meloni Vini	798
Nasco di Cagliari Gutta'e Axina, Villa di Quartu	804
Naturalis Historia, Mastroberardino	712
Nausica, Vini Classici Cardone	747
Navicchio, Il Conte	640
Nearco, Tenuta Col d'Orcia	521
Nebbiolo d'Alba, Marziano ed Enrico Abbona	75
Nebbiolo d'Alba, Destefanis	117
Nebbiolo d'Alba, Giacomo Grimaldi	39
Nebbiolo d'Alba, Hilberg - Pasquero	131
Nebbiolo d'Alba, Fabrizio Pinsoglio	61
Nebbiolo d'Alba, Poderi Colla	27
Nebbiolo d'Alba, Porello	54
Nebbiolo d'Alba, Flavio Roddolo	113
Nebbiolo d'Alba, Terre del Barolo	66
Nebbiolo d'Alba, Vielmin	62
Nebbiolo d'Alba Bric du Nota, Antica Casa Vinicola Scarpa	126
Nebbiolo d'Alba Bric Merli, Malabaila	156
Nebbiolo d'Alba Bricco Reala, Bel Colle	149
Nebbiolo d'Alba Bricco S. Giacomo, Ascheri	46
Nebbiolo d'Alba Ca Veja, Paitin	124
Nebbiolo d'Alba Cascinotto, Claudio Alario	74
Nebbiolo d'Alba Cumot, Bricco Maiolica	75
Nebbiolo d'Alba Giachét, Sinaglio	28
Nebbiolo d'Alba La Perucca, Eugenio Bocchino	160
Nebbiolo d'Alba La Val dei Preti, Matteo Correggia	51

Nebbiolo d'Alba Le Ombre, Luigi Pira	141
Nebbiolo d'Alba Mompissano, Cascina Chicco	50
Nebbiolo d'Alba Occhetti, Prunotto	27
Nebbiolo d'Alba Ochetti, Renato Ratti	96
Nebbiolo d'Alba Parigi, Mauro Sebaste	28
Nebbiolo d'Alba Piadvenza, Casavecchia	158
Nebbiolo d'Alba S. Rocco, Giuseppe Mascarello e Figlio	105
Nebbiolo d'Alba Sansivé, Raffaele Gili	60
Nebbiolo d'Alba Sorì Coppa, Tenuta Langasco	154
Nebbiolo d'Alba V. Bricco dell'Asino, Pira	78
Nebbiolo d'Alba V. di Lino, Cascina Val del Prete	130
Nebbiolo d'Alba V. Tavoleto, Tenuta Carretta	129
Nebbiolo d'Alba Valmaggiore, Bruno Giacosa	122
Nebbiolo d'Alba Valmaggiore, Giacomo Grimaldi	39
Nebbiolo d'Alba Valmaggiore, Mario Marengo	93
Nebbiolo d'Alba Valmaggiore, Luciano Sandrone	42
Nebbiolo dei Colli del Limbara Karana, Cant. Soc. Gallura	801
Nebidu, Mura	802
Nebiosè, F.lli Ferrero	160
Negroamaro, Vinicola Mediterranea	756
Negroamaro E lo Veni, Leone de Castris	751
Neitea, Mormoraia	582
Nemo, Castello di Monsanto	469
Nepas Rosso, Alessandro e Gian Natale Fantino	109
Nerello Cappuccio, Benanti	782
Nerello Mascalese, Abbazia Santa Anastasia	768
Nerello Mascalese, Benanti	782
Nero, Conti Zecca	746
Nero d'Avola, Abbazia Santa Anastasia	768
Nero d'Avola, Adragna	788
Nero D'Avola, Fattorie Azzolino	767
Nero d'Avola, Baglio Hopps	771
Nero d'Avola, Benanti	782
Nero d'Avola, Centonze	788
Nero d'Avola, Curatolo	785
Nero d'Avola, Feudo Montoni	783
Nero d'Avola, Feudo Principi di Butera	767
Nero d'Avola, Fondo Antico	781
Nero d'Avola, Martorana	783
Nero d'Avola, Aziende Vinicole Miceli	780
Nero d'Avola, Morgante	770
Nero d'Avola, Cantine Rallo	773
Nero d'Avola, Terre di Salemi	787
Nero D'avola, Girolamo & C. Tola	787
Nero d'Avola Cabernet, Carlo Pellegrino	773
Nero D'Avola e Merlot, Girolamo & C. Tola	787
Nero D'avola e Syrah, Girolamo & C. Tola	787
Nero d'Avola Mandrarossa, Settesoli	775
Nero d'Avola Ragabo, Martorana	783
Nero d'Avola Sel. Speciale, Feudo Montoni	783
Nero d'Ombra, Mirabella	208
Nero della Cervara Sel., Todini	675
Nero della Greca, Cardeto	668
Nero della Spinosa, Fattoria Colle Verde	604
Nero di Nubi, Farnetella	586
Nero Ibleo, Gulfi	784
Nerobaroni, Gulfi	784
Nerobufaleffj, Gulfi	784
Nieddera Rosso, Attilio Contini	791
Niergal, Pravis	234
Nikà, Case di Pietra	786
Niteo, Giuseppe Vezzoli	198
Nivola Lambrusco Scuro, Chiarli 1860	446
Noà, Cusumano	779
Noans, La Tunella	406
Nobile di Montepulciano, Avignonesi	542
Nobile di Montepulciano, Bindella	543
Nobile di Montepulciano, Boscarelli	543
Nobile di Montepulciano, Canneto	610
Nobile di Montepulciano, Fattoria del Cerro	544
Nobile di Montepulciano, Contucci	610
Nobile di Montepulciano, Corte alla Flora	611
Nobile di Montepulciano, Dei	544
Nobile di Montepulciano, Fattoria La Braccesca	545
Nobile di Montepulciano, La Calonica	546
Nobile di Montepulciano, La Ciarliana	546
Nobile di Montepulciano, Lodola Nuova - Tenimenti Ruffino	547
Nobile di Montepulciano, Nottola	611
Nobile di Montepulciano, Fattoria di Paterno	611
Nobile di Montepulciano, Poggio alla Sala	611
Nobile di Montepulciano, Poliziano	547
Nobile di Montepulciano, Redi	548
Nobile di Montepulciano, Salcheto	548
Nobile di Montepulciano, Terra Antica	612
Nobile di Montepulciano, Tenuta Valdipiatta	549
Nobile di Montepulciano, Villa Sant'Anna	550
Nobile di Montepulciano Asinone, Poliziano	547
Nobile di Montepulciano Briareo, Redi	548
Nobile di Montepulciano Calvano, Fattoria di Gracciano	611
Nobile di Montepulciano Gersemi, Fassati	545
Nobile di Montepulciano I Quadri, Bindella	543
Nobile di Montepulciano La Villa, Tenimenti Angelini	536
Nobile di Montepulciano Pasiteo, Fassati	545
Nobile di Montepulciano Pietra del Diavolo, Il Faggeto	611
Nobile di Montepulciano Poggio Tocco, Le Tre Berte	549
Nobile di Montepulciano Ris., Canneto	610
Nobile di Montepulciano Ris., Fattoria del Cerro	544
Nobile di Montepulciano Ris., Contucci	610
Nobile di Montepulciano Ris., Corte alla Flora	611
Nobile di Montepulciano Ris., Dei	544
Nobile di Montepulciano Ris., Fattoria di Gracciano	611
Nobile di Montepulciano Ris., Fattoria La Braccesca	545
Nobile di Montepulciano Ris., La Calonica	546
Nobile di Montepulciano Ris., La Ciarliana	546
Nobile di Montepulciano Ris., Lodola Nuova - Tenimenti Ruffino	547
Nobile di Montepulciano Ris., Fattoria di Paterno	611
Nobile di Montepulciano Ris., Poggio alla Sala	611
Nobile di Montepulciano Ris., Salcheto	548
Nobile di Montepulciano Ris., Terra Antica	612
Nobile di Montepulciano Ris., Tenuta Valdipiatta	549
Nobile di Montepulciano Salarco Ris., Fassati	545
Nobile di Montepulciano Salco, Salcheto	548
Nobile di Montepulciano Simposio, Tenimenti Angelini	536
Nobile di Montepulciano Terre di Rubinoro, Redi	548
Nobile di Montepulciano V. d'Alfiero, Tenuta Valdipiatta	549
Nobile di Montepulciano V. del Nocio, Boscarelli	543
Nobile di Montepulciano V. del Nocio Ris., Boscarelli	543
Nobile di Montepulciano Vecchia Cant., Redi	548
Nobile di Montepulciano Vign. Antica Chiusina, Fattoria del Cerro	544
Nobile di Montepulciano Vigna del Fattore, Nottola	611
Nobile di Montepulciano Vigneto Antica Chiusina, Fattoria del Cerro	544
Nogarole Brut, Bruno Agostinetto	334
Noi Due, Saputi	653
Noriolo, Cant. Soc. Dorgali	794
Nosiola, Pojer & Sandri	232
Nosiola Le Frate, Pravis	234
Nosside, Statti	761
Notarpanaro, Cosimo Taurino	745
Notturno Sangiovese, Drei Donà Tenuta La Palazza	443
Novai, Marco Donati	237
Nuhar, Tenute Rapitalà	768
Nume, Cottanera	769
Numero Sei, Sassotondo	587
Nuragus di Cagliari Pedraia, Cant. Soc. di Santadi	797
Nuragus di Cagliari Perlas, Cantine di Dolianova	793
Nuragus di Cagliari S'Elegas, Antonio Argiolas	799
Nuragus di Cagliari Salnico, F.lli Pala	800
Nuvola Démi Sec, Bersi Serlini	207
O'feo Nero d'Avola, Cantine Foraci	785
O.P. Pinot Nero Brut P. Rosè, Gancia	56
Oblin Blanc, Isidoro Polencic	375
Oblin Ros, Isidoro Polencic	375
Obsession, Villa Vignamaggio	507
Occhiorosso, Luigi Cataldi Madonna	702
Offida Passerina Ninfa Ripana, La Cant. dei Colli Ripani	648
Offida Pecorino Ciprea, San Savino - Poderi Capecci	649
Offida Pecorino Crivellino, La Fontursia	655
Offida Pecorino Fiobbo, Aurora	643
Offida Pecorino Le Merlettaie, Ciù Ciù	643
Offida Pecorino Podere Colle Vecchio, Cocci Grifoni	655
Ognissanti Passito, Amistani Guarda	348
Oirad, Ferruccio Deiana	800
Olivar, Cesconi	235
Olivella, Migliarese	694
Olmaia, Tenuta Col d'Orcia	521
Olmera, Santo Stefano	294
Olpaio, Rubbia Al Colle	621
Oltre Vittorio Puiatti Bianco, Puiatti	360
OP Barbera, Ca' del Gè	222
OP Barbera, Isimbarda	210
OP Barbera, Montelio	192
OP Barbera, Tenuta Pegazzera	188
OP Barbera Becco Giallo, Podere San Giorgio	211
OP Barbera Campo del Marrone, Bruno Verdi	185
OP Barbera Campo Rivera, Pietro Torti	222
OP Barbera Cascina Bellaria, Marchesi di Montalto	201
OP Barbera Clà, Vercesi del Castellazzo	204
OP Barbera Frizzante, Monterucco	219
OP Barbera I Due Draghi, Tenuta La Costaiola	202
OP Barbera Olmetto, Bellaria	187
OP Barbera Piccolo Principe, Cabanon	221
OP Barbera Ris. Vigna Pivena, Monsupello	215
OP Barbera Roccolo del Casale, Cant. Soc. La Versa	211
OP Barbera Roncolongo, Bisi	209
OP Barbera Sel. Dino Torti, Tenimenti Castelrotto - Torti	222
OP Barbera Vigna Preda, Vanzini	225
OP Barbera Vignamarona, Ca' Tessitori	217
OP Barbera Vignole, F.lli Guerci	218
OP Bonarda, Pietro Torti	222
OP Bonarda Campo del Monte, Agnes	208
OP Bonarda Cresta del Ghiffi, Agnes	208
OP Bonarda Fatila, Vercesi del Castellazzo	204
OP Bonarda Frizzante, Cant. Soc. La Versa	211
OP Bonarda Frizzante, Montelio	192
OP Bonarda Frizzante, Tenuta Pegazzera	188
OP Bonarda Frizzante, Quaquarini	184
OP Bonarda Frizzante, Vanzini	225
OP Bonarda Frizzante Ca' Bella, Cant. Soc. La Versa	211
OP Bonarda La Rubiosa, Le Fracce	188
OP Bonarda Luogo della Milla, Vercesi del Castellazzo	204
OP Bonarda Mazzolino, Tenuta Mazzolino	194
OP Bonarda Millenium, Agnes	208
OP Bonarda Possessione del Console, Agnes	208
OP Bonarda Riva Zingari, Ca' del Santo	222
OP Bonarda Staffolo, Anteo	207
OP Bonarda Vigna Matta, Bagnasco	225
OP Bonarda Vignazzo, Agnes	208
OP Bonarda Vivace, Riccardo Albani	186
OP Bonarda Vivace, Ca' del Gè	222
OP Bonarda Vivace, Tenimenti Castelrotto - Torti	222
OP Bonarda Vivace, F.lli Guerci	218
OP Bonarda Vivace, Tenuta Il Bosco	226
OP Bonarda Vivace, Isimbarda	210
OP Bonarda Vivace Dardo, Frecciarossa	187
OP Bonarda Vivace Giada, Tenuta La Costaiola	202
OP Bonarda Vivace La Brughera, F.lli Giorgi	184
OP Bonarda Vivace Le Cento Pertiche, Clastidio Ballabio	218
OP Bonarda Vivace Possessione di Vergombera, Bruno Verdi	185
OP Bonarda Vivace V. Il Modello, Monterucco	219
OP Bonarda Vivace Vigna Bricco della Sacca, Fiamberti	217
OP Bornarda Vivace La Bria, Bellaria	187
OP Brut Cl. Anteo, Anteo	207

OP Brut Cl. Blanc de Blancs, Ruiz de Cardenas	189
OP Brut Cl. Ris. Ca' del Tava, Monsupello	215
OP Brut Cl. Vergomberra, Bruno Verdi	185
OP Buttafuoco Casa del Corno, F.lli Giorgi	184
OP Buttafuoco Frizzante, Bagnasco	225
OP Buttafuoco Roccolo delle Viole, Cant. Soc. La Versa	211
OP Buttafuoco Vigna Pregana, Quaquarini	184
OP Buttafuoco Vigna Solenga, Fiamberti	217
OP Buttafuoco Vivace, Tenuta La Costa	218
OP Buttafuoco Vivace La Manna, F.lli Giorgi	184
OP Cabernet Sauvignon Aplomb, Monsupello	215
OP Cabernet Sauvignon Corvino, Tenuta Mazzolino	194
OP Cabernet Sauvignon Ligna, Tenuta Pegazzera	188
OP Cabernet Sauvignon Primm, Bisi	209
OP Chardonnay, Ca' Tessitori	217
OP Chardonnay, Cant. Soc. La Versa	211
OP Chardonnay Blanc, Tenuta Mazzolino	194
OP Chardonnay Costa Soprana, Bellaria	187
OP Chardonnay Dama Bianca, Podere San Giorgio	211
OP Chardonnay Elaisa, Carlo Conte Giorgi di Vistarino	225
OP Chardonnay La Collegiata, Tenuta Pegazzera	188
OP Chardonnay Monsaltus, Marchesi di Montalto	201
OP Chardonnay Senso, Monsupello	215
OP Cortese, Montelio	192
OP Malvasia Dolce Frizzante, F.lli Giorgi	184
OP Malvasia Frizzante, Tenuta Il Bosco	226
OP Malvasia Il Raro, Ca' di Frara	204
OP Moscato, Ca' Montebello	219
OP Moscato La Volpe e L'Uva, Anteo	207
OP Moscato Passito Apricus, F.lli Guerci	218
OP Pinot Grigio, Bagnasco	225
OP Pinot Grigio, Cabanon	221
OP Pinot Grigio, Cant. Soc. La Versa	211
OP Pinot Grigio, Podere San Giorgio	211
OP Pinot Grigio, Bruno Verdi	185
OP Pinot Grigio Levriere, Le Fracce	188
OP Pinot Grigio Rusan, Cant. di Casteggio	218
OP Pinot Grigio V. T., Ca' di Frara	204
OP Pinot Nero, Frecciarossa	187
OP Pinot Nero, Isimbarda	210
OP Pinot Nero, La Marzuola	217
OP Pinot Nero, Pietro Torti	222
OP Pinot Nero, Vanzini	225
OP Pinot Nero 3309, Monsupello	215
OP Pinot Nero Baloss, Ruiz de Cardenas	189
OP Pinot Nero Bellarmino, Tenuta La Costaiola	202
OP Pinot Nero Blau, Quaquarini	184
OP Pinot Nero Brumano, Ruiz de Cardenas	189
OP Pinot Nero Brut Cl., Marco Giulio Bellani	218
OP Pinot Nero Brut Cl., Cant. Soc. La Versa	211
OP Pinot Nero Brut Cl., Monsupello	215
OP Pinot Nero Brut Cl., Tenuta Pegazzera	188
OP Pinot Nero Brut Cl. Carta Oro, Cant. Soc. La Versa	211
OP Pinot Nero Brut Cl. Gianfranco Giorgi, F.lli Giorgi	184
OP Pinot Nero Brut Cl. Mill. Elith, F.lli Giorgi	184
OP Pinot Nero Brut Classese, Cant. Soc. di Broni	217
OP Pinot Nero Brut Classese, Monsupello	215
OP Pinot Nero Brut Haris, Tenuta La Costaiola	202
OP Pinot Nero Brut Martinotti, Anteo	207
OP Pinot Nero Brut Martinotti, Cant. Soc. di Broni	217
OP Pinot Nero Brut Martinotti, Tenuta Pegazzera	188
OP Pinot Nero Brut Martinotti Incontro, F.lli Giorgi	184
OP Pinot Nero Ca' dell'Oca, Anteo	207
OP Pinot Nero Cà Nuè, Marchesi di Montalto	201
OP Pinot Nero Cl. Nature, Monsupello	215
OP Pinot Nero Costarsa, Montelio	192
OP Pinot Nero Cuvée Bussolera Extra Brut, Le Fracce	188
OP Pinot Nero Extra Brut Cl. Anteo Nature Ecru, Anteo	207
OP Pinot Nero Extra Brut Cl. Gianfranco Giorgi, F.lli Giorgi	184
OP Pinot Nero Extra Dry Cl. Anteo Rosè, Anteo	207
OP Pinot Nero Giorgio Odero, Frecciarossa	187
OP Pinot Nero in bianco Frizzante, Tenuta Pegazzera	188
OP Pinot Nero in Bianco Frizzante, Quaquarini	184
OP Pinot Nero in bianco Gugiarolo, Vercesi del Castellazzo	204
OP Pinot Nero in bianco Querciolo, Doria	201
OP Pinot Nero in bianco Sillery, Frecciarossa	187
OP Pinot Nero in bianco Vivace, Isimbarda	210
OP Pinot Nero in rosa Brut Cl., Marco Giulio Bellani	218
OP Pinot Nero Martinotti Monte Calvo, Cant. Soc. La Versa	211
OP Pinot Nero Noir, Tenuta Mazzolino	194
OP Pinot Nero Pernice, Carlo Conte Giorgi di Vistarino	225
OP Pinot Nero Petrae, Tenuta Pegazzera	188
OP Pinot Nero Re Nero, Podere San Giorgio	211
OP Pinot Nero Sel. Dino Torti, Tenimenti Castelrotto - Torti	222
OP Pinot Nero Vigna Miraggi, Ruiz de Cardenas	189
OP Riesling Italico, Ca' del Gè	222
OP Riesling Italico, Quaquarini	184
OP Riesling Renano, Monsupello	215
OP Riesling Renano Apogeo, Ca' di Frara	204
OP Riesling Renano Attimo, Tenuta La Costaiola	202
OP Riesling Renano Gli Orti, Frecciarossa	187
OP Riesling Renano Landò, Le Fracce	188
OP Riesling Renano Roncobianco, Doria	201
OP Riesling Renano V. Costa, Bruno Verdi	185
OP Riesling Renano Vigna Martina, Isimbarda	210
OP Rosso Articioc, Marco Giulio Bellani	218
OP Rosso Bohemi, Le Fracce	188
OP Rosso Bronis, Cant. Soc. di Broni	217
OP Rosso Cardinale, Tenuta Pegazzera	188
OP Rosso Cavariola Ris., Bruno Verdi	185
OP Rosso Cirgà, Le Fracce	188
OP Rosso Costa del Morone, Riccardo Albani	186
OP Rosso Custiò, Ca' Montebello	219
OP Rosso Garboso, Le Fracce	188
OP Rosso Great Ruby Vivace, Monsupello	215
OP Rosso Il Frater, Ca' di Frara	204
OP Rosso Il Frater Ris., Ca' di Frara	204
OP Rosso Infernot, Cabanon	221
OP Rosso La Vigna Bricca, Tenuta La Costaiola	202
OP Rosso Le Praielle, Frecciarossa	187
OP Rosso Luzzano 270 Ris., Castello di Luzzano	225
OP Rosso Magister, Quaquarini	184
OP Rosso Monplò, Isimbarda	210
OP Rosso Montezavo Ris., Isimbarda	210
OP Rosso Mosaico Ris., Monsupello	215
OP Rosso Pezzalunga, Vercesi del Castellazzo	204
OP Rosso Ris., La Marzuola	217
OP Rosso Ris. Monte Acutello, Fiamberti	217
OP Rosso Ris. Solarolo, Montelio	192
OP Rosso Roncorosso, Doria	201
OP Rosso Solarolo Ris., Montelio	192
OP Rosso V. Casa Corno, F.lli Giorgi	184
OP Rosso Vigna della Casona Ris., Riccardo Albani	186
OP Rosso Villa Odero Ris., Frecciarossa	187
OP Sangue di Giuda, Tenuta La Costa	218
OP Sangue di Giuda Acqua Calda, Quaquarini	184
OP Sangue di Giuda Dolce Paradiso, Bruno Verdi	185
OP Sangue di Giuda Frizzante, F.lli Giorgi	184
OP Sauvignon, Cant. di Casteggio	218
Opera Bianco, Mamete Prevostini	199
Opera Prima XIV, I Paglieri	34
Oppidum, Ciù Ciù	643
Oracolo, Poggio Amorelli	480
Orazio, Fontanavecchia	724
Orbaio, Redi	548
Orcia Cenerentola, Casato Prime Donne Donatella Cinelli Colombini	523
Orcia Guardiavigna, Podere Forte	489
Orcia Petrucci, Podere Forte	489
Orcia Rosso Capitoni, Sedime	614
Orcia Rosso Invidia, Trequanda	622
Ordine del Toson d'Oro Rosato, Castello di Ama	495
Oreno, Tenuta Sette Ponti	592
Orfeo, Vinagri	756
Ori di Taranto, Mille Una	746
Ornellaia, Tenuta dell' Ornellaia	470
Oro, Alessandro Moroder	625
Oro dei Saraceni, Cave di Moleto	129
Oro del Cedro V. T., Fattoria Lavacchio	615
Orpello, Tenuta Bacco e Petroio	622
Orvietano Rosso Torre Sant'Andrea, Cristine Vaselli	683
Orvieto Cl. Poggio Calvelli, La Carraia	669
Orvieto Cl. Secco, Tenuta Le Velette	670
Orvieto Cl. Sup., Tenuta di Salviano	676
Orvieto Cl. Sup. Calcaia, Barberani - Vallesanta	667
Orvieto Cl. Sup. Campo del Guardiano, Palazzone	670
Orvieto Cl. Sup. Colbadia, Cardeto	668
Orvieto Cl. Sup. Decugnano dei Barbi, Decugnano dei Barbi	669
Orvieto Cl. Sup. Febeo, Cardeto	668
Orvieto Cl. Sup. L'Armida, Cardeto	668
Orvieto Cl. Sup. Matricale, Vaglie	659
Orvieto Cl. Sup. Pourriture Noble, Decugnano dei Barbi	669
Orvieto Cl. Sup. Terre Vineate, Palazzone	670
Orvieto Cl. Torre Sant'Andrea, Cristine Vaselli	683
Orvieto Cl. Vigna Tragugnano, Sergio Mottura	684
Orvieto Cl. Vigneto Torricella, Bigi	668
Orvieto Secco, Sergio Mottura	684
Osar, Masi	327
Ostrea Grigia, Mormoraia	582
Ottavianello, Sergio Botrugno	753
Ottavianello Dedalo Torre Guaceto, Accademia dei Racemi	748
Ottocento Liberty, Luigi Spertino	104
P. Brut, Zonin	296
P. di Conegliano Brut, Collalbrigo	346
P. di Conegliano Brut Bubbly, Zardetto Spumanti	293
P. di Conegliano Brut San Salvatore, Conte Collalto	333
P. di Conegliano Brut Vigna del Cuc Case Bianche, Martino Zanetti	349
P. di Conegliano Extra Dry, Bepin de Eto	320
P. di Conegliano Extra Dry, Conte Collalto	333
P. di Conegliano Extra Dry, G. B. Cerletti Scuola Enol. di Conegliano	346
P. di Conegliano Extra Dry Cuvée Oro, Carpenè Malvolti	346
P. di Conegliano Frizzante Brioso, Zardetto Spumanti	293
P. di Conegliano Tranquillo, Bepin de Eto	320
P. di Conegliano Tranquillo Lungo, Zardetto Spumanti	293
P. di Conegliano Valdobbiadene Extra Dry, Gregoletto	304
P. di Conegliano Valdobbiadene Extra Dry, Masottina	318
P. di Conegliano Valdobbiadene Tranquillo, Gregoletto	304
P. di Conegliano Zeroventi Dry, Zardetto Spumanti	293
P. di Valdobbiadene Bosco di Gica Brut, Adami	343
P. di Valdobbiadene Brut, F.lli Bortolin Spumanti	335
P. di Valdobbiadene Brut, Bortolomiol	336
P. di Valdobbiadene Brut, Sorelle Bronca	344
P. di Valdobbiadene Brut, Canevel Spumanti	336
P. di Valdobbiadene Brut, Il Cardo	351
P. di Valdobbiadene Brut, Col Vetoraz	337
P. di Valdobbiadene Brut, De Faveri	352
P. di Valdobbiadene Brut, Le Bellerive - Angelo Ruggeri	337
P. di Valdobbiadene Brut, Nino Franco	338
P. di Valdobbiadene Brut, Santa Eurosia	339
P. di Valdobbiadene Brut, Tanorè	340
P. di Valdobbiadene Brut Barreta, Merotto	347
P. di Valdobbiadene Brut Crede, Desiderio Bisol & Figli	335
P. di Valdobbiadene Brut Cuvée del Fondatore, Spumanti Valdo	351
P. di Valdobbiadene Brut Cuvée di Boj, Spumanti Valdo	351
P. di Valdobbiadene Brut Fagher, Le Colture	338
P. di Valdobbiadene Brut Jeio, Desiderio Bisol & Figli	335
P. di Valdobbiadene Brut Quartese, Ruggeri & C.	339
P. di Valdobbiadene Brut Rive di S. Floriano, Nino Franco	338
P. di Valdobbiadene Dry, F.lli Bortolin Spumanti	335
P. di Valdobbiadene Dry, Bortolomiol	336

P. di Valdobbiadene Dry, Merotto 347
P. di Valdobbiadene Dry Cruner, Le Colture 338
P. di Valdobbiadene Dry Funer, Le Bellerive - Angelo Ruggeri 337
P. di Valdobbiadene Dry Garnei, Desiderio Bisol & Figli 335
P. di Valdobbiadene Dry Giardino, Adami 343
P. di Valdobbiadene Dry Millesimato, Col Vetoraz 337
P. di Valdobbiadene Dry Millesimato, Santa Eurosia 339
P. di Valdobbiadene Dry Primo Franco, Nino Franco 338
P. di Valdobbiadene Dry S. Stefano, Ruggeri & C. 339
P. di Valdobbiadene Dry Salis, Desiderio Bisol & Figli 335
P. di Valdobbiadene Dry Sel., Tanorè 340
P. di Valdobbiadene Extra Dry, Bruno Agostinetto 334
P. di Valdobbiadene Extra Dry, F.lli Bortolin Spumanti 335
P. di Valdobbiadene Extra Dry, Bortolomiol 336
P. di Valdobbiadene Extra Dry, Sorelle Bronca 344
P. di Valdobbiadene Extra Dry, Canevel Spumanti 336
P. di Valdobbiadene Extra Dry, Il Cardo 351
P. di Valdobbiadene Extra Dry, Col Vetoraz 337
P. di Valdobbiadene Extra Dry, De Faveri 352
P. di Valdobbiadene Extra Dry, Le Bellerive - Angelo Ruggeri 337
P. di Valdobbiadene Extra Dry, Santa Eurosia 339
P. di Valdobbiadene Extra Dry, Tanorè 340
P. di Valdobbiadene Extra Dry Colbelo, Merotto 347
P. di Valdobbiadene Extra Dry dei Casel, Adami 343
P. di Valdobbiadene Extra Dry Dirupo, Andreola Orsola 347
P. di Valdobbiadene Extra Dry Giall'Oro, Ruggeri & C. 339
P. di Valdobbiadene Extra Dry Giustino B., Ruggeri & C. 339
P. di Valdobbiadene Extra Dry Il Millesimato, Canevel Spumanti 336
P. di Valdobbiadene Extra Dry Particella 68, Sorelle Bronca 344
P. di Valdobbiadene Extra Dry Pianer, Le Colture 338
P. di Valdobbiadene Extra Dry Rù, F.lli Bortolin Spumanti 335
P. di Valdobbiadene Extra Dry San Venanzio, Casa Coste Piane 351
P. di Valdobbiadene Extra Dry Sel. Banda Rossa, Bortolomiol 336
P. di Valdobbiadene Extra Dry Vign. del Faé, Canevel Spumanti 336
P. di Valdobbiadene Extra Dry Vign. del Fol,
    Desiderio Bisol & Figli 335
P. di Valdobbiadene Frizzante, Col Vetoraz 337
P. di Valdobbiadene Frizzante, Le Bellerive - Angelo Ruggeri 337
P. di Valdobbiadene Frizzante Il Ponteggio, Bortolomiol 336
P. di Valdobbiadene Frizzante Mas, Le Colture 338
P. di Valdobbiadene Frizzante Sur Lie, Casa Coste Piane 351
P. di Valdobbiadene Frizzante Vign. di S. Biagio, Canevel Spumanti 336
P. di Valdobbiadene Sur Lie, Adami 343
P. di Valdobbiadene Tranquillo, Il Cardo 351
P. di Valdobbiadene Tranquillo, Santa Eurosia 339
P. di Valdobbiadene Tranquillo, Tanorè 340
P. di Valdobbiadene Tranquillo Canto Fermo, Bortolomiol 336
P. di Valdobbiadene Tranquillo Giardino, Adami 343
P. di Valdobbiadene Tranquillo La Bastia, Ruggeri & C. 339
P. di Valdobbiadene Tranquillo Masaré, Le Colture 338
P. di Valdobbiadene Tranquillo Molera, Desiderio Bisol & Figli 335
P. di Valdobbiadene Tranquillo Romit, Andreola Orsola 347
P. di Valdobbiadene Tranquillo Sassi Bianchi, Nino Franco 338
P. di Valdobbiadene Tranquillo Tresiese, Col Vetoraz 337
P. di Valdobbiadene Tranquillo V.ID.OR., De Faveri 352
P. Extra Dry, Serafini & Vidotto 315
P. Extra Dry, Zardetto Spumanti 293
P. Special Cuvée Extra Dry, Zonin 296
Pagadebit di Romagna, Calonga 443
Pagello, Vini Pallavicini 689
Pagliatura, Fattoria di Magliano 512
Palafreno, Querciabella 504
Palazzo della Torre, Allegrini 294
Paleo Bianco, Le Macchiole 470
Pallagrello Bianco del Ventaglio, Castello Ducale 713
Pantelleria Bianco Secco, Agricola Bonsulton 786
Pantelleria Secco Yrnm, Aziende Vinicole Miceli 780
Papiano di Pantelleria, Villa Papiano 447
Pardàli Cabernet Sauvignon, Valetti 345
Parrina Bianco, La Parrina 554
Parrina Rosso, La Parrina 554
Parrina Rosso Muraccio, La Parrina 554
Parrina Rosso Ris., La Parrina 554
Passamante, Masseria Li Veli 741
Passatempo, Azzoni Avogadro Carradori 654
Passerina del Frusinate, Casale della Ioria 680
Passito, Il Mosnel 206
Passito, Tordimaro 678
Passito Anima Mundi, La Cant. dei Colli Ripani 648
Passito Bianco, Ca' La Bionda 299
Passito Bianco, Marion 319
Passito Bianco, Ciccio Zaccagnini 697
Passito di Corzano, Fattoria Corzano e Paterno 571
Passito di Erbaluce Autunno degli Artisti, Bianchi 142
Passito di Pantelleria, Agricola Bonsulton 786
Passito di Pantelleria, Cantine Colosi 785
Passito di Pantelleria, Marco De Bartoli 771
Passito di Pantelleria, Cantine Rallo 773
Passito di Pantelleria Ben Ryé, Tenuta di Donnafugata 772
Passito di Pantelleria Bukkuram, Marco De Bartoli 771
Passito di Pantelleria Mare d'Ambra, Cantine Rallo 773
Passito di Pantelleria Mueggen, Benanti 782
Passito di Pantelleria Nes, Carlo Pellegrino 773
Passito di Pantelleria Nikà, Case di Pietra 786
Passito di Pantelleria Nun, Aziende Vinicole Miceli 780
Passito di Pantelleria Solidea, Solidea 787
Passito di Pantelleria Tanit, Aziende Vinicole Miceli 780
Passito Esperidio, Lo Sparviere 203
Passito Monte delle Fontane, Tezza 343
Passito Passut, Santo Stefano 294
Passito Re Sol, Luigi Brunelli 322
Passito Rosso, Ciccio Zaccagnini 697
Passito Suavis, Sarchese Dora 704
Passo Rosso, Stefano Accordini 320
Passomaggio, Abbazia Santa Anastasia 768
Passopisciaro, Tenuta di Trinoro 584

Passrì Pineto, Marenco 143
Paterno, Trappolini 682
Paterno II, Il Paradiso 579
Pathos, Santa Barbara 627
Patriglione, Cosimo Taurino 745
Pàtrimo, Feudi di San Gregorio 723
Paule Calle, Francesco Candido 751
Pazzesco, Castello del Trebbio 615
Pecorino Contesa, Contesa di Rocco Pasetti 704
Pecorino Fattoria Pasetti, Franco Pasetti 700
Pelago, Umani Ronchi 644
Pen. Sorr. Gragnano, De Falco 728
Penisola Sorrentina Gragnano, Cantine Grotta del Sole 720
Peperino, Teruzzi & Puthod 583
Pepestrino, Fattoria di Felsina 485
Pepita Bianco, Gaspare Di Prima 787
Pepita Rosso, Gaspare Di Prima 787
Percarlo, San Giusto a Rentennano 501
Perdaudin Passito, Angelo Negro & Figli 117
Perelle, Josef Niedermayr 256
Perlato del Bosco Rosso, Tua Rita 591
Permartina, Vallona 437
Pernicolò, Fattoria San Francesco 758
Pesanella, Castello di Monterinaldi 616
Petelia, Roberto Ceraudo 760
Petit Verdot, Casale del Giglio 681
Petra Rosso, Petra 620
Petranera, Le Crete 677
Petraro, Roberto Ceraudo 760
Petroio Primo, Tenuta Bacco e Petroio 622
Petroso Merlot, Vigneto delle Terre Rosse 466
Pezzolo Cabernet Sauvignon, Tenuta Pandolfa 451
Pfefferer, Stephan Ramoser - Fliederhof 264
Phigaia After the Red, Serafini & Vidotto 315
Pian del Conte, Fattoria Sorbaiano 610
Piandorino, Pian dell'Orino 608
Pianetta di Càgnore, Antico Terreno Ottavi 650
Piano del Cipresso, Fattoria di Terrabianca 568
Piantonaia, Podere Poggio Scalette 503
Piave Cabernet, Conte Collalto 333
Piave Cabernet Ardesco, Sorelle Bronca 344
Piave Cabernet Franc, Casa Roma 327
Piave Cabernet Le Ronche, Santo Stefano 294
Piave Cabernet Ornella, Ornella Molon Traverso 317
Piave Cabernet Podere Torrai Ris., Conte Collalto 333
Piave Cabernet Sauvignon, Giorgio Cecchetto 352
Piave Cabernet Sauvignon ai Palazzi Ris., Masottina 318
Piave Cabernet Sauvignon Mormorò, Bortolomiol 336
Piave Cabernet V. Tilia, Villa Brunesca 347
Piave Chardonnay, Casa Roma 327
Piave Chardonnay, Conte Collalto 333
Piave Chardonnay ai Palazzi Ris., Masottina 318
Piave Chardonnay La Cesura, Italo Cescon 349
Piave Chardonnay Ornella, Ornella Molon Traverso 317
Piave Chardonnay Prà Longo, Santo Stefano 294
Piave Chardonnay Terre Nobili, Santo Stefano 294
Piave Merlot, Casa Roma 327
Piave Merlot, Conte Collalto 333
Piave Merlot ai Palazzi Ris., Masottina 318
Piave Merlot Ornella, Ornella Molon Traverso 317
Piave Merlot Rosso di Villa, Ornella Molon Traverso 317
Piave Pinot Grigio, Casa Roma 327
Piave Pinot Grigio ai Palazzi, Masottina 318
Piave Raboso, Casa Roma 327
Piave Raboso, Giorgio Cecchetto 352
Piave Raboso Gelsaia, Giorgio Cecchetto 352
Piave Raboso La Cesura, Italo Cescon 349
Piave Raboso La Potestà, Bonotto delle Tezze 352
Piave Raboso Ornella, Ornella Molon Traverso 317
Pico, La Biancara 295
Piemonte Alta Langa Brut Giulio Cocchi, Cantine Bava 70
Piemonte Alta Langa Brut Rosé Giulio Cocchi, Cantine Bava 70
Piemonte Alta Langa Carlo Gancia Cuvée del Fondatore, Gancia 56
Piemonte Alta Langa Cuvée Aurora, Vigne Regali 144
Piemonte Alta Langa Talento Brut, Fontanafredda 140
Piemonte Barbera, Einaudi 77
Piemonte Barbera, Valditerra 162
Piemonte Barbera Briccobotti, Pira 78
Piemonte Barbera Bunéis Gianni Zonin Vineyards,
    Castello del Poggio 130
Piemonte Barbera Elisa, La Colombera 145
Piemonte Barbera Mounbè, Cascina Ulivi 162
Piemonte Barbera Quass, Pecchenino 77
Piemonte Bonarda, Cascina Gilli 62
Piemonte Brachetto, Cascina Fonda 102
Piemonte Brachetto, Piero Gatti 136
Piemonte Brachetto Ca' du Sindic,
    Sergio Grimaldi - Ca' du Sindic 137
Piemonte Brachetto Carlotta, Ermanno e Alessandra Brema 88
Piemonte Brachetto Forteto Pian dei Sogni, Forteto della Luja 101
Piemonte Brut M. Cl. La Bernardina, Ceretto 25
Piemonte Chardonnay, Tenuta Olim Bauda 88
Piemonte Chardonnay Armonia, Colonna 152
Piemonte Chardonnay Butàs, La Guardia 118
Piemonte Chardonnay Casot dan Vian, Scagliola 48
Piemonte Chardonnay Costebianche, Coppo 55
Piemonte Chardonnay Crevoglio, Borgo Maragliano 100
Piemonte Chardonnay Diversamente, Garetto 23
Piemonte Chardonnay Galet, Marenco 143
Piemonte Chardonnay Giarone, Bertelli 72
Piemonte Chardonnay Innuce, Malgrà 104
Piemonte Chardonnay L'Altro, Pio Cesare 26
Piemonte Chardonnay La Sabauda, Contratto 55
Piemonte Chardonnay Le Aie, Cascina Roera 73
Piemonte Chardonnay Lidia, La Spinetta 58
Piemonte Chardonnay Mej, Caudrina 67

Piemonte Chardonnay Monteriolo, Coppo 55
Piemonte Chardonnay Plenilunio, Michele Chiarlo 47
Piemonte Chardonnay Riserva della Famiglia, Coppo 55
Piemonte Chardonnay Robi & Robi, L'Armangia 56
Piemonte Chardonnay Roleto, Araldica - Il Cascinone 59
Piemonte Chardonnay Thou Bianc, Cantine Bava 70
Piemonte Chardonnay V. Levi, Sciorio 73
Piemonte Chardonnay Villa Delfini, La Guardia 118
Piemonte Cortese Balera, Icardi 67
Piemonte Grignolino, Pelissero 148
Piemonte Grignolino, Tenuta San Sebastiano 102
Piemonte Grignolino La Capletta, Casalone 101
Piemonte Grignolino Sansoero, Marchesi Alfieri 134
Piemonte Moscato, Piero Gatti 136
Piemonte Moscato d'Autunno, Paolo Saracco 69
Piemonte Moscato Passito, Cascina Fonda 102
Piemonte Moscato Passito Avié, Cascina Castlèt 72
Piemonte Moscato Passito IL, I Vignaioli di S. Stefano 137
Piemonte Moscato Passito L'Altro Moscato,
   Tenuta Cisa Asinari dei Marchesi di Gresy 32
Piemonte Moscato Passito La Bella Estate, Terre da Vino 43
Piemonte Moscato Passito Passrì di Scrapona, Marenco 143
Piemonte Muscatel Tardì, Batasiolo 90
Pier delle Vigne, Cant. Coop. Botromagno 743
Pietracupa, Fattoria Montecchio 621
Pietraforte del Carobbio, Carobbio 555
Pietranera, Marco De Bartoli 771
Pietro, Le Filigare 468
Pieve Alta Chardonnay, La Berta 435
Pignacolusse, Jermann Vinnaioli 388
Pignocco Rosso, Santa Barbara 627
Pignoletto Vivace, Vallona 437
Pilin, Castellari Bergaglio 84
Pinea, Sergio Botrugno 753
Pinèro, Ca' del Bosco 196
Pino & Toi, Maculan 290
Pinodisé, Contadi Castaldi 182
Pinot Bianco, Cant. Prod. di Cormons 370
Pinot Bianco, Costozza - Conti da Schio 298
Pinot Bianco, Gregoletto 304
Pinot Bianco, Roncùs 361
Pinot Bianco, Jermann Vinnaioli 388
Pinot Bianco Principe di Corleone, Pollara 786
Pinot Brut, Masottina 318
Pinot Grigio, Conti Bossi Fedrigotti 242
Pinot Grigio, Sant'Elena 393
Pinot Grigio, Leonardo Specogna 382
Pinot Grigio, Jermann Vinnaioli 388
Pinot Grigio Corte Le Marsure, Teresa Raiz 403
Pinot Grigio Olivers, Pierpaolo Pecorari 421
Pinot Grigio Prà Longo, Santo Stefano 294
Pinot Grigio Ronco Calaj, Russolo 422
Pinot Grigio Sialis, Franco Terpin 418
Pinot Nero, Ca' del Santo 222
Pinot Nero, Poderi di San Pietro 209
Pinot Nero, Pojer & Sandri 232
Pinot Nero, San Vettore 502
Pinot Nero, Serafini & Vidotto 315
Pinot Nero, Vallarom 229
Pinot Nero Camerti, Tenuta Corini 667
Pinot Nero Grifo Nero, Russolo 422
Pinot Nero Il Nero, Ca' del Santo 222
Pinot Nero in bianco, Giuseppe Guglielmini 222
Pinot Nero L'Arturo, Ronco Calino 182
Pinot Nero Sebino, Ricci Curbastro 186
Pinot Nero Sel., Pojer & Sandri 232
Pinot Nero Torre di Borea, Conti Formentini 416
Pinot Nero Vigna Baragazza,
   Tenuta di Bagnolo dei Marchesi Pancrazi 542
Pinot Nero Vigneto Consola, Castello della Sala 662
Pinot Nero Villa di Bagnolo,
   Tenuta di Bagnolo dei Marchesi Pancrazi 542
Pix Merlot, Boccadigabbia 631
Planargia Alvarega, Columbu 802
Planargia Murapiscados, Gianvittorio Naitana 803
Platone, Tenute Albano Carrisi 740
Plissé Traminer, Bertelli 72
Pluminus, Ferruccio Deiana 800
Poch ma Bon Passito, Cascina Pellerino 118
Podalirio, Querceto di Castellina 481
Podere Brizio, Roberto Bellini 605
Podere Fontarca, Tenimenti Luigi D'Alessandro 490
Podere Il Bosco, Tenimenti Luigi D'Alessandro 490
Podere Ispoli Rosso, Ispoli 573
Podere Le Rocce, Le Filigare 468
Podernovo, Castello delle Regine 658
Poesia d'Inverno Vino da Uve Stramature,
   Ist. Prof. per l'Agricoltura e l'Ambiente 441
Poggiassai, Fattorie Chigi Saracini 485
Poggio a Tramontana, Fattoria del Cerro 544
Poggio ai Chiari, Colle Santa Mustiola 599
Poggio alla Badiola, Castello di Fonterutoli 478
Poggio Argentato, Le Pupille 509
Poggio Belvedere, Arnaldo Caprai - Val di Maggio 665
Poggio Bestiale, Fattoria di Magliano 512
Poggio Canneto, Carini 672
Poggio Cavalluccio, Tenuta Roccaccia 562
Poggio Cosmiano, Tenuta di Poggio Cosmiano 614
Poggio Golo, Fattoria del Cerro 544
Poggio Granoni, Farnetella 586
Poggio l'Aiole, Castello di Modanella 570
Poggio Madrigale, Di Filippo 676
Poggio Maestrino, Erik Banti 585
Poggio Montino, Castello di Modanella 570
Poggio Muralto, Rio Grande 671
Poggio Solivo, Ca' del Vispo 576

Poggioaicozzi, Tenuta Cortina e Mandorli 612
Pojer & Sandri Extra Brut, Pojer & Sandri 232
Pojo di Lupo, COS 782
Polito, Il Lebbio 578
Polveriera Rosso, Piovene Porto Godi 344
Polzina, Barone Pizzini 193
Pomele, Falesco 688
Pomino Bianco, Marchesi de' Frescobaldi 494
Pomino Il Benefizio, Marchesi de' Frescobaldi 494
Pomino Rosso, Marchesi de' Frescobaldi 494
Porticato Bianco, Colle di Maggio 690
Portico Rosso, Vignaiolo Giuseppe Fanti 236
Portulano, Rosa del Golfo 738
Possessioni Bianco Serègo Alighieri, Masi 327
Pourriture Noble, Petreto 465
Praepositus Weiss, Abbazia di Novacella 282
Prato Grande Chardonnay, Tenuta De Angelis 629
Pratobianco, Torre Fornello 455
Pratto, Ca' dei Frati 212
Predaia Rosso, Santa Sofia 323
Pregio del Conte, Saladini Pilastri 651
PreposITURA, Ist. Agrario Prov. San Michele all'Adige 244
Priante, Castel di Salve 756
Prima Causa, La Selva 613
Prima Luce Passito, Ottella 316
Primamateria, Poggerino 568
Primitivo, Cant. Coop. Botromagno 743
Primitivo, Vini Classici Cardone 747
Primitivo, Castello Monaci 750
Primitivo, Conti Zecca 746
Primitivo, Cant. Due Palme 740
Primitivo, Le Fabriche 755
Primitivo, Paradiso 753
Primitivo, Rosa del Golfo 738
Primitivo del Tarantino, I Pastini - Carparelli 754
Primitivo di Manduria, Felline 748
Primitivo di Manduria, Vinicola Miali 749
Primitivo di Manduria Archidamo, Pervini 749
Primitivo di Manduria Dolce Naturale Chicca, Vigne & Vini 745
Primitivo di Manduria Dunico Millennium
   Masseria Pepe, Accademia dei Racemi 748
Primitivo di Manduria Elegia, Cons. Prod. Vini e Mosti Rossi 755
Primitivo di Manduria Giravolta Tenuta Pozzopalo,
   Accademia dei Racemi 748
Primitivo di Manduria Memoria, Cons. Prod. Vini e Mosti Rossi 755
Primitivo di Manduria Ognisole, Feudi di San Gregorio 723
Primitivo di Manduria Papale, Vigne & Vini 745
Primitivo di Manduria Primo Amore, Pervini 749
Primitivo di Manduria Santera, Leone de Castris 751
Primitivo di Manduria Terre di Don Peppe,
   Cant. Soc.Coop. del Locorotondo 747
Primitivo di Manduria Zinfandel Sinfarosa,
   Accademia dei Racemi 748
Primitivo Dolce Naturale, Vinicola Mediterranea 756
Primitivo La Rena, Leone de Castris 751
Primitivo Maestro, Borgo Canale 743
Primitivo Mater, Vinicola Miali 749
Primitivo Mo e Mo, Borgo Canale 743
Primitivo Portile Masseria Pepe, Accademia dei Racemi 748
Primitivo Primaio, Vini Classici Cardone 747
Primitivo Punta Aquila, Tenute Rubino 739
Primitivo Scalee, Vinicola Mediterranea 756
Primitivo Sigillo Primo, Antica Masseria del Sigillo 744
Primitivo Tatu, Vigne & Vini 745
Primitivo Terre Mediterranee, Zonin 296
Primitivo Terre Rosse, Morella 754
Primitivo Torre Sgarrata, Bepin de Eto 320
Primitivo Vecchia Torre, Cant. Soc. Coop. Leverano 754
Primitivo Visellio, Tenute Rubino 739
Primitivo Zinfandel, Vigne & Vini 745
Primoquarto Rosso, Aziende Vinicole Miceli 780
Primosole Rosso, Bianchi 142
Primovolo, Villa Giada 57
Princeps, Castello delle Regine 658
Priore, La Brugherata 212
Priscus, Fattoria di Presciano 614
Privilegia Rosso, Giuseppe Lonardi 301
Promis, Cà Marcanda 475
Prosecco Brut Rustico, Nino Franco 338
Prospero, Borgo Canale 743
Provincia di Pavia Uva Rara, Frecciarossa 187
Prugnolo, Di Majo Norante 698
Prulke, Zidarich 385
Prunaio, Viticcio 508
Puer sed Formosus, Gostolai 804
Puglia Bianco, Torre Quarto 741
Puglia Chardonnay Sannà, Borgo Canale 743
Puglia Rosso, Le Fabriche 755
Pulleraia, Agricoltori del Chianti Geografico 495
Pupà Pepu, Roberto Bellini 605
Puro Sangue, Livernano 567
Quadrimendo, Vitanza 610
Quarantale, Rosa del Golfo 738
Quarto di Luna, Cantine Grotta del Sole 720
Quarto di Sole, Cantine Grotta del Sole 720
Quarto Ducale, Torre Quarto 741
Quattro Mori, Castel De Paolis 686
Quattrocentenario, Castello della Paneretta 466
Querciagrande, Podere Capaccia 616
Querciolaia, Mantellassi 513
Querciolaia, Castello di Querceto 503
Querciolo, Teresa Raiz 403
Quercus, Villa 203
Quirico, Pietracupa 717
Racemo Rosso, L'Olivella 692
Radaia, La Parrina 554

Radames, Antichi Poderi Jerzu	794
Raddese, Vignavecchia	569
Rafé Vign. di Costa Bianca, Cascina Gilli	62
Raim, Tenute Sella & Mosca	790
Rainero, Castello di Meleto	498
Rairi Moscato, Tenuta dei Fiori	49
Rambaldo VIII, Conte Collalto	333
Ramì, COS	782
Rapace, Uccelliera	537
Rasa di Marmorata, Tenuta Le Quinte	693
Ré, La Corte	755
Re Sole, Stefano Mancinelli	654
Reale, La Castellina	597
Realgar, Alessandro Secchi	250
Recioto dei Capitelli, Roberto Anselmi	307
Recioto della Valpolicella, Corte Sant'Alda	302
Recioto della Valpolicella, Musella	319
Recioto della Valpolicella, Trabucchi	297
Recioto della Valpolicella Cl., Lorenzo Begali	321
Recioto della Valpolicella Cl., F.lli Bolla	352
Recioto della Valpolicella Cl., Brigaldara	321
Recioto della Valpolicella Cl., Corte Lenguin	350
Recioto della Valpolicella Cl., Corte Rugolin	300
Recioto della Valpolicella Cl., F.lli Degani	301
Recioto della Valpolicella Cl., Aleardo Ferrari	350
Recioto della Valpolicella Cl., Le Ragose	312
Recioto della Valpolicella Cl., Angelo Nicolis e Figli	323
Recioto della Valpolicella Cl., Novaia	302
Recioto della Valpolicella Cl., Santa Sofia	323
Recioto della Valpolicella Cl., Villa Bellini	326
Recioto della Valpolicella Cl., Viviani	314
Recioto della Valpolicella Cl. Acinatico, Stefano Accordini	320
Recioto della Valpolicella Cl. Amabile degli Angeli, Masi	327
Recioto della Valpolicella Cl. BG, Tommaso Bussola	311
Recioto della Valpolicella Cl. Campo Casalin I Castei, Michele Castellani	300
Recioto della Valpolicella Cl. Capitel Monte Fontana, F.lli Tedeschi	324
Recioto della Valpolicella Cl. Casotto del Merlo, Giuseppe Campagnola	299
Recioto della Valpolicella Cl. Domini Veneti, Cant. Soc. Valpolicella	312
Recioto della Valpolicella Cl. El Rocolo, Manara	322
Recioto della Valpolicella Cl. Francesca Finato Spinosa, Villa Spinosa	314
Recioto della Valpolicella Cl. Giovanni Allegrini, Allegrini	294
Recioto della Valpolicella Cl. La Roggia, F.lli Speri	324
Recioto della Valpolicella Cl. La Rosta, F.lli Degani	301
Recioto della Valpolicella Cl. Le Arele, Giuseppe Lonardi	301
Recioto della Valpolicella Cl. Le Brugnine, Massimino Venturini	326
Recioto della Valpolicella Cl. Le Calcarole, Roberto Mazzi	313
Recioto della Valpolicella Cl. Le Novaje, Novaia	302
Recioto della Valpolicella Cl. Le Traversagne, Le Salette	295
Recioto della Valpolicella Cl. Le Vigne Ca' del Pipa, Michele Castellani	300
Recioto della Valpolicella Cl. Maddalena, I Scriani	347
Recioto della Valpolicella Cl. Monte Faustino, Giuseppe Fornaser	350
Recioto della Valpolicella Cl. Pal Sun, Raimondi - Villa Monteleone	328
Recioto della Valpolicella Cl. Pergole Vece, Le Salette	295
Recioto della Valpolicella Cl. TB, Tommaso Bussola	311
Recioto della Valpolicella Cl. V. Alte, F.lli Zeni	289
Recioto della Valpolicella Cl. Vign. Le Tordare, Ca' La Bionda	299
Recioto della Valpolicella Cl. Vigneti di Moron Domini Veneti, Cant. Soc. Valpolicella	312
Recioto della Valpolicella l'Eremita, Ca' Rugate	307
Recioto della Valpolicella Re Teodorico, Giacomo Montresor	342
Recioto della Valpolicella Roccolo Grassi, Roccolo Grassi	303
Recioto della Valpolicella Tesauro, Cant. Soc. della Valpantena	341
Recioto della Valpolicella Valpantena, Cant. Soc. della Valpantena	341
Recioto della Valpolicella Valpantena Brolo delle Giare, Tezza	343
Recioto di Gambellara, La Biancara	295
Recioto di Gambellara Cl. Riva dei Perari, Luigino Dal Maso	306
Recioto di Gambellara Podere il Giangio Aristòs, Zonin	296
Recioto di Soave, Monte Tondo	330
Recioto di Soave Acinatium, Suavia	331
Recioto di Soave Case Vecie, Cecilia Beretta	341
Recioto di Soave Cl., Santa Sofia	323
Recioto di Soave Cl. Acinatium, Suavia	331
Recioto di Soave Cl. Corte Pittora, Cant. del Castello	329
Recioto di Soave Cl. Le Sponde, Coffele	330
Recioto di Soave Col Foscarin, Gini	308
Recioto di Soave Etichetta Bianca, Le Mandolare	309
Recioto di Soave Etichetta Nera, Le Mandolare	309
Recioto di Soave I Capitelli, Roberto Anselmi	307
Recioto di Soave La Broia, Roccolo Grassi	303
Recioto di Soave La Perlara, Ca' Rugate	307
Recioto di Soave Le Colombare, Leonildo Pieropan	331
Recioto di Soave Oro, Umberto Portinari	309
Recioto di Soave Renobilis, Gini	308
Recioto di Soave Rocca Sveva, Cant. di Soave	329
Recioto di Soave S. Zeno, Fasoli	292
Recioto di Soave Santa Croce, Tenuta Faltracco	310
Recioto di Soave Sur Lie Ardens, Cant. del Castello	329
Recioto di Soave V. Marogne, Tamellini	332
Reciso, Pietro Beconcini	619
Red Angel, Jermann Vinnaioli	388
Red Branko, Branko - Igor Erzetic	371
Redigaffi, Tua Rita	591
Refolà Cabernet Sauvignon, Le Vigne di San Pietro	333
Refosco, Marco Felluga	393
Refosco Campo della Stafula, Brojli - Franco Clementin	424
Refosco P. R., Villa Brunesca	347
Refosco P. R., Villa Frattina	404
Refosco P. R. Bottaz, Venica & Venica	384
Refosco P. R. I Legni, Russolo	422
Refosco P.R. Lucia Galasso, Giovanni Crosato	427
Refosco P. R. Panta Rei, Pierpaolo Pecorari	421
Regaleali Bianco, Tasca d'Almerita	778
Regaleali Rosato, Tasca d'Almerita	778
Regaleali Rosso, Tasca d'Almerita	778
Reggiano Assolo, Ermete Medici & Figli	451
Reggiano Lambrusco Bianco Spumante Brut Arita, Moro - Rinaldini	462
Reggiano Lambrusco Inchiostro Cant. del Gallo, Cantine Cooperative Riunite	458
Reggiano Lambrusco Piazza San Prospero, Ca' de' Medici	462
Reggiano Lambrusco Secco, Ermete Medici & Figli	451
Reggiano Lambrusco Secco Concerto, Ermete Medici & Figli	451
Regina del Bosco, Fattoria Dezi	651
Renè, Cascina Pellerino	118
Resico, San Luciano	539
Retiko, Grigoletti	240
Rêve Chardonnay di Villa Angela, Ercole Velenosi	626
Ribballa di Càgnore, Antico Terreno Ottavi	650
Ribeca, Firriato	776
Ribolla Gialla, Le Due Torri	429
Ribolla Gialla, Gravner	391
Ribolla Gialla, I Feudi di Romans - Lorenzon	414
Ricciobianco, Lanciola	511
Richenza, Vigna Petrussa	411
Riesling Brut M. Cl., La Palazzola	674
Riesling Frizzante, Giuseppe Guglielmini	222
Riesling Renano Podere Valtini, Molino dei Lessi	251
Riflesso Antico, Lorella Ambrosini	588
Riggiano, Casetto dei Mandorli	461
Rigoletto Passito, Zenato	316
Rimitivo Primaio, Vini Classici Cardone	747
Riné, Cantrina	183
Ripa, Podere Sopra la Ripa	587
Ripa delle Mandorle, Castello di Vicchiomaggio	507
Ripa delle More, Castello di Vicchiomaggio	507
Ris. del Governatore Extra Brut, Bortolomiol	336
Risveglio Chardonnay, Cascina Montagnola	153
Ritratto Bianco, La Vis/Valle di Cembra	234
Ritratto Rosso, La Vis/Valle di Cembra	234
Rivarossa, Schiopetto	362
Riviera del Garda Bresciano Gropèl, Comincioli	224
Riviera del Garda Bresciano Pedemut, Comincioli	224
Riviera del Garda Bresciano Sulèr, Comincioli	224
Riviera Ligure di Ponente Ormeasco, Calleri	166
Riviera Ligure di Ponente Ormeasco, Giampaolo Ramò	179
Riviera Ligure di Ponente Ormeasco Sup., Nicola Guglierame	179
Riviera Ligure di Ponente Ormeasco Sup. Le Braje, Tommaso e Angelo Lupi	174
Riviera Ligure di Ponente Pigato, A Maccia	175
Riviera Ligure di Ponente Pigato, Anfossi	178
Riviera Ligure di Ponente Pigato, Laura Aschero	174
Riviera Ligure di Ponente Pigato, Maria Donata Bianchi	170
Riviera Ligure di Ponente Pigato, BioVio	178
Riviera Ligure di Ponente Pigato, Calleri	166
Riviera Ligure di Ponente Pigato, Cascina Feipu dei Massaretti	166
Riviera Ligure di Ponente Pigato, Colle dei Bardellini	172
Riviera Ligure di Ponente Pigato, Le Rocche del Gatto	167
Riviera Ligure di Ponente Pigato, Tommaso e Angelo Lupi	174
Riviera Ligure di Ponente Pigato, Sancio	180
Riviera Ligure di Ponente Pigato, Terre Bianche	171
Riviera Ligure di Ponente Pigato, Cascina delle Terre Rosse	172
Riviera Ligure di Ponente Pigato, La Vecchia Cantina	167
Riviera Ligure di Ponente Pigato, Claudio Vio	177
Riviera Ligure di Ponente Pigato Costa de Vigne, Alessandri	175
Riviera Ligure di Ponente Pigato Le Petraie, Tommaso e Angelo Lupi	174
Riviera Ligure di Ponente Pigato Le Russeghine, Bruna	176
Riviera Ligure di Ponente Pigato Saleasco, Calleri	166
Riviera Ligure di Ponente Pigato U Bacan, Bruna	176
Riviera Ligure di Ponente Pigato Vigna La Torretta, Colle dei Bardellini	172
Riviera Ligure di Ponente Pigato Vigna Proxi, La Rocca di San Nicolao	170
Riviera Ligure di Ponente Pigato Villa Torrachetta, Bruna	176
Riviera Ligure di Ponente Rossese, A Maccia	175
Riviera Ligure di Ponente Rossese, Anfossi	178
Riviera Ligure di Ponente Rossese, Bruna	176
Riviera Ligure di Ponente Rossese, Cascina Feipu dei Massaretti	166
Riviera Ligure di Ponente Rossese, La Rocca di San Nicolao	170
Riviera Ligure di Ponente Vermentino, Laura Aschero	174
Riviera Ligure di Ponente Vermentino, Maria Donata Bianchi	170
Riviera Ligure di Ponente Vermentino, Calleri	166
Riviera Ligure di Ponente Vermentino, Cascina Praié	178
Riviera Ligure di Ponente Vermentino, Colle dei Bardellini	172
Riviera Ligure di Ponente Vermentino, Tenuta Giuncheo	168
Riviera Ligure di Ponente Vermentino, Le Rocche del Gatto	167
Riviera Ligure di Ponente Vermentino, Tommaso e Angelo Lupi	174
Riviera Ligure di Ponente Vermentino, La Rocca di San Nicolao	170
Riviera Ligure di Ponente Vermentino, Sancio	180
Riviera Ligure di Ponente Vermentino, Terre Bianche	171
Riviera Ligure di Ponente Vermentino, Cascina delle Terre Rosse	172
Riviera Ligure di Ponente Vermentino, La Vecchia Cantina	167
Riviera Ligure di Ponente Vermentino, Claudio Vio	177
Riviera Ligure di Ponente Vermentino Eclissi, Tenuta Giuncheo	168
Riviera Ligure di Ponente Vermentino I Muzazzi, Calleri	166
Riviera Ligure di Ponente Vermentino Le Palme, Tenuta Giuncheo	168
Riviera Ligure di Ponente Vermentino Le Serre, Tommaso e Angelo Lupi	174
Riviera Ligure di Ponente Vermentino V. Proxi, La Rocca di San Nicolao	170
Riviera Ligure di Ponente Vermentino Vigna U Munte, Colle dei Bardellini	172
Robanera, Cantine Cavicchioli & Figli	462
Robbio, Villa Frattina	404
Roccagiglio, Adragna	788
Roccato, Rocca delle Macìe	481

Rocceto, Il Toppello	662
Roccia Rosso, Cant. Soc.Coop. del Locorotondo	747
Roero, Giovanni Almondo	115
Roero, Funtanin	52
Roero, Filippo Gallino	52
Roero, Angelo Negro & Figli	117
Roero, Cascina Pellerino	118
Roero, Fabrizio Pinsoglio	61
Roero, Cascina Val del Prete	130
Roero Arneis, Bel Colle	149
Roero Arneis, Cornarea	156
Roero Arneis, Matteo Correggia	51
Roero Arneis, Funtanin	52
Roero Arneis, Filippo Gallino	52
Roero Arneis, Bruno Giacosa	122
Roero Arneis, F.lli Giacosa	122
Roero Arneis, Raffaele Gili	60
Roero Arneis, Malvirà	53
Roero Arneis, Marchesi di Barolo	40
Roero Arneis, Stefanino Morra	61
Roero Arneis, Pio Cesare	26
Roero Arneis, Mauro Sebaste	28
Roero Arneis, Enrico Serafino	156
Roero Arneis, Vielmin	62
Roero Arneis Anterisio, Cascina Chicco	50
Roero Arneis Boneur, Cascina Pellerino	118
Roero Arneis Bricco Cappellina, Gianni Voerzio	99
Roero Arneis Bricco delle Ciliegie, Giovanni Almondo	115
Roero Arneis Camestrì, Porello	54
Roero Arneis Capural, Montaribaldi	35
Roero Arneis Daivej, Deltetto	51
Roero Arneis Gianat, Angelo Negro & Figli	117
Roero Arneis Liffrei, Valerio Aloi	160
Roero Arneis Luet, Cascina Val del Prete	130
Roero Arneis Merica, Cascina Ca' Rossa	50
Roero Arneis Perdaudin, Angelo Negro & Figli	117
Roero Arneis Pierin di Soc, Funtanin	52
Roero Arneis Pradvaj, Malabaila	156
Roero Arneis Re Cit, Monchiero Carbone	53
Roero Arneis Renesio, Malvirà	53
Roero Arneis S. Michele, Deltetto	51
Roero Arneis Saglietto, Malvirà	53
Roero Arneis San Servasio, Marsaglia	157
Roero Arneis Sernì, Michele Taliano	116
Roero Arneis Sorilaria, Araldica - Il Cascinone	59
Roero Arneis Trinità, Malvirà	53
Roero Arneis V. Elisa, Paitin	124
Roero Arneis V. Sparse, Giovanni Almondo	115
Roero Arneis Vign. Malinat, Fabrizio Pinsoglio	61
Roero Arneis Vign. S. Pietro, Stefanino Morra	61
Roero Arneis Vigna Canorei, Tenuta Carretta	129
Roero Audinaggio, Cascina Ca' Rossa	50
Roero Braja, Deltetto	51
Roero Bric Angelino, Raffaele Gili	60
Roero Bric Torretta, Porello	54
Roero Bric Valdiana, Giovanni Almondo	115
Roero Bricco Morinaldo, Valerio Aloi	160
Roero La Rocca, Vielmin	62
Roero Leoni, Cascina Pellerino	118
Roero Mompissano, Cascina Ca' Rossa	50
Roero Montespinato, Cascina Chicco	50
Roero Monvijé, Bel Colle	149
Roero Printi, Monchiero Carbone	53
Roero Ròche d'Ampsèj, Matteo Correggia	51
Roero Ròche dra Bòssora, Michele Taliano	116
Roero Srai, Stefanino Morra	61
Roero Srù, Monchiero Carbone	53
Roero Sup., Cornarea	156
Roero Sup., Filippo Gallino	52
Roero Sup., Malvirà	53
Roero Sup., Stefanino Morra	61
Roero Sup. Bric Paradiso, Tenuta Carretta	129
Roero Sup. Bricco Barbisa, Funtanin	52
Roero Sup. Brich d'America, Marsaglia	157
Roero Sup. Castelletto, Malabaila	156
Roero Sup. Giovanni Almondo, Giovanni Almondo	115
Roero Sup. Mombeltramo, Malvirà	53
Roero Sup. Pasiunà, Enrico Serafino	156
Roero Sup. Sodisfà, Angelo Negro & Figli	117
Roero Sup. Trinità, Malvirà	53
Roero Torretta, Porello	54
Roero Valmaggiore, Cascina Chicco	50
Roero Vicot, Cascina Pellerino	118
Rôl, Eddi Luisa	398
Rolenzo, San Lorenzo	618
Romagnano Bianco, Colacicchi	680
Romagnano Rosso, Colacicchi	680
Romalbo, Cima	513
Romeo, Castel Noarna	239
Romio, Terragens Fine Wines - Volo Rosso	433
Romito del Romitorio, Castello Romitorio	534
Romitorio di Santedame, Tenimenti Ruffino	564
Ronc, Paolo Rodaro	366
Ronchedone, Ca' dei Frati	212
Ronchello, Majolini	205
Ronco dei Ciliegi, Castelluccio	446
Ronco del Re, Castelluccio	446
Ronco delle Ginestre, Castelluccio	446
Ronco Nolè Rosso, Di Lenardo	389
Roncùs Bianco Vecchie Vigne, Roncùs	361
Rondinaia, Castello del Terriccio	482
Rondon, Colmello di Grotta	388
Rosa del Golfo, Rosa del Golfo	738
Rosa di Montacuto, Alessandro Moroder	625
Rosa di Selva, Borgo Canale	743
Rosato Amistà, Val di Neto	764
Ross'Oro, Villa Cilnia	464
Rosserto Bianco, Giovanni Manzone	110
Rossese di Dolceacqua, Giovanna Maccario	180
Rossese di Dolceacqua, Terre Bianche	171
Rossese di Dolceacqua Bricco Arcagna, Terre Bianche	171
Rossese di Dolceacqua Sup. Vigneto Arcagna, Giobatta Mandino Cane	171
Rossese di Dolceacqua Sup. Vigneto Morghe, Giobatta Mandino Cane	171
Rossese di Dolceacqua Vigneto Pian del Vescovo, Tenuta Giuncheo	168
Rosso, Girolamo & C. Tola	787
Rosso A. D., Doria	201
Rosso A.D., Doria	201
Rosso Archè, Val di Neto	764
Rosso Avignonesi, Avignonesi	542
Rosso Caparzo Sangiovese, Tenuta Caparzo	517
Rosso Carolin, Armando Martino	736
Rosso Carpino, Il Carpino	415
Rosso Conero, Fazi Battaglia	630
Rosso Conero, Lanari	624
Rosso Conero, Malacari	655
Rosso Conero, Maurizio Marchetti	624
Rosso Conero, Alessandro Moroder	625
Rosso Conero, F.lli Zaccagnini & C.	652
Rosso Conero Adeodato, Monteschiavo	636
Rosso Conero Adino, Spinsanti	628
Rosso Conero Camars, Spinsanti	628
Rosso Conero Cimerio Ris., Terre Cortesi Moncaro	639
Rosso Conero Conti Cortesi, Monteschiavo	636
Rosso Conero Cùmaro, Umani Ronchi	644
Rosso Conero Dorico, Alessandro Moroder	625
Rosso Conero Fibbio, Lanari	624
Rosso Conero Fructus, Conte Leopardi Dittajuti	642
Rosso Conero Grigiano, Malacari	655
Rosso Conero Grosso Agontano Ris., Gioacchino Garofoli	635
Rosso Conero Julius, Silvano Strologo	629
Rosso Conero Marro, Alberto Serenelli	625
Rosso Conero Passo del Lupo Ris., Fazi Battaglia	630
Rosso Conero Piancarda, Gioacchino Garofoli	635
Rosso Conero Pigmento, Conte Leopardi Dittajuti	642
Rosso Conero Poggio al Cerro, Poggio Montali	654
Rosso Conero Rubjo, Piersanti	656
Rosso Conero S. Lorenzo, Umani Ronchi	644
Rosso Conero Sassi Neri, Fattoria Le Terrazze	642
Rosso Conero Serrano, Umani Ronchi	644
Rosso Conero Traiano, Silvano Strologo	629
Rosso Conero Varano, Alberto Serenelli	625
Rosso Conero Vigneti del Coppo, Conte Leopardi Dittajuti	642
Rosso Conero Vigneti del Parco Ris., Terre Cortesi Moncaro	639
Rosso Conero Villa Bonomi Ris., Maurizio Marchetti	624
Rosso Conero Visions of J, Fattoria Le Terrazze	642
Rosso Corte dell'Abbà, Villa Frattina	404
Rosso Costozza, Costozza - Conti da Schio	298
Rosso degli Appiani, San Giusto	614
Rosso dei Frati Priori, Uberti	198
Rosso del Bepi, Giuseppe Quintarelli	313
Rosso del Castellazzo, Vercesi del Castellazzo	204
Rosso del Gatto, Le Rocche del Gatto	167
Rosso del Gnemiz, Ronco del Gnemiz	420
Rosso del Palagio, Castello Il Palagio	617
Rosso del Pievano, La Pieve	515
Rosso del Pivier, Cesconi	235
Rosso del Postiglione, Perusini	381
Rosso del Presidente, Fatascià	777
Rosso del Senatore, Fattoria dell' Aiola	483
Rosso del Soprano, Palari	775
Rosso della Fabriseria, F.lli Tedeschi	324
Rosso delle Chiaie, Giovanni Palombo	681
Rosso di Alberico, La Brugherata	212
Rosso di Campomaggio, Castellani	615
Rosso di Casale Marchese, Casale Marchese	685
Rosso di Luna, Monzio Compagnoni	220
Rosso di Marco, Marco De Bartoli	771
Rosso di Montalcino, Altesino	605
Rosso di Montalcino, Argiano	605
Rosso di Montalcino, Castello Banfi	515
Rosso di Montalcino, Fattoria dei Barbi	516
Rosso di Montalcino, Brunelli - Le Chiuse di Sotto	605
Rosso di Montalcino, Castello di Camigliano	516
Rosso di Montalcino, Canalicchio di Sopra	605
Rosso di Montalcino, Tenuta Caparzo	517
Rosso di Montalcino, Casanova di Neri	517
Rosso di Montalcino, Casanuova delle Cerbaie	518
Rosso di Montalcino, Casisano Colombaio	518
Rosso di Montalcino, Castiglion del Bosco	519
Rosso di Montalcino, Tenuta Col d'Orcia	521
Rosso di Montalcino, Collelceto	606
Rosso di Montalcino, Tenuta di Collosorbo	522
Rosso di Montalcino, Corte Pavone	606
Rosso di Montalcino, Andrea Costanti	522
Rosso di Montalcino, Tenuta Di Sesta	523
Rosso di Montalcino, Casato Prime Donne Donatella Cinelli Colombini	523
Rosso di Montalcino, Donna Olga	524
Rosso di Montalcino, Fanti - La Palazzetta	524
Rosso di Montalcino, Fanti - San Filippo	525
Rosso di Montalcino, Fattoi	606
Rosso di Montalcino, Tenuta Il Greppo	526
Rosso di Montalcino, Il Palazzone	527
Rosso di Montalcino, Tenuta Il Poggione	528
Rosso di Montalcino, La Fornace	607
Rosso di Montalcino, Podere La Fortuna	528
Rosso di Montalcino, La Gerla	529
Rosso di Montalcino, La Poderina	529
Rosso di Montalcino, La Rasina	607

Rosso di Montalcino, La Togata - Tenuta Carlina	530
Rosso di Montalcino, Le Chiuse	530
Rosso di Montalcino, Le Gode di Ripaccioli	607
Rosso di Montalcino, Le Macioche	607
Rosso di Montalcino, Lisini	531
Rosso di Montalcino, Mastrojanni	532
Rosso di Montalcino, Mocali	608
Rosso di Montalcino, Cant. di Montalcino	608
Rosso di Montalcino, Tenute Silvio Nardi	532
Rosso di Montalcino, Siro Pacenti	533
Rosso di Montalcino, Palazzo	608
Rosso di Montalcino, Pian dell'Orino	608
Rosso di Montalcino, Piancornello	609
Rosso di Montalcino, Agostina Pieri	609
Rosso di Montalcino, Poggio Antico	533
Rosso di Montalcino, Poggio di Sotto	609
Rosso di Montalcino, Poggio San Polo	609
Rosso di Montalcino, Castello Romitorio	534
Rosso di Montalcino, Podere Salicutti	534
Rosso di Montalcino, Solaria - Cencioni	535
Rosso di Montalcino, Talenti	536
Rosso di Montalcino, Tenimenti Angelini	536
Rosso di Montalcino, Uccelliera	537
Rosso di Montalcino, Tenuta Val di Cava	537
Rosso di Montalcino, Visconti	538
Rosso di Montalcino, Vitanza	610
Rosso di Montalcino Banditella, Tenuta Col d'Orcia	521
Rosso di Montalcino Calbello, Andrea Costanti	522
Rosso di Montalcino Ginestreto, Eredi Fuligni	525
Rosso di Montalcino Il Roccolo, Oliveto	608
Rosso di Montalcino La Caduta, Tenuta Caparzo	517
Rosso di Montalcino Pietranera, Centolani	520
Rosso di Montalcino Poggio Salvi, Tenuta Il Greppo	526
Rosso di Montalcino Ris., Cerbaia	606
Rosso di Montalcino Tenuta Friggiali, Centolani	520
Rosso di Montalcino Tirso, Villa Le Prata	538
Rosso di Montalcino V. del Cassero Ris., Tenuta di Collosorbo	522
Rosso di Montalcino V. della Fonte, Ciacci Piccolomini D'Aragona	521
Rosso di Montepulciano, Avignonesi	542
Rosso di Montepulciano, Canneto	610
Rosso di Montepulciano, Carpineto	503
Rosso di Montepulciano, Contucci	610
Rosso di Montepulciano, Corte alla Flora	611
Rosso di Montepulciano, La Calonica	546
Rosso di Montepulciano, La Ciarliana	546
Rosso di Montepulciano, Nottola	611
Rosso di Montepulciano, Poggio alla Sala	611
Rosso di Montepulciano, Poliziano	547
Rosso di Montepulciano, Redi	548
Rosso di Montepulciano, Salcheto	548
Rosso di Montepulciano, Tenuta Valdipiatta	549
Rosso di Montepulciano, Villa Sant'Anna	550
Rosso di Montepulciano Fosso Lupaio, Bindella	543
Rosso di Montepulciano Lupaio, Il Faggeto	611
Rosso di Montepulciano Poggio Tocco, Le Tre Berte	549
Rosso di Montepulciano Sabazio, Fattoria La Braccesca	545
Rosso di Montepulciano Selciaia, Fassati	545
Rosso di Montepulciano Vecchia Cant., Redi	548
Rosso di Nero, Ist. Prof. per l'Agricoltura e l'Ambiente	441
Rosso di Sera, Fattoria Poggiopiano	575
Rosso di Turi, Feotto dello Jato	787
Rosso di Valpanera, Valpanera	426
Rosso di Villa Ris., Ornella Molon Traverso	317
Rosso Faye, Pojer & Sandri	232
Rosso Fiorentino, Cennatoio Intervineas	556
Rosso Fogliano, Bisci	637
Rosso Gli Affreschi, Tenuta di Blasig	412
Rosso Golfo dei Poeti, La Felce	179
Rosso Gravner, Gravner	391
Rosso Io, Ca' di Frara	204
Rosso La Tia, Traversa - Cascina Bertolotto	143
Rosso Maradea, Val di Neto	764
Rosso Orvietano Il Tordimaro, Tordimaro	678
Rosso Ottella, Ottella	316
Rosso Outsider, Arnaldo Caprai - Val di Maggio	665
Rosso Piceno, Aurora	643
Rosso Piceno, Boccadigabbia	631
Rosso Piceno, Castello Fageto	645
Rosso Piceno, Cocci Grifoni	655
Rosso Piceno, Tenuta De Angelis	629
Rosso Piceno, Fattoria Laila	638
Rosso Piceno, Saladini Pilastri	651
Rosso Piceno, Santa Cassella	647
Rosso Piceno, Villa Pigna	655
Rosso Piceno Bacchus, Ciù Ciù	643
Rosso Piceno Bulciano, Fattoria di Forano	626
Rosso Piceno Casa Nostra, Vallerosa Bonci	633
Rosso Piceno Castru Vecchiu, Saputi	653
Rosso Piceno Colle Ambro, Gioacchino Garofoli	635
Rosso Piceno Collemura, San Savino - Poderi Capecci	649
Rosso Piceno di Gino, Fattoria San Lorenzo	638
Rosso Piceno Duca Guarnerio, Capinera	641
Rosso Piceno Farnio, Gioacchino Garofoli	635
Rosso Piceno Fontursio, La Fontursia	655
Rosso Piceno GrAnarijS, Rio Maggio	640
Rosso Piceno Grizio, Fonte della Luna - Medoro Cimarelli	656
Rosso Piceno Grotte sul Mare, Vinicola del Tesino	634
Rosso Piceno Il Maschio da Monte, Santa Barbara	627
Rosso Piceno Il Moro, Cavallaro	655
Rosso Piceno Lyricus, Colonnara Viticoltori in Cupramontana	632
Rosso Piceno Marinus, Il Conte	640
Rosso Piceno Montenereto, Saputi	653
Rosso Piceno Montesecco, Montecappone	635
Rosso Piceno Morellone, Le Caniette	648
Rosso Piceno Nero di Vite, Le Caniette	648
Rosso Piceno Ophites, San Giovanni	644
Rosso Piceno Orum Sup., Ciù Ciù	643
Rosso Piceno Regina del Bosco, Fattoria Dezi	651
Rosso Piceno Roccaviva, Terre Cortesi Moncaro	639
Rosso Piceno Rosso Bello, Le Caniette	648
Rosso Piceno Rosso Bello Memoria Storica N° 1, Le Caniette	648
Rosso Piceno Rusus, Castello Fageto	645
Rosso Piceno Santa Maria d'Arco, Enrico Ceci	656
Rosso Piceno Sup., Aurora	643
Rosso Piceno Sup., Tenuta De Angelis	629
Rosso Piceno Sup. Castellano, La Cantina dei Colli Ripani	648
Rosso Piceno Sup. Gotico, Ciù Ciù	643
Rosso Piceno Sup. Il Brecciarolo, Ercole Velenosi	626
Rosso Piceno Sup. Leo Guelfus, San Giovanni	644
Rosso Piceno Sup. Leo Ripanus, La Cantiina dei Colli Ripani	648
Rosso Piceno Sup. Naumachos, Vinicola del Tesino	634
Rosso Piceno Sup. Oro, Tenuta De Angelis	629
Rosso Piceno Sup. Picus, San Savino - Poderi Capecci	649
Rosso Piceno Sup. Roggio del Filare, Ercole Velenosi	626
Rosso Piceno Sup. Rosso del Nonno, San Giovanni	644
Rosso Piceno Sup. V. Monteprandone, Saladini Pilastri	651
Rosso Piceno Sup. V. Montetinello, Saladini Pilastri	651
Rosso Piceno Talliano, Laurentina	639
Rosso Piceno Tenuta Pongelli, Bucci	645
Rosso Piceno Transone, La Cant. dei Colli Ripani	648
Rosso Piceno V. Piediprato, Saladini Pilastri	651
Rosso Piceno Villa Forano, Fattoria di Forano	626
Rosso Poculum, Agnes	208
Rosso San Lorenzo, San Lorenzo	663
Rosso Sergio, Michele Castellani	300
Rosso Sorbus, Tenuta di Collosorbo	522
Rosso Valletta, Firmino Miotti	291
Rosso Vigliano, Vigliano	603
Rosso Virzì, Spadafora	777
Rossole, Borgo Salcetino	565
Rossonero, Leone Conti	439
Rossore, Iuli - Ca.Vi.Mon.	69
Rouchet Briccorosa, Antica Casa Vinicola Scarpa	126
Rouge du Prieur, Institut Agricole Régional	16
Rovai, Ca' del Vispo	576
Rovaio, La Lastra	580
Rozzano, Villa Pigna	655
Rubacuori Passito da Uve Stramature, Poderi Morini	441
Rubbio, Palazzone	670
Rubinia, La Montina	202
Rubino, La Palazzola	674
Rubino, Maurizio Marconi	649
Rubis, Mille Una	746
Rubizzo, Rocca delle Macìe	481
Rubrum, Il Carpino	415
Ruché di Castagnole M.to Bric Majoli, Dacapo	22
Ruché di Castagnole M.to 'Na Vota, Cantine Sant'Agata	138
Ruché di Castagnole M.to Pro Nobis, Cantine Sant'Agata	138
Rumpotino, Rubbia Al Colle	621
Runcu Brukau, Claudio Vio	177
Rupestro, Cardeto	668
Rupino V. di Cembra, La Vis/Valle di Cembra	234
S. Agata dei Goti Falanghina, Mustilli	722
S. Agata dei Goti Piedirosso, Mustilli	722
S. Agata dei Goti Rosso Conte Artus, Mustilli	722
S'Arai, F.lli Pala	800
S. Gimignano Rosso, Signano	619
S. Gimignano Rosso Acantho, Casa alle Vacche	577
S. Gimignano Rosso Folgore, Giovanni Panizzi	583
S. Gimignano Rosso Il Botticello, San Quirico	618
S. Gimignano Rosso Il Casato, Baroncini	576
S. J., Eredi Fuligni	525
Sabiniano di Casanova, Podere La Chiesa	622
Sabòt, Fattoria di Romignano	604
Saccaia, Piero Mancini	796
Saeculum, Riseccoli	602
Saffredi, Le Pupille	509
Sagana, Cusumano	779
Saggio Sangiovese, Ciù Ciù	643
Saia Grande, Maurigi	779
Salae Domini, Antonio Caggiano	724
Salamartano, Fattoria Montellori	494
Salento Primitivo, Alessia Imperatori	753
Salento Rosso, Vini Classici Cardone	747
Salento Rosso Mjère, Michele Calò & Figli	756
Salgalaluna Bianco, Aziende Vinicole Miceli	780
Salice Salentino, Casa Vinicola Apollonio	750
Salice Salentino, Castello Monaci	750
Salice Salentino, Alessia Imperatori	753
Salice Salentino, Lomazzi & Sarli	754
Salice Salentino Anticaia, Cant. Coop. Sandonaci	756
Salice Salentino Anticaia Ris., Cant. Coop. Sandonaci	756
Salice Salentino Bianco Donna Lisa, Leone de Castris	751
Salice Salentino Bianco Portafalsa, Francesco Candido	751
Salice Salentino Cantalupi Ris., Conti Zecca	746
Salice Salentino Morgana Alta Ris., Masseria Li Veli	741
Salice Salentino Pezzo Morgana, Masseria Li Veli	741
Salice Salentino Puteus, Mocavero	755
Salice Salentino Ris., Francesco Candido	751
Salice Salentino Rosato Le Pozzelle, Francesco Candido	751
Salice Salentino Rosso, Cosimo Taurino	745
Salice Salentino Rosso Cantalupi, Conti Zecca	746
Salice Salentino Rosso Donna Lisa Ris., Leone de Castris	751
Salice Salentino Rosso Ris., Cantele	744
Salice Salentino Rosso Te Deum Laudamus Casale Bevagna, Accademia dei Racemi	748
Salice Salentino Rosso Vecchia Torre, Cant. Soc. Coop. Leverano	754
Salice Salentino Selvarossa Ris., Cant. Due Palme	740
Salivolpe, Tenimenti Angelini	536
Sallier de La Tour, Sallier de La Tour	784
Saltapicchio Sangiovese, Boccadigabbia	631
Salvanél, Castel Noarna	239

Sammarco, Castello dei Rampolla 556
San Brunone, Querciavalle 487
San Carlo, Barone Pizzini 193
San Colombano Monastero di Valbissera,
  Poderi di San Pietro 209
San Colombano Rosso di Valbissera, Poderi di San Pietro 209
San Colombano Roverone, Enrico Riccardi 225
San Colombano Vigna Battaia, Giuseppe Guglielmini 222
San Donato, Tenuta di Bagnolo dei Marchesi Pancrazi 542
San Dordi, Casa Roma 327
San Gimignano Rosso San Biagio, F.lli Vagnoni 584
San Gioan I Carati, Pasini Produttori 224
San Giorgio, Lungarotti 675
San Giusto, San Giusto 614
San Leopardo,
  Belisario Cant. Soc. di Matelica e Cerreto d'Esi 636
San Leopoldo, Tenuta Il Poggione 528
San Lorenzo, Sassotondo 587
San Marino Brugneto, Cons. Vini Tipici di San Marino 462
San Marino Tessano Ris., Cons. Vini Tipici di San Marino 462
San Marsan Bianco, Bertelli 72
San Marsan Rosso, Bertelli 72
San Martino, Villa Cafaggio 560
San Martino della Battaglia Campo del Soglio,
  Cantine Colli a Lago 220
San Pio, Mastrojanni 532
San Rocco, Feudo Principi di Butera 767
San Severo Bianco Candelaro, D'Alfonso del Sordo 752
San Severo Rosato Posta Arignano, D'Alfonso del Sordo 752
San Severo Rosso Posta Arignano, D'Alfonso del Sordo 752
San Verano, Agri Peccioli 613
San Vincenzo, Roberto Anselmi 307
San Vito di Luzzi Rosato, Luigi Vivacqua 762
San Vito di Luzzi Rosso, Luigi Vivacqua 762
San Zio, Cantine Leonardo da Vinci 593
Sancta Catharina, Dei 544
Sandiavolo, Canonica a Cerreto 598
Sangervasio Rosso, San Gervasio 554
Sangiovese, Tenuta Bacco e Petroio 622
Sangiovese, Castello delle Regine 658
Sangiovese, Di Majo Norante 698
Sangiovese, La Palazzola 674
Sangiovese, Castello di Monastero 486
Sangiovese, Palazzone 670
Sangiovese, San Lorenzo 618
Sangiovese Chiostro, San Lorenzo 663
Sangiovese di Romagna, Umberto Cesari 436
Sangiovese di Romagna, Leone Conti 439
Sangiovese di Romagna Amarcord d'un Ross Ris., Treré 442
Sangiovese di Romagna Auriga, Stefano Ferrucci 436
Sangiovese di Romagna Ca' Grande, Umberto Cesari 436
Sangiovese di Romagna Campo Rosso Ris.,
  Tenuta Poggio Pollino 460
Sangiovese di Romagna Canova, Tenuta Pandolfa 451
Sangiovese di Romagna Domus Caia Ris., Stefano Ferrucci 436
Sangiovese di Romagna I Probi di Papiano, Villa Papiano 447
Sangiovese di Romagna Le Iadi Ris., Paolo Francesconi 440
Sangiovese di Romagna Le Papesse di Papiano, Villa Papiano 447
Sangiovese di Romagna Olmatello Ris., La Berta 435
Sangiovese di Romagna Pergami Ris., Tenuta Amalia 459
Sangiovese di Romagna Prugneto, Poderi dal Nespoli 438
Sangiovese di Romagna Ris., Tenuta Ca' Lunga 459
Sangiovese di Romagna Ris., Umberto Cesari 436
Sangiovese di Romagna Ris., La Macolina 459
Sangiovese di Romagna Ris., Tre Monti 445
Sangiovese di Romagna Ris., Tenuta Uccellina 462
Sangiovese di Romagna Riserva della Beccaccia, Tenuta Valli 444
Sangiovese di Romagna Riserva della Beccaccia Ris.,
  Tenuta Valli 444
Sangiovese di Romagna Sup., Tre Monti 445
Sangiovese di Romagna Sup. Aulente, San Patrignano 439
Sangiovese di Romagna Sup. Avi Ris., San Patrignano 439
Sangiovese di Romagna Sup. Baccanale, Tenuta Diavoletta 457
Sangiovese di Romagna Sup. Beccaccio, Poderi Morini 441
Sangiovese di Romagna Sup. Calisto, Stefano Bertì 442
Sangiovese di Romagna Sup. Centurione, Stefano Ferrucci 436
Sangiovese di Romagna Sup. Ceregio, Fattoria Zerbina 440
Sangiovese di Romagna Sup. Ceregio V. Querce,
  Fattoria Zerbina 440
Sangiovese di Romagna Sup. Fermavento, Giovanna Madonia 433
Sangiovese di Romagna Sup. Gaudentia, Tenuta Godenza 459
Sangiovese di Romagna Sup. Il Bruno, Calonga 443
Sangiovese di Romagna Sup. Il Colombarone, Tenuta La Viola 457
Sangiovese di Romagna Sup. Il Palazzetto, Tenuta Valli 444
Sangiovese di Romagna Sup. Il Tibano, Tenuta Valli 444
Sangiovese di Romagna Sup. La Badia Ris., Tenuta La Viola 457
Sangiovese di Romagna Sup. Le Case Rosse, Tenuta Amalia 459
Sangiovese di Romagna Sup. Le Grillaie, Celli 432
Sangiovese di Romagna Sup. Le Grillaie Ris., Celli 432
Sangiovese di Romagna Sup. Le More, Castelluccio 446
Sangiovese di Romagna Sup. Mastro Guido, Tenuta Diavoletta 457
Sangiovese di Romagna Sup. Michelangiolo Ris., Calonga 443
Sangiovese di Romagna Sup. Millennium Ris.,
  Fattoria Camerone 458
Sangiovese di Romagna Sup. Mirus Ris., Tenuta Godenza 459
Sangiovese di Romagna Sup. Mistero, Tenuta Ca' Lunga 459
Sangiovese di Romagna Sup. Nonno Rico Ris., Poderi Morini 441
Sangiovese di Romagna Sup. Ombroso Ris.,
  Giovanna Madonia 433
Sangiovese di Romagna Sup. Poderepozzo Le Betulle,
  Leone Conti 439
Sangiovese di Romagna Sup. Pruno Ris.,
  Drei Donà Tenuta La Palazza 443
Sangiovese di Romagna Sup. Ravaldo, Stefano Berti 442
Sangiovese di Romagna Sup. Romio,
  Terragens Fine Wines - Volo Rosso 433

Sangiovese di Romagna Sup. Romio Ris.,
  Terragens Fine Wines - Volo Rosso 433
Sangiovese di Romagna Sup. Rosso del Camerone
  Ris., Fattoria Camerone 458
Sangiovese di Romagna Sup. Rosso del Montale, Tenuta Valli 444
Sangiovese di Romagna Sup. Santodeno, Poderi dal Nespoli 438
Sangiovese di Romagna Sup. Scabi, San Valentino 452
Sangiovese di Romagna Sup. Solano, La Berta 435
Sangiovese di Romagna Sup. Terra di Corvignano
  Ris., San Valentino 452
Sangiovese di Romagna Sup. Thea, Tre Monti 445
Sangiovese di Romagna Sup. Torre di Ceparano,
  Fattoria Zerbina 440
Sangiovese di Romagna Sup. Torre di Oriolo, Poderi Morini 441
Sangiovese di Romagna Sup. Tre Rocche,
  Casetto dei Mandorli 461
Sangiovese di Romagna Sup. V. del Molino, Fattoria Paradiso 432
Sangiovese di Romagna Sup. V. delle Lepri Ris.,
  Fattoria Paradiso 432
Sangiovese di Romagna Sup. V. dello Sperone, Treré 442
Sangiovese di Romagna Sup. VignalMonte, Podere Vecciano 459
Sangiovese di Romagna Sup. Villa Rasponi Ris.,
  Colonna - Vini Spalletti 462
Sangiovese di Romagna Sup. Zarricante Ris., San Patrignano 439
Sangiovese di Romagna Tito San Martino, Tenuta Amalia 459
Sangiovese di Romagna V. del Generale Ris.,
  Casetto dei Mandorli 461
Sangiovese di Romagna V. del Monte, Treré 442
Sangiovese di Romagna V. delle Iadi Ris., Paolo Francesconi 440
Sangiovese di Romagna V. di Cambro, Tenuta Poggio Pollino 460
Sangiovese di Romagna Vign. Il Prugneto, Poderi dal Nespoli 438
Sangiovese Don Camillo, Farnese 703
Sangiovese Farneto Valley, Farnese 703
Sangiovese Merlot Pieve di Spaltenna, Castello di Meleto 498
Sangiovese Moggio, San Savino - Poderi Capecci 649
Sangiovese Vigna La Pieve, Fanini 661
Sangioveto, Badia a Coltibuono 496
Sanleone, Fattoria Castello Sonnino 612
Sannio Aglianico, Cantine Caputo 712
Sannio Aglianico, Colli Irpini 718
Sannio Aglianico, Corte Normanna 716
Sannio Aglianico Clanius, Cantine Caputo 712
Sannio Aglianico Tre Pietre, Corte Normanna 716
Sannio Agliatico Clanius, Cantine Caputo 712
Sannio Barbera Barbetta Vàndari, Antica Masseria Venditti 726
Sannio Bianco, Antica Masseria Venditti 726
Sannio Falanghina, Colli Irpini 718
Sannio Falanghina, Di Meo 721
Sannio Falanghina, Feudi di San Gregorio 723
Sannio Falanghina La Palombaia, Corte Normanna 716
Sannio Falanghina Opera, Fattoria Torre Gaia 727
Sannio Falanghina Simposium, Colli Irpini 718
Sannio Falanghina Vigna delle Ginestre V.T., De Lucia 727
Sannio Fiano Colle di Tilio, La Guardiense 727
Sannio Greco Koinè, Fattoria Torre Gaia 727
Sannio Rosso, Antica Masseria Venditti 726
Sant'Agata dei Goti Aglianico Cesco di Nece, Mustilli 722
Sant'Amato, Fattoria Montellori 494
Sant'Antimo Ateo, Ciacci Piccolomini D'Aragona 521
Sant'Antimo Ca' del Pazzo, Tenuta Caparzo 517
Sant'Antimo Cabernet Sauvignon Camigliano,
  Castello di Camigliano 516
Sant'Antimo Colvecchio, Castello Banfi 515
Sant'Antimo Cum Laude, Castello Banfi 515
Sant'Antimo Do, Il Paradiso di Frassina 607
Sant'Antimo Excelsus, Castello Banfi 515
Sant'Antimo Fabius, Ciacci Piccolomini D'Aragona 521
Sant'Antimo Fontanelle Chardonnay, Castello Banfi 515
Sant'Antimo Gea, Il Paradiso di Frassina 607
Sant'Antimo La Fortuna, Podere La Fortuna 528
Sant'Antimo Pietradonice, Casanova di Neri 517
Sant'Antimo Rosso, Fanti - San Filippo 525
Sant'Antimo Rosso Romito del Romitorio,
  Castello Romitorio 534
Sant'Antimo Serena Sauvignon Blanc, Castello Banfi 515
Sant'Antimo Summus, Castello Banfi 515
Sant'Antimo Tavernelle, Castello Banfi 515
Sant'Efeis, Cant. Soc. della Trexenta 799
Sant'Ippolito, Cantine Leonardo da Vinci 593
Santa Brigida, Fattoria La Ripa 467
Santa Brigida, Masseria Monaci 742
Santa Cecilia, Planeta 774
Santa Chiara, Tenuta Terre Nobili 765
Santa Cristina, Marchesi Antinori 492
Santa Giulia, Cristine Vaselli 683
Santagostino Bianco Baglio Soria, Firriato 776
Santagostino Rosso Baglio Soria, Firriato 776
Santo Pellegrino, La Ciarliana 546
Santomío Rosso, Giacomo Montresor 342
Santufili, Mocavero 755
Saraceno, Coop. Svevo - Lucera 754
Saramago, Ca' Ronesca 383
Sarastro, Morgassi Superiore 85
Sardegna Semidano Sup. Puisteris, Cant. Soc. Il Nuraghe 803
Sarica Rosso, Pisoni 234
Sarmaro Bianco, Curatolo 785
Sartiano, Bigi 668
Sassello, Castello di Verrazzano 506
Sassicaia, Tenuta San Guido 471
Sassoalloro, Tenuta Il Greppo 526
Sassobucato, Russo 590
Sassòne, Spinsanti 628
Sassotondo Rosso, Sassotondo 587
Satrico, Casale del Giglio 681
Sauvignon, Nicola Balter 241
Sauvignon, Casa Roma 327

Sauvignon, Casale del Giglio	681
Sauvignon, Weingut Falkenstein	278
Sauvignon, Farnetella	586
Sauvignon, La Cappuccina	308
Sauvignon, Camillo Montori	699
Sauvignon, Pojer & Sandri	232
Sauvignon, Villa Brunesca	347
Sauvignon, Jermann Vinnaioli	388
Sauvignon Del Frate, Triacca	215
Sauvignon Ghiaiolo, Orlandi Contucci Ponno	705
Sauvignon Kolàus, Pierpaolo Pecorari	421
Sauvignon Montesanto, Bonotto delle Tezze	352
Sauvignon Ornella, Ornella Molon Traverso	317
Sauvignon Sansaia, Giacomo Montresor	342
Sauvignon Vulcaia, Inama	317
Sauvignon Vulcaia Fumé, Inama	317
Savuto, Odoardi	762
Savuto Sup. Vigna Mortilla, Odoardi	762
Saxa Calida, Il Paradiso	579
Scaloti, Cosimo Taurino	745
Scannagallo, Fattoria Santa Vittoria	601
Scarlet, Pasqualetti Viticoltori	613
Scasso dei Cesari, Tenuta di Valgiano	511
Scasso del Bugiardo, Tenuta di Valgiano	511
Scavigna Pian della Corte, Odoardi	762
Scavigna Vigna Garrone, Odoardi	762
Scheria Rosso, Pietratorcia	727
Schiaccianoci, Vigne & Vini	745
Schiaffo, Colacicchi	680
Schiava della Bergamasca, Cant. Soc. Bergamasca	210
Schiava della Bergamasca, Cant. Soc. Val San Martino	223
Schiccato, Nobile Prima	491
Schidione, Tenuta Il Greppo	526
Schietto Rosso, Spadafora	777
Schietto Syrah, Spadafora	777
Schioppettino, Borgo Conventi	387
Schioppettino, Vignai da Duline	420
Sciara di Villagrande Rosso, Barone di Villagrande	776
Scioppettino Picotis Grand Cru, Livon	419
Scirus, Le Sorgenti	465
Scrio, Le Macchiole	470
Scuderie del Cielo Bianco, Filomusi Guelfi	707
Scurati, Ceuso	766
Scyri, COS	782
Sedàra, Tenuta di Donnafugata	772
Seduzione, Eubea	734
Seifile, Fiorenzo Nada	147
Selciaio, Il Toppello	662
Selvascura, Guicciardini Strozzi - Fattoria Cusona	578
Selvatelle, Azienda Agricola Il Colle	616
Semifonte di Semifonte, Castello di Vicchiomaggio	507
Ser Gioveto, Rocca delle Macìe	481
Ser Niccolò Solatio del Tani, Machiavelli	575
Ser Piero, Cantine Leonardo da Vinci	593
Serafina, Poderi di San Pietro	209
Seragio, Granducato	562
Seraselva, Poggio al Sole	592
Serpico, Feudi di San Gregorio	723
Serra delle Querce, D'Angelo	733
Serralori Rosato, Antonio Argiolas	799
Serrata di Belguardo, Tenuta Belguardo	508
Serrone, Castello Fageto	645
Sette Chiese, Demetrio Serracavallo	760
Sette Pievi, Vigne dei Boschi	458
Sghiras, Le Sorgenti	465
Shahrazad, Mille Una	746
Shahryar, Mille Una	746
Shams, Ajello	774
Shàrjs, Livio Felluga	371
Shiraz, Casale del Giglio	681
Shiraz, Colle San Lorenzo	684
Shiraz Cabernet Sauvignon, Cantine San Marco	685
Sibiola Rosato, Cantine di Dolianova	793
Siepi, Castello di Fonterutoli	478
Sigillo Primo Chardonnay, Antica Masseria del Sigillo	744
Sigillo Rosso, Avide	770
Signorelli, La Calonica	546
Signorio Rosso, Barone La Lumia	784
Sikélios Rosso, Tenuta Scilio	785
Similoro Bianco, Malena	759
Simut, Monteacuto	224
Sinfarosa Primitivo, Accademia dei Racemi	748
Sirio, Vignalta	334
Sirius, Tenuta Giuncheo	168
Siùm, La Viarte	409
Sizzano, Bianchi	142
Sizzano, Dessilani	79
Soave, La Cappuccina	308
Soave, Tamellini	332
Soave Cl., Cant. del Castello	329
Soave Cl., Coffele	330
Soave Cl., Gini	308
Soave Cl., Guerrieri Rizzardi	289
Soave Cl., Bruno Martinelli	349
Soave Cl., Leonildo Pieropan	331
Soave Cl., Prà	310
Soave Cl., Suavia	331
Soave Cl. Anguane, Tamellini	332
Soave Cl. Brognoligo, Cecilia Beretta	341
Soave Cl. Ca' Vecchie I Fossili, Cant. di Montecchia	348
Soave Cl. Ca' Visco, Coffele	330
Soave Cl. Calvarino, Leonildo Pieropan	331
Soave Cl. Capitel Alto, Giacomo Montresor	342
Soave Cl. Capocolle, Lenotti	345
Soave Cl. Clivus, Cant. Soc. di Monteforte d'Alpone	349
Soave Cl. Colle S. Antonio, Prà	310
Soave Cl. Corte Menini, Le Mandolare	309
Soave Cl. Il Nicolaio, Roncolato	351
Soave Cl. Il Roccolo, Le Mandolare	309
Soave Cl. Il Vicario, Cant. Soc. di Monteforte d'Alpone	349
Soave Cl. in Casette Foscarin, Monte Tondo	330
Soave Cl. La Froscà, Gini	308
Soave Cl. Le Bine, Tamellini	332
Soave Cl. Monte Carbonare, Suavia	331
Soave Cl. Monte Fiorentine, Ca' Rugate	307
Soave Cl. Monte Grande, Prà	310
Soave Cl. Monte Tondo, Monte Tondo	330
Soave Cl. Monteforte, Santi	297
Soave Cl. Montefoscarino, Santa Sofia	323
Soave Cl. Monteleon, Roncolato	351
Soave Cl. Pressoni, Cant. del Castello	329
Soave Cl. Rocca Sveva, Cant. di Soave	329
Soave Cl. San Michele, Ca' Rugate	307
Soave Cl. Sanfederici, Santi	297
Soave Cl. Sup. Acini Soavi, Cant. del Castello	329
Soave Cl. Sup. Alzari, Coffele	330
Soave Cl. Sup. Anguane, Tamellini	332
Soave Cl. Sup. Bucciato, Ca' Rugate	307
Soave Cl. Sup. Ca' Visco, Coffele	330
Soave Cl. Sup. Contrada Salvarenza Vecchie Vigne, Gini	308
Soave Cl. Sup. Costeggiola, Guerrieri Rizzardi	289
Soave Cl. Sup. La Froscà, Gini	308
Soave Cl. Sup. La Rocca, Leonildo Pieropan	331
Soave Cl. Sup. Le Rive, Suavia	331
Soave Cl. Sup. Monte Alto, Ca' Rugate	307
Soave Cl. Sup. Monte Carbonare, Suavia	331
Soave Cl. Sup. Monte Carniga, Cant. del Castello	329
Soave Cl. Sup. Monte Casarsa, Tenuta Faltracco	310
Soave Cl. Sup. Monte Grande, Prà	310
Soave Cl. Sup. Monte Pressoni, Cant. del Castello	329
Soave Cl. Sup. Pieve Vecchia, Fasoli	292
Soave Cl. Sup. Sereole, Bertani	311
Soave Cl. Sup. V. Ronchetto, Umberto Portinari	309
Soave Cl. Sup. Valentina, Bruno Martinelli	349
Soave Cl. Sup. Vign. Calvarino, Leonildo Pieropan	331
Soave Cl. Sup. Vign. di Foscarino, Inama	317
Soave Cl. Sup. Vign. Du Lot, Inama	317
Soave Cl. Sup. Vign. in Casette Foscarin, Monte Tondo	330
Soave Cl. Sup. Vign. La Rocca, Leonildo Pieropan	331
Soave Cl. Sup. Vign. Monte Foscarino Le Bine, Giuseppe Campagnola	299
Soave Cl. V. Ronchetto, Umberto Portinari	309
Soave Cl. Vign. di Ca' de Napa Domini Veneti, Cant. Soc. Valpolicella	312
Soave Cl. Vign. di Montegrande, Pasqua Vigneti e Cantine	342
Soave Cl. Villa Rasina, Cant. di Soave	329
Soave Cl. Vin Soave, Inama	317
Soave Mito, Monte Tondo	330
Soave Partenio, Corte Sant'Alda	302
Soave Sup. Fontégo, La Cappuccina	308
Soave Sup. La Broia, Roccolo Grassi	303
Soave Sup. Monte Ceriani, Tenuta Sant'Antonio	304
Soave Sup. S. Brizio, La Cappuccina	308
Soave Sup. Sagramoso, Pasqua Vigneti e Cantine	342
Soave Sup. San Brizio, La Cappuccina	308
Soave Sup. Santo Stefano, Umberto Portinari	309
Soave Sup. V. Albare Doppia Maturazione Ragionata, Umberto Portinari	309
Soave V. Albare Doppia Maturazione Ragionata, Umberto Portinari	309
Soave Vign. Terrelunghe, Agostino Vicentini	346
Sodole, Guicciardini Strozzi - Fattoria Cusona	578
Sogno di Dama, Barone La Lumia	784
Sol Doré, Provenza	195
Solace, Paradiso	753
Solaia, Marchesi Antinori	492
Solalto, Le Pupille	509
Solare, Capannelle	497
Solare, La Pierotta	620
Solarianne, Solaria - Cencioni	535
Solarolo, Poderi di San Pietro	209
Solatia, Tenimenti Ruffino	564
Solatio, Borgo Casignano	599
Solativo, Ferrando	89
Soldati La Scolca Brut, La Scolca	159
Sole dei Padri, Spadafora	777
Sole di Dario, Cantrina	183
Sole di Sesta, Cottanera	769
Sole e Vento, Marco De Bartoli	771
Solengo, Argiano	605
Solesine, Bellavista	195
Solinero, Tenute Rapitalà	768
Solitario, Cascina delle Terre Rosse	172
Solo, Di Palma	734
Solo Chardonnay, Castello di Monastero	486
Solo Sangiovese, Fattoria Dezi	651
Soloio, Casa Emma	466
Solomalvasia, Cantine San Marco	685
Solopaca Rosso Bosco Caldaia, Antica Masseria Venditti	726
Solopaca Rosso Guiscardo, Corte Normanna	716
Soloshiraz, Cantine San Marco	685
Sono Montenidoli, Montenidoli	581
Soremidio, Sant'Isidoro	694
Sorì di Bertolotto Vin Blanc, Traversa - Cascina Bertolotto	143
Sortì, Roberto Zeni	245
Sotsàs, Maso Cantanghel	231
Sottobosco, Palagetto	582
Sovana Rosso Aleatico Ris., Tenuta Roccaccia	562
Sovana Rosso La Roccaccia, Tenuta Roccaccia	562
Sovana Rosso Sup. Franze, Sassotondo	587
Sovana Rosso Sup. Franze, Sassotondo	587
Sovenigo, Delai	224

Spargolo, Famiglia Cecchi	479		TdF Bianco Curtefranca, Bersi Serlini	207
Spigau Crociata, Le Rocche del Gatto	167		TdF Bianco Curtefranca, Ca' del Bosco	196
Spirto, Sant'Agnese	615		TdF Bianco Curtefranca, Contadi Castaldi	182
Spumante Cl. Brut Roccolo delle Rose, Cant. Soc. La Versa	211		TdF Bianco Curtefranca, Enrico Gatti	197
Spumante Cl. Cuvée Extra Dry Testarossa, Cant. Soc. La Versa	211		TdF Bianco Curtefranca, Ricci Curbastro	186
Spumante Extra Brut Vign. del Convento, F.lli Bortolin Spumanti	335		TdF Bianco dei Frati Priori, Uberti	198
Spumante M. Cl. Brut Ris. Giuseppe Contratto, Contratto	55		TdF Bianco Dossi delle Querce, F.lli Berlucchi	193
Squinzano Rosso, Cant. Due Palme	740		TdF Bianco Favento, Ferghettina	197
Stàngja Rosso, Franco Visintin	394		TdF Bianco Febo, Le Cantorie	219
Stefano Antonucci Rosso, Santa Barbara	627		TdF Bianco Il Dossello, Lo Sparviere	203
Stefano Ferrucci Vino da Uve Stramature, Stefano Ferrucci	436		TdF Bianco Le Arzelle, Guido Berlucchi & C.	194
Stella del Teso, Fattoria del Teso	541		TdF Bianco Manca Pane, Contadi Castaldi	182
Sterpigno Merlot, Giovanna Madonia	433		TdF Bianco Marengo, Villa	203
Stielle, Rocca di Castagnoli	500		TdF Bianco Maria Medici, Uberti	198
Stignano, San Vincenti	501		TdF Bianco Palazzina, Mirabella	208
Stoppa, La Stoppa	452		TdF Bianco Pian della Villa, Villa	203
Stravino di Stravino, Pravis	234		TdF Bianco Pio Elemosiniere, Bredasole	205
Strinà Passito, Manara	322		TdF Bianco Rampaneto, Cavalleri	196
Stroncoli, Giacomo Marengo	539		TdF Bianco Solicano, Bonomi - Tenuta Castellino	192
Su Baroni, Vitivincola Su Baroni	803		TdF Bianco Sottobosco, Ronco Calino	182
Su Gucciu, Gostolai	804		TdF Bianco Sulìf, Il Mosnel	206
Sud, Le Vigne di San Pietro	333		TdF Bianco Uccellanda, Bellavista	195
Suffragium, Claudio Morelli	634		TdF Bianco Vign. Palanca, La Montina	202
Sul Bric, Franco M. Martinetti	144		TdF Bianco Vigna Bosco Alto, Ricci Curbastro	186
Sulana, Baglio Hopps	771		TdF Chardonnay, Ca' del Bosco	196
Sulky, Sardus Pater	797		TdF Chardonnay Polzina, Barone Pizzini	193
Sumanero, Santa Barbara	756		TdF Curtefranca Bianco, Bellavista	195
Suolo, Argiano	605		TdF Gatti Bianco, Enrico Gatti	197
Syrae, Pravis	234		TdF Rosso, Bonomi - Tenuta Castellino	192
Syrah, Baglio Hopps	771		TdF Rosso, CastelFaglia	190
Syrah, Castagnoli	477		TdF Rosso, Cavalleri	196
Syrah, Feotto dello Jato	787		TdF Rosso, Ferghettina	197
Syrah, Castelli del Grevepesa	572		TdF Rosso, La Montina	202
Syrah, Isole e Olena	467		TdF Rosso, Lantieri de Paratico	185
Syrah, Aziende Vinicole Miceli	780		TdF Rosso, Ronco Calino	182
Syrah, Planeta	774		TdF Rosso, San Cristoforo	220
Syrah, Poggio al Sole	592		TdF Rosso, Villa	203
Syrah, Castello di Poppiano	552		TdF Rosso Augustus, Uberti	198
Syrah, Sallier de La Tour	784		TdF Rosso Baldoc, Cornaleto	216
Syrah, Streda in Belvedere	622		TdF Rosso Capineto, Bonomi - Tenuta Castellino	192
Syrah, Vallarom	229		TdF Rosso Colzano, Lantieri de Paratico	185
Syrah, Villa Pillo	502		TdF Rosso Curtefranca, Barone Pizzini	193
Syrah Case Via, Tenuta Fontodi	557		TdF Rosso Curtefranca, F.lli Berlucchi	193
Syrah Cicogna, Domenico Cavazza & F.lli	306		TdF Rosso Curtefranca, Bersi Serlini	207
Syrah Mandrarossa, Settesoli	775		TdF Rosso Curtefranca, Ca' del Bosco	196
Taburno Coda di Volpe, Ocone	728		TdF Rosso Curtefranca, Enrico Gatti	197
Taburno Coda di Volpe Amineo, Cant. del Taburno	714		TdF Rosso Curtefranca, Le Cantorie	219
Taburno Falanghina, Cant. del Taburno	714		TdF Rosso dei Dossi, La Montina	202
Taburno Falanghina, Fattoria La Rivolta	725		TdF Rosso Fontecolo, Il Mosnel	206
Taburno Falanghina Folius, Cant. del Taburno	714		TdF Rosso Gradoni, Villa	203
Taburno Falanghina Vigna del Monaco, Ocone	728		TdF Rosso Il Sergnana, Lo Sparviere	203
Tal Lûc, Lis Neris	421		TdF Rosso Maniero, Mirabella	208
Talenti Rosso, Talenti	536		TdF Rosso Ruc di Gnoc, Majolini	205
Talento Banfi Brut M. Cl., Vigne Regali	144		TdF Rosso Santella del Gröm, Ricci Curbastro	186
Talento Brut Etichetta Argento, Pittaro	366		TdF Rosso Vino del Cacciatore, Lo Sparviere	203
Talento Brut Etichetta Oro, Pittaro	366		Tegolaia, Travignoli	614
Talento Brut Ris., Desiderio Bisol & Figli	335		Tegolaro, Carini	672
Talia, Salvatore Murana	778		Tegolaro Sel. Dedicata Armando, Carini	672
Tamino, Morgassi Superiore	85		Tela di Ragno, Mocavero	755
Tamurro Nero, Tenuta Le Querce	731		Templaria, Cantine di Castignano	631
Tanca Su Conti, Cant. Soc. della Trexenta	799		Tener Brut N. M., Vigne Regali	144
Tanè, Cant. Valle dell'Acate	766		Tenores, Tenute Dettori	798
Tarabuso, Torre Quarto	741		Tenuta Albrizzi, Cant. Due Palme	740
Taras, Tenute Albano Carrisi	740		Tenuta Belguardo, Tenuta Belguardo	508
Tarasco Passito, Cornarea	156		Tenuta Casabianca, Fattoria Casabianca	553
Tarlo Rosso, Anzivino	82		Tenuta di Testarossa Bianco, Franco Pasetti	700
Tassinaia, Castello del Terriccio	482		Tenuta di Trinoro, Tenuta di Trinoro	584
Tato, Sant'Elena	393		Tenuta San Michele, Barone Scammacca del Murgo	788
Tauleto Sangiovese, Umberto Cesari	436		Teodoro, Tenuta Le Calcinaie	581
Tauleto Sel. Umberto Cesari, Umberto Cesari	436		Teresa Manara Chardonnay, Cantele	744
Taurasi, Cant. del Barone	726		Teresa Manara Rosso, Cantele	744
Taurasi, D'Antiche Terre - Vega	727		Tergeno, Fattoria Zerbina	440
Taurasi, La Casa dell'Orco	719		Teroldego, Marion	319
Taurasi, Pietracupa	717		Teroldego Armilo, Nilo Bolognani	235
Taurasi, Urciuolo	727		Teroldego Lagrein, Villa Corniole	251
Taurasi, Villa Raiano	722		Teroldego Rotaliano, Cant. Rotaliana	238
Taurasi Fatica Contadina, Terredora	718		Teroldego Rotaliano, Marco Donati	237
Taurasi Macchia dei Goti, Antonio Caggiano	724		Teroldego Rotaliano, F.lli Dorigati - Metius	238
Taurasi Piano di Montevergine, Feudi di San Gregorio	723		Teroldego Rotaliano, Cipriano Fedrizzi	252
Taurasi Piano di Montevergine Ris., Feudi di San Gregorio	723		Teroldego Rotaliano, Foradori	239
Taurasi Radici, Mastroberardino	712		Teroldego Rotaliano, Zanini	252
Taurasi Ris., Di Meo	721		Teroldego Rotaliano Bagolari, Marco Donati	237
Taurasi Ris., Marianna	726		Teroldego Rotaliano Bottega de' Vinai,	
Taurasi Selve di Luoti, Feudi di San Gregorio	723		Cavit - Consorzio di Cantine Sociali	246
Taurasi Vigna Cinque Querce, Salvatore Molettieri	719		Teroldego Rotaliano Bottega Vinai, Cavit -	
Taurasi Vigna Cinque Querce Ris., Salvatore Molettieri	719		Consorzio di Cantine Sociali	246
Taurasi Vigna Macchia dei Goti, Antonio Caggiano	724		Teroldego Rotaliano Braide,	
Taurì, Antonio Caggiano	724		Concilio/Vigneti delle Meridiane	248
Tazzelenghe, Jacùss	424		Teroldego Rotaliano Canevarie, Cant. Rotaliana	238
Tazzelenghe Ris., Tenuta Beltrame	355		Teroldego Rotaliano Clesure, Cant. Rotaliana	238
TdF Bianco, Guido Berlucchi & C.	194		Teroldego Rotaliano Diedri Ris., F.lli Dorigati - Metius	238
TdF Bianco, Bonomi - Tenuta Castellino	192		Teroldego Rotaliano Due Vigneti, Cipriano Fedrizzi	252
TdF Bianco, CastelFaglia	190		Teroldego Rotaliano Le Cervare, Zanini	252
TdF Bianco, Cavalleri	196		Teroldego Rotaliano Maso Camorz, Endrizzi	244
TdF Bianco, Battista Cola	216		Teroldego Rotaliano Maso Cervara,	
TdF Bianco, Ferghettina	197		Cavit - Consorzio di Cantine Sociali	246
TdF Bianco, Lantieri de Paratico	185		Teroldego Rotaliano Pini, Roberto Zeni	245
TdF Bianco, Lo Sparviere	203		Teroldego Rotaliano Ris., Cant. Rotaliana	238
TdF Bianco, Ronco Calino	182		Teroldego Rotaliano Sangue del Drago, Marco Donati	237
TdF Bianco, Villa	203		Teroldego Rotaliano Sup., Gaierhof	241
TdF Bianco Antica Cant. Fratta, Guido Berlucchi & C.	194		Terra Antica, Terra Antica	612
TdF Bianco Campolarga, Il Mosnel	206		Terra Calda Rosso, Ca' de' Medici	462
TdF Bianco Colzano, Lantieri de Paratico	185		Terra dei Rovi Rosso, Luigino Dal Maso	306
TdF Bianco Convento dell'Annunciata, Bellavista	195		Terra di Lavoro, Galardi	723
TdF Bianco Curtefranca, Barone Pizzini	193		Terraccia, Demetrio Serracavallo	760
TdF Bianco Curtefranca, F.lli Berlucchi	193		Terraforte, Castello di Lispida	305

Terralba, Castello di Lispida	305
Terras Rosso, Josto Puddu	804
Terrato, Il Mandorlo	573
Terre Brune, Cant. Soc. di Santadi	797
Terre d'Agala, Duca di Salaparuta - Vini Corvo	769
Terre del Guiscardo, Antica Masseria del Sigillo	744
Terre del Volturno Aglianico Zicorrà, Cantine Caputo	712
Terre del Volturno Casavecchia Rosso, Cantine Caputo	712
Terre di Galatrona, Fattoria Petrolo	471
Terre di Ginestra 651, Calatrasi - Accademia del Sole	780
Terre di Ginestra Nero d'Avola, Calatrasi - Accademia del Sole	780
Terre di Maria, Maurigi	779
Terre di S. Nicola Rosso, Di Filippo	676
Terre di Sofia, Maurigi	779
Terre di Tufi, Teruzzi & Puthod	583
Terre Lontane, Librandi	759
Terresicci, Cantine di Dolianova	793
Terricci, Lanciola	511
Terso Bianco, Marchesi Fumanelli	350
Tertium, Cant. Cerveteri	683
Testal, Angelo Nicolis e Figli	323
Testamatta, Bibi Graetz	600
Tiare Bluv Grand Cru, Livon	419
Tigiolo, Lorenzo Begali	321
Tignanello, Marchesi Antinori	492
Timorasso, Morgassi Superiore	85
Tindaro Torre Sgarrata, Bepin de Eto	320
Tinorso, Poggio Capponi	612
Tinscvil, Castello di Monsanto	469
Titanium, Podere San Giorgio	211
Tiziano, Rietine	500
Tizzonero, La Carraia	669
Toar, Masi	327
Tor di Nubia Nero D'Avola, Marchesi Platamone	786
Torcicoda, Tormaresca	752
Torcularia Bianco, Carra	445
Torgiano Cabernet Sauvignon, Castello di Antignano - Brogal Vini	672
Torgiano Rosso Ris. Santa Caterina, Castello di Antignano - Brogal Vini	672
Torgiano Rosso Rubesco, Lungarotti	675
Torgiano Rosso Vigna Monticchio Ris., Lungarotti	675
Tormaresca Chardonnay, Tormaresca	752
Tormaresca Rosso, Tormaresca	752
Tornamagno, Colonnara Viticoltori in Cupramontana	632
Torraccia, Villa Simone	688
Torre del Noce Bianco, Marco Donati	237
Torre della Sirena, Conti Sertoli Salis	214
Torre di Ciardo, Marchesi Torrigiani	468
Torre di Re, Luciano Landi	628
Torre Ercolana, Colacicchi	680
Torre Maggiore, Fattoria Le Poggette	677
Torre Pasolina, Vini Pallavicini	689
Torre Testa, Tenute Rubino	739
Torri Bianche, Le Due Torri	429
Torrione, Fattoria Petrolo	471
Toscoforte, Castello di Poppiano	552
Traicolli, Poderi Morini	441
Traluce, Tenuta Le Velette	670
Trames, Tenuta Pegazzera	188
Traminer, Ornella Molon Traverso	317
Traminer, San Vettore	502
Traminer Aromatico, Jermann Vinnaioli	388
Tramonto d'Oca, Poggio Bonelli	487
Tranùi, Fattorie Azzolino	767
Trasgaia, Villa Trasqua	598
Tre Filer, Ca' dei Frati	212
Tre Fonti, Tenuta Valdipiatta	549
Trebbiano, Tenuta di Capezzana	474
Trebbiano d'Abruzzo, Barone Cornacchia	710
Trebbiano d'Abruzzo, Fattoria Buccicatino	708
Trebbiano d'Abruzzo, Luigi Cataldi Madonna	702
Trebbiano d'Abruzzo, Contesa di Rocco Pasetti	704
Trebbiano d'Abruzzo, Fattoria La Valentina	707
Trebbiano d'Abruzzo, Lepore	698
Trebbiano d'Abruzzo, Gianni Masciarelli	706
Trebbiano d'Abruzzo, Camillo Montori	699
Trebbiano d'Abruzzo, Bruno Nicodemi	702
Trebbiano d'Abruzzo, Terra d'Aligi - Spinelli	696
Trebbiano d'Abruzzo, Edoardo Valentini	701
Trebbiano d'Abruzzo, Villa Medoro	696
Trebbiano d'Abruzzo Aldiano, Cantina Tollo	708
Trebbiano d'Abruzzo Altare, Marramiero	705
Trebbiano d'Abruzzo Anima, Marramiero	705
Trebbiano d'Abruzzo Colle della Corte, Orlandi Contucci Ponno	705
Trebbiano d'Abruzzo Colle Maggio, Torre Zambra	710
Trebbiano d'Abruzzo Colle Morino, F.lli Barba	710
Trebbiano d'Abruzzo Colle Secco, Cantina Tollo	708
Trebbiano d'Abruzzo Dama, Marramiero	705
Trebbiano d'Abruzzo Diogene, Torre Zambra	710
Trebbiano d'Abruzzo Farneto Valley, Farnese	703
Trebbiano d'Abruzzo Fonte Cupa, Camillo Montori	699
Trebbiano d'Abruzzo Le Vigne, Faraone	700
Trebbiano d'Abruzzo Marina Cvetic, Gianni Masciarelli	706
Trebbiano d'Abruzzo Matté, Chiusa Grande	709
Trebbiano d'Abruzzo Natum, Agriverde	703
Trebbiano d'Abruzzo Pietrosa, Sarchese Dora	704
Trebbiano d'Abruzzo Preludio, Valori	706
Trebbiano d'Abruzzo Riseis, Agriverde	703
Trebbiano d'Abruzzo Sel., Bruno Nicodemi	702
Trebbiano d'Abruzzo Vigna Franca, F.lli Barba	710
Trebbiano di Romagna V. del Rio, Tre Monti	445
Trebiano V. T., Castello dei Rampolla	556
Trentino Bastie Alte Rosso, Maso Bastie	249
Trentino Bianco Aura, Vallis Agri	230
Trentino Bianco Castel San Michele, Ist. Agrario Provinciale San Michele all'Adige	244
Trentino Bianco Thamè, Cant. Rotaliana	238
Trentino Bianco Villa Margon, Lunelli	247
Trentino Cabernet, Cesconi	235
Trentino Cabernet, F.lli Dorigati - Metius	238
Trentino Cabernet, Grigoletti	240
Trentino Cabernet, Cant. Toblino	229
Trentino Cabernet Fratagranda, Pravis	234
Trentino Cabernet Pianilonghi, de Tarczal	232
Trentino Cabernet Sauvignon, Accademia del Vino Cadelaghet	251
Trentino Cabernet Sauvignon, de Tarczal	232
Trentino Cabernet Sauvignon, Maso Martis	248
Trentino Cabernet Sauvignon, Molino dei Lessi	251
Trentino Cabernet Sauvignon, Vallis Agri	230
Trentino Cabernet Sauvignon Marognon Ris., Longariva	243
Trentino Cabernet Sauvignon Maso Kinderlait Ris., Endrizzi	244
Trentino Cabernet Sauvignon Ritratti, La Vis/Valle di Cembra	234
Trentino Cabernet Sauvignon Rosso di Pila, Maso Cantanghel	231
Trentino Chardonnay, Accademia del Vino Cadelaghet	251
Trentino Chardonnay, Riccardo Battistotti	240
Trentino Chardonnay, Cesconi	235
Trentino Chardonnay, Dalzocchio	252
Trentino Chardonnay, de Tarczal	232
Trentino Chardonnay, Maso Furli	237
Trentino Chardonnay, Maso Martis	248
Trentino Chardonnay, Pisoni	234
Trentino Chardonnay, Ist. Agrario Provinciale San Michele all'Adige	244
Trentino Chardonnay, Arcangelo Sandri	251
Trentino Chardonnay, Armando Simoncelli	243
Trentino Chardonnay, Cant. Toblino	229
Trentino Chardonnay Bottega Vinai, Cavit - Consorzio di Cantine Sociali	246
Trentino Chardonnay Campo Grande, Castel Noarna	239
Trentino Chardonnay Costa Erta, Gaierhof	241
Trentino Chardonnay di Faedo, Graziano Fontana	231
Trentino Chardonnay I Giardini, Zanini	252
Trentino Chardonnay L'Incanto, Maso Martis	248
Trentino Chardonnay L'Opera, Grigoletti	240
Trentino Chardonnay Praistel, Longariva	243
Trentino Chardonnay Ritratti, La Vis/Valle di Cembra	234
Trentino Chardonnay Robur, Vignaiolo Giuseppe Fanti	236
Trentino Chardonnay Vign. Capitel, Armani	293
Trentino Chardonnay Vigna Brioni, Vallarom	229
Trentino Chardonnay Vigna Piccola, Maso Cantanghel	231
Trentino Chardonnay Villa Gentilotti, Lunelli	247
Trentino Chardonnay Villa Margon, Lunelli	247
Trentino Lagrein, Casata Monfort	251
Trentino Lagrein, Arcangelo Sandri	251
Trentino Lagrein, Armando Simoncelli	243
Trentino Lagrein di Faedo, Graziano Fontana	231
Trentino Lagrein Rosato, F.lli Dorigati - Metius	238
Trentino Lagrein Scuro, Cant. Toblino	229
Trentino Marzemino, Cant. Soc. di Avio	228
Trentino Marzemino, Riccardo Battistotti	240
Trentino Marzemino, Conti Bossi Fedrigotti	242
Trentino Marzemino, Cant. d'Isera	233
Trentino Marzemino, de Tarczal	232
Trentino Marzemino, Grigoletti	240
Trentino Marzemino, Letrari	242
Trentino Marzemino, Longariva	243
Trentino Marzemino, Cant. Soc. di Nomi	252
Trentino Marzemino, Armando Simoncelli	243
Trentino Marzemino, Enrico Spagnoli	233
Trentino Marzemino d'Isera Husar, de Tarczal	232
Trentino Marzemino dei Ziresi, Cavit - Consorzio di Cantine Sociali	246
Trentino Marzemino Don Giovanni, Enrico Spagnolli	233
Trentino Marzemino Etichetta Verde, Cant. d'Isera	233
Trentino Marzemino Maso Romani, Cavit - Consorzio di Cantine Sociali	246
Trentino Marzemino Poiema, Eugenio Rosi	249
Trentino Marzemino Sel., Letrari	242
Trentino Marzemino Sup. Etichetta Verde, Cant. d'Isera	233
Trentino Marzemino Verdini, Riccardo Battistotti	240
Trentino Marzemino Vigna Fornas, Vallis Agri	230
Trentino Marzemino Vigne Autari, Cant. di Ala	250
Trentino Merlot, Cesconi	235
Trentino Merlot, de Tarczal	232
Trentino Merlot, Armando Simoncelli	243
Trentino Merlot, Cant. Toblino	229
Trentino Merlot, Vallis Agri	230
Trentino Merlot, Vinicola Aldeno	250
Trentino Merlot Antica Vigna di Nomì, Grigoletti	240
Trentino Merlot Borgo Sacco, Vallis Agri	230
Trentino Merlot Campiano, de Tarczal	232
Trentino Merlot Ris., Gaierhof	241
Trentino Merlot Tajapreda, Maso Cantanghel	231
Trentino Merlot Tovi, Longariva	243
Trentino Moscato Giallo, Nilo Bolognani	235
Trentino Moscato Giallo, de Tarczal	232
Trentino Moscato Giallo, Enrico Spagnolli	233
Trentino Moscato Giallo, Vinicola Aldeno	250
Trentino Moscato Giallo Le Comete, Cant. Soc. di Nomi	252
Trentino Moscato Rosa, Riccardo Battistotti	240
Trentino Moscato Rosa, Letrari	242
Trentino Moscato Rosa, Roberto Zeni	245
Trentino Müller Thugau Vigna delle Forche V. di Cembra, La Vis/Valle di Cembra	234
Trentino Müller Thurgau, Nilo Bolognani	235
Trentino Müller Thurgau, Casata Monfort	251
Trentino Müller Thurgau, Arcangelo Sandri	251
Trentino Müller Thurgau, Enrico Spagnolli	233
Trentino Müller Thurgau, Cant. Toblino	229

848

Trentino Müller Thurgau, Villa Corniole 251
Trentino Müller Thurgau Bottega de' Vinai,
  Cavit - Consorzio di Cantine Sociali 246
Trentino Müller Thurgau dei Settecento, Gaierhof 241
Trentino Müller Thurgau di Faedo, Graziano Fontana 231
Trentino Müller Thurgau I Fiori del Trentino,
  Cant. Soc. di Nomi 252
Trentino Müller Thurgau La Rupe, Cant. Rotaliana 238
Trentino Müller Thurgau Le Croci, Roberto Zeni 245
Trentino Müller Thurgau Sup. dei Settecento, Gaierhof 241
Trentino Müller Thurgau Zeveri,
  Cavit - Consorzio di Cantine Sociali 246
Trentino Nosiola, Accademia del Vino Cadelaghet 251
Trentino Nosiola, Nilo Bolognani 235
Trentino Nosiola, Castel Noarna 239
Trentino Nosiola, Cesconi 235
Trentino Nosiola, Marco Donati 237
Trentino Nosiola, Vignaiolo Giuseppe Fanti 236
Trentino Nosiola, Pisoni 234
Trentino Nosiola, Enrico Spagnolli 233
Trentino Nosiola, Cant. Toblino 229
Trentino Nosiola Casot, Castel Noarna 239
Trentino Nosiola Maso Nero, Roberto Zeni 245
Trentino Nosiola V. di Cembra, La Vis/Valle di Cembra 234
Trentino Pinot Bianco, Cant. Soc. di Avio 228
Trentino Pinot Bianco, de Tarczal 232
Trentino Pinot Bianco, Letrari 242
Trentino Pinot Bianco,
  Ist. Agrario Provinciale San Michele all'Adige 244
Trentino Pinot Bianco, Armando Simoncelli 243
Trentino Pinot Bianco Pergole, Longariva 243
Trentino Pinot Bianco Sortì, Roberto Zeni 245
Trentino Pinot Grigio, Cesconi 235
Trentino Pinot Grigio, F.lli Dorigati - Metius 238
Trentino Pinot Grigio,
  Ist. Agrario Provinciale San Michele all'Adige 244
Trentino Pinot Grigio, Cant. Toblino 229
Trentino Pinot Grigio, Villa Corniole 251
Trentino Pinot Grigio Agiato, Cant. d'Isera 233
Trentino Pinot Grigio Bottega Vinai,
  Cavit - Consorzio di Cantine Sociali 246
Trentino Pinot Grigio Castel Pietra, Cant. Soc. di Nomi 252
Trentino Pinot Grigio Graminè, Longariva 243
Trentino Pinot Grigio La Rupe, Cant. Rotaliana 238
Trentino Pinot Grigio Maso Guà,
  Concilio/Vigneti delle Meridiane 248
Trentino Pinot Grigio Ritratti, La Vis/Valle di Cembra 234
Trentino Pinot Grigio Vigna Reselé, Vallis Agri 230
Trentino Pinot Nero, Accademia del Vino Cadelaghet 251
Trentino Pinot Nero, Cant. Soc. di Avio 228
Trentino Pinot Nero, Dalzocchio 252
Trentino Pinot Nero, Maso Martis 248
Trentino Pinot Nero, Enrico Spagnolli 233
Trentino Pinot Nero, Cant. Toblino 229
Trentino Pinot Nero, Vallarom 229
Trentino Pinot Nero Bottega Vinai,
  Cavit - Consorzio di Cantine Sociali 246
Trentino Pinot Nero di Faedo, Graziano Fontana 231
Trentino Pinot Nero Maso Montalto, Lunelli 247
Trentino Pinot Nero Maso Poli, Gaierhof 241
Trentino Pinot Nero Spiazol, Roberto Zeni 245
Trentino Pinot Nero Zabini, Maso Cantanghel 231
Trentino Rebo, Cant. d'Isera 233
Trentino Rebo, F.lli Dorigati - Metius 238
Trentino Rebo, Pisoni 234
Trentino Rebo, Cant. Toblino 229
Trentino Riesling, Pelz & Piffer 251
Trentino Rosso Esegesi, Eugenio Rosi 249
Trentino Rosso Maso Le Viane, Lunelli 247
Trentino Rosso Monastero,
  Ist. Agrario Provinciale San Michele all'Adige 244
Trentino Rosso Mori Vecio, Concilio/Vigneti delle Meridiane 248
Trentino Rosso Navesèl, Armando Simoncelli 243
Trentino Rosso Ris., Cant. Soc. di Avio 228
Trentino Rosso Sentieri Sel. 907, Cant. d'Isera 233
Trentino Rosso Tre Cesure Ris., Longariva 243
Trentino Sauvignon, Nilo Bolognani 235
Trentino Sauvignon, Cesconi 235
Trentino Sauvignon, Concilio/Vigneti delle Meridiane 248
Trentino Sauvignon, Maso Furli 237
Trentino Sauvignon, Cant. Toblino 229
Trentino Sauvignon Cascari, Longariva 243
Trentino Sauvignon di Faedo, Graziano Fontana 231
Trentino Sauvignon Vigneto Ronchi, Roberto Zeni 245
Trentino Sauvignon Villa San Nicolò, Lunelli 247
Trentino Sorni Bianco Maso Poli, Gaierhof 241
Trentino Sortì, Roberto Zeni 245
Trentino Traminer, Maso Bastie 249
Trentino Traminer, Pojer & Sandri 232
Trentino Traminer Aromatico, Casata Monfort 251
Trentino Traminer Aromatico, Cesconi 235
Trentino Traminer Aromatico, Maso Furli 237
Trentino Traminer Aromatico, Arcangelo Sandri 251
Trentino Traminer Aromatico, Cant. Toblino 229
Trentino Traminer di Faedo, Graziano Fontana 231
Trentino Vendemmia Tardiva, Cant. Soc. di Avio 228
Trentino Vino Santo, Pisoni 234
Trentino Vino Santo, Francesco Poli 252
Trentino Vino Santo, Giovanni Poli 252
Trentino Vino Santo, Cant. Toblino 229
Trentino Vino Santo Aréle, Cavit - Cons. di Cantine Sociali 246
Trento Abate Nero Extra Dry, Abate Nero 245
Trento Brut, Nicola Balter 241
Trento Brut, Cant. di Ala 250
Trento Brut, Cesarini Sforza 246
Trento Brut, Maso Martis 248

Trento Brut, Armando Simoncelli 243
Trento Brut Firmato, Cavit - Cons. di Cantine Sociali 246
Trento Brut Letrari Ris., Letrari 242
Trento Brut M. Cl., Roberto Zeni 245
Trento Brut Maximum, Ferrari 247
Trento Brut Perlé, Ferrari 247
Trento Brut Perlé Rosé, Ferrari 247
Trento Brut Ris., Abate Nero 245
Trento Brut Ris., Letrari 242
Trento Brut Ris., Maso Martis 248
Trento Brut Rosé, Ferrari 247
Trento Démi Sec, Ferrari 247
Trento Extra Brut, Abate Nero 245
Trento Graal Brut Ris., Cavit - Cons. di Cantine Sociali 246
Trento Methius Ris., F.lli Dorigati - Metius 238
Trescone, Lamborghini - La Fiorita 671
Tretarante, Mille Una 746
Trianon, Poderi di San Pietro 209
Tricorno, Castello di Poppiano 552
Trincerone, Tenuta Valdipiatta 549
Triskelè, Duca di Salaparuta - Vini Corvo 769
Tristo di Elisena, Castello Fageto 645
Triusco, Rivera 379
Tu Chiamale se Vuoi Emozioni Lato B, Leone Conti 439
Tuderi, Tenute Dettori 798
Tumoli Grillo, Curatolo 785
Turriga, Antonio Argiolas 799
Tuvara, Alberto Loi 792
U' Summarill, Coop. Svevo - Lucera 754
Ucelut Bianco, Alessandro Vicentini Orgnani 402
Umbria Aleatico Bartolomeo, Cant. dei Colli Amerini 658
Umbria Bianco Luna, Terre de' Trinci 663
Umbria Rosso Cajo, Terre de' Trinci 663
Umbria Rosso Vaglie, Vaglie 659
Umbria Sangiovese, Bigi 668
Umbria Sangiovese, La Carraia 669
Umbria Sangiovese Torraccio, Cant. dei Colli Amerini 658
Umbria Torrello, Tordimaro 678
Umbria Vin Santo, Goretti 673
Uva Rara, La Marzuola 217
V. del Mandorlo, Fattoria Montellori 494
V. del Moro, Fattoria Montellori 494
V. del Picchio, Moro - Rinaldini 462
V. l'Apparita Merlot, Castello di Ama 495
V. Vecchia, Perinelli 461
V. Virzì Rosso, Spadafora 777
Vadum Caesaris, Vallarom 229
Val d'Arbia, Castello di Volpaia 569
Val di Chiana Grechetto, Fattoria Santa Vittoria 601
Val di Cornia Aleatico, Jacopo Banti 472
Val di Cornia Aleatico, Bulichella 588
Val di Cornia Aleatico Sciatà, Jacopo Banti 472
Val di Cornia Aleatico Stillo, Petricci e Del Pianta 621
Val di Cornia Bianco Eliseo, Gualdo del Re 589
Val di Cornia Bianco Tuscanio, Bulichella 588
Val di Cornia Bianco Vignanuova, Incontri 589
Val di Cornia Centomini, Jacopo Banti 472
Val di Cornia Col di Pietre Rosse, Bulichella 588
Val di Cornia di Casetta Bianco, Petricci e Del Pianta 621
Val di Cornia Gualdo del Re, Gualdo del Re 589
Val di Cornia Il Peccato Barrique, Jacopo Banti 472
Val di Cornia Il Peccato Rosso, Jacopo Banti 472
Val di Cornia Lorenzo degli Incontri, Incontri 589
Val di Cornia Rivellino, Daniele Rocchi 614
Val di Cornia Rosso, Le Volpaiole 595
Val di Cornia Rosso Barbicone, Russo 590
Val di Cornia Rosso Ceppitaio, Russo 590
Val di Cornia Rosso I'Rennero, Gualdo del Re 589
Val di Cornia Rosso Rubino, Bulichella 588
Val di Cornia Rosso Rubizzo, Incontri 589
Val di Cornia Rosso Tabarò, Lorella Ambrosini 588
Val di Cornia Rosso Tuscanio, Bulichella 588
Val di Cornia Subertum, Lorella Ambrosini 588
Val di Cornia Trafui, Jacopo Banti 472
Val di Cornia Valentina, Gualdo del Re 589
Val di Cornia Vermentino, Daniele Rocchi 614
Val di Cornia Vermentino Ildebrandino, Incontri 589
Val di Cornia Vermentino Poggio Angelica, Jacopo Banti 472
Val di Miez, Roncùs 361
Val Polcèvera Rosso Treipaexi, Enoteca Andrea Bruzzone 179
Valcalepio Bianco, Cant. Soc. Bergamasca 210
Valcalepio Bianco, Bonaldi - Cascina del Bosco 226
Valcalepio Bianco, Castello di Grumello 221
Valcalepio Bianco, Il Calepino 189
Valcalepio Bianco, La Tordela 214
Valcalepio Bianco, La Rocchetta 226
Valcalepio Bianco, Cant. Soc. Val San Martino 223
Valcalepio Bianco Arlecchino, Tallarini 221
Valcalepio Bianco Gonzaghesco, Le Corne 221
Valcalepio Bianco Vescovado, La Brugherata 212
Valcalepio Moscato di Scanzo Passito Doge,
  La Brugherata 212
Valcalepio Moscato Passito, La Tordela 214
Valcalepio Rosso, Cant. Soc. Bergamasca 210
Valcalepio Rosso, Bonaldi - Cascina del Bosco 226
Valcalepio Rosso, Castello di Grumello 221
Valcalepio Rosso, Il Calepino 189
Valcalepio Rosso, La Tordela 214
Valcalepio Rosso, La Rocchetta 226
Valcalepio Rosso Akros Ris., Cant. Soc. Bergamasca 210
Valcalepio Rosso Arlecchino, Tallarini 221
Valcalepio Rosso Colle del Calvario, Castello di Grumello 221
Valcalepio Rosso Messernero Ris., Le Corne 221
Valcalepio Rosso Ris., La Tordela 214
Valcalepio Rosso Ris., Cant. Soc. Val San Martino 223
Valcalepio Rosso Ris. Doglio, La Brugherata 212

Valcalepio Rosso Ris. Vigna del Conte,
Cant. Soc. Bergamasca 210
Valcalepio Rosso Riserva Akros Vigna La Tordela,
Cant. Soc. Bergamasca 210
Valcalepio Rosso San Giovannino Ris., Tallarini 221
Valcalepio Rosso Surie, Il Calepino 189
Valcalepio Rosso Vescovado, La Brugherata 212
Valcanzjria, Gulfi 784
Valdadige Chardonnay Piccola Botte, Armani 293
Valdadige Pinot Grigio, Santa Margherita 347
Valdadige Pinot Grigio Vign. Corvara, Armani 293
Valdadige Quaiare, Le Fraghe 291
Valdadige Terra dei Forti Enantio, Letrari 242
Valdadige Terra dei Forti Sauvignon
Campo Napoleone, Armani 293
Valdenrico Passito, Rovellotti 87
Valdichiana Luna di Monte, San Luciano 539
Valentino Brut Ris. Elena, Podere Rocche dei Manzoni 112
Valeo, Odoardi 762
Valle Cupa, Casa Vinicola Apollonio 750
Valle d'Aosta Blanc de Morgex et de La Salle,
Cave du Vin Blanc de Morgex et de La Salle 18
Valle d'Aosta Blanc de Morgex et de La Salle,
Maison Albert Vevey 20
Valle d'Aosta Blanc de Morgex et de La Salle M. Cl.,
Cave du Vin Blanc de Morgex et de La Salle 18
Valle d'Aosta Blanc de Morgex et de La Salle Rayon,
Cave du Vin Blanc de Morgex et de La Salle 18
Valle d'Aosta Blanc de Morgex et de La Salle Vini Estremi,
Cave du Vin Blanc de Morgex et de La Salle 18
Valle d'Aosta Chambave Moscato Passito,
La Crotta di Vegneron 17
Valle d'Aosta Chambave Muscat, La Crotta di Vegneron 17
Valle d'Aosta Chambave Rouge Quatre Vignobles,
La Crotta di Vegneron 17
Valle d'Aosta Chardonnay, Anselmet 19
Valle d'Aosta Chardonnay, Di Barrò 20
Valle d'Aosta Chardonnay Barrique, Institut Agricole Régional 16
Valle d'Aosta Chardonnay Cuvée Frissonnière
Les Crêtes, Les Crêtes 17
Valle d'Aosta Chardonnay Cuvée Frissonnière
Les Crêtes Cuvée Bois, Les Crêtes 17
Valle d'Aosta Chardonnay Élevé en Fût de Chêne, Anselmet 19
Valle d'Aosta Donnas, Caves Cooperatives de Donnas 20
Valle d'Aosta Donnas Napoleone,
Caves Cooperatives de Donnas 20
Valle d'Aosta Fumin, F.lli Grosjean 19
Valle d'Aosta Fumin, La Crotta di Vegneron 17
Valle d'Aosta Fumin Vigne La Tour, Les Crêtes 17
Valle d'Aosta Gamay, F.lli Grosjean 19
Valle d'Aosta Gamay, Lo Triolet 18
Valle d'Aosta Malvoisie, La Crotta di Vegneron 17
Valle d'Aosta Mayolet, Costantino Charrère 16
Valle d'Aosta Müller Thurgau, Institut Agricole Régional 16
Valle d'Aosta Müller Thurgau, La Crotta di Vegneron 17
Valle d'Aosta Müller Thurgau, Gabriella Minuzzo 20
Valle d'Aosta Nus Malvoisie Flétrì, La Crotta di Vegneron 17
Valle d'Aosta Nus Rouge, La Crotta di Vegneron 17
Valle d'Aosta Nus Rouge, Lo Triolet 18
Valle d'Aosta Petite Arvine, F.lli Grosjean 19
Valle d'Aosta Petite Arvine, Institut Agricole Régional 16
Valle d'Aosta Petite Arvine Vigne Champorette, Les Crêtes 17
Valle d'Aosta Pinot Gris, Institut Agricole Régional 16
Valle d'Aosta Pinot Gris Élevé en Fût de Chêne, Lo Triolet 18
Valle d'Aosta Pinot Gris Lo Triolet, Lo Triolet 18
Valle d'Aosta Pinot Noir, Anselmet 19
Valle d'Aosta Pinot Noir, F.lli Grosjean 19
Valle d'Aosta Pinot Noir, Institut Agricole Régional 16
Valle d'Aosta Pinot Noir, Gabriella Minuzzo 20
Valle d'Aosta Pinot Noir Élevé en Barrique, F.lli Grosjean 19
Valle d'Aosta Pinot Noir Vigne La Tour, Les Crêtes 17
Valle d'Aosta Prëmetta, Costantino Charrère 16
Valle d'Aosta Torrette, Costantino Charrère 16
Valle d'Aosta Torrette, F.lli Grosjean 19
Valle d'Aosta Torrette Sup., Di Barrò 20
Valle d'Aosta Torrette Sup. Élevé en Fût de Chêne, Anselmet 19
Valle d'Aosta Torrette Vigne Les Toules, Les Crêtes 17
Valle del Crati, Demetrio Serracavallo 760
Valle del Crati Ris., Demetrio Serracavallo 760
Vallocaia, Bindella 543
Valmora Rosso Terre di Braccio, Cantine Perusia 678
Valpantena Ripasso Falasco, Cant. Soc. della Valpantena 341
Valpantena Ritocco, Cant. Soc. della Valpantena 341
Valpantena Secco Bertani, Bertani 311
Valpantena Sup., Cant. Soc. della Valpantena 341
Valpolicella, Poggio Toccalta 352
Valpolicella Ca' Fiui, Corte Sant'Alda 302
Valpolicella Cl., Stefano Accordini 320
Valpolicella Cl., Allegrini 294
Valpolicella Cl., Brigaldara 321
Valpolicella Cl., Luigi Brunelli 322
Valpolicella Cl., Corte Rugolin 300
Valpolicella Cl., F.lli Degani 301
Valpolicella Cl., Le Ragose 312
Valpolicella Cl., Giuseppe Lonardi 301
Valpolicella Cl., Angelo Nicolis e Figli 323
Valpolicella Cl., Novaia 302
Valpolicella Cl., Le Salette 295
Valpolicella Cl., Santa Sofia 323
Valpolicella Cl., F.lli Speri 324
Valpolicella Cl., Massimino Venturini 326
Valpolicella Cl., Villa Spinosa 314
Valpolicella Cl., Viviani 314
Valpolicella Cl. Campo S. Lena, Raimondi - Villa Monteleone 328
Valpolicella Cl. Capitel della Crosara, Giacomo Montresor 342
Valpolicella Cl. I Roccoli, Villabella 345

Valpolicella Cl. Il Brolo, Villa Bellini 326
Valpolicella Cl. Montegradella, Santa Sofia 323
Valpolicella Cl. Primo Ripasso Castelliere delle Guaite,
Giacomo Montresor 342
Valpolicella Cl. Santepietre, Lamberti 348
Valpolicella Cl. Sup., F.lli Degani 301
Valpolicella Cl. Sup., La Giaretta 348
Valpolicella Cl. Sup., Giuseppe Lonardi 301
Valpolicella Cl. Sup., Roberto Mazzi 313
Valpolicella Cl. Sup., Angelo Nicolis e Figli 323
Valpolicella Cl. Sup., Zenato 316
Valpolicella Cl. Sup. Acinatico, Stefano Accordini 320
Valpolicella Cl. Sup. Antanel, Villa Spinosa 314
Valpolicella Cl. Sup. Ca' Carnocchio, Le Salette 295
Valpolicella Cl. Sup. Campo Casal Vegri, Ca' La Bionda 299
Valpolicella Cl. Sup. Campo Morar, Viviani 314
Valpolicella Cl. Sup. Campo Praesel, Luigi Brunelli 322
Valpolicella Cl. Sup. Campo S. Vito, Raimondi - Villa Monteleone 328
Valpolicella Cl. Sup. Capitel dei Nicalò, F.lli Tedeschi 324
Valpolicella Cl. Sup. Cicilio, F.lli Degani 301
Valpolicella Cl. Sup. Corte Colombara, Tenute Galtarossa 325
Valpolicella Cl. Sup. di Ripasso, Corte Rugolin 300
Valpolicella Cl. Sup. I Cantoni, Novaia 302
Valpolicella Cl. Sup. I Pianeti Il Sestante, Tommasi Viticoltori 325
Valpolicella Cl. Sup. I Progni, Le Salette 295
Valpolicella Cl. Sup. I Quadretti, La Giaretta 348
Valpolicella Cl. Sup. Il Taso, Villa Bellini 326
Valpolicella Cl. Sup. Jago, Villa Spinosa 314
Valpolicella Cl. Sup. La Casetta di Ettore Righetti
Domini Veneti, Cant. Soc. Valpolicella 312
Valpolicella Cl. Sup. La Roverina, F.lli Speri 324
Valpolicella Cl. Sup. Le Morete, Manara 322
Valpolicella Cl. Sup. Le Portarine, Le Bertarole 347
Valpolicella Cl. Sup. Le Sassine, Le Ragose 312
Valpolicella Cl. Sup. Le Solane, Santi 297
Valpolicella Cl. Sup. Marogne, F.lli Zeni 289
Valpolicella Cl. Sup. Monte Cà Paletta, Giuseppe Quintarelli 313
Valpolicella Cl. Sup. Monte Riondo, Bertani 311
Valpolicella Cl. Sup. Montegradella, Casa Vinicola Sartori 349
Valpolicella Cl. Sup. Montepalà, Aleardo Ferrari 350
Valpolicella Cl. Sup. Pariondo, Luigi Brunelli 322
Valpolicella Cl. Sup. Poiega, Guerrieri Rizzardi 289
Valpolicella Cl. Sup. Ripassa, Zenato 316
Valpolicella Cl. Sup. Ripasso, I Scriani 347
Valpolicella Cl. Sup. Ripasso, Tommasi Viticoltori 325
Valpolicella Cl. Sup. Ripasso, Villabella 345
Valpolicella Cl. Sup. Ripasso I Castei, Michele Castellani 300
Valpolicella Cl. Sup. Sant'Urbano, F.lli Speri 324
Valpolicella Cl. Sup. Seccal, Angelo Nicolis e Figli 323
Valpolicella Cl. Sup. Semonte Alto, Massimino Venturini 326
Valpolicella Cl. Sup. Squarano, Marchesi Fumanelli 350
Valpolicella Cl. Sup. TB, Tommaso Bussola 311
Valpolicella Cl. Sup. Terre di Cariano, Cecilia Beretta 341
Valpolicella Cl. Sup. Vign. di Ravazzol, Ca' La Bionda 299
Valpolicella Cl. Sup. Vign. di Torbe Domini Veneti,
Cant. Soc. Valpolicella 312
Valpolicella Cl. Sup. Vign. La Cengia, Lorenzo Begali 321
Valpolicella Cl. Sup. Vign. Poiega, Roberto Mazzi 313
Valpolicella Cl. Sup. Vign. Rafael, Tommasi Viticoltori 325
Valpolicella Cl. Sup. Vigne Alte, F.lli Zeni 289
Valpolicella Cl. Sup. Vigneti di Purano Le Bine,
Giuseppe Campagnola 299
Valpolicella Cl. Sup. Villa Borghetti, Pasqua Vigneti e Cantine 342
Valpolicella Rio Albo, Ca' Rugate 307
Valpolicella Sup., Marion 319
Valpolicella Sup., Musella 319
Valpolicella Sup., Poggio Toccalta 352
Valpolicella Sup. Campo Lavei, Ca' Rugate 307
Valpolicella Sup. Campo Torbian, Luigino e Marco Provolo 303
Valpolicella Sup. Idea Bacco, Agostino Vicentini 346
Valpolicella Sup. La Bandina, Tenuta Sant'Antonio 304
Valpolicella Sup. Mithas, Corte Sant'Alda 302
Valpolicella Sup. Monti Garbi, Tenuta Sant'Antonio 304
Valpolicella Sup. Ripasso, Corte Sant'Alda 302
Valpolicella Sup. Ripasso Rocca Sveva, Cant. di Soave 329
Valpolicella Sup. Rocca Sveva, Cant. di Soave 329
Valpolicella Sup. Roccolo Grassi, Roccolo Grassi 303
Valpolicella Sup. Sagramoso, Pasqua Vigneti e Cantine 342
Valpolicella Sup. Sagramoso Ripasso, Pasqua Vigneti e Cantine 342
Valpolicella Sup. San Raffaele, Monte Tabor 348
Valpolicella Sup. Terre del Cereolo, Trabucchi 297
Valpolicella Sup. Terre di S. Colombano, Trabucchi 297
Valpolicella Sup. Vign. di Monte Lodoletta, Romano Dal Forno 296
Valpolicella Valpantena Sup. Brolo delle Giare, Tezza 343
Valpolicella Valpantena Sup. Monte delle Fontane, Tezza 343
Valpolicella Vign. Boccascalucce, Agostino Vicentini 346
Valtellina Prestigio, Triacca 215
Valtellina Prestigio Millennium, Triacca 215
Valtellina Sforzato, Pietro Nera 219
Valtellina Sforzato, Triacca 215
Valtellina Sforzato Albareda, Mamete Prevostini 199
Valtellina Sforzato Canua, Conti Sertoli Salis 214
Valtellina Sforzato Ronco del Picchio, Fay 213
Valtellina Sforzato San Domenico, Triacca 215
Valtellina Sfursat, Nino Negri 191
Valtellina Sfursat, Aldo Rainoldi 191
Valtellina Sfursat 5 Stelle, Nino Negri 191
Valtellina Sfursat Fruttaio Ca' Rizzieri, Aldo Rainoldi 191
Valtellina Sfurzat Vin da Ca', Plozza 226
Valtellina Sup. Capo di Terra, Conti Sertoli Salis 214
Valtellina Sup. Casa La Gatta, Triacca 215
Valtellina Sup. Corte della Meridiana, Conti Sertoli Salis 214
Valtellina Sup. Corte di Cama, Mamete Prevostini 199
Valtellina Sup. Crespino, Aldo Rainoldi 191
Valtellina Sup. Fracia, Nino Negri 191
Valtellina Sup. Giupa, Caven Camuna 226

Valtellina Sup. Grumello, Conti Sertoli Salis 214
Valtellina Sup. Grumello Sassorosso, Nino Negri 191
Valtellina Sup. Inferno, Aldo Rainoldi 191
Valtellina Sup. Inferno Al Carmine, Caven Camuna 226
Valtellina Sup. Inferno Efesto, Pietro Nera 219
Valtellina Sup. Inferno Mazer, Nino Negri 191
Valtellina Sup. Inferno Prodigio, F.lli Bettini 226
Valtellina Sup. Inferno Ris. Barrique, Aldo Rainoldi 191
Valtellina Sup. La Scala Ris., Plozza 226
Valtellina Sup. Prugnolo, Aldo Rainoldi 191
Valtellina Sup. Quadrio, Nino Negri 191
Valtellina Sup. Ris. Grumello, Plozza 226
Valtellina Sup. Ris. La Gatta, Triacca 215
Valtellina Sup. Ris. Triacca, Triacca 215
Valtellina Sup. Sassella, Conti Sertoli Salis 214
Valtellina Sup. Sassella, Triacca 215
Valtellina Sup. Il Glicine, Fay 213
Valtellina Sup. Sassella Le Tense, Nino Negri 191
Valtellina Sup. Sassella Ris., Aldo Rainoldi 191
Valtellina Sup. Sassella Sommarovina,
  Mamete Prevostini 199
Valtellina Sup. Sfursat, F.lli Bettini 226
Valtellina Sup. Signorie Ris., Pietro Nera 219
Valtellina Sup. Valgella Ca' Morei, Fay 213
Valtellina Sup. Valgella Carteria, Fay 213
Vareij Rosso, Hilberg - Pasquero 131
Varenne, Drei Donà Tenuta La Palazza 443
Varius, Cantele 744
Varramista, Varramista 613
Varrone V. del Centenario, Ist. Prof. per l'Agricoltura e l'Ambiente 441
Vasario, Fattoria del Buonamico 540
Vassilla Bianco, Do Ville 413
Vecchio Samperi Ris. 30 Anni Solera, Marco De Bartoli 771
Vedetta, Botrona 620
Velenosi Brut M. Cl., Ercole Velenosi 626
Velitrae Bianco, Colle di Maggio 690
Velitrae Rosso, Colle di Maggio 690
Velo di Maya, Alfiero Boffa 135
Vencaia Bianco Terre di Braccio, Cantine Perusia 678
Vendemmia Tardiva, Canneto 610
Vendemmia Tardiva, Cascina Fonda 102
Vendemmia Tardiva Mandrarossa, Settesoli 775
Venegazzù della Casa, Conte Loredan Gasparini Venegazzù 344
Veneroso, Tenuta di Ghizzano 561
Venus, Marchesi Platamone 786
Vepraio, Nobile Prima 491
Ver Sacrum, San Savino - Poderi Capecci 649
Verbeia, Piero Gatti 136
Verdàc, Eugenio Collavini 380
Verdicchio Castelli di Jesi Cl. Passito Arché, Monteschiavo 636
Verdicchio dei Castelli di Jesi, Fattoria Laila 638
Verdicchio dei Castelli di Jesi, Mario Lucchetti 654
Verdicchio dei Castelli di Jesi Cl., Bucci 645
Verdicchio dei Castelli di Jesi Cl., Luciano Landi 628
Verdicchio dei Castelli di Jesi Cl., Maurizio Marchetti 624
Verdicchio dei Castelli di Jesi Cl., Sartarelli 647
Verdicchio dei Castelli di Jesi Cl. Bacco, Coroncino 652
Verdicchio dei Castelli di Jesi Cl. Borgo, Maurizio Marconi 649
Verdicchio dei Castelli di Jesi Cl. Casa Lisà, F.lli Zaccagnini & C. 652
Verdicchio dei Castelli di Jesi Cl. Crocetta Ris., Cavallaro 655
Verdicchio dei Castelli di Jesi Cl. del Pozzo Buono, Vicari 655
Verdicchio dei Castelli di Jesi Cl. di Gino, Fattoria San Lorenzo 638
Verdicchio dei Castelli di Jesi Cl. Ghibellino, Benito Mancini 654
Verdicchio dei Castelli di Jesi Cl. Le Gemme,
  Mario & Giorgio Brunori 654
Verdicchio dei Castelli di Jesi Cl. Le Giuncare Ris., Monteschiavo 636
Verdicchio dei Castelli di Jesi Cl. Le Vaglie, Santa Barbara 627
Verdicchio dei Castelli di Jesi Cl. Le Vele,
  Terre Cortesi Moncaro 639
Verdicchio dei Castelli di Jesi Cl. Loretello, Laurentina 639
Verdicchio dei Castelli di Jesi Cl. Luzano, Marotti Campi 641
Verdicchio dei Castelli di Jesi Cl. Maestro di Staffolo
  Ris., F.lli Zaccagnini & C. 652
Verdicchio dei Castelli di Jesi Cl. Montesecco, Montecappone 635
Verdicchio dei Castelli di Jesi Cl. Nidastore, Santa Barbara 627
Verdicchio dei Castelli di Jesi Cl. Nidastore Vigne Alte,
  Santa Barbara 627
Verdicchio dei Castelli di Jesi Cl. Pignocco, Santa Barbara 627
Verdicchio dei Castelli di Jesi Cl. Plenio Ris., Umani Ronchi 644
Verdicchio dei Castelli di Jesi Cl. Romitello delle Mandriole
  Ris., Colonnara Viticoltori in Cupramontana 632
Verdicchio dei Castelli di Jesi Cl. Salmariano Ris., Marotti Campi 641
Verdicchio dei Castelli di Jesi Cl. San Sisto Ris.,
  Fazi Battaglia 630
Verdicchio dei Castelli di Jesi Cl. Serra Fiorese Ris.,
  Gioacchino Garofoli 635
Verdicchio dei Castelli di Jesi Cl. Stefano Antonucci,
  Santa Barbara 627
Verdicchio dei Castelli di Jesi Cl. Sup., F.lli Zaccagnini & C. 652
Verdicchio dei Castelli di Jesi Cl. Sup. Casal di Serra,
  Umani Ronchi 644
Verdicchio dei Castelli di Jesi Cl. Sup. Cimaio, Casalfarneto 650
Verdicchio dei Castelli di Jesi Cl. Sup.
  Contrada Balciana, Sartarelli 647
Verdicchio dei Castelli di Jesi Cl. Sup. Corona Reale,
  Maurizio Marconi 649
Verdicchio dei Castelli di Jesi Cl. Sup. Fontelleccio,
  Poggio Montali 654
Verdicchio dei Castelli di Jesi Cl. Sup. Fontevecchia,
  Casalfarneto 650
Verdicchio dei Castelli di Jesi Cl. Sup. Frà Moriale,
  Fonte della Luna - Medoro Cimarelli 656
Verdicchio dei Castelli di Jesi Cl. Sup. Gaiospino, Coroncino 652
Verdicchio dei Castelli di Jesi Cl. Sup. Grancasale,
  Casalfarneto 650
Verdicchio dei Castelli di Jesi Cl. Sup. Il Coroncino, Coroncino 652

Verdicchio dei Castelli di Jesi Cl. Sup. Le Case, Vallerosa Bonci 633
Verdicchio dei Castelli di Jesi Cl. Sup. Le Moie, Fazi Battaglia 630
Verdicchio dei Castelli di Jesi Cl. Sup. Macrina,
  Gioacchino Garofoli 635
Verdicchio dei Castelli di Jesi Cl. Sup. Massaccio,
  Fazi Battaglia 630
Verdicchio dei Castelli di Jesi Cl. Sup. Nativo, Monteschiavo 636
Verdicchio dei Castelli di Jesi Cl. Sup.
  Ori di Verdicchio, Piersanti 656
Verdicchio dei Castelli di Jesi Cl. Sup.
  Pallio di S. Floriano, Monteschiavo 636
Verdicchio dei Castelli di Jesi Cl. Sup.
  Pier delle Vigne, F.lli Zaccagnini & C. 652
Verdicchio dei Castelli di Jesi Cl. Sup. Podium,
  Gioacchino Garofoli 635
Verdicchio dei Castelli di Jesi Cl. Sup. S. Michele,
  Vallerosa Bonci 633
Verdicchio dei Castelli di Jesi Cl. Sup. Salmàgina,
  F.lli Zaccagnini & C. 652
Verdicchio dei Castelli di Jesi Cl. Sup. San Nicolò,
  Mario & Giorgio Brunori 654
Verdicchio dei Castelli di Jesi Cl. Sup.
  Santa Maria d'Arco, Enrico Ceci 656
Verdicchio dei Castelli di Jesi Cl. Sup.
  Sapore di Generazioni, Maurizio Marconi 649
Verdicchio dei Castelli di Jesi Cl. Sup. Stracacio, Coroncino 652
Verdicchio dei Castelli di Jesi Cl. Sup. Sultano, Umani Ronchi 644
Verdicchio dei Castelli di Jesi Cl. Sup. Tavignano,
  Lucangeli Aymerich di Laconi 653
Verdicchio dei Castelli di Jesi Cl. Sup.
  Tenuta del Cavaliere, Maurizio Marchetti 624
Verdicchio dei Castelli di Jesi Cl. Sup. Tralivio, Sartarelli 647
Verdicchio dei Castelli di Jesi Cl. Sup. Tùfico V. T.,
  Colonnara Viticoltori in Cupramontana 632
Verdicchio dei Castelli di Jesi Cl. Sup. Verde
  Ca' Ruptae, Terre Cortesi Moncaro 639
Verdicchio dei Castelli di Jesi Cl. Sup.
  Vigna delle Oche, Fattoria San Lorenzo 638
Verdicchio dei Castelli di Jesi Cl. Sup. V. San Marco,
  Colonnara Viticoltori in Cupramontana 632
Verdicchio dei Castelli di Jesi Cl. Sup. Vignamato, Amato Ceci 656
Verdicchio dei Castelli di Jesi Cl. Sup. Villa Bianchi,
  Umani Ronchi 644
Verdicchio dei Castelli di Jesi Cl. Sup. Villa Talliano,
  Benito Mancini 654
Verdicchio dei Castelli di Jesi Cl. Titulus, Fazi Battaglia 630
Verdicchio dei Castelli di Jesi Cl. Viatorre, Vallerosa Bonci 633
Verdicchio dei Castelli di Jesi Cl. Vigna delle Oche Ris.,
  Fattoria San Lorenzo 638
Verdicchio dei Castelli di Jesi Cl. Vigna Novali Ris.,
  Terre Cortesi Moncaro 639
Verdicchio dei Castelli di Jesi Cl. Vigneto di Tobia, Laurentina 639
Verdicchio dei Castelli di Jesi Cl. Villa Bucci Ris., Bucci 645
Verdicchio dei Castelli di Jesi Lailum, Fattoria Laila 638
Verdicchio dei Castelli di Jesi Passito Onyr, Marotti Campi 641
Verdicchio dei Castelli di Jesi Passito Rojano,
  Vallerosa Bonci 633
Verdicchio dei Castelli di Jesi Passito Sanctorum,
  Colonnara Viticoltori in Cupramontana 632
Verdicchio dei Castelli di Jesi Passito Tordiruta,
  Terre Cortesi Moncaro 639
Verdicchio di Matelica, Bisci 637
Verdicchio di Matelica Aja Lunga, Del Carmine 653
Verdicchio di Matelica Cambrugiano Ris.,
  Belisario Cant. Soc. di Matelica e Cerreto d'Esi 636
Verdicchio di Matelica Casa Fosca Sotto le Querce,
  Enzo Mecella 633
Verdicchio di Matelica Collestefano, Collestefano 630
Verdicchio di Matelica La Monacesca, La Monacesca 637
Verdicchio di Matelica Mirum, La Monacesca 637
Verdicchio di Matelica Mirum Ris., La Monacesca 637
Verdicchio di Matelica Petrara, Del Carmine 653
Verdicchio di Matelica Ris., Bisci 637
Verdicchio di Matelica Terre di Valbona,
  Belisario Cant. Soc. di Matelica e Cerreto d'Esi 636
Verdicchio di Matelica Vigneti Belisario,
  Belisario Cant. Soc. di Matelica e Cerreto d'Esi 636
Verdicchio di Matelica Vigneti del Cerro,
  Belisario Cant. Soc. di Matelica e Cerreto d'Esi 636
Verdicchio di Matelica Vigneto Fogliano, Bisci 637
Verdiso, Conte Collalto 333
Verduno Basadone, Castello di Verduno 150
Verduno Pelaverga, Bel Colle 149
Verduno Pelaverga, G. B. Burlotto 150
Verduno Pelaverga, Terre del Barolo 66
Verduzzo del Piccolo Campo, Brojli - Franco Clementin 424
Verduzzo Friulano, Russiz Superiore 361
Verduzzo Friulano Passito, Ronco dei Pini 411
Verduzzo Limine, Podere del Ger 405
Verduzzo Soandre, Bosco del Merlo 288
Verduzzo Trevigiano Passito, Casa Roma 327
Vermentino, Serraiola 550
Vermentino di Gallura Cucaione, Piero Mancini 796
Vermentino di Gallura Funtanaliras, Cant. Soc. del Vermentino 795
Vermentino di Gallura Gemellae, Cant. Soc. Gallura 801
Vermentino di Gallura Hysonj, Pedra Majore 795
Vermentino di Gallura I Graniti, Pedra Majore 795
Vermentino di Gallura Mavriana, Cant. Soc. Gallura 801
Vermentino di Gallura Piras, Cant. Soc. Gallura 801
Vermentino di Gallura S'Eleme, Cant. Soc. del Vermentino 795
Vermentino di Gallura Saraina, Piero Mancini 796
Vermentino di Gallura Sienda, Mura 802
Vermentino di Gallura Sup. Aghiloa, Cant. Soc. del Vermentino 795
Vermentino di Gallura Sup. Canayli, Cant. Soc. Gallura 801
Vermentino di Gallura Sup. Hysonj, Pedra Majore 795
Vermentino di Gallura Sup. Monteoro, Tenute Sella & Mosca 790

Vermentino di Gallura Sup. Saruinas, Andrea Depperu	802
Vermentino di Gallura Vigna 'Ngena, Capichera	791
Vermentino di Sardegna, Piero Mancini	796
Vermentino di Sardegna, Gigi Picciau	802
Vermentino di Sardegna, Tenute Soletta	793
Vermentino di Sardegna Arvali, Ferruccio Deiana	800
Vermentino di Sardegna Boghes, Giovanni Cherchi	801
Vermentino di Sardegna Cala Silente, Cant. Soc. di Santadi	797
Vermentino di Sardegna Costamolino, Antonio Argiolas	799
Vermentino di Sardegna Crabilis, F.lli Pala	800
Vermentino di Sardegna Donnikalia, Ferruccio Deiana	800
Vermentino di Sardegna La Cala, Tenute Sella & Mosca	790
Vermentino di Sardegna Le Conche, Pedra Majore	795
Vermentino di Sardegna Le Sabbie, Meloni Vini	798
Vermentino di Sardegna Naeli, Cantine di Dolianova	793
Vermentino di Sardegna Pigalva, Giovanni Cherchi	801
Vermentino di Sardegna Prendas, Cantine di Dolianova	793
Vermentino di Sardegna Tanca Sa Contissa, Cant. Soc. della Trexenta	799
Vermentino di Sardegna Tuvaoes, Giovanni Cherchi	801
Vermentino di Sardegna Villa Solais, Cant. Soc. di Santadi	797
Vermentino Nero, Cima	513
Vermiglio, Andrea Costanti	522
Vernaccia di Oristano, Attilio Contini	791
Vernaccia di Oristano, Josto Puddu	804
Vernaccia di Oristano Antico Gregori, Attilio Contini	791
Vernaccia di Oristano Ris., Attilio Contini	791
Vernaccia di S. Gimignano, Ca' del Vispo	576
Vernaccia di S. Gimignano, Casa alle Vacche	577
Vernaccia di S. Gimignano, Vincenzo Cesani	577
Vernaccia di S. Gimignano, Granducato	562
Vernaccia di S. Gimignano, Il Lebbio	578
Vernaccia di S. Gimignano, Il Paradiso	579
Vernaccia di S. Gimignano, La Lastra	580
Vernaccia di S. Gimignano, Tenuta Le Calcinaie	581
Vernaccia di S. Gimignano, Mormoraia	582
Vernaccia di S. Gimignano, Palagetto	582
Vernaccia di S. Gimignano, Giovanni Panizzi	583
Vernaccia di S. Gimignano, Pietrafitta	618
Vernaccia di S. Gimignano, San Lorenzo	618
Vernaccia di S. Gimignano, San Quirico	618
Vernaccia di S. Gimignano, Teruzzi & Puthod	583
Vernaccia di S. Gimignano, F.lli Vagnoni	584
Vernaccia di S. Gimignano Abbazia di Monteoliveto, Fattoria Il Palagio	490
Vernaccia di S. Gimignano Alata, La Rampa di Fugnano	580
Vernaccia di S. Gimignano Biscondola, Il Paradiso	579
Vernaccia di S. Gimignano Carato, Montenidoli	581
Vernaccia di S. Gimignano Crocus, Casa alle Vacche	577
Vernaccia di S. Gimignano Dometaia Ris., Baroncini	576
Vernaccia di S. Gimignano Fiore, Montenidoli	581
Vernaccia di S. Gimignano Hydra, Il Palagione	579
Vernaccia di S. Gimignano I Macchioni, Casa alle Vacche	577
Vernaccia di S. Gimignano La Gentilesca, Fattoria Il Palagio	490
Vernaccia di S. Gimignano Le Grillaie, Melini	563
Vernaccia di S. Gimignano Mocali, F.lli Vagnoni	584
Vernaccia di S. Gimignano Mocali Ris., F.lli Vagnoni	584
Vernaccia di S. Gimignano Perlato, Guicciardini Strozzi - Fattoria Cusona	578
Vernaccia di S. Gimignano Poggio ai Cannici Sovestro, Baroncini	576
Vernaccia di S. Gimignano Ris., Guicciardini Strozzi - Fattoria Cusona	578
Vernaccia di S. Gimignano Ris., La Lastra	580
Vernaccia di S. Gimignano Ris., Mormoraia	582
Vernaccia di S. Gimignano Ris., Palagetto	582
Vernaccia di S. Gimignano Ris., Giovanni Panizzi	583
Vernaccia di S. Gimignano Sanice, Vincenzo Cesani	577
Vernaccia di S. Gimignano Tradizionale, Montenidoli	581
Vernaccia di S. Gimignano Tropie, Il Lebbio	578
Vernaccia di S. Gimignano V. ai Sassi, Tenuta Le Calcinaie	581
Vernaccia di S. Gimignano V. Borghetto, Pietrafitta	618
Vernaccia di S. Gimignano Vigna a Rondolino, Teruzzi & Puthod	583
Vernaccia di S. Gimignano Vigna in Fiore, Ca' del Vispo	576
Vernaccia di S. Gimignano Vigna La Costa Ris., Pietrafitta	618
Vernaccia di S. Gimignano Vigna Santa Chiara, Palagetto	582
Versato Merlot del Veneto, Santa Margherita	347
Versoio, Mantellassi	513
Vesco Bianco, Cantine Rallo	773
Vesco Rosso, Cantine Rallo	773
Vespa Bianco, Bastianich	405
Vespa Rosso, Bastianich	405
Vespolino, Vercesi del Castellazzo	204
Vespro, Contrada Castelletta	653
Vesuvio Lacryma Christi Rosso, Cantine Caputo	712
Vesuvio Lacryma Christi Rosso, De Falco	728
Vi Ogni è, La Rampa di Fugnano	580
Viburnum, Vignai da Duline	420
Vico, I Campetti	617
Vigna Adriana, Castel De Paolis	686
Vigna al Cavaliere, Michele Satta	476
Vigna Alta, Badia di Morrona	621
Vigna dei Pini, D'Angelo	733
Vigna del Cavaliere, Casale Marchese	685
Vigna del Feudo, Felline	748
Vigna del Gobbio, Antica Tesa	216
Vigna del Vassallo, Paola Di Mauro	686
Vigna dell'Erta, Vigliano	603
Vigna dell'Iris, Artimino	596
Vigna Hortulus, Castagnoli	477
Vigna Mazzì, Rosa del Golfo	738
Vigna Verdana Ascevi, Ascevi - Luwa	415
Vigna Vescovi, F.lli Zaccagnini & C.	652
Vignamaggio, Villa Vignamaggio	507
Vignamare, Tommaso e Angelo Lupi	174
Vignanova, Coop. Agricola Valdarnese	621
Vignaricco Rosso, Conte D'Attimis-Maniago	357
Vigne d'Oro, Avide	770
Vigneti delle Meridiane Teroldego Cernidor, Concilio/Vigneti delle Meridiane	248
Vigneti delle Meridiane Trentino Chardonnay Ravina, Concilio/Vigneti delle Meridiane	248
Vigneti delle Meridiane Trentino Merlot Ris., Concilio/Vigneti delle Meridiane	248
Vigneto del Solleone, Fattoria San Lorenzo	638
Vigneto La Gavina, Famiglia Cecchi	479
Vigorello, San Felice	488
Villa Angela Chardonnay, Ercole Velenosi	626
Villa Bernetti, Tenuta Vitereta	604
Villa Caracciolo, Cantine Lento	761
Villa Castiglioni, Bisci	637
Villa di Corsano, Cant. di Montalcino	608
Villa Fidelia Rosso, Sportoletti	673
Villa Gemma Bianco, Gianni Masciarelli	706
Villa Giona, Villa Giona	350
Villa Noce Nero d'Avola, Cant. Soc. La Torre	787
Villa Sparina Brut M. Cl., Villa Sparina	86
Villa Tulino Bianco, Colle di Maggio	690
Villa Tulino Rosso, Colle di Maggio	690
Villamaura Syrah, Gaspare Di Prima	787
Vin Brusco del Solatio, F.lli Vagnoni	584
Vin de La Sabla, Costantino Charrère	16
Vin Les Fourches, Costantino Charrère	16
Vin Ruspo, Fattoria Ambra	473
Vin Ruspo, Tenuta di Capezzana	474
Vin Ruspo, Castelvecchio	596
Vin Santo, Castello d' Albola	565
Vin Santo, Avignonesi	542
Vin Santo, Castello di Cacchiano	601
Vin Santo, Caparsa	566
Vin Santo, Fattoria Fabbri	600
Vin Santo, Fattoria di Gracciano	611
Vin Santo, Tenuta Il Corno	572
Vin Santo, Poggio a Poppiano	552
Vin Santo, San Giusto a Rentennano	501
Vin Santo, Fattoria Santa Vittoria	601
Vin Santo, Fattoria del Teso	541
Vin Santo, Villa Sant'Anna	550
Vin Santo Chianti Cl., Villa Sant'Andrea	618
Vin Santo Colli Fiorentini, Lanciola	511
Vin Santo del Chianti, Fattoria Petrolo	471
Vin Santo del Chianti, Castello Uzzano	506
Vin Santo del Chianti Cl., Badia a Coltibuono	496
Vin Santo del Chianti Cl., Castello della Paneretta	466
Vin Santo del Chianti Cl., Rocca di Castagnoli	500
Vin Santo del Chianti Cl., Rocca di Montegrossi	601
Vin Santo del Chianti Cl., Castello di Volpaia	569
Vin Santo del Chianti Classico, Villa Vignamaggio	507
Vin Santo del Chianti Rufina, Frascole	491
Vin Santo dell'Empolese, Fattoria Montellori	494
Vin Santo della Rufina, Fattoria Selvapiana	564
Vin Santo di Carmignano Ris., Tenuta di Capezzana	474
Vin Santo di Montepulciano Sangallo, Fattoria del Cerro	544
Vin Santo Dolce Sinfonia, Bindella	543
Vin Santo Eletto, Pucciarella	677
Vin Santo Lamole di Lamole, S. M. Tenimenti Pile e Lamole	499
Vin Santo Le Solaie, Tenuta Cortina e Mandorli	612
Vin Santo Occhio di Pernice, Avignonesi	542
Vin Santo Tegrino d'Anchiano, Cantine Leonardo da Vinci	593
Vineargenti Rosso, Bosco del Merlo	288
Vino degli Orti, Matijaz Tercic	417
Vino del Maso Rosso, Marco Donati	237
Vino della Pace, Cant. Prod. di Cormons	370
Vino di Bianca, Marisa Pouchain Taffuri	693
Vino Passito Sibilla Appenninica, Le Caniette	648
Vinsanto del Chianti Cl., Castello Il Palagio	617
Vintage Tunina, Jermann Vinnaioli	388
Vintàn, San Patrignano	439
Vioca di Plaia, Calatrasi - Accademia del Sole	780
Viogner, Terre di Salemi	787
Vite Bianca, Ornella Molon Traverso	317
Vite Rossa, Ornella Molon Traverso	317
Vitiano, Falesco	688
Vito Arturo, Le Fonti	615
Vivaldaia, Villa Pillo	502
Vocato, Villa Cilnia	464
Volgente Rosso, Mazziotti	691
Vulcaia Après Passito, Inama	317
Were Dreams, Now It Is Just Wine!, Jermann Vinnaioli	388
Wildbacher, Conte Collalto	333
Xyris Filtrato di Lacrima, Marotti Campi	641
Yanna, Villa di Quartu	804
Ylenia, Fatascià	777
Yngram, Hofstätter	281
Zaccagnini Brut Ris., F.lli Zaccagnini & C.	652
Zagaia Frizzante, Baraccone	461
Zagarolo Sup., Federici	694
Zagarolo Sup., Giancarlo Loreti	694
Zagros, San Giovanni	644
Zarachè, Franco Pasetti	700
Zeii, San Giovanni	644
Zephyro Rosato, Vintripodi Calabria	764
Zero - D'Orta-De Conciliis, Viticoltori De Conciliis	720
Zilath Bianco, Casale dei Cento Corvi	691
Zilath Rosso, Casale dei Cento Corvi	691
Zinfandel, Conti Zecca	746
Zinfandel, La Corte	755
Zipolo, Il Conte	640

INDEX OF PRODUCERS

A Maccia	175	Ascevi - Luwa	415
Abate Nero	245	Ascheri	46
Abbazia di Novacella	282	Aschero, Laura	174
Abbazia Santa Anastasia	768	Attems, Conti	390
Abbona, Anna Maria	80	Aurora	643
Abbona, Marziano ed Enrico	75	Avanzi	221
Abrigo, F.lli	158	Avide	770
Abrigo, Orlando	146	Avignonesi	542
Accademia dei Racemi	748	Avio, Cantina Sociale di	228
Accademia del Vino Cadelaghet	251	Azelia	63
Accordini, Stefano	320	Azzolino, Fattorie	767
Accornero e Figli, Giulio	151	Azzoni Avogadro Carradori	654
Adami	343	Bacco e Petroio, Tenuta	622
Adanti, Agricola	659	Badia a Coltibuono	496
Adragna	788	Badia di Morrona	621
Agareno	785	Baglio Hopps	771
Agnes	208	Bagnasco	225
Agostinetto, Bruno	334	Bagnolo dei Marchesi Pancrazi, Tenuta di	542
Agri Peccioli	613	Baldizzone - Cascina Lana, Antonio	161
Agricoltori del Chianti Geografico	495	Balter, Nicola	241
Agriverde	703	Banfi, Castello	515
Aia della Macina, Podere	585	Banti, Erik	585
Aiola, Fattoria dell'	483	Banti, Jacopo	472
Ajello	774	Baraccone	461
Alario, Claudio	74	Barattieri di San Pietro, Conte Otto	454
Albani, Riccardo	186	Barba, F.lli	710
Albano Carrisi, Tenute	740	Barberani - Vallesanta	667
Alberice	429	Barberis, Osvaldo	158
Albola, Castello d'	565	Barbi, Fattoria dei	516
Alessandri	175	Barisél, Cascina	54
Alessandria, F.lli	149	Barni	46
Alessandria, Gianfranco	106	Baroncini	576
Alessandro di Camporeale	783	Barone Cornacchia	710
Alfieri, Marchesi	134	Barone Pizzini	193
Allegretti	736	Barone Ricasoli	496
Allegrini	294	Barsento	755
Almondo, Giovanni	115	Basciano, Fattoria di	570
Aloi, Valerio	160	Basilisco	732
Altare - Cascina Nuova, Elio	89	Basilium	736
Altesino	605	Bastianich	405
Alzatura, Tenuta	677	Batasiolo	90
Ama, Castello di	495	Battistotti, Riccardo	240
Amalia, Tenuta	459	Baudana, Luigi	139
Ambra, Fattoria	473	Bava, Cantine	70
Ambrosini, Lorella	588	Beato Bartolomeo Da Breganze, Cantina	346
Amistani Guarda	348	Beconcini, Pietro	619
Andreas Berger -Thurnhof	259	Befehlhof, Oswald Schuster	286
Anfossi	178	Begali, Lorenzo	321
Angoris, Tenuta di	428	Beghelli, Giuseppe	458
Anselmet	19	Bel Colle	149
Anselmi, Roberto	307	Bel Sit	157
Antano, Fattoria Milziade	676	Belguardo, Tenuta	508
Anteo	207	Belisario Cantina Sociale di Matelica e Cerreto d'Esi	636
Antica Masseria del Sigillo	744	Bellani, Marco Giulio	218
Antica Tesa	216	Bellaria	187
Antichi Vigneti di Cantalupo	87	Bellavista	195
Antico Terreno Ottavi	650	Bellei, Francesco	434
Antinori, Marchesi	492	Bellini, Roberto	605
Antonelli - San Marco	665	Beltrame, Tenuta	355
Antoniolo	81	Benanti	782
Antonutti	401	Benotto, Carlo	71
Anzivino	82	Bepin de Eto	320
Apollonio, Casa Vinicola	750	Bera, F.lli	125
Aquila del Torre	403	Beretta, Cecilia	341
Araldica - Il Cascinone	59	Bergaglio, Nicola	83
Argiano	605	Bergamasca, Cantina Sociale	210
Argiolas, Antonio	799	Berlucchi, F.lli	193
Armani	293	Berlucchi & C., Guido	194
Artimino	596	Bersano & Riccadonna	125

Bersi Serlini	207	Bronca, Sorelle	344
Berta, Guido	163	Broni, Cantina Sociale di	217
Bertani	311	Brovia	64
Bertelli	72	Bruna	176
Berti, Stefano	442	Brunelli, Luigi	322
Bettini, F.lli	226	Brunelli - Le Chiuse di Sotto	605
Bettoni Cazzago, Conti	218	Brunnenhof	285
Biancara, La	295	Brunori, Mario & Giorgio	654
Bianchi	142	Bucci	645
Bianchi, Maria Donata	170	Buccicatino, Fattoria	708
Bibbiano, Tenuta di	597	Buiatti, Livio e Claudio	356
Bibi Graetz	600	Buiatti, Olivo	357
Bidoli, Vini	430	Bulichella	588
Bigi	668	Buonamico, Fattoria del	540
Bindella	543	Buondonno	477
BioVio	178	Buranco	173
Bisci	637	Burlotto, G. B.	150
Bisi	209	Bussia Soprana	160
Bisol & Figli, Desiderio	335	Busso, Piero	120
Bisson, Enoteca	169	Bussola, Tommaso	311
Blasig, Tenuta di	412	Butussi, Valentino	380
Blason	429	Buzzinelli, Maurizio	368
Boccadigabbia	631	Ca' Bianca	29
Bocchino, Eugenio	160	Ca' Bolani	364
Boeri, Alfonso	158	Ca' d'Gal	136
Boffa, Alfiero	135	Ca' de' Medici	462
Boglietti, Enzo	90	Ca' dei Frati	212
Bolla, F.lli	352	Ca' dei Mandorli	157
Bolognani, Nilo	235	Ca' del Baio	146
Bonaldi - Cascina del Bosco	226	Ca' del Bosco	196
Bondi, Cascina	162	Ca' del Gè	222
Bonomi - Tenuta Castellino	192	Ca' del Santo	222
Bonotto delle Tezze	352	Ca' del Vént	219
Bonsulton, Agricola	786	Ca' del Vispo	576
Borgo Canale	743	Ca di Bon	429
Borgo Casignano	599	Ca' di Frara	204
Borgo Conventi	387	Ca' La Bionda	299
Borgo dei Posseri	250	Ca' Lojera	213
Borgo del Tiglio	367	Ca' Lunga, Tenuta	459
Borgo di Colloredo	697	Ca' Lustra	292
Borgo Maragliano	100	Cà Marcanda	475
Borgo Salcetino	565	Ca' Montebello	219
Borgo San Daniele	367	Ca' Rome' - Romano Marengo	30
Borgo Scopeto	483	Ca' Ronesca	383
Borgogno & Figli, Giacomo	38	Ca' Rossa, Cascina	50
Borin	305	Ca' Rugate	307
Boroli	25	Ca' Selvatica	460
Bortolin Spumanti, F.lli	335	Ca' Tessitori	217
Bortolomiol	336	Ca' Tullio	354
Bortolusso, Emiro Cav.	363	Ca' Viola	76
Boscarelli	543	Cabanon	221
Boschis, Francesco	159	Caccese, Paolo	368
Bosco, Nestore	701	Cacchiano, Castello di	601
Bosco, Rosa	394	Caccia al Piano 1868	595
Bosco del Merlo	288	Caggiano, Antonio	724
Botromagno, Cantina Cooperativa	743	Calatrasi - Accademia del Sole	780
Botrona	620	Calleri	166
Botrugno, Sergio	753	Calò & Figli, Michele	756
Boveri, Luigi	71	Calonga	443
Boveri, Renato	114	Camerone, Fattoria	458
Bovio, Gianfranco	91	Camigliano, Castello di	516
Bracco, Alfredo	428	Campagnola, Giuseppe	299
Braida	132	Camposilio	600
Bredasole	205	Canalicchio di Sopra	605
Brema, Ermanno e Alessandra	88	Canato, Marco	164
Brezza & Figli, Giacomo	38	Candido, Francesco	751
Bricchetto, Cantina del	161	Cane, Giobatta Mandino	171
Bricco del Cucù	44	Canevel Spumanti	336
Bricco Maiolica	75	Caniette, Le	648
Bricco Mondalino	151	Canneto	610
Bricco Rocche - Bricco Asili	63	Canonica a Cerreto	598
Brigaldara	321	Cantarutti, Alfieri	419
Brigl, Josef	254	Cantele	744
Broglia - Tenuta La Meirana, Gian Piero	84	Cantina Cerquetta	692
Brojli - Franco Clementin	424	Cantina del Barone	726

Cantina del Castello	329	Castel Noarna	239
Cantina del Pino	31	Castel Ringberg & Kastelaz Elena Walch	280
Cantina del Taburno	714	Castel Ruggero	493
Cantina di Ala	250	Castel Sallegg - Graf Kuenburg	285
Cantina di Montecchia	348	CastelFaglia	190
Cantina di Soave	329	Castelgiocondo	519
Cantina Gries/Cantina di Bolzano	259	Castellada, La	390
Cantina Rotaliana	238	Castellani	615
Cantina Sociale della Valpantena	341	Castellani, Michele	300
Cantine Cooperative Riunite	458	Castellare di Castellina	478
Cantine del Notaio	733	Castellari Bergaglio	84
Cantrina	183	Castelli del Duca	434
Capannelle	497	Castello dei Rampolla	556
Caparra & Siciliani	763	Castello del Poggio	130
Caparsa	566	Castello del Trebbio	615
Caparzo, Tenuta	517	Castello della Paneretta	466
Capezzana, Tenuta di	474	Castello della Sala	662
Capichera	791	Castello delle Regine	658
Capinera	641	Castello di Antigniano - Brogal Vini	672
Capodilista, Giordano Emo	288	Castello di Bossi	484
Caprai - Val di Maggio, Arnaldo	665	Castello di Fonterutoli	478
Caputo, Cantine	712	Castello di Grumello	221
Cardeto	668	Castello di Lispida	305
Cardinali	437	Castello di Luzzano	225
Cardo, Il	351	Castello di Neive	161
Cardone, Vini Classici	747	Castello di Razzano, Tenuta	29
Carini	672	Castello di Spessa	360
Carlo di Pradis	369	Castello di Tassarolo	164
Carlozadra	199	Castello di Verduno	150
Carmignani, Gino Fuso	540	Castello Ducale	713
Carobbio	555	Castello Fageto	645
Carpenè Malvolti	346	Castello Monaci	750
Carpineta Fontalpino	484	Castelluccio	446
Carpineti, Marco	691	Castelrotto - Torti, Tenimenti	222
Carpineto	503	Castelvecchio	414
Carpino, Il	415	Castelvecchio	596
Carra	445	Castelvecchio	571
Carretta, Tenuta	129	Castiadas, Cantina Sociale di	792
Carussin	163	Castiglion del Bosco	519
Casa alle Vacche	577	Castiglioni, Tenuta	551
Casa Emma	466	Castignano, Cantine di	631
Casa Roma	327	Cataldi Madonna, Luigi	702
Casa Zuliani	387	Caudrina	67
Casabianca, Fattoria	553	Cavalchina	332
Casale dei Cento Corvi	691	Cavallaro	655
Casale del Giglio	681	Cavalleri	196
Casale della Ioria	680	Cavallotto, F.lli	65
Casale Marchese	685	Cavazza & F.lli, Domenico	306
Casale Mattia.	693	Cave di Moleto	129
Casalfarneto	650	Cave du Vin Blanc de Morgex et de La Salle	18
Casalone	101	Caven Camuna	226
Casaloste, Fattoria	555	Caves Cooperatives de Donnas	20
Casanova della Spinetta	622	Cavicchioli & Figli, Cantine	462
Casanova di Neri	517	Cavit - Consorzio di Cantine Sociali	246
Casanuova delle Cerbaie	518	Cecchetto, Giorgio	352
Casata Monfort	251	Cecchi, Famiglia	479
Casavecchia	158	Cecchini, Marco	386
Cascina Adelaide	154	Ceci, Amato	656
Cascina Ballarin	91	Ceci, Enrico	656
Cascina Bongiovanni	64	Cecilia	595
Cascina Castlèt	72	Cella di San Michele, La	164
Cascina Feipu dei Massaretti	166	Celli	432
Cascina La Maddalena	132	Cennatoio Intervineas	556
Cascina Montagnola	153	Centolani	520
Cascina Nuova, La	223	Centonze	788
Cascina Praié	178	Ceralti	596
Cascina Roera	73	Ceraudo, Roberto	760
Case di Pietra	786	Cerbaia	606
Caseo	183	Cerbaiona	520
Casetto dei Mandorli	461	Ceretto	25
Casisano Colombaio	518	Cerro, Fattoria del	544
Castagnoli	477	Cerveteri, Cantina	683
Casteggio, Cantina di	218	Cesanese del Piglio, Cantina Sociale	693
Castel De Paolis	686	Cesani, Vincenzo	577
Castel di Salve	756	Cesari, Umberto	436

Cesarini Sforza	246
Cescon, Italo	349
Cesconi	235
Ceuso	766
Charrère, Costantino	16
Cherchi, Giovanni	801
Chiappini, Giovanni	595
Chiara, La	159
Chiarieri	710
Chiarli 1860	446
Chiarlo, Michele	47
Chicco, Cascina	50
Chigi Saracini, Fattorie	485
Chionetti & Figlio, Quinto	76
Chiorri	678
Chiusa Grande	709
Ciabrelli, Fattoria	726
Ciacci Piccolomini D'Aragona	521
Cieck	24
Cigliuti, F.lli	120
Cima	513
Cinqueterre, Cantina	180
Cinti, Floriano	453
Ciolli, Cantine	693
Cisa Asinari dei Marchesi di Gresy, Tenuta	32
Ciù Ciù	643
Clastidio Ballabio	218
Clerico, Domenico	106
Co.di.vin. - Tenuta Di Maria	788
Cocci Grifoni	655
Coffele	330
Cogno, Elvio	127
Col d'Orcia, Tenuta	521
Col di Bacche	604
Col Vetoraz	337
Cola, Battista	216
Colacicchi	680
Coletti Conti, Antonello	691
Collalbrigo	346
Collalto, Conte	333
Collavini, Eugenio	380
Collazzi, Fattoria	603
Colle Bereto	616
Colle dei Bardellini	172
Colle di Maggio	690
Colle Duga	369
Colle Manora	131
Colle Massari	475
Colle San Lorenzo	684
Colle Santa Mustiola	599
Colle Verde, Fattoria	604
Collelceto	606
Collelungo, Podere	479
Collestefano	630
Colli a Lago, Cantine	220
Colli Amerini, Cantina dei	658
Colli di Lapio - Clelia Romano	717
Colli Irpini	718
Colli Ripani, La Cantina dei	648
Collosorbo, Tenuta di	522
Colmello di Grotta	388
Colognole	617
Colombera, La	145
Colombo - Barone Riccati, Il	105
Colonna	152
Colonna - Vini Spalletti	462
Colonnara Viticoltori in Cupramontana	632
Colosi, Cantine	785
Còlpetrone	664
Columbu	802
Colutta	395
Comelli, Paolino	386
Comincioli	224
Concilio/Vigneti delle Meridiane	248
Consorzio Viticoltori Associati del Vulture	730
Contadi Castaldi	182
Conte, Il	640
Conte D'Attimis-Maniago	357
Conte Giorgi di Vistarino, Carlo	225
Conte Leopardi Dittajuti	642
Conte Spagnoletti Zeuli	738
Conte Zandotti	689
Conterno, Aldo	107
Conterno, Giacomo	107
Conterno, Paolo	108
Conterno Fantino	108
Contesa di Rocco Pasetti	704
Conti, Leone	439
Conti Bossi Fedrigotti	242
Conti Formentini	416
Conti Zecca	746
Contini, Attilio	791
Contrada Castelletta	653
Contratto	55
Contucci	610
Convento Muri-Gries, Cantina	260
Coop. Svevo - Lucera	754
Coos, Dario	399
Coppo	55
Corini, Tenuta	667
Corino, Giovanni	92
Cormons, Cantina Produttori di	370
Cornaleto	216
Cornarea	156
Coroncino	652
Correggia, Matteo	51
Corte alla Flora	611
Corte d'Aibo	449
Corte Gardoni	340
Corte Lenguin	350
Corte Manzini	438
Corte Marzago	351
Corte Normanna	716
Corte Pavone	606
Corte Rugolin	300
Corte Sant'Alda	302
Cortese, Giuseppe	33
Cortina e Mandorli, Tenuta	612
Corzano e Paterno, Fattoria	571
COS	782
Costanti, Andrea	522
Costaripa	200
Coste Piane, Casa	351
Costozza - Conti da Schio	298
Cottanera	769
Crosato, Giovanni	427
Cucco, Cascina	139
Curatolo	785
Curto, Francesca e Giambattista	784
Cusmano, Tenuta	692
Cusumano	779
D'Alessandro, Tenimenti Luigi	490
D'Alfonso del Sordo	752
D'Ambra Vini d'Ischia	715
d'Amico, Paolo	682
D'Angelo	733
D'Antiche Terre - Vega	727
d'Isera, Cantina	233
Dacapo	22
Dal Fari	364
Dal Forno, Romano	296
Dal Maso, Luigino	306
Dall'Asta, Cantine	461
Dalzocchio	252
Damilano	39
De Angelis, Tenuta	629
De Bartoli, Marco	771
De Battè, Walter	176
De Conciliis, Viticoltori	720
De Falco	728

De Faveri	352	Fattoria di Bagnolo	510
De Lucia	727	Fattoria di Fiano	599
de Tarczal	232	Fattoria di Magliano	512
Decugnano dei Barbi	669	Fattoria di Romignano	604
Degani, F.lli	301	Fattoria La Rivolta	725
Degiorgis, Sergio	103	Fattoria Mancini	646
Dei	544	Fattoria Paradiso	432
Deiana, Ferruccio	800	Fattoria San Lorenzo	638
Del Carmine	653	Fattoria Zerbina	440
Delai	224	Favaro	163
Deltetto	51	Fay	213
Depperu, Andrea	802	Fazi Battaglia	630
Dessilani	79	Federici	694
Destefanis	117	Fedrizzi, Cipriano	252
Dettori, Tenute	798	Felce, La	179
Dezi, Fattoria	651	Felline	748
Di Barrò	20	Felluga, Livio	371
Di Filippo	676	Felluga, Marco	393
Di Fonti	489	Felsina, Fattoria di	485
Di Lenardo	389	Feotto dello Jato	787
Di Majo Norante	698	Ferghettina	197
Di Mauro, Paola	686	Ferrando	89
Di Meo	721	Ferrara, Benito	725
Di Palma	734	Ferrari	247
Di Prima, Gaspare	787	Ferrari, Aleardo	350
Di Sesta, Tenuta	523	Ferraris, Roberto	22
Diavoletta, Tenuta	457	Ferrero, F.lli	160
Dievole, Fattoria di	598	Ferrucci, Stefano	436
Do Ville	413	Feudi di San Giuliano	784
Doglia, Gianni	157	Feudi di San Gregorio	723
Dolianova, Cantine di	793	Feudi di Zangara	784
Donatella Cinelli Colombini, Casato Prime Donne	523	Feudo Montoni	783
Donati, Marco	237	Feudo Principi di Butera	767
Donda, Giovanni	354	Fiamberti	217
Donna Olga	524	Ficomontanino	599
Donnafugata, Tenuta di	772	Fidanza, Fabio	155
Dorgali, Cantina Sociale	794	Fiegl	391
Doria	201	Filippino, Domenico	161
Dorigati - Metius, F.lli	238	Filomusi Guelfi	707
Dorigo, Girolamo	358	Fiorini, Valentino	627
Drei Donà Tenuta La Palazza	443	Firriato	776
Drius, Mauro	370	Flino, Cascina	158
Duca della Corgna	660	Florio, Cantine	772
Duca di Salaparuta - Vini Corvo	769	Foffani	426
Due Palme, Cantina	740	Folonari, Tenute Ambrogio e Giovanni	493
Due Torri, Le	429	Fonda, Cascina	102
Egger-Ramer	284	Fondo Antico	781
Einaudi	77	Fontana, Graziano	231
Endrizzi	244	Fontana Candida	687
Enoteca Andrea Bruzzone	179	Fontanabianca	121
Enotria, Cantina	763	Fontanafredda	140
Erede di Armando Chiappone	162	Fontanavecchia	724
Erioli	457	Fonte della Luna - Medoro Cimarelli	656
Ermacora, Dario e Luciano	406	Fontodi, Tenuta	557
Erste & Neue	268	Fontursia, La	655
Erzetic, Branko - Igor	371	Foraci, Cantine	785
Eubea	734	Foradori	239
Fabbri, Fattoria	600	Forano, Fattoria di	626
Faccoli & Figli, Lorenzo	220	Forchir	430
Falesco	688	Forlini Cappellini	180
Falkenstein, Weingut	278	Fornaser, Giuseppe	350
Fanini	661	Forte, Podere	489
Fanti, Vignaiolo Giuseppe	236	Forteto della Luja	101
Fanti - La Palazzetta	524	Fossacolle	606
Fanti - San Filippo	525	Fraghe, Le	291
Fantinel	423	Francesconi, Paolo	440
Fantino, Alessandro e Gian Natale	109	Frascole	491
Faraone	700	Frecciarossa	187
Farnese	703	Freddano	678
Farnetella	586	Frentana, Cantina Sociale	710
Fasoli	292	Frescobaldi, Marchesi de'	494
Fassati	545	Fucci, Elena	730
Fatascià	777	Fuligni, Eredi	525
Fattoi	606	Fumanelli, Marchesi	350
Fattoria Castellina	595	Funtanin	52

Gabbas, Giuseppe	796
Gabutti - Franco Boasso	140
Gaggino	163
Gaggioli - Vigneto Bagazzana, Maria Letizia	466
Gagliardo, Gianni	160
Gagliole	597
Gaiano, Tenuta	49
Gaierhof	241
Gaja	33
Galardi	723
Gallino, Filippo	52
Gallura, Cantina Sociale	801
Gancia	56
Garetto	23
Garitina, Cascina	59
Garofoli, Gioacchino	635
Gastaldi	121
Gatti, Enrico	197
Gatti, Piero	136
Germano, Ettore	141
Ghio e Figli, Domenico	45
Ghisolfi, Attilio	109
Ghizzano, Tenuta di	561
Giacomelli	179
Giacosa, Bruno	122
Giacosa, Carlo	34
Giacosa, F.lli	122
Gigante, Adriano	381
Gili, Raffaele	60
Gillardi, Giovanni Battista	80
Gilli, Cascina	62
Gini	308
Giorgi, F.lli	184
Giovinale, Cascina	162
Gironda, La	162
Giuncheo, Tenuta	168
Giustiniana, La	85
Godenza, Tenuta	459
Gojer Glögglhof, Franz	260
Goretti	673
Gostolai	804
Gotto d'Oro	692
Gracciano, Fattoria di	611
Gradis'ciutta	416
Gradizzolo	460
Gradnik Eredi, Gradimiro	428
Graf Pfeil Weingut Kränzel	272
Gran Furor Divina Costiera, Cantine	715
Granducato	562
Grasso	786
Grasso, Elio	110
Grasso, Mauro	155
Grasso, Silvio	92
Gravner	391
Gregoletto	304
Greppone Mazzi - Tenimenti Ruffino	526
Grevepesa, Castelli del	572
Grigoletti	240
Grillo, Iole	408
Grimaldi, Giacomo	39
Grimaldi - Ca' du Sindic, Sergio	137
Grosjean, F.lli	19
Grotta del Sole, Cantine	720
Guado al Melo, Podere	596
Guado al Tasso, Tenuta	469
Gualdo del Re	589
Guardia, La	118
Guerci, F.lli	218
Guerrieri	646
Guerrieri Rizzardi	289
Guglielmini, Giuseppe	222
Guglierame, Nicola	179
Guicciardini Strozzi - Fattoria Cusona	578
Gulfi	784
Gumphof, Markus Prackwieser	275
Haas, Franz	277
Haderburg, Weingut	279
Happacherhof - Istituto Tecnico Agrario, Maso	285
Hastae	47
Hauser, Ester	656
Hilberg - Pasquero	131
Hofstätter	281
Hohler, Karin e Remo	58
Humar, Marcello e Marino	417
I Balzini	594
I Campetti	617
I Feudi di Romans - Lorenzon	414
I Girasoli di Sant'Andrea	678
I Giusti e Zanza	492
I Pastini - Carparelli	754
I Scriani	347
I Sodi	601
I Vignaioli di S. Stefano	137
Icardi	67
Il Borro, Tenuta	604
Il Bosco, Tenuta	226
Il Calepino	189
Il Carnasciale, Podere	514
Il Chioso	178
Il Colle, Azienda Agricola	616
Il Colombaio di Cencio	497
Il Corno, Tenuta	572
Il Faggeto	611
Il Feuduccio di Santa Maria d'Orni	709
Il Greppo, Tenuta	526
Il Grillesino	600
Il Lebbio	578
Il Mandorlo	573
Il Marroneto	606
Il Molino di Grace	557
Il Mosnel	206
Il Nuraghe, Cantina Sociale	803
Il Palagio, Castello	617
Il Palagio, Fattoria	490
Il Palagione	579
Il Palazzino, Podere	498
Il Palazzone	527
Il Paradiso	579
Il Paradiso di Frassina	607
Il Poggiarello	453
Il Poggiolo	527
Il Poggione, Tenuta	528
Il Pratello	447
Il Tagliato	602
Il Torchio	168
Illuminati, Dino	699
Imperatori, Alessia	753
Inama	317
Incontri	589
Institut Agricole Régional	16
Ippolito 1845	763
Isabella	119
Isimbarda	210
Isola	448
Isole e Olena	467
Ispoli	573
Istituto Professionale per l'Agricoltura e l'Ambiente	441
Iuli - Ca.Vi.Mon.	69
Jacùss	424
Jerzu, Antichi Poderi	794
Kante	385
Keber, Edi	372
Keber, Renato	428
Kettmeir	269
Kitzmüller, Thomas	428
Klosterhof, Tenuta	285
Köfererhof	283
Kössler - Praeclarus	255
Kuenhof - Peter Pliger	267
L'Armangia	56

L'Olivella	692	La Viola, Tenuta	457
La Barbatella, Cascina	126	La Vis/Valle di Cembra	234
La Berta	435	La Zucca	119
La Boatina	372	Laila, Fattoria	638
La Braccesca, Fattoria	545	Laimburg, Cantina	282
La Brancaia	566	Lamberti	348
La Brugherata	212	Lamborghini - La Fiorita	671
La Calonica	546	Lambruschi, Ottaviano	169
La Caplana	155	Lamoretti, Isidoro	460
La Cappella, Podere	591	Lanari	624
La Cappuccina	308	Lanciola	511
La Carletta	619	Landi, Luciano	628
La Carraia	669	Langasco, Tenuta	154
La Casa dell'Orco	719	Lano, Gianluigi	26
La Castellina	597	Lantieri de Paratico	185
La Chiesa, Podere	622	Laurentina	639
La Ciarliana	546	Lavacchio, Fattoria	615
La Corte	755	Le Bellerive - Angelo Ruggeri	337
La Costa, Tenuta	218	Le Bertarole	347
La Costaiola, Tenuta	202	Le Boncie, Podere	598
La Crotta di Vegneron	17	Le Calcinaie, Tenuta	581
La Fornace	607	Le Calvane	551
La Fortuna, Podere	528	Le Cantorie	219
La Gerla	529	Le Capannacce	599
La Ghersa	103	Le Chiuse	530
La Giaretta	348	Le Chiusure	225
La Giribaldina	48	Le Cinciole	559
La Guarda	223	Le Colture	338
La Guardiense	727	Le Corne	221
La Lastra	580	Le Corti, Fattoria	574
La Leccia, Castello	597	Le Crete	677
La Loggia	617	Le Due Terre	409
La Lumia, Barone	784	Le Fabriche	755
La Macolina	459	Le Filigare	468
La Madonnina - Triacca	602	Le Fonti	615
La Marcellina	558	Le Fracce	188
La Marzuola	217	Le Gode di Ripaccioli	607
La Massa	558	Le Macchiole	470
La Meridiana, Tenuta	116	Le Macioche	607
La Monacesca	637	Le Marchesine	223
La Montecchia	328	Le Monde, Vigneti	404
La Montina	202	Le Poggette, Fattoria	677
La Novella, Tenuta	602	Le Pupille	509
La Palazzola	674	Le Querce, Tenuta	731
La Parrina	554	Le Quinte, Tenuta	693
La Pertica, Cascina	206	Le Ragose	312
La Pierotta	620	Le Rocche del Gatto	167
La Pietra del Focolare	173	Le Sorgenti	465
La Pieve	515	Le Tende	348
La Poderina	529	Le Terrazze, Fattoria	642
La Querce	510	Le Velette, Tenuta	670
La Rajade	384	Le Volpaiole	595
La Rampa di Fugnano	580	Lebovitz	216
La Rasina	607	Lenotti	345
La Regola	617	Lento, Cantine	761
La Rendola	553	Lentsch, Hartmann	284
La Ripa, Fattoria	467	Leonardo da Vinci, Cantine	593
La Sala	574	Leone de Castris	751
La Sansonina	315	Lepore	698
La Selva	613	Lequio, Ugo	123
La Smilla	155	Lequio - Prinsi, Ottavio	123
La Stellata	605	Les Crêtes	17
La Stoppa	452	Letrari	242
La Togata - Tenuta Carlina	530	Leverano, Cantina Sociale Cooperativa	754
La Tordela	214	Librandi	759
La Torre, Cantina Sociale	787	Lignano, Castello di	81
La Torre, Fattoria	610	Lis Neris	421
La Torretta, Tenuta	460	Lisini	531
La Tosa	454	Livernano	567
La Tunella	406	Livon	419
La Valentina, Fattoria	707	Lo Sparviere	203
La Versa, Cantina Sociale	211	Lo Triolet	18
La Viarte	409	Loacker Schwarzhof	261
La Vigna	217	Locorotondo, Cantina Soc.Cooperativa del	747
La Vigna, Podere	607	Lodola Nuova - Tenimenti Ruffino	547

Loi, Alberto	792	Maso Martis	248
Lomazzi & Sarli	754	Masottina	318
Lonardi, Giuseppe	301	Masseria Felicia	728
Longariva	243	Masseria Li Veli	741
Loredan Gasparini Venegazzù, Conte	344	Masseria Monaci	742
Loreti, Giancarlo	694	Mastroberardino	712
Lucangeli Aymerich di Laconi	653	Mastrojanni	532
Lucchetti, Mario	654	Masut da Rive	398
Luce	531	Mattiello, Natalino	298
Luisa, Eddi	398	Maurigi	779
Luisin, Cascina	31	Mayr - Erbhof Unterganzner, Josephus	262
Lun, Cantina H.	274	Mazzi, Roberto	313
Lunelli	247	Mazziotti	691
Lungarotti	675	Mazzolino, Tenuta	194
Lupi, Tommaso e Angelo	174	Mecella, Enzo	633
Luretta	444	Medici & Figli, Ermete	451
Lusenti, Gaetano	455	Meleto, Castello di	498
Maccario, Giovanna	180	Melini	563
Macchialanzi	596	Meloni Vini	798
Macellio - Renato Bianco, Podere	155	Meroi, Davino	358
Machiavelli	575	Merotto	347
Maculan	290	Miali, Vinicola	749
Madonia, Giovanna	433	Miani	359
Maffini, Luigi	713	Miceli, Aziende Vinicole	780
Magnàs	373	Midolini	395
Maiano, Tenuta	612	Migliarese	694
Majolini	205	Mille Una	746
Malabaila	156	Minuzzo, Gabriella	20
Malacari	655	Miotti, Firmino	291
Malena	759	Mirabella	208
Malenchini	594	Mocali	608
Malfatti, Costanza	512	Mocavero	755
Malgrà	104	Moccagatta	35
Malojer Gummerhof, R.	261	Modanella, Castello di	570
Malvirà	53	Molettieri, Salvatore	719
Manara	322	Molino, Mauro	93
Mancina, La	450	Molino dei Lessi	251
Mancinelli, Stefano	654	Molon Traverso, Ornella	317
Mancini, Benito	654	Monastero, Castello di	486
Mancini, Piero	796	Monchiero Carbone	53
Mandolare, Le	309	Mondo, Franco	164
Mandrolisai, Cantina Sociale del	804	Monfalletto - Cordero di Montezemolo	94
Mannucci Droandi	613	Monrubio, Cantina	660
Mantellassi	513	Monsanto, Castello di	469
Manzocco, Giulio	373	Monsupello	215
Manzone, Giovanni	110	Montalcino, Cantina di	608
Marangona	223	Montalto, Marchesi di	201
Marchesi di Barolo	40	Montanine, Fattoria	603
Marchesi Platamone	786	Montaribaldi	35
Marchesi Torrigiani	468	Montauto, Castello di	618
Marchetti, Maurizio	624	Monte Cicogna	200
Marconi, Maurizio	649	Monte delle Vigne	459
Marenco	143	Monte Pugliano	727
Marengo, Giacomo	539	Monte Rossa	190
Marengo, Mario	93	Monte Tabor	348
Marianna	726	Monte Tondo	330
Marinig, Valerio	410	Monteacuto	224
Marion	319	Montecalvi	602
Mariotto, Claudio	145	Montecappone	635
Marotti Campi	641	Montecchio, Fattoria	621
Marramiero	705	Montechiari, Fattoria di	541
Marsaglia	157	Monteforte d'Alpone, Cantina Sociale di	349
Martinelli, Bruno	349	Montelio	192
Martinetti, Franco M.	144	Montellori, Fattoria	494
Martini, Lorenz	284	Montemaggio, Fattoria di	616
Martini & Sohn, K.	255	Montenidoli	581
Martino, Armando	736	Montenisa	219
Martorana	783	Montepeloso	590
Mascarello, Bartolo	40	Monterinaldi, Castello di	616
Mascarello e Figlio, Giuseppe	105	Monterucco	219
Masciarelli, Gianni	706	Montesalario	596
Masi	327	Monteschiavo	636
Maso Bastie	249	Montevertine	567
Maso Cantanghel	231	Montevetrano	721
Maso Furli	237	Monti	111

Monti, Antonio e Elio	709	Palazzo	608
Monticello, Il	177	Palazzone	670
Montiverdi	601	Pallavicini, Vini	689
Montori, Camillo	699	Palombo, Giovanni	681
Montresor, Giacomo	342	Panizzi, Giovanni	583
Monzio Compagnoni	220	Panzanello	559
Morandina, La	68	Paradiso	753
Morassino, Cascina	32	Parusso, Armando	111
Morella	754	Pasetti, Franco	700
Morelli, Claudio	634	Pasini Produttori	224
Morellino di Scansano, Cantina Cooperativa del	586	Pasqua Vigneti e Cantine	342
Morgante	770	Pasqualetti Viticoltori	613
Morgassi Superiore	85	Paterno, Fattoria di	611
Morini, Poderi	441	Paternoster	731
Moris Farms	514	Pavia e Figli, Agostino	23
Mormoraia	582	Pecchenino	77
Moroder, Alessandro	625	Pecorari, Pierpaolo	421
Morra, Stefanino	61	Pedra Majore	795
Moschioni, Davide	365	Pegazzera, Tenuta	188
Mosole	350	Pelissero	148
Mossio, F.lli	133	Pellegrino, Carlo	773
Mottura, Sergio	684	Pellerino, Cascina	118
Mulino delle Tolle	355	Pelz & Piffer	251
Mumelter, Georg	262	Perdarubia	803
Mura	802	Perinelli	461
Murana, Salvatore	778	Perrone, Elio	68
Musella	319	Perticaia, Podere	664
Mustilli	722	Pertinace, Vignaioli Elvio	148
Mutti	138	Perusia, Cantine	678
Muzic	430	Perusini	381
Nada, Ada	147	Pervini	749
Nada, Fiorenzo	147	Petra	620
Naitana, Gianvittorio	803	Petreto	465
Napolitano, F.lli	736	Petricci e Del Pianta	621
Nardi, Tenute Silvio	532	Petriolo, Fattoria di	599
Ne. Ne.	156	Petroio, Fattoria di	486
Negri, Nino	191	Petrolo, Fattoria	471
Negro & Figli, Angelo	117	Petrucco	359
Nera, Pietro	219	Petrussa	410
Nervi	82	Pfeifer Pfannenstielhof, Johannes	263
Nicodemi, Bruno	702	Piaggia	563
Nicolis e Figli, Angelo	323	Pian dell'Orino	608
Niedermayr, Josef	256	Pian delle Vigne	608
Niedrist, Ignaz	257	Piancornello	609
Nino Franco	338	Piane, Le	154
Nittardi, Fattoria	480	Picciau, Gigi	802
Nobile Prima	491	Picech - Le Vigne del Ribél, Roberto	374
Nomi, Cantina Sociale di	252	Pierazzuoli, Enrico	473
Nössing - Hoandlhof, Manfred	267	Pieri, Agostina	609
Nottola	611	Pieropan, Leonildo	331
Novaia	302	Piersanti	656
Oasi degli Angeli	632	Pietra Porzia, Tenuta di	692
Oberto, Andrea	94	Pietracupa	717
Ocone	728	Pietrafitta	618
Oddero, F.lli	95	Pietratorcia	727
Odoardi	762	Pieve de' Pitti	622
Oliena, Cantina Cooperativa di	804	Pieve del Vescovo	676
Olim Bauda, Tenuta	88	Pighin, F.lli	401
Oliveto	608	Pile e Lamole, S. M. Tenimenti	499
Oppizzi	461	Pinni, Tenuta	422
Orciaverde	597	Pinsoglio, Fabrizio	61
Orlandi Contucci Ponno	705	Pio Cesare	26
Ornellaia, Tenuta dell'	470	Pioiero	164
Orsola, Andreola	347	Piona, Albino	351
Orsolani	134	Piovene Porto Godi	344
Ortaglia	593	Pira	78
Ottella	316	Pira, Luigi	141
Pacenti, Siro	533	Pira & Figli - Chiara Boschis	41
Pacherhof	283	Pisanu	803
Pacina	598	Pisoni	234
Paglieri, I	34	Pittaro	366
Paitin	124	Planeta	774
Pala, F.lli	800	Plattner - Waldgries, Heinrich	263
Palagetto	582	Plozner	423
Palari	775	Plozza	226

Podere Capaccia	616
Podere del Ger	405
Podere Terreno alla Via della Volpaia	616
Podere Vecciano	459
Poderi Colla	27
Poderi dal Nespoli	438
Poderi di San Pietro	209
Poderi Marcarini	95
Podversic, Damijan	392
Poggerino	568
Poggi, Giorgio	345
Poggio, Paolo	155
Poggio a Poppiano	552
Poggio al Sole	592
Poggio alla Sala	611
Poggio Amorelli	480
Poggio Antico	533
Poggio Argentiera	509
Poggio Bertaio	661
Poggio Bonelli	487
Poggio Capponi	612
Poggio Cosmiano, Tenuta di	614
Poggio di Sotto	609
Poggio Le Volpi	687
Poggio Montali	654
Poggio Pollino, Tenuta	460
Poggio Romita, Fattoria	621
Poggio Saccone	594
Poggio San Polo	609
Poggio Scalette, Podere	503
Poggio Toccalta	352
Poggiopiano, Fattoria	575
Pojer & Sandri	232
Polencic, Aldo	374
Polencic, Isidoro	375
Poli, Francesco	252
Poli, Giovanni	252
Poliziano	547
Pollara	786
Pontoni, Flavio	427
Poppiano, Castello di	552
Porcu, F.lli	803
Porello	54
Portinari, Umberto	309
Pouchain Taffuri, Marisa	693
Prà	310
Pradio	356
Pratesi	474
Prattico, Fattoria	728
Pravis	234
Presciano, Fattoria di	614
Prevostini, Mamete	199
Primosic	392
Princic, Alessandro	375
Principe Banfi Podere Pio IX	220
Principiano, Ferdinando	112
Produttori Andriano, Cantina	254
Produttori Burggräfler, Cantina	275
Produttori Colterenzio, Cantina	258
Produttori Cornaiano, Cantina	256
Produttori Cortaccia, Cantina	273
Produttori del Barbaresco	36
Produttori del Gavi	86
Produttori di Merano, Cantina	276
Produttori Nalles Niclara Magrè, Cantina	277
Produttori Nebbiolo di Carema, Cantina dei	57
Produttori San Paolo, Cantina	257
Produttori Santa Maddalena/Cantina di Bolzano, Cantina	264
Produttori Termeno, Cantina	281
Produttori Valle Isarco, Cantina	272
Provenza	195
Provolo, Luigino e Marco	303
Provveditore	620
Prunotto	27
Pucciarella	677
Puddu, Josto	804
Puiatti	360
Punset	161
Pupillo	788
Puri Charlotte	694
Quaquarini	184
Quarello, Carlo	70
Quartu, Cantina di	804
Querceto, Castello di	503
Querceto di Castellina	481
Querciabella	504
Querciavalle	487
Quintarelli, Giuseppe	313
Quistello, Cantina Sociale Cooperativa di	224
'R Mesueto	179
Raccaro, Dario	376
Raimondi - Villa Monteleone	328
Rainoldi, Aldo	191
Raiz, Teresa	403
Rallo, Cantine	773
Rametz, Castello	285
Ramò, Giampaolo	179
Ramoser - Fliederhof, Stephan	264
Ramoser Untermoserhof, Georg	265
Rapitalà, Tenute	768
Ratti, Renato	96
Redi	548
Revelli, Eraldo	159
Revello, F.lli	96
Ribote	159
Riccardi, Enrico	225
Ricchi	223
Ricchino - Tiziana Menegaldo	158
Ricci Curbastro	186
Riecine	499
Rietine	500
Riforma Fondiaria, Cantina Cooperativa della	755
Rinaldi, Giuseppe	41
Rinaldini, Moro -	462
Rio Grande	671
Rio Maggio	640
Riosto, Podere	461
Ripe, La	656
Riseccoli	602
Ritterhof, Tenuta	269
Rivera	379
Rocca, Albino	36
Rocca, Bruno	37
Rocca Bernarda	407
Rocca delle Macìe	481
Rocca di Castagnoli	500
Rocca di Fabbri	666
Rocca di Montegrossi	601
Rocca di San Nicolao, La	170
Roccaccia, Tenuta	562
Rocche Costamagna	97
Rocche dei Manzoni, Podere	112
Rocchetta, La	226
Rocchi, Daniele	614
Roccolo Grassi	303
Rockhof	286
Rodaro, Paolo	366
Roddolo, Flavio	113
Romitorio, Castello	534
Roncada	376
Roncaia, La	400
Roncal, Il	365
Ronchi	154
Ronchi di Manzano	396
Ronco Calino	182
Ronco dei Pini	411
Ronco dei Tassi	377
Ronco del Gelso	377
Ronco del Gnemiz	420

Ronco delle Betulle	396	Sant'Antonio, Tenuta	304
Ronco Vieri	400	Sant'Appiano, Fattoria	594
Roncolato	351	Sant'Elena	393
Roncùs	361	Sant'Isidoro	694
Rontana	458	Santa Barbara	627
Rosa del Golfo	738	Santa Barbara	756
Rosi, Eugenio	249	Santa Cassella	647
Rosso, Giovanni	164	Santa Caterina	180
Rottensteiner, Hans	266	Santa Eurosia	339
Rottensteiner, Heinrich & Thomas	265	Santa Lucia	753
Roveglia, Tenuta	224	Santa Lucia	603
Rovellotti	87	Santa Lucia, Fattoria	615
Rovero, F.lli	30	Santa Margherita	347
Rubbia Al Colle	621	Santa Maria La Palma, Cantina Sociale	790
Rubino, Tenute	739	Santa Sofia	323
Ruffino, Tenimenti	564	Santa Vittoria, Fattoria	601
Ruggeri	678	Santadi, Cantina Sociale di	797
Ruggeri & C.	339	Santarosa	448
Ruggeri Corsini	113	Sante Marie	619
Ruiz de Cardenas	189	Santi	297
Russiz Superiore	361	Santini, Enrico	476
Russo	590	Santo Stefano	294
Russolo	422	Santo Stefano, Fattoria	602
Saccoletto, Daniele	163	Saputi	653
Saffirio, Josetta	160	Saracco, Paolo	69
Saladini Pilastri	651	Sarchese Dora	704
Salcheto	548	Sardus Pater	797
Salette, Le	295	Sarotto, Roberto	161
Salicutti, Podere	534	Sartarelli	647
Sallier de La Tour	784	Sartori, Casa Vinicola	349
Salviano, Tenuta di	676	Sassotondo	587
Salvioni - La Cerbaiola	535	Satta, Michele	476
Sammarco, Ettore	728	Savignola Paolina	505
San Cristoforo	220	Scacciadiavoli	666
San Fabiano - Borghini Baldovinetti, Fattoria	464	Scagliola	48
San Fabiano Calcinaia	482	Scagliola e Figlio, Giacomo	156
San Felice	488	Scammacca del Murgo, Barone	788
San Fereolo	78	Scamuzza, La	152
San Francesco, Fattoria	758	Scarbolo	402
San Gervasio	554	Scarpa, Antica Casa Vinicola	126
San Giorgio, Podere	211	Scarzello e Figli, Giorgio	42
San Giorgio a Lapi	620	Scavino, Paolo	65
San Giovanni	644	Schiopetto	362
San Giusto	614	Schmid - Oberrautner, Anton	266
San Giusto a Rentennano	501	Schwanburg, Castello	278
San Guido, Tenuta	471	Scilio, Tenuta	785
San Leonardo, Tenuta	228	Sciorio	73
San Lorenzo	709	Scolca, La	159
San Lorenzo	618	Scrimaglio, Franco e Mario	127
San Lorenzo	663	Scubla	407
San Luciano	539	Scuola Enologica di Conegliano, G. B. Cerletti	346
San Luigi, Podere	561	Sebaste, Mauro	28
San Marco, Cantine	685	Secchi, Alessandro	250
San Michele, Podere	619	Sedime	614
San Michele a Torri	619	Seghesio, F.lli	114
San Michele all'Adige, Istituto Agrario Provinciale	244	Sella	100
San Michele Appiano, Cantina Produttori	258	Sella & Mosca, Tenute	790
San Patrignano	439	Selvapiana, Fattoria	564
San Quirico	618	Selvole, Castello di	488
San Romano	79	Serafini & Vidotto	315
San Savino - Poderi Capecci	649	Serafino, Enrico	156
San Sebastiano, Tenuta	102	Serenelli, Alberto	625
San Simone	430	Serracavallo, Demetrio	760
San Valentino	452	Serraiola	550
San Vettore	502	Sertoli Salis, Conti	214
San Vincenti	501	Sesti - Castello di Argiano	609
San Vito	450	Sette Ponti, Tenuta	592
Sancio	180	Settesoli	775
Sandonaci, Cantina Cooperativa	756	Signano	619
Sandoni, Virgilio	458	Silva, Giovanni	24
Sandri, Arcangelo	251	Simon di Brazzan	428
Sandrone, Luciano	42	Simoncelli, Armando	243
Sant'Agata, Cantine	138	Sinaglio	28
Sant'Agnese	615	Skerk	429
Sant'Andrea, Cantina	690	Solaria - Cencioni	535

Soletta, Tenute	793	Terre Rosse, Cascina delle	172
Solidea	787	Terredora	718
Sölva - Niklaserhof, Josef	270	Terriccio, Castello del	482
Sölva & Söhne, Peter	270	Teruzzi & Puthod	583
Sonnino, Fattoria Castello	612	Teso, Fattoria del	541
Sopra la Ripa, Podere	587	Tezza	343
Sorbaiano, Fattoria	610	Tiefenbrunner	273
Sottimano	124	Tirolensis Ars Vini	286
Spadafora	777	Tizzano	435
Spadaio e Piecorto	595	Toblino, Cantina	229
Spagnolli, Enrico	233	Todini	675
Sparviero, Casale dello	597	Tola, Girolamo & C.	787
Specogna, Leonardo	382	Tollo, Cantina	708
Speri, F.lli	324	Tommasi Viticoltori	325
Spertino, Luigi	104	Toppello, Il	662
Spezia, Stefano	221	Tordimaro	678
Spinetta, La	58	Tormaresca	752
Spinsanti	628	Tornano, Castello di	601
Spoletoducale	674	Toros, Franco	379
Sportoletti	673	Torraccia del Piantavigna	159
Statti	761	Torraccia di Presura	505
Steinhauserhof	285	Torre Fornello	455
Stelitano	758	Torre Gaia, Fattoria	727
Streda in Belvedere	622	Torre Quarto	741
Stroblhof	284	Torre Rosazza	397
Strologo, Silvano	629	Torre Zambra	710
Sturm, Oscar	378	Torrevento	742
Su Baroni	803	Torti, Pietro	222
Suavia	331	Trabucchi	297
Subida di Monte	378	Tramonti	598
Suveraia	612	Trapani, Cantina Sociale di	781
Tacchino, Luigi	60	Trappolini	682
Talenti	536	Travaglini, Giancarlo	83
Taliano, Michele	116	Traversa - Cascina Bertolotto	143
Tallarini	221	Travignoli	614
Tamburello	786	Tre Berte, Le	549
Tamellini	332	Tre Monti	445
Tanorè	340	Trecciano, Tenuta di	620
Tasca d'Almerita	778	Trequanda	622
Taschlerhof	268	Treré	442
Taurino, Cosimo	745	Trexenta, Cantina Sociale della	799
Tedeschi, F.lli	324	Triacca	215
Telaro	716	Trinoro, Tenuta di	584
Tenimenti Angelini	536	Tua Rita	591
Tenuta Bonzara	449	Turco, Innocenzo	180
Tenuta dei Fiori	49	Uberti	198
Tenuta del Portale	732	Uccelliera	537
Tenuta dell'Arbiola	135	Uccelliera, Fattoria	600
Tenuta Faltracco	310	Uccellina, Tenuta	462
Tenuta La Volta - Cabutto	43	Ulivi, Cascina	162
Tenuta Pandolfa	451	Umani Ronchi	644
Tenuta Valli	444	Umbria Viticoltori Associati	677
Tenute Galtarossa	325	Unterortl-Castel Juval, Tenuta	271
Teracrea, Tenuta	349	Urciuolo	727
Tercic, Matijaz	417	Uzzano, Castello	506
Terenzi, Giovanni	694	Vaglie	659
Terlano, Cantina	279	Vagnoni, F.lli	584
Terpin, Franco	418	Vajra, G. D.	44
Terra Antica	612	Val del Prete, Cascina	130
Terra d'Aligi - Spinelli	696	Val delle Corti	617
Terrabianca, Fattoria di	568	Val di Cava, Tenuta	537
Terragens Fine Wines - Volo Rosso	433	Val di Neto	764
Terralba	45	Val San Martino, Cantina Sociale	223
Terre Bianche	171	Valchiarò	425
Terre Cortesi Moncaro	639	Valdarnese, Cooperativa Agricola	621
Terre da Vino	43	Valdipiatta, Tenuta	549
Terre de' Trinci	663	Valditerra	162
Terre degli Svevi	735	Valdo, Spumanti	351
Terre del Barolo	66	Valentini, Edoardo	701
Terre del Carpine	677	Valetti	345
Terre del Cesanese	693	Valfieri	74
Terre di Salemi	787	Valgiano, Tenuta di	511
Terre di Santa Maria	785	Vallarom	229
Terre di Shemir	788	Valle	427
Terre Nobili, Tenuta	765	Valle del Sole	604

Valle dell'Acate, Cantina	766	Villa Chiopris	427
Valle Reale	710	Villa Cilnia	464
Vallechiesa, Casale	692	Villa Corniole	251
Vallerosa Bonci	633	Villa Crespia - F.lli Muratori	217
Valli Unite	157	Villa dal Ferro Lazzarini	318
Vallis Agri	230	Villa di Corlo	460
Vallona	437	Villa di Quartu	804
Vallone, Agricole	754	Villa Fiorita	157
Valori	706	Villa Frattina	404
Valpane, Cantine	163	Villa Giada	57
Valpanera	426	Villa Giona	350
Valpolicella, Cantina Sociale	312	Villa La Selva, Fattoria	472
Valtenesi - Lugana, Cantine	222	Villa Le Prata	538
Valtidone, Cantina Sociale	457	Villa Matilde	714
Vanzini	225	Villa Medoro	696
Varaldo, Rino	37	Villa Papiano	447
Varramista	613	Villa Pigna	655
Vaselli, Cristine	683	Villa Pillo	502
Vecchia Cantina, La	167	Villa Raiano	722
Vecchie Terre di Montefili	560	Villa Russiz	363
Veglio, Mauro	97	Villa Sandi	346
Vegni - Capezzine	600	Villa Sant'Andrea	618
Velenosi, Ercole	626	Villa Sant'Anna	550
Vellano, Pierino	156	Villa Simone	688
Velona, La	609	Villa Sparina	86
Venditti, Antica Masseria	726	Villa Spinosa	314
Venica & Venica	384	Villa Trasqua	598
Venosa, Cantina di	735	Villabella	345
Venturini, Massimino	326	Villagrande, Barone di	776
Vercesi del Castellazzo	204	Villanova, Tenuta	389
Verdi, Bruno	185	Vinagri	756
Vermentino, Cantina Sociale del	795	Vinchio - Vaglio Serra, Cantina Sociale di	153
Verrazzano, Castello di	506	Vini e Mosti Rossi, Consorzio Produttori	755
Vevey, Maison Albert	20	Vini Tipici di San Marino, Consorzio	462
Vezzoli, Giuseppe	198	Vinicola Aldeno	250
Viberti, Eraldo	98	Vinicola del Tesino	634
Viberti, Osvaldo	98	Vinicola Falcone	783
Vicara	133	Vinicola Mediterranea	756
Vicari	655	Vinnaioli, Jermann	388
Vicchiomaggio, Castello di	507	Vintripodi Calabria	764
Vicentini, Agostino	346	Vio, Claudio	177
Vicentini Orgnani, Alessandro	402	Viola & Figli, Luigi	764
Vidon, Alessandra	430	Visconti	538
Vidussi, Gestioni Agricole	362	Visconti Podere Sant'Onorata	220
Vie di Romans	399	Visintin, Franco	394
Vielmin	62	Visintini, Andrea	382
Vietti	66	Vistorta - Brandino Brandolini d'Adda	413
Vigliano	603	Vitanza	610
Vigna Angeli	430	Vitereta, Tenuta	604
Vigna del Lauro	379	Viticcio	508
Vigna Petrussa	411	Viticoltori di Caldaro, Cantina	271
Vigna Rionda - Massolino	142	Vivacqua, Luigi	762
Vigna Traverso	412	Vivaldi - Arunda	276
Vignai da Duline	420	Viviani	314
Vignale, Il	128	Voerzio, Gianni	99
Vignalta	334	Voerzio, Roberto	99
Vignamaggio, Villa	507	Volpaia, Castello di	569
Vignavecchia	569	Volpe Pasini	425
Vigne dei Boschi	458	Von Braunbach	280
Vigne del Pareto	128	Vosca, Francesco	429
Vigne di San Pietro, Le	333	Wandanna	610
Vigne di Zamò, Le	397	Zaccagnini, Ciccio	697
Vigne Fantin Noda'r	408	Zaccagnini & C., F.lli	652
Vigne Regali	144	Zanetti, Martino	349
Vigne & Vini	745	Zanini	252
Vigneti Massa	115	Zardetto Spumanti	293
Vigneto delle Terre Rosse	466	Zemmer - Kupelwieser, Peter	274
Vigneto Due Santi	290	Zenato	316
Vignole	613	Zeni, F.lli	289
Villa	203	Zeni, Roberto	245
Villa Bellini	326	Zidarich	385
Villa Brunesca	347	Zito, Vinicola	763
Villa Cafaggio	560	Zof	383
Villa Calcinaia	603	Zonin	296
Villa Casale	603	Zuani	418